# HANDBOOK
## OF
# INFORMATION SECURITY

**Threats, Vulnerabilities, Prevention, Detection, and Management**

## Volume 3

**Hossein Bidgoli**
Editor-in-Chief
*California State University*
*Bakersfield, California*

WILEY

John Wiley & Sons, Inc.

*Library of Congress Cataloging-in-Publication Data:*

The handbook of information security / edited by Hossein Bidgoli.
      p. cm.
   Includes bibliographical references and index.
      ISBN-13: 978-0-471-64830-7, ISBN-10: 0-471-64830-2 (CLOTH VOL 1 : alk. paper)
      ISBN-13: 978-0-471-64831-4, ISBN-10: 0-471-64831-0 (CLOTH VOL 2 : alk. paper)
      ISBN-13: 978-0-471-64832-1, ISBN-10: 0-471-64832-9 (CLOTH VOL 3 : alk. paper)
      ISBN-13: 978-0-471-22201-9, ISBN-10: 0-471-22201-1 (CLOTH SET : alk. paper)
      1. Internet–Encyclopedias.   I. Bidgoli, Hossein.
TK5105.875.I57I5466   2003
004.67'8'03–dc21

                                                                    2002155552

Printed in the United States of America

10  9  8  7  6  5  4  3  2  1

To so many fine memories of my mother, Ashraf, my father, Mohammad, and my brother, Mohsen, for their uncompromising belief in the power of education.

# About the Editor-in-Chief

**Hossein Bidgoli, Ph.D.**, is professor of Management Information Systems at California State University. Dr. Bidgoli helped set up the first PC lab in the United States. He is the author of 43 textbooks, 27 manuals and over five dozen technical articles and papers on various aspects of computer applications, information systems and network security, e-commerce and decision support systems published and presented throughout the world. Dr. Bidgoli also serves as the editor-in-chief of *The Internet Encyclopedia* and the *Encyclopedia of Information Systems*.

The *Encyclopedia of Information Systems* was the recipient of one of the *Library Journal's* Best Reference Sources for 2002 and *The Internet Encyclopedia* was recipient of one of the PSP Awards (Professional and Scholarly Publishing), 2004. Dr. Bidgoli was selected as the California State University, Bakersfield's 2001–2002 Professor of the Year.

# Editorial Board

# Contents

## Part 3: Standards and Protocols for Secure Information Transfer

## Volume II: Information Warfare: Social, Legal, and International Issues; and Security Foundations

## Part 1: Information Warfare

# Volume III: Threats, Vulnerabilities, Prevention, Detection, and Management

## Part 1: Threats and Vulnerabilities to Information and Computing Infrastructures

## Part 2: Prevention: Keeping the Hackers and Crackers at Bay

# Part 3: Detection, Recovery, Management, and Policy Considerations

## CONTENTS

# Contributors

**Tarek F. Abdelzhaer**
University of Virginia
*Security and Web Quality of Service*

**Dawn Alexander**
University of Maryland
*Protecting Web Sites*

**Edward Amoroso**
AT&T Laboratories
*Network Attacks*

**Michael R. Anderson**
SCERC
*Computer Forensics—Computer Media Reviews
in Classified Government Agencies*

**Nadeem Ansari**
Wayne State University
*Home Area Networking*

**Amy W. Apon**
University of Arkansas
*Public Network Technologies and Security*

**Onur Ihsan Arsun**
Isik University, Turkey
*Security Insurance and Best Practices*

**Vijay Atluri**
Rutgers University
*Mobile Commerce*

**Pierre Balthazard**
Arizona State University
*Groupware: Risks, Threats, and Vulnerabilities
in the Internet Age*

**William Bard**
The University of Texas, Austin
*Digital Communication*

**William C. Barker**
National Institute of Standards and Technology
*E-Government Security Issues and Measures*

**Kent Belasco**
First Midwest Bank
*Online Retail Banking: Security Concerns, Breaches,
and Controls*

**István Zsolt Berta**
Budapest University of Technology and Economics,
Hungary
*Standards for Product Security Assessment*

**Bhagyavati**
Columbus State University
*E-Mail and Instant Messaging*

**Hossein Bidgoli**
California State University, Bakersfield
*Guidelines for a Comprehensive Security System
Internet Basics*

**Gerald Bluhm**
Tyco Fire & Security
*Patent Law*

**Andrew Blyth**
University of Glamorgan, Pontypridd, UK
*Computer Network Operations (CNO)*

**Robert J. Boncella**
Washburn University
*Secure Sockets Layer (SSL)
Wireless Threats and Attacks*

**Charles Border**
Rochester Institute of Technology
*Client-Side Security*

**Nikita Borisov**
University of California, Berkeley
*WEP Security*

**Noureddine Boudriga**
National Digital Certification Agency and University
of Carthage, Tunisia
*Forensic Computing
IPsec: AH and ESP
Security Policy Guidelines
Server-Side Security*

**Sviatoslav Braynov**
University of Illinois, Springfield
*E-Commerce Vulnerabilities*

**Susan W. Brenner**
University of Dayton School of Law
*Cybercrime and the U.S. Criminal Justice System*

**Roderic Broadhurst**
University of Hong Kong, Hong Kong
*Combating the Cybercrime Threat: Developments
in Global Law Enforcement*

**Christopher L. T. Brown**
Technology Pathways
*Evidence Collection and Analysis Tools*

**Duncan A. Buell**
University of South Carolina
*Number Theory for Information Security
The Advanced Encryption Standard*

**Levente Buttyán**
Budapest University of Technology and Economics,
Hungary
*Standards for Product Security Assessment*

**Jon Callas**
PGP Corporation
*E-Mail Security*

**L. Jean Camp**
Harvard University
*Peer-to-Peer Security*

**Randy Canis**
Greensfelder, Hemker & Gale, P.C.
*Copyright Law*

**Lillian N. Cassel**
Villanova University
*Security and the Wireless Application Protocol*

**Tom S. Chan**
Southern New Hampshire University
*Spyware*

**Steve J. Chapin**
Syracuse University
*Forensic Analysis of Windows Systems*

**Thomas M. Chen**
Southern Methodist University
*Electronic Attacks*

**Hamid Choukri**
Gemplus & University of Bordeaux, France
*Fault Attacks*

**Chao-Hsien Chu**
Pennsylvania State University
*Hacking Techniques in Wired Networks*

**Fred Cohen**
University of New Haven
*The Use of Deception Techniques: Honeypots
and Decoys*

**J. Philip Craiger**
National Center for Forensic Science and
University of Central Florida
*Computer Forensics Procedures
and Methods*
*Law Enforcement and Digital Evidence*

**Lorrie Faith Cranor**
Carnegie Mellon University
*P3P (Platform for Privacy Preferences Project)*

**Marco Cremonini**
University of Milan, Italy
*Contingency Planning Management*
*Network-Based Intrusion Detection Systems*

**Dipankar Dasgupta**
University of Memphis
*The Use of Agent Technology for Intrusion
Detection*

**Magnus Daum**
Ruhr University Bochum, Germany
*Hashes and Message Digests*

**Jaime J. Davila**
Hampshire College
*Digital Divide*

**S. De Capitani di Vimercati**
Università di Milano, Italy
*Access Control: Principles And Solutions*

**Mathieu Deflem**
University of South Carolina
*Law Enforcement and Computer Security
Threats and Measures*

**Lynn A. DeNoia**
Rensselaer Polytechnic Institute
*Wide Area and Metropolitan Area Networks*

**David Dittrich**
University of Washington
*Active Response to Computer Intrusions*
*Hackers, Crackers, and Computer Criminals*

**Hans Dobbertin**
Ruhr University Bochum, Germany
*Hashes and Message Digests*

**Hans-Peter Dommel**
Santa Clara University
*Routers and Switches*

**Matthew C. Elder**
Symantec Corporation
*Electronic Attacks*

**Mohamed Eltoweissy**
Virginia Tech
*Security in Wireless Sensor Networks*

**David Evans**
University of Virginia
*Hostile Java Applets*

**G. E. Evans**
Queen Mary University of London Intellectual
Property Research Institute, UK
*Online Contracts*

**Ray Everett-Church**
PrivacyClue LLC
*Privacy Law and the Internet*
*Trademark Law and the Internet*

**Seth Finkelstein**
SethF.com
*Electronic Speech*
*The Digital Millennium Copyright Act*

**Susanna Frederick Fischer**
Columbus School of Law, The Catholic University
of America
*Internet Gambling*

**Dario V. Forte**
University of Milan, Crema, Italy
*Forensic Analysis of UNIX Systems*

**Allan Friedman**
Harvard University
*Peer-to-Peer Security*

**Song Fu**
Wayne State University
*Mobile Code and Security*

**G. David Garson**
North Carolina State University
*E-Government*

**Karin Geiselhart**
University of Canberra and Australian National
University, Canberra, Australia
*International Security Issues of
E-Government*

**Craig Gentry**
DoCoMo USA Labs
*IBE (Identity-Based Encryption)*

**Michael Gertz**
University of California, Davis
*Database Security*

**Robert Gezelter**
Software Consultant
*Internet E-Mail Architecture*
*OpenVMS Security*

**April Giles**
Independent Consultant
*Protecting Web Sites*

**Julia Alpert Gladstone**
Bryant University
*Global Aspects of Cyberlaw*

**James E. Goldman**
Purdue University
*Firewall Architectures*
*Firewall Basics*

**Nicole Graf**
University of Cooperative Education,
Germany
*Security Architectures*

**Sven Graupner**
Hewlett-Packard Laboratories
*Web Services*

**Robert H. Greenfield**
Computer Consulting
*Security in Circuit, Message, and Packet Switching*

**Steven J. Greenwald**
Independent Information Security Consultant
*S/MIME (Secure MIME)*

**Qijun Gu**
Pennsylvania State University
*Hacking Techniques in Wired Networks*

**Mohsen Guizani**
Western Michigan University
*TCP over Wireless Links*

**Harald Haas**
International University Bremen (IUB),
Germany
*Air Interface Requirements for Mobile Data
Services*

**Mohamed Hamdi**
National Digital Certification Agency, Tunisia
*Forensic Computing*
*Security Policy Guidelines*

**David Harley**
NHS Connecting for Health, UK
*E-Mail Threats and Vulnerabilities*

**Jan Ll. Harris**
Salford University, UK
*Hacktivism*

**Robert W. Heath Jr.**
The University of Texas, Austin
*Digital Communication*

**Peter L. Heinzmann**
University of Applied Sciences, Eastern Switzerland
*Security of Broadband Access Networks*

**Kenneth Einar Himma**
University of Washington
*Active Response to Computer Intrusions*
*Legal, Social, and Ethical Issues of the Internet*
*Hackers, Crackers, and Computer Criminals*

**Chengdu Huang**
University of Virginia
*Security and Web Quality of Service*

**Ali Hushyar**
San Jose State University
*Multilevel Security Models*

**Renato Iannella**
National ICT Australia (NICTA)
*Digital Rights Management*

**Cynthia E. Irvine**
Naval Postgraduate School
*Quality of Security Service: Adaptive Security*
*Security Policy Enforcement*

**Gene Itkis**
Boston University
*Forward Security Adaptive Cryptography: Time
Evolution*

**William K. Jackson**
Southern Oregon University
*E-Education and Information Privacy and Security*

**Charles Jaeger**
Southern Oregon University
*Cyberterrorism and Information Security*
*Spam and the Legal Counter Attacks*

**Sushil Jajodia**
George Mason University
*Intrusion Detection Systems Basics*

**Markus Jakobsson**
Indiana University, Bloomington
*Cryptographic Privacy Protection Techniques*
*Cryptographic Protocols*

**Abbas Jamalipour**
University of Sydney, Australia
*Wireless Internet: A Cellular Perspective*

**Jiwu Jing**
Chinese Academy of Sciences, Beijing, China
*Information Assurance*

**Ari Juels**
RSA Laboratories
*Encryption Basics*

**Jonathan Katz**
University of Maryland
*Symmetric Key Encryption*

**Charlie Kaufman**
Microsoft Corporation
*IPsec: IKE (Internet Key Exchange)*

**Doug Kaye**
IT Conversations
*Web Hosting*

**Rick Kazman**
University of Hawaii, Manoa
*Risk Management for IT Security*

**Wooyoung Kim**
University of Illinois, Urbana-Champaign
*Web Services*

**Nancy J. King**
Oregon State University
*E-Mail and Internet Use Policies*

**Jerry Kindall**
Epok Inc.
*Digital Identity*

**Dominic Kneeshaw**
Independent Consultant, Germany
*Security Architectures*

**David Klappholz**
Stevens Institute of Technology
*Risk Management for IT Security*

**Graham Knight**
University College, London, UK
*Internet Architecture*

**Prashant Krishnamurthy**
University of Pittsburgh
*Wireless Network Standards and Protocol (802.11)*

**Christopher Kruegel**
Technical University, Vienna, Austria
*Host-Based Intrusion Detection*

**Priya Kubher**
Wayne State University
*Home Area Networking*

**Stan Kurkovsky**
Central Connecticut State University
*VPN Architecture*

**Selahattin Kuru**
Isik University, Turkey
*Security Insurance and Best Practices*

**Zenith Y. W. Law**
JustSolve Consulting, Hong Kong
*Fixed-Line Telephone System Vulnerabilities*

**Margarita Maria Lenk**
Colorado State University
*Asset–Security Goals Continuum: A Process for Security*

**Arjen K. Lenstra**
Lucent Technologies Bell Laboratories
and Technische Universiteit Eindhoven
*Key Lengths*

**Albert Levi**
Sabanci University, Turkey
*Digital Certificates*

**Timothy E. Levin**
Naval Postgraduate School
*Quality of Security Service: Adaptive Security*

**John Linn**
RSA Laboratories
*Identity Management*

**Helger Lipmaa**
Cybernetica AS and University of Tartu,
Estonia
*Secure Electronic Voting Protocols*

**Peng Liu**
Pennsylvania State University
*Hacking Techniques in Wired Networks*
*Information Assurance*

**David J. Loundy**
Devon Bank University College of Commerce
*Online Stalking*

**Michele Luglio**
University of Rome Tor Vergata, Italy
*Security of Satellite Networks*

**Chester J. Maciag**
Air Force Research Laboratory
*Forensic Analysis of Windows Systems*

**Normand M. Martel**
Medical Technology Research Corp.
*Medical Records Security*

**Prabhaker Mateti**
Wright State University
*Hacking Techniques in Wireless Networks*
*TCP/IP Suite*

**Cavan McCarthy**
Louisiana State University
*Digital Libraries: Security and Preservation*
*Considerations*

**Patrick McDaniel**
Pennsylvania State University
*Computer and Network Authentication*

**J. McDermott**
Naval Research Laboratory
*The Common Criteria*

**David E. McDysan**
MCI Corporation
*IP-Based VPN*

**Daniel J. McFarland**
Rowan University
*Client/Server Computing: Principles and Security*
*Considerations*

**Matthew K. McGowan**
Bradley University
*EDI Security*

**John D. McLaren**
Murray State University
*Proxy Firewalls*

**A. Meddeb**
National Digital Certification Agency and University
of Carthage, Tunisia
*IPsec: AH and ESP*

**Mark S. Merkow**
University of Phoenix
*E-Commerce Safeguards*

**M. Farooque Mesiya**
Rensselaer Polytechnic Institute
*Mobile IP*

**Pascal Meunier**
Purdue University
*Cracking WEP*
*Software Development and Quality Assurance*

**Mark Michael**
Research in Motion Ltd., Canada
*Physical Security Measures*
*Physical Security Threats*

**Pietro Michiardi**
Institut Eurecom, France
*Ad Hoc Network Security*

**Brent A. Miller**
IBM Corporation
*Bluetooth Technology*

**Refik Molva**
Institut Eurecom, France
*Ad Hoc Network Security*

**Robert K. Moniot**
Fordham University
*Software Piracy*

**Roy Morris**
Capitol College
*Voice-over Internet Protocol (VoIP)*

**Scott Nathan**
Independent Consultant
*Corporate Spying: The Legal Aspects*

**Randall K. Nichols**
The George Washington University
*Wireless Information Warfare*

**Daryle P. Niedermayer**
CGI Group Inc.
*Security in Circuit, Message, and Packet*
*Switching*

**Peng Ning**
North Carolina State University
*Intrusion Detection Systems Basics*

**M. S. Obaidat**
Monmouth University
*Digital Watermarking and Steganography*
*Forensic Computing*
*IPsec: AH and ESP*
*Security Policy Guidelines*

*Server-Side Security*
*Wireless Local Area Networks*
*VPN Basics*
**S. Obeidat**
Arizona State University
*Wireless Local Area Networks*
**Stephan Olariu**
Old Dominion University
*Security in Wireless Sensor Networks*
**G. Massimo Palma**
Università degli Studi di Milano, Italy
*Quantum Cryptography*
**Cynthia Pandolfo**
Villanova University
*Security and the Wireless Application Protocol*
**Raymond R. Panko**
University of Hawaii, Manoa
*Computer Security Incident Response
    Teams (CSIRTs)*
*Digital Signatures and Electronic Signatures*
*Internet Security Standards*
**G. I. Papadimitriou**
Aristotle University, Greece
*VPN Basics*
*Wireless Local Area Networks*
**C. Papazoglou**
Aristotle University, Greece
*VPN Basics*
**S. Paraboschi**
Università di Bergamo, Italy
*Access Control: Principles and Solutions*
**Radia Perlman**
Sun Microsystems Laboratories
*PKI (Public Key Infrastructure)*
**Sebastien Petit**
Gemplus, France
*Smart Card Security*
**Thomas L. Pigg**
Jackson State Community College
*Conducted Communications Media*
**Mark Pollitt**
DigitalEvidencePro
*Law Enforcement and Digital Evidence*
**A. S. Pomportsis**
Aristotle University, Greece
*VPN Basics*
**Daniel N. Port**
University of Hawaii, Manoa
*Risk Management for IT Security*
**Stephanie Porte**
Gemplus, France
*Smart Card Security*
**Dennis M. Powers**
Southern Oregon University
*Cyberlaw: The Major Areas, Development,
    and Information Security Aspects*
**Anupama Raju**
Western Michigan University
*TCP over Wireless Links*
**Jeremy L. Rasmussen**
Sypris Electronics, LLC
*Password Authentication*

**Indrajit Ray**
Colorado State Univesity
*Electronic Payment Systems*
**Julian J. Ray**
University of Redlands
*Business-to-Business Electronic
    Commerce*
**Drummond Reed**
OneName Corporation
*Digital Identity*
**Slim Rekhis**
National Digital Certification Agency and University
    of Carthage, Tunisia
*Server-Side Security*
**Jian Ren**
Michigan State University, East Lansing
*Managing A Network Environment*
**Vladimir V. Riabov**
Rivier College
*SMTP (Simple Mail Transfer Protocol)*
**Marcus K. Rogers**
Purdue University
*Internal Security Threats*
**Pankaj Rohatgi**
IBM T. J Watson Research Center
*Side-Channel Attacks*
**Arnon Rosenthal**
The MITRE Corporation
*Database Security*
**Emilia Rosti**
Università degli Studi di Milano, Italy
*IP Multicast and Its Security*
**Neil C. Rowe**
U.S. Naval Postgraduate School
*Electronic Protection*
**Bradley S. Rubin**
University of St. Thomas
*Public Key Algorithms*
**K. Rudolph**
Native Intelligence, Inc.
*Implementing a Security Awareness
    Program*
**B. Sadoun**
Al-Balqa' Applied University, Jordan
*Digital Watermarking and Steganography*
**Akhil Sahai**
Hewlett-Packard Laboratories
*Web Services*
**Antonio Saitto**
Telespazio, Italy
*Security of Satellite Networks*
**Atul A. Salvekar**
Intel Corporation
*Digital Communication*
**Pierangela Samarati**
Università di Milano, Italy
*Access Control: Principles and Solutions*
*Contingency Planning Management*
**Shannon Schelin**
The University of North Carolina, Chapel
    Hill
*E-Government*

**William T. Schiano**
Bentley College
*Intranets: Principals, Privacy, and Security Considerations*

**Matthew Schmid**
Cigital, Inc.
*Antivirus Technology*

**E. Eugene Schultz**
University of California–Berkeley Lab
*Windows 2000 Security*
*Denial of Service Attacks*

**Mark Shacklette**
The University of Chicago
*UNIX Security*

**P. M. Shankar**
Drexel University
*Wireless Channels*

**J. Eagle Shutt**
University of South Carolina
*Law Enforcement and Computer Security Threats and Measures*

**Nirvikar Singh**
University of California, Santa Cruz
*Digital Economy*

**Robert Slade**
Vancouver Institute for Research into User Security, Canada
*Computer Viruses and Worms*
*Digital Courts, the Law and Evidence*
*Hoax Viruses and Virus Alerts*

**Nigel Smart**
University of Bristol, UK
*Elliptic Curve Cryptography*

**Richard E. Smith**
University of St. Thomas
*Multilevel Security*

**Min Song**
Old Dominion University
*Mobile Devices and Protocols*

**Mike Speciner**
Independent Consultant
*Data Encryption Standard (DES)*

**Richard A. Spinello**
Boston College
*Internet Censorship*

**Lee Sproull**
New York University
*Online Communities*

**Evdoxia Spyropoulou**
Technical Vocational Educational School of Computer Science of Halandri, Greece
*Quality of Security Service: Adaptive Security*

**William Stallings**
Independent Consultant
*Kerberos*
*Operating System Security*

**Mark Stamp**
San Jose State University
*Multilevel Security Models*

**Philip Statham**
CESG, Cheltenham, Gloucestershire, UK
*Issues and Concerns in Biometric IT Security*

**Charles Steinfield**
Michigan State University
*Click-and-Brick Electronic Commerce*
*Electronic Commerce*

**Ivan Stojmenovic**
University of Ottawa, Cananda
*Cellular Networks*

**Robin C. Stuart**
Digital Investigations Consultant
*Digital Evidence*

**M. A. Suhail**
University of Bradford, UK
*Digital Watermarking and Steganography*

**Wayne C. Summers**
Columbus State University
*Local Area Networks*

**Jeff Swauger**
University of Central Florida
*Law Enforcement and Digital Evidence*

**Mak Ming Tak**
Hong Kong University of Science and Technology, Hong Kong
*Fixed-Line Telephone System Vulnerabilities*

**Thomas D. Tarman**
Sandia National Laboratories
*Security for ATM Networks*

**Paul A. Taylor**
University of Leeds, UK
*Hacktivism*

**Dale R. Thompson**
University of Arkansas
*Public Network Technologies and Security*

**Jimi Thompson**
Southern Methodist University
*Electronic Attacks*

**Stephen W. Thorpe**
Neumann College
*Extranets: Applications, Development, Security, and Privacy*

**Amandeep Thukral**
Purdue University
*Key Management*

**Michael Tunstall**
Gemplus & Royal Holloway University, France
*Fault Attacks*
*Smart Card Security*

**Okechukwu Ugweje**
The University of Akron
*Radio Frequency and Wireless Communications Security*

**István Vajda**
Budapest University of Technology and Economics, Hungary
*Standards for Product Security Assessment*

**S. Rao Vallabhaneni**
SRV Professional Publications
*Auditing Information Systems Security*

**Nicko van Someren**
nCipher Plc., UK
*Cryptographic Hardware Security Modules*

**Phil Venables**
Institute of Electrical and Electronics Engineers
*Information Leakage: Detection and
Countermeasures*

**Giovanni Vigna**
Reliable Software Group
*Host-Based Intrusion Detection Systems*

**Linda Volonino**
Canisius College
*Security Middleware*

**Richard P. Volonino**
Canisius College
*Security Middleware*

**Ashraf Wadaa**
Old Dominion University
*Security in Wireless Sensor Networks*

**Blaze D. Waleski**
Fulbright & Jaworski LLP
*The Legal Implications of Information Security:
Regulatory Compliance and Liability*

**Jonathan Wallace**
DeCoMo USA Labs
*Anonymity and Identity on the Internet*

**Siaw-Peng Wan**
Elmhurst College
*Online Retail Banking: Security Concerns, Breaches,
and Controls*

**Yongge Wang**
University of North Carolina, Charlotte
*PKCS (Public-Key Cryptography Standards)*

**John Warren**
University of Texas, San Antonio
*Groupware: Risks, Threats, and Vulnerabilities
in the Internet Age*

**James L. Wayman**
San Jose State University
*Biometric Basics and Biometric Authentication*

**Edgar R. Weippl**
Vienna University of Technology, Austria
*Security in E-Learning*

**Stephen A. Weis**
MIT Computer Science and Artificial Intelligence
Laboratory
*PGP (Pretty Good Privacy)*
*RFID and Security*

**Susanne Wetzel**
Stevens Institute of Technology
*Bluetooth Security*

**A. Justin Wilder**
Telos Corporation
*Linux Security*

**Raymond Wisman**
Indiana University Southeast
*Search Engines: Security, Privacy, and Ethical
Issues*

**Paul L. Witt**
Texas Christian University
*Internet Relay Chat*

**Avishai Wool**
Tel Aviv University, Israel
*Packet Filtering and Stateful Firewalls*

**Cheng-Zhong Xu**
Wayne State University
*Mobile Code and Security*

**Xu Yan**
Hong Kong University of Science and Technology,
Hong Kong
*Fixed-Line Telephone System Vulnerabilities*

**Mustafa Yildiz**
Isik University, Turkey
*Security Insurance and Best Practices*

**Adam L. Young**
Cigital, Inc.
*Trojan Horse Programs*

**Meng Yu**
Monmouth University
*Information Assurance*

**Sherali Zeadally**
Wayne State University
*Home Area Networking*

**Jingyuan Zhang**
University of Alabama
*Cellular Networks*

**Xukai Zou**
Purdue University
*Key Management*
*Public Key Standards: Secure Shell*

**William A. Zucker**
Gadsby Hannah LLP
*Corporate Spying: The Legal Aspects*

# Preface

*The Handbook of Information Security* is the first comprehensive examination of the core topics in the security field. *The Handbook of Information Security*, a 3-volume reference work with 207 chapters and 3300+ pages, is a comprehensive coverage of information, computer, and network security.

**The primary audience** is the libraries of 2-year and 4-year colleges and universities with computer science, MIS, CIS, IT, IS, data processing, and business departments; public, private, and corporate libraries throughout the world; and reference material for educators and practitioners in the information and computer security fields.

**The secondary audience** is a variety of professionals and a diverse group of academic and professional course instructors.

Among the industries expected to become increasingly dependent upon information and computer security and active in understanding the many issues surrounding this important and fast-growing field are: government, military, education, library, health, medical, law enforcement, accounting, legal, justice, manufacturing, financial services, insurance, communications, transportation, aerospace, energy, biotechnology, retail, and utility.

Each volume incorporates state-of-the-art, core information, on computer security topics, practical applications and coverage of the emerging issues in the information security field.

This definitive 3-volume handbook offers coverage of both established and cutting-edge theories and developments in information, computer, and network security.

This handbook contains chapters by global academic and industry experts. This handbook offers the following features:

1) Each chapter follows a format including title and author, outline, introduction, body, conclusion, glossary, cross-references, and references. This format allows the reader to pick and choose various sections of a chapter. It also creates consistency throughout the entire series.

2) The handbook has been written by more than 240 experts and reviewed by more than 1,000 academics and practitioners from around the world. These experts have created a definitive compendium of both established and cutting-edge theories and applications.

3) Each chapter has been rigorously peer-reviewed. This review process assures accuracy and completeness.

4) Each chapter provides extensive online and off-line references for additional readings, which will enable the reader to learn more on topics of special interest.

5) The handbook contains more than 1,000 illustrations and tables that highlight complex topics for further understanding.

6) Each chapter provides extensive cross-references, leading the reader to other chapters related to a particular topic.

7) The handbook contains more than 2,700 glossary items. Many new terms and buzzwords are included to provide a better understanding of concepts and applications.

8) The handbook contains a complete and comprehensive table of contents and index.

9) The series emphasizes both technical as well as managerial, social, legal, and international issues in the field. This approach provides researchers, educators, students, and practitioners with a balanced perspective and background information that will be helpful when dealing with problems related to security issues and measures and the design of a sound security system.

10) The series has been developed based on the current core course materials in several leading universities around the world and current practices in leading computer, security, and networking corporations.

We chose to concentrate on fields and supporting technologies that have widespread applications in the academic and business worlds. To develop this handbook, we carefully reviewed current academic research in the security field from leading universities and research institutions around the world.

Computer and network security, information security and privacy, management information systems, network design and management, computer information systems (CIS), decision support systems (DSS), and electronic commence curriculums, recommended by the Association of Information Technology Professionals (AITP) and the Association for Computing Machinery (ACM) were carefully investigated. We also researched the current practices in the security field carried out by leading security and IT corporations. Our research helped us define the boundaries and contents of this project.

## TOPIC CATEGORIES

Based on our research, we identified nine major topic categories for the handbook.

- Key Concepts and Applications Related to Information Security
- Infrastructure for the Internet, Computer Networks, and Secure Information Transfer
- Standards and Protocols for Secure Information Transfer
- Information Warfare
- Social, Legal, and International Issues

- Foundations of Information, Computer, and Network Security
- Threats and Vulnerabilities to Information and Computing Infrastructures
- Prevention: Keeping the Hackers and Crackers at Bay
- Detection, Recovery, Management, and Policy Considerations

Although these topics are related, each addresses a specific concern within information security. The chapters in each category are also interrelated and complementary, enabling readers to compare, contrast, and draw conclusions that might not otherwise be possible.

Though the entries have been arranged logically, the light they shed knows no bounds. The handbook provides unmatched coverage of fundamental topics and issues for successful design and implementation of a sound security program. Its chapters can serve as material for a wide spectrum of courses such as:

Information and Network Security

Information Privacy

Social Engineering

Secure Financial Transactions

Information Warfare

Infrastructure for Secure Information Transfer

Standards and Protocols for Secure Information Transfer

Network Design and Management

Client/Server Computing

E-commerce

Successful design and implementation of a sound security program requires a thorough knowledge of several technologies, theories, and supporting disciplines. Security researchers and practitioners have had to consult many resources to find answers. Some of these resources concentrate on technologies and infrastructures, some on social and legal issues, and some on managerial concerns. This handbook provides all of this information in a comprehensive, three-volume set with a lively format.

## Key Concepts and Applications Related to Information Security

Chapters in this group examine a broad range of topics. Theories, concepts, technologies, and applications that expose either a user, manager, or an organization to security and privacy issues and/or create such security and privacy concerns are discussed. Careful attention is given to those concepts and technologies that have widespread applications in business and academic environments. These areas include e-banking, e-communities, e-commerce, e-education, and e-government.

## Infrastructure for the Internet, Computer Networks, and Secure Information Transfer

Chapters in this group concentrate on the infrastructure, popular network types, key technologies, and principles for secure information transfer. Different types of communications media are discussed followed by a review of a variety of networks including LANs, MANs, WANs, mobile, and cellular networks. This group of chapters also discusses important architectures for secure information transfers including TCP/IP, the Internet, peer-to-peer, and client/server computing.

## Standards and Protocols for Secure Information Transfer

Chapters in this group discuss major protocols and standards in the security field. This topic includes important protocols for online transactions, e-mail protocols, Internet protocols, IPsec, and standards and protocols for wireless networks emphasizing 802.11.

## Information Warfare

This group of chapters examines the growing field of information warfare. Important laws within the United States criminal justice system, as they relate to cybercrime and cyberterrorism, are discussed. Other chapters in this group discuss cybercrime, cyberfraud, cyber stalking, wireless information warfare, electronic attacks and protection, and the fundamentals of information assurance.

## Social, Legal, and International Issues

Chapters in this group explore social, legal, and international issues relating to information privacy and computer security. Digital identity, identity theft, censorship, and different types of computer criminals are also explored. The chapters in this group also explain patent, trademark, and copyright issues and offer guidelines for protecting intellectual properties.

## Foundations of Information, Computer, and Network Security

These chapters cover four different but complementary areas including encryption, forensic computing, operating systems and the common criteria and the principles for improving the security assurance.

## Threats and Vulnerabilities to Information and Computing Infrastructures

The chapters in this group investigate major threats to, and vulnerabilities of, information and computing infrastructures in wired and wireless environments. The chapters specifically discuss intentional, unintentional, controllable, partially controllable, uncontrollable, physical, software and hardware threats and vulnerabilities.

## Prevention: Keeping the Hackers and Crackers at Bay

The chapters in this group present several concepts, tools, techniques, and technologies that help to protect information, keep networks secure, and keep the hackers and computer criminals at bay. Some of the topics discussed include physical security measures; measures for protecting client-side, server-side, database, and medical records; different types of authentication techniques; and preventing security threats to e-commerce and e-mail transactions.

## Detection, Recovery, Management, and Policy Considerations

Chapters in this group discuss concepts, tools, and techniques for detection of security breaches, offer techniques and guidelines for recovery, and explain principles for managing a network environment. Some of the topics highlighted in this group include intrusion detection, contingency planning, risk management, auditing, and guidelines for effective security management and policy implementation.

## Acknowledgments

Many specialists have helped to make the handbook a resource for experienced and not-so-experienced readers. It is to these contributors that I am especially grateful. This remarkable collection of scholars and practitioners has distilled their knowledge into a fascinating and enlightening one-stop knowledge base in information, computer, and network security that "talks" to readers. This has been a massive effort, as well as a most rewarding experience. So many people have played a role, it is difficult to know where to begin.

I would like to thank the members of the editorial board for participating in the project and for their expert advice on selection of topics, recommendations of authors, and review of the materials. Many thanks to the more than 1,000 reviewers who provided their advice on improving the coverage, accuracy, and comprehensiveness of these materials.

I thank my senior editor, Matt Holt, who initiated the idea of the handbook. Through a dozen drafts and many reviews, the project got off the ground and then was managed flawlessly by Matt and his professional team. Many thanks to Matt and his team for keeping the project focused and maintaining its lively coverage.

Tamara Hummel, editorial coordinator, assisted the contributing authors and me during the initial phases of development. I am grateful for all her support. When it came time for the production phase, the superb Wiley production team took over. Particularly, I want to thank Deborah Schindlar, senior production editor. I am grateful for all her hard work. I thank Michelle Patterson, our marketing manager, for her impressive marketing campaign launched on behalf of the handbook.

Last, but not least, I want to thank my wonderful wife, Nooshin, and my two children, Mohsen and Morvareed, for being so patient during this venture. They provided a pleasant environment that expedited the completion of this project. Mohsen and Morvareed assisted me in sending out thousands of e-mail messages to authors and reviewers. Nooshin was a great help in designing and maintaining the authors' and reviewers' databases. Their efforts are greatly appreciated. Also, my two sisters, Azam and Akram, provided moral support throughout my life. To this family, any expression of thanks is insufficient.

Hossein Bidgoli
California State University, Bakersfield

# Guide to The Handbook of Information Security

*The Handbook of Information Security* is a comprehensive coverage of the relatively new and very important field of information, computer, and network security. This reference work consists of three separate volumes and 207 different chapters on various aspects of this field. Each chapter in the handbook provides a comprehensive overview of the selected topic, intended to inform a broad spectrum of readers, ranging from computer and security professionals and academicians to students to the general business community.

This guide is provided to help the reader easily locate information throughout *The Handbook of Information Security*. It explains how the information within it can be located.

## Organization

This is organized for maximum ease of use, with the chapters arranged logically in three volumes. While one can read individual volumes (or articles) one will get the most out of the handbook by becoming conversant with all three volumes.

## Table of Contents

A complete table of contents of the entire handbook appears in the front of each volume. This list of chapter titles represents topics that have been carefully selected by the editor-in-chief, Dr. Hossein Bidgoli, and his colleagues on the editorial board.

## Index

A subject index for each individual volume is located at the end of each volume.

## Chapters

The author's name and affiliation are displayed at the beginning of the chapter.

All chapters in the handbook are organized in the same format:

**Title and author**
**Outline**
**Introduction**
**Body**
**Conclusion**
**Glossary**
**Cross-References**
**References**

## Outline

Each chapter begins with an outline that provides a brief overview of the chapter, as well as highlighting important subtopics. For example, the chapter "Internet Basics" includes sections for Information Superhighway and the World Wide Web, Domain Name Systems, Navigational Tools, Search Engines, and Directories. In addition, second-level and third- level headings will be found within the chapter.

## Introduction

Each chapter begins with an introduction that defines the topic under discussion and summarized the chapter, in order to give the reader a general idea of what is to come.

## Body

The body of the chapter fills out and expands upon items covered in the outline.

## Conclusion

The conclusion provides a summary of the chapter, highlighting issues and concepts that are important for the reader to remember.

## Glossary

The glossary contains terms that are important to an understanding of the chapter and that may be unfamiliar to the reader. Each term is defined in the context of the particular chapter in which it is used. Thus the same term may be defined in two or more chapters with the detail of the definition varying slightly from one chapter to another. The handbook includes approximately 2,700 glossary terms. For example, the chapter "Internet Basics" includes the following glossary entries:

**Extranet** A secure network that uses the Internet and Web technology to connect two or more intranets of trusted business partners, enabling business-to-business, business-to-consumer, consumer-to-consumer, and consumer-to-business communications.

**Intranet** A network within the organization that uses Web technologies (TCP/IP, HTTP, FTP, SMTP, HTML, XML, and its variations) for collecting, storing, and disseminating useful information throughout the organization.

## Cross-References

All chapters have cross-references to other chapters that contain further information on the same topic. They appear at the end of the chapter, preceding the references. The cross-references indicate related chapters that can be consulted for further information on the same topic. The handbook contains more than 1,400 cross-references in all. For example, the chapter "Computer Viruses and Worms" has the following cross references:

Hackers, Crackers and Computer Criminals, Hoax Viruses and Virus Alerts, Hostile Java Applets, Spyware, Trojan Horse Programs.

## References

The references in this handbook are for the benefit of the reader, to provide references for further research on the given topic. Review articles and research papers that are important to an understanding of the topic are also listed. The references typically consist of a dozen to two dozen entries, and do not include all material consulted by the author in preparing the chapter.

# PART 1

# Threats and Vulnerabilities to Information and Computing Infrastructures

# Internal Security Threats

Marcus K. Rogers, *Purdue University*

## INTRODUCTION

The threat of attacks on the information systems of businesses and institutions has become such a persistent issue that we have almost come to accept it as part of doing business in the new digital age (Carnegie-Mellon, 2004; Conte, 2003). Granted, risk has always been inherent in any business enterprise. What is unusual is the defeatist attitude that has emerged that assumes we cannot do anything about information security threats or, more precisely, risks. We have been led to believe that the most serious threat comes from the stereotypical young socially dysfunctional male sitting in front of the family computer until the wee hours of the morning wrecking havoc on governments and the corporate world[1] (Denning, 1999; Rogers & Ogloff, 2003). The media also paint a dismal picture regarding the current state of information security preparedness. Vendors bombard us with marketing perpetuating the myth that we are helpless at the hands of these marauders—unless, of course, we buy their product. It is no wonder we feel overwhelmed and somewhat despondent. The truth is much more positive than the bleak picture painted by those with hidden and sometimes not-so-hidden agendas. As other chapters state, we can employ numerous strategies and security controls to reduce the risks to an acceptable level.

A crucial factor to consider in our efforts to combat or coexist in the digital world is that insiders account for the lion's share of the risk-faced-by businesses and institutions. The threat from inside an organization has historically accounted for the majority of the loss suffered by businesses (Conte, 2003; Messmer, 2003). The insider threat is not an artifact of technology or even the Internet. The banking industry is a prime example of a sector that has been plagued by internal fraud and theft since the beginning of its existence. Corporate espionage has relied on insiders to gain access to trade secrets and other

intellectual property long before computer systems entered the business environment.

This chapter closely examines internal security threats and attempts to shed light on how to deal with the associated risk. The thesis is that dealing with internal threats requires a sociotechnical approach. Despite assertions to the contrary by various authors, internal threats, or information security in general, are as much a sociological–psychological cultural issue as it is a technical problem. Simply throwing more money at technical solutions or drafting more draconian policies will not solve the problem; it may, in fact, exacerbate the issue. We must delve into the hazy world of sociology, criminology, and psychology and, using this as a filter, develop practical risk mitigation strategies using all of the domains of information security and assurance as discussed in the other chapters of this book (e.g., technical, administrative–operational, environmental–physical). A good portion of this chapter is devoted to providing some insight into the motivations and characteristics of malicious insiders. Once we understand what makes these individuals tick, we can start determining effective strategies to deal with the problem and, it is hoped, mitigate some of the risk. I begin the discussion by defining the term *internal* and then examine how big the problem is, who are the internal threats, what motivates these individuals to breach the trust of their employers, and what mitigation strategies can be used to reduce the risk to an acceptable level. A basic framework of useful strategies is also provided to assist organizations kick-start their efforts in dealing with this real but manageable issue. The reader needs to be forewarned that there is no panacea for internal threats; due diligence and a reasonable security posture across all domains are still required.

### Operational Definition

The word *insider* can have multiple definitions. According to Webster's Dictionary, an insider is defined as "an officer of a corporation or others who have access to private information about the corporation's operations, especially

---

[1] I purposely use masculine pronouns in this chapter because hacking is still a male-dominated activity.

information relating to profitability." Definitions related to malicious insiders, however, can be thought of in both legal terms and more technical terms. Law enforcement tends to define insiders based on a violation of trust in the business sense, whereas technologists focus on threat agents that by virtue of their position, have trust (e.g., users, system administrators) and then choose to abuse that trust (Nuemann, 1999). For the purposes of this chapter, I combine aspects of both the legal and technical definitions. A good starting definition was presented at the Rand 2000 workshop on insider threats to information systems: "Any authorized user who performs unauthorized actions" (Anderson et al., 2000, p. 21). This definition is more suited to the information technology (IT) domain in general and to the risk analysis and risk mitigation process specifically. The workshop also provided a working definition of insider threat: "Any authorized user who performs unauthorized actions that result in loss of control of computational assets" (Anderson et al., 2000, p. 21). To be relevant to the nonmilitary, nonintelligence community as well, I add "actions resulting in unauthorized disclosure of information, and actions negatively impacting the confidentiality, authenticity, and availability of information systems and assets." The operational definition of a malicious insider for our discussion thus becomes:

> Any authorized user who performs unauthorized actions that result in loss of control of computational assets, or actions resulting in unauthorized disclosure of information, and actions negatively impacting the confidentiality, authenticity, and availability of information systems and information assets.

Given the multitude of possible threat agents in the IT realm, the definition sets the parameters for our discussion and ensures that we are comparing the proverbial apples to apples. As Shaw, Ruby, and Post (1998) indicated, the terms *insider* and *internal* depend on the context of the employment relationship. Depending on the relationship, an insider could be a consultant hired to perform some temporary duty, a permanent contract worker, a part-time or full-time employee, or even an ex-employee. The term *insider* or *internal* is best thought of as referring to a continuum of possible relationships that share the common trait of entering into a trust relationship with an organization in which there is some assumed or implied loyalty based on being hired or entering into a contractual relationship. Our operational or working definition is further constrained by the criteria that the individual intentionally harmed or tried to harm the organization. This places errors and omissions out of scope for our discussion.[2]

## EXTENT OF THE PROBLEM

Historically, insider threats have plagued the business environment and as such are not unique to IT or the use of IT in the current business environment (Mesmer, 2003).

Although most organizations, especially the financial industry, have employed preventative and detective controls such as background checks, separation of duty, double-entry bookkeeping, and so on, internal fraud, abuse, and malfeasance are still significant threats and pressing issues that have by no means been sufficiently mitigated (Department of Defense, 2000; Randazzo, Keeny, Cappell, & Moore, 2004).

To have any kind of meaningful discussion regarding insider threats, it is important that we try to get a handle on the scope and magnitude of the problem. Unfortunately, this is easier said than done. Obtaining meaningful and accurate statistics is problematic in the area of information assurance and security in general. Despite Computer Security Institute/Federal Bureau of Investigation (CSI/FBI) surveys and studies conducted by consulting companies and vendors, we do not have reliable or valid statistics. The annualized impact of information security breaches has been reported as ranging from $300 million to more than $12 billion. The majority of the studies that are available bemoan the fact that they either have a small sample size in comparison to the population of interest (e.g., 500 respondent companies) or very poor response rates (i.e., less than 10%). This seriously undermines the ability to generalize the findings to the population or even a specific industry.

It would seem that the majority of those organizations that have suffered losses due to information security breaches are not overly eager to either make the fact public or even admit it to any third-party despite assurances of anonymity and confidentiality (Gordon, Loeb, Lucyshyn, & Richardson, 2004). The FBI and the National Information Protection Center (NIPC) have gone on record stating that the majority of successful attacks go unreported.

If we have a lack of reliable statistics, how do we go about estimating the size of the problem? One logical strategy is to look at trends over time. Using this strategy, we can use studies that despite other shortcomings have been conducted over a reasonable period of time. The CSI and the San Francisco field office of the FBI have been conducting a computer crime and information security survey since 1995. The latest survey, despite finding a drop in the volume of attacks and the amount of financial loss (total reported for 2003/2004 was $141,496,560), found that attacks were evenly split between those originating from the outside and those from the inside (Gordon et al., 2004). This trend of insider attacks has been maintained, more or less, over the last 7 years. Whitman (2003) reported that in his study, the insider abuse of Internet access was ranked second only to virus attacks. A recent United Kingdom Department of Trade and Industry/ Price Waterhouse Coopers survey reported that, on average, large businesses suffered one information security attack per week, with insider abuse accounting for 64% of the known breeches (Helsby, 2003).

Most studies are quick to point out that contrary to the commonly held notion, the outsider accounts for at least 50% of the attacks. This assertion requires further scrutiny. Although respondents are able to provide numbers related to attacks, it is not clear whether a simple port scan is included in the raw total provided. It is also unclear

---

[2] Although errors and omission are serious and costly problems, they are dealt with in other chapters.

whether the respondents have the ability to accurately monitor insider abuses or attacks because the majority of their security controls are outward facing (e.g., demilitarized zone [DMZ] firewalls, border intrusion detection systems). The postmortem resulting from the distributed DoS attacks in early 2002 revealed that if organizations had been monitoring information leaving their networks, they would have been able to detect the presence of zombie systems and thus prevented or at least drastically reduced the impact that these attacks had on the Internet and other businesses.

We also need to differentiate between sheer numbers of attacks and the actual negative impact of the events. Studies have concluded that insider attacks, although less in volume, have a far greater economic impact on the organization. An FBI study determined that the average cost for an outside attack was $56,000, whereas the cost from an insider attack was $2.5 million. Intuitively this makes sense; malicious insiders know where the "treasures" are. Depending on their current or former role, they have or had more access privileges than someone external to the company. They may also know more about the infrastructure's strengths and weaknesses, thus increasing the likelihood of the attack being successful. The literature on traditional white-collar crime also supports the idea that insider incidents are more costly than outsider criminal activity (Bishop, 2004).

Other studies have indicated that employees in general are the greatest risk faced by most organizations. The American Society for Industrial Security (ASIS) has concluded from its studies that malicious insiders pose the most significant risk to businesses (Verton, 2003). A study conducted in 2003 by Information Technology Association reported that 90% of workers would tell a stranger their password in return for receiving a free pen (Wade, 2004). Another study conducted in England found that 70% of the 200 workers approached at the subway stations verbally gave their passwords to a stranger in exchange for a candy bar (Wade, 2004).

It is clear that insider abuse and malfeasance is very costly to businesses and organizations. The insider threat accounts for a significant portion of today's business risk and, as indicated by the various studies, can seriously undermine consumer and shareholder confidence.

## CHARACTERISTICS AND MOTIVATIONS

Simply recognizing that insider threats are a serious problem is not sufficient if we are to deal with risk effectively. To mitigate the risk, we must understand that we are dealing with a social–psychological phenomenon as much as a technical issue. We need to gain some insight into who these malicious insiders are, what makes them tick, why they choose to betray the trust of their employers, which if any patterns of behavior are common, and so on. Once we gain insight into the personality characteristics and traits, we can then use this knowledge to develop effective risk mitigation strategies. As Sun Tzu indicated in the sixth century B.C., to be successful in battle, we must understand the enemy (Tzu, 1983).

It needs to be made clear that personality traits and characteristics are potential risk factors, and the mere fact that an individual possess a "risky" trait does not in and of itself mean they are a criminal or will become a criminal. Psychology is an inexact science at best; although human resources (HR) prescreening procedures and processes often look for flagged characteristics, it would be unethical and foolish to deny someone employment or access based solely on the results of these tests. It would be equally unwise, however, to ignore completely the body of research that has concluded that there is a positive correlation between these "at-risk traits" and deviance. Therefore, a balance between ethical treatment, common sense, and good management practices is required.

Unfortunately, there have only been one or two published studies on IT malicious insiders. The most referenced study is that by Shaw et al. (1998). This study focused on individuals whose intent was to cause some damage to the organization after they were already hired. The study concluded that there was no generic malicious insider typology. The malicious insiders ranged from disgruntled employees or ex-employees who acted out of anger and revenge to actual "moles" planted to conduct industrial espionage on behalf of a competitor or foreign national government (Shaw et al., 1998). The study went on to develop a taxonomy of insiders that highlighted the intent and assumed motivation of the insiders.

Despite the various types of insiders identified, several common risk factors were identified. The research concluded that individuals attracted to information and computer technology careers often:

1. were introverted,
2. had difficulty with interpersonal skills,
3. displayed addictivelike attachments to technology,
4. had loose ethical boundaries and a diminished sense of loyalty,
5. had an unrealistic sense of entitlement (narcissism),
6. exhibited a lack of empathy, and
7. expressed anger toward authority.

The authors cautioned that many of these individual traits are fairly common in the general population as well (e.g., introversion) and that the characteristics are only risk factors indicating the potential or proneness to deviant behavior. These risk factors, when combined with certain other variables (e.g., work stress, personal relationship stress, money problems), increased the probability that the individual would act inappropriately and attack the systems or technology of their employers (Shaw et al., 1998). The mere presence of these traits does not indicate that someone is a criminal or deviant.

The study further related that some of the insider attacks were motivated by greed and financial gain, but these were often combined with other factors and rarely occurred in isolation (Shaw et al., 1998). The study unveiled a rather complex relationship between risk factors possessed by individuals in the IT industry, environmental variables and stressors, poor management practices, and insecure internal IT infrastructures. These factors together make up a critical path for insider attacks. This critical path has many junctures at which an observant manager can intervene and possibly head off an attack. As the authors of the study concluded, technical solutions alone will not address the issue of insider attacks because this is a social–psychological and managerial problem. The solution therefore lies in better management awareness of the dangerous insider warning signs and employee assistance programs that allow employees to better deal with stressors.

Other studies, although not focusing specifically on insiders, have concluded that individuals engaging in deviant computer behaviors in general have significantly different characteristics than the noncomputer deviant public. In studies focusing on self-reported computer crime, it was concluded that computer criminals had significantly higher amoral dishonest tendencies than the general public, were more introverted, were less likely to make moral decisions based on social norms, and were less open to experience (i.e., more rigid thinking) (Rogers, Smoak, & Jia, 2004).

The study, although exploratory, does indicate that the computer underground community has some discriminating personality characteristics. The findings regarding the moral decision process (Rogers et al., 2004) and the diminished sense of empathy and loyalty (Shaw et al., 1998) are interesting. As the workforce in IT becomes increasingly transient, reciprocal loyalty between the employee and the employer are negatively affected. We no longer expect to join an organization upon graduation and remain with that company until we retire. An IT professional in today's environment is lucky to remain with the same organization for 2 years or more. This constant uncertainty has lead to many professionals taking on the consultant mind-set of working for themselves with 1- to 2-year contracts. This mentality leads to an attitude of looking out for number one, with little or no concern to the well-being of other employees or the company. As Shaw et al. (1998) indicated, this lack of loyalty is a serious risk factor. The transient professional phenomenon also exacerbates the lack of empathy common in some IT professionals. The finding that hackers also use less social norms when weighing the moral correctness of some choice or behavior only increases the potential of the other risk factors (Rogers et al., 2004).

### Insiders versus Outsiders

There are certain characteristics inherent to an insider that differentiates them from outside attackers (Wood, 2000). By examining these differences, it becomes clear why malicious insiders are such a risk and why internal threats have a high impact. By default, insiders are trusted; they are already on our systems and usually within or behind most of technical security controls. They usually have some type of authority on the systems they plan to attack. In some cases, this authority is highly privileged (e.g., systems administration). This authority allows the insider either to abuse that privilege or gain higher privileges through some means (e.g., social engineering, shoulder surfing, sniffers, and so on).

Insiders possess characteristics or attributes that not only differentiate them from other types of threat agents but that also increase the impact and likelihood of success of their attack (e.g., trusted accounts, access to systems).

These attributes are grouped into access, knowledge, privileges, skills, risk, tactics, motivation, and process (Wood, 2000). The attribute of knowledge is important; insiders have the potential to be very knowledgeable regarding the systems they wish to attack. This knowledge can include information related to documentation, standards, security controls, policies, backdoors, as well as the location of sensitive or business-critical information. Armed with this kind of knowledge, the impact and the chances of conducting a successful attack are greatly increased (Wood, 2000).

Wood (2000) hypothesized that insiders also have skills directly related to the systems that they target. In most cases, the insiders go after information contained on systems that they are familiar with or have some basic skills on. This restriction of attacking within their domain of expertise or confidence provides a starting point for investigating insider attacks. If the attack is directed at only a subset of a much larger pool of systems, this may be an indication of an insider. This restricted attack domain is very unlike outside attackers who tend to use automated attack tools that target multiple operating system and application vulnerabilities and are not tied to the domain of expertise of the actual attacker.

Insiders are thought to operate alone to reduce the risk of being caught (Wood, 2000). This characterization may be valid for certain classes of insiders, but in some instances the insider is reacting emotionally, and the risk of being caught does not factor into the thought process. The more rational inside attacker (e.g., corporate espionage, greed motivated) may be more risk adverse, but without more research, this is just speculation.

The tactics used by insiders varies considerably and are tied to the motivation of the attacker (Wood, 2000). These motivations include greed, revenge, espionage, and ego stroking. Using tactics to determine the source of attack can be tricky because the motivations are similar to those possessed by outside attackers. Tactics need to be looked at in the overall context of the attack and not viewed in isolation from the other data collected.

Once an individual decides to launch an attack, the method is similar to that of outside attackers, except that less time is spent enumerating systems and potential targets. The insider, due to his inside knowledge of the internal network, usually has a target predetermined and launches into the attack with only a minimal amount of presurveillance. Wood (2004) argued that the insider uses a predictable process of target identification, operational planning, and finally the attack. Research, on the other hand, indicates that most of the identification and planning occurs over an extended interval of time while the individual rehearses the attack mentally. This extended time frame may differentiate the insider from the outsider who usually works within a tighter time frame; in some cases, the time from system enumeration to attack is within minutes.

An overlooked characteristic of insider attacks is that once the source of an attack has been identified as being internal, the insider can be more easily arrested and prosecuted than an outsider attack. The insider is usually physically present. The same luxury does not apply with outsiders who may be geographically distant from the victim or, in some cases, citizens of countries hostile to the victim's country or residents of countries with little or no cyber crime laws. These factors make the prosecution of external attackers much more difficult. The fact that insiders are usually part of the staff allows for more successful intervention and mitigation strategies (Shaw et al., 1998).

# INSIDER TYPOLOGY

To appreciate fully the risk presented by insiders, it is necessary to break the group into subcategories. The choice of exact categories is somewhat arbitrary. For the purposes of this chapter, I use the following:

- Disgruntled employees
- Hackers
- Criminals (organized and individual)
- Spies (corporate and foreign national)
- Terrorists (foreign and domestic)

These are somewhat fluid categories and are not consider mutually exclusive. In some cases, an individual may migrate between two or more groups during his tenure with an organization (e.g., hackers to disgruntled employee).

## Disgruntled Employees

Although no current systematic studies regarding the actual number or impact of attacks on IT systems have been undertaken (at least none have been published in open sources), there are a plethora of media reports from which to draw. The Computer Crime and Intellectual Property Section (CCIPS) of the U.S. Department of Justice, which is in charge of the federal prosecution of computer crimes, keeps a publicly available database of current cases. This database lists various details about the cases: the relationship of the accused to the victim, whether it is a person or organization, dollars lost, target (e.g., private, public, or public safety), and type of perpetrator (e.g., juvenile, group, or international). According to the CCIPS, there were five cases between 2000 and 2004 in which the suspect was classified as a disgruntled employee with total losses of more than $13 million, and 16 cases that were classified as insider attacks in general (Department of Justice, 2004).

The generic disgruntled employee is the most common type of an inside attacker (Anderson et al., 2000; Department of Justice, 2004). The category covers current employees, ex-employees, contractors, and consultants. As Shaw et al. (1998) indicated, the disgruntled employee also causes a considerable amount of damage. I use the term *generic* here to indicate that the insider is primarily motivated by anger and frustration and seeks revenge on the employer or former employer. The primary motivation is not financial, although causing the employer or ex-employer a significant amount of direct and indirect financial loss plays into the revenge scenario. These individuals already have the trust of the organization, accounts on the systems they attack, and they know what IT assets are most business critical. As stated previously, these factors cause these attacks to be the most costly both economically and from a public relations perspective. It is an interesting phenomenon that the public seems more sympathetic to an organization that was victimized by an external attacker than by an attack from someone internal.

The key element with this group is that the individual feels resentment toward the organization whether that resentment is well founded or not. With the recent trend of downsizing, offshoring of technology-related jobs, and lack of long-term job security, the number of disgruntled employees is expected to increase and accordingly so does the risk of revenge attacks. As research has indicated, stress, whether personal or job related, is a critical factor in insider attack chain of events. A recent survey indicated that the majority of IT employees are dissatisfied with their jobs and uncertain about their job future (Glen, 2003). This creates a large pool of potential attackers.

The nature of the relationship between the attacker and the victim, employee and employer, makes it difficult to protect against this type of attacker. The key here is the word *difficult*, not impossible, as I discuss in the mitigation strategies section.

## Hackers

The category of *hacker* refers to individuals internal to an organization who have or are sympathetic to the hacker mentality or ethos. This mentality is characterized by a disregard for convention and rules, loose ethical boundaries, ambiguous morality, disregard for private property, and an innate curiosity (Gordon & Ma, 2003; Rogers et al., 2004). These individuals believe that rules do not apply to them and that there should be no restrictions on what information is available to them. They also believe that information, regardless of its level of business sensitivity, should be shared with the outside world, especially with their hacking friends (Shaw et al., 1998).

Studies indicate that greed, revenge, or monetary considerations are not this group's primary motivator. The hacker need not be stressed or disgruntled to carry out an attack, although this can compound the situation, causing the attacks to be more reckless or damaging. The primary need here is for ego stroking or the satiation of innate curiosity. This is coupled with a disdain for authority.

Many individuals in the hacker group have access to the latest attack tools and information on system vulnerabilities and exploits. Armed with these weapons, the internal network becomes their playground or test environment, without much thought to the direct or collateral damage that they might inflict (e.g., DoS attacks, database corruption).

Hackers may inadvertently expose an organization to the risk of outsider attacks as well. Posturing and one-upmanship are common behaviors within the hacker culture. Bragging or taunting by an internal hacker can cause external hackers to retaliate by attacking the internal hacker's source location (i.e., domain or ISP address). The internal hacker may also divulge, intentionally or unintentionally, an organization's vulnerabilities to the outside world while in chat rooms or messaging sessions. Once these vulnerabilities are known, the likelihood that an organization will be attacked increases

(Gordon & Ma, 2003). The hacker may set up a "playground" or "sandboxes" where his fellow outside hackers may play to prove their skills or impress other hackers, thus becoming a member of the in crowd. Having unauthorized or unknown individuals on an internal network or sensitive systems is a bad situation because these individuals now have a toehold inside the organization, and this can be used to wreck havoc internally or as a launching pad for attacking other organizations, sites, and systems.

Although the primary risk is damage inflicted by the hackers themselves, a secondary risk from this group is the liability incurred if these individuals conduct attacks against other parties while on company time or using an organization's systems. This type of activity can result in the victim suing both the individual and that individual's employer. With more serious attacks, computer equipment used by the hacker but belonging to the company can be seized by law enforcement. Although there are no hard numbers to point to, it is assumed that the economic and public relations impact of this secondary risk is serious. Media headlines and anecdotal evidence support this contention.

Interestingly, reported cases of insider hackers have revealed that many of these individuals were terminated from previous jobs because of their behavior and irresponsible attitude toward information assets and data. This fact was unknown to their current employer despite having conducted background checks and speaking with references prior to hiring the individual. The importance of proper employment screening is discussed in the mitigation section.

## Criminals

This category has two subgroupings, petty criminals and professional criminals. Petty criminals are individuals who display criminal behavior or intent but do not derive the majority of their livelihood from criminal activities. Professional criminals derive the majority of their income from their criminal activities and, in some cases, have ties back to organized or quasi-organized crime. The fact that a criminal element exists within our organizations should come as no surprise to anyone. As stated earlier, fraud, embezzlement, murder, larceny, and other crimes have been part of the business environment for decades. Computers, databases, and the Internet are merely tools used by these individuals to assist them in their criminal endeavors (Post, Shaw, & Ruby, 1998; Rogers & Ogloff, 2003).

Petty criminals take advantage of opportunities that present themselves at the workplace and do not usually join an organization with the intent to steal from them. Once employed, they take advantage of lax security and opportunities to conduct criminal activities. The recently released U.S. Secret Service CERT/CC study on insider threats indicated that with insider attacks against financial institutions, 81% of attacks were planned in advance, or someone else had fore knowledge that the attack was coming (e.g., friends, family, coworkers; Randazzo et al., 2004).

Petty criminals generally tend to take advantage of opportunities that arise. Given the overall lack of security controls inside most companies, numerous "opportunities" present themselves. These include physical access to money, negotiables, and classified or business sensitive data, as well as technological opportunities (e.g., unsecured databases and transaction logs). This group's timing of attacks and criminal activity may have some loose association with environmental variables such as general stress in the work environment, pending layoffs, or corporate restructuring, but the fact that these conditions lead to opportunities to commit crime is believed to be more important than the actual stress itself.

Professional criminals join an organization with criminal intent in mind. These individuals target companies that they have preselected as victims. The goal for these individuals is to steal assets, money, credit card numbers, intellectual property, and, a more recent trend, personal information for identity theft to sell on the black market. Post et al. (1998) referred to this group as career criminals and indicated that they are cold and calculating and that their actions are not correlated with any perceived wrongs against them by the organization.

It is speculated that organized crime has a presence inside of many strategic companies. This speculation does not take any great stretch of the imagination because with any good business organization, organized crime would be remiss if it did not take advantage of new technologies and opportunities. Although exact statistics on organized crime's infiltration are unknown, the law enforcement community spends a great deal of its time and money on this problem (Department of Homeland Security [DHS], 2003). The increase in virus and worm activity in the past few years has fueled speculation that organized crime in Russia and other Eastern European countries may be at the source. The DHS has issued several advisories hinting at the link of organized crime and virus activity. These advisories warn companies to be aware of concerted attacks against key industry leaders such as Microsoft. The U.S. National Counterintelligence Executive, which heads up all U.S. national counterintelligence activities, has publicly discussed the threat of IT insiders with links to organized crime groups.

## Spies

Criminals, in the traditional sense, are not the only groups with which organizations need to be concerned; corporate- and state-sponsored espionage is a very real problem (Rosner, 2001). As with the other types of criminal activity discussed thus far, incidents of foreign governments and other companies spying on competitors, enemies, and allies are not new. The aircraft manufacturing and atomic energy sectors have historically been prime targets for countries trying to gain either an economic or strategic advantage. Several countries are on record as "spying" on foreign business people entering their countries.

The U.S. Department of Energy (DOE) has been a large target for Chinese spies in the past. In many of the reported cases, operatives were placed inside the DOE in research-related positions. These insiders gathered information and then leaked it back to their respective handlers or fled the United States all together. The use of moles or insiders is not restricted to any particular business sector or industry. Even the FBI has been victimized by spies among its ranks, who have sold classified information to foreign governments.

The motivation for this group is varied; it may be patriotic, financial, or revenge, for example. Government organizations have exerted a great deal of effort lately to identify risk models of traits and characteristics related to IT personnel becoming a risk to national security. Both the U.S. Secret Service and the Department of Defense have conducted studies on the social–psychological traits of high-risk insiders. These studies have corroborated the findings of Shaw et al. (1998).

Historical precedent in the IT industry indicates that espionage is a real threat. Corporate espionage and the gray area of competitive intelligence took advantage of several of the dot-com companies' unique business models and assets during the boom of 1999–2001. The heavy reliance on intellectual assets or property as opposed to tangible assets made technology-related companies prime targets. Intellectual property and trade secrets were the lifeblood of these businesses, many not having any real tangible assets for venture capitalists or investors to value them by once an initial public offering was made. Most valuations during this period were based solely on the intellectual property of the employees or owners.

A recent article in *Labor Law Journal* stressed the significant risk related to loss of trade secrets due to both foreign and domestic espionage (Kovach, Pruett, Samuels, & Duvall, 2004). The authors indicated that the most common threat is employees who take trade secrets with them to a competitor when leaving an organization. This can occur by individuals physically taking something, but in most cases, it is the knowledge they have acquired while employed by the company that is of value. In many high-profile legal battles, one party has accused the other of purposely hiring away individuals or teams of individuals to gain access to the competitor's intellectual property or trade secrets. The issue of insiders is so great that *American Banking Journal* has released several checklists to assist banks in dealing with the threat of insiders divulging proprietary customer information and intellectual property to hackers and competitors.

The competitive intelligence (CI) industry relies heavily on insiders. CI can best be described as activities or practices that walk a thin line between legal and illegal or moral and amoral business practice and are specifically designed to gather intelligence about competitors. CI deals primarily with open-source intelligence via Web sites and the media, as well as through loose-lipped employees (or those with an axe to grind). Many involved in CI are ex-government intelligence operatives, however, who have other, more dubious methods in their repertoire (Rosner, 2001). Recruiting insiders or placing plants or moles is not uncommon, given the potential monetary gains from the information gathered about a competitor.

## Terrorists

The final category discussed in this chapter is terrorists' use of insiders. Traditional terrorist groups, both foreign and domestic, have used whatever means they have at their disposable to carry out their mission (Reich, 1990).

Because of the asymmetric nature of the conflicts in which these groups are involved (e.g., small groups taking on nation states or, in the case of eco-terrorism, taking on big business), having people on the inside, either spies or simply individuals sympathetic to the group's cause, is a tactical advantage. History is filled with stories of insiders and spies who aided terrorist groups either directly (planting bombs) or indirectly (providing intelligence or other vital information about a target and, in many cases, funneling money to support the cause).

The harbingers of doom who predict a "Cyber Waterloo" or "Digital Pearl Harbor" speculate that these terrorist groups will use their battle-tested techniques against critical infrastructures and the Internet. Although information warfare is now part of military strategy and has been used by United Nations forces in Bosnia and by the United States in Desert Shield, Desert Storm, and the current war on terrorism, there are few if any examples in the open media of terrorists attacking critical infrastructures. To be considered a terrorist attack, the motivation and objectives of the group behind the attack must be taken into consideration. A 14-year-old defacing the Department of Defense Web site is not a cyber terrorist attack, despite what popular media would have us think. Terrorism is defined by the motivation and the desired effect of the act. In most cases, this includes the use of violence or the threat of violence to coerce the public in furthering a political or social objective (FBI, 1999). A legitimate example of cyber terrorism would be if Hezbollah were able to hack into the air traffic control systems of the Los Angeles International Airport and cause planes to crash in order to destabilize the U.S. economy and terrify the U.S. population. Despite the lack of concrete examples, society's dependence on the Internet and technology almost guarantees that terrorist groups will focus attention on the cyber world.

The risk of the terrorist insider is considerable. Terrorism, whether foreign or domestic in origin, deals with ideologies and often fanaticism. Terrorists are highly motivated individuals who are willing to risk everything for their cause. Being sensitive to an ideology may have no outward manifestation that could be used to distinguish someone as a risk. Terrorists are patient and often think in terms of years or decades. Planting someone inside a high-tech company or organization who becomes part of the critical infrastructure with the goal of having that person work for several years until the timing is right is not outside normal terrorist practices (Pearlstein, 1991).

Terrorists take advantage of the openness of democratic countries like the United States. The traditional freedoms and personal rights inherent in societies and cultures based on the democratic ideology make it difficult to combat terrorism inside the borders. The recent trend of offshoring high-tech jobs to countries with known ties to terrorist groups or, at the very least, to countries with active terrorist groups operating inside of their sovereign domain only exacerbates the problem and greatly increases the likelihood if not the impact of terrorist insiders.

Although several types of insiders have been discussed (i.e., disgruntled employees, hackers, criminals, spies, terrorists), the limited data indicate that the disgruntled employee is by far the most likely threat and historically has the biggest impact. Using a standard risk management formula, the risk of insiders is also by far the highest of all categories:

$$Risk = f\ [threat \times vulnerability \times likelihood \times impact]$$

Given this high risk, the remainder of this discussion focuses on the disgruntled employee.

# FACTORS AND CAUSES

Understanding the factors that may be directly or indirectly responsible for the insider threat should allow us to choose better mitigation strategies and, in some cases, be preventative and proactive rather than being solely reactive as we currently are. At a high level, the factors can be categorized as business culture and society. Under the heading of business culture, we have subcategories of ethics and morals and a transient workforce. Society is subdivided into economy, morality, and social learning. Because the focus of this chapter is to provide a broad overview of internal threat, it only scratches the surface with this section.

## Business Culture

Business culture here refers to the current business environment that is predominant in the United States, if not globally. Similar to the convergence of technology, business practices are less polarized today than they were a decade ago. The availability of information, together with media saturation, has harmonized many of today's industries and, by default, the businesses operating in these industries (e.g., telecomm, automotive, defense, hydroelectric, financial). Other critics blame deregulation as leading to a dog-eat-dog, cutthroat mentality, where the bottom line is the sole focus.

### Ethics and Morality

Examples of corporate immorality and a lack of ethics are numerous today. It may be that the media and, by extension, the public are more sensitive and that the actual number of unethical businesses is not greater than before; this is, however, a rather dubious line of reasoning, one often used by those who find themselves under scrutiny. Regardless of whether there is more or less unethical corporate behavior, the perception exists that it has increased (Green, 2004). To the public and ergo to employees, perception becomes reality. Images and headlines of corrupt corporate executives, companies being fined by regulators for questionable practices, and corporate executives receiving multimillion-dollar severance packages or bonuses while the company is laying off its employees, closing operations, or filing for bankruptcy protection only reinforces the notion that the corruption is rampant and that the end justifies the means. Unfortunately, employees look to executive management and their supervisors for indications of what is and is not acceptable behavior. If the perception is that ethical behavior is not rewarded or is in fact detrimental to one's career growth, less ethical behaviors become reinforced.

The end results of questionable ethics in the business environment are unethical employees and a disaffected workforce at best, and disgruntled employees who feel no sense of loyalty to their employers at worst (Glen, 2003).

## Transient Workforce

The phenomena of an uncertain economy, poor corporate governance, downsizing, and cheap labor in foreign countries has contributed to the transient workforce that we see in today's business world. The IT and manufacturing industries have been hard hit by offshoring of jobs to foreign countries. Although the practice is understandable from a purely business decision in some cases, the fallout is fewer jobs and little security. The high-tech industry has many examples of employees of 15 or more years being laid off and competing for low-paying jobs with recent college grads because their company now outsources to a cheaper, foreign-based company.

A recent study conducted in the United Kingdom reported that 20% of the workforce is planning a job change in the year 2005 (City & Guild, 2004). This is double the amount from the previous year's study. The same survey predicted that in the next 20 years, workers will have, on average, 19 job changes in their career lifetime. The U.S. Department of Labor describes the current workforce as dynamic, a term that describes situations in which employees consider their tenure at a company to be 2 to 3 years.

The net result of this temporary employment and constant job-hopping is an erosion of any feeling of trust, commitment, or loyalty between employee and employer. Without these internal factors acting as barometers for gauging appropriate behaviors, individuals are more apt to engage in questionable behaviors and to feel less guilt in doing so because they are able to rationalize the behavior by saying, "I don't owe the employer anything."

## Society

The business culture is only one area influencing our behaviors. Cultural and societal norms play an important role in acting as filters for what is right and wrong, ethical and unethical, and morally correct. Researchers, religious leaders, and politicians have bemoaned the decline of morality and ethical behavior in modern society. The Federal Communications Commission in the United States has gone on the offensive to curtail questionable behavior in the broadcast media. To capture a total picture of factors influencing questionable behavior involving technology, we need to look at the backdrop on which these behaviors evolve.

### Economy

It is too easy to blame societal woes on external factors such as the economy: "If only the economy were better, we would not have x or y." With regard to internal security threats, however, the exact influence of the economy is unknown. It is well documented that economic factors exert a large impact on our daily lives. The stressors related to unemployment or underemployment negatively affect marital relations and feelings of general self-worth. What is interesting is that, in general, increases in crime rates are not correlated with tougher economic conditions. Although hard economic conditions further the mentality to succeed at any cost in some people, others merely become resolute and take on a second or third job to make ends meet.

It is unrealistic to think that the factors discussed in this chapter exist in a vacuum; in the real world, the variables interact in numerous ways. We must consider the combination and interactions of variables or factors. When we look at tough economic times combined with decreased feelings of loyalty and models of less-than-ethical behavior, the combined effect is significantly greater than any individual variable. Acknowledging that the economy is merely one factor in a model of causality comprising several factors places the appropriate emphasis on economic conditions without placing blame squarely on the shoulders of constantly varying economic conditions.

### Morality

Among the causal factors is the decline in social morality in general, not only in the business culture. Some have argued that the moral apathy is rampant in today's society. The strong moral compass of yesteryear seems to have been replaced by a more hedonistic model in which individualism and personal needs takes precedent over the collective societal need.

Moral ambiguity may also be part of the problem. Insider attacks, like other forms of white-collar crime, are seen as less insidious; no "real" person was victimized. By attacking a computer system and the organization owning the data or system, no person has been physically hurt (in most cases). The crime is based on a violation of trust or power as opposed to violence directed at any one person. Because of the abstraction attached to who or what is the victim, society has tended to be somewhat ambiguous in its reaction to these crimes (Green, 2004). Whether these actions are wrong is not so black and white. The media are responsible for contributing to this ambiguity by downplaying the seriousness and magnitude of the problem. A prime example of people's ambiguity toward this kind of criminal behavior has been the recent court cases in which CEOs were charged with misuse of corporate funds. Many of the cases tried by jury ended in a mistrial, as the jurors could not come to a proper decision.

### Social Learning

Researchers who specialize in examining the possible roots of deviant and criminal behavior have concluded that such behavior, like other behaviors, is learned. Learning a criminal behavior is based on positive and negative reinforcement and reciprocity between the individual and the environment (we act on and influence our environment, and the environment acts on and influences us). Learning occurs against a backdrop of our social circles and culture. Although the actual learning process is not clear, differential reinforcement, differential association, imitations, and definitions are believed to be principal components (Akers, 1998).

Social-learning theory states that people become involved with and continue to exhibit deviant or criminal behaviors because they associate with other individuals who share a similar opinion about nonconforming behaviors (Akers, 1998). The group shares a common definition of what is moral, ethical, or right and wrong, often directly or indirectly at odds with the views held by society at large. An individual may be reinforced for deviant behavior either directly (e.g., monetary rewards, status, power, ego stroking) or vicariously (e.g., popular media and the general public's glorification of organized crime). Although one may experience some negative reinforcement or punishment (e.g., being arrested, going to jail), the balance between the negative and the positive reinforcement is in favor of the positive. The individual may also witness significant others either carrying out deviant behaviors directly or condoning them in others. This reinforcement can be as subtle as an offhand comment such as how "smart" the crook was or that a hacker was "really gutsy."

As already discussed, certain elements in our society have different views regarding moral and ethical IT behavior. There are numerous role models for IT deviance, and the negative consequences to such behavior are often overshadowed by the media attention and occasional "folk hero" status bestowed on the perpetrator by segments of the IT community (Rogers & Ogloff, 2003). Even when an individual goes to jail, there is a good chance that if the case was a big enough media event, the person will be better off financially than before the incident. The financial gain comes about with books, speaking tours, consulting opportunities, and even lucrative employment opportunities. Despite the supposed repugnance we feel toward insiders who attack systems, our overt actions tend to reveal that in some cases our definitions of what is right and wrong, good and bad, are fuzzy when technology is involved.

The issues of software piracy and copyright violations have highlighted the gray area associated with online- and technology-related activities (Gattiker & Kelley, 1999). Recent studies by software vendor associations and the recording industry concluded that the majority of people have committed software piracy or knowingly violated copyright laws. One study gave the prevalence of these behaviors to be approximately 60% of the respondents in the survey. Obviously, all the elements to learn criminal insider behavior are present in today's society and work culture; maybe a better question to ask is why isn't everyone involved in this deviant behavior?

## MITIGATION

Now that the reader is truly convinced that the sky is falling, let's take off the Chicken Little costume and look at what we can do to reduce the risk of this very real threat. As stated earlier, risk is inherent with everything we do in life and certainly with all business activities and ventures. The mere existence of risk should not preclude us from carrying on a business or embarking on something new. What risk does is force us to consider strategies to reduce the risk to an acceptable or a tolerable level. This level is not static and fluctuates with the various economic conditions, business trends, consumer attitudes, regulations, and shareholder and investor confidence.

Using our basic understanding of what motivates, drives, and reinforces malicious insiders, we can have an honest examination and discussion on how we effectively and efficiently begin dealing with the problem. Although there is no magic bullet that will completely negate the threat of insiders, some basic strategies can greatly reduce the likelihood and the impact of an insider incident. The strategies need to be considered within the context that information security and assurance require a holistic approach. If we believe the current surveys, we are spending more money now on technical security controls than ever before, yet attacks on our systems are increasing annually, as is the cost of these attacks. A good example is viruses; they have plagued the IT world for nearly 20 years at the time of this writing. Businesses and individual users are constantly updating antivirus signatures and buying the latest and greatest antivirus engines, yet viruses and malware cost businesses millions of dollars a year in lost productivity and damages.

The following strategies attempt to either lessen the direct and indirect impact of insiders or reduce the probability of an attack. This is accomplished by reducing opportunities for and reinforcement of deviant behaviors, increasing the level of effort necessary to commit a successful attack, or identifying patterns of at-risk behaviors before a catastrophic event occurs. Other chapters go into much more detail on specific safeguards and controls (see Part 2), and thus only a high-level discussion is provided here.

Any truly effective mitigation strategy needs to incorporate multiple layers of defense from various control domains. Here the discussion is broken down into the following domains:

- Operational and Administrative
- Environmental and Physical
- Technical and Logical
- Education, Training, and Awareness

## Operational and Administrative

A logical place to begin is the operational and administrative domain. To assist in reducing internal threats, controls need to concentrate on possible motives for the threat and stress diligence in identifying and possibly screening out potential problems before they arise. This domain can also help to reduce the opportunity or, at the very least, increase the work effort, of the attack to the point that an individual loses interest. As previously mentioned, we deal with insiders on a personal basis daily, often in both the physical and the technical–virtual sense. These individuals have some degree of interaction with HR, management, and fellow employees, and stakeholders should capitalize on these.

We have all heard how policies are the cornerstone to effective IT security. Although this is true, a policy is inanimate; it is a document, plain and simple. A document does not actively scan a network for noncompliance, nor does it trigger any alarms during an attack. The document provides for legal and contractual sanctions against someone found to be in violation of the policy. It is more an exercise in demonstrating due diligence on behalf of the executive and legal counsel than a risk-mitigation tool.

A policy also authorizes certain actions that are designed to be preemptive as opposed to the more common position of simply reacting to an event after the fact. Policies should drive out standards and procedures that proscribe certain duties, responsibilities, and job functions. These active components are truly designed to reduce risk in an active manner.

One of the most logical procedures that should be followed is actual background checks of employees before making offers of employment. Few companies actually carry out proper background checks or even bother to contact references the applicant has provided. The excuses most commonly given are the view that it is a violation of the applicant's right to privacy and the cultural myth that one is not allowed to say anything negative or positive about any former employee, so why ask? Neither of these beliefs is accurate. Conditions for employment can stipulate that an individual provide proof of a clean background or criminal record check. If the applicant feels that this is an invasion of privacy or does not wish to divulge such information, he or she can choose to withdraw the application. Having an applicant sign a waiver indicating that the company can contact references and former employers to discuss work history is a feasible solution to the second issue. As Post et al. (1998) indicated, the majority of insiders have histories of similar behavior with past employers. In many cases, if someone had spoken with the last employer and previous coworkers, this information would have surfaced, saving the current company millions of dollars in the more extreme cases.

Once an employee is hired, there should be periodic criminal record checks and security clearance reviews. This is especially important if a person enters a company in a relatively junior position and then works his or her way to a more senior position. Most organizations that conduct background and criminal record checks do so only during the initial employee-screening procedure, yet there are numerous examples in which employees have risen through the ranks to increasing positions of trust only to have their personal life place them in a position where an insider attack appears to be a solution to their problems (e.g., increasing gambling debts, alcoholism, drug abuse, relationships with individuals in organized crime or terrorists groups). Periodic and promotional checks would have brought these risk factors to light, allowing management to be proactive (e.g., by providing employee assistance programs or terminating or reassigning the employee).

As Shaw et al., (1998) concluded, it is rare that an individual spontaneously attacks a system. The critical path model makes it clear that precipitating risk factors and a buildup over time culminates in an individual striking out in desperation. Management and supervisors need to be better trained to recognize at-risk individuals and warning signs that something is wrong. As the CERT/CC Secret Service survey found, before an attack occurred, other parties were aware that something was going to happen (Kimberland, 2004). The current "crisis only" management style, in which management ignores a situation until it becomes a crisis, is neither proactive nor effective. HR needs to provide training and education to management-level personnel to ensure that they have the proper skills to perform their duties and responsibilities effectively. Employees in general need to be trained to spot problems and informed of the protocol to use in the event that they feel intervention is required. Early intervention is one of the best methods to avoid attacks (Department of Defense, 2000).

Effective administrative tools that increase the work effort required for an attack and remove opportunity include separation of duties among employees[3] and the compartmentalization of and access to information and data. Separation of duties has been reasonably effective in the financial and health insurance industry. By splitting key duties between one or more individuals, an attacker would have to be in collusion with at least one other employee to mount a successful attack. This greatly reduces the probability that an attack will occur, and if the individual acts alone, the impact will be limited. This administrative control is hard to implement, however. With today's modern operating systems, it is difficult to have the sufficient level of granularity of roles and privileges to have effective separation of duties.

Flow of information related to new hires and terminations is another extremely important area. It is not unusual for security reviews and audits to discover active accounts belonging to individuals who have left the company several months or even a year earlier. The timely assigning and, possibly more important, rescinding of privileges and deactivation of accounts is crucial to maintain proper access controls. Regular reviews regarding the workflow of this type of information between HR and systems administrators are vital.

Organizations need to be proactive in dealing with job and career satisfaction as well (Post et al., 1998; Quigley, 2002; Randazzo et al., 2004; Wade, 2004). Not only is minimizing the chances of an attack important, but the economic impact of an employee simply leaving a company and going elsewhere is roughly 3 times the person's annual salary (taking into consideration lost productivity and search and screening for a replacement). Simple steps such as biweekly "bull sessions" with upper management, confidential feedback via intranet Web page, and easy access to employee assistance programs can help alleviate some feelings of frustration and can identify employees with issues that need to be dealt with before a crisis occurs.

Standard operational and administrative mitigation strategies for internal threats should include (but not be limited to) the following:

1. Have clearly articulated and enforceable policies, standards, and procedures related to information security and assurance.
2. Ensure that all employees, contractors, vendors, and consultants are familiar with the company's policies, standards, and procedures.
3. Conduct proper preemployment screening, including criminal record checks and reference verification.
4. Have periodic security clearance reviews of employee backgrounds (especially upon promotion or job reassignment).
5. Separate duties in job functions and responsibilities among employees.
6. Follow clear information workflows for hiring, reassignment, and termination practices.
7. Provide proper training for management-level employees.
8. Provide easy and confidential access to employee assistance programs.
9. Provide an employee satisfaction feedback mechanism.

## Environmental and Physical

Although most of the literature on information security in general and internal threats specifically stresses administrative and operational controls, we must not neglect the more basic physical controls. Removing or reducing the opportunity is an effective strategy. As with other areas of information security, all the pieces of the puzzle must be in place, or we do not have the full security and assurance picture. The key these days is to have complementary security controls or, at the very least, defense in depth. Defense in depth leverages the strengths of each defensive layer, while minimizing the weakness of any individual layer (e.g., policies, procedures, and physical isolation of key systems).

Where applicable, we should endeavor to ensure that our systems and data are physically protected from both insiders and outsiders. Unfortunately, this is not happening in the majority of businesses today. Placing servers, switches, routers, and access control systems in common areas (e.g., bathrooms, lunchrooms, open cubicles) with no boundaries from the employees is not a good business practice. All the logical security in the world is useless if someone can just walk off with the system or physically access or damage it.

A good rule of thumb is that if someone has physical access to a system, it is vulnerable. Obviously, a certain number of people need access for troubleshooting, hardware upgrades, and so on. As with access to information, physical access to systems should be based on the rule of least privileges. Systems must be placed in secure areas, and access to these areas needs to be justified before it is granted.

Often evidence related to an event exists physically on a system, whether it is in a log or event file or some other audit or accountability output (assuming the business has turned on these functions). Most attackers realize the forensic importance of these logs and audit trails and will attempt to delete or somehow alter them, hoping to cover their electronic tracks. Most rootkit or Trojan horse programs have built in routines to seek these files out and destroy or obfuscate the malicious activity. If these trails are on insecure systems, an insider can damage the system (e.g., remove the drive) or use a boot device (e.g., CD, diskette, firewire drive) to bypass the default security and audit software, alter the logs, and reset the system. By booting the system in this manner, they have blinded the operating system and filesystem from their activities and destroyed or altered the evidence. To overcome this

---

[3] Readers need to be cautious here because separation of duties alone does not negate risk; it only means that collusion must occur for the attack to be successful. In some cases, it is not difficult to find several disgruntled employees willing to join forces in a malicious act against an employer.

threat, some organizations are looking to distributed, encrypted, and authenticated logging systems. In this case, logs do not exist on the same system that produces them, and in some instances, the logs are mirrored on multiple systems, making it difficult to erase them completely.

Various studies have concluded that the review and monitoring of logs is an essential component to any insider threat mitigation strategy (Anderson et al., 2000; Randazzo et al., 2004). This assumes, however, that the integrity of these data is known or can somehow be validated. Without proper physical security, this becomes impossible.

Systems left unattended with no passwords are another physical security vulnerability that insiders take advantage of to initiate an attack or gather information. Remember, the attacker is inside and can physically walk around and see whose system has been left unattended with the user still logged on. Why crack passwords or use buffer overflows that can be logged when you can simply walk over to a machine whose user has authority to perform whatever function you are seeking.

Assume you can trust no one, verify those whom you have to trust (e.g., system administrators), and monitor everything, keeping log and audit data securely and digitally signed. At the very minimum, organizations need to review their physical security within the context of attacks originating from the inside as well as the outside. By increasing the difficulty of physical access, the attacker is forced to attack a system(s) logically where event logs and audit trails can be generated, monitored, and analyzed for evidence of whom is responsible or that an attack is imminent.

Systems and data also need to be grouped together logically, based on the sensitivity of the information; the commingling of sensitive information with nonsensitive information, although universal, only compounds the problem. Mixing of information leads to uneconomical solutions; we pay to protect information that is not sensitive. It also results in allowing logical and physical access to systems by individuals of different trust levels—a direct violation of formal models of access control (e.g., Bell laPadula).

Standard physical and environmental strategies should include (but not be limited to) the following:

1. Restrict access to business-critical or business-sensitive systems.
2. Physically group systems according to criticality and sensitivity of information they contain.
3. Use distributed, encrypted, and authenticated audit and event logging.
4. Ensure that bios and screensaver passwords are enabled on all workstations.
5. Conduct weekly physical security sweeps.
6. Enact a clean desk policy to prevent the inadvertent disclosure of information, including hard copies.

## Technical and Logical

One would assume that using technical and logical security controls as a method for mitigating the insider threat would be relatively simple (Caloyannides & Landwehr, 2000). We already spend large sums of money on technical safeguards directed at securing the outside edges of our networks. However, the majority of network security postures have hard crusty outsides and soft mushy insides. Businesses tend to turn technical controls such as firewalls and intrusion detection systems outward-facing to protect them from the "bogeyman" on the outside. We need to take these external-facing safeguards and countermeasures and focus them internally as well (Caloyannides & Landwehr, 2000).

To be worthwhile and not simply a knee-jerk reaction or band-aid solution to a perceived symptom, technical controls need to be implemented in a manner that produces multiple layers of protection (e.g., implementing several layers of firewalls, intrusion detection systems, filtering routers). The goal is to decrease the opportunity, increase the work effort, and significantly increase the risk of getting caught, thus negatively affecting reinforcement. This defensive in-depth strategy takes advantage of the different strengths and weaknesses that each control has. The idea is to maximize the strengths, increase the odds of detection if prevention fails, and minimize the weaknesses of each individual control. The approach is akin to the concept of gestalt whereby the whole is greater than the sum of its parts.

Similar to the steps required to ensure that we have adequate protection from the outside, we first have to understand the deficiencies of our internal coverage. A risk analysis needs to be conducted, and the results must be fed into a risk-management process to determine the most pressing issues from a risk and business–cost benefit analysis perspective. The output from the analysis is used to derive a project-management strategy to begin implementing the recommendations.

It is crucial that a proper risk-management strategy be in place before implementing any additional controls on the environment. With limited budgets and manpower, the general principle of proportionality needs to be followed; our expenditures in both time and money are proportional to the risk. It is illogical to spend tens of thousands of dollars securing information available to the public or that, if compromised, will have an extremely small impact. Having said this, certain regulatory compliance issues force organizations to take measures regardless of the direct level risk or impact to the company directly (e.g., Health Insurance Portability and Accountability Act[HIPAA], Sarbanes-Oxley[SOX]). In those cases, the regulatory penalties need to be factored into the risk analysis model.

Standard technical and logical strategies should include (but not be limited to) the following:

1. Enable audit and event logging on key systems.
2. Monitor and audit event data on a daily basis.
3. Use a combination of host- and network-based intrusion detection systems.
4. Segment the network into different trust domains (either at the network level or by use of firewalls; e.g., finance, HR, Web development).
5. Implement identity management systems to control access and privileges.

6. Implement role-based access control throughout the enterprise.
7. Use Virtual Private Networks for communications and access between domains of higher trust.
8. Install antivirus software on all systems, ensuring that both engine and signatures are updated automatically.
9. Use at least two-factor authentication to prevent easily guessed passwords and sharing of passwords.
10. Encrypt sensitive data both in transit and in storage.
11. Conduct periodic user-account reviews to identify unneeded or tombstone accounts.
12. Keep up to date with critical operation system patches.
13. Conduct periodic internal security reviews.

## Education, Training, and Awareness

The last control area focuses on removing or reducing the motive for the attack and making employees and managers more sensitive to the warning signs of an impending problem. At the most basic level, the problem of insider attacks is a people issue, not a technology issue (Department of Defense, 2000). This is an issue of aberrant human behavior and deviance that is not unique to technology. Although many in the IT security field claim that information security and assurance is a hardware–software–firmware problem, it is also a peopleware problem (Rogers, 2004). If we continue to focus solely on administrative, technical, and physical controls, we are missing a quarter of the formula. It has been suggested that if we were able to eliminate all users, then we have a chance at being secure. Obviously, this cannot happen because technology is a tool for users, not vice versa. It therefore behooves us to look at dealing with people's behaviors, modifying the behaviors where necessary, and providing opportunities for employees to be part of the solution as opposed to being the problem.

Education, training, and awareness can play a large part in being proactive toward information security and assurance in general (Department of Defense, 2000; Quigley, 2002). Unfortunately, this area receives the least attention. Most companies that have responded to surveys report a disturbing lack of education or awareness training. Strangely enough, several national studies have reported that companies that had been victims of information security attacks in the preceding year reported cutting funding to education and training during that year (Chief Security Officer, 2003).

Respondents that reported having education and training programs usually employ computer-based training that is at best a conglomeration of PowerPoint-like slides or talking heads. Furthermore, the tests the employees are required to take to prove they understand the material are too simple and designed to satisfy a legal responsibility or to protect the employer from liability as opposed to being a learning evaluation and assessment tool. It is no wonder that companies and employees are skeptical about taking part in training and awareness programs. These poorly designed programs result in the self-perpetuating notion that education and awareness training is a waste of time and money. What is required is proper training and education that follows the principles of outcome-based learning, instructional design, and proper pedagogical evaluation and assessment.

The one-size-fits-all solution toward education and training has undermined any potential benefits. Contrary to popular belief, the different user communities within an organization require different education and training approaches. Administrative support personnel, help desk, internal audit, and HR have different functions, different levels of technical skill, and deal with different classifications of data. The education and training programs need to take these differences into consideration. Although there should be common goals for these efforts (better information security awareness, a security mindset while dealing with technology in general, and an understanding of the corporate policies and procedures), how this is accomplished will have to be tailored to the audience. One possible rule of thumb across all potential audiences is that if the message is made personal and individuals understand how they are directly affected, they will be easier to engage and more motivated to pay attention and change some of their behaviors. Focusing directly on the problem at hand, given findings that many insiders discussed their malicious intentions with other people before an attack means that if these people (to whom the attack was disclosed) would have acted in an appropriate manner, the attack could have been prevented and some type of intervention initiated.

Standard education training and awareness strategies should include (but not be limited to) the following:

1. Executives should truly back and support initiatives.
2. Tailor education and training programs to specific business units and user roles (e.g., help desk, HR, tech support, data entry).
3. Develop proper evaluation and assessment techniques to determine the effectiveness of the initiatives and of employee learning.
4. Utilize multimodal education and learning programs (e.g., computer based, brown bag lunch, intranet sites, newsletters).
5. Mandate remedial training for noncompliance.
6. Offer ongoing training and education efforts throughout the tenure of employees.

## CONCLUSION

This chapter focused on providing insight into of the real risk of insider attacks on IT systems. Armed with this knowledge, organizations should be better able to mitigate this risk. The internal threat, has been classified as the most serious threat facing businesses that have any level of IT infrastructure. The exact toll that information security attacks have on organizations is not known (Gordon et al., 2004). The various studies that have looked at IT attacks have been plagued by design and methodological problems, small sample sizes, research bias, and poor response rates. Despite these shortcomings, a general trend has emerged: the volume of attacks is increasing as are the costs to businesses.

Contrary to popular belief, the sources of attacks on IT systems, networks, and data are not always external. We have fallen under the spell of mass media and vendors who have directed our attention away from inside threats—the historical cause of the majority of incidents—to the evil outsider, from whom, by the way, vendors can protect us for the right price. Realistically, the focus should be on individuals with whom the organization has a trusted relationship—namely employees, ex-employees, contractors, consultants, and sometimes vendors. It is the very nature of having a trusted relationship between the victim and the attacker increases in the impact of these attacks. Insiders are behind physical and technical defensive controls. The enemy does not have to breach the walls; we have invited them in, and they live among us.

The psychological makeup, characteristics, and motivations of inside attackers are fairly well understood. This kind of deviant behavior has followed businesses into the cyber world from the real world of traditional white-collar crimes such as fraud and embezzlement. Individuals drawn to the IT field share certain common characteristics that, when combined with environmental stressors, increase the chances that an attack will be directed internally. The malicious insider is driven by greed, anger, frustration, financial gain, ideology, and, in some cases, psychopathologies.

Of the various types of insider attackers, the most common is the disgruntled employee. The causes of the deviant behavior include today's perceived unethical business culture, society's moral ambiguity toward technology-based deviance, lack of loyalty and trust between employee and employer, and learned social behavior that is inadvertently reinforced by society.

The chapter was more heavily weighted in favor of examining the behavioral sciences aspect of internal threats than the technical controls that might be implemented. The rationale for this is that if we do not sufficiently understand the sociopsychological aspects of insider threats, we are wasting our time, money, and resources implementing band-aid solutions and focusing on symptoms and not the root causes.

The chapter painted a bleak picture of the state of internal threats and how they are normally dealt with or, more precisely, not dealt with but swept under the rug. There is no quick fix. To deal effectively with internal threats, organizations need to undertake a holistic approach to the problem. The approach must include mitigation strategies from the following domains: administrative–operational, physical–environmental, technical–logical, and education, training, and awareness. As with IT security in general, an organization is only as strong as its weakest link. An insider wishing to attack your system will find that weak link.

Although not reaching a consensus on the exact cause and impact of insider attacks, the literature reviewed for this chapter does conclude that education, training, and awareness provide the best near- and long-term return on security investment. Yet businesses spend the least amount of their budgets on this domain and consider it to be a necessary evil required to demonstrate diligence and compliance with various regulations. This myopic view must change if we are to reduce internal threats.

Cartoonist Walt Kelly, creator of the comic strip *Pogo*, summed it up best when he wrote, *"We have met the enemy and he is us."*

## GLOSSARY

**Social Engineering**   Successful or unsuccessful [attempts] to influence a person(s) either to reveal information or act in a manner that would result in unauthorized access to or use of an information system, network, or data.

## CROSS REFERENCES

See *Corporate Spying: The Legal Aspects; Hackers, Crackers and Computer Criminals; Information Leakage: Detection and Countermeasures; Risk Management for IT Security.*

## REFERENCES

Akers, R. (1998). *Deviant behavior: A social learning approach.* Belmont, NY: Wadsworth.

Anderson, R. H., Bozek, T., Longstaff, T., Meitzler, W., Skroch, M., & Wyk, K. V. (2000). *RAND Research on mitigating the insider threat to information systems.* Retrieved September 2, 2004, from http://www.rand.org/publications/CF/CF163/index.html

Bishop, T. (2004). *Association of certified fraud examiners 2004: Report to the nation on occupational fraud and abuse.* Retrieved August 1, 2004, from http://www.cfenet.com/resources/RttN.asp

Caloyannides, M., & Landwehr, C. (2000). *Can technology reduce the insider threat?* Retrieved August 1, 2004, from http://www.rand.org/publications/CF/CF163/CF163.appd.pdf

Carnegie-Mellon. (2004). *2004 e-crime watch survey shows significant increase in electronic crimes.* Retrieved September 22, 2004, from http://www.cert.org/about/ecrime.html

Chief Security Officer. (2003). *CSO 2003 Information security survey.* Retrieved September 8, 2004, from http://www.csoonline.com

City and Guild. (2004, Spring/Summer). The future of work, *Broadsheet*, 2.

Conte, J. M. (2003). *Cybersecurity: Looking inward internal threat evaluation.* Retrieved September 2, 2004, from http://www.giac.org/certified_professionals/practicals/gsec/3110.php

Denning, D. (1999). *Information warfare and security.* Reading, MA: Addison Wesley.

Department of Defense. (2000). *DoD insider threat mitigation: Final report of the insider threat integrated process team.* Retrieved September 2, 2004, from http://akss.dau.mil/servlet/ActionController?screen=Policies&Organization=6&Career=52

Department of Homeland Security. (2003). The national strategy to secure cyberspace. Retrieved September 2, 2004, from http://www.dhs.gov/interweb/assetlibrary/National_Cyberspace_Strategy.pdf

Department of Justice. (2004). *Computer crime intrusion cases.* Retrieved September 1, 2004, from http://www.cybercrime.gov/cccases.html

Federal Bureau of Investigation. (1999). *Terrorism in the USA*. Retrieved September 1, 2004, from http://www.fbi.gov/publications/terror/terror99.pdf

Gattiker, U., & Kelley, H. (1999). Morality and computers: Attitudes and differences in moral judgments. *Information Systems Research, 10*, 233–254.

Glen, P. (2003). Job satisfaction survey 2003. *Computerworld, 37*, 1–2.

Gordon, L., Loeb, M., Lucyshyn, W., & Richardson, R. (2004). *2004 CSI/FBI computer crime and security survey*: Computer Security Institute.

Gordon, S., & Ma, Q. (2003, September). *Convergence of virus writers and hackers*. Paper presented at the 12th Annual Virus Bulletin Conference, Toronto, Canada.

Green, S. (2004). Moral ambiguity in white collar criminal law. *Notre Dame Journal of Law Ethics and Public Policy, 18*, 501–519.

Helsby, R. (2003). *Price Waterhouse Coopers economic crime survey*: Price Waterhouse Coopers.

Kimberland, K. (2004). *SEI press release: Secret service and CERT coordination center release comprehensive report analyzing insider threats to banking and finance sector*. Retrieved September 22, 2004, from http://www.sei.cmu.edu/about/press/insider-threat-release.html

Kovach, K., Pruett, M., Samuels, L., & Duvall, C. (2004). Protecting trade secrets during employee migration: What you don't know can hurt you. *Labor Law Journal, 55*, 69–84.

Messmer, E. (2003). *Security experts: Insider threat looms largest*. Retrieved December 8, 2003, from http://www.nwfusion.com/news/2003/1208infowar.html

Nuemann, P. (1999). *Research and development initiatives focused on preventing, detecting, and responding to insider misuse of critical defense information systems*. Retrieved September 2, 2004, from http://www.rand.org/publications/CF/CF151/index.html

Pearlstein, R. (1991). *The mind of the political terrorist*. Wilmington, DE: Scholarly Resources.

Post, J., Shaw, E., & Ruby, K. (1998, September). *Information terrorism and the dangerous insider*. Paper presented at the InfowarCon'98, Washington, DC.

Quigley, A. (2002). *Inside job: Ex-employees and trusted partners may pose the greatest threats to network security*. Retrieved September 2, 2004, from http://delivery.acm.org/10.1145/510000/505290/p20-quigley.pdf

Randazzo, M., Keeney, M., Cappell, D., & Moore, A. (2004). *Insider threat study: Illicit cyber activity in the banking and finance sector*. Retrieved September 2, 2004, from http://www.secretservice.gov/ntac_its.shtml

Reich, W. (1990). Understanding terrorist behavior: The limits and opportunities of psychological inquiry. In M. Reich (Ed.), *Origins of terrorism: Psychologies, ideologies, theories and states of mind* (pp. 261–280). New York: Cambridge University Press.

Rogers, M., & Ogloff, J. (2003, Winter). Understanding computer crime: A comparative analysis of convicted Canadian computer and general criminals. *Canadian Journal of Police and Security Services: Practice, Policy and Management*, 366–376.

Rogers, M., Smoak, N., & Jia, L. (2005). Self-reported criminal computer behavior: A big-5, moral choice and manipulative Exploitive Behavior Analysis. Submitted for publication.

Rosner, B. (2001). HR should get a clue: Corporate spying is real. *Workforce, 80*(4), 72–75.

Shaw, E., Ruby, K., & Post, J. (1998). *The insider threat to information systems: The psychology of the dangerous insider*. Retrieved April 13, 2004, from http://rf-web.tamu.edu/security/secguide/Treason/Infosys.htm

Tzu, S. (1985). *The art of war* (J. Clavell, Ed.) New York: Delacorte Press.

Verton, D. (2003). *Thwart insider abuse*. Retrieved September 1, 2004, from http://www.computerworld.com

Wade, J. (2004). The weak link in IT security. *Risk Management Magazine, 51*, 32–37.

Whitman, M. (2003). Enemy at the gate: Threats to information security. *Communications of the ACM, 46*, 91–95.

Wood, B. (2000). *An insider threat model for adversary simulation*. Retrieved 2004 from http://www.rand.org/publications/CF/CF163/CF163.appb.pdf

# Physical Security Threats

Mark Michael, *Research in Motion Ltd., Canada*

## INTRODUCTION

For our purposes, information is digital, represented by zeroes and ones in storage or transmission media. Those ones and zeroes can be threatened by unauthorized changes or use incited by other ones and zeroes; cyberthreats may arrive as basic digital commands or as malware, such as viruses. The concern in this chapter is all other threats to information. This takes us into areas sometimes classified as environmental security, personnel security, or administrative security. The corresponding countermeasures are discussed in the separate chapter on physical security measures in this *Handbook* and numerous additional chapters cited in that chapter.

The first area of concern here is physical threats to the continued existence of information in uncorrupted form, for they endanger the integrity and availability of information. Those threats can be to any part of the physical support structure of information:

1. storage media and transmission media, which hold the representation of information as ones and zeroes;
2. machines (including their software) that can read, write, send, or receive information;
3. supporting documentation, which may, for instance, hold crucial instructions or reveal passwords;
4. utilities—electrical power, communication services, and water (for air conditioning and fire suppression);
5. buildings and the controlled environment they provide; and
6. humans and the knowledge they possess to run the system.

Physical threats to sustaining information run the gamut from a scratch on a CD-ROM to the destruction of a data storage facility, from no electrical power to too much power, from fire to ice, from thieves to Mother Nature. The discussion of this area is broken into two major areas in this chapter. The first is fundamental threats, those involving the necessities of life for information—suitable electrical power, environmental conditions, and the like. The second major area involves the kinds of disasters that carry one or more of the fundamental threats.

Even if information is preserved in uncorrupted form, there is a second area of concern: information may be misappropriated, threatening its confidentiality and authorized usage. By its unique nature, information may be replicated, the original copy remaining available and unchanged while a duplicate copy goes elsewhere. Copying a file is one of the most obvious means of attack, but wiretapping, electronic surveillance, or merely looking over one's shoulder may be equally compromising. Well-meaning employees may unwittingly reveal sensitive information on a newsgroup or to a persuasive adversary. An increasing problem is that of acceptable use of information resources, notably access to the Internet and e-mail service.

Physical threats can occur anywhere an organization's information resources reside. The ubiquity of mobile computing and the ease with which storage media can be transported pose challenges unlike those faced by, for example, a bank guarding its money. Even when machines and media remain secured, human knowledge is a mobile resource at risk. Thus, certain physical threats are not constrained by a geographic footprint.

Some physical threats to information, such as fire and theft, predate the digital age. Others, such as anthrax and car bombs, are much newer. Some, such as natural disasters, are more formidable than any cyberthreat.

## FUNDAMENTAL THREATS TO SUSTAINING INFORMATION

This chapter organizes into five categories threats that could compromise the continued existence of information in its intended form:

1. loss of or physical damage to components of the information support structure;
2. anomalies in electrical power;
3. foreign substances, including dust and chemicals;
4. inappropriate humidity and temperature; and
5. the passage of time, which conspires with the other threats and presents a distinct threat as well.

## Loss of Resources

The most obvious threat to an information resource is its loss. Humans may cause loss by misplacing or accidentally discarding something or by deliberately stealing or destroying it. Weather and geologic events are other causes. There are spontaneous failures due to normal (or, perhaps, accelerated) wear and tear.

Physical damage is another obvious threat, but it may not be obvious from a visual or performance standpoint. In some cases, it is progressive, with total failure awaiting one more straw on the camel's back.

The ones and zeroes that represent digital information depend on an extensive support structure. Therefore, the availability or integrity of information is endangered by loss or physical damage to any of the following:

1. storage media and transmission media, which hold the representation of information as ones and zeroes;
2. machines (including their software) that can read, write, send, or receive information;
3. supporting documentation, which may, for instance, hold crucial instructions or reveal passwords;
4. utilities—electrical power, communication services, and water (for air conditioning and fire suppression);
5. buildings and the controlled environment they provide; and
6. humans and the knowledge they possess to run the system.

### Interruption of Utilities

Sustaining information requires electrical power, communication services, and water. In most cases, an organization is at the mercy of one or more external agencies for these utilities. Each agency may be a cooperative venture, may be directly controlled by a government, may be a corporate monopoly operating with government oversight, or may be one among many competing companies. The dependability of these agencies and the likelihood of interruptions due to forces of nature vary widely from region to region, even from neighborhood to neighborhood. Some elements of the world's infrastructure—roads, bridges, railroads, and buildings—age in ways obvious to the casual observer. Others, such as water, sewer, telecommunications, and electrical networks, age more invisibly and often receive less attention as a result. In the United States, deregulation of and competition among electric companies has fostered an unwillingness for any company to upgrade transmission capacity that can be used by its competitors.

Although a few electrical utilities are "islands," most are tied into a massive grid. The conundrum is this: the large, interconnected networks fashioned to allow power demands to be met by sharing power resources are precisely what allow one mountain climber to bring down all the other climbers roped together. The year 2003 brought reminders of this: a massive power outage in North America affecting 50 million people, followed soon afterward by blackouts in the United Kingdom and Italy. Many had thought power disruptions on this scale were no longer a threat. In fact, the strain placed on the world's aging electrical systems seems only to worsen.

In the case of the North American blackout, human error has been well documented to be a contributing factor (see U.S.–Canada Power System Outage Task Force, 2004). Obviously, human error will never be eliminated; utilities can only strive to prevent, catch, or compensate for such errors. Perhaps the most important lesson to be learned is that there will always be some new combination of circumstances that may fall outside the range of what the best system can handle. Deliberate sabotage, either by physical or computer attack, has long been feared as a possibility. Certainly, there are many natural events that can cause power failures on a variety of scales regardless of the system. These include:

1. ice storms and snowstorms
2. windstorms (including tornadoes and hurricanes)
3. earthquakes
4. fires
5. solar flares (see the section on Power Fluctuations)

A generalization that can be made is that large-scale outages tend to take longer to fix and, therefore, have more consequences. One is that battery-based backup power supplies are more likely to fail before power is restored. If the outage lasts days, even backup generators may run out of fuel, which often must be pumped from holding tanks to delivery trucks. Just getting to work may be a challenge for employees who normally depend on electric trains or traffic signals. Even if one company has done its part to stay operational, its continued functioning may be impossible or moot if another company has not had the same foresight.

Whereas an electrical system can be restricted to a single building, telecommunications is, by definition, about connectivity. Loss of telecommunications capabilities effectively nullifies any facility whose sole purpose is to serve the outside world. The difficulty may originate internally or externally. In the latter case, an organization must depend on the problem-solving efficiency of another company. In situations in which voice and data are carried by two separate systems, each is a possible point of failure. Although continuity of data transfer is the highest priority, maintenance of voice communications is still necessary to support the computing environment. Sometimes overlooked is the fact that some alarm systems can be disabled by cutting telephone lines.

Despite the interconnected nature of telecommunication systems, problems typically do not cascade the way electrical problems do. Hence, they rarely strike an entire system. The exceptions (e.g., the loss of all toll-free service by one phone company) have tended to be the result of a software problem. On certain holidays (e.g., Mother's Day in the United States), a spike in the number of calls taxes transmission capacity. The clogging of phone lines is even more severe during local emergencies, and this can have a ripple effect as calls are rerouted. This applies even to cellular communications. Or cellular services could be shut down, as occurred on September 11, 2001, for fear they might be used to trigger bombs (a technique used later in Madrid). Disruptions in service are frequently due to underground lines being accidentally dug up by construction workers. It is not uncommon for large areas to experience lines downed by windstorms or ice storms. Systems dependent on satellite transmission can also be affected by weather; dishes may be damaged by wind or rendered temporarily inoperable by a thick blanket of snow or ice. Solar flares (discussed later) can affect satellite and radio communications, especially at high latitudes.

### Loss of Media and Hardware

Small, unattached items are the easiest to lose, either through theft or accident. In the information processing domain, removable storage media fits this description. As the data density of removable storage media increases, so does the volume of information that can be stored on one item and, therefore, the ease with which a vast amount of information can be stolen or misplaced. Particularly at risk to accidental loss problem are the tiny solid-state forms of removable storage, such as *USB (universal serial bus) flash memory*.

By comparison, stealing hardware usually involves removing bigger, more obvious objects, such as computers and peripherals, with the outcome being more apparent to the victim. Yet by some accounts, the second costliest type of attack on information resources after viruses is theft of laptop computers; off-site location of these provides increased opportunity for theft. Garfinkel (2002) reported thefts of *(RAM) random access memory*. If some but not all RAM is removed from a machine, the loss in performance might initially go unnoticed.

The loss of more old-fashioned forms of media can still affect operations. For instance, a map of an Intranet's topology may be easier to scan visually from a giant printout than from an electronic version. In some cases, crucial information may have been written down and never stored online. In some cases, physical damage to items can be more insidious than outright loss. The reason is that the damage may not be externally visible and performance may degrade in ways that are not immediately evident.

## Inappropriate Forces on Media and Hardware

Physical damage can result from various causes. Here the focus is on the effects of inappropriate forces applied to media and machines. Although computers and their components have improved considerably in shock resistance, there are still many points of potential failure due to shock. Hard drives and laptop *LCD (liquid crystal display)* screens remain particularly susceptible. More insidious are protracted, chronic vibrations. These can occur if fixed equipment must be located near machinery, such as *(HVAC) heating, ventilation, and air conditioning* equipment or a printer. Mobile equipment that is frequently in transit is also at higher risk. Persistent vibrations can loosen things, notably screws, that would not be dislodged by a sharp blow.

Removable storage media are more vulnerable to damage because they are more mobile and delicate. They can be damaged by bending, even if they appear to return to their original shape. Optical media, for instance, can suffer microscopic cracking or delamination (separation of layers). Cracks or delamination may also allow the incursion of air and the subsequent deterioration of the reflective layer. In this regard, DVDs are more susceptible to flexing than are CDs; this is because DVDs have a protective layers on both sides of the data layer whereas a CD has a single, sturdier protective layer. On the other hand, CDs are more easily damaged by scratching on the label side; this is because there is very little protecting the data layer from that side.

Scratches and cracks on the bottom side of a disc (the side facing the laser) will interfere with reading data. Claims have been made that DVDs' more robust error-correction schemes (with an increased proportion of non-data bits) should, in theory, more than compensate for the increased data density (i.e., increased number of bits affected by a given scratch), making them more forgiving of a scratch than would be a CD. In practice, anecdotal experience of lending libraries seems to indicate that DVDs are more problematic with regard to scratching. In addition, a minute off-centering of an attached label would cause greater instability and, therefore, a greater likelihood of data error with a DVD than with a CD because of the former's higher rotational speed.

Although physical shocks can affect magnetic media by partially rearranging ferromagnetic particles, a far more common cause for magnetic realignment is, of course, magnetic fields. Earth's magnetic field, averaging about 0.5 Gauss at the surface, does no long-term, cumulative damage to magnetic media. Certain electrical devices pose hazards to magnetic media; among these are electromagnets, motors, transformers, magnetic imaging devices, metal detectors, and devices for activating or deactivating inventory surveillance tags. (X-ray scanners and inventory surveillance antennae do not pose a threat.) *Degaussers (bulk erasers)* can produce fields in excess of 4,000 Gauss, strong enough to affect nearby media not intended for erasure. Although magnetic media are the obvious victims of magnetic fields, some equipment can also be damaged by strong magnetic fields.

### Loss of Human Resources

Despite their flaws, humans have always been recognized as an essential resource. Before the 2001 attacks on New York and Washington, D.C., however, the sudden disappearance of large numbers of personnel was simply not anticipated by most business continuity planners or disaster recovery planners. All planners, whether focused on preservation of processes or assets, now have a different outlook on the preservation of life.

Aside from mass slaughter, there are other circumstances in which human resources may be lacking. Severe weather may preclude employees from getting to work.

Labor disputes may result in strikes. These may be beyond the direct control of an organization if the problems are with a vendor from whom equipment has been bought or leased or with a contractor to whom services have been outsourced. A different kind of discontinuity in human expertise can come with a change of vendors or contractors or with the replacement of a large group of workers in one country with workers in another country.

Even the temporary absence or decreased productivity of individuals soon adds up to a major business expense. Employers may be held responsible for a wide range of occupational safety issues. Some general health issues that may arise are sick-building syndrome (symptoms arising from toxic mold) and legionnaire's disease (a form of pneumonia transmitted via mist and sometimes associated with large air-conditioning systems). Those specific to the computing environment include:

1. carpal tunnel syndrome (from repetitive actions, notably typing);
2. back and neck pain (from extended use of improper seating);
3. eye strain and headaches (from staring at a computer screen for long periods) ); and
4. pooling of blood in the legs and increased intraspinal pressure (from sitting for extended periods).

There is currently no consensus on the long-term effects of *extremely low-frequency (ELF)* emissions (below 300 Hz), magnetic fields emitted by a variety of devices, including high-tension lines and *cathode ray tube (CRT)* monitors (but not LCD displays). Laboratory tests with animals have found that prolonged exposure to ELF fields may cause cancer or reproductive problems. Studies of pregnant CRT users have produced conflicting data.

Health worries with regard to cellular phones had mostly been dispelled, but a recent report of the (U.K.) National Radiological Protection Board (2005) calls for caution and continued research. Specific concerns involve *third-generation (3G)* phones, which omit higher levels of radiation; greater sensitivity of children and other groups to radio waves; longer lifetime exposures for those who begin using cellular phones in childhood; and a lack of very long-term data due to the newness of the technology.

Although the World Health Organization acknowledges the need for continued research in certain areas, its latest position is that there is no evidence of health risks associated with electromagnetic field exposures below the levels set forth by the International Commission on Non-Ionizing Radiation Protection (1998).

The heat produced by a laptop computer is sufficient that warnings have been issued against using one on bare skin and against falling asleep while having one in a lap. A recent study indicated that the heat could affect male fertility.

## Power Anomalies

Electrical power is to electrical equipment what oxygen is to humans. Obviously, a complete loss of power (discussed earlier) precludes the operation of electrical devices and causes the loss of any information stored in volatile memory. But the quantity and quality of electricity supplied to equipment are important, too. Just as humans can suffer, even die, from too much or too little air pressure, electrical equipment may malfunction or be permanently damaged when fed the wrong amount of current or voltage. This accounts for approximately half of computer data loss. Just as a properly pressurized atmosphere may carry constituents harmful to the immediate or long-term health of people, problems can arise when the power being supplied to a computer is itself conveying "information" in conflict with the digital information of interest. Often forgotten is that the power supply is also crucial for support equipment, such as HVAC and some types of monitoring devices.

### Power Fluctuations

Even under normal conditions, the power grid will deliver *transients* created as part of the continual balancing act performed in distributing power. Loose connections, wind, tree limbs, and errant drivers are among the causes of irregularities.

Low-voltage equipment such as telephones, modems, and networks are susceptible to small changes in voltage. Integrated circuits operate on very low currents (measured in milliamps); they can be damaged by minute changes in current. Power fluctuations can have a cumulative effect on circuitry over time, termed *electronic rust*. Of the data losses due to power fluctuations, about three fourths of culpable events are drops in power.

Both the power grid and communications can be affected by so-called *space weather*. Earth's magnetic field captures high-energy particles from the solar wind, shielding most of the planet while focusing it near the magnetic poles. Communications satellites passing between oppositely charged "sheets" of particles (seen as the Aurorae Borealis and Australis) may suffer induced currents, even arcing; one was permanently disabled in 1997. A *surge* (sudden increase in current) due to a 1989 geomagnetic storm blew a transformer, which in turn brought down the entire HydroQuébec electric grid in 90 seconds. The periods of most intense solar activity generally coincide with Solar Max, when the cycle of sunspot activity peaks every 10.8 years (on the average). The most recent peak was in July 2000. That said, some of the largest flares ever recorded occurred in October 2003 (and did adversely affect air traffic control at high latitudes).

A more frequent source of surges is lightning. In addition to direct hits on power lines or a building, near misses can travel through the ground and enter a building via pipes, telecommunication lines, or nails in walls. Even cloud-to-cloud bolts can induce voltage on power lines.

Although external sources are the obvious culprits, the reality is that most power fluctuations originate within a facility. A common circumstance is when a device that draws a large inductive load is turned off or on; thermostatically controlled devices, such as fans and compressors for cooling equipment, may turn off and on frequently.

### Electrostatic Discharge (ESD)

A type of power fluctuation worthy of special note can be created on a very local scale. An ESD of *triboelectricity* (static electricity) generated by friction can produce *electromagnetic interference* (discussed later) or a *spike* (momentary increase in voltage) of surprisingly high voltage. Among factors contributing to a static-prone environment are low relative humidity (possibly a consequence of heating) and synthetic fibers in floor coverings, upholstery, and clothing.

Especially at risk is integrated circuitry that has been removed from its antistatic packaging just before installation. In actuality, just opening the cover of a computer increases the vulnerability of the components inside. Estimates on the voltage threshold at which damage to electronic circuitry can occur vary by an order of magnitude—not surprising given the variety of circuits in use. Some present-day electronic components can be damaged by charges as low as 10 volts, and technology in development will be even more sensitive to discharges. At a few thousand volts, monitors, disk drives, and printers can malfunction and a computer system may shut down.

There is more agreement on voltage thresholds that relate to human perception. The minimum voltages at which a discharge can be felt and heard are in the ranges of 1,500 to 3,000 and 3,000 to 5,000 volts, respectively. Humans can generate more than 10,000 volts, enough to produce a visible blue spark. The point is this: the most likely delivery system for a discharge is a human, yet a human may deliver a charge that is both damaging and imperceptible. See Electrostatic Discharge Association (2001) for a thorough introduction to ESD.

### Electromagnetic Interference (EMI)

Digital and analog information is transmitted over conductive media by modulating an electrical current or is broadcast by modulating an electromagnetic wave. Even information intended to remain within one device, however, may become interference for another device. All energized wires have the potential to broadcast, and all wires, energized or not, may receive signals. The messages may have no more meaning than the "snow" on a television screen. Even with millions of cell phones on the loose, much of the *"electromagnetic smog"* is incidental, produced by devices not designed to broadcast information.

The terms EMI and *RFI (radio frequency interference)* are used somewhat interchangeably. Electrical noise usually indicates interference introduced via the power input, although radiated energy may have been among the original sources of the noise; this term is also used with regard to small spikes. *EMC (electromagnetic compatibility)* is a measure of a component's ability neither to radiate electromagnetic energy nor to be adversely affected by electromagnetic energy originating externally. Good EMC makes for good neighbors. The simplest example of incompatibility is crosstalk, when information from one cable is picked up by another cable. By its nature, a digital signal is more likely to be received noise-free than an analog signal.

EMI from natural sources is typically insignificant (background radiation) or sporadic (like the pop of distant lightning heard on an amplitude modulated radio). Occasionally, solar flares, discussed earlier, can muddle or even jam radio communications on a planetary scale, especially at Solar Max. Fortunately, a 12-hour window for such a disruption can be predicted days in advance.

Most EMI results from electrical devices or the wires between. Power supply lines can also be modulated to synchronize wall clocks within a facility; this information can interfere with the proper functioning of computer systems. For radiated interference, mobile phones and other devices designed to transmit signals are a major hazard; according to Garfinkel (2002), they have triggered explosive charges in fire-extinguisher systems. Major high-voltage power lines generate fields so powerful that their potential impact on human health has been called into question. Motors are infamous sources of conducted noise, although they can radiate interference as well.

## Foreign Substances

Foreign substances—those that don't belong in the information processing environment—range from insects down to molecules that are not native to the atmosphere. They can damage information resources in subtle, perhaps unseen ways. Often damage results from the combination of a normal motion (e.g., rotation of a disk) and an inappropriate substance.

The most prevalent threat is dust. Even fibers from fabric and paper are abrasive and slightly conductive. Worse are finer, granular dirt particles. Manufacturing by-products, especially metal particles with jagged shapes, are worse yet. A residue of dust can interfere with the process of reading from media. Media other than solid-state media incorporate some kind of moving part. It is the combination of motion with foreign particles that is particularly damaging. Dirty magnetic tape can actually stick and break. Rotating media can be ground repeatedly by a single particle; a head crash is a possible outcome.

A massive influx of foreign particles can overwhelm the air-filtering capability of HVAC systems, which can in turn result in adverse temperature or humidity (or both). Potential causes include:

1. a controlled implosion of a nearby building
2. a catastrophic collapse (e.g., occurred near the World Trade Center)
3. a volcanic eruption
4. a dust storm
5. a massive wildfire
6. a windstorm carrying debris left over from a massive wildfire (as happened weeks after the major fires in California in 2003)

Dust surges that originate within a facility due to construction or maintenance work are not only more likely than nearby catastrophes; they can also be more difficult to deal with because there may be no air filter between the source and the endangered equipment. A common problem occurs when the panels of a suspended ceiling are lifted and particles rain fall onto equipment and media.

Keyboards are convenient input devices—for dust and worse. The temptation to eat or drink while typing only grows as people increasingly multitask. Food crumbs are stickier and more difficult to remove than ordinary dust. Carbonated drinks are not only sticky, but also far more corrosive than water. In industrial contexts, other hand-borne substances may also enter.

Some airborne particles are *aerosols* (liquid droplets suspended in air). Those produced by industrial processes may be highly corrosive. A more common and particularly pernicious aerosol is grease particles from cooking, perhaps in an employee lunchroom; the resulting residue may be less obvious than dust and cling more tenaciously.

Smoke consists of gases, particulates, and possibly aerosols resulting from *combustion* (rapid oxidation, usually accompanied by glow or flame) or *pyrolysis* (heat-induced physiochemical transformation of material, often prior to combustion). The components of smoke, including that from tobacco products, pose all the hazards of dust and may be corrosive as well.

Removable storage media often leave the protection of a controlled environment. They can suffer damage from contact with solvents or other chemicals. CDs and, even more so, DVDs can be harmed by chemicals in the markers and label adhesives not specially designed for them. (Recall that any label can be hazardous to a DVD because the slightest imbalance will have more serious consequences due to the higher rotational speed of DVDs.) Solid-state memory devices, such as USB flash memory, have cases that can easily admit water and other foreign substances.

There is an ever-growing list of potential chemical, biological, and radiological contaminants, each posing its own set of dangers to humans. Most are eventually involved in storage or transportation mishaps. More and more are intentionally used in a destructive fashion. Even if humans are the only component of the computing environment that is threatened, normal operations at a facility must cease until any life- or health-threatening contamination is removed.

One of the most common chemicals on the planet is water. Although essential to human life, water is a well-known threat to most objects of human design. Damage to paper products and the like is immediate. Mold and mildew will begin growing on certain damp materials. Sooner or later, most metals corrode (sooner if other substances, such as combustion by-products, are present).

The most critical problem is in energized electrical equipment. Water's conductive nature can cause a *short circuit* (a current that flows outside the intended path). When the improper route cannot handle the current, the result is heat, which will be intense if there is *arcing* (a luminous discharge from an electric current bridging a gap between objects). This may melt or damage items, even spawn an electrical fire.

## Inappropriate Humidity and Temperature

The threat from high humidity is akin to the threat from water—no surprise given that relative humidity is a measure of the atmosphere's water content as a percentage of the maximum possible (at the current ambient temperature). For electrical equipment, the most common problem is the long-term corrosive effect. If condensation forms, however, it brings the dangers posed by water. Magnetic media deteriorate by *hydrolysis*, in which polymers "consume" water; the binder ceases to bind magnetic

particles to the carrier and sheds a sticky material (which is particularly bad for tapes). Obviously, the rate of decay increases with humidity (and, as for any chemical process, temperature). Formation of mold and mildew can damage paper-based records, furniture, and so on. It can also obstruct reading from optical media. A bigger concern for optical media is corrosion of the metallic reflective layer. In tropical regions, there are even documented cases of fungi burrowing in CDs and corrupting data; high humidity promotes the fungal growth.

On the other hand, very low humidity may change the shape of some materials, thereby affecting performance. A more serious concern is that static electricity is more likely to build up in a dry atmosphere. If not actively controlled, humidity tends to drop when air is heated.

The internal temperature of equipment can be significantly higher than that of the room air. Although increasing densities have brought decreasing currents at the integrated-circuit level, dissipation of heat is still a major concern. If a cooling system fails, a vent is blocked, or moving parts create abnormal friction, temperature levels can rise rapidly. In some facilities, HVAC equipment is an essential support component for maintaining the security of information. After the attack on the Pentagon, continued computer operations hinged on stopping the hemorrhage of chilled water for climate control.

Excessively high temperatures can decrease computer performance, sometimes in ways that are not immediately evident; the resources might continue to operate, but with unreliable results. The point at which permanent damage begins depends on the type of resource, as detailed in Table 1. The severity of the damage increases with temperature and exposure time. Media may be reconditioned to recover data, but the success rate drops rapidly above these thresholds. Magnetism—the essence of much data storage—can be affected by temperatures higher than those listed; therefore, damage to magnetic media occurs first in the carrier and binding materials. On the other hand, silicon—the foundation of current integrated circuitry—will lose its semiconductor properties at significantly lower temperatures than what it takes to melt the solder that connects a chip to the rest of the computer.

**Table 1** Temperature Thresholds for Damage to Computing Resources

| Component or Medium | Sustained Ambient Temperature at Which Damage May Begin |
|---|---|
| Flexible disks, magnetic tapes, etc. | 38°C (100°F) |
| Optical media | 49°C (120°F) |
| Hard-disk media | 66°C (150°F) |
| Computer equipment | 79°C (175°F) |
| Thermoplastic insulation on wires carrying hazardous voltage | 125°C (257°F) |
| Paper products | 177°C (350°F) |

Source: Data taken from National Fire Protection Association (2003).

To put these temperatures in perspective, some heat-activated fire-suppression systems are triggered by ambient temperatures (at the sensor) as high as 71°C (160°F). Even in temperate climates, the passenger compartment of a sealed automobile baking in sunlight can reach temperatures in excess of 60°C (140°F). If media or a mobile computer is directly in sunlight and absorbing radiant energy, the heating is more rapid and pronounced, especially if the encasing material is a dark color, which, in the shade, would help radiate heat. (Direct sunlight is bad for optical media even at safe temperatures.)

Although excessive heat is the more common culprit, computing equipment also has a minimum temperature for operation. Frigid temperatures can permanently damage mobile components (e.g., the rechargeable battery of a laptop computer), even when (in fact, especially when) they are not in use. Plastics can also become more brittle and subject to cracking with little or no impact.

## Time

Time is the enemy of all things made by humans, and stored information is no exception. Time is the ally of all threats that have hidden, cumulative effects: heat, high humidity, foreign substances, power spikes, magnetic and electromagnetic fields, vibrations, and so forth.

The most destructive handmaidens of time are inappropriate temperature and humidity. Even atmospheric conditions that would be acceptable for day-to-day storage and usage of media in the short run will degrade media of all types in the long run. Although some information is only of transitory value, other data, such as official records of births, deaths, marriages, and transfers of property ownership, should be kept in perpetuity. When archiving media for long periods, a new consideration enters into the picture: potential chemical interaction between the media and its storage container. Time magnifies everything that can do harm. Even low-grade vibrations will eventually loosen connections or misalign read-write heads, for example.

Projected life spans for properly archived media are considered to be 5 to 10 years for floppy diskettes, 10 to 30 years for magnetic tapes, and 20 to 30 years for optical media (International Advisory Committee for the UNESCO Memory of the World Programme, 2000). These estimates are conservative to ensure creation of a new copy before degradation is sufficient to invert any bits. For optical media, life expectancies are extrapolated from accelerated aging tests based on assumptions and end-of-life criteria that may be invalid.

Optical media incorporating dyes are also subject to degradation from exposure to light. Numerous factors influence longevity. Write-once formats have greater life expectancies than rewriteable formats. It is known that the bit-encoding dye phthalocyanine (appearing gold or yellowish green) is less susceptible than cyanine (green or blue-green) to damage from light after data has been written; yet manufacturers' claimed life expectancies of up to 300 years are not universally accepted. What appears to be a major determiner of longevity is the original quality of the stored data. This in turn depends on the quality of the blank disc, the quality of the machine writing the data, and

speed at which data was written. Hartke (2001) gave an enlightening look at the complexities of the longevity issue.

Although the physical degradation of information has been around since the days of cave art, a new threat has emerged now that the Information Age is decades old: technological obsolescence. Successive generations of information-storage technology have resulted in data lost because no one thought to convert the data to a new format when the hardware, supporting software, or human expertise associated with the old storage format faded into oblivion.

Vital records of types enumerated earlier are easy to keep in mind when a new storage format comes along; although the costs of converting to the new format may be high, there are always benefits in terms of storage space and access time. Data gathered for other reasons, perhaps as part of a scientific or socioeconomic study, is particularly susceptible to eventual loss due to (temporary) disinterest. Human knowledge often follows a waterfall model, dropping from current and interesting to outdated and uninteresting to archaic and irretrievable. In many cases, the old information then becomes of interest again, precisely because it *is* old. Unfortunately, it is not always possible to anticipate which information will someday be useful, perhaps after being ignored for several techno-generations.

# DISASTERS AND THE THREATS THEY BRING

The fundamental threats discussed so far and combinations there of often arrive courtesy of a disaster of natural or human origin. Given the variety of disasters, the focus here is on four majors areas: fire, flooding, storms, and geologic events. Obviously, similar combinations of threats accompany bombings, vehicle crashes, and other calamities.

Disasters of a regional scale can disrupt society in a variety of ways, even if a particular facility remains physically unscathed. These include the following:

1. disruption of electrical power
2. disruption or overwhelming of communications lines
3. loss of water (needed for air conditioning and fire safety)
4. inability of employees to get to work

## Fire

Throughout history, fire has been one of the most important threats to human life, property, and activity when measured in terms of frequency, potential magnitude, and rapidity of spread. Fire presents a bundle of the previously mentioned environmental threats. By definition, combustion involves chemical and physical changes in matter—in other words, destruction of what was. Even away from the site of actual combustion, heat can do damage, as detailed earlier. Smoke can damage objects far from the site of combustion. More critical to humans are the irritant, toxic, asphyxial, and carcinogenic properties of smoke; it is the leading cause of death related to fire. With the advent of modern synthetic materials, fires can now produce deadlier toxins. Hydrogen cyanide, for instance, is approximately 25 times more toxic than carbon monoxide.

Sometimes the cure can be worse than the disease. If water is the suppressing agent, it can wreak havoc on adjacent rooms or lower floors that suffered no fire damage at all. Some modern fire suppressants decompose into dangerous substances; this is discussed in more detail in the chapter on physical security measures in this *Handbook*. A comprehensive tome on fire is Cote (2003).

## Flooding

Invasive water may be the result of nature or human action. It may rise from below, fall from above, or strike laterally. The force of moving water and debris can do structural damage directly or indirectly, by eroding foundations. In some cases, natural gas lines are broken, which feed electrical fires started by short-circuiting.

Most flood damage, however, comes from the water's suspended load of particles. Whereas falling water, say, from a water sprinkler or a leaking roof, is fairly pure and relatively easy to clean up, floodwater is almost always muddy. Fine particles (clays) cling tenaciously, making cleanup a nightmare. A dangerous biological component may be present if sewage removal or treatment systems back up or overflow or if initially safe water is not drained promptly. Another hazard is chemicals that may have escaped containment far upstream.

When flooding or subsequent fire has disabled HVAC systems in the winter, ice formation has sometimes added further complications. Freezing water wedges items apart. Obviously, recovery is delayed further by the need to first thaw the ice.

As many have learned too late, much flood damage occurs in areas not considered flood-prone. Government maps depicting flood potential are not necessarily useful in assessing risk, because they can quickly become outdated. One reason is construction in areas with no recorded flood history. Another is that urbanization itself changes drainage patterns and reduces natural absorption of water.

Small streams react first and most rapidly to rainfall or snowmelt. Even a highly localized rain event can have a profound effect on an unnoticed creek. Perhaps the most dangerous situation is in arid regions, where an intermittent stream may be dry or nearly dry on the surface for much of the year. A year's worth of rain may arrive in an hour. Because such flash floods may come decades apart, the threat may be unrecognized or cost-prohibitive to address.

Usually, advance warning of floods along large rivers is better than for the small rivers that feed them. Having a larger watershed, large rivers react more slowly to excessive rain or rapidly melting snow. Formation of ice jams, breaking of ice jams, structural failure of dams, and landslides or avalanches into lakes, however, can cause a sudden, unexpected rise in the level of a sizeable river.

Coastal areas are occasionally subjected to two other types of flooding. The storm surge associated with a hurricane-like storm (in any season) can produce profound and widespread damage, but advanced warning is usually sufficient to allow for appropriate preparations.

Moving at 725 km (450 miles) per hour on the open ocean, *tsunamis* (seismic sea waves) caused by undersea earthquakes or landslides can be higher than storm surges. Monitors at sea together with computer modeling have aided in posting or canceling some tsunami warnings. However, near-shore events allow little time for warnings. Tsunamis most often strike coastlines on the Pacific Rim because the "Ring of Fire" is responsible for much of Earth's strongest seismic activity. However, the largest recorded tsunami occurred in the Indian Ocean on December 26, 2004. An even larger (and rarer) *megatsunami* would affect much of the Atlantic if a particular volcano in the Canary Islands collapses all at once.

An urban area is at the mercy of an artificial drainage system, the maintenance of which is often at the mercy of a municipality. A violent storm can itself create enough debris to diminish greatly the system's drainage capacity.

Not all flooding originates in bodies of water. Breaks in water mains can occur at any time, but especially during excavation or winter freeze-thaw cycles. Fire hydrants can be damaged by vehicles. Pipes can leak or commodes overflow. Although safest from rising water, the top floor is the first affected if the roof leaks, collapses, or is blown away.

## Storms

Storms are one obvious source of flooding. Storms are singled out here because they may have other consequences resulting from:

1. wind or windblown debris
2. excessive weight of snow or ice accumulating on roofs
3. lightning strikes

The heat from lightning can ignite a fire or can physically destroy through explosive expansion. Even a near miss can induce massive power surges. Even if a lightning bolt is not triggered, an electrical storm produces huge charged fields.

Ice storms and high winds frequently cause tree limbs to fall on power lines, cutting the municipal source of electricity. Satellite dishes can be damaged by wind or temporarily disabled by a thick layer of ice or snow.

## Geological Events

Geological hazards fall into a number of categories. These events are far more unpredictable than meteorological events, although some, notably landslides and mudslides, may be triggered by weather. Earthquakes can have widespread effects on infrastructure. The damage to an individual structure may depend more on *where* it was built than on *how*. Buildings on fill dirt are at greater risk because of potential *liquefaction*, in which the ground behaves like a liquid. Earthquake predictions are currently vague as to time and location.

Landslides and mudslides are more common after earthquakes and rainstorms, but they can also occur with no obvious triggering event. Anticipating where slides might occur may require professional geological consultation. As an illustration, a cliff with layers of clay dipping toward the face of the cliff is an accident waiting to happen.

Volcanic ash is one of the most abrasive substances in nature. It can occasionally be carried great distances and in great quantities. It may thoroughly clog up HVAC air filters between outside and inside air domains, or people may track it into a building. Most volcanic eruptions are now predictable.

## PHYSICAL MEANS OF MISAPPROPRIATING RESOURCES

To this point, the chapter has looked at threats, perhaps from disasters, that endanger the availability of information in uncorrupted form. In some cases, we have referred to "losses" of information. Although such losses are *a priori* threats to availability, if the loss is due to theft, it may also threaten confidentiality or authorized usage. Thus far, humans have been treated as essential, albeit imperfect, components of the information support structure. The chapter now considers humans as an internal or external threat. Obviously, people can intentionally or accidentally endanger information by means of the basic environmental threats discussed up until now. Instead, we focus on the misappropriation of assets that can be possessed in some sense—physical objects, information, and computing power.

In addition to the possible impact on availability and integrity, human acts of misappropriation may compromise other security goals: confidentiality, authentication, and authorization. Misuse may entail use by the wrong people or by the right people in the wrong way. The transgressions may be without malice. Current attitudes toward intellectual property rights are a major societal problem. A pilferer of "excess" computing power may view his or her actions as a "victimless crime." In other cases, insiders create new points of presence (and, therefore, new weak points) in an attempt to possess improved, legitimate access. See Skoudis (2002) or the separate chapters on corporate espionage and on internal security measures for discussions of many of these issues.

### Unauthorized Movement of Resources

For computing resources, theft comes in several forms. Outsiders may break or sneak into a facility. Insiders may aid a break-in, may break into an area or safe where (or when) they are not entitled to access, or they may abuse access privileges that are a normal part of their job. Physical objects may be removed. Information, whether digital or printed, is subject to *theft by copying*, when it is duplicated or merely memorized, with the original object staying in place.

A different situation is when items containing recoverable data have been intentionally discarded or designated for recycling. The term *dumpster diving* conjures up images of an unauthorized person recovering items from trash bins outside a building (although perhaps still on an organization's property). In fact, discarded items can also be recovered from sites inside the facility by a malicious insider. At the other extreme, recovery could, in theory, take place thousands of miles from the point at which an object was initially discarded. A large fraction of the "recycled" components from industrialized countries actually end up in trash heaps in Third World countries. The legality of dumpster diving depends on local laws and on the circumstances under which an item was discarded and recovered.

Perhaps the most obvious candidate for theft is removable storage media. As the data density of removable storage media increases, so does the volume of information that can be stored on one item and, therefore, the ease with which a vast amount of information can be stolen. Likewise, downloading from fixed media to removable media can also be done on a larger scale, facilitating theft by copying.

By comparison, stealing hardware usually involves removing bigger, more obvious objects, such as computers and peripherals, with the outcome being more apparent to the victim.

### Unauthorized Connections and Use

*Wiretapping* involves making physical contact with guided transmission media for the purposes of intercepting information. Wired media are relatively easy to tap, and detection (other than visual inspection of all exposed wires) may be difficult.

According to Tapanes and Carroll (1999), "Although it was initially thought that optical fiber transmission would be inherently secure, it has now been shown that it is relatively easy to 'tap' information out of an optical fiber with negligible interference to the optical signal." This can be accomplished by bleeding off less than 1% of the light, an amount less than normal operational variations. There are two ways to do this. *Macro-bending* involves flexing the cable in the way a road would curve, then suitably aligning an optical detector. *Micro-bending* consists of creating ripples in the surface of an otherwise straight (and perhaps fully coated) cable by clamping onto it a device with ridges; the optical detector is incorporated into the clamp.

A specific type of wiretapping is a *keyboard monitor*, a small device interposed between a computer and its keyboard that records all keystrokes. The attacker (or suspicious employer) must physically install the item and access it to retrieve stored data. (Hence, keyboard logging is more often accomplished by software.)

A variation on wiretapping is to use connectivity hardware already in place, such as a live, unused local area network (LAN) wall jack; a live, unused hub port; a LAN-connected computer that no longer has a regular user; or a computer in use but left unattended by the user currently logged on. For the perpetrator, these approaches involve varying degrees of difficulty and risk. The second approach may be particularly easy, safe, and reliable if the hub is in an unsecured closet, the connection is used for sniffing only, and no one has the patience to check the haystack for one interloping needle.

Phone lines are connectivity hardware that is often overlooked. A naïve employee might connect a modem to an office machine so it can be accessed (for legitimate reasons) from home. This gives outsiders a potential way around the corporate firewall. Even information technology (IT) administrators who should know better leave "backdoor" modems in place, sometimes with trivial or no password protection. Sometimes the phone service itself is a resource that is misappropriated. Although less common now, some types of *PBX (private branch exchange)* can be hacked, allowing an attacker to obtain free long-distance service or to mount modem-based attacks from a "spoofed" phone number. See also the separate chapter on telephone system vulnerabilities.

A final asset is an adjunct to the phone service. Employee voice mail, even personal voice mail at home, has been compromised for the purpose of obtaining sensitive information (e.g., reset passwords).

Appropriate access through appropriate channels does not imply appropriate use. One of the biggest productivity issues nowadays is employee e-mail and Internet surfing unrelated to work. If prohibited by company policy, this can be viewed as misappropriation of equipment, services, and, perhaps most important, *time*. Although text-based e-mail is a drop in the bucket, downloading music files can "steal" considerable bandwidth; this is especially a problem at those academic institutions where control of students' Internet usage is minimal.

## Eavesdropping

*Eavesdropping* originally meant listening to something illicitly. Although capture of acoustic waves (perhaps with an infrared beam) is still a threat, the primary concern in the computing environment involves electronically capturing information without physical contact. Unguided transmission media such as microwave (whether terrestrial or satellite), radio (the easiest to intercept), and infrared (the hardest to intercept) should be considered fair game for outsiders to eavesdrop; such transmissions must be encrypted if security is a concern.

Among guided transmission media, fiber optic cable stands alone for its inability to radiate or induce any signal on which to eavesdrop. Therefore, the interesting side of eavesdropping is tempest emissions. Electrical devices and wires have long been known to emit electromagnetic radiation, which is considered "compromising" if it contains recoverable information. Mobile detectors have been used to locate radios and televisions (where licensing is required) or to determine the stations to which they are tuned. Video displays (including those of laptops) are notorious emitters; inexpensive equipment can easily capture scan lines, even from the video cable to an inactive screen.

The term *tempest* originated as the code word for a U.S. government program to prevent compromising emissions. (Governments are highly secretive in this area; contractors need security clearance to learn the specifications for equipment to be tempest-certified.) Related compromising phenomena are as follows:

1. *hijack*—signals conducted through wires (and perhaps the ground, as was noted during World War I),
2. *teapot*—emissions intentionally caused by an adversary (possibly by implanted software), and
3. *nonstop*—emissions accidentally induced by nearby radio frequency sources.

One attack is to irradiate a target to provoke resonant emissions—in other words, intentional nonstop. (This is analogous to how an infrared beam can expropriate acoustic information.) Interestingly, equipment certified against passive tempest eavesdropping is not necessarily immune to this more active attack. (Compare the infrared device to a parabolic microphone, which is merely a big ear.) Although these emissions were formerly the concern only of governments, increasingly less expensive and more sophisticated equipment is making corporate espionage a growing temptation and concern. An excellent introduction to this area is chapter 15 of Anderson (2001). A well-known portal for tempest information is McNamara (2002). See also the chapter in this *Handbook* on electronic protection.

## Social Engineering and Information Mining

Human knowledge is an asset less tangible than data on a disk but worth possessing, especially if one is mounting a cyberattack. An attacker can employ a variety of creative ways to obtain information. *Social engineering* involves duping someone else to achieve one's own illegitimate end. The perpetrator—who may or may not be an outsider—typically impersonates an insider having some privileges ("I forgot my password..."). The request may be for privileged information ("Please remind me of my password...") or for an action requiring greater privileges ("Please reset my password..."). Larger organizations are easier targets for outsiders because no one knows everyone in the firm. Less famous than social engineering are methods of mining public information. Some information must necessarily remain public, some should not be revealed, and some should be obfuscated.

Domain name service information related to an organization—domain names, IP (Internet protocol) addresses, and contact information for key IT personnel—must be stored in an online *"whois" database*. If the name of a server is imprudently chosen, it may reveal the machine's maker, software, or role. Such information makes the IP addresses more useful for cyberattacks. Knowing the key IT personnel may make it easier to pose as an insider for social-engineering purposes.

Currently, the most obvious place to look for public information is an organization's own Web site. Unless access is controlled so that only specific users can view specific pages, anyone might learn about corporate hardware, software, vendors, and clients. The organizational chart and other, subtler clues about corporate culture may also aid a social-engineering attack. Of course, this information and more may be available in print.

Another dimension of the Internet in which one can snoop is newsgroup bulletin boards. By passively searching these public discussions (*"lurking"*), an attacker might infer which company is running which software on which hardware. He or she may instead fish actively for information. An even more active approach is to provide disinformation, leading someone to incorrectly configure a system. See also the chapter in this *Handbook* on information leakage.

## Acceptable Use

A growing problem is that of improper use of resources by those who are authorized to use them as an essential part of work-related duties. Before the Digital Age, infractions would have been on the level of personal phone calls and photocopying. Now there are far more ways to misuse information resources, and the consequences can be much greater. The most pressing problem now is personal Internet access in the workplace. Volonino and Robinson (2004) cited two studies that quantify the magnitude of the problem. One, by IDC Research, estimated that 30% to 40% of workplace Internet usage in 2003 was not work related. In another, Websence claims that *cyberslacking* costs U.S. businesses $85 billion per year in lost productivity.

Forms of inappropriate use include:

1. accessing confidential data for personal reasons,
2. downloading pirated music or software,
3. launching cyberattacks or enabling resources to become launching points for attacks by others,
4. downloading pornography,
5. creating a hostile work environment because of downloaded materials, and
6. exchanging information in connection with criminal activities (e.g., fraud or money laundering).

The consequences of these inappropriate uses include:

1. lost productivity due to time misspent,
2. expended bandwidth and therefore reduced speed for authorized services,
3. legal action based on employee claims of a hostile work environment,
4. legal action based on violation of intellectual property rights,
5. legal action based on the use of resources (even if by outsiders) in illegal activities, and
6. damage to an organization's reputation.

Beyond the obvious waste of time for which employees are being compensated, there may also be a significant impact on an organization's available bandwidth. In some institutions, the (often illegal) downloading of entertainment media has, in some cases, exceeded the volume of all other Internet traffic. From a practical standpoint, inbound or outbound Internet traffic can be selectively blocked, filtered, or *shaped;* the last is the least intrusive because it limits the portion of bandwidth that can be consumed by certain services but not prohibit them entirely.

The direct impact on the bottom line is not the only consequence of improper use. Legal precedent has established that a company that does not actively prevent inappropriate behavior by its employees within the job's time-space domain is seen as promoting that misconduct and may be held liable for it; this is the principle of *respondeat superior*. Violation of intellectual property rights is one concern. When the Internet activity of some employees offends other employees, a company is likely to incur legal action for neglecting its duty of care obligations to employees by allowing the creation of a hostile work environment. Chapter 6 of Volonino and Robinson (2004) is a brief but excellent introduction to the concept of acceptable use.

## CONCLUSION

In the era of digital information, physical threats tend to receive less attention than threats mounted via cyberspace. Yet physical threats can have effects as profound or even more profound than cyberattacks.

The scope of physical threats is wider than is immediately evident. It concerns an organization's resources, wherever they go. An asset often forgotten is employees' knowledge. Equally important are their intentions. Thus, any employee may pose or mitigate a physical threat.

Ultimately, physical threats can come in any shape at any time. Aside from the human attacker's penchant for exploiting the element of surprise, nature and human error can be just as unpredictable. A single year (2003) saw tropical storms form in the North Atlantic more than a month before and a month after "hurricane season," California's worst wildfires rage after "fire season," some of the most powerful solar flares erupt in an "off year," power grids fail on a scale that "was never supposed to happen again," and hazardous debris rain down from a disintegrating space shuttle *Columbia* during reentry.

## GLOSSARY

**Class A Fire**   Fire involving ordinary combustibles (e.g., wood, paper, and some plastics).

**Class B Fire**   Fire involving flammable or combustible liquid or gas (e.g., most solvents).

**Class C Fire**   Class A or Class B fire amid energized electrical wiring or equipment, which precludes the use of extinguishing agents of a conductive nature (e.g., water or foam).

**Combustible**   Capable of burning at normal ambient temperature (perhaps without a flame).

**Electrical Noise**   electromagnetic interference, especially interference conducted through the power input, or minor spikes.

**Electromagnetic Interference (EMI)**   Undesired electrical anomalies (imperfections in the desired waveform) due to externally originating electromagnetic energy, either conducted or radiated.

**Flammable**   Capable of burning with a flame; for liquids, having a flash point below $38°C$ ($100°F$).

**Heating, Ventilation, and Air Conditioning (HVAC)**   Equipment for maintaining environmental air characteristics suitable for humans and equipment.

**Radio Frequency Interference (RFI)**   Sometimes used as a synonym for EMI, but technically the subset of EMI due to energy in the "radio" range (which includes frequencies also classified as microwave energy).

**Sag** or **Brownout**   A drop in voltage.

**Smoke**   Gaseous, particulate, and aerosol by-products of (imperfect) combustion.

**Spike, Transient,** or **Transient Voltage Surge (TVS)**   A momentary (less than 1 cycle) increase in voltage.

**Surge**   A sudden increase in electrical current; also used for spike, because the two often arrive together.

**Tempest** or **Compromising Emissions**   Electromagnetic emanations from electrical equipment that carry recoverable information, popularly referred to by the code word for a U.S. government program to combat the problem.

## CROSS REFERENCES

See *Corporate Spying: The Legal Aspects; Electronic Protection; Fixed-Line Telephone System Vulnerabilities; Information Leakage: Detection and Countermeasures; Internal Security Threats; Physical Security Measures.*

## REFERENCES

Anderson, R. (2001). *Security engineering: A guide to building dependable distributed systems.* New York: Wiley.

Cote, A. E. (Ed.). (2003). *Fire protection handbook (2003 ed.).* Quincy, MA: National Fire Protection Association.

Electrostatic Discharge Association. (2001). *Fundamentals of ESD.* Retrieved January 12, 2005, from http://www.esda.org/basics/part1.cfm

Garfinkel, S., with Spafford, G. (2002). *Web security, privacy, and commerce.* Sebastapol, CA: O'Reilley & Associates.

Hartke, J. (2001). *Measures of CD-R longevity.* Retrieved November 11, 2004, from http://www.mscience.com/longev.html

International Advisory Committee for the UNESCO Memory of the World Programme staff. (2000). *Memory of the world: Safeguarding the documentary heritage.* Retrieved November 11, 2004, from http://webworld.unesco.org/safeguarding/en

International Commission on Non-Ionizing Radiation Protection. (1998). Guidelines for Limiting Exposure to Time-Varying Electric, Magnetic, and Electromagnetic Fields (up to 300 GHz). *Health Physics, 75,* 494–522. Retrieved December 6, 2003, from http://www.icnirp.de/documents/emfgdl.pdf

McNamara, J. (2002). *The unofficial tempest information page.* Retrieved December 6, 2003, from http://www.eskimo.com/~joelm/tempest.html

National Fire Protection Association. (2003). *Standard for the protection of electronic computer/data processing equipment* (NFPA 75, 2003 ed.). Quincy, MA: Author.

National Radiological Protection Board. (2005). *Mobile phones and health.* Retrieved January 12, 2005, from http://www.nrpb.org/press/press_releases/2005/press_release_02_05.htm

Skoudis, E. (2002). *Counter hack: A step-by-step guide to computer attacks and effective defenses.* Upper Saddle River, NJ: Prentice Hall PTR.

Tapanes, E., & Carroll, D. (1999). *Securing fibre optic communication links against tapping.* Retrieved December 2, 2004, from http://www.fft.com.au/products/FOSL_WP.PDF

U.S.–Canada Power System Outage Task Force. (2004). *Final report on the August 14, 2003 blackout in the United States and Canada: Causes and recommendations.* Retrieved November 11, 2004, from https://reports.energy.gov/BlackoutFinal-Web.pdf

Volonino, L., & Robinson, S. R. (2004). *Principles and Practices of Information Security.* Upper Saddle River, NJ: Pearson Prentice Hall.

## FURTHER READING

Future Fibre Technologies. (2003). *Fibre optic secure link.* Retrieved December 2, 2004, from http://www.fft.com.au/products/fosl.shtm

International Electrotechnical Commission. (2001). *Information technology equipment-safety—part 1: General requirements* (IEC 60950–1, Ed. 1). Geneva: International Electrotechnical Commission.

National Computer Security Center. (1991). *A guide to understanding data remanence in automated information systems, version 2* (NCSC-TG-025). Retrieved December 6, 2003, from http://www.radium.ncsc.mil/tpep/library/NCSC-TG-025.2.pdf

Rittinghouse, J. W., & Hancock, W. M. (2003). *Cybersecurity operations handbook.* Burlington, MA: Elsevier Digital Press.

Svenson, P. (2004). *CDs and DVDs not so immortal after all.* Retrieved October 23, 2004, from http://www.cnn.com/2004/TECH/ptech/05/06/disc.rot.ap/index.html

# Fixed-Line Telephone System Vulnerabilities

Mak Ming Tak and Xu Yan, *Hong Kong University of Science and Technology*
Zenith Y. W. Law, *JustSolve Consulting, Hong Kong*

## INTRODUCTION

Since their invention in 1876, fixed-line telephone networks have evolved from copper wires to a web of sophisticated fiber optic and digital devices linking people and businesses all over the world. At present, the voice over Internet protocol (VoIP) service is accelerating its pace of diffusion. Owing to growing scale and increasing complexity, the fixed-line telephone system represents serious risk-management issues. The frequency with which unauthorized individuals hack into telephone systems is alarming. As portals to the world community, vulnerabilities inherent in fixed-line telephone systems can provide opportunities for terrorism, industrial espionage, and malicious hacking.

Although fixed-line telephone systems have been subject to increased security breaches in recent years, few studies have been conducted in this area. This chapter makes an important contribution to research in telephone security and related issues. It provides an overview of the economic, political, social, and financial implications of a secured fixed-line telephone system and then addresses the threats and vulnerabilities of traditional and emerging systems. Finally, countermeasures to vulnerabilities are reviewed.

## IMPLICATIONS OF A SECURE FIXED-LINE TELEPHONE SYSTEM

The fixed-line telephone remains the primary medium of communication in today's society. In many countries, telephone service is considered a basic human need, along with food, water, and electricity. Because of its importance, disruption or unavailability of telephone service has a significant impact on society. Disruption of service not only limits people's ability to communicate with others, it also has serious economic, political, social, and financial implications.

### Economic Implications

Telephone systems, along with other telecommunication systems, play a significant role in economic development. Chakraborty and Nandi (2003) found a positive causal relationship between teledensity and gross domestic product (GDP), that is, the growth in telephone penetration rate leads to growth in the GDP. The telephone network acts as a platform or infrastructure for other value-added services such as telemarketing, facsimile, toll-free service, telephone banking and business transaction, and, importantly, Internet access. Therefore, a secure and robust telephone system has significant implications to a nation's economy.

### Political Implications

Telephone service is heavily regulated by the government because it is arguably an essential element of a nation's infrastructure. Ensuring the universal availability of a reliable and secure telephone service is part of the political commitments of many governments. Normally, the telephone company is bound by a contractual agreement with the government, and any violation of services will be subject to civil lawsuit raised by the contracted parties. In many countries, the telephone company is required to submit monthly reports detailing the cause of any disruptions that may have occurred.

### Social Implications

The public's reliance on the telephone service cannot be understated. Telephone service remains the primary means of communication. The use of telephone service ranges from personal communication to requesting assistance in the event of an emergency.

An example of the significance of telephone service to a city is the fire that disabled a central office in downtown Toronto, Canada, for more than 6 hours on July 17, 1999. The accident affected more than 110,000 phone lines and brought chaos to the city, as all essential services such as emergency calls to hospitals and police stations were suspended during the period (Cribb & Lu, 1999).

## Financial Implications

Finally, failure of a telephone system also has direct impact on finance. Many business transactions rely on the telephone for placing, confirming, and closing an order. In addition, many financial services rely on the public switched telephone network (PSTN) for data transmission.

In the case of Toronto fire, the stock market lost nearly $1 billion dollars (Canadian) as traders were unable to place or confirm transactions. An AT&T system crash on January 15, 1990, caused by a faulty system bug, led to nearly $60 million (U.S.) in lost revenue, as well as intangible damage to reputation and customer confidence (Ryan & Ryan, 1997).

## VULNERABILITIES OF TRADITIONAL FIXED-LINE TELEPHONE SYSTEMS

Given the significant implications of the fixed-line telephone system, it is crucial to protect the network from attacks and from failures ranging from system bugs to improper operation. Various threats and vulnerabilities exist in the following main components of a traditional telephone system:

1. Customer equipment
2. Cabling
3. Switching facilities
4. Signaling and protocol standards
5. Value-added voice service facilities

Key terms presented in this chapter are defined in the following paragraphs.

*Hacking* means gaining access to a system or its data, or even modifying a system from the basic configuration, with or without authorization. A hacker is one who attempts to perform the task. If the hacker's access is legitimate, meaning the actions are taken with the intention of helping the system owner to identify security flaws, the hacker is referred to as a "white-hat hacker," "sneaker," or "ethical hacker." Otherwise, the hacker is referred to as "black-hat hacker" or "cracker," and the activity is regarded as an illegitimate criminal act.

*Phreaking* refers to manipulating a telephone system for actions considered criminal, such as making free calls or having calls charged to another account.

*War dialing* is the action of dialing a given list or range of phone numbers and recording those that answer with handshake tones—a predetermined signal used to establish connections between two terminal devices (and so might be entry points to computer or telecommunication systems). It can detect modem, fax, or private branch exchanges (PBXs) tones and log each one separately for nefarious purposes.

*Wiretapping* is a physical action in which an alternate connection is made on the telephone wire or at the central office to eavesdrop on the telephone conversation.

*Social engineering* is a practice for obtaining sensitive computer information through interaction with users. It includes methods such as stealing user IDs and passwords from garbage or memos. The attacker may also masquerade as a technical support worker and request the victim to reveal his or her user ID and password for future intrusion.

*Packet sniffing* is reviewing the contents of network traffic using analyzing software. By capturing live network traffic, it may be possible to decode packet information for illegitimate purposes.

*Denial of service (DoS)* is a type of attack on a network system that causes service disruptions. DoS can be initiated by a single entity or by multiple entities (distributed DoS) working to disable the victim's network system by overloading available resources.

*A brute-force attack* is a password-reviewing technique that makes sequential attempts of various possibilities until a password is revealed.

## Customer Equipment Vulnerabilities
### Phone Handset
The phone handset is basic equipment consisting of an earpiece, a mouthpiece, and a key pad that enables the user to access basic telephone services. Because of its simplistic design, the handset possesses little or no security mechanism and is therefore the most vulnerable item in the telephone system. For example, the handset does not have any authentication mechanism in place to identify users. Also, it can easily be tapped for eavesdropping (Freeman, 1999).

### Fax Machine
The fax machine is a device for transmitting a written document over telephone lines. Like a telephone handset, a fax machine also provides opportunities for fraud and intrusion. The current fax standard defined by the International Telecommunications Union (ITU) has not incorporated any authentication standard to verify the fax message's origination as well as its recipients. As a result, anyone can fax fake or altered documents. Faxed documents may also be accidentally sent to a wrong number or person, allowing personal, privileged, or confidential information to fall into the wrong hands without the sender's knowledge (Orvis & Lehn, 1995).

### Modem
The Modulator/Demodulator (modem) is a hardware device that converts digital computer signals into analog signals for transmission over a telephone network. Because of the high penetration rate and low cost of the telephone network, the modem was a popular choice for data access

from the 1960s to late 1990s. The typical transmission rate for a modem is 56 kbps.

Modems, aside from being used for data transmission, are also used for connection with the PBX to enable the direct inward dial (DID) service, which allows each internal telephone station to connect the external caller directly. This service, however, has raised security risks. Because the human operator involved in the call connection is bypassed, the DID service allows the outside caller to contact the internal parties directly without being screened by an operator. Additionally, because the DID service is exposed to the public at all times, hackers and phreakers can use their own modems to seek entry points at the perimeters of targeted networks by using techniques such as war dialing.

Modems can also be used to send and receive facsimiles by using fax software such as Symantec WinFax or HylaFAX. Unfortunately, these have the same security vulnerabilities from the facsimile.

## Cabling Vulnerabilities

### Local Loop

In order to provide telephone service to the customer, a local loop is needed to connect the telephone handset with the Central Offices (CO) or Class 5 switches. To ease the equipment installation, service provision, troubleshooting, and expansion, the physical telephone line of a local loop is divided into different segments. Each segment is terminated at the Intermediate Distribution Frame (IDF) and is then consolidated at the Main Distribution Frame (MDF). Both the IDFs and the MDFs are unmanned facilities (or simply a cabinet) located in an open area or inside a locked room in a building.

The IDF and MDF, while allowing the telephone company to provide new services and repatch the faulty telephone wire quickly, do have their drawbacks. Both the IDF and the MDF consist of rows of connectors and the connections are cramped close together for space-saving purposes. As time goes by and these distribution frames are not managed properly, the frame will be filled with loose wires, making troubleshooting and provisioning vulnerable to accidental disconnection or faulty installation.

Another known vulnerability is using the *linesmen handset* at the distribution frames. Because the local loops are running electrical signal with no encryption, there is no protection in place for unauthorized tapping or interception. The issue becomes even worse when linesmen handsets can be easily acquired from specialty stores or assembled according to schematics available on the Internet, making the padlock in front of the distribution frames the only real protection.

### Trunks

Trunks are used to interconnect switches of different types, such as Class 5 "ingress" and "egress" switches, Class 4 tandem switches, PBXs, and COs, to form a telephone server infrastructure. The media used may be wire-pair cables, fiber optic cables, microwave radio, or satellite channels. Under normal circumstances, trunks along with the phone company's Class 4 and Class 5 switches, are safeguarded within the CO premises with proper access control such as a security guard and locks. Threats such as fire, accidents, internal vandalism, physical attacks, sabotage, and unauthorized eavesdropping on the trunk are possible, however, and should not be underestimated (Simonds, 1996).

Another issue of concern about the vulnerabilities of the trunk relates to PBXs, where the security of the trunk and other telecommunication devices has often been neglected. In many small to medium-sized companies, it is common to see that the PBX and trunk cables are freely exposed in an open area and are subject to accidental cable cut or vandalism.

## Telephone Switching Facilities Vulnerabilities

### PBX

The PBX, or private area branch exchange (PABX), is a phone switch used for a private telephone network within an enterprise. Users of the PBX can share a certain number of outside lines to save the line subscription fee. The PBX also allows an enterprise to customize additional features such as specific dialing plans for its internal phone system. For example, the PBX makes it easier to call someone within a PBX because the number a user needs to dial is typically just three or four digits.

PBX is one of the most commonly used systems and also one of the most vulnerable systems. The most commonly met vulnerabilities are as follows:

**Public availability of password**—PBX administrators or contractors may use the default password provided by the manufacturers rather than change it to a private one. Because default passwords are publicly available on line, it is easy for phreakers to access the PBX for foul play (National Institute of Standards and Technology, 2001). A sample Web site (http://www.cirt.net/cgi-bin/passwd.pl) lists out the default passwords of various systems, including PBXs.

**Hacking via remote access**—Another common vulnerability of the PBX is the fact that it can be hacked via remote management access. To consolidate resources, some companies outsource the maintenance of PBX to vendors or contractors. Normally these vendors and contractors monitor the PBX remotely. This remote management capability has enabled phreakers and hackers to gain illegitimate access to PBX through methods such as social engineering or war dialing and to conduct the following illegal activities:

*Toll fraud*—Toll fraud is accomplished by modifying PBX configurations so that one can charge long-distance calls and teleconference services to a victim's account. Toll fraud is the number-one issue facing PBXs users. In the United States alone, toll fraud accounted for $4 billion annual loss to private enterprises and carriers (Tipton & Krause, 2003).

Motivations for toll fraud range from inability or unwillingness to pay for long-distance services to attempts to hide identity when engaging in criminal activities. Toll fraud is achieved by the following methods:

- Social engineering—toll fraud can be achieved by simply borrowing the victim's phone or obtaining sensitive PBX information from the victim. Social engineering is common in companies that have not deployed network class of services to block long-distance calls on public-access phone stations.

- Theft of service—toll fraud can also be achieved through internal and external theft. Internal employees may abuse PBX for long-distance services; the service can also be abused by phreakers who manipulate the PBX by scanning its maintenance ports or the PBX direct inward system access ports.

*Using the compromised PBX as a relay to attack other victims*—When compromised, an Internet protocol (IP)–enabled PBX can be used to hide a phreaker's tracks or to conduct activities such as a DoS attack.

*Illegal access to automatic call distribution (ACDs)*—Most PBXs offer an ACD feature such as silent monitoring to display customer-related information or capture audio records for authentication or training purposes. By allowing this information to fall into the hands of phreakers or hackers, a company may suffer sabotage or industrial espionage.

*Unauthorized access to private information, such as customer account details and PBX system configurations*—Compromised information, such as PBX system configurations, users' password, or users' voice mail information, allows phreakers and hackers to gain knowledge of the PBX system or user accounts for future reintrusion purposes.

These are only a few examples of PBX vulnerabilities. To combat exploitation of PBX by illegitimate means, the National Institute of Standards and Technology of the U.S. Department of Commerce (2001) has published a paper offering instructions for conducting PBX vulnerability analysis.

## Centrex

Centrex stands for central office exchange. This system provides virtual PBX service over a public telephone network for small companies. Centrex offers two significant advantages over PBX: reduced space and maintenance requirements. Because Centrex offers similar features to PBX, it has essentially the same types of vulnerabilities (Abrahams & Lollo, 2003).

## PSTN

PSTN is the aggregation of the public circuit-switched telephone networks throughout the world. The PSTN typically consists of switches of various classes and types, such as tandem exchanges, toll exchanges, local exchanges, and COs. The PSTN provides a rich set of services, procedures, and functions to data, voice, and teleconferencing users through a bundle of protocols, software, and other related products. These make PSTN vulnerable to security threats, however. Given that today's feature-rich telephone network involves a high degree of complexity with numerous functionalities, it is increasingly difficult for the developer to test new equipment and software adequately before installation. As a result, software anomalies, or bugs, may exist and lead to irregular functioning of the telephone system. In addition to technical challenges, PSTN is also subject to external threats such as fire, destruction

of COs, terrorism, and sabotage (Mazda, 1996). These vulnerabilities are discussed in other sections of this chapter.

## Telephone Signaling Protocol and Standard Vulnerabilities

### Signaling System 7 (SS7)

SS7 is used among telephone companies' central offices to set up calls, indicate their status, and disable calls when they are completed (Rowe, 2001). The SS7 standard offers the following features (Russell, 1998):

**Open Standards**—SS7 is an open standard that is approved by the ITU. The standard guarantees interoperability among SS7-compliant equipment within a PSTN.

**Separation of voice and data path**—SS7 uses separate lines to set up calls used for voice and for data transmission, which can improve the efficiency of networks (Rowe, 2002).

**Packet switching**—SS7 uses packet switching to carry multiple voice signaling information over a single channel.

**Advanced Intelligent Network (AIN)**—AIN provides database querying and programming capability to the PSTN through the SS7 network. The new programming platform allows the telephone company to create value-added services such as calling cards, automatic billing, caller ID, toll-free (800/888) calling, toll (900) calling, local number portability (LNP), and short messaging service (SMS).

Although the implementation of SS7 has significantly enhanced PSTN services, it has also brought additional security problems (Casey, 1996; Lorenz, Moore, Manes, Hale, & Shenoi, 2001). The following vulnerabilities related to SS7 have been identified.

**Easy access to SS7 information**—Because SS7 was designed for a closed community, the standards developers were primarily concerned with high availability and redundancy, which enables the network to protect itself against system failure. However, the U.S. Telecom Act of 1996 and the emergence of VoIP have brought unforeseen threats to the signaling environment. According to the act, the incumbent carriers must open their SS7 networks to all other carriers for unbundling fees as low as $10,000. Similar deregulation is occurring worldwide. Unregulated access may enable a terrorist organization or hacker to disrupt the network by injecting malicious code in the wider connected PSTN, thereby placing national security at risk. The growing interoperation between VoIP services and the SS7 network has also brought unprecedented instability to this once closed environment because of the different signaling systems used (International Engineering Consortium [IEC], 2004).

**Network intrusion**—With an SS7-compliant system, telephone users can access automated telephone services all the time. Currently, the SS7 system uses a touch-tone password authorization scheme for customer authentication. However, because the touch-tone system offers only 10 combination tones (0–9) with password length from 4 to 8 digits, it is insufficient to implement complexity sufficient to combat today's cyber criminals. With today's powerful toolkits, a customer password can be easily discovered with the help of a brute-force attack method, that is, using a computer system to scan through all combinations of 4 to 6 digits. Once the password has been obtained, customer information is typically accessed within a short period of time, and the privileged services can be abused by unauthorized sources.

**Malicious coding attacks**—Formerly, there were a small number of telephone system manufacturers, which made it possible to test and modify new applications rigorously before their delivery to a telephone company. SS7 has provided a common platform for application development that has encouraged other new players to develop applications. As a result, new suppliers and manufacturers no longer test applications thoroughly before making their products available to customers. Some cite insufficient staffing, funding, and resources as the reason for this; others indicate that intense competition makes rigorous testing cost-prohibitive (IEC, 2004). This practice has made the PSTN increasingly vulnerable to unexpected errors or bugs that may cause system failure. In extreme cases, these bugs will be exploited by hackers to disrupt the normal operation of the telephone system.

## Value-Added Voice Service Facility Vulnerabilities

Value-added voice services are highly susceptible to attacks from phreakers and hackers. The following value-added voice services are most vulnerable to attacks.

### Voice Mail

Voice mail is a common feature available in PBX and Centrex systems to record messages of unanswered calls. Because of the inherent weakness of short passwords, phreakers can easily gain illegal access to the victim's voice mailbox using social engineering, brute-force attacks, or common password dictionary attacks (a way of guessing the password by using victims' personal information such as birthdays or telephone numbers). Through the compromised voice mail, phreakers can review private voice massages. In extreme cases, phreakers can falsify messages or overload the voice mail system using DoS attacks and message flooding.

### Interactive Voice Response System (IVRS)

IVRS is an auto-answering system providing a hierarchical voice menu system to manage incoming calls. Similar to the voice mail system, extensive planning and programming are required for the logic and the flow of sequences. Because IVRS is a software program, it is vulnerable to system malfunctions and anomalies resulting from improper programming and installation (White, et al., 2001).

### Calling Cards

Calling cards allow users to make long-distance phone calls by charging a prepaid or preregistered account. Although the service has created substantial cost savings and convenience for phone users, calling cards are among the services that are most vulnerable to toll fraud.

Because the password of a calling card normally has only 4 to 6 digits, phreakers can easily hack it if the card is stolen or the information is disclosed. The password can also be retrieved by redialing the last number of the phone or simply by watching the number on the phone display while the victim enters the information.

## VULNERABILITIES OF THE EMERGING TELEPHONE TECHNOLOGY
### Voice Over Internet Protocol

VoIP technology allows users to make telephone calls over an Internet connection instead of a traditional analogue telephone line. To make a call, users can use a computer or a phone with a special adaptor. The adaptor works as an interface between the telephone and the Internet. The user can also download a "soft phone" on the computer desktop and dial by clicking on the key displayed on the soft phone, just as one would normally do using a real telephone.

VoIP represents the technology trend of digital convergence: By converting the analogue voice signal into IP packets, traditional analogue telephone service is transformed into data communication. VoIP may offer new features and services that are not available with traditional phones. For example, a voice message can be attached to an e-mail as a voice file and can be delivered to the receiving party's e-mail box. VoIP can also facilitate the portability of telephone service. For example, a user can use VoIP service through an adaptor wherever he or she travels as long as an Internet connection is available.

The convergence of voice and data communications has enabled VoIP to become a powerful and economic way of communication. At the same time, this has raised new concerns regarding telephone system vulnerabilities because VoIP has inherited the vulnerabilities associated with both telephone and data networks. The U.S. Defense Information Systems Agency (DISA) has identified and summarized these vulnerabilities as follows (DISA, 2004):

**Sniffing**—Sniffing can result in disclosure of confidential information, unprotected user credentials, and the potential for identity theft. It also allows sophisticated malicious users to collect information about users' VoIP systems that can be used to mount an attack on other systems or on data that might not otherwise be vulnerable. IP networks differ from circuit-switched networks because information is sent over commonly accessible paths. All the tools needed for sniffing, including H.323 and SIP plugins for packet sniffers, are available on open-source Web sites.

**DoS**—The traditional system (separate data and voice networks) enables an organization to maintain voice communications even when the data network fails. With the implementation of VoIP in a converged network, a DoS attack could be effective because the overly congested traffic of packets as a result of DoS attack will affect the quality of service necessary for VoIP to be functional.

**Traffic flow disruption**—Because data packets do not flow over a dedicated connection for the duration of a session, phreakers or hackers could manipulate the route of packets and cause delay in certain paths, forcing the packets to take a different path. This results in two vulnerabilities. The first enhances sniffing vulnerability because a phreaker could detect a preferred location to place a sniffing device. The second enhances the DoS vulnerability. When such an attack is applied to a VoIP network, quality of service may diminish noticeably. Additionally, VoIP may suffer the following vulnerabilities (Federal Communications Commission [FCC], 2004; Gruener, 2004):

- Some VoIP services may be suspended during power outages, and the service provider may not have backup power supplies. In traditional telephone systems, the power is supplied by the service provider via the telephone line and normally is not affected by outage of the users' private power supply.
- It may be difficult for some VoIP services to connect seamlessly with an emergency dispatch center (e.g., the 911 service center in the United States) or for emergency service providers to identify the location of VoIP emergency service callers because VoIP supports geographic portability of end users whereas traditional telephony is fixed to a specific location.
- The difficulty in identifying the caller's location may open a door for hackers or phreakers to hide themselves. It makes crimes such as telemarketing fraud difficult to combat.
- VoIP providers may or may not offer directory assistance or white page listings because some VoIP services use numbering systems different from that of the traditional telephone system.
- A growing trend in VoIP is the scourge of spam. Spam is no longer confined to the e-mail world, it is making its way into VoIP. It is easy for spammers to configure scripts to call VoIP numbers and transmit messages. Compared with e-mail spam, VoIP spam is more harmful because the gateways are hit directly, which leads to traffic disruption and degrades quality of real-time voice communications.
- Control of enterprise PBX is moving from private dedicated voice networks onto IP networks, so PBX and telephony systems are now vulnerable to the same sort of hacking that the IP-based services have experienced. In the world of VoIP, PBX serves as a server or gateway, which implies that the hackers and phreakers may gain access more easily to internal telephone systems.
- VoIP phone, similar to other IP-enabled devices, lacks protection against malicious attacks. A recent study from Secure Lab demonstrated that some VoIP phones are susceptible to DoS attacks and ARP (address resolution protocol) spoofing, allowing "man-in-the-middle" attacks including data interception and packet injection, making IP phones vulnerable to wiretapping and Trojan horse attacks (ICT Security, 2004).

Generally speaking, VoIP network security refers to both voice-packet and IP security. The former focuses on application concerns and the latter on a transport or network security. At the application level, a system that provides a layer of abstraction protecting the application from potential vulnerabilities of the underlying operation system is needed. At the transport, or OS, level, high-performance encryption technologies and clustering technologies are needed (Malaney, 2004). Controlling security at these levels of the VoIP environment may require network redesign or reengineering, which will affect the architecture of the network supporting the VoIP environment.

Even though today's data network technology (e.g., firewalls) may provide adequate protection for VoIP traffic within the protected infrastructure, implementing such proper security measures is both expensive and complicated (Mier, Birdsall, & Thayer, 2004).

## COUNTERMEASURES FOR TELEPHONE SYSTEM VULNERABILITIES

Given the seriousness of the telephone system vulnerability, critical countermeasures must be taken to guarantee the security of the telephone system. In the context of digital convergence, the security of the telephone system can be enhanced by taking almost all technical precautions for data communications security, such as encryption. Because these technical solutions are elaborated on in Volume III of this *Handbook*, this chapter simply highlights countermeasures from legal and managerial perspectives.

### Countermeasures from the Legal Perspective: The U.S. Case

Telephone security, especially the protection of personal privacy, has been a significant issue since the invention of the device. To collect evidence and criminal intelligence, law enforcement officials have widely adopted techniques such as wiretapping to monitor suspected criminals' telephone conversations. Although the technique has been proven effective, questions on what and how the information should be collected were raised. In the United States, individuals' privacy is protected by the Fourth Amendment of the U.S. Constitution:

> The right of the people to be secure in their persons, houses, papers, and effects, against unreasonable searches and seizures, shall not be violated, and no warrant shall issue, but upon probable cause, supported by Oath or affirmation, and particularly describing the place to be searched, and the persons or things to be seized.

The U.S. Supreme Court has had to balance law enforcement's reasonable needs against the rightful privacy needs of the public. Because the Supreme Court was uncertain whether telephone lines should be protected from wiretapping, telephone wires could be tapped by anybody without obtaining a warrant from the courts. This situation was not changed until the publication of the Communications Act of 1934. A provision in Section 605 of the act provided that "no person not being authorized by the sender shall intercept any communications and divulge or publish [its] existence, contents, substance, purport, effect, or meaning. . . ." The telephone was defined as one of the communications in the act and was therefore under protection. In accord with the Supreme Court, however, wiretapping by the federal government without a warrant was legal until the "expectation of privacy" cases in 1967, when the Court decided that a communication is private when at least one party has such expectation. At that time, the Court prohibited interception by government and electronic eavesdropping of aural communications carried by common carriers. In response to the Court's decision, Congress passed two federal laws protecting communications from eavesdroppers while the communications were in transit from the sender to the receiver or in storage. These two laws are the Omnibus Crime Control and Safe Streets Act (Crime Control Act) of 1968 and the Electronic Communications Privacy Act (ECPA) of 1986. Later, these two laws were balanced by the Communications Privacy Act for Law Enforcement Act (CALEA) of 1994.

Title III of the Crime Control Act of 1968 is also known as Wiretap Act of 1968 and is codified at 18 USC §§ 2510-21. Title III explicitly states that to protect privacy rights, all wiretaps require a court order and careful supervision by a federal court. In 1986, the Wiretap Act of 1968 was updated by the Electronic Communications Privacy Act (ECPA), codified at 18 USC §§ 2510-21 and 2710-10. According to the ECPA, the coverage of protection was extended from "in transit" to "in storage" and from public common carriers to all private networks. In 1996, the ECPA was updated in light of the dramatic change in computing and telecommunications technologies, especially the Internet. Electronic mail (e-mail) was included for protection, and enforcement was extended to all carriers in addition to the common carrier.

The ECPA of 1996 narrowed the definition of the contents of communication, however. At present, it includes only "information concerning the substance, purport, or meaning of the communication" and excludes the protection from "interception or disclosure," "information about the identities of the parties," or "the existence of the communication." In recent years, this exception has been used several times to track threatening e-mail messages (Black, 2002).

The last section of the ECPA, Title I, provides for Enforcement of the Communications Assistance for Law Enforcement Act (CALEA) of 1994, also called the Digital Telephone Act. Background for the Congress to enact the CALEA included the fact that the rapid advances experienced in telecommunications technology had affected law enforcement's ability to conduct court-approved wiretaps and other forms of electronic surveillance. In the CALEA, Congress urged all communications service providers to ensure that law enforcement personnel are able to continue legal interceptions of communications and electronic surveillance. To ensure this, all telecommunications carriers are required by CALEA to ensure that their equipment, facilities, and services are capable of meeting law enforcement assistance criteria specified in Section 103 of CALEA. They are also required to disclose detailed subscriber account information, including communicators' identities and addresses. However, "information services," "private networks," and the "interconnection services and facilities" are excluded from the Section 103 requirements (Black, 2002).

The U.S. laws reviewed here have provided a transparent legal framework that guarantees the security of the telephone system by balancing user privacy and public safety. At the same time, carriers can use the need to protect network security as an excuse to defend their interests, including monopoly status. One relevant case was the 1968 Carterfone decision. The Carterfone was a device developed by Carter Electronics of Texas. It was a small box used to connect radio calls to a fixed-line network. It was simply nonelectrical equipment that connected the two systems acoustically. AT&T responded by threatening to disconnect the service of any users who used Carterfone; its rationale was the need to maintain the security of the network. In fact, the main purpose was to defend its monopoly of end-to-end telecommunications service and equipment. Carter sued AT&T and won after AT&T failed to demonstrate how the Carterfone could threaten network security. Accordingly, in its 1968 decision, the FCC decided that equipment manufactured independently could be attached to the network provided that an interface device was used to protect the network from harm (Black, 2002; Temin, 1987).

## Countermeasures from the Managerial Perspective

Given the sophistication of current telephone networks, it is not an exaggeration to claim that it is impossible to eliminate all vulnerabilities. From the managerial perspective, the goal of a successful security guarantee is to ensure noninterruption of system operation by minimizing threats and vulnerabilities to the extent that the cost and complexity of countermeasures are justifiable.

Because the term *security* is highly subjective, it is up to individual companies to formulate their own security strategies. The following tips should nonetheless be constructive to formulate an effective security strategy.

### Define a Plan, Rules, and Procedures

A security strategy starts with a plan to identify resources that require protection. Resources, from a general perspective, refer to tangible or physical items with associated values. In reality, intangible resources such as company financial information, sensitive documents, and mission-critical services should also be included. Additionally, during the identification process, information such as equipment description and specification, equipment location, and individual's responsibility should also be defined.

Once the resources have been identified, assessment of the degree of protection is required. At this stage, considerations such as the resource's criticality to the business operation, available budget, government regulations, corporate requirements, industry standard practices, possible threats and vulnerabilities of the resource, and damages if resources cease to operate are reviewed and assessed.

Finally, on the basis of the assessment, rules and procedures are designed and formulated. The complexity may vary, but ease of deployment should be taken into consideration. Sufficient authentication, records, and logs should be generated for future cross-reference and trace.

## Security System Planning

A secure telephone system is subject to proper planning. In the case of VoIP, it is critical that all systems in the VoIP infrastructure are designed with network security in mind, with security features built directly into the system from the beginning. Information technology managers must first think carefully about the degree of security that their systems and applications can provide: are they based on a highly scalable and reliable OS? Are they built using a secured application programming language and protocol? Only by looking at security from the inside out and by choosing a technology vender that builds systems and solutions in the same manner can IT managers successfully steer security and deliver the degree of reliability the user expects. It is the IT manager's job to look for vendors that can offer not only best methods and practices for tailoring the OS to its environment but also security architectures to build on (Malaney, 2004).

## Proper Equipment Protection

In addition to proper rules and procedures, resources should be provided with proper protection and maintenance. In the case of VoIP, for example, a network administrator must ensure that all critical VoIP network and server components are located in a secured area and restrict access to server rooms and network-wiring closets to trusted authorized personnel only. A network administrator must also ensure that telephony terminals (IP phones) do not display the network IP configuration information on their displays (DISA, 2004).

Because online intrusion and sabotage have become more serious since the advent of the Internet, a proper suite of security infrastructures such as firewall, authentication server, and proxy server should be put in place to protect vital company resources. Some vital features to include in a proper VoIP protection environment are as follows (Mier, 2004):

- VoIP call control, that is, the ability to deploy network address translation and tunnel call control through the firewall
- Transmission control protocol (TCP) intercept, which ensures that TCP connections are completed and can prevent certain DoS assaults on the call manager
- Secure skinny call-control protocol (Secure SCCP) support, which uses a TCP connection rather than user datagram protocol (UDP) and encrypts call control information

As to the VoIP handset, the following features are recommended:

- Phone software upgrades that allow handset software or firmware to fix bugs
- Secure real-time transport protocol (RTP) support, a feature to prevent the VoIP conversations from being intercepted by unauthorized sources

The guideline prepared by the the U.S. Air Force can also be used for reference (Department of the Air Force, 1997).

## Contingency Planning

Regardless of how reliable and sophisticated the equipment, it is always subject to breakage and failure. Equipment failure can cause catastrophic disruption of business. Because it is impossible to predict the exact time equipment failure will occur, a good security strategy must include a comprehensive contingency plan.

A well-designed contingency plan is based on the following considerations:

**Tolerable downtime**—How long can the resource realistically be disabled before causing extensive damage to business? The shorter the downtime, the more sophisticated and costly the backup strategy will be.

**Available resources**—What resources are available to implement the backup strategy?

Once these have been determined, security personnel can determine the appropriate backup strategies (e.g., periodic backup, equipment redundancy, or disaster recovery and business continuity planning).

## Periodic Inspection

A successfully designed security strategy needs to be inspected periodically. This makes it possible to identify security flaws quickly and then solve them immediately. For example, the underlying OS of the VoIP is usually the target of an attack. One step that can be taken is to ensure that periodic updates and security patches are applied to any system on the network. The susceptibility to DoS attacks, viruses, and worms can be partially mitigated by a well-maintained OS platform.

A security inspection can be conducted internally or externally: an internal inspection minimizes leaks of sensitive information and is less costly; an external inspection minimizes internal conflicts of interest and provides a subjective assessment with fresh ideas from outside.

Finally, companies are also encouraged to deploy international standards such as ISO 17799 (http://www.iso.org/iso/en/CombinedQueryResult.CombinedQueryResult?queryString=17799 or http://www.17799.com) to enforce the company in taking a structured and standardized approach to security.

## Commitment at All Levels

With poor personnel commitment to security, any security strategy will be doomed to fail. Relevant employees at all levels need to understand and follow the rules involved in enforcing a security strategy.

## Continuous Improvement

Last but not least, a successful security strategy is a continuous improvement and refinement process. Because new technologies constantly emerge, security personnel must continuously improve and revise strategy to accommodate change.

Numerous Web sites provide useful information for the security staff to update their knowledge. A sampling of these includes the following:

- The International Engineering Consortium (http://www.iec.org) provides a profound resource on understanding the latest technologies with tutorials and illustrations.
- The U.S. government's Computer Security Resource Center (http://csrc.nist.gov) has information on various security issues faced by the U.S. government as well as recommendations on strengthening the security of computer and telephone systems.
- The U.S. Computer Emergency Response Team Co-ordination Center (http://www.cert.org) provides the most updated security vulnerability information regarding viruses, worms, and so forth.

# CONCLUSION

The fixed-line telephone is considered an essential public service. In many countries, universal service obligation enforces the provision of standard telephone services to all residents. The security of the fixed-line telephone service is therefore of significant importance.

Fixed-line telephone security is a complicated issue that is subject to technical, legal, and managerial effects. This chapter has provided a panoramic review of its vulnerabilities. It has also reviewed certain countermeasures dealing with the security issue, mainly from legal and managerial perspectives. Nonetheless, what this chapter includes addresses only a fraction of what these systems encounter today. In the specific context of digital convergence, service providers must face the fact that the emerging technologies such as VoIP are going to raise increasing concerns regarding telephone system vulnerabilities. In the meantime, because of resource constraints, service providers must strike a balance between security and financial resources. In this sense, it may not be an exaggeration to claim that defending telephone system security is a war without end.

# GLOSSARY

**CERT/CC**   CERT Coordination Center, the first computer security incident response team, registered with the U.S. Patent and Trademark office as service trademarks of Carnegie Mellon University.

**International Telecommunication Union (ITU)**   Headquartered in Geneva, Switzerland, this international organization allows governments and the private sector to coordinate global telecommunications networks and services.

**Public Switched Telephone Network (PSTN)**   The international telephone system based on copper wires carrying analog voice data. Newer telephone networks are based on digital technologies, such as ISDN and VoIP. Telephone service carried by the PSTN is often called plain old telephone service (POTS).

**Signaling System 7 (SS7)**   A signaling system used among telephone company central offices to set up calls, indicate their status, and terminate calls when they are completed.

**T1**   A full-duplex digital transmission facility composed of transmission media and regenerators that carry one DS1 signal.

**Voice Over Internet Protocol (VoIP)**   Also called IP telephony, VoIP refers to the act of sending voice signals over a network that uses IP protocol.

**War Dialer**   A software program used to find entry into telecommunications systems.

# CROSS REFERENCES

See *Hackers, Crackers and Computer Criminals; Physical Security Measures; Physical Security Threats; Voice Over Internet Protocol (VoIP)*.

# REFERENCES

Abrahams, J. R., & Lollo, M. (2003). *Centrex or PBX: The impact of IP*. Boston: Artech House.

Black, S. K. (2002). *Telecommunications law in the Internet age*. San Francisco: Morgan Kaufmann.

Casey, T. A., Jr. (1996). *The advanced intelligent network—a security opportunity*. Communication Systems Division, GTE Government Systems Corporation.

Chakraborty, C., & Nandi, B. (2003). Privatization, telecommunications and growth in selected Asian countries: An econometric analysis. *Communications & Strategies, 52*, 31–47.

Cribb, R., & Lu, V. (1999, July 17). No dialing, no dollars as blast pulls plug on phone system. *Toronto Star*. Retrieved June 15, 2005, from http://64.233.179.104/search?q=cache:8G6zlmwYnowJ:www.hope-tindall.com/peter/1999july.htm+No+dia-ling,+no+dollars+as+blast+pulls+plug+on+phone+sy-stem.+Toronto+Star.&hl=zh-TW

Defense Information Systems Agency. (2004, January 13). *Voice over Internet protocol (VoIP) security technical implementation guide* (ver. 1, release 1). Arlington, VA: Field Security Operations of the Defense Information Systems Agency of the United States.

Department of the Air Force. (1997). On-hook telephone security guidelines. *Communications and Information* (Air Force Manual 33-274). Retrieved from http://www.stormingmedia.us/48/4894/A489404.html

Federal Communications Commission. (2004, February 11). *FCC Consumer Facts: VoIP/Internet Voice*. Retrieved May 30, 2005, from the FCC Web site: http://ftp.fcc.gov/cgb/consumerfacts/voip.html

Freeman, R. L. (1999). *Fundamentals of telecommunications*. Wiley: New York.

Gruener, W. (2004). Experts: Future of VoIP challenged by prices, spam. Retrieved June 15, 2005, from *Tom's Hardware Guide*, http://www.tomshard-ware.com/hardnews/20041007_122306.html

ICT Security. (2004, July 9). *Data threats over Internet protocol*. Retrieved October 20, 2004, from http://www.transafrica2000.com/cgi-bin/newsread.cgi

International Engineering Consortium. (2004). *Access mediation: Preserving network security and integrity*. Retrieved June 15, 2005, from http://www.iec.org/online/tutorials/acrobat/acc_med.pdf

Lorenz, G., Moore, T., Manes, G., Hale, J., & Shenoi, S. (2001, June). Securing SS7 telecommunications networks. *Proceedings of the Second Annual IEEE Systems,*

*Man, and Cybernetics Information Assurance Workshop*, West Point, New York.

Malaney, R. (2004). Controlling threats to VoIP in the Office. Retrieved September 24, 2004, from http://www.fiercevoip.com

Mazda, F. F. (1996). *Switching systems and applications*. Oxford: Focal Press.

Mier, E., Birdsall, R., & Thayer, R. (2004). *Breaking through IP telephony*. Retrieved October 20, 2004, from http://www.nwfusion.com/reviews/2004/0524 voipsecurity.html

National Institute of Standards and Technology, U.S. Department of Commerce. (2001, April). PBX vulnerability analysis. Finding holes in your PBX before someone else does (Special publication 800-24). Gaithersburg, MD: Author. Retrieved May 30, 2004, from http://csrc.nist.gov/publications/nistpubs/800-24/sp800-24pbx.pdf

Orvis, W. J., & Lehn, A. L. V. (1995). *Data security vulnerabilities of facsimile machines and digital copiers (Computer Incident Advisory Capability Report No. UCRL-AR-118607/CIAC-2304)*. Retrieved June 15, 2005, from http://www.ciac.org/ciac/documents/CIAC-2304_Vulnerabilities_of_Facsimilie_Machines_and_Digital_Copiers.pdf

Rowe, S. H., II. (2001). *Telecommunications for managers*. Upper Saddle River, NJ: Prentice Hall.

Russell, T. (1998). *Signaling system #7*. New York: McGraw-Hill.

Ryan, D. J., & Ryan J. J. C. H. (1997). INFOSEC and INFOWAR: The protection of information assets and systems. Retrieved June 15, 2005, from http://www.julieryan.com/BOOK1297.html

Simonds, F. (1996). *Network security—data and voice communications*. New York: McGraw-Hill.

Temin, P. (1987). *The fall of the Bell system: A study in prices and politics*. Cambridge: Cambridge University Press.

Tipton, H. F., & Krause, M. (2003). *Information security management handbook* (4th ed., Vol. 4). New York: Auerbach.

White, G. B., Archer, K. T., Core, J., Cothren, C., Davis, R. L., DiCenso, D. J., Good, T. J., & Williams, D. E. (2001). *Voice and data security*. Indianapolis: Sams.

## FURTHER READING

Bellamy, J. C. (2000). *Digital telephony* (3rd ed.). New York: Wiley.

European Parliament. (1998). An appraisal of the technologies of political control: Updated executive summary prepared as a background document for the September 1998 part-session. Retrieved October 24, 2004, from http://www.europarl.eu.int/stoa/publi/166499/execsum_en.htm

Kabay, M. E. (1996). *The NCSA guide to enterprise security: Protecting information assets*. New York: McGraw-Hill.

# E-Mail Threats and Vulnerabilities

David Harley, *NHS Connecting for Health, UK*

## INTRODUCTION

The classic information technology (IT) security tripod model (integrity, confidentiality, and availability) applies as much to e-mail as it does to other areas of information management, and the medium is subject to a range of problems. Johnson (2000) categorized these as follows:

- **Eavesdropping.** This exploits susceptibility to network sniffing and other breaches of confidentiality.
- **Impersonation/identity theft.** Even though well-managed organizations use authentication to regulate access to services, many e-mail-related Internet services such as SMTP (simple mail transfer protocol) are highly vulnerable to such abuses as impersonation by forging e-mail headers. Although identity theft is an ongoing problem, the less glamorous problem of impersonation by spam and mass mailer viruses is a more persistent problem and a constant drain on resources and patience.
- **Denial of service (DoS).** This may be accomplished either by deliberate action such as e-mail traffic volume attacks (mail bombing and subscription bombing, for example) or as an accidental result of inappropriate action by legitimate software or authorized users (mail loops, poorly configured filters, inappropriate mass mailing), or incidental action such as direct harvesting attacks (DHA) by spamming software. In the latter case, the intention is not normally to bring down systems deliberately, but the sheer volume of traffic may result in unavailability of services. At times, of course, there might be an intention to mount a secondary DoS attack from compromised systems, such as distributed DoS (DDoS) attacks, often on sites with high profiles and low popularity: the Novarg (MyDoom) virus, for instance, attempted to launch attacks from infected machines on a number of vendor sites including Microsoft and SCO (F-Secure, 2004), and attacks on anti-spam sites are commonplace (Hypponen, 2003).
- **System integrity.** E-mail attacks may impair system integrity in a number of ways, notably by the transmission of malicious software such as viruses and Trojan horses.

Johnson (2000) described a number of technologies such as encryption, authentication, anonymity protocols, and technologies that are considered elsewhere in this *Handbook*. In this overview, however, I deal primarily with technologies that address direct e-mail abuse such as malicious software and spam.

## SOCIAL AND ANTISOCIAL E-MAIL ISSUES

As Michel Kabay (1996) pointed out, there are also a number of social issues associated with e-mail use and management:

- "Flaming" (intemperate language in the heat of the moment), inappropriately targeted humor or vulgarity, gossip and other indiscretions that can result in bad feeling, communications breakdowns, and even implication of the employer in libel action.
- Careless targeting of e-mail responses can result in inappropriate leakage of confidential or sensitive information inside and beyond the organization's perimeter.
- Relations between the employer and employees can be damaged by unclear policies and perceived rights to individual privacy.
- End users can send unconsidered mail that puts them in breach of copyright and data protection laws, and other legislation that restricts how data can be used and reused.

Many of these problems are best dealt with on a policy level, and I include a lengthy consideration of e-mail-related policy management at the end of this chapter.

## Malware

A full taxonomy of malware types is beyond the scope of this chapter, in which they are considered only in the context of e-mail transmission. Fuller taxonomical issues were addressed by Harley, Slade, and Gattiker (2001), and Thompson (2002) addressed specific virus taxonomies. Other chapters in this *Handbook* deal at length with other malware issues.

## E-Mail and Early Viruses

Although e-mail as a virus vector is mostly associated popularly with recent mass-mailer epidemics, viruses have actually been associated with e-mail almost since the first replicative malware.

## Boot Sector Infectors

Most of the effective early viruses were boot sector infectors (BSIs) and master boot record (MBR) infectors. Some of these are still occasionally reported. They do not normally spread via e-mail, however, but rather when a system is booted with an infected diskette. However, it is possible to transport such viruses in dropper form or as a disk image. These methods are normally associated with intentional transfer by mutual consent, but it is not impossible or unknown for malware to use them as a direct propagation channel.

## File Viruses

File viruses (parasitic viruses) infect files by attaching themselves to them in some way, so that when the file is run, the virus code is also run. They're far less common than in the early days, but are still found "in the wild" (for a full consideration of this concept, see http://csrc.nist.gov/nissc/1997/proceedings/177.pdf) and can be spread by e-mail. An interesting phenomenon sometimes reported is the infection of a modern mass mailer virus/worm by an older parasitic virus such as CIH, perhaps better known but misleadingly renamed as Chernobyl (Symantec, 2004)—the virus has no known intended connection with the Chernobyl disaster, but was "catchily" renamed by an antivirus vendor long after a common name had been assigned to it, in defiance of accepted practice. Some types of virus, such as companion and cluster viruses, use different infection mechanisms, but the precise mechanics need not concern us here.

## File and Boot (Multipartite) Viruses

File and boot viruses, because they use both methods of infection, can, in principle, be spread by e-mail. These are often referred to as multipartite viruses, although strictly speaking, this term refers to a virus that uses more than one infection method, not only to viruses that infect program files and boot sectors (Harley et al., 2001).

## Macro Viruses

Macro viruses normally infect documents: technically, they might be regarded as a special case of file virus. Most macro viruses infect Microsoft Word or Excel documents, but there are other vulnerable applications, not all of which are Microsoft Office applications. They can be multiplatform—most of the very few viruses to cause problems on Macintoshes in recent years have been macro viruses rather than Macintosh-specific malware (Harley, 1997)—and some can affect more than one application. Macro viruses are particularly likely to be a problem in relation to applications that, like those that are part of the Microsoft Office software suite, store macros in data files. Macro viruses are still commonly found transmitted by e-mail but are much less prevalent than they were in the mid- to late 1990s.

## Script Viruses

Script viruses are self-contained miniprograms in VBscript, Javascript, and so on and are often found as embedded scripts in some form of HTML (hypertext markup language) file (as well as in some types of formatted e-mail). They may also be transmitted as e-mail attachments.

## Mass Mailers

Mass mailers are a class of malware designed explicitly to spread via e-mail that maximize their own spread by seeking new target addresses from a victim's address book, files on an infected system, and other sources such as Web pages, and these are considered at length later in the chapter. They generally rely on social engineering (a term applied to a variety of attacks exploiting human weakness and gullibility rather than technological loopholes) to persuade the recipient to execute the malicious program.

Recent examples of social engineering in mass mailer dissemination are included in the next section and involve a form of impersonation on the part of the virus (the real sender of the e-mail) to dupe the recipient into thinking the attachment is safe to open, or at least interesting enough to be worth the risk. Most recent mass mailers are spoofing viruses: that is, they forge e-mail headers.

## Spoofing Viruses

The adjective *spoofing* was formerly applied to viruses that exploit a characteristic of an antivirus program to hide their presence from that program. The term is now more often applied to e-mail viruses (or worms) that forge message headers (especially the "From:" and "Reply-to:" fields) to obscure the real source of the viral e-mail or to dupe the recipient into running the viral attachment. The term is often abbreviated to *spoofer,* and the antonym is *nonspoofer* or *nonspoofing virus.* Spoofing viruses often insert addresses they find in the Windows Address Book or elsewhere on the infected hard disk, or an address from a list carried in the body of the virus, or an address simply made up. Thus, the message arrives looking as if it were sent by Person A, when it really comes from Person B. This not only causes mischief by blaming the wrong person for having an infected PC, it also makes it harder to trace the owner of the system that is really infected. Sometimes, however, a different form of spoofing is used. A popular alternative form is for the message to masquerade as a message from a vendor (especially Microsoft!) or a system administrator, passing off the attachment as a systems or application patch or as an important message. Yet another alternative is to disguise the message as being from someone the recipient doesn't know and as being intended for a completely different recipient, but suggesting that the content of the attachment is something particularly interesting or desirable. Recently popular forms of this particular trick include suggesting that the attachment consists of erotic photographs. It may also be suggested that the attachment:

- Is a returned message from the targeted recipient,
- Contains information pertaining to the recipient's being investigated by a law enforcement agency
- Is a photograph of the recipient
- Contains password information
- Contains a mail message intended for the targeted recipient that has been received in error by the apparent sender.

Although antivirus vendor sites such as F-Secure (http://www.f-secure.com/v-descs/), McAfee/AVERT (http://vil.nai.com/vil/default.asp), and Symantec (http://securityresponse.symantec.com/) include information about specific forms of message used by individual mass mailers such as Sobig, MyDoom, Bagle, and Netsky to trick the recipient into opening the attachment, it is not feasible to address all the possible social-engineering tricks available to an imaginative virus writer.

## Network Worms

Network worms are usually distinguished from e-mail viruses, as well as from conventional viruses, by the fact that they don't attach themselves to a legitimate program, although they do replicate across networks. This distinction is somewhat contentious, however. Network worms are usually self-launching—that is, they do not require direct user action in order to execute—and don't spread by e-mail or not only by e-mail. (Network worms that also spread by e-mail would be better described as hybrid.) Examples include the Code Red family, Slammer, Blaster, and Welchia/Nachi. Mass mailers are also frequently referred to as worms but are not usually self-launching, although some e-mail viruses do exploit misconfigured or unpatched mail software to execute without direct human intervention.

## Hybrid and Multipolar Malware

Although Nimda is sometimes taken to be part of the Code Red family, it is actually a hybrid virus, a network worm that can also be spread by e-mail. Malware like this, combining multiple attack vectors, is sometimes referred to as convergent, blended, or multipolar (Harley, 2002b).

## E-Mail Viruses and Worms

Most mass mailers—the type of virus most commonly encountered currently in the context of e-mail—occupy somewhat fuzzy middle ground between conventional viruses (because they replicate), worms (because they do not attach themselves to a legitimate program), and Trojans (because they trick the recipient into running malicious programs, thinking they do something desirable). In fact, there can be considerable overlap between these types. (Trojans are considered in more detail later.) Melissa, for example, was a macro virus but also one of the first effective e-mail worm–mass mailers (although claims that it was *the* first are untenable). It tricked the recipient into opening a document that then ran code, much as the **CHRISTMA EXEC** worm had in 1987 (Slade, 1996). It infected other documents (and so can be described as a true virus) but also made use of e-mail to trick the recipient into furthering its spread. More recent mass mailers tend to rely on persuading the victim to run stand-alone code, but some also use software vulnerabilities as an additional entry point, and some mass mailers are also viruses, or drop viruses or other malware—especially Trojans such as keyloggers and backdoors—as part of the replicative mechanism.

The mass mailer problem is seriously compounded by the poor option sets or local configuration of some filtering and antivirus products and services, especially gateway products. There are many circumstances under which generation of multiple alerts or any alert at all is incorrect behavior, most notably when the message that accompanies a mass mailer is known to forge message headers. An infected message should only be returned to the sender if it can be ascertained with reasonable certainty that the address in the From: and Reply-To: fields is not forged. Even then, it should not be returned with the uncleaned attachment, as often happens with filters that don't recognize specific viruses (either generic filters or mail transfer agents [MTAs] bouncing an undeliverable message). It isn't possible, however, for automated software to ascertain the real sender with this degree of confidence in the case of most modern spoofing viruses. Indeed, even inspection by eye often fails to do this reliably. As a result, antivirus services often inform the wrong person that their system is infected and similarly mislead the intended recipient, leading to panic on the part of the wrongly blamed system's owner and ill feeling between apparent sender and intended recipient; it may even lead to legal action (Harley, 2003b).

A high proportion of current infected e-mail traffic carries spoofing malware, so although it is responsible behavior to advise someone with an infected system when there is no doubt about the correct identification of the infected system, it is appropriate to do so only when the detected malware is known *not* to spoof headers. Many products and services cannot discriminate between viruses in this sense, even though they can identify the actual name of the virus correctly. The recipient should only receive a message if the removal of the viral code leaves a disinfected and useful object to be forwarded (as is the case with macro viruses) or if the forwarded message is a legitimate and intended communication from the sender.

Most e-mail-borne viruses are not "infective" in the sense of attaching to a legitimate object. The message is initiated and controlled by the virus author, not the owner of the infected system, who is usually unaware of the presence and transmission of the malware. The "infected" file contains no legitimate code, so disinfection is effectively the same as deletion. There is therefore no reason to forward the message and no point (except advertising the product) in advising the intended recipient of the interception, certainly if the originating e-mail account cannot be accurately ascertained.

Unfortunately, many scanning services cannot distinguish cases in which it isn't appropriate to send an alert or forward a message or when the malware is known to forge headers; therefore, they are unable to modify their own behavior accordingly. In fact, some services cannot even be configured to stop alerts or forwarding. As a result, it can happen at times that the impact of secondary traffic from filtering and antivirus services vastly exceeds that of "real" mass mailers and spam (Harley, 2004).

## The Malware Author's Dilemma

The malware writer has a significant barrier to overcome if his (or her) program is to spread beyond his own development environment. Malicious programs are harmless unless they are executed. How does the programmer get his code run on someone else's system? All malware exploits one or more vulnerabilities. These may consist of programming bugs and errors and other software vulnerabilities in a victim system, or of a lack of caution and skepticism in a human victim, allowing them to be tricked into running unsafe programs, or in some cases, of a combination of the two.

"Self-launching" code exploits bugs such as buffer overflows that can allow code to be run where it shouldn't be. No action from the victim is necessary (Harley et al., 2001). The "Internet Worm" or "Morris Worm" of 1988 is as good an example as the more recent MSBlaster or Code Red worms—possibly better, in that one of the vulnerabilities it exploited was in *sendmail* (Hruska, 1992), whereas recent network worms have tended to exploit vulnerabilities in applications other than e-mail such as IIS or SQLServer. Mass mailers have in some cases, however, exploited vulnerabilities in mail applications, notably Outlook and Outlook Express (Microsoft, 1999). There is a minor distinction to be drawn here between instances in which malware exploits miscoding and instances in which malware exploits (not necessarily intentionally) incautiously configured systems (as when MS Office applications are set to allow macros to auto-execute or mail clients are set to run attachments automatically).

"User-launched" code relies on persuading the victim to execute a malicious program, using social engineering in the general sense of psychological manipulation (Harley et al., 2001).

Hybrid malware combines both the self-launching and user-launched approaches, thus maximizing the potential for spread. E-mail-borne malware is often hybrid. It uses a bug such as those in some versions of Outlook that allow code to be run just by previewing a message, or the facility for auto-executing macros in Word or Excel, thus requiring no intervention from the victim. However, it also hedges its bets by using what is often called social engineering to persuade the victim to conspire in his own downfall by running an attachment. Such manipulation might persuade an unwary or unsophisticated computer user to open an executable file under the impression it is a game or screensaver or even a data file. Most data files can't carry executable code but Microsoft Office documents can, in the form of macros, and a PostScript file contains both programming instructions and data. This issue has long been recognized in antivirus circles but has recently been revisited in more general security circles, notably on some specialist mailing lists. Not everyone realizes that a screensaver (.SCR) is an executable program with the same format as an .EXE file, not a simple graphics file, and there are a multitude of well-documented ways in which an executable file might be "disguised" as a data file. For example, by using the "double file name extension" technique (examplefile.doc.scr) to hide the real file-type, or by presenting it as a self-extracting or self-decrypting archive file.

## Trojan Horses

A Trojan horse (or simply a Trojan) tricks the victim into running its code by masquerading as something else (a desirable program). Most e-mail worms also do this, so they meet the definition of a Trojan, but they also replicate, so they belong in the virus family. (In fact, there is an argument for claiming that viruses belong to the Trojan family, although to do so is not particularly helpful in practical terms, because it tends to increase confusion among nonexperts.)

Trojans tend to be destructive to data or cause leakage of information (or both). They may include, among other payloads, the following:

- Damage to or loss of files and file systems
- Allowing access to the network via network shares
- Opening ports to allow traffic through the Internet gateway
- Sending passwords or data back to an unauthorized person
- Altering the configuration of a victim system
- Causing advertisements to pop up
- Track which Web sites the victim visits and which passwords they use

Their main weakness as an e-mail-borne threat is that they are usually reliant on the quality of the social engineering in the accompanying message to gain a foothold on the system, and they cannot self-replicate even when they do gain a foothold (Harley, 2002). They include a wide variety of subclasses according to functionality including, among others the following:

- Destructive (Trojans that trash or overwrite files or file systems, most commonly)
- Backdoors (Trojans that attempt to open a connection to the victim computer from a remote system, for whatever purpose)

- Password stealers and keyloggers
- Porndialers
- DDoS agents
- Rootkits (Trojanized versions of system files)

Grimes (2001) also considered a class of program he called parasites. Although these include such privacy-invasive nuisances as programs that "call home" and pass on marketer-friendly data (often installed as part of a more-or-less legitimate and authorized program installation), there is also an argument for including objects with similar potential functionality such as adware, single-pixel GIFs (graphics interchange format), malicious cookies, and Web bugs that can be accessed via e-mail incorporating active-content.

## Antimalware Solutions

The most effective answer to viruses is, of course, antivirus software, deployed not only at the desktop but also on Web servers, file servers, and, most relevant to this chapter, at the e-mail gateway. There are two main approaches to e-mail gateway-hosted virus management: generic- and virus-specific. Generic virus management largely consists of discarding or quarantining objects that are capable of carrying or consisting entirely of a predetermined range of malicious code. In e-mail terms, this range usually consists of file attachments of file types often used by the writers of mass mailer viruses, including .PIF, .SCR, .VBS, .EXE, .BAT, .COM, and so on, although exactly which file types are blocked will depend partly on local usage. For instance, most sites do not block Microsoft Office documents, even though they are commonly associated with the passing of macro viruses, since legitimate business processes would suffer seriously from the blocking of legitimate documents. Issues regarding the relative risks of common file types are examined in considerable detail in a Technical Note published by the United Kingdom's National Infrastructure Security Coordination Centre (NISCC, 2004; see Table 1).

Virus-specific software detects (obviously) known, specific viruses. A consideration of the precise mechanisms for such detection is beyond the scope of this chapter but is based on a process of comparing code-bearing objects to a database of definitions (sometimes, not altogether correctly, referred to as signatures), so that (in principle) a new definition is required for each new virus or variant. In practice, the use of augmented detection by heuristic analysis and of generic drivers that are capable of catching some currently unknown variations and variants sometimes lessens the impact of brand-new malware. However, the need still exists for updating antivirus software with the latest definitions (sometimes incorrectly referred to as signatures) as soon as they become available. Gateway systems and services should also be implemented with due regard to the need for configurability and appropriate alerting and forwarding mechanisms arising from the increase in header-spoofing mass mailers and allied problems, as described earlier and (at far greater length) by Harley (2003a, 2003b).

The range and speed of the spread of malicious code (e-mail-borne or not) also necessitates good systems and software patching practice at the server, desktop, and application levels, as well as supplementary measures such as the blocking of vulnerable ports and services wherever possible and applicable. It is no longer realistic to consider virus management in complete isolation from other security technologies such as perimeter and desktop firewalls, intrusion detection systems, and intrusion prevention software. Policy and education remain a sometimes neglected but nonetheless essential component of a holistic security posture.

Although encryption is an essential adjunct to confidentiality in e-mail, it may also form part of the problem regarding the transfer of malicious code, and virus writers have made frequent use of the popular confusion between "encrypted" and "safe." The fact that a message or attachment is encrypted tells us nothing about whether it is infected. In most environments, encryption can be a barrier to effective gateway scanning, forcing the enterprise to rely on desktop scanning as a last-ditch defense, notwithstanding the difficulties of maintaining desktop security products in large or fragmented corporate environments. Viruses such as Netsky and Bagle that present as encrypted .ZIP files indicate that even a comparatively trivial form of encryption can present challenges to conventional antivirus that have not yet been completely addressed. Indeed, generic filters that regulate the introduction of executable attachments can often be circumvented simply by zipping the viral program.

Public key infrastructure (PKI) can, if rigorously applied, have benefits in terms of control of mass mailers and some forms of spam by making it harder for a message using deception and forgery as a means of delivery to survive an authentication mechanism. Applied purely as a means of managing e-mail abuse, however, it constitutes a somewhat expensive form of white-listing.

## Anti-Trojan Software

Most antivirus software detects a sizeable proportion of Trojans, joke programs, and similar nuisances, but antivirus vendors are not usually brave enough to claim that they can detect all known Trojans. There are a number of reasons for this, including the following:

- Difficulties in formal definition—the definition of a Trojan relies, in part, on the perception of the victim, a factor often not susceptible to automated code or text analysis
- The fact that it is immeasurably easier to write trivial nonreplicative malware and introduce minor variants
- The lack of a more or less universal Trojan-specific mechanism for sharing samples with trusted vendors and researchers comparable to those that exist for virus sample sharing

Unfortunately, the same caveats tend to apply to the producers of Trojan-specific scanners, and rivalry between some Trojan specialists and the antivirus industry further complicates the issue.

**Table 1** Categorization of Attachment Types by Risk Level

| Risk Level | Attachment Type |
|---|---|
| Very High Risk | This category includes<br>• file types almost never exchanged legitimately by e-mail but that are executable file types used by mass mailers (e.g., .PIF, .LNK,.BAT, .COM, .CMD, .SHS). These file types should be blocked in all but the most exceptional circumstances. The .EXE file type is also heavily used by mass mailers and is frequently blocked by generic filters for this reason. However, it is included in the High Risk category rather than Very High Risk because it is possible and may be convenient for legitimate .EXE files to be exchanged, so blocking must remain a local decision<br>• file names with double extensions, especially when one type is a non-executable and the last one is not (e.g., myfile.txt.pif)<br>• file types that don't match the file name extension, when the file type is more dangerous than the file name extension suggests<br>• file names with double or multiple extensions in which an attempt has been made to mask the presence of the real file type (e.g., by inserting several spaces between the penultimate extension and the real, final extension)<br>• files with a deceptive icon suggesting a non-executable file type<br>• file names that include the characters {}, suggesting an attempt to disguise an executable file type by using its CLSID (class ID extension) |
| Medium-High Risk | This category includes<br>• file types heavily used by mass mailers but that may also be exchanged legitimately (e.g., .EXE, .SCR, .VBS) It may be decided locally not to block these types for the following reasons: .EXE attachments may denote data rather than a "real" executable, but in the form of a program file; e.g., self-decompressing archive files and self-decrypting files are often convenient because they do not oblige the recipient to own the archiving or encryption utility that generated them. It is hard to imagine that any organization still considers the attractions of exchanging fluffy screensavers to be worth the risk of allowing .SCR files, but again the final decision must be local. Earlier mass mailers were very often VBScript files, and new .VBS mass mailers are still seen from time to time, but it can also happen that such scripts are used to install system patches, for example. Nonetheless, it is strongly recommended that if any of these file types must be allowed and exchanged by e-mail, that stringent precautions be taken to ensure that only trusted and trustworthy code is allowed through<br>• compressed archive files, especially the .ZIP file type characteristic of PKZip and WinZip, pose an increasing risk, convenient as they are. Some generic filters are unable to check inside a compressed file for the presence of archived executables, although virus-specific software is almost always capable of scanning the contents of a .ZIP file (and a variety of other archive formats). However, virus-specific scanners are not able to scan the contents of encrypted archives in real time and have been forced to apply less satisfactory search criteria as more viruses have exploited this loophole. Also, multiply-nested archives containing unusually large compressed files may constitute an effective denial of service attack on antivirus scanners and e-mail servers. |
| Medium Risk | This category includes<br>• file types not frequently used by mass mailers but capable of carrying executable/malicious code. Most file infectors, (e.g., Trojans) would be caught by the previous categories, but documents that can contain macros (especially MS Office documents) fall here. Note that exchange of some documents will often be seen as having too heavy an impact on normal business practices to override the moderate increase in security (.DOC, .XLS), but others may be borderline high risk, such as those file types associated with Microsoft Access. People don't exchange full databases as often as they do more concise forms of data. |
| Medium-Low Risk | This category includes<br>• executable files of types not currently associated with virus action or that are associated only with extinct viruses or zoo viruses; especially proof-of-concept viruses that exist only "to show it's possible" |
| Low Risk | This category includes<br>• non-executables. Technically, this should be "no risk." However, it is impractical to prove automatically that a file contains no executable code. |
| Uncategorized | This category includes<br>• files with executability or infective status that is unknown and can't be determined<br>• files of unknown file type (or no explicit file type: Macintosh users are frequently penalized by generic checkers by the fact that Mac data files are often not given a file name extension).<br>• encrypted files<br>• archives that can't be unpacked (fully or at all) for scanning<br>Note that the last two categories can be said to include some file types in preceding categories; however, no presumptions are made in this case about file name extensions. |

# SPAM AND RELATED E-MAIL ABUSE

The term *spam* is applied to a number of abuses involving the indiscriminate use of e-mail or newsgroup postings, although use of the term as applied to newsgroup abuse is largely overlooked nowadays except by Usenet junkies. E-mail spam includes the following:

- **Unsolicited commercial e-mail (UCE; junk mail).** This term is applied to any unsolicited advertising. Most spam is disseminated with the intention of advertising a product or service, but other motivations may exist. Although the term can be and is applied to all unsolicited advertising, it is useful to discriminate between honest advertising (from more or less legitimate and reputable organizations using more or less legitimate direct-marketing techniques) and advertising that includes a degree of deception not only in the content but also in the delivery mechanism. Reputable organizations generally conform to regulatory legislation. As well as being reasonably restrained in their claims regarding the products they are advertising, they obey (increasingly restrictive) laws.
- **Unsolicited bulk e-mail (UBE).** UBE is sent in bulk to many addresses. It may be and often is commercial, and so is essentially a superset of UCE.

The term spam is applied to many divergent forms of unsolicited bulk e-mail. Most sources (especially antispam vendors) suggest that well over 50% of all e-mail is now junk mail (some estimates suggest a much higher proportion, and almost all sources indicate continuing growth).

The term is still applied to bulk postings to Internet newsgroups (Usenet) but is now most commonly applied to unsolicited commercial and other bulk e-mail. It often involves advertising products or services but may also be applied to many other types of unsolicited mail, including the following (some of these categories often overlap with other categories of e-mail abuse considered here and may not always be considered "real" spam):

- Financial marketing messages that may or may not be genuine
- Product-oriented messages (general goods or services ranging from antivirus products to fake diplomas and qualifications by way of septic tanks and timeshare apartments)
- Illegal products or services (e.g., illicit drugs, pirated software)
- Pornographic spam
  - Hardcore
  - Softcore
  - Deviant
  - Legal/illegal (The implications of legality may be far-reaching; for instance, processing of pedophilic content can, if not conducted in accordance with law enforcement guidelines, expose the recipient of such material to legal action.)
- Offers of spamming software and services
- Health (diet-related, "improvement" of physical assets, medical supplies)
- Spiritualism/organized religion
- Other soapboxing from individuals with religious, moral, or other preoccupations and obsessions
- Fraud
  - Pyramid and MLM (multi-level marketing) schemes
  - 419s (discussed later)
  - Credit card scams
- Leisure messages (prizes, online games, electronic greeting cards using wormlike replicative techniques to spread)
- Surveys
- Begging letters

Some find it useful to distinguish between "amateur" spam or unsolicited junk mail (commercial or otherwise) and "professional" or "hardcore" spam, which is not only unsolicited but includes a degree of deception—not only in its content but also with regard to origin. The following definition covers most of the bases:

> Unsolicited and usually unwanted mail (of disproportionately greater benefit to the sender than to the recipient), often for advertising purposes, sometimes fraudulent, and generally including some degree of deception as to the source and purpose of the mail, such as forged From: fields, misleading Subject: fields, fake "opt-out" mechanisms that don't work or are used only to validate the address as a potential spam target, misleading pseudo-legal statements, and obfuscation of the originator of the spam mail.

Other commentators have made similar implicit assumptions about the nature of spam (Schwartz & Garfinkel, 1998).

*Revenge spamming* is a term sometimes applied to the implication of disliked persons or groups (especially an antispammer) in spamming activities by using their site as a relay, fraudulently inserting their details into the mail headers, using their details in the body of the message, and so on. The victim of this sort of revenge spam subsequently becomes the victim of various sanctions applied by groups and individuals who are violently opposed to spamming. This form of abuse is closely allied to other forms of impersonation where offensive or inappropriate mail is manipulated to make it look as if it came from someone else.

Some junk mail is clearly not expected to achieve anything other than annoying or in some way distressing the recipient, although in some instances antisocial messages may be sent as a "probe" to test spamming software or to validate an address. However, malware writers are increasingly making use of spamming techniques to inject viruses, worms, and Trojan horses into the wild. Not only do they use deceptive headers and content to trick the recipient into opening the mail and running the malicious program attached, but they also use spammerlike forgery of mail headers to disguise the true whereabouts and ownership of the infected system. They also use built-in SMTP servers to maximize spread and cover their tracks in a manner highly reminiscent of some spamming tools.

## Spam and Malware

A correlation has recently been noted between virus writing and spamming (Hypponen, 2003). Some mass mailers and Trojans install software on infected systems that allow them to be used as open relays or open proxies by spammers, so that infected machines can be used to relay spam, increasing the potential spam processing rate and the difficulty of tracing the real source of a spammed message. Because most corporate organizations nowadays maintain reasonable antivirus precautions—at least on the e-mail gateway and preferably on the desktop as well—home computer systems are far more vulnerable to being exploited in this way. As long as most home computer users fail to install, configure, or maintain antivirus software correctly, it is probable that spammers will continue to make use of this approach.

Some malware is also known to install Web server processes on infected home machines for the distribution and advertising of products and services, which in themselves are often illegal. There have also been reports of infected systems being used to mount DoS attacks against antispam sites. Some malware forwards e-mail addresses and other information that may subsequently be used for spamming purposes. However, mass-mailing malware also uses techniques analogous to those used by spambots to harvest target e-mail addresses not only from the victim's Windows address book but also often from other files and system areas such as Word documents, HTML files, Web caches, and so on. Mass mailers often use header forgery to spoof addresses and disguise the source of the infected mail and avoid early detection by gateway filters by using varying ("polymorphic") subject lines, message content, and made-up source addresses. The use by mass-mailer viruses of their own internal SMTP engines or known relays to self-disseminate also makes it harder to trace the source of infective mail or the footprint of the virus in the infected mail system. These spamlike techniques suggest increasing cross-pollination not only between virus and malware technology and spamming technology but also between the malware authors and spammer communities (EEMA, 2003).

## Chain Letters, Chain E-Mails, and Hoaxes

A chain letter is, in its broadest sense, any message that includes a request for the recipient to forward it. Terrestrial chain letters usually ask the recipient to forward a set number of copies, but chain e-mail usually asks the recipient to forward to "everyone they know" or "everyone in their address book" or "everyone who might use the Internet." The common denominator is that circulation increases in a geometric progression.

Chain letters are not necessarily hoaxes but frequently contain some deceptive content, either through a deliberate attempt to mislead or because of a misunderstanding of the issue in question. Fact is frequently mixed in with fiction to add circumstantial credibility. It's possible for purely factual material to be forwarded in this way, of course, but in general, responsible (or for-fee) distributors of quality information tend to use less intrusive forms of dissemination.

On its Hoaxbusters Web site, the U.S. Department of Energy's Computer Incident Advisory Capability (CIAC) describes chain letters as having a tripartite structure: hook, threat, and request (CIAC, 2004). Although it is not always straightforward to separate these elements, they do seem to be common to most chain letters, electronic or otherwise.

The hook is there, like a riff in a popular song, to catch the recipient's interest and consists of an eye-catching tag such as "Free trainers!" or "Virus alert" and perhaps some expansion of the theme. It exploits some basic psychological issue such as greed and self-interest, fear of technology and its consequences, or sympathy with the unfortunate (Harley, 2000). A threat inherent in this message pressures the recipient into passing on the message.

- Sometimes the threat is simply that if the mark doesn't forward the mail, they will miss out on some personal advantage: for instance, offers of free cell phones, sports gear, and so forth in return for meeting or exceeding a required number of forwarding. Less blatantly, a chain mail may exploit the desire to please, the chance to earn "brownie points" or a competitive advantage while doing something responsible and helpful, or the fear of being thought mean or uncharitable or unsympathetic (Harley & Gattiker, 2002).

- Direct threats may be used, somewhat in the fashion of older terrestrial chain mail, that describe how recipients who neglected to forward the letter met with misfortune or even death. More modern, less superstitious variations include threats to deluge the target's mailbox with spam or viruses.

- It is more common for chain e-mail to use indirect threats that are not necessarily explicitly stated. For instance, behind virus hoaxes, there is the implicit threat of widespread damage and inconvenience personally and to all Internet users.

- Some chain mail makes an overt emotional appeal such as that made by political petitions (e.g., those concerning the treatment of Afghan women under the Taliban or opposition to the war with Iraq) or solicitations to forward e-mail to attract funding for cancer research. The threat is that if the mail is not forwarded, political injustice, cancer, or an individual's suffering will continue unchecked, or a little boy's dying wish won't be granted. The common denominator is that all representatives of this class of nuisance ask the recipient to keep the chain going by forwarding e-mail, so that some undesirable outcome will be avoided.

The request expresses the "core function" of the chain letter: that is, to replicate by forwarding. The use of the term *replicate* is not accidental: chain letters, especially virus hoaxes, are sometimes considered to be "memetic viruses" (Gordon, Ford, & Wells, 1997) or "viruses of the mind" (these common expressions and concepts largely originate in the writings and theories of biologist Richard Dawkins). Instead of the code used by computer viruses, which replicates by infection, chain letters rely on persuading the recipient to pass the message on to others. They often have a "payload" that results in the useless consumption of bandwidth through the replication of hoax e-mail, personal fear caused by scare stories with no basis in fact, and, in some instances, the erasure of legitimate software incorrectly identified as "viruses." However, they masquerade as an appeal to "help" others by disseminating "information," whereas cancer-victim hoaxes ask you to generate money for medical research by forwarding identical messages, and others appeal to self-interest by offering money or free goods or services (clothes, cell phones, holidays, and so on).

Chain letters can be said to fall into three main classes:

- Pure fiction, intended to trick the victim into forwarding a chain letter and bolster the self-image of the originator by "proving" the stupidity of others. This class includes many virus hoaxes and other hoaxes related to security—sometimes to other aspects of information security, but often to personal security such as vulnerability to robbery or personal attack. This latter class of hoax includes elements of the urban legend, especially those urban legends that have a gory or otherwise horrific element.

- Some hoaxes might be better described as semihoaxes, as they may be based on misunderstanding a real issue. Some virus hoaxes may fall into this class but so do other hoaxes such as widespread stories about highway speed cameras and telephone scams. However, a hoax with no basis in fact may nevertheless acquire a patina of circumstantial support as it passes from person to person. Such messages often originate from or are perpetuated by (for example) consultants, journalists, and others who are perceived, often inaccurately, as speaking authoritatively or from a position of exceptional knowledge. Rosenberger and others sometimes describe this as False Authority Syndrome (Harley et al., 2001).

More rarely, a security alert or other form of chain letter may be reasonably accurate in its content, but the form of transmission is inappropriate. Hoaxes and chain letters are not easy to manage using automatic software, although some sites do attempt to manage it using keyword filtering, Bayesian methods, and other analytical techniques. However, these can lead to an unacceptably high false positive rate. In general, this is an area where good policy and education works best, with good information resources as backup.

## E-Mail Fraud

The following subclassifications are by no means all-inclusive but do include some major current abuses.

**Password Stealing.** Attempts to gain password information, either by social engineering, the enclosure of some form of Trojan horse, or a combination of both, have long been associated with e-mail (Gordon & Chess, 1998) and the use of particular Internet Service Providers (ISP); American Online (AOL) users have been particularly victimized. However, this class of abuse is by no means ISP specific and can involve attempts to gain other types of information.

**Phishing.** This form of fraud, which may be regarded as a special case of the preceding category, has become increasingly prevalent in recent years. In its most usual current form, it masquerades as a communication from a banking establishment asking the recipient to reenter their banking details into a form that appears to be generated at a legitimate bank site. Variations include the exploitation of cross-site scripting vulnerabilities, setting up a spoof Web site, and persuading the recipient to download and run a mass mailer such as Mimail or a Trojan horse program. Although some definitions emphasize the element of Web site spoofing, there is a certain amount of crossover here between several types of e-mail abuse. At the moment, the efficacy of such frauds tends to be diluted by ineffective targeting, but it would be naïve to assume that fraudsters won't find ways of improving their credibility. It is not unlikely that this type of identity fraud will mutate into other business areas and target other types of data. Figures published regularly by the Anti-Phishing Working Group on their web site (http://www.apwg.org) suggest that the dissemination of phishing scams is currently rising very quickly, and that the number of victims remains significant.

**Pyramid Schemes and MLM.** Pyramid schemes are based on the principle that the recipient of the e-mail sends money to a number of people, who send money to more people, who send money to more people ad infinitum. The idea is that eventually the recipient's name will rise to the top so that he or she, too, will receive money. They are generally associated with the selling of some token product or service. However, they make a profit only for the originator of the scam. Such scams often claim to be more or less legitimate MLM operations. Ponzi schemes are another type of fake "investment" widely advertised by e-mail. Note that scam e-mails of this sort are often widely spammed, although they will usually need to point to a temporary but legitimate mailbox somewhere to which the money is directed. The mathematical model of some pyramid schemes resembles the model for the distribution of chain letters, especially those that specify the number of addresses to which you should forward them. This class of abuse is considered at some length by Barrett (1996).

**419s (Advance Fee Fraud).** 419 frauds (also known as Advance Fee Frauds or Nigerian scams; the name derives from the section of the Nigerian Criminal Code dealing with fraud) are a long-standing type of scam that can be disseminated by fax, letter, and so on, but is nowadays most often seen as e-mail. They constitute the largest proportion of current e-mail fraud and work, broadly, as follows. The target receives an unsolicited communication containing a business proposal, which often involves some form of money laundering or similar illegal operation, although if the proposal is obviously illegal, it usually includes an attempt at moral justification. Variations are endless, but may include the following:

- A request for help from political refugees to get their family and their money out of a wartorn (usually African) country

- A request for help with the distribution of money for charitable purposes
- A request for assistance from a bank or other official with transferring money obtained more or less illicitly from the government
- A request to stand as "next of kin" for the purposes of claiming the estate of a dead foreigner who has died intestate
- Notification of a lottery win

At some point, the victim is asked to pay advance fees of some sort (e.g., for tax, legal fees, bribes, or as evidence of good faith) or to give sensitive information about their own financial accounts. Some individuals have lost many thousands of dollars in this way.

These communications often but by no means always derive from Nigeria or another African state but may originate or appear to originate from any part of the world. They often offer an URL (uniform resource locator) pointing to a convincing but not necessarily relevant or genuine news item as circumstantial evidence.

419s are often regarded as indistinguishable from spam, and there are indeed many points of similarity. Like spammers, 419 perpetrators use target addresses harvested directly or indirectly from Web sites, newsgroups, mailing lists, and so on. However, they tend not to manipulate message headers so heavily, possibly because they need to maintain some sort of contact with the victim, although the contact point may be buried in the body of the message rather than the header, which may contain a forged address. They also make heavy use of "disposable" free e-mail accounts from Web mail providers: These are easily blocked when complaints are received but also quite difficult to trace and less susceptible to automatic detection by filters that rely on header anomalies. They are, however, fairly susceptible to detection by filtering on key words and phrases. Address information, text, and scam ideas are heavily recycled and exchanged, and some kinds of stereotyped "business English," names, and event information are frequently reencountered by the dedicated 419-trapper.

419 fraudsters, like spammers, generally use a scattergun approach. The messages are mailed to anyone whose address is harvested, irrespective of their likely interest, on the assumption that one or two potential victims will bite and make it worth the minimal initial investment required from the perpetrator. However, there seem to be many "gangs," individuals, and countries operating this form of organized crime. It is strongly recommended that individuals, and the organizations they belong to, should *not* respond directly to such communications unless asked to by law enforcement agencies.

There are a number of possibilities for dealing directly with 419s received. Individuals may be encouraged simply to delete them, of course, or report them to their local IT helpdesk or security administrator, who may be authorized to take immediate action to block, send alerts, and advise law enforcement, as well as finding it useful to monitor incoming fraudulent mail to keep records and to track trends in 419 technology and psychology. If a reporting mechanism exists, it is useful to include the whole message and full headers, but the From:, To:, and Subject:

fields are the minimum likely to be needed for reactive blocking by domain or sender.

Possible direct action includes the following:

- Forward the e-mail to the abuse@[domain] account for the domains mentioned in the e-mail headers and in the message body, including full message headers.
- Forward to an appropriate law enforcement agency: any local agency will give advice on how best to do this, but some national resources are included in the Further Reading section of this chapter. The 419 Coalition Web site (419 Coalition, 2004) includes contact addresses for several countries.
- In the event of a 419 with a likely Nigerian connection, file a complaint with the Nigerian Embassy or High Commission and with the Central Bank of Nigeria (info@cenbank.org).
- Where loss has occurred, a complaint can be filed with the Nigerian Economic and Financial Crimes Commission (EFCC; info@efccnigeria.org). In many countries, it is also possible to report cases of contact and actual loss to national law enforcement agencies, as well as to the local police.

However, the sheer scale of this problem means that none of these parties will necessarily take action in every case, and if there has been no return communication with the fraudster, it is unlikely that there will be any direct response.

## Threats and Extortion

There are as many possibilities for persuading or bullying an e-mail recipient into inappropriate and self-destructive behavior, as many as human ingenuity and gullibility can accommodate. A recently common attack on individuals (especially those within corporate environments) is to send mail claiming to be able to take over their system and threatening to delete files or to unleash viruses or pornographic e-mail onto the individual's machine unless they pay a (comparatively small) sum (CNN, 2003).

This form of attack is difficult to address by technical means and is better addressed by corporate policy and education. It is noteworthy that the efficacy of this particular attack relies implicitly on organizational security being draconian and blame oriented. Security is often improved by encouraging the end user to report incidents and breaches without fear of unjust retribution (Harley, 1998).

## MailBombing

This term is applied when an individual (or sometimes a site) is bombarded with e-mail messages, constituting a form of DoS attack and invasion of privacy.

## Subscription Bombing

This term is applied when rather than directly bombarding a target individual or site with e-mail, as in mailbombing, the target is subscribed to numerous mailing lists, especially high-volume lists. List-processing software nowadays includes a verification and confirmation mechanism by which an applicant subscriber is required to confirm their wish to subscribe. However, commercial mailing lists are not always so scrupulous.

## E-MAIL ABUSE AND POLICY-BASED SOLUTIONS

The following suggested policy outlines will not work for everyone in all respects but highlight and to some extent address most of the core issues (Harley et al., 2001).

### Acceptable Use of Facilities and Resources

Policies addressing the use and abuse of company resources may cover the use of E-mail, Internet messaging, and access to the World Wide Web and other resources owned by the employer specifying that they are intended for work purposes only, or for nonwork purposes in moderation, according to local practice. Access should not be permitted to such resources that customarily carry pornographic material, pirated software, and other illegitimate information and resources, such as malicious software (binaries or source code) including viruses, Trojan Horses, Backdoor/Remote Access Tools, password cracking tools, and hacking tools. Special considerations may apply regarding the use of Web-hosted mail services (and related or somewhat similar services such as Usenet, Internet Messaging, and Chat services).

All use of company facilities should be required to be in accordance with:

- All binding laws, including but not restricted to
  - data protection legislation
  - copyright legislation
  - legislation concerned with unauthorized access or modification to systems or data
  - trade secrets legislation
  - antidiscrimination legislation
  - obscenity/pornography legislation (especially legislation relating to child pornography and pedophilia)
- All internal policies
- Other policies and agreements by which the company is bound

It might be considered appropriate here to proscribe the use of company resources for administration of private business ventures.

### Acceptable Use of E-Mail

Staff using a company e-mail account, or other messaging facility, need to be aware that what they write will be seen to represent the views and policies of the company. They should therefore be required to conform to appropriate standards of accuracy, courtesy, decency, and ethical behavior and to refrain from the dissemination of inappropriate mail content.

Inappropriate behavior exposes the employee and the company to accusations of libel and defamation, harassment and discrimination, copyright infringement, invasion of privacy, and so on. Employees are therefore required to act in accordance with the company's published policies as well as all applicable legislation and other binding agreements.

The company is probably not able or obliged to maintain constant surveillance of employees' use of its facilities, especially where use is not specifically authorized or is misused, but employees should not assume an automatic right to privacy. Mail may be monitored or checked from time to time for reasons of maintaining network support or security or for other reasons, as well as for ensuring that it meets prescribed standards of conduct, including the following:

- E-mail should not be used as if it were a secure communications channel for the transmission of sensitive information or messages. Use of encryption, however, should be in accordance with the company's policy and practice.
- There should be no sharing of games, joke programs, screensavers, and so on. Any attachment is potentially hostile, irrespective of what it claims to be or the perceived trustworthiness of the source.
- On no account should an end user be allowed to disable or reduce the functionality of security software without authorization.
- End users should be expected to use the corporate standard antivirus package. Systems running unsupported security packages and other applications should be regarded as unprotected; this may have general support implications, as well as the obvious security implications.

### Hoax Management and Chain Mail Policy

Chain e-mail is a drain on network resources, system resources, and support staff. Any mail that includes a request to forward widely and inappropriately should be regarded with suspicion. Originating or forwarding mail that carries some sort of threat against recipients who don't forward it in turn should be regarded as a disciplinable offense.

On no account should mail that warns of viruses, Trojan horses, and other security threats be forwarded without checking and authorization from the local IT unit, however apparently trustworthy or senior the source, unless they are specifically qualified and authorized to do so.

Some virus hoaxes may have been intended to discourage the forwarding of previously existing chain letters. This is not an acceptable reason for passing on a hoax or chain letter, and it may be worth addressing the issue specifically.

Passing on warnings about hoax warnings can be a difficult area. Some individuals and groups have recommended passing on information about hoaxes and chain letters back to other recipients of a hoax or chain letter and, in some extreme instances, to everyone in the recipient's address book.

- Passing on an explanatory message with instructions to the recipient to forward indiscriminately (or to a fixed number of people) is simply a chain letter and should not be regarded as acceptable.

Passing back an explanatory message to other hoax recipients may be justifiable if there are only a few of them and if it is reasonable to assume that they'll receive more benefit than annoyance from the information. Even then, the information should be accurate and subject to the approval of the appropriate manager.

- Not all hoaxes are security-related. Appeals to forward mail to raise money for a worthy cause (for example), even if not actually a hoax, may not be an appropriate use of company resources. End users should be educated to be skeptical, rather than believing that everything heard from Web sites, colleagues, newsgroups, or the media is true, or completely true.

## Antispam Policies

Employees should be strictly forbidden to use company resources for the dissemination of inappropriate mass e-mail for private or work-related purposes. Mailing lists specifically set up for dissemination of particular types of work-related information are an exception, if the type of information broadcast is appropriate to the list. However, spamming a mailing list should never be considered appropriate.

Employees should be expected to react appropriately to spam by reporting and forwarding it to the appropriate quarter and following their advice on what further action to take, if any. Direct response to spam (including angry replies or following instructions to unsubscribe) can cause more damage than ignoring or simply deleting offending messages and should be discouraged or controlled, subject to local policy.

Spoofing, or forging mail headers, in the headers of e-mail or news postings should be forbidden, whether as a means of disguising the source of mass e-mail (there is no legitimate business reason for doing this) or as a means of making it more difficult for spammers to harvest an address. Exceptions may be made for manipulating the address (as in the interpolation of spaces or the substitution of AT and DOT for @ or the period character) to make it harder for automatic harvesting software to recognize a valid address. Spoofing likely to ease the spoofer's burden of junk mail at the expense of other legitimate users should be seriously discouraged. The use of anonymous e-mail should be considered specifically and according to local practice.

Advice should be available to end users on minimizing exposure to junk mail. Some research (Center for Democracy and Technology, 2003) suggests that the most common means for address-harvesting is from the Web, so measures that might be explored include the following:

- not publishing e-mail addresses unnecessarily on the Web, and obfuscating addresses where they *do* need to be published on Web sites (this is a measure to avoid the automated harvesting of e-mail addresses by spammers and should not be confused with the forging of e-mail headers, which is generally deprecated)
- placing restrictions on membership of and specific posts to newsgroups, Web forums, and mailing lists from work addresses except as required for work purposes

It also makes sense at an administrative and technical level to consider mitigating the impact of Direct Harvesting Attacks by mandating account names that may be less susceptible to automated guessing (dictionary) attacks than obvious formats like [firstname][surname-initial]@ or [firstname-initial][surname]@, and by specifying appropriate MTA configurations to counteract brute-force guessing attacks (e.g., by flagging traffic patterns that suggest such an attack preparatory to blocking the domain).

## Codes of Conduct

All staff should be required to meet prescribed ethical standards, but particular attention should be paid to staff with special skill sets and corresponding privileges (technical management, management information systems personnel). It might be specified that all staff are expected to conform with the following strictures, which are staples of many codes of conduct used by IT professional peer organizations:

- Promote public health and safety
- Respect the legitimate rights of others—property rights, copyrights, intellectual property, and so on
- Comply with and maintain knowledge of standards, policies, legislation
- Exert due care and diligence
- Refuse inducements
- Avoid disclosing confidential information
- Avoid conflicts of interest
- Avoid representing customers financially inappropriately
- Conform to and maintain relevant professional standards in e-mail
- Advance public and customer knowledge
- Support fellow professionals
- Not exceed their own expertise or authority
- Upgrade skills where opportunities exist
- Accept professional responsibility; follow through and do not offload inappropriately or evade responsibility by blaming others
- Access systems, data, resources only when authorized and when appropriate

## CONCLUSION

As I write this (August 2004), MessageLabs (http://www.messagelabs.com/) tells me that the ratio of spam to legitimate e-mail is around 1 in 1.4, while virus-infected traffic is in the proportion 1/14.7. On the Postini Web site (http://www.postini.com/stats/), it is estimated that an average 30% of an e-mail server's capacity is taken up with Direct Harvesting Attacks. The Anti-Phishing Working Group (http://www.antiphishing.org/) reports a "huge increase in the volume of phishing attacks." Obviously, these figures are highly variable and based on reports from their respective customers/members; how well they represent all Internet messaging is open to discussion. Equally obviously, even as the rest of us have taken to the Internet in general and e-mail in particular, the bad guys have quickly spotted its potential for exploitation, to the point where legitimate traffic is increasingly swamped by e-mail abuse. These problems are accentuated by the essential insecurity of core messaging protocols, although the impact of these vulnerabilities can be mitigated by the application of encryption and authentication protocols such as Transport Layer Security (TLS), further supported by abuse-specific technologies such as antivirus (in its many forms) and antispam technologies such as those described in this chapter. It can nonetheless be assumed that spammers, virus writers, and other undesirables will continue to waste their energy and creativity on new ways to evade these technologies, at least as long as home users fail to protect themselves and businesses fail to supplement technical measures with education and policy.

# GLOSSARY

**419 (Nigerian Scam, Advance Fee Fraud)**  A fraudulent communication, today mostly e-mail, that attempts to persuade the target to take part in a (sometimes frankly illegal) scheme to transfer large sums of money to an account in the target's country, in return for a percentage of those funds. The victim is persuaded to part with sensitive financial information or funds upfront for taxes, bribes, and so on, but never sees any return. A common variation is to persuade the victim that they've won a lottery but are required to pay local taxes before they receive their "win."

**Acceptable Use Policy (AUP)**  Guidelines for users on what constitutes acceptable usage of a system, network services, and so on.

**Blacklisting**  In spam management, the blocking or other special treatment of messages with particular attributes, for example, originating from a known spam-friendly e-mail address or domain.

**Chain Letter**  Originally a letter promising good luck if you pass it on to others or misfortune if you don't, thus breaking the chain. Hoax virus alerts are a special case of electronic chain mail: the recipient is urged to pass on the warning to everyone he knows.

**Denial of Service (DoS) Attack**  An attack that compromises the availability of system services, and therefore of data. DoS attacks in the e-mail context often consist of attempts to overwhelm a mail server or individual's ability to handle mail by sheer volume of traffic, or to exceed an individual's quota of incoming e-mail (e.g., by mail-bombing or subscription bombing).

**Direct Harvest Attack (DHA)**  An attempt to harvest target e-mail addresses for spam or virus dissemination purposes, often by brute force guessing of account names.

**eSMTP**  Based on standard SMTP, but includes an enhanced command set that adds some of the functionality of more powerful protocols, notably X.400. However, it does not significantly increase security in the context of e-mail abuse as considered here.

**Ethics**  Moral philosophy dealing with human conduct and character. In the context of practical computer ethics, we are mostly concerned with "normative ethics," the establishment of a code of values based on accepted social norms, but applied specifically to the use of computers.

**File Type**  In the virus context, especially with reference to mass mailers, the important characteristic of a file type is whether it is executable—that is, whether it contains executable code, and that is the use of the term in this chapter. The file type may be indicated by the file name extension, and much generic filtering is based on checking that attribute, but a virus writer can change the extension to mislead the target. Some filters check file headers, which is generally more accurate but requires considerably more work and maintenance.

**Hybrid Malware**  Malware that can gain a foothold and execute on a target system both by exploiting a vulnerability in software and by using social engineering to track the system user, thus combining both the self-launching and user-launched approaches.

**Malware**  Malicious code such as viruses and Trojan horses.

**Mass Mailer**  A malicious program of which the main or only infection mechanism is to mail itself out to e-mail addresses found on an infected system in the hope of persuading the recipient by social engineering into executing an attached copy of the mass mailer. (Some mass mailers may also use software vulnerabilities to force execution of embedded code without the intervention of the recipient.)

**Message Headers**  The part of an e-mail message that contains information as to the identities of the sender and the intended recipient, where replies should be sent, and information about the route the message has taken to get from one party to the other. However, a very high proportion of e-mail abuse is enabled by the ease with which headers can be forged (either manually or automatically).

**Ponzi Schemes**  A fraudulent scheme by which the victim is persuaded to "invest" money. As the number of participants increases, the fraudster uses money sent by later investors to pay off early investors and build up numbers and confidence in the scheme, until he chooses to disappear with the money. The Internet offers virtually costless administration of such schemes.

**Post Office Protocol (POP)**  A protocol that allows a client machine to transfer e-mail from a server. Mail received via this protocol evades central malware management measures if applied only to an SMTP service, and unless the client machine has up-to-date desktop antivirus, it becomes vulnerable to mass mailers and other incoming e-mail abuse. Some organizations address this potential weakness by blocking port 110, thus blocking the service.

**Pyramid Schemes**  An allegedly profitable scheme by which one person sends money to a number of people who send money to a number of people ad infinitum. A common variation is to disguise this (generally illegal) scheme as a legitimate scheme to buy and sell mailing lists, software, T-shirts, and so on.

**Realtime Blackhole List (RBL)**  A list of mail sources (usually IP addresses) associated with spam and continuously maintained by the addition and removal of addresses as appropriate as a commercial or voluntary service.

**Scam**  An attempt to con money or services or information out of the victim. Scams always involve an element of deception and may be distributed as a chain letter, among other means (including spam). 419s and phishing scams are particularly common at present.

**Self-Launching Malware**  Malware, especially a worm, that exploits a vulnerability in software or operating systems rather than social engineering to gain a foothold and execute on a target system.

**Signature**  *See* Virus Definition

**Simple Mail Transfer Protocol (SMTP)**  A core e-mail standard that is not, in itself, significantly secured against header forgery or breaches of confidentiality and therefore open to a variety of forms of e-mail abuse.

**Social Engineering**  A term applied to a variety of attacks that rely on exploiting human weakness rather than technological loopholes. Often specifically applied to password stealing but also to manipulation of an e-mail recipient into running an attached malicious program.

**Spam**  Unsolicited electronic mail, especially commercial or junk e-mail. Also applied to the practice of posting large numbers of identical messages to multiple newsgroups. *Hardcore* or *professional* spam are terms sometimes applied to junk mail including a measure of deception (forged headers, misleading or even fraudulent content) and incorporates techniques intended to evade gateway filters and other antispam measures. The term derives, probably via a Monty Python sketch, from the canned meat marketed by Hormel. The company is understandably sensitive about the use of the name in the context of e-mail abuse.

**Unsolicited Bulk E-Mail (UBE)**  A term sometimes used synonymously with *spam*.

**Unsolicited Commercial E-mail (UCE)**  Large subset of UBE with an overt commercial agenda. This term is also sometimes used synonymously with *spam*.

**User-Launched Malware**  Malware that relies on social engineering to persuade a human victim to execute it.

**Virus Definition**  A scan string or algorithm used by a virus-specific scanner to recognize a known virus. Sometimes referred to as a signature (but not altogether correctly), which in antivirus is usually taken to refer to matching a static string, a technique that has not been much used in that context for many years.

**Virus-Specific Scanner**  An antivirus scanner that checks an infectable object for indications that it is infected by a known virus, rather than for generic indications of possible infection. Essentially, it looks for matches to a virus definitions database. Sometimes referred to as a known virus scanner or, less correctly, as a signature scanner.

**Vulnerability**  Condition of an asset where a risk-reducing safeguard has not been applied or is not fully effective in reducing risk. Sometimes used less formally to refer simply to a flaw, especially a programming error, which may require application of a patch.

**Webmail**  A generic term applied to e-mail that, irrespective of the underlying mail transfer protocol, is accessed via a Web interface. Some mail services are only accessible by this means (e.g., Hotmail, Bigfoot), but many ISPs include an additional Web interface facility as a courtesy to allow their customers to access their mail on systems other than their own PCs. From a security standpoint, a major corporate problem with Web mail stems from the fact that it is less susceptible to central filtering for viruses and other forms of abuse. However, many of the bigger providers apply their own antivirus and antispam measures.

**White-listing**  In spam management, allowing only mail from approved sources through to the protected mailbox.

**Worm**  A replicative, malicious program. The term is particularly applied to malware that spreads across networks and does not infect another program parasitically (as opposed to "true" viruses). The term is also often applied to mass mailers.

# CROSS REFERENCES

See *Computer and Network Authentication; Computer Viruses and Worms; Encryption Basics; Hoax Viruses and Virus Alerts; Trojan Horse Programs.*

# REFERENCES

419 Coalition. (2004). Retrieved August 18, 2004, from http://home.rica.net/alphae/419coal/

Barrett, D. J. (1996). *Bandits on the information superhighway*. Sebastopol, CA: O'Reilly & Associates.

Center for Democracy and Technology. (2003). Retrieved August 18, 2004, from http://www.cdt.org/speech/spam/030319spamreport.shtml

CIAC. (2004). Hoaxbusters Web page of the U.S. Department of Energy's Computer Incident Advisory Capability (CIAC). Retrieved August 18, 2004, from http://hoaxbusters.ciac.org/HBHoaxInfo.html#what

CNN. (2003). Retrieved August 18, 2004, from http://www.cnn.com/2003/TECH/internet/12/29/cyber.blackmail.reut/

EEMA. (2003). In "Spam and e-mail Abuse Management." Retrieved August 18, 2004, from https://www.eema.org/

F-Secure. (2004). Retrieved August 18, 2004, from http://www.f-secure.com/v-descs/novarg.shtml; http://www.f-secure.com/v-descs/mydoom_b.shtml

Gordon, S., & Chess, D. (1998). Where there's smoke, there's mirrors: The truth about Trojan horses on the Internet. Retrieved August 18, 2004, from http://www.research.ibm.com/antivirus/SciPapers/Smoke/smoke.html

Gordon, S., Ford, R., & Wells, J. (1997). Hoaxes and hypes. In *Proceedings of the Seventh Virus Bulletin International Conference* (pp. 49–66). Abingdon, England: Virus Bulletin.

Grimes, R. A. (2001). *Malicious mobile code—virus protection for Windows*. Sebastopol, CA: O'Reilly & Associates.

Harley, D. A. (1997). Macs and macros: The state of the Macintosh nation. In *Proceedings of the Seventh International Virus Bulletin Conference* (pp. 67–98). Abingdon, England: Virus Bulletin.

Harley, D. A. (1998). Refloating the *Titanic*—Dealing with social engineering attacks. In *EICAR 98 Conference Proceedings* [Compact disc]. EICAR.

Harley, D.A. (2000). The e-mail of the species—Worms, chainletters, spam and other abuses. Reserve paper for 2000 Virus Bulletin International Conference. Retrieved from mailto:davida.harley@gmail.com

Harley, D. A. (2002). Trojans. In *Maximum security* (pp. 351–377). Indianapolis, IN: SAMS.

Harley, D. A. (2003a). Virus incident management at the gateway. Retrieved August 18, 2004, from http://www.aavar.org/avar2003/presentations/David_Harley.pdf

Harley, D. A. (2003b). Fact, fiction and managed anti-malware services—vendors, resellers, and customers divided by a common language. In *Proceedings of the 13th Virus Bulletin International Conference*. Abingdon, England: Virus Bulletin.

Harley, D. A. (2004, January). Fighting the epidemic. *SC Magazine*, 28–29.

Harley, D. A., & Gattiker, U. (2002). Man, myth, memetics and malware. In *Proceedings of the 2002 EICAR conference*. [Compact Disk] EICAR.

Harley, D. A., Slade, R. M., & Gattiker, U. (2001). *Viruses revealed*. Berkeley, CA: Osborne.

Hruska, J. (1992). *Computer viruses and anti-virus warfare*. Chichester, England: Ellis Horwood.

Hypponen, M. (2003). *F-Secure Corporation's data security summary for 2003: The year of the worm*. Retrieved August 18, 2003, from http://www.f-secure.com/2003/

Johnson, K. (2000). *Internet e-mail protocols—a developer's guide*. Reading, MA: Addison-Wesley.

Kabay, M. E. (1996). *The NCSA guide to enterprise security*. New York: McGraw-Hill.

Microsoft. (1999, December 7). *Windows Security Update*. Retrieved August 18, 2004, from http://www.microsoft.com/windows98/downloads/contents/wucritical/scriptlet/default.asp

National Infrastructure Security Co-ordination Centre. (2004, March 19). *Guidance on handling files with possible malicious content* (Technical Note 03/04). Retrieved August 18, 2004, from http://www.uniras.gov.uk/l1/l2/l3/tech_reports/NTN0304.pdf

Schwartz, A., & Garfinkel, S. (1998). Stopping spam. Sebastopol, CA: O'Reilly & Associates.

Slade, R. (1996). *Robert Slade's guide to computer viruses*. New York: Springer.

Symantec. (2004). Retrieved August 18, 2004, from http://securityresponse.symantec.com/avcenter/venc/data/cih.html

Thompson, R. (2002): Virus varieties. In S. Bosworth & M. E. Kabay (Eds.), *Computer security handbook* (4th ed., 9.4–9.8). New York: Wiley.

## FURTHER READING

Harley, D. A. (2002). The future of malicious code: Predictions on blended threats, e-mail exploits, social engineering and more. *Information Security, 5*(5), 36–38.

Hughes, L. (1998) *Internet e-mail: Protocols, standards, and implementation*. Norwood, MA: Artech.

Loshin, P., & Hoffman, P. (1999) *Essential E-mail Standards: RFCs and Protocols Made Practical*. Hoboken, NJ: Wiley.

Rhoton, J. (2000) *Programmer's Guide to Internet Mail*. Woburn, MA: Digital Press.

### Spoofing Mass Mailers

Burrell, B. (2004) *The plague of viruses that send e-mail with forged "From:" fields*. Retrieved June 25, 2005, from http://www.itd.umich.edu/virusbusters/forged_from.html

### Information on E-mail Spoofing

Burrell, B. (2003). Retrieved June 25, 2002, from http://www.itd.umich.edu/virusbusters/forged_spam.html

CERT. (2002). Retrieved June 25, 2002, from http://www.cert.org/tech_tips/email_spoofing.html

### Policy Resources

Flynn, N. (2001), *The ePolicy handbook*. New York: Amacom.

Flynn, N., & Kahn, R. (2003), *E-mail rules: A business guide to managing policies, security, and legal issues for e-mail and digital communications*. New York: Amacom.

Overley, M. R. (2000) *E-Policy: How to develop computer, e-mail and internet guidelines to protect your company and its assets*. New York: Amacom.

Wood, C. C. *Information security policies made easy*. See http://www.informationshield.com/products.html (retrieved June 25, 2005).

### E-mail Cryptography/Confidentiality Resources

Blum, R. (2001) *Open source e-mail security*. Indianapolis: SAMS.

Schneier, B. (1995) *E-mail security*. New York: Wiley.

### Virus Information Resources

*Virus Bulletin* is a specialist monthly publication that runs a major yearly virus and spam-related conference. Its Web site (http://www.virusbtn.com/resources/links/index.xml) links to a wide range of resources, including antivirus vendors, virus information databases, and so on.

*WildList International* tracks viruses in the wild: http://www.wildlist.org/
http://www.wildlist.org/faq.htm

### Anti-Virus Vendors' Information Databases

http://www.sophos.com/
http://www.f-secure.com/
http://viruslist.com/
http://www.symantec.com/
http://www.mcafee.com/
http://www.complex.is
Microsoft's Antivirus Defense-in-Depth Guide: http://www.microsoft.com/technet/security/guidance/avdind_0.mspx

### Trojan Information Resources

This site is comprehensive but no longer updated: http://www.simovits.com/trojans/trojans.html

Other sites specializing in Trojans and related issues include:
http://www.moosoft.com/products/cleaner/search/
http://anti-trojan.com/

http://www.chebucto.ns.ca/~rakerman/trojan-port-table.html

http://anti-trojan-security.com/

## Spam

Antivirus companies with an antispam product include Symantec (http://www.symantec.com), Sophos (http://www.sophos.com), and NAI (http://www.nai.com). Although not exactly an antivirus company, Sybari (www.sybari.com) also has virus and spam management products.

Brightmail (anti-virus and antispam managed services): http://www.brightmail.com/

Exiscan (patch to exim that supports several antivirus packages, SpamAssassin, Brightmail spam management, etc.): http://duncanthrax.net/exiscan-acl/

Mailscanner (free, highly configurable antispam product from University of Southampton, includes capacity to plug in antivirus scanning and works with SpamAssassin): http://www.sng.ecs.soton.ac.uk/mailscanner/

MessageLabs (antivirus and antispam managed services): http://www.messagelabs.com/ and http://www.messagelabs.com/binaries/aspammerintheworks.pdf

SpamAssassin open source filtering product: http://eu.spamassassin.org/index.html

Spamcop (spam reporting, spam-blocking service) FAQ; http://www.spamcop.net/fom-serve/cache/1.html

## Reading E-Mail Headers

http://www.haltabuse.org/help/headers/

http://www.spamcop.net/fom-serve/cache/19.html

http://www.stopspam.org/e-mail/headers.html

http://www.umich.edu/~virus-busters/full_email.html

## Spam Management Information, Discussion, and Resources

http://www.cauce.org <http://www.cauce.org/>

http://www.cauce.org/about/resources.shtml#web

http://www.claws-and-paws.com/spam-l/<http://www.claws-and-paws.com/spam-l/>

http://combat.uxn.com/

http://www.elsop.com/wrc/complain.htm

http://www.emailabuse.org/

http://www.euro.cauce.org/

http://www.junkbusters.com/

http://www.mail-abuse.org/

http://www.samspade.org/

http://law.spamcon.org/

http://www.spamfree.org/

http://www.spamhaus.org/

## Newsgroups

Discussion of how to combat spam: news.admin.net-abuse.policy

Discussion of Usenet spam: news.admin.net-abuse.usenet

Discussion of e-mail spams: news.admin.net-abuse.email

All other spam issues: news.admin.net-abuse.misc

## Phishing

Anti-Phishing Working Group: http://www.antiphishing.org/apwg.htm

Internet Fraud Complaint Center (Joint venture between the FBI and the National White Collar Crime Center): http://www.ifccfbi.gov/index.asp

## Multilevel Marketing

http://www.mlmsurvivor.com/

http://www.mlmwatch.org/

http://www.mlmwatchdog.com/

http://www.quackwatch.org/01QuackeryRelatedTopics/mlm.html

## 419 Information

Alert mailing list: http://arachnophiliac.com/hoax/419-Alert.htm

The 419 Coalition Web site: http://home.rica.net/alphae/419coal/

419 fraud site: http://www.419fraud.com/

419 samples and lottery winner variants: http://www.data-wales.co.uk/nigerian.htm

International Investigation Services with searchable database: http://www.superhighway.is/iis/index.asp

NCIS, the National Criminal Intelligence Service, has a West African Organised Crime Section: http://www.ncis.co.uk/waocu.asp. In case of loss, they can be contacted on 020 7238 8012 or at victim@spring39.demon.co.uk.

Nigerian letter scam links page: http://www.geocities.com/acidtestgpts/nigerian_letter_scam_links.htm

Scamwatch: http://www.scamwatch.com/scam_reports/scam_directory.html

Searchable database: http://arachnophiliac.com/hoax/419_search.htm

The West African Organised Crime Section of the National Criminal Intelligence Service has a Web site at http://www.ncis.co.uk/waocu.asp. A local contact for 419 reporting can be obtained from +44 (0) 20 7238 8012. NCIS will offer assistance to people losing money to 419 fraud via waocs@ncis.gov.uk.

UK Metropolitan Police general fraud information: http://www.met.police.uk/fraudalert/. Their 419 information page is at http://www.met.police.uk/fraudalert/419.htm

UK National Hi-Tech Crime Unit has a 419 page, plus information on other forms of IT-related fraud and other crime: http://www.nhtcu.org/

UK Specialist Crime OCU Fraud Squad: +44 (0) 20 7230 1220

USA Secret Service 419 page: http://www.secretservice.gov/alert419.shtml

## Hoaxes, Urban Legends, and Memetic Malware (Web Pages)

http://ciac.llnl.gov/ciac/

http://www.f-secure.com/

http://hoaxbusters.ciac.org/

http://www.korova.com/

http://www.nai.com/

http://www.snopes.com/

http://www.sophos.com

http://www.stiller.com/

http://www.symantec.com/
http://www.urbanlegends.com
http://www.urbanlegends.com /afu.faq
http://urbanlegends.miningco.com/
http://www.vmyths.com

## Memetics

Blackmore, Susan. (1999). *The Meme Machine*. Oxford: Oxford University Press.

Brodie, Richard. (1996). *Virus of the Mind: The New Science of the Meme*. Integral Press.

Dawkins, Richard. (1991). "Viruses of the Mind." Retrieved 25, June, 2005, from http://cscs.umich.edu/~crshalizi/Dawkins/viruses-of-the-mind.html

Dawson, R. "The Selfish Gene," "River Out of Eden," "Unweaving the Rainbow" (social biology, memetics, and specific material on chain letters).

Harley, D. (1997). Dealing with Internet Hoaxes/Alerts. Retrieved January 1, 2004, from http://www.arachnophiliac.com/

Harley, David. (2001). E-Mail Abuse—Internet Chain Letters, Hoaxes and Spam. Retrieved January 1, 2004, from http://www.arachnophiliac.com/

http://www.urbanlegends.com/afu.faq/intro.html

http://www.arachnophiliac.com/hoax/index.htm#papers

http://arachnophiliac.com/files/av/VB2001_Electronic_Ephemera-1.01.pdf

Kaminski, J. (1997). Multiplatform Attack—In the land of the Hoaxes. In *Proceedings of the 1997 Virus Bulletin International Conference*.

Overton, M. (2000). Safe Hex in the 21st Century—Part 1. *Virus Bulletin*, June 2000, pp. 16–17.

Overton, M. (2000). Safe Hex in the 21st Century—Part 2. *Virus Bulletin*, July 2000, pp. 14–15.

# E-Commerce Vulnerabilities

Sviatoslav Braynov, *University of Illinois, Springfield*

## INTRODUCTION

E-commerce has both promises and dangers. One promise is to dramatically change the way business is conducted by lowering the costs, reaching larger markets, and creating new distribution channels and new forms of business interaction. One danger is that the more successful e-commerce becomes, the more likely it is to attract abusive actions, fraud, and deception. Every year, companies and customers lose billions of dollars from fraudulent transactions, credit card abuse, and identity theft.

What makes e-commerce extremely vulnerable to computer attacks is the fact that the three main components of every commercial activity—the agents, the process, and the commodity—can all be digital. This means that agents can be spoofed or impersonated, the process can be hijacked or altered, and the digital commodity can be stolen.

The security of e-commerce systems, however, is not a new topic. It touches on many aspects of computer and network security; the three basic security components (CIA), confidentiality, integrity, and availability, continue to play a basic role. Buffer overflows, misconfigured access controls, default configurations of Web servers, improper input validation, and race conditions, to name just a few, are typical vulnerabilities causing enormous damage every year because of loss of reputation, revenue loss, leakage of confidential information, loss of consumer base, and so on.

In this chapter, I refrain from repeating common network, server-side, or client-side vulnerabilities because they are discussed in other parts of this *Handbook*. Instead, I focus on vulnerabilities specific to online business, such as e-shoplifting, credit card fraud, online auction fraud, and nonrepudiation of digital transactions. I also discuss how trust and reputation management can be useful safeguards against online fraud.

## E-SHOPLIFTING

E-shoplifting differs from traditional shoplifting in that an attacker uses computer or network vulnerabilities to commit fraud. For example, an attacker can use software exploits to steal a product, buy a product at a fictitious price (sometimes even at a negative price), or use a fictitious identity.

Although e-commerce Web sites can be compromised by standard exploits such as buffer overflows and password cracking, some attacks are specific to the nature of e-commerce. At the heart of every e-commerce Web site is online shopping, materialized as a shopping cart application. The shopping cart is one of the central applications in e-commerce and obviously the most common target for e-shoplifting. The purpose of the shopping cart is to maintain a session with customers and allow them to select and save items that interest them. The basic objective is to organize session management, state tracking, and front-end interface and navigation. Shopping carts also need to be properly integrated with online catalogs, payment gateways, and back-end databases.

There are also off-the-shelf shopping carts provided by third-party vendors. Many of them do not come with security guaranties and may contain loopholes. Even reliable shopping carts can open security holes if not properly configured and integrated with a database and a payment gateway. For example, McClure et al. (2003) reported a vulnerability in the Viva Merchant shopping cart, which when not properly integrated with VeriSign's PayFlow payment system, allows an attacker to save and edit the HTML (hypertext markup language) code of the final checkout page, bypassing the credit card validation process. The main vulnerabilities in shopping cart implementation are caused by the following:

- Poor input validation
- Poor session management

## Poor Input Validation

Poor input validation is probably the major culprit for many vulnerabilities in computer and network security. Race conditions, buffer overflows, and many TCP (transfer control protocol) attacks, for example, are based on poor input validation. I skip the basics of poor input validation and focus on vulnerabilities specific to Web-based e-commerce applications.

### Hidden Fields

This is an application level vulnerability in which hidden fields in HTML forms convey important information, such as price, user ID, and so on. For example, online catalogs may have their prices stored as hidden fields in an HTML form. An attacker can then save the catalog page, change the value of hidden fields to manipulate prices, and send the manipulated form via a POST request to the server-side application responsible for the form processing. The process of finding hidden fields could even be automated. For example, McClure et al. (2003) points to the possibility of using search engines to find hidden fields in a business Web site.

### Bypassing Client-Side Validation

Client-side input validation is vulnerable to attacks in which the attacker edits the HTML source code to alter or remove the validation process. For example, if a shopping cart performs input validation via JavaScript or VBScript code, the attacker can read and alter the code to bypass validation.

### Lack of Input Sanitization

Usually, two main input validations need to be performed: validation of the size of the data received and validation of its format and content. If the input is not properly sanitized for meta-characters, such as "|", "&", "%", "+", an attacker can insert malicious code to achieve remote command execution. For example, an attacker can insert the pipe character followed by a malicious command into an input field of a shopping cart, or directly into the URL (uniform resource locator) string.

## Poor Session Management

Because of the statelessness of HTTP (hypertext transfer protocol) and the multiuser nature of e-commerce sites, session management is required to segregate users and prevent unauthorized access. Session management usually refers to the process of tracking users' sessions and states. The Web application creates an ID for a user and subsequently binds every HTTP request with the user's identity. In this way, every user interacts with the application via a separate session, and the application keeps track of current users and their relative progress (whether the user is in the authentication stage, in the product selection stage, or in the checkout stage).

Improperly implemented session management could lead to session hijacking (i.e., taking over an existing active session, bypassing the authentication process, and gaining access to a machine). In computer security, hijacking is most commonly used to describe the process of taking over a TCP connection by sequence guessing. In e-commerce, however, session hijacking is application oriented and refers to the process of impersonating an authorized user. In practice, there are three basic ways to track a user, and therefore three ways to hijack a session: cookies, URL session tracking, and hidden form elements.

### Cookies

Cookies could be used to store session IDs. There are two types of cookies: persistent and nonpersistent. A persistent cookie is stored on the client's hard drive, and an attacker who has access to the client machine can easily access the cookie. A nonpersistent cookie is stored in memory and is more difficult to access.

With the help of special programs called sniffers, cookies can also be pulled off the wire as they travel between the client and the server. Another attack is to guess a cookie. An attacker can visit an e-commerce site numerous times and get an idea of session IDs and cookie values. If the attacker successfully guesses a cookie, he or she can impersonate a valid user and gain access to the user's account.

To make the guessing of cookies difficult, session IDs must be unique long numbers. If a session ID is serially incremented or if it follows a specific time pattern, an attacker can generate an identifier that coincides with the identifiers of a current user.

**URL Session Tracking.** Another method of session tracking is placing the session ID in the URL. Because session identifiers are visible and transmitted in the clear, they are much easier to guess. The best defense against URL session tracking is to use long randomlike session IDs.

**Hidden Form Elements.** Some e-commerce Web sites prefer to pass session IDs as hidden form elements. This means that whenever the user hits the submit button, his or her session ID is sent back to the Web application. Obviously, an attacker can change the hidden element to impersonate a valid user.

To better protect against session hijacking, Cole (2002) recommended using two types of session IDs: one session ID for viewing information and another for updating information. The session ID for viewing information can be valid for about an hour and must expire as soon as the user logs off. The session ID for updating information, however, should be valid for only a few minutes.

## CREDIT CARD PAYMENTS

Today, credit and debit cards are the most popular way for paying over the Internet. For that reason, I focus mainly on credit card vulnerabilities. Although credit cards are not usually used for business to business (B2B) transactions involving larger dollar amounts, such transactions are usually carried out over well-protected private financial networks, which present relatively low security risks.

## Traditional Credit Card Fraud

The major risk in credit card payments comes from the possibility of stealing and misusing a credit card number. Credit card fraud existed long before the advent of e-commerce, and credit card numbers have been stolen with nontechnical means such as stealing records from a business, bribing an employee, social engineering, and trash rummaging (dumpster diving).

Credit card numbers can also be stolen by using portable electronic devices known as skimmers. Once a credit card is swiped through the device, all the information contained on the magnetic stripe is captured. The device can sometimes store the details of up to 150 cards. Some devices are equipped with a button that can immediately erase all of the collected data when pressed, effectively eliminating any evidence of the crime.

A fraudulent skimmer can be used in many ways. It can be carried in the pocket of a waiter or a corrupt cashier. The card is swiped twice: once through the legitimate machine and once through the skimmer. A skimmer can also be connected to a phone line between the phone jack and the credit card machine itself. When a consumer swipes his or her credit card to make a purchase, the fraudulent skimmer captures the credit card information.

## Online Credit Card Fraud

There is a common misconception that a credit card number can be stolen while it travels over the Internet. With the development of secure cryptographic protocols for electronic payments, such as Secure Electronic Transaction (SET), secure socket layer (SSL) and transport layer security (TLS), VISA 3-D Secure, and MasterCard SPA, the chances of an attacker intercepting a credit card number are virtually zero. Traditional transactions carried over the phone, for example, present a much greater security risk and are much easier to eavesdrop. In addition, the benefits of capturing a single credit card number are outweighed by its costs, thereby presenting little economic incentive.

What the Internet makes possible, however, is the stealing of credit card numbers on a large scale. A popular example is that of a 19-year-old Russian named Maxim who broke into CDUniverse and stole more than 300,000 credit card numbers in 1999. He posted 25,000 of the numbers on the Web, causing a lot of problems for customers, CDUniverse, and credit card companies.

In general, credit card numbers could be stolen on a large scale by the following means:

- **Breaking into an organization's computers.** A successful attack against a corporate computer, however, is not sufficient to gain access to credit card numbers, which are usually encrypted. If weak encryption is used, an attacker can download credit card numbers to his or her computer and try an offline attack against the cryptosystem, possibly lasting several months.

- Setting up a fake Web site or spoofing a reputable business. Many different kinds of Web spoofing can be used, including IP (Internet protocol) spoofing and DNS (domain name server) poisoning. Cole (2002) described an interesting type of Web spoofing attack. An attacker sets up a fake Web site using a domain name similar to that of a reputable business. Because the fake Web site looks like the original, a user goes through the fraudulent site clicking on the items he or she wants to purchase. During the checkout stage, the site collects the credit card information, gives the user a cookie, and puts up a message, "This site is currently experiencing problems. Please try again later." When the user comes back, the fraudulent site receives the cookie, knows that this user has already been fooled, and automatically redirects the user to the original Web site.

The skills required to steal credit card information online and sell or exchange such information have been limited to a relatively small number of online criminals. A recent report by the Honeynet project (http://www. honeynet.org/papers/profiles/cc-fraud.pdf), however, reveals a rather worrying tendency to automate credit card fraud. Honeynet researchers monitored a dozen Internet relay chat (IRC) channels because traffic for these channels passed through an IRC proxy on a compromised host. The researchers found that criminals (commonly known as carders) automated many stages of credit card fraud by running software robots called *bots*. IRC bots were run on several IRC channels to automate merchant site identification, target exploitation, card validation, and card verification. These IRC bots were capable of remotely accessing a common database containing vulnerable target merchant Web sites. The robots also had access to a database of known exploits that could be used to compromise a Web site. By automating credit card fraud and making it available to less skilled individuals, such tools present a significant security threat.

## Identity Theft and Identity Management

Security vulnerabilities and the pervasiveness of computer systems that host personal information (e.g., names, social security numbers [SSNs], dates of birth, card account numbers, driver's license numbers) have considerably increased the risk of identity theft. According to the Identity Theft and Assumption Deterrence Act, enacted by the U.S. Congress in 1998 (http://www. ftc.gov/os/statutes/itada/itadact.htm), identity theft is an offense when someone "knowingly transfers or uses, without lawful authority, a means of identification of another person with the intent to commit, or to aid or abet, any unlawful activity that constitutes a violation of Federal law, or that constitutes a felony under any applicable State or local law." A recent survey by the Federal Trade Commission (FTC; http://www.ftc.gov/os/2003/09/synovatereport .pdf) shows that identity theft is the fastest growing crime in the United States, with 9.9 million complaints for the year 2002.

In an attempt to fight the growing crime of identity theft, California has recently passed a new law (California Civil Code Section 1798) that forces organizations to notify state residents when a computer security breach has permitted the release of personal information to unauthorized recipients.

Although identity theft is more general than credit card fraud and includes stealing different forms of personal identification, credit card fraud remains the most prevalent form. The problem is that credit card numbers usually come with their owners' names, addresses, and other information. Once this information is stolen, an attacker can impersonate the victim to open an account in an online auction, to buy or sell over the Internet, and so forth. In the largest online-fraud case prosecuted to date, Teresa Smith pleaded guilty in December 2002 to defrauding more than 200 people through $800,000 worth of computer sales (Lee, 2003).

Computer and network security is only part of the problem with identity theft. An attacker can break into a corporate computer and steal SSNs, credit card numbers, addresses, and other personal information. The information can also be intercepted when it travels unencrypted over the Internet. Unfortunately, there is no special protection against identity theft, and general security measures apply.

Another problem is the lack of clear understanding of the notion of digital identity and identity management. Identity management usually refers to processes, tools, and policies governing the creation, maintenance, and termination of a digital identity. Traditionally, identity management has been a component of system security. With the increased pervasiveness and richness of the Internet, however, many assumptions and policies regarding digital identity and identity management need to be revisited and redefined.

Recently, many companies and organizations have made a push toward a federated identity management. The reason is that digital-identity information is scattered across the Internet in isolated databases. Two major initiatives, Liberty 1.0 and the Microsoft .NET Passport, have been proposed. Both support the idea of federated identity (Costa, 2002), which allows a user to visit several Web sites with a single sign-on. For example, with the Microsoft .NET Passport, the user profile is stored on a Microsoft server that (with the user's approval) shares the information with participating Web sites. However, this raises some doubts as to whether digital identity services provide sufficient protection of privacy. Users can easily lose the ability to control how and to what extent personal information is shared with marketing firms, governmental agencies, and other third parties.

Unlike the Microsoft .NET Passport, Liberty Alliance does not centralize personal information with Liberty 1.0. Instead, information is distributed across a large network of participating companies (e.g., Citigroup, General Motors Corp., Sony Corp., Sun Microsystems, American Express, Ford, and Nokia), which together form the Liberty Alliance Network. Liberty Alliance also allows users to decide whether to link their accounts to other participating sites. For example, users can choose to opt out and not link their accounts to a specific site. The main difference between the Microsoft .NET Passport and Liberty Alliance is that Microsoft keeps all the data about individual users to itself, whereas Liberty Alliance allows data to be owned by many Web sites.

# PROTECTING CREDIT CARD PAYMENTS
## Secure Electronic Transactions

In January 1996, Visa, MasterCard, Microsoft, Netscape, and other companies agreed on a joint standard for on-line electronic payments called Secure Electronic Transactions (SET). The agreement came after several years of fighting over incompatible standards such as Secure Transaction Technology (STT), proposed by VISA and Microsoft, and secure electronic payment protocol (SEPP), proposed by MasterCard, Netscape, IBM, and others. To coordinate their efforts, VISA and MasterCard established in 1997 an independent company, SETCo, expected to promote and approve extensions and modifications to SET.

SET is not intended to be a general-purpose payment protocol; it is restricted to payment card applications. The most important advantage of SET is the separation of transactional and financial information. Transactional information (items being ordered, types of shipping, and so forth) is supposed to be private between the customer and the merchant. Financial information (e.g., customer account number, mode of payment) is expected to be private between the customer and his issuer (the customer's financial institution). A serious problem with all other payment systems is that they do not separate these two types of information, allowing a merchant to access financial information and an issuer to access transactional information. The way other payment protocols work is to submit both transactional and financial information (eventually encrypted) to the merchant, who then forwards them to the issuer. Such a scheme creates opportunities for abuse from both the merchant and the issuer. For example, a dishonest merchant can abuse the financial information by selling it to third parties, or the issuer can keep a record of the spending habits of their customers, thereby violating their privacy.

The core feature of SET, separating financial from transactional information, is called a dual signature. Figure 1 shows how a dual signature is composed.

The transactional information and the financial information are separately hashed, and the resulting digests are concatenated. A new hash is computed on the concatenation, which is then signed with the sender's private key. The transactional information, Digest 2, and the dual signature are sent to the merchant, whereas the financial information, Digest 1, and the dual signature are sent to the financial institution. The merchant can verify the dual signature without being able to access the financial information. Likewise, the financial institution can verify the dual signature without having the transactional

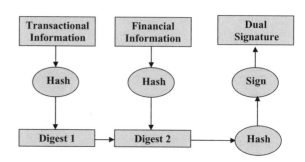

**Figure 1:** Composing a dual signature.

information. The dual signature can be thought of as an extension of the standard digital signature, which links an identity to a message. The dual-signature mechanism, however, extends the idea further by allowing an identity to be linked to a message, without having to see the message content.

Despite the fact that SET is the most secure credit-card payment protocol developed so far, it has not enjoyed wide market acceptance. The first problem with SET was its complex specification. Initially, it came with several weighty volumes of specification, resulting in expensive software development and testing. The second barrier to SET was its reliance on the well-developed public key infrastructure (PKI) and specifically on a certification authority hierarchy (O'Mahony, Peirce, & Tewari, 2001). The full specification and the current status of SET can be found at the SETCo Web site (http://www.setco.org).

## Secure Socket Layer and Transport Layer Security

SSL and TLS provide basic security services for online credit card payments. First, the communication between the merchant and the customer is encrypted, so that an attacker cannot intercept the credit card numbers. Second, the merchant is authenticated (customer authentication is optional) to prevent spoofing attacks, where an attacker sets up a fake merchant server. Because SSL and TSL are covered in depth in other chapters of this *Handbook,* I do not provide a technical description here. For good technical coverage of SSL and TLS, see Rescorla (2001).

## VISA 3-D Secure

Starting in 2001, VISA required all its merchants to follow specific security rules. For example, they must install a firewall, encrypt stored and transmitted data, keep security patches up to date, and so forth.

VISA has also introduced 3-D Secure (http://international.visa.com), a TLS-based protocol that provides confidentiality of information, ensures payment integrity, and authenticates cardholders. 3-D Secure works as follows:

1. When checking out, the cardholder supplies billing and payment card information to merchant server plug-in (MPI) software.
2. The MPI contacts the Visa directory server to determine whether authentication services are available for the cardholder.
3. The Visa directory server checks card participation with the issuer (the customer's financial institution).
4. The issuer confirms the credit card transaction.
5. The Visa directory server instructs the MPI on how to contact the access control server (ACS) of the associated issuer.
6. MPI redirects the credit card holder to the issuer ACS. The issuer ACS requests a username and a password from the credit card holder. Upon successful authentication, the ACS redirects the customer to the MPI.
7. The merchant confirms the transaction and issues a receipt.

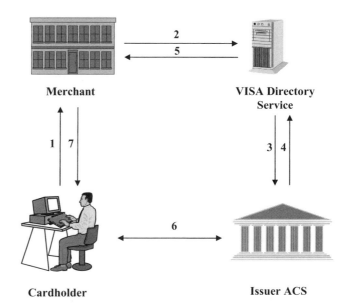

**Figure 2:** VISA 3-D Secure.

The main steps of the protocol are shown in Figure 2.

One advantage of 3-D Secure is that it creates an online receipt that is (a) approved by the cardholder, (b) digitally signed by the issuer after verification of the cardholder's identity, and (c) stored by the merchant to serve as a proof of purchase.

Another advantage of 3-D Secure is the centralization of the authentication process that is controlled and run by VISA. Such a solution relieves merchants from the necessity to deploy specialized authentication software, reduces the merchant's responsibility, and decreases the chances of errors. A drawback of 3-D Secure is its reliance on an extensive infrastructure, involving ACSs and directory servers. Compared with SET, however, 3-D Secure is more lightweight and requires much less investment. Only the future will tell whether and when it will become an accepted standard.

## MasterCard SPA

Secure Payment Application (SPA) is a MasterCard security solution to the cardholder authentication problem. At the heart of MasterCard's SPA is a unique transaction token generated each time a registered accountholder initiates an electronic transaction. The token is called the accountholder authentication value (AAV). It incorporates information specific both to the transaction and the cardholder's identity, thereby binding the cardholder to a particular transaction.

SPA requires the cardholder, his issuer, and the merchant to use client software known as the SPA applet. In addition, the issuer is required to implement an SPA server that is responsible for generating AAVs. SPA consists of the following main steps:

1. When purchasing from a merchant that supports the SPA program, the SPA applet of the merchant requests authentication information from the cardholder. At this point, the cardholder is asked to authenticate with a secret password.

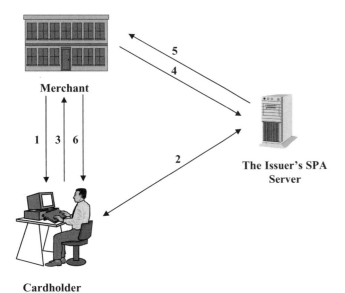

**Merchant**

**The Issuer's SPA Server**

**Cardholder**

**Figure 3:** *MasterCard SPA* (Secure Payment Application).

2. The cardholder SPA applet sends this information to the SPA server, which verifies the cardholder's identity, generates a unique AAV, and sends it back to the cardholder.

3. The cardholder SPA applet sends the AAV to the merchant's site.

4. The merchant performs a regular authorization request by sending the AAV number to the issuer.

5. If the verification is successful, the issuer sends a response back to the merchant.

6. Finally, the merchant confirms the transaction and issues a receipt to the cardholder.

The main steps of the protocol are shown in Figure 3.

Both VISA 3-D Secure and MasterCard SPA provide valuable security measures to improve online authentication and reduce e-commerce chargebacks and electronic fraud. A brief comparison between 3-D Secure and SPA is provided in Table 1.

## PayPal Security

Before PayPal (http://www.paypal.com) was established in 1999, it was impossible for individuals to accept credit card payments over the Internet. Today, PayPal is the largest peer-to-peer payment service that significantly simplifies electronic payments. To transfer money between two individuals, PayPal requires only that individuals have an e-mail address and a credit card or a bank account.

The security PayPal provides is twofold. First, when a person registers a bank account with PayPal, the company verifies that the person is an authorized user of the account without calling the bank. This is done by initiating two credits for less than $1 to the account. After that PayPal asks the user to confirm the value of the transactions. The intuition is that only an authorized user can access the account to get the value of the transactions.

Second, PayPal requires authorization for transactions greater than $200, thereby limiting the possibility for credit card fraud. PayPal does not implement any special security mechanisms to protect credit card payments, however. Instead, it relies exclusively on reversibility of credit card transactions, and some fraudulent transactions may not be reversible. For example, a person could transfer money from his or her bank account to another person's account. After the transaction is verified by PayPal and before the money is actually transferred, the person can immediately withdraw the money from the account, thereby leaving nothing to be transferred.

## Check Digit Algorithm (ISO 2894)

Although widely available, the check digit algorithm is not well known. The algorithm provides a basic check of

**Table 1** A Comparison Between 3-D Secure and SPA (Secure Payment Application).

|  | 3-D Secure | SPA |
|---|---|---|
| **Cardholder registration** | Requires registration | Requires registration |
| **Client-side software** | Does not require client-side software for the cardholder | Requires downloading the SPA applet, which can increase the length of the registration process and introduce incompatibility issues |
| **Protection against spoofing the authentication site** | Uses only user name and password | Uses additional personal greeting created during the registration process to reduce the possibility of spoofing |
| **Automatic form filling** | Not available | Available through the SPA applet |
| **Shopping at multiple sites** | The cardholder is required to authenticate him- or herself at every site | The cardholder may be required to authenticate only once and can then buy products from different sites |
| **Additional services** | Limits itself to providing cardholder authentication and payment services | The SPA applet allows a wide range of additional services, such as transaction reporting, storage of passwords, electronic bill presentment and payment, and so on |

whether a credit card number is valid. The purpose of the algorithm is not to authorize a credit card transaction but to provide a first line of defense against misspellings and wrong input. The algorithm works as follows:

1. Multiply every digit in the credit card number by its weight. The weights are either 1 or 2 depending on the position of the digit. If the card has an even number of digits, the first digit has a weight of 2, otherwise it has a weight of 1. Weights alternate: 1,2,1,2 . . . . . , or 2,1,2,1 . . .
2. If the weighted value of a digit exceeds 9, subtract 9.
3. Add together the weighted values of all digits, modulo 10.
4. If the credit card number is correct, the result must be 0.

Again, the algorithm performs a very basic check. Further authorization is needed to validate a credit card.

## One-Time-Use Credit Card Numbers

Many credit card companies are already practicing the so called one-time credit card number. The idea is to issue for every transaction a one-time number, not to be reused for a period of some time. After the number has been spent, it offers no value and does not need special protection. One-time numbers resemble the digital coins used by digital payment systems, such as ECash, NetCash, and so on. A one-time credit card number, however, does not have the cryptographic protection of digital coins, such as a bank signature, encryption with a session key, and so forth.

One-time credit card numbers are issued by client-side wallets. For example, Discover offers a wallet called Discover Deskshop, which runs permanently on the client computer. Whenever the wallet discovers an HTML form asking for the user's name, address, and credit card information, a small pop-up window asks the user for permission to fill out the form automatically. After receiving the user's permission, the wallet authenticates the user by asking him to enter a password and automatically generates a single-use credit card number.

## ONLINE AUCTIONS

The increasing popularity of online auctions makes them an attractive playground for online fraud. Complaints about online auction transactions have skyrocketed, accounting for 90% of the Internet fraud reports made to the Internet Fraud Watch in the first half of 2002, compared with 70% in 2001 (http://www.fraud.org). According to a report by the FTC (http://www.ftc.gov), the most typical auction fraud cases are as follows:

- Failure to send merchandise, especially high-ticket goods such as computers, plasma televisions, and diamond jewelry
- Sending something of lesser value than advertised
- Failure to deliver in a timely manner
- Failure to disclose all relevant information about a product or terms of sale

## Basic Auction Types

Although there are numerous auction rules, most online auctions are direct or close implementations of the four basic auction types: English, Dutch, first-price sealed-bid, and second-price sealed-bid (also called the Vickrey auction after its author William Vickrey, a Nobel Prize laureate in economics in 1996). In the English auction, each bidder is free to raise his or her bid. When no bidder is willing to do so, the highest bidder wins at the price of the bid. In the Dutch auction, the seller continuously lowers the price until one of the bidders agrees to the price and purchases the item. In the first-price sealed-bid auction, each bidder submits a bid only once, without knowing the other bids. The highest bidder wins and pays his or her price. The second-price sealed-bid auction is similar to the first-price sealed-bid auction except that the winner pays the price of the second highest bid.

One particular advantage of the Vickrey auction is the simplicity of the bidders' optimal strategies. Whereas other auction types require complex bidding strategies involving speculation and counterspeculation, in the Vickrey auction, it is a dominant strategy to bid the maximum a bidder is willing to pay, that is, the value of the item.

There are three types of parties involved in online auctions: auctioneers, bidders, and intermediaries. Any of these is a potential security threat. In general, online auction fraud can be divided into three major groups: cheating auctioneers, cheating bidders, and cheating intermediaries.

## Cheating Auctioneers

Insincerity of the auctioneer is a problem for many online auctions and especially for Vickrey auctions. The possibility of a cheating auctioneer was pointed out as early as 1961, when Vickrey's seminal paper (1961) appeared. The problem is that the auctioneer can overstate the second highest bid in an attempt to squeeze the maximum profit from the winner. The scheme works only in situations in which the winner cannot verify the second highest bid. To solve the problem, digital signatures can be used so that the auctioneer can present the second highest bid to the winner. The other three auctions (English, Dutch, and first-price sealed-bid) are not vulnerable to such a scheme, because the winner gets the item at the price of his or her bid.

The auctioneer can also cheat by using shills, fake bidders who bid aggressively to make the real bidders increase their bids. The scheme works only for the English auction, where bidders can observe each other's bids. Instead of injecting shills, the auctioneer can place a bid under a changed identity. Such aggressive overbidding, however, is not always safe for the auctioneer who, after placing a bid, could win his or her own auction.

Another possibility for a dishonest auctioneer is to peek at bidding proxies, which have been widely used by many auctions, such as eBay, Amazon, UBid, and so on. Proxy bidding is an automated service provided by the auction site that bids on behalf of a user. Users specify the maximum price they are willing to pay, and the proxy monitors the auction by automatically placing bids just high enough to beat the last bid. The problem with proxy bidding is that a cheating auctioneer can extract the maximum price from a proxy and place a shill bid just below it, thereby squeezing the maximal bid from the winner.

The power of auctioneers to run and control the auction gives them an enormous potential for committing fraud. Obviously, it is not possible to cover all the various online auction vulnerabilities. To give an idea of the scope of the problem, I briefly mention a few more possibilities for a cheating auctioneer:

- The auctioneer can open a sealed bid and inform a collaborating bidder of the amounts bid by their competitors.
- The auctioneer can award the auction item to somebody other than the winner, when auctions have private bids.
- The auctioneer can manipulate the bidding time.
- The auctioneer can drop some bids and claim that they never arrived.

Some of these problems could be fixed with properly designed cryptographic auctions, discussed in a separate section.

## Cheating Bidders

Auctions in general and online auctions in particular are susceptible to bidder collusion. Bidder collusion is more a protocol weakness than an implementation vulnerability. In bidder collusion, several bidders coordinate their bid prices in an attempt to win an auction at an artificially low price. Bidder collusion is possible only in the English and Vickrey auctions. The following example illustrates the problem. Suppose that, in an English auction, Alice, Bob, and Charlie are willing to pay maximal prices of $10, $5, and $5, respectively. If they bid honestly, Alice will win the auction at the price of $10. By colluding, they can decide that Alice will bid $3 and everyone else will bid $2. In this case, Alice wins and pays $3, creating an extra benefit of $7 that can be split between the members of the colluding group.

A bidder could also break into an auction server and manipulate or peek at prices. Given the level of security of many auction houses and the fact that such an attack needs a proper time synchronization, cheating by breaking into an auction server remains a rather theoretical possibility.

A more realistic attack is a denial of service against an auction server, when an attacker or a group of attackers slows down the server by sending an overwhelming number of requests. Because bidding is time sensitive, this could manipulate the auction results.

Another possibility for a dishonest bidder is to intercept and drop packets containing his or her opponent's bids. Obviously, such a scheme works even when the bids are encrypted. To avoid such problems, Monderer and Tennenholtz (1999) proposed a distributed protocol in which it is in the best interest of every agent to follow the protocol. The basic assumption is that the communication network is $k$-connected. That is, there are at least $k$ disjoint paths between any two nodes, allowing a bid to be duplicated and sent along many paths. Monderer and Tennenholtz's solution, however, is vulnerable to distributed attacks in which several nodes collude and drop packets simultaneously. The problem is that every k-connected graph has a set of critical nodes, the removal of which makes the graph disconnected.

Another possibility for cheating is using false-name bids in combinatorial auctions. A conventional auction sells a single item at a time, whereas a combinatorial auction sells multiple items and allows bidders to bid for a combination of items. In false-name bidding, a bidder registers under more than one name and profits by submitting several bids at once. That is, instead of bidding on a single combination of items, the bidder simultaneously bids on several combinations using fictitious names. False-name bidding is difficult to detect because identifying each user on the Internet is virtually impossible. The possibility for false-name bids was first pointed out by Sakurai, Yakoo, and Matsubara (1999). The authors proposed an auction protocol, called leveled division set, which is robust against false-name bids.

## Cheating Intermediaries

Among the most popular fraud schemes involving intermediaries are fake escrow services. Escrow services are used to enable a transaction between two parties that do not trust each other, by putting the money with the escrow service while the goods are being exchanged. In some way, an escrow service can be viewed as a trusted third party. The problem, reported by the FTC, is that people posing as legitimate auction participants, both buyers and sellers, have been setting up fake escrow services and insisting that the opposite party use the service. In her *New York Times* article, Lee (2003) reported a case in which a man from Arizona lost more than $50,000 when he tried to buy a BMW using a fraudulent escrow service called Premier-Escrow.com. The FTC filed a restraining order against the service on April 22, 2003.

## Cryptographic Auctions

Franklin and Reiter (1995a) first presented the basic problems with online auction security and proposed to solve them using four basic security requirements to online sealed-bid auctions:

1. Bids must remain secret until the auction is closed.
2. The auction must implement a nonrepudiation mechanism to ensure that a payment can be collected from winning bidders.
3. Because of the secrecy of bids, the auction should allow an outside observer to verify the validity of the auction.
4. An auction has to protect the identity of bidders and winners. That is, they must remain anonymous.

To meet these requirements, they proposed a distributed auction service. The auction ensures the validity of the outcome, despite malicious cooperation of arbitrarily many bidders and fewer than one-third of auction servers. The auction is based on a cryptographic technique known as *threshold secret sharing* (Shamir, 1979).

A $(t, n)$-threshold secret sharing scheme is a method of breaking a secret $s$ into $i$ shares, so that any $t + 1$ shares are sufficient to reconstruct the secret $s$, but $t$ or fewer shares give no information about $s$. In a subsequent work, Franklin and Reiter (1995b) extended this technique to allow for verifiable signature sharing in which a digital signature is shared among $n$ holders and can be reconstructed only by at least $t + 1$ holders.

The protocol proposed by Franklin and Reiter (1995a) works as follows. Bidders share their bids among $n$ auction servers. Once the bidding period is closed, the auction servers can reconstruct each bid and jointly determine the winner, using verifiable signature sharing. The secrecy of each bid is guaranteed until bidding is closed, because servers do not collude in the bid reconstruction. Even if $t$ (roughly one third of $n$) auction servers collude, they still cannot reconstruct the bid.

Another alternative to Franklin and Reiter's protocol is threshold cryptography (Desmedt, 1994), in which a message can be decrypted only with the cooperation of a threshold number of auction servers. Threshold cryptography can also be used for winner determination, in which the cooperation of a threshold number of auction servers is required to sign a message with the auction house's private key. One important problem with threshold cryptography is that it is computationally intensive, allowing a malicious bidder to launch a denial of service attack by submitting a large number of bids.

Another important aspect of cryptographic auctions is nonmalleability. The concept of a nonmalleable auction was first introduced by Dolev, Dwork, and Naor (1991) and is illustrated by the following example. Municipality $M$ has voted to construct a new elementary school and advertises in the appropriate journals. The advertisement consists of a public key $E$, to be used for encrypting bids, and a fax number to which encrypted bids must be sent. Company $A$ places a bid of \$1,500,000 by faxing E(1,500,000). The public-key cryptosystem is nonmalleable if having access to E(1,500,000), a competing company $B$ cannot generate a bid E($\beta$), $\beta < 1,500,000$, without knowing the plaintext 1,500,000.

A cryptographic auction does not necessarily preserve the privacy of the participants' inputs. The information about the amount a bidder submits and his or her identity need to be kept private, otherwise they could be used to manipulate the results of an auction or even the results of future auctions. Consider the following example, given by Naor et al. (1999). A company places a bid of \$1,000 on a single unit Vickrey auction and wins. The second highest is only \$600, which means that the company pays \$600. The next month, the same company is participating in an identical auction, run by the same auctioneer, for a second unit of the same product. This time, the auctioneer sets a reserve price of \$999, thereby forcing the company to bid \$1,000.

Naor et al. (1999) proposed a privacy-preserving auction protocol that solves such problems. They use a new auction party, called the auction issuer, that generates the programs for computing the auction, without taking active part in the auction. The auction issuer is not a trusted third party but is assumed not to collude with the auctioneer.

Obviously, the assumption that the issuer does not collude with the auctioneer cannot be satisfied in many real-life situations, thereby limiting the applicability of issuer-based online auctions. To fix the problem, Brandt (2002) proposed an auction protocol that does not need an auctioneer at all. In the protocol, a bidder distributes shares of his bid among all bidders. The bidders then jointly compute the selling price and the winner, without uncovering any additional information. The auction results cannot be manipulated by cheating bidders, although they can perform a denial of service attack on the auction.

## The Cocaine Auction Protocol

Although security and privacy are desirable properties of online auctions, they have to be used with caution. The problem is that privacy-preserving auctions can easily be abused or used for illicit purposes. Stajano (2002) described the so-called cocaine auction protocol, which leaves no traces of illegal activity. The point is that full anonymity combined with good cryptography considerably limits the ability to monitor, prevent, and detect illegal activities.

In the cocaine auction protocol, the auctioneer sells a shipment of cocaine to several dealers. Because the stakes are high and the participants are shady, nobody trusts anybody, and everybody wants maximum anonymity and security. Stajano showed that with appropriately chosen cryptographic techniques, the auction can be organized to ensure the anonymity of bidders and the privacy of their bidding amounts. In the example given, even the auctioneer is not able to find the identity of the winner before committing to sale.

Although the cocaine auction protocol only points out the theoretical possibility of abuse, a report by Greg Sandoval (1999) on CNET News.com showed an actual incident in which marijuana had been put up for sale on eBay, with bids reaching \$10 million. Fortunately, the auction was discovered and shut down.

# NONREPUDIATION
## Concept and Definition

The term *nonrepudiation* was first coined in the 1988 ISO (International Standards Organization) Open Systems Interconnection Security Architecture standard (ISO 7498-2). Nonrepudiation is typically understood as a security service that counters repudiation. In the context of computer and network security, repudiation refers to a denial of one of the parties involved in a communication in having participated in all or part of the communication (ISO 7498-2). For example, a party could deny the sending, the receipt, or the content of a message, the delivery time, and so on. This definition is formulated with communication in mind and does not encompass all aspects of e-commerce repudiation. In e-commerce, there are many more possibilities for repudiation: repudiation of an offer, payment, delivery, expected quality, and so on. It seems more appropriate to define repudiation in e-commerce as *a denial of an action in a transaction taken by a party in the transaction*. The action is by no means limited to communication.

Under common law, repudiation usually has two interpretations. It can refer to the legitimate right of a party to refuse the validity of a transaction (if the other party breached the transaction, for example). In another interpretation, repudiation refers to the wrongful refusal by a party to follow a transaction. Throughout this chapter, I use repudiation as a wrongful refusal.

One problem with e-commerce transactions is that they are relatively easy to repudiate. The problem stems from the ease with which an electronic transaction can be formed and conducted. All customers have to do to repudiate a transaction, for instance, is call their credit card company and say that they never hit the submit button, that something went wrong during the checkout process, or that somebody else misused their personal information to commit fraud. Every year, companies are suffering million-dollar losses from credit card chargebacks. A chargeback is a reversal of a transaction initiated by a customer who may feel cheated by the merchant (e.g., for nondelivery, inferior quality). Chargebacks open large opportunities for fraud by dishonest customers who can victimize merchants by wrongful repudiation. The burden of proving the transaction usually is carried by the merchant, who has to perform additional bookkeeping and logging at extra cost.

Nonrepudiation must not be confused with preventing a party from repudiating a transaction. After all, a party always has the right to dispute a transaction or part of it. Instead of deterring repudiation, nonrepudiation aims at collecting evidence that can help in a subsequent dispute resolution. In other words, the objective of nonrepudiation is to guard against false or wrongful denial of a transaction by providing strong and substantial evidence to a dispute-resolution authority.

## Types of Nonrepudiation

In general, one can differentiate between repudiation of an electronic contract or part of it and a repudiation of the contract execution. Any contract, electronic or not, requires three basic elements: (a) offer, (b) acceptance, and (c) consideration—a promised exchange of value (Garfinkel & Spafford, 2002). Therefore, we may have repudiation of an offer, repudiation of an acceptance, or repudiation of consideration. In the context of electronic contracts, the three contract elements are usually represented as electronic messages. Treating electronic contracts as messages allows us to reduce the concept of contract repudiation to simple message repudiation. Correspondingly, message repudiation has two basic types: repudiation of origin and repudiation of delivery.

*Repudiation of origin* occurs when the recipient claims to have received the message, but the sender denies sending it. Another variant is when the recipient claims to have received a message different from what the sender claims to have sent. Another possibility is to have a disagreement between sender and receiver over the date or time the message was sent.

Repudiation of origin may be caused by different events: The sender (or the recipient) may be misinformed or may lie; communication errors may occur; or a third party may maliciously or unintentionally interfere with the communication.

*Repudiation of delivery* occurs when the sender claims to have sent the message, but the recipient denies receiving it; the sender claims to have sent a message different from what the recipient claims to have received; or the sender and the recipient claim different date or time of receiving the message.

The repudiation of delivery could be triggered by the same events as the repudiation of origin: misinformation, lying, communication error, or a third-party intervention.

## Mechanisms for Nonrepudiation

One convenient mechanism for nonrepudiation of origin is for the sender to digitally sign the message. Care has to be taken to ensure that the receiver possesses the correct cryptographic key and that the sender's key has not been revoked or compromised. The digital signature of the sender constitutes a nonrepudiation record, proving both the message integrity and the identity of the sender.

One disadvantage of this mechanism is its reliance on PKI, which includes a complex infrastructure of certification authorities and mechanisms for key generation, storing, and revocation. Reliance on PKI makes this mechanism impractical for small transactions in which the cost of PKI outweighs the cost of the transaction.

To minimize the number of certified public keys that need to be managed, Ford and Baum (2001) proposed a trusted third party (TTP) to vouch for the source of the message. In this case, the message is signed by a TTP, after authenticating the source and the content of the message. The authentication can be based on local security services, such as Kerberos, VPN (virtual private network), and so on.

To support nonrepudiation of delivery, the recipient may digitally sign an acknowledgment containing a copy or a digest of the original message. There are several standards, such as S/MIME (secure multipurpose Internet mail extension), PGP/MIME, and OpenPGP that provide a digitally signed receipt mechanism. Alternatively, the recipient can use a TTP to sign the acknowledgment. The involvement of TTPs in nonrepudiation not only decreases the burden of PKI but also provides stronger evidence in case of dispute. Clearly, in a dispute between a sender and a recipient, the evidence collected by a TTP will be given greater weight than the evidence collected locally by each party.

Time stamping is another mechanism supporting nonrepudiation of origin and delivery. Time stamps can be created by parties to a transaction, TTPs, or to communication services.

Nonrepudiation requires record collection and retention. This may include Web server logs, transaction information, acknowledgment messages, and so on. Depending on the legal context, records often need to be retained for a long period, even for years. Another important point is that nonrepudiation records are often an attractive target for attacks. Therefore, dedicated servers and special security measures are needed to protect nonrepudiation data.

The repudiation problem is alleviated a bit by the E-SIGN (Electronic signatures in Global and National Commerce Act, enacted by the Congress in 2000). E-SIGN stipulates that many electronic contracts do not require writing to be considered valid. There are a few exceptions to this rule, related to transactions with higher degrees of risk. According to E-SIGN, signatures are needed if a transaction involves transfer of land, sales of goods priced over $500, fulfillment periods longer than 1 year, or the assignment of intellectual property.

Another important feature of E-SIGN is the broad meaning and interpretation of the notion of signature. For example, according to E-SIGN, hitting the "I agree" button counts as a valid electronic signature (not necessary digital). Therefore, from a nonrepudiation standpoint, a Web server log may suffice in providing evidence.

# TRUST AND REPUTATION

The main challenge faced by many e-commerce users is trust: whom to trust, when to trust, and to what extent to trust. The problem is that the Internet is open to a variety of interactions with complete strangers, having no records of previous transactions. After a customer has paid for a product, the seller may never deliver, may deliver with considerable delay, or may deliver an inferior-quality product. The number of consumer complaints about fly-by-night Internet scams is continuously growing, thereby destroying the consumers' trust in online business.

There is a significant difference between trust in physical markets and trust in e-commerce. Building and maintaining trust in electronic markets is more difficult without face-to-face interaction (Rocco, 1998), partner identity, and a clearly defined legal framework. In online markets, it may not be possible to track down or even to identify a party in a transaction. A software agent, for example, may act on behalf of different human users at different moments in time, thereby making it difficult to relate its behavior to one physical entity.

In general, trust can be defined as a willingness of a party, called trustor, to depend on another party, called trustee, for an action that is important for the trustor. The need for trust arises in cases where the trustor does not have full control over the trustee (or such control is prohibitively expensive). The trustor may then choose to depend on the trustee in the hope that the trustee will behave favorably.

Contrary to general understanding, complete trust is not necessary for successful e-commerce. Braynov and Sandhom (2002) proved that market efficiency does not require complete trustworthiness. Untrustworthy agents could transact as efficiently as trustworthy agents, provided that they have sufficient information about each other's trustworthiness. In other words, if economic agents have accurate estimates of each other's trustworthiness, then the amount of trade, the social welfare, and the individual utilities are maximized. Therefore, what really matters is not the actual level of trustworthiness but the accuracy of information. A market in which agents are trusted to the degree they deserve to be trusted is as efficient as a market with complete trustworthiness.

The problem with trust information, however, is not an easy one. Collecting, aggregating, and analyzing information about an individual's past behavior is costly and requires an infrastructure. Likely, the burden of such costs is not commensurate with the benefits of individual market transactions, and a third party is needed to collect trust information.

The current market solution to this problem is provided by reputation systems (Resnick, Zeckhauser, Friedman, & Kuwabara, 2000). A reputation system is an information repository run by a third party. The repository collects information about a business entity and produces a reputation rating for the entity. What makes reputation systems particularly useful is the ability of an individual to check the reputation of a business before starting a transaction with that business.

Reputation systems are provided by either large market-making companies, such as eBay and Amazon, or by independent companies, such as BizRate. For example, eBay runs a point-based reputation system in which a market participant accumulates points from the comments of people who interacted with him. The points are 1 for a positive feedback, 0 for a neutral comment, and –1 for a negative comment. The reputation rating is calculated as the sum of all points during the past 6 months.

Reputation systems often have the following vulnerabilities:

- **Fake transactions.** Two friends may decide to make fake transactions, rating each other with high scores so as to inflate their reputation ratings.
- **Fake identities.** Even if we allow two individuals to rate each other only once, they can easily evade detection by registering with multiple identities. Moreover, a person who has accumulated a very low reputation rating can switch to another username and start with the clear reputation of a beginner.
- **Manipulation.** The formula for calculating reputation ratings can easily be abused. Zacharia (1999) pointed to the following example. Suppose that a user carries out 100 transactions and cheats in 20 of them. His reputation rank is $80 - 20 = 60$. In other words, a user may cheat on eBay 20% of the time and still maintain a monotonically increasing reputation value with a rate of 60%. To fix the problem, Zacharia (1999) proposed a nonlinear formula for calculating reputations, which takes into account not only the nature of a comment (positive, negative, neutral) but also the reputation of the person submitting the comment.

Other problems with reputation systems are as follows:

- **Lack of portability.** A reputation rank from eBay cannot be used in Amazon and vice versa.
- **Difficulty of obtaining negative feedback.** People are more willing to provide positive feedback than negative feedback (Resnick et al., 2000).
- **Small coverage.** Current reputation systems cover only a small part of all users.
- **Correlated information** (Schillo, Funk, & Rovastos, 1999). Several comments can refer to the same piece of evidence, thereby inflating a reputation rating.

To overcome some problems with reputation systems, Braynov et al. (2002) proposed a market protocol in which parties truthfully report their degree of trustworthiness, that is, information regarding their abilities, intentions, quality of delivered products, and so on. The protocol is self-enforcing, which means that it is in the best interest of each party to report truthfully. The main advantage of the protocol is that it does not require a trusted third party or an information collection.

Another solution to the problem of trust and reputation is a separating auction (Braynov & Sandholm, 2003), which separates trustworthy from untrustworthy bidders. In a separating auction, the auctioneer offers bidders to choose from two auctions with different rules. The auction rules are specially chosen, so that all trustworthy bidders choose the same auction, and all untrustworthy bidders choose the other. Moreover, the separating auction is incentive compatible. That is, even if untrustworthy bidders know that they are participating in a separating auction, they will not change their choice. A separating auction helps the auctioneer identify the trustworthiness of each bidder and run the auction efficiently.

## CONCLUSION

Security of e-commerce applications is an important factor for the success of e-commerce. When performing a transaction, users need to be confident that the Web site is a legitimate business and will deliver as promised, that their credit card numbers are securely stored, and that their privacy is guaranteed.

Although e-commerce security is inseparable from computer and network security, it differs in many respects. First, e-commerce security requirements are different from those for businesses without direct exposure to the Internet. Second, e-commerce has its own interaction protocols (online auctions, for example) that require special security measures. Third, the stakes are high when it comes to individual or corporate assets, such as personal identity, private information, credit card numbers, or being directly exposed to the Internet.

In this chapter, I briefly discussed specific e-commerce vulnerabilities and measures that can be deployed to prevent online fraud. Because of the large variety of e-commerce fraud, this survey is by no means exhaustive. Security reports constantly inform about new vulnerabilities or new sophisticated attack tools and scams. It is our belief, however, that despite security incidents, e-commerce remains a relatively safe and promising area.

## GLOSSARY

**Dual Signature**  A digital signature method used in SET to sign two related messages.

**E-shoplifting**  Shoplifting in which an attacker uses computer or network vulnerabilities to commit commercial fraud.

**Identity Theft**  An offense when someone knowingly transfers or uses, without lawful authority, a means of identification of another person with the intent to commit, or to aid or abet, any unlawful activity.

**Internet Relay Chat (IRC)**  A program that supports online conversations among users who can talk in groups or in private over channels that are devoted to specific topics.

**Public Key Infrastructure (PKI)**  The set of services that support the wide-scale use and management of cryptographic keys, signatures, and encryption.

**Repudiation**  A denial of an action in a transaction taken by a party in the transaction.

**Reputation System**  A database containing users' reputation rankings.

**Secure Electronic Transaction (SET)**  A protocol for secure credit card payments over the Internet.

**Secure Socket Layer and Transport Layer Security (TLS)**  Protocols used to encrypt and authenticate sessions across a network.

**Shopping Cart**  An application that maintains a session with customers and allows them to select and save items that interest them.

**Spoofing**  A variety of techniques used to assume a false identity.

## CROSS REFERENCES

See *Digital Identity; Digital Signatures and Electronic Signatures; Electronic Commerce; Electronic Payment Systems; Encryption Basics; Secure Sockets Layer (SSL).*

## REFERENCES

Braynov, S., & Sandholm, T. (2002a). Contracting with uncertain level of trust. *Computational Intelligence, 18,* 501–514.

Braynov, S., & Sandholm, T. (2002b). Trust revelation in multiagent interaction. *Proceedings of CHI'02 Workshop on The Philosophy and Design of Socially Adept Technologies* (pp. 57–60).

Braynov, S., & Sandholm T. (2003). Auctions with untrustworthy bidders. Presented at the *IEEE Conference on E-Commerce.*

Cole, E. (2002). *Hackers beware.* Berkeley, CA: New Riders.

Costa, D. (2002, October 15). Identity crisis. *PC Magazine.*

Desmedt, Y. (1997). Some recent research aspects of threshold cryptography. In M. Mambo, E. Okamoto, E. Davida (Eds.). *Information Security, First International Workshop* (pp. 158–173).

Dolev, D., Dwork, C., & Naor, M. (1991). Non-malleable cryptography. *Proceedings of the 23rd ACM Symposium on Theory of Computing* (pp. 542–552).

Ford, W., & Baum, M. (2001). *Secure electronic commerce.* Prentice Hall.

Franklin, M., & Reiter, M. (1995a). The design and implementation of a secure auction service. *Proceedings of the IEEE Symposium on Security and Privacy* (pp. 2–14).

Franklin, M., & Reiter, M. (1995b). Verifiable signature sharing. In L. Guillou & J. Quisquarter (Eds.). *Lecture Notes in Computer Science* (Vol. 921, pp. 5–63). New York: Springer-Verlag.

Garfinkel, S., & Spafford, E. (2002). *Web security, privacy and commerce.* Cambridge, MA: O'Reilly and Associates.

Lee, J. (2003, May 1). U.S. and states join to fight internet-auction fraud. *New York Times*.

McClure, S., Shah, S., & Shah, S. (2003). *Web hacking.* Addison-Wesley.

Monderer, D., & Tennenholtz, M. (1999). Distributed games: From mechanisms to protocols. *Proceedings of the American National Conference on Artificial Intelligence* (pp. 32–37).

O'Mahony, D., Peirce, M., & Tewari, H. (2001). *Electronic payment systems for e-commerce*. Boston: Artech House.

Rescorla, E. (2001). *SSL and TLS: Designing and building secure systems*. Boston: Addison-Wesley.

Resnick, P., Zeckhauser, R., Friedman, E., & Kuwabara, K. (2000). Reputation systems. *Communications of the ACM, 43*, 45.

Rocco, E. (1998). Trust breaks down in electronic contexts but can be repaired by some initial face-to-face contact. *Proceedings of ACM CHI 98 Conference on Human Factors in Computing Systems* (pp. 496–502).

Sakurai, Y., Yokoo, M., & Matsubara, S. (1999). A limitation of the generalized Vickrey auction in electronic commerce: Robustness against false-name bids. *Proceedings of the American National Conference on Artificial Intelligence* (pp. 86–92).

Sandoval, G. (1999). eBay auction goes up in smoke. Retrieved September 23, 1999, from CNET News.com: http://news.cnet.com/news/0-1007-202-123002.html

Schillo, M., Funk, P., & Rovastos M. (1999). Who can you trust: Dealing with deception. In *Proceedings of the Second Workshop on Deception, Fraud, and Trust in Agent Societies* (pp. 95–106).

Shamir, A. (1997). How to share a secret. *Communications of the ACM, 22*, 612–613.

Stajano, F. (2002). *Security for ubiquitous computing*. New York: John Wiley & Sons.

Vickrey, W. (1961). Counterspeculations, auctions, and competitive sealed tenders. *Journal of Finance, 16*, 15–27.

Zacharia, G. (1999) Trust management through reputation mechanisms. In *Proceedings of the Second Workshop on Deception, Fraud, and Trust in Agent Societies* (pp. 163–167).

## FURTHER READING

Yokoo, M., Sakurai, Y., & Matsubara, S. (2001). Bundle design in robust combinatorial auction protocol against false-name bids. *Proceedings of the International Joint Conferences on Artificial Intelligence*, 1095–1101.

# Hacking Techniques in Wired Networks

Qijun Gu, Peng Liu, and Chao-Hsien Chu, *Pennsylvania State University*

## INTRODUCTION

Nowadays, wired networks, especially the Internet, have already become a platform to support not only high-speed data communication, but also powerful distributed computing for a variety of personal and business processes every day. However, the principles for designing and developing a network mainly targeted at providing connection and communication capabilities, until a series of security "disasters" happened on the Internet recently as shown in Figure 1. As a result, without making security an inherent part of the network design and development process, existing networks are very vulnerable to cyberattacks because of various security vulnerabilities. Such vulnerabilities, when being exploited by the hacker, can motivate the development of a variety of hacking techniques. These hacking techniques directly lead to cyber attacks; and these cyberattacks have become a more and more serious threat to our society.

To better protect networks, this chapter attempts to give an overview on a variety of hacking techniques. No wonder, as the better we understand the hacker, the better networks can be protected. This chapter will focus on the objectives, principles, functionalities, and characteristics of different types of hacking techniques in wired networks, but will not address detailed and in-depth hacking processes, which can be found in several other chapters in this *Handbook*. In addition, we only discuss well-known and published vulnerabilities and attacks. Most of these attacks have been prevented by the improved protocols and systems. Although it is not possible to identify all vulnerabilities and attacks, this chapter will provide in-depth discussions on the common characteristics of cyberattacks, the structure and components of cyberattacks, and the relationships among cyberattacks. These discussions can help security professionals grasp the soul of a new cyberattack in an easier and quicker way.

This chapter is organized as follows. First, the principles of hacking are summarized. We overview the common hacking procedures, review mostly used hacking toolkits, and illustrate how these tools are employed in hacking. Second, we discuss how hacking techniques can be used to conduct attacks on the Internet infrastructure. Third, we discuss how hacking techniques can be used to construct attacks on end systems of the Internet. Fourth, we discuss how hacking techniques can be used to conduct attacks on enterprise network systems. Finally, we conclude this chapter.

## PRINCIPLES OF HACKING

In this chapter, attacks and hacking techniques are two different concepts that are, nevertheless, closely related to each other. An *attack* typically goes through several steps or phases. In each phase, some attack *actions* will be carried out by the hacker, and these attack actions will typically involve the use of one or more hacking techniques. The hacking techniques involved in different attack phases could be different. Moreover, an attack or hacking (software) tool may cover several phases of an attack and involve multiple hacking techniques.

### Seven Steps of Hacking

No matter how to hack or attack a network, the attacker always takes certain procedures to accomplish his or her objectives. In general, these procedures fall in one of the following seven steps (Boulanger, 1998): reconnaissance, probe, toehold, advancement, stealth, listening post, and takeover, where each step is enabled or helped by its previous steps and prepares for its following steps. These seven steps can serve as a procedural classification of hacking techniques because the hacking techniques used in each step are for the same purpose and share many common characteristics.

#### Reconnaissance

Reconnaissance is to gather information of the target system or network. The information of interest may include

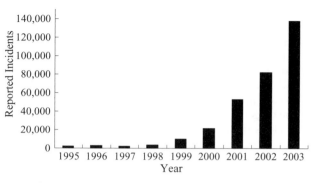 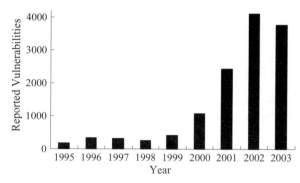

**Figure 1:** Reported incidents and vulnerabilities from 1995 to 2003 (CERT/CC Statistics 1988–2003, 2004).

host names, host addresses, host owners, host machine types, host operating systems, network owners, network configurations, hosts in the networks, list of users, and so on. An intruder may start with searching the Internet for references to the target to find the domain information of the target. Then the intruder can obtain further information about other machines within that domain such as their host names and network addresses. For example, the intruder can analyze the target Web pages to gather useful information about the users of the target system, because most Web pages contain user information, such as contact e-mails or some personal information (name, address, phone number, etc.). If the intruder obtains a user account in the target system, he or she can begin to guess the password. Sometimes, the intruder can even directly contact a person through phone or e-mail to acquire the person's account information.

### Probe

Probe is to detect the weaknesses of the target system in order to deploy the hacking tools. After gathering enough information of the target, the intruder begins to probe the perimeter of the system for potential weaknesses. He or she can utilize remote exploit tools, which enable the intruder to conduct security surveys and automatically collect and report security-related vulnerabilities of remote hosts and networks. Using these hacking tools, the intruder can find out the remote services the target is providing, such as World Wide Web (WWW), file transfer protocol (FTP), simple mail transfer protocol (SMTP), finger, or X server, by scanning the hosts of the target network. In addition, the intruder can obtain such information as machine names, software names, and version numbers. Then, he or she can refer to the known vulnerabilities of the detected services for further exploitation.

### Toehold

Toehold is to exploit security weaknesses and gain entry into the system. Once a vulnerability is found, the intruder will first exploit this vulnerability to build a connection (or session) between his or her machine and the target host and then remotely execute hostile commands on the target. (For example, the intruder can generate an X terminal emulation on his or her own display.) In this way, a toehold into the target network has been established and the intruder can go further to compromise the system. Gaining entry into the system, the intruder can also search for

more critical system information. If the current user id (UID) is for a privileged user, the intruder will jump to the stealth step; otherwise, the intruder will get into the advancement phase.

### Advancement

Advancement is to advance from an unprivileged account to a privileged one. In this step, the intruder uses local exploit tools to obtain additional information of the target, such as configuration errors and known vulnerabilities of the operating system. Once a local vulnerability has been found, the intruder can advance from an unprivileged UID to a root UID. Then, with the highest level of privileges, the intruder can fully control the target system, steal sensitive data, maliciously modify files, and even delete the entire file system.

### Stealth

Stealth is to hide the penetration tracks. During the probing phase, the intrusion actions are likely to be logged by intrusion detection systems, and during the phases of toehold and advancement, the intruder may leave his or her activities in the system log. Hence, to hide, the intruder will access the local log files and modify the corresponding log entries to remove the traces and avoid detection. The intruder may further replace the system binary code with a malicious version to ensure future unlogged and undetected access to the compromised system.

### Listening Post

An intruder installs backdoors to establish a listening post. In this step, the intruder inserts some malicious programs into the system, such as a stealth tool, a backdoor tool, and a sniffer. These programs ensure that the intruder's future activities will not be logged. They report false information on files, processes, and status of the network interface to the administrators. They also allow the intruder to access the compromised system through the backdoor. With the sniffer tool, the intruder can capture the traffic on the network interfaces. By logging the network traffic of interests, the intruder can better monitor and control the compromised system.

### Takeover

Takeover is to expand control (or infection) from a single host to other hosts on a network. From the listening post, the intruder can sniff a lot of important information about other hosts on the network, such as user names and passwords. The intruder can also obtain information in several other ways. For example, he or she can check some specific configuration files (e.g., /.rhosts) of the compromised host and find mutually trusted hosts. With this information, the intruder can retake the previous steps to break into other hosts. In this way, the intruder can expand his or her control to the whole network.

## Overview of Hacking Toolkits

In a broad sense, hacking toolkits not only include the software developed for attacks, but also the human activities for the collection of sensitive information and the penetration into the target systems. In the following, we discuss 14 types of representative hacking software and approaches.

### Scanners

A scanner is a tool to obtain information about a host or a network. It is developed to probe networks and report security-related information. A scanner is used by both security administrators for securing networks and systems and hackers for breaking into. Scanners can be broken down into two categories: network auditing tools and host-based auditing tools. Network auditing tools are used to scan remote hosts ("Nessus," 2004; "Network Mapper [NMAP]," 2004; "Security Administrator Tool," 1995). For example, NMAP is a free open-source utility for network exploration and security auditing. It can rapidly scan large networks and single hosts. NMAP uses raw Internet protocol (IP) packets to determine which hosts are available on the network, the services those hosts are offering, the operating systems they are running, the types of packet filters/firewalls in use, and so forth. Host-based auditing tools, working in a local system, are used to scan a local host and report its security vulnerabilities ("Computer Oracle," 1993; "Tiger," 1994). For example, the Computer Oracle and Password System (COPS) package ("Computer Oracle") can help identify file permission problems, easy-to-guess passwords, known vulnerable services, and improperly configured services.

### Sniffers and Snoopers

A sniffer monitors and logs network data [16]. The network traffic that passes through a host's network interface usually contains user name-password pairs as well as other system information that would be useful to an intruder. In a network where data is transmitted without encryption, an intruder with physical access to the network can plug in a sniffer to monitor the network traffic and obtain necessary information to access other hosts in the network. A snooper, also known as spyware, monitors a user's activities by snooping on a terminal emulator session, monitoring process memory, and logging a user's keystrokes [26]. By watching the user's actions, an intruder can obtain useful information to attack other users on the computer or even other systems in the network.

### Spoofing Tools

In a network, a data packet always contains the source address field, which can expose the source of the intruder if he or she sends malicious packets. Hence, to hide and avoid detections, the intruder uses spoofing tools to forge another source address that is usually the address of another host or a nonexistent address. The spoofed address can be an IP address or a physical address, depending on the type of the network. Another usage of spoofing tools is to gain access to a network from outside. If the firewall of the target network is not configured to filter out incoming packets with source addresses belonging to the local domain, it is possible for an intruder to inject packets with spoofed inner addresses through the firewall.

### Trojan Horse

The concept of Trojan horse comes from the legend in which the Greeks sneaked into the Trojan city by hiding in a huge, hollow wooden horse and defeated the Trojans. A Trojan horse in a computer system is thus defined as a malicious, security-breaking program that is a piece of executable code hiding in a normal program. When the normal program is opened or executed, the hidden code will perform some malicious actions silently, such as deleting critical system files. The Trojan horse is spread in a disguised way. It presents itself as a game, a Web page, or a script that attracts people. It may come from an e-mail with your friend as the sender or an online advertisement. But if the receiver opens it, the malicious code will commit the unsolicited actions.

### Password Crackers

A password cracker is used to find a user's password ("John the Ripper," 2004; "Password Cracker," 2004). It is used by both computer crackers and system administrators for recovering unknown or lost passwords. There are three major types of crack approaches. The first type is the smart guessing cracker, which infers or guesses the password based on user's information, such as user name, birthday, and phone number. The second is the dictionary-based cracker, which generates a large set of possible passwords, called a *dictionary*, from a collection of words and phrases. These two types of crackers are smart and quick, but may not work if the password is randomly generated. The third type is to enumerate and test all possible passwords in a brute-force way. When the password is extremely long, the last type of password cracker will usually take a tremendous amount of time.

### Denial of Service Tools

A denial of service (DoS) tool is used by an attacker to prevent legitimate users from using their subscribed services. DoS attacks aim at a variety of services and accomplish the objective through a variety of methods ("Denial of Service Attacks," 2001). Attackers can flood the target network, thereby throttling legitimate network traffic; can disrupt connections between two machines, thereby denying access to the service; can prevent a particular individual from accessing the service; and can disrupt the service to a specific system or person. Different from an inappropriate use of resources, DoS tools explicitly and intentionally generate attack packets or disrupt connections. For example, they can consume scarce or nonrenewable resources with a large number of Internet control message protocol (ICMP) echo packets, suppress network connectivity with

SYN flooding, alter network configuration by changing routing information, or even physically destroy network components.

## Stealth and Backdoor Tools

Backdoors are programs furtively installed in the target system. They are malicious replacements of critical system programs that provide authentication and system reporting services. Backdoor programs provide continued and unlogged use of the system when being activated, hide suspicious processes and files from the users and system administrators, and report false system status to the users and system administrators. They may present themselves as an existing service, such as FTP, but implant a function to accept controls and execute commands from the intruder. They can also be a new service that may be neglected because they hide their processes and do not generate noticeable network traffic.

## Malicious Applets and Scripts

A malicious applet or script is a tiny piece of code that is written in Web-compatible computer languages, such as Java, Jscript, and Vbscript. The code is embedded in a Web page, an e-mail, or a Web-based application. When a person accesses the Web page or opens the e-mail, the code is downloaded to his or her personal computer and executed. The code may misuse the computer's resources, modify files on the hard disk, send fake e-mails, or steal passwords.

## Logic Bombs

A logic bomb is a piece of code surreptitiously inserted into an application to perform some destructive or security-compromising activities when a set of specific conditions are met. A logic bomb lies dormant until being triggered by some event. The trigger can be a specific date, the number of execution times (of the code), a random number, or even a specific event such as deletion of a specific file. When the logic bomb is triggered, it will usually do something unsolicited, such as deleting or changing files. Logic bombs may be the most insidious attack because they may do a lot of damage before being detected.

## Buffer Overflow

A buffer overflow tool launches attacks by inserting an oversized block of data into a program's input buffer or stack to enable an intruder to execute a piece of malicious code or destroy the memory structure (Cowan, Wagle, Pu, Beattie, & Walpole, 2000). When a program receives a block of input data, it puts the data into its input buffer. Without the boundary checking, the intruder can write data past the end of the buffer and overwrite some unknown space in the memory. At the same time, the intruder carries the malicious code in the oversized data block. If the unknown space is a part of the system stack that records the return addresses, the overwritten part may change the normal return address to the address pointing to the malicious code. Hence, when the return address is fetched for execution, the malicious code, instead of the original code, will be executed.

## Bugs in Software

A piece of software is vulnerable once it is released. First, it typically contains unknown bugs. The more complex it is, more bugs it may have. If an intruder finds a bug before it is fixed or patched, he or she can exploit it to hack a system. For example, the unchecked buffer size is a bug for possible buffer overflow attacks. Second, for the purpose of developing software, the developers usually write some codes for debugging. These debugging codes generally give the developers a lot of authorities. If these codes are not removed from the released version, the intruder can utilize them for attack.

## Holes in Trust Management

Trust management is crucial for a large-scale security system. Due to the complexity of trust management, mistakes in managing and configuring trust relationships may occur in many cases and leave holes for an intruder to gain authorized access as an unauthorized user. For example, logic inconsistence could be such a hole. If we assume that there are three parties, an intruder, a database, and a school, the database trusts the school, but does not trust the intruder. However, if the school trusts the intruder (who may be an adolescent student), the intruder can access the database through the school.

## Social Engineering

Social engineering is a tactic to acquire access information through talking and persuasion. The target person is a user who can access the computer system desired by the intruder. The intruder may pretend to be a salesperson, a consultant, a listener, a friend of the user, or any role that the user does not suspect when they are chatting and exchanging information. The intruder thus can obtain valuable information, such as passwords, to gain access to the system.

## Dumpster Diving

Trash is not trash in the eyes of a serious hacker. Trash usually contains shattered and incomplete information. The intruder can sift through the garbage of a company to find and recover original information so that he or she can break into the company's computers and networks. Sometimes, the information is used as an auxiliary to help intrusion, such as making social engineering more credible.

# Classifications of Hacking Toolkits

Each of the hacking toolkits can help hackers achieve certain objectives. They may be applied in different hacking phases, provide different information, and be used in different attack scenarios. Accordingly, we classify them and illustrate how they may be used.

## Procedural Classification

As shown in Table 1, a hacking toolkit can be used in one or several penetration steps, and different penetration steps usually need a different set of hacking toolkits. In the reconnaissance step, an intruder wants to gather information about the target system or network and needs scanners to collect information of computers, user accounts,

**Table 1** Procedural Classification

| Procedures | Toolkits |
|---|---|
| Reconnaissance | Scanners, social engineering, dumpster diving |
| Probe | Scanners, sniffers |
| Toehold | Spoofing tools, malicious applets and scripts, buffer overflow tools, password crackers, software bugs, Trojan horses, holes in trust management |
| Advancement | Password crackers, software bugs |
| Stealth | Stealth and backdoor tools |
| Listening post | Stealth and backdoor tools, sniffers and snoopers, Trojan horses |
| Takeover | Scanners, sniffers, spoofing tools, malicious applets, buffer overflow tools, password crackers, and so on |

**Table 2** Functional Classification

| Functions | Toolkits |
|---|---|
| Information gathering | Scanners, sniffers, backdoors, social engineering, dumpster diving |
| Remote exploit | Spoofing tools, malicious applets, buffer overflow tools, Trojan horses, holes in trust management |
| Local exploit | Password crackers, software bugs |
| DoS | Denial of service tools |

and services of the target. The intruder may also apply social engineering and dumpster diving to facilitate the information collection. Then, in the second step, the intruder probes the system for weakness and uses scanners and sniffers to capture the activities of the target system and network and to analyze possible security holes and vulnerabilities.

Knowing the weakness, the intruder tries to gain entry into the system. In this step, the useful toolkits include spoofing tools, malicious applets, buffer overflow tools, password crackers, and so on. These tools enable the intruder to break into the system remotely or to obtain authorized local access. Once inside the system, he or she tries to advance from an unprivileged account to a privileged account. In this step, the intruder can first find some system files containing the information of privileged accounts and then use password crackers to get the name–password pairs. The intruder can also exploit the system bugs to advance his or her privileges.

At this point, the system is under control. The intruder hurries to hide any traces before the administrators find him or her. So the intruder will use stealth and backdoor tools to remove any traces while continuing access to the system. To keep monitoring the hacked system, the intruder establishes a listening post and uses sniffers and backdoor tools to watch system activities and report crucial information, so that he or she can fully control the compromised system and prepare for further attacks.

Finally, the intruder expands his or her control from a single host to other hosts in the network. The previously described tools will be used again. Scanners, sniffers, spoofing tools, malicious applets, buffer overflow tools, and password crackers are all necessary tools for the intruder to break into other hosts.

### Functional Classification

According to the functions of the hacking toolkits, they can be broken into four categories, information gathering tools, remote exploit tools, local exploit tools, and DoS tools as shown in Table 2.

Information gathering tools are used to obtain the target's system information before and after an attack. These tools include scanners, sniffers, and backdoors. Before an attack, scanners and sniffers are mostly used to detect the target's vulnerabilities, whereas after an attack the intruder will monitor the compromised system's activities and keep the control of the victim by installing sniffers and backdoors.

To break into a system and obtain the desired privileges, the intruder needs either remote or local exploit tools. If the intruder does not have any account in the target system, he or she will use remote exploits tools that enable penetration into a remote host. Spoofing tools, malicious applets, and buffer overflow tools are mostly employed. These tools allow the intruder to compromise the target without much prior knowledge about the target.

If the intruder has already had a local account, he or she can use local exploit tools to gain higher privileges in the computer. The intruder can use password crackers to guess the password of the root account. If the intruder succeeds, he or she can gain the root privilege. Another method is to exploit system bugs or unremoved debugging codes. These system holes enable the intruder to execute programs with only an unprivileged account.

The fourth category is denial-of-service tools. DoS tools will typically apply some information gathering (or reconnaissance) techniques first. But instead of trying to break into the target system, as both remote exploit tools and local exploit tools want to do, DoS tools try to disrupt the services provided by the target system.

## ATTACKS AGAINST THE INTERNET INFRASTRUCTURE

It is difficult to give a precise meaning of the Internet infrastructure. In general, the infrastructure includes all hardware and protocols that support the communication between two hosts inter networks, such as routers, gateways, fibers, and cables (as hardware) and transmission control protocol (TCP), ICMP, and border gateway protocol (BGP). In this section, we use several representative attacks to demonstrate the principles of infrastructure-oriented attacks, which may directly impact our daily usage of the Internet. Readers can identify other similar attacks against the Internet infrastructure.

Figure 2 shows the daily activity on the Internet, for example, browsing a Web page. In this browsing procedure,

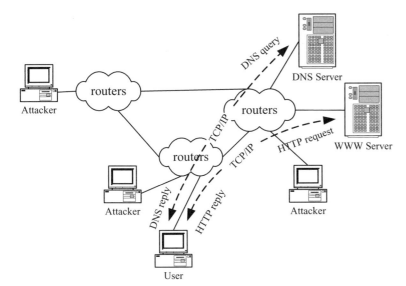

**Figure 2:** Surfing the Internet.

a user first puts the text-based uniform resource locator (URL) of the Web page into the browser. That computer then sends a domain name system (DNS) query to the corresponding DNS server to resolve the IP address of the Web server and starts a hypertext transfer protocol (HTTP) session with the Web server to retrieve the Web page. The HTTP session is based on the TCP/IP communication, which ensures the feasibility and reliability of the browsing. The Web page is retrieved in a series of data packets, which are routed through a sequence of routers according to their embedded IP headers. In this process, three basic components of the Internet are involved, that is, DNS, TCP/IP, and routing. Accordingly, in the following sections, we discuss attacks against these components launched by attackers in different domains and networks.

## Attacks against DNS

The DNS is a distributed database to provide mapping between host names and IP addresses. A domain name is divided into a series of zones separated by periods, and all names form a name tree. For example, www.mysite.com is a domain name in which "com" is one of the root zones of the name tree, "mysite" is a branch of "com", and "www" is a branch of "mysite." A DNS server resides at a certain level of the name tree and contains name–address mapping information of some zones and the corresponding subzones.

Forward DNS mapping means that a host queries the DNS server for the address of a domain name. Inverse DNS mapping means address-to-name mapping, that is, a host queries for the domain name of an address. The response to a DNS query may contain the address or the name that is desired, a pointer to the proper DNS server if the information is not contained within the current zone, or an error indication if the record requested does not exist. The mapping can be multi-names to multi-addresses and vise versa. In general, hosts that use the DNS maintain a local cache to record returned DNS entries. All these records contain a time-to-live field set by the creator. At the end of that period, the cached record must be discarded.

Bellovin (1995) identified a famous DNS attack. The essence of the DNS attack lies in the attacker controlling a DNS server for the target zone and being able to make any malicious forward and inverse mapping. Consequently, the attacker can make the target host believe that a remote host is trusted. In the early Berkeley version of UNIX, an attacker could exploit this attack to gain access to the target host from an untrusted host. To illustrate this, assume that the target host is "target.com" with IP address 190.190.190.190, the attacker's host is "attack.com" with IP address 180.180.180.180, and the target host trusts "trust.com." Before an attack, the attacker changes the inverse mapping so that the attacker's IP address is associated with "trust.com." When the attacker attempts to "rlogin" to "target.com" from the attacker's machine, the target machine will try to validate the name of the attacker's machine, that is, it sends the DNS server a query with the attacker's IP address. However, because the DNS has been modified by the attacker, the DNS server will reply to the target host that 180.180.180.180 is associated with the domain name "trust.com." Hence the target host believes that one of its trusted hosts, i.e. "trust.com," is trying to connect. Thus the remote login is accepted and the attacker obtains the access. Forward DNS mapping can also fail because a compromised DNS server can return false IP addresses.

The attacker can also exploit the DNS attack to go inside a victim's network ("DNS Attack Scenario," 1996). To illustrate, assume that "trust.com" and "target.com" are in the same network segment. The attacker first makes a name-to-address mapping so that "attack.com" has two IP addresses: the IP address of "target.com," namely 190.190.190.190, and its own IP address 180.180.180.180. If, on host "trust.com," the victim occasionally visits a Web page on "attack.com," an embedded malicious applet may be downloaded to the victim's browser and run. The applet asks to create a network connection to "attack.com." The victim's Java virtual machine first looks up the address of "attack.com" to make sure that the applet does come from "attack.com." Not surprisingly, the Java virtual machine will get the IP address pair (190.190.190.190, 180.180.180.180) and it will compare this address pair with the address of the machine from which the applet came, that is, 180.180.180.180. Because the pair includes the address 180.180.180.180, the Java virtual machine allows the connection. However, the Java virtual machine actually connects to the first address, namely 190.190.190.190 (i.e., "target.com"). Hence, the attacker now gets into the victim's network with a connection from an inside host "trust.com" to another inside host "target.com."

## Attacks against TCP/IP

TCP/IP is the basis for data transmission in the Internet. The TCP/IP suite includes a set of protocols to control and guarantee worldwide information exchange, such as the TCP protocol, the routing information protocol (RIP), and the ICMP. Despite inspiring features, the security flaws inherent in the TCP/IP suite are exploited by attackers to disrupt the Internet. Although we cannot enumerate all the attacks related to TCP/IP, we discuss several widely known TCP/IP vulnerabilities in this section.

At the TCP layer, an attacker can predict the TCP sequence number to construct a TCP packet without receiving any response from the server and thus impersonate a trusted host (Bellovin, 1989). A normal TCP connection is established according to the three-way handshake protocol. The client sends to the server a SYN message that includes an initial sequence number $SN_C$. The server acknowledges it and replies with a SYN message that includes its current sequence number $SN_S$ and a piggybacking ACK with $SN_C$. The client acknowledges this reply by sending an ACK message with $SN_S$. If the procedure succeeds, a TCP connection is established and the client starts to send data packets. If the value of $SN_S$ is generated in a predictable way, for example, $SN_S$ is increased by a constant amount every second, the intruder can impersonate a trusted host. In particular, the intruder first sends to the server a SYN message with a spoofed source address that belongs to a host trusted by the server. Although the server replies to the trusted host and the intruder may not receive the reply, the intruder can still forge the ACK message with the predicted $SN_S$. Hence, even if the trusted host does not request any TCP connection, the intruder can still successfully establish one connection in the name of the trusted host.

An attacker can also hijack a TCP connection to disconnect the target from the server (Joncheray, 1995). First, the attacker sniffs for packets belonging to the connection between the client and the server. Thus, he or she can obtain the corresponding IP addresses, port numbers, and sequence numbers. Then, the attacker waits to get a packet whose ACK flag is set from the target to the server. The acknowledgment number $SN_S$ in the packet is the sequence number of the next packet that the target is expecting. The attacker thus forges a packet using the server's address as the source address and the client's address as the destination address. In the packet, the reset (RST) flag is set and the sequence number is set to $SN_S$. When the target receives the packet, the TCP connection is reset and thus disconnected.

At the IP layer, the attacker can exploit the holes inside the ICMP protocol for attack (Bellovin, 1989). One such attack is involved with the ICMP redirect message, which is used by gateways to advise hosts of better routes. If an intruder wants to set up a false route for the target, he or she first penetrates into or claims to be a secondary gateway available to the target. Then the intruder sends a false TCP open-connection packet to the target with a spoofed source address, which is the IP address of a trusted host. The target will reply to the trusted host by finding a route through the primary gateway. During the process, the intruder sends a false redirect message, which refers to the bogus connection from the trusted host, through the secondary gateway, and to the target. This packet appears to be a legitimate ICMP control message, and thus the target will accept this routing change. If the target updates its routing table accordingly, future traffic from the target to the trusted host will be directed to the secondary gateway, which is under control of the intruder. Then, the intruder may proceed to spoof the trusted host and establish connections to the target.

ICMP may also be used for distributed denial-of-service (DDoS) attacks ("CERT Advisory CA-1998-01," 2000). In an IP network, a packet can be directed to an individual machine or broadcast to the entire network. When a packet is sent to an IP broadcast address from a machine in the local network, that packet will be delivered to all machines on that network. Hence, when an attacker sends an ICMP echo request packet to a network in which the destination address is the network broadcast address and the source address is the target's address, any machine on the network will send an ICMP echo reply packet back to the target after receiving the broadcast ICMP packet. Therefore, the amount of ICMP echo traffic directed to the target could be large enough to degrade the network performance and cause DoS on the target.

## Attacks against BGP

Internet routing is classified as intradomain routing and interdomain routing. The BGP is the interdomain routing protocol for routing between autonomous systems (ASs), also known as routing domains. An AS uses the BGP protocol to announce its IP address ranges, which include the IP prefixes of its inner networks, to its neighbor ASs. Each AS also announces the IP ranges it learns from its neighbors.

As part of the TCP/IP protocol suite, BGP is subject to all the TCP/IP attacks, such as IP spoofing and session stealing. Attacks against BGP mainly target the provision of false routing information to the network (Murphy, 2003). Attackers can achieve this objective in multiple ways. Because BGP routing data are carried in clear text, it is very easy for attackers to obtain the content and thus take further steps. Because BGP uses TCP connections, the attacker can insert bogus but believable BGP messages into the communication channels between BGP peers. For example, to achieve this, an outside attacker can exploit the hacking technique of TCP sequence number prediction. Moreover, BGP speakers themselves can inject bogus routing information, either by masquerading as another legitimate BGP speaker or by directly distributing unauthorized routing information. Because BGP does not have peer entity authentication, the man-in-the-middle attack can be easily done. Because BGP does not provide protection against deletion and modification of messages, attackers can change or delete interdomain routing information. If an attacker removes the relevant routing information of a particular network from the information base maintained by the relevant BGP speakers, other networks of the Internet will not be able to reach this network because they can get only incomplete routing information. If an attacker alters the information so that the route to a network is changed, then packets destined to that network may be forwarded through the detoured route. As a consequence, traffic to that network could be delayed by a longer than expected period of time or they may never reach the destination. If the route is detoured to the attacker, traffic will be forwarded to the adversary. The attacker can also announce a piece of false information saying that an AS originates a network, and then packets for that network may not be deliverable.

## ATTACKS AGAINST END SYSTEMS OF THE INTERNET

In this section, we summarize the most famous recent attacks across the Internet, as summarized in Table 3. In contrast to the previous sections, in which attacks were against the infrastructure of the Internet, the attacks in this section take advantage of the Internet infrastructure and target hosts or end systems of the Internet. Most of these attacks exploit vulnerabilities in software, operating systems, and protocols above the transport layer. They impacted hundreds and thousands of computers connected to the Internet.

### Morris Worm

On the evening of November 2, 1988, a self-replicating program was released to attack the Internet (Seeley, 1990). The program, later called the Morris worm, invaded VAX and Sun-3 computers running versions of Berkeley UNIX and used their resources to attack more computers. Within the space of hours this program had spread across the United States, infecting thousands of computers and making many of them unusable due to the burden of its activity. Although the worm was designed to spread

itself to as many computers as possible and took only a tiny process to be unnoticeable, it did work strikingly due to mistakenly underestimating its spreading power and overload. As time went on, some of these affected machines became so loaded with running processes (because they were repeatedly affected) that they were unable to continue any processing. Some machines failed completely when their swap space or process tables were exhausted.

The worm has two parts, a main program and a vector program. At first, the worm starts stealthily on a VAX or Sun-3 computer. It gathers the information of authorized user accounts from the file "passwd." Then it begins to break into user accounts. It chooses a possible password based on either the user information or a dictionary. It then encrypts the candidate password and compares the result to the list of encrypted passwords kept in the "passwd" file. If it succeeds in finding a username–password pair, it will go on to break into other hosts using these cracked user accounts.

To break into a remote host, the worm selects a host whose name is contained in a specific set of local files, such as "hosts.equiv", ".rhosts" and ".forward", and tries "rsh", "fingerd", or "sendmail" to execute a malicious process on the remote host. Through "rsh", it establishes a connection from the remote host to the current host, copies the vector program to the remote host, and then compiles and runs it. The vector program in turn copies the whole worm to the remote host and thus generates a new worm on the remote host. For "fingerd", it exploits the buffer overflow bug by sending a specific string of 536 bytes to the fingerd daemon. The string overflows the daemon's input buffer and changes the stacked return address for executing the worm's self-regeneration process. For "sendmail", the worm takes advantage of a piece of unremoved debugging code. The worm sends to the remote host an e-mail message with the DEBUG flag set and a carefully constructed recipient string. This string can pass the body of the message to a command interpreter that will execute a malicious process embedded in the message body on the remote host.

Once the worm resides on a remote host, the whole process starts over again. In addition, the worm takes several measures to avoid local detection. For example, it sets its

**Table 3** Major Attacks against End Systems before 2004

| Names | Date | Target systems |
|---|---|---|
| Morris | November 2, 1988 | VAX and Sun-3 running Berkeley UNIX |
| Melissa | March 26, 1999 | Systems running Microsoft Word 97 and Word 2000 |
| Sadmind | May 8, 2001 | Systems running unpatched Microsoft IIS or Solaris up to version 7 |
| Code Red I | June 19, 2001 | Microsoft Windows NT 4.0, Windows 2000, and other systems with IIS 4.0 or |
| Code Red II | August 6, 2001 | IIS 5.0 enabled and indexing services installed |
| Nimda | September 18, 2001 | Systems running Microsoft Windows 95, 98, ME, NT, and 2000 with IIS |
| SQL Slammer | January 25, 2003 | Systems running Microsoft SQL Server 2000 and Microsoft Desktop Engine (MSDE) 2000 |
| W32/Blaster | August 11, 2003 | Systems running Microsoft Windows NT 4.0, Microsoft Windows 2000, Microsoft Windows XP, and Microsoft Windows Server 2003 with Remote Procedure Call |

process name as "sh", forces the core dump size to zero, deletes the copied programs, and so on.

## Melissa

On March 26, 1999, a Microsoft Word 97 and Word 2000 macro virus named Melissa propagated widely via e-mail attachments ("CERT Advisory CA-1999-4," 1999). Its widespread attack affected a variety of sites throughout the Internet. Human actions, for example, a user opening an infected Word document, are typically required for this virus to propagate. Nevertheless, it is possible that under some mailer configurations, a mailer might automatically open an infected document received in the form of an e-mail attachment. This macro virus is not known to exploit any new vulnerability. Although the primary propagation mechanism of this virus is via e-mail, any way of transferring files can also propagate the virus.

In the Melissa attack, the e-mail attachment is a .DOT Word document that contains a piece of malicious macro code. If an infected document in Word97 or Word2000 is opened, the embedded macro code will infect the "Normal.dot" template and cause any documents referencing this template to be infected with this macro virus. If the infected document is opened by another user, the macro virus included in the document will be executed. Indirectly, this virus could cause serious denial of service on mail servers. Many large sites have reported performance degradation with their mail servers as a result of the propagation of this virus.

The Melissa macro virus propagates in the form of an e-mail message containing an infected Word document as an attachment. The e-mail message contains a specific subject header "Important Message From <name>," where <name> is the full name of the user sending the message. The body of the message contains two sections. The first section contains the deceiving text "Here is that document you asked for . . . don't show anyone else ;-)." The next section is a Word document that contains references to some pornographic Web sites.

The malicious code embedded in the attachment is actually a piece of Visual Basic for applications (VBA) code associated with the "document.open" method. When a user opens an infected .doc file with Microsoft Word97 or Word2000, the macro virus is immediately executed if macros are enabled. Upon execution, the virus first lowers the macro security settings to permit all macros to run when documents are opened in the future. Then the macro checks the registry key to decide if the system is already infected. If not, the virus proceeds to propagate itself by sending an e-mail message in the format described above to the first 50 entries in every Microsoft Outlook messaging application programming interface (MAPI) address book. For successful propagation, the infected machine should have Microsoft Outlook installed. The macro then infects the "Normal.dot" template file, and as a result, any newly created Word document will be infected. Since unpatched versions of Word97 may trust macros in templates, the virus may be executed without warning. Finally, if the minute of the hour matches the day of the month at this point, the macro inserts into the current document the message "Twenty-two points, plus triple-word-score, plus fifty points for using all my letters. Game's over. I'm outta here."

Melissa is not the only (macro) virus that propagates itself through e-mail attachments. There are many other viruses like Melissa, such as the I Love You virus (in 2000) and MyDoom (in 2004).

## Sadmind

On May 8, 2001, a self-propagating malicious worm, Sadmind/IIS, was created ("CERT Advisory CA-1999-16," 2000). The worm uses two vulnerabilities to compromise systems and deface Web pages. It affects systems running unpatched Microsoft Internet Information Server (IIS) and systems running unpatched Solaris up to version 7. Intruders can use the vulnerabilities exploited by this worm to execute arbitrary code with root privileges on vulnerable Solaris systems and arbitrary commands with the privileges of the IUSR_machinename account on vulnerable Windows systems.

To compromise the Solaris systems, the worm exploits a buffer overflow vulnerability in the Solstice sadmind program. It overwrites the stack pointer within a running sadmind process. Because sadmind is installed as a root, it is possible for the attacker to execute arbitrary code with root privileges on a remote machine. Then the worm automatically propagates itself to other vulnerable Solaris systems. It adds "++" to the ".rhosts" file in the root user's home directory and modifies the "index.html" file on the host Solaris system after compromising 2,000 IIS systems. It also establishes a root shell listening on TCP port 600, creates certain directories to hold the worm, and runs some processes.

After successfully compromising the Solaris systems, the worm installs software to attack Microsoft IIS Web servers. It uses a vulnerability of the IIS systems, that is, an intruder can encode the relative reference with certain Unicode characters to execute arbitrary commands with the privileges of the IUSR_machinename account on vulnerable Windows systems. If an IIS is compromised, the worm will modify the corresponding Web pages.

## Code Red I and Code Red II

In 2001, two worms exploited the same vulnerability to disturb the Internet: Code Red I on July 19 and Code Red II on August 6 ("CERT Advisory CA-2001-19," 2002). Both of them exploited the vulnerability of buffer overflow bugs in Microsoft IIS Indexing Service DLL. They affected Microsoft Windows NT 4.0 with IIS 4.0 or IIS 5.0 enabled and Index Server 2.0 installed, Windows 2000 with IIS 4.0 or IIS 5.0 enabled and Indexing services installed, and other systems running IIS. More than 250,000 hosts suffered from their attack.

Both worms attempt to connect to TCP port 80 on a randomly chosen host to find a Web service. Upon a successful connection to port 80, the attacking host sends a crafted HTTP GET request to the victim, attempting to exploit a buffer overflow bug in the Indexing Service. If the exploit is successful, these two worms begin their execution on the victim host. Unpatched IIS 4.0 and 5.0 servers with Indexing service installed will almost certainly be compromised.

Code Red I changes all Web pages requested from the victim server with a default language of English. Servers configured with a non-English language will not experience any change in the served content. The other worm activity occurs based on the day of the month of the system clock. On Days 1–19, the infected host will attempt to connect to TCP port 80 of randomly chosen IP addresses to further propagate the worm. On Days 20–27, a packet-flooding denial of service attack will be launched against a particular fixed IP address. On Day 28 to the end of the month, the worm sleeps, with no active connections or denial of service.

Compared with Code Red I, Code Red II goes beyond defacing Web pages. It exploits the vulnerability to execute arbitrary codes in the LocalSystem security context. If the default system language is Chinese, 600 threads will be spawned to scan for 48 hours. Otherwise, 300 threads will be created that will scan for 24 hours. It copies "%SYSTEM%\CMD.EXE" to "root.exe" in the IIS scripts and MSADC folders. It places "CMD.EXE" in a publicly accessible directory to allow an intruder to execute arbitrary commands on the compromised machine with the privileges of the IIS server process. It creates a Trojan horse copy of "explorer.exe" and copies it to "C:\" and "D:\". The Trojan horse "explorer.exe" calls the real "explorer.exe" to mask its existence and creates a virtual mapping that exposes the "C:" and "D:" drives. Hence, Code Red II causes system-level compromise and leaves a backdoor on machines running Windows 2000.

## Nimda

On September 18, 2001, a worm, named W32/Nimda or Concept Virus (CV) v.5, propagated in the Internet to attack systems running Microsoft Windows 95, 98, ME, NT, and 2000 ("CERT Advisory CA-2001-26," 2001). With the worm, intruders can execute arbitrary commands within the LocalSystem security context on machines running unpatched versions of IIS. In the case in which a client is compromised, the worm will run with the same privileges as the user who triggered it. The infected computers may suffer from DoS caused by network scanning and e-mail propagation.

Once running on the victim machine, the worm visits all directories in the system (including all those accessible through file sharing) and writes a multipurpose Internet mail extension (MIME)-encoded copy of itself to the disk using file names with ".eml" or ".nws" extensions (e.g., "readme.eml"). When a directory containing Web content (e.g., HTML or active server page files) is found, a snippet of Javascript code is appended to every one of these Web-related files for propagation. The worm also enables the sharing of the "C:" drive as C$, creates a guest account on Windows NT and 2000 systems, adds this account to the administrator group, and replaces existing binaries with their Trojan horse versions.

The worm spreads in multiple ways. First, it can propagate via an e-mail that contains a base64-encoded attachment, named "readme.exe". Because Internet Explorer 5.5 SP1 or earlier renders will automatically run the enclosed attachment, the worm infects the receiving computer. The worm also contains code to resend the infected e-mail messages every 10 days. The target e-mail addresses are found from the user's Web cache and the e-mails retrieved via the MAPI service. Second, it propagates via open network sharing. Users on another system can trigger the worm in their own computers if they open a copy of the worm or execute the Trojan horse versions of the legitimate applications in the shared folder. Third, it propagates via browsing compromised Web sites. Because the worm adds a piece of Javasript code to all the Web files it finds, a user browsing Web content on the infected system may download a copy of the worm, which may be automatically executed and thus infects the system. Fourth, the worm exploits the Microsoft IIS 4.0 / 5.0 directory traversal vulnerabilities as the Code Red worm and scans for the backdoors left by Code Red II and sadmind/IIS worms to propagate.

## SQL Slammer

On January 25 2003, a worm referred to as SQL Slammer, W32.Slammer, or Sapphire caused varied levels of network performance degradation across the Internet ("CERT Advisory CA-2003-04," 1999). The worm affects Microsoft SQL Server 2000 and Microsoft Desktop Engine (MSDE) 2000. The high volume of user datagram protocol (UDP) traffic generated by the infected hosts may lead to performance degradation against Internet-connected hosts or those computers that stay on the same network of a compromised host.

The worm exploits the vulnerability of stack buffer overflow in the Resolution Service of Microsoft SQL Server 2000 and MSDE 2000 so that an intruder can execute arbitrary code with the same privileges as the SQL server. It may be possible for an attacker to subsequently leverage a local privilege escalation exploit to gain administrator access to the victim system.

Once the worm compromises a machine, it will try to propagate itself. The worm will craft UDP packets of 376 bytes and send them to randomly chosen IP addresses on port 1434. If such a packet is sent to a vulnerable machine, the victim machine will become infected for further propagation.

## W32/Blaster

On August 11, 2003, a worm, named W32/Blaster, was launched ("CERT Advisory CA-2003-20," 1999). It affects computers running Microsoft Windows NT 4.0, Microsoft Windows 2000, Microsoft Windows XP, and Microsoft Windows Server 2003. This worm exploits a vulnerability in the Microsoft Remote Procedure Call (RPC) interface. This vulnerability affects a distributed component object model (DCOM) interface with RPC, which listens on TCP/IP port 135. This interface handles the DCOM object activation requests that are sent by client machines to the server. Due to incorrect handling of malformed messages exchanged over TCP/IP, an attacker can use buffer overflow to execute arbitrary code with system privileges or cause denial of service.

Upon successful execution, the worm attempts to retrieve a copy of the file "msblast.exe" from the compromising host. Once this file is retrieved, the compromised system runs it and begins scanning for other vulnerable systems to compromise in the same manner. In the course of propagation, the TCP session to port 135 is used to execute the attack. The worm also has the ability to launch a TCP SYN flood DoS attack against "windowsupdate.com".

## ATTACKS AGAINST ENTERPRISE NETWORK SYSTEMS

An enterprise network system refers to all hardware and software that construct the network infrastructure of a company to support its business. Generally, the network is composed of an internal network and some connections to the Internet. It can permit flexible communications among a wide range of individuals and enterprises, thereby enabling more convenient and efficient business operations. However, it can also expose the enterprise systems to a much wider variety of attacks than they previously faced (Landwehr & Goldschlag, 1997). If sensitive information is disclosed or improperly modified, or if critical services are denied to the enterprise or its customers, the security of the enterprise network system will be breached. In this section, we give an overview of the possible vulnerabilities of enterprise network systems and the corresponding security mechanisms.

### Attacks against Private Networks

In this scenario, the network is mainly a local area network (LAN) inside a company, which connects and supports communication among all divisions of the company, for example, headquarters, sales, R&D, and factories. Business information from outside goes through leased telephone, mail, or fax and is entered (by human operators) into the system. Office operations and word processing are handled with in-house servers and clients (personal computers [PCs]) that are connected by an in-house LAN. There are no external network connections to the LAN.

This type of network is typically hacked from inside. An authorized user or administrator can incorrectly configure authorized software, which results in misdelivery of messages. A user can load arbitrary software into a computer through a diskette and introduce malicious codes to the enterprise system. Users can attach their own modems to their PCs and open a backdoor to the private LAN through the leased telephone lines. It is also possible that an intruder gains physical access to the private network lines and eavesdrops on parts of the private network.

### Attacks against Private Networks with Web Service

In this scenario, a Web site is added to the private network as an interface for customers to place orders through the Internet. On the site, customers can review information about product specifications, new product announcements, company telephone numbers, and so on. In addition, the Web site can also provide HTML forms to take orders. This entails implementation of interactive scripts on the existing Web server, which can provide a path for the orders to be placed into the private network.

The Web server, as long as it provides information, is vulnerable to denial of service attacks that originate in the Internet. If there is a bug in the Web server that can be invoked by Internet users, such as a buffer overflow bug, the Web server may be taken by attackers. If the Web server is hosted by an Internet service provider (ISP), attackers can penetrate into the ISP's system to take control of the server and modify the Web content. Some vulnerabilities come from nontechnical operations in the WWW environment. For example, competitors or vandals could set up Web sites with similar names and place bogus information on them.

Unless specific measures are implemented to authenticate customers and protect their communications with the server, the order information that the server sends to the order-taking staff may be forged, and outsiders may be able to forge order information that seems to come from the Web site. Valid but unsafe scripts can permit an outsider to take over a Web site and thereby alter the information it provides, generate false requests, close it down, or initiate other malicious actions.

### Attacks against Firewalls and Virtual Private Networks

In this scenario, to ensure security, firewalls are added to protect the internal network. However, this is not absolutely safe. If the firewall is not carefully configured, it may provide a false sense of security and permit outsiders to hack internal systems. An inadequately configured firewall can make internal hosts visible to the outside world, may pass traffic from untrusted hosts and ports that are supposed to be blocked, and may provide an incorrect proxy server that lets malicious traffic into the internal network. Insiders can invoke malicious software to leak information or import malicious codes. Administrators and users may install tools on systems so that they can work remotely and conveniently. These tools may become backdoors for outside intruders.

A company may have several private networks allocated across separated locations. A virtual private network consists of a set of corporate sites and internal networks. Each site manages its own Internet connection and runs an encrypting firewall so that traffic between any pair of sites is encrypted and the Internet works as a transmission medium. The network is virtually private in that only the packet headers containing routing information are exposed to public view; however, it is still not private in the sense that it contains no leased private lines. Although communication over the Internet can be flexible, the Internet does not guarantee quality and security. Depending on the ISP and the Internet backbone, delays may occur in delivering important messages or cause serious degradation of performance. Furthermore, more internal corporate information is flowing over the Internet and open to interception, although they are encrypted. Without careful configuration and usage of cryptographic techniques, such as weak encryption and short keys, critical information may still be decrypted by a malicious third party.

## CONCLUSION

In this chapter, we discussed a variety of hacking techniques. From the functionalities, objectives, and principles of different hacking techniques, we can summarize that vulnerabilities of a network or system always come from two major factors: technical factors and human factors. The technical factors refer to those imperfect designs of networks and systems, such as unencrypted data, unprotected communications, buffer overflow problems, and software bugs. These deficiencies provide holes through which intruders can penetrate into the system. The human factors are another important perspective. For example, users' incautious talk can become the source to disclose critical information about network and system. Inappropriate use of the system may let attackers sneak in. Insiders may be the most serious threats to the system.

## ACKNOWLEDGEMENTS

This work was partially supported by NSF ANI-0335241, NSF CCR-0233324, and Department of Energy Early Career PI Award.

## GLOSSARY

**Autonomous system (AS)** A collection of routers under a single administrative authority, using a common interior gateway protocol for routing packets.

**Border gate protocol (BGP)** A protocol that distributes routing information to the routers, which connect autonomous systems.

**Domain name** A series of alphanumeric strings separated by periods that is used to name organizations and computers and addresses on the Internet.

**Domain name system (DNS)** A general-purpose distributed, replicated, data query service chiefly used on the Internet for translating hostnames into Internet addresses.

**Firewall** A router or computer software that prevents unauthorized access to private data (as on a company's local area network or intranet) by outside computer users (as on the Internet).

**Hypertext transfer protocol (HTTP)** A protocol used to request and transmit files, especially Web pages and Web page components, over the Internet or other computer network.

**Internet control message protocol (ICMP)** An Internet protocol that allows for the generation of error messages, test packets, and informational messages related to IP.

**Internet protocol (IP)** A connectionless, best-effort packet-switching protocol that provides packet routing, fragmentation, and reassembly through the data link layer.

**Internet service provider (ISP)** A company that provides other companies or individuals with access to, or a presence on, the Internet.

**Listening post** A center for monitoring electronic communications (as of an enemy).

**Plaintext** The unencrypted form of an encrypted message.

**Private network** A network composed of point-to-point leased lines between sites.

**Router** A device that forwards packets between networks based on network layer information and routing tables, which are often constructed by routing protocols.

**Routing information protocol (RIP)** A distance vector routing protocol that distributes routing information to the routers within an autonomous system.

**Transmission control protocol (TCP)** A protocol for the Internet to obtain data from one network device to another by using a retransmission strategy to ensure that data will not be lost in transmission.

**Uniform resource locator (URL)** A way of specifying the location of an object, typically a Web page, on the Internet. It has two parts separated by a colon. The part before the first colon specifies the protocol. The part after the colon is the pathname of a file on the server.

**User datagram protocol (UDP)** A connectionless protocol in the transport layer layered on top of the IP protocol that provides simple but unreliable datagram services.

**Virtual private network** A network composed of several subprivate networks connected through a public network (such as the Internet). The network traffic is encrypted in the IP layer so that secure connections among the subprivate networks are provided through the insecure public network.

## CROSS REFERENCES

See *Computer Viruses and Worms; Hackers, Crackers and Computer Criminals; Hacking Techniques in Wireless Networks; TCP/IP Suite.*

## REFERENCES

Bellovin, S. (1995). Using the domain name system for system break-ins. *Proceeding of the 5th UNIX Security Symposium*, pp. 199–208, Salt Lake City, Utah, USA.

Bellovin, S. M. (1989). Security problems in the TCP/IP protocol suite. *ACM SIGCOMM Computer Communication Review, 19*, 32–48.

Boulanger, A. (1998). Catapults and grappling hooks: The tools and techniques of Information warfare. *IBM System Journal, 37*, 106–114.

*CERT advisory CA-1998-01 Smurf IP denial-of-service attacks.* (2000). Retrieved May 20, 2004, from http://www.cert.org/advisories/CA-1998-01.html

*CERT advisory CA-1999-04 Melissa macro virus.* (1999). Retrieved May 20, 2004, from http://www.cert.org/advisories/CA-1999-04.html

*CERT advisory CA-1999-16 buffer overflow in Sun Solstice AdminSuite daemon sadmind.* (2000). Retrieved May 20, 2004, from http://www.cert.org/advisories/CA-1999-16.html

*CERT advisory CA-2001-19 "Code Red" worm exploiting buffer overflow in IIS indexing service DLL.* (2002). Retrieved May 20, 2004, from http://www.cert.org/advisories/CA-2001-19.html

*CERT advisory CA-2001-26 Nimda worm.* (2001). Retrieved May 20, 2004, from http://www.cert.org/advisories/CA-2001-26.html

*CERT advisory CA-2003-04 MS-SQL server worm.* (2003). Retrieved May 20, 2004, from http://www.cert.org/advisories/CA-2003-04.html

*CERT advisory CA-2003-20 W32/Blaster worm.* (2003). Retrieved May 20, 2004, from http://www.cert.org/advisories/CA-2003-20.html

*CERT/CC statistics 1988-2003.* (2004). Retrieved May 20, 2004, from http://www.cert.org/stats/cert_stats.html

*Computer Oracle and Password System.* (1993). Retrieved May 20, 2004, from http://www.fish.com/cops/

Cowan, C., Wagle, F., Pu, C., Beattie, S., & Walpole, J. (2000). Buffer overflows: Attacks and defenses for the vulnerability of the decade. *Proceeding of DARPA Information Survivability Conference and Exposition,* pp. 119–129, Anaheim, CA, USA.

*Denial of service attacks.* (2001). Retrieved May 20, 2004, from http://www.cert.org/tech_tips/denial_of_service.html

*DNS attack scenario.* (1996). Retrieved May 20, 2004, from http://www.cs.princeton.edu/sip/news/dns-scenario.html

*Ethereal.* (2004). Retrieved May 20, 2004, from http://www.ethereal.com/.

*John the Ripper password cracker.* (2004). Retrieved May 20, 2004, from http://www.openwall.com/john/

Joncheray, L. (1995). Simple active attack against TCP. *Proceedings of the 5th USENIX UNIX Security Symposium,* Salt Lake City, Utah, USA.

Landwehr, C. E., & Goldschlag, D. M. (1997). Security issues in networks with Internet access. *Proceedings of the IEEE, 85,* 2034–2051.

Murphy, S. (2003). *BGP security vulnerabilities analysis.* Retrieved May 20, 2004, from http://www.ietf.org/internet-drafts/draft-ietf-idr-bgp-vuln-00.txt

*Nessus.* (2004). Retrieved May 20, 2004, from http://www.nessus.org

*Network Mapper (NMAP).* (2004). Retrieved May 20, 2004, from http://www.insecure.org/nmap/

*Password cracker.* (2004). Retrieved May 20, 2004, from http://www.pwcrack.com/index.shtml

*Security administrator tool for analyzing networks.* (1995). Retrieved May 20, 2004, from http://www.fish.com/satan/

Seeley, D. (1990). *The Internet worm of 1988.* Retrieved May 20, 2004, from http://world.std.com/~franl/worm.html

*Spytech.* (2004). Retrieved May 20, 2004, from http://www.spytech-web.com/

*Tiger.* (1994). Retrieved May 20, 2004, from http://savannah.nongnu.org/projects/tiger/

# Hacking Techniques in Wireless Networks

Prabhaker Mateti, *Wright State University*

## INTRODUCTION

Wireless networks broadcast their packets using radio frequency (RF) or optical wavelengths. A modern laptop computer can listen in. Worse, attackers can manufacture new packets on the fly and persuade wireless stations to accept their packets as legitimate. In this chapter, the term *hacking* is used as follows:

**hacker** *n*. [originally, someone who makes furniture with an axe] **1.** A person who enjoys exploring the details of programmable systems and how to stretch their capabilities, as opposed to most users, who prefer to learn only the minimum necessary. **2.** One who programs enthusiastically (even obsessively) or who enjoys programming rather than just theorizing about programming. **3.** A person capable of appreciating hack value. **4.** A person who is good at programming quickly. **5.** An expert at a particular program, or one who frequently does work using it or on it; as in "a Unix hacker." (Definitions 1 through 5 are correlated, and people who fit them congregate.) **6.** An expert or enthusiast of any kind. One might be an astronomy hacker, for example. **7.** One who enjoys the intellectual challenge of creatively overcoming or circumventing limitations. **8.** *[deprecated]* A malicious meddler who tries to discover sensitive information by poking around.

Hence "password hacker," "network hacker." The correct term for this sense is cracker. (From *The Jargon Dictionary* http://info.astrian.net/jargon/)

This chapter describes Institute of Electrical and Electronics Engineers (IEEE) 802.11–specific hacking techniques that attackers have used and suggests various defensive measures. It is not an overview of security features proposed in WPA or IEEE 802.11i and does not consider legal implications or the intent behind such hacking, whether malevolent or benevolent. The chapter's focus is on describing techniques, methods, analyses, and uses that were unintended by the designers of IEEE 802.11.

## WIRELESS LAN OVERVIEW

This section provides a brief overview of wireless local area networks (WLAN) and emphasizes how its features help an attacker. It assumes that the reader is familiar with the transmission control protocol/Internet protocol (TCP/IP) suite (see, e.g., Mateti, 2003).

IEEE 802.11 refers to a family of specifications (http://www.ieee802.org/11/) developed by the IEEE for over-the-air interface between a wireless client and an access point (AP) or between two wireless clients. To be

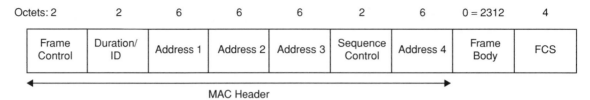

**Figure 1:** An IEEE 802.11 frame.

called 802.11 devices, they must conform to the medium access control (MAC) and physical layer specifications. The IEEE 802.11 standard covers the physical (Layer 1) and data link (Layer 2) layers of the OSI Model. This chapter is mainly concerned with the MAC layer and not the variations of the physical layer known as 802.11a/b/g.

## Stations and Access Points

A wireless network interface card (adapter) is a device, called a *station,* providing the network physical layer over a radio link to another station. An *access point* is a station that provides frame distribution service to stations associated with it. The AP itself is typically connected by wire to a LAN.

The station and AP each contain a network interface that has a MAC address, just as wired network cards do. This address is a 48-bit number, unique worldwide, that is assigned to it at the time of manufacture. The 48-bit address is often represented as a string of six octets separated by colons (e.g., 00:02:2D:17:B9:E8) or hyphens (e.g., 00-02-2D-17-B9-E8). Although the MAC address as assigned by the manufacturer is printed on the device, the address can be changed in software.

Each AP has a 0- to 32-byte-long service set identifier (SSID) that is also commonly called a network name. The SSID is used to segment the airwaves for usage. If two wireless networks are physically close, the SSIDs label the respective networks and allow the components of one network to ignore those of the other. SSIDs can also be mapped to virtual LANs; thus, some APs support multiple SSIDs. Unlike fully qualified host names (e.g., gamma.cs.wright.edu), SSIDs are not registered, and it is possible that two unrelated networks use the same SSID.

## Channels

The stations communicate with each other using RFs between 2.4 and 2.5 GHz. Neighboring channels are only 5 MHz apart. Two wireless networks using neighboring channels may interfere with each other.

## Wired Equivalent Privacy

Wired equivalent privacy (WEP) is a shared-secret key encryption system used to encrypt packets transmitted between a station and an AP. The WEP algorithm is intended to protect wireless communication from eavesdropping. A secondary function of WEP is to prevent unauthorized access to a wireless network. WEP encrypts the payload of data packets. Management and control frames are always transmitted in the clear. WEP uses the RC4 encryption

algorithm. The shared-secret key is either 40 or 104 bits long. The system administrator chooses the key. This key must be shared among all the stations and the AP using mechanisms that are not specified in the IEEE 802.11.

## Infrastructure and Ad Hoc Modes

A wireless network operates in one of two modes. In the *ad hoc* mode, each station is a peer to the other stations and communicates directly with other stations within the network. No AP is involved. All stations can send beacon and probe frames. The ad hoc mode stations form an independent basic service set (IBSS).

A station in the *infrastructure* mode communicates only with an AP. Basic service set (BSS) is a set of stations that are logically associated with each other and controlled by a single AP. Together they operate as a fully connected wireless network. The BSSID is a 48-bit number of the same format as a MAC address. This field uniquely identifies each BSS. The value of this field is the MAC address of the AP.

## Frames

Both the station and AP radiate and gather 802.11 frames as needed. The format of frames is illustrated in Figure 1. Most of the frames contain IP packets. The other frames are for the management and control of the wireless connection.

There are three classes of frames (Figure 2). The *management* frames establish and maintain communications. These are the association request, association response, reassociation request, reassociation response, probe request, probe response, beacon, announcement traffic indication message, disassociation, authentication, deauthentication types. The SSID is part of several of the management frames. Management messages are always sent in the clear, even when link encryption (WEP or WPA) is used, so the SSID is visible to anyone who can intercept these frames.

The *control* frames help in the delivery of data.

The *data* frames encapsulate the OSI network layer packets. These contain the source and destination MAC address, the BSSID, and the TCP/IP datagram. The payload part of the datagram is WEP-encrypted.

## Authentication

Authentication is the process of proving identity of a station to another station or AP. In the open-system authentication, all stations are authenticated without any checking. A Station A sends an authentication management frame that contains the identity of A to Station B.

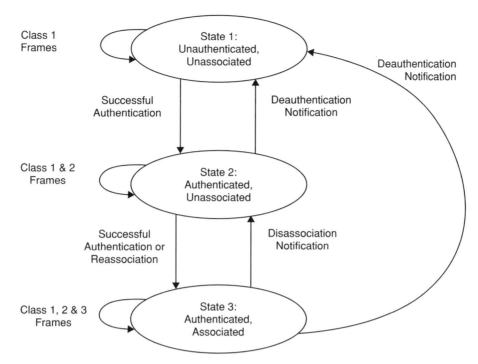

**Figure 2:** States and services.

Station B replies with a frame that indicates recognition, addressed to A. In the closed-network architecture, the stations must know the SSID of the AP to connect to the AP. The shared-key authentication uses a standard challenge and response along with a shared secret key.

## Association

Data can be exchanged between the station and AP only after a station is associated with an AP in the infrastructure mode or with another station in the ad hoc mode. All the APs transmit beacon frames a few times each second that contain the SSID, time, capabilities, supported rates, and other information. Stations can choose to associate with an AP based on the signal strength and other characteristics of each AP. Stations can have a null SSID that is considered to match all SSIDs.

The association is a two-step process. A station that is currently unauthenticated and unassociated listens for beacon frames. The station selects a BSS to join. The station and the AP mutually authenticate themselves by exchanging authentication management frames. The client is now authenticated but unassociated. In the second step, the station sends an association request frame, to which the AP responds with an association response frame that includes an association ID to the station. The station is now authenticated and associated.

A station can be authenticated with several APs at the same time but associated with at most one AP at any time. Association implies authentication. There is no state in which a station is associated but not authenticated.

## WIRELESS NETWORK SNIFFING

*Sniffing* is eavesdropping on the network. A (packet) *sniffer* is a program that intercepts and decodes network traffic broadcast through a medium. Sniffing is the act by a Machine S of making copies of a network packet sent by Machine A intended to be received by Machine B. Such sniffing, strictly speaking, is not a TCP/IP problem, but it is enabled by the choice of broadcast media, Ethernet, and 802.11 as the physical and data link layers.

Sniffing has long been a reconnaissance technique used in wired networks. Attackers sniff the frames necessary to enable the exploits described in later sections. Sniffing is the underlying technique used in tools that monitor the health of a network. Sniffing can also help find the "easy kill," as in scanning for open access points that allow anyone to connect; capturing passwords used in a connection session that does not even use WEP; or in telnet, rlogin, and ftp connections.

It is easier to sniff wireless networks than wired ones. It is easy to sniff the wireless traffic of a building by setting up shop in a car parked in a lot as far away as a mile or while driving around the block. In a wired network, the attacker must find a way to install a sniffer on one or more of the hosts in the targeted subnet. Depending on the equipment used in a LAN, a sniffer needs to be run either on the victim machine on which the traffic is of interest or on some other host in the same subnet as the victim. An attacker at large on the Internet has other techniques that make it possible to install a sniffer remotely on the victim machine.

## Passive Scanning

Scanning is the act of sniffing by tuning to various radio channels of the devices. A *passive* network scanner instructs the wireless card to listen to each channel for a few messages. This does not reveal the presence of the scanner.

An attacker can passively scan without transmitting at all. Several modes of a station permit this. There is a mode called *RF monitor* mode that allows every frame appearing on a channel to be copied as the radio of the station tunes to various channels. This is analogous to placing a wired Ethernet card in promiscuous mode, which is not enabled by default. Some wireless cards on the market today have disabled this feature in the default firmware. One can buy wireless cards with firmware and corresponding driver software that together permit reading of all raw 802.11 frames. A station in *monitor* mode can capture packets without associating with an AP or ad hoc network. The so-called promiscuous mode allows the capture of all wireless packets of an associated network. In this mode, packets cannot be read until authentication and association are completed. An example sniffer is Kismet (http://www.kismetwireless.net). An example wireless card that permits RF monitor modes is Cisco Aironet AIR-PCM342.

## Detection of SSID

The attacker can discover the SSID of a network usually by passive scanning because the SSID occurs in the following frame types: beacon, probe requests, probe responses, association requests, and reassociation requests. Recall that management frames are always in the clear, even when WEP is enabled.

On a number of APs, it is possible to configure so that the SSID transmitted in the beacon frames is masked or even to turn off beacons altogether. The SSID shown in the beacon frames is set to null in the hope of making the WLAN invisible unless a client already knows the correct SSID. In such a case, a station wishing to join a WLAN begins the association process by sending probe requests because it could not detect any APs via beacons that match its SSID. If the beacons are not turned off and the SSID in them is not set to null, an attacker obtains the SSID included in the beacon frame by passive scanning.

When the beacon displays a null SSID, there are two possibilities. Eventually, an associate request may appear from a legitimate station that already has a correct SSID. There will be an associate response frame from the AP to such a request. Both frames will contain the SSID in the clear, and the attacker sniffs these. If the station wishes to join any available AP, it sends probe requests on all channels and listens for probe responses that contain the SSIDs of the APs. The station considers all probe responses, just as it would have with the nonempty SSID beacon frames, to select an AP. Normal association then begins. The attacker waits to sniff these probe responses and extract the SSIDs.

If beacon transmission is disabled, the attacker has two choices. The attacker can keep sniffing, waiting for a voluntary associate request to appear from a legitimate station that already has a correct SSID and sniff the SSID as described earlier. The attacker can also choose to probe actively by injecting frames that he or she constructs and then sniffs the response (described in a later section). When these methods fail, SSID discovery is done by *active* scanning (see Wireless Network Probing later in the chapter).

## Collecting MAC Addresses

The attacker gathers legitimate MAC addresses for use later in constructing spoofed frames. The source and destination MAC addresses are always in the clear in all the frames. There are two reasons an attacker would collect MAC addresses of stations and APs participating in a wireless network. First, the attacker wishes to use these values in spoofed frames so that his station or AP is not identified. Second, the targeted AP may be controlling access by filtering out frames with MAC addresses that were not registered.

## Collecting the Frames for Cracking WEP

The goal of an attacker is to discover the WEP shared secret key. Often, the shared key can be discovered by guesswork based on a certain amount of social engineering regarding the administrator who configures the wireless LAN and all its users. Some client software stores the WEP keys in the operating system registry or initialization scripts. In the following section, it is assumed that the attacker was unsuccessful in obtaining the key in this manner. The attacker then employs systematic procedures in cracking the WEP. For this purpose, a large number (millions) of frames needs to be collected because of the way WEP works.

The wireless device generates on the fly an initialization vector (IV) of 24 bits. Adding these bits to the shared secret key of either 40 or 104 bits, we often speak of 64- or 128-bit encryption. WEP generates a pseudo-random key stream from the shared secret key and the IV. The CRC-32 checksum of the plain text, known as the integrity check (IC) field, is appended to the data to be sent. It is then exclusive-ORed with the pseudo-random key stream to produce the cipher text. The IV is appended in the clear to the cipher text and transmitted. The receiver extracts the IV, uses the secret key to regenerate the random key stream and exclusive-ORs the received cipher text to yield the original plaintext.

Certain cards are so simplistic that they start their IV as 0 and increment it by 1 for each frame, resetting in between for some events. Even the better cards generate weak IVs from which the first few bytes of the shared key can be computed after statistical analyses. Some implementations generate fewer mathematically weak vectors than others do.

The attacker sniffs a large number of frames from a single BSS. These frames all use the same key. The mathematics behind the systematic computation of the secret shared key from a collection of cipher text extracted from these frames is described elsewhere in this volume. What is needed, however, is a collection of frames that were encrypted using "mathematically weak" IVs. The number of encrypted frames that were mathematically weak is a small percentage of all frames. In a collection of a million frames, there may only be a hundred mathematically weak frames. It is conceivable that the collection may take a few hours to several days, depending on how busy the WLAN is.

Given a sufficient number of mathematically weak frames, the systematic computation that exposes the bytes of the secret key is intensive. However, an attacker can employ powerful computers. On an average personal computer, this may take a few seconds to hours. The storage of the large numbers of frames is in the range of several hundred megabytes to a few gigabytes. An example of a WEP cracking tool is AirSnort (http://airsnort.shmoo.com).

## Detection of Sniffers

Detecting the presence of a wireless sniffer, who remains radio-silent, through network security measures is virtually impossible. Once the attacker begins probing (i.e., by injecting packets), the presence and the coordinates of the wireless device can be detected.

# WIRELESS SPOOFING

Well-known attack techniques known as spoofing occur both in wired and wireless networks. The attacker constructs frames by filling selected fields that contain addresses or identifiers with legitimate-looking but nonexistent values or with values that belong to others. The attacker would have collected these legitimate values through sniffing.

## MAC Address Spoofing

Attackers generally desire to be hidden, but the probing activity injects frames that are observable by system administrators. The attacker fills the sender MAC address field of the injected frames with a spoofed value so that his equipment is not identified.

Typical APs control access by permitting only those stations with known MAC addresses. Attackers either have to compromise a computer system that has a station or they spoof with legitimate MAC addresses in frames that they manufacture. MAC addresses are assigned at the time of manufacture, but setting the MAC address of a wireless card or AP to an arbitrary chosen value is a simple matter of invoking an appropriate software tool that engages in a dialog with the user and accepts values. Such tools are routinely included when a station or AP is purchased. The attacker, however, changes the MAC address programmatically, sends several frames with that address, and repeats this with another MAC address. In a period of a second, this can happen several thousand times.

When an AP is not filtering MAC addresses, there is no need for attackers to use legitimate MAC addresses. In certain attacks, however, attackers need to have a large number of MAC addresses than they can collect by sniffing. Random MAC addresses are generated. Not every random sequence of 6 bytes is a MAC address, however. The IEEE assigns globally the first 3 bytes, and the manufacturer chooses the last 3 bytes. The officially assigned numbers are publicly available. The attacker generates a random MAC address by selecting an IEEE-assigned 3 bytes appended with an additional 3 random bytes.

## IP Spoofing

Replacing the true IP address of the sender (or, in rare cases, the destination) with a different address is known as IP spoofing. This is a necessary operation in many attacks. The IP layer of the operating system (OS) simply trusts that the source address, because it appears in an IP packet, is valid. It assumes that the packet it received was indeed sent by the host officially assigned that source address. Because the IP layer of the OS normally adds these IP addresses to a data packet, a spoofer must circumvent the IP layer and talk directly to the raw network device. Note that the attacker's machine cannot simply be assigned the IP address of another host X using `ifconfig` or a similar configuration tool. Other hosts, as well as X, will discover (through address resolution protocol [ARP], for example) that there are two machines with the same IP address.

IP spoofing is an integral part of many attacks. For example, an attacker can silence Host A from sending further packets to Host B by sending a spoofed packet announcing a window size of zero to A as though it originated from B.

## Frame Spoofing

In this case, an attacker injects frames that are valid by 802.11 specifications but with content that is carefully spoofed. Frames themselves are not authenticated in 802.11 networks, so when a frame has a spoofed source address, it cannot be detected unless the address is wholly bogus. If the spoofed frame is a management or control frame, no encryption is necessary. If it is a data frame, perhaps as part of an ongoing man-in-the-middle attack, the data payload must be properly encrypted.

Construction of the byte stream that constitutes a spoofed frame is a programming matter once the attacker has gathered the needed information through sniffing and probing. There are software libraries that ease this task, such as libpcap (http://sourceforge.net/projects/libpcap/), libnet (http://libnet.sourceforge.net/), libdnet (http://libdnet.sourceforge.net/), and libradiate (http://www.packetfactory.net/projects/libradiate).

The difficulty here is not in the construction of the contents of the frame but in getting it radiated (transmitted) by the station or an AP. This requires control over the firmware and driver of the wireless card that may sanitize certain fields of a frame. Therefore, the attacker selects his equipment carefully. Currently, there are off-the-shelf wireless cards that can be manipulated. In addition, the construction of special-purpose wireless cards is within the reach of a resourceful attacker.

# WIRELESS NETWORK PROBING

Even though attackers gather a considerable amount of information regarding a wireless network through sniffing, without revealing their wireless presence, there are pieces that may still be missing. Attackers then send artificially constructed packets to a target that triggers useful responses. This activity is known as probing or active scanning. The target may discover that it is being probed and may even be a *honey pot* (www.honeynet.org/) target carefully constructed to trap the attacker. The attacker would try to minimize this risk.

## Detection of SSID

Detection of SSID is often possible by simply sniffing beacon frames as described in a previous section. If beacon transmission is disabled and the attacker does not wish to patiently wait for a voluntary associate request to appear from a legitimate station that already has a correct SSID or probe requests from legitimate stations, the attacker will resort to probing by injecting a probe request frame that contains a spoofed source MAC address. The probe response frame from the APs will contain, in the clear, the SSID and other information similar to that in the beacon frames had they been enabled. The attacker sniffs these probe responses and extracts the SSIDs.

Some models of APs have an option to disable responding to probe requests that do not contain the correct SSID. In this case, the attacker determines a station associated with the AP and sends the station a forged disassociation frame where the source MAC address is set to that of the AP. The station will send a reassociation request that exposes the SSID.

## Detection of APs and Stations

Every AP is a station, so SSIDs and MAC addresses are gathered as described earlier. Certain bits in the frames identify that the frame is from an AP. If we assume that WEP is either disabled or cracked, the attacker can also gather the IP addresses of the AP and the stations.

## Detection of Probing

Detection of probing is possible. The frames that an attacker injects can also be heard by the intrusion detection systems (IDS) of hardened wireless LAN. Global positioning satellite (GPS)–enabled equipment can identify the physical coordinates of a wireless device through which the probe frames are being transmitted.

## AP WEAKNESSES

APs have weaknesses that are due both to design mistakes and to user interfaces that promote weak passwords and other problematic issues. Many publicly conducted war-driving efforts (www.worldwidewardrive.org) in major cities around the world have demonstrated that a large majority of the deployed APs are poorly configured, most with WEP disabled and configuration defaults, as set up by the manufacturer, untouched.

## Configuration

The default WEP keys used are often too trivial. Different APs use various techniques to convert the user's keyboard input into a bit vector. Usually 5 or 13 ASCII printable characters are directly mapped by concatenating their ASCII 8-bit codes into a 40-bit or 104-bit WEP key. A stronger key can be constructed from an input of 26 hexadecimal digits. It is possible to form an even stronger104-bit WEP key by truncating the MD5 hash of an arbitrary length pass phrase.

## Defeating MAC Filtering

Typical APs permit access only to those stations with known MAC addresses. This is easily defeated by attackers who spoof their frames with a MAC address that is registered with the AP from among those collected by sniffing. That a MAC address is registered can be detected by observing the frames from the AP to the stations.

## Rogue AP

APs that are installed without proper authorization and verification that overall security policy is obeyed are called *rogue* APs. Valid users install and use them. Such APs are configured poorly, and attackers will find them.

## Trojan AP

An attacker sets up an AP so that the targeted station receives a stronger signal from it than it would receive from a legitimate AP. If WEP is enabled, the attacker would have already cracked it. A legitimate user selects the Trojan AP because of the stronger signal, then authenticates and associates. The Trojan AP is connected to a system that collects the IP traffic for later analyses. It then transmits all the frames to a legitimate AP so that the victim user does not recognize the ongoing man-in-the-middle attack. The attacker can steal the user's password and network access and compromise the user's system to gain root access. This attack is called the *evil-twin attack*.

It is easy to build a Trojan AP because an AP is a computer system optimized for its intended application. A general purpose PC with a wireless card can be turned into a capable AP. An example of such software is HostAP (http://hostap.epitest.fi). Such a Trojaned AP would be formidable.

## EQUIPMENT FLAWS

A search on the Security Focus Web site (http://www.securityfocus.com) with key words "access point vulnerabilities" will show that numerous flaws in equipment from well-known manufacturers are known. For example, one AP crashes when a frame is sent to it that has the spoofed source MAC address of itself. Another AP features an embedded TFTP (trivial file transfer protocol) server. By requesting a file named config.img via TFTP, an attacker receives the binary image of the AP configuration. The image includes the administrator's password required by the hypertext transfer protocol (http) user interface, the WEP encryption keys, MAC address, and SSID. Yet another AP returns the WEP keys, MAC filter list, and the administrator's password when sent a user datagram protocol (UDP) packet to port 27155 containing the string gstsearch.

It is not clear how these flaws were discovered. The following is a likely procedure: Most manufacturers design their equipment so that its firmware can be flashed to the field with a new and improved version. The firmware images are downloaded from the manufacturers' Web site. The central processing unit used in the APs can be easily recognized, and the firmware can be systematically disassembled, revealing the flaws at the assembly-language level. Comprehensive lists of such equipment flaws are likely circulating among the attackers.

## DENIAL OF SERVICE

A *denial of service* (DoS) attack occurs when a system is not providing services to authorized clients because of resource exhaustion by unauthorized clients. In wireless networks, DoS attacks are difficult to prevent; it is also difficult to stop an ongoing attack, and the victim and its clients may not even detect it. The duration of such DoS may range from milliseconds to hours. A DoS attack against an individual station enables session hijacking.

## Jamming the Air Waves

A number of consumer appliances such as microwave ovens, baby monitors, and cordless phones operate on the unregulated 2.4-GHz RF. An attacker can unleash large amounts of noise using these devices and jam the airwaves so that the signal-to-noise ratio drops so low, the wireless LAN ceases to function. The only solution to this is RF proofing the surrounding environment.

## Flooding with Associations

The AP inserts the data supplied by the station in the association request into a table called the *association table* that the AP maintains in its memory. IEEE 802.11 specifies a maximum value of 2,007 concurrent associations to an AP. The actual size of this table varies among AP models. When this table overflows, the AP refuses further clients. Having cracked WEP, an attacker authenticates several nonexisting stations using legitimate-looking but randomly generated MAC addresses. The attacker then sends a flood of spoofed associate requests so that the association table overflows. Enabling MAC filtering in the AP will prevent this attack.

## Forged Dissociation

The attacker sends a spoofed disassociation frame where the source MAC address is set to that of the AP. The station is still authenticated but needs only to reassociate and sends reassociation requests to the AP. The AP may send a reassociation response accepting the station and the station can then resume sending data. To prevent reassociation, the attacker continues to send disassociation frames for a desired period.

## Forged Deauthentication

The attacker monitors all raw frames collecting the source and destination MAC addresses to verify that they are among the targeted victims. When a data or an association response frame is observed, the attacker sends a spoofed deauthentication frame where the source MAC address is spoofed to that of the AP. The station is now unassociated and unauthenticated and needs to reconnect. To prevent a reconnection, the attacker continues to send deauthentication frames for a desired period. The attacker may even rate limit the deauthentication frames to avoid overloading an already congested network. The mischievous packets of disassociation and deauthentication are sent directly to the client, so that they will not be logged by the AP or IDS, and neither MAC filtering nor WEP protection will prevent it.

## Power Saving

Power conservation is important for typical station laptops, so they frequently enter an 802.11 state called Doze. An attacker can steal packets intended for a station while the station is in the Doze state.

The 802.11 protocol requires a station to inform the AP through a successful frame exchange that it wishes to enter the Doze state from the Active state. Periodically, the station awakens and sends a PS-Poll frame to the AP. In response, the AP will transmit the packets that were buffered for the station while it was dozing. Attackers can spoof the polling frame, causing the AP to send the collected packets and flush its internal buffers. Attackers can repeat these polling messages so that when the legitimate station periodically awakens and polls, the AP will inform that there are no pending packets.

# MAN-IN-THE-MIDDLE ATTACKS

The term *man-in-the-middle* (MITM) attack refers to the situation in which an attacker on Host X inserts X into all communications between Hosts B and C, and neither B nor C is aware of the presence of X. All messages B sends do reach C, but via X, and vice versa. The attacker can observe the communication or modify it before sending it out. An MITM attack can break connections that are otherwise secure. At the TCP level, secure socket shells (SSHs) and virtual private networks (VPNs), for example, are prone to this attack.

## Wireless MITM

Assume that Station B was authenticated with C, a legitimate AP. Attacker X is a laptop with two wireless cards. Through one card, he will present X as an AP. Attacker X sends deauthentication frames to B using the C's MAC address as the source and the BSSID he has collected. B gets deauthenticated and begins a scan for an AP and may find X on a channel different from C. There is a race condition between X and C. If B associates with X, the MITM attack succeeded. X will retransmit the frames it receives from B to C, and then the frames it receives from C to B after suitable modifications.

The package of tools called AirJack (see http://802.11ninja.net/airjack) includes a program called `mon-key_jack` that automates the MITM attack. This is programmed well so that the odds of it winning in the race condition just described are improved.

## ARP Poisoning

ARP cache poisoning is an old problem in wired networks. Wired networks have deployed mitigating techniques, but the ARP poisoning technique is reenabled in the presence of APs that are connected to a switch–hub along with other wired clients.

ARP is used to determine the MAC address of a device with a known IP address. The translation is performed with a table lookup. The ARP cache accumulates as the host continues to network. If the ARP cache does not have an entry for an IP address, the outgoing IP packet is queued, and an ARP request packet broadcasts essentially the following request: "If your IP address matches this target IP address, then please let me know what your Ethernet address is." The host with the target IP is expected to respond with an ARP reply, which contains the MAC address of the host. Once the table is updated because of having received this response, all the queued IP packets can be sent. The entries in the table expire after a set time to account for possible hardware address changes for the same IP address. This change may have happened, for example, because the network interface card was replaced.

Unfortunately, ARP does not provide for any verification that the responses are from valid hosts or that it is receiving a spurious response as if it had sent an ARP request. *ARP poisoning* is an attack technique exploiting this lack of verification. It corrupts the ARP cache that the OS maintains with wrong MAC addresses for some IP addresses. An attacker accomplishes this by sending an ARP reply packet that is deliberately constructed with a "wrong" MAC address. The ARP is a stateless protocol. Thus, a machine receiving an ARP reply cannot determine whether or not the response is due to a request it sent.

ARP poisoning is one of the techniques that enables the MITM attack. An attacker on Machine X inserts himself between two hosts B and C by (a) poisoning B so that C's IP address is associated with X's MAC address, (b) poisoning C so that B's address is associated with X's MAC address, and (c) relaying the packets X receives.

The ARP poison attack is applicable to all hosts in a subnet. Most APs act as transparent MAC layer bridges, and so all stations associated with it are vulnerable. If an AP is connected directly to a hub or a switch without an intervening router and firewall, all hosts connected to that hub or switch are also susceptible. Note that recent devices aimed at the home consumer market combine a network switch with maybe four or five ports, an AP, a router, and a digital subscriber line (DSL) or cable modem connecting to the Internet at large. Internally, the AP is connected to the switch. As a result, an attacker on a wireless station can become a MITM between two wired hosts, one wired and one wireless, or two wireless hosts. The tool called Ettercap (see http://ettercap.sourceforge.net) is capable of performing ARP poisoning.

## Session Hijacking

This section is based on the white paper by Fleck and Dimov (2001). *Session hijacking* occurs in the context of a "user," whether human or computer. The user has an ongoing connection with a server. Hijacking is said to occur when an attacker causes a user to lose its connection, and the attacker assumes its identity and privileges for a period of time.

An attacker temporarily disables the user's system, for example, by a DoS attack or a buffer overflow exploit. The attacker then takes the identity of the user. The attacker then has gained all the access that the user has. When the attacker is done, he stops the DoS attack and lets the user resume. The user may not detect the interruption if it lasts no more than a couple of seconds. Such hijacking can be achieved by using a forged disassociation DoS attack.

Corporate wireless networks are often set up so that the user is directed to an authentication server when his station attempts a connection with an AP. After the authentication, the attacker employs the session hijacking described earlier using spoofed MAC addresses.

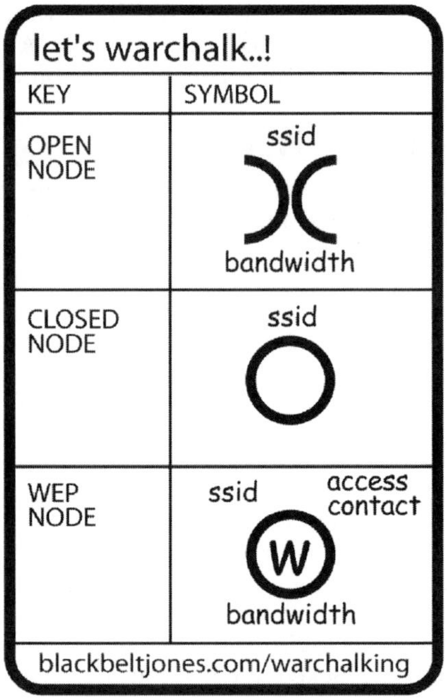

**Figure 3:** War chalking symbols.

## WAR DRIVING

Equipped with wireless devices and related tools, and driving around in a vehicle or parking at interesting places with a goal of discovering easy-to-get-into wireless networks, is known as war driving. War drivers (http://www.wardrive.net) define war driving as "The benign act of locating and logging wireless access points while in motion." This benign act is, of course, useful for attackers.

### War Chalking

War chalking is the practice of marking sidewalks and walls with special symbols to indicate that wireless access is nearby so that others do not need to go through the trouble of making the same discovery (Figure 3). A search on Google (http://www.google.com) with key words "war-driving maps" will produce a large number of hits. Yahoo! Maps can show "Wi-fi Hotspots" near an address you give.

### Typical Equipment

Typical war-driving equipment consists of a laptop computer system or a personal digital assistant (PDA) with a wireless card, a GPS, and a high-gain antenna (Figure 4). Typical choice of an operating system is Linux or FreeBSD where open-source sniffers (e.g., Kismet) and WEP crackers (e.g., AirSnort) are available. Similar tools (e.g., Net-Stumbler) that run on Windows are available.

War drivers need to be within the range of an AP or station located on the target network. The range depends on the transmit output power of the AP and the card and the gain of the antenna. Ordinary AP antennae transmit their signals in all directions. Often these signals reach beyond the physical boundaries of the intended work area, perhaps to adjacent buildings, floors, and parking lots. With the typical 30-mW wireless cards intended for laptops, the range is about 300 feet, but in 2004 there were wireless

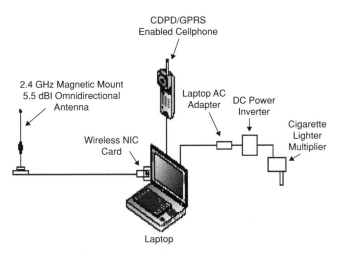

**Figure 4:** War drivers' equipment.

cards for laptops on the market that had 200-mW cards. Directional high-gain antennae and an RF amplifier can dramatically extend the range.

# WIRELESS SECURITY BEST PRACTICES

This section describes best practices in mitigating the problems described throughout the chapter.

## Location of APs

APs should be topologically located outside the perimeter firewalls. Wireless network segments should be treated with the same suspicion as is the public Internet. Additionally, it is important to use directional antennae and physically locate them in such a way that the radio-coverage volume is within the control of the corporation or home.

## Proper Configuration

Statistics collected by Worldwide Wardrive (http://www. worldwidewardrive.org) show that a distressingly large percentage of APs are left configured with the defaults. Before a wireless device is connected to the rest of the existing network, proper configuration of the wireless device is necessary. The APs come with a default SSID, such as "Default SSID," "WLAN," "Wireless," "Compaq," "intel," and "linksys." The default passwords for the administrator accounts that configure the AP via a web browser or SNMP are well known for all manufacturers. A proper configuration should change these to difficult-to-predict values.

Note that the SSID serves as a simple handle, not as a password, for a wireless network. Unless the default SSID on the AP and stations is changed, SSID broadcasts are disabled, MAC address-filtering is enabled, the WEP is enabled, and an attacker can use the wireless LAN resources without even sniffing.

The configuration via Web browsing (HTTP) is provided by a simplistic Web server built into an AP. Often this configuration interface is provided via both wired connections and wireless connections. The Web server embedded in a typical AP does not contain secure HTTP, so the

password that the administrator submits to the AP can be sniffed. Web-based configuration via wireless connections should be disabled.

WEP is disabled in some organizations because this allows higher throughput. Enabling WEP encryption makes it necessary for the attacker intending to WEP crack to sniff a large number of frames. The higher the number of bits in the encryption, the larger the number of frames that must be collected. The physical presence in the radio range of the equipment for long periods increases the odds of his equipment being detected. WEP should be enabled.

The IEEE 802.11 does not describe an automated way to distribute the shared-secret keys. In large installations, manual distribution of keys each time they are changed is expensive. Nevertheless, the WEP encryption keys should be changed periodically.

## Secure Protocols

If WEP is disabled or after it is cracked, an attacker can capture all TCP/IP packets by radio-silent sniffing for later analyses. All wired-network attacks are possible. There are real-time tools that analyze and interpret the TCP/IP data as they arrive. All protocols that send passwords and data in the clear must be avoided. This includes the rlogin family, telnet, and POP3. Instead, one should use SSH and VPN. In general, when a wireless segment is involved, one should use end-to-end encryption at the application level in addition to enabling WEP.

## Wireless IDS

A wireless intrusion detection system (WIDS) is often a self-contained computer system with specialized hardware and software to detect anomalous behavior. The underlying software techniques are the same hacking techniques described earlier. The special wireless hardware is more capable than the commodity wireless card of various actions, including implementation of the RF monitor mode, detection of interference, and keeping track of signal-to-noise ratios. It also includes GPS equipment so that rogue clients and APs can be located. A WIDS includes one or more listening devices that collect MAC addresses, SSIDs, features enabled on the stations, transmit speeds, current channel, encryption status, beacon interval, and so on. Its computing engine is powerful enough to dissect frames and WEP decrypt into IP and TCP components. These can be fed into TCP/IP-related intrusion detection systems.

Unknown MAC addresses are detected by maintaining a registry of MAC addresses of known stations and APs. Frequently, a WIDS can detect spoofed known MAC addresses because the attacker could not control the firmware of the wireless card to insert the appropriate sequence numbers into the frame.

## Wireless Auditing

Periodically, every wireless network should be audited. Several audit firms provide this service for a fee. A security audit begins with a well-established security policy. A policy for wireless networks should include a description of the geographic volume of coverage. The main goal of an audit is to verify that there are no violations of the policy. To this end, the typical auditor employs the tools and techniques of an attacker.

## Newer Standards and Protocols

Many improvements in wireless network technology have been proposed through proprietary channels (e.g., Cisco lightweight extensible authentication protocol) as well as through the IEEE. The new IEEE 802.11i (ratified in June 2004) enhances the current 802.11 standard to provide improvements in security. These include port-based access control for authentication, temporal key integrity protocol for dynamic changing of encryption keys, and wireless robust authentication protocol. An interim solution proposed by vendors is the Wi-Fi protected access (WPA), a subset of 802.11i, which is now available in some products. Time will tell whether these can withstand future attacks.

## Software Tools

This section describes a collection of cost-free tools that can be used both as attack tools and as audit tools.

- AirJack (http://802.11ninja.net/airjack) is a collection of wireless card drivers and related programs. It includes a program called monkey_jack that automates the MITM attack. Wlan_jack is a DoS tool that accepts a target source and BSSID to send continuous deauthenticate frames to a single client or an entire network (broadcast address). Essid_jack sends a disassociate frame to a target client in order to force the client to reassociate with the network, thereby giving up the network SSID.
- AirSnort (http://www.airsnort.shmoo.com) can break WEP by passively monitoring transmissions and computing the encryption key when enough packets have been gathered.
- Ethereal (http://www.ethereal.com) is a LAN analyzer, including wireless LAN. One can interactively browse the capture data, viewing summary and detail information for all observed wireless traffic.
- FakeAP (http://www.blackalchemy.to/project/fakeap) can generate thousands of counterfeit 802.11b APs.
- HostAP (http://www.hostap.epitest.fi) converts a station that is based on Intersil's Prism2/2.5/3 chipset to function as an AP.
- Kismet (http://www.kismetwireless.net) is a wireless sniffer and monitor. It passively monitors wireless traffic and dissects frames to identify SSIDs, MAC addresses, channels, and connection speeds.
- Netstumbler (http://www.netstumbler.com) is a wireless AP identifier running on Windows. It listens for SSIDs and sends beacons as probes searching for access points.
- Prismstumbler (http://prismstumbler.sourceforge.net) can find wireless networks. It constantly switches channels and monitors frames received.
- The Hacker's Choice organization (http://www.thc.org) has LEAP Cracker Tool suite that contains tools to break

Cisco LEAP. It also has tools for spoofing authentication challenge packets from an AP. The WarDrive is a tool for mapping a city for wireless networks with a GPS device.
- StumbVerter (http://www.sonar-security.com/sv.html) is a tool that reads NetStumbler's collected data files and presents street maps showing the logged WAPs as icons, the color and shape of which indicate WEP mode and signal strength.
- Wellenreiter (http://www.wellenreiter.net) is a WLAN discovery tool. It uses brute force to identify low-traffic APs while hiding the real MAC address of the card it uses. It is integrated with GPS.
- WEPcrack (http://www.wepcrack.sourceforge.net) cracks 802.11 WEP encryption keys using weaknesses of RC4 key scheduling.

## CONCLUSION

This chapter is an introduction to the techniques attackers use on wireless networks. Regardless of the protocols, wireless networks remain potentially insecure because an attacker can listen in without gaining physical access. In addition, the protocol designs were security-naïve. The chapter has described several existing tools that implement attack techniques to exploit the weaknesses in the protocol designs. The integration of wireless networks into existing networks has also been done carelessly. Finally, the chapter concluded with several best practices that can mitigate the insecurities.

## GLOSSARY

**Access Point (AP)**   Any entity that has station functionality and provides access to the distribution services, via the wireless medium for associated stations.

**Association Table**   The association table is within an AP and controls the routing of all packets between the AP and the wireless devices in a WLAN.

**Basic Service Set (BSS)**   A collection, or set, of stations that are logically associated with each other and controlled by a single AP. Together, they operate as a fully connected wireless network.

**Basic Service Set Identifier (BSSID)**   A 48-bit identifier used by all stations in a basic service set as part of the frame header.

**Beacon**   A wireless LAN frame broadcast by APs that signals their availability.

**Evil-Twin Attack**   An evil twin is an unauthorized AP, the goal of which is to masquerade as an existing legitimate or authorized AP. The evil twin AP is designed and located so that client stations receive stronger signals from it. Legitimate users are lured into the evil twin and unknowingly give away user IDs and passwords.

**Independent BSS**   (IBSS) Usually an ad hoc network; in an IBSS, all of the stations are responsible for sending beacons.

**Service Set Identifier (SSID)**   An identifier that is up to 32-bytes long. All APs and stations within the same wireless network use the same SSID.

**Social Engineering**   Coined in jest, this term refers to all nontechnical methods of collecting information about a person so that the passwords the person may choose can be predicted. The methods of collection range from dumpster diving, analyzing publicly available information, to making phone calls impersonating others.

**Wired Equivalent Privacy (WEP)** A shared-secret key encryption system used to encrypt packets transmitted between a station and an AP.

## CROSS REFERENCES

See *Computer Viruses and Worms; Denial of Service Attacks; Hackers, Crackers, and Computer Criminals Hacking Techniques in Wireless Networks; Trojan Horse Programs; WEP Security.*

## REFERENCES

Fleck B., & Dimov, J. (2001, October). Wireless access points and ARP poisoning: Wireless vulnerabilities that expose the wired network. Retrieved January 20, 2004, from http://www.cigitallabs.com/resources/papers/download/arppoison.pdf

Mateti, P. (2003). TCP/IP suite. In H. Bidgoli (Ed.), *The Internet encyclopedia.* New York: John Wiley.

## FURTHER READING

Bellardo, J., & Savage, S. (2003). 802.11 denial-of-service attacks: Real vulnerabilities and practical solutions. Proceedings of Usenix 2003. Retrieved January 20, 2004, from http://www.cs.ucsd.edu/users/savage/papers/ UsenixSec03.pdf

Edney J., & Arbaugh, W. A. (2003). *Real 802.11 security: Wi-Fi protected access and 802.11i.* Reading, MA: Addison Wesley.

Farshchi, J. (2003, November 5). Wireless intrusion detection systems. Retrieved January 20, 2004, from http://www.securityfocus.com/infocus/1742

Flickenger, R. (2003). *Wireless hacks: 100 industrial-strength tips & tools.* Sebastopol, CA: O'Reilly & Associates.

Gast, M. S. (2002). *802.11 wireless networks: The definitive guide.* Sebastopol, CA: O'Reilly & Associates.

Gupta, V., Krishnamurthy, S., & Faloutsos, M. (2002, October). Denial of service attacks at the MAC layer in wireless ad hoc networks. Proceedings of 2002 MILCOM Conference, Anaheim, CA.

Hurley, C., Puchol, M., Rogers, R., & Thornton, F. (2004). *WarDriving: Drive, detect, defend, a guide to wireless security.* Syngress.

Institute of Electrical and Electronics Engineers. (n.d.). *IEEE 802.11 standards documents.* Retrieved January 20, 2004, from http://standards.ieee.org/wireless/

Karygiannis, T., & Owens, L. (2002, November). Wireless network security: 802.11, Bluetooth and handheld devices (National Institute of Standards and Technology Special Publication 800-48). Retrieved January 20, 2004, from http://cs-www.ncsl.nist.gov/publications/nistpubs/800-48/NIST_SP_800-48.pdf

Moskowitz, R. (n.d.). Debunking the myth of SSID hiding. Retrieved on March 10, 2004, from http://www.icsalabs.com/html/communities/WLAN/wp_ssid_hiding.pdf

Potter, B., & Fleck, B. (2002). *802.11 security.* Sebastopol, CA: O'Reilly & Associates.

Stallings, W. (2001). *Wireless communications & networks.* Prentice Hall.

War-chalking. (n.d.). Retrieved on January 20, 2004, from http://www.warchalking.org

Wright, J. (n.d.). Detecting wireless LAN MAC address spoofing. Retrieved on January 20, 2004, from http://home.jwu.edu/jwright/

Stallings's (2001) book is a broad introduction to wireless communications including electrical signal theory, TCP/IP suite, IEEE 802.11, and Bluetooth. Gast's (2002) book is devoted to 802.11. The report by Karygiannis and Owens (2002) is a gentle introduction to wireless security. Potter and Fleck's (2002) book is about network security in general (in spite of its title) and covers several Unix-like OS. The book by Edney and Arbaugh (2003) is an advanced technical book aimed at wireless-networking professionals and covers 802.11i and WPA.

The Wireless LAN Security (802.11)/Wardriving and Warchalking Web site (http://802.11-security.com) is a rich collection of links. A Wikipedia page (http://en.wikipedia.org/wiki/IEEE_802.11) shows promise of becoming a living free encyclopedia on wireless networks.

The research paper by Bellardo and Savage (2003) provides an experimental analysis of denial of service attacks at the wireless MAC level. This paper also describes a method of transmitting arbitrary frames even while the wireless card firmware attempts to sanitize the frame content. The article by Farshchi (2003) is a nontechnical overview of the capabilities of wireless intrusion detection systems. The book by Hurley, Puchol, Rogers, and Thornton (2004) is about war driving.

# Computer Viruses and Worms

Robert Slade, *Vancouver Institute for Research into User Security, Canada*

## INTRODUCTION

Computer viruses are unique among the many security problems in that the fact that someone else is infected increases the risk to you. However, viruses also seem to be surrounded by myths and misunderstandings. It is hoped this chapter will help to set the record straight.

## History of Computer Viruses and Worms

Many claims have been made for the existence of viruses prior to the 1980s, but, so far, these claims have not been accompanied by proof. The Core Wars programming contests did involve self-replicating code, but usually within a structured and artificial environment.

The general perception of computer viruses, even among security professionals, has concentrated on their existence in personal computers (PCs) and particularly Wintel-type systems. This is despite the fact that Fred Cohen's seminal academic work took place on mainframe and minicomputers in the mid-1980s. The first e-mail virus was spread in 1987. The first virus hoax message (then termed a *metavirus)* was proposed in 1988. Even so, virus and malicious software (malware) research has been neglected, possibly because malware does not fit easily into the traditional access control security models.

There is some evidence that the first viruses were created during the 1980s. At least two Apple II viruses are known to have been created in the early 1980s. However, it was not until the end of the decade (and 1987 in particular) that knowledge of real viruses became widespread, even among security experts. For many years boot sector infectors and file infectors were the only types of common viruses. These programs spread relatively slowly, were primarily distributed on floppy disks, and were thus slow to disseminate geographically. However, these viruses tended to be very long lived.

During the early 1990s, virus writers started experimenting with various functions intended to defeat detection. (Some forms had seen limited trials earlier.) Among these were polymorphism, to change form in order to defeat scanners, and stealth, to attempt to confound any type of detection. None of these virus technologies had a significant impact. Most viruses using these so-called advanced technologies were easier to detect because of a necessary increase in program size.

Although demonstration programs had been created earlier, the mid-1990s saw the introduction of macro and script viruses in the wild. These were initially confined to word processing files, particularly files associated with the Microsoft Office suite. However, the inclusion of programming capabilities eventually led to script viruses in many objects that would normally be considered to contain data only, such as Excel spreadsheets, PowerPoint presentation files, and e-mail messages. This fact led to greatly increased demands for computer resources among antiviral systems, because many more objects had to be tested, and Windows OLE (Object Linking and Embedding) format data files presented substantial complexity to scanners. Macro viruses also increase new variant forms very quickly, because the virus carries its own source code and anyone who obtains a copy can generally modify it and create a new member of the virus family.

E-mail viruses became the major new form in the late 1990s and early 2000s. These viruses may use macro capabilities, scripting, or executable attachments to create e-mail messages or attachments sent out to e-mail addresses harvested from the infected machine. E-mail viruses spread with extreme rapidity, distributing themselves worldwide in a matter of hours. Some versions create so many copies of themselves that corporate and even service provider mail servers are flooded and cease to function. E-mail viruses are very visible and so tend to be identified within a short space of time, but many are macros or scripts, and so generate many variants.

With the strong integration of the Microsoft Windows operating system with its Internet Explorer browser, Outlook mailer, Office suite, and system scripting, recent viruses have started to blur the normal distinctions. A document sent as an e-mail file attachment can make a call to a Web site that starts active content that installs a remote access tool acting as a portal for the client portion of a distributed denial of service network. Indeed, not only are viruses starting to show characteristics that are similar to each other, but functions from completely different types of malware are beginning to be found together in the same programs, leading to a type of malware convergence.

Recently, many security specialists have stated that the virus threat is reducing because, despite the total number of virus infections being seen, the prevalent viruses are now almost universally e-mail viruses and therefore constitute a single threat with a single fix. This ignores the fact that, although almost all major viruses now use e-mail as a distribution and reproduction mechanism, there are a great many variations in the way e-mail is used. For example, many viruses use Microsoft's Outlook mailer to spread and reproduction can be prevented simply by removing Outlook from the system. However, other viruses may make direct calls to the Mail Application Programming Interface (MAPI), which is used by a number of mail user programs, whereas others carry the code for mail server functions within their own body. A number of e-mail viruses distribute themselves to e-mail addresses found in the Microsoft Outlook address book files, whereas others may harvest addresses from anywhere on the computer hard drive or may actually take control of the Internet network connection and collect contact data from any source viewed online.

Because the work has had to deal with detailed analysis of low-level code, virus research has led to significant advances in the field of forensic programming. However, to date computer forensic work has concentrated on file recovery and decryption, so the contributions in this area likely still lie in the future.

Many computer pundits, as well as some security experts, have proposed that computer viruses are a result of the fact that currently popular desktop operating systems have only nominal security provisions. They further suggest that viruses will disappear as security functions are added to operating systems. This thesis ignores the fact, well established by Cohen's research and subsequently confirmed, that viruses use the most basic of computer functions and that a perfect defense against viruses is impossible. This is not to say that an increase in security measures by operating system vendors could not reduce the risk of viruses: the current danger could be drastically reduced with relatively minor modifications to system functions.

It is going too far to say (as some have) that the very existence of viral programs, and the fact that both viral strains and the numbers of individual infections are growing, means that computers are finished. At the present time, the general public is not well informed about the virus threat, and so more copies of viral programs are being produced than are being destroyed.

Indeed, no less an authority than Fred Cohen has championed the idea that viral programs can be used to great effect. An application using a viral form can improve performance in the same way that computer hardware benefits from parallel processors. It is, however, unlikely that viral programs can operate effectively and usefully in the current computer environment without substantial protective measures being built into them. A number of virus and worm programs have been written with the obvious intent of proving that viruses could carry a useful payload, and some have even had a payload that could be said to enhance security. Unfortunately, all such viruses have created serious problems themselves.

## Virus Definition

A computer virus is a program written with functions and intent to copy and disperse itself without the knowledge and cooperation of the owner or user of the computer. A final definition has not yet been agreed upon by all researchers. A common definition is, "a program which modifies other programs to contain a possibly altered version of itself." This definition is generally attributed to Fred Cohen from his seminal research in the mid-1980s, although Cohen's actual definition is in mathematical form. Another possible definition is an entity that uses the resources of the host (system or computer) to reproduce itself and spread, without informed operator action.

Cohen is generally held to have defined the term *computer virus* in his thesis (published in 1984). (The suggestion for the use of the term virus is credited to Len Adleman, his seminar advisor.) However, his original definition covers only those sections of code that, when active, attach themselves to other programs. This, however, neglects many of the programs that have been most successful "in the wild." Many researchers still insist on Cohen's definition and use other terms such as *worm* and *bacterium* for those viral programs that do not attack programs. Currently, viruses are generally held to attach themselves to some object, although the object may be a program, disk, document, e-mail message, computer system, or other information entity.

Computer viral programs are not a natural occurrence. Viruses are programs written by programmers. They do not just appear through some kind of electronic evolution. Viral programs are written, deliberately, by people. However, the definition of *program* may include many items not normally thought of in terms of programming, such as disk boot sectors and Microsoft Office documents or data files that also contain macro programming.

Many people have the impression that anything that goes wrong with a computer is caused by a virus. From hardware failures to errors in use, everything is blamed on a virus. A virus is not just any damaging condition. Similarly, it is now popularly believed that any program that may do damage to your data or your access to computing resources is a virus. Viral programs are not simply programs that do damage. Indeed, viral programs are not always damaging, at least not in the sense of being deliberately designed to erase data or disrupt operations. Most viral programs seem to have been designed to be a kind of electronic graffiti: intended to make the writer's mark in the world, if not his or her name. In some cases a name is displayed, on occasion an address, phone number, company name, or political party.

## Is My Computer Infected? What Should I Do?

Many books and articles contain lists of symptoms to watch for to determine whether your computer is infected. These signs include things such as running out of memory space, running out of disk space, the computer operating slower than normal, files changing size, and so forth. In fact, many factors will create these same effects, and current viruses seldom do. The best way to determine whether you have been infected by a virus is to get and use an antiviral scanner. In fact, get more than one. With the rapid generation of new viruses these days, it is quite possible for a maker of antivirus software to make mistakes in updating signatures. Therefore, having a second check on a suspected virus is always a good idea.

One scanner for the Wintel platform is F-PROT. It is available in a DOS version, free of charge from www.f-secure.com. (Look under Downloads and Tools.) Although a DOS scanner has some limitations in a Windows environment (particularly with a New Technology File System [NTFS] under Windows XP), it will still be able to identify infected files and is quite good at picking out virus infections within e-mail system files (the files of messages held on your computer).

Another scanner available for free is AVG, from www.grisoft.com. This one also does a good job of scanning and will even update itself automatically (although that feature is problematic on some machines).

The various commercial antiviral producers generally produce trial versions of their software, usually limited in some way. Sophos and Avast have been very good in this regard.

In regard to the suggestion to use more than one scanner, it should be noted that a number of successful software publishers have included functions that conflict with software from other vendors. These products should be avoided, because of the previously noted possibility of failure in a single protection program. The use of free software, and purchase of software from companies that provide such free versions, is recommended, because the existence of these free scanners, and their use by other people, actually reduces your risk, because there will be fewer instances of viruses reproducing and trying to spread.

Readers may be surprised at the recommendation to use free software: there is a general assumption that commercial software must be superior to that provided free of charge. It should be noted that the author of this chapter is a specialist in the evaluation of security and, particularly, antiviral software and has published more reviews of antiviral software than any other individual. The reader can be assured that it can be proven that, in the case of antiviral software, free software is as effective, and in some cases superior to, many very expensive products.

## TROJAN HORSES, VIRUSES, WORMS, RATs, AND OTHER BEASTS

Malware is a relatively new term in the security field. It was created to address the need to discuss software or programs that are intentionally designed to include functions for penetrating a system, breaking security policies, or carrying malicious or damaging payloads. Because this type of software has started to develop a bewildering variety of forms, such as backdoors, data diddlers, distributed denial of service (DDoS), hoax warnings, logic bombs, pranks, remote access Trojans (RATs), Trojans, viruses, worms, and zombies, the term malware has come to be used for the collective class of malicious software. The term is, however, often used very loosely simply as a synonym for virus, in the same way that virus is often used simply as a description of any type of computer problem. This chapter will attempt to define the virus and worm problem more accurately, and to do this we need to describe the various other types of malware.

Viruses are the largest class of malware, both in terms of numbers of known entities and in impact in the current computing environment. Viruses, therefore, tend to be synonymous, in the public mind, with all forms of malware.

Programming bugs or errors are generally not included in the definition of malware, although it is sometimes difficult to make a hard and fast distinction between malware and bugs. For example, if a programmer left a buffer overflow in a system and it creates a loophole that can be used as a backdoor or a maintenance hook, did he or she do it deliberately? This question cannot be answered technically, although we might be able to guess at it, given the relative ease of use of a given vulnerability.

In addition, it should be noted that malware is not just a collection of utilities for the attacker. Once launched, malware can continue an attack without reference to the author or user and in some cases will expand the attack to other systems. There is a qualitative difference between malware and the attack tools, kits, or scripts that have to operate under an attacker's control and that are not considered to fall within the definition of malware. There are gray areas in this aspect as well, since RATs and DDoS zombies provide unattended access to systems, but need to be commanded to deliver a payload.

### Trojans

Trojans, or Trojan horse programs, are the largest class of malware in terms of numbers of different entities produced. However, the term is subject to much confusion, particularly in relation to computer viruses.

A Trojan is a program that pretends to do one thing while performing another, unwanted action. The extent of the pretense may vary greatly. Many of the early PC Trojans relied merely on the filename and a description on a bulletin board. Login Trojans, popular among university student mainframe users, mimicked the screen display and the prompts of the normal login program and could, in fact, pass the username and password along to the valid login program at the same time as they stole the user data. Some Trojans may contain actual code that does what it is supposed to be doing while performing additional nasty acts that it does not tell you about.

An additional confusion with viruses involves Trojan horse programs that may be spread by e-mail. In years past, a Trojan program had to be posted on an electronic bulletin board system or a file archive site. Because of the static posting, a malicious program would soon be identified and eliminated. More recently, Trojan programs have been distributed by mass e-mail campaigns, by posting on Usenet newsgroup discussion groups, or through automated distribution agents (bots) on Internet relay chat (IRC) channels. Because source identification in these communications channels can be easily hidden, Trojan programs can be redistributed in a number of disguises, and specific identification of a malicious program has become much more difficult.

Some data security writers consider that a virus is simply a specific example of the class of Trojan horse programs. There is some validity to this usage because a virus is an unknown quantity that is hidden and transmitted along with a legitimate disk or program, and any program can be turned into a Trojan by infecting it with a virus. However, the term *virus* more properly refers to the added, infectious code rather than the virus/target combination. Therefore, the term *Trojan* refers to a deliberately misleading or modified program that does not reproduce itself.

A major aspect of Trojan design is the social engineering (fraudulent or deceptive) component. Trojan programs are advertised (in some sense) as having a positive component. The term *positive* can be in dispute, because a great many Trojans promise pornography or access to pornography, and this still seems to be depressingly effective. However, other promises can be made as well. A recent e-mail virus, in generating its messages, carried a list of a huge variety of subject lines, promising pornography, humor, virus information, an antivirus program, and information about abuse of the recipient's e-mail account. Sometimes the message is simply vague, and relies on curiosity.

Social engineering really is nothing more than a fancy name for the type of fraud and confidence games that have existed since snakes started selling apples. Security types tend to prefer a more academic sounding definition, such as the use of nontechnical means to circumvent security policies and procedures. Social engineering can range from simple lying (such as a false description of the function of a file), to bullying and intimidation (to pressure a low-level employee into disclosing information), to association with a trusted source (such as the user name from an infected machine).

## Worms

A worm reproduces and spreads, like a virus and unlike other forms of malware. Worms are distinct from viruses, though they may have similar results. Most simply, a worm may be thought of as a virus with the capacity to propagate independently of user action. In other words, they do not rely on (usually) human-initiated transfer of data between systems for propagation, but instead spread across networks of their own accord, primarily by exploiting known vulnerabilities in common software.

Originally, the distinction was made that worms used networks and communications links to spread and that a worm, unlike a virus, did not directly attach to an executable file. In early research into computer viruses, the terms *worm* and *virus* tended to be used synonymously, it being felt that the technical distinction was unimportant to most users. The technical origin of the term *worm program* matched that of modern distributed processing experiments: a program with segments working on different computers, all communicating over a network (Shoch & Hupp, 1982).

The first worm to garner significant attention was the Internet Worm of 1988, discussed in detail later in this chapter. Recently, many of the most prolific virus infections have not been strictly viruses, but have used a combination of viral and worm techniques to spread more rapidly and effectively. LoveLetter was an example of this convergence of reproductive technologies. Although infected e-mail attachments were perhaps the most widely publicized vector of infection, LoveLetter also spread by actively scanning attached network drives, infecting a variety of common file types. This convergence of technologies will be an increasing problem in the future. Code Red and a number of Linux programs (such as Lion) are modern examples of worms. (Nimda is an example of a worm, but it also spreads in a number of other ways, so it could be considered to be an e-mail virus and multipartite as well.)

## Viruses

A virus is defined by its ability to reproduce and spread. A virus is not just anything that goes wrong with a computer, and virus is not simply another name for malware. Trojan horse programs and logic bombs do not reproduce themselves.

A worm, which is sometimes seen as a specialized type of virus, is currently distinguished from a virus because a virus generally requires an action on the part of the user to trigger or aid reproduction and spread. The action on the part of the user is generally a common function, and the user generally does not realize the danger of the action or the fact that he or she is assisting the virus.

The only requirement that defines a program as a virus is that it reproduces. There is no necessity that the virus carries a payload, although a number of viruses do. In many cases (in most cases of "successful" viruses), the payload is limited to some kind of message.

A deliberately damaging payload, such as erasure of the disk or system files, usually restricts the ability of the virus to spread because the virus uses the resources of the host system. In some cases, a virus may carry a logic bomb or time bomb that triggers a damaging payload on a certain date or under a specific, often delayed, condition.

Because a virus spreads and uses the resources of the host, it affords a kind of power to software that parallel processors provide to hardware. Therefore, some have theorized that viral programs could be used for beneficial purposes, similar to the experiments in distributed processing that are testing the limits of cryptographic strength. (Various types of network management functions, and updating of system software, are seen as candidates.) However, the fact that viruses change systems and applications is seen as problematic in its own right. Many viruses that carry no overtly damaging payload still create problems with systems. A number of virus and worm programs have been written with the obvious intent of proving that viruses could carry a useful payload and some have even had a payload that could be said to enhance security. Unfortunately, all such viruses have created serious problems themselves. The difficulties of controlling viral programs have been addressed in theory, but the solutions are also known to have faults and loopholes.

## Logic Bombs

Logic bombs are software modules set up to run in a quiescent state, but to monitor for a specific condition, or set of conditions, and to activate their payload under those conditions. A logic bomb is generally implanted in or coded as part of an application under development or maintenance. Unlike a RAT or Trojan, it is difficult to implant a logic bomb after the fact. There are numerous examples of this type of activity, usually based upon actions taken by a programmer to deprive a company of needed resources if employment was terminated.

A Trojan or a virus may contain a logic bomb as part of the payload. A logic bomb involves no reproduction and no social engineering.

A persistent legend in regard to logic bombs involves what is known as the salami scam. According to the story, this involves the siphoning off of small amounts of money (in some versions, fractions of a cent) credited to the account of the programmer, over a very large number of transactions. Despite the fact that these stories appear in a number of computer security texts, the author has a standing challenge to anyone to come up with a documented case of such a scam. Over a period of 8 years, the closest anyone has come is a story about a fast food clerk who diddled the display on a drive-through window and collected an extra dime or quarter from most customers.

## Other Related Terms

Hoax virus warnings or alerts have an odd double relation to viruses. First, hoaxes are usually warnings about new viruses: new viruses that do not, of course, exist. Second, hoaxes generally carry a directive to the user to forward the warning to all addresses available to them. Thus, these descendants of chain letters form a kind of self-perpetuating spam.

Hoaxes use an odd kind of social engineering, relying on people's naturally gregarious nature and desire to communicate, and on a sense of urgency and importance, using the ambition that people have to be the first to provide important new information.

Hoaxes do, however, have common characteristics that can be used to determine whether their warnings may be valid:

- Hoaxes generally ask the reader to forward the message
- Hoaxes make reference to false authorities such as Microsoft, AOL, IBM, and the FCC (none of which issue virus alerts) or to completely false entities

- Hoaxes do not give specific information about the individual or office responsible for analyzing the virus or issuing the alert
- Hoaxes generally state that the new virus is unknown to authorities or researchers
- Hoaxes often state that there is no means of detecting or removing the virus.
- Many of the original hoax warnings stated only that you should not open a message with a certain phrase in the subject line. (The warning, of course, usually contained that phrase in the subject line. Subject-line filtering is known to be a very poor method of detecting malware.)
- Hoaxes often state that the virus does tremendous damage and is incredibly virulent
- Hoax warnings very often contain A LOT OF CAPITAL LETTER SHOUTING AND EXCLAMATION MARKS!!!!!!!!!!
- Hoaxes often contain technical-sounding nonsense (technobabble), such as references to nonexistent technologies such as nth complexity binary loops

It is wisest, in the current environment, to doubt all virus warnings, unless they come from a known and historically accurate source, such as a vendor with a proven record of providing reliable and accurate virus alert information or preferably an independent researcher or group. It is best to check *any* warnings received against known virus encyclopedia sites. It is also best to check more than one such site: in the initial phases of a fast burner attack, some sites may not have had time to analyze samples to their own satisfaction, and the better sites will not post information they are not sure about. A detailed treatment of hoax warning viruses is found in another chapter in this *Handbook*.

RATs are programs designed to be installed, usually remotely, after systems are installed and working (and not in development, as is the case with logic bombs and backdoors). Their authors would generally like to have the programs referred to as remote administration tools to convey a sense of legitimacy.

When a RAT program has been run on a computer, it will install itself in such a way as to be active every time the computer is started subsequent to the installation. Information is sent back to the controlling computer (sometimes via an anonymous channel such as IRC) noting that the system is active. The user of the command computer is now able to explore the target, escalate access to other resources, and install other software, such as DDoS zombies, if so desired.

DDoS is a modified denial of service (DoS) attack. DoS attacks do not attempt to destroy or corrupt data, but attempt to use up a computing resource to the point at which normal work cannot proceed. The structure of a DDoS attack requires a master computer to control the attack, a target of the attack, and a number of computers in the middle that the master computer uses to generate the attack. These computers between the master and the target are variously called agents or clients, but are usually referred to as running zombie programs. The existence of a large number of agent computers in a DDoS attack acts to multiply the effect of the attack and also helps to hide the identity of the originator of the attack.

There is a lot of controversy over a number of technologies generally described as adware or spyware. Most people would agree that the marketing functions are not specifically malicious, but what one person sees as aggressive selling another will see as an intrusion or invasion of privacy.

Shareware or freeware programs may have advertising for a commercial version or a related product, and users may be asked to provide some personal information for registration or to download the product. For example, an unregistered copy of the WinZip archiving program typically asks the user to register when the program is started, and the free version of the QuickTime video player asks the user to buy the commercial version every time the software is invoked. Adware, however, is generally a separate program installed at the same time as a given utility or package and continues to advertise products, even when the desired program is not running. Spyware is, again, a system distinct from the software the user installed and passes more information than simply a user name and address back to the vendor: often these packages will report on Web sites visited or other software installed on the computer and possibly compile detailed inventories of the interests and activities of a user.

The discussion of spyware often makes reference to cookies or Web bugs. Cookies are small pieces of information in regard to persistent transactions between the user and a Web site, but the information can be greater than the user realizes, for example in the case of a company that provides content, such as banner ads, to a large number of sites. Cookies, limited to text data, are not malware and can have no executable malicious content. Web bugs are links on a Web page or embedded in e-mail messages that contain links to different Web sites. A Web bug therefore passes a call, and information, unknown to the user, to a remote site. Most commonly a Web bug is either invisible or unnoticeable (typically it is 1 pixel in size) to avoid alerting the user to its presence.

There is a persistent chain letter hoax that tells people to forward the message because it is part of a test of an e-mail tracking system. Although all such chain letter reports to date are false, such a system has been implemented and does use Web bug technology. The system is not reliable: Web bugs in e-mail rely on an e-mail system calling a Web browser function, and although this typically happens automatically with systems such as Microsoft's Outlook and Internet Explorer, a mailer such as Pegasus requires the function call to be established by the user and warns the user when it is being invoked. On susceptible systems, however, a good deal of information can be obtained: the mail system noted can frequently obtain the Internet protocol (IP) address of the user, the type and version of browser being used, the operating system of the computer, and the time the message was read.

Pranks are very much a part of the computer culture, so much so that you can now buy commercially produced joke packages that allow you to perform "Stupid Mac (or PC or Windows) Tricks." There are numberless pranks available as shareware. Some make the computer appear to insult the user; some use sound effects or voices; some use special visual effects. A fairly common thread running through most pranks is that the computer is, in some way, nonfunctional. Many pretend to have detected some kind of fault in the computer (and some pretend to rectify such faults, of course making things worse). One entry in the virus field is PARASCAN, the paranoid scanner. It pretends to find large numbers of infected files, although it does not actually check for any infections.

Generally speaking, pranks that create some kind of announcement are not malware: viruses that generate a screen or audio display are actually quite rare. The distinction between jokes and Trojans is harder to make, but pranks are intended for amusement. Joke programs may, of course, result in a denial of service if people find the prank message frightening.

One specific type of joke is the easter egg, a function hidden in a program and generally accessible only by some arcane sequence of commands. These may be seen as harmless, but note that they do consume resources, even if only disk space and also make the task of ensuring program integrity much more difficult.

## FIRST GENERATION VIRUSES

Many of the books and articles that are currently available to explain about viruses were written based on the research that was done on the first generation of viruses. Although these programs are still of interest to those who study the internal structures of operating systems, they operated much differently than the current crop of malicious software. First generation viruses tended to spread very slowly, but to hang around in the environment for a long time. Later viruses tended to spread very rapidly, but also to die out relatively quickly.

### Boot Sector Viruses

Viruses are generally partly classified by the objects to which they attach. Worms may be seen as a type of virus that attaches to nothing.

Most desktop computer operating systems have some form of boot sector, a specific location on the disk that contains programming to bootstrap the startup of a computer. Boot-sector infectors (BSIs) replace or redirect this programming to have the virus invoked, usually as the first programming running on the computer. Because the minimal built-in programming of the computer simply starts to read and execute material from a specific location on the disk, any code that occupies this location is run. BSIs copy themselves onto this location whenever they encounter any new disk.

Boot-sector infectors would not appear to fit the definition of a virus infecting another program, because BSIs can be spread by disks that do not contain any program files. However, the boot sector of a normal MS-DOS disk, whether or not it is a system or bootable disk, always contains a program (even if it only states that the disk is not bootable), and so it can be said that a BSI is a true virus.

The terminology of BSIs comes from MS-DOS systems, and this leads to some additional confusion. The physical first sector on a hard drive is not the operating-system boot sector. On a hard drive, the boot sector is the first logical sector. The number one position on a hard drive is the master boot record (MBR). Some viral programs, such as the Stoned virus, always attack the physical first sector: the boot sector on floppy disks and the master boot record on hard disks. Thus viral programs that always attack the boot sector might be termed pure BSIs, whereas programs such as Stoned might be referred to as an MBR type of BSI. The term *boot-sector infector* is used for all of them, though, because all of them infect the boot sector on floppy disks.

## File Infecting Viruses

A file infector infects program (object) files. System infectors that infect operating system program files (such as COMMAND.COM in DOS) are also file infectors. File infectors can attach to the front of the object file (prependers), attach to the back of the file and create a jump at the front of the file to the virus code (appenders), or overwrite the file or portions of it (overwriters). A classic is Jerusalem. A bug in early versions caused it to add itself over and over again to files, making the increase in file length detectable. (This has given rise to the persistent myth that it is a characteristic of a virus that it will fill up all disk space eventually: by far the majority of file infectors add minimally to file lengths.)

## Polymorphic Viruses

Polymorphism (literally many forms) refers to a number of techniques that attempt to change the code string on each generation of a virus. These vary from using modules that can be rearranged to encrypting the virus code itself, leaving only a stub of code that can decrypt the body of the virus program when invoked. Polymorphism is sometimes also known as self-encryption or self-garbling, but these terms are imprecise and not recommended. Examples of viruses using polymorphism are Whale and Tremor. Many polymorphic viruses use standard mutation engines such as MtE. These pieces of code actually aid detection because they have a known signature.

A number of viruses also demonstrate some form of active detection avoidance, which may range from disabling of on-access scanners in memory to deletion of antivirus and other security software (Zonealarm is a favorite target) from the disk.

## Virus Creation Kits

The term *kit* usually refers to a program used to produce a virus from a menu or a list of characteristics. Use of a virus kit involves no skill on the part of the user. Fortunately, most virus kits produce easily identifiable code. Packages of antiviral utilities are sometimes referred to as tool kits, occasionally leading to confusion of the terms.

## MACRO VIRUSES

A macro virus uses macro programming of an application such as a word processor. (Most known macro viruses use Visual Basic for Applications (VBA) in Microsoft Word: some are able to cross between applications and function in, for example, a PowerPoint presentation and a Word document, but this ability is rare.) Macro viruses infect data files and tend to remain resident in the application itself by infecting a configuration template such as Microsoft Word's NORMAL.DOT. Although macro viruses infect data files, they are not generally considered to be file infectors: a distinction is generally made between program and data files. Macro viruses can operate across hardware or operating system platforms as long as the required application platform is present. (For example, many Microsoft Word macro viruses can operate on both the Windows and the Macintosh versions of Microsoft Word.) Examples are Concept and CAP. Melissa is also a macro virus, in addition to being an e-mail virus: it mailed itself around as an infected document.

Viruses contained in test or data files had been both theorized and tested prior to the macro viruses that used VBA. DOS batch files had been created that would copy themselves onto other batch files, and self-reproducing code had been created with the macro capabilities of the Lotus 1-2-3 spreadsheet program, but these were primarily academic exercises.

Macro viruses are not currently a major class of malware and are certainly nothing in comparison to e-mail viruses and network worms. However, increasing numbers of applications have macro programming capabilities, and it is possible that macro viruses may become a problem again as the computing environment changes.

## What Is a Macro?

As noted above, a macro is a small piece of programming contained in a larger data file. This differentiates it from a script virus that is usually a standalone file that can be executed by an interpreter, such as Microsoft's Windows Script Host (.vbs files). A script virus file can be seen as a data file in that it is generally a simple text file, but it usually does not contain other data and generally has some indicator (such as the .vbs extension) that it is executable. Loveletter is a script virus.

## Free Technology to Avoid Macro Viruses

A recommended defense is MacroList, written by A. Padgett Peterson. This is a macro itself, available for both Wintel and Macintosh machines. It will list all the macros in a document. Because most documents should not contain macros, any document that does should either have a really good reason for it or be looked at with suspicion. You can find MacroList at www2.gdi.net\ ~padgett\index.htm.

## E-MAIL VIRUSES

With the addition of programmable functions to a standard e-mail user agent (usually Microsoft's Outlook), it became possible for viruses to spread worldwide in mere hours, as opposed to months.

### The Start of E-Mail Viruses: Melissa

Melissa was far from the first e-mail virus. The first e-mail virus to successfully spread in the wild was the CHRISTMA exec, in the fall of 1987. However, Melissa was certainly the first of the fast burner e-mail viruses and the first to come to wide public attention.

The virus, generally referred to as W97M.Melissa, is a Microsoft Word macro virus. The name "Melissa" comes from the class module that contains the virus. The name is also used in the registry flag set by the virus.

The virus is spread, of course, by infected Word documents. What has made it the "bug du jour" is that it spreads *itself* via e-mail. Melissa was originally posted to the alt.sex newsgroup. At that time it was LIST.DOC and purported to be a list of passwords for sex sites.

If you get a message with a Melissa-infected document, do whatever you need to do to invoke the attachment, and have Word on your system as the default program for .doc files, Word starts up, reads in the document, and the macro is ready to start.

Assuming that the macro starts executing, several things happen.

The virus first checks to see if Word 97 (Word 8) or Word 2000 (Word 9) is running. If so, it reduces the level of the security warnings on Word so that you will receive no future warnings. In Word97, the virus disables the Tools/Macro menu commands, the Confirm Conversions option, the Microsoft Word macro virus protection, and the Save Normal Template prompt. It upconverts to Word 2000 quite nicely and there disables the Tools/Macro/Security menu.

Specifically, under Word 97 it blocks access to the Tools|Macro menu item, meaning you cannot check any macros. It also turns off the warnings for conversion, macro detection, and to save modifications to the NORMAL.DOT file. Under Word 2000 it blocks access to the menu item that allows you to raise your security level and sets your macro virus detection to the lowest level, that is, none. Because the access to the macro security menu item is blocked, you must delete the infected NORMAL.DOT file to regain control of your security settings. Note that this will also lose all of your global templates and macros. Word users who make extensive use of macros are advised to keep a separate backup copy of a clean NORMAL.DOT in some safe location to avoid problems with macro virus infections.

After this, the virus checks for the HKEY_CURRENT_USER\Software\Microsoft\Office\Melissa?\ registry key with a value of "...by Kwyjibo." (The "kwyjibo" entry seems to be a reference to the "Bart the Genius" episode of the *Simpsons* television program where this word was used to win a Scrabble match.)

If this is the first time you have been infected, then the macro starts up Outlook 98 or higher, in the background, and sends itself as an attachment to the top 50 names in *each* of your address lists. (Melissa will not use Outlook Express. Also, Outlook 97 will not work.) Most people have only one (the default is "Contacts"), but if you have more than one then Outlook will send more than 50 copies of the message. Outlook also sorts address lists such that mailing lists are at the top of the list, so this can get a much wider dispersal than just 50 copies of the message/virus.

Once the messages have been sent, the virus sets the Melissa flag in the registry and looks for it to check whether to send itself out on subsequent infections. If the flag does not persist, then there will be subsequent mass mailings. Because the key is set in HKEY_CURRENT_USER, system administrators may have set permissions such that changes made are not saved, and thus the key will not persist. In addition, multiple users on the same machine will likely each trigger a separate mailout, and the probability of cross infection on a common machine is very high.

Because it is a macro virus, it will infect your NORMAL.DOT and will infect all documents thereafter. The macro within NORMAL.DOT is "Document_Close()" so that any document that is worked on (or created) will be infected when it is closed. When a document is infected, the macro inserted is "Document_Open()" so that the macro runs when the document is opened.

Note that not using Outlook does not protect you from the virus, it only means that the 50 copies will not be automatically sent out. If you use Word but not Outlook, you will still be infected and may still send out infected documents on your own. Originally the virus would not invoke the mailout on Macintosh systems. However, infected documents would be stored, and, recently, when Outlook became available for Macs, there was a second wave of Melissa mailings.

The message appears to come from the person just infected, of course, since it really is sent from that machine. This means that when you get an infected message, it will probably appear to come from someone you know and deal with. The subject line is "Important Message From: [name of sender]" with the name taken from the registration settings in Word. The text of the body states "Here is that document you asked for...don't show anyone else ;-)." Thus, the message is easily identifiable: that subject line, the very brief message, and an attached Word document (file with a .doc extension to the filename).

However, note that, as with any Microsoft Word macro virus, the source code travels with the infection, and it was very easy for people to create variations of Melissa. Within days of Melissa there was a similar Excel macro virus, called Papa.

One rather important point: the document passed is the active document, not necessarily the original posted on alt.sex. So, for example, if I am infected, prepare some confidential information for you in Word, and send you an attachment with the Word document, containing sensitive information that neither you nor I want made public and you read it in Word, and you have Outlook on your machine, then that document will be mailed out to the top 50 people in your address book, and so forth.

## How to Avoid E-Mail Viruses

It really is very simple to avoid e-mail viruses: do not double-click on any attachments that come with your e-mail. We used to say not to run any programs that came from someone you do not know, but many e-mail viruses spread using the identity of the owner of the infected computer, so that is no longer any protection. Do not run anything you receive, unless you know from some separate verification that this person intended to send you something, that it is something you need, and that the person sending it is capable of protecting themselves from infection.

It is also somewhat safer to use a mail program other than Outlook, because some versions of Outlook allowed attachments to run even before the user read the message to which they were attached.

# WORMS (FIRST AND THIRD GENERATION)

In autumn 1988, the Internet/UNIX/Morris worm did not actually bring the Internet in general and e-mail in particular to the proverbial grinding halt. It was able to run and propagate only on machines running specific versions of the UNIX operating system on specific hardware platforms. However, given that the machines that are connected to the Internet also comprise the transport mechanism for the Internet, a minority group of server-class machines, thus affected, degraded the performance of the Net as a whole. Indeed, it can be argued that despite the greater volumes of mail generated by Melissa and LoveLetter and the tendency of some types of mail servers to achieve meltdown when faced with the consequent traffic, the Internet as a whole has proved to be somewhat more resilient in recent years.

During the 1988 mailstorm, a sufficient number of machines had been affected to impair e-mail and distribution-list mailings. Some mail was lost, either by mailers that could not handle the large volumes that backed up or by mail queues being dumped in an effort to disinfect systems. Most mail was substantially delayed. In some cases, mail would have been rerouted via a possibly less efficient path after a certain time. In other cases, backbone machines, affected by the problem, were simply much slower at processing mail. In still others, mail routing software would crash or be taken out of service, with a consequent delay in mail delivery. Ironically, electronic mail was the primary means that the various parties attempting to deal with the trouble were trying to use to contact each other.

In many ways, the Internet Worm is the story of data security in miniature. The Worm used trusted links, password cracking, security holes in standard programs, standard and default operations, and, of course, the power of viral replication.

Big Iron mainframes and other multiuser server systems are generally designed to run constantly and execute various types of programs and procedures in the absence of operator intervention. Many hundreds of functions and processes may be running all the time, expressly designed neither to require nor report to an operator. Some such processes cooperate with each other; others run independently. In the UNIX world, such small utility programs are referred to as daemons, after the supposedly subordinate entities that take over mundane tasks and extend the power of the "wizard," or skilled operator. Many of these utility programs deal with the communications between systems. *Mail*, in the network sense, covers much more than the delivery of text messages between users. Network mail between systems may deal with file transfers, the routing of information for reaching remote systems, or even upgrades and patches to system software.

When the Internet Worm was well established on a machine, it would try to infect another. On many systems, this attempt was all too easy, because computers on the Internet are meant to generate activity on each other, and some had no protection in terms of the type of access and activity allowed.

The finger program is one that allows a user to obtain information about another user. The server program, fingerd, is the daemon that listens for calls from the finger client. The version of fingerd common at the time of the Internet Worm had a minor problem: it did not check how much information it was given. It would take as much as it could hold and leave the rest to overflow. "The rest," unfortunately, could be used to start a process on the computer, and this process was used as part of the attack. This kind of buffer overflow attack continues to be very common, taking advantage of similar weaknesses in a wide range of applications and utilities.

The sendmail program is the engine of most mail-oriented processes on UNIX systems connected to the Internet. In principle, it should only allow data received from another system to be passed to a user address. However, there is a debug mode that allows commands to be passed to the system. Some versions of UNIX were shipped with the debug mode enabled by default. Even worse, the debug mode was often enabled during installation of sendmail for testing and then never turned off.

When the Worm accessed a system, it was fed with the main program from the previously infected site. Two programs were used, one for each infected platform. If neither program could work, the Worm would erase itself. If the new host was suitable, the Worm looked for further hosts and connections.

The program also tried to break into user accounts on the infected machine. It used standard password-cracking techniques such as simple variations on the name of the account and the user. It carried a dictionary of words likely to be used as passwords and would also look for a dictionary on the new machine and attempt to use that as well. If an account was cracked, the Worm would look for accounts that this user had on other computers, using standard UNIX tools.

Following the Internet Worm, and a few similar examples in late 1988 and early 1989, worm examples were very infrequent during the 1990s.

By spring 2001, a number of examples of Linux malware had been seen. Interestingly, although the Windows viruses generally followed the CHRISTMA exec style of having users run the scripts and programs, the new Linux worms were similar to the Internet/Morris/UNIX worm in that they rely primarily on bugs in automatic networking software.

The Ramen worm makes use of security vulnerabilities in default installations of Red Hat Linux 6.2 and 7.0 using specific versions of the wu-ftp, rpc.statd, and LPRng programs. The worm defaces Web servers by replacing index.html and scans for other vulnerable systems. It does this initially by opening an file transfer protocol (FTP) connection and checking the remote system's FTP banner message. If the system is vulnerable, the worm uses one of the exploitable services to create a working directory and then downloads a copy of itself from the local (attacking) system.

Lion uses a buffer overflow vulnerability in the bind program to spread. When it infects, Lion sends a copy of output from the ifconfig command /etc/passwd and /etc/shadow to an e-mail address in the china.com domain. Next the worm adds an entry to etc/inetd.conf and restarts inetd. This entry would allow Lion to download components from a (now closed) Web server located in China. Subsequently, Lion scans random class B subnets in much the same way as Ramen, looking for vulnerable hosts. The worm may install a rootkit onto infected systems. This backdoor disables the syslogd daemon and adds a trojanized ssh (secure shell) daemon.

Code Red uses a known vulnerability to target Microsoft IIS (Internet Information Server) Web servers. Despite the fact that a patch for the loophole had been available for 5 months prior to the release of Code Red, the worm managed to infect 350,000 servers within 9 to 13 hours.

When a host gets infected, it starts to scan for other hosts to infect. It probes random IP addresses but the code is flawed by always using the same seed for the random number generator. Therefore, each infected server starts probing the same addresses that have been done before. (It was this bug that allowed the establishment of such a precise count for the number of infections.)

During a certain period of time the worm only spreads, but then it initiates a DoS attack against www1.whitehouse.gov. However, because this particular machine name was only an overflow server, it was taken offline prior to the attack and no disruptions resulted. The worm changed the front page of an infected server to display certain text and a background color of red, hence the name of the worm.

Code Red definitely became a media virus. Although it infected at least 350,000 machines within hours, it had probably almost exhausted its target population by that time. In spite of this, the Federal Bureau of Investigation held a press conference to warn of the worm.

Code Red seems to have spawned quite a family, each variant improving slightly on the random probing mechanism. In fact, there is considerable evidence that Nimda is a descendent of Code Red.

Nimda variants all use a number of means to spread. Like Code Red, Nimda searches random IP addresses for unpatched Microsoft IIS machines. Nimda will also alter Web pages to download and install itself on computers browsing an infected Web site using a known exploit in Microsoft Internet Explorer's handling of Java. Nimda will also mail itself as a file attachment and will install itself on any computer on which the file attachment is executed. Nimda is normally e-mailed in HTML format and may install automatically when viewed using a known exploit in Microsoft Internet Explorer. Nimda will also create e-mail and news files on network shares and will install itself if these files are opened.

# DETECTION TECHNIQUES

All antiviral technologies are based on the three classes outlined by Fred Cohen in his early research. The first type performs an ongoing assessment of the functions taking place in the computer, looking for operations known to be dangerous. The second checks regularly for changes in the computer system where changes should occur only in-

frequently. The third examines files for known code found in previous viruses.

Within these three basic types of antiviral software, implementation details vary greatly. Some systems are meant only for use on standalone systems, whereas others provide support for centralized operation on a network. With Internet connections being so important now, many packages can be run in conjunction with content scanning gateways or firewalls.

## String Search (Signature-Based)

Scanners examine files, boot sectors, and memory for evidence of viral infection. They generally look for viral signatures, sections of program code that are known to be in specific viral programs but not in most other programs. Because of this, scanning software will generally detect only known viruses and must be updated regularly. Some scanning software has resident versions that check each file as it is run.

Scanners have generally been the most popular form of antiviral software, probably because they make a specific identification. In fact, scanners offer somewhat weak protection, because they require regular updating. Scanner identification of a virus may not always be dependable: a number of scanner products have been known to identify viruses based on common families rather than definitive signatures.

## Change Detection (Integrity Checking)

Change detection software examines system and program files and configuration, stores the information, and compares it against the actual configuration at a later time. Most of these programs perform a checksum or cyclic redundancy check that will detect changes to a file even if the length is unchanged. Some programs will even use sophisticated encryption techniques to generate a signature that is, if not absolutely immune to malicious attack, prohibitively expensive, in processing terms, from the point of view of a piece of malware.

Change detection software should also note the addition of completely new entities to a system. It has been noted that some programs have not done this and allowed the addition of virus infections or malware.

Change detection software is also often referred to as integrity-checking software, but this term may be somewhat misleading. The integrity of a system may have been compromised before the establishment of the initial baseline of comparison.

A sufficiently advanced change-detection system, which takes all factors including system areas of the disk and the computer memory into account, has the best chance of detecting all current and future viral strains. However, change detection also has the highest probability of false alarms, because it will not know whether a change is viral or valid. The addition of intelligent analysis of the changes detected may assist with this failing.

## Real-Time Scanning

Real-time, or on-access, scanning is not really a separate type of antivirus technology. It uses standard signature scanning, but attempts to deal with each file of object as it is accessed or comes into the machine. Because on-access scanning can affect the performance of the machine, vendors generally try to take shortcuts to reduce the delay when a file is read. Therefore, real-time scanning is significantly less effective at identifying virus infections than a normal signature scan of all files.

Real-time scanning is one way to protect against viruses on an ongoing basis, but it should be backed up with regular full scans.

## Heuristic Scanning

A recent addition to scanners is intelligent analysis of unknown code, currently referred to as heuristic scanning. It should be noted that heuristic scanning does not represent a new type of antiviral software. More closely akin to activity monitoring functions than traditional signature scanning, this looks for suspicious sections of code that are generally found in viral programs. Although it is possible for normal programs to want to "go resident," look for other program files, or even modify their own code, such activities are telltale signs that can help an informed user come to some decision about the advisability of running or installing a given new and unknown program. Heuristics, however, may generate a lot of false alarms and may either scare novice users or give them a false sense of security after wolf has been cried too often.

## Permanent Protection

The ultimate objective, for computer users, is to find some kind of antiviral system that you can set and forget: that will take care of the problem without further work or attention on your part. Unfortunately, as previously noted, it has been proved that such protection is impossible. On a more practical level, every new advance in computer technology brings more opportunity for viruses and malicious software. As it has been said in political and social terms, so too the price of safe computing is constant vigilance.

## Vaccination

In the early days of antiviral technologies, some programs attempted to add change detection to every program on the disk. Unfortunately, these packages, frequently called vaccines, sometimes ran afoul of different functions within normal programs that were designed to detect accidental corruption on disks. No program has been found that can fully protect a computer system in more recent operating environments.

Some vendors have experimented with an autoimmune system, whereby an unknown program can be sent for assessment, and, if found to be malicious, a new set of signatures created and distributed automatically. This type of activity does show promise, but there are significant problems to be overcome.

## Activity Monitoring (Behavior-Based)

An activity monitor performs a task very similar to an automated form of traditional auditing: it watches for suspicious activity. It may, for example, check for any calls to format a disk or attempts to alter or delete a program file while a program other than the operating system is in control. It may be more sophisticated and check for any program that performs direct activities with hardware, without using the standard system calls.

Activity monitors represent some of the oldest examples of antiviral software and are usually effective against more than just viruses. Generally speaking, such programs followed in the footsteps of the earlier anti-Trojan software, such as BOMBSQAD and WORMCHEK in the MS-DOS arena, which used the same "check what the program tries to do" approach. This tactic can be startlingly effective, particularly given the fact that so much malware is slavishly derivative and tends to use the same functions over and over again.

It is, however, very hard to tell the difference between a word processor updating a file and a virus infecting a file. Activity monitoring programs may be more trouble than they are worth because they can continually ask for confirmation of valid activities. The annals of computer virus research are littered with suggestions for virus-proof computers and systems that basically all boil down to the same thing: if the operations that a computer can perform are restricted, viral programs can be eliminated. Unfortunately, so is most of the usefulness of the computer.

## PREVENTION AND PROTECTION TECHNIQUES

In regard to protection against viruses, it is germane to mention the legal situation with regard to viruses. Note that a virus may be created in one place and still spread worldwide, so issues of legal jurisdiction may be confused. In addition, specific activity may have a bearing: in the United States it may be legal to write a virus, but illegal to release it. However, in the first 16 years of the existence of viruses as a serious occurrence in the computing environment, only five people have been convicted in court of writing computer viruses, and in all five cases the defendants entered guilty pleas. Therefore, it is as well not to rely on criminal prosecutions as a defense against viruses.

The converse, however, is not true. If you are infected with a virus, and it can be demonstrated that your system subsequently sent a message that infected someone else, you may be legally liable. Thus, it is important to protect yourself from infection, even if the infection will not inconvenience you or cause loss to your business.

Training and some basic policies can greatly reduce the danger of infection. The following are a few guidelines that can really help in the current environment:

- Do not double-click on attachments.
- When sending attachments, be really specific when describing them.
- Do not blindly use Microsoft products as a company standard.
- Disable Windows Script Host. Disable ActiveX. Disable VBScript.
- Disable JavaScript. Do not send HTML formatted e-mail.
- Use more than one scanner and scan everything.

There are now companies that will provide insurance against virus attacks. This insurance is generally an extension of business loss-of-use insurance, and potential buyers would do well to examine the policies very closely to see the requirements for making a claim against it and also conditions that may invalidate payment.

Unfortunately, the price of safe computing is constant vigilance. Until 1995 it was believed that data files could not be used to transport a virus. Until 1998 it was believed that e-mail could not be used to automatically infect a machine. Advances in technology are providing new viruses with new means of reproduction and spread. Two online virus encyclopedias are listed in the Further Reading section and information about new viruses can be reliably determined at these sites.

## NON-PC PLATFORM VIRUSES

As noted, many see viruses only in terms of DOS or Windows-based programs on the Intel platform. Although there are many more PC viruses than on other platforms (primarily because there are more PCs in use than other computers), other platforms have many examples of viruses. Indeed, I pointed out earlier that the first successful viruses were probably created on the Apple II computer.

CHRISTMA exec, the Christmas Tree Virus/Worm, sometimes referred to as the BITNET chain letter, was probably the first major malware attack across networks. It was launched on December 9, 1987, and spread widely on BITNET, EARN, and IBM's internal network (VNet). It has a number of claims to a small place in history. It was written, unusually, in Restructured Extended Executor (REXX), a scripting system used to aid with automating simple user processes. It was mainframe-hosted (on Virtual Machine/Conversational Monitor System [VM/CMS] systems) rather than microcomputer-hosted, quaint though that distinction sounds nowadays when the humblest PC can run UNIX.

CHRISTMA presented itself as a chain letter inviting the recipient to execute its code. This involvement of the user leads to the definition of the first e-mail virus, rather than a worm. When it was executed, the program drew a Christmas tree and mailed a copy of itself to everyone in the account holder's equivalent to an address book, the user files NAMES and NETLOG. Conceptually, there is a direct line of succession from this worm to the social engineering worm/Trojan hybrids of today.

In the beginning of the existence of computer viruses actually proliferating in the wild, the Macintosh computer seemed to have as many interesting viruses as those in the DOS world. The Brandau, or "Peace" virus, became the first to infect commercially distributed software, and the nVIR virus sometimes infected as many as 30% of the computers in a given area. However, over time it has become evident that any computer can be made to spread a virus, and the fact that certain systems have more than others seems to be simply a factor of the number of computers of a given type in use.

## CONCLUSION

Malware is a problem that is not going away. Unless systems are designed with security as an explicit business requirement, which current businesses are not supporting through their purchasing decisions, malware will be an increasingly significant problem for networked systems.

It is the nature of networks that what is a problem for a neighboring machine may well become a problem for local systems. To prevent this, it is critical that the information security professional help business leaders recognize the risks incurred by their decisions and help to mitigate those risks as effectively and economically as possible. With computer viruses and similar phenomena, each system that is inadequately protected increases the risk to all systems to which it is connected. Each system that is compromised can become a system that infects others. If you are not part of the solution, in the world of malware, you are most definitely part of the problem.

## GLOSSARY

**Terms derived from the "Glossary of Communications, Computer, Data, and Information Security Terms" posted online at http://victoria.tc.ca/techrev/secgloss.htm and http://sun.soci.niu. edu/~rslade/secgloss.htm.**

**Activity Monitor** A type of antiviral software that checks for signs of suspicious activity, such as attempts to rewrite program files, format disks, and so forth. Some versions of activity monitor will generate an alert for such operations, whereas others will block the behavior.

**Change Detection** Antiviral software that looks for changes in the computer system. A virus must change something, and it is assumed that program files, disk system areas, and certain areas of memory should not change. This software is very often referred to as integrity-checking software, but it does not necessarily protect the integrity of data, nor does it always assess the reasons for a possibly valid change. Change detection using strong encryption is sometimes also known as authentication software.

**False Negative** There are two types of false reports from antiviral software: false negatives and false positives. A false negative report is when an antiviral reports no viral activity or presence when there is a virus present. References to false negatives are usually only made in technical reports. Most people simply refer to an antiviral missing a virus. In general security terms, a false negative is called a false acceptance, or Type II error.

**False Positive** The second kind of false report that an antiviral can make is to report the activity or presence of a virus when there is, in fact, no virus. False positive has come to be very widely used among those who know about viral and antiviral programs. Very few use the analogous term, *false alarm*. In general security terms, a false positive is known as a false rejection, or Type I error.

**Heuristic** in general, heuristics refer to trial-and-error or seat-of-the-pants thinking rather than formal rules. In antiviral jargon, however, the term has developed a specific meaning regarding the examination of program code for functions or opcode strings known to be associated with viral activity. In most cases, this is similar to activity monitoring but without actually executing the program; in other cases, code is run under some type of emulation. Recently the meaning has expanded to include generic signature scanning meant to catch a group of viruses without making definite identifications.

**Macro Virus** A macro is a small piece of programming in a simple language used to perform a simple, repetitive function. Microsoft's Word Basic and VBA macro languages can include macros in data files and have sufficient functionality to write complete viruses.

**Malware** A general term used to refer to all forms of malicious or damaging software, including viral programs, Trojans, logic bombs, and the like.

**Multipartite** Formerly a viral program that would infect both boot sectors and files, the term now refers to a virus that will infect multiple types of objects or that reproduces in multiple ways.

**Payload** This term is used to describe the code in a viral program that is not concerned with reproduction or detection avoidance. The payload is often a message but is sometimes code to corrupt or erase data.

**Polymorphism** Techniques that use some system of changing the form of the virus on each infection to try and avoid detection by signature scanning software. Less sophisticated systems are referred to as self-encrypting.

**Scanner** A program that reads the contents of a file looking for code known to exist in specific viral programs. Also known as a signature scanner.

**Stealth** Various technologies used by viral programs to avoid detection on disk. The term properly refers to the technology and not a particular virus.

**Trojan Horse** A program that either pretends to have or is described as having a (beneficial) set of features but that, either instead or in addition, contains a damaging payload. Most frequently the usage is shortened to Trojan.

**Virus** A final definition has not yet been agreed upon by all researchers. A common definition is, "a program which modifies other programs to contain a possibly altered version of itself." This definition is generally attributed to Fred Cohen, although Cohen's actual definition is in mathematical form. Another possible definition is "an entity which uses the resources of the host (system or computer) to reproduce itself and spread, without informed operator action."

**Wild, in the** A jargon reference to those viral programs that have been released into, and successfully spread in, the normal computer user community and environment. It is used to distinguish those viral programs that are written and tested in a controlled research environment, without escaping, from those which are uncontrolled "in the wild."

**Worm** A self-reproducing program that is distinguished from a virus by copying itself without being attached to a program file or that spreads over computer networks, particularly via e-mail. A recent refinement is the definition of a worm as spreading without user action, for example by taking advantage of loopholes and trapdoors in software.

## CROSS REFERENCES

See *Hackers, Crackers, and Computer Criminals; Hoax Viruses and Virus Alerts; Hostile Java Applets; Spyware; Trojan Horse Programs.*

## FURTHER READING

*Are good viruses still a bad idea?* Retrieved March 2004, from http://www.frisk.is/~bontchev/papers/goodvir.html.

Bidgoli, H. (Ed.). (2002). *Encyclopedia of information systems*. San Diego, CA: Academic Press.

Cohen, F. (1994). *A short course on computer viruses* (2nd ed.). New York: Wiley.

Ferbrache, D. (1992). *A pathology of computer viruses*. London: Springer-Verlag.

*F-Secure/Data fellows virus encyclopedia*. Retrieved March 2004, from http://www.f-secure.com/v-descs/.

Gattiker, U., Harley, D., & Slade, R. (2001). *Viruses revealed*. McGraw-Hill, New York

Highland, H. J. (1990). *Computer virus handbook*. New York: Elsevier Advanced Technology.

Hruska, J. (1992). Computer viruses and anti-virus warfare (2nd ed.). London: Ellis Horwood.

IBM Research Papers. Retreived March 2004, from http://www.research.ibm.com/antivirus/

Kane, P. (1994). *PC security and virus protection handbook*. New York: M&T Books.

Lammer, V. (1993). *Survivor's guide to computer viruses*. Abingdon, UK: Virus Bulletin.

Shoch, J.F., & Hupp, J.A., (1982, March). The "worm" programs—early experience with a distributed computation of the ACM, 25 (3), 172-180.

Slade, R. M. (1996). *Robert Slade's guide to computer viruses* (2nd ed.). New York: Springer-Verlag.

Solomon, A. (1991). *PC viruses: Detection, analysis and cure*. London: Springer-Verlag.

Solomon, A. (1995). *Dr. Solomon's virus encyclopedia*. Aylesbury, UK: S&S International PLC.

*Sophos virus encyclopedia*. Retrieved March 2004, from http://www.sophos.com/virusinfo/analyses/.

Tipton, H., & Krause, M. (Eds.). (2003). *Information security management handbook* (4th ed., vol. 4). Auerbach: Malware.

Vibert, R. S. (2000). *The enterprise anti-virus book*. Braeside, Canada: Segura Solutions.

# Trojan Horse Programs

Adam L. Young, *Cigital, Inc.*

## INTRODUCTION

In computer security, a *Trojan horse* is defined as a segment of executable code that performs some function that the user does not expect and that resides in a program. A Trojan can be placed in the program when the program is compiled or can be added to the program after it is compiled.

The term *Trojan horse* carries with it a very negative connotation due to the abundance of deployed Trojan horses that have been designed to subvert computer systems. At the very least, a Trojan horse may be nothing more than a nuisance, and at worst a Trojan horse can completely undermine the integrity of the machine that it resides on. An example of a Trojan that is merely an annoyance is the cookie monster Trojan that prompts the user to enter the word "cookie" periodically. An example of a rather common form of malicious Trojan is *spyware* (which may be integrated into a program or may be standalone) that is deployed by a software vendor that sends private information pertaining to the user back to the vendor for marketing and development purposes. Some malicious Trojans nefariously log the keystrokes of users to a hidden file and are referred to as keyboard loggers or password snatchers. These Trojans allow the perpetrator to impersonate other users when the hidden file is later obtained.

This chapter covers the history of Trojan horse programs and also describes several classes of Trojan horse attacks. The chapter concludes with several defenses that can be used to help mitigate the risk of Trojan horse attacks.

## Laying Siege to Troy

The term *Trojan horse* is a fitting one for describing malicious software and is based on a Greek myth. According to legend, the Greeks were unable to penetrate the city of Troy using siege machines and other weapons of war. So, they devised a plan. They built a huge wooden horse with a hollow belly and filled it with Greek warriors that were poised for attack. The Greeks pushed the horse to the outskirts of Troy and then sailed away. The Trojans assumed that it was a peace offering and brought the horse inside the city to celebrate the presumed departure of the Achaeans. The citizens rejoiced and drank heavily throughout the evening and much of the night. The Greek warriors took the city by surprise under cover of dark.

One often hears the term *logic bomb* within the context of malicious software attacks. A logic bomb is a portion of code in an application or operating system that remains dormant for a specified period of time or until a particular event occurs that causes it to perform some predefined action. This action is often referred to as the payload of the malware. As a result, certain Trojan horses are logic bombs and vice versa. However, a Trojan can cause perpetual damage such as wasting central processing unit (CPU) cycles by performing useless computations on a regular basis. Such a Trojan is not a logic bomb.

## How Trojans Differ from Viruses and Worms

Trojan horses differ from computer viruses and worms because they do not replicate. A computer virus is a program that replicates by infecting programs and requires some form of user action to propagate. A worm, however, may or may not infect programs and often does not require any explicit user intervention to replicate. Worms typically replicate and spread much faster than computer viruses. Slightly different definitions of a virus and a worm have appeared over the years, but no one would argue that a Trojan horse does not replicate.

Trojan horse programs can be roughly divided into those that are deployed by modifying source code and those that are deployed by manually infecting the host executable in much the same way that an executable is infected with a virus. The former deployment method assumes that the Trojan author has the luxury of modifying the original source code to contain the Trojan horse program and that the Trojan author can then compile and deploy the apparently innocent program. This option is not always possible, and so malware authors sometimes resort to modifying preexisting binary executables. The programs that are modified in this way are typically popular programs that are subsequently made available for download or operating system programs that reside on a machine that is under attack.

## HISTORY OF TROJAN HORSES
### Early Investigations into Abnormal Finite Automata

The notion of unusual or abnormal finite automata can be traced back to 1949 when John von Neumann presented lectures that encompassed the theory and organization of complicated automata (von Neumann, 1949). The notes corresponding to these lectures were later reprinted (von Neumann, 1966). In these lectures, Neumann postulated that a computer program could reproduce itself. In retrospect, it is remarkable how soon after the notion of the stored program concept the notion of self-replicating programs was investigated. Neumann is credited for promoting the notion of storing programs in memory (as opposed to using punch cards).

Bell Laboratories employees eventually gave life to Neumann's notion of self-replicating machines in the 1950s in a game dubbed *core wars*. In this game, two programmers would unleash software organisms and watch as the programs attempted to lay claim to the address space in which they fought. The core wars were described in a May 1984 issue of *Scientific American* (Dewdney, 1984).

The core wars were a way to model and observe highly simplistic forms of artificial life. These life forms would fight for resources, namely processor time and memory, within the core. The programs that were unleashed were written in a very simple assembly language for an equally simple virtual machine. Some programs fared better against some programs yet were vulnerable to others. It may well be that the earliest analog to a Trojan horse was evident as a program in core wars. There were programs that replicated in an attempt to overwrite the other hostile program in the core. There were also bomber programs that did not replicate at all but rather bombed locations outside of the bomber program. The bombing operation could be as simple as overwriting a memory location with binary zeros. Many of the ingredients for a Trojan were present since, at least with respect to the enemy program, the bomber was a malicious program that did not replicate.

### Early Military Awareness Due to Shared-Resource Machines

The notion of a Trojan horse as we know it today can be traced back to the late 1960s. The concept of multiuser operating systems grew out of the need to make efficient use of expensive computing machinery. Prior to this, physical controls were used to maintain the security of batch processing machines, yet the effectiveness of such controls began to wane as soon as programs from different users began sharing memory on a single computer.

When the military began utilizing multiuser and networked operating systems, security issues surrounding these systems came to a head. Petersen and Turn addressed computer subversion in an article that was published in the proceedings of the AFIPS Conference (Peterson & Turn, 1967). The question of security control in resource-sharing systems was the focus of series of events in 1967. The Advanced Research Projects Agency (ARPA) was asked to form a task force to study and recommend hardware and software safeguards to protect classified information in multiaccess resource-sharing computer systems. This would be used to protect information from the lowest to the highest security levels—for example, unclassified, classified, secret, and top secret where top secret is the highest security level. The task force contained a technical panel that included, among others, James P. Anderson and Daniel J. Edwards. RAND published the report of the task force under ARPA sponsorship (Ware, 1970).

The RAND report defines *deliberate penetration* to be a deliberate and covert attempt to (a) obtain information contained in the system, (b) cause the system to operate to the advantage of the threatening party, or (c) manipulate the system to make it unreliable or unusable by the legitimate operator. The report notes that deliberate efforts to penetrate secure systems can either be active or passive: *passive* methods include monitoring electromagnetic emanations and wiretapping, whereas *active* methods involve attempting to enter the system to obtain data files or to interfere with files or the system. The discussion of subversion cites the AFIPS paper (Peterson & Turn, 1967).

A class of active infiltration that is identified in the report is the exploitation of *trapdoor* entry points into the system to bypass the security facilities to permit direct access to data. A trapdoor entry point is often created deliberately during the design and development stage to simplify the insertion of authorized program changes by legitimate system programmers and is closed prior to operational use. The report also notes the risk of implicit trapdoors that may result from improper system design. Finally, the report notes the possibility of an agent operating within a secure organization. It is noted that such an agent may attempt to create a trapdoor that can be exploited at a later date.

The actual phrase *Trojan horse* appeared in a computer security technology planning study that was prepared for the U.S. Air Force (USAF) by James P. Anderson (1972). The report addressed the growing security concerns of the USAF and suggested ways that the Air Force could prepare for attacks, from both inside and outside, against the USAF computing infrastructure. The report cited several issues that fueled the need for the study.

The first concern was that there was a growing requirement to provide shared use of computer systems that contained different classification levels and need-to-know requirements in a user population that was not uniformly cleared. In some systems, particularly those found in the

USAF Data Services Center at the Pentagon, users were permitted and encouraged to directly program the system for their applications. It is due to this kind of use that weaknesses in the technical foundation of security were most acutely felt.

An issue that compounded the security risk was the growing pressure to interconnect separate but related computer systems into increasingly complex computer networks. At that time the security issues surrounding multiuser systems and interconnected computers received nowhere near the amount of attention that it gets from the open research community today. In the same vein as the RAND study, the Anderson report identifies the threat of a single user that operates as a hostile agent. It is noted that such an agent can simply modify an operating system to bypass or suspend security controls. This fact, coupled with the fact that the implementation of the operating system was outside USAF control, contributed strongly to the reluctance to certify the security of the systems that were used at the time.

A number of specific threats are articulated in an appendix of the Anderson report titled, "Security Threats and Penetration Techniques." The section titled "Trojan Horse" identifies a trapdoor that is embedded in a program that appears to be so useful that the user will use it even though it may not have been produced under the user's control. A hypothetical Trojan is detailed that records the user ID and passwords to a file and it is noted that this file may be accessible to the perpetrator. A footnote attributes the Trojan horse attack to D. J. Edwards (from the National Security Administration [NSA]).

The Anderson report also describes the notion of a *clandestine code change* in which code that contains trapdoors is injected into the system for exploitation by the perpetrator. Section 1.3 describes a trapdoor that can be installed when the implementers are not cleared and that is activated by some unique string of input characters that is presented by a collaborating user. The report foreshadowed much of the computer security threats that we face today and was of paramount importance in shedding light on the issue of malicious software.

The Bell and LaPadula model (BLP) was devised to control access of a set of active entities to a set of passive (i.e., protected) entities based on some security policy (Bell & LaPadula, 1976). Active entities are called subjects (e.g., programs) and passive entities are called objects (e.g., data files). The two effects that an access can have on an object are the extraction of information (observing) and the insertion of information (altering).

The BLP *-property (pronounced "star-property") was devised primarily to counter the Trojan horse threat for high-assurance, military systems. A simplified version of the Bell and LaPadula *-property is as follows. The *-property holds if: in any state, if a subject has simultaneous observe access to object $o_1$ and alter access to object $o_2$ then the security level of $o_2$ is greater than or equal to the security level of $o_1$. The reader is referred to the original technical report for the complete version of this definition.

The discussion thus far has focused on the theoretical notion of a Trojan horse. In the early 1970s, an actual Trojan horse was inserted into Multics binary code and was distributed to all sites. Paul Karger and Roger Schell (1974) give a description of this Trojan. The paper details a penetration exercise of Multics on a HIS 6180 computer. The range of possible Trojan horse attacks was expanded in the work of Gus Simmons, which is the subject of the next section.

## The Trojan Threat to Nuclear Arms Control Verification Systems

Gus Simmons investigated a highly specialized form of Trojan horse attack in the 1970s. The attack constituted a Trojan horse that resided within a cryptographic algorithm and deviated significantly from the Trojans that had been foreseen at the time. The Trojan was number theoretic in nature and was designed for the sole purpose of covertly transmitting information outside of its host.

Simmons' research grew out his analysis of cryptographic protocols that were designed to verify the compliance of the Strategic Arms Limitation Treaty II (SALT II), a treaty that was intended to control the nuclear arms race. This work forms the cornerstone for the theory of subliminal channels and is regarded as seminal with respect to cryptographic protocol failures and trust-related issues for black-box (e.g., microchip) cryptosystems. It is instructional to cover the origin of this interesting cryptographic phenomenon (Simmons, 1994).

In 1978, the Carter administration was seriously considering the adoption of a national security protocol that was designed to allow Russia to verify how many nuclear missiles the United States had fielded in the 1,000 U.S. silos without exposing which silos were actually armed. To constitute an acceptable solution to Russia, the compliance messages would have to be digitally signed in a way that would not be possible for the United States to forge. At any given time the United States was permitted to have 100 missiles residing in randomly chosen silos. Any more than this would be a violation of the SALT II treaty (Simmons, 1998).

The scheme that the Carter administration was endorsing was often referred to in the press as the missile shell game. This is because the 100 missiles would be shuttled randomly using trucks among the 1,000 Minuteman silos on a continual basis. It was envisioned that these trucks would even haul fake payloads, such as water, to conceal whether a given payload actually contained a live missile. This was necessary because the trucks could be observed via spy satellites. However, simply hauling fake loads would of course not be enough. The trucks would all have to exhibit the same acceleration, lest they be distinguished using elementary kinematics.

The proposed solution, one that would allow Russia to verify the number of missiles that the United States had placed afield, utilized both sensors and cryptographic devices. The sensors were to be placed in the silos. The data acquired by the sensors would indicate the presence or absence of a missile in a given silo, thus constituting a single bit of information. This bit had to be protected so that it could not be forged or falsely attributed. Both countries agreed that the sensor technology was acceptable. Gravimetric sensors could be used to detect underground features versus voids, tilt sensors could also be used, and so forth. In the proposed solution, each country would provide its own cryptographic algorithm.

This problem was being solved at about the same time that the Diffie-Hellman key exchange was devised. Symmetric ciphers were the norm at that time. The basic idea was to have the cipher use a secret key to encrypt a message. Both the ciphertext and plaintext would be output by the device. Signature verification amounted to decrypting the ciphertext and comparing the result to the plaintext. Implicit in this approach was that it should not be possible to leak information in each ciphertext. The ability to do so could potentially compromise the identity of the silo and give the enemy the opportunity to launch a devastating first strike.

As the story goes, the NSA viewed the SALT II treaty as an opportunity to learn more about the state of cryptography in Russia. It was suggested that the Russians devise their own cipher to place inside the device. Simmons saw the peril in this approach. He called for a meeting with the NSA, armed with the fact that the recently discovered Rabin cipher could be used inside the device to leak a single bit to the Russians. To sign a message in Rabin, the message is transformed into a square modulo the public key. A square root of the message is then computed using the two prime factors of the public key. Four square roots exist and so any of the four square roots can be used as the signature on the message. This was an incredibly important discovery. It implied that for certain appropriately designed algorithms that could be placed in the device, elbowroom exists to leak information unbeknownst to the United States. Exactly two of these roots can safely be used to leak a single bit. These two roots are the ones that have a Jacobi symbol of 1. Had this channel actually been exploited, the code to do so would constitute a Trojan horse program.

This was conveyed to the NSA and the response was largely that of disinterest. They indicated that they would never approve of such a cipher and said that a 1-bit channel is insignificant. Ten bits would allow the unambiguous identification of a given silo because $2^{10} = 1024 > 1000$. Ultimately, it was the projected cost of the solution and not this channel that caused the whole idea to be abandoned.

The cryptographic Trojan that Simmons envisioned was sound in design and constituted a plausibility result: namely that by carefully crafting a backdoor into a cryptographic treaty compliance algorithm, the enemy could learn the location of the missiles to enable a devastating first strike. This type of Trojan horse was far off the beaten path from the Trojans that were envisioned at the time. It involved a carefully selected cryptographic algorithm to subliminally leak information and was nontrivial in every respect, especially considering the fact that ad hoc symmetric ciphers were the bread and butter of the cryptographic research community at that time.

Simmons continued to explore the implications of subliminal channels with respect to computer security. He proposed what is now known as the *prisoner's problem* (Simmons, 1984). This problem is not to be confused with the prisoner's dilemma from game theory. In the prisoner's problem, Alice and Bob are in prison and they want to coordinate an escape plan. They are permitted to digitally sign messages to each other but are not allowed to give each other ciphertexts. The warden actively monitors the messages that they send to one another and verifies the signatures. A message is not forwarded unless the corresponding signature is valid. The problem is to devise a way for Alice and Bob to communicate privately without the warden knowing about it by sending signed messages to one another, where the subliminal message is contained in the signature. This eliminates the use of trivial encodings in the actual messages that are signed. As it turns out, the prisoner's problem can be solved for quite a number of digital signature algorithms including ElGamal and the digital signature algorithm (DSA).

The solution to the prisoner's problem can be applied to carry out rather devastating Trojan horse attacks against smart cards. The purpose of this attack is to leak the private signing key of the user to the manufacturer of the smart card. The algorithm that transmits information over the subliminal channel can be embedded within a digital signing algorithm, which in turn is implemented within a smart card. So, code within the smart card can be regarded as Alice, the manufacturer can be regarded as Bob, and the unwary user of the smart card can be regarded as the warden. Simmons described an attack in which the smart card transmits the bits of the user's DSA private key to the manufacturer through the signatures that the card produces. The manufacturer can obtain these signed messages if and when they become public (Simmons, 1993).

The idea that advanced and customized Trojan horses can be devised specifically for attacking certain cryptographic algorithms contributed heavily to the development of other types of Trojan horses and viruses. It became apparent that cryptography itself could be employed by Trojan horses to strengthen the attacks that they mounted against their hosts. The areas that explore this possibility have been dubbed cryptovirology (Young & Yung, 1996a) and kleptography (Young & Yung, 1996b). Asymmetric cryptography is the central enabling technology for such Trojan horse attacks.

A cryptotrojan is a Trojan horse that contains and uses the public key of its author. The private key is kept private by the author and is not included in the Trojan. This makes it possible for the Trojan to perform trapdoor one-way operations as part of its payload using the public key. Only the author can reverse these trapdoor one-way operations because only the author knows the private key. No matter how carefully the Trojan is analyzed, the private key will not be revealed. Cryptovirology attacks are interesting because it is not enough to be the world's greatest antiviral expert to reverse their effects. It is necessary to be the world's greatest cryptanalyst.

## TYPES OF TROJAN HORSE ATTACKS

It is difficult at best to devise a strict hierarchy of Trojan horse attacks that is organized according to what the Trojan horses do. By definition, a Trojan horse program is *already inside* the system in question, so its capabilities are bounded only by the access controls placed on its host. This is the primary restriction that is placed on the capabilities of a Trojan horse program. In the most general sense, a Trojan can do *anything* to the system that its host is permitted to do.

However, the ability to do anything to the host system by no means implies that Trojans can be safely designed (from the attacker's perspective) to do anything. A secondary design-level restriction that is placed on a Trojan horse is the fact that the host program may be under constant surveillance. This occurs when heuristic activity monitors that, for example, execute from within the safety of the operating system kernel attempt to identify if the program misbehaves. Activity monitors observe, record, and attempt to interpret the actions of the host program on a regular basis (some even have automated response systems). A Trojan horse program that causes the host to behave in a noticeably suspicious way may reveal the presence of the Trojan.

## Malicious versus Benign Trojan Horses

Many databases on computer viruses, worms, and Trojan horses categorize malware as being malicious or benign. A benign Trojan is one that, for instance, presents a modal dialog box saying "Happy Halloween" every October 31. Whereas it may be argued that such a Trojan is benign in many respects, it is perhaps safest to say that it is malicious. Such a Trojan demands the user's attention and should not be in the system in the first place.

The view that is adopted here is that any Trojan horse is malicious because by definition it has a payload that does something that the user does not expect. This implies that, for example, the insertion into a program of a dummy variable that is never used constitutes a Trojan. After all, an unused variable may end up wasting space on the stack in random access memory (RAM).

In this study, Trojan horses are identified as being either overt or covert in their operation. The hierarchy that is given in the next section is not meant to supersede any existing formal characterizations of Trojan horses. Rather, it is intended to convey the types of Trojans that are employed time and time again by computer assailants.

## An Attempt to Categorize Trojans

Depending on the attacker's goal, it may be possible to carry out a Trojan horse attack covertly. This type of attack is ideal from the attacker's perspective, especially when the attack is a perpetual one, because the Trojan attracts little attention and is therefore more likely to survive. Examples of covert attacks include information theft, subtle information alteration, and subtle resource usage.

In a covert information theft attack, the Trojan transmits stolen information from the host system to the author of the Trojan. This can be the login/password pair of a user, for instance. In an information alteration attack, the state of the host machine is changed in a way that is likely to go unnoticed for a prolonged period of time. For instance, fractions of a cent may be siphoned off from the payroll accounts of employees and moved into a secret account that the Trojan author has access to (*salami slicing* attack). Also, the Trojan may attempt to utilize the resources to which the host machine has access. For instance, the Trojan horse author may try to get several host machines

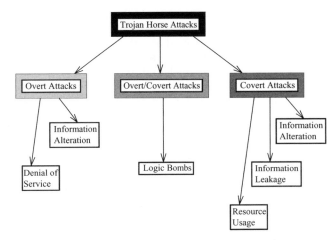

**Figure 1:**  Hierarchy of Trojan horse attacks.

to solve an instance of a hard problem, such as breaking a password by brute force, and later send the broken password to the author if it is found. These computations would utilize the CPU in small increments to go unnoticed. In this particular attack, the Trojan horse steals CPU time to solve a problem that would be difficult, if not impossible, to solve on a single machine.

Some types of Trojan horses are unavoidably overt in nature. For example, a purely destructive Trojan that deletes the hard drive would hardly go unnoticed once the deletion occurs. This is a form of overt information alteration. Another form of overt attacks is a denial of service (DoS) attack. A DoS attack denies users or processes access to a service. Overt Trojan horse attacks often (but not always) lead to the discovery of the Trojan soon after the attack is carried out. In contrast, a Trojan with a covert payload may carry out the attack for months or even years without notice.

Given these two extremes, it makes sense to divide Trojans into those that operate in secret and those that by design will not go unnoticed (see Figure 1). There are, however, some discrepancies between the covert attacks on the right and the overt attacks on the left that bear mentioning. A parallel can be drawn between DoS attacks and covert resource usage. From the perspective of the operating system kernel, peripheral devices provide a service to user processes. A line printer lets a process print data out on paper. A hard disk lets processes store data in nonvolatile memory. A form of denial of service against a process is denying network access, preventing writes to disk, and so on. So, overt DoS attacks and covert resource usage both affect services, yet they do so in fundamentally different ways. In a DoS attack, users and user processes are denied access to a service, whereas in a covert resource usage, a service is utilized slowly over time by the Trojan horse program.

Another aspect to note is the absence of information leakage in the overt attacks category. The reason for this is that there is often little reason for a Trojan horse to attract attention when all it has to do is leak information to the attacker.

There are a variety of ways to covertly transmit information. In some cases, it may be possible to establish a network connection and simply transmit the sensitive information to the attacker. Yet subtler methods exist to do this. For example, the data can be *steganographically* encoded into images or sound files that are normally sent out. When cryptosystems are involved, the data can be sent via a subliminal channel, and so on.

Observe that there is a generic heading for overt/covert attacks utilizing a *logic bomb*. This category is intended to encompass any attack that does not directly fall under the previously mentioned categories. Almost all Trojan horse payloads activate under a prescribed set of conditions and so a category encompassing overt/covert logic bombs addresses most of these other forms of attack.

A good example of a logic bomb is the cookie monster Trojan that ran on PDP machines (Harley, Slade, & Gattiker, 2001). Its name derives from the Cookie Monster on the television show *Sesame Street*. This Trojan would flash the message "I want a cookie" to the user on the monitor. The word "cookie" had to be fed to the program to keep it quiet. This type of Trojan horse payload is clearly overt in nature. A cookie monster virus was also reported (McAfee & Haynes, 1989).

This middle category is also meant to encompass Trojan horses that may or may not be covert in nature. For example, the Trojan called *Trojan.Download.Revird* (Symantec, 2003a) may be covert or overt depending upon the savvy of the computer user. This Trojan terminates processes belonging to security and monitoring applications. The Trojan horse titled *Backdoor.Gaster* terminates predefined processes as well (Symantec, 2003b). The act of terminating processes may be overlooked by the average user yet be detected by more observant users. These Trojans also contain backdoor functionality that is designed to permit the author to perform functions on the host machine. In this case, whether the Trojan is overt is at the discretion of the attacker that executes commands remotely via the Trojan.

## COVERT TROJAN HORSE ATTACKS

A covert Trojan horse attempts to perform some function on the host machine in such a way that the operation of its payload is overlooked by the human user and by processes on the machine. Some defensive actions, such as killing security processes and deleting security-related files, might be overt enough to be noticed. However, this category may be loosely defined as encompassing those Trojan horses that are intended to go unnoticed.

### Covert Information Alteration

There are a great number of possible covert information alteration attacks. An offensive tactic against military simulation systems is to introduce small errors into the experimental simulations to produce erroneous outputs. Other less spine-chilling and more nefarious attacks include remapping two keys on the keyboard. For example, a Trojan could with some small probability register a Y as the received keystroke instead of T when the user presses the T key. The desired effect is to frustrate the user into thinking that the letter T was mistyped. Such an attack is covert if the probability of remapping is so small that the user dismisses it as a random yet irritating occurrence.

An interesting example of covert information alteration is a salami-slicing Trojan that steals from the payroll accounts of employees. The first case of this may well be an urban legend. However, there do exist concrete sources that at least pinpoint when the attack allegedly occurred. A brief description of this attack appeared in an article dated November 3, 1987 (Makin, 1987). The article described a talk given by Sergeant Ted Green of the Ontario Provincial Police. Green described several logic-bomb attacks and other attacks against systems.

One attack was a Trojan horse that was clearly intended to achieve financial gain. An employee of a bank is said to have carried out an attack in which $70,000 was accumulated by funneling a few cents out of every account into his own (Neumann, 1987). This type of attack is called a salami-slicing attack (Parker, 1976) since small portions of money are purloined from numerous accounts. Stealing in small increments is necessary to prevent employees from noticing that their paychecks are a tiny bit less than they should be.

### Covert Information Leakage

A covert information leakage attack is one in which malware transmits sensitive information outside the host system in an inconspicuous fashion. Early examples of covert information transmission include the password-pilfering Trojan mentioned in the Anderson report and the findings of Gus Simmons. However, in this section a bit more light is shed on the subject.

A well-known measure to protect against Trojan horses is to encapsulate programs into small domains that are given the minimal amount of rights necessary to perform their tasks. However, even when encapsulated, a program may have access to secret parameters that are passed to it by a caller. A Trojan in the program may retain the information for later use or transmit the data to the Trojan horse author. A program that is not able to transmit or store its parameters is said to be *confined*. The *confinement problem* is the problem of confining a program as such to eliminate the possibility of subversion. Lampson (1973) first explored the intricacies of this problem.

An inconspicuous way of leaking information via a Trojan horse is through the use of a *covert channel*. A covert channel is a channel that was not originally designed to transfer information at all. A concrete example will go a long way to explain what a covert channel is. Suppose that Alice and Bob are connected to a computer that is running a multiuser operating system. In a secure operating system that can be used for sensitive (e.g., military) applications, it should not be possible for a process that Alice is running to transmit information covertly to a process that Bob is running. But, suppose that a printer is connected to this machine. Each process can make an operating system call to print data. This call will return a result code indicating success or failure. The result code will also indicate if the printer is busy printing out a document. Alice's process can utilize a special communication protocol to speak with a process that Bob is running. For example, printing out two short documents with a brief pause in between could correspond to a binary "1" and printing out one document could be a binary "0." Bob's process calls the operating system routine in a busy waiting fashion to receive bits from Alice's process.

A *timing channel* is a special type of covert channel. For example, a Trojan may execute in such a way that its running time is proportional to some confidential value $x$, which it reads. By measuring the running time on a clock that operates independent of the system, the Trojan horse author can determine the value of $x$ (D. E. Denning, 1983).

A channel that is related to a covert channel is a *subliminal channel* (Simmons, 1984). Typically, the term *subliminal channel* is used to refer to an information transmission channel that can be used to send information out of (or potentially into) a cryptosystem. A covert channel, on the other hand, is somewhat broader in scope. It has been shown that subliminal channels can be used to securely and subliminally leak private keys outside of cryptosystems in a way that is very robust against reverse engineering and that cannot, under reasonable intractability assumptions, be detected (Young & Yung, 1996b). This area of research has been dubbed *kleptography*.

Finally, *steganography* is the study of encoding data in other forms in a way that is not detectable. For instance, steganographic techniques allow a particular binary string to be encoded into certain graphics and sound files when there exists some leeway in terms of how the multimedia information is encoded. Steganography differs from cryptography because it does not provide for confidentiality; if the adversary knows which bits correspond to the steganographically encoded message, then the plaintext will be revealed. The challenge is to make these bits indistinguishable from bits that are normally present. The secure use of steganographic techniques usually involves encrypting the plaintext message and then steganographically encoding the resulting ciphertext.

Entire volumes could be written on the subject of covert information leakage, and the notions presented here are merely the tip of the iceberg. The bottom line is that it is very difficult to prevent information leakage (proactive) and to detect information leakage when it occurs (reactive). Research is ongoing in this area, and it encompasses both new ways to covertly leak information as well as new ways to counter clandestine information leakage.

## Covert Resource Usage

Covert resource usage is loosely defined as the use of the host machine and associated peripherals in a way that is likely to go unnoticed. This includes but is not limited to the CPU, RAM, disk space, and so on. A general-purpose computing machine is a resource all by itself and has value to an attacker irrespective of the data that it processes and contains.

A good example of covert resource usage is a Trojan horse program that tries to solve an instance of an intractable problem. For example, it could try to solve an instance of the traveling salesman problem or some type of optimization problem. It could also be used for the purposes of breaching security by doing a brute-force key search, and so forth.

Steve White investigated the possibility of using viruses to conduct key searches. In particular, he observed that a virus could try to determine the Data Encryption Standard (DES) key that was used to produce a particular symmetric encryption (White, 1990). Trojans can be used to steal CPU time to try to factor composites, compute discrete logarithms, and so on. In general, this type of Trojan needs to salami-slice the CPU usage so that the attack can be carried out for a prolonged period of time without notice.

# OVERT TROJAN HORSE ATTACKS

Overt Trojan horses carry out attacks that will more than likely be noticed when they occur. The distinction is often subtle, because some Trojans delete files belonging to antiviral programs, which is an offensive tactic, but the overall rationale is defensive in nature. Overt Trojan horse attacks are offensive attacks, for the most part.

## Overt Information Alteration

A classic overt information alteration attack is the deletion of data, although many other forms of malicious information alteration exist. The business of deleting data on a hard disk is subtle because a single write to disk will not necessarily destroy all traces of the previously stored binary digits. If not done properly, people that specialize in digital forensics may be able to recover the original data. The standard approach to deleting information on silicon platters is to overwrite with zeros, then overwrite with ones, then overwrite with zeros, and so on. Usually more than five iterations of this are performed to ensure that the ions on the surface of the disk do not reveal their original orientations.

The ChinaTalk Trojan is an Apple Macintosh Trojan that mounts an overt information alteration attack. The system extension containing the Trojan is advertised as being a sound driver for a female voice that is compatible with the MacInTalk program (Wilding & Skulason, 1992). However, the Trojan erases the hard disk.

## Denial of Service

The subject of DoS attacks is not treated in detail here because a chapter in this *Handbook* is dedicated to this subject. Trojans can carry out DoS attacks, so the subject must be addressed here.

The notion of a DoS attack within the context of application programs was originally defined as follows (Needham, 1993). A contractor uses a client, the network, and a server to provide a service to a given customer. In a DoS attack, service is denied to the customer, not to the client. DoS attacks may consist of destroying or disabling the client. They may also involve interfering with the network traffic or with the server. Needham was the first researcher to investigate the effects of DoS attacks in the application layer. He focused mainly on end-to-end solutions for a given application.

DoS attacks have been carried out on the Internet to bring down various Internet and Web services. A particular type of DoS attack, called a *distributed denial of service attack*, is geared toward disrupting a service by overloading servers with packet requests and the like. Multiple machines located at multiple locations typically carry out these types of attacks. The machines submit packet requests (or some similar disruptive function) simultaneously to the target machine to disrupt service. A challenge in defending against this type of attack is distinguishing legitimate packet requests from the packets involved in the attack (e.g., packets that originate from Trojans residing on the machines). There has been a significant amount of research into countering this threat.

A cryptovirus attack can be regarded as a form of DoS attack (Young & Yung, 1996a). The payload of a cryptovirus (or cryptotrojan) encrypts critical data files on the host machine using the public key of the virus author. This public key is contained within the virus. If the critical data files are not backed up, then the host data files are effectively lost to the victim. This is due to the fact that an analysis of the virus will only reveal the public encryption key and not the needed private decryption key. The author of the virus can therefore hold these data ransom in return for the private decryption key.

Although there is no "service" involved in this scenario, the attack is nonetheless reminiscent of a DoS attack. For example, in a DoS attack that involves making packet requests, service can be restored when the bogus requests cease. In a cryptovirus extortion attack, the author can restore the critical data by revealing the private decryption key. This differs greatly from an overt information alteration attack that simply destroys data.

# DEFENSES AGAINST TROJAN HORSE PROGRAMS

There are several challenges surrounding the design of robust Trojan horse programs and designing algorithms to detect Trojans wherever present. The first part of this section covers the issue of string matching. Antivirus programs often use string matching to positively identify viruses and Trojan horse programs. The development of antiviral string-matching programs led to the development of polymorphic viruses, which are viruses that are specifically designed to foil string-matching programs. The notion of polymorphism is a very general one and has been applied to the design of Trojan horses. For example, the Trojan horse program *Backdoor.Smorph* uses polymorphic techniques (Lancaster University, 2001).

## Scanners

Consider a case in which a moderately sized Trojan horse has been discovered and analyzed by antivirus experts. When some or all of its binary code stays the same when the infected program is run, then there exists a simple way to detect the Trojan whenever it appears in plaintext form. The basic method for doing so is called *pattern matching* (Cohen, 1986). The idea is to take a string of bytes from the malware that is invariant across invocations of the malware and use it to find other instances of the malware. By checking an executable for the presence of this substring, it can be determined whether the executable is infected. Antiviral programs called *scanners* perform this scanning process. If the string is sufficiently long and the pattern it contains is unique, this method will detect the presence of the malware in infected programs. This approach is not

flawless since the string may appear naturally in certain programs. As a result, this method sometimes produces false positives.

However, this method can never produce a false negative when used to identify known Trojans. Stealth techniques are an exception to this rule because they have the potential to alter the scanner's perception of the true binary data in the program. This is due to the fact that a stealthy Trojan horse (or virus) reroutes operating systems calls so that a disk read will reveal an image of the original uninfected sectors of the disk to the caller. So, with the exception of stealth techniques and the like, string matching is performed correctly every time and an invariant string from the malware will never be missed.

A countermeasure to scanners is to design a Trojan horse program so that it does not contain any of the strings contained in the database. This is incredibly easy for an attacker to do: the attacker inserts the Trojan into a host program and then subjects the program to all available antivirus tools to see if the Trojan is found. A scanner is capable of detecting a deployed Trojan only after the needed search string is included in the list of search strings. It is often the case that a new Trojan is detected only after it mounts a successful attack against a host. Consequently, scanners are not very proactive in identifying Trojan horse programs and viruses. The measure is occasionally proactive because a new Trojan sometimes reuses the code of other Trojans or contains trivial modifications and as a result succumbs to an existing search string.

## Polymorphic Code

A straightforward countermeasure to scanners is designing malware that modifies its own coding sequence. In laboratory experiments, Fred Cohen produced viruses that had no common sequences of over 3 bytes between each subsequent generation by using encryption (Cohen, 1986, 1987). Cohen referred to such viruses as *evolutionary viruses*, but they are more commonly referred to as *polymorphic viruses*.

Numerous polymorphs have appeared in the wild. For example, the Tremor virus is a polymorphic virus that has almost 6 trillion forms (Slade, 1994). A polymorphic program typically consists of two parts: a header and a body. When dormant, the body remains in encrypted form. When activated, the header decrypts the body of the malware. Once the body is decrypted, the header transfers control to the body. The body then performs the normal malware operations. When the body is finished, it sends control to the host program.

The header stores the symmetric key needed to decrypt the body. At periodic intervals, the malware can choose a new symmetric key randomly, replace the key in the header with it, and make sure that the body of the malware is encrypted under the new key. The problem now, from the perspective of the malware author, is that scanners can successfully search for the decryption header.

Malware authors have a variety of methods for changing the appearance of the decryption header as well. Some approaches for this are more effective than others. One obvious method is to employ several different ciphers and randomly select among them. This is a good approach but may in some cases lead to unacceptably large viruses.

Another common approach is to weave dummy instructions between the instructions that constitute the decryption algorithm. Most processors support a NOP instruction that literally does nothing. It is shorthand for no-operation and has many uses. On reduced instruction set computing (RISC) machines, these instructions cause the program to wait until all pending bus activity is completed. This allows synchronization of the pipeline and prevents instruction overlap. It is not uncommon on complex instruction set computing (CISC) machines to see NOP instructions woven within the sections of a switch statement to improve the performance of the instruction cache by aligning each section on a new cache line.

There are also a number of arithmetic dummy instructions. For instance, the additive identity element 0 can be used in an *add* instruction. The multiplicative identity element 1 can be used in a *multiply* instruction, and so on. There are dummy instructions for logical operations such as *or* as well.

Another type of dummy instruction is any instruction that operates on registers that are not used in the underlying algorithm. For example, many algorithms do not require the use of all of the data registers at once on the target microprocessor. In this case, the addition, multiplication, and so forth of any number in that register has a null effect. All of these dummy instructions have the potential to foil string-matching scanners.

There exist a number of tools that antiviral analysts use that specifically search for such dummy instructions. These tools typically have false positive rates that are very high and as a result make them unsuitable for use by the average user. They nonetheless greatly minimize the time needed for skilled analysts to find polymorphic code.

A better way to obfuscate the decryption header is to replace instructions with other instructions that perform the same operation and to exploit the fact that many instructions can be reordered without affecting the overall correctness of the algorithm (Skardhamar, 1996). Register usage is another aspect that is easily randomized. On the Motorola 68000 processor, there are eight general-purpose data registers. A given decryption algorithm may only require the use of four data registers. There are 8 choose 4 ways of selecting four distinct registers from the set of eight registers.

It has been observed that, because many viruses execute before the host, it is often possible to positively identify polymorphic viruses by letting them decrypt themselves (Nachenberg, 1997). The general idea behind this heuristic is to emulate the operation of the host program for the first few thousand or so instructions and then scan the resulting executable for the presence of known polymorphic viruses. The method is called *generic decryption* and involves three components: a CPU emulator, an emulation control module, and a scanner. The CPU emulator is designed to emulate a particular CPU such as a Pentium IV processor. The emulation control module determines such things as how many instructions will be emulated and is also responsible for making sure that no damage is done to the underlying machine as a result of the presence of malware. For example, writes to the disk may be prevented or otherwise contained. The scanner is applied to the code at regular intervals during the emulation to attempt to detect malicious software. Generic decryption can be performed on the fly along with traditional scanning methods to help identify polymorphic malware that is present at the beginning of programs.

Using generic decryption to scan the first several thousand instructions in a program is particularly useful in finding polymorphic Trojans that gain control soon after the program is executed. This applies to Trojans that have been appended to the host program after it was compiled and to Trojans that are inserted into the source code near the beginning of the program.

A countermeasure to generic decryption is to make the malware decrypt its body with some fixed probability. The malware could generate a random number and with some probability not decrypt its main body at all. For example, when the malware gains control in a given invocation of the host program, it could roll a six-sided die. If the result is "1" then the malware could decrypt itself and then go about its normal activity. If the result is not "1" then it could simply send control back to the host.

Another countermeasure to generic decryption is to make the malware gain control at a randomly determined offset within the host program. Implementing this countermeasure is more complicated than it seems because simply overwriting portions of the host will likely lead to crashes. When a Trojan is appended to a preexisting program, the bulk of the Trojan can be stored at the end of the host program. The problem then remains to modify the host to send control to the Trojan. One approach to accomplishing this is to choose an offset within the host randomly and overwrite the code at that location with a jump instruction. The original code would need to be stored within the Trojan, and the overlaid jump instruction would send control to the Trojan unconditionally. When the Trojan finishes executing, it repairs the host by overwriting the jump instruction with the original host code and then sends control back to where it normally would have been.

This approach is not without its risks, however. The jump instruction and the Trojan code that follows it should preserve the state of the program. Register values should be pushed onto the stack, and so on, and popped when the Trojan completes. Also, if the jump instruction is too long, it might overwrite code that forms an entry point for another jump instruction within the host. This could cause the host program to crash as a result of the inserted jump instruction. The Trojan would have to heuristically analyze the host to make certain that this cannot occur. If the host were naturally polymorphic, this analysis would be just as hard as the problem faced by antiviral programs. Finally, race conditions could cause faulty behavior within the host. If the jump instruction were written over an atomic action that operates on a semaphore and if the Trojan's code exacerbates the race condition, then the infected host could crash or produce erroneous results. There are numerous other problems that could result as well. For example, the inserted jump could cause a digital signature verification to fail, cause a checksum to fail, and so on.

Another general heuristic for detecting polymorphic malware is to look for changes in memory where the code for the currently running executable resides (Symantec, 1999). Symantec developed a tool that interprets the program one instruction at a time and takes note of every byte in the program's code space that changes. This method is a solid countermeasure, but has certain weaknesses. For example, it is possible to make the Trojan utilize multiple encryption layers with decryption headers in the host. These small headers can decipher the rest of the binary executable and therefore almost every byte of the program in memory can be changed. Another issue to deal with is programs that spawn child programs. For example, processes could *fork* and *exec* (e.g., in the UNIX operating system), thereby creating more heap zones that need to be analyzed.

## Heuristic Activity Monitors

The ability to patch operating-system routines provides a good approach to assessing abnormal program behavior. An interrupt activity monitor works by loading antiviral interrupt handlers soon after the computer is booted. These handlers are collectively managed and typically span several different operating system routines. When they gain control from an operating system call, they analyze the circumstances surrounding the call and often maintain state information across calls. Heuristic activity monitors are useful for proactively detecting new Trojans and viruses that have been released. To address the threat of viruses, they have been designed to look for attempts to write to any sector containing executable code such as device drivers, boot sectors, and so on (McAfee & Haynes, 1989; Spafford, Heaphy, & Ferbrache, 1990). Monitors are equally useful in detecting certain actions that are characteristic of Trojans. They take note of such things as suspicious network activity, attempts to delete sectors, and attempts to reformat mounted volumes.

Activity monitors typically create audit trails of certain events that occur in the system. Users and system administrators can later analyze these audit trails to look for security breaches. Audit trails often have the potential to reveal the sequences of events leading up to an attack. When a suspicious event is about to occur (e.g., by intercepting a system call), some activity monitors will proactively display a message to the user that implicates the calling program. The monitor may request permission from the user to allow the suspicious event to occur. This way, users have a chance to stop a Trojan or virus before it adversely affects the underlying system.

The alerts from an activity monitor are very effective at identifying self-replicating code. However, the alerts often arise when a software patch is applied or when a new program is compiled. Another case is when a program utilizes a copy protection scheme that causes the program to write to itself. This happened in an old version of WordPerfect (McAfee & Haynes, 1989).

One of the dangers in using activity monitors is that if the alerts occur too frequently, the user may become desensitized to them. Too many alerts create a situation akin to crying wolf. This makes it more likely that users will allow a Trojan or virus to attack the system down the road because agitated users may eventually disable or ignore the alerts altogether. Unlike scanners, activity monitors are designed to identify both existing and future malware and, as a result, activity monitors are prone to yield false negative results.

## Code Signing and Security Kernels

Although heuristic activity monitors provide a solid line of defense, they are after all only heuristic in nature. Another measure that can be taken to minimize the Trojan horse threat is to utilize strong authentication techniques. This approach combines the notion of a secure kernel with digital signatures (P. J. Denning, 1988). In this method, the kernel stores the root and certificate authority digital certificates of the public key infrastructure (PKI) used to certify the application that is to be run. The manufacturer digitally signs the application and releases it along with the digital signature and certificate that are needed to verify the signature. When the user runs the application, the certificate and signature are given to the kernel. The kernel verifies the authenticity of the certificate using the internally stored certificate authority certificate and also checks a certificate revocation list if necessary. Once the certificate is deemed valid, it is used to verify the signature on the application. The application is run if and only if the certificate and signature are valid (D. E. Denning, 1983). When a signature is valid, it is overwhelmingly certain that a Trojan (or virus) was not placed within the program after the software manufacturer released it.

This form of integrity checking, if implemented properly, will never produce false positive results. If the digital signature is invalid, then without a doubt the application has been changed. However, there is a negligible chance that a false negative will result. A malicious user or program can change an application and still have the signature verify correctly with negligible probability. This type of defense is likely to be utilized more and more as time goes on and as PKIs become more widespread.

## CONCLUSION

A study of Trojan horses was presented that is based on how inconspicuous a given Trojan horse is. Insomuch as possible, the set of Trojan horses was partitioned into those that are intended to act covertly and those that are unavoidably overt in their actions. This contrasts with typical classifications that identify Trojans as being malicious or benign, for some (arguably vague) definition of benign. Several types of covert attacks and overt attacks were identified. Some of these attacks are advanced because they utilize modern concepts in cryptography and steganography. It is essential to understand how attackers think, what they seek, and what tools they have at their disposal to minimize the Trojan horse threat.

## GLOSSARY

**Certificate Revocation List (CRL)** A CRL is used by a certification authority to publicly disclose key pairs that have been revoked. It lists revoked key pairs and is digitally signed by the certification authority. A CRL is typically updated on a regular basis (e.g., every day or two).

**Cryptotrojan** A Trojan horse program that contains and uses the public key of its author (or more generally any public key).

**Cryptovirus** A computer virus that contains and uses the public key of its author (or more generally any public key).

**Data Encryption Standard (DES)** A standardized symmetric cipher with a 64-bit block size. It has been replaced by the Advanced Encryption Standard.

**Intractable Problem** A problem is intractable if in general it cannot be solved efficiently. A problem cannot be solved efficiently if there does not exist a probabilistic poly-time Turing machine that solves it.

**Logic Bomb** Code surreptitiously inserted into a program that causes it to perform some destructive or security-compromising activity whenever a specified condition is met.

**Malware (Malicious Software)** Examples of malware include computer viruses, worms, and Trojan horses.

**Public Key Infrastructure (PKI)** An infrastructure that is designed to distribute the public keys of users securely, thereby avoiding man-in-the-middle attacks.

**Subliminal Channel** A communications channel, usually within cryptosystems, that when utilized allows information to be transferred in secret without hindering the normal operation of the cryptosystem.

**Trojan Horse** A code segment that is appended, designed, or integrated into another program that does something that the user does not expect.

# CROSS REFERENCES

See *Computer Viruses and Worms; Hackers, Crackers and Computer Criminals; Hoax Viruses and Virus Alerts; Hostile Java Applets; Spyware.*

# REFERENCES

Anderson, J. P. (1972). *Computer security technology planning study* (ESD-TR-73-51, vol. 2). Hanscom Air Force Base, MA: HQ Electronic Systems Division.

Bell, D. E., & LaPadula, L. J. (1976). Secure computer system: Unified exposition and multics interpretation (MTR-2997). MITRE Corporation.

Cohen, F. (1986). *Computer viruses*. Ph.D. thesis, University of Southern California, ASP Press.

Cohen, F. (1987). Computer Viruses: Theory and experiments (IFIP-TC11). *Computers and Security, 6*, 22–35.

Denning, D. E. (1983). *Cryptography and data security*. Reading, MA: Addison-Wesley.

Denning, P. J. (1988). The science of computing: Computer viruses. *American Scientist, 76*, 236–238.

Dewdney, A. K. (1984). Computer recreations: In the game called Core War hostile programs engage in a battle of bits. *Scientific American, 250*(5), 14–22.

Harley, D., Slade, R., & Gattiker, U. E. (2001). *Viruses revealed*. New York: Osborne/McGraw-Hill.

Karger, P. A., & Schell, R. R. (1974). *Multics security evaluation: Vulnerability analysis*. (ESD-TR-74-193, vol. 2).

Hanscom Air Force Base, MA: HQ Electronic Systems Division.

Lampson, B. W. (1973). A note on the confinement problem. *Communications of the ACM, 16*(10), 613–615.

Lancaster University. (2001). *Backdoor.Smorph, Trojan found at Lancaster University*. Retrieved from http://www.lancs.ac.uk/iss/a-virus/v-smorph.htm.

Makin, K. (1987, November 3). *Globe and Mail*.

McAfee, J., & Haynes, C. (1989). *Computer viruses, worms, data diddlers, killer programs, and other threats to your system*. St. Martin's Press.

Nachenberg, C. (1997). Computer virus-antivirus coevolution. *Communications of the ACM, 40*, 46–51.

Needham, R. M. (1993). Denial of service. *Proceedings of the First ACM Conference on Computer and Communications Security*, pp. 151–153. ACM Press.

Neumann, P. G. (1987). Logic bombs and other system attacks—in Canada. *The Risks Digest, 5*(63).

Parker, D. B. (1976). *Crime by computer*. Charles Scribner's Sons.

Petersen, H. E., & Turn, R. (1967). System implications of information privacy. *Proceedings of the AFIPS Spring Joint Computer Conference*, vol. 30, pp. 291–300. AFIPS Press.

Simmons, G. J. (1984). The prisoners' problem and the subliminal channel. *Advances in Cryptology—Crypto '83*, pp. 51–67. New York: Plenum Press.

Simmons, G. J. (1993). Subliminal communication is easy using the DSA. *Advances in Cryptology—Eurocrypt '93*. Lecture Notes in Computer Science, vol. 765, pp. 218–232. New York: Springer-Verlag.

Simmons, G. J. (1994). Subliminal channels: Past and present. *IEEE European Transactions on Telecommunication, 5*, 459–473.

Simmons, G. J. (1998). The history of subliminal channels. *IEEE Journal on Selected Areas in Communication, 16*, 452–462.

Skardhamar, R. (1996). *Virus detection and elimination*. San Diego, CA: Academic Press.

Slade, R. (1994). *Robert Slade's guide to computer viruses*. New York: Springer-Verlag.

Spafford, E. H., Heaphy, K. A., & Ferbrache, D. J. (1990). A computer virus primer. In P. J. Denning (Ed.), *Computers under attack: Intruders, worms, and viruses*. New York: Addison-Wesley.

Symantec Corporation. (1999). Understanding and managing polymorphic viruses. *The Symantec Enterprise Papers*.

Symantec Corporation. (2003a). *Security response: Trojan.download.revird*. Retrieved December 27, 2003, from http://securityresponse.symantec.com/avcenter/venc/data/trojan.download.revird.html

Symantec Corporation. (2003b). Security response: Backdoor.Gaster. Retrieved December 29, 2003, from http://securityresponse.symantec.com/avcenter/venc/data/backdoor.gaster.html

Von Neumann, J. (1949). *Theory and organization of complicated automata*. Unpublished manuscript (lecture notes).

Von Neumann, J. (1966). Transcripts of lectures given at the University of Illinois (A. W. Burks, Ed.). Part 1, pp. 29–87.

Ware, W. H. (Ed.). (1970). *Security controls for computer systems* (R-609). Santa Monica, CA: RAND.

White, S. R. (1990). Covert distributed processing with computer viruses. *Advances in Cryptology—Crypto '89*. Lecture Notes in Computer Science, vol. 435, pp. 616–619. New York: Springer-Verlag.

Wilding, E. (Ed.), & Skulason, F. (Tech. Ed.). (1992, August). [Entire issue]. *Virus Bulletin*.

Young, A. L., & Yung, M. M. (1996a). Cryptovirology: Extortion-based security threats and countermeasures. *Proceedings of the IEEE Symposium on Security and Privacy*, pp. 129–141. Los Alamitos, CA: IEEE Press.

Young, A. L., & Yung, M. M. (1996b). The dark side of black-box cryptography, or: Should we trust Capstone? *Advances in Cryptology—Crypto '96*. Lecture Notes in Computer Science, vol. 1109, pp. 89–103. New York: Springer-Verlag.

## FURTHER READING

Grimes, R. A. (2001). *Malicious Mobile Code*. O'Reilly & Associates, Inc.

Harley, D. Slade, R., Gattiker, U. E. (2001). *Viruses Revealed*. Osborne/McGraw-Hill.

Slade, R. (1994). *Robert Slade's Guide to Computer Viruses*. Springer-Verlag.

Young, A., Yung, M. (2004). *Malicious Cryptography: Exposing Cryptovirology*. John Wiley & Sons.

# Hoax Viruses and Virus Alerts

Robert Slade, *Vancouver Institute for Research into User Security, Canada*

## INTRODUCTION

On occasion, you will find messages circulating by e-mail, alerting the reader to a new virus, usually virulent and fast-spreading. Called variously virus warning hoaxes, hoax virus warnings, hoax viruses, metaviruses, meme viruses, or simply hoaxes, these messages are false alarms and yet, in a sense, are viruses themselves. Hoaxes attempt to convince the readers to forward multiple copies to other recipients, thus taking up bandwidth, disk space, time, and attention. At times, hoaxes create more problems than computer viruses themselves.

## Memes

In *The Selfish Gene*, Richard Dawkins (1990) expanded on the idea of a meme: an idea that has some perceived value and so, like a useful gene, it is passed along from person to person and generation to generation.

In the case of genes, the value tends to be expressed tautologically: if the gene has value it will benefit the organism and thus increase the chances of being passed on. In the case of memes, the value tends to be subjective and perceived by the individual. Thus, a meme may have an entertainment value, or even one of simple novelty, and thus get passed on. This is very much the case with chain letters in general and virus hoaxes in particular. Virus hoaxes are therefore sometimes referred to as meme viruses, or mind viruses.

## Social Engineering

Broadly, social engineering is the attacking or penetrating of a system by tricking or subverting operators or users, rather than by means of a technical operation. Even more generally, it is the use of fraud, spoofing, or other social or psychological measures to get legitimate users to break security policy.

A major aspect of maliciously programmed software (malware) design is the social engineering component. Trojan horse programs are advertised as having a positive component. E-mail viruses, in generating infected messages, may carry lists of a variety of subject lines, promising pornography, humor, virus information, an antivirus program, and information about abuse of the recipient's e-mail or bank account. Sometimes the message is simply vague and relies on curiosity.

Social engineering really is nothing more than a fancy name for the type of fraud and confidence games that have existed since snakes started selling apples. Social engineering can range from simple lying (such as a false description of the function of a file), to bullying and intimidation (to pressure a low-level employee into disclosing information), to association with a trusted source (such as the user name from an infected machine), to dumpster diving (to find potentially valuable information people have carelessly discarded), to shoulder surfing (to find out personal identification numbers and passwords).

In specific relation to virus warning hoax messages, those who create them rely on human tendencies to want to pass on the latest news (particularly about disasters), to be helpful to other users, and to perform easy actions (such as forwarding messages) rather than more difficult ones (such as verifying facts).

## RELATED ITEMS

Virus hoaxes are far from being the only unwanted e-mail messages. There are a number of types of missives that are equally annoying and that involve factors that are a part of hoaxes. Studying these items helps direct us in regard to policies and means of identification of hoaxes.

## Spam

Spam is a term applied to a number of abuses involving the indiscriminate use of e-mail or newsgroup postings to broadcast advertising, propaganda, self-promotion, or even nonsense. Although the term is most closely associated in the public mind with advertising, other specific activities are multiposting or cross posting to mailing lists or newsgroups, commercial postings, off-topic postings, mailbombing, unsolicited commercial e-mail, junk mail, or unsolicited bulk e-mail.

Frequent topics of spam are advertising, promotion of pornographic sites or services, promotion of consumer items (frequently with attendant fraud), aggression, denial of service by flooding systems with unwanted mail, libel, mischief, fraud (pyramid schemes are a particular favorite), malware distribution, propaganda or political activism, begging letters, sales of spamming service itself, and gambling.

Spammers use a variety of technical means to produce a large number of messages. Most recently it has become clear that viruses or Trojan programs are being used to install backdoors or remote control programs on unguarded home computers and that these are being used as relay networks to create masses of spam that cannot be traced to the originator. (In addition, these spam networks are sometimes being used to distribute initial releases of new e-mail viruses.) Virus hoaxes attempt to do the same thing by having recipients generate more copies of the message because they are under the impression that it is legitimate information.

## Chain Letters

A simple definition of the chain letter can be found in *Oxford Reference Dictionary*: "a letter of which the recipient is asked to make copies and send these to others, who will do the same." Webster's offers a slightly more complex definition: "a letter directing the recipient to send out multiple copies so that its circulation increases in a geometric progression as long as the instructions are carried out." These definitions offer a starting point for considering the mechanism that the chain letter author seeks to exploit.

The U.S. Department of Energy Computer Incident Advisory Capability (CIAC) http://www.ciac.org/ciac) describes the chain letter as having a tripartite structure: hook, threat, and request. Although it is not always straightforward to separate these elements, they do seem to be common to most chain letters, electronic or otherwise. Certainly, all three components are present in virus hoaxes.

The hook is there to catch your interest. Some of the ways in which it might do this include an appeal to greed, fear of technology (our primary topic, virus hoaxes) and the consequences of its perversion or breakdown, sympathy, luck, or important social matters or changes. In some cases the hook is simple interest or curiosity, such as chain letters promoting urban legends or lists of jokes.

The threat is there to persuade you to keep the chain going. Traditional chain letters threaten bad luck, loss of money, loss of sexual activity or attractiveness, or even death. Virus hoaxes threaten the destruction of systems: physical damage, file trashing, or leakage of confidential data. One chain letter ironically threatens unlimited spam if you do not forward it. Others are more subtle: if you do not pass it on, you will miss out on the opportunity to make money or to earn the undying gratitude of your friends. Sometimes the threat is to others: if you do not forward the letter, a little boy's dying wish will not be honored or cancer will continue to flourish. The threat may be implicit or explicit.

Sometimes it pays to look for operative form, not specific content. Most chain letters share some common characteristics. The request is the core function of the chain letter. That purpose is to have you replicate the letter by forwarding it to your friends and acquaintances. The term *replicate* is not used lightly. Chain letters, especially virus hoaxes, are the meme viruses, or viruses of the mind, that we spoke of earlier. Instead of using the infective code used by computer viruses, chain letters rely on suggesting to the recipients that they pass the message on to others.

Virus hoaxes ask you to help others by disseminating information. Cancer victim hoaxes ask you to generate money for medical research by forwarding identical messages. However, the common aim in each case is not to inform, to improve society, or even to sell a product: it is (purely or primarily) self-replicative.

Mailing list sales pyramid schemes ask you to send money, add yourself to the list, and sell on the list or another token product. These schemes are fraudulent. Frequently the messages contain specious claims that, because of a certain twist, they are legal and will provide the promised revenue. All are illegal in most developed countries. All are based on a premise that can be demonstrated to fail in practice.

The following are some of the more common e-mail chain letters you might encounter. Most chain letters circulating on the Internet today are variants of these. Many varieties add their own commentaries or embellish the original letters.

Bill Gates and Microsoft are not going to give you $1,000 for forwarding copies of e-mail. Disney definitely is not going to give you a free vacation. There is no baby food company issuing checks from a class-action suit. There is no kidney theft ring in New Orleans, Detroit, New York City, or anywhere else for that matter. No one is waking up in a bathtub full of ice. (The U.S. National Kidney Foundation has issued repeated appeals for actual victims of kidney thefts to come forward with their stories. None have.)

Yet another form of chain letter appears to be superficially less destructive, in that it purports to be spreading friendship or luck as you pass it on. However, the messages often contain vague, but nonetheless disturbing, threats that the reader will somehow lose providence or companionship if the message is not passed along to others. This may be the most insidious form of chain letter.

## Urban Legends

Urban legends may differ from hoaxes in intent, but contain similar characteristics. The alt.folklore.urban Frequently Asked Questions (FAQs) describe a number of relevant factors: urban legends usually contain elements of humor or horror (the horror often punishing someone who flouts society's conventions), they make a good story, and they do not have to be false, although most are (urban legends often have a basis in fact).

Clearly urban legends resemble hoax chain letters in several respects, according to this definition. Both hoaxes and urban legends often derive from unknown originators and diverge into variant forms. Both have a hook (they make a good story). Both may contain a threat: in the case of the urban legend, the threat is often implicit in the reinforcement of conventional behavior. Both may have a basis in fact, an aspect that is often overlooked in discussions of hoax alerts. The biggest difference is that the urban legend does not carry an overt replicative function: the further dissemination of the story depends largely on its storytelling appeal, rather than an explicit request.

# VIRUS WARNING HOAXES

Hoax virus warnings or alerts have an odd double relation to viruses. First, hoaxes are usually warnings about new viruses: new viruses that do not, of course, exist. Second, hoaxes generally carry a directive to the user to forward the warning to all addresses available to them. Thus these descendants of chain letters form a kind of self-perpetuating spam. Hoaxes use an odd kind of social engineering, relying on people's naturally gregarious nature and desire to communicate, and on a sense of urgency and importance, using the ambition that people have to be the first to provide important new information.

## The Concept and the Metavirus

The first outline of the idea that would become known as the hoax virus warning or metavirus dates back to early 1988. In response to a draconian suggestion for virus protection, Jeffrey Mogul noted that making such recommendations spuriously would be a good way to create more trouble than viruses themselves. He asked the forum to consider the consequences of creating a message that read:

> WARNING! A serious virus is on the loose. It was hidden in the program called 1987TAXFORM that was on this bboard last year.

> This virus does several nasty things:

> (1) Copies itself into several important system programs so that it will propagate to other disks
> (2) Copies itself into your own data files so that it can infect system programs on other systems
> (3) Keeps track of the files you encrypt and mails copies of the cleartext to a bboard in Iowa and a computer at the NSA
> (4) Randomly garbles files so that you don't necessarily know they are damaged

> By now, it is possible that your system is infected even if you didn't download this program, since you could easily have been infected indirectly.

> The only safe way to protect yourself against this virus is to print all your files onto paper, erase all the disks on your system with a demagnetizer, buy fresh software disks from the manufacturer, and type in all your data again. But FIRST! send this message to everyone you know, so that they will also follow these steps to protect themselves.

(The original message can be read at http://catless. ncl.ac.uk/Risks/6.23.html#subj3.1.) Mogul noted that the metavirus only took minutes to produce and did not require any knowledge of programming at all. Thus, a completely unskilled person would be able to create a potentially enormous problem with an absolutely minimal expenditure of effort.

## Mike RoChenle

Within that same year, the first example of the hoax virus was seen. A message did the rounds on Fidonet electronic bulletin boards, purporting to be from someone who had all of his data and programs corrupted, several times in succession, by a virus. According to the notice, the virus copied itself to other systems over a "modem sub-carrier" on the 2,400 bps (the message made the common mistake of referring to "baud") modems, which were relatively new at the time.

The missive went on to state that the subcarrier was used for debugging read-only memory (ROM) and modem registers, and therefore a modem could become infected. The program was then supposed to attach to incoming data and infect the hard drive.

All of this description is, of course, utter nonsense. There is no subcarrier on such modems, ROM is not (or was not, at the time) subject to online debugging, and registers do not have enough space to store a virus. The only way for a virus to attach to incoming data would be to inject bits or bytes into the data stream, and this would result in random noise.

It all sounds very good, and technical, though. This type of technobabble is characteristic of virus hoaxes.

The message was signed by Mike RoChenle. This choice of name was probably a play on IBM's then-new microchannel bus architecture.

## The First Hoax: Good Times

Good Times is probably the most famous of all false alerts and was certainly the earliest that was widely distributed. Some controversy persists over the identity of the originators of the message, but it is possible that it was a sincere, if misguided, attempt to warn others. The hoax probably started in early December 1994. In 1995, the Federal Communications Commission (FCC) variant of the hoax began circulating.

The Good Times alert was mostly likely started by a group or an individual who had seen a computer failure without understanding the cause and associated it with an e-mail message that had "Good Times" in the subject line. (In fact, there are indications that the message started out on the America Online [AOL] system, and it is known that there are bugs in AOL's mail software that can cause the program to hang.) The announcement states that there was a message, identified by the title of "Good Times," that, when read, would crash your computer. The message was said to be a virus, even though there was nothing viral about that sort of activity (even if it were possible).

At the time of the original Good Times message, e-mail was almost universally text-based. Other chapters in this book discuss the possibility of American National Standards Institute (ANSI) bombs and other text-based malicious software. Suffice it to say that the possibility of a straightforward text message carrying a virus in an infective form is remote. The fact that the warning contained almost no details at all should have been an indication that the message was not quite right. It provided no information on how to detect, avoid, or get rid of the virus, except for its warning not to read messages with "Good Times" in the subject line. (The irony of the fact that many of the warnings contained these words in the subject seems to have escaped most people.)

Pathetically (and far from uniquely), a member of the VX community produced a Good Times virus. Like the virus named after the older Proto-T hoax, the "real" Good Times was an uninteresting specimen, having nothing in common with the original alert. It is generally known as GT-Spoof by the antivirus community and was hardly ever found in the field.

The heyday of the Good Times virus (in terms of its maximum impact) and its primary variants was around 1994–1995, though close variants continued to appear for many years.

The Good Times FAQ has not been updated for several years, but remains an excellent source of information, not only on the hoax itself, but also on the hoax phenomenon. The FAQ's influence on later writers and researchers is as profound as the hoax itself was on the content of later hoaxes. The original document seems to have been abandoned, but there are copies of it at http://www.claws-and-paws.com/virus/faqs/gtfaq.shtml, http://www.wap.org/info/techstuff/good-times-virus-hoax-faq.txt, and http://www.cityscope.net/hoax1.html.

## The JPEG Hoax and Graphics Viruses

The Joint Photographic Experts Group (JPEG) virus hoax is a straightforward prank, released on April 1 of both 1994 and 1995. The announcement was rather carefully crafted of technobabble that recalled, for example, the data overrun bug in sendmail that was used by the Internet Worm. The warning was said to be the result of research by Dr. Charles Forbin. Charles Forbin is the main character in the science-fiction book *Colossus* and the movie *The Forbin Project*. (That story is along the usual computer-takes-over-the-world line.)

Although the announcement of the JPEG virus was an obvious hoax, the concept of a virus hidden in a graphics file is a complex one. In general, the data in a graphics file would never be executed as a program and therefore would be of no use as a viral vector. During 1994, however, a .GIF (graphics interchange format) file caused much alarm when posted to a Usenet newsgroup. The file header contained a very odd section of data, with suspicious text references. Those who examined it ultimately decided that the file was harmless and that this file was possibly a hoax aimed at a select and suspicious few on the nets. This should not, however, be interpreted as meaning that JPEGs are always safe. Apart from the well-known double extension trick (virusfile.jpg.exe, for instance) which has been used by real viruses several times already, a file with a filename whose extension really is .JPG or an icon suggesting an association with a graphics program is not necessarily what it appears to be. A true JPEG is not an executable file and cannot be executed: it can only be displayed by a suitable graphics application.

Such an application will not execute an .EXE masquerading as a .JPG, but a command shell may interpret the filename correctly as an executable file irrespective of its extension.

## The Use of Real Files

A more recent example of a hoax, SULFNBK.EXE, got a number of people to clear this legitimate utility off their machines.

The origin was likely the fact that the Magistr virus targets Windows system software, and someone with an infection did not realize that the file is actually present on all Windows 98 and Windows 2000 systems.

When people received this warning, the fact that they actually found this file on their computers lent credence to the warning, and most forwarded the warning with their own personal endorsement. Subsequent hoaxes have used this pattern of referring to a real (albeit little known) file. Rather ironically, one such hoax made reference to a database engine file that was part of the Microsoft Office suite. It was later found that this particular file did have a security loophole, although it was never used by any virus.

# CHARACTERISTICS AND IDENTIFICATION

As we have seen, hoax warnings can come in a variety of forms and with a variety of justifications. In addition, it is easy to either modify an existing hoax warning or to create a new one with a few moments' thought.

Hoaxes do have common characteristics that can be used to determine whether their warnings are valid. Example text from actual hoax viruses is included to demonstrate some of the attributes under discussion. Hoaxes generally ask the reader to forward the message, making the reader the infectious agent.

> California (also known as **Wobbler**): "Please pass this message on to all your contacts and anyone who uses your e-mail facility.... Forward this letter to as many people as you can."

> Bug's Life: "Please pass it on to anyone you know who has access to the Internet.... Please copy this information and e-mail it to everyone in your address book. We need to do all we can to block this virus...pass this information on to your friends, acquaintances and work colleagues."

> Budweiser Frogs: "Please distribute this message.... Please share it with everyone that might access the Internet. Once again, pass this along to EVERYONE in your address book so that this may be stopped."

> It Takes Guts to Say Jesus: "Pass this warning along to EVERYONE in your address book and please share it with all your online friends ASAP so that this threat may be stopped."

> It Takes Guts to Say Jesus Variant: "Please practice cautionary measures and tell anyone that may have access to your computer. Forward this

warning to everyone that might access the Internet."

Hoaxes make reference to false authorities such as Microsoft, AOL, IBM, and the FCC (none of which issue virus alerts) or to completely false entities.

California (also known as Wobbler): "IBM and AOL have announced that it is very powerful, more so than Melissa [The same hoax contained an internal contradiction]... information was announced yesterday morning from Microsoft."

Bug's Life: "This information came from Microsoft yesterday.... AOL has confirmed how dangerous [the virus] is."

Budweiser Frogs: "This information was announced yesterday morning from Microsoft."

It Takes Guts to Say Jesus: "... was announced yesterday morning from IBM; AOL states that this is..."

Hoaxes do not give specific information about the individual or office responsible for analyzing the virus or issuing the alert. A real warning worth receiving will tell you what the virus infects, how it activates, what actions to take to avoid activating it, how to get rid of it, what antiviral programs will detect it (and by what name), which Web sites to go to for more information or updates, the company or person responsible for this report, and much more hard data as well.

Hoaxes generally state that the new virus is unknown to authorities or researchers. This is probably an attempt to dissuade readers from contacting real authorities and finding out that the warning is false. In the case of any real virus, samples are generally obtained and analyzed within hours.

California (also known as Wobbler): "Not many people seem to know about this yet so propagate it as fast as possible.... This is a new, very malicious virus and again, not many people know about it."

Bug's Life: "As far as we know, the virus was circulated yesterday morning. It's a new virus, and extremely dangerous."

Budweiser Frogs: "IT JUST WENT INTO circulation yesterday, as far as we know.... This is a new, very malicious virus and not many people know about it."

Win a Holiday: "This is a new, very malicious virus and not many people know about it."

Hoaxes often state that there is no means of detecting or removing the virus.

California (also known as Wobbler): "There is no remedy."

Death Ray: "'So how do you protect yourself? I wish I knew,' said Heriden. 'You either stop using the Internet or you take your chances until we

can get a handle on this thing and get rid of it for good.'"

Budweiser Frogs: "A very dangerous virus and that there is NO remedy for it."

Many of the original hoax warnings stated only that you should not open a message with a certain phrase in the subject line. (The warning, of course, usually contained that phrase in the subject line. Subject line filtering is known to be a very poor method of detecting malware.)

California (also known as Wobbler): "Very Urgent VIRUS(s) Warning with titles: 'Win a Holiday' OR 'California.'"

PenPal Greetings: "If anyone receives mail entitled: PENPAL GREETINGS! please delete it WITHOUT reading it."

Budweiser Frogs: "Also do not open or even look at any mail that says 'RETURNED' or 'UNABLE TO DELIVER.'" [At that time, those were common subject lines for email rejection notices.]

It Takes Guts to Say Jesus: "If you receive an E-mail titled, 'It Takes Guts to Say "Jesus."'"

Hoaxes often state that the virus does tremendous damage and is incredibly virulent, often including damage to hardware. Some viruses can, and will, erase data on your computer, sometimes to the extent of overwriting everything on the hard disk. There is no known virus that actually damages hardware, and most researchers believe it would be pointless to try and create such a beast, since any possible damage to hardware that can be accomplished with software would be very hardware-specific.

Death Ray: "But suffice it to say that the virus affects the computer's hardware, creating conditions that lead to dangerous short circuits and power surges. The end result? Explosions— powerful explosions. And millions of Internet users are at risk."

California (also known as Wobbler): "It will eat all your information on the hard drive and also destroys Netscape Navigator and Microsoft Internet Explorer."

Bug's Life: "Once opened, you will lose EVERYTHING on your PC. Your hard disk will be completely destroyed."

Budweiser Frogs: "This virus will attach itself to your computer components and render them useless."

It Takes Guts to Say Jesus: "It will erase everything on your hard drive.... Some very sick individual has succeeded in using the reformat function from Norton Utilities causing it to completely erase all documents on the hard drive.... It destroys Macintosh and IBM compatible computers."

A.I.D.S. Hoax: "IT WILL ATTACH ITSELF INSIDE YOUR COMPUTER AND EAT AWAY AT YOUR MEMORY. THIS MEMORY IS IRREPLACEABLE. THEN WHEN IT'S FINISHED WITH MEMORY IT INFECTS YOUR MOUSE OR POINTING DEVICE. THEN IT GOES TO YOUR KEY BOARD AND THE LETTERS YOU TYPE WILL NOT REGISTER ON SCREEN. BEFORE IT SELF TERMINATES IT EATS 5MB OF HARD DRIVE SPACE AND WILL DELETE ALL PROGRAMS ON IT AND IT CAN SHUT DOWN ANY 8 BIT TO 16 BIT SOUND CARDS RENDERING YOUR SPEAKERS USELESS."

As you can see in the previous example, hoax warnings very often contain A LOT OF CAPITAL LETTERS, SHOUTING, AND EXCLAMATION MARKS!!!!!!!!!!

E-mail or Get a Virus: "IM SORRY GUYS>>I REALLY DONT BELIEVE IT BUT SENDING IT TO YALL JUST IN CASE!!!!!!!!!!!!"

California, (also known as Wobbler): "Remember, DO NOT DOUBLE CLICK THE FILE!!!"

Win a Holiday: "If you receive an email titled 'WIN A HOLIDAY' DO NOT open it."

Bug's Life: "DO NOT OPEN IT UNDER ANY CIRCUMSTANCES."

Hoaxes often contain technical-sounding nonsense (technobabble), such as references to nonexistent technologies such as nth complexity binary loops.

## PROTECTION AND POLICY

It is wisest, in the current environment, to doubt all virus warnings unless they come from a known and historically accurate source, such as a vendor with a proven record of providing reliable and accurate virus alert information or preferably an independent researcher or group. It is best to check *any* warnings received against known virus encyclopedia sites. It is best to check more than one such site: in the initial phases of a fast-burner attack, some sites may not have had time to analyze samples to their own satisfaction, and the better sites will not post information they are not sure about.

To deal with hoaxes, you should appoint a competent person to verify potential hoaxes as required by checking signatures, personally contacting trusted individuals, and checking reliable sources and uniform resource locators (URLs). It makes sense for this person to have in-depth knowledge of computer software and hardware and, even better, real virus and antivirus technology, so that he or she can evaluate a wide range of reported threats from his or her own knowledge and experience. Alternatively, you could outsource this function to your antivirus vendor or some other suitably qualified third party.

You should have policies in place that discourage people from passing on virus alerts (even real ones), chain letters, and so on and absolutely forbid them to do so without having them verified. Be as general as possible in your definitions: you do not want people who would

recognize a Good Times clone easily to fall victim nevertheless to a chain letter hoax, so discourage unverified mass mail-outs rather than just discouraging the passing on of virus alerts.

## CONCLUSION

Despite the complete lack of technical work or programming involved, hoax virus alerts can frequently cause serious trouble. They overload mail queues, contribute to spam, waste bandwidth, consume time and attention, and may, on occasion, cause users to cripple their own machines. Teaching users to recognize and ignore, or at least test, hoaxes is a worthwhile use of security awareness time.

## GLOSSARY

**American National Standards Institute (ANSI) Bomb** In ANSI bombs, the use of certain codes (escape sequences, usually embedded in text files or e-mail messages) remaps keys on the keyboard to commands such as "delete" or "format." ANSI is a short form that refers to the ANSI screen formatting rules. Many early MS-DOS programs relied on these rules and required the use of the ANSI.SYS file, which also allowed keyboard remapping. The use of ANSI.SYS is now very rare.

**ASCII Files** ASCII files are files consisting of only ASCII characters and generally only the printable characters. With effort, it is possible to write program files for Intel-based computers consisting only of printable characters. (An example is the EICAR Standard Antivirus Test File.) Windows batch (BAT) files and Visual Basic Script files are also typically pure text and program files, but are interpreted rather than being executed as object code.

**Hoax** Literally, a joke, fraud, or other form of spoofing. The term *hoax* has developed a specific technical meaning in virus research in reference to a form of chain letter carrying a false warning of a nonexistent virus. Originally (1988) referred to in the research community as a metavirus, this type of activity was more widely seen in the late 1990s. Hoaxes are characterized by a lack of technical detail and valid contact information, references to false authorities, warnings of extreme damage that the putative virus will cause, all uppercase "SHOUTING" and exclamation marks in the text and frequently statements that the virus is too new or spreading too rapidly for legitimate virus researchers to know anything about. The one universal factor in hoaxes is the attempt to have the reader forward the message to all friends, relatives, and contacts, which is, of course, the viral component: the hoax message uses the user to retransmit and spread.

**Mailbomb** (n.) Excessively large volume of e-mail (typically many thousands of messages) or one large message sent to a user's e-mail account for the purpose of crashing the system or preventing genuine messages from being received. (v.) To send a mailbomb.

**Mail Storm** A condition in which many redundant messages are generated and sent, generally resulting from automated mail handling (such as vacation autoresponders replying to automatic forwarding mailing lists). Most modern mail systems have capabilities for dealing with common causes of mail storms.

**Malware** A collective term including the many varieties of deliberately malicious software, that is, software written for the purpose of causing inconvenience, destruction, or the breaking of security policies or provisions. Malware is generally considered to include programs such as distributed denial of service (DDoS) clients (or zombies), logic bombs, remote access Trojans (RATs), Trojan horses, viruses, and worms. Malware is generally not considered to include unintentional problems in software, such as bugs, or deliberately written software that is not intended to do harm, such as pranks.

**Social Engineering** Social engineering is attacking or penetrating a system by tricking or subverting operators or users, rather than by means of a technical attack. More generally, the use of fraud, spoofing, or other social or psychological measures to get legitimate users to break security policy.

**Spam** (v.) To indiscriminately send unsolicited, unwanted, irrelevant, or inappropriate messages, especially commercial advertising in mass quantities. In sufficient volume, spam can cause denial of service. (n.) Electronic junk mail.

Yes, the term spam, used in reference to masses of unwanted e-mail or newsgroup postings, does derive from SPAM the canned meat. There is an opinion that says the term was used because spam pretends to be information in the same way that SPAM pretends to be . . . well, Hormel is a good sport about the neologistic appropriation of their trade name, so we will not belabor the point, beyond noting that the same speculation also makes an analogy between nonsense content and fat content. Hormel says, "We do not object to use of this slang term [spam] to describe [unsolicited commercial email (UCE)], although we do object to the use of our product image in association with that term. Also, if the term is to be used, it should be used in all lower-case letters to distinguish it from our trademark SPAM, which should be used with all uppercase letters."

The more commonly accepted derivation is that the term derives from a Monty Python sketch involving a restaurant where the menu items contain increasing amounts of SPAM, and the Viking clientele eventually drown out all dialogue by singing about "SPAM, SPAM, SPAM, SPAM, SPAM, SPAM, SPAM, SPAM" in a kind of conversational denial of service.

**Viral** Having the features of a virus, particularly self-reproduction.

**Virus** A self-replicating and propagating program, usually operating with some form of input from the user, although generally the user is unaware of the intent of the virus. Often considered to be a self-propagating Trojan horse composed of a mission component, a trigger component, and a self-propagating component. A final definition has not yet been agreed upon by all researchers. A common definition is, "a program which modifies other programs to contain a possibly altered version of itself." This definition is generally attributed to Fred Cohen, although Dr. Cohen's actual definition is in mathematical form. Another possible definition is, "an entity which uses the resources of the host (system or computer) to reproduce itself and spread, without informed operator action."

## CROSS REFERENCES

See *Computer Viruses and Worms; Hackers, Crackers and Computer Criminals; Hostile Java Applets; Spyware; Trojan Horse Programs.*

## REFERENCES

Dawkins, R. (1990). *The selfish gene* (2nd ed.). New York: Oxford University Press.

Gattiker, U., Harley, D., & Slade, R. (2001). *Viruses revealed*. New York: McGraw-Hill.

*Oxford English Reference Dictionary* (2nd Rev edition (October 1, 2002). J. Pearsall & B. Trumble (Eds). Oxford University Press.

Security Glossary. Retrieved May 14, 2005, http://victoria.tc.ca/techrev/secgloss.htm and http://sun.soci.niu.edu/~rslade/secgloss.htm.

Slade, R., Harley, D., & Gattiker, U. (2001). *Viruses revealed*. New York: McGraw-Hill Ryerson/Osborne.

Slade, R. M. (1996). *Robert Slade's guide to computer viruses* (2nd ed.). New York: Springer-Verlag.

Spam and the Internet. Retrieved May 14, 2005, from http://www.spam.com/ci/ci_in.htm.

## FURTHER READING

*A to Z Hoax's.* (n.d.). Retrieved March 2004, from http://www.virusassi.st/atoz.htm.

*H-05 Internet Hoaxes: PKZ300, Irina, Good Times, Deeyenda, Ghost.* (1996, November 20). Retrieved March 2004, from U.S. Department of Energy Computer Incident Advisory Capability Web site: http://ciac.llnl.gov/ciac/bulletins/h-05.shtml.

*Information about hoaxes.* (n.d.) Retrieved March 2004, from U.S. Department of Energy Computer Incident Advisory Capability's Hoaxbusters Web site: http://hoaxbusters.ciac.org/HBHoaxInfo.html.

*Les Jones' Good Time FAQ.* (n.d.). Retrieved March 2004, from http://www.claws-and-paws.com/virus/faqs/gtfaq.shtml.

*What should I know about virus hoaxes?* (2002, May 29). Retrieved March 2004, from University of Pennsylvania's Web site: http://www.sas.upenn.edu/computing/help/Server/virus_info.html.

# Hostile Java Applets

David Evans, *University of Virginia*

## INTRODUCTION

Java was introduced in 1995 as both a high-level programming language and an intermediate language, Java Virtual Machine language (JVML, sometimes called *Java byte codes*), and execution platform, the Java Virtual Machine (Java VM), designed for secure execution of programs from untrusted sources in Web browsers (Gosling, 1995). These small programs that are intended to execute within larger applications are known as *applets*. Java runs on a wide range of platforms scaling from the Java Card smart card environment (Chen, 2000) to the Java 2 Enterprise Edition (J2EE) for large component-based enterprise applications (Singh, Stearns, Johnson, & the Enterprise Team, 2002). This chapter focuses on the Java 2 Platform, Standard Edition (J2SE), which is the most common platform for desktop applications and servers, including Web browsers. Most of the security issues are the same across all Java platforms, however. Because of the limited functionality of the Java Card environment, some of the security concerns with the standard edition do not apply; the added complexity of J2EE raises additional security issues (Gong, Ellison, & Dageforde, 2003).

The Java programming language adopted most of the syntax of C++ and semantics of Scheme. Because the Java programming language does not provide the type unsafe features of C++ (including pointer arithmetic and unchecked type casts), programs written in the Java programming language (and compiled correctly and executed in a correct virtual machine implementation) can guarantee certain security properties. However, because applets are transmitted as JVML, there is no guarantee that Java applets were created using the Java programming language. JVML programs can be created using a compiler for a different programming language or edited directly. Hence, all security claims made for executing Java applets are based solely on the mechanisms provided by JVML and the Java VM execution platform.

The Java Virtual Machine attempts to provide security properties that enable code from untrusted sources to be safely executed. It confines executing applets to a *virtual playpen* (sometimes called a *sandbox*) that limits what they can do and mediates access to external resources according to a policy. Malicious applets can attempt to behave in ways that are detrimental to the host. The most serious malicious applets find a way to circumvent Java's security mechanisms and gain complete control of the host machine. These attack applets depend on exploiting a vulnerability in a Java implementation. Other classes of malicious applets may disturb the victim without circumventing Java's security mechanisms by behaving in an annoying or disruptive way that is within the behaviors permitted by the policy.

The next section of this chapter presents an overview of Java's security mechanisms. Next, we provide an overview of the Java security model. The next section describes Java's mechanisms for low-level code safety necessary to ensure that malicious applets cannot circumvent high-level security mechanisms. The third section describes Java's high-level code safety mechanisms that can impose a policy on an applet execution. The fourth section discusses hostile applets that behave maliciously without circumventing Java's security mechanisms, and the fifth section considers exploit applets that damage the victim by circumventing Java security mechanisms. The sixth section concludes.

## JAVA SECURITY OVERVIEW

Security in Java is based on a model in which code executes in a virtual machine that mediates access to critical system resources. Instead of executing directly on the host machine and having access to all resources a user-level process can access on the machine, a Java applet executes inside the Java VM. The Java VM itself is typically a user-level process running on the host machine, so its access is limited by the underlying operating system according to the permissions assigned to its process owner. The Java VM, however, places additional constraints on what the applets it executes may do. In particular, it mediates access to system resources that are considered security critical.

The Java VM executes programs written in JVML, a stack-based language with a relatively small and simple instruction set. Although they are often produced from a Java programming language program by a Java compiler, JVML programs can be produced manually or from some other language by a compiler that targets JVML.

Java security depends crucially on knowing that the only way an applet can manipulate controlled resources is through Java application program interface (API) method calls that perform security checks before permitting security-critical operations. Hence, we can divide Java security mechanisms into two categories:

• *Low-level* code safety mechanisms designed to ensure that all manipulations of critical resources are performed only through Java API calls
• *High-level* code safety mechanisms designed to enforce an access control policy on resource manipulations done through Java API calls

Java's security model has evolved since the initial 1.0 release. Java 1.0 distinguished local trusted code from untrusted applets but did not provide any mechanisms for signing code or applying different policies to different external code. Java 1.1 introduced code signing whereby cryptographically signed applets could execute as trusted code. The Java 2 platform provided richer mechanisms for access control and policy association. It allows different policies to be associated with different applets running in the same Java VM. Except when specifically noted, this chapter describes the security model provided by version 1.4.2 of the Java 2 platform.

The next sections describe what low-level code safety and policy-specific code safety involve, first describing Java's mechanisms for providing low-level code safety and second describing Java's mechanisms for providing policy-specific code safety.

## Low-Level Code Safety

Low-level code safety ensures that all resource manipulation is done through standard method calls. It is necessary to prevent malicious applets from circumventing Java's security mechanisms. Low-level code safety requires *type safety*, *memory safety*, and *control flow safety*.

Type safety means that data values are always manipulated in a type-consistent way. All values in Java have a type, and different operations are possible on different types. For example, integers can be added and object references can be dereferenced but integers cannot be dereferenced. If it were possible to dereference integer values or to perform arithmetic operations on object references, it would be possible to manipulate arbitrary locations in memory, thereby circumventing Java's security mechanisms. For example, if type safety is not enforced, an applet could create an integer constant that corresponds to the address where the security policy is stored and then use that integer as an object to change the security policy.

Memory safety means that reads and writes to memory must be within the storage allocated for an object. Without memory safety, a malicious applet could access memory beyond the range allocated for an object to change the value of some other value. The standard stack smashing buffer overflow attack (Aleph One, 1996) operates this way: by writing data beyond the space allocated for an object, the attacker can overwrite the return address on the stack and inject malicious code into memory. Memory safety prevents this class of attacks in Java, because it should not be possible for a malicious applet to write to memory beyond the allocated space for an object.

Control flow safety ensures that execution jumps are always to valid locations. In Java, this means that execution may not jump into the middle of a method but only to the beginning. Without control flow safety, a malicious applet could jump directly to security critical code inside an API method, thereby circumventing the security checks that must be done before performing the critical operation.

## High-Level Code Safety

High-level code safety is concerned with controlling access to security-critical resources. Unlike low-level code safety, which is necessary to ensure that security mechanisms are not circumvented and essentially the same mechanisms are necessary to enforce *any* security policy, high-level code safety enforces a resource control policy that will vary by users, systems, and applications. Enforcement is done using a straightforward reference monitor: before an applet attempts a security critical operation, checks are performed to determine whether the intended operation is permitted by the policy. If the check fails, the security critical operation is not permitted and a security exception is raised. A policy is associated with code using a ClassLoader, which controls how new classes are loaded into a Java VM.

The two main challenges in high-level code safety are defining a policy that allows enough access to enable applets to do useful things and associating the appropriate policy with particular code. Later sections in this chapter describe the permissions that can be granted in Java to control access to system resources, describe how policies for different applets and executions are defined using those permissions and how a particular policy is associated with an executing class, and explain Java's mechanisms for enforcing those policies.

## LOW-LEVEL CODE SAFETY MECHANISMS

Java enforces low-level code safety using a combination of static and dynamic checks. Static checks are performed by the Java bytecode verifier before a Java class file is loaded into the Java virtual machine; dynamic checks are performed by the Java virtual machine to check certain properties before an instruction that could violate low-level code safety is executed.

### Bytecode Verification

The Java bytecode verifier statically checks certain properties of Java class files before they are loaded into the virtual machine (Lindholm & Yellin, 1999). It checks that the class file is in the correct format and that it contains the data it should. Most important, it checks properties of the class file that are necessary for low-level code safety. The bytecode verifier by itself is not sufficient to completely guarantee low-level code safety, but it does establish properties that in combination with the run-time checks are enough to provide low-level code safety. These properties include ensuring that values of the appropriate types are on the stack before every instruction and that a value stored in a memory location is treated as the same type of value when it is loaded.

The bytecode verifier simulates execution of a JVML program. In general, checking low-level code safety is an undecidable problem that requires reasoning about all possible executions of a program. To enable efficient verification, Java's bytecode verifier makes some conservative assumptions and puts off checking certain instructions (e.g., as type casts and array fetches) until run time. The conservative assumptions mean that there are some safe programs that the verifier will reject, but that there are no unsafe programs that are accepted by a correctly implemented verifier. One assumption made by the bytecode verifier is that the type stored in a particular local memory location is the same throughout a procedure's execution. This, along with a few other similar assumptions, means that the bytecode verifier can simulate execution without needing to follow any backward jumps (e.g., loop repetitions) and that each method call can be checked based only on the type signature, without any need to simulate the method body for each call site.

If the verifier finds a type violation or an instruction that would cause a stack overflow or underflow, it raises an exception and the code will not be loaded to execute in the Java VM. If the code is accepted by the verifier, it means that all operations except checked casts and array assignments are type safe, all jumps are to valid locations, and all memory loads and stores are either to valid locations or are done through instructions that will be checked for memory safety at run time.

## Run-Time Checks

Because of the limits of static analysis, some type and memory safety properties cannot be checked by the bytecode verifier. These properties must be checked at run time by the Java VM. Run-time checking is typically simpler and hence less prone to vulnerability than static checking, but it imposes an execution time penalty because the checking is done during the program execution. The other disadvantage of run-time checking is that problems will not be detected until the program has already begun executing.

Array fetches and stores in Java use load and store instructions that expect an array and an integer index value that identifies the array element on the stack. Memory safety depends on the index being within the array bounds. Arbitrary computations can calculate the index value, so it is impossible for the bytecode verifier to determine whether the index is within range. Hence, the Java VM must check at run time that all array indexes are within bounds. If the index is not in bounds, an

ArrayIndexOutOfBoundsException is raised and the attempted array access is prevented.

Type casts are necessary in Java to change the apparent type of an object to a subtype of its apparent type. The actual type of the object must be a subtype of the cast type, but it is not always possible to determine the actual type of an object at verification time. For type casts that are not known to be safe at compile time, the Java compiler produces a checkcast instruction that changes the apparent type of an object for bytecode verification but is checked at run time to ensure that the actual type of the object matches the cast type.

The final run-time low-level code safety check performed by the Java VM is for stores into elements of array parameters. Java's type system allows an array of type S elements to be passed as a parameter whose type is an array of T elements if S is a subtype of T. However, if the method body stores a value of type T into the array, it may not be of type S and would violate the array element type. The verifier checks the method body according to the apparent type of the array parameter, but the actual type is not known at verification time. Hence, the array store must be checked at run time. If the type of the value stored in the array is not a subtype of the actual element type of the array, the array store is prohibited and an ArrayStoreException is raised.

In conjunction with the bytecode verifier, the run-time safety checks provided by the Java VM are designed to ensure that Java applets cannot violate type safety, memory safety, or control flow safety. As long as they are implemented correctly (see the Violating Low-Level Code Safety section for a discussion of hostile applets that exploit bugs in the bytecode verifier) and the assumptions they make about the computing environment are true (that section includes a description of an example attack that depends on violating those assumptions), they prevent hostile applets from being able to manipulate resources without going through the high-level code safety mechanisms.

## HIGH-LEVEL CODE SAFETY MECHANISMS

Low-level code safety mechanisms prevent hostile applets from circumventing the high-level code safety mechanisms provided by the Java VM. Those high-level code safety mechanisms are designed to impose a policy on an executing applet that limits its access to system resources. Depending on the level of trustworthiness associated with the applet, a different policy may apply that enables and disables permissions appropriately. The next sections describe the types of policies Java can impose and how they are defined, how a particular policy is associated with code, and how the Java VM enforces a high-level code safety policy on an execution.

## Permissions

A Java policy specifies what actions an applet may perform. Particular actions require specific permissions. If an applet attempts an action but does not have the associated permission, the action will not be permitted and a security exception is raised.

Java supports 19 permission classes for specifying different actions; many of these permissions can be parameterized (Sun 2002a). For example, the java.io. FilePermission class represents permissions related to file input and output. An instance of the class is a pathname and a set of actions (selected from read, write, execute, and delete) permitted for that pathname.

This summarizes all the permissions that can be granted by a Java security policy. Many of the permissions are inherently dangerous: if they are granted, a hostile applet could use them to obtain other permissions. For example, granting the ReflectPermission permits an applet to use Java's reflection methods to access field and call methods without normal access checks being performed. A hostile applet could use this permission to manipulate other resources in ways that circumvent the security policy. For example, reflection could be used to invoke the private java.io.File.delete0 method to delete a file regardless of whether the applet has the required permission (normally, the java.io.File.delete method first checks whether the caller has permission to delete the file and then invokes delete0 to delete the file). The permission RuntimePermission.setSecurityManager allows an applet to replace the security manager with a custom security manager, thereby circumventing any checking done by the original security manager.

## Policies

When loading a class in Java, a subclass of the abstract class, ClassLoader, is responsible for creating the association between the loaded class and its protection domain. These static permissions are associated with the class at run time through a protection domain (PD). Each Java class will be mapped to one PD, and each PD encapsulates a set of permissions. A PD is determined based on the person running the code, the code's signers, and the code's origin. If two classes share the same context (principal, signers, and origin), they will be assigned to the same PD, because their set of granted permissions will be the same.

Policies are sets of rules that determine whether a particular action is permitted. To assign permissions, the class loader checks the security policy defined, and the policy grants specific permissions to code based on certain code attributes and then associates the permissions with the class by a PD. Prior to J2SE 1.4, permissions were assigned statically at load time by default, but now dynamic security permissions are supported (Sun, 2003). This provides more flexibility but increases complexity and makes reasoning about security policies difficult.

Java policies are defined by specifying the permissions granted in a policy file. The policy file specifies permissions to be granted based on properties of an execution: the origin of the code, the digital signers of the code (if any), and who is executing the code. A user can edit the policy files with a normal text editor or the PolicyTool. Java's policies are also affected by a system-wide properties file, java.security, that specifies paths to other policy files, a source of randomness for the random number generator, and other important properties. These security properties should not need to change often, but they are important in understanding how the policy is configured. Changes to this file could greatly influence the system's policy, since a user could change which files are used for the actual policy in this file.

The policy file contains a list of grant entries. Each grant entry identifies a context that determines when the grant applies and then lists a set of permissions that are granted in that context. The context may specify the signers of the code (a list of names, all of whom must have signed the code for the context to apply), the origin of the code (code base uniform resource locator [URL]), and one or more principals (on whose behalf the code is executing). If no principals are listed, the context applies to all possible principals.

The following is an example grant entry:

```
grant signedBy "John" {
        permission java.io.FilePermission
            "C:\\temp\\*", "read, write";
};
```

This grants all applets signed by "John" permission to read and write files in the C:\temp\ directory. The grant entry

```
grant codebase "http://www.cs.virginia.edu",
  principal javax.security.auth.x500
        .X500Principal "cn=evans" {
    permission java.io.FilePermission
            "/usr/evans/*",
            "read, write";
};
```

grants applets from URLs within the www.cs.virginia.edu domain permission to read and write files in the /usr/evans/ directory when they are running on behalf of principal "evans."

Java is installed with one system-wide policy file, but if a user adds his or her own policy file, that file will also be taken into account. The granted permission set is the union of the permissions granted in all the policy files, so the default permission is the union of both of these policy files' granted permissions. This is dangerous, because a user may have a difficult time of actually determining what permissions are actually being granted. Further, it means a user can make the policy less restrictive than the system policy but cannot make the policy more restrictive.

Because most users are unlikely to change the security policy themselves, hostile applets target the default system security policy. Sun's default Java security policy (J2SE 1.4.2) grants all permissions to code loaded from the lib/ext subdirectory of the Java installation on the local file system and grants several permissions to all applets (including untrusted applets):

- Listen on unprivileged ports (port numbers 1024–65535)
- Stop its own thread
- Read standard system properties including the Java version and vendor and operating system

In addition, most containers permit applets to make network connections back to their originating host.

Everything else such as file system operations, network sockets (except to the originating host), and audio is forbidden.

## Enforcing Policies

The Java VM enforces policies on executions using the SecurityManager, which uses the AccessController class to check that code has the necessary permission before a controlled operation is executed. When a controlled operation is requested in Java, the call to the SecurityManager's CheckPermission method simply calls on the AccessController and the AccessController grants or denies access according to the applicable security policy based on the code's protection domain, as determined from its associated ClassLoader. Security depends on the Java API calling the appropriate SecurityManager check method before every controlled operation and on the checking code associating the correct policy with the executing code.

When deciding to grant a permission to execute a requested action, the AccessController must determine which policy should apply to the request. Because code with different trust levels may be executing in the same Java VM, associating a policy with a request requires examining the stack to determine which code is responsible for the request. Every thread's stack consists of a set

**Table 1** Java Permissions

| Resource | Permission Class (Target) | Actions Controlled |
|---|---|---|
| General Resources | AllPermission | All permissions. Granting AllPermission effectively turns off all access control security. |
| | SecurityPermission | Altering the security policy including setting the policy, setting security properties, and retrieving private keys. |
| | UnresolvedPermission | Used to represent permissions that are not resolved until run time (actual permission class does not exist when the policy is initialized). |
| | AuthPermission | Managing credentials and invoking code using a different identity. |
| File System | FilePermission | Reading, writing, executing, and deleting files. |
| Network | SocketPermission | Creating network sockets. Controls the ability to connect to specific hosts and ports and to listen on local ports. |
| | NetPermission | Various network actions: control how authentication is done, stream handling, and requesting passwords. |
| | SSLPermission | Accessing SSL session contexts. |
| Display | AWTPermission (showWindow-WithoutWarning, readDisplayPixels) | Creating pop-up windows that are not marked with a warning that indicates that they were created by an untrusted program; examine pixels on the display. |
| System Clipboard | AWTPermission (accessClipboard) | Reading from and writing to the system clipboard. |
| Keyboard, Mouse | AWTPermission (listenToAllAWTEvents, accessEventQueue, createRobot) | Examining, altering, and creating events in the system event queue. |
| System Properties | PropertyPermission | Reading and writing system properties (environment variables). |
| Speaker, Microphone | AudioPermission | Playing and recording sounds. |
| Printer | RuntimePermission (queuePrintJob) | Sending jobs to the printer. |
| Application-Specific Resources | SQLPermission | Accessing the SQL log. |
| | ServicePermission, Delegation Permission | Using and delegating Kerberos services. |
| | PrivateCredentialPermission | Accessing private credentials associated with a specific subject. |
| Java-Specific Resources | LoggingPermission | Altering system logging levels. |
| | ReflectPermission | Using Java reflection to directly access fields and methods in a class. (Allows code to access private methods and fields.) |
| | RuntimePermission | Creating class loaders, setting class loader contexts, changing the security manager, altering threads, dynamic loading. |
| | SerializablePermission | Alter the way objects are serialized by overriding the serialization methods. |

of stack frames built by a sequence of method calls. The AccessController must not only verify that the current stack frame has the required permission but also that the previously invoked stack frames have the permission. In this way, previously called methods cannot gain privileges by calling higher privileged code.

When the AccessController performs a security check, it examines the call stack to determine which protection domain should apply and then checks if it grants the appropriate permissions. This is known variously as *stack introspection* (Wallach, Balfanz, Dean, & Felten, 1997), *stack inspection* (McGraw & Felten, 1999), and *stack walking*. Because every Java method belongs to a class and there is a protection domain associated with every class, each stack frame has an associated protection domain. A frame may also have dynamically granted permissions. If any stack frame has not been granted the permission for the requested access, then the request will be denied by throwing an exception. The AccessController checks permissions by calling a method to indirectly return an object encapsulating the current protection domains on the stack and then checking the associated permissions.

## MALICIOUS BEHAVIOR

The simplest strategy for an attacker is to attempt to achieve the attack goals without violating the security policy. If the attacker's goal is just to obtain free computing resources or annoy the victim, then it is possible to do so without circumventing any security mechanisms. This section considers hostile applets that have negative consequences without needing to violate typical security policies.

### Exploiting Weak Policies

The challenge in defining a good security policy is to disallow all undesirable behavior while permitting all useful behavior. It is impossible to define a policy that does this exactly—all policies must either allow some undesirable behavior, disallow some useful behavior, or both. This is especially problematic when a generic, one-size-fits-all policy is applied to all applets, regardless of their intended purpose. For example, it would be appropriate (and necessary) for a chat-room applet to send data entered by the user over the network, but it may be unacceptable for a mortgage calculator applet to do so.

The default policy for typical Java implementations allows untrusted applets to perform many potentially detrimental actions. For example, standard security policies permit untrusted applets to make any number of network connections to the originating host and transmit any amount of data to the network. Because very few users are likely to customize their policy settings, a hostile applet that does these things without violating the default security policy is likely to succeed in victimizing most users who execute it.

### Consuming Resources

Java's standard security manager supports only absolute permissions: an action is either permitted or not; if the action is permitted, it is always permitted. This means that Java security policies provide no constraints on resource consumption, beyond what the underlying operating system provides. On typical consumer operating systems, such as Windows XP, there are no per-process resource constraints, so an untrusted Java applet could effectively consume all available system resources. Although we know of no cases in which a malicious resource consumption attack was discovered in the wild, one can imagine hostile applets designed to consume excessive amounts of almost any machine resource.

An applet that enters an infinite loop will continue to consume processor cycles as long as it executes. How damaging this is depends on the operating system's scheduler. On an operating system without preemptive multitasking (e.g., the Macintosh before OS X), a process that enters an infinite loop can prevent any other process from executing. With more recent operating systems and virtual machines, the processing time allotted to a given process is controlled by the operating system. Hence, even if a thread enters an infinite loop, it will be preempted by the operating system and another thread will be given a chance to execute. Nevertheless, hostile applets can still consume substantial central processing unit (CPU) cycles on modern operating systems. An attacker can use the stolen CPU cycles to perform a computation valuable to the attacker on the victim's machine such as attempting to do a brute-force key search.

A thread that is set to the highest priority (MAX_PRIORITY) will be given all available CPU cycles by most schedulers. Java applets can also create new threads to consume more host resources. Normally, when a browser leaves a Web page, all the applets running on that page will be terminated. This is done by the containing application invoking each thread's stop method. However, since an applet can override the stop method (e.g., to do nothing), it is possible for a hostile applet to continue executing after the browser leaves its page. Recent implementations (e.g., Netscape Navigator 7.1) mitigate this attack by forcing the threads to terminate after the page is left even if their stop method does not.

Hostile applets could also consume other system resources such as memory (by allocating objects in a loop and holding live references to them to prevent the garbage collector from reclaiming the storage) and the display (by creating windows to fill the screen). If the security policy permits the applet to open a file for writing, the applet may write as much data as it wants to the file, filling up the victim's disk. If any network connections are permitted, the applet can send data at the maximum rate possible and consume much of the victim's network bandwidth. Mark LaDue's collection of hostile applets provides examples of many different resource consumption attacks (LaDue, 2004).

### Countermeasures

Because there are no permissions associated with consuming CPU cycles, creating threads, consuming memory, and creating windows (except for creating windows without warning markings), none of these attacks can be mitigated using standard Java security policies. Attacks that consume network or file system resources can be prevented by prohibiting all network or file system access, but there is no way to define a policy that allows an applet to open a network connection without also allowing it to send unlimited amounts of data over that connection.

One strategy to limit the damage resource consumption attacks can accomplish is to use the underlying operating system to place limits on the total resources consumed by the Java VM. An operating system with a preemptive scheduler, such as Windows XP, will be less vulnerable to a CPU consumption attack because even if the hostile applet is able to consume all available cycles of the Java VM, it will not receive more system CPU cycles than the Java VM is allocated. Operating systems can also place limits on the memory, network bandwidth, and other resources a process may consume. This can prevent the hostile applet from interfering substantially with non-Java applications running on the host but does not prevent it from interfering with the execution of other Java applets.

Java VM implementations could also monitor resource consumption and terminate applets that are exceeding set resource limits. Accounting for resource consumption by individual applets is not necessarily straightforward, however, because applets may interact in ways that make it difficult to account for which applet is responsible for a particular resource use. JRes is a resource accounting mechanism that can be implemented on top of a Java VM (Czajkowski & von Eicken, 1998). It accounts for CPU, memory, and network use by individual threads and allows a user to enforce a policy that takes actions when a thread exceeds usage limits.

Accounting for memory consumption is difficult because the thread that allocates an object may not be the thread responsible for it remaining in memory. Code from one applet may hold references to objects created by other applets, and a memory consumption attack could exploit this by holding on to references to objects created by another applet. Price, Rudys, and Wallach (2003) developed a technique for accounting for memory consumption by applets by modifying a garbage collector to measure the amount of storage attributable to each applet.

A more general defense strategy is to extend Java's security mechanisms to support more expressive policies. Java policies are limited by the defined permissions, but more fundamentally they are limited by the need to insert calls to SecurityManager checks in the Java API before every controlled operation. This means extending Java to support permissions associated with allocating memory, consuming processor cycles, reading or writing bits to a file (as opposed to opening a file for reading or writing), or transmitting data over the network (on a socket that is already open) would involve a substantial performance penalty. The costs associated with checking the permissions would be necessary for every operation, regardless of whether the policy in effect places any constraints on consumption of that resource. One solution to this is to use an *inlined reference monitor* (Erlingsson, 2003). This approach involves inserting checking code directly into an untrusted applet (or a policy-specific Java API). The inserted checking code performs the necessary security checks to enforce a policy before each security-critical action. Because the checking code is inserted to enforce

a specific policy, it is possible to express a large class of policies that provide arbitrary constraints on use and consumption of any resource visible through code instructions. Two systems that adopt this approach to provide fine-grained policies on Java applets are Naccio (Evans & Twyman, 1999) and SASI (Erlingsson & Schneider, 1999).

# CIRCUMVENTING POLICIES

This section describes several strategies a hostile applet may use to circumvent Java's security mechanisms. In McGraw and Felten's (1999) terminology, these are known as *attack applets*. The attacker's goal is to be able to perform some action that is not permitted by the safety policy. An attacker may be able to circumvent those mechanisms by finding a way to violate low-level code safety properties, by exploiting a vulnerability in the Java VM to make it associate the wrong policy with the executing code, or by exploiting a flaw in the Java API implementation that allows a critical resource to be manipulated without checking the appropriate permission.

## Violating Low-Level Code Safety

A hostile applet can violate low-level code safety by exploiting a bug in the bytecode verifier that allows type-unsafe code to pass verification. At least 4 of the 31 known Java security bugs (13%) from February 1996 to December 2003 were due to bugs in the bytecode verifier that allows code that violates type safety to execute in a Java VM (Sun 2002b, 2004). These bugs often involve mistakes in implementing the verification of complex instructions. For example, a bug in the Java bytecode verifier found in 2001 involving the invokespecial instruction (Sun, 2002c) affected many implementations of the Java VM and could be exploited to violate type safety ("Last Stage of Delirium," 2002). Exploiting a bytecode verifier bug to achieve a hostile goal is generally possible if the attacker can obtain two references to the same object with different apparent types. The hostile applet can then proceed to access fields of the object through either reference. If the types of the fields of the first reference type and the second reference type are different, the attack can access arbitrary locations in memory by following references in the actual type that correspond to integers in the apparent type.

A hostile applet may also circumvent Java's security mechanisms by violating control flow safety. Multiple bugs have been found within the implementation of the exception-handling mechanism of Java. One flaw in exception-handling subroutines was discovered in the Microsoft Java VM in 1999 ("Last Stage of Delirium," 2002). The jsr and ret instructions are used to implement final clauses in Java. Control flow safety depends on the correct return addresses being on the stack when the ret instruction executes. A flaw in the bytecode verifier allowed an applet to use two jsr instructions to put two addresses on the stack and then to use a swap instruction to exchange the addresses (a correct verifier implementation would disallow this). Then, the swapped return address is used by the ret instruction to return to the instruction that is now referenced by the address. The verifier verifies the method as if the correct return were done. In this case, violating control flow safety leads to the ability to violate type safety because after the switched return, the stack can contain values of different types than is expected by the verifier's analysis.

Another strategy for violating low-level code safety is to break one of the assumptions the verifier relies on. For example, bytecode verification for type safety assumes that values in memory cannot be altered except through Java instructions. This seems like a reasonable assumption because all memory allocated to the applet is controlled by the Java VM process, so as long as the operating system provides virtual memory, it should be impossible for another process to alter values in the memory accessible to an executing applet. However, it is possible for this assumption to be violated if bits in memory flip due to faulty hardware. Govindavajhala and Appel (2003) invented an attack based on violating this assumption. By filling memory with objects of a particular type, they were able to create a situation in which a random bit flip had a high probability (about 70%) of being exploitable by a hostile applet to violate type safety. After type safety is violated in this way, the hostile applet can change the value stored in arbitrary locations in memory. For example, an attacker could replace the reference to the current security manager with null, thereby circumventing all successive policy checking. Random bit flips can be induced in typical memory hardware simply by heating the memory chips (e.g., with a light bulb or hair dryer). This requires physical access to the host machine, which may not be likely for remote desktop attacks, but is a serious concern for Java VMs that attempt to execute isolated applets on smart cards to which a potential attacker readily has physical access.

## Policy Association

A hostile applet can obtain permissions beyond its trust level if it can confuse the Java VM into assigning it to the wrong protection domain. When a class is loaded, the protection domain is assigned based on the apparent origin of the code, its signers, and the principal executing the code. If a hostile applet can either alter the ClassLoader associated with a particular class or forge the origin or signers of a class, it can prevent the Java VM from associating the appropriate policy with the code.

Vulnerabilities in Java's class-loading mechanism have been fairly common. Four of the 31 known Java security bugs are directly attributable to ClassLoader issues (Sun 2002b, 2004). Java 1.0 assumed that all code loaded from a trusted path (set by the CLASSPATH environment variable) was fully trusted and obtained all permissions. The Java 2 platform treats code loaded on the CLASSPATH as any other application but uses the bootclasspath to identify fully trusted code. This is necessary to bootstrap the class loader, but poses the risk that an attacker who can store a file on the bootclasspath can circumvent all access controls.

The ClassLoader is also responsible for ensuring that there are never two different classes loaded with the same name. If this property is violated, low-level code safety properties can be violated because the two classes will type check according to their matching names, but may be implemented differently.

## Security Checking

Security checking happens when Java API methods call SecurityManager check methods before performing critical operations. A hostile applet may be able to exploit mistakes in the way the Java API calls those methods or in the way the checks are implemented to circumvent an intended security policy. Types of possible flaws in Java security implementations include allowing access to a protected resource indirectly without the necessary security checking (e.g., an applet can read a protected file by instead loading a font with a peculiarly constructed name), race conditions that allow system changes to occur between the time a check is made and the protected resource is used (e.g., a file is checked and then replaced with a symbolic link before it is opened), or checks that make incorrect assumptions about resources.

One example of an exploitable security checking flaw was the Java domain name sytem (DNS) bug discovered by Drew Dean, Ed Felten, and Dan Wallach (1996). The security policy permitted an applet to open network connections to its originating host. However, connections were checked based on the DNS name, not the Internet protocol (IP) address. Netscape Navigator 2.0's Java implementation would use DNS to look up a list of IP addresses corresponding to the originating host and a list of IP addresses corresponding to the host the applet is attempting to connect to and would allow the connection if there are any common IP addresses between the two lists. An attacker who can create bogus DNS mappings can then exploit this flaw to connect to arbitrary network hosts.

## Defenses

The best defense against hostile applets that exploit vulnerabilities in the Java VM implementation is to obtain a Java VM implementation with no bugs. Of course, producing bug-free code is beyond our current capabilities, so it is worth considering techniques that can mitigate the damage a hostile applet can produce if it successfully circumvents Java's security mechanisms. Below, we describe five approaches.

**Virus Scanners.** Traditional virus scanners analyze untrusted programs to see if they contain strings that match a database of known hostile programs. Although commercial virus scanners focus on Windows platform exploits, most do include some hostile Java applets in their virus database (McAfee, 2004; Symantec, 2004). The string-matching approach works against known threats but provides little protection against new attacks.

**Malicious Behavior Detectors.** To detect attacks from unknown threats, the system must observe the behavior and identify behavior that is likely to be malicious. Because several Java applets may be running concurrently in one Java VM, it is awkward to apply standard intrusion-detection techniques to detect anomalous behavior of Java applets. The actions caused by a particular applet are not clear, because applets may interact through shared data structures and multiple threads. Soman, Krintz, and Vigna (2003) proposed a thread-level auditing facility for a Java VM that enables precise accounting for actions and detection of malicious behavior from Java applets. Note, however, that this assumes the hostile applet is not able to violate type safety, because an attack applet that could do so could also interfere with the auditing mechanisms.

**Firewalls.** Firewalls monitor network traffic and can prevent harmful incoming packets from reaching system applications and harmful outgoing packets from reaching the network. Firewalls can prevent hostile applets from behaving harmfully in the same way they would prevent other applications from doing so. A firewall can also be designed to prevent potentially hostile Java applets from executing by blocking Java applets when they arrive on the network (Martin, Rajagopalan, & Rubin, 1997).

**Isolation.** Another approach is to execute possibly hostile applets in an isolated environment. Malkhi, Reiter, and Rubin (1998) propose running untrusted applets on a dedicated machine. The interface to the applet will appear in the users' browser in a way that provides users with the illusion that it is running on their own machine. Because the applet is executing on a separate machine and has only limited access to the outside world through the network, it cannot carry out any hostile actions on the user's machine. If a dedicated machine is not available, similar security properties can be achieved by executing untrusted applets in a way that isolates their effects. Liang, Venkatakrishnan, and Sekar (2003) describe a system that allows untrusted programs to execute in an environment in which all changes they make to the system are recorded. When the execution completes, the user can inspect the changes and decide whether to approve them.

**Proof-Carrying Code.** The size and complexity of the Java VM make implementing a correct Java VM difficult, so one approach to improving security is to reduce the complexity of the trusted computing base. Proof-carrying code attempts to do that by using a small and simple verifier to check a proof that is included with an untrusted program (Necula, 1997; Necula & Lee, 1996). Because it is easier to check a proof than to create one, the trusted computing base can be reduced by requiring programs to provide a proof that they satisfy required security properties. Automatically producing proofs of complex security policies and representing proofs in a condensed way remain challenging research problems, however.

## CONCLUSION

Although numerous hostile applets have been proposed by security researchers, hostile applets are very rare in the wild. Reports of intentionally hostile Java applets are rare and only minor incidents have been reported. Compared to the damage caused by e-mail worms, viruses that exploit buffer overflows in Windows and common server applications, and cross-site scripting attacks, the actual damage caused by hostile Java applets is miniscule. Symantec's security response site reports 44 threats discovered in January 2004, none of which involved Java. Their entire database includes only two Java applet attacks that have been found in the wild: Java.Nocheat and Trojan.ByteVerify. Both are exploit applets that exploited a vulnerability in the Java VM included with Microsoft Internet Explorer (Microsoft, 2003). No significant damage

was caused by either attack, and fewer than 50 infections were known.

The lack of instances of actual Java applet attacks is not terribly surprising given the motivations and technical capabilities of most malicious attackers. E-mail worms are comparatively very easy to write and far more effective in causing damage; buffer overflow attacks require a bit more sophistication but can be created by nonexperts using widely available tools and can readily give the attacker complete control over the victim's machine. By contrast, most Java exploits depend on subtle flaws in the bytecode verifier or class-loading mechanisms, which are both harder to identify and often difficult to exploit even after the flaw is identified. As a result, most of the work on finding vulnerabilities in Java has been done by nonmalicious researchers interested in improving the security of the platform, not by malicious attackers interested in causing harm.

Java's security mechanisms are certainly not perfect, and there are many ways a malicious applet can cause harm. Some of these exploit vulnerabilities in Java implementations to violate low-level code safety and enable the attacker to circumvent the security mechanisms; others work within the security mechanisms but exploit weak policies that provide insufficient limits on resource consumption and access. Ongoing work in industry and academic research labs is developing techniques for efficiently enforcing precise policies that can control resource consumption, accurately account for resources consumed by applets, and execute untrusted programs in protected environments. As with most security issues, understanding new attacks leads to new work on defensive countermeasures, and new defensive countermeasures lead to new approaches to attacks.

## GLOSSARY

**Applet**   Small program intended for execution inside a container (e.g., a Web browser).

**Control Flow Safety**   Property of a platform or programming language that ensures that attempts to jump to instruction addresses always jump to valid locations.

**Denial-of-Service Attack**   Attack intended to prevent legitimate users from accessing a resource.

**Dynamic Checking**   Analysis done on program executions.

**Java Platform**   Platform that includes the Java virtual machine intended for executing programs written in JVML.

**Java Virtual Machine Langauge (JVML)**   Stack-based intermediate language.

**Low-Level Code Safety**   Properties necessary to prevent circumvention of high-level security mechanisms. Comprises type safety, memory safety, and control flow safety.

**Malicious Code**   Code created with the intention of causing harm to someone who executes it.

**Memory Safety**   Property of a platform or programming language that ensures that attempts to read and write to memory are to valid locations.

**Safety Policy**   Set of rules that specify behavior that is permitted. If the safety policy is enforced correctly, programs are prevented from actions that are not permitted by the policy.

**Static Checking** Analysis done by examining programs directly without executing them.

**Type Safety** Property of a platform or programming language that ensures that values of a particular type can only be used with operations that expect values of that type. In particular, type safety prevents forging pointers.

**Virtual Machine** A program that provides an abstract platform for executing programs to enable portability, simplicity, and security. The Java virtual machine interprets programs written in JVML.

## CROSS REFERENCES

See *Computer Viruses and Worms; Hackers, Crackers and Computer Criminals; Hoax Viruses and Virus Alerts; Mobile Code and Security; Spyware; Trojan Horse Programs.*

## REFERENCES

Aleph One. (1996). Smashing the stack for fun and profit. *Phrack Magazine, 7*(49). Retrieved from http://www.insecure.org/stf/smashstack.txt

Chen, Z. (2000). *Java card technology for smart cards: Architecture and programmer's guide.* Reading, MA: Addison-Wesley.

Czajkowski, G., & von Eicken, T. (1998, October). *JRes: A resource accounting interface for Java.* Proceedings of ACM Conference on Object-Oriented Programming Systems, Languages and Applications.

Dean, D., Felten, E., & Wallach, D. (1996, May). *Java security: From HotJava to Netscape and beyond.* IEEE Symposium on Security and Privacy, Oakland, CA.

Erlingsson, Ú. (2003). *The inlined reference monitor approach to security policy enforcement* (Technical Report 2003-1916). Ph.D. thesis, Department of Computer Science, Cornell University, Ithaca, NY.

Erlingsson, Ú., & Schneider, F. B. (1999, September). *SASI enforcement of security policies: A retrospective.* Proceedings of the New Security Paradigms Workshop.

Evans, D., & Twyman, A. (1999, May). *Policy-directed code safety.* Proceedings of the IEEE Symposium on Security and Privacy.

Gong, L., Ellison, G., & Dageforde, M. (2003). *Inside Java 2 platform security: Architecture, API design, and implementation* (2nd ed.) Reading, MA: Addison-Wesley.

Gosling, J. (1995, February). *Java: An overview* (Sun Microsystems White Paper). Santa Clara, CA: Sun Microsystems.

Govindavajhala, S., & Appel, A. (2003, May). Using memory errors to attack a virtual machine. *IEEE Symposium on Security and Privacy.*

LaDue, M. (2004). *A collection of increasingly hostile applets.* Retrieved from http://www.cigital.com/hostile-applets/

Last Stage of Delirium Research Group. (2002, October). *Java and virtual machine security: Vulnerabilities and their exploitation techniques.* Retrieved from http://www.lsd-pl.net/documents/javasecurity-1.0.0.pdf

Liang, Z., Venkatakrishnan, V. N., & Sekar, R. (2003, December). *Isolated program execution: An application transparent approach for executing untrusted programs.* 19th Annual Computer Security Applications Conference.

Lindholm, T., & Yellin, F. (1999). *The Java virtual machine specification* (2nd ed.). Reading, MA: Addison-Wesley.

Malkhi, D., Reiter, M., & Rubin, A. (1998, May). *Secure execution of Java applets using a remote playground.* Proceedings of the 1998 IEEE Symposium on Security and Privacy.

Martin, D. M., Jr., Rajagopalan, S., & Rubin, A. (1997). *Blocking Java applets at the firewall.* Internet Society Symposium on Network and Distributed Systems Security.

McAfee Security. (2004, January). *Virus information library.* Retrieved from http://us.mcafee.com/virusInfo/

McGraw, G., & Felten, E. (1999). *Securing Java: Getting down to business with mobile code.* New York: Wiley.

Microsoft. (2003, June 27). *Flaw in Microsoft VM could enable system compromise* (Microsoft Security Bulletin MS03-011). Redmond, WA: Author.

Necula, G. (1997). *Proof-carrying code.* Proceedings of the 24th Annual ACM SIGPLAN-SIGACT Symposium on Principles of Programming Languages.

Necula, G., & Lee, P. (1996). *Safe kernel extensions without run-time checking.* Proceedings of the Second USENIX Symposium on Operating Systems Design and Implementation.

Price, D. W., Rudys, A., & Wallach, D. S. (2003). *Garbage collector memory accounting in language-based systems.* 2003 IEEE Symposium on Security and Privacy, Oakland, CA.

Singh, I., Stearns, B., Johnson, M., & the Enterprise Team. (2002). *Designing enterprise applications with the J2EE platform.* Reading, MA: Addison-Wesley.

Soman, S., Krintz, C., & Vigna, G. (2003). *Detecting malicious Java code using virtual machine auditing.* Proceedings of the 12th USENIX Security Symposium.

Sun Microsystems. (2002a). *Permissions in the Java 2 SDK.* Retrieved from http://java.sun.com/j2se/1.4.2/docs/guide/security/permissions.html

Sun Microsystems. (2002b, November 19). *Chronology of security-related bugs and issues.* Retrieved from http://java.sun.com/sfaq/chronology.html

Sun Microsystems. (2002c). *Sun security bulletins article 218.* Retrieved from http://sunsolve.sun.com/pub-cgi/retrive.pl?doc=secbull/218

Sun Microsystems. (2003). *Java 2 platform, standard edition: 1.4.2 API specification.* Retrieved from http://java.sun.com/j2se/1.4.2/docs/api/

Sun Microsystems. (2004, January). *Sun alert notifications.* Retrieved from http://sunsolve.sun.com/pub-cgi/search.pl, category:security java

Symantec Corporation. (2004, January). *Virus threats page.* Retrieved from http://www.symantec.com/avcenter/vinfodb.html

Wallach, D. S., Balfanz, D., Dean, D., & Felten, E. W. (1997, October). *Extensible security architectures for Java.* Proceedings of the 16th Symposium on Operating Systems Principles.

# Spyware

Tom S. Chan, *Southern New Hampshire University*

## INTRODUCTION

Computer viruses were first widely seen in the late 1980s. They are mysterious and headline grabbing. Every time a new virus hits, it makes the news if it spreads quickly (Brain, 2004). In the past few years, a new class of malicious programs called spyware has emerged. Spyware is not a virus but behaves more like a Trojan horse. Although no data are damaged, it runs quietly in the background without a user's knowledge and forwards information to the spyware's owner. Spyware is just as malicious as a virus but it is generally less well known. In fact, the ICSA Labs Annual Virus Prevalence Survey (2003) does not tabulate spyware as a separate statistical category. Spyware programs are currently embedded in hundreds of popular shareware and even commercial software products. By the latest estimate, about 15% of notebooks and 20% of desktops are infected ("PC Pitstop statistics," 2004). Recently, EarthLink, an Internet service provider (ISP), started to offer its subscribers free online spyware scanning. It discovered over 2 million spyware programs and 9 million cookies in 426,500 scans (Borland, 2004a)!

## TECHNICAL ASPECTS OF SPYWARE
### Definition of Spyware

Although arguments abound on its precise definition, literally spyware is ware that spies on you. Consequently, the main issue regarding spyware centers on the matter of privacy. Webopedia (2004) defines spyware as

> any software that covertly gathers user information through the user's Internet connection without his or her knowledge, usually for advertising purposes. Spyware applications are typically bundled as a hidden component of freeware or shareware programs that can be downloaded from the Internet. Once installed, the spyware monitors user activity on the Internet and transmits that information in the background to someone else.

Based on functionality, spyware can be classified as loggers and trackers. A common type of logger is a key logger. It runs silently in the background and records key strokes and mouse clicks on a computer. The data can then be played back to reconstruct what a user did. Apart from key loggers, there are also loggers for e-mails and chats. Key loggers are famous because they are most common and are notorious for stealing passwords and credit card numbers. Different from loggers, trackers monitor usage habits and store them as statistical data for reporting. The data may be a person's surfing habits, usage of a particular program, or a particular function in the program.

### How Does Spyware Work?

Technically, spyware is not a virus, so it is undetected by antiviral programs. By definition, viruses damage data on a computer and replicate themselves. Spyware operates in stealth. Although spyware damages no data, it quietly copies itself onto a computer, runs as a background task, and forwards information about the user to its owner without the user's knowledge. Spyware technically has two components. In the foreground, it is a core program that is visible and provides useful functions. In the background, there is a spying program that monitors and forwards information. Spyware can exist in any form of executable programs, including applications, installers, ActiveX, plug-ins, scripts, or applets.

Spyware usually does not collect personal information, but only general demographics and surfing habits. Information gathered is potentially being sold and resold and combined with other databases to build up profiles of users and usage habits. Correlating with personal data such as name, address, e-mail address, age, gender, income, and credit history, they can be very powerful marketing tools. Naturally, to properly correlate information, data sent to the spyware server must be uniquely identifiable. There are many ways to create such globally unique identifiers (GUIDs). They are usually created during spyware installation and stored in the user's computer. Every time the spyware uploads information, the identifier is also attached for proper updating to the user's record. Although software coded identifiers are commonly employed, a computer's chip ID, network card, and Internet protocol (IP) address can all be used for identification and tracking purposes (Center for Democracy and Technology, 2001).

## How Does One Get Infected?

The signs are subtle at first. Typically, the computer is slower than usual, the browser seems to behave differently, or sometimes users are redirected to a site without reason. Recall all those free software utilities, screensavers, games, and MP3s downloaded from the Internet? Spyware programs are found in hundreds of freeware, shareware, and even some commercial software (Labriola, 2002). They are installed silently and automatically. How? For example, a user downloads what is apparently a free and useful software utility. Typically, he or she installs the program without reading the license agreement carefully enough. When the program is installed, it bundles in something extra. Usually, this is a plug-in designed for downloading advertisements or forwarding information. However, sometimes, even when the software is removed, the computer will still send information in the background. Why? The uninstall removes only the core program but not its spying components.

How could they do this? The Uniform Computer Information Transactions Act (UCITA, 2001) was passed in 2001 to facilitate e-commerce. Basically, it is traditional commercial law with a digital twist. Software distributors can use clickwrap licenses as a convenient way to license its software to end users on the Internet. When a user agrees to the end user license agreement (EULA), that user is legally bound by its terms (see Figure 1). The spyware's EULA is supposed to include clauses that the software gathers information for statistical purposes or product improvement. But, the EULA may also be worded to contain so much information that it is difficult to read, or the information gathering clauses are obscure and ambiguous. Furthermore, a majority of users accept the EULA without understanding its implications. Many users become angry when discovering their freeware contains spyware. Yet, most users remain unaware and are subject to customer profiling without their knowledge.

Another way to get infected can be as simple as visiting a Web site or viewing an e-mail that requires downloads to view or use its contents. The download may be automatic, without a user's consent or knowledge. More typically, a pop-up window will appear and ask for consent. These spyware programs are known as drive-by or pop-up downloads. Apart from software, spyware can also be constructed with hardware. Hardware tools are commercially available to record key strokes, either as an inline add-on or as a direct build-in. Spying features can also be built into other hardware devices. For example, one disk drive can copy data from the other drives on a small computer system interface (SCSI) bus, microphones and cameras can be bugged, sound cards can use speakers as input devices and modems can record conversations that take place on the same phone line. These devices can capture millions of bits of information and then download later either locally or via a wired or wireless network. They are designed to be obscure and often remain unnoticed by users.

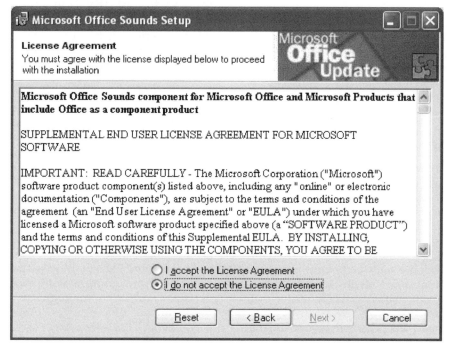

**Figure 1:** An example of a EULA from a Microsoft Office add-in.

## SPYWARE FROM A SOCIAL PERSPECTIVE
### Who Is Doing the Spying and Why?

Why do companies make software with spyware? It is simple: for money, of course. Why do consumers tolerate them? Well, that is simple too. Downloads are free, and consumers may not have the awareness or sophistication. Free software downloaded from the Internet could have a hidden price, often in the form of pop-up ads or information gathering opposed by privacy advocates. Spyware vendors are typically third-party marketing firms who prepare advertising campaigns for many of the world's largest corporations. Originally, the marketers wanted to know general demographics on the where, when, and how long questions. In many ways, information gathered is similar to the Nielsen rating in TV broadcasting. However, marketers are always hungry for more and better information. With GUID assignments, consumers can be tracked and provided with highly targeted advertisements. For example, if marketers know that a user is looking for a new car because the user visited vehicle information sites, they can provide, or bombard, that user with car makers', local dealers', and finance companies' pop-up ads. By targeting specifically to consumers who are likely to be interested rather than to just anyone who passes by, these advertisements can be much more cost effective.

Many spyware vendors acknowledge that they monitor browsing habits, click through rates, and query strings and even information from form fields that might contain very personal information such as when one is performing medical or financial transactions. In their defense, software companies have been forced to experiment with new business models to survive the dot-com bust. In general, a marketing firm will approach a struggling software company that is pressed for money and offer to sponsor it financially. Of course, it will agree to bundle spyware programs in its products. Some popular software may be spyware free. For technical reasons or business partnership, the software comes bundled with programs from another company, that is, a third party, that happens to contain spyware. Finally, marketing firms can set up, develop, and market their own software to the general public. The objective is to find as many ways as possible to distribute and install the spyware program.

### A Short History of Spyware

Spyware can be traced back to a more humble and benign beginning as cookies and advertising-supported spyware, or adware. Cookies are pieces of information generated by a Web server and stored in the user's computer. They are text files implemented to allow client-side customization. However, cookies can be used to track users' habits and behavior. Adware, on the other hand, is advertising supported software. They are software programs that can be downloaded free from the Internet, but contain banner advertisement pop-ups that create revenues for their owners or sponsors.

Cookies are, by design, accessible only to the site that generates them, and one Web site cannot interpret the cookie set by another. However, most ad banners now generate third-party cookies. Third-party cookies are set by a Web site located elsewhere rather than the visiting site. DoubleClick gained notoriety in 2001 by exploiting the cookie design. It ran ad banners on affiliate sites from its servers remotely and used those servers to set and read cookies. By placing ads on thousands of Web sites, the DoubleClick servers can read cookies set by any of them. Similar to placing a network of sensors on the ocean floor to track submarines, it can track Web surfers from site to site. The DoubleClick affair is a major milestone in spyware development. It places the conflicts between online privacy, spying, and business practice in center stage, and we will explore this case in more detail later.

The benign adware became malignant spyware with the rise of malicious mobile code in the late 1990s (Nachenberg, 1999). The introduction of Java in 1995 changed the world of computing forever. Mobile codes are downloadable executable programs, such as Java applets and Active X components. These programs have codes written and stored on a server somewhere and download to clients on demand. Spyware is a form of malicious mobile code. Because they are programs instead of text, spyware programs are functionally much more powerful than cookies. They can be written to perform tasks such as logging and tracking. Around this time, we also saw the introduction of Back Orifice, a remote administrated Trojan horse, or RAT (Internet Security Systems, 1998). RAT runs like a server on the infected computer, allowing a remote administrator to control and monitor the system over a network. With this open access, that person can do virtually anything on the computer! This advance ushered in spyware that can be extremely dangerous. The threats go from spying and annoyances to outright criminal activities.

## THE EFFECTS OF SPYWARE
### Privacy in the Information Age?

In this Information Age, personal information is a highly valued commodity. It is captured and compiled, bought and sold in ways never imagined before. Studies indicate privacy is the major concern for online shoppers, and it is also a top reason why many still avoid the Internet (Berman & Mulligan, 1999). Many users expect their online activities to be anonymous and private. They are not. It is very possible to record and access virtually all online activities. The level of privacy one can expect from offline activities usually is clear from the nature of that activity. Online activities are less obvious. The Electronic Communications Privacy Act (ECPA, 1986) states that it is not illegal for anyone to view or disclose an electronic communication if the communication is readily accessible to the public. Online privacy is actually a false impression as information is routed over a vast global network passing through many different computer systems on its way to the destination. Each of these systems is owned and operated by different entities totally capable of capturing and storing the online communication.

The buying and selling of consumer information has been ongoing for a long time, for years prior to the Internet. Technology simply allows for more effective sorting and cross referencing. It empowers businesses to intelligently target consumers. Rather than sending many advertisements to consumers who are uninterested, businesses can tailor messages to those who are interested. It is possible to argue that this is win–win for everybody (Simons, 1997). Businesses can spend less by not sending advertising to people who have no interest in their products, and consumers are not bombarded with pop-ups that they do not want.

In the end, online privacy really is a matter of philosophy, that is, whether one should care if someone is tracking one's movements on the Internet. It may be true that privacy in this age is an idealistic illusion anyway. Naturally, spyware vendors claim only demographic information is collected, and the data are for the sole purpose of providing better products and services. Regardless, one cannot help but feel creepy about having a piece of software in one's computer that, while possibly doing something noble, is collecting who knows what information, sending it to someone, for who knows what reason?

Transactions in the Information Age are faceless, and online commerce is based on blind trust in a certain sense. However, when a person gives out a credit card online, that person has a good idea what information is given and to whom. One has total control. It is a very different matter with spyware that could record a trail of a person's activity everywhere, regardless of that person's intent and without his or her consent. Finally, the concern over spyware can best be summed up by this testimony before the U.S. Congress: "What the growing arrays of invasive program have in common is a lack of transparency and an absence of respect for users' ability to control their own computers and Internet connections" (Berman, 2004).

## Annoyances to Dubious Practices

In the early days of computing, software programs were often shared among developers. In fact, the Internet is built upon the tradition of open source software or freeware. Many software makers today have incorporated open source in their products and have adapted the concept into their business models. Freeware helps a corporation to reduce costs, thereby positioning itself better in emerging markets. It also reenergizes development efforts that are building better products (MacKenze, 2001). Although not all freeware contains spyware, even for freeware that does, given its contributions, one should be willing to put up with some intrusion and annoyance to subsidize its development. After all, one is getting something useful free of charge. It is only fair that software makers get something in return for all of their hard work.

Adware typically falls under a different and more benign category. However, what if it is a 10-year-old who is surfing on the Internet and what if the advertisement is pornographic? With the dot-com bubble burst in 2000, many software companies have been forced to experiment with new business strategies to fight for survival. The postapocalyptic shakeout has drastically reduced the amount of free-flowing venture capital. Companies are looking to make money any way they can—pushing the very limits of acceptable business practices.

In a U.S. securities filing, it was disclosed that the Kazaa file-swapping program had quietly bundled software from Brilliant Digital Entertainment that would create a peer-to-peer (P2P) distribution network. When activated, the program used individual users' bandwidth, drive space, and process cycles to distribute paid commercial content for Brilliant's clients and possibly run computing tasks for those clients (Borland, 2002). The Brilliant plan was the most ambitious yet from a string of companies that have tried to make money off the millions of people who are downloading free music. Nearly all of the file-swapping programs are now routinely bundled with spyware. In this new twist, Brilliant actually gained authorization through EULA to use the user's computing resources.

Recently, spyware threw the world of e-commerce into chaos. Some file-swapping services used spyware to redirect commissions for online purchases from the rightful recipients to themselves (Schwartz & Tedeschi, 2002). How did this scheme work? For example, a consumer bought a DVD on buy.com through a referral Web site. The referral site was supposed to receive a sale commission. The spyware inserted or substituted the uniform resource locator (URL) of the referral site with its own. The commission went to the file-swapping services. The story quoted a spyware developer, who said, "While I agree that this is really a bit of a scam, it is a way for us to pay salaries while not adversely affecting our users." The spyware vendors naturally used the EULA defense. Although clickware agreements have generally been upheld by courts, courts have also ruled that unconscionable provisions in a contract are not enforceable.

Spying software has been around for a long time. Typically, it is installed by the computer's owner. The motives can be individual security and recording, protecting a child by monitoring his or her Internet use, or employee monitoring because of an increase in cyberloafing and lawsuits. Recently, a company, Lover Spy, offered a way for jealous lovers, and anyone else, to spy on the computer activity of their partners by sending an electronic greeting, the equivalent of a thinking-of-you card, doubled as a spying device (Abreu, 2003). Naturally, the software violated the ECPA as it amounted to illegal wire tapping. There is a big difference between recording one's own conversations as compared to recording others' conversations without their consent.

Variations of these scenarios have proliferated across the Internet thanks to an emerging breed of opportunistic e-companies that keep pushing and testing the limits on acceptable business practices. The resulting potential for abuse, affecting millions of Internet users, resulted in increasing calls for government intervention. At the same time, marketing experts are questioning whether such intrusive tactics are effective. These practices inflict serious damage to brand reputations, and it has been noted that several companies that began the trend have already gone out of business (Konrad, 2002).

## Security and Performance Degradations

Privacy and annoyance aside, spyware can cause a whole range of problems. Because of its stealthy nature, a spyware program's codes may be poorly written and inadequately tested. This will open up security holes in the infected system enabling hackers to break in. Even if security is not compromised, spyware degrades system performance and can induce random crashes. Like any program, spyware takes up resources such as memory, processing, and bandwidth, taking them away from other more important programs. Spyware can thus cause a noticeable addition in load. Sometimes, the added load can severely impact a system's functionality. In general, the older or less powerful a computer is, the greater the impact that can be expected.

The list of possible problems caused by spyware includes the following:

- Web accessing slow down
- "Blue Screen of Death" in Windows
- Computer locking up
- System start-up problems
- Windows not shutting down properly
- Computer slowdown because of all of the applications running in the background.

Spyware is a fully functional executable program that takes on a user's authorization abilities, including auto install and auto update privileges. The program can replace system files with its own version, reset the auto signature, even disable the uninstall features. Once installed, the majority of spyware cannot be deleted by normal methods. It leaves residual components behind to continue monitoring the system, communicating with its server and trying to reinstall itself.

Spyware infection could have potentially very serious consequences. To start with, most ISPs have limitations in their user agreements. Could spyware cause a violation of a user agreement? After all, the ISPs are probably paying the real price because they supply the required bandwidth. Thus, would a subscriber be responsible for compensating the ISP for use of its network by a spyware program? What if the spyware uses a computer in committing fraudulent acts? Will its owner then be liable for contributory negligence? Perhaps a most severe danger appears when the file-swapping spyware stores illegal content such as child pornography in a computer. Has its owner become an accomplice to a criminal act?

Because of the potential liability, spyware is a major concern for corporations. When spyware programs are downloaded unwittingly by employees surfing the Internet, the program may be able to bypass the corporate firewall. This is because firewalls are generally designed to keep hackers out and not communications initiated from within. For a corporation that invests a huge sum in security, this is just an unacceptable risk. Most corporations now have strict Internet-use policy regarding spyware and the incorporation of antispying utilities as standard features.

## The Good Spyware?

Any powerful tool can be used both for good and evil. Spyware can actually be good. One example is the use of intelligent agents, or bots. They are software programs that act on behalf of the user. They are characterized by the ability to operate autonomously. Once started, no further interventions are required from the user. Intelligent agents are now being used for a variety of purposes such as network management. An administrator can use intelligent agents to observe operations, monitor resources, and even configure the network. The agents can focus on the connection nodes in the network infrastructure, such as bridges, hubs, routers, and switches. Operating autonomously, an agent travels from node to node, collects status information, maintains and configures, and then reports back to the network server. Such an approach can greatly lessen both the server's load and network traffic (Lewis, 1999).

Another important spyware characteristic, the tracking ability, can also have a positive application. With the Internet becoming the medium for commercial transactions, some kind of identification and tracking technology makes e-commerce more secure. Microsoft and Intel claimed that devices such as the GUID (Lefevre, 1999) and chip ID (Niccolai, 1999) were not designed to invade privacy, but rather to enable the establishment of accountability, protection of ownership, and tracking of lost data. Government and businesses are the main proponents of Internet tracking technology because the ability to verify a person's identity can greatly reduce cybercrime and fraud.

## LEGAL RAMIFICATIONS
### DoubleClick Inc. Privacy Litigation

Although the legality of spyware's EULA as a business contract has generally been upheld, the practices must still be confined within privacy laws. In response to complaints, a class action was brought in 2000 on behalf of computer users who had cookies placed on their computers by DoubleClick and who had their Web site movements tracked. The suit alleged DoubleClick violated 18 U.S.C. 2701—the Electronic Communications Privacy Act, 18 U.S.C 2510—the Federal Wiretap Act, and 18 U.S.C. 1030—the Computer Fraud and Abuse Act (CFAA). The case was decided in favor of DoubleClick on its motion to dismiss for failure to state a claim on which relief can be granted (In re DoubleClick Inc., 2001).

ECPA is designed to target computer hacking. It prohibits the interception and disclosure of wire, oral, or electronic communications. The complainant charged that DoubleClick's information gathering and cookies placement were unauthorized access. DoubleClick claimed that its information gathering was authorized and paid for by the Web sites. This authorization caused the actions to fall outside the ECPA scope. DoubleClick also claimed cookies placement did not fall under the ECPA because they were not "storage by an electronic communication service" (Robinson, 2003a).

The Federal Wiretap Act provides for criminal punishment and civil actions against any person who intentionally intercepts oral, wire, or electronic communications, except where one of the parties consents to the interception. DoubleClick claimed that its affiliate sites consented to the interception of the electronic communication and therefore the action was exempt from the law. The court found that information submission by computer users was intended for DoubleClick's affiliate sites. As a party to the communications, the sites consented to DoubleClick's access.

CFAA imposes liability on anyone who intentionally accesses a computer without authorization and by doing so steals anything of value worth more than $5,000 in any 1-year period. DoubleClick did not claim the cookie was not an unauthorized access but there was no loss claimed. The court agreed and determined no user's loss met the threshold amount. The court also indicated that users had the ability to stop the cookies with browser settings or they could have opted-out from DoubleClick's Web site (Robinson, 2003b).

## Guideline for Business Practices

In August 2002, an agreement between 10 states attorneys general and DoubleClick Inc. was published (NYSOAG, 2002). While winning the court case, DoubleClick wanted to avoid further legal actions as the states began investigations to determine if DoubleClick's practices violated state consumer protection and privacy laws. The terms of the agreement included disclosure practices, notice, data use, data minimization and purging, data sharing, access, notice of changes, and verification.

The settlement terms provided a guideline of acceptable business practice. DoubleClick agreed to the following:

- Disclose the use of its cookies, data gathering, and business practices on its Web site.
- Require the affiliated sites to post a privacy statement that clearly and conspicuously discloses what data are collected, how they are used, how the user can opt-out, and how the user can get to DoubleClick's privacy statement.
- Only collect and use data as it discloses and not include personal identifiable or sensitive data. It will also take reasonable measures to educate clients in practices that promote privacy.
- Only keep 3 months of collected information on its secure servers and archive older data for no longer than 30 months.
- Not share the information it retrieves for one client with any other person except as directed by that client.
- Offer the user a means to delete the user's data and instructions to configure browsers to block the cookies.
- Notify users at least 7 days before changes take effect and offer the user an option to receive e-mail notification of any change.
- Retain an independent firm to audit compliance with these terms.

The operating principle entails notice to consumers about the collection, use, and disclosure of information. The Federal Trade Commission (FTC) issued a report in 2000 identifying five principles of Fair Information Practices: notice, choice, access, security, and enforcement. It recommended that Web sites give a clear and conspicuous notice of their information practices. If Web sites and online marketers comply with these principles, they will not be subject to civil sanctions (FTC, 2000).

# COUNTERMEASURES FOR SPYWARE
## Cookie Screeners

Cookie preference can be set from a browser. One has the ability to accept all, some, or none of the incoming cookies. Many users disable all cookies. This may not be advisable as many sites require a session cookie to fully function. Session cookies are generally safe because they expire as soon as one leaves the Web site. Another alternative is to use the "warn before accepting" feature to screen cookies manually. However, this could lead to one getting bombarded by cookie prompts wherever one is surfing. A site can create a privacy policy that refers to the intended usage of cookies. In the newer Web browsers, users can import privacy settings and set their preferences based upon the privacy policy of the target site (Bowman, 2001). The browser will reject cookies automatically for sites without a policy or sites for which the policy is not confined within its setting. Users will see on the status bar an indication of a detected conflict.

## Ad and Pop-Up Blockers

Ad blockers are programs that suppress the download and display of advertisement images and pop-ups. They key on certain strings of code in Web pages that indicate ads are present and then screen them out before they are downloaded. By avoiding the often annoying banner ads and bandwidth hogging multimedia, ad blockers improve a browser's performance and usability. Users can have a more positive experience, and it also keeps hard drives clear of unnecessary files. Some ad blockers can also improve privacy by limiting the information given out. On the minus side, ad blockers have a subtle skewing effect because they drop images from a Web page.

Ad blockers are available for both Netscape and Internet Explorer. Although they have been around for a long time, ad blockers are not widely installed because of the extra work required. Furthermore, they sometimes prevent users from getting to a legitimate site. On a separate note, some sites are fighting back against the ad blockers with anti-ad blockers. If the site detects that the surfer is using an ad blocker, it sends a message telling the surfer that he or she is not allowed to view the site content until the ad blocker is turned off (Perera, 2001).

## Antispyware Scanners

The best defense against spyware is to know one's system. Open the Windows Task Manager by pressing Ctrl-Alt-Delete to check the lists of programs running in the computer. One can also use the Add/Remove Programs if any spyware is listed. Some spyware programs may include uninstallers, but most do not. To remove spyware manually can be a very tricky and technically challenging process. It is necessary to search and remove all spyware files and registries from the hard drives. However, in some cases, it might be impossible to remove the spyware from an infected machine without reformatting the hard drive and reinstalling the operating system.

The easiest and safest way to remove spyware is to use an antispyware program. These programs are very

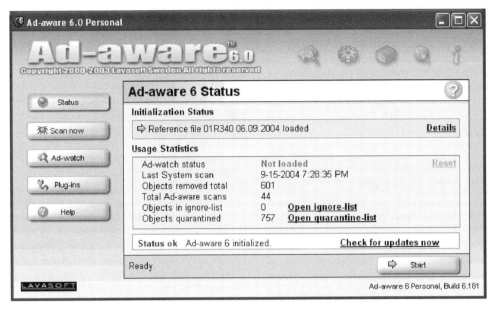

**Figure 2:**   Ad-aware, an example of antispyware program.

similar to antivirus software. Because spyware is technically not a virus, antivirus software currently does not offer protection against them. Antispyware software works in much the same way as antivirus software. It scans the computer looking for files associated with known spyware programs. After the scan, the software quarantines potential problems and allows users to decide what programs should be removed (see Figure 2). The software also scans for cookies. Depending on the individual, tolerance for advertising-related cookies may be high.

Antispyware software is signature-based. A signature is the fingerprint that captures the unique code patterns or actions of a given attack. However, these systems can only deal with known attacks. They cannot detect and prevent unknown attacks. Like antivirus software, they rely on a database of known spyware signatures. Furthermore, new spyware programs are released onto the unsuspecting public frequently. Similar to updating the antiviral signature files on a regular basis, it is necessary to keep the spyware reference file current.

Taking advantages of consumers' fear of spyware, unfortunately, there are a number of deceptive programs claiming to remove spyware. These products do not always do the job that they claim. Even worse, they are themselves spyware or use spyware tactics to promote their products (Borland, 2004a, 2004b). As always, buyers beware. Consumers simply need to be careful and do research to ensure that they can trust the source of any software before installing it on the computer. Of course, they should also contact authorities such as the FTC if they think their privacy has been violated.

## Firewalls and Intrusion Detection Systems

To complement and increase protection, signature-based systems should be incorporated with behavioral-based protection to form a secure environment. In a behavioral model, the focus is on user behavior and not on a specific signature. The goal is to distinguish between malicious and nonmalicious behaviors, monitoring and blocking suspicious sites, and user activities.

A firewall is only a part of a complete network security solution. An intrusion detection system (IDS) can be installed to complement a firewall (see Figure 3). An IDS is designed to detect unauthorized access attempts. It monitors network traffic or system conditions. An IDS is policy based. It requires a policy database that defines bad behavior. With this database, it learns what normal activities are. It then monitors changes to the norm that would suggest an intrusion or suspicious activity.

As many spyware programs can install themselves while one surfs the Internet, installing a personal firewall can offer some protections. Typically, these firewalls block programs from communicating with the Internet without a user's permission or a user can quarantine the IP address of known spyware servers. Firewalls can also alert users to any attempts to access the computer while the user is surfing online. It also informs users if any program on the computer is attempting to send data out without authorization.

## Safe and Sane Browsing

Firewalls are not designed to prevent software installed internally from doing what it is supposed to. Their function is to keep external intruders out. The ultimate countermeasure against malicious code is the practice of safe and sane browsing habits. It goes without saying that one should read the EULA with greater care. Spyware often entices users with the offer of something free. Look past them. There are plenty of freeware programs that are safe and clean. Using only applications downloaded from reliable sources will minimize the risk. Unfortunately, as a product becomes more popular, it seems inevitable that it will be targeted by spyware.

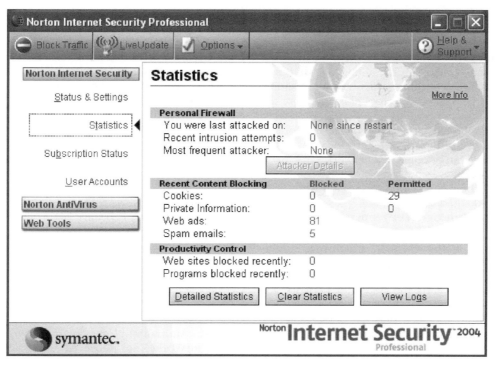

**Figure 3:** Norton Internet Security, an example of a personal firewall.

Another step in preventing spyware is to adjust the browser's Internet Security settings. Security should be set to medium or higher with the following options for ActiveX controls and plug-ins:

- Disable initialization and scripting ActiveX controls that are not marked as safe
- Prompt signed and disable unsigned download of ActiveX controls
- Prompt running of ActiveX controls and plug-ins
- Prompt scripting ActiveX controls marked as safe

## CONCLUSION

The clouds of war are gathering on the spyware front. In the beginning, a few individuals and companies produced software to erase banner ads or block cookies. Spyware vendors reacted with a new tactic. They bundle their programs along with freeware available on the Internet. These piggybacking tactics are now common practices. File-swapping programs are routinely bundled with advertising spyware. As concern increases, 2002 saw a huge increase in antispyware purchases by corporations and in new vendors springing up with products aimed at eradicating spyware (Borland, 2001, 2003). Naturally, spyware vendors countered with new means of distribution, from disabling antispyware programs (SpywareInfo, 2002) to an unusual tactic: lawsuits (Festa, 2003). Granted, software vendors may have a legal or even legitimate right to use spyware to subsidize free services. It too is in their interests not to have the practices become extreme or they may "kill the goose that lays the golden eggs."

Apart from ongoing legislation (Bono, 2003), the World Wide Web Consortium (W3C) recently approved a technology called the Platform for Privacy Preferences (P3P) as a standard that would help consumers choose how much of their personal information to divulge online (W3C, 2004). With the P3P specification, a site can use an extensible markup language (XML) file to describe how it intends to use personal data during and after a user's session. Meanwhile, a consortium of private companies is trying to create standard definitions of spyware by defining what is acceptable, and what is not, and giving best practices recommendations to the companies that want to avoid having their products labeled as spyware (COAST, 2004). For network administrators, one should keep abreast of current technical developments by subscribing to weekly spyware alerts (ExtremeTech, 2004). Furthermore on the policy front, the U.S. Senate also has an active and ongoing agenda on spyware ("Spyware, Communication Hearing," 2004). With the commercialization of the Web, the Internet is no longer the wild frontier that it once was. Just as the West was tamed, time and progress will inevitably force civility upon the online community, through self-censorship, court litigation, or government legislation.

## GLOSSARY

**ActiveX**  ActiveX is a Microsoft technology for plug-ins that provides added software to the computer when a Web page is accessed.

**Applet**  Applets are small downloadable Java programs embedded in Web pages that allow for enhanced animation and user interactivity.

**Bots**  A bot or robot is a program that can be directed to automatically perform tasks, such as search and collect information on the Internet.

**Clickwrap License** A clickwrap license is used on the Internet when a surfer clicks "I accept" to agree to the Web site's terms and conditions of use online.

**Extensible Markup Language (XML)** Extensible markup language (XML) is a meta-language that provides a format for describing structured information so that it can be shared by cross-platform applications.

**Firewall** A firewall is a defense shield for the network. It allows users to establish rules to determine what traffic should be allowed in or out of the network

**Installer** An installer is a small program that helps guide users through the setup of the application when it is started up for the first time.

**Internet Service Provider (ISP)** An Internet service provider is a company that provides customers and businesses access to the Internet.

**Intrusion Detection System (IDS)** An intrusion detection system monitors network traffic and flags suspicious activities and alerts the system or network administrator.

**Opt-out** An opt-out assumes that the consumers approve the collection of their personal information, as compared to an opt-in, which requires the data collector to get specific permission.

**Peer-to-Peer (P2P) Network** A peer-to-peer network is a network with two or more personal computers sharing files and access to devices without requiring a separate network server.

**Plug-in** Plug-ins are additional pieces of software that add extra capabilities to the Web browser, for example, enable it to view movies.

**Privacy** Privacy is different from security. It is a person's right to control the provision and use of information about oneself.

**Script** Scripts are a list of commands. Like batch or macro processing, they can be executed automatically without user interaction.

**Security** Security for a computing system means that the information on the system is protected from unauthorized disclosure or modification.

**Trojan** Trojan horses are impostors, files that claim to be something desirable but are malicious in reality. Unlike viruses, Trojans do not replicate themselves.

**Virus** A computer virus is a program written to alter the way a computer operates without the permission or knowledge of the user.

**World Wide Web Consortium (W3C)** World Wide Web Consortium is an open and nonproprietary forum for industry and academia setting standards regarding Web technologies.

## CROSS REFERENCES

See *Computer Viruses and Worms; Corporate Spying: The Legal Aspects; Electronic Commerce; Mobile Code and Security; Privacy Law and the Internet; Trojan Horse Programs.*

## REFERENCES

Abreu, E. (2003, September 30). E-spying on your lover could be illegal — Experts. *Reuters News Service.*

Berman, J. (2004). *Prepared statement on the Spy Block Act before U.S. Congress.* Washington, D.C.: Center for Democracy and Technology.

Berman, J., & Mulligan, D. (1999). Privacy in the digital age: Work in progress. *Nova Law Review, 23*(2). Retrieved May 14, 2005, from 05/14/2005 http://www.cdt.org/publications/lawreview/1999nova.shtml

Bono, M. (2003, July 28). *Bono introduces SPI Act to protect Internet users from downloading unwanted spyware* [Press Release].

Borland, J. (2001, May 14). *Spyware piggybacks on Napster rivals.* CNET News.com.

Borland, J. (2002, April 3). *Kazaa exec defends stealth network.* CNET News.com.

Borland, J. (2003, February 24). *Spike in spyware accelerates arms race.* CNET News.com.

Borland, J. (2004a, February 4). *Spyware cure may cause more harm than good.* CNET News.com.

Borland, J. (2004b, February 11). *Anti-spyware vendors come under fire.* CNET News.com.

Bowman, L. (2001, August 11). *Privacy experts rip IE cookie cutter.* ZDNet News.

Brain, M. (2004). *How computer viruses work.* HowStuffWorks Inc. Retrieved July 8, 2004, from http://www.howstuffworks.com/virus.htm

Center for Democracy and Technology. (2001). *Intel Pentium III processor serial number.* Washington, D.C.

COAST. (2004). Consortium of Anti-Spyware Technology Vendors. Retrieved July 8, 2004, from http://www.coast-info.org/index.htm

Electronic Communications Privacy Act, 18 U.S.C. §§ 2510-21, 2701-11 (1986).

ExtremeTech. (2004). *Weekly spyware alert.* Retrieved July 8, 2004, from http://www.extremetech.com

Federal Trade Commission. (2000). *Privacy online: Fair information practices in the electronic marketplace, a report to Congress.* Washington, DC. Retrieved July 8, 2005, from http://www.ftc.gov/reports/privacy2000/privacy2000text.pdf

Festa, P. (2003, October 22). *See you later, anti-gators?* CNET News.com.

ICSA. (2003). *The 9th annual virus prevalence survey report.* Herndon, VA: TruSecure Corporation. Retrieved July 8, 2004, from http://www.icsalabs.com/2003avpsurvey/index.shtml

In re DoubleClick Inc. Privacy Litigation, U.S. District Court, Southern District of New York (March 2001).

Internet Security Systems. (1998, August 6). *Cult of the Dead Cow Back Orifice Backdoor* [ISS security alert advisory]. Retrieved July 8, 2004, from http://xforce.iss.net/xforce/alerts/id/advise5

Konrad, R. (2002, June 26). *Reality check: Does adware work?* CNET News.

Labriola, D. (2002, March). Is Media Player spyware? *PC Magazine.* Retrieved May 14, 2005, from http://www.extremetech.com/article2/0,1558,3995,00.asp?kc=ETNKT0209KTX1K0100361

Lefevre, G. (1999, March 6). *Microsoft's GUID sparks fears of privacy invasion.* CNN.com.

Lewis, L. (1999). *Service level management for enterprise networks.* Norwood, MA: Artech House.

MacKenze, A. (2001). Open source software: When is a tool? What is a commodity? *Science as Culture, 10,* 541–553.

Nachenberg, C. (1999). *Mobile code threats, Fact or friction.* Paper presented at International Virus Prevention Conference. Vancouver, Canada.

Niccolai, J. (1999, January 22). *Intel to add personal ID numbers to chips.* CNN.com.

NYSOAG. (2002, August 26). *Agreement between DoubleClick Inc. and ten states attorneys general.* New York: State Office of Attorney General.

*PC Pitstop statistics: Spyware and adware.* (2004). Retrieved July 8, 2004, from http://www.pcpitstop.com/research/spyware.asp.

Perera, R. (2001, October 2). *Web advertisers strike back at ad filters.* IDG News.

Robinson, S. (2003a, February 25). U.S. Information Security Law, Part I. Security Focus. Retrieved May 14, 2005, from http://www.securityfocus.com/infocus/1669.

Robinson, S. (2003b, April 1). U.S. Information Security Law, Part II. Security Focus. Retrieved May 14, 2005, from http://www.securityfocus.com/infocus/1681

Schwartz, J., & Tedeschi, B. (2002, September 27). New software quietly diverts sales commissions. *New York Times.*

Simons, J. (1997). Psst, You Want Free Internet? *U.S. News & World Report, 122*(1). Retrieve 05/14/2005 from http://www.usnews.com/usnews/biztech/articles/970113/archive_005973.htm.

Spyware, Communication Hearing before the U.S. Senate Committee on Commerce, Science & Transportation (March 23, 2004).

SpywareInfo (2002, April 22). *Urgent Warning. Spyware Weekly.* April 22, 2002. Retrieved July 8, 2004, from http://www.spywareinfo.com/newsletter/archives/april-2002/04222002.html.

Uniform Computer Information Transactions Act. (2002). National Conference of Commissioners on Uniform State Laws.

Webopedia. (2004). *Spyware.* Retrieved July 8, 2004, from http://www.webopedia.com/TERM/s/spyware.html.

World Wide Web Consortium (W3C). (2004). *W3C P3P 1.1 first public working draft.* Cambridge, MA: Author. Retrieved July 8, 2004, from http://www.w3.org/TR/P3P11/.

# Mobile Code and Security

Song Fu and Cheng-Zhong Xu, *Wayne State University*

## INTRODUCTION

Mobile code, as its name implies, refers to programs that function as they are transferred from one machine to the other. Code mobility opens up vast opportunities for the development of distributed applications and it has been widely exploited. For example, script programs in ActiveX or Javascript are mobile codes that are widely used to realize dynamic and interactive Web pages. One of the most practical uses of such mobile codes is validating on-line forms. That is, a Javascript code embedded in hypertext markup language (HTML) form pages can help check what a user enters into a form, intercept a form being submitted, and ask the user to retype or fill in the required entries of a form before resubmission. The use of the mobile codes not only avoids the transmission of intermediate results back and forth from client to server and reduces the consumption of network bandwidth and server processing power, but also enhances the responsiveness of the user inputs.

Java applets are another form of mobile codes that empower Web browsers to run general-purpose executables that are embedded in HTML pages. When a page that contains an applet is accessed via a Java-enabled browser, the applet's code is downloaded and executed by the browser's Java Virtual Machine (JVM). Java applets of early days were more Web-page-enhancement oriented. Recent years have seen the increasing popularity of the technology in business, scientific, and visualization applications, according to the Java Applet Rating Service.

Java applets are limited to one-hop migration from Web server to client. Like mobile script codes, applet migration deals with the transfer of code only. A more flexible form of migration is a mobile agent that has as its defining trait the ability to travel from machine to machine autonomously, carrying its code as well as data and running state. An agent is a sort of active software object that has autonomy, acting on behalf of its owners. Agent autonomy is derived from artificial intelligence and is beyond the scope of this chapter.

Because of the unique properties of autonomy and proactive mobility, mobile agents have been the focus of much speculation and hype in the past decade. Lange and Oshima (1999) specifically identified seven good reasons for mobile agents: reducing network load, overcoming network latency, encapsulating protocols, asynchronous execution, dynamic adaptation, naturally heterogeneous, and robust and fault-tolerant. Although none of the individual advantages represents an overwhelming motivation for their adoption, their aggregate advantages facilitate many network services and applications (Chess, Harrison, & Kershenbaum, 1995).

In an open environment, mobile code can be written by anyone and executed on any machine that provides remote executables hosting capability. In general, the system needs to guarantee the mobile code is executed under a controlled manner. Its behaviors should not violate the security policies of the system. For mobile agents that are migrated from one system to another, they may carry private information and perform sensitive operations in the execution environment of the residing hosts. An additional security concern is their privacy and integrity. It deals with protecting the sensitive components of an agent from being discovered and tampered with by malicious hosts.

Because mobile agents offer the highest degree of flexibility for the organization of mobility-aware distributed applications and their deployment raises more security concerns than other forms of code mobility, this chapter focuses on mobile agent systems and related security measures. In this chapter, we review the existing techniques and approaches to enhance security for mobile code systems. We classify the types of mobile code and discuss its security issues in the remainder of this section. We then present a survey of some mobile code systems, discuss the design issues in constructing a mobile code system, focus on the research challenges in tackling the security problems for mobile code, describe existing techniques to protect agent hosts and mobile agents, and conclude.

## History of Code Mobility

The concept of code mobility is nothing new. It is rooted back to the early worm programs (Shoch & Hupp, 1982) for resource management in distributed systems. Internet Worm (Spafford, 1989) spawned copies of them onto the Internet upon arrival or upon a simple user action. It is an example of malicious mobile code that tends to break system security measures and gain access to system resources illegitimately.

Mobile codes are not necessarily hostile. Several early mechanisms and facilities were designed and implemented to move code among the nodes of a network to realize execution control. Examples are remote batch job submission (Boggs, 1973) and the use of PostScript (1985) to control printers. In the research work on distributed operating systems, an important problem is to support the migration of active processes and objects (along with their state and associated code) at the operating system level. In particular, *process migration* (Milojicic et al., 2000) concerns the transfer of an operating system process from the machine where it is running to a different one. There are implementations such as Sprite (Ousterhout et al., 1988), Mach (Accetta et al., 1986), and MOSIX (Barak & Litman, 1985) at the kernel level and Condor (Litzkow, Livny, & Mutka, 1988) and LSF (Zhou et al., 1993) at the user level; see (Milojicic, Douglis, & Wheeler, 1999) for a comprehensive review. *Active messages* migrate in a network, carrying program code to be executed on remote computers. They were introduced in the early systems such as Chorus (Banino, 1986). A later approach is by *mobile objects*, which encapsulate data along with the set of associated operations. Object migration makes it possible to move objects among address spaces, implementing a finer grained mobility with respect to process-level migration. For example, Emerald provides object migration at any level of granularity ranging from small, atomic data to complex objects (Jul et al., 1988). Emerald does not provide complete transparency because the programmer can determine objects' locations and may request explicitly the migration of an object to a particular node. An example of a system that provides transparent migration is COOL (Habert, Mosseri, & Abrossimov, 1990). COOL is able to move objects among address spaces without user intervention or knowledge. Java Remote Method Invocation (RMI, n.d.) realizes object mobility by passing objects as arguments in remote object invocation. *Mobile agents* grew out of early code mobility technologies. With mobile agents, execution entities including the program code, data, and running state can be dispatched and roam across networks in a proactive manner. It thus has more autonomy compared with other forms of mobile codes. Mobile agent technology has been implemented in a number of distributed systems; see the Survey of Representative Systems section for details.

By utilizing the code mobility technology, active networks visualize the network as a collection of active routers that can perform any computations and a collection of active packets that carry code and are indeed programs (Tennenhouse et al., 1997; Campbell et al., 1999). In some architectures, the executable code is placed in active routers and packets carry some identifiers to indicate which code should be executed on their behalf. They provide the programmable environments using the concept of network layer processing.

## Types of Mobile Code

Traditionally, applications in distributed environments are structured using the client/server paradigm, in which client and server processes communicate with each other by *message passing* or *remote procedure calls* (RPC). This execution model is usually synchronous, that is the client suspends itself after sending a request to the server, waiting for the results of the call (Birrell & Nelson, 1984). Java RMI is an instance of the RPC model. In *code on demand* (COD), a client process requires a remote program, which is downloaded to the client's local executing environment. It is a pull-based approach to perform alien codes. Java applets are a popular implementation of this model. Another execution model exploiting mobility is called *remote evaluation* (REV). In REV, instead of invoking a remote procedure, a client sends its own procedure code to a server and requests the server to execute it and return the results (Stamos & Gifford, 1990). Compared with COD, REV is a push-based execution model. Active messages and active networks are such examples. Although remote execution only allows for code mobility, the concept of a mobile agent supports process mobility; that is, program executions may migrate among networked hosts. For migrating agents, not only code but also their state information has to be transferred to the destination. Figure 1 illustrates these four mobile code paradigms.

## Security Concerns

The introduction of mobile code in a network raises several security issues. In a completely closed local area network, administrated by a single organization, it is possible to trust all machines and the software installed on them. Users may be willing to allow arbitrary mobile code to execute on their machines and dispatch their code to execute on remote hosts. However, in an open environment, such as the Internet, it is entirely possible that hosts belong to different administrative domains. In such cases, they will have much lower levels of mutual trust. As a result, several types of security problems may arise:

- Hosts are exposed to the risk of system penetration by malicious mobile code, which may leak sensitive information.
- Sensitive data contained within an agent dispatched by a user may be compromised, due to eavesdropping on insecure networks or if the agent executes on a malicious host.

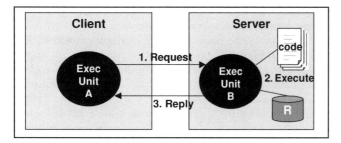

(a). Remote procedure calls (RPC)

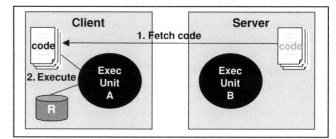

(b). Code on demand (COD)

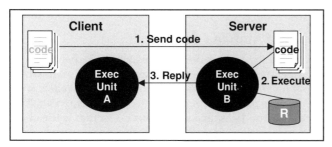

(c). Remote evaluation (REV)

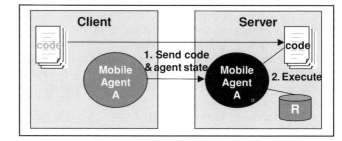

(d). Mobile agent (MA)

**Figure 1:** Mobile code paradigms.

• The code, control flow, and results of a mobile agent could be altered by hosts for malicious purposes. An agent may suffer from denial of execution on a host.

• Mobile code may launch denial of service attacks on hosts, whereby it exhausts server resources and prevents other requests from processing.

A mobile code system must provide certain security mechanisms for detecting and preventing such attacks. These include privacy mechanisms to protect secret data and code, authentication mechanisms to establish the identities of communicating parties, and authorization mechanisms to provide mobile code with controlled access to server resources.

## A SURVEY OF MOBILE CODE SYSTEMS
### A System Structure for Code Mobility

A mobile code system is composed of a collection of servers hosting the executing units of mobile code. Figure 2 illustrates the modeling of such a system. Each executing unit contains a code segment, which provides the static description of the mobile code's behavior, a state including an execution state and a data space, and an itinerary that lists the sequence of servers to be visited in its lifetime. The data space is the set of references to objects that are accessed by the mobile code. The execution state contains private data that cannot be shared and the control information for the execution of mobile code. Mobile code needs to access the server resources to complete its computation. These resource proxies will contact the mobile code computational environment using predefined access protocols. The computational environment serves to provide applications with the capability to relocate their components on different servers dynamically.

Hence, it leverages off the communication channels managed by the network operating system and of the low-level resource access provided by the core operating system to handle the relocation of code, and possibly of state, of the hosted mobile code.

## Taxonomy of Code Mobility Mechanisms

Mobile code is an active entity that travels across a network. Here we discuss mobile code in a broad way. It may be a sequence of instructions or an object or agent that can be transferred among distributed hosts. Mobile code carries its program, data, and even execution state in its life cycle. There are two categories of mobility, in terms

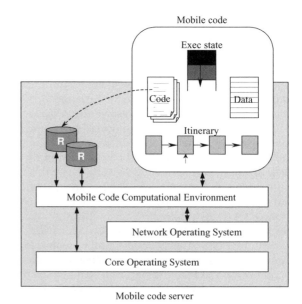

**Figure 2:** A mobile code system.

of the constituents of mobile code that can be migrated. *Strong mobility* is the ability of a mobile code system that allows migration of both the code and the execution state of the mobile code to a different host. The underlying system captures the entire mobile code's state and transfers it together with the code segment to the next server in the itinerary. Once the mobile code is received at its new location, its state is restored. From a programmer's perspective, this scheme is quite attractive because capturing, transferring, and restoring the complete state of mobile code is realized transparently by the underlying system. However, providing this transparency in heterogeneous environments at least requires a global model of mobile code state and a transfer syntax for this information. Moreover, a mobile code system must provide functions to externalize and internalize the state information. Few languages allow an externalizing state at such a high level. Besides, strong mobility may be a very time-consuming and expensive operation due to the large size of the mobile code state. In contrast, *weak mobility* only allows code transfer to a remote host. Although code may be accompanied by some initialization data, no migration of execution state is involved. As a consequence, the programmer is responsible for encoding the relevant state of mobile code in the program variables and for specifying a start method that decides where to continue execution after migration based on the encoded state information. Therefore, weak mobility puts an additional burden on the programmer and makes mobile code programs more complicated.

There are two approaches to realize strong mobility: migration and remote cloning. The migration mechanism suspends a mobile code, transmits it to the destination host, and then resumes its execution. Migration can be either proactive or reactive. In proactive migration, the time and destination for migration are determined autonomously by the mobile code. In reactive migration, movement is triggered by a host that the mobile code is residing on. The remote cloning mechanism creates a copy of the mobile code at a remote host. Remote cloning differs from the migration mechanism in that the original mobile code is not detached from its current host. As in migration, remote cloning can be either proactive or reactive.

As for the weak mobility, a mobile code system can either fetch the code to be dynamically linked and executed or ship such code to another host. The code can be migrated either as stand-alone code or a code fragment. Stand-alone code is self-contained and will be used to instantiate a new execution entity on the destination host. However, a code fragment must be linked in the context of already running code and eventually executed. Weak mobility can be either synchronous or asynchronous, depending on whether the mobile code requesting the transfer suspends or not until the code is executed.

According to the number of servers that mobile code visits in its lifetime, mobility can be single hop or multihop. With the single-hop scheme, mobile code is transferred from its origin to a destination server, where it completes its computation and ends itself. A Java applet is such an example. In contrast, multihop mobility allows the execution of mobile code to span several hosted servers. The sequence of visits is determined by the mobile code's itinerary. Mobile agents utilize multihop mobility to roam in networks while carrying out tasks on behalf of their owners.

## Survey of Representative Systems

Several industrial and academic research groups have been investigating and building mobile code systems. In this section, we present an overview for a representative subset of them, mainly focusing on their architecture, migration and communication mechanisms, and security measures. These systems are arranged approximately in chronological order of development.

***Telescript.*** Telescript (White, 1995), developed by General Magic, includes an object-oriented, type-safe language for agent programming. Telescript servers, which are called *places*, offer services by installing stationary agents to interact with visiting agents. Agents can move by using the go primitive, which implements a proactive migration mechanism. A send primitive is also available, which implements remote cloning. Telescript supports strong mobility for agent transfer. In the absolute migration (by the go primitive), the destination host specified by the domain name system (DNS)-based hostname is required. The name of another co-located agent or resource is needed to provide for a relative migration (by the meet primitive). Co-located agents can invoke each other's methods for communication. An event-signaling facility is also available.

Security has been one of the driving factors in the language design. Telescript provides significant support for security (Tardo & Valente, 1996), including an access control mechanism similar to capabilities. Each agent and place has an associated authority. A place can query an incoming agent's authority and potentially deny the agent's entry or restrict the agent's access rights. The agent is issued a permit, which encodes its access rights, resource consumption quotas, and so forth. The system terminates an agent that exceeds its quota and raises an exception when it attempts an unauthorized operation.

***Agent Tcl.*** Agent Tcl (Gray, 1996; Kotz et al., 1997), developed by Dartmouth College, provides a Tcl interpreter extended with support for strong mobility. Agents are implemented by UNIX processes running the language interpreter. Agents can jump to another host, fork a cloned agent at a remote host, or submit code to a remote host. In the first case, an absolute migration enables the movement of a whole Tcl interpreter along with its code and execution state. In the second case, a proactive remote cloning mechanism is implemented. In the third case, code shipping of stand-alone code is supported by asynchronous and immediate execution. Agents have location-dependent identifiers based on DNS hostnames, which therefore change upon migration. Interagent communication is accomplished either by exchanging messages or by setting up a stream connection. Event-signaling primitives are available, but events are currently identical to messages.

Agent Tcl uses the Safe Tcl execution environment to provide restricted resource access (Levy & Ousterhout, 1995). It ensures that agents cannot execute dangerous operations without the appropriate security mediation. The system maintains access control lists at a coarse granularity, by which all agents arriving from a particular host are subjected to the same access rules. Agent Tcl calls upon external programs, such as Pretty Good Privacy (PGP), to perform authentication when necessary and to encrypt data in transit. However, cryptographic primitives are not available to the agent programmers.

**Concordia.** Concordia, developed by Mitsubishi Electric (1997), is a framework for developing and executing agent applications. Each node in a Concordia system consists of a Concordia server that executes on top of a JVM. Like most Java-based systems, it provides agent mobility using Java's serialization and class-loading mechanisms and does not capture execution state at the thread level. An agent object is associated with a separate Itinerary object, which specifies the agent's migration path (using DNS hostnames) and the methods to be executed at each host. The directory manager maintains a registry of application services, which enables mobile agents to locate the Concordia server on each host. Two forms of interagent communication are supported in Concordia: asynchronous event signaling and agent collaboration. It also addresses fault tolerance requirements via proxy objects and an object persistence mechanism that is used for reliable agent transfer. And it also can be used by agents or servers to create checkpoints for recovery purposes.

Concordia's security model provides support for three types of protection: agent transmission protection, agent storage protection, and server resource protection (Walsh, Paciorek, & Wong, 1998). Secure Sockets Layer version 3 (SSLv3) is exploited to create authentication and encryption services for agent migration. When an agent is stored, its information is encrypted and written to persistent stores. The agent's information includes its bytecodes, internal states, and travel status. It is encrypted by a symmetric key encryption algorithm. Concordia's resource protection is built upon the standard Java SecurityManager class. The security policy for a server is stored in a file called the permissions file. The access requests of an agent are controlled based on the identity of the user on whose behalf the agent is executing.

**Aglets.** Aglets Workbench (1998) is a Java-based mobile code system developed by IBM Tokyo Research Laboratory. Executing units, which are called *aglets*, are threads in a Java interpreter, called *aglet contexts*, located on different network hosts. Weak mobility is supported by the underlying Java Virtual Machine. Two migration primitives are provided in the system. The primitive `dispatch` performs code shipping of stand-alone code to the context. The primitive `retract` exercises code fetching of stand-alone code and is used to force an aglet to return to the requesting context. Mobile code is shielded by proxy objects, which provide language-level protection as well as location

transparency. Message passing is the only mode of communication and aglets cannot invoke each other's methods. Messages are tagged objects and can be synchronous, one-way, or future-reply.

A security model for the Java Aglets supports architectural definition of the policies (Karjoth, Lange, & Oshima, 1997). The policy specifies the actions that an aglet can take. In the policy database, the context administrator combines principals that denote aglet groups and privileges into rules. On the other hand, the aglet owner can establish a set of security preferences that will be honored by the visited contexts. They are rules specifying who may access/interact with an aglet on its itinerary. For instance, *allowances* are preferences dealing with the consumption of resource, such as CPU time or memory. A secure channel established between the source and the destination contexts protects aglet migration. The integrity of aglet data is ensured by computing a secure hash value that allows the destination context to perform tampering detection. Cryptograph techniques are applied to make aglet transit confidential.

**Ajanta.** Ajanta (Tripathi et al., 1999) is an object-oriented mobile agent system developed by University of Minnesota. Each server in Ajanta maintains a domain registry, which keeps track of agents executing on it. Accesses to server resource are realized by proxy interposition between the resource and client agents. Instead of offering direct access to a resource, an agent is given a proxy managed by the server. Ajanta provides various primitives to control an agent. The callback functions, such as `arrive` and `depart` methods, define the agent behavior during different phases of its life cycle. They can be overridden by agent programmers for different applications. An agent itinerary records the list of servers to be visited before completing its tasks. Ajanta introduced the concept of abstract migration patterns, which simplifies the construction of complex itineraries by composition of some basic patterns.

In Ajanta security architecture (Karnik & Tripathi, 2000), each agent carries a tamper-proof certificate, called its credentials, signed by its owner. It contains the agent's name and the names of its owner and creator. The agent-server interactions are controlled by an authentication protocol based on a challenge-response mechanism. Resource access is granted according to the identity of the agent's owner and an access control list. Agent migration is protected by a secure transfer protocol. An agent image, including its state and code, is selectively hiding and exposing parts of it to different agent servers it visits. Cryptographic techniques are applied to ensure integrity of the agent's read-only states.

**Naplet.** The Naplet system is a Java-based experimental framework in support of adaptive distributed applications (Xu, 2002). It was developed by Wayne State University. The Naplet system is built upon two first-class objects: *Naplet* and *NapletServer*. The former is an abstract of agents that defines hooks for application-specific functions to be performed on the servers and itineraries to be followed by the agent. The latter is a dock of naplets. It provides naplets with a protected runtime environment within a Java Virtual Machine. The interagent communication can be asynchronous persistent, by the post-office-like message delivery. Also, a synchronous transient communication mechanism between naplets is provided by NapletSocket (Zhong, Shen, & Xu, 2004). It builds atop of conventional socket and transmission control protocol/Internet protocol (TCP/IP), featuring a reliable and secure connection migration mechanism for mobile agents. A traveling naplet is traced by using the naplet trace information maintained by the NapletManager of a server.

The services available to alien naplets can be run in one of the two modes: *privileged* and *nonprivileged*. The privileged services are protected by proxies: the ServiceChannel objects. The ResourceManager allocates a privileged resource when a naplet request is granted and the access control is done based on naplet credentials in the allocation of service channels. The Naplet system manages resources by applying an owner-based access control mechanism (Xu & Fu, 2003). When a naplet lands on a server, the naplet presents its owner's credentials for authentication. If this process succeeds, a *Subject* instance will be constructed for the naplet to confine its authorized permissions. Then, the server delegates the naplet execution to the subject of the naplet itself. To ensure the safety of naplet itineraries, a formal itinerary reasoning method was proposed (Lu & Xu, 2005). The authors developed a structured agent itinerary language and its operational semantics. The itinerary constraint satisfaction problem was tackled by itinerary reasoning. In addition, a role-based access control model was extended to support the specification and enforcement of spatio-temporal constraints on resource accesses (Fu & Xu, 2005). The formal model and reasoning approach ensure that permissions authorized to a naplet will be valid only for a specific period of time and the naplet access history influences the authorization of permissions with spatial requirements.

## Standardization Efforts

Mobile-code-based programming is a new paradigm for distributed processing. However, the differences among mobile code systems prevent interoperability and proliferation of this technology. To promote both interoperability and system diversity, there are various standardization efforts in this field, for example, by the Object Management Group (OMG, n.d.) and by the Foundation for Intelligent Physical Agents (FIPA, n.d.). The Mobile Agent System Interoperability Facility (MASIF) by OMG specifies a standard for agent management, tracking, and transport (Milojicic et al., 1998). The common object request broker architecture (CORBA) implementations are utilized to fulfill the agent security requirements, including authentication and access control. Although the publication is one of the earliest and best known in agent standardization, the document has not had much public scrutiny yet. Few mobile agent systems have implemented the MASIF standard. FIPA is an active standardization group working in the area of intelligent agents. By 2004, 96 specifications

had been proposed. The FIPA standard specifies an abstract architecture that can be used to develop an agent platform. It also provides specifications for the issues of agent communication, agent management, and several agent-based applications. The security mechanisms are mainly for communication message protection and they are not comprehensive.

# DESIGN ISSUES IN MOBILE CODE

Mobile code can move from one host to another during its lifetime. A mobile agent is a special type of mobile code and it provides a general approach to code mobility. The execution autonomy and proactive multihop migration enable a mobile agent to be an appealing paradigm for developing wide-area distributed applications. An agent-based system is made up of many parts, including the two primary components: agents and execution platforms. An agent can move among networked hosts, perform its tasks, and communicate with other agents or its owner. To construct an efficient and secure mobile agent system, several key design issues must be properly tackled. In this section, we discuss the design choices for mobility, communication, naming, and security in mobile agent systems. These techniques are also applicable to other mobile code systems with proper modification.

## Migration

The defining trait of mobile agents is their ability to migrate from host to host. Thus, support for agent mobility is a fundamental requirement of the agent infrastructure. An agent can request its host server to transfer it to some remote destination. The agent server must then deactivate the agent, capture its state, and transmit it to the server at the remote host. The destination server must restore the agent state and reactivate it, thus completing the migration.

The image of an agent includes all its code and data, as well as the execution state of its thread, also referred to as its thread-level context. At the lowest level, this is represented by its execution context and call stack. If this can be captured and transmitted along with the agent, that is, strong mobility, the destination server can reactivate the thread at precisely the point at which it requested the migration. This can be useful for transparent load balancing, because it allows the system to migrate processes at any time to equalize the load on different servers. An alternative is to capture execution state at a higher level, in terms of application-defined agent data. The agent code can then direct the control flow appropriately when the state is restored at the destination. This is weak mobility and only captures execution state at a coarse granularity, for example, function level, in contrast to the machine instruction-level state provided by the thread context.

Most current agent systems execute agents using commonly available virtual machines or language environments, which do not usually support thread-level state capture. The agent system developer could modify the virtual machines for this purpose, but this renders the system incompatible with standard installations of those virtual machines. Because mobile agents are autonomous, migration only occurs under explicit programmer control, and thus state capture at arbitrary points is usually unnecessary. Most current systems therefore rely on coarse-grained execution state capture to maintain portability.

Another issue in achieving agent mobility is the transfer of agent code. One possibility is for the agent to carry all its code as it migrates. This allows the agent to run on any server that can execute the code. Some systems do not transfer any code at all; instead, they require that the agent's code be preinstalled on the destination server. This is advantageous from a security perspective, because no foreign code is allowed to execute. However, it suffers from poor flexibility and limits its use to closed, local networks. In a third approach, the agent does not carry any code but contains a reference to its *code base*, which is a server providing its code upon request. During the agent's execution, if it needs to use some code that is not already installed on its current server, the server can contact the code base and download the required code. This is often referred to as code on demand (Carzaniga, Picco, & Vigna, 1997).

## Communication

Agents need to communicate with other agents residing on the same or remote host for cooperation. An agent can invoke a method of another agent or send it a message if it is authorized to do so. In general, agent messaging can be peer-to-peer or broadcast. Broadcasting is a one-to-many communication scheme. It allows a single agent to post a message to a group of agents and is a useful mechanism in multiagent systems. Interagent communication can follow three different schemes (Aglets, 1998):

- *Now-type messaging*. This is the most popular and commonly used communication scheme. A now-type message is synchronous and further execution is blocked until the receiver of the message has completed the handling of the message and replied to it.
- *Future-type messaging*. A future-type message is asynchronous and the current execution is not blocked. The sender retains a handle, which can be invoked in the future to obtain the result. Because the sender does not have to wait until the receiver responds and sends the reply, this messaging scheme is flexible and particularly useful when multiple agents communicate with one another.
- *One-way-type messaging*. A one-way-type message is asynchronous and the current execution is not blocked. The sender will not retain a handle for this message, and the receiver will never have to reply to it. This messaging scheme is similar to the mail-box-based approach and it is convenient when two agents are allowed to engage in a loosely connected conversation in which the message-sending agent does not expect any replies from the message-receiving agent.

To support agent communication during migration, one approach is to exploit the mailbox-like asynchronous persistent communication mechanisms to forward messages to the new destination host of an agent. In this way, an agent can send messages to others no matter whether its communication parties are ready. Asynchronous persistent communication is widely supported by existing mobile agent systems; see (Wojciechowski, 2001) for a recent comprehensive review of location independent communication protocols between mobile agents. Another way is to apply the synchronous transient communication mechanisms, in which agents communicate with each other only when both parties are ready. This is particularly useful for some parallel applications, which need frequent synchronization in the execution of cooperative agents. Socket over TCP is an example that ensures instantaneous communication in distributed applications. By migrating agent sockets transparently, an agent can continue communicating with other agents after movement (Zhong, Shen, & Xu, 2004).

## Naming and Name Resolution

Various entities in a mobile agent system, such as agents, agent servers, resources, and users need to be assigned names that can identify them. An agent should be uniquely named, so that its owner can communicate with or control it while it migrates on its itinerary. For example, a user may need to contact his or her shopper agent to update some preferences it is carrying or simply recall it back to the home host. Agent servers need names so that an agent can specify its desired destination when it migrates. Some namespaces may be common to different entities; for example, agents and agent servers may share a namespace. This allows agents to uniformly request either migration to a particular server or co-location with another agent with which it needs to communicate.

During the execution of a mobile agent system, there must be a mechanism to find the current location of an entity, given its name. This process is called name resolution. The names assigned to entities may be location dependent, which allows easier implementation of name resolution. Systems such as Agent Tcl (Gray, 1996) and Aglets (1998) use such names, based on hostnames and port numbers, and resolve them using the DNS. In such systems, when an agent migrates, its name changes to reflect the new location. This makes agent tracking more cumbersome. Therefore, it is desirable to provide location-transparent names at the application level. This can be done in two ways. The first is to provide local proxies for remote entities, which encapsulate their current location. The system updates the location information in the proxy when the entity moves, thus providing location transparency at the application level. For example, Voyager (1997) uses this approach for agent tracking, although its agent servers are identified using location-dependent DNS names. An alternative is to use global, location-independent names that do not change when the entity is relocated. This requires the provision of a name service that maps a symbolic name to the current location of the named entity. Ajanta uses such global names for referring to all types of entities uniformly (Karnik & Tripathi, 1998).

## Security

To design a secure mobile agent system, we have to consider the security problem in three areas, as illustrated in

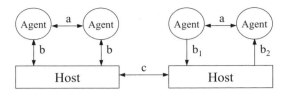

**Figure 3:** The security problems of a secure mobile system are in three areas: (a) interagent security, (b) agent–host security, and (c) interhost security.

Figure 3: (a) interagent security, (b) agent–host security, and (c) interhost security. Although the security issues associated with areas (a) and (c) can be solved with conventional security mechanisms, such as those applied in today's client/server systems, agent–host security requires specific treatment. In agent–host security, we can distinguish two aspects: (b1) host security and (b2) agent security. The former addresses the problem of how to protect agent servers against malicious actions of untrusted mobile agents, and the latter is concerned with the protection of agents against manipulation caused by malicious hosts. To ensure the secure access of server resources, traditional security techniques such as authentication, authorization, access control, and sandboxes are still applicable. But different from the conventional distributed systems, an agent server will accommodate agents arriving from remote hosts. Therefore, it is relatively difficult to identify the principal of an agent. The authorization scheme based on code source in the mobile code systems, such as Java applets, is not able to effectively authenticate a mobile agent (Xu & Fu, 2003). Instead, we can identify the owner of an agent by certain credentials, which are carried by the agent and signed by its owner. Thus, access privileges are granted to the agent based on its owner's principal. Other approaches against attacks of malicious agents include using secure languages or isolated address spaces and applying audition and contract mechanisms.

The inequality between mobile agents and servers in terms of controlling capability complicates the tasks of protecting agents against malicious hosts. An agent executes its program within the environment of a host. The host has full control over the agent action. It may eventually understand the program and therefore change it in any way it wants. It is almost impossible to ensure the correct interpretation and execution by the host (Farmer, Guttman, & Swarup, 1996b). However, Sander and Tschudin (1998a) proposed an approach to agent protection of applying encrypted techniques. Until now, there has been no general solution to ensure the secure agent execution on untrusted hosts. Broadly speaking, there are two ways to protect mobile agents: prevention or detection.

Prevention mechanisms strive to make it infeasible or impossible for a host to understand and manipulate the program of an agent during its execution. Static components, such as the program instructions, can be encrypted and signed to ensure their privacy and integrity. Fully protecting a mobile code program is an elusive and open research problem. But we can adopt some techniques that use complexity to make it computationally infeasible,

if not impossible, to tamper with or inspect an agent program. Detection mechanisms enable a mobile agent's owner to identify that an attack has occurred on the mobile agent. This can be useful in judging the validity of results that an agent has accumulated, but only after the fact. The most useful detection mechanisms let the owner discover the actual identity of a remote host or aid partially in authenticating the intermediate results produced by the visited hosts.

# RESEARCH CHALLENGES OF MOBILE AGENT SECURITY

Mobile agents provide an efficient approach to construct distributed applications. However, this paradigm will not be widely accepted unless its security problems are solved. Protecting the agents and execution platforms in an open environment is nontrivial. Many research challenges are introduced due to the special features of agent mobility.

## Protection of Agent Hosts

To prevent untrusted agents from accessing server resources, we have to deduce the identity of each incoming agent. This process is called authentication. However, in a mobile agent system, authentication is complicated by the fact that an agent may traverse multiple hosts and network channels that are secured in different ways and are not equally trusted (Lampson et al., 1992). In addition, agent image, including its code, data, and state, may be tampered with during its execution on visited hosts. The authentication process can only identify the owner of an agent. This is not sufficient to ensure the trust of it, because a migrating agent can become malicious by virtue of its state getting corrupted (Farmer, Guttman, & Swarup, 1996b). Traditional security mechanisms control agent operations based on the agent identity and certain security policies. Consequently, a protection scheme that takes the dynamic behaviors of each running agent into account cannot be enforced. The requirement "an agent with identity $i$ cannot access resource $r$ if it has already accessed $r$ before (maybe on a previously visited host)" is an example of such a protection scheme. So, the existing security techniques have great limitations and novel approaches should be devised to accommodate these requirements.

## Protection of Mobile Agents

Protecting mobile agents from malicious hosts is more challenging than protecting the server resource. As an agent migrates from host to host accumulating partial results, it is vulnerable to malicious manipulation by a visited host. Multiple remote hosts may even collude to attack a mobile agent. The degree of vulnerability depends on the security requirements of different applications, but we can classify agent vulnerabilities in a broad way: inspection, tampering, replay, and denial of service.

*Inspection.* In many applications, the code and state of agents need to be confidential. Algorithms that the agent program uses to perform tasks might be proprietary, and the partial results accumulated from visited hosts might be considered private or proprietary. One barrier to achieving such confidentiality of code and state is that the instructions of agent program must be available for execution on a remote host. Enforcing a security policy that disallows the host's inspection of some parts of the program while allowing it to read and execute others is very difficult, if not impossible.

*Tampering.* Tampering vulnerabilities in mobile agents are similar to inspection ones: a portion of an agent program, including its execution state, may change as the agent moves from host to host, but general security requires that other portions remain immutable. The constant portions include the partial results obtained from visited hosts as well as certain algorithms that might also require immutability to guarantee fair computational results across all remote hosts. Each remote host expects to be able to load a mobile code for execution. Thus, a remote host could potentially read each instruction and modify the agent program before it migrates to a new host. To combat the tampering threats in an untrusted execution environment is a research challenge. Some cryptographic techniques might be used to provide partial solutions.

*Replay or denial of execution.* Replay attacks occur when a remote host reexecutes a mobile agent in an attempt to infer the semantics of the agent program or to gain extra profits. Effective countermeasures to replay attacks have not been developed. Like any other software system, mobile agents are susceptible to denial-of-execution attacks: a remote host can simply refuse to execute an agent program, thus causing the corresponding application to abnormally terminate. In other cases, a remote host could intercept and deny the mobile agent's requests to databases or other external information sources. Novel methods tackling the denial of execution also need to be proposed for ensuring agent execution.

## Secure Agent Communication and Navigation

Mobile agents are created by their owners to perform certain tasks. Agents may communicate with each other to synchronize their operations or exchange execution results. When agents roam around an open environment, security of agent communication is a great challenge. The conventional way to keep messages confidential is to use cryptographic techniques. Either the symmetric key or the public key mechanisms is able to encrypt the message contents. However, mobile agents may execute on untrusted hosts. So, it is not secure to let agents carry the private keys that are inherited from their owners or generated for communication sessions. As a consequence, the encryption/decryption algorithms are not effective.

Another difficulty posed by multihop migration of agents is how to trace a roaming agent. It is relatively easy to find an agent in a single administrative domain, as certain global information is available. When it comes to a system covering multiple administrative domains, it is hard to let hosts trust each other to provide information of their residing agents. This is particularly difficult when malicious hosts forge false tracing records for private interests.

## Secure Control of Cloned Agents

A mobile agent encompasses its program code, execution state, and data and carries out its computation on networked hosts. This paradigm facilitates the development of applications for parallel computing. For instance, a coordinator agent may generate multiple worker agents to execute the same program on different hosts, similar to the single program multiple data (SPMD) model. Each worker agent performs its tasks and sends back the results to the coordinator (Xu & Wims, 2000). A convenient approach to realize this is by agent cloning, which generates a copy of a mobile agent. However, cloned agents may introduce additional security problems. To distinguish cloned agents from the original ones, they should be assigned different names or identities, so they will have different message digests. This requires the host where the original agent resides to re-sign the cloned agent with its owner's private key. As we know, it is quite insecure to have an agent carry secret keys in an open, untrusted environment. An alternative is to clone a mobile agent as an exact copy of the original one. The message digest is also copied without change. But the problem with this approach is that we cannot distinguish them, which results in the difficulty of authentication and access control of the cloned versions. Another challenge introduced by agent cloning is authorizing cloned agents. They should be granted the same privileges as their original or a restricted subset. For the latter case, defining this subset to satisfy the security and application requirements is a critical problem.

# AGENT HOST PROTECTION

Agent hosts are the major component of a mobile agent system. They provide an execution environment for mobile agents and accommodate agents that may come from different remote hosts. Agents perform their tasks by accessing host resources. The access requests are issued by agents that may or may not be acting for legitimate users. Malicious agents may attempt to exercise unauthorized operations, exhaust host services or even break down the system. Agent host protection strives to ensure agent behaviors abide by the security policies specified by the system administrator and agents cannot execute dangerous operations without the appropriate security mediation.

## Security Requirements

Mobile agents residing on a host may come from different remote hosts. They may traverse multiple hosts and network channels that are secured in different ways and are not equally trusted. To protect hosts from attacks by malicious or malfunctioned agents in an open environment, the following security requirements should be fulfilled.

- The identity of an agent needs to be determined before allowing it to access to sensitive resources. This is realized by the agent authentication mechanisms. With the generated identity information, a host can tell whether an access request is from an agent executing on behalf of a legitimate user.

- An agent cannot be authorized more permissions than those delegated from its owner. Agents roam around networks to perform tasks for their owners. To complete these tasks, agent owners delegate part or all of their privileges to their agents (privilege delegation), whose behaviors are restricted by those permissions. When an agent lands on a remote host, it is granted a set of permissions (agent authorization) according to the delegation from its owner principal.

- An agent behavior must conform to the security policy of a visited host. Agents can only access the resources allowed by their authorized permissions (agent access control), whereas other operations will result in security exceptions. A mobile agent may malfunction after being tampered with by a malicious host visited in its itinerary. This type of agent also poses a great security threat to the entire system. To control their actions appropriately, we need a coordinated access control scheme that takes the dynamic behaviors that agents have performed since their creation into account when making access control decisions.

## Agent Authentication

Authentication is the process of deducing which principal has made a specific request and whom a mobile agent represents. Lampson proposed a theory for authentication in distributed environments (Lampson et al., 1992). It is based on the notion of principal and a *speaks-for* relation between principals. A simple principal either has a name or is a communication channel, whereas a compound principal can express delegated authority. A principal's authority is authenticated by deducing other principals that it can speak for.

Based on this authentication theory, Berkovits, Guttman, and Swarup (1998) designed an authentication scheme for mobile agent systems. In this framework, five types of atomic principals are specified: authors, senders, programs, agents, and places. They represent the persons who write the agent programs, who send the agent on their behalf, the agent programs, agents themselves, and the servers where agents are executed. Compound principals can be built from public keys and atomic principals. When an author creates a program, he or she constructs a state appraisal function, which detects whether the program state has been corrupted. A sender permission list (SPL) is attached to the program to determine which users are permitted to send the resulting agent. A complementary mechanism is provided by issuing a sender permission certificate (SPC) by the author to allow new users to become the agent senders. In creating a mobile agent, its sender specifies another appraisal function to verify the integrity of the agent's state. The sender also appends a place permission list (PPL), which determines which places are allowed to run the resulting agent on behalf of its sender. Similar to an SPC, a place permission certificate (PPC) will be issued if the sender decides to add a new acceptable place.

During agent migration, a migration request will be sent from the current place to the destination place. The request contains the agent principal, its current state, the principal of the current place, and principals on behalf of whom the current and destination places execute the agent. The semantics of a request is determined by the handoff or delegation relationship between the agent and places. When the destination place receives a request to execute an agent, it will check the author's signature on the agent program and the sender's signature on the agent itself. Then, the place will authenticate the principal, on behalf of whom it will execute the agent as indicated in the request, according to the agent's PPL and PPCs. Once the authentication process is completed, the agent is appended with the corresponding principal.

This agent authentication scheme assumes the executing hosts are trustworthy. Otherwise, the migration requests communicated between places may contain false information, which misleads the authentication procedure of the destination place. In addition, the scheme is only applicable to mobile agents with proactive migration, in which the agent sender can predict the sequence of hosts on the agent journey. For places that an agent reactively migrates to, the authentication procedure cannot succeed according to the agent's PPL and PPCs. One solution to this problem is to apply public key-based authentication. For example, a Kerberos-like protocol was developed to authenticate mobile devices by Harbitter and Menasce (2001). This approach can be adapted for mobile agent authentication by modeling a mobile device by an agent.

## Privilege Delegation and Agent Authorization

A mobile agent can travel across a network in pursuit of its designated tasks. On each host in its itinerary, an agent needs to be granted certain privileges to execute its program. Privilege delegation specifies the set of permissions that its owner allows it to carry out the tasks. At the same time, the executing host needs to determine which privileges can be granted based on the agent's request and the host's security policy.

Farmer, Guttman, and Swarup (1996a) exploited *state appraisal functions* to specify permissions delegated from agent authors and owner to their agents. State appraisal is to ensure that an agent has not been somehow subverted due to alterations of its state information. A state appraisal function computes a set of privileges to request, as a function of the agent state, when it arrives at a new host. After the state appraisal has determined which permissions to request, the authorization mechanism on the host determines which of the requested permissions will be granted. So, an agent's privileges on an executing host are determined by its current state. An agent whose state violates an invariant will be granted no privileges, whereas an agent whose state fails to meet some conditional factors may be granted a restricted set of privileges. In this way, a host can be protected from attacks that alter the agent states maliciously. In addition, the author and owner of an agent can ascertain that it will not be misused in their name by enforcing state invariants.

Before an agent is dispatched from its home host, both its author and owner impose appraisal functions. The author-supplied function max will return a maximum safe set of permits. An owner applies state constraints, functions, to reduce liability or control costs. When the author and owner each digitally sign the agent, their respective appraisal functions are protected from undetectable modification. An agent platform uses the functions to verify the correctness of an incoming agent's state and to determine which permissions the agent can possess during execution. Permissions are issued by a platform based on results of the appraisal functions and the platform's security policy. State appraisal provides a convenient approach to delegate privileges to an agent from its owner. But, it is not clear how well the theory will hold up in practice, because the state space for an agent could be quite large. Although appraisal functions for obvious attacks can be easily formulated, more subtle attacks may be significantly hard to foresee and detect. From the perspective of a host, it cannot trust the results of the appraisal functions when the mobile agent comes from an untrusted source. As a result, the approach by state appraisal functions has not had practical application in the existing mobile code systems, and there is no recent work following this direction.

## Agent-Oriented Access Control

After a host establishes the principal of a mobile agent, the agent may attempt to access system resources, such as files or network sockets. It is not appropriate to grant all permissions to an agent, because the agent may come from a malicious user or through untrusted networks. Access control tries to restrict the actions of an agent to protect a host system.

For a secure system, access control is usually realized by enforcing a security policy, which is a set of access rules, in a reference monitor. However, access control for the mobile agent systems differs from the traditional access control model in many ways. First, there is no fixed set of resources that a host can administer. Different hosts may possess different resources. An access control mechanism cannot rely on controlling requests for specific resources. It should be applicable to any resource that a host may define. Second, the access control model should allow the customization of access control policies from one host to another, one mobile program to another, and one source to another. At the same time, the permission management cannot be too complicated. Third, a mobile agent may have visited multiple hosts before arriving at the current one and its operations may depend on its access history. Therefore it is necessary to integrate spatial information and access history in the secure mobile agent system.

Java has become a popular programming language in the development of mobile agent systems. A practical approach is to utilize the special security mechanisms provided by Java to design an agent-oriented access control scheme. Pandey and Hashii (2000) proposed an approach that allowed a host to protect and control the local resource that external Java programs could access. In their scheme, a site uses a declarative policy language to specify a set of constraints on accesses to local resources and the conditions under which they will be applied. A set of code transformation tools enforces these constraints on an external Java program by integrating the code and checking access constraints into the program and the host's resource definitions. Execution of the resulting modified mobile program satisfies all access constraints,

thereby protecting the host's local resource. Because this approach does not require resource access to make an explicit call to the reference monitor, as implemented in the Java run-time system, the approach does not depend on a particular implementation of the run-time system. However, this approach applies binary editing to modify an agent's program, which leads to violation of the agent's integrity. Moreover, it is not orthogonal to code obfuscation, in which an agent's program is encrypted to achieve privacy and integrity. Xu and Fu (2003) proposed a fine-grained access control mechanism for mobile agent systems by using the Subject-based control in Java. After successful authentication, an agent is associated with a *Subject* instance, which confines the access permissions authorized to the agent. Access control is performed by the Java runtime environment (JRE) and customized SecurityManagers.

Edjlali, Acharya, and Chaudhary (1998) described a history-based access control scheme for mobile code security. It maintains a selective history of the access requests made by individual mobile programs and uses this information to improve the differentiation between safe and potentially dangerous accesses. The permissions granted to a program depend on its identity and behaviors, in addition to some discriminators, such as the location it is loaded from or the identity of its author. When a request is made to a protected resource, a *Deed* security event is prompted. Handlers can be associated with security events. They maintain an event history and check whether it satisfies user-specified constraints. If the checking fails, the handler issues a security-related exception. The access-control policies of the system consist of one or more handlers, which are grouped together. Handlers belonging to a single policy maintain a common history and check common constraints. They ensure the security of access operations.

Although this mechanism considers the dynamic actions of an agent in controlling access requests, it is useful only for applications with one-hop migration, for example, the Java applets, because the history information and security events are maintained and processed by the local handlers. In addition, the request history was not clearly defined, which results in the difficulty of deriving its properties and verifying the soundness of this approach. This access control scheme is essentially a trace-based control in execution monitoring (Soman, Krintz, & Vigna, 2003; Gao, Reiter, & Song, 2004). Like other trace-based approaches, it is difficult for the execution history to record all the security-relevant operations of an agent when *covert channels* exist. A covert channel is a path of communication that is not intended for information transfer at all (Lampson, 1973). For example, an unauthorized agent may manipulate a restricted resource by accessing its attributes or some temporary file. In this way, the history-based access control is circumvented. A recent research work was conducted by Fu and Xu (2005) in which they formally defined an access history model for mobile computing and proposed a coordinated access control model to specify and reason about the spatial safety property of a mobile code. Their goal is to leverage and enforce the security policies in which the control of a mobile code's accesses depends not only on its current request but also on its behaviors in the past and maybe on different hosts.

## Proof-Carrying Code

Proof-carrying code (PCC) is a software mechanism that allows a host to determine with certainty that it is safe to execute a program supplied by an untrusted source (Necula, 1997). The basic idea of PCC is that the code producer is required to provide an encoding of a proof that his or her code adheres to the security policy specified by the code consumer. The proof is encoded in a form that can be transmitted digitally. Therefore, the code consumer can quickly validate the code using a simple, automatic, and reliable proof-checking process.

A typical PCC session requires five steps to generate and verify the PCC. It works as follows:

- A PCC session starts with the code producer preparing the untrusted code to be sent to the code consumer. The producer adds annotations to the code, which can be done manually or automatically by a tool such as a certifying compiler. These annotations contain information that helps the code consumer to understand the safety-relevant properties of the code. The code producer then sends the annotated code to the code consumer to execute it.
- The code consumer performs a fast but detailed inspection of the annotated code. This is accomplished by using a program, called VCGen, which is a component of the consumer-defined safety policy. VCGen performs two tasks. First, it checks simple safety properties of the code. For example, it verifies that all immediate jumps are within the code-segment boundaries. Second, VCGen watches for instructions whose execution might violate the safety policy. When such an instruction is encountered, VCGen emits a predicate that expresses the conditions under which the execution of the instruction is safe. The collection of the verification conditions, together with some control flow information, makes up the *safety predicate*, and a copy of it is sent to the proof producer.
- Upon receiving the safety predicate, the proof producer attempts to prove it. In the event of success, it sends an encoding of a formal proof back to the code consumer. Because the code consumer does not have to trust the proof producer, any system can act as a proof producer.
- Then, the code consumer performs a proof validation. This phase is performed using a proof checker. The proof checker verifies that each inference step in the proof is a valid instance of one of the axioms and inference rules specified as part of the safety policy. In addition, the proof checker verifies that the proof proves the same safety predicate generated in the second step.
- After the executable code has passed both the VCGen checks and the proof check, it is trusted not to violate the safety policy. It can thus be safely installed for execution, without any further need for run-time checking.

In PCC, a proof-generating compiler emits a proof of security along with the machine code. And a type checker can verify the code and proof efficiently to allow a safe agent to execute remotely. Recent research on PCC focuses on how to reduce the size of a consumer's trusted code base (TCB), which constitutes the security policy (Necula & Schneck, 2002; Schneck & Necula, 2002). This is achieved by removing the safety proof rules from TCB, while allowing the producer to provide its own proof rules with soundness guaranteed.

Although PCC leverages mobile code by generating a machine-checkable proof of its safety, there are problems associated with this approach. First, the proof of security is relative to a given security policy. In a system where there are many security policies or where the policy is not known beforehand, policy negotiation is necessary. This poses insecurity because the code consumers need to reveal their security policies to code producers that they may not trust. In addition, the consumers deal with binary code, which makes it difficult for them to statically verify its safety satisfaction. This practical difficulty limits the application of PCC to primarily type and memory safety properties. Sekar et al. (2003) combined the ideas of PCC and executing-monitoring and proposed the model-carrying code (MCC) approach, which allows runtime enforcement of safety policies. As a result, the code consumer can define flexible policies for more safety properties. Automatic proof generation is just one concern. Colby et al. (2000) designed a PCC certifying compiler that generates safety proofs with certain automation for a subset of the Java programming language. We can find that the certifying compilers are language dependent and complicated. In general, however, the proof generation is similar to program verification and is not completely automatable. It requires a level of sophistication and familiarity with automatic reasoning and inference mechanisms that exceeds the capabilities of most programmers.

## MOBILE AGENT PROTECTION

Mobile agents are autonomous entities encapsulating the program code, data, and execution state. Agents are dispatched by their owners for special purposes and they may carry some private information and secrete execution results. When agents are transferred in a network, they are exposed to the threats discussed in the network security. In addition, agent execution on malicious hosts is more risky. They may be inspected, tampered with, or reexecuted for the hosts' covert interests. In this section, we focus on the techniques and mechanisms to protect mobile agents in an open environment.

### Security Requirements

A mobile agent is vulnerable to various types of security threats. These include passive attacks, such as eavesdropping and traffic analysis, and active attacks, such as impersonation, message modification, deletion, or forging. Passive attacks are difficult to detect, but can usually be protected against using traditional cryptographic mechanisms. In contrast, active attacks are relatively easy to detect cryptographically, but they are difficult to prevent altogether. Host–host communication often contains sensitive agent data. Therefore, the agent migration process must incorporate confidentiality, integrity, and authentication mechanisms. Most of these requirements can be tackled by various techniques for secure communication (Ford, 1994), which have already been proposed.

When an agent performs tasks on a host's execution environment, its internals are in effect exposed to that host. A malicious host can read or tamper with sensitive information stored in the agent, deny agent execution, or replay it multiple times. The agents' code can also be altered, so that it will perform malicious or malfunctioned actions during the following execution. It is almost impossible to provide a general approach to guarantee that an agent will not be deliberately modified, although some partial solutions have been proposed (Farmer, Guttman, & Swarup, 1996b). Several mechanisms using cryptographic techniques at the hardware level, software levels, or both can make it difficult for attacks by malicious hosts to achieve their objectives. The integrity and privacy of agent execution on different hosts should also be ensured.

## Integrity Detection

Detection mechanisms aim at identifying illegal modifications of agent code, state, and execution flow. This is useful in judging the validity of execution results as an agent returns to the home host or in determining the trust of agent information by a host.

Mechanisms for detecting illicit mobile code manipulationt can be as simple as *range checkers*, which verify the values of variables within the agent program and state, or certain timing constraints. We can also embed *function monitors* into the agent programs, and they are called upon in execution of the program to give assurance that the agent executes correctly. Sophisticated approaches include the appraisal functions in state appraisal mechanisms (discussed in the Privilege Delegation and Agent Authorization section), which check the integrity of agent states by enforcing certain invariants.

Vigna (1998) proposed execution tracing to detect unauthorized modifications of an agent through the faithful recording of the agent's behavior during its execution on each remote host. This scheme requires each host involved to create and retain a nonrepudiatable *trace* of operations performed by the agent while residing there and to submit a cryptographic hash of the trace upon conclusion as a trace summary. A trace is composed of a sequence of statement identifiers and host signature information. It is a partial or complete snapshot of the agent's execution actions. The signature of the platform is needed only for those instructions that depend on interactions with the computational environment maintained by the host. For instructions that rely only on the values of internal variables, a signature is not required and, therefore, is omitted in the trace. The host then forwards the trace and state to the next remote host in the agent itinerary. Vigna also described a protocol for detecting agent tampering by these signed execution traces. Upon the completion of an agent itinerary, the agent's home host verifies the program execution, if it believes that the program has been incorrectly manipulated. The home host simulates the agent execution and asks a remote host for traces from the point at which the agent decided to migrate to that host. The remote host will have difficulty in repudiating the request from the owner because it has cryptographically signed and forwarded its trace to the next host. However, this mechanism is not foolproof. A remote host could manipulate the agent program and hide the changes in the traces forwarded to the next host. Kassab and Voas (1998) proposed a similar approach that transmits protective assertions of an agent to its owner to verify the integrity of agent state. The assertions reveal the owner-specified agent state snapshots throughout its execution on a host. They also can monitor the execution environment by providing the resource information for the agent owners to determine the timing of agent migration to fulfill the overall agent computation. Like the execution tracing, protective assertions are not foolproof. Even with the assertions, it is still possible to clone agents, remove assertions, lie to agents, or tamper with agent communication.

Yee (1997) presented two ways to detect tampering by malicious hosts. The first method involves the use of partial result authentication codes (PRACs). An agent is sent out with a set of secret keys $k_1, \ldots, k_n$. At server $i$, the agent uses key $k_i$ to sign the result of its execution there, thereby producing a PRAC, and then removes $k_i$ from its state before moving to the next server. This means that a malicious server cannot forge the partial results from previous hosts; at worst, it could only remove them from the agent. The PRACs can allow the agent's owner, who also possesses $k_1, \ldots, k_n$, to automatically cryptographically verify each partial result contained in a returning agent. The property that these messages guarantee is perfect forward integrity, that is, if a mobile agent visits a sequence of servers $s_1, \ldots, s_n$, and the first malicious server is $s_c$, then none of the partial results generated at server $s_i$, $i < c$, can be forged. However, if the tampering occurs simply through dishonest interactions with the running agent, this scheme will not automatically detect it. Again, we must rely on the suspicions of the agent's owner to make the PRACs examined —the PRACs will all be cryptographically valid, although one or more may not be semantically valid.

Yee (1997) also proposed a speculative approach to detecting this semantic tempering based on computationally sound proofs (Micali, 1994). For a program $x$, let $y$ be an execution trace for $x$. Now, the host could send $y$ back to the owner to verify it. But the execution traces might be so large that their transmission is costly in terms of network bandwidth. Instead, the host can encode $y$ as a *holographic proof* $y'$ that was the result of running $x$. The proof $y'$ has the property that the owner only needs to examine a few bits of $y'$ for its verification. The server then uses a tree-hashing scheme to hash the proof down to a small root value, which is then transmitted back to the owner, who gets some confidence that $y$ was correct. The main problem of this scheme is the burden placed on the server. The construction of holographic proof $y'$ is an NP-complete problem, which makes this approach impractical, particularly when the trace $y$ is already too large to be simply transmitted back to the owner.

The *detection objects* idea was proposed by Meadows (1997) to detect possible modifications to the mobile agent data state. These are dummy data items or attributes that will not be modified by the hosts performing the agent

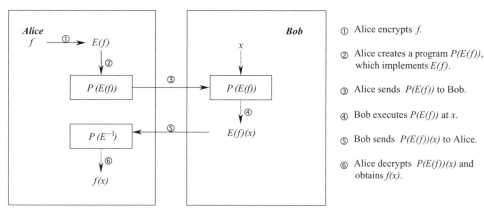

**Figure 4:** Computing with encrypted functions.

execution for legitimate work. If the detection objects have not been modified, then one can have reasonable confidence that legitimate data also have not been corrupted. For a detection object to work, it is necessary that hosts for mobile agents not be aware which are the detection objects. This approach seems to be simple and effective. However, a general mechanism to construct detection objects is hard to design, because hosts can apply data flow analysis to discern the dummy data and so the detection objects should be application-program dependent.

## Cryptographic Protection of Mobile Agents

To protect mobile agents from malicious attacks by untrusted hosts, we can apply cryptographic techniques to encrypt agent program and data or mask their semantics, so that it is difficult for a host to understand or even know what is running. One possible approach is to adopt tamper-proof hardware. This kind of device executes agents in a physically sealed environment, which makes the agent code and state inaccessible to hosts, and the agent integrity and privacy can be easily ensured. Software-based approaches include computing with encrypted functions and code obfuscation. They change agent programs by different methods and provide agent protection to a certain extent.

**Tamper-Proof Hardware** Tamper-proof hardware, such as secure processors (Lie et al., 2000), smart cards (Bieber et al., 2000), and secure coprocessors (Yee, 1994), offer an attractive approach to both detection and prevention of attacks on agent execution. It provides a trustworthy computing environment at remote hosts. A mobile agent program can perform cryptographic operations on a host, and in most cases, the crypto keys will be hidden from that host. The tamper-proof hardware can encrypt and digitally sign program code, execution state, and partial results prior to transmitting them to a subsequent host. Alternatively, this hardware can also securely provide critical algorithms to an agent program in hardware form, which would virtually guarantee that the algorithms could not be inspected or modified. For example, the signature algorithm of an agent can be executed within this hardware using the agent's private key, so that the secret key is protected by making it available only when decrypted inside the trusted hardware.

Despite these strengths, tamper-proof hardware is not a general solution to secure mobile agent applications. They extend the hardware infrastructure to each remote host in a way that limits the agent's ability to migrate. This will work only for applications in which tamper-proof hardware can be deployed throughout a controlled network, such as a closed corporate system or secure military network.

**Computing with Encrypted Functions** Encrypted computing applies cryptographic techniques to provide execution privacy by transforming functions into encrypted forms that become part of an agent program and reveal no information about the original function. Figure 4 shows the principle of encrypted computing. Here, Alice has a secrete function $f$ that wants to run on Bob's machine using some input $x$ provided by Bob. To prevent Bob from understanding or modifying function $f$, Alice encrypts $f$ using her private key and an encryption scheme $E$ to obtain a new program $P(E(f))$ for computing $E(f)$. Then, she sends this program to Bob, who receives the program and runs it on his input $x$. The program produces an encrypted result $E(f)(x)$, which Bob sends back to Alice. Finally, Alice runs a decryption program $P(E^{-1})$ on result $E(f)(x)$ to obtain the desired value $f(x)$. In this way, Bob is able to do useful computation without learning either the function $f$ or the final result $f(x)$. With this approach, an agent's computation would be kept secret from the executing host, as the sensitive information is carried by the agent. For instance, the means to produce a digital signature can thereby be given to an agent without revealing its private key. This scheme is referred to as computing with encrypted functions (CEF) (Sander & Tschudin, 1998a). However, a malicious host is still able to use the agent to produce a signature on arbitrary data. This leads to a security flaw in agent execution. To tackle this problem, Sander and Tschudin (1998b) suggested incorporating undetachable signatures to encrypted computing.

CEF can also be extended to *function hiding*, where the result $f(x)$ is returned to Bob after being decrypted by Alice (Sander & Tschudin, 1998c). Function hiding can be used to protect intellectual property from theft and piracy. Suppose function $f$ is some proprietary algorithm that Alice has developed for solving a problem of interest to many people. With function hiding, Alice can embed the encrypted function $P(E(f))$ in an agent program and let users run it on their own machines using their own input. The program will produce encrypted results, which users can ask Alice to decrypt. In this way, Alice can protect her intellectual property for algorithm $f$ and at the same time charge users for its use.

Although the idea of computing with encrypted functions is straightforward, the challenge is to find appropriate encryption schemes that can transform functions as intended. It remains an interesting research topic. Sander and Tschudin (1998b) developed homomorphic encryption schemes to encrypt a polynomial function's coefficients and function composition to mask the semantics of rational functions. However, these schemes only provide limited functionality. They were later improved by the authors to provide noninteractive evaluation of all functions that can be represented by circuits of logarithmic depth (Sander, Young, & Yung, 1999). Cachin, Camenisch, Kilian, and Müller (2000) further generalized this to arbitrary functions, provided they can be represented by a polynomial-size circuit.

However, there exists a serious drawback for this type of protection: no information about the encrypted functions must leak to the host and only the originator may receive any output. If a malicious host observes the output of the computation, it can probe the agent function by simulating its computation on different inputs and observing the corresponding outputs. This problem was addressed by Algesheimer (2001) who introduced a software-based secure computation service as a minimally trusted third party for secure mobile agent execution. This approach is based on encrypting a binary digital circuit that realizes the agent computation. However, it is only suitable for small parts of an agent application, because the costs of constructing such circuits are prohibitive for large applications. Yee (2003) proposed a different approach to detecting the simulation attacks made by malicious hosts. It is based on the one-way program state transitions by using monotonic bits (once set, they can never be cleared). There is a third-party detection program, which is trusted by the mobile agents, to monitor their execution state transitions. When it finds inconsistency in the one-way state transitions, a simulation attack is detected.

**Code Obfuscation** To protect the privacy of programs, *code obfuscation* uses heuristic techniques to modify the program for computing a function (Libes, 1993). It transforms the program into an equivalent "messy" form, which is quite hard to reverse engineer, but performs the same function as the original one. Collberg and Thomborson (2002) have explored the approaches to code obfuscation and classified them into three types: lexical, control, and data transformations.

*Lexical transformations* change the way that code appears to a malicious attacker. For example, we can remove the source code formatting information sometimes available from Java bytecode or scramble identifier names to make a program look different. In general, lexical transformations are simple to apply, but have relatively low potency because the structure information of the code and data is still mostly preserved and can be eventually understood in spite of the lexical alteration.

*Control transformations* aim to obscure the control-flow of the original program. They rely on the existence of opaque predicates. A predicate is opaque if its outcome is known at the obfuscation time, but is difficult for the deobfuscator to deduce. Given such opaque predicates, it is possible to construct obfuscating transformations that break up the control flow of a program. Examples of control transformations include *computation transformations*, which convert the apparent computation being performed by the program to another equivalent one. For example, we can change a program by using more complicated but equivalent loop conditions, converting a sequential program into a multithreaded one by using automatic parallelization techniques, and so forth. *Aggregation transformations* alter the original code by breaking the abstraction barriers represented by procedures and other control structures, for example, inlining subroutine calls and outlining sequences of statements and interleaving methods. *Ordering transformation* modifies the order of statements, blocks, or methods within the code, while maintaining data dependencies.

*Data transformations* obscure the data structures used by the program. For example, *storage and encoding transformations* change the usual ways to encode and store data items in a program, such as by splitting variables and converting static to procedural data. *Aggregation transformations* alter the way data items are grouped together by restructuring arrays, merging scalar variables, and more. *Ordering transformations* randomize the order in which data are stored in the program.

Compared with encrypted computing, code obfuscation has the advantage of being more generally applicable, because it can be applied to any computation that can be expressed as a program. However, these schemes are based on heuristic methods and they are not as provably secure as the encrypted computation. Hohl (1998) proposed *time-limited blackbox* security to tackle this problem by introducing an interval for each obfuscated code. It realizes the protection of mobile agents from malicious hosts by "messing-up" the agent code and data to make them hard to analyze and then attaching an expiration date to indicate its protection interval. The mess-up algorithm is essentially the same as an obfuscation transformation. And the approach does not assume it is impossible for an attacker to analyze the agent program, but the analysis simply takes time. So, after creating an obfuscated version of the agent, the agent owner adds the desired protection interval to the current time to get an expiration date. During the execution of the agent, a digital signed certificate including the expiration date information must be presented to any other party with which it wants to communicate. If it indicates that the agent has already expired in checking its certificate, communication is refused by others. The expiration date protects the agent even if it migrates to another host. When the agent needs to extend its life for certain reasons, it can get extended by returning to its owner, or some other trusted hosts, which can reobfuscate it using different random parameters for the mess-up algorithms, and then issue a new expiration date.

The time-limited blackbox scheme is an applicable method to ensure agent privacy during its lifetime. It combines the code obfuscation mechanisms with the dynamics of agent behaviors. However, one serious drawback to this technique is the lack of an approach to quantify the protection interval provided by the obfuscation algorithms, thus making it difficult to apply in practice. Furthermore, no techniques are currently known for establishing the lower bounds on the complexity for an attacker to reverse engineer an obfuscated program.

There is much research work in this field aimed at the construction of an obfuscating compiler, because an efficient method for obfuscating programs is an important precondition for its usability for mobile agents. A final point to this research was reached when Barak et al. (2001) proved that the existence of such a compiler is impossible as long as one requires the resulting program to have a virtual black box property. This result does not mean that any research in these fields is obsolete. There is still hope to find function-hiding schemes such as homomorphic encryption, but they would not offer an efficient way to construct an obfuscating compiler.

# CONCLUSIONS

Mobile code is a promising solution to the design and implementation of wide-area distributed applications, because it overcomes many of the drawbacks of the traditional client/server approach. A critical issue in the construction of mobile code systems is to open system resource and application services to visiting mobile code in a controlled manner. Security is a great concern for the successful deployment of large-scale mobile code systems.

In this chapter, we review the existing techniques and approaches to enhance security for mobile code. We group them into two broad categories: protection of executing hosts and protection of mobile code. Although we focus on the security issues for a mobile agent, which is one type of mobile code, these mechanisms are also applicable to other types of mobile codes, because agent migration mechanisms provide a general approach to code mobility.

Mobile code security is an interesting and important research area. A large number of techniques have been proposed to protect mobile code systems. However, there are still many critical issues that remain unsolved. For instance, the protection of mobile code against inspection and tampering in an open environment is still a great challenge. The combination of encrypted functions and simulation attack detection provides a possible solution. Much research work has been conducted on related topics. However, issues such as constructing cost-efficient encryption schemes for function transformation and minimizing the trusted third party in replay detection still need to be tackled.

# GLOSSARY

**Code Mobility** The mechanisms that move code among different computational environments.
**Execution State** Control and internal data associated with the executing unit, for example, the program counter or the call stack.

**Host Protection** The mechanisms that protect the host resources from unauthorized accesses by malicious or malfunctioned mobile code.
**Mobile Agent** A mobile software program that moves around the networks to complete a predefined task autonomously. The data and execution states of a mobile agent also move, along with the agent program.
**Mobile Code Authentication** The process of establishing the identity of mobile code.
**Mobile Code Authorization** The process of establishing the set of rights associated with mobile code.
**Mobile Code Platform** A computational environment that hosts and executes mobile code. It provides some low-level services and controls access to underlying resources of the host.
**Mobile Code Protection** The mechanisms that ensure the privacy, integrity, and functionality of mobile code.
**Strong Mobility** Mobile code systems supporting strong mobility enable an executing unit to move as a whole by retaining its execution state across migration.
**Weak Mobility** Mobile code systems supporting weak mobility enable the transfer of application code toward or from a different host. At destination, the code may be run into a newly created executing unit or it may be linked into an already running one.

# CROSS REFERENCES

See *Computer and Network Authentication; Encryption Basics; Hostile Java Applets; The Use of Agent Technology for Intrusion Detection*.

# REFERENCES

Accetta, M., Baron, R., Bolosky, W., Golub, D., Rashid, R., Tevanian, A., et al. (1986). *Mach: A new kernel foundation for UNIX development*. In Proceedings of the USENIX 1986 Summer Conference, Atlanta, GA.

Aglets. (1998). IBM Aglets documentation Web page. Retrieved Oct. 20, 2004, from http://www.trl.ibm.com/aglets/documentation_e.htm

Algesheimer, J., Cachin, C., Camenisch, J., & Karjoth, G. (2001). *Cryptographic security for mobile code*. Proceedings of IEEE Symposium on Security and Privacy, Oakland, CA (pp. 2–11).

Banino, J. (1986). Parallelism and fault tolerance in chorus. *Journal of Systems and Software, 6(1)*, 205–211.

Barak, B., Goldreich, O., Impagliazzo, R., Rudich, S., Sahai, A., Vadhan, S., et al. (2001). On the (Im) possibility of Obfuscating Program. *CRYPTO 2001*, Lecture Notes in Computer Science (Vol. 2139, pp. 1–18). New York: Springer-Verlag.

Barak, A., & Litman, A. (1985). MOS: A multicomputer distributed operating system. *Software - Practice and Experience, 15(8)*, 725–737.

Berkovits, S., Guttman, J., & Swarup, V. (1998). Authentication for mobile agents. In G. Vigna (Ed.), *Mobile agent and security*. Lecture Notes in Computer Science (Vol. 1419, pp. 114–136). New York: Springer-Verlag.

Bieber, P., Cazin, J., Girard, P., Lanet, J. L., Wiels, V., & Zanon, G. (2000). *Checking secure interactions of smart* card applets. Proceedings of the 6th European Symposium on Research in Computer Security (ESORICS 2000), Toulouse, France (pp. 1–16).

Birrell, A. D., & Nelson, B. J. (1984). Implementing remote procedure calls. *ACM Transactions on Computer Systems, 2*(1), 39–59.

Boggs, J. (1973). *IBM remote job entry facility: Generalize subsystem remote job entry facility* (IBM Technical Disclosure Bulletin 752). Armonk, NY: IBM.

Cachin, C., Camenisch, J., Kilian, J., & Müller, J. (2000). *One-round secure computation and secure autonomous mobile agents.* Proceedings of the 27th Colloquium on Automata, Languages and Programming (ICALP), Geneva. Lecture Notes in Computer Science. (Vol. 1853, pp. 512–523) New York: Springer-Verlag.

Campbell, A. T., De Meer, H. G., Kounavis, M. E., Miki, K., Vicente, J. B., & Villela, D. (1999). A survey of programmable networks. *ACM SIGCOMM Computer Communication Review, 29*(2), 7–23.

Carzaniga, A., Picco, G. P., & Vigna, G. (1997). *Designing distributed applications with a mobile code paradigm.* Proceedings of the 19th International Conference on Software Engineering, Boston, MA.

Chess, D., Harrison, C., & Kershenbaum, A. (1995). *Mobile agents: Are they a good idea?* (IBM Research Report RC 19887). Yorktown Heights, NY: T.J. Watson Research Center.

Colby, C., Lee, P., Necula, G. C., Blau, F., Plesko, M., & Cline, K. (2000). *A certifying compiler for Java.* Proceedings of the ACM SIGPLAN 2000 on Programming Language Design and Implementation, British Columbia, Canada.

Collberg, C. S., & Thomborson, C. (2002). Watermarking, tamper-proofing, and obfuscation- tools for software protection. *IEEE Transactions on Software Engineering, 28*(8), 735–746.

Edjlali, G., Acharya, A., & Chaudhary, V. (1998). *History-based access control for mobile code.* Proceedings of ACM Conference on Computer and Communications Security, San Francisco, CA (pp. 38–48).

Farmer, W., Guttman, J., & Swarup, V. (1996a). *Security for mobile agents: Authentication and state appraisal.* Proceedings of the 4th European Symposium on Research in Computer Security (ESORICS '96), Rome, Italy (pp. 118–130).

Farmer, W. M., Guttman, J. D., & Swarup, V. (1996b). *Security for mobile agents: Issues and requirements.* Proceedings of the 19th National Information Systems Security Conference, Baltimore, MD, (pp. 591–597).

Foundation for Intelligent Physical Agents. (n.d.). Retrieved Oct. 20, 2004, from http://www.fipa.org/

Fu, S., & Xu, C. Z. (2005). *A coordinated spatio-temporal access control model for mobile computing in coalition environments.* Proceedings of the 19th International Parallel and Distributed Processing Symposium (IPDPS '05), Denver, CO.

Gao, D., Reiter, M. K., & Song, D. (2004). *Gray-box extraction of execution graphs for anomaly detection.* Proceedings of the 11th ACM Conference on Computer and Communications Security (CCS' 04), Washington DC.

Gray, R. S. (1996). *Agent tcl: A flexible and secure mobile agent system.* Proceedings of the 4th Annual Tcl/Tk Workshop (TCL '96), Monterey, CA.

Habert, S., Mosseri, L., & Abrossimov, V. (1990). *COOL: Kernel support for object-oriented environments.* Proceedings of the Conference on Object-Oriented Programming Systems, Languages, and Applications (OOPSLA) (Vol. 25, pp. 269–277). New York: ACM Press.

Harbitter, A., & Menasce, D. A. (2001). *The performance of public key-enabled kerberos authentication in mobile computing applications.* Proceedings of the 8th ACM Conference on Computer and Communications Security (CCS '01), Philadelphia, PA.

Hohl, F. (1998). Time limited blackbox security: Protecting mobile agents from malicious hosts. In G. Vigna (Ed.), *Mobile agent and security.* Lecture Notes in Computer Science (Vol. 1419, pp. 92–113). New York: Springer-Verlag.

Java Remote Method Interface (RMI). (n.d.). Retrieved on Oct. 20, 2004 from http://java.sun.com/products/jdk/rmi/

Jul, E., Levy, H., Hutchinson, N., & Black, A. (1988). Fine grained mobility in the Emerald system. *ACM Transactions on Computer Systems, 6*(*1*), 109–133.

Karjoth, G., Lange, D. B., & Oshima, M. (1997). A security model for aglets. *IEEE Internet Computing, 1*(4), 68–77.

Karnik, N., & Tripathi, A. (1998). *Agent server architecture for the Ajanta mobile agent system.* Proceedings of the International Conference on Parallel and Distributed Processing Techniques and Applications (PDPTA '98), Las Vegas, NV (pp. 66–73).

Karnik, N., & Tripathi, A. (2000). *A security architecture for mobile agents in Ajanta.* Proceedings of the International Conference on Distributed Computing Systems (ICDCS '00), Taiwan, China (pp. 402–409).

Kassab, L. L., & Voas, J. (1998). *Agent trustworthiness.* Proceedings of the ECOOP Workshop on Distributed Object Security and 4th Workshop on Mobile Object Systems: Secure Internet Mobile Computations (pp. 121–133). INRIA, France.

Kotz, D., Gray, R., Nog, S., & Rus, D. (1997). Agent Tcl: Targeting the needs of mobile computers. *IEEE Internet Computing, 1*(*4*), 58–67.

Lampson, B. (1973). A note on the confinement problem. *Communications of the ACM on Operating Systems, 16*(*10*), 613–615.

Lampson, B., Abadi, M., Burrows, M., & Wobber, E. (1992). Authentication in distributed systems: Theory and practice. *ACM Transactions on Computer Systems, 10*(4), 265–310.

Lange, D. B., & Oshima, M. (1999). Seven good reasons for mobile agents. *Communications of the ACM, 42*(*3*), 88–89.

Levy, J. Y., & Ousterhout, J. K. (1995). *A safe tcl toolkit for electronic meeting places.* Proceedings of the 1st USENIX Workshop on Electronic Commerce, New York, NY (pp. 133–135).

Libes, D. (1993). *Obfuscated C and other mysteries.* New York: Wiley.

Lie, D., Thekkath, C. A., Mitchell, M., Lincoln, P., Boneh, D., Mitchell, J. C., & Horowitz, M. (2000). *Architectural support for copy and tamper resistant software.*

Architectural Support for Programming Languages and Operating Systems, Cambridge, MA (pp. 168–177).

Litzkow, M., Livny, M., & Mutka, M. W. (1988). *Condor: A hunter of idle workstations*. Proceedings of the 8th IEEE International Conference on Distributed Computing Systems, San Jose, CA (pp. 104–111).

Lu, S., & Xu, C.-Z. (2005). *A formal framework for mobile agent itinerary specification, safety reasoning, and logic analysis*. Proceedings of the International Workshop on Mobile Distributed Computing (MDC '05), Columbus, OH.

Meadows, C. (1997). *Detecting attacks on mobile agents*. Proceedings of DARPA Workshop on Foundations for Secure Mobile Code, Monterey, CA.

Micali, S. (1994). *CS proofs*. Proceedings of the 35th IEEE Symposium on Foundations of Computer Science, Santa Fe, NM (pp. 436–453).

Milojicic, D., Breugst, M., Busse, I., Campbell, J., Covaci, S., Friedman, B., et al. (1998). *MASIF the OMG mobile agent system interoperability facility*. Proceedings of the International Workshop on Mobile Agents (MA' 98), Stuttgart, Germany.

Milojicic, D., Douglis, F., & Wheeler, R. (1999). *Mobility: Processes, computers, and agents*. Reading, MA: Addison-Wesley.

Milojicic, D., Douglis, F., Panedeine, Y., Wheeler, R., & Zhou, S. (2000). Process migration. *ACM Computing Surveys, 32(3)*, 241–299.

Mitsubishi Electric. (1997). *Concordia: An infrastructure for collaborating mobile agents*. Proceedings of the 1st International Workshop on Mobile Agents (MA '97), Berlin, Germany.

Necula, G. C. (1997). *Proof-carrying code*. Proceedings of the 24th ACM SIGPLANSIGACT Symposium on Principles of Programming Langauges (POPL '97), Paris (pp. 106–119).

Necula, G. C., & Schneck, R. R. (2002). *Proof-carrying code with untrusted proof rules*. Proceedings of the 2nd International Software Security Symposium.

Object Management Group. (n.d.). Retrieved on Oct. 20, 2004 from http://www.omg.org/

Ousterhout, J. K., Cherenson, A. R., Douglis, F., Nelson, M. N., & Welch, B. B. (1988). The Sprite network operating system. *IEEE Computer, 21*(2), 23–38.

Pandey, R., & Hashii, B. (2000). Providing fine-grained access control for Java programs via binary editing. *Concurrency: Practice and Experience, 12*(14), 1405–1430.

PostScript. (1985). *PostScript language reference manual*. Reading, MA: Adobe Systems Inc., Addison-Wesley.

Sander, T., & Tschudin, C. (1998a). Protecting mobile agents against malicious hosts. In G. Vigna (Ed.), *Mobile agent and security*. Lecture Notes in Computer Science (Vol. 1419, pp. 44–60). New York: Springer-Verlag.

Sander, T., & Tschudin, C. (1998b). *Towards mobile cryptography*. Proceedings of the IEEE Symposium on Security and Privacy, Oakland, CA.

Sander, T., Young, A., & Yung, M. (1999). *Non-interactive cryptocomputing for $NC^1$*. Proceedings of the IEEE Symposium on Foundations of Computer Science (FOCS '99), New York City, NY.

Schneck, R. R., & Necula, G. C. (2002). *A gradual approach to a more trustworthy, yet scalable, proof-carrying code*.

Proceedings of the Conference on Automated Deduction (CADE '02), Copenhagen, Denmark.

Sekar, R., Venkatakrishnan, V. N., Basu, S., Bhatkar, S., & DuVarney, D. C. (2003). *Model-carrying code: A practical approach for safe execution of untrusted applications*. Proceedings of the 9th ACM Symposium on Operating Systems Principles (SOSP '03), Bolton Landing, New York.

Shoch, J. F., & Hupp, J. A. (1982). The "Worm" programs: Early experience with a distributed computation. *Communications of the ACM, 25(3)*, 172–180.

Soman, S., Krintz, C., & Vigna, G. (2003). *Detecting malicious Java code using virtual machine auditing*. Proceedings of the 12th USENIX Security Symposium, Washington, DC.

Spafford, E. H. (1989). The Internet worm: Crisis and aftermath. *Communications of the ACM, 32(6)*, 678–687.

Stamos, J. W., & Gifford, D. K. (1990). Remote evaluation. *ACM Transactions on Programming Languages and Systems, 12(4)*, 537–565.

Tardo, J., & Valente, L. (1996). *Mobile agent security and Telescript*. Proceedings of IEEE COMPCON Spring '96, Santa Clara, CA (pp. 58–63).

Tennenhouse, D. L., Smith, J. M., Sincoskie, D. W., Wetherall, D. J., & Minden, G. J. (1997). A survey of active network research. *IEEE Communications Magazine, 35(1)*, 80–86.

Tripathi, A. R., Karnik, N. M., Vora, M. K., Ahmed, T., & Singh, R. D. (1999). *Mobile agent programming in Ajanta*. Proceeedings of the 19th International Conference on Distributed Computing Systems (ICDCS '99), Austin, TX (pp. 190–197).

Vigna, G. (1998). Cryptographic traces for mobile agents. In G. Vigna (Ed.), *Mobile agent and security*. Lecture Notes in Computer Science (Vol. 1419, pp. 137–153). New York: Springer-Verlag.

Voyager. (1997). *ObjectSpace Voyager core package technical overview*. ObjectSpace Inc. Retrieved Oct. 20, 2004, from http://www.objectspace.com/voyager/ whitepapers

Walsh, T., Paciorek, N., & Wong, D. (1998). Security and reliability in Concordia. Proceedings of the 31st Hawaii International Conference on Systems Sciences, Kohala Coast, HI (pp. 44–53).

White, J. E. (1995). *Mobile agents* (White Paper). General Magic. Retrieved on Oct. 20, 2004 from http://sherry. ifi.unizh.ch/white96mobile.html

Wojciechowski, P. T. (2001). *Algorithms for location-independent communication between mobile agents*. Proceedings of AISB Symposium on Software Mobility and Adaptive Behavior, University of York, United Kingdom (pp. 10–19).

Xu, C.-Z. (2002). *Naplet: A flexible mobile agent framework for network-centric applications*. Proceedings of the 2nd Workshop on Internet Computing and e-Commerce (ICEC '02). Fort Lauderdale, FL.

Xu, C.-Z., & Fu, S. (2003). *Privilege delegation and agent-oriented access control in naplet*. Proceedings of the International Workshop on Mobile Distributed Computing (MDC '03), Providence, RI.

Xu, C.-Z., & Wims, B. (2000). Mobile agent based push methodology for global parallel computing.

*Concurrency: Practice and Experience, 14(8)*, 705–726.

Yee, B. (1994). *Using secure coprocessors*. Unpublished PhD thesis, Carnegie Mellon University.

Yee, B. (1997). A sanctuary for mobile agents. In *Secure Internet programming: Security issues for mobile and distributed objects* (pp. 261–273). New York: Springer-Verlag.

Yee, B. (2003). *Monotonicity and partial results protection for mobile agents*. Proceedings of the 23rd Int'l Confer-ence on Distributed Computing Systems (ICDCS '03), Providence, RI.

Zhong, X., Shen, H., & Xu, C.-Z. (2004). *A reliable and secure connection migration mechanism for mobile agents*. Proceedings of International Workshop on Mobile Distributed Computing (MDC '04), Tokyo, Japan.

Zhou, S., Zheng, X., Wang, J., & Delisle, P. (1993). Utopia: A load sharing facility for large, heterogeneous distributed computer systems. *Software - Practice and Experience, 23(12)*, 1305–1336.

# Wireless Threats and Attacks

Robert J. Boncella, *Washburn University*

## INTRODUCTION

### Wireless Security Requirements

The security requirements for wireless devices are the same as for wired devices. The minimal requirements for communication security are confidentiality, integrity, and availability. This is sometimes referred to as the CIA requirement.

*Confidentiality* is keeping your secrets secret. Attackers who try to break confidentiality are trying to find out something that you don't want them to know.

*Integrity* is making sure that your data are what they are supposed to be. Someone who changes or destroys data compromises integrity.

*Availability* is the property that allows people to get at the data they need when they need it. Denial of service (DoS) attacks that try to bring a network or server down are attacks on availability.

A secure communication channel will ensure these requirements. In addition, wireless communication security should include techniques that allow for the authentication of both the sender and receivers of a message and techniques by which nonrepudiation of a message is guaranteed.

An *attack* on a wireless network is an attempt to exploit a particular vulnerability or number of vulnerabilities that exist in the wireless communication medium. A successful attack will compromise any single or perhaps all of the assurances of either confidentiality, integrity, or availability of the information being transmitted using wireless technology. For detailed discussions of information security, see Whitman and Mattord (2003).

### Threats

For wireless communications, a threat is an object, person, or other entity that represents a danger to the assurance of security for a communication channel. Particular threats to wireless communication are device theft, malicious hackers, malicious code, theft of service, and espionage, both foreign and domestic. An instance of a threat is referred to as *threat agent*. Of all possible threat agents, the majority will be hackers. There is a classification of hackers that helps to define the degree of threat to a wireless system.

### Types of Hackers

Wireless local area network (LAN) security has vulnerabilities that are simple for hackers to create automated tools to exploit those vulnerabilities. The barrier to entry for wireless hackers is low. All that is needed is a computer and a wireless client card. Because of the way that wireless LANs work, hackers do not even have to try getting into your network. An improperly configured network will allow even the most inept hacker access. Unauthorized users, or hackers, can be divided into four categories:

1. **Accidental users:** Accidental users are just regular people. Their computers are configured to join any network that can be detected and will have them. Most newer laptops with onboard wireless are configured to seek public "hot spots" automatically. It is a wireless vulnerability when wireless networks are not configured to keep out people who aren't even *trying* to break into a network.

2. **Script kiddies:** This is a derogatory term that refers to people who want to be hackers but don't have much talent. They have downloaded some publicly available tools and know how to use them but they do not know how they work. Even the least knowledgeable script kiddie can wreak havoc with a poorly configured network.

3. **Casual hackers:** This type of hacker knows how the exploit tools work. They are able to decode a wireless packet log and draw conclusions based on what they find. Their interest in your network is casual, however. They are not getting paid to hack a system; they are just looking for a challenge. The casual hacker is capable but will pursue targets of opportunity.

4. **Skilled hackers:** Skilled hackers are capable and determined. They might be getting paid to try to break into a network. They might have a grudge or just like a challenge. They might have written one of the

common utilities but do not rely on it. They can exploit cryptographic weaknesses that require patience and insight. These hackers are rare compared with the other categories.

When securing a wireless network, a decision will be made as to which of these types of hackers you will defend against.

### Hacker Tools—Freeware

As of the writing of this chapter, there are a number of freeware hacking tools available that will exploit the vulnerabilities of a wireless network. Following is a brief list of the name of hacking tools and brief description of their capabilities. This set of tools is used on the wireless protocol 802.11. It is certain that as security measures increase to reduce the vulnerabilities exploited by these tools, new hacking tools and methods will emerge. In the future hacker, tools will undoubtedly be devised to exploit the vulnerabilities in the Bluetooth protocol and handheld devices as well.

**NetStumbler**   Freeware wireless access point identifier; listens for service set identifiers (SSIDs) and sends beacons as probes searching for access points

**Kismet**   Freeware wireless sniffer and monitor; passively monitors wireless traffic and sorts data to identify SSIDs, MAC addresses, channels, and connection speeds

**Wellenreiter**   Freeware wireless LAN (WLAN) discovery tool; uses brute force to identify low traffic access points; hides the real MAC; integrates with global positioning system (GPS)

**THC-RUT**   Freeware WLAN discovery tool; uses brute force to identify low traffic access points

**Ethereal**   Freeware WLAN analyzer; interactively browses the capture data, viewing summary and detail information for all observed wireless traffic

**WEPCrack**   Freeware encryption breaker; cracks 802.11 wired equivalent privacy (WEP) encryption keys using the latest discovered weakness of RC4 key scheduling

**AirSnort**   Freeware encryption breaker; passively monitoring transmissions, computing the encryption key when enough packets have been gathered

**HostAP**   Converts a WLAN station to function as an access point; available for WLAN cards that are based on Intersil's Prism2/2.5/3 chipset

## Vulnerabilities

A vulnerability is a weakness or fault in the communication medium or protocol that allows one or more of the assurances for a secure channel to be compromised. Most of the vulnerabilities that exist for wireless medium are the result of the medium itself. In particular, because the transmissions are broadcast, they are freely available to anyone who has the appropriate equipment. Specifically, wireless networks are vulnerable to:

unauthorized access to a firm's computer or voice (Internet protocol [IP] telephony) network through wireless connections, potentially bypassing any firewall protections

identity theft of legitimate users to use on internal or external corporate networks

violation of the privacy of legitimate users and tracking of their physical movements

deployment of unauthorized equipment (e.g., client devices and access points) to gain surreptitious access to sensitive information

use of wireless connections to connect to other agencies for the purposes of launching attacks and concealing their activity

use of a third-party untrusted wireless network services to gain access to a firm's network resources

the capture of sensitive information that is not encrypted (or that is encrypted with poor cryptographic techniques) and that is transmitted between two wireless devices may be intercepted and disclosed

DoS attacks directed at wireless connections or devices

having sensitive data corrupted during improper synchronization

having handheld devices easily stolen and revealing sensitive information

having data extracted from improperly configured devices, without detection

viruses or other malicious code that may corrupt data on a wireless device and be subsequently introduced to a wired network connection

interlopers, from inside or out, who may be able to gain connectivity to network management controls and thereby disable or disrupt operations

internal attacks via ad hoc transmissions

For the details of the vulnerabilities of wireless networks, see Boncella (2002) and Nichols and Lekkas (2002).

## TAXONOMY OF ATTACKS

Wireless network attacks can be classified into passive and active attacks. These two broad classes are then subdivided into other types of attack, defined as follows.

### Passive Attack

An attack in which an unauthorized party gains access to an asset but does not modify its content (e.g., eavesdropping). Passive attacks can be either eavesdropping or traffic analysis (sometimes called traffic flow analysis). These two passive attacks are described as follows.

**Traffic analysis:** When carrying out traffic analysis, the attacker gains intelligence by monitoring the transmissions attempting to identify patterns of communication. Intelligence may be contained in the frequency of the flow of messages between the sender and receiver.

**Eavesdropping:** The attacker monitors transmissions for message content. This type of attack can be carried in either a passive or active mode.

Passive attacks are attempts to compromise the confidentiality requirement of secure communications.

## Active Attack

An active attack is one by which an unauthorized party makes modifications to a message, data stream, or file. It is possible to detect this type of attack, but it may be unpreventable. Active attacks may take the form of one of four types (or in combination): masquerading, replay, message modification, or DoS. These types of attacks are defined as follows:

**Masquerading:** The attacker impersonates an authorized user and thereby gains certain unauthorized privileges. This type of attack is an attempt to compromise the integrity requirement of a secure communication.

**Replay (man in the middle):** The attacker monitors transmissions (passive attack) and retransmits messages as the legitimate user. This type of an attack is an attempt to compromise both the confidentiality and integrity requirements.

**Message modification:** The attacker alters a legitimate message by deleting, adding to, changing, or reordering it. This type of attack is an attempt to compromise the integrity requirement of a secure communication.

**Denial-of-service:** The attacker prevents or prohibits the normal use or management of communications facilities. This type of attack is an attempt to compromise the availability requirement of a secure communication.

Examples of passive and active attacks against wireless networks are presented in the next section.

## ATTACKS AGAINST WIRELESS NETWORKS

The discussion of attacks against wireless networks is organized around three types of wireless networks. First is a presentation of the types of attacks that can be carried out against 802.11 wireless networks, followed by the kinds of attacks that can be carried out against personal area networks that use the Bluetooth protocol. Finally, there is a presentation of the types of attacks that can be carried out against handheld devices (e.g., personal digital assistants [PDAs] and smart phones).

The following is an adaptation of information contained in two very detailed technical reports. The interested reader is referred to National Institute of Standards and Technology (2002) and Welch and Lathrop (2003). Each of these reports contains comprehensive bibliographies and provides an excellent foundation for anyone wishing to pursue the details of wireless threats and attacks. In addition, they provide suggestions on appropriate controls for these risks and attacks. Many of these controls are discussed in related articles in the *Handbook of Information Security*.

**Table 1** Key Characteristics of 802.11 Wireless Local Area Networks

| Characteristics | Description |
| --- | --- |
| Physical Layer | Direct sequence spread spectrum (DSSS), frequency hopping spread spectrum (FHSS), orthogonal frequency division multiplexing (OFDM), infrared (IR) |
| Frequency Band | 2.4 GHz (ISM band) and 5 GHz (UNII band) |
| Data Rates | 1 Mbps, 2 Mbps, 5.5 Mbps (802.11b), 11 Mbps (802.11b), 54 Mbps (802.11a) |
| Data and Network Security | RC4-based stream encryption algorithm for confidentiality, authentication, and integrity. Limited key management (AES is being considered for 802.11i.) |
| Operating Range | Up to 300 feet indoors depending on interior wall construction, 1,500 feet outdoors, but with high gain directional antennas to 20 miles |
| Pros | Ethernet speeds without wires; many products from many companies; wireless client cards and access point costs are decreasing |
| Cons | Poor security in native mode; throughput decrease with distance and load |

## Against 802.11 Networks

### 802.11 Overview

The development of WLAN technology started in the mid-1980s when the Federal Communications Commission (FCC) first made the radio frequency (RF) spectrum available to industry. Early on (1980s to mid-1990s), growth was relatively slow. Since then, WLAN technology has experienced tremendous growth. An important factor in this growth was the increased bandwidth made possible by the IEEE 802.11 standard. Table 1 lists some key characteristics of the 802.11 standard.

### Passive Attacks

**Interception and Monitoring of Wireless Traffic.** It is an easy matter to intercept and monitor network traffic that is using a wireless LAN. The attacker needs to be within range of an access point (approximately 300 feet for 802.11b). The advantage that a wireless intercept has over a wired intercept is a wired attack requires the placement of a monitoring agent on the compromised system. Although all a wireless intruder needs is access to the wireless network's data stream that is being broadcast via an RF signal.

A normal installation of 802.11b yields a maximum range of 300 feet. A directional antenna can dramatically extend either the transmission range or reception range of 802.11b devices. As a result, enhanced equipment will enhance the risk. Access points transmit their signals in a circular pattern; as a result, the 802.11b signal can inadvertently extend beyond the physical boundaries of the area it is intended to cover. This signal can be intercepted outside buildings or through floors in multistory buildings. Careless antenna placement can cause the 802.11b signal to propagate beyond physical boundaries for which it was intended.

### Traffic Analysis

Traffic analysis is a technique by which the attacker can determine the load on the wireless network by the number and size of packets being transmitted. Traffic analysis allows the attacker to obtain three forms of information. First, the attacker identifies that there is activity on the network. A significant increase in the amount of network activity would serve as an indicator for the occurrence of something out of the ordinary course of events. Second, the identification and physical location of wireless access points (APs) in the surrounding area can be determined from traffic analysis. Access points may be configured to broadcast their SSIDs to identify themselves to wireless nodes desiring access. The SSID is a parameter configured in the wireless card's driver software. This allows a wireless station to access a particular AP. By broadcasting this information, access points allow anyone in their area to identify a particular AP on the basis of that AP's SSID. Using a directional antenna in conjunction with GPS, not only will an attacker know there is an AP in the area, the attacker can also obtain the physical location of the access point.

The third piece of information that an attacker may learn through traffic analysis is the type of protocols being used in the transmissions. This knowledge is obtained based on the size and the number of packets in transmission over a period of time. An example of this attack is the analysis of a transmission control protocol (TCP) three-way handshake. TCP synchronizes the communication between two end nodes by transmitting a series of three packets. The sender transmits a synchronize (SYN) packet to let the receiver know it wants to communicate, to provide it with the sender's initial sequence number, and to pass other parameters used in the protocol. The receiver then replies with its initial sequence number and an acknowledgement of the original sender's sequence number (SYN + ACK). Finally, the original sender transmits an acknowledgment of the receiver's initial sequence number (ACK) and then the transmission of application data between the two nodes may commence. Each packet used in the three-way handshake is a fixed size in terms of the number of bytes transmitted. This sequence is depicted in Figure 1.

Because of the easily identifiable size of the SYN/SYNACK/ACK packet sequence followed by a sequence of several large packets, it would indicate that the network stations are communicating using TCP/IP as their underlying protocol. This information about the protocol being used can then be used to carry out attacks that exploit the knowledge of TCP/IP header information.

### Passive Eavesdropping

The attacker passively monitors a wireless session. Assuming that the session is not encrypted, and quite often

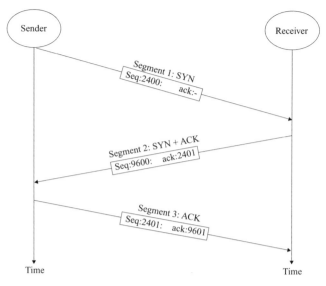

**Figure 1:** Three-Way Handshake

this is the case, an attacker can gain two types of information from passive eavesdropping. First, the attacker can read the data transmitted in the session. Second, the attacker can gather useful information by examining the packets in the session. In particular, the packet's source, destination, size, number, and time of transmission will be available to the attacker. The impact of this type of attack is twofold: The first effect is on the privacy of the information; the second is that the information obtained from the packet headers can be used for other types of attacks.

### Active Eavesdropping Using Partially Known Plaintext

An attacker monitors the wireless session as described in passive eavesdropping . In this case the transmission is encrypted using WEP. Unlike passive eavesdropping, the attacker not only listens to the wireless connection but also injects messages into the communication medium to determine the contents of messages. Required for this attack is access to the transmission and access to partially known plaintext such as a destination IP address. The destination IP address is not difficult to obtain by other means. The transmissions between the access point and the device uses WEP, which in turn uses a cyclic redundancy check (CRC) to verify the integrity of the data in the packet. The attacker can modify messages (even in encrypted form) so that changing data in the packet (i.e., the destination IP address or destination TCP port) cannot be detected via CRC. This requires the attacker to determine the bit difference between the data they want to inject and the original data. This is not difficult to accomplish.

An example of active eavesdropping with partially known plaintext is IP spoofing. The attacker changes the destination IP address of the packet to the IP address of a host they control. In the case of a modified packet, when it does not arrive at the destination, the authentic receiving node will request a resend of the packet. Hence, the attack will not be apparent to the sender and receiver.

Initially, security had been a weakness of the 802.11 standard. WEP standard is easily compromised through cryptoanalysis. However, new methods of encryption have been developed, such as WiFi (wireless fidelity) protected access (WPA) for small offices and home office wireless networks (see http://support.microsoft.com/?kbid=815485) and the 802.11i standard (see http://csrc.nist.gov/wireless/ and http://www.drizzle.com/~aboba/IEEE/0.

## Active Attacks

### Masquerade Examples

**Malicious Association.** Attackers can either force stations to connect to an undesired 802.11 network or alter the configuration of a station to force it to operate in an ad hoc networking mode. Ad hoc networks are self-organizing mobile wireless communication networks. They operate in a completely distributed manner and are independent of preexisting network infrastructure. Each network node acts as a router and helps to forward traffic toward its destination.

Using the freeware HostAP, an attacker can convert an attacking station to operate as a functioning access point. When the victim's station broadcasts a probe to associate with an access point, the attacker's access point responds to the victim's request for association and begins a connection between the two. If necessary, the attacker's AP may provide an IP address to the victim's workstation. Once the AP and station are associated, the attacker can exploit all vulnerabilities on the victim's station. If the victim's station is laptop, the attacker may install the HostAP firmware or any other laptop configuration or programmatic changes.

**MAC Spoofing and Identity Theft.** Securing wireless LANs with authentication based on a list of authorized MAC addresses provides a low level of security. However, MAC addresses are not intended for use as security measures. Attackers can easily change the MAC address of their station or access point and hence change their "identity," defeating MAC-address-based authentication. Software tools such as Kismet or Ethereal allow attackers to easily pick off the MAC addresses of an authorized user. The attacker can then assume the identity of that user by asserting the stolen MAC address as his or her own. The attacker then connects to the wireless LAN as an authorized user.

**Insertion Attacks.** Another type of masquerade attack is the insertion attack. Insertion attacks are based on deploying unauthorized devices or creating new wireless networks without going through security process and review. These devices can either be clients or access points.

**Unauthorized Clients.** An attacker can connect a wireless client, generally a laptop or PDA, to an access point without authorization. This can be done in one of two ways: the AP has no SSID or the SSID can be hacked. Access points can be configured to require a SSID for client access. SSID is a configurable identification that allows clients to communicate with an appropriate access point. With proper configuration, only clients with the correct SSID can communicate with access points. In effect, SSID acts as a single shared password between access points and clients. The AP can be configured to have a blank SSID or to broadcast its SSID; in effect the access point has no SSID. If there is no SSID, an intruder can connect to the AP simply by enabling a wireless client to communicate with the access point. This simply means that the client is within range of the AP. If the AP does have a required SSID, it may be compromised in several ways.

### Brute Force Attacks Against Access Point SSIDs

Access points come from the manufacturer with default SSIDs. If these are not changed, these units are easily compromised. Following is a list of default SSIDs for a given manufacturer:

"tsunami"—Cisco
"101"—3Com
"RoamAbout Default Network Name"—Lucent/Cabletron
"Compaq"—Compaq
"WLAN"—Addtron
"intel"—Intel
"linksys"—Linksys
"Default SSID" and "Wireless"—Other manufacturers

If WEP is disabled, these SSIDs go over the air as clear text. This allows the SSID to be captured by anyone monitoring the network's traffic.

Most access points use a SSID that is shared with all connecting wireless clients. Brute force dictionary attacks attempt to compromise this key by methodically testing every possible SSID. The intruder gains access to the access point once the SSID is guessed.

SSIDs can also be compromised through other means. A compromised client—either hacked or, in the case of a laptop, stolen—can expose the access point. Not changing the SSIDs on a frequent basis or when employees leave the organization also opens the access point to attack.

**Unauthorized or Renegade Access Points.** An organization may not be aware that internal employees have deployed wireless capabilities on their network. This lack of awareness could lead to the previously described attack, with unauthorized clients gaining access to corporate resources through a rogue access point. Organizations need to implement policy to ensure secure configuration of access points, plus an ongoing process in which the network is scanned for the presence of unauthorized devices.

### Replay Attack Examples

**Man-in-the-Middle Attacks (against a virtual public network [VPN]).** A man-in-the-middle attack can break a secure VPN connection between an authorized station and an access point. By inserting a malicious station between the victim station and the access point, the attacker becomes the "man in the middle." The attacker tricks the station into believing that he (or she) is the access point and tricks the access point into thinking he is the station.

This attack begins by forcing a connected station to reauthenticate with the access point. The station must respond to a random challenge from the access point, and the access point must respond to a successful challenge response with a success packet.

The attacker passively observes the station as it connects to the access point, and the attacker collects the authentication information, including the username, server name, client and server IP address, the ID used to compute the response, and the challenge and associate response. The attacker then tries to associate with the access point by sending a request that appears to be coming from the authenticated station. The access point sends the VPN challenge to the authenticated station, which computes the required authentic response and sends the response to the access point. The attacker observes the valid response. The attacker then acts as the access point in presenting a challenge to the authorized station. The station computes the appropriate response, which is sent to the access point. The access point then sends the station a success packet with an imbedded sequence number. The attacker captures this packet. After capturing all this data, the attacker then has what is needed to complete the attack and defeat the VPN.

### Denial-of-Service Attack Examples

**Jamming.** DoS attacks are also applied to wireless networks. In this case, legitimate traffic cannot reach clients or the access point because illegitimate traffic overwhelms the transmission frequencies. An attacker with the proper equipment and tools can easily flood the 2.4-GHz frequency. This corrupts the signal until the wireless network ceases to function. Cordless phones, baby monitors, and other devices that operate on the 2.4-GHz band can disrupt a wireless network using this frequency. These DoSs can originate from outside the work area serviced by the access point or can inadvertently arrive from other 802.11b devices installed in other work areas that degrade the overall signal.

**Exploiting Wireless Protocols.** Attackers can launch more sophisticated DoS attacks by configuring a station to operate as an access point. As an access point, the attacker can flood the airwaves with persistent disassociate commands that force all stations within range to disconnect from the wireless LAN.

Another variation is when the attacker's AP broadcasts periodic disassociate commands every few minutes that causes a situation where stations are continually kicked off the network, reconnected, and kicked off again. Attackers are now abusing the extensible authentication protocol (EAP) to launch DoS attacks. There are several forms of DoS attacks from various ways an attacker can manipulate EAP protocols by targeting wireless stations and access points with log-off commands, start commands, premature successful connection messages, failure messages, and other modifications of the EAP protocol. The details of the number of these types of attacks may be found at http://www.drizzle.com/~aboba/IEEE/.

### Additional Attacks

**Client-to-Client Attacks.** Two wireless clients can talk directly to each other forming an ad hoc network. Because they can bypass an access point, users need to protect clients from each other.

**File Sharing and Other TCP/IP Service Attacks.** Wireless clients running TCP/IP services such as a Web server or file sharing are open to the same exploits and misconfigurations as any user on a wired network; for example, anonymous FTP.

**DoS.** A wireless device can flood other wireless clients with bogus packets, creating a DoS attack. Further, duplicate IP or MAC addresses, both intentional and accidental, can cause disruption on the network.

**Misconfiguration.** Many APs ship in an unsecured configuration in order to emphasize ease of use and deployment. Understanding wireless security risks and proper configuration for each unit prior to deployment are required. These access points will remain at a high risk for attack or misuse.

**Client-Side Security Risk.** Clients connected to an access point store sensitive information for authenticating and communicating to the access point. This information can be compromised if the client is not properly configured. For example, Cisco client software stores the SSID in the Windows registry, and the WEP key in the firmware, where it is more difficult to access. Lucent/Cabletron client software stores the SSID in the Windows registry. The WEP key is stored in the Windows registry, but it is encrypted using an undocumented algorithm. 3Com client software stores the SSID in the Windows registry. The WEP key is stored in the Windows registry with no encryption.

## Against Bluetooth Networks

### Bluetooth Overview

Bluetooth is an open standard for short-range digital radio. Bluetooth is a wireless protocol used for PANs (personal area networks). This protocol provides fast and reliable transmission for voice and data. There are several IEEE specifications associated with Bluetooth (IEEE 802.15.1). The interested reader is referred to http://grouper.ieee.org/groups/802/15/pub/Tutorials.html for more detail. Bluetooth may be employed to connect any Bluetooth enable device to any other Bluetooth enable device. An example would be the connection between a PDA and a mobile phone. The goal of Bluetooth is to connect disparate devices together (e.g., PDAs, cell phones, printers, faxes, mouse, and central processing unit) wirelessly in a small environment such as an office or home.

Bluetooth is a standard that is intended to

Eliminate wires and cables between both stationary and mobile devices

Facilitate both data and voice communications

Offer the possibility of ad hoc networks and deliver synchronicity between personal devices

Bluetooth is designed to operate in the unregulated ISM (industrial, scientific, medical applications) band. The characteristics of Bluetooth are summarized in Table 2.

**Table 2** Key Characteristics of Bluetooth Technology

| Characteristics | Description |
|---|---|
| Physical Layer | Frequency hopping spread spectrum (FHSS) |
| Frequency band | 2.4–2.4835 GHz (ISM band) |
| Hop frequency | 1,600 hops/sec |
| Data rates | 1 Mbps (raw); higher bit rates are anticipated |
| Data and network security | Three modes of security (none, link-level, and service level), two levels of device trust, and three levels of service security; stream encryption for confidentiality, challenge-response for authentication; personal identification number–derived keys and limited management |
| Operating range | About 10 meters (30 feet); can be extended to 100 meters |
| Throughput | Up to approximately 720 kbps |
| Pros | No wires and cables for many interfaces; ability to penetrate walls and other obstacles; costs are decreasing; low power and minimal hardware |
| Cons | Possibility for interference with other ISM band devices; relatively low data rates; signals leak outside desired boundaries |

Bluetooth-enabled devices, if they are in range of each other, are able to locate each other. However, making connections with other devices and forming piconets requires user action. Bluetooth networks maintain a master–slave relationship maintained between the network devices. Up to eight Bluetooth devices may be networked together in a master–slave relationship, called a *piconet*. The master device controls and sets up the network (including defining the network's hopping scheme). Devices in a Bluetooth piconet operate on the same channel and follow the same frequency-hopping sequence. A slave in one network can act as the master for other networks creating a chain of networks. This is referred to as a "scatter-net," which allows several devices to be internetworked over an extended distance. This topology may change during any given session as a device moves toward or away from the master device in the piconet. As the topology and the relationships of the devices in the immediate piconet change, so does the scatter-net.

Mobile routers are required for this changing topology. Mobile routers control the flow of data between devices that are capable of supporting a direct link to each other. As devices move about in a random fashion, these networks must be reconfigured on the fly. The routing protocols Bluetooth employs allow it to establish and maintain these shifting networks.

## Passive Attacks
**Eavesdropping.** Authorized remote users pose a threat to Bluetooth networks. These users may employ nonsecure links. When they transmit their user IDs and passwords, a malicious user can easily capture them using a network sniffer. Because this will be a RF transmission, it is an easy matter to intercept the transmission. Further, a device or link can be compromised. If a link is compromised, it allows a malicious user to monitor data traffic. If a device is compromised, it may allow the malicious user to request and receive data. In addition, if the malicious user obtains knowledge of the user IDs and passwords on a targeted network, then a compromised device can be used in an active attack to gain access to a network that the device may be using for its data source.

## Active Attacks
**Masquerade.** A trait of Bluetooth that makes this compromise unique is that the Bluetooth network requires device—and not user—authentication to access resources. Once the device is authenticated, it is automatically connected to resources without the need for subsequent authentication. As a result, a compromised device can gain access to the network and compromise both the network and devices on the network.

**Man in the Middle.** In the man-in-the-middle attack, the man in the middle obtains the security encryption key that a network device uses to monitor traffic between itself and another network device. The attack requires Device A to separately share its unit key (a static key unique to each device) with Device C and Device B at the same time. The connections between Devices A and B and between Devices A and C may be completely unrelated. Once Device C knows the unit key, it can use a fake device address to calculate the encryption key and monitor traffic between Devices A and B without their knowledge. The man-in-the-middle attack does not require costly or special equipment. A knowledgeable malicious user who has access to the unit key and who can mimic a Bluetooth address to generate the encryption key can conduct the attack. Attacks such as these use a priori knowledge of the targeted Bluetooth devices.

Figure 2 illustrates the attack. A trusted PDA (Device A) shares proprietary information with a trusted laptop (Device B). During the connection with Device B, Device A connects to an untrusted PDA (Device C) to share personal contacts in A's PDA address book. Once Device C makes the connection to A, C now becomes the man-in-the-middle and can monitor the traffic between Devices A and B by using Device A's unit key and a fake address. The biggest danger in such monitoring is that the owner(s) of Device A or B may never realize that the information is being compromised.

To date, no software is available for monitoring such intrusions, and Bluetooth devices are invisible to network administrators.

**Message Modification.** Message modification involves the alteration, addition, or deletion of information, which is then passed through the network without the user's or network administrator's knowledge. This may result in the

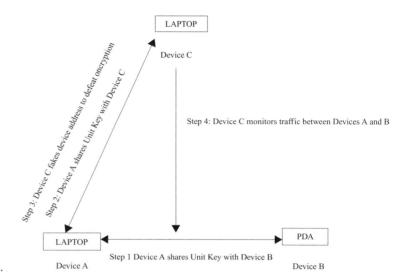

**Figure 2:** Bluetooth Man-in-the-Middle Attack.

corruption of an organization's or user's data. Information that is subject to corruption includes files on the network and data on user devices. This attack can be carried out by a malicious user who might employ an untrusted device, such as a PDA, to access the address book of another PDA or laptop. Rather than copying the information, the attacker may alter the information or may even delete the information completely. If undetected, such attacks could result in the agency (or user) losing confidence in its data and system.

**Denial of Service.** Bluetooth devices are also susceptible to signal jamming. Bluetooth devices share bandwidth with microwave ovens, cordless phones, and other wireless networks and thus are vulnerable to interference. Attackers can interfere with the flow of information by using devices that transmit in the 2.4-GHz ISM band. In particular, if the routing protocols are disrupted, this will prevent ad hoc network devices from negotiating the network's dynamic topologies.

Remote users must contend with the same interference that users experience in the office. Further, because the remote environment is uncontrolled, remote devices are more likely to be in close proximity to devices (e.g., other Bluetooth and ISM band devices) that are intentionally or unintentionally jamming their signals.

Another threat associated with ad hoc devices is a battery exhaustion attack. This attack attempts to disable a device by draining its battery. A malicious user continually sends requests to the device asking for data transfers (assuming the user is part of the network topology) or asking the device to create a network. Although this type of attack does not compromise network security, it ultimately prevents the user from gaining access to the network, because the device cannot function.

## Against Handheld Devices

### Handheld Devices Overview
Wireless handheld devices range from simple one- and two-way text messaging devices to Internet-enabled PDAs, tablets, and smart phones. They have become indispensable tools and competitive business advantages for the mobile workforce. The use of these devices introduces new security risks. Because these devices may have their own IP addresses, they can become the targets of attacks. At present, handheld devices have different capabilities and uses from those of personal computers. The differences between handheld devices and personal computers that affect security are as follows:

The small size, relatively low cost, and constant mobility of handheld devices make them more likely to be stolen, misplaced, lost, or more easily concealed.

Because they have limited computing power and memory, encryption with long key lengths is too time-consuming to be practical. However, as technology associated with these devices evolves, this will become less of a limitation.

Synchronization software allows handhelds and PCs to exchange information. When this exchange takes place, the information can be vulnerable to attack. The PC and the handheld device face different threats and require different security controls for those threats. However, both must provide the same level of security to protect information.

Wireless handheld devices are often used for both personal and business data. Users may purchase these devices without conferring with the network administrator or chief security officer. The result is users who may not be aware of the security implications of their using handhelds in the work environment.

Handheld devices provide multiple access points (e.g., the user interface, expansion modules, wireless modems, Bluetooth, infrared ports, and 802.11 connectivity). An attacker can exploit these access points. In addition, handheld devices have limited capabilities in authenticating the devices with which they exchange data.

Handheld users can access the Internet through wireless modems or WISP (wireless Internet service providers). This allows these users to upload or download data to and from other computers without complying without having to go through their organization's firewall.

Handheld operating systems and their applications have not been thoroughly field tested to expose potential vulnerabilities.

The increased computing power and the ease with which handhelds can access networks and exchange data with other handheld devices introduce new security risks to computing. As handheld devices increase their networking capabilities, the vulnerabilities they introduce into the computing environment will also increase.

### Passive Attacks

**Eavesdropping.** Most handheld devices are shipped with connectivity that is enabled by default. These default configurations are not in the most secure setting. For example, PDAs can beam information from an IR port to another PDA IR port to exchange contact information easily and automatically, including information such as telephone numbers and mailing addresses. This is a useful feature, but generally the data is unencrypted, and any user who is in close proximity to the handheld device and has the device pointed in the right direction can intercept and read the data. The probability of eavesdropping occurring without the victim's knowledge is relatively low. However, a handheld using Bluetooth that is not configured properly is vulnerable to having a user with a Bluetooth-enabled device pull data from the device. Similarly, an 802.11-enabled device with an insecure P2P setting may also expose data to another 802.11-enabled device.

### Active Attacks

**Masquerade.** A compromised handheld—generally stolen or cloned devices—may attempt to synchronize with a networked PC; alternatively, a compromised PC may try to synchronize with a PDA. In either case, the attacker is attempting to gain access to the user's network by pretending to be a legitimate device on that network.

PDAs can synchronize with a networked PC using remote connections, dialing either directly to a corporate facility or through a WISP. The modems allow users to dial into an access server at their office or use third-party WISPs. Dial-up capability introduces risks. Dialing into a corporate facility requires a handheld device synchronization server; otherwise, the remote PDA must derive synchronization service by connecting to a PC that is logged on using the remote client's ID and password. If the PC is not at least configured with a password-protected screensaver, it is left vulnerable to anyone with physical access to the PC. Because the WISP is an untrusted network, establishing a remote connection requires additional security mechanisms to ensure a secure connection.

Another means for synchronizing data is through a wireless Ethernet connection. Users can synchronize data from any networked work space. The data that crosses the network are as secure as the network itself and may be susceptible to network traffic analyzers or sniffers.

**Denial of Service.** Handheld devices can be the targets of DoS attacks. Trojan horses, worms, viruses, and other malware can affect the availability of a network. Viruses have not been widely considered a security threat in PDAs or handhelds because of their limited memory and processing power. However, as their technology advances, this will no longer be a deterrent to the type of malware that now is a threat to PCs.

Smart phones may lose network connectivity when they travel outside a cell coverage area. They also lose access when cell phone jammers are used. Commercially available jammers can be used by restaurants and theaters to block cell phone communications. This is often done without notifying the cell phone users. Malicious users may use these cell phone jamming devices. Jamming devices can carry out these attacks by broadcasting transmissions on cellular frequencies that nullify the actual cellular tower transmissions. The jammed cell phone will not be able to communicate.

Cell phones, smart phones, and text pagers are able to send text messages, from 110 to 160 characters in length depending on the carrier, to other cell phones by using short message service (SMS). To send and receive SMS text messages, phone users usually have to pay a monthly fee to their service provider or a small fee for each text message beyond a preset monthly limit. Text messages can also be sent from a cellular service provider's Web page, by visiting Web sites that allow users to send text messages free of charge from e-mail applications. Text messages rely on the service provider's network and are not encrypted, and no guarantees exist on quality of service. Cell phones and text-messaging devices can be spammed with text messages until their mailbox is full, and the user is no longer able to receive new text messages unless previously stored e-mails are deleted.

As third-generation (3G) development progresses and 3G phones become more prevalent, agencies will need to be aware of the security issues that arise. One potential security issue is that a 3G mobile device, when connected to an IP network, is in the "always-on" mode. This mode alleviates the need for the device to authenticate itself each time a network request is made. However, the continuous connection also makes the device susceptible to attack. Moreover, because the device is always on, the opportunity exists to track users' activities, and this may violate their privacy.

### Future Threats and Attacks Against Handheld Devices

As the technology used in handheld devices evolves, their vulnerabilities will increase. The interested reader is referred to the SANS Information Security Reading Room (http://www.sans.org/rr/) to stay informed of the current state of security with regard to handheld devices. As the threats and attacks become apparent, appropriate controls will be used to mitigate these threats and attacks.

## SUMMARY

The information security requirements for wireless devices are the same as for wired devices. The requirements for information security are confidentiality, integrity, and availability. The foregoing discussion provided an overview of the threats, vulnerabilities, and attacks to which wireless networks can be subjected. These exploit the technology that is used to implement wireless information networks. Currently, there are controls that mitigate these threats, vulnerabilities, and attacks. As this technology evolves, new exploits will be carried out against wireless networks and, accordingly, new controls will be put in place to counter these exploits. That is the price paid for the convenience of this form of communication.

# GLOSSARY

**802.11i–802.11i** A developing IEEE standard for security in a wireless local area network (WLAN). A subset of 802.11i called Wi-Fi Protected Access will be available for use in the early part of 2003.

**Advanced Encryption Standard (AES)** A symmetric key encryption technique that will replace the commonly used DES standard. It was the result of a worldwide call for submissions of encryption algorithms issued by the National Institute of Standards and Technology in 1997 and completed in 2000. The winning algorithm, Rijndael, was developed by two Belgian cryptologists, Vincent Rijmen and Joan Daemen. AES provides strong encryption in various environments: standard software platforms, limited space environments, and hardware implementations.

**Direct-Sequence Spread Spectrum (DSSS).** A transmission technology used in WLAN (wireless local area network) transmissions in which a data signal at the sending station is combined with a higher data rate bit sequence, or chipping code, that divides the user data according to a spreading ratio. The chipping code is a redundant bit pattern for each bit that is transmitted, which increases the signal's resistance to interference. If one or more bits in the pattern are damaged during transmission, the original data can be recovered due to the redundancy of the transmission.

**Frequency Hopping Spread Spectrum (FHSS)** A spread spectrum modulation technique in which the transmitter frequency hops from channel to channel in a predetermined but pseudo-random manner. The signal is de-hopped at the receiver by a frequency synthesizer controlled by a pseudo-random sequence generator synchronized to the transmitter's pseudo-random generator. In essence, frequency hopping is a type of radio communications in which the transmitter and receiver hop in synchronization from one frequency to another according to a prearranged pattern.

**ISM Band** ISM is an acronym for industrial, scientific, and medical. This refers to the unlicensed radio bands that are typically unused due to interference from medical, industrial, and scientific equipment. Technologies such as Bluetooth and wireless local area networks use these bands because no governmental approval is needed for transmission, making it significantly cheaper. Although interference is still an issue, technologies for overcoming it are built into most technologies using these bands. Frequencies in this band are 2.4 GHz to 2.4835 GHz and are unlicensed.

**Infrared or Infrared Radiation (IR)** Energy in the region of the electromagnetic radiation spectrum at wavelengths longer than those of visible light but shorter than those of radio waves. These frequencies can be used for wireless transmissions.

**MAC Address** Also known as hardware address or Ethernet address. This is a unique identifier specific to the network card inside the computer. It allows for the authentication so that the computer is allowed to access the network. MAC Addresses are of the form XX-XX-XX-XX-XX-XX, where the X's are either digits or letters from A–F.

**Orthogonal Frequency Division Multiplexing (OFDM)** A transmission technique that utilizes multiple carriers to divide the data across the available spectrum. Interference will degrade only a small portion of the signal and has no or little effect on the remainder of the frequency components; the overall benefit is greater throughput under more diverse situations.

**Rivest Cipher #4 (RC4)** A variable length, secret key stream cipher. RC4 is intended as an alternate to DES and is approximately 10 times faster than DES. The exportable, 40-bit length version, used in Netscape secure sockets layer, has been broken by at least two separate organizations.

**Radio Frequency (RF)** The 10-kHz to 300-GHz frequency range that can be used for wireless communication. The term RF is usually used to distinguish signals transmitted to and from the satellite from signals processed at other frequencies within the same communication system (e.g., intermediate frequencies).

**UNII Band (Unlicensed National Information Infrastructure)** An FCC regulatory domain for 5-GHz wireless devices. UNII bands are 100 MHz wide and divided into four channels when using 802.11a OFDM modulation.

**Virtual Public Network (VPN)** One or more wide area network (WAN) links over a shared public network, typically over the Internet or Internet protocol backbone from a network service provider, that simulates the behavior of dedicated WAN links over leased lines.

**Wide Area Network (WAN)** A physical or logical network that provides data communications to a larger number of users than are usually served by a local area network (LAN) and is usually spread over a larger geographic area than that of a LAN.

# CROSS REFERENCES

See *Bluetooth Security; Bluetooth Technology; Hacking Techniques in Wireless Networks; WEP Security; Wireless Network Standards and Protocol (802.11).*

# REFERENCES

Boncella, R. J. (2002). Wireless security: An overview. *Communications of the AIS, 9,* Article 15. Retrieved March 5, 2003, from http://cais.isworld.org/

Nichols, R., & Lekkas, P. (2002). *Wireless security models, threats and solutions.* New York: McGraw-Hill.

National Institute of Standards and Technology. (2002, November). *Wireless network security: 802.11,*

*Bluetooth, and handheld devices* (NIST Special Publication 800-48).

SANS Information Security Reading Room http://www.sans.org/rr/ (date of access: June 7, 2004).

Welch, D., & Lathrop, S. (2003). *A survey of 802.11a wireless security threats and security mechanisms* (Technical Report ITOC-TR-2003-101). Retrieved February 14, 2003, from http://www.itoc.usma.edu/Documents/ITOC_TR-2003-101_(G6).pdf

Whitman, M., & Mattord, H. (2003). *Principles of information security*. Boston: Course Technology.

## FURTHER READING

Flickenger, R. (2003). *Wireless hacks: 100 industrial-strength tips & tools*. Cambridge, MA: O'Reilly and Associates.

Gast, M. (2002). *802.11 wireless networks: The definitive guide.* Cambridge, MA: O'Reilly and Associates.

WAP Forum. (2002). *Wireless application protocol WAP 2.0* (WAP Forum Technical White Paper). Retrieved October 1, 2002, from http://www.wapforum.org/what/WAPWhite_Paper1.pdf

# WEP Security

Nikita Borisov, *University of Illinois at Urbana-Champaign*

## INTRODUCTION

The IEEE (Institute of Electrical and Electronics Engineers) 802.11 standard is the most popular mechanism for wireless networking. First standardized in 1997 (IEEE Computer Society, 1997), it has grown to many millions of deployed nodes and more than a billion-dollar annually industry. The use of a wireless medium presented new security threats because anyone within transmission range of the network could both eavesdrop on the network traffic and inject malicious contents. To address these threats, the 802.11 standard incorporated the wired equivalent privacy (WEP) protocol with the goal of preventing casual eavesdropping and providing a level of security similar to wired networks. It was discovered, however, that WEP contained numerous security flaws and in fact did not meet any of its goals. Attackers could easily exploit these flaws, and tools automating some of the attacks were made widely available. Responding to this security failure, the 802.11i task group was formed to redesign the 802.11 security suite. The group produced two standards, a short-term solution designed to run on existing hardware with only a firmware upgrade and a long-term solution using industry-standard tools and providing a higher margin of security. These standards are currently in the process of being deployed.

This chapter examines the design of WEP, the vulnerabilities contained therein, and how they are fixed by the new protocols. It also discusses why the vulnerabilities exist and how they could have been avoided.

## BACKGROUND

The IEEE 802.11 standard (IEEE Computer Society, 1999) specifies the wireless communication protocol for local area networks (LANs). It is intended to provide a compatible replacement for other 802 protocols, such as 802.3 (Ethernet; IEEE Computer Society, 1985). The standard specifies the physical and data-link layers in the Open System Interconnection (OSI) model (ISO, 1992); as with 802.3, it is most commonly used with transmission control

protocol/Internet protocol (TCP/IP) for the higher layers. The physical layer specification has been amended several times to support different transmission media and data rates; our discussion focuses on the data-link specification, because the physical layer is not used for security.

### Overview

The standard defines communication between *stations* (STAs), which include any equipment capable of speaking the 802.11 protocols. Commonly, communication is managed by one or more *access points* (APs), which control network parameters, mediate most communications between STAs, and forward data to other APs or other networks. There is also a mode of communication where non-AP STAs communicate directly with each other, called *ad hoc* mode. However, *managed* networks are much more common. A group of APs might form an extended service set (ESS), providing unified distribution services for all STAs within the set (i.e., creating a LAN).

To participate in a managed 802.11 network, an STA first performs discovery to find out which APs are within communication range and then selects the best AP according to criteria such as ESSID, signal strength, and any other user-defined parameters. It then proceeds to *associate* with the AP, registering itself for communication.

The upper network layers access the distribution services of 802.11 by sending packets, also known as MSDUs (MAC [media access control] service data units). These MSDUs are processed by the MAC layer and translated (with potential fragmentation) into protocol data units (MPDUs, also called frames), which are then transmitted over the wireless medium (with retransmissions, if necessary). The MPDUs are reassembled into MSDUs and passed back to the upper network layers of the receiving STA. STAs may also exchange management frames to implement coordination functions in the MAC protocol.

### Wireless Security Threats

Before discussing wireless threats, we identify several goals of secure communications. One is *confidentiality*, protecting the privacy of the transmitted data from eavesdroppers. Another is *access control*, restricting the use of the network to only those authorized. Access control is also necessary for accounting and logging—charging users for access and keeping track of which users are responsible for which actions. *Integrity protection* ensures that communications are not maliciously corrupted or subverted. A special form of integrity protection is *replay protection*, ensuring that an attacker cannot send old messages and have them accepted as new ones. Replayed actions may have effects that go beyond what was intended and can be damaging. A final goal is to protect from *denial of service*, where an attacker may prevent legitimate users from being able to communicate using the network.

It would be wrong to say that these goals are fully addressed in wired networks; certainly, the number of solutions aimed to address these issues at layers of the network above data link provides ample evidence to the contrary. However, the use of a wireless medium changes the context of the underlying security threats and renders some common security solutions ineffective.

An important example is tiered risk management, found in many corporate security architectures. Insiders are considered to present a low or medium security risk; highly sensitive data are protected by solutions operating at other layers, and other data are left basically unprotected. Outsiders are considered a high risk, but their physical access to the corporate network is prevented by a security perimeter, and remote access is mediated through a firewall, defending against most kinds of security threats.

The use of a wireless medium allows anyone within range to receive and transmit data, however. The 802.11 range is rated to extend anywhere from 100 to 1,500 feet, depending on potential interference. Experiments with directional antennae show that an amplified receiver with a direct line-of-sight can extend this range to several miles. Securing a large enough perimeter to cover the entire range is impractical, and hence the possibility of malicious users of the local network must be addressed. Effectively, the wireless medium removes the distinction between outsiders and insiders.

We briefly address the feasibility of attacking 802.11 networks, as the expensive hardware required to attack wireless protocols has sometimes been cited as a defense against attacks. In the case of 802.11, attacks may be carried out using inexpensive and readily available 802.11 end-point hardware. Although the standard interfaces to this hardware may not be sufficient for certain attacks, experience suggests that even attacks requiring low-level modifications to the protocol are possible (Bellardo & Savage, 2003). Further, many of the 802.11 end points use upgradeable firmware; a significant but feasible engineering effort could reprogram it to perform attacks. Such reprogramming could then be part of a kit, fully automating the process of exploiting vulnerabilities and making attacks accessible to even the most novice users (mirroring the experience we have seen with software exploits).

# WIRED EQUIVALENT PRIVACY

To address the security concerns listed in the previous section, the 802.11 standard included a protocol titled wired equivalent privacy. Before discussing the details of the protocol, it is helpful to understand what its security goals were. The name of the protocol suggests that it focuses on privacy (confidentiality). The standard also contains a *shared key* authentication method, which makes use of WEP, to provide access control. Integrity protection is not discussed in the standard, although the actual protocol does include an integrity checking mechanism. The standard claims to provide security "equivalent to that provided by the physical security attributes inherent to a wired medium," which should reasonably include access control, integrity protection, and confidentiality. The 802.11 standard does not address denial of service, as such denial is easiest to carry out by a physical layer attack (jamming) and is therefore impossible to protect from at the data-link layer where 802.11 operates.

The standard lists five properties of the WEP algorithm that can be assumed to be design goals: reasonably strong, with the security relying on the difficulty of a brute-force search to recover the secret key; self-synchronizing for each message; efficient to implement in hardware or software; exportable, complying with the U.S. export control requirements; and optional. The export requirements of the time mandated that keys no longer than 40 bits be used in any software or hardware to be exported outside the United States. We will see in our description how these goals constrained the design of WEP.

## WEP Protocol

The WEP protocol defines an algorithm to cryptographically encode and decode MPDUs. The WEP encoding process happens before an MPDU is sent over the wireless medium; it makes use of an encryption algorithm to encipher the data. The encryption relies on a secret key, shared between the sender and receiver. Possession of the key allows the legitimate receiver to decipher the data and recover the original MPDU, whereas an eavesdropper within range but without the key should not be able to decode the message, preserving the privacy of the communications.

The encoding procedure is shown in Figure 1. The sender first must generate a 24-bit value called the *initialization vector* (IV). The IV is then concatenated with the shared key and used as input to a *pseudo-random number generator* (PRNG) by the name of RC4 (Rivest, 1992) to generate enough bytes to encode the length of the MPDU, plus 4 bytes for the *integrity check value* (ICV). The

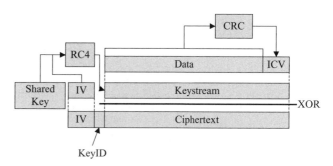

**Figure 1:** Wireless equivalent privacy encoding algorithm. CRC: Cyclic Redundancy Check; ICV: Integrity Check Value; IV: Initialization Vector; XOR: Exclusive OR

contents of the MPDU is then subjected to the integrity algorithm to produce the ICV. The ICV is concatenated with the MPDU, and together they are exclusive-OR ed with the output of the PRNG to produce a *ciphertext*. The final data frame contains the IV, followed by a byte specifying a key ID (used to select from a set of shared keys), and then the ciphertext.

The decoding is similar, with the receiver using the IV value in the frame together with the shared key to generate the same stream of bytes using the PRNG. The ciphertext is then exclusive-OR ed with the PRNG stream to recover the plaintext. Finally, the integrity algorithm is applied to the data portion of the plaintext to recompute the ICV, and that value is compared with the one sent with the packet. If they match, the MPDU is accepted; otherwise, it is discarded and an error is logged.

## PRNG

The salient component is the PRNG RC4, also known as a *stream cipher*. The PRNG takes an input key and generates a sequence of bytes called the *keystream*. Given the same input, the PRNG will always produce the same output, which is how the receiver is able to recover the original plaintext. The security condition of the PRNG is that its output be computationally indistinguishable from random data, which means that given certain output bytes in the keystream produced by the PRNG, it is infeasible to determine what the other bytes might be. (A corollary is that it is impossible to deduce the PRNG input from an output sequence.) A sequence of plaintext exclusive-OR ed with a sequence of random bytes carries no information other than the length; hence, an eavesdropper without a key will not be able to learn anything about the contents of the plaintext. If used properly, stream ciphers can ensure that the only way to learn the contents of the encrypted message is to perform an exhaustive search of all the possible values of the key. To achieve this level of security, it is important never to use the same keystream to encrypt the same message; otherwise, the results are catastrophic. Someone in possession of two ciphertexts encoded with the same keystream can perform a simple algebraic transform and learn a lot about the plaintexts.

$$C_1 \oplus C_2 = (P_1 \oplus PRNG) \oplus (P_2 \oplus PRNG) = P_1 \oplus P_2$$

(Here we use $\oplus$ to denote the exclusive-OR operation.) The keystream is canceled out, leaving only the exclusive-OR of the two plaintexts. Knowledge of one plaintext immediately reveals the other, but even with both plaintexts unknown, simply knowing something about the expected distribution of the contents of $P_1$ and $P_2$ (such as that they both contain English text) can help recover the contents of both.

To address this issue, WEP introduces an IV. The standard recommends choosing a different IV for each MPDU. This varies the input key to the PRNG, producing a different keystream each time. Effectively, WEP uses a different key to encrypt each frame, except that a part of the key is public and included in the frame. If a secure PRNG is used, the public part of the key does not invalidate the security of the encryption because an eavesdropper would still need to search exhaustively through all possibilities

of the secret part of the key to recover the keystream. However, flaws in the IV implementation fail to prevent keystream reuse fully and create vulnerabilities, as discussed later. (We also discuss recently discovered flaws in the RC4 PRNG that allow attackers to use a known part of a key to gain information about an unknown part.)

The use of RC4 PRNG here is motivated by the design goals we listed earlier. Above all else, RC4 is simple to implement in both hardware and software and is extremely efficient, running at several times the speed of other common ciphers such as DES (National Bureau of Standards, 1977). It had been in use since 1987, analyzed in the open cryptography community since 1994, and considered reasonably strong; RC4 is also used in the Secure Sockets Layer/Transport Layer Security (SSL/TLS) (Dierks & Allen, 1999) standard to secure Web browsing. The use of the IV makes the protocol self-synchronizing because the IV is included in the packet. Finally, RC4 supports a flexible key length of 1 to 256 bytes; this means that it is easier to make exportable. WEP used a key with 40 secret bits and 24 known ones (the IV). Performing an exhaustive search through the space of $2^{40}$ keys was out of reach of casual attackers at the time of the design. As computing power grew and export restrictions were lifted, a common extension came into use increasing the key length to 128 bits, with 104 unknown.

## ICV

The integrity algorithm used is CRC-32. Cyclic Redundancy Check(CRC) is often used for integrity checking as it is quite good at detecting errors. However, we will see later that CRC-32 is poor at defending against deliberate modifications. It is not clear that deliberate modifications were considered part of the threat model because integrity protection is never stated as a desired security goal. The fact that the ICV is only computed when WEP is used, as well its name, suggest, however, that integrity protection was indeed its purpose. Regardless, integrity protection is important to provide equivalent security to that of wired networks; we discuss the consequences of ineffective integrity protection later.

### Shared Key Authentication

Before association, an STA must authenticate itself to the AP. The 802.11 standard describes two authentication methods: *open system* authentication and *shared key* authentication. Open system performs no authentication; it is a placeholder method used when no actual authentication is desired. Shared key authentication asks the STAs to prove knowledge of a secret shared key before authenticating. The authenticating node issues a challenge, which is a sequence of 128 random bytes. The response to the challenge is a frame WEP-encoded with the shared key, using the 128 challenge bytes as the plaintext. The authenticator then verifies that the encrypted contents match the original challenge and declares the authentication successful if they do.

## VULNERABILITIES

Unfortunately, the design of WEP included numerous vulnerabilities and has been shown to achieve none of its security goals. Here we discuss the vulnerabilities, grouping them into categories based on the design flaw that caused them.

## Keystream Reuse

As discussed earlier, using the same keystream to encrypt two MPDUs reveals information about the plaintext, motivating the use of IVs. However, the way that IVs are implemented in WEP fails to prevent keystream reuse and thus leaves open the possibility of attack.

The length of the IV is 24 bits, which means there are only $2^{24}$ possibilities for the value. At the maximum MSDU length of 2,304 bytes, this allows for at most 36GB of data to be transmitted, which would take about 8 hours at the maximum data rate of 802.11b of 11 Mbps. In practice, many MSDUs are smaller, so the expected time to exhaust the IV space will range from a few hours for busy installations to a few days for less busy ones. Unless the shared key is changed more frequently than this interval, the same pair of key and IV values, and hence the same PRNG keystream, will be reused for multiple encoded frames, leaking information about the original data.

Most installations do not perform key changes often enough to avoid this vulnerability. Worse, the same shared key will frequently be used by multiple STAs, increasing the likelihood of IV collisions. This vulnerability is exacerbated by a common implementation strategy for choosing IVs. When the hardware is initialized, it sets the IV to 0 and then increments it with each subsequent frame. Because STAs are often laptops and PDAs, which are reset frequently, low-numbered IVs occur much more often, once again lowering the time to wait for a collision. Note that a common suggestion of picking random IVs for each message fares little better because randomly picked IVs for a single station will likely have a collision within a few thousand packets according to the birthday paradox.

To make decoding easier, an attacker can introduce known plaintext into the system by, for example, sending large mail messages to be read over the wireless connection, injecting data from outside networks, or exploiting the authentication method (see "Authentication" later in this chapter). When the plaintext of one frame is known, the contents of another frame with the same IV can be immediately determined, as long as that frame is the same length or shorter. Essentially, knowing both the plaintext and the ciphertext allows the attacker to learn the PRNG keystream bytes associated with that IV and decrypt other messages that use the same IV. When enough plaintext–ciphertext pairs are known, either from the injection strategies listed earlier or from recovering the plaintext through statistical techniques, the attacker can create a dictionary of IV values and corresponding keystreams. A sufficiently long-lived shared key will provide enough time to collect a complete dictionary (of size 36 GB), enabling the attacker to decrypt all traffic instantly.

## Integrity Vulnerabilities

As we alluded to earlier, the integrity algorithm used in WEP, CRC-32, is ineffective against deliberate modifications. CRC-32 has two basic flaws: it is unkeyed, and it is linear. The former flaw means that anyone can compute the CRC-32 of a given sequence of bytes. This is enough to be able to modify the contents of a WEP-encoded frame, the contents of which are known.

For a given message $M$, the WEP encoding of it will be

$$IV \,||\, keyid \,||\, (M \,||\, CRC(M)) \oplus RC4(key, IV).$$

An attacker who knows $M$ can compute the CRC of $M$ and use that to recover the full RC4 keystream. To modify the message to be $M'$, the attacker computes $CRC(M')$ and then creates the following message:

$$IV \,||\, keyid \,||\, (M' \,||\, CRC(M')) \oplus RC4(key, IV).$$

This will work for any messages $M'$ as long as it is as long as $M$ or shorter. (Longer messages would require more keystream bytes.)

If an attacker does not know the contents of $M$, he can still modify it by exploiting the linearity of CRC-32. Linearity in this case means that:

$$CRC(A \oplus B) = CRC(A) \oplus CRC(B).$$

Suppose that an attacker wanted to flip bit $i$ of the message $M$, the contents of which he does not know. He would then construct a $\delta_i$ of the same length as $M$ (which *is* known), with all but the $i$-th bit set to 0. He then constructs a message as follows:

$$IV \,||\, keyid \,||\, (M \,||\, CRC(M)) \oplus RC4(key, IV) \oplus (\delta_i \,||\, CRC(\delta_i)).$$

When the message is then decoded by the receiver, the recovered plaintext will be

$$(M \,||\, CRC(M)) \oplus RC4(key, IV) \oplus (\delta_i \,||\, CRC(\delta_i)) \oplus RC4(key, IV)$$
$$= (M \,||\, CRC(M)) \oplus (\delta_i \,||\, CRC(\delta_i)) = M \oplus \delta_i \,||\, CRC(M) \oplus CRC(\delta_i)$$
$$= M \oplus \delta_i \,||\, CRC(M \oplus \delta_i).$$

Therefore, the CRC computed over $M \oplus \delta_i$ will be the same as the CRC contained in the packet, and the receiver will accept $M$ with the $i$-th bit flipped.

In this way, the attacker can flip arbitrary bits, or sets of bits, and adjust the ICV to match. This ability to modify messages can be used to corrupt transmitted data or perform more sophisticated attacks we describe later. In most cases, for the modified packet to be accepted, the original must not be received at the destination. This can be done either opportunistically, modifying each frame that the attacker received but the destination did not (because of nonuniform interference) or by directed jamming. Another trick is to rely on the retransmission mechanisms of 802.11 and jam only a portion of the packet during the first transmission attempt. On the retry attempt, another portion is jammed, such that the receiver discards both frames, but the attacker knows the contents of the entire frame. This approach avoids the difficult task of sending a jamming signal and receiving data at the same time. An attacker can also perform a man-in-the-middle attack, masquerading as the AP to the user and as the user to the AP and forwarding packets between them. This setup gives the attacker complete freedom to drop, forward, or modify packets.

## Integrity-Based Attacks

The lack of effective integrity protection can be leveraged as a stepping point to mount other attacks. The main problem is that of interaction between layers of the network stack because not all of them are resilient to malicious modifications at the lower layers. Integrity-based attacks can be used not only to interfere with the functionality provided by these upper layers but also to violate the security guarantees of the lower layers. As examples, we show here several ways in which integrity attacks can be used to violate confidentiality.

One such attack makes use of the context in which 802.11 networks are commonly employed. Many wireless LANs are used to provide connectivity to the Internet; this means that one legitimate function of the access point is to decrypt a WEP-encoded packet and forward it over IP to some destination on another network. An attacker can exploit this functionality to be able to decrypt IP packets transmitted over the wireless network. If the destination address of a packet is known, a modification attack as described earlier can be used to change the address specified in the IP header to be one controlled by the attacker (using some tricks to update properly the encrypted IP header checksum). The modified packet will now be forwarded to the attacker's host, and the plaintext will be revealed. Note that for this attack it is not necessary to use jamming or other techniques to ensure that the original frame is not received because WEP does not offer replay protection. The only sequencing element in the WEP-encoded frame is the IV, but as 802.11 does not mandate that IVs be changed with every packet, a compliant AP must accept two frames using the same IV in order not to violate legitimate semantics. Therefore, both versions of the frame will be accepted, with the first one going to the legitimate destination and the second sent to the attacker.

Another class of integrity-based attacks is reaction attacks. These attacks rely on observing the responses of higher layer processes to injected data and using them to learn some information. One example is a TCP-checksum-based reaction attack. TCP uses a one's complement checksum, which has the property that if two bits that are 16-bit positions apart in the packet are flipped, the checksum will remain the same if and only if the original bits were different. An attacker wanting to learn information about the packet's contents can modify the encrypted version by flipping 2 bits, using the integrity attack. A TCP packet with a valid checksum will be accepted at the destination and cause an ACK packet to be returned; packets with invalid checksums will be silently ignored. The two kinds of events can easily be distinguished by an attacker and therefore reveal one bit of information. Iterating this attack can reveal the entire contents of a TCP packet starting with 16 known bits.

Another version of a reaction attack uses the ICV itself. It requires a short message that once again has an easily observable result, such as a DHCP discover message or an ICMP echo request, and enough known keystream to encrypt this message. It can then learn another byte of the keystream by encoding a version of the message 1 byte longer, guessing the extra byte necessary to encrypt the last byte of the CRC. If the guess is correct, the ICV will be correct, and a response will be observed; otherwise, we can assume that the guess was wrong and try another one. This way the correct byte will be learned after about 128 guesses on average; at that point, we can inductively apply the attack to learn further bytes of the keystream.

## RC4 Attack

In 2001, a new weakness in the WEP PRNG algorithm, RC4, was discovered (Fluher, Mantin, & Shamir, 2001). The weakness is that for a certain class of "weak keys," the first bytes of output would show a significant correlation to the key material. This weakness is particularly problematic because of the way that WEP uses RC4, namely, that the first 3 bytes of the key (the IV) are public and change with each frame, whereas the rest are secret. The weak key class is such that it can be identified from the known part of the key, and the correlation can be used to learn information about the secret part from the first byte of output, which is usually easy to predict. (This is not a coincidence; the attack was designed with WEP in mind.) Each weak key provides a different sample point to compute the correlation; when enough of them have been observed, the key material may be recovered. Researchers at AT&T Labs built a proof-of-concept implementation of this attack (Stubblefield, Loannidis, & Rubin, 2002). They showed that the attack is viable and can successfully recover the shared key after watching 5 million to 6 million packets. They also suggested optimizations that can reduce the amount of necessary data by making assumptions about the key, for example, that it is ASCII text. Although their code was never released, an independent implementation of the same attack is widely distributed (Schmoo Group, 2001). This is by far the easiest to carry out and the most devastating of all the attacks on WEP because recovery of the shared key immediately circumvents all of the WEP security measures. Fortunately, it admits a simple fix: Some newer 802.11 firmware versions avoiding choosing IVs that result in weak keys and therefore are invulnerable to the attack.

## Authentication

The shared key authentication method in WEP works by verifying knowledge of the shared WEP key. The AP sends a challenge text of 128 random bytes and asks the responder to send the same bytes in a WEP-encoded frame. The problem with this approach is that a listener watching an authentication exchange will know both the plaintext of the challenge and the ciphertext contained in the response. This will allow him to learn the keystream associated with the IV picked by the responder. Knowing the keystream has two consequences: the ability to decrypt messages sent with that IV and the ability to send WEP-encoded messages of the same length or shorter. In particular, the latter ability can be used to respond to new authentication challenges. The attacker is restricted to using the same IV as the responder, but the lack of replay protection in WEP means that the authenticating STA must accept the response.

Hence, the authentication method is entirely ineffective. Worse, authentication sequences are a reliable source of known plaintext, which may be useful to decrypt other messages. It is worth noting that even if a more secure authentication method were used, WEP would still not provide effective access control because of the confidentiality and integrity vulnerabilities. An attacker wishing to gain access to the network could simply hijack a legitimate connection by modifying messages sent by the end points to contain the desired data. Effective integrity protection is a prerequisite to any access control scheme.

## DEPLOYMENT

The 802.11 standard has enjoyed wide acceptance in both commercial and home markets. Its long deployment history provides a number of lessons about the effects of the design decisions and the needs of the users. One lesson is that in a large portion of networks, WEP was never even turned on. One reason for this is that most 802.11 equipment is not configured to use WEP directly out of the box. Part of the appeal of 802.11 technology, especially in home markets, is that it requires little or no configuration to provide wireless service. Users are left with little incentive to learn how to set up WEP when the network is already functional. Furthermore, properly configuring WEP can be cumbersome because all nodes in an 802.11 LAN must have a shared secret key to connect. With most equipment, the only way to do this is to enter the shared key manually on all nodes. For large networks, this had two negative implications: the significant overhead required to configure all of the STAs with the correct key and the loss of security because many people knew the shared key and it was hard to change. Further, as we saw, a single shared key means that IV reuse happens much more frequently.

Some solutions emerged to provide different key management alternatives. Typically, a login-style approach was used. Users had to authenticate with an ID and a password before connecting to the network, and the authentication process would be used to derive a session key that was used for WEP encryption. This solution avoided a number of WEP vulnerabilities as the session keys were short-lived enough to sidestep the IV collision problems. Because this approach was not part of the 802.11 specification, however, it took the form of vendor-specific extensions and interfered with the interoperability of equipment from different vendors.

A compatible approach to key management and access control moved the login-style authentication to a higher layer of the protocol stack. After association, a login process, usually through a Web browser, would be required before an STAs packets would be forwarded by the AP. This style of authentication is especially popular at hotspots where users have to pay for network access, with the login exchange being replaced by a credit card transaction. Because there was no protection at the link layer, however, no confidentiality was provided, and the authenticated connection could easily be hijacked to gain unauthorized access.

Other common security extensions included increasing the key length to 104 bits from 40 as cryptographic export regulations were changed and providing access control by maintaining a list of authorized MAC addresses (although the latter extension has dubious security because MAC addresses are neither encrypted nor authenticated).

Although none of the extensions provided a comprehensive solution to the WEP security problems, their preponderance pointed to a need for an improved 802.11 security suite.

## NEW PROTOCOLS

The 802.11 committee formed Task Group i to design such a suite. The goals of the group were to address confidentiality vulnerabilities in 802.11, to provide effective integrity protection, to prevent replay attacks, and to integrate with the 802.1X (IEEE Computer Society, 2001) standard for authentication, access control, and key management. Because of the large amount of deployed 802.11 hardware, the task group produced two new protocols: temporal key integrity protocol (TKIP) to be used for the interim, which could run on existing hardware with only a firmware update, and countermode/CBC-MAC protocol, a more complete redesign using state-of-the-art cryptographic tools.

### TKIP

TKIP is built as a wrapper around WEP, using it as a primitive. The main design goal of TKIP was to correct the known security flaws of WEP while preserving the ability to implement it on most existing devices. TKIP uses an extended IV that is 48 bits long to avoid keystream reuse problems; it includes a message integrity code (MIC) called Michael to prevent integrity-based vulnerabilities. It also uses a mixing function to derive the RC4 key from the extended IV and temporal key to avoid correlations between the IV and the key, avoiding the RC4 weakness.

Let us first look at the TKIP mixing function. It starts with the transmitter address (TA), the temporal key (TK), and the TKIP sequence counter (TSC) as input. The TSC is a 48-bit value, starting at 0 and incremented with each frame; a receiver will drop any frames with out-of-sequence TSC values preventing replay attacks. The TK is a 128-bit value obtained from 802.1X; it is guaranteed to be fresh with each new authentication. Hence, the combination (TA, TK, TSC) is guaranteed to be unique for each frame.

The mixing function has two phases. The first phase uses only the 32 most significant bits of the TSC and produces an 80-bit intermediate value. The second phase uses the intermediate value and the entire TSC to produce a 128-bit RC4 key. This split-phase design is used so that the first phase can be only executed once every $2^{16}$ frames, and the second phase can be made fast. The first 3 bytes of the RC4 key consist of the first 2 bytes of TSC and a special byte designed to avoid the weak RC4 key classes. These bytes are transmitted in the clear in the frame, as with WEP. The upper 4 bytes of the TSC are then included in an added field of the MPDU, indicated by a reserved field. A receiver will possess all 6 bytes of the TSC and hence be able to recover the RC4 key and decrypt the contents.

The MIC is a simple 64-bit integrity code calculated over the data (as well as the source and destination addresses, to prevent redirection attacks) using a shared secret MIC key. The MIC key is derived from the 802.1X mechanism, and a different key is used for both directions of the communication. It provides only weak integrity protection because of the constraints imposed by existing hardware, and a relatively small number of attempted forgeries can be used to bypass the MIC. To avoid this problem, the revised standard calls for limiting the rate of MIC failures to one per minute. If this rate is exceeded, the association is terminated and a new authentication is performed, generating a new MIC key. This decision strikes a balance between integrity protection and potential denial of service.

## CCMP

CCMP is the long-term security solution for 802.11. It uses the advanced encryption standard (AES National Institute of Standards and Technology, 2001) in CCM mode (Whiting, Housely, & Ferguson, 2002), which provides both encryption and integrity protection. CCMP uses a temporal key, derived from 802.1X authentication, along with a nonce constructed from a 48-bit packet number and incremented with each packet, to encrypt and authenticate the plaintext MPDU. In addition, the integrity component of CCM is also performed over the MAC header to authenticate the values contained therein.

AES is a widely analyzed encryption standard, so it is expected to provide strong confidentiality protection. The CBC-MAC construction of CCM provides strong integrity protection, so both confidentiality and integrity attacks should be infeasible. The combination of countermode AES and CBC-MAC used by CCM is itself analyzed by Jonsson (2002) and is shown to be secure. The packet number provides replay protection; a packet number is not allowed to repeat until the temporal key is changed. AES and CCM can be implemented quickly in both hardware and software, so it should be feasible to incorporate them into new equipment; the updated security suite will require support of CCMP.

## CONCLUSION

The WEP security suite is a well-known example of a security failure. It is important to understand not only how WEP failed, as we discussed in detail here, but also why it failed and how those failures could have been prevented.

### Lessons

Two main problems caused the vulnerabilities of WEP. The first is a misapplication of cryptographic primitives. The keystream reuse attacks resulted from insufficient care that was taken to prevent IV collisions. Arguably, the RC4 vulnerability could have been prevented by using a more appropriate primitive. This demonstrates a need for greater involvement of expert cryptographers in the design of secure protocols.

The other problem is the mistaken set of goals. Of course, any standard must limit its goals to succeed. However, some of the goals left out in WEP are essential to security. The lack of integrity protection as an explicit goal leads to a number of active attacks compromising not only integrity but confidentiality as well. The decision to leave key management out of the standard meant that the only option for installations with interoperable hardware was either not to use WEP at all or to use an insecure

shared key known to all users. There is also a feeling that WEP was not designed to be very secure, suggested by the phrase "casual eavesdropper." However, automation can render even the most complex attacks accessible to casual users. Right now WEP can be easily defeated with off-the-shelf equipment and freely available software (The Schmoo Group, 2001). Any limitation of goals must be accompanied with an explicit and careful examination of what is being given up and what the implications are.

### Future Designs

In this section, we list several design principles that we believe would have prevented the vulnerabilities in WEP.

- Use appropriate cryptographic primitives and designs.
- Study and imitate similar protocols. The IPSEC (Internet protocol security: Kent & Atkinson, 1998a, 1998b) suite of protocols has similar goals to WEP, and some of the attacks on WEP such as reaction attacks first appeared in the context of IPSEC (Bellovin, 1996).
- Design security with context in mind. From the perspective of a link-layer protocol, integrity protection may not seem important; however, in the context of interacting with IP, integrity attacks can be used to violate confidentiality.
- Employ cryptographic expertise. Because many networking protocols require some security design, such design is too often carried out by network engineers without formal training in the area. A cryptography expert would have immediately noticed the problems of keystream reuse and the ineffectiveness of the ICV checksum.
- Properly set security goals. Any secure communications protocol should provide at least confidentiality, integrity, and replay protection.
- Do not avoid solving hard problems. Key management is complicated, and there is an argument to leave its definition outside the standard. However, the lack of standard definition resulted in primitive and insecure key management schemes being widely used, and not until the 1 [802.11i] standard is widely adopted can we expect sophisticated and interoperable key management solutions to exist.
- Be conservative in your security design. Security is an elusive target, and unforeseen future problems can have devastating effects on a standard, as the WEP experience clearly demonstrates. One good example of conservative design is CCMP; whereas TKIP addresses the vulnerabilities of WEP, CCMP is a more comprehensive and conservative solution and stands a better chance of providing security in the long term.

## GLOSSARY

**802.11**  Institute of Electrical and Electronic Engineers standard for wireless local area network communications.

**Access Point (AP)**  A station managing and mediating network connectivity for a group of stations.

**Advanced Encryption Standard (AES)** A block cipher standardized by the National Institute of Standards and Technology.

**Block Cipher** An encryption algorithm that encrypts a fixed-length sequence of bytes.

**Ciphertext** A message encrypted with a cipher.

**CRC-32** A checksum used to detect errors in transmitted data.

**Initialization Vector (IV)** A value used to select a per-packet key to be used with RC4.

**MAC Protocol Data Unit (MPDU)** A sequence of bytes passed to the MAC layer from an upper layer.

**MAC Service Data Unit (MSDU)** A sequence of bytes sent over the physical layer by the MAC layer.

**Media Access Control (MAC)** The layer that controls framing and transmission of packets on the physical layer. WEP operates at the MAC layer.

**Plaintext** Readable data before encryption or after decryption.

**Pseudo-Random Number Generator (PRNG)** An algorithm to generate a continuous unpredictable stream of bytes.

**RC4** A PRNG used to create a stream cipher used by WEP.

**Station (STA)** Any equipment speaking the 802.11 protocol.

**Stream Cipher** An encryption algorithm that encrypts an stream of bytes of arbitrary length, usually implemented using a PRNG and exclusive-OR.

## CROSS REFERENCES

See *Computer and Network Authentication; Encryption Basics; Wireless Channels; Wireless Network Standards and Protocol (802.11).*

## REFERENCES

Bellovin, S. M. (1996). Problem areas for the IP security protocols. In *6th USENIX Security Symposium*. San Jose, CA: USENIX.

Dierks, T., & Allen, C. (1999). The TLS protocol version 1.0. RFC2246. The Internet Society.

Fluthrer, S., Mantin, I., & Shamir, A. (2001). Weaknesses in the key schedule algorithm of RCA. In *8th Annual Workship on Selected Areas of Cryptography*. Springer-Verlag.

IEEE Computer Society. (1985). Carrier sense multiple access with collision detection (CSMA/CD; IEEE Standard 802.3).

IEEE Computer Society. (1997). Wireless LAN medium access control (MAC) and physical layer (PHY) specification (IEEE Standard 802.11).

IEEE Computer Society. (1999). Wireless LAN Medium access control (MAC) and physical layer (PHY) specification (IEEE Standard 802.11).

IEEE Computer Society. (2001). Port-based network access control (IEEE Standard 802.1X).

International Standardization Organization (1992). ISO open system interconnection—basic reference model (2nd ed.) ISO/TC 97/SC 16(ISO CD 7498-1).

Jonsson, J. (2002). The security of CTR + CBC-MAC. In 9th Annual Workshop on *Selected Areas of Cryptography*, St. John's, Newfoundland: Springer-Verlag.

Kent, S., & Atkinson, R. (1998a). IP authentication header. Internet Request for Comment RFC 2402, Internet Engineering Task Force.

Kent, S., & Atkinson, R. (1998b). IP encapsulating security payload (ESP). Internet Request for Comment RFC 2406, Internet Engineering Task Force.

National Bureau of Standards. (1977). Data encryption standard (Federal Information Processing Standards Publication 46). Gaithersburg, MD: National Institute of Standards and Technology.

National Institute of Standards and Technology (2001). Announcing the advanced encryption standard (AES) (Federal Information Processing Standards Publication 197). Gaithersburg, MD: National Institute of Standards and Technology.

Rivest, R. L. (1982). *The RC4 Encryption Algorithm*. Bedford, MA: RSA Data Security.

Stubblefield, A., Ioannidis, J., & Rubin, A. (2002). Using the Fluhrer, Mantin, and Shamir attack to break WEP. In *2002 Network and Distributed Systems Security Symposium*. Internet Society.

The Shmoo Group. (2001). Airsnort homepage. Retrieved from http://airsnort.shmoo.com August 2005 accessed.

Whiting, D., Housely, R., & Ferguson, N. (2002). AES encryption and authentication using CTR mode and CBC-MAC (IEEE Document 802.11-02/001r2).

## FURTHER READING

Arbaugh, W. A. (2001). An inductive chosen plaintext attack against WEP/WEP2 (IEEE Document 802.11-01/230).

Arbaugh, W. A., Shankar, N., Wan, Y. J., & Zhang, K. (2002). Your 802.11 wireless network has no clothes. Volume 9, no. 6. *IEEE Wireless Communications*.

Bellardo, J., & Savage, S. (2003). 802.11 denial-of-service attacks: Real vulnerabilities and practical solutions. In *USENIX Security Symposium*, Washington, DC: The USENIX Association.

Borisov, N., Goldberg, I., & Wagner, D. (2001). Intercepting mobile communications: The insecurity of 802.11. In *7th Annual International Conference on Mobile Computing and Networking*. Association for Computing Machinery.

Cam-Winget, N., Housley, R., Wagner, D., & Walker, J. (2003). Security flaws in 802.11 data link protocols. *Communications of the ACM*, 46(5), 35–39.

Walker, J. R. (2000). Unsafe at any key size; an analysis of the WEP encapsulation (IEEE Document 802.11-00/362).

# Bluetooth Security

Susanne Wetzel, *Stevens Institute of Technology*

## INTRODUCTION

In 1998, the five computer and telecommunication companies Ericsson, IBM, Intel, Nokia, and Toshiba formed an alliance to develop and promote a wireless communication technology that became known as Bluetooth. Since then, the membership of the Bluetooth Special Interest Group has increased significantly, and both the number of as well as the market for Bluetooth products have increased considerably.

Bluetooth was designed to be a short-range, low-cost technology eliminating wires and cables between devices such as personal digital assistants (PDAs), cell phones, printers, faxes, headsets, cars, and turnstiles. A particular focus in the design of the communication technology was to not require a fixed infrastructure but to allow for ad hoc networking instead, that is, to enable Bluetooth devices to communicate with each other in dynamically changing constellations. Consequently, these manifold advantages over other (wireless) communication standards and technologies allow for a large set of new applications of the Bluetooth technology in today's society. These applications range from personal area networks (e.g., a headset and PDA that are wirelessly connected to a cell phone) to various office or home settings (e.g., computers, printers, keyboards, and fax machines being connected without cables).

However, at the same time, this new technology and functionality is a double-edged sword in that it not only provides its users with increased possibilities but also introduces additional security risks because of its wireless ad hoc nature. The Bluetooth specification therefore also provides mechanisms to secure the functionality of the system. The security mechanisms currently defined in the Bluetooth baseband specification are aimed to provide confidentiality and authentication on the wireless radio link; that is, the security mechanisms are implemented to thwart the danger of unauthorized devices eavesdropping on communication between other Bluetooth devices or engaging in communication under false identities. Other security needs (e.g., end-to-end security on the application layer) are not addressed in the specification.

Since the first publication of the Bluetooth specification in 1999 (Bluetooth, 1999a, 1999b, 2001, 2003), various weaknesses in the specified Bluetooth security mechanisms have been discovered. The main attacks can roughly be categorized into three classes: eavesdropping and impersonation, location attacks, and cipher vulnerabilities.

Jakobsson and Wetzel (2001) described how attackers can steal keys from victim devices of their choice and how this in turn enables attackers not only to impersonate a victim device (i.e., produce correctly formatted and encrypted messages on behalf of a victim's device) but also to eavesdrop on the conversation between two or more devices. Kügler (2003) improved on the man-in-the-middle scenario introduced by Jakobsson and Wetzel by exploiting the Bluetooth connection-establishment procedures. Shaked and Wool (2005) described optimizations for the personal identification number (PIN) cracking and discussed methods to force devices to repeat the pairing process.

By means of a location attack, an attacker can track and profile the geographic locations of victim devices. In Gehrmann, Persson, and Smeets (2004) and Jakobsson and Wetzel (2001), attacks are presented that allow easy mapping of the physical whereabouts of users carrying Bluetooth-enabled devices but yet do not require a major investment in building a large infrastructure for the tracking.

The feasibility of the impersonation and eavesdropping attacks is contingent on certain conditions that are discussed later. By contrast, the location attack is a practical attack because it can be carried out without requiring any major effort. Although some of the attacks could be thwarted relatively easily by employing simple countermeasures, others would necessitate major changes in not only the Bluetooth baseband but also higher layers of the Bluetooth protocol stack.

The Bluetooth specification defines the stream cipher $E_0$, which allows for key lengths ranging from 8 to 128 bits. However, Jakobsson and Wetzel (2001) and Saarinen (2001) have both shown that the strength of the cipher will not exceed 100 bits. Furthermore, using a time–space trade-off (Jakobsson & Wetzel, 2001), an attack with a time and memory complexity of $2^{66}$ can be devised. Hermelin and Nyberg (1999) presented an attack to recover the initial state from the keystream generator requiring $O(2^{64})$ operations and the knowledge of $O(2^{64})$ keystream bits. Ekdahl and Johansson (2000) reduced this to $O(2^{61})$ operations and $O(2^{50})$ keystream bits. Fluhrer and Lucks (2001) described an analysis that allows one to determine the cipher key from known keystream bits in time $O(2^{84})$ $(O(2^{73}))$ at the cost of knowing 132 $(2^{43})$ keystream bits. Using 128 keystream bits, Krause (2002) devised an attack to derive the internal state with $O(2^{77})$ operations. Lu, Meier, and Vaudenay (2004a, 2004b) presented correlation attacks. Their best conditional correlation attack is the first practical attack on Bluetooth encryption. Using the first 24 bits of $2^{23.8}$ frames, determining the encryption key requires $2^{38}$ operations. In Armknecht (2002), Armknecht and Krause (2003), and Courtois (2003) introduced an alternative attack on the keystream generator by solving a system of nonlinear equations over the finite field GF(2). The major drawback of the latter approach is that it is not yet known how many keystream bits are needed to carry out the attack successfully.

This chapter begins by reviewing the relevant aspects of the Bluetooth specification and focuses on describing the specified Bluetooth security concepts and mechanisms. It then details the various security weaknesses that are known so far, followed by some countermeasures for some of the attacks that may be integrated in the Bluetooth specification in the future. This chapter closes with a comparison of the security mechanisms in IEEE (Institute of Electrical and Electronics Engineers) 802.11b and Bluetooth. This chapter is based on the general introduction to Bluetooth provided in the chapter on "Bluetooth Technology" and makes reference to the chapters "Wireless Networks Standards and Protocols (802.11)," "WEP Security," and "Cracking WEP," which provide a detailed discussion of the security mechanisms and shortcomings in the IEEE 802.11b standard.

## DETAILS OF THE BLUETOOTH SPECIFICATION

Bluetooth operates in the unlicensed 2.4-GHz frequency band. The technology allows for transmission speeds up to 1 Mbps, achieving a throughput of up to 721 kbps. To reduce signal interference and collision, Bluetooth employs frequency-hopping with 1,600 hops per second (which translates into 625 $\mu$s per hop). Based on a pseudorandom pattern, the hops are evenly distributed over 79 channels that are displaced by 1 MHz each. Depending on their power level, Bluetooth devices have an operating range of 0.1 to 100 m. The specification distinguishes three classes: Class 1 devices have a maximum power output of 100 mW and an expected range of 100 m (300 feet), whereas Class 2 (3) devices operate with a maximum power output of 2.5 mW (1 mW) resulting in an expected range of 10 m (10 cm).

The formed wireless local area networks—the *piconets*—can be of either permanent or temporary nature and consist of one master and up to seven active slaves (see Figure 1). The device first initiating a connection

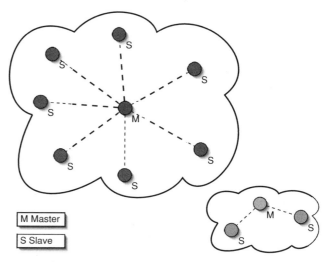

**Figure 1:** Piconets with two and seven slaves.

automatically becomes the master of the piconet. Subsequently, devices can agree on switching roles. Each device can be active in only one piconet at a time. By means of time multiplexing, a device, however, can participate in two or more overlaying piconets. Although a device can be master for only one piconet, a device can act as master in one piconet and slave in other piconets or as only slave in several piconets. A group of piconets with connections between the different piconets is referred to as scatternet (see Figure 2).

Each Bluetooth device is characterized by a unique 48-bit device address, the so-called *Bluetooth device address* (BD_ADDR). Every Bluetooth unit also has an internal clock (CLK) that determines the timing as well as the hopping of the transceiver. The clock is a 28-bit counter with a clock rate of 3.2 kHz.

Several states of operation of Bluetooth devices are defined to support the functionality of establishing a piconet, adding additional devices or removing devices from a piconet. A Bluetooth device can be in one of two major

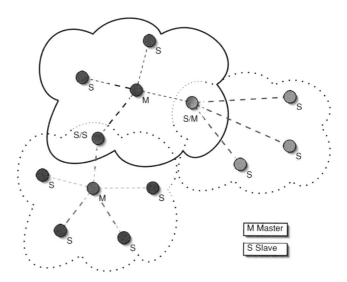

**Figure 2:** Scatternet.

states, *standby* or *connection*, or one of the seven interim substates: *page, page scan, inquiry, inquiry scan, master response, slave response*, and *inquiry response*. By means of the inquiry procedures, devices in the range yet unknown to the inquiring device are discovered. The inquiring device will learn their device addresses and clocks. Devices may be in one of two modes, the *discoverable* and *nondiscoverable modes*. A device must be in discoverable mode for it to respond to inquiry messages. With the paging procedures, an actual connection can be established based on the knowledge of the Bluetooth device address of an already discovered device. A Bluetooth device can be in either *non-connectable* or *connectable* mode. When in the former, the device will not respond to paging.

To establish and maintain a connection, the master and the slave devices must synchronize to the same hopping sequence. During inquiry and paging, only 32 of the 79 frequencies are used for the hopping sequences, which all have a short period of length 32. The pseudorandom inquiry-hopping sequences are determined by the inquire access code and the clock of the discovering device. For the paging procedures, the respective hopping sequence is based on the device address and clock of the paged device. Once connected, the channel-hopping sequence makes use of all 79 channels. It exhibits a very long period. The master's clock and device address determine the sequence.

During inquiry, the responding device communicates its clock to the inquiring device. Subsequently, the master will use that clock for paging the slave. Once a connection is established, the master clock is communicated to the slaves. To synchronize their clocks to the master clock, the slaves then add an offset to their native clocks. The offsets have to be updated regularly as the clocks are free running and thus tend to drift. Because the channel access code is sufficient for synchronization once a connection is established, any periodic master transmission can be used for that purpose. To compensate drifts during paging, the paging device will transmit not just on the hop frequency $f(k)$ based on the clock estimate $k$ of the paged device but also on frequencies just before and after that. Although the paged device hops to the next frequency only every 1.28s, the paging device increases its hop rate to 3,200 hops/s (i.e., hops to the next frequency every 312.5 $\mu$s). The 32 dedicated paging hop frequencies are divided in two so-called trains, A and B, of 16 frequencies each. Train A includes the frequencies $f(k-8)$, $f(k-7), \ldots f(k), \ldots f(k+7)$ that surround the predicted frequency $f(k)$, Train B contains the more distant hops $f(k-16)$, $f(k-15), \ldots f(k-9)$, $f(k+8), \ldots f(k+15)$. The paging will first repeat Train A for $N$ times or until a response is obtained. If no response is received, Train $B$ is tried for $N$ times. If still no response is obtained, this procedure is repeated until a timeout occurs. $N$ depends on when the slave will enter the page scan substate and is either 128 or 256. Once the master (i.e., paging device) receives a response from the paged device, the master will respond with a *frequency-hopping synchronization* (FHS) packet containing the master's clock setting.

Data packets sent on a particular piconet channel consist of a 72-bit access code, a 54-bit header, and a payload of up to 2,745 bits. The access code is of particular interest because it is used for synchronization and identification

purposes. Moreover, it is used as a signaling message during inquiry and paging. Three types of access codes are defined: *channel access code* (CAC), *device access code* (DAC), and the *inquiry access code* (IAC). The CAC identifies a particular piconet and as such is included in all packets sent in the piconet. During paging, the DAC is used to address devices. The IAC is used to discover other Bluetooth devices in range. While the IAC is common to all devices, both the CAC as well as the DAC are determined as a deterministic function of the master's respectively paged device's unique Bluetooth device address. It is important to note that the access code is always transmitted in the clear. (For further details on the Bluetooth specification, see Bluetooth, 1999a, 1999b, 2001, 2003.)

## Bluetooth Security Mechanisms

The immanent risk of wireless ad hoc communication is that unauthorized devices listen in to ongoing communication or actively engage themselves in communication with other devices. The Bluetooth specification defines countermeasures in the baseband and thus provides authentication and encryption on the link layer. Consequently, the security mechanisms currently defined in the Bluetooth specification do not provide true end-to-end security. Rather, it is necessary to have additional security measures implemented on higher layers of the protocol stack (e.g., on the application layer) to achieve stronger means of security.

This section provides a brief introduction to the core security concepts defined in the Bluetooth specification. The description focuses on the concepts needed to discuss the weaknesses in the Bluetooth specification described. For a more detailed description, refer to the specification (see Bluetooth, 1999a, 1999b, 2001, 2003). This section first focuses on security policies, then describes the authentication and encryption mechanisms, and finally details the pairing procedure used for key establishment.

### Bluetooth Security Modes

In the Bluetooth specification, the Generic Access Profile not only defines generic procedures for discovery of Bluetooth devices and link management but also determines three modes of security for the use of Bluetooth devices:

**Security Mode 1** is the nonsecure mode. A device in Mode 1 will not initiate any security procedures on the link layer; that is, authentication and encryption are bypassed. This mode is suitable in settings that do not require any security.

**Security Mode 2** enforces service-level security; that is, authentication or encryption are not initiated at the time the link is established but may be requested at channel or connection establishment. This mode provides flexibility in that it allows the security to depend on the requirements of the requesting channel or service.

**Security Mode 3** provides link-level security. A device in Mode 3 will initiate authentication or encryption, or both before the link setup is completed. Depending on the settings of connecting devices, the Bluetooth device in Mode 3 may reject connection.

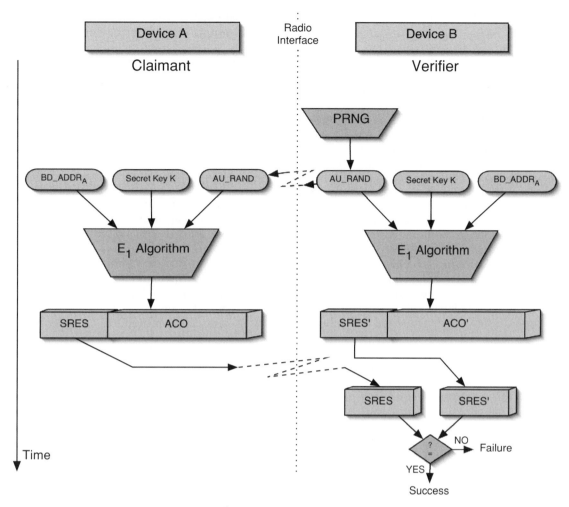

**Figure 3:** Authentication.

## Authentication

The authentication mechanism implemented in Bluetooth is a two-pass challenge–response protocol. Devices are authenticated by means of verifying their knowledge of a shared secret key $K$. The protocol provides unilateral authentication; that is, one device (claimant) authenticates itself to another device (verifier). Mutual authentication can be achieved by repeating the protocol with roles exchanged.

In the first pass of the authentication protocol (see Figure 3), the verifier (Device $B$) sends the 128-bit challenge (random number $AU\_RAND$) to the claimant (Device $A$). Using the challenge $AU\_RAND$, its own 48-bit device address $BD\_ADDR$, and the shared secret $K$, the claimant uses the $E_1$ algorithm ($E_1$ is a modification of the block cipher algorithm SAFER+) to compute the 128-bit result $(SRES\|ACO) = E_1(AU\_RAND, BD\_ADDR, K)$.

In the second pass of the protocol, the claimant sends the 32 most significant bits $SRES$ of the result to the verifier. The verifier performs the same computation as the claimant. The claimant is authenticated if the $SRES$ received from the claimant is identical to the one computed by the verifier. The 96-bit $ACO$ (authentication ciphering offset) is retained for a subsequent generation of an encryption key.

If authentication fails, the specification requires a waiting interval to pass before a new attempt can be made. To prevent an attacker from testing the correctness of keys by means of repeated authentications, the waiting interval is increased exponentially.

## Encryption

The Bluetooth specification employs baseband encryption to thwart the risk of unauthorized eavesdropping on the wireless link. The packet payload is encrypted by XORing the payload bits with the keystream output of the stream cipher $E_0$. The ciphertext bits are sent to the receiving device, which also computes the same stream cipher output. The encrypted payload is decrypted by XORing the encrypted payload bits with the keystream output.

The steam cipher $E_0$ determines the keystream sequence upon input of the 48-bit master device address, the master clock, as well as an encryption key $K_C$. Using the key-generation algorithm $E_3$, the encryption key $K_C$ is computed from the current link key (see the next subsection), the ciphering offset $COF$, and a 128-bit random number $EN\_RAND$. The master issues $EN\_RAND$ and transmits it in clear to all communicating devices. Depending on whether encryption operates in point-to-point or point-to-multipoint fashion, the $ACO$ is used as *COF*, or the master device address determines the *COF*.

To support different effective encryption key sizes (necessary because of different local jurisdictions and export regulations for cryptographic products), within $E_0$ the key $K_C$ is first transformed into a key $K'_C$ with an effective key-size between 8 and 128 bits.

Subsequently, the stream cipher $E_0$ uses four linear feedback shift registers (LFSRs) followed by a finite state machine (combining the outputs of the LFSRs) to determine the key-stream sequence, which in turn is used to encrypt the packet payload. The LFSRs as well as the 4-bit determining the feedback for the finite state machine (the *summation combiner*) are reinitialized for each packet; that is, a new key stream is generated for each payload.

In general, encryption can be initiated once an (unilateral) authentication has been completed successfully. Encryption can be requested by either the master or the slave. Once the devices have agreed on a key length to be used, the encryption will be initiated by the master device. The setup of an encrypted link will fail in case one device is not able to support the key size requested by the other device.

The Bluetooth specification allows for three settings regarding baseband encryption. *Encryption Mode 1* is the default setting in which no encryption is performed on any traffic. While in *Encryption Mode 2*, only point-to-point encryption is supported (i.e., broadcast messages are not encrypted). In *Encryption Mode 3*, all messages are encrypted.

## Keys and Key Establishment

Previous discussions have already generally referred to a secret key shared between different devices, respectively, the link key. This section describes how these keys as well as other keys used in related contexts are established.

When communication is first initiated between devices that have not yet been exposed to each other, then these devices do not yet share a common secret key. Rather, they must be paired; that is, a shared secret key, the *link key*, must first be established to allow authenticated and/or private connections between these devices in the future. The link-key generation and distribution defined in the Bluetooth specification 1.0B works in five steps:

1. Generation of an initialization key
2. Authentication
3. Generation of a link key
4. Exchange of link key
5. Authentication

Starting with the Bluetooth Specification 1.1, the authentication in Step 2 was eliminated and instead the link key is generated immediately after the initialization key is established in Step 1.

When two devices that have previously been paired reinitiate communication after the conclusion of a previous session, they may set up a new link key using either the previously shared link key, or (as when they meet for the first time) negotiate a new one.

**Establishing an Initialization Key.** The initialization key is a temporary key that is established to allow encryption and decryption of information in the subsequent steps of the link-key generation process. It is discarded once a link key is successfully established.

- In the Bluetooth specification 1.0B, the initialization key between two devices is established in two steps: the generation of the key followed by a verification step that uses the defined authentication protocol.

  1. At first, one device chooses a random number $IN\_RAND$ and transmits it to the other device. Using algorithm $E_{22}$, both Bluetooth devices then compute an initialization key $K_{init}$ as a function of a shared PIN, the Bluetooth device address $BD\_ADDR$ of the device that received the random number, and the random number itself.

  2. To verify that both devices hold the same key, mutual authentication is performed using the newly derived initialization key $K_{init}$ as key $K$ for the authentication procedure. This step is deemed successful if the corresponding results in each round match. It should be noted that using the term *authentication* in this context is not in the sense of the word as it is generally used in cryptography. Rather, it means verification and is done to ensure that both sides not only hold the same key (that is, to prevent errors) but also to prevent man-in-the-middle attacks, which are discussed later.

- Starting with the Bluetooth specification 1.1, the initialization key is derived from a Bluetooth device address $BD\_ADDR$, a PIN code, and a random number $IN\_RAND$ using the algorithm $E_{22}$. If both devices have a fixed PIN, the devices cannot be paired. If both devices have a variable PIN, the Bluetooth device address of the device that did not generate the random number will be used to compute the initialization key. If only one device has a fixed PIN, then the other device's Bluetooth device address will be used to determine the initialization key (see Figure 4).

  The verification step previously used to ensure that both devices hold the same initialization key has been eliminated.

**Link-Key Generation.** The actual link-key generation step is the same for all Bluetooth specifications published to date (see Bluetooth, 1999a, 1999b, 2001, 2003). It distinguishes two cases:

1. When one of the devices involved in the link-key generation protocol has limited memory resources, the unit key of the respective device will be used as the link key for the two parties. The unit key of a device is generated and stored in nonvolatile memory once a device is in operation for the first time. It will rarely be changed afterwards. Using the previously established initialization key, the Bluetooth Device $B$ with limited memory resources encrypts its unit key $K_B$ (by XORing the unit key and initialization key together) and

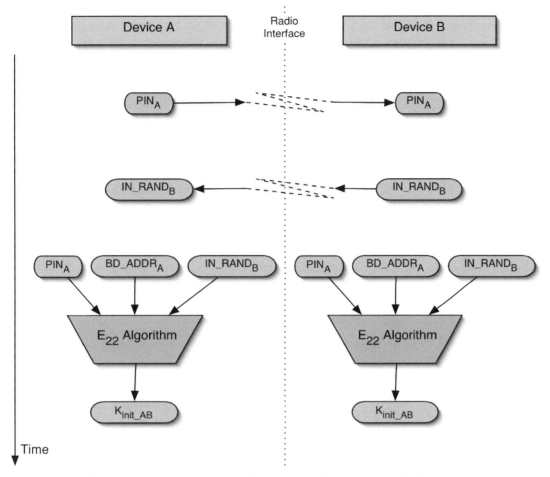

**Figure 4:** Establishing an initialization key (Bluetooth Specification 1.1).

transmits the resulting ciphertext to Device $A$. The receiving unit $A$ uses the initialization key $K_{init\_AB}$ to decrypt the received message. Subsequently, the unit key $K_B$ of Device $B$ with limited memory resources is used as link key $LK\_K_{AB}$ for Devices $A$ and $B$ (see Figure 5).

2. When both Devices $A$ and $B$ have sufficient memory resources, the devices establish a *combination key* as their link key (see Figure 6):

(a) Both devices choose random numbers, $LK\_RAND_A$ and $LK\_RAND_B$, respectively. Using algorithm $E_{21}$, the Device $A$ ($B$) then computes $LK\_K_A$ ($LK\_K_B$) as a function of $LK\_RAND_A$ ($LK\_RAND_B$) and its own unique device address.

(b) $A$ and $B$ encrypt their random numbers $LK\_RAND_A$ and $LK\_RAND_B$ using the previously established initialization key and exchange the resulting ciphertexts.

(c) Both devices decrypt the received ciphertexts using the symmetric initialization key. Because the devices know each others' unique Bluetooth device address, they can now compute the other party's contribution $LK\_K_B$ ($LK\_K_A$). Both units determine the link key as $LK\_K_A \oplus LK\_K_B$.

In both cases, a mutual verification is performed (using the authentication procedure with link key $K_{AB}$ as $K$) to confirm the success of the link-key generation, that is, to verify that both devices hold the same link key.

Whenever deemed necessary, the combination-key method can also be used to exchange a new link key by using the old link key (instead of the initialization key) in Steps (b) and (c) to encrypt the random numbers and decrypt the received ciphertexts. Changing a link key when it is the unit key of a device with limited memory resources is more cumbersome. The corresponding device is not only required to change its unit key but must also renegotiate the new link key with devices with which it was previously paired.

A previous section describes how the encryption key is derived from a link key in point-to-point communication. In case of a point-to-multipoint configuration, the master may request all slaves to use a *master link* key (and thus also a common encryption key) instead of pairwise link keys to avoid capacity loss. Using two random numbers, the master first computes the master link key as output of the algorithm $E_{22}$. For each slave to receive the master link key, the master will choose a random number and transmit it to the respective slave. Using $E_{22}$ with its random number and link key as input, each slave computes an *overlay*. The master will then send the XOR of the master link key and the overlay to the slave. Each slave can recalculate the master key $K_{master}$

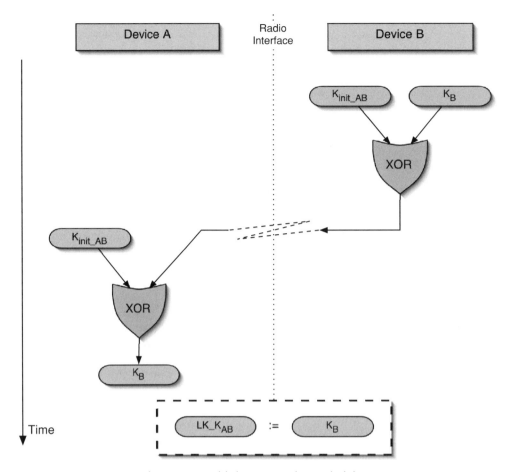

**Figure 5:**  Establishing a unit key as link key.

because it knows the individual overlays. Mutual authentication is performed to ensure that all slaves hold the same master link key. Figure 7 summarizes the dependencies in establishing the different keys.

Rather than discussing further details on the algorithms (e.g., $E_0$, $E_1$, $E_{22}$), the interested reader is referred to the specification (Bluetooth, 1999a, 1999b, 2001, 2003).

## Security Architectures and Access Policies

Although not yet defined in the Bluetooth specification, the Bluetooth Security Special Interest Group (SIG) has outlined some sample security architectures and access policies based on the security mechanisms defined in the Bluetooth baseband specification. In addition to the three security modes introduced earlier, the descriptions in Gehrmann, Persson, and Smeets (2004), Müller (1999), and Bluetooth SIG Security Export Group (2002) distinguish two levels of trust and three levels of service security.

A trusted device is a device that is given unconditional access to all services on a host. It assumes previous authentication and negotiation of a link key. By contrast, an untrusted device does not have a permanent connection, resulting in only limited access to services. These properties can be further refined by defining them not per device but per service or groups of services instead.

Services fall into one of the following three security levels: Level 1 services are those services that require both authorization and authentication; automatic access is granted to trusted devices only. Level 2 services require authentication only, and Level 3 services are open to all devices.

The architectures in Gehrmann, Persson, and Smeets (2004), Müller (1999), and Bluetooth SIG Security Export Group (2002) define individual settings for access policies of different services, thus providing selected access to some services without granting access to others. The architectures furthermore account for the facts that higher layer protocols (i.e., above L2CAP) may or may not be Bluetooth-specific and may even have their own security features. The architectures are designed such that lower layers do not need to be aware of security settings and policies at higher layers of the Bluetooth protocol stack.

## SECURITY WEAKNESSES IN THE BLUETOOTH SPECIFICATION

This section reviews the security vulnerabilities in the Bluetooth baseband specification that have been published to date. First it focuses on the eavesdropping, impersonation and location attacks detailed in (Gehrmann & Nyberg, 2001; Jakobsson & Wetzel, 2001). It then

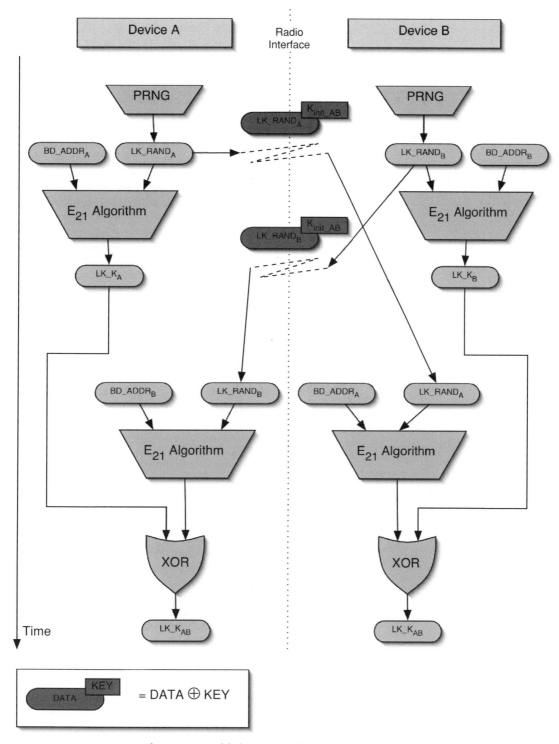

**Figure 6:** Establishing a combination key as link key.

discusses *man-in-the-middle* attacks (Jakobsson & Wetzel, 2001; Kügler, 2003) and reviews the shortcomings of the Bluetooth stream cipher $E_0$ identified in Armknecht (2002), Armknecht and Krause (2003), Courtois (2003), Ekdahl and Johansson (2000), Fluhrer and Lucks (2001), Hermelin and Nyberg (1999), Jakobsson and Wetzel (2001), and Krause (2002). It also provides an overview of other vulnerabilities such as the lack of integrity protection, battery draining as well as attacks due to implemen-

tation flaws and bad handling (Digital, 2003; Karygiannis & Owens, 2002). The section closes with a brief discussion on the feasibility of the various attacks.

## Eavesdropping and Impersonation

As discussed earlier, the Bluetooth baseband specification defines two ways for establishing a link key, which is subsequently used for authentication purposes and serves as the basis for determining encryption keys.

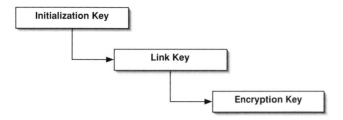

**Figure 7:** Dependencies between the different keys.

If one of the communicating devices has insufficient memory resources, the unit key of the respective device will be established as the link key for the two communicating devices. As a consequence, all devices that have ever been paired with the device (exhibiting limited memory resources) can impersonate that device at any time. Furthermore, any one of these devices can eavesdrop on any communication that involves the device with limited memory resources, including past communication, if recorded.

In the case in which a link key different from the unit key is established between the communicating devices, the security of the procedure is based on the secure establishment of an initialization key. In turn, the security of the initialization key depends solely on the secrecy of the PIN, because the other inputs needed for generating a secret initialization key (random number and the respective Bluetooth device addresses) are either publicly known or communicated in the clear. If no PIN is available (in which case zero may be taken as the default) or if the PIN is transmitted in the clear between the devices, then the PIN is known to the attacker. Furthermore, even if the PINs are communicated between units in a secure way, an attacker can still determine the correct PIN in the case where short or weak PINs are used by observing or participating in the communication on the wireless link and using the acquired information to search exhaustively through all possible PINs.

Jakobsson and Wetzel (2001) distinguished between a passive attacker, who only listens in on two Bluetooth devices communicating on the wireless link, and an active attacker, who engages in a protocol with the victim device to determine the secret PIN.

**Passive Attack.** Here, the attacker listens in on the wireless link while two devices engage in the key-establishment protocol described earlier. The attacker guesses a PIN and verifies the correctness of the guess by performing the authentication step (i.e., the second step in the key-establishment process) using the random string that was communicated in the clear. If the result is correct, then his guess is correct with high probability. Starting with the Bluetooth specification 1.1, the authentication step after establishing the initialization key has been eliminated. Consequently, the attacker must guess a PIN, compute both a candidate initialization and link key, and check the correctness by means of the recorded authentication protocol following establishment of the link key.

**Active Attack.** Instead of obtaining a challenge–response transcript by listening in on the communication between victim devices, the attacker actively engages in obtaining a transcript. The attacker first guesses a PIN and computes an initialization key (as well as the corresponding link key in Bluetooth specifications 1.1 and 1.2). Then, the attacker initiates the authentication protocol with the victim device by sending a challenge. The victim device uses the correct key to compute the corresponding response. By means of this transcript, the attacker can check the correctness of his guess.

Once an attacker has obtained at least one challenge–response transcript from the victim, he can exhaustively search through all PINs up to a certain length by repeatedly verifying the correctness of the PIN guesses using the transcript. Once the correct PIN is found, the attacker not only knows the correct initialization key but also the link and encryption keys and, consequently, can eavesdrop on encrypted communication between the victim devices.

Shaked and Wool (2005) described optimizations for the PIN cracking and discussed methods to force devices to repeat the pairing process since obtaining a challenge–response transcript requires for an attacking device to be in proximity of the victim device upon exchange of the messages.

## Location Attacks

The second type of attack described by Jakobsson and Wetzel (2001) concerns the disclosure of location information of victim devices. By capturing information that uniquely identifies or that can be traced back to a certain Bluetooth device, an attacker can easily record crucial traffic and movement patterns in his neighborhood of interest. The Bluetooth identities may eventually be mapped to human identities using additional information available through other contexts such as, for example, consumers disclosing their identity by paying for a purchase by credit card.

Jakobsson and Wetzel (2001) described two types of attacks violating location privacy. The first attack exploits the fact that devices in discoverable mode will always respond to inquiry messages transmitting their identity—that is, their unique Bluetooth device address—in the clear on the baseband. An attacker can therefore determine the whereabouts (location and movements) of victim devices by maintaining geographically distributed devices that continuously inquire about all devices entering within their reach and recording the identities given in the responses. Consequently, an attacker can easily establish timing, traveling, and moving patterns, such as to what devices appeared where at what time, and which devices were in close proximity to each other on a repeated basis or have traveled together to certain locations or for extended periods of time. Gehrmann and Nyberg (2001) described a similar attack for devices that are in connectable mode. Upon recognizing its DAC, a victim device will reveal its presence by responding with its DAC to a paging message.

For the first attack to succeed, the victim device is required to be in discoverable or connectable mode. By contrast, the second attack described by Jakobsson and Wetzel (2001), which violates location privacy, works regardless of what mode a victim device is in. It is solely based on the fact that once devices have established a piconet, when communicating, these devices will address each other using a particular CAC. The CAC is associated with each message transmitted in the piconet. An attacker can easily intercept messages along with the corresponding CACs by eavesdropping on the baseband. As a consequence, an attacker can monitor victim devices based on the CAC because it is deterministically computed from the master unit's unique Bluetooth device address. Even though there is no 1–1 mapping between a particular CAC and a Bluetooth device address (i.e., several Bluetooth device addresses map to the same CAC), this limitation is of theoretical interest only because the probability of two randomly selected devices colliding is very small.

## Man-in-the-Middle Attacks

Jakobsson and Wetzel (2001) described man-in-the-middle attacks (RSA Laboratories, 2005) in which the attacker contacts two victim devices, pretending to be the other Bluetooth device. Consequently, each Bluetooth device believes that the other device initiated the communication and, upon successful connection setup, both devices believe they are communicating with the other. In fact, each device is communicating with the attacker who controls the message flow between the attacked devices. Jakobsson and Wetzel (2001) suggested that the attacked devices either both be slaves or masters to avoid jamming on the radio link. In case either device requests link encryption, it is assumed that the attacker has previously obtained the link key. Alternatively, the attacker can enforce the negotiation of a new link key by having the devices pretend to each other that the key has been lost.

Kügler (2003) improved on these attacks in that victim devices do not have to take on the same roles. Although both devices use the same channel-hopping sequence, the attacker forces the devices to use a different offset in the sequence not only to avoid jamming but also to allow the interception and relay of communication. The attack exploits the fact that a paging device must send paging requests repeatedly because it is unknown to the paging device when the paged device will begin scanning for paging requests. By quickly replying to the original paging requests, an attacker can first establish a connection with the paging device and then do the same with the paged device. In the case of encrypted links, the man-in-the-middle attacker can manipulate ciphertexts employing methods introduced in Borisov, Goldberg, and Wagner (2001).

## Cipher Vulnerabilities

Attacks on the Bluetooth stream cipher $E_0$ are discussed in numerous sources (Armknecht, 2002; Armknecht & Krause, 2003; Courtois, 2003; Ekdahl & Johansson, 2000; Fluhrer & Lucks, 2001; Hermelin & Nyberg, 1999; Jakobsson & Wetzel, 2001; Krause, 2002). In Jakobsson and Wetzel (2001) two types of attacks are described. In the first one, an attacker guesses the contents of three smaller LFSRs and determines the content of the fourth one by reverse engineering. This type of attack was independently put forward by Saarinen (2001). The correctness of the guess is verified by comparing the resulting output string with the actual output. This method requires the knowledge of 128 bits of ciphertext and known plaintext. The complexity of the attack is in the order of $2^{100}$ operations.

The second attack is a birthday-type attack (Golić, 1997). In a precomputation phase, an attacker randomly selects a number of internal states of the cipher, computes the corresponding output keystream, and stores them in a database. Subsequently, observed keystreams are compared with the stored keystreams. A collision is expected with each the number of stored keystreams and the number of observed keystreams being in the order of $2^{66}$.

Further attacks on the Bluetooth encryption scheme have been published by Ekdahl and Johansson (2000) as well as Hermelin and Nyberg (1999). Both attacks show how to recover the initial state from the keystream generator. Whereas the attack by Hermelin and Nyberg (1999) requires $O(2^{64})$ work and the knowledge of $O(2^{64})$ keystream bits, Ekdahl and Johansson (2000) were able to reduce that to $O(2^{61})$ work and $O(2^{50})$ keystream bits by exploiting weak linear correlations between the outputs of the LFSRs and the actual keystream output. The main shortcoming of these attacks is that they require the knowledge of a very large amount of consecutive keystream output.

Subsequently, Fluhrer and Lucks (2001) published an analysis of the Bluetooth encryption scheme that allows an attacker to determine the cipher key from known keystream bits. If 132 keystream bits are available, the attack runs in time $O(2^{84})$. This can be reduced to $O(2^{73})$ at the cost of knowing $2^{43}$ keystream bits. In guessing initial states of the cipher and checking for consistency, the attack takes the same basic approach as in Jakobsson and Wetzel (2001) and Saarinen (2001). However, in taking advantage of additional dependencies in the stream cipher, Fluhrer and Lucks (2001) were able to improve the performance of the attack. The most efficient attack known in this context to date was devised by Krause (2002). The attack derives the internal state using 128 keystream bits and $O(2^{77})$ operations.

Lu et al. (2005) first presented a practical attack on Bluetooth encryption. Their best conditional correlation attack determines the encryption key for two-level $E_0$ with $2^{38}$ computations using the first 24 bits of $2^{23.8}$ frames. The attack exploits a flaw in the resynchronization of $E_0$ (see Lu and Vaudenenay, 2004a, 2004b).

Armknecht (2002) introduced an alternative attack on the keystream generator by solving a system of nonlinear equations over the finite field GF(2). Using linearization, the system can be transformed into a system of linear equations with at most $2^{24.056}$ unknowns that can be solved in practice with about $2^{70.341}$ operations. In Armknecht and Krause (2003) this was later reduced to $2^{23.07}$ unknowns and $2^{67.58}$ operations. The major drawback of this attack, however, is that it is not yet known how many keystream bits are needed to obtain sufficiently many linearly independent equations. Courtois (2003) showed that given $2^{23.4}$ consecutive keystream bits, some of the equations exhibit a recursive structure that can be exploited to mount the actual attack with $2^{49}$ operations (assuming a precomputation step in the order of $O(2^{28})$).

## Other Vulnerabilities

**Lack of Integrity Protection.** The Bluetooth specification does not provide for any cryptographic mechanisms that could be used to ensure that data has not been altered during transmission without authorization. Although the cyclic redundancy check (CRC) defined in the specification can be successfully employed to detect random transmission errors, it does not provide adequate protection against deliberate modifications (Karygiannis & Owens, 2002). Borisov et al. (2001) have shown how data and the corresponding CRC can be manipulated accordingly.

**Battery Draining.** Because of the ad hoc nature of the Bluetooth technology, a malicious device can carry out a DoS type attack. Keeping a victim device active—for example, by continuously sending requests to the victim device—will quickly drain the battery of the victim device (Karygiannis & Owens, 2002).

**Bluesnarf, Bluejacking, Backdoor, and Bluebug.** Recently, some serious flaws in the authorization and data transfer mechanisms of some Bluetooth-enabled devices have been reported (Digital, 2003). These vulnerabilities are not due to weaknesses in the Bluetooth security mechanisms but result from design errors and implementation flaws.

In Bluejacking, the attacker abuses the pairing protocol in that a user-definable name field (up to 248 characters) is used to pass on unwanted messages. The Bluesnarf attack allows a malicious device to connect to a victim device and gain access to data even in restricted areas without alerting the owner of the victim device. In a Backdoor attack, an attacker first establishes a trust relationship with a victim device and then deletes it from the list of paired devices. Consequently, the attacker can continue to access any of the resources it had used before. The Bluebug attack establishes a serial profile connection to the victim device, thus allowing an attacker to make unauthorized phone calls, read and send short message service (SMS) messages, and connect to data services.

## Discussion on the Feasibility of the Attacks

The attack by Lu, Meier, and Vaudenay is the only practical attack on the Bluetooth encryption known to date. Because of their complexity, all other attacks on the Bluetooth stream cipher described so far are of theoretical interest only.

By contrast, all the location attacks are practical attacks. They can be carried out easily because they require only the recording of information sent in the clear over the wireless Bluetooth link.

The feasibility of the impersonation and eavesdropping attacks is contingent on the transmission of the PIN in the clear or the use of short PINs. In practical applications, this is not likely to impose any limitations. Typically, a PIN consists of four decimal digits. This is due to the fact that in case the PINs are not sent over the wireless link, a user will have to enter them manually into at least one of the devices. Entering long PINs is not just cumbersome, but doing so without errors is nontrivial (Gehrmann, Mitchell, & Nyberg, 2004).

## COUNTERMEASURES TO THE VULNERABILITIES IN BLUETOOTH SECURITY

Since the discovery of the attacks on the Bluetooth Security mechanisms, various countermeasures and improvements have been proposed (e.g., Bluetooth, 2002; Gehrmann, Mitchell, & Nyberg, 2004; Gehrmann & Nyberg, 2001; Hermelin & Nyberg, 1999; International Organization for Standardization, 2003; Jakobsson 2001; Jakobsson & Wetzel, 2001; Jakobsson & Wetzel, 2003; Kügler, 2003; Larsson, 2001; Xydis, 2001). However, aside from recommending the employment of application layer security as well as the use of sufficiently long and robust PINs, encouraging the pairing of devices to be done in only private places, and discouraging the use of unit keys as link keys (Bluetooth, 2002, 2003; Xydis, 2001), any of the other discussed improvements have yet to be implemented in the Bluetooth specification (Bluetooth, 2003). They include methods to protect unit keys, prevent location and man-in-the-middle attacks, as well as improvements for establishing the link keys. This section briefly describes the suggested solutions. For a detailed description, refer to the respective publications.

**Protecting Unit Keys.** Jakobsson and Wetzel (2001) addressed the problem that devices with limited memory resources disclose their unit keys to other devices during pairing. To counteract the risk of impersonation, the authors proposed using the device's unit key as well as the Bluetooth device address of the other party as seed to a pseudorandom generator. The generated keys do not need to be stored because they can be recomputed easily whenever needed.

**Pseudonyms to Avoid Location Attacks.** The location attack described earlier takes advantage of the fact that either the unique Bluetooth device address or an access code that is deterministically generated from the unique Bluetooth device address is transmitted in the clear on a regular basis. Introducing an *anonymity mode* (Gehrmann & Nyberg, 2001; Jakobsson & Wetzel, 2001; Jakobsson & Wetzel, 2003) allows the use of random pseudonyms $BD\_ADDR\_ALIAS$ instead of the unique Bluetooth device address $BD\_ADDR$ to avoid the attack.

**Preventing Man-in-the-Middle Attacks.** The man-in-the-middle attacks described in Jakobsson and Wetzel (2001) can be addressed by implementing policies strictly governing which device may take what role (master versus slave) in which situations. The attacks described by Kügler (2003) can be avoided by enforcing the synchronization of the devices not just to the same hopping sequence but also to the same offset within the hopping sequence. This requires the perfect synchronization of the slaves to the clock of the master device.

**Improved Link-Key Establishment.** The Bluetooth specification (Bluetooth, 2001, 2003) indicates that the procedure for establishing the link key could be improved by using methods to exchange and establish keys on higher layers of the protocol stack. These methods have not yet been specified. With manual key exchange (Gehrmann, Mitchell, & Nyberg, 2004; Gehrmann & Nyberg, 2001; International Organization for Standardization, 2003; Jakobsson, 2001; Larsson, 2001) and key exchange based on an infrastructure (Gehrmann & Nyberg, 2001), two possible approaches have been discussed in literature. The latter suggests the use of the IEEE 802.1X standard (which includes mechanisms for key exchange and authentication based on the IETF Extensible Authentication Protocol (EAP)) to allow the reuse of existing key infrastructures for Bluetooth. The manual key-exchange methods allow for ad hoc key establishment and use manual transfers of data to authenticate a key exchange such as, for example, the Diffie-Hellman key exchange.

## COMPARISON OF SECURITY MECHANISMS IN BLUETOOTH AND IEEE 802.11B

The two technologies, Bluetooth and IEEE 802.11b, have similarities in that both are wireless technologies operating in the 2.4-GHz band. The technologies are different because the focus of 802.11b is on a planned, fixed infrastructure, such as local area network access, whereas Bluetooth is a low-cost and low-power technology focusing on spontaneous wireless communication with other devices in smaller personal area networks. Furthermore, Bluetooth has a smaller range than 802.11b. Despite the differences, the technologies are compared more and more often (e.g., Oraskari, 2001; Silicon Wave, 2001; Xydis, 2001) and not seldomly compete with each other. In particular, this also extends to the security in both technologies.

The chapters on "Wireless Networks Standards and Protocols (802.11)", "WEP Security", and "Cracking WEP" introduce and discuss the security mechanisms and shortcomings of the IEEE 802.11b standard in great detail. The two security shortcomings that are most commonly referred to when comparing Bluetooth and 802.11 concern the problems of eavesdropping and false authentication.

**Eavesdropping.** In IEEE 802.11b, originally the Wired Equivalent Privacy (WEP) algorithm was used to encrypt the data on the wireless link. The core component of WEP is the stream cipher RC4, which is widely used in software applications. It is the mode of operation that is used in WEP that makes RC4 insecure. In the 802.11b implementation, each mobile device shares a secret key (the WEP key) with an access point. (In practice, all mobile stations and the access points often share one common secret key.) RC4 is initialized with the WEP key and a public 24-bit initialization vector. The RC4-generated keystream is XORed with the plaintext to generate the ciphertext. Knowing a plaintext–ciphertext pair, an attacker can determine the corresponding keystream. XORing two ciphertexts that were encrypted using the same IV yields the XOR of the two plaintexts. Because of the low entropy of most messages, it is then possible to infer information about the

two plaintext messages. Even though the IV is changed on a message basis, a busy access point will repeat using the same IV within a short period of time (Borisov et al., 2001). Furthermore, Fluhrer, Mantin, and Shamir (2001) described an attack on the RC4 key scheduling algorithm in WEP that allows the complete recovery of the shared secret key. It should be noted that in response to these attacks, the Wi-Fi Alliance introduced the Wi-Fi Protected Access (WPA), which includes the Temporal Key Integrity Protocol (TKIP) to replace WEP (as well as 802.1X-based user authentication).

As described earlier, Bluetooth uses the stream cipher $E_0$, and the encryption keys are derived from the shared link keys of the communicating devices. Although, the attacks on the cipher exhibit a complexity higher than the one for the attacks on RC4, this nevertheless bears the potential risk of more efficient attacks (Jakobsson and Wetzel, 2001). Furthermore, Bluetooth is vulnerable to attacks during pairing that eventually allow eavesdropping. If an attacker can record, guess, or steal the PIN, he will be able to derive the link key and thus determine the encryption keys.

**Authentication.** Like Bluetooth, 802.11b supports device authentication by means of a challenge–response protocol. Upon receiving a random 128-bit challenge, the claimant computes the response by XORing the challenge with a string formed by the shared secret and a public initialization vector. By recording both the challenge and the response and XORing them together, an attacker can easily determine the string formed by the shared secret and the public initialization vector. This information can subsequently be used to impersonate the victim device (Arbaugh, Shankar, & Wan, 2002).

As discussed earlier, the claimant applies the $E_1$ algorithm (which is based on SAFER+) to the shared link key, the Bluetooth device address, and the challenge to compute a 128-bit-long result. Only the 32 most significant bits of the result will be sent to the verifier. An attacker will be able to impersonate a victim device if he can determine the respective link key (e.g., by stealing, guessing, or recording the PIN during pairing). Clearly, if unit keys are used as link keys, all devices knowing the link key can impersonate the device to which this unit key belongs.

## CONCLUSION

The discussions in this and other chapters in this book show that both IEEE 802.11b and Bluetooth have security shortcomings that must be addressed. While many researchers in both the IEEE 802.11b community as well as the Bluetooth Security SIG are continuously working on improving the security mechanisms in these standards, this undertaking has proved to be very difficult.

## GLOSSARY

**Bluetooth** A short-range wireless communication technology which operates in the unlicensed 2.4-GHz band.

**Bluetooth Device Address (BD_ADDR)**  A 48-bit address that uniquely characterizes a Bluetooth device.

**Channel Access Code (CAC)**  A code that identifies a particular piconet. It is derived from the master's Bluetooth device address.

**Connectable Device**  A Bluetooth device that will respond to pairing requests.

**Cyclic Redundancy Check (CRC)**  The method used to detect random transmission errors.

**Device Access Code (DAC)**  A code that is used during paging to address a device. It is determined from the master's unique BD_ADDR.

**Discoverable Bluetooth Device**  A Bluetooth device that will respond to inquiry messages.

**Inquiry Access Code (IAC)**  A code that is used in inquiry procedures.

**IEEE 802.11b**  Specification for wireless local area networks operating in the 2.4 GHz band, providing an 11 Mbps transmission rate.

**Impersonation**  An attack which allows a malicious Bluetooth device to produce correctly formated and encrypted information on behalf of a victim device or to eavesdrop on the conversation between two or more devices.

**Link Key**  A secret key that is known by two devices and used to to authenticate the devices to each other, respectively, determine the common secret encryption key.

**Location Attack**  An attack that allows an attacker to identify and determine geographic location information of a victim device.

**Man-In-the-Middle Attack**  An attack in which the attacker intercepted the keys and is impersonating the victim devices.

**Master**  The device in a piconet that provides the synchronization reference, that is, the common clock and frequency hopping pattern.

**Piconet**  A Bluetooth wireless local area network that consists of one master and up to seven active slaves.

**Scatternet**  A group of piconets with connections among various piconets.

**Slave**  Any other device in a piconet that is not the master but is connected to the master of the piconet.

## CROSS REFERENCES

See *Bluetooth Technology; Encryption Basics; Wireless Network Standards and Protocol (802.11); WEP Security; Cracking WEP.*

## REFERENCES

Arbaugh, W., Shankar, N. & Wan, Y. C. J. (2002). Your 802.11 wireless network has no clothes. IEEE Wireless Communications Magazine, Vol. 9, pp. 44–51, Dec. 2002.

Armknecht, F. (2002). A linearization attack on the Bluetooth key stream generator. Retrieved from http://eprint.iacr.org/2002/191

Armknecht, F., & Krause, M. (2003). Algebraic attacks on combiners with memory. *Lecture Notes in Computer Science: Volume 2729. Proceedings of Crypto 2003* (pp. 162–175). New York: Springer-Verlag.

Bluetooth. (1999a). Specification of the Bluetooth System. Specification Volume 1, v.1.0B. Retrieved from http://www.bluetooth.com

Bluetooth. (1999b). Specification of the Bluetooth System. Specification Volume 2, v.1.0B. Retrieved from http://www.bluetooth.com

Bluetooth. (2001). Specification of the Bluetooth System. Specification v.1.1. Retrieved from http://www.bluetooth.com

Bluetooth. (2003). Specification of the Bluetooth System. Specification v.1.2. Retrieved from http://www.bluetooth.com

Bluetooth FAQ—Security. Retrieved from http://www.bluetooth.com/bluetoothguide/faq/5.asp

Bluetooth SIG Security Expert Group. (2002). Bluetooth Security White Paper. Retrieved from http://www.bluetooth.com

Borisov, N., Goldberg, I., & Wagner, D. (2001) Intercepting mobile communications: The insecurity of 802.11. *ACM MOBICOM 2001: Proceedings of the 7th Annual International Conference on Mobile Computing and Networking* (pp. 176–194).

Courtois, N. (2003). Fast algebraic attacks on stream ciphers with linear feedback. *Lecture Notes in Computer Science: Volume 2729. Proceedings of Crypto 2003* (pp. 176–194). New York: Springer-Verlag.

Digital, A. L. (2003). Retrieved from http://www.bluestumbler.org

Ekdahl, P., & Johansson, T. (2000). Some results on correlations in the Bluetooth stream cipher. *Proceedings of the 10th Joint Conference on Communications and Coding* (pp. 210–224).

Fluhrer, S. R., Mantin, I., & Shamir, A. (2001). Weaknesses in the key scheduling algorithm of RC4. *Lecture Notes in Computer Science: Volume 2259. Proceedings of SAC 2001* (pp. 1–24). New York: Springer-Verlag.

Fluhrer, S. R., & Lucks, S. (2001). Analysis of the $E_0$ encryption system. *Lecture Notes in Computer Science: Volume 2259. Proceedings of SAC 2001* (pp. 38–48). New York: Springer-Verlag.

Gehrmann, C., Mitchell, C. J., & Nyberg, K., (2004). Manual authentication for wireless devices. *CryptoBytes*, 7, 29–37. Bedford, MA: RSA.

Gehrmann C., & Nyberg, K. (2001). Enhancements to Bluetooth baseband security. *Proceedings of Nordic Workshop on Secure IT Systems* (pp. 39–53).

Gehrmann, C., Persson, J., & Smeets, B. (2004). *Bluetooth security*. London: Artech House.

Golić, J. Dj. (1997). Cryptanalysis of alleged A5 stream cipher. *Lecture Notes in Computer Science: Volume 1233. Proceedings of Eurocrypt 1997* (pp. 239–255). New York: Springer-Verlag.

Hermelin, M., & Nyberg, K. (1999). Correlation properties of the bluetooth combiner. *Lecture Notes in Computer Science: Volume 1787. Proceedings of ICISC 1999* (pp. 17–29). New York: Springer-Verlag.

International Organization for Standardization. (2003). Information technology—security techniques—entity authentication. Part 6: Mechanisms using manual data transfer (ISO/IEC 1st CD9798-6). Geneva.

Jakobsson, M. (2001). Method and Apparatus for Immunizing against offline Dictionary Attacks. U.S. Patent Application 60/283,996.

Jakobsson, M., & Wetzel, S. (2001). Security weaknesses in Bluetooth. *Lecture Notes in Computer Science: Volume 2020. Proceedings of CT-RSA 2001* (pp. 176–191). New York: Springer-Verlag.

Jakobsson, M., & Wetzel, S. (2003). Method and apparatus for ensuring security of users of Bluetooth™ -enabled devices. U.S. Patent 6,574,455.

Karygiannis, T., & Owens, L. (2002). Wireless network security: 802.11, Bluetooth and handheld devices. National Institute of Standards and Technology (Publication No. 800-48). Retrieved from http://csrc.nist.gov/publications/nistpubs/800_48/NIST_SP_800–48.pdf

Krause, M. (2002). BDD-based cryptanalysis of keystream generators. *Lecture Notes in Computer Science: Volume 2332. Proceedings of Eurocrypt 2002* (pp. 222–237). New York: Springer-Verlag.

Kügler, D. (2003). Man-in-the-middle attacks on Bluetooth. *Lecture Notes in Computer Science: Volume 2742. Proceedings of FC 2003* (pp. 149–161). New York: Springer-Verlag.

Larsson, J.-O. (2001). Higher layer key exchange techniques for Bluetooth security. *Open Group Conference*.

Lu, Y., Meier, W., & Vaudenay, S. (2005). The conditional correlation attack: A practical attack on Bluetooth encryption. *Lecture Notes in Computer Science: Volume 3621. Proceedings of Crypto 2005* (pp. 97–117). New York: Springer-Verlag.

Lu, Y., & Vaudenay, S. (2004a). Faster correlation attack on Bluetooth keystream generator E0. *Lecture Notes in Computer Science: Volume 3152. Proceedings of Crypto 2004* (pp. 407–425). New York: Springer-Verlag.

Lu Y., & Vaudenay, S. (2004b). Cryptanalysis of the Bluetooth keystream generator two-level E0. *Lecture Notes in Computer Science: Volume 3329. Proceedings of Asiacrypt 2004* (pp. 483–499). New York: Springer-Verlag.

Müller, T. (Ed.). (1999). Bluetooth security architecture (white paper, revision 1.0), Bluetooth SIG. Retrieved from http://www.bluetooth.com

Oraskari, J. 2001. Bluetooth versus WLAN IEEE 802.11x. (Technical Report). Helsinki, University of Technology, Technical Report.

RSA Laboratories. (2005). Frequently asked questions about today's cryptography. Retrieved from http://www.rsasecurity.com/rsalabs/faq/

Saarinen, M. (2000). Retrieved from http://www.mail-archive.com/cryptography-research%40senator-bedfellow.mit.edu/msg00110.html

Shaked, Y., & Wool, A. (2005). Cracking the Bluetooth PIN. *Proceedings of the 3rd International Conference on Mobile Systems, Applications, and Services* (pp. 39–50). Seattle: ACM and USENIX.

Silicon Wave. (2001). Bluetooth and 802.11 compared. (White Paper). Retrieved from http://whitepapers.silicon.com/0,39024759,60063845p-3900066.9.00.html

The official Bluetooth SIG Web site; Retrieved from http://www.bluetooth.com

Vainio, J. T. (2000). Bluetooth security. *Proceedings of Helsinki University of Technology, Telecommunications Software and Multimedia Laboratory, Seminar on Internetworking: Ad Hoc Networking*. Retrieved from http://www.niksula.cs.hut.fi/~jiitv/bluesec.html

Xydis, T. G. (2001). Security comparison: Bluetooth communications vs. 802.11. (white paper Bluetooth SIG). Retrieved from http://www.bluetooth.com

# Cracking WEP

Pascal Meunier, *Purdue University*

## INTRODUCTION

The Burlington Northern and Santa Fe Railway Company (BNSF) U.S. railroad uses Wi-Fi (wireless fidelity) to run "driverless" trains (Smith, 2003). Home Depot (Luster, 2002), BestBuy (Computerworld, 2002; Sandoval, 2002), and Lowes (Ashenfelter, 2003) were famous for being targeted by hackers sitting in the parking lots and eavesdropping on traffic to cash registers, and even accessing their networks through their wireless networks. The U.S. Navy was reportedly interested in deploying 802.11b technology to control warships (Cox, 2003). There are many possible functional benefits of using wireless LAN technology; in most cases, however, a successful malicious attack could have disastrous consequences. The designers of the 802.11b standard provided the wired equivalent privacy (WEP) as a defense.

The details of the 802.11b standard were revealed to the world much as a surprise. Although the development process followed standard IEEE practice and was "open" as per the limited IEEE meaning, it failed to produce a specification without vulnerabilities. One reason is that instead of using free "Request for Comments" (RFC), documentation for the 802.11b standard was available for reading only for people with deep pockets. The latest design documents were available only to a few paying participants (i.e., companies) at a moderately high cost (more than a thousand dollars for a "subscription"). Old documentation (if you could figure out what you needed to order and how to order it from the IEEE Web site) was available only with fees of several hundred dollars. Some "standards" are little more than editorial instructions to add, modify, or delete sections of the 802.11-1999 standard to

re-create the standard or a "kit" to assemble your own documentation. PDF format downloads required agreeing with restrictive terms of use. These factors made academic or third-party reviews of the standard difficult, especially when compared to the "RFC" model.

The 802.11 committee knew internally about several security issues that were discussed privately (Walker, 2000) but "lived in sin" (sic) without correcting them (Walker, 2001). The Institute of Electrical and Electronics Engineers made the 802 standards "available" to the public for free in mid-2001, with the limitations that (a) they are only free after they are 6 months old; (b) drafts are still for sale; and (c) the documents are made available under a license prohibiting redistribution, and IEEE reserves the right to withdraw them at any time, and thus using them as references is problematic. The access difficulties that were in place during the design of 802.11b are similarly present for the new 802 standards; free public access is only available after it's too late.

The goal of WEP was to provide wired-equivalent protection. Regardless of arguments as to what is "wired equivalent," it is clear that the protection was insufficient for many uses (for which it provided a false sense of security) but better than nothing. However, surveys throughout the world show that only about a quarter to a third of wireless access points use WEP (Hamilton, 2002; Pickard & Cracknell, 2001, 2003; Tam, Shek, & Wo Sang, 2002). It is likely that many replaced WEP altogether with virtual private networks (VPN) solutions, but most simply didn't bother enabling WEP because it is not enabled by default. Therefore, this chapter applies to a third or less of deployed access points and should be read by those considering enabling WEP. Because 802.11b has been widely deployed, a lot of hardware (mainly access points) is not upgradable, and budgets are tight, WEP will persist for some time.

For the purposes of this chapter, WEP will have been "cracked" whenever one of its uses will have been defeated; therefore, there are many ways of cracking WEP, depending on the objective and the network configuration. The reader is refered to the "WEP Security" chapter of this book for the detailed description of the security objectives of WEP and its vulnerabilities. The main points of these vulnerabilities are briefly reviewed here as necessary for the discussions with a focus on scenarios, strategies, and tactics for efficiently breaking WEP and the countermeasures that apply. The reader is reminded that there are easier and more effective ways to wreak havoc on wireless networks than completely cracking WEP or wireless protected access (WPA), as described in "Hacking Techniques in Wireless Networks" of this *Handbook* and demonstrated by Bellardo (2003).

Although this chapter could be seen as a hacker tutorial, the plethora of automated cracking tools demonstrates that these tricks are already known. This chapter should help convince the reader of the practicality of cracking WEP because of defects in the standard as well as implementation and configuration defects. Awareness of these issues should help to improve the security of deployed networks.

## WIRELESS THREATS

The wireless medium is characterized by the near-impossibility of establishing a clear physical security boundary. Bigger and better antennas can be used to overcome distance or a weak signal. Moreover, a malicious person can direct high-energy signals toward a wireless node to disrupt communications. As a result, the medium is open to most attackers in the neighborhood of a wireless node. The use of directional antennas and the minimum power required for communications (several manufacturers of 802.11b equipment allow the power to be adjusted) are sensible precautions for minimizing these risks. The location of the access points can be chosen to provide minimal power outside the area physically secured ("spillage"), and so on; the reader is referred to the chapter "Wireless Threats and Attacks" in this *Handbook*. However, the open nature of the medium mandates cryptographic mechanisms to defend against the following threats.

### Denial-of-Service Attacks

Flooding the medium with data is an obvious attack given its open nature. More clever flood attacks will attempt to get wireless nodes to respond or will attempt to exhaust resources on the access points or other nodes.

### Integrity Attacks

If packets can be captured (and preferably prevented from reaching their destination) and then reinjected in the medium, they can be modified to change their meaning. This can be used to redirect traffic for later analysis or make the traffic go through an unencrypted network (e.g., as part of cracking WEP), for replay attacks, or for man-in-the-middle attacks. WEP should prevent the modification of frames.

### Confidentiality Attacks

This is the same as eavesdropping, or "sniffing." Presumably the traffic contains passwords, authentication tokens, and other confidential information such as illnesses, beliefs, preferences, relationships, or banking information. Network cards typically support a mode of operation called "promiscuous." In this mode, all frames available on the medium are captured. Even if the driver provided by the vendor does not allow this mode, alternative drivers supporting this mode are available for most wireless cards. WEP encryption should prevent the contents of frames from being revealed to bystanders (aka sniffers) who obtain the ciphertext.

### Authentication and Accountability Attacks

Mechanisms to defend against these issues will establish some means of authenticating users. Attacks can then be made against the authentication mechanism. Moreover, attacks launched against third parties from the wireless network, or against other users, will be attributed respectively to the owner of the network or to a user whose authentication secrets were stolen. This provides anonymity for the attacker and evades or reassigns accountability for the attacks. This is a significant threat for business models where anonymous consumers (e.g., travelers in airports, users in hotels and fast food and coffee shops) are provided with wireless Internet access.

## DESIGN WEAKNESSES

The 802.11b standard and its implementations have several possible layers of security. Unfortunately, many of these are fairly weak and provide nearly equal inconvenience to users and attackers; good security mechanisms should inconvenience attackers much more than users.

WEP is a stream cipher, using RC-4 to produce a stream of bytes that are XORed with the plaintext. The input to the stream cipher algorithm is an "initial value" (IV) sent in plaintext and a secret key. The IV is 24 bits long. The length of the secret is either 40 or 104 bits, for a total length for the IV and secret of 64 or 128 bits. Marketing publicized the larger number, implying that the secret was a 64- or 128-bit number, in a classical case of deceptive advertising (24 fewer bits make the encryption 16.8 million times weaker than advertised!).

Many problems in WEP derive from the fact that given an IV and secret, the stream of bytes produced is always the same. Whereas a stream can be of any size in theory (up to a point when it will repeat), WEP never needs more than 1,500 bytes (the maximum Ethernet frame size). A sequence of bytes of some finite, size, part of a stream produced with a cipher, an IV, and a secret, is called a pad. The 24-bit IV provides 16,777,216 ($256 ^3$) possible streams, so all the WEP pads can fit inside 25,165,824,000 bytes (23.4 GB). If an IV is ever reused, then the pad is the same, which leads to some interesting attacks (described later);

knowing all the pads is equivalent to knowing the 40- or 104-bit secret. These weaknesses are present regardless of whether the secret is 40- or 104-bits long. Furthermore, the improper use of RC4 in WEP results in the problem known as "weak IVs" (see "Key Recovery Attacks" later in the chapter); when weak IVs are used, information about the secret can be leaked.

Cracking WEP can be accomplished through passive or active attacks (see the "Wireless Threats and Attacks" chapter). Active attacks increase the risk of being detected but are more capable. An active attack can be used to stimulate traffic, in order to collect more pads and uses of weak IVs, or can redirect and modify traffic. Some attacks described herein require only one pad.

## SSID, BSSID, ESSID

A collection of stations (or nodes) communicating wirelessly together is known as a *basic service set* (BSS). To differentiate between other in-range BSSs and their own, stations use an identifier called BSSID, which has the format of a MAC address. When there is a dedicated access point (AP; this situation is called the *infrastructure mode*), the BSSID is usually the MAC address of the AP. Sophisticated APs have the capability of handling several BSSs with different BSSIDs and appear as several virtual APs. In the absence of a dedicated access point (ad hoc mode), the stations use a random number as the BSSID.

The *service set ID* (SSID) is commonly known as the network name. ESSID is sometimes used to refer to the SSID used in the context of an *extended service set* (ESS). An ESS is composed of several BSSs joined together. This network composition is transparent for the end user, who is only aware of the SSID; however, the traffic in an ESS may be using several BSSIDs if there are several APs in it.

To help users locate available networks, the SSID is regularly broadcasted using "beacon frames." A security option offered by several vendors is the "closed network." The choice of this term was highly misleading, because "closed network" is also used to define networks that are protected by various means so that they only allow access to authorized users. However, in the context of 802.11b, it simply means that the SSID is not broadcast anymore (cf. vendors manuals; this is easily confirmed by using a sniffer; see also Arbaugh, Shankar, & Wan, 2001). This is an attempt at security through obscurity, to make the presence of the network less obvious. With or without WEP, however, a BSSID can be found as soon as a single frame is sent by any member station. This is sufficient to start accumulating information for cracking WEP, even if the matching SSID is unknown. Moreover, the mapping between SSIDs and BSSIDs is revealed by several management frames that are not encrypted. This issue is independent from other 802.11b security issues such as cracking WEP.

Stations looking for an access point send the SSID they are looking for in a "probe request." Access points can answer with a "probe reply" frame, which contains the SSID and BSSID pair. Moreover, stations wanting to become part of a BSS send an association request frame, which also contains the SSID/BSSID pair in clear text. So do reassociation requests (described later) and their response.

Therefore, the SSID remains secret only on closed networks with no activity.

## MAC Address–Based Access and Association Control

This security mechanism is not part of WEP but is often mentioned as mitigating WEP weaknesses. The way it is defeated enables several other attacks described later in this chapter. It is therefore appropriate to discuss it. The objective of this mechanism is to establish a list of hardware authorized to use the wireless network and to deny access to all others. Each Ethernet (and wireless) interface is given a unique MAC address at the time of manufacture, with blocks of addresses assigned to specific manufacturers (IEEE, 2004). The MAC address is then used for addressing packets. It was thought that screening packets for those containing an authorized MAC address would only allow authorized hardware to associate with a BSS. However, the MAC addresses are sent in plaintext and aren't secret; it is fairly easy to create a program that will collect all the MAC addresses in use in a BSS (Meunier et al., 2002; see the tools in the section "Implementation Weaknesses"). The question is whether a wireless card can be made to use another MAC address instead of the one assigned to it. This depends on the drivers; those provided by the manufacturers sometimes allow it. However, freely available operating systems typically have drivers capable of doing so (Meunier et al., 2002). Therefore, defeating MAC-based access control is not difficult.

## Authentication and Association

The 802.11b standard (see IEEE 802.11-1999 and 802.11b-1999; both documents are needed as 802.11b-1999 is really a set of editorial changes to 802.11-1999) specifies that to become part of a BSS, a station must first authenticate itself to the network (the authentication mechanism is determined by the access point) and then request association to a specific access point (see sections 5.4.2 and 5.4.3 of IEEE 802.11-1999). The access point is in charge of authentication and accepting the association of the station. However, as in 3.2, the MAC address is trusted as giving the correct identity of the station or access point. There is no way for a station to know whether it is talking to a proper access point; that is, the access points do not authenticate themselves to the stations. Likewise, an access point doesn't know whether a message really originated from a given station. Therefore, any station can impersonate another station or access point and attack or interfere with the authentication and association mechanisms. The impersonation is trivial because the identification (source and destination) fields of the frames are not protected or verifiable in any way.

One type of management frame sent by access points is the disassociation and deauthentication frame (see the section IEEE 802.11-1999 later in the chapter). A station receiving one of those frames must redo the authentication and association processes if it wishes to communicate again. Therefore, with a single short frame, an attacker can delay the transmission of data and require the station and real access point to redo these processes, which take several frames to perform. This is an asymmetric denial-of-service vulnerability. Its efficiency was demonstrated by Bellardo (2003), although it seems to have been used in the black hat community before that report. The tool KisMAC implements it.

Authentication is done simply by a station providing the correct SSID or through shared key authentication. The optional shared key authentication process requires a station to encode with WEP a challenge text provided by the access point. An eavesdropper therefore gains both the plaintext and the ciphertext and can perform a known plaintext attack. Because WEP encryption uses the XOR operation, the ciphertext XORed with the plaintext yields the pad for the IV that was used. An eavesdropper can collect pads for each possible IV. By sending deauthentication frames regularly, an attacker can collect pads.

Note that the choice of the IV for the encryption is under the control of the client stations, so an eavesdropper needs only to listen to one authentication exchange to be able to authenticate itself as well, using the same IV and pad. An attacker can also pretend to be an access point and run a cycle of authentication and deauthentication to collect all the pads from other stations. Even if the real access points do not require shared-key authentication, the attacker can require it while faking being an access point. In this manner, an attacker can enlist stations into providing pads.

## Single Pad Attacks

Given the knowledge of a single IV and matching pad, an attacker can authenticate itself to an ESS or BSS, as described in the previous section. From that point a class of attacks can be launched, requiring only the knowledge of a single pad. Examples of this class of attacks are those that require only sending packets (without needing a response), such as ICMP Smurf or TCP (transfer control protocol) SYN floods, and for which receiving replies is not required. UDP services on any host reachable from the wireless network can also be attacked as UDP does not require the establishment of a connection; some UDP attacks do not require the capability to receive replies. For UDP services, if the length of the reply can tell success or failure, it is conceivable that brute-force attacks could be launched.

Single-pad attacks are also possible if replies can be received elsewhere by the attacker. This involves using a spoofed IP address; the packets injected by Malory will contain as source IP address, the address of the accomplice. The responses provided by the victims will be routed to the accomplice, who can then forward them to Malory, or Malory could be using a host with two interfaces. An interesting scenario is the one where an access point is connected to the local area network (LAN), behind a simple firewall that protects a resource from Malory. For simplicity, we assume that there is a single firewall separating the LAN from the Internet and that this firewall will reject incoming traffic to some combinations of {port, protocol, address} but will let through outgoing traffic, that is, from the inside network to an outside Internet provider address. Malory can inject packets on

the wireless network (and therefore the LAN) and collect the answers through the accomplice. The consequences of this attack are that UDP replies can be obtained unencrypted; TCP sessions can be established with sensitive services intended to be protected by the firewall; intrusion detection systems located at the firewall or in a demilitarized zone (see Glossary) will most likely ignore responses originating from internal hosts, so the attacks can proceed undetected at this level. For all practical purposes, in this configuration WEP has been completely defeated.

This attack can be prevented by providing a firewall for the wireless network with a rule to refuse packets that do not contain source addresses within the wireless network's range. A less elegant and flexible solution, but one that negates many advantages of hacking the wireless network, is to connect access points outside the Internet firewall (as if they were part of the Internet). This last solution can also negate some advantages of the wireless network for legitimate users.

Some access points allow administrative access from the wireless network or offer services on a UDP port (e.g., Apple base stations listen on UDP port 192). One-packet attacks directed against these services could exploit vulnerabilities to disable the access point or make it difficult to use. Administrative access to access points should be disabled from the wireless network. Not all access points support this feature.

## Pad Collection Attack

A problem with the shared-key authentication pad collection attacks is that the length of the pad is limited. With the knowledge of only an in-use valid IP address on the wireless network, pads of maximum length can be collected. This requires sending packets from the Internet to that IP, using an accomplice or a host with two network interfaces. To bypass any firewall, a number of fake responses can be sent; which ones work depends on the firewall. Malory chooses the plaintext and watches the corresponding encrypted wireless traffic for packets of matching length, which are destined to the BSSID (MAC address) of the host using that IP. The plaintext XORed with the cryptotext provides the pad for that IV. If the BSSID is not known, packets of various unlikely lengths can be sent until the attacker observes matching traffic destined to a single BSSID. Defense against this attack requires a stateful firewall, which will distinguish and block fake responses by keeping track of whether the destination host really made a prior request to the source IP of the packets. A variation of this allows a more sophisticated attacker to launch chosen plaintext attacks against the encryption itself; this attack may be useful against encryptions superseding WEP as well.

## Initial Value Collisions

IV collisions produce identical WEP keys when the same IV is used with the same shared secret key for more than one data frame; therefore, the pad is the same, which helps in cracking WEP. In practice, however, few attackers, if any, aim at collecting instances of collisions.

# Key Recovery Attacks

## Brute Force

Brute-force attacks on WEP are possible with commodity hardware against the 40-bit secret key, although it still requires patience (weeks) at the time of this writing, assuming a single computer is used. Brute-force attacks against 104-bit encryption are out of reach of current attackers, probably for the next 25 years or more.

## Dictionary Attacks

See "Implementation Weaknesses" subsections in "Newsham 21-Bit Attack" and "Dictionary Attacks" later in this chapter.

## Weak Keys, aka Weak IVs

This attack is based on the examination of how RC4 operates. In WEP, IVs and secret are simply concatenated to generate the RC4 encryption key. In a first stage, data structures in the RC4 algorithm are initialized based on the encryption key (IV + secret); this process is called the *key scheduling algorithm*. In a second stage, values in the data structures are used to produce pseudo-random numbers. The first byte output has a relatively simple dependency on the contents of that data structure (the "S" array); as a result, the first byte output leaks information. The attack is based on the finding that when certain keys (called "weak keys") are used in the key scheduling algorithm, the initial contents of the "S" array are not scrambled appropriately. Parts of the array are dependent on certain bits of the key, and it is possible for the first byte output to reveal those parts of the array. When this happens ("resolved condition"), the first byte output by RC4 is statistically biased toward a specific value (Fluhrer, Mantin, & Shamir, 2001). Because the secret part doesn't change and the IV is known, by passively (listening only) collecting the first byte of many packets, statistics reveal the bias. For statistical reasons, the number of packets needed to perform the attack is variable, and there is some uncertainty about the process. This attack can be performed not only on WEP but also on other applications in which RC4 is used in a similar manner.

The practicality of this attack was demonstrated by Stubblefield, Ionnidis, and Rubin (2001). To find the first byte produced by RC4, we need to XOR the first byte of the plaintext (which we don't know) and the first byte of the ciphertext (which can be sniffed). However, the first byte of wireless packets is almost always 0xAA because of 802.2 encapsulation of IP and ARP traffic (Stubblefield et al., 2001; RFC [Request for Comment] 1042). All that is necessary for this attack is the collection of the first encrypted octet of several million packets, with the matching IVs. The free tools WEPcrack (Rager, 2001) and Airsnort (Bruestle, Hegerle, & Snax, 2001a) implement this attack. About 5 million to 10 million packets need to be collected, after which the key can be recovered in under a second. Because this attack is passive, it can take a long time to succeed if there is little traffic. Some means of generating traffic, as described in the other sections, could be used in that case.

The time required for cracking WEP with this method is highly variable (Bruestle, Hegerle, & Snax, 2001b), in part because of random use of IVs and uneven distribution of weak IVs and because there is only a 5% chance that an IV and first encrypted byte will expose information about the secret. The KisMAC tool will attempt to find packets that cause responses and reinject them into the network to create more traffic and, it is hoped, collect weak IVs faster (Rossberg, 2003). This greatly speeds up cracking (an hour) but might trigger IDS alarms because it is abnormal traffic. Whereas this attack cannot be discovered, some wireless cards no longer generate weak IVs (given a secret, weak IVs can be listed; WEPcrack can do this). Some Lucent devices are known to have stopped generating weak IVs (Rossberg, 2003). This demonstrates that other vendors should be able to do the same and make this attack ineffective.

# Integrity Attacks

This is based on a CRC checksum weakness (Borisov, Goldberg, & Wagner, 2001) and is reviewed in the chapter on WEP security in this *Handbook*. Given the knowledge of the plaintext, a WEP-protected message can be changed at will. With only partial knowledge, that part of the message can be changed (Borisov et al., 2001). The proposed scenario in Borisov et al. (2001) is the interception of a message, somehow blocking its delivery (perhaps by pretending to be an access point), followed by modification and reinjection.

## Redirection Attack

Malory knows that Alice is exchanging information with Bob, and wants to eavesdrop on the WEP-encrypted exchange, perhaps capturing passwords or interesting information or in preparation for a replay attack. If Malory somehow knows or guesses the BSSID of Alice's station and either its IP address or the IP address of Bob's host somewhere on the Internet, he doesn't need to find the secret key or collect pads. Malory can sniff messages and change the destination IP address to a host he controls somewhere on the Internet (accomplice). If Malory knows the IP address of Alice's station, he waits for an incoming packet for Alice, changes the destination to that of the accomplice, and reinjects it. If Malory knows the IP address of Bob's host, he captures messages from Alice, changes the destination to that of the accomplice, and reinjects it until one of the messages was indeed for Bob. Malory then gets the missing IP address from the decrypted packets sent to his host.

Malory is now able to redirect all packets between Alice and Bob to his host; all packets have been decrypted on the way by an access point. Therefore, with only the knowledge of Alice's BSSID and one IP address and knowing nothing about IVs and secret key, the attacker can get a complete transcript of Alice's exchanges, including any passwords she sent. Perhaps she was doing her banking online, accessing her e-Bay account, or sending and receiving e-mail. Note that Bob could be another wireless user and does not need to be on the Internet; note also that any intervening firewalls (not shown) are likely to let this outgoing traffic through.

As a variation, assume that Malory knows only the network address of Alice's or Bob's host. He can redirect packets to a network where he has a sniffer configured to intercept these packets, so it is not necessary to know an exact IP address initially. Of course, if Malory's station can fake being an access point and get chosen by Alice's software (e.g., better signal), Malory is now able to change the exchanges completely and mount man-in-the-middle attacks. In addition, Malory can also collect pads because he has both the ciphertext and plaintext of all messages, in the future allowing him more convenient, stealthy, direct decoding and use of the wireless network, but this is a minor point because WEP has already been completely defeated. The only defense against this is to use another encryption layer, such as SSL (secure sockets layer; https) or ssh, or one of the replacements for WEP.

### WEP Proxy Attack

A variation on this and "single pad" attacks (discussed earlier) uses a host on the Internet that acts somewhat like a proxy for Malory. The scenario involves a resource protected from the Internet by a firewall but accessible from a wireless network. In this case, there would be a rule on the firewall that would prevent the resource from sending packets to the Internet, so a single-pad attack would fail. However, Malory knows a single pad and IV and with them sends packets to the resource or service without spoofing his IP address on the wireless network. Replies are then sent to his station, which is unable to decrypt the WEP packets. Malory modifies the destination and source IP addresses and the CRC checksum and then sends the packets to an accomplice or a host that he controls somewhere on the Internet. The firewall lets them through because the source IP address is not that of the protected resource. By accessing his host through another network connection (e.g., Malory is a competitor next door to Alice's company offices), Malory is able to conduct full TCP exchanges with the protected resource. A countermeasure for this scenario is placing the wireless access point outside the firewall, as if it were part of the Internet.

## IMPLEMENTATION WEAKNESSES
### Restricted IV Selection

Some access points (old Cisco firmware, notably) produced IVs using only 18 of the 24-bit space, which increased the probability of collisions (reuses) and lowered the storage requirement for all pads from 23.4 GB to a mere 366 MB (Meunier et al., 2002). In this case, users should ensure that access point firmware is up-to-date.

## IV Selection

Random IV selection results in random reuses of IVs (collisions), which allow more attacks. However, collecting all pads is slower with random IV selection. Some manufacturers select IVs simply sequentially, so that collecting all pads is a simple matter of running through the count of IVs. The worst selection method is through a flawed random number generator, which may be unable to generate some IV values or which repeats some values more often. In practice, however, the IV selection method (apart from *restricted IV selection*) has had little impact on the attacks mounted to crack WEP.

### Newsham 21-Bit Attack

Some manufacturers generate WEP keys from text in an effort to increase ease of use. However, the algorithm used produces only keys in a 21-bit space instead of 40-bit. As a result; brute-force cracking of WEP is 2^19 (524,288) times faster; that is, it takes less than a minute on commodity hardware (Newsham, 2001). The tool KisMAC implements this attack; according to the tool's documentation, Linksys and D-link products seemed to be vulnerable but not 3Com and Apple (Rossberg, 2003).

### Dictionary Attacks

Again, because some manufacturers generate WEP keys from text, in an effort to increase ease-of-use, some users configure them with dictionary words. Therefore, classic dictionary attacks are possible if one knows the algorithm used to generate the key from text.

## AUTOMATED WEP CRACKERS AND SNIFFERS

Wireless networks, and wireless security in general, can be evaluated, tested, and optimized using these tools. At a minimum, organizations should perform mapping of access points connected to their network or located inside their physical perimeter, to identify rogue access points and verify that WEP (or even better, WPA) is enabled (Byers & Kormann, 2003). This is a likely risk, as demonstrated by reports of a theft in the banking arm of the Israeli Postal Authority through a rogue access point (Evron, 2004).

### AiroPeek

AiroPeek, reviewed by Held (2002), is a commercial, easy-to-use, flexible, and sophisticated analyzer. Although it can capture and export packets, it is not a cracking tool. It is a useful tool for the system administrator or network architect wanting to diagnose wireless networks, including their signal strength, transmission speed (speed degrades as strength becomes lower), and coverage. As discussed earlier, using the minimum power necessary can decrease risks.

### WEPCrack

This is an implementation of the FMS attack (see "Key Recovery Attacks" earlier in the chapter). It captures and logs weak IVs and the first encrypted byte of the packets.

### AirSnort

This is also an implementation of the FMS attack (see "Key Recovery Attacks" earlier in the chapter). It runs under LINUX and uses a passive (sniffing) approach.

### NetStumbler

This is a popular network discovery tool, with GPS support. It does not perform any cracking. A MacOS equivalent is named "iStumbler."

## KisMAC

This is a MacOS X tool for network discovery and cracking WEP with several methods. It can use two wireless cards at the same time (the Airport card and another in a PCMCIA slot) to do packet reinjection (Rossberg, 2003). It is not related to Kismet.

## Kismet

This is a "Swiss Army knife," supporting many cards and providing information on GPS, SSIDs, IP ranges of networks, Cisco infrastructure information, connection speeds, and more (Kershaw, 2002). It runs on Linux.

## BSD-Airtools

These tools implement the attacks discussed here (e.g., weak IVs, Newsham 21-bit attack), as well as functionality similar to that of NetStumbler, for BSD-based operating systems (Dachboden Labs, n.d.).

## ALTERNATIVES TO WEP

By the time that the WEP vulnerabilities were announced, Cisco already had alternatives ready for sale, practically cornering the secure wireless network: LEAP (lightweight extensible authentication protocol) with RADIUS, and a line of VPN products. During the public outcry over WEP, Cisco felt a need to respond because of its role in the IEEE committees developing the 802.11 standard; however, the answers simply stated that Cisco's separately sold products were not vulnerable (Cisco, 2002a). Cisco admitted already knowing about deficiencies in WEP but kept them secret instead of changing the work of the 802.11b committee (Cisco, 2002b). These answers were somewhat disingenuous because they implied that anyone wanting the security already expected from WEP had to buy additional Cisco products and that the market who already bought into wireless technology, believing it reasonably secure, found itself hostage. Several of the following subsections describe 802.1x-related technologies (based on the extensible authentication protocol, EAP). The reader is referred to the treatment of 802.1x in Gast (2002). There are several design flaws in the combination of the IEEE 802.1X and IEEE 802.11 protocols that permit man-in-the-middle and session hijacking attacks (Mishra & Arbaugh, 2002), so these solutions should not be considered as robust as a full VPN (discussed in more detail later in this section).

## LEAP

LEAP is a proprietary, closed solution that was stated (without much detail) by Cisco as unaffected by WEP vulnerabilities (Cisco, 2002). LEAP conducts mutual authentication, so the client is assured that the access point is an authorized one. It uses per-session keys that can be renewed regularly. This makes the collection of a pad or weak IVs more difficult, and the secret key can be changed before the collection is complete. The user is authenticated instead of the hardware, so MAC address access-control lists are not needed. LEAP requires an authentication server (RADIUS) to support the access points; during authentication, the access points relay messages between clients and the server.

LEAP, as all password-based schemes, was shown to be vulnerable to dictionary attacks should user passwords be guessable (Wright, 2003). LEAP access points don't use weak IVs, but because they use MS-CHAP v2, show the same weaknesses as MS-CHAP (Wright, 2003). There are many variants of the EAP, such as EAP-TLS and PEAP (protected EAP).

## PEAP

Protected EAP is a proprietary 802.1x authentication type, like LEAP. PEAP is supported by the Cisco licensing scheme known as CCX (Cisco Compatible Extensions) version 2. It uses one-time passwords and digital certificates and so is more complex to deploy and manage than LEAP.

## EAP FAST

EAP flexible authentication via secure tunneling (FAST; Cam-Winget et al. 2004) fixes security weaknesses present in LEAP. It combines the ease of use of LEAP with the security of PEAP. This Cisco proprietary solution is licensed through the CCX v.3 specification (Cox, 2004).

## WPA

The public outcry over WEP resulted in the development of Wi-Fi protected access, a stopgap solution that solves issues related to the WEP encryption itself but without solving issues with the management of frames. It can be supported by most of the 802.11b hardware. In WPA, the IVs are larger, the shared key is used more rarely, and "temporal keys" are used to encrypt packets instead. WPA is reviewed in other chapters of this *Handbook*. As with all password schemes, dictionary passwords must be avoided.

## VPNs

VPNs can solve the issues related to WEP but are an additional expense, put an additional load on system administrators, and may not scale well to some network architectures in large enterprises. The total cost to an enterprise may be similar to that of a LEAP solution.

## CONCLUSION

In conclusion, WEP cracking is made easier through a combination of design flaws, implementation flaws, and deployment configurations that facilitate powerful attacks. Some protections against WEP cracking are provided through firmware updates that disable the FMS (weak IV) vulnerability, fix implementation flaws, or implement WPA instead of WEP. In particular, all new purchases should be checked for compliance or upgradability with the newer wireless protected access or the full 802.11i standards; however, this does not resolve all wireless risks. In addition, the connection of access points to any internal networks should be mediated via a properly configured firewall, and the wireless network should be audited for issues such as rogue access points and dictionary attacks. Nevertheless, even with all these precautions, DoS attacks against wireless infrastructure remain easy, so this threat should be evaluated against the goals and requirements of the wireless deployment. The deployment and usage cost (someone has to review rules and alerts) of a wireless monitoring and intrusion detection system should be compared with the protected value of the assets reachable through the wireless network, and the added value of the wireless network.

## GLOSSARY

**Demilitarized Zone (DMZ)**   Jargon to designate a sub-network that is exposed to both external (Internet) and internal hosts but separated from them by firewalls. This is a useful configuration for Web servers and similar services. In the context of this chapter, the demilitarized zone would be sandwiched in-between the Internet and the internal network. Sometimes the DMZ is outsourced to Internet service providers.

**Firewall**   A host that can block unwanted traffic from reaching a network. Most firewalls use static rules that apply only to a single packet. Stateful firewalls remember properties of prior packets to make the decision to block or allow packets.

**Intrusion Detection System (IDS)**   This refers to programs such as Snort, possibly running on dedicated hosts. The goals of IDS are to detect network traffic, host behavior, or activity that indicates recon or attacks in progress. The bane of IDS are false positives and semi-important warnings, which require analysts to sift through alerts and decide which ones require action. IDSs require monitoring, adjustment, and response; they are therefore expensive to operate. However, high-value targets and goals can justify them.

## CROSS REFERENCES

See *Encryption Basics; WEP Security; Wireless Network Standards and Protocol (802.11); Wireless Threats and Attacks.*

## REFERENCES

Arbaugh W. A., Shankar N., & Wan Y. C. J. (2001). Your 802.11 wireless network has no clothes. *Proceedings of the First IEEE International Conference on Wireless LANs and Home Networks.*

Ashenfelter, D. (2003). Waterford men hacked store files, FBI alleges; laptop setup used for system access, agent tells court. Retrieved from http://www. freep.com/news/locoak/nhack11_20031111.htm

Borisov, N., Goldberg, I., & Wagner, D. (2001). Intercepting mobile communications: The insecurity of 802.11. *Proceedings of the 7th Annual Conference on Mobile Computing and Networking* (pp. 180–188).

Bruestle, J., Hegerle, B., & Snax (2001a). AirSnort. Retrieved from http://airsnort.shmoo.com

Bruestle, J., Hegerle, B., & Snax (2001b). Shmoo Airsnort FAQ. Retrieved from http://airsnort.shmoo.com/faq.html

Byers, S., & Kormann, D. (2003). 802.11b access point mapping. *Communications of the ACM* [Special issue: Wireless networking security],

*46*, 41–46. Retrieved from http://delivery.acm.org/ 10.1145/770000/769824/p41-byers.pdf?key1=769824& key2=2728696701&coll=GUIDE&dl=ACM&CFID= 16819563&CFTOKEN=55360594

Cam-Winget, N., McGrew, D., Salowey, J., & Zhou, H. (2004). EAP flexible authentication via secure tunneling (EAP-FAST) (IETF Internet Draft). Retrieved from http://www.ietf.org/internet-drafts/draft-cam-winget-eap-fast-00.txt

Cisco. (2002a). Cisco comments on recent WLAN security paper from University of Maryland (Cisco product bulletin 1327). Retrieved from http://www.cisco.com/ warp/public/cc/pd/witc/ao350ap/prodlit/1327_pp.htm

Cisco. (2002b). Cisco Aironet security solution provides dynamic WEP to address researchers' concerns (Cisco product bulletin 1281). Retrieved from http://www.cisco.com/warp/public/cc/pd/witc/ao350ap/ prodlit/1281_pp.htm

ComputerWorld. (2002). Hackers say holes exposed retail data. Retrieved from http://www.cnn.com/2002/TECH/ internet/05/08/retail.security.idg/

Cox, J. (2003). Navy prepares to navigate with wireless LANs; warships will feature 802.11b wireless systems, allowing captains to command the entire ship from anywhere on board. Retrieved from http://www.pcworld.com/news/article/0,aid,109053,00. asp

Cox, J. (2004, February 12). Cisco proposes EAP FAST wireless security protocol. Network World Fusion. Retrieved from http://www.nwfusion.com/news/ 2004/0212cisietf.html

Dachboden Labs. (n.d.). BSD-airtools. Retrieved from http://www.dachb0den.com/projects/bsd-airtools.html

Evron, G. (2004). Israeli post office break-in. Retrieved from http://www.math.org.il/post-office.html

Fluhrer S., Mantin, I., & Shamir, A. (2001). Weaknesses in the key scheduling algorithm of RC4. Presented at the Eighth Annual Workshop on Selected Areas in Cryptography.

Gast, M. S. (2002). In M . Loukides (Ed.), *802.11 Wireless Networks, the definitive guide.* Sebastopol, CA: O'Reilly & Associates.

Hamilton, T. (2002, September 10). Insecure wireless networks exposed. *Toronto Star.* Retrieved from http://www.wirelessfriendly.com/pdf/Sep-10-02%20 Toronto%20Star%20Article.PDF

Held, G. (2002). Focus on AiroPeek. *International Journal of Network Management, 12,* 331–335.

Institute of Electrical and Electronics Engineers. (2004). IEEE OUI and Company_id assignments. Retrieved from http://standards.ieee.org/regauth/oui/index.shtml

Kershaw, M. (2002, March 4). LINUX 802.11b and wireless (in)security. Retrieved from http://www. linuxsecurity.com/feature_stories/wireless-kismet. html

Meunier, P., Nystrom, S., Kamara, S., Yost, S., Alexander, K., Noland, D., & Crane, J. (2002, June). *ActiveSync, TCP/IP and 802.11b wireless vulnerabilities of WinCE-based PDAs.* Presented at the Eleventh IEEE International Workshops on Enabling Technologies: Infrastructure for Collaborative Enterprises (WETICE'02). Pittsburgh, PA.

Mishra, A., & Arbaugh, W. A. (2002). *An initial security analysis of the IEEE 802.1X standard* (Technical Report CS-TR-4328,UMIACS-TR-2002-10). University of Maryland.

Newsham, T. (2001). *Cracking WEP keys*. Presented at Blackhat 2001, Las Vegas, NV. Retrieved from http://www.lava.net/~newsham/wlan/WEP_password_cracker.ppt

Pickard, T., & Cracknell, P. (2001). Out of thin air; a wireless network security survey of London. Retrieved from http://www.rsasecurity.com/solutions/wireless/whitepapers/ORTHUS_WP_1101.pdf

Pickard, T., & Cracknell, P. (2003). The wireless security survey of London 2002. RSA security. Retrieved from http://www.rsasecurity.com/solutions/wireless/whitepapers/CLWS_WP_0203.pdf

Rager, A. T. (2001). *WEPcrack*. Retrieved from http://wepcrack.sourceforge.net

Rossberg, M. (2003). *KisMAC: A wireless stumbler for MacOS X*. Retrieved from http://www.binaervarianz.de/projekte/programmieren/kismac/

Sandoval, G. (2002). Security causes Best Buy register ban. Retrieved from http://zdnet.com.com/2100-1105-898775.html

Stubblefield, A., Ioannidis, A., & Rubin, A. (2001, August 21).*Using the Fluhrer, Mantin, and Shamir attack to break WEP* (ATT Labs Technical Report, TD4ZCPZZ, Revision 2).

Tam, A., Shek, J., & Wo Sang, Y. (2002). War driving in Hong Kong. Retrieved from the Professional Information Security Association Web site: http://www.pisa.org.hk/event/wardriving2002-07.pdf

Walker, J. (2000). *Unsafe at any key size*. Submission to 802.11 committee IEEE 802.11/00-362.

Walker, J. (2001). *Overview of 802.11 security*. Presentation to the 802.15.3 committee. Retrieved from http://grouper.ieee.org/groups/802/15/pub/2001/Mar01/01154r0P802-15_TG3-Overview-of-802-11-Security.ppt

Wright, J. (2003). *Weaknesses in LEAP challenge/response*. Presented at Defcon 2003. Retrieved from http://home.jwu.edu/jwright/presentations/asleap-defcon.pdf

## FURTHER READING

Fiore, F., & Francois, J. (2002). Unwitting collaborators, part 6: Wireless insecurity. Retrieved from http://www.informit.com/isapi/product_id~{578B0F83-0A40-4DAF-AEF6-913010 96A52C}/content/articlex.asp

# Denial of Service Attacks

E. Eugene Schultz, *University of California-Berkeley Lab*

## WHAT ARE DoS ATTACKS?

### Background

News about some kind of disruption or prolonged outage of computing services due to malicious activity or programs seems to surface almost every day. In late 2001, for example, a flood of network traffic brought the *New York Times* network to a standstill. Earlier that year, the Web server of the Computer Emergency Response Team Coordination Center (CERT/CC) was brought down by a denial of service (DoS) attack. A series of DoS attacks in February 2000 brought down numerous systems used by ZDnet, eTrade, Amazon.com, eBay, and others, severely disrupting these companies' ability to conduct e-business transactions. Other large companies that have been successfully targeted for DoS attacks include Microsoft and Yahoo!

Although the public may not know exactly what DoS attacks are, many members of the Internet community have experienced such attacks. CloudNine, an Internet service provider (ISP), went out of business. Several media sources attributed CloudNine's business failure to a series of DoS attacks that this ISP encountered. About the same time that CloudNine went out of business, the University of Colorado shut down what was then the Internet's oldest Internet relay chat server because of repeated DoS attacks.

DoS attacks have grown from a relatively rare phenomenon to a frequent occurrence in recent times. Whereas 10 or 15 years ago DoS attacks were relatively unheard of, the relative proportion of DoS attacks has in recent years increased dramatically. CERT/CC has repeatedly stated that more DoS attacks are reported to this organization than any other single type of attack.

The 2004 E-Crime Watch survey by CSO magazine/U.S. Secret Service/CERT Coordination Center revealed that 43.6% of all attacks reported to the CERT Coordination Center are DoS attacks (see http://www.cert.org/about/ecrime.html).

First we turn our attention on how DoS attacks can be distinguished from other types of undesirable events and other types of attacks.

### Distinguishing DoS Attacks

#### DoS Attacks versus Other Damaging and Disruptive Events

What distinguishes DoS from other damaging and disruptive events? Although experts often disagree concerning the answer to this question, there is little disagreement with the premise that many DoS attacks are designed to disrupt, overwhelm, or damage computing resources and data. The fact that so many of these attacks are *designed* to cause disruption, damage, and so forth implies *intention* on the part of the attacker(s). Many disruptive and damaging events occur in normal computing environments. Examples include allowing disks to fill up; running software with bugs that cause the software to crash frequently; misconfiguring routers, firewalls, and domain name service (DNS) servers; faulty system configurations that result in floods of broadcasts or other undesirable results; and faulty network configurations that result in poor traffic flow. These events do not normally constitute DoS attacks, however, because they are the result of human error, not an attack. Human error is in fact a far greater cause of loss in the computing world than intentional attacks (Schultz & Shumway, 2001). Still, DoS attacks are a major (and ever growing) source of concern.

Other kinds of attacks are not specifically designed to produce DoS, yet they result in DoS. A good example is the MSBlaster worm that exploited a vulnerability in the interface between the remote procedure call (RPC) and the distributed component object model (DCOM) in several types of Windows operating systems (Schultz, 2003). Although this worm was designed primarily to infect systems, it clogged many organizations' networks with the traffic it created. Computer outages at numerous power plants in the northeastern United States in the summer of 2003 were, for example, attributed to MSBlaster.[1] The point here is that an attack does not have to intentionally cause DoS to result in a DoS attack.

### DoS Attacks versus Other Types of Attacks

DoS attacks are at least to some degree different from other types of attacks. Information security has three widely recognized goals[2]—confidentiality of data; integrity of data and systems; and availability of data, systems, networks, and services. DoS attacks target primarily availability. To this end, DoS attacks can be distinguished from attacks geared toward copying or stealing confidential data or tainting the integrity of data and/or systems. DoS attacks can, however, overlap with attacks on integrity—someone who breaks into a system and changes key parameters in critical system files to out-of-range values is in effect attacking not only the integrity of the system but also its availability. Depending on the particular changes made, the victim system might not only crash but may not even be bootable—something that is likely to constitute a serious loss of availability over a prolonged period of time.

## Motivations for Launching DoS Attacks

Why do attackers launch DoS attacks? Although we cannot usually be sure of the exact motives of anyone who launches a DoS attack, case studies in which DoS attacks' origins have been traced to individuals indicate that in many cases DoS attacks are launched with one or more of the following, distinct motives.

### Retribution, Hostility, or Frustration

The perpetrator may be an employee or ex-employee of a corporation who perceives that she or he has not been treated fairly. The perpetrator may accordingly try to get even with the person or organization perceived as causing the inequity. In one case a database programmer wiped out the entire customer database of an insurance company in retaliation for his employment having been terminated. In another more recent case, Timothy Lloyd was convicted and sentenced to 41 months in jail for planting a "time bomb"[3] in the network of his employer, Omega Engineering, causing what his company claimed was many millions of dollars in damages (see http://www.nwfusion.com/news/2002/0304lloyd.html). Lloyd apparently planted the time bomb because of growing frustration due to what he perceived as diminishing ability to influence his work environment.

### Need to Gain Recognition or Regain Lost Status

Sometimes perpetrators launch DoS attacks, usually in the form of some kind of sabotage, then rush in and solve the problem they have introduced quickly in the hope of being recognized as a "hero." Because they have created the problem, they can quickly solve it. Having quickly solved it makes them appear to have incredible abilities.

### Political Activism

In some cases, the perpetrator of a DoS attack may be politically motivated; the DoS attack(s) may represent an attempt to register a protest against the actions and/or policies of a particular organization or government. In 1989, for example, a perpetrator launched a worm called "WANK" (Worms Against Nuclear Killers) to protest the U.S. National Space Aeronautics Administration's (NASA's) impending launch of a rocket containing a nuclear-powered energy generator. Many information security experts also predict that widespread attacks on computers and networks can and will be launched by organizations such as the one reportedly responsible for the September 11 attacks.

### Gaining Control Over Computing Resources

Perpetrators of DoS attacks have sometimes launched attacks to monopolize computing resources. Chat channel users (often but not always members of the "hacker" community) have, for instance, initiated DoS attacks to take over chat channels. Owners of certain Web sites have reportedly brought down competing Web sites for extended periods.

### Avoiding Detection

Another reason for launching DoS attacks is to masquerade actions performed on computing systems. A perpetrator intent on attacking numerous hosts within a network may, for example, be aware that syslog (system logging) is enabled on the potential target hosts and that the syslog output is sent to a central server. The perpetrator may thus launch a DoS attack on the central server to avoid being detected.

### Extortion

Individuals have in some cases threatened others with DoS attacks unless the potential victim paid them a sum of money. Although extortion has in the past not been one of the greatest motivators for DoS attacks (or in this case, *threatened* DoS attacks), the number of cases in which threats of DoS attacks are made to extort money from others appears to be growing in recent years.

---

[1] MSBlaster also launched an intentional DoS attack on Microsoft's Windows Update site, http://www.windowsupdate.microsoft.com

[2] Many experts feel that focusing exclusively on these goals represents too narrow a view of the goals of information security, however. They assert that other goals such as nonrepudiation of actions and transactions (i.e., being unable to deny that one has initiated an action, business order, and so forth) and accountability (i.e., having records of each user's actions performed on computing systems and networks) are also among the major goals of information security.

---

[3] A time bomb is a destructive program that activates when the system clock reaches a certain time.

### Attacking for the Sake of Attacking

Yet another motivation for initiating DoS attacks has been to bring systems or services down simply for the sake of doing so—a manifestation of "electronic vandalism."

### Fame and Glory

Sometimes individuals have launched DoS attacks to gain notoriety—to bring them attention (often thereby elevating their status in hacker circles).

### Information Warfare[4] or Economic Espionage

In a number of cases, individuals have initiated DoS attacks as part of an apparent information warfare or industrial espionage effort. When the U.S. military bombed Yugoslavia in 1999, for example, individuals within Yugoslavia countered by launching flooding attacks against U.S. military systems in the Pentagon. A similar scenario occurred in 2001 after a U.S. spy plane crash-landed within the territory of the Peoples Republic of China (PRC). For weeks, DoS and other attacks on U.S. computing systems originated from IP addresses within the PRC.

Now that we have explored the reasons for perpetrating DoS attacks, let's focus on why attempted DoS attacks have such a high probability of succeeding.

## Why DoS Attacks Succeed

DoS attacks are not only frequent, but they often succeed. Why do DoS attacks succeed as often and well as they do? Let's consider several explanations.

### The Nature of the Internet

The Internet itself has limited and consumable resources (Houle, Weaver, Long, & Thomas 2001). The Internet's infrastructure consists of huge numbers of hosts and networks, both of which have limited resources. Any limitation (e.g., a relatively slow processor) in a system or device is thus a potential "weak link" in a DoS attack. Additionally, Internet security is interdependent. The security of one host or device depends on the security of others. A host that is reasonably secure one day can be taken over by an attacker and used to launch attacks at other hosts, including hosts within the same network in which a certain consistent level of security is presumed to exist.

Many if not most protocols and services do not incorporate protections against DoS attacks. If you look at the RFCs (Requests for Comments; see http://www.ietf.org) for networking protocols and services, you'll see that many of them address numerous security concerns but that few include mechanisms for staving off DoS attacks. Patches that fix vulnerabilities in major implementations of these protocols and services often have been developed as an afterthought, but add-ons seldom address software problems as effectively as addressing requirements during the initial development cycle. One of the best examples of a protocol that offers little protection against DoS attacks

is the ICMP (Internet message control protocol). ICMP incorporates virtually no reliability mechanisms; it is sessionless, connectionless, and unreliable. It is often easy to simply flood another system with various types of ICMP traffic, causing a certain service or often the system itself to hang or crash. Other protocol implementations are often done based on false assumptions. Ethernet implementation, for example, is often based on the assumption that oversized Ethernet packets will not be created and sent, something that is not necessarily true.

### Bug-Ridden Software

Numerous vulnerabilities in many software products have been identified over the years. Many of these vulnerabilities can be exploited to produce DoS conditions. Buffer overflow attacks, to be covered shortly, provide one of the best examples. Many programs and routines with operating systems do not perform appropriate bounds checking on input that they receive, opening the door for a variety of DoS and other types of attacks. Worse yet, certain vendors' products, most notably Microsoft's (e.g., Microsoft operating systems and Microsoft's Internet Explorer), are interrelated; failure in the functionality of one can result in massive failure. Their products are deployed so much that they comprise what functionally constitutes an information technology monoculture. When there is a DoS susceptibility problem in one product, many related products have an elevated susceptibility to DoS attacks, leading to greater potential for disruption.

### Increased Popularity of DoS Attacks Within the Hacking Community

Whereas break-ins were in many respects the modus operandi within the "hacking community" several years ago, DoS attacks are ostensibly now more valued within this community. With a single DoS attack, an attacker can cause considerable trouble, thus gaining considerable notoriety within this community. Consider the recognition that "Mafia Boy," a Canadian teenager, gained after he reportedly initiated successful DoS attacks against several companies that made front-page news in February 2000.

### Slowness in Recognizing the Problem

Software is to a certain degree unreliable; among other things, it is subject to crashes and it may not perform the functions it is intended to perform (Neumann, 1994). It is often easy to confuse software unreliability with the results of DoS attacks. Additionally, for many years, people did not take DoS threats seriously because other problems such as break-ins into systems caused more loss and disruption at that time.

Corporations are not deploying necessary countermeasures. A report written by the National Academy of Science's Computer Science and Telecommunications Board (CSTB) asserts that U.S. corporations are not deploying security countermeasures needed to defend their computing assets from cyberattacks (National Academy of Sciences, 2002). This failure to adopt necessary measures also elevates the likelihood of successful DoS attacks.

We'll now consider the amount of damage and disruption that DoS attacks cause or potentially *can* cause.

---

[4] Information warfare is using the computing capabilities of one organization or country to gain an advantage over adversaries. Typically, this involves (among other things) attempting to disrupt and disable the adversary's computing capabilities.

## The Toll

Losses associated with any type of information security attack are difficult to pinpoint with any precision. Consider that one estimate of the collective losses due to the distributed DoS attacks (to be covered shortly) against several U.S. corporations in February 2000 was $5 billion. Regardless of whether this estimate can be taken literally, one thing is sure: the victim companies undoubtedly experienced a sufficient level of financial loss to evoke concern on the part of management because of the threat to each company's bottom line. DoS-related losses are generally attributable to a number of sources, including:

**Down Time in Business-Related or Other Critical Systems.** This source of loss constitutes an operational disruption that generally has the worst impact in billing and other types of financial systems in which down time of only a few minutes can be financially costly. Consider also the impact on safety of a DoS attack on a flight control or plant process control system. Disruption of ongoing computing operations not only means that personnel time will be wasted, but also that somehow the down time will be made up in a manner that does not conflict with ongoing computing operations. This is often a far greater problem than anyone other than operations specialists and senior-level management can readily understand.

**Cost of Response.** The cost of investigating and repairing the problem adds up quickly. Manpower, particularly time devoted by technical staff, is by no means cheap. Finding the cause of a successful DoS attack and correcting the problem can involve a significant manpower investment. Additionally, because it is frequently so difficult to trace the real origin of DoS attacks,[5] investigations of the cause of DoS attacks are often more lengthy and complicated than for other types of attacks.

**Legal Costs.** Although legal costs associated with DoS attacks have been relatively rare so far, the fact that eTrade was sued by a customer who complained that he suffered stock market losses as a result of the DoS attack against this company is significant. The cost of prosecuting suspected perpetrators of DoS attacks could also add to the financial toll of such attacks.

**Loss of Customer or Third-party Partner Confidence and Reputation.** Disruption of access to services that customers and/or third-party business affiliates experience negatively impact confidence in the service supplier or other organization that experiences a DoS attack.

Interestingly, of the three major goals of information security—confidentiality, integrity, and availability—availability is sometimes the most overlooked. Confidentiality breaches can allow valuable or private information to fall into the wrong hands, integrity compromises can cause people to doubt data and whether systems and network devices are working properly, but interruption of availability can completely disrupt computing operations. Given the complete dependence of so many organizations on computing, the amount of loss and disruption can be huge.

DoS attacks are not likely to affect every type of site and organization equally. The next subsection discusses the types of sites that are most likely to be most negatively impacted by these attacks.

## What Types of Sites Are Most Vulnerable?

Although predicting the magnitude of loss resulting from a DoS or any other form of attack is by no means an exact science, some types of sites and computing environments are more likely to suffer damage and loss than others. The amount of probable loss depends on the types of damage and disruption (as discussed earlier) as well as factors such as the impact of down time upon an organization's business or mission. As mentioned previously, even a short down time in a billing system can have adverse consequences for an institution. Someone from a stock brokerage firm that was one of the first to offer Internet-based transactions to customers told me that a certain newspaper reporter monitored that firm's Web site on a 24/7 basis and wrote a news article whenever the Web server was not functional. *As a general rule, the more critical continuity of services and operations are to an organization and the more mission critical the type of operational services, the more adverse the potential impact of DoS attacks is.*

The following are some representative types of sites that tend to be more vulnerable to DoS attacks than others:

- Financial institutions and financial transaction processing centers
- Stock and commodities trading centers
- Military operations control centers
- Transportation control centers (particular air traffic control centers, airports, and space flight centers)
- Emergency response operations centers
- Telecommunications operations centers
- Plant process control centers
- Security operations command centers
- Hospitals and health clinics

Although it is true that risk due to the threat of DoS attacks is considerably elevated in gigantic organizations with large, continuity-dependent operations centers, DoS-related risk in small to medium-sized businesses is also often high. Why? Because small to medium-sized businesses may operate with a minimum of monetary reserves or may face tight deadlines that affect the survival of the business. A DoS-related incident may be sufficient to disrupt operations to the point of forcing a smaller company out of business.

Now that we have considered the basics of DoS attacks and their impact, it is time to consider the types of DoS attacks that can be found on the Internet and elsewhere.

---

[5] In many DoS attacks, the source (origination) address in packets sent to victim systems is spoofed (falsified), making tracing the real origin of the attack more difficult. "Spoofing" means using an IP source address other than the real address of the machine from which this kind of attack is launched.

# TYPES OF DoS ATTACKS

To date, numerous high-level types of DoS attacks have been identified. Many classifications of the types of these attacks have been published. Hussein, Heidemann, and Papadopoulos (2003) have proposed classifying these attacks in terms of header contents, ramp-up behavior (all-at-once vs. gradual), and spectrum (single or multisource). The following is a classification of DoS attacks based on real-life observation. Categories may overlap with each other and are by no means mutually exclusive of each other. Types of DoS attacks include the following:

## Hardware and Software Sabotage

In a sabotage attack, someone attempts to damage one or more hardware components or something related to the software within one or more systems. Normally a hardware attack requires physical access to hardware components. Someone who gains direct access to a system could, for example, damage the keyboard, video display terminal, any peripheral device such as an attached printer or mouse, or the central processing unit (CPU) by deliberately dropping any of them. Alternatively, someone with physical access to a UNIX or LINUX machine may be able to boot the system in single-user mode, thereby gaining complete control over the system (often without having to even enter a password). Another kind of sabotage attack involves integrity compromises in routers, firewalls, DNS servers, or ordinary systems (including applications that run on systems). An attacker can use methods such as exploiting unsecured Simple Network Management Protocol (SNMP) access to a router to alter an access control list (ACL) that rejects certain incoming traffic or crafting bogus DNS query replies that populate the cache of a DNS server with garbage entries, resulting in network failure. Critical system configuration files, binaries, databases, and so forth in virtually any system are also at risk of unauthorized alteration as a result of a wide variety of attacks, including breaking into a system, leaving the system dysfunctional, or causing it to crash.

## Shut-Down or Slow-Down Attacks

Shut-down attacks are similar to sabotage attacks, except that the goal of a shut-down attack is not to cause damage but simply to take one or more systems down. The attacker might power the system down or remotely cause it to shut down by invoking a remote shut-down function. As mentioned previously, however, a nongraceful shut down can easily also result in damage to hard drives. Additionally, a perpetrator can slow down a system or network without shutting any system or device down. Although potentially less damaging to an organization's operational and business needs, a slow-down attack can nevertheless fulfill the intentions of someone bent on getting even with an organization or individuals.

## Flooding Attacks

In flooding attacks, someone or a program running on behalf of someone sends so many packets or data that they overwhelm the receiving system, service, or application. The best known form of flooding attack is probably a SYN flooding attack in which the three-way handshake involved in establishing a TCP (transmission control protocol) connection is misused. Normally in the first part of this handshake, a system sends a SYN packet to another system. If a malicious system sends many SYN packets without responding to the target system's response, the target system may tie up system resources (e.g., space in the process table) waiting for the malicious system's response.

## System Resource Starvation Attacks

As mentioned previously, types of DoS attacks may overlap with each other. The previously mentioned SYN flooding attack is a flooding attack that results in resource starvation. Consider also the effect of running the following routine on a UNIX or LINUX system:

```
while true
do
mkdir foo
chdir foo
done
```

In many UNIX and LINUX systems, this will generate so many i-nodes (file system objects that hold file parameters such as ownerships and permissions, times of access and modification, and the size of each file) that the system may run out of resources and crash. Another type of resource starvation attack is a snork attack. In this kind of attack, a perpetrator sends a specially crafted UDP packet to a particular port, causing the victim system to use 100% of its CPU for an extended period of time.

## Buffer Overflow Attacks

In a buffer overflow attack, a program writes too much data into a buffer compared witih the amount of memory allocated. Examples of buffer overflow attacks include sending a message with an excessively long subject line or using FTP (the file transfer protocol) to request a file with an excessively long name or to change directories, again with an excessive number of characters in the argument that follows the cd command. The excess input may be written into memory, overwriting data that control the execution path for the program that is running, seizing control of the execution of the program, and running rogue commands or programs (often with superuser-level privileges) instead. Each program runs by sequentially executing CPU instructions. The sequence order of these instructions is kept in the extended instruction counter (also known as the EIP register) that controls program execution, specifying the address of each subsequent instruction that is to be executed. The extended instruction counter is modified whenever there is a jump instruction or a function is called. When a function has been run, the extended instruction counter needs to know where to go when the function has been run. It does this by putting the return address for the function call into the stack, a special area of memory used to hold arguments for functions, register values, and other variables that enable it to go to the instruction immediately after the one that has called the function that has just been run. Attackers can send specially constructed input that spills over into memory, overwriting the return address within the stack. Once the called function is through running, the special input is loaded into the EIP register in an attempt to make overflow code (i.e., code that is inserted after the data designed to exceed the allocated buffer size) to be run in lieu of the normal process code. Note that the heap, an area in memory similar to the stack but designed to store dynamic variables, can also be targeted in a buffer overflow attack.

Any rogue commands or programs in a buffer overflow attack can be used for a variety of malicious purposes, including causing DoS on the victim or other hosts. In many instances, however, an attacker's attempt to overflow a buffer to run rogue commands or program goes awry. The attacker may, for example, miscalculate the allocated buffer size, spilling garbage data as well as specially crafted input designed to overwrite the stack's return address into memory. The result may be that the application that is running (and possibly also the system itself) may crash. In recent years, a large number of buffer overflow attacks that have caused DoS were not specifically designed to do so; DoS has been an unintended by-product of these attacks.

## Packet Fragmentation Attacks

Sometimes in the course of networking, packets that are too large for routers or other network devices to handle are created and then sent over the network. Certain kinds of network devices, routers in particular, often cannot deal with such oversized packets. Packets are often consequently fragmented (broken into smaller pieces); each packet fragment will travel over the network until it reaches the destination system. If everything goes well, the destination system will then combine the fragment into one packet so that it can process the packet data appropriately. Numerous DoS attacks abuse packet fragmentation in one way or another such that the receiving system processes fragmented packets in a manner that causes it to hang or crash. One possible attack, for example, is to simply flood a system with fragmented packets. Another is to send fragments that overlap with each other in what is called a *Teardrop attack,* in which the overlapping packet fragments cause the reassembled packet to have values that are out of the permissible range. If the receiving system is not programmed to check and drop fragments constructed in this manner, it will go into an abnormal operating condition and crash. Yet other examples are the "Ping-of-Death" and "SSPing" attack in which a Windows 95/98/NT system is sent a series of fragmented IP packets. When the system combines the fragments, they now form a larger packet than the system can process, causing the system to freeze. "Jolt" and "Jolt2" attacks are similar, except that in these attacks multiple identical fragments are sent to the victim system (which in this case needs to be a Windows 95/98/NT or 2000 system), causing massive CPU overutilization.

## Malformed Packet Attacks

In malformed packet attacks, the problem is that the program that implements a particular network service

```
1/02–16:01:36.792199 222.41.41.204:2022 -> 192.210.132.28:21

TCP TTL:24 TOS:0x0 ID:39426

**UAPRSF**** Seq: 0x27896E4 Ack: 0xB35C4BD Win: 0x404
```

**Figure 1:** A Christmas Tree packet.

has not been written to detect and screen out malformed packets. RFCs define how packets for various networking protocols should be formed. Normal network programs form and then send packets that conform to these RFCs. An attacker can, however, use such a program to send packets with unconventional ("illegal") values, possibly that are out of range or are missing entire fields, to crash victim systems because they "spin out of control," possibly overallocating memory or using all available CPU. An example is a "Land attack" in which an attacker sends one or more packets that have the same source and destination addresses, something that confuses the receiving system to the point that it crashes. Another example is a "Bubonic attack" in which a barrage of pseudo-random TCP packets with identical TCP sequence numbers, source and destination ports, and other packet header information is sent to a victim Windows 2000 system and certain versions of Linux, causing it to crash. Still another example is a "Christmas Tree attack" in which the attacker sends a packet with every option set for a particular protocol being used. The most common type of Christmas Tree packet has all the TCP flags (e.g., SYN, URG, PUSH, FIN) set. If the operating system of the target host has weaknesses in its TCP/IP stack implementation, the packet may crash or disable the system. Figure 1 shows a Christmas Tree packet captured by Snort, an intrusion detection tool, sent from IP address 222.41.41.204 to 192.210.132.28. Note in the beginning of the bottom line that all TCP flags, URG (U), ACK (A), PSH (P), RST (R), SYN (S), and FIN (F), are set.

## "Boomerang" Attacks

In a "boomerang attack," the attacker spoofs the IP address of the host that is the intended victim. The attacker sends packets that elicit some kind of reply. If the attacker sends enough packets initially, a large volume of replies is returned to the victim, causing it to hang or crash. A representative type of boomerang attack is the "Smurf attack" in which the attacker sends many ping packets to systems within a network. A ping request in effect asks, "Are you there?" Each pinged host replies, but each reply goes to the intended victim, overwhelming it.

## Premature Session Termination

A TCP session keeps going until one of the hosts that is part of the session sends a TCP packet with the FIN (for "finish") or RST (for "reset") flag set. An RST terminates the session immediately. Any host involved in a TCP session must augment by one the packet sequence number of the most recent packet sent by the other host; a wrong packet sequence number causes the receiving host to drop the packet for being out of sequence. In various TCP implementations, however, a receiving host may receive a packet sequence number within a certain range from the sending host; the packet sequence number is not quite correct, but the receiving host will accept it anyway. This allows an attacking host to fabricate packets bearing the source IP address of one host that has an ongoing TCP session with another host and with the RST flag set and then send them to the other host. These packets have a range of packet sequence numbers. If one of these packet sequence numbers is within an acceptable range, the receiving host will accept the packet, causing the connection to be reset—in other words, causing DoS. The border gateway protocol (BGP), which runs over TCP, appears to be most affected by this vulnerability.

## Distributed Denial of Service (DDoS) Attacks

In DDoS attacks, an attacker plants programs ("zombies") that unleash a DoS attack (e.g., by releasing a huge volume of packets within a network or by releasing malformed or fragmented packets when they receive a signal from a specialized machine called the "handler"). Normally there are multiple handlers, one for each part of the victim network. Each handler receives its signal from a master system that starts the DDoS attack. The zombies and handlers are normally installed in systems well in advance of the intended date on which the DDoS attack is to occur. Figure 2 depicts a network in which zombies and a handler have been installed in a small network. The master is not shown here because the master is often outside of the victim network.

A set of conventions (e.g., special types of pinglike conventions) is typically used to keep the zombies and handlers and also the handlers and master in touch with each other before the attack is launched. This also enables the attacker to inventory how many zombies and handlers are in place and functional. In 2001, CERT/CC was the victim of a DDoS attack in which a vast number of large,

fragmented UDP packets was sent to its Web port from numerous zombies. Web servers can usually deal with IP packet reassembly in a reasonable and efficient manner. Packet fragments must be stored until the servers receive every packet fragment; however, storing packet fragments in this manner consumes system resources. When too many packet fragments arrived, the Web server was overwhelmed, causing it to crash and resulting in a prolonged outage.

DDoS attacks constitute a particularly high level of threat because of the potential for massive outages. Nondistributed attacks are far less likely to cause a catastrophic condition—to reach a threshold necessary to disrupt traffic flow throughout an entire network, for example. Individual systems can do only so much, and networks and the systems therein have built-in mechanisms to correct errors and unusual conditions up to a certain point. So, for instance, when one machine is flooding another with packets, the latter is likely to send ICMP "source quench" packets that suppress the former's packet sending. However, many systems—in this case, zombies—working in orchestration to attack the network are too much for normal correction mechanisms. In one case, an attacker installed more than 100 zombies within an organization's network. When the zombies released a massive barrage of packets, the entire network went dead and could not be used for several days while technical people attempted to diagnose what was wrong and to bring the network back up. Many types of DDoS programs use stealth techniques to hide the presence of zombies and handlers, as well as to make the network communications between both unreadable through the use of encryption. Some recent types of DDoS programs even wait to create zombies; they create a process on each compromised system that later creates zombie programs, making detection of zombies even more difficult. The sheer number of DDoS

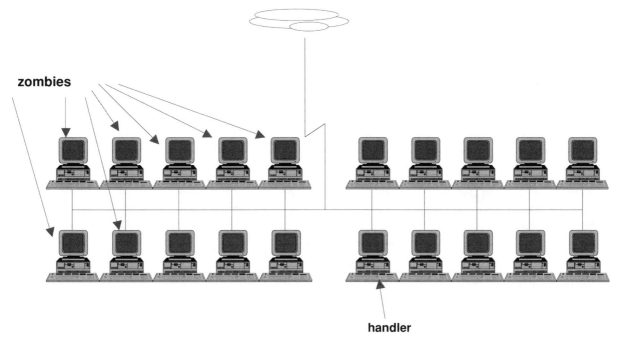

**Figure 2:** How zombies and a handler might be planted in a small network.

tools (Trinoo, Stacheldracht, Tribe Flood Network [TFN] and its many variants, Shaft, and more) freely available on the Internet is another factor that elevates the level of threat from DDos attacks.

We've seen that there are many types of DoS attacks, each with potentially debilitating effects. Let's move on to the practical application of this chapter, namely how to prevent these kinds of attacks in the first place.

# PREVENTION OF DoS ATTACKS

What can an organization do to prevent DoS attacks? This section addresses this topic by considering a number of alternatives. These alternatives are not necessarily mutually exclusive.

## Risk Management Considerations

As mentioned earlier, DoS attacks are likely to be successful for many reasons. It follows that preventing DoS attacks altogether is no easy task. From a risk management perspective, therefore, a mitigation strategy that dictates prevention at all costs is not only likely to be unrealistic from a technical perspective but also is likely to entail excessive cost in a cost–benefit analysis. A more realistic strategy is to determine the types of DoS attacks that could occur, the likelihood of occurrence of each, and the expected loss. Countermeasures that mitigate risk could then be deployed on a priority basis, with the risks that compromise the largest expected loss addressed before others until available resources are exhausted. So if, for example, extended down time for billing systems due to sabotage or shut-down attacks were considered the greatest risk, priority in resource allocation could be devoted to controls that counter this threat. Classic risk management models would generally dictate this type of approach. Although this approach seems intuitive, it is at least to some degree flawed by inherent limitations of risk assessment methods. Simply put, these methods (especially quantitative risk assessment methods) imply a level of objectivity and precision that are simply not present. Furthermore, new instantiations of DoS attacks are constantly emerging, changing the relative risk of each identified source. Finally, although virtually every information security professional agrees that some form of risk analysis and risk management occurs in the course of conducting information-security-related activity, the more formal the risk analysis and risk management method deployed, the more cumbersome and costly these methods are. By the time the results of these methods are available, the results are already likely to be out of date. In short, classic risk-management-based methods of dealing with DoS threats are not likely to be effective.

What is the alternative? One of the most popular is the "due care" or "baseline controls" approach in which an organization learns of the controls posture of other peer organizations and tries to deploy roughly the same controls posture. "Controls posture" means the type and amount of controls deployed. If, for example, other responsible peer organizations deploy a certain set of business continuity measures (as discussed shortly), an organization could exercise due care by deploying the same measures. One of the chief advantages of the due care approach is that organizations tend to adjust their controls posture based on real outcomes. If a financial organization does not deploy adequate perimeter control measures (e.g., firewalls), security-related costs due to intrusions, successful DoS attacks, and so forth can become intolerably high, prompting the organization to tighten its perimeter security. The due care approach tends also to be financially less costly; it can be based on normative data concerning actual controls deployment from various sectors, including the government, financial, transportation, and manufacturing sectors. On the other hand, many information security professionals are skeptical of this approach, which they often claim is too general to work in specific organizations that have specific business and security needs.

The debate between advocates of classic risk-based methods and the due care approach will continue to rage. Nevertheless, some kind of risk management activity is necessary to deal with DoS threats. At a minimum, organizations need to anticipate and prepare for worst-case DoS scenarios. Sadly, most organizations do not realize just how much disruption to ongoing operations and the financial impact of worst-case scenarios until after they occur. Consider, too, how little prepared most organizations currently are for a massive cyberterrorist attack designed to produce widespread disruption and panic.

## Policy Considerations

Policy is in many respects the beginning point in countering DoS attacks. An organization's information security policy must at a minimum delineate baseline security measures needed to fend off DoS as well as other types of attacks. Policy provisions must also spell out actions (e.g., whether to bring in law enforcement) that are and are not to be taken in case of DoS attacks as well as punishments for employees, contractors, and others who initiate such attacks. Service providers (e.g., ISPs) and third-party business partners should establish clear expectations concerning the level of security to be provided for customers and business affiliates. One of the best ways to communicate these expectations is through policy statements that can be communicated to employees through memoranda, Web site postings, e-mail messages, and so forth.

## Business Continuity Measures

Given the vulnerability of today's systems, networks, and software to DoS attacks, it is naïve to assume that these attacks can be prevented altogether. Fallback measures, measures that enable an organization to carry on its business despite computing and network outages, are thus essential. Business continuity measures collectively provide a strong but by no means complete way of minimizing the impact of disasters, including many types of DoS attacks. Some of the major types of business contingency measures include the following:

### Hot Sites

Hot sites are computing sites to which current computing operations can be rolled over in case of outage or disruption. The beauty of hot sites is that if set up properly, they provide an almost seamless method of operational continuity, although they tend to be rather financially costly. One limitation is that rolling operations over to a hot site will not do much good if a massive network attack such as a flooding attack occurs. Network operations within a hot site may be normal, but trying to send traffic to hosts outside the network is a different matter.

### Warm Sites

Warm sites do not have all of the necessary hardware and software to allow for a fast rollover of operations to a backup site, but they have the necessary information technology (IT) infrastructure. Warm sites thus generally provide a reasonably fast and efficient way of moving operations to a backup site without all the financial costs of hot sites. Just as in the case of hot sites, however, warm sites are not effective when certain kinds of DoS attacks occur.

### Cold Sites

With cold sites, operations cannot be immediately rolled over to cold sites. Cold sites must first be brought into operational status by bringing in the needed hardware, software, and personnel to get computing operations going again.

## Uninterruptable Power Supplies (UPSs)

UPSs are attached to computing systems and network devices in a manner such that if an electrical failure occurs, the computer or device keeps running because of availability of UPS-supplied power. The cost of UPSs has declined over the years to the point that UPSs are widely used in many organizations.

## Failover Systems and Devices

Failover systems and devices are redundant to those they support, such that if the primary system or device goes down, the failover one is immediately used. Failover systems are particularly important whenever there is a single point of failure, such as a firewall or router; single points of failure often exacerbate the impact of DoS attacks. Although deploying failover systems and devices is one of the best single countermeasures against DoS attacks, this approach, like the others, is not perfect. An attacker could, for example, initiate an attack on a primary system, causing partial but not complete resource starvation. This system may thus continue to operate without any rollover.

## Firewalls

Firewalls are systems located between two networks that analyze and selectively handle (e.g., filter out, allow to pass through) traffic. Firewalls put up a barrier to attacks and undesirable types of network traffic. To the degree that DoS attacks can be prevented in the first place, properly configured firewalls are in many experts' minds the best single defense against this kind of attack. Although there are many types of firewalls and various depths at which firewalls can analyze and handle traffic, the ability to filter traffic (i.e., allow it through or reject it) is the most basic firewalling function for stopping DoS attacks. Firewalls

can, for example, block all incoming echo requests. One of the easiest types of DoS attacks to perpetrate is to send echo requests to another system. That system will reply with echoes that go right back to the original system, something that will trigger more replies, and so on, until both systems are flooded to the point of crashing. Using a firewall to block all incoming traffic destined for the echo port (TCP and UDP port 7) goes a long way in preventing echo storm attacks initiated from outside a network. They can also drop fragmented packets, although as mentioned previously, dropping fragmented packets also has its downsides, considering the percentage of Internet packets that is fragmented. Higher ended firewalls such as application firewalls can even analyze incoming input such as user input to applications that could cause a variety of undesirable outcomes, including DoS, and drop such input before it can reach the intended victim(s). Additionally, firewalls should block all incoming packets that have IP source addresses of hosts within an organization's internal network. This will keep spoofed packets that are so frequently used in DoS attacks out of one's network.

## Routers

If properly configured, routers can serve as "low-level firewalls." They can filter packets according to their source and destination IP addresses, ports, and so forth. They can also drop fragmented packets.[6] In so doing, routers can also help prevent certain types of DoS attacks. Additionally, RFC 1812 (http://www.ietf.org/rfc/rfc1812.txt?number=1812) specifies router options than can substantially reduce the probability of successful DoS attacks against an internal network. This RFC states that routers must include an option to turn off forwarding network-prefix-directed broadcasts. Routers may also have the ability of disabling receiving network-prefix directed broadcasts on network interfaces. RFC 2644 (see http://www.ietf.org/rfc/rfc2644.txt?number=2644) updates this previous RFC by specifying that routers must deny both forwarding and receiving directed broadcasts by default.

## Host-Based Measures

In addition to network-based measures, several host-based measures can be effective in countering DoS attacks. These include the following:

### Packet Filters and Personal Firewalls

Packet filters and personal firewalls are like miniature firewalls that run on systems to protect them from undesirable traffic. Packet filters are often more basic in that they allow or deny traffic based on rules such as the source of the traffic or the destination port. Personal firewalls generally go farther; they not only serve as packet filters but can also often block dangerous programs from being downloaded from Web sites, stop malformed packets from reaching a system, provide detailed log data, and so forth. One of the chief advantages of both is that they work

---

[6] Given that a reasonably large proportion of packets that traverse the Internet are fragmented, however, dropping such packets is often not regarded as a viable solution.

regardless of whether an attack has been initiated from outside or inside a network. If configured properly, they (like firewalls and screening routers) block traffic that if allowed through would result in DoS as well as other undesirable outcomes. Additionally, hosts can be configured to not respond to dangerous kinds of incoming packets, such as broadcasted ICMP echo packets, something that for all practical purposes achieves the same kinds of benefits that packet filters and personal firewalls deliver.

### Limiting Services

Many network services have vulnerabilities that leave the systems on which these services run vulnerable to DoS attacks. The recently mentioned echo service is one such service. The SNMP service is another. An attacker may be able to flood a system with SNMP traffic, causing it to crash. Other services that have proven especially conducive to DoS attacks include the character generator (chargen), WINS (the Windows Internet name service), POP (post office protocol), RPC (the remote procedure call), the NetBIOS session service in Windows systems, and IMAP (the Internet message application protocol). Running only the services necessary for business and operational needs is a good way of limiting the potential for successful service-related DoS attacks.

### Patch Installation

Many vulnerabilities that if exploited can result in DoS have surfaced over the years. Attackers generally begin attacking by remotely scanning systems for vulnerabilities, then follow up with attacks that exploit the vulnerabilities they have discovered.

Most operating system and applications vendors produce patches, software, and other solutions that correct the vulnerabilities. Promptly installing patches is thus one of the best ways to prevent DoS attacks.

## Quality of Service (QoS) Mechanisms

QoS (not to be confused with DoS) mechanisms have been developed to improve the quality of networking. These mechanisms include (among other things) a range of architectures, protocols, and routing mechanisms to boost performance and reliability. Another such mechanism, network admission control, restricts network connectivity to any network entity other than devices with integrity. One of the many benefits of the use of QoS is to make networks less vulnerable to DoS attacks. On the other hand, although QoS mechanisms thus potentially provide another defense against DoS attacks, they are generally rather difficult to set up and use.

## Intrusion Detection

Intrusion detection in simple terms is the process of discovering unauthorized use of computers and networks. Intrusion detection systems (IDSs) are somewhat limited in dealing with DoS attacks because they are post hoc in nature; they tell you that something is wrong only *after* something bad occurs (Endorf, Schultz, & Mellander, 2004). Nevertheless, IDSs can be useful in helping prevent DoS attacks in that once they detect a DoS attack against one system, the data about the origin of the attack can be used to block ("shun") the IP address of the apparent

attacking system at the entrance to a network (i.e., by modifying access control lists in the router or firewall), thus helping prevent further attacks of this nature.

## Intrusion Prevention

In intrusion prevention, systems resource requests to a host that are initiated by applications are analyzed in real time. These requests are either allowed or rejected according to the particular application security policy that is in effect. If, for example, a host receives a potentially destructive file system manipulation request, or so much data that some of it is likely to be written into memory, or a request to do something that is potentially dangerous on the network, or to potentially cause an application to go into an abnormal state, or to bypass security operations, or something similar, the IPS stops the request from being carried out. Many IPSs have a central server that performs intrusion detection analysis to discover new attacks that might potentially be destructive. The server then determines the requests that are associated with any new attacks and updates the appropriate application security policy accordingly. Finally, it sends a policy update to clients. In this manner, hosts can be spared from the effects of DoS and many other types of attacks.

The notion of warding off the effects of attacks has considerable intuitive appeal. There is usually no good reason for a system to keep reacting to input that will eventually exhaust its memory or that will spill over into memory. Additionally, "zero day" attacks (attacks that surface for the first time) are not nearly as much of a problem with IPSs as with IDSs because most IPs do not rely on exact signatures of attacks for their functionality. IPSs also tend to be fairly easy to run and maintain and also generally have a relatively small impact on system and network performance.

Like everything else, however, IPSs are no panacea. For one thing, they are heavily reliant on changes in systems, but there are generally so many changes and combinations of changes that they often deal with these in a less than optimal manner. False alarms can be catastrophic in that they can produce what in effect amounts to DoS, because an IPS will initiate measures such as denying suspicious data transfers from other hosts to protect the host on which it runs. The data input could, however, not only be legitimate but also essential for business continuity. In fact, in many respects IPSs provide an almost ideal opportunity for a perpetrator who knows the particular type of input that would cause hosts to go into defensive mode, thereby bringing computing operations to a standstill. IPS technology is also still rather crude; some IPSs have rather limited capabilities. Finally, the financial cost of IPSs is also generally fairly high. Still, intrusion prevention technology holds considerable promise in countering DoS attacks, and IPSs are likely to continue to have even better capabilities over time.

Note that some operating system vendors such as Microsoft are planning to build something that is similar to intrusion prevention capabilities into their products. The operating system itself, not a program such as an IPS program that runs on top of the operating system, will recognize requests and conditions that are potentially harmful and will neither allow such requests to be processed

**Table 1** Preventative Measures against DoS Attacks

| Preventative Measure(s) | Function or Mechanism | Effectiveness |
| --- | --- | --- |
| Business continuity measures | Varied (ranges from simple hardware solutions to an entire hot or cold site) | Medium to high |
| Firewalls | Varied, ranging from packet filtering to connection analysis and management | High |
| Routers | Packet filtering | Medium to high |
| Packet filters and personal firewalls | Packet filtering and logging (plus additional functions in personal firewalls) | High |
| Limiting services | Reducing the probability that services that can be exploited in DoS attacks run | High |
| Patch installation | Correcting vulnerabilities | High |
| QoS mechanisms | Varied (throughput regulation, allocating priorities to network applications, and so forth) | Medium to high |
| Intrusion detection | Detecting attacks | Low to medium |
| Intrusion prevention | Detecting and stopping their effects or shutting off the source | Medium to high |
| Third-party software | Varied (anti-DoS, virus and worm detection and eradication, integrity checking, and so forth) | Variable (depends on type and quality of software) |
| Use of Security Operations Centers | Quickly detect and shut off DoS attacks | High |

nor allow potentially catastrophic system conditions to develop. This approach goes hand-in-hand with ongoing research on system survivability—building systems that are healthy and that try to stay that way.

## Third-Party Software Tools

A variety of third-party software tools may potentially prevent at least some kinds of DoS attacks. The previously mentioned packet filters and personal firewalls are readily recognizable examples of such tools, but there are many others too. Arbor Networks, for example, has created software that uses network probes to create a baseline of network activity. Departures from the baseline constitute abnormal activity, something that evokes an alert. DeepNines Technologies' product, Security Platform, helps prevent exploitation of router and switch vulnerabilities that could result in a variety of undesirable outcomes, including DoS. This product in effect puts a layer of security in front of routers and switches. Antivirus software can also help prevent DoS by detecting and eradicating self-reproducing programs such as viruses, as well as many Trojan horse programs that users would otherwise download into their systems. Special software such as vulnerability scanners can detect DDoS zombies and handlers through methods such as determining whether certain ports known to be used by DDoS tools are listening for input. For example, many versions of Trinoo utilize UDP port 27444 by default. If port 27444 on a system is listening, a Trinoo zombie may be installed on that system. (Note that the netstat command will also list listening ports on a system.) Other software uses cryptographic algorithms to detect changes in files and directories, some of which may be due to insertion of malicious programs that can cause systems and applications to crash or hang. Simply having software that can detect the presence of DoS tools does little good, however. It is necessary not

only to use this software systematically at defined intervals but also to ensure that the integrity of these tools is intact. Attackers love to modify these tools to make them unable to detect anything. Keeping these tools offline and loading them only long enough to run them is the wisest course of action.

## Security Operations Centers

Finally, an organization can set up security operations centers (SOCs) to quickly detect and respond to DoS and other types of attacks. SOCs can be both external and internal to an organization's network. If SOC staff find a new attack, they can quickly take action such as changing router rules to cut off subsequent traffic from the attacking site(s). Distributing SOCs throughout a network can substantially increase their effectiveness. An SOC can, for instance, be located in a part of a network that is experiencing a DoS attack that renders networking useless. The SOC in this part of the network will be effectively neutralized, but SOCs in other parts of the network are likely to still be operable to the point that each can defend its part of the network against the DoS attack that is occurring.

Table 1 summarizes the types of preventative measures that can be used against DoS attacks and the relative effectiveness of each.

## CONCLUSION

By now you should realize that DoS attacks constitute an extremely serious problem that has proven costly to many organizations. If anything, the problem is likely to become worse because systems, networks, applications, and the Internet itself are not really built to withstand these or many other type of attacks. With the increased threat of terrorist attacks also comes the possibility that terrorist organizations will launch DoS attacks to accomplish some of their purposes. Yet the Internet community depends on continuous computing and network services. What strategic directions can we take?

Unfortunately, there is no silver bullet. Many technical solutions, some of which are better than others, are available, yet they are unlikely in-and-of-themselves to solve the problem. Widespread cooperative effort might, however, help considerably. Under the initiative of the U.S. government, numerous Information Analysis and Sharing Centers (ISACs) have been formed for various sectors (e.g., financial, energy) of industry. ISAC members share information under a nondisclosure agreement, including information concerning attacks such as DoS attacks that they have experienced, and work on common solutions. Passing appropriate legislation would also constitute an important, additional solution for the DoS attack threat. Government representatives need to take the threat of these attacks more seriously and must draft and pass legislation designed to punish perpetrators of DoS and other kinds of cyberattacks. At the same time, government must seriously consider putting more pressure on ISPs to assume more responsibility for Internet security. If pressed, ISPs could block a greater amount of dangerous Internet traffic to reduce the amount of DoS attack-generated traffic. Considerably more funding for research on detection and prevention of DoS attacks would also constitute a big step forward. Research on system resilience and survivability conducted at institutions such as the University of New Mexico and the Software Engineering Institute of Carnegie Mellon University is already providing answers to what must be done in systems to reduce susceptibility to a wide range of catastrophes, including attacks such as DoS attacks. However, the ultimate responsibility belongs to senior management. Senior management must pay more attention to DoS attacks, particularly to the real level of risk that they pose. Senior management must then determine what the worst-case DoS scenarios are and ensure that their organizations are adequately prepared to deal with them.

The good news is that appropriate measures for preventing DoS attacks are not radically different from those for preventing other kinds of security-related attacks. Key measures include creating a sound information security policy and procedures, adopting the necessary technical countermeasures, being vigilant in detecting and analyzing anomalies, and responding promptly and effectively to incidents that occur.

## GLOSSARY

**Baseline Controls**　An approach to information security in which an organization learns of the controls posture of other peer organizations and tries to deploy roughly the same controls posture.

**Boomerang Attack**　A type of DoS attack in which the attacker spoofs the IP address of the host that is the intended victim; the attacker sends packets that elicit some kind of reply, but if the attacker sends enough packets initially, a large volume of replies is returned to the victim, causing it to hang or crash.

**Bubonic Attack**　A type of attack in which a barrage of pseudo-random TCP packets with identical TCP sequence numbers, source and destination ports, and other packet header information is sent to a victim Windows 2000 system and certain versions of Linux, causing the system to crash.

**Buffer Overflow Attack**　A type of attack in which a program receives too much input for the amount of memory allocated.

**Christmas Tree Attack**　An attack in which the attacker sends a packet with every option set for the TCP protocol.

**Cold Sites**　Operational sites to which computing operations are transferred after they are brought into operational status.

**CPU Hog**　A Windows NT Trojan horse program that feeds its process threads at the expense of other, unprivileged threads, causing the system to crash several seconds after this program starts to run.

**Denial of Service (DoS) Attacks**　Attacks are designed to disrupt, overwhelm, and/or damage computing resources and data.

**Distributed Denial of Service (DDoS) Attacks**　Attacks in which an attacker plants cooperative programs designed to unleash a massive DoS attack against a network.

**Due Care**　See baseline controls.

**Failover Systems and Devices**　Redundant systems and devices that are immediately used if the primary system or device goes down.

**Handler**　A type of program in a DDoS attack that controls zombies that have been planted in systems.

**Hot Sites**　Computing sites to which current computing operations can be rolled over in case of outage or disruption.

**Jolt and Jolt2 Attacks**　Attacks in which multiple identical fragments are sent to the victim system, causing massive CPU overutilization.

**Land Attack**　An attack in which an attacker sends one or more packets that have the same source and destination addresses, confusing the receiving system to the point that it crashes.

**Master**　A type of program in a DDoS attack that controls handlers that have been planted in systems.

**Packet Fragmentation Attacks**　Attacks in which packets are fragmented (broken into smaller pieces) in such a way that the receiving system processing them hangs or crashes.

**Ping-of-Death**　An attack in which a Windows 95/98/NT system is sent a series of fragmented IP packets that when combined form a packet larger than the system can process, causing the system to freeze.

**RAID (Redundant Array of Independent Drives)**　A hardware solution that allows uninterrupted access to data on disks if one disk fails.

**Shaft**　A type of DDoS tool.

**Security Operations Center**　A center within or outside of a network created for the purpose of identifying and quickly shutting off attacks.

**Shut-Down Attacks**　Attacks in which the purpose is to shut down but not delay systems or networks.

**Slow-Down Attacks** DoS attacks in which the purpose is to delay but not shut down processing activities of systems and/or networks.

**Smurf Attack** An attack in which the attacker sends many spoofed ping packets to one or more systems within a network, causing the victim(s) to become overwhelmed with replies.

**Spoofing** Using an IP source address other than the real address of the machine launching this kind of attack.

**SSPing** An attack in which a Windows 95/98/NT system is sent a series of fragmented IP packets that when combined form a packet larger than the system can process, causing the system to freeze.

**Stacheldracht** A type of DDoS tool.

**Teardrop Attack** A type of DoS attack in which the overlapping packet fragments cause the reassembled packet to have out-of-range values. If the receiving system is not programmed to check and drop fragments constructed in this manner, it will go into an abnormal operating condition and crash.

**Tribe Flood Network (TFN)** A type of DDoS tool.

**Trinoo** A type of DDoS tool.

**TFTP (Trivial File Transfer Protocol)** A protocol designed for efficient but not secure file transfer.

**UDP (User Datagram Protocol)** A protocol that is sessionless, connectionless, and unreliable.

**Uninterruptable Power Supply (UPS)** A hardware device attached to computing systems and network devices in a manner such that if an electrical failure occurs, the computer or device keeps running because of availability of UPS-supplied power.

**Warm Site** A backup recovery site that has the same basic information technology infrastructure as the original site but does not have all of the necessary hardware, software, and personnel.

**Zombie** A type of program in a DDoS attack that launches the attack after its handler instructs it to do so.

## CROSS REFERENCES

See *Active Response to Computer Intrusions; Firewall Basics; Hackers, Crackers and Computer Criminals; Intrusion Detection Systems Basics; Risk Management for IT Security.*

## REFERENCES

Endorf, C., Schultz, E. E., & Mellander, J. (2004). *Intrusion detection and prevention*. New York: McGraw-Hill.

Houle, K. J., Weaver, G.M., Long, N., & Thomas, R. (2001). *Trends in denial of service attack technology*. CERT Coordination Center.

Hussein, A., Heidemann, J., & Papadopoulos, C. (2003). A framework for classifying denial of service attacks. In *Proceedings of the ACM 2003 Conference on Applications, Technologies, Architectures, and Protocols for Computer Communications*, Karlsruhe, Germany (pp. 99–110).

National Academy of Sciences. (2002). *Cybersecurity today and tomorrow: Pay now or pay later*. Retrieved from http://www7.nationalacademies.org/cstb/pub_cybersecurity.html

Neumann, P. G. (1994) *Computer-related risks*. Reading, MA: Addison-Wesley.

Schultz, E. E. (2003, October). The MSBlaster worm: Going from bad to worse. *Network Security*, pp. 4–8.

Schultz, E. E., & Shumway, R. M. (2001). *Responding to incidents: A strategic guide for handling system and network security breaches*. Indianapolis, IN: New Riders.

# Network Attacks

Edward Amoroso, *AT&T Laboratories*

## INTRODUCTION

One of the earliest malicious attacks on a modern communications network was the infamous frequency spoof (at 2600 Hz) designed to trick Bell System circuit-switching equipment into providing a free phone call ("Toll Fraud Device," 1993). The attack was astonishingly simple to accomplish; it provided a clear gain to the intruder (monetary, in this case), and it turned out to be incredibly difficult for phone companies to actually fix. These basic attributes are still considered—from the perspective of an intruder—to be desirable. In fact, many modern intruders still trace their first recognition of computer-based attacks to this simple phone spoof and its associated simplicity, gain, and difficulty in remediation.

Our familiar anecdote demonstrates a basic presumption in this chapter—namely that although network technology will certainly evolve, the underlying principles of attacking such technology will remain firm. Therefore, this chapter concentrates on the fundamental and foundational principles of network attack. Such treatment ensures longevity and continued relevancy of this information as network infrastructure shifts in whatever direction users and network service providers determine. Wireless data and voice networking (e.g., 802.11), as well as multiprotocol label switching (MPLS), are two examples of newer technologies that can be attacked in essentially the same manner as previous networking methods.

### Underlying Network Infrastructure Model

Many models of networks are available in the literature, most based on the traditional International Standards Organization (ISO)—Open Systems Interconnect (OSI) seven-layer model (Tannenbaum, 1998). Although I maintain rough consistency in the discussions of this well-known model, I choose to explain network attacks in the context of a much simpler three-level model—one specially designed to be consistent with typical attacks carried out frequently on networks of diverse means, including ones carrying data, voice, and video over various packet, cell, and circuit switches technologies.

The first level of this simple model includes all underlying infrastructure elements that enable network communications. This level, referred to as the *network infrastructure* level (see Figure 1), includes all of the procedural, provisioning, monitoring, and other operational components that support network communications. This level is especially important because most practical attacks on networks include steps related to reconnaissance, social engineering, and other exploits focused at underlying operations. Many attackers claim that this level is easiest to target (see, for example, Kevin Mitnick's [2002] remarks).

The next level, referred to as *network protocol*, includes all of the various protocol services consistent with the ubiquitous Internet protocol (IP) services. IP security attacks involving service destination or source port weaknesses, as well as any destination or source address-level weaknesses, are included at this level. This level in our model is generally addressed almost *exclusively* in most treatments on network attacks. Such orientation stems from the plethora of weaknesses identified in the past decades for protocol services. Many real attacks have been created at this level, as one might expect. It is worth noting, by the way, that alternate non-IP protocols at this level (e.g., Signaling System 7) will not be specifically acknowledged but are nonetheless vulnerable to similar problems.

The third level, referred to as the *network applications* level, involves all software application-based vulnerabilities that are typically targeted by worms and network viruses. In recent years, such services have dominated network security. In essence, end-point vulnerabilities are increasingly being targeted over a network. This involves the network as a transport medium for attack steps rather than as the target of such attacks. Figure 1 depicts our simple network model.

The remainder of this chapter presents and discusses a collection of representative network attacks at

| Network Applications | Level 3 | Worms, Viruses, etc. |
| Network Protocol | Level 2 | IP, TCP, UDP, etc. |
| Network Infrastructure | Level 1 | Management, etc. |

**Figure 1:** Simple network model.

each of these three levels. As suggested earlier, I focus on foundational issues in each attack, including some suggestions for proper security remediation in practice.

# NETWORK INFRASTRUCTURE ATTACKS

The underlying infrastructure supporting modern networking is often ignored, especially in academic treatments of network security. This is unfortunate because the messiness inherent in supporting practical infrastructure offers the intruder amazing opportunities for exploit. Consider, for example, the aggressive treatment afforded public key cryptography in the mid-1990s. Academia—and, of course, the so-called dot-com companies of the Internet bubble era—recognized immediately the potential for such elegant technology in the provision of electronic commerce services. Software products, services, and entire companies thus sprung up in anticipation of this seemingly obvious technology path. The problem is that few of these groups recognized the extreme difficulty inherent in building a sustainable supporting infrastructure. As a result, the relatively disappointing public key infrastructure (PKI) that has only partially emerged across the globe can be directly traced to the complexity and other problems associated with building network infrastructure.

This section outlines several common types of attacks that occur repeatedly in such infrastructure systems. Our two selected attacks start with the softest of the infrastructure underbelly of any network: the people. Social engineering is shown to be an effective and technology-independent means for gaining unauthorized access, information, and other desirable assets from some network target. The second attack selected involves attacks directed specifically at the supporting devices. In the early days of networks, these would have been circuit switches; today, they are routers.

## Remote Access Through Social Engineering

Social engineering is arguably the most effective means for intentionally causing serious problems to a network infrastructure. No network service provider on the globe has been successful in totally removing the human element from its infrastructure (a common goal driven by intense cost pressures). As a result, attackers have long recognized that any people tasked with providing assistance do exactly that: They will provide assistance. And it is exactly this assistance that is so attractive to intruders.

Most examples of social engineering involve simply calling into a help desk and lying through one's teeth. The attacker obtains, for example, credentials for some employee of Company XYZ through a simple business card or Web search. The attacker then calls Company XYZ's network help desk posing as this targeted employee. It

isn't difficult to imagine getting all sorts of useful network information through this means. Another twist on this notion involves tricking the intruder masquerading not as a user or some system but as the help desk itself.

One example of this sort of social-engineering attack is the well-known password phishing expedition aimed at any Internet service provider offering e-mail service to a large number of users (see Figure 2). The way it works is simple: the intruder starts by identifying a large block of potentially valid email addresses. This can be accomplished in any number of ways—perhaps the most trivial being a handcrafting of likely handles appended to the service provider's domain name. Thus, we can imagine a block of target emails addresses as follows: aaa@isp.com, aab@isp.com, aac@isp.com, and so on. (I will leave it as an exercise to the reader to devise any number of more clever means for creating such a target list.)

The next step in the attack involves a crafting of some official-looking message that is sent to the block of crafted e-mails. The message should be sent from an authoritative source e-mail address, generally one that includes phrases like "admin" or "sysop" in the handle. These are pretty easily obtained from so-called anonymous e-mail providers such as Yahoo! or Hotmail. The content of the message is always pretty much the same in a password phishing scam: the user is asked to provide username and password information back to the administrator to maintain the accuracy of the account. It's always worded to sound mundane, but firm, and it usually suggests that nonaction will result in lost use of the account. Better phishing attacks include forms that users simply fill out—this certainly makes things more convenient.

Consider that if the intruder sent 10,000 such messages to a block of target crafted addresses. If we suppose that one tenth of the crafted addresses actually have associated users, then we can conclude that a thousand users get this message. If we presume that 99% of all users are smart enough to ignore or delete such a request, then we can conclude that 1% will respond. The intruder thus obtains 100 usernames and passwords.

To combat this problem, one might imagine a service provider being on the lookout for such phishing. This can be done by training users to ignore such phony messages. Expecting more than 99% compliance is not realistic, however. It can also be done by deliberately inserting bogus e-mail accounts that will automatically receive such phishing inquiries. This helps identify the problem when it is occurring but does little to stop it. In the end, such social-engineering attacks represent fundamental weaknesses in networking technology, and it is unlikely that this will change in the coming decades.

## Router Attacks

The most traditional of network infrastructure attacks are those that target specific equipment embedded in the underlying transport architecture. In the era of circuit switching, this involved attacks aimed at complex switches such as the AT&T 4ESS gateways. Security teams for network service providers focused in those days on ensuring that dial access maintenance ports were all sufficiently protected on these switches. Most people knew at

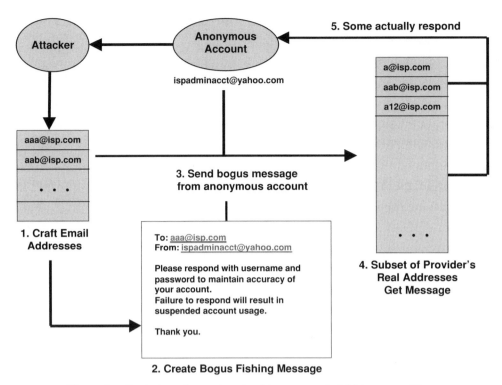

**Figure 2:** Depiction of steps involved in password phishing expedition.

the time that the only means for such protection was to remove such dial access entirely.

More recently, as circuit switching has been replaced with packet-based routed infrastructure, attacks must now be addressed that target specific devices in the packet switching network. Most likely, these devices are routers, and although they are not as complicated as circuit switches, they are just as vulnerable to direct attacks. In fact, given the degree to which routers can dynamically interact with their environment, one might argue that they are more vulnerable than traditional circuit switches. The key weakness lies in the common method of establishing trivial connectivity controls around routers. Many router administrators, for instance, continue to allow Telnet or SNMP (simple network management protocol) access for remote management. Even in environments where more secure remote access methods are used, vulnerabilities remain.

Additionally, because routers exist in so many locations, their physical security comes immediately into question. Traditional circuit switched service providers hid their equipment in bunker-like central offices. Modern routed infrastructure generally involves routers located in all sorts of unprotected locations.

It is precisely this physical weakness that brings to mind an attack that can have devastating consequences for any network infrastructure. The attack exploits the common mechanism in routers that allows administrators to recover access to their device in the event of a forgotten or lost password. The most familiar method for such recovery involves cycling power on the device and then interrupting the subsequent reboot sequence. This interruption provides the physical intruder, presumably standing there in front of the router console, with the

ability to direct the device to resume its reboot sequence without requesting that the existing password be issued. Once the router does come up, the physical intruder can simply set the password to whatever is desired. The reader can easily imagine the mischief that can ensue given this newly established intruder-set password.

Methods for preventing such an attack are generally mundane in nature. Routers in network infrastructure must be physically protected, a notion that is often foreign in many environments designed to assume a common cooperative environment. Furthermore, carefully designed programs of configuration management and system administration are required to ensure that router management processes are sufficiently robust to avoid sloppy access controls, weak logging, and an insecure routed network.

## NETWORK PROTOCOL ATTACKS

Network technology is built on the notion of protocol. The stepwise interaction between remote entities to accomplish some task is the essence of networking, and this will remain true well into the future. One great distinction that must be made in any taxonomy of network protocols involves the freedoms afforded participants in the various steps they accomplish. On one hand, certain protocols do not allow much in the way of such freedoms. Infrastructure is generally centralized in such cases, and any changes from the strict rules embedded in the protocol will cause immediate breakage. Traditional circuit switching worked this way, and it had clear security advantages. One end of a circuit switched interaction could not simply decide to play the protocol in a different way. Things would break.

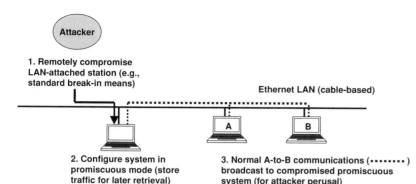

**Figure 3:** Sniffing on a compromised local area network station.

On the other hand, we have protocols that allow considerable freedoms on the part of its participants. IP environments, for example, allow the end-point participants to configure, initiate, and respond in manners that are casually specified in documents called (appropriately) Request for Comments (RFCs). If, for example, some system administrators decide to run Telnet services on port 500 over transmission control protocol (TCP), rather than the recommended port 23, then so be it. Certainly, this can cause problems for end users, but herein lies the attractiveness of such freedoms from a security perspective.

This section outlines six popular and well-known approaches to causing problems in an IP-type protocol environment. All of these attack strategies exploit the freedoms afforded participants in such environments. In particular, I illustrate the popular use of so-called sniffing, scanning, spoofing, flooding, and crafting approaches. For completeness, I also explain some security problems emergent in the control plane associated with the Internet.

## Network Sniffers

The concept of listening in over a shared communication medium is as old as the party lines that operated over telecommunications. That is, when groups of users have shared access to the same transmission lines, the opportunity for eavesdropping will always arise. Law enforcement pushes this notion in traditional telephony wiretapping, albeit using somewhat unconventional means.

For network attackers, the rise and usage of so-called sniffing methods seem to have paralleled the success of Ethernet and IP technologies. Both have seen amazing growth in the past decades and both are well suited to snooping over shared media. In fact, the design of both technologies explicitly relied on entities having the ability to examine communications and make local decisions about whether the information should be passed along, kept, or both. Because this local decision is based entirely on the integrity of deciding entity, it is easily abused.

The most common means for network sniffing involves simply configuring a station on an Ethernet local area network (LAN) in so-called promiscuous mode. This is often considered fine in local workgroups where such behavior is assumed or at least tolerated. The security issues arise when some external entity manages to penetrate this cozy arrangement with a sniffer that leaks confidential information outside the trusted workgroup. This is generally

done via some quiet insertion into a compromised LAN station—most likely on a cable-based Ethernet—in which the compromised station taps the A-to-B communication on the LAN (see Figure 3).

The obvious means for dealing with this specific sniffing threat is to configure the LAN in a so-called smart hub arrangement, which is essentially nothing more than a star configuration of multiple LAN segments. This is intended to provide privacy for A-to-B communications by segmenting the broadcast domain. Attackers are wise to this approach, however, and merely direct their attention toward embedding sniffers into the LAN management device itself. In fact, in the excellent book *@Large* (Freeman and Mann, 1998), an account is offered of a young hacker who manages to place sniffers onto actual Internet backbone routers, a feat that offers endless passwords and other interesting information. In the end, the only true means for countering this sort of attack is encryption. The difficulty associated with properly deploying modern encryption technology on a LAN, or any other type of network infrastructure, is thus most unfortunate.

## Network Scanning

Scanning is a network management technique that allows for remote determination of certain properties in the equipment or software of interest. Managers can first scan network-connected systems to determine whether they are capable of responding—an obviously important question in any network management setting. Scanning can also be done to determine the types of services that are remotely accessible from these target systems. In a typical IP environment, this involves attempts to attach to different listener programs—called daemons or services—on specifically named ports.

For all the reasons that scanning is powerful and useful for network managers, it is also powerful and useful for intruders. The first step in most nontrivial remote attacks involves the initiation of a scan from some reasonably hidden origination point toward the infrastructure of interest. (Note the use of the term *reasonably hidden* because scanning is so prevalent on the Internet today that a scan from some known source will probably go unnoticed and thus carries almost total impunity to the scanner.) In any event, the notion of "doorknob rattling" comes to mind in the implementation of a scan. The goal is to create a listing of each and every service being accepted on the target network interfaces. For IP services, this means checking

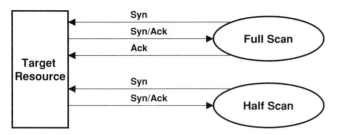

**Figure 4:** Full and half scanning techniques.

each of the roughly 130K ports associated with the TCP and UDP (user datagram protocol), as well as any other protocols that may be of interest.

Most scans fall into one of two categories. They are either aggressive in their operation, generally taking little or no steps to be stealthy and leaving a clear footprint of operation for any system managers who may be watching. These scanners are fine when used in the context of an information security and protection program. Most of them initiate a so-called *full scan* and complete the three-step TCP handshake when connecting to target resources. (Translated: Good guys doing approved scanning don't have to hide.) The second category of scanning involves slightly more stealth design. Some such scanners employ a so-called *half scan* technique in which the scanner initiates the familiar TCP handshake but then does not complete the final step in the process. Presumably, this will reduce the visibility of the scan in any associated log files (see Figure 4).

One of the more prevalent means for scanning in a modern Intranet environment today involves scanning for 802.11 or WiFi (wireless fidelity) access. This follows the basic premise established earlier—namely that an intruder can simply attempt to connect to infrastructure of interest with the intention of rattling the doorknobs. With the massive proliferation of WiFi hotspots, many set up with little or no authentication, the use of scanners as a first step toward determining connectivity profiles for companies is only likely to grow.

Many experts recommend that the best way to deal with the threat of scanning is simply to expect it. In fact, by proactively scanning one's own infrastructure with the expressed purpose of understanding the access footprint, one can more easily understand any exposure. Certainly, for services that simply must be allowed for open access, scanners will find them, but in cases when such services might be removed or minimized, proactive scanning will help define the problem to be solved. Deception offers a slightly more creative but far less mature option for network managers. In a deceptive scheme (e.g., see Fred Cohen's Deceptive Toolkit, n.d.,), scanners are duped into finding open services that are specifically installed to deceive. Time will tell whether such approaches can become practical.

## Address Spoofing

IP carries with it the source addressing baggage one often finds in any connectionless environment; that is, packets can be injected into a network with arbitrary—even bogus—source address information. So just as with paper letters in a postal service environment, the "from" information is less critical to the delivery algorithms than the "to" information. This allows for a standard sort of attack strategy in which the intruder forges the source address information in the packets associated with the attack.

A common forgery strategy involves an intruder specifically setting a source address to some designated alternate. This has the consequence of directing all return packets to that designated source address, but in volume-based attacks such as a denial of service, this may not matter. In addition, in some convoluted cases, one could employ a timing-based attack in which the packets are sent off with a forged source address, and then the intruder times the responses and guesses as to the types of information required in the response.

The well-known sequence number attack works in this fashion. Intruders pick the source IP address of some dupe system—presumably one with privileges that are based on its address. The intruder then floods the dupe system with packets so that it cannot be reached effectively once the attack has begun. As a final preparation, the intruder establishes a rhythm with the actual target system, watching the response sequence numbers in the TCP handshake. Once the rhythm is determined, the intruder quickly changes its source to the dupe, sends a sequence number guess as the dupe, and then hopes that connectivity is established (see Figure 5).

In truth, this attack does not work as effectively in recent years because so many systems have effectively removed source address-based authentication. Furthermore, TCP implementations have improved recently to the point where greater randomization is ensured in successive sequence number provisions. Nevertheless, the overall attack concept remains sound—and in any protocol where endpoints are authenticated based on address information, weaknesses emerge.

## Network Floods

One of the great axioms of network communications is that if a set of entities exceeds the capacity of their shared channel, delays will occur. This is true for the same reason that busy highways slow down when the traffic gets too heavy. Service providers combat this problem by a variety of methods ranging from over-designing available capacity to installation of clever routing methods to shift

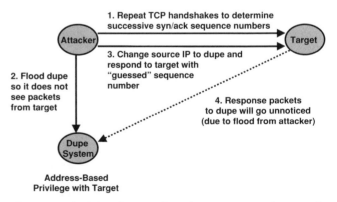

**Figure 5:** Traditional timing-based sequence number attack.

volume from heavily trafficked channels to less busy ones. In traditional telecommunications, for example, it is not uncommon to route voice calls from one busy region to another that might be less busy (perhaps the region is still largely asleep!).

Attackers also recognize this basic axiom of communication and have, as a result, devised attacks that are intended to overwhelm some channel. The target channel might be the transport systems for inbound and outbound IP communications for a business, or it could be the company Web site, or it could be some telephony systems, IP-based or otherwise. In each of these cases, the intruder tries to create a so-called denial of service effect by creating larger volumes of flow than the channel can handle.

One clever method for achieving this effect involves a so-called redirection attack. This involves an intruder first finding some large number of systems that are vulnerable to a remote code insertion. Commercial operating systems often allow arbitrary execution of code through sloppy programming. The most visible such sloppiness involves programmers forgetting to check boundary conditions properly for all input–output routines. The result is that attackers can exploit a buffer overflow condition, after which the target machine transfers execution to some designated address, which the intruder has already loaded with the software intended for execution.

In any event, once the remote code insertion has been done to a large number of systems, the denial of service generally proceeds as follows: The inserted code will have been designed to attack at some designated time a target system. The attack will include large flows of information; because a large number of distributed systems were set up in this manner, they will all collectively begin to overwhelm the target system (see Figure 6).

Unlike the previous attacks cited in this chapter, distributed denial of service continues to be a lethal and difficult to prevent attack strategy. Most network security managers deal with the problem by ensuring ample capacity in all critical communications channels. This can be expensive, not to mention being somewhat ineffective if the denial of service is truly excessive. One attack that has been particularly insidious in this regard involves spam e-mail being sent to a target by this series of hacked dupes. As one would guess, e-mail systems are typically designed to deal with a reasonable volume spike—perhaps some number of times greater than the normal load. Because it is expensive to extend e-mail-processing capability, most companies do not overdo this spare capacity. Thus, denial of service attacks aimed at such infrastructure can often gum up and slow down organizational e-mail.

## Crafted Packets

The final protocol attack strategy examined here involves the intentional crafting of sent packets in such a manner as to confuse the receiving endpoint. As you would guess, these packets would be crafted to be either malformed or to employ some sort of logic that the software developers of the receiving code might not have considered. This strategy is more often than not a hit-or-miss sort of method, one that requires a test bed where the intruder can try various combinations of malformation.

Familiar heuristics used in the creation of malformed packets include changes to packet size (larger or smaller), changes in packet payload, or, more commonly, changes in the packet header. Sometimes the change to a packet header involves some logic that is more than random malformation. If the source IP address of some packet that is coming in-bound to Organization X is, in fact, an Organization X source address, then the packet may be malformed. Similarly, if the source IP address of some packet exiting Organization X is not an Organization X source address, then something might be wrong as well.

Perhaps the most common sort of crafted packet involves attackers playing with the various flag options that exist in an IP header. These flag options that enable TCP/IP communications are designed to allow protocol designers to ensure, effectively and predictably, two-way communication handshakes, as in the TCP sequence. Consider, for example, what happens if these flags are jumbled or set to irrational combinations. The result will depend on the strength with which the implementation has considered such possibilities. An example of such an attack is the familiar Christmas tree attack, in which all of the flags in the IP header are set (i.e., lit up like a Christmas tree).

Combatting this sort of attack is generally quite simple. First of all, protocol implementations must be robust enough to consider all combinations of possible packet configuration. This is true even when the associated protocol specification might be silent on such decisions. Second, simple intrusion detection processing, perhaps even within the packet filtering functionality of a router or firewall, can trivially check for many of the absurd logical conditions inherent in this strategy. Perhaps this is, in fact,

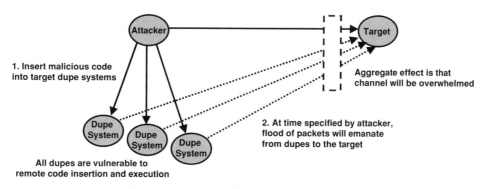

1. Insert malicious code into target dupe systems

Aggregate effect is that channel will be overwhelmed

2. At time specified by attacker, flood of packets will emanate from dupes to the target

All dupes are vulnerable to remote code insertion and execution

**Figure 6:**  Distributed denial of service attack.

one of the few scenarios where intrusion detection can be counted on to reliably protect infrastructure.

# APPLICATION-BASED NETWORK WORMS AND VIRUSES

Metcalf's famous remark about the value of networks rising exponentially with the value of its end points can be appended here for security. That is, the value of a network to an intruder also rises exponentially with the target value of its endpoints. As such, we must acknowledge that application software vulnerabilities on a network create opportunities for attack. Because these attacks are unrelated to the underlying characteristics of the network, we treat them separately in our model.

Arguably, the most dramatic new challenge in security involves the myriad software vulnerabilities that have arisen in off-the-shelf code from major vendors. This has included office automation software, network utilities, operating system routines, Web-based utilities, and on and on. Nothing seems to have been immune. Dijkstra (1982) predicted this effect many years ago in the majority of his musings, but perhaps even Dijkstra would have been surprised by the intensity with which such programming shortcomings have damaged our infrastructure.

This section outlines the basic characteristics of recent popular worms and viruses. I examine the Morris worm of 1988, which effectively brought down the Internet. I also look at the SoBig, Slammer, and Nachi worms of 2002. These provide good insight into the design and associated effect of such worms on network infrastructure.

## Simple Worm Schema

In 1988, a then-graduate student from Cornell University named Robert Morris Jr. created a worm program that he unleashed—apparently with no intent to harm—onto the Internet. Clearly, the Internet was a much less content-rich environment at the time, and the World Wide Web had yet to be deployed in the form we recognize today. Nevertheless, the worm had a broad-reaching impact on Internet operations and caused an unprecedented amount of trouble across the global infrastructure.

Perhaps most notable about the Morris worm of 1988 was the simplicity in its design. Detailed forensic analyses of the code are already well documented (see Denning, 1989) and are thus considered well beyond the scope of this chapter. The basic schema involved in the Morris worm, however, would come to be seen over and over in subsequent decades of malicious worm design. It is thus instructive to examine this high-level schema with the intention of understanding its power and basic operation.

At the root of the Morris worm is a simple recursive three-step process that astounds most observers on first glance. We say that it astounds because most observers expect something considerably more complex. Following are the three steps in trivial pseudo code:

```
Worm {
    Step 1: Find Networked System X
    Step 2: Copy Worm Over Network to X
    Step 3: Remotely Execute Worm on X
    }
```

Let's consider each of the simple steps in the schema: First, the worm tries to find some system that it can reach over a network. This could be done dynamically by actually initiating a scan or search; alternatively, it might be done in a local manner by consulting some appropriate file or database of remote systems. It might even use some algorithm to create well-formed addresses of some randomly targeted systems. In an IP environment, the requisite address-generating code can be surprisingly compact and efficient (as was the case in the Slammer worm, discussed later).

The second step in the worm schema involves finding some way to copy the worm code over a network and onto the target system. In the more open and friendlier era of the 1980s and early 1990s, traditional Berkeley UNIX-style R-series commands might have been used to accomplish this task. Today, with the advent of the Internet firewall, the more likely arrangement involves exploiting a known vulnerability in an Internet-visible system. Further, broadband-connected PCs are an attractive target in this regard. Once the vulnerability—perhaps a buffer overflow—is exploited, the worm copies itself onto the now-compromised system. The irony here is that the security team closes the front door to such remote copy, only to find that software bugs in commercially procured systems provide an alternate path in.

The third step in the worm schema is often done automatically. That is, the inserted code might be set up to wreak havoc from the target system at some designated time, controlled by a simple timer in the code. In certain cases, one could imagine a remote command from the attacker being sent to the exploited system; as noted earlier, in friendlier times, R-series commands provided a convenient means for such remote execution. Firewalls have made this all but disappear.

Effective security fixes to worms of this type are few and far between. Most security teams simply practice their response procedures to the point where they can minimize the duration from detection time to taking action. Obviously, the best way to stop worms of this sort is to remove the exploitable vulnerabilities from software being run in enterprise systems. This is easier said than done.

## Denial of Service Worms

On January 25, 2003, at roughly midnight in New York, a lethal worm—subsequently dubbed Slammer—injected itself onto the Internet infrastructure, taking roughly 3 minutes to reach many tens of thousands of vulnerable computer systems. Slammer exploited a buffer overflow vulnerability (what else?) in Microsoft's SQL database code. The worm executed via UDP port 1434 and produced a bounce effect with UDP packets flying around networks at a dizzying pace causing a severe denial of service effect. All day on the 25th and well into the 26th, corporations and agencies scrambled to figure out what to do. Few decent solutions were immediately available.

The root cause of the Slammer worm was buggy Microsoft code. No amount of debate can alter that fact; this is not to suggest that Microsoft is solely to blame for all the worm problems that have ensued across the global network community. Yet, Slammer clearly exploited a Microsoft coding error. Microsoft has since announced a major corporate program called the Trusted Computing Initiative (see Dijkstra, 1982), and this author applauds such efforts. Nevertheless, considerable buggy software remains from all vendors, including Microsoft, and this is a legitimate cause for concern for information technology, network, and security managers.

The practical six-step approach to mitigating worms like Slammer is worthy of some attention here. Our discussion is based on experiences dealing with corporate and government chief security officers throughout 2003 and into 2004. Most of the groups we queried converged on these six simple steps in a roughly similar manner, suggesting that the following may constitute the beginnings of a best practice. Note that the process described here is generally followed in a stepwise manner, with successive steps highly interleaved.

*Step 1: Address Filtering.* When a worm hits a local area network and begins to have a negative effect (e.g., performance problems, outages), the first order of business must be to restore order. Source IP addresses can be easily determined to be infected and must be filtered immediately. This can be done via access control list rules on LAN switches, routers, or firewalls. Organizations are advised to plan for this in advance.

*Step 2: Service Filtering.* If the worm is particularly pervasive, network and security managers might decide to filter at the service level. This involves dropping packets based on the service port (usually TCP or UDP) or defined protocol. For Slammer, this meant dropping SQL traffic between sites, workgroups, locations, or LANs.

*Step 3: Traffic Monitoring.* This step really interleaves with all the others, but it became particularly important once filtering has been out in place. If all is done properly, the effects of the worm should dampen immediately, or at least become contained within the confines of each filtering chokepoint. For example, if LAN X is spewing out Slammer packets and is then isolated via a filter, the packets should no longer have any effect on the rest of the enterprise. LAN X might still see problems, however.

*Step 4: Software Patching.* The introduction of well-tested patches obviously relies on cooperation and fast response from the targeted software vendor. Once filters have isolated worm activity to LANs, it should *in theory* be relatively easy to go in and patch any computers that remain infected—in theory because sometimes these systems are not so easily located. Most tools for remote management of systems do not query or store information like the reach number of the system owner, the location in some packed laboratory where an infected server or PC might be located, or where the key might be to open the door to that laboratory. These are mundane concerns certainly, but when neglected, they greatly complicate the patch process.

*Step 5: Forensic Analysis.* This step is optional. In my experience, most organizations are desperate to understand the details of the worm that has hit their infrastructure. While patches are being done, forensic analysis often

ensues. This is actually an important step because it provides hints as to any residual effects or variants that should be planned for.

*Step 6: Service and User Remediation.* Any time filtering is put in place, users or groups will invariably begin to experience problems. After all, the filtering is shutting down services. If this causes no problems, then arguably the service should not have been allowed in the first place. So the last step we will mention here involves dealing with the business effects of the filters. Usually, this involves expediting the patching and then restoring service to the affected group.

## Misguided Ethical Worms

The last example discussed in this chapter involves the misguided notion of using worms to produce a purported beneficial result. This vigilante notion was realized in the summer of 2003 with the Nachi worm that exploited a vulnerability in Microsoft's remote procedure call (RPC) code. The Nachi worm came in through the traditional TCP port 135 associated with RPC but used ICMP (Internet control message protocol) type 8 packets (echo request) to find target systems. Amazingly, the purpose of Nachi was to deliver the required Microsoft patch. The problem is that the ICMP traffic began to bounce all over enterprise and wide area networks causing a gradual denial of service result for many, many companies and agencies.

One technique that offers considerable potential early warning security benefit for managers involves monitoring network traffic to detect anomalies. The idea is that by watching traffic on a real-time basis and creating baseline profiles of what is considered normal, the analyst might be able to detect changes quickly and accurately. As an example, consider that Figure 7 shows the ICMP traffic that AT&T engineers watched on a collection of IP transport links on its backbone on the day that preceded Nachi's expansive growth. Nothing particularly interesting is occurring and (although not evident from the diagram) the histogram demonstrates little change from previous hours.

As the hours progressed, the AT&T security operations center detected a gradual change in this ICMP profile for these circuits. By 06:00 Greenwich mean time on the 18th—8 hours later—the histogram had changed dramatically. This change is particularly important because it precedes the Nachi infection of most business and agency network by many hours (even days). Figure 8 shows the changed histogram, which depicts the stark changes in ICMP traffic that Nachi caused.

## CONCLUSION AND FURTHER READING

Networks will continue to dominate computing usage and societal infrastructure into the foreseeable future. In addition, malicious attacks on infrastructure will continue to grow in their intensity and vigor (see recent works in this area including Hansche, Berti, & Hare, 2004; Kaufman, Perlman, & Speciner, 2002). Putting these two observations together underscores the importance of continued vigilance in network security.

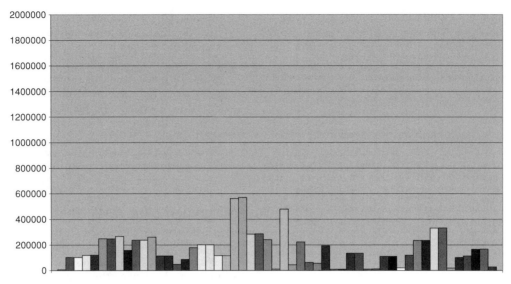

**Figure 7:** Normal Internet control message protocol traffic just prior to Nachi's growth (08/17/03—22:00 Greenwich mean time).

In this short final section, I comment on two issues that require much greater attention in the coming years. First, I illustrate the security problems inherent in efforts at ubiquitous networking—the "an IP address on every microwave oven" activity. Second, I comment on the problems associated with the clear lack of diversity that exists in our software infrastructure with the underlying architecture dominated by a single approach from a single off-the-shelf software vendor.

## Ubiquitous Networked Devices

The effect here should be obvious: currently, worms and viruses cause problems on servers, PCs, and related network devices. Increasingly, this is also becoming a problem for voice telephony systems that use IP infrastructure. If the often-discussed ubiquity of networked entities across a greater range of devices (e.g., household utilities) becomes a reality, we can expect these security attacks to cause problems on such devices as well. Certainly, the likelihood that exploitable vulnerabilities will exist in future network microwave ovens, home alarm systems, automobiles, and airplanes will be high. As such, we can expect that worms will travel across this new network grid with a ferocity that will at least match what we've seen to date.

## Lack of Diversity

It goes without saying that diverse populations are always more robust that monocultures. This implies that as global infrastructure continues to evolve, additional thought should be placed on whether planned diversity at the application, operating system, and network layers is desirable.

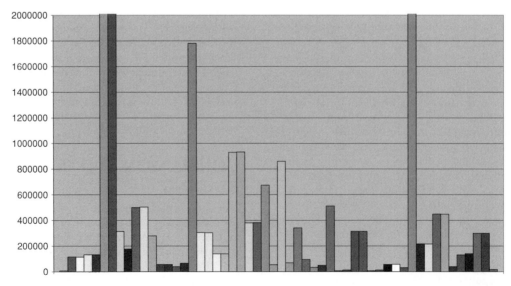

**Figure 8:** Nachi-affected normal Internet control message protocol traffic (08/18/03—06:00 Greenwich mean time).

## GLOSSARY

**Attack** The malicious exploitation of some vulnerability.

**Denial of Service** A condition in which malicious action prevents authorized use of a service.

**Flood** A volume-based attack designed to overwhelm a target.

**Scanning** A systematic technique for checking elements of a target set.

**Social Engineering** An attack technique designed to exploit human frailty and shortcomings.

**Spoofing** A malicious means for unauthorized use of an identity.

**Virus** A maliciously created program that propagates and replicates.

**Worm** A virus that can self-propagate and replicate.

## CROSS REFERENCES

See *Access Control: Principles and Solutions; Computer Viruses and Worms; Denial of Service Attacks; Firewall Basics; Hackers, Crackers and Computer Criminals; Routers and Switches.*

## REFERENCES

Note that these references include, for the most part, more mature publications; this reflects the observation that the majority of the huge tomes on network attacks found in most bookstores provide precious little new insight into the network attack problem.

Cohen, F. (n.d.) Deception toolkit (DTK). Retrieved from http://www.all.net

Denning, P. (1989, March/April). The Internet worm. *American Scientist*, 126–128.

Dijkstra, E. (1982). *Selected writings on computing.* New York: Springer-Verlag.

Freeman, C., & Mann, T. @*Large*. 1998.

Hansche, S., Berti, J., & Hare, C. (2004). *Official (ISC2) guide to the CISSP exam*. Auerbach.

Kaufman, C., Perlman, R., & Speciner, M. (2002). *Network security: Private communication in a public world* (2nd ed.). Englewood Cliffs, NJ: Prentice Hall.

Mitnick, K. (2002). *The Art of Deception*. New York: Wiley.

Tannenbaum, A. (1998). *Computer networks*. Upper Saddle River, NJ: Prentice Hall.

Toll Fraud Device. *2600: The Hacker Quarterly, 10*, 42.

# Fault Attacks

Hamid Choukri, *Gemplus & University of Bordeaux, France*
Michael Tunstall, *Gemplus & Royal Holloway, University of London*

## INTRODUCTION

One of the first examples of faults being injected in a microchip was accidental. It was noticed that radioactive particles produced by elements present in the packaging material (May & Woods, 1978) caused faults in chips. Uranium-235, Uranium-238, and Thorium-230 was present that decays to Lead-206. The process released alpha particles that created a charge in sensitive areas of the chip causing bits to flip. These elements were only present in 2 or 3 parts per million, but this was sufficient to have an effect on the behavior of the chip.

Subsequent research included studying the effects of cosmic rays on semiconductors (Ziegler, 1979). Cosmic rays are weak at ground level because of the earth's atmosphere. The probability of a fault produced in an integrated circuit is therefore very small, but the more random access memory (RAM) a computer has, the higher the chance of a fault occurring (i.e., it becomes more likely that a fault will occur in one RAM cell). This also provoked a great deal of research by organizations such as NASA and Boeing as the effects of cosmic rays become more pronounced in the upper atmosphere and space.

Most of the work on fault resistance was motivated by this vulnerability to charged particles. A great deal of research has gone into "hardening" electronic devices to be able to function in harsh environments. This has mainly been done using simulators to model a circuit and then to study the effect of randomly induced faults.

Various methods have since been discovered to induce a fault in a chip, but all the different methods have similar effects on the behavior of the chip. An example of such a method is the use of a laser to imitate the effect of charged particles (Habing, 1992). The various faults that can be produced have been characterized to enable suitable protective measures to be designed.

The first published attack that used a fault to derive secret information from a chip was DeMillo, Boneh, and Lipton (1997). This attack was against the RSA public-key cryptographic algorithm when calculated using the Chinese remainder theorem. If the calculation is disturbed in a certain way, the two large prime numbers, on which the security of the algorithm rests, can be derived. This led to attacks being published on other cryptographic algorithms.

A great deal of research had already been conducted into fault analysis. Practical countermeasures that can be used to protect systems against fault-attacks have already largely been defined.

## FAULT INJECTION

The increasingly high-speed, high-integration density and reduced power consumption have made electronic circuits increasingly sensitive to fault-injection techniques.

### Method of Fault Injection

Various methods of fault injection can be used to influence what is happening in a chip.

### Particle Accelerator

A particle accelerator is a device used in nuclear physics that produces a beam of high-speed particles (e.g., neutrons, protons, ions). These particles are used as projectiles to "bombard" atoms and to disintegrate them. A particle accelerator was the method used initially to simulate faults generated in space on electronic circuits because it was able to create the same effect. However, a particle accelerator is expensive and therefore not available to everybody. This is more of an aggressively hostile environment rather than a mechanism for injecting precise faults.

### Variations in the Supply Voltage

This method of fault injection uses a variation of the power voltage during a short period of time so that the processor misinterprets an instruction or a variable. This method is widely known in the smart-card industry but does not often appear in the literature.

## Variation in the External Clock

The object of this fault-injection method is to vary the external clock in such a way that the operating speed of the electronic circuit is reduced or to introduce a false cycle that could push the circuit into an abnormal operating condition.

## Temperature

The circuit designer defines upper and lower temperature thresholds between which the circuit will function correctly. The goal of this method of fault injection is to change the temperature (Skorobogatov, 2002) until it exceeds the threshold defined by the designer, after which faults may occur in the circuit (Govindavajhala & Appel, 2003).

## White Light

All electric circuits are sensitive to light because of the photoelectric effect. Current induced by photons can induce a fault if a circuit is exposed to intense light for a brief period of time. This can be used as an inexpensive method of fault induction (Anderson & Skorobogatov, 2002).

## Laser Light

A laser can reproduce a wide variety of faults and can be used to simulate (Habing, 1992) the fault-injection effects of particle accelerators (Fouillat, 1990; Pouget, 2000). The effects produced are similar to white light because faults are also due to current induced by the photoelectric effect. The advantage of a laser over white light is that laser light is directional and can therefore be used to target a small area of a circuit.

## The Effects of Different Types of Faults

A fault can arise in the chip through two main effects that the previously described physical stimuli can produce in semiconductors. A current can be induced via a physical effect (e.g., the photoelectric effect, ionization) that can

be sufficient to cause a fault. Alternatively, a defect can be created in the structure of the semiconductor (usually permanent). These two types of faults can be classed as destructive and transient (or provisional) faults and can cause different effects in the silicon.

## Destructive Faults

There are four types of destructive faults, classified in the following manner:

1. **Single Event Burnout Faults (SEB):** These involve a parasitic thyristor being formed in the MOS (metal oxide semiconductor) power transistors (Kuboyama, Matsuda, Kanno, & Ishii, 1992; Stassinopoulos et al., 1992). This can cause thermal runaway in the circuit causing its destruction.

2. **Single Event Snap Back Faults (SES):** SES faults (Koga & Kolasinski, 1989) are due to a self-sustained current produced by a parasitic bipolar transistor in MOS transistor channel N. This type of fault is not likely to occur in technologies with a low supply voltage.

3. **Single Event Latch-Up Faults (SEL) (Figure 1):** SEL faults (Adams, Daly, Harboe-Sorensen, Nickson, Haines, Schafer, et al., 1992; Fouillat, 1990) are produced in an electronic circuit by the creation of a self-sustained current, through the releasing of PNPN parasitic bipolar transistors in CMOS (complementary metal oxide semiconductor) technology. This can potentially destroy the circuit.

4. **Total Dose Rate:** This type of fault (Cazenave et al., 1998) is due to a progressive degradation of the electronic circuit through exposure to a hostile environment, which can cause defects in the circuit (Rax, Lee, Johnston, & Barnes, 1996).

## Provisional Faults

Provisional faults have a reversible effect, and the circuit will return to its original mode after the system is reset or the corrupted area is changed by another part of the circuit.

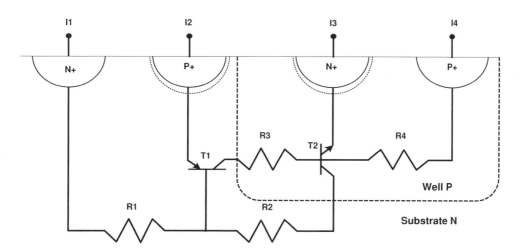

**Figure 1:**   Single event latch-up—parasitic transistors T1 and T2.

**Single Event Upsets (SEU):** These involve flipping in the logical state of the cell to its complementary state. The transition can be temporary if the fault is produced in a dynamic system, or permanent if it appears in a static system. The single event upset was first noticed during a space mission in 1975 (O'Gorman, 1994; Pickel & Blandford, 1978) and generated a need for research into the mechanisms by which faults could be created in chips. The SEUs can also manifest as a variation in an analogue signal such as the supply voltage or the clock signal.

**Multiple Event Upsets (MEU):** The MEU faults are a generalization of the SEU faults. The fault consists of several SEUs that occur simultaneously. A high circuit integration density is a factor that can provide conditions favorable to the generation of this type of fault.

**Dose Rate Faults:** Faults produced by the total dose rate (Koga, Looper, Pinkerton, Stapor, & McDonald, 1996) are caused by the impact of several particles whose individual effect is negligible. However, the cumulative effect of their effects generates a sufficient disturbance for a fault to be induced in the circuit.

When using fault-injection methods to perform a fault attack, it is the provisional faults that are usually of greater interest. They allow for faults in numerous different configurations to be attempted before the desired effect is achieved. It also means that the system is functional after the attack has finished. A destructive fault can easily render the device under attack unusable, as described in the section on destructive faults.

## FAULT ANALYSIS

The first example of a fault attack was published in DeMillo et al. (1997), which was an attack against implementations of RSA using the Chinese remainder theorem. Since then, numerous papers have been published on attacks against various different cryptographic algorithms. More recently, a paper was published attacking the Java virtual machine on a personal computer (PC; Govindavajhala & Appel, 2003).

Most of these publications concern themselves with attacking secure tokens that generally have a relatively simple communication protocol. This makes finding the moment in time where a successful fault attack can be made far easier than for more complex systems such as a PC. In devices with simple protocols, there will generally exist an "execute algorithm" command that will give an indication of precisely when the algorithm of interest executes. With complex systems such as a PC, it becomes much more problematic due to system interrupts, multitasking, and so on. Even when the process to be attacked can be readily located, the precision required by some theoretical attacks is next to impossible to realize. What follows is a description of some of the fault-based attacks that have been published.

### Transferring Secret Data

One of the simplest types of fault attack to understand is the injection of a fault during the transfer of secret data

**Table 1** Shamir Data Encryption Standard (DES) Attack

| Input | DES Key | | | | | | | | | Output |
|---|---|---|---|---|---|---|---|---|---|---|
| M → | $K_0=$ | XX | XX | XX | XX | XX | XX | XX | XX | →$C_0$ |
| M → | $K_1=$ | XX | XX | XX | XX | XX | XX | XX | 00 | →$C_1$ |
| M → | $K_2=$ | XX | XX | XX | XX | XX | XX | 00 | 00 | →$C_2$ |
| M → | $K_3=$ | XX | XX | XX | XX | XX | 00 | 00 | 00 | →$C_3$ |
| M → | $K_4=$ | XX | XX | XX | XX | 00 | 00 | 00 | 00 | →$C_4$ |
| M → | $K_5=$ | XX | XX | XX | 00 | 00 | 00 | 00 | 00 | →$C_5$ |
| M → | $K_6=$ | XX | XX | 00 | 00 | 00 | 00 | 00 | 00 | →$C_6$ |
| M → | $K_7=$ | XX | 00 | 00 | 00 | 00 | 00 | 00 | 00 | →$C_7$ |

from one part of data memory to another, although the implementation is far from trivial. One published attack (Biham & Shamir, 1997) assumes the transferring of a data encryption standard (DES) key from the EEPROM (electrically erasable and programmable memory) to the RAM in a smart card. If the value of parts of the key can be changed to a fixed value (1 byte at a time, for example), a method of deriving the key can be found. The attack operates as follows.

The DES algorithm can be executed with message m to obtain ciphertext $c_0$. During the transfer of the DES key to RAM, 1 byte of the key is changed to a fixed value, and the DES executed with the result is noted. The same thing is done with 2 bytes being set to a fixed value, then with 3, and so on. This continues until the vast majority of the key has a fixed and, therefore, a known value. This procedure is shown in Table 1, where $c_n$ represents the ciphertext of an unknown key with $n$ bytes set to a fixed value (00 has been chosen for this example). Once these data have been collected, they can be used to derive the DES key.

To find $K_7$, there are 128 possible values for the first byte of the DES key, which can searched through until M produces $C_7$. Although a byte is changed, only 128 values are possible because the least significant bit is the parity bit. After this, $K_6$ can be found by searching through the 128 possible values for the second byte because the first byte will be known. Finding the entire key will require the searching through a reduced key space of 1,024 keys.

This type of attack can also be used where unknown data is manipulated with a known algorithm. The efficiency of this type of attack depends on the amount of data that is changed by injecting a fault (and also that the value it takes is known). If it is possible to change 1 bit at a time, it would be necessary to generate 56 values for the ciphertexts. The processing a posteriori becomes trivial because the bits can be read directly from the faulty ciphertexts. If a ciphertext is identical to the previous ciphertext, then forcing the bit to zero has caused no change, so its value was already zero. If a change occurred, however, then the bit had been set to one before being forced to zero.

A continuation of this idea was published in Paillier (1999) in which the assumption is made that random bits of the key would move from 1 to 0 or from 0 to 1 with given probabilities. This provides a more complicated algorithm for deriving the key and allows for more liberty in the type of fault that can be created in the key. Unfortunately, there is nothing to suggest that modern semiconductors can be made to behave in this fashion.

## RSA

The first published attack based on fault induction appeared in DeMillo et al. (1997) and described a method of retrieving the secret keys from a faulty execution of the RSA algorithm (Rivest, Shamir, & Adleman, 1978) calculated using the Chinese remainder theorem. This is achieved with the following calculations, where the signature (S) is generated from a message (m) using a secret key (d) in the following manner (a certain familiarity with the algorithm is assumed):

$$S_q = m^{d \mod (q-1)} \mod q$$
$$S_p = m^{d \mod (p-1)} \mod p$$

These two values are then combined to produce a signature using the formula:

$$S = S_q + ((S_p - S_q)(q^{-1} \mod p) \mod p)q$$

If a fault is produced in the calculating device during the calculation of $S_p$ or $S_q$, the prime numbers that form $n$ in the calculation of RSA can be derived by the formula:

$$\gcd(S - S', n) = \gcd(a(S - S'), n)$$
$$= q$$

This assumes that the fault was created during the generation of $S_q$. If the fault was induced during the calculation of $S_p$, the formula would produce $p$.

This is the simplest fault attack to implement once a method of fault injection has been found. This is because the two exponentiations to calculate $S_p$ and $S_q$ will take a significant amount of time to calculate when compared with the whole algorithm, and any fault during this time will produce an exploitable result.

## DES

Another example of an attack against a cryptographic algorithm is that of attacking the 15th round of the DES algorithm during its execution. DES is a 16-round secret key algorithm based on a Feistel structure. The attack described here is a specific version of the attack described in Biham & Shamir, 1997, which is based on 1-bit changes at a random point in the DES algorithm. A version of this attack can be derived in which the fault is injected into the 15th round of the DES.

If a simplified version of the last round of the DES is considered (Figure 2), it can be used to show what happens if the previous round has not executed properly. In Figure 2, the bitwise permutations have been removed to simplify the explanation because they do not change the theory (even if they complicate an actual implementation).

The outputs of the last round can be expressed as:

$$R_{16} = S(R_{15} \oplus K_{16}) \oplus L_{15}$$
$$= S(L_{16} \oplus K_{16}) \oplus L_{15}$$

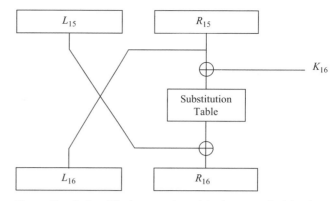

**Figure 2:** A simplified expression of the last round of the data encryption standard algorithm.

If a fault occurs during the execution of the 15th round, that is, the calculation of $R_{15}$, such that $R_{15}$ is changed to become $R_{15}'$, then we can show that:

$$R_{16}' = S(R_{15}' \oplus K_{16}) \oplus L_{15}$$
$$= S(L_{16}' \oplus K_{16}) \oplus L_{15}$$

If we xor the values of $R_{16}$ and $R_{16}'$ together, we get:

$$R_{16} \oplus R_{16}' = S(L_{16} \oplus K_{16}) \oplus L_{15} \oplus S(L_{16}' \oplus K_{16}) \oplus L_{15}$$
$$= S(L_{16} \oplus K_{16}) \oplus S(L_{16}' \oplus K_{16})$$

This gives a relationship in which only the value for the 16th subkey is unknown; all the other variables are given directly as an output of the DES. For each substitution table used in the last round of the DES, this relationship will be true. An exhaustive search of the 64 possible values that validate this equation can be conducted for each of the 6 bits corresponding to the input of each substitution table. This will give approximately $2^{18}$ hypotheses for the last subkey leading to an exhaustive search of $2^{26}$ DES keys to find the whole key.

In practice, it is simplest to conduct the attack several times either at different positions in the 15th round or with a varying message. When the lists of possible hypotheses are generated, the actual subkey will be present in the intersection of all the sets of hypotheses.

If the difference between the two output values for a given substitution table ($R_{16}$ and $R_{16}'$) is zero, then all the possible values of $K_{16}$ for that substitution table will be valid. This means that it is advantageous to induce a fault as early as possible in the 15th round so that the effect of the fault is spread to as many substitution tables as possible in the 16th round.

A more powerful attack was published in Piret and Quisquater (2003), which can be applied to all secret key algorithms. The details of this attack are beyond the scope of this chapter and are referred to as further reading.

## The Java Sandbox

The Java sandbox is an environment in which applets are run where they have no direct access to the computer's resources, the idea being that an applet need not be trusted as the system renders it incapable of behaving maliciously.

Java programs are commonly used on the Internet, where an applet is downloaded and executed on a PC to achieve a given effect on the Web page being observed.

A relatively recent paper (Govindavajhala & Appel, 2003) describes a fault attack on a PC to break the Java sandbox to be able to execute arbitrary code. This was done by using a spotlight to heat up the RAM used by the PC to the point where a fault, in this case a bit flip, was likely to occur within the computer's RAM.

A special applet was loaded into the computer's memory and the computer's RAM heated up to the point where some bits would change their value. The fault that was expected was that the address of a function called by the applet would have 1 bit complemented, so that the address called was $\pm 2^i$, where $i$ varies between 1 and 32 (the computers word size). A different function can be placed at all these addresses with a different function interface to the one normally called.

This allows a function to be created in which the data type can be masked to another type, which is normally forbidden by the Java sandbox. For example, an integer can be masked to a pointer. This will permit the applet to have read and write access to an arbitrary address in the RAM. This can be used to adjust a field in the systems security manager to allow the applet any rights it desires.

## COUNTERMEASURES

Because the identification of faults is a problem in electronic systems, several studies of circuit-hardening methods have been carried out. These solutions help circuits to avoid, detect, or correct faults. The countermeasures that can be applied to hardware and software will be treated separately for clarity.

### Hardware

Hardware protection is generally implemented by the chip designer and can be divided into two categories, the first being active protections that aim to detect any external intrusion to thwart any invasive attacks. These include the following:

- Light detectors detect changes in the gradient of light.
- Supply voltage detectors make it possible to detect any abrupt variation in the applied potential to ensure that

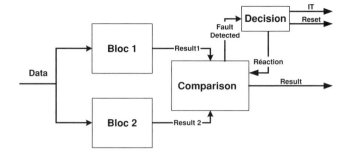

**Figure 3:** Simple duplication with comparison.

the voltage is within the limits of functionality of the electronic circuit.

- Frequency detectors impose a maximum operating frequency outside of which the electronic circuit will reset itself.
- Active shield is a metal mesh that covers the entire chip and has data passing continuously across it. If there is a disconnection or modification of this mesh, the chip does not operate. This is primarily a countermeasure against probing, although it makes fault injection more difficult as it is harder to locate specific blocks in a circuit.
- Hardware redundancy including the following:
  **Simple duplication with comparison (SDC; Figure 3)** —consists of the duplication of hardware blocks followed by a test processed by the comparison block. When the results of the two blocks do not match, a fault-detected status is transmitted to the decision block.

  Two types of reaction can be implemented: a hardware reset or the activation of an interruption that triggers dedicated countermeasures. This type of duplication protects against single focused errors and only permits the detection of the event. A retroaction signal can be enabled to stop the resulting transmission of the output to the exterior, which may otherwise be exploitable.

  **Multiple duplication with comparison (MDC; Figure 4)**—each hardware block is duplicated in at least three blocks. The comparison block detects any mismatch between the blocks and

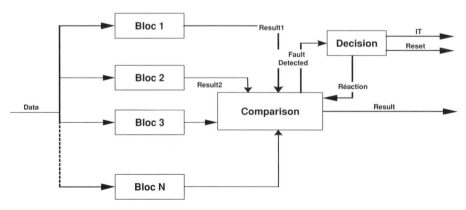

**Figure 4:** Multiple duplication with comparison.

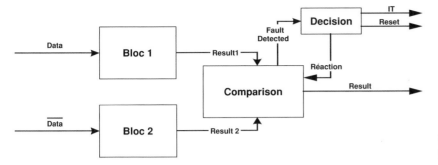

**Figure 5:** Simple duplication with complementary redundancy.

transmits the fault-detected status to the decision block.

As noted previously, two types of reaction could be implemented, a hardware reset or the activation of an interruption. The difference with respect to the SDC is the possibility to correct the fault detected with the feedback signal that can permit a majority vote on the correct exit signal.

**Simple duplication with complementary redundancy (SDCR; Figure 5)**—this is based on the same principles as SDC, but the two blocks manage complemented signals. When the result of the two blocks' results do not mismatch, the comparison block transmits an error status to the system, which manages the state by triggering a hardware reset or activating an interrupt. This type of duplication protects against multiple focused errors because it is difficult to inject two errors with complementary effects, but this type of protection only permits the error detection in the same manner as SDC.

**Dynamic duplication (Figure 6)**—consists of multiple redundancies with a decision module, which switches the selected module when the fault is detected. The vote block is a switching circuit, which transmits the correct result in agreement with the comparison block. The corrupted blocks are disabled so these results are not transmitted. This type of implementation permits detection and subsequent reaction to the detected error (Losq, 1975).

**Hybrid Duplication (Figure 7)**—consists of a combination of multiple duplications with complementary redundancy and a dynamic duplication.

This type of implementation protects against single and multiple focused fault injection because it is difficult to inject a multiple fault with complementary effects.

• Protection using time redundancy:

**Simple time redundancy with comparison (Figure 8)**—consists of processing each operation twice and comparing the results (Anghel & Nicolaidis, 2000). This type of implementation protects against single and multiple time synchronized errors, but it is only capable of detecting faults. The reaction is limited to disabling the transmission of the corrupted results.

**Multiple time redundancy with comparison (Figure 9)**—is based on the same principle used by simple time redundancy with comparison but the result is processed more than twice. This type of implementation detects and reacts to single and multiple fault injections.

**Recomputing with swapped operands (Figure 10)**—this consists of recomputing the operation with the operand's little endian bits and big endian bits swapped. The result is swapped and compared to detect the presence of a fault.

This type of protection has the advantage of desynchronizing two processes that makes it difficult to

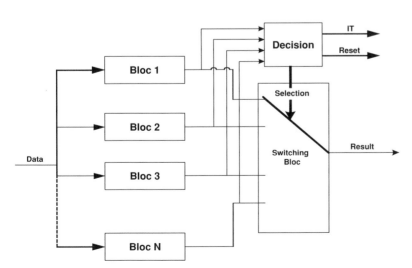

**Figure 6:** Dynamic duplication.

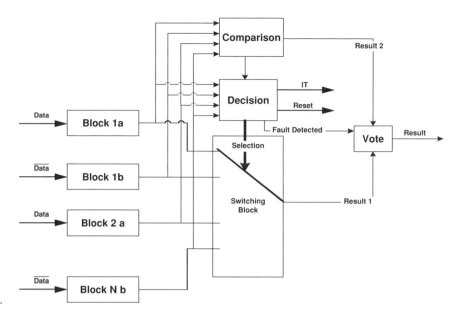

**Figure 7:** Hybrid duplication.

inject an exploitable fault without detection. It protects against single and multiple time synchronized errors.

**Recomputing with shifted operand (Figure 11)—** described in Patel & Fung (1982) where the operations are recomputed by shifting the operand by a given number of bits. The result is shifted and compared with the original one.

**Recomputing with duplication and comparison (Figure 12)—**is a combination of time redundancy and hardware redundancy. This type of implementation is the best protection against single, multiple, and time-synchronized faults, but the time penalty and increase in block size limits its use.

• Protection by information redundancy by mechanisms such as the Hamming code (Lima et al., 2000), single and multiple error checking and correction. These techniques protect systems and in some cases allow the recovery from fault injection (Pflanz, Walther, Galke, & Vierhaus, 2002). The typical example is checksums attached to each machine word in RAM or EEPROM to ensure integrity.

The second type of hardware protection mechanisms consists of passive protections that increase the difficulty of successfully attacking a device. These protections can be self-activated or managed by the software application programmer. These include the following:

**Random Delay:** This utilizes mechanisms that introduce fake or random cycles during code processing.

**Encrypting RAM Content:** The random access memory is a working area where the secret and sensitive data are manipulated. The attacker could potentially exploit any fault injected during the data processing. The encryption mechanism encrypts the manipulated data so as to decorrelate it from its actual value. A fault that has a known effect on unencrypted RAM will not have the same effect on an algorithm being executed using this RAM.

**Bus Encryption or Scrambling:** This allows the transmitted data to be decorrelated from its real value (as for the RAM).

**Passive Shield:** In this case, a full metal mesh covers some sensitive parts of the circuit, which makes light attacks,

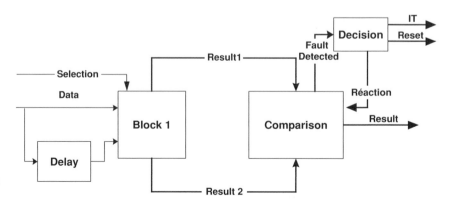

**Figure 8:** Simple time redundancy with comparison.

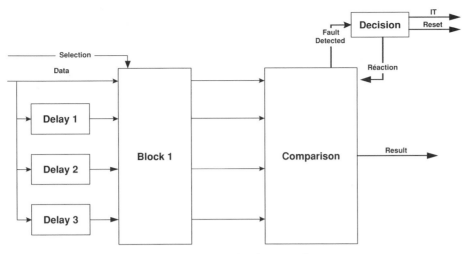

**Figure 9:** Multiple time redundancy with comparison.

for example, more difficult because the shield needs to be removed before the attack can proceed.

**Unstable Internal Frequency Generation (Figure 13):** This protects against attacks that need to be synchronized with a certain event because a given event will occur at different times when replayed.

## Software

Software countermeasures are implemented on a system that could be subject to fault attacks because of a lack of hardware countermeasures or as protection against future attack techniques that may be able to defeat the hardware countermeasures currently present. The advantage of software countermeasures is that they do not increase the block size of the hardware, although they do affect the execution time of the functions to which they are applied.

**Checksums:** Checksums can be implemented in software. This is often complementary to hardware checksums because they can be applied to buffers of data rather than to machine words.

**Randomized Execution:** If the order of independent operations in an algorithm is randomized, it becomes difficult to predict what it is doing at any given time. When a fault is injected, there is no guarantee what function it will affect. For most fault attacks, this countermeasure

will only slow down a determined adversary because a fault can eventually be positioned in the desired place.

**Variable Redundancy:** This is the repeating of variables so that if one variable is changed via a fault, it will be possible to detect this event as the two variables will be different. Following this, the decision can be made to return an error or restart the process concerned. As for the hardware countermeasures described, this is merely a method of detection and cannot rectify the fault.

**Execution Redundancy:** The repeating of algorithms and comparing the results to verify that the correct result is generated. As with the hardware countermeasures, this is usually more secure if the second calculation is different from the first (for example, its inverse) so that two identical faults cannot be used to mislead the detection mechanisms. This is ideal in the case of the RSA algorithm when it is used to generate signatures, as the verification can be done extremely quickly (because the public exponent is usually a small number).

The same methods of data redundancy that are used in hardware can be implemented in software. The problem then becomes one of execution time rather than block size because some of the hardware designs proposed

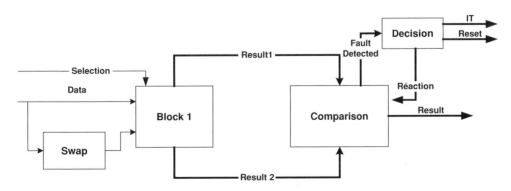

**Figure 10:** Recomputing with swapped operands.

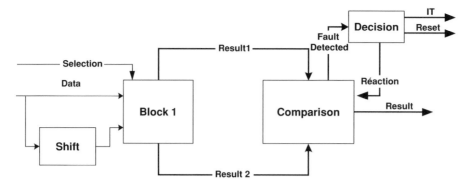

**Figure 11:**   Recomputing with shifted operand.

become extremely time-consuming when implemented in software.

The countermeasures discussed here need to be implemented in such a way that they do not create another avenue of attack. In Yen and Joye (2000), an attack is described that uses the fault countermeasures present to derive information about the secret key used in an RSA implementation. The attack assumes that the attacker is able to change arbitrary bits of the secret key used during the calculation of an RSA signature from a 0 to a 1. If the signature is then verified, it will be supplied if correct or an error status given if incorrect. If the signature is supplied, the attacker knows that a given bit is equal to 1 because no effect was produced. If the signature was withheld, the attacker will know that the bit attacked was changed from a 0 to a 1. Although the fault model used is not very realistic, this chapter does highlight the importance of the care required when designing robust countermeasures because they may allow other attacks to be implemented.

# CONCLUSION

The attacks presented in this chapter can be easily defeated by using some of the countermeasures described in the previous section. Using such countermeasures will usually increase the cost of the system being developed because the development process will cost more due to the increased complexity. The resulting system will be slower and might have an increased data block-size depending on which countermeasures are used.

With secure devices, such as smart cards, this is not a problem because the product is designed to be a tamper-resistant device. It is important that the device resist these attacks even if the performance suffers to some extent. Therefore, countermeasures are usually implemented in both hardware and software.

In more general systems, such as the PC, this becomes much more problematic. Any implementation in hardware is going to drive up the cost. Because the PC

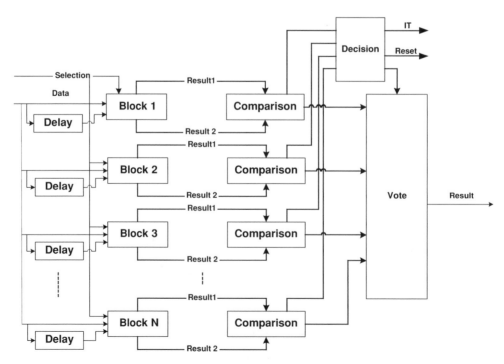

**Figure 12:**   Recomputing with duplication with comparison.

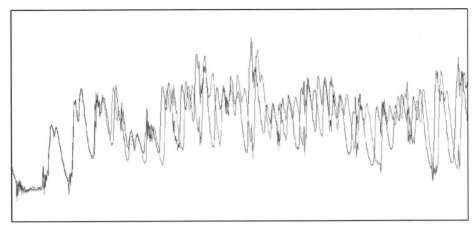

**Figure 13:** Unstable internal frequency generation as seen in the current consumption of a chip.

market is cost driven, this will reflect directly in the sales of the product. In the case of sensitive processes such as the Java Sandbox (as described previously), countermeasures need to be implemented in software to ensure that the system is always secure.

## GLOSSARY

**Ciphertext** In cryptography, this is the result of encoding a plaintext message.

**Chinese Remainder Theorem** A method of speeding up the RSA signature scheme.

**External Clock** The clock signal provided to a device from the exterior used to govern the speed of the device or synchronize communication protocols (or both).

**Feistel Structure** A structure used in secret key cryptography (see Figure 2).

**Internal Clock** The clock generated within a device to render it independent of an external clock.

**Plaintext** In cryptography, this is the original message before it has been encoded.

**Public Key** One of the pair of keys used in public key encryption.

**Public Key Cryptography** A cryptographic technique that uses two keys, a public key and a private key.

**Private Key** One of the pair of keys used in public key encryption.

**Secret Key** The key that is shared between two parties in secret key encryption.

**Secret Key Cryptography** A cryptographic technique that uses a single key for both encryption and decryption.

**Thyristor** A device similar to a diode, with an extra terminal that is used to turn it on. Once activated, the thyristor will remain on as long as a significant current flows through it. If the current falls to zero, the device switches off.

## CROSS REFERENCES

See *Cryptographic Hardware Security Modules; Data Encryption Standard (DES); Encryption Basics; Physical Security Measures; Physical Security Threats; Side-Channel Attacks.*

## REFERENCES

Adams, L., Daly, E. J., Harboe-Sorensen, R., Nickson R., Haines J., Schafer W., et al. (1992). A verified proton induced latchup in space. *IEEE Transactions on Nuclear Science, 39,* 1804.

Anderson, R., & Skoroboatov, S. (2002). Optical fault induction attacks. In S. B. Kaliski Jr., C. K. Koç, D. Naccache, & C. Paar (Eds.), *Lecture Notes in Computer Science: Volume 2523. Cryptographic Hardware and Embedded Systems—CHES 2002* (pp. 2–12). New York: Springer-Verlag.

Anghel, L., & Nicolaidis, M. (2000, March). Cost reduction and evaluation of a temporary fault detecting technique. In *Proceedings of DATE, Conference IEEE* (pp. 591–597).

Biham, E., & Shamir, A. (1997). Differential fault analysis of secret key cryptosystems. In B. Kaliski Jr. (Ed.), *Lecture Notes in Computer Science: Volume 1294. CRYPTO 97* (pp. 513–525). New York: Springer-Verlag.

Cazenave, P., Fouillat, P., Montagner, X., Barnaby, H., Schrimpf, R. D., Bonora, L., et al. (1998). Total dose effects on gate controlled lateral PNP bipolar junction transistors. *IEEE Transactions on Nuclear Science, 45,* 2577–2583.

DeMillo, R. A., Boneh, D., & Lipton, R. J. (1997). On the importance of checking computations. In W. Fumy (Ed.), *Lecture Notes in Computer Science: Volume 1233. EUROCRYPT'97 Proceedings* (pp. 37–55). New York: Springer-Verlag.

Fouillat, P. (1990). *Contribution à l'étude de l'interaction entre un faisceau laser et un milieu semiconducteur. Applications à l'étude du Latchup et à l'analyse d'états logiques dans les circuits intégrés en technologie CMOS.* Unpublished doctoral dissertation, Université Bordeaux I.

Govindavajhala, S., & Appel, A. W. (2003). Using memory errors to attack a virtual machine. In *2003 IEEE Symposium on Security and Privacy.*

Habing, D. H. (1992). The use of lasers to simulate radiation-induced transients in semiconductor devices and circuits. *IEEE Transactions on Nuclear Science, 39,* 1647–1653.

Koga, R., & Kolasinski, W. A. (1989). Heavy ion induced snapback in CMOS devices. *IEEE Transactions on Nuclear Science, 36,* 2367–2374.

Koga, R., Looper, M. D., Pinkerton, S. D., Stapor, W. J., & McDonald, P. T. (1996). Low dose rate proton irradiation of quartz crystal resonators. *IEEE Transactions on Nuclear Science, 43,* 3174–3181.

Kuboyama, S., Matsuda, S., Kanno, T., & Ishii, T. (1992). Mechanism for single-event burnout of power MOSFETs and its characterization technique. *IEEE Transactions on Nuclear Science, 39,* 1698–1703.

Lima, F., Costa, E., Carro, L., Lubaszewski, M., Reis, R., Rezgui, S., & Velazco, R. (2000). Designing and testing a radiation hardened 8051-like micro-controller. In *3rd Military and Aerospace Applications of Programmable Devices and Technologies International Conference* (Vol. 1).

Losq, J. (1975). Influence of fault detection and switching mechanisms on reliability of stand-by systems. In *Digest 5th International Symp Fault-Tolerant Computing* (pp. 81–86).

May, T., & Woods, M. (1978). A new physical mechanism for soft errors in dynamic memories. In *16th International Reliability Physics Symposium.*

O'Gorman, T. J. (1994). The effect of cosmic rays on soft error rate of a DRAM at ground level. *IEEE Transactions on Electronics Devices, 41,* 553–557.

Paillier, P. (1999). Evaluating differential fault analysis of unknown cryptosystems. In H. Imai & Y. Zheng (Eds.), *Lecture Notes in Computer Science: Volume 1560. Public Key Cryptography (PKC '99)* (pp. 235–244). New York: Springer-Verlag.

Patel, J. H., & Fung, L.Y. (1982). Concurrent error detection in ALU's by recomputing with shifted operands. *IEEE Transactions on Computers, C-31,* 589–595.

Pflanz, M., Walther, K., Galke, C., & Vierhaus, H. T. (2002). On-line detection and correction in storage elements with cross-parity check. In *Proceedings of the Eighth IEEE International On-Line Testing Workshop (IOLTW'02)* (pp. 69–73).

Pickel, J. C., & Blandford, J. T., Jr. (1978). Cosmic ray induced errors in MOS memory circuits. *IEEE Transactions on Nuclear Science, NS-25,* 1166–1171.

Piret, G., & Quisquater, J. J. (2003). A differential fault attack technique against SPN structures, with application to the AES and KHAZAD. In C. D. Walter, C. K. Koc, & C. Paar (Eds.), *Lecture Notes in Computer Science: Volume 2779. Cryptographic Hardware and Embedded Systems CHES 2003* (pp. 77–88). New York: Springer-Verlag.

Pouget, V. (2000*). Simulation expérimentale par impulsions laser ultra-courtes des effets des radiations ionisantes sur les circuits intégrés.* Unpublished doctoral dissertation, Université de Bordeaux I.

Rax, B. G., Lee, C. I., Johnston, A. H., & Barnes, C. E. (1996). Total dose and proton damage in optocouplers. *IEEE Transactions on Nuclear Science, 43,* 3167–3173.

Rivest, R. L., Shamir, A., & Adleman, L. M. (1978). Method for obtaining digital signatures and public-key cryptosystems. *Communications of the ACM, 21,* 120–126.

Skorobogatov, S. (2002, June). Low temperature data remanence in static RAM (Technical Report UCAM-CL-TR-536). Cambridge, England. University of Cambridge.

Stassinopoulos, E. G., Brucker, G. J., Calvel, P., Baiget, A., Peyrotte, C., & Gaillard, R. (1992). Charge generation by heavy ions in power MOSFETs, burnout space predictions and dynamic SEB sensitivity. *IEEE Transactions on Nuclear Science, 39,* 1704–1711.

Yen, S.-M., & Joye, M. (2000). Checking before output may not be enough against fault-based cryptanalysis. In *IEEE Transacctions on Computers, 49,* 967–970.

Ziegler, J. (1979). Effect of cosmic rays on computer memories. *Science, 206,* 776–788.

## FURTHER READING

National Institute of Standards and Technology. (n.d.). Federal Information Processing Standards, Data Encryption Standard (DES) (FIPS publication 46-3). Retrieved December 21, 2004, from http://csrc.nist.gov/publications/fips/fips46-3/fips46-3.pdf

# Side-Channel Attacks

Pankaj Rohatgi, *IBM T. J. Watson Research Center*

## INTRODUCTION

Maintaining information integrity and confidentiality is a core security requirement in most systems. These goals are typically realized using a combination of techniques such as authentication, discretionary and mandatory access control, use of high-assurance trusted components, encryption, integrity tags, and secure communication protocols.

In most commercial environments, however, these generic techniques are applied and analyzed only with respect to an abstract model of the system being protected. Thus, gaps between the model and actual implementation can open up a system to attacks that its designers never anticipated. Poorly designed and implemented systems have numerous gaps and security vulnerabilities. For example, many abstract models assume a secure operating environment, but the actual implementations run in low-assurance environments. Such implementations can be easily compromised by attacking the operating environment. Sometimes the abstract models do not fully specify the error conditions and appropriate responses. This leads to attacks such as Bleichenbacher's (1988) attack on RSA Cryptography Standard PKCS #1, where sensitive information can be extracted by analyzing the error messages returned by the implementation. In many instances, because of poor quality control, the actual functionality of an implementation differs from its specification. Some of these errors may permit an attacker to mount data-driven attacks; carefully chosen data could be used to subvert the implementation via buffer overflows, script injection, and so on.

Poorly designed and implemented systems are expected to be insecure, but most well-designed and implemented systems also have subtle gaps between their abstract models and their physical realization due to the existence of side channels. A side channel is a potential source of information flow from a physical system to an adversary, beyond what is available via its abstract model. These side channels could be as subtle as externally observable timing of certain operations, the electromagnetic (EM) radiation emanating from the computing equipment, the power being consumed by the equipment, the analog signals being propagated on the communication and ground lines and other conducting surfaces attached to it, the acoustic emanations from mechanical components and peripherals, the light and heat emanating from the equipment and peripheral devices, and so on. All these side channels have been demonstrated to provide enough information to break system security. Given their amazing power, it is hardly surprising that, for decades, governments everywhere have used such attacks for espionage while keeping all information about this topic highly classified (e.g., see NSA, 1982). Over time, information about such attacks slowly leaked into the public domain. For example, the book *Spycatcher* (Wright, 1987) describes several side-channel attacks that were allegedly performed by MI5, the security service of the United Kingdom. These included the ENGULF operation that exploited the sound of the rotors of a Hagelin ciphering machine used in the Egyptian Embassy during the Suez Crisis and the STOCKADE operation that exploited the electromagnetic echoes of the input teleprinter in the output of a ciphering machine used in the French Embassy. Technical details about side-channel attacks are only recently being rediscovered in the public domain.

The first technical works on side channels in the public domain focused on leakage from computing peripherals. For example, van Eck (1985) showed that EM emanations from computer monitors could be captured at a distance and used to reconstruct the information being

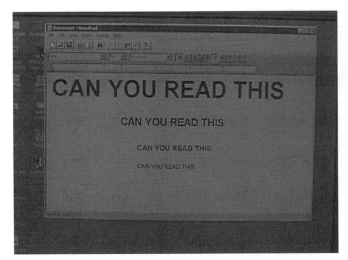 

**Figure 1:** Computer display (left) and reconstruction (right).

displayed. For example, Figure 1 shows a Microsoft Word document being displayed on a computer monitor on the left and its reconstruction from EM emanations on the right. As this example shows, even if a computer system has perfect access control on who gets to access documents, a side channel can easily subvert this control. Subsequently, Kuhn and Anderson (1998) re-created van Eck's attack and showed how a Trojan horse could use EM emanations to leak information deliberately from a monitor without detection. In addition, as a defensive measure, they created special fonts that have substantially reduced EM leakage characteristics so that they are not easily reconstructible by van Eck's attack. Other side-channel attacks on peripherals include optical attacks that use the flicker of a screen to reconstruct its contents (see Kuhn, 2002), the flicker of light emitting diodes (LEDs) to derive information being processed in a device (see Loughry & Umphress, 2002), the timing of keystrokes during password entry to get information about the password (see Song, Wagner, & Tian, 2001), and acoustic emanations from mechanical peripherals such as keyboards to extract what is being typed (see Asonov & Agrawal, 2004) and from dot-matrix printers to reconstruct what is being printed.

This chapter focuses on various side-channel attacks against cryptographic implementations and hardware rather than peripherals. The reason for this focus is that cryptography is part of the foundation for building secure systems, and protecting cryptographic implementations is a prerequisite for building a truly secure system.

## TIMING ATTACKS

The idea of using timing of operations as a cryptanalytic tool was proposed by Kocher (1996), who showed how it could be used to attack implementations of Diffie-Hellman, RSA, DSS, and other cryptographic algorithms. Before timing attacks were discovered, designers of cryptographic implementations focused primarily on performance and employed many optimizations to reduce unnecessary computation. These resulted in implementations that executed different sets of instructions and had different timings for different values of the secret key and the input data, even if the data and key sizes were fixed. Timing variation can exist even in the absence of explicit optimizations because different processing sequences can lead to different timing behavior from the hardware and the operating environment. For example, timing variation due to variable cycle instructions, pipeline stalls, hardware cache misses, page faults, and so on are strongly dependent on the processing sequence.

I now illustrate how operation timing can be used to attack cryptographic implementations by means of a simple example (Kocher, 1996).

### Timing Attack Example

Modular exponentiation is a core operation in several public-key cryptosystems such as RSA, and Diffie-Hellman, DSS. For example, in RSA, signing a message $M$ is done by first creating a padded hash $L$ of the message and then computing the signature

$$S = L^d \bmod N,$$

where $d$ is a $w$-bit-long secret exponent and $N$ is the public modulus (see Chapter 77). In practice, there are many techniques to compute this exponentiation efficiently, such as the use of the Chinese remainder theorem, Montgomery multiplication, and sliding windows. For this example, however, I focus on the simplest technique, the square and multiply algorithm shown in Figure 2.

In this algorithm, the main time-consuming steps in each iteration of the loop consist of computing a multiprecision modular square operation ($S = S * S \bmod N$)

```
Square-and-Multiply(inputs: L, d, N: output: S)
    S=1;
    for i = 1 to w do
        S = S * S  mod N        // SQUARE
        if (i'th most significant bit of d is 1)
            S = S * L  mod N // CONDITIONAL MULTIPLY
        endif
    endfor
    return S;                    // S = L ^d mod N
end Square-and-Multiply
```

**Figure 2:** Square and multiply algorithm for computing $S = L^d \bmod N$.

and conditionally computing a multiprecision modular multiplication operation ($S = S * L \bmod N$) if the $i$th most significant bit of $d$ is 1. The exponentiation algorithm is just a sequence of these modular square and modular multiply operations. Note that if the sequence of modular squares and modular multiplies becomes known, $d$ will be revealed.

In theory, even if an adversary can invoke the RSA exponentiation operation multiple times with known but random values $L_1, L_2, \ldots, L_q$ and obtain the corresponding signatures $S_1, S_2, \ldots, S_q$, it is computationally infeasible to determine $d$. In practice, however, the adversary could measure the timings $T_1, T_2, \ldots, T_q$ for each of these signature computations, which for simplicity can be assumed to be the sum of the times taken by the constituent modular square and modular multiply operations.

If the timings of the modular square and modular multiply operations were independent of the operand(s) being squared and multiplied (or dependent on their bit length), then the timing information would not reveal any compromising information. At best, the hamming weight $HW$ of $d$ can be determined, but that is not a security exposure. Most multiprecision modular square and multiplication implementations show a timing dependence on the operands, however. For example, Kocher (1996) reported that the RSAREF software on a PC exhibited the following behavior for 512-bit arithmetic: the timings for a modular multiplication with random operands was approximately normally distributed with $\mu = 1167.8\ \mu s$, $\sigma = 12.01\ \mu s$, whereas for fixed operands, the timing variation is less than 1 $\mu s$.

Kocher (1996) showed how this timing information can be exploited by an adversary to extend a correct guess of $k$ bits of $d$ by 1 more bit. The adversary can apply this process iteratively, starting from $k = 1$ to recover $d$ completely using the same timing samples. The technique works as follows.

The adversary has two hypotheses for the $(k + 1)$th bit: $H_0$ for the bit being 0 and $H_1$ for it being 1. Under both $H_0$ and $H_1$, for any input $L$, the adversary can completely simulate the square-and-multiply algorithm up to the squaring operation of the $(k + 2)$ nd iteration. Given knowledge of the implementation, he could then accurately determine the time taken by this partial computation and, given the overall timing, also determine the time taken by the remaining suffix of the computation that he cannot fully simulate. Thus, under hypothesis $H_0$, on inputs $L_1, L_2 \ldots, L_q$, the adversary has a list of potential timings $T_1^{k0}, T_2^{k0}, \ldots, T_q^{k0}$ for the suffix of the computation and for hypothesis $H_1$, he has a corresponding list of timings $T_1^{k1}, T_2^{k1}, \ldots, T_q^{k1}$.

The main step in this attack is to use a statistical technique to determine which list of timings (and hence which hypothesis) is more likely to be correct. In fact, hypothesis testing based on statistical tests on side-channel signals is a core step in most side-channel attacks. The following elementary fact from probability theory and the simplifying assumption about the pseudorandomization properties of RSA modular arithmetic are relevant here:

**Fact 1:** *Let X and Y be independent random variables having variance Var(X) and Var(Y), respectively. Let Var(X + Y) be the variance of their sum and Var(X − Y) be the variance of their difference, then Var(X + Y) = Var(X − Y) = Var(X) + Var(Y).*

**Pseudorandomization Assumption:** *The timing of any modular squaring or multiplication operation in the computation of $L^d$ for random L and random RSA modulus N, using the Square-and-Multiply Algorithm, is independent of the timing of any combination of other modular squaring or multiplication operations in the computation.*

The idea behind this assumption is that successive values of $S$ in each iteration are derived from earlier values by a process of modular squaring and multiplication by $L$. Because $L$ and $N$ are random, this process randomizes the bit patterns within $S$ and hence the timing, which is highly dependent on the bit pattern. Similar arguments regarding properties of modular division by $L$ and of square roots modulo $N$ apply regarding the bit-pattern relationships between later values of $S$ and the earlier values. In practice, this assumption is only a simplifying approximation because successive values can be weakly related (see Schindler, 2002; Schindler & Walter, 2003).

I now argue that the correct hypothesis can be determined with high probability by comparing the variance of the sequence $T_1^{k0}, T_2^{k0}, \ldots, T_q^{k0}$ with the variance of $T_1^{k1}, T_2^{k1}, \ldots, T_q^{k1}$ for sufficiently large $q$. The correct hypothesis is one for which the corresponding timing sequence has *lower* variance. Let $T0$ be the random variable denoting the timing estimate of the computation's suffix reached under hypothesis $H_0$ on random input $L$ and $T1$ be the corresponding random variable for $H_1$. Let the hamming weight of the suffix of $d$ from bits $(k + 2)$ to $w$ be $HW_{k+2}$. There are two cases:

**Case 1:** $H_0$ is correct. In this case, $T0$ is the actual time taken by the suffix of the computation consisting of $HW_{k+2}$ multiplies and $(w - k - 2)$ squares. If $Var_M$ and $Var_S$ are the variances of the modular multiply and modular square operation for random inputs, then by the pseudorandomization assumption and Fact 1, the variance of $T0$ should be $(w - k - 2) * Var_S + HW_{k+2} * Var_M$. However, $T1$ is a faulty estimate that is derived from an incorrect hypothesis that the $(k + 1)$st bit of $d$ is 1 when it is actually 0. In this case, $T1$ is actually $T0 - MultiplyF(k + 1) + SquareC(k + 2) - SquareF(k + 2)$, where $MultiplyF(k + 1)$ is the time taken by the multiply operation that was wrongly assumed to have occurred at iteration $(k + 1)$, $SquareF(k + 2)$ is the time taken by the subsequent squaring operation at iteration $(k + 2)$ that was assumed to have occurred but actually occurred with a different operand, and $SquareC(k + 2)$ is the time taken by the actual squaring operation that occurred in iteration $(k + 2)$. By the pseudorandomization assumption and extensions, all these times—$T0$, MultiplyF$(k + 1)$, SquareC$(k + 2)$, and SquareF$(k + 2)$—are independent so the variance of $T1$ is the variance of $T0$ plus $Var_M + 2 * Var_S$. Thus, variance of $T1 = (w - k) * Var_S + (HW_{k+2} + 1) * Var_M$. Hence, the variance of timing for the correct hypothesis is lower.

**Case 2:** $H_1$ is correct. By a similar reasoning, the variance of $T1$ will be $(w - k - 2) * Var_S + HW_{k+2} * Var_M$. $T_0$ will be $T1 + MultiplyC(k + 1) + SquareC(k + 2) - SquareF(k + 2)$, where $MultiplyC(k + 1)$ is the time for the actual multiply operation at iteration (k + 1) that was not accounted for in $T0$ and $SquareC(k + 2)$ is the timing for the actual squaring operation at iteration (k + 2), whereas $SquareF(k + 2)$ is the timing of the squaring operation with the wrong operand that was assumed by the faulty hypothesis. Thus, variance of $T0$ will be variance of $T1$ plus $Var_M + 2* Var_S$ or $(w - k)* Var_S + (HW_{k+2} + 1)*Var_M$. Again, the variance of timing for the correct hypothesis is lower.

This analysis shows that picking the correct hypothesis is simply a matter of comparing the variances of the sequences $T_1^{k0}, T_2^{k0}, \ldots, T_q^{k0}$ and $T_1^{k1}, T_2^{k1}, \ldots, T_q^{k1}$. Kocher (1996) also proved that with $q = O(w)$ timing samples, this procedure will identify the correct hypothesis with high probability. However, just having high probability of success in each step is not enough for a process that has to iterate the step $w$ times. One simple solution is to require a larger number of timings so that the chances of making even one mistake in any of the $w$ iterations remains small. However, this is not necessary, because this iterative process of deriving successive bits of $d$ has a *self-correcting property*. Note that for the correct hypothesis on (k + 1) bits the variance $Var_{k+1} = (w - k - 2)* Var_S + HW_{k+2}* Var_M$, which is a steadily decreasing function of $k$. However, for an incorrect hypothesis that agrees with the correct hypothesis only up to some bit $i < k + 1$, the variance will keep decreasing till the $i$th iteration (although the hypothesis is still correct) and reach $Var_i$, but subsequently the variance will start rising at every iteration. In fact, each subsequent iteration $j$ (where $j > i$) would raise the variance by $Var_S + F_j* Var_M$, where $F_j$ is the $j$'th bit of the false hypothesis because of the subtraction of an incorrect squaring time and possibly an incorrect multiplication time. Thus, if an incorrect hypothesis is ever selected, the mistake will become apparent in subsequent iterations because the variance will start to increase rather than decrease. Such a mistake can be easily corrected by backtracking.

## Extensions, Countermeasures, and Further Reading

So far we have ignored the timing noise and variations and measurement errors that inevitably arise when measuring the timing of operations on a remote system under varying load. It turns out that it is still possible for statistical techniques to overcome the effect of the added timing noise at the cost of requiring many more timing samples. A simple rule of thumb is that if the added noise reduces the signal-to-noise ratio by a factor of $n$, then the number of samples needed for the attack have to increase by a factor of $n^2$.

The earlier example shows how to attack an RSA implementation based on modular exponentiation with the square-and-multiply algorithm. In practice, for reasons of efficiency, RSA is rarely implemented in this manner. Typical implementation optimizations include Chinese remainder theorem coupled with Montgomery arithmetic and sliding windows. To see how RSA implementations used in practice can be attacked, the reader is encouraged to read the work of Dhem et al. (1998), which shows how RSA implementations using Montgomery multiplication

can be attacked; the work of Schindler (2000) for RSA with Chinese remainder theorem; and the work of Brumley and Boneh (2003), which shows how the RSA implementation in the widely deployed OpenSSL software can be remotely attacked.

An obvious countermeasure against timing analysis is to ensure that the timing of an operation is fixed. However, there are many cases where fixing the operation timing is not feasible or practical. For example, the timing leakage from an implementation may depend on the specifics of the hardware, operating system, and so on, and creating tailor-made implementations for every single platform is not commercially viable. In such cases, an alternative is to develop an implementation in which the timing is either independent of secret information such as keys or is dependent only on a limited amount of information about the keys, and disclosure of that limited information is safe. One way to achieve this for RSA is by using blinding (see Kocher, 1996), where for a message $L$, the RSA signature operation is carried out not on $L$ but on $L \times R^e(modN)$, for a randomly selected $R$. The correct signature is then recovered by multiplying the result by $R^{-1}$. This way, the actual RSA operation is being performed on random data that is unknown to the attacker. At best, the attacker can use timing to figure out the probability distribution of the timing of the RSA operation with the secret key on random data. This is hardly a secret; for example, if the hamming weight of the secret exponent $d$ is known, this distribution can be predicted analytically from the timing distribution of modular squares and multiplies using the pseudorandomization assumption.

## POWER ANALYSIS ATTACKS

A few years after the discovery of timing attacks, Kocher, Jaffe, and Jun (1998; see also Kocher, Jaffe, and Jun, 1999) introduced power analysis, a far more devastating type of side-channel attack that has had a profound impact on the entire smart-card industry. This attack extracts information from cryptographic devices by analyzing their instantaneous power consumption. For many large systems using filtered power supplies, this may not be an issue. The filters substantially reduce the information available externally, and bypassing them may require physical access to the system that the adversary may not have. However, such attacks are a big problem for tamper-resistant devices that are required to withstand physical attacks and an even bigger problem for chip cards that are further constrained to draw power from an untrusted terminal without further filtration. Although the first power analysis attacks were mounted against chip cards, there has been recent interest and success in attacking other devices such as FPGAs (see McDaniel, 2003; Örs, Oswald, & Preneel, 2003; Standaert et al., 2003).

Power analysis attacks are easy to mount against chip cards. An attacker can attach a current probe inside the card terminal to tap the power line that feeds the chip card and connect the probe to a digital oscilloscope. In addition, the attacker may need to install additional software and hardware components to trigger the digital oscilloscope to collect samples of the power signal at the right time. The power signal is sampled at a frequency

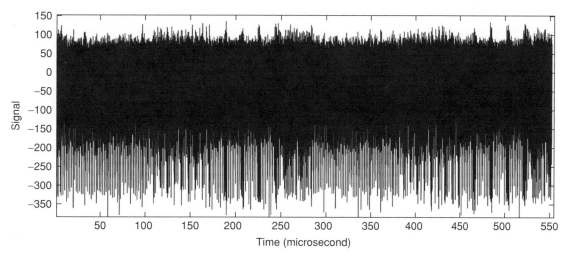

**Figure 3:** Power signal showing two rounds of DES.

## Information Within Power Consumption Signals

Compared with the timing side channel, the power consumption signal from even a single simple operation contains an overwhelming amount of information. For example, a short computation involving a few hundred instructions could generate several tens of thousands of power samples. By plotting these power samples with respect to time, we can view the power consumption characteristics of the computation at different times at various levels of granularity.

At the macrolevel, that is, when we plot the power signal over a longer period of time, one can easily discern the structure of the execution sequence, because the shape of the power consumption signal depends on the execution sequence. For instance, iterations of a loop or a repeated sequence of similar operations show up as a repeating structure in the power signal. The example in Figure 3 shows a power signal during two rounds of a

DES computation (see also Chapter 113). The two rounds, which are executed in the time intervals (0,250) $\mu s$ and (280, 530) $\mu s$ are clearly visible as a repeating shape, the signal in between being the interround key rotation. Within each round, three regions showing different power consumption characteristics are clearly visible. From 0 to 110, $\mu s$ are eight similar structures corresponding to the selection of the key for each of the 8 S-Boxes; from 110 to 175, $\mu s$ are the 8 S-Box lookups; and from 175 to 250, $\mu s$ is the P permutation, which shows up as four similar structures, one for each byte of the permutation computation.

At the microlevel, that is, when we zoom into a small portion of the computation, we can view the cycle and instruction level power function. The power consumption for each clock cycle and instruction has a basic shape that is determined by the current and a limited prior history of values, addresses, and location (ROM, EEPROM, or RAM) of the code, and the addresses, values, and location of the operands and results. This basic shape is further perturbed to some extent by noise. For example, Figure 4 shows cycle-level details during the key-selection process. The signal shows a repeating seven-cycle pattern, formed

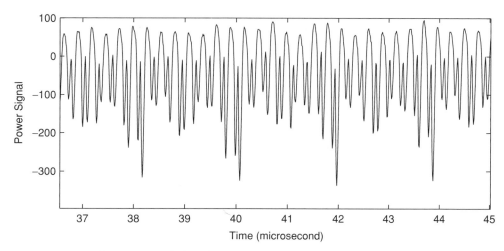

**Figure 4:** Cycle-level details during DES round key selection.

```
DES-CheckParity(byte Key[8])
    for i = 8 down to 1
            parity=0;
            for j = 8 down to 1
                    if (bit j of Key[i] is set) // CONDITIONAL
                            parity = parity+1    // OPERATION
                    endif
            endfor
            if (parity is even) parity_error();
    endfor
end DES-CheckParity
```

**Figure 5:** DES parity-check algorithm.

by an instruction to test a bit from the key to move it to carry, followed by an instruction that shifts the carry bit into the accumulator. This operation is repeated until all key bits for an S-box are selected. The large dips in the power signal corresponds to the cycle in which the key is accessed from RAM during the bit test.

## Simple Power Analysis

*Simple power analysis* (SPA) uses the shape of the power signal during a single execution of a cryptographic algorithm to extract information about the secret key. The shape of the power signal can leak information about the key in many ways. If an implementation performs key-dependent conditional operations, then the shape of the power signal can reveal the execution sequence and hence the values of the key-dependent conditions. For example, in the RSA square and multiply algorithm, the sequence of modular squares and multiplies is key-dependent. Because the implementation of modular squaring can be different from modular multiplication, the square-and-multiply sequence and hence the secret exponent may be discernable from the power signal. SPA may also be possible if an implementation manipulates key-dependent data using instructions that leak a lot of information into the power channel. For example, in some chip-cards, instructions affecting the carry bit leak its value in the power channel.

The following example based on the DES algorithm shows just how devastating such SPA attacks can be. DES uses a 56-bit key, but according to its specification, these 56 bits must be stored in 8 bytes using a parity code; that is, the seven most significant bits of each byte hold consecutive bits of the key and the 8th bit must hold the parity bit for that byte. Many implementations of DES check the parity code for the key before using it, and the sample code for one such checking routine is shown in Figure 5.

At first glance, this parity-check routine seems acceptable, apart from a minor issue of leakage of the key's total hamming weight from timing. However, under a power analysis attack, it becomes trivial to determine whether the conditional operation on each bit of the 8-byte key is executed. If it is, then that iteration of the loop will require additional instructions, take longer, and be easily distinguishable from an iteration in which the operation is not executed. For example, Figure 6 shows a processed power signal during three iterations of the outer loop (for 3 bytes of key). There are eight peaks seen for each iteration of the outer loop corresponding to the iterations of the inner loop. The signal during an inner iteration when the key bit is 1 is longer and different from an iteration when the bit is 0, and the bits of these 3 key bytes can be read directly from the power trace!

## Differential Power Analysis

Although SPA is a very strong attack, it requires some easily observable information leakage in the power signal. This makes it easy to defend against. With a little work, most algorithms can be implemented using low-leakage instructions and a fixed instruction execution sequence. This fixes most of the factors that affect the power signal at any cycle, such as the current and prior values, addresses, and location of code. When such implementations are executed with different keys and data, the only variation possible at a cycle level would be due to variation in the prior and current values or addresses of operands and results. Such a variation produces only a minor variation in the shape of the power signal at that cycle, and such minor variations are easily obscured by noise. Therefore, little usable information is available by inspecting a single power sample, and SPA becomes ineffective.

To overcome such a defense, Kocher et al. (1998) also proposed *differential power analysis* (DPA), a far more sophisticated attack technique based on statistical analysis of a large number of power traces with different data. The technique combines statistical hypothesis testing together with details of the algorithm being attacked to derive information about the secret keys. The basic premise for a DPA attack is that the shape of the power signal of an instruction that is processing an operand or result depends on (or correlates with) the individual bits of the value and address of the operand or result. Although such

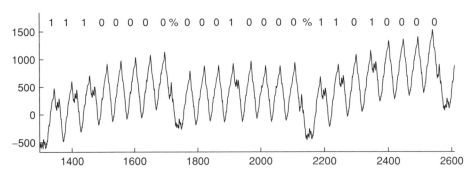

**Figure 6:** Simple power analysis attack on DES-check-parity.

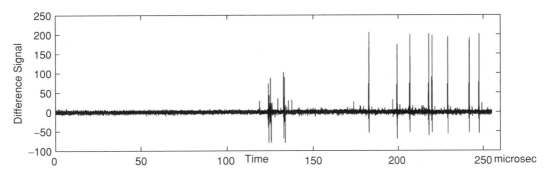

**Figure 7:** Differential power analysis difference signal for correct hypothesis.

a dependence on a particular bit may be small and easily masked by the values of other bits and by noise, the right statistical test will average out and remove these masking influences to expose the correlation, given enough power samples.

We now illustrate DPA by describing how the attack works for DES. Let us assume an adversary who can observe multiple invocations of DES on a chip card with random but known inputs and can collect the power traces. Given the inputs, one can simulate the DES algorithm till the first key-dependent operation, which happens to be the 8 S-Box table lookups. Each S-Box table lookup involves 6 bits of the unknown key, 6 data bits chosen from the input, and produces a 4-bit output. Let us focus on how DPA can extract the 6-bit key, $k_1$ used in the first S-Box S1. According to the DES specification, if $j$ denotes the 6-bit data fed to S1 and $r$ denotes the 4-bit output, then $r = S1[k_1 \oplus j]$.

The adversary does not know $k1$ and thus cannot compute $r$. However, because $k1$ lies in the range $(0, \ldots, 63)$ and the adversary can form 64 hypotheses or guesses $h_0 : k_1 = 0, h_1 : k_1 = 1, \ldots, h_{63} : k_1 = 63$, for its value. For any given hypothesis $h_i$, for any DES invocation with known input, the adversary can predict the value of $r$ under $hi$ and, in particular, predict the first bit of $r$. Based on this prediction of the bit under hypothesis, $h_i$, he can group all the $n$ power signals he has $[p_0(t), p_1(t), \ldots, p_n(t)]$ into two bins $B_i^0$ and $B_i^1$ corresponding to the predicted bit, being 0 and 1, respectively, under hypothesis $h_i$. This partitioning of power signals into two bins can be done for each of the 64 hypotheses.

Now, for each hypothesis $h_i$, the adversary can compute the mean difference signal $D_i(t)$, which is just the mean of the signals in $B_i^1$ minus the mean of the signals in $B_i^0$;

that is,

$$D_i(t) = \frac{\sum_{k \in B_i^1} p_k(t)}{|B_i^1|} - \frac{\sum_{k \in B_i^0} p_k(t)}{|B_0^i|},$$

where $|B_i^0|$ and $|B_i^1|$ denote the number of signals that fall in bins $B_i^0$ and $B_i^1$, respectively.

Now, consider the case when the hypothesis $h_i$ is correct. In this case, the adversary has correctly partitioned the power signals $p_0(t), p_1(t), \ldots, p_n(t)$ into the two bins $B_i^0$ and $B_i^1$ based on the actual bit of $r$. Because $r$ is part of the DES specification, that bit must be created and manipulated by any DES implementation in the first round. Because the power signal is correlated with this bit wherever it is used, there will be a small difference between the signals in bins $B_i^0$ and $B_i^1$ at times when this bit is used in the computation. With large enough $n$, the averaging operation will remove the noise, and $D_i(t)$ will show peaks during the time the bit is used and will be close to zero at other times. This is exactly what occurs in practice, as shown in Figure 7, which is a plot of $D_i(t)$ for the right hypothesis in an actual attack.

In the case when a hypothesis $h_j$ is incorrect, the partitioning of signals into bins is incorrect. Although significant exceptions arise in practice, for the sake of simplicity, we can assume that a partitioning based on a wrong hypothesis is like a random partitioning of the power signals. Then the two bins $B_j^0$ and $B_j^1$ contain just a random set of power signals, and their averages will simply be the average of a random collection of signals. Thus, $D_j(t)$ will be a signal that is close to zero with small fluctuations due to noise remaining after the averaging of signals. A typical plot of $D_j(t)$ for a wrong hypothesis $h_j$ is shown in Figure 8. Notice that we do get some peaks even for

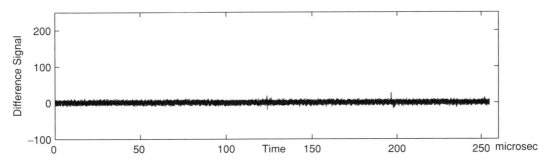

**Figure 8:** Differential power analysis difference signal for wrong hypothesis.

a wrong hypothesis, because a partition based on a false assumption on $k_1$ is not an entirely random partition of signals. This is because an S-box lookup operation is not random enough to produce completely unrelated outputs for two related inputs. Thus, a wrong hypothesis may also have smaller peaks at places where the right hypothesis has large peaks.

Using this technique, we can determine the right hypothesis for $k_1$ by selecting the signal $D_i(t)$, which has obvious peaks that dominate those in all other $D_j(t)$s. The full DPA attack consists of using the same technique for each of the 8 S-Boxes in the first round using the same set of power samples. This yields the 48 bits of key used in the first round. The remaining 8 key bits can be extracted using a similar attack on the second round because knowing the key bits used in the first round, we can simulate the algorithm up to the S-Box lookup in the second round. Note that the DPA attack described here was based only on the specification of the DES algorithm and did not require any knowledge of the implementation. This property of being able to attack completely unknown implementations is a major advantage of DPA-style attacks and the main reason that such attacks have such a major impact on the chip-card industry.

## EM ANALYSIS

Of the many side channels, the EM side channel has had the longest history of rumors and leaks associated with its use for espionage. It is well known that defense organizations were concerned to contain EM emanations from their equipment and facilities and that much research in this area was classified as part of TEMPEST (see NSA,1982). This view was reinforced by the work of van Eck (1985), who demonstrated that EM emanations from computer monitors made them vulnerable to eavesdropping from a distance. However, the first openly published works on EM analysis of cryptographic devices by Quisquater and Samyde (2001) and Gandolfi, Mourtel, and Olivier (2001) were limited to chip cards and required an adversary to be in close proximity to the chips being attacked. In fact, the best attacks required the decapsulation of the chip packaging and the careful positioning of microantennas on the passivation layer of the chip substrate. Subsequently, the work of Agrawal, Archambeault, Rao, and Rohatgi (2002) removed these limitations and showed why these rumors and precautions were fully justified: they showed that EM analysis provides an avenue for attacking cryptographic devices from a distance where the power line is inaccessible and also that EM emanations can leak information not readily available from the power side channel.

### Understanding EM Emanations

There are two broad classes of EM emanations:

**1. Direct Emanations:** These result from *intentional* current flows within circuits. In CMOS circuits, these flows consist of short bursts of current with sharp rising edges that occur during the switching operation and result in emanations observable over a wide frequency band. Often, higher frequency emanations are more useful to the attacker because there is substantial noise and interference in the lower frequency bands. In complex circuits, it may be diffcult to isolate direct emanations because of interference from other signals. Reducing such interference requires tiny probes positioned close to the signal source or special filters to separate the desired signal from other interfering signals.

**2. Unintentional Emanations:** Most modern devices pack a large number of circuits and components in a very small area and suffer from numerous unintentional electrical and electromagnetic couplings between components. The vast majority of these couplings are small, do not affect the functioning of these devices, and are typically ignored by circuit designers. Such couplings, however, are a rich source of compromising emanations. These emanations manifest themselves as *modulations* of the carrier signals generated, present, or introduced within the device. Typical sources of such carriers include the harmonic-rich clock signal(s) and signals used for internal and external communication. Depending on the type of coupling, the carrier can be *amplitude modulated* or *angle modulated* (e.g., FM) by the sensitive signal, or the modulation could be more complex. If a modulated carrier can be captured, the sensitive signal can be recovered by an EM receiver tuned to the carrier frequency and performing the appropriate demodulation.

Initial published work on EM analysis by Quisquater and Samyde (2001) and Gandolfi et al. (2001) focused exclusively on direct emanations. However, because of the difficulty of isolating direct emanations, the resulting attacks required careful EM probe positioning, close physical proximity, and even chip decapsulation to be effective. Unlocking the power of the EM side-channel requires the exploitation of unintentional emanations rather than direct emanations. This is because some modulated carriers are much stronger and propagate much farther than direct emanations. This enables attacks to be carried out at a distance without resorting to any invasive techniques.

### EM Attack Equipment

Like power analysis, an EM attack system requires sample-collection equipment such as a digital oscilloscope. The *critical* piece of equipment for EM attacks is a tunable receiver–demodulator that can be tuned to various modulated carriers and can perform demodulation to extract the sensitive signal. High-end receivers such as the Dynamic Sciences R-1550 (see Dynamic R-1550, n.d.) are ideal for this purpose because they cover a wide band and offer a large selection of bandwidths and demodulation options. However, such receivers tend to be expensive, even when purchased secondhand. Those on low budgets can construct their own receiver for under $1,000 by using commonly available low-noise electronic components, common lab equipment, and demodulation software, but this approach can become inconvenient because of the need for frequent calibration. Once the best signal to attack is identified, a custom, nontunable receiver–demodulator for the attack can be built quite cheaply, however. Picking up EM signals also requires the use of EM field probes and antennas appropriate for the band being considered, but such items are not expensive and can even be constructed at very low cost.

## EM Attacks on an RSA Accelerator

An example illustrates the power of the EM side channel. This example show how EM analysis can compromise a commercial, PCI–based SSL/RSA accelerator, R, (a pseudonym to protect vendor identity) installed in an Intel-based server and rated to perform 200, 1,024-bit cathode ray tube–based RSA private key operations per second. The server has been programmed to invoke R repeatedly to perform modular exponentiation with a given ciphertext, modulus, and exponent.

Mounting a power attack on such a system is not feasible in real life because the server's power supply is well filtered. Bypassing the filter to mount a power-analysis attack would require physical access to R, which an adversary may not have. Also, even if R is vulnerable, a timing attack given perfect timing information, converting this to a practical attack requires substantially more samples, time, and effort. This is because the timing data obtained by interacting with the server will be inaccurate and noisy due to random delays introduced by network latency, server load, server OS, server-to-R communication, and so on. Compensating for this timing inaccuracy could easily necessitate one or more orders of magnitude increase in the number of timing samples required because this number is inversely proportional to the square of the signal-to-noise ratio.

The situation changes dramatically when EM emanations are considered. Even though R is inside a closed server, a large number of carriers are available on the outside. This is the case not only for R but also for many other RSA accelerators, including some designed to meet the tamper-resistance standard of FIPS. One typically finds many high-energy carriers at multiples of the accelerator's clock frequency and several intermediate-strength *intermodulated* carriers at other frequencies. These intermodulated carriers arise due to nonlinear interactions among the various carriers present within the accelerator's operating environment. The presence of so many signals permits a variety of attacks to be mounted at various distances from the device.

Even at distances of 50 feet and through walls and glass, one can capture high-energy emanations from R.

These are mostly modulated carriers at the odd harmonics of R's internal clock. AM demodulating of these carriers yields signals where the start and end of the modular exponentiation is clearly delimited. These signals greatly enhance the timing attack on R by substantially reducing the need for additional samples to eliminate timing noise. An EM detector stationed inconspicuously in another room, 40 to 50 feet away, could precisely measure RSA operation timing, regardless of network, server, or communication latency. Such an EM-enhanced timing attack still has a few disadvantages. First, a large number of invocations are needed to mount the timing attack even with perfect timing information. Second, the attack does not work if the software controlling R implements the simple data-blinding countermeasure against RSA timing analysis.

If, on the other hand, the adversary can get a small EM capturing–retransmitting device within 4 to 5 feet from R, he will have a wide range of EM attacks at his disposal, including attacks that work with a single invocation and attacks that bypass the data-blinding defense. Although the details of possible attacks are beyond the scope of this book (see Agrawal, Archambeault, Chari, Rao, & Rohatgi, 2003, for more details), the reader will appreciate this situation by looking at the quality of information about RSA internals that is available in these EM emanations.

Figure 9 shows the signal obtained by AM demodulating a 461.46-Mhz intermodulated carrier with a band of 150 Khz for a period of 2.5 ms during which R computes two successive and identical 2048-bit modular exponentiations with a 12-bit exponent. For clarity, the figure shows an average taken over ten signal samples. One can clearly see a basic signal shape repeated twice, with each repetition corresponding to a modular exponentiation. The first repetition spans the time interval from 0 to 1.2 ms and the second from 1.2 to 2.4 ms. The signal also shows the internal structure of the exponentiation operation. From time 0 to 0.9 ms, R receives the exponentiation request and performs some precomputation to initialize itself to exponentiate using the Montgomery method. The actual 12-bit exponentiation takes place approximately from time 0.9 to 1.2 ms. A closer inspection of this region reveals substantial information leakage, which is beneficial to an

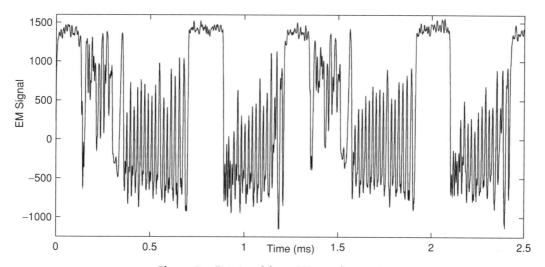

**Figure 9:** EM signal from SSL accelerator R.

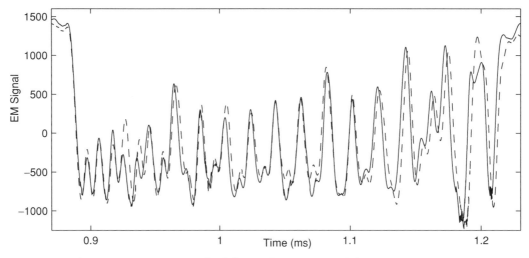

**Figure 10:** Two EM signals, different data, same modulus, same exponent.

adversary. Figure 10 plots an expanded view of this region for two exponentiation requests that have the same modulus and exponent but different data. The two signals are plotted in different line styles (solid and broken). From the start, one can see that the two signals go in and out of alignment because of data-dependent timing of the Montgomery multiplications employed by this implementation. This data dependence of the Montgomery multiply operation provides the basis for most of the attacks against R (see Borovik & Walter, 1999; Schindler, 1999; Walter & Thompson, 2001).

At intermediate distances of 10 to 15 feet, the level of noise increases significantly, but simple statistical attacks on R are still feasible and require a few thousand samples. However, attacks that are limited to one or a few samples become much harder and quickly start approaching the limits of even the advanced signal analysis techniques, such as template attacks described later.

## Multiplicity of EM Channels

One aspect of the EM side channel is that several EM signals can be isolated from any device. Earlier work on EM analysis showed that different placements of microantennas on the chip surface yielded different signals, emphasizing different circuitry. Later work showed that multiple modulated carriers were available from any device, and demodulating different carriers resulted in visibly different EM signals. This multiplicity of EM signals raises several interesting questions. One question is whether such a multiplicity is beneficial to an attacker; that is, do different signals provide different types of information, or is there just one type of information leakage that happens to be present with differing magnitudes within different EM signals? Another important question is whether the EM side channels as a whole are any better than the power side channel; that is, are EM attacks still useful when the power side channel is available?

These questions was answered in the affirmative by Agrawal, Archambeault, Rao, and Rohatgi (2002). They performed a differential power analysis attack (DPA) as well as differential electromagnetic attacks (DEMA) on the same DES implementation using three EM signals obtained by demodulation of three carriers. The peaks in the difference signal for the correct key hypothesis for these four attacks were not similar and not always at the same instant. This showed that the leakage of the predicted bit in the DES implementation was not identical in the four side channels. In particular, there were cases when some EM channels showed the leakage of the bit, but this leakage was absent in the power channel. More important, they demonstrated that an implementation that resisted power analysis with a reasonably large number of samples could be broken efficiently using an EM channel. Subsequently, Agrawal, Rao, and Rohatgi (2003) also showed that one can improve DPA-style attacks by combining information from multiple side-channel signals; for example, a power and an EM signal.

## ADVANCED SIDE-CHANNEL ANALYSIS TECHNIQUES

Most power- or EM-based side-channel attacks have been based on analysis techniques that are closely related to the SPA and DPA techniques outlined earlier. The core principle behind SPA and variants is that compromising information is readily observable from individual samples. The principle behind DPA is that even the tiniest leakage in the side-channel signal, which is easily masked by noise, can be exposed by applying a statistical approach that uses a large enough number of samples to average out the noise. Viewed in this light, techniques such as higher order DPA (HO-DPA; see Chari, Jutla, Rao, & Rohatgi, 1999; Kocher et al., 1999; Messerges, 2000), which requires leakage analysis over multiple time instants; the inferential power analyis technique (IPA) of Fahn and Pearson (1999), which uses averaging to profile locations where key bits are manipulated and SPA to extract key bits; the multiexponent single-data technique (MESD) of Messerges, Dabbish, & Sloan (1999); and the noisy equation-solving approach of Biham and Shamir (1999) also fall into the class of techniques based on noise reduction by averaging.

Although averaging over side-channel samples to eliminate noise has advantages, such an approach does not consider the large amount of information present in each sample that is not readily accessible via SPA. In addition, an assumption that once SPA is not possible, DPA or averaging-style attacks are the only possibility leads to false conclusions regarding the security of some implementations. Another limitation of the SPA- or DPA-based techniques is that they are designed for analyzing a single side channel. There can be many cases in which the attacker could collect signals from multiple channels such as multiple EM channels and the power side channel. Ideally, the attacker would combine the information available from multiple channels to perform a side-channel attack.

Addressing these limitations of SPA- and DPA-style techniques requires the use of advanced side-channel analysis techniques that borrow many concepts from information theory and from signal detection and estimation theory. In this chapter, I outline one such technique, known as template attacks and proposed by Chari, Rao, and Rohatgi (2002), that, at least in theory, can extract all the information from each side-channel signal. Some of the theoretical underpinnings behind template attacks have also been used by Agarwal, Rao, and Rohatgi (2003) to design multichannel attacks, but I do not cover them in this chapter.

## Template Attacks

Template attacks attempt to extract the maximum amount of information from each side-channel sample to attack implementations in which the adversary is limited to one or only a few compromising samples. Many such implementations can be found in applications in which SPA is not possible and higher level protocols limit the number of samples an adversary can collect with a given key as part of a DPA countermeasure. Such situations also arise naturally in the case of stream ciphers.

Consider an implementation of the stream cipher RC4. Although there are cryptanalytic results on RC4 based on minor statistical weaknesses, none of these is useful for side-channel attacks. RC4 has been attacked when used in poorly designed wireless networking protocols such as IEEE 802.11, but it is fairly safe when used properly—that is, when initialized by a *fresh* secret key for each session. In fact, in a well-designed system, RC4 implementations are also easy to secure against SPA- and DPA-style attacks. This is because initializing the 256-byte internal state of RC4 with a secret key is simple enough to be implemented using low-leakage instructions in a key-independent manner. This makes SPA unlikely. After initialization, the only secret is the internal state. However, this secret state evolves rapidly as the cipher outputs more bytes. This rapidly evolving secret state is outside the control of the adversary. This provides inherent immunity against statistical attacks such as DPA because the adversary cannot freeze the active part of the state to collect multiple samples to eliminate the noise. For RC4, the best that an adversary can hope for is to obtain a *single* sample of the side-channel leakage during the key initialization phase and attempt to recover the key from that single sample.

Thus, it may appear that reasonable RC4 implementations may be immune to side-channel attacks. This is not the case, however. In fact, Chari et al. (2002) implemented RC4 on a smart-card and showed that while the implementation was clearly resistant to SPA, it could still be broken using a single sample by the *template attack* technique described next.

## Template Attack Technique

A key requirement for template attacks is that the adversary should have a programmable experimental device identical to the device being attacked. Although such an assumption is limiting, it is practical in many cases, especially if an adversary has access to another device from the same manufacturing run or if the adversary has shared access to the same device but is limited to execute algorithms with only his own keys.

Assume we have a device performing one of $K$ possible operation sequences. For example, these could be the executions of the same code for $K$ different values of some key bits. An adversary who gets a sample $S$ of the side-channel during this operation wishes to identify exactly which of the $K$ operation sequences produced $S$, or at least to significantly reduce the set of possibilities. We'll call this the *sample classification problem*.

In signal-processing, it is customary to model the observed sample as a combination of an intrinsic signal component generated by the operation and a noise component that is intrinsically generated or ambient. Whereas the signal component is the same for repeated invocations of the operation, the noise component is best modeled as a random sample drawn from a noise-probability distribution. This distribution depends on several factors such as the type of operation being performed and the physical operating environment. It is well known (see Van Trees, 1968) that the optimal approach for solving the sample-classification problem is to use the maximum-likelihood approach; that is, the best guess is to pick the operation such that the probability of the observed-noise component in $S$ is maximized. Computing this probability requires the adversary to precisely model both the intrinsic signal and the noise-probability distribution for each of the $K$ operations. Let us refer to these models for intrinsic signals and noise-probability distributions as *templates*. Once each of the $K$ templates for the different operations is available, the sample-classification problem can be solved using maximum likelihood.

Translating this theoretical technique into an attack presents several practical problems. The first is to obtain templates without complete and detailed physical specifications of the device to be attacked or even full access to it. This problem can be addressed by having an experimental device, identical to the one to be attacked, to build the templates that are needed. Although no two devices are truly identical, devices with the same hardware revision number are similar enough for this technique to work.

The second problem is the difficulty in estimating the noise-probability distribution because the noise is a real valued function of time. Even band-limited noise needs to be modeled as a $T$-dimensional vector of reals in a certain range, where $T$ depends on the Nyquist sampling rate and the parts of the signal needed for classification. Even assuming some smoothness properties for noise, estimating the probability density function over this huge domain becomes infeasible when $T$ is large. Luckily, modeling the noise of physical systems is a well-studied problem in signal detection and estimation theory (see Van Trees, 1968), and several accurate and computationally feasible noise models are available. For example, in the RC4 attack, the *Multivariate Gaussian Noise* model was found to be sufficient, whereas simpler models based on univariate statistics gave poor results. Most of the effort in estimating the multivariate Gaussian noise distribution goes toward computing the pairwise noise correlations for the $T$ points, which require around $O(T^2)$ work.

The third problem is that in cryptographic settings, the key-finding problem does not directly translate into a sample-classification problem because the value of $K$, the entire key space, is huge. Clearly, building a template for each possible cryptographic key is infeasible. The solution is to meld the basic sample-classification approach with details of the cryptographic operation being attacked. The result is a process of *iterative classification* of the signal from a signal-processing viewpoint and an *extend-and-prune* strategy from the perspective of searching the key space. The adversary uses the experimental device to identify a small prefix $S_0$ of the sample $S$, depending only on a few unknown key bits $K_0$. Using the experimental device, he builds templates for $S_0$ with each possible value for $K_0$. Using these templates, he classifies $S_0$, that is, prunes the set of possibilities for the values of $K_0$ being used in $S_0$ to a small number. Then, in the next iteration, a longer prefix $S_1$ of $S$ involving additional key bits $K_1$ is considered. Each remaining possible value of $K_0$ is then extended by all possible values of $K_1$, and templates are constructed for these key values using the longer prefix. Again, the sample $S$ is used to prune the set of possible values for both $K_0$ and $K_1$. This process is repeated with longer and longer prefixes of $S$ until all the key bits are covered and a manageable size set of possibilities for the entire key remains. The actual key can then be identified from this set by testing with known inputs–outputs.

The success of this strategy critically depends on how effectively the pruning process reduces the combinatorial explosion in the extension process. In general, the extent of information leakage from an implementation on a particular device inherently places theoretical bounds on the success of the template attack; the best an adversary can do is to approach this theoretical bound by building extremely accurate templates. In the particular case of cryptographic algorithms implemented on CMOS devices, the chances of success are likely to be good because of the twin properties of *contamination* and *diffusion*. Contamination refers to key-dependent leakages that can be observed over multiple cycles in a section of computation. In CMOS devices, direct manipulation of the key bits makes them part of the device state, and these state leakages can persist for several cycles. Additionally, other variables affected by the key, such as key-dependent table indices and values, cause further contamination at other cycles. The extent of contamination determines the level of success in pruning candidates for fresh key bits introduced in the expansion phase. However, if two keys are almost the same, even with contamination, pruning at this stage may not be able to eliminate one of them. Diffusion is the well-known cryptographic property wherein small differences in key bits are increasingly magnified in subsequent portions of the computation. Even when certain candidates for key bits are not eliminated because of contamination effects, diffusion will ensure that closely spaced keys will be pruned rapidly at later stages.

## Template Attack on RC4

I now describe how template attacks apply against RC4's state initialization routine. RC4 operates on a 256-byte state table $T$ to generate a pseudorandom stream of bytes that is then exclusive-OR'ed (XORed) with the plaintext.

Table $T$ is initially fixed, and in the state initialization routine, a variable length key (1–256 bytes) is used to update $T$ using the following pseudocode:

```
i1 = 0
i2 = 0
for ctr = 0 to  255
  i2 = (key[i1] + T[ctr] + i2) mod  256
  swap_byte(T[ctr], T[i2]);
```

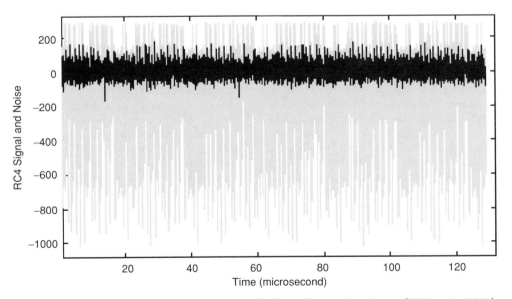

**Figure 11:** Power signal (gray) and noise (black) during first six iterations of RC4 state initialization loop.

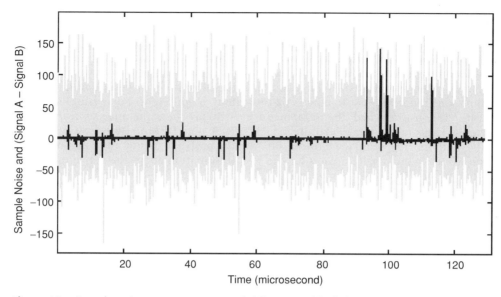

**Figure 12:** Sample noise (gray) versus signal differences (black) between Keys A and B in the first six rounds.

```
i1 = (i1 + 1) mod (key_data_len)
endfor
```

A portion of the corresponding power side-channel signal (plotted in gray) and the sample noise (plotted in black) for the first six iterations of the loop is shown in Figure 11.

First, it needs to be verified that simple side-channel analysis techniques will not work on this implementation. This can be easily seen in Figure 12, which plots the noise level for the first six iterations in a power sample in gray and plots in black the difference between the signals for two keys, A and B, that differ only in the first byte. The figure clearly shows that the level of noise in the first iteration (time 0 to 20 $\mu s$) far exceeds the differences between the signals for Keys A and B in that iteration, so SPA cannot be used to determine which key byte was used in the first iteration. In fact, in the original template attack paper, it was stated that averages of several tens of samples would be needed to reduce the level of noise below the signal differences.

RC4 is, however, an ideal candidate for template attacks. It is evident from inspecting the previous code that the key byte used in each iteration causes substantial contamination. The loading of the key byte, the computation of index i2 and the use of i2 in swapping the bytes of the state table $T$ all contaminate the side-channel at different cycles in the iteration. Further, the use of i2 and the state in subsequent iterations and the fact that RC4 is a well-designed stream cipher quickly propagate small key differences and cause diffusion. This analysis is borne out in practice as is shown in Figure 13, which plots the signal for the first six iterations for Key A in grey and the difference between the signals for Key A and Key B

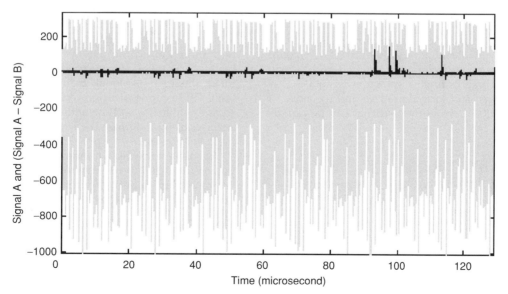

**Figure 13:** Signal for Key A (gray) versus signal differences (black) between Keys A and B in first six rounds.

in black. Keys A and B differ only in the first byte, and a small difference signal is clearly visible in the figure in the first iteration (0 to 20 $\mu s$). The important point to note is that even though the magnitude of the difference signal is small in the first iteration, significant differences appear at many different places in the first iteration, which indicates good contamination. The next point to note is that by the time the fifth iteration is reached, the difference signal has become quite large, indicating good diffusion.

As stated by the authors, the template attacks on this implementation works by building templates for the signal and noise for around 42 sample points in each iteration of RC4 state initialization routine. These are the points where significant differences arise for different keys, as shown in Figure 13. The authors first attempted to used statistical models that treated these 42 points independently, that is, looked only at means and standard deviations of the samples at each of the 42 points and reported good results for distinguishing between widely different key bytes but poor results for distinguishing between key bytes that are close. Subsequently, the authors used the multivariate Gaussian noise model and claimed that with this approach there is only a 5% to 6% error rate when trying to determine the value of the key byte.

With the multivariate approach, small-sized keys can be extracted even by using the drastic pruning strategy of retaining only one possibility for the key byte at each iteration. If the key is small, this key extraction process takes only a few iterations, and the overall error, bounded by the sum of the errors in each iteration, will still be small. For example, one can do better than 60% (total error = $1 - (0.94)^8 \leq 0.4$) for about 8 bytes of key material.

The authors argued that with a little more effort, much better results can be obtained. For example, more candidates for the key byte can be retained at the end of each pruning stage, and this can significantly reduce the probability of error. The authors estimated that with a slight modification of the maximum likelihood method, one could retain at most 1.3 hypotheses (on average) for the key byte and have 98.67% guarantee that the correct byte is retained. Using this modification independently in each iteration, one can correctly classify keys of size $n$ bytes with expected success probability around $(100$ to $1.33n)\%$ while retaining at most $(1.3)^n$ candidates. The authors also claim that actual results will be better than these estimates since the templates can be built on longer and longer prefixes and, because of the diffusion in RC4, errors made earlier can be rapidly eliminated.

## COUNTERMEASURES

Among the various side channels, the timing side channel carries the least amount of information and is the easiest to defend against. In an earlier section, I have already discussed the main countermeasures, which include fixing the timing of an operation or making it dependent on only a limited amount of secret information that is safe to disclose.

However, the power and EM side-channels carry such large amounts of information that multiple nontrivial countermeasures are usually required to block possible power and EM analysis attacks. Power and EM side-channel attacks share many of the same characteristics with respect to the analysis techniques employed and the characteristics of information leakages that are exploited, although the specific leakages in each of these channels may be different. For example, SPA and SEMA are essentially the same analysis technique, as is the case for DPA and DEMA. Both power and EM channels have the property that at any time instant, they provide some information about the active internal state of the device being attacked. Thus, the countermeasures against power and EM analysis are often similar or are directed toward achieving similar goals.

One way to classify countermeasures against EM and power analysis is based on where they are implemented, that is, in hardware or in software. Another way to classify these countermeasures is with respect to the specific attack that they prevent. In all cases, the goal is to degrade substantially the side-channel information available to the adversary to the extent that the attacks become impractical.

Hardware countermeasures are designed to reduce the leakage with respect to the noise and to introduce an element of unpredictability or randomness in the operations and into the side channel. Steps to reduce the leakage include circuit redesign to prevent instructions from leaking excessive information on operands in the side channels; external and internal shielding and isolation to prevent coupling effects between components and to attenuate compromising signals; the use of alternate semiconductor logics, such as current mode logic; sense-amplifier-based logic (see Tiri, Akmal, & Verbauwhede, 2002 ); and dual-rail, self-timed logic (see Moore, Anderson, Cunningham, Mullins, & Taylor, 2002) to reduce variability and information in the power signal. Steps to increase noise involve implementing cryptographic algorithms into hardware so that a large number of steps get executed in parallel, the addition of active noise generators, and the capability to busy-idle other components while a sensitive computation is being executed. Several hardware countermeasures also involve randomization that reduces the effectiveness of SPA and DPA attacks and can also be viewed as another means to add noise. These include introducing random jitter into the clock, randomizing the number of cycles taken by instructions, and other measures to make alignment of signals from multiple invocations difficult. Other randomization techniques involve randomly scrambling buses and the addresses and data in RAM at each reset to randomize the leakage characteristics of an implementation.

Although hardware countermeasures are useful in reducing the signal-to-noise ratio (see Mangard, 2004), they are rarely sufficient to prevent practical side-channel attacks that use additional signal processing and a larger number of samples (see Clavier, Coron, & Dabbous, 2000). Thus, in practice, additional software countermeasures are invariably required. Software countermeasures against single-sample attacks such as SPA are usually simpler and easier to implement than countermeasures against multisample statistical attacks such as DPA. One countermeasure against SPA is to have the implementation to use low-leakage instructions and to have a fixed execution sequence independent of the key. However, in cases when the algorithm requires a lot of key-dependent processing, this needs to be masked by appropriate use of dummy instructions. For example, for point multiplication in elliptic curves that is usually implemented via a double-and-add algorithm (analogous to the square-and-multiply algorithm), one can always carry out the add operation and throw the results if the operation was not needed. However, extensive use of dummy operations have significant performance costs, and there is also a danger that if the same set of dummy operations is used with the same key (e.g., in elliptic curve point multiplication or in RSA exponentiation), they could be identified by applying statistical techniques to multiple invocations. In such cases, approaches that randomize the algorithm have been employed to protect against SPA as well as multisample statistical attacks.

Protecting against statistical attacks that utilize multiple samples can be tricky. One countermeasure suggested by Kocher et al. (1999) is to refresh the secret key in a highly nonlinear fashion after every run so that the limited knowledge gained by the adversary from a single sample is not useful for subsequent runs. Updating keys may not be practical in many applications, and the main approach for defending static keys is the extensive use of randomization within the implementation to degrade substantially the attacker's ability to eliminate noise via averaging.

For public-key algorithms, some of these randomization techniques include performing the computation on randomly blinded but functionally equivalent values and representations of data and keys in public-key algorithms such as RSA (see Kocher et al., 1999) or elliptic curves (see Coron, 1999). Another approach has been to randomize the algorithm itself, that is, the internal steps of the algorithm are randomized in a manner that it produces the right output from input data and key, but the internal randomization makes SPA or DPA analysis infeasible. The core idea in all these algorithms is that exponentiation (or point multiplication) with a fixed exponent (or fixed scaler) can be done using addition or addition–subtraction chains, and there are potentially a large number of chains that could achieve the same result. By carefully and randomly selecting the specific addition or addition–subtraction chain to use for each invocation, an implementation could avoid SPA and DPA attacks. Examples of this approach include the work of Liardet and Smart (2001); Oswald and Aigner (2001); Ha and Moon (2002); Walter (2002); and Itoh, Yajima, Takenaka, and Torii (2002). Although such countermeasures have been shown to be useful against straightforward SPA- and DPA-style attacks, they have a poorer track record when more sophisticated side-channel attacks are considered that either tailored specifically for the countermeasure (see, e.g., Walter, 2004) or use a more sophisticated analysis using techniques based on hidden Markov models (see Karlof & Wagner, 2003).

In most secret-key algorithms, the lack of an algebraic structure usually makes such blinding and algorithm randomizing techniques inapplicable, and data-masking techniques are required. Conceptually, these masking techniques are similar to secret-sharing techniques (see Chari et al., 1999), where each data item $d$ in the original algorithm is replaced by $k$ random shares $d_1, d_2, \ldots, d_k$, and any $k - 1$ shares do not yield any information on $d$. Any computation on $d$ in the original algorithm is replaced by $k$ computations on $k$ shares $d_1, d_2, \ldots, d_k$, in a manner that maintains the relationship between the algorithmic data items and the shares. A special case of this approach for the case of $k = 2$ with shares created using EXOR (i.e., $d = d_1 \oplus d_2$) was independently proposed by Goubin and Patarin (1999) and applied to DES. With masking, attacks have to consider the joint statistics of at least $k$ points in the signal where the $k$ shares are being manipulated and perform a kth-order DPA-style attack. Such an attack is much harder than a DPA attack because, first, if the $k$ shares are being manipulated in parallel by hardware, then isolating the individual signals for the operations may be possible only by carefully positioned EM probes, and if these $k$ shares are being manipulated at different times during the computation, then figuring out these exact times may require considerable effort. Even if these diffculties could be overcome, the results of Chari et al. (1999) show that the number of samples required for a kth-order DPA attack grows exponentially in $k$. This technique does have several drawbacks. For instance, if special hardware is not available and share manipulation needs to be done sequentially by a central processing unit, this countermeasure reduces the efficiency of the computation by at least a factor of $k$. Also, different types of operations may require different types of shares, and converting from one type of shares to another may require creation of randomized conversion tables in RAM, which is a scarce resource in chip cards. There have also been other attempts to perform data masking without incurring these penalties, but these approaches have met with limited success, and some of these implementations have been broken.

# FURTHER READING

This chapter is just an introduction to the newly emerging and rapidly advancing field of side-channel cryptanalysis. Since its inception, there has been a large body of work done on side-channel attacks and countermeasures for almost all cryptographic algorithms. One of the best sources of information on the work done in this field can be found in the *Proceedings of the Cryptographic Hardware and Embedded Systems* (CHES) conferences, which have been held every year since 1999 (see CHES 1999, 2000, 2001, 2002, 2003). In this section, I briefly describe some exciting new directions in side-channel analysis and its linkages with other more traditional forms of security analysis.

## Reverse Engineering Using Side Channels: First Steps

One exciting new research direction is the use of side channels as tools for reverse-engineering implementations of secret algorithms. Despite mounting evidence that home-grown cryptographic algorithms are likely to be much less secure than publicly vetted ones, many vendors have persisted in deploying secret algorithms in chip cards, relying on the fact that these implementations will be hard to reverse engineer and hence to cryptanalyze. However, it turns out that using one or more side channels and some domain knowledge, it becomes possible to reverse engineer an implementation and recover the secret algorithm. Quisquater and Samyde (2002) showed an example in which this was done using neural nets. Roman Novak, in a series of articles (Novak 2003a, 2003b, 2003c), showed how side-channel information was used to reverse engineer the secret COMP128-2 algorithm used within SIM cards for authentication and key generation in GSM networks. Although current results may not be general enough to threaten all secret implementations, over time, side-channel–driven reverse-engineering techniques will likely improve.

## Combining Side Channels with Invasive or Fault Attacks

Chapter 161 described many examples of how cryptographic implementations could be attacked by injecting faults. There is also a significant body of attacks, both invasive and noninvasive, that combine techniques using fault injection with side-channel information to yield more effective attacks. A simple example would be to use a high-information side channel, such as the power channel, to precisely time a fault injection (e.g., a clock or power glitch or a light attack) so that the resulting fault occurs at a part of the computation that the attacker can easily exploit. For example, for a RSA private-key operation using the Chinese remainder theorem, the power sample could be used to ensure that the fault is injected during one of the two modular exponentiation operations, thereby revealing the factorization of the modulus. A much more precise attack on the DES algorithm involves causing a fault after the first round at exactly the point where the loop variable for the number of rounds is being compared against 16. In such an attack, the fault causes the DES implementation to perform only one round instead of 16, thereby revealing substantial information about the secret key. The attack can then be repeated with different data and at different numbers of rounds to extract the full key.

## Active Side-Channel Attacks

For many years, there has been anecdotal evidence about a class of active attacks that drive a signal into a device and observe information as a modulation in the reaffected signal emanating from the device. One such example is given in the book *Spycatcher* (Wright, 1987), in which the Russians were alleged to have planted a bug in the Great Seal of the United States in the U.S. Embassy in Moscow in the early 1950s. The bug could capture nearby conversations and modulate an incoming electromagnetic beam with the audio signal. More recently, there has been speculation linking the terms *NONSTOP* and *HIJACK*, the definitions of which are still classified, to such attacks (see Kelsey, Schneier, Wagner, & Hall, 2000). Over the coming years, we expect technical details about such attacks to emerge in the public domain.

## Combining Classical and Side-Channel Cryptanalysis

Another exciting area of research involves combining classical and side-channel cryptanalysis to achieve practical results that neither technique can achieve in isolation. Many cryptographic algorithms such as DSS, RSA, and DES are vulnerable to cryptanalytic attacks if a small portion of either the private key or an ephemeral key is disclosed (see Boneh, Durfee, & Frankel, 1998; Howgrave-Graham & Smart, 2001) or if information about intermediate results such as internal collisions (see Schramm, Wollinger, & Paar, 2003) or hamming weights becomes known (see Klima & Rosa, 2002). In the traditional cryptanalysis model, this information is not readily available. Side-channel analysis has the potential to extract such information leading to combined side-channel and cryptanalytic attacks. Conversely, the extensive use of side-channel-analysis countermeasures is severely limiting the information available to an attacker via side channels and, over time, side-channel attacks will have to borrow increasingly from techniques and results used for more traditional cryptanalysis (e.g., see Walter, 2003).

## Connections Between Side-Channel and Covert-Channel Analysis

An interesting connection exists between side-channel and covert-channel analysis that is done in the context of high-assurance systems. High-assurance systems that implement a mandatory access control policy are required to ensure that certain information flows be disallowed, even if the sending and receiving party wish to communicate; for example, if the sender is a highly privileged Trojan horse attempting to leak information to a less privileged receiver. To circumvent these restrictions in such a scenario, the parties attempt to convey information in subtle ways (akin to side channels) and the system must be designed to limit even these subtle covert channels, which is akin to side-channel countermeasures but much more difficult because the parties are deliberately trying to leak information.

## GLOSSARY

**Differential Electromagnetic Analysis (DEMA)** A type of EM analysis attack that performs statistical analysis on a large number of EM traces to extract secret information.

**Differential Power Analysis (DPA)** A type of power analysis attack that performs statistical analysis on a large number of power-consumption traces to extract secret information.

**EM Analysis** A type of attack that utilizes information available from the electromagnetic emanations from a device (i.e., the EM side channel) to extract secret information.

**Power Analysis Attack** A type of attack that utilizes information available from the instantaneous power consumption of a device (i.e., the power side channel) to extract secret information.

**Side Channel** A source of additional information about the internal workings of a physical device above and beyond what is permitted by its specification. Examples of side channels include the timing of device operations, its instantaneous power consumption, and the acoustic and electromagnetic emanations from the device.

**Simple Electromagnetic Analysis (SEMA)** A type of EM analysis attack that uses easily visible structural features from one or a few EM traces to extract secret information.

**Simple Power Analysis (SPA)** A type of power analysis attack that uses easily visible structural features from one or few power-consumption traces to extract secret information.

**Template Attack** A type of side-channel attack that extracts secret information from one or a few side-channel signals collected from a device by using side-channel signal-and-noise models developed using an identical test device.

**Timing Attack** A type of attack that utilizes information available from the timing of operations (i.e., the timing side channel) to extract secret information from a device.

## CROSS REFERENCES

See *Cryptographic Hardware Security Modules; Data Encryption Standard (DES); Encryption Basics; Physical Security Measures; Physical Security Threats.*

## REFERENCES

Agrawal, D., Archambeault, B., Chari, S., Rao, J. R., & Rohatgi, P. (2003). Advances in side-channel cryptanalysis: Electromagnetic analysis and template attacks. *RSA Laboratories Cryptobytes, 6.* Retrieved Jan. 15, 2004, from http://www.rsasecurity.com/rsalabs/cryptobytes/CryptoBytes_March_2003_lowres.pdf

Agrawal, D., Archambeault, B., Rao, J. R., & Rohatgi, P. (2002). The EM side-channel(s). In B. Kaliski, C. K. Koc, & C. Paar (Eds.), *Proceedings of CHES 2002* Lecture Notes in Computer Science (Vol. 2523, pp. 29–45). Springer.

Agrawal, D., Archambeault, B., Rao, J. R., & Rohatgi, P. (2003). Multichannel attacks. In C. D. Walter, C. K. Koc, & C. Paar (Eds.), *Proceedings of CHES 2003. Lecture Notes in Computer Science* (Vol. 2779, pp. 2–16). Springer.

Asonov, D., & Agrawal, R. (2004). Keyboard acoustic emanations. Retrieved June 7, 2004 (a version of this paper also appeared in the 2004 IEEE Symposium on Security and Privacy, May 2004) from http://www.almaden.ibm.com/software/quest/Pulications/papers/ssp04.pdf

Biham, E., & Shamir, A. (1999). Power analysis of the key scheduling of the AES candidates. Retrieved Jan. 15, 2004, from http://csrc.nist.gov/CryptoToolkit/aes/round1/conf2/papers/biham3.pdf

Bleichenbacher, D. (1998). Chosen ciphertext attacks against protocols based on the RSA encryption standard PKCS #1. In H. Krawczyk (Ed.), *Proceedings of Advances in Cryptology CRYPTO '98. Lecture Notes in Computer Science* (Vol. 1462, pp. 1–12). Springer.

Boneh, D., Durfee, G., & Frankel, Y. (1998). An attack on RSA given a small fraction of the private-key bits. In K. Ohta & D. Pei (Eds.), *Proceedings of ASIACRYPT 1998. Lecture Notes in Computer Science* (Vol. 1514, pp. 25–34). Springer.

Borovik, A. V., & Walter, C. D. (1999, July). A side-channel attack on Montgomery Multiplication (Private technical report). Datacard Platform Seven Limited.

Brumley, D., & Boneh, D. (2003). Remote timing attacks are practical. *Proceedings of the 12th USENIX Security Symposium, USENIX Association* pp. 1–14.

Chari, S., Jutla, C. S., Rao, J. R., & Rohatgi, P. (1999). Towards sound approaches to counteract power-analysis attacks. In M. Wiener (Ed.), *Proceedings of Advances in Cryptology, CRYPTO '99. Lecture Notes in Computer Science* (Vol. 1666, pp. 398–412). Springer.

Chari, S., Rao, J. R., & Rohatgi, P. (2002). Template attacks. In B. Kaliski, C. K. Koc, & C. Paar (Eds.), *Proceedings of CHES 2002. Lecture Notes in Computer Science* (Vol. 2523, pp. 13–28). Springer.

Clavier, C., Coron, J.- S., & Dabbous, N. (2000). Differential power analysis in the presence of hardware countermeasures. In C. K. Koc, & C. Paar (Eds.), *Proceedings of CHES 2000. Lecture Notes in Computer Science* (Vol. 1965, pp. 252–263). Springer.

CHES. (1999). C. K. Koc & C. Paar (Eds.), *Proceedings of CHES 1999. Lecture Notes in Computer Science* (Vol. 1717). Springer.

CHES. (2000). C. K. Koc & C. Paar (Eds.), *Proceedings of CHES 2000. Lecture Notes in Computer Science* (Vol. 1965). Springer.

CHES. (2001). C. K. Koc, D. Naccache, & C. Paar (Eds.), *Proceedings of CHES 2001. Lecture Notes in Computer Science* (Vol. 2162). Springer.

CHES. (2002). B. Kaliski, C. K. Koc, & C. Paar (Eds.), *Proceedings of CHES 2002. Lecture Notes in Computer Science* (Vol. 2523). Springer.

CHES. (2003). C. D. Walter, C. K. Koc, & C. Paar (Eds.), *Proceedings of CHES 2003. Lecture Notes in Computer Science* (Vol. 2779). Springer.

Coron, J.- S. (1999). Resistance against differential power analysis for elliptic curve cryptosystems. In C. K. Koc & C. Paar (Eds.), *Proceedings of CHES 1999. Lecture Notes in Computer Science* (Vol. 1717, pp. 292–302). Springer.

Dhem, J.- F., Koeune, F., Leroux, P.- A., Mestre, P., Quisquater, J.- J., & Willems, J.- L. (1998). A practical implementation of the timing attack. In J.-J. Quisquater & B. Schneier (Eds.), *Proceedings of CARDIS 1998. Lecture Notes in Computer Science* (Vol. 1820). Springer.

Dynamic R1550. (n.d.) Dynamic Sciences International. R 1550 Receiver. Specifications retrieved Jan. 15, 2004, http://www.dynamic-sciences.com/r1550.html

Fahn, P. N., & Pearson, P. K. (1999). IPA: A new class of power attacks. In C. K. Koc & C. Paar (Eds.), *Proceedings of CHES 1999. Lecture Notes in Computer Science* (Vol. 1717, pp. 173–186). Springer.

Gandolfi, K., Mourtel, C., & Olivier, F. (2001). Electromagnetic analysis: Concrete results. In C. K. Koc, D. Naccache, & C. Paar (Eds.), *Proceedings of CHES*

*2001. Lecture Notes in Computer Science* (Vol. 2162, pp. 251–261). Springer.

Goubin, L., & Patarin, J. (1999). DES and differential power analysis (the "duplication" method). In C. K. Koc & C. Paar (Eds.), *Proceedings of CHES 1999. Lecture Notes in Computer Science* (Vol. 1717, pp. 158–172). Springer.

Ha, J.- C., & Moon, S.- J. (2002). Randomized signed-scaler multiplication of ECC to resist power attacks. In B. Kaliski, C. K. Koc, & C. Paar (Eds.), *Proceedings of CHES 2002. Lecture Notes in Computer Science*, (Vol. 2523, pp. 551–563). Springer.

Howgrave-Graham, N., & Smart, N. P. (2001). Lattice attacks on digital signature schemes. *Designs, Codes and Cryptography, 23*, 283–290.

Itoh, K., Yajima, J., Takenaka, M., & Torri, N. (2002). DPA countermeasures by improving the window method.

Kelsey, J., Schneier, B., Wagner, D., & Hall, C. (2000). Side channel cryptanalysis of product ciphers. *Journal of Computer Security, 8*, 141–158. (Also available at http://www.cs.berkeley.edu/daw/papers/sidechan-final.ps; retrieved June 15, 2004).

Klima, V., & Rosa, T. (2002). Further results and considerations on side-channel attacks on RSA. In B. Kaliski, C. K. Koc, & C. Paar (Eds.), *Proceedings of CHES 2002. Lecture Notes in Computer Science* (Vol. 2523, pp. 244–259). Springer.

Kocher, P. C. (1996). Timing attacks on implementations of Diffie–Hellman, RSA, DSS, and other systems. In N. Koblitz (Ed.), *Advances in Cryptology—CRYPTO '96. Lecture Notes in Computer Science* (Vol. 1109, pp. 104–113). Springer-Verlag.

Kocher, P. C., Jaffe, J., & Jun, B. (1998). Introduction to differential power analysis and related attacks. Retrieved Jan. 15, 2004, from http://www.cryptography.com/resources/whitepapers/DPATechInfo.PDF

Kocher, P. C., Jaffe, J., & Jun, B. (1999) Differential power analysis. In M. Wiener (Ed.), *Proceedings of Advances in Cryptology CRYPTO '99. Lecture Notes in Computer Science* (Vol. 1666, pp. 388–397). Springer-Verlag.

Kuhn, M. G., & Anderson, R. J. (1998). Soft Tempest: Hidden data transmission using electromagentic emanations. In D. Aucsmith (Ed.), *Information Hiding 1998. Lecture Notes in Computer Science* (Vol. 1525, pp. 124–143). Springer-Verlag.

Kuhn, M. G. (2002). Optical time-domain eavesdropping risks of CRT displays. *Proceedings of 2002 IEEE Symposium on Security and Privacy* (pp. 3–18). IEE Computer Society.

Liardet, P.- Y., & Smart, N. P. (2001). Preventing SPA/DPA in ECC systems using the Jacobi form. In C. K. Koc, D. Naccache, & C. Paar (Eds.), *Proceedings of CHES 2001. Lecture Notes in Computer Science* (Vol. 2162, pp. 391–401). Springer.

Loughry, J., & Umphress, D. A. (2002). Information leakage from optical emanations. *ACM Transactions on Information Systems Security, 5*, 262–289.

Mangard, S. (2004). Hardware countermeasures against DPA—A Statistical analysis of their effectiveness. *Proceedings of the RSA Conference 2004 Cryptographers' Track. Lecture Notes in Computer Science* (Vol. 2964, pp. 222–235). Springer.

McDaniel, L. (2003). An investigation of differential power analysis attacks on FPGA-based encryption systems. Master's thesis, Virginia Polytechnic Institute and State University. Retrieved June 15, 2004, from http://scholar.lib.vt.edu/theses/available/etd-06062003-163826/unrestricted/Larry_McDaniel.pdf

Messerges, T. S. (2000). Using second-order power analysis to attack DPA resistant software. In C. K. Koc & C. Paar (Eds.), *Proceedings of CHES 2000. Lecture Notes in Computer Science* (Vol. 1965, pp. 238–251). Springer.

Messerges, T. S., Dabbish, E. A., & Sloan, R. H. (1999). Power analysis attacks of modular exponentiation in smartcards. In C. K. Koc & C. Paar (Eds.), *Proceedings of CHES 1999. Lecture Notes in Computer Science* (Vol. 1717, pp. 144–157). Springer.

Moore, S., Anderson, R., Cunningham, P., Mullins, R., & Taylor, G. (2002). Improving smart card security using self-timed circuits. In *Proceedings of 8th IEEE International Symposium on Advanced Research in Asynchronous Circuits and Systems*, IEEE Computer Society, ed. pp. 211–218.

Novak, R. (2003a). Side-channel attack on substitution blocks. In J. Zhou, M. Yung, & Y. Han (Eds.), *International Conference on Applied Cryptography and Network Security, ACNS 2003. Lecture Notes in Computer Science* (Vol. 2846, pp. 307–318). Springer.

Novak, R. (2003b). Sign-based differential power analysis. *Proceedings of the 4th International Workshop on Information Security Applications, WISA 2003. Lecture Notes in Computer Science* (Vol. 2908, pp. 203–216). Springer.

Novak, R. (2003c). Side-channel based reverse engineering of secret algorithms. In B. Zajc (Ed.), *Proceedings of the 12th International Electrotechnical and Computer Science Conference, ERK 2003* (pp. 445–448).

NSA. (1982) NACSIM 5000. Retrieved Jan. 15, 2004, from http://cryptome.org/nacsim-5000.htm

Örs, S. B., Oswald, E., & Preneel, B. (2003). Power-analysis attacks on an FPGA—First experimental results. In C. D. Walter, C. K. Koc, & C. Paar (Eds.), *Proceedings of CHES 2003. Lecture Notes in Computer Science* (Vol. 2779, pp. 35–50). Springer-Verlag.

Oswald, E., & Aigner, M. (2001). Randomized addition–subtraction chains as a countermeasure against power attacks. In C. K. Koc, D. Naccache, & C. Paar (Eds.), *Proceedings of CHES 2001. Lecture Notes in Computer Science* (Vol. 2162, pp. 39–50). Springer.

Quisquater, J.- J., & Samyde, D. (2001). Electromagnetic analysis (EMA): Measures and countermeasures for smart cards. *Proceedings of e-Smart 2001. Lectures Notes in Computer Science* (Vol. 2140, pp. 200–210). Springer.

Quisquater, J.- J., & Samyde, D. (2002). Automatic code recognition for smart cards using a Kohonen neural network. In *Proceedings of CARDIS '02* (pp. 51–58). USENIX Association.

Schindler, W. (2000). A timing attack against RSA with Chinese remainder theorem. In C. K. Koc & C. Paar (Eds.), *Proceedings of CHES 2000. Lecture Notes in Computer Science* (Vol. 1965, pp. 109–124). Springer.

Schindler, W. (2002). A combined timing and power attack. In P. Paillier & D. Naccache (Eds.), *Proceedings* of PKC 2002. *Lecture Notes in Computer Science* (Vol. 2274, pp. 263–279). Springer.

Schindler, W., & Walter, C. D. (2003). More detail for a combined timing and power attack against implementations of RSA. In K. G. Paterson (Ed.), *Proceedings of Cryptography and Coding, 9th IMA International Conference. Lecture Notes in Computer Science* (Vol. 2898, pp. 245–263). Springer.

Schramm, K., Wollinger, T. J., & Paar, C. (2003). A new class of collision attacks and its application to DES. In *Proceedings of FSE 2003. Lecture Notes in Computer Science* (Vol. 2887, pp. 206–222). Springer Verlag.

Song, D. X., Wagner, D., & Tian, X. (2001). Timing analysis of keystrokes and timing attacks on SSH. *Proceedings of 10th USENIX Security Symposium* (pp. 337–352) USENIX Association.

Standaert, F.- X., van Oldeneel tot Oldenzeel, L., Samyde, D., Quisquater, J.- J., & Legat, J.- D. (2003). Power analysis of FPGAs: How practical is the attack? *Proceedings of the International Conference on Field Programmable Logic and Applications FPL (2003). Lecture Notes in Computer Science* (Vol. 2778, pp. 701–711). Springer.

Tiri, K., Akmal, M., & Verbauwhede, I. (2002). A dynamic and differential CMOS logic with signal independent power consumption to withstand differential power analysis on smart cards. *Proceedings of 28th European Solid-State Circuits Conference* (pp. 403–406).

van Eck, W. (1985). Electromagnetic radiation from video display units: An evesdropping risk? *Computers and Security, 4,* 269–286.

Van Trees, H. L. (1968). *Detection, estimation, and modulation theory, Part I.* New York: Wiley.

Walter, C. D. (2002). MIST: An efficient, randomized exponentiation algorithm for resisting power analysis. *Proceedings of CT-RSA 2002. Lecture Notes in Computer Science* (Vol. 2271, pp. 53–66). Springer.

Walter, C. D. (2003). Seeing through MIST given a small fraction of an RSA private key. *Proceedings of CT-RSA 2003. Lecture Notes in Computer Science* (Vol. 2612, pp. 391–402). Springer.

Walter, C. D. (2004). Issues of security with the Oswald–Aigner exponentiation algorithm. *Proceedings of CT-RSA 2004. Lecture Notes in Computer Science* (Vol. 2964, pp. 208–221). Springer.

Walter, C. D., & Thompson, S. (2001). Distinguishing exponent digits by observing modular subtractions. In D. Naccache (Ed.), *Proceedings of CT-RSA 2001. Lecture Notes in Computer Science* (Vol. 2020, pp. 192–207) Springer.

Wright, P. (1987). *Spycatcher: The candid autobiography of a senior intelligence offcer.* New York: Viking.

# PART 2

# Prevention: Keeping the Hackers and Crackers at Bay

# Physical Security Measures

Mark Michael, *Research in Motion Ltd., Canada*

## INTRODUCTION

There are different ways to subdivide the field of information security. This *Handbook*, for instance, is broken into hundreds of interrelated chapters. This particular chapter views information security as being composed of only two parts: cybersecurity and physical security.

Cybersecurity protects information assets in the form of ones and zeroes against threats that come in the form of other ones and zeroes designed to cause unauthorized changes in or to make unauthorized use of an information asset. A virus is an example of a cyberthreat, and virus-protection software is a corresponding cyberdefense.

The role of physical security is to protect the physical expression of information. It must do this in two distinct ways. The first goal is to sustain the data by protecting its entire physical support structure, specifically:

1. hardware, in the broadest sense—storage and transmission media and information processing machines;
2. environmental infrastructure—electrical power, communication services, buildings, and environmental controls; and
3. humans and the information they possess to run the system.

Thus, to guard information assets, we must guard all of these resources. This very broad view of physical security encompasses topics sometimes classified as environmental, personnel, and administrative security.

The second goal is to prevent the misuse of information. Misuse can be accidental or intentional, malicious or well meaning. It may come in the form of vandalism, theft, theft by copying, or theft of services.

These two goals, sustaining information and preventing its misuse, can only be achieved by an appropriate combination of devices and policies. Proper practices cannot replace expensive security equipment, but improper practices can render that equipment useless.

Because physical security predates cybersecurity, it is better understood. This does not imply it is easier to maintain. For instance, an absolute defense against unauthorized modification of a file by a cyberattack is to store the file on a CD-ROM. On the other hand, we cannot stop a rocket-propelled grenade from destroying the disk. We could preemptively save a backup copy at a distant location, but if an employee is forced at gunpoint to turn it over, any confidential information on it will be irreversibly compromised. This illustrates that physical security is, in a way, an intractable problem.

Traditionally, physical security defended against such things as thieves and fires. Over time, suspicious powders and car bombs have been added to the list. Information's unlimited ability to be reproduced means it can be stolen in ways unlike physical objects. In many cases, the modern *virtual workplace* renders obsolete the classical concept of a "perimeter" to be guarded. Even if employees leave all physical resources at the office, their knowledge remains with them; sensitive information could be revealed by extortion or by an indiscreet question posted on a newsgroup. Thus, physical security of information has grown from its simple, ancient roots into a modern, highly complex field.

As with the chapters in this *Handbook*, physical security and cybersecurity overlap and complement one another. Where an organization's control over the physical resources ends, packet filtering and the like must take over. When cyberdefenses are strengthened, physical vulnerabilities become more inviting targets and vice versa. Physical security and cybersecurity often parallel each other; we see analogous concepts in both domains, such as access control, key management, and defense in depth. In some places, such as biometrics and smart cards, physical security and cybersecurity converge. In other places, they work together. Encryption and tracking software, for example, can mitigate the theft of a laptop. Conversely, a slip on one side can cause a fall on the other. A password that should serve as a cyberdefense may be compromised if it is written down and stolen.

This chapter separates physical security measures into two major categories. The first category includes two long-time concerns of generic physical security: physical access and fire. The second category recognizes the special nature of digital information—sustaining information assets in an uncorrupted form requires the existence of a diverse support structure. A final section deals with remediation measures that can be applied if necessary. The chapter starts, however, with a section providing some perspective on physical security threats, risks, and measures.

## OVERVIEW OF THE PHYSICAL SECURITY DOMAIN

Digital information is central to this *Handbook*. It is also central to business processes. Figure 1 portrays this centrality of information from the standpoint of physical security. Information assets are supported by physical resources on one hand and support deliverables and more abstract corporate assets on the other hand.

This is not to diminish the role of cybersecurity but to provide a context. From the physical security perspective, what are threatened are the physical resources on which information assets rely. (An introduction to physical security threats is contained in a separate chapter in this *Handbook*.) What are really endangered are the activities that rely on the confidentiality, integrity, availability, and authentication of information and that are essential for the continued well-being of the organization.

Security planning begins with an obvious question: *What are the assets to be guarded?* For our purposes, we seek to protect not only the information but also the support structures that must be maintained to sustain the integrity, availability, and confidentiality of the information. By implication, protecting the entire base in Figure 1 serves (along with cyberdefenses) to protect the assets in the top of the diagram, some of which are intangible.

## The Temporal Dimension of Physical Security

Having determined what is to be protected, the next step is to assess the risks associated with those assets. Although a separate chapter in this *Handbook* deals with risk assessment and risk management, to discuss physical security measures here, we must still consider the question: *What is likely to go wrong in the future?* This immediately brings to mind another question: *What has gone wrong in the past?* Because looking back in time is infinitely easier than looking forward, the temptation is to "fight the last war," a trap that has snared many a general; a reminder is the sequence of low-tech forms of attack mounted by Iraqis seeking to expel high-tech invaders. An understanding of past disasters is essential but not sufficient. Not all that *will* happen (in your neighborhood or in the world) *has* happened. Many events are common enough that we can reasonably trust probability tables constructed for them. Others calamities have yet to be invented. To expand George Santayana's famous quote, those who are ignorant of history are doomed to repeat it, but those who live in the past are also doomed.

The key to preventing physical breaches of confidentiality, integrity, and availability of information resources is to anticipate as many bad scenarios as possible. A common flaw is to overlook plausible combinations of concurrent problems, such as the incursion of water at the same time backup power is needed. Another error is to become frozen in time, forgetting to reassess assets and the threat space periodically.

Past history has taught us that preventing *all* bad events in the future is impossible, regardless of the time, effort, and money invested in preventive measures. There *will* be failures. For integrity and availability of resources, redundancy can be used as a safety net when the worst-case scenario becomes reality, allowing one to "go back in time" to some extent. Unfortunately, there is no comparable way to undo a breach of confidentiality.

The temporal dimension of physical security can be looked at another way. On one hand, there are discrete events that support physical security measures, such as the installation of a lock on a door or the instatement of a policy that the door should be locked. On the other

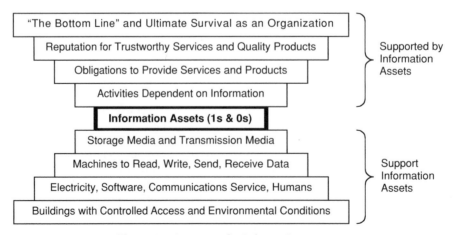

**Figure 1:** A context for information assets.

hand, there is the continual vigilance needed to consistently abide by the policy and use the lock.

This highlights how two disparate components of physical security measures—objects (perhaps incorporating software) and policies—are intertwined. Consequently, we discuss the associated policies as we introduce objects. (A separate chapter in this *Handbook* deals with security policy guidelines at length.)

## The Spatial Dimension of Physical Security

Having contemplated what bad things might happen to our assets, it is time to ask the question: *Where are the assets located?* Formerly, to answer the question, one relied entirely on a manual inventory. Now there are asset management tools that can track the location and migration of hardware and software. These can manage software licenses and monitor security policy violations, such as unauthorized software or outdated virus definitions. (See, for example, Absolute Software, 2003.)

Clearly, the location of any asset influences which defenses can be put in place. For example, the options for guarding a laptop are different than for guarding a server. More important is how the location of an asset influences the risks associated with it and therefore the defenses that *should* be employed. Therefore, whenever practical, it is better to ask the question: *Where* should *the assets be located?* Choosing an asset's location can dramatically influence the probability that it will be subjected to certain attacks. Therefore, physical security planning would best begin before there were any assets to protect and would dictate where and in what manner they should reside. At various points later, this chapter discusses good and bad locations for mobile assets. For now, the focus is on how the earliest stages of physical security planning for fixed assets should, to the extent possible, take to heart the cliché, "Location, location, location."

Locating a facility in a particular region is usually done with an eye on the bottom line. A variety of regional characteristics influence the difficulty of maintaining physical security and can ultimately affect profit: the availability of electrical power and a skilled workforce; the frequency of earthquakes, hurricanes, tornadoes, or wildfires; and the likelihood of terrorism, civil unrest, or regional conflict. The natural traits will stay fairly constant, whereas the political, social, and economic ones may vary dramatically over time.

Locating a facility at a specific site within a region may have an even more profound influence on total risk. New factors, such as topography and neighbors, enter into the equation at this level. A small difference in elevation can make a big difference where flood plains and storm surges are concerned. Higher terrain may initially look safer than a valley but may be dealt bigger surprises resulting from steep land gradients. The ground underneath may hold more surprises, such as an old mine, which may cause subsidence. Nearby rail lines, highways, airports, massive electrical lines, natural gas pipelines, and even major water mains pose potential threats. Control over security will be different if the facility is owned, leased, or shared with other tenants. In any case, neighboring establishments may be high-profile targets, have hazardous operations, or produce abundant electromagnetic pollution. Choosing to have no close neighbors may have long-term consequences if high-risk establishments later occupy adjoining parcels of land. Being in an isolated area has implications for emergency services. Even in an established neighborhood, municipal emergency services may have inadequate equipment, personnel, or response time.

Locating assets within a building should, in a perfect world, influence its architecture and construction. Even if a business cannot control building design, there is still much that can be done to locate resources judiciously. Critical departments and support equipment (including backup power) should be in the safer areas, not in the basement or on the top floor. Within departments, the most crucial resources should preferably be placed away from windows and overhead plumbing. Safes for any on-site backups or essential printed documents should be in windowless, interior rooms with high fire ratings. Flammable and hazardous materials should be isolated to the extent possible.

Once assets have been located (either in the sense of discovering their location or in the sense of specifying their location), the physical perimeter of the organization must be defined; beyond some point, the responsibility for physical security switches to others, for example, *ISPs (Internet service providers)* and civil authorities. This footprint (often a collection of widely scattered toe prints), determines where and what kinds of physical access controls can be installed.

Mobile assets complicate the spatial dimension of physical security. Beyond the traditional, well-guarded perimeter is a vast, diffuse, and ever-changing virtual perimeter that encompasses the organization's assets, wherever they may go.

## The Human Dimension of Physical Security

Information exists to serve humans, and certain humans are employed for the express purpose of information processing; therefore, security planning must ask the question: *Who should have what kind of access to each information asset?* For cybersecurity, this is a complex issue. For instance, different employees may have different create, read, modify, and delete privileges for different files within a single data set. For physical access, the situation is simpler because the granularity is cruder. Once a person is given physical access to a computer, cybersecurity must take over to control access more finely.

Defining allowable access is an exclusionary act, but our intent for the moment is not to focus on the people who are being kept at bay. Rather, we want to consider those people who form an essential part of the support structure in the base of Figure 1. As such, humans are universally regarded as the weak link in security. Their detrimental action or inaction may be accidental or deliberate. In every role where people are needed as a resource, they may alternatively serve as klutz, saboteur, or thief.

Humans transcend space and time in the sense that they can carry potentially compromising knowledge within them to places where there are no corporate laptops or disks, and that knowledge may persist beyond their employment at (or even the existence of) an organization.

The human dimension of physical security is governed (to the extent possible) by establishing, articulating, implementing, enforcing, and periodically reviewing policies and educating employees accordingly. A classical view is that corporate respect for the importance of security must start at the top of the organization and be communicated downward through the chain of command. Corporations have taken a number of approaches to enhance security awareness, including the following:

1. publishing policies in handbooks, memos, and similar materials;
2. requiring courses (perhaps self-study) before activating user accounts; and
3. periodically testing employees for knowledge of policies.

See also the separate chapter in this *Handbook* on security awareness.

Enforcement is far more difficult than training. Chapter 8 of Wylder (2004) discusses the various past approaches to enforcement and the problems each has encountered. He advocated and details a "bottom-up" approach that emphasizes personal accountability; in a nutshell, a personal security plan is created and incorporated into employee performance assessments. This approach makes security more analogous to occupational health and safety, where employers and employees share responsibility for maintaining an appropriate work environment.

In the end, the employees' competence and trustworthiness are invaluable defenses. The former is much easier to ensure than the latter. Managers at all levels must understand that most attacks are from within and must guard against provoking negative attitudes toward the organization. (See the separate chapter on internal security threats in this *Handbook*.)

## The Financial Dimension of Physical Security

Security planning must, of course, consider the expense of security measures. This naturally leads to another question: *What are the guarded assets worth?* In attempting to answer this question, it is essential to distinguish between the cost to create or restore information and the ultimate value of the information in a larger context.

In some sense, the ones and zeroes that make up digital information have no cost. The cost begins with the media on which data are stored or over which it is transmitted. These media depend on machines that can read from and write to storage media or send and receive information. These in turn rely on appropriate electrical power, telecom service, software, and human expertise; in many cases, the human effort needed to create the information in the first place is the biggest expense per byte. All of this rests on an environment with suitable temperature, humidity, and isolation from unauthorized access. Thus, the cost of creating and the burden of physically protecting information come from the large base of Figure 1, the physical resources that support the ones and zeroes in question.

Strictly speaking, digital information has no inherent value. A particular sequence of ones and zeroes might, in theory, represent part of the description of a trade secret, a copyrighted song, a compromising photograph, or a patented computer program. The ones and zeroes only have a value in some context, their value being defined by how they are used. Thus, the motivation for protecting and the consequences of failing to protect information come from the wide range of tangible and intangible corporate assets dependent on information, represented in the top of Figure 1. Admittedly, an estimation of an asset's value may be fairly unreliable, especially for a less tangible asset. But measuring a potential loss in monetary terms helps to justify an investment in security measures.

It is often said that the cost of protecting an asset should not exceed the value of the asset. It would be more precise to say that the cost of protecting an asset against a particular type of attack should not exceed the liability if the attack succeeds. That liability may be many orders of magnitude greater than the cost of the asset. The marginal cost of creating a customer's bank account may be relatively small. The impact could be huge if an unauthorized person were to drain the account or if sensitive financial information were revealed to the public. An organization failing to exercise *due diligence may be* subject to lawsuits, fines, or other legal sanctions. Even the financial losses directly related to a failure to maintain physical security may be small compared with the consequences of a loss of clients' confidence in an organization.

As a practical matter, the probability of each type of potential breach of physical security must also be factored in when comparing the potential liability incurred by the breach with the expense of preventing that particular event. This allows one to compute the (probabilistically) *expected* benefit of adopting a security measure. As mentioned earlier, the probabilities of some events will be more difficult to estimate than others.

For a more extensive discussion of the financial side of information security, see the separate chapters on risk assessment and risk management and on security insurance and best practices in this *Handbook*.

## CONTROLLING PHYSICAL ACCESS AND FIRE

An age-old role of physical security is to control access to valuables. This alone is a multifaceted task, involving barriers, lighting, surveillance, detectors, and alarms. In the particular context of guarding information resources, additional issues arise, such as disposal of media, espionage, and appropriate use.

Another traditional role of physical security is to deal with the threat of fire, a bane of humans since before there were doors and locks. There are several sides to this issue as well—prevention, mitigation, detection, and suppression. Again, some aspects of fire control pertain specifically to the information-processing environment. Measures that might be adequate in a general setting would be inappropriate for the protection of delicate equipment and media.

For several reasons, certain aspects of fire control are discussed along with physical access control. One is that barriers and openings influence the movement of both humans and fire, though in different ways. Another is that providing means of quick egress in times of fire is inherently at odds with restricting free egress to prevent the unauthorized removal of information. Finally, the enlightened approach to security management integrates detection and alarm systems for intrusion and fire.

Controlling access by humans and fire takes many forms. Some, such as locks and nonflammable materials, are preventive in nature. Others, such as "Authorized Personnel Only" and "No Smoking" signage, serve as deterrents only. Still others, such as motion sensors and smoke alarms, allow for detection and reaction if prevention and deterrence fail.

## Barriers and Openings

The most fundamental protection against intruders is to put obstacles in their way. In doing so, we must not unreasonably impede authorized access or emergency egress. In theory, barriers are preventive measures. In reality, they are merely deterrents. To paraphrase General George C. Patton, any security device designed by humans can be defeated by humans. Each has its own weaknesses to attacks by stealth or force. The context will determine which type of attack is more likely. Stealthy attacks usually require more expertise and time. Forceful attacks are simpler, but typically are noisier and require larger tools. POA Publishing (2003) has numerous comparisons (some the result of research at Sandia Laboratories) of the time required for and the noise produced by various types of attacks on different kinds of walls, doors, windows, and locks.

The openings required for the passage of people, air, and utilities are the most obvious potential weak points, where penetration by people, foreign particles, and fire is easier. In some cases, however, walls have turned out to be easier to breach than locked doors. Doors tend to get the most attention when it comes to protection, but windows, even if sealed shut, are relatively "open" compared with the more impermeable surrounding walls. Some of the unseen openings are easy to overlook, especially below raised floors (common in computing centers) and above suspended ceilings (common in many rooms). These include passages for power and communication lines, water and sewer lines, and ventilation.

### Layers

The barriers to intrusion form layers, from the campus boundary to buildings to rooms to safes. Using each layer effectively to protect the information processing environment provides defense in depth.

The outermost barrier can be established at the property line. The sensitivity of a facility may require a wall or fencing. If vehicles must be permitted on the property, the potential for car or truck bombs may require strict control of which vehicles can drive or park where; permanent barriers, pop-up barriers, swing-down arms, "wrong-way" tire-puncturing spikes, and guard houses are possible traffic controls.

The second barrier is buildings. Exterior architecture and landscaping should avoid providing easy access to windows and roofs or obscuring public view of entrances. Regional and seasonal considerations should influence grounds maintenance. In colder climes, security-aware architecture may be nullified if snow is allowed to drift up toward windows or near entrances. In all climates, external construction materials should inhibit ignition by external fires. In dry regions, special care should be taken to keep away from buildings any vegetation with the potential to fuel wildfires. Roofs often have service hatches (e.g., to afford servicing of external components of an air conditioning system). Any roof or windows that might reasonably be accessed via a portable ladder should be protected accordingly.

The third barrier is the surfaces of individual rooms. Floors and ceilings are often forgotten. In the case of a dropped ceiling or raised floor, the hidden space should not extend above or below multiple rooms if the intention is that access to each room be controlled separately. It is at the level of rooms or groups of rooms that fire divisions (discussed later) are created.

Within rooms, specific resources may be stored within safes or locked cabinets. An alternative is for a resource to incorporate its own defenses. (See the following section.)

These layers need not restrict access the same way. In some settings, stringent controls at the outmost layer may obviate the need to "recheck" people once they are inside. A more orthodox scheme is to tighten security closer to sensitive resources.

### Approaches to Physical Access Control

At some facilities, only entrance to areas and/or contact with information resources is controlled. When removal of materials (or copies thereof) is a concern, controlling egress should be equally important. There are several philosophical approaches to controlling physical contact with and movement of resources. These methods can be used in combination with one another:

1. Physical contact with a resource is restricted by putting it in a locked cabinet, safe, or room; this would deter even vandalism.

2. A machine may be accessed, but it is secured (perhaps permanently bolted) to an object that is difficult to move; this would deter theft. In a variation of this, movement of an object is allowed, but a motion-sensed alarm sounds.

3. Contact with a machine is allowed, but a security device controls the power switch.

4. A machine can be turned on, but logging on requires a user identification process, possibly involving a password or a biometric device. Related to this is the idea of having the computer "locked" by software (perhaps a password-protected screensaver) while the user is away from the machine.

5. A resource is equipped with a tracking device so that a sensing portal can alert security personnel or trigger an automated barrier to prevent the object from being moved out of its proper security area.

6. An object, either a resource or a person, is equipped with a tracking device so that his, her, or its current position can be monitored continually.

7. Resources are merely checked in and out by employees, for example by scanning barcodes on items and ID cards, so administrators know at all times of who has what but not necessarily where they have it.

Information's special nature—its ability to be copied— makes it a special security challenge. Information is subject to *theft by copying*: the original copy remains, another copy is expropriated. Controlling the movement of media owned by a corporation would, in itself, not preclude the use of media brought in by an outsider or insider to hold a copy of information. The motive of an insider may be benign (perhaps copying information for convenience, not subterfuge), but the result may still pose a potential hazard.

It is sometimes appropriate for an organization to allow public access to some of its computers. Such computers should be on a separate *LAN (local area network)*, isolated from sensitive resources. Furthermore, to avoid any liability issues, the public should not be afforded unrestricted access to the Internet.

Mobile computers are a special problem because they are popular targets for theft; by some accounts, this is the second costliest type of attack on information assets after viruses. Rittinghouse (2003) suggested that employees sign an acknowledgment of additional precautions to be taken with off-site use of mobile devices. When a laptop must be left unattended, it should be kept in a locked cabinet or car trunk or, at the very least, hidden from the view of passersby. The suggestion to "disguise" a laptop by *not* carrying it in a case designed for it runs contrary to proper practice for protecting the machine from accidental blows and the like. Some hardware devices specific to deterring laptop theft are security cables (for locking the laptop to a less movable object) and alarms.

The prudent assumption is that a laptop will eventually be accessed by an unauthorized person. In addition to hardware or software controls for logging in, portable machines should have all stored sensitive data encrypted. There are also software products for helping recover or control stolen laptops. One application has the laptop periodically report its serial number to a central monitoring center. If necessary, the laptop can be traced to its current location. The software is supposed to remain hidden and resident, even if a drive is formatted or the operating system is reinstalled. (See Absolute Software, 2003.)

Another approach is to "sacrifice" hardware but preserve the confidentiality of information by turning the extreme portability of data to an advantage. More and more high-density, removable storage options are available, including (re)writeable optical media and removable solid-state memory such as *USB (universal serial bus) flash memory*. If data are stored only on the media, theft of the machine from a vehicle or room will not compromise the data. There are several problems with this. First, it may be difficult to ensure that no remnant of the data is stored with or within a laptop. (See the separate chapter on computer forensics procedures and methods in this *Handbook*

for a thorough discussion of how an operating system may create echoes of files.) If there really is no copy of a file on a machine, then the machine is removed as a locus of backup data.

The small size that makes portable media so convenient to carry also makes them easy to lose. To counter this, some versions have been worn as a necklace or incorporated in larger items such as pens, watches, and Swiss Army knives, which makes them a little harder to misplace.

## Physical Access Control Devices

There are a multitude of devices for keeping people out of areas or containers, ranging from padlocks to enclosures with two doors. Fundamental to most systems are the following:

1. an immovable barrier (e.g., a wall) with an opening,

2. a door or comparable part that can be moved to block or to expose the opening, and

3. a way of securing the "door" to the barrier, typically with a bolt or latch.

The bolt used to secure a door is usually either a *latchbolt* or a *deadbolt*. The former provides greater convenience as it is spring-loaded and beveled, so it slides into the *strike* when the door is pulled closed. The latter provides greater security because it requires an additional separate action after the door is closed to move the bolt into the strike. Bolts controlled electrically may be either *fail-safe* (opening if power fails) or *fail-secure* (remaining closed if power fails).

Traditional mechanical locks using metal keys are still common and may be adequate in certain situations. They certainly are better than nothing (as is often the case with wiring cabinets). As with encryption, security is no better than key management. Policy guidelines in this connection include the following:

1. special security for the key cabinet,

2. logs of who has which key(s),

3. periodic inventories of keys, duplicates, and blanks,

4. stampings of "Do not duplicate" on keys, and

5. the absence of room or name identification on keys.

Comparable precautions must be taken with combinations, personal identification numbers, badges, and cards of various types.

*EAC (electronic access control)* systems typically involve a central point of control and monitoring. EAC systems may provide the following features:

1. being able to lock and unlock doors remotely,

2. being able to log who has entered,

3. being able to preclude access by specific persons (perhaps everyone),

4. knowing when a room is legitimately occupied so intrusion-detection devices can be deactivated (preferably automatically), and

5. knowing in times of emergency where people remain.

The actual identification mechanism may be the use of some kind of card or *PIN (personal identification number)*. The most promising new technology appears to be *biometric devices*. A major advantage of these is that they depend on a physiological or behavioral characteristic, which cannot be forgotten or lost and which is difficult to forge. There are a wide range of available technologies, which are the subject of the separate chapter on biometric basics and authentication in this *Handbook*; consequently, the many types of biometric devices are not detailed here.

Table 1 lists a selection of the more common components of physical access control systems other than biometric devices. Some, such as door closers, must be used in conjunction with other measures.

It is not practical here to enumerate the various techniques for defeating each of the various access control devices listed in Table 1. POA Publishing LLC (2003, p. 60) lists the average time it takes to neutralize surreptitiously several kinds of standard locks via different techniques. Whereas most of us probably think of picking a lock or shimming a latchbolt (stereotypically, with a credit card) as the usual attacks on locks, most people do not have the right skills or tools for a stealthy attack. Consequently, most attacks are by force. The most vulnerable type of lock is the kind that incorporates the key mechanism in

**Table 1** Nonbiometric Physical Access Control Components

| Access Control Type | Characteristics |
|---|---|
| *Badge, Visitor's Pass* | Worn by authorized persons, checked by security guards (and perhaps other employees). For employees, should feature a photograph. Features to prevent forgery should be incorporated. |
| *Mechanical Key Lock* | Requires inserting and turning a metal key with a specific configuration. Among various subtypes, *pin-tumbler* offers better protection than *warded*, *wafer*, or *lever* locks. |
| *Combination Lock* | Mechanical version involves turning a dial to certain positions. Electronic version requires typing a specific sequence on a keypad. |
| *Card Reader* | Activated upon insertion of a smart card or swiping of a card with a magnetic strip or bar code. May also incorporate a keypad for entering a personal identification number. Alternatively, may sense a proximity card without contact. |
| *Hollerith Card* | Holes in card are read by passage of light or contact brushes. Now used only for hotel security. |
| *Swipe Card* | Slid through a reader. Can utilize a magnetic strip or a bar code. Can be used in conjunction with a personal identification number. *Magnetic watermarked* subtype has magnetic strip embedded, not added on to outside. *Infrared shadow* subtype is transparent to infrared light, has embedded bar code. |
| *Proximity Card* | Embedded circuitry emits frequencies that can be detected by a reader when the card is near. Reader can be hidden in a wall. Card can remain inside clothing. Suffers less wear than a swipe card. Same principle can be applied to automobile access. |
| *Memory Card* | Contains memory circuitry to carry a user's identification information. *Intelligent* (or *protected* or *segmented*) subtype has logic to control memory access. |
| *Smart Card* | Contains both memory for a user's identification information and processing power to run related security protocols. |
| *Stairtower Lock* | Frame-mounted hybrid electric device. Allows door handle to operate if power fails. Designed for emergency egress. |
| *Magnetic Lock* | Electromagnet installed on door frame plus strike plate on door. Always a fail-safe device. *Direct hold* subtype is surface-mounted on the secure side of door and door frame. *Shear* (or *concealed*) subtype is embedded within door and door frame. |
| *Electric Strike Lock* | Solenoid moves a strike from door frame into door. No wiring in door required. Can be fail-safe or fail-secure, use a latch bolt or deadbolt. |
| *Electric Lockset* | Similar to a mechanical lockset but with solenoid action in place of key action. Can be fail-safe or fail-secure. |
| *Door Closer* | Automatically pulls a door shut after it has been opened. |
| *Turnstiles, Revolving Doors* | Used as a choke point (possible with a programmed time delay and sensors in walls) to prevent entry by two people at once ("piggybacking" or "tailgating"). |
| *Mantrap* (or *Double Vestibule Portal*) | Glassed enclosure with two doors that cannot be open simultaneously. Prevents "piggybacking." |
| *Dispensable Barriers* | Foam, fog, or entangling devices deployed when intrusion is detected. (A "reactive-preventive" measure.) |

the door knob, common in residential use, because it can easily succumb to an attack by force.

All parts of an opening and its closure are fair game for attacks. Exposed hinges are easy to remove. A strike that is weak or weakly attached will give way under the force of a quickly moving shoulder. The bolt can be exposed by prying a flimsy door jam or "peeling" poorly constructed doors or walls. The locking mechanism itself can succumb to particular types of drilling, punching, hammering, and wrenching.

Conventional methods are not the only ways to defeat locks. One example of an unconventional attack involves a famous maker of U-locks intended for locking bicycles to immovable objects. For decades, these have featured impressive-looking, hard-to-duplicate cylindrical keys. However, the plastic barrel of a disposable pen will also open the locks.

Another design flaw involves a swipe-card system in which an electrically activated lever pushes open a miniature door so that the latchbolt of the lock can pass unimpeded, allowing the full-sized door to be pulled open. Because the lever and miniature door are not linked, the electrical system has no indication that the latter has been propped open by an inconspicuously placed paperclip. Even security guards, seeing the light on the lock indicate that a swipe card is needed, dutifully swipe their cards, hear the lever activate, and never realize they could have pulled the door open without swiping a card.

In assessing a candidate for a security device or architecture, the time, resources, and sophistication of a likely hypothetical attacker must be correlated with both the overall security scheme *and* the assets it protects. The lower the level of surveillance, the greater the opportunity to attack. The bigger prize, the greater the enticement to attack.

### Emergency Egress

To this point, we have dodged a ticklish issue: The same principles of controlling entrance to areas can be applied to controlling egress—except in times of fire or other emergency. Allowing quick escape is inherently at odds with checking to see who and what is leaving a building. With an EAC, a person would not be required to use a swipe card to exit; therefore, there would be no record of precisely who exited.

Knowing how to escape from a fire is of the utmost importance because human life has greater value than any other assets. Fire evacuation maps and procedures should be posted, and evacuation should be practiced. When the general power supply is cut, signs above and pointing toward exits must stay illuminated, and some of the lighting along escape routes should also stay on. Ideally, additionally lighting should come on when a fire has been detected to help evacuees see through smoke.

Fire doors must be latched in fail-safe mode, require only a single action to use, and must incorporate door closers. In particular, emergency exits cannot consist of a sequence of two doors (as in a mantrap, for instance).

Despite good design, instances continue to occur in which well-marked emergency exits have been found to be blocked or locked when the need for them arises. One

reason for nullifying a door's panic hardware is that the doors were being used for other reasons, perhaps being propped open, thereby creating the threat of unauthorized entry. If emergency doors are *alarmed*, misuse of the doors should be rare. If misuse of the doors cannot be prevented by connecting them to alarms, then personnel must be educated as to the threats from such misuse. In any case, all employees must know where the emergency exits are, and maintenance personnel must understand the importance of keeping those exits functional.

Governmental regulations may mandate accommodations for persons who have problems with mobility. In the United States, the Americans with Disabilities Act requires that sight-impaired people be able to understand what to do upon touching door hardware, that exit signage meet certain visibility criteria, that exits be usable by weak and wheelchair-bound persons, and that doorways provide at least 32 inches of clearance.

It is possible to install a delayed-egress device on a fire door. The delay can be as long as 15 seconds. *CCTV (closed-circuit television) and* remote control of the exit by a guard can be implemented. In such case, the CCTV signal should not be delayed by transmission over low-bandwidth voice communication lines. See Konicek and Little (1997) and National Fire Protection Association (2003b).

### Fire Mitigation

Although fire prevention typically receives more attention in the media, fire mitigation is arguably more important. This is because, despite the best precautions to prevent the accidental ignition of a fire within a facility, a fire may have an external or deliberate origin. Mitigation requires greater planning and expense. The key ideas are to erect fire-resistant barriers and to limit fuel for the fire between the barriers.

For computing environments, the choice of construction materials, design, and techniques for mitigating the spread of fire should exceed the minimum standards dictated by local building codes. Because fires can spread through unseen open spaces, including ventilation systems, a *computing area* is defined to be all spaces served by the same *HVAC (heating, ventilation, and air-conditioning)* system as a computing room. Air ducts within that system should have smoke dampers. The computing area must be isolated in a separate *fire division*. This means the walls must extend from the structural floor to the structural ceiling of the computer area and have a *one-hour rating* (resistance to an external fire for 1 hour). Care should be taken to ensure that openings where pipe and cables pass through the fire-resistant boundaries of the separate fire division are sealed with material that is equally fire-resistant.

Many fires affecting a computer area do not actually originate in that area. Even if a fire does not technically spread into a computing area, its products—heat, smoke, and *soot* (carbon deposits)—may. Consequently, the level of fire protection beyond the computing area is still of critical concern. *Fully sprinklered* buildings (protected by sprinkler systems throughout) are recommended. Concern should extend beyond the building if it is located in an area with high hazards, such as chemical storage or periodically dry vegetation. In the latter case, an important barrier to fire is a *firebreak* around the building created by removal of any vegetation likely to fuel a fire.

The standards prescribed by the National Fire Protection Association (2003a) for fire protection of computing equipment put forth specifications for wall coverings, carpet, and furnishings (which are relaxed in fully sprinklered buildings). Additional prescribed limitations on which other materials can be present in a computer area do not take into account that even high-hazard areas have computers present. In interpreting those standards, one should determine which dangerous materials are absolutely essential for operations and work to minimize any unnecessary hazards. Due to their potential contribution to fire (as well as being a more likely starting point for a fire), materials that could contribute to a *Class B* fire (e.g., including solvents, paints) should not be stored in a computing area except in a fireproof enclosure. Materials that could contribute to a *Class A* fire, such as paper, should be kept to the minimum necessary.

Raised floors are standard features of many computer facilities, allowing for cables to connect equipment without the need to cover cables to prevent fraying and electrical shorting. The use of junction boxes below the floor should be minimized, however. The needed equipment for lifting the heavy removable panels to gain access to the space between the raised floor and the structural floor must be easy to locate, even in the event of a fire.

## Fire Prevention

In attempting to prevent an accidental fire from ever getting started, the two things best to avoid are high temperatures and low ignition points. It is usually possible to exclude highly flammable materials from the computing environment. Overheating, on the other hand, is a possibility in almost any electrical device and many mechanical devices. In some cases a cooling system has failed or has been handicapped. In other cases, a defective component generates abnormal friction. The biggest threat comes from short circuits; the resulting resistance may create a small electric heater or incite arcing.

Some factors that may lead to a fire, such as short circuits within a machine or a wall, are beyond our control. Yet many precautions can be taken to lessen the chances of a fire. Vents should be kept unobstructed and air filters clean. Power circuits should not be asked to carry loads in excess of their rated capacity. Whenever possible, wires should run below a raised floor rather than on top of it. If wires must lie on a floor where they might be stepped on, a sturdy protective cover must be installed. In any case, wires should be protected from fatiguing or fraying. See National Fire Protection Association (2003a) for fire prevention guidelines for the computing environment. As of this writing, the newest electrical code pertaining specifically to computing equipment is from the International Electrotechnical Commission (2001).

Many fires are actually the culmination of a protracted process. In some cases, a material smolders for hours before the first flame appears. Therefore, another preventive measure is for employees to use their eyes, ears, noses,

and brains. Damage to a power cord can be observed if potential trouble spots are checked. Uncharacteristic noises from a component may be symptomatic of a malfunction. The odor of baking thermoplastic insulation is a sign that things are heating up.

A common, sudden cause of fire is lightning. See the later section, Lightning Precautions, for references on lightning protection systems.

## Lighting and Surveillance

Whereas barriers can be an obstacle to intrusion, they can also be an aid to it. If, for example, an entrance is sheltered, an intruder has a better chance of picking a lock unobserved. Consequently, one of the principles of *CPTED (crime prevention through environmental design)* is to increase the perception of *natural surveillance*, that is, a clear line of sight between the honest and the dishonest. There are several applications of this principle. Outside, fences, doors, and windows should not be obscured by hedges. The architectural design should also present an unobstructed view of doors and windows. Within the workplace, an open design can discourage certain kinds of activities. See Crowe (2004) for a broader discussion of CPTED.

Organized surveillance can be done in person (by stationed or roving guards) or remotely (by camera). In any case, if potential perpetrators are aware of the surveillance, then it can serve as a deterrent, not just as a reactive measure.

CCTV or digital cameras may or may not be monitored by humans in real time, but some form of recording should be done in any case. Digital cameras can be integrated with motion-detection software so that continual human monitoring of screens is not required. Obviously, real-time monitoring in some form affords the opportunity to interrupt malfeasance before it is completed. Even in such cases, a recording serves as evidence in legal proceedings. Recording can be done on analog tape or digitally on hard drives. To the extent possible, care should be taken to install cameras in a way that makes it difficult to disable them or their communication link with a monitor or recorder.

Lighting and surveillance go hand in hand. Whether achieved remotely by cameras or in person, surveillance is aided by lighting. Therefore, good lighting is a deterrent to crime. Although continual illumination is generally preferred, motion-triggered lighting may have more of a deterrent effect in situations where its activation would be noticed by others more readily than would be the actions of an intruder; an example would be where there are rows of shelving or equipment racks blocking natural surveillance. The most effective type of lighting to support color CCTV cameras is metal halide lamps because they imitate daylight well; however, they are the most expensive type to install and maintain. See Chapter 5 of Cumming (1992) for a comprehensive introduction to CCTV and types of lighting.

Even if surveillance is not a concern, to help prevent accidents, some lighting should remain on outside business hours; it should remain on even if the municipal power supply fails and should not be controllable by any publicly accessible switches. Moreover, additional lighting triggered by a fire or other emergency should aid escape despite the presence of smoke.

## Detectors and Alarms

When prevention and deterrence fails, the next line of defense is to discover, report, and react to fire or unauthorized access. Whether for intrusion or fire, all alarm systems should adhere to the following principles:

1. The functioning of detectors and alarms should not depend on the municipal power supply, which can be disrupted; the control unit should indicate status of municipal and backup power.
2. The remote reporting by detectors should not depend on exposed communication lines that can be cut; alternatives available include radio, microwave, cellular, and satellite communication links.
3. Sensing and reporting should be *zoned,* meaning that responders know an event's location within a facility;

ideally, the monitor panel should provide specific information, such as whether a door is still ajar.

### Intrusion Detection

There is a wide variety of devices for detecting unwanted intrusions in the form of unauthorized entry or activity. Table 2 outlines the basic characteristics of the main types. Devices should be chosen based on their reliability, features, and cost and on the kind of threat anticipated. The primary consideration, however, is the intended protection pattern. Some devices are strictly for monitoring outdoor areas, perimeters, indoor areas, or items; other types can be used in multiple applications.

Not indicated in Table 2 is the full litany of strengths and weaknesses of the various types of sensors, that is, what causes them to issue false alarms or to ignore suspect events. A very thorough reference for explicit characteristics of sensors is Cumming (1992). Table 11-1 in Fennelly (2004) gave recommendations based on an extensive list of factors affecting sensors usage.

**Table 2** Comparison of Intrusion Detection Sensors

| Sensor Type | Characteristics |
| --- | --- |
| PIR (Passive Infrared) | "Sees" change in heat characteristic of human movement. Limited range. |
| Glass Break | "Hears" 3- to 5-kHz sound frequencies and "feels" 200-Hz seismic shock frequencies characteristic of glass breaking; has replaced foil strips previously common on windows. |
| Acoustic | Microprocessor analyzes shapes of sound frequency to discriminate between breaking glass and other sounds. Best when placed opposite the window to be protected |
| Audio | Reacts to and perhaps records the audible range (20–20,000 Hz). Can be attached to a fence to "hear" sound of it being cut. |
| Shock | Attached directly to pane of glass. Subtype generating piezo-electric current can protect only one pane. Subtype in which a circuit is "shaken" open can protect nearby panes as well. |
| Vibration | Reacts to vibrations from forced entry (other than glass breaking). |
| Electromechanical | Motion breaks or completes an electrical circuit. Largely obsolete. Many subtypes, including pressure mats; metallic foil on windows; door or window switches; and window screens, wooden lattices, or door paneling incorporating fine, easily broken wires. |
| Ultrasonic | Uses the Doppler effect to detect motion by noting changes in reflections of 19.2-kHz sounds. Limited range. (Can be adjusted to detect air convection from fire but may be triggered by ventilation system.) Not fooled by movement outside protected room. |
| Microwave | Similar in principle to an ultrasonic sensor but using higher frequency waves that will penetrate nonmetallic construction. Can be used outside without being inhibited by weather. Can protect perimeters (narrow beam) or areas (wide beam). |
| Capacitance | Detects changes in capacitive coupling between a ground and an energy-radiating antenna. Very limited range, obsolete except for protecting an individual object. |
| Photoelectric | Reacts to interference with a beam of light, preferably infrared. Outdoors, weather can interfere with its proper operation. |
| Chemical | Detects human effluvia. Vapor trace analyzer subtype can test for explosives, inflammables, and drugs. |
| Balanced Pressure | Notes changes in differential pressure in liquid-filled tubes buried under soil. Hard (e.g., frozen) soil may prevent triggering. Nearby traffic may cause false alarms. |
| Leaky Coax | Detects changes in standing pattern of electronic signal emitted by a buried coaxial cable with (partially) stripped shielding. More reliable than balanced pressure sensor. |
| Fiber Optic Cable Vibration | Cable can be attached to fences, walls, rooftops, ducts, or pipes or can be buried in ground. Software monitoring changes in signal transmitted through the cable can be "tuned" to ignore certain types of vibrations. Protection extends the entire length of the cable. |

Many sensors have added or optional features (not listed here) that improve their sophistication. It should be noted that the *integration*—not simply the *usage*—of two or more technologies can dramatically improve reliability, that is, the likelihood of detecting all and only unwanted intrusions.

Security guards are listed neither in Table 1 as an access control device (although they are often used to check badges) nor in Table 2 as a detection device (although they often check articles brought in or out). They can also be used in both capacities and also to respond to unauthorized entry or behavior. Guard service is frequently outsourced, a practice that requires depending on the competence and trustworthiness of another organization. Choosing good security guards directly may be a riskier proposition, as determining the reputation of an established security firm is easier than checking the background of each applicant for a security position. Moreover, agencies specializing in physical security provide extensive experience and specialized knowledge, not just expediency. Rittinghouse (2003) reported that it is "extremely rare" that an outsourcing security company is the problem when there is an internal or external breach of security.

The principle of natural surveillance effectively makes every employee (or, for that matter, helpful nonemployee) a quasi-guard. Those whose primary job function is not security can use a *duress alarm* to send a signal to a security specialist or law enforcement agency to indicate that help is needed. This can be of a fixed nature, such a hidden button a bank teller might use, or can be on a wearable, wireless device. All employees need to know how intruders might enter, how to recognize intruders, and how to react—whom to call and what to do until they arrive. Dealing with intruders is a lengthy subject in itself. A comprehensive list of appropriate actions is given in Chapter 143 of Tyska and Fennelly (2000).

Custodial personnel may need additional training and oversight. They often work at night, a time favored by certain types of intruders. Cleaning crews also are prone to breach security protocols to streamline their work, for example, by leaving offices open and unattended for periods of time. For this reason, education should be reinforced by spot checks to see what is actually going on.

## Fire Detection

Automatic fire detectors should be placed on the ceilings of rooms as well as in hidden spaces (e.g., below raised floors and above suspended ceilings). The number and positioning of detectors should take into account the location of critical items, the location of potential ignition sources, and the type of detector. Fire detectors are based on several technologies, outlined in Table 3.

Of the technologies listed, the continuous air-sampling smoke detector is particularly appropriate for computing facilities because it can detect very low smoke concentrations and report different alarm levels.

For high-hazard areas, there are also automatic devices for detecting the presence of combustible vapors or abnormal operating conditions likely to produce fire. Said another way, they sound an alarm *before* a fire starts.

Some fire detectors, especially the fusible type, are integrated into an automatic fire-suppression system. This means that the first alarm could be the actual release of an extinguishing agent (hence the water-flow detector). Because an event triggering a fire may also disrupt the electrical supply, fire detectors must be able to function during a power outage. Many fire detectors are powered by small batteries, which should be replaced on a regular schedule. Some components of detectors, such as the radioisotope in an ionizing smoke detector, have a finite life span; the viability of such a detector cannot be determined by pushing the "test" button, which merely verifies the health of the battery. Such detectors must be replaced according to the manufacturer's schedule.

**Table 3** Comparison of Fire Detection Technology

| Detector Type | Characteristics |
|---|---|
| *Fixed-Temperature* | Triggered at a specific temperature. |
| | *Fusible* subtype has metal with a low melting temperature. |
| | *Quartzoid bulb* subtype completes an electrical circuit when a liquid-filled bulb breaks. |
| | *Line* subtype completes an electrical circuit when insulation melts. |
| | *Bimetallic* subtype completes a circuit by bending of bonded metals that expand differently. |
| *Rate-Compensation* | Triggers at a lower temperature if the temperature rise is faster. |
| *Rate-of-Rise* | Reacts to a rapid temperature rise, typically 7–8°C (12–15°F) per minute. |
| *Electronic Spot-Type Thermal* | Uses electronic circuitry to respond to a temperature rise. |
| *Flame* | "Sees" radiant energy. Good in high-hazard areas. |
| | *Infrared* subtype may be fooled by sunlight. |
| | *Ultraviolet* subtype may be affected by smoke. |
| *Smoke* | Usually detects fires more rapidly than heat detectors. |
| | *Ionizing* subtype uses a small radioactive source (common in residences). |
| | *Photoelectric* subtype detects obscuring or scattering of a light beam. |
| | *Cloud chamber* subtype detects formation of droplets around particles in high humidity. |
| | *Continuous air-sampling* subtype can detect very low smoke concentrations. |
| *Water Flow* | Reacts to the activation (or malfunction) of a sprinkler system. |

## Fire Suppression

The delicate nature of information resources presents special challenges for firefighting. It is preferable to extinguish a fire with specialized, on-site equipment rather than high-volume fire hoses. Local fire departments should always be informed of any special fire hazards they might encounter on a call. Likewise, they should be made aware of sensitive equipment and media, as well as the fire controls in place (Newman, 2003). Depending on how many operations are automatic, certain employees (enough so that an adequate number are always on duty) must be trained to perform extra duties, including the following:

1. calling emergency officials,
2. shutting off electricity and natural gas,
3. altering the air flow (if HVAC is powered from outside the immediate area) so that either smoke is exhausted or it is prevented from spreading inside, and
4. operating special fire systems (e.g., hoses, wheeled portable units, manually controlled sprinklers).

Fire-suppression systems generally release water, dry chemical, or gaseous agents. The release can be from portable devices, from a centralized distribution system of pipes (perhaps with hoses that will be manually directed), or from modular devices in fixed locations. Fire can be extinguished by displacing oxygen, by breaking the chemical reaction, by cooling the fire's fuel below its point of ignition, or by a combination of these.

Any fire in a computing environment should be considered a *Class C* fire because of the presence of electricity. Electrical power should be cut as soon as possible, regardless of whether a conductive fire-suppression agent is used, because any electrical shorting will work against the suppressant. Obviously, automatic fire-suppression systems must be able to function independent of the facility's main power supply.

When possible, it is preferable to extinguish a fire immediately with portable extinguishers aimed at the base of the fire before it can grow. Each device should have one or more letters on the label, indicating the class(es) of fires on which it can be used. For most computing facilities, a dry chemical extinguisher rated A-B-C will cover all situations. The dry chemical will leave a residue, but if the fire can be caught early, this is a small price to pay. All personnel should be acquainted with the location and proper use of portable fire-suppression devices. If more than one type is available, they must know which type is suitable for which kinds of fires.

Countermeasures must match the potential conflagration, both in quantity and quality. The presence of flammable materials requires greater suppression capacity. In addition, special tools and techniques are needed for special fires. A *Class D* fire, involving combustible metals such as magnesium, requires the application of a metal-specific *dry powder*, so named to distinguish its purpose from that of ordinary dry chemical with B-C or A-B-C ratings. (Rechargeable batteries in laptops do not contain enough lithium to require special treatment in case of a fire.) Recently certified, specialized (wet chemical) extinguishing equipment should be installed if there is the potential of a *Class K* fire, involving cooking equipment using oils and fats at high temperature.

### Total Flooding with Gaseous Agents

*Total flooding* seeks to release enough of a gaseous agent to alter the entire atmosphere of a sealed area (with openings totaling no more than 1% of the total surface area of the enclosure). The term *clean agent* is often used to indicate that the gas itself leaves no residue (although its decomposition by-products will). Ordinarily, the air-agent mixture alone would be safe for humans, but fires always produce toxic smoke.

Consequently, the best protocol is to have an alarm continuously announce the impending release of a flooding agent, allow a reasonable time period for personnel to evacuate and seal the area, and sound a second alarm to announce the actual release. Occupants of those areas must understand the different alarms, must know how to proceed when the first alarm sounds, and must appreciate the seriousness of that environment. (A short science lesson might help.) Doors must be self-closing and have *panic hardware* for easy exit. Warning signs must proclaim the special nature of the area. Self-contained breathing equipment must be available for rescuing people.

The sudden release of a highly pressurized gaseous agent has several side effects. The gas undergoes a dramatic decrease in its temperature. Reportedly, skin in direct contact with a release could suffer frostbite. Equipment could suffer as well. The force of the exhaust is considerable and should be taken into account when placing the vents. The noise of a release is loud but does not impair hearing.

Gaseous fire-suppression systems can be either centralized or decentralized. Centralized systems are generally custom-fitted for a particular installation. A network of pipes delivers the suppressant from a single tank to multiple nozzles operating simultaneously. This is the more traditional and common approach.

Decentralized systems are modular, so there is greater flexibility in placing the individual units or repositioning them (on expert advice) if the layout of a facility changes. Independent units each have a tank, triggering device, and nozzle; they can be equipped for remote triggering or monitoring. On the negative side, the individual units, being self-contained, are heavier and bulkier than the outlets and pipes of a centralized system. Therefore, they must be supported from a structural ceiling rather than a suspended ceiling. Moreover, each cylinder must be anchored very securely to prevent the force of release from turning the cylinder into a projectile upon the release of gas.

Gaseous agents that have been used in total flooding fire-suppression systems in computing facilities include carbon dioxide, argon, nitrogen, *halogenated agents (halons)*, newer replacements for halons, and mixtures of these. (Pure $CO_2$ at the concentration needed for total flooding is hazardous to humans.)

### Halon

For decades, the fire-suppression technique of choice in computing facilities was total flooding with Halon 1301, also known as bromotrifluoromethane, or $CBrF_3$. (Halon 1211, a liquid streaming agent, was also used in portable extinguishers.) Because of their ozone-depleting nature, proportionally worse than chlorofluorocarbons (CFCs), halons were banned by the Montréal Protocol of 1987. Disposal and recycling of Halon 1301 must be performed by experts, because it is contained under high pressure. Consult Halon Recycling Corporation (HRC; 2002) for advice and contacts. Although no new halons are being produced, existing systems may remain in place, and the use of recycled Halon 1301 in new systems is still allowed by the protocol (on a case-by-case basis) for "essential" use (not synonymous with "critical" as used by the HRC). Because the world's supply has been decreasing since 1994, a concern when relying on Halon 1301 is its future availability.

Halon 1301's effectiveness is legendary. One factor is its high *thermal capacity* (ability to absorb heat). More important, it also appears to break the chemical chain reaction of combustion. Although the mechanism by which it does this is not perfectly understood (nor, for that matter, is the chemistry of combustion), the dominant theory proposes that the toxins into which it decomposes at about 482°C (900°F) are essential for chemical inhibition. The chemistry and other aspects of halons are discussed in the chapter "Halogenated Agents and Systems" in Cote (2003).

In low-hazard environments, a concentration of approximately 5% Halon 1301 by volume suffices. Short-term exposure at this level is considered safe but not recommended for humans; dizziness and tingling may result. An even lower concentration is adequate when the Halon 1301 is delivered with a dry chemical that inhibits reignition. Regardless of the concentration applied, immediately after exposure to Halon 1301 (perhaps from an accidental discharge), a victim should not be given adrenaline-like drugs because of possibly increased cardiosensitivity. The real risk comes when fire decomposes Halon 1301 into deadly hydrogen fluoride, hydrogen chloride, and free bromine. Fortunately, these gases, being extremely acrid, are easy to smell at concentrations of just a few parts per million.

### Alternatives to Halon

In addition to the natural inert gases, there are numerous gaseous replacements for Halon 1301 in the general category of halocarbon agents. Subcategories include hydrofluorocarbons (HFCs), hydrochlorofluorocarbons (HCFCs), perfluorocarbons (PFCs and FCs), and fluoroiocarbons (FICs). Neither these nor blends of them seem to be as effective; that is, more of the substance is needed to achieve the same end. One of the most popular and effective alternatives is HFP, also designated $C_3HF_7$, HFC-227ea, or 1,1,1,2,3,3,3-heptafluoropropane and sold under the names FM-200 (a trademark of Great Lakes Chemical Corporation) and FE-227 (a trademark of Dupont). According to Sheinman (2004), more than twice as much HFP (by weight or volume) is required as Halon 1301; moreover, it produces 5 to 8 times as much hydrogen fluoride gas, not surprising given its chemical formula. The search for better clean agents continues. See National Fire Protection Association (2000b) for guidelines regarding clean agents and (United States) Environmental Protection Agency (2003) for a listing of alternatives.

### Water-Based Suppression

Despite its reputation for doing as much damage as fire, water is coming back in favor—more so in Europe than in North America. Because water's corrosive action (in the absence of other compounds) is slow, computer equipment that has been sprinkled is not necessarily damaged beyond repair. In fact, cleanup from water can be much simpler and more successful than from other agents. Water also has an outstanding thermal capacity.

Misting is now used as an alternative to Halon 1301. The decreased droplet size in mists (compared with ordinary sprays) makes them more effective in extracting heat. The explosive expansion of the steam contributes to displacing oxygen at the place where the water is being converted to steam, namely the fire. (Steam itself has been used as a suppressant.) See for example, Fleming (1999).

To reduce the risk of accidental leakage, recommendations have traditionally specified *dry pipe* systems, in which pipes for hose, sprinkler, or mist systems remain dry until needed. In fact, leakage from wet pipe systems is very rare; damage from washroom incidents is far more likely. See, for instance, Mangan (2002).

There has also been research with chemically enhanced water mists, but this is not yet in common use. Sheinson (2004) reported on tests with a combination water mist and HFC-227ea, the two individual Halon alternatives found to be most effective by the (U.S.) Navy Technology Center for Safety and Survivability.

## Reuse or Disposal of Media

At some point in time, every piece of storage media of every type will cease to play its current role. It may be reused to store new information, it may be recycled into a new object, or it may be "destroyed" in some sense (probably not as thoroughly as by incineration). If the media is to be used by another individual not authorized to access the old information, the user of that information may very well think to purge it from the media. In the case of recycling or destruction, the original user of the media may assume that no attempt to access the old information will be made after it leaves his or her possession. This is a foolhardy assumption. The term *dumpster diving* usually conjures up images of an outsider pillaging items that have been "thrown out" and are no longer in a secure area. It could just as easily involve an insider scrounging within a trash receptacle in a building for discarded documents, media, and equipment to recover information. Thus, media must be sanitized, by another person with more expertise in that area, regardless of whether it is to be reused or discarded. The only difference is that care must be taken *not* to damage the media in the former case but not the latter.

For printed media holding sensitive information, reuse is not an option. Some shredders are worthless, slicing pages into parallel strips, which can be visually "reassembled." At the other extreme is government equipment that liquefies documents to the point that they cannot be recycled (due to the destruction of the paper fibers). In between are crosscut shredders that produce tiny pieces of documents—a reasonable approach.

For magnetic media, one of the best known vulnerabilities comes from "deleting" a file, which really only changes a pointer to the file. There are commercial, shareware, and freeware tools for (repeatedly) overwriting files so that each byte is replaced with random garbage. Echoes of the original information may remain in other system files, however. Another potential problem is that sectors that have been flagged as bad might not be susceptible to overwriting. Special, drive-specific software should be used to overwrite hard drives because each has its own way of using hidden and reserved sectors.

Even after all sensitive bytes have been overwritten by software, there may still be recoverable data, termed *magnetic remanence*. One reason that write heads shift position over time is that the position where new bytes are written does not perfectly match where the old bytes were written. Hence, the use of a *degausser (bulk eraser)* is generally recommended. Some models can each accommodate a wide range of magnetic media, including hard drives, reel or cartridge tape, and boxed diskettes. Degaussers are rated in Gauss (measuring the strength of the field they emit), in Oersteds (measuring the strength of the field within the media they can erase), or in dB (measuring on a logarithmic scale the ratio of the remaining signal to the original signal on the media). A degausser generates heat rapidly and cannot be operated continuously for long periods; it should be equipped with an automatic shut-off feature to prevent overheating. Even degaussing may leave information retrievable by an adversary with special equipment. If a hard drive is not to be reused, then grinding off the surface is an option.

Guidelines for sanitizing write-once or rewritable optical media are not as clear. In theory, even write-once disks can be overwritten. But from what has been said about magnetic media, it is unadvisable for any optical media to be erased for reuse. Two "folk remedies," breaking the disk or placing it in a microwave oven for 2 seconds, should *not* be used. Another suggestion, scratching, may be ineffective because there are commercial products and services for repairing scratched disks by polishing. Therefore, if complete destruction of the disk is not possible, it should be ground to the point of obliterating the layer on which the data are actually stored.

For maximum security in reusing or disposing of media, learn to think forensically. If a government agency could recover information from your media, so could a sufficiently sophisticated adversary. See, for example, the section on disk forensics in the separate chapter on forensic computing; even more detail is provided by the section on analysis of a forensic image in the chapter on computer forensics procedures and methods.

## Espionage and "Loose Lips"

Although there are separate chapters in this *Handbook* on corporate espionage, internal security threats, and information leakage, the three topics are unified here to focus on the physical security aspects and to illustrate that there is a spectrum of ways confidentiality can be compromised. An attacker may act unaided, may exploit mistakes made by others, or may dupe others into being unwitting

accomplices. For some threats, there are technological countermeasures. For the threats that exploit human failings, the articulation, implementation, and enforcement of a security policy and a thorough security-awareness training program are essential.

There are several ways to eavesdrop in the broadest sense. One of the easiest is to passively intercept any information that is intentionally broadcast. Because of their inherent vulnerability to interception, wireless digital transmissions should be encrypted (a cyberdefense) and analog voice communication should be scrambled if confidentiality, integrity, or authentication is desired.

Even electronic equipment *not* designed to broadcast information does produce unintended, compromising emanations, often termed *tempest emissions* (after the U.S. government TEMPEST program to combat the problem). For instance, inexpensive equipment can be used to "receive" the display from a computer monitor. Of the guided transmission media, unshielded twisted-pair cabling emits most readily, and fiber optic cable does not emit. A thorough treatment of this threat and the range of countermeasures can be found in the separate chapter on electronic protection in this *Handbook*.

*Wiretapping* originally referred to making a surreptitious (perhaps legal) connection with telephone lines, often with a transmitting device. More sophisticated equipment (e.g., a nonlinear junction detector or a telephone analyzer) is generally expensive. See Purpura (2002). Telephone-system vulnerabilities are dealt with extensively in a separate chapter in this *Handbook*. A more general concern is unauthorized physical contact with any guided transmission media for the purposes of intercepting information.

Wired media are relatively easy to tap. A reactive measure is to detect a tap using *time-domain reflectometry* (sending a pulse down the wire and analyzing the signal that bounces back) together with a baseline reading of cable in an "inviolate" state. A preventive measure is to enclose in pipes all cables that are not in secured spaces; the pipes should themselves be protected against tampering. See the separate chapter on conducted communication media in this *Handbook*.

Contrary to what is claimed by some photonics texts and experts, fiber optic cable can be tapped. One defense against this is to employ *optical time-domain reflectometry*, which is analogous to the electronic version mentioned earlier. However, this may not be able to detect the small loss of light required to obtain meaningful information from a line. An alternative is a relatively new technique to detect physical disturbances in the cable that do not even involve a loss of light. (The same principle can be employed to protect a variety of items, even very large ones, by attaching a nondata fiber optic cable; see the last line in Table 2.) This form of defense is discussed in Tapanes (1999).

Connecting to a network, whether copper-based or fiber-optic, is easiest at unguarded standard points of access. Examples are an unused network jack left active (perhaps with an unused computer still in place) and the proverbial router in the unlocked closet. Defenses are to secure wiring cabinets and to establish and enforce policies that remove or nullify access points as soon as they are not needed; computers that are no longer needed on the LAN should be locked away and have their hard drives sanitized.

A slightly different issue is employees' installing unauthorized modems, sometimes to facilitate work-related activities (Skoudis, 2000). These can provide entrée to an attacker who would otherwise be stopped by a firewall. Checking for these can be done either by visually inspecting every computer or by war-dialing company extensions.

A particularly easy attack is to use a computer to which an authorized user has already logged on. The defense is the establishment and enforcement of policies requiring "locking" a computer when unattended and prohibiting the "sharing" of an account.

Almost as good is learning a password by *"shoulder surfing"* or by finding one written down. This highlights the challenges of physical and personnel security. Automatic, iron-clad cyberenforcement of policies dictating the length, composition, or lifespan of passwords is trivial. On the other hand, enforcing a policy such as, "Eat it if you write it down," is essentially impossible to enforce. At the same time, stringent password policies commonly result in passwords that are hard to remember and short-lived, thereby provoking users to write them down.

A less haphazard way of gaining unauthorized access to resources is *social engineering*, the art of conning others into revealing sensitive information. The victim usually realizes the information is privileged, but the perpetrator successfully conveys the impression that he or she is entitled to the information. This is more likely to occur in large institutions, where it is difficult to know all of one's coworkers. Social engineering can be done in person, over the phone, or via the Internet. An Internet forum is a very likely place where "loose lips" can "sink ships." In fact, an attacker might infer a great deal about corporate clients, hardware, software, and configurations simply by *"lurking,"* without contributing to an online conversation. All employees who know anything that might be useful to a potential attacker need awareness training with regard to social engineering, indiscreet usage of newsgroup bulletin boards, and so forth. For both of these, sample scenarios should be described.

Sample scenarios can also help with awareness training in the sensitive area of malicious insiders. Smaller institutions in which everyone knows everyone else are especially likely to have coworkers who are overly trusting of one another. The corporate culture should foster "collegial paranoia" without breeding mistrust among coworkers. Physical security is just another problem that needs to be attacked with teamwork, a highly valued corporate virtue. That means that everyone should expect cooperation from everyone else in adhering to physical security protocols. For instance, anyone asking to "borrow" someone else's account should expect to be turned down. System administrators should not assign a common account name and password to a group of people, because this complicates tracing malfeasance to a single person. Policies must be communicated and justified. Policies that are considered to be frivolous or unnecessarily restrictive tend to be ignored or circumvented (e.g., doors will be propped open).

Ultimately, the goodwill of employees is priceless. All managers must be careful not to turn employees against the organization either by how they treat subordinates or by how they behave in the workplace.

## Acceptable Use

An increasingly nagging and complex issue is the personal use of information resources by those who are authorized to use the resources as an essential part of their work-related duties. It is typically done without malice or any thought that it has any significant adverse impact on the organization. In the digital information age, however, inappropriate use of resources has far more legal and ethical implications than older forms of misbehavior, such as photocopying body parts.

Currently, the most pressing problem is how employees abuse Internet access in the workplace. Volonino and Robinson (2004) cited two studies that quantify the magnitude of the problem. One, by IDC Research, estimates that 30% to 40% of workplace Internet usage in 2003 was not work related. In another, Websence claims that *cyberslacking* costs U.S. businesses $85 billion per year in lost productivity. It should come as no surprise, then, that surveys of U.S. companies indicate the proportion monitoring employees' Internet activities is about 63%, 80% for larger companies.

Beyond the obvious waste of time for which employees are being compensated, there may also be a significant impact on an organization's available bandwidth. In academic institutions with lax controls over student usage, the (often illegal) downloading of entertainment media has, in some cases, exceeded the volume of all other Internet traffic. From a practical standpoint, inbound or outbound Internet traffic can be selectively blocked, filtered, or *shaped*. Of these, shaping is the least intrusive approach because it limits the portion of bandwidth that can be consumed by certain services while not prohibiting them entirely.

The direct impact on the bottom line is not the only consequence of improper use. Legal precedent has established that a company that does not actively prevent inappropriate behavior by its employees within the job's time-space domain is seen as promoting that misconduct and may be held liable for it under the principle of *respondeat superior*. Although violation of intellectual property rights is one concern, the behavior most likely to incur legal action is the creation of a hostile work environment when the Internet activity of some employees offends other employees. For a company to defend legally its *duty of care* obligations to employees, it must establish a well-written *AUP (acceptable-Use Policy)*, communicate it clearly to employees, and enforce it consistently.

Checking on employees' computer usage is easy. In addition to monitoring e-mail passing through their hardware, companies also use *activity monitors*, that is, software to record keystrokes (*keyloggers*), to capture screen displays, or to log time spent on Internet chatting, game playing, and the like. Some activity monitors can be set up to alert administrators to inappropriate behavior or to block use of certain applications or Web sites. Some products claim they cannot be detected, located, deactivated, or removed, even by experienced users. Other products exist to detect or even block any keylogging software.

**Table 4** Comparison of Surge Protectors

| Surge Protector Type | Characteristics |
| --- | --- |
| MOV (Metaloxide Varistor) | Inexpensive, easy to use, but progressively degrades from even minor surges (possibly leading to a fiery demise). |
| Gas Tube | Reacts quickly, can handle big surges, but may not deactivate until an alternating circuit polarity flip (which may mean the computer shuts down in the meantime). |
| SAD (Silicon Avalanche Diode) | Faster than an MOV (1 ns vs. 5 ns) but has a limited power capacity. |
| Reactive Circuit | Also smoothes out noise but can only handle *normal-mode* surges (between hot and neutral lines) and may actually cause a *common-mode* surge (between neutral and ground lines), which is thought to be the more dangerous type of surge for desktop computers. |

(Activity monitoring as described actually covers a small fraction of the spectrum of security-related behavior.)

Trickier than enforcement is the establishment of an AUP that strikes the right balance. Some employers prohibit even personal e-mail to an employee's spouse saying, "I have to work late," a practice this spouse has found to be both ironic and very inconveniencing. Others seem not to care about misuse of resources until glaring abuses arise. Neither policy extreme is optimal; research has shown that productivity is actually best when employees are allowed modest time for personal e-mail and Internet access.

Depending on the jurisdiction and circumstances, companies may be required to announce monitoring of employees' usage of their resources. For example, by the U.K. Data Protection Act of 1998, covert monitoring is only allowed if there are clear grounds for suspecting criminal activity. If activity monitoring is used, the notification of employees (whether legally required or not) may create some animosity but much less so than when it is eventually discovered that secret monitoring has been in effect. It is best to spell out both what an employer expects in the way of behavior and what employees might expect with regard to what they may see as their "privacy." In practice, monitoring should be used to control problems before they get out of hand, not to ambush employees.

A thorough introduction to the subject is contained in Chapter 6 ("Acceptable-Use Policies") of Volonino and Robinson (2004).

# SUSTAINING INFORMATION ASSETS

Wheras controlling physical access and fire are security concerns relative to any valuable asset, digital information assets have their own special requirements. The continued existence of such assets in an accurate, accessible state depends on the electrical power supply, communications services, a functioning workforce, and an environment free of inappropriate temperature, humidity, forces, and substances. Measures must be taken to meet all of these physical needs.

## Power Maintenance and Conditioning

The most basic necessity for the functioning of an electronic information environment is maintenance of power. Merely having power is not enough: It must be the right kind of power. *Power conditioning* refers to smoothing out the irregularities of that power. Although maintaining power is clearly the highest priority, power conditioning is discussed first because power maintenance devices can also condition power.

### Surge Protectors and Line Filters

A *surge protector* is designed to protect against sudden increases in current. It forms a third line of defense, the circuit breaker being the second. Neither should be counted on to protect against the ultimate power surge, a direct hit by lightning, which is discussed later. Surge protectors are currently based on four technologies, described in Table 4.

Metal oxide varistor (MOV), gas tube, and silicon avalanche diode (SAD) surge protectors short out the surge and isolate it from the protected equipment. The reactive-circuit type uses a large inductance to spread a surge out over time. All should have lights to indicate if they are in functioning order. MOVs and SADs are the types preferred for computing environments because of their reaction times. All surge protectors require a properly grounded electrical system to do their job.

*Line filters* clean power at a finer level, removing electrical noise entering through the line power. Their concern is not extreme peaks and valleys in the alternating current (AC) sine wave but modulation of that wave. Their goal is to restore the optimal sine shape. Power purity can also be fostered by adding circuits rather than filters. The most important precaution is to keep large machinery off any circuit powering computing equipment. If possible, it is preferable to have each computer on a separate circuit.

Any energized wire emits electromagnetic radiation, and any wire (energized or not) can act as an antenna. Thus, electrical devices have an inherent potential to interfere with one another by broadcasting and receiving conflicting "information." Government regulations limit how much *RF (radio frequency)* radiation computers and other electronic devices may emit and where they may be used. To achieve *EMC (electromagnetic compatibility)* in components, there are specially designed, conductive enclosures, gaskets, meshes, pipes, tapes, and sprays. The simplest EMC measure is to use shielded cables and keep them separated to prevent crosstalk. Devices designed to be RF emitters, such as mobile phones, should be kept away from computers with sensitive data.

For an annotated bibliography of EMC publications, see Gerke (2003). An especially important reference regarding grounding and EMC is Institute of Electrical and Electronic Engineers (1999).

## Lightning Precautions

Lightning can be surprisingly invasive, penetrating where rain and wind do not. Moreover, it does not always hit the most "logical" target, and it can arrive unexpectedly. A bolt was documented to have traveled horizontally 16 km (10 miles) before landfall; it appeared to come out of a blue sky when, in reality, it originated in a cloud hidden behind a hill.

At home, there are surge protectors for power, telephone, and cable TV lines; however, during an electrical storm, there is no substitute for disconnecting computers from both the electric grid and communication lines.

Few businesses will be willing to disconnect thusly whenever the potential for lightning exists. Consequently, the first line of defense for a large building should be a lightning protection system. See National Fire Protection Association (2000a) and International Electrotechnical Commission (1993) for different viewpoints on lightning protection systems.

As another precaution against lightning, magnetic media and sensitive equipment should be kept away from metal objects, especially structural steel and the components of a lightning arresting system. On the other hand, storage *within* a metal container affords the same protection that passengers enjoy within the metal body of an automobile; this is called the *skin effect* because the current passes only through the outer skin of the metal. (The rubber tires would need to be a mile thick to provide equivalent protection.)

## Controls for Electrostatic Discharge (ESD)

An *electrostatic discharge* results from the same segregation of positive and negative charges that spawn lightning. Although highly localized, it is nevertheless a potentially serious form of excess power. When not discharged, static electricity can attract contaminants.

The dangers of static electricity can be reduced by inhibiting its buildup, providing ways for it to dissipate gradually (rather than discharge suddenly), or insulating vulnerable items. General techniques for discouraging the buildup of static electricity include the following:

1. Properly bond components and ground equipment.
2. Keep the relative humidity from dropping too low (below 40%).
3. Avoid the use of carpets and upholstery with synthetic fibers, or spray them with antistatic sprays.
4. Use antistatic tiles or carpets on floors.
5. Do not wear synthetic clothing and shoes with soles prone to generating charges.
6. Use an *ionizer*, which sends both positive and negative ions into the air as a neutralizing influence.

It is also advisable to keep computers away from metal surfaces or to cover metal surfaces with dissipative mats or coverings.

Electronic circuitry becomes exposed to a possible ESD from a human as soon as the case of a computer is open. It is most at risk when it is encased in neither a computer nor its antistatic shipping container. The following precautions should be taken when installing integrated circuits and cards:

1. Work on an antistatic mat.
2. Use an antistatic "garment" such as a bracelet or strap for wrists and ankles, glove, finger cot, or smock.
3. Attach the computer, antistatic mat, and antistatic garment to a common, reliable ground.
4. Avoid touching any conducting surface of a card or chip.
5. Do not set a component on a synthetic or other static-prone surface.

See Electrostatic Discharge Association (2001) for a sequence of Web pages introducing ESD and its control.

## Uninterruptible Power Supplies (UPS)

Although an *uninterruptible power supply*, by definition, counteracts a loss of power, it typically provides surge protection as well. This is accomplished by means of separate input and output circuits, the input circuit inducing current in the output circuit. A UPS may also incorporate noise filtering. UPS systems fall into three categories.

An *online* system separates the input and output with a buffer, a battery that is constantly in use and (almost) constantly being charged. This is analogous to a water tank providing consistent water pressure, regardless of whether water is being added to it. This is the original and most reliable design for a UPS. In the strictest sense, this is the only truly uninterruptible power supply; its transfer time (defined below) is 0 ms.

An *offline* system sends the primary current straight through in normal circumstances but transfers to backup power if its detection circuit recognizes a problem with the primary power. The problem might be a complete drop in primary power, but it might also be a spike, a surge, a *sag* (drop in voltage), or electrical noise.

A *line interactive* system is similar to an offline system, but its output waveform will be a sine wave (as is the input waveform) rather than a square or step wave.

Aside from its basic type, the most important characteristics of a UPS are its:

1. *capacity*—how much of a load it can support (measured in volt-amps or watts);
2. *voltage*—the electromotive force with which the current is flowing (measured in volts);
3. *efficiency*—the ratio of output current to input current (expressed as a percentage);
4. *backup time*—the duration during which it can provide peak current (a few minutes to several hours);
5. *transfer time*—the time from the drop in primary power until the battery takes over (measured in milliseconds);
6. *battery life span*—how long it is rated to perform as advertised;

7. *battery type*—a small Ni-MH (nickel metal hydride) battery may support an individual machine, whereas lead-acid batteries for an entire facility may require a room of their own; and

8. *output waveform*—sine, square, or step (also known as a modified sine) wave.

Another consideration is the intended load: *resistive* (as a lamp), *capacitive* (as a computer), or *inductive* (as a motor). Because of the high starting current of an inductive load, the components of an offline UPS (with its square or step wave output) would be severely damaged. Actually, an inductive load will still have a similar but less severe effect on other types of UPS systems (with sine wave output).

Some UPS systems have features such as scalability, redundant batteries, or redundant circuitry. Especially important is interface software, which can:

1. indicate the present condition of the battery and the main power source,

2. alert users when backup power is in operation (so that they can manually shut equipment down gracefully), or

3. actually initiate a controlled shutdown of equipment prior to exhaustion of backup power.

This last feature is critical on those occasions (e.g., fires and floods) when power must suddenly be cut; this includes disconnecting a UPS from its load. (Emergency lighting and fire detection and suppression systems must, of course, have self-contained power sources and remain on.) Any intentional disruption of power should be coordinated with computers via software to allow them to power down gracefully.

The existence of any UPS becomes moot whenever someone accidentally flips the wrong switch. The low-cost, low-tech deterrent is switch covers, available in stock and custom sizes.

Large battery systems may generate hydrogen gas, pose a fire hazard, or leak acid. Even a sealed, maintenance-free battery must be used correctly. It should never be fully discharged, it should always be recharged immediately after usage, and it should be tested periodically.

Most UPS systems have backup times designed only to allow controlled shutdown of the system so that no data are lost or equipment damaged. For continued operation during extended blackouts, a backup generator system will also be necessary. It is tempting to place large UPS systems and generators in a basement, but that can backfire if the power outage is concurrent with water entering the building. It is important to anticipate plausible combinations of calamities.

A UPS should come with a warranty for equipment connected to it. However, the value of any lost data is typically not covered.

When limited resources do now allow for all equipment to be on a UPS, the process of deciding which equipment is most critical and therefore most deserving of guaranteed power continuity should consider two questions. First, if power is lost, will appropriate personnel still receive automated notification of this event? Second, is the continued functioning of one piece of equipment moot if another component loses power?

See Kozierok (2004) for a sequence of Web pages introducing the various aspects of the subject.

## Communications

An essential part of information processing is communication between machines near and far. Whereas the robustness of an Intranet is often under an organization's own control, communication beyond a single campus typically depends on an ISP. Politically, operationally, and economically, it may make sense to have a single ISP. From the standpoint of robustness, however, it is better to have at least two service providers and to have their respective cables exit the organization's physical perimeter by different routes (so that any careless excavation cannot damage both lines). Internally, the organization must be able to switch critical services promptly from one provider to the other.

Less glamorous but also essential is basic voice communication. Increasingly, this may be a service handled by *VoIP (Voice over IP)*. Thus, a lack of Internet service automatically implies a lack of voice communication. Although a separate chapter in this *Handbook* details telephone vulnerabilities, we discuss here the difficulties of providing backup voice communication channels.

Cellular communication is an obvious alternative to wired phone service. But phone systems in general become overloaded and may sustain damage as a result of a major event. Or cellular services could be shut down, as occurred on September 11, 2001, for fear they might be used to trigger bombs (a technique used later in Madrid).

Another alternative emergency communication system would be a battery-powered, two-way radio that broadcasts on a frequency monitored by emergency agencies; this may require a governmental license. In any case, RF-emitting devices must not be active near equipment that could suffer from the emissions. Chapter 12 of Garcia (2001) discusses the use of radios as standard tool of security guards; she suggests a minimum of four to six channels as a defense against jamming.

Physical security doesn't stop at the door. Events outside—riots, dust storms, rolling brownouts—can disturb operations inside. Physical security policies must provide for timely, two-way flow of information; for example, monitoring of weather forecasts and prompt reporting of internal incidents to relevant authorities.

## The Physical Needs of Information Assets

In addition to electrical and communication needs, media and information processing equipment have a number of physical requirements:

1. temperature and humidity that are neither too high nor too low,

2. an environment free of deleterious particles and chemicals (including water), and

3. "TLC" (tender loving care)—freedom from physical abuse.

HVAC systems should have independently controlled temperature and relative humidity settings. Each variable should be monitored by a system that can issue alerts when problems arise. Ideally, HVAC units should be installed in pairs, with each unit being able to carry the load of the other should it malfunction. For large, critical facilities, HVAC should be protected from sabotage. In particular, air intakes should be viewed as potential entry points for dangerous airborne substances. If information processing equipment is to be kept running during a loss of municipal power, then provisions should be made for backup power and, if required for cooling, water supplies for HVAC systems.

Standards for long-term preservation of data stored in magnetic or optical format are far stricter than guidelines for ordinary usage. As a sample, for archival storage, the prescribed allowable temperature variation in 24 hours is a mere $\pm 1°C$ (2°F). See International Advisory Committee for the UNESCO Memory of the World Programme (2000) for detailed preservation guidelines. One such guideline is that magnetic media, both tapes and disks, be stored in an upright orientation (i.e., with their axes of rotation horizontal). The exclusion of light is important for extending the useful life of writeable optical media, which incorporate dyes. All media should be stored in containers that will not chemically interact with the media. In general, the desired storage temperature and humidity for long-term preservation are much lower than what is allowable for daily usage of media. Projected life spans for properly archived media are considered to be 5–10 years for floppy diskettes, 10–30 years for magnetic tapes, and 20–30 years for optical media. These estimates are conservative to ensure creation of a new copy before degradation is sufficient to invert any bits.

For optical media, life expectancies are extrapolated from accelerated aging tests based on assumptions and end-of-life criteria that may be invalid. Numerous factors influence longevity. Write-once formats have greater life expectancies than rewriteable formats. It is known that the bit-encoding dye phthalocyanine (appearing gold or yellowish green) is less susceptible than cyanine (green or blue-green) to damage from light after data has been written. Manufacturers' claimed life expectancies of up to 300 years, however, are not universally accepted.

What appears to be a major determiner of longevity is the original quality of the stored data. This in turn depends on the quality of the blank disc (which can vary greatly), the quality of the machine writing the data, and speed at which data was written. For example, recording data at a slower speed does not necessarily imply a better job will be done; lasers calibrated for high-speed recording will "over burn" at a very low recording speed. Actual testing is necessary to ensure that the machine and batch of media being used is producing a good representation of the data. Hartke (2001, 1998) gave an enlightening look at the complexities of this particular issue and at broader quality issues for both magnetic and optical media.

All archived data of critical importance should be sampled periodically and backed up *well before* the rate of correctable errors indicates that data might be unrecoverable at the next sampling. A related concern when longtime storage is involved is technological obsolescence. Even physically perfect data have been effectively lost because it outlived the software or hardware needed to read it. Therefore, before its storage format becomes obsolete, the data must be converted to an actively supported format.

There are devices or consumable products for cleaning every type of storage medium and every part of a computer or peripheral device. Backup tapes that are frequently overwritten should be periodically removed from service to be tested on a *tape certifier*, which writes sample data to the tape and reads it back to detect any errors; some models incorporate selective cleaning as an option. Read-write heads for magnetic media typically need to be cleaned far more often than the medium that moves by them. For optical media, keeping discs clean is usually the concern. Compressed air should not be used, as the resulting drop in temperature produces a *thermal shock* (rapid temperature change) for the disc. In some cases, CDs or DVDs that have been scratched on the *bottom* side (the side read by the laser) may be rehabilitated by products or services that polish that surface.

Evidence seems to indicate that DVDs are more easily made unreadable by scratching them on the bottom side. The construction technique of DVDs (the data layer being sandwiched between two protective layers) eliminates one problem of CDs, namely that the seemingly "safe" label side of a CD is actually more vulnerable to scratching; this is because it is right next to the data layer.

On the down side, DVDs' construction requires lamination that is more susceptible to flexing than for CDs. Hence, DVDs should never be stored in CD cases, which do not provide adequate support. Furthermore, care should be taken to depress the button of the hub lock fully before attempting to remove a DVD from its case and to avoid any flexing of the disk. Both DVDs and CD should be stored vertically and should not be stored in envelopes (especially ones with plastic windows). See Svenson (2004).

DVDs seem to be more sensitive to chemicals in the form of markers and label adhesives. Actually, labels for DVDs should be avoided as the slightest imbalance will have more serious consequences because of the higher rotational speed of DVDs. The alternative is to use specialized equipment to print labels directly on DVDs.

Keeping a computing area free of foreign particles requires multiple defenses. Air filters should remove fine dust particles because outdoor dust is brought in on clothes and shoes. Filters must be cleaned or replaced on a regular schedule. Periodically, air-heating equipment should be turned on briefly even when not needed. This is to burn off dust incrementally that would otherwise accumulate and be converted to an appreciable amount of smoke when the equipment is activated for the first time after a long period of disuse. Vacuuming of rooms and equipment should also involve filters. Food, drink, and tobacco products should be banned from the computing area. Maintenance and construction workers (whether they are employees or not) must be made of aware of the dangers posed by dust, even from something as simple as accessing the space above a suspended ceiling. When dust-producing activities are anticipated, other employees should know to take precautions, such as installing dust covers on equipment.

An often-overlooked environmental parameter is the ambient magnetic field. Earth's contribution to the magnetic field is too weak to cause short-term or even long-term damage to magnetic media. However, degaussers and any other equipment that produce strong magnetic fields should be kept in a room separate from any media not scheduled to be erased. Although the intensity of most magnetic fields decreases rapidly with distance, it is exceedingly difficult to shield against them.

Likewise, computers should be kept away from sources of vibrations, including printers. If this cannot be arranged, vibration-absorbing mats can be placed under the computer or the offending device.

With the upsurge in mobile computing has come an increased incidence of damage from shock, vibration, dust, water, and extremes of temperature and humidity. One survey found that 18% of corporate laptops in "non-rugged" applications had suffered substantial damage (averaging about half the purchase price). Several precautions that should be taken with laptops are as follows:

1. transporting it only in a case designed for that purpose;
2. making sure it is off (not just in standby mode) when it is stored in its case (to avoid overheating);
3. not leaving it where it is subjected to temperature extremes (such as an unoccupied car);
4. not subjecting it to moisture, dust, food, or drink; and
5. being careful not drop, bang, or jostle it.

## Ruggedization

An alternative to pampering a device is to make it more resistant to hazards. Laptops and other mobile devices can be *ruggedized* by adding characteristics such as the following:

1. having an extra-sturdy metal chassis, possibly encased in rubber;
2. being shock- and vibration-resistant (with a floating *LCD (liquid crystal display)* panel or gel-mounted hard drive);
3. being rainproof, resistant to high humidity, and tolerant of salt fog;
4. being dustproof (with an overlay panel for the LCD screen);
5. being able to withstand temperature extremes and thermal shock; and
6. being able to operate at high altitude.

Touchscreens, port replicators, glare-resistant coatings for the LCD screen, and modular components are available on some models. Some portable ruggedized units resemble a suitcase more than a modern laptop.

Ruggedization techniques can also be used for any computer that must remain in areas where explosions or other harsh conditions may be encountered. Accessories available are ruggedized disk drives, mouse covers, transparent keyboard covers, and sealed keyboards (some of which can be rolled up). Some biometric devices can be used in demanding environments.

## Hardening Facilities

On a larger scale, facilities can be reinforced to withstand known local hazards. This can be done in a structural sense (preferably at the time of construction) or by internal design. In times of impending disaster, additional protective measures can be taken.

Facilities housing hazardous materials are required to take extra precautions, not the least of which is training its personnel in handling the materials and dealing with mishaps. Every organization should endeavor to determine which hazardous materials are located in nearby enterprises so precautions can be taken as well. Unfortunately, any nearby major transportation route will likely carry a wider array of substances with toxic, corrosive, or explosive potential, and it is impossible to know in advance what might leak or ignite in case of an accident.

The focus here is on two particular types of natural disasters because of their potential to do substantial damage: geologic events and weather events. The frequency and severity of these are well known to be related to geographic location. That said, all facilities, regardless of the locale, should take certain standard precautions. This is because earthquake-like forces and destructive weather can occur anywhere. For example, buildings have collapsed for a wide variety of reasons, ranging from snow accumulation above to watermain breaks below. Even if your building does not collapse, a nearby collapse has a seismic impact on the immediate vicinity. (Even the initial crashes into the World Trade Center registered on seismographs.)

### Preparing for Geologic Events

In regions of the world having a well-known history of frequent earthquakes, planning for the inevitable is second nature. Complacency prevails where damaging earthquakes strike decades or centuries apart; earthquake survivability features may not be required by building codes or may not be calculated to be cost-effective. Fortunately, some cities in seismically dormant areas are waking up to the importance of earthquake precautions.

Regardless of construction techniques, how the occupants furnish buildings is largely their own responsibility. Some precautions can be taken with relatively little expense or intrusion to normal operations. Following are three suggestions from Garfinkel (2002) based on the simple principle that objects will move and perhaps fall from high places to lower places:

1. Place computers under sturdy tables, not on high surfaces or near windows.
2. Do not place heavy objects so that they could fall onto computers.
3. Restrain the possible movement of computers with bolts and other equipment.

The first two recommendations also help in case damaging wind or the force of an external explosion blows out a window or damages a roof. The last could also serve as a theft deterrent, depending on the type of restraint used. There are also relatively easy ways to secure things other than computers. For example, bookcases can be bolted to walls so they cannot topple, and books can be restrained by removable bars or straps. In the newly opened Computer History Museum in Mountain View, California (10 miles from the infamous San Andreas Fault), some fragile items are bolted down, and others are prevented from shaking off shelves by fittings on the front of the shelves (Ward 2004).

Currently, the forecasting of earthquakes is not well focused in space or time coordinates. The only certainty is that major shocks are always followed by aftershocks. Therefore, a partially damaged building should not be entered without professional advice on how it is likely to react to an aftershock that could be nearly as strong as the original quake. Tsunamis that accompany earthquakes (under or near water) or landslides (under or into water) can travel across an entire ocean. National and regional tsunami warning systems have been developed and have alerted threatened regions minutes, even hours ahead of time. Unfortunately, as the world learned after the December 26, 2004, Indian Ocean tsunami spawned by the quake off Sumatra, only the systems in the Pacific Ocean are operational.

Volcanic activity, on the other hand, can be anticipated with some accuracy, and advanced warning of eruptions has saved lives. Precautions to protect against an influx of ash may be required hundreds of kilometers downwind of an explosive eruption. For threats from lava, the Japanese have had some success with constructing structures to divert lava flows. In most areas that might be engulfed by lava, evacuation is the only defense.

Landslides and mudslides may not have the heat (and eventual permanence) of lava, but they can move more rapidly, arrive with less warning, and occur in many more locations than lava. The triggering event (if any) may be an earthquake, a soaking rain, or a combination of the two. Often, there is evidence of slow, subtle movement before a collapse. Consequently, monitoring of weather, soil conditions, and any changes in potentially threatening slopes may give enough warning to evacuate.

## Preparing for Weather Events

Many regions of the world are subject to seasons when monsoons, hurricanes (typhoons), tornadoes, damaging hail, ice storms, or blizzards are more likely to occur. But global climate change has already resulted in more frequent extreme weather events and more of them occurring outside their customary seasons and regions. In 2003, one tropical storm formed in the North Atlantic more than a month before "hurricane season" and another formed more than a month after. The following year, Brazil was struck by the first recorded South Atlantic hurricane.

Even if an event arrives in its proper season, that arrival may be unexpected. In general, the larger the scale of the weather event, the farther in advance it can be anticipated. Despite dramatic advances in the accuracy and detail of regional forecasting, the granularity of current weather models does not allow precise forecasting of highly localized phenomena beyond saying, "Small, bad things may happen within this larger area." As the probability of any specific point in that area being hit with severe weather is small, such generalized warnings often go unheeded. Even if a warning is noted, there may not be time to "board up the windows."

Consequently, some standing precautions should be taken regardless of severe-weather history of a locale. These precautions can serve in case of other disasters as well. For example, fitted covers for equipment can be quickly deployed to protect against falling water from a damaged roof, overhead pipe leaks, or sprinkler systems. They can also be used as dust covers when equipment is moved or stored, during construction work, or when the panels of a suspended ceiling need to be lifted. Keeping critical resources away from windows and off top floors is a good precaution in any location, but particularly in areas where fierce winds could breach the windows, walls, or roofs.

Similarly, all facilities—but especially those in flood-prone areas—should keep critical resources out of the lowest level or any level below ground level. This is because flooding can occur from a broken water main in any region of the world. Water detectors should be placed above and below a raised floor to monitor the rise of water. A sensor that is lower than the lowest energized wire should trigger an automatic power shutdown.

Hurricane-prone jurisdictions are increasingly requiring ever sturdier construction; design consideration should also be given to efficiently protecting windows in advance of an approaching storm. Advanced warning of hurricanes is now adequate to evacuate personnel, crucial media, and perhaps small equipment. In fact, one suite of hurricane-related commercial products can predict peak winds, wind direction, and the arrival time of damaging winds at specific locations.

While protecting against potential wind damage is important, more damage actually comes from the associated flooding. This may be from a storm surge, but stalled storms that have lost their "punch" (in terms of wind speed) have inundated areas far inland. In either case, it is difficult to imagine the level to which water might rise during a once-in-a-lifetime event.

Facilities in tornado-prone regions should provide for emergency shelter. This involves two things. The first is to construct or at least identify a safe place within the facility, preferably within each building, so that people are not required to walk far, especially outside. The other requisite is universal knowledge of where to go. Because tornadoes still, on occasion, arrive with little or no warning, everyone must be ready to move at a moment's notice.

The actual formation of small, intense weather events can be detected by modern radar, and warnings of potential and imminent danger can be obtained through a variety of means. There are radio receivers that respond specifically to warnings transmitted by meteorological agencies or civil authorities. The Internet itself can be the messenger. One mode of notification is e-mail. Other services run in the background on a client machine, checking with a specific site for the latest information. Some of these services are free (although accompanied by advertising banners).

It is now possible to receive automated alerts regarding impending adverse *space weather*, that is, electromagnetic anomalies originating with solar flares and potentially disruptive of communications and power networks (especially at high latitudes). The service can be tailored with regard to the means of notification (e-mail, fax, or pager), the type of event expected (radio burst, geomagnetic impulse, and so forth), and the threshold at which a warning should be reported. See Space Environment Center (2002).

## Human Health and Safety

Human health and safety should be valued above any other asset. The protection of humans is mandated by laws, insurance companies, and the simple fact that employees are needed to make things work. Some concerns are common to any indoor workplace. We have already dealt with defenses against fire and unauthorized intrusion. Even authorized personnel occasional "go postal" (a phrase deriving from several instances involving postal workers shooting coworkers). Dealing with emergencies such as these as well as events involving hazardous materials requires advanced planning and training of personnel.

As with media and machines, humans need reasonable environmental conditions, but humans have their own set of susceptibilities. *Sick building syndrome* may be manifested by a variety of symptoms, including nausea, headaches, dizziness, fatigue, and irritations of the eyes, nose, and throat. The most common cause is poor ventilation combined with indoor air pollution from office supplies and equipment as well as furnishings and construction materials, notably insulation. Minimizing the sources of such pollution may not be as practical as improving ventilation and air filtration, either by means of the HVAC system or standalone devices. Another threat is the growth of bacteria or toxic mold from excessive humidity, possibly localized to areas such as washrooms. Eradication of toxic mold can be an expensive, disruptive process. On the other hand, maintaining the proper humidity and ventilation can result in *legionnaire's disease*, a form of pneumonia transmitted via mist and sometimes associated with large air-conditioning systems; contaminated water in these systems is the suspected source of the *Legionella pneumophilia* bacteria.

Other dangers are more specific to those who work with computers. These include:

1. carpal tunnel syndrome (from repetitive actions, notably typing);
2. back and neck pain (from extended use of improper seating);
3. eye strain and headaches (from staring at a computer screen for long periods); and
4. pooling of blood in the legs and increased intraspinal pressure (from sitting for extended periods).

The defense against these is to combine proper equipment, proper relative positioning of equipment and body parts, and proper use of body parts.

Human-friendly appointments pertinent to an information processing facility include the following:

1. a negative-tilt platform for the keyboard or mouse;
2. a specially shaped keyboard or mouse (preferably large and not curved);
3. a comfortable, adjustable chair with lumbar support;
4. appropriately aimed or diffused lighting, a matte working surface, a monitor hood, or a screen covering that reduces glare (and, therefore, eyestrain); and
5. a document holder, positioned in line with the monitor.

Among behavior patterns beneficial to healthy computer usage are the following:

1. sitting at arms' length from the monitor with feet flat on the floor and thighs parallel to the ground;
2. *dynamic sitting*, that is, not staying in a fixed position for a long time;
3. keeping shoulders, arms, hands, and fingers relaxed;
4. using arm motion (from the elbow) rather than wrist motion to move a mouse;
5. taking frequent *microbreaks*, resting on palm supports; and
6. being continually aware of one's own body.

Two extensive sources of information on computer workstation ergonomics can be found at (United States) Centers for Disease Control (2000) and Cornell Human Factors and Ergonomics Research Group (2004).

It is known that people with pacemakers should avoid devices creating strong magnetic fields, such as degaussers.

There is currently no consensus on the long-term effects of *ELF (extremely low-frequency)* emissions (below 300 Hz), magnetic fields emitted by a variety of devices, including high-tension lines and *cathode ray tube* (CRT) monitors (but not LCD displays). Laboratory tests with animals have found that prolonged exposure to ELF fields may cause cancer or reproductive problems.

Studies of pregnant CRT users have produced conflicting data. Pending conclusive evidence, some recommend keeping 60 cm (2 ft) away from such monitors, which may not be practical.

A recent report of the (United Kingdom) National Radiological Protection Board (2005) has raised new concerns about the potential health effects of cellular phones. In particular, it has been suggested that children limit use of the devices for voice communication and rely primarily on text-messaging.

Although the World Health Organization acknowledges the need for continued research in certain areas, its latest position is that there is no evidence of health risks associated with EMF exposures *below* the levels set forth by the International Commission on Non-Ionizing Radiation Protection (1998).

The heat produced by a laptop computer is sufficient that warnings have been issued against using one on bare skin and against falling asleep while having one in a lap. A recent study indicated that the heat could affect male fertility.

# RECOVERING FROM BREACHES OF PHYSICAL SECURITY

Disaster is in the eye of the beholder. If it's *your* hard drive that crashes while holding unique data, it's a disaster. Other events, such as the destruction of an entire building, may be far more disastrous in one sense; yet with the proper planning, an organization might continue to function with no loss of data or services.

Disaster recovery can take as many forms as the disasters themselves. A single event may be handled in different ways or may require a combination of remedies. Data and services replicated elsewhere may be called into service. Media and equipment may be rehabilitated on- or off-site. Simultaneously, operations may be (partially) restored on-site or transferred off-site. In most disaster-recovery planning, the first priority is maintaining operations or restoring them as soon as possible. A variety of services can be contracted to resume operations or to rehabilitate damaged media, equipment, and buildings. Some are mobile facilities. (See the separate chapter in this *Handbook* on contingence planning management.)

## Redundancy

Redundancy is the safety net for ensuring integrity and availability of resources, but not confidentiality; some damage, such as the revelation of personal information, can never be undone. Redundancy can be viewed as a preventive measure in that it prevents a permanent or extended loss of information or services. In fact, redundancy only pays dividends when other defenses have failed to prevent some calamity. In that sense, exploiting redundancy is a reactive measure. Redundancy cannot succeed without a combination of foresight and discipline. An organization must envision the potential need for redundancy and must consistently adhere to proper practices.

Because of the many facets of the computing environment, redundancy takes many forms. We have already seen that a loss of electrical power can be counteracted, perhaps with severe limits on capacity and duration, and that redundancy in regard to communications services can also be achieved.

Possibly the first type of redundancy that springs to mind is backing up data. If only a single copy of information exists, it may be difficult, if not impossible, to reconstruct it with complete confidence in its validity. Not to be overlooked are system software and configurations and any documents needed to restore systems expeditiously.

There are a wide variety of schemes for creating backups. Many are based on some type of high-density tape. Capacities for some are measured in terabytes. The backup procedure can be either manual or automated. However, the former approach is subject to human error or simple neglect. The latter approach is safer, but the system should issue a notification if it encounters problems while performing its duties. Backups can be made, managed, and used remotely. Some systems allow access to other cartridges while one cartridge is receiving data. Reliability and scalability are important features to consider

when choosing a system. As mentioned earlier, tapes that are subjected to repeated reuse should periodically be tested and, if necessary, cleaned by a tape certifier.

Ideally, backups should be kept far enough away from the site of origin that a single storm, forest fire, earthquake, or dirty bomb could not damage both locations. At a bare minimum, backups should be kept in a safe which is fireproof, explosion-resistant, and insulated so that heat is not conducted to its contents. Backups that are going off-site (perhaps via the Internet) should be encrypted. In all cases, access to backups should be restricted to authorized personnel.

Point-in-time recovery requires not only periodic backups but also continual logging of changes to the data since the last complete backup so that files can be reconstructed to match their last version. Although the need to backup digital information is well recognized, essential printed documents are sometimes overlooked. These can be converted to a more compact medium (e.g., microfilm).

The ultimate redundancy is a *hot site*, ready to take over operations. This does not need to be owned outright because services of this sort can be contracted. Furthermore, there are many levels of readiness (warm site, cold site) and concomitant expense. Again, refer to the separate chapter on contingence planning management in this *Handbook*.

## Restoration

We concentrate here on the physical aspects of rehabilitating buildings, equipment, and media. Professional disaster recovery services should always be employed for this purpose. Because such specialized companies are not based in every city, however, their response time does not match that of emergency personnel. Yet for many physical disasters, the first 24 hours are the most important in limiting progressive damage, for example, from water and smoke. Consequently, knowledge of what to do during that crucial time frame is essential. Good references in this regard are McDaniel (2001) and the three separate links on "What to do in the first 24 hours!" (for electronics; for magnetic, optical, information media; and for documents and vital records) at the press releases Web site of BMS Catastrophe (2002).

### Recovering from Fire Damage

Even when a fire has been put out, new problems arise—and can intensify as time passes. By-products of the fire, perhaps because of the type of suppressant used, may be toxic to humans or corrosive to equipment. As soon as practical after a fire has been extinguished, thorough ventilation should take place. Only appropriately trained and equipped experts should enter to begin this dangerous procedure. Aside from the initial health hazard, improper procedures may worsen the situation. For example, active HVAC equipment and elevators might spread contamination to additional areas.

Once air quality has returned to a safe level, resources should be rehabilitated. In some cases, equipment will never again be suitable for regular use; however, it may be brought to a condition from which any unique data can be backed up. The same is true of removable storage media. Paper documents can be restored provided they have not become brittle.

The combustion by-products most devastating to electronic equipment are corrosive chloride and sulfur compounds. These reside in particulate residue, regardless of whether dry chemical (which itself leaves a film) or a clean agent (a somewhat misleading term) was applied. In either case, time is of the essence in preventing the progression of damage. Some types of spray solvents may be used for preliminary cleanup. In the case of fire suppression by water, the procedures outlined in the following paragraphs should be followed.

### Recovering from Water Damage

The first rule of rehabilitating electrical equipment exposed to water is to disconnect it from its power source. Energizing equipment before it is thoroughly dried may cause shorting, damage, and fire. The second rule is to expedite the drying process to prevent the onset of corrosion. Low ambient humidity speeds drying, whereas high humidity (and, even more so, dampness) speeds the corrosive action of any contaminants. If the HVAC system cannot (or should not) be used to achieve a relative humidity of 40% to 50%, then wet items should be moved to a location where this can be done. Actively applying heat significantly above room temperature must be done with caution. (See the separate chapter on physical security threats in this *Handbook* for temperatures at which damage can occur to media and equipment.) Handheld dryers can be used on low settings. An alternative is aerosol sprays that have a drying effect. Even room-temperature air moved by fans or compressed air at no more than 3.4 bar (50 psi) can be helpful. In any case, equipment should be opened up as much as possible for the greatest effect. Conversely, equipment should not be sealed, because this may cause condensation to develop inside. Low-lint cotton-tipped swabs may be used to dab water from hard-to-reach areas.

### Recovering from Other Events

Because of the tremendous variety of characteristics of modern contaminants, a facility contaminated by chemical, biological, or radiological agents should not be reentered until local authorities and appropriately trained professionals give clearance. Some contaminants, such as sarin gas, dissipate on their own. Some, such as anthrax spores, require weeks of specialized decontamination. Others, such as radiation, effectively close down an area indefinitely.

One helpful action that can be taken during egress or remotely as soon as possible is to shut down air circulation equipment because it will tend to distribute airborne particles or molecules.

## CONCLUSION

Physical security tends to receive less attention than it deserves. Yet cybersecurity depends on it. The two sides of security must be balanced to defeat malicious insiders and outsiders. Ultimately, physical security is the greater challenge, because nature can be the biggest foe. Physical security involves a broad range of topics outside the normal sphere of IT expertise. Consequently, to obtain the best protection, professionals in other fields should be consulted with regard to HVAC, fire detection and suppression, power maintenance and conditioning, physical access control, forensic science, managerial science, and disaster recovery. A basic understanding of how these areas relate to physical security facilitates communication with consultants. Combining knowledge with the imagination to expect the unexpected leads to better physical security planning and practice.

The scope of physical security is wider than is immediately evident. It concerns an organization's resources, wherever they go. An asset often forgotten is employees' knowledge. Equally important are their intentions. Thus, physical security involves everyone, all the time. It relates to intangibles such as trust and privacy, and it must look inward as well as outward.

## GLOSSARY

**Bolt**   A bar that slides into a *strike* to attach a movable object (e.g., a door) to an immovable object (e.g., a door frame).

**Class A Fire**   Fire involving ordinary *combustibles* (e.g., wood, paper, and some plastics).

**Class B Fire**   Fire involving *flammable* or *combustible* liquid or gas (e.g., most solvents).

**Class C Fire**   *Class A* or *Class B* fire amid energized electrical wiring or equipment, which precludes the use of extinguishing agents of a conductive nature (e.g., water or foam).

**Clean Agent**   Gaseous fire suppressant that technically leaves no residue; residues will result when the agent breaks down under the heat of combustion.

**Combustible**   Capable of burning at normal ambient temperature (perhaps without a flame).

**Degausser** or **Bulk Eraser**   Alternating current-powered device for removing magnetism. (*Degausser* is often applied specifically to wands that rid cathode ray tube monitors of problems displaying colors. The term *bulk eraser* indicates that data are wiped en masse rather than sequentially.)

**Electrical Noise**   Electromagnetic interference, especially interference conducted through the power input, or minor *spikes*.

**Electromagnetic Interference (EMI)**   Undesired electrical anomalies (imperfections in the desired waveform) due to externally originating electromagnetic energy, either conducted or radiated.

**Flammable**   Capable of burning with a flame; for liquids, having a flash point below 38°C (100°F).

**Halon** or **Halogenated Agent**   *Clean agent* formed when one or more atoms of the halogen series (including bromine and fluorine) replace hydrogen atoms in a hydrocarbon (e.g., methane).

**Heating, Ventilation, Air-Conditioning (HVAC)**   Equipment for maintaining environmental air characteristics suitable for humans and equipment.

**Line Filter**   Device for "conditioning" a primary power source (i.e., removing electrical noise).

**Radio Frequency Interference (RFI)**   Sometimes used as a synonym for *EMI*, but technically the subset of

EMI due to energy in the "radio" range (which includes frequencies also classified as microwave energy).

**Sag** or **Brownout**   A drop in voltage.

**Smoke**   Gaseous, particulate, and aerosol by-products of (imperfect) combustion.

**Spike, Transient,** or **Transient Voltage Surge (TVS)**   Momentary (less than 1 cycle) increase in voltage.

**Strike**   The socket into which a *bolt* slides when locking a door, etc.

**Surge**   A sudden increase in electrical current; also used for *spike* because the two often arrive together.

**Uninterruptible Power Supply (UPS)**   Device to provide battery power as a backup in case the primary source of power failures.

## CROSS REFERENCES

See *Biometric Basics and Biometric Authentication; Conducted Communications Media; Contingency Planning Management; Corporate Spying: The Legal Aspects; Electronic Protection; Fixed-Line Telephone System Vulnerabilities; Forensic Computing; Implementing a Security Awareness Program; Information Leakage: Detection and Countermeasures; Internal Security Threats; Physical Security Threats; Risk Management for IT Security; Security Insurance and Best Practices.*

## REFERENCES

Absolute Software. (2003). *AbsoluteTrack: Secure Computer Asset Tracking Solution*. Retrieved January 12, 2005, from http://www.absolute.com/PDF/AbsoluteTrack_WP.pdf

BMS Catastrophe. (2002). *BMS CAT Response: What to Do in the First 24 Hours*. Retrieved October 23, 2004, from http://www.bmscat.com/were/press.shtml

Centers for Disease Control. (2002). *Computer Workstation Ergonomics*. Retrieved October 23, 2004, from http://www.cdc.gov/od/ohs/Ergonomics/compergo.htm

Cornell Human Factors and Ergonomics Research Group. (2004). *Cornell University Ergonomics Web site*. Retrieved October 23, 2004, from http://ergo.human.cornell.edu

Cote, A. E. (Ed.). (2003). *Fire Protection Handbook (2003 ed.)*. Quincy, MA: National Fire Protection Association.

Crowe, T. (2004). Crime prevention through environmental design strategies and applications. In L. J. Fennelly (Ed.), *Effective physical security (3rd ed., pp. 49–99)*. Burlington, MA: Elsevier Butterworth-Heinemann.

Cumming, N. (1992). *Security: A guide to security system design and equipment selection and installation*. Stoneham, MA: Butterworth-Heinemann.

Electrostatic Discharge Association. (2001). *Fundamentals of ESD*. Retrieved January 12, 2005, from http://www.esda.org/basics/part1.cfm

Environmental Protection Agency. (2003). *Halon substitutes under SNAP as of August 21, 2003*. Retrieved October 23, 2004, from http://www.epa.gov/ozone/snap/fire/halo.pdf

Fennelly, L. J. (2004). *Effective physical security (3rd ed.)*. Burlington, MA: Elsevier Butterworth-Heinemann.

Fleming, J. W. (1999). Chemical fire suppressants: How can we replace halon? *Proceedings of the Fall Technical Meeting of the Eastern States Section of the Combustion Institute* (pp. 16–23). Raleigh, NC: The Combustion Institute.

Garcia, M. L. (2001). *The effective evaluation of physical protection systems*. Woburn, MA: Butterworth-Heinemann.

Garfinkel, S., with G. Spafford. (2002). *Web security, privacy, and commerce*. Sebastapol, CA: O'Reilly & Associates.

Gerke, K. (2003). *Bibliography of EMC publications*. Retrieved October 23, 2004, from http://emiguru.com/biblio.htm

Halon Recycling Corporation. (2002). *Halon recycling corporation homepage*. Retrieved October 23, 2004, from http://www.halon.org

Hartke, J. (1998). *Duplication quality tips (2nd ed.)*. Marlborough, MA: Media Sciences.

Hartke, J. (2001). *Measures of CD-R longevity*. Retrieved October 23, 2004, from http://www.mscience.com/longev.html

Institute of Electrical and Electronic Engineers. (1999). *Recommended practice for powering and grounding electronic equipment* (IEEE Standard 1100-1999). Piscataway, NJ: IEEE Standards Department.

International Advisory Committee for the UNESCO Memory of the World Programme staff. (2000). *Safeguarding the documentary heritage*. Retrieved October 23, 2004, from http://webworld.unesco.org/safeguarding/en

International Commission on Non-Ionizing Radiation Protection. (1998). Guidelines for limiting exposure to time-varying electric, magnetic, and electromagnetic fields (up to 300 GHz). *Health Physics, 75*, 494–522. Retrieved October 23, 2004, from http://www.icnirp.de/documents/emfgdl.pdf

International Electrotechnical Commission. (1993). *Information technology equipment-safety—part 1: General principles, section 1: Guide A: selection and protection levels for lightning protection systems* (IEC 61024–1–1—Ed. 1.0). Geneva: Author.

International Electrotechnical Commission. (2001). *Information technology equipment-safety—part 1: General requirements* (IEC 60950–1—Ed. 1). Geneva: Author.

Konicek, J., & Little, K. (1997). *Security, ID systems and locks: The book on electronic access control*. Woburn, MA: Butterworth-Heinemann.

Kozierok, C. M. (2004). *Uninterruptible power supplies*. Retrieved October 23, 2004, from http://www.pcguide.com/ref/power/ext/ups/index-c.html

Mangan, J. F. (2002). Cutting edge protection for information technology hardware is old hat. *Insurance Advocate, 111*(43), 12.

McDaniel, L. D. D. (Ed.). (2001). *Disaster restoration guide for disaster recovery planners* (rev. no. 10). Fort Worth, TX: Blackman-Mooring Steamatic Catastrophe.

National Fire Protection Association. (2000a). *Standard for installation of lightning protection systems* (NFPA 780; 2000 ed.). Quincy, MA: Author.

National Fire Protection Association. (2000b). *Standard for clean agent fire extinguishing systems* (NFPA 2001; 2000 ed.). Quincy, MA: Author.

National Fire Protection Association. (2003a). *Standard for the Protection of Electronic Computer/Data Processing Equipment* (NFPA 75; 2003 ed.). Quincy, MA: Author.

National Fire Protection Association. (2003b). *Life safety code* (NFPA 101; 2003 ed.). Quincy, MA: Author.

National Radiological Protection Board. (2005). *Mobile phones and health*. Retrieved January 12, 2005, from http://www.nrpb.org/press/press_releases/2005/press release_02_05.htm

Newman, R. C. (2003). *Enterprise security*. Upper Saddle River, NJ: Prentice Hall.

POA Publishing. (2003). *Asset protection and security management handbook*. Boca Raton, FL: Auerbach.

Purpura, P. (2002). *Security and loss prevention* (4th ed.). Woburn, MA: Butterworth-Heinemann.

Rittinghouse, J. W., & Hancock, W. M. (2003). *Cybersecurity operations handbook*. Burlington, MA: Elsevier Digital Press.

Sheinson, R. S., et al. (2004). *Heptafluoropropane with Water Spray Cooling System as a Total Flooding Halon 1301 Replacement: System Implementation Parameters*. Retrieved July 18, 2005, from http://fire.nist.gov/bfrlpubs/fire04/PDF/f04027.pdf

Skoudis, E. (2002). *Counter hack: A step-by-step guide to computer attacks and effective defenses*. Upper Saddle River, NJ: Prentice Hall PTR.

Space Environment Center. (2002). *Space environment center space weather alerts*. Retrieved December 6, 2003, from http://www.sec.noaa.gov/alerts/register.html

Svenson, P. (2004). *CDs and DVDs not so immortal after all*. Retrieved October 23, 2004, from http://www.cnn.com/2004/TECH/ptech/05/06/disc.rot.ap/index.html

Tapanes, E., & Carroll, D. (1999). *Securing fibre optic communication links against tapping*. Retrieved December 2, 2004, from http://www.fft.com.au/products/FOSL_WP.PDF

Tyska, L. A., & Fennelly, L. J. (2000). *Physical security: 150 things you should know*. Woburn, MA: Butterworth-Heinemann.

Volonino, L., & Robinson, S. R. (2004). *Principles and practices of information security*. Upper Saddle River, NJ: Pearson Prentice Hall.

Ward, Bob (Ed.). (2004). Silicon Valley Museum Celebrates History of Computing. *Computer, 37*, (10) 15–19.

Wylder, J. (2004). *Strategic information security*. Boca Raton, FL: Auerbach.

## FURTHER READING

Future Fibre Technologies. (2003). *Fibre optic secure link*. Retrieved December 2, 2004, from http://www.fft.com.au/products/fosl.shtm

International Standards Organization. (2000). *Information technology—Code of Practice for Information Management* (ISO/IEC 17799:2000). Geneva: Author.

# RFID and Security

Stephen A. Weis, *MIT Computer Science and Artificial Intelligence Laboratory*

## INTRODUCTION

Radio frequency identification (RFID) technology has the potential to greatly impact inventory control, supply chain management, and retail sales applications by lowering costs and raising efficiency. Although some form of RFID systems has been used for decades, modern innovation and open technology standards are lowering costs to the point where it will be economical to use RFID for everyday consumer applications. By enabling digital naming of common items, RFID may facilitate an "Internet of things" by associating arbitrary data with physical objects. However, widespread adoption of RFID systems may both positively and negatively affect the security of an RFID-enabled infrastructure.

The most basic building blocks of RFID systems are small devices that broadcast identifying via radio frequency (RF) signals. These devices are called RFID transponders or tags. RFID tags are part of a greater system of RFID reading devices (or simply readers) and databases that facilitate automatic identification of objects. This definition encompasses a broad range of tag technologies, differing in power sources, operating frequencies, and functionalities.

A variety of applications employ RFID systems. For example, RFID tags are used frequently for supply chain management, retail inventory control, automated payment systems, and more recently for anticounterfeiting. RFID systems offer both cost benefits and efficiency gains in these applications.

However, there may be security risks associated with RFID systems of which users should be cognizant. Specifically, insecure RFID systems may facilitate corporate espionage, violate individual privacy rights, or create a false sense of authentication. Fortunately, there are security countermeasures that may address some of the potential risks.

This chapter offers a brief history of RFID under History of Radio Frequency Identification and a system primer under Radio Frequency Identification System Primer. Adversarial Model and Attacks discusses several security risks that may be present in an insecure system. Finally, Security Countermeasures offers countermeasures that may limit potential security risks.

## HISTORY OF RADIO FREQUENCY IDENTIFICATION
### Early RFID

The origin of RFID technology lies in the 19th century. Luminaries of that era made great scientific advances in electromagnetism. Of particular relevance to RFID are Michael Faraday's discovery of electronic inductance, James Clerk Maxwell's formulation of equations describing electromagnetism, and Heinrich Rudolf Hertz's experiments validating Faraday and Maxwell's predictions. Their discoveries laid the foundation for modern radio communications.

A precursor to automatic radio frequency *identification* systems were automatic object *detection* systems. One of the earliest patents for such a system was a radio transmitter for an object detection system designed by John Logie Baird in 1926 (Baird, 1926). More well known is Robert Watson-Watt's 1935 patent for a radio detection and ranging system, or RADAR.

One of the first applications of a RFID system was in identifying friend or foe (IFF) systems deployed by the British Royal Air Force during World War II (Royal Air Force, 2004). IFF allowed radar operators and pilots to automatically distinguish friendly aircraft from enemies via RF signals. This system helped prevent friendly fire incidents and rapidly identified enemy aircraft. Advanced IFF systems are used today in aircraft and munitions, although much of the technology remains classified.

Clearly, security is crucial in an IFF system. Adversaries with the ability to forge IFF signals represent a dire threat because it could allow an enemy to disguise themselves as friendly forces. Even without the ability to actively forge IFF signals, a passive eavesdropper could derive sensitive logistics and deployment data by extracting the contents of legitimate IFF signals. It would be truly devastating if an enemy could use a military's IFF system against itself. In fact, in World War II both sides were able to track and target enemy aircraft by their IFF signals, leading to an arms race of IFF systems and countermeasures. Although less dire, similar threats may exist in unprotected commercial systems and are discussed later in this chapter.

## Uniform Product Codes

In terms of commercial applications, RFID systems may be considered an instance of a broader class of automatic identification (Auto-ID) systems. Auto-ID systems essentially attach a name or identifier to a physical object by some means that may be automatically read. This identifier may be represented optically, electromagnetically, or even chemically.

Perhaps the most successful and well-known auto-ID system is the universal product code (UPC). The UPC is a one-dimensional, optical bar code encoding product and brand information but no unique identifying information. UPC labels can be found on most consumer products in the United States. Similar systems are deployed worldwide.

The UPC was specified by the Uniform Code Council (UCC), a standards body originally formed by members of the grocery manufacturing and food distribution industries (Uniform Code Council, 2004). A precursor body to the UCC first met in 1969 to discuss the need for an interindustry auto-ID system. By 1973, a one-dimensional (or linear) bar code design was chosen. In 1974, a supermarket in Ohio scanned the first UPC-labeled product: a package of Wrigley's gum.

Adoption of the UPC grew steadily throughout the following years, to the point where UPC bar code scanners are found in a vast majority of large American retailers. Today, over 5 billion bar codes are scanned around the world each day. Shipping and transit companies, such as United Parcel Service, Federal Express, and the United States Postal Service, commonly use two-dimensional bar codes, which can carry more data in a smaller surface area. Consumers may even print their own two-dimensional bar code postage stamps (Stamps.com, 2004), possibly including cryptographic properties (Tygar & Yee, 1993).

Optical bar codes offer faster, more reliable, and more convenient inventory control and consumer checkout. Several weaknesses of optical bar codes are that they require line-of-sight and may be smudged or obscured by packaging. In most circumstances, optical bar codes still require some human manipulation to align a bar code label with a reader. Supermarket shoppers have certainly experienced a checker struggling to scan an optical bar code.

## Modern RFID

Auto-ID systems that transmit data via RF signals do not have the same performance limitations as optical systems. Data may be read without line-of-sight and without human or mechanical intervention. A key advantage in RF-based auto-ID systems is parallelism. Modern RFID systems may offer read rates of hundreds of items per second.

Two early examples of RFID applications are the automatic tracking of train cars and shipping containers.

Sturdy, self-powered RFID devices could be used in these applications, because the per-item value and physical size could accommodate more bulky and expensive tags. These RFID systems helped automatically track and locate shipments of goods.

RFID began to be used for lower-value items in other industries, for example, tracking automotive parts and, surprisingly, cattle. The value of cows and auto parts is still high enough to justify the use of more robust and expensive RFID technologies. RFID-based contact-less smart cards have been used for years, particularly in Europe, for applications like toll booth passes, ski-lift passes, or building access control. Again, these are essentially low-volume, high-value applications.

These applications also illustrated some of the shortcomings of RFID. For instance, some RFID technologies do not operate well in proximity to liquids or metals. Each different technology has its own strengths and weaknesses, including variations in cost, size, power requirements, and environmental limits. There is no "one size fits all" RFID technology. The term actually describes an entire array of technologies, which are each applicable to different types of applications. "RFID Taxonomy" offers more detailed discussion of these various technologies.

Although RFID continues to lower the costs of tracking high-value items, an untapped and lucrative market lies in tracking everyday consumer goods. A low-cost RFID tag incorporated into consumer product packaging could lower retail sales costs and customer checkout time. EPC Global, an RFID standards body, is currently developing a specification for an electronic product code, or EPC (EPC Global, 2004), as a replacement for the ubiquitous UPC. In the past, the lack of an open standard was a barrier to RFID adoption. The EPC standard and, to some extent, the ISO-18000 standard (International Standardization Organization, 2003) will make it easier for users to integrate their RFID systems.

The potential for EPC is huge. Globally, over 5 billion bar code transactions are conducted daily (Uniform Code Council, 2004). Even miniscule savings per transaction could translate into a huge aggregate cost savings. The market has already begun to adopt low-cost RFID on a large scale. According to Mario Rivas, the executive vice president of Philips Semiconductor, his company has already shipped 1 billion RFID chips (RFID Privacy Workshop at MIT, 2003). In 2003, razor manufacturer Gillette placed a single order of up to 500 million low-cost RFID tags (RFID Journal, 2003).

Wal-Mart, the world's largest retailer, is starting to adopt RFID technology in its supply chain. Because of Wal-Mart's large size and close integration with suppliers, this move may be a major driving force for industry to embrace RFID. The U.S. Department of Defense, Postal Service, and Food and Drug Administration have all shown interest in RFID as well and may lead adoption by government agencies.

In the context of security, the limited scale of high-value RFID applications limited their vulnerability. Parties typically deployed and used their own devices rather than passing them through the supply chain. If necessary, these devices could devote adequate resources to security mechanisms, although they were often used in closed environments where security was less of a concern.

EPC tags represent a new threat. Tags are intended to change hands as products pass through manufacturers, wholesalers, transit providers, retailers, consumers, and even recyclers. These tags will not be rugged, expensive devices used in, for example, railway tracking. Rather, EPC-style tags will be cheap, disposable devices that can be easily incorporated into plastic or cardboard packaging.

The sheer size of the EPC market may expose new security risks not present in other RFID applications. Consumers may carry numerous RFID tags, perhaps unknowingly. In contrast to the relatively closed manufacturing or logistics environments, retail RFID infrastructures will be exposed to the public. This could expose security and privacy holes, unless proper countermeasures are employed. Adversarial Models and Attacks and Security Countermeasures discusses these risks and countermeasures further.

## Related Work

A growing body of material deals with RFID security and privacy research. The Auto-ID Labs (Auto-ID Labs, 2004) conduct ongoing general research into low-cost RFID systems. Rivest, Sarma, Weis, and Engels present overviews of RFID security issues and propose counter measures in Sarma, Weis, and Engels (2002), Weis, Sarma, Rivest, and Engels (2002), and Weis (2003). Molnar and Wagner examine RFID privacy issues in the library setting (2004). Juels and Pappu present several security proposals regarding RFID-tagged currency (2003), which is analyzed for weaknesses by Avoine (2004). Juels, Rivest, and Szydlo offer a "blocker tag" to protect consumer privacy (2003).

Feldhofer, Dominikus, and Wolkerstorfer describe low-cost cryptographic implementations appropriate for RFID (2004). Several relevant technical and policy papers were presented at the RFID Privacy Workshop at MIT (2003), notably by Ohkubo, Suzuki, and Kinoshita (2003) and by Inoue and Yasuura (2003). An article by Avoine and Oechslin deals with RFID traceability (2005). Articles by Henrici and Müller address RFID privacy issues and propose countermeasures (2004a, 2004b).

## RADIO FREQUENCY IDENTIFICATION SYSTEM PRIMER
### System Components

Often, discussion of RFID technology, especially in the press, tends to focus only on tag devices. RFID is actually a complete system that includes not only tags but also other important components. RFID systems are composed of at least three core components:

1. RFID tags, or transponders, carry object-identifying data.
2. RFID readers, or transceivers, read and write tag data.
3. Databases associate arbitrary records with tag-identifying data.

### Tags

Tags are attached to all objects to be identified in an RFID system. A tag is typically composed of an antenna or coupling element and identification circuitry. Modern EPC designs tend to implement identification functionality using a silicon microchip supporting both computation and storage. Other designs may be "chipless" or have identifying information hard-wired at fabrication time. Differences between types of tags and tag technologies are discussed further in "RFID Taxonomy."

### Readers

RFID readers communicate with tags through an RF channel. This channel may provide power to what are called *passive* tags. Readers may have internal storage, processing power, or network connectivity. A reader may be a simple conduit to an outside database or may store all relevant data locally.

An important characteristic of some types of RFID reader/tag communications is an asymmetry in directional channel strength. The reader-to-tag, or *forward*, channel signal is often much stronger than the tag-to-reader, or *backward*, channel. This can be an issue in protocols that transmit sensitive data over the forward channel, because the forward channel signal can be monitored from long distances.

Tag readers may come in many forms. They may be a handheld device or integrated into a "smart shelf" or pallet. The cellular phone manufacturer Nokia is already offering RFID-reading functionality in some of its cell phones (Nokia, 2004). If EPC-type tags become highly successful, interesting and useful consumer applications might arise. If this occurs, RFID reading functionality might become a common feature on cellular phones, PDAs, or other handheld computing devices.

### Databases

RFID databases associate arbitrary records with tag identifying data. These records may contain product information, tracking logs, sales data, or expiration dates. Independent databases may be built throughout a supply chain by unrelated users or may be integrated in a centralized or federated database system.

Databases are assumed to have a secure connection to readers. Although there are scenarios where readers may not be trusted, it is often useful to collapse the notions of reader and database into one entity. For example, if tags contain all relevant product information, there is no need to make a call to an off-site database.

### RFID Taxonomy

Because RFID encompasses a broad spectrum of technologies, it is useful to introduce a taxonomic organization to describe and differentiate various types of systems. Security issues will be more relevant to certain classes of tags, so it is beneficial to introduce the vocabulary necessary to identify which tags are vulnerable to which attacks.

#### Passive, Semipassive, and Active

It is useful to separate types of tags by their power source and means of transmission. A tag's power source

**Table 1** Passive, Semipassive, and Active Tag Types

| Tag Type | Passive | Semipassive | Active |
|---|---|---|---|
| Power source | Harvesting RF energy | Battery | Battery |
| Communication | Response only | Response only | Respond or initiate |
| Max range | 10 m | 100 m | 1,000 m |

and means of transmission determine its range, performance, lifetime, and cost. There are three types of classifications based on these attributes: active, semipassive, and passive.

Active tags have their own source of power, such as a battery, and may initiate communication to a reader or other active tags. Semipassive tags have a battery, but may not initiate communication. Passive tags have neither their own power source nor the ability to initiate communication. Passive tags will harvest energy from the incoming RF communication signal. Table 1 depicts these tag types and their potential operating ranges.

### Class 0 Through Class 4

Another useful method of classifying tags is by their functionality. EPC Global offers five broad classes of tag based on functionality (EPC Global, 2004). Similar classes are presented in Weis (2003). This article offers five class definitions loosely based on the definitions appearing in other literature.

**Class 0**: Class 0 tags are the simplest tag, offering only passive "electronic article surveillance," or EAS. EAS tags do not contain unique identifying data, but rather simply announce their presence. EAS tags are often found on compact disks and books.

**Class 1:** Class 1 tags store unique identifying read-only data. In contrast to EAS tags, each Class 1 tag can have its own personal serial number. Class 1 tags will tend to be passively powered but could also be semipassive or active.

**Class 2:** Class 2 tags have write-once read-many (WORM) or rewritable memory. These tags may be used as logging devices and can emulate Class 1 tags. They may have a passive, semipassive, or active power source.

**Class 3:** Class 3 tags contain on-board environmental sensors and may store data without the presence of a reader. These tags can be considered part of a "sensor net." Class 3 tags are necessarily semipassive or active.

**Class 4:** Class 4 tags may initiate communications and form ad hoc networks with other tags. These tags are necessarily active. Functionally, Class 4 tags lie in the realm of "smart dust" (Pister, 2004).

These classes are summarized in Table 2. The most challenging security problems arise in Class 1 and particularly Class 2 devices. EAS tags are so limited in function that there are neither major security concerns nor the resources for security measures. Class 3 and Class 4 tags are relatively powerful devices that can employ more standard cryptographic primitives and protocols applicable. The vulnerability "sweet spot" lies in Class 1 and Class 2 tags, which can contain sensitive data, yet lack security resources.

### Radio Spectrum

There are RFID systems that operate at a variety of radio frequencies, each with their own operating range, power requirements, and costs, as shown in Table 3. This chapter is largely concerned with ultra-high-frequency (UHF) tags operating in the 868- to 956-MHz range, because they will be one of the most pervasive types of tags and have a longer operating range. Table 3 compares some of the properties of low-frequency (LF) and high-frequency (HF) passive tags with UHF passive tags.

## Example EPC Tag Specification

To give a perspective on the resources available in a low-cost EPC-type RFID tag, this section offers a hypothetical tag specification. This specification represents the types of resources that may be available on a tag costing US$0.05–$0.10 in the near future.

## ADVERSARIAL MODEL AND ATTACKS
### Adversarial Model

Prior to discussing classes of potential attacks against RFID systems, we first offer a model for different types of adversaries. This model categorizes attackers by their read and write access to tag communication channels and data. We classify this access in three broad categories: physical, logical, and signal.

Physical read access means that an attacker has direct access to physical data stored on a tag. This access may be in the form of a logic probe, an electron

**Table 2** Tag Functionality Classes

| Class | Nickname | Memory | Power Source | Features |
|---|---|---|---|---|
| 0 | Antishoplift tags | None | Passive | Article surveillance |
| 1 | EPC | Read-only | Passive | Identification only |
| 2 | EPC | Read/write | Passive | Data logging |
| 3 | Sensor tags | Read/write | Semipassive | Environmental sensors |
| 4 | Smart dust | Read/write | Active | Ad hoc networking |

**Table 3** Tag Operating Frequencies

| Range Class | LF | HF | UHF |
|---|---|---|---|
| Frequency range | 120–140 MHz | 13.56 MHz | 868–956 MHz |
| Maximum range | 3 m | 3 m | 10 m |
| Typical range | 10–20 cm | 10–20 cm | 3 m |

microscope, or through electromagnetic TEMPEST-style attacks (National Security Agency, 1982). Any number of physical attacks, such as those described by Anderson and Kuhn, might be deployed (1997).

Physical read access does not imply any write capabilities. By contrast, an attacker with physical write access can store arbitrary data on a tag but cannot necessarily read tag contents. This access may be achieved through some form of electromagnetic attack that could physically wipe out or overwrite tag data.

A weaker class of attackers will have what we call logical access, meaning they have access to the contents of messages sent to and from a tag. Logical read access means essentially eavesdropping. This attacker can read message contents but may or may not have the ability to modify them. An attacker with logical write access can inject well-formed messages into communication protocols but might not necessarily be able to read any traffic. In other words, logical write access implies having the ability to forge arbitrary messages.

We can consider having logical read and write access on the forward channel, the backward channel, or both. Because the forward, reader-to-tag channel is typically much stronger, having backward logical access will imply having forward logical. Thus, we can consider there being two meaningful classes: logical and the weaker forward logical.

A yet weaker class of adversaries has only what is termed *signal* access. Attackers with signal read access can only detect the presence of messages. Again, this can be

**Table 4** An Example EPC Tag Specification

| | |
|---|---|
| Storage | 128–512 bits of read-only storage |
| Memory | 32–128 bits of volatile read-write memory |
| Gate Count | 1,000–10,000 gate equivalents |
| Security Gate Budget | 200–2,000 gate equivalents |
| Operating Frequency | UHF 868–956 MHz |
| Forward Range | 100 m |
| Backward Range | 3 m |
| Read Performance | 100 read operations per second |
| Cycles per Read | 10,000 clock cycles |
| Tag Power Source | Passively powered via RF signal |
| Power Consumption per Read | 100 $\mu$W |
| Features | Anticollision support random number generator |

**Table 5** Attacks and Their Corresponding Access Levels

| Attack | Read Access Level | Write Access Level |
|---|---|---|
| Tag cloning | Physical or logical | Physical |
| Privacy attack/spoofing | Logical | Logical |
| Short-range eavesdropping | Logical | None |
| Long-range eavesdropping | Forward logical | None |
| Traffic analysis | Signal | None |
| Tag manufacture | None | Physical |
| Message forging | None | Logical |
| Denial of service | None | Signal |

broken down to a weaker forward signal subclass. Signal-only readers cannot understand the contents of a given message so are limited to traffic analysis.

Signal write access implies the ability to inject noise into the communication channel. It may also be broken down into a forward signal write subclass. However, in this case, forward signal write access will imply full signal write access rather than vice versa. Signal write attackers are limited to denial of service and jamming attacks, because they do not have the ability to form meaningful messages.

Attackers may have different combinations of these levels of read or write access or none at all. Table 5 lists the access level requirements for several attacks and abilities. For example, an adversary with forward logical read access and no write access can conduct long-range eavesdropping, whereas an adversary with only physical write access can manufacture his or her own tags. The attacks themselves are discussed at length in the following section.

## Attacks

### Espionage

Perhaps the biggest security concerns in RIFD systems are espionage and privacy threats. As organizations adopt and integrate RFID into their supply chain and inventory control infrastructure, more and more sensitive data will be entrusted on RFID tags. As these tags inevitably end up in consumer hands, they could leak sensitive data or be used for tracking individuals.

An attacker needs only forward logical read access to eavesdrop from long range. The forward channel will actually provide power to passive tags. A consequence is that this signal will be quite strong and, depending on the eavesdropper's receiver, may be monitored from a range up to 100–1,000 m. Although this reveals only one side of a communication protocol, some simple anticollision protocols will actually echo sensitive tag data over the forward channel.

A spy could sit outside with an antenna and monitor the contents of an RFID-enhanced warehouse or retail store. Tabulated over time, this data might be used to track movements of supplies or calculate sales information. There is little risk of detection for this type of long-range attacker.

Fortunately, tag protocols may be designed with these threats in mind to ensure that sensitive data is not sent over the forward channel. These protocols may still be vulnerable to short-range eavesdroppers with full logical read access. In practice, attackers with full logical read access must be within 1–10 m of the tags and so are much easier to detect.

Although short-range eavesdropping requires physical access, it can still be a threat in many settings. For example, a corporate spy could carry a monitoring device while a retail store conducts its daily inventory. Alternatively, a spy could simply place bugging devices that log protocol transmissions.

Espionage need not be passive. Attackers with both logical read and write access can actively query tags for their contents. Rather than waiting to eavesdrop on legitimate readers, an active attacker could simply conduct tag read operations herself. (To clarify our attack model, it requires logical write access to send a query to a tag—the write is to the communication channel and not to the tag.) Active attackers may be easy to detect in a closed retail or warehouse environment. It is a different case with individuals carrying RFID tags in the open.

Both eavesdropping and active queries pose threats to individual privacy. RFID tags can be embedded in clothes, shoes, books, key cards, prescription bottles, and a slew of other products. Many of these tags will be embedded without the consumer ever realizing they are there. Without proper protection, a stranger in public could tell what drugs you are carrying, what books you are reading, and perhaps even what brand of underwear you prefer.

In addition to leaking sensitive data, individuals might be physically tracked by the tags they carry. Of course, individuals can already be tracked by their cellular phones. Unlike a cell phone, which is only supposed to be able to be tracked by a cellular provider, RFID tags might be tracked by anyone (granted, within a relatively short read range). Readers will be cheap to acquire and easy to conceal. It is not unreasonable to imagine that a small organization could cover an urban area with RFID readers fairly cheaply. People interested in this data might be criminals, marketers, politicians, or other unsavory characters.

Clearly, tracking someone is trivial if an attacker is able to actively query unique identifying numbers from tags. Even if unique serial numbers are removed from tags, an individual might be tracked by the constellation of brands they carry. A unique fashion sense might let someone physically track you through an area by your set of favorite brands.

Constellation tracking begins to fall in the realm of traffic analysis. In the parlance of our attack model, these are attackers with signal read access. They can detect the presence of messages but not their contents. This is a weaker class of attacks but may be particularly worrisome for drug manufacturers or military RFID users.

## Forgery

Rather than simply trying to glean data from legitimate tags, adversaries might try to imitate tags to readers. RFID systems are currently being used for access control and payment systems. Most notably is the Mobil SpeedPass, which is an RFID keychain fob that allows purchases at Mobil gas stations (Mobile Speedpass, 2004). RFID tags are also being integrated into casino chips and other token systems. An adversary with the ability to forge tags could produce counterfeit products, clone access-control devices, or make decoy tags to mask thefts.

Illustrating the threat of forgery, Mandel, Roach, and Winstein, three undergraduate students at the Massachusetts Institute of Technology, were able to clone the new RFID student identification cards issued at MIT (2004). The MIT ID cards are used to access buildings and to make purchases on campus. The attack took "a couple weeks" and cost about US$30 to produce a prototype clone. Subsequent clones, capable of spoofing several identities, could be produced for less than US$1. Especially concerning is that despite the fact that the cards must be read from a range of a couple *inches* in practice, they were able to read them from a range of several *feet*.

Depending on the environment, adversaries might have logical write or both logical read and write access. This means that an adversary could send messages to tags or readers and potentially receive any responses. Some forgery attacks might also involve attackers with physical write access, which are able to overwrite existing tag data. Forgers with both physical read and write access to tags have the ability to fully clone existing tags.

Some proposals call for RFID devices to be used for an anticounterfeiting. An example is a recent proposal by the U.S. Food and Drug Administration (FDA) to attach RFID tags to prescription drug bottles (Food and Drug Administration, 2004). These tags would effectively act as a pedigree, providing a pointer to the history of a particular bottle of drugs. Rather than try to simply sell counterfeit drugs, a thief might steal the legitimate drugs and replace them with a decoy—in other words, a swapping attack. With RFID tags, the decoy counterfeit drugs must have the same pedigrees as the originals.

This attack cannot be prevented when an attacker has physical read access to pedigrees or can actually remove the pedigree labels from the originals. In most cases, drugs would be sealed in a box and an attacker would only have logical access to them. This is still a risk if an attacker can quickly scan data from legitimate tags and write that data to clones attached to counterfeit drugs. Then a thief could carry out a swapping attack.

Another swapping attack is one where a thief drops an RFID tagged product into a shielded foil bag. Such bags are often sold with complimentary potato chips. The thief could then replace the stolen products with an RFID-emulating decoy. In systems using RFID-reading "smart shelves" and automated checkout, it would appear that the stolen goods are still on the shelf. Unlike the counterfeit drug scenario, this decoy could be significantly more powerful than the tags it emulates (as long as it is cheaper than the value of the stolen goods).

An attack called *skimming* is a threat to RFID-based proximity access control cards or RFID-labeled tokens like casino chips. In skimming attacks, a snoop scans a victim's casino chip, subway card, or key card in an insecure location. The skimmer can then produce a clone and use the victim's credentials at an access-control point or charge goods to the victim's account.

This attack creates a race condition between the legitimate device and the clone. Whoever uses it first will gain access, whereas the second will be detected as a fraud. Unfortunately, the attacker has the upper hand, because he or she knows when and where he or she scanned a legitimate device. For example, scanning someone's subway card as they leave the station means you can probably use a clone to board the next train without much risk of getting caught.

### Sabotage

Weaker attackers with only signal write access may be able to sabotage RFID systems or conduct denial of service attacks. Adversaries with signal write access can attempt to jam tag responses or cause delays in anticollision algorithms. Attackers with logical write access could also poison RFID databases by introducing fake tag data into a system.

Denial of service and poisoning attacks are trivial to detect in other types of auto-ID systems. It is easier to catch someone scribbling over an optical bar code or pasting on a homemade bar code. This is more difficult with a wireless interface. Someone can carry concealed devices that carry out automatic attacks or even place data bomb devices that can independently carry out a denial of service attack. Left unprotected, the data in a retail store or warehouse could be wiped out.

Poisoning is a particular nuisance. Someone could hide dummy devices around a warehouse or store that respond to readers with fake ID numbers. These devices could operate intermittently, rotate through fake ID values, or learn legitimate values to spoof. These responses would be intended to confuse or slow down automated inventory control systems. Such devices could be made very difficult to locate, especially in an environment crowded with many other tags.

Powerful electromagnetic signals might be used in a destructive denial of service attack. Very strong signals could physically destroy RFID tags. Fortunately, attempting these attacks from long range would require so much power that it would affect other electronic components and be easily detected. A less destructive attack would be to simply broadcast noise on RFID frequencies. This could temporarily disable a critical point in a supply chain, at least until the source signal is located.

Although these denial of service and sabotage attacks may seem to be simply nuisances, they could represent serious risks. This is especially true in defense or medical applications. For example, the U.S. Department of Defense is moving toward RFID-based logistics control. An attack against the RFID infrastructure could delay crucial shipments of war materiel or slow down troop deployments.

# SECURITY COUNTERMEASURES

There is a variety of RFID security mechanisms and countermeasures to combat the attacks discussed under Adversarial Model and Attacks. No single tool will protect RFID systems from all threats or will be applicable to all types of RFID systems. Rather, a spectrum of tools can be chosen per application depending on cost, performance, and security requirements.

## Cryptographic

Cryptographic primitives may be used to protect tag security. Encrypting messages between tags and readers makes them unreadable to eavesdroppers. In the parlance of Adversarial Model and Attacks, encryption reduces logical read access to signal read access. Similarly, authenticating messages can effectively drop logical write access (i.e., the ability to transmit valid messages) to signal write access.

Advanced and expensive RFID devices can support strong cryptography. These devices may have internal power sources, ample gate counts, large memories, and tamper-resistant packaging. They can perform the complex operations necessary to engage in standard cryptographic protocols. The security assumptions made in this setting do not differ much from other distributed computing environments. At the very least, expensive RFID devices can support the functionality of a smart card.

Security issues of smart cards or other distributed devices are well studied and are the subject of a large body of literature. For this reason, this chapter focuses primarily on lower-cost devices. This chapter also does not discuss securing communications between tag readers and back-end databases. Although interesting engineering issues do exist, the reader-to-database connection is analogous to a typical Internet connection.

The low-cost RFID setting presents more difficult problems. These devices can carry sensitive data but are not advanced enough to employ strong cryptography. Because low-cost tags will typically be passively powered via an RF signal, they cannot have an on-board clock or compute anything in the absence of a reader. Cost restrictions will limit the number of logic gates available for security features. Performance requirements will determine available computation time. The hypothetical low-cost specification in Table 4 illustrates some of the practical limitations one might expect in a low-cost, EPC-style RFID tag.

Implementing an asymmetric cryptosystem based on modular arithmetic, like RSA, is completely infeasible in a low-cost tag. Just storing an RSA public key would dwarf a low-cost tag's resources. Despite efficiency gains, performing large field modular arithmetic is simply too computationally intensive for a cheap tag.

Even a relatively lightweight asymmetric cryptosystem like NTRU (Hoffstein, Pipher, & Silverman, 1998) is still too costly to implement on an EPC tag. That being said, much progress has been made in recent years in shrinking the implementation footprint of NTRU, notably developments by the Worcester Polytechnic Institute's Cryptography and Information Security Group (2004). Regardless, an NTRU implementation suitable for a consumer RFID tags is still several years away.

Standard symmetric algorithms do not fare much better. Hardware implementations of DES take tens of thousands of gates, which are orders of magnitude more than what can be expected on a cheap tag. The same applies for standardized hash functions like SHA-1, which is optimized for software. AES is more hardware friendly and recent implementations take only several thousand gates (Feldhofer et al., 2004). These implementations may eventually be cheap enough for low-cost tags.

Accepting these limitations for the near future, securing tags may need to rely on weaker cryptographic primitives. One simple approach is to use a "hash-lock," proposed by Weis, Sarma, Rivest, and Engels (2002). A reader will lock a tag by selecting a random key and storing its one-way hash value on the tag. This value is referred to as a meta-ID. While locked, tags will respond to all queries with this meta-ID value. Unauthorized read queries sent by logical write adversaries or queries observed by logical read adversaries will only reveal a tag's meta-ID. All other commands issues by adversaries with logical write access will be ignored. To unlock a tag, the reader will simply send the key to the tag, and the tag will verify the key is the meta-ID's hash preimage.

Tags could still be tracked by their static meta-ID values. To combat tag tracking, a randomized hash-lock variant can return a different meta-ID value on each query. Hash-locks require the implementation of a one-way hash function, and randomized hash-locks require an additional random number generator (RNG). Hardware-based RNGs are fairly simple and low cost. However, cost-effective one-way hash functions still need to be designed.

A security mechanism proposed independently by Weis (2003) and by Molnar and Wagner (2004) is to use a tag-side RNG as a one-time pad source. A tag will generate a random value and transmit it over the backward channel. The reader can then XOR this value with message contents to be transmitted over the forward channel. Recall that the backward channel range is much shorter than the forward channel range. This scheme would offer protection from forward-logical readers but not full logical readers. This idea has been adopted in some proposed industry standards (EPC Global, 2004).

Another approach is Juels's "minimalist cryptography" (2004a). Tags using minimalist cryptography are preloaded with a set of keys that can each be used once. Each time a valid reader accesses a tag, it can refresh a tag's key list. Juels also offers the notion of "yoking proofs" (2004b). A yoking proof can be generated by reading two nearby tags within a predefined period, then later presented as proof that the tags were once in proximity. This might be useful in proving that a tag passed an inventory control checkpoint.

Juels, Rivest, and Szydlo introduce the notion of a "blocker tag" (2003), which is a device that can be carried by individuals to protect personal privacy. The blocker will disrupt the unauthorized readers' anticollision protocols and prevent them from reading nearby tags. Legitimate readers will still be able to read their own tags. Blocker tags or similar privacy agents can be incorporated into cellular telephones, PDAs, or other portable computing devices.

## Physical

The most difficult attacks to defend against are physical attacks against the RFID hardware itself. If attackers have physical access to a tag over a long period, they can subject it to many different physical attacks that can reveal an entire tag's contents. Tamper-resistance countermeasures, such as electromagnetic shielding, environmental sensors, self-destruct mechanisms, or robust packaging, are expensive to implement.

In fact, most tamper resistance is difficult to implement in the relatively expensive smart-card setting. Many can be defeated by low-cost attacks, such as those studied by Cambridge University's TAMPER lab (Anderson & Kuhn, 1997). For these reasons, many low-cost RFID users should concede that someone who is able to physically possess a tag will have complete physical read and write access. An implication is that tags cannot be trusted with long-term or shared secrets. If they did, compromising a single tag could compromise every tag with the same secret.

However, there are some low-tech and low-cost physical countermeasures and design practices that can help protect RFID systems. First, it is advantageous to embed a tag inside a consumer product or within a shipping container rather than simply affixing it to the outside. This makes it more difficult for vandals and thieves to physically tamper with tags, because it involves destroying the product packaging. For example, someone could not simple peel off an RFID sticker and replace it with a new one.

A second design practice is to embed place tags in prominent positions on a package. If a tag is placed, for example, on the lower rear corner of a box, someone might be able to remove or destroy it and replace it on a shelf without detection. For instance, someone could place a foil sticker over an RFID tag to mask it from readers. This would be easier to detect if the tag were prominently located on a package.

Two other useful tools are to include printed tag management data inside a package and to incorporate a physical contact channel in a tag. Printed management data can be used to manually corroborate a tag's authenticity and to reset a tag that has been accidentally or maliciously locked. This management data would only be accessible to someone in possession of a tag. A similar idea is proposed by Juels and Pappu for verifying RFID-tagged Euro banknotes (2003).

A physical contact channel, such as is found in a smart card, is another mechanism that allows legitimate tag owners to reset or "imprint" their tags. Accessing the physical contact channel could be a slow, costly, and easily detectable operation that attackers could not carry out in public.

Although these physical design features may seem trivial in some aspects and could be defeated by a determined attacker, they are low-cost mechanisms that could raise the cost of conducting a widespread attack. However, these design properties are of little value without an adequate detection and response system.

## Detection, Response, and Diversification

There is no single "silver bullet" countermeasure that will address all potential RFID security threats. Any security mechanism should be considered part of a greater overall security system. Cryptographic and physical countermeasures will be most effective when coupled with detection and response systems and other orthogonal security measures.

In a retail setting, RFID users should be prepared to detect potential attacks against tagged merchandise and respond appropriately. This includes detecting both unauthorized reader transmissions and physical attacks against the tags embedded in merchandise themselves. Any monitoring systems will be useful only if someone can quickly respond to detected attacks. One analogy is a CCTV video camera in a retail store. Simply recording footage may be useful for retrospective forensics but cannot stop attacks in progress. Someone needs to actively monitor video footage and quickly respond to shoplifters or other attackers.

The notion of detection and response may seem like simple common sense. Unfortunately, there are many misconceptions about the security of RFID systems. For instance, automated, wireless supermarket checkout systems are often proposed as a potential RFID application. The misconception is that such a system could effectively run with little human intervention or monitoring; that RFID tags will effortlessly detect shoplifters and could not be manipulated to enable fraud.

In reality, a store with an automated checkout system would need a standard security staff and would also need to actively monitor for attacks against its RFID infrastructure. The danger is that the presence of an RFID system could lull users into a false sense of security. Another fallacy is that RFID tags alone could be simply embedded into luxury items and could not be forged. The reality is that a skilled hobbyist could probably forge most commercial RFID tags over a weekend, as was illustrated by Mandel, Roach, and Winstein (2004).

For this reason, RFID users should also consider a policy of security diversification. RFID systems should be coupled with other orthogonal security measures such that the failure of one will not affect the others. For example, optical bar codes coupled with RFID can provide secondary authentication and key recovery data and function as a backup in the event of a denial of service attack. Similarly, anticounterfeiting tags should be combined with special dyes, laser engraving, chemical taggants, or other existing anticounterfeiting technology. Essentially, the sum of orthogonal security systems may be greater than their individual parts.

## CONCLUSION

RFID systems literally have the potential to revolutionize supply-chain management and retail sales, yielding economic benefits for manufacturers, retailers, and consumers alike. However, like many new technologies, RFID may create new security threats. If not properly addressed, these threats could limit the long-term success of RFID. Fortunately, prudent security measures may mitigate these threats, while preserving most economic benefits. We hope this chapter offers perspective into some potential RFID security problems and provides users and system designers insight into securing RFID systems.

## GLOSSARY

**Active Tag**  A tag with its own battery that can initiate communications.

**Advanced Encryption Standard**  A government-approved symmetric encryption algorithm that is the successor to DES.

**Automatic Identification**  Auto-ID systems automatically identify physical objects through optical, electromagnetic, or chemical means.

**Backward Channel**  The communication channel from tag to reader.

**Data Encryption Standard**  A government-approved symmetric encryption algorithm, now deprecated by AES.

**Electronic Article Surveillance**  An RF device that announces its presence but contains no unique identifying data. EAS tags are frequently attached to books or compact disks.

**Electronic Product Code**  A low-cost RFID tag designed for consumer products as a replacement for the UPC.

**Forward Channel**  The communication channel from reader to tag.

**High Frequency**  This is at the frequency of 13.56 MHz.

**Identify Friend or Foe**  Advanced RFID systems used to automatically identify military aircraft.

**Logical Access**  Adversaries with logical read or write access have the ability to receive or transmit messages between tags and readers.

**Low Frequency**  This includes the range 120–140 KHz.

**Linear Bar Code**  A one-dimensional optical bar code used for auto-ID.

**Passive Tag**  A tag with no on-board power source that harvests its energy from a reader-provided RF signal.

**Physical Access**  Adversaries with physical read or write access have direct physical access to tags and can read or write arbitrary tag data.

**Reader**  An RFID transceiver, providing read and possibly write access to RFID tags. Radio Frequency Identification describes a broad spectrum of devices and technologies and is used to refer both to individual tags and overall systems.

**Semipassive Tag**  A tag with an on-board power source that is unable to initiate communications with a reader.

**Signal Access**  Adversaries with signal read access can detect but not understand messages between tags and readers. Adversaries with signal write access can transmit signals on communication channels but cannot form valid messages.

**Skimming Attack**  Scanning a legitimate tag and using its contents to produce a forgery.

**Swapping Attack**  Stealing RFID-tagged items and replacing them with counterfeit items labeled with forged tags.

**Tag**  An RFID transponder, typically consisting of an RF coupling element and a microchip that carries identifying data. Tag functionality may range from simple identification to being able to form ad hoc networks.

**Uniform Code Council**  A standards committee originally formed by grocery manufacturers and food distributors that designed the UPC bar code.

**Ultra-High Frequency** This includes the range 868–956 MHz.

**Universal Product Code** A one-dimensional, optical bar code found on many consumer products.

## CROSS REFERENCES

See *Access Control: Principles and Solutions; Computer and Network Authentication; Cryptographic Privacy Protection Techniques; Encryption Basics; Privacy Law and the Internet; Radio Frequency and Wireless Communications Security.*

## REFERENCES

Anderson, R., & Kuhn, M. (1997). Low cost attacks on tamper resistant devices. In *Lecture notes in computer science, vol. 1361: International Workshop on Security Protocols* (pp. 125–136).

Auto-ID Labs. (2004). *Webpage*. Retrieved November 14, 2004, from http://www.autoidlabs.org

Avoine, G. (2004). Privacy issues in RFID banknote protection schemes. *Smart Card Research and Advanced Application Conference (CARDIS)*.

Avoine, G., & Oechslin, P. (2005). RFID traceability: A multilayer problem. *Financial Cryptography*, submitted for publication.

Baird, J. L. (1926). British Patent #292,185.

EPC Global. (2004). *Webpage*. Retrieved November 14, 2004, from http://www.epcglobalinc.org

Feldhofer, M., Dominikus, S., & Wolkerstorfer, J. (2004). Strong authentication for RFID systems using the AES algorithm. In *Cryptographic Hardware in Embedded Systems*.

Food and Drug Administration. (2004). *Combating counterfeit drugs* (Technical Report). Washington, DC: United States Department of Health and Human Services.

Henrici, D., & Müller, P. (2004a). Hash-based enhancement of location privacy for radio-frequency identification devices using varying identifiers. *Workshop on Pervasive Computing and Communications Security*, 149–153.

Henrici, D., & Müller, P. (2004a). Tackling security and privacy issues in radio frequency identification devices. In *Lecture notes in computer science, vol. 3001: Pervasive computing* (pp. 219–224).

Hoffstein, J., Pipher, J., & Silverman, J. H. (1998). NTRU: A ring-based public key cryptosystem. In *Lecture notes in computer science, vol. 1423: Algorithmic number theory* (pp. 267–288).

Inoue, S., & Yasuura, H. (2003). *RFID privacy using user-controllable uniqueness*. RFID Privacy Workshop at MIT.

International Standardization Organization. (2003). *RFID for item management* [FDIS 18000-3:2003(E)]. Draft version.

Juels, A. (2004a). Minimalist cryptography for RFID tags. *Security in Communication Networks*.

Juels, A. (2004b). "Yoking Proofs" for RFID tags. In *Pervasive computing and communications workshop*. New York: IEEE Press.

Juels, A., & Pappu, R. (2003). Squealing euros: Privacy-protection in RFID-enabled banknotes. In *Lecture notes in computer science, vol. 2742: Financial cryptography* (pp. 103–121).

Juels, A., Rivest, R. L., & Szydlo, M. (2003). The blocker tag: Selective blocking of RFID tags for consumer privacy. In *Computer and Communications Security* (pp. 103–111). New York: ACM Press.

Mandel, J., Roach, A., & Winstein, K. (2004). *MIT proximity card vulnerabilities*. Retrieved November 14, 2004, from http://web.mit.edu/keithw/Public/MIT-Card-Vulnerabilities-March31.pdf

Mobile Speedpass. (2004). *Webpage*. Retrieved November 14, 2004, from http://www.speedpass.com

Molnar, D., & Wagner, D. (2004). Privacy and security in library RFID: Issues, practices, and architectures. In *Computer and Communications Security*. New York: ACM Press.

National Security Agency. (1982). *TEMPEST fundamentals* (Technical Report). Retrieved November 14, 2004, from http://www.politrix.org/foia/nsa/nsa-tempest.htm

Nokia. (2004). *Nokia mobile RFID kit*. Retrieved November 14, 2004, from http://www.nokia.com/nokia/0,,55738,00.html

Ohkubo, M., Suzuki, K., & Kinoshita, S. (2003). *Cryptographic approach to "Privacy-Friendly" tags*. RFID Privacy Workshop at MIT.

Pister, K. (2004). *Smart dust: Autonomous sensing and communications in a cubic millimeter*. Retrieved November 14, 2004, from http://robotics.eecs.berkeley.edu/~pister/SmartDust/

RFID Journal. (2003). Gillette confirms RFID purchase. In *RFID Journal*. Retrieved November 14, 2004, from http://www.rfidjournal.com/article/articleview/258/1/1/

RFID Privacy Workshop at MIT. (2003). *Various speakers*. Retrieved August 28, 2004, from http://www.rfidprivacy.org

Royal Air Force. (2004). *Royal Air Force history*. Retrieved November 14, 2004, from http://www.raf.mod.uk/history/line1940.html

Sarma, S. E., Weis, S. A., & Engels, D. W. (2002). RFID systems and security and privacy implications. In *Lecture notes in computer science, vol. 2523: Cryptographic hardware in embedded systems* (pp. 454–470).

Stamps.com. (2004). *Webpage*. Retrieved November 14, 2004, from http://www.stamps.com

Tygar, J. D., & Yee, B. (1993). *Cryptography: It's not just for electronic mail anymore* (Carnegie Mellon University Technical Report CS-93-107).

Uniform Code Council. (2004). *Webpage*. Retrieved November 14, 2004, from http://www.uc-council.org

Uniform Code Council. (2004). *Frequently asked questions*. Retrieved November 14, 2004, from http://www.uc-council.org/ean_ucc_system/stnds_and_tech/eanucc-faq.html

Vajda, I., & Buttyan, L. (2003). Lightweight authentication protocols for low-cost RFID. In *Ubiquitous Computing (UBICOMP)*.

Weis, S. A., Sarma, S. E., Rivest, R. L., & Engels, D. W. (2002). Security and privacy aspects of low-cost radio frequency identification systems. In *Lecture notes in computer science, vol. 2802: Security in pervasive computing* (pp. 201–212).

Weis, S. A. (2003). *Security and privacy in radio-frequency identification devices*. Unpublished masters thesis, Massachusetts Institute of Technology, Cambridge, MA.

Worcester Polytechnic Institute. (2004). *Cryptography and Information Security Group webpage*. Retrieved November 14, 2004, from http://www.ece.wpi.edu/Research/Crypt/

# Cryptographic Privacy Protection Techniques

Markus Jakobsson, *Indiana University, Bloomington*

## INTRODUCTION

As we move toward a society with more and more information being produced and processed, privacy issues will become increasingly important to understand and address. Although much of the information in question has been available in one form or another long before the information age, it is the ease with which it can be collected and processed—and the amount of it that can be obtained—that poses a threat to privacy. The threats to a person's or company's privacy are numerous and not always easy to anticipate without careful analysis. This chapter strives to describe and exemplify potential privacy threats to clarify what types of threats might be avoided by means of legislation and what types of threats appear better to counter by means of technology. Examples of possible techniques are given. This chapter also describes when privacy (as opposed to the lack thereof) may become a threat to society and how this may be addressed.

An example of a privacy threat is *traffic analysis*. This is the term used to refer to determining who is interacting with whom. Clearly, at a time when all communication was done in person or by messenger, it would be very easy for an observer to infer who in a village interacts with whom but at the cost of following the person of interest around. The use of electronic communication has made this collection of information easier to perform even on a large scale: the phone company could easily determine who calls whom, when, for how long, and how often, as could any other entity able to access the databases of the phone company. Although this ability typically is used by law enforcement to monitor and track known criminals and their associates, it is clear that it could in principle be used to monitor anybody and everybody. Most people would not consider this an immediate threat to their privacy, thinking that if the government wanted to harm them, there would be easier ways to do so. However, if traffic analysis could be done easily and without the possibility of detection (perhaps by a simple modification of the code of a telephone switch), then it could be used by one organization to spy on another, whether for military or commercial reasons, or for an individual or organization to determine the behavior

and preferences of other individuals. The same goes for the Internet traffic, only that the network component that would be modified may be a router and not a switch. For wireless traffic, it may suffice to eavesdrop on broadcast packets.

Although data packets are often encrypted, control packets almost never are, and knowledge of the contents of control packets could allow the eavesdropper to infer communication patterns. If mechanisms for preserving privacy were implemented and put in place, the efforts of an attacker could be frustrated or prevented.

Another example of a situation where there is a potential privacy threat concerns payment patterns. It is entirely feasible that credit card companies establish profiles relating to their cardholders' spending patterns, using this information to determine who is likely to belong to certain groups of interest. The spending patterns of a person are clearly helpful to establish whether this person is likely to be interested in a new product, thereby allowing more precise targeted advertising. At first, this may also not sound threatening to many people, who may even feel that the relevant product advertisements may be of benefit. However, most people would agree that the existence of a database listing many of their purchases (by amounts, time, and vendor) is harmful to their privacy and particularly so if this database would fall into the wrong hands. This would allow potential employers and insurance companies to study the lifestyles of applicants, possessive ex-boyfriends to determine where their former girlfriends shop and eat, and burglars to determine when their potential victims are on vacation. The more detailed the payment data is, the clearer the picture of a person becomes. For example, although most hotel bills do not state what movie a person watched in his or her room, the price is stated. Because movies of different categories are often priced differently, this would allow a snooper with access to a hotel bill to potentially determine what type of movie the person watched. This, of course, constitutes an invasion of the privacy of the hotel guest. Even though payment information may be possible to protect by means of laws and auditing in situations with a small number of market players (major banks and clearinghouses), it becomes increasingly harder the more other companies and individuals obtain access to the information. The SET protocol strives to limit such leaks of information on the path to the bank/clearinghouse by means of encryption. Other payment schemes (to be reviewed in detail later) even limit the amount of information the bank and the clearinghouse would learn. Such techniques guard against accidental leaks of information from otherwise well-behaving banks and clearinghouses, as well as against intentionally abusive information usage. Although the schemes that are to be presented do not necessarily conform to current banking requirements, they are interesting in that they demonstrate the possibilities of anonymous payment schemes.

Although legislation may protect abuse of private information in many instances, there are other cases where it will be more difficult; consequently, technical solutions increase in importance. An example where technical solutions may be of benefit, whereas legislation may not, relates to wireless devices that operate in the unlicensed spectrum. This means that they use radio frequencies that are allowed to be used by everybody and where, accordingly, anybody could in principle obtain transmitted information, if within the range of a transmitter. Such information may identify the device or the type of the device. In turn, if an attacker manages to associate the identity of a device with the identity of its owner (we describe a few ways later), this would allow an attacker to automatically determine the location of a given person at a certain time. This can have severe repercussions on the privacy of users of such devices. Even if an attacker cannot infer the identity of a wireless device but only its type, this may also be used to uniquely identify the person carrying such devices—we also explain how this can be done in more detail. In such instances, the potential attacker may not necessarily be a large organization but perhaps instead a misbehaving individual, thereby reducing the benefits of legislation. Moreover, attacks on privacy are very hard to detect: they constitute theft of information and leave few, if any, immediate traces. Attacks that leave no evidence are not meaningful to legislate against, as there would be no way of catching wrongdoers. This is the situation where technical solutions are preferred.

In this chapter, the technical means to prevent assaults on privacy are described, after a detailed description of some common privacy problems. It is interesting to see that in settings where privacy protection was an afterthought, or perhaps not even considered at all, it becomes difficult to later implement privacy. This stresses the need to understand and consider privacy issues at an early phase in the design of a system. However, privacy is a thornier issue than most people may think at first: if a system with perfect privacy is designed and employed, this may grant criminals undesirable abilities. Consider, for example, a hypothetical payment system where it is impossible to determine who pays whom (such schemes have been proposed and are described and explained). This may at first seem like an appealing idea, especially considering the scenarios previously described. At a second glance, though, we can see that it would provide blackmailers and kidnappers an excellent way of collecting

their ransoms and would therefore stimulate these types of crimes. Clearly, many situations may require what we call "controlled privacy": privacy that is offered to some users under certain conditions but which can be selectively revoked by a privileged entity under certain other conditions.

Taking a look at the bigger picture relating to privacy, we note that Webster defines the word *privacy* as either "(a) the quality or state of being apart from company or observation," or "(b) freedom from unauthorized intrusion." We previously mentioned both of these types of privacy (and the lack thereof), focusing on an attacker learning information about a victim (which relates to the first type of privacy) and then using this to make a decision about or somehow affect this person (which relates to the second type of privacy). The technical emphasis of this chapter is placed on the former type of privacy concern: trying to prevent information to leak. However, it is important to note that if systems are designed to avoid privacy vulnerabilities of the second type, this automatically reduces the incentives for an attacker to attempt to learn user information that was not intended for it—a privacy vulnerability of the first type. As an example of this, let us assume for a moment that there was a good way to avoid spam. This would reduce the incentives of attackers of privacy (the spammers in this case) to obtain information about users (their e-mail addresses and likely preferences). This suggests that it may be important to study the big picture to successfully address privacy concerns.

The remainder of this chapter is aimed toward giving an understanding of various problems relating to privacy, along with some proposed approaches. It is in no way exhaustive but rather attempts to illustrate the important issues using a small set of examples.

# WHERE IS PRIVACY IMPORTANT?
## Privacy of Actions

There are many instances where a person performs an action and wishes the nature of this not to become revealed. An example of this is Web browsing: a user visits a sequence of sites and wishes that the administrators of these sites do not learn about the other sites visited or that anybody else learns this information. For example, a user may first visit a site describing a certain disease and then a site belonging to an insurance company. He may wish for the insurance company not to know of his concern about the disease in question (Jakobsson, Jagatic, Stamm, 2005).

In contrast to the individual's privacy wishes, there are good commercial reasons to establish who visits what sites and when—even the order may be relevant, as knowing what a user may be interested in next may help in deciding which banner ads to select at a given site. Although this may not be of concern to users as long as they are only known by a pseudonym (e.g., their IP address or a particular third-party cookie), it is clear that once a link is established between a pseudonym and a user identity, this association would always remain. For example, if a user ever purchases an item using a credit card, gives his or her home or e-mail address, or otherwise identifies him- or herself at one of these sites, the association between pseudonym and identity has been made. Although the privacy policy of the site in question may forbid this, there is no known way for a user to verify the compliance, and privacy policies are routinely broken. The information may leak because of technical flaws, human error, a change or breach of policy, and more. Thus, a cautious user may wish to prevent linking between sites, or linking to his identity where not necessary.

A technical approach to solve this problem is to use a traffic anonymizer. This is a construction that disassociates the IP address from the request sent to a site by replacing these with temporary pseudonyms and then sending out the request with this pseudonym. When the response associated with a certain pseudonym comes back, this pseudonym is replaced with the real identifier and the response sent to this location. This way, a user can browse Web sites without revealing his identity. However, it is clear that the anonymizer now becomes a "bottleneck" of information: it will potentially be able to determine the entire sequence of sites a user visits. By using a sequence of anonymizers, in combination with encryption techniques, this problem can be avoided. This construction was introduced by Chaum in 1981 and is referred to as a *mix network*. Let us look at how one can implement a mix network.

Assume that the mix network consists of three anonymizers or mix servers. Each one of them has a public key and a secret key. Let's denote the three public keys by $pk_1$, $pk_2$, and $pk_3$. Assume further that Alice wishes to anonymously send a message $m$ to Bob. For simplicity, we can assume that $m$ includes a header that states for whom the message is intended (Bob); the remainder of the message may be encrypted using Bob's public key, but it does not have to be. Now, Alice encrypts the message using $pk_3$. Let us call the resulting ciphertext $c_3$. Then she encrypts $c_3$ using $pk_2$. We call the result $c_2$. Finally, she encrypts $c_2$ using $pk_1$, resulting in a ciphertext $c_1$. She sends $c_1$ to the first mix server, who also receives many other ciphertexts from other users concerned with their privacy.

The first mix server takes all the ciphertexts it receives and decrypts them using its secret key $sk_1$. He then randomly reorders the resulting ciphertexts and forwards this new list to the second mix server. (We note that the message that Alice wants to send to Bob now has been decrypted to be $c_2$, because the encryption of the first mix server has been removed.)

The second mix server takes all the ciphertexts it received from the first mix server and decrypts them by using $sk_2$. He then randomly reorders the resulting ciphertexts and passes the new list on to mix server three. (Now, the message Alice wants to send to Bob has been "peeled off" so that it equals $c_3$.)

The third mix server, finally, decrypts all the ciphertexts it received and reorders the results. The mixing is completed. Now, all the resulting messages are ready to be sent to their corresponding recipients. They all receive them from the third mix server, and nobody knows who originated them. In fact, all three mix servers need to collude and let each other know what random permutations they used, or otherwise it will not be possible for either of them—or anybody else—to determine what input item to the first mix server corresponds to what output item of the third mix server. Now, this is a bit of a simplification. For this really to work, at least if an encryption method such as RSA were to be used, one has to add a random pad each time before encrypting. In other words, when Alice encrypts $m$, she would first attach a first random number and then encrypt using $pk_3$, then attach a second random number and encrypt using $pk_2$, and then finally attach a third random number and encrypt using $pk_1$. When a mix server decrypts, it throws away the random pads and then reorders the remaining elements. Why is this necessary? Otherwise, an attacker could look at all the outputs of a given mix server, encrypt those values with the mix server's public key, and compare the results to the input of the mix server; that would reveal which random permutation the mix server used. This is no longer possible if the messages are padded, as the attacker cannot guess the random pads and therefore cannot encrypt in the "same way" as the originators. Therefore, he cannot compare encrypted messages to determine the permutation.

There are many other ways of performing mixing, but we do not go into detail about these here but only give pointers to further reading at the end of the chapter. Another technical solution to obtain communication privacy is the so-called *crowd*, which was proposed by Reiter and Rubin.

Another type of action that a user may wish to keep secret is whom he or she is paying and when, as this may reveal his or her preferences and interests, as well as other information, such as his location. We describe various approaches to implement (various degrees of) privacy in payment schemes. In particular, we describe one classic payment scheme based on so-called *blind signature* and one payment scheme based on signatures for which some third party can revoke privacy.

## Privacy of Communicated Data

The most commonly known form of privacy is that which relates to communicated data. In fact, the field of cryptography has arisen from the need to send messages without these being intercepted and read by an adversary. Whereas other aspects of cryptography are all children of the 20th century (and later), encryption existed long before computers did. As computers became commonplace, this increased the "firepower" of an attacker who wishes to break an encryption scheme. Clearly, if a computer can try all possible decryption keys within a reasonable amount of time, that makes the encryption effort meaningless. However, the security of a cipher is not only a matter of the number of possible keys (i.e., the key lengths) but also a matter of the design of the cipher. If you compare two secure ciphers, you often find that they may require different key lengths to maintain the same security level, simply because of the different structures they use. There is no simple way to evaluate the security of a given cipher, and the best known ways involve public scrutiny. Thus, to determine the required key lengths for a certain cipher and a particular application, it is best to see what the most recent key-length recommendations are.

It is, however, important to realize that encryption is not a panacea. There are many applications where it is not possible to use encryption or where the problem of establishing or distributing keys makes it practically infeasible to do so. One example is the sending of control data between routers. This is data that indicates for whom a message is intended, how to process it, as well as information about network topology changes. The control data may contain information about the identity of the next router on the path of the packet, the intended recipient, or the priority of the packet. Although the payload of a packet can be encrypted, one faces practical difficulties if one attempts to encrypt control information, especially in a setting where network nodes move relative to each other (e.g., an ad hoc network). This is so since it is of importance to propagate the control data to a large set of network nodes, some of whose identities may not be known to the originator of the data.

Although the control data may not reveal anything about the nature of a message itself, it is sometimes sufficient for an attacker to know who is communicating with whom to draw conclusions regarding the likely data content; this is particularly so if he can observe the actions of either party at the same time as he can observe the exchange of information. As an example, if an observer knows that a certain party is interacting with a known dissident, he could guess that they share opinions, independently of the actual message contents. Thus, although anonymizers may be used to prevent certain types of traffic analysis, there are other possible leaks of information—such as route requests—that one must also consider.

Exposure of control information also allows a potential attacker to determine network topologies in an ad hoc network, which could be used to later attack and partition the network. Although in principle, one could let all routers use the same decryption keys (to simplify the key establishment issue), this only provides security as long as one of the servers is not compromised or the contents of the ciphertexts are otherwise inferred from the behavior of the routers. For example, if an attacker can observe encrypted ciphertext along with the behavior of the nodes (i.e., to what other router the packet is sent), then it may be possible to infer the meaning of the ciphertext from the associated actions.

To make things worse, it is the case that encryption sometimes does not hide the secret information—no matter how good the cipher is. Assume that we wish to protect the privacy of a user by not allowing an attacker to determine the user's actions. To that extent, say that we encrypt the user's identity. However, this in itself does not safeguard privacy, especially if one uses a deterministic encryption scheme (e.g., AES or RSA without random padding). This is so because the encryption of the identity would be the same for each interaction and therefore come to constitute a pseudonym of the user. Much as social security numbers do not reveal anything about the person they are associated with but still become

associated with the person with repeated usage, we therefore have that encrypted identities can become pseudonyms. To avoid such a problem, one could instead use what is referred to as a *probabilistic encryption scheme*, which uses different random components for different invocations, thereby producing different ciphertexts. An example of a probabilistic encryption scheme is El Gamal encryption.

## Database Privacy

There are many examples of situations in which the contents of a database need to be protected against unauthorized access. One such example relates to medical data: it is important to prevent unauthorized persons from accessing such a database, as it is equally important to allow authorized users instant access to information associated with their patients. This poses a difficult problem, given the very large number of professionals potentially needing access to information. Although it is possible that the patient has (or knows) information allowing the access to records, there are certainly cases where it must be possible to gain access to parts of a patient's medical record without help from the patient. In some situations, it is necessary that this access be instantaneous. Securing a database of this type corresponds to several security issues, namely those of authentication, access control, audit control, and data integrity. Authentication is required to determine that a person is who he or she claims to be and can be addressed using password techniques or token-based authentication techniques. Access control is needed because not everybody has access to all information, but certain types of information may only be accessible by certain groups of people. Audit control is used to determine exactly who accessed what, which can be useful to detect and trace unwanted behavior. As data is sent over a network, the integrity of the data becomes important to verify; digital signatures may be used to this extent.

It is clear that to protect the information of databases, it is important to be able to allow access only to privileged persons. As described previously, this amounts to verifying the credentials of people attempting to access the database. Still, this does not protect the data against being read by insiders (e.g., administrators of the database) or otherwise accessed by malware that infects the machine that controls the database. It is important to provide protection against such attacks as well.

A common cryptographic technique to solve this problem is to break up the stored information in portions and store the portions in different places. A straightforward way of doing this would be to select some $k$ random values of the proper length and XOR all of these to a given piece of data. The resulting value is stored on one machine, and the $k$ random values on some other $k$ machines. Although this would make the "legitimate access" somewhat more cumbersome in that a privileged party would have to present valid credentials to all of the $k + 1$ different machines to retrieve information from the database, it also significantly frustrates the efforts of an infiltrator. This is so because he or she would have to corrupt all

$k + 1$ machines to be able to recover the secret data from its shares: combining any fewer shares simply results in a random value.

For reasons of robustness against failures of some of the machines involved, it may be beneficial not to require all portions to reconstitute a stored piece of data; conversely, it is important that more than just one portion is needed or the privacy benefits of distribution evaporate. A common technique to distribute secret information uses a technique introduced by Adi Shamir and is referred to as *Shamir secret sharing*. Here, to encode a piece of information (which we call $y_0$) using this technique, one chooses random coefficients of a $k$th degree polynomial $f(x)$ such that $y_0 = f(0)$. Different points on the curve are stored in different locations—say that we store $2k$ such points. If one can access $k + 1$ of these points, it is easy to determine the polynomial and compute $y_0 = f(0)$; however, with fewer points, all values of $y$ are equally likely. In this way, it becomes necessary for an attacker to corrupt a majority of servers storing points (or shares) to be able to compute the value $y_0$.

To further enhance the protection of the information, one can use a technique such as the one proposed by Herzberg et al., in which the individual portions get modified over time in a way that does not alter the secret data. This can be thought of as continually selecting new polynomials whose only thing in common is that they intersect the $y$ axis in the same point, which can be done by adding a random polynomial intersecting $x = y = 0$ to the old polynomial. This technique allows protection against an attacker who compromises all servers but not at the same time. As long as fewer than $k$ servers are corrupted between any updates of the polynomials, this renders old shares meaningless to the adversary.

Another approach to secure a database against unauthorized access is to encrypt its contents. For general cases, though, this does not solve the problem in itself, as the decryption key needs to be stored somewhere to allow authorized users to access the data. It is not practical to give the decryption keys to authorized users, as this would require a lot of trust in these people—and their systems! However, in some applications, it is a meaningful approach. One such relates to privacy of forensic data. Assume that some forensic data would be kept about anybody spending time in a prison, making the tracing of repeat offenders easier given some amount of tissue found on a crime scene. Along with the forensic data, one may wish to store information relating to the person's criminal history, descriptions of his or her behavior and acquaintances, and so on. This is information that must be accessible to law enforcement, where relevant, but not to others. Some information that one may wish to store in such a record could have commercial value, such as information on the medical history of the person and forensic data from which one could potentially infer an increased risk of certain diseases. The leak of information could hurt the person associated with the record but also people mentioned therein—such as acquaintances of a person convicted of a crime: they may not wish it to be publicly known that they have associated with a criminal.

Although one could address this problem in the same way as for medical data, another possibility to allow only law enforcement access to data of a given person— and only if they found tissue from this person on a crime scene—is to treat the genetic information in the tissue sample as a cryptographic key used to access the remaining data, as described in an article by Bohannon, Jakobsson, and Srikwan (2000). This interpretation of genetic information as a cryptographic key must be done in a way that allows the recovery of information even if the tissue sample is old or partly damaged, the processing is partially error prone, or there is another way in which a perfect match cannot be obtained. Conversely, it is not desirable to allow access given a poor match between the correct "tissue key" and that presented, because this would otherwise reduce the effective length of the encryption keys and make exhaustive search easy.

Another issue relating to privacy of stored data is the requirement of being able to erase data once it is no longer needed. This is known to be a difficult problem, as common storage media (including RAM!) get "imprinted" with the data the store if they store it for extended periods of time. Although this imprinted data is not readable by means of conventional methods, it may be readable using high-precision analysis methods. This would allow a corporate spy to obtain secret information from discarded hard drives of a competitor, even if these have been reformatted or the data overwritten multiple times. A solution to this problem has been proposed by Di Crescenzo, Ferguson, Impagliazzo, and Jakobsson (1999). This solution is based on having some potentially very small quantity of storage for which erased data can never be retrieved; using this small quantity of storage, this ability to securely erase is expanded using encryption-related techniques, allowing any quantity of data stored on normal storage media to be safely erased. Several possible implementations of the small memory at the heart of this construction are proposed in the article. One of them is based on smart cards that get physically destroyed and replaced to securely erase; another is based on using a redundant format to store the "core" erasable data and frequently modifying the representation of this data (to avoid burning it into memory) without changing the data itself. This could be done by storing a random number and another number such that the two add up to the "core" number to store. Every so often, we would change the two numbers (without changing the sum), which would make sure that neither number burns in.

## Privacy of Location

Many telephony service providers are starting to offer location services, helping users find places of interest. The typical situation is where a user wishes to know his own whereabouts relative to some known location or possibly relative to some other person who agrees to be located by him or her.

This is in contrast to the typical location privacy breach, where the whereabouts of a user is tracked by some other user or organization, without the knowledge or consent of the person tracked. This attack may have profound implications in terms of privacy. First of all, the location of a person, in particular when considered along with the time of the day, may reveal the activity of the person, which may be much more of an intrusion than location alone. Second, by considering the location over time of many people, it is possible to determine who is associating with whom and when. It is clear how this would affect the privacy of individuals, but it goes further than that. It also affects the privacy of organizations: consider a scenario in which one organization can determine with whom executives of a competitor are meeting. Finally, it also has detrimental political and military effects, given that the lack of location privacy of a person (or a person likely to be in the same surroundings, such as a spouse or a bodyguard) may increase the risk of assassinations, blackmail, and other undesirable events.

Although everybody using a cellular phone today is constantly revealing his or her approximate location (to allow the closest base station to locate him or her and be able to establish connections), this information is not easily accessible to third parties. In other words, the location information can for many practical reasons be considered to remain private unless the base stations are untrustworthy or corrupted. The problem is exasperated in settings with peer-to-peer communication, such as Bluetooth. In the current specifications of Bluetooth, devices may query other devices in their proximity for identifying information, whether the static "device addresses" identifying devices or user-friendly names associated with devices (e.g., "Joe's phone" or the phone number associated with it). It is also possible to infer the device identities from the so-called channel access code, an identifier used to tell communicating devices for whom a transmitted message is intended. This allows a snooper to determine the location of a given user, as described in more detail in the chapter on Bluetooth security. In a setting where a company has a large number of Bluetooth sensors spread over a city, perhaps to provide users with some service delivered by means of Bluetooth, it will be trivial to carefully map where a given user is at any time—without the knowledge or approval of the user.

The problem of location privacy remains even in settings where devices do not have unique identifiers or where the identifiers are so short that large numbers of devices would share the same identifier. An example of this is RFID tags, which is short for radio frequency identification tags. These are the electronic counterparts of bar codes and are already found on most garments, where they are used to avoid shoplifting. Within the next few years, they are predicted to become truly pervasive.

Current RFID tags are so computationally limited that they can do little else than just respond with their identity when paged by a reader. If devices were to use identities whose length is about 100 bits, this would allow (by far) all RFID tags to have unique identifiers—which is a threat to privacy as much as it is practical in terms of tagging different items. For many purposes, shorter identifiers would suffice to implement wanted applications. One could argue that very short tags would not result in a loss of privacy, because a very large number of items and users

would carry the same bit string. However, even if tags were very short (say 5 to 10 bits long), which would result in numerous "collisions," this would not in itself safeguard the privacy of the person carrying the tags, as it would be highly unlikely for several individuals to carry around exactly the same set of tags. Thus, an attacker querying all RFID tags for their identities would be able to create temporary profiles of the people carrying the tags, thereby allowing him or her to shadow his or her victims at a very low cost. Although, again, this would require having access to or temporary control of a large set of readers, this is not an unlikely scenario, especially if peer-to-peer applications using RFID tags were to be developed and become popular.

Several techniques have been proposed to address the potential privacy problems that come with RFID tags. It is rumored that by 2007, high-denomination Euro bills would be equipped with RFID tags; this could present problems both relating to privacy of individuals (as described before) as well as problems relating to robberies of "rich victims." In an article by Juels and Pappu (2003), a technique is described that prevents spurious tracking of bills, while still allowing legitimate entities (e.g., stores) to verify the information stored in the tags. In this proposal, all identifying information would be encrypted using El Gamal encryption techniques. To avoid having the ciphertexts become static pseudonyms associated with the tags they are carried on, techniques for re-encryption of ciphertexts can be used to transform ciphertexts over time. Given an El Gamal ciphertext and the corresponding public key, one can compute a new and independent El Gamal ciphertext that represents the same plaintext but without needing access to the decryption key. This allows selected (and trusted) access points to "rename" tags, thereby creating a dynamic appearance of an otherwise static identity—the identifying information corresponding to the plaintext. Only some party with access to the appropriate secret key can decrypt the ciphertexts to obtain this information. The proposed scheme would allow a limited tracking of bills and could allow merchants to verify the authenticity of bills but would prevent unauthorized access to information.

Many applications using RFID tags have been proposed, apart from those of labeling clothes and currency. For example, labeling all recyclable material with information indicating the type of material it is made of has been proposed—this would allow for a very straightforward sorting of recycled goods, in which a reader would query items of their types, and the items would be processed accordingly. Moreover, RFID tags are already being used for inventory control and tracking and to identify pets and are likely to soon be used on merchandise to include purchase information, warranties, and more. To prevent intrusions into location privacy, one could use a re-encryption technique such as that proposed for Euro bills. However, because it is highly unlikely that the authorities who oversee all these different uses of RFID tags would be able to collaborate and trust each other to the extent that they would use the same secret key for decryption, it is very likely that different types of items would use different public keys. This poses a new problem: if different types of items would use different public keys, an attacker could potentially profile people using the public keys assigned to the devices as pseudonyms. These public keys would then constitute recognizable identifiers, even if the ciphertexts are re-encrypted over time. In an article by Golle et al. a new type of encryption scheme was proposed, allowing re-encryption of ciphertexts without the knowledge of the corresponding public keys. This means that a party can re-encrypt a ciphertext, thereby creating a new and independent ciphertext that corresponds to the same plaintext, without needing access to neither the public nor the secret key associated with the ciphertext and without being able to infer what the plaintext is. This would allow tagging of items corresponding to different and independent authorities and jurisdictions and would protect the privacy of owners of such devices.

A third example of a privacy-enhancing technology is the so-called RFID blocker tag, which was proposed by Juels, Rivest, and Szydlo (2004). A blocker tag is an RFID tag that responds to all queries, thereby identifying itself as an RFID tag of all existing identities. In effect, this hides any other device in the neighborhood of the blocker tag, protecting users from being identified from the tags they carry. To avoid interference with legitimate queries, the blocker tags may block queries of only certain types; for example, it may block only queries to devices with an identifier that starts with a zero.

## Privacy Against Intrusion

As mentioned, the word *privacy* has two separate meanings, one related to observation and one based on intrusion. We briefly discuss the latter here. This is not to have an exhaustive description of various interpretations of the word but rather to recognize the relation between the two forms of privacy.

A common example of a case where people lack privacy against intrusion is that of telemarketing. Another related example is that of spam or unsolicited e-mail. Although it is clear that companies performing unwanted telemarketing campaigns benefit from knowledge of whom to target (as a way of improving the accuracy of the campaign), there is not quite the same issue when it comes to spam. This is the case because spam is virtually free to send. However, to successfully send spam, one needs to know e-mail addresses of the people to target; this can also be seen as a form of consumer information, along with information of likely preferences. Thus, for both of these types of intrusion of privacy, we can see that the party performing the "attack" benefits from knowledge of information about users. Thus, if this type of information is allowed to leak from other applications (which is a privacy problem of the other type), the severity and ease of the attempts increase. There is, in other words, a causal link between privacy (observation) and privacy (intrusion).

The connection between the two types of privacy is stronger than that. The desire of telemarketers and spammers to profile users fuels the need for information and therefore may cause attacks on users in which their private information gets extracted or observed. Assume for a moment that we could find a technically convincing method of discouraging or preventing spam. This may then, as a result, avoid attacks in which user information is stolen. More in particular, preventing breaches of privacy of the type related to intrusion may also to some extent prevent attacks on the privacy of the type related to observation. This suggests that to protect user information against unwanted observation attempts, it is a meaningful strategy to make such information less useful. Of course, there may be more direct ways of preventing leaks of information, but these two approaches could be considered independently.

There are recent examples of legislative attempts to stop telemarketing and spam. The latter type of attempt states that it is illegal to send spam to or from an entity located in California; it is up to a potential spammer to determine whether a potential recipient is indeed in California. This is likely to be very difficult, if at all possible. In combination with the fact that many spammers may be hard to locate or operate from outside borders where the legislation is meaningful, it may be the case that the efficacy of the legislation is not the desired solution and therefore technical solutions are instead required.

There are many attempts to prevent spam. Some solutions, such as one developed by researchers at Microsoft (The Penny Black Project, 2000), require a fee for each e-mail sent, allowing recipients to claim money for unwanted e-mails he or she receives and thereby placing an economic burden onto the sender. Another approach is to require a computational effort for each e-mail sent, as suggested by Dwork and Naor (1992). This approach makes it easy to send reasonable numbers of messages from a computer but difficult to send truly large number of messages. To avoid difficulties of sending large quantities of wanted messages, there are proposed methods for users to opt in, thereby reducing the computational burden of the sender. A third approach is to accept e-mails only from people on a white list (i.e., a list of preestablished senders). This requires some form of setup to establish such a list and may not be suitable for people who want to be able to receive e-mails from people with whom they have not previously communicated.

## CONTROLLED PRIVACY
### Encryption with Privacy Control

To avoid criminals using encryption methods and a public key infrastructure (PKI) put in place for use by honest citizens, it has been proposed that everybody use techniques that allow for some government agencies to decrypt selected communication when needed. Although many people think this is reasonable, there are two arguments against such a solution. One concerns the risk of surveillance of honest as well as dishonest citizens; the other relates to the possibility that criminals use additional encryption techniques once they have established contact with each other, thereby making decryption impossible.

Another use of *escrowing techniques*, as these techniques are often referred to, is for corporate use to allow a company to retrieve the e-mails of selected employees, whether the employees pass away, refuse to give out the information, or simply forget passwords needed to access it. These techniques may be used to allow a company to retrieve plaintext messages for encrypted communication and encrypted stored data. Here, the risk of "duplicate" encryption, as above, appears less pressing.

There are three principal techniques to approach the problem. In the first technique, first proposed by Micali and Shamir, a set of trustees store shares of the secret keys of all people whose public keys are certified. If a person refuses to send in these secret key shares, he or she will not obtain a certificate on his public key. Once a sufficient number of the trustees agree that a particular ciphertext should be decrypted, they can do so in collaboration with each other and in a way that does not reveal any secret key shares to anybody who does not already have this information. Only the selected ciphertexts will be decrypted, and the privacy of the remaining ciphertexts will not be affected.

A second approach is as follows: if Alice wants to encrypt a message for Bob, she encrypts the message for Bob using his public key, obtaining a first ciphertext. Then Alice encrypts the same message using the public key of the trustee (which must be known by everybody beforehand) and attaches this second ciphertext to the first one. In addition, Alice produces and attaches a cryptographic proof that the two ciphertexts correspond to the same plaintext—to avoid an attack in which the message to Bob has some other contents than the message accessible by the trustee. This proof, which does not reveal any part of the plaintext, can be verified by anybody, including the operator of the communication media between Alice and Bob. If the proof is not correct, then the information will not be transmitted. This approach allows the trustee to decrypt selected ciphertexts and does not require users to deposit shares of their secret keys with trustees. Just as in the first approach, the trustee may correspond to several independent trustees that each store a portion of the "main trustee's" secret key—thereby, a sufficient number of these trustees are required to decrypt any message.

A third technique relies on tamperproof hardware to work. This is the technique corresponding to the Clipper Chip, a government attempt at controlled privacy for encryption. This technique has certain vulnerabilities. For example, if criminals manage to tamper with the hardware used for encryption and decryption, they can prevent their messages from being read by a trustee. The Clipper Chip implementation also was found to have weaknesses, which were described by Blaze (1994).

## Payments with Privacy Control

Digital signatures can be used in payment schemes to allow a bank to authenticate withdrawn funds. Let us consider how this can be done by using RSA signatures. An RSA signature on a message $m$ of some appropriate format is a value $s = m^d \bmod N$ such that $m = s^e \bmod N$, where $e$ and $N$ are public values associated with the signer and $d$ is secret and only known by the signer. Here, the signer may be the bank. Thus, for a person to withdraw \$1 (say) from his bank account, he would identify himself to the bank and prepare a random message $m$ for the bank to sign. The bank then produces the signature $s$ on this message $m$ and sends it to the user withdrawing the funds. The user can later spend the money by sending the pair $(m,s)$ to a store, who can verify that $s$ is a valid signature on $m$, meaning that this is a valid \$1 bill withdrawn from the bank that produced the signature. The store would send in $(m,s)$ to the bank at some point, at which time the bank would credit its account with \$1. To spend \$10, ten such transcripts would be used; alternatively, a different type of signature could be used for each denomination. This simple system does not offer any privacy, though, as the bank will be able to determine where withdrawn funds were spent. Note that it is not possible to forge money without being able to forge signatures, as both stores and banks will verify the correctness of signatures before accepting the payments in question.

It is possible to construct a system where a person can withdraw funds from an account and later spend these in a way that makes it impossible to link the purchase to the withdrawal and therefore to the identity of the account owner. One way to achieve this involves so-called blind signatures. To obtain a blind RSA signature on a message $m$, the withdrawer would select a random value $r$ and compute $m' = r^e m \bmod N$, which is sent to the bank. If $r$ is a uniformly distributed random value, each value $m'$ is equally likely to correspond to each possible value $m$, so the bank would not be able to infer $m$ from $m'$. However, the bank can sign $m'$ by computing $s' = m'^d \bmod N$. This is sent to the withdrawer after he has identified himself—this is necessary for the bank to withdraw the funds from the appropriate account. The user making the withdrawal would then compute $s = s'/r \bmod N$, which equals $(r^e m)^d/r \bmod N = m^d \bmod N$. This gives him a correct signature $s$ on the message $m$. He can later spend the money in the same way as previously described, that is, by sending $(m,s)$ to the store. When the store sends in this pair to the bank, it is not possible for the bank to associate it with any particular withdrawal. This is a system that was proposed by Chaum, Fiat, and Naor (1990).

However, although this system offers privacy to all honest users, it also offers privacy to dishonest users. For one thing, unless the store sends in the transcript $(m,s)$ to the bank immediately, there is a risk that the user would spend the same money in another store—simply by sending another store the same transcript. To avoid massive overspending (that cannot be traced to the perpetrator!), the bank therefore needs to keep a list of all deposited pairs $(m,s)$ and credit only the first store to send in a valid pair of this format. To allow stores to send in payments in batches (which results in cost savings as well as faster transactions), several systems were proposed in which a payment could be traced to the withdrawer if and only if it is spent twice (or more). Such schemes are based on Shamir's secret sharing scheme: for each payment, a point on a line has to be given out, where the store selects the $x$ coordinate of the point. If only one point is given, this does not reveal where the line intersects the $y$ axis, but if two or more points are given out, this can easily be computed. Here, the point where the line intersects the $y$ axis is selected to encode the identity of the withdrawer. If he spends the funds only once (as he is supposed to), then his privacy remains perfect; otherwise, he "signs his own confession."

This scheme has a problem, as first noted by von Solms and Naccache (1992): a criminal, such as a kidnapper or a blackmailer, can demand untraceable ransoms. This would work as follows: the attacker selects a value $m$ and blinds it as above, obtaining a value $m'$. Only the attacker knows the value $r$. He gives $m'$ to his victim, who uses it in a withdrawal from his account, sending $s'$ to the attacker. The attacker unblinds $s'$, obtaining $s$. Now, he can spend the pair $(m,s)$, but this pair cannot be traced back to the values $(m',s')$ seen by his victim and the bank. To avoid this type of attack, one could imagine a type of payment scheme where a trustee can remove the privacy selectively, much like what was previously described for escrow encryption. Many approaches of how to do this have been suggested; an example is described by Jakobsson and Yung (1997).

The perhaps most extreme attack on a payment system is one in which an attacker forces the bank to give him its secret signing key, after which he can mint his own money by producing bank signatures on his own. It is difficult to defend against such an attack without affecting the privacy of honest users. Another type of attack might involve money-laundering or crooks selling stolen goods or laundering phishing revenue. In all of these cases, it is important to be able to trace the payments by selectively removing the privacy.

The scheme described by Jakobsson and Yung (1997) avoids the "bank robbery" attack, along with other attacks in which an attacker attempts to abuse the privacy of the system. This is achieved by the bank maintaining a log in which it enters information relating to each legitimate withdrawal; if the bank is robbed, each deposited payment is then compared against the list of legitimate withdrawals. If no match is found, then the deposit must be minted by the attacker. However, without access to the database in which all logs are kept, it is not possible to determine who pays whom. But can we trust the keeper of the database, then? The point is that we do not have to. Just as a mix network can disassociate an input ciphertext from an output plaintext by use of multiple servers, encryption, and permutation, according to the same principles, one can store the logs, allowing a payment to be traced only if all servers were to collaborate. Some of these servers would belong to a bank and others to a consumer organization, with the goal of protecting the privacy of all honest consumers. This is a somewhat simplified description, and we refer to the full chapter for more details.

## CONCLUSION: FURTHER READING

There are a large number of research papers on mix networks, which discuss many other features than the basic privacy feature. One common feature is *robustness*. This means that if a mix server is dishonest and tries to replace some of the items it receives with other (appropriately formatted) items, then this will not go unnoticed. This is important if the mix network is to be used in, for example, an election. To vote, a user would encrypt his or her vote multiple times and then send the result to the first mix server. The last mix server would output his or her vote, along with everybody else's vote, but in random order. But if a mix server could replace any (or all) of its input items with whatever is preferred, and this is undetectable, then malicious mix servers could manipulate the election. For examples of mix networks of this type, we refer the reader to articles by Abe (1999); Jakobsson, Juels, and Rivest (2002); and Neff (2001). Many of these proposals use El Gamal encryption instead of RSA, which has the benefit that random padding is not necessary, and it is not necessary to use different public keys for the different mix servers, but one can encrypt plaintexts using only one public key (associated with the mix network as such). We refer to the chapter on encryption for details on El Gamal encryption and to the previously mentioned articles for details on how to employ this.

Many researchers and practitioners are concerned with location privacy. One forum where these issues are discussed and addressed is the IETF working group named *geopriv*. A good place to catch up on legislative attempts to address the problem is the wireless location pages of the Center for Democracy and Technology.

For an overview of issues relating to escrow encryption, we refer the interested reader to the Cryptography Project at Dorothy Denning's Web page; and for an excellent set of pointers on RFID security, we suggest the RFID Privacy and Security pages at RSA Security.

## GLOSSARY

**Anonymizer** A technique to obtain communication privacy by reordering input elements, in combination with potential decryption or re-encryption operations. See also Mix Network.

**Asymmetric** In the context of encryption, a type of cryptographic system in which a participant publishes an encryption key and keeps private a separate decryption key. These keys are respectively referred to as public and private. RSA and El Gamal encryption are examples of asymmetric systems. Asymmetric is synonymous with public key.

**Ciphertext** The data conveying an encrypted message.

**Decryption** The process of obtaining a readable message (*a* plaintext) from an encrypted transformation of the message (a ciphertext).

**Encryption** The process of rendering a message (a plaintext) into a data string (a ciphertext) with the aim of transmitting it privately in a potentially hostile environment.

**Escrow Encryption** Encrypting data in a way that law enforcement is able to decrypt it. If used in a commercial setting, the employer of a sender or recipient of data may be the party with access to decryption (apart from the recipient of the ciphertext)

**Key** A short data string parameterizing the operations within a cipher or cryptosystem and whose distribution determines relationships of privacy and integrity among communicating parties.

**Location Privacy** Not being able to infer location of a victim, whether absolute or relative to some other user.

**Mix Network** A network consisting of a set of servers, so-called mix servers, each acting as an anonymizer. A mix network creates a privacy guarantee as long as not a large portion of the mix servers is corrupted, where this portion typically is all of the available servers.

**Plaintext** A message in readable form, prior to encryption or subsequent to successful decryption.

**Privacy** Defined by *Webster's Dictionary* as either "(a) the quality or state of being apart from company or observation," or "(b) freedom from unauthorized intrusion."

**Private Key** In an asymmetric or public key cryptosystem, the key that a communicating party holds privately and uses for decryption or completion of a key exchange.

**Public Key** In an asymmetric or public key cryptosystem, the key that a communicating party disseminates publicly. In the context of encryption, a type of cryptographic system in which a participant publishes an encryption key and keeps private a separate decryption key. These keys are respectively referred to as public and private. RSA is an example of a public-key system. Public key is synonymous with asymmetric.

**Radio Frequency ID Tag** A small computer with a radio unit, allowing other units to send data to and receive data from the tag. They are typically embedded in clothing for theft protection but are entering the consumer market in more and more aspects and merchandise.

**RSA** A public key cryptosystem in very wide use today, as in the secure sockets layer protocol. RSA can also be used to create and verify digital signatures.

# CROSS REFERENCES

See *Anonymity and Identity on the Internet; Encryption Basics; Privacy Law and the Internet; RFID and Security; Spam and the Legal Counter Attacks.*

# REFERENCES

Abe, M. (1999). Mix-networks on permutation networks. In *Advances in Cryptology—Proceedings of Asiacrypt'99*, (vol. 1716, pp. 258–273).

Anonymizer. (2000). *Online privacy and security homepage.* Retrieved September 1, 2004, from www.anonymizer.com.

Blaze, M. (1994). *Protocol failure in the escrowed encryption standard.* In *Proceedings of the 2nd ACM Conference on Computer and Communications Security.* New York: ACM Press.

Bohannon, P., Jakobsson, M., & Srikwan, S. (2000). Cryptographic approaches to privacy in forensic DNA databases. *Public Key Cryptography, 1751,* 373–390.

Brands, S. A. (1993). *An efficient off-line electronic cash system based on the representation problem.* Amsterdam: Centrum voor Wiskunde en Informatica (CWI).

Chaum, D., Fiat, A., & Naor, M. (1990). Untraceable electronic cash. In *Lecture notes in computer science* (vol. 403, pp. 319–327).

Chaum, D. L. (1981). Untraceable electronic mail, return addresses, and digital pseudonyms. *Communications of the ACM, 24*(2), 84–88.

Di Crescenzo, G., Ferguson, N., Impagliazzo, R., & Jakobsson, M. (1999). How to forget a secret (Extended abstract). In *Stacs'99—16th Annual Symposium on Theoretical Aspects of Computer Science* (vol. 1563, pp. 500–509).

Dwork, C., & Naor, M. (1992). Pricing via processing or combating junk mail. In *Advances in Cryptology—Crypto'92.* New York: Springer-Verlag.

Golle, P., Jakobsson, M., Juels, A., & Syverson, P. (2004). Universal re-encryption for mixnets. In *Topics in Cryptology—Proceedings of CT-RSA 2004* (vol. 2964, pp. 163–178).

Herzberg, A., Jarecki, S., Krawczyk, H., & Yung, M. T. (1995). Proactive secret sharing or: How to cope with perpetual leakage. In *Advances in Cryptology—Crypto '95* (vol. 963, pp. 339–352).

Jakobsson, M., Jagatic, T., & Stamm, M. (2005). Phishing for Clues, www.browser-recon.info

Jakobsson, M., Juels, A., & Rivest, R. (2002). Making mix nets robust for electronic voting by randomized partial checking. USENIX'02.

Jakobsson, M., & Yung, M. (1997). Distributed "magic ink" signatures. In *Lecture notes in computer science, vol. 1233: Eurocrypt '97.* New York: Springer-Verlag.

Juels, A., & Pappu, R. (2003). Squealing euros: Privacy protection in RFID-enabled banknotes. *Proceedings of Financial Cryptography, 2742,* pp. 103–121.

Juels, A., Rivest, R. L., & Szydlo, M. (2003). The Blocker Tag: Selective Blocking of RFID Tags for Consumer Privacy. In *Proceedings of the 8th ACM Conference on Computer and Communications Security.* New York: ACM Press.

Micali, S., & Rivest, R. L. (2002). Micropayments revisited. In *RSA-CT* 2002 (pp. 149–163).

Neff, C. A. (2001). A verifiable secret shuffle and its application to e-voting. In *Proceedings of the 8th ACM Conference on Computer and Communications Security.* New York: ACM Press.

Reiter, M. K., & Rubin, A. D. (1998). Crowds: Anonymity for Web transactions. *ACM Transactions on Information and System Security, 1,* pp. 66–92.

RFID Privacy and Security. (2000). *RSA security homepage.* Retrieved September 5, 2004, from http://www.rsasecurity.com/rsalabs/node.asp?id=2115

Secure Electronic Transactions (SET). (2000). *Homepage.* Retrieved January 2, 2003, from http://www.ieee-security.org/Cipher/Newsbriefs/1996/960213.cards.html

Shamir, A. (1979). How to share a secret. *Communications of the ACM, 22*(11), pp. 612–613.

Shamir, A. (1995). *Partial key escrow: A new approach to software key escrow*. Paper presented at the NIST Key Escrow Standards meeting, The Weizmann Institute.

The Center for Democracy and Technology. (2000). *Homepage*. Retrieved September 3, 2004, from www.cdt.org/privacy/issues/location/

The Cryptography Project. (2000). *Homepage*. Retrieved September 5, 2004, from www.cosc. georgetown.edu/~denning/crypto/

The IETF GeoPriv Working Group. (2000). *Homepage*. Retrieved September 4, 2004, from *www.ietf. org/html.charters/geopriv-charter.html*

The Penny Black Project. (2000). *Homepage*. Retrieved September 5, 2004, from http://research. microsoft.com/research/sv/PennyBlack/

von Solms, S., & Naccache, D. (1992). On blind signatures and perfect crimes. *Computers and Security, 11*(6). pp. 581–583.

# Cryptographic Hardware Security Modules

Nicko van Someren, *nCipher Plc., UK*

## INTRODUCTION

Previously we have seen how cryptography can be used to secure information in computer systems and networks. Encryption with a symmetric cipher can allow data at rest on a computer disc to be protected against those who do not have the key. Encryption with public key ciphers allow data to be sent across a network by any party such that only the designated recipient can make use of it. Message authentication codes can be used to detect when data have been altered and digital signatures can be used to check the origin of a message. Unfortunately, all of these tools are of limited use if either their cryptographic keys or the implementations of the algorithms or protocols are compromised.

## Threat Models

For many people, the most commonly assumed threat is that of an external attacker. Some villain or malicious hacker will try to access your computer system through the network and, should he or she find a way in, will steal your data, deface your Web site, and publish your customers' private data to all and sundry. This is, however, not the biggest threat for many high-value systems. Whereas the external attackers tend to be opportunistic and often no more damaging than vandals or petty thieves, a bigger danger comes from internal attacks.

Internal attackers have, in general, an easier task and more to gain. They often know a great deal about the system. They may know where the valuable data are stored,

how they are processed, and over which protocols they are moved. Furthermore, these attackers are likely to know which are the really valuable data. To make matters worse, a distressingly large number of computer networks within large companies rely heavily on perimeter security, and those inside the network face far fewer hurdles when attempting an attack. Based on FBI statistics of companies reporting computer crimes, the number of attacks from insiders and the number of attacks from outsiders are roughly equal (Gordon, Loeb, Lucyshyn, & Richardson, 2004).

In many high-security systems, no individual is implicitly trusted. In a bank, it is rare for a single individual to be authorized to carry out high-value transactions without a second person's confirmation. In theory, the system administrators of computer systems should not be able to authorize the actions that are facilitated by those systems; after all, these actions may involve the transfer of large values and that is not the sort of thing a lowly sys-admin is allowed to authorize at all, let alone facilitate without the confirmation of a second signatory. Unfortunately, in many modern computer systems, the system administrators have near total control of all the data on every server they administer. In particular, if all the cryptography in the system is carried out in software, using keys that are stored on the computer system itself, then they have absolute control over the signing and decryption of messages. In a large organization with many administrators, a significant number of people may have access to all the data necessary to carry out fraudulent acts, and it is often impractical to require high-level vetting of all staff.

There is another class of threat that may need to be considered: the case in which the legitimate user is the expected attacker. In the case of Digital Rights Management systems such as the conditional access control for a satellite or cable TV service, the goal is to stop the parties who purchases service from gaining access to more service than they are paying for even when the content is broadcast. In such a situation, the users can become the attackers, either for individual use or with intent to supply the service (or access to the service) to other people. In this scenario the users can generally expect that any attack they carry out will pass unnoticed, whereas the system administrator who attaches a logic analyzer to the server is going to need to have a good excuse!

One remaining consideration regarding threats is to look at the difference between the allowing and attacker to use a key transiently versus allowing the attacker to get hold of the key material. In the former case, it may be possible to limit the damage once the attack is detected. On the other hand, in the latter case it may be hard to detect that the attacker was in the system, and, depending on the nature of the protocol, possession of the key may allow the decryption of both past and future traffic.[1]

## The Strength of the Attacker

When considering the threat from an attacker, it is important to understand the resources available to an attacker as well as the level of access to the system with which the attacker starts. Aucsmith (1996) proposed a taxonomy of attackers ranging from the remote exploiter (I) through those who can install malicious software (II), past those who can gain low level access, without (IIIa) or possibly with (IIIb) use of specialized debugging tools, and right up to those who have complex hardware analysis tools such as bus probes and logical analysers (IIIc). (Anderson Kuhn (1997) presented a similar taxonomy.) When considering what level of security is appropriate, we need to understand against what are we protecting ourselves. It is fair to say that if an attacker has a great deal to gain from breaking the system, she will use every tool at her disposal. If the attacker is already an authorized user of the system (as an insider), she will likely be at least IIIb, and, should she be a system administrator with access to the machine room, she may well be IIIc.

## The Need for Hardware Security Modules

If a system's software cannot be trusted, because the attacker either may have root privileges or simply have unfettered access to the system, then we cannot rely on the system to keep our keys or process our cryptographic functions. If the system's bus can be probed, we must avoid sending key material over the bus. If the attacker can install software or hardware to record keystrokes, we cannot use the standard keyboard for entering key material unless the keys are themselves encrypted. In general, if the attacker can control the machine, we must not use that machine to handle our cryptography.

If we cannot trust the host, we must look elsewhere for something else to which we can entrust our keys. The idea of a hardware security model is to separate out the cryptographic key storage and processing functions into a device that we do trust. Such a device should have a simple and strictly defined interface, and if physical access is an issue, it should also resist tampering.

# LIMITATIONS OF SOFTWARE SECURITY

To understand properly both the benefits and the limitations of hardware security modules (HSMs), it is important to understand the limitations of security both for the software systems that run on the host that uses the HSM and for the firmware inside it. In this section, I discuss some of the issues surrounding software security and look at how this affects the design and use of HSMs.

## General-Purpose Operating Systems versus Security Kernels

It is generally said that complexity and security do not mix.[2] When one examines modern, general-purpose computer operating systems, they are very complex indeed, which leads one to believe that it will be very hard to make them secure. Experience shows this to be the case. Besides the simple complexity of general-purpose operating systems (OSs), other factors often conspire to reduce the overall security of the system. OSs are designed first and foremost for factors such as performance, flexibility, and usability, with security not being a primary consideration at the outset. If one wants maximal security, then security must be the primary design goal and all other design criteria must lose out when a compromise has to be made.

## Key-Finding Attacks

Unintended accessibility of information in any security system is usually a bad thing. Just how bad this is depends on the information and the extent to which an attacker can make use of this. Usually allowing read-write access is worse than allowing read-only access, because there is more scope for manipulation of the data. Usually transient access to data is less useful to an attacker than long-term access, because in the former case the attacker only gains sight of that data that is in the system in the transient period when he has access. In the case of cryptographic key material, however, short-term, read-only access of data can be enough to compromise the entire system. This is because in many cryptographic systems, loss of the private keys leads to a total breakdown in security.

Over the years, some programmers have relied on "security through obscurity" to hide important keys in system. The theory goes that finding a few hundred bytes of key material inside a few hundred megabytes of runtime data would be an impossible task for any transient attacker. Unfortunately, research has shown (Shamir & van Someren, 1999) that not only is key material particularly dangerous to lose, it is also particularly easy to find among large bodies of data. The higher than usual

---

[1] The widely used (SSL) Secure Socket Layer protocol is generally used in a mode that provides no "forward secrecy," and as such possession of the key is sufficient to decrypt previously recorded traffic as well as new data from the network.

[2] It is not clear who first said this, so I have no specific reference, but any security expert worth her salt will agree.

entropy of cryptographic key material compared with normal data, along with other mathematical characteristics, makes keys particularly easy to find in software systems.

## Physical Access

Perhaps the most important limitation of software security is the most obvious one: it is only really effective against software attacks. If the attacker has physical access to the system being attacked and is not adverse to shutting that system down, almost any software security can be overcome. The attacker can simply extract the hard discs from the system and examine them using another computer without regard for any supposed access control. The lower layers of the OS can be altered, consistency checks bypassed, and "Trojan horse" software inserted. When the attacker can gain this level of access, it is virtually impossible to stop him from extracting cryptographic key material from the system. Even with supposedly "tamper-resistant" software, attack mechanisms more normally associated with hardware such as fault induction attacks (Anderson & Kuhn, 1997) can be used to save the effort of having to reverse engineer the software.

In the face of an attacker with physical access, security can only properly be maintained with the use of special-purpose equipment that provides physical protection of cryptographic keys as well as logical protection against software attacks.

## PHYSICAL SECURITY CONSIDERATIONS

When dealing with hardware security devices, the physical security of the device is of great importance. We need to consider both the intrinsic security of the device (how well does it resist attack) and its extrinsic security (how easy is it for the attacker to get to the device). Most digital certificate authorities surround their hardware security modules with stringent physical security measures,[3] so many of the attacks that might be possible against such devices become completely impractical. A balance of intrinsic and extrinsic security must be struck against the convenience to the user and other practical considerations.

## Form Factors

When dealing with the extrinsic security of an HSM, one key issue is the form factor of the device. The common "smart card" can be used as a limited hardware security module, and there are devices in the form of (PCMCIA) Personal Computer Memory Card International Association cards or "dongle" devices that attach to a host through the universal serial bus (USB) port. Such devices may well provide much of the key storage and cryptographic processing needed for many security applications. It is important to remember, however, that they are small and light enough to be carried away unnoticed. This may be a

benefit in some situations, for instance, when the cryptographic keys need to be controlled by an individual who does not want to let the keys out of sight at any time, but for keys belonging to an institution such a small-form factor may be an outright liability. At the other extreme, many HSMs designed for the banking market not only are shipped as standard 19-inch rack-mount units to be physically bolted to a rack but also are actually loaded with internal weights to make them more difficult to carry.[4] Such bulky devices can provide added physical protection simply by virtue of having more mass, as well as being able to dissipate the heat from more powerful processors, but are essentially useless as personal authentication tokens.

## Tamper Evidence

The lowest level of physical "protection" offered by most cryptographic modules is *tamper evidence*; that is, the device is designed to show permanent signs of tampering if physically attacked. The idea is that in many situations, simply knowing that a key has been compromised is sufficient to allow keys to be revoked, and for some applications in which the threat is expected to come from external sources, physical attacks are unlikely. Technologies for tamper evidence include the following:

- *Tamper-evident labels*: If the device resides inside some enclosure that could be opened, it is useful to be able to see that the seal has been broken. Tamper-evident labels usually are formed by having more than one layer to the label and by having the adhesive that bonds the label to the device be stronger than the adhesive bonding the layers together. When any attempt is made to remove the label, it will tend to come apart. Ensuring that the separation of the layers is highly visible (e.g., by making the parting of the layers reveal some writing) allows tampering to be recognized. It is important with tamper-evident labeling that the attacker cannot obtain authentic-looking replacement labels. As such, these labels often are made with holographic markings to make them hard to reproduce.

- *Conformant coatings*: These coatings cover all the sensitive parts of the device with a layer of material that binds to those parts and can be used to show tampering. In the simplest form, a spray paint that tends to flake if disturbed when dry can be used because matching the paint afterward is notoriously hard. Often, thicker coatings are used to make any attempt to patch up the damaged layer show up as a change in the relief of the layer.

- *Fragile or brittle parts*: Simply constructing parts of the device with fragile or brittle parts can be used to show signs of tampering. Barbed parts can allow an enclosure to be closed once, but an attempt to open the enclosure again will likely break the part so that it cannot be closed again.

---

[3] At least one digital certificate authority keeps the hardware security modules for its root signing keys in the bottom of a disused mine shaft, and another makes use of an old Cold War–era missile base.

[4] The ISO 13491 (International Standards Organization, 2000) standard for banking secure cryptographic devices states that one way to comply with the physical security characteristics requirements is for the device to weigh at least 40 kg or for it to be locked to something that weighs at least 40 kg.

Although tamper evidence is sufficient in some circumstances, its major drawback is simply that someone must regularly inspect the device for signs of tampering. If the device usually resides inside another machine (e.g., a computer server), it may be inconvenient to inspect the parts regularly, and this means that tampering may go unnoticed for extended periods, allowing the attacker time to exploit the compromise.

## Tamper Resistance

If it is not practical to inspect a device regularly for signs of tampering, or if the consequences of any tampering are negative even on a short time scale, then it is important for HSMs to resist attempts to penetrate them. As a result, most key storage devices attempt to provide some degree of tamper resistance to stop an attacker gaining access to the sensitive material inside.

Tamper-resistance strategies can be loosely divided into two methods. The device can be put inside a strongbox that is hard to compromise, or alternatively the device itself can be made of material that is hard to compromise or for which any physical attack is likely to damage the device irreparably, to the point that it will be useless. Both of these approaches have their merits, and sometimes they are used in conjunction with each other.

Placing the device in a strong container can be a simple way to render tamper resistant an existing design with relatively little effort. People have been making strongboxes for millennia, and the technology is fairly well understood. Metals that are resistant to drilling and cutting are in common use in all sorts of security devices. In the simplest case, some sort of safe can be used to lock up the sensitive parts of the device, although most existing safe designs need to be compromised slightly to allow for electrical connections to enter. A downside to simply locking up the device is that an attacker who can pick the locks (or in the case of an insider attack, one who has the key) can open the box and tamper directly with the circuits. This type of tampering is hard to detect if the device is designed to be opened, and if it is carried out before the device is put into service, it is possible to compromise the device for easier attack at a later date. Therefore, it is more common to place the device in a box that is designed to be closed and never opened again. Such boxes can be welded shut, closed with adhesives (some of which are stronger than welding), or closed using interference fitting in which two parts that would not fit together at the same temperature are heated or cooled differentially to make them fit during closing. Any of these techniques can be used to render the box difficult to open.

Although putting the device into a strong box is simple and often effective, it is also costly and cumbersome. Drill-resistant steel is heavy, and dealing with welding or interference fitting while ensuring that no parts are damaged by heat can be a difficult process. As a result, a more frequently used approach is to "pot" or encase all the security-critical components of the device in some material that can been molded around the components. The material is usually a mixture of a binding resin and a "loading" of some sort of hard or abrasive material. The loading makes the material hard to mill through and also will tend to damage the circuitry underneath when attacked. Careful choice of resin to make it similar to the plastic casing of integrated circuits means that chemical attacks on the resin will also permanently damage the Integrated Circuit (ICs) in the device. The resin is also chosen to adhere to the chips inside the device better than the chips adhere to the circuit board and potentially can be made to adhere to the cases of the chips more strongly than the pins of the chip adhere to the case, meaning that any attempt to break off the potting will damage the chips, the board, or both.

Some cryptographic devices are manufactured as a single integrated circuit rather than a circuit board holding many parts. This is most commonly seen in devices such as smart cards but is also increasingly common in other sorts of small personal authentication devices. In general, such monolithic devices are inherently tamper resistant because it requires a fair amount of skill and equipment to get at the insides of such devices. That said, these small and usually relatively cheap devices are often deployed in more hostile environments in which the holder of the device is the potential attacker (e.g., conditional access [CA] systems for satellite television). In these circumstances, the attacker has a fair amount of scope for probing the device to get it to reveal its keys, and it is therefore desirable to take extra precautions. The exact nature of the precautions taken in smart cards for conditional access systems tend to be closely guarded secrets because they are of commercial importance both to the content providers relying on the system and to the vendors of the CA systems. This is one of the few areas of cryptographic security that still regularly attempts "security through obscurity."

## Tamper Reaction

When it comes to placing cryptographic devices in situations when attackers have extended, unfettered access to the HSM when the attackers potential gain is high, or when the potential loss from a successful attack is high, actively detecting signs of tampering and destroying the keys when attacked makes sense. This sort of tamper reaction is desirable in devices that store monetary value on behalf of some party not in control of the HSM (e.g., with electronic postal franking machines) and with devices in various military situations (e.g., containers for launch codes for missiles). Tamper reaction is also used in a variety of banking applications.

There are many ways to detect signs of tampering with a device, just as there are many ways to attack devices. As new attacks have been invented, so new means of detecting have to be invented. Chaum (1984) discussed a number of fundamental approaches to tamper reaction in detail; listed here are some of the most common tamper-detection techniques with discuss their benefits and drawbacks.

- *Reactive membranes*: Probably the most commonly used tamper-detection mechanism is to wrap the device tightly in a mesh of conductors with electrical characteristics that will change if any of the conductors are broken or shorted together. The mesh is commonly provided in the form of a membrane that is embedded into potting similar to that used to make devices tamper resistant. An attempt to compromise the potting will, with high probability, either break some of the conductors in the mesh or short some of them together, thereby changing the resistance of the mesh in a measurable manner. One of the major drawbacks of the reactive membrane is that because the detector must measure the membrane resistance, a current must be flowing through the membrane, which in turn requires power to be consumed. By making the membrane of high overall resistance, this power consumption can be kept low.

- *Glass plates*: A variation on the reactive membrane is to place conductors on the inside surface of a brittle tempered glass plate. Because the conductors lie on the inside of the plate, an attacker will need to get through the plate to attempt to bypass the detection circuits. By using a carefully tempered glass, it can be made to shatter completely if compromised; this makes it difficult to penetrate without detection. On the downside, along with all the drawbacks of the usual reactive membranes, glass plates are heavy and fragile, which means that they are not useful for any device that might need to be portable.

- *Tilt switches*: When dealing with devices that an attacker might deem to be portable, from the point of view of theft of the device, tilt switches can be used to attempt to detect movement of the device. There are several types of tilt switch in use; mercury switches are still the simplest and cheapest, but they are increasingly being replaced by ball-bearing switches or solid-state devices because of environmental concerns and regulations surrounding the use of mercury. Tilt switches can be useful for detecting movement of the HSM, but they can have trouble in locations where they may be subjected to environmental vibration. This can result from something as benign as a springy raised floor in a machine room or from minor earthquakes. This has prompted some manufacturers to provide a "California" setting for their HSM to reduce the sensitivity or entirely disable the motion switches when the device is deployed in an earthquake-prone area.

- *Temperature sensors*: Some types of memory device can have their contents frozen when the device is made cold enough. The effect of this is that other tamper-reaction triggers might not be able to erase the keys stored in the device. As a result, many devices contain temperature sensors that detect cooling of the device and treat this as an attack, allowing the keys to be erased before the device gets too cold to react. Many devices also detect rising temperatures that might be indicators of friction from abrasion, heat from soldering, or some other sort of attack. The use of temperature sensors is not without its problems, however. Famously, the original IBM 4758 security module was fitted with a temperature sensor that was sensitive enough that extended transit by air freight or storage in an unheated facility could cause the device to erase all of its keys; IBM ended up redesigning the packaging of the device to include packs of gel with a large thermal mass to mitigate the problem.

- *Voltage measurement*: All of the sensors mentioned so far require electrical power to operate, and similarly any reaction to the attack will require some energy. Removing the power source would therefore prevent tamper detection and reaction; thus, it is important also to detect when an attacker is attempting to remove the power prior to an attack. This is usually done by constantly monitoring the input voltage to the device and triggering a reaction if the power level goes outside the expected range. Most tamper-reactive devices have external batteries to power the detection circuits when the host device is powered down, but they also contain some sort of internal capacitor to allow reaction after the batteries have been disconnected. Because the removal of the power supply is treated as an attack, great care should be taken when changing the battery!

- *Radiation detectors*: There is some evidence that exposure of memory chips to certain types of ionizing radiation can cause the memory chips to permanently retain their memory state. Some devices detect this sort of radiation before burn-in occurs and erasure of the keys before the radiation has any effect.

Once an attack has been detected, a tamper-reactive device must react in some way. Because the goal is to keep the attacker from getting hold of the keys, clearly the keys need to be destroyed. Unfortunately, this is often not as simple as writing different values into the memory that held the keys. Many memory devices are physically changed by storing the same data for a long period of time; as a result, even if the key material has been deleted, it may be possible to discover the values that previously resided in the chip. To combat this, the device might continually cycle the contents of the memory to ensure that the same data do not reside in the same place for too long. (Gutmann, 1996, presented a good analysis of this subject.)

Another mode of tamper response, which is not so common in commercial systems but is allegedly popular in the military and diplomatic sector, is to use explosive charges to destroy the memory devices. Care needs to be taken with this sort of approach, not only for the obvious reason of accidental triggering, but also because naïve implementations will not necessarily destroy enough of the chip to prevent extraction of the data. In the commercial world, explosive destruction of the memory devices is also unpopular for fear of product-liability consequences.

Although the primary response of tamper reaction is usually to destroy key material, it is not uncommon for HSMs to disable themselves permanently. This is because if the attacker does succeed in compromising the device, it might be possible to alter the firmware programs inside the device to change the protection characteristics of the device and then try to put the unit back into service. If a device was attacked while in transit from manufacturer to customer, then destruction of keys would not be an issue, but leaving the device in a permanently compromised state would allow an easier attack after the end user had generated keys inside the device.

## Side-Channel Attack Resistance

The previous three sections considered ways to protect against an attacker set on extracting the keys directly from memory of the device. It has, however, been known for some time that there are other channels by which to extract key material. These *side channels* can allow for indirect determination of either the key material or the plaintext of messages without direct access to the inside of the HSM.

The topic of side-channel attacks is too extensive to be exhaustively discussed here, but the general class of attack can be summarized as measuring some observable facet of the HSM that is affected by the data the HSM is processing when the HSM is carrying out operations on data of interest. There is anecdotal evidence that this technique goes back to the 1950s when Western intelligence operators discovered that some Eastern bloc encrypting teletype machines emitted broad radio frequency (RF) interference correlated to the key presses of the operator superimposed onto the encrypted signal on the wire. The British referred to this type of attack as a Tempest attack, and since the 1950s, Western intelligence services have spent a fair amount of effort ensuring that their equipment does not emanate any unwanted RF interference. Since then, a variety of side channels has been discovered, analyzed, and occasionally exploited.

To understand why side-channel attacks work, it is worth observing that, in the absence of explicit measures to avoid them, the paths through a body of code or the actions of a logic circuit are dependent on the data being processed. The classic "square and multiply" technique for exponentiation, used in the majority of public key cryptosystems, will perform a number of squaring operations that depends on the key size, but the multiply operations will only occur once for each set bit in the exponent, and the exponent is often the private key. If it is possible to tell when the processor is multiplying and when it is squaring, the key material can be discovered. Similar attacks exist against common ways of implementing block ciphers.

Closely related to the original Tempest attack is the general class of electromagnetic (EM) radiation side channels. As anyone who used an early PC anywhere near an AM radio will know, computers emit RF signals that can be picked up at some distance. In the absence of explicit countermeasures, emanations are usually correlated with what the processor is doing and, as noted earlier, this leaks key material.

Another side channel that has proven effective in the analysis of items such as smart cards, to which the attacker can often gain physical access, is the power line. The current consumed by the device (and, in the absence of a perfect power source, the line voltage) depends on which parts of the circuit are active at any given time. In the case of a smart card carrying out an RSA signature, the multiply and square phases of exponentiation may well take different amounts of power, and this allows an attacker to read the key bits off the power line. Power analysis has also been used for attacks against smart cards used in conditional access systems for satellite television.

When the path through a body of code is data dependent, not only does the processor activity look different with different data but also the time taken to execute the code can change. This leads to the class of attacks known as timing attacks (Kocher, 1996), which have been successfully performed against targets as diverse as Web servers and smart cards.

Given a side channel that is known to be leaking information, there are various ways an attacker can exploit it. In the simplest cases, it is sometimes possible to analyze a single run of the code to get the key. If this is not possible, then the averaging of a large number of runs of the same system with the same data will allow the signal-to-noise ratio to be improved because the noise will not be correlated between runs, but the signal will be, so the former will tend to cancel out, and the latter will tend to reinforce itself. As a result, countermeasures to power line or RF emission attacks that simply filter the signal will tend to fail if the attack can run the system over and over again with the same data. Another approach to analyzing a side channel is to measure the signal with a number of different inputs (usually with the same key) and examine the differences in behavior. So-called *differential* side-channel attacks can be particularly effective (see Kocher, 1999).

There many other variants on side-channel attacks. Multiple channels can be used simultaneously (Agrawal, 2003), and a wide variety of methods of statistical analysis has been offered for extracting key information from signals (Brier, Clavier, & Olivier, 2004; Chari, Rao, & Rohatgi, 2002; Karlof & Wagner, 2003). A full analysis of side-channel attacks is outside the scope of this chapter, but it should be noted that in the face of these, it is generally accepted that simply attempting to damp the leaked side-channel information is insufficient. As long as there is a signal, lowering the signal-to-noise ratio will simply require more samples to be taken. As such, it is generally accepted that devices performing cryptographic computations should be designed from the start to try to avoid internal activity directly correlated to key or cleartext data. In general, there are two approaches to this. First, one can attempt to randomize the signal using methods including *blinding* of the message or key material (Kocher & Jaffe, 2001; Kocher, 1996) or randomly permuting the execution order within the code. These methods have costs associated with the blinding process and with upsetting data flows in randomized orders. Second, the system can be designed to attempt to make the signal constant, for instance, by having code that has the same execution time or hardware that consumes the same amount of power irrespective of the data. Naturally, such systems must always take the longest time or consume the greatest amount of power, which may be problematic in some situations. Despite these drawbacks, protection against side-channel attacks is important given that they have been successfully applied to a number of systems.

## Limitations

When building an HSM, it is easy to get carried away and put in every conceivable protection against every possible attack. It should be noted, however, that (a) it is probably not possible to build a truly *tamper-proof* device, and (b) it is probably not necessary either. Ultimately, from a financial point of view, there is little case for spending more on the protection mechanism than the amount of loss that would occur were the protection to be compromised. If a satellite TV company stands to lose $10 million from piracy of its signals, then spending 20 million to combat this does not make commercial sense. Spending on protection needs to consider the cost of protection, the cost resulting from an attack, and the probability that a successful attack will occur. Thus, the majority of HSMs that are sold into the commercial world tend to be tamper resistant rather than tamper reactive, but they are then locked into a rack, which is placed in a locked cage that is bolted to the floor of a machine room which itself has good physical security. In such a scenario, a theoretical attack involving grinding down potting and applying logic probes becomes impractical. On the other hand, it has been shown (Anderson & Kuhn, 1997) that on some systems, attacks can be carried out surprisingly cheaply when appropriate precautions have not been taken by the device manufacturer.

## VALIDATION AND STANDARDS

When users of HSMs are making decisions about which type to use, the quality of the security provided by the device is of paramount importance. Because most users have neither the skills nor the resources to evaluate products in detail, and because they do not usually wish simply to rely on the assertions of the HSM vendor, independent validation of such devices is important. For it to be possible to carry out a meaningful comparison, different HSMs should be tested against the same standard, and a number of standards have emerged for this purpose. The various standards differ in approach and in what they compare, but each gives a yardstick by which to measure various products. To date, two standards have emerged as widely accepted: FIPS 140-2 and Common Criteria.

### FIPS 140

Probably the most widely used accepted standard for evaluating HSMs is the Federal Information Processing Standard (FIPS) 140-2 standard (National Institute for Standards and Technology [NIST], 1999) published by the U.S. government. NIST is part of the U.S. Commerce Department's Technology Administration and its Computer Security Division, in conjunction with the Communications Security Establishment (CSE) of the government of Canada, run the Cryptographic Module Validation Program. The original version of the standard, FIPS 140-1, was published in January 1994 and was superseded by FIPS 140-2 in May 2001.

FIPS 140 specifies four security levels for validation with progressively more demands and restrictions to provide progressively higher levels of security.

- Level 1 primarily involves testing that the cryptographic algorithms provided by the module perform correctly with standard test vectors. At this level, the certification is a statement that the device performs as described rather than making any assertions about security. There are no physical security requirements at this level.
- Level 2 may be applied to hardware or software, but when hardware is being evaluated, it must provide a degree of tamper evidence or tamper resistance. Level 2 also requires at a minimum a role-based authentication system that separates the duties of the general user and the *crypto officer* and provides for the possibility of a maintenance role. The cryptography used in the access control system must be built using FIPS-approved algorithms such as Data Encryption (DES) or Advanced Encryption Standard (AES), Secure Hash Algorithm (SHA)-1 and Digital Signature Algorithm (DSA), or Rivest, Shamir and Adleman (RSA).
- Level 3 raises the bar still further by requiring enhanced physical security, usually in the form of strong tamper resistance, to prevent an attacker from gaining access to the critical internal circuitry. Rather than relying on role-based authentication, an identity-based authentication system must be used, and then any authenticated identity must be authorized to carry out requested operations. Level 3 also places requirements on the movement of security-critical data, specifying that such data must only pass in and out of the device through dedicated channels that do not pass through any other computer system or through the usual channels in an encrypted form. In the case of direct entry of key material, it should be provided using a secret sharing or split knowledge scheme. Only FIPS-approved algorithms may be supported by the HSM.
- Level 4 is currently the highest security level in FIPS 140. It requires that the device be not merely tamper resistant but also reactive to a variety of types of attack including physical penetration, manipulation of environmental conditions, and altering of the electrical environment in which the device is operating. Formal definitions of the design and modes of operation of the device are required, along with evidence that the implementation meets these definitions.

Although the FIPS 140 standard is driven by the U.S. and Canadian governments, it has become a de facto standard internationally in many industries such as banking and finance. The FIPS 140 standard lays out a set of hurdles that the HSM must cross to be validated, which, in a risk-adverse environment, is comforting.

### Common Criteria

Another validation program frequently applied to hardware security devices is called Common Criteria for Information Technology Security Evaluations, often referred to as just Common Criteria or simply as CC.

The Common Criteria standards were set up jointly by the governments of the United States, Canada, the United Kingdom, France, Germany, and the Netherlands to develop a harmonized set of security criteria for Information Technology (IT) products. Starting work in 1993, the first version (v1) of the standard was published in 1996 and extensively updated (v2) in 1998. In 1999, it was adopted by the ISO as International Standard 15408 and had minor updates (v2.1) (Common Criteria, 1999) later that year.

CC lays out a common evaluation methodology (CEM) for evaluating a target of evaluation (TOE), which need not necessarily be a security device but may be some larger system that has security components. It describes a number of classes of functionality that might be evaluated including security audit, communication, cryptographic support, user data protection, identification and authentication, security management, privacy, protection of the TOE security functions (TSF), resource utilization, access to the TOE, and trusted paths and channels. Each of these classes is broken down into subclasses; for instance, cryptographic support is broken down into cryptographic key management and cryptographic operations. Within each subclass, the standard defines what issues need to be considered when evaluating the target.

One notable difference between CC and FIPS 140 is that whereas FIPS 140 proscribes a number of functions and types of protection, CC describes a methodology and a detailed list of areas for examination but does not lay down what exactly the target must do. For a target to be evaluated, it must be considered in the context of a protection profile (PP), which states what the target aims to do. A vendor of a product is at liberty to have its product evaluated against any PP it sees fit. This approach has both benefits and drawbacks. In the context of complex systems such as public key infrastructure products, it is unrealistic to expect the standards organizations to lay down in detail what exactly the product must do and how it should do it. On the other hand, the fact that similar products may have been evaluated against different protection profiles makes direct comparison of their evaluations more difficult. Furthermore, because it is often up to the system vendor to write the PP against which the product will be evaluated, there is an argument that "of course it will pass." Since 2001, NIST has worked to develop standardized protection profiles for a number of product areas from which vendors can derive their own more detailed profiles, but it is still occasionally joked that the standard is so open, it would be possible to achieve a high CC assurance level on a soft drink can.

When the CEM is applied to a TOE in the context of a PP,[5] there are seven evaluation assurance levels, EAL1 up to EAL7, that can be granted. These differ both in terms of the depth of review and the level of formality applied to both design and revue processes. The seven levels are defined as follows:

*EAL1*: Functionally tested
*EAL2*: Structurally tested
*EAL3*: Methodically tested and checked
*EAL4*: Methodically designed, tested, and reviewed
*EAL5*: Semiformally designed and tested
*EAL6*: Semiformally verified design and tested
*EAL7*: Formally verified design and tested

Although the two standards are not directly comparable, for the reasons listed here, it is probably the case that if four protection profiles were derived from the FIPS 140 standard for each of the four FIPS levels, these would result in evaluations to EAL1 for FIPS 140 level 1, EAL3 for FIPS level 2, EAL4 for FIPS level 3, and EAL6 or EAL7 for FIPS level 4.

---

[5] The CC documents define nearly 200 acronyms.

# MANAGEMENT

One of the main uses of HSMs is to look after keys critical to business processes in large IT systems. As with any component of a large IT system, the HSM needs to be managed and maintained by the system administrators and so do the keys. To make matters more complex, the security-critical nature of the data in the HSM may mean that those who are trusted to maintain most of an organization's IT infrastructure may not be trusted to look after all the keys held by an HSM.

The general problem of management of IT components is beyond the scope of this chapter, but it is worth addressing the specific problems associated with the management of HSMs and the keys they hold.

## Backup and Recovery

One of the most fundamental and routine IT management tasks is the backup of critical data and the provisioning for its recovery in case of data loss. Data on servers are habitually backed onto removable storage devices such as tape, but data embedded in a physical security device cannot be so easily copied. After all, the whole point of putting the data in an HSM is to stop it being copied. There are various approaches to dealing with this issue. Some HSM vendors provide a mechanism to connect two of their devices together and "clone" the contents of one into the other, providing suitable authorization has been granted. This means that the user will need to buy multiple devices and find a physically secure location in which to store the backup. An alternative to this is to encrypt the key material with other keys and take backups of the encrypted data. Of course, this latter approach simply moves the problem to one of backing up the wrapper key, but backing up a single, long-term key is a problem that can be solved out of hand; once done, the regularly used application keys can be backed up in encrypted form on a more regular basis (because these are the keys that are likely to change on a regular basis). It should be noted that it is not just the keys that need to be backed up but also all the access control information that goes with those keys, and the binding between these must be maintained if security is to be preserved, so the tuples of keys and access information should be both encrypted and signed before backing up.

## Scalability

When structuring IT systems, it is important to consider how the system will scale should it need to grow. Being able to provide the same service from a number of machines, possibly in different physical locations, can allow for higher throughput; with servers geographically distributed, it can provide better latency as well. Unfortunately, when it comes to dealing with cryptographic systems, this requires replicating keys across multiple devices, but data replication for sensitive material such as keys is complex. As with the problem of backup and recovery, a preshared wrapper key can help with this problem, but care must be taken to ensure that only authorized devices can receive wrapped keys; otherwise, there is a danger that an attacker might obtain an unauthorized device and fool the system into duplicating important keys into the attackers hands.

## Resilience

As with scalability and backup, resilience to localized failures is an important part of any business system. Again, as with scalability and backup, the solution is to replicate data into many places and yet again care needs to be taken when doing this with information as sensitive as cryptographic keys. The same techniques and the same caveats apply as before.

## Multiparty Control

There is a second aspect to resilience that has nothing to do with computer failure: resilience against people failure, either accidental or malicious. It is desirable to make it difficult for a single person, or even a small set of people, to compromise the security of the system. Attackers may well be insiders to the system, and even in the absence of malice, the operators might simply get things wrong. Furthermore, sometimes people simply cease to be available; they may have quit or been fired; they may be sick or have died. Critical business systems must be resilient against such people failures. The importance is all the greater when the people concerned are the administrators or overseers of the system because attacks by individuals in this group are potentially much more damaging, and the inability for this group to act can lead to an inability for a business to function.

The general technique used to be resilient against the incompetence or malice of a subset of users is called *multiparty control*. If a system is built such that more than one person is required to authorize an operation, a single person cannot cause problems. In the field of cryptography, a great deal of time and effort has been put into the subject of secure distributed computation and threshold cryptography, but if we have access to a trusted hardware security module, we do not need any of that; we can simply assemble the keys inside the HSM and require it to enforce the appropriate policy. We may require any arbitrarily sized subset of the authorized operators to present credentials before an operation is allowed to proceed. If the size of the subset is greater than one, no single person can carry out the operation, and, in general, requiring a set of size $K$ protects against the failure of $K-1$ people. If the required number of people is less than the total number of operators, there is also resilience against the system failing when not all the operators are available.

Having said that threshold cryptography is unnecessary to provide multiparty control, certain simple tools such as threshold-based secret sharing (see Shamir, 1979, for the canonical system for this), when implemented inside the HSM, can nonetheless be used straightforwardly to provide exactly the desired effect without having to resort to complex multiparty computation protocols.

## ACCESS CONTROL ENFORCEMENT

Protecting keys is a desirable goal, but it may all be for nothing if there is no control over who can do what with the key. If an attacker can ask an HSM to decrypt a message, there may be no need to get the key itself; use of the key is sufficient. As a result, one of the most important functions of the HSM is to enforce an access-control policy. In general, the problem of access-control can be summed up thus: given a user $U$, bearing credentials $C_U$, wishing to carry out an action $A$ with parameter set $(p)$ when the policy for authorization is $P$, an enforcement function $E(U, C_U, A, (p), P)$ should return either the result of $A(p)$ or indicate an authorization failure, depending on the parameters. Of course, this oversimplifies the problem massively; not only have entire theses been written on how to implement $E()$, but the nature of the credentials $C_U$ and the best way to represent the policy $P$ are also controversial.

## Authenticating Users to an HSM

At first sight, authentication to an HSM looks similar to any other authentication operation, but in practice we have the opportunity to implement more rigorous controls given a hardened environment in which to operate.

For small personal devices such as smart cards, a simple password or PIN (personal identification number) might suffice, but rather than comparing the password to a value stored inside the device, we can use it to derive a cryptographic key with which we can encrypt the user's keys stored inside the device. This allows us to bind more tightly the authentication and authorization operations because in the absence of the correct password, the user's keys cannot be decrypted.

With larger HSMs, it is common to have multifactor authentication such as requiring the presence of a token and a passphrase, requiring of the users something that they *have* as well as something that they *know*. Again, we can store an encrypted key on the token, encrypted with a key derived from the passphrase, and we can use that key on the token to encrypt the data inside the HSM. Thus, even if the HSM were compromised, the contents of its long-term memory would not reveal any key material without also having the token and PIN. It would of course be possible to extend this to also require a biometric authentication, requiring of the users something that they *are* as well as things they *know* and *have*. This, however, is unusual, largely because if multiparty control is properly implemented with two-factor authentication and appropriate operational measures are taken to control who gets access to the system, further technological controls are probably unnecessary.

## Policy Representation

Probably the most difficult problem in any access control system is coming up with a means of representing policies that is rich enough to allow for any reasonable policy while at the same time being simple enough that those people setting the policy can actually be confident that the policy they wrote matches the policy they sought.

Historically, many HSM vendors have tended to err toward not providing enough flexibility in their access control mechanisms. Because many of the common application programming interfaces (APIs) used by HSM vendors (e.g., PKCS#11, discussed in the next section) evolved from interfaces designed for personal tokens, they often only provide the flexibility needed for the simplest form of use; keys have one owner, and that owner gets to use the key. Removal of the key from the device might be controlled by an administrative role of some sort, but in that case, the policy under which the key can get exported tends to be either predefined or taken from a limited set of policies (e.g., export it wrapped under any key or export to any module from the same vendor).

More modern HSMs, and some with their heritage rooted in the mainframe world, provide a more complete "access control list" based authorization system possibly coupled with cryptographic wrapping bound into the user authentication phase as described earlier (Smith and Weingart, 1999, go into some detail on this). In the Access Control List (ACL) model, a list of tuples representing patterns to match against the operation requested, and patterns describing allowable credentials defines what operations are allowed. When the user requests an operation, credentials must also be presented and the operation is only allowed if both the operation and the credentials match patterns in the same list entry. Sometimes list entries can also indicate that operations may be delegated by an authorized party.

Although a powerful access control list based system is a powerful model, it is easy for the complexity to escalate to a point where it can be confusing, leading to the wrong policy being requested, in which case the wrong policy will be rigorously enforced. Bond (2004) concluded in his section on "The Future of APIs" that rich interfaces such as nCipher's nCore (discussed in the next section) are so complex that only a few users can fully understand them. Although the flexibility is doubtless a good thing to have, it is usually well worth making full use of any management tools or abstractions provided by the supplier whenever possible.

# APPLICATION PROGRAMMING INTERFACES

The nature of the protection afforded by an HSM is affected to a large extent not just by the management interface and access control model but also by the nature of the API available for interacting with the HSM. Whereas some APIs concentrate on controlling who can access the keys, others concentrate more on controlling what operations can be performed with a given key. Some HSMs offer APIs that allow for the functionality protected by the HSM to be expanded, and others offer only predefined sets of operations; these sets may be either primitive cryptographic functions or compound operations implementing whole sections of protocols.

Another cleavage line in the set of available APIs is between those APIs that aim to provide unified support across a set of various brands of HSM and those that are vendor-specific. Those that offer a unified view make it easier for developers to build products that can support a variety of HSMs but at the cost of usually only supporting the lowest common denominator of functionality. On the other hand, the vendor-specific APIs can allow for detailed access to the unique functions provided by a specific type of HSM, although in the process locking the user into using that particular brand. Some vendors offer both proprietary and generic APIs (usually by providing a mapping from the former to the latter), which gives the developer the choice.

Although it is not possible to give an exhaustive catalogue of all the APIs available on all HSMs, in this section I present outlines of some of the more common APIs and also discuss some of the security issues that arise from their designs.

## Standard APIs

As mentioned earlier, using a standardized API to access an HSM allows a developer to program to a single API without needing to know the specifics of the particular HSM that an end customer will end up using. That is the theory, at least; in practice, some of the API specifications are sufficiently loose that extensive testing against individual brands of HSM may be needed to ensure compatibility.

### PKCS#11

Public Key Cryptographic Standard number 11 (RSA Laboratories, n.d.), or PKCS#11 as it is commonly known, is one of a set of standards published by RSA Security and bears the subtitle "Cryptographic token interface standard." As the name suggests, it was originally designed for accessing cryptographic *tokens*, HSMs targeted at authenticating an individual user at a client machine. It is closely based on the original (and originally proprietary) API for access to the Luna cryptographic token (discussed later) from the now-defunct company Chrysalis ITS (whose products are carried on by SafeNet), and it is occasionally referred to as *Cryptoki*, the name of the Chrysalis interface.

Although PKCS#11 was originally designed to interface to simple user tokens, it is now widely used both for accessing key storage devices used by PKI software and for accessing the keys used by servers implementing the secure socket layer (SSL) protocol. It is commonly held that the interface is not well suited to server-side applications because its design is targeted as a more single-user, single-process, single-threaded model. That said, the API is widely adopted by both HSM vendors and application software authors and as such is probably the most widely used API for HSMs. It is supported by everything from high-performance server-oriented HSMs to USB connected key-ring tokens.

The PKCS#11 API separates out the role of the security officer, who is responsible for initializing the token, from the normal users who generate and use keys. The API allows for the management of data and certificate objects as well as keys, and like most of the standard APIs, it is largely focused on controlling *who* can access a key rather than limiting *what* can be done with the key. Keys have associated with them a few access control bits that determine which operations can be carried out with that key, but essentially the access control is all or nothing.

### MS-CAPI

In 1996, Microsoft introduced the Microsoft Crypto API, often referred to as MS-CAPI. The design at that time served two goals: first, it provided a common interface to a variety of hardware and software implementations of cryptographic functions; and second, it provided a single place where Microsoft could attempt to enforce the export control restrictions that the U.S. State Department applied at that time to all cryptographic systems. The MS-CAPI model allows applications to communicate with the core libraries, which in turn communicate with *Crypto service providers* (CSPs), which either implement the cryptographic functions in software or communicate with an HSM. The core library requires all CSPs to be digitally signed, and by using different signing keys for regular and "export" (e.g., weakened) CSPs, Microsoft was able to offer a solution[6] to the export control problem while still shipping the same versions of the applications that used MS-CAPI to all countries.

MS-CAPI provides a similar set of functions to PKCS#11, although it does not separate out the roles of security officer and normal user. The model presented is somewhat better suited to multiapplication and multi-threaded situations, but it still provided an all-or-nothing access model. MS-CAPI has occasionally been criticized for the fact that the default access control settings for new keys are too permissive, allowing private keys to be exported by any user who gained control. In practice, this is only the case when using the software CSPs, and most vendors who provide CSPs for accessing their HSMs use more secure defaults.

## CDSA

The Common Data Security Architecture (CDSA)(Open Group, n.d.) was originally created by Intel, although it was subsequently handed over to the Open Group and much of the source code made freely available.

CDSA aims to provide a broad framework in which keys, certificates, and security policies can be managed. This breadth leads to a level of complexity of interface (if not of design), which is probably the reason that CDSA is not more widely adopted. As of the time of writing, Apple Computers is the only company making widespread use of CDSA (it is the core of the security framework in Apple's OS X operating system). CDSA is also starting to gain a certain amount of traction among users of Linux because both the specification and large bodies of source code are freely available.

As with MS-CAPI, and most implementations of PKCS#11, CDSA makes use of cryptographic service providers to interface to specific types of HSM. Unfortunately, the interface provided at this level does little more than the functions offered by PKCS#11, and as a result of this and the slow uptake of the API, most HSM support for CDSA is provided using a mapping layer between PKCS#11 and CDSA and using standard PKCS#11 CSPs.

## Proprietary APIs

Many, if not most, HSM vendors offer a proprietary API for communicating with their hardware. Each of these APIs tends to reflect the particular focus of the company selling the devices.

Thales (formerly Zaxus, formerly Racal), Hewlett Packard's Atalla division (formerly part of Compaq, which acquired it from Tandem), and Eracom all offer their own APIs, which have a strong focus toward the processing of messages to and from automated teller machines (ATMs), point-of-sale terminals, and electronic funds transfer systems, owing much to the VISA security module specifications set out by VISA in the 1980s. To this end, they tend to be more concerned with controlling what can be done with keys and data than who can do it. Although secondary controls are present to prevent the unauthorized movement of keys from device to device, it is expected that the HSM will be attached to a secured host machine and as such keys can generally be used for any operation for which the key is authorized without further controls.

### IBM's Common Cryptographic Architecture (CCA)

The IBM 4758 HSM (see from http://www.ibm.com/security/cryptocards) offers the common cryptographic architecture (CCA) as its API. CCA is worthy of note primarily for its long heritage, being derived from the Intergrated Cryptographic Services Facility API on IBM's OS/390 mainframes, which in turn was derived from the Transaction Security Services API. Like many of the other APIs on devices targeted at the finance and payments industries, CCA makes heavy use of symmetric encryption in its key management architecture and provides relatively little in the way of control of who can do what, although it does benefit from some role management related to facilities provided by OS/390. The underlying IBM 4758 hardware is in fact capable of much more, but CCA hides much of this functionality; if the user wishes to access the hardware at a lower level, then they need to use the User Defined eXtensions (discussed later in this section).

### nCipher's nCore API

The API provided by nCipher Corporation (http://www.ncipher.com) for their nForce and nShield HSMs (see from http://www.ncipher.com/nshield/) is different from most of the APIs provided by the vendors of hardware for the financial services sector. Rather than implementing complex protocols inside the standard HSM firmware, the nCore API offers a wide range of cryptographic primitives, similar to the sets offered by APIs such as PKCS#11 and MS-CAPI. Unlike those APIs, however, nCore provides a rich access control system to limit who can perform what operations using a key and allows for the delegation of subsets of those rights. The access-control policy for any given key is determined by the party that creates the key (although the security officer who initialized the module can require certain module-wide constraints).

As well as offering mechanisms to constrain who can do what with each key managed through the API, nCore can generate certificates signed by the module to attest to the state of the HSM and to show that a given module generated a given key with a given access control policy at the time of creation. This is useful both for audit purposes and also to allow a degree of remote management for the devices because it allows for the creation of strongly authenticated connections to the HSM from elsewhere.

## User Configurable HSMs

With the exception of some early smart card devices, almost all HSMs execute a set of firmware that is preprogrammed into the device. Most vendors provide a mechanism to upgrade the firmware, and most vendors,

---

[6] The solution is in practice ineffective because the signature verification keys can easily be altered; see Shamir and van Someren (1999).

if offered enough money, will add custom functionality to the HSM for specific customers. That said, having the vendor alter the firmware for a customer can be a slow process, can invalidate any existing certification of the hardware, and can leave the customer beholden to the vendor when upgrades are needed in the future. To better deal with this, some HSMs can have additional functionality added to them by the user in the field, without recourse to the HSM vendor.

The IBM 4758 software architecture is layered to make it easier to achieve the highest level of FIPS 140 validation. A two-level boot loader (half in Read Only Memory (ROM) half in FLASH memory) is used to start an operating system that is in turn used to start an application. The implementation of the CCA exists as an application in this model but it is possible for the user to replace either the application using IBM's User Defined eXtensions (n.d.) or to replace the operating system and the applications sitting on top of it.

The nShield HSM offered by nCipher (see from http://www.ncipher.com/nshield/) also has the option of allowing user applications to be loaded into it using nCipher's Secure Execution Engine (SEE) technology (n.d.) Unlike the IBM 4758, in which layers must be replaced, SEE allows for a user application to be loaded on top of existing functionality while still allowing the underlying functions to be accessed from the host machine. The application code (known as an *engine*) running in SEE has essentially the same API available to it when running inside the HSM as it would have running on the host but with two important differences. First, the application when loaded is afforded the same physical and logical protection as a loaded key. Second, the engine and its separately loadable configuration *user data* must be digitally signed, and the signatures are used by the rich access control model in the nCore API to determine what the code is allowed to do with the key.

The trust model adopted by nCipher is different from the model used by the IBM 4758. With the IBM hardware, the chain of trust for the authentication starts with a key held by IBM; they sign the operating system, and the OS determines what keys are acceptable for signing the application. With the standard operating system, the application signing key is also rooted with IBM. In the nCipher model, the code may be signed by anyone (although the security officer has a say regarding whether it can be loaded). Once loaded, however, the application code is not capable of doing anything with the keys that it would not have been able to do running outside the box unless the access control lists for those keys explicitly delegate rights to the party that signed the application. This, in practice, makes for a much more flexible system for protecting access because different applications can be run on the same HSM but not be able to access each other's keys.

## API Attacks and Defenses

There is often a close mapping between the API presented to the programmer and the set of functions that an HSM is capable of performing. Although in some cases there is a mapping layer, it is usually the case that the vendor exposes a primitive interface that gives access to the basic functional building blocks. (Bond [2004] pointed out that when the vendor assumes the user cannot access the device at this low level, there is added potential for attack.) Because the low-level API represents the *front door* to the HSM, there has been a certain amount of work on examining these APIs to try to find ways to make HSMs allow misuse of the keys that they hold.

The majority of the work in this area has been targeted at APIs for financial transaction processing. This is not just because there is more money to be made here but also because they tend to be oriented toward implementing parts of a protocol rather than simply controlling who can use them. This is largely a result of these protocols being based on symmetric encryption systems and the fact that in such systems both ends of a channel hold the same key gives potential for abuse.

Both Bond (2001a, 2004) and Clulow (2003a) have uncovered flaws in the transaction sets specified for various means of validating the (PINs) of the user of a credit or ATM card. The attacks allow for the recovery of the PIN value by manipulating parameters to the PIN validation commands that would normally remain constant for all calls to the function in any particular installation.

Bond (2001b, 2004) also discussed a number of other types of attack that stem from the need for the APIs to maintain a degree of backward compatibility, a feature that often leads to flaws being perpetuated. In analyzing the CCA, Bond showed that in migrating from 56-bit Data Encryption Standard (DES) to 112-bit triple DES. IBM had not forced the two single DES keys used for triple. DES to be bound together, allowing an attack in which the two halves of the key could be attacked independently. Other modes of attack include using the ability in some APIs to cast a key from one type to another, allowing a key known in one context to be misused in another.

In the arena of nonfinancial APIs, there has been less success so far. This is due in part to the differing nature of the protection for which the design aims. Many of the generic APIs simply aim to control who gets to use a key and to stop the key material being exposed. In asymmetric crypto systems, this is often sufficient and is also sufficiently simple that it is relatively easy to achieve. That said, Clulow (2003b) raised some questions regarding the security of PKCS#11.

At the forefront of API analysis is the field of automated attacks using theorem proving. Although it is essentially impossible to prove absolute security of an API against as-yet-unknown attacks, it has been shown that APIs can be attacked in much the same way that cryptographic protocols can be attacked. Work at MIT by Youn (2004) and ongoing work at Cambridge by Anderson, Bond, and Clulow seem to be bearing fruit in this area.

## EXAMPLES OF HSMS

It is hard to provide an exhaustive and current list of available HSMs in what is a rapidly changing market. Not only do vendors bring out new models and retire old ones every few years, but the ownership of some of the companies involved is also fairly rapidly shifting. At the time of this writing, the Atalla brand has changed hands three times since 1987, the Chrysalis brand twice in the last 3 years, and the Racal brand twice in the last 5 years. Therefore, in this section, I merely aim to provide a representative sample of the HSMs in the market rather than any attempt at providing a definitive catalogue.

## Public Key Infrastructure–Focused HSMs

Various vendors offer HSMs focused on storing the keys that underpin public key infrastructure solutions.

### AEP

AEP Systems in Dublin purchased the SureWare Keyper line of HSMs previously offered by Baltimore Technologies back in 2002. These devices, evolved from products originally sold by Zergo (which merged with Baltimore in 1999), offer PKCS#11 and MS-CAPI interfaces and deliver protection up to FIPS 140-2 level 4. Form factors include external HSMs connecting to the host computer via Ethernet or Peripheral Component Interconnect (PCI) cards that fit internally to the host computer.

### nCipher

nCipher Corporation was founded in the United Kingdom in 1996 and offers the nShield line of HSMs for protecting keys with FIPS 140-2 level 3 certification. The devices are offered in external, Ethernet-connected form or internal device with either a PCI interface or a SCSI peripheral interface (the latter in a 5.25-inch form factor that fits into a standard disc-drive bay). The devices all offer access through PKCS#11, MS-CAPI, Java CAPI, and half a dozen other application-specific APIs as well as nCipher's own nCore API. They also offer advanced capabilities for remote management, clustering, load balancing, and fail-over.

### Safenet

SafeNet offers the Luna CA line of HSMs originally offered by Chrysalis ITS, which was purchased by Rainbow Technologies, who was in turn purchased by SafeNet in 2003. Most of the Luna line exists in the form of a small card with PCMCIA form factor, a hang over from its origin as a personal authentication token for laptops (an adaptor is provided to allow connection to a PCI bus). The lowest level API exposed on the Luna card is PKCS#11 as that API was derived from the original Luna Cryptoki API, although MS-CAPI is offered as an alternative on Windows platforms. The Luna cards are available in FIPS 140 level 2 and level 3 forms. SafeNet also offers the network-attached Luna SA.

## Performance Devices

A number of vendors offer high-performance cryptographic accelerators, mostly targeted at dealing with the computationally intensive public key cryptographic operations involved in setting up secure network sessions with protocols such as SSL and Internet protocol security (IPSec). For the most part, these products are not true HSMs because they do not provide any security, they merely accelerate computations that would otherwise be carried out on the host computer. There are, however, a few products on the market that deliver both secure key management and acceleration. nCipher was

the first company to offer such a product with its nForce product line introduced in 1997, and more recently Sun Microsystems has started to sell its Sun Cryptographic Accelerator 4000 for accelerating SSL connections to its line of enterprise Web servers.

## HSMs for Payment Processing

The market for payments-specific HSMs is dominated by three players, each of which has dominance in different parts of the world. Hewlett-Packard's Atalla brand of security processors, known as the Ax100 range, are network-attached devices aimed at the ATM/EFT/POS banking sector and have a large installed base in North America. Thales e-Security offers its HSM 7000 and HSM 8000 ranges of products for the same market, and with very similar functionality, with market dominance in Europe and Africa. Eracom Technologies offers its ProtectHost and ProtectServer product lines (network connected, although the ProtectServer is available as a PCI card as well) to the same customers and has considerable presence in Asia and Australasia. Although there is considerable variation in the size, shape, and connection options among these products, the functionality offered is largely similar because it is driven by the requirements of the major credit card companies and interbank transaction networks. nCipher also offers a variant of the nShield called the payShield, which delivers the same payment processing functions but is otherwise identical to the nShield.

## Programmable HSMs

For customers who wish to secure their own custom protocols or have their own applications run inside the HSM, there is a fairly limited selection.

The IBM 4758 offers the ability to replace the application with the customer's own application, but only by disposing of the standard functionality. Replacing the application wholesale means that the developer must re-create a fair amount of functionality, which makes development for the 4758 cumbersome; indeed, Bond (2004, p. 54) suggested that IBM subsidize the sale of the 4758 hardware because it expects to make the money back consulting on how to customize the device to meet the customers needs.

The main alternative to the 4758 is the nCipher nShield with its Secure Execution Engine (SEE; nCipher, n.d.) capability. This allows custom code to be loaded alongside the standard key management and crypto functionality, allowing the developer to take full advantage of its access-control mechanisms, state attestation, and FIPS-validated crypto algorithm implementations. The SEE model splits the application into two parts, the *engine* and the *user data*, each of which must be signed. The former is machine code for the processor inside the HSM (an ARM or a PowerPC, depending on the model) and the later is data that will be interpreted by the engine. The engine and user data may be supplied by different parties, in which case the acceptable signers of the engine must be identified within the signed user data. The trust placed in the SEE application by the underlying access-control system is based on the signature on the user data. This allows both the arrangement in which the engine is a user program and the user data is some configuration for that program or the arrangement in which the engine is an interpreter or vitrual machine and the user data is the end-user supplied program (nCipher offers a Java Virtual Machine as an engine).

## Trusted Platform Modules and the Trusted Computing Group

So far, most of the discussion in this chapter has related to hardware security modules that are attached as peripherals to existing systems. The Trusted Computing Group (TCG; http://trustingcomputedgroup.org) is an organization that aims to bring together technology companies to allow trusted platform modules (TPM) to be built into every PC and to thereby deliver some of the functionality of an HSM inside each machine.

The TCG (previously known as the Trusted Computing Platform Alliance or TCPA) proposes a specification for a TPM that can carry out a minimal set of cryptographic functions that allow code running on the PC to prove its integrity to others and to allow that code to have exclusive access to its own set of cryptographic keys managed by the TPM. Each TPM is capable of computing hash functions over sections of the code before it is run and will contain keys that it can use to attest to the integrity of this code. It will also hold a confidentiality key that it will use to unwrap other keys on behalf of the applications and grant them access to those keys if the code is authentic.

Although there are clearly benefits to such a device, from a security point of view the system is controversial for a number of reasons. The first reason is historical; the original TCPA specification did not simply grant access to keys if code was not authentic, it refused to allow the code to run at all. Because in their original model what was "authentic" was determined at the sole discretion of the TCPA and its members, it meant that a machine so equipped could be configured to only run code with the TCPA's say-so. This led to a public relations nightmare, and the TCPA rewrote the specification, changed its name, and started again. Unfortunately, it is still somewhat tainted by the past.

The second main reason for controversy regarding the TCG is the general feeling that users stand to lose control over their own data. One of the main uses for the TPM is to enforce digital rights management (DRM), allowing the source of some digital content to proscribe that only authorized applications will be able to access that content. Although the content might be copyrighted music of films, it would also be possible to use the system on word processor documents and e-mail. Such a system would be able to enforce control of the content over and above the extent provided by copyright law, denying users *fair use*. Furthermore, the vendor of a word processing system would be able to build an application that would never allow documents to be exported into other applications; a source of potential concern when one of the supporters of the TCG is also the dominant vendor of word processor software and has been previously found guilty of monopolistic practices.

It seems likely that despite these concerns, TPMs shall become commonplace in PCs, in the corporate environment if not at home. The benefits to a business of knowing that corporate secrets can be kept secure is significant, especially as various regulatory requirements increasingly mandate more secure storage of sensitive data such as financial records, health care data, and personal information.

## CONCLUSION

Hardware security modules are an essential part of any cryptographic security system that needs to resist competent attackers. From signing of e-mail for a single user to logging onto a remote network through to high throughput e-Commerce servers and certificate authorities in public key infrastructures, the HSM plays an important role when cryptography is used for business. We have seen that the soft security of implementing cryptography on general-purpose computer operating systems does not deliver the security needed when there is likely to be a concerted attack.

The physical security afforded by an HSM provides a barrier to access even when the attacker may have direct access to the device. Although no HSM is perfectly impenetrable (and any HSM vendor who says otherwise is not to be trusted), it is possible to provide enough of a barrier to make it uneconomic or impractical to attack the system by breaking into the HSM. Evaluating the security, both physical and logical, of these modules is a complex task, but in most cases the standard validation programs offered in the form of FIPS 140-2, and to an extent the Common Criteria, mean that most users will be able to compare commercial products on a fairly level playing field.

From the practical point of view, when it comes to deploying hardware security modules, it is important to consider the operational issues. Having a secure backup and recovery program in case of disaster is important, but it must not be so cumbersome as to be impractical. Similarly, any deployment of HSMs needs to be able to scale with business needs and be resilient against the failures of both hardware and people. Finally, it must be possible for those responsible for setting security policies to be able to describe the requirements and have the HSM enforce the policy, preferably with as much of the policy as possible enforced cryptographically rather than programmatically.

## GLOSSARY

**Authentication**  The process of establishing the identity of an on-line entity.

**Cryptography**  The science of constructing mathematical systems for securing data.

**PKI (Public Key Infrastructure)**  Enables the users of a public network such as the Internet to exchange data and information in a secure fashion. This is done through the use of a public and a private cryptographic key pair that is obtained through a trusted authority.

**Side-channel**  A source of additional information about the internal workings of a physical device above and beyond what is permitted by its specification.

**SSL (Secure Sockets Layer)**  A computer networking protocol that provides authentication of, confidentiality of, and integrity of information exchanged by means of a computer network.

**Tamper resistance device**  A device that is difficult to be compromised or broken into.

# CROSS REFERENCES

See *Fault Attacks; Physical Security Measures; Physical Security Threats; PKI (Public Key Infrastructure); Side-Channel Attacks; The Common Criteria.*

# REFERENCES

Agrawal, D., Rao, J. R., & Rohatgi, P. (2003). Multi-channel attacks. In *Fifth Workshop on Cryptographic Hardware and Embedded Systems (CHES 2003), LNCS 2779* (pp. 2–16).

Anderson, R., & Kuhn, M. (1997). Low cost attacks on tamper resistant devices. In *IWSP: International Workshop on Security Protocols, LNCS.*

Aucsmith, D. (1996). Tamper resistant software. *Lecture Notes in Computer Science: Information Hiding, 1174,* 317–333.

Bond, M. (2001a). Attacks on cryptoprocessor transaction sets. *Lecture Notes in Computer Science, 2162,* 220–234.

Bond, M. (2004). *Understanding security APIs.* Unpublished doctoral thesis, Cambridge University.

Bond, M. (2004, June). Unwrapping the chrysalis. Technical report, Cambridge University Computer Laboratory. Retrieved from http://www.cl.cam.ac.uk/TechReports/UCAM-CL-TR-592.pdf

Bond, M., & Anderson, R. (2001b). API-level attacks on embedded systems. *Computer, 34*(10):67–75.

Brier, E., Clavier, C., & Olivier, F. (2004). Sixth Workshop on Cyptographic Hardware and Embedded System (CHES 2004), LNCS 3156 (pp. 16–29).

Chari, S., Rao, J. R., & Rohatgi, P. (2002). Forth Workshop on Cryptographical Hardware and Embedded System (CHES 2002), LNCS 2523 (pp. 13–28).

Chaum, D. (1984). Design concepts for tamper responding systems. In D. Chaum (Ed.), *Advances in Cryptology: Proceedings of Crypto '83* (pp. 387–392). New York: Plenum.

Clulow, J. (2003a). *The Design and Analysis of Cryptographic Application Programming Interfaces for Security Devices.* Unpublished master's thesis, University of Natal, Durban. Retrieved from http://www.cl.cam.ac.uk/jc407/Dissertation.pdf

Clulow, J. (2003b). On the security of pkcs#11. In *Fifth Workshop on Cryptographic Hardware and Embedded Systems (CHES 2003), LNCS 2779* (pp. 411–425).

Common criteria for information technology security evaluation version 2.1. (1999). Retrieved from http://www.commoncriteriaportal.org/

Gordon, L., Loeb, M., Lucyshyn, W., & Richardson, R. (2004). Ninth annual CSI/FBI computer crime and security survey (Technical report). Computer Security Institute.

Gutmann, P. (1996, July). Secure deletion of data from magnetic and solid-state memory. In *Proceedings of the Sixth Annual USENIX Security Symposium, focusing on applications of cryptography, July 22–25, 1996, San Jose, California* (pp. 77–89). Berkeley, CA, USA. USENIX.

IBM. (n.d.). Custom programming—IBM PCI cryptographic coprocessor. Retrieved from http://www-03.ibm.com/security/cryptocards/overcustom.shtml

International Organization for Standardization. (2000). *ISO 13491: Banking—Secure cryptographic devices (retail).* Geneva: International Organization for Standardization.

Karlof, C., & Wagner, D. (2003, September). Hidden markov model cryptanalysis. In *Fifth Workshop on Cryptographic Hardware and Embedded Systems (CHES 2003), LNCS 2779* (pp. 17–24).

Kocher, P. C., & Jaffe, J. M. (2001), Secure modular exponentiation with leak minimization for smartcards and other cryptosystems. U.S. Patent no. 6,298,442.

Kocher, P., Jaffe, J., & Jun, B. (1999). Differential power analysis. In M. J. Wiener (Ed.), *Lecture Notes in Computer Science: Advances in Cryptology: Proceedings of Crypto '99* (Vol. 1666, pp. 388–397).

Kocher, P. C. (1996). Timing attacks on implementations of Diffie-Hellman, RSA, DSS, and other systems. *Lecture Notes in Computer Science* (Vol. 1109, pp. 104–113).

Microsoft. The Microsoft CryptoAPI. Retrieved from http://msdn.microsoft.com/library/en-us/security/security/cryptography_portal.asp

National Institute for Standards and Technology. (1999). Security requirements for cryptographic modules (FIPS PUB 140-2).

nCipher Corporation. (n.d.). The Secure Execution Engine (SEE). Retrieved from http://www.ncipher.com/technologies/see.html

RSA Labratories. PKCS#11: Cryptographic token interface standard. Retrieved from http://www.rsasecurity.com/rsalabs/pkcs/pkcs-11/

Shamir, A. (1979). How to share a secret. *Communications of the ACM, 22,* 612–613.

Shamir, A., & van Someren, N. (1999). Playing "hide and seek" with stored keys. *Lecture Notes in Computer Science: Financial Cryptography, 1648,* 118–124.

Smith, S. W., & Weingart, S. (1999). Building a high-performance, programmable secure coprocessor. *Computer Networks, 31,* 831–860.

The Open Group. The Common Data Security Architecture (CDSA). Retrieved from http://www.opengroup.org/security/l2-cdsa.htm

Youn, P. (2004). *The Analysis of Cryptographic APIs Using the Theorem Prover Otter.* Unpublished master's thesis of engineering, Massachusetts Institute of Technology.

# Smart Card Security

Michael Tunstall, *Gemplus, France, and Royal Holloway, University of London*
Sebastien Petit and Stephanie Porte, *Gemplus, France*

## INTRODUCTION

The sheer convenience of smart cards has contributed to their becoming more and more prevalent in a number of sectors today. We use them to withdraw money, to make telephone calls, to access buildings, to pay for goods, or to authenticate ourselves to a computer.

### Birth of the Smart Card

Banking needs were the real motivation behind the introduction of the smart card's ancestor, the credit card (Rankl & Effing, 2002). The main objective was to protect payment systems against fraud. The first credit cards were quite simple; only information such as the card's issuer, the cardholder's name, and the card number was printed or embossed on the card. These systems relied on a visual verification for security (security printing and signature field, for example), and as a consequence, the security of the system relied mainly on the traders that accepted the card. Because of the payment cards' increasing popularity, it became evident that this was not enough to prevent the system being defrauded. The first improvement appeared with the addition of a magnetic stripe on the back of the card. This allowed data storage in a machine-readable form, making it easier to process transactions. The identification of the cardholder was achieved via either a signature or a personal identification number (PIN). Even though magnetic stripes cards are still commonly used worldwide, they suffer from a crucial weakness: data stored on them can be read, deleted, copied, and replaced easily with the appropriate equipment. One solution would be to allow payment only where transactions can be validated online, but this is not always possible because of the high cost of the necessary infrastructure and the low speed of such transactions.

Patents were filed in several different countries at the end of the 1960s and the beginning of the 1970s on the idea of using plastic cards to carry microchips (Jürgen Dethloff and Helmut Grötrupp in Germany and Roland Moreno in France). In 1974 the first prototype appeared that functioned as a memory card. Two years later the first microprocessor card based on a Motorola chip was developed. However, many new problems had to be solved before manufacturing in large quantities with acceptable quality and prices enabled the smart card to become a viable product.

The French telecommunications industry saw this new technology as an opportunity to reduce fraud and vandalism in coin-based phone booths. In 1980 the French General Direction of Telecommunication (DGT for short) replaced all French phone booths with new ones equipped with a smart card reader. To make a telephone call a "telecarte" is required. It is initially credited with a fixed number of units that are reduced depending on the cost of each call made.

The telecarte's success succeeded in convincing banking organizations that the smart card could be used in payment systems. In 1985, French banks agreed on a common payment system based on smart cards, resulting in the Carte Bleue. The idea has since spread all around the world and in 1994 was adopted by Europay, MasterCard, and Visa International.

Smart cards have also been used in health care, transport, pay TV, access control, electronic purse, and identity applications and the number of different uses is always increasing.

### Different Types of Smart Cards

Since their first appearance smart cards have been compared with personal computers. In fact, the more complicated smart cards have a central processing unit (CPU), an operating system, and different types of memories, exactly like a computer. To satisfy the different requirements of the various applications, a number of different types of smart cards are in common usage.

- **Memory-only cards:** Such cards only have memory that can be written to once. They are mainly used to decrement units previously stored in memory, an example being prepaid phone cards.

- **Memory cards with logic:** Data stored in this type of cards are protected with logic, increasing security as discussed later in this chapter. Such cards can be reloaded with updated values because they include a high counting capacity. These cards are commonly used for public telephony. In addition to a standard counter function, some applications require a dynamic authentication between the card and the terminal. The logic can have an embedded cryptographic algorithm with a state machine to control it.

- **Microprocessor cards:** A microprocessor is embedded into the card to manage and compute data. Such cards contain a dedicated program (e.g., an operating system software) in the read only memory (ROM), which manages other memory areas such as the random access memory (RAM) and nonvolatile memory, or the electrically erasable programmable read only memory (EEPROM), where personalization data is usually stored. The amount of ROM and EEPROM is very small and is expressed in kilobytes; the same is true for the RAM (usually expressed in few thousands of bytes). The amount of memory available in smart cards is increasing all the time as advances in technology allow more transistors to be included in the same surface area. Some chip manufacturers also propose different types of memories such as external RAM and flash, granting extra data storage areas.

- **Contactless smart cards:** Such cards can be based on either a microcontroller or a memory chip. Communications are performed via an antenna glued inside the card's plastic body. Transactions use various different radio frequencies, depending on application requirements. For example, some frequencies require the card to be within 10 cm and others a few meters from the reader. Contactless cards are usually used in applications requiring high flow and low reader maintenance, like transport or identification applications.

- **Dual interface cards:** These cards are able to communicate both in contact and contactless modes. Two types of products are available:

1. Cards with two chips present in the card. One chip is a normal smart card chip and functions via the normal contacts. The second chip is a contactless one with its own specific communication interface, such as MIFARE (MIFARE, 2000). These chips are independent and do not share resources.

2. Cards with one chip that have both interface integrated on the silicon, although the interfaces may be separated logically within the chip.

Dual interface cards are generally designed to support more than one application, for example, access control cards with transport ticketing or e-purse.

## Smart Card Architecture

What follows is a summary of some of the important points in smart card architecture (as there is not enough space to treat the whole subject); the interested reader is referred to Dhem and Feyt (2001) for more details.

### Microcontrollers

Unlike memory cards and magnetic stripe cards that are totally passive, the microprocessor embedded in the card can manipulate and control all the data present in the card. Smart card processors are usually derived from well-known microcontrollers.

The 8-bit microprocessors traditionally used in smart cards are based on complex instruction set computer (CISC) architecture. They are often inspired by Motorola's 6805 or Intel's 8051 core with improvements to permit further optimization of the embedded software. Recently, new 32-bit architectures have appeared. Such processors mainly use an ARM or MIPS's core architecture and instruction sets. However, for example, the STMicroelectronics SmartJ ST22 is based on the company's own 32-bit RISC processor, the NEC V-Way range of products use a V850 32-bit RISC processor, and Atmel provides a ARM 32-bit Thumb Core–based product.

### Cryptographic Coprocessors

To offer authentication, confidentiality, or integrity services, smart cards must have enhanced arithmetic computation capabilities. For this purpose, dedicated coprocessors that will perform computationally intensive operations are appended to the CPU. These coprocessors are used to perform operations such as modular exponentiation that are needed for tasks like digital signature generation or ciphering/deciphering. The card's main processor (microcontroller) presents the data to be manipulated to the cryptoprocessor and retrieves the result when it becomes available via the data bus.

An algorithm that is often implemented in a coprocessor is RSA (Rivest, Shamir, & Adleman, 1978), as otherwise routines to manipulate the large numbers required will greatly increase the cards' execution time. The data encryption standard (Federal Information Processing Standard 46-3, 1999) algorithm is often seen in coprocessors to help increase performance, and more recently advanced encryption standard (Federal Information Processing Standard 197, 2001) implementations are also appearing on the market. These coprocessors can increase the smart cards' performance but the chip size and the power consumption also increase. This means that chips with coprocessors are more expensive and are not ideal in environments where the amount of current available is severely limited.

### Random Number Generators

Random number generators are usually included in smart cards, as unpredictable numbers are an important element in many secure protocols. A true random number generator is based on a signal generated from an analog device, such as a noisy resistor, which is then treated to make sure that even if the analog device is not performing as expected the output will still appear to be random. The correct functioning of the chip as a whole under varied environmental conditions is important, but this is critical for random number generation, because the quality of random numbers generated can have a profound effect on cryptographic schemes and thus on the overall security of the systems in which the smart card operates. Random number generators are designed to function correctly for a large range of environmental conditions, including temperature, supply voltage, and so on. Pseudorandom number generators are often included based on linear feedback shift registers (LFSRs) but are deterministic over time and are not usually used for secure implementations.

## Smart Card Standardization

In the late 1980s, the number of smart card applications forced emergence of international standards on this technology. The International Organization for Standardization (ISO) defines all the basic characteristics of smart cards. The main body of smart card specifications is present in the ISO/IEC 7816 standards, whereas the contactless specifications are described in ISO/IEC 14443 and ISO/IEC 15693 standards.

### Physical Properties

A smart card as defined in the ISO standards is a rectangular card with round edges. A chip is inserted in the front side and it can have one (or more) magnetic strip(s) on the back. The card's form and contact positions are respectively specified in the ISO 7816-1 and ISO 7816-2 standards respectively. See Figure 1.

### Electrical Properties

The integrated circuit is a 1- to 30-mm$^3$ silicon chip. This circuit is located in a micro module and the chip is no longer visible (see Figure 2). In accordance with ISO 7816-2, the micromodule contains an array of eight contacts, only five of which are connected to the chip.

The standard voltage supplied to the smart card is 5 V, with a possible variation of approximately 10%. For GSM applications a voltage range between 3 and 5 V is required, as cellular phone components function with a 3-V power supply. Smart cards rely totally on the card reader for their power supply they do not have their own power supply because of size constraints.

The operating system must also attempt control of the smart card's current consumption. Smart cards are

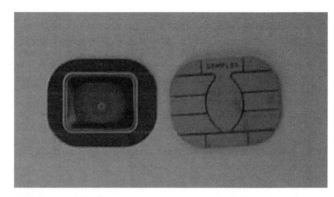

**Figure 2:** A front and rear of a micromodule before it is set into a plastic card.

generally not aware of how much current they consume and the operating system's programmer has to be aware of what functions are called as some will consume more than others. Banking applications, such as EMV2000 (EMVCo, 2004), limit the current consumption to 50 mA. GSM applications are limited to 4, 6, or 10 mA depending the standard that is being implemented. All peripherals have specific power consumption when activated and used. Cryptographic coprocessors and some hardware countermeasures need more power in comparison to the rest of the system. These features may be disabled on some smart cards in order to reduce the current consumption and comply with the associated standard. Recent smart card microcontrollers include a hardware mechanism that automatically adapts the internal clock frequency so that the current consumption is always compliant with the required levels directed by the standards.

### Communication

Smart card terminals use a simple protocol to communicate with the microchip embedded in smart cards. Every time the card is inserted into a terminal it is reset. After the voltage supply, the clock, and the reset signal have been applied, the card sends an answer to reset (ATR) to the terminal via the I/O pin. This data contains a series of bytes that define the parameters and communication protocol that can be used by the card during the session, as specified in the ISO 7816-3 standard. The terminal has the ability to change the communication protocol, transaction speed, or other parameters by sending a protocol type selection (PTS) command to the card. The PTS will specify a set of parameters within the boundaries set by the card in the ATR. After the protocol has been established, the terminal can begin to send commands to the card using the application protocol data unit format (APDU). These exchanges are depicted in Figure 3.

### Operating System

At present a smart card operating system will be in one of two classes: either an operating system especially designed for a dedicated application (also called a native OS) or a Java card operating system that can host several applications. Each application is handled by an applet and several applets can be loaded onto the Java card at a given time. The operating system chosen is closely related to the chip's characteristics; for example, Java cards require

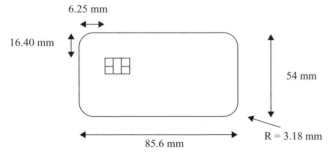

**Figure 1:** Classic shape and dimensions of a smart card.

6.25 mm

16.40 mm

54 mm

R = 3.18 mm

85.6 mm

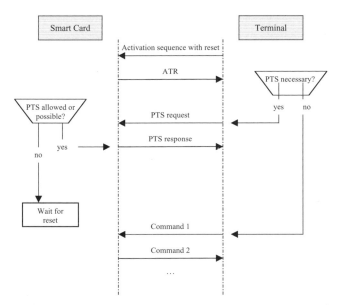

**Figure 3:** Communication initialization between a smart card and a reader.

much more memory to house the virtual machine, applets, and all the functions the user could call. The Java card operating systems correspond to a proprietary implementation of a standardized API edited by SUN Microsystems (Java card specifications, 2004). This allows interoperability of applications: any applet based on the Java card API can be loaded on to any Java card smart card without the need to be concerned about the implementation of other card components by the manufacturer.

Smart card operating systems have become more and more complex as more versatility is required. As a consequence, it is becoming increasingly difficult to implement a secure architecture on modern chips. The aim of the Java card standards is to simplify this problem by allowing one applet to be designed per application that will be secure on all Java cards.

## HARDWARE SECURITY

Hardware specific security features are necessary to prevent a range of attacks against the smart card. These attacks can potentially endanger the security of the system and expose the intellectual property information relating to chip design and embedded software. Attacking the hardware can range from observing the layout of the chip to altering the chip to try and change its behavior. These attacks are usually expensive because of the equipment required, and the attacks themselves are difficult to realize because of the precision required.

### Chip Decapsulation and Silicon Preparation

As described in the introduction, a smart card is made of a silicon chip attached to a façade containing the contacts and covered with an epoxy resin (referred to as a glop-top), which is then glued into a plastic card. To access the silicon the attacker has to remove most of the epoxy resin that covers the chip. This operation can be performed using hot fuming nitric acid. At this stage the features can

be seen on some, generally older, chips. A polyimide layer is sometimes used to make it difficult to see the surface of the chip; this can be removed with chemicals such as ethylendiamine. Just above the metal layers (i.e., the active part of the chip) is the passivation layer, which needs to be removed to directly access the chip internals. This is a thin layer directly over the chip dedicated to protect it during manufacturing. It can either be removed with an etching process using hydrofluoric acid or perforated with an ablation laser to access the active parts of the chip. The complete removal of the passivation layer and or layers of silicon is attempted only to aid in the analysis of the hardware, as after etching the chip is normally nonfunctional because of the aggressive nature of hydrofluoric acid.

### Chip Reverse Engineering

*CARD DATA SECURITY*

Once the chip has been revealed the easiest form of analysis is to simply look at it. The various different blocks can often be identified (see Figure 4).

Reverse engineering targets the internal design by such methods to understand how a given chip or block work. Malicious attackers can use this sort of information to improve their own knowledge of chip design and find potential weaknesses in the chip, which may allow them to compromise the chip's integrity.

In modern smart cards various features that are used to inhibit reverse engineering are implemented using glue logic: [important blocks are laid out in a randomized fashion, which make it difficult to identify blocks.] ③ This technique increases the size of the block where it is implemented and is thus not used in the design of large blocks such as the ROM and EEPROM.

**Figure 4:** A chip surface with readily identifiable features.

## Retrieving Data from Memory

Some of the most valuable data are usually stored inside the ROM of the chip, as it contains the proprietary smart card operating system. Once this program has been extracted it is possible for an attacker to run it inside a debugger tool and understand how the card works. It is also likely to contain proprietary countermeasures, which are jealously guarded by each manufacturer, being one of the main differentiating features of smart cards.

There are three types of ROM technology that have to be approached in different ways to try and retrieve the information stored in them:

1. Diffused ROM can be read by optical analysis, as there is a visible difference between a 1 and a 0 bit value. This is because a connection is visible that will return a signal when it is read for a value of 1 and be absent for a value of 0.
2. Ionic implanted ROM can also be read after a chemical staining process. Ions are present in zones representing a 1 and absent otherwise. A simple inspection will reveal none of the contents but a staining process can stain the ions, producing a visible difference.
3. Metal ROM also hides the values stored as all that is visible is a metal grid to which connections come to represent the values for a 0 or a 1 (i.e., the presence or absence of this connector). The contents can be made visible via a parallel polishing process to expose the metal contacts by removing the top layer so the connectors are visible. This is a difficult process to realize, so this is the hardest ROM to read of those presented here.

Reading the chips' nonvolatile memory is a harder task; simple optical analysis is not enough. One possible way is to probe the data bus when the data are accessed and transferred. For example, a secret key stored in EEPROM has to be read and loaded in RAM to be used. Placing microscopic needles on the data bus and reading the value as it is transferred can achieve this.

In general chip manufacturers scramble the ROM and EEPROM (both data and address) so that it is difficult to interpret any data read from these memories areas. Buses can also be buried in deeper metal layers that will make it harder to access without rendering the chip nonfunctional.

## Chip Modification Techniques

Reading the chip passively can produce interesting results. More powerful attacks are possible by modifying the way a chip works. A focused ion beam (FIB) can be used to add or remove conductive material on a chip. This can allow modification of the connections in different parts of a chip to modify its internal working. One possible use of this sort of attack is to reconnect blown fuses inside the chip to revive a test mode. Some chip manufacturers use a test mode where it is possible to read and write all the memory available while a fuse is present. Once the fuse is blown inside the chip (before the chip leaves the chip manufacturer's factory) this mode is no longer available. In more recent smart cards this system is no longer used because of the potential security risk involved.

Another method of modifying the chip is by cutting parts of it. This can be done with a FIB or a laser (the relatively inexpensive solution). When cutting areas of a chip it is possible to remove security sensors (light and/or voltage sensors to allow more aggressive fault attacks, for example) or the random number generator to set the number read to a fixed value. It is difficult to conduct this sort of attack and still have a functioning chip at the end of this process, as the resulting behavior cannot always be predicted.

Glue logic or obfuscated design can be used to protect against these kinds of attacks, as if an attacker cannot reverse engineer the map of a chip, he or she will not be able to successfully modify a given part of it.

## Hardware Countermeasures

The chip countermeasures can be categorized into three different types:

1. **Design:** As previously described, the chip design includes such countermeasures as glue logic, obfuscated logic, and buried buses. If buses or other key features are buried in the deeper metal layers they become much harder to identify and influence. The scrambling of nonvolatile memory, buses, and logic can stop—or render too expensive—the reverse engineering of embedded software or chip design techniques.
2. **Silicon features:** Some chips include a shield that involves adding a metal layer above the functional metal layers. This acts to hide the design of the chip. A sensor can also be added to detect the presence of this shield that will prevent the chip from working if it is damaged. Features of this nature can be used over the entire chip or over specific parts that are deemed to be the most sensitive, or the whole chip as in Figure 5.
3. **Anomaly detectors:** There are usually different types of anomaly detectors present in the smart card. These are used to detect unusual events in the voltage or clock supplied to the card. They also monitor the smart card's environment, for example, the temperature, so that the card remains within the range within which it functions correctly. When unusual conditions are detected the chip will cease to function until the effect has been removed (i.e., a reset or an infinite loop is initiated when the sensor is activated).

## SIDE CHANNEL ANALYSIS

Sensitive systems that are based on smart cards use well-studied and well-developed cryptosystems. Generally these cryptosystems have been subject to rigorous mathematical analysis in the effort to uncover weaknesses in the system. Therefore the cryptosystems used in smart cards are not usually vulnerable to these types of attacks. Because smart cards are small, physical objects that can actually be carried around in one's pocket, adversaries have turned to different mechanisms of attack. Side channel analysis is a class of attacks that seek to deduce

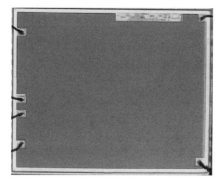 

**Figure 5:** A chip with an active shield present and removed. Removing a shield using hydrofluoric acid renders the chip nonfunctional but allows the layout to be determined.

information in a less direct manner by extracting secret information held inside the devices, such as smart cards, via the monitoring of information that leaks naturally during its operation. The main physical properties that side channel analysis targets are timing, power consumption, and electromagnetic emanations. Each of these forms of attack are detailed below.

## Timing Analysis

Timing analysis basically involves observing the amount of time it takes to calculate certain operations. By monitoring the length of time that a command operates on a piece of the data, deductions can be made about what data are actually being manipulated within the smart card. As the command is sent to the I/O pad, the time it takes is recorded with an oscilloscope. There are also some proprietary smart card readers that can record how many clock cycles a given command takes. Figure 6 shows the execution of the RSA signature command. The upper trace shows the I/O of the command. The lower trace

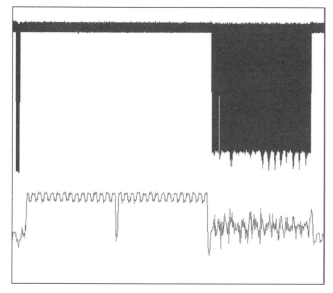

**Figure 6:** The execution of an RSA signature command. The upper trace is the I/O and the lower trace is the corresponding current consumption.

shows the corresponding current consumption. The APDU sent can be seen on the left with the response from the card on the right of the trace. Given the sampling frequency the number of clock cycles for the command can be calculated.

An attack of this type can be launched against against a command that will verify a PIN value. Although most PIN verifications have a counter that limits the number of times a false PIN can be entered, that will be ignored for the sake of this example. If we assume that the PIN is a four-decimal digit value, the amount of tries to search through all of the possible values of the PIN would take 10,000 commands. If the command is implemented in the most obvious fashion it will take the first digit of the presented PIN value and check this against the first digit of the actual PIN value, returning an error if they are different. This is then repeated with the second digit, the third digit, and then the fourth digit.

To find the first digit an attacker needs to try all 10 possible values for the first digit and record the time it took for the card to respond. The time corresponding to the correct value of the first digit will have a slightly larger time than those for which the first digit is incorrect. This is because the first digit will be evaluated as being correct so rather than exiting straight away the second digit will be evaluated before exiting. To find the PIN value under these conditions the attacker need to search through only 40 different values.

## Simple Power Analysis

The most basic form of power analysis known as simple power analysis (SPA) involves simply watching the power consumption via an oscilloscope and making deductions about secret data based on the observations. A widely known attack involves observing the execution of a modular exponentiation. The power traces observed can be used to aid in the derivation of the exponent used in the calculation. This technique can be applied to many algorithms, one of which is the RSA algorithm for signature generation. Figure 6 depicts an attack of this form on RSA. The lower trace shows the current consumption for the command performing modular exponentiation. This particular command is calculated using the Chinese remainder theorem (CRT), and here both exponentiations can be clearly seen.

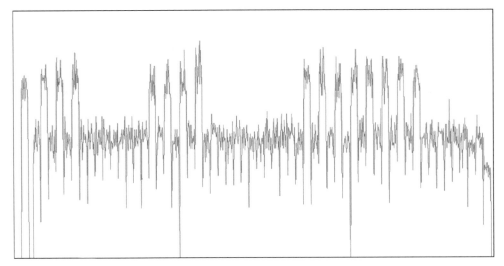

**Figure 7:** The current consumption of an unprotected RSA implemented using the square and multiply algorithm. It should be noted this is taken from old smart card and modern smart cards are unlikely to show such a marked difference.

A closer look at these exponentiations can potentially reveal more information on the secret data being manipulated. An example of the current consumption of a smart card during the execution of a modular exponentiation is shown in Figure 7.

Looking closely at the acquired data we can see a series of events in the current consumption. There are two types of event at two different current consumption levels each bounded by a short dip in the current consumption. This corresponds well with the simplest algorithm for calculating a modular exponentiation: the square and multiply algorithm. Where the key is read bit by bit, a 0 results in a square being performed on the message and a 1 gives a square followed by multiplication with the original message. Given the ratio of the two features we can assume that the feature with the lower power consumption represents the square and the higher power consumption represents the multiplication. From this the beginning of the exponent can be read from the current consumption; in this case the key used is F00F000FF00, which is expressed in hexadecimal.

This class of attacks can be extremely efficient, because only a single current consumption acquisition is required. However, this example presents the simplest possible algorithm for the RSA and it is performed on a chip that is used for demonstrating how this sort of attack works. Attacks conducted on modern smart cards are unlikely to reveal such a marked difference between a square and a multiple. A strong mathematical background and a great deal of experience is often required to make any headway as the algorithm used needs to be reverse engineered before the attack can be realized. In reality, algorithms used in modern smart cards are not susceptible to this sort of attack.

## Statistical Power Analysis

A more powerful form of power analysis attack is known as statistical power analysis [further subcategorized as differential power analysis (DPA) and correlation power analysis (CPA)]. In this attack the smart card is run many times with different inputs. For each input the corresponding power consumption is captured and statistical analysis is performed on the data gathered to infer information about the secret information held inside the card. These techniques require many more acquisitions than with simple power analysis and a certain amount of treatment a posteriori.

Statistical power analysis is a method of exploiting the slight differences in the power consumption of a smart card between different executions of the same commands. The first implementation of this type of attack is known as DPA (Kocher, Jaffe, & Jun, 1999). Statistical power attacks are based on the relationship between the current consumption of the hamming weight of the data manipulated at a particular point in time. The variation in current consumptions is extremely small and acquisitions cannot be interpreted individually as the information will be lost in noise added during the acquisition. The small differences produced can be seen in Figure 8.

Differential power analysis works by amplifying the differences in the current consumption, such as those visible in Figure 8. A bit that is manipulated by the chip will produce a slight difference in the current consumption of the chip that will not occur if it is not modified. If two average curves are produced (one where the bit is modified and one where it is not), the effect of the modified bit on the current consumption becomes visible in a fashion similar to that shown in Figure 9. A peak in this waveform will occur at the moment the bit used to divide the acquisitions into two sets was manipulated. This occurs because the rest of the data are assumed to be average and the difference between the two averages will tend to be zero.

Correlation power analysis (Brier, Clavier, & Olivier, 2003) attacks smart cards in a similar way to DPA. CPA uses the correlation between the current consumption

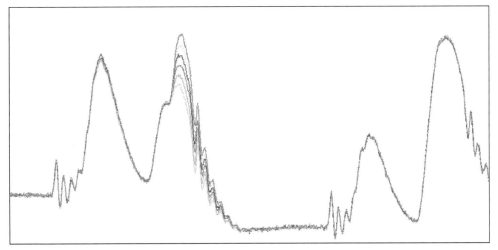

**Figure 8:** Overlaid acquisitions of the current consumption produced by the same instruction, but with varying data. The data-dependant part of these acquisitions can be seen toward the center of the image where the maximum current consumption varies considerably. The non-data-dependant part is almost identical from one acquisition to another. The difference in current consumption is not always as visible as in the above image.

and the machine word being manipulated at a given point in time. It is for this reason that it is more complete, as the assumption that all the data manipulated at a given time are random apart from the predicted bit made in DPA attacks does not always hold.

To calculate a correlation waveform a number of acquisitions of the current consumption are made during the execution of a given command. Assuming that all the acquisitions are synchronized, the correlation between the current consumption and a set of data is calculated for every point of the acquisition. This generates a waveform such as Figure 9, where we have the correlation

coefficient plotted against time. Where the correlation coefficient starts to approach 1 we can assume that the data manipulated by the chip at this point in time correspond to the set of data with which the correlation was calculated. If the set of data do not correspond with the data manipulated the correlation coefficient will stay close to 0.

Using this method we have a way of knowing when we have predicted what data are being manipulated by the smart card at a certain time. This sort of attack technique is generally used against secret key algorithms but there are numerous other situations where this method

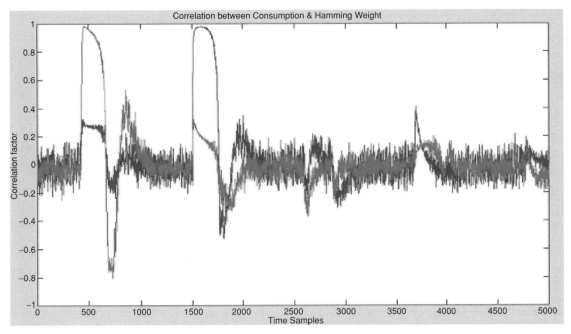

**Figure 9:** Two examples of correlation curves. The correlation approaches 1 where the series of data used to correlate with the current consumption corresponds to the data being manipulated by the smart card.

could be applicable, such as the reverse engineering of the structure of a command.

If, for example, the current consumption of a smart card is acquired during the first round of the AES algorithm, information can be deduced about the key being used. During the first round of the AES there will be an XOR with the first subkey (in fact the key itself from which the rest of the subkeys are derived) followed by the round functions (shift row, byte sub, and mix column). If we consider the first byte of the message we need concern ourselves only with the XOR of the first byte of the subkey and the byte subfunction. The shift row function is a bytewise permutation and will have no effect on our calculations.

So, for each byte we have the simple transformation, assuming the implementation is on an 8-bit chip architecture of a given byte ($x$) to its value after the byte subfunction ($y$) as follows:

$$y = S(x \oplus K)$$

where $K$ represents the relevant key byte. A series of acquisitions are carried out for each of the possible values of $x$, giving a series of current consumption waveforms, each with a corresponding value of $x$. The series of data $y$ is calculated for each of the possible values of $K$, giving us 256 different possible series of data for $y$.

The aim is to predict the output of the byte subfunction by taking into account all the possible values of $K$. A correlation waveform is calculated from the current consumption acquisitions and each of the possible series of $y$, producing 256 different correlation waveforms. Each point in a given correlation waveform will correspond to the correlation of the current consumption and the series of values of $y$ calculated at that specific time.

The correct series of values of $y$ will include some correlation peaks, consisting of values close to 1. The time at which these correlation peaks occur corresponds to where the data $y$ are manipulated during the command. This shows which value of $K$ has been used with the first byte of the message.

If this is repeated for each byte of the message fed into the algorithm the entire key can be deduced. Generally, the data acquisition will be large enough that it will include the whole of the first round so it is only the a posteriori processing that needs to be repeated.

As with simple power analysis this type of attack requires a strong mathematical background and experience in signal processing. The countermeasures that are present in modern smart cards are usually more than adequate to prevent the realization of these attacks. The countermeasures themselves are covered in more detail below.

## Electromagnetic Analysis

Electromagnetic analysis (Gandolfi, Mourtel, & Olivier, 2001) differs from power analysis only in the way which data are acquired. After this all the a posteriori treatment remains the same. The attacks described above for simple power analysis and statistical power analysis will function in the same manner for electromagnetic acquisitions as for current consumption acquisitions.

**Figure 10:**  Electromagnetic probing of a chip.

However, different things are possible via electromagnetic analysis as the probe is very small when compared to the size of the chip. This can be seen in Figure 10, where a probe is shown above an opened smart card chip. The probe is of an equivalent size to the chip's features, which can be seen as blocks on the chip's surface. This means that the probe can be placed just above a given feature to try and get a strong signal from this part of the chip (i.e., the cryptocoprocessor) during the generation of an RSA signature.

This technique can also be used to overcome some hardware countermeasures such as current scramblers. Unfortunately, it is much more complicated to realize, as the chip needs to be open as in Figure 10; otherwise the signal is not strong enough for any information to be deduced. The tools required to capture this information are also more complex as the current consumption can be measured by reading the potential difference over a resistor in series with the smart card. To measure the electromagnetic changes involves a suitable probe (the probe in Figure 10 is handmade) and amplifiers so that an oscilloscope can detect the signal.

## Countermeasures

The discussion of countermeasures has been left until the end of the section as the majority of the countermeasures used protect against more than one category of attack.

- **Constant time:** Code written on a smart card should execute with no variation in the amount of time it takes for a given command to execute, or at the very least not bear any relation to any secret data held within the card. This is to prevent timing attacks and some forms of simple power analysis, as it is difficult to see where data-dependent decisions take place.

- **Randomization:** Data manipulated by the smart card is often randomized in some way so that the data manipulated is hidden from an observer. This can take various forms depending on what is to be protected. The most frequently used example of this is that of masking data (XOR) with a random value and manipulating the masked data and the random in such a way that the XOR of the two values is the desired result. This means that the current consumption is at all times decorrelated with the data being manipulated in the secure algorithms. In the case of the RSA algorithm the parameters used can be randomized in such a way that the result is correct modulo $n$ but the exponent is not the secret key. This sort of countermeasure prevents side channel attacks as it removes the relationship between the current consumption and the data sent to the smart card.

- **Desynchronization:** This is the addition of code that serves no purpose other than to add random amounts of time to the command length. Their purpose is not to prevent timing attacks but to make it difficult to conduct a statistical power analysis. To produce such an attack all the acquisitions need to be synchronized where the correlation peak is expected. If the acquisitions are desynchronized with the others then it adds an extra nontrivial exercise to resynchronize all the acquisitions. This can be implemented in hardware or software. In hardware, this can be achieved by introducing clock cycles where the CPU does either nothing or something of no consequence at random points during the command. The second version being preferable as it disguises these events in the current consumption, making them harder to remove as they are harder to distinguish from the real code being executed. In software, loops of a random length can be added to various points to desynchronize the code. Delays in software are not as efficient as those implemented in hardware as they are larger and are therefore easier to remove.

Another method of introducing desynchronization is by using an unstable internal clock that desynchronizes the current consumption waveforms as shown in Figure 11.

It is usual to implement all of the above countermeasures so that it becomes a near impossible task to break the algorithm. It is possible to remove certain countermeasures but the combination of all of them will present a complex challenge.

## FAULT ANALYSIS

In recent years fault analysis has come to the foreground as a possible means of attacking devices such as smart cards. The vast majority of articles written on this subject discuss very specific faults (usually a bit-flip in a specific variable) that are extremely difficult to produce. However, there have been several attacks published that have enough freedom in the type of fault required that they can be realized with current fault injection methods.

### Injection Techniques

There are several ways to induce faults in smart cards that have been discussed in the literature (Anderson & Skoroboatov, 2002), the most frequently discussed being fault induction by light and glitches.

Inducing a fault with a light source involves opening the smart card to expose the surface of the chip. This means that a certain amount of equipment that is not generally available is required to carry out this sort of attack. Once the chip is open, a strong light source is used on a portion of the chip during the execution of the command under attack. Because of the photoelectric effect this may cause an unusual event inside the chip, changing its behavior. The advantage of this technique is that it is generic and will have some effect against all chips, except when detected by light sensors.

Creating a fault using a glitch involves finding a signal that can be sent to the card on one of the contacts that will produce an anomalous event in the card. Examples of this include raising the voltage of the reset contact slightly or reducing the voltage of the power supply given to the card over a short period of time. The advantage of using a glitch is that it is relatively simple and inexpensive to develop a tool for injecting a fault. However, a new glitch has to be found for each new chip and there is no guarantee that an exploitable glitch will be found.

It should also be noted that while these attacks work in theory, smart cards include sensors that are designed to detect when a chip is being attacked. This results in the chip resetting itself or becoming unresponsive until

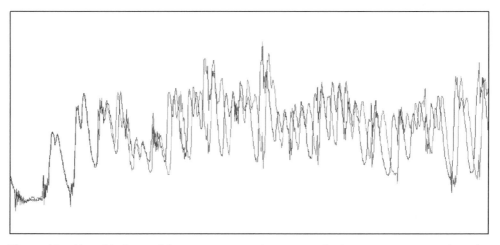

**Figure 11:** Unstable internal frequency generation as seen in the current consumption of a chip.

reset. If a fault induction method has an overly aggressive effect it can overstress the chip, rendering it nonfunctional and increasing the difficulty of attacks requiring a high degree of precision.

When a fault injection method is being researched the majority of attempts will either be detected by the card's sensors or have no visible effect. It is only occasionally that a fault will produce a detectable anomalous event. From this point it can take a lot of work to try and exploit this, which is often not possible.

Once a method of fault induction has been found, the implementation of attacks such as those described in the examples below become realizable. However, there do exist numerous fault attacks that require a much higher degree of precision, which will remain problematic unless a particular fault effect has been found.

There are attacks based on the perturbation of one specific opcode (one command word as interpreted by the chip processor) during the execution of sensitive code such as a cryptographic algorithm. These types of attacks are more difficult to carry out, as the moment in time where the opcode is executed can only be approximately located by SPA techniques. This means that often numerous attempts are made before the correct moment in time is found. Other types of attack present in the literature specify a control over the fault produced that cannot be achieved with the precision of current techniques, such as being able to temporarily complement a given bit in a given variable. If the effect of a fault is well understood, complex attacks can be designed around them but the effect has to be well understood.

## Attacking an Algorithm

The first published attack (DeMillo, Boneh, & Lipton, 1997) using fault attack techniques was against the RSA algorithm when implemented using the Chinese remainder theorem. This publication was purely theoretical and did not talk about how to implement these attacks against an actual system or device. It is, however, a relatively easy attack to implement once a method of fault induction is found because of the quantity of possible faults that will produce a usable result.

When the RSA algorithm is calculated in this manner, two modular exponentiations are calculated with some key elements, the results of which are referred to as $S_p$ and $S_q$ and are derived from the plaintext and the two large primes, $p$ and $q$, upon which the security of RSA reposes. The results of these two modular exponentiations are combined to produce the result ($S$). A summary of these calculations follows. A certain familiarity with the algorithm as specified in Rivest, Shamir, and Adleman (1978) is assumed.

The private key consists of two large primes ($p$ and $q$) from which the other key elements are calculated as follows:

$$D_q = d \bmod (q - 1)$$
$$D_p = d \bmod (p - 1)$$
$$I_q = q^{-1} \bmod p$$

where $d$ is the private key in the standard RSA algorithm. To calculate a signature using these elements two modular exponentiations are done with the message ($m$) in the following manner:

$$S_q = m^{D_q} \bmod q$$
$$S_p = m^{D_p} \bmod p$$

These two values are then combined to produce a signature using the formula

$$S = S_q + [([(S_p - S_q)]I_q \bmod p)] q$$

The advantage in doing this is that each modular exponentiation is half the size it would be if the Chinese remainder theorem were not used, leading to a significant gain in performance.

The attack consists of injecting a fault during the calculation of $S_p$ or $S_q$ to produce a different signature. If, for example, $S_q$ is changed to $S_p$ producing signature S′ then we obtain the following:

$$\gcd[(S - S'), n)] = \gcd[(a[(S - S')], n)] = q$$

This provides an extremely rapid method of deriving the prime numbers upon which the security of the algorithm is based. As stated above, once a method of fault injection is found this attack can be realized relatively easily. However, the fault itself is difficult to find and characterize so that such an attack can be carried out.

## Countermeasures

Fault attacks are a very powerful class of attacks once a method of fault injection has been found that can produce a known effect within the smart cards. Some countermeasures against such attacks are often present in smart card implementations for integrity purposes and just need to be extended to protect sensitive data.

- **Hardware sensors:** The best defense is high-quality sensors that can prevent undesired effects being produced within the chip. However, it is often considered prudent to include a certain level of software countermeasures in case new methods of fault injection are discovered. In the case of the smart card, sensors to detect variations in light, external clock, voltage, and temperature are often present to prevent undesired effects in the chip.

- **Checksums:** Sensitive data can be associated with checksum of a sufficient complexity that the probability that there is an undetected fault becomes negligible. This checksum can be verified every time the data is moved from one type of memory to another.

- **Redundancy:** A certain amount of redundancy is required in the code so that any fault that occurs will either be detected or have no effect on the program. This includes such things as having two variables to represent important values in memory and running an algorithm's inverse after it has been executed to verify no fault occurred. This countermeasure is especially pertinent when applied to the example attack given, as the inverse of the RSA signature generation algorithm does not take much time when compared to the length of the algorithm already executed.

# APPLICATION AND PROTOCOL SECURITY

Although smart card security is based on low-level security as discussed in previous sections, the whole system needs to be secure or the problem is merely displaced. The following sections detail some of the considerations that need to be made when designing a secure system based on smart cards and a more detailed look at the 3G standards for use in mobile networks. The 3G standards explicitly assume that smart cards implement countermeasures to prevent all currently known attacks against smart cards.

## General Smart Card Security

As with all secure systems the protocols and cryptographic primitives need to be secure. The same problems are present with a smart card–based system as any other secure protocol. The most well-known example of this was the use of the Comp128 authentication algorithm in the original GSM application. An attack was developed based on the structure of the substitution tables that enabled the key to be derived with several days of computation. This enabled cards to be cloned, which created some problems with fraud. If the clone was used in a foreign country the network could not detect its presence for several days, as it took a while for the billing information to get to the affected operator.

It is possible to implement anything imaginable (memory permitting) on a smart card but the calculation speed can be a limiting factor. A smart card will accept a clock of between 1 and 5 MHz and has a slow communication protocol and should therefore not be used for time critical processes unless security is required. To counteract this problem many chip manufacturers are offering chips with faster internal clocks. Coupled with the fact that the use of 16- and 32-bit architectures is becoming more common, the smart cards' processing power is steadily increasing. In the future it will be possible to have more and more complex processes. A demonstration of this was given at Cartes 2003 (Cryptomotion, 2003), where a card was presented by Gemplus capable of deciphering a music CD in real time based on a chip with a fast internal clock. A proprietary communication protocol was also used as the existing standard protocols are slow.

The communication between a smart card and a reader can be spied on relatively easily. Tools for logging and modifying the communication between the two entities are available via the Internet (Season 2 interface, 2004) and were developed to attack television systems. For this reason the communication between the smart card and its host should be viewed as insecure and the protocol designed accordingly. Some standards, such as the global platform (Global Platfom, 2004), allow for a secure channel to be created between the card and the computer piloting the reader to prevent this sort of spying from taking place.

When sensitive data are being manipulated a smart card needs to have a suitable backup mechanism that will ensure that the data are changed correctly. Smart cards are totally dependent on their environment to provide a clock and a power supply that can be removed at any time. In old implementations it was sometimes possible to prevent the smart card from updating the EEPROM, which can cause security problems when updating PIN counters, for example. A system needs to be in place whereby the EEPROM will be updated after a reset if the power supply is interrupted. If an EEPROM write is interrupted, the data being written may be in an invalid state. This is done by backing up data, modifying it and then validating the modification. To prevent this mechanism from causing problems during the normal functioning of a card, mechanisms also need to be in place that are able to return to a normal state (i.e., if a transaction is left unfinished the smart card will need to be able to return to the state it was in before the transaction started). This is to prevent the card becoming useless as otherwise it may be waiting for commands to finish the current transaction and not respond correctly to the normal command set. This process is termed *rollback*.

There are new developments that can change the security considerations in smart card–based applications. In Praca and Barral (2001) various additions to the smart card are proposed to help alleviate some of the security problems present with smart cards. Most of the ideas that would dramatically increase the cost of making them and so such complicated smart cards have thus far not been produced. One of the ideas presented was to have a screen embedded in the smart card that would display the balance on an electronic purse or show the amount being charged to the card. Currently when a transaction takes place it would be feasible to display an incorrect amount to the user so that the user authorizes the transaction but charges a different amount to the card. A display would prevent this from happening as the card would be able to confirm the amount being asked. Other ideas include integrating power sources and biometric sensors that, although potentially useful, have yet to become part of a product.

A fairly recent product (SUMO, 2002) that is a continuation of Pinocchio, mentioned in Praca and Barral (2001), has been produced that is able to store a very large amount of information. Numerous flash memories were embedded in a plastic card body that allowed a memory of 224 Mb to be achieved. This creates some new practical and security problems. A proprietary protocol needs to be used to allow for the amount of data that will be traveling between the reader and the smart card. If the information is not going to be freely available the flash memory needs to be protected so that dumping the flash memories does not reveal its contents.

This highlights some of the security considerations that need to be taken into account when designing a secure system based on smart cards. The points mentioned are by no means exhaustive. The interested reader is referred to Rankl and Effing (2002) for a more complete and in-depth discussion of the issues of application and protocol security with regard to smart cards.

## 3G Network Security

At the end of 1998 several working groups were launched to specify the security of the 3G system. The aim was to

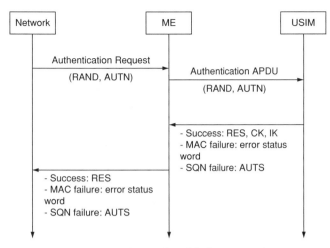

**Figure 12:** The 3G handshake protocol.

provide a replacement for the existing GSM network protocols (referred to as 2G). Most of documents issued by these workgroups are available online at the 3GPP Web site (3GPP, 2004).

In a 3G network, mutual authentication is performed (i.e., both user and network have to authenticate to each other). This is the most sensitive operation in a 3G network as it identifies the client for billing purposes. To initiate an authentication handshake, two values are sent by the network (the operator) to the USIM (the smart card supporting the 3G standards, equivalent to the SIM used in 2G networks). This consists of a random 128-bit random number (RAND) and an authentication number (AUTN). Figure 12 presents a summary of this handshake protocol. The USIM will take the values supplied by the network and calculate a response (RES) and some session keys (CK and IK) that are passed back to the mobile equipment (ME) and the network. These values depend on a 128-bit key that is stored in the USIM and is known by the network. The response will also state whether the USIM has authenticated the network based on information in the AUTN value. The network will then check that the value for RES is the correct value for the USIM that it is addressing.

The calculation of the RES value is done using an algorithm based on the AES (FIPS-197) called Milenage, although operators are free to replace this with a proprietary algorithm. The specification for this algorithm is also available on the 3GPP Web site. This represents a complete change in philosophy when compared to the 2G

algorithms that are still kept secret. The reason behind this is that Comp128 (used in 2G networks to authenticate the client) was a secret proprietary algorithm that was eventually broken, which has left many network operators wary of trusting proprietary algorithms. Milenage can be customized by each operator so that it is possible for each operator to derive a different version of the algorithm. For security reasons, the manner in which the algorithm can be modified is defined in the 3GPP technical report on the algorithm.

Figure 13 shows the structure of the AUTN value sent by the network that contains the sequence number (SQN, XOR-enciphered with the anonymity key AK), the 2-byte authentication management field (AMF), and the 8-byte MAC field. These data are used by the USIM to authenticate the network as presented in Figure 12.

The AMF field contains some information that can be used by the USIM but is not involved in the security of the protocol and is therefore not discussed here. The MAC value is verified by the USIM to verify the authenticity and the integrity of the RAND value. The algorithm for generating this depends on the values of RAND, SQN, and the secret key held in the USIM. This makes it difficult to make the card think it is communicating with a network unless the secret key is known. The SQN value is a sequence number that prevents message sequences being replayed as the card will return an error unless a new SQN value is presented, and that varies according to parameters determined by the network operator. Again, the algorithm for deriving this value is reliant on the secret key held in the smart card, which makes it difficult to forge. This is important, as the anonymity key (AK) is optional.

After authentication algorithm has taken place the session keys (CK and IK) are used to encipher the communication using an algorithm based on Kasumi. This algorithm is also available in the 3GPP specifications. This algorithm is implemented in the mobile device as it is not necessary to secure the session keys in the same way as for the fixed secret key that identifies the client. The session keys constantly change and are therefore of use only for a very short period of time.

The 3G standards also specify that the smart card implementations of the Milenage algorithm must be resistant to side channel analysis such as SPA or DPA. If an attacker succeeds in retrieving the client's key, he or she might be able to produce a clone of the client's card that can then be used to make phone calls at the expense of that client.

In this protocol the smart card provides a secure means of storing the client's secret key to prevent fraud (i.e., the client is authenticated by the network for billing purposes). Mobile devices are not currently considered secure and until this is achieved it would not be wise to store sensitive information in them. A second, purely practical, reason also exists. Smart cards provide a mechanism of personalizing mobile devices that is totally under the control of the network operator. This means that subscribers can be provided with mobile devices made in the same factory but that are made individual by smart cards owned and managed by the operator.

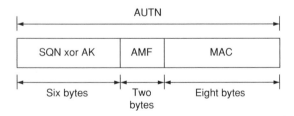

**Figure 13:** The authentication data sent to the USIM by the network.

# OTHER USES

A smart card can be used as a secure token in many other ways. The previous example is given because the mobile phone smart card application is familiar to everyone.

Other implementations include the OYSTER (OYSTER, 2004) system used in the London Underground to replace tickets. This is a contactless smart card that is able to hold details of a client's season tickets and pre-paid fares. This is most likely a smart card based on a MIFARE chip, where different keys are needed to read or write to various memory locations (i.e., essentially a contactless memory card). The communication between the card and the reader is also enciphered to prevent replay attacks.

Another common use of smart cards is in bankcards to provide a higher level of security than is available with just a magnetic strip. The most widely used standard for bankcards is EMV (EMVCo, 2004), which provides a worldwide standard for smart card payment systems. Each card contains a certificate that is used to prove that the payment was made with a given card. The card is also able to assess the risk of any given situation, following a set of rules determined by the bank in question to determine whether certain types of payment are permitted. For example, only a certain number of offline payments are permitted before the card will insist that the payment be made online to have the bank's authorization, the aim being to minimize the loss in the case of a stolen card as the bank will be able to tell the card to stop functioning once the transaction is online.

# SECURITY EVALUATION

Evaluation standards have been developed to guarantee a certain level of security and to provide a method of comparing the security of one product with that of another. There are two main standards that exist to evaluate the security of a given product: Common Criteria (CC) and the Federal Information Processing Standard (FIPS).

## Common Criteria

Common Criteria was created to ensure that an evaluation standard existed that fulfills the needs of consumers, sponsors, developers, the evaluation laboratory (Information Technology Security Evaluation Facility, ITSEF), and the certification body. The product, or component, subject to evaluation is usually named the TOE, which stands for target of evaluation. Several documents specify the TOE security environment (i.e., the security aspects of the environment in which the TOE is expected to be used). Such documents should include three items:

1. A description of threats to the assets against which specific protection within the TOE or the environment is required.
2. A description of assumptions: security aspects of the environment in which the TOE will be used or is intended to be used.
3. A description of organizational security policies: security policy rules with which the TOE must comply.

The evaluation assurance level (EAL) provides an increasing scale that balances the level of assurance obtained with the cost and feasibility of acquiring that degree of assurance. The different possible levels of EAL are given in the Common Criteria security assurance requirements (CCIMB-99-033, 1999). Each EAL level gives a different security level as more and more different elements are included in the evaluation.

The first certification recognition agreement was the Senior Official Group for Information Security of the European Commission. Twelve Europeans countries signed this agreement in March 1998. Six countries, France, Germany, Australia and New Zealand, Canada, the United States, and the United Kingdom, signed a new agreement, the Mutual Recognition Agreement, in October 1998 that covers Common Criteria Certificates from EAL1 to EAL4. This means that in these countries a certificate for a product rated EAL1 to EAL4 will be valid in all the others; a certificate of a higher level than 4 is considered to be equivalent to EAL4. These certificates are used as a means of ranking products with regard to security.

## FIPS 140-2

The FIPS 140-2 is an American standard that specifies the security requirements that will be satisfied by a cryptographic module used within a security system protecting sensitive but unclassified information. Four increasing, qualitative levels of security, which cover a wide range of potential applications and environments in which cryptographic modules may be employed, are provided. The security requirements are related to the secure design and implementation of the cryptographic module and include the following:

- cryptographic module specifications,
- cryptographic module ports and interfaces,
- roles, services, and authentication,
- finite state model,
- physical security,
- operational environment,
- cryptographic key management,
- electromagnetic interference and electromagnetic compatibility (EMI/EMC),
- self-tests,
- design assurance, and
- mitigation of others attacks.

To validate FIPS 140-2 and other cryptographic standards, the National Institute of Standards and Technologies (NIST) and the Communications Security Establishment (CSE) of the Canadian government created the Cryptographic Module Validation Program (CMVP). The goal of the CMVP is to promote the use of validated cryptographic modules and provide federal agencies with a security metric to use in procuring equipment containing validated cryptographic modules. The module's validation is performed by independent, accredited testing laboratories.

# CONCLUSION

Various different attacks against smart cards with their corresponding countermeasures have been described. It is normal to implement all of the countermeasures described, which makes it exceedingly difficult to implement these attacks on all but the oldest of smart cards. A high degree of knowledge is required in a multitude of domains (e.g., electronics, mathematics, silicon technology, and protocols) and it is unusual to find someone with sufficient knowledge to design and implement these attacks on their own. It generally requires a well-funded team to realize the majority of the attacks presented and the current state of the art in countermeasures is making even this extremely difficult. The design of new attacks and countermeasures is a field of ongoing research to make sure that such attacks are not possible outside of the smart card industry.

A smart card can provide a high level of security but it is not necessarily a trivial solution to a given security problem. Care needs to be taken to make sure that it is properly integrated. The security issues presented cover the hardware and signal/protocol levels of smart cards as well as application-level issues. The reader is encouraged to consult other sources such as Rankl and Effing (2002) for a more complete description.

One of the current areas of research in the smart card industry is that of the Java card, which has only been briefly mentioned in this chapter. The Java card standard (Java Card Specifications, 2004) provides a system where applets can be loaded onto the smart card and each one is executed separately as an application. The security of each application rests on the security of the lower levels (i.e., the functions called by the virtual machine that interprets the applet). The presence of different Java card applets raises new issues. For example, if two applets are present the card's resources need to be shared securely (e.g., making sure that one applet cannot read or manipulate the data of another applet). The virtual machine also needs to be secured against the loading of potentially hostile applets so that any attempts to directly access the card's resources can be prevented. A great deal of research is also devoted to making these cards efficient, as implementing a virtual machine adds to the load on the processor, slowing down the computation speed. These are just a couple of examples to show the sort of problems that can arise, as a thorough discussion of the Java card is beyond the scope of this chapter.

# GLOSSARY

**Chinese Remainder Theorem**   A method of speeding up the RSA signature scheme.
**Ciphertext**   In cryptography, this is the result of encoding a plaintext message.
**Complementary Metal Oxide Semiconductor (CMOS)** An electronic gate formed by joining a positive MOS and a negative MOS transistor together in a complementary fashion. This is the prevalent technology in microelectronic circuit design.
**Electrically Erasable and Programmable Memory**   A rewritable memory technology that will maintain its

state without any power. An EEPROM cell can be updated 10,000–100,000 times.
**External Clock**   The clock signal provided to a device from the exterior used to govern the speed of the device and/or synchronize communication protocols.
**FIPS Approved**   NIST cryptographic standards are specified in Federal Information Processing Standards publications. The term *FIPS approved* indicates something that is either specified in a FIPS or adopted in a FIPS and specified either in an appendix to the FIPS or in a document referenced by the FIPS.
**Internal Clock**   The clock generated within a device to render it independent of an external clock.
**Linear Feedback Shift Register**   A register where bits are shifted and XOR ed with each other to create a value that will change with each clock cycle. For a register of size $n$ the same value will reappear after $2^n$ updates after having passed through every other possible value. Used as pseudorandom number generators.
**Metal Oxide Semiconductor (MOS)**   A polycrystalline silicon gate over silicon dioxide. A positive MOS (PMOS) gate is a transistor where a positive voltage on the gate will turn the transistor on, a negative voltage will turn the transistor off. A negative MOS (NMOS) gate is the inverse.
**Personal Identification Number**   A four-digit number commonly used in smart cards to authenticate a user.
**Plaintext**   In cryptography, this is the original message before it has been encoded.
**Private Key**   One of the pair of keys used in public key encryption.
**Public Key**   One of the pair of keys used in public key encryption.
**Public Key Cryptography**   A cryptographic technique that uses two different keys, a public key and a private key.
**Secret Key**   The key that is shared between two parties in secret key encryption.
**Secret Key Cryptography**   A cryptographic technique that uses a single key for both encryption and decryption.
**Subscriber Identity Module**   A small smart card that contains a subscriber's identity key allowing them to securely authenticate with a mobile network. Most commonly used in GSM networks.

# CROSS REFERENCES

See *Cryptographic Hardware Security Modules; Fault Attacks; Physical Security Measures; Physical Security Threats; Side-Channel Attacks; The Common Criteria.*

# REFERENCES

3GPP. (2004). *3GPP specifications*. Retrieved November 24, 2004, from http://www.3gpp.org/ftp/Specs/html-info/TSG-WG–S3.htm
Anderson, R., & Skoroboatov, S. (2002). Optical fault induction attacks. In S. B. Kaliski, Jr, Ç. K. Koç, D. Naccache, & C. Paar (Eds.), *Lecture notes in computer science, vol. 2423: Cryptographic hardware and embedded systems* (pp. 2–12). New York: Springer-Verlag.

Brier, E., Clavier, C., & Olivier, F. (2004). *Lecture notes in computer science, vol. 3156: Cryptogaphic hardware and embedded systems-CHES 2004* (pp. 16–29). New York: Springer-Verlag.

CCIMB-99-033 (1999). Common Criteria part 3: Security assurance requirements. Retrieved November 24, 2004, from http://www.commoncriteriaportal.org/public/files/ccpart3v21.pdf

Cryptomotion. (2003). *Review*. Retrieved November 24, 2004, from http://www.prnewswire.co.uk/cgi/news/release?id=112260

DeMillo, R. A., Boneh, D., & Lipton, R. J. (1997). On the importance of checking computations. In W. Fumy (Ed.), *Lecture notes in computer science, vol. 1233: Proceedings of EUROCRYPT '97* (pp. 37–55). New York: Springer-Verlag.

Dhem, J.-F., & Feyt, N. (2001, November–December). Hardware and software symbosis helps smart card evolution. *IEEE Micro, 21*(6), pp. 14–25.

EMVCo. (2004). *Homepage*. Retrieved November 24, 2004, from http://www.emvco.com/

Federal Information Processing Standards 197. (2001). Advanced Encryption Standard (AES). *FIPS publication 197*. Retrieved November 24, 2004, from http://csrc.nist.gov/publications/fips/fips197/fips-197.pdf

Federal Information Processing Standards 46-3. (1999). Data Encryption Standard (DES). *FIPS publication 46-3*. Retrieved November 24, 2004, from http://csrc.nist.gov/publications/fips/fips46-3/fips46-3.pdf

Gandolfi, K., Mourtel, C., & Olivier, F. (2001). Electromagnetic analysis: Concrete results. In Ç. K. Koç, D. Naccache, & C. Paar (Eds.), *Lecture notes in computer science, vol. 2162: Cryptographic hardware and embedded systems-CHES 2001* (pp. 251–261). New York: Springer-Verlag.

Global Platfom. (2004). *Homepage*. Retrieved November 24, 2004, from http://www.globalplatform.org

Java Card Specifications. (2004). *Homepage*. Retrieved November 24, 2004, from http://java.sun.com/products/javacard/index.html

Kocher, P., Jaffe, J., & Jun, B. (1999). Differential power analysis. In M. Wiener (ed.), *Lecture notes in computer science, vol. 1666: Advances in cryptology, Proceedings of CRYPTO '99* (pp. 388–397). New York: Springer-Verlag.

MIFARE. (2004). *Homepage*. Retrieved November 24, 2004, from http://www.mifare.net

OYSTER. (2004). *Homepage*. Retrieved November 24, 2004, from http://tube.tfl.gov.uk/content/tickets/oyster.asp

Praca, D., & Barral, C. (2001). From smart cards to smart objects: The road to new smart card technologies. *Computer Networks, 36*(4), 381–389.

Rankl, W., & Effing, W. (2002). *Smart card handbook* (2nd ed.). New York: John Wiley & Sons.

Rivest, R. L., Shamir, A., & Adleman, L. M. (1978). Method for obtaining digital signatures and public-key cryptosystems. *Communications of the ACM, 21*(2), 120–126.

Season 2 Interface. (2000). Retrieved November 24, 2004, from http://www.maxking.co.uk/season2.htm

SUMO. (2002). Retrieved November 24, 2004, from http://www.computerweekly.com/Articles/2002/04/16/186504/Sumosmartcardtohandleheavyappsload.htm

# Client-Side Security

Charles Border, *Rochester Institute of Technology*

## INTRODUCTION

Although large organizations spend millions of dollars every year to secure the periphery of their networks through the use of firewalls, a technological solution that controls the actions of insiders has thus far proved elusive. According to Thompson and Ford (2004), "The issue is trust. Insiders must be trusted to do their jobs; applications must be trusted to perform their tasks. The problem occurs when insiders—be they users or applications—intentionally, or unintentionally, extend trust inappropriately." Client-side security involves finding ways to control the ability of insiders to extend the trust relationship that they acquire as insiders in ways that are detrimental to the overall security of the network. Because a wholly technological solution has remained beyond the reach of developers, managers of both information technology professionals and other employees must work together to develop a solution that involves not only technology but also improving user awareness through policies, procedures, and user education.

Client-side security is a particularly important topic now. Many of the most damaging attacks to hit organizational networks have succeeded based on the exploitation of attack vectors that circumvent firewalls placed on the periphery of networks. Malicious code arrives either as attachments to routine e-mail messages or by being released inside the periphery of protected networks by infected laptop computers or mobile devices. It is particularly difficult to apply a technological solution to these types of attack vectors because they rely on the assistance of naïve or malicious users with direct access to the inside of organizational networks.

Although technology can be our most valuable aid to secure networks from many attacks, managerial solutions such as the promulgation of acceptable use policies and user education programs can be the most effective solution to these types of attacks.

This chapter provides a rationale for maintaining the security of client computers and outlines some of the most important precautions that can be taken to protect networks from attacks based on exploitation of insecure clients. This is accomplished first by discussing some of the characteristics of recent client-based attacks followed by a discussion of the relevant characteristics of clients and how this affects the techniques that must be used to protect them. Securing clients on an organizational network from attack involves tools and techniques that can be grouped in four areas:

- *Deployment*. The deployment of known and well-understood operating systems and applications in a managed and secure fashion
- *Management*. Management and maintenance of the currency of applications and operating systems through the secure and organized deployment of patches and updates to organizational computing resources
- *Monitoring*. The development and implementation of tools and techniques to monitor application and resource use to ensure that the consistency of configuration and exposure to vulnerability are within organizational guidelines
- *Improving user awareness*. Making users aware of their rights and responsibilities as they relate to the security of the network

Securing the client side of a network involves more than securing all the operating systems on all the clients on that network. The goal of a client-side security program is a general hardening of the interior of a network that, when combined with a strong perimeter, is part of a layered approach to overall network security. Client-side security is a process that involves the entire life cycle of network resources.

Many of the tools and techniques mentioned in this chapter are more thoroughly discussed in other chapters of this book. When possible, this chapter contains cross-references to both other chapters and Web sites that the reader might find useful.

## WHY WORRY ABOUT THE SECURITY OF CLIENTS?

According to the F-Secure Corporation (2004), on January 25, 2003, around 4:31 UTC, the importance of controlling the configuration of clients on large organizational networks was driven home by the onset of the Slammer worm. The Slammer worm exploited a vulnerability in a common component in many Microsoft products, the Microsoft Desktop Engine (MSDE), which caused compromised clients to put all their considerable resources to work trying to contact other MSDE engines. The resulting surge in traffic was the biggest attack up to that date and spread around the globe in about 15 minutes. The net result of this surge in traffic was a denial of service that slowed down Internet-based communications worldwide. The reason this attack was so problematic had nothing to do with the attack itself; rather, that it affected far more machines than most administrators expected it to affect was of significance. Most administrators knew and in many cases had patched the most important of the SQL Server servers (the most well known of the MSDE-based applications) on their networks. (A patch had been available for 26 days.) But the small clients, desktop and laptop computers—the configuration of which administrators had long ago lost control of— brought down many networks. In an era of trusting the security of a network to server-side security and controlling the perimeter through firewalling, this attack forced administrators to rethink their previous strategies and to attempt to regain control of the configuration of clients.

The basic techniques used to maintain the security of a large network of clients and servers are not very different from those used to maintain strictly server-side security. Client-side security is not about technical revolutions; it is about cultural revolutions. It requires the same thinking that goes into securing servers against crackers applied to securing clients, with one huge exception. When maintaining the security of servers from attack, we have three important assets on our side: a relatively small number of hosts to worry about, a better trained user at the console, and a tradition of concern to fall back on. This is not the case with client-side security. The main difference between server-side security and client-side security is that when we attempt to secure clients from attack, we must attempt to deal with our history of relations with the users at the keyboard. An educated and responsible user community is our best and last hope for securing our networks from client-based attacks. And it is here where our collective history of neglecting user concerns and not investing in user training comes home to roost.

## RFC 2196 *Site Security Handbook*

Before an effective client-side security plan can be developed, some very basic and very fundamental questions need to be addressed. These questions relate primarily to the role of information in the organization and the types of security exposures that are most relevant for a given network. RFC 2196 edited by B. Fraser (1997) from the Internet Engineering Task Force (IETF) outlines the following as the more important questions that must be addressed in a site security handbook.

1. *Identify what you are trying to protect.* Client-side security is primarily about protecting the ability of users to use technology to accomplish their jobs. Users who must stop working while a virus is being cleaned off their computer or a group of users who are unable to access a server because a workstation in their workgroup is infected with a virus are not able to do their jobs, and the huge investment their organization has made in technology is not returning anything to the organization. Users who lose all the important files on their computer and do not have backup copies might have permanently damaged their careers. As organizations integrate technology more closely into their business process, the ability of users to access technology becomes crucial for them to do their jobs and for the organization as a whole to accomplish its goals and objectives.

2. *Determine what you are trying to protect it from.* Client-side security has many aspects. You might be trying to protect users of the network from the malicious attempts of others within or outside the organization to access personal or sensitive files. You also might be trying to protect users from a virus that they might unknowingly download from malicious Web sites. Although these are two very different goals, they are not mutually exclusive and are both part of a comprehensive client-side security program.

3. *Determine how likely the threats are.* Information technology (IT) managers and security administrators must be cognizant of both technical and societal indicators that might have a bearing on the likelihood of an attack. Threats to an organizational network can originate from either inside or outside the network. The likelihood of malicious outsiders targeting your organization for exploitation can have more to do with random chance, or the perceptions of activists on the other side of the globe, than it does with anything you can control. Some of the factors that should be included in the process of identifying the likelihood of attacks from outsiders include the organization's current level of security, the ease with which the organization has been attacked in the past, the type of transactions for which the organization uses the Internet (information only versus online transactions), and the history of the organization's involvement in activities that might be considered controversial by the hacking community.

Threats from users inside an organization can be either malicious or accidental in nature and far more damaging in extent. Insider users are granted much more access to organizational resources and have a better understanding of the role of specific information sources in the organization. IT managers and security administrators must be cognizant of the relationship between the organization and its insiders and the effect that any changes might have on the motivation of insiders either to damage information resources maliciously or accidentally.

For detailed information on this topic, please consult Chapter 81, Hackers, Crackers, and Computer Criminals, and Chapter 82, Hacktivism.

4. *Implement measures that will protect your assets in a cost-effective manner.* A balance must be found between the cost of protecting information assets and the value of those assets to the organization. This balance must be informed by a thorough understanding of the role of information technology in the organization and the public's perception of the organization.

5. *Review the process continuously and make improvements each time a weakness is found.* The current

paradigm for client-side security is a continual battle between malicious crackers and system administrators. The results of the battle thus far have been a draw, with system administrators frantically blocking ports and upgrading software and crackers honing their techniques in search of the elusive zero-day attack (an attack on a vulnerability that has not previously been realized). This paradigm requires that system administrators continuously review the processes by which they secure their networks and continuously improve those processes that are found lacking.

## TYPES OF ATTACKS

Before you can gain an adequate understanding of how to secure clients from attack, you need to have a conceptual understanding of the different types of attacks that might be executed.

In the most general terms, the goal of any client-side security program is to protect client computers from being used as the platform for launching two general types of attacks: those that attempt to gain inappropriate access to resources located directly on the local host and those that attempt to use the trust relationship of the local host to attack other resources either within or outside the network. When we look at the security architecture common to most networks, the two most relevant design elements we see are a reliance on securing the network by securing the perimeter through the use of firewalls at all points of connection with the Internet, and the reliance on the idea that requests for resources originating from within the network can be trusted more than requests for resources originating from outside the network (see Figure 1). This architecture falls apart in the face of attacks that either originate on the inside from a malicious user or are released on the inside of the network by a naïve user who uses a mobile computing device as both an office workstation during the day and a home workstation in the evening.

## HOW CAN CRACKERS ACCOMPLISH THEIR GOALS?

The technique that crackers rely on revolves around finding a way to escalate the permissions at which their processes are run. This can be accomplished in only two ways: either users of trusted computers are somehow induced to extend the trust relationship they have as insiders to a cracker's program by running that program, or the cracker exploits software vulnerabilities that exist in the operating system or application software on the computer to do

other things. John Pescatore (2003) of the Gartner Group has developed what he refers to as "a taxonomy of software vulnerabilities" that divides vulnerabilities into two broad groups and two subcategories:

1. *Software defects*.
   a. *Coding flaws*. Vulnerabilities can be incorporated into well-designed programs through the accidental inclusion of coding mistakes.
   b. *Design flaws*. Vulnerabilities can be designed into applications as the applications iterate through the design process.
2. *Configuration errors*.
   a. *Dangerous/unnecessary services*. Ease of administration and security can come into conflict and result in the deployment of additional services that then can be used as part of an exploit.
   b. *Access administration errors*. Although the deployment of permission structures sounds like a simplistic operation, it can become very complex as the size of a user community grows in both geographic and temporal diversity.

Protecting client computers from these two groups of software vulnerabilities requires two very different approaches. Software defects are very difficult for individual users to find out about and hence to protect themselves from. Commercially developed and open-source software is conventionally tested for usability long before it is released to the general public. The problem with the software defects that crackers exploit is that such defects do not affect the general use of the software (those defects are usually caught in testing). They involve the internal workings of the software with which users seldom if ever interact. From the user's perspective, the software appears to work fine, in spite of the presence of design or coding flaws.

Configuration errors are much more common and potentially much more dangerous because they provide a means for the normal operating procedures of the computer to be turned against the user or organization. One reason configuration errors are common revolves around the conflict between the incentives developers have to make their software as flexible as possible as soon as it is installed and the needs of system administrators for a secure deployment. This leads to an initial installed configuration that has more available services running than is strictly necessary—exactly the wrong scenario for a secure configuration. (The ideal for a secure configuration is that only those services required for users to accomplish their specific jobs be running at any given time.)

## CLASSES OF CLIENTS

One of the more recent trends that makes securing all clients more important is the growing number of always-on connections to the Internet. Always-on connections are provided as part of an organizational network, a Small Office/Home Office (SOHO) setup, or a home computer connected to the Internet through a high-speed cable modem or Digital Subscriber Line (DSL). The first class of client computers that must be secured encompasses those

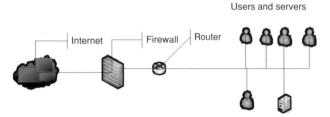

**Figure 1:** Common network architecture.

that are physically connected to the Internet through their connection to a parent organization network. As members of a larger network, they are nominally protected from attack by firewall devices located at the perimeter of the network, and, more important, they are protected by having access to a group of IT personnel who are responsible for seeing that the client operating systems and application software are kept up-to-date and can be relied on to intervene when problems arise.

The second class of clients are those that are owned by individuals and are used to connect SOHO computers directly to the Internet through DSL or cable modem systems. In the past, most of these computers connected to the Internet through an Internet service provider (ISP) by using dial-up modems and actively disconnected when the connection was no longer needed so that the phone line could be used for voice connections. When these computers connect to the Internet through DSL or cable modems, they are frequently left on and are connected to the Internet all the time. According to a study by the National Cyber Security Alliance by America Online, Inc., the owners of these always-on computers are not well educated about the perils of viruses and worms and do little to prevent their computers from becoming vehicles for attacking others computers. "The vast majority of subjects (86%) said they felt their computer was very or somewhat safe from online threats, however only 11% had a safe broadband connection—with a properly and safely configured firewall, recently upgraded anti-virus protection, and, if children were present in the household, parental controls" (National Cyber Security Alliance, 2003, p. 4). This class of computers presents a very different set of problems when it comes to client security. The reason relates to the lack of support users have from any IT personnel.

Although securing SOHO-based computers from exploitation by crackers might seem irrelevant to an organizational client-side security program, this is not the case for two very important reasons: many of the computers that connect to the Internet through unfiltered DSL or cable modem connections are in reality laptops owned by large organizations that are brought home at night by members of the organization, or they are exploited as e-mail relay agents to generate spam, which then floods organizational e-mail systems.

# ACTIVE CONTENT AND CLIENT-SIDE SECURITY

Much of what is considered cool on the Internet is a new class of content called *active content*. Active content consists of small applications or applets that users actively download from Web sites or that are downloaded automatically when a Web site is first accessed. These small applications then generate dancing hippos (for example) by running a small program on the client computer rather than on the server that provides the content. The problem with active content is that users have little if any idea what the active content actually will do before they run these applications or programs. The only effective security that exists between the client computer and the arbitrary application developed by someone the user doesn't know and

whose code the user has not evaluated in any fashion is that provided by the security settings of the browser in which the processes will execute or the language in which the application is written.

Rolf Oppliger (2003) of eSECURITY.com has developed a list of the types of active content that are designed to interact with client workstations: binary mail attachments, helper applications and plug-ins, scripting languages, Java applets, and ActiveX controls. He points out that one of the most dangerous things that a user can do on a networked computer is download an unknown piece of software and execute it locally. Most operating system software places little restraint on an authenticated user's ability to execute programs. Although this is the desired situation in most circumstances (it enables users to run the applications they need to do their jobs), when users download and execute programs from unknown sources, they are placing themselves, and all the systems that they are attached to them by their network, in the hands of a stranger.

For detailed information on this topic, please consult Volume III, Part 1 of this handbook: Threats and Vulnerabilities to Information and Computing Infrastructures. Also, see chapter 145, Computer Viruses and Worms, chapter 146, Trojan Horse Programs, chapter 148, Hostile Java Applets, and chapter 149, Spyware.

## Binary Mail Attachments

It has become standard procedure for users to rely on e-mail attachments to send small programs to friends and coworkers over the Internet. These programs are usually attached to ordinary e-mail messages and enter the destination network as binary files. These binary files can be images or formatted text messages, and they can be based on the multipurpose Internet mail extension (MIME) standard or be basically anything the sender wants to attach. The problem is that hackers can send executable files that, when clicked by the recipient, automatically execute with the same rights as the recipient. In effect, recipients are then running a program whose source they may or may not know and whose purpose and the ways in which it interacts with the client workstation and others on the users' network are not understood. For some time, this has been one of the main means of transmitting Trojan horse viruses. Browsers and e-mail clients can easily be configured to open a message box asking the user for confirmation to run the file instead of automatically executing files like this, but many users have determined for themselves that the convenience of automatic execution outweighs the potential risk. Although many users have received extensive instruction not to execute attachments sent to them from unknown sources, the trick for the hacker is to find a way to increase the probability that some users will execute the file. Crackers have become very adept at preying on people's natural curiosity and baser instincts to induce users to execute binary attachments. Some of the more intriguing means through which this has been attempted in the past include using a subject line message of "I love you," "pictures of Anna Kournikova attached," or "an urgent message from the University Registrar."

## Helper Applications and Plug-Ins

In the early days of browser development, browsers were able to work with only a few types of files (basically, American Standard Code for Information Interchange [ASCII], Hypertext Markup Language [HTML], graphics interchange format [GIF], and Joint Photographic Experts Group [JPEG] files), but users wanted to do more with their browsers. The natural solution was to develop helper applications that had their own address space. When a specific type of file was called, the helper apps automatically ran and processed the file. Although this provided a fairly extensible workaround, Netscape developed a different version of the same idea called plug-ins. Plug-ins do the same thing as helper applications, but they share the address space of the browser. To make it easier for users to obtain and use the correct plug-in or helper application, browsers were configured to prompt the user for a specific plug-in when they encountered a new file type. This opened a huge security hole that was quickly exploited by crackers. Crackers discovered that users who were prompted to download and install a new plug-in would do it with very little consideration of the developer of the plug-in or the veracity of the code. Crackers developed Web sites to exploit the gullibility of users and to prompt them to install plug-ins developed by the crackers that allowed the crackers to gain control over client workstations.

The problem of unauthenticated plug-ins remains. And although users have become somewhat more sophisticated about installing plug-ins from companies they do not know, crackers continue to use this technique successfully.

## Scripting Languages

Another way to extend the functionality of browsers is to configure them to support the execution of scripting languages on the client. Although several powerful scripting languages can be supported by browsers (JavaScript, Jscript, VBScript), the security of each of these languages can be gauged, in its most basic form, by the existence of capabilities that allow them to operate outside their own "sandbox" (the operating environment of the browser), such as the ability to open other files or establish network connections that can be exploited by crackers to accomplish their goals. The problem with this idea is that the intentionally limited capabilities of a scripting language need not be used to attack a client machine directly; instead, they can be used to increase the sophistication of a social engineering attack and therefore the likelihood that the cracker can trick the user into doing something that the scripting language by itself cannot do.

JavaScript, when run in a Netscape Navigator browser, has the following security-related restrictions placed on it:

- It is unable to read or write files.
- There is no access to file system information.
- It can't execute programs or system commands.
- It is able to make network connections only to the computer from which the code was downloaded.
- There are restrictions to the access of <form> data.

Wagner and Wyke (2000) also point out that while JavaScript is somewhat secure, as outlined earlier, it is still subject to many of the same issues as any other programming language, such as infinite loops, stack overflows, infinite modal dialogs, and use of all available memory. Even though a JavaScript program that runs into these problems could be dismissed as poorly coded, the net result to a user is a denial of service that incapacitates the browser and requires that it be manually shut down. In the early days, the preceding security restrictions were sufficient to prevent many of the hacks that had surfaced, but this has not continued to be the case. The reason for this is twofold: the browsers in which the applets are run have proved to be less secure than they should be, and the ability of the JavaScript to create cute and enticing applets has been used as part of social engineering schemes to lure unsuspecting users to Web sites containing malicious code.

### Java Applets

The Java programming language and Java applets (small Java programs that can be run only within a Java-enabled Web browser) were designed with a dynamic, extensible security architecture. The boundary between untrusted source code and the resources of the host system is contained by three distinct layers: the Security Manager, the Class Loader, and the Verifier. Included in the Java language are such useful technologies as cryptography, authentication, authorization, and support for public key infrastructures.

### ActiveX Controls

ActiveX controls are essentially Component Object Model (COM) objects that support the IUnknown interface. They can be used to enhance the usability of Web pages and can be made to be relatively secure. The problem arises in that they can, either through malice or by accident, be made extremely insecure. According to Microsoft (2004a), ActiveX controls must be designed from the beginning to be secure, and the onus is on the programmer to make them secure. Once a control is initiated, it can be repurposed (used in ways that you did not intend) by any application that can gain the control's class identifier (CLSID). Because all ActiveX controls are Microsoft Win32 components, they are not limited to any sandboxing limitations and can be made to run without any restrictions. They therefore can be made to modify any of the settings in the local registry or the file system.

## SECURING CLIENTS

This section discusses some of the tools and techniques used to enhance the security of clients in an organizational network. To effectively secure a network of clients from attack requires attention to be paid to those clients throughout their effective life. They should be deployed with a well-known operating system, antivirus program, personal firewall, and applications properly installed and configured. They need to be maintained and managed throughout their effective lifetime with patches and upgrades automatically installed. And their configuration, access to the network, and exposure to vulnerabilities need to be monitored through periodic host scans and a program of vulnerability management.

Julia H. Allen and the Computer Emergency Response Team Coordination Center (CERT/CC) at Carnegie Mellon University have developed a list of practices to be followed to enhance client security (Allen, 2001). The list of practices are not specific to any one operating system but represent generic good practices that should be followed at any installation where client-side security is an issue. Their goal in developing these practices was to secure clients in the following ways:

- To provide a backup to the failure of perimeter defenses as well as provide a first line of defense against internal threats
- To assist in the early recognition of security incidents and thereby enhance the ability to respond to those incidents and prevent their occurrence in the future
- To promote consistency of configuration and deployment across clients and thereby make it easier to identify behavior that is outside the norm and potentially indicative of an attack

Their recommendations are based on the premise that client-side security is not only about technology. The approach that CERT/CC advocates for effective client-side security is a holistic approach that recognizes the vital role that users play in the securing of computer networks, and it can be divided into four separate areas: planning, configuring, maintaining, and improving user awareness.

## Initial Deployment

The initial deployment of clients to a network is a very important time because it is the only time when system administrators can feel entirely comfortable with their configuration. To make the initial deployment as effective and secure as possible, the following areas need to be covered.

### Planning

Security cannot be added onto a deployment of user workstations. For security to be effective, it must be planned in from the onset. Many questions need to be asked regarding the deployment of individual computers, but they revolve around gaining an understanding of exactly what the purpose of each computer is and deploying that computer with only the required services enabled to support that purpose. The following questions can be helpful in the planning phase:

- What will the computer be used for?
- What types of information will be stored on the computer?
- What types of information will be processed on the computer?
- What are the security requirements for the information to be processed on the computer?
- How will the computer interact with other computers on the network?

- What users will have access to the computer, what configuration changes will they be able to make to the computer, and how are the users related?
- What trust relationship will this computer have with other computers on the network?

The answers to these questions will help determine the operating system and application software configuration that a computer will require. Having a thorough, well-documented deployment plan enables you to make the correct decisions in balancing usability and security.

### Configuring

It is vitally important that new clients not be released onto the network without a tested and thoroughly understood initial operating system and application software configuration. The initial configuration should have all vendor updates installed and browsers configured with only those services required to enable users to perform their tasks. Many client-side security problems can be avoided by deploying computers with secure configurations, including encrypted authentication, virus protection, and personnel firewalls.

### Virus Protection

Virus protection software must be a part of every client configuration. It should be installed with an up-to-date signature file prior to placing the device on the network, and new updates must be implemented as soon as they become available. Because new virus signatures cannot be developed prior to a virus appearing on the Internet, virus protection software is always somewhat out of date. There are, however, enough old viruses on the Internet at any given time that virus protection software is a requirement for every client connection.

For detailed information on this topic, please consult the chapter titled Antivirus Technology.

### Personal Firewalls

The traditional model of deploying firewalls at the periphery of networks is not effective in the face of attacks that crackers send into the interior of networks as e-mail attachments and those that are released on the internal side of networks by malicious or naïve users. To safeguard client workstations more fully requires the deployment of firewalls on all computing devices that can be monitored and configured centrally.

For detailed information on this topic, please consult Volume III, Chapter 175, Firewall Basics, Chapter 176 Firewall Architectures, Chapter 177, Packet Filtering and Stateful Firewalls, and Chapter 178 Proxy Firewalls.

### Intrusion Detection

Although intrusion detection systems have been likened to dashboard indicators on cars, which go on only after the damage is done, they still have a valuable role to play in the overall securing of computer networks. As more work is done on the actual means by which attacks occur, intrusion detection systems will become more reliable in their ability to analyze network traffic and system configuration information and therefore better able to apply that baseline information against the current conditions to judge if an attack is actually occurring.

For detailed information on this topic, please consult Volume III, chapter 183, Intrusion Detection Systems Basics, chapter 184, Host-Based Intrusion Detection Systems, chapter 185, Network-Based Intrusion Detection Systems, chapter 186, The Use of Agent Technology for Intrusion Detection, and chapter 194, Use of Data Mining for Intrusion Detection.

## User Authentication

User authentication is the basis for all security in a networked environment. There are four processes involved in securely granting access to network resources. Users must *identify* themselves to the system. This is usually accomplished through the use of a user name but might also be accomplished through something that the user has, such as an identification card. Users must then *authenticate*, or prove their asserted identity, to the system. Although this is usually accomplished through a password, the use of biometrics such as hand geometry or fingerprint or retinal scans is becoming more common. Linked to a valid account are all the *authorizations* or privileges that accrue to an identity. Once a user's identity has been proved and the privileges ascertained, the final step in the process is the granting of *access* to actual resources. There are a number of variations or extensions to the preceding general scheme. Two-factor authentication requires that users have both a user name and password as well as an access token to authenticate. One of the problems with two-factor authentication is that it can be difficult and expensive to equip all the potential access points to a network with hardware that can authenticate the access token as a legitimate access token. One of the ways around this is the use of time-based authentication codes that are recalculated every minute on both the host and a credit-card-sized authenticator that the user must possess.

For detailed information on this topic, please consult Volume III, chapter 164, Password Authentication, and chapter 165, Computer and Network Authentication. For more information on biometrics and their use, please see Volume III, chapter 167, Biometric Basics and Biometric Authentication, chapter 168, Issues and Concerns in Biometric IT Security, and chapter 174, Applications of Biometrics in Financial Security Transactions.

## Client-side Security in a Microsoft Environment

The means and the extent of security settings available in a Microsoft Windows environment are very much dependent on the type of network involved and the relationship of the client to that network. Although it is beyond the scope of this chapter to discuss the specifics of the many Microsoft Windows client operating systems and the different types of domains to which they can be joined, the following subsections outline some of the issues involved with Microsoft Windows XP clients, Microsoft Windows 2000 and Windows 2003 Server servers, and Active Directory domains.

## Microsoft Windows XP Clients in Active Directory Domains

Windows XP clients in Active Directory domains are the typical configuration in a Microsoft enterprise environment. Windows XP is the current release of the Microsoft Windows client operating system, and it provides a very sophisticated interface between the user and the network. The Active Directory is a database of user information that uses an implementation of the Lightweight Directory Access Protocol (LDAP) to access a centralized store of information and configuration settings that is replicated to computers called *domain controllers*. Domain controllers not only store this database but also handle such administrative tasks as user authentication and authorization services.

One of the many other interesting functions that domain controllers provide as part of the logon process is to push out to clients a series of user and environment configuration settings called Group Policy Objects (GPOs). GPOs can be used to apply and maintain a consistent set of security settings or policies across a network of clients and servers from a central location. Recognizing that many people are ambivalent about the role that Microsoft products have played in many of the security problems that have plagued the Internet recently, Microsoft has developed a set of recommendations for securing Windows XP in an Active Directory environment (Microsoft, 2004b). These security settings can be imported into GPOs by using templates and applied to all or some of the clients on a Microsoft network. Although most of the settings have to do with fairly esoteric areas of securing network communications, many have to do with more basic ideas.

Microsoft recommends evaluating whether to implement security settings through GPOs in more than 200 areas. Some of those areas include the following:

- *Password settings.* How often should passwords be changed? When changing passwords, what restrictions are placed on these changes?
- *Account lockout policy.* What should the computer do when a user tries unsuccessfully to log on? Should it allow the user another try, and if so, how many?
- *Audit policy.* What events should the computer record and save to log files? What should happen when the log files become full? How often should the log files be reviewed and analyzed?
- *User rights.* What rights should the local user have on the local computer? Should users have the right to install new software? The right to change the system time? The right to back up or restore files?
- *Login messages.* What message should be displayed at login (for example: "This system is restricted to authorized users. Individuals attempting unauthorized access will be prosecuted.")?

## Microsoft Windows XP Clients in Stand-Alone Environments

Without the network infrastructure that an Active Directory environment provides, the options for implementing security settings on Windows XP clients are much more limited. Each Windows XP client, however, has at least one Local Group Policy Object (LGPO) that can be used to implement some security-related settings. The limitations relate to the ways in which the client interacts with the network and Active Directory. All of the previously referenced settings are still possible.

For detailed information on this topic, please consult Volume II, chapter 130, Operating System Security, chapter 135, Windows 2000 Security; very good sources on the Web include http://www.windowsecurity.com/ and http://www.microsoft.com/security/default.mspx.

### Client-side Security in a UNIX/Linux Environment

Although most of the more serious worms and viruses have had the greatest impact on Microsoft Windows–based clients, it is important for users and administrators responsible for the security of UNIX/Linux-based clients to be concerned with the security of their computers. This is particularly the case as more mature, higher quality, graphical user interfaces have made more practicable the deployment of UNIX/Linux-based computers as clients for less experienced users.

Many of the basic ideas behind securing a UNIX/Linux computer are the same as securing any other: use strong passwords and authentication, keep installed applications revisions up-to-date, only deploy those services that are necessary for users to accomplish their tasks, use personal firewalls, and use antivirus software. The most significant difference between securing Microsoft Windows and Apple Macintosh computers and securing UNIX/Linux computers is the lack of a single, centralized company that can be expected to provide many of the software updates for the UNIX/Linux operating system and applications. To maintain the security of applications with UNIX/Linux clients, users must have a deeper understanding of their computer and the applications that are running on it. They also must be aware of security warnings from many more organizations. A user running an Apache Web server as a personal Web server on an Intel-based computer using Mandrake as an operating system needs to pay attention to security warnings from both Apache and Mandrake, and it might not be the case that Mandrake would warn the user of problems with the Apache Web server.

Because of the long history of UNIX/Linux as an enterprise operating system, many Web-based resources provide information on securing UNIX/Linux clients. Some of the better ones include the following: the Computer Emergency Response Team (CERT) Coordination Center of Carnegie Mellon University in conjunction with the Australian Computer Emergency Response Team (AusCERT) has published a UNIX Security Checklist with an extensive set of potential vulnerabilities, scripts, and white papers that detail both the vulnerabilities and steps that can be taken to remediate them (http://www.cert.org/tech_tips/usc20_full.html). A very good place to learn the latest in Linux security advisories and to find out about new open-source and proprietary security applications is http://www.linuxsecurity.com/. A Linux Security Quick Reference guide and a Quick Start guide also can quickly get you organized (http://www. linuxsecurity.com/docs/).

For detailed information on this topic, please consult Volume II, chapter 130, Operating System Security, chapter 132, UNIX Operating System Security, and chapter 133, Linux Operating System Security.

### Client-side Security in a Mac OS X Environment

Mac OS X is a version of UNIX originally developed based on the BSD UNIX family, and it provides users with a very stable and reliable platform. Mac OS X is well supported with both printed and online resources to help users better secure their computers. Some of the better online resources related to Mac OS X security include the following: *An Introduction to Mac OS X Security* (http://developer.apple.com/internet/security/ securityintro.html), *A Security Primer for Mac OS X* (http:// www.macdevcenter.com/pub/a/mac/2004/02/20/security. html), and *Macintosh OS X Security: Understanding the Platform and Usage* (http://www.securemac.com/ macosxsecurity.php). As originally installed, Mac OS X is a very secure operating system that Apple does a very good job maintaining by releasing timely patches as needed. There are, however, certain practices that must be implemented to maintain the security of most Mac OS X computers. The most important security practice that can be applied to any computer, including a Macintosh, is the use of strong passwords. The default configuration of Mac OS X has the root account disabled and instead utilizes a very sophisticated graphical user interface (GUI) that assumes the capabilities of root (by invoking SUDO) when root access is required. Although access to the root account can be accomplished without much technical sophistication, this is actively discouraged by Apple based on the fear that users might then use the root account as their normal account and expose themselves to hacks based on processes being run as root. As initially installed, very few services operate in Mac OS X. Although it is relatively easy to enable additional services, such as Windows file sharing and remote access, it is very important for users to understand how the services work and the implications of the additional services before they enable them. Mac OS X comes with a personal firewall that enables users to limit the ports through which their Mac is listening for connections. The firewall is called ipfw (IP firewall) and can be enabled from the Sharing Preferences pane in the System Preferences application. Finally, as with other operating systems, it is vitally important that the user install and keep current antivirus software. Although traditionally most antivirus software was written for MS Windows operating systems, the attack vectors used by crackers now are beginning to span platforms, and vendors are now developing antivirus software specifically for Mac OS X.

For detailed information on this topic, please consult Volume II, chapter 130, Operating System Security, chapter 132, UNIX Operating System Security, and chapter 133, Linux Operating System Security.

## Maintenance

Computer operating systems, software applications, and hardware are very complex systems with substantial

**Table 1**

| Company | Product Name | Product URL |
|---|---|---|
| Ecora | Patch Manager | http://www.ecora.com/ecora/ |
| Shavlik | HFNetChkPro | http://www.shavlik.com/ |
| St. Bernard | UpDate Expert | http://www.stbernard.com/ |
| Patchlink | Update | http://www.patchlink.com/ |
| Configuresoft | ECM | http://www.configuresoft.com/ |

market incentives for vendors to get a product released quickly to market. The combination of complexity of configuration and market incentive for early release creates a situation in which many of the defects in hardware and software are not discovered until after release. Vendors usually respond to this by releasing updates for newly discovered flaws that must be installed with administrator or superuser access permissions. Although several systems attempt to make this process as automated as possible, they are not infallible and can introduce new problems in the process of resolving others.

According to Allen (2001), some of the more common problems with the current update/patch deployment process relate to the following:

- It is impossible for all clients on a network to receive and install the update at exactly the same time; therefore, there will be a period during which different machines are operating with different configurations. This can lead to data corruption (depending on the nature of the update/patch), inconsistent operation, or worse.
- Some of the vendors, and many of the users, do not know how to use authentication via encryption appropriately to deploy updates/patches to users. This leaves users wide open to crackers deploying Trojan horses and viruses through the social engineering practice of sending them to users disguised as updates/patches deployed by a vendor they know and trust.
- To install some updates, it is necessary that the host be taken offline or restarted before the update can take effect. The unavailability of the host during this time can cause problems depending on the services it provides to other members of the network.
- With the plethora of updates/patches that have been released recently, it is virtually impossible for network administrators to evaluate them effectively before they are installed. The time pressure that this has induced for system and network administrators can force them to violate good practice for update deployment and install

updates without properly researching and testing them in their own environment.

## Automated Patch and Update Management

Passive patch management techniques might not be as effective as required in dealing with the large-scale deployment of necessary patches. According to a survey done by Theo Forbath of the Product Strategies and Architecture Practice of WiPro Technologies (2005), enterprises spent on average $297 on each Windows client and $343 on each Open Source System per year to apply patches in 2004. Although the tidal wave of patches has not let up since then, the use of automated patch management tools has greatly increased. Several products are available that automate the patching process either as stand-alone tools or as part of asset and configuration tool sets. The key functionality of these systems is the ability to analyze systems remotely for installed patches and to push required patches out to individual computers. There are several closed-source automated patch management products available. Table 1 provides only a short list.

## Automated Application Deployment

Another topic of importance during the maintenance phase of client-side security is the automated deployment of new and modified applications. As with patch and update management, the goal is to deploy applications in a secure, manageable, and consistent fashion to groups and subgroups within an organization with little if any user involvement. A valuable resource in both understanding the available technology and finding vendors for closed- and open-source products is AppDeploy.com (http://www.appdeploy.com/).

This site does not sell products but instead serves as a central point for information dissemination. Other companies that sell products that provide application deployment and client management functionality include those listed in Table 2.

**Table 2**

| Company | Product Name | Product URL |
|---|---|---|
| Altiris | Client Management | http://www.altiris.com/ |
| BMC Software | Marimba Client Management | http://www.bmc.com/ |
| Tally Systems | Cenergy Client Management Suite | http://www.tallysystems.com/ |
| Hewlett-Packard | Client Manager Suite | http://www.hp.com/ |

# Monitoring

One of the maxims of computer security is that if a cracker gains physical access to the console, that cracker owns the computer. With client-side security, that is the situation we face everyday. With that in mind, an important part of a comprehensive client-side security program is the monitoring of clients and the users that use them. Monitoring in this case involves several activities, some technological and others more managerial in nature.

## Vulnerability Management

The incredible proliferation of vulnerabilities and the speed at which exploits have been developed have created a situation in which it is no longer possible to deploy all patches as soon as they are available. Administrators are forced to prioritize and accept a certain degree of exposure to vulnerabilities at any given time. Determining which vulnerabilities to patch immediately and which can be safely ignored until several patches can be deployed at once is a managerial decision that should be made based on a thorough knowledge of the degree of exposure and the risk that putting off deploying a patch incurs.

## Host Scanning

Given the degree of physical access that users have to the clients that are to be secured, it is crucial that the currency of configuration be monitored on a periodic basis. This can take the form of the deployment of a closed-source hardware-based tool such as Foundstone's Enterprise Manager (http://www.foundstone.com/). This tool continually scans the devices on a network and compares any vulnerabilities it finds to a vulnerability database that prioritizes vulnerabilities based on their potential impact to the specific network and automatically takes remedial actions. Although this degree of sophistication comes at a significant price, less sophisticated but still effective host scanners can either be developed in-house based on such tools as SuperScan (also from Foundstone, but freely downloadable), Nmap (freely downloadable from http://www.insecure.org/tools.html), or Nessus (also freely downloadable from http://www.insecure.org/tools.html).

## Host-Based Intrusion Detection Systems

No matter how secure a network of clients is, crackers will attempt to search for and exploit vulnerabilities. Although it is possible to manage your direct exposure to vulnerabilities and attempt to keep that exposure within a set of guidelines, it is becoming impossible to be impervious to exploits and still remain connected to the Internet. With this in mind, the deployment of host-based intrusion detection systems should be part of a client-side security program. Host-based intrusion detection systems enable network and system administrators to develop historic baseline information regarding the expected use or configuration of resources on a network when the resource is in a known state. This baseline can then be compared to a current state to determine whether there is cause to suspect an ongoing cracking incident. The problem with these systems is that they have the potential to overwhelm network and system administrators with false positives and false negatives. Although this should not obviate their use, administrators need to be aware of this limitation as they begin to determine the configuration of the devices.

Many closed-source host-based intrusion detection systems are currently on the market either as stand-alone programs or as part of an enterprise security service. Also, many open-source programs are available that can provide an acceptable level of security, including Snort (available at http://www.snort.org/) and Tripwire (available at http://www.tripwire.com/).

For detailed information on this topic, please consult Volume III, chapter 190, Intrusion Detection Basics, chapter 191, Host-Based Intrusion Detection Systems, chapter 192, Network-Based Intrusion Detection Systems, chapter 193, Use of Agent Technology for Intrusion Detection, and chapter 194, Use of Data Mining for Intrusion Detection.

## Procedures

As the complexity of computer networks and individual computers grows, it is ever more important that they be managed according to a set of procedures that are well understood by those affected by them. Although it might have been possible in the past for a group of system administrators and desktop support personnel to keep track of the individual configuration of each client workstation on their network, the growing complexity of operating systems and the ubiquity of computing across the enterprise obviates this practice. One of the keys to the securing of a network of computers is to develop and then securely deploy standardized configurations to all the devices on the network. Although this cold, hard rule can be softened somewhat by the development of several different configurations for different user groups, the proliferation of active content and the reliance on social engineering and adeptness at getting past perimeter defenses of the current crop of viruses and worms require that greater control be exercised over client configurations. This can be accomplished only by regularizing the means through which we interact with users, and client configurations, through the use of procedures.

The software engineering community has long worked to improve the processes that organizations use as a way to enhance the products that those organizations produce. From their efforts, a Capability Maturity Model (CMM) has been developed and refined (Carnegie Mellon Software Engineering Institute, n.d.). This same thinking is now being applied to the deployment of many information technology–related processes by Frank Niessink and his associates (Niessink, Clerc, & van Vliet, 2004). They are in the process of developing an IT service CMM that is designed to aid organizations in both gauging the current maturity of their IT services and in understanding how to improve the way that IT services are provided. The IT service CMM is composed of five levels, only three of which are currently defined. An organization that scores high on the IT service CMM will be able to deliver reliable IT services tailored to the needs of their customers in a reliable and consistent fashion as well as continuously improve those services over time.

Level 1 of the IT service CMM is the ad hoc level where services are delivered as well as possible with little thought to consistency or learning from past mistakes. Level 2 is the repeatable level. Basic service management policies are in place and attempts are made to build on past successes to deliver services more effectively in a repeatable fashion. Level 3 involves the development of documentation and service definitions to enhance the organization's ability to deliver consistent services. In level 4, the focus shifts to the development of quantitative measures of service delivery process and quality. The final level involves the development of feedback loops that build upon the efforts of the previous level to improve the quality of service delivery continuously.

For detailed information on this topic, please consult Volume III, chapter 205, Managing a Network Environment, chapter 210, Multilevel Security, and chapter 211, Multilevel Security Models.

## Improving User Awareness

At the end of the day, there is no way that the security of client workstations with access to the Internet can be maintained from a central location. It is ultimately the responsibility of the users of a system to keep that system secure. One of the most important and most easily ignored aspects of client-side security relates to training users to both maintain their systems and to avoid doing things that could put their systems and, by extension, the entire network in jeopardy. Many IT organizations have a continuing relationship with the users of their systems to help them to utilize their IT systems more effectively. Part of any IT training program needs to include a discussion of the user's responsibility to maintain the security of clients used on a daily basis. This discussion can take place as a face-to-face discussion, and it can also be a mediated discussion that takes place through mailings, Intranet Web sites, or newsletters. Because the threats to which clients are exposed change every day, provisions should be made for an ongoing training and education program designed to keep users up-to-date on ways in which technology can be used to make them more productive and to alert them to new threats and hacking techniques.

For detailed information on this topic, please consult Volume III, chapter 197, Implementing a Security Awareness Program.

## Policies

The front line in this effort is the development and promulgation of an acceptable use policy (AUP) for all users. It is unreasonable to expect users to "just know" what their rights and responsibilities are as they relate to client-side security. What is expected of the users of a workstation and their role in securing a network from malicious code must be spelled out in detail, and users must be asked to acknowledge having read and understood the policy. Policies developed for this purpose should not take the form of commandments from on high; instead, they should emphasize the "we're all in this together" aspect of security and provide users with available means for asking legitimate questions when they arise. According to CERT (2003), the following practices are very important in the development of an AUP:

- *Gain management-level support.* In many cases, the detection of violations of the provisions of an AUP falls under the aegis of the IT department, whereas the enforcement falls under the aegis of management or human resources. This situation requires that management be brought in early in the development of the AUP.

- *Designate an individual with responsibility for the development, maintenance, and enforcement of the AUP.* In many cases, a chief information officer (CIO), rather than a system administrator, is given the responsibility for developing, maintaining, and enforcing the AUP. A CIO is better positioned to have the organization-wide perspective that makes a more effective AUP and also has the authority to better enforce it across organizational lines.

- *Develop the policy with participation from all stakeholders.* A policy developed with input from those it affects is both more likely to prevent those actions it seeks to prevent and allow users the freedom they need to accomplish their tasks.

- *Explain the policy to users and train them to follow it.* The introduction of an AUP to an existing organization can force changes in user behavior that might initially be challenged. An organization that both explains a new AUP to users and trains them periodically to work within its guidelines is much more likely to have a successful implementation.

- *Document user acceptance of the policy.* Documenting the acceptance by users of a new AUP enables the organization to enforce the AUP with less chance of litigation. Documenting acceptance of the AUP on an ongoing basis further bolsters the importance of the AUP in the organization's standing.

- *Provide explicit reminders at each login.* At each login, a banner should be displayed that reminds the user of the existence of the AUP and the function, ownership, and consequences of unauthorized access that are used to monitor user compliance.

- *Maintain the policy to reflect changes in your business and the technologies that you utilize.* Because businesses and their use of technology evolve over time, the AUP should also evolve to reflect any changes. This is particularly important now as more organizations implement mobile and wireless networking devices.

Lawrence (2002) discusses the cross-functional aspect of AUP development and points out that the following groups should be involved: human resource and legal departments to cover liability issues, marketing and strategic planning groups to ensure positive use of the tools, and information technology and information security to ensure security and the efficient use of the technological tools.

The AUP should outline for users what is and what is not allowed for them to do with their computers, the consequences of violating the policy, and the means by which their actions will be monitored to ensure that they are not violating the policy. It should outline what maintenance procedures are the responsibility of the user and the types of applications that can be used on the computer. It should also inform users of their rights and responsibilities in relation to e-mail attachments and active content. The AUP should be reviewed on a periodic basis, and users should acknowledge the policy as part of their periodic review process. There are many sources of information available on the Web for templates and guides to aid in the construction of an AUP.

For detailed information on this topic, please consult Volume III, chapter 206, E-Mail and Internet Use Policies, chapter 208, Security Policy Guidelines, and chapter 213, Security Policy Enforcement.

# CONCLUSION

*Client-side security* is an overarching term that covers the tools and techniques used to secure client computers on organizational networks from attacks originating on the inside or outside of the network. Rather than a single technology, client-side security is a process that involves the deployment of several different technologies, managerial policies, and procedures. The client-side security tools and techniques can be grouped into four different areas:

- *Deployment.* The deployment of known and well-understood operating systems and applications in a managed and secure fashion
- *Management.* Management and maintenance of the currency of applications and operating systems through the secure and organized deployment of patches and updates to organizational computing resources
- *Monitoring.* The development and implementation of tools and techniques to monitor application and resource use to ensure that the consistency of configuration and exposure to vulnerability are within organizational guidelines
- *Ensuring user awareness.* Making users aware of their rights and responsibilities as they relate to the security of the network

Securing the client side of a network involves more than securing all the operating systems on all the clients on that network. The goal of a client-side security program is a general hardening of the interior of a network that, when combined with a strong perimeter, is part of a layered approach to overall network security.

# GLOSSARY

**Acceptable Use Policy (AUP)** A document that outlines the rights and responsibilities of computer users for organizational assets. Some questions to answer in an AUP include: Are e-mail communications considered private, or are they subject to monitoring by managers? Can users freely browse the Internet, or are they restricted in the sites that they may visit? What are the responsibilities of users for maintaining their own workstations?
**Active Content** Portions of Web sites that are either interactive or dynamic. Usually, active content is downloaded as a small program from the Web site and executed on the client computer.
**Application** A program designed to perform a specific function.

**Authentication** The process of ascertaining whether someone or something is who they assert that they are. Many times this is done through the use of a combination of a user name and password for a computer user.
**Client-Side Security** A combination of the tools and techniques used to control access to and the configuration of client computers in a network environment.
**Firewall** Usually located between a network and the Internet, a firewall is a set of programs that examines each packet of information being sent out or coming in and compares it to a set of rules. A firewall is used to prevent users from sending unauthorized information out from a network and to prevent unauthorized packets from coming into a network.
**Host-Based Security** A synonym for *client-side security*.
**Host Scanning** An automated process used to check individual computers for configuration problems and available services.
**Internet Service Provider (ISP)** An organization that provides access to the Internet for computer users.
**Intrusion** When an unauthorized user gains access to computing resources either inside or outside a network.
**Information Technology Capability Maturity Model (IT CMM)** A set of best practices for the delivery of information technology services.
**Patch Management** The processes (both managerial and technological) used to aid in the deployment of software upgrades.
**Personal Firewall** A firewall that is installed on an individual workstation that is designed to halt the spread of unwanted programs.
**Services** A general term used to refer to capabilities a server computer offers to other computers.
**Small Office/Home Office (SOHO)** Many people now work out of their homes or from offices not located at the home location of their employers. These offices are usually connected to their parent office by either a DSL or cable modem connection to the Internet.
**Virus** An unwanted self-replicating program that attempts to spread from one computer to others.
**Vulnerability** A weakness in a process or program that could be exploited by attackers to do damage.
**Vulnerability Management** The processes (both managerial and technological) used to aid in the management of weaknesses in organizations. Although primarily used to discuss avenues of attack that exist in computing systems, this term could also refer to physical facilities.
**Worm** A self-replicating virus that does not alter files.

# CROSS REFERENCES

See *Computer Viruses and Worms; Denial of Service Attacks; Hostile Java Applets; Intrusion Detection Systems Basics; Protecting Web Sites; Trojan Horse Programs.*

# REFERENCES

Aberdeen Group. (2003). *Patch management.* Retrieved July 31, 2004, from http://www.aberdeen.com/2001/research/06030015.asp.

Allen, J. H. (2001). *The CERT guide to system and network security practices*. Indianapolis, IN: Addison-Wesley.

Apple Computer Corporation. (2004). *An introduction to Mac OS X security for Web developers*. Retrieved January 3, 2005, from http://developer.apple.com/internet/security/securityintro.html.

AusCERT. (2001). *UNIX security checklist V2.0*. Retrieved January 3, 2005, from http://www.cert.org/tech_tips/usc20_full.html.

Carnegie Mellon Software Engineering Institute. (n.d.). *Getting started with CMMI adoption*. Retrieved January 3, 2005, from http://www.sei.cmu.edu/cmmi/adoption/cmmi-start.html.

CERT. (2003). *Develop and promulgate an acceptable use policy for workstations*. Retrieved January 3, 2005, from http://www.cert.org/security-improvement/practices/p034.html.

Fraser, B. (Ed.). (1997). *Site security handbook IETF 2196*. Retrieved January 3, 2005, from http://www.ietf.org/rfc/rfc2196.txt?number=2196.

F-Secure Corporation. (2004). *F-Secure Corporation's data security summary for 2004: The year of phishing, professional virus writing, and arrests*. Retrieved January 3, 2005, from http://www.f-secure.com/2004/.

Forbath, Theo, Patrick Kalaher, and Thomas O'Grady (2005). *The total cost of security patch management: A comparison of Microsoft Windows and Open Source Software*. Retrieved June 25, 2005, from http://download.microsoft.com/download/1/7/b/17b54d06-1550-4011-9253-9484f769fe9f/TCO_SPM_Wipro.pdf.

Fraser, B. ed. (1997). *Site Security Handbook*. Internet Engineering Task Force. Retrieved June 25, 2005, from http://www.ietf.org/rfc/rfc2196.txt?number=2196.

Kermadec, F. J. (2004, February 20). *A security primer for Mac OS X*. Retrieved January 3, 2005, from http://www.macdevcenter.com/pub/a/mac/2004/02/20/security.html.

Lawrence, P. (2002, March). *Acceptable use: Whose responsibility is it?* Retrieved January 3, 2005, from http://www.sans.org/rr/papers/2/3.pdf.

Microsoft Corporation. (2004a). *Designing secure ActiveX controls*. Retrieved January 3, 2005, from http://msdn.microsoft.com/library/default.asp?url=/workshop/components/activex/security.asp.

Microsoft Corporation. (2004b). *Windows XP security guide*. Retrieved January 3, 2005, from http://www. microsoft.com/downloads/details.aspx?FamilyID=2d3e25bc-f434-4cc6-a5a7-09a8a229f118&displaylang=en.

Morrison, J. (2004, June). Blaster revisited. *ACM Queue*, 2(4). Retrieved January 3, 2005, from http://www.acmqueue.org/modules.php?name=Content&pa=showpage&pid=159.

National Cyber Security Alliance (2004). AOL/NCSA Online Safety Study. Retrieved June 25, 2005, from http://www.staysafeonline.info/news/safety_study_v04.pdf

Niessink, F., Clerc, V., & van Vliet, H. (2004, June 24). *The IT service capability maturity model*. Retrieved January 3, 2005, from http://www.itservicecmm.org/doc/itscmm-0.4.pdf.

Oppliger, R. (2003). *Client-side security*. Retrieved January 3, 2005, from http://www.ifi.unizh.ch/~oppliger/Presentations/WWWSecurity2e/sld160.htm.

Pescatore, J. (2003). *Taxonomy of software vulnerabilities*. Gartner Group, Stamford, CT.

Russell, R., et al. (2002). *Hack proofing your network* (2nd ed.). Rockland, MA: Syngress Publishing.

SecureMac.com. (n.d.). *Macintosh OS X security: Understanding the platform and usage*. Retrieved January 3, 2005, from http://www.securemac.com/macosxsecurity.php.

Thompson, H. H., & Ford, R. (2004, June). The insider, naivety, and hostility: Security perfect storm? *ACM Queue*, 2(4). Retrieved January 3, 2005, from http://www.acmqueue.org/modules.php?name=Content&pa=showpage&pid=164.

Wagner, R. & Wyke, R. A. (2000). *Javascript unleashed* (3rd ed.). Indianapolis, IN: Sams.

## FURTHER READING

For further information on concentrating security devices on the periphery of networks, please see Lindquist, C. (2004). *The world is your perimeter*. Retrieved January 3, 2005, from http://www.csoonline.com/read/020104/perimeter.html.

For more information on firewalls and their deployment, please see Robinson, C. (2002). *Best practices for firewall deployments*. Retrieved January 3, 2005, from http://www.csoonline.com/analyst/report563.html.

For more information on the importance of involving employees at all levels in the securing of organizations, please see CIO, Inc. (2002). The Security Revolution. Retrieved June 25, 2005, from http://www.csoonline.com/whitepapers/061502security.

# Server-Side Security

Slim Rekhis and Noureddine Boudriga, *National Digital Certification Agency and University of Carthage, Tunisia*
M. S. Obaidat, *Monmouth University*

## SERVER VULNERABILITIES

Securing a server is a difficult and challenging task that cannot be fully accomplished. Introducing an additional solution to enhance a server's security can increase vulnerability and exposure to further threats. One answer to the problem is to understand server vulnerabilities and start implementing a risk-mitigation approach. In general, server security vulnerabilities might exist in three main areas: installed software, defined and enforced security policies, and used protocols.

## Software Vulnerabilities

Operating systems, services, and applications are all subject to specification, configuration, or implementation flaws that can generate embedded security vulnerabilities. The latter, when exploited, can grant intruders the opportunity to gain the privileges under which the related programs are running, thus reducing the security of the server and the entire network. Examples of software vulnerabilities include *buffer overflow, race conditions*, and *special character processing* (Cowan, et al., 2000). Whereas the first type of vulnerability is caused by poor bounds checking on the user input, the second represents an undesirable situation that can occur when a program attempts to perform operations that should be done in a proper order, and the last mainly affects the scripts that can be subverted by passing arbitrary inputs to yield the control of the system to intruders.

Examples of buffer overflow vulnerability involve the one found in the WebDAV component in Microsoft IIS Web Server 5.0 (Wood, 2003), which allows remote intruders to execute arbitrary commands under the server security context of the Internet Information Server (IIS) service. An example of a race condition is present in the Samba daemon (Vulnerability Information Center, 2004), which allows local attackers to overwrite files on the server when writing REG files (i.e., text files that contain registry information and have the file extension .reg). Security administrators should be aware of the potential vulnerabilities, particularly when they are deploying their own developed tools.

The most reliable way for security administrators to react against the preceding weaknesses is to keep the server up-to-date with software suppliers' fixes and patches. Careful consideration should be made, particularly when a deployed software component is developed by the company itself without security awareness. Meanwhile, tools such as Cqual (Foster, 2002), MOPS (Chen & Wagner, 2002), Flawfinder, and ELF Finder (DaCosta, Dahn, Mancoridis, & Prevelakis, 2003) are useful to scan (usually during program compiling) source code for patterns of known flaws such as buffer overflow or format string problems. Other vulnerabilities (e.g., general logic errors) are more tedious to identify during program compilation. Therefore, server vulnerabilities represent a hard challenge to address. A good way to ensure their mitigation is provided through complementing the automated verification of software with manual extensive testing and continuous monitoring.

## Server Security Policies

Even if security solutions such as antivirus software (AV) and intrusion detection systems (IDSs) are deployed, security breaches remain persistent because system owners and operators might misuse the system and security standards. To ensure that a system is used in an effective and productive way without exposing it to the realm of intruders, a security policy should be defined, including a strategy to protect and maintain the availability of the organizational resources. An example of writing an information security policy that is compliant with the BS7799 standard is provided in NHSnet (2004). The use of a security policy helps considerably in preventing configuration inconsistencies and can shorten reaction time to incidents. However, defining a security policy is not sufficient for good protection. The policy should also be valid, consistent, well understood, and correctly enforced by server operators. A simple modification in the configuration of a security component without an understanding of the organizational security objectives can expose the whole network to harmful security weaknesses.

In practice, security specialists have noticed that a high percentage of server security vulnerabilities are caused by problems related to security policy. For instance, testing new software components on a public online server can add a temporary privileged user with a weak password. Obviously, this can temporarily introduce a flaw that exposes the server to attacks. Another example is a vulnerability found in Windows NT Server Service Pack 6 (Syed, 2002). It enables a valid user, whose permission for changing passwords is revoked (here, the administrator is supposed to apply the local policy, "User cannot change password"), to still change his or her password through IIS 4.0 Web service by using the following uniform resource locator (URL): http://iisserver/iisadmpwd/aexp3.htr. Therefore, defining a security policy should be done carefully to prevent the introduction of inconsistencies that can alter the protection policy and strategy.

## Protocol Vulnerabilities

Protocols are extremely hard to design in a correct and secure manner, even if the goal is straightforward. Any design flaw that has a relationship with security can lead to damaging impact on the protocol usage. Often, during the design phase of a security solution, administrators select the security technology required to implement the organizational policy but neglect to consider the protocol features. Consequently, if security administrators rely on vulnerable protocols, they might see their network resources, including servers, become victims of attacks.

In practice, a lot of powerful security attacks have emerged because of vulnerabilities in protocols; particularly for those protocols developed with no security features. Transmission control protocol/Internet protocol (TCP/IP) represents a common example of such protocols. One of its most fascinating security holes is based on a sequence-number prediction used to construct TCP/IP packets without the need for any response from the server (Bellovin, 1989). Such a weakness enables an intruder to spoof a trusted host and perform malicious actions on the server. Another way to compromise servers is through routing protocols. Routing Information Protocol (RIP), for instance, propagates routing information and updates the gateways routing tables without checking the received information. An intruder can send erroneous routing information to the gateways on a given path and induce them to build incorrect routing paths with the purpose of deviating all packets issued from the server (and addressed to a legitimate host) to the intruder's machine.

Cryptographic protocols are widely used to guarantee security properties, such as authentication or secrecy in the information exchange between servers and their users. Despite the fact that they use secure cryptographic primitives, several protocols have been declared insecure because of design flaws. For instance, servers that rely on an authentication protocol such as the *Needham-Schroeder public key authentication protocol* (Needham & Schroeder, 1978) can easily be compromised using the *Lowe's attack* (Lowe, 1995), where an intruder can start a legitimate session with user A and impersonates it to mislead user B in a second session.

## SERVER SECURITY ISSUES

It is obvious from the previous section that securing a server requires significant effort because the weakest neglected point can be a source of access. In fact, protecting a server from attacks implies considering issues including security policy, user management, security auditing, system configuration, and log management. An overview of these issues is discussed in this section.

### Server Security Policies

The use of a security policy helps prevent configuration inconsistencies and helps administrators react efficiently to security incidents. A security policy is a progressive document that aims to protect an organization's information security systems, delimit acceptable uses, elaborate on personnel training plans for security policy enforcement, and enforce security measures. Because organizations are facing different types of threats, server security policies should be customized to the organization's need to cope with its business activity, information infrastructure, and resource sensitivity. Consider the case of remote-server administration. For instance, say organization A could prohibit a given activity after identifying the relevant need and consequent risk, whereas organization B could allow the activity but constrain it to strong requirements (e.g., restricting access to specific source IP domains or defining access timetables). Organization C could allow such activity using a weak authentication with user name and password. Canavan (2003) presents a guide to develop organizational security policies and describes the elements to be considered during its design and maintenance.

Security policies need to be reviewed on a regular basis and also on the occurrence of situations when new vulnerabilities are of concern. Such occurrences can require changing security rules, developing new plans, modifying practices, or restructuring security information services. For example, a vulnerability revealed in Cisco switch and router IOS (ITSS Information Security Services, 2003) leads these devices to be victims of denial of service attacks, if exploited. It can be dealt with through the upgrade or the acquisition of a new IOS. A more straightforward solution is to modify the organization's security policy by implementing appropriate ingress filtering.

Finally, it is worth mentioning that ideally a security policy should be sufficiently clear and comprehensive. It should come with a set of procedures for maintaining and evaluating its effectiveness. Similar to a software specification, it should satisfy a set of properties and requirements (e.g., validation, verification, modularity, completeness, and consistency). However, because of the occurrence of threats and unpredicted vulnerabilities, modifications and monitoring represent serious challenges.

## Management of Users

Users are the most active participants in server activity. Locally and remotely, they can abuse, misuse, or compromise server security. To prevent damages and reduce the consequent risk of their uses, users should be managed effectively. Default configurations of services and applications often include default accounts with known passwords, as well as active guest accounts. These are commonly known and widely used by the intruder community. They can be worked out using tools that make it easier to penetrate a system (e.g., the Default Account Database as provided by Swordsoft, which includes approximately 1,500 default passwords), if configured by default. Moreover, some users such as e-mail server subscribers can be granted access to the system to perform a very restrictive activity (e.g., sending and receiving e-mails). Because their number is large, an administrator should be aware of the potential risks that such users can generate and should not allow them to get interactive shells. More common user-management issues are related to how account passwords are set. Weak parameters in the choice of password should be avoided, particularly when these parameters correspond to length, complexity, aging, reuse possibility, number of failed attempts accepted, and change authority. Thus, password-checking software could be used to reject all passwords that do not satisfy a predefined password policy.

Granting full trust to a server user who has been authenticated can cause major concerns because an unauthorized user can, for example, take control of an active session while its legitimate user is away. To reduce this risk, the server operating system can be configured to lock any user session after an idle period. Such a solution can be insufficient in highly sensitive contexts. More elaborate solutions can be provided, including smart cards and hardware tokens, which can be used to lock the system when the owners extract them from the computer device. User passwords can be replaced or complemented with more secure solutions such as a private key stored inside cryptographic tokens, one-time password systems, and biometric solutions (Obaidat & Sadoun, 1999). Even though these solutions are expensive and require significant effort to be integrated, they can be justified in many situations.

## Auditing Server Security

From the moment a server risk-mitigation plan is enforced in an organization and a security policy including procedures and configuration settings is established, a security audit needs to be begun and continuously conducted on the server because it remains necessary to verify whether the security policy is being enforced correctly. Auditing aims to check that no breaches in the server configuration have been introduced during system operation and that the server is sufficiently protected. Depending on the practices and activities affecting the server, a security audit needs to be performed on a regular basis and whenever undesired conditions are observed.

During the audit procedures, the system configuration, operating system, services, and applications need to be examined carefully with an understanding of the impact of each component on the security of others.

Verifying software vulnerabilities is very important, and any neglected vulnerability can call into question the overall server security. A remote vulnerability that grants unprivileged access to a server can enable an intruder to exploit a local vulnerability on that server to gain privileged access and affect its neighborhoods, especially if sniffed data can reveal relevant information (e.g., clear passwords or a trusted relation is established between the server and its neighbors). Multiple software tools can help considerably in checking the security of a server under audit against the presence of known vulnerabilities, as they are described in general information sources, such as National Institute of Standards and Technology (NIST), Computer Emergency Response Team (CERT), Australian CERT (AusCERT), Bugtraq, and Security Focus. Some of these sources (e.g., NIST) maintain a security vulnerabilities metabase that can be interrogated online, allows the download of supporting new software, and provides flexible search capabilities and links for patch information.

To check whether security measures taken to protect a server have really protected the server, the security audit should try to identify whether the server has been targeted or subverted by intruders. To this aim, the set of available logs (these should cover network logs because an intruder might have cleaned the server log content before leaving the machine) have to be examined, statistical analysis performed, anomalies detected, and alerts correlated to identify attack scenarios and decide the appropriate countermeasures. Remote penetration testing complements the local vulnerability auditing. A series of remote attacks can be conducted against the server by a trusted user that behaves exactly like an intruder. Methods, techniques, and tools used for penetration testing are described in McClure, Scambray, and Kurtz (2003), where the authors demonstrate how to defend against a large number of security attacks.

However, because most security threats are generated by insiders, penetration testing is insufficient to defend against vulnerabilities. Therefore, a security audit should also cover personnel misuse and hardware failures. International security standards such as ISO 19977 identify the range of controls to be performed on the information systems.

## System Configurations

Protecting the server from attacks caused by poor or wrong configuration is a challenging task. A system configuration involves setting file and program ownerships and permissions, activating and deactivating software components and add-ons, restricting access to the system, and so forth. A security administrator needs to implement an accurate configuration to prevent attacks. Thus, only minimal software functionalities are activated, minimal effort is spent in administering security, and minimal risk is assumed. Vulnerabilities could flow out from bugs in the software components, the related programs, or the used libraries. Consequently, any component (e.g., add-on, add-in, and script) that is not needed should be deactivated, if not uninstalled. Program privileges also play an important role because the program might grant its privileges to an intruder, if subverted or exploited. An example of such a problem occurs when an administrator configures a Web server to run under the root user. In that case, any subversion of the Web daemon (e.g., PHF attack; NMRC 2003) can lead to the execution of the intruder's commands under root privileges. Guidelines for securing and hardening these are widely available on the Internet. Some tools were developed to make the process easy and to automate the set of tasks to be used for such purposes. The tool XPLizer, for instance, is a front-end tool designed to provide a graphical user interface (GUI) for fixing some of the most common security problems in Microsoft Windows, whereas Languard Network Security Scanner helps considerably in auditing the configuration part of Windows systems.

## Management of Logs

Log files represent the most common source for detecting suspicious behaviors and intrusion attempts. The efficiency of these files is strictly affected by any failure or attack on the related data collection mechanisms and any weakness in protecting their output. Log protection is very important in that intruders can access these files or the utilities that manage them to remove information, alter signs of malicious activity, or even add erroneous information to these files.

Log file protection can be altered because of badly configured access permissions, storage in public areas, and insecure transfer to remote hosts, in addition to any successful penetration of the system that hosts the log files. Logging data locally is easy to configure; it allows instantaneous access, although it is less secure because the log content can be lost whenever the server is compromised. On the other hand, remote log storage protects against this threat, but requires strengthening the communication security medium, using, for example, a separate subnet path or an encryption mechanism. The logging mechanism is also subject to denial of service attacks. In Linux systems, for example, an intruder could fill the Syslog output files until the logging partition becomes overloaded. This forces the logging process to stop. In Windows NT systems, the logging process starts to overwrite old files when the available storage is filled. Solutions to avoid this include compression, periodic remote transfer, and a warning report if logs reach their size limits.

Choosing the kind of information to log is an important issue. A security administrator should be aware of the resources required to store the generated files and must read, understand, and interpret log-file contents without being swamped with data. In fact, mechanical interpretation of log content can become boring, requiring

a look into a lexicon to understand the meaning of the records. Windows Server 2003, for instance, uses failure code 3221225578 with event ID 680 to denote that a wrong NTLM authentication occurred, where the user name is correct but the password is wrong. To enhance the significance of the generated log files, a security administrator should consider using log-dedicated tools that automate some operations, including content aggregation, automated interpretation, and statistics generation. GFI's LANGuard SELM, for instance, is a tool specialized in monitoring Windows security event logs, with centralization of alerts and reporting capabilities.

When deciding how long a log file is kept available, first consider the file's category and content. An error or a warning log generated a month ago, for example, is irrelevant today because errors that are faced today can be completely different from past errors or because system components might have been updated.

It is worthwhile to complement the log management with a verification mechanism to ensure that log content is consistent, meaningful, and useful when trying to conduct a forensic examination following a security incident.

# PROTECTING SERVERS FROM OVERLOAD

One important challenge that server-security administrators face is the guarantee of server availability, especially when servers are very much in demand. Server overload should be correctly managed to avoid being a victim of worsening quality of service (QoS), where client response time is increasing and the target begins reaching a denial of service. To protect servers from overload, simply bounding the flow rate is inefficient, but different actions should be taken, including traffic shaping, load controlling, and policy management.

## Traffic Shaping

Because server overload is generally caused by uncontrolled reception of client requests, controlling the overload can start at the network entry to the server. Shape the traffic flow to meet server performance by delaying excess traffic using buffering, queuing mechanisms, and request rejection. Such mechanisms are currently available in different networks such as Asynchronous Transfer Mode (ATM) networks, where in addition to resource management techniques that include virtual paths and connections admission control, traffic shaping has been implemented through two main traffic-shaping algorithms: the *leaky bucket algorithm* and *token bucket* (Li & Stol, 2002). The token bucket, for example, is a formal definition of the transfer rate using a formula involving three components: burst size, mean rate, and a time interval. The burst size denotes the traffic quantity that can be sent within a given unit of time without scheduling.

Incoming network traffic to a server can be arranged into different classes, where incoming packets are mapped to their corresponding classes. Various types of parameters can be used to define the set of classes depending on the granularity of the classification. These include the server-side IP addresses or services (user datagram protocol [UDP] and transmission control protocol [TCP] ports), client IP addresses, DiffServ bits, client socket connections, and processes that will be generated on servers when processing packet content. Traffic classification plays an important role in reducing the complexity of eliminating malicious activity. For example, to protect a server from a SYN flood attack (Kargl, Maier, & Weber, 2001), a traffic class should be defined based on TCP SYN packets. For example, an e-commerce firm that wants the company Web site to be continually available to high-paying customers even under heavy loads might define traffic classes based on ordering requests. This is a high-gain criterion that imposes costly traffic processing to differentiate between classes.

## Load Controlling

Classifying traffic is not enough to reduce or avoid overload on the supervised server. It should be complemented by a load-controlling mechanism based on well-defined and reliable traffic metrics. Once a packet is mapped to its corresponding class, the set of load metrics associated with that class are assessed to decide which action should be taken against that packet. Load indicators and metrics can be defined based on static or dynamic observations of the system capacity. With static controlling, a priori resource bounds are generally imposed (e.g., maximum number of client socket connections, maximum incoming packet rate). These metrics should be carefully defined to compromise between resource underuse and resource exhaustion. A particular static metric can be expressed in the form of *processing packet X gets Y% of the CPU* (Welsh & Culler, 2002). These metrics are based on resources accounting and assume that the controller has an exact and up-to-date idea of the server's resource status. Static metrics definition seems to work well with services that have an a priori knowledge of the resources required.

In dynamic controlling, a load controller is aware of the server's capacity and adjusts the used metrics actively based on the observed system's behavior and performance. To use dynamic controlling effectively, appropriate parameters should be taken into consideration to provide system stability and reduce false interpretations. For example, a minimal amount of time may be imposed on the load controller between metrics changes. Another load-controlling parameter can be defined by the minimal variation of the observed metric value that should be noticed before switching metrics.

## Policy Management

Policy management is partly the administratively configurable part of the overload protection component. It defines the metrics values, describes the server reactions, and specifies whether specific measures should be taken when the load controller metrics reach their limits. Policy management can, for example, state to refuse additional SYN packets when the number of service-connection attempts has reached its throughput limit $Y$ within an observed $Z$ seconds. This is a straightforward and naive policy rule that can be associated with static load controlling. Another policy can specify that the system should begin trying to adjust the priorities of a traffic class under a heavy load from a value $X$ to value $Y$ if the server resource $Z$ has reached its limit value $W$. When the system becomes overloaded, the set of new connections corresponding to the assigned traffic class can then be refused.

QGuard (Jamjoom & Reumann, 2000) provides a differentiation treatment for incoming traffic based on the adjustment of the priority or admission control parameters. It divides the system capacity to grant more importance than preferred server clients and enables protection against SYN floods and the ping of death.

## Protecting from Denial of Service

Denial of service (DoS) attacks attempt to deprive systems and applications from needed resources to prevent them from providing their services. Consequently, a server that is a victim of such an attack will appear unreachable to its users. Recently, DoS attacks have evolved into more intense and damaging attacks, including distributed DoS (DDoS) attacks that use many compromised servers to launch coordinated DoS attacks against single or multiple targets. The most famous event illustrating such attacks occurred in February 2000, when a variant of the Smurf and DoS attacks was conducted against Yahoo!, Buy.com, and Amazon.com. A DDoS attack starts by installing a master program on a compromised server to hide the intruder. At a later time, the master program initiates a coordinated attack performed by a set of agents (called zombies) installed on a set of compromised distributed sites. Intermediate systems/nodes called reflectors can be used to hide the identity of the intruder or to amplify the attack.

DDoS attacks have become easier to conduct. Many variants of DDoS attack tools exist today such as the Triple Flood Network (TFN) tool that supports Internet Control Message Protocol (ICMP) floods, SYN floods, UDP floods, and Smurf-style attacks. A more complex variant, called TFN2K, makes its recognition more difficult by using encryption and by communicating over multiple transport protocols, including TCP and UDP.

To protect servers against DoS attacks, many proposals have been made, but they don't completely solve the issue. Protection mechanisms include packet filtering, automated attack detection, and security vulnerability fixing. With packet filtering, end routers apply ingress packet filtering to allow only server-supported protocols and to deny security-critical services, suspicious identified source IP domains and services, directed broadcasts (RFC 2644), and forged IP addresses (RFC 2267). Routers should be monitored to update their filtering rules because intruders' techniques and behaviors evolve.

Automated attack detection is benefited by the fact that DoS attacks disrupt server resources (e.g., memory occupancy, processor utilization, network buffer) conspicuously. Therefore, end system resources should be continuously monitored and alerts should be instantaneously issued to enable a very quick reaction.

Security vulnerability fixing is achieved through the following actions: (1) servers should be configured carefully and securely; (2) unnecessary network services should be permanently deactivated; and (3) highly available services should be patched with all available security fixes.

Protection from DoS is sometimes insufficient, especially in cases where packets are spoofed. Many research proposals are making considerable effort to identify the real sources of packets. Savage and associates (Savage, Wetherall, Karlin, & Anderson, 2000) have used a probabilistic packet-marking scheme to enable tracing packets back to their source after an attack has occurred. Song and Perrig (2001) have enhanced the marking scheme and provided an efficient mechanism to authenticate the packet marking such that a compromised router cannot forge markings of other routers on the path connecting the intruder to the target server. Bellovin (2000) enabled ICMP messaging to be emitted randomly by routers along the path to a destination. This reduces the computation complexity but increases the overall network traffic. Finally, Snoeren et al. (2002) enabled single traceback IP packets by generating audit trails for traffic within the network.

## SERVER SCRIPTING ISSUES

A script is generally referred to as an external program component used to create dynamic content without modifying the server code. Its use is of great importance in Web development. Perl, PHP, Active Server Pages (ASP), and JavaServer Pages (JSP) are examples of server-side scripting languages. Common gateway interface (CGI) represents another way to achieve this end (see Figure 1). A CGI defines an interface between the server and external programs and enables a Web page to call programs written in any language. Because security vulnerabilities can be easily introduced in any step during the life cycle of a script (e.g., design, encoding, configuration), enabling the running of insecure programs on the server can increase the risk of attacks. There is no denying that the content of this section is extremely suitable for Web servers; nevertheless, it can be applied to any server that uses scripts.

### Risk Mitigation in the Use of Scripts

The installation and use of scripts and external programs should be done with maximum attention to reduce their potential damage risk. To do so, the script should be checked against poor programming practices that can lead to known vulnerabilities such as buffer overflow or misuse of characters input (e.g., metadata that can involve the execution of unexpected system commands).

Server-side include (SSI), which is Perl-based coding that enables dynamic information to be gathered from servers at the time the Web pages are generated (i.e., at the last modification time), can be the root of potential vulnerabilities that intruders can easily exploit. A buffer overrun in Microsoft FrontPage server extensions, for instance, allows code execution (Microsoft Corporation, 2004). The key idea for protection is to disable SSI whenever possible

as well as any other external program or script kept available for remote use on the server.

Server administrators need to keep track of all the scripts installed on the server. A single directory such as cgi-bin can be set, for example, for serving all the scripts. The access to this directory should then be controlled to detect any malicious creation or nonpermissible execution attempts. Integrity-checking tools can also be used to track any unauthorized changes. All users should be prohibited from seeing the directory's contents, and none of the script backups (e.g., *.cgi.bak, *.cgi~) should be left in that directory.

Another issue related to scripts is granting privileges. Requested script permissions should be restricted to allow the execution of scripts only by the user under which the process is invoked. Moreover, the user IDs granted to these scripts and programs should be different from those under which the service software that accommodates the scripts runs.

In cases in which a script needs to grant supplementary privilege to its users without allowing them much more than required, the script can be made *suid* (a practice specific to UNIX systems). This should be used only if necessary, and the need for it ought to be carefully evaluated. A weakness in making a script *suid* allows an intruder to access not only the set of files of the script owner but also any other file that could be accessed by the user on whose behalf the script is running.

### Writing Safe CGI Scripts

A CGI script works as follows. First, it processes the client input taken from the Web server while the script is invoked. Then, it executes and returns the related results to the Web server, which combines this result with the requested HTML page and returns it to the client. Despite its power, a CGI script can introduce security holes on the server. Such holes can be grouped into three categories: system information leaking, access grant to internal and undesirable system commands, and system resource exhaustion. To overcome these holes, security measures should be taken both when configuring the server to accommodate the scripts and during the CGI script encoding.

When encoding a script, the script developer must be aware of the security issues related to the selected language. CGI scripts can be written using compiled languages such as C or interpreted languages such as Perl. Interpreted languages make it easy to pass data to the system shell and wait for the output. Unfortunately, they might introduce a risky security hole because an intruder can pass arbitrary string commands as input to be executed by the shell. Moreover, because the source

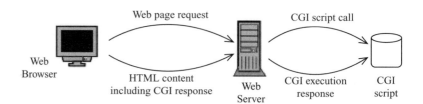

**Figure 1:**   Common gateway interface operation.

code for interpreted scripts is accessible, this makes it easier to find a bug to exploit. In this context, compiled languages are more difficult to subvert. The complexity of the compiled languages makes it also more difficult to find an embedded bug to exploit.

Once the coding language is chosen, the script developer should be aware of the possible unexpected user input that can contain shell metacharacters. To illustrate this issue, let's discuss the following Perl script, which can be used to send an e-mail after filling out a form.

```
$mail_to = $input{email_address};
open (MAIL, "|/path_to/sendmail $mail_to");
print MAIL "To: $mailto\n FROM: The Web user\n\n";
close MAIL;
```

The first instruction affects the variable *mail_to*, an e-mail address that the user of the form inserts in the appropriate field. Then, the command *sendmail* followed by variable *mail to* is started and the body of the mail is printed. Finally, the *sendmail* command is closed.

The developer here assumes that the user will always input an e-mail address. Such a statement can easily introduce a security weakness because an intruder can, for example, introduce the following string:

myname@mailserver.com; mail myname@mailserver.com < /etc/passwd"

When appended to the *sendmail* command, this input will also e-mail the content of the /etc/passwd file. To avoid such a situation, it is, in general, inappropriate to pass commands through a shell; rather, it is recommended to pass arguments directly to external programs as separate elements in a list. In all cases, the pattern of the user input should be matched against the set of undesirable shell metacharacters (see Kamthan, 1999) and removed or corrected, if necessary. The first instruction of the previous example can be complemented as follows to ensure that the user has entered a valid e-mail address:

```
$mail_to = $input{email_address};
if ($mail_to = ~/[;<>\*\|\'&\$!#\(\)\[\]\{\}:"'\n\r]){
    &return_error (500, "Invalid Address", "invalid email characters");
    }
else {...}
```

## Reducing CGI Risk Using Wrappers

Reducing these risks requires an administrator to be familiar with coding languages and to be able to spend a long period of time analyzing them. In some circumstances, when a provider allows its customers to upload their own scripts, checking scripts against security weaknesses is difficult.

A common solution to this problem is the use of wrappers on the server. Wrappers allow changing the user under which the script is running to prevent damages if the script is broken. Wrappers perform additional security checks before they allow scripts to be executed. They can also put restrictions on scripts to access limited parts of the file.

CGIWrap is a popular CGI wrapper. It runs any CGI script as its file owner, performs a set of security checks, and blocks the script execution if any of the checks fail. But it cannot guarantee that no misuse of the resources was done (e.g., a script is generating e-mails or introducing errors in the server logs), and it does not prevent a subverted CGI script from manipulation of the user's home directory under which it is running. It also cannot check whether scripts running with the same user permission are interfering with each other (e.g., a script is deleting another script's database entries). Another popular wrapper is suEXEC, which allows users to run scripts as the owner mentioned in the Apache server's configuration file. It also runs a series of approximately 20 security checks.

## ACCESS CONTROL

Apart from security efforts that aim at providing the needed protection of the delivered content, there must be requirements regarding the assurance of interacting principals' identities. Obviously, access control is of great importance to prevent unauthorized operations and malicious uses of server resources. After describing the types of access control, we discuss the set of widely used methods in practice.

### Types of Access Control

The literature distinguishes three types of access control mechanisms that are used to protect systems from unauthorized access (Kraft, 2002; Weber, 2003; Obaidat & Sadoun, 1997). They are called discretionary access control (DAC), mandatory access control (MAC), and role-based access control (RBAC). The first class works by assigning privileges on objects to subjects. The access is based on the identity of the involved user, the access mode, and the requested object. Because DAC allows an object's owner to grant or revoke a privilege to another subject, it requires that all operations be set only by the administrator. To this limitation, one can add that DAC is also limited by the cascade of positive and negative rules that can lead to contradictions. Nevertheless, DAC is widely used because of its effectiveness and simplicity. Access control lists (ACLs) represent the most popular implementation of DAC.

MAC bases its decision on the sensitivity level relating to the information content of the objects and the formal authorization of subjects to access information. A lattice of information sensitivity is first established and a security level is then assigned to each object and subject, called classification and clearance, respectively. A subject is typically authorized to read classified information, which is lower or equal to its clearance and is disallowed to introduce modifications on the classified information only if its clearance is equal or higher. MAC policy is well suited for rigid environments with a centralized information owner; but, on the other hand, it is unsuited for services that are processing unclassified information and presents a problem when there are multiple instances of objects that are classified differently despite their same meaning.

RBAC techniques have shown their effectiveness in managing security in dynamic environments, such as commercial contexts. RBAC works by defining roles and assigning the appropriate users to them. The roles are created based on the user activity on the system, and they are updated by granting or revoking new permissions as new system components are added or removed. Typically, a role can hold many users, and a user can be assigned many roles. Similarly, a role can hold several permissions, and a permission can be allocated to many roles. Roles introduce great simplicity in managing server security, and users can be reassigned easily to new roles as their responsibilities or categories change. With RBAC, an administrator can grant the minimal necessary privileges to a system's users. In contrast with MAC policy, RBAC can support abstract permissions (e.g., cipher, decipher, generate key, recover key) rather than generic read and write permissions.

Other models of access control have emerged, including the Clark-Wilson model for the preservation of integrity and the Chinese Wall model for the preservation of confidentiality by preventing conflict of interest in commercial activities. Details on these models can be found in Yao (2003).

## IP-Based Control

Various fields and traffic characteristics within the TCP/IP protocol can serve as a basis for access control. A server inspects the traffic received to extract the subject's information. Examples of subject IDs involve the requested service (TCP or UDP port number), protocol identifier at the transport layer, and IP source address. Once the subject ID is extracted, a list is used to deduce whether the client is allowed to use the local resource. This access control is widely implemented in basic solutions, terminal servers, and routers. It is simple, easy to implement, and can cope with the possibility of managing the whole network identity. Nevertheless, the level of user-identity assurance is low (e.g., users that connect from the same machine look the same) and the server administrator may be brought to manage a huge amount of meaningless subject identities. The reasons for this include the use of proxies and Network Address Translation, which allows a great number of users to share the same IP address. In addition, the lack of security in the TCP/IP protocol suite can misrepresent identification results. An intruder can forge an IP address to gain unauthorized access to the server or can substitute an identity for a legitimate user and behave maliciously to induce the server administrator to deny the corresponding IP address. Doing so is a form of DoS. Some access control solutions rely on, in addition to TCP/IP identifiers, the use of the host name (e.g., domain name system [DNS] name, NetBIOS name), which is being used by the user

that connects to the server. This is also inefficient because it does not point out which user is accessing the server.

Although the discussed solution is the easiest access control method, it is better to use it only in situations where the level of security requirements is reasonably low or when the security is handled jointly with other solutions (e.g., firewall, authentication server). The Linux TCP Wrapper is an example that provides an efficient IP-based access control mechanism in addition to its capability of logging requests. Its daemon *tcpd* checks the *hosts.allow* file and the *hosts.deny* file before granting or denying access. The two files mark which hosts are allowed to access which network services and keep the list of which hosts are denied.

## Name-Based Control

With the previous control scheme, the server was able to identify the host initiating connections and not the users themselves. With *name-based* access control, subjects should provide valid information (e.g., user names and passwords) on their IDs to the server so the server can decide whether the subject is authorized to access its resources. On the server side, a naming scheme such as uniform resource names (URNs; RFC 1737) should be used to map subject IDs to the real users efficiently. The notion of groups, which can be a set of users granted the same privilege, is used to reduce administration efforts in allocating authorizations. Permission for users with similar privileges is granted or denied to the entire group, instead of applying it separately to each user. Nevertheless, administrators should be aware of the potential weaknesses that can be introduced if a user is included simultaneously in groups having different privileges. Name-based access control can become a hard task to manage, especially when the number of clients is high or growing at a fast rate. Moreover, users are forced to manage a lot of IDs, especially when every server they are connecting to uses its own ID database.

To overcome these shortcomings, some solutions that rely on centralized authorities to verify user identity have been developed. Microsoft Passport represents such a solution. It allows a user to access sites that have implemented the Passport Single Sign-In using a single sign-in (SSI) name and password. Other solutions such as Terminal Access Controller Access Control System Plus (TACACS+) and Remote Authentication Dial-In User Service (RADIUS) rely on the use of authentication services. They receive the user ID from the server and send it back to make the authorization decision (e.g., accept, reject, or change password).

Separate management of user IDs requires that each site that stores user IDs deploy efficient security mechanisms. However, although such approaches are more practical than the distributed approaches, they can lead to damages in the case where a user gained access to the user IDs database.

## Access Control and Scripts

The use of scripts is a suitable solution to strengthen and customize the access-control mechanism previously presented. Suppose a server provides name-based access control to its users, and the users have specified at the time of their subscription whether they are connecting from a laptop or a desktop computer. To enforce the reliability of the access-control mechanism, a script can be implemented to record the IP addresses of the machines from which the connections are initiated. After verifying the user login and password, the script checks the stored mobility attribute of the user and its current IP address. If the attribute is set to false information, this could mean that an intruder has stolen the user account and used it to connect with a spoofed source IP address. Therefore, the script can initiate countermeasures such as sending an e-mail to the system administrator, logging the observation, or locking the account. Obviously, these measures are commonly implemented in reactive intrusion-detection systems, but they can be used to provide efficient access control. Scripts play an important role in enriching the authorization rules needed to maintain access control.

## Certificate-Based Access Control

X.509 certificates provide support for access control because they bind the owner identity, a private key, and the related public key (the private key is kept secret by its owner). A trusted certificate authority digitally signs each issued certificate after appending a set of attributes, including the user identity. The access control is then performed by first ensuring that the user mentioned in the certificate owns the corresponding private key. This is done typically by asking the user to digitally sign a message with its private key. Once the message is received, the server accesses the user certificate and starts signature verification. This includes validation of the certificate, decryption of the signature, and computation of the message hash. To test the validity of a user's certificate, a set of checks has to be performed, including the certificate integrity (using the public key of the certificate issuer), the chain of trust (i.e., if the signature really has been issued by the certificate authority, and if the certificate authority is trusted), and the certificate's expiration time.

Even if all the quoted tests have succeeded, the certificate can be meaningless if the certificate issuer has revoked it (for reasons that are described in RFC 3280). To determine the certificate status, the server typically downloads a certificate revocation list (CRL) that has a list containing the serial numbers of all revoked certificates. This list is issued periodically to enable clients to access up-to-date information. All the certificates and the CRL are made available through public directories, generally using Lightweight Directory Access Protocol (LDAP) or Web servers.

Despite its high level of subject identity assurance, certificate usage requires the availability of a whole infrastructure (LDAP server, certificate authority, revocation lists) to guarantee the availability of the publication service. The use of CRL technology implies that there is always a short period between revocation requests and CRL publication during which the certificate holder might still use its private key and temper access control. Also, processing a CRL generates problems in terms of server resources and traffic usage because CRLs can become very large. To overcome this limitation, the use of Online

Certificate Status Protocol (OCSP) has emerged. A user sends a request for certificate status to the OCSP server to receive the certificate status instantaneously. Another security issue regarding the use of public-key infrastructure is that a certificate's validity is dependent on all its parents' issuers, including intermediate certificate authorities and the root certificate authority.

Certificate-based access control is useful to authenticate users. It also can be used to authorize the execution of actions within the server. To state whether a user has the required rights to perform an action, one idea is to append the user rights, roles, and authorization information to the certificate based on the X.509 version 3 extensions. But this is quite undesirable because the authorization information, user identity, and user public key do not have the same life duration. Furthermore, the certificate issuer might not have enough information on the authorizations accorded to users. Another solution to this problem proposes a role-based access-control infrastructure using X.509 public-key certificates and attributes certificates that can be used to store users' roles and authorizations (Zhou & Meinel, 2004).

# GUIDELINES FOR IMPROVING SERVER SECURITY

As outlined previously, securing servers is subject to many challenges. Thus, administrators need a set of guidelines to follow to simplify their tasks and reduce the likelihood of introducing potential security weaknesses. The content of this section is written with the help of many references available on Web sites belonging to CERT, the SANS Institute, and the University of Minnesota.

## Server-Side Security Practices

Effective security practices involve managing accounts, hardening installations, fixing vulnerabilities, configuring files and directories access permissions, managing logs, and performing backups.

### Account Management

Unauthorized users can put the security of the server's information in danger if they successfully access it. To avoid such circumstances, administrators should carefully consider account management, including the following points:

- Because the security policy states that only authorized users can access server resources, the server should be configured to authenticate all users who attempt to access it.
- The security policy should describe under what conditions user accounts are created, modified, and deleted. Refer to a set of administrative practices to specify requirements regarding users' usage of passwords. For example, they should be prohibited from exposing their passwords.
- A password policy should be stated and enforced. It includes rules related to password length, complexity (generally, alphanumeric and special characters are recommended), aging, possibility of reuse, and timetables

access. Such parameters depend heavily on the context and frequency of the server use, account types (e.g., administrator accounts have different lifetimes than user accounts), and risk associated with password compromise.

- Default accounts and groups should be renamed or disabled whenever possible to avoid their use by intruders. Moreover, old, unused, and unnecessary accounts should be disabled, if not deleted.

- Accounts that do not require an interactive login (e.g., user mail accounts) should not be permitted to get a command shell.

- Assembling users into appropriate groups and assigning group-based privileges should be used whenever possible, particularly when the number of users per group is important. Particular attention should be paid to users who belong to distinct groups.

- Server administrators should be ensured that the password policy is followed by users when they change their passwords. Password auditing tools or cracks can be used by administrators if it is permitted by the security policy to ensure password robustness.

- Whenever possible, system account settings should be configured to reject passwords that are not in accordance with the password policy and deny login and lock the account after a predefined number of failed attempts.

- Users should be requested through formal procedures to lock access to the system whenever they leave it and configure their system to be locked after an idle period of time.

- An administrator account should be used only if necessary. In the case where different administrative accounts are used, they should be named differently to better distinguish each administrator activity. Moreover, default administrator accounts should be renamed whenever possible.

- Anonymous access should be restricted whenever possible. Guest accounts should be renamed and, if possible, disabled.

## Secure Installation and Vulnerability Fixing

To cope with the occurrence of new vulnerabilities on operating systems and applications, vendors and security groups release patches, fixes, and updates. The following practices can help secure servers:

- Security updates on production servers should follow a policy that defines their periodicity, the required testing phases, the documentation of these operations, and the required user privileges.

- Administrators should install and run up-to-date versions of operating systems and applications. They should use packages that are actively supported by their providers for security updates and vulnerability fixing.

- Only needed services should be installed on servers; unnecessary features must be disabled, and configurations should respond to security constraints. Moreover, any required feature should be limited, and all recommended patches have to be applied.

- Applications and services should run with the lowest required privileges to reduce potential damages if they are compromised.

- Necessary and unsecured services such as file transfer protocol (FTP), telnet, and simple network management protocol (SNMP) should be replaced by more secure services. For example, *SSH* can be used instead of *rlogin* and *ftps* instead of *ftp*.

- Often, vendors provide update utilities that automatically connect, download, and install packages. Because these utilities do not usually cope with administrator privileges, they should be disabled whenever it is possible to download and install updates manually. Such prevention reduces potential damages if a server is compromised.

- Up-to-date scanners of vulnerabilities should be actively used to find the latest common and most critical vulnerabilities. Examples of scanners include IIS Internet Scanner and Nessus.

- A risk-mitigation strategy is highly recommended to implement to study the possible attack scenarios and reduce the cost relative to the security measures that can be applied against threats.

- In the case where a trust relationship is defined between servers, configurations should be reviewed carefully. An intruder can use the trust relationship to access another host from a compromised host.

## Files and Directories Access Permission

The following practices help set the most accurate file and directory permissions to reduce security breaches and maintain integrity and secrecy:

- The installed operating system (OS) should be provided with a secure file system, and the disk partitions should be formatted using the most secure available file formats (e.g., NTFS for Windows systems and EXT3 for Linux).

- File and folder permissions as well as access should be configured with the lowest required rights (e.g., public scripts should be configured to be modified by their owner only, and the log files permissions should be set to append only whenever possible).

- Access to files and directories storing OS configurations should be restricted to administrators only, with even the read privilege revoked from others.

- Attention should be given to access-control inheritance when creating or appending new files and directories. The best way is to let access-control propagate down directory hierarchies.

- When the relationship between users is complex or when secrecy must be maintained, encryption should be used to protect sensitive data.

- File-sharing services should be disabled whenever possible. File and folder shares should be reduced whenever unneeded, and access permissions should be configured to maximum security levels. File owners should know how the system should behave to satisfy local-access and shared-access permissions.

- Remote registry access should be minimized, restricted, and generally allowed only for administration purposes.

- In UNIX and Linux file systems, the use of *suid* files should be refused, unless required. An audit of these files should be periodically performed.

## Logging Configuration

Managing logs effectively should help administrators detect signs of intrusion, evaluate system performance, and detect faults. The following practices are recommended:

- Security policy should define explicitly the use of logs, their period of availability (depending on their category), and the relevant responsibilities. Logged activities should include administrative operations (e.g., account creations), successful and unsuccessful connections, remote and local connections information (e.g., IP address, requested service), authentication information (e.g., used account name, failed or successful attempts), and unsuccessful file accesses.
- If permitted by the logging mechanism, the level of detail should be set so that only useful information is recorded. Log files as well as their locations should be protected by defining the most restrictive access permissions to prevent them from being illegitimately modified. The access to the utilities that can modify these logs should be restricted.
- Public servers such as Web and FTP servers should maintain logs relative to user activities, including the rejected and dropped requests.
- Server logs should be rotated periodically to avoid the saturation or the alteration of system resources. If permitted by the logging mechanism, the log file content should be split into many fragments in a way that makes it easy to find any record inside the log.
- Whenever required, log files can be compressed to save storage space.
- Log files should be stored into a secure location. Keeping logs locally is not secure because they can be altered whenever the server is compromised. It is worthwhile to transfer them securely to a more secure place. The use of remote logging (e.g., *Syslog* service) is very helpful.
- Security personnel should be trained to review server logs on a regular basis and ensure that logs are recorded in accordance with the security policy and any time it is needed (e.g., in cases where an anomaly is perceived).
- The system clock should provide the correct time to ensure accurate results when correlating the different log outputs issued from different network sources. Protocols such as Network Time Protocol (NTP) can be used to synchronize server clocks.
- Procedures to handle situations where breaches are detected should be prepared in advance. Moreover, security personnel should be trained to use forensic-data-collection mechanisms and extract evidences and preserve them from being altered.
- Server security administrators should periodically conduct a security audit to evaluate the security practices and locate potential weaknesses in configurations. To do so, administrators can use software to correlate and analyze server logs and should rely on their intuition and skills to find anomalies.

## Performing Backups

Providing a service without developing backup and restoration plans can be inappropriate. The following practices enable administrators to perform efficient backups and help them restore the system state after the occurrence of critical incidents:

- Administrators should create a backup and restoration plan based on the following queries: what (file identification), where (backup media), when (backup periodicity), and how (type of backup) to backup.
- Scheduled backup creation should be constrained by the required time to perform the backup, the storage space needed, and the complexity of restoring files from backups.
- Server administrators should be informed about their responsibility regarding backups and restoration activities.
- Backups should be performed periodically in accordance with the defined schedule.
- Performing backups locally on the server does not require additional security mechanisms to protect data that traverse the network. But it increases the needed effort because it requires managing different storage media at each workstation. If backups are centralized, secrecy and integrity of the transferred files should be guaranteed. Appropriate tools (e.g., Amanda and Arkeia) should be used to help implement the defined backup scheme.
- After the creation of backup files on given media, the files should remain encrypted and the media should be documented along with the restoration guidelines.
- A copy of the backup tools should be stored offline because they cannot be trusted after the server that stores them is targeted by security attacks.
- The set of media as well as backup and recovery processes should be tested periodically to enhance the restoration ability and detect potential backup deficiencies.
- Servers that provide highly available services and whose content changes often should be fully replicated on a backup machine that can be plugged into the network directly in case an incident occurs.
- Reuse of backup media outside the backup activity should be done prior to their secure deletion.

## Effective Use of Security Software

Relying on the set of built-in system tools and services is insufficient to guarantee an acceptable system security level. Supplementing the protection mechanisms with additional security solutions as described here is essential:

- It is highly recommended to install up-to-date antivirus software with filtering capabilities on servers that are used to store user data content (e.g., public FTP servers, e-mail servers, and Web servers with personal user directories). In cases where the security policy allows the server to initiate connections, the server should be configured to periodically look up updates on virus signatures and detection algorithms. In other cases, a security administrator should perform this role.

- The real-time capturing of state features (e.g., system performance, processes, and files) and the monitoring of any potential deviation of the expected behavior should be implemented. This includes the use of host-based or application-based intrusion detection systems (IDSs). Moreover, network-based IDSs should be installed on the most sensitive network segments to monitor the network traffic for suspicious events. It should generate alerts and take a snapshot of any suspicious activity as soon as it happens.

- Because network firewalls are not able to prevent local attacks (those issued from internal users or from compromised neighborhood servers), the deployment of local server firewalls is recommended. These firewalls should be configured with a total understanding of legitimate server traffic.

- Reactive IDSs (e.g., snort-inline) can complement the set of protection mechanisms because they can take countermeasures on the detection of intrusions (e.g., active connections killing and router ACL updating). They should be used carefully to prevent DoS attacks. In all cases, the set of countermeasures should follow an a priori response policy (e.g., when, what, and how long a countermeasure is applied).

- The use of integrity-checking software should complement the intrusion-detection effort because it can be applied to static content (e.g., configuration files, administrative binary commands) to detect changes. Use integrity-checking software carefully to avoid confusing legitimate and malicious file modification.

- Remote privileged access to the server should be reduced as much as possible. When used, the access should be strictly controlled using IP filtering tools, utilities, and encryption. Secure Shell (SSH) and virtual private networks (VPNs) can be used to encrypt the user session traffic (including login and password) and provide lower-level traffic encryption, respectively.

- Authentication techniques should be used on the server based on server activity. For example, usually a public Web server does not require the same level of authentication as a remote administration server does. Virtual local area networks should be used whenever possible because they represent another type of efficient access control that can be implemented in networks.

- Servers should implement data encryption for sensitive data to avoid illegal reading and retrieving if the server is compromised. For example, a Web server that uses X.509 certificates should store its corresponding private key privately in a ciphered form (e.g., PKCS#1).

## Infrastructure Countermeasures

Protecting an information system by applying the strongest security measures can be insufficient to guarantee that once the security policy is violated, an efficient and accurate incident response can be undertaken

quickly. Mandia and Prosise (2003) defined an incident-response methodology and described a set of goals. We describe a series of considerations to be made prior to a server incident occurrence so that administrators can minimize the impact of the incident, determine the relevant causes and effects, track intruders, provide accurate reports, and finally promote prevention and detection:

- The first consideration relates to host security. The set of used applications, services, and operating systems should have been well patched and verified against potential security exploits. All supplementary security functions such as logging, filtering, wrapping, and controlling access need to be implemented even if they are repetitive. It is also important to decide from the beginning which protocols and activity to log.

- The second consideration relates to the network. Some network-based security schemes measure the adequacy of countermeasures when they are installed. The network architecture and topology configured should be favorable to monitoring. For example, it is better to install a Linux Syslog server in the internal network stub to avoid the destruction of log content if an intruder takes control of the public network.

- The third consideration relates to network protocols. Protocols that are more secure, in the sense that they provide an accurate representation of participant identity and activity, should be used because they present more meaningful proof of intruder activity and identity.

- The fourth consideration relates to the expert team qualified to perform incident response and forensic investigation. Preparing the team should involve considering the needed hardware and software, appropriate policies, operating procedures, and staff training.

- Finally, the fifth consideration relates to the legal environment. Any security measure should be governed by law because any omission can expose the person responsible for server security to legal repercussions. This is important because it is essential to find the proof for law-enforcement agencies to track intruders. For example, if the country laws state that a lawful electronic certificate involves only X.509 certificates, an authentication server that uses SPKI certificates will be unable to prove the identity of the user that has been accepted by the system.

## ADVANCED ISSUES

Various advanced issues present challenges for server-side security, including remote authoring, transaction security, and server protection from user-side holes. Because the latter issue can be considered as part of the former issues, we describe in the following subsection the remote authoring and transaction security challenges.

## Remote Authoring and Administration

Remote authoring is the ability to write and store a resource (e.g., HTML file, database entry) in the storage area of a remote server. This process can initiate a distributed interactivity between users and servers. Distributed authoring on the Web requires scaling the content across the resources, users, and transaction rates. Supporting these requirements can demand a decentralized repository with an easy-to-use, standard, multiuser, and multiversion interface. Access is required based on open and nonproprietary document formats. Hypertext transfer protocol (HTTP) fulfills some of these goals and requirements as a remote procedure call protocol. It is stateless and relatively secure. However, HTTP is not sufficient to support remote authoring on the Web. One important limitation is the HTTP POST method, which can be used to invoke any operation on the server. The POST method ends up being a security hole through which any operation can be executed. Trying to analyze POST message bodies to determine which operations are being performed is extremely difficult.

Therefore, HTTP provides no means for organizing the complex content that is typical of a Web server supporting multiple applications. It does not provide any way to link multilevel security documents. The solution is to improve HTTP to satisfy remote authoring needs. Web-distributed authoring and versioning (Web-DAV) is an example of a solution that provides new methods to extend HTTP functionality. Despite its advantages, HTTP does not accommodate easily adding new methods because interactions between headers and methods should be explicitly defined. However, server security and access control benefit from adding new methods.

## Server-Side Transactions Security

To process transactions securely, a server might need to be able to evaluate credentials and set up credential acceptance policies; it should also be able to export parts of its acceptance policies to users who ask for explanations. In addition, the server administrator needs to have a clear understanding of the services the server provides and the roles a user could assume when accessing the services. The response to a transaction depends on the role of the user, who is initiating the transaction.

When a set of credentials is submitted with a transaction (or request for a service), the server might need to decrypt, parse, and determine whether a credential has been revoked by its issuer before processing the related transaction. This can induce a translation of the credential formats into the internal language used for reasoning by the server.

The translated credentials along with the classification of a transaction under process might need to be submitted to a knowledge base describing the server's credential acceptance policy. Often, the set of eligible roles can be passed because it is to the server's application. It is beyond the scope of this chapter to discuss several important issues, including the authentication of a transaction initiator to one of the individuals mentioned in the credential, role conflict, credential translation, and policy explanation.

## GLOSSARY

**CGI Wrapper** A script that prevents users of common gateway interface (CGI) scripts from compromising the security of the Web server. This is usually achieved by running a series of security checks on the invoked script, restricting the script access, or even denying the script access to the user's home directory.

**Common Gateway Interface (CGI)** An interface between the Web server and external programs called gateways. It enables a server to return dynamic Web content by calling programs written in any language and sending their output back to the browser.

**EXT3** A file system common to Linux that adds speed, reliability, and support for large drives in comparison to old UNIX file systems. It adds journaling to enhance recovery after crashes or data loss.

**Network Address Translation (NAT)** A protocol that enables networking resources to use a set of Internet Protocol (IP) addresses for internal traffic and a second set for external traffic.

**Server-Side Include (SSI)** Enables dynamic Web pages to be created by inserting hypertext markup language (HTML) comment commands within static HTML files. Theses commands are processed by the server when Web pages are requested by the client. Can be used to call external programs such as common gateway interface (CGI) scripts.

**Simple Network Management Protocol (SNMP)** It provides information exchange between two SNMP entities about configuration and resource status.

**Traffic Shaping** A mechanism that adjusts the network-flow characteristics to guarantee performance and quality of service (e.g., avoid overload) while meeting the requirements of the server, network, and resources.

**Uniform Resource Name (URN)** It represents a name assigned to an Internet resource. URNs are maintained using naming services and are designed to have a long lifetime.

**Virtual Local Area Network (VLAN)** This concept is defined in RFC 3069. It represents a subgroup of network computers (including any network hardware) that behaves as if they are connected to the same wire, although in fact they belong to different physical networks.

## CROSS REFERENCES

See *Access Control: Principles and Solutions; Client-Side Security; Computer Security Incident Response Teams (CSIRTs); Protecting Web Sites; Security and Web Quality of Service.*

## REFERENCES

Bellovin, S. M. (1989). Security problems in the TCP/IP protocol suite. *Computer Communications Review,* 2(19), 32–48.

Bellovin, S. M. (2000). *ICMP traceback messages—Internet draft.* Retrieved June 8, 2004, from http://www.research.att.com/~smb/papers/draft-bellovin-itrace-00.txt

Burke, J. (2003). *Windows forensic how-to: Incident response plan for abuse of corporate assets*. Retrieved June 2005, from http://www.giac.org/practical/GSEC/Joe_Burke_GSEC.pdf

Canavan, S. (2003). An information security policy development guide for large companies. *Information Security Reading Room*.

CERT. (2000). *Configure computers for file backups*. Retrieved June 10, 2004, from http://www.cert.org/security-improvement/practices/p071.html

CERT. (2001a). *Configure computers for user authentication*. Retrieved June 10, 2004, from http://www.cert.org/security-improvement/practices/p069.html

CERT. (2001b). *Keep operating systems and applications software up to date*. Retrieved June 10, 2004, from http://www.cert.org/security-improvement/practices/p067.html

CERT. (2001c). *Manage logging and other data collection mechanisms*. Retrieved June 10, 2004, from http://www.cert.org/security-improvement/practices/p092.html

Chen, H., & Wagner, D. (2002, November 18–22). MOPS: An infrastructure for examining security properties of software. *ACM Conference on Computer and Communications Security (CCS '02)*.

Cowan, C., Beattie, S., Kroah-Hartman, G., Pu, C., Wagle, P., & Gligor, V. (2000). SubDomain: Parsimonious server security. *14th USENIX Systems Administration*.

DaCosta, D., Dahn, C., Mancoridis, S., & Prevelakis, V. (2003). Characterizing the "security vulnerability likelihood" of software functions. *International Conference on Software Maintenance (ICSM '03)*.

Foster, J. F. (2002). *Type qualifiers: Lightweight specifications to improve software quality*. Unpublished doctoral dissertation, University of California, Berkeley.

ITSS Information Security Services. (2003). Denial of service in Cisco IOS caused by IPv4 packets. Retrieved June 5, 2004, from http://securecomputing.stanford.edu/alerts/cisco-ios-17jul2003.html

Jamjoom, H., & Reumann, J. (2000). *QGuard: Protecting Internet servers from overload* (Tech. Rep. No. CSE-TR-427-00). University of Michigan.

Kamthan, P. (1999). CGI security: Better safe than sorry. Retrieved June 5, 2004, from http://tech.irt.org/articles/js184/

Kargl, F., Maier, J., & Weber, F. (2000). Protecting Web servers from distributed denial of service attacks. *International World Wide Web Conference*, 514–524.

Kraft, R. (2002). Research and design issues in access control for network services on the Web. *The 3rd International Conference on Internet Computing, 3*, 542–548.

Li, F. Y., & Stol, N. (2002). QoS provisioning using traffic shaping and policing in 3rd-generation wireless networks. *IEEE Wireless Communications and Networking Conference (WCNC), 17*(21), 139–143.

Lowe, G. (1995). An attack on the Needham-Schroeder public-key authentication protocol. *Information Processing Letters, 56*(3), 131–133.

Mandia, K., & Prosise, C. (2003). Introduction to the incident response process. In *Incident Response and Computer Forensics* (2nd ed., pp. 11–32). New York: McGraw-Hill Osborne Media.

McClure, S., Scambray, J., & Kurtz, G. (2003). *Hacking exposed: Network security secrets and solutions* (4th ed.). New York: McGraw-Hill Osborne Media.

Microsoft Corporation. (2004). *Microsoft Security Bulletin MS03-051. Buffer overrun in Microsoft FrontPage Server Extensions could allow code execution*. Retrieved June 8, 2004, from http://www.microsoft.com/technet/security/bulletin/MS03-051.mspx

Needham, R. M., & Schroeder, M. D. (1978). Using encryption for authentication in large networks of computers. *Communications of the ACM, 21*(12), 993–999.

NHSnet. (2004). Information security policy. Retrieved June 5, 2004, from http://www.nhsia.nhs.uk/nhsnet/pages/connecting/hospices/High_Level_InfoPolicy_PCT.pdf.

NMRC. (2003). The hack FAQ: Web browser as attack tool. Retrieved June 7, 2004, from http://www.nmrc.org/pub/faq/hackfaq/hackfaq-09.html

Obaidat, M. S., & Sadoun, B. (1997). Verification of computer users using keystroke dynamics (Part B). *IEEE Transactions on Systems, Man, and Cybernetics, 27*(2), 261–269.

Obaidat, M. S., & Sadoun, B. (1999). Keystroke dynamics based identification. In Anil Jain et al. (Eds.), *Biometrics: Personal identification in networked society* (pp. 213–229). MA: Kluwer Academic Publishers.

Savage, S., Wetherall, D., Karlin, A., & Anderson, T. (2000). Practical network support for IP traceback. *2000 ACM SIGCOMM Conference*, 295–306.

Snoeren, A. C., Partridge, C., Sanchez, L. A., Jones, C. E., Tchakountio, F., Schwartz, B., Kent, S. T., & Strayer, W. T. (2002). Single-packet IP traceback. *IEEE/ACM Transactions on Networking (ToN), 10*(6), 721–734.

Song, D. X., & Perrig, A. (2001). Advanced and authenticated marking schemes for IP traceback. *IEEE Infocomm*, 878–886.

Syed, M. A. (2002). NT users can bypass password changing policy via IIS. Retrieved June 6, 2004, from http://www.securiteam.com/windowsntfocus/5NP082A6KM.html.

Thiagarajan, V. (2003). *Information security management—BS 7799.2:2002—audit check list*. Retrieved June 11, 2004, from http://www.sans.org/score/checklists/ISO_17799_checklist.pdf

University of Minnesota, Office of Information Technology. (2003). *Server installation security guidelines*. Retrieved June 10, 2004, from http://www1.umn.edu/oit/security/ServerInstall.pdf

Vulnerability Information Center. (2004). *Samba smbd buffer overflow and race condition vulnerabilities*. Retrieved June 5, 2004, from http://www3.ca.com/securityadvisor/vulninfo/Vuln.aspx?ID=7286

Weber, H. A. (2003). Role-based access control: The NIST solution. Retrieved June 9, 2004, from http://www.giac.org/practical/GSEC/Hazen_Weber_GSEC.pdf

Welsh, M., & Culler, D. (2002). Overload management as a fundamental service design primitive. *Tenth ACM SIGOPS European Workshop*.

Wood, M. (2003). *WebDAV buffer overflow vulnerability revisited*. Retrieved June 5, 2004, from http://www.frame4.com/php/modules.php?name=News&file=printpdf&sid=468

Yao, W. T. (2003). *Trust management for widely distributed systems*. Unpublished doctoral dissertation, Jesus College, University of Cambridge, England.

Zhou, W., & Meinel, C. (2004). Implement role based access control with attribute certificates. *IEEE International Conference on Advanced Communication Technology (ICACT2004)*, 536–541.

# Protecting Web Sites

Dawn Alexander, *University of Maryland*
April Giles, *Johns Hopkins University*

## INTRODUCTION
### Current State of the Internet

Protecting Web sites from Web defacements is an important topic these days with the rapid rise in Internet usage and its increasing contribution to world trade through e-commerce and information exchange. As of September 2002, Nua Internet surveys indicated that the number of people using the Internet is estimated to be 605.60 million worldwide (Nua Internet, 2004). According to the On-line Computer Library Center, the number of Web sites has also shown tremendous growth over the past several years, with estimates that there were 8.4 million Web sites in 2001 (*On the size of the World Wide Web*, n.d.).

With total Internet usage growing significantly, there are correspondingly growing risks when someone "hacks" or breaks into a Web site. In 2001, a study of businesses by University of California economist Frank Bernhard estimated that approximately 6% of revenue is lost to problems caused by hackers (DeLong, 2001). It is hard to estimate how many hackers are on the Internet currently because of its relatively open accessibility. However, Peter Allor of ISS's X-Force Threat Analysis Division suggests that up to 3 million people as of 2003 can be classified as hackers (Niccolai, 2003). These hackers are very active. According to Lawrence K. Gershwin, U.S. National Intelligence Officer for Science and Technology, in a 2001 report for the Joint Economic Committee, "Cyber Threat Trends and U.S. Network Security," results of the HoneyNet project conducted by an independent group of security professionals indicate that "the average computer placed on the Internet will be hacked in about 8 hours. University networks are even worse, with an unsecured computer system being hacked in only about 45 minutes" (Gershwin, 2001).

Similar to other Web security threats, Web defacements are increasing significantly over time. An analysis completed by security consultancy group mi2g Ltd. reported in InfoWorld that more than 40,000 Web defacements occurred through September 2002, which surpassed total 2001 incidents of 31,322. This was an exponential increase from 2000 when 7821 Web defacements

were reported (Legard, 2002). Although the total number of reported Web defacements remains miniscule in comparison to the total number of estimated Web sites, the rapidly growing risks are of tremendous concern to many citizens, officials, businesses, and security professionals.

### Threat Agents

Who is doing such hacking damage over the Internet? Those with hacking capability do not have to use it negatively, but can help to improve the body of knowledge. Jim Wagner (2002) of Internetnews.com describes three types of hackers:

- *White hats.* People who help identify computer system vulnerabilities to improve the security of the Internet and who conduct only "ethical" or legal hacking.
- *Black hats.* People who hack illegally for destructive purposes or as thieves, also known as "crackers."
- *Gray hats.* People who provide information regarding vulnerabilities that could result in hacking activity both to the public (and thus potential crackers) as well as to vendors (so vendors can address how to mitigate the vulnerability).

The potentially damaging activities of black hats are the focus of this chapter, and we refer to these people as hackers. Why are these hackers wreaking havoc? Many hackers view Web defacement as an invigorating challenge, especially the teens and young adults who traditionally do this for fun and bragging rights.

Other groups such as organized crime hack as another way to get money illegally. For example, they might extort an organization by threatening to put illegally hacked credit card data on a defaced Web site unless paid hush money.

Extremist political groups might hack Web sites to terrorize opponents. For example, defacing an opponent's Web site communicates that the political group is the one in control.

Hacking activity negatively impacts global citizens at large in several ways. One is economic because the 6%

revenue impact discussed earlier is ultimately paid for by consumers and citizens as companies pass-through these costs. Also, hacking lowers the trust factor, which is key for the success of open systems such as the Internet. Unsecured Web sites are the easiest targets for hackers. This is similar to physical security in that most intruders follow the path of least resistance to gain access and inflict damage.

## Chapter Scope and Goals

This chapter focuses on protecting Web sites primarily from Web defacements by looking more closely at vulnerabilities, threats/attacks, and countermeasures from an independent viewpoint. Thus, it does not include extensive discussion regarding a variety of important security measures that are also part of the overall solution to improving Web security. The intended audience is security professionals and students who are interested in learning more about the impact of Web defacements on protecting Web sites.

## BACKGROUND
### Internet Overview

The Internet consists of all the computers and their connections that provide a method for people to communicate. The World Wide Web (WWW) or Web is a component of the Internet. The Web includes a set of rules or protocols regarding how computers communicate and the tools used for the connections.

When people communicate by using the Web, a series of commands is provided to a Web server, which houses the Web site. The Web server interprets these commands and returns the requested information through individual Web browsers, the most typical examples of which are Microsoft Internet Explorer and Netscape Navigator.

A Web site is a specific location on the World Wide Web that is identifiable by its uniform resource locator (URL). The Web site is composed of a variety of files in formats such as Hypertext Markup Language (HTML), Extensible Markup Language (XML), Java, ActiveX, common gateway interface (CGI), RPL, or WSOP that are viewed using a browser.

Also, several interfaces with Web servers enable data to be processed successfully (see Figure 1). One example is the Web server interface with the application server, which enables the user request to be processed. Interfacing with the application server is a database server with which the Web server interacts to obtain stored data such as contact information during an e-commerce transaction. Also, an authentication server can be included in the network to confirm that the user and session identification information is valid. This is important protection for financial services Web sites through which users can complete monetary transactions.

Figure 1 illustrates the path of communication used to obtain financial data from the user application at the desktop to the Web site.

Requests and responses are most often exchanged on the Web through the use of Hypertext Transfer Protocol (HTTP). A good description of HTTP is a stateless protocol

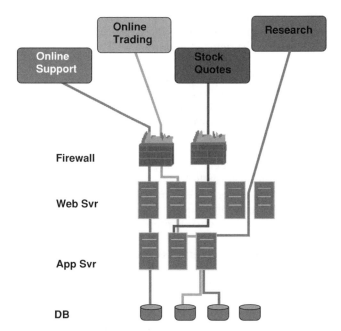

**Figure 1:** Interfaces with Web servers.
*Source:* Retrieved January 26, 2004, from www.nextslm. org/images/measure.gif.

that "defines how messages are formatted and transmitted, and what actions Web servers and browsers should take in response to various commands" (Webopedia. com, n.d). However, for transactions involving commerce, HTTP is too open and does not adequately protect private data. For these transactions, Secure HTTP is used because it ensures that data are sent securely over the Web. It supports encryption without requiring public keys. Also, it can be recognized when the URL address identifier changes from HTTP to HTTPS.

## Web Defacement Attacks

Web defacement occurs when a perpetrator accesses a Web site and changes it. This is a problem for a Web site owner because the Web site cannot be used as intended, plus there is the "embarrassment" factor and its impact on customers, partners, and others.

Web defacement attacks have been around as long as the Web has but are occurring with increasing frequency. For example, a group named Attrition has been credited with maintaining the largest archive of Web site defacement information (Attrition.org: About us, n.d.). Some of the more recognizable defacements archived there include BWI Airport, the security organization SANS Institute, and the *New York Times* Business Section.

### The BWI Airport Defacement
The BWI Airport Web site was defaced on September 27, 2001, and credit for this act was given to tty0 (Attrition. org: BWI Airport defaced, n.d.). The timing of the attack was unnerving because it was so close to 9/11. This defacement was recognizable to those who viewed it, but Attrition raised a good point when mentioning that a bigger problem could have been caused if unrecognizable

changes were made. For example, chaos could result if flight information was surreptitiously modified (Attrition. org: BWI Airport defaced, n.d.).

### The SANS Institute Defacement

The SANS Institute is a leading security organization that describes itself as "the most trusted and by far the largest source for information security training and certification in the world" (SANS Institute, n.d.). The Web site of the SANS Institute was defaced on July 13, 2001, with credit for the defacement given to Fluffi Bunni, who asked, "Would you really trust these guys to teach you security?" (Attrition.org: SANS Institute defaced, n.d.). This is a clear example that defacement is an ongoing challenge for even the most ostensibly prepared organizations.

### The *New York Times* Business Section Defacement

The *New York Times* Business Section Web site was defaced on February 15, 2001, and credit was attributed to Sm0ked Crew (Attrition.org, n.d.). One interesting point regarding this defacement was that the Sm0ked Crew mentioned Attrition.org in their defacement message (see Figure 2), although Attrition.org disclaimed all prior knowledge or support.

### What Types of People Are Committing Web Defacements?

Young people, some of whom develop vast computer skills at early ages, are a prime group believed to commit a significant number of defacements. It seems to be a badge of accomplishment that they wear to represent the number of defacements they completed, and for some it is surely a game.

Organized crime organizations worldwide has been accused of numerous Web defacements. This appears to be another channel for their illegal activities to make money and terrorize people.

Another potential group to which organizations must be sensitive is employees. Tensions stemming from the weak economy that result in higher layoff activity and much heavier workloads for remaining employees can contribute to employee dissatisfaction. Disgruntled employees are likely to have easier access to corporate Web sites than outsiders.

Political extremists are another group that has been known to commit Web defacements as part of cyberwar.

## VULNERABILITIES, THREATS/ATTACKS, AND COUNTERMEASURES

Within the security realm it is generally agreed that there are two key components of an attack: vulnerability and threat. As a security professional it is crucial that you understand the difference between a vulnerability and a threat. A clear and concise perception of these terms is necessary to build a comprehensive security plan across multiple distributed applications, services, and appliances. When taking on the daunting task of providing a secure wrapper for a product for which you have had no input on the security design (commercial off-the-shelf products), identifying the relevant design attributes of the product might well be more important than environmental factors in determining what security strategy to employ.

A *vulnerability* can be defined as "a component inherent within the design that can be exploited." Contrary to claims by some product developers, *vulnerabilities exist in every product*. For example, company A designs and develops a steel enclosure, whose function is to protect tangibles. Vulnerabilities exist within aluminum, which may be conducive to rust formation, which weakens protection capabilities of the enclosure. Software vulnerabilities can be characterized as singular or combinational (as well as explicit or implicit). Singular vulnerabilities are

THE-REV | SPLURGE

Sm0ked crew is back and better than ever!

Well, admin I'm sorry to say but you just got sm0ked by splurge.
Don't be scared though, everything will be all right, first
fire your current security advisor, he sux.

I would like to take this spot to say I'm sorry to attrition.org
I do mean it man, and I want to thank them for everything they have done for me.
http://www.attrition.org

Hey thanks Rev for teaching me how to hack IIS, you da man!!!

Shouts To: Downkaos, datagram, Italguy
gorro, Silver Lords, Hi-Tech Hate, Fux0r,
prime suspectz, WFD, and Hackweiser.

questions email us at: sm0kedcrew@hushmail.com

**Figure 2:** *New York Times* Business Section defacement.
*Source:* Retrieved January 26, 2004, from www. attrition.org

caused by one known factor, for example, buffer overflow. Combinational vulnerabilities are caused by a set of occurrences that happen simultaneously and that lead to an unintended consequence.

Most vulnerabilities are well known within the security community. Why, then, are they so prevalent within most products? Because businesses develop products to make a profit, and the time it takes to move a product from the drawing board to market is a critical component in the amount of profit that can be made. Consequently, testing for product vulnerabilities is often seen as a profit-*reducing* activity that increases time to market or reduces time available to implement new features. It is our job as security professionals to recognize that vulnerabilities will always exist and to ensure that our security wrappers address these vulnerabilities as appropriate to meeting our business objectives.

A *threat* can be defined as "one or more actions that have a potential to harm." It is important to realize that the potential for harm is not restricted to just the product, but extends throughout all of the components that interface with the product. Consequently, when developing a threat profile, it is imperative to develop a clear understanding of and to identify all product interfaces. An example of a threat is applying an acidic solution to an aluminum enclosure. This could potentially harm not only the enclosure, but all of its contents and anyone who might come in contact with the contaminated enclosure. Software threats typically include actions that intentionally (or unintentionally) alter software functionality from what was originally intended. Actions that exploit software bugs (errors in coding), insecure network conditions, application architecture, configuration capabilities, active built-in tests (BIT), and enabled fault isolation tests (FIT) are all considered software threats.

It is apparent that vulnerabilities and threats are very closely related. It is important to remember that a threat cannot occur without at least one vulnerability. Also, security strategies protect against threats (as defined by security policy and ultimately business objectives) not vulnerabilities. Ideally, vulnerabilities should be eradicated within the design process.

Now that we have a clear understanding of threats, vulnerabilities, and threat agents, let's apply that knowledge to several prevalent threats that exist in our current Web-based environment. In response to increasing Internet-based attacks, several groups were formed to identify vulnerabilities and assist businesses in defining appropriate security measures to protect their strategic Web-based assets. One notable project that started in September 2000 is the Open Web Application Security Project (OWASP). The primary purpose of OWASP is to provide an open-source knowledge base of Web application security issues (Donaldson, 2002). OWASP (OWASP, 2003) has gathered several Web application security data from multiple sources and created a top 10 vulnerability list. It is modeled on the SANS/FBI Top 20 Internet Vulnerability list (Sans Institute, 2003, October 8), but OWASP focuses on Web application security vulnerabilities. Combining the OWASP top 10 list with actual field-based experiences led to the development of the top 5 list

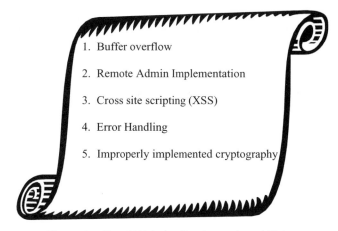

1. Buffer overflow
2. Remote Admin Implementation
3. Cross site scripting (XSS)
4. Error Handling
5. Improperly implemented cryptography

**Figure 3:** Top 5 Web application vulnerabilities. *Source:* April Giles, 2004.

shown in Figure 3. A cursory explanation of the included vulnerabilities follows.

## Buffer Overflow

A *buffer* is a container (memory block) that holds data. A buffer overflow vulnerability exists when an application does not verify that data inserted by the user fit within the boundary of the buffer established by the designer of the application. Mark Donaldson (2002) presents an excellent analogy:

> A buffer overflow is very much like pouring ten ounces of water in a glass designed to hold eight ounces. Obviously, when this happens, the water overflows the rim of the glass, spilling out somewhere and creating a mess. . . . The glass represents the buffer and the water represents the application or user data.

What happens to the data as they overflow the container? One possibility is that the data could overwrite an area within memory that contains code for another program, causing anomalous behavior, system crashes, or malicious code execution. Also, the data could overwrite existing data within the executing program, causing the application to execute with altered data.

C and C++ do not have automatic bounds checking on buffers; therefore, no programming error is returned to the designer when the program is compiled. Example:

```
void buffer overflow (void)
{
    char buffer[8];
    int i;
    for ( i = 0; i < 16; i++);
    {
            buffer[i];
    }
}
```

Notice that there is no out-of-bounds checking code included in the preceding function. Normally, exceeding buffer boundaries causes a program to crash with a segmentation fault error. Usually, this code alone will not create a security vulnerability. Conditions that are required for a vulnerability to exist are the following:

- The threat agent must be able to control data written into the buffer.
- The threat agent must know which variables are stored after the buffer and whether these variables are security sensitive.

Countermeasures for buffer overflows are as follows:

- Designers and programmers should review their code to ensure buffer overflows are not inherent within their programs.
- Programmers should utilize languages such as Java, Perl, or Python, which provide automatic buffer boundary checking.
- Programmers or security professionals could utilize automated source code checkers to review code line by line to check for potential buffer overflow conditions. However, source code reviewers still require manual resources because automated results almost always include false positives.

The Computer Emergency Response Team (CERT), Bugtraq, application developers, and equipment manufacturers report numerous newly discovered vulnerabilities every day. SecureNet Solutions VulnerabilityAlert database compiles vulnerability alerts from more than 1200 sources. Figure 4 is an overview of compiled statistics.

## Remote Admin Implementation

In today's highly distributed workplace a network administration team will often be accountable for multiple sites. Most businesses have networking services at more than one location. Small and medium-sized businesses (and a surprising number of banks) typically have their entire Internet presence hosted offsite and administered by people not directly employed by the organization. These circumstances require an employee acting as an in-house administrator or central administrator to make configuration changes by remote access. *Remote admin implementation* is an inability of an interface to authenticate a user such that an attacker can exploit account administration authorization processes to gain unlawful privileges to the system. Often, remote interfaces are designed on the premise that some other product will provide the security required to maintain a trusted environment. Designers assume that only authorized individuals will have access to the interface, although unfortunately this is almost never the case.

For example, say a shopping cart application provides an administrative interface that is accessed through HTTP (unencrypted) without security precautions such as a lockout for multiple unsuccessful login attempts, an access control list in accordance with security policy, logging of unsuccessful attempts to administer application, or logging of successful administrative logins. If a threat agent is able to penetrate the designer's perceived protected environment, the insecure shopping cart administrative interface, and the processes in place for implementation, can be the vulnerabilities that can lead to successful exploitation of the rest of the network. For example, if the threat agent gained access to the network through a firewall misconfiguration, it might discover the password on the administrative interface by brute force and eventually gain access to sensitive customer data, as well as to other applications and data on the server.

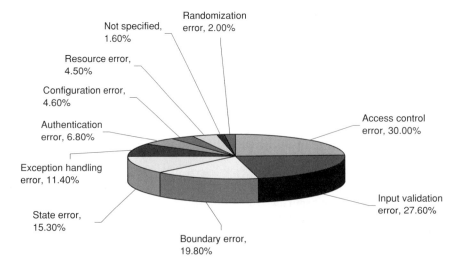

**Figure 4:** 2001–2002 Vulnerability Alert[SM] summary.
*Source:* SecureNet Solutions Report, 2003.

Countermeasures for remote admin implementation are as follows:

- If possible, involve security professionals in the design stage of sensitive interfaces.
- Verify that only authorized administrators can make changes to your site.
- Make sure insecure services (HTTP, File Transfer Protocol, telnet, any "R" service, or Simple Network Management Protocol) are replaced with more secure services (HTTPS, sFTP).
- Ensure lockout mechanisms for multiple login attempts are activated.
- Persuade designers to include a minimum wait time (10–20 seconds) before allowing successive login attempts.
- Ensure login passwords are a minimum of nine characters (preferably not in the dictionary) and include at least one nonstandard character (!@#$%).
- Use stronger authentication when feasible.
- Use firewalling/filtering to reduce the set of systems or users that can directly access the administration functionality.

## Cross-Site Scripting

One of the main advantages of using HTML can also be its principal disadvantage—the ability to run code dynamically. The default configuration of most Web browsers is set to run whatever arbitrary code is downloaded from Web servers. A primary function of a dynamic Web site is to interpret scripts and tags that alter client presentation of a page, modify the page's performance, or otherwise interfere with its normal operation in a way defined by the injected code. Cross-site scripting (XSS) occurs when either a browser or a Web application executes injected code forwarded by the server or client browser (hence, the *cross* designation). XSS is successful because it exploits trust between the client (end user) and the server (Web application).

OWASP splits XSS attacks into two categories: stored and reflected. In a stored attack, injected code is permanently saved on target servers, in databases, or in a message log. Reflected attacks occur when a user clicks a link or activates rogue code by selecting a submit button that is embedded with malicious code. Results of successful XSS attacks are the same whether they are stored or reflected. The only difference is how the injected code arrives at the server. XSS attacks are easy to implement and are therefore prevalent throughout the Internet. A threat agent has nothing but time and opportunity to find vulnerable areas within a designer's program to insert malicious code. A designer, on the other hand, deals with time to market pressure demanding the release of feature-abundant software . . . yesterday.

For example, an attacker might construct a malicious link such as this:

```
<A HREF="http://sample.com/comment.cgi?
mycomment=<SCRIPT>malicious code</SCRIPT>">
  Click here</A>
```

When a trusting user clicks this link, the URL sent to example.com includes the malicious code. If the Web server sends a page back to the user including the value of *mycomment*, the malicious code might be executed unexpectedly on the client. This example also applies to untrusted links followed in e-mail or newsgroup messages.

Countermeasures for XXS vulnerabilities include the following:

- Client-side users should disable scripting languages in their browsers. If not feasible, design the Web site not to use or to minimize scripting and investigate application firewall solutions.
- In the age of utilizing search engines such as Google, Yahoo!, and Dogpile to peruse the Internet, a user should carefully scrutinize a link before clicking. Remember that these search engines do not certify the Web sites, but simply forward users blindly, assuming a trusted environment.
- Users should access security-sensitive sites directly instead of by following links from unknown sources or untrusted sites. For example, users should not trust a link to their banking site that is in an e-mail message. Users should always access their banking site directly.
- By using manual and automated means, designers should verify that unauthorized tags are not present within their code. This activity should be scheduled on a regular basis after the code goes live (Carnegie Mellon University, 2000).

## Error-Handling Problems

Anyone who has ever surfed the Net has run into an occasional error page (401, 404). Out of memory, system call failure, network timeout, and null pointer exceptions are just a few of the many error conditions that can occur during normal Web application operation. Error pages are necessary to inform the user that a process did not execute in the manner that was expected. But in an error message, just how much information do you provide the user? What about those error messages that are not meant to be viewed by the user that end up being displayed in the client browser window? Ordinarily, information is a very important feedback mechanism for applications. Error-handling vulnerabilities exploit feedback mechanisms so that system information is divulged to the external client. System information can be exploited when a threat agent footprints a victim in this way in preparation for a more costly attack.

For example, a threat agent selects Victim.com as the target. The threat agent inputs a URL known not to exist, for example, http://www.victim.com/this-wont-work.html.

An error message is returned that might contain information about the type of Web server and even its software version number. For an attacker, this is very useful information that could be combined with data from any of the public vulnerability databases (for example, CERT, Bugtraq), which provide a comprehensive data catalog of existing relevant Web server vulnerabilities. Figure 5 shows an actual example taken from a daily news site.

daily news

```
Warning: Too many connections
in /web/include/classes/DBConnect_GFN.inc on line 14

Warning: mysql_query(): supplied argument is not a valid MySQL-Link
resource in /web/include/classes/DBConnect_GFN.inc on line 35
Too many connections
Warning: mysql_query(): supplied argument is not a valid MySQL-Link
resource in /web/include/classes/DBConnect_GFN.inc on line 35
Too many connections
Warning: mysql_num_rows(): supplied argument is not a valid MySQL
result resource in /web/include/classes/StoryFetch.inc on line 23
Fatal error in class StoryFetch [1]
```

**Figure 5:** Example error page.
*Source:* Daily News Site.

Countermeasures for error-handling problems include the following:

- Verify that there is a defined error-handling process in place that reflects the organization's security policy.
- Test each error condition and verify that the return data do not divulge sensitive system information.
- Ensure that software is designed not to release non-user-input-related error details to the client browser.
- Verify that data requiring protection is secured utilizing the "deny access until specifically granted" paradigm.
- Utilize simple, not overly informative, error message feedback mechanisms.

## Improperly Implemented Cryptography

Need to secure data? Just encrypt it, you might suggest. It's not that simple though (see Part 3, chapter 109, "Encryption Basics," for more information on encryption). Encrypting Web-based data is a task that should be performed only by those well versed in cryptography and only when this level of protection is warranted according to the business security policy. Most Web applications have a need to store credit card data, passwords, user account records, or proprietary information. Encryption techniques are often the protection of choice for these types of data. Generally, the use of cryptographic techniques can generate a false sense of security. Developers could become careless about securing other aspects of the site that are required for successful encryption implementation. OWASP concludes that the following are the most commonly overlooked areas:

- *Insecure storage of keys.* Whether the technology applied is asymmetric or symmetric, both still depend on the secrecy of the private key. Most private keys are encrypted with a password and stored on the owner's hard disk drive, resulting in vulnerability to attack either directly or through the network. Therefore, it is imperative that the private key is stored securely. Following are methods of storing a key securely:

- Ensure that comprehensive authentication and authorization processes are implemented on both receiving and transmitting devices.
- Implement physical access controls.
- Consider storing the key in a tamper-resistant device.
- Use passwords with high entropy (number of different equiprobable key states).
- Limit access to the key file to authorized administrators.
- Protect backup media with the same vigor as primary media.
- *Improper storage of secrets in memory.* When programs are loaded, code and data are placed in temporary storage areas (cache, random access memory, virtual memory). It is possible that remnants of a private key can be discovered and/or removed from these temporary storage areas.
- *Poor sources of randomness.* Randomness is a key component of Web server session key development. Cryptographic keys need to be as random as possible so that it is unfeasible to reproduce or predict them. Developers should take steps to ensure that random function calls actually generate unpredictable results.
- *Failure to encrypt critical data.* Choosing which data to encrypt should be methodical, well organized, and based on a security policy that reflects business objectives.
- *Attempting to invent a new encryption algorithm.* Cryptography is not a science for the light-hearted. Very few people can create a secure algorithm.
- *Failure to include support for encryption key changes and other required maintenance procedures.*

Countermeasures for improper cryptography implementation are as follows:

- Ensure that a specific rationale exists for encryption technology instead of hash technology.
- Consider splitting the master secret into three locations and assembling it at run time.

## WEB SITE SECURITY ASSESSMENT

Determining whether a Web site is secure can be a long, arduous, expensive undertaking. Literally hundreds of new application and operating system (OS)–based vulnerabilities are discovered monthly. Also, many security resources are available that identify and explain vulnerabilities found within the most common commercial software products. Manually verifying each vulnerability could prove to be an insurmountable task.

Consequently, several companies have developed tools that perform an automated vulnerability scan (AVS). An AVS enables application and Web services developers to automate the discovery of security vulnerabilities as they construct applications. Some AVSs also include instructions on how to remediate found vulnerabilities. Application return on investment (ROI) and overall organizational security are improved significantly (multiplied by three less cost) when vulnerabilities are discovered and remediated early in the development process.

Security professionals can also make use of AVSs during the assessment process.

It is imperative, however, that a security professional understand the difference between a vulnerability scan and a vulnerability assessment. A vulnerability scan takes an objective view of the system and compares it to a specific set of criteria (i.e., a list of recently released vulnerabilities). A vulnerability assessment reviews the results of a vulnerability scan to filter out false positives and also to develop and perform specific manual tests for obscure and emerging vulnerabilities that might have escaped detection by automated testing. Individual security professionals might have their own methods of performing a vulnerability assessment (as guided by the organizational security policy), but vulnerability scans often are completed by defined criteria within a software product base.

A general guide for completing a Web site vulnerability assessment is as follows:

1. *Determine what* secure *means to the organization.* Review the organization's security policy to determine what level of assurance is necessary as defined by the accepted (by executive stakeholders) security policy. Review any departmental charters that exist for indications and clarifications of authority boundaries.

2. *Define a scope and goals.* Identify what is included in the scope of the WSA. For example, a Web application might consist of the following components:
   - data,
   - database,
   - back-end systems,
   - front-end systems,
   - web server, and
   - user interface code.

   On which section will assessment resources be focused? Be careful not to bite off more than you can chew. In other words, each component will require a defined set of resources—make sure that resources are available to fulfill the steps required to complete each of the selected sections.

   What is the purpose of the Web site security assessment (WSA)? What do you hope to accomplish? It's absolutely imperative that a security professional and developer understand the goals of the WSA; after all, how is it possible to know when you are finished if you have not clearly defined what finished means? Understand your goals for a WSA, and make sure that all involved with the execution of the WSA understand what you hope to achieve by completing the assessment. Also, remember that goals must be achievable. For example, *find all existing vulnerabilities* is not an achievable goal because there will always be unknown vulnerabilities.

3. *Develop a project plan.* A WSA does not succeed without an accurate, comprehensive, approved project plan. A project plan should define a work breakdown structure that details WSA tasks to a functional level while identifying expected achievements (milestones) by WSA participants. It should clearly define all resources (personnel, software, hardware,

bandwidth) and time required for successful project completion.

4. *Obtain approval for the project plan.* A security professional should ensure that the scope and the project plan are approved by C level management prior to initiating assessment. Approval should be in writing; otherwise, the security professional might fall prey to prosecution by multiple laws such as the Computer Security Act, Digital Millennium Copyright Law, and the Economic Espionage Act, among others.

   Understanding results. Now that all of the tasks have been completed, what actions should be taken? What does it all mean in relationship to the big picture? Remediation of known vulnerabilities should be completed by the information technology staff under supervision of the security professional. A remediation plan should be developed to include resources and tasks that validate remediation and a check for possible side effects (ensure the baseline system is intact). Defining the results as they apply to the big picture can be accomplished only with the assistance of a senior stakeholder. A security professional should strive to reformat the results such that a clear, concise overview of the problems found can be presented to the stakeholder along with possible long-term solutions. In some cases the senior stakeholder will decide to accept the risks uncovered by the assessment. In other cases the stakeholder will decide to mitigate the risk by purchasing cyberinsurance. In either case, strategic decisions are made in accordance with business objectives.

5. *Decide whether to use a consultant or in-house staff.* Decisions on whether WSAs should be completed by a consultant or in-house security professionals depend on two factors:
   - Is a competent and trustworthy consultant available?
   - Are trained in-house resources available?

   A complete project plan identifies all resources required to complete the assessment. The project plan should clearly identify whether sufficient resources are available in-house. Remember that trust is purely subjective. Sure, certain qualities (experience, good references from similar-sized organizations, financial stability, staff certification) provide a warm and fuzzy feeling about a consultant's capability, but ultimately the stakeholder should decide whether the consultant has the capability to reduce organizational risk by identifying vulnerabilities.

6. *Implement a maintenance plan.* An organization's security policy should define how often each Web application component is assessed. Vulnerability scans should occur more frequently than vulnerability assessments. Vendors often provide software maintenance packages that automatically evaluate and update compiled applications. Custom applications (e.g., user interfaces) should be reviewed on a regular basis. Also, the appropriate security review should occur before changes are made in the operational environment, including Web application modification or creation, system configuration, and/or administrator procedures.

7. *Estimate cost and time involved.* The project plan should have been completed in enough detail to provide a clear indication of labor and material costs. Often, the project plan ultimately defines the scope of the project by using a cost analysis. For each component, it is important to realize that the sooner the vulnerability is found, the less costly it will be to the organization.

## CONCLUSION

Key points to remember regarding Web site protection are as follows:

- The problem of Web defacements is growing very aggressively and demands initiative on the part of security professionals in terms of action and education of others to address this significant threat.
- Security professionals must work together to encourage the development of more up-front, secure programs and network products.
- Security professionals must band together to identify and share information about vulnerabilities, encouraging vendors to introduce fixes quickly.
- All who interact with and use Web sites must be diligent about implementing effective countermeasures to address vulnerabilities, threats, and attacks.

In terms of the future of Web site defacement, the risk presented by threat agents can change. For example, we hope that the work of organizations such as the SANS Institute and InfraGard (a public–private partnership to secure the critical infrastructures of the United States), which have conducted poster contests featuring computer security education topics for young people, will result in less hacking activity among that group (Infragard.net, 2004). What will probably not change in the short to midterm is the frequency of hacker activity and Web defacements. Unfortunately, as soon as more stringent security measures are put in place, crackers make it their business to break the new security measures. Thus, everyone must be ever vigilant, constantly taking security to the next and higher levels.

## GLOSSARY

**Black Hat**   People who hack illegally for destructive purposes or as thieves, also known as crackers.
**Buffer Overflow**   A condition that exists when an application does not verify that data inserted by the user are within the boundary established by the designer of the application.
**Hacker**   Someone who breaks into a Web site.
**Internet**   The Internet consists of all the computers and their connections that provide a method for people to communicate.
**Threat**   Actions that have a potential to harm.
**Vulnerability**   A set of conditions within a product that can be exploited, whether it arises by design or from an implementation error.

**Web Defacement**   An attack that occurs when a perpetrator accesses a Web site and changes it.
**Web Site**   A specific location on the World Wide Web that is identifiable by its uniform resource locator (URL).
**World Wide Web**   A component of the Internet that includes a set of rules or protocols regarding how computers communicate and the tools used for the connections so that people can share information.

## CROSS REFERENCES

See *Client-Side Security; Hackers, Crackers and Computer Criminals; Network Attacks; Server-Side Security.*

## REFERENCES

*Attrition.org: About us.* (n.d.). Retrieved January 26, 2004, from http://attrition.org/attrition/about.html

*Attrition.org: BWI Airport defaced.* (n.d.). Retrieved January 26, 2004, from http://attrition.org/security/commentary/bwiair.html

*Attrition.org: SANS Institute defaced.* (n.d.). Retrieved January 26, 2004, from http://attrition.org/security/commentary/sans.html

Carnegie Mellon University. (2000, February). *CERT advisory CA-2000-02 malicious HTML tags embedded in client Web requests.* Retrieved January 10, 2004, from http://www.cert.org/advisories/CA-2000-02.html

Curphey, M., et al. (2000, February). *A guide to building secure Web applications.* Retrieved January 12, 2004, from http://prdownloads.sourceforge.net/owasp/OWASPGuideV1.1.1.pdf?download

DeLong, D. (2001, February 8). *Hackers said to cost U.S. billions.* Retrieved January 26, 2004, from http://www.newsfactor.com/perl/story/7349.html

Donaldson, M. (2002, April 3). *Inside the buffer flow attack: Mechanism, method, and prevention.* Retrieved January 10, 2004, from http://www.sans.org/rr/papers/46/386.pdf

Gershwin, L. (2001, June 21). *Statement for the record to the Joint Economic Committee cyber threat trends and U.S. network security.* Retrieved January 26, 2004, from http://www.fas.org/irp/congress/2001hr/062101_gershwin.html

*How many online?* (n.d.). Retrieved January 26, 2004, from http://www.nua.ie/surveys/how_many_online/

Legard, D. (2002, September 30). *Web site defacements rise in September.* Retrieved January 26, 2004, from http://www.infoworld.com/articles/hn/xml/02/09/30/020930hndeface.html

Niccolai, J. (2003, April 4). *Security incidents skyrocket.* Retrieved January 26, 2004, from http://pcworld.shopping.yahoo.com/yahoo/article/0,aid,110140,00.asp

*On the size of the World Wide Web.* (n.d.). Retrieved January 26, 2004, from http://www.pandia.com/sw-2001/57-Websize.html

OWASP. (2003, January 13). *Top ten Web application security vulnerabilities.* Retrieved January 12, 2004, from http://aleron.dl.sourceforge.net/sourceforge/owasp/ OWASPWebApplicationSecurityTopTen-Version1. pdf

*SANS Institute.* (n.d.) About the SANS Institute. Retrieved January 26, 2004, from http://www.sans.org/ aboutsans.php

*SANS Institute.* (2003, October 8). International consortium releases list of the top twenty Internet security vulnerabilities. Retrieved January 26, 2004, from http:// www.sans.org/top20/pressrelease03.pdf

Wagner, J. (2002, February 1). *Giving hackers their due.* Retrieved January 26, 2004, from http://www.isp-planet.com/news/2002/hackers_020201.html

Webopedia.com. (n.d.). *HTTP definition.* Retrieved February 29, 2004, from http://www.pcWebopeida.com/ TERM/H/HTTP.html

# Database Security

Michael Gertz, *University of California, Davis*
Arnon Rosenthal, *The MITRE Corporation*

## INTRODUCTION

In the past three decades, database systems have evolved from specialized applications to fundamental components of today's computing infrastructures. Many organizations in industry, government, and research sectors rely on database systems to manage, share, and disseminate various forms of data in an effective and reliable manner. In fact, the most valuable assets of many organizations are their data, and the loss of hardware or software is often easier to overcome than the loss of data that have been collected and maintained over many years. As our society becomes increasingly dependent on information, the protection of data against various security threats becomes an important mission for database designers, developers, and administrators. Threats to database security typically concern the integrity, secrecy, and availability of data. They are characterized as follows:

- *Data integrity* refers to the requirement that the data residing in a database system are protected from improper modifications. The integrity is violated if unauthorized changes are made to the data through either intentional or accidental operations, including the insertion, deletion, and modification of data. Violations of database integrity, if not corrected, can result in erroneous or inaccurate decisions that are based on the improperly modified data.

- *Data secrecy* refers to the protection of sensitive data from unauthorized disclosure. An unauthorized, accidental, or unanticipated disclosure of confidential data can result in the loss of confidence in the data provider or even in legal actions against the organization maintaining the data.

- *Data availability* refers to the requirement that data are available to users and applications that have the legitimate right and authorization to access or modify the data. Loss of data availability can result in the unavailability of services and applications that operate on the database.

Database systems offer several countermeasures to protect data against these types of security threats. Countermeasures include (1) access controls that ensure that all accesses to data occur exclusively according to the rules described by security policies specifying certain security goals; (2) flow controls that regulate the distribution and flow of information among accessible objects; (3) inference control that aims at protecting data from indirect detection; and (4) encryption of data. The effective realization of countermeasures is driven by security policies and data security principles. A *security policy* is a (formal) statement or rule that partitions the states of a system into secure and nonsecure states. *Data security principles* guide the design and realization of database security policies. In particular, these principles include the following:

- *Least privilege.* Users and applications should be given those privileges they need to complete their tasks. That is, if an entity does not need to operate on some data managed by the database, this entity should not have the right or authorization to operate on that data.

- *Reconstruction of events.* Improper behavior of a user or application that leads to a violation of database security should be detected, thus preventing future (accidental or intentional) misuse of privileges and making individuals accountable for their operations on the data. In an ideal setting, events should be monitored and a misuse of privileges should be prevented rather than only detected after the event(s) happened.

These principles, among others, equally apply to the more general context of computer security (see, e.g., Bishop, 2003; Landwehr, 2001), in particular to operating systems security and network security.

In this chapter, we give an overview of the database security aspects that address the preceding security threats and principles, and we discuss how security aspects are realized in current database technology. Our focus is on relational database management systems (RDBMSs) because these are (and will be for the foreseeable future) the major type of database system used in the industry, government,

380

and research sectors. In the section entitled Database Security Models and Mechanisms, we present the principles and components of database security models. We discuss in detail discretionary access control, which is supported by all major relational RDBMSs and included in the structured query language (SQL). We then discuss the main usage of role-based access control and outline mandatory access control as it is realized in some RDBMSs. We conclude this section with a discussion of security mechanisms that support the different access controls.

In the section entitled Database Security Design, we focus on security design aspects of databases. Too often, database security mechanisms are implemented in an ad-hoc fashion, without well-defined security design guidelines and security policies on hand. In this section, we also compare the security design for databases with the design of secure systems and outline database security design tasks, with a particular focus on nonidealized settings.

Finally, in the section entitled Database Security Evaluation and Reconfiguration, we approach the different aspects of database security at a more practical level. In today's world, data, applications, and security requirements change while a system is in service. Thus, database systems require continuous monitoring for vulnerabilities, misuse, and other types of system weaknesses security threats can expose. We outline several approaches to evaluate the security of a database system and to restore security.

As indicated earlier, in this chapter, we exclusively focus on security aspects in relational databases. A more comprehensive framework detailing security aspects related to other types of database systems, including object-oriented databases and statistical databases, can be found in the textbook by Castano, Fugini, Martella, and Samarati (1995).

# DATABASE SECURITY MODELS AND MECHANISMS
## Overview

A security model provides a semantically rich set of concepts and tools to (formally) specify and analyze security policies. Security models for database systems are not that different from general computer security models except that they place more emphasis on the modeling of access controls and less emphasis on user identification, authorization, and data encryption. In general, *access controls* are concerned with security policies that describe the principles on which access to objects is granted or denied (see also Access Controls: Principles and Solutions, chapter 168). There are several reasons for the importance of access controls in database systems. First, database systems manage many different types of objects (relations, views, stored procedures, and so forth) and at different levels of granularity (relation, tuple, attribute value). Second, database objects can be composed of other objects. For example, database views can refer to relations and other views. Third, standard read/write operations assumed in many security models translate into operations to create, delete, update, alter, and read database objects at different levels of granularity.

For database management systems, one can distinguish among three approaches to access controls: *discretionary access control*, *mandatory access control*, and *role-based access control*. Discretionary access control (DAC) is based on the concept of object ownership and mechanisms with which object owners can assign privileges to users, including policies on the administration of privileges. Almost all of today's RDBMSs provide means to specify and enforce security policies through discretionary access control. We focus on the basic concepts of DAC and in particular its realization in SQL in the section entitled Discretionary Access Control.

Mandatory access control (MAC), on the other hand, is based on labeling data objects with security classes and assigning security clearances to users. System-wide policies, which cannot be changed by individual users, then specify whether a user with a given clearance can read and/or write an object that has a given security label. The objective of the policies is to ensure that a user who does not have the necessary clearance can never obtain sensitive data, an important security requirement typically found in data management scenarios in the military. Mandatory access control is discussed in the section entitled Mandatory Access Control.

Role-based access control (RBAC), the third type of access control relevant to database systems, is concerned with aggregating access privileges into named entities (called roles) and assigning such entities to individual users, groups of users, and other roles. Although RBAC can be used to simulate DAC and MAC, in practice it is primarily used to manage effectively access privileges in RDBMSs comprising large amounts of objects and users and applications operating on these objects. In the section entitled Role-Based Access Control, we give a brief overview of RBAC and outline how RBAC is typically used to administer privileges.

No matter which type of access control is used, one must eventually map access policies to database security mechanisms that implement the policies to prevent and detect improper accesses. In the section entitled Database Security Mechanisms, we give an outline of the mechanisms available in RDBMSs and discuss how such mechanisms are used to enforce access control.

## Discretionary Access Control

In the DAC model, access control is based on object ownership. Privileges on objects are granted to other entities at the discretion of the object owner. Formally, a discretionary access policy consists of a set of policy assertions. An assertion is a Six-tuple $<u, o, t, s, p, f>$, stating that user $u$ (grantor) has granted operation $o$ on object $t$ to user $s$ (grantee). The optional component $p$ is a predicate and can define conditions on system or environmental variables to enable the specification of context-dependent access control. For example, Bertino, Bettini, Ferrari, and Samarati (1996) describe how such predicates can formulate temporal conditions and how such conditions can be embedded into access control mechanisms for database systems. Beznosov (2002) proposes a CORBA-like architecture in which various attribute providers can be called to provide information the policies need. $f$ is a Boolean value and states whether user $s$ can further transfer $<o, t, p, f>$ to other users, and thus enables the specification of access administration.

In the context of relational databases, a few aspects of a discretionary access policy are worth mentioning. First, underlying access control in general and DAC in particular is the notion of *authorization identifier* (*AuthID*), which is either the identifier of a database user or a role name. According to the SQL:1999 standard (Melton & Simon, 2001), when an SQL session is initiated (e.g., an application connects to the database), the authorization identifier is determined in an implementation-defined manner. For the previous form of access policy, this means that the grantor is a database user and the grantee is an AuthID; that is, either a database user or a role. Second, in addition to object privileges, there are also *system privileges* for operations on a database as a whole or on objects of a particular type. For example, to create an AuthID, table, database file, or role, or to start up or shut down the database, the AuthID performing the operation must have respective system privileges. Typically, only administrative personnel possess such system privileges. As an example, Oracle 9i supports more than 100 system privileges.

Discretionary access control is included in the current SQL standard (SQL:1999) and is supported by all major commercial and public domain RDBMSs that offer security. The SQL GRANT command has the following syntax:

object-relational database management systems, such as Oracle or DB2, support more object privileges than RDBMSs that do not provide any object-relational features, such as user-defined data types or methods. In the following, we concentrate on the discussion of privileges related to tables and views because these object types are supported by all RDBMSs.

The following object privileges can be specified for a table using a GRANT statement:

- select [{columns}]. The grantee has the privilege to read the specified columns. If no column is given, the grantee is allowed to read all columns, even those added later through an ALTER TABLE statement.
- insert [{columns}]. The grantee is allowed to insert rows with values for the named columns into the table. If no column is specified, values for all columns can be inserted.
- update [{columns}]. The semantics of this privilege is analogous to the insert [{columns}] privilege.
- delete. The grantee has the privilege to delete rows from the table.
- references [{columns}]. The grantee is allowed to define foreign keys (in another table) that refer to the specified columns.

In SQL terminology, a view is a table that is derivable from other tables, which can be previously defined views

---

GRANT <PRIVILEGES> TO <GRANTEE>[{,<GRANTEE>}] [WITH GRANT OPTION]

---

A GRANT statement specifies which AuthID(s) are allowed to execute which SQL commands. If the WITH GRANT OPTION is specified, each AuthID different from a role is allowed to further grant the privilege(s) to other AuthIDs. If the privileges to be granted are all system privileges, these privileges are enumerated (e.g., create user, create table, alter database). Because system privileges are often related to administrative tasks, some RDBMSs, such as Oracle, use the clause WITH ADMIN OPTION if a grantee is allowed to further grant the privileges. If the GRANT statement specifies object privileges to be granted, these are numerated in the form of comma-separated <OBJECT PRIVILEGE> ON <OBJECT NAME> clauses.

Only AuthIDs with the following certain privileges can execute a GRANT statement: (1) the grantor has created (hence owns) the database object; (2) the grantor has received the privilege(s) with respective administrative options; or (3) the grantor has received the privileges GRANT ANY PRIVILEGE (for system privileges) or GRANT ANY OBJECT PRIVILEGE (for object privileges). Thus, the semantics of the SQL GRANT statement clearly resembles the semantics of the $<u, o, t, p, f>$ components of a discretionary access policy, as introduced earlier. We should mention, however, that neither the SQL standard nor any existing RDBMS supports the specification of a predicate $p$ as part of a discretionary access policy.

The object privileges available in existing RDBMSs vary from system to system, depending on the types of objects supported in the different systems. For example,

or base tables. Views are either implemented by (1) query modification, in which the defining view query is translated into a query on the underlying base tables, or (2) view materialization, which involves physically storing the result when the view is first queried (see, e.g., Ramakrishnan & Gehrke, 2003; Elmasri & Navathe, 2004). Privileges on views can be granted in the same way as privileges on tables can be. A user creating a view must have the system privilege CREATE VIEW and at least the select privilege on all base tables and views referred to in the view query. If a user grants the privilege to insert, update, or delete rows from a view to another AuthID, this AuthID must have respective privileges on the base tables underlying the view. We talk more about views as important security mechanisms in the following sections.

There are some interesting aspects worth mentioning regarding granting privileges on database objects. If a user wants to grant all privileges on an object to an AuthID, instead of enumerating all these object privileges, the user can simply specify ALL PRIVILEGES ON <OBJECT NAME> in the <PRIVILEGES> clause. Different RDBMSs, however, associate different sets of privileges with the ALL PRIVILEGES clause. For example, in Oracle, granting all privileges on a table to an AuthID not only includes the object privileges listed earlier, but also the privileges to create an index on that table and to alter the table definition (i.e., column definitions, integrity constraints). If a set of privileges needs to be granted to all AuthIDs known to a database system, the keyword PUBLIC can be specified. Of course, this type of GRANT statement has to be used with care.

Another type of object supported by many RDBMSs is stored procedures as programming language extensions to SQL. Stored procedures are typically used for the development of database applications and functionality within the RDBMS. They enable bundling logically related procedures and functions in the form of packages. Triggers are stored procedures that execute program code whenever some specified database action occurs. A user defining a stored procedure must have the system privilege CREATE PROCEDURE. If a procedure operates on database objects, such as tables or views, or it invokes other procedures and functions, the user must have respective privileges on these objects. Some systems, such as Oracle, require that such privileges be explicitly granted to the user and not through a role. A user can grant access to a procedure to other users using the object privilege EXECUTE. This is the only privilege a grantee needs to invoke a procedure defined by another user.

To revoke system, object, or administrative privileges from users and roles, SQL provides the REVOKE statement, which has the following form:

The precise semantics associated with revoking administrative, object, and system privileges heavily depends on the type of object, nature of the authorizer (role or user), and RDBMS used. For example, if a user holds the privilege to create an index on a table and then this privilege is revoked, what happens to the index? Another scenario is when a user has been granted the REFERENCES privilege and has used this privilege to define a foreign key constraint on one of the user's tables. In Oracle, for example, this constraint is deleted if the privilege is revoked from the user. The SQL:1999 standard and several other works describe a precise semantics for the revocation of privileges in different settings (e.g., Bertino, Jajodia, & Samarati, 1995; Bertino, Jajodia, & Samarati, 1999). However, it is good practice to consult the documentation accompanying individual RDBMSs for the precise semantics of the REVOKE statement.

We conclude this subsection with a final remark on DAC in RDBMSs. In principle, DAC is based on the concept of *ownership-based administration*. That is, the creator (and thus owner) of an object has all privileges on that object and can grant such privileges to other users. Only when all objects in a database system are owned by

REVOKE [GRANT OPTION FOR | ADMIN OPTION FOR] <PRIVILEGES> FROM <GRANTEE> [CASCADE]

The command is used to (1) revoke grant options on system or object privileges (i.e., the grantee received the privileges with a grant or admin option) and (2) revoke system or object privileges from the grantee. Recall that a user who has received a privilege with a grant or admin option can further grant this privilege to other users. This is a case in which the CASCADE option can be used. When this clause is specified in a REVOKE statement, the listed privileges are revoked from all users who currently possess these privileges based on a GRANT command previously issued by the user who now issues the REVOKE command. If a user has been granted the same privilege from different users, no single REVOKE command is sufficient to revoke the privilege from that user. Figure 1 illustrates the behavior of the CASCADE option.

Assume user John has granted a privilege P with grant option to both Paul and Peter, who, in turn, both granted privilege P with grant option to Mary. The edge numbers indicate the points in time the respective grant statements have been issued. Mary has granted privilege P to Tom at time point 40. If John revokes P from Peter using the CASCADE option, Mary still possesses the privilege P; so does Tom because his privilege P is based on a grant Mary got at time point 30. Tom, however, would lose privilege P if John (or Paul) would revoke P from Mary using the CASCADE option.

a single user and this user grants privileges to other users (without allowing them to further grant these privileges) can we talk about *centralized access administration*. The latter scenario is typical for most database settings in practice where all applications operate on a schema owned by a single user. Such a setting naturally requires that authorization identifiers and privileges associated with these applications are properly managed, an aspect we discuss next.

## Role-Based Access Control

Database systems that serve as the back end to large-scale information system infrastructures, for example, those used in supply chain management or customer relationship management, typically support dozens, sometimes more than a hundred, different applications. Administration of the database privileges the numerous applications users need to perform all the activities corresponding to their job descriptions can be a daunting task. This holds in particular for database environments where the same user is supposed to have access to different applications and the tasks associated with the applications require different privileges. Clearly, it is not a good strategy to simply grant users all the database privileges they need to use all applications with which they are supposed to work.

Roles provide an effective means to administer database privileges in such settings. Conceptually, a *role* is a named collection of privileges and can be granted to AuthIDs, optionally with the permission to grant this role to other users. Because roles can be granted to roles as well, it is possible to specify role hierarchies. But roles provide further important functionality in administering AuthIDs and the jobs and tasks that are associated with AuthIDs.

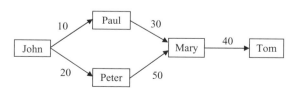

**Figure 1:** (Cascading) revocation of privileges.

In a database system, there are typically different types of users. One can broadly classify database users as (1) application owners, that is, users who own database objects as part of an application, (2) end users who operate on application objects but do not own any object in the database, and (3) administrators. With a given application, different tasks are associated, each task requiring the execution of specific operations and accesses to application objects. Based on these tasks, roles are defined that precisely describe the privileges necessary and are sufficient for an end user to execute a task. Roles determined by an application owner are then assigned to end users by the application owner. Roles associated with administrators primarily contain system privileges to manage physical and logical database components, such as data files, users, and security mechanisms. In summary, roles provide an important means to define application-specific security and to manage privileges dynamically based on application-specific tasks.

In the past decade, there have been several developments and advancement in role-based access control (RBAC) models. RBAC models are not specifically aimed at database systems but provide a general type of access model that can be used in combination with discretionary or mandatory access controls. In fact, based on a seminal paper published by Sandhu, Coyne, Feinstein, and Youman (1996) proposing a family of models known as RBAC96, Osborn, Sandhu, and Munawer (2000) show that RBAC96 can be configured to model DAC or MAC. One of the recent developments in RBAC is the adoption of a consensus standard model by the U.S. National Institute of Standards and Technology (NIST) (Ferraiolo, Sandhu, Gavrila, Kuhn, & Chandramouli, 2001; Sandhu, 2001). In the following, we outline some properties of RBACs in RDBMSs. Though somewhat outdated, Ramaswamy and Sandhu (1998) give a more detailed overview of how major commercial RDBMSs support different features of RBACs.

The concept of roles has also been adopted for the SQL:1999 standard. There, the CREATE ROLE statement is used to define a role. Some systems allow adding an authentication clause to the definition of a role. This authentication can be based on passwords users give if they want to assume that role, or the identification can occur externally, for example, through the operating system. As illustrated in the section entitled Discretionary Access Control, the GRANT command is used to assign privileges to roles. Because roles can be granted to other roles, role hierarchies can be built in which roles with more (powerful) privileges form the upper part of such a hierarchy. The concepts underlying role hierarchies and the administration of such hierarchies are discussed in detail by Ferraiolo et al. (2001) and Sandhu (1998).

In an RDBMS, there are typically several predefined roles. Many of them concern administrative tasks. A set of default roles can be assigned to a database user when the user is created using the CREATE USER statement. Other roles that have been created and granted to a user can be enabled by the user on demand through the SQL statement SET ROLE <role name>. Although several roles can be accessible to a user, according to the SQL:1999 standard, a user can hold exactly one role at a time. Given that a user can enable or disable roles, an important security design aspect is that only those roles are enabled that are necessary and sufficient to perform the operations in the current application context. Such a design is typically guided by higher level security policies that precisely describe which roles (and thus privileges) are required for which application-specific tasks and who is allowed to activate which roles at which times.

This aspect is also related to the security principle of *separation of duties*, which states that no single user should be able to tamper with the integrity of the data, but several users must collude to violate the integrity of data. To support this principle in the context of RBAC, it thus must be possible to impose constraints on role relationships and role activations. Although neither the SQL standard nor existing commercial RDBMSs support this principle, in practice, it can be realized by using stored procedures for enabling and disabling roles. Such procedures then can be called from within applications, and database users are prevented from issuing SET ROLE statements during sessions. In respective procedures, the current role setting and constraints implementing the previously mentioned higher level policies on role relationships are then checked and enforced.

## Mandatory Access Control

Mandatory access control (MAC) is based on system-wide policies that cannot be changed by individual users. MAC, first introduced by Bell and LaPadula (1976), plays an important role in environments where data can be classified (e.g., based on its sensitivity) and users are cleared (e.g., based on their trustworthiness not to disclose sensitive information). In the following, we give a brief overview of MAC and outline how it is supported by commercial RDBMSs. We refer readers interested in the details of MAC to Castano et al. (1995). Bertino et al. (1995) give an excellent overview of MAC and the underlying multilevel relational data model. Several comprehensive articles addressing multilevel secure databases can be found in Abrams, Jajodia, and Podell (1995).

In MAC, each database object is assigned a security class, and each subject is assigned a clearance for a security class; subjects are active entities, for example, users, which operate on the objects. The policies specify whether a subject with a given clearance can read or write an object that has a given security class. The objective of the policies is to prevent the flow of information from sensitive objects to less sensitive objects.

In MAC, policies are based on *access classes*, each of which is a class comprising a *security level* and a set of *categories*. Security levels build a hierarchically ordered set. For example, in the military domain, security levels often include Top Secret (TS), Secret (S), Confidential (C), and Unclassified (U), forming a hierarchy with TS > S > C > U. A set of categories is simply a subset of an unordered set of named entities that represent, for example, application domains or departments of an organization and depend on the considered environment.

In a military environment, such categories can include NATO, Air Force, Army, and so forth. An access class $AC_1$ = $(L_1,C_1)$ with security level $L_1$ and set of categories $C_1$ is said to *dominate* an access class $AC_2$ = $(L_2,C_2)$ with security level $L_2$ and set of categories $C_2$, denoted $AC_1 > AC_2$, if and only if $L_1 \geq L_2$ and $C_1 \supseteq C_2$. Two access classes $AC_1$ and $AC_2$ are said to be incomparable if neither $AC_1 \geq AC_2$ nor $AC_2 \geq AC_1$ holds. Thus, access classes are partially ordered. Based on the concept of access classes, the following two principles are employed by all security models that enforce MAC policies.

*No read-up* (also known as the *Simple Security Property*), meaning a subject can read only those objects whose access class is dominated by the access class of the subject. For example, a subject with security level TS can read a table that has security level C, but a subject with security level C is not allowed to read a table with security level TS.

*No write-down* (also known as the *\*-Property*), meaning a subject can only write those objects whose access class dominates the access class of the subject. For example, a subject with security level S is allowed to write only objects with security level equal to or greater than S.

For a RDBMS to support MAC, a security class must be assigned to each database object, which can be a table, a row, or even individual column values, depending on the policy employed. In general, the application of MAC to relational data leads to the concept of *multilevel relations*, which are tables in which users with different security levels see different collections of rows when they access the same table. We refer the reader interested in the concepts (and problems) of multilevel relational databases to Abrams et al. (1995). In the following, we outline how a flavor of MAC is supported in some commercial RDBMSs, here Oracle9i. Before we do so, we should mention that no major RDBMS fully supports MAC mainly because MAC needs to be applied to a complete computing infrastructure from the top to the bottom. That is, mandatory access control and multilevel security must be realized at all layers, including the operating system, network components, and application components. For example, in military environments, security levels are generally physically isolated. MAC policies specified at the RDBMS level thus must be applied appropriately at the operating system layer as well, physically separating data that have different security classes. Trusted operating system infrastructures are essential in this context.

In practice, the realization of MACs at all levels is not only very costly but also requires substantial system administration skills and sophisticated security management tools for MAC; the latter is almost nonexistent. However, to provide customers with some flavor of MAC (and some of its functionality), some RDBMS vendors provide additions to traditional DAC. For example, in Oracle9i, row-level access control is supported with the virtual private database (VPD) technology. VPD provides fine-grained access control that is context dependent and row based (Levinger, 2002; Nanda, 2004). This technique is known as *Oracle Label Security* (*OLS*), first introduced in Oracle8i Release 3.

OLS is a set of procedures and constraints that are built into the database engine, and it enforces row-level access control on a single table. Following is a brief summary of how an OLS policy is realized.

First, after initializing (naming) a security policy, the administrator defines security levels. Each level is associated with a policy and has a name; security levels describe the sensitivity of table data, such as "Confidential" or "Public." Then, compartments can be defined. Compartments correspond to categories and enable a refined access to rows of a table within a level. The purpose of compartments is the same as that of categories introduced earlier in the context of access classes. OLS also allows defining user groups as another way to restrict access within a level, in particular when there are hierarchies of users. After this, labels are defined. Labels are a combination of security levels, compartments, and groups. Whereas a label must contain one security level, compartments and groups are optional. A label thus can be viewed as an access class that determines the types of access required for users to the table data. Each label is assigned a number, which must be unique among all the security policies in the database.

In the next step, the label policy is applied to a given table, realizing read and write control for users. This step adds an extra column to the table. Attribute values correspond to the labels introduced earlier; this extra attribute can be hidden from users. Figure 2 is an example of a table that manages information about projects. Two levels have been specified: Public and Confidential, and each row has a label (attribute ProjectLabel). Now one needs to define which users have which types of access within the policy. This is done by assigning labels to database users; a label specifies a maximum read level and maximum/minimum write levels. Respective levels refer to the security levels introduced previously and can be refined by adding compartments. For example, a maximum read level "Internal:Finance" specifies that the user is allowed to read documents (rows) whose label is equal or less than the security level "Internal" and that belong to the compartment "Finance." Finally, once all users have been assigned labels, these users then are granted discretionary access privileges (select, insert, update, delete) to that table.

As indicated earlier, OLS works in combination with regular discretionary access control. Within the Oracle database engine, security enforcement works as follows. If a user issues an SQL statement, this statement is first processed as in standard DAC, as outlined in the following section, Database Security Mechanisms. After this,

| ProjectID | ProjectName | Level | ProjectLabel |
|-----------|-------------|-------------|--------------|
| 1 | WideStreets | Public | 100 |
| 2 | HighWalls | Confidential | 200 |
| 3 | LargeSUVs | Confidential | 200 |
| 4 | OilDrill | Confidential | 200 |

Figure 2: Example of a table to which a row-level security policy has been applied.

a so-called VPD SQL modification occurs in which the SQL statement is refined in a way such that only those rows whose row label satisfies the read/write label specified for the user are retrieved. The latter step thus realizes fine-grained access control. We refer the reader interested in all the details of Oracle's Label Security to Levinger (2002).

## Database Security Mechanisms

To support an access control model, an RDBMS has to provide database mechanisms implementing the access policies specified in that model. The purpose of a security mechanism is to enforce one or more security policies. Current database technology provides several types of security mechanisms that differ in functionality, efficiency, and flexibility. In the following paragraphs, we outline the basic properties of the mechanisms available in database systems with a focus on authentication and in particular access control mechanisms.

The process used to determine that a user is who he or she claims to be is called *authentication* (see, e.g., chapter 169, Password Authentication, and chapter 170, Computer and Network Authentication in this handbook). All RDBMSs provide authentication mechanisms that prevent unauthorized users from using the database system and specific application components realized in the database. Authentication can even be applied to the enabling of roles, as discussed in the section entitled Role-Based Access Control. One can broadly distinguish between three authentication mechanisms for database systems: internal authentication, application-based authentication, and operating system (OS)–based authentication. Internal authentication mechanisms are part of the RDBMS functionality for which a user has to give a user name and password to connect to the database. Only if the user is known to the database (i.e., the authentication information is stored in the RDBMS system catalog) is the user authorized to use the database. OS-based authentication is a combination of an authentication mechanism provided by the OS that hosts the RDBMS and the authentication mechanism provided by the RDBMS. Once a user is authenticated by the OS, the user can connect to the database. In the context of large-scale database systems that manage several applications, application-based authentication is the most prominent approach in which authentication is accomplished at the application level using third-party mechanisms external to the RDBMS. Kerberos-based authentication is a popular technique of that type (see chapter 63, Kerberos). We refer the reader interested in a detailed discussion of the different authentication models supported by some of today's commercial RDBMSs to respective system documentation such as for Oracle Advanced Security and Microsoft SQL Server.

Once a user has been authenticated, the RDBMS authorization mechanisms govern the user's database operations and accesses. In the section entitled Discretionary Access Control, we discussed the realization of DAC in databases using the GRANT command. The specification of an access policy using the GRANT statement and subsequent access controls are realized by mechanisms as follows.

All system and object privileges a user (or more generally, an AuthID) has received are recorded in the system catalog. That is, whenever a valid GRANT or REVOKE statement is issued, modifications to system catalog tables are performed. Now consider the scenario in which a database user submits an SQL statement in a database session, for example, through an application. Note that in a session an AuthID is associated with the user and that an active role is associated with that AuthID. The SQL statement is passed to the query compiler component of the RDBMS, which verifies the syntax and semantics of the statement for correctness. In particular, it verifies whether the AuthID that issued the SQL statement has the privilege to execute the statement and to perform accesses to database objects (tables, attributes, views) referred to in the statement. For this, the query compiler uses the parse tree for the SQL statement, and it queries the system catalog to check for respective permissions associated with the AuthID. Thus, the GRANT command results in a *compile-time* approach for access control. That is, authorization occurs during the verification of an SQL statement. A REVOKE statement results in the deletion of respective entries from the system catalog.

Views provide another important mechanism to prevent users from accessing data they are not supposed to access. The usage of views as access control mechanisms was first suggested in the 1970s by Stonebraker (1975). Recall that a view definition is a named query and that the view definition as well as object privileges on views that have been granted to AuthIDs are recorded in the system catalog. If an AuthID submits an SQL statement that refers to a view, checking proper object privileges on the view occurs in the same manner as described previously, that is, during the compilation of the SQL statement. Views provide for much finer access control to tables and other views because one can precisely specify rows and columns to select in the query by using a WHERE clause and subqueries in the view definition. Thus, views provide a *data-dependent access control mechanism* in which the data an AuthID can access are determined based on the data stored in base tables.

Many of today's RDBMSs provide programming language extensions to SQL, such as stored procedures or embedded SQL. These extensions can be used to realize sophisticated security and access control mechanisms. Although these mechanisms provide for more functionality, their design and usage is nontrivial and requires a very good knowledge about the security requirements of applications and the RDBMS's environment. Stored procedures can realize security mechanisms that are not possible through using only GRANT/REVOKE statements and views. Because stored procedures offer programming language constructs, such a loops, if-then-else blocks, and calls to other procedures, they are in particular useful for implementing *context-dependent* access controls. Recall that context-dependent access uses information about the context in which a data access or an operation on the database occurs. This can include time information, that is, when an SQL statement has been issued, information about previous statements the AuthID has issued, or information about other current activities in the database system. Stored procedures can be used to realize many features of access control that are not supported by current RDBMS access control models, including negative authorizations, separation of duty in the context of role-based access control, and context-, resource-, and data-dependent access control policies. The drawbacks of more expressive and flexible mechanisms, of course, are higher design and maintenance costs and difficulty in understanding the system behavior, as well as some performance impact on the database.

All mechanisms discussed previously are *preventive mechanisms* in that they check at the compile time of an SQL statement whether an AuthID is authorized to execute the statement. Most RDBMSs also support *detection mechanisms* that are realized through *auditing*. Although auditing can occur at many places in an information system infrastructure, that is, at the application, network, and database layers, in this chapter we are mainly concerned with auditing database activities. An RDBMS naturally supports the logging of all database operations and activities in the form of database logs (Weikum & Vossen, 2002; Gray & Reuter, 1993). Although such logs, which record database activities in typically proprietary data formats, are mainly used for database recovery purposes, several federal and government regulations require the archiving of such logs for reporting purposes (see, e.g., Nanda & Burleson, 2003). Database logs can be analyzed using tools (e.g., Oracle's LogMiner; Rich, 2003) to check for possible access violations and other types of potential security breaches. In addition to database logs, some RDBMSs also provide for recording information in audit tables. That is, the database administrator (DBA) can specify users or types of accesses on database objects that are to be audited, and respective audit information is recorded in audit tables. Audit information can readily be queried and analyzed using SQL and thus provides another useful setting for realizing detection mechanisms in a database.

# DATABASE SECURITY DESIGN

Database design is concerned with accurately modeling an organization's information needs, and then implementing the model as a high-performance relational database. Numerous textbooks concentrate on the various database design approaches, concepts, and techniques (e.g., Batini, Ceri, & Navathe, 1992; Ramakrishnan & Gehrke, 2003; Elmasri & Navathe, 2004), but very few include database security design aspects. Only Castano et al. (1995) give a very detailed, though idealized, description of the different steps and approaches in database security design. In the following sections, we give an overview of the different practical database security design aspects, how they relate to system security design approaches, and how database and security design tasks interact with each other.

The enterprise's security administration goal is to find an optimal mix of benefit (convenient operation) and risk. They might configure jobs so that few people have access to sensitive data. For example, commercial processes deliberately minimize the number of people able to change payment information, whereas military processes split tasks to execute at a single security level. At the level of privilege administration, job redesign is rarely an option. In this case, the ideal is to allow each user exactly the accesses needed for legitimate tasks. This ideal cannot be attained, for several reasons:

- It is normally too difficult to determine *exactly* which actions are appropriate for a job.
- The policy might not have access to context information (e.g., location of the user, which middleware-resident function made the request, which stage of the task the user is currently executing) or might be unable to express subtle choices even for the context it does have.
- Administrators are overburdened and often choose coarse granule privileges on database objects, such as table rather than column. Even when they have been conscientious, they will rarely bother to revoke privileges that are no longer needed.
- The cost to the administrator or the organization of improper denial is high, so the administrators grant extra privileges. For example, as new applications are added, the administrator does not want repeated calls that development has stopped because of lack of access privileges.

The following section, Protecting the RDBMS, discusses some practical aspects of protecting an RDBMS. The section entitled Designing Security Policies examines the design of access policies on data, at successively greater levels of detail. The section Security Policy Implementation outlines the steps of implementing security policies on a given RDBMS.

## Protecting the RDBMS

Despite some marketing claims, RDBMS products can be hacked or bypassed. This section briefly discusses attacks that cause unexpected behavior. Following are some considerations one has to keep in mind when protecting an RDBMS:

- *With any complex software system, poor configuration practices cause vulnerability* (see, e.g., Newman, 2004; Theriault & Newman, 2001). Passwords might be unchanged from vendor defaults or database tables are left accessible to Public. The sheer complexity of RDBMS configuration parameters exacerbates the problem. Security configuration and management software can help administrators in analyzing and keeping track of security settings.
- *The database administrator has excessive privileges.* Administrators' actions require auditing in a trail not under their control.
- *By penetrating the underlying operating system, an attacker can copy, change, or delete database files.* Significant skill is required to execute such types of attacks.

Penetrating a system in ways that keep applications working to hide the penetration can be particularly difficult. To avoid tampering with files, data, and query results, several products offer encryption techniques, and researchers have proposed schemes for digital signatures to authenticate query results (e.g., Devanbu, Gertz, Martel, & Stubblebine, 2003). However, the performance effect might be serious.

- *Applications that construct queries on the fly can be fooled into constructing improper requests.* "SQL injection" techniques apply when an application constructs an SQL query on the fly, for example, by inserting a user-supplied value into a query string (Anley, 2002; Boyd & Keromytis, 2004). A malicious user can manipulate quotation marks to insert additional SQL statements. This problem can be addressed by coding standards on query builders or (more secure but less flexible) by having the user supply parameters to a precompiled query.

A strategy of defense in depth is appropriate, for example, placing the RDBMS server behind a firewall or limiting the number of accounts authorized to submit SQL statements. In system terms, RDBMSs provide a layer of protection even after the operating system has been penetrated. The reader might also wish to examine general advice on using security software systems and components residing at the network, operating, or application layer of a computing system discussed in detail elsewhere in this handbook.

Also note that several security standards (though not specific to RDBMSs) help customers and vendors focus on protection requirements and provide design and implementation strategies for a secure (database) system. These include the DoD criteria (U.S. Department of Defense, 1985); various documents published by the NIST Computer Security Resource Center (CSRC; http://csrc.nist.gov/), which are also available as part of the NCSC & DoD Rainbow series through the Network Security Library (NSL) at http://secinf.net/; the *Site Security Handbook* (Fraser, 1997); and the Common Criteria for Information Technology Security Evaluation (*Common Criteria*, 2004). Most database vendors furthermore provide extensive documentation on how to secure system components that interact with a database system and database applications, including application servers and network components.

## Designing Security Policies

Today's RDBMSs offer considerable flexibility in protecting data from inappropriate access by authorized users. To harness this power, one must first *model the data to be protected*; then *define what access is permissible*. Thus, data administration practices and artifacts must be understood to practice security design, implementation, and administration.

There is a vast body of data administration literature in the context of database systems (see references given at the beginning of the section entitled Database Security Design), with many proposed methodologies. A typical idealized story goes like this: an idealized picture of an enterprise assumes that system development begins with comprehensive analyses of available technologies and user requirements. Requirements are then elaborated to functional requirements, architectures, descriptions of business processes, and lists of individual transactions. Based on all this knowledge, one derives a conceptual design for a database and then an implementation design, which is carefully mapped to the process descriptions. At the same time, one examines security requirements, including both organizational needs and applicable laws and regulations, carefully mapping them to all the preceding information.

From this, one gets a security policy expressed in terms of a *conceptual model*, a model that models the problem domain. An *implementation model* tells about the implementation in a given computing system, for example, which data are physically stored, what is the interface to a service. Concepts useful for categorizing information are also defined (e.g., Financial, Medical) and carefully mapped to individual data elements. One further assumes that these models and mappings are kept in well-managed repositories, and whenever a change is desired, the various models are changed, too. Unfortunately, we are unaware of any large organization that conforms to this ideal. Few organizations capture and maintain all the artifacts formally, but they still guide designers. In the following paragraphs, we describe a simple picture that seems to capture the essence, without proposing a specific formalism.

Most data systems are designed or understood using a series of models, each an elaboration of higher level ones. For example, many approaches suggest having an external layer, a conceptual layer, and a physical implementation layer. By looking at any layer, one gets a specification (possibly very vague) covering the data in the system. There is a mapping of objects in each layer $L_i$ to objects at the next most detailed level $L_{i+1}$. A security policy defined in terms of objects at layer $L_i$ needs to be implemented by a policy on $L_{i+1}$. Furthermore, if $L_{i+1}$ identifies more detailed granules of data (e.g., attributes as well as entities), more detailed policies can be written. Layers can also elaborate sets of information that are not intended as structural units. For example, one layer can require auditing of access to "sensitive medical information," deferring to the next layer the definition of what information is medical and what is sensitive. The relationships of entities and attributes to "sensitive" and "medical" are important metadata and capture the mappings between levels.

Data administration often begins with naming large categories of data that a system is to manage, with later layers identifying entities and attributes that constitute, for example, medical or financial information. The policy front is similar. An organization is likely to have policies driven by upper management statements, phrased in terms of a high-level model. Lower-level models add flesh to the concepts used by upper management. In addition to categorizing data, it is also important to categorize users and privileges, for example, in the form of user groups and roles (see the section entitled Role-Based Access Control). In both cases, the category is given a name and a human-understandable membership criterion, for example, a group of DrugResearchers (scientists or statisticians engaged in drug research) or Check-Out role (privileges needed to check a patient out of the hospital). A policy then delegates a role to a group, that is, asserts that it is appropriate for its members to have those rights. Our formulation is intended to maximize the amount that can be handled by routine judgments and minimize the policy decisions that need careful consideration. It also guides maintenance decisions as the system evolves. It is crucial to set up a process by which user needs are learned, groups and roles designed, and policy decisions made. Some approaches to designing roles and groups appear in the literature. For example, an extension of Entity-Relationship (ER) modeling concepts to address security and authorization features has been proposed by Oh and Navathe (1995). Approaches to modeling roles and role relationships have been proposed by Neumann and Strembeck (2002) and Epstein and Sandhu (1999, 2001). In general, important (application-specific) tasks should be identified and described—the privileges needed for a task are assigned to a role. Some roles might correspond to "natural" groups of resources, such as Medical Records, and new kinds of records need to be appropriately characterized. It is essential that the *meaning* of each group and role be explained, in human-understandable form, independent of its current membership. This explanation is particularly important for evolution as new job titles, tasks, and data are created.

For each substantive policy determined during the previously described steps, one also needs a policy on required strength of implementation. Such a specification is likely to be done by categorizing policies and having a treatment for each category, which might include default treatments. For example, some U.S. government agencies require various degrees of physical and logical separation between classified data and systems accessed by users with low or no security clearances. The next section discusses the core issues in actually implementing policies in terms of the mechanisms provided by an RDBMS.

## Security Policy Implementation

The final step in database security design is the actual implementation of the database using a particular RDBMS. That is, the database schema and security policies (specified at the finest level of granularity) are transformed into the implementation data model, which in the context of this chapter is the relational model. Several tools exist that automate this process at least for a conceptual database schema formulated as an ER or Unified Modeling Language (UML) diagram. The transformation of a database schema results in a set of tables and views. Furthermore, the roles determined during the policy design phase are specified using the CREATE ROLE command (see the section entitled Role-Based Access Control), individual database users are created (including appropriate user authentication mechanisms), and privileges and roles, including the administration of privileges, are assigned to users using the GRANT command. For security policies that include predicates, either views or procedural security mechanisms (see the section entitled Database

Security Mechanisms) are created. If security policies furthermore include accountability aspects, such as what users issued what operation on objects at what time, auditing mechanisms are initialized as well. In cases in which procedural security mechanisms, such as stored procedures and triggers are used, the performance impact of these mechanisms on the operation of the database system should be verified and compared with the performance and functional requirements of the database stated during the requirements analysis.

Once all security mechanisms have been created, it is important to verify (at least partially) the security mechanisms for correctness and completeness. That is, based on the security threats identified prior to the policy design phase, privileges assigned to users and roles that operate on sensitive data should be verified to determine whether they correctly reflect all the requirements stated (at all model levels). For this, documents that focus on the security design and evaluation of systems provide important and useful guidelines in verifying the correct mapping and realization of requirement and policies using the different levels of abstraction employed during policy design and implementation (see references at the end of the section entitled Protecting the RDBMS).

## DATABASE SECURITY EVALUATION AND RECONFIGURATION

From a security point of view, in an ideal setting (1) database applications and users have precisely all the privileges to perform their tasks and (2) all operations on the database and objects can be traced back to users. In practice, however, this is rarely the case. There are several reasons for this. Many database settings are dynamic; new applications and middleware components are added, underlying database structures are changed, or security settings are modified to accommodate new or changing requirements (e.g., to address performance). Even if a database has been designed and implemented following the security design steps outlined in the previous section, security requirements, policies, and mechanisms can become outdated. Thus, the security settings of the database might not correctly reflect current (now implicit) security policies and requirements.

Assume a setting where a database serves as the back end to several applications. One might want to ask the following security-related questions: What are the potential vulnerabilities of the database? Are there database users who misuse their privileges and thus might cause a threat to the security of the database? If the answer to either of the two questions is positive, a follow-up question then is: How can the current database security mechanisms be reconfigured to exclude these vulnerabilities? A brute force approach, as often suggested in the literature, is to perform an extensive auditing of all database actions and to analyze audit logs for possible vulnerabilities and insider misuse. Without further guidance, such an approach is unrealistic and impractical for databases that mange hundreds of tables, views, and stored procedures, and a high volume of transactions is constantly executed against the database.

In the following sections, we outline an approach for the evaluation and reengineering of the security of a database. The approach is based on a data-centric view to database security and employs a technique called focused auditing.

## Database Security Evaluation

The first phase in evaluating the security of a database for possible vulnerabilities and insider misuse is the inspection of the current database security mechanisms. All database users, including their database privileges, are verified against current security requirements and expectations. Information about database users, their privileges, and association with database roles can easily be obtained from the database's data dictionary. This simple inspection, which resembles a reverse engineering of security policies in a database system, not only leads to valuable insights into the current security setting of a database, but it also provides an up-to-date picture of the state of access controls in a database. Results of this analysis include (1) database user accounts (AuthIDs) that have been associated with applications and that are not needed anymore (e.g., they have been used during some test phase), and (2) privileges and role associations that do not reflect current information needs for users or applications. For example, several commercial RDBMSs come with preinstalled database accounts. If these accounts (AuthIDs) are not used, they should be deleted (or deactivated) in order to not cause a possible entry point for attacks. In general, the outcome of this evaluation phase should be a revised (conceptual) security design that formulates current access policies and roles and associates privileges and roles with users (AuthIDs).

Now assume that the privileges associated with AuthIDs have been verified to be sound and complete; that is, they reflect all the accepted information needs of users and applications. Consider the scenario in which a database user has been granted the privilege to select rows from a table, say, a table with customer information. If this table contains millions of rows and the application in which the user is operating on this table serves a specific task, the access privilege might be too coarse grained. That is, the user is supposed to retrieve only data about specific customers but has been granted the privilege to perform selections on all customers. Such a discrepancy between the granularity of privileges assigned to a user and operations supposed to be executed by the user can result in insider misuse. Ideally, one would like to know what users are executing what types of operations on what database objects based on the privileges they have been assigned.

To address the issue of possible insider misuse, in the following, we outline the concept of *focused auditing* (see also Gertz & Csaba, 2003, for more details). In this approach, auditing of database events is tailored to a few tables that contain sensitive data (e.g., as determined during policy design). That is, initially auditing focuses on data and not that much on users. Respective audit logs are analyzed to determine which users operate on the tables using which types of operations. Note that we specifically refer to audit logs and not general database logs that are used for transaction management and recovery purposes. Audit logs contain only information about specified database events of interest and they can easily be queried. Database logs, on the other hand, contain information about all database events, and the analysis of log data requires separate data extraction and analysis tools. All major RDBMS provide tools and SQL commands to manage the auditing of operations on tables. Through these tools, access frequencies and other temporal properties of accesses to a table can be determined, for example, during what time period(s) what accesses (insert, update, delete, select) occurred. Although most RDBMS tools provide for statement-level auditing, that is, they record what AuthIDs executed what operation at what time, in most systems, fine-grained access audit information can be obtained only using triggers. Fine-grained audit information includes information about individual tuples that have been inserted, deleted, and updated.

In the focused auditing approach, fine-grained access information to tables of interest is recorded in extra tables. The data are accumulated over a period of time and are analyzed using SQL queries and reporting tools. Results include access frequencies of operations (grouped by AuthIDs), average and median values of attributes being updated, and aggregated properties of tuples inserted and deleted. Different grouping criteria of access data recorded in these tables enable administrators to inspect different aspects of accesses to the underlying table; such aspects include AuthID-specific aspects, that is, what AuthID performed what types of operations, and data-specific aspects, that is, how did tuples and attribute values evolve over time. This information then again is compared to the security requirements formulated during the security policy design phase. Administrators can easily expand the focus of the auditing to other (semantically related) tables and AuthIDs.

In summary, the idea of the security evaluation approach is first to establish a focus that consists of one or more sensitive tables, perform a fine-grained auditing of operations on these tables using triggers, and use the obtained audit data to further explore the behavior of AuthIDs with respect to other database objects. Such focused auditing can naturally be used to investigate possible or potential scenarios for insider misuse (see, e.g., Chung, Gertz, & Levitt, 1999).

## Security Reconfiguration Through User and Data Profiling

Security reconfiguration of a database encompasses the definition of views, roles, and procedural access control mechanisms that provide for access control that is more fine-grained than simple object privileges assigned to users and roles using the GRANT command. In addition to deleting or deactivating unused AuthIDs and revoking unused privileges from users and roles, security reconfiguration tries to adhere to the least privilege principles.

That is, although an AuthID has been granted privileges to perform insert, update, delete, or select operations on a table, based on the information obtained through fine-grained auditing, these operations should be applied only to certain rows in a table or in a specific context.

Audit information about accesses is used in two ways: to create *data profiles* and *user profiles*. A data profile describes the current state of attribute values in a table and includes information about the distribution of attribute values, minimum and maximum values for attributes, and occurrences of null values (if permitted by the table specification). It also includes information about how attribute values evolve over time, for example, in the context of update operations. The information can be presented to the administrator based on different grouping criteria on access measures, and it can be appropriately visualized to provide the administrator with a complete picture of the data in a table. What role does a data profile play in the context of database security? First, if data values are observed that clearly represent outliers (e.g., a value for a salary attribute that is 10 times the maximum of the other salary values), integrity constraints can be added to the audited table to prevent such erroneous data values in the future. Obviously, removing existing erroneous table entries and attribute values requires "cleaning" the data, a typical activity in data quality frameworks (Johnson & Dasu, 2003). Second, even if no outliers are observed, integrity constraints that might have been neglected or not known during the design of the database can be added; these then better describe admissible values or further restrict admissible values. In both cases, additional integrity constraints, which are either added to the table specification or specified in the form of triggers, prevent future data entries that might be caused by accidental or malicious modifications of table data.

User profiles are much harder to derive from audit data. The goal of a user profile is to describe the behavior of a database user (or more generally, an AuthID) in terms of insert, update, delete, and select operations against one or more tables. The area of profiling users operating on database objects is relatively unexplored, and we thus give only some ideas of how profiles can be obtained. If audit data includes information about the user performing the operation, frequencies and time windows for the different operations can be established. For example, a profile might include the statement that a user executes between 70 and 100 select operations between 9 a.m. and 2 p.m. If this behavior corresponds to the expected behavior, a respective security mechanism can be implemented that detects deviations from this behavior. The mechanism can be a stored procedure or function through which the select operation occurs (see the section entitled Database Security Mechanisms). A user profile can include statements at different levels of granularity, for example, the user behavior on a daily basis or an hourly basis. It can simply include access frequencies or might include profiles of the data accessed by the user, as described earlier. A user profile can include statements about accesses to one or more tables and might even include information about which accesses occur together, for example, in the context of user transactions. There is no limit to what a user profile can contain. However, based on the audit data available, different levels of granularity can be established and an increasing set of tables can be audited through the focused auditing approach, thus providing an administrator with a means to verify the behavior of a user incrementally and to configure security mechanisms that guard against deviations from the behavior determined by profiles. Eventually, user profiles can be compared and similarity measures can be established, thus providing a means to discover roles from individual user behaviors. Similar profiles indicate similar necessary privileges, which thus can be specified in the form of roles.

In general, although all the preceding analysis and profiling tasks can be done using the functionality supported by today's RDBMSs, tools are needed that provide administrators with a comprehensive and flexible way to configure, manage, and analyze audit data and to (semi-)automatically translate audit results, such as data and user profiles, into respective security mechanisms.

# CONCLUSIONS AND FUTURE DIRECTIONS

Today's computing systems are not secure. This holds for network components, operating systems, and database systems. A significant amount of work on securing networks and operating systems has been done, for example, in the context of intrusion detection systems (Intrusion Detection Systems Basics, chapter 191) or code analysis. Security for relational database systems, on the other hand, has mainly focused on providing access control mechanisms, which in today's relational database systems are primarily realized through granting privileges to users, specifying roles, and occasionally through using stored procedures. This is despite the fact that there has been a tremendous amount of research and proposals on more sophisticated security mechanisms and access controls for database systems. We therefore envision the following future directions in database security research and development.

First, in addition to security products at the network and operating system layer that try to detect security breaches, an intrusion and misuse detection system *within* an RDBMS might add another layer of defense against security threats. Such a system would monitor the behavior of users and their operations on sensitive data and establish user and data profiles from which security mechanisms are automatically derived. Such a system would be a significant step toward dealing with insider misuse. Note that insider misuse is a type of security breach that is most frequently observed in existing systems (Anderson, 1999; Neumann, 1999; Power, 2002).

Second, most of the existing commercial database products provide means to manage application logic within the database. For example, Java programs can be called from within SQL queries and stored procedures; such programs can even call functions and procedures external to the RDBMS. As RDBMSs are able to manage more and more types of objects and become programming platforms, richer access control and information flow models are needed that go beyond operations on just database tables and views.

Third, although current RDBMSs provide database designers and developers with several types of security mechanisms, there is a lack of support for security design, administration, and management tools. Tools are needed to support all database security design tasks and furthermore help and guide administrators in maintaining the security of the database through monitoring, auditing, and analyzing the collected data.

In summary, we envision several opportunities for tool developers to provide (database) administrators and security personnel with comprehensive and flexible database security configuration, management, and analysis tools that help these users to better deal with the complexity and diversity of security aspects in today's large-scale and mission-critical database systems.

## ACKNOWLEDGMENTS

The work by Michael Gertz was partially supported by the National Science Foundation under Grant No. IIS-0242414.

## GLOSSARY

**Access Control** A framework to specify and reason about security policies that describe the principles on which access to objects is granted or denied.

**Auditing** The process of analyzing a (database) system to determine which actions took place and who performed them.

**AuthID** The authorization identifier uniquely identifies a database user or a role name in a database system. It is determined by a system in an implementation-dependent manner.

**DAC** Discretionary access control (DAC) is based on the concept of object ownership and mechanisms that allow owners to assign privileges to users, including policies on the administration of privileges.

**Data Dictionary** A relational database management system maintains all information (metadata) about logical and physical database objects in a data dictionary (also called system catalog).

**Least Privilege** The principle of least privilege states that a subject should be given only those privileges that it needs to complete its tasks.

**MAC** When a system mechanism controls access to an object and an individual user cannot alter that access, the control is mandatory access control (MAC). This type of access control is typically based on system-wide security policies.

**Policy** A (security) policy describes constraints placed on entities and actions in a system; a policy is independent of the system mechanisms that enforce the policy.

**RBAC** Role-based access control (RBAC) is concerned with aggregating access privileges into named entities (roles) and assigning such entities to individual users, groups of users, or other roles.

**Security Mechanism** A security mechanism implements a security policy to prevent and/or detect improper accesses that violate the policy.

**Separation of Duties** The principle of separation of duties (or privileges) states that a system should not grant permission based on a single condition.

**Stored Procedure** A stored procedure is a program that is executed through a single SQL statement that can be locally executed and completed within the process space of the database server.

**Trigger** A trigger is a type of stored procedure that describes database actions to be executed when certain database events occur.

**View** A view is a table that is derivable from other database tables, which can be previously defined views or base tables. A view is specified through an SQL query.

## CROSS REFERENCES

See *Access Control: Principles and Solutions; Auditing Information Systems Security; Security Policy Guidelines*.

## REFERENCES

Abrams, M. D., Jajodia, S., & Podell, H. J. (Eds.). (1995). *Information security: An integrated collection of essays*. New York: Wiley-IEEE Computer Society Press.

Anderson, R. (1999). RAND Corporation: Research and development initiatives focused on preventing, detecting, and responding to insider misuse of critical information systems. *Conference Proceedings* CF-151-OSD.

Anley, C. (2002). *Advanced SQL injection in SQL Server applications*. Next Generation Security Software Ltd. Retrieved June 30, 2005 from http://www.ngssoftware.com/papers/advanced_sql_injection.pdf

Batini, C., Ceri, S., & Navathe, S. B. (1992). *Conceptual database design: An entity-relationship approach*. Redwood City: Benjamin/Cummings.

Bell, D. E., & LaPadula, L. J. (1976). *Secure computer systems: Unified exposition and multics interpretation* (Technical Report). Bedford, MA: MITRE Corporation.

Bertino, E., Bettini, C., Ferrari, E., & Samarati, P. (1996). A temporal access control mechanism for database systems. *IEEE Transactions on Knowledge and Data Engineering, 8*(1), 67–80.

Bertino, E., Jajodia, S., & Samarati, P. (1995). Database security: Research and practice. *Information Systems, 20,*(7), 537–556.

Bertino, E., Jajodia, S., & Samarati, P. (1999). A flexible authorization mechanism for relational database systems. *ACM Transactions on Information Systems, 17*(2), 101–140.

Beznosov, K. (2002). Object security attributes: Enabling application-specific access control In middleware. R. Meersman and Z. Tari (Eds.) *4th International Symposium on Distributed Objects and Applications (DOA),*

Lecture Notes in Computer Science 2519, (693–710), Springer.

Bishop, M. (2003). *Computer security: Art and science.* Boston: Addison-Wesley.

Boyd, S. W., & Keromytis, A. D. (2004). SQLrand: Preventing SQL injection attacks. In *Proceedings of Applied Cryptography and Network Security*, Second International Conference, ACNS 2004, Lecture Notes in Computer Science 3089, Springer.

Castano, S., Fugini, M., Martella, G., & Samarati, P. (1995). *Database security.* Boston: Addison-Wesley.

Chung, C., Gertz, M., & Levitt, K. (1999). A misuse detection system for database systems (pp. 159–178). In M. E. van Biene-Hershey and Strous (Eds.) *integrity and internal control, IFIP TC11 working group 11.5, Third working conference an integrity and internal control in information system.* Kluwer Academic Publishers.

*Common Criteria for Information Technology Security Evaluation (Version 2.2).* (2004). Retrieved June 30, 2005 from http://niap.nist.gov/cc-scheme/cc_docs/cc_v2_part1.pdf

Devanbu, P., Gertz, M., Martel, M., & Stubblebine, S. G. (2003). Authentic data publication over the Internet. *Journal of Computer Security, 11*(3) 291–314.

Elmasri, R., & Navathe, S. B. (2004). *Fundamentals of database systems* (4th ed.). Addison-Wesley.

Epstein, P., & Sandhu, R. (1999). A UML-based approach to role engineering. *Proceedings of the Fourth Workshop on Role-Based Access Control.* 135–143, NewYork: ACM.

Epstein, P., & Sandhu, R. (2001). Engineering of role/permission assignments. *Proceedings of the 17th Annual Computer Security Applications Conference (ACSAC)* 127–136 IEEE Computer Society.

Ferraiolo, D. F., Sandhu, R., Gavrila, S., Kuhn, D. R., & Chandramouli, R. (2001). Proposed NIST standard for role-based access control. *ACM Transactions on Information and System Security, 4*(3), 224–274.

Fraser, B. (1997). *Site Security Handbook* (Request for Comments (RFC) 2196). Network Working Group, Internet Engineering Task Force. Retrieved June 30, 2005 from http://www.ietf.org/rfc/rfc2196.txt

Gertz, M., & Csaba, G. (2003). Monitoring mission critical data for integrity and availability In *5th International IFIP TC-11 WG 11.5 Working Conference on Integrity and Internal Control* (pp. 189–201). Kluwer Academic Publishers.

Gray, J., & Reuter, A. (1993). *Transaction processing: concepts and techniques.* San Francisco: Morgan Kaufman.

Johnson, T., & Dasu, T. (2003). Data quality and data cleaning: An overview. *Proceedings of the ACM SIGMOD International Conference on Management of Data.* p. 681, NewYork: ACM.

Landwehr, K. (2001). Computer security. *International Journal of Information Security, 1*, 3–13.

Levinger, J. (2002). *Oracle label security administrator's guide, release 2 (9.2), part number A96578-01.* Redwood Shores, CA: Oracle Corporation.

Melton J., & Simon, A. R. (2001). SQL 1999-Understanding Relational Language Components, (2nd Edition) San Francisco: Morgan Kaufman.

Nanda, A. (2004, March/April). Oracle's row-level security gives users their own virtual private databases. *Oracle Magazine.*

Nanda, A., & Burleson, D. (2003). *Oracle privacy security auditing (includes Federal Law Compliance with HIPAA, Sarbanes-Oxley and the Gramm-Leach-Bliley Act GLB).* Kittrell, NC: Rampant TechPress.

Neumann, P. G. (1999). *The challenges of insider misuse.* Paper prepared for the Workshop on Preventing, Detecting, and Responding to Malicious Insider Misuse, August 16–18, 1999, at RAND, Santa Monica, CA. Retrieved from http://www.csl.sri.com/users/neumann/pgn-misuse.html

Neumann, G., & Strembeck, M. (2002). A scenario-driven role engineering process for functional RBAC roles. *Proceedings of the 7th ACM Symposium on Access Control Models and Technologies*, 33–42. NewYork: ACM

Newman, A. (2004). Six security secrets attackers don't want you to know. *DB2 Magazine 9*(2).

Oh, Y., & Navathe, S. (1995). SEER: Security enhanced entity-relationship model for modeling and integrating secure database environments. In M. Papazoglou (Ed.), *OOER'95: Object-Oriented and Entity-Relationship Modeling, 14th International Conference, Lecture Notes in Computer Science, 1021* (pp. 170–180). Springer.

Osborn, S., Sandhu, R., & Munawer, Q. (2000). Configuring role-based access control to enforce mandatory and discretionary access control policies. *ACM Transactions on Information and Systems Security, 3*(2), 85–106.

Power, R. (2002). 2002 CSI/FBI computer crime and security survey. Computer Security Institute.

Ramakrishnan, R., & Gehrke, J. (2003). *Database management systems* (3rd ed.). New York: McGraw-Hill.

Ramaswamy, C., & Sandhu, R. (1998). Role-based access control features in commercial database management systems. In *21st National Information Systems Security Proceedings: Papers.* Retrieved June 30, 2005, from http://csrc.nist.gov/nissc/1998/papers.html

Rich, K. (2003). Oracle Database Utilities. Part No. B10825. Oracle Corporation, Redwood City.

Sandhu, R. (1998). Role activation hierarchies. In *Proceedings of the 3rd ACM Workshop on Role-Based Access Controls,* 33–40. NewYork: ACM

Sandhu, R. (2001). Future directions in role-based access control models. Keynote lecture at 2nd International Workshop on Mathematical Methods, Models, and Architectures for Computer Network Security, *Lecture Notes in Computer Science 2776,* Springer. Retrieved June 16, 2005, from http://www.list.gmu.edu/confrnc/misconf/mms01-rbac-future.pdf

Sandhu, R., Coyne, E. J., Feinstein, H. L., & Youman, C. E. (1996). Role-based access control models. *IEEE Computer, 29*(2), 38–47.

Sandhu, R., & Samarati, P. (1994, September). Access control: Principles and practice. *IEEE Communications Magazine,* 40–48.

Stonebraker, M. (1975). Implementation of integrity constraints and views by query modification. *Proceedings of the 1975 ACM SIGMOD International Conference on Management of Data,* 65–78. NewYork: ACM

Theriault, M. L., & Newman, A. (2001). *Oracle security handbook: Implement a sound security plan in your Oracle environment.* New York: McGraw-Hill Osborne.

U.S. Department of Defense. (1985). *Trusted computer system evaluation criteria* (DoD 5200.28 - STD). Retrived June 30, 2005, from http://www.radium.ncsc.mail/tpep/library/rainbow/5200.28-STD.htmal.

Weikum, G., & Vossen, G. (2002). *Transactional information systems.* Morgan Kaufman.

# Medical Records Security

Normand M. Martel, *Medical Technology Research Corp.*

## INTRODUCTION

The patient health record is a sensitive collection of information. It is meant to serve in part as a reference for medical providers but as more records become electronic, the patient health record creates potential liability concerns for those involved with its use and safe-keeping.

According to the Health Information Portability and Accountability Act (HIPAA), security and privacy legislation passed by the United States Department of Health and Human Services (HHS), the keepers of health records are required to take the necessary steps needed to protect the confidentiality and integrity of the patient health record. Keepers of health records can reduce and control their liability through a combination of best practices and ongoing employee training.

### The Diversity of Health Data

The patient health record consists of a diverse set of data resulting from the broad range of purposes, providers, and services the patient encounters in the process of seeking out and obtaining medical care. The patient health record might include benefits enrollment and evidence of insurability, the record of encounter, claims and claims processing, lab requests, test results, and financial information.

Over time, each entity involved in the medical process has discovered what systems and documentation best suit its needs. The end result is that the patient health record becomes an amalgam of information. No one part of the record can fulfill all needs of all medical service providers.

### The Paradox of Health Data

To be useful, the patient health record must be as current, coherent, and complete as possible. The information in the patient health record needs to be considered private, yet, to serve its purpose and furnish medical providers with vital information, the patient health record must be readily available at the various points of service. Therein lies the patient health record paradox: making the data readily available is contradictory to securing the data and limiting liability regarding inappropriate use or disclosure of the patient information. This conflict means care providers must perform a balancing act, weighing the protection of the patient's privacy against the doctor's urgent need to access that same data to provide timely, cost-effective, and reliable medical services.

### The Value of Health Data in an Information Society

The worth of health record data is incalculable, because health record data represent aspects of people's lives that include finances, life–death control, and a physiological life history. Patients value the information because the data describe and represent their physical selves. The insurer and claims processing entities place financial value on the data because they are the lifeblood of their existence. Researchers and clinicians value the data because they can contain hints regarding unresolved or undiscovered problems and their treatments.

## HEALTH RECORDS

The technology explosion that began in the 1990s and continues today has included a transition from the traditional, paper-based health record to the present-day electronic health record (EHR). It is necessary to examine the looming transition of the EHR to the portable health record (PHR) and explore some of the hurdles that must be overcome to reach this new plateau.

## Traditional Paper Record: Pros and Cons

The traditional, paper-based record is attractive because it is easy to create, moderately easy to store, and easily referenced. This type of record is unaffected by power outages and other disturbances that plague the technology of today.

The chain-of-custody and security aspects of the paper-based health record are fairly easy and straightforward to control. It is pretty simple, for example, to number an original document and then log whom you have faxed copies of this document to. The unique station signatures of the sending and receiving FAX machines combined with a document serial number easily identity the source and the recipient of a paper-based record.

One of the major drawbacks to the paper-based health record is the difficulty in correlating the diverse data and parts of the record. Another drawback relates to controlling who has viewed a document. Although a document can be identified by a unique set of markings, it is difficult to determine how many people have viewed the document and when it was viewed. Yet another difficulty lies in the medium itself, the paper. Paper records do not last very long unless stored under ideal conditions. They are easily destroyed by fire, water, smoke, and sunlight. Further, paper records are not easily mined or searched, resulting in a tedious analysis and collection process when such a search is required.

Although it can be argued that technology alone has brought about the EHR, the issues created by the short-comings of a scattered and diverse paper record have also contributed to the quest for a better mousetrap. Regardless of the triggering causes, the EHR is an evolutionary change that dramatically influences how records are kept, what data are kept as part of the record, and how long the data are kept. The EHR also enables data to be more easily accessed, used, and possibly abused.

## Structure and Functions of the Electronic Health Record

The EHR is not a single document but rather it is an eclectic collection of items, including the benefits application and enrollment forms, patient encounter records, medical history, lab test orders, test results, x-ray images, MRI images, prescriptions, patient claims, and other items needed to handle the various aspects of providing medical care.

Understanding the structure of the EHR (HL7 2004) provides a basis from which to break apart and handle the vast collection of information. Segregating the information into functional areas provides a means to manage each area and reduces the amount of information that could be needlessly exposed to an entity that did not require the information. An example of a logical breakdown is the separation of claims and claim processing data from lab requests and lab results. By separating the data by logical function, a researcher, for instance, could obtain collections of demographics data and lab results while not receiving specific, patient-identifying data referred to as Individually Identifiable Health Information (IIHI) in the HIPAA legislation (HHS, 2001). If the EHR is

segregated, the researcher is also shielded from the claims and claim processing data, further reducing the exposure of the source data because the irrelevant information is excluded from the research data right from the start.

A simple compartmentalization of the data leads to reduced data exposure and therefore reduces the risk associated with maintaining and distributing these data. Segregation of the health record causes a reduction in data that are disseminated, which in turn results in greater data security and more control over what is handed off to other entities, sharing only what is necessary.

## Electronic Health Record: Pros and Cons

Because the EHR makes it so easy to obtain, mine, and disseminate health record data, the mere existence of the EHR introduces a security, chain of custody, and right-to-privacy dilemma. Data are so easily and readily copied and transferred, it is hard to know who has seen what and when. It can be difficult to determine how many copies of a document or e-mail have been distributed and to whom this information has been distributed. Because there is no fading or loss of quality in the copies, the health record documents can be copied, transferred, and stored indefinitely with no loss of data quality or resolution. Further, there are presently no identifying marks on a document and no controls in place to identify which of multiple copies is truly the original, unaltered copy. These ease-of-use and ease-of-distribution features endowed by the present technology have paved the way for the right-to-privacy issues that have become the catalyst for change.

The proliferation of health data and the apparent disregard for patient privacy have led HHS to pass legislation aimed specifically at protecting the privacy of individuals by ensuring that there are nominal privacy and security constraints placed on what the HIPAA legislation calls "covered entities" (HHS, 2001), which include insurance companies and health care providers.

Although the EHR is a security nightmare for some, it is a goldmine for others. Researchers, drug developers, and device development companies are all looking at the wealth of new data as the "promised land" of research. Some of the insurance companies and clearinghouses have started mining their data and selling access and reports regarding these data to outside firms. This practice has caused further right-to-privacy concerns.

One anticipated advantage of moving to an EHR remains to be seen: a reduction in medical errors resulting from documents that are easier to read than the typical physician's hand-scrawled notes and prescriptions. A July 2004 Boston Globe article (Kowalczyk, 2004) cited HHS secretary Tommy Thompson as stating that the adoption of the EHR remained low (fewer than 13% of hospitals in the United States) and that, to date, there have been no notable reductions in medical errors resulting from the increased use of technology in U.S. hospitals.

## Future Direction: Portable Health Record (PHR)

A PHR is an EHR with a major philosophical change: ownership and responsibility for the integrity of the record shifts from the service providers to the patient. Patients now carry the EHR on their person via some convenient portable means. The PHR must be available at all times to medical providers for them to provide medical care. It is important to note that medical providers are no longer responsible for collecting and collating the record but rather the patient is now the party responsible for this activity.

The shift to patient-kept records introduces many issues: Do the various service providers keep copies of the record as the record is created? Who backs up the data in the PHR? If the patient is responsible for backing up the data, how does the patient go about it? What happens if the patient forgets or loses the PHR? What happens if the PHR cannot be read successfully? What happens if there is a local copy of data and those data conflict with the contents of the cached copy of the record? Who resolves discrepancies in the record? When and how are discrepancies discovered and resolved? Do the data in the PHR need to be stored in an encrypted form? If so, under what conditions do the data get encrypted and what triggers or allows the data to be decrypted? If the patient supplies part of the key needed to decrypt the data in the PHR, what happens if the patient is unable to supply the missing key component? How does the medical professional override the encryption/protection in an emergency situation?

Other issues that plague the introduction of the PHR include the cost of hardware. Who pays for the initial media needed to cover all of the patients? How and when are those media distributed to all patients? How are the initial data accumulated to produce the initial copy of the PHR? What about standards for the health record and their interfaces? The HL7 standard has not yet been adopted by all major stakeholders, namely the software vendors, physicians, hospitals, insurance carriers, and others. So, if records are stored on external media, what format are the data stored in? What applications can read/write these media? Is portability provided between likely different record management systems?

PHR solutions are presently aimed at portable rewriteable devices such as Smart Media, USB Key Chain Drives, Compact Flash, Secure Digital Cards, and Micro CDs. The number and mix of suggested solutions are very large. This diverse set of technologies combined with the lack of standardized techniques for encrypting and protecting the information on portable media makes it difficult for the industry to begin adopting some standard form of PHR that is acceptable and usable by all the medical entities as well as all of the patients.

The issues behind the PHR are just beginning to surface. It is likely to take a while for them to be worked out. After all, the adoption of the EHR by all covered entities has been slow at best (Larson, 2004; iHealth Beat, 2003a; iHealth Beat, 2003b). The medical software industry feels that cost has hampered the current adoption rate and places the rate at between 20 and 25% at the time of this writing. President Bush has offered a lofty goal of a 50–75% adoption rate by 2008 (Health Data Management, 2004). Combining financial pressures, litigation pressure, and the passing of the HIPAA legislation seems to have triggered more entities to move to the electronic record by placing a significant financial burden on entities for not acting. Since the passing of the HIPAA legislation, the EHR adoption rate has increased from an estimated 5–10% to the currently estimated 20–25% range (Health Data Management, 2003). But most medical industry experts consider this rate to be very slow.

## ELECTRONIC HEALTH RECORD STANDARDS BODIES

The introduction of the U.S. HIPAA legislation prepared the way for an EHR. The expected increase in use and importance of the EHR in turn presents the need for a standard method of information interchange. The need to represent the patient record in a common, clear, and concise manner is complicated by the security and privacy requirements. Without some form of standardization, many industry experts believe that the goal of data interchange while maintaining record security would be extremely difficult if not impossible to attain.

Although there are several standards bodies around the world working on aspects of an EHR, two organizations are becoming increasingly important in providing a standardized means of electronic health information interchange. These two groups are the American National Standards Institute (ANSI) X12N committee and Health Level Seven (HL7). By welcoming this pair of well-established and broad-based international groups, the HHS hopes to leverage the groups' momentum to increase the portability and interoperability of the various portions of the EHR in addition to making the standards internationally appealing.

### ANSI X12N

On February 4, 1991, an ANSI working group formed to standardize the insurance claims processing portion of the EHR. After the passing of the HIPAA legislation, the ANSI X12N committee realigned itself and approved a new standard on February 6, 2002, designed to harmoniously interact with the HL7 EHR standard. X12N and HL7 were sanctioned by HHS as a viable basis upon which entities can build secure records storage and records interchange platforms.

The purpose and charter of the X12N committee is best described on the committee's Web site, which can be found at http://www.x12.org. The purpose and scope of the X12N committee is stated as follows:

- Develops and maintains X12 electronic data interchange (EDI) and XML standards, standards interpretations, and guidelines as they relate to all aspects of insurance and insurance-related business processes
- Includes development and maintenance activities relating to property, casualty, health care, life, annuity, reinsurance, pensions, and reporting to regulatory agencies. Insurance subcommittee initiatives also include all products and services, such as government health care programs such as Medicare
- Serves as a liaison with complementary insurance standards bodies, such as HL7, to coordinate standards development activities

This list clearly defines the boundary between X12N and HL7 and enables a synergistic relationship to be formed between X12N and HL7.

## Health Level Seven (HL7)

HL7 defines itself on its Web site at http://www. hl7.org as follows:

> There are several health care standards development efforts currently under way throughout the world. Why then, embrace HL7? HL7 is singular as it focuses on the interface requirements of the entire health care organization, while most other efforts focus on the requirements of a particular department. Moreover, on an ongoing basis, HL7 develops a set of protocols on the fastest possible track that is both responsive and responsible to its members. The group addresses the unique requirements of already installed hospital and departmental systems, some of which use mature technologies.
>
> While HL7 focuses on addressing immediate needs, the group continues to dedicate its efforts to ensuring concurrence with other United States and international standards development activities. Argentina, Australia, Canada, China, Czech Republic, Finland, Germany, India, Japan, Korea, Lithuania, The Netherlands, New Zealand, Southern Africa, Switzerland, Taiwan, Turkey, and the United Kingdom are part of HL7 initiatives. Moreover, HL7 is an ANSI-approved Standards Developing Organization (SDO). HL7 strives to identify and support the diverse requirements of each of its membership constituencies: users, vendors, and consultants. Cognizant of their needs, requirements, priorities, and interests, HL7 supports all groups as they make important contributions to the quality of the organization. The committee structure, balanced balloting procedures, and open membership policies ensure that all requirements are addressed uniformly and equitably with quality and consistency.

## SECURITY CONCERNS

EHR security can be looked at from two perspectives. The first perspective is the privacy concern. Privacy control translates into having the ability to log and control access to the EHR so that access to which information and when is identifiable. The other perspective looks at the data from the data integrity point of view. This view questions which data are valid and unaltered, who produced the data, when was the data produced, and whether the data are part of or related to the correct patient entity.

## Who Has Access to Health Records?

The first entity concerned with the health record is the source of the data—the patient. Because the data are a representation of the patient, the patient owns the data or at least the right to control who sees and uses the data.

HIPAA was introduced to address this precise set of concerns.

Access to the record can be controlled by segregating the record into logical parts or sections. Each section of the record is in turn identified by the needs and characteristics of the person or entity accessing that specific section of the record.

The first-tier consumers in the access chain of the health record are the service providers, including hospitals, nurses, and clinical staff; physicians and their office staff; the pharmacy and pharmacist; outsourcers such as encoders and transcribers; labs and lab employees; specialists such as cardiologists, neurologists, and neonatal staff; and front desk and billing staff.

The secondtier consumers are drug and medical device researchers. They do not require immediate access to the record and typically do not provide immediate benefit to the patient. Instead, these second-tier members provide benefit by developing new drugs and therapies based on the data derived from a collection of patient records.

The third tier in the chain consists of people who are paramount to obtaining and paying for care but do not directly provide the care. These entities include the records management outsourcers, billing staff, plan sponsors such as an employer, and the plan payers such as the insurers and clearinghouses.

Fourth are those entities that are beyond those with immediate need yet still require direct access to portions of the EHR. These entities are incidental and ancillary users of the data and include financial auditors, accreditation and government agencies, law enforcement and legal agencies, and health care/data registries.

Finally, there are entities that do not require direct access to the data but possess some or all of the data and are in some way related to the entities enumerated above. An example of this type of entity is an off-site, data storage company. A storage entity could possess all the records, yet never need to access those records.

## Identifying Threats to the Security of the EHR

Given the wide array of health data producers and users, it seems that the number of threats to the EHR is limitless. A classification of threats by groups and types of threats begins to establish boundaries to the problem.

For the purposes of this article and the security model to be presented, threats are broadly classified as internal threats and external threats. Each threat category is a combination of physical threats, equipment threats, environmental threats, and people-centric threats. This classification model separates the threats by those an individual or organization can control and minimize (internal) and those that cannot be controlled by an individual or an organization (external). Refer to the chapters on physical security threats and internal security threats for a more in-depth look at various threats and their potential impact on the infrastructure, data, and the entities that retain and manage the data.

Internal threats are generally classified by industry experts as the most likely means by which data will be or can be compromised. A recent incident at Los Alamos Lab in New Mexico is a case in point (Associated Press, 2004). At the time of this writing, five employees had been fired after classified disks turned up missing at the lab. This type of security breach is preventable and demonstrates the need for sound security practices, which includes employee education and monitoring employees for conformance to security rules.

Examples of external threats include natural disasters such as hurricanes, fire, earthquakes, and terrorist attacks. To be effective, security planning must consider internal and external threats. Even though no set of measures will be able to prevent all breaches, security measures and practices must provide the foundation needed to at least minimize the occurrence and enable the detection and isolation of the inevitable breach.

## Internal Threats

Internal threats to the EHR can be separated into the following groups: loss of or loss of use of infrastructure, the misuse of the EHR, or the alteration of the EHR contents. The internal threats against infrastructure can be dealt with through environmental controls, physical access controls, logical access controls, and implementable and sustainable use policies (Associated Press, 2004). Loss of use can be mitigated with backup and redundant systems and a solid disaster avoidance and recovery plan.

Day-to-day security operations are manageable through the use of industry best practices, including updating technology against blended threats and constant training of staff. The staff needs to be aware and continually updated to guard against the new and evolving threats in addition to the old tricks such as social engineering and phishing tactics (Blau, 2004) used to harvest preattack knowledge. One slip by an employee could easily arm potential attackers with node, login, and/or password information, which could then be expanded upon once an attack is undertaken. A small knowledge breach could then cascade into a total system failure. The techniques used to protect the infrastructure must guard against this type of scenario and isolate any damage that could be done in the event of a security breach.

## External Threats

Many external threats are similar or identical to internal threats, but the external category introduces a new layer of issues. The control of the data is in someone else's possession, yet HIPAA mandates control of the data's integrity and confidentiality.

Some of the external threat issues stem from the transmission of the EHR via physical systems and media such as in data backup, data archiving, and e-mail. The transmission and sharing of the EHR to provide services to the patient (such as claims processing and lab tests) is another exposure. Because one entity must interface with others to complete its service mission, this causes numerous new vulnerabilities to surface. In the delivery of medical services, one entity must give up control over some portion of the EHR to other entities via the transmission of a copy of the data and must trust those entities to implement the same level of care to protect the integrity of the EHR.

Being able to correctly identify and deal with external interactions requires a virtual paper trail also known as a chain of custody. To have any notion about who is accessing what, an entity first needs to know what it is giving, to whom it is giving it, and under what circumstances it is delivering the various pieces of information.

## THE SECURITY SOLUTION

Security is difficult to manage but it must be dealt with. Needs and users constantly evolve and the technology providing the access and services is always in flux. There are many users, ongoing threats to security, and a chain of custody of unknown length. Nevertheless, it is possible to adopt a set of best practices and a security policy that provide a reasonably stable work and record environment.

Note that an entity is not freed from its responsibilities to provide adequate security because of cost factors (Grove, 2003). HIPAA mandates due care and reasonable practices regardless of their cost. Failure to meet the HIPAA criteria makes the organization or individual liable and positioned for fines.

Before undertaking any security planning, an individual or organization should undertake an assessment of their position, exposure, risk, and tolerance to each of these issues. The entity securing something needs to decide what that something is, how valuable that something is, and how much the entity is willing to pay in terms of labor and money to achieve the desired level of protection. An example of this would be a two-physician office choosing to install the ZoneLabs personal firewall on their personal office PC versus a large hospital installing an industrial-strength firewall appliance to protect upwards of 2000 PCs. An entity must be sure that the effort being expended to secure an asset has a reasonable rate of return on the investment.

Two fundamental principles of the security model presented here are those of "least privilege" and "proactive measures." In the least privilege part of the model, access to a resource or data is not granted to anyone unless their position demonstrates a need to know. In other words, a consumer must prove that access to a specific piece of data is required to perform a defined job and then access is made available by another action, otherwise access to that data is denied by default. In the proactive measures portion of the model, precautions are demonstrated through the use of updating systems and user training even though new threats may not be actively deployed. In other words, even though the latest Bagel Worm hasn't entered the infrastructure, the patches against the new Bagel Worm variant are applied under the assumption that it is just a matter of time before the infection is attempted.

The least privilege concept is easier to adopt and administer by instituting role- or group-based policies. By using roles, only the role and the elements associated with the role need to be clearly identified. Then, because the actual implementation occurs for a role, the issue of maintaining a plethora of individual users is reduced to assigning the user to the proper group or role.

Next, the physical plant and user access are tightly controlled and monitored. The network, systems, applications, databases, and other software components must be secured and addressed in the security policy. For more information, refer to Network Security, Firewalls, Operating System Security, Linux Operating System Security,

Windows 2000 Security, Database Security, and other similar chapters in this publication.

## The Virtual Policy Notebook

To improve chances of successfully conforming to the HIPAA requirements and maintaining a secure yet usable computing infrastructure, document processes and procedures in one place and make these data available to everyone in the organization. For example, begin by creating a virtual policy notebook on your Intranet and placing references to the policy or procedures within. For maximum effectiveness, make this information widely available to all employees and partners via the organization's intranet home and portal Web pages. The policies and procedures must be easily found and must be easy to follow and adhere to. If the policy or procedure is too difficult to uphold, it will be short-circuited and thus weaken the security policy.

## Security Step By Step

In conjunction with reading the step-by-step guideline below, an entity must perform a risk assessment and/or a gap analysis. The best time for an entity to assess what its needs are and how much it is willing to spend in hours and dollars to attain the desired level of protection is before the security planning process even begins.

The following step-by-step guideline is aimed at large organizations, but the steps can be abbreviated or collapsed with other steps as necessary for smaller installations.

1. To begin, identify where the buck stops. HIPAA states that security responsibility must be assigned, in writing, to an individual. Responsibility cannot be assigned to a group. This individual must also have the authority to act on and enforce the policy.
2. Create, document, and deploy a formal security program.
   a. Draft an organization-wide physical security plan. Ensure that the daily operational procedures include data backup in case your infrastructure is compromised.
   b. Create an effective disaster recovery plan and constantly test it.
   c. Put active physical access controls in place.
      i. Limit unauthorized access.
      ii. Allow authorized access on a need-to-know basis.
      iii. Verify access authorization before physical access occurs.
   d. Include a manual sign-in procedure for all nonemployees.
   e. Physically secure key computer equipment to prevent theft.
   f. Record all the serial numbers of the infrastructure equipment.
   g. Create a policy and procedures addressing portable computer loss and theft and potential confidentiality issues (such as, all patient data must be stored in encrypted form on portable media).
   h. Physically secure computer workstation locations (install door locks and other methods to restrict access to the physical equipment).
   i. Restrict unauthorized personnel from accessing the workstations.
   j. Ensure workstations have physical controls to prevent unauthorized access (use biometrics, tokens, key fobs, or other physical means to authenticate the user standing in front of the workstation).
   k. Use screen savers with timely, automatic password activation.
   l. Use monitors or alarms to prevent unauthorized entry into the workstation areas.
   m. Keep system logs and make the logging procedure somewhat pessimistic. Decide who screens the logs, what they are screened for, and what will happen if various scenarios occur. Keeping logs is pointless if no one ever screens them or does anything with them.
   n. Secure computer media (CDs, USB drives, keychain drives, tapes, disks, printouts, etc.).
   o. Block screens from unauthorized viewing.
   p. Create a policy governing regular maintenance of the computer systems and data communication network components. Be sure the policy addresses virus updates, upgrades, patches, and critical fixes.
   q. Environmentally protect the computer and data communications hardware.
   r. Create policies addressing the proper use of the Internet.
   s. Prohibit and monitor for the downloading of unauthorized software and unauthorized data (use proxy servers, stateful inspection firewalls, and system logs).
   t. Address the issues of data access, destruction, theft, or breach of confidentiality by terminated employees.
   u. Put employee termination procedures in writing.
   v. Ensure that the termination procedures address long absences such as pregnancy, disability, military duty, and educational leave.
   w. Be sure the termination procedure addresses removal of the user from lists, user accounts, badges, cards, keys, portable computers, and other access devices.
   x. Ensure your termination procedure requires employees to maintain confidentiality after departure.
3. Perform a facility-wide risk analysis annually.
   a. Identify the assets that need protection.
   b. Identify key or reasonably anticipated threats to the security and confidentiality of individual health data.
   c. Assess the probability of security threats occurring and the degree of risk involved.
   d. Ensure physical safeguards are in place to protect the computer system and databases.
4. Institute top-level policies and procedures to cover common workplace conditions and the work environment.

a. Design an emergency mode of operation for computer systems, medical workstations, and data communications.

b. Ensure safety policies and procedures address the processing of health record information.

c. Institute policies and procedures that address access control management.

d. Ensure policies and procedures are in place for background and reference checks for all personnel.

e. Create a workstation use policy.

f. Design a sanctions and credentialing policy for all personnel.

g. Ensure policies and procedures are in place governing the receipt and removal of hardware and software into and out of the facility (including portable computers and media storage).

5. Create an operational personnel security policy.

6. Require all employees to sign a statement acknowledging their responsibility for safeguarding confidential information upon employment or receiving access authorization.

7. Be sure that all personnel, including maintenance, students, temporary, and part-time help, are included in the policy. Access must be timed to coincide with the personnel's service period. Use automatic expiration of accounts and access where possible so that inactive or terminated personnel are locked out of various systems in a timely manner.

8. Maintain access authorization records.

9. Perform personnel background checks before granting access authorization and ensure that personnel wear prominently displayed identification badges.

10. In the medical staff bylaws, specify responsibilities of the physicians regarding protecting health data confidentiality.

11. Create a workstation access policy that addresses the following:
   • Role-based or user-based access
   • How to obtain authorization for the use and disclosure of medical information
   • Who grants or changes access authorization and under what conditions
   • Different access levels based on use model and roles
   • Special protection for sensitive information (such as mental health and AIDS/HIV)
   • Patient- and physician-specific access to health records
   • An override that would allow a health record to be accessed in an emergency situation (creating a common or symmetrical access key, for instance, in case the doctor and primary key are not available in an emergency)

12. Create a current password system that enforces the following:
   • Regular expiration of passwords so that passwords that are no longer in use are removed from authorization
   • Restrictions on password reuse

   • Composition of strong passwords but strong only to the point where users can remember them under stressful conditions and do not need to resort to writing down their password
   • No "sharing" of passwords
   • Signed user statements pertaining to the proper use of passwords
   • An audit capability for monitoring compliance
   • Timely automatic deactivation of access controls

13. Provide an ongoing, computer-access training program.
   a. The awareness program must require that all employees, even management personnel, attend. The programs can be self-paced, Web-based training applications, making it easier for the users to comply with the training requirements.
   b. Create a training system that has an automated training record. A Web-based application could, for instance, tailor its training to the target employee and role, prompt a user to run through quick role-specific refreshers, and then update the training record, indicating that the user had complied with the requirements. This allows employees to receive timely training relevant to their specific position within the organization and prevents the class-type setting from interfering with work schedules and personal preferences.
   c. Ensure that the training addresses the following:
      • Firewall, virus protection, and patch policy
      • Login success/failure
      • How to report discrepancies
      • Password maintenance and retention periods

14. Create chain-of-trust agreements with data-sharing partners.

15. Acknowledge entity-specific identity for access and log the access at the record level as a minimum.

16. Use an automatic log-off capability when the system is used by other partners or organizations.

17. Use a combination of secrets to control access (a secret you know and something you have). The first secret can be the traditional password and the second element can be one of Biometrics, Token, or FOB.

18. Create policies and procedures for processing health records, including the following:
   • Receiving routine and nonroutine information
   • Processing the information
   • Storing the information
   • Disseminating the information (including protection and training against social engineering tactics)
   • Transmitting the information
   • Purging or disposal processes and timelines
   • Retention management

19. Have policies and procedures to provide data integrity, including full auditing of all elements, writing to records, using hashes, and providing digital certificates so that record integrity is maintained as the records pass through the chain of custody.

20. Put a process in place to allow patients to determine and amend inaccurate or incomplete information in their health record.

21. Establish processes to conduct computer system audits. (This process needs to indicate who performs the audits and how often and also needs to document how violations are documented and corrected.) Auditing should include the following:
    - Daily computer operations
    - Software management access and controls
    - Maintenance review and testing of security features for hardware and software
    - Inventory management
    - Virus protection management

22. Establish a security management process.
    a. Create an incident-reporting process and test its operational status.
    b. Address specific actions to take in response to reported incidents.
    c. Create and train an incident response team.
    d. Ensure the team and the systems provide the necessary information that can quickly identify what data may have been exposed or compromised during an incident. Use security consultants to test the systems security, plans, and incident response teams.

23. Establish policies and procedures to safeguard patient privacy for all telemedicine processes.

24. Include safeguards in the authentication process to protect data integrity and confidentiality, including the following:
    a. Provide an opportunity for the author to review for accuracy and completeness before signing.
    b. Assign a unique user ID. or access code.
    c. Maintain signed user statements attesting that no one else will use their personal signature.
    d. Establish quality controls to ensure the accuracy of health record entries that are not authenticated.
    e. Require professional titles to accompany signatures.
    f. Enable a user to affix document identifiers and/or attributes to the document.
    g. Get medical staff endorsement to use electronic signatures.
    h. Establish and manage electronic signature rules and regulations.
    i. Purge electronic signature capability upon termination of employment or revocation of a privilege.

25. Ensure there is a policy for correcting the health record.
    a. Uniquely identify and separate the corrected documentation from the original documentation.
    b. Offer a process for patients to request corrections of their record.
    c. Maintain documentation for patient requests and correction activity.
    d. Disseminate information to the public pertaining to the patient request/review/correction process.

26. Create a retention policy that addresses electronically maintained records.
    a. Ensure that the electronic storage media last for the entire retention period.
    b. Protect confidentiality concerns.
    c. Determine how to secure data placed on an unsecured or portable machine. Should the data be encrypted? What happens if the portable unit is lost or compromised?
    d. Check that each of the various media can be cleaned or securely erased once the retention period expires.

27. Establish a release-of-information policy that addresses electronically maintained records.
    a. Verify authority for the release.
    b. Create a training process for the proper release of medical information.

28. Institute a facsimile (fax) process policy.
    a. Put a confidentiality notice on the fax cover sheet.
    b. Have the fax process take place in a secure area.
    c. Take precautions so that the fax reaches the proper recipient.
    d. Limit fax transmissions.
    e. Maintain a log of all fax processes.

29. Create an e-mail policy.
    a. Make e-mail messages concerning patient diagnosis or treatment part of the health record.
    b. Obtain patient consent to use email containing patient information.
    c. Take appropriate measures to protect the integrity and confidentiality of email messages.

## Summary and Recommendations: Service Providers

In the United States, government health ministries and departments, health care institutions, and health care practitioners can no longer be treated as having unique sets of requirements for record keeping and data security. The climate of the Internet and information security has come to the point where all entities need a hybrid defense system composed of multiple tiers of security. Everyone must protect themselves against blended threats (Puran, 2003) as well as the social engineering attacks that are possible and occur on a daily basis.

To attain a reasonable level of security and protection of the data and systems hosting these data, an entity needs a security plan and the commitment and ability to articulate this plan. Further, the plan needs to be communicated to all employees as part of an ongoing education program. As part of the security training program, employees need to be informed and taught the best practices needed to defend against security breaches and how to handle the inevitable breach.

Keeping the employees and security plan up-to-date requires an ongoing education as technology is constantly evolving as are the threats to security. Because the threats continually evolve, the security system and the employee training can be modeled after an organism. That is, the security system and employee training constantly evolve to provide effective defense against a constantly changing adversary.

## Recommendations: Patients

According to Beth Givens (1998), patients have the right to access their records. Patients need to obtain copies of their records, screen them for accuracy, and correct any errors. Patients need to be on the lookout for any potential abuse of their records or information. Before a visit, a patient can submit a letter to the medical provider to limit the collection, use, disclosure, and retention of the data to whatever matter is at hand and to prevent excess dissemination of data. The service entities must be held accountable for the dissemination of data and the secondary uses of that data.

The bottom line is that patients need to treat their health record just as they would treat their financial data—with great care. Unfortunately, in the modern era of technology, the policy for a patient has to be: provide and release information to various entities on an as-needed basis and ensure that the data has a limited lifespan by specifying retention and validity periods in your permissions and disclosure documents. By placing your desires in writing and providing detail to the patient disclosure and permissions documents, the amount of data and the amount of time that the data floats around in the system will be minimized.

## REGULATIONS, POLICIES, AND ORGANIZATIONS
### United States National Regulations (HIPAA)

With the passing of the HIPAA legislation (HHS, 2001, HHS, 2003), and the high visibility and exposure of health records created through the movement to electronic-based records (Gue, 2003), all those involved with health records must now meet stringent security requirements and be held liable for the unintended disclosure of any or all of the data. For more background on the legal and liability aspects of health records, refer to the Regulatory Applications and Liability Considerations chapter in this publication.

The complete text of the HIPAA legislation can be found in the Federal Register (45 CFR parts 160, 162, and 164). At the time of this writing, almost all of the conformance deadlines for the privacy rule have passed for most medical-related and insurance entities. Additionally, most covered entities must be in compliance with the final security rule by April 21, 2005. The small health plans (those with annual receipts of $5 million or less) have an extra year, with the deadline extended to April 21, 2006.

Refer to the Security Solution of this chapter for a description of a methodology that can be adopted to help an organization achieve both the security rule and privacy rule conformance. Even if a health care entity has missed all of the HIPAA conformance deadlines, the HIPAA legislation is clear. HIPAA mandates that a health care entity must complete its obligation regardless of cost. A health care entity must act swiftly to complete its obligation and eliminate future liabilities.

### Standards Organizations

ANSI X12N—An ANSI working group standardizing the electronic health record and insurance claims processing (http://www.x12.org/x12org/subcommittees/sc_home.cfm?strSC=N).

DCC—Dental Content Committee (http://www.ada.org). This group was formed to create a uniform record format for dental records.

HL7—Health Level Seven (http://www.hl7.org). Various organizations exist and are aimed at helping medical entities over the hurdles involved with electronic health records. A major effort to standardize the electronic health record has been under way for many years. Health Level Seven, a nonprofit group, spearheads this effort.

NCPDP—National Council for Prescription Drug Programs (http://www.ncpdp.org). This group absorbed the HIPAA-regulated portion of the electronic health record as it relates to prescription drugs.

NIST—National Institute of Standards. NIST maintains various standards and best practices documents. The documents are available to the public at no charge and are typically the result of federally funded academic research projects.

NUBC—National Uniform Billing Committee (http://www.nubc.org). This group was formed to create a uniform and simplified billing form and process for healthcare. The passing of the HIPAA ruling made this work critical to success.

NUCC—National Uniform Claims Committee (http://www.nucc.org). This group was formed to create a uniform and simplified claims form and process for healthcare. The passing of the HIPAA ruling altered this group's charter to focusing on the administrative simplification section of the HIPAA ruling.

### Oversight Bodies

Numerous oversight bodies exist in the United States alone and there are considerably more bodies internationally. A small sample of the more prominent United States organizations is presented here to provide an overview of the groups and their respective position within the system. This is not a comprehensive list.

HHS—Health and Human Services (http://www.hhs.gov). The HHS is the driving force and the department with the responsibility and authority for HIPAA regulations and HIPAA compliance. The department might also have the authority to enforce and fine nonconformers, but at the time of this writing that is not yet the case.

CMS—Centers for Medicare and Medicaid Services (http://www.cms.hhs.gov/hipaa). According to its Web site, the CMS (formerly the Healthcare Finance Authority or HCFA) is responsible for implementing various unrelated provisions of HIPAA. CMS is presently focused on health insurance reform with respect to HIPAA and it is also focused on administrative simplification. Refer to the CMS Web site to explore their charter and efforts in more detail.

ADA—American Dental Association. The ADA believes that dental data are not really part of standard health data. For the purposes of the health record and HIPAA, the ADA was granted the notion that the dental portion of the record is a separate and isolated component and deserves different treatment. The standards groups have provided for layered records and layered security and the ADA controls the dental-related portion of the content.

JCAHO—Joint Commission on Accreditation of Healthcare Organizations. The JCAHO is the national watchdog body that oversees the operations of hospitals, clinics, and other medical facilities. The JCAHO is responsible for making sure that these entities follow rules and regulations and that they have proper process and procedures in place to protect patients as well as patient records. The JCAHO is most concerned with the process and adherence to the process than to the details of the security process.

## Grassroots Privacy Groups

American Civil Liberties Union (http://www.aclu.org). The ACLU is a large organization that is extremely active in seeking the protection of an individual's rights with regard to various U.S. civil liberties.

Association of American Physicians and Surgeons (http://www.aapsonline.org). The Association of American Physicians and Surgeons (AAPS) is a nonpartisan professional association of physicians in all types of practices and specialties across the country. The group writes collectively to inform online readers about the AAPS view on various topics. The group published a Patient Bill of Rights and advocates the freedom of choice and right to privacy of the individual.

Hep-C Alert—The Hep-C Alert group (http://www.hep-c-alert.org/links/medprivacy.html) is mainly focused on the right to privacy for people with hepatitis C. Although the group focuses on a specific disease, its Web site has good tips on securing health records and has several good references to other groups and locations for further assistance.

Medical Privacy Coalition (http://www.medicalprivacycoalition.com/index.php). The group is a national partnership of organizations concerned about the threat to Americans' fundamental right to protect their medical information.

## Patient Advocacy Groups

National Coalition for Patient Rights (http://www.nationalcpr.org). This is a nonprofit patient rights group located in Lexington, MA. The current status of the group is unknown.

North Dakota Medical Association (http://www.ndmed.com/index.html). A North Dakota-based patient advocacy and resource group.

Patient Rights Clearinghouse (http://www.privacyrights.org/Medical.htm). This is a nonprofit patient rights and consumer advocacy group located in San Diego, California. It is currently active.

Stateside Associates (http://www.stateside.com/management/specialty/healthcare.shtml). This group consists of advocates, lobbyists, and many others. The group has an active subgroup aimed at online advocacy for patient rights and also tries to keep site members and clients informed about various grassroots efforts via their Grassroots and Grasstops education programs and services.

Universal Health Care Action Network (http://www.uhcan.org). A Cleveland, Ohio-based national advocacy network that also supports activist groups.

# GLOSSARY

**CEs** Covered Entities is a term defined by HIPAA to mean hospitals, clinics, insurers, and other similar entities that are part of the care delivery and care payment system.

**Electronic Health Record** This term refers to the computer-based or electronic version of the patient health record.

**HHS** In the context of this book, the United States Department of Health and Human Services is a government agency that is responsible for sponsoring, implementing, and enforcing the HIPAA legislation.

**HIPAA** The Health Insurance Portability and Accountability Act is a term that refers to a two-part legislation covering the privacy and security of the patient health (data) record.

**HL7** Health Level Seven is the name of a nonprofit group that develops electronic medical record standards. It is also the brand name by which a collection of the protocols is known.

**IIHI** The Individually Identifiable Health Information is the term assigned by HIPAA to any of the elements of the patient health record that can uniquely identify an individual.

**Patient Health Record** This is the term used to identify the collection of diverse material that comprises the patient medical record. This collection includes dental records, medical records, lab tests, claims, insurance-related documents, and other similar material. The recent migration to the more general term *health* from *medical* is intended to make the diversity of the data more obvious.

**Phishing** The term *phishing* is a degenerate spelling of the word *fishing* and is used by the security industry to represent the technique of illegally obtaining critical user information such as social security numbers, birthdays, bank account numbers, and so on through means such as spoofed Web pages. The data obtained by the fishing expedition is then used to commit illegal acts such as assuming another's identity.

**Portable Health Record** This term refers to the future incarnation of the patient health record where the record is likely to be possessed and maintained by the patients themselves.

**Threats** The term threat in this context refers to environmental or electronic threats that raise the probability of compromising data which is part of the patient health record.

**USB** The Universal Serial Bus is a personal computer standard that enables simplified connectivity of various devices to the computer such as micro disk drives, key chain drives, and human interface devices.

**X12N** The ANSI standards group that addresses the insurance and claims processing portion of the patient health record.

# CROSS REFERENCES

See *Legal, Social, and Ethical Issues of the Internet; Privacy Law and the Internet; Security Policy Guidelines; The Legal Implications of Information Security: Regulatory Compliance and Liability*

# REFERENCES

Associated Press. (2004). *Five fired at Los Alamos lab,* September 15, 2004. Retrieved January 2, 2005, from http://www.wired.com/news/privacy/0,1848,64973,00. html

Blau, J. (2004). *Deutsche Bank hit again by phishing attack,* August 25, 2004. Retrieved January 2, 2005, from http://www.computerworld.com/printthis/2004/ 0,4814,95471,00.html

Givens, B. (1998). *Privacy Rights Clearinghouse—Ten privacy principals for health care,* November 6, 1998. Retrieved January 3, 2005, from http://www. privacyrights.org/ar/privprin.htm.

Grove, T. (2003). *Phoenix Health Systems—Summary analysis: The Final HIPAA security rule.* Retrieved January 3, 2005, from http://www.hipaadvisory.com/ regs/finalsecurity/summaryanalysis.htm

Gue, D. G. (2003). *Phoenix Health Systems—The HIPAA Security Rule* (*NPRM*): Overview. Retrieved January 3, 2005, from http://www.hipaadvisory.com/regs/ securityoverview.htm

Health Data Management. (2003). *The scales are tipping,* May 13, 2003. Retrieved January 3, 2005, from http:// www.healthdatamanagement.com/html/supplements/ tepr03/teprNewsStory.cfm?DID=10153

Health Data Management. (2004). *Bush records goal a tough target,* June 23, 2004. Retrieved January 3, 2005, from http://www.healthdatamanagement.com/ html/PortalStory.cfm?type=trend&DID=11718

HHS (2001). US Department of Health and Human Services—Federal Register—Monday, February 26, 2001—45 CFR parts 160 and 164—*Standards for Privacy of Individually Identifiable Health Information; Final Rule;* http://www.hhs.gov/ocr/hipaa/finalreg.html

HHS (2003). US Department of Health and Human Services—Federal Register—Thursday February 20, 2003—45 CFR parts 160, 162, and 164—*Health Insurance Reform: Security Standards; Final Rule;* http:// www.cms.hhs.gov/hipaa/hipaa2/regulations/security/ default.asp

iHealth Beat. (2003a). *Computerized record adoption on the rise, but barriers remain,* October 22, 2003. Retrieved January 3, 2005, from http://www. ihealthbeat.org/index.cfm?Action=dspItem&itemID= 100118

iHealth Beat. (2003b). *WSJ looks at plan to stimulate EHR adoption,* January 16, 2003. Retrieved January 3, 2005, http://www.ihealthbeat.org/index.cfm?Action=dspItem &itemID=98880

Kowalczyk, L. (2004). *US pushes digital health records. The Boston Globe,* July 22, 2004, p. C5.

Larson, J. (2004). *Medical records go online,* October 14, 2004. Retrieved January 3, 2005, from http:// www.azcentral.com/arizonarepublic/business/articles/ 1014integreat14.html

Puran, Ranjeev (2003). Beyond Conventional Terrorism... *The Cyber Assault.* Retrieved May 25, 2005, from https://www.sans.org/rr/whitepapers/threats/931. php

# FURTHER RESOURCES

ANSI (2004). X12N Electronic health record Standard; http://www.x12.org

Bird, T, Callas, J. (2003). *PGP—The HIPAA security rule and PGP Corporation,* June 2003. Retrieved January 2, 2005, from http://www.pgp.com

hcPro's Healthcare Marketplace (2004). http://www. hcmarketplace.com; online resource providing a wide variety of publications and information concerning Medical Records, Compliance Audits, Patient Safety, and similar topics.

Healthcare Informatics Online (2004). http://www. healthcare-informatics.com; Healthcare Informatics is an industry-specific publication with an online searchable edition containing industry-specific articles. Various articles describe actual scenarios and case studies concerning the deployment of the electronic health record, data privacy, and information security.

HHS (2001, 2003). US Department of Health and Human Services—Federal Register—Monday, February 26, 2001—45 CFR parts 160 and 164—*Standards for Privacy of Individually Identifiable Health Information; Final Rule* and Federal Register Thursday February 20, 2003—45 CFR parts 160, 162, and 164—*Health Insurance Reform: Security Standards; Final Rule;* http://www.hhs.gov/ocr/hipaa/finalreg. html

HL7 (2004). Health Level Seven (HL7) and the Electronic health record Standard; http://www.hl7.org

iHealthBeat (2004). iHealthBeat is an online medical-industry specific publication regularly reporting on the state of various web and online-centric technologies as well as industry-impacting trends and news; http://www.ihealthbeat.org

MITRE (2004). The Common Vulnerabilities and Exposures Web Site (CVE); http://www.cve.mitre.org

NCVHS (2004). The National Council in Vital and Health Statistics—A public advisory body to the Secretary of the U.S. Dept of Health and Human Services in the area of health data and statistics; http://www.ncvhs.hhs.gov

SANS (2004). SysAdmin, Audit, Network, and Security Institute (SANS) and the keepers of the Internet Storm Center; http://www.sans.org and http://isc.sans.org. A large collection of useful security-related information can be browsed in the SANS reading room; http://www.sans.org/rr.

The University of Miami (2004). Privacy/Data Protection Project; http://privacy.med.miami.edu/glossary/ xd_dsmo.htm

# Access Control: Principles and Solutions

S. De Capitani di Vimercati and S. Paraboschi, *DTI–Università di Milano, Italy*

Pierangela Samarati, *DIGI–Università di Bergamo, Italy*

## INTRODUCTION

An important requirement of any system is to protect its *data* and *resources* against unauthorized disclosure (*secrecy* or *confidentiality*) and unauthorized or improper modifications (*integrity*), while at the same time ensuring their availability to legitimate users (*no denial-of-service* or *availability*) (Samarati & De Capitani di Vimercati, 2001). The problem of ensuring protection has existed since information has been managed. However, as technology advances and information management systems become more and more powerful, the problem of enforcing information security also becomes more critical. The increasing development of information and communication technology has led to the widespread use of computer systems to store and transmit information of every kind, offering concrete advantages in terms of availability and flexibility but at the same time posing new serious security threats and increasing the potential damage that violations may cause. Today more than ever organizations depend on the information they manage. A violation to the security of the information may jeopardize the whole system and cause serious damage. Hospitals, banks, public administrations, and private organizations all depend on the accuracy, availability, and confidentiality of the information they manage. Just imagine what could happen, for example, if an organization's data were improperly modified, were not available to the legitimate users because of a violation blocking access to the resources, or were disclosed to the public domain.

A fundamental component in enforcing protection is represented by the *access control* service, whose task is *to control every access to a computer system and its resources and ensure that all authorized and only authorized accesses can take place*. To this purpose, every management system usually includes an access control service that establishes the kinds of rules that can be stated, through an appropriate specification language, and then enforced by the access control mechanism enforcing the service. By using the provided interface, security administrators can specify the access control policy (or policies) that should be obeyed in controlling access to the managed resources.

The definition of access control policies to be fed into the access control system is far from a trivial process.

One of the major difficulties lies in the interpretation of real-world security policies, which are often complex and sometimes ambiguous, and in their translation in well-defined unambiguous rules enforceable by the computer system. Many real-world situations have complex policies, where access decisions depend on the application of different rules coming, for example, from laws, practices and organizational regulations. A security policy must capture all the different regulations to be enforced and, in addition, must consider all possible additional threats because of the use of computer systems. Given the complexity of the scenario, it is therefore important that the access control service provided by the computer system be expressive and flexible enough to accommodate the different requirements that may need to be expressed, while at the same time be simple both in terms of use (so that specifications can be kept under control) and implementation (so to allow for its verification).

An access control system should include support for the following concepts/features:

*Accountability and reliable input*. Access control must rely on proper input. This simple principle is not always obeyed by systems allowing access control rules to be evaluated on the basis of possibly unreliable information. This is, for example, the case of *location-based* access control restrictions, where the access decision may depend on the IP from which a request originates, a piece of information that can be easily faked in a local network, thus fooling access control (allowing nonlegitimate users to acquire access despite the proper rule enforcement). This observation has been traditionally at the basis of requiring proper user authentication as a prerequisite for access control enforcement (Sandhu & Samarati, 1997). Although more recent approaches may remove the assumption that every user is authenticated (e.g., by allowing credential-based access control), still the assumption that the information on which access decision is taken must be correct indeed continues to hold.

*Support for fine and coarse specifications*. The access control system should allow rules to be referred to specific accesses, providing fine-grained reference to the subjects and objects in the system. However, fine-grained specifications should be supported but not forced. In fact, requiring the specification of access rules with reference to every single user and object in the system would make the administration task a heavy burden. Besides, groups of users and collections of objects often share the same access control requirements. The access control system should then provide support for authorizations specified for groups of users, groups of objects, and possibly even groups of actions (Jajodia, Samarati, Sapino, & Subrahmanian, 2001). Also, in many organizational scenarios, access needs may be naturally associated with *organizational activities*; the access control system should then support authorizations referred to organizational roles (Sandhu, Coyne, Feinstein, & Youman, 1996).

*Conditional authorizations.* Protection requirements may need to depend on the evaluation of some conditions (Samarati & De Capitani di Vimercati, 2001). Conditions can be in the simple form of system's predicates, such as the date or the location of an access (e.g., "Employees can access the system *from 9 a.m. to 5 p.m.*"). Conditions can also make access dependent on the information being accessed (e.g., "Managers can read payroll data of *the employees they manage*").

*Least privilege.* The least privilege principle mandates that every subject (active entity operating in the system) should always operate with the least possible set of privileges needed to perform its task. Obedience to the least privilege requires both static (policy specification) and dynamic (policy enforcement) support from the access control system. At a static level, least privilege requires support of *fine-grained authorizations*, granting each specific subject only those specific accesses it needs. At a dynamic level, least privilege requires restricting processes to operate within a *confined set of privileges*. Least privilege is partially supported within the context of *roles*, which are essentially privileged hats that users can take and leave (Sandhu et al., 1996). Authorizations granted to a role apply only when the role is active for a user (i.e., when needed to perform the tasks associated with the role). Hence, users authorized for powerful roles do not need to exercise them until those privileges are actually needed. This minimizes the danger of damage because of inadvertent errors or by intruders masquerading as legitimate users. Least privilege also requires the access control system to discriminate between different processes, even if executed by the same user, for example, by supporting authorizations referred to specific applications or *applicable only during the execution of specific programs*.

*Separation of duty.* Separation of duty refers to the principle that no user should be given enough privileges to misuse the system (Sandhu, 1990). Although separation of duty is better classified as a policy specification constraint (i.e., a guideline to be followed by those in charge of specifying access control rules), support of separation of duty requires the security system to be expressive and flexible enough to enforce the constraints. At a minimum, fine-grained specifications and least privilege should be supported; *history-based authorizations*, making one's ability to access a system dependent on previously executed accesses, are also a convenient means to support separation of duty.

*Multiple policies and exceptions.* Traditionally, discretionary policies have been seen as distinguished into two classes: *closed* and *open* (Samarati & De Capitani di Vimercati, 2001). In the more popular closed policy, only accesses to be authorized are specified; each request is controlled against the authorizations and allowed only if an authorization exists for it. By contrast, in the open policy (negative), authorizations specify the accesses that should not be allowed. All access requests for which no negative authorization is specified are allowed by default.

*Policy combination and conflict resolution.* If multiple modules (e.g., for different authorities or different domains) exist for the specification of access control rules, the access control system should provide a means for users to specify how the different modules should interact, for example, if their union (maximum privilege) or their intersection (minimum privilege) should be considered. Also, when both permissions and denials can be specified, the problem naturally arises of how to deal with *incompleteness*, that is, existence of accesses for which no rule is specified, and *inconsistency*, that is, the existence of accesses for which both a denial and a permission are specified. Dealing with incompleteness—requiring the authorizations to be complete would be very impractical—requires support of a *default* policy either imposed by the system or specified by the users. Dealing with inconsistencies requires support for *conflict resolution* policies. Different conflict resolution approaches can be taken, such as the simple *denials take precedence* (in the case of doubt access is denied) or *most specific* criteria that make the authorization referred to the more specific element (e.g., a user is more specific than a group, and a file is more specific than a directory). Although among the different conflict resolution policies that can be thought of (see Samarati & De Capitani di Vimercati, 2001, for a deeper treatment) some solutions may appear more natural than others, none of them represents "the perfect solution." Whichever approach we take, we will always find one situation for which the approach does not fit. Therefore any conflict resolution policy imposed by the access control mechanism itself will always be limiting. Conversely, support of negative authorizations is not free, and there is a price to pay in terms of authorization management and less clarity of the specifications. However, the complications brought by negative authorizations are not because of negative authorizations themselves but rather the different semantics that the presence of permissions and denials can have in the different real-world scenarios and requirements that may need to be captured. There is therefore a trade-off between expressiveness and simplicity. Consequently, current systems try to keep it simple by adopting negative authorizations for exception support, imposing specific conflict resolution policies, or supporting a limited form of conflict resolution.

*Administrative policies.* As access control systems are based on access rules defining which ones are (or are not) to be allowed, an administrative policy is needed to regulate the specification of such rules, that is, define who can add, delete, or modify them. Administrative policies are one of the most important, though less understood, aspects in access control. Indeed, they have usually received little consideration, and, although it is true that a simple administrative policy would suffice for many applications, it is also true that new applications (and organizational environments) would benefit from the enrichment of administrative policies. In theory, discretionary systems can support different kinds of administrative policies: *centralized*, where a privileged user or group of them is reserved the privilege of granting and revoking authorizations; *hierarchical/cooperative*, where a set of authorized users is reserved the privilege of granting and revoking authorizations; *ownership*, where each object is associated with an owner (generally the object's creator) who can grant to and revoke from others the authorizations on its objects; and *decentralized*, where, extending the previous approaches, the owner of an object (or its administrators) can delegate other users the privilege of specifying authorizations, possibly with the ability of further delegating it. For its simplicity and large applicability the ownership policy is the most popular choice in today's systems (see Access Control in Operating Systems). Decentralized administration approaches can be instead found in the database management system contexts (see Access Control in Database Management Systems). Decentralized administration is convenient because it allows users to delegate administrative privileges to others. Delegation, however, complicates the authorization management. In particular, it becomes more difficult for users to keep track of who can access their objects. Furthermore, revocation of authorizations becomes more complex.

In the remainder of this chapter, after a brief overview of the basic concepts about access control policies (Access Control Policies), we survey the access control services provided by some of the most popular operating systems (Access Control in Operating Systems), database management systems (Access Control in Database Management Systems), and network solutions (Access Control for Internet-Based Solutions). Although clearly their characteristics will vary from one class to the other as their focus is different (e.g., database management systems focus on the data and rely on the operating systems for low level support), it will be interesting to see how they accommodate (or do not accommodate) the features introduced above. Also, it will be noticed how, while covering a feature in some way, some systems take unclean solutions that may have side effects in terms of security or applicability, aspects that then should be taken into account when using the systems.

## ACCESS CONTROL POLICIES

An access control policy must capture all the different regulations to be enforced and, in addition, must also consider possible additional threats because of the use of a computer system. Traditionally, access control policies can be grouped into three main classes:

*Discretionary (DAC) (authorization-based) policies* control access based on the identity of the requestor and on access rules (authorizations) stating what requestors are (or are not) allowed to do.

*Mandatory (MAC) policies* control access based on mandated regulations determined by a central authority.

*Role-based (RBAC) policies* control access depending on the roles that users have within the system and on rules stating what accesses are allowed to users in given roles.

Discretionary and role-based policies are usually coupled with (or include) an *administrative policy* that defines who can specify authorizations/rules governing access control. Because the access control services described in the following sections are based on discretionary policies, we now focus on such a kind of policies.

A simple way to represent a set of authorizations for their enforcement consists in using an access *control matrix*. First proposed by Lampson (1974) for the protection of resources within the context of operating systems, and later refined by Graham and Denning (1972), the model was subsequently formalized by Harrison, Ruzzo, and Ullmann (HRU model) (1976), who developed the access control model proposed by Lampson to the goal of analyzing the complexity of determining an access control policy. The name access matrix derives from the fact that the authorizations holding at a given time in the system are represented as a matrix. The matrix therefore gives an abstract representation of protection systems. In particular, the state of the system is represented by a triple $(S, O, A)$, where $S$ is the set of subjects, $O$ is the set of objects (often the set $S$ is considered as a subset of $O$), and $A$ is a matrix whose rows correspond to subjects, columns corresponds to objects, and the entry $A[s,o]$ includes the privileges (i.e., read, write, own, and execute) that $s$ can exercise on $o$. By simply providing a framework where authorizations can be specified, the model can accommodate different privileges. For instance, in addition to the traditional read, write, and execute actions, *ownership* (i.e., property of objects by subjects), and *control* (to model father–children relationships between processes) can be considered.

Figure 1 illustrates a simple example of access matrix. Because the access matrix is usually large and sparse, its storage implies a waste of memory space. There are three basic approaches of implementing the access matrix in a practical way:

*Authorization table.* Store a table of nonnull triples of the form $(s,a,o)$. It is especially used in database management systems (DBMSs), where authorizations are stored as catalogs.

|  | fileA | fileB | programC |
|---|---|---|---|
| **Alice** | own write read | write | execute |
| **Bob** | read | read | execute read write |
| **Eve** | read | read |  |

**Figure 1:** An example of access matrix.

*Access control lists (ACLs).* Each object is associated with an ACL that specifies which users have which access modes on it.

*Capability lists (tickets).* Each user is associated with a capability list that specifies the objects that the user can access and the access modes the user can exercise on them.

Intuitively, an entry in the authorization table corresponds to a cell in the matrix, an ACL corresponds to a column of the matrix, and a capability corresponds to a row of the matrix.

Figure 2 illustrates the authorization table, ACLs, and capability lists corresponding to the access matrix in Figure 1. ACLs and capabilities have dual advantages and disadvantages: the ACL approach provides efficient per-object access, whereas the capability approach provides efficient per-subject access. In particular, in the ACL approach, by looking at an object's ACL, it is easy to determine which actions subjects are currently authorized for that object. Determining all accesses for which a subject is authorized would require instead the examination of all the ACLs. Conversely, in a capability-based approach it is easy to review all accesses that a subject is authorized to perform by simply examining the subject's capability list. However, determination of all subjects who can access a particular object requires examination of each and every subject's capability list. A number of capability-based computer systems were developed in the 1970s but did not prove to be commercially successful. As we will see, modern operating systems typically take the ACL-based approach.

# ACCESS CONTROL IN OPERATING SYSTEMS

We describe access control services in two of the most popular operating systems: Linux (e.g., www.redhat.com, www.linux-mandrake.com, www.suse.com) and Microsoft Windows 2000/XP (www.microsoft.com).

## Access Control in Linux

We use Linux as a modern representative of the large family of operating systems deriving from Unix. We signal the features of Linux that are absent in other operating systems of the same family.

Apart from specific privileges such as access to protected TCP ports, the most significant access control services in Linux are the ones offered by the file system. The file system has a central role in all the operating systems of the Unix family, as files are used as an abstraction for most of the system resources.

### User Identifiers and Group Identifiers

Access control is based on a user identifier (UID) and group identifier (GID) associated with each process. A UID is an integer value unique for each username (login name), where the association between usernames and UIDs is described in file /etc/passwd. A user connecting to a Linux system is typically authenticated by the login process, invoked by the program managing the communication line used to connect to the system (getty for serial lines, telnetd for remote telnet sessions). The login process asks the user for a username and a password and checks the password with its hash stored in read-protected file /etc/shadow; a less secure and older alternative stores hashed password in the readable-by-all file /etc/passwd. When authentication is successful, the login process sets the UID to that of the authenticated user, before starting an instance of the program described in the user entry in /etc/passwd (typically a shell, like /bin/bash). Users in Linux are members of groups. Every time a user connects to the system, together with the UID, a primary GID is set. The primary GID value to use at login is defined in file /etc/passwd. Group names and additional memberships in groups are defined in file /etc/group. Command *newgrp* allows users to switch to a new primary GID. If a user is listed in /etc/group as belonging to the new group, the request is immediately executed; otherwise, for groups having a hashed password in /etc/group, the primary GID can be changed after the password has been correctly

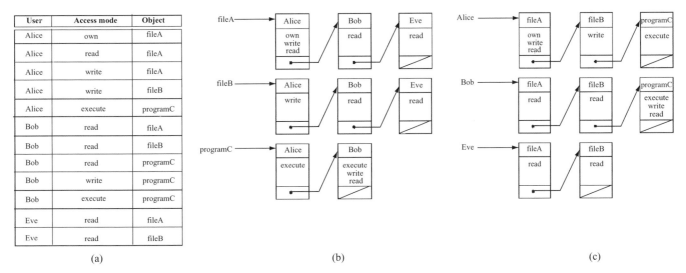

Figure 2: Authorization table (a), ACLs (b), and capabilities (c) for the matrix in Figure 1.

returned. However, group passwords are deprecated, as they easily lead to lapses in password management.

Processes are usually assigned the UIDs and GIDs of the parent processes, which implies that processes acquire the UIDs and GIDs associated with the login names with which sessions have been started. The process UID is the central piece of information for the evaluation of the permitted actions. There are many operations in the system that are allowed only to a user that has zero as the value of its UID. By convention, user *root* is associated with UID value zero and represents the owner of the system, who supervises all the activities. For instance, the TCP implementation allows only user *root* to open ports below 1024.

### Files and Privileges

In the Linux file system, each file is associated with a UID and a GID, which typically represent the UID and primary GID of the process that created the file. UID and GID associated with a file can be changed by commands *chown* and *chgrp*. Each file has associated a list of nine privileges: *read*, *write*, and *execute*, each defined three times, at the level of *user*, *group*, and *other*. The privileges defined at the level of *user* are the actions that will be permitted to processes having the same UID as the file; the privileges defined at the level of *group* are granted to processes having the same GID as the file; the privileges at the level of *other* are for processes that share neither UID nor GID with the file. The privileges are commonly represented by the *ls -l* command as a string of nine characters (preceded by a character representing the file type). Each privilege is characterized by a single letter: r for *read*; w for *write*; x for *execute*; the absence of the privilege is represented by character -. The string presents first the *user* privileges and then *group* and finally *other*. For instance, rwxr-xr-- means that a process having as UID the same UID as the file has all the three privileges, a process with the same GID can read and execute (but not write) the file, and remaining processes can only read the file. When a user belongs to many groups, all the corresponding GIDs are stored in a list in the process descriptor beside the primary GID; other operating systems of the Unix family stored only the primary GID within the process descriptor. All the groups in the list are then considered: if the GID of the file is the primary GID, or appears anywhere in the list, group access privileges apply.

The semantics of privileges may be different depending on the type of the file on which they are specified. In particular, for directories, the *execute* privilege represents the privilege to access the directory; *read* and *write* privileges permit respectively to read the directory content and to modify it (adding, removing, and renaming files). Privileges associated with a file can be updated via the *chmod* command, which is usable by the file owner and by user *root*.

### Additional Security Specifications

The file system offers three other file privileges: *save text image* (sticky bit), *set user ID* (setuid), and *set group ID* (setgid). The *sticky bit* privilege is useful only for directories, where it allows only the owner of the file, owner of the directory, and root to remove or rename the files contained in the directory, even if the directory is writable by all. The *setuid* and *setgid* privileges are particularly useful for executable files, where they permit to set the UID or GID of the process that executes the file to that of the file itself. These privileges are often used for applications that require a higher level of privileges to accomplish their task (e.g., users change their passwords with the *passwd* program, which needs read and write access on file /etc/shadow). Without the use of these bits, enabling a process started by a normal user to change the user's password would require explicitly granting the user the write privilege on the file /etc/shadow. Such a privilege could, however, be misused by users who could access the file through different programs and tamper with it. The *setuid* and *setgid* bits, by allowing the *passwd* program to run with root privilege, avoid such security exposure. It is worth noticing that, although providing a necessary security feature, the *setuid* and *setgid* solutions are themselves vulnerable as the specified programs run with root privileges—in contrast to the least privilege principle, they are not confined to the accesses needed to execute their task—and it is therefore important that these programs be *trusted* (Samarati & De Capitani di Vimercati, 2001).

The *ext2* and *ext3* file systems, the most common in Linux implementations, offer additional boolean attributes on files. Among them, there are attributes focused on low-level optimizations (e.g., a bit requiring a compressed representation of the file on the disk) and two privileges that extend access control services: *immutable* and *append-only*. The *immutable* bit specifies that no change be allowed on the file; only the user *root* can set or clear this attribute. The *append-only* bit specifies that the file can be extended only by additions at the end; this attribute can also be set only by *root*. Attributes are listed by command *lsattr* and are modified by command *chattr*.

### IP-Based Security

Linux offers several utilities that base authentication on IP addresses. All of these solutions should be used with care, as IP addresses can be easily spoofed in a local network (Bellovin, 1989) and therefore fool the access control system. For this reason, they are not enabled by default. Among these utilities, *rsh* executes remote shells on behalf of users; *rcp* executes copies involving the file systems of machines in a network; NFS permits to share portions of the file system on the network. For these applications, access control typically is based on a few relatively simple textual files, which describe the computers that can use the service and the scope of the service; patterns can be used to identify ranges of names or addresses, and groups may be defined, but overall the access control features are basic. Secure solutions of the above applications (such as the *ssh* application and the *scp* program offered within the same package) offer a greater degree of security, at the expense of computational resources, configuration effort, and in general less availability.

### Evaluation of Linux Access Control

We briefly evaluate the access control features of Linux in terms of the principles presented in the introduction.

*Accountability and reliable input*: the operating system allows the use of reliable and strong authentication solutions; some of the access control mechanisms, like those based on IP security, show limited protection. The various Linux distributions have evolved on this respect and the standard configuration typically does not activate the weak solutions (indeed, for a relatively inexperienced Linux user, the activation of insecure services may require a significant effort).

*Support for fine-grained and coarse-grained specifications*: the Linux operating system essentially offers access control only at the level of files/directories; protection privileges (like setuid/setgid and access to network resources) also suffer of a limited granularity. It is possible to introduce applications within the Linux operating system that protect their resources with a finer granularity, but the native operating system support is limited.

*Conditional authorizations*: it is possible to specify in a declarative way protection, specifying, for example, patterns of IP addresses and DNS identifiers; protection of files does not permit the use of conditions or declarative mechanisms.

*Least privilege*: because fine-grained authorizations are not supported, Linux can offer a limited support to the least privilege principle; theoretically, the use of groups can be used to approximate the presence of many different access requirements for different users, but in practice this strategy does not work very well and is not scalable.

*Separation of duty*: the presence of an all-powerful *root* user represents the approach against which this principle is directed.

*Multiple polices and exceptions*: the access control services offered by Linux do not support this requirement.

*Policy combination and conflict resolution*: conflicts may arise when privileges represent conflicting requirements; for instance, a user may not have the privilege to access a directory, but it may be the owner of a file contained within it. In Linux, the user is not allowed to access the file, unless she has the *execute* privilege on all the directories present in the path. The presence of symbolic links complicates the matter, because a single resource can be identified by different paths. The path used to identify the resource has to be completely accessible by the user to permit access to the resource. The conflict resolution mechanism is ad hoc and is not flexible.

*Administrative polices*: administration is based on the identification of a resource owner, together with the presence of an all-powerful root user.

Overall, Linux shows its lineages and represents a modern version of an operating system that was created when security was not as important as it is today. A lot of effort is currently being directed at designing Linux components that are able to overcome these limits and to let it become the core of complex computer architectures (e.g., the Security Enhanced Linux initiative and many others). For a role as a specialized server, the limitations of the design are probably under control; for Linux to be an effective solution for the construction of multiuser information systems, the development of novel access control services is probably required.

## Access Control in Windows

We now describe the characteristics of the access control model of the Microsoft Windows 2000/XP operating system (msdn.microsoft.com). Most of the features we present were already part of the design of Microsoft Windows NT; we will clarify the features that were not present in Windows NT and were introduced in Windows 2000. We use the term Windows to refer to this family of operating systems. We do not consider the family of Windows 95/98/ME operating systems.

### Security Descriptor

One of the most important characteristics of the Windows operating system is its object-oriented design. Every component of the system is represented as an object, with attributes and methods. In this scheme, it is natural to base access control on the notion that objects can be *securable*; that is, they can be characterized by a *security descriptor* that specifies the security requirements of the object (this corresponds to implementing access control with an access control list approach [Samarati & De Capitani di Vimercati, 2001], equivalent to the nine-character string in Unix). Almost all of the system objects are *securable*: files, processes, threads, named pipes, shared memory areas, registry entries, and so on. The same access control mechanism applies to all of them.

Any subject that can operate on an object (user, group, logon session, etc.) is represented in Windows by a *Security Identifier* (SID), with a rich structure that manages the variety of active entities. The main components of the *security descriptor* are the SIDs of the owner and of the primary group of the object and two access control lists: a *Discretionary Access Control List* (DACL) and a *System Access Control List* (SACL).

### Access Control Element

Each access control list consists of a sequence of *Access Control Elements* (ACEs). An ACE is an elementary authorization on the object, with which it is associated by way of the ACL; the ACE describes the subject to which the authorization applies, the action (operation) that the subject can execute on the object, the type (allow, deny, or audit), and several flags (to specify the propagation and other ACE properties). The subject (called *trustee* in Windows) is represented by a SID. The action is specified by an *access mask*, a 32-bit vector (only part of the bits are currently used; many bits are left unspecified for future extensions). Half of the bits are associated with access rights valid for every object type; these access rights can be divided into three families as follows:

*Generic*: *read*, *write*, *execute*, and the union of all of them.

*Standard*: *delete*, *read_control* (to read the security descriptor), *synchronize* (to wait on the object until a signal is generated on it), *write_dac* (to change the DACL), and *write_owner* (to change the object's owner).

*SACL*: *access_system_security* (a single access right to modify the SACL; the right is not sufficient, as the subject must also have the SE_SECURITY_NAME privilege). It cannot appear in a DACL.

The remaining 16 bits are used to represent access rights specific to the object type (directory, file, process, thread, etc.). For instance, for directories access rights *open*, *create_child*, *delete_child*, *list*, *read_prop*, and *write_prop* apply. Active directory services, described under "Fine Granularity Access Control," are the base for the introduction of object-specific ACEs.

## Access Token

Each process or thread executing in the system is associated with an *Access Token,* an object that describes the security context. An access token describing the user is created after the user has been authenticated and is then associated with every process executing on behalf of the user. The access token contains the SID of the user's account, SIDs of the groups that have the user as a member, a *logon* SID identifying the current logon session, a list of the privileges held by the user or the groups, an owner SID, the SID of the primary group, and the default DACL to use when a process creates a new object without specifying a security descriptor. In addition, there are other components that are used for changing the identifiers associated with a process (called *impersonation* in Windows) and to apply restrictions.

## Evaluation of ACLs

When a thread makes a request to access an object, its access token is compared with the DACL in the security descriptor. If the DACL is not present in the security descriptor, the system assumes that the object is accessible without restrictions. Otherwise, the ACEs in the DACL are considered one after the other, and for each one the user and group SIDs in the access token are compared with the SID in the ACE. If there is a match, the ACE is applied. Order in the DACL is extremely important. The first ACE that matches will apply or deny the access rights in it. The following matching ACEs will only be able to allow or deny the remaining access rights. If the analysis of the DACL terminates and no allow/deny has been obtained for a given access right, the system assumes that the right is denied (closed policy). As an example, with reference to Figure 3, for user Bob the second ACE will apply (as it matches the group in the thread's access token) denying Bob the execute and write accesses on object1. The approach of applying the first ACE encountered corresponds to the use of a "position-based" criterion for resolving possible conflicts (Samarati & De Capitani di Vimercati, 2001). Although simple, this solution is quite limiting. First, it gives the users specifying the policy the complete burden of solving each specific conflict that may arise (not allowing them to specify generic high level rules for that). Second, it is not suitable if a decentralized administration (where several users can specify authorizations) should be accommodated. Also, users should have explicit direct write privilege on the DACL to properly order the ACEs. However, doing so it would be possible for them to abuse the privilege and set the ACL in an uncontrolled way.

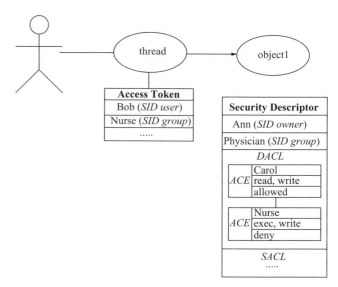

**Figure 3:** Access control in Windows.

It is worth noting how an empty DACL (which returns no permissions) will deny all users the access to the object, whereas a null DACL (which returns no restrictions) would grant them all. Then, attention must be paid to the difference between the two.

The object creator sets the DACL. When no DACL is specified, the default DACL in the access token is used by the system. The SACL is a sequence of ACEs like the DACL, but it can only be modified by a user having the administrative privilege SE_SECURITY_NAME and describes the actions that have to be logged by the system (if the ACE for a given access right and SID is positive, the corresponding action must be logged; if it is negative, no trace will be kept); the access control system records access requests that have been successful, rejected, or both, depending on the value of the flags in the ACE elements in the SACL. Each monitored access request produces a new entry in the *security event log*.

## System Privileges

A system privilege in Windows is the right to execute privileged operations, such as making a backup, debugging a process, increasing the priority of a process, increasing the quota, and creating accounts. All these operations are not directly associated with a specific system object, and ACEs cannot conveniently represent them in an object security descriptor. System privileges can be considered as authorizations without an explicit object. System privileges can be associated with user and group accounts. When a user is authenticated by the system, the access token is created; the access token contains the system privileges of the user and of the groups in which the user is a member. Every time a user tries to execute a system privileged operation, the system checks if the access token contains the adequate system privilege. System privileges are evaluated locally; a user can then have different system privileges on different nodes of the network.

## Impersonation and Restricted Tokens

Impersonation is a mechanism that permits threads to acquire the access rights of a different user. This feature is similar to the *setuid* and *setgid* services of Linux, where the change in user and group identifier permits programs invoked by a user to access protected resources. In Windows, impersonation is also an important tool for client–server architectures. The server uses impersonation to acquire the security context of the client when a request arrives. The advantage is that, in a network environment, a user will be able to consistently access the resources for which the user is authorized, and the system will be better protected from errors in the protocol used for service invocation or in the server application.

Each process has an access token (created at logon) built from the profile of the authenticated user. An impersonating thread has two access tokens, the primary access token that describes the access token of the parent process and the impersonation access token that represents the security context of a different user. Obviously, impersonation requires an adequate system privilege.

Windows 2000 introduced primitives for the creation of restricted tokens. A restricted token is an access token where some privileges have been removed or restricting SIDs have been added. A restricting SID is used to limit the capabilities of an access token. When an access request is made and the access token is compared with the ACEs in the ACL, each time there is a match between the restricting SID in the token and the SID in an ACE, the ACE is considered only if it denies access rights on the object.

## Inheritance

Some important securable objects contain other securable objects. As an example, folders in the NTFS file system contain files and other folders; registry keys contain subkeys. This containment hierarchy puts in the same containers objects that are often characterized by the same security requirements. Then, it is extremely convenient to permit an automatic propagation of security descriptions from an object to all the objects contained within it (cf. Introduction, support of abstractions). This feature is realized in Windows by access control *inheritance*.

A difference exists between Windows NT and Windows 2000 and later with respect to inheritance. In Windows NT there was no distinction between direct and inherited ACEs; in addition, ACEs were inherited by an object only when the object was created or when a new ACL was applied onto an object. The result was that a change in an ACE was not propagated down the hierarchy to the object that had inherited it. In Windows 2000 and later, propagation is automatic (as users would probably expect). In addition, Windows 2000 gives higher priority to ACEs directly defined on the specific objects by putting the inherited ACEs at the end of the DACL.

In Windows 2000 and later, three flags characterize every ACE. The first flag is active if the ACE has to be propagated to descendant objects. The second and third flag are active only if the first flag is active. The second flag is active when the ACE is propagated to child objects without activating the first flag, thus blocking propagation to the first level. The third flag is active when the ACE is not applied to the object itself. In addition, in the security descriptor of a securable object there is a flag that permits disabling the application of inherited ACEs to the object.

## Fine Granularity Access Control

Another innovation of Windows 2000 is the introduction of a fine-grained access model, which supports the Windows object model. There are two different solutions. The first solution is applicable to directory services objects and uses new ACE types defining access rights on specific object properties. These ACEs are based on an object structure that extends the regular ACE with two GUID parameters (a GUID is the general object identifier). The first GUID represents the specific property, property set, or child object for which the ACE is defined. The second represents the object that can inherit the ACE.

The second solution is the one offered within Active Directory services by the *controlAccessRight* object. The object specifies access rights on object properties or on user-defined actions. The object is then referenced within an ACE inserted in the DACL of the object itself.

## Evaluation of Windows Access Control

As we did with Linux, we evaluate Windows access control services along the principles presented in the Introduction.

*Accountability and reliable input*: the operating system allows the use of reliable and strong authentication solutions. Because of its dominance of the desktop platform, many providers of authentication mechanisms focus their products on the Windows platform. Because of the need to avoid obstacles to its use by inexperienced users, the standard configuration of the Windows platform presents choices that are questionable from a security perspective, but it is possible to create resilient solutions with a careful configuration.

*Support for fine-grained and coarse-grained specifications*: the security model permits the definition of authorizations at different granularities.

*Conditional authorizations*: the Windows security model is based on the construction or inheritance of a concrete ACL for every resource that needs to be protected. Conditions are not supported.

*Least privilege*: to realize this principle, the security administrator has to carefully design the security policy.

*Separation of duty*: the separation between the DACL and SACL is the basis for the construction of a system where the administrator actions are monitored. Nonetheless, the system administrator has complete control over the local system.

*Multiple policies and exceptions*: the Windows security model supports exceptions, in the form of positive and negative authorizations. There is no explicit support for multiple policies, except the combination that may occur because of authorization inheritance.

*Policy combination and conflict resolution*: when there is the need to combine policies, for example, when for an object there are explicit and inherited authorizations, Windows considers the position in the ACL (between two conflicting authorizations, the first one wins). Because inherited authorizations are considered after the locally specified ones, the inherited policies are dominated by those specified on the object or nearer to the object.

*Administrative polices*: administration is based on the ownership of resources, together with the presence of an administrator able to define policies for all the resources of the system.

Overall, the Windows security model is quite powerful, but given its reliance on the position of authorizations within the ACL to solve conflicts, it is more adequate as an enforcement mechanism rather than a policy definition language; it appears an interesting opportunity that is the design of tools that is able to represent policies at an abstract level and then to map the defined policy in the terms that are adequate for the Windows mechanism.

## ACCESS CONTROL IN DATABASE MANAGEMENT SYSTEMS

Database management systems (DBMSs) usually provide access control services in addition to those provided by the underlying operating systems (Castano, Fugini, Martella, & Samarati, 1995). DBMS access control allows references to the data model concepts and the consequent specification of authorizations dependent on the data and on the applications. Most of the existing DBMSs (e.g., Oracle Server, SQL Server, and Postgres) are based on the relational data model and on the use of Structured Query Language (SQL) as the data definition and manipulation language (Atzeni, Ceri, Paraboschi, & Torlone, 1999). The SQL standard provides commands for the specification of access restrictions on the objects managed by the DBMS. We here illustrate the main SQL facilities with reference to the latest version of the language, namely SQL:1999 (ISO International Standard, 1999).

### Security Features of SQL

SQL access control is based on *user* and *role* identifiers. User identifiers correspond to login names with which users open the DBMS sessions. DBMS users are defined by the DMBS in an implementation-dependent way and are usually independent of the usernames managed by the operating system; SQL does not define how OS users are mapped to SQL users. Roles, introduced in SQL:1999, are "named collections of privileges" (Sandhu, Ferraiolo, & Kuhn, 2000), that is, named virtual entities to which privileges are assigned; by activating a role, users are enabled to execute the privileges associated with the role.

Users and roles can be granted authorizations on any object managed by the DBMS, namely tables, views, columns of tables and views, domains, assertions, and user-defined constructs such as user-defined types, triggers, and SQL-invoked routines. Authorizations can also be granted to public, meaning that they apply to all the user and role identifiers in the SQL environment. Apart from the drop and alter statements—which permit deletion and modification of the schema of an object and whose execution is reserved to the object's owner—authorizations can be specified for any of the commands supported by SQL, namely *select*, *insert*, *update*, and *delete* for tables and views (where the first three can refer to specific columns) and *execute* for SQL-invoked routines. In addition, other actions allow controlling references to re-

sources; they are as follows: *reference*, *usage*, *under*, and *trigger*. The *reference* privilege, associated with tables or attributes within, allows reference to tables/attributes in an integrity constraint: a constraint cannot be checked unless the owner of the schema in which the constraint appears has the *reference* privilege on all the objects involved in the constraint. The reason for this is that constraints may affect the availability of the objects on which they are defined, and therefore their specification should be reserved to those explicitly authorized. The *usage* privilege, which can be applied to domains, user-defined types, character sets, collations, or translations, allows the use of the object in one's own declarations. The *under* privilege can be applied to a user-defined type and allows subjects to define a subtype of the specified type. The *trigger* privilege, referred to a table, allows the definition of a trigger on the table.

In addition to authorizations to execute privileges on the different objects of the database management system, SQL also supports authorizations on roles. In particular, roles can be granted to other users and roles. Granting a role to a user means allowing the user to activate the role. Granting a role $r'$ to another role $r$ means permitting $r$ to enjoy the privileges granted to $r'$. Intuitively, authorizations of roles granted to roles introduce chains of roles through which privileges can flow. For instance, consider the case in Figure 4 where the rightmost three nodes are users, the remaining three nodes are roles and an arc corresponds to an authorization of the incident node on the role source of the arc (e.g., Ann has an authorization for the Admin_Supervisor role). Although each of the users will be allowed to activate the role for which it has the authorization (directly connected in our graph) it will enjoy the privileges of all the roles reachable through a chain. For instance, when activating role Admin_Supervisor, Ann will also enjoy, in addition to the privileges granted to this role, the privileges granted to roles Secretary and Accountant.

### Access Control Enforcement

A pair <uid, rid> always identifies the subject making a request, where *uid* is the SQL session user identifier (which can never be null) and *rid* is a role name, whose value is initially null. Both the user identifier and the role identifier can be changed via commands set session authorization and set role, respectively, whose successful execution depends on the specified authorizations. In particular, enabling a role requires the current user to have the authorization for the role. The current pair *<uid, rid>* can also change upon execution of an SQL-invoked routine, where it is set to the owner of the routine (cf. "Views and Invoked Routines"). An *authorization stack* (maintained using a "last-in, first-out" strategy) keeps track of

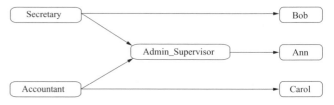

**Figure 4:**  An example of role chains in SQL.

the sequence of pairs <uid, rid> for a session. Every request is controlled against the authorizations of the top element of the stack. Although the subject is a pair, like for authorizations and ownership, access control always refers to either a user or a role identifier in mutual exclusion: it is performed against the authorizations for *uid* if the *rid* is null; it is performed against the authorizations for *rid*, otherwise. In other words, by activating a role a user can enjoy the privileges of the role while disabling her own. Moreover, at most one role at a time can be active: the setting to a new role rewrites the *rid* element to be the new role specified.

## Administration

Every object in SQL has an owner, typically its creator (which can be set to either the current_user or current_role). The owner of an object can execute all privileges on it or a subset of them in case of views and SQL-invoked routines (cf. "Views and Invoked Routines"). The owner is also reserved the privilege to drop the object and to alter (i.e., modify) it. Apart for the drop and alter privileges, whose execution is reserved to the object's owner, the owner can grant authorizations for any privilege on its objects, together with the ability to pass such authorizations to others (grant option).

A grant command, whose syntax is illustrated in Figure 5, allows granting new authorizations for roles (enabling their activation) or for privileges on objects. Successful execution of the command requires the grantor to be the owner of the object on which the privilege is granted or to hold the grant option for it. The specification of all privileges, instead of an explicit privilege list, is equivalent to the specification of all the privileges, on the object, for which the grantor has the grant option. The with hierarchy option (possible only for the *select* privilege on tables) automatically implies granting the grantee the *select* privilege on all the (either existing

or future) subtables of the table on which the privilege is granted. The with grant option clause (called with admin option for roles) allows the grantee to grant others the received authorization (as well as the grant option on it). No cycles of role grants are allowed.

The revoke statement allows revocation of (administrative or access) privileges previously granted by the revoker (which can be set to the current_user or current_role). Because of the use of the grant option and the existence of derived objects (see "Views and Invoked Routines"), revocation of a privilege can possibly have side effects, because there may be other authorizations that depend on the one being revoked. Options cascade and restrict dictate how the revocation procedure should behave in such a case: cascade recursively revokes all those authorizations that should no longer exist if the requested privilege is revoked; restrict rejects the execution of the revoke operation if other authorizations depend on it. To illustrate, consider the case where user Ann creates a table and grants the select privilege, and the grant option on it, to Bob and Carol. Bob grants it to David, who grants it to Ellen, and to Frank, who grants it to Gary. Carol also grants the authorization to Frank. Assume for simplicity that all these grant statements include the grant option. Figure 6(a) illustrates the resulting authorizations and their dependencies via a graph reporting a node for every user and an arc from the grantor to the grantee for every authorization. Consider now a request by Ann to revoke the privilege from Bob. If the revoke is requested with option cascade, the authorizations granted by Bob (who would not hold anymore the grant option for the privilege) will be revoked, causing the revocation of David's authorization, which will recursively cause the revocation of the authorization David granted to Ellen. The resulting authorizations (and their dependencies) are illustrated in Figure 6(b). Note that no recursive revocation is activated for Frank as, even if the authorization he

---

```
grant all privileges | <action>
on [ table ] | domain | collation | character set | translation | type <object name>
to <grantee> [{<comma> <grantee>}...]
[ with hierarchy option ]
[ with grant option ]
[ granted by <grantor> ]
```

```
grant <role granted> [{ <comma> <role granted>}...]
TO <grantee> [{ <comma> <grantee>}...]
[ with admin option ]
[ granted by <grantor> ]
```

```
revoke [ grant option for | hierarchy option for ] <action>
on [ table ] | domain | collation | character set | translation | type <object name>
from <grantee> [ { <comma> <grantee> }...]
[ granted by <grantor> ]
cascade | restrict
```

```
revoke [ admin option for ]
<role revoked> [ { <comma> <role revoked> }... ]
from <grantee> [ { <comma> <grantee> }... ]
[ granted by <grantor> ]
cascade | restrict
```

**Figure 5:** Syntax of the grant and revoke SQL statements.

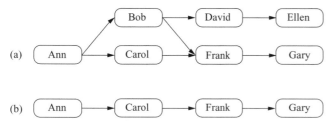

**Figure 6:** A graphical representation of authorizations before (a) and after (b) a cascade revocation.

received from Bob is deleted, Frank still holds the privilege with the grant option (received from Carol). By contrast, if Ann were to request the revoke operation with the `restrict` option, the operation would be refused because of the authorizations dependent on it (those which would be revoked with the `cascade` option).

### Views and Invoked Routines

A special consideration must be devoted to authorizations for derived objects (views) and SQL-invoked routines, where the case can be that the owner creating them does not own the underlying objects used in their definition.

A view is a *virtual* table derived from base tables and/or other views. A view definition is a SQL statement whose result defines the content of the view. The view is virtual because its content is not explicitly stored but it is derived, at the time the view is accessed, by executing the corresponding SQL statement on the underlying tables. A user/role can create a view only if it has the necessary privilege on all the views, or base tables, directly referenced by the view. The creator receives on the view the privileges that it holds on all the tables directly referenced by the view. Also, it receives the grant option for a privilege only if it has the grant option for the privilege on all the tables directly referenced by the view. If it holds a privilege on the view with the grant option, the creator can grant the privilege (and the grant option) to others. The grantees of such privileges need not hold the privileges on the underlying tables to access the view; access to the view requires only the existence of privileges on the view. Intuitively, the execution of the query computing the view is controlled against the authorizations of the view's owner (similar to what the *suid* bit does in Unix). Also, views provide a way to enforce finer grained access (on specific tuples). For instance, a user can define a view `EU_Employees` on table `Employees` containing only those rows for which the value of attribute `nationality` is equal to `EU`. She can then grant other users the *select* privilege on the view, thus allowing (and restricting) them access to information on employees within the European Union. Views are the only means to bypass an *all tuples* or *no tuple* access on tables. Although convenient, views are, however, simply a trick for enforcing content-dependent fine-grained access control (which is not the main reason why they were developed) and as such result are limiting for this purpose: a different view should be defined for any possible content-dependent access restriction that should be enforced.

A SQL-invoked routine is an SQL-invoked procedure, or a SQL-invoked function, characterized by a header and a body. The header consists of a name and a possibly empty list of parameters. The body may be specified in SQL or, in the case of external routines, written in a host programming language. At object creation time, a user is designated as the *owner* of the routine. Analogous to what is required for views, to create a SQL-invoked routine, the owner needs to have the necessary privileges for the successful execution of the routine. The routine is dropped if at any time the owner loses any of the privileges necessary to execute the body of the routine. When a routine is created, the creator receives the *execute* privilege on it, with the grant option if it has the grant option for all the privileges necessary for the routine to run. If the creator of a routine has the *execute* privilege with the grant option, she can grant such a privilege, and the grant option on it, to other users/roles. The *execute* privilege on a SQL routine is sufficient for these other users/roles to run the routine (they need not have the privileges necessary for the routine to run; only the creator does). Intuitively, SQL routines provide a service similar to the *setuid/setgid* privileges in Linux and impersonation in Windows (controlling privileges with respect to the owner instead of the caller of a procedure).

### Evaluation

We now evaluate SQL access control services along the principles presented in the Introduction.

*Accountability and reliable input*: DBMSs typically employ an authentication mechanism separate from that of the operating system on which the system executes. This permits a greater flexibility and independence from the specific operating system. Authentication usually is based on the use of passwords, but the model is compatible with other approaches and it is quite common to protect access to the database from the outside, allowing access only from specified network nodes.

*Support for fine-grained and coarse-grained specifications*: views and stored procedures are powerful tools that permit representation of the security policy with fine granularity.

*Conditional authorizations*: views permit the introduction of authorizations on table portions specified by a query, fully satisfying this principle.

*Least privilege*: the SQL access model satisfies this principle with roles, which are acquired dynamically before accessing a protected resource and should be immediately released.

*Separation of duty*: the database administrator has complete control over the DBMS.

*Multiple policies and exceptions*: the current access control model only envisions positive authorizations.

*Policy combination and conflict resolution*: policy combination may arise because of the presence of many users able to give privileges for access to their resources. Because there are no negative authorizations, policy combination is trivial, as it only requires for each user to add all the privileges obtained from any user in the system.

*Administrative policies*: the SQL access control model clearly identifies the possibility to grant the privilege to pass to other users the authorization that a user has received, implementing a delegation model.

Overall, the SQL access model presents several features that characterize it as a modern access control solution.

## ACCESS CONTROL FOR INTERNET-BASED SOLUTIONS

We here survey the most common security features for Internet-based solutions. Again, we illustrate the most popular representative of the different families. We therefore look at TCPD for Internet service access, at Apache for Web-based solutions, and at the Java 2 security model.

```
#hosts.allow
in.ftpd: ALL: mail -s "remote ftp attempt from %h" admin)
#hosts.deny
ALL: ALL
```

### TCPD

The `tcpd` program (`www.porcupine.org/wietse`) is a wrapper program that is normally used in Unix-like operating systems to monitor incoming requests for Internet services such as `telnet`, `finger`, and `ftp`, among others. `tcpd` is activated by the `inetd` process every time a request for service is received on a port. Upon activation, `tcpd` logs the request (recording the timestamp, the client host name, and the name of the requested service) as specified in `etc/syslog.conf` and evaluates files `/etc/hosts.allow` and `/etc/hosts.deny` (which are the files where access control rules are specified) to determine whether the request should be granted or denied. Each of these files include zero or more *access rules* of the form

*service_ list* : *client_ list* [ : *shell_ command* ] ,

where *service_list* is a list of service daemons (e.g., `ftpd`, `telnetd`, and `fingerd`); *client_list* is a list of host names, host addresses, or patterns; and *shell_command* is an optional shell command that must be executed every time the rule is matched. Wildcards can be used in place of a specific service/client to denote a set of them. For instance, wildcard `ALL` matches with any service/client, whereas `LOCAL` matches any host whose name does not contain a dot character. Patterns are partial host/address specification and are used to refer, in a convenient way, to groups of hosts or addresses (all those matching with the pattern). Typically a pattern specifies only the most generic part of a host/address identifier (namely the rightmost elements for symbolic addresses and the leftmost elements for numeric IPs), thus denoting a whole subnetwork of machines. In other words, a symbolic pattern begins with a dot character and matches all host names whose rightmost components equal those specified. For instance, patterns `.it` or `.acme.com` will match all machines in the `it` domains or within the `acme.com`

subnetwork, respectively. Conversely, a numeric pattern ends with a dot character and matches all host addresses whose leftmost fields equal those specified. For instance, pattern `159.155.` will match all machines in the `159.155.` subnetwork.

The difference between files `hosts.allow` and `hosts.deny` is that `hosts.allow` expresses permissions (i.e., which hosts should be allowed access to the mentioned services), whereas `hosts.deny` expresses denials.

The access control process performs first an evaluation of `hosts.allow`. If a matching rule is found access is granted (and the shell command executed, if any). Otherwise, `hosts.deny` is evaluated and, if a matching rule is found, access is denied (and the shell command executed, if any). The fact that the evaluation order is established by the mechanism implies that only this single predefined conflict resolution policy is supported. If no rule is found in either file, the access is granted (open policy by default). As an example, we consider the specification in Figure 7, which denies all accesses but `ftp`. The shell command in the permission, executed in correspondence of `ftp` requests, sends an e-mail message to the system administrator signaling the ftp request from client `%h`, where the symbolic name `%h` is expanded to the client host name or IP address.

Overall, the access control model is relatively simple and all its features are present in the host-based access control of Apache. For this reason, we omit the evaluation on the principles.

### Apache Access Control

The Apache HTTP server (www.apache.org) allows the specification of access control rules via a per-directory configuration file usually called `.htaccess` (Apache, 2005). The `.htaccess` file is a text file including access control rules (called *directives* in Apache) that affect the directory in which the `.htaccess` file is placed and, recursively, directories below it. See Evaluation of .htaccess

```
SetEnvIf Referer www.mydomain.org internal_site
AuthName "user-based restriction"
AuthType Basic
AuthUserFile /home/mylogin/.htpasswd
AuthGroupFile /home/mylogin/.htgroup
Order Deny,Allow
Deny from all
Allow from acme.com
Allow from env= internal_site
Require valid-user
Satisfy any
<FilesMatch public_access.html>
 Allow from all
</FilesMatch>
```

**Figure 7:** A simple example of the TCPD configuration files.

files. Figure 7 illustrates a simple example of the .htaccess file.

Access control directives, whose specification is enabled via module mod access, can be either *host based* (they can refer to the client's host name and IP address, or other characteristics of the request) or *user based* (they can refer to usernames and groups thereof). We start by describing such directives and then illustrate how the .htaccess files that include them are evaluated.

### Host-Based Access Control

Host-based directives resemble and enrich the security specifications of the tcpd solution examined earlier. Both permissions and denials can be specified, by using the Allow (for permissions) and Deny (for denials) directives, which can refer to location properties or environment variables of the request. *Location-based* specifications have the following form:

Allow from *host-or-network*/all
Deny from *host-or-network*/all,

where *host-or-network* can be a domain name (e.g., acme.com), an IP address or IP pattern (e.g., 155.50.), a network/netmask pair (e.g., 10.0.0.0/255.0.0.0), or a network/*n* mask size, where *n* is a number between 1 and 32 specifying the number of high-order 1 bits in the netmask. For instance, all the following definitions are equivalent: 10.0.0.0/8 and 10.0.0.0/255.0.0.0. Alternatively, value all denotes all hosts on the network.

*Variable-based* specifications have the following form:

Allow from env = *env-variable*
Deny from env = *env-variable*,

where *env-variable* denotes an environment variable. The semantics is that the directive (allow or deny) applies if *env-variable* exists. Apache sets environment variables based on different attributes of the HTTP client request, using the directives provided by module mod_setenvif. The attributes may correspond to various HTTP request header fields (see RFC 2616; Fielding et al., 1999) or to other aspects of the request. The most commonly used request header field names include User-Agent (typically the browser originating the request) and Referer (the URI of the document from which the URI in the request was obtained). For instance, in Figure 7 directive SetEnvIf sets "internal_site" if the referring page was in the www.mydomain.org Web site. The "Allow from env = internalsite" directive, then, permits access if the referring page matches the given URI.

Access control evaluates the content of file .htaccess to determine whether a request should be granted or denied. The Order directive controls the order in which the Deny and Allow directives must be evaluated (thus allowing users to dictate the conflict resolution policy to be applied) and defines the default access state. There are three possible orderings:

Deny, Allow: the deny directives are evaluated first, and access is allowed by default (open policy). Any client that does not match a deny directive *or* matches an allow directive is granted access.

Allow, Deny: the allow directives are evaluated first and access is denied by default (closed policy). Any client that does not match an allow directive *or* matches a deny directive is denied access.

Mutual-failure: only clients that do not match any Deny directive *and* match an Allow directive are allowed access.

For instance, the .htaccess file in Figure 7 states that all hosts in the acme.com domain and requests with a referring page in the www.mydomain.org Web site are allowed access; all other hosts are denied access.

### User-Based Access Control

In additions to host-based access control rules, Apache includes a module, called mod_auth, that enables user authentication (based on usernames and passwords) and enforcement of user-based access control rules. Usernames and associated passwords are stored in a text *user file*, reporting pairs of the form *"username:MD5-encrypted password."* Command htpasswd is used to modify the file (i.e., add new users or change passwords) as well as to create/rewrite it (a -c flag rewrites the file as new). The command has the following form:

htpasswd [-c] *filename username*,

where *filename* is the full path name of the user file and *username* is the name of the created user. Upon entering the command, the system will ask to specify the password (as usual, asking its input twice to avoid insertion errors). An alternative to the text user file provided by module mod_auth is given by modules mod_auth_db and mod_auth_dbm. With these modules, the usernames and passwords are stored in Berkeley DB files and DBM type database files, respectively.

To define user-based restrictions, a name can be given to the portion of the file system that requires authentication. This portion, called *realm*, corresponds to the subtree rooted at the directory containing the .htaccess file.

The main directives to create realms are as follows:

AuthName, to give a name to the realm. The realm name will be communicated to users when prompted for the login dialog (e.g., as in Figure 8).

AuthType, to specify the type of authentication to be used. The most common method implemented by mod_auth is Basic, which sends the password from the client to the server unencrypted (with a base64 encoding). A more secure, but less common, alternative is the Digest authentication method, implemented by module mod_auth_digest, which sends the server a one-way hash (MD5 digest) of the username:password pair. This Digest authentication method is supported only by relatively recent versions of browsers (e.g., Opera, MS Internet Explorer, Amaya, Mozilla, and Netscape since version 7).

AuthUserFile, to specify the absolute path of the file that contains usernames and passwords. Note that the user file containing names and passwords does not need to be in the same directory as the .htaccess file.

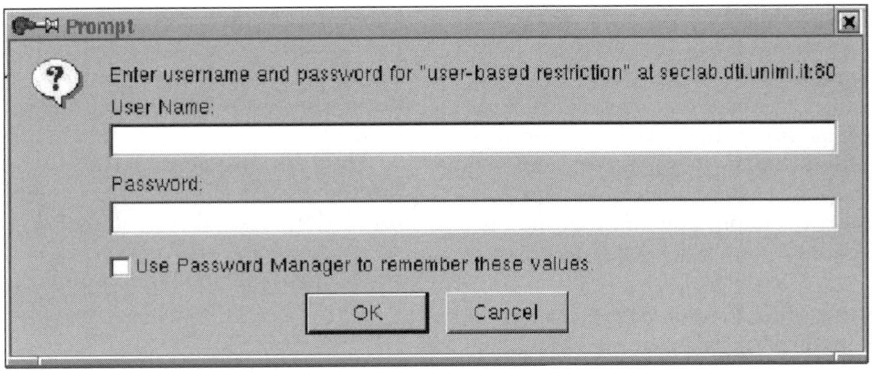

**Figure 8:** An example of dialog box that prompts for username and password.

AuthGroupFile, to specify the location of a *group file*, and therefore provide support for access rules specified for groups. The group file is a list of entries of the form group-name: username1 username2 username3... where *group-name* is the name associated with the group to which the specified usernames are declared to belong, and each of the usernames appearing in the list must be in the user file (i.e., be an existing username).

The four directives above allow the server to know where to find the usernames and passwords and what authentication protocol has to be used. User-based access rules are specified with a directive require that can take the following three forms:

require user *username1 username2...usernameN*
    Only usernames *"username1 username2...usernameN"* are allowed access.
require group *group1 group2...groupM*
    Only usernames in groups *"group1 group2...groupM"* are allowed access.
require valid-user
    Any username in the user file is allowed access

### Host-Based and User-Based Interactions and Finer-Grained Specifications

Host- and user-based access directives are not mutually exclusive and they can both be used to control access to the same resources. Directive Satisfy allows the specification of how the two sets of directives should interact. Satisfy takes one argument whose value can be either all or any. Value all requires both user-based and host-based directives to be satisfied for access to be granted, whereas for value any, it is sufficient that either one is satisfied for access to be granted.

As already said, all the directives specified in .htaccess apply to the file system subtree rooted at the directory that contains the specific .htaccess file unless overridden. In other words, a .htaccess file in a directory applies to all the files directly contained in the directory and recursively propagates to all its subdirectories unless a .htaccess has been specified for them (*most specific takes precedence*). Apache 1.2 and later support finer-grained rules allowing the specification of access directives on a per-file basis by includ-

ing FilesMatch section of the form "<FilesMatch *reg-exp>directives</FilesMatch>*," with the semantics that the directives included in the FilesMatch section apply only to the files with a name matching the regular expression specified. Also, directives can be specified on a per-method basis by use of a Limit section of the form "<Limit *list of access methods>directives</Limit>*," with the semantics that the directives included in the Limit section apply only to the accesses listed (again overriding the directives specified in the .htaccess file). As an example, directive

```
<Limit get post put>
  require valid-user
</Limit>
```

would allow any authenticated user to execute methods get, post, and put. The directive does not apply to other operations.

### Evaluation of .htaccess Files

As mentioned previously, file .htaccess is used to control accesses to the files in a directory. Therefore, whenever an access request to a file is submitted, the Apache HTTP server starts checking in the top directory for a .htaccess file and then checks each subdirectory down to and including the directory where the requested file is stored. All .htaccess files found during this process (called *directory walk*) are processed and merged, thus resulting in a set of directives that apply to the requested file. More precisely, the directives specified in the .htaccess files have to be processed if they belong to the categories (AuthConfig, FileInfo, Indexes, Limit, and Options) listed in the AllowOverride list specified in a server configuration file. These directives are then merged according to the most specific principle; that is, directives within .htaccess files in subdirectories may change or nullify the effects of the directives within .htaccess files of parent directories. As an example, suppose that the access request for http://acme.com/Department1/welcome.html resolves to the file/home/myaccount/www/Department1/welcome.html and that statement AllowOverride All has been specified. In this case, the Apache HTTP server merges *all* directives included in the .htaccess files of directories: /; /home; /home/myaccount; /home/myaccount/www; and /home/myaccount/www/Department1.

## Evaluation of the Apache Model

We now evaluate the Apache access control model along the principles presented in the Introduction.

*Accountability and reliable input*: the Apache server supports a few alternatives for authentication; an issue that often has to be faced is the inadequate support that often Internet browsers provide and that may require use of a weak solution in order not to penalize a portion of users.

*Support for fine-grained and coarse-grained specifications*: as was shown, the model permits use of a flexible granularity in the specification of authorizations.

*Conditional authorizations*: patterns may be used for addresses, host names, and resource identifiers.

*Least privilege*: the flexibility in the specification of authorizations permits identification of the specific resource portions that a user should access.

*Separation of duty*: the environment where the system is configured is completely separated from the HTTP requests that represent the way the system is accessed. The use of privileges on the file system may permit the construction of a partitioned system, with well-identified responsibilities for the different owners of resources exported by the server.

*Multiple policies and exceptions*: the Apache model contains positive and negative authorizations, and it also allows the specification of multiple policies.

*Policy combination and conflict resolution*: the Apache model offers flexibility in the choice of the policy combination that has to be used.

*Administrative polices*: an administrative policy may be realized using the access control services of the file system where the resources are stored together with the .htaccess file representing the security policy. Within the Apache model it is possible to specify which is the domain of options that a more specific policy can override.

Overall, the access control model of Apache presents many interesting features and is a powerful solution that has aimed to satisfy the requirements of modern access control solutions.

## Java 2 Security Model

Java is both a modern object-oriented programming language and a complex software architecture. Java has been developed by Sun Microsystems and is currently one of the most important solutions for the construction of applications in a network environment. Java offers sophisticated solutions for the design of distributed and mobile applications, where the software can be partitioned on distinct nodes and downloaded from one node to be executed on another.

Since its introduction, Java designers have carefully considered the security implications of an architecture where executable code could be downloaded from the network, possibly from untrusted hosts. The first security model of Java, the one associated with Java Development Kit version 1.0 (JDK 1.0), was based on the construction of a *sandbox*, a restricted environment for the execution of downloaded code, with rigid restrictions on the set of local resources that could be used (e.g., with no access to the file system and with limits on network access).

The main problem of JDK 1.0 security model was the limited granularity and the availability of a single policy for all downloaded code. JDK 1.0 would let programmers revise the access control services and implement their own version, but the implementation of access control services is complex, expensive and delicate, making it unfeasible for most applications.

The evolution of Java to version 2 gave the opportunity to revise the security model and significantly improve it. We describe the Java 2 security architecture. A full and authoritative description of the architecture appears in Gong (1999).

We observe that the security services of Java are not related to the access control system of the host operating system. This design choice derives from the requirement to make Java a fully portable execution environment that does not depend on the services of the underlying system. The Java environment will have to be properly protected on the host system, as write access to the implementation of the Java Virtual Machine, or to its configuration, would permit bypassing of any security mechanism within the Java environment.

We focus the presentation on the security model that associates permissions with pieces of Java code. This code-centric model adequately supports the security of mobile code. We do not describe the *Java Authentication and Authorization Service* (JAAS, since Java 2 v. 1.4 integrated with the JDK), a set of Java packages that offers services for user authentication and management of access control rights. JAAS extends the native Java 2 security model, using all the mechanisms presented here.

## Security Policy

The security policy describes the behavior that a Java program should exhibit. Each security policy is composed of a list of entries (an access control list) that define the permissions associated with Java classes and applications. There is a standard security policy defined for the whole Java installation, and each user can personalize it, extending the ACL in several ways, for example, writing a specific file in the personal home directory. A policy object represents the security policy.

Each entry in the security policy describes a piece of Java code and the permissions that are granted to it. Each piece of Java code is described by a URL and a list of signatures (represented in Java by a `CodeSource` object). The URL can be used to identify both local and remote code; with a single URL it is also possible to characterize single classes or complete collections (packages, JAR files, directory trees). The signatures may be applied on the complete URL or on a single class within a collection. Because URLs may identify collections, it is important to support implication among `CodeSource` objects (e.g., `http://www.xmlsec.org/classes/` implies `http://www.xmlsec.org/classes/xml.jar`).

## Permissions

Permissions describe the access rights that are granted to pieces of Java code. Each permission is represented by an instance of the abstract class `Permission`. Permissions are typically represented by a target and an action (e.g., file target `/tmp/javaAppl/buffer` and action `write`). There are permissions that are characterized only by the target, with no action (e.g., target `exitVM` for the execution of `System.exit`). The `Permission` class is specialized by many concrete classes, which define a hierarchy. Direct descendants of `Permission` are `FilePermission` (used to represent access rights on files), `SocketPermission` (used to control access to network ports), `AllPermission` (used to represent with a single permission the collection of all permissions), and `BasicPermission` (typically used as the base class for permissions with no action).

The current security model considers only positive permissions. The rationale is that the evaluation is more efficient and the model is clearer for the programmer. However, no fundamental restriction has been introduced and the model could evolve to support negative authorizations (in a future version of Java, or in an ad hoc security mechanism built for a specific application).

It is also interesting to note that permissions refer to classes and not to instance objects. A model granting permissions to objects would have offered finer granularity, but it would have also been more difficult to manage. Specifically, objects exist only at run-time, whereas the security policy is static and it is not convenient to specify in it permissions at the level of objects.

To manage sets of permission, the Java model offers class `PermissionCollection`, which groups permissions of the same category (e.g., file permissions). Class `Permissions` represents collections of `PermissionCollection` objects, that is, collections of collections of `Permission` objects.

## Access Control

In the Java 2 architecture, permissions are not directly associated with classes. Class `ProtectionDomain` realizes the link between classes and permissions. The security policy specifies permissions for a URL, which may correspond to many classes; all the classes refer to the same protection domain. There is a predefined *system* domain that associates permission `AllPermissions` with all the classes in the core of the Java architecture.

In Java 2, access control is realized at two levels: `SecurityManager` and `AccessController`. At the higher level, class `SecurityManager` is responsible for evaluating access restrictions and is invoked whenever permissions have to be verified. In JDK 1.0 the class was abstract, forcing each Java implementation to provide its own realization. In Java 2 the class is concrete and a standard implementation is part of the run-time environment. The main method of class `SecurityManager` is `checkPermission`. In JDK 1.0 the check on permissions was realized by ad hoc methods (e.g., to check for read permission on a file, method `checkRead` was used). Java 2 maintains all the previous methods for backward compatibility, but it uses a single method `checkPermission` for every permission type. This increases the flexibility of the security model, as the introduction of novel permissions can be managed with relative ease, without the need to modify the implementation of the `SecurityManager`.

Method `checkPermission` determines whether the permission that appears as first parameter of the method is granted. If the check is successful, the method returns the control to the caller; otherwise it generates a security exception.

Method `checkPermission` in the standard `SecurityManager` immediately calls method `checkPermission` of class `AccessController`. Class `AccessController` is a final (i.e., unmodifiable) class that represents the security policy that Java 2 supports by default. This distinction into two levels is motivated by two conflicting requirements, each managed at a separate level. On the one hand, there is the need for flexibility, for applications that may need a different security policy; for these applications it would be possible to realize a specialized implementation of the `SecurityManager` class that would then be automatically invoked for security checks by Java classes (which call the services of the `SecurityManager`). On the other hand, applications may prefer to have a guarantee that the security model used is the default one for Java 2; in this case, applications may opt to refer directly to the services of the `AccessController` class.

Access control is evaluated in the execution environment, which is characterized by an array of `ProtectionDomain` objects. There may be more than one `ProtectionDomain` object as Java classes may invoke the services of classes that belong to different domains. The problem is then to decide how to consider the permissions of different domains in the execution environment. The solution used in Java 2 is to consider as applicable only those permissions that belong to the intersection of all the domains. Consequently, when `checkPermission` runs, it considers all the `ProtectionDomain` objects and if there is at least one domain that has not been granted the permission being checked, a security exception is generated. The rationale for this policy is that this is the safest approach, realizing the least privilege principle.

There is an exception to the above behavior, which requires the use of method `doPrivileged` of class `AccessController`. Method `doPrivileged` creates a separate execution environment, which considers only the permissions of the `ProtectionDomain` associated with the code itself. The goal of this method is analogous to that of the *setuid* mechanism in Linux, where the privileges of the owner of the code are granted to the user executing it. For instance, a `changePassword` method that requires write permission on a password file can be realized within a `doPrivileged` method. The advantage of this mechanism with respect to the *setuid* mechanism is that in Java it is possible to restrict with a very fine granularity the Java statements that have to be executed in a privileged mode, whereas in Linux the privileges of the owner are available to the executor for the complete run of the program (in contrast to the *least privilege* principle). Finally, we consider how the security model integrates with the inheritance mechanism that characterizes the Java object model. Two classes where one is a specialization of the other may belong to distinct domains. When a method of a subclass is invoked, the effective `ProtectionDomain` is the one where the method is implemented; if the method is simply inherited from the superclass, with no redefinition, the domain of the superclass is considered; if the method is redefined in the subclass, the domain of the subclass is instead used by the `checkPermission` method.

### Evaluation of Java Access Control Model

We now evaluate the Java access control model along the principles presented in the Introduction.

*Accountability and reliable input*: the Java environment supports many alternatives for authentication, with a rich collection of solutions that include support for PKI, hardware access control devices (e.g., smart cards and cryptographic tokens), and biometrics.

*Support for fine-grained and coarse-grained specifications*: privileges can be defined at several levels, depending on the needs of the application.

*Conditional authorizations*: patterns can be used to identify resources; resources are organized in hierarchies and it is possible to specify the privilege at an arbitrary level of the hierarchy.

*Least privilege*: the flexibility in the specification of authorizations permits identification of the specific resource portions that a user has to access, satisfying this principle. The mechanism of impersonation has also been introduced to satisfy this principle.

*Separation of duty*: this principle is applied in many contexts, for example, in the identification of the protection domains that characterize the access profiles needed for distinct activities.

*Multiple policies and exceptions*: the current security model allows only the definition of positive authorizations, for efficiency reasons. It is possible to implement several policy evaluation mechanisms, depending on the requirements of the application, with a considerable degree of flexibility.

*Policy combination and conflict resolution*: the combination of policies occurs when combining the protection domains of separate classes or when considering the policies defined at distinct levels of the class hierarchy. Because of the absence of negative authorizations, the combination of policies is relatively simple to manage.

*Administrative polices*: the owner of the Java execution environment is able to specify the policy that the system will have to follow.

Overall, the access control model of Java is a modern and complex solution that considers all previous research and implementation experience of previous systems and adapts the access control principles to the needs of a sophisticated execution environment. This adaptation has produced a flexible system that requires a significant learning effort to be exploited at its full potential. Current Java applications do not typically use all the features presented above, and the definition of a complex policy is a task that requires careful analysis, but in this way the Java environment is ready to be used for the construction of modern applications, possibly using additional support tools able to provide a higher level description of the access control policy.

## CONCLUSIONS

In this chapter we have discussed the basic concepts of access control and illustrated the main features of the access control services provided by some of the most popular operating systems, database management systems, and network-based solutions. Hinting at the principles and how they are (or are not) satisfied by current approaches, the chapter can be useful to both those interested in access control development, who may get an overview of a wide array of solutions in many different contexts, and to those end users who need to represent their protection requirements in their systems and, by knowing their strengths and weaknesses, can make more proper and secure use of it.

## ACKNOWLEDGMENTS

We thank the anonymous referees for helpful comments and suggestions. This work was supported in part by the European Union within the PRIME Project in the FP6/IST Programme under contract IST-2002-507591 and by the Italian MIUR within the KIWI and MAPS projects.

## GLOSSARY

**Authentication**   Means of establishing the validity of a claimed identity.

**Authorization**   The right granted to a user to exercise an action (e.g., read, write, create, delete, and execute) on certain objects.

**Availability**   A requirement intended to guarantee that information and system resources are accessible to authorized users when needed.

**Confidentiality**   The assurance that private or confidential information not be disclosed to unauthorized users.

**Data Integrity**   A requirement that information is not modified improperly.

**Discretionary Access Control**   Policies control access based on the identity of the requestor and on access rules stating what requestors are (or are not) allowed to do.

**Group**   A set of users.

**Integrity**   Information has integrity when it is accurate, complete, and consistent. (See *data integrity* and *system integrity*).

**Mandatory Access Control**   Policies control access based on mandated regulations determined by a central authority.

**Role**   A job function within an organization that describes the authority and responsibility related to the execution of an activity.

**Role-Based Access Control**   Policies control access depending on the roles that users have within the system and on rules stating what accesses are allowed to users in given roles.

**Secrecy**   A requirement that released information be protected from improper or unauthorized release.

**Security**   The combination of integrity, availability, and secrecy.

**Security Mechanism** Low-level software and/or hardware functions that implement security policies.

**Security Policy** High-level guidelines establishing rules that regulate access to resources.

**Subject** An active entity that can exercise access to the resources of the system.

**User** A person who interacts directly with a system.

## CROSS REFERENCES

See *Computer and Network Authentication; Database Security; Linux Security; Password Authentication; Unix Security; Windows 2000 Security.*

## REFERENCES

Apache (2005). *HTTP server version 2.0.* http://httpd. apache.org/docs-2.0/en.

Atzeni, P., Ceri, S., Paraboschi, S., & Torlone, R. (1999). *Database systems—Concepts, languages and architectures.* New York: McGraw-Hill.

Bellovin, S. M. (1989). Security problems in the TCP/IP protocol suite. *Communication Review, 19*(2), 32–48.

Castano, S., Fugini, M. G., Martella, G., & Samarati, P. (1995). *Database security.* Boston: Addison-Wesley.

Coar, K. (2000). *Using .htaccess files with apache.* http:// apache-server.com/tutorials/ATusing-htaccess. html

Fielding, R., Gettys, J., Mogul, J., Frystyk, H., Masinter, L., Leach, P., & Berners-Lee, T. (1999). *Hypertext Transfer Protocol—HTTP/1.1.* http://www.rfc-editor.org/rfc/rfc2616.txt

Gong, L. (1999). *Inside Java 2 platform security.* Boston: Addison-Wesley.

Graham, G. S., & Denning, P. J. (1972). Protection principles and practice. In *Proceedings of the Spring Jt. Computer Conference* (Vol. 40, pp. 417–429). Montvale, NJ: American Federation of Information Processing Societies Press.

Harrison, M. H., Ruzzo, W. L., & Ullman, J. D. (1976). Protection in operating systems. *Communications of the ACM, 19*(8), 461–471.

ISO International Standard. (1999). Database Language SQL—Parts 1–5. ISO/IEC 9075.

Jajodia, S., Samarati, P., Sapino, M. L., & Subrahmanian, V. S. (2001). Flexible support for multiple access control policies. *ACM Transactions on Database Systems, 26*(2), 18–28.

Lampson, B. W. (1974). Protection. In *5th Princeton Symposium on Information Science and Systems* (pp. 437–443). *ACM Operating Systems Review, 8*(1):18–24.

Samarati, P., & De Capitani di Vimercati, S. (2001). Access control: Policies, models, and mechanisms. In R. Focardi & R. Gorrieri (Eds.), *Lecture notes in computer science: Vol. 2171: Foundations of security analysis and design.* New York: Springer-Verlag.

Sandhu, R. (1990). Separation of duties in computerized information systems. In *Proceedings of the IFIP WG11.3 Workshop on Database Security.* The Netherlands: North-Holland.

Sandhu, R., Coyne, E. J., Feinstein, H. L., &Youman, C. E. (1996). Role-based access control models. *IEEE Computer, 29*(2), 38–47.

Sandhu, R., Ferraiolo, D., & Kuhn, R. (2000). The NIST model for role-based access control: Towards a unified standard. In *Proceedings of the Fifth ACM Workshop on Role-Based Access Control* (pp. 47–63). New York: ACM Press.

Sandhu, R., & Samarati, P. (1997). *CRC handbook of computer science and engineering* (pp. 1929–1948). Boca Raton, FL: CRC Press.

# Password Authentication

Jeremy L. Rasmussen, *Sypris Electronics*

## INTRODUCTION

The ancient folk tale of "Ali Baba and the Forty Thieves" mentions the use of a password. In this story, Ali Baba finds that the phrase "open sesame" magically opens the entrance to a cave where the thieves have hidden their treasure. Similarly, modern computer systems use passwords to authenticate users and allow them entrance to system resources and data shares on an automated basis. The use of passwords in computer systems can be traced to the earliest time sharing and dial-up networks. There is no evidence that passwords were used before this in purely batch systems.

The security provided by a password system depends on the passwords being kept secret at all times. Thus, a password is vulnerable to compromise whenever it is used, stored, or even known. In a password-based authentication mechanism implemented on a computer system, passwords are vulnerable to compromise because of the following exposure areas of the password system:

1. Passwords are initially assigned to users when they are enrolled on the system. The threat here is that a default password can be guessed and used by an attacker before it is changed by the authorized user. In addition, an attacker could trick a system administrator or user to reset an account password to a default state, allowing an avenue for compromise.

2. Passwords are stored in a "password database" by the system. The threat here is that if an attacker could access the database, he could compromise the security of the passwords stored in it.

3. Passwords are remembered by users. Because of the limitations of human memory, users often choose weak or easily guessed passwords that can be compromised by attackers.

4. Passwords are entered into the system by users at authentication time. Whenever passwords are entered, an attacker could use a keystroke logger, sniffer, or other device to capture the password and replay it later.

Because of these factors, a number of protection schemes have been developed for maintaining password security. These include implementing policies and mechanisms to ensure "strong" passwords, encrypting the password database, and simplifying the sign-on and password synchronization processes. Without a "defense in depth" approach to securing passwords—that is, implementing each of the preceding methods to provide several layers of security—system administrators could be leaving their systems open to attack.

## TYPES OF IDENTIFICATION/ AUTHENTICATION

Access control is the security service that deals with granting or denying permission for subjects (for example, users or programs) to use objects (other programs or files) on a given computer system. Access control can be accomplished through hardware or software features, operating procedures, management procedures, or a combination of these. Access control mechanisms are classified by their ability to verify the authenticity of a user. The three basic verification methods are (1) what you have (e.g., smart card or token), (2) what you are [e.g., biometric fingerprint (see Figure 1) or iris pattern], or (3) what you know (e.g., PIN or password).

Of all verification methods, passwords are probably weakest because of the exposure factors enumerated above, yet they are still the most widely used method in systems today because password verification schemes are easily programmed and maintained in automated

**Figure 1:** A biometric fingerprint reader (photo courtesy of Biometric Access Corporation).

systems. To guarantee strong authentication, a system ought to combine two or more of these verification factors. For example, to access an ATM, one must have a bank card and know one's personal identification number (PIN).

## HISTORY OF PASSWORDS IN MODERN COMPUTING

Conjecture as to which system was the first to incorporate passwords has been discussed by several computing pioneers on the Cyberspace History List-Server (CYHIST) [URL: http://maelstrom.stjohns.edu/archives/cyhist.html]. However, no one has provided any concrete evidence to support one system or another as the progenitor. The consensus opinion favors the Compatible Time Sharing System (CTSS) developed at the Massachusetts Institute of Technology (MIT) Computation Center beginning in 1961. As part of Project MAC (Multiple Access Computer) under the direction of Professor Fernando J. "Corby" Corbató, the system was implemented on an IBM 7094 and reportedly began using passwords by 1963. According to researcher Norman Hardy, who worked on the project, the security of passwords immediately became an issue as well: "I can vouch for some version of CTSS having passwords. It was in the second edition of the CTSS manual, I think, that illustrated the login command. It had Corby's user name and password. It worked—and he changed it the same day."

Passwords were widely in use by the early 1970s as the "hacker" culture began to develop, possibly in tacit opposition to the ARPANET (the precursor to the Internet). By the 1980s, there were published accounts of how passwords had been used to access systems either by guessing or using system default passwords. In the 1990s, sophisticated password cracking tools began to appear. Incidentally, the technical knowledge required to use such tools did not increase. On the contrary, these tools are simple to use and widely available for free on the Internet (see Figure 2).

Now, with the explosion of the World Wide Web, the use of passwords and the quantity of confidential data that those passwords protect have grown exponentially. But just as the 40 thieves' password protection system was breached (the cave could not differentiate between Ali Baba's voice and those of the thieves), computer password systems have also been plagued by a number of vulnerabilities. The history of password authentication is replete with examples of weak, easily compromised systems. In general, "weak" authentication systems are characterized by protocols that either leak the password directly over the network or leak sufficient information while performing authentication to allow intruders to deduce or guess at the password.

The U.S. Department of Defense Computer Security Center (CSC) recognized this problem and published the *Password Management Guideline* (also known as the "Green Book") in 1985 "to assist in providing that much needed credibility of user identity by presenting a set of good practices related to the design, implementation and use of password-based user authentication mechanisms." The Green Book outlined a number of steps that system security administrators should take to ensure password security on the system and suggests that, whenever possible, they be automated. These include the following "ten commandments" of passwords:

1. System security administrators should change the passwords for all standard user ids before allowing the general user population to access the system.
2. A new user should always appear to the system as having an "expired password" that will require the user to change the password by the usual procedure before receiving authorization to access the system.
3. Each user id should be assigned to only one person. No two people should ever have the same user id at the same time or even at different times. It should be considered a security violation when two or more people know the password for a user id.
4. Users need to be aware of their responsibility to keep passwords private and to report changes in their user status or suspected security violations. Users should also be required to sign a statement to acknowledge understanding of these responsibilities.
5. Passwords should be changed on a periodic basis to counter the possibility of undetected password compromise.
6. Users should memorize their passwords and not write them on any medium. If passwords must be written, they should be protected in a manner that is consistent with the damage that could be caused by their compromise.
7. Stored passwords should be protected by access controls provided by the system, by password encryption, or by both.
8. Passwords should be encrypted immediately after entry, and the memory containing the plaintext password should be erased immediately after encryption.
9. Only the encrypted password should be used in comparisons. There is no need to be able to decrypt passwords. Comparisons can be made by encrypting the password entered at login and comparing the

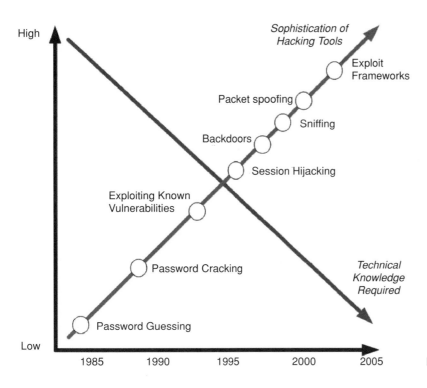

Figure 2: Proliferation of hacking tools.

encrypted form with the encrypted password stored in the password database.

10. The system should not echo passwords that users type in, or at least should mask the entered password (e.g., with asterisks).

## PASSWORD SECURITY—BACKGROUND
### Information Theory

According to fundamental work in information theory performed by Claude Shannon during the 1940s, we find that a password is only as good as its entropy. Entropy is a measure of uncertainty. According to Shannon's theorems, the quality of a password (i.e., that which keeps an attacker from guessing it) is not necessarily a function of the length of a password or the number of symbols used in it. Rather, it is determined by how many different possible passwords there are and how frequently each is used. The following illustrates this.

Say a user is filling out a form on a Web page (Fig. 3). The form has a space for "Sex" and leaves six characters for entering either "female" or "male" before the entry is encrypted and sent to the server. If we consider each character is a byte (8 bits), then $6 \times 8 = 48$ bits will be sent for this response. Is this how much information is actually contained in the field, though? Clearly, there is only *1 bit* of data represented by the entry—a binary value—either male or female. That means there is only one bit of entropy (or uncertainty), and there are 47 bits of *redundancy* in the field. This redundancy could be used by a cryptanalyst (someone who analyzes cryptosystems) to find regularities between the unencrypted and encrypted text, perhaps allowing him to crack the key and reveal the entire entry.

The same concept applies to password security. A longer password is not necessarily a better password.

Rather, a password that is difficult to guess (that is, one that has high entropy or appears "random") is best. This usually comes from a combination of factors (see "Guidelines for Selecting a Strong Password"). The probability that any single attempt at guessing a password will be successful is one of the most critical factors in a password system. This probability depends on the size of the password space and the statistical distribution within that space of passwords that are actually used.

However, over the past several decades, *Moore's law* has made it possible to use brute force methods to crack password spaces of larger and larger entropy. This, combined with the fact that there is a limit to the entropy that the average user can remember, means that nowadays passwords are more at risk than ever. A user cannot typically

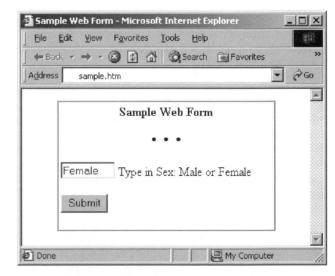

Figure 3: Sample Web page entry form.

remember a 32-character password, but that is what is required to have the equivalent strength of a 128-bit key. Recently, password cracking tools have advanced to the point of being able to crack nearly anything a system could reasonably expect a user to memorize (see "Password Length and Human Memory").

## Cryptographic Protection of Passwords

In early password systems, the most basic and least secure method of authentication was to store passwords in plaintext in a database on a server. During authentication, the client would send her password to the server, and the server would compare this against the stored value. Obviously, however, if the password file were accessible to unauthorized users, the security of the system could be easily compromised.

In later systems, developers discovered that a server did not need to store a user's password in plaintext form to perform password authentication. Instead, the user's password could be transformed through a one-way function, such as a *hashing* function, into a random looking sequence of bytes. Such a function would be difficult to invert. In other words, given a password, it would be easy to compute its hash, but given a hash, it would be computationally infeasible to derive the password from it (see "Hashing"). Authentication would consist merely of performing the hash function over the client's password and comparing it to the stored value. The password database itself could be made accessible to all users without fear of an intruder being able to steal passwords from it.

According to Cambridge University professor of computing Roger Needham, the Cambridge Multiple Access System (CMAS), which was an integrated online–offline terminal or regular input-driven system, may have been among the earliest to implement such one-way functions. It first went online in 1967 and incorporated password protection. According to Needham: "In 1966, we conceived the use of one-way functions to protect the password file, and this was an implemented feature from day one."

## Hashing

A hash function is an algorithm that takes a variable length string as input and produces a fixed length value (the hash) as output. The challenge for a hashing algorithm is to make this process irreversible; that is, finding a string that produces a given hash value should be very difficult. It should also be difficult to find two arbitrary strings that produce the same hash value.

Also called message digests or fingerprints, several one-way hash functions are in common use today. Among these are Secure Hashing Algorithm No. 1 (SHA-1) and Message Digest No. 5 (MD5). The latter was invented by Ron Rivest for RSA Security, Inc. and produces a 128-bit hash value. See Table 1 for an example of output generated by MD5. SHA-1 was developed by the U.S. National Institute of Standards and Technology (NIST) and the National Security Agency (NSA) and produces 160-bit hash values. SHA-1 is generally considered more secure than MD5 because of its longer hash value. The longer the output, the harder it is to find a collision (that is, another input that hashes to the same value). Note however that in 2005, researchers from Shandong University in China demonstrated successful collision attacks against both MD5 and SHA-1, signifying that these may no longer be considered secure schemes for hashing passwords.

Microsoft Windows XP uses one-way hash functions to store password information in the Security Account Manager (SAM). There are no Windows32 Applications Programming Interface (API) function calls to retrieve user passwords because the system does not store them. It stores only hash values. However, even a hash-encrypted password in a database is not entirely secure. A cracking tool can compile a list of, say, the one million most commonly used passwords and compute hash functions from all of them. Then the tool can obtain the system account database and compare the hashed passwords in the database with its own list to see what matches. This is called a "dictionary attack" (see "Password Cracking Tools").

To make dictionary attacks more difficult, some systems use what is called a "salt." A salt is a random string that is concatenated with a password before it is operated on by the hashing function. The salt value is then stored in the user database, together with the result of the hash function. Using a salt makes dictionary attacks more difficult, as a cracker would have to compute the hashes for all possible salt values.

A simple example of a salt would be to add the time of day; for example, if a user logs in at noon using the password "pass," the string that would be encrypted might be "1p2a0s0s." By adding this randomness to the password, the hash will actually be different every time the

**Table 1** Output from the MD5 Test Suite

| Input String | Fixed Length Output Message Digest |
|---|---|
| "" (no password) | d41d8cd98f00b204e9800998ecf8427e |
| "a" | 0cc175b9c0f1b6a831c399e269772661 |
| "abc" | 900150983cd24fb0d6963f7d28e17f72 |
| "message digest" | f96b697d7cb7938d525a2f31aaf161d0 |
| "abcdefghijklmnopqrstuvwxyz" | c3fcd3d76192e4007dfb496cca67e13b |
| "ABCDEFGHIJKLMNOPQRSTUVWXYZabcdefghijklmno pqrstuvwxyz0123456789" | d174ab98d277d9f5a5611c2c9f419d9f |
| "12345678901234567890123456789012345 678901234567890123456 78901234567890" | 57edf4a22be3c955ac49da2e2107b67a |

user logs in (unless it is at noon every day). Whether a salt is used and what the salt is depends on the operating system and the encryption algorithm being used. In the FreeBSD operating system, for example, there is a function called `crypt` that uses the DES, MD5, or Blowfish algorithms to hash passwords and can also use three forms of salts.

Hashing addresses the storage issue, but it does not address another weakness, in a networked environment—it is difficult to transmit the password securely to the server for verification without it being captured and reused, perhaps in a replay attack. To avoid revealing passwords directly over an untrusted network, computer scientists have developed challenge–response systems. At their simplest, the server sends the user some sort of challenge, which would typically be a random string of characters, called a *nonce*, that changes with time. The user then computes a response, usually some function based on both the challenge and the password. This way, even if the intruder captured a valid challenge–response pair, it would not help him gain access to the system, because future challenges would be different and require different responses.

These challenge–response systems are sometimes referred to as one-time password (OTP) systems. Bellcore's S/KEY is one such system in which a one-time password is calculated by combining a seed with a secret password known only to the user and then applying a secure hashing algorithm a number of times equal to the sequence number. Each time the user is authenticated, the sequence number expected by the system is decremented, thus eliminating the possibility of an attacker trying a replay attack using the same password again.

## PASSWORD CRACKING TOOLS
### Password Cracking Approaches

As mentioned above, passwords are typically stored as values hashed with one-way functions. In other words, this entire book could be hashed and represented as 8 bytes of gibberish. There would be no way to use these 8 bytes of data to obtain the original text. However, password crackers know that people do not use whole books as their passwords. The majority of passwords are 4 to 12 characters in length. Passwords are also, in general, not just random strings of symbols. Because users need to remember them, passwords are usually words or phrases of significance to the user. This is an opportunity for the attacker to reduce the search space.

An attacker might steal a password file, or sniff the network segment and capture the user id–password hash pairs during logon and then run a password cracking tool on them. Because it is impossible to decrypt a hash back to the password, these programs will try a dictionary attack first to look for collisions. The program guesses a password; for instance, the word *Dilbert*. The program then hashes *Dilbert* and compares the hash to one of the hashed entries in the password file. If it matches, then that password hash represents the password *Dilbert*. If the hash does not match, the program takes another guess. Depending on the tool, a password cracker will try all the words in a dictionary, all the names in a phone book, and so on. Again, the attacker does not need to know the

original password, just a password that hashes to the same value.

This is analogous to the "birthday paradox," which is an old parlor trick that says, "If you get 25 people together in a room, the odds are better than fifty-fifty that two of them will have the same birthday." How does this work? Imagine a person meeting another on the street and asking him his birthday. The chances of the two having the same birthday are only 1/365 (0.27%). Even if one person asks 25 people, the probability is still low. But with 25 people in a room together, each of the 25 is asking the other 24 about their birthdays. Each person only has a small (less than 5%) chance of success, but trying it 25 times increases the probability significantly.

In a room of 25 people, there are 300 possible pairs ($25 \times 24/2$). Each pair has a probability of success of $1/365 = 0.27\%$, and a probability of failure of $1 - 0.27\% = 99.726\%$. Calculating the probability of failure: $99.726\%^{300} = 44\%$. The probability of success is then $100\% - 44\% = 56\%$. So a birthday match will actually be found five of nine times. In a room with 42 people, the odds of finding a birthday match rise to 9 of 10. Thus, the birthday paradox is that it is much easier to find two arbitrary values that match than it is to find a match to some particular value.

If the first wave of dictionary guesses fails to produce any passwords for the attacker, the cracking program will try a *hybrid* approach of different combinations, such as forward and backward spellings of dictionary words, additional numbers and special characters, or sequences of characters. The goal here again is to reduce the cracker's search space by trying "likely" combinations of known words. Note that cracking programs are very clever about guessing hacker jargon, so do not assume that "h@ck0rz" would be a sufficiently obscure form of "hackers," if that were your password.

Only after exhausting both of these avenues will the cracking program start in on an exhaustive or brute force attack on the entire password space. The program also remembers the passwords it has already tried and will not need to recheck these either during the search.

### Rainbow Tables

An alternative to cracking passwords is simply to know all of them ahead of time. Modern techniques make use of prodigiously large tables that list all possible password hash values and allow quick lookup and retrieval. These are known as Rainbow Tables. The idea here is that you are trading off space for time. You could implement a hash-and-check operation with a very small amount of memory; however, you are the mercy of your processing speed. Conversely, with enough storage space, you could access a table of every possible hash value for passwords of a given length and on a particular system (for example, all of the older LanMan type Windows passwords), and then processing speed would be inconsequential. There are techniques for looking up things very quickly in large tables.

Computer scientist Philippe Oechslin demonstrated this at the Crypto 2003 Conference. Using 1.4 GB of data (two CD-ROMs), he showed that he could crack 99.9% of all alphanumerical Windows passwords hashes in 13.6 seconds. Subsequently, Zhu Shuanglei published code and a tool called RainbowCrack that allows anyone to generate his or her own Rainbow Tables for all sorts of hashing algorithms. There are Web sites where you can download the Rainbow Tables people have generated using RainbowCrack, and there are various forums where people trade Rainbow Tables they have custom-generated.

## Password Retrieving Approaches

Before a password cracking program can begin its work, the attacker must first retrieve the password hashes for the program to decipher. Several programs, such as L0phtcrack, have built-in mechanisms to do this. A sophisticated attacker will not try to guess passwords by entering them through the standard user interface, because the time to do so is prohibitive, and most systems can be configured to lock out a user after too many wrong guesses.

On Microsoft Windows systems, obtaining the password hashes requires the administrator privilege to read them from the database in which they are stored. This is usually somewhere in the system registry. To access them, a cracking tool will attempt to dump the password hashes from the Windows registry on the local machine or over the network if the remote machine allows network registry access. The latter requires a target Windows machine name or IP address.

Another method is to access the password hashes directly from the file system. On Microsoft Windows systems, this is the SAM. Because Windows locks the SAM file where the password hashes are stored in the file system with an encryption mechanism known as SYSKEY, it is impossible to read them from this file while the system is running. However, sometimes there is a backup of this file on tape, on an emergency repair disk (ERD), or in the repair directory of the system's hard drive. Alternately, a user may boot from a floppy disk running another operating system such as Linux and be able to read password hashes directly from the file system. This is why security administrators should never neglect physical security of systems. If an attacker can physically access a machine, she can bypass the built-in file system security mechanisms (see "Recovering Windows Passwords").

Todd Sabin released a free utility called PWDUMP2 that can dump the password hashes on a local machine if the SAM has been encrypted with the SYSKEY utility that was introduced in Windows NT Service Pack 3 and is also used in Windows 2000. Once a user downloads the utility, she can follow the instructions on the Web page to retrieve the password hashes, load the hashes into a tool such as L0phtcrack, and begin cracking them.

## Password Sniffing

Instead of capturing the system user file (SAM on Windows or /etc/passwd or /etc/shadow on UNIX/Linux), another way of collecting user IDs and passwords is through sniffing network traffic. Sniffing uses some sort of software or hardware wiretap device to eavesdrop on network communications, usually by capturing and deciphering communications packets. According to Peiter "Mudge" Zatko, who authored L0phtcrack: "Sniffing is slang for placing a network card into promiscuous mode so that it actually looks at all of the traffic coming along the line and not just the packets that are addressed to it. By doing this one can catch passwords, login names, confidential information, etc."

L0phtcrack offers an SMB Packet Capture function to capture encrypted hashes transmitted over a Windows network segment. On a switched network, a cracker will only be able to sniff sessions originating from the local machine or connecting to that machine. As server message block (SMB) session authentication messages are captured by the tool, they are displayed in the SMB Packet Capture window. The display shows the source and destination IP addresses, the user name, the SMB challenge, the encrypted LAN manager hash, and the encrypted NT LAN manager hash, if any. To crack these hashes, the tool saves the session and then works on the captured file.

## Bypassing Password Security

Limiting physical access to computer systems is still an important way to protect password-enabled systems. Norwegian software developer Petter Nordahl-Hagen built a resource (The Offline NT Password Editor) for recovering Windows passwords on work stations. His approach bypasses the NTFS file permissions of Windows NT, 2000, and XP by using a Linux boot disk that allows one to reset the administrator password on a system by replacing the hash stored in the SAM with a user-selected hash. His program has even been shown to work on Windows XP systems with SYSKEY enabled. An MS-DOS version also exists, as does a version that boots from CD-ROM instead of floppy disk. Thus, physical access to the workstation can mean instant compromise, unless, perhaps the system BIOS settings are also password protected and do not allow a user to boot from floppy or CD-ROM. However, several attacks against BIOS settings have also been published. These include the following:

- Using a manufacturer's backdoor password to access the BIOS.
- Using password cracking software.
- Resetting the CMOS using the jumpers or solder beads.
- Removing the CMOS battery for at least 10 min.
- Overloading the keyboard buffer.
- Using a professional service.

## Types of Password Cracking Tools

Password cracking tools can be divided into two categories—those that attempt to retrieve system level login passwords and those that attack the password protection mechanisms of specific applications. The first type includes programs such as L0phtcrack, Cain & Abel, and John the Ripper. Some sites for obtaining password cracking tools for various platforms, operating systems, and applications are included in the "Software Tool References" section at the end of this chapter.

The Russian company ElcomSoft has developed a range of programs that can crack passwords on Microsoft Office encrypted files, WinZip or PKZip archived files, or Adobe Acrobat (PDF) files. The U.S. federal government charged ElcomSoft with violating the Digital Millennium Copyright Act of 1998 for selling a program that allowed people to disable encryption software from Adobe Systems that is used to protect electronic books. The case drew attention after ElcomSoft programmer Dmitry Sklyarov was arrested at the DefCon IX convention in July 2001. A jury later acquitted Sklyarov and ElcomSoft. Although the jury agreed that ElcomSoft's product was illegal, they decided to acquit because they believed the company did not mean to violate U.S. law.

## PASSWORD SECURITY ISSUES AND EFFECTIVE MANAGEMENT
### Enforcing Password Guidelines

The FBI and the Systems Administration and Networking Security (SANS) Institute maintain a Web page summarizing the "Twenty Most Critical Internet Security Vulnerabilities." The majority of successful attacks on computer systems via the Internet can be traced to exploitation of security flaws on this list. From the beginning, one of the items on this list has been "accounts with no passwords or weak passwords." In general, these accounts should be removed or assigned stronger passwords.

In addition, accounts with built-in or default passwords that have never been reconfigured create vulnerabilities because they usually have the same password across installations of the software. Attackers will look for these accounts, having found the commonly known passwords published on hacking Web sites or some other public forum. Therefore, any default or built-in accounts also need to be identified and removed from the system or reconfigured with stronger passwords.

With the proliferation of wireless systems, the default configuration vulnerability has become an even bigger issue. For instance, a user who installs a new wireless router at his home and keeps the out-of-the-box settings is susceptible to being compromised. The device will likely have a default service set identifier (SSID), which would attract would-be snoopers because it shows the system has not been customized. Next, after instantly gaining access to the unsuspecting user's network, the interloper could point his browser to the default network address for configuring the router and use the default user id–password that is published on the vendor's Web site. Within moments, the attacker could have changed the router settings, created a denial of service, or performed other malicious acts because of the user never changing his default settings.

The list of common vulnerabilities and exposures (CVE) maintained by the MITRE Corporation (http://www.cve.mitre.org) provides a taxonomy for more than 3,000 well-known attacker exploits (and some 4,500 others that are currently under consideration). Among these, more than 500 have to do with password insecurities. The following provides a few examples:

- CVE-1999–0366: "In some cases, Service Pack 4 for Windows NT 4.0 can allow access to network shares using a blank password, through a problem with a null NT hash value."

- CVE-1999–1104: "Windows 95 uses weak encryption for the password list (.pwl) file used when password caching is enabled, which allows local users to gain privileges by decrypting the passwords."

- CVE-1999–1298: "Sysinstall in FreeBSD 2.2.1 and earlier, when configuring anonymous FTP, creates the ftp user without a password and with/bin/date as the shell, which could allow attackers to gain access to certain system resources."

- CVE-2000–0267: "Cisco Catalyst 5.4.x allows a user to gain access to the 'enable' mode without a password."

- CVE-2000–0981: "MySQL Database Engine uses a weak authentication method which leaks information that could be used by a remote attacker to recover the password."

- CVE-2000–1187: "Buffer overflow in the HTML parser for Netscape 4.75 and earlier allows remote attackers to execute arbitrary commands via a long password value in a form field."

- CVE-2001–0465: "TurboTax saves passwords in a temporary file when a user imports investment tax information from a financial institution, which could allow local users to obtain sensitive information."

- CVE-2002-0911: "Caldera Volution Manager 1.1 stores the Directory Administrator password in cleartext in the slapd.conf file, which could allow local users to gain privileges."

- CAN-2003-0601: "Workgroup Manager in Apple Mac OS X Server 10.2 through 10.2.6 does not disable a password for a new account before it is saved for the first time, which allows remote attackers to gain unauthorized access via the new account before it is saved."

- CAN-2003-0745: "SNMPc 6.0.8 and earlier performs authentication to the server on the client side, which allows remote attackers to gain privileges by decrypting the password that is returned by the server."

- CVE-2004-0031: "PHPGEDVIEW 2.61 allows remote attackers to reinstall the software and change the administrator password via a direct HTTP request to editconfig.php."

[Note: CVE indicates the item is on the recognized list, whereas CAN means it is a candidate for inclusion.]

SANS suggests that to determine if your system is vulnerable to such attacks, you need to be cognizant of all the user accounts on the system. First, the system security administrator must inventory the accounts on the system and create a master list. This list should include even intermediate systems, such as routers and gateways, as well as any Internet connected printers and print controllers. Second, the administrator should develop procedures for adding authorized accounts to the list and for removing accounts when they are no longer in use. The master list should be validated on a regular basis. In addition, the administrator should run some password strength checking tool against the accounts to look for weak or nonexistent passwords. A sample of these tools is noted under References at the end of this chapter.

Many organizations supplement password control programs with procedural or administrative controls that ensure that passwords are changed regularly and that old passwords are not reused. If password aging is used, the system should give users a warning and the opportunity to change their passwords before they expire. In addition, administrators should set account lockout policies that lock out a user after a number of unsuccessful login attempts and cause him or her to have his password reset.

Microsoft Windows 2000 and Windows XP include built-in password constraint options in the "Group Policy" settings. An administrator can configure the network so that user passwords must have a minimum length, a minimum and maximum age, and other constraints. It is important to require a minimum age of a password.

## Guidelines for Selecting a Strong Password

The following outlines the minimal criteria for selecting "strong" passwords:

- The goal is to select something easily remembered but not easily guessed.
- Length:
  - Windows systems: seven characters or longer
  - UNIX, Linux systems: eight characters or longer
- Composition:
  - Mixture of alphabetic, numeric, and special characters (e.g., #, @, or !)
  - Mixture of upper- and lowercase characters
  - No words found in a dictionary
  - No personal information about the user (e.g., any part of the user's name, a family member's name, or the user's date of birth, Social Security number, phone number, or license plate number)
  - No information that is easily obtained about the user, especially any part of the user id
  - No commonly used proper names such as local sports teams or celebrities
  - No easily recognized keyboard patterns such as 12345, sssss, or qwerty
  - Try misspelling or abbreviating a word that has some meaning to the user (Example: "How to select a good password?" becomes "H2sagP?")

## Password Aging and Reuse

To limit the usefulness of passwords that might have been compromised, it is suggested practice to change them regularly. Many systems force users to change their passwords when they log in for the first time, and again if they have not changed their passwords for an extended period (say, 90 days). In addition, users should not reuse old passwords. Some systems support this by recording the old passwords, ensuring that users cannot change their passwords back to previously used values, and ensuring that the user s' new passwords are significantly different from their previous passwords. Unfortunately, such systems usually have a finite memory (say, the past 10 passwords), and users can circumvent the filtering controls by changing their password 10 times in a row until it is the same as the previously used password.

It is recommended that, at a predetermined period of time prior to the expiration of a password's lifetime, the user id it is associated with be notified by the system as having an "expired" password. A user who logs in with an id having an expired password should be required to change the password for that user id before further access to the system is permitted. If a password is not changed before the end of its maximum lifetime, it is recommended that the user id it is associated with be identified by the system as "locked." No login should be permitted to a locked user id, but the system administrator should be able to unlock the user id by changing the password for that user id. After a password has been changed, the lifetime period for the password should be reset to the maximum value established by the system.

## Social Engineering

With all the advances in technology, the oldest way to attack a password-based security system is still the easiest: coercion, bribery, or trickery against the users of the system. Social engineering is an attack against people rather than machines. It is an outsider's use of psychological tricks on legitimate users of a computer system, usually to gain the information (e.g., user ids and passwords) needed to access a system. The notorious hacker Kevin Mitnick, who was convicted on charges of computer and wire fraud and spent 59 months in federal prison, told a congressional panel that he rarely used technology to gain information, whereas he employed social engineering techniques almost exclusively.

According to a study by British psychologists, people often base their passwords on something obvious and easily guessed by a social engineer. Around 50% of computer users base them on the name of a family member, a partner, or a pet. Another 30% use a pop idol or sporting hero. Another 10% of users pick passwords that reflect some kind of fantasy, often containing some sexual reference. The study showed that only 10% use cryptic combinations that follow all the rules of "tough" passwords.

The best countermeasures to social engineering attacks are education and awareness. Users should be instructed never to tell anyone their passwords. Doing so destroys accountability, and a system administrator should never need to know it either. In addition, users should never write down their passwords. A clever social engineer will find it if it is hidden under a mouse pad or inside a desk drawer.

### Some Examples of Social Engineering Attacks
**"Appeal to Authority" Attack.** This is impersonating an authority figure or else identifying a key individual as a supposed acquaintance to demand information. For example, a secretary receives a phone call from someone claiming to be the IT manager. He or she requests the secretary's user id and password or provides a new password that must be set immediately because "there has been a server crash in the computer center and we need to reset everyone's account." Once he or she has complied, the hacker now has a valid user id and password to access the system.

**"Fake Web Site" Attack.** The same password should not be used for multiple applications. Once a frequently used password is compromised, all of the user's accounts could be compromised. A good social engineering attack might be to put up an attractive Web site with titillating content, requiring users to register a username and password to access the "free" information. The attacker would record all passwords (even incorrect ones, which a user might have mistakenly entered thinking of another account), and then use those to attack the other systems frequented by the user. The Web site could even solicit information from the users about their accounts—for example, what online brokerage, banking, and e-mail accounts they use. Web site operators can always keep a log of IP addresses used to access the site and could go back to attack the originating system directly.

**"Phishing" Attack.** Similar to the fake Web site, phishing schemes typically send an official looking email to the victim informing her about a security problem with her bank or email account, and asking her to reconfirm her personal data via a secure link. The URL appears as if it takes her to the correct Web site, but it actually redirects her to the ISP of the attacker, where he collects her user id, password, and sometimes other private data such as credit card or Social Security numbers.

**"Dumpster Diving" Attack.** Many serious compromises are still caused by contractors and third parties throwing away draft instruction manuals or development notes with user ids and passwords in them. Social engineers may employ "dumpster diving," that is, digging through paper printouts in the trash looking for such significant information to gain system access.

## Single Sign-on and Password Synchronization

One issue that has irritated users in large secure environments is the increasing number of passwords they have to remember to access various applications. A user might need one password to log into his work station, another to access the network, and yet another for a particular server. Ideally, a user should be able to sign on once, with a single password, and be able to access all the other systems on which he or she has authorization.

Some have called this notion of single sign-on the "Holy Grail" of computer security. The goal is admirable—to create a common enterprise security infrastructure to replace a heterogeneous one. It is currently being attempted by several vendors through technologies such as the Open Group's distributed computing environment (DCE), MIT's Kerberos, Microsoft's Active Directory, and public key infrastructure (PKI)–based systems. However, few, if any, enterprises have actually achieved their goal. Unfortunately, the task of changing all existing applications to use a common security infrastructure is very difficult, and this has further been hampered by a lack of consensus on a common security infrastructure. As a result, the disparate proprietary and standards-based solutions cannot be applied to every system. In addition, there is a risk of a single point of failure. Should one user's password be compromised, it is not just his local system that can be breached but the entire enterprise.

Password synchronization is another means of trying to help users maintain the passwords that they use to log onto disparate systems. In this scheme, when users periodically change their passwords, the new password is applied to every account the user has rather than just one. The main objective of password synchronization is to help users remember a single, strong password. Password synchronization purports to improve security because synchronized passwords are subjected to a strong password policy, and users who remember their passwords are less likely to write them down.

The following guidelines should be used to mitigate the risk of a single system compromise being leveraged by an intruder into a network wide attack:

- Very insecure systems should not participate in a password synchronization system.
- Synchronized passwords should be changed regularly.
- Users should be required to select strong (hard to guess) passwords when synchronization is introduced.

## UNIX/Linux Specific Password Issues

Traditionally on UNIX and Linux platforms, user information (including passwords) was kept in a system file called /etc/passwd. The password for each user is stored as a hash value. Despite the password being encoded with a one-way hash function and a salt as described earlier, a password cracker could still compromise system security if she obtained access to the /etc/passwd file and used a successful dictionary attack. This vulnerability has been mitigated simply by moving the passwords in the /etc/passwd file to another file, usually named /etc/shadow and making this file readable only by those who have administrator (also called root) access to the system.

In addition, UNIX or Linux administrators should examine their password file (as well as the shadow password file when applicable) on a regular basis for potential account level security problems. In particular, it should be examined for

- accounts without passwords,
- UIDs of 0 for accounts other than root (which are also superuser accounts),
- GIDs of 0 for accounts other than root (generally, users do not have group 0 as their primary group), and
- other types of invalid or improperly formatted entries.

Note: User names and group names in UNIX and Linux are mapped into numeric forms (UIDs and GIDs, respectively). All file ownership and processes use these numerical names for access control and identity determination throughout the operating system kernel and drivers.

Under many UNIX and Linux implementations (via a shadow package), the command pwck will perform some simple syntax checking on the password file and can identify some security problems with it. pwck will report invalid usernames, UIDs and GIDs, null or nonexistent home directories, invalid shells, and entries with the wrong number of fields (often indicating extra or missing colons and other typos).

## Microsoft Specific Password Issues

Windows uses two password functions: a stronger one designed for Windows NT, 2000, and XP systems and a weaker one, the LAN Manager hash, designed for backward compatibility with older Windows 9X networking login protocols. The latter is case insensitive and does not allow passwords to be much stronger than seven characters, even though they may be much longer. These passwords are extremely vulnerable to cracking. On a standard desktop PC, for example, L0phtcrack can try every short alphanumeric password in a few minutes and every possible keyboard password (except for special ALT-characters) within a few days. Some security administrators have dealt with this problem by requiring stronger and stronger passwords; however, this comes at a cost (see "An Argument for Simplified Passwords").

In addition to implementing policies that require users to choose strong passwords, the Computer Emergency Response Team (CERT) Coordination Center provides guidelines for securing passwords on Windows systems:

- Using SYSKEY enables the private password data stored in the registry to be encrypted using a 128-bit cryptographic key. This is a unique key for each system. However, as mentioned in "Bypassing Password Security" above, physical access to the computer and an alternate boot disk can bypass this protection.

- By default, the administrator account is never locked out, so it is generally a target for brute force logon attempts of intruders. It is recommended to rename the account in User Manager. It may also be desirable to lock out the administrator account after a set number of failed attempts over the network. The NT Resource Kit provides an application called passprop.exe that enables administrator account lockout except for interactive logons on a domain controller.

- Another alternative that avoids all accounts belonging to the administrator group being locked over the network is to create a local account that belongs to the administrator group, but is not allowed to log on over the network. This account may then be used at the console to unlock the other accounts.

- The guest account should be disabled. If this account is enabled, anonymous connections can be made to Windows computers.

- The Emergency Repair Disk should be secured, as it contains a copy of the entire SAM database. If a malicious user has access to the disk, he or she may be able to launch a crack attack against it.

## How Long Should Your Password Be?

Say you start with a typical password of six characters. When you enter this into your computer's authentication mechanism, it is normally hashed and stored in a database. Because an attacker cannot try to guess passwords at a high rate through the standard user interface (the time to enter them is prohibitive, and most systems can be configured to lock out the user out after

consecutive wrong attempts), one may assume that the attacker will get them either by capturing the system password file or by sniffing the network to capture login packets.

There are, of course, many other factors to be considered here. What operating system is it? What algorithm is being used for the hash? Is there a salt? What characters will be used for inputting the password? None of these, however, will greatly affect the time needed for brute forcing all possible combinations of passwords. All an attacker really needs is one password to gain entry to a system. If there are 1,000 users on the system, he needs only to capture 0.1% of the passwords to gain entry.

Nevertheless, let us make an assumption about which characters will be used as input for a password. Each character in a password is a byte. The keyboard has 95 possible choices for each of the six password characters; this makes the password space $95^6 = 735,091,890,625$ combinations.

According to the Web site www.top500.org, several supercomputer clusters in the world can perform in excess of teraflops; that is, a million million floating point operations per second. That is only the publicized machines. It has been conjectured that agencies such as the National Security Agency (NSA) have code breaking machines that could hash and check passwords at a rate in excess of 1 billion per second, assuming there are 1,000 floating point operations required to perform a hash and check operation. The actual number, given an elegant implementation, could be somewhat lower than this. Note, as discussed in the Rainbow Tables section above, if it is possible to generate a Rainbow Table for the hashes used in the system, the time to "crack" passwords will be an order of magnitude faster—perhaps only a few seconds. However, many systems, such as Linux, use a salt to randomize the stored password hash. The time-memory trade-off technique used in generating Rainbow Tables is not practical when this type of hash is used.

How fast, then, could a high-powered attacker check every possible combination of six-character passwords? $735,091,890,625/1,000,000,000 =$ about 12 min (see Table 2).

Mind you, this is the time needed to use brute force for every possible combination of passwords. As we said earlier, password crackers will first use dictionary and hybrid attacks before resorting to brute force. Thus, if your password is weak (that is, easily guessed and not sufficiently random), the time to crack it could be much shorter.

What if the system forces users to have a seven-character password? Then it would take the attacker 19 hr to use brute force for every possible password. Many Windows networks fall under this category because of backward compatibility issues. Passwords on these systems cannot be much stronger than seven characters. Thus, it can be assumed that every password sent on a Windows system using the old LAN manager hashes could be cracked within a day.

What if the system enforces eight-character passwords? Then it would take the attacker 77 days to use brute force to obtain them all. If a system's standard policy is to require users to change passwords every 90 days, this would not be sufficient. So, it appears a nine-character

**Table 2** Password-Cracking Times of a Mythical Supercomputer[a]

| #Chars | #Combinations | Time to Crack (hrs) |
|---|---|---|
| 0 | 1 | 0.0 |
| 1 | 95 | 0.0 |
| 2 | 9025 | 0.0 |
| 3 | 857375 | 0.0 |
| 4 | 81450625 | 0.0 |
| 5 | 7737809375 | 0.0 |
| 6 | 735091890625 | 0.2 |
| 7 | 69833729609375 | 19.4 |
| 8 | 6634204312890620 | 1842.8 |
| 9 | 6.E+17 | 2.E+05 |
| 10 | 6.E+19 | 2.E+07 |
| 11 | 6.E+21 | 2.E+09 |
| 12 | 5.E+23 | 2.E+11 |
| 13 | 5.E+25 | 1.E+13 |
| 14 | 5.E+27 | 1.E+15 |
| 15 | 5.E+29 | 1.E+17 |
| 16 | 4.E+31 | 1.E+19 |

Note: Printable ASCII characters are in codes 32 through 126. ASCII codes 0–31 and 127 are unprintable characters, and 128–255 are special ALT characters that are not generally used for passwords. This leaves 95 printable ASCII characters that are usually used for password generation.

[a] Assume 1 billion hash and check operations per second.

password should be sufficient for today. Fortunately, this is still within the constraints of human memory.

## PASSWORD LENGTH AND HUMAN MEMORY

Choosing a longer password does not help much on systems with limitations such as the LAN Manager hash issue. It also does not help if a password is susceptible to a dictionary or hybrid attack. It only works if the password appears to be a random string of symbols, but that can be difficult to remember. A classic study by psychologist George Miller showed that humans work best with the magic number 7 ($\pm 2$). So it stands to reason that once a password exceeds nine characters, the user is going to have a hard time remembering it.

Here is one idea for remembering a longer password. Security professionals generally advise people never to write down their passwords. But the user could write down half of it—the part that looks like random letters and numbers—and keep it in a wallet or desk drawer. The other part could be memorized—perhaps it could be a misspelled dictionary word, the initials of an acquaintance, or something similarly memorable. When concatenated together, the resulting password could be much longer than nine characters, and therefore presumably stronger.

Some research has shown that the brain remembers images more easily than letters or numbers. Thus, a number of new schemes use sequences of graphical symbols for passwords. For example, a system called PassFace, developed by RealUser, replaces the letters and numbers in

passwords with sequences or groups of human faces. It is one of several applications that rely on graphical images for the purpose of authentication. Another company, Passlogix, has a system in which users can mix drinks in a virtual saloon or concoct chemical compounds using an onscreen periodic table of elements as a way to log onto computer networks.

## AN ARGUMENT FOR SIMPLIFIED PASSWORDS

Employing all of the guidelines for a strong password (length, mix of upper- and lowercase, numbers, punctuation, no dictionary words, no personal information, and so on) as outlined in this chapter may not be necessary after all.

According to security expert and Cybertrust Chief Technology Officer Peter Tippett, statistics show that strong password policies work only for smaller organizations. Suppose a 1,000-user organization has implemented such a strong password policy. On average, only half of the users will actually use passwords that satisfy the policy. Perhaps if the organization frequently reminds its users of the policy, and implements special software that will not allow users to have "weak" passwords, this figure can be increased to 90%. It is rare that such software can be deployed on all devices that use passwords for authentication; thus there are always some loopholes. Even with 90% compliance, this still leaves 100 easily guessed user id–password pairs. Is 100 better than 500? No, because either way, an attacker can gain access. When it comes to strong passwords, anything less than 100% compliance allows an attacker entry to the system.

Second, with modern processing power, even strong passwords are no match for current password crackers. The combination of 4-GHz clock speed desktop computers and constantly improving hash dictionaries and algorithms means that, even if 100% of the 1,000 users had passwords that met the policy, a password cracker might still be able to defeat them. Although some user id–password pairs may take days or weeks to crack, approximately 150 of the 1,000, or 15%, can usually be brute forced in a few hours.

In addition, strong passwords are expensive to maintain. Organizations spend a great deal of money supporting strong passwords. One of the highest costs of maintaining IT help desks is related to resetting forgotten user passwords. Typically, the stronger the password (i.e., the more random), the harder it is to remember. The harder it is to remember, the more help desk calls result. Help desk calls require staffing, and staffing costs money. According to estimates from such technology analysts as the Gartner Group and MetaGroup, the cost to businesses for resetting passwords is between $50 and $300 per computer user each year.

So, for most organizations, the following might be a better idea than implementing a strong password policy: simply recognize that 95% of users could use simple (but not basic) passwords—that is, good enough to keep a casual attacker (not a sophisticated password cracker) from guessing them within five attempts while sitting at a keyboard. These could be four or five characters (no names or initials) and changed perhaps once a year. In practical terms, this type of password is equivalent to the current "strong" passwords. The benefit is that it is much easier and cheaper to maintain.

Under this scenario, a system could still reserve stronger passwords for the 5% of system administrators who wield extensive control over many accounts or devices. In addition, a system should make the password file very difficult to steal. Security administrators should also introduce measures to mitigate sniffing, such as network segmentation and desktop automated inventory for sniffers and other tools. Finally, for the strongest security, a system could encrypt all network traffic with IPSec on every desktop and server.

Dr. Tippett states: "If the Promised Land is robust authentication, you can't get there with passwords alone, no matter how 'strong' they are. If you want to cut costs and solve problems, think clearly about the vulnerability, threat and cost of each risk, as well as the costs of the purported mitigation. Then find a way to make mitigation cheaper with more of a security impact."

# CONCLUSION

Passwords have been widely used in computing systems since the 1960s, and password security issues have followed closely behind. Now, the increased and very real threat of cyber crime necessitates higher security for many networks that previously seemed safe. Guaranteeing accountability on networks—that is, uniquely identifying and authenticating users' identities—is a fundamental need for modern e-commerce. Strengthening password security should be a major goal in an organization's overall security framework. Basic precautions (policies, procedures, filtering mechanisms, encryption) can help reduce risks from password weaknesses. However, lack of user buy-in and the rapid growth of sophisticated cracking tools may make any measure taken short lived. Additional measures, such as biometrics, certificates, tokens, smart cards, and other means can be very effective for strengthening authentication, but the trade-off is additional financial burden and overhead. It is not always an easy task to convince management of inherent return on these technologies, relative to other system priorities. In these instances, organizations must secure their passwords accordingly and do the best they can with available resources.

# GLOSSARY

**Access Control**  The process of limiting access to system information or resources to authorized users.

**Accountability**  The property of systems security that enables activities on a system to be traced to individuals who can then be held responsible for their actions.

**ARPANET**  The network first constructed by the Advanced Research Projects Agency of the U.S. Department of Defense (ARPA), which eventually developed into the Internet.

**Biometrics**  Technologies for measuring and analyzing living human characteristics, such as fingerprints, especially for authentication purposes. Biometrics are seen as a replacement for or augmentation of password security.

**Birthday Paradox**  The concept that it is easier to find two unspecified values that match than it is to find a match to some particular value. For example, in a room of 25 people, if 1 person tried to find another person with the same birthday, there would be little chance of a match. However, there is a very good chance that some pair of people in the room will have the same birthday.

**Brute Force**  A method of breaking decryption by trying every possible key. The feasibility of a brute force attack depends on the key length of the cipher and on the amount of computational power available to the attacker. In password cracking, tools typically use brute force to crack password hashes after attempting dictionary and hybrid attacks to try every remaining possible combination of characters.

**Cipher**  A cryptographic algorithm that encodes units of plaintext into encrypted text (or *ciphertext*) through various methods of diffusion and substitution.

**Ciphertext**  An encrypted file or message. After plaintext has undergone encryption to disguise its contents, it becomes ciphertext.

**Compatible Time Sharing System**  An IBM 7094 time-sharing operating system created at MIT Project MAC and first demonstrated in 1961. May have been the first system to use passwords.

**Computer Emergency Response Team**  An organization that provides Internet security expertise to the public. CERT is located at the Software Engineering Institute, a federally funded research and development center operated by Carnegie Mellon University. Its work includes handling computer security incidents and vulnerabilities and publishing security alerts.

**Crack, Cracking**  Traditionally, using illicit (unauthorized) actions to break into a computer system for malicious purposes. More recently, either the art or science of trying to guess passwords, or copying commercial software illegally by breaking its copy protection.

**Dictionary Attack**  A password cracking technique in which the cracker creates or obtains a list of words, names, and so on, derives hashes from the words in the list, and compares the hashes with those captured from a system user database or by sniffing.

**Entropy**  In information theory, a measure of uncertainty or randomness. The work of Claude Shannon defines it in bits per symbol.

**Green Book**  The 1985 U.S. DoD CSC-STD-002–85 publication *Password Management Guideline*, which defines good practices for safe handling of passwords in a computer system.

**Hybrid Attack**  A password cracking technique that usually takes place after a dictionary attack. In this attack, a tool will typically iterate through its word list again using adding certain combinations of a few characters to the beginning and end of each word prior to hashing. This attempt gleans any passwords that a user has created by simply appending random characters to a common word.

**Kerberos** A network authentication protocol developed at MIT to provide strong authentication for client–server applications using secret key cryptography. It keeps passwords from being sent in the clear during network communications and requires users to obtain "tickets" to use network services.

**Message Authentication Code** A small block of data derived by using a cryptographic algorithm and secret key that provide a cryptographic checksum for the input data. MACs based on cryptographic hash functions are known as HMACs.

**Moore's Law** An observation named for Intel cofounder Gordon Moore that the number of transistors per square inch of an integrated circuit has doubled every year since integrated circuits were invented. This "law" has also variously been applied to processor speed, memory size, and so on.

**Nonce** A random number that is used once in a challenge–response handshake and then discarded. The one-time use ensures that an attacker cannot inject messages from a previous exchange and appear to be a legitimate user (see **Replay Attack**).

**One-Time Password** Also called OTP. A system that requires authentication that is secure against passive attacks based on replaying captured reusable passwords. In the modern sense, OTP evolved from Bellcore's S/KEY and is described in RFC 1938.

**One-Way Hash** A fixed sized string derived from some arbitrarily long string of text, generated by a formula in such a way that it is extremely unlikely that other texts will produce the same hash value.

**Orange Book** 1983 U.S. DoD 5200.28-STD publication, *Trusted Computer System Evaluation Criteria*, which defined the assurance requirements for security protection of computer systems processing classified or other sensitive information. Superseded by the Common Criteria.

**Password Synchronization** A scheme to ensure that a known password is propagated to other target applications. If a user's password changes for one application, it also changes for the other applications that the user is allowed to log onto.

**Phishing** A play on "fishing," the idea that bait is thrown out in hopes that some victim will be tempted into biting. In a phishing scheme, an attacker sends an email falsely claiming to be an established legitimate enterprise in an attempt to entice the user into providing private information that will be used for identity theft.

**Plaintext** A message or file to be encrypted. After it is encrypted, it becomes *ciphertext*.

**Promiscuous Mode** A manner of running a network device (especially a monitoring device or sniffer) in such a way that it is able to intercept and read every network packet, regardless of its destination address. Contrast with nonpromiscuous mode, in which a device only accepts and reads packets that are addressed to it.

**Rainbow Table** Based on the work of Philippe Oechslin and Zhu Shuanglei, a lookup table that takes advantage of the time–memory trade-off to break passwords. In other words, by listing every possible hash value and providing a quick means for lookup/retrieval, it can break any possible password for a particular system and algorithm.

**Replay Attack** An attack in which a valid data transmission is captured and retransmitted in an attempt to circumvent an authentication protocol.

**Salt** A random string that is concatenated with a password before it is operated on by a one-way hashing function. It can prevent collisions by uniquely identifying a user's password, even if another user has the same password. It also makes hash matching attack strategies more difficult because it prevents an attacker from testing known dictionary words across an entire system.

**Secure Shell** An application that allows users to login to another computer over a network and execute remote commands (as in rlogin and rsh) and move files (as in FTP). It provides strong authentication and secure communications over unsecured channels.

**Secure Sockets Layer** A network session layer protocol developed by Netscape Communications Corp. to provide security and privacy over the Internet. It supports server and client authentication, primarily for HTTP communications. SSL is able to negotiate encryption keys as well as authenticate the server to the client before data are exchanged.

**Security Account Manager** On Windows systems, the secure portion of the system registry that stores user account information, including a hash of the user account password. The SAM is restricted via access control measures to administrators only and may be further protected using SYSKEY.

**Shadow Password File** In the UNIX or Linux, a system file in which encrypted user passwords are stored so they are inaccessible to unauthorized users.

**Single Sign-On** A mechanism whereby a single action of user authentication and authorization can permit a user to access all computers and systems on which that user has access permission, without the need to enter multiple passwords.

**Sniffing** The processes of monitoring communications on a network segment via a wiretap device (either software or hardware). Typically, a sniffer also has some sort of "protocol analyzer" that allows it to decode the computer traffic on which it is eavesdropping and make sense of it.

**Social Engineering** An outside hacker's use of psychological tricks on legitimate users of a computer system to gain the information (e.g., user ids and passwords) needed to gain access to a system.

**SYSKEY** On Windows systems, a tool that provides encryption of account password hash information to prevent administrators from intentionally or unintentionally accessing these hashes using system registry programming interfaces.

## CROSS REFERENCES

See *Access Control: Principles and Solutions; Computer and Network Authentication; Encryption Basics; Hackers, Crackers and Computer Criminals; Hashes and Message Digests.*

# REFERENCES

Brotzman, R. L. (1985). *Password management guideline* (Green Book). Baltimore, MD: Department of Defense Computer Security Center, Fort George G. Meade.

Brown, A. (2002). *U.K. study: Passwords often easy to crack*. Retrieved January 3, 2005, from http://www.cnn.com/2002/TECH/ptech/03/13/dangerous.passwords/index.html

CERT Coordination Center. (2002). *Windows NT configuration guidelines*. Retrieved January 3, 2005, from http://www.cert.org/tech_tips/win_configuration_guidelines.html

CYHIST. (2004). *Cyberspace history list-server*. Retrieved January 2, 2005, from http://maelstrom.stjohns.edu/archives/cyhist.html

SANS Institute. (2005). *The twenty most critical Internet security vulnerabilities*. Retrieved January 3, 2005, from http://www.sans.org/top20.htm

Tippett, P. (2001). Stronger passwords aren't. *Information Security*. Retrieved January 2, 2005, from http://www.infosecuritymag.com/articles/june01/columns_executive_view.shtml

Zatko, P. "Mudge" (1999a). *L0phtCrack 2.5 Readme.doc*. Boston, MA: L0pht Heavy Industries, Inc. [now @stake, Inc.].

# SOFTWARE TOOL REFERENCE

Cain & Abel (computer software). Retrieved 2005 from http://www.oxid.it

Cracklib and associated PAM modules (computer software). Retrieved 2005 from http://www.kernel.org/pub/linux/libs/pam/Linux-PAM-html/pam.html

ElcomSoft (computer software). Retrieved 2005 from http://www.elcomsoft.com/prs.html

Intertek (computer software). Retrieved 2005 from http://www.intertek.org.uk/downloads

John the Ripper (computer software). Retrieved 2005 from http://www.openwall.com/john

LC5 (L0phtcrack 5) (computer software). Retrieved 2005 from http://www.atstake.com

Microsoft Baseline Security Analyzer V1.2.1 (computer software). Retrieved 2005 from http://www.microsoft.com/technet/security/tools/mbsahome.mspx

NT Password Recovery (computer software). Retrieved 2005 from http://home.eunet.no/~pnordahl/ntpasswd/

Npasswd (computer software for SunOS 4/5, Digital UNIX, HP/UX, and AIX). Retrieved 2005 from http://www.utexas.edu/cc/UNIX/software/npasswd

Pandora (computer software). Retrieved 2005 from http://www.nmrc.org/project/pandora/index.html

Passfilt (computer software). Retrieved 2005 from http://support.microsoft.com/kb/q161990/

Passlogix (computer software). Retrieved 2005 from http://www.passlogix.com

Project RainbowCrack (computer software). Retrieved 2005 from http://www.antsight.com/zsl/rainbowcrack

PWDUMP2 (computer software). Retrieved 2005 from http://www.bindview.com/Support/RAZOR/Utilities/Windows/pwdump2_readme.cfm

RealUser (computer software). Retrieved 2005 from http://www.realuser.com

# FURTHER READING

Barbalace, R. J. (1999). *How to choose a good password (and why you should)*. Retrieved January 2, 2005, from http://www.mit.edu/afs/sipb/project/doc/passwords/passwords.html

Bobby, P. (2000). *Password cracking using focused dictionaries*. Retrieved January 2, 2005, from http://www.totse.com/en/hack/hack_attack/162116.html

Botzum, K. (2001). *Single sign on—A contrarian view*. Retrieved January 3, 2005, from http://www7b.software.ibm.com/wsdd/library/techarticles/0108_botzum/botzum.html

Curry, D. A. (1990). *Improving the security of your UNIX system*. Retrieved January 3, 2005, from http://www.alw.nih.gov/Security/Docs/UNIX-security.html

Donovan, C. (2000). *Strong passwords*. Retrieved January 2, 2005, from http://www.giac.org/pratical/GSEC/Craig_Donovan_GSEC.pdf

Frisch, A. (2002). *Essential system administration* (3rd ed.). Sebastopol, CA: O'Reilly & Associates.

Jablon, D. P. (1997). Extended password key exchange protocols immune to dictionary attack. In *Proceedings of the 6th Workshop on Enabling Technologies*. Infrastructure for Collaborative Enterprises, Institute of Electrical and Electronics Engineers, Inc. Retrieved online January 3, 2005, from http://csdl2.computer.org/persagen/DLAbsToc.jsp?resourcePath=/dl/proceedings/&toc=comp/proceedings/wetice/1997/7967/00/7967toc.xml&DOI=10.1109/ENABL.1997.630822

LabMice.net (2003). *How to Bypass BIOS Passwords*. Retrieved January 3, 2005, from http://labmice.techtarget.com/articles/BIOS_hack.htm

Litchfield, D. (2002). *Hackproofing Oracle application server (a guide to securing Oracle 9)*. Retrieved January 3, 2005, from http://www.nextgenss.com/papers/hpoas.pdf

Luby, M., & Rackoff, C. (1989). A study of password security. *Journal of Cryptology, 1*(3), 151–158.

McGraw, G., & Viega, J. (2000). *Protecting passwords: Part 1*. Retrieved January 2, 2005, from http://www-106.ibm.com/developerworks/library/s-pass1

Morris, R. T., & Thompson, K. (1979). Password security: A case history. *Communications of the ACM, 22*(11). Retrieved January 3, 2005, from http://portal.acm.org/citation.cfm?id=359168.359172.

Netscape. (2002). *Choosing a good password*. Retrieved January 2, 2005, from http://channels.netscape.com/ns/browsers/sec_password.jsp

Nomad, S. (1997). *The unofficial NT hack FAQ*. Retrieved January 2, 2005, from http://www.secinf.net/windows_security/The_Unofficial_NT_Hack_FAQ

Oechslin, Philippe (2003). *Making a faster cryptanalytic time-memory trade-off*. Retrieved August 1, 2005, from http://lasecwww.epfl.ch/pub/lasec/doc/Oech03.pdf

Raymond, E. S. (1998). A brief history of hackerdom. *In Open sources: Voices from the open source revolution* (1st ed.). Sebastopol, CA: O'Reilly & Associates.

Russell, R. (Ed.). (2002). *Hack proofing your network.* Rockland, MA: Syngress.

Sanjour, J., Arensburger, A., & Brink, A. (2000). *Choosing a good password.* Retrieved January 2, 2005, from http://www.cs.umd.edu/faq/Passwords.shtml

Schneier, B. (2000). *Secrets & lies: Digital security in a networked world.* New York: John Wiley & Sons.

Smith, R. E. (2001). *Authentication: From passwords to public keys.* Boston, MA: Addison Wesley Longman.

Zatko, P. "Mudge" (1999b). *Vulnerabilities in the S/KEY one time password system.* Retrieved January 3, 2005, from http://www.UNIX.geek.org.uk/~arny/junk/skeyflaws.html

# Computer and Network Authentication

Patrick McDaniel, *Pennsylvania State University*

Authentication is the process by which the identity of an entity is established. Authenticating entities present credentials, such as passwords or certificates, as evidence of their identity. The entity is deemed authentic where presented credentials are valid and sufficient. Note that authentication does not determine which entities should be given access but only verifies that an entity is who they claim to be. However, it is only after an entity is authenticated that their rights to resources can be assessed (through authorization). Hence, failure to correctly authenticate users on the Internet can leave on-line resources vulnerable to misuse.

This article considers the semantics, methods, and mechanisms for authentication on the Internet. The goals and principles of authentication are illustrated through several expository systems. The embodied trust, operation, and limitations of these systems are explored. This article is concluded with a number of axioms for the selection and use of authentication systems on the Internet.

## AUTHENTICATION

An authentication process establishes the identity of some entity under scrutiny. For example, a traveler authenticates herself to a border guard by presenting a passport. Possession of the passport and resemblance to the attached photograph is deemed sufficient proof that the traveler is the identified person. The act of validating the passport (by checking a database of known passport serial numbers) and assessing the resemblance of the traveler is a form of authentication.

On the Internet, authentication is somewhat more complex; network entities do not typically have physical access to the parties they are authenticating. Malicious users or programs may attempt to obtain sensitive information, disrupt service, or forge data by impersonating valid entities. Distinguishing these malicious parties from valid entities is the role of authentication, and is essential to network security.

Successful authentication does not imply that the authenticated entity is given access. An authorization process uses authentication, possibly with other information, to make decisions about whom to give access. For example, not all authenticated travelers will be permitted to enter the country. Other factors, such as the existence of visas, past criminal record, and political climate will determine which travelers are allowed to enter the country.

Although the preceding discussion has focused on *entity authentication*, it is important to note that other forms of authentication exist. In particular, *message authentication* is the process by which a particular message is associated with some sending entity. Message authentication is a continuous process, where the sender of each new message must be constantly evaluated. Such evaluation is typically performed with respect to some identity previously authenticated (i.e., through entity authentication). This article restricts itself to entity authentication, deferring discussion of forms to other entries in this encyclopedia.

## Meet Alice and Bob

Authentication is often illustrated through the introduction of two protagonists, Alice and Bob. In these descriptions, Alice attempts to authenticate herself to Bob. Note that in practice, Alice and Bob may not be users but computers. For example, a computer must authenticate itself to a file server prior to being given access to its contents. Independent of whether Alice is a computer or person, she must present evidence of her identity. Bob evaluates this evidence, commonly referred to as a credential. Alice is deemed authentic (is authenticated) by Bob if the evidence is consistent with information associated with her claimed identity. The form of Alice's credential determines the strength and semantics of authentication.

The most widely used authentication credential is a password. To illustrate, UNIX passwords configured by system administrators reside in the `/etc/passwd` file. During the login process, Alice (a UNIX user) types her password into the host console. Bob (the authenticating UNIX operating system) compares the input to the known password. Bob assumes that Alice is the only entity in possession of the password. Hence, Bob deems Alice authentic because she is the only one who could present the password credential.

Note that Bob's assertion that Alice is the only entity who could have supplied the password is not strictly accurate. Passwords are subject to *guessing* attacks. Such an attack continually retries different passwords until the authentication is successful. Many systems combat this problem by disabling authentication of that identity after a threshold of failed authentication attempts. The more serious *dictionary* attack makes use of the UNIX password file itself. Passwords are not stored in their original form. The password and a random salt value are cryptographically hashed and the result is stored. Because the hash function is guaranteed to be noninvertible, someone who gains access to the password file cannot trivially recover the passwords. However, a malicious party who obtains the password file can mount a dictionary attack by comparing hashed, salted password guesses against the password file's contents. Such an attack bypasses the authentication service and hence is difficult to combat. Recent systems have sought to mitigate attacks on the password file by placing the password hash values in a highly restricted *shadow password* file.

Passwords are subject to more fundamental attacks. In one such attack, the adversary simply obtains the password from Alice directly. This can occur when Alice "shares" her password with others or when she records it in some obvious place (e.g., on her PDA). Such attacks illustrate an axiom of security: a system is only as secure as the protection afforded to its secrets. In the case of authentication, failure to adequately protect credentials from misuse can result in the compromise of the system.

The definition of the identity has historically been controversial. This is largely because authentication does not truly identify physical entities but associates some secret or (presumably) unforgeable information with a virtual identity. Hence, for the purposes of authentication, any entity in possession of Alice's password is Alice. The strength of authentication is determined by the difficulty with which a malicious party can circumvent the authentication process and incorrectly assume an identity. In our above example, the strength of the authentication process is largely determined by the difficulty of guessing Alice's password. Note that other factors, such as whether Alice chooses a poor password or writes it on the front of the monitor, will determine the effectiveness of authentication. The lesson here is that authentication is as strong as the weakest link; failure to protect the password either by Alice or the host limits the effectiveness of the solution.

Authentication on the Internet is often more complex than suggested by the previous example. Often, Alice and Bob are not physically colocated. Hence, both parties will wish to authenticate each other. In our above example, Alice will wish to ensure that she is communicating with Bob. However, no formal process is needed; because Alice is sitting at the terminal, she assumes that Bob (the host) is authentic.

On the Internet, it is not always reasonable to assume that Alice and Bob have (or can) established some relationship prior to communication. For example, consider the case where Alice is purchasing goods on the Internet.

Alice goes to Bob's Web server, identifies the goods she wishes to purchase, provides her credit card information, and submits the transaction. Alice, being a cautious customer, wants to ensure that this information is only being given to Bob's Web server (i.e., authenticate the Web server). In general, however, requiring Alice to establish a direct relationship with each vendor from whom she may purchase goods is not feasible (e.g., not feasible to establish passwords for each Web site out-of-band).

Enter Trent, the trusted third party. Logically, Alice appeals to Trent for authentication information relating to Bob. Trent is trusted by Alice to assert Bob's authenticity. Therefore, Bob need only establish a relationship with Trent to begin communicating with Alice. Because the number of widely used trusted third parties is small (on the order of tens), and every Web site establishes a relationship with at least one of them, Alice can authenticate virtually every vendor on the Internet.

## CREDENTIALS

Authentication is performed by the evaluation of credentials supplied by the user (i.e., Alice). Such credentials can take the form of something you know (e.g., password), something you have (e.g., smartcard), or something you are (e.g., fingerprint). The credential type is specific to the authentication service and reflects some direct or indirect relationship between the user and the authentication service.

Credentials often take the form of shared secret knowledge. Users authenticate themselves by proving knowledge of the secret. In the UNIX example above, knowledge of the password is deemed sufficient evidence to prove user identity. In general, such secrets need not be statically defined passwords. For example, users in one-time password authentication systems do not present knowledge of secret text but identify a numeric value valid only for a single authentication. Users need not present the secret directly but demonstrate knowledge of it (e.g., by presenting evidence that could only be derived from it).

Secrets are often long random numbers and thus cannot be easily remembered by users. For example, a typical RSA private-key is a 1024-digit binary number. Requiring a user to remember this number is at the very least, unreasonable. Such information is frequently stored in a file on a user's host computer, a PDA, or other nonvolatile storage. The private key is used during authentication by accessing the appropriate file. However, private keys can be considered "secret knowledge" because the user presents evidence external to the authentication system (e.g., from the file system).

Credentials may also be physical objects. For example, a smartcard may be required to gain access to a host. Authenticity in these systems is inferred from possession rather than knowledge. Note that there is often a subtle difference between the knowledge and possession based credentials. For example, it is often the case that a user-specific private key is stored on an authenticating smartcard. In this case, however, the user has no ability to view or modify the private key. The user can only be authenticated via the smartcard issued to the user. Hence, for the purposes of authentication, the smartcard is identity; no amount of effort can modify the identity encoded in the smartcard.[1]

Biometric devices measure physical characteristics of the human body. An individual is deemed authentic if the measured aspect matches previously recorded data. The accuracy of matching determines the quality of authentication. Contemporary biometric devices include fingerprint, retina, or iris scanners and face recognition software. However, biometric devices are primarily useful only where the scanning device is trusted (i.e., under control of the authentication service). Although biometric authentication has seen limited use in the Internet, it is increasingly used to support authentication associated with physical security (i.e., governing clean room access).

Credential use is subject to eavesdropping and replay. For example, any adversary can watch a user type a password from across the room. The adversary later uses the password to gain access to the system. This problem only gets worse in networks: anyone who can get access to the messages used to authenticate users could potentially reuse the data to masquerade as a legitimate user. Such attacks are mitigated in authentication systems by requiring *freshness*. Freshness guarantees that the use of a credential is bounded in time and hence could not possibly be replayed. The following sections demonstrate several methods for achieving freshness.

Multifactor authentication systems use more than one system to authenticate the user. For example, some systems require both a password and a token to prove identity. These systems can significantly increase the difficulty of attacks on the authentication. It is much harder to eavesdrop a password and a steal a token than it is to do one or the other. Multifactor systems have been seen as valuable way to increase security while maintaining the simplicity and ease of use of traditional authentication mechanisms and have been widely adopted in corporate environments.

Credentials need not identify a particular entity but can be used to prove some characteristic of a community. For example, a concert ticket serves as a credential that the owner has paid or received permission to the show. *Reverse turning tests* use tasks that cannot easily be performed by a computer (e.g., such as extracting text from complex images). The correct answer shows that a human was involved. Such tests are useful in preventing online "scripted" attacks.

## Authentication Services

A number of general purpose services have been developed to support authentication, credential maintenance, access control, and accounting. For example, RADIUS-, DIAMETER-, and LDAP-based authentication services have been widely deployed on the Internet. Networks subscribing to these services defer all authentication related activities to these centralized services. Each such system can supports a range of authentication services and protocols appropriate for the served environment.

In addition to authentication, these services typically implement access control for the controlled environment. *Access control* regulates access to valued infrastructure or data. For example, all users are authenticated when entering most networks. However, this (typically) does not give total access to the entire network. An access control service determines, based on the identity established via authentication, which services that entity user has a right to access (e.g., file servers and printers). How access control is performed and results presented to the network is beyond the scope of this chapter.

Authentication services exist to simplify network management. Because of the way technology has evolved, the diverse services comprising a network often require different methods of authentication. Supporting the many authentication methods required by an environment (or many instantiations of a single authentication service) can be enormously costly. Administrators can vastly simplify the administrative process by managing a single database of identities in the authentication services. The services can use whatever credentials are deemed necessary, so long as they are supported by the authentication service. Similarly, new applications can be developed and easily integrated with the existing authentication service through well-defined interfaces. Existing authentication services (nearly) universally support the authentication services defined in this article.

# WEB AUTHENTICATION

One of the most prevalent uses of the Internet is Web browsing. Users access the Web via specialized protocols that communicate HTML and XML requests and content. The requesting user's Web browser renders received content. However, it is often necessary to restrict access to Web content. Moreover, the interactions between the user and a Web server are often required to be private. One aspect of securing content is the use of authentication to establish the true or virtual identity of clients and Web servers.

## Password-Based Web Access

Web servers initially adopted well-known technologies for user authentication. Foremost among these was the use of passwords. To illustrate the use of passwords on the Web, the following describes the configuration and use of *basic authentication* in the Apache Web server (Apache, 2002). Note that the use of basic authentication in other Web servers is largely similar.

Access to content protected by basic authentication in the Apache Web server is indirectly governed by the password file. Web site administrators create the password file (whose location is defined by the Web site administrator) by entering user and password information using the `htpasswd` utility. It is assumed that the passwords are given to the users using an *out-of-band channel* (e.g., via e-mail or phone).

In addition to specifying passwords, the Web server must identify the subset of Web content to be password protected (e.g., set of protected URLs). This is commonly performed by creating a `.htaccess` file in the directory

---

[1] In practice, contemporary smartcards can be modified or probed. However, because such manipulation often takes considerable effort and sophistication (e.g., use of an electron microscope) such attacks are beyond the vast majority of attackers.

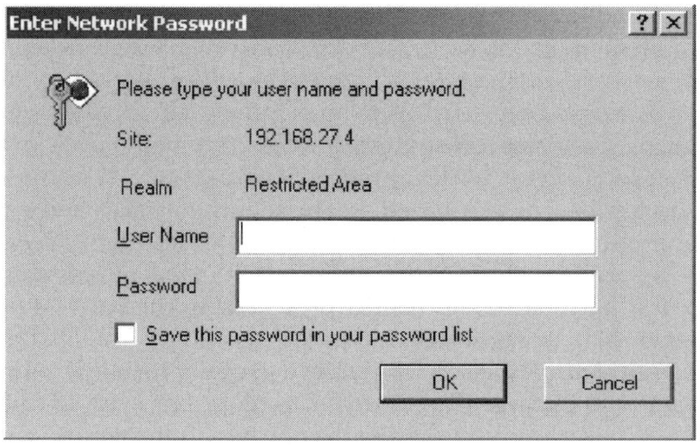

**Figure 1:** Password Authentication on the Web

to be protected. The `.htaccess` file defines the authentication type and specifies the location of the relevant password file. For example, located in the content root directory, the following `.htaccess` file restricts access to those users who are authenticated via password.

```
AuthName "Restricted Area"
AuthType Basic
AuthUserFile /var/www/Webaccess
require valid-user
```

Users accessing protected content (via a browser) are presented with a password dialog (e.g., similar to the dialog depicted in Figure 1). The user enters the appropriate username and password and, if correct, is given access to the Web content.

Because basic authentication sends passwords over the Internet in clear-text, it is relatively simple to recover them by eavesdropping on the HTTP communication. Hence, basic authentication is sufficient to protect content from casual misuse but should not be used to protect valuable or sensitive data. However, as is commonly found on commercial Web sites, performing basic authentication over more secure protocols (e.g., see "SSL") can mitigate or eliminate many of the negative properties of basic authentication.

Many password-protected Web sites store user passwords (in encrypted form) in *cookies* the first time a user is authenticated. In these cases, the browser automatically submits the cookie to the Web site with each request. This approached eliminates the need for the user to be authenticated every time she visits the Web site. However, this convenience has a price. In most single-user operating systems, any entity using the same host will be logged in as the user. Moreover, the cookies can be easily captured and replayed back to the Web site (Fu, Sit, Smith, & Feamster, 2001).

Digest authentication uses *challenges* to mitigate the limitations of password-based authentication (Franks et al., 1999). Challenges allow authenticating parties to prove knowledge of secrets without exposing (transmitting) them. In digest authentication, Bob sends a random number (*nonce*) to Alice. Alice responds with a hash of the random number and her password. Bob uses Alice's password (which only he and Alice know) to compute the correct response and compares it to the one received from Alice. Alice is deemed authentic if the computed and

received responses match (because only Alice could have generated the response). Because the hash, rather than the secret, is sent, no adversary can obtain Alice's password from the response.

## Single Sign-On

Password authentication is the predominant authentication method on the Web. Users register a username and password with each retailer or service provider with which they do business. Hence, users are often faced with the difficult and error-prone task of maintaining a long list of usernames and passwords. In practice, users avoid this maintenance headache by using the same passwords on all Web sites. However, this allows adversaries who gain access to the user information on one site to impersonate the user on many others.

A *single sign-on* system (SSO) defers user authentication to a single, universal authentication service. Users authenticate themselves to the SSO once per session. Subsequently, each service requiring user authentication is redirected to a SSO server that vouches for the user. Hence, the user is required to maintain only a single authentication credential (e.g., SSO password). Note that the services themselves do not possess user credentials (e.g., passwords) but simply trust the SSO to state which users are authentic.

Although single sign-on services have been used for many years (e.g., see "Kerberos" below), the lack of universal adoption and cost of integration has made their use in Web applications highly undesirable. These difficulties have led to the creation of SSO services targeted specifically to authentication on the Web. One of the most popular of these systems is the *Microsoft Passport* service (Microsoft, 2002). Passport provides a single authentication service and repository of user information. Web sites and users initially negotiate secrets during the Passport registration process (i.e., user passwords and Web site secret keys). In all cases, these secrets are known only to the Passport servers and the registering entity.

Passport authentication proceeds as follows. Users requesting a protected Web page (i.e., page that requires authentication) are redirected to a Passport server. The user is authenticated via a Passport supplied login screen. If successful, the user is redirected back to the original Web site with an authentication *cookie* specific to that site. The cookie contains user information and site specific information encrypted with a secret key known only to the site and the Passport server. The Web site decrypts and validates the received cookie contents. If successful, the user is deemed authentic and the session proceeds. Subsequent user authentication (with other sites) proceeds similarly, except that the login step is avoided. Successful completion of the initial login is noted in a session cookie stored at the user browser and presented to the Passport server with later authentication requests.

Although SSO systems solve many of the problems of authentication on the Web, they are not a panacea. By definition, SSO systems introduce a single point of trust for all users in the system. Hence, ensuring that the SSO is not poorly implemented, poorly administered, or malicious is essential to its safe use. For example, Passport has been shown to have several crucial flaws (Kormann & Rubin,

2000). Note that although existing Web-oriented SSO systems may be extended to support mutual authentication, the vast majority have yet to do so.

## Certificates

Although passwords are appropriate for restricting access to Web content, they are not appropriate for more general Internet authentication needs. Consider the Web site for an on-line bookstore *examplebooks.com*. Users wishing to purchase books from this site must be able to determine that the Web site is authentic. If not authenticated, a malicious party may impersonate *examplebooks.com* and fool the user into exposing his credit card information.

Note that most Web-enabled commercial transactions do not authenticate the user directly. The use of credit card information is deemed sufficient evidence of the user's identity. However, such evidence is typically evaluated through the credit card issuer service (e.g., checking that the credit card is valid and has not exceeded its spending limit) before the purchased goods are provided to the buyer.

The dominant technology used for Internet Web site authentication is public key certificates. Certificates provide a convenient and scalable mechanism for authentication in large distributed environments (such as the Internet). Note that certificates are used to enable authentication of a vast array of other non-Web services. For example, certificates are often used to authenticate electronic mail messages (see "PGP" below).

Certificates are used to document an association between an identity and a cryptographic key. Keys in public key cryptography are generated in pairs; a public and private key (Diffie & Hellman, 1976). As the name would suggest, the public key is distributed freely, and the private key is kept secret. To simplify, any data signed (using a digital signature algorithm) by the private key can be validated using the public key. A valid digital signature can be mapped to exactly one private key. Therefore, any valid signature can only be generated by some entity in possession of the private key. Conversely, keys in secret cryptography use a single shared secret key. Although often more efficient public key algorithms, secret key cryptography requires the communicating parties negotiate a secret before communicating.

Certificates are issued by *certification authorities* (CA). The CA issues a certificate by signing an identity (e.g.,

domain name of the Web site), validity dates, and a Web site's public key. The certificate is then freely distributed. A user validates a received certificate by checking the CA's digital signature. Note that most browsers are installed with a collection of CA certificates that are invariantly trusted (i.e., do not need to be validated). For example, many Web sites publish certificates issued by the Verisign CA (Verisign, 2002), whose certificate is installed with most browsers. In its most general form, a system used to distribute and validate certificates is called a *public key infrastructure* (PKI).

Certificate technologies such as those supported by PGP are the basis of S/MIME standards (Dusse et al., 1998). S/MIME defines protocols, data structures, and certificate management infrastructures for authentication and confidentiality of MIME (multipurpose Internet mail extensions) data. These standards are being widely adopted as a means to secure personal and enterprise e-mail.

## SSL

Introduced by Netscape in 1994, the Secure Socket Layer (SSL) protocol uses certificates to authenticate Web content. In addition to authenticating users and Web sites, the SSL protocol negotiates an ephemeral secret key. This key is subsequently used to protect the integrity and confidentiality of all messages (e.g., by encrypting the messages sent between the Web server and the client). SSL continues to evolve. For example, the standardized and widely deployed TLS (transport layer security) protocol is directly derived from SSL version 3.0.

The use of SSL is signaled to the browser and Web site through the `https` URL protocol identifier. For example, Alice enters the following URL to access a Web site of interest:

```
https://www.example.com/
```

In response to this request, Alice's browser will initiate a SSL handshake protocol. If the Web site is correctly authenticated via SSL, the browser will retrieve and render Web site content in a manner similar to HTTP. Authentication is achieved in SSL by validating statements signed by private keys associated with the authenticated party's public key certificate.

Figure 2 depicts the operation of the SSL authentication and key agreement process. The *SSL handshake*

**Figure 2:** The SSL Protocol: Alice (the client) and Bob (the server) exchange an initial handshake identifying the kind of authentication and configuration of the subsequent session security. As dictated by the authentication requirements identified in the handshake, Alice and Bob may exchange and authenticate certificates. The protocol completes by establishing a session-specific key used to secure (e.g., encrypt) later communication.

*protocol* authenticates one or both parties, negotiates the cipher suite policy for subsequent communication (e.g., selecting cryptographic algorithms and parameters), and establishes a *master secret*. All messages occurring after the initial handshake are protected using cryptographic keys derived from the master secret.

The handshake protocol begins with both Alice (the end user browser) and Bob (the Web server) identifying a cipher suite policy and session identifying information. In the second phase, Alice and Bob exchange certificates. Note that policy will determine which entities require authentication: as dictated by policy, Alice and/or Bob will request an authenticating certificate. The certificate is validated upon reception (e.g., issuance signature checked against CAs whose certificate is installed with the browser). Note that in almost all cases, Bob will be authenticated, but Alice will not. In these cases, Bob typically authenticates Alice using some external means (only when it becomes necessary). For example, online shopping Web sites will not authenticate Alice until she expresses a desire to purchase goods, and her credit card number is used to validate her identity at the point of purchase.

Interleaved with the certificate requests and responses is the server and client key exchange. This process authenticates each side by signing information used to negotiate a session key. The signature is generated using the private key associated with the certificate of the party to be authenticated. A valid signature is deemed sufficient evidence because only an entity in possession of the private key could have generated it. Hence, signed data can be accepted as proof of authenticity. The session key is derived from the signed data, and the protocol completes with Alice and Bob sending *finished* messages.

## HOST AUTHENTICATION

Most computers on the Internet provide some form of *remote access*. Remote access allows users or programs to access resources on a given computer from anywhere on the Internet. This access enables a promise of the Internet: independence from physical location. However, remote access has often been the source of many security vulnerabilities. Hence, protecting these computers from unauthorized use is essential. The means by which host authentication is performed in large part determines the degree to which an enterprise or user is protected from malicious parties lurking in the dark corners of the Internet. This section reviews the design and use of the predominant methods providing host authentication.

### Remote Login

Embodying the small, isolated UNIX networks of old, *remote login* utilities allow administrators to identify the set of hosts and users that are deemed "trusted." Trusted hosts are authenticated by source IP address, hostname, and/or username only. Hence, trusted users and hosts need not provide a username or password.

The `rlogin` and `rsh` programs are used to access hosts. Configured by local administrators, the `/etc/ hosts. equiv` file enumerates hosts/users that are trusted. Similarly, the `.rhosts` file contained in each

users home directory identifies the set of hosts trusted by an individual user. When a user connects to a remote host with a remote login utility, the remote login server (running on the accessed host) scans the `hosts.equiv` configuration file for the address and username of the connecting host. If found, the user is deemed authentic and allowed access. If not, the `.rhosts` file of the accessing user (identified in the connection request) is scanned and access is granted where the source address and username is matched.

The remote access utilities do not provide strong authentication. Malicious parties may trivially forge IP addresses, DNS records, and usernames (called *spoofing*). Although recent attempts have been made to address the security limitations of the IP protocol stack (e.g., IPsec and DNSsec), this information is widely accepted as untrustworthy. Remote access tools trade off security for ease of access. In practice, these tools often weaken the security of network environments by providing a vulnerable authentication mechanism. Hence, the use of such tools in any environment connected to the Internet is considered extremely dangerous.

### SSH

The early standards for remote access, `telnet` and `ftp`, authenticated users by UNIX password. Although the means of authentication were similar to terminal login, their use on an open network introduces new vulnerabilities. Primarily, these utilities are vulnerable to password sniffing. Such attacks passively listen on the network for communication between the host and the remote user.[2] Because passwords are sent in the clear (unencrypted), user-specific authentication information could be recovered. For this reason, the use of these utilities as a primary means of user access has largely been abandoned.[3]

The secure shell (SSH) (Ylonen, 1996) combats the limitations of standard tools by performing cryptographically supported host and/or user authentication. Similar to SSL, a byproduct of the authentication is a cryptographic key used to obscure and protect communication between the user and remote host. SSH is not vulnerable to sniffing attacks and has been widely adopted as a replacement for the standard remote access tools.

SSH uses public key cryptography for authentication. Upon installation, each server host (host allowing remote access via SSH) generates a public key pair. The public key is manually stored at each initiating host (host from which a user will remotely connect). Note that unlike SSL, SSH uses public keys directly rather than issued certificates. Hence, SSH authentication relies on the due diligence of host administrators to maintain the correct set of host keys.

---

[2] The physical media over which many local network communication occurs is Ethernet. Because Ethernet is a broadcast technology, all hosts on the local network (subnet) receive every bit of transmitted data. Obviously, this approach simplifies communication eavesdropping. Although eavesdropping may be more difficult over nonbroadcast media (e.g., switched networks), it is by no means impossible.

[3] `ftp` is frequently used on the Web to transfer files. When used in this context, `ftp` generally operates in *anonymous* mode. `ftp` performs no authentication in this mode, and the users are often restricted to file retrieval only.

SSH initiates a session in two phases. In the first phase, the server host is authenticated. The initiating host creates the SSH session by requesting remote access. To simplify, the requesting host generates a random session key, encrypts it with the received host public key of the server, and forwards it back to the server.[4] The server recovers the session key using its host private key. Subsequent communication between the hosts is protected using the session key. Because only someone in possession of the host private key could have recovered the session key, the server is deemed authentic.

The second phase of the SSH session initialization authenticates the user. Dictated by the configured policy, the server will use one of the following methods to authenticate the user:

- *.rhosts file*: as described for the *remote access* utilities, it simply tests whether the accessing user identifier is present in the .rhosts file located in the home directory of the user.
- *.rhosts with RSA*: similar to previous but requires that the accessing host is authenticated via a known and trusted RSA public key.
- *password authentication*: prompts the user for local system password. The strength of this approach is determined by the extent to which the user keeps the password private.
- *RSA user authentication*: authenticates via a user-specific RSA public key. Of course, this requires that the server be configured with the public key generated for each user.

Note that it is not always feasible to obtain the public key of each host that a user will access. Host keys may change frequently (as based on an administrative policy), be compromised, or accidentally deleted. Hence, where the remote host key is not known (and the configured policy allows it), SSH will simply transmit it during session initialization. The user is asked if the received key should be accepted. If accepted, the key is stored in the local environment and is subsequently used to authenticate the host.

Although the automated key distribution mode does provide additional protection over conventional remote access utilities (e.g., eavesdropping prevention), the authentication mechanism provides few guarantees. A user accepting the public key knows little about its origin (e.g., is subject to forgery and man-in-the-middle attacks). Hence, this mode may be undesirable for some environments.

## One-Time Passwords

In a very different approach to combating password sniffing, the S/Key system (Haller, 1994) limits the usefulness of recovered passwords. Passwords in the S/Key system

are valid only for a single authentication. Hence, a malicious party gains nothing by recovery of a previous password (e.g., via eavesdropping of a telnet login). Although on the surface one-time password approach may seem to require that the password be changed following each login, the way in which passwords are generated alleviates the need for repeated coordination between the user and remote host.

The S/Key system establishes an ordered list of passwords. Each password is used in order and only once and then discarded. Although the maintenance of the password list may seem like an unreasonable burden to place on a user, the way in which the passwords are generated makes it conceptually simple. Essentially, passwords are created such that the knowledge of a past password provides no information on future passwords. However, if one knows a secret value (called a seed value), then all passwords are easily computable. Hence, although an authentic user can supply passwords as they are needed, a malicious adversary can only supply those passwords that have been previously used (and are no longer valid).

In essence, the S/Key system allows the user to prove knowledge of the password without explicitly stating it. Over time, this relatively simple approach has been found to be extremely powerful and is used as the basis of many authentication services. For example, RSA's widely used SecurID combines a physical token with one-time password protocols to authenticate users (RSA, 2002).

## Kerberos

The Kerberos system (Neuman and Ts'o, 1994) performs *trusted third party* authentication. In Kerberos, users, hosts, and services defer authentication to a mutually trusted key distribution center (KDC). All users implicitly trust the KDC to act in their best interest. Hence, this approach is appropriate for localized environments (e.g., campuses and enterprises) but does not scale well to large, loosely coupled communities. Note that this is not an artifact only of the Kerberos system but true of any trusted third party approach; loosely coupled communities are unlikely to universally trust any single authority.

Depicted in Figure 3, the Kerberos system performs mediated authentication between Alice and Bob through a two-phase exchange with the KDC. When logging onto the system, Alice enters her username and password.

Alice's host sends the KDC her identity. In response, the KDC sends Alice information that can be understood only by someone in possession of the password (i.e., is encrypted with a key derived from the password). Included in this information is a ticket granting ticket (TGT) used later by Alice to initiate a session with Bob. Alice is deemed authentic because she is able to recover the TGT.

At some later point, Alice wishes to perform mutual authentication with another entity, Bob. Alice informs the KDC of this desire by identifying Bob and presenting the previously obtained TGT. Alice receives a message from the KDC containing the session key and a ticket for Bob. Encrypting the message with a key known only to Alice ensures that its contents remain confidential.

Alice then presents the ticket included in the message to Bob. Note that the ticket returned to Alice is opaque;

---

[4] In reality, the server initially transmits a short-term public key in addition to the host key. The requesting host encrypts the random value response with both keys. The use of the short-term keys prevents adversaries from recovering the content of past sessions should the host key become compromised.

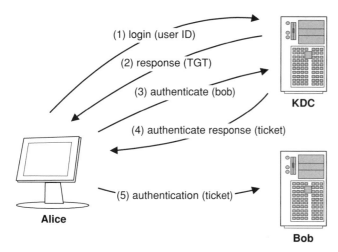

(1) login (user ID)

(2) response (TGT)

(3) authenticate (bob)

(4) authenticate response (ticket)

**KDC**

(5) authentication (ticket)

**Alice**

**Bob**

**Figure 3:** Kerberos Authentication: Alice receives a ticket-granting-ticket (TGT) after successfully logging into the Kerberos Key Distribution Center (KDC). Alice performs mutual authentication with Bob by presenting a ticket obtained from the KDC to Bob. Note that Bob need not communicate with the KDC directly; the contents of the ticket serve as proof of Alice's identity.

its contents are encrypted using a key derived from Bob's password. Therefore, Bob is the only entity that can retrieve the contents of the ticket. Because later communication between Alice and Bob uses the session key (given to Alice and contained in the ticket presented to Bob), Alice is assured that Bob is authentic. Bob is assured that Alice is authentic because Bob's ticket explicitly contains Alice's identity.

One might ask why Kerberos uses a two-phase process. Over the course of a session, Alice may frequently need to authenticate a number of entities. In Kerberos, because Alice obtains a TGT at login, later authentication can be performed automatically. Thus, the repeated authentication of users and services occurring over time does not require human intervention; Alice types in her password exactly once.

Note that a KDC authenticates users only within its *realm*. Users and services in different realms would seem not to be able to authenticate each other. However, protocol extensions allow interrealm authentication by cross registering KDCs. A user contacts its local KDC, which acts as an introducer to the foreign KDC, which in turn enables authentication of the entities as above.

Because of its elegant design and technical maturity, the Kerberos system has been widely accepted in local environments. Historically common in UNIX environments, it has recently been introduced into other operating systems (e.g., Windows 2000 and XP).

## Pretty Good Privacy

As indicated by the previous discussion of trusted third parties, it is often true that two parties on the Internet will not have a direct means of performing authentication. For example, a programmer in Great Britain may have no formal relationship with a student in California. Hence, no trusted third party exists to which both can defer authentication. A number of attempts have been made to address

this problem by establishing a single public key infrastructure spanning the Internet. However, these structures require users to directly or indirectly trust CAs whose operation they know nothing about. Such assumptions are inherently dangerous and have been largely rejected by user communities.

The Pretty Good Privacy (PGP) system (Zimmermann, 1994) takes advantage of informal social and organization relationships between users on the Internet. In PGP, each user creates a self-signed PGP certificate identifying a public key and identity information (e.g., e-mail address, phone number, and name). Users use the key to sign the keys of those users that they trust. Additionally, they obtain signatures from those users who trust them. The PGP signing process is not defined by PGP. Users commonly will exchange signatures with friends and colleagues.

The keys and signatures defined for a set of users defines a *Web of trust*. Upon reception of a key from a previously unknown source, an entity will make a judgment of whether to accept the certificate based on the presence of signatures by known entities. A certificate will likely be accepted if a signature generated by a trusted party (with known and acceptable signing practices) is present. Such assessment can span multiple certificates, where signatures create trusted linkage between acceptable certificates. However, because trust is not frequently transitive, less trust is associated with long chains. PGP certificates are primarily used for electronic mail, but have been extended to support a wide range of data exchange systems (e.g., Internet newsgroups).

## IPsec

IPsec (Kent & Atkinson, 1998) is emerging as an important service for providing security on the Internet. IPsec is not just an authentication service but also provides a complete set of protocols and tools for securing IP-based communication. The IPsec suite of protocols provides host-to-host security within the operating system implementation of the IP protocol stack. This has the advantage of being transparent to applications running on the hosts. A disadvantage of IPsec is that it does not differentiate between users on the host. Hence, although communication passing between the hosts is secure (as determined by policy), little can be ascertained as to the true identity of users on those hosts.

The central goal of IPsec was the construction a general purpose security infrastructure supporting many network environments. Hence, IPsec supports the use of an array of authentication mechanisms. IPsec authentication can be performed manually or automatically. Manually authenticated hosts share secrets distributed via administrators (i.e., configured manually at each host). Identity is inferred from knowledge of the secret. Session keys are directly or indirectly derived from the configured secret.

The Internet security association key management protocol (ISAKMP) defines an architecture for automatic authentication and key management used to support the IPsec suite of protocols. Built on ISAKMP, the Internet key exchange protocol (IKE) implements several protocols for authentication and session key negotiation. In these protocols, IKE negotiates a shared secret and policy between authenticated end points of an IPsec connection. The resulting IPsec security association (SA) records the result of IKE negotiation and is used to drive later communication between the end points.

The specifics of how authentication information is conveyed to a host are a matter of policy and implementation. However, in all implementations, each host must identify the keys or certificates to be used by IKE authentication. For example, Windows XP provides dialogs used to enter preshared keys. These keys are stored in the Windows registry and are later used by IKE for authentication and session key negotiation. Note that how the host stores secrets is of paramount importance. As with any security solution, users should carefully read all documentation and related security bulletins when using such interfaces.

## Wireless Networks

Wireless networks are quickly becoming ubiquitous. The ability to get access to the Internet anywhere and at any time is permitting new applications and easing our online and physical lives. However, wireless networks introduce enormous security risks. The omnipresence of wireless permits anyone within range some level of access to sensitive assets. In short, the security perimeter on which much of traditional network security is based has completely disappeared. This has caused security personnel, developers, and researchers to reevaluate the methods and policies used to govern the digital domain. This is particularly true of authentication.

Wireless networks are defined by the mode in which they operate. There are two predominant modes in use today: *ad hoc* and *infrastructure*. In an ad hoc mode, the hosts in the wireless network form a peer-to-peer physical routing infrastructure. That is, each host acts as a router for the other hosts in the network by passing packets between themselves and local *access points* (devices that route packets between wireless and physical networks). In infrastructure mode, every host must communicate directly with an access point. As it introduces fewer security and performance concerns and is generally simpler to administer, infrastructure mode is more popular. Independent of the mode, either the access points or peer hosts authenticate new hosts before they are allowed entry into a secure wireless network.

The simplest form of wireless authentication is MAC (media access control) authentication. Each physical network device (e.g., network card) is programmed with a unique MAC address. Because this is guaranteed to be unique, it can be used to identify the devices that should be allowed on the network (e.g., employee laptops). The authenticating device simply looks at the MAC address included in each packet. If it is on the list of "approved" devices, the packet is allowed. Note that this is not very secure but prevents hosts from inadvertently gaining access to the network. MAC addresses can be trivially spoofed, and moderately sophisticated users easily bypass such authentication measures.

The wired equivalent privacy (WEP) protocol was introduced to solve some of the security issues associated with wireless networks. The WEP protocol aims only to prevent unauthorized parties from gaining access to the network or manipulating packets on the network. WEP assumes all authorized entities have access to a cryptographic key shared by all authorized parties. In practice, this key is typically generated from a password or pass phrase entered into some host configuration dialog. WEP specifies how the key is used to encrypt and provide integrity checks for the packet payload. Hence, the WEP key (or password) is used as a credential—access to the password is deemed sufficient proof of identity as an authorized user.

WEP suffers from two central limitations. First, the protocol has a critical design flaw that leaves the WEP key vulnerable to exposure. This exploit is available in several widely available hacker tools and has led to the decline of the protocol's use. A second limitation was that the protocol did not identify a particular user or host. Hence, it is difficult to perform accounting and user logging in environments that use WEP as the sole authentication mechanism.

The 802.11i standards are designed to address the security limitations of WEP. In addition to addressing transport security (e.g., encryption key management), these standards define a framework for wireless authentication. The authentication framework standard, called 801.1x, provides an architecture in which centralized services authenticate hosts through access points. Existing authentication services can be used for authenticating the hosts (e.g., Kerberos and certificates), and the standard defines how these methods will be performed in the wireless network.

The centerpiece of the 802.1x standard is the EAP (extensible authentication Protocol). EAP is a challenge-response protocol run over secured transport service such as TLS/SSL. Once the secure transport protocol is established, other authentication services such as Kerberos or RADIUS are used to complete authentication. Developed by the CISCO Corporation, LEAP is an instance of the EAP protocol. Wireless clients (e.g., Laptops, PC, handhelds) use the LEAP protocol to communicate with RADIUS-enabled gateway devices. Typically, the gateway devices are wireless base stations that connect the wireless network to local wired networks.

## Interactive Media

The growth of the Internet has spawned many new ways of communicating. Internet messaging, voice-over-Internet protocol, digital conferencing, collaborative tools, and other media have hastened changes in the way we interact with people all over the globe. However, with these new media comes the need for authentication: we must ensure that we are exposing our data and ourselves only to authenticated users and services.

The H.323 protocol is the dominant tool for interactive media on the Internet. H.323 is a suite of media protocols that control the signaling and data transmission in media calls. The session initialization protocol (SIP) is an evolving framework for IP-based media signaling and is seen as a replacement for much of H.323. Both H.323 and SIP allow the gatekeeper servers to integrate external authentication services such as RADIUS. Hence, as is the trend on general computing systems, the media applications most frequently defer authentication to specialized services.

# CONCLUSION

The preceding sections described but a small fraction of the vast array of available authentication services. Given the huge number of alternatives, one might ask, "which one of these systems is right for my environment?" The following presents several guidelines for the integration of an authentication service with applications and environments.

- *Don't try to build a custom authentication service*. Designing and coding an authentication service is inherently difficult. This fact has been repeatedly demonstrated on the Internet; bugs and design flaws are occasionally found in widely deployed systems, and several custom authentication services have been broken in a matter of hours. It is highly likely that there exists an authentication service that is appropriate for a given environment. For all of these reasons, one should use services that have been time tested.
- *Understand who is trusted by whom*. Any authentication system should accurately reflect the trust held by all parties. For example, a system that authenticates students in a campus environment may take advantage of local authorities. In practice, such authorities are unlikely to be trusted by arbitrary end points in the Internet. Failure to match the trust existing in the physical world has ultimately led to the failure of many services.
- *Evaluate the value of the resources being protected and the strength of the surrounding security infrastructure*. Authentication is only useful when used to protect access to a resource of some value. Hence, the authentication service should accurately reflect the value of the resources being protected. Moreover, the strength of the surrounding security infrastructure should be matched by authentication service. One wants to avoid "putting a steel door in a straw house." Conversely, a weak or flawed authentication service can be used to circumvent the protection afforded by the surrounding security infrastructure.
- *Understand who or what is being identified*. Identity can mean many things to many people. Any authentication service should model identity as is appropriate for the target domain. For many applications, it is often not necessary to map a user to a physical person or computer but treat them as distinct, largely anonymous entities. Such approaches are likely to simplify authentication and provide opportunities for privacy protection.
- *Establish credentials securely*. Credential establishment is often the weakest point of a security infrastructure. For example, many Web registration services establish passwords through unprotected forms (i.e., via HTTP). Malicious parties can trivially sniff such passwords and impersonate valid users. Hence, these sites are vulnerable even if every other aspect of security is correctly designed and implemented. Moreover, the limitations

of many credential establishment mechanisms are often subtle. One should be careful to understand the strengths, weaknesses, and applicability of any solution to the target environment.
- *Authenticate all hosts in wireless environments*. Wireless networks vastly complicate network security. The loss of the traditional security perimeter caused by ubiquitous access mandates that strong protections be put in place to prevent authorized entities from gaining access. Authentication is a necessary component of such protections.

In the end analysis, an authentication service is one aspect of a larger framework for network security. Hence, it is necessary to consider the many factors that contribute to the design of the security infrastructure. It is only from this larger view that the requirements, models, and design of an authentication system emerge.

# GLOSSARY

**Authentication** The process of establishing the identity of an online entity.

**Authorization** The process of establishing the set of rights associated with an entity.

**Certificate** A digitally signed statement associating a set of attributes with a public key. Most frequently used to associate a public key with a virtual or real identity (i.e., identity certificate).

**Credential** Evidence used to prove identity or access rights.

**Malicious Party** Entity on the Internet attempting to gain unauthorized access, disrupt service, or eavesdrop on sensitive communication (syn: adversary, hacker).

**Secret** Information known only to and accessible by a specified (and presumably small) set of entities (e.g., passwords and cryptographic keys).

**Trusted Third Party** An entity mutually trusted (typically by two end points) to assert authenticity or authorization or perform conflict resolution. Trusted third parties are also often used to aid in secret negotiation (e.g., cryptographic keys).

**Web of Trust** Self-regulated certification system constructed through the creation of ad hoc relationships among members of a user community. Webs are typically defined through the exchange of user certificates and signatures within the Pretty Good Privacy (PGP) system.

# CROSS REFERENCES

See *Digital Certificates; Kerberos; PGP (Pretty Good Privacy); Secure Shell (SSH); Secure Sockets Layer (SSL)*.

# REFERENCES

Apache. (2002). Retrieved May 22, 2002, from http://httpd.apache.org/

Diffie, W., & Hellman, M. E. (1976). New directions in cryptography. *IEEE Transactions on Information Theory, 6*, 644–654.

Dusse, S., Hoffman, P., Ramsdell, B., Lundblade, L., & Repka. L. (March 1998). *S/MIME Version 2 message specification.* Internet Engineering Task Force, RFC 2311.

Franks, J., Hallam-Baker, P., Hostetler, J., Lawrence, S., Leach, P., Luotonen, A., & Stewart, L. (1999). *HTTP authentication: Basic and digest access authentication.* Internet Engineering Task Force, RFC 2617.

Fu, K., Sit, E., Smith, K., & Feamster, N. (2001). *Dos and don'ts of client authentication on the Web.* Paper presented at the 10th USENIX Security Symposium.

Haller, N. M. (1994). The S/key one-time password system. In *Proceedings of 1994 Internet Society Symposium on Network and Distributed System Security* (pp. 151–157).

Kent, S., & Atkinson, R. (1998). *Security architecture for the Internet protocol.* Internet Engineering Task Force, RFC 2401.

Kormann, D. P., & Rubin, A. D. (July, 2000). Risks of the Passport single signon protocol. *Computer Networks, 33,* 51–58.

Microsoft. (2002). Retrieved May 22, 2002, from http://www.passport.com/

Neuman, B. C., & Ts'o, T. (1994). Kerberos: An authentication service for computer networks. *IEEE Communications, 32(9),* 33—38.

RSA. (2002). *RSA SecurID Authentication.* Retrieved August 21, 2002, from http://www.rsasecurity.com/node.asp?id=1156

Verisign Homepage. (2002). Retrieved May 22, 2002, from http://www.verisign.com/

Ylonen, T. (1996). SSH—Secure login connections over the Internet. In *Proceedings of 6th USENIX Security Symposium* (pp. 37–42).

Zimmermann, P. (1994). *PGP user's guide.* Cambridge, MA: MIT Press.

# Antivirus Technology

Matthew Schmid, *Cigital, Inc.*

## INTRODUCTION

This chapter addresses the technologies and techniques being used in the fight against malicious software. The roots of this battle can be found in software designed to detect and eliminate computer viruses, though as this chapter illustrates, this 1.5 billion dollar industry has progressed far beyond the simple scanning techniques often associated with antivirus products (Gartner, 2002). A constant game of cat-and-mouse between the antivirus industry and malicious software authors has resulted in comprehensive tools designed to protect users from harm and equally sophisticated malicious software that attempts to evade detection and spread voraciously throughout the Internet.

Throughout this chapter the term *antivirus* refers to anything designed to combat a variety of malicious threats, including computer viruses, worms, Trojan horses, spyware, and other digital pests. Detailed information on various types of malicious software can be found elsewhere in this *Handbook*, and the distinctions will be largely ignored in this chapter except when necessary to the discussion (please refer to the chapters on Computer Viruses and Worms, Trojan Horse Programs, and Spyware). Many of the technologies described originated as countermeasures to computer viruses and have since been adapted to protect against new classes of malicious threats. Before delving into the details of how antivirus software works, it is important to understand what this technology is being used to accomplish.

## Antivirus Goals

Antivirus technology has the common goal of protecting users from undesired damage, disclosure, or loss of data and computing resources because of the introduction of malicious software. This objective can be further subdivided into goals that address the different stages of a malicious threat. The four subgoals of antivirus software can be expressed as blocking the introduction of malicious software, detecting the presence of malicious software, preventing damage caused by the execution of malicious software, and recovering from an attack.

### Blocking Malicious Threats

The first line of defense against malicious software includes tools and approaches that prevent these threats from ever executing on a protected computer system. Because of the growth of the Internet and the connectedness of today's computer systems, the spread of malicious software is no longer limited by geographical bounds. Unlike the early days of computer viruses, when malicious software was spread almost exclusively through the use of floppy disks, today's antivirus software must address numerous points of entry including e-mail, Web browsers, Internet enabled services, and shared file systems.

There are two basic approaches that antivirus software can use to prevent malicious programs from being introduced: they can block programs that are known to be malicious or they can allow only a set of programs that are known to be benign. These practices are respectively known as blacklisting and whitelisting. A more advanced approach to blocking malicious software involves trying to determine whether an unknown program is malicious or benign. This method is further discussed under "Heuristic Virus Detection."

### Detecting Malicious Software

The detection and identification of malicious software is essential to both blocking its introduction and cleaning up after an attack. There is an important distinction between detection and identification: detection implies only determining the existence of a malicious threat, whereas identification involves matching the malicious software to a previously known example of this attack. Many modern antivirus products contain techniques capable of both the identification of known malicious threats and the detection of previously unknown malicious software. The accuracy of both identification and detection techniques is a large component of the overall effectiveness of an antivirus product, and improvement in these capabilities is a fertile area for ongoing research. Techniques for the detection and identification of malicious software are described in detail later in this chapter.

### Tolerating Malicious Software

Despite the best efforts of antivirus software and practices, some malicious threats slip by these defenses. Virus writers continue to develop new malicious programs that are able to evade existing antivirus software—at least until the vendor is able to distribute updates designed to catch a new threat. The time between the development of a new virus and the release of a corresponding antivirus update is a window of opportunity during which a virus may spread unchecked.

Because the development of new malicious software that evades detection is likely to continue in the near future, antivirus researchers have created defensive measures designed to limit the damage that can be done by malicious software without requiring its detection. Designing protection that does not interfere with the operation of benign software applications is a challenging task.

### Recovering from an Attack

In addition to detecting and identifying malicious software, most antivirus tools include mechanisms for helping users to remove threats from their systems and to repair files that may have been damaged. Successful recovery from a malicious software attack is dependent on many factors and may not be possible in all situations. Accurate identification of the malicious threat is important to most recovery approaches. In the case of computer viruses that infect executable programs or documents, it is essential that all traces of the virus be removed to prevent further infection. Maintaining the integrity of the program or document during virus removal can be a difficult process to automate.

## ANTIVIRUS TECHNOLOGIES AND TECHNIQUES

Technologies for protecting users from malicious threats have evolved significantly since the mid-1990s. The goal of this section is to provide the reader with a basic idea of how existing antivirus techniques work and thereby facilitate a better understanding of the capabilities of antivirus software and the challenges that are faced by the antivirus industry. Although commercial antivirus products contain proprietary technologies and varying methods for protecting against malicious threats, the goal of this section is to cover the core techniques that are common across many of these solutions.

### Signature Scanning

Signature scanning is the most common, accurate, and effective technique currently used in the fight against malicious software. It is the method employed by the earliest antivirus software and it continues to be an important piece of all comprehensive antivirus products. The goal of signature scanning is to examine a *target* for the presence of a *signature* that is used to indicate infection by a malicious program (Computer Knowledge, 2001). The target can be any type of data file, though it is often a program or other executable. The signature is a set of characteristics that can uniquely identify a malicious program.

Early virus signatures were often as simple as a string of bytes taken from a malicious program. The antivirus scanner then searches the target for this string. If the

**Table 1** Simple Virus Signature

| Virus Name: | W32.Sample.A |
| --- | --- |
| Byte Signature: | 0A 8E 91 82 86 4C D2 |

scanner finds the string, then it assumes that the target is infected with the virus. If the string is not found, then the target is assumed to be free of this particular virus. Table 1 shows a fictitious example of a basic virus signature.

Although the process of scanning for virus signatures sounds fairly simple, getting it to work accurately and efficiently in practice is not quite so easy.

### The Signature Development Process

The process of building a virus signature begins with the capture of a specimen. The virus specimen can come from any number of sources. Many infected executables are submitted to antivirus companies by customers every day. The antivirus company examines these programs to determine whether they actually are infected with a virus. If they are infected, and the virus is not one that has been seen before, then they may decide to generate a new signature.

The first step is to get the virus to propagate to other hosts. This may be as simple as running the virus (in a controlled environment) and looking to see if any files on the system have changed because of the infection. For viruses that are more particular about which files they will infect and/or when they will propagate it may require manual analysis of the virus to determine how it can be forced to spread under laboratory conditions.

After the virus has propagated to several additional files, the antivirus vendor can begin to look for a suitable signature. The signature must exist across all of the examples of the infected programs, must not exist in any known benign programs, and should serve as a unique identifier for this particular virus (signatures that match more than one virus are often desirable, but they must be augmented with information that can be used to distinguish one match from another). The large and continually growing number of software programs in the world makes finding a valid signature a difficult task. Many antivirus venders evaluate each signature against a huge collection of benign programs to ensure that it is unlikely to show up accidentally.

Once the virus signature has been verified to be unique, it needs to be made available to the antivirus program. Most of today's virus scanners use the Internet to receive signature updates. After receiving the new signature, the antivirus program is ready to protect against this most recent threat. To facilitate updates, modern antivirus software is separated into two main components: the analysis engine and the virus database (Muttik, 2000). The database contains information on how to detect and remove viruses. It may contain both information specific to particular viruses and data that can be used to address families or classes of malicious software. The analysis engine is a software program that knows how to use the information in the virus database to search for and remove malicious software. In many antivirus implementations, the boundary between the analysis engine and the virus database is somewhat blurred because the database may actually contain code modules used for detecting certain viruses. This provides the flexibility to easily extend the antivirus software to handle new threats without directly updating the analysis engine.

To improve efficiency, the antivirus industry has managed to automate a significant portion of the signature development process. Researchers at IBM explored the creation of an antivirus system capable of analyzing viruses and generating signatures with minimal human interaction (Kephart, 1994). This work has since been expanded into Symantec's *Digital Immune System*, which automates the detection, analysis, and response to over 85% of the virus specimens they receive (Symantec, 2001). This level of automation leaves virus analysts with more time to address more complicated threats and reduces the overall amount of time required to release updates that can counter newly discovered malicious software.

## Improved Signature Scanning

Scanning an entire file for a sequence of bytes is a time- and processor-intensive operation that is not feasible in many antivirus scenarios. A modern computer system with a typically sized hard drive contains tens of thousands of files. Scanning each of these for all of the signatures in the signature database would take far more time than most people are willing to wait. Fortunately, this level of thoroughness is rarely required. By paring down the number of files that need to be examined and the areas within a file that need to be analyzed, it is possible to greatly reduce the amount of time needed to scan a hard drive effectively. Time is also a key consideration when antivirus software performs on-access scanning (looking for malicious code when a file is accessed or executed) or when antivirus software is deployed as part of a network gateway. Significant performance degradation is unacceptable in these situations.

To reduce the performance cost of signature scanning, antivirus software limits the types of files that are scanned and the areas of these files that are examined (Network Associates, 2002). The signature for a particular virus is expanded to include additional information on where to look for that virus. Viruses that infect executable programs are only searched for in files of an appropriate type. Likewise, macro virus signatures are not applied to executable files. Limiting scanning by file type can greatly reduce the search space with only a small impact on the effectiveness of a scanner.

Even with these reductions, scanning a large file can still be a time-consuming operation. Signature scanning can be refined further by limiting the areas of a file that are examined to those that are most likely to contain the signature. Each signature is tailored to include information that instructs the scanner on where to look for that particular virus. For example, some viruses may only infect the header section of an executable program. Others may be found immediately at the program's entry point (the location in the file where program execution begins). The signature may also restrict the size of the area that is

**Table 2** More Sophisticated Virus Signature

| Virus Name: | W32.Sample.A |
| --- | --- |
| Byte Signature: | 0A 8E 91 82 86 4C D2 |
| File Types: | Executable files |
| Scan Region: | Program entry point |
| Scan Length: | 112 bytes |

scanned. Table 2 illustrates how a virus signature can be refined to include additional information.

The efficiency of signature scanning can be greatly increased by using more detailed virus signatures. Unfortunately, this also has the effect of making virus signatures less resilient to small variations in the virus. These variations may be because of the virus itself (in the form of metamorphism), may be the result of a malicious individual making modifications to an existing virus, or may be because of infection by more than one virus. If a virus signature consists of a sequence of instructions at a particular location in an executable file, a slight change to the virus that leaves this sequence intact, but moves the location of the virus by a few bytes, may result in a failure to detect the variant.

## Evading Signature Detection

A major goal of virus writers has been to develop malicious software that cannot be detected by the simple, but effective, signature scanning approach favored by the antivirus industry. One of the most common techniques used by viruses is to attempt to avoid detection by hiding their actual code from the antivirus scanner. Polymorphic viruses, which first began to appear in the wild in 1991 (Nachenberg, 1996), vary their appearance with each new host they infect. This is often accomplished through using simple encryption algorithms with variable keys to make signature detection more difficult (Ludwig, 1995). These viruses typically contain a simple symmetric encryption/decryption algorithm that is executed early in the program and used to decrypt the main body of the virus. When the virus infects a new target, it chooses a new key, infects the target, and then encrypts the body of the virus. The result is an obfuscated virus body that contains no recognizable signatures.

A major weakness of polymorphism is that the decryption algorithm itself cannot be encrypted (it must be able to execute). This makes it a good candidate for a virus signature. One way that virus writers have tried to counter this detection technique is by introducing metamorphic viruses. These viruses further disrupt signature scanning by actually altering their own executable code as they infect new hosts (Ször & Ferrie, 2001). Typically, metamorphic viruses modify their own code by adding new instructions that do not have any real effect on the execution of the virus. Table 3 illustrates how a metamorphic engine might alter the instructions in a virus (and disrupt its signature) without actually affecting the semantics of the code. The ineffective instructions are marked as NOP.

A more sophisticated metamorphic program might reorder instructions or substitute equivalent (but different)

**Table 3** Metamorphic Virus Example

| Original Code | Metamorphic Code | Comments |
|---|---|---|
| mov eax, 5 | mov eax, 5 | |
| add eax, ebx | push ecx | NOP |
| call [eax] | pop ecx | NOP |
| | add eax, ebx | |
| | swap eax, ebx | NOP |
| | swap ebx, eax | NOP |
| | call [eax] | |
| | nop | NOP |

instructions. A metamorphic virus may apply these alterations to its entire body (including the code for performing the metamorphosis), or it may consist of a polymorphic virus that uses metamorphism to disguise only its decryption algorithm. A recent study (Christodorescu & Jha, 2004) found that simple obfuscating transformations were enough to confuse several popular antivirus products. Fortunately for the antivirus industry, the difficulty of writing a robust metamorphic virus has limited their number.

## Advanced Scanning Techniques

Addressing the threat of polymorphic and metamorphic viruses required changes to how virus scanning is performed. Simply updating the database of virus signatures would not work against these new attacks. The success of polymorphic viruses led to an increase in the use of polymorphism and to the development of virus writing tools that assisted others in the creation of hard-to-detect malicious software. To deal with these new threats, the antivirus industry turned to a novel antivirus technique that became known as generic decryption (Nachenberg, 1997).

The idea was to allow a program to execute for a short period of time before applying traditional signature scanning to the program's image in memory. If the virus code was executed during this time, it would perform the decryption operation itself, exposing the virus body to the antivirus software. To do this safely required that the program's execution was emulated rather than actually executed on the computer. Although computationally expensive, this improvement to signature scanning was very effective at dealing with polymorphic viruses.

Metamorphic viruses continue to be a dangerous threat even today. Although approaches to detecting them do exist, the methods are often time consuming and failure prone. Inexact string matching algorithms are one technique that can be used to identify metamorphic viruses. A signature based on inexact matching allows for some of the variations introduced by metamorphic viruses and incorporates wildcards in the byte signature (Harley, Slade, & Gattiker, 2001; Kumar & Spafford, 1992). If the sequence of bytes in the signature is A B C, the signature must be able to match the sequence A [bogus instructions] B [bogus instructions] C (as in the example in Table 3). Accounting for this type of inexact match requires a more sophisticated scanning engine and is potentially more prone to false positives. There is also a

significantly greater chance that an inexact signature may inadvertently match a benign program than that an exact signature (with the same number of instructions) will do so. Researchers in both industry and academia continue to search for a solution for effectively detecting metamorphic viruses.

Another improvement made to antivirus scanning engines is the ability to analyze compressed or archive files. Archive files contain collections of other files that are bundled together for easier transport. The problem with archives is that they may contain infected files and analyzing their contents requires the antivirus engine to support multiple extraction algorithms. Most antivirus solutions are able to handle common archive and compression formats, but proprietary formats may prevent analysis, and files that have been encrypted and protected with a password or key cannot be analyzed.

## Heuristic Virus Detection

Although signature scanning is an effective approach to detecting known malicious software, it is notoriously poor at detecting novel malicious programs. As previously discussed, virus signatures are designed to accurately identify a particular malicious program. The result is that even minor variations to a virus may result in it slipping by scanners unnoticed. Likewise, there is almost no chance of detecting a newly created malicious program with existing signatures.

Signature scanning forces the antivirus industry to react to each new threat that is discovered. The use of the Internet for malicious code propagation has dramatically reduced the amount of time that it takes for a virus to spread, thereby reducing the amount of time that antivirus companies have to release new signatures. Although the spread of viruses that require human interaction to propagate may still be contained by rapid response to new threats, the growing problem of malicious software that propagates on its own clearly requires a new approach. The recent outbreak of the Sapphire worm spread to over 90% of vulnerable hosts in about 10 minutes (Moore et al., 2003). A reactive approach to defending against these threats is clearly inadequate.

Heuristic virus detection refers to techniques used to detect malicious software based on a set of rules rather than using predefined signatures (Symantec, 1997). The goal is to develop measurements that can be used to indicate whether a program is infected with a virus without needing prior knowledge of that virus. Heuristic scanners look for common characteristics of viruses that have been defined by experts or discovered through machine learning. By applying these rules to an unknown program, the heuristic engine makes an educated guess as to whether the unknown program is infected with a virus.

A heuristic scanning engine may examine a suspicious file for dozens or even hundreds of signs of infection. The exact nature of what today's antivirus software looks for is a closely guarded trade secret and is a major differentiator among antivirus products. A few examples of signs of infection that may be used by heuristic scanners include the following:

- The location of the program's entry point
- The permissions of each section of a program (read, write, and/or execute)
- The presence/absence of certain patterns of instructions
- ASCII strings that may be included in the program

Although none of these rules may be very reliable when used alone, combined they provide a capable method of detecting the presence of malicious software. Although difficult to thoroughly evaluate, antivirus vendors claim that modern heuristics are capable of detecting over 80% of newly emerging threats (Symantec, 1997). As new malicious software is released, heuristic engines may be updated with additional rules based on information from these latest examples.

### Advantages

Heuristic virus detection has the potential to greatly improve protection against new and unknown malicious software. A strong heuristic engine would be capable of detecting most threats without requiring frequent updates from the antivirus vendor. This provides a great advantage against fast-spreading viruses that propagate before a detection signature can be distributed to the scanning software. Heuristics may also prove more effective against polymorphic and metamorphic viruses that are designed to thwart signature detection. A heuristic scanning engine may actually look for signs of this behavior. For example, determining that a program is capable of modifying its own code may be viewed as suspicious. When found in conjunction with other unusual properties, this may provide enough information to assume that the program is hostile.

### Disadvantages

Several unsolved problems with heuristic virus scanning have kept the technology from playing a more significant role in many antivirus products. Heuristic techniques are generally more likely than signature scanning to falsely determine that a program is malicious. This is because heuristics look for indicators that a program is malicious rather than identifying the presence of a particular virus. Though the designers of heuristic algorithms strive to keep false positives to a minimum, occasionally legitimate programs will appear to contain malicious behavior. For example, a program that automatically decrypts itself when executed may be flagged as suspicious even though it may be perfectly benign. With most heuristic techniques, it is possible to tune the sensitivity of the algorithm to favor increased detection capabilities or a lower false positive rate. Some antivirus products even allow the users to adjust these parameters themselves.

The use of rules rather than signatures also means that heuristic scanners can detect that a program may be malicious, but it cannot identify the threat by name. In some cases, heuristic scanners may be able to determine that a virus appears related to a known family of viruses. Although this may not seem like a significant shortcoming, it is, however, a barrier to user acceptance. Heuristic engines may also face difficulties in removing the virus infections that they detect because they do not have specific

enough information about the threat. Without this additional information, the virus scanner risks damaging the file or failing to remove all of the malicious content.

Analyzing a file with a heuristic engine can also be time and processor intensive. Although some heuristics may be relatively easy to calculate, others may require reading and analyzing a significant portion of the program file. The amount of time required for heuristic analysis will affect the acceptance of the solution.

Finally, as in the case with signature scanning, virus writers have the advantage of being able to test their viruses against existing heuristic engines before actually releasing a new malicious program on the Internet. Although a good set of heuristic rules is more difficult to evade than a virus signature, through trial and error a virus writer may be able to produce something that cannot be detected by available heuristic scanners. By not publicizing their heuristic scanning rules, antivirus vendors make the virus writers' task more difficult though not insurmountable.

### Future of Heuristics

In a seminal paper on computer viruses, Cohen (1987) showed that it is theoretically impossible to develop an algorithm that can differentiate between viruses and nonviruses based on examination. The author reasons that if we assume the existence of an algorithm for detecting a particular virus, then the virus could use that same algorithm to examine itself and propagate if and only if the algorithm does not identify the program as a virus. The resulting contradiction in logic proves the impossibility of designing such an algorithm: the program will act as a virus when it is not identified as a virus and will fail to exhibit virus behavior when it is identified as a virus. More recent work (Chess & White, 2000) uses a similar argument to prove that there exist viruses for which no error-free detection algorithm can be developed. Although these papers focus on the theoretical limits of virus detection rather than the practical aspects of the problem, they do effectively demonstrate that the perfect virus detection tool can never exist.

For the reasons discussed in this chapter, heuristic virus scanning will not replace signature scanning anytime soon. Antivirus vendors look to heuristics as a technology that can augment traditional signature scanning and can hopefully improve protection against new threats. Reactive approaches to detecting known threats remain the best way of identifying common viruses, and with reductions in the amount of time required to generate and distribute virus signatures, it is an effective solution in most instances. The use of heuristic virus scanners does further raise the bar for virus writers, making it more difficult for a novice virus writer to create a virus that will not be detected by existing antivirus products. It also offers a level of protection against new threats that is otherwise nonexistent.

## Integrity Checking and Code Signing

Verifying the integrity of data and program files has been shown to be useful for virus detection and for identifying other malicious activity. The goal is to alert the user to any unusual changes that are made to the file system. Although the contents of data files are changed frequently, most executable files are modified only during software upgrades. Any unauthorized changes to an executable file may indicate infection by a virus.

Integrity verification programs, such as Tripwire (Kim & Spafford, 1994), use cryptographic hashing to establish a baseline for file contents. Files are hashed again either when accessed or at a predetermined time, and the hash values are compared. Any changes to the hash values indicate that a file's contents have been altered. This simple approach is fairly effective at detecting viruses that infect executable files, though it is less useful for detecting viruses that hide in frequently modified data files (as is often the case with macro viruses). To get the most out of an integrity checking program, it is essential that the system is clean from malicious software when the initial hash values are established and that the cause of all integrity violations is determined. Integrity checking can serve as a useful heuristic for detecting and containing malicious software outbreaks before updated signatures can be obtained.

Digital signatures can also be used to verify the integrity and source of software that is downloaded over the Internet. Technology such as Microsoft's Authenticode packages software with a digital signature that can be used to help in deciding whether to trust a particular program (Grimes, 2001). Prior to executing the software, the signing certificate is displayed, and the user is given a choice of whether to proceed. If any changes have been made to the software, then the signature is rendered invalid.

The downside of this approach is that signed code is not necessarily safe. The signature only tells you what certificate was used—it says nothing about the trustworthiness of the signer or the behavior of the signed software. Obtaining a code-signing certificate is easy, and if users are not discriminating in whom they decide to trust, then code signing offers little or no protection.

## Scanning on Demand

The scanning techniques described previously can be made more effective and efficient by performing them only when needed. On-access (or on-demand) scanning invokes the antivirus engine at the point when a user accesses a potentially dangerous file. For data files this means prior to being read and for executable files it takes place just prior to execution. Because it is performed while a user is accessing a file, on-access virus scanning must be very fast to minimize the latency that is introduced. If a virus is detected, the scanner can block the user's access to the file, preventing the spread of the virus. Some antivirus products combine integrity checking with on-access scanning to prevent repeating the examination of a file that has not changed.

### Behavior Monitoring

The techniques examined so far are based on the static analysis of files and simple processor emulation. Dynamic antivirus technologies differ in that they monitor the behavior of a program while it is executing. It is often easier to determine what a program is doing by observing its interaction with the system rather than trying to predict its behavior by analyzing it statically. Because dynamic approaches are watching program behavior, they are typically heuristic in nature. An example of a heuristic that is sometimes employed is to watch for programs that are writing to other executable files. This unusual behavior may indicate that a virus is infecting a new host—or it may be the benign actions of a programming language compiler. If a program is believed to be a virus, it can be terminated by the antivirus software to prevent further damage.

A different dynamic approach that some antivirus products take is to restrict an application's behavior based on a predefined policy. The objective is to limit a program's access to system resources while still enabling it to execute. This technique, often referred to as running an application in a *sandbox*, can be applied to all programs or only to suspicious applications. The most well-known example of a sandbox is probably that implemented by the Java virtual machine (JVM). Beginning with Java 2, the JVM is capable of enforcing fine-grained policies on all executing Java programs and applets (McGraw & Felten, 1999). The sandbox policy can be used to specify which system resources should be made available to the Java program and how the program can use them.

Although this discussion focused on the Java sandbox, researchers have shown that a similar model can be enforced by the native operating system (Goldberg, Wagner, Thomas, & Brewer, 1996), and sandbox technology is beginning to emerge in commercial tools. A sandbox can be very effective at containing potentially malicious code while enabling it to execute in a safe environment. A significant weakness of using a sandbox is the difficulty in defining an appropriate policy for each target program. If the sandbox policy is too permissive, malicious software can still damage the system; however, if the policy is too restrictive, the program will not be able to access the resources necessary to run. Each application may require its own custom sandbox policy, resulting in an administrative nightmare. Researchers continue to explore effective techniques for implementing this promising technology in a noninvasive manner (Balfanz & Simon, 2000; Weber, Schmid, Geyer, & Schatz, 2002).

## Virus Removal and Recovery

In addition to detecting viruses, most antivirus solutions incorporate technology to disinfect files that have been compromised. The goal of disinfection (or cleaning) is to remove any dangerous components of the virus from the infected file and to restore the file to working order. This means repairing infected executables so that they will run correctly and removing viral code from data files without corrupting the file. Virus removal is a valuable feature of antivirus software because otherwise the file must be restored from a backup or may be lost entirely. The ability to clean files is less important in a tool that is being used to block viruses from entering an organization but may be essential when being used to recover from a virus outbreak.

Cleaning or removing viruses is closely tied to virus detection and identification. Cleaning engines are similar to scanning engines in their ability to perform both generic cleaning and virus-specific cleaning. Antivirus companies are able to reduce the size and complexity of their product by designing cleaning techniques that can be applied to large families of viruses rather than requiring a unique approach to cleaning each infection. The balance that companies try to achieve is to cover the vast majority of viruses with a few generic disinfection routines and develop virus-specific techniques only when needed. Modern antivirus scanners are able to use generic methods of disinfection over 50% of the time when dealing with new executable viruses and as often as 90% of the time with new macro viruses (Muttik, 2000).

The process of cleaning data files and executable files is quite different because of the structure of these files and the methods used during infection. In the case of many macro viruses, cleaning is as simple as deleting the macros that contain the malicious code. Cleaning viruses from an executable can be a much more complicated endeavor. All executable viruses alter the infected program's control flow to take control at some point during execution (typically the virus takes control near the beginning of the program). If a cleaning tool were to simply remove or overwrite the virus code, then the executable, though rendered harmless, would fail to run. To make the host program functional again, the disinfection routine must reverse the changes made during the infection process.

Some viruses intentionally make the disinfection process more difficult for antivirus software. These viruses may encrypt or even overwrite portions of the host file that they infect. Removing the virus can result in lost data or a program that will not run. In most cases, it is possible to derive an effective algorithm for removing a virus from an executable by carefully studying how the infection routine works. Preparing and distributing custom disinfection routines is costly, however, and tends only to be done for the most prevalent viruses.

In the worst-case scenario, recovering from a virus infection may require a complete reinstallation of the operating system and may even require hardware replacement. One of the most critical factors in limiting the damage that can be done by malicious code is restricting the privileges granted to the program when it is executed. Most viruses are executed with the same privileges that the user is granted. This means that if a user running as an administrator on a Microsoft Windows NT/2000/XP machine (or *root* on a UNIX-based system) accidentally launches a virus, it can perform all of the actions available to that user. Viruses executed with elevated privileges can make changes to the operating system, can disable antivirus software, and can install stealthy *rootkits* that provide attackers with access to the machine. Particularly dangerous viruses have even been known to install themselves into the persistent RAM found on peripherals such as graphics cards (Hoglund & McGraw, 2004). Fortunately, the damage done by most viruses is fairly limited, and antivirus products are often successful in removing them.

# ANTIVIRUS POLICIES AND PRACTICES

The technologies discussed in this chapter are most effective when deployed according to established best practices and placed within the context of an organizational security policy. Defining a policy designed to minimize the threat posed by viruses and malicious software is essential to maintaining a secure environment. Users are very likely to inadvertently introduce viruses into an organization unless proper policies are in place and vigorously enforced. Preventing viral outbreaks in the workplace can be accomplished only through a combination of technical and nontechnical solutions. Home users must also be vigilant in practicing safe Internet behavior. This section will describe key elements of protecting both homes and businesses from computer viruses (for a broader look at security policies, refer to the chapter on Security Policy Guidelines).

## Deploying Antivirus Solutions

By now the reader should have a good idea of how existing antivirus solutions can protect them from viruses and other malicious software. Deploying antivirus solutions on all general-purpose computer systems is the best approach to preventing viral infections for both home and business users. In addition to installing antivirus software on desktops, it is also a good practice for organizations to incorporate antivirus solutions at all entry points to the network. Mail servers, FTP servers, and other gateways should all be protected.

Installing solutions from multiple vendors rather than selecting a single antivirus solution for the entire enterprise can improve the odds of detecting and stopping a virus. These solutions should be deployed in a layered fashion to ensure that a virus must make it past several antivirus solutions to succeed. For example, an organization may deploy one company's product at the network gateway and a different company's product on users' computers. Deploying more than one antivirus solution on a particular machine should generally be avoided as it may result in incompatibilities that could render one or both solutions ineffective.

Antivirus solutions that employ signature detection must be kept up to date if they are to detect newly discovered threats. Most antivirus products are able to obtain updates across the Internet. The update schedule may either be periodic or triggered by the vendor's release of new signature information. In either case, it is important to verify that the antivirus solution is able to receive updates and is not blocked by a firewall or other network restriction. Not all antivirus products that include heuristic detection engines have them enabled by default. As discussed previously, heuristics currently offer the best form of protection against unknown viruses and should therefore be enabled when available. Files flagged as potentially malicious by a heuristic engine should be treated as dangerous unless proven otherwise.

## Awareness

Most users are aware of the dangers of malicious software because of the high-profile news coverage of computer viruses and worms during the past several years. Unfortunately, merely knowing about these threats is not enough to prevent people from becoming victims. Teaching people the basics of *how* viruses propagate and what they should watch out for can help them to avoid attacks. Deep technical knowledge of how viruses work is not a requirement and providing too much information may be counterproductive.

People are often tricked into opening e-mail attachments because they appear to have been sent by someone they trust. Users can be made less susceptible to these attacks by learning that viruses often use this method of social engineering as a way of spreading across the Internet (Harley et al., 2001). Similarly, the installation of unauthorized software must be actively discouraged. Malicious threats that arrive through Web browsers are particularly dangerous because many people believe that Web browsing is inherently safe. They often do not realize that ActiveX controls and signed Java applets can be every bit as damaging as an e-mail attachment or downloaded program. Improving the awareness of how malicious threats are introduced can reduce the success rate of many common attacks.

## Enforceable Security Policies

Whenever possible, users should be prevented from making decisions that impact organizational security. When given the choice between security and interesting functionality, people often make the wrong choice. This is where antivirus technology can provide valuable assistance by enforcing organizational policies. Antivirus software is often capable of quarantining potentially dangerous attachments and preventing users from installing and running unauthorized software. Rather than just telling people not to install ActiveX controls, most Web browsers support the central administration of policies that enforce this guideline. There are analogous methods of addressing macro and script viruses. It is important that this functionality is mandatory and cannot be easily circumvented by the end user.

## Updates and Operating Systems

The choice of an operating system will have a significant impact on how susceptible the system is to viruses and other malicious threats. The emphasis on usability and interoperability in the most popular operating systems often opens these systems to attack, as by far the most common family of operating systems, Microsoft Windows and its associated software, has been the victim of numerous high-profile attacks. Although vendors are often quick to respond to significant outbreaks, the rapid spread of malicious software across the Internet can occur long before an appropriate patch becomes available. Selecting a less common operating system such as Mac OS X, Linux, or another UNIX-based operating system may reduce the likelihood of being attacked by viruses or worms, but these systems are certainly not immune to the malicious software problem. In environments where high availability is a requirement, the best solution is often to deploy multiple operating systems with the knowledge that it is unlikely for a single attack to succeed against all.

Ensuring that the operating system and its software are kept up to date with the latest patches, revisions, and service packs is paramount to preventing malicious software attacks. Many widespread viruses and worms enter systems through known vulnerabilities that can be eliminated with freely available vendor-supplied patches. System administrators and home users should keep their computers secure by routinely verifying that they have installed all available updates. To help users with this otherwise time-consuming task, many operating systems and applications are able to determine when updates are available by communicating with the vendor over an Internet connection. For example, Microsoft Windows provides the *Windows Update* service, which can automatically detect, download, and install important operating system upgrades (Thurrott, 2004).

As mentioned previously, performing routine tasks as a user that does not possess administrative or root privileges can prevent viruses from inflicting the most serious damage. Even home users should resist the urge to always run as an administrator as most applications do not require elevated privileges to function. Although antivirus technology can help to prevent attacks from succeeding, it is best to employ a layered system of defenses. If an administrative account is compromised by malicious software, then the possibilities for damage or information theft are endless.

## SUMMARY

This chapter has explained the goals of antivirus software and has introduced the technologies and practices that support these goals. Antivirus software is an important countermeasure to dangerous malicious software that can spread rapidly across the Internet. Recent improvements in antivirus technology provide better protection than ever against new or unknown malicious software. By providing an understanding of how antivirus software works, it should be more apparent why viruses and other threats continue to plague today's computer systems. Knowing the strengths and weaknesses of these solutions will enable users to make better informed decisions when choosing an antivirus solution and should provide a context for understanding new technological advances being made in this field. Computer users must also understand that antivirus technology is only one element in the fight against viruses and other malicious threats. The best protection from viruses and other malicious software comes from a combination of technology, policies, and practices. By following the guidelines provided in this chapter and installing strong antivirus solutions, most computer virus infections can be prevented.

## GLOSSARY

**Executable** The compiled binary image of a program that is loaded into memory and executed by the processor.

**Heuristic** A set of rules or guidelines that can be used to infer the presence or absence of malicious software.

**Macro Virus** A computer virus that is written in an interpreted application macro language. The host of a macro virus is typically a document rather than a program executable.

**Signature**   A set of characteristics that can be used to uniquely identify an element of malicious software.

**Virus**   A program that can "infect" other programs by modifying them to include a possibly evolved copy of itself (Cohen, 1987).

**Worm**   A self-replicating computer program that typically spreads via computers connected to the Internet. Unlike a virus, a computer worm does not necessarily infect a benign host program.

## CROSS REFERENCES

See *Computer Viruses and Worms; Hoax Viruses and Virus Alerts; Hostile Java Applets; Spam and the Legal Counter Attacks; Trojan Horse Programs.*

## REFERENCES

Balfanz, D., & Simon, D. (2000). WindowBox: A simple security model for the connected desktop. In *Proceedings of the 4th USENIX Windows System Symposium*, Seattle, WA.

Chess, D., & White, S. (2000). An undetectable computer virus. In *Proceedings of the 2000 Virus Bulletin Conference*, Orlando, FL.

Christodorescu, M., & Jha, S. (2004). Testing malware detectors. In *Proceedings of the 2004 ACM SIGSOFT International Symposium on Software Testing and Analysis*, Boston, MA.

Cohen, F. (1987). Computer viruses: Theory and experiments. *Computers and Security, 6*(1), 22–35.

Computer Knowledge. (2001). *Virus tutorial: Scanning.* Retrieved October 15, 2004, from http://www.cknow.com/vtutor/vtscanning.htm

Gartner. (2002). *Total worldwide security software market revenue forecast by segment*. Gartner Press Room. Retrieved October 21, 2004, from http://www.dataquest.com/press_gartner/quickstats/security.html

Goldberg, I., Wagner, D., Thomas, R., & Brewer, E. (1996). A secure environment for untrusted helper applications: Confining the wily hacker. In *Proceedings of the 1996 USENIX Security Symposium*, San Jose, CA.

Grimes, R. (2001). *Malicious mobile code: Virus protection for Windows* (pp. 358–361). Sebastopol, CA: O'Reilly.

Harley, D., Slade, R., & Gattiker, U. (2001). *Viruses revealed: Understand and counter malicious software* (pp. 158–159, 406–410). Los Angeles, CA: McGraw-Hill.

Hoglund, G., & McGraw, G. (2004). *Exploiting software: How to break code* (pp. 408–429). Boston: Addison-Wesley.

Kephart, J. (1994). A biologically inspired immune system for computers. In *Proceedings of the Fourth International Workshop on Synthesis and Simulation of Living Systems* (pp. 130–139). Cambridge, MA: MIT Press.

Kim, G., & Spafford, E. (1994). Writing, supporting, and evaluating Tripwire: A publicly available security tool. In *Proceedings of the 1994 USENIX Applications Development Symposium* (pp. 89–107), Toronto, Canada.

Kumar, S., & Spafford, E. (1992). A generic virus scanner in C++. In *Proceedings of the 8th Computer Security Applications Conference* (pp. 210–219), Los Alamitos, CA.

Ludwig, M. (1995). *The giant black book of computer viruses* (pp. 425–467). Arizona: American Eagle.

McGraw, G., & Felten, E. (1999). *Securing Java: Getting down to business with mobile code* (pp. 95–114). New York: John Wiley & Sons.

Moore, D., Paxson, V., Savage, S., Shannon, C., Staniford, S., & Weaver, N. (2003). *The spread of the Sapphire/Slammer worm*. Technical Report, Cooperative Association for Internet Data Analysis, Berkeley, CA.

Muttik, I. (2000). Stripping down an AV engine. In *Proceedings of the 2000 Virus Bulletin Conference* (pp. 59–68), Orlando, FL.

Nachenberg, C. (1996). Understanding and managing polymorphic viruses. The Symantec Enterprise Papers, Volume XXX.

Nachenberg, C. (1997). Computer virus-antivirus coevolution. *Communications of the ACM, 40*(1), 46–51.

Network Associates. (2002). *Advanced virus detection scan engine and DATs*. Executive White Paper. Retrieved October 15, 2004, from http://www.networkassociates.com/us/local_content/white_papers/wp_scan_engine.pdf

Symantec. (1997). Understanding heuristics: Symantec's bloodhound technology. Symantec White Paper Series, Volume XXXIV.

Symantec (2001). The digital immune system. Technical Brief. Retrieved October 15, 2004, from http://securityresponse.symantec.com/avcenter/reference/dis.tech.brief.pdf

Ször, P., & Ferrie, P. (2001). Hunting for metamorphic. In *Proceedings of the 2001 Virus Bulletin Conference* (pp. 123–144), Prague, Czech Republic.

Thurrott, P. (2004). *What you need to know about Windows update services*. Windows IT Pro, InstantDoc #41969. Retrieved October 20, 2004, from http://www.windowsitpro.com

Weber, M., Schmid, M., Geyer, D., & Schatz, M. (2002). A toolkit for detecting and analyzing malicious software. In *Proceedings of the 2002 Annual Computer Security Applications Conference*, Las Vegas, NV.

# Biometric Basics and Biometric Authentication

James L. Wayman, *San Jose State University*

## INTRODUCTION

Biometric authentication is the automatic recognition of individual persons based on distinguishing biological (usually anatomical) and behavioral traits. The field is a subset of the broader field of human identification science. Example technologies include, among others, fingerprinting, face recognition, hand geometry, speaker recognition, and iris recognition. At the current level of technology, DNA analysis is a laboratory technique not fully automated and requiring human processing, so it not considered biometric authentication under this definition. Some techniques (such as iris recognition) are more biologically based, some (such as signature recognition) are more behaviorally based, but all techniques are influenced by both behavioral and biological elements.

Biometric authentication is frequently referred to as simply biometrics, although this latter word has historically been associated with the statistical analysis of general biological data. The word *biometrics*, like *genetics*, is usually treated as singular. It first appeared around 1980 in the vocabulary of physical and information security as a substitute for the earlier descriptor, *automatic personal identification*, which was in use in the 1970s. Biometric systems recognize "persons" by recognizing "bodies." The distinction between person and body is subtle but is of key importance in understanding the inherent capabilities and limitations of these technologies. In our context, biometrics deals with computer recognition of patterns created by human behaviors and biological structures and is usually associated more with the field of computer engineering and statistical pattern analysis than with the behavioral or biological sciences.

Today, biometrics is being used to recognize individuals in a wide variety of contexts, such as computer and physical access control, law enforcement, voting, border crossing, social benefit programs, and driver licensing.

## FUNDAMENTAL CONCEPTS

It has been recognized since 1970 that the three pillars of personal identification are as follows: "What you have (keys and tokens), what you know (PINS and passwords), and what you are (biometrics)" (IBM, 1970). Biometric technology, this last pillar, can be used alone, but is generally combined in access control systems with the other forms of identification (PINs, passwords, or physical tokens). Physical access control applications using biometrics can currently be found at airports, amusement parks, consumer banking kiosks, international ports of entry, universities, office buildings and secured government facilities. When used to control access to information systems, biometrics becomes a technology important to the field of information security.

The perfect biometric measure for all applications would be distinctive (different across users), repeatable (similar across time for each user), accessible (easily displayed to a sensor), acceptable (not objectionable to display by users), and universal (possessed and observable on all people). Unfortunately, no biometric measure has all of the above properties; there are great similarities among different individuals, measures change over time, some physical limitations prevent display, "acceptability" is in the mind of the user, and not all people have all characteristics. Practical biometric technologies must compromise on every point. Consequently, the challenge of biometric deployments is to develop robust systems to deal with the vagaries and variations of human beings.

Biometric systems verify claims (test hypotheses) regarding the source of a biometric pattern in the database. The claim can be made by the person presenting a biometric sample (e.g., "I am the source of a biometric data record in the database") or about the source by another actor in the system (e.g., "She is the source of a biometric data record in the database"). The claims can be positive (e.g., "I am the source of a biometric record in the database") or negative (e.g., "He is not the source of a biometric record in the database"). Claims can be specific (e.g., "I am the source of biometric record A in the database") or unspecific (e.g., "I am not the source of any biometric record in the database"). Any combination of specific or unspecific, positive or negative, or first or third person is possible in a claim.

Systems requiring a positive user claim to a specific enrollment record treat the biometric pattern as an attribute of the record. These systems "verify" that the biometric attribute in the claimed enrollment record matches the sample submitted by the user and are called "verification" systems. Some systems, such as those for social service and driver's licensing, verify negative user claims of no biometric pattern already in the database by treating the biometric pattern as a record identifier or pointer. These systems search the database of biometric pointers to find one matching the submitted sample and are called "identification" systems. However, the act of finding an identifier (or pointer) in a list of identifiers also verifies an unspecific claim of enrollment in the database, and not finding a pointer verifies a negative claim of enrollment. Consequently, the differentiation between "identification" and "verification" systems is not always clear and these terms are not mutually exclusive.

In the simplest systems, "verification" of a positive claim to a specific enrollment record might require the comparison of submitted samples to only the biometric attributes in the single claimed record. For example, a user might claim to be the source of the hand geometry record stored on an immigration card, such as the INSPASS card used by the United States government since 1994 to facilitate airport immigration by frequent air travelers. To prove the claim to being the source of the enrolled identity, the user would insert the card into a card reader that reads the record and then place his/her hand on the hand geometry reading device. The system compares the hand geometry recorded on the card to that of the hand placed on the reader. If the two measures are reasonably close, the system concludes that the user is indeed the source of the record on the card and therefore should be afforded the rights and privileges associated with the card.

Simple "identification" might require the comparison of the submitted biometric samples to all of the biometric identifiers stored in the database. The State of California requires applicants for social service benefits to verify the negative claim of no previously enrolled identity in the system by submitting fingerprints from both index fingers. Depending on the specific automated search strategy, these fingerprints might be searched against the entire database of enrolled benefit recipients to verify that there are no matching fingerprints already in the system. If matching fingerprints are found, the enrollment record pointed to by those fingerprints is returned to the system administrator to confirm the rejection of the applicant's claim of no previous enrollment.

These are examples of the simplest systems. More advanced systems might use comparisons with multiple enrolled records for verification of a claimed identity or only a very limited number of comparisons for identification among all the enrolled records. There is no dependable relationship between verification or identification and the number of comparisons that the system is required to make.

Information security systems generally use biometrics to verify positive user claims to be the source of a specific or unspecific enrollment record in the database. These systems are commonly called verification systems regardless of the search strategy and architecture employed. If a claim to enrollment is verified, authorizations associated with the verified or identified enrollment record can then be applied with confidence to the requested activities, such as computer logon. Although hybrid systems—verifying at the time of enrollment the negative claim that a subject is not already in the database and then verifying in later encounters positive claims of enrollment—are also possible, they are not currently widespread.

Biometric technologies are playing a growing role in information security systems today to connect users to system authorizations through verification of claims of enrolled identity. The argument can be made that biometric measures more closely link the authentication process to the human user than "what you have" or "what you know." Biometric measures are not as easy to transfer, forget, or steal as PINs, passwords, and tokens and so may increase the security level of systems employing them. Biometrics can be combined with PINs and tokens into "multifactor" systems for added security should the PINs or tokens be stolen or compromised.

## A SHORT HISTORY

The science of recognizing people based on physical measurements owes to the French police clerk Alphonse Bertillon, who began his work in the late 1870s (Beavan, 2001; Cole, 2001). The Bertillon system involved multiple measurements, including height, weight, the length and width of the head, width of the cheeks, and the lengths of the trunk, feet, ears, forearms, and middle and little fingers. Categorization of iris color and pattern was also included in the system. By the 1880s, the Bertillon system was in use in France to identify repeat criminal offenders. Use of the system in the United States for the identification of prisoners began shortly thereafter and continued into the 1920s.

Although research on fingerprinting by a British colonial magistrate in India, William Herschel, began in the late 1850s, knowledge of the technique did not become known in the western world until the 1880s (Faulds, 1880; Herschel, 1880), when it was popularized scientifically by Sir Francis Galton (1888) and in literature by Mark Twain (1893). Galton's work also included the identification of persons from profile facial measurements.

By the mid-1920s, fingerprinting had completely replaced the Bertillon system within the U.S. Bureau of Investigation (later to become the Federal Bureau of Investigation). Research on new methods of human identification continued, however, in the scientific world. Handwriting analysis was recognized by 1929 (Osborn, 1929) and retinal identification was suggested in 1935 (Simon & Goldstein, 1935)

None of these techniques are "automatic," however, so none meet the definition of biometric authentication being used in this article. Automatic techniques require automatic computation. Work in automatic speaker recognition can be traced directly to experiments with analog filters done in the 1940s (Potter, Kopp, & Green, 1947) and early 1950s (Chang, Pihl, & Essignmann, 1951). With the computer revolution picking up speed in the 1960s, speaker (Pruzansky, 1963) and fingerprint (Trauring, 1963a) pattern recognition were among the very first applications in automatic signal processing. By 1963, a "wide, diverse market" for automatic fingerprint recognition was identified, with potential applications in "credit systems" and "industrial and military security systems" and for "personal locks" (Trauring, 1963b). Computerized facial recognition research followed (Bledsoe, 1966; Goldstein, Harmon, & Lesk, 1971). In the 1970s, the first operational fingerprint and hand geometry systems were fielded, results from formal biometric system tests were reported (Wegstein, 1970), measures from multiple biometric devices were being combined (Fejfar, 1978; Messner, Cleciwa, Kibbler, & Parlee, 1974), and government testing guidelines were published (National Bureau of Standards, 1977). In the 1980s, fingerprint scanners and speaker recognition systems were being connected to personal computers to control access to stored information. Based on a concept patented in the 1980s (Flom & Safir, 1987), iris recognition systems became available in the mid-1990s (Daugman, 1993). Today there are close to a dozen approaches used in commercially available systems, utilizing hand and finger geometry, iris and

fingerprint patterns, face images, voice and signature dynamics, computer keystroke, and hand vein patterns.

## SYSTEM DESCRIPTION
### Overview

Given the variety of applications and technologies, it might seem difficult to draw any generalizations about biometric systems. All such systems, however, have many elements in common. Biometric samples are acquired from a person by a sensor. The sensor output is sent to a processor that extracts the distinctive but repeatable measures of the signal (the "features"), discarding all other components. The resulting features can be stored in the database as a template or compared to a specific template, many templates, or all templates already in the database to determine if there is a match. A decision regarding the identity claim is made based on the similarity between the sample features and those of the template or templates compared.

Figure 1 illustrates this information flow, showing a general biometric system consisting of data collection, transmission, signal processing, storage, and decision subsystems. This diagram illustrates both enrollment and operation of systems designed for verifying specific or unspecific, positive or negative claims of enrollment. In the following sections, we go through each of these subsystems in detail.

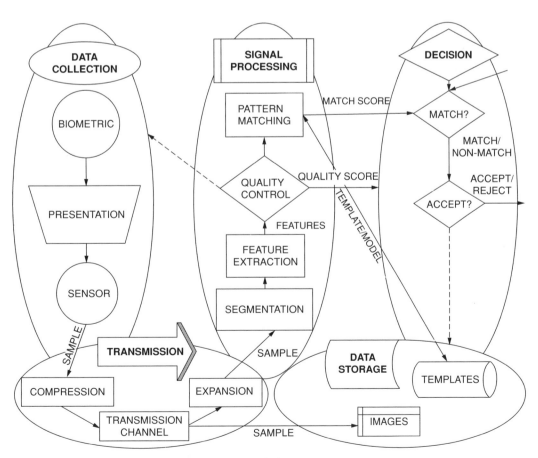

**Figure 1:** Example biometric system.

## Data Collection

Biometric systems begin with the collection of a signal from a behavioral/biological characteristic. As data from a biometric sensor can be one- (speech), two- (fingerprint), or multidimensional (handwriting dynamics), we are not generally dealing with images. To simplify our vocabulary, we refer to raw signals simply as samples.

Key to all systems is the underlying assumption that the signal from the biometric characteristic being observed is both distinctive between individuals and repeatable over time for the same individual. Therefore, it is desirable that there be as much variation between individuals and as little variation within an individual as possible. The challenges of measuring and controlling these variations begin in the data collection subsystem.

The user's characteristic must be observed by a sensor, such as a microphone, CCD-based fingerprint scanning chip, digital camera, or computer keyboard. In systems where a user seeks verification of a positive claim to an enrolled identity, the user can cooperatively present the characteristic to the sensor. The act of presenting a biometric measure to a sensor introduces a behavioral component to every biometric method as the user must interact with the sensor in the collection environment. The output of the sensor is the combination of (1) the biometric measure, (2) the way the measure is presented, and (3) the technical characteristics of the sensor. All measurements and decisions made by the system will be based on this sensor output. Both the repeatability and the distinctiveness of the measurement are negatively impacted by changes in any of these three factors. If a system is to exchange data with other systems, the presentation and sensor characteristics must be standardized to ensure that biometric characteristics collected with one system will match those collected on the same individual by another system.

## Transmission

Some biometric systems collect data at one location but process it at another. If a great amount of data is involved, data compression may be required to conserve transmission bandwidth. It is not usual that raw biometric data is stored, but those systems requiring sample storage do so in a compressed format. Figure 1 shows compression and transmission occurring before signal processing or sample storage. The transmitted or stored compressed data must be expanded before further use. The process of compression and expansion generally causes quality loss in the restored signal, with loss increasing with higher compression ratios. An interesting area of research is in finding, for a given biometric technique, compression methods with minimum negative impact on the subsequent signal processing activities. Interestingly, limited compression has been seen in many cases to improve the performance of the pattern recognition software, as information loss in the original signal is generally in the less repeatable high-frequency components.

## Signal Processing

The biometrics signal processing subsystem is composed of four modules: segmentation, feature extraction, quality control, and pattern matching. The segmentation module must determine if biometric signals exist in the received data stream (signal detection) and, if so, extract the signal from the surrounding noise. If the segmentation module fails to properly detect or extract a biometric signal, we say that a failure-to-acquire has occurred.

The feature extraction module must process the signal in some way to preserve or enhance the between-individual variation (distinctiveness) while minimizing the within-individual variation (nonrepeatability). The output of this module are numbers that, although called biometric features, may not have direct biological or behavioral interpretation. For example, the numerical values developed by a facial recognition system do not indicate the width of the lips, length of the nose, or the distances between the eyes and the mouth but rather represent the face in a more abstract, mathematically based way.

The quality control module must do a statistical "sanity check" on the extracted features to make sure they are not outside population statistical norms. If the sanity check is not successfully passed, the system may be able to alert the user to resubmit the biometric pattern. If the biometric system is ultimately unable to produce an acceptable feature set from a user, a failure-to-enroll or a failure-to-acquire will be said to have occurred. Failure-to-enroll/acquire may be because of failure of the segmentation algorithm, in which case no feature set will be produced. The quality control module might even impact the decision process, directing the decision subsystem to adopt higher requirements for matching a poor-quality input sample, for instance.

The pattern matching module compares sample feature data with previously enrolled feature data (templates) from the database and produces a numerical comparison score. When both template and features are vectors, the comparison may be as simple as a Euclidean distance. Neural networks or statistical measures, such as likelihood ratios, might be used instead. Regardless of what pattern matching technique is used, templates and features from samples will never exactly match because of the repeatability issues already discussed. Consequently, the matching scores determined by the pattern matching module will have to be interpreted by the decision subsystem.

In more advanced systems, such as speaker verification, the enrollment templates might be models of the feature generation process—very different data structures than the observed features. The pattern matching module determines the consistency of the observed features with the stored model. Some pattern matching modules may even direct the adaptive recomputation of features from the input data to see if better matches might be made through small adjustments to the input data.

## Decision

The decision subsystem is considered independently from the pattern matching module. The decision subsystem might make a simple match or no match determination by comparing the output score from the pattern matching module against a predetermined threshold value. The ultimate acceptance or rejection of a user's identity claim might be based on multiple match/no match decisions from multiple measures or from some dynamically determined, user-dependent, or measure-dependent decision criteria. For instance, common decision policies will accept a user transaction if a match occurs in any of three attempts or against any one of several stored templates.

The decision module might also direct operations to the stored database, storing features as templates during enrollment, updating templates in the database after a successful transaction, calling up additional templates for comparison in the pattern matching module, or directing a database search.

Because input samples and stored templates will never exactly match, the decision modules will make mistakes—wrongly rejecting a correctly claimed identity of an enrolled user or wrongly accepting the identity claim of an impostor. Thus, there are two types of errors: false rejection and false acceptance. These errors can be traded off against one another to a limited extent: decreasing false rejections at the cost of increased false acceptances and vice versa. In practice, however, inherent within-individual variation (nonrepeatability) limits the extent to which false rejections can be reduced, short of accepting all comparisons. The decision policies regarding match/no match and the accept/reject criteria are specific to the operational and security requirements of the system and reflect the ultimate cost and likelihood of errors of both types.

Because of the inevitability of false rejections, all biometric systems must have exception handling mechanisms in place. If exception handling mechanisms are not as strong as the basic biometric security system, a vulnerability will result. High numbers of falsely rejected transactions may overload even strong exception handling mechanisms and lower the responsiveness of system management to potential attacks on the system. Consequently, a high false rejection rate can lead not only to user inconvenience and operational delays but to a compromise in system security as well.

The false acceptance rate measures the percentage of "zero effort" impostor transactions that result in access to the system. The false acceptance rate should never be confused with the probability that a successful transaction is actually fraudulent. This latter probability depends on both the false acceptance rate and the percentage of all transaction attempts that are actually by impostors. Depending on the application and how alarms are handled, even a 20% false acceptance rate (which indicates an 80% probability of intercepting an impostor) may be low enough to decrease the frequency of attacks on the biometric system to the point that there are no successful impostor transactions. Truly determined fraudsters might find other entry points, including the exception handling mechanism, more appealing than the biometric portal.

Consequently, the security level provided by a biometric system might be as sensitive to the false rejection rate as to the false acceptance rate. Sound practice would indicate that we not rely on a single biometric safeguard to catch every impostor, not place extreme emphasis on attaining near-zero false acceptance rates, and continue to couple biometrics with other methods, such as PINs and passwords.

## Storage

The remaining subsystem to be considered is that of storage. The processed features or the feature generation model of each user will be stored or "enrolled" in a database for future comparison by the pattern matcher to incoming feature samples. Systems for verifying negative claims of identity require a centralized database (or the equivalent, linked decentralized databases) of all enrolled templates to verify a claim that a person is not enrolled in the system. Such systems generally return the records of any previous enrollments found, so are called identification systems as previously discussed. Large-scale identification systems generally partition the database using factors such as gender or age so that not all centrally stored templates need be examined to establish that a person is not in the database. Such systems are sometimes loosely called one-to-$N$ to indicate that a submitted sample must be compared to multiple enrollment templates or models.

For systems only verifying positive claims to a specific identity, the database of templates may be distributed on a magnetic stripe, optically read or smartcards carried by each enrolled user; no centralized database need exist. Such positive verification systems are sometimes loosely called one-to-one to indicate that biometric samples might be compared to the templates or models of only the single claimed identity. However, verification systems based on likelihood estimation techniques compare samples not only to the claimed enrollment templates, but also to the templates of other users or to background models so might not really be one to one.

Although distributed storage is possible, positive claim verification systems might use a centralized, encrypted database to prevent creation of counterfeit cards or to reissue lost cards without re-collecting the biometric measures.

The original biometric measurement, such as a fingerprint pattern, is generally not reconstructable from the stored templates. However, if access can be had to unencrypted templates, it is quite possible for a knowledgeable hacker in possession of an identical system to construct an artifact capable of regenerating the accessed template. Although this artifact will not have the exactly the same visible pattern as the original biometric sample, the biometric system will generate the same template. For this reason, biometric templates must always be protected as sensitive data and will generally require encryption, even when stored on user-controlled cards. The decision to maintain a centralized template database for verification applications should be done with an assessment of the privacy and security risks should the database be compromised.

Biometric templates are created using the proprietary feature extraction algorithms of the system vendor. Consequently, biometric systems are not currently interoperable at the level of the feature vector. To support interoperability (for instance, to allow future use of legacy data), it may be necessary to store raw data, usually in

**Table 1** Biometric Template Sizes

| Device | Size in Bytes |
|---|---|
| Fingerprint | 200–1,000 |
| Speaker | 100–6,000 |
| Finger geometry | 14 |
| Hand geometry | 9 |
| Face | 100–3,500 |
| Iris | 512 |

compressed form. Of course, unauthorized access to raw biometric data can allow for compromise through the construction of artifacts or through replay attacks. Unlike PINs and passwords, however, raw biometric data cannot be changed at the request of the user. Consequently, the storage of raw biometric data presents particular security and liability concerns.

Table 1 shows some example unencrypted template sizes for various biometric devices.

## PERFORMANCE TESTING

Biometric devices and systems might be tested in many different ways. Types of testing include the following: technical performance; reliability, availability, and maintainability (RAM); vulnerability; security; user acceptance; human factors; cost/benefit; and privacy regulation compliance.

Technical performance has been the most common form of testing since the mid-1970s. Technical tests are generally conducted with the goal of predicting system performance with a target population in a target environment, but historically, extrapolation of results from a test environment to the real world has been difficult.

Technical tests can be either closed-set or open-set. A closed-set test assumes that all users are enrolled in the system and does not acknowledge the existence of impostors. A closed set test returns the rank of the true comparison when an input sample is compared to all of the enrolled patterns. Closed-set tests measure the probability that the true pattern was found at rank $k$ or better in the search against the database of size $N$. In any test, the rank $k$ probability is dependent on the database size, decreasing as the database size increases.

An open-set test does not require that all input samples be represented by a pattern in the enrolled database and measures all comparison scores against a score threshold. An open-set test returns, as a function of the threshold, the probability of either missing a true comparison (the false nonmatch rate) or matching a wrong comparison (the false match rate). Open-set measures are independent of the size of the database searched, converging to the correct estimator as the test size increases. Examples of both open-set and closed-set tests are found in the literature, but as most applications must acknowledge the potential for impostors, open-set results are of the greater practical value to the system designer or analyst.

To make test results more predictive of real-world performance, testing best practices are developing (Mansfield & Wayman, 2002). Metrics generally collected in open-set technical tests are as follows: failure-to-enroll, failure-to-acquire, false match, false non-match, and throughput rates. Failure-to-enroll rate is determined as the percentage of all persons presenting themselves to the system in good faith for enrollment who are unable to do so because of system or human failure. Failure-to-acquire rate is determined as the percentage of "good faith" presentations by all enrolled users that are not acknowledged by the system. The false non-match rate is the percentage of all users whose claim to identity is not accepted by the system. This will include failed enrollments and failed acquisitions, as well as false nonmatches against the user's stored template. The false match rate is the rate at which zero-effort impostors making no attempt at emulation are incorrectly matched to a single, randomly chosen false identity. Because false match/nonmatch rates are competing measures, they can be displayed together on a decision error trade-off (DET) curve.

The throughput rate is the number of persons processed by the system per minute and includes both the human/machine interaction time and the computational processing time of the system.

## Types of Technical Tests

Three types of technical tests have been described: technology, scenario, and operational (Philips, Martin, Wilson, & Przybocki, 2000).

**Technology Test.** The goal of a technology test is to compare competing algorithms from a single technology, such as fingerprinting, against a standardized database collected with a universal sensor. There are competitive, government-sponsored technology tests in speaker verification (National Institute of Standards and Technology, 2003), facial recognition (Philips, Grother, Bone, & Blackburn, 2002), and fingerprinting (Maio, Maltoni, Wayman, & Jain, 2002)

**Scenario Test.** Although the goal of technology testing is to assess the algorithm, the goal of scenario testing is to assess the performance of the users as they interact with the complete system in an environment that models a real-world application. Each system tested will have its own acquisition sensor and so will receive slightly different data. Scenario testing has been performed by a number of groups, but few results have been published openly (Bouchier, Ahrens, & Wells, 1996; Mansfield, Kelly, Chandler, & Kane, 2000; Rodriguez, Bouchier, & Ruehie, 1993).

**Operational Test.** The goal of operational testing is to determine the performance of a target population in a specific application environment with a complete biometric system. In general, operational test results will not be repeatable because of unknown and undocumented differences between operational environments. Further, "ground truth" (i.e., who was actually presenting a good faith biometric measure) will be difficult to ascertain. Because of the sensitivity of information regarding error rates of operational systems, few results have been reported in the open literature (Wayman, 2000).

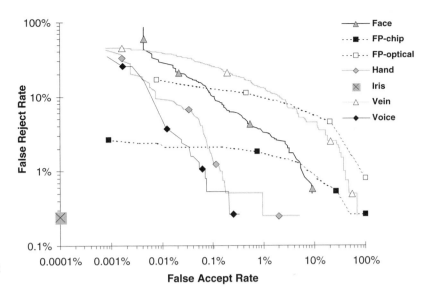

**Figure 2:** Detection error trade-off curve: best of three attempts.

Regardless of the type of test, all biometric authentication techniques require human interaction with a data collection device, either standing alone (as in technology testing) or as part of an automatic system (as in scenario and operational testing). Consequently, humans are a key component in all system assessments. Error, failure-to-enroll/acquire and throughput rates are determined by the human interaction, which in turn depends on the specifics of the collection environment. Therefore, little in general can be said about the performance of biometric systems or, more accurately, about the performance of the humans as they interact with biometrics systems.

## The National Physical Lab Tests

A study by the UK National Physical Laboratory, Mansfield et al. (2000), looked at eight commercially available biometric products in a scenario test designed to emulate access control to computers or physical spaces by scientific professionals in a quiet office environment. A more detailed description of the products, test environment, and volunteer population is available in the original report.

The false accept/false reject DET under a "three-tries" decision policy for this test is shown in Figure 2. The false rejection rate includes failure-to-enroll/acquire rates in its calculation.

Figure 2 allows estimation of the false rejection rate for each of the tested products for any required false acceptance rate but only for this test environment and this set of test subjects. The figure does not show the decision thresholds required to attain those false acceptance rates. The tested products may not be representative of the technology in general and it is not possible to extrapolate these results to any other application environment or set of test subjects. For example, the figure shows that it is possible for National Physical Laboratory users of hand geometry to attain a 1% false rejection rate at a 0.1% false acceptance rate in this environment. A failure-to-enroll was considered as a false rejection in the computation of this figure. These results relate to the average error rates

over all users. Individual users may have error rates considerably above or below the averages.

It is also important to note that the National Physical Laboratory results do not tell us about the user error rates with technologies such as PINs and tokens, generally thought to be competitors of biometrics. Determining the strength of biometrics relative to the other mechanisms for personal identification is an unresolved research issue.

The National Physical Laboratory study also established the access control transaction times for these users with the various biometric devices in this office environment, shown as Table 2.

In Table 2, the term *PIN?* indicates whether the transaction time included the manual entry of a four-digit identification number by the user. These times referred only to the use of the biometric device and did not include actually accessing a restricted area.

## BIOMETRICS AND INFORMATION SECURITY

Hopefully it is clear by this point that biometrics can have an important role in information security, being much more closely linked to a user and more difficult to forget,

**Table 2** Transaction Times in Office Environment

| | Transaction Time (seconds) | | | |
|---|---|---|---|---|
| **Device** | **Mean** | **Median** | **Minimum** | **PIN?** |
| Face | 15 | 14 | 10 | No |
| Fingerprint—optical | 9 | 8 | 2 | No |
| Fingerprint—chip | 19 | 15 | 9 | No |
| Hand | 10 | 8 | 4 | Yes |
| Iris | 12 | 10 | 4 | Yes |
| Vein | 18 | 16 | 11 | Yes |
| Speaker | 12 | 11 | 10 | No |

give away, or lose than a token, a PIN, or a password. Use of biometrics can provide additional evidence that an authorization credential is being presented by the person to whom it was issued. However, biometric technologies do not represent a silver bullet eliminating PINs, passwords, and tokens while resolving all security issues.

In architecting a system for verifying a positive claim to identity, we must decide whether each person's biometric template will be carried by the person themselves on a token or whether the template will be stored centrally in a database linked to the point of service by a communications system. The former approach has positive implications for privacy (Kent & Millett, 2003), but will require some form of key, such as a PIN or a password, to unlock the biometric measure that will be encrypted on the token. Consequently, all the issues regarding data security on tokens, as considered elsewhere in this *Handbook*, still exist.

If biometric templates are stored centrally, several different questions arise:

1. Will the sample be sent to the central system or will the central system pass the template to the point of service for processing? In either case, some strong form of encryption will be required to protect the data during transmission.
2. If the data are sent from the point of service to the central site, will it be in raw form or processed into features? If processed into features prior to transmission, computational power and knowledge of the feature extraction algorithm will be required at each point of service but transmission bandwidth will be reduced.
3. How will the encrypted data be unencrypted when necessary for comparison?
4. How will the user trust the point of service to be legitimate and not to be storing the biometric data after transmission?

Although these issues are not insurmountable, they demonstrate that use of biometrics does not eliminate the usual security issues.

It has been well known since the 1970s that biometric devices can be fooled by forgeries (Lummis & Rosenberg, 1972; National Bureau of Standards, 1977; Raphael & Young, 1974). In a system for verifying positive claims of identity, spoofing is the use of a forgery of another person's biometric measures. In a system for verifying a negative claim, spoofing is an attempt to disguise one's own biometric measure. Forging biometric measures of another person is more difficult than disguising one's own measures but is quite possible nonetheless. Several studies (Blackburn, Bone, Grother, & Phillips, 2000; Matsumoto, Matsumoto, Yamada, & Hoshino, 2002; Thalheim, Krissler, & Ziegler, 2002; van der Putte & Keuning, 2000) discuss ways by which facial, fingerprint, and iris biometrics can be forged. Speaker recognition systems can make forgery difficult by requesting the user to say numbers randomly chosen by computer. However, the current state of technology does not provide reliable "liveness testing" to ensure that the biometric measure is both from a living person *and* not a forgery.

The use of biometrics does not reduce the need to fully vet all applicants for authorizations. A biometric system can neither verify the external truth of the enrolled identity itself nor establish the link automatically to an external identity with complete certainty. Determining a user's "true" identity, if required, is done at the time of enrollment through trusted external documentation, such as a birth certificate or driver's license. The biometric measures link the user to an enrolled identity and associated authorizations that are only as valid as the original determination process.

Not all systems, however, have a requirement to know a user's true name or identity. Biometric measures can be used as anonymous and pseudoanonymous identifiers and consequently have intriguing potential for privacy enhancement of authorization systems.

All biometric measures may change over time, because of aging of the body, injury, or disease. Therefore, reenrollment may be required. If true identity or continuity of identity is required by the system, reenrollment must necessitate presentation of trusted external documentation. Both enrollment and reenrollment also require the physical presence of the enrolling person before the enrolling authority. Otherwise, there is no way to determine that the enrolled biometric measure came from the body of the person presenting it.

## EXAMPLE APPLICATIONS

San Jose State University has been using hand geometry readers for around-the-clock, controlled, secure access to the Computer and Telecommunications Center since 1993. About 125 employees are enrolled in the system and log a combined 500 entrance events each day at the three entrances. The system records all events on a central PC, allowing management to audit after-hour access to the Center.

Employees enter a four-digit PIN into the system and place their right hand down on a reflective platen. Infrared light reflects vertically off the platen, but not the skin, allowing a "shadow" of the hand without texture information to be imaged. Additionally, a mirror reflects light horizontally across the top of the hand, supplying a second two-dimensional shadow of the side of the hand. These two, two-dimensional images are reduced using image processing techniques to a 9-byte sample, the values of which cannot be directly related to finger lengths, widths, or other anatomical measures. If the sample is "close enough" in Euclidean distance to the 9-byte template stored at enrollment, the door strike opens and access is permitted. Upon successful use, the system automatically updates the stored template by averaging in the newly acquired sample. The threshold used to determine "close enough" can be set individually, if necessary, to accommodate anyone having unusual difficulty using the system. The entire access process takes just a few seconds and the false rejection of daily (and therefore, habituated) users of the system is exceedingly rare.

Impostors would need both a valid PIN and the correct hand shape to gain access to the system. PIN guessing can be prevented by locking the system or alarming after some number of consecutive access failures.

The hand readers at each door cost about U.S.$1500 in 2005. Some additional items, such as electrically activated door strikes, cabling, and request-to-exit switches must be purchased and installed. The door strikes are controlled and powered directly from the hand reader unit. Although the units can stand alone, a central PC is usually desirable for event logging and for networking multiple units into a single template database. University management has been quite pleased with the cost, efficiency, and security of the system.

We can classify this as an application to verify a positive claim of identity, with trained, habituated users in an unsupervised office environment. The system is used only by employees of the Computer and Telecommunications Center, so is not a "public" application. It serves as a good cost, performance, and procedure model only for proposed applications with these same characteristics.

Since 1997, Purdue Employees Federal Credit Union (PEFCU) in West Lafayette, Indiana, has been using fingerprint verification to replace PINs at nine automatic teller machines (ATMs) kiosks. About 11,500 customers (20% of the PEFCU membership) are enrolled in the system, generating about 28,000 biometrically enabled transactions per month. Customers electing to use fingerprinting can enroll in the system at the central office by presenting any two fingers to an optical scanner. Customers with poor fingerprints because of age or occupation, and customers not wishing to participate, can continue to use traditional PINs at all PEFCU ATMs.

The scanner takes a digital image of the fingerprint, which is converted into a numerical structure based on the patterns in the fingerprint ridges. The numerical structure, but not the original fingerprint image, is stored in a central database. After enrollment, customers can withdraw or deposit cash or apply for loans presenting their ATM card with either enrolled fingerprint to the kiosk scanner. No PIN entry is required. To guide users in the proper placement of the finger, a display screen on the kiosk shows the user the image of the presented fingerprint and an image of an ideally placed finger. The numerical structure extracted from the presented fingerprint is compared to that in the central database stored under the entered user name. Close similarity between the stored and presented structures verifies that the user is the source of the claimed enrollment record and is, therefore, the authorized ATM card holder.

The fingerprinting technology is estimated to represent only a small fraction of the total $70,000 cost of the ATM kiosk. No case of fraud owing to misuse of the fingerprinting system has ever been reported. Incidence of fraud originating from fingerprint-equipped ATMs is currently less than 5% of the fraud rate on other ATMs operated by PEFCU. The credit union is currently expanding the fingerprint system to traditional teller lines to eliminate the need for enrolled users to present photo identification when making withdrawals.

We can classify this use by PEFCU as an application to verify a positive claim of identity, with habituated and nonhabituated users in an unsupervised indoor or outdoor environment. The system is used by a wide cross section of credit union customers, so can be called a public application. Consequently, we would expect the PEFCU application to be more challenging than the San Jose State University Computer Center application with its more controlled population and environment.

# BIOMETRICS AND PRIVACY

The concept *privacy* is highly culturally dependent. Legal definitions vary from country to country and, in the United States, even from state to state (Alderman & Kennedy, 1995). A classic definition is the intrinsic "right to be let alone" (Warren & Brandeis, 1890), but more modern definitions include informational privacy: the right of individuals "to determine for themselves when, how and to what extent information about them is communicated to others" (Westin, 1967). Both types of privacy can be impacted positively or negatively by biometric technology.

## Intrinsic (or Physical) Privacy

Some people see the use of biometric devices as an intrusion on intrinsic privacy. Touching a publicly used biometric device, such as a fingerprint or hand geometry reader, may seem physically intrusive, even though there is no evidence that disease can spread any more easily by these devices than by door handles. People may also object to being asked to look into cameras or to stand still while giving an iris or facial image.

Not all biometric methods require physical contact. A biometric application that replaced the use of a keypad with the imaging of an iris, for instance, might be seen as enhancing of physical privacy.

If biometrics are used to limit access to private spaces, then biometrics can be more enhancing to intrinsic privacy than other forms of access control, such as keys, which are not as closely linked to the holder

There are people who object to use of biometrics on religious grounds: Some Muslim women object to displaying their face to a camera and some Christians object to hand biometrics as the Biblical "the sign of the beast." In response, it has been noted (Seildarz, 1998) that a theistic interpretation would more properly consider biometric patterns to be marks given by God.

It can be argued (Locke, 1690; Baker, 2000) that a physical body is not identical to the person that inhabits it. Whereas PINs and passwords identify persons, biometrics identifies the body. Some people are uncomfortable with biometrics because of this connection to the physical level of human identity, the possibility of nonconsensual collection, and the impossibility of changing biometric measures if stolen. Biometric measures could allow linking of the various "persons" or psychological identities that each of us choose to manifest in our separate dealings within our social structures. Biometrics, if universally collected without adequate controls, could aid in linking employment records to health history and church membership, for example. This leads us to the concept of "informational privacy."

## Informational Privacy

With notably minor qualifications, biometric features contain no personal information whatsoever about the user. This includes no information about health status, age, nationality, ethnicity, or gender. Consequently, this also limits the power of biometrics to prevent underage access to pornography on the Internet or to detect voting registration by noncitizens.

No single biometric measure has been demonstrated to be distinctive or repeatable enough to allow the selection of a single person out of a very large database. However, when aggregated with other data, such as name, telephone area code, or other even weakly identifying attributes, biometric measures can lead to *unique* identification within a large population. For this reason, databases of biometric information must be treated as personally identifiable information and protected accordingly.

Biometrics can be directly used to enhance informational privacy. Use to control access to and promote accountability with databases containing personal and personally identifiable data can enhance informational privacy. The use of biometric measures, in place of name or social security number, to anonymize personal data, is privacy enhancing.

## SUGGESTED RULES FOR SECURE USE OF BIOMETRICS

From what has been discussed thus far, we can develop some reasonable rules for the use of biometrics for logical and physical access control and similar applications.

1. Never participate in a biometric system that allows either remote enrollment or reenrollment. Such systems have no way of connecting a user with the enrolled biometric data, so the purpose of using biometrics to connect the user more closely to the authentication mechanism is lost.

2. Biometric measures can reveal your identity only if they are linked at enrollment to your name, social security number, or other closely identifying information. Without that linkage, your biometric measures are anonymous.

3. Remember that biometric measures cannot be reissued if stolen or sold. Do not enroll in a nonanonymous system unless you have complete trust in the system administration.

4. All biometric access control systems must have "exception handling" mechanisms for those that either cannot enroll or cannot reliably use the system. If you are uncomfortable with enrolling in a biometric system for verifying positive claims of identity, insist on routinely using the "exception handling" mechanism instead.

5. The most privacy enhancing biometric systems are those in which each user controls his/her own template.

6. Because biometric measures are not perfectly repeatable, are not completely distinctive, and require specialized data collection hardware, biometric systems are not useful for tracking people within large populations. Anyone who really wants to physically track the movements of a person in a large population will use credit card, phone records, or cell phone emanations instead. But over a small population, biometric measures are distinctive and repeatable enough to provide

accountability for activities such as accessing stored information. Consequently, the technology itself should not be feared. In the proper applications, biometrics can be used as a strongly privacy enhancing technology.

## CONCLUSIONS

Automated methods for human identification have a history predating the digital computer age. For decades, mass adoption of biometric technologies has appeared to be just a few years away (Raphael & Young, 1974), yet even today, difficulties remain in establishing a strong business case, in motivating consumer demand, and in creating a single system usable by all sizes and shapes of persons. Nonetheless, the biometric industry has grown at a steady pace as consumers, industry, and government have found appropriate applications for these technologies. Although the privacy implications continue to be debated, biometrics can be used in privacy enhancing applications. Only time will tell if biometric technologies will receive widespread application in the area of information security.

## GLOSSARY

**Biometrics** The automatic recognition of living persons based on distinguishing traits.

**Decision** A determination of probable validity of a subject's claim to an identity or no identity in the system.

**Enrollment** A subject presenting (or being presented) to a biometric system for the first time, creating an identity within the system, and submitting biometric samples for the creation of biometric measures to be stored with that identity.

**Failure-to-Acquire rate** The percentage of transactions for which the system cannot obtain a usable biometric sample.

**Failure-to-Enroll rate** The percentage of a population for which the system cannot create a usable template.

**False Acceptance Rate** The expected proportion of transactions with wrongful claims of identity (in a positive ID system) or nonidentity (in a negative ID system) that are incorrectly confirmed. In applications to verify positive claims, the FAR will be dependent upon the false match rate and the system policy specifying how many attempts will be allowed to prove the claimed identity. In negative identification systems, the FAR may include the failure-to-acquire rate and the false nonmatch rate.

**False Match Rate** The false match rate is the expected probability that an acquired sample will be falsely declared to match to a single, randomly-selected, non-self template or model.

**False Nonmatch Rate (FNMR)** The false nonmatch rate is the expected probability that an acquired sample will be falsely declared not to match a template or model from the same user.

**False Rejection Rate (FRR)** The expected proportion of transactions with truthful claims of identity (in a positive ID system) or nonidentity (in a negative ID system) that are incorrectly denied. In positive identification systems, the FRR will include the failure-to-enroll and the failure-to-acquire rates, as well as the false nonmatch rate.

**Features** A mathematical representation of the information extracted from the presented sample by the signal processing subsystem that will be used to construct or compare against enrolment templates. Biometric features generally have no direct anatomical meaning.

**Identifier** An identity pointer, such as a biometric measure, a PIN (personal identification number), or a name.

**Identity** An information record about a person, perhaps including attributes or authorizations, or other pointers, such as names or identifying numbers.

**Matching Score** A measure of similarity or dissimilarity between a presented sample and a stored template or model.

**Models** Mathematical representation of the generating process for biometric measures.

**Negative Claim of Identity** The claim that a subject is not known to or enrolled in the system. As an example, social service systems open only to those not already enrolled require all applicants to make negative claims to any existing identity in the system.

**Positive Claim of Identity** The claim that a subject is enrolled in or known to the system. A specific positive claim of identity will be accompanied by an identifier in the form of a name, PIN, or identification number. Common access control systems are an example. An unspecific positive claim of identity will not require any identifier be given other than the biometric sample. "PIN-less" verification systems are an example.

**Sample** A biometric signal presented by the subject and captured by the data collection subsystem. (E.g., voice signals, fingerprints, and face images are samples)

**Template** A subject's stored reference measure based on features extracted from samples.

**Transaction** An attempt by a subject to prove a claim of identity or nonidentity by consecutively submitting one or more samples, as allowed by the system policy.

**Verification** Proving as truthful a subject's claim to an identity in the system.

**Zero-Effort Impostor** a fraudulent or opportunistic user who submits their own biometric measure without alteration in an attempt to make a positive claim to another, randomly chosen identity.

## CROSS REFERENCES

See *Computer and Network Authentication; Issues and Concerns in Biometric IT Security; Password Authentication.*

## REFERENCES

Alderman, E., & Kennedy, C. (1995). *The right to privacy.* New York: Vintage.

Baker, L. R. (2000). *Persons and bodies: A constitution view.* Cambridge, UK: Cambridge University Press.

Beavan, C. (2001). *Fingerprints.* New York: Hyperion.

Blackburn, D., Bone, M., Grother, P., & Phillips, P. J. (2001). *Facial recognition vendor test 2000: Evaluation report.* Retrieved January 25, 2004, from http://www.frvt.org

Bledsoe, W. W. (1966). *Man–machine facial recognition: Report on a large-scale experiment.* Palo Alto, CA: Panoramic Research, Inc.

Bouchier, F., Ahrens, J., & Wells, G. (1996). *Laboratory evaluation of the IriScan Prototype Biometric Identifier.* Retrieved July 11, 2004, from at http://infoserve.library.sandia.gov/sand_doc/1996/961033.pdf

Chang, S. H., Pihl, G. E., & Essignmann, M. W (1951). Representations of speech sounds and some of their statistical properties. *Proceedings of the Institute of Electrical and Electronic Engineers*, IRE, New York, NY:147–153.

Cole, S. (2001). *Suspect identities.* Cambridge, MA: Harvard University Press.

Daugman, J. (1993). High confidence visual recognition of persons by a test of statistical independence. *Transactions on Pattern Analysis and Machine Intelligence, 15*, 1148–1161. [Retrieved July 1, 2004, from http://www.cl.cam.ac.uk/users/jgd1000/PAMI93.pdf]

Faulds, H. (1880). On the skin furrows of the hand. *Nature, 22*, 605. [Retrieved July 11, 2004, from http://www.scafo.org/library/100101.html]

Fejfar, A. (1978, May). *Combining techniques to improve security in automated entry control.* Paper presented at Carnahan Conference on Crime Countermeasures, Mitre Corp. MTP-191, University of Kentucky.

Fejfar, A., & Myers, J. W. (1977, July). The testing of three automatic identity verification techniques. In *Proceedings of the International Conference on Crime Countermeasures*, Oxford, UK.

Flom, L., & Safir, A. (1987). Iris recognition system, U.S. Patent 4,641,349.

Galton, F. (1888). On personal identification and description. *Nature, 21/28*, 201–202. [Retrieved July 11, 2004, from http://www.scafo.org/library/100801.html]

Goldstein, A. J., Harmon, L. D., & Lesk, A. B. (1971). Identification of human faces. *Proceedings of the Institute of Electrical and Electronic Engineers, 59*, 748–760.

Herschel, W. J. (1880). Skin furrows of the hand. *Nature, 23*, 76.

IBM. (1970). *The considerations of data security in a computer environment* (Report G520-2169). White Plains, NY: Author.

Kent, S. T., & Millett, L. I. (2003). *Who goes there? Authentication through the lens of privacy.* Washington, DC: National Academies Press. [Retrieved July 11, 2004, from http://books.nap.edu/html/whogoes/]

Locke, J. (1690). *An essay concerning human understanding* (Book 2, Chapter 27). [Retrieved July 11, 2004, from http://www.ilt.columbia.edu/publications/locke_understanding.html]

Lummis, R. C., & Rosenberg, A. (1972). Test of an ASV method with intensively trained professional mimics. *Journal of the Acoustical Society of America, 51*, 131.

Maio, D., Maltoni, D., Wayman, J., & Jain, A. (2002). FVC2000: Fingerprint verification competition. *Transactions on Pattern Analysis and Machine Intelligence, 24*, 402–411.

Mansfield, A. J., Kelly, G., Chandler, D., & Kane, J. (2000). *Biometric product testing final report.* Retrieved

July 11, 2004, from http://www.cesg.gov.uk/site/ast/biometrics/media/BiometricTestReportpt1.pdf

Mansfield, A. J., & Wayman, J. L. (2002). *Best practices for testing and reporting biometric device performance, issue 2.0*. U.K. Biometrics Working Group. Retrieved July 11, 2004, from http://www. cesg.gov.uk/site/ast/biometrics/media/BestPractice.pdf

Matsumoto, T., Matsumoto, H., Yamada, K., & Hoshino, S. (2002, January). *Impact of artificial 'gummy' fingers on fingerprint systems*. In Proceedings of SPIE, 4677, San Jose, CA.

Messner, W. K., Cleciwa, C. A., Kibbler, G. O. T. H., & Parlee, W. L. (1974). Research and development of personal identify verification systems. In *Proceedings 1974 Carnahan and International Crime Countermeasures Conference*, University of Kentucky, Laxington, KY.

Osborn, S. (1929). *Questioned documents*. Chicago: Nelson-Hall.

National Bureau of Standards. (1977). *Guidelines for evaluation of techniques for automated personal identification*. (Federal Information Processing Standard Publication 48). Washington, DC: Author.

National Institute of Standards and Technology. (2003). *Speaker recognition evaluation*. Retrieved July 11, 2004, from http://www.nist.gov/speech/tests/spk/2003/index.htm

Philips, P. J., Grother, P., Bone, M., & Blackburn, D. (2002). Facial recognition vendor test 2002. Retrieved July 11, 2004, from http://www.frvt.org/DLs/FRVT_2002_Evaluation_Report.pdf

Phillips, P. J., Martin, A., Wilson, C. L., & Przybocki, M. (2000). An introduction to evaluating biometric systems. *Computer, 33*, 56–63. Retrieved July 11, 2004, from www.frvt.org/DLs/FERET7.pdf

Potter, R. K., Kopp, G. A., & Green, H. C. (1947). *Visible speech*. New York: van Nostrand Co.

Pruzansky, S. (1963). Pattern-matching procedure for automatic talker recognition. *Journal of the Acoustical Society of America, 26*, 403–406.

Raphael, D. E., & Young, J.R. (1974). *Automated personal identification*. Palo Alto, CA: SRI International.

Rodriguez, J. R., Bouchier, F., & Ruehie, M. (1993). *Performance evaluation of biometric identification devices*. Albuquerque: Sandia National Laboratory Report SAND93-1930.

Seildarz, J. (1998, April 6). [Letter to the editor]. *Philadelphia Inquirer*.

Simon, C., & Goldstein, I. (1935). A new scientific method of identification. *New York State Journal of Medicine, 35*, 901–906.

Thalheim, L., Krissler, J., & Ziegler, P. (2002). Biometric access protection devices and their programs put to the test. *C T Magazine, 11*, 114. Retrieved July 11, 2004, from www.heise.de/ct/english/02/11/114.

Trauring, M. (1963a). On the automatic comparison of finger ridge patterns. *Nature, 197*, 938–940.

Trauring, M. (1963b). Automatic comparison of finger ridge patterns. *Hughes Research Laboratory Report, 190*.

Twain, M. (1893). Pudd'nhead Wilson. In *The Century*, serialized *47(2)–48(2)*. New York: The Century Company.

van der Putte, T., & Keuning, J. (2000). Biometrical fingerprint recognition: Don't get your fingers burned. In *IFIP TC8/WG.8., Fourth Working Group Conference on Smart Card Research and Advanced Applications* (pp. 289–303). Retrieved July 11, 2004, from http://www.keuning.com/biometry/Biometrical_Fingerprint_Recognition.pdf

Warren, S., & Brandeis, L. (1890). The right of privacy. *Harvard Law Review, 4*, 193. Retrieved July 11, 2004, from www.louisville.edu/library/law/brandeis/privacy.html.

Wayman, J. L. (2000). Evaluation of the INSPASS hand geometry data. In J. L. Wayman (Ed.), *U.S. National Biometric Test Center Collected Works: 1997–2000*. San Jose: San Jose State University.

Wegstein, J. (1970). Automated fingerprint identification. *National Bureau of Standards Technical Note*, Gaithersburg, MD. 538.

Westin, A. (1967). *Privacy and freedom*. Boston: Atheneum.

# Issues and Concerns in Biometric IT Security

Philip Statham, *CESG, U.K.*

## INTRODUCTION

Biometrics, literally *the measure of life*, is used here to refer to the automated recognition of individuals based on their behavioral and biological characteristics. Examples of behavioral characteristics are signature and keystroke dynamics; biological characteristics include fingerprints, iris patterns, and hand geometry. Voice recognition is an interesting case as it is a combination of biological and behavioral characteristics.

This basic ability to recognize individuals can be used as part of an authentication process to control access to assets or services. What constitutes authentication will depend on the application. Typically we think of physical or logical access control applications, where authentication serves to ensure that access is only granted to previously enrolled authorized users. It is easy to overlook the significance of the enrollment stage. Not only does enrollment play a vital part in the integrity of the authentication process, but its actual function may depend on the application. In some cases an important part of the enrollment process will be to ensure that an intending enrollee is not already enrolled in the application, perhaps under another name or identity. Biometrics can provide a valuable tool to guard against so-called multiple identity frauds in applications offering beneficial services such as welfare payments, driving licenses, passports, and visas. This type of check has proved exceedingly hard to do successfully without recourse to biometrics. In reality, few applications will use biometrics solely for what we might term this *negative identification* function—most applications that make use of negative identification also implement the more familiar authentication function as well.

It is important to realize that biometrics, in common with other forms of authentication, is not a security panacea. It can only play a useful role as one component of a holistic security strategy. Knowledge of biometric functionality and technology, with its strength and limitations, will allow prospective implementers to appreciate whether and how biometrics can provide security to their applications and to determine what other issues need to be addressed by the system security policy to meet the overall security requirements.

The security assurance of an authentication mechanism is ultimately limited by its integrity. For password mechanisms, the integrity is mainly defined by the password space, the strength of the password hashing algorithm, and of course the secrecy of the password itself. For token-based authentication, integrity is determined by the difficulty of acquiring or forging the token. Both passwords and tokens offer indirect forms of authentication, whereas biometrics involves an intrinsic property of the individual and offers a direct form of authentication and a strong binding to that individual.

This intrinsic property and the personal nature of the biometric data raise another significant distinction between biometrics and other authentication technologies, namely that of the privacy issues surrounding the capture, storage, and use of personal data. The use of biometrics brings with it the need to safeguard the biometric data beyond that necessary to protect the integrity of the authentication mechanism itself. In many countries, personal data protection legislation is in place that applies to biometric data. Even where this is not so, if widespread user acceptance of biometrics is to be attained, implementers will probably need to adopt codes of practice that will give similar protection to biometric data.

To provide implementers, legislators, and end users with the confidence that applications employing biometrics are designed, implemented, and operated in a secure way, security evaluation to accredited standards will be needed. The International Common Criteria Security Evaluation Scheme (ISO 15408, 1999) is the ISO standard for security evaluation of products and systems. Standards for Common Criteria Biometric product and system evaluation are currently under development by the biometrics community as an important step in providing confidence in the security of biometric systems deployed in the future.

This chapter explores the information security issues around the use of biometric technology for human authentication. It addresses some major concerns that have been raised both by prospective implementers and also by the end user community. Most people's knowledge of biometrics is limited to what they have seen in films and on TV and read in the printed media. This inevitably gives rise to some misconceptions in terms of both what biometrics

is capable of doing and also to fears that are not always well founded in reality. Nevertheless, some concerns are genuine and need to be tackled squarely by the biometrics community. Solutions are readily available to some of these but, as we will see, there are areas where much further research and development will be needed to provide the necessary confidence. Not all the solutions are technical in nature; some involve the sensible and sensitive application of procedural measures, including codes of best practice, which have a legislative underpinning in some countries.

## Biometric Source Feature and Biometric Image—A Note on Terminology

We frequently use the terms *biometric source feature* and *biometric image* (sometimes just image) in this chapter. The biometric source feature is the biometric as it exists on or with the user; the image is the form that the biometric source feature takes when it is recorded by the biometric capture device. Frequently this will actually be an image (e.g., for fingerprint, iris, hand, and face) but in some cases it will be audio (e.g., for voice) or a pattern of movement (e.g., for signature). However, in this chapter, for simplicity, we use the term *image* regardless of the actual form, unless explicitly stated otherwise. Of course, in all cases, the image data is conveyed within the biometric system by electrical signals. Note that the unqualified term *feature* is often used in biometric literature to refer to extracted data from the image that is actually used for the biometric comparison process, either directly or encoded and stored in the form of a biometric template. Occasionally in this chapter we use feature in its generic English language sense (e.g., "security feature"), which we trust will be clear from the surrounding context.

## AUTHENTICATION, IDENTIFICATION, AND VERIFICATION

These terms are widely used in the biometrics literature and elsewhere, unfortunately with no consistency of meaning. Sometimes the words are used interchangeably for a single concept. In other instances, the same word is used to express entirely different concepts in different publications. This results in widespread confusion. This chapter does not seek to resolve these conflicts (which would be impossible), nor to claim supremacy over definitions or use elsewhere. We are concerned here simply with explaining how the terms are used in this chapter, in a way we hope is at least reasonable and internally consistent. We use authentication as a general description for the overall process of authorizing a person before granting access to assets or beneficial services. The U.K.'s e-Government Unit (e-Government, 2002), in one of its strategy framework and policy guidelines documents, recognizes two stages in the overall process as follows:

Registration: This is the process by which a user gains a credential such as a username or digital certificate for subsequent authentication. It may require the user to present proof of real-world identity (such as a birth certificate or passport) and/or proof of other attributes depending on the intended use of the credential (e.g., proof that an individual works for a particular organization). Registration can be associated with a real-world identity or can be anonymous or pseudonymous.

Authentication: The process by which the electronic identity of a user is asserted to, and validated by, an information system for a specific occasion using a credential issued following a registration process. It may also involve establishing that the user is the true holder of that credential, by means of a password or biometric. A client is required to authenticate their electronic identity in order to use some of the services available through UKonline.

This gives a flavor of the meaning that we can accept here, but we note that the terms *verification* and *identification* have assumed a special significance in the context of biometrics:

Verification: The biometric process of determining the validity of a claim of identity. Conceptually this may be thought of as the one-to-one process of comparing a submitted biometric sample against the biometric reference template of a single enrollee whose identity is being claimed to determine whether it matches the enrollee's template. Note, however, that this description should not be taken to infer anything about the internal processes of a specific biometric system implementation (which could involve multiple comparisons).

Identification: The biometric process that results in the return of an identifier or a pointer to an identity (which may be empty). Conceptually this is a one-to-many process of comparing a submitted biometric sample against all or a set of biometric templates in the template database to determine which—if any—template it matches and, where a match is found, to return the identity of the enrollee whose template was matched; otherwise a null match.

For further information on biometric terminology see the Glossary.

## PERFORMANCE AND SECURITY

The capture and matching of biometric characteristics is an imperfect process. There are a number of sources of variability, including those resulting from changes in the capture device and of the environment in which the source features are captured, though in many cases the main variability results from changes in the biometric source feature itself and the interaction of the subject with the system. The effect of this variability is to lead to uncertainty in matching decisions, which in turn sets limitations on the performance achievable. The principal factors are the (undesirable) differences among biometric samples captured from the same individual, and the (desirable) differences among biometric samples captured from different individuals. Typically, these two groups do not occupy completely disjoint sets in the decision space, leading to decision errors.

At the heart of a biometric system are the biometric matching algorithm and the associated decision process, whose functions are to make comparisons between pairs of biometric features extracted from biometric samples and to determine whether they form a matching pair. Usually, one member of the pair is a reference derived from a stored template, whereas the other is derived from the "test" sample. Because an exact match is unlikely, even when the samples do come from the same person, the overall process involves firstly calculating a score that indicates how close the match is to perfection. The system decision policy defines a predetermined score that will be used to delineate between match and nonmatch for the system—commonly referred to as the threshold for the system. In many cases the threshold score will be constant for all enrollees, but more complex scenarios are possible (e.g., individual thresholds set for each enrollee).

Four outcomes are possible at the matching level, two representing correct decisions and two incorrect (i.e., error) conditions.

1. *Matching Level—Correct Decisions*
   - True Match—The decision process correctly determines that the test and reference features do come from the same source feature of a single individual.
   - True Nonmatch—The decision process correctly determines that the test and reference features do not come from the same source feature of a single individual.
2. *Matching Level—Incorrect Decisions*
   - False Match—The decision process incorrectly determines that the test and reference features match, whereas in fact the test and reference features DO NOT come from the same source feature of a single individual.
   - False Nonmatch—The decision process incorrectly determines that the test and reference features do not match, whereas in fact the test and reference features DO come from the same source feature of a single individual.

When measured statistically over large numbers of subject comparisons, these parameters can be expressed in terms of true match rate (TMR), false match rate (FMR), true nonmatch rate (TNMR), and false nonmatch rate (FNMR). Many discussions of matching level performance concentrate on the error conditions—FMR and FNMR.

At the system level, performance is characterized in terms of the evaluation of claims in regard to the application, with the result that the system either accepts or rejects the claim. All biometric systems evaluate claims, the precise formulation of the claim being dependent on the function or functions of the system. Claims can be explicit or implicit, positive or negative; claims may be made by the subjects whose biometrics are tested or on behalf of the subjects. In the latter case, a claim may be regarded as a hypothesis that the biometric system is being used to evaluate. Examples of claims are as follows:

- I am John Doe (positive explicit claim by subject).
- I am not Jane Doe (negative explicit claim by subject).
- I have previously enrolled in the system (positive implicit claim by subject).

- I have not previously enrolled in the system (negative implicit claim by subject).
- Check whether the subject is enrolled in the system [positive implicit claim (hypothesis) about subject].

The list above is not exhaustive but it covers many cases in practice.

Note: Biometric systems for which claims (hypotheses) are made about the subjects rather than by the subjects are often covert (e.g., surveillance systems) or have some covert function in addition to their overt function. In such cases it would be disingenuous to regard the subject as having made any claim.

The system evaluates these claims, which it may do correctly or incorrectly. This gives rise to the corresponding system-level performance parameters: true accept rate (TAR), false accept rate (FAR), true reject rate (TRR), and false reject rate (FRR). As previously, many discussions of system-level performance concentrate on the error conditions—FAR and FRR.

It is important to realize that the relationship between the algorithmic matching error rates FMR and FNMR and the application-level error rates FAR and FRR is not necessarily simple or invariant. In particular, where negative claims are being evaluated, the intuitive relationships between FMR and FAR, and FNMR and FRR, are inverted and become relationships between FNMR and FAR, and FMR and FRR. This will have ramifications when it comes to determining the relevance of the various error rates to security considerations, which are application dependent.

It will be apparent that as the threshold score is adjusted the error rates will change. In particular it will be possible to trade off (at the system level) the FAR against the FRR. Figure 1 is extracted from a report on a biometric device performance test conducted in 2001 at the U.K. National Physical Laboratory (Mansfield, Kelly, Chandler, & Kane, 2001). It illustrates the relationship between the FAR and FRR with threshold score as the parameter for a number of different biometric technologies under test conditions in the laboratory.

Although it is evident that errors are likely to have security ramifications, it is not immediately obvious how to characterize the errors in security terms for two reasons:

1. The relevance of errors will be highly dependent on the application—in particular on the function that the biometric element is performing and the likely consequences of any errors that occur.
2. It is not obvious how to relate error rates in biometric authentication to error rates that occur with other forms of authentication.

At this point we discuss two generic classes of application for the purpose of illustrating the significance of FAR and FRR in each case.

## Positive Identification and Verification Applications

Examples of this type of application include physical access control to a building and logical access control to an IT workstation. They are intended to allow convenient access to authorized persons while preventing access by unauthorized persons. The effect of false accept errors is to allow casual impostors a chance to gain unauthorized access. System implementers who are familiar with conventional password/PIN access and are capable of assessing the risk associated with casual attacks on these mechanisms will be seeking advice on what FAR they should be aiming for to achieve comparable levels of protection with biometric access control. Intuitively, we feel that there is a connection between password space and FAR, because both parameters characterize the effective

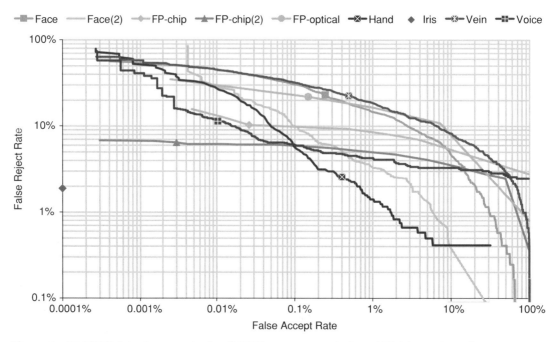

**Figure 1:**   FAR/FRR detection error trade-off (DET) curves—results from NPL biometric performance tests.

**Table 1** Biometric Strength of Function Against False Accept Rate—Access Control (BEM, 2002)

| FAR | Strength |
| --- | --- |
| 1 in 100 | Basic |
| 1 in 10,000 | Medium |
| 1 in 1,000,000 | High |

discrimination of their respective mechanisms. However, the attack profiles are not well matched because attackers cannot perform a biometric exhaustion attack in the way that they could on a password. This infers that applying a simple one-to-one equivalency between FAR and password [e.g., password space of 10,000 (four-digit PIN) is equivalent to FAR of 1 in 10,000] would not be correct because the susceptibility of the biometric to retries is low compared to the password case (see Table 1). Discussion among security specialists who are experienced in both biometric and password authentication mechanisms have resulted in the figures suggested in Table 1 for biometric security strength of function related to FAR.

The ratings basic, medium, and high are the three levels recognized by Common Criteria for the strength of function of a mechanism where the security protection depends on a probabilistic mechanism. Passwords and PINs fall into this class. For comparison, a four-digit PIN is rated as a basic strength mechanism under Common Criteria.

False reject errors are generally a usability issue for an access control application. If the FRR is excessive, the system may become unusable. However, if usability problems cause the decision threshold to be changed to reduce the FRR, the FAR may increase, which will of course reduce the security strength. Therefore, inadequate FRR may indirectly result in compromises of the FAR and hence the strength of function. System implementers will need to ensure that when the threshold is adjusted to achieve an acceptable FRR, the corresponding FAR still satisfies the strength of function requirement for the application.

## Negative Identification Applications

A typical important requirement of such a system is the ability to detect attempts by individuals to enroll multiple times on the system using different identities. Traditional countermeasures involve extensive document checks, which are slow, expensive, and prone to error. Forged documents are also a common problem, which can render the checking process ineffective. Biometric checking is an attractive alternative because it can offer a quick, direct means of checking for multiple identities based on individuals' intrinsic biometric characteristics.

During enrollment, a person's biometric characteristic or characteristics are captured and are checked against the enrollment database of biometric templates to ensure that the enrollment is unique to the application. Limitations in the effectiveness of the check will be determined by the FNMR in this case because a false nonmatch error means that a prior enrollment for an individual has been missed, giving rise to the acceptance of a false claim

(corresponding to a false accept error). False match errors give rise to false alarms, which are false rejections of true claims (corresponding to false reject errors) and which will be at least inconvenient and, more seriously, could lead to enrollees being falsely accused of fraud.

System implementers will need to balance the conflicting requirements to detect fraud attempts while minimizing false alarms. One concern with this type of application is that it may be easier for a malevolent user to force an FNMR error (i.e., failure to match against a previous enrolled template) than it would be to force an FMR error (i.e., an apparent match between two different individuals). This is particularly true for behavioral biometrics and for unsupervised system operations. Note that this underlines the importance of providing proper supervision for such applications.

It should be noted that few applications are likely to operate exclusively in a negative id functional mode. This mode of operation is typically characteristic of the enrollment stage; operational use usually involves either positive identification or verification functional mode, although applications may use both positive and negative functional modes in normal operation to keep a continuing check on multiple identities. Indeed some applications may use a combination of positive identification, verification, and negative identification to meet complex, multifunction requirements.

## Measuring Biometric System Performance

Biometric system performance can be characterized by many parameters including failure and error rates for enrollment, acquisition, verification, and so on as well as speed factors such as throughput. We are interested here in the performance factors that have a direct effect on security, which we characterized earlier by error rates of the biometric algorithms FMR and FNMR and the system application-level decision error rates: FAR and FRR. For a specific application, these error rates relate to the security of the application against attempts by opportunistic impersonators. They might be viewed in a similar light to the protection that the password space gives against opportunistic attacks on a password-based mechanism. Note that the analogy should not be stretched too far, because the biometric is not subject to the same kind of exhaustion attack that a password would be.

As described previously, these rates are interdependent and can be traded off against each other by adjusting the decision threshold. The relationship between FAR and FRR can be determined as the threshold is adjusted and the results are typically plotted as a receiver operating characteristic (ROC) curve or detection error trade-off (DET) curve, where environmental and other test conditions are kept constant. Note that ROC and DET curves plot the same data but are displayed in a different way. The ROC curve plots true accept rate against FAR, whereas the DET curve plots FRR (1-true accept rate) against FAR. DET curves are often preferred because they make it easier to see performance differences between similarly performing biometric algorithms or systems. Logarithmic scaling is commonly used to plot the whole range of error rates while emphasizing the important region at the lower end of the range. As the threshold is adjusted to lower the FAR, then the FRR inevitably rises; similarly adjusting the threshold to lower the FRR results in a rise in FAR. Figure 1 shows DET curves for a number of biometric devices from biometric performance tests undertaken in 2001 at the U.K. National Physical Laboratory.

A major difficulty is that these error rates cannot be determined by theoretical analysis of the matching algorithm. Biometric error rates are crucially dependent on the distribution and variability of the relevant biometric source feature among human beings in general and the members of the user group in particular. Errors are also influenced by user behavior; how technically literate, patient, and cooperative they are and the incentives to be recognized (or not to be recognized) according to the outcome.

Realistic performance measurements can be obtained only through practical measurement at our present level of understanding of biometric technology and applications. As with other probabilistic testing, accurate results necessitate large numbers of independent trials, which means large numbers of test subjects. Cost and complexity normally limit the accuracy that can be achieved practically. To illustrate the problem, if we wish to confirm a claimed FAR of 1% to a 90% confidence level, at least 300 independent tests must be performed without any false matches occurring. To preserve proper sample independence, 600 test subjects would be needed, assuming that each subject can only provide one independent biometric sample. In many tests, compromises are often tolerated in the interest of practicability. For example, increasing the number of tests by matching each subject against all other subjects allows 600 subjects to generate (600 × 599)/2 cross matches.

Performance testing has been characterized (Phillips, Martin, Wilson, & Pryzbocki, 2000) into three categories as follows:

1. Technology Testing—to determine the performance of the image feature extraction and matching algorithm of a biometric device. This is usually done offline, using a database of test images captured on a standard capture device. Technical testing is often done by external organizations to compare the performance of different algorithms or by developers to measure improvements in performance of an algorithm under development. However, technology testing could be used for other purposes (e.g., to compare the performance of different capture devices when using the same algorithm and database).

2. Scenario Testing—To determine the performance of a complete biometric system in a predetermined, modeled environment. This is done using live capture of the biometric characteristics of an appropriately selected test population. Scenario testing may be conducted
   - to predict the performance of a biometric system in a future live application and
   - to compare the performance of different biometric systems under the same test conditions.

3. Operational Testing—To measure the real performance of a biometric system in operational use.

Each of the test types serves useful but different purposes. Technical testing is typically used as a research and development tool to measure the performance of the core algorithms and to stimulate improvements in biometric technology. Scenario testing may seek to emulate an operational environment to predict the performance of the operational system. Or it may be used in an attempt to rank similar systems under controlled conditions that have some recognizable relevance to real-life situations. Operational testing is not generally feasible for comparative testing because the conditions of use of different applications are not usually sufficiently alike to allow meaningful comparison of results.

## Performance Test Results Available in the Public Domain

A number of organizations have conducted biometric tests and published results in the public domain, some on a regular basis. The following paragraphs detail some well-known examples.

### Facial Recognition Vendor Test

Under the auspices of the U.S. National Institute of Standards and Technology (NIST), and with sponsorship and support of many other organizations, the U.S. government has conducted a regular series of tests of facial recognition algorithms. These tests began in the 1990s as the FAce REcognition Test (FERET) tests and were updated in 2000, 2002, and 2005 to become the Face Recognition Vendor Test (FRVT). The organizers supply a large test corpus of facial images comprising many individuals, including multiple (different) images of the same individual. Developers are provided with a copy of the corpus and are invited to test their recognition algorithms against the images using specified protocols and to report the results back to the organizers—hence the "vendor test" alluded to in the name. The results are analyzed by the FRVT team, who alone know the so-called ground truth (i.e., which images correspond to which individuals). The results are reported on the FRVT Web site (see FRVT, 2005, for further information). Note that FRVT 2005 was the latest test at the time of publication of this article, but the interested reader should check the FRVT Web site for the most recent test report. The FRVT is an example of technology testing.

### Fingerprint Verification Competition

This is a technology test of fingerprint algorithms organized by the University of Bologna, Italy. The test is conducted using several databases of fingerprint images, each collected with a different fingerprint reader. More recently a database comprising synthesized fingerprint images produced by an algorithm developed at the University of Bologna has been included. Fingerprint Verification Competition (FVC) is run as a competition where fingerprint algorithm developers from commerce and academe are invited to submit algorithms in a specified standard form that allows them to be embedded in a test harness developed by the university. The published protocol for the test describes the methodology that will be used and the parameters to be measured in the test. The organizers conduct the testing against the test databases and report the results on the FVC Web site. A simple alphanumeric coding within the results identifies the algorithms. Competitors may identify their products with the results if they wish, or they may choose to remain anonymous. At the time of writing, FVC 2000, FVC 2002, and FVC 2004 results have been published. Again, the reader should visit the FVC Web site to determine the current status of the FVC tests—see FVC (2000), FVC (2002), and FVC (2004).

### NPL Biometric Product Test

This test, conducted by the U.K. National Physical Laboratory, is an example of a scenario test. It is an output from the U.K. Government Biometrics Working Group, sponsored by CESG, the U.K. Information Assurance Technical Authority, and forms a companion document to the best practice testing methodology (Mansfield, 2002). The NPL test was performed mainly to validate the methodology, but at the same time to generate results that could be used as representative of the performance of commercial products available at the time. The NPL test covers a range of common biometric technologies, and the results are available on the CESG Web site (see Mansfield, Kelly, Chandler, & Kane, 2001, for further details).

### Other Biometric Tests in the Public Domain

Other biometrics tests include the ICBA Face Verification Contest on the Banca dataset (ICBA, 2004) and SVC 2004 First International Signature Recognition Competition (SVC, 2004).

## SPOOFING, MIMICRY, AND LIVENESS DETECTION

Spoofing is the name usually given to an attempt by a person to fool a biometric system by presenting to the system an artifact that bears a copy of a biometric source feature. The motivation could be to impersonate another individual or to appear not to be the actual person who is presenting the biometric. It is a concern for biometric technology that utilizes biological source features such as fingerprints, iris patterns, and face and hand geometry. In these cases the artifact takes a tangible form. This may be contrasted with attacks against behavioral biometric systems that involve behavioral copying, which we term *mimicry*.

The main motivation for spoofing is likely to be an impostor who wishes to appear to be an enrollee. The remainder of this section addresses the issue of spoofing from this standpoint, though readers should bear in mind possible alternative motivations and their ramifications.

Successful spoofing undermines the binding between the extracted biometric features used within the biometric system for the recognition process and the individual who possesses the corresponding biometric source feature. It is the presumed strength of this binding that is often the principal motivation for using biometrics, so a demonstrable weakness in this area must be regarded as a serious matter. A number of studies have been conducted that have demonstrated the potential susceptibility to spoofing attacks of some commercial biometric products under carefully controlled conditions (Gunnerson, 1999; Matsumoto, Matsumoto, Yamada, & Hoshino, 2002; Thalheim, Krissler, & Ziegler, 2002; Van der Putte & Keuning, 2000; Willis & Lee, 1998).

For positive identification or verification applications, spoofing involves the following three steps: (1) capturing the biometric source feature belonging to an enrollee, (2) manufacturing an artifact containing a copy of the captured biometric source feature, and (3) presenting the artifact to the biometric system to be identified or verified as the enrollee. Separating the attack into three steps is a useful precursor to an analysis of the range of difficulties and possible countermeasures. An understanding of the various issues will help implementers to assess the risks for their applications and to provide appropriate safeguards.

For negative identification applications, there is no requirement to copy an enrollee; quite the opposite in fact—the aim is to avoid being linked to an existing enrollee. In this case the artifact would contain source features that do not correspond to an enrollee. These could be obtained by copying as before except that a nonenrollee would be used as the target, or perhaps the creation of a fictitious source feature, which is nevertheless realistic enough to be accepted by the biometric system. In some cases a deliberate change in the presentation of the source feature to the biometric system may be sufficient to cause nonrecognition.

## Capturing the Biometric Characteristics Belonging to an Enrollee

Biometric characteristics cannot be regarded as secret, but their capture will pose varying degrees of difficulty. Faces are easy to photograph; fingerprints can be lifted from residual images left on smooth surfaces; voices can be captured on tape or other audio recorder. Other biometrics images will be harder to capture without the use of sophisticated equipment (e.g., retinal images). It should be noted that many biometric systems do not use high-resolution capture devices, so covert image capture may not need to be to a high standard. Some devices using optical images do not use visible wavelengths, so this will impose additional difficulties for image capture, particularly where covert capture is involved, which will often be the case. With cooperation from the target enrollee the capture process is likely to be much easier, of course.

Fingerprints are often thought to be especially susceptible to capture because of the potential availability of latent images. However, this has to be set against the additional difficulty of identifying the required image (perhaps from a multitude of different prints), finding an image containing sufficient detail, and converting the latent image into a form that will be suitable to copy to an artifact. Although Van der Putte and Keuning (2000) and Matsumoto et al. (2002) have addressed the use of latent fingerprint images, it is believed that their experiments may have involved cooperation, which greatly simplifies the process. All in all, the difficulty of image capture should not be underestimated. What may appear to be a straightforward process from theoretical considerations often presents far greater problems in the context of real-world situations.

Capturing the biometric source feature directly from the intended target is only one way on which the images may be acquired. Other possible examples include stored images that may be retrieved from the biometric system, biometric templates that may be reverse engineered to provide workable images, and electrical signals flowing between components of the system containing biometric images that may be captured and converted to an appropriate form to copy to an artifact. We consider security issues associated with data storage and transfer in more detail later.

## Manufacturing an Artifact Containing a Copy of the Captured Biometric Source Feature

As with the capture process this stage will have varying degrees of difficulty depending on the nature of the source feature and the form of presentation. For a fingerprint, the aim will be to manufacture a fake finger or fingertip containing a copy of the captured fingerprint; for a face recognition system a photograph or a mask with a copy of the appropriate biometric source feature. For an iris system the impostor might seek to use a photographic image of the target iris.

## Presenting the Artifact to the Biometric System at a Later Time to Be Identified or Verified as the Enrollee

This might be regarded as the easy bit, but it is also the time of highest risk for the would-be impostor. It is where he or she will discover how effective the artifact is and whether the attack will be detected. Unlike a remote attack, the impostor must be present in person.

The success (or otherwise) will depend on a combination of factors involving both the sophistication and realism of the artifact and the countermeasures implemented by the biometric system. It is impossible to be very specific about this. Note that countermeasures include both technical antispoofing measures implemented by the system and also procedural measures put in place by the system operators. Supervised operation will generally make successful spoofing attacks much more difficult, with the attendant higher risk of detection.

## Countermeasures to Spoofing

Countermeasures to spoofing can be broadly split into technical and procedural measures and technical measures divided into image quality control and liveness checking.

When a biometric source feature is presented to the capture device of a biometric system, the system has broadly two ways of assessing its integrity. One is to subject the biometric image to quality control checks to assess whether the image is of the form that corresponds to the biometric source feature expected. For example, is this image that of a fingerprint? Does it have the characteristic source features of a face: is it a voice or is it just noise? These are the types of questions that the image quality control process should pose before accepting the image for the biometric matching process. It may surprise readers, but some systems have considerable difficulty in this area and are liable to accept images for matching that bear little resemblance to plausible biometric characteristics. Extreme examples of this would be the acceptance of a null image or an image comprising only noise.

The second way is to assess the integrity of the biometric source feature itself—not the image—does the biometric source feature come from a real person? This is what is often termed *liveness checking*. Although liveness checking is logically distinct from image quality control, the image may also contain information relevant to liveness checking and will therefore sometimes play a part in the liveness check.

### Biometric Image Quality Control

Image quality control is an important issue, particularly at the enrollment stage. The ability of a biometric system to distinguish between large numbers of enrollees can be quantified at one basic level by its FAR. For example if the FAR is 1%, we are saying that the template space (the biometric equivalent of the password space) effectively contains only about 100 distinguishable cells, and enrollees will be placed in one or other of these cells. The discrimination capability will be limited by the number of different feature states that are present in the biometric image and the ability of the biometric system to recognize and record those feature states. The more feature states that are present and recorded, the more likely that the individual will be distinguishable from others. The discrimination capability can be impaired both by reducing the number of feature states present or by failing to properly record those feature states that are present. Poor quality control of images, particularly enrollment images, will compromise the discrimination capability of the biometric system.

Image quality is an attribute that is dependent both on the quality of the user's biometric characteristics and on the performance of the image capture process. The system of course cannot do anything about the former, but it should at least be able to assess the quality of the image and issue a warning if there is insufficient detail to maintain the predetermined discrimination requirements and FAR. Images with little or no discernable biometric detail should not be accepted. If a poor or null image is accepted for enrollment, and if the identity of the individual concerned becomes known, he or she will be an easy target to attack. The system administrator may be able to find out if such targets exist. This has a positive side in that a diligent administrator could notice that an enrollment was weak and call in the individual for reenrollment; the negative side is that an untrustworthy administrator could use knowledge of a weak enrollment to exploit the system.

Further image quality control checks can be done on the image format: essentially, does the image represent a plausible biometric source feature of the modality in question? Does it look like a fingerprint? Face? Iris? Checks of this kind can help ward off attempts to enroll simple or bogus images in the system to provide an easy route to attack at a later time. These checks can also form part of the liveness checking countermeasures.

Figures 2–5 show some examples of images that were accepted for enrollment by some commercial biometric products in tests conducted in the CESG biometrics lab in 2003. We have done similar tests on a number of products and we believe that the results are fairly typical of current biometric technology.

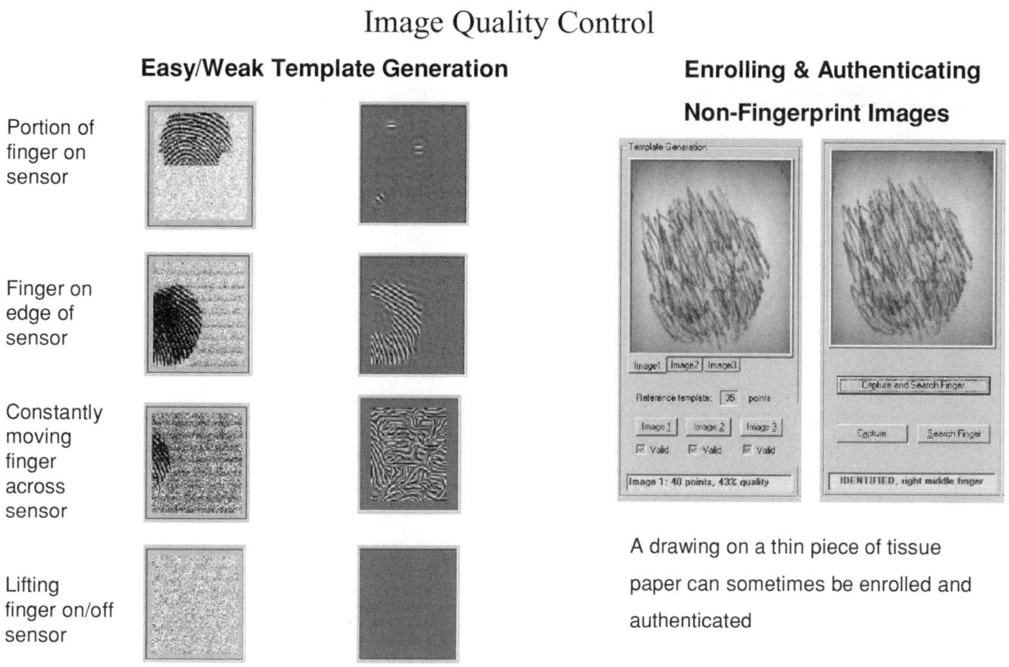

## Image Quality Control

**Easy/Weak Template Generation**     **Enrolling & Authenticating Non-Fingerprint Images**

Portion of finger on sensor

Finger on edge of sensor

Constantly moving finger across sensor

Lifting finger on/off sensor

A drawing on a thin piece of tissue paper can sometimes be enrolled and authenticated

**Figure 2:** Examples of poor and simple images that can be enrolled in some fingerprint systems.

## Face Recognition

### Image Acquisition Criteria

Enrolling Simple/Easy Images

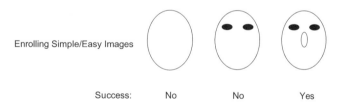

Success:          No              No              Yes

**Figure 3:** What is a face? Example of what one facial recognition system will enroll.

## Iris Recognition Image Quality

### Control Test

**Caricature iris image accepted for enrolment and identification by one iris recognition system**

**Figure 4:** Image quality control test of an iris recognition system.

Signature Enrolment Image Quality Test

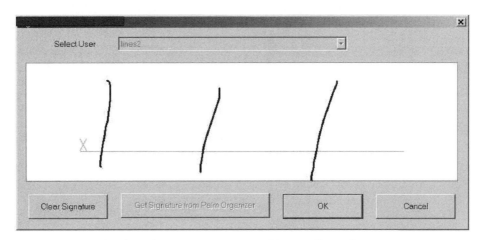

**Figure 5:** Example of simple "signature" accepted for enrollment by one signature recognition system.

## Liveness Checking

Liveness checking is the normal countermeasure to the threat of spoofing. The biometric system measures properties of the biometric source feature that help to provide confidence that the source feature is a genuine human feature and not an artifact.

Liveness checking may tackle the problem of artifacts from two basic directions as follows: (1) looking for specific properties of liveness (we will call this the positive approach) and (2) looking for (the absence of) specific properties of known spoof attacks (we will call this the negative approach). Table 2 shows some of the candidate properties for positive liveness testing.

An example of the negative approach applied to fingerprint artifact would be to look for the specific properties of known fingerprint artifacts. The Van der Putte and Keuning (2000) studies used silicone rubber, whereas Matsumoto et al. (2002) used gelatin for making their fingerprint artifacts. Detection and rejection of these materials would constitute a negative liveness check.

**Table 2** Liveness Test Measures

| Properties | Involuntary Signals |
|---|---|
| *Physical:* weight, density, elasticity | *Pulse* |
| | *Blood pressure* |
| *Electrical:* capacitance, resistance, impedance | *Blood flow* |
| | *Heat & thermal* |
| *Visual:* color, opacity, appearance, shape | *gradients* |
| | *Transpiration* |
| *Spectral:* transmittance, reflectance, absorbance | *Perspiration* |
| | ECG–electrical signals generated by the heart |
| | EEG–brain wave signals |
| *Body fluid:* oxygen, blood constituents, DNA | |

In practice, positive and negative approaches may be combined, with knowledge of known spoofing attacks being used to help define and delimit the positive liveness characteristics being searched for. So a liveness check might measure the electrical capacitance and resistance of the applied finger and compare the values with those expected for silicone rubber and gelatin, as well as for a human finger. Here the information afforded by the known attacks can be used to assist in discriminating between the live finger and fingers made from silicone rubber and gelatin. The weakness of the negative approach is that, although it may provide good discrimination against known artifact materials, it may not be so effective in detecting an artifact made from a different material.

How liveness checking is implemented will depend on the biometric modality and the biometric image capture technology. The techniques may involve hardware- or software-based detection or both in combination. Optical fingerprint devices often use electrodes or electrically sensitive coatings on the surface of the reader platen that are used to measure physical properties of the skin, the subcutaneous tissue, or the underlying bulk finger. Charge coupled device (CCD) fingerprint readers could use coatings, but coatings might upset the image capture mechanism; alternatively the matrix of CCD cell contacts could be used as electrodes for liveness detection, or separate electrodes could be used that do not form part of the CCD array to act as generators and detectors of liveness signals and responses.

Current facial recognition systems typically use no hardware other than the usual biometric image capture camera or cameras. In this case the liveness checking is reliant on the normal signals captured as part of the biometric enrollment or verification process. Software techniques analyze the images looking for signs of liveness, such as head movement, facial expression changes, 3D effects, or some other property. Methods may also include challenge–response actions (e.g., ask subjects to smile) and "negative" checking for known properties of predictable spoofs such as photographs or masks.

Iris recognition systems may look for spontaneous eye or pupil movement that are characteristic of a live eye and for specular reflections of light or infrared radiation from the surface of the eye, which will permit the distinguishing of live eyes/iris from photographs.

Hand geometry readers typically make use of the three-dimensional properties of live hands to discriminate against two-dimensional spoofs such as photographic images or cardboard cutouts. They may also use conductivity measurements on the hand as an additional safeguard against the spoof hands made from artificial materials such as metals, plastics, or other materials having the "wrong" conductivity.

Some voice recognition systems claim to be able to detect and distinguish voice recordings from live voices, though details of how this is done are not known and, at the time of writing, no independent corroboration of the claims had been reported.

The above examples are by no means comprehensive. Product developers are often reluctant to reveal details of their liveness checking techniques as they feel that keeping the information confidential helps to frustrate attempts by attackers to defeat systems. At the present level of knowledge and deployment of biometric technology, this view is probably correct. In the longer term, however, as the deployment of biometric systems increases and knowledge of potential and actual vulnerabilities becomes more widely disseminated, this policy will eventually become unsustainable, and possibly counterproductive, because it may inhibit wider analysis and research, which could lead to the development of improved countermeasures.

It is important to distinguish between detecting the presence of a live person and detecting a live biometric source feature. To be effective, biometric liveness checking must address the latter rather than the former.

Experience indicates that product developers do not always recognize this distinction. We call this essential property *simultaneity*, meaning that liveness checking must occur at the same place and time as the biometric image capture. If not, it indicates only that a live person was present in the vicinity of the capture device at the time of capture.

Paradoxically, some apparently sophisticated liveness checking techniques fail this simple test. Consider, for example, detecting the presence of a live finger by measuring pulse, temperature, and/or properties that lie behind the surface of the fingerprint. These techniques are sometimes promoted as effective measures against simple two-dimensional fingerprint artifacts or fake fingers. However, the fact that the measurements utilize properties of the finger that lie behind the biometric source feature itself means that they may fail the simultaneity test. They may not be effective against an artifact constructed from a lamina containing a copied fingerprint stuck over the tip of a live finger. The liveness check may "see" the underlying live finger but may fail to detect that the biometric source feature captured does not come from this live finger!

Figure 6 shows some sample lamina artifact fingerprint images alongside the genuine images. The fingerprints were cooperatively obtained and constructed in the CESG laboratories using household materials. They were used to successfully spoof several commercial fingerprint products, including a number that made claims to liveness checking. Some of these checks probably failed for the reason described in the previous paragraph.

Software-based liveness checking techniques that work directly from captured biometric image data have an advantage, because, by definition, they are working on the same data that are used for the biometric recognition process—they pass the simultaneity test. However, the image alone may not contain much information relevant to liveness checking. Sometimes liveness indications can be

## Lamina Fingerprint Artifacts

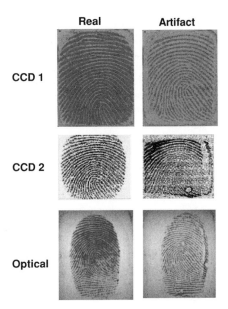

Successful enrollment and authentication with lamina fingertip artifacts

Note: This is a cooperative effort

**Figure 6:** Example of the use of lamina fingerprint artifacts on three fingerprint systems using CCD and optical technologies.

obtained from the dynamic changes and variations occurring in a sequence of images. Some interesting original research into fingerprint liveness checking is reported by Derakhshani, Schuckers, Hornak, and O'Gorman (2003). They used a neural network to distinguish the temporal changes in the fingerprint images from live fingers and artifacts based on perspiration emanating from the pores in the finger while the finger is in contact with the reader. Although individuals differ in their amounts of perspiration and the effect is also dependent on environmental conditions, the researchers were able to clearly distinguish between the live fingers and the artifacts (which included cadaver fingers). One practical difficulty they found was the increased capture time required to register the necessary changes for the liveness check. The author is not aware that this research has yet carried through to implementation in any commercial fingerprint product.

Liveness detection usually entails the use of additional information to that used for the biometric recognition process. Dedicated sensors at the capture station may gather this, or the normal biometric capture sensor may be used. The choice will often depend on the form of the liveness checking information and hence the suitability of the biometric sensor to capture and convey it. Noncontact optical systems (e.g., face and iris) typically use the same camera (or cameras) for liveness detection as they do for the biometric source feature capture. Contact systems (e.g., fingerprint and hand) typically make use of the contact to measure different types of information than is used for the recognition process and often use dedicated sensors for this task.

One negative aspect of liveness checking is the increased likelihood of rejection of legitimate users. This is a factor of any image integrity mechanism, where the natural variations in source feature properties and presentation are not always clearly distinguishable from the properties of artifacts.

## Mimicry

Mimicry is the copying of human behavioral characteristics by another human being. Instead of copying the biological source features of an enrollee onto an artifact, the impostor learns to copy the behavioral characteristics of the enrollee and is able to reproduce them to the biometric system when required. Biometric characteristics that are amenable to mimicry are known as behavioral biometrics, common examples being signature and voice. Note that classifying a biometric source feature as behavioral does not mean that copying is restricted to mimicry—a voice could be copied using a tape recorder or by impersonation. The former would constitute an artifact, the latter mimicry.

Actually voice is a problematic case, as it does not fit comfortably into either the biological or behavioral camp. It possesses strong characteristics of both. Physiology of the vocal folds, head, throat, and chest cavities determine basic parameters. However, there are clearly strong behavioral components from familial influences, location and environment of upbringing, voice training, occupation, and so on. From a biometric standpoint, whether the

biological or behavioral factors predominate will depend both on the individual and on the modus operandi of the biometric voice algorithm. Voice is usually placed in the behavioral category probably because of our awareness of the strong behavioral component in everyday life and our common experience of voice impersonators in the entertainment industry.

Impostors are unlikely to mount attacks using mimicry on biologically based biometrics such as fingerprint or iris. Because mimicry does not involve the use of any technology, it may be perceived to be easier, which might result in a higher incidence of impostor attacks against systems employing behavioral biometrics.

Liveness checking measures plainly cannot help to detect impostor attacks using mimicry. Countermeasures should focus on increasing the ability to distinguish between genuine users and impostors. This includes improved technical performance, making better use of physical discrimination where there are biological as well as behavioral components of the biometric source feature (e.g., voice). Supervision can also help as mimics may exhibit unnatural or suspicious conduct when attempting mimicry. Adding a challenge–response process, where information known only to the legitimate user is asked for, may be an effective countermeasure to impostors using mimicry (and other forms of attack).

## Miscellaneous Advice

- Do not accept images of insufficient quality for enrollment—this is fundamental. If the enrollment quality is low, the security will be low (and the performance will be bad too!).

- Do not accept images for matching until liveness checks are satisfied (obviously!).

- Do not tell users why they failed, directly or indirectly. There may be several barriers (e.g., multiple stages of biometric process or biometric and PIN). Make sure users are allowed to attempt all barriers even if they fail an early one. Letting impostors know prematurely, or reporting which barrier they fail, will allow them to tackle the barriers one at a time, facilitating their attack.

- Ensure that failure time is independent of reason for failure. This is an extension of the previous case. If failure times are dependent on reason, impostors may determine the reason, hence which of the barriers they are failing. They can then tackle the barriers one at a time.

- Do not tell failed users how close they were to succeeding. Telling impostors how well they are doing (i.e., their score) will help them to perfect their attack.

- Report liveness check failures to the administrator and record details in the audit trail. The details could include the biometric feature details where available. Fear of detection and apprehension are powerful deterrents.

- Always supervise enrollment using competent trusted staff—if you care about security.

- Use supervised operation if possible. Supervision is not infallible, but it is a strong weapon against spoofing and mimicry attacks (and other security threats). We cannot repeat this too often.

# PROTECTING DATA WITHIN THE BIOMETRIC SYSTEM

Biometric systems are also IT systems. As with other IT systems, biometric systems are susceptible to compromise by attacks on the IT infrastructure and the data that flows around or are stored in the system. Biometric data may need protection to protect both the integrity of the biometric authentication mechanism and the confidentiality of the users' biometric data. Other security relevant data such as acceptance thresholds and accounting and audit data may also need to be protected. Protection is typically provided by a combination of procedural and technical measures. Technical security measures include access control and cryptographic mechanisms to safeguard data integrity and confidentiality. Procedural measures include security clearance for administrative and operating staff and auditing as part of the system security policy. We examine these measures in more detail in this section, indicating the threats that each one counters and how they relate to different implementation scenarios.

## Template Integrity

Biometric templates are fundamental to the integrity of the authentication process. If templates can be tampered with or replaced without detection, then the authentication cannot be trusted. Untrustworthy templates could occur for one or more of several different reasons:

- Accidental corruption because of a malfunction of the system hardware or software.
- Intentional modification of a bona fide template by an attacker.
- The substitution of a biometric template corresponding to the attacker, in place of the template of an authorized enrollee.
- The addition of a biometric template (and other associated data) corresponding to the attacker to create a bogus additional "enrollment" on the system.

Equally, if the biometric sample is tampered with during operational use, for example, by substituting a biometric sample corresponding to that of an authorized enrollee in place of the live sample of the attacker, a compromise will occur.

To maintain authentication integrity, the biometric system needs to be able to verify the integrity of the templates it is using. Cryptographic techniques, including digital signature and encryption, can be used for this purpose. We draw a distinction between the approaches to note that encryption is not necessary to protect the *integrity* of the template—digital signing is sufficient. Until the template is signed, it is susceptible to undetected modification, so the signing process should be applied as early as possible in the life of the template, preferably immediately on successful enrollment. The security assurance provided by the cryptographic algorithm used and the signing procedures can be assessed through a security evaluation procedure such as Common Criteria evaluation.

During operational use, the system should verify the integrity of the template before it is used as the reference for a biometric matching process. If the integrity check fails, the authentication process should be stopped and an alert message issued to the operator. Appropriate log information should also be recorded. Integrity checking can also be performed as part of a regular offline audit task to validate the continuing integrity of the template database.

Use of digitally signed templates may have performance advantages over encryption, as only the signature has to be checked, which is likely to be a less computationally intensive activity than decryption. For the case of an application involving one-to-many comparisons with a large database, this saving could be highly significant. Note, however, that digital signing does not protect the confidentiality of the template.

## Template Confidentiality

Biometric templates contain personal information that is used to recognize individuals—this is the purpose of the template in the biometric recognition process. Although current privacy principles advocate separation between personal and nonpersonal data, in some cases templates also contain other personal data about individuals. There is at least an obligation—in some countries it is a legal requirement—to protect the storage of biometric templates from disclosure to others without the permission of the subjects. Methods of protection range from procedural measures embodied in codes of conduct to technical measures that could include access control and data encryption. What measures are appropriate will be determined by a number of factors, including the amount and type of data, the security provided by the physical environment of the system, the trustworthiness of the system administrators and operators, and technical access control measures implemented by the system.

Where encryption is used to protect templates, it can also serve the function of integrity protection (see "Template Integrity"). This dual benefit may be a motivating factor, but there are some disadvantages. As mentioned previously, use of template encryption is likely to add administrative and performance overheads. It will usually be necessary to remove the encryption from the template prior to matching, although we note that in one practical implementation, iris recognition templates can be encrypted in such a way that the matching process can be performed directly between the encrypted template and an identically encrypted sample, thus avoiding the decryption overhead (Iridian, 2004). However, it is generally believed that the encryption is not strong, when judged from the conventional cryptographic standpoint. One reason for this belief is that the required properties for biometric matching and strong cryptography are in direct conflict.

For biometric matching, a small change in the source data must result in a small change in the matching score; for cryptography, a small change in the source data must result in an unpredictable (random) change in the output data. An encryption algorithm that satisfied the required cryptographic characteristic would therefore be thought to be inherently unsuitable for generating encrypted data that could be used directly for the biometric matching/scoring process.

Typically we would expect that biometric templates will have to be decrypted prior to matching taking place. This could impose substantial performance penalties on large-scale applications where one-to-many identification functionality is provided, particularly where population-sized databases are involved and results are needed quickly. Various practical expedients might be employed, such as the use of an unencrypted cache of templates, though these solutions inevitably involve some security compromises.

## Transitory Data and Data Flow Protection

In operational use, biometric data will exist within the components and will flow between the various components of the biometric system. At some stages it will probably of necessity be in unencrypted form (e.g., during the matching process). Fortunately, these stages are brief and deeply embedded in the hardware and software. Normally, physical protection will be used to keep this ephemeral data safe. One readily identifiable danger point is the data flow between the biometric capture device and the rest of the biometric system. In many cases the capture device is a separate hardware component linked by a cable to the IT components of the biometric system. The cable carries the biometric images, which, if captured, could be used to mount a replay attack on the system. It would be the equivalent of tapping into the keyboard cable of a workstation and reading passwords or other data.

The capture device signals may be protected by procedural, physical, or logical measures. Procedural measures imply supervised operation to prevent a signal capture attack being mounted. Physical protection is the usual method for a self-contained biometric system (such as typically used on a door entry application) where the capture device and the matching components together with the interconnecting paths carrying biometric data are all contained in a single enclosure that employs appropriate tamper-resistant construction and an alarm. Connections from this unit to the outside world will need alternative protection measures. For other applications, where the capture device is separated from the rest of the system, an armored cable may be deemed adequate, particularly if combined with a tamper alarm.

In many cases, logical protection will be called for. Logical protection usually involves cryptography to encrypt or sign data flowing from the capture device. The arguments for signature versus encryption are similar to the case for template protection. To ensure that captured templates cannot be replayed at a later time, some element of uniqueness will be needed (e.g., unique session keys or cryptographic time stamping). Where biometric capture devices are remote from the matching components, signals may have to flow across networks, possibly public networks. Under these circumstances the signal path is wholly untrusted, and appropriate logical measures to protect the confidentiality and integrity of the biometric data will be necessary. These measures will usually involve encrypting the data flowing across the network.

## Reverse Engineering of Templates

It is frequently stated by protagonists of biometric technology that biometric templates cannot be reverse engineered to reveal the original biometric characteristics of the individual. This is a typical rejoinder to criticism from privacy advocates who express concerns about the potential disclosure of personal information from biometric systems. Both the claims and the responses need some further consideration as they relate to and confuse a number of distinct issues.

The statement about reverse engineering is literally true. The biometric template contains a coded subset of information derived from the individual's biometric characteristics, intended for use by the biometric system for the purpose of identifying or verifying the identity of the individual. Much of the data present in the original captured image of the source feature is discarded and is not present in the template; therefore the original image cannot be recreated. Note that it is the absence of data, and not the encoding, that prevents the reverse engineering. It would in principle be possible to define a template format that did containing all the necessary information to allow the recreation of an original image, but in practice this would largely defeat the purpose of the template, which is the efficient storage of identifying features for the matching process.

The corollary to the argument is that the template clearly does contain sufficient information to identify or verify the identity of the individual. This brings into question the real basis of the concern expressed by the privacy lobby—is it a concern about recreating the image itself, or is it really a disguised concern about the possibility of using the template data to synthesize an artifact that could be used to perpetrate an identity theft?

A significant issue therefore is whether it might be possible to reverse engineer the template to produce a workable artifact that might succeed in spoofing the biometric system (note: we do not address the concern about direct replay of the template through electronic injection—this issue is addressed under "Template Integrity"). Because the template, by definition, contains all the information needed by the system for matching, in principle it should be possible to reconstruct an artifact containing an image that would result in the extracted features matching those on the stored template, at least on the system concerned or possibly one using the same biometric technology. A masters thesis by Hill (2001) documents an investigation of the issue of "adequate" image reconstruction and comes to the conclusion that it is indeed possible. The approach used by Hill was to develop an image model for the biometric and then seed the model with many sets of parameters, using the same biometric technology from which the template was taken, testing and tuning the parameters until an adequately matching template was created.

In summary we can say the reverse engineering a template to produce a replica of a biometric source image is not a real possibility, but it may not be necessary to do this to create a successful artifact. The concern expressed by the privacy advocates seems to be misdirected—biometric characteristics are not secret anyway. They are open and liable to capture and copying onto an artifact. The real issues that need to be addressed are those of protecting biometric systems against spoofing and other attacks that make use of captured biometric characteristics, and the application system security policies and procedures that safeguard user's private data from unwarranted disclosure.

## Latent and Residual Images Within the Biometric System

Latent images within the biometric system are images of biometric characteristics that are physically deposited on the biometric system capture device. This is limited to contact-based biometrics such as fingerprints. In some cases it may be possible for an impostor to reactivate a previously deposited latent image and gain access as that individual. Various techniques to enhance latent images and make them accepted by some biometric systems have been investigated (Matsumoto, Matsumoto, Yamada, & Hoshino, 2002; Van der Putte & Keuning, 2000). Where successful, this indicates a design weakness in specific cases, which the biometric system developers should address. Other safeguards include ensuring regular cleaning of the capture device.

We use the term *residual images* to refer to images that may be held in internal system memory. During the normal operation, biometric images will exist transiently in system memory. After the biometric recognition process is completed, whether successful or not, residual images should be removed from the system. If these images are not purged, there is a potential risk that insecure system software could allow the previous user's residual image to be passed to the feature extraction and matching process. This has been noted in one case of a system under test (A. J. Mansfield, private communication, 2001). The potential problem of failing to purge residual images is a system design and implementation issue that should be investigated as part of a security evaluation process.

Note that we have intentionally excluded the subject of latent and other images captured outside the biometric system and used to construct artifacts or to aid mimicry. This is an inherent issue for biometrics that is not under the control of system designers, implementers, or operators, and the security implications must be addressed (see "Spoofing, Mimicry, and Liveness Detection").

## Binding Biometric Templates to Applications

In addition to their role in protecting the integrity of biometric templates, cryptographic techniques can also be used to bind templates to biometric applications. This binding has been proposed as a solution to user concerns that their biometric data may be "leaked" to other organizations or applications without their consent or used for different functions than were declared when they were enrolled. Binding can be applied in a structured way to limit the use of template data to specific functions within the overall application space as well as to prevent unauthorized use in other organizations. Once again, digital signatures and encryption can be used as mechanisms, and in specific cases, both may be used in concert to meet the limitation of use and confidentiality requirements according to the application environment.

Let us consider a simple example. Biometric authentication is to be used in an application family comprising several different applications, each of which needs user consent for use of their biometric data. Each application also needs specific user-related information, which is associated with the corresponding coded biometric feature data stored in the biometric template. Separate checksums are used to bind the user application data to the biometric feature data for each application. Before using the biometric template data, an application verifies the relevant checksum and proceeds only if the checksum is valid. The whole template, including all the associated data fields, is encrypted for storage purposes to prevent compromise of confidentiality should the database be compromised or data leakage occur. Of course, this scenario only works in a cooperative environment. The checksums are used here as a technical underpinning to a system security policy.

In a complex application/function environment, the template data can be wrapped in a series of envelopes whose structure matches the structure of the environment, with judicious use of cryptographic signing and encryption according to the protection required.

A more comprehensive description of the principles and techniques, and their potential uses, can be found in Soutar (2002).

## MISCELLANEOUS TOPICS

This section contains a collection of biometric security related subjects that do not fit comfortably under the main headings previously. Though not generally new, they are mostly of the status of research and development topics with few if any implementations in the world at the time of writing.

## Biometric Encryption and Templateless Biometrics

Conventional data encryption uses symmetric or asymmetric key cryptography. With symmetric key cryptography, the same cipher key is used to encrypt and decrypt the data, so both sender and recipient must possess the key. The security depends on a number of factors, including the encryption algorithm and the key structure and length, and is ultimately limited by the security afforded by the means of distribution and storage of the key. Asymmetric key cryptography, usually known as public key cryptography, uses a pair of cipher keys that are mathematically bound to each other. One key is called the public key because it is made available to anyone who needs to use it. The other key is known as the private key, which is known only to the owner of the corresponding public key. The owner must ensure that the private key is protected from disclosure. The public key of the intended recipient is used to encrypt the data and only the matching private key of the recipient can be used to decrypt the data.

The technique of public key cryptography can also be used to digitally sign data for the purpose of validating its source. In this case, the data is signed by means of a checksum secured by the sender's private key. The received checksum can be decrypted only with the corresponding public key, thus validating its source and its integrity (note: this assumes the availability of a trusted confirmation of ownership of the public key). Note that the two approaches can be combined to protect confidentiality, integrity, and validation of source.

A problem with both symmetric and asymmetric key cryptography is that of storing the private key securely. Keys are very long and randomly formed, which makes it impractical for people to memorize them. Normally they are stored in the machine used for the cipher processing, and their security is protected by an access control mechanism that is triggered by a user password or phrase. This is a recognized weak point and has motivated the search for a more secure mechanism. Biometric authentication could be used in place of a password to release the key, and this may have security benefits, but it does not address the security problem of protecting the stored key from a technical or hacking attack. Researchers have proposed the more radical approach of using biometric characteristics to directly generate cipher keys or to bind traditional cipher keys to biometric characteristics in a combination that can be unlocked only by presenting the biometric, thereby protecting the keys from conventional forms of attack.

Tomko, Soutar, and Schmitt (1996, 1997), in two closely related U.S. patents, describe a proposed scheme for binding fingerprint image data to a cipher key such that the finger image is required to release the key. The advantage claimed for using an intermediate key, rather than directly generating the key from the finger image, is that the key can be changed if required (e.g., if a specific key is compromised) by reenrolling the finger and binding it to a different key. These patents do not address the problem of variability of the captured fingerprint features. A later patent (Soutar, Roberge, Stolanov, Gilroy, & Vijaya-Kumar, 2001) and a companion article (Soutar, Roberge, Stolanov, Gilroy, & Vijaya-Kumar, 1999) describe a modified proposal that uses data filtering to optimize the ability to discriminate between different individuals, with the robustness to deal with the expected variability of multiple samples from the same individual. The author is not aware of any demonstrators or commercial products that make use of these techniques at the time of writing, therefore the efficacy and practicability of the approach remains to be established.

If biometric systems that do not need to store templates can be realized, such systems might help to overcome some of the privacy concerns that surround the use of biometrics with template databases and the associated fears of template theft or nonconsensual use. Such systems might generate a unique and repeatable user key directly from the presented source biometric, and the biometric data could then be discarded. Tomko (2002) explores these privacy concerns and advocates the use of templateless biometrics for "biometric encryption." Once again though, the practicability of the proposals remains to be demonstrated. Also, Tomko's article covers only a limited range of applications. It does not address, for example, the use of biometrics for passports, visas, and other applications where there will be a need for centralized databases of enrollees to check for attempts to establish multiple identities.

## Multimodal Biometrics

Biometric modalities relate to the biometric source feature used; for example, fingerprint, iris, face, voice, and so on are examples of biometric modalities. Many biometric systems use a single modality, but there is increasing interest in multimodal biometrics using two or more modalities for a single identification or verification. There is also the related case of using two or more instances of a single modality (e.g., two irises or four fingerprints), though there is no universal agreement as to whether this case falls within the definition of multimodal biometrics. Ross and Jain (2003) certainly include this latter case in their analysis of multimodal data fusion. A detailed discussion of multimodal biometric systems is complicated by the many possible ways that the results from the various modalities can be used to make a final decision. This will usually be determined by the underlying reasons that the implementers had for adopting the multimodal approach, as well as specific details of the application. Some of these issues are discussed in the next section.

### Why Multimodal Biometrics?

There are three main reasons for the employment of multimodal biometrics:

- To improve the performance of the system, through reduced system error rates.
- To increase the robustness of the system in dealing with users who cannot be enrolled with a specific modality or who cannot use the system subsequent to enrollment; such failures may be permanent (e.g., lack of the requisite biometric source feature or disability) or temporary (e.g., through illness or injury).
- To increase the resistance to spoofing attacks.

Note that the performance and robustness arguments are usually mutually exclusive (i.e., one cannot normally realize both improved performance and increased robustness at the same time). From an information security standpoint, it is the increased resistance to spoofing attacks and the potential for improved performance that are most relevant, the latter because a reduction in error rates usually translates into an increase in security against a number of forms of attack (see "Performance and Security").

However, multimodal biometrics also have significant attendant disadvantages as follows:

- Increased cost for the multiple capture devices and the supporting infrastructure and the operating costs.
- Increased storage requirement for the biometric data, which can cause particular difficulties where the data is stored in a user-held token as a bar code or in a smartcard.
- Where the application requires users to be enrolled in more than one modality, users may experience more difficulty in successful enrollment in all modalities, and the proportion of failures to enroll will increase.
- Enrollment time will generally increase so enrollment throughput will decrease.

- Similarly, throughput during normal use will normally decrease.

In referring to multimodal biometrics, there is often a tacit assumption that end users will be required to enroll in more than one modality. Some applications, however, may employ multimodal biometrics to overcome problems of robustness and usability that frequently occur for certain users when a single biometric modality is used. In these applications various enrollment strategies may be adopted (e.g., users may be enrolled in all modalities where possible or a reduced set of modalities where difficulties with specific modalities are experienced). Alternatively, users may be required to enroll in only one modality, perhaps there may be a preferred modality and a fallback modality, or users may be allowed to choose their preferred modality. The security implications of the various strategies will clearly need to be considered. Although it is not possible to be definitive here with the wide range of possible options, as a general principle and following normal security assessment practice, the overall security achieved will normally correspond to that of the least secure modality or modality combination permitted.

Note that the use of multimodal biometrics may give rise to adverse user reactions, either inherently from the feeling of greater intrusiveness or simply through a worsening of the user experience resulting from the greater complication of use and the increased time taken to interact with the biometric system.

## Using Multimodal Biometrics to Improve Performance—Data Fusion

One reason for using multimodal biometrics is to improve on the recognition performance achievable with a single biometric modality. This entails combining the biometric data from each modality through a process of data fusion. Ross and Jain (2003) provide a comprehensive analysis, classifying the various ways in which the multimodal biometric data can be combined, which includes combining multiple samples of a single modality as well as samples of different modalities and the use of multiple algorithms on a single biometric source feature. Combination strategies include decision-based fusion, score-based fusion, and feature-based fusion, which are described further:

1. Decision-based fusion. The match/no match decisions of each of the modalities are combined in "and" or "or" combination or through majority voting in cases where three or more modalities are involved. This is the simplest approach but rarely provides optimal results. As pointed out by Daugman (2004), using the "and" combination will typically decrease the FAR at the expense of increased FRR, whereas using the "or" combination will decrease the FRR at the expense of increased FAR. For decision-based fusion, Daugman shows that often the overall performance is degraded by the addition of the poorer performance devices, although an improvement may sometimes be realized by a suitable adjustment of the threshold setting for each modality. A more detailed discussion of this and other combinatorial aspects of iris recognition can be found in Daugman (2000).

2. Score-based fusion. The matching scores of the individual modalities are combined to produce a composite score and the match/no match decision is made on the basis of a combined threshold. This case has been subject to a number of investigations, including those by Ross and Jain (2003), Griffin (2003b), Griffin (2003c), and Sedgwick (2003), which seek to determine the optimum basis for combining the scores and the resulting benefits to performance. Ross and Jain show the practical results for fusing normalized scores from face, hand, and fingerprint modalities in various combinations and illustrate the improvement in the resulting ROC for the fused scores. Griffin and Sedgwick use broadly similar approaches—to normalize the scores from the individual modalities (typically, scores generated by biometric matching algorithms are to arbitrary scales) and to express the score in terms of the probabilities that a particular score would result from an authorized user or alternatively from an impostor. These probabilities can be derived directly from the ROC or DET (i.e., error) curves for the individual biometric modalities. Once the scores are expressed in terms of probabilities, a probability density function for each modality can be derived from the corresponding DET curve and the functions optimally combined to give the probability density function relationship for the fused multimodal biometric. This composite curve can be inverted to derive a corresponding ROC or DET curve that represents the performance of the optimally fused multimodal biometric. This approach can be extended to more than two modalities to achieve further gains in performance.

The analyses depend on a number of assumptions, including the absence of correlation between the biometric characteristics of the modes used and the availability of suitable ROC or DET curves for the individual modes. This raises a number of issues that will need to be addressed before the fused results can be used with confidence for a target multi-modal application, including the following:

- The accuracy and confidence limits of the individual ROC/DET curves.
- The effect of errors and uncertainties in the individual ROC/DET curves for each modality on the combined performance of the multimodal system.
- The need for consistency between the conditions under which the individual curves were determined and those of the multimodal target application.

In particular, the consistency issue could raise many difficulties because of the number of variables that are involved, including population demographics, ethnicity, behavior, environmental conditions, enrollment policies, and verification policies (e.g., numbers of attempts allowed). Unless all the factors mirror the target application conditions, the validity of the fused results will be questionable for the target domain and will probably only ultimately be resolvable by a test of the application itself.

3. Feature-based fusion. In principle, it would be possible to combine the features from individual modalities

into an agglomerated "super" biometric. Ross and Jain argue that feature-based fusion should be the optimum approach. However, it is not clear how this would be implemented in practice, because the feature set for each modality is generally completely distinct and intimately bound to the biometric algorithm. It is difficult to conceive of a single generic algorithm that could universally (and optimally) handle the composite feature set resulting from several different modalities, other than by dealing with each of the feature subsets separately, in which case the approach would degenerate to the score-based fusion example previously. There are no biometric systems using feature-based fusion known to the author.

Using multiple instances of the same mode (e.g., fingerprints and irises) can fulfill the same role as the use of multimodal biometrics, namely performance gains or increased robustness. The score-based fusion approach could be used to fuse the scores from two or more biometric characteristics; alternatively, feature-based fusion may be a workable alternative in this case. Due regard will need to be taken of the degree of correlation between the individual source features. In practice, with fingerprints there is evidence of some correlation, at least at the major characteristic level (arch, loop, and whorl). This will reduce the benefit of the fusion process somewhat. Left eye/right eye iris patterns for individuals are thought to be uncorrelated.

It is worth noting that fusion models described in this section may not adequately reflect the more complex scenarios that often occur in real-world applications, where decision policies may involve a combination of technical and human factors. For example, a multimodal application may use a single biometric initially. If this gives as sufficiently good matching score, the user may be admitted without any further test. If not, recourse may be made to a second or third biometric for confirmation. The process may also include nonbiometric factors (e.g., a token or password). In this example the fusion operation is performed by the operator, as directed by the system security policy, rather than technically by the biometric system itself.

## BIOMETRIC SECURITY CONCERNS

This section provides a brief inventory of security related concerns about biometrics that are commonly heard from implementers and users. Some concerns result from misconceptions of what biometrics can and cannot be used for; others are genuine and need to be addressed by developers, implementers, and system owners as appropriate. Some of the issues raised here relate problems that have already been addressed in previous sections, possibly cast in a different guise. Where appropriate, readers will be directed to other parts of this chapter for further information. Inevitably, some concerns are not fully resolved at the present state of the art, a reality that is not unique to biometric technology of course.

## Biometrics Do Not Provide Absolute Identification

This is so obviously true that it seems to need no further comment, yet on numerous occasions, proposed solutions to serious problems (e.g., crime and terrorism) involve the use of biometrics in ways that would appear to depend on the ability to provide absolute identification of persons or intent.

In reality, biometric systems can only identify/verify individuals who have been previously enrolled, or indicate that they are not recognized as having been enrolled. Applications can use this functionality in various ways; for example, to verify an individual's identity and to open a gate or to raise an alert when a nonenrolled individual is detected. The feasibility and effectiveness of the application will depend on the technology, environment, and other details of the implementation.

Biometric authentication addresses only part of the overall authentication framework (see "Authentication, Identification, and Verification"). Nonbiometric credentials are needed to establish absolute identity at the point of enrollment and the credentials should be selected to provide confidence at an assurance level deemed appropriate for the application (e.g., birth certificate, utility bills, and peer endorsement).

## Biometrics Are Not Secret

Biometric characteristics are often readily observed and do not possess equivalent secrecy. They may also be captured with varying degrees of difficulty.

The strength of an authentication mechanism is measured by its integrity. For password mechanisms, the integrity is ultimately dependent on the secrecy of the password, which once disclosed is easy to exploit. For a token, the integrity is dependent on the difficulty of acquiring a genuine token or making a usable copy. For a biometric, the integrity is dependent on the difficulty of capturing the biometric characteristics of a target and then constructing an artifact that will spoof the system. Both these stages require some effort and expertise and biometric systems should be designed to reject artifacts. However, we know from practical experiments that detection of artifacts is not always as effective as we might hope, and so this issue is a genuine concern. At the current state of the art, it would likely preclude the use of biometrics as the sole authentication mechanism for high-security applications. A methodology for comparing the strengths and weaknesses of the various authentication technologies is not currently available, and it is therefore difficult to rank this concern quantitatively against equivalent concerns over weak or carelessly protected passwords or lost, stolen, or forged tokens.

## Biometrics Do Not Possess the Equivalent Level of Randomness That Passwords Have

People are rather alike and their biometric characteristics therefore lack true randomness. This concern relates to the perceived limitation in the variability of human biometric characteristics when compared to the randomness available with a password mechanism. In reality, it is well known that passwords lack randomness too, because they are typically easy or familiar words and phrases chosen by users to be memorable. Even machine-generated passwords normally make concessions to memorization requirements and therefore lack true randomness. Password cracking programs make use of this lack of randomness to conduct ordered attacks on password files.

Interestingly, biometric template sizes are usually larger than password lengths, which might be taken as a counterargument to the concern expressed, though this is not very meaningful without further information on how much of the template space is actually usable and how uniformly distributed is the occupancy of the template space. Our current understanding of biometric algorithm behavior and human source feature randomness and variation does not allow us to resolve this issue analytically.

The substantive concern here is to the true discrimination performance of the biometric system. This can only be determined through the use of performance testing that is able to explore the interaction of the human and system parameters and thereby determine the real discrimination capability. The results are expressed in terms of statistical error rates such as false match rate and false nonmatch rate (see "Measuring Biometric System Performance"). Intending implementers will need to assess the acceptable error rates for the application and determine whether a biometric system can meet them. The mode of use and the number of users will also have to be considered. For systems involving identification (with their one-to-many comparisons), error rates that may be acceptable for a small number of enrollees can rapidly become intolerable as the enrollee numbers increase. This is likely to be a significant problem for large-scale public domain applications where there may be many millions of enrollees, which will probably limit the choice of biometric technologies to those capable of extremely high levels of discrimination. Multimodal biometrics may offer a possible alternative approach here.

## Biometrics Cannot Be Changed When Compromised

This is often expressed in words such as "If my password is compromised I can change it, but I can't change my biometric if that is compromised." Taken literally this is a true statement, but the cases are not exactly equivalent, as exploitations involve quite different orders of difficulty. Furthermore, the unadorned statement conceals a number of subtle issues that bear more detailed examination, including the meaning of "biometric" in this context, what it is that is "compromised" and how the compromise might occur, and finally what cannot be "changed"? "Biometrics" could refer to the biometric source feature on the person, the image captured and possibly recorded by the biometric system, or the biometric template containing the coded biometric data.

It seems that the substantive concern here is the threat of identity theft through compromise and the perceived inability to solve the problem through a change of biometric. The following paragraphs explore some of the different forms of compromise that might occur together with possible solutions. It will be seen that, in some cases, solutions are readily available, but in other cases there are residual concerns that need further research and development effort.

### Compromise Through Use of an Artifact

Here we are referring to the exploitation of the biometric source feature (which is generally not secret anyway) through the capture of the feature and the construction of an artifact with similar characteristics. The two basic issues are as follows:

- How easy is it to capture the biometric characteristics?
- How easy is it to construct an artifact that can spoof the biometric system?

If successful, then, at a minimum, that user on that system is compromised. But the situation is actually worse than that, because once the system has been shown to be vulnerable to spoofing, every enrolled user is at risk of compromise in the same way. Reenrolling the compromised user (using an alternate biometric source feature if available) will not resolve the fundamental problem. Other biometric systems using the same technology may also be vulnerable, which further increases the scope of the potential problem.

Solutions to the spoofing issue include supervised operation and liveness detection built into the biometric system. Note that the difficulty of capture of biometric characteristics and the construction and employment of artifacts should not be underestimated, particularly where this needs to be done covertly as will often be the case in reality.

For further information, see "Spoofing, Mimicry, and Liveness Detection."

### Compromise Through Capture/Replay of Signals

If undetected, this attack may be used repeatedly and will compromise that user on that system. However, once in place, other users on the compromised connection may also be captured and the set of compromised users is liable to grow. Once discovered, the attack may be disabled for all compromised users, provided that the capture devices can be protected in future from similar attacks.

Various countermeasures are possible, including physical hardware protection, variable signal encryption, and challenge/response operation. For further information see "Transitory Data and Data Flow Protection."

### Compromise of Template Integrity

A template compromise may involve the replacement or modification of the stored biometric template of an enrolled user to substitute the template of an unauthorized user or the addition of the template of an unauthorized user. In the former case, the impostor would assume the identity of an authorized user and be able to perform any actions permitted to that user. However, the authorized user might thereafter be unable to access the system and this could lead to the discovery of the compromise. Adding a new template would effectively illegally enroll the impostor on the system. Existing users would be unaffected, which may lessen the chance of detection. For these forms of attack to be successful the integrity of the template database would have to be seriously undermined. These compromises can be prevented by employing well-known data protection techniques including access control measures to templates and template protection, either through checksumming (integrity) or data encryption (integrity and confidentiality). For further information, see "Template Integrity."

### Cancelable Biometrics—A Generic Solution?

The use of cancelable biometrics has been proposed by Ratha, Connell, and Bolle of IBM (2002) as a generic solution to the "biometrics cannot be changed when compromised" problem. The user's captured biometric image is distorted in a repeatable but nonreversible manner before template generation. If the biometric is compromised, the user is reenrolled using a different distortion characteristic.

The proposal needs to be examined in the context of the various compromises that may occur to determine which problems cancelable biometrics addresses and what benefits it offers over other available solutions. Cancelable biometrics do not address spoofing/mimicry as that issue involves copying of the original biometric characteristics, which is outside the envelope of the protection afforded by the variable distortion characteristic. The approach seems to apply to protection against the threat of compromise by theft of the biometric template, which will be subject to change when a user is reenrolled with a new distortion characteristic. However, as we have already seen, traditional integrity protection measures already address this issue (see "Template Integrity" and "Template Confidentiality"). A compromised template can be re-signed if necessary to cancel a compromised one. A possible advantage of the "cancelable biometrics" approach is that it does not incur the overheads of a cryptographic solution; in particular it avoids the decryption step, which may speed up the matching process. This could be significant in large-scale identification (one-to-many comparison) or negative identification applications.

Note that the distorted image must preserve the general characteristics of the original if an existing biometric matching algorithm is to be used and should not cause the typical differences between multiple samples from the same individual to be amplified. The use of distorted biometric images may affect the performance of biometric algorithms, and system performance should be measured with image distortion in operation and not inferred from performance figures obtained using undistorted images.

## Biometrics May Not Offer Nonrepudiation

This concern is raised by those seeking an authentication mechanism that can bind (usually in a legally enforceable sense) a transaction to an individual and who believe that biometrics may not be able to meet the requirement. We also include in the analysis here the opposite concern—that biometrics does not offer repudiation—also voiced to the effect that, although biometric authentication is in reality imperfect, it might attain a spurious legal validity, which could result in false accusations being made against innocent individuals that would be very difficult to refute. The latter concern may have been fueled by historical cases of transactions involving ATMs (cash dispensers), which the account holders contested, but the banks maintained must have been made by the account holders because of the infallibility of the ATM transaction security safeguards. Following several cases successfully defended by the banks, weaknesses in the ATM security procedures were eventually uncovered that indicated how fraudulent transactions could in fact have been perpetrated.

Without wishing to enter a debate on whether repudiation or nonrepudiation is desirable or undesirable attributes for biometrics, we can say that, for authentication mechanisms, these characteristics depend principally on the following considerations:

- The ability of the authentication mechanism to discriminate between individuals.
- The strength of binding between the authentication data and the individual in question.
- Technical and procedural vulnerabilities that could undermine the intrinsic strength of the binding.
- Informed consent of the individual at the time the authentication is given.

Authentication mechanisms invariably have weaknesses in one or more of the above areas. Passwords and tokens can usually meet the first criterion without difficulty but typically are weak on the second because they are indirect forms of authentication that bear no intrinsic link to the individual concerned. The binding depends solely on procedural discipline. Biometrics have somewhat complementary characteristics. Their discrimination capabilities depend on the technology used and on other, application-related, factors, and are quantified in terms of the error rates (FAR and FRR), which set the fundamental limits. However, their key benefit lies in the area of the second criterion, the binding between the authentication data and the individual. Because the biometric characteristics are an intrinsic part of the individual, this binding is strong, which contrasts with the situation for passwords and tokens.

Regardless of their respective merits in discrimination and binding, in practice all applications of authentication technology suffer from procedural and technical vulnerabilities in their implementation and operation. Some of the technical vulnerabilities that biometric systems can suffer from are described in other sections of this chapter.

Password and token authentication are also subject to technical weaknesses in design, construction, and operation. However, their technical shortcomings are usually overshadowed by their susceptibility to procedural security failures caused by compromise, loss, theft, and misuse.

The final important factor is informed consent. The "informed" is important, because there are situations where an individual could give consent based on false or inadequate information. If the declared use of the system does not correspond to its actual use, the consent is not informed and therefore not valid. This can also apply in situations where consent is given but the functionality of the system subsequently changes significantly, thereby invalidating the original consent.

If legally valid nonrepudiation is to be attained for biometric authentication, the wide range of issues noted above must be adequately addressed. Nonrepudiation requirements must be determined and the authentication mechanism matched to the requirement. A proper procedural framework will need to be put in place, which may involve legal accreditation (e.g., as for digital signature legislation). The availability of such a legally accepted and enforceable framework will effectively determine the nonrepudiation status of an application. Note that if nonrepudiation is not achieved, the risk of "bad" transactions is transferred to the service provider and away from the service user.

It is the opinion of the author, at the time of writing, that the state of the art of biometric technology in respect of technical issues of performance and security will make it unlikely that authentication of individuals, based solely on the recognition of their biometric characteristics could attain a legally acceptable nonrepudiation status in the near future.

## Biometric Characteristics May Be Collected Accidentally or Covertly Without Consent

Users may be concerned that their biometric characteristics might be captured without their consent or even knowledge and that they might thereby unintentionally initiate an action or conduct a transaction. There are clear risks in the use of biometrics for surveillance, where biometric characteristics may be captured without the knowledge or consent of the subjects. This can also occur in nonbiometric cases (e.g., CCTV surveillance and telephone recording), and there are often legal constraints on the employment of such systems and the use of the data. In most cases, there will be a requirement to make subjects aware of the existence and purpose of the system, and this may be enough to legitimize its use, though if the data are also to be used for biometric identification purposes, further legal restrictions related to personal data protection issues are likely to be in force.

Even in cases where biometrics are not used explicitly for the purpose of surveillance, advances in technology might lead to problems of accidental capture and processing of biometric data without consent. With increasing emphasis on ease of use, and on needing less overt actions by the user, the risk of inadvertent operation may rise. Research under way into biometric technologies that can operate at greater distances from users may exacerbate this kind of problem. Owners and operators of biometric applications will need to ensure that transactions cannot be triggered without explicit consensual authorization from the user. The consent might involve a deliberate user action such as the insertion of a card or typing in a personal identification number.

The available technology most likely to be involved in covert collection is facial or voice recognition. In the future, gait recognition may be added to the list, though for now this is a research topic. For surveillance operations, the performance levels of these technologies impose severe limitations on their effectiveness as surveillance tools. The future potential must however be recognized and biometric applications subject to appropriate legal and procedural constraints. In many applications, prior consultation with citizens and the prominent display of information notices may serve to allay fears. Where people can perceive some benefit to themselves (e.g., reduction in crime) they may support the implementation of biometric surveillance systems, providing that adequate safeguards to protect the privacy and civil rights of citizens are in place. Conversely, there have been some notable examples of bad practice where biometric surveillance systems that have been used without adequate openness and consultation and have resulted in substantial public disquiet and opposition.

## Biometric Identity Theft

This is a frequently expressed concern. Users know that passwords can easily be changed and tokens revoked, so compromise, loss, or theft are temporary and soluble problems. With biometrics, however, the user cannot change his or her biometrics at will; at most a few changes would be possible (e.g., reenroll different fingers). A biometric identity theft then might be a permanent handicap.

It has to be said that this is a real issue, though those who raise the concern do not always understand it in detail. Biometric theft could occur in a number of ways including the following:

- Copying the original biometric source feature (which is not secret).
- Accessing a stored image on a biometric system.
- Intercepting a path carrying the image from the capture device.
- Reconstructing an image by reverse engineering an acquired template.

Also, if a stolen template includes associated data, then the associated data could be used separately and independently of the biometric data. Any user credentials or alternative authentication data (e.g., password) might be used to compromise the system or the user without exploiting the biometric data. The degree of compromise would depend on the data and the protective measures in place to prevent exploitation of captured data.

The solutions depend on the nature of the biometric data stolen. Stored images or templates can be protected by encryption. Data intercepted between the capture device and the rest of the system could also be protected by cryptography, but here unique session keys would be necessary (e.g., through time stamping) to prevent the data being replayed successfully. If stolen image data are used to construct an artifact, then liveness testing could be used to ensure that the biometric is actually being submitted from a person.

Stolen templates and template data can be rendered innocuous through the use of cryptographically based integrity checking or encryption. Alternatively, cancelable biometrics have been mooted to overcome the threat of a stolen template. However, although this might offer some protection against reverse engineering the template, it does not protect against direct copying of the original biometric source feature. See also "Protecting Data Within the Biometric System" and "Biometrics Cannot Be Changed When Compromised."

## Will I Know When and How My Biometric Has Been Used?

This is related to the covert use of biometrics (see "Biometric Characteristics May Be Collected Accidentally or Covertly Without Consent") and to functional creep in applications. It is important to realize that authentication does not necessarily imply consent, and it is consent that is the issue of concern here. Any application could be affected though the concern will grow with wider deployment of biometric systems and the opportunities and motivation for sharing biometric data increase.

Biometric applications using different modalities will not be able to share biometric data, which will act as one limiting factor. Depending on future template and image standards, applications using similar technologies from different companies may be able to share data. The desire for integration and interoperability of biometric systems is likely to grow and will act as a driver for standardization.

Functional creep and data sharing are not concerns that are limited to biometric systems. They are common experiences in the modern world with interconnection of systems, and address and lifestyle information is routinely traded as marketing commodities. Biometric data sharing may therefore be seen as an extension to existing personal data sharing, but its singular role as a symbol and authenticator of human identity may render it peculiarly sensitive. This is likely to become an increasing problem as the use of biometrics for authentication grows. With the widespread use of networked applications, the opportunities for sharing data will increase and controls will be harder to enforce.

Legal and procedural constraints are the first line of defense against functional creep and covert capture. In Europe, the Data Protection Directive and the resulting national legislation requires that the storage and processing of personal data is justified, that the data are adequately protected from disclosure, and that the purpose and operation of the system are declared to both the information commissioner and also to the users. Changes in functionality are not allowed unless approved by the resubmission and registration of the system.

Audit trails can provide users with evidence of proper implementation of the system privacy policy and any violations that may have occurred.

Technology can provide solutions by cryptographic binding of templates to specific applications, but successful employment will also depend on strict procedural enforcement. It should be noted that, typically, biometric data will exist (transiently) in clear form within the biometric system to allow the matching process to take place. See "Protecting Data Within the Biometric System" for further details.

# SECURITY EVALUATION AND CERTIFICATION OF BIOMETRIC SYSTEMS

The purpose of security evaluation and certification is to provide assurance to users of IT systems that the system will provide adequate protection against identified security threats under operational conditions. The first step is to define the scope of the problem by describing the system and the environment in which it will operate. This will usually serve to limit the possible range of threats (for example, some threats may be removed or nullified by virtue of the external environment in which the system will operate). The remaining threats that may exist within the defined environment can then be cataloged and a description provided as to how the system as a whole will deal with each threat. This is usually through a combination of technical and procedural countermeasures, the latter of which are addressed by the system security policy and the associated operating procedures.

## Common Criteria Evaluation and Certification

This overall security specification provides the reference for the security evaluation. Historically there has been a gradual transition from national schemes, such as the "Orange Book," developed in 1983 by the National Security Agency for U.S. government use, and the European ITSEC Scheme of 1991 to the present International Common Criteria Security Evaluation Scheme introduced in 1998 and supported by Europe, the United States, and many other nations. Common Criteria is an International Standard (ISO 15408, 1999).

There are three fundamental elements of the evaluation:

- Specifying what is to be evaluated—this is the reference for the evaluation and is usually called the security target.
- Specifying how rigorous the evaluation is to be—this is dependent on how much confidence is needed in the results of the evaluation and is called the assurance level.
- Specifying how the evaluation will be done—this is called the methodology.

The security target encompasses the subjects listed in the opening paragraph of the section. The assurance level allows us to vary the rigor that will be applied to the evaluation. The rigor should be matched to the level of risk to be determined through a risk assessment process, which usually includes such factors as consequences of security failures, motivation and expertise of likely attackers, time and opportunity available to launch an attack, and cost of launching an attack. High levels of rigor are extremely costly to implement in evaluations and it would clearly not be cost effective to use a uniformly high level for all evaluation regardless of the assessed risk. Under Common Criteria, seven Evaluation Assurance levels (EAL1 to EAL 7 in ascending level of rigor) are recognized. At EAL 1, the evaluation is mainly concerned with checking the high level design of the system security features and functional testing; at EAL 7, there is a requirement for formal design and development techniques to be used to specify and construct the system and mathematical proof of correctness of the implementation of the security functions in the delivered system.

The methodology describes the way in which the evaluation will be performed. A mutual recognition agreement between participating nations provides a basis for accepting the results of the evaluation across national borders. To facilitate this, a common evaluation methodology (CEM) has been developed to help ensure uniform evaluation standards. At the time of writing, the CEM applies to EAL 1 to EAL 4 only, so above the EAL 4 assurance level, national schemes still determine their own methodologies. The main reason for this is that higher assurance level evaluations are more usually employed for critical government system evaluations. Sovereign nations jealously guard their own critical evaluation methodologies, which they may not always wish to share with other nations; equally they may not be willing to accept practices used elsewhere, as they would have to do if they agreed to recognize and accept a common methodology.

The Common Criteria scheme operates in a number of participating countries and is controlled by national certification authorities, which are normally government bodies. Commercial laboratories, licensed by the certification authority in the country in which they operate, usually perform the evaluations. The certification authority monitors the evaluations performed by the licensed laboratories in that country. Upon successful completion of an evaluation, the certification body issues a certificate for the evaluated product or system.

## Biometrics and Common Criteria Evaluation

Common Criteria and the CEM are generic standards for security evaluations, although they are broadly suitable for the evaluation of biometric security functionality. Biometric specialists have recognized that biometric systems embody some special considerations for which the generic Common Criteria methodology provides little explicit guidance. This could lead to important aspects of biometric security evaluation not being addressed adequately by evaluators and certifiers who lacking specialist knowledge of security relevant aspects of biometric technology.

Recognition of these difficulties led to the creation of an informal Biometric Evaluation Methodology (BEM) Working Group. The BEM Working Group drew its membership from a pool of interested and informed biometric and security specialists, who developed and published in August 2002 the first released version of the Biometric Evaluation Methodology (BEM, 2002). This document has subsequently been submitted to the Common Criteria Development Board (CCDB) with a view to its adoption as a standard within the (ISO 15408, 1999) Common Criteria Standard.

To provide acceptable security standards for government use, both the U.S. and U.K. governments have developed Biometric Device Protection Profiles for use with Common Criteria evaluations (CESG, 2001; NIAP, 2003).

A Protection Profile is a standard security specification for a class of security products. It contains an inventory of security functions and assurance requirements, determined by experts in the field to be a useful standard for a security evaluation. Products that have been evaluated and certified against the same Protection Profile can be broadly regarded as having the same security features (more accurately to conform to the set of standards defined in the Protection Profile).

At the time of writing two biometric products had successfully achieved EAL 2 Common Criteria Certification (Common Criteria, 2001, 2003). The first evaluation predates the biometric specific methodology development work described above; in fact experience gained during that evaluation helped to inform the methodology work. The second evaluation made use of the methodology and the then-extant draft Protection Profiles informally and without making any specific claims of compliance.

## AUDITING OF BIOMETRIC SYSTEMS

According to the dictionary definition, audit is concerned with the inspection, verification, and correction of business systems. For an IT system, an audit depends on the prior recording of relevant data, and the integrity of the audit process is of course dependent, among other things, on the integrity of this data.

In many instances auditing of a biometric system will parallel that of other IT systems, but here are some auditing processes that are specific to the biometric functions, and these specific features can play a part in inspecting, verifying, and correcting security functioning and help to underpin the system security policy. Although auditing could apply to any stage, including testing and operations, in practice it normally refers to the operational conditions, which is the assumption made in this section.

In a biometric system the principal source of data for the audit is likely to be the system log, which should carry a record of security relevant activities and transactions. However other sources of data can also provide useful information—biometric data images and templates are examples. The following paragraphs list some ways on which log and other data can be used to monitor and improve security. Clearly, any specific analysis can only be performed if the relevant source data are available; the natural corollary being that system owners must ensure that the relevant data are recorded to provide the necessary input for the analysis that they wish to perform.

Information that may be relevant to security audit includes the following:

- Biometric template data.
- Biometric "image" data and features, particularly for failure events.
- Failure events (e.g., rejections).
- Security parameter access and changes.

Recorded events should include date and time information and be associated with a specific user, operator, or administrator where known.

## Monitoring and Maintaining System Performance

Biometric system performance parameters are usually set to an acceptable compromise between security and usability. As we have already seen, more stringent criteria for FAR come at the cost of increased FRR. Fortunately, it is often the case that access control systems having the highest security requirements in regard to FAR also have relatively small numbers of authorized users, and the users will generally be expected to be more security aware, cooperative, and tolerant of problems than the average person.

One difficulty that system administrators face is knowing whether the security standards set at the time of installation have become eroded with the passage of time. This can occur for a number of reasons, including technical factors such as equipment deterioration, procedural relaxations in enrollment security criteria, matching decision threshold adjustments or similar, or simply through growth in size of the enrollee database. It is possible that, unknowingly, some enrollee templates closely match other enrollees or that certain enrollees have poor-quality enrollments that make them relatively easy targets for a would-be impersonator, should the resemblance become known.

Using the enrolled template database, it is possible to run offline tests that compare all the templates against each other and report matching scores, indicating if any abnormally close matches exist between enrollees or, worse, whether certain users' templates match well against a number of other users. Such instances can arise occasionally through the inherent characteristics of a particular enrollee's source biometric or more likely through a failure of quality control at enrollment. In many cases, reenrollment of such users will resolve the problem and restore the system security level. If users' biometric "images" or features are recorded during normal use, or when failures occur, these can be used to further enhance performance monitoring and to aid the investigation and diagnosis of problems (see also below). Comparisons between multiple samples and the template for the same enrollee can show occurrences of wider than normal variations, which may signal a need for reenrollment or retraining of the enrollee.

## Detecting and Diagnosing System Problems

Checking the system log may reveal current or incipient problems. For example, if biometric images or features are logged when failures occur, these can be used individually to investigate and diagnose specific failures or collectively to indicate trends that may presage more serious problems. Once again it must be emphasized that analysis can be performed only on data that have been collected and that requirements for monitoring and analysis should therefore be used to inform decisions on the data that will be logged.

## Security Monitoring

A system log that records security relevant information can be a valuable tool for monitoring security problems.

We have already seen this in the context of performance monitoring. Analysis of log records can reveal a user who persistently has problems using the system, most likely for an innocent reason (indicating that the user may need to be reenrolled), but could also be a sign that a directed attack has taken place; at least it highlights a problem that merits further investigation.

Auditing is limited to highlighting problems after the event; it cannot normally prevent them happening (but see "Countermeasures Against Spoofing Attacks"). However, auditing is a powerful tool because of the aggregation of information and evidence. Detailed analysis can provide an insight into problems and suspicious activity that would be unlikely to be detected from isolated events. Because of this evidential trail, an audit log is an obvious target for an attacker, who is likely to want to hide the traces of an attack. Thus the system log will need to be protected against unauthorized access, modification, or destruction, and consideration should also be given to protecting historical archives, where long-term analysis is called for.

## Countermeasures Against Malicious Operator and Administrator Actions

Most security countermeasures are directed against impostors and other attackers, with a tacit assumption that operation and administration staff are trustworthy. Indeed it is difficult to guard against corrupt administrators, as their legitimate duties generally require them to have access to security relevant functionality and to sensitive data and parameters. For biometric systems, administrators will often be responsible for setting matching decision thresholds and usually need access and update other security-sensitive enrollment data. Furthermore a corrupt administrator could enroll an impostor directly, bypassing any technical security countermeasures (such as spoofing detection).

A security audit is one of the few tools that can provide some safeguard (or at least deterrence) against the malevolent administrator, with the proviso that the integrity of logged information must be protected. The association of an administrator with a security relevant event (e.g., the modification of a security parameter) can act as a powerful deterrent to a corrupt administrator. Because of the administrator privileges, special measures will be needed to protect the log data from modification or deletion. One possibility is role separation; operations administrators who can enroll users and who have access to security parameters but not to the log records and log administrators who have access to the log records but cannot enroll users and have no access to security parameters. Hostile administrator actions would require conspiracy if they were to be perpetrated without a telltale record appearing in the log.

## Countermeasures Against Spoofing Attacks

A number of studies have concluded that spoofing biometric devices using artifacts is sometimes possible (see "Spoofing, Mimicry, and Liveness Detection" for further information). What these studies do not always indicate is that using artifacts often involves greater difficulties than occur with the presentation of genuine live source biometrics. Typically, intricate manipulations and repeated failures over an extended time period precede successful acceptance. This is most marked when liveness detection measures are employed, even if these are not completely effective. Armed with this knowledge, the biometric system developer could include measures that monitor the progress of image acquisition, and use an "intelligent" approach to help distinguish genuine attempts from spoof attacks. In its most basic form this could be a simple timeout—timeouts are often employed in the biometric capture process but normally it seems they are used to reset internal devices and software for technical reasons rather than as a security measure.

The approach outlined here would be possible and probably useful. It has similarities with the normal audit function in that it examines historical events and pieces together information from individual but related items of data. In this case it is looking for aberrant activity during the image acquisition phase. Because of the much reduced time scale compared to a conventional audit, it could be used to monitor the acquisition process during operational use, and we therefore call it "real-time auditing." A real-time audit could provide an additional countermeasure to liveness checking against spoofing attacks. Such an approach would not be foolproof of course and would sometimes signal events as suspicious that were in fact innocent examples of real difficulty of use that occur occasionally for genuine users. The author is not aware of any biometric systems that currently implement such a strategy as a countermeasure to spoofing attacks.

# BIOMETRIC STANDARDS

Standards activities are often taken to be a sign of a maturing technology, and in the case of biometric technology this maturity began around 2000 with several important initiatives from the user community, government, and industry practitioners. Early standards activities were fragmentary, but a more coordinated picture is now emerging with industry-sponsored groups giving way to the formal international standards community. The following sections list the principal biometric standards activities and provide a historical outline, from parochial beginnings to the international arena.

## X9.84—Biometric Information Management and Security

The financial services community, looking forward to the use of biometric authentication for electronic commerce applications and access control, recognized that biometric security issues would need to be addressed and brought into line with existing security practice in the finance sector. A task force was established under the X9 committee of TC 68, the Financial Services standards group within the US ANSI standards organization. The first version of X9.84—Biometric Information Management and Security was published in 2001. It contained not only "best practice" procedural and management advice for handling biometric data but also provided a set of standard biometric objects and data structures defined in terms of Abstract Syntax Notation (ASN.1) schema. In addition, X9.84 2001 specified the requirements for the cryptographic protection of biometric data. A revised version, X9.84 2003, incorporated other new standards work on CBEFF and OASIS XCBF (see below) to update its data object definitions. For further information see Griffin (2003a).

## BioAPI—Biometric Applications Programming Interface

The BioAPI Consortium was formed by a group of biometrics companies who perceived the need for interoperability standards for building biometric systems that would provide plug-and-play capability. Vendor independent standards are recognized as important drivers for the growth of the marketplace for a technology. Customers are more likely to invest in biometric technology if they have the confidence that they will not risk becoming locked in to a single vendor.

BioAPI comprises a standard suite of software. API calls for implementing the basic functions of a biometric system. It builds on and supersedes a number of earlier initiatives on biometric APIs. It is vendor and modality neutral, though it is limited to the high-level function calls and does not address the low-level device driver interface. Several versions were developed within the BioAPI Consortium, and an open source reference implementation has been produced. Later, BioAPI was transferred to the ANSI INCITS M1 Committee and became a U.S. national standard in 2003. It has since moved into the international standards arena through the ISO SC 37 Biometric Standards Committee (see below). For further information see BioAPI (2001) and ANSI (2002).

## CBEFF—Common Biometric Exchange Framework Format

CBEFF was developed by a government/industry working body under the joint sponsorship of the U.S. National Institute of Standards and Technology (NIST) and the Biometric Consortium. Originally it was conceived to specify and hence promote common formats for the core biometric recognition data (e.g., fingerprint minutiae, facial features, and iris patterns) in the interest of interoperability. However, it did not (at the time) prove possible to achieve the necessary consensus of opinion among the participants on the desirability or feasibility of core biometric data standardization. Several issues stood in the way, including the proprietary nature of such data and the concern that standardizing at the core data level might impede future developments and improvements in biometric technology.

In the event CBEFF went ahead as a metadata specification to facilitate the exchange of biometric data among applications, services, and organizations. The metadata comprises a header to the biometric data block, which contains the core biometric recognition data and is undefined. The header provides a detailed description of the data that is the subject of the exchange, which includes practically everything necessary to classify the data and its quality, so that it may be correctly read and interpreted by the recipient. It also includes an indication of the organization that originated the data, termed the patron by CBEFF. Patrons are required to register through an approved registration authority, which provides the unique registration number that is included in the CBEFF header.

As happened with BioAPI, CBEFF was moved into the ANSI INCITS M1 committee to become a U.S. national standard and later into the international standards arena through ISO, SC 37; see "ISO SC 37—Biometric Standards"). For further information, see NIST (2001).

## OASIS XCBF—XML Common Biometric Format

OASIS exists to map data specifications appearing in other standards into an XML representation. XCBF defines a common set of secure XML encodings for the patron formats specified in CBEFF. The XCBF XML encodings are based on the ASN.1 schema defined in ANSI X9.84:2003 *Biometrics Information Management and Security*. For further information see OASIS (2003).

## International Biometric Standards

The terrorist attacks of 11 September 2001 produced a strong impetus to subsequent international biometric standards activities. They galvanized activity and provided focus and acceleration to a number of preexisting programs aimed at improving border security. It also reinforced the view that biometric authentication could play a vital role in helping to achieve these objectives. Passports, visas, and other border control programs incorporating biometrics were in the planning stages and some were already operational in a number of countries, and standards were needed to ensure interoperability between the biometric technologies being implemented under future programs.

### ICAO—International Civil Aviation Organization

ICAO is responsible for standards for machine-readable travel documents including passports. ICAO is a recognized standards body operating under the ISO SC 17—Cards and Personal Identification Subcommittee. ICAO was charged with the responsibility for defining requirements for biometrically enabled passports, which included not only the biometric element but also the associated chip-based technology and the supporting document and electronic security infrastructure. In this key central position, ICAO has taken on the dual role of a driver for international biometric standards development and a major customer for the standards. The short time scales associated with the introduction of biometric passports has imparted a sense of urgency to the standards development work. For further information see ICAO (2004).

### ISO SC 37—Biometric Standards

To bring together some of the existing work on biometric standards and promote the rapid progress of international biometric standards, the U.S. ANSI standards organization approached ISO in 2002 with a proposal for a dedicated ISO subcommittee to move the development of international biometric standards forward in support

the upcoming programs on biometrics in travel documents. Following a successful international ballot, the ISO SC 37 Biometric Standards Committee was inaugurated in December 2002. The stated objectives were as follows:

> .... to ensure a high priority, focused, and comprehensive approach worldwide for the rapid development and approval of formal international biometric standards. These standards are necessary to support the rapid deployment of significantly better, open systems standard-based security solutions for purposes such as homeland defense and the prevention of ID theft.

The core activities are those concerned with interoperability. SC 37 has inherited CBEFF and BioAPI from ANSI INCITS M1 and is developing them to meet the criteria for wide international acceptability

The activities are divided into six working groups as follows:[1]

**WG 1 Harmonized Biometric Vocabulary**— "To ensure an agreed and common use of terms and definitions throughout all SC 37 International Standards. The group should be considerate in choosing terms of the problems of translating to other languages, and should take account of the current ISO/IEC International Standards and related documentation."

**WG 2 Biometric Technical Interfaces**—"To consider the standardization of all necessary interfaces and interactions between biometric components and sub-systems, including the possible use of security mechanisms to protect stored data and data transferred between systems. To consider the need for a reference model for the architecture and operation of biometric systems in order to identify the standards that are needed to support multivendor systems and their application." Current activities are focused on

- Biometric Application Programming Interface (BioAPI) and
- Common Biometric Exchange Formats Framework (CBEFF).

**WG 3 Biometric Data Interchange Formats**—"To consider the standardization of the content, meaning, and representation of biometric data formats which are specific to a particular biometric technology. To ensure a common look and feel for Biometric Data Structure standards, with notation and transfer formats that provide platform independence and separation of transfer syntax from content definition." At the time of writing (June 2005), current activities include

- Part 1 Framework,
- Part 2 Finger Minutiae Data,
- Part 3 Finger Pattern Spectral Data,
- Part 4 Finger Image Data,

---

[1] The descriptions of the working groups are drawn from the WG official Terms of Reference.

- Part 5 Face Image Data,
- Part 6 Iris Image Data,
- Part 7 Signature/sign Image Time Series Data,
- Part 8 Finger Pattern Skeletal Data,
- Part 9 Vascular Image Data,
- Part 10 Hand Geometry Silhouette Data, and
- Part 11 Signature/sign Processed Dynamic Data.

**WG 4  Biometric Profiles for Interoperability and Data Interchange**—"To consider the need for and approach to standardization of profiles for biometric applications." Current activities include

- Biometric Reference Architecture,
- Biometric Based Verification and Identification of Employees in a Highly Secure Environment, and
- Biometric Based Verification and Identification of Seafarers.

**WG 5  Biometric Performance Testing**

- Part 1 Principles and Framework.
- Part 2 Test Methodologies (technology, and scenario testing).
- Part 3 Specific Testing Methodologies (biometric modalities).
- Part 4 Performance and Interoperability Testing of Interchange Formats.
- Part 5 Framework for Biometric Device Performance Evaluation for Access Control.

**WG 6  Cross Jurisdictional and Societal Aspects**—"To study the scope and approach to cross-jurisdictional aspects in the application of ISO/IEC biometrics standards. This could include the safe operation of biometric systems, the use of technical measures such as privacy maintaining and enhancing technologies, and development of codes of practice." Current activity is aimed at the development of a Technical Report on Cross-Jurisdictional and Societal Aspects of Implementations of Biometric Technology.

See ISO (SC 37) for further information on SC 37 activities.

## International Biometric Security Standards

Most of the biometric standards activities have not been directly aimed at security; in fact the terms of reference of SC 37 explicitly exclude biometric security standards, which are deemed to lie within the scope of SC 27, IT Security Techniques. International biometric security standards are less advanced than the other areas of standards. A brief listing of those activities known to the author at the time of writing follows.

The furthest advanced activity is probably that being undertaken within the TC 68 committee—a recasting of ANSI X9.84 2003 into the international domain, where it has been given the following reference: ISO 19092. The original X9.84 document has been separated into two parts as follows:

- 19092—1 Security Framework, and
- 19092—2 Cryptographic Requirements.

### SC 27—IT Security Techniques

At the time of writing a set of studies on aspects of biometric security and security evaluation have begun in SC 27. There is at present only one formally identified biometric standards project, 19792. The list includes the following:

- ISO/IEC WD 19792 Information technology—Security techniques—Framework for Security Evaluation and Testing of Biometric Technology.
- Biometric Security Management.
- Biometric Authentication.
- ISO/IEC NP 24745 Information technology—Biometric template protection.

Some of these informal studies may lead to projects in due course. For further information on SC 27 activities see ISO, SC 27.

## ACKNOWLEDGMENTS

The author gratefully acknowledges all the many biometric specialists whose referenced work has informed this article but are too numerous to name individually. However, particularly thanks is due to the following for providing valuable information, papers, and figures in response to direct requests and who are, in alphabetical order:

Paul Griffin of Identix Inc., Minnetonka, Minnesota, for the papers on multimodal data fusion (Griffin, 2003b, 2003c).

Matthew Lewis of CESG, who conducted the vulnerability assessment program and provided the illustrations on biometric images and artifacts.

Nigel Sedgwick of Cambridge Algorithmica Ltd., Beaconsfield, U.K., for the paper on multimodal data fusion and for making it publicly available on the Cambridge Algorithmica Web site (Sedgwick, 2003).

Colin Soutar of Bioscrypt Inc., Mississauga, Ontario, Canada, who provided papers on biometric encryption and key management and copies of several BioScrypt U.S. patent documents (various, see references).

## GLOSSARY

This glossary includes not only terms used in the chapter but also a selection of other terms in common use. It draws on several sources, principally Mansfield & Wayman (2002) and BEM (2002). These were in turn derived from an earlier glossary jointly developed by the U.K.-based Association for Biometrics (AfB) and the U.S.-based International Computer Security Association (ICSA).

At the time of writing, a biometric vocabulary of terms and definitions is in preparation by the ISO. This forms part of the broader development of biometric standards taking place within ISO/IEC JTC-1 SC 37—the Committee for Biometric Standards. Where possible, the terms and definitions in this glossary reflect the current ISO draft, but the reader is cautioned that the ISO work is at an early stage and the final terms and definitions in the ISO vocabulary standard may be significantly different. The entries are grouped logically rather than alphabetically.

## General Terms

**Attempt**    The submission of a biometric sample to a biometric system for identification or verification. A biometric system may allow more than one attempt to identify or verify.

**Behavioral Biometrics**    Biometrics characterized by a behavioral trait that is learned and acquired over time (e.g., a signature). See also Biological Biometrics.

**Biological Biometrics**    Biometrics characterized by a biological or physical trait that is inherited (e.g., fingerprints, iris patterns). See also Behavioral Biometrics.

**Biometric**    Adjective; pertaining to biometrics.

**Biometric System**    An automated system that evaluates claims of identity through the automated recognition of individuals based on their behavioral and biological characteristics

**Biometrics**    The automated recognition of individuals based on their behavioral and biological characteristics.

**Capture Device**    The physical hardware device used for biometric capture.

**Claim**    Assertion or hypothesis regarding the identity of a subject. A claim may be made by or on behalf of the subject. The role of the biometric system is to evaluate the claim and return a response (usually to the claimant). There are many possible formulations of claims, illustrations of which are given in the following examples.

*Positive claim of identity*: The subject claims (either explicitly or implicitly) to be enrolled in or known to the system. An explicit claim might be accompanied by a claimed identity in the form of a name or personal identification number (PIN). Access control systems are a typical example.

*Negative claim of identity*: The subject claims (either implicitly or explicitly) not to be known to or enrolled in the system. Enrollment in social service systems open only to those not already enrolled is an example.

*Explicit claim of identity:* In applications where there is an explicit claim of identity or nonidentity, the submitted sample needs to be matched against just the enrolled template for that identity. Conceptually, the accept/reject decision depends on the result of a one-to-one comparison.

*Implicit claim of identity*: In applications where there is an implicit claim of identity or nonidentity, the submitted sample may need to be matched against many enrolled templates. In this case the decision depends on the result of many comparisons (i.e., a one-to-many search), and the response is an identifier or pointer to an identity, which may be empty if no matching template is found.

*Genuine claim of identity:* A truthful, positive claim about identity in the system made by or on behalf of the subject. The truthful claim leads to a comparison of a sample with a truly matching template.

*Impostor claim of identity:* A false, positive claim about identity in the system made by or on behalf of the subject. The false claim of identity leads to the comparison of a sample with a nonmatching template.

**Enrollee**    A subject with a stored biometric template in a biometric system.

**Enrollment**    The process of collecting biometric sample(s) from a subject, and the subsequent preparation and storage of template(s) and associated data representing the subject's identity.

**Genuine Attempt**    A single good faith attempt by a subject to match his or her own stored template.

**Identification**    Evaluation by a biometric system of an implicit claim of identity made by or on behalf of the subject, resulting in the return of an identifier or a pointer to an identity (which may be empty). In identification systems, the claim may be positive or negative with regard to an enrolled identity. Conceptually, identification may be thought of as involving a one-to-many search of the entire enrolled database, though biometric systems may use internal strategies that avoid exhaustive searches.

**Impostor**    An individual making a false claim about his or her own identity to a biometric system.

**Impostor Attempt**    A single zero-effort attempt, by a subject "unknown to the system," to match a stored template.

*Unknown to the system*: A subject is known to the system if (1) the subject is enrolled and (2) the enrollment affects the templates of other enrollees in the system. An enrolled subject can be considered unknown with reference to other enrollees only if the other templates are independent and not influenced by this enrollment. Eigenface systems using all enrolled images for creation of the basis images, and cohort-based speaker recognition systems, are two examples for which templates are dependent. Such systems cannot treat any enrolled subject as unknown with reference to the other templates.

*Zero-effort attempts*: An impostor attempt is classed as zero-effort if the subject submits their own biometric feature as if they were attempting successful verification against their own template. In the case of dynamic signature verification, an impostor would therefore sign his or her own signature in a zero-effort attempt. In such cases, where impostors may easily imitate aspects of the required biometric, a second impostor measure based on "active impostor attempts" may be required. However, defining the methods or level of skill to be used in active impostor attempts is outside the scope of this definition.

**Multimodal Biometrics**    Biometrics that uses samples captured from more than one biometric modality (e.g., fingerprint and hand geometry); some definitions also include the case of multiple source features of the same modality (e.g., two different fingers).

**Transaction** An attempt by a subject to validate a claim of identity or nonidentity by consecutively submitting one or more samples, as allowed by the system decision policy.

**Verification** Evaluation by a biometric system of an explicit claim of identity made by or on behalf of the subject, resulting in either acceptance or rejection of the claim. Conceptually, verification may be thought of as a one-to-one process involving a comparison of the submitted sample biometric source feature to the enrolled template for the claimed identity. Note, however, that biometric verification systems may employ internal strategies involving multiple template comparisons.

## Biometric Data Terms

**Biometric Characteristic** Biological or behavioral characteristic that a subject presents to the data collection subsystem (e.g., fingerprint, iris, face, and voice are examples of source features or biometric characteristics).

**Channel Effects** The changes imposed on the presented signal in the transduction and transmission process because of the sampling, noise, and frequency response characteristics of the sensor and transmission channel.

**Decision** A determination by the system of the probable validity of a claim to identity/nonidentity made by or in reference to the subject.

**Features** A mathematical representation of the information extracted from the presented biometric characteristic by the signal processing subsystem that will be used to construct or compare against enrollment templates (e.g., minutiae coordinates, principal component coefficients, and iris codes are features).

**Matching Score** A measure of the similarity between features derived from a presented biometric charactristic and a stored template or a measure of how well these features fit a user's reference model. A match/nonmatch decision may be made according to whether this score exceeds a decision threshold.

**Presentation Effects** A broad category of variables impacting the way in which the users' biometric characteristics are displayed to the sensor; for example, in facial recognition, pose angle and illumination; in fingerprinting, finger rotation and skin moisture. In many cases, the distinction between changes in the fundamental biometric characteristics (see Template Aging and the presentation effects may not be clear (e.g., facial aging versus expression in facial recognition, or throat infection vs. behavioral pitch change in speaker verification systems).

**Sample** One instance of a source feature presentation to the data collection subsystem.

**Template/Model** A user's stored reference measure based on features extracted from enrollment samples. The reference measure is often a template comprising the biometric features for an ideal sample presented

by the user. More generally, the stored reference will be a model representing the potential range of biometric features for that user. In this chapter, we use template to include model.

**Template Aging** The gradual change of an enrollee's biometric source feature(s), which may require periodic reenrollment to update the enrollee's reference template.

**Threshold** A parameter value used to convert a matching score to a decision. A threshold change will usually change both FAR and FRR—as FAR decreases, FRR increases.

## Biometric Performance and Error Terms

**Detection Error Trade-Off Curves** In the case of biometric systems, a modified ROC curve known as a detection error trade-off curve is often preferred. A DET curve plots error rates on both axes, giving uniform treatment to both types of error. The graph can then be plotted using logarithmic axes. This spreads out the plot and distinguishes different well-performing systems more clearly. DET curves can be used to plot matching error rates (false nonmatch rate against false match rate) as well as decision error rates (false reject rate against false accept rate).

**Failure to Acquire Rate** The expected proportion of transactions for which the system is unable to capture or locate an image or signal of sufficient quality. The failure to acquire rate may depend on adjustable thresholds for image or signal quality.

**Failure to Enroll Rate** The expected proportion of the target population for whom the system is unable to generate repeatable templates. This will include those unable to present the required biometric source feature, those unable to produce an image of sufficient quality at enrollment, and those who cannot reliably match their template in attempts to confirm that the enrollment is usable. The failure to enroll rate will depend on the enrollment policy. For example, in the case of failure, enrollment might be reattempted at a later date.

**False Accept Rate** The expected proportion of transactions with wrongful claims of identity (in a positive id system) or nonidentity (in a negative Id system) that are incorrectly confirmed. A transaction may consist of one or more wrongful attempts dependent on the decision policy. A false acceptance is often referred to in the mathematical literature as a type II error. Note that acceptance always refers to the claim regarding the subject.

**False Match Rate** The false match rate is the expected probability that a sample randomly selected from the target population will be falsely declared to match a single randomly selected nonself template. (A false match is sometimes called a false positive in the literature.)

**False Nonmatch Rate** The false nonmatch rate is the expected probability that a sample randomly selected from the target population will be falsely declared not to match a template of the same measure from the same subject supplying the sample. (A false nonmatch is sometimes called a "false negative" in the literature.)

**False Reject Rate**    The expected proportion of transactions with truthful claims of identity (in a positive Id system) or nonidentity (in a negative Id system) that are incorrectly denied. A transaction may consist of one or more truthful attempts dependent on the decision policy. A false rejection is often referred to in the mathematical literature as a type I error. Note that rejection always refers to the claim regarding the subject.

**Receiver Operating Characteristic Curves**    Receiver operating characteristic (ROC) curves are an accepted method for summarizing the performance of imperfect diagnostic, detection, and pattern matching systems. An ROC curve plots, parametrically as a function of the decision threshold, the rate of false positives (i.e., impostor attempts accepted) on the $x$ axis, against the corresponding rate of true positives (i.e., genuine attempts accepted) on the $y$ axis. ROC curves are threshold independent, allowing performance comparison of different systems under similar conditions or of a single system under differing conditions.

## Biometric Security Relevant Terms

**Biometric Evaluation Methodology**    Document produced by an international group of experts describing a methodology for the security evaluation of biometric products and systems under the ISO 15408 Common Criteria evaluation scheme.

**Common Criteria**    An international scheme for the security evaluation and certification of IT products and systems.

**Threat**    An intentional or unintentional potential event that could compromise the security integrity of a biometric system.

**Vulnerability**    A flaw in the system concept, design, and implementation or a failure in operation that, if exploited intentionally or inadvertently, could compromise the security functionality of a biometric system.

**Weak Template**    A template created from a noisy, poor-quality, highly varying, or null image, which exhibits abnormally high error rates during match operations compared to other templates.

## CROSS REFERENCES

See *Auditing Information Systems Security; Biometric Basics and Biometric Authentication; Computer and Network Authentication; Password Authentication; Privacy Law and the Internet.*

## REFERENCES

ANSI. (2002). *Information technology—BioAPI Specification document number: ANSI/INCITS 358-2002*. Retrieved June 7, 2005, from http://webstore.ansi.org/ansidocstore/product.asp?sku=ANSI+INCITS+358-2002

BEM. (2002, August). *Biometric Evaluation Methodology Supplement version 1.0*. Retrieved June 7, 2005, from http://www.cesg.gov.uk

BioAPI. (2001). *BioAPI specification version 1.1 and BioAPI reference implementation version 1.1*. Retrieved June 7, 2005, from www.bioapi.org

CESG. (2001, September). *Biometric device protection profile*. (UK Government Biometrics Working Group. Draft Issue 0.82). Retrieved June 7, 2005, from http://www.cesg.gov.uk [follow the biometrics link from the home page]

Common Criteria. (2001, June). *BioScrypt Enterprise for NT logon version 2.1.3; Common Criteria EAL2 Certificate*. Retrieved June 7, 2005, from http://www.cse-cst.gc.ca/en/services/ccs/bioscrypt.html

Common Criteria. (2003, October). *KnoWho Authentication Server v1.2.2 and Private ID v2.1.15; Common Criteria EAL2 Certificate*. Retrieved June 7, 2005, from http://www.dsd.gov.au/infosec/evaluation_services/epl/biometric/Iridian_KnoWhoAuthServer.html

Daugman, J. (2000). *Biometric decision landscapes*. Cambridge: The Computer Laboratory. Retrieved June 3, 2005, from http://www.cl.cam.ac.uk/TechReports/UCAM-CL-TR-482.pdf

Daugman, J. (2004). *Combining multiple biometrics*. Cambridge: The Computer Laboratory. Retrieved June 7, 2005, from http://www.cl.cam.ac.uk/users/jgd1000/combine/combine.html

Derakhshani, R., Schuckers, S. A. C., Hornak, L. A., & O'Gorman, L. (2003). Determination of vitality from a non-invasive biomedical measurement for use in fingerprint scanners. *Pattern Recognition, 36*, 383–396.

e-Government. (2002, September). *Registration and authentication—e-Government strategy framework policy and guidelines v3.0*. Retrieved June 3, 2005, from http:// www.cabinetoffice.gov.uk/e-government/docs/responsibilities/document_library/pdf/registration_auth_policy_fw.pdf

FRVT. (2005). *Face recognition vendor test 2005*. Retrieved June 7, 2005, from http://www.frvt.org/FRVT2005/default.aspx

FVC. (2000). *Fingerprint verification competition 2000*. Retrieved June 7, 2005, from http://bias.csr.unibo.it/fvc2000/

FVC. (2002). *Fingerprint verification competition 2002*. Retrieved June 7, 2005, from http://bias.csr.unibo.it/fvc2002/

FVC. (2004). *Fingerprint verification competition 2004*. Retrieved June 7, 2005, from http://bias.csr.unibo.it/fvc2004/

Griffin, P. (2003a). *Biometric information management and security*. Retrieved June 7, 2005, from http://asn-1.com/x984.htm

Griffin, P. (2003b). *How to fuse two biometrics together*. Identix Corporate Research Center Preprint RDNJ-03-0065. Minnetonka, MN: Identix Inc.

Griffin, P. (2003c). *Optimal biometric fusion for identity verification*. Identix Corporate Research Center Preprint RDNJ-03-0064. Minnetonka, MN: Identix Inc.

Gunnerson, G. (1999). Are you ready for biometrics? *PC Magazine, 18*, 160.

Hill, C. J. (2001). *Risk of masquerade arising from the storage of biometrics*. Retrieved June 7, 2005, from http://chris.fornax.net/biometrics.html

ICAO. (2004). *Biometrics deployment of machine readable travel documents* (Technical Report Version 2). Retrieved June 7, 2005, from http://www.icao.int/mrtd/biometrics/recommendation.cfm

ICBA. (2004). *Face verification contest on the Banca dataset*. Retrieved June 7, 2005, from http://www.ee.surrey.ac.uk/banca/icba2004/messer-icba04.pdf

Iridian. (2004). *Iridian KnoWho and PrivateID technology*. Retrieved June 7, 2005, from http://www.iridiantech.com

ISO 15408. (1999). *Common Criteria for Information Technology Security Evaluation*. Retrieved June 7, 2005, from http://csrc.nist.gov/cc/index.html

ISO. (n.d.). *SC 27 IT security techniques*. Retrieved June 3, 2005, from http://www.iso.org/iso/en/CatalogueListPage.CatalogueList?COMMID=143&scopelist=PROGRAMME

ISO. (n.d.). *SC 37 Biometric standards*. Retrieved June 3, 2005, from http://www.iso.org/iso/en/CatalogueList Page.Catalogue List? COMMID=5537&scopelist=PROGRAMME

Mansfield, A. J., & Kelly, G., Chandler, D., & Kane, J. (2001). *CESG/BWG biometrics test programme—Biometric product testing final report issue 1.0*. Teddington, Middlesex: National Physical Laboratory. Retrieved June 7, 2005, from http://www.cesg.gov.uk [click on biometrics link]

Mansfield, A. J., & Wayman. J. L. (2002). *Best practices in testing and reporting performance of biometric devices*. Retrieved June 3, 2005, from http://www.cesg.gov.uk [click on biometrics link]

Matsumoto, T., Matsumoto, H., Yamada, K., & Hoshino, S. (2002). *Impact of artificial "gummy" fingers on fingerprint systems*. Presented at SPIE, Optical Security and Counterfeit Detection Techniques IV, Jan 2002. Retrieved June 3, 2005, from http://crypto.csail.mit.edu/classes/6.857/papers/gummyslides.pdf

NIAP. (2003). U.S. government verification mode biometric protection profile for medium robustness environments. Retrieved June 3, 2005, from http://www.niap.nist.gov/cc-scheme/pp/PP_VID1022.html

NIST. (2001). *Common biometric exchange framework format, NISTIR 6529*. Retrieved June 7, 2005, from www.nist.gov/cbeff

OASIS. (2003). *XCBF XML common biometric format*. Retrieved June 7, 2005, from http://www.oasis-open.org/committees/tc_home.php?wg_abbrev=xcbf

Phillips, P. J., Martin, A., Wilson, C., & Pryzbocki, M. (2000). An introduction to the evaluation of biometric systems. *IEEE Computer, 33*(2), 56–63. Retrieved June 3, 2005, from http://www.frvt.org/DLs/FERET7.pdf

Ratha, N. K., Connell, J. H., & Bolle, R. M. (2001). Enhancing security and privacy in biometrics-based authentication systems. *IBM Systems Journal, 40*, (3). Retrieved June 3, 2005, from http://www.research.ibm.com/journal/sj/403/ratha.pdf

Ross, A., & Jain, A.K. (2003). Information fusion in biometrics. *Pattern Recognition Letters, 24,* 2115–2125. Retrieved June 7, 2005, from http://www.csee.wvu.edu/~ross/pubs/RossFusion_PRL03.pdf

Sedgwick, N. (2003). *The need for standardization of multi-modal biometric combination*. Retrieved June 7, 2005, from http://www.camalg.co.uk/s03017_pr0/begin.html

Soutar, C. (2002). *Template Protection and Usage version 1.3* (NIST/BC Biometric Interoperability, Performance and Assurance Working Group). Retrieved June 3, 2005, from http://www.ncits.org/tc_home/m1htm/docs/m1020219.pdf

Soutar, C., Roberge, D., Stolanov, A., Gilroy, R., & Vijaya-Kumar, B. (1999). *Biometric encryption*. Retrieved June 7, 2005, from http://www.bioscrypt.com/technology/white_papers.shtml

Soutar, C., Roberge, D., Stolanov, A., Gilroy, R., & Vijaya-Kumar, B. (2001, April). *Method for secure key management using a biometric*. U.S. Patent 6,219,794 B1. Retrieved June 7, 2005, from http://www.bioscrypt.com/technology/intel_property.shtml#corealg

SVC. (2004). *First international signature recognition competition*. Retrieved June 7, 2005, from http://www.cs.ust.hk/svc2004/icba2004paper.pdf

Thalheim, L., Krissler, J., & Ziegler, P.-M. (2002). Body check: Biometric access protection devices and their programs put to the test. *C'T Magazine, 11,* 114. Retrieved June 7, 2005, from http://www.heise.de/ct/english/02/11/114/

Tomko, G. (2002). The threats associated with template-based biometric identification. *World Data Protection Report, 2*(10). 27–31.

Tomko, G. J., Soutar, C., & Schmitt, G. J. (1996, July). *Fingerprint controlled public key cryptographic system*. U.S. Patent 5,541,994. Retrieved June 7, 2005, from http://www.bioscrypt.com/technology/intel_property.shtml#corealg

Tomko, G. J., Soutar, C., & Schmitt, G. J. (1997, October). *Biometric controlled key generation*. U.S. Patent 5,680,460. Retrieved June 7, 2005, from http://www.bioscrypt.com/technology/intel_property.shtml#corealg

Van der Putte, T., & Keuning, J. (2000). *Biometrical fingerprint recognition: Don't get your fingers burned*. Presented at the Fourth Working Conference on Smart Card Research and Advanced Applications, IFIP TC8/WG8.8.

Willis, D., & Lee, M. (1998, June). Six biometric devices point the finger at security. *Network Computing*. Retrieved June 3, 2005, from http://www.nwc.com/910/910r1.html

# Firewall Basics

James E. Goldman, *Purdue University*

## INTRODUCTION

When an organization or individual links to the Internet, a two-way access point out of and into their information systems is created. To prevent unauthorized activities between the Internet and the private network, a specialized hardware, software, or software–hardware combination known as a firewall is often deployed.

## Overall Firewall Functionality

Firewall software often runs on a dedicated server between the Internet and the protected network. Firmware-based firewalls and single-purpose dedicated firewall appliances are situated in a similar location on a network and provide similar functionality to the software-based firewall. All network traffic entering the firewall is examined, and possibly filtered, to ensure that only authorized activities take place. This process may be limited to verifying authorized access requested files or services, or it may delve more deeply into content, location, time, date, day of week, participants, or other criteria of interest. Firewalls usually provide a layer of isolation between the inside, sometimes referred to as the "clean" network, and the outside or "dirty" network. They are also used, although less frequently, to separate multiple subnetworks so as to control interactions between them. Figure 1 illustrates a typical installation of a firewall in a perimeter security configuration.

A common underlying assumption in such a design scenario is that all of the threats come from the outside network or the Internet, but many modern firewalls provide protection against insiders acting inappropriately and against accidental harm that could result from internal configuration errors, viruses, or experimental implementations. Research consistently indicates that 70–80% of malicious activity originates from insiders who would normally have access to systems both inside and outside

of the firewall. In addition, outside threats may be able to circumvent the firewall entirely if dial-up modem access remains uncontrolled or unmonitored, if radiolocal area networks or similar wireless technology is used, or if other methods can be used to co-opt an insider, to subvert the integrity of systems within the firewall, or to otherwise bypass the firewall as a route for communications. Incorrectly implemented firewalls can exacerbate this situation by creating new, and sometimes undetected, security holes or by creating such an impediment to legitimate uses that insiders subvert its mechanisms intentionally. It is often said that an incorrectly configured and maintained firewall is worse than no firewall at all because it gives a false sense of security.

The advantages of firewalls are as follows:

1. When properly configured and monitored, firewalls can be an effective way to protect network and information resources.
2. Firewalls are often used to reduce the costs associated with protecting larger numbers of computers that are located inside it.
3. Firewalls provide a control point that can be used for other protective purposes.

The disadvantages of firewalls are as follows:

1. Firewalls can be complex devices with complicated rule sets.
2. Firewalls must be configured, managed, and monitored by properly trained personnel.
3. A misconfigured firewall gives the illusion of security.
4. Even a properly configured firewall is not sufficient or complete as a perimeter security solution. A total security solution typically also includes intrusion detection/prevention systems, vulnerability assessment

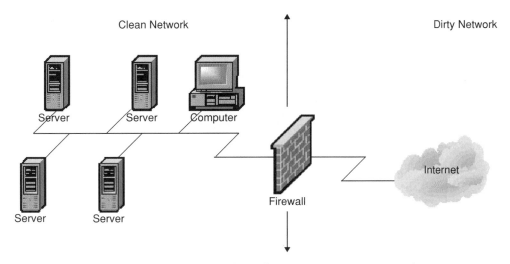

**Figure 1:** Typical installation of a firewall in a perimeter security configuration.

technology, and antivirus technology. According to the Computer Security Institute, 80% of successful network attacks either penetrate or avoid firewall security.

5. The processing of packets by a firewall inevitably introduces latency that, in some cases, can be significant.

6. Firewalls often interfere with network applications that may expect direct connections to end user workstations such as voice-over-Internet protocol (IP) phones and virtual private networks (VPNs) as well as some collaborative tools such as instant messenger and video and audio conferencing software.

7. The level to which firewalls inspect the data contained with packets varies widely. Although some firewalls only filter packets based on source and destination addresses, other firewalls perform much more comprehensive packet inspection on the contents of those packets.

8. Firewalls cannot prevent vulnerabilities introduced directly at client computers such as malicious code,

e-mail attacks, and Web-based Trojans. Such Trojan programs can then launch attacks within the internal network, undetected by the perimeter-based firewall.

# FIREWALL FUNCTIONALITY
## Background

Network communication between computers, whether or not that communication is through a firewall, is most often organized into layers according to the open systems interconnect (OSI) model. Figure 2 illustrates basic firewall functionality and technology categories in terms of the OSI model.

Firewalls were initially introduced as application level programs running over standard operating systems. As a result, these firewall programs were easily bypassed by directly attacking the vulnerabilities of the underlying TCP/IP stack and native operating system. Such operating

| OSI Model Layer | Firewall Functionality | Firewall Technology | |
|---|---|---|---|
| 7 Application | Application level proxies forward and reverse proxies | Proxy Servers | Switched Firewalls Air Gap Technology |
| 6 Presentation | | Firewall Appliances | |
| 5 Session | Stateful firewall | | |
| 4 Transport TCP/UDP | Port filtering circuit level proxy | | |
| 3 Network IP | Packet filtering address filtering packet filtering firewall | Router | |
| 2 Data link | | | |
| 1 Physical | | | |

**Figure 2:** Basic firewall functionality and technology versus the OSI model.

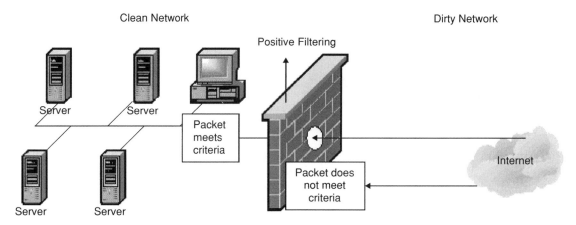

**Figure 3:** Positive filtering.

systems were sometimes referred to as nonhardened operating systems. Firewalls conforming to this type of configuration are sometimes referred to as first-generation firewalls.

Today, most firewalls use hardened operating systems and are run as single programs on a dedicated computing device or hardware firewall appliance. As a result, it is more difficult to attack firewalls through the underlying vulnerabilities of operating systems and network protocols. Firewalls conforming to this architecture are sometimes referred to as second-generation firewalls.

Firewalls basically act as filters. They either allow or disallow a given packet based on rules contained in a filter table. At the highest level, filtering is either positive or negative. Positive filters allow traffic to pass through the firewall if those packets meet the criteria listed in the filter table and block all traffic that does not. Negative filters prevent any traffic that meets criteria on filter tables from passing through the firewall and allows all traffic to pass that does not. Firewall rules are processed in a serial fashion. Initially, the first rule in a firewall is generally to block all traffic, followed by exception rules allowing those packets specified in the filter table (positive filtering). Conversely, the first rule could be to allow all traffic to pass through the firewall followed by exception rules in a filter table specifying which traffic must be blocked (negative filtering). Filters can be applied as easily to traffic going

from internal (secure) networks to the Internet (nonsecure) as they can be from the Internet into the secure internal networks. Which packets get allowed and disallowed in either direction can vary based on the order in which the firewall rules are processed. As a result, firewall rule logic can be extremely complicated and must be tested carefully. Figure 3 illustrates positive and Figure 4 illustrates negative filtering.

A given firewall may, but does not necessarily, offer any or all of the following functions.

## Bad Packet Filtering

The first type of filtering normally done is to remove bad packets, sometimes also referred to as misshapen packets. Such abnormal packets are often used to look for vulnerabilities or to launch attacks such as denial of service attacks or distributed denial of service attacks. Bad packet filtering can be, and often is, implemented in a router, sometimes referred to as a filtering router, that faces the dirty network. However, it is highlighted here as an initial firewall function to assure that it is not overlooked. More specific examples of bad packets are packet fragments, packets with abnormally set flags, time-to-live (TTL) fields, abnormal packet length, or Internet control message protocol (ICMP) packets. The overall purpose in removing such "trash" initially is that the processing

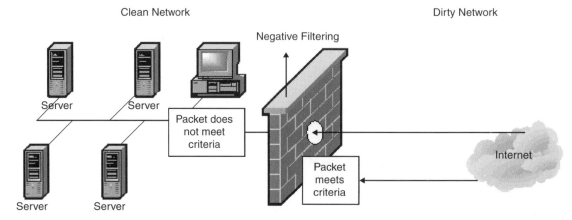

**Figure 4:** Negative filtering.

intensive firewall can spend its time only looking at legitimate (although not necessarily authorized) packets.

## Address Filtering

This function can, and perhaps should, be performed by a device other than the firewall, such as a border router. Based on address filter tables containing allowed or disallowed individual or groups (subnets) or addresses, address filtering blocks all traffic that contains either disallowed source or destination addresses. Address filtering by itself may not provide adequate protection because it is too large a granularity for some protective requirements.

## Port Filtering

Port filtering goes beyond address filtering, examining to which function or program a given packet applies. For example, file transfer protocol (FTP) typically uses ports 20 and 21, inbound electronic mail (simple mail transfer protocol; SMTP) typically uses port 25, and inbound nonencrypted Web traffic (hypertext transfer protocol; HTTP) typically uses port 80. Attacks are often targeted and designed for specific ports. Port filtering can be used to ensure that all ports are disabled except those that must remain open and active to support programs and protocols required by the owners of the inside network. Static port filtering leaves authorized ports open to all traffic all the time, whereas dynamic port filtering opens and closes portions of protocols associated with authorized ports over time as required for the specifics of the protocols.

## Domain Filtering

Domain filtering applies to outbound traffic headed through the firewall to the Internet. Domain filtering can block traffic with domains that are not authorized for communications or can be designed to permit exchanges only with authorized "outside" domains.

## Network Address Translation

When organizations connect to the Internet, the addresses they send out must be globally unique. In most cases, an organization's Internet service provider specifies these globally unique addresses. Most organizations have relatively few globally unique public addresses compared with the actual number of network nodes on their entire network.

The Internet Assigned Numbers Authority has set aside the following private address ranges for use by private networks: 10.0.0.0 to 10.255.255.255, 172.16.0.0 to 172.31.255.255, and 192.168.0.0 to 192.168.255.255.

Traffic using any of these "private" addresses must remain on the organization's private network to interoperate properly with the rest of the Internet. Because anyone is welcome to use these address ranges, they are not globally unique and therefore cannot be used reliably over the Internet. Computers on a network using the private IP address space can still send and receive traffic to and from the Internet by using network address translation (NAT). An added benefit of NAT is that the organization's private network is not as readily visible from the Internet.

All of the work stations on a private network can share a single or small number of globally unique assigned public IP address(es) because NAT mechanism maintains a table that provides for translation between internal addresses and ports and external addresses and ports. These addresses and port numbers are generally configured so as not to conflict with commonly assigned transmission control protocol (TCP) port numbers. The combination of the shared public IP address and a port number that is translated into internal address and port numbers via the translation table allows computers on the private network to communicate with the Internet through the firewall. NAT can also run on routers, dedicated servers, or other similar devices, and "gateway" computers often provide a similar function.

Dynamic NAT entries are created automatically in the NAT table as the firewall or router receives packets that require NAT translation. Dynamic NAT entries are purged after a preset period. For mapping addresses on a more permanent basis through the firewall, static NAT entries can be manually entered into the NAT table and must be manually removed as well. Most firewalls provide some type of NAT functionality as illustrated in Figure 5.

## Data Inspection

The primary role of many firewalls is to inspect the data passing through it using a set of rules that define what is and is not allowed through the firewall and then to act appropriately on packets that meet required criteria. The various types of firewalls, described in the next section, differ primarily in what portions of the overall data packet are inspected, the types of inspections that can be done, and what sorts of actions are taken with respect to those data. Among the data elements that are commonly inspected are the following:

- IP address
- TCP port number
- User datagram protocol port number
- Data field contents

Contents of specific protocol payloads, such as HTTP, to filter out certain classes of traffic (e.g., streaming video, voice, and music), access requests to restricted Web sites, information with specific markings (e.g., proprietary information), and content with certain words or page names.

## Virus Scanning and Intrusion Detection

Some firewalls also offer functionality such as virus scanning and intrusion detection. Advantages of such firewalls include the following:

- "One-stop shopping" for a wide range of requirements
- Reduced overhead from centralization of services
- Reduced training and maintenance

Disadvantages include the following:

- Increased processing load requirements
- Single point of failure for security devices

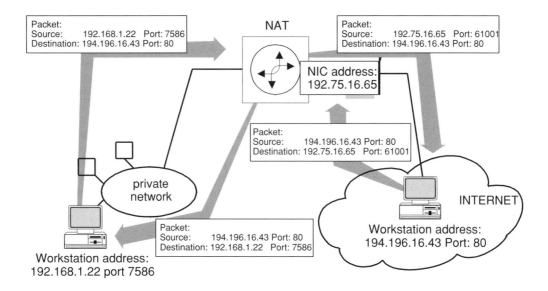

| Private Source IP Address | Private Source Assigned Port ID |
|---|---|
| 192.168.1.22 | 61001 |
| 192.168.1.23 | 61002 |
| 192.168.1.24 | 61003 |
| 192.168.1.25 | 61004 |
| ..and so on.. | ..and so on.. |

GOLDMAN & RAWLES: ADC3e
FIG. 09-13

**Figure 5:** NAT functionality.

- Increased device complexity
- Potential for reduced performance over customized sub-solutions

## Other Functions

Some firewalls also offer such functions as the following:

- Virtual Private Networks (VPN): VPN functionality, allowing secure communication over the Internet, was typically provided by separate, dedicated devices (VPN traffic would have to be decrypted from the VPN tunnel and then passed through a separate firewall for filtering. By combining the VPN functionality with the firewall functionality on a single box, the process is somewhat simplified)
- Usage monitoring, traffic monitoring, and traffic logging: these functions provide usage statistics that can be valuable for capacity planning and also provide information to troubleshoot problems or spot potential abuse
- Protection against some forms of IP address spoofing
- Protection against denial of service attacks

## FIREWALL TYPES

Another difficulty with firewalls is that there are no standards for firewall types, configuration, or interoperability. As a result, users must often be aware of how firewalls work to use them, and owners must be aware of these issues to evaluate potential firewall technology purchases. Many different devices can all be called firewalls, but that does not imply that these devices provide identical or even similar functionality. Firewall types and configuration are explained in the next few sections.

## Bastion Host

Many firewalls, whether software or hardware based, include a bastion host—a specially hardened server or a trusted system designed so that the functionality of the device cannot be compromised by attacking vulnerabilities in the underlying operating system or software over which its software runs. Specifically, the bastion host employs a secure version of the operating system with the most recent patches, security updates, and minimum number of applications to avoid known and unknown vulnerabilities. A bastion host is nothing more than the platform on which the firewall software is installed, configured, and executed. Once configured with firewall software, the

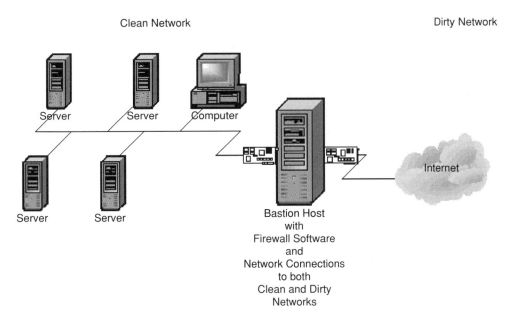

**Figure 6:** Bastion host.

bastion host sits between clean and dirty networks providing a perimeter defense as illustrated in Figure 6.

## Packet Filtering Firewalls

Every packet of data on the Internet can be identified by a source address (IP address) normally associated with the computer that issued the message and the destination address (IP address) normally associated with the computer to which the message is bound. These addresses are included in a portion of the packet called the header.

A packet filter can be used to examine the source and destination address of every packet. Network access devices known as routers are among the commonly used devices capable of filtering data packets. Filter tables are lists of addresses with data packets and embedded messages that are either allowed or prohibited from proceeding through the firewall. Filter tables may also limit the access of certain IP addresses to certain services and subservices. This is how anonymous FTP users are restricted to only certain information resources. It takes time for a firewall server to examine the addresses of each packet and compare those addresses to filter table entries. This filtering time introduces latency to the overall transmission time and may create a bottleneck to high volumes of traffic. Hardware implementations of such filters are often used to provide low latency and high throughput.

A filtering program that only examines source and destination addresses and determines access based on the entries in a filter table is known as a network-level filter or packet filter. The term network level or network layer in this case refers to the network layer or Layer 3 of the OSI Model (see Figure 2) where IP addresses reside in the TCP/IP protocol stack.

Packet filter gateways can be implemented on routers. This means that an existing piece of technology can be used for dual purposes. Maintaining filter tables and access rules on multiple routers is not a simple task and

packet filtering of this sort is limited in what it can accomplish because it only examines certain areas of each packet. Dedicated packet-filtering firewalls are usually easier to configure and require less in-depth knowledge of protocols to be filtered or examined. One easy way that many packet filters can be defeated by attackers is a technique known as IP spoofing. Because these simple packet filters make all filtering decisions based on IP source and destination addresses, an attacker can often create a packet designed to appear to come from an authorized or trusted IP address, which will then pass through such a firewall unimpeded.

Packet filtering is illustrated in Figure 7.

## Circuit-Level Gateways and Proxies

Circuit-level proxies or circuit-level gateways provide proxy services for transport layer (Layer 4) protocols such as TCP. Socks, an example of such a proxy server, creates proxy data channels to application servers on behalf of the application client. Socks uniquely identifies and keeps track of individual connections between the client and server ends of an application communication over a network. Like other proxy servers, both a client and server portion of the Socks proxy are required to create the Socks tunnel. Some Web browsers have the client portion of Socks included, whereas the server portion can be added as an additional application to a server functioning as a proxy server. The Socks server would be located inside an organization's firewall and can block or allow connection requests, based on the requested Internet destination, TCP port ID, or user identification. Once Socks approves and establishes the connection through the proxy server, it does not care which protocols flow through the established connection. This is in contrast to other more protocol-specific proxies such as Web proxy, which only allows HTTP to be transported, or WinSock Proxy, which only allows Windows application protocols to be transported.

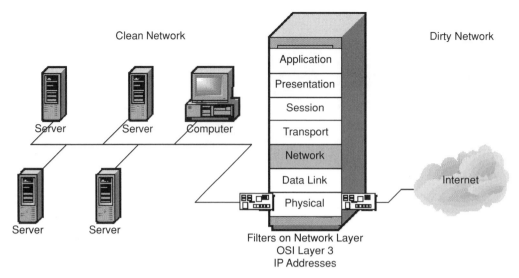

**Figure 7:**   Packet filtering firewall.

Because all data go through Socks, it can audit, screen, and filter all traffic in between the application client and server. Socks can control traffic by disabling or enabling communication according to TCP port numbers. Socks4 allowed outgoing firewall applications, whereas Socks5 supports both incoming and outgoing firewall applications, as well as authentication.

The key negative characteristic of Socks is that applications must be "socksified" to communicate with the Socks protocol and server. In the case of Socks4, this meant that local applications had to be recompiled using a Socks library that replaced its normal library functions. However, with Socks5, a launcher is employed that avoids "socksification" and recompilation of client programs that in most cases do not natively support Socks. Socks5 also uses a private routing table and hides internal network addresses from outside networks. Figure 8 illustrates Circuit level gateways and proxies.

## Application Gateways

Application gateways are concerned with what services or applications a message is requesting in addition to who is making that request. Connections between requesting clients and service providing servers are created only after the application gateway is satisfied as to the legitimacy of the request. Even once the legitimacy of the request has been established, only proxy clients and servers actually communicate with each other. A gateway firewall does not allow actual internal IP addresses or names to be transported to the external nonsecure network, except as this information is contained within content that the proxy does not control. To the external network, the proxy application on the firewall appears to be the actual source or destination, as the case may be.

Application-level filters, sometimes called assured pipelines, application gateways, or proxy servers, go beyond port-level filters in their attempts to control packet

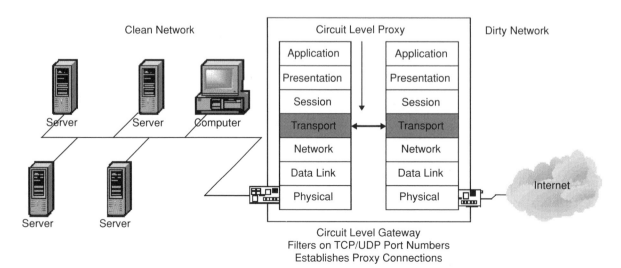

**Figure 8:**   Circuit-level gateways and proxies.

flows. Whereas port-level filters determine the legitimacy of the IP addresses and ports within packets, application-level filters are intended to provide increased assurance of the validity of packet content in context. Application-level filters typically examine the entire request for data rather than just the source and destination addresses. This ability to examine the entire contents of a data packet in the context of its intended application is sometimes referred to as deep packet inspection. Controlled files can be marked as such, and application-level filters can be designed to prevent those files from being transferred, even within packets authorized by port-level filters. Of course, this increased level of scrutiny comes at the cost of a slower or more expensive firewall.

Proxies are also capable of approving or denying connections based on directionality. Users may be allowed to upload but not download files. Some application-level gateways have the ability to encrypt communications over these established connections. The level of difficulty associated with configuring application-level gateways versus router-based packet filters is debatable. Router-based gateways tend to require a more intimate knowledge of protocol behavior, whereas application-level gateways deal predominantly at the application layer of the protocol stack. Proxies tend to introduce increased latency compared with port-level filtering. The key weaknesses of an application-level gateway is their inability to detect embedded malicious code such as Trojan horse programs or macro viruses and the requirement of more complex and resource intensive operation than lower level filters.

Certain application-level protocols commands that are typically used for probing or attacking systems can be identified, trapped, and removed. For example, SMTP is an e-mail interoperability protocol that is a member of the TCP/IP family and used widely over the Internet. It is often used to mask attacks or intrusions. Multipurpose internet mail extension (MIME) is another method that is often used to hide or encapsulate malicious code such as Java applets or ActiveX components. Other application protocols that may require monitoring include but are not limited to World Wide Web protocols such as HTTP, telnet, ftp, gopher, and Real Audio. Each of these application protocols may require its own proxy, and each application-specific proxy must be designed to be intimately familiar with the commands within each application that will need to be trapped and examined. For example an SMTP proxy should be able to filter SMTP packets according to e-mail content, message length, and type of attachments. A given application gateway may not include proxies for all potential application layer protocols. Figure 9 illustrates application gateway functionality.

## Trusted Gateway

A trusted gateway or trusted application gateway seeks to relieve all the reliance on the application gateway for all communication, both inbound and outbound. In a trusted gateway, certain applications are identified as trusted and are able to bypass the application gateway entirely and are able to establish connections directly rather than be executed by proxy. In this way, outside users can access information servers and Web servers without tying up the proxy applications on the application gateway. These servers are typically placed in a demilitarized zone (DMZ) so that any failures in the application servers will grant only limited additional access to other systems. Figure 10 illustrates a trusted gateway only. See the chapter on firewall architectures for further discussion on DMZs.

## Stateful Firewalls

Rather than simply examining packets individually without the context of previously transmitted packets from the same source, stateful firewalls, sometimes referred to as stateful multiplayer inspection firewalls, store information about past activities and use this information to test future packets attempting to pass through. Stateful firewalls typically review the same packet information as normal simple packet filtering firewalls such as

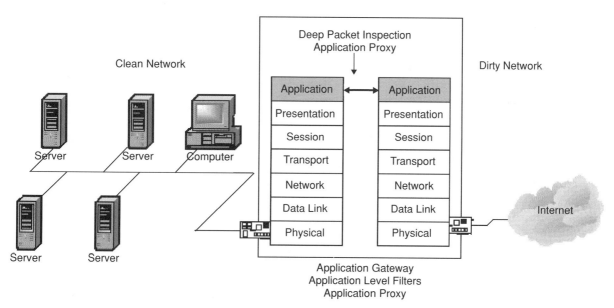

**Figure 9:** Application gateway.

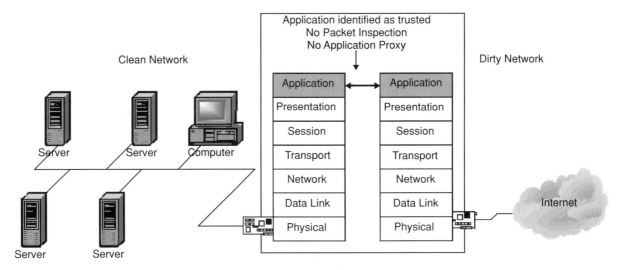

**Figure 10:** Trusted gateway.

source address, destination address, protocol, port, and flags; however, they also record this information in a connection state table, also referred to as a dynamic state table, before sending the packet on. This table will have an entry for each valid connection established over a particular reference frame. The multiplayer aspect of their functionality refers to the fact that they filter packets at the network, transport, session (connection), and application layers. Although stateful firewalls filter applications and evaluate application packet contents, they do not provide application specific proxies. They combine the functionality of network packet filters, circuit level gateways, and application level gateways while adding the connection oriented stateful inspection.

Some stateful firewalls keep sequence number information to validate packets even further, so as to protect against some session hijacking attacks. As each packet arrives to a stateful firewall, it is checked against the connection table to determine whether it is part of an existing connection. The source address, destination address, source port, and destination port of the new packet must match the table entry. If the communication has already been authorized, there is no need to authorize it again and the packet is passed. If a packet can be confirmed to belong to an established connection, it is much less costly to send it on its way based on the connection table rather than re-examine the entire firewall rule set. This makes a stateful firewall faster then a simple packet filtering firewall for certain types of traffic patterns, because the packet filtering firewall treats each connection as a new connection. Additionally, because there is a "history" in the state tables, flags can be analyzed to ensure the proper sequence as in the TCP connection handshake, and the stateful firewall can drop or return packets that are clearly not a genuine response to a request.

As a result, stateful firewalls are better able to prevent some sorts of session hijacking and man-in-the-middle attacks. Session hijacking is very similar to IP spoofing, described earlier, except that it hijacks the session by sending forged acknowledgment (ACK) packets so that the victimized computer still thinks it is talking to the legitimate intended recipient of the session. A man-in-the-middle attack could be seen as two simultaneous session hijackings. In this scenario, the hacker hijacks both sides of the session and keeps both sides active and appearing to talk directly to each other when, in fact, the man-in-the-middle is examining and potentially modifying any packet that flows in either direction of the session. Figure 11 illustrates the basic functionality of a stateful firewall.

## Internal Firewalls

Not all threats to a network are perpetrated from the Internet by anonymous attackers, and firewalls are not a stand-alone, technology-based quick fix for network security. In response to the reality that most losses because of computer crime involve someone with inside access, internal firewalls have been applied with increasing frequency. Internal firewalls include filters that work on the data link, network, and application layers to examine communications that occur only within internal networks. Internal firewalls also act as access control mechanisms, denying access to applications for which a user does not have specific access approval. To ensure the confidentiality and integrity of private information, encryption and authentication may also be supported by firewalls, even during internal communications.

## Virtual Firewalls and Network-Based Firewall Services

Virtual firewalls, also known as virtual firewall systems, provide a single, centralized point of control over multiple distributed firewalls. As enterprise networks have grown in both scale and complexity, it has become more difficult to manage increasing numbers of firewalls on an individual basis. As a result, centralized firewall management systems have been developed. Each individual firewall is able to be configured uniquely with its own policies and rule sets. The area of protection provided by each firewall is referred to as its security domain or risk domain. All

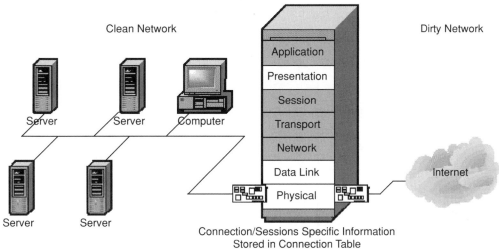

**Figure 11:** Stateful firewall.

of the configuration for the distributed firewalls can be done from a single, centralized location. A third party service provider, such as an Internet VPN provider, may provide virtual firewall services, otherwise known as network-based firewall services.

## Switched Firewalls—Air Gap Technology

Some vendors try to assert the strength of their protection by using widely known terms such as switched firewalls and *air gap* to characterize their protective mechanisms. One example of such a technology provides the same separation of the clean and dirty networks as firewalls. A hardware-based network switch is at the heart of this technology. The premise of creating a physical disconnection between the clean or secure network (Intranet) and the nonsecure or dirty network (Internet) is accomplished by connecting a server on the Internet connection that will receive all incoming requests. This server will connect to an electronic switch that strips the TCP headers and stores the packet in a memory bank, and then the switch disconnects from the external server and connects with the internal server. Once the connection is made, the internal server recreates the TCP header and transmits the packet to the intended server. Responses are made in the reverse order. The physical separation of the networks and the stripping of the TCP headers remove many of the vulnerabilities in the TCP connection-oriented protocol. Of course this provides little additional protection over other firewalls at the content level because content-level attacks are passed through the so-called air gap and responses are returned.

By utilizing high speed switches for the rule checking and packet forwarding, switched firewalls, also known as switch-accelerated firewalls, are able to filter and forward packets at multigigabit speeds. In some switched firewall architectures, separate dedicated devices sometimes referred to as switched firewall directors perform firewall control functions such as policy and session management, connection table management, and packet handling rules

specification, thus freeing the dedicated separate switched firewall to perform only rule checking and packing forwarding. In some cases, applications specific filtering is provided on the air gap technology. Such devices may be referred to as application firewall appliances or air gap application firewalls. Figure 12 illustrates air gap functionality.

There is a protective device that is highly effective at limiting information flow to one direction. The so-called digital diode technology is applied in situations in which the sole requirement is that no information be permitted to leak from one area to the other while information is permitted to flow in the other direction. An example would be the requirement for weather information to be available to military planning computers without the military plans being leaked to the weather stations. This sort of protection typically uses a physical technology such as a fiber optic device with only a transmitter on one end and receiver on the other end to provide high assurance of traffic directionality.

## Small Office Home Office Firewalls

As telecommuting has boomed and independent consultants have set up shop in home offices, the need for firewalls for the small office home office (SOHO) market has grown as well. These devices are often integrated with integrated services digital network-based multiprotocol routers that supply bandwidth on demand capabilities for Internet access. Some of these SOHO firewalls offer sophisticated features such as support for virtual private networks at a reasonable price. The most expensive of these costs less than $3,000 and some simpler filtering firewalls cost as little as $100. Some of these devices combine additional functionality such as network address translation, built in hub and switch ports, and load balancing in a combined hardware–software device known as a security appliance. Often digital subscriber line (DSL) or cable modems include firewall functionality because of their "always on" connection status.

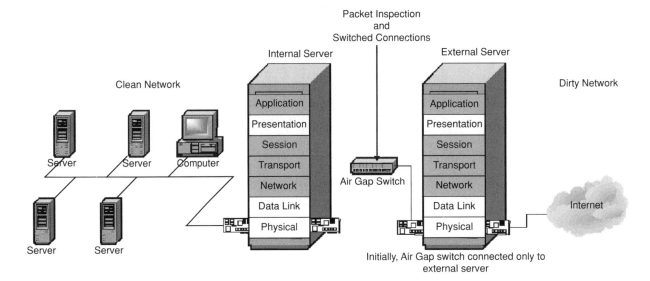

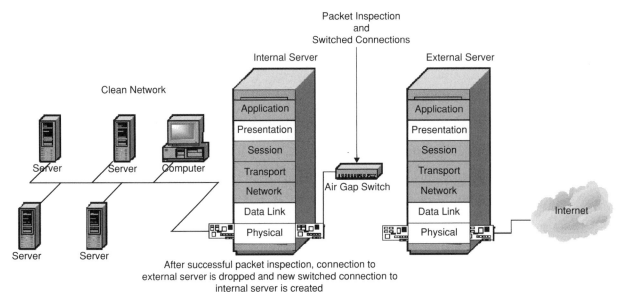

**Figure 12:** Air gap functionality.

Software-only solutions are also available. These products are installed on every computer and provide firewall-like functionality to each work station, thereby effectively eliminating client-side vulnerabilities that may bypass server-based or perimeter firewalls. Additional benefits are that each workstation has an extremely inexpensive solution and that protection can be customized at the system level. The problem is that this requires all users to be firewall administrators for their computers, losing the economy of scale that was one of the original benefits associated with firewalls.

## FIREWALL FUNCTIONALITY AND TECHNOLOGY ANALYSIS

Commercially available firewalls usually employ either packet filtering or proxies as firewall architecture and add an easy-to-use graphical user interface (GUI) to ease the configuration and implementation tasks. Some firewalls even use industry standard Web browsers as their GUIs. Several certifying bodies and internationally accepted criteria are available to certify various aspects of firewall technology. Common Criteria Evaluation Assurance Level (EAL) 4 has been certified on some firewalls. These evaluation criteria are officially known as "Common Criteria for Information Technology Security Evaluation" ISO/IEC 15408 (2000). In addition ICSA (International Computer Security Association) Labs, a division of TruSecure Corporation, offers certification of a variety of security technology including firewalls.

In general, certification seeks to assure the following:

- That firewalls meet the minimum requirements for reliable protection
- That firewalls perform as advertised
- That Internet applications perform as expected through the firewall

Table 1 summarizes some of the key functional characteristics of firewall technology.

**Table 1** Sample Functional Characteristics of Firewall Technology.

| Firewall functional characteristic | Explanation/importance |
|---|---|
| Encryption | Allows secure communication through firewall. Encryption schemes supported: DES, 3DES, and AES Encryption key length supported: 40, 56, 128, 168, 256 bits |
| Virtual Private Network (VPN) support | Allows secure communication over the Internet in a virtual private network topology VPN Security protocols supported: IPSEC and SSL |
| Application proxies supported | How many application proxies are supported? Internet application protocols (HTTP, SMTP, FTP, telnet, NNTP, WAIS, SNMP, rlogin, ping traceroute)? Real Audio? How many controls or commands are supported for each application? |
| Proxy isolation | In some cases, proxies are executed in their own protected domains to prevent penetration of other proxies or the firewall operating system should a given proxy be breached. |
| Operating systems supported | Unix and varieties; Windows NT, 2000, and XP |
| Virus scanning included | Because many viruses enter through Internet connections, the firewall is a logical place to scan for viruses. |
| Web tracking | To ensure compliance with corporate policy regarding use of the World Wide Web, some firewalls provide Web tracking software. The placement of the software in the firewall makes sense because all Web access must pass through the firewall. Access to certain uniform resource locators (URLs) can be filtered. |
| Violation notification | How does the firewall react when access violations are detected? Options include SNMP traps, e-mail, pop-up windows, pagers, reports. |
| Authentication supported | As a major network access point, the firewall must support popular authentication protocols and technology. |
| Network interfaces supported | Which network interfaces and associated data link layer protocols are supported? |
| System monitoring | Are graphical systems monitoring utilities available to display such statistics as disk usage or network activity by interface? |
| Auditing and logging | Is auditing and logging supporting? How many different types of events can be logged? Are user-defined events supported? Can logged events be sent to SNMP managers? |
| Attack protection | Following is a sample of the types of attacks that a firewall should be able to guard against: TCP denial of service attack, TCP sequence number prediction, source routing and RIP attacks, EGP infiltration and ICMP attacks, authentication server attacks, finger access, PCMAIL access, DNS access, FTP authentication attacks, anonymous FTP access, SNMP access remote access remote booting from outside networks; IP, MAC, and ARP spoofing and broadcast storms; trivial FTP and filter to and from the firewall, reserved port attacks, TCP wrappers, gopher spoofing, and MIME spoofing. |
| Attack retaliation/counterattack | Some firewalls can launch specific counterattacks or investigative actions if the firewall detects specific types of intrusions. |
| Administration interface | Is the administration interface graphical in nature? Is it forms based? |

Abbreviations: ARP = address resolution protocol; DNS = domain name server; EGP = exterior gateway protocol; DES = data encryption standard; FTP = file transfer protocol; HTTP = hypertext transfer protocol; ICMP = Internet control message protocol; IP = Internet protocol; MAC = media access control; MIME = multipurpose Internet mail extension; NNTP = network news transfer protocol; RIP = routing information protocol; SMTP = simple mail transfer protocol; SNMP = simple network management protocol; TCP = transmission control protocol; WAIS = wide area information services.

# CONCLUSION

Firewalls are an essential and basic element of many organizations' security architecture. Nonetheless, technology must be chosen carefully to ensure that it offers the required functionality, and firewalls must be arranged into properly designed enterprise firewall architectures and properly configured, maintained, and monitored. Even in the best circumstances, firewalls should be seen as a relatively small solution within the overall information protection challenge and should not be considered sufficient on their own.

# GLOSSARY

**Address Filtering**  A firewall's ability to block or allow packets based on Internet protocol addresses.

**Air Gap Technology**  Switched connections established to connect external and internal networks that are not otherwise physically connected.

**Application-Level Gateway**  Application-level filters examine the entire request for data rather than only the source and destination addresses.

**Bastion Host**  Hardened server with trusted operating system that serves as the basis of the firewall.

**Circuit-Level Proxies**  Proxy servers that work at the circuit level by proxying such protocols as file transfer protocol.

**Demilitarized Zone (DMZ)**  A neutral zone between firewalls or between a packet filtering router and a firewall in which mail and Web servers are often located.

**Domain Filtering**  A firewall's ability to block outbound access to restricted sites.

**Dual-Homed Host**  A host firewall with two or more network interface cards with direct access to two or more networks.

**Firewall**  A network device capable of filtering unwanted traffic from a connection between networks.

**Internal Firewall**  Firewalls that include filters that work on the data link, network, and application layers to examine communications that occur only on an organization's internal network, inside the reach of traditional firewalls.

**Multitiered DMZ**  A DMZ that segments access areas with multiple layers of firewalls.

**Network Address Translation**  A firewall's ability to translate between private and public globally unique Internet protocol addresses.

**Packet Filtering Gateway**  A firewall that allows or blocks packet transmission based on source and destination Internet protocol addresses.

**Port Filtering**  A firewall's ability to block or allow packets based on transmission control protocol port number.

**Proxy Server**  Servers that break direct connections between clients and servers and offer application and circuit layer specific proxy services to inspect and control such communications.

**Screened Subnet**  Enterprise firewall architecture that creates a DMZ.

**Stateful Firewall**  A firewall that monitors connections and records packet information in state tables to make forwarding decisions in the context of previous transmitted packets over a given connection.

**Trusted Gateway**  In a trusted gateway, certain applications are identified as trusted, are able to bypass the application gateway entirely, and are able to establish connections directly rather than by proxy.

# CROSS REFERENCES

See *Firewall Architectures; Packet Filtering and Stateful Firewalls; Proxy Firewalls.*

# FURTHER READING

Canavan, J. E. (2001). *Fundamentals of network security.* Boston: Artech House.

CERT Coordination Center. (1999, July 1). *Design the firewall system.* Retrieved January 1, 2004, from http://www.cert.org/security-improvement/practices/p053.html

Check Point Software Technologies. (1999, June 22). *Stateful inspection firewall technology tech note.* Retrieved June 2, 2004, from http://www.checkpoint.com/products/downloads/Stateful_Inspection.pdf

Edwards, J. (2001, May 1). Unplugging cybercrime. *CIO Magazine.* Retrieved March 1, 2004, from http://www.cio.com/archive/050100/development.html

Enterprise Technology. (2001, October). *Keeping a safe distance.* Retrieved January 2, 2004, from http://www.avcom.com/et/online/2001/oct/keeping.html

Goldman, J. E., & Rawles, P. T. (2001). *Applied data communications: A business oriented approach* (3rd ed.). New York: John Wiley & Sons.

Hurley, M. (2001, April 4). *Network air gaps—Drawbridge to the backend office.* Retrieved January 2, 2004, from http://rr.sans.org/firewall/gaps.php

NetGap. (n.d.). *SpearHead Security Web site.* Retrieved January 2, 2004, from http://www.spearheadsecurity.com/products.shtml

Scheer, S. (2001, January 10). *Israeli start-up may thwart Internet hackers.* Retrieved January 2, 2004, from http://staging.infoworld.com/articles/hn/xml/01/01/10/010110hnthwart.xml?Tem

Senner, L. (2001, May 9). *Anatomy of a stateful firewall.* Retrieved January 2, 2003, from http://rr.sans.org/firewall/anatomy.php

Whale Communications. *Air gap technology.* Retrieved January 2, 2004, from http://www.whalecommunications.com/fr_0300.htm

# Firewall Architectures

James E. Goldman, *Purdue University*

## INTRODUCTION

When an organization or individual links to the Internet, it creates a two-way access point in and out of their information systems. To prevent unauthorized activities between the Internet and the private network, a specialized hardware, software, or software–hardware combination known as a firewall is often deployed.

## Brief Review of Firewall Functionality

Firewall software often runs on a dedicated server between the Internet and the protected network. Firmware-based firewalls and single-purpose dedicated firewall appliances are situated in a similar location on a network and provide similar functionality to the software-based firewall. All network traffic entering the firewall is examined, and possibly filtered, to ensure that only authorized activities take place. This process may be limited to verifying authorized access to requested files or services, or it may delve more deeply into content, location, time, date, day of week, participants, or other criteria of interest. Firewalls usually provide a layer of isolation between the inside, sometimes referred to as the "clean" network, and the outside or "dirty" network. They are also used, although less frequently, to separate multiple subnetworks so as to control interactions among them. Figure 1 illustrates a typical installation of a firewall in a perimeter security configuration.

A common underlying assumption in such a design scenario is that all of the threats come from the outside network or the Internet, but many modern firewalls provide protection against insiders acting inappropriately and against accidental harm that could result from internal configuration errors, viruses, or experimental implementations. Research consistently indicates that 70–80% of malicious activity originates from insiders who would normally have access to systems both inside and outside of the firewall. In addition, outside threats may be able to circumvent the firewall entirely if dial-up modem access remains uncontrolled or unmonitored or wireless local area networks (LANs) or similar wireless technology are used. Other methods can be used to co-opt an insider, subvert the integrity of systems within the firewall, or otherwise bypass the firewall as a route for communications.

Incorrectly implemented firewalls can exacerbate this situation by creating new, and sometimes undetected, security holes or by creating such an impediment to legitimate uses that insiders subvert its mechanisms intentionally. It is often said that an incorrectly configured and maintained firewall is worse than no firewall at all because it gives a false sense of security.

Advantages of firewalls include the following:

1. When properly configured and monitored, firewalls can be an effective way to protect network and information resources.
2. Firewalls are often used to reduce the costs associated with protecting larger numbers of computers that are located inside it.
3. Firewalls provide a control point that can be used for other protective purposes.

Disadvantages of firewalls include the following:

1. Firewalls can be complex devices with complicated rule sets.
2. Firewalls must be configured, managed, and monitored by properly trained personnel. Distributed or network-based firewalls are more comprehensive in terms of detection ability but far more complex in terms of configuration and systems administration.

**515**

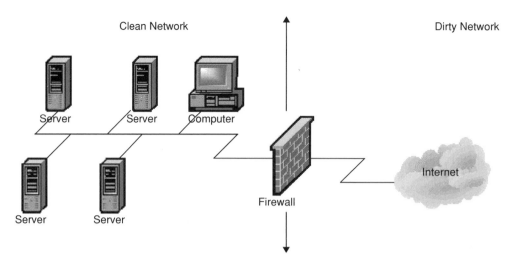

Clean Network                                                          Dirty Network

**Figure 1:** Typical installation of a firewall in a perimeter security configuration.

3. A misconfigured firewall gives the illusion of security.

4. Even a properly configured firewall is not sufficient or complete as a perimeter security solution. A total security solution typically also includes intrusion detection/prevention systems, vulnerability assessment technology, and antivirus technology. According to the Computer Security Institute, 80% of successful network attacks either penetrate or avoid firewall security.

5. The processing of packets by a firewall inevitably introduces latency that, in some cases, can be significant.

6. Firewalls often interfere with network applications that may expect direct connections to end user work stations such as voice-over-Internet protocol (IP) phones and some VPNs (virtual private networks) as well as some collaborative tools such as instant messenger and video and audio conferencing software.

7. The level to which firewalls inspect the data contained within packets varies widely. Whereas some firewalls only filter packets based on source and destination addresses, other firewalls perform much more comprehensive packet inspection on the contents of those packets. This could perhaps more properly be classified as a choice in level of capability as opposed to being considered strictly as a disadvantage. Stateful firewalls can add this deep packet inspection capability. More and more protocols are embedded within or tunnel over port 80 (HTTP) as accessed via a Web browser. Deep packet inspection or content inspection is required to peer within the outer protocol to examine packet contents. Data streams are often encrypted, preventing the firewall from thoroughly inspecting them.

8. Firewalls do not necessarily prevent vulnerabilities introduced directly at client computers such as malicious code, e-mail attacks, and Web-based Trojans. Such Trojan programs can then launch attacks within the internal network, undetected by the perimeter-based firewall. Prevention of such vulnerabilities is typically handled by packet filters or routers that set rules to deny certain types of internal and egress communications. For instance, a rule can be set to disallow outbound ICMP, spoofed source addresses, out-of-range internal addresses, and so on.

## REQUIREMENTS ANALYSIS FOR FIREWALL ARCHITECTURES
### Importance of Understanding Security Requirements

The term firewall architecture refers to the physical and logical arrangement of firewalls in relation to each other, to the information assets (usually servers) they are protecting, and to other security-related devices such as intrusion detection systems.

Which firewall architecture is correct for a given scenario depends on the unique security requirements of that scenario. Although security requirements analysis is beyond the scope of this chapter, the bulleted list below gives a high-level view of the kinds of issues that must be thoroughly understood before a particular firewall architecture can be chosen.

• Asset identification—what are you trying to protect? Where is the information to be protected stored?

• Vulnerability analysis—how might the information be accessed by unauthorized parties?

• Threat analysis—who might want to potentially use the information in an unauthorized manner? Where are these individuals located? Internally? Known external locations? Unknown external locations?

• Risk analysis—what is the likelihood that a given threat will attack a given asset via a given vulnerability?

• Protective measures analysis—what can be done to mitigate a given risk? Is the cost of the protective measure justifiable given the value of the asset?

• Cost—how much will alternative choices in firewall architectures cost? How much functionality/security is gained for a given increase in cost among alternative firewall architecture choices?

# Clean Networks and Dirty Networks

Security requirements analysis often uses terms such as clean networks and dirty networks to define the scenarios into which firewalls are deployed. To assure the proper placement of firewalls, or to assure the proper selection of a firewall architecture, one must first understand where the boundaries of clean and dirty networks exist, as this is where firewalls and other security devices must be placed. The terms clean and dirty networks might lead one to believe that there are only two polarized categories of risk: clean, or totally secure and trusted, and dirty, totally nonsecure and untrusted. In fact there can be many interim categories of risk environments in between these two poles.

# Risk Domains

Risk domains, also known as security domains or security zones, consist of a unique group of networked systems sharing common elements of exposure/risk and often also sharing common business functions as well. These common business functions and risks are identified during initial risk analysis or assessment. Risk domains are differentiated or isolated from each other based on the differences in risks associated with each risk domain. Because each risk domain has unique business functions and risks, it would stand to reason that each should have a uniquely designed set of security policies, security control processes, and security technology to offer the required level of security for that particular risk domain. Risk domains are important to security analysts because of their use as a means to determine security strategies and technology. Firewall placement will depend largely on the boundaries of an enterprise's risk domains. As a result, risk domain identification is directly related to the selection of the preferred firewall architecture.

# Requirements versus Firewall Functionality

Once security requirements have been determined and risk domains have been defined, these requirements must be matched against available firewall functionality. Not all firewalls offer identical functionality. In some cases, additional security technology such as intrusion detection systems or VPN servers might be deployed. However, the list below summarizes typical security functionality offered by firewalls.

## Bad Packet Filtering

The first type of filtering normally done is to remove bad packets, sometimes also referred to as misshapen packets. Such abnormal packets are often used to look for vulnerabilities or to launch attacks such as denial of service attacks or distributed denial of service attacks. Bad packet filtering can be, and often is, implemented in a router, sometimes referred to as a filtering router, that faces the dirty network. However, it is highlighted here as an initial firewall function to assure that it is not overlooked. More specific examples of bad packets are packet fragments, packets with abnormally set flags, time-to-live (TTL) fields, abnormal packet length, or Internet control message protocol (ICMP) packets. The overall purpose in removing such "trash" initially is that the processing intensive firewall can spend its time only looking at legitimate (although not necessarily authorized) packets.

## Address Filtering

This function can, and perhaps should, be performed by a device other than the firewall, such as a border router. Based on address filter tables containing allowed or disallowed individual or groups (subnets) of addresses, address filtering blocks all traffic that contains either disallowed source or destination addresses. Address filtering by itself may not provide adequate protection because it is too large a granularity for some protective requirements.

## Port Filtering

Port filtering goes beyond address filtering, examining to which function or program a given packet applies. For example, file transfer protocol (FTP) typically uses ports 20 and 21, inbound electronic mail (simple mail transfer protocol; SMTP) typically uses port 25, and inbound nonencrypted Web traffic (hypertext transfer protocol; HTTP) typically uses port 80. Attacks are often targeted and designed for specific ports. Port filtering can be used to ensure that all ports are disabled except those that must remain open and active to support programs and protocols required by the owners of the inside network. Static port filtering leaves authorized ports open to all traffic all the time, whereas dynamic port filtering opens and closes portions of protocols associated with authorized ports over time as required for the specifics of the protocols.

Ephemeral ports are port numbers that are temporarily assigned by the computer's IP protocol stack to client-side connections from a predetermined range of available port numbers. Ephemeral port numbers are reused, so a given client will not always have the same ephemeral port number. These are typically assigned to the client-side connection when that client initiates an outbound connection for a remote service. BSD Unix uses ports 1024 to 4999 and Windows uses 1024 to 5000 as their default ephemeral port allocation. The implication for firewall port filtering of ephemeral ports is that when the requested remote service attempts to respond to the requesting client behind the firewall, that firewall must enable or leave open that ephemeral port number so that the return traffic can reach the requesting client. Whereas ephemeral port ranges are not typically service port addresses, they are often blocked or disabled by firewalls.

## Domain Filtering

Domain filtering applies to outbound traffic headed through the firewall to the Internet. Domain filtering can block traffic with domains that are not authorized for communications or can be designed to permit exchanges only with authorized "outside" domains.

## Network Address Translation

When organizations connect to the Internet, the addresses they send out must be globally unique. In most cases, an organization's Internet service provider specifies these globally unique addresses. Most organizations have relatively few globally unique public addresses compared with the actual number of network nodes on their entire network.

The Internet Assigned Numbers Authority has set aside the following private address ranges for use by private networks: 10.0.0.0 to 10.255.255.255, 172.16.0.0 to 172.31.255.255, and 192.168.0.0 to 192.168.255.255. Traffic using any of these "private" addresses must remain on the organization's private network to interoperate properly with the rest of the Internet. Because anyone is welcome to use these address ranges, they are not globally unique and therefore cannot be used reliably over the Internet. Computers on a network using the private IP address space can still send and receive traffic to and from the Internet by using network address translation (NAT). An added benefit of NAT is that the organization's private network is not as readily visible from the Internet.

All of the work stations on a private network can share a single or small number of globally unique assigned public IP address(es) because NAT mechanism maintains a table that provides for translation between internal addresses and ports and external addresses and ports. These addresses and port numbers are generally configured so as to not to conflict with commonly assigned transmission control protocol (TCP) port numbers. The combination of the shared public IP address and a port number that is translated into internal address and port numbers via the translation table allows computers on the private network to communicate with the Internet through the firewall. NAT can also run on routers, dedicated servers, or other similar devices, and "gateway" computers often provide a similar function.

Dynamic NAT entries are created automatically in the NAT table as the firewall or router receives packets that require NAT translation. Dynamic NAT entries are purged after a preset period. For mapping addresses on a more permanent basis through the firewall, static NAT entries can be manually entered into the NAT table and must be manually removed as well. Most firewalls provide some type of NAT functionality.

### Data Inspection

The primary role of many firewalls is to inspect the data passing through it using a set of rules that define what is and is not allowed through the firewall and then to act appropriately on packets that meet required criteria. The various types of firewalls, described under "Virus Scanning and Intrusion Detection," differ primarily in what portions of the overall data packet are inspected, the types of inspections that can be done, and what sorts of actions are taken with respect to that data. Among the data elements that are commonly inspected are the following:

- IP address,
- TCP port number,
- user datagram protocol port number,
- data field contents, and
- contents of specific protocol payloads, such as HTTP, to filter out certain classes of traffic (e.g., streaming video, voice, and music), access requests to restricted Web sites, information with specific markings (e.g., proprietary information), and content with certain words or page names.

### Virus Scanning and Intrusion Detection

Some firewalls also offer functionality such as virus scanning and intrusion detection. Advantages of such firewalls include the following:

- "one-stop shopping" for a wide range of requirements,
- reduced overhead from centralization of services, and
- reduced training and maintenance.

Disadvantages include the following:

- increased processing load requirements,
- single point of failure for security devices,
- increased device complexity, and
- potential for reduced performance over customized subsolutions.

### Other Functions

Some firewalls also offer such functions as the following:

- Virtual private networks (VPN)—VPN functionality, allowing secure communication over the Internet, was typically provided by separate, dedicated devices. VPN traffic would have to be decrypted from the VPN tunnel (or secure, encrypted end-to-end connection) and then passed through a separate firewall for filtering. By combining the VPN functionality with the firewall functionality on a single box, the process is somewhat simplified.
- Usage monitoring, traffic monitoring, and traffic logging—these functions provide usage statistics that can be valuable for capacity planning and also provide information to troubleshoot problems or spot potential abuse.
- Protection against some forms of IP address spoofing.
- Protection against denial of service attacks.

## ENTERPRISE FIREWALL ARCHITECTURES
## Conceptual Design Options of Firewall Architectures

Firewalls, or any security technology for that matter, are virtually useless without associated security policies and the requisite education and communication that are associated with those policies. Before considering alternative enterprise firewall architectures, the information security analyst must be sure that the policies to be implemented on that enterprise firewall architecture are clearly understood and rigorously enforced.

Before the correct physical firewall architecture for a given situation can be determined, alternative conceptual design options for firewall architectures must be analyzed. At a high level, there are really two alternative conceptual philosophies to firewall architecture design: defense in depth security and perimeter security.

### Defense in Depth

A defense in depth design philosophy proposes multiple levels of security devices such as firewalls and intrusion detection devices. The greater the value of the information assets within a given risk domain, the greater the number of layers of security technology must be penetrated to reach those information assets. Such a philosophy would seem to assume that intrusion or attack is as likely to come from someone inside a corporate network as from outside that network. Defense in depth at its extreme would propose server-specific firewalls protecting individual servers. In a physical or building security metaphor, defense in depth would propose biometric locks on every door throughout a building not just on the outside doors.

## Perimeter Security

A perimeter security design philosophy draws an imaginary line, or moat, around the perimeter of the risk domain it is seeking to protect. An underlying design assumption in perimeter security is that threats to the information assets within the protected risk domain are only likely to come from outside that risk domain. Individual servers within a risk domain are typically not specifically or individually protected. All of the emphasis is on building impenetrable perimeter security architecture. In a physical or building security metaphor, perimeter security would have biometric access to the outside doors or armed guards protecting the entrance to the building, but no further security within the building.

## Firewall Architecture Design Elements

Once an overall security or firewall philosophy has been determined, key decisions remain to be made regarding the number and location of these firewalls in relation to the Internet and a corporation's public and private information resources. Each of the alternative enterprise firewall architectures explored in this section attempt to segregate three distinct networks or risk domains:

1. The Internet or other "dirty" networks: contains legitimate customers and business partners as well as hackers.

2. The DMZ(s), otherwise known as the screened subnet, neutral zone, or external private network: contains Web servers and mail servers among other information assets.

3. The internal private network, otherwise known as the secure network or intranet: contains most valuable corporate information.

The firewall architectures described in the following sections represent generalized designs or approaches to firewall architecture design. They are not necessarily mutually exclusive. Elements of various firewall architectures described below may be combined to properly meet the security requirements of a particular risk domain. For example, packet-filtering routers could easily, and correctly, be added to any of the other firewall architectures described. Likewise, server- or host-specific firewalls could easily be added to other firewall architectures as well.

# PACKET-FILTERING ROUTERS
## Functionality

Packet-filtering routers or border routers are often the first devices that face the Internet or dirty network from an organization network perspective. These packet-filtering routers first remove all types of traffic that should not even be passed to the firewalls. This process is typically fast and inexpensive because it involves only simple processes that are implemented in relatively low-cost hardware. Examples of removed packets include packet fragments, packets with abnormally set flags, TTL, abnormal packet length, or ICMP packets, all of which could potentially be used for attacks or to exploit known vulnerabilities, and packets from or to unauthorized addresses and ports. Figure 2 illustrates a packet-filtering router architecture.

Advantages of packet-filtering routers are as follows:

- Perimeter routers can easily perform this task.
- Fast processing.
- No additional expense or specialized equipment.
- Filter tables listing bad packets to remove are relatively static; not a lot of maintenance involved.

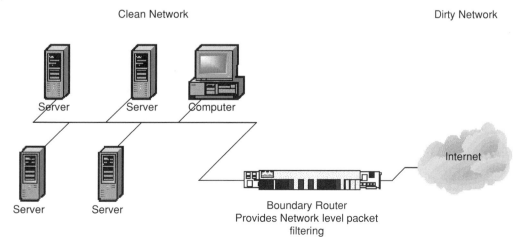

**Figure 2:** Packet-filtering router architecture.

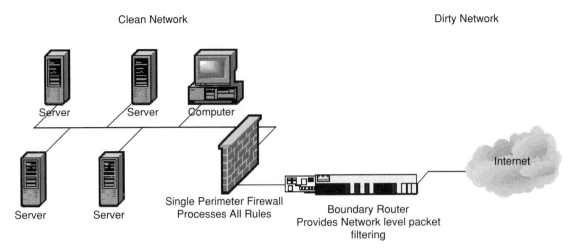

**Figure 3:** Perimeter firewall architecture.

Disadvantages of packet-filtering routers are as follows:

- Should not be mistaken as a replacement for a firewall.
- Processor speed and memory on the router must be properly sized to handle required throughput.
- Filter tables must be manually maintained.

## PERIMETER FIREWALL ARCHITECTURE
### Functionality

The perimeter firewall architecture represents the physical implementation of the perimeter security conceptual design described previously. It was, and in some cases still is, the most commonly implemented firewall architecture. All rules processing and packet filtering is performed on the perimeter firewall. It is very important that firewall rules are carefully configured and tested because there is no additional security provided once past the perimeter firewall. A perimeter firewall architecture implies that all information assets within a risk domain protected in this manner are of equal value and face equal risk. Figure 3 illustrates a perimeter firewall architecture.

One advantage of perimeter firewall architecture is that it is relatively simple to configure and manage and disadvantages include the following: a single point of security implies a single point of failure, and all information assets within risk domain are at risk if perimeter security is breached.

## SERVER/HOST FIREWALL ARCHITECTURE
### Functionality

The server/host firewall architecture is also known as a screened host architecture. This architecture can be used in combination with other architectures such as the perimeter, DMZ, and multitiered DMZ. A server/host firewall is often software based and resides/executes on the application server that it is protecting. It is sort of a personal bodyguard for the application server within an otherwise secure environment.

TCPWrapper is just one example of a Unix-based program that could be considered a limited function server/host firewall software program. It is a utility that can intercept and log any requests for TCP services. It could be considered a "shim" program, much like a proxy server that sits between the computer connection requesting the service and the actual service itself on the server computer. Server/host firewall software programs such as TCPWrapper may provide some or all of the following functionality:

- Attempts to detect IP address spoofing by performing what is known as a double-reverse lookup of the IP address to ensure that the IP address and hostname match the domain name service (DNS) entry. DNS is a service that translates between commonly remembered names such as www.wiley.com and an IP address such as 128.210.114.39.
- Performs address and service filtering to be sure that the requested connection is allowed or authorized.
- Logs the connection.
- Completes the connection to the requested service.

Server/host firewalls such as TCPWrapper often run directly on application servers. Microsoft's ISA (Internet Security & Acceleration) server, formerly known as Microsoft Proxy Server, is another example of a software-based firewall package that can run on an application server. This makes them distinct from other software-based firewalls that require a dedicated server. Checkpoint would be an example of such a software-based dedicated server firewall. Figure 4 illustrates a server/host firewall architecture.

Advantages of server/host firewall architecture include the following:

- Relatively easy to install and configure.
- Adds server-specific incremental protection to other firewall architectures.

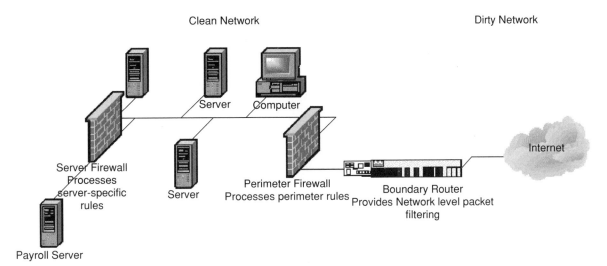

**Figure 4:** Server/host firewall architecture.

Disadvantages of server/host firewall architecture include the following:

- Ongoing maintenance/management can become difficult as the numbers of individual server/host firewalls are installed unless some type of centralized firewall management system is utilized.

# SCREENED SUBNET FIREWALL ARCHITECTURE
## Functionality

Rather than using only the packet-filtering router as the front door to the DMZ, a second firewall is added behind the packet-filtering router to further inspect all traffic bound to or from the DMZ. The initial application gateway or firewall still protects the perimeter between the DMZ and the intranet or secure internal network.

A DMZ is considered a neutral or safe zone. Outbound communications from the clean network to the Internet can go through proxy servers in the DMZ. The general public accessing this network from the Internet would only be able to access servers located in the DMZ. The DMZ contains mail, Web, and often e-commerce servers. Servers located behind the DMZ firewall on the clean network would not be accessible by the general public from the Internet. Figure 5 illustrates a screened subnet (DMZ) firewall architecture. Although this logical diagram would suggest that multiple distinct firewalls are required to establish a DMZ, this is actually not the case. Numerous vendors sell "multilegged" (multiple interface) firewalls that allow both DMZ or Internet-accessible networks as well as clean or protected networks to be physically attached to a single firewall device.

Advantages of DMZ firewalls include the following:

- Provides flexibility especially for Internet based applications such as e-mail, Web services, and e-commerce.
- Allows servers that must be accessible to the Internet while still protecting back office services on the secure internal network or Intranet.

Disadvantages of DMZ firewall include the following:

- More complicated rule configuration means more likelihood of errors.

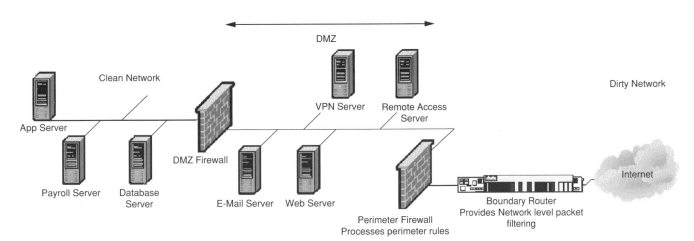

**Figure 5:** Screened subnet (DMZ) firewall architecture.

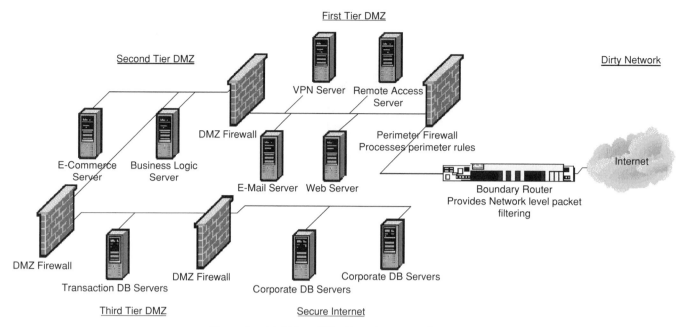

**Figure 6:** Multititiered/distributed DMZ architecture.

- Applications running in DMZ may still need access to servers/resources in the secure internal network.
- Once through the server between the DMZ and the internal network, there is no further protection or differentiated levels of security.

## MULTITIERED/DISTRIBUTED DMZ ARCHITECTURE
### Functionality

As e-commerce and e-business have proliferated, the need for e-commerce servers to access more and more secure information from database and transaction servers within the secure intranet has increased proportionately. As a result, the number of connections allowed through firewalls into the most secure areas of corporate networks has increased dramatically. In response to this phenomenon, the model of a multitiered DMZ has developed. Such a scenario really builds on the DMZ architecture by adding additional tiers to the DMZ, each protected from other tiers by additional firewalls. Typically, the first tier of the DMZ closest to the Internet would contain only the presentation or Web portion of the e-commerce application running on Web servers.

A firewall would separate that first tier of the DMZ from the second tier that would house the business logic and application portions of the e-commerce application typically running on transaction servers. This firewall would have rules defined to only allow packets from certain applications on certain servers with certain types of requests through from the first-tier DMZ to the second-tier DMZ. The third (most secure) tier of the DMZ is similarly protected from the second tier by a separate firewall. The servers in the third-tier DMZ would be database servers and should contain only the data necessary to complete requested e-commerce transactions. Finally, as

in the screened subnet firewall architecture, a firewall would separate the third-tier DMZ from the intranet, or most secure corporate network. Figure 6 illustrates the multitiered/distributed firewall architecture.

Advantages of multitiered/distributed firewall architecture include the following:

- When combined with screened host/server specific firewalls, a multitiered DMZ firewall architecture provides good protection for back office systems such as payroll and inventory servers.
- A multitiered DMZ system provides the greatest level of flexibility and highest number of risk domains thus providing ability for optimal placement of information resources.

Disadvantages of multitiered/distributed firewall architecture include the following:

- Each additional level of firewalls adds a level of complexity in terms of rule configuration and opportunity for configuration errors that can lead to security breaches.
- There is obviously a proportional increase in expense for each level of security/DMZ added.

## AIR GAP ARCHITECTURE
### Functionality

A hardware-based network switch is at the heart of the air gap architecture. The premise of creating a physical disconnection between the clean or secure network (intranet) and the nonsecure or dirty network (Internet) is accomplished by connecting a server on the Internet connection that will receive all incoming requests. This server will connect to an electronic switch that strips the TCP headers and stores the packet in a memory bank, and then the switch disconnects from the external server and connects with the internal server. Once the connection is made, the internal server recreates the TCP header and transmits the packet to the intended server. Responses are made in the reverse order. The physical separation of the networks and the stripping of the TCP headers remove many of the vulnerabilities in the TCP connection-oriented protocol. Of course this provides little additional protection over other firewalls at the content level because content-level attacks are passed through the so-called air gap and responses are returned.

By utilizing high-speed switches for the rule checking and packet forwarding, switched firewalls, also known as switch-accelerated firewalls, are able to filter and forward packets at multigigabit speeds. In some switched firewall architectures, separate dedicated devices sometimes referred to as switched firewall directors perform firewall control functions such as policy and session management, connection table management, and packet handling rules specification, thus freeing the dedicated separate switched firewall to perform only rule checking and packing forwarding. In some cases, application-specific filtering is provided on the air gap technology. Such devices may be referred to as application firewall appliances or air gap application firewalls. Figure 7 illustrates an air gap architecture.

Advantages of air gap architecture include the following:

- Provides switched connections between clean and dirty networks, thereby creating a physical gap or moat between the two.
- High-speed network switches at the heart of the air gap architecture provide high throughput.

Disadvantages of air gap architecture include the following:

- Effectiveness of the architecture is still dependent on the effectiveness of the packet filtering rules within the air gap device.
- Deep packet inspection or content/application specific inspection cannot be assumed.
- Vendors loosely interpret the term *air gap technology*. Specific functionality of any given device should not be assumed.

## CONCLUSION

There is no single firewall architecture that is the correct choice for all security scenarios. Firewall architectures

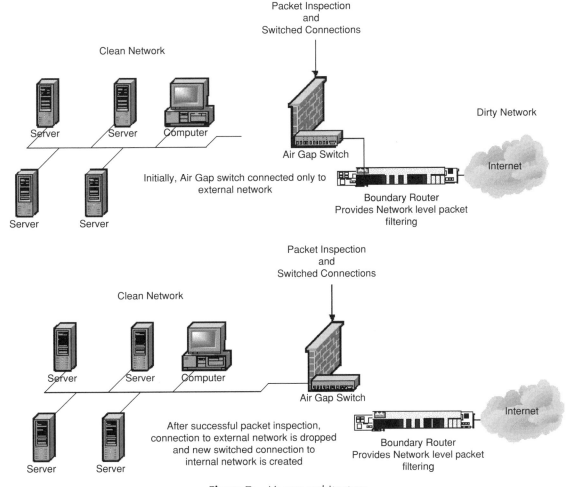

**Figure 7:** Air gap architecture.

vary primarily in the number of firewalls employed and the placement of those firewalls relative to each other, the information resources they are trying to protect, and the dirty networks or threats they are trying to protect the information resources from. A thorough security requirements analysis is prerequisite to firewall architecture choice. Such a security requirements analysis must start with a detailed understanding of the applications that must be secured. Firewalls, and their arrangement in a particular architecture, are just one piece of the overall security framework puzzle.

## GLOSSARY

**Address Filtering**　A firewall's ability to block or allow packets based on Internet protocol addresses.
**Air Gap Technology**　Switched connections established to connect external and internal networks that are not otherwise physically connected.
**Application-Level Gateway**　Application-level filters examine the entire request for data rather than only the source and destination addresses.
**Bastion Host**　Hardened server with trusted operating system that serves as the basis of the firewall.
**Circuit-Level Proxies**　Proxy servers that work at the circuit level by proxying such protocols as File Transfer Protocol.
**Demilitarized Zone (DMZ)**　A neutral zone between firewalls or between a packet filtering router and a firewall in which mail and Web servers are often located.
**Domain Filtering**　A firewall's ability to block outbound access to restricted sites.
**Dual-Homed Host**　A host firewall with two or more network interface cards with direct access to two or more networks.
**Ephemeral Ports**　Port numbers that are temporarily assigned to client-side connections from a predetermined range of available port numbers.
**Firewall**　A network device capable of filtering unwanted traffic from a connection between networks.
**Internal Firewall**　Firewalls that include filters that work on the data-link, network, and application layers to examine communications that occur only on an organization's internal network, inside the reach of traditional firewalls.
**Multitiered DMZ**　A DMZ that segments access areas with multiple layers of firewalls.
**Network Address Translation**　A firewall's ability to translate between private and public globally unique Internet Protocol addresses.
**Packet-Filtering Gateway**　A firewall that allows or blocks packet transmission based on source and destination Internet Protocol addresses.
**Port Filtering**　A firewall's ability to block or allow packets based on Transmission Control Protocol port number.
**Proxy Server**　Servers that break direct connections between clients and servers and offer application and circuit layer specific proxy services to inspect and control such communications.
**Screened Subnet**　Enterprise firewall architecture that creates a DMZ.

**Stateful Firewall**　A firewall that monitors connections and records packet information in state tables to make forwarding decisions in the context of previous transmitted packets over a given connection.
**Trusted Gateway**　In a trusted gateway, certain applications are identified as trusted, are able to bypass the application gateway entirely, and are able to establish connections directly rather than by proxy.

## CROSS REFERENCES

See *Firewall Basics; Packet Filtering and Stateful Firewalls; Proxy Firewalls.*

## FURTHER READING

Bittard, C. (2003, April). *Security infrastructure technology overview*. Retrieved January 2, 2003, from http://www.evidian.com

Canavan, J. E. (2001). *Fundamentals of network security.* Boston: Artech House.

CERT Coordination Center. (1999, July 1). *Design the firewall system*. Retrieved January 2, 2004, from http://www.cert.org/security-improvement/practices/p053.html

Check Point Software Technologies. (1999, June 22). *Stateful inspection firewall technology tech note*. Retrieved January 2, 2004, from http://www. checkpoint. com/products/downloads/Stateful_Inspection.pdf

Cisco Systems. (2003). *PIX 500 series firewalls*. Retrieved January 2, 2003, from http://www.cisco.com

Dubrawsky, I. (2003, July). *Firewall evolution—Deep packet inspection* Retrieved January 2, 2004, from http://www.securityfocus.com/infocus/1716

Edwards, J. (2001, May 1). *Unplugging cybercrime*. Retrieved January 2, 2003, from http://www.cio.com/archive/050100/development.html

Garfinkel, S., & Spafford, G. (2003). *Practical Unix and Internet security* (3rd ed.). Sebastapol, CA: O'Reilly.

Goldman, J. E., & Rawles, P. T. (2004). *Applied data communications*: *A business oriented approach* (4th ed.). New York: John Wiley & Sons.

Hurley, M. (2001, April 4). Network air gaps—Drawbridge to the backend office. Retrieved January 2, 2003, from http://rr.sans.org/firewall/gaps.php

Intoto, Inc. (2002). *Virtual firewalls white paper*. Retrieved January 2, 2003, from http://www.intotoinc.com

Keeping a safe distance. (2001, October). *Enterprise Technology*. Retrieved January 2, 2004, from http://www.avcom.com/et/online/2001/oct/keeping.html

Mercadet, R. (2003, February). *From DMZ to DdMZ*. Retrieved January 2, 2004, from http://www.evidian.com

NASA. (2003, September). *Wireless firewall gateway white paper*. Retrieved January 2, 2003, from http://www.nas.nasa.gov

NetGap. (n.d.). *SpearHead Security Web site*. Retrieved January 2, 2004, from http://www.spearheadsecurity.com/products.shtml

Nortel Networks. (2001). Alteon switched firewall. Retrieved January 2, 2004, from www.nortelnetworks.com

Poynter, I., & Doctor, B. (2003, January). *Beyond the firewall: The next level of network security*. Retrieved January 3, 2004, from http://www.stillsecure.com

Qwest. (2001, June). *Leveraging network based firewall services in your next generation wide area network solution*. Retrieved January 2, 2004, from http://www.qwest.com

Ramsey, J. (2003, July). *Client-side vulnerabilities: Meet your network's weakest link*. Retrieved January 2, 2003, from http://www.secureworks.com

Scheer, S. (2001, January 10). *Israeli start-up may thwart Internet hackers*. Retrieved January 2, 2003, from http://staging.infoworld.com/articles/hn/xml/01/01/10/010110hnthwart.xml?Tem

Senner, L. (2001, May 9). *Anatomy of a stateful firewall*. Retrieved January 2, 2002, from http://rr.sans.org/firewall/anatomy.php

Trlokom. (2003). *Beyond perimeter firewalls and intrusion detection systems*. Retrieved January 2, 2004, from http://www.trlokom.com/white_paper/distributed_firewall. php

Whale Communications. *Air gap technology*. Retrieved January 2, 2004, from http://www.whalecommunications.com/fr_0300.htm

Whale Communications. (2003, January). *E-gap application firewall appliance: A technical overview*. Retrieved January 2, 2004, from http://www.whalecommunications.com

# Packet Filtering and Stateful Firewalls

Avishai Wool, *Tel Aviv University, Israel*

## INTRODUCTION

The Internet is like a system of roads that transport packets of data from one computer network to another, using the transmission control protocol/Internet protocol (TCP/IP) protocol suite. However, not all IP traffic is welcome everywhere. Most organizations need to control the traffic that crosses into and out of their networks: to prevent attacks against their computer systems, to prevent attacks originating from their network against other organizations, to prevent attacks originating from inside of the organization against other parts of the organization (insider threat, i.e., an employee in finance trying to get into the human resources department network), and to conform with various policy choices. The firewall is the primary control point for these tasks. It is typically the first filtering device that sees IP packets that attempt to enter an organization's network from the outside, and it is typically the last device to see an exiting packet. It acts like the security guard at the entrance to a building: It is the firewall's job, using the *policy* it is configured to use, to make a filtering decision on every packet that crosses it: either to let it pass or to drop it.

For the firewall to perform its job, several conflicting issues need to be addressed:

1. The firewall must be able to *observe all the traffic*: obviously, a firewall cannot control traffic that bypasses it.

2. The firewall must be able to *differentiate* among various types of traffic and apply the appropriate filtering decisions.

3. The firewall must *work fast* enough so that it does not become a bottleneck.

### Observe All Traffic

To address the first issue, a firewall needs to be placed at a *choke point* on the network, through which all controlled traffic has to travel. In a typical setup the firewall is connected to the communication line going to the organization's Internet service provider (ISP). If the organization is large, with multiple Internet connections, there should be a firewall attached to each connection. The only way to ensure that unauthorized traffic cannot bypass the firewall is by an administrative policy that forbids adding Internet connections without authorization.

### Differentiate

The firewall must be able to distinguish between packets that conform to the corporate policy (and should be let through) and the rest (which should be dropped). For this, the policy needs to be encoded in a language that the firewall's software can understand. This encoding is usually done via a sequence of *rules* that describe various cases. The sequence of rules is usually called a *rule base*. A rule base has to have a policy decision for every possible type of packet the firewall will ever encounter: this is usually done by listing all the special cases, followed by a catch-all default rule. The default rule should implement a safe stance of "what is not explicitly allowed should be dropped": almost all firewalls have such a default "out of the box," but some exceptions do exist, in which case the administrator needs to add a safe default rule manually.

Each rule makes reference to values that distinguish one packet from another. The common *match fields* in firewall rules refer to a packet's source and destination IP addresses, protocol, and source and destination port numbers. These are fields that appear in a packet's IP header or in the TCP/User Datagram Protocol (UDP) headers as appropriate. However, some firewalls look deeper into the packet and are able to interpret the semantics of specific protocols such as Simpal Mail Transffer Protocol (SMTP) (e-mail), Hyper Text Transffer Protocol (HTTP) (Web browsing), and so on. Most firewalls are also capable of filtering based on a packet's *direction*: which network interface card the packet is crossing, and whether the packet is crossing the interface from the network into the firewall ("inbound") or vice versa ("outbound").

Most firewalls implement *first match semantics*: This means that the firewall tries to match a packet against all the rules in the rule base, in sequence. When if it finds the first rule that that matches all the match fields in the packet, it stop and makes the filtering decision according to that rule. Therefore, more specific rules need to be listed higher up in the rule base.

## Work Fast

Packet matching in firewalls involves matching on many fields from the TCP, UDP, and IP packet header. With available bandwidth increasing rapidly, very efficient matching algorithms need to be deployed in modern firewalls to ensure that the firewall does not become a bottleneck. There is an inherent trade-off between speed and differentiation capabilities: a firewall that looks deeper into each packet spends more time on it. The standard solution that practically all firewalls adopt is to start with the five basic fields (protocol number, source and destination IP addresses, and source and destination port numbers). The advantage of these five fields is that they are in fixed positions in the packet headers, their contents are standardized and simple, and they describe a packet fairly well: the IP addresses show where the packet is going and where it is coming from, and the combination of protocol and port numbers show what the packet is trying to achieve. The combination of protocol and port numbers is called a *service*: From a firewall's perspective, the HTTP service is defined by protocol = TCP, destination port = 80, and any source port. Beyond these five basic fields, there is a great variability between vendors and configuration choices, because looking deeper into the packets is service dependent and often computationally expensive. Common solutions offload the service dependent filtering to additional dedicated machines that are situated behind (or next to) the firewall (e.g., an e-mail filter that scans for viruses, an HTTP filter that strips Java applets and malformed URLs).

## BASIC PACKET FILTERING
### What Is It?

Most first generation firewalls used *basic packet filtering*. Basic packet filtering means the following:

1. The firewall keeps no *state*. The filtering decision is made separately for every packet and does not take into account any earlier decisions made on related packets.
2. The filtering decision is based only of the five basic fields: source and destination IP addresses, protocol, and source and destination port numbers (for protocols that have port numbers).

The typical actions that a basic packet filter can take are as follows:

1. Pass: let the packet through.
2. Drop: do not forward the packet. No indication is sent back to the sender.

3. Reject: Same as Drop, except that a special ICMP packet is sent back to the sender informing it that the packet was filtered.

In addition, it is usually possible to *log* the action: write an entry in a log file with the details of the packet, the decision, the rule that caused the decision, and so on. Logging is very useful for debugging and for identifying concentrated attacks. However, logging should be used with care, as it can be very expensive: disk-write rates are orders of magnitude slower than network transmission rates. When the network is subjected to a denial of service (DoS) attack, and the firewall is bombarded with packets that are being dropped, the firewall itself may crash under the load if it attempts to log too many of the packets.

Basic packet filtering can still be found in free firewalls such as `iptables/netfilter` (Netfilter 2004) and `IP-Filter` (Reed 2005) in their standard configuration, and also in routers that implement access lists. However, such "pure" packet filters are becoming rare: `netfilter` can be used with the `conntrack` module, which is stateful, and Cisco provides add-on modules that make their access control lists stateful as well.

## Limitations of Basic Packet Filtering

Most of the useful Internet services are bidirectional: data are sent from one computer to another, and responses (*return traffic*) are sent back. This is always the case for TCP-based services—at the very least, every TCP packet must be acknowledged by its recipient. For the sake of simplicity, in this section we focus on TCP traffic. Obviously, for a bidirectional service to work correctly, both traffic directions have to be allowed to cross the firewall.

The combination of packets going in both directions is called a TCP *flow*. There is always one end point (computer) that initiates a flow (sends the first packet)—this end point is called the *client*, and the other is called the *server*. A TCP flow is characterized by four attributes: the IP addresses of the two end points, and the two ports being used. However, the specification of a TCP service typically only identifies the destination port. For example, a telnet connection is almost always on TCP port 23. So a typical telnet *server* listens on port 23. However, a telnet *client* may use any port number on its end point—and typically, this port number is chosen dynamically at run time and is essentially unpredictable. If the firewall is a basic packet filter, the unpredictability of the client's port number makes it almost impossible to let the flow cross the firewall without introducing risky side effects.

To illustrate the problem, let us continue with the telnet example. Suppose we want to allow a telnet flow between a client at IP address 1.1.1.1 and a server at 2.2.2.2. Assume further that the client is inside the organization's network and the server is outside. Client-to-server packets look like this:

Source IP = 1.1.1.1, Destination IP = 2.2.2.2,
Source Port = NNN, Destination Port = 23,

where NNN is an arbitrary number selected by the client. Conversely, return traffic, from the server to the client, swaps IP addresses and port numbers and looks like this:

Source IP = 2.2.2.2, Destination IP = 1.1.1.1,
Source Port = 23, Destination Port = NNN

(for the same port number NNN). Now consider this flow from the firewall's point of view. The person writing the rules to allow this flow knows the end points' IP addresses and knows that the telnet port is 23. But he or she does not know the client's source port (NNN), which is selected dynamically at run time. So to allow both directions of traffic through the firewall, he or she needs to write two basic filtering rules:

1. Permit TCP packets from 1.1.1.1, to 2.2.2.2, with any source port and destination port 23.
2. Permit TCP packets from 2.2.2.2, to 1.1.1.1, with source port 23 and any destination port.

Unfortunately, rule 2, which matches packets based on their source port, is extremely risky. Remember that the source port is under the packet sender's control. An attacker on machine 2.2.2.2 can craft packets with source port 23, destination IP 1.1.1.1, and a destination port of his choice. Packets crafted this way will cross the firewall because they match the second telnet rule—and then access a *non-telnet* port! Thus, we see that basic filtering rules that are intended to allow outbound telnet also allow inbound TCP on *any* destination port as a side effect.

This type of risk is unavoidable for a basic packet filter. Because the firewall does not keep state, it does not "remember" whether a telnet flow is already established and what source port number the client selected. Thus, the firewall has to rely on source port filtering—which, as we just saw, is unreliable and risky.

Therefore, essentially all modern firewalls go beyond basic packet filtering and are *stateful*. Stateless filtering can still be found (e.g., in routers), but these devices should not be perceived as "real" firewalls and should only be used in relatively safe environments, such as within an organization's internal network, to separate departments from each other.

## STATEFUL PACKET FILTERING
### What Is It?

To address the limitations of basic packet filtering, nearly all the firewalls on the market nowadays are stateful. This means that the firewall keeps track of established flows, and all the packets that belong to an existing flow, in both directions, are allowed to cross the firewall.

To do this, the firewall keeps an entry in a *cache* for each open flow. When the first packet of a new flow is seen by the firewall (this is the so-called SYN packet in a TCP flow), the firewall matches it against the rule base. If there is a rule that allows the packet across, the firewall inserts a new entry into the cache. This entry includes both end points' IP addresses and, important, both port numbers. The port number information was not fully known when the administrator wrote the rules—however, when the flow is being set up, both port numbers are known, because they are listed in the packet's TCP header.

When a subsequent packet reaches the firewall, the firewall checks whether an entry for the flow it belongs to already exists in the cache. If the flow is listed in the cache, the packet is allowed through immediately. If no such flow exists, then the packet is matched against the rule base and is handled accordingly.

When the flow is torn down (triggered by a so-called FIN packet), the firewall removes the cache entry, thereby blocking the flow. Typically the firewall also has a timeout value: if a flow becomes inactive for too long, the firewall evicts the entry from the cache and blocks the flow. Therefore, we see that the first packet of a flow effectively opens a hole in the firewall, and the cache mechanism allows the return traffic to go through this hole.

## Advantages of Stateful Filtering

The main advantage of a stateful firewall is that it is inherently more secure. The firewall administrator no longer needs to write broad (and insecure) source filtering rules to allow the return traffic: he or she only needs to list the attributes of the flow's first packet in the rule base, and the cache mechanism takes care of the rest. The hole that is created is only large enough for this particular flow and does not introduce side effects. Furthermore, the hole is temporary: once the flow is torn down, the hole is closed.

An additional benefit is that the rule base is shorter: a single rule is enough to describe a flow, whereas a basic packet filter needs two rules for the same flow. Writing and managing fewer rules mean less work for the administrator and fewer chances to make mistakes.

Finally, this mechanism provides a significant performance boost. With appropriate data structures, a cache lookup can be made very efficiently (e.g., by using a hash table or search tree). Matching a packet against the rule base is usually a much slower operation (although, as we shall see under Matching Algorithms, it does not have to be slow).

## Limitations of Stateful Filtering

An established flow is allowed through the firewall only as long as it has an entry in the cache. Therefore, if the cache entry is removed while the flow is still active, all remaining traffic will be dropped, and the connection will break. This can happen in two common situations:

1. Cache table overflow: the cache table grows dynamically, as more connections are activated concurrently. A firewall protecting a busy network may need to keep hundreds of thousands of established flows in its cache. If the firewall does not have sufficient memory and the cache overflows its capacity, then the firewall will start evicting cache entries, causing connections to drop. Note that causing a cache table overflow can be a type of denial of service (DoS) attack: If an attacker floods the firewall with connections, the firewall would drop legitimate network connections.
2. Time-out too short: As we noted, the cache entry is removed when a flow is intentionally torn down and also if it is inactive for more than a certain time. If the time-out period is set too short, then the cache entry may be evicted simply because the flow was quiet for too long. Firewalls typically have sensible default values for their timeout parameters, but occasionally a connection is

dropped for this reason: a typical example is a telnet or ssh connection, which sends no traffic if the person at the terminal stops typing. For this reason, well-designed ssh clients use the protocol's "NOOP" packets to keep the connection alive even if the user stops typing. This is a sensible feature for any protocol that needs to cross a firewall.

## Dynamic Port Selection

As we noted, a firewall identifies a service based on the port numbers it uses. Implicit in this mechanism is the assumption that the port numbers, at least on the server side, are *fixed* and known in advance to the firewall administrator. Unfortunately, this assumption is not universally true.

There exist services, which we call *multichannel services*, which dynamically select both the server and client ports numbers. Most streaming audio services work this way and so does the very common file transfer protocol (FTP). A typical multichannel service has a control channel that uses a fixed port number (e.g., TCP port 21 for FTP). Within the application layer protocol running over the control channel, the communicating hosts dynamically agree on a port number for a data channel, over which they transfer the bulk of their data.

To support such services, the firewall is forced to parse the application layer protocols, keep additional state for such connections, and dynamically open the ports that were negotiated. This usually means that the firewall vendor needs to add special program code to handle each multichannel service it wishes to support: it is not something that the firewall administrator can add on her own by adding rules to the rule base.

## MATCHING ALGORITHMS

> *This section discusses the internal algorithmics of firewalls, and assumes some mathematical background. Readers who are primerily interested in using and configuring firewalls may skip this section.*

As discussed, most modern firewalls are stateful. This means that after the first packet in a network flow is allowed to cross the firewall, all subsequent packets belonging to that flow, and especially the return traffic, are also allowed through the firewall. This statefulness is commonly implemented by two separate search mechanisms: (1) a slow algorithm that implements the "first match" semantics and compares a packet to all the rules and (2) a fast state lookup mechanism that checks whether a packet belongs to an existing open flow.

In many firewalls, the slow algorithm is a naive linear search of the rule base, whereas the state lookup mechanism uses a hash table or a search tree. This is the case for the open source firewalls `pf` (Benzedrine 2004) and `iptables/netfilter` (Netfilter 2004). Note that this two-part design works best on long TCP connections, for which the fast state lookup mechanism handles most of the packets. However, connectionless UDP and ICMP traffic, and short TCP flows (like those produced by HTTP

V1.0), only activate the "slow" algorithm, making it a significant bottleneck. The rest of this section explores this "slow" packet matching algorithm.

Here is a mathematical way of looking at the firewall packet matching problem: given a packet, find the first rule that matches it on $d$ fields from its header. Every rule consists of set of ranges $[l_i, r_i]$ for $i = 1, \ldots, d$, where each range corresponds to a field in a packet header. The field values are in $0 \le l_i, r_i \le U_i$, where $U_i = 2^{32} - 1$ for 32-bit IP addresses, $U_i = 65535$ for 16-bit port numbers, and $U_i = 255$ for 8-bit ICMP message type or code. Note that we are assuming that the field values are all numeric, which is reasonable for header fields but less so for data within the packet payload. The number of fields to be matched ($d$) in this representation is typically $d = 4$ (for TCP, UDP, and ICMP protocols) or $d = 2$ if the matching is limited to IP addresses when the protocol does not have (or does not expose) any port numbers (e.g., when filtering encrypted IPSec traffic)

Viewed this way, we can give the packet matching problem a geometric interpretation. Each packet is a point in $d$-dimensional space: each header field corresponds to a dimension. Each rule is now a $d$-dimensional "box," and we have $N$ such boxes (rules) that may overlap each other, with a higher priority given to boxes (rules) that are listed first. Under this interpretation, the matching problem is now to find the highest priority box that contains a given $d$-dimensional point.

It is difficult for people to visualize four-dimensional space. But in two dimensions the analogy is quite natural. Think of a plane, with the $x$ axis corresponding to the source IP address and the $y$ axis corresponding to the destination IP address. In this view, a rule is a rectangle: all points whose $x$ value is in some range and whose $y$ value is in some other range. If one of the fields is a "don't care," we just end up with a very wide (or very tall) rectangle. A rule base with $N$ rules now becomes a collection of overlapping rectangles. When two rectangles overlap, one hides parts of the other. Now think of all the "PASS" rules as having a white color and all the "DROP" rules as having a black color. Viewed from above, the full set of $N$ rectangles subdivides the plane into a patchwork of rectangles and rectangle fragments (that are just smaller rectangles), some white and some black. Given a particular point, with some $x/y$ coordinates (= source/destination IP addresses), which rectangle does it belong to and what color is that rectangle? This is called a *point location* problem.

In addition to being elegant, this geometric view has great algorithmic importance. Computer scientists working in the field of computational geometry have studied point location problems for several decades and have come up with some very efficient algorithms. Some algorithms are limited to two dimensions, but there are algorithms that deal with arbitrary $d$-dimensional problems as well.

Usually, these algorithms have two parts: The first part preprocesses the colored patchwork plane into a data structure that supports fast searches. This is done once, when the rule base is created. The size of the search data structure often grows rather large. The second part is a very fast lookup through the data structure. The search is done on every point lookup query (i.e., for every packet to be matched). Usually we do not care so much about how long the preprocessing takes, as long as it is "within reason." What we do care about are (1) getting blazingly fast lookups, because the lookup rate has to be as fast as the rate of arriving packets, and (2) the size of the search data structure: if it is too large to fit in main memory, the filtering rate will drop rapidly because of disk accesses or page faults.

One successful application of geometric algorithms to the firewall packet matching problem can be found in Rovniagin and Wool (2004). As we mentioned previously, stateful firewalls have a slow algorithm that compares a packet to each rule in sequence and then a fast state lookup algorithm for open flows. In Rovniagin and Wool (2004) the authors show that "slow" algorithms do not need to be slow. They demonstrated an algorithm (called GEM, for geometric efficient matching) that does lookups in $O(\log N)$ time and has an $O(N^4)$ search data structure size. More important, though, is that they implemented the algorithm as an extension to the Linux `iptables` firewall and tested it. They showed that, for example, on 5000-rule rule bases, the data structure reached only some 13 MB, which easily fits into the main memory of modern computers. They report that the GEM algorithm sustained a matching rate of more than 30,000 packets per second, with 10,000 rules, without losing packets, on a standard 2.4-GHz PC running RedHat Linux 9.0. This is at least 10 times faster than the rate achieved by the regular `iptables`. The interested reader is referred to Rovniagin and Wool (2004) and the references therein for further details.

## COMMON CONFIGURATION ERRORS

The protection that firewalls provide is only as good as the policy they are configured to implement. Once a company acquires a firewall, a systems administrator must configure and manage it according to a security policy that meets the company's needs. Configuration is a crucial task, probably the most important factor in the security a firewall provides (Rubin, Geer, & Ranum, 1997).

Network security experts generally consider corporate firewalls to be poorly configured, as witnessed in professionally oriented mailing lists such as Firewall Wizards (1997–2004). This assessment is indirectly affirmed by the success of recent worms and viruses such as Blaster (CERT Coordination Center, 2003) and Sapphire (Moore et al., 2003), which a well-configured firewall could easily have blocked.

In this section we focus on rule sets for Check Point's FireWall-1 product (www.checkpoint.com) and specifically on 12 possible misconfigurations that would allow access beyond a typical corporation's network security policy.

### Rule Set Complexity

Firewall administrators are intuitively able to classify a rule set as "complicated" or "simple." To quantify this intuition into a concrete measure of complexity, Wool (2004a) suggests the following measure of rule-set complexity:

$$RC = Rules + Objects + Interfaces (Interfaces-1)/2,$$

where RC denotes rule complexity, Rules denotes the raw number of rules in the rule set, Objects denotes the number of network objects, and Interfaces denotes the number of interfaces on the firewall. The rationale for this measure is as follows: counting the number of rules is obvious and adding the number of objects is useful because a Check Point rule can refer to a great number of network objects (subnets and groups of these) that significantly increase its complexity. Finally, if the firewall has $i$ interfaces then the number of different interface-to-interface paths through the firewall is $i(i - 1)/2$, and the number of paths increases the complexity of the rule base.

## Which Configuration Errors to Count?

To quantify the quality of a firewall configuration, we must define what constitutes a configuration error. In general, the definition is subjective, because an acceptable policy for one corporation could be completely unacceptable for another. Wool (2004a) counted as errors only those configurations that represented violations of well-established industry practices and guidelines (Cheswick, Bellovin, & Rubin, 2003; Zwicky, Cooper, & Chapman, 2000). Note that these are not the only dangerous configuration mistakes an administrator may make—many others are possible. The misconfigurations listed here should only serve as a *baseline* of things to avoid rather than an exhaustive list. The following 12 items counted as configuration errors:

1. *No stealth rule*. To protect the firewall itself from unauthorized access, it is common to have a "stealth" rule of the form: "From anywhere, to the firewall, with any service, drop." The absence of such a rule to hide the firewall counted as a configuration error.

2–4. *Check Point implicit rules*. In addition to the regular user written rules, the Check Point FireWall-1 GUI has several checkboxes that produce implicit rules. These rules control both the Internet's domain name service (DNS) separately over TCP and UDP and the Internet control message protocol (ICMP). However, the implicit rules are very broad, basically allowing the service at hand from anywhere to anywhere. Because DNS is one of the most attacked services (SANS Institute, 2003), writing narrow, explicit rules for it is more secure. Likewise, with any-to-any ICMP, attackers can scan the internal net and propagate worms such as Nachi/Welchia. Each of the three possible implicit rules—DNS-TCP, DNS-UDP, and ICMP—counted as one error.

5. *Insecure firewall management*. Access to the firewall over insecure, unencrypted, and poorly authenticated protocols—such as telnet, FTP, or x11—counted as one error.

6. *Too many management machines*. Firewalls should be managed from a small number of machines. Allowing management sessions from more than five machines was counted as a configuration error. Although this threshold is somewhat subjective, most experts agree that it is reasonable.

7. *External management machines.* An error was counted if machines outside the network's perimeter could manage the firewall. The preferred way for administrators to manage the firewall from home is from the "inside" through a virtual private network.

8. *NetBIOS service.* NetBIOS is a set of services that Microsoft Windows operating systems use to support network functions such as file and printer sharing. These frequently attacked services are very insecure (SANS Institute, 2003). Allowing any NetBIOS service to cross the firewall in any direction counted as an error.

9. *Portmapper/Remote Procedure Call service.* The portmapper daemon assigns TCP ports to implement RPC services, a Unix mechanism that has a long history of being insecure. Among other services, RPCs include the Network File System protocol, which potentially exposes all the organization's file system. Allowing traffic to the portmapper (TCP or UDP on port 111) counted as an error.

10. *Zone-spanning objects.* A Check Point network object is a named definition of a set of IP addresses. Zone-spanning objects include addresses that reside on more than one "side" of the firewall—for example, some IP addresses internal to the firewall and others external. Note that a firewall with more than two interfaces has more than just an inside and an outside—each interface defines another "side." Zone spanning objects cause many unintended consequences when used in firewall rules. For example, when administrators write a rule, they usually assume that the object is either internal or external, and this assumption affects how they write the rule. Zone spanning objects break this dichotomy—with disastrous results. Any use of zone spanning objects in the rule set counted as an error.

11. *"Any" service on inbound rules.* Allowing "Any" service to enter the network is a gross mistake, because "Any" includes numerous high-risk services, including NetBIOS and RPC services. Allowing such access was counted as an error.

12. *"Any" destination on outbound rules.* Because internal users typically have unrestricted access to the Internet, outbound rules commonly allow a destination of "Any." Unfortunately, firewalls commonly have more than two network interfaces. The typical usage of a third interface is to attach a demilitarized zone (DMZ): a subnet dedicated to the corporation's externally visible servers. In such cases, free Internet access also gives internal users free access to the servers in the DMZ. Worse, it often allows the DMZ servers free access to the internal network, because the predefined "Any" network object is inherently zone spanning (see "Direction-Based Filtering"). Therefore, allowing such access counted as an error.

Item 12 is probably the most subjective error counted. It is possible to safely use a destination of "Any" by carefully adding other rules that restrict the unwanted access. Nevertheless, finding "destination = Any" outbound rules in a firewall audit should, at least, raise a warning flag.

## Results and Analysis

Figure 1 shows the raw distribution of configuration errors reported in Wool (2004a), based on a survey of real corporate firewall configurations. The results can be characterized only as dismal. Most of the errors appeared in most of the firewalls studied: in fact, 9 of the 12 errors appeared in more than half the firewalls.

Even if we discount the two most frequent errors (items 10 and 12), which may be somewhat controversial, the results show that almost 80% of firewalls allow both the "Any" service on inbound rules (item 11) and insecure access to the firewalls (item 5). These are gross mistakes by any account. In fact, only one of the firewalls exhibited only a single misconfiguration. All the other firewalls could have been easily penetrated by both unsophisticated attackers and mindless automatic worms.

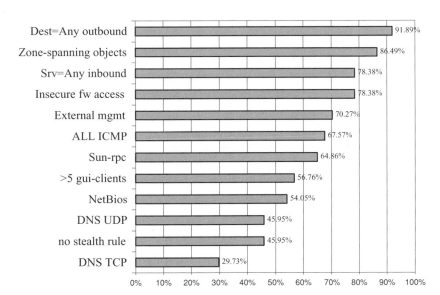

**Figure 1:** Distribution of configuration errors.

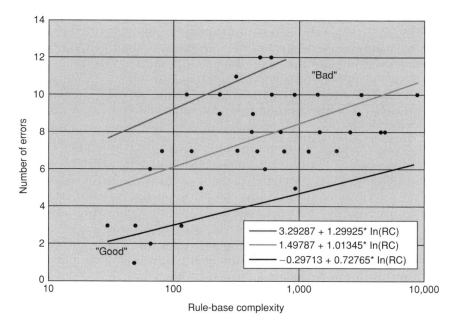

**Figure 2:** Number of errors as a function of rule set complexity. The RC scale is logarithmic. The middle line represents the least-squares fit, and the top and bottom lines represent one standard deviation above and below the least-squares fit line.

## Complexity Matters: Small Is Beautiful

The study in Wool (2004a) examined several possible factors that influence the distribution of configuration errors. The study found that the firewall's operating system was mostly irrelevant and that later firewall software versions had slightly fewer mistakes. However, the most significant factor was shown to be the firewall rule set's complexity, as quantified by the RC measure.

Figure 2 shows a scatter plot of the number of errors versus RC. The RC measure showed a wide range in complexity values. The average RC was 1,121, the lowest value was 30, and the highest was an astonishing 8,521. Although the plot is fairly sparse, the empty lower right quadrant indicates that there are no good high-complexity rule sets. The only reasonably well configured firewalls—three errors or less—are very simple, with RC values under 100. However, a small and simple rule set is no guarantee of a good configuration. The figure shows that a small rule set can be configured quite badly: there are two configurations with RC values under 100 but with six or more errors.

In fact, the RC measure yields a crude but fairly accurate prediction of the number of configuration errors: a linear regression shows that a rule set of complexity RC is predicted to have about $\ln(RC) + 1.5$ errors—this is the formula for the central line in Figure 2.

The conclusion to draw here is obvious: limiting a firewall's rule set complexity as defined by RC is safer. Instead of connecting yet another subnet to the main firewall and adding more rules and more objects, it is preferable to install a new, dedicated firewall to protect only that new subnet. Complex firewall rule sets are apparently too complex for administrators to manage effectively.

## DIRECTION-BASED FILTERING
### Background

Beyond the standard header fields, most firewalls are also capable of filtering based on a packet's *direction*: which

network interface card the packet is crossing and whether the packet is crossing the interface from the network into the firewall or vice versa. We call these last capabilities *direction-based filtering*.

Taking a packet's direction into account in filtering rules is extremely useful: it lets the firewall administrator protect against source address spoofing, write effective egress filtering rules, and avoid unpleasant side effects when referring to subnets that span the firewall. Unfortunately, the firewall's definition of a packet's direction is different from what users normally assume. If interface eth0 connects the firewall to the internal network, then, from a user's perspective, "inbound on eth0" is actually "outbound" traffic. This discrepancy makes it very confusing for firewall administrators to use the packet direction correctly and creates a significant usability problem.

Most firewall vendors (exemplified by Cisco and Lucent) seem to be unaware of the usability issues related to direction-based filtering. These vendors simply expose the raw and confusing direction-based filtering functionality to the firewall administrators. A notable exception is Check Point. To avoid the usability problem, Check Point chooses to keep its management interface simple and hide the direction-based filtering functionality in such a way that most users are essentially unable to use it (indeed, many users do not even know that a Check Point FireWall-1 can perform direction-based filtering).

As we saw earlier in this chapter, many firewalls are enforcing poorly written rule sets, and in particular direction-based filtering is often misconfigured or entirely unused. We suspect that direction-based filtering is underutilized in great part because of the usability problem associated with the vendor's configuration tools.

## Why Use Direction-Based Filtering?
### Antispoofing

It is well known that the source IP address on an IPv4 packet is not authenticated. Therefore, a packet's source address may be spoofed (forged) by attackers in an attempt to circumvent the firewall's security policy (cf. Zwicky et al., 2000). For instance, consider the very common firewall rule "From IP addresses in `MyNet`, to anywhere, any service is allowed." Assuming that `MyNet` is behind the firewall, this rule is supposed to allow all outbound traffic from hosts in `MyNet`. However, an attacker on the Internet may spoof a packet's source address to be inside `MyNet` and set the destination address to some IP address behind the firewall. Such a spoofed packet would clearly match the above rule and be allowed to enter. Obviously, the attacker will not see any return traffic, but damage has already been done: this is enough to mount a denial of service (DoS) attack against hosts behind the firewall and is sometimes enough to hijack a `TCP` session (Bellovin, 1989).

The main defense against such spoofing attacks, at the perimeter firewall, is based on direction-based filtering. Legitimate packets with source IP addresses that belong to `MyNet` should only enter the firewall from its internal interface. Therefore, giving the rule a direction would cause spoofed packets not to match and to be dropped by a subsequent rule.

### Egress Filtering

The primary goal of a firewall is to protect the network behind it. However, it is also important to filter egress traffic—traffic that exits the network. Otherwise, the network may become a launching point of attacks, and in particular DoS attacks, against other organizations on the Internet or against other zones in the internal network. During such attacks, the attacking host often sends spoofed packets to conceal its true location. Such an attack can come from a compromised host on the internal network or from any other network that is routing through the internal network (e.g., a business partner). A well configured firewall can prevent most DoS attacks originating behind it. This is called egress filtering.

Again, because the problem at hand is rooted in source address spoofing, the most effective way to combat it in IPv4 is by direction-based filtering. The solution outlined in the previous section essentially works as an egress filtering rule too: if the *only* packets that are allowed to enter the firewall via its internal interface (on their way out) are those packets with source address in `MyNet`, then the firewall will drop all the spoofed DoS attack packets. This forces the attacker to use legitimate source addresses and makes the attack host easier to trace back.

Note that when we talked about antispoofing, we dealt with protecting the internal network. Egress filtering deals with protecting other networks from being attacked from the internal network. But because both problems are manifestations of source address spoofing, the solution is very similar and utilizes direction-based filtering.

See SANS Institute (2000) and Edmead (2002) for recommendations on how to write effective egress filtering rules for various types of firewalls. The same recommendations also appear in RFC 2827 (Ferguson & Senie, 2000). Interestingly, the language in the RFC speaks of *ingress* filtering, because it is written for an audience of Internet service providers to whom source spoofed traffic is inbound. This is another illustration of the confusion surrounding packet directions (more on this in the next sections).

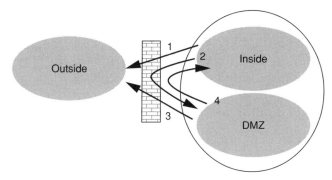

**Figure 3:** The side effects of zone spanning definitions when the rule is "From `MyNet` to Anywhere with Any service" and `MyNet` includes both the inside and the DMZ subnets. Arrow 1 indicates the intended traffic, arrows 2 and 4 indicate side effects. Arrow 3 could be either intended or a side effect; however, current best practices suggest not to allow unrestricted outbound traffic from the DMZ.

### Zone Spanning

Firewall administrators often define objects that span more than one zone ("side") of the firewall. A typical case is to define the `MyNet` group so that it contains both the internal net and the DMZ (see Figure 3). When the `MyNet` group is zone spanning, the rule "from MyNet to Anywhere with Any Service" has some unintended side effects, in addition to the spoofing vulnerability we discussed. Specifically, the rule now allows all traffic between the DMZ and the internal network, in both directions, because both subnets belong to `MyNet` and both subnets obviously belong to "Any." This defeats the whole purpose of having a DMZ, because a compromised machine in the DMZ has full access to the internal network. Additionally, the rule also allows unrestricted outbound traffic to originate from the servers in the DMZ, which is not considered prudent (cf. Wool, 2002).

The best way to avoid such side effects is to completely eradicate zone spanning definitions, at least in "pass" rules. Unfortunately, zone spanning definitions are often convenient and intuitive, so avoiding them may be difficult. In particular, the "Any" built-in definition is zone spanning.

A less draconian measure would be to set the direction on the rule, as we suggested before. For instance, if the rule is applied only to traffic leaving the firewall via its external interface, then traffic between the DMZ and Inside zones will not match the rule and will be dropped (assuming that the firewall has no other matching rules that allow the traffic and a default DENY policy rather than default ALLOW.)

## Usability Problems with Direction-Based Filtering

As we saw, direction-based filtering is a highly useful technique to combat various types of spoofing attacks. Unfortunately, though, configuring firewalls to actually use direction-based filtering seems to involve a significant usability problem. This problem is caused by the clash between the user's global, network-centric stance and the firewall's local, device-centric stance. There is

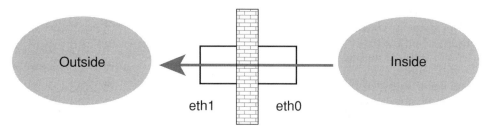

**Figure 4:** A traffic flow that it outbound and is both inbound on `eth0` and outbound on `eth1`.

ample anecdotal evidence supporting the existence of this difficulty on firewall mailing lists such as Firewall Wizards (1997–2003) and, indirectly, in the amount of documentation devoted to explaining the use of direction-based filtering.

To a firewall administrator, IP addresses are usually split into two disjoint sets: "inside" invariably means "my protected network" and "outside" is the rest of the Internet. Traffic directions such a "inbound" draw their meaning from this dichotomy. When there are other networks involved, such as DMZs, the distinctions blur somewhat, because the DMZ can be viewed as part of either the inside or the outside. Still, an inbound flow of traffic is always understood to be traffic flowing from a less trusted IP address to a more trusted IP address, the latter being within the organization's perimeter.

To the firewall, however, "inbound on interface `eth0`" means "crossing interface `eth0` from the adjacent network into the firewall." This may completely contradict the user's notion of "inbound": If `eth0` connects the firewall to the internal, protected network, then "inbound on `eth0`" is actually "outbound" traffic (see Figure 4). Furthermore, the *same* outbound traffic is both "inbound on `eth0`" and "outbound on `eth1`," assuming that `eth1` is the external interface. This discrepancy makes it very confusing for firewall administrators to use the packet direction correctly.

Note that the difficulty is not merely syntactic or specific to a particular firewall vendor's configuration language. A typical firewall is not aware of the levels of trust given to the networks attached to each of its interfaces. Absent of such global knowledge, the *only* way to specify a direction for traffic flowing through the firewall is device-centric per interface. This implies that, *unavoidably*, the definitions in the firewall configuration language will often clash with the users' understanding. Wool (2004b) includes a detailed critique of several vendor's approaches to direction-based filtering and suggests possible improvements.

## ADVANCED FIREWALL MANAGEMENT
### Higher Level Configuration

As we have seen already, firewall configuration is a difficult task for humans to do well, as evidenced by the poor state of firewall configurations observed in Wool (2004a). A significant part of the problem is that the configuration is done at a very low level of abstraction, dealing with IP addresses (or groups) and services, with no higher level of abstraction available. Because the syntax and semantics of the rules and their ordering depend on the firewall product/vendor, this is akin to the dark ages of software, where programs were written in assembly language and thus the programmer had to know all the idiosyncrasies of the target processor.

These problems get even worse for medium or large companies, which use more than a single firewall, or use routers for internal packet filtering tasks. These filtering devices divide the company's intranets into multiple *zones*. In this case, the security policy is typically realized by *multiple* rule bases, located on multiple firewalls that connect the different zones to each other. Thus, the interplay between these rule bases must be carefully examined so as not to introduce security holes. It is easy to see how rapidly the complexity of designing and managing these rules grows, as intranets get more complex.

The *Firmato* prototype (Bartal, Mayer, Nissim, & Wool, 2004) was built to address these difficulties. *Firmato* is a multivendor firewall rule compiler. Its input comprises a security policy and a description of the network topology on which the policy is to be enforced. This information is written in *Firmato*'s model description language (MDL). The compiler parses this input, transforms the data through several compilation phases, and produces firewall rules in the supported vendor's configuration languages. *Firmato* has the following distinguishing properties:

- Separate the security policy design from the firewall/router vendor specifics. This allows a security administrator to focus on designing an appropriate policy without worrying about firewall rule complexity, rule ordering, and other low-level configuration issues. It also enables a unified management of network components from different vendors and a much easier transition when a company switches vendors.

- Separate the security policy design from the actual network topology. This enables the administrator to maintain a consistent policy in the face of intranet topology changes. Furthermore, this modularization also allows the administrator to reuse the same policy at multiple corporate sites with different network details, or to allow smaller companies to use default/exemplary policies designed by experts.

- Generate the firewall configuration files automatically from the security policy, simultaneously, for multiple gateways. This reduces the probability of security holes introduced by hard-to-detect errors in firewall-specific configuration files.

- Automatically assign directions to all the rules, through the use of a *routing aware* algorithm. This implies that antispoofing is turned on all the time, and requires no user intervention. Therefore, the *Firmato* approach side-steps the whole usability issue associated with direction-based filtering, by letting the compiler compute the correct direction for each rule.

In Bartal et al. (2004) the authors describe their modeling framework and algorithms. They report that a prototype system was built and supported several commercially available firewall products. This prototype was used to control an operational firewall for several months. It seems that the *Firmato* approach is an important step toward streamlining the process of configuring and managing firewalls, especially in complex, multifirewall installations.

## Firewall Analysis

Understanding the deployed firewall policy can be a daunting task. Administrators today have no easy way of answering questions such as "can I telnet from here to there?" or "from which machines can our DMZ be reached, and with which services?" or "what will be the effect of adding this rule to the firewall?" These are basic questions that administrators need to answer regularly to perform their jobs, and sometimes more importantly, to explain the policy and its consequences to their management. There are several reasons why this task is difficult, including the following:

1. Firewall configuration languages tend to be arcane, very low level, and highly vendor specific.
2. Vendor-supplied GUIs require their users to click through several windows in order to fully understand even a single rule: at a minimum, the user needs to check the IP addresses of the source and destination fields, and the protocols and ports underlying the service field.
3. Firewall rule bases are sensitive to rule order. Several rules may match a particular packet, and usually the first matching rule is applied—so changing the rule order, or inserting a correct rule in the wrong place, may lead to unexpected behavior and possible security breaches.
4. Alternating PASS and DROP rules create rule bases that have complex interactions between different rules. What policy such a rule base is enforcing is hard for humans to comprehend when there are more than a handful of rules.
5. Packets may have multiple paths from source to destination, each path crossing several filtering devices. To answer a query the administrator would need to check the rules on all of these.

The Fang research prototype (Mayer, Wool, & Ziskind, 2000) was designed and built to address these difficulties. This work was subsequently commercialized into the Firewall Analyzer (Algorithmic Security Firewall Analyzer, 2004; Wool, 2001), which currently support several of the leading firewall vendors. The design goals for these systems were as follows:

1. Use an adequate level of abstraction: The administrator should be able to interact with the tool on the level at which the corporate security policy is defined or expressed. In a large network, the tool should allow the administrator to quickly focus on important security aspects of testing.
2. Be comprehensive: A partial or statistical analysis is not good enough. A firewall with even a single badly written rule is useless if an attacker discovers the vulnerable combination of IP addresses and port numbers.
3. Do no harm: Policy analysis should be possible without having to change or tinker with actual network configurations, which in turn might make the network vulnerable to attacks.
4. Be passive: Policy analysis should not involve sending packets, and should complement the capabilities of existing network scanners.

The first generation Fang prototype (Mayer et al., 2000) interacted with the administrator through a query-and-answer session, using a simple GUI. This GUI let the administrator compose a query through a collection of menus, and displayed the results of the query. Fang demonstrated, for the first time, that static firewall policy analysis was possible and an important task. However, the most important lesson learned from Fang was that users often *do not know what to query*.

Therefore, in subsequent generations of the tool, human input is limited to providing the firewall configuration, and the analysis is fully automated from that point on. Instead of a manually written topology file, the Firewall Analyzer accepts the firewall's routing table. Instead of the point-and-click interface, it automatically issues all the "interesting" queries. Work on this topic is still ongoing, and improvements are added at a rapid pace. The reader is referred to Algorithmic Security Firewall Analyzer (2004) and Wool (2001) for further details.

## GLOSSARY

**Action**  The decision of a firewall rule, such as Pass, Drop, Reject, and Log.

**Basic Packet Filter**  A firewall or router that matches packets only according to their header fields, without keeping any state.

**Demilitarized Zone**  A subnet that is accessible from outside the perimeter (usually contains public servers) and is semitrusted.

**Direction-Based Filtering**  The firewall's ability to match packets based on the network interface card they are crossing and the direction (into or out of the firewall).

**First-Match Semantics**  Among all the rules that match a given packet, take the action stated in the first rule.

**Packet Matching**  The process of comparing packets to all the rules in the rule base, and optionally to the state, and finding the action to take.

**Policy** The organization's choices of which types of packets are allowed to cross into or out of the network. Encoded as a rule base.

**Rule Base** An ordered list of rules that instruct the firewall what to do. Each rule describes a set of packets and an action for this set.

**Spoofing** Forging the source IP address of a packet to bypass the firewall rules or to avoid detection.

**Stateful Firewall** A firewall that matches packets based on their headers and also on the state (or history), such as whether the packet belongs to an open flow.

**Zone** A collection of subnets, which are located behind one of the firewall's network interface cards.

**Zone Spanning** A subnet definition that contains IP addresses, which are located in more than one zone. Considered harmful.

## CROSS REFERENCES

See *Firewall Architectures; Firewall Basics; Proxy Firewalls.*

## REFERENCES

Algorithmic Security Firewall Analyzer. (2004). Retrieved January 2, 2005, from http://www.algosec.com

Bartal, Y., Mayer, A., Nissim, K., & Wool, A. (2004, November). Firmato: A novel firewall management toolkit. *ACM Transactions of Computer Systems, 22*(4): 381–420 [An earlier version appeared *in Proceedings of the 20th IEEE Symposium on Security and Privacy,* 1999.]

Bellovin, S. M. (1989). Security problems in the TCP/IP protocol suite. *Computer Communications Review, 19*(2), 32–48.

Benzedrine. (2004). *OpenBSD packetfilter (pf)*. Retrieved January 2, 2004, from http://www.benzedrine.cx/pf.html

CERT Coordination Center. (2003, August 11). *CERT advisory CA-2003-20: W32/Blaster Worm*. Retrieved January 2, 2004, from http://www.cert.org/advisories/CA-2003-20.html

Chapman, D. W., & Fox, A. (2001). *Cisco secure PIX firewalls*. New York: Cisco Press.

Cheswick, W. R., Bellovin, S. M., & Rubin, A. (2003). *Firewalls and Internet security: Repelling the wily hacker* (2nd ed.). Boston: Addison Wesley.

Edmead, M. T. (2002, January). Egress filtering. *TISC Insight, 4*(1). Retrieved January 2, 2004, from http://www.tisc2001.com/newsletters/41.html

Ferguson, P., & Senie, D. (2000, May). *Network ingress filtering: Defeating denial of service attacks which employ IP source address spoofing* (Internet Engineering Task Force RFC 2827). Retrieved January 2, 2004, from http://www.ietf.org/rfc/rfc2827.txt [An earlier document is RFC 2267, January 1998.]

Firewall Wizards. (1997–2004). Electronic mailing list. Retrieved January 2, 2004, from http://honor.icsalabs.com/mailman/listinfo/firewall-wizards

Fulmer, C. (2004). *Firewall product overview*. Retrieved January 3, 2004, from http://www.thegild.com/firewall/

Held, G., & Hundley, K. (1999). *Cisco access lists*. New York: McGraw-Hill.

Mayer, A., Wool, A., & Ziskind, E. (2000). Fang: A firewall analysis engine. In *Proceedings of the IEEE Symposium on Security and Privacy* (pp. 177–187). New York: IEEE Press.

Moore, D. et al. (2003). The spread of the Sapphire/Slammer worm. Retrieved January 2, 2004, from http://www.caida.org/outreach/papers/2003/sapphire/sapphire.html

Netfilter. (2004). *Linux netfilter/iptables*. Retrieved January 2, 2004, from http://www.netfilter.org/

Reed, D. (2005). *FreeBSD IP filter*. Retrieved January 2, 2004, from http://coombs.anu.edu.au/~avalon/

Rovniagin, D., & Wool, A. (2004). The geometric efficient matching algorithm for firewalls. In *Proceedings of the 23rd Convention of IEEE*. New York: IEEE Press.

Rubin, A., Geer, D., & Ranum, M. (1997). *Web security sourcebook*. New York: John Wiley & Sons.

SANS Institute. (2000, February). *Egress filtering, v. 0.2*. Global Incident Analysis Center. Retrieved January 2, 2004, from http://www.incidents.org/protect/egress.php

SANS Institute. (2003). *The twenty most critical Internet security vulnerabilities, v. 4.0*. Retrieved January 2, 2004, from http://www.sans.org/top20/

Welch-Abernathy, D. D. (2002). *Essential CheckPoint Firewall 1: An installation, configuration, and troubleshooting guide*. Boston: Addison-Wesley.

Wool, A. (2001). Architecting the Lumeta firewall analyzer. In *Proceedings of the 10th Usenix Security Symposium* (pp. 85–97). New York: Usenix Association.

Wool, A. (2002, August). Combating the perils of port 80 at the firewall. *The Magazine of USENIX & SAGE, 27*(4), 44–45.

Wool, A. (2004a). A quantitative study of firewall configuration errors. *IEEE Computer 37*(6): 62–67.

Wool, A. (2004b). The use and usability of direction-based filtering in firewalls. In *Computers & Security 23*(6): 459–468. New York: Elsevier.

Zwicky, E. D., Cooper, S., & Chapman, D. B. (2000). *Building Internet firewalls* (2nd ed.). Sebastopol, CA: O'Reilly.

# Proxy Firewalls

John D. McLaren, *Murray State University*

## INTRODUCTION

As network security issues continue to dominate the world of networking, new devices and software are constantly surfacing. Proxy firewalls are just one of the players that are receiving more attention lately. Proxies have been around for a long while, but their primary purpose historically has been to serve as Web accelerators.

The endless variety of the application layer contents make it ripe for potential security vulnerabilities; there is a need for more detailed traffic analysis. Things such as viruses and spam cannot be discovered using simple packet-filtering firewalls. The solution to issues such as these is application layer and proxy firewalls.

Like most hot subjects, proxies are often misunderstood. There is considerable variation in the definition of firewalls that work at the application layer. Proxy firewalls not only provide the capability to examine the application data in detail, making decisions in terms of whether to drop or accept a packet, but they also are able to modify the packet. Proxy firewalls stand between the client and the server, providing a totally separate connection.

## PROXY TERMINOLOGY

In the modern telecommunications world of technobabble, there are many terms that are used in a variety of connotations. *Proxy* is one of these terms. Before we begin a discussion of what might be considered a proxy firewall, it might be a good idea to clear the air on the potential contexts that will be involved. This section attempts to define some of the key terms, and later sections further distinguish proxy firewall functions through examples.

### Houston, We Have a Proxy

In August 2003, Russian cosmonaut Yuri Malenchenko married Ekaterina Dmitriev. However, it was an unconventional wedding. Yuri was on board the International Space Station, and said his "I dos" via videolink. The wedding was a modern example of a proxy marriage—a wedding ceremony where a third party stands in for one or the other of the principals.

Using a video link-up between the station and the wedding hall, Malenchenko, with his best man, fellow astronaut Ed Lu, appeared in his formal flight uniform. Following Texas' proxy marriage law, the marriage ceremony proceeded with one of Yuri's friends, a Russian flight surgeon, standing in for him in Houston. There was even a life-size cutout of the groom placed at the reception to great the guests.

Throughout history, proxies have stood in for their counterparts. In the 18th and early 19th centuries, when duels were fairly common, it was traditional to select someone to act as a proxy for one of the principals. In the case that one of principals was rendered incapable of performing their part, the proxy would stand in. The practice of proxy weddings was quite common in WWI, when soldiers returned to combat after a short leave only to discover that their loved one was with child. A proxy wedding helped save the bride's reputation. Napoleon married Marie Louise, his second wife, by proxy in 1810 and Italian immigrants to Australia were marrying girls back in Italy by proxy until as late as 1976.

What does all this have to do with proxy firewalls? Not a lot. However, with today's confusion about telecommunication and networking terminology, it is good to have one definition that we can depend on. The term *proxy* is used in a variety of connotations, and its definition changes almost daily. Proxy is in the same nebulous position as terms such as *firewall* and *gateway*. New software and new appliances are appearing regularly that use the term *proxy* when describing their functions—such as proxy firewall.

Topics such as state firewalls can be accurately described in terms of their functions. The topic of proxy firewalls will encompass a much wider range of definitions. Therefore, this chapter spends some considerable time providing the user with a set of terms used to help distinguish one proxy firewall from another.

One key characteristic distinguishes a proxy from any other firewall. Like the stand-in groom from the Malenchenko wedding, the proxy *stands in* for one of the parties. In our connotation, the parties are the client and the server. The proxy will be between them so that there is never any direct communications between the client and the server. *This is a very important distinction. Whenever the term proxy is used, it should at least imply that the system being discussed can serve as an intermediary between client and server. Throughout the rest of the chapter, this characteristic is referred to as the SiG (Stand-in Groom).*

## Definition of Firewall

Because the topic of this chapter is proxy firewalls, let us also define *firewall*. It is generally accepted that a firewall is a system that sits between two networks—one assumed to be trusted and the other untrusted. The system monitors traffic passing between the two networks. In this context, firewalls are choke points—a place in a network topology through which traffic is forced to pass. This allows the traffic to be analyzed and manipulated, based on the analysis. Certainly, if a proxy has the SiG characteristic that we have defined previously, it must also be a choke point. Therefore, any proxy is also a firewall by definition. As shown, it may not be a choke point for *all* traffic between two networks, but certainly it will serve that function for *some* traffic.

## The Application Layer Gateway

In some sources, we find an application layer gateway defined as a machine that is surrounded by a firewall on either side, and neither of the firewalls will forward any packets unless those packets are to or from the gateway. For example, to transfer a file from inside to outside, the file must first be transferred to the gateway machine, at which point the file is accessible to be read by the outside. To access any machine on the outside, you must first log into the gateway. In this scenario, the application is ultimately performed by the gateway, so the gateway can be said to be working at the application layer. However, the gateway is *not* performing as a real-time SiG—so some may not refer to it as a proxy. An SMTP server falls into this category, performing a store-and-forward type operation.

## The Application Layer Firewall

An application layer firewall is simply a firewall that has the capabilities to look into the application layer of a packet. This is often a characteristic that is associated with proxies by default. Because a proxy is a SiG, it must evaluate the application request by the client and translate that request into its own application request to the server.

Many firewalls have the capability to analyze application-layer information. Even iptables has the ability to associate related FTP data connections, which requires at least partial analysis of the FTP control application data. So, in itself, application-layer analysis does not identify a

proxy, and an application-layer firewall will not necessarily be a proxy.

## The NAT-ing Firewall

A NAT-ing firewall (network address translation) will substitute its IP for the client's IP (Layer 3). A PAT-ing firewall (port address translation) will do the same for ports (Layer 4). Because a proxy is creating an entirely new conversation with the server on behalf of the client, the source IP address must obviously be changed. It is most likely that the source port will be replaced as well. Therefore, a proxy server performs NAT functions by default. Actually, the proxy takes this process one step further because it creates an entirely new connection (e.g., new three-way handshake). In most cases, this means entirely new header contents for Layers 3 and up.

In summary then, let us go forth with the following understanding: A proxy is a SiG. Because the proxy is relaying application requests, it must work at the application layer, and it must be a choke point (firewall) for at least *some types* of traffic. In the next section, we look at more specific characteristics of proxies and then take a look at the different categories.

## WHY AND WHEN TO USE A PROXY
### Goals of a Proxy Firewall

A proxy is an application that accesses a server *for* the client. It serves to isolate a client from a server. One of the primary goals of using a proxy server is that both parties (client and server) avoid a peer-to-peer connection. Strictly speaking, a proxy server is both a server *and* a client.

The process is fairly simple:

1. The client accesses the proxy with a request that is to be forwarded to the server.
2. The proxy then forwards the request to the server, making changes to the request as specified by the proxy configuration.
3. The server responds to the request by sending information back to the proxy.
4. The proxy then forwards that reply on to the client, again making changes to the response as specified by the proxy rule set.

To the user, it appears that he or she is talking directly to the real server. To the server, it appears that he or she is talking to the proxy and has no knowledge of the real user.

Proxy servers are often bundled with firewalls, creating a bit of confusion as to which does what. The primary differences can be summarized in the layers at which each works. A packet-filtering firewall operates at the network and transport layers of the OSI model, whereas proxy servers work at the application layer.

Each layer of a packet adds complexity to the packet. The more layers a packet has, the more permutations that are possible and the more complex the software that analyzes it must be. The Layer 3 and Layer 4 headers are very predictable and have only a finite set of possible permutations. Application-layer protocols have considerably more possible entries, and these entries can often be extended in an indefinite fashion. Once the application layer is involved, the possible permutations grow extremely large, and analyzing the information therein can become quite involved and consume considerable processor time.

Packet filters check each packet against a set of filtering rules based on information contained in Layers 3 and 4. For example, it is an easy matter for a packet-filtering firewall to block traffic based on source or destination IP or the service involved. Packet-filtering firewalls have the advantage of speed when compared to a proxy firewall. One situation that should definitely be avoided is using a proxy firewall when a packet-filtering or stateful firewall could accomplish the same task.

Proxy servers are different from a packet-filtering or stateful firewall in that they break the direct link between client and server. They start by performing network address translation, mapping the client's IP address to the address of the proxy. They continue to analyze the client's requests embedded in the application layer, as well as the server's responses. Because they operate at the application layer of the OSI model, proxy servers are capable of much more detailed analysis. A given proxy will be a specialist in a single application protocol such as HTTP, FTP, SMTP/POP, NNTP, and so on. The degree to which a proxy can be configured is only limited to the same extent as the potential application layer content.

## Advantages of Proxy Firewalls

Before considering the use of a proxy firewall, one should review a proxy's potential capabilities versus the needs of the network in terms of both security and functionality. The following is a list of functions that proxies are most often used to accomplish.

### Conceal Internal Clients

Because the proxy creates a new connection for the client, the client's identity is concealed. This type of function resembles NAT. However, proxies go beyond simply remapping IP addresses. The headers in the packets coming from a proxy are totally rebuilt based on the proxy's TCP stack. Using proxies will help reduce the threat from hackers who monitor network traffic in an attempt to gather information about computers on internal networks. NAT and PAT firewalls are simpler systems and can accomplish this task rather well. Therefore, if this is the *only* reason you are considering a proxy firewall, you should probably rethink your plan.

### Block URLs

This is one of the conceived uses of Web proxy servers. The goal is to block users from visiting certain URLs, which are specified as either IP addresses or DNS names. However, this function is very unreliable unless the administrator is diligent. He or she must keep up with domain name changes and their IP counterparts. Just entering domain names in a "forbidden list" will still allow users to enter IP addresses directly into their browser. A packet-filtering firewall can block access to given IPs or domain names.

Unless you need to be able to look at the exact complete URL being accessed, a packet-filtering firewall would be a more efficient solution.

### Block and Filter Content

In terms of internal network security, it is important to prevent malicious content from entering. This is an application firewall function. Proxy firewalls can be configured to scan for potential damaging payloads, such as Java applets, ActiveX controls, or any executables. This filtering can be extended to spam as well (although spam is much harder to define and fingerprint).

### Improve Security

With proxies, security policies can be much more powerful and flexible because of all of the information in the packets can be used to write the rules that determine how packets are handled by the gateway. A variety of time-based access rules is available with most proxies.

### Authenticate Users

Most modern proxy products provide at least some form of user authentication. The simplest provision might utilize the operating system's authentication capabilities, but most today will provide alternate, standardized choices. Many firewalls (and even some routers) can provide user authentication services as well.

### Perform More Advanced Logging

Because proxy servers examine application-layer data, they are privy to more information—and any combination of this additional information can be logged. This additional logging can help identify and isolate new security problems, such as application-level attacks. Some proxy systems even provide a degree of intrusion detection system (IDS)—notifying the administrator when a particular signature is discovered.

### Improve Performance

Actually, proxy servers were originally developed as a way to speed up communications on the Web by storing a site's most popular pages in cache. Proxies can be used as intermediate caching servers and as load-balancing systems—providing controlled access to a server bank. Caching proxies can also work in "clusters" to provide more efficient Web content delivery throughout areas of the Internet. Under this same category, a proxy firewall can actually be used to improve network throughput when properly coupled with a packet-filtering firewall. The firewall can simply route the packets that have to do with a given application directly to the proxy. This will allow the firewall filters to be less complex. The total number of rules does not decrease, but the load is distributed.

## Disadvantages of Proxy Firewalls

Let us now take a look at the other side of the coin—what negative issues are normally associated with proxy firewalls?

## Reduced Performance

If throughput is already an issue, you probably do not want to put a proxy in the path of all traffic. Proxies can severely reduce performance. Newer technologies have helped to reduce this issue considerably, but it is still a basic fact that proxies must evaluate a lot of information—requiring more system resources than a packet-filtering firewall.

## A Proxy for Each Application

An application-layer proxy firewall is typically written around a single application. In general, you will need a different proxy for each application you intend to proxy (although they can run on the same machine). There will be some lag time between when a new application appears and when a proxy server is available for that application.

## Not Immune to OS Problems

A proxy server runs on an existing platform (e.g., Linux and Microsoft). Therefore, it is dependent on that operating system's strength and vulnerable to its weaknesses. If the system needs to be patched, the proxy will have to go down. Some specialized proxies are starting to appear as appliances.

## Complex

Proxy firewalls are inherently more complex than their packet-filtering and even stateful counterparts. Most proxies can be set up and running easily in their default configuration, but to use them in a more advanced configuration often introduces a considerable level of complexity. If you employ a proxy to serve your clients, you will also need to configure the clients.

## Single Point of Failure

If your proxy firewall is situated such that all traffic is routed through it, it will obviously be a key point of failure. Most often, a proxy is set up to handle traffic for only a specific application or set of applications. We look at several topological arrangements under "System Configuration."

## Inability to Handle Encryption

A proxy cannot handle authentication and encryption because the keys are held by the end nodes.

# PROXY CHARACTERISTICS AND CAPABILITIES

## Building a Proxy

To better understand the characteristics of a proxy, it might help to examine the functions that are desirable in a proxylike system. Keep in mind our key characteristic of a proxy (SiG): the proxy is an intermediary between the client and the server. The intermediary will fashion the client's requests into a format that is satisfactory to the proxy.

## Proxy Firewall Characteristics

Let us begin by dividing the desired capabilities into two categories—those that are fairly easy to incorporate and those that are more complex.

Those capabilities that are easily realized are as follows:

- User authentication: our system more than likely will require some sort of user authentication whenever they log in. We could customize this in a variety of ways—selecting the encryption technique and setting requirements in terms of password characteristics.

- User account control: it may be that we would like to control the available applications based on individual users. This is a standard control in any multiuser system. Users can be restricted in terms of which programs they are allowed to launch, what times and days they are allowed to use the system, and what percentage of the system resources they can consume.

- Logging: standard system logging can be employed, allowing us to record the applications run by each user, time of day, and length of time they spend using each application, as well as nonapproved operations that they may be attempting.

- Encryption: if we employ a system such as Secure Shell for users logging in, we will have encryption on the local network to prevent advantages that might be obtained from sniffing and session hijacking. Externally, we can employ a variety of systems, such as Secure Sockets Layer or even VPNs in selected situations.

All of these capabilities are fairly easy to implement in a system such as Linux. PAM modules can be customized to provide authentication and account control. The standard syslog system can be set up to provide adequate logging, and SSH can provide our local encryption.

Those capabilities *not* so easily realized are as follows:

- Better logging: when we analyze the system's built-in logging capabilities, we realize that we can easily determine when a user is running a particular application—such as a browser. However, the basic logging does not provide the facility for actually determining *what or where* the user is browsing. In other words, there is no built-in, easy-to-use logging facility that allows us to log application-layer information. Most browser clients keep a browse history, which is stored in the user's home directory by default. The administrator could customize this setting, making the browse history either accessible only by the admin or at least copied to a file that is only accessible to admin. This allows us to determine and log the destination IPs and URLs but still no detailed application data.

- More granular restrictions: restricting access to particular sites means that our system will probably have to include firewall capabilities of some sort. In a Linux system, this might be accomplished through ipchains or iptables. The addition of firewall functionality will further increase our logging capabilities as well.

- Log management: the result of all this logging will obviously generate a mass of disjunctive logs that must be somehow assimilated chronologically as well as divided by user. A set of customized scripts could undoubtedly accomplish this for the administrator but at the expense of time and effort.

- User interface: providing a seamless user interface would not be so simple. The user may not be familiar with the pseudoproxy system at all, and the tools available for Internet access may be as foreign as well. To overcome this problem and make the connection seamless would require custom applications. For example, a custom browser would be written that performed automatic login and automatic startup of the browser application on the pseudoproxy and then received and displayed the returning information. The custom application would be designed to look and act just like the browser application to which the user was accustomed. (There would *still* be an obvious delay, however.)

- Application-layer filtering: with all of these enhancements to our pseudoproxy, there is still one major difference. There is no application-layer analysis. We have *control* over the application, who can run it, how it is run, and when it is run but no real analysis of the actual application-layer data. For example, in the case of Web browsing, we may wish to monitor and control the sites visited as well as the types of material retrieved. Adding a packet-filtering or stateful firewall (e.g., iptables) could monitor, and control Web access based on site identity (i.e., domain names and IP addresses) but could not provide controls based on specific content at the application layer.

All of these characteristics are typical of the capabilities of a proxy firewall. Some of the same characteristics are available without using specific proxy application software, but many are not. In addition, the system designed from the beginning as a proxy will integrate these functions in a more efficient fashion.

One other note: we are demanding much more of the system when its set up as this pseudoproxy because it must actually run the application for each user as well as deliver the full content (including graphics) to the user. With a standard proxy server, the application is run on the user's system and only the connection is managed by the proxy.

## Summary of Capabilities

- Those capabilities that are also achievable with a packet filter are as follows:
  - Source/destination IP address
  - Current day/time
  - Destination port
  - Protocol (FTP, HTTP, SSL)
- Those achievable with only application-layer information are as follows:
  - Source/destination domain
  - Regular expression match of requested domain
  - Words in the requested URL
  - Words in the source or destination domain
  - Command/method (e.g., FTP PORT, HTTP GET, or HTTP POST)
  - Client/browser type
- Those achievable through OS capabilities or additional applications are as follows:
  - Identification of user (e.g., use of the Ident protocol)
  - Username/password pair

This last category is mostly about identification and authentication—typically an important characteristic of a proxy system. A proxy server should never be used in a public environment (e.g., an ISP) without a sophisticated access control system. Ideally, the proxy server should not be used in *any* environment without some kind of basic authentication system. It is amazing how fast other Internet users will find your proxy and use it to relay requests through your cache or disguise their real identity.

The source IP address of a request that originates from a multiuser system will only identify the system itself, not the user specifically. To solve this problem, the *ident* protocol was created. The Ident protocol is a mechanism that can be used on any multiuser system to more positively identify the source of an incoming request. When the proxy accepts a connection, it can connect back to the multiuser system and find out which user just connected.

If you want to track Internet usage, it is best to get users to log into the proxy server whenever they want to access the Internet. You can then use a statistics program to generate per-user reports, no matter which machine on your network a person is using. User authentication can be custom code that is part of the proxy software, or it can utilize the operating system's user authentication tools or third-party modules could be used (PAM modules, for example). Any proxy administrator should inquire as to the type of authentication available on a proxy package that is being considered for use.

## Proxy Protocols

Because different Internet services require different protocols, the proxy application must be able to converse in the appropriate protocol(s). A proxy server may run only a single protocol to handle a single service, or it may run a variety of service protocols.

Each layer of a packet adds complexity to the packet. The more layers a packet has, the more permutations that are possible, and the more complex the software that analyzes it must be. If the application layer is involved, the possible permutations grow extremely large.

The Layer 3 and Layer 4 headers are very predictable and have only a very finite set of possibilities. The application-layer protocols have considerably more possible entries, and these entries can often be extended in an indefinite fashion. Therefore, the software that analyzes application-level protocols must be, by nature, considerably more complex.

The appearance of new application-layer protocols is quite commonplace. Notable examples recently include protocols for music, video, conferencing, and file sharing. The appearance of new applications provides a serious challenge for the proxy administrator that is endeavoring to keep his users satisfied while maintaining a given level of security. In many cases, there is not a proxy server available for a new application and the administrator has a limited set of choices:

- Write his/her own proxy server for the new application
- Do not permit the new application
- Permit the new application to run *around* the proxy

Off-the-shelf proxy systems are typically designed with a particular set of application protocols in mind (the minimum usually includes HTTP and FTP). It is important that any administrator entertaining the use of a proxy become aware of the restrictions that any given product might impose. Determine your application needs and then choose a proxy that will provide the necessary capabilities and flexibility.

## TYPES OF PROXIES

In this section, we continue our definitions by looking into current terminology concerning *types* of proxies. The following proxy-related systems are discussed:

- Store-and-forward
- Application-level proxy
- Circuit-level proxy
- Forward proxy
- Reverse proxy
- Proxy firewalls
- Caching/Web-caching proxy
- Proxy appliances/application filters

### Store-and-Forward Servers

Some services, such as SMTP, NNTP, and NTP, provide proxylike functions by default. These services are all designed so that messages (e-mail messages for SMTP, Usenet news postings for NNTP, and clock settings for NTP) are received by a server and then stored until they can be forwarded. In SMTP, the e-mail messages are forwarded directly to the e-mail message's destination. For NNTP and NTP, the messages are forwarded to all neighbor servers. Obviously, each of these servers creates a new connection, acting as a proxy for the original sender or server.

The primary difference between a store-and-forward server and a conventional proxy server is that one works in real time. The proxy server performs SiG services as they are requested. A store-and-forward server performs the requested services at its own convenience and the convenience of the recipient.

### Application versus Circuit-Level Proxies

An application-level proxy is one that is aware of the particular application and makes decisions based on the contents of the application layer. The circuit-level proxy completes the connection independent of the contents of the application layer.

At one end of the spectrum, an SMTP server that performs store-and-forward must be totally aware of the contents of the application data to deliver the e-mail. At the other end, a circuit-level proxy such as SOCKS will be concerned only with IP addresses and port numbers.

A circuit-level proxy is often referred to as a gateway. It is slightly more complex than a state firewall in that it *monitors* the sessions as they progress. A simple state firewall will add a session to its state table and then allow or reject future packets based on whether they match one of the entries. A circuit-level proxy will continue to monitor the traffic within an established state (circuit) to verify the transmission of additional packets.

Remember, even though the circuit-level proxy is *like* a state firewall, it is *still a proxy*. This means that

as a proxy, it will *stand between* the client and server (i.e., there is no direct connection between client and server).

Beyond this, there is a lot of disparity in exactly how deep into the packet the circuit-level proxy will venture. For example, WinGate 3.0 (which is based on SOCKS) is considered to be a circuit-level proxy; it uses only packet information from Layers 3 and 4 (source and destination ports indicating the application), whereas flags and sequence numbers are used to indicate the connection. Conversely, the Cisco series of PIX firewalls can (and often do) look into the application layer to maintain complex connections, such as FTP and H.323.

Circuit-level proxies are popular because once they are configured, they can be used to proxy most Internet protocols, such as IMAP, LDAP, POP3, SMTP, FTP, and HTTP. They can even be used to proxy Internet protocols secured with SSL.

Whereas SOCKS attempts to provide a single, general proxy, a system such as Trusted Information Systems Firewall Toolkit (TIS FWTK) provides individual proxies for the most common Internet services. The philosophy behind such a system is to use small separate programs for each application but at the same time employ a common configuration file.

TIS FWTK uses the destination port and the source address of the connection as an indicator of where the new connection should be sent. This means that the only way a client can specify a different destination is to connect to a different port on the proxy. Obviously, this makes *plug-gw* inappropriate for many types of services.

In general, the two terms (i.e., circuit level, application level) are really related to the *depth* to which a program looks into the packets. The term *proxy* can be applied to a variety of systems that typically scrutinize traffic more extensively than packet-filtering or state firewalls. Circuit-level proxies would be considered to be at the simplistic end of the range, and application-level proxies would be further up the chain of complexity.

Circuit-level proxies will not provide the level of monitoring and control of an application-level proxy, but they can be beneficial in many ways, as follows:

- Secures addresses from exposure: remember that even circuit-level proxies are *proxies* (i.e., they have the SiG characteristic). There is no direct connection between an application client and an application server. Proxy servers hide the address structure of the network and make it difficult to access confidential information.
- Offers a high degree of flexibility: because circuit-level proxies communicate at the session layer, they support a multiprotocol environment. As new Internet services are added, circuit-level proxies automatically support them. Also, configuring clients to work with circuit-level proxies is much simpler than application-level proxies. Client software no longer needs to be configured on a case-by-case basis. With Microsoft's Proxy Server, for example, once WinSock Proxy software has been installed onto a client computer, client software such as the Windows media player, Internet relay chat (IRC), or telnet will perform just as if it were directly connected to the Internet.

• Ease of configuration: although application-level proxies are considered highly secure, they do require a high degree of technical configuration and support. Circuit-level proxies were developed to resolve this problem.

## Forward versus Reverse Proxies

These two terms are used to describe whether the proxy is set up to protect the client or the server. If the proxy is set up to protect the client, it is said to be a *forward proxy*. The idea of the forward proxy began to appear with the infusion of firewalls as choke points between private trusted networks and the Internet. The proxies provided safe Internet access to inside users.

If the proxy is set up to protect the *server*, it is a *reverse proxy*. A reverse proxy is typically set up outside the firewall to represent a secure content server to clients on the Internet (or at least outside the trusted network). This will prevent unnecessary direct connections to the server's data. The reverse proxy can also improve performance by caching often-accessed information and by performing load balancing.

Proxies can be set up to provide both forward and reverse functions. However, physical placement of a proxy machine in terms of a company's firewall could dictate its use.

## Application Firewalls

Security threats on the Internet are constantly becoming more specialized. The Layer 3 and layer 4 vulnerabilities are finite. At this point, the vulnerabilities in these layers have been well published. Modern firewalls and educated administrators have evolved to defend against this finite set of possibilities. Now the attackers are turning to the packet's payload and new application-layer protocols—providing them with an almost infinite set of possibilities.

This attack specialization has spawned a variety of new products (both software and hardware) designed to deal with a particular category of attacks.

One example of specialized protection is in the area of viruses being delivered as part of the application payload—e-mail and Web content are two primary cases. Numerous software products have appeared over the last few years that can be integrated with an SMTP's functions. The payloads that are destined to be processed by an SMTP can be preexamined by one of these products to remove malicious content. In some circles, a product such as this is considered a specialized proxy firewall. As we have already discussed, an SMTP server is in itself a proxy and a choke point of sorts. Adding this new type of capability to the SMTP server certainly promotes it to application firewall level.

## Caching Proxies/Web-Caching Proxies

A Web cache sits between Web servers and the client(s). It monitors requests for Web objects (e.g., HTML pages, images, scripts). When the Web server responds with the object, the caching proxy saves a copy locally. Whenever another request arrives for the same object, the caching proxy will deliver the local copy, saving the time and bandwidth of an additional connection to the server. The advantages of a caching proxy are obvious: the client will realize a reduced latency, there will be less traffic generated, and the proxy will have fewer connections to create and maintain.

An organization might use a caching on a reverse proxy to help speed access to its own Web servers and as a type of load balancing. On a forward proxy, caching might be used to speed up access for local users as well as reduce bandwidth needs on the connection to the Internet.

## PROXY CONFIGURATIONS

As we have seen, proxy servers can provide a considerable level of security. However, these capabilities do not come easily. Proxy firewalls are among the most difficult systems to configure properly and, once configured, they cannot be left to run without constant attention. There are several configuration topics that must be carefully considered. This section breaks these topics into two categories: system configuration and network configuration.

## System Configuration

A proxy server will typically be installed on a dual-homed machine that has been thoroughly hardened. The machine will be connected in such a way that it is available on one side for the clients and the other side for the servers (more on the placement of the proxy in the next section). The proxy server evaluates requests from the client, deciding which of these to forward. Assuming a request is approved, the proxy will then communicate with the real server, forwarding the client's requests and then relaying the server's replies back to the client. In the situation where the proxy is the only machine communicating with the Internet, it is the only machine that requires a public IP address. Therefore, it is natural to use private address ranges for the internal machines.

Proxy servers are based entirely on software—no special hardware is required. Obviously, the speed of the system and its interfaces will ultimately determine how much traffic it can handle and how many connections it can proxy simultaneously. Sophisticated proxy systems avoid user frustration and their shortcomings when dealing with an unknown operating system. The user has the illusion of dealing directly with the server with a minimum of interaction with the proxy itself. The proxy server and proxy client software are exactly what makes this possible. There are a number of issues that will influence the selection, configuration, and topological placement of a proxy system.

### Scalability

Proxy servers must grow with network needs. Additional network clients will require additional bandwidth and more proxy connections. Multiple "parallel" proxies can be configured to handle increased load. Alternately, the administrator can configure individual proxies for different network segments, and these can be customized to support the particular segment's needs. Additionally, proxy servers can be divided according to the applications that they serve.

## New Applications

New network applications will require new proxy plug-ins or custom coding. Keep in mind that application-level proxies are configured to work on an application-by-application basis. When an application arises that is not supported by your proxy server, there are a few options, as follows:

- Disallow the service
- Upgrade the proxy (either through an available plugin or through custom coding)
- Route the service around the proxy (i.e., do not proxy that service)
- Use a circuit-level proxy for that service

## Client Configuration

Remember that application-level proxies will typically have two components—the proxy server component and the client component. The client software must know how to contact the proxy server rather than the designated server. Some applications come with this capability built in (e.g., CERN compatible browsers). However, most do not, particularly new applications. Alternately, a circuit-level proxy can be used (e.g., SOCKS), and a one-time client configuration will satisfy future applications.

The problem of client configuration is one of volume. Typically, the client component for a proxy aware application is simple to install and, once running, works without incident. However, installing the client component companywide might be a daunting task. Some proxy systems provide an automatic delivery mechanism to handle this task—typically through the client's browser.

Because of the considerable time requirement that client configuration entails, the administrator should evaluate prospective proxy packages with this task in mind.

## Caching Service

If your proxy is functioning as a reverse proxy for your own set of Web servers, or if you want to speed up Web responses for your clients, you will undoubtedly want to configure caching service. There are numerous considerations involved with caching.

Most proxy server packages provide an easy initial caching setup. As long as there are no problems, this default caching configuration may be satisfactory. If problems do arise, however, it can be extremely difficult to troubleshoot. To effectively judge the performance impact of proxy caches, one needs to take into consideration the interactions among HTTP, TCP, and the network environment. (Before attempting to configure and fine-tune a Web caching system, the administrator should review the work done in proxy cache testing by Cáceres, Douglis, Feldmann, Glass, and Rabinovich at the AT&T research labs.)

Another often-overlooked concern of caching is the legal aspects—caching copyrighted material. At this point in time, there is a lot of uncertainty regarding the rights of the Web page owners and those engaged in caching. Undoubtedly, there will be cases in the future that address this issue.

## Building the Firewall

Just as with any firewall, a proxy firewall will have a rule set—commonly referred to as the access control. Most of the proxy systems have some form of GUI for setting up the most common rules, such as URL filtering, but setting up detailed custom rule sets will typically be as complex as configuring any firewall. The more filtering that can be done *before* the packet reaches the proxy, the easier it will be to build the proxy's access-control rule set. Layers 3 and 4 filtering will be done more efficiently with a packet or stateful firewall.

Filtering application-layer information is considerably more difficult than filtering Layer 3 or 4 information because of the almost limitless range of possible content. Rules written with one intention in mind can often lead to unpredictable results. Only thorough testing can provide some degree of confidence in a particular rule set. As with packet-filtering firewalls, always start with the "deny all, accept by exception" philosophy. It will be far better to open new doors based on friendly user requests than to discover you have exploitable holes from unfriendly attackers.

## Proxy Vulnerabilities

In addition to the configuration considerations listed herein, the proxy administrator needs to be aware of the specialized vulnerabilities introduced through the use of *any* proxy system.

Whenever you have a proxy system that is a choke point for all traffic in and out of your network, you are setting up a single point of failure. If your proxy crashes, your network could be totally cut off from the Internet.

One might argue that such a problem exists with *any* choke point—such as a router or packet-filtering firewall. However, failover with these devices is a fairly common utility, built into the system by design. Proxy-server failover is typically a responsibility designated to the administrator. There are a number of ways to implement proxy failover:

- Provide multiple proxies working in parallel. This will also provide a degree of load-sharing capabilities
- Alternate routes can be provided that are enabled only when the proxy fails. This type of functionality would typically be realized by allowing the router to make the decision based on the "availability" of the proxy.
- Fix it. Both of the previous solutions obviously reduce the security of your network. If the proxy is considered to be an important security cornerstone in your network, then any time you allow traffic to go around it you are compromising your security intentions. Having a spare proxy, ready to come online (either automatically or manually) would be the best choice. Redundancy is an excellent solution on paper but often is economically unfeasible.

The proxy server stands to protect, but what protects the proxy server? As we have already mentioned, a proxy server should be installed on only the most robust and hardened system. Nonetheless, proxy servers can still fall victim to any number of problems that typically afflict

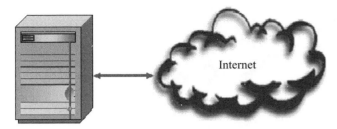

**Figure 1:** Single-homed proxy.

any complex application software. The most common of these today is the buffer overflow. The impact of a buffer overflow can vary from server malfunctioning to server crash to providing an attacker with a command line. As with all key systems and servers, the administrator must stay informed as to the latest vulnerabilities and apply all security patches.

Ideally, a single host would be used for each proxy service. This would make it easier to administer and control the service in question. Advancements in computer speed and storage have led to systems that provide multiple services on a single machine, however, and this has become the normal approach. Keep in mind the old adage about keeping all of your eggs in one basket. Putting a number of proxy services on a single host creates a single point of failure.

## Network Configuration

A proxy server can work with a single network connection (as in Figure 1). However, in the case of the single connection, traffic is not *forced* to go through the proxy. In some circles, such a setup would probably not qualify as a proxy *firewall*.

A common example of a proxy with a single network connection could be an SMTP server. The user sends a composed e-mail message to the SMTP server. The SMTP server then transfers the message to the appropriate destination SMTP server, which then passes the message to the recipient user. In this case, the SMTP servers at both ends are acting as proxy servers. Because they handle the e-mail messages, they can be used to perform filtering operations—shielding the recipient from dangerous or unwanted contents (malicious code or spam).

Alternately, a similar situation is shown in Figure 2. In this case, the proxy is probably multihomed (alternatively, it could have a single interface with two IP addresses), but both of its interfaces are connected to the Internet. Such a proxy can serve as what is typically referred to as an *anonymous proxy*. It provides a SiG for Internet users who would like to conceal their machine specifics, such as IP address, operating system, browser, and so on.

Because anonymous proxy servers are an SiG and create an entirely new connection on behalf of the user, they hide the user's IP address and other OS fingerprinting information. Most anonymous proxy servers can be used for any kind of services that are normally accessed through a browser, such as Web mail, Web chat rooms, FTP archives, and so on.

One might question why anonymous proxies even exist—what is the economical advantage? Following are some of the reasons such a service might be provided:

- As part of an ISP's service (helps to reduce their traffic as well, because of caching)
- As part of "bundled services," for example, with an e-mail account
- A way to deliver advertising or spam

The anonymous proxy service is also available as a charged service—anonymous proxying offered with a monthly fee—playing strong on the "anonymous" and "private" functions. There is even software that will do the work of finding an appropriate anonymous proxy server and then connecting to it automatically whenever one uses their browser.

Any user intending to use an anonymous proxy should be aware of one important issue—whether or not the proxy is truly anonymous. Though the proxy may create an entirely new connection, it may also include the user's IP in the payload of new packets. For example, in the following proxy connection where the proxy is forwarding a request to a Web site from a user, we see that part of the content is the user's IP (192.168.1.2 in this case):

```
X-Forwarded-For: 192.168.1.2..
```

Obviously, this type of service is not totally anonymous.

If the proxy is set up on a dual-homed machine, the machine may also be set to either provide IP forwarding (i.e., as a router). For example, in Figure 3, a dual-homed proxy is set up as the *only* path between a local network and the Internet. If the proxy does not allow IP forwarding, then the proxy software must process *all* packets, rebuild them, and deliver them. If IP forwarding is allowed (as illustrated in Figure 4), the packets can be *selectively* processed. The routing process occur first, and then packets are either routed *around* the proxy or *through* the proxy.

Finally, the proxy could be a separate machine that has packets selectively routed to it by a router or dual-homed bastion host, as shown in Figure 5. Functionally, this setup is the same as that shown in Figure 4, but now the functions are provided by individual machines, and the routing function will likely be provided by an appliance. Obviously, this arrangement could help alleviate the "single point of failure" issue discussed earlier.

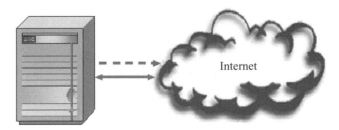

**Figure 2:** Anonymous proxy.

**Figure 3:**   Dual-homed proxy without IP forwarding.

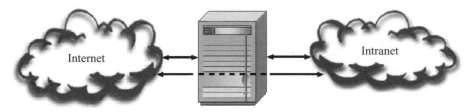

**Figure 4:**   Dual-homed proxy with IP forwarding.

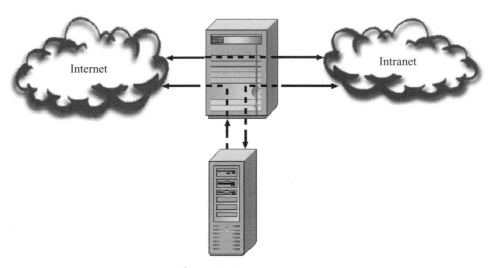

**Figure 5:**   Separate proxy.

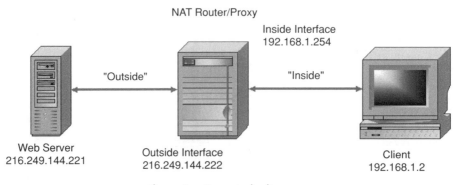

**Figure 6:**   Case-study diagram.

**Table 1.** NAT-Only Inside Traffic

| # | Source IP | Destination IP | Size | Protocol | Sequence # |
|---|-----------|----------------|------|----------|------------|
| 1 | 192.168.1.2 | 216.249.144.221 | 78 | TCP HTTP | S=1531784746 |
| 2 | 216.249.144.221 | 192.168.1.2 | 82 | TCP HTTP | S=2805436594 |
| 3 | 192.168.1.2 | 216.249.144.221 | 70 | TCP HTTP | S=1531784747 |
| 4 | 192.168.1.2 | 216.249.144.221 | 449 | TCP HTTP | S=1531784747 |
| 5 | 216.249.144.221 | 192.168.1.2 | 1494 | TCP HTTP | S=2805436595 |
| 6 | 192.168.1.2 | 216.249.144.221 | 70 | TCP HTTP | S=1531785126 |
| 7 | 192.168.1.2 | 216.249.144.221 | 78 | TCP HTTP | S=1542623850 |
| 8 | 216.249.144.221 | 192.168.1.2 | 82 | TCP HTTP | S=2805611041 |
| 9 | 192.168.1.2 | 216.249.144.221 | 70 | TCP HTTP | S=1542623851 |
| 10 | 192.168.1.2 | 216.249.144.221 | 601 | TCP HTTP | S=1542623851 |
| 11 | 216.249.144.221 | 192.168.1.2 | 1518 | TCP HTTP | S=2805611042 |
| 12 | 192.168.1.2 | 216.249.144.221 | 70 | TCP HTTP | S=1542624382 |
| 13 | 216.249.144.221 | 192.168.1.2 | 1518 | TCP HTTP | S=2805612490 |
| 14 | 192.168.1.2 | 216.249.144.221 | 70 | TCP HTTP | S=1542624382 |
| 15 | 216.249.144.221 | 192.168.1.2 | 206 | TCP HTTP | S=2805613938 |
| 16 | 192.168.1.2 | 216.249.144.221 | 70 | TCP HTTP | S=1542624382 |

# CASE STUDY: TRAFFIC ANALYSIS OF A PROXY OPERATION

This analysis compares a NAT-only connection with a connection through a proxy. The network layout is shown in Figure 6. In the first set of captures (Tables 1 and 2), the middle machine is serving as a NAT router. In the second set of captures (Tables 3 and 4), the middle machine is serving as a proxy. The operation performed is the same in both cases—the client is accessing a Web page on the server and then a cookie is transferred.

First let us analyze the general traffic pattern. The operation performed by the client was identical in both cases—a browser was used to open a single page on the server and a cookie was transferred. In the first set of captures, there is a NAT-ing router between the client and the server. In the second set, there is a proxy between the client and the server.

In both cases, the client's IP address is replaced by the router/proxy's IP address. The client is 192.168.1.2 and the Web server is 216.249.144.221. The outside IP address of the router/proxy is 216.249.144.222, and the inside address is 192.168.1.254. So, as the client's traffic is relayed onto the outside network, the 192.168.1.2 address is replaced by the 216.249.144.222 address. In both cases, the outside conversation is between .221 and .222.

The inside conversation varies, however. In the NAT-only scenario, the client uses the specific IP address of the server as the destination. When the proxy is involved, however, the client speaks directly to the proxy. This indicates that the client must be configured to translate any given set of browser requests into requests directed to the proxy. This is done in the browser settings.

The next thing that is quite obvious from the NAT-only scenario to the proxy scenario is the difference in the inside traffic. In the case of the proxy, there is considerably

**Table 2.** NAT-Only Outside Traffic

| # | Source IP | Destination IP | Size | Protocol | Sequence # |
|---|-----------|----------------|------|----------|------------|
| 1 | 216.249.144.223 | 216.249.144.221 | 78 | TCP HTTP | S=1531784746 |
| 2 | 216.249.144.221 | 216.249.144.223 | 82 | TCP HTTP | S=2805436594 |
| 3 | 216.249.144.223 | 216.249.144.221 | 70 | TCP HTTP | S=1531784747 |
| 4 | 216.249.144.223 | 216.249.144.221 | 449 | TCP HTTP | S=1531784747 |
| 5 | 216.249.144.221 | 216.249.144.223 | 1494 | TCP HTTP | S=2805436595 |
| 6 | 216.249.144.223 | 216.249.144.221 | 70 | TCP HTTP | S=1531785126 |
| 7 | 216.249.144.223 | 216.249.144.221 | 78 | TCP HTTP | S=1542623850 |
| 8 | 216.249.144.221 | 216.249.144.223 | 82 | TCP HTTP | S=2805611041 |
| 9 | 216.249.144.223 | 216.249.144.221 | 70 | TCP HTTP | S=1542623851 |
| 10 | 216.249.144.223 | 216.249.144.221 | 601 | TCP HTTP | S=1542623851 |
| 11 | 216.249.144.221 | 216.249.144.223 | 1518 | TCP HTTP | S=2805611042 |
| 12 | 216.249.144.221 | 216.249.144.223 | 1518 | TCP HTTP | S=2805612490 |
| 13 | 216.249.144.223 | 216.249.144.221 | 70 | TCP HTTP | S=1542624382 |
| 14 | 216.249.144.221 | 216.249.144.223 | 206 | TCP HTTP | S=2805613938 |
| 15 | 216.249.144.223 | 216.249.144.221 | 70 | TCP HTTP | S=1542624382 |
| 16 | 216.249.144.223 | 216.249.144.221 | 70 | TCP HTTP | S=1542624382 |

**Table 3.** Proxy Inside Traffic

| # | Source IP | Destination IP | Size | Protocol | Sequence # |
|---|---|---|---|---|---|
| | **Packets 1-3: Handshake between client and proxy** | | | | |
| 1 | 192.168.1.2 | 192.168.1.254 | 78 | IP TCP | S=2555300348 |
| 2 | 192.168.1.254 | 192.168.1.2 | 78 | IP TCP | S=2132876752 |
| 3 | 192.168.1.2 | 192.168.1.254 | 70 | IP TCP | S=2555300349 |
| | **Packets 4 and 5: Client request and proxy ACK** | | | | |
| 4 | 192.168.1.2 | 192.168.1.254 | 474 | IP TCP | S=2555300349 |
| 5 | 192.168.1.254 | 192.168.1.2 | 70 | IP TCP | S=2132876753 |
| | **Packets 6 and 7: Proxy response and client ACK** | | | | |
| 6 | 192.168.1.254 | 192.168.1.2 | 1518 | IP TCP | S=2132876753 |
| 7 | 192.168.1.2 | 192.168.1.254 | 70 | IP TCP | S=2555300753 |
| | **Packets 8-10: FIN Sequence** | | | | |
| 8 | 192.168.1.254 | 192.168.1.2 | 104 | IP TCP | S=2132878201 |
| 9 | 192.168.1.2 | 192.168.1.254 | 70 | IP TCP | S=2555300753 |
| 10 | 192.168.1.2 | 192.168.1.254 | 70 | IP TCP | S=2555300753 |
| | **Packets 11-13: Handshake between client and proxy for next connection** | | | | |
| | **This second connection is to transfer a cookie. Follows the same general pattern.** | | | | |
| 11 | 192.168.1.254 | 192.168.1.2 | 70 | IP TCP | S=2132878235 |
| 12 | 192.168.1.2 | 192.168.1.254 | 70 | IP TCP | S=2555300754 |
| 13 | 192.168.1.2 | 192.168.1.254 | 78 | IP TCP | S=2560783519 |
| 14 | 192.168.1.254 | 192.168.1.2 | 78 | IP TCP | S=2132834458 |
| 15 | 192.168.1.2 | 192.168.1.254 | 70 | IP TCP | S=2560783520 |
| 16 | 192.168.1.2 | 192.168.1.254 | 626 | IP TCP | S=2560783520 |
| 17 | 192.168.1.254 | 192.168.1.2 | 70 | IP TCP | S=2132834459 |
| 18 | 192.168.1.254 | 192.168.1.2 | 1518 | IP TCP | S=2132834459 |
| 19 | 192.168.1.2 | 192.168.1.254 | 70 | IP TCP | S=2560784076 |
| 20 | 192.168.1.254 | 192.168.1.2 | 104 | IP TCP | S=2132835907 |
| 21 | 192.168.1.2 | 192.168.1.254 | 70 | IP TCP | S=2560784076 |
| 22 | 192.168.1.254 | 192.168.1.2 | 1518 | IP TCP | S=2132835941 |
| 23 | 192.168.1.2 | 192.168.1.254 | 70 | IP TCP | S=2560784076 |
| 24 | 192.168.1.254 | 192.168.1.2 | 230 | IP TCP | S=2132837389 |
| 25 | 192.168.1.2 | 192.168.1.254 | 70 | IP TCP | S=2560784076 |
| 26 | 192.168.1.2 | 192.168.1.254 | 70 | IP TCP | S=2560784076 |
| 27 | 192.168.1.254 | 192.168.1.2 | 70 | IP TCP | S=2132837549 |
| 28 | 192.168.1.2 | 192.168.1.254 | 70 | IP TCP | S=2560784077 |

**Table 4.** Proxy Outside Traffic

| # | Source IP | Destination IP | Size | Protocol | Sequence # |
|---|---|---|---|---|---|
| | **Packets 1-3: Proxy Handshake with Web server** | | | | |
| 1 | 216.249.144.222 | 216.249.144.221 | 78 | TCP HTTP | S=2125937178 |
| 2 | 216.249.144.221 | 216.249.144.222 | 82 | TCP HTTP | S=3048224752 |
| 3 | 216.249.144.222 | 216.249.144.221 | 70 | TCP HTTP | S=2125937179 |
| | **Packet 4: Proxy relays client request to Web server** | | | | |
| 4 | 216.249.144.222 | 216.249.144.221 | 538 | TCP HTTP | S=2125937179 |
| | **Packets 5-8: Web server responds with data and proxy ACK's** | | | | |
| 5 | 216.249.144.221 | 216.249.144.222 | 1518 | TCP HTTP | S=3048224753 |
| 6 | 216.249.144.221 | 216.249.144.222 | 94 | TCP HTTP | S=3048226201 |
| 7 | 216.249.144.222 | 216.249.144.221 | 70 | TCP HTTP | S=2125937647 |
| 8 | 216.249.144.222 | 216.249.144.221 | 70 | TCP HTTP | S=2125937647 |
| | **Proxy relaying second request from client** | | | | |
| | **Connection continues and transfers cookie** | | | | |
| 9 | 216.249.144.222 | 216.249.144.221 | 690 | TCP HTTP | S=2125937647 |
| 10 | 216.249.144.221 | 216.249.144.222 | 1518 | TCP HTTP | S=3048226225 |
| 11 | 216.249.144.221 | 216.249.144.222 | 1518 | TCP HTTP | S=3048227673 |
| 12 | 216.249.144.221 | 216.249.144.222 | 230 | TCP HTTP | S=3048229121 |
| 13 | 216.249.144.222 | 216.249.144.221 | 70 | TCP HTTP | S=2125938267 |
| 14 | 216.249.144.222 | 216.249.144.221 | 70 | TCP HTTP | S=2125938267 |
| 15 | 216.249.144.222 | 216.249.144.221 | 70 | TCP HTTP | S=2125938267 |

more traffic. Also note the protocol. Despite the fact that the operation is intended to be HTTP (Web browser), the protocol in use is simply TCP. All data transferred between the client and the proxy is considered to be TCP payload. The extra traffic is primarily because of the fact that each request and response requires a new connection (and handshake), and there must be additional acknowledgments.

If you look at the NAT-only connection, you will see that the traffic on the outside connection precisely mirrors the traffic on the inside connection—right down to the packet sizes. The only thing changed about the packets is the source IP address. (Of course, the TTL is decremented and the data link layer information is modified.)

## Details on the Proxy Scenario

Packets 1–5 are used to connect to the proxy and send the request. The reader will note that the protocol listed on the inside traffic is just TCP. This is because the proxy is listening on Port 3128 rather than Port 80, and the protocol analyzer does not associate Port 3128 with HTTP protocol. However, the application-layer data in the packets from the client to the proxy are *identical* to those that would have been sent directly to the server.

Notice that the request from the proxy to the server (Packet 4) is 474 bytes. The same request in the NAT situation is 449 bytes. The difference is because of the fact that the destination-machine information must be included in the payload rather in the header.

The first part of the request in the NAT-only scenario is as follows:

```
GET / HTTP/1.1..
Connection: Keep-Alive
User-Agent: Mozilla/5.0 (compatible; Konqueror/2.2-11; Linux)
```

The first part of the request in the proxy scenario is as follows:

```
GET / http://216.249.144.221:80/ HTTP/1.1
Connection: Keep-Alive
User-Agent: Mozilla/5.0  (compatible; Konqueror/2.2-11; Linux)
```

The additional information is indicated in bold and totals 25 bytes (474–449).

After this initial request to the proxy server, the proxy server relays that request onto the Web server. This can be seen in the outside traffic, Packets 1–4. Packet 5 is then the response (which is too large to fit in one packet, so is extended to Packet 6).

Note also that as the request gets relayed from the proxy to the Web server, the request packet grows in size from 474 to 538 bytes. This difference is because of the fact that the proxy includes the client's IP address in the payload. Compare the original request to the relayed request as follows:

Inside (only the tail shown)
```
... ALJLJ
```
Outside (only the tail shown)
```
  ALJLJ
Via: 1.1 Inside1:3128 (Squid/2.4.STABLE1)
X-Forwarded-For: 192.168.1.2
Host: 216.249.144.221
Cache-Control: no-cache,  max-age=259200
Connection: keep-alive
```

All of the portion in bold is added by the proxy. The portion that is not bolded was part of the original request, but the proxy moved it to this position. The total additional bytes are 89. However, the additional 25 bytes that were part of the original request can now be removed, because the proxy is talking directly to the server. This leaves $89 - 25 = 64$ additional bytes ($538 - 474 = 64$).

This response received by the proxy is then passed onto the client. This traffic can be seen on this inside listing and is represented by Packets 6–9. Packets 6 and 8 are the actual data corresponding to Packets 5 and 6 of the outside traffic, and Packets 7 and 9 are the client's acknowledgements to the proxy. Note again the change in the size of the packets. The proxy received a 1,518-byte packet and a 94-byte packet, but it passed on a 1,518-byte packet and a 104-byte packet. This difference is because of a number of changes and additions the proxy makes to the packet. An example of one addition is shown below in the packet that is relayed (showing that the proxy is indicating that the information is *not* cached):

```
Cache-Control: p 43 61 63 68 65 2D 43 6F 6E 74 72 6F 6C 3A 20 70
rivate..X-Cache: 72 69 76 61 74 65 0D 0A 58 2D 43 61 63 68 65 3A
 MISS from Insid 20 4D 49 53 53 20 66 72 6F 6D 20 49 6E 73 69 64
e1..Proxy-Connec 65 31 0D 0A 50 72 6F 78 79 2D 43 6F 6E 6E 65 63
tion: keep-alive 74 69 6F 6E 3A 20 6B 65 65 70 2D 61 6C 69 76 65
......<!--... W 0D 0A 0D 0A 0D 0A 3C 21 2D 2D 0D 0A 09 20 20 57
```

The next transfer follows the same general procedure. One key issue to note, however, is that the proxy–client connection is closed in the interim. Packets 10–12 on the inside traffic represent the FIN handshake sequence. Packets 13–15 represent the three-way handshake for the next connection (cookie transfer). Note that the connection remains persistent on the outside traffic, never closing until Packets 13–15.

One last lesson that this capture can verify is the complete reconstruction of the connection. It is obvious that the source IP address is changed (in both the NAT-only and in the proxy scenarios), but note that the sequence numbers are also changed in the proxy scenario but remain the same in the NAT-only scenario.

# CONCLUSION

A proxy firewall is first and foremost a *proxy*. It serves as a SiG, standing between the server and the client. Because it establishes a new connection with the server on behalf of the client, the connection parameters (e.g., source IP and port) are replaced with its own. By default, the proxy performs a type of network address and port address translation (NAT and PAT).

Second, a proxy firewall is a firewall. Because certain types of traffic are funneled through the proxy, it is a choke point. It also makes decisions concerning clients' requests and servers' responses based on a rule set (i.e., access-control list).

A proxy should probably be considered if you need:

- More advanced control over client access to the Internet: use a forward proxy
- More advanced control over access to your servers: use a reverse proxy
- To improve performance: use a caching proxy
  - Better service for your clients when accessing outside servers
  - Better service for your customers accessing your servers
  - Reduced traffic

A proxy should probably *not* be considered if you just need:

- To shield internal machine information (e.g., IPs): consider a NAT-ing firewall
- To limit Internet access to clients based on the client identity, protocol, or time of day. These things can all be done more efficiently with packet-filtering and stateful firewalls.

When considering a proxy, there are some key issues of which you should be aware:

- Proxies are generally designed for a single application, and each new application will require a new proxy. Alternatively, you can use a circuit-level proxy, but it will not provide the same degree of control.
- Clients must be configured. No matter what type of proxy you use to protect your clients, the client machines will almost invariably need to be modified in some way.

Be sure to examine the client needs before committing to a particular proxy and include the time needed for setting up the clients in your implementation estimation.

- Logs can get out of hand and rule sets can get quite complex. For simple operations, default proxy settings will suffice, but when advanced functions are needed, defining rule sets can become intimidating and resultant logs can quickly become overwhelming.
- Caching issues can further complicate matters. If one of the reasons for using a proxy is performance, you will undoubtedly be caching. Like rule sets, default caching can be simple. However, advanced caching techniques are new and many aspects yet undocumented. Additionally, one should be aware of the legal ramifications involved.

In conclusion, before considering a proxy firewall, be sure your security needs warrant the additional effort and cost involved with such a decision. Do not underestimate the time necessary for both setup and maintenance. Finally, always check for the latest products available. There may be an application-layer firewall appliance specifically designed for your need.

# GLOSSARY

**Application-Layer Firewall**   Any firewall that has the capability to examine application-layer data.

**Application-Level Proxy**   A proxy that is designed around a particular application and has the capabilities to analyze traffic involved with that application.

**Caching Proxy**   A proxy that caches client requests. When identical requests occur, the proxy will provide the reply from its own cache.

**Circuit-Level Proxy**   A proxy that is not concerned with the application but simply creates an intermediate connection—separating client from server.

**Firewall**   A system that has the capability to analyze traffic passing through it, make decisions based on a set of rules that determine whether the traffic should be passed, dropped, or modified.

**Forward Proxy**   A proxy that is installed to protect the client.

**Network Address Translation**   Changing the source and/or destination IP address of a packet.

**Port Address Translation**   Changing the source and/or destination port of a packet.

**Proxy**   A system the stands between the client and a server, creating a new connection on behalf of the client.

**Proxy Appliance**   A proxy that is built as its own box. These are fairly new to the market and primarily supplement SMTP servers to check for viruses.

**Reverse Proxy**   A proxy that is installed to protect the server.

**Store-and-Forward Server**   A type of proxy that does not necessarily operate in real time, such as an SMTP server.

**Web Accelerator**   A proxy that is installed to provide improved Web performance, primarily by caching Web content.

# CROSS REFERENCES

See *Firewall Architectures; Firewall Basics; Packet-Filtering and Stateful Firewalls*.

## FURTHER READING

Chappell, L. A., & Tittel, E. D. (2002). *Guide to TCP/IP*. Course Technology.

Forouzan, B. A. (2003). *TCP/IP protocol suite*. New York: McGraw-Hill.

Holden, G. (2004). *Guide to Firewalls and Network Security*. Course Technology.

Kaufman, Perlman, & Speciner (1995). *Network Security*. Prentice Hall.

Larson, E. (2000). *Web Servers, Security, and Maintenance*. Prentice Hall.

Northcutt, Zeltser, Winters, Frederick, & Ritchey (2003). *Inside Network Perimeter Security*. New Riders.

Sheldon & Cox (2001). *Windows 2000 Security Handbook*. Osborne/McGraw-Hill.

Shinder, T. W., & Shinder, D. L. (2001). *ISA Server 2000*. Syngress.

Tipton & Krause (2000). *Information Security Management Handbook*. Auerbach.

Zeigler, R. L. (2002). *Linux Firewalls*. New Riders.

Zwicky, Cooper, & Chapman (2000). *Building Internet Firewalls*. Sebastopol, CA: O'Reilly.

*Online Material*
(all online sources were last accessed by this author in October 2003)
General Information:
http://wp.netscape.com/proxy/v3.5/evalguide/criteria.html
http://service.real.com/help/library/whitepapers/rproxy/htmlfiles/proxy22.htm
http://www.novell.com/info/collateral/docs/4621235.02/4621235.html
http://www.ctlinc.com/Pages/News_CTL.html
http://www.winproxy.com/english/products/AVStripper/pd_avstripper_en.asp

Installing and setting up the Linux proxy firewall:
http://new.linuxnow.com/docs/content/Firewall-HOWTO-html/Firewall-HOWTO-12.html

Shareware and Freeware Proxies:
http://www.hairy.beasts.org/fk/competition.html
http://www.solsoft.org/nsm/
http://www.obtuse.com/juniper/
http://www.opensourcefirewall.com/trex.html
http://www.delegate.org/delegate/

SOCKS:
http://www.socks.permeo.com/
http://www.inet.no/dante/

Squid was the proxy used to generate the captures included in this paper. For more information on setting up your own Squid proxy:
General Page:
http://www.squid-cache.org/

Programmer's Guide:
http://www.squid-cache.org/Doc/Prog-Guide/prog-guide.html
Used as a reverse proxy:
http://secinf.net/unix_security/Linux_Administrators_Security_Guide/Linux_Administrators_Security_Guide_Proxy_software.html

TIS FWTK Home Site:
http://fwtk.intrusion.org/fwtk/
Anonymous/Public Proxy Servers:
http://www.publicproxyservers.com/index.html
http://www.inetprivacy.com/a4proxy/anonymous-proxy-faq.htm
http://www.anonymous-surfing-web.com/
Automatic Public Proxy Software:
http://www.winnowsoft.com/anonymous-proxy.htm
http://www.publicproxyservers.com/index.html

Web Caching:
http://www.cs.wisc.edu/~cao/WISP98/html-versions/anja/proxim_wisp/index.html

Legal Considerations:
http://www.mnot.net/cache_docs/

The Houston Proxy Marriage
MSNBC:
http://www.msnbc.com/news/950579.asp

# E-Commerce Safeguards

Mark S. Merkow, *University of Phoenix Online*

## INTRODUCTION

Consumer identity and payment card data are under attack. The very connectedness that enables e-commerce also threatens its existence. Between the new hoards of personal identifying data collected for the electronic exchange of goods and services and the organized attacks and attackers trying to separate consumers from their money, effective e-commerce safeguards are needed more than ever. Although some online merchants continue to have an "it can't happen to me" mentality and ignore or treat casually the handling of consumer information and transaction information, e-commerce will remain vulnerable, and without sufficient self-enforcement activities in place, the credit card associations and governments around the world will mandate and impose regulations that may be a cure worse than the original disease.

Although safeguarding e-commerce is a set of activities and technologies that can succeed, it is neither cheap nor easy to do. Effective safeguards can only be achieved once it is clear to the site operators what threats are present, how likely will an attack succeed, and what is the value of the asset that may be successfully compromised. This risk analysis is mandatory to determine where to start and what controls or countermeasures are needed.

An approach to risk analysis that is often successful takes into account industry best practices, specific information related to the site, an internal review of practices, and a gap analysis to determine where improvements can be made.

## CONSUMER CONCERNS ABOUT E-COMMERCE TRANSACTIONS

Electronic commerce asks consumers to make a leap of faith, trusting that the data they input is kept as safe as data collected in a face-to-face point of sale (POS) transaction.

Questions that customers often ask related to security and privacy include the following:

- How secure is the merchant's Web site?
- Does the merchant safeguard my information?
- Can my information be intercepted along the way to the merchant?
- Is the information I give the merchant private?
- Can I view the names and information of other customers?
- How does the merchant know that I am who I say I am?
- What if someone has stolen my payment information?
- What does the merchant's Web site allow me to do?
- Will my information be used for a purpose I did not authorize?

Merchants must be prepared to respond to these concerns and be certain that safeguards are in place to counter the risks and threats ever present in e-commerce systems.

## E-COMMERCE RISK ASSESSMENT PRINCIPLES AND RECOMMENDATIONS

Clearly, there is more to safeguarding e-commerce than technology alone—effective controls take into account the three elements of people, process, and technology. To address the people and process sides, it is essential to fully understand your own e-commerce operations and to document your processes and systems. New security tools arrive on the scene daily, but these tools are only as good as the security policies and procedures behind them.

Any discussion about security must include basic principles that often have nothing to do with security products or services you will ultimately purchase or build. Common sense tells you to protect those things you value. One basic principle of security states that you should protect your assets just a *little better* than your neighbors protect theirs. Consider The Club, which is used to lock a steering wheel of parked car to deter car theft. Given a long line of parked cars, a thief will opt to steal the one that is easiest to steal, whereas those with a Club would force the thief to spend time defeating its security. The goal is to maximize damage while minimizing the time it takes to carry out the misdeed. The same holds true for information protection—the more you deter thefts, the lower the likelihood that you'll be victimized.

Another basic principle states that different types of information call for different types of protection. Think about your information assets and the promises you have made to your customers to protect their private, sensitive, and confidential data. Once again, we're referring to instilling—and maintaining—the highest possible levels of the confidence and trust that keeps your customers coming back for more.

The best approach to security that you can take is a practical and realistic one. First, you must realize that there is no such thing as absolute security. The best you can accomplish is a mix of controls that implement the principle of defense in depth, whereby the weaknesses of any controls are countered by the strengths of one or more other overlapping controls (Merkow & Breithaupt, 2004). This concept is illustrated under security conscious e-commerce network architecture.

Risk planning and risk management are central themes to securing e-commerce systems and sales channels. Once risks are well understood, there are three possible outcomes: (1) mitigate (counter) the risks, (2) insure against the consequence should the risk be exploited, and (3) accept the risk and manage the consequences.

Not all risks are the same. When developing e-commerce security solutions, it is critical to understand that spending more on securing an asset than the intrinsic value of the asset is an irresponsible use of resources. As an example, buying a $500.00 safe to protect $200.00 of jewelry makes no practical sense. The same is true when protecting electronic assets; thus it is vital to understand that all security work is a careful balance of risks and rewards. The advice and best practices described here apply more the merchant who is personally responsible for the e-commerce technical architecture and less so for the home office merchant who uses a third-party hosting service for catalogs, shopping carts, and payment processors or those who primarily conduct business using auction sites or hosted marketplaces.

## RECOMMENDATIONS FOR HOME OFFICE E-COMMERCE MERCHANTS

For people who are starting out in e-commerce and for those who have successfully built their business and plan on maintaining their sites on an externally hosted service provider, here's a short list of recommended practices to assure your business viability and maintain your customer's trust:

- **Develop internal controls**—Work with your accountant and lawyer to best understand your responsibilities with the handling of customer personal information and credit card information and make sure that your

employees clearly understand these principles. Many internal controls rely on the principle of separation of duties to make certain that no single person has excessive authority to control a financial transaction from start to end and lead to abuses.

- **Protect your PCs**—Make certain that your operating system patches are up to date and your system is set up to automatically let you know when a new patch is available, make sure you have a personal firewall that is running in a state that provide the bare minimum access that is needed, and, make sure that the software is kept up to date and do the same with antivirus software.

- **Protect your network**—If you have an always-on broadband connection and you're sharing it with other PCs in your home or small office, make certain that router security controls are implemented and working. If you are using a wireless (Wi-Fi) LAN, extra controls are needed to protect against information leakage.

- **Keep regular backups**—Even when all the controls in the world are implemented, some disasters still are not prevented, so make certain that you keep regular backups of all business critical files and maintain your backups off-site from where you conduct your business.

- **Shred everything**—Don't make the mistake of recycling paperwork that contains anything related to customer data or business sensitive data. Dumpster divers do not need more reasons to continue their nefarious ways.

## E-COMMERCE SAFEGUARDS BEGIN WITH BUILDING TRUST

With a risk management mindset and a security program in place that addresses the fundamental needs that one practiced in the art would expect to see in place, the focus on e-commerce security becomes a natural extension of the overall internal IT security practice. Major e-commerce concerns are related to providing open Internet access from noncustomers (browsers), customers, and unwanted traffic from hackers, proper separation of processing to reduce the likelihood of an attack's success, and a set of internal controls that assure that no single person inside the company has excessive authority to compromise the systems or deny their accessibility.

Once a merchant has the requisite trust in their own capabilities, their network can then be extended to external users and can begin to build a system of consumer trust. Following are some recommendations and industry best practices to make certain all three elements of the security implementation triad (people, process, and technology) are properly addressed so that a chain of consumer trust can begin to build.

Beyond recommendations and safeguards, the payment card industry has also issued guidelines and best practices for e-commerce security. At the end of this article you'll find a laundry list of these best practices.

## A SECURE PAYMENT PROCESSING TECHNICAL ENVIRONMENT

One common theme that is central to any payment processing environment is the security of the environment

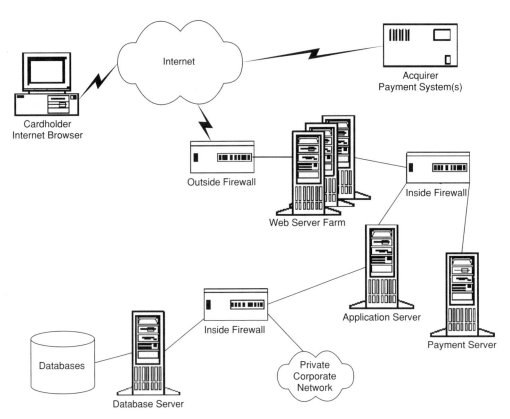

**Figure 1:** A "security conscious" payment processing environment.

in which payments are made. Safeguarding a payment card handling system requires both secure architectures to assure network and server-based security, and they require the use of complex cryptography protocols running atop the network layer—primarily at the application layer. Many of today's payment protocols incorporate multiple forms of applied cryptography for its functions.

A payment processing system necessarily requires a secure zone that is far away from the Internet connection. The best approach for creating these zones uses what are called three-tier or *n*-tier architectures.

Security experts embrace three-tier systems for Internet, intranet, and extranet applications. When they are present, these three tiers—Web server(s), application server(s), and database server(s)—greatly reduce many of the threats to production back office systems and networks and empower you to perform an excellent job of "border protection." These concepts arise from industry best practices and recommendations from security experts around the world. Because by definition your e-commerce site must be "security conscious," you are advised to utilize these principles as much as possible in your own designs. Figure 1 illustrates one example of *n*-tier network architecture that is well suited for e-commerce and payment processing applications.

Figure 1 illustrates how it is possible to add security as traffic moves beyond the Web servers into deeper tiers. As you move through the inner firewalls, you can turn off protocols that do not belong there. You can also enforce the use of trusted hosts to help prevent unwanted requests from processing.

For performance reasons and the lack of any need for specific protection, you might opt to keep your materials "intended for the public" directly within the file systems of the Web servers themselves. Normally, this will only include information that people could otherwise locate via your other advertising channels (catalogs, images, marketing brochures, etc.) Any dynamically generated data (stored billing and shipping information, etc.) should be kept as far out of reach from the Internet as possible.

Furthermore, any data that your customers supply via Web-based forms should immediately be removed from the Web server through as many firewalls as needed to safely secure it. It is these data that thieves want, so you must be extra careful with its handling. This is the most fundamental security precaution that you can take. Never store anything on the Web server itself because you can never really be sure the server will remain constantly in your control. Should a man-in-the-middle attack occur, perhaps a few Web pages will be spoofed, but your important assets will remain secure. Never operate your Common Gateway Interface (CGI) or Active Server Pages (ASP) scripts on the Web server that is handling public HTTP traffic. Rather, move them to the application zone or tier to make it harder for hackers who take over the Web server to learn useful information about back office operations and databases. The idea here is to limit the damage from a successful attack on the Web tier by not permitting any peeking into other network zones that contain valuable company assets.

Another sound measure you can take is to switch the protocols your network supports as you move backward. Because of inherent HTTP protocol vulnerabilities, you do not want it running past the outer firewall. Permitting HTTP routing into the back office places you at risk of hackers tunneling through HTTP to try and take over another server. Cut them off at the knees. Consider using protocols like MQSeries, Java Server Pages (JSPs), RMI, socket connections via TCP, or COM/DCOM on the Windows server to gain access to services residing on the application tier. From the application tier to the database tier, switch the protocols on the firewalls again, only allowing open database connectivity (ODBC) and Java database connectivity (JDBC) for SQL server, native database clients (e.g., Sybase's OpenClient and Oracle's SQL*Net), and message queuing protocols, such as Microsoft's MSMQ and IBM's MQSeries.

With the three-tier approach you can begin to see how to add still more layers of security both between and within each tier. Before the outer firewall, consider using intrusion detection systems to scan for known attack signatures and to automatically alert those in charge of the network—in real time. Using cryptography for security both at the transport layer and the application layer is also possible without rewriting programs. Furthermore, the Secure Sockets Layer (SSL) protocol for encrypted communications of information—running atop the architecture described—can help turn your e-commerce site into a genuine citadel.

Trusted hosts are another security measure that you may elect to use. Using access control lists (ACLs) on your application servers helps to thwart attempts at running or installing programs without the authority to do so. If your application software can somehow be identified as legitimate and trusted, you add still another layer of protection to your resources. Yet another approach might use server-to-server authentication with digital certificates to provide two-way assurances that application requests and responses are legitimate.

Fixed (static) access control information (database login ids and passwords stored as parameters and database connection strings) that you store on your servers should be kept in the most obscure forms possible. Never leave this type of information in the clear anywhere on the file systems. Move them to registries on the operating system in encrypted forms or encrypt the configuration files themselves. Even if the server is hijacked, the attacker will still have a hard time accessing other systems or doing anything destructive.

On the database tier, consider encrypting the contents—at the field level, the row level, the table level, or at the entire database level. Different data elements call for different situations, so analyze your needs carefully. Where audit trails of activity are crucial, turn on database auditing to help in monitoring activity or for prosecution purposes.

## ADDITIONAL SERVER CONTROLS

You've seen the practices of switching protocols and closing ports on firewalls, but there is still more to do at the server level:

- Make certain that your e-commerce servers and any payment system processors are running on separate servers that are insulated from both the Internet and from other domains within your organization. Remove all unnecessary server software that is not specifically for operational purposes. This may include language compilers, Perl/CGI/PHP libraries, administrative utilities, and factory-supplied logins and passwords.

- Firewalls should disallow FTP, telnet, or requests on any open ports.
- Do not operate software such as FTP, telnet, or e-mail systems on any e-commerce server or Web server hardware. Instead use a separate server for these functions.
- Whenever remote operations (telnet, xterm, etc.) are needed, make sure the Secure Shell (SSH) and Secure Copy (SCP) are used. These protocols secure the data in transmission using encryption.
- Make sure HTTP and merchant server software (catalog and shopping cart software) are protected against hostile browsers by keeping your Web servers patched with all the latest patches, and monitor the security advisories for newly discovered vulnerabilities and patches on common Web server software implementations

## RECAPPING NETWORK SECURITY RESPONSIBILITIES

Failing to consider security as part of the support and operations of e-commerce systems is the Achilles heel in many organizations. It is easy to locate examples of how organizations undermine expensive security measures because of poor documentation, old user accounts, conflicting software, or poor control of maintenance accounts.

In general, system support and operations staff need to be able to identify security problems, respond appropriately, and inform appropriate individuals. A wide range of possible security problems exist. Some will be internal to custom applications, whereas others apply to off-the-shelf products. Additionally, problems can be software or hardware based. Small systems are especially susceptible to viruses, whereas networks are particularly susceptible to hacker attacks, which can be targeted at multiple systems. System support personnel should be able to recognize attacks and know how to respond.

The more responsive and knowledgeable system support and operation staff personnel are, the less user support will be provided informally. The support other users provide is important, but they may not be aware of the "whole picture."

## SOFTWARE SUPPORT

Software is the heart of an organization's computer operations, whatever the size and complexity of the system. Therefore, it is essential that software function correctly and be protected from corruption. There are many elements of software support.

One is controlling what software is used on a system. If users or systems personnel can load and execute any software on a system, the system is more vulnerable to viruses, to unexpected software interactions, and to software that may subvert or bypass security controls. One method of controlling software is to inspect or test software before it is loaded (e.g., to determine compatibility with custom applications or identify other unforeseen interactions). This can apply to new software packages, to upgrades, to off-the-shelf products, or to custom software, as deemed appropriate. In addition to controlling the loading and execution of new software, organizations should also give care to the configuration and use of powerful system utilities. System utilities can compromise the integrity of operating systems and logical access controls.

Viruses take advantage of the weak software controls in personal computers. Also, there are powerful utilities available for PCs that can restore deleted files, find hidden files, and interface directly with PC hardware, bypassing the operating system. Some organizations use personal computers without floppy drives to have better control over the system. There are several widely available utilities that look for security problems in both networks and the systems attached to them. Some utilities look for and try to exploit security vulnerabilities.

A second element in software support can be to ensure that software has not been modified without proper authorization. This involves the protection of software and backup copies. This can be done with a combination of logical and physical access controls.

Many organizations also include a program to ensure that software is properly licensed, as required. For example, an organization may audit systems for illegal copies of copyrighted software. This problem is primarily associated with PCs and LANs but can apply to any type of system.

## CONFIGURATION MANAGEMENT

Closely related to software support is configuration management—the process of keeping track of changes to the system and, if needed, approving them. Configuration management normally addresses hardware, software, networking, and other changes; it can be formal or informal. The primary security goal of configuration management is ensuring that changes to the system do not unintentionally or unknowingly diminish security. Some of the methods discussed under software support, such as inspecting and testing software changes, can be used.

For networked systems, configuration management should include external connections. Is the computer system connected? To what other systems? In turn, to what systems are these systems and organizations connected? Note that the security goal is to know what changes occur, not to prevent security from being changed. There may be circumstances when security will be reduced. However, the decrease in security should be the result of a decision based on all appropriate factors.

A second security goal of configuration management is ensuring that changes to the system are reflected in other documentation, such as the contingency plan. If the change is major, it may be necessary to reanalyze some or all of the security of the system.

## BACKUPS

Support and operations personnel and sometimes users back up software and data. This function is critical to contingency planning. Frequency of backups will depend on how often data changes and how important those changes are. Program managers should be consulted to determine what backup schedule is appropriate. Also, as a safety measure, it is useful to test that backup copies are actually usable. Finally, backups should be stored securely, as appropriate.

Users of smaller systems are often responsible for their own backups. However, in reality, they do not always perform backups regularly. Some organizations, therefore, task support personnel with making backups periodically for smaller systems, either automatically (through server software) or manually (by visiting each machine).

## CONTROLS

Media controls include a variety of measures to provide physical and environmental protection and accountability for tapes, diskettes, printouts, and other media. From a security perspective, media controls should be designed to prevent the loss of confidentiality, integrity, or availability of information, including data or software, when stored outside the system. This can include storage of information before it is input to the system and after it is output.

The extent of media control depends on many factors, including the type of data, the quantity of media, and the nature of the user environment. Physical and environmental protection is used to prevent unauthorized individuals from accessing the media. It also protects against such factors as heat, cold, or harmful magnetic fields. When necessary, logging the use of individual media (e.g., a tape cartridge) provides detailed accountability—to hold authorized people responsible for their actions.

Marking: Controlling media may require some form of physical labeling. The labels can be used to identify media with special handling instructions, to locate needed information, or to log media (e.g., with serial/control numbers or bar codes) to support accountability. Identification is often by colored labels on diskettes or tapes or banner pages on printouts. If labeling is used for special handling instructions, it is critical that people be appropriately trained. The marking of PC input and output is generally the responsibility of the user, not the system support staff. Marking backup media (disks, tapes, etc.) can help prevent them from being accidentally overwritten.

- Logging: The logging of media is used to support accountability. Logs can include control numbers (or other tracking data), the times and dates of transfers, names and signatures of individuals involved, and other relevant information. Periodic spot checks or audits may be conducted to determine that no controlled items have been lost and that all are in the custody of individuals named in control logs. Automated media tracking systems may be helpful for maintaining inventories of tape and disk libraries.

- Integrity Verification: When electronically stored information is read into a computer system, it may be necessary to determine whether it has been read correctly or subject to any modification. The integrity of electronic information can be verified using error detection and correction or, if intentional modifications are a threat, cryptographic-based technologies.

- Physical Access Protection: Media can be stolen, destroyed, replaced with a look-alike copy, or lost. Physical access controls that can limit these problems include locked doors, desks, file cabinets, and safes. If the media requires protection at all times, it may be necessary to actually output data to the media in a secure location (e.g., printing to a printer in a locked room instead of to a general purpose printer in a common area). Physical protection of media should be extended to backup copies stored offsite. They generally should be accorded an equivalent level of protection to media containing the same information stored onsite. (Equivalent protection does not mean that the security measures need to be exactly the same. The controls at the offsite location are quite likely to be different from the controls at the regular site.)

- Environmental Protection: Magnetic media, such as diskettes or magnetic tape, require environmental protection, because they are sensitive to temperature, liquids, magnetism, smoke, and dust. Other media (e.g., paper and optical storage) may have different sensitivities to environmental factors.
- Transmittal: Media control may be transferred both within the organization and to outside elements. Possibilities for securing such transmittal include sealed and marked envelopes, authorized messenger or courier, or U.S. certified or registered mail.
- Disposition: When media is disposed of, it may be important to ensure that information is not improperly disclosed. This applies both to media that is external to a computer system (such as a diskette) and to media inside a computer system, such as a hard disk. The process of removing information from media is called sanitization.

Three techniques are commonly used for media sanitization: overwriting, degaussing, and destruction. Overwriting is an effective method for clearing data from magnetic media. As the name implies, overwriting uses a program to write (1s, 0s, or a combination) onto the media. Common practice is to overwrite the media three times. Overwriting should not be confused with merely deleting the pointer to a file (which typically happens when a delete command is used). Overwriting requires that the media be in working order. Degaussing is a method to magnetically erase data from magnetic media. Two types of degausser exist: strong permanent magnets and electric degaussers. The final method of sanitization is destruction of the media by shredding or burning.

Many people throw away old media, believing that erasing the files alone has made the data irretrievable. In reality, however, erasing a file simply removes the pointer to that file. The pointer tells the computer where the file is physically stored. Without this pointer, the files will not appear on a directory listing. This does not mean that the file was removed. Commonly available utility programs can often retrieve information that is presumed deleted.

# DOCUMENTATION

Documentation of all aspects of computer support and operations is important to ensure continuity and consistency. Formalizing operational practices and procedures with sufficient detail helps to eliminate security lapses and oversights, gives new personnel sufficiently detailed instructions, and provides a quality assurance function to help ensure that operations will be performed correctly and efficiently.

The security of a system also needs to be documented. This includes many types of documentation, such as security plans, contingency plans, risk analyses, and security policies and procedures. Much of this information, particularly risk and threat analyses, has to be protected against unauthorized disclosure. Security documentation also needs to be both current and accessible. Accessibility should take special factors into account (such as the need to find the contingency plan during a disaster).

Security documentation should be designed to fulfill the needs of the different types of people who use it. For this reason, many organizations separate documentation into policy and procedures. A security procedures manual should be written to inform various system users how to do their jobs securely. A security procedures manual for systems operations and support staff may address a wide variety of technical and operational concerns in considerable detail.

# MAINTENANCE

System maintenance requires either physical or logical access to the system. Support and operations staff, hardware or software vendors, or third-party service providers may maintain a system. Maintenance may be performed on site, or it may be necessary to move equipment to a repair site. Maintenance may also be performed remotely via communications connections. If someone who does not normally have access to the system performs maintenance, then a security vulnerability is introduced.

In some circumstances, it may be necessary to take additional precautions, such as conducting background investigations of service personnel. Supervision of maintenance personnel may prevent some problems, such as "snooping around" the physical area. However, once someone has access to the system, it is very difficult for supervision to prevent damage done through the maintenance process.

Many computer systems provide maintenance accounts. These special login accounts are normally preconfigured at the factory with preset, widely known passwords. One of the most common methods hackers use to break into systems is through maintenance accounts that still have factory-set or easily guessed passwords. It is critical to change these passwords or otherwise disable the accounts until they are needed. Procedures should be developed to ensure that only authorized maintenance personnel can use these accounts. If the account is to be used remotely, authentication of the maintenance provider can be performed using callback confirmation. This helps ensure that remote diagnostic activities actually originate from an established telephone number at the vendor's site. Other techniques can also help, including encryption and decryption of diagnostic communications; strong identification and authentication techniques, such as tokens; and remote disconnect verification.

Larger systems may have diagnostic ports. In addition, manufacturers of larger systems and third-party providers may offer more diagnostic and support services. It is critical to ensure that these ports are only used by authorized personnel and cannot be accessed by hackers.

# INTERDEPENDENCIES

Support and operations components coexist in most computer security controls.

- Personnel: Most support and operations staff have special access to the system. Some organizations conduct background checks on individuals filling these positions to screen out possibly untrustworthy individuals.

- Incident handling: Support and operations may include an organization's incident handling staff. Even if they are separate organizations, they need to work together to recognize and respond to incidents.
- Contingency planning: Support and operations normally provides technical input to contingency planning and carries out the activities of making backups, updating documentation, and practicing responding to contingencies.
- Security awareness, training, and education: Support and operations staff should be trained in security procedures and should be aware of the importance of security. In addition, they provide technical expertise needed to teach users how to secure their systems.
- Physical and environmental: Support and operations staff often control the immediate physical area around the computer system.
- Technical controls: The technical controls are installed, maintained, and used by support and operations staff. They create the user accounts, add users to access control lists, review audit logs for unusual activity, control bulk encryption over telecommunications links, and perform the countless operational tasks needed to use technical controls effectively. In addition, support and operations staff provide needed input to the selection of controls based on their knowledge of system capabilities and operational constraints.
- Assurance: Support and operations staff ensure that changes to a system do not introduce security vulnerabilities by using assurance methods to evaluate or test the changes and their effect on the system. Operational assurance is normally performed by support and operations staff.

## COST CONSIDERATIONS

The cost of ensuring adequate security in day-to-day support and operations is largely dependent upon the size and characteristics of the operating environment and the nature of the processing being performed. If sufficient support personnel are already available, it is important that they be trained in the security aspects of their assigned jobs; it is usually not necessary to hire additional support and operations security specialists. Training, both initial and ongoing, is a cost of successfully incorporating security measures into support and operations activities.

Another cost is that associated with creating and updating documentation to ensure that security concerns are appropriately reflected in support and operations policies, procedures, and duties.

## PAYMENT CARD BEST PRACTICES

Because credit card fraud most affects credit card issuers and merchant banks, Visa and Mastercard have published a set of "best practices" for merchants to follow when accepting their branded products for payment.

Some of these best practices include the following:

1. Limit personnel access to data and database systems: Merchants should restrict physical access to the servers running the e-commerce database system only to permit staff with direct operational duties. By limiting the duties that operational staff may perform, the merchant ensures that only authorized personnel have access to the data, perform cryptographic support functions, and manage keys. Active password management or smart card authentication or both can further protect data storage systems. Only staff with direct responsibility for payment processing should have access to payment information, and only to the extent authorized by the customer, such as for shipping orders or customer service. This includes limiting access to the customer's password, user id, and the "cookie" that the merchant may place on the customer's home PC.

2. Physically segregate the data: Separate the database platform from devices that interface with the network. The server or database containing customer information should be physically isolated from all other data to prevent commingling of sensitive data with maintenance programs or files associated with online processing. This separation can be achieved using three- or $n$-tier client–server computing architecture design best practices.

3. Remove unneeded data: Regularly inspect the server and application systems and remove trace files, log files, and system dumps. Also, delete data from inactive accounts both from customers and from internal users who leave the organization. Merchants sometimes create files that contain unencrypted customer data. The frequent removal of such transient data reduces the risk of its compromise. Maintaining information about inactive accounts also exposes the customer data to unnecessary risks. Obsolete files should be deleted as part of a regular maintenance schedule.

4. Protect the network with a firewall: Use a dedicated server residing on a secure back office network protected with a firewall between the back office and the Internet. A firewall protects data by imposing logical and physical network controls that separate and protect the database platform from the open network interface and the internal processing platforms, preventing intrusion both from without and within. The merchant's server should reside on a trusted network that uses internal and non-Internet routable IP addresses to move the data from the Web servers through to the database platform through as many network firewalls as necessary to protect the application servers, cryptographic processors, point of sale systems, and database servers from malicious or knowledgeable insider attacks.

5. Keep security prevention up to date: Merchants must regularly update security patches and antivirus software because new threats and vulnerabilities continually emerge. Additionally, merchants should regularly test security systems and employ the use of intrusion detection systems (IDSs) in parallel to perimeter firewalls to detect patterns of an attack or anomalous behavior that can in turn be blocked or force an alert for human investigation.

6. Encrypt all sensitive cardholder data before transmitting: Merchants should encrypt all transmitted cardholder data by using industry-accepted

encryption technology such as Secure Electronic Transaction (SET™) or Secure Sockets Layer (SSL). Never use electronic mail to transmit sensitive or private information in the clear because the potential for abuse is rampant.

7. Encrypt stored account data: Store all sensitive cardholder data and back-up files only in encrypted forms using industry-accepted and tested software and algorithms suitable for secret information. These include triple data encryption standard (3DES), advanced encryption system (AES), or other common, secure cryptographic applications. Sensitive data is at risk of exposure whenever other internal or external systems access the database on which it is stored. Therefore, merchants should store all cardholder data in encrypted form. To further limit exposure, merchants also should encrypt backup files, including files not accessible via the Internet and files stored offsite.

8. Protect encryption keys: Generate and store encryption and communication keys in a secure hardware device, often called a hardware security module (HSM). Secure key generation and storage ensures the safety of the keys and allows merchants securely to manage their databases, backup files, and transmissions.

9. Encrypt and decrypt data securely: To protect the value of the encryption key, support encryption and decryption only within a secure hardware device. Using an HSM to perform encryption and decryption isolates encryption keys within a tamper-resistant security module, minimizing the chance of their exposure in clear form. This technique has the additional benefit of more rapid data access, because hardware-based cryptographic modules often process keys considerably faster than software-based modules.

10. Use sufficiently strong keys: Use keys based on current industry standards, such as double-length keys for 3DES. As technology improves, the relative strength of any encryption key weakens. Merchants should upgrade their cryptographic systems to support algorithms with key management capable of safeguarding sensitive data from possible attack.

11. Use dual control to manage cryptographic keys: Split the knowledge of key components among multiple security or key signing officers. A single staff member performing key management functions should never have sole access to encrypted data, the operation of the platform, maintenance responsibilities, or other support functions. Control and custody of key components should be divided between at least two, but preferably three, security officers. No single officer should have direct knowledge of the others' key components, passwords, PINs, or other secret information used in the key management process to install, transmit, destroy, or generate cryptographic keys. HSMs typically enforce this policy through their normal operations.

12. Do not display data on a Web page: If a merchant obtains a customer's payment information and keeps it on file, the merchant should not display this information on a Web page when the customer signs in during subsequent visits but should rather display only the last four digits of the card number.

13. Protecting Customer Privacy: Privacy is one of the foremost concerns of Internet shoppers. Merchants should adhere to these general concepts when developing privacy and information management policies:

   - Recognize the interest and concerns of the customer in developing information management principles. Many customers appreciate the product and service offerings they receive from merchants, particularly when merchants tailor such offerings to their individual needs. However, merchants should remain sensitive to the privacy expectations of their customers.
   - Develop procedures to safeguard the security of customers' personal information and to govern access to and use and disclosure of personal information.
   - Merchants should ensure that customer information is securely stored and that such data are available only to those employees who have a legitimate business need and authorization to access the data. Merchants should inform all employees who have access to customer data of the merchant's policies and responsibilities regarding the use of the data.
   - Use accurate record-keeping procedures. Merchants should ensure that personal information used to provide enhanced customer satisfaction, increased fraud protection, and targeted marketing programs should be pertinent to these purposes, accurately recorded, and up to date.
   - Merchants who intend to send promotional materials to customers using personal information should inform the customers in advance and give them opportunity to decline (i.e., opt out). Merchants should determine a reasonable means of informing customers consistent with their own practices and programs.
   - Remain flexible in responding to changing customer needs and expectations regarding privacy as the payment services business continues to evolve.
   - Merchants should continuously seek to ensure that their information management practices keep pace with customer needs as technological advancements drive changes in the payment services industry.

14. Disclosing your privacy policy to customers: Here are some examples of situations where merchants should provide special disclosure statements to customers:

   - A limitation of the applicability of the privacy provisions by country or region.
   - Part of the Web site is directed to children or information is collected from online visitors actually known to be children.
   - Information that can identify an individual may be used by the merchant to market products or services to that individual.
   - The disclosure of information that can identify an individual is required to gain access to any part of the Web site.
   - Information that can identify an individual may be collected by or shared with other organizations by direct interaction with visitors to the merchant's Web site.

- The merchant collects passive information (including cookie information) that is linked to a name or similarly specific identifier.
- The merchant uses the information it collects for any purpose other than those for which the information was submitted.

## CONCLUSION

You have seen how safeguarding e-commerce can only be achieved by paying close attention to all elements of operational security—people, processes, and technology carefully balanced to achieve the desired state to not only protect but also to enable new e-commerce opportunities. With confidence that e-commerce sites are operated with a high level of security consciousness, the possibilities for growth and expansion are unbounded.

Minding the store using the recommendations and best practices you have read about here can help you establish the model of excellence in e-commerce to which most merchants aspire.

## GLOSSARY

**Authenticate** To establish the validity of a claimed user or object.

**Availability** Assuring information and communications services will be ready for use when expected. One of the three goals of information security (also see Integrity and Confidentiality).

**Compromise** An intrusion into a computer system where unauthorized disclosure, modification, or destruction of sensitive information may have occurred.

**Computer Abuse** The willful or negligent unauthorized activity that affects the availability, confidentiality, or integrity of computer resources. Computer abuse includes fraud, embezzlement, theft, malicious damage, unauthorized use, denial of service, and misappropriation.

**Computer Fraud** Computer-related crimes involving deliberate misrepresentation or alteration of data to obtain something of value.

**Computer Security Intrusion** Any event of unauthorized access or penetration to an information system.

**Confidentiality** Assuring information will be kept secret, with access limited to appropriate persons. One of the three goals of information security (also see Integrity and Availability).

**Countermeasures** Action, device, procedure, technique, or other measure that reduces the vulnerability of an information system. Countermeasures that are aimed at specific threats and vulnerabilities involve more sophisticated techniques as well as activities traditionally perceived as security.

**Cracker** A malicious or inquisitive meddler who tries to discover information by poking around (also see Hacker).

**Denial of Service** Action(s) that prevent any part of an information system from functioning in accordance with its intended purpose.

**Fault Tolerance** The ability of a system or component to continue normal operation despite the presence of hardware or software faults.

**Firewall** A system or combination of systems that enforces a boundary between two or more networks. Gateway that limits access between networks in accordance with local security policy. The typical firewall is an inexpensive micro-based UNIX box kept clean of critical data, with many modems and public network ports on it, but just one carefully watched connection back to the rest of the cluster.

**Hacker** A person who enjoys exploring the details of computers and how to stretch their capabilities. A person who enjoys learning the details of programming systems and how to stretch their capabilities, as opposed to most users who prefer to learn only the minimum necessary.

**Hacking** Unauthorized use or attempts to circumvent or bypass the security mechanisms of an information system or network.

**Host** A single computer or workstation; it can be connected to a network.

**Information Assurance (IA)** Information operations that protect and defend information and information systems by ensuring their availability, integrity, authentication, confidentiality, and nonrepudiation. This includes providing for restoration of information systems by incorporating protection, detection, and reaction capabilities.

**Information Security** The result of any system of policies and/or procedures for identifying, controlling, and protecting from unauthorized disclosure, information whose protection is authorized by executive order or statute.

**Integrity** One of the three goals of information security to assure that information will not be accidentally or maliciously altered or destroyed.

**Network** Two or more machines interconnected for communications.

**Network Security** Protection of networks and their services from unauthorized modification, destruction, or disclosure, and provision of assurance that the network performs its critical functions correctly and there are no harmful side effects. Network security includes providing for data integrity.

**Nonrepudiation** To repudiate means to deny that one participated in a transaction. Nonrepudiation eliminates the possibility to repudiate their involvement. Typically this is performed using cryptographic values and digital signatures.

**Penetration** The successful unauthorized access to an automated system.

**Penetration Testing** The portion of security testing in which the evaluators attempt to circumvent the security features of a system. The evaluators may be assumed to use all system design and implementation documentation that may include listings of system source code, manuals, and circuit diagrams. The evaluators work under the same constraints applied to ordinary users.

**Perimeter-Based Security** The technique of securing a network by controlling access to all entry and exit points of the network. Usually associated with firewalls and/or filters.

**Personnel Security** The procedures established to ensure that all personnel who have access to any classified information have the required authorizations as well as the appropriate clearances.

**Physical Security**  The measures used to provide physical protection of resources against deliberate and accidental threats.

**Proxy**  A firewall mechanism that replaces the IP address of a host on the internal (protected) network with its own IP address for all traffic passing through it. A software agent that acts on behalf of a user; typical proxies accept a connection from a user, make a decision as to whether the user or client IP address is permitted to use the proxy, perhaps does additional authentication, and then completes a connection on behalf of the user to a remote destination.

**Risk Assessment**  A study of vulnerabilities, threats, likelihood, loss or impact, and theoretical effectiveness of security measures. The process of evaluating threats and vulnerabilities, known and postulated, to determine expected loss and establish the degree of acceptability to system operations.

**Risk Management**  The total process to identify, control, and minimize the impact of uncertain events.

**Router**  An interconnection device that is similar to a bridge but serves packets or frames containing certain protocols. Routers link LANs at the network layer.

**Security Architecture**  A detailed description of all aspects of the system that relate to security, along with a set of principles to guide the design. A security architecture describes how the system is put together to satisfy the security requirements.

**Security Audit**  A search through a computer system for security problems and vulnerabilities.

**Security Countermeasures**  Countermeasures that are aimed at specific threats and vulnerabilities or involve more active techniques as well as activities traditionally perceived as security

**Security Incident**  Any act or circumstance that involves classified information that deviates from the requirements of governing security publications. For example, compromise, possible compromise, inadvertent disclosure, and deviation.

**Security Perimeter**  The boundary where security controls are in effect to protect assets.

**Security Policies**  The set of laws, rules, and practices that regulate how an organization manages, protects, and distributes sensitive information.

**Security Policy Model**  A formal presentation of the security policy enforced by the system. It must identify the set of rules and practices that regulates how a system manages, protects, and distributes sensitive information.

**Security Requirements**  Types and levels of protection necessary for equipment, data, information, applications, and facilities.

**Security Service**  A service, provided by a layer of communicating open systems, which ensures adequate security of the systems or of data transfers.

**Security Violation**  An instance in which a user or other person circumvents or defeats the controls of a system to obtain unauthorized access to information contained therein or to system resources.

**Secure Sockets Layer**  A session layer protocol that provides authentication and confidentiality to applications.

**Threat**  The means through which the ability or intent of a threat agent to adversely affect an automated system, facility, or operation can be manifest. A potential violation of security.

**Threat Assessment**  Process of formally evaluating the degree of threat to an information system and describing the nature of the threat.

**Trojan Horse**  An apparently useful and innocent program containing additional hidden code that allows the unauthorized collection, exploitation, falsification, or destruction of data.

**Virus**  A program that can "infect" other programs by modifying them to include a possibly evolved copy of itself.

**Vulnerability**  Hardware, firmware, or software flow that leaves an information system open for potential exploitation. A weakness in automated system security procedures, administrative controls, physical layout, internal controls, and so forth that could be exploited by a threat to gain unauthorized access to information or disrupt critical processing.

# CROSS REFERENCES

See *E-Commerce Vulnerabilities; Electronic Commerce; Firewall Basics; Risk Management for IT Security; Security Architectures.*

# FURTHER READING

Ghosh, A. (1998). *E-commerce security: Weak leaks, best defenses*. New York: Wiley Computer Books.

Greene, T. (2004). *Computer security for the home and small office*. Berkeley, CA: Apress.

Greenstein, M., & Vasarhelyi, M. (2001). *Electronic commerce: security, risk management, and control* (2nd ed.), New York: McGraw-Hill/Irwin.

Gutzman, A. (2002). *Unforeseen circumstances: Strategies and technologies for protecting your business and your people in a less secure world*. New York: American Management Association.

Huston, B. (2001). *Hack proofing your e-commerce site*. Rockland, MA: Syngress.

Mastercard. (2002). *Mastercard website security information site*. Retrieved January 2, 2004, from http://www.mastercardmerchant.com/preventing_fraud/website_security.html

Merkow, M., & Breithaupt J. (2000). *Complete guide to Internet security*. New York: AMACOM.

Merkow, M., & Breithaupt, J. (2004). *Computer security assurance using the common criteria*. New Jersey: Thomson-Delmar Learning.

Merkow, M., Breithaupt, J., & Wheeler, K. (1998). *Building SET applications for secure transactions*. New York: John Wiley & Sons.

NIST Special Publication 800-12. (2004). *Introduction to computer security: The NIST handbook*. Retrieved January 3, 2004, from http://csrc.nist.gov/nistpubs/800-12

Pfleeger, C., & Pfleeger, S. (2002). *Security in computing* (3rd ed.). New York: Prentice Hall.

Visa. (2003). *Visa cardholder information security program website*. Retrieved January 2, 2004, http://usa.visa.com/business/merchants/cisp_merch.html#b

Whitman, M., & Mattord, H. (2002). *Principles of information security*. New York: Course Technology.

# Digital Signatures and Electronic Signatures

Raymond R. Panko, *University of Hawaii*

## INTRODUCTION

When we send letters, we sign them to indicate that they are from us. When we sign contracts, we are expressing our willingness to abide by the terms of the contract. We cannot later repudiate the contract because our signature binds us. Signing is also possible in the electronic world, and it generally serves the same purposes.

There are three related terms we use in this article. An *electronic signature* (e-signature) is any signing method that is used with computers and networks. It is the broadest concept. It includes such things as clicking a button to indicate that we accept the terms of a program's end user licensing agreement.

More narrowly, there are two general ways to add signature blocks to outgoing messages. Digital signatures are signature blocks created with public key encryption. Message authentication codes (MACs) also are per-message signature blocks, but they are created using symmetric key encryption. MACs are also called key-hashed message authentication codes (HMACs).

In our discussion, we begin with the narrowest and most familiar technology, digital signatures. We then discuss MACs and, finally, electronic signatures broadly.

## BACKGROUND
### Applicant, Verifier, and True Party

A prime reason for electronic signing is authentication. In authentication, there are two main parties. The *verifier* wishes to determine the identity of the *applicant* —the party wishing to have his or her identity authenticated. Applicants are sometimes called supplicants.

In addition, the *true party* is the person the applicant claims to be. (The applicant may be an impostor.) The person who signs the document is the *signatory*; this may be the true party or someone authorized by the true party to sign for the true party.

### Key-Based Authentication

As discussed in the chapter on authentication, authentication can be based on something the person knows (such as a reusable password), something a person is (biometrics), or some other distinguishing characteristic.

Digital signatures and MACs are based on the applicant knowing a secret key. Digital signatures are based on public/private encryption key pairs and require the applicant to know the true party's private key. MACs require the person wishing to be authenticated to know the symmetric key the true party shares with the verifier.

### Threat Model

In normal authentication, the biggest danger is that the *applicant* is an impostor who tries to impersonate the true party in one or more transactions. This danger also is a key element in electronic signature threat models.

In addition, there is a danger that the true party will later falsely repudiate messages and contracts that he or she signed electronically, claiming that these were signed by an impostor. Against this threat, we would like to have nonrepudiation, that is, the ability to provide proof that the true party actually did sign the messages or contracts.

In simple authentication, the *verifier* is assumed to be the "good guy." However, electronic signatures should also protect the true party from verifier malfeasance. For instance, the verifier might fabricate a message or contract, add a false signature, and then claim that the true party sent the signed message or contract.

While the true party and verifier are communicating, an *attacker in the middle* may insert a single fabricated message into an ongoing dialog. Or an attacker in the middle might delete a message or simply replay an earlier message. Initial authentication at the start of a dialog will not protect against such attacks.

# DIGITAL SIGNATURES

Digital signatures are used in message-by-message authentication. A digital signature is a block of bits attached to each outgoing message to prove the sender's identity. This greatly reduces attacker-in-the-middle threats. A digital signature also provides nonrepudiation on a message-by-message basis. Figure 1 illustrates the process of creating and verifying digital signatures.

## Creating the Digital Signature

The sender creates a message to be sent. In cryptographic terminology, this is the plaintext or original plaintext. The name is a bit misleading because the message may not be limited to text, but for historical reasons, the term plaintext remains in use.

The sender/applicant will have to sign something (encrypt it with his or her private key) for authentication to be possible. However, public key encryption is very processing intensive, so it can only be used on small blocks of bits—not on large messages.

## Hashing to Produce a Message Digest

To create something small to sign, the sender's software first hashes the original plaintext message. Hashing is a mathematical process that can be applied to a string of bits of any length and that will produce a result (called a hash) that has the same short length no matter how long the input string is. For instance, the MD5 hashing algorithm always produces a hash of 128 bits, whereas the SHA-1 hashing algorithm always produces a hash of 160 bits. So message digests will be either 128 bits or 160

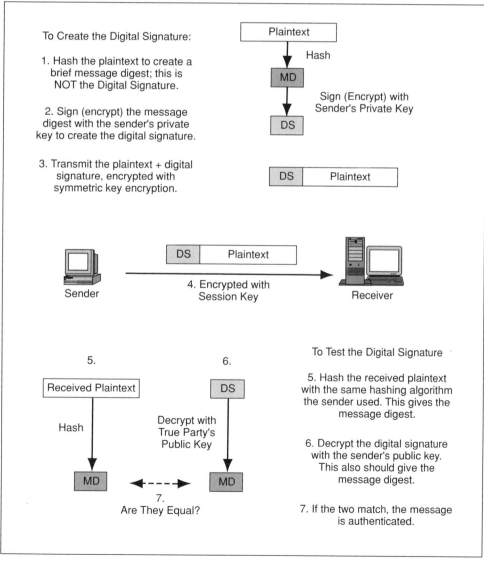

**Figure 1:** Digital signature creation, transmission, and verification. From *Corporate Computer and Network Security* (p. 258), by R. Panko, 2004, Upper Saddle River, N.J: Prentice-Hall. Reprinted with permission.

bits, depending on which of these hashing algorithms is used.

The hash of the original plaintext is called the message digest. The message digest is not the digital signature itself but rather the basis for creating the digital signature.

### Signing the Message Digest to Produce the Digital Signatures

The applicant/sender wishes to authenticate himself or herself using something only the true party should know. This is the true party's private key. If someone is given a public key/private key pair, he or she should guard the private key jealously. However, their public key is not secret and can be shared freely.

Therefore, the applicant/sender signs the message digest with his or her private key, that is, encrypts the message digest with his or her private key. The result of this encryption is the digital signature.

### Transmission with Confidentiality

After creating a digital signature, the applicant/sender creates a composite message by concatenating the bits of the digital signature to the bits of the original plaintext message. We call this the composite message. (Terminology here is not standardized.)

Next, the applicant/sender normally encrypts the composite message with the symmetric key that he or she shares with the verifier/receiver. This provides confidentiality, meaning that no one can read the original plaintext en route. Note that this step has nothing to do with authentication, and it is possible to wish to have authentication without confidentiality. However, confidentiality is normally desired during transmission.

Symmetric key encryption is used rather than public key encryption because the composite message may be quite long. As noted earlier, public key encryption is unfeasible for long messages. Symmetric key encryption, in contrast, is efficient enough for longer messages.

The applicant/sender now transmits the composite message encrypted with symmetric key encryption to the verifier/receiver. This message cannot be read en route by an attacker in the middle.

The verifier/receiver decrypts the transmitted message using the symmetric key it shares with the applicant/sender. This restores the composite message.

## Verifying the Digital Signature

Now it is time for the verifier/receiver to verify the authenticity of message. This involves recomputing the message digest in two ways and comparing the results.

One way to recompute the message digest is to rehash the original plaintext. The applicant/sender hashed the original plaintext message to create the digital signature. The verifier/receiver rehashes the original plaintext message using the same algorithm the applicant/sender used. Hashing is a repeatable process, meaning that the verifier/receiver will get the same resulting hash the applicant/sender obtained. This, of course, is the message digest.

The second way is to decrypt the digital signature. The digital signature was created by encrypting the message digest with the true party's private key. The verifier/receiver, in turn, decrypts the digital signature with the true party's public key, which is widely known. Public

key encryption is reversible, so this decryption will give the message digest.

In the final step, the verifier/receiver compares the two computed message digests. If they are the same, then the digital signature was created with the true party's private key. If the message digest was encrypted with an impostor's private key, decrypting the digital signature with the true party's public key would not give the message digest. Only the true party would know the true party's private key, so the message is authenticated.

## Benefits and Issues

### Benefits

Digital signatures provide three important benefits. One is message-by-message authentication. This guards against the insertion of a fabricated message in a dialog's message stream by an attacker in the middle.

A second benefit is message integrity, that is, proof that a message has not been tampered with en route. If an attacker has deliberately modified a message or if there has been a technical transmission error, the two message digests will not match. The verifier/receiver will discard the message.

The third benefit is nonrepudiation. If the message was signed by the true party, then the true party cannot disclaim responsibility for the message without arguing that he or she lost control of the private key, which itself may be considered negligence. If a private key is stolen, of course, it can be used as a rubber stamp to sign documents. However, for nonrepudiation, the verifier/receiver must keep the original composite message so that authentication can be verified in court or by an expert.

### Issues

Digital signature verification requires the verifier/receiver to know the true party's public key. This seems simple, but it is fraught with danger. For instance, suppose the applicant/sender sends the verifier/receiver a public key claiming that it belongs to the true party. If the applicant/sender is an impostor, of course, he or she will send his or her own public key rather than the true party's public key. If the verifier/receiver accepts this impostor's public key as the true party's public key, the impostor will be "verified" as the sender of all messages. This is public key deception.

To guard against such deception, the verifier/receiver must get the true party's public key from a trusted third party. As discussed in the chapter on public key infrastructures (PKIs), organizations called certificate authorities (CAs) provide such information in the form of digital certificates. To use digital signature authentication, the verifier/receiver needs to get the true party's digital certificate from a trusted certificate authority.

There is a great deal of confusion about digital certificates. The main thing to keep in mind is that the essential information that digital certificates provide is the true party's name and the true party's public key. Anyone claiming to be the named true party should be able to create digital signatures that can be tested with the public key enclosed in the digital certificate.

A digital certificate generally does not vouch for the trustworthiness of the party named in the digital certificates. Although some CAs provide compensation to victims if a named party behaves badly, few do. Vouching for trustworthiness is not what digital certificates are designed to do. Digital certificates are designed to tell you the public key of the named party.

At the same time, companies and individuals who do behave badly may have their certificates revoked before the expiration date on the digital certificate. CAs maintain certificate revocation lists (CRLs) of such digital certificates.

Of course, if the verifier/receiver contacts the certificate authority, the authority will not send the verifier/receiver a revoked certificate. However, it is crucial for the verifier/receiver who gets the digital certificate from another party, for instance, the applicant/sender, to check the certificate authority's CRL to be sure that the certificate has not been canceled.

The certificate authority also has a private key and a public key. The CA adds a digital signature to every certificate it creates, signed with the CA's private key. Popular CAs have public keys that are well known, so it is easy for verifier/receivers to check any digital certificate sent to them. As noted earlier, digital signatures provide message integrity, ensuring that the digital certificate has not been modified, say by entering an impostor's public key in place of the true party's public key.

In practice, every browser today comes with the ability to read digital signatures automatically, without the user's intervention. Browsers also come with the public keys of several root certificate authorities, so they can also handle most digital certificates. What the user sees is merely a notification that a particular document came from a particular, named entity. When this notice appears, the user can feel confident that the message really did come from that person or organization.

# MESSAGE AUTHENTICATION CODES (MACs)

Message authentication codes (MACs) are similar to digital signatures. Both are blocks of bits appended to original plaintext messages. However, although digital signatures are created using public key encryption, MACs are created using symmetric key encryption. Figure 2 illustrates the creation, transmission, and use of message authentication codes.

## Why MACs?

### Speed

The main advantage of MACs over digital signatures is processing speed. Public key encryption used in digital signatures is very slow, even if only the message digest is encrypted. In contrast, the symmetric key encryption used in message authentication codes requires far less processing time. Quite simply, MACs place much less of a load on the machines of both the applicant/sender and the verifier/receiver.

### Symmetric Key

The applicant/sender and the verifier/receiver share a single key in symmetric key encryption. Each uses this key both to create MACs and to verify MACs.

Often, the symmetric key used for MAC authentication is different from the symmetric key used for confidential transmission. In such cases, the two parties have at least two symmetric keys that they share.

## Creating a Message Authentication Code

To create a MAC, the applicant/sender again begins with the message to be sent—the original plaintext. Next, the applicant/sender appends the symmetric key to be used in MAC creation to the original plaintext message.

Next, the sender hashes the combined original plaintext and symmetric key with either MD5 or SHA-1 to create a hash of 128 bits or 160 bits, respectively. This hash is the message authentication code. To transmit the message, the applicant/sender appends the MAC to the original plaintext message. This is the composite message that actually will be transmitted.

Next, for confidentiality, the applicant/sender normally encrypts the composite message with a different symmetric key shared by the two parties. The applicant/sender then transmits the resultant cipher text. Interceptors will not be able to decrypt the cipher text back to plaintext because interceptors will not have the shared symmetric key used for confidentiality.

## Verifying the MAC

The verifier/receiver undoes the encryption for confidentiality by decrypting the cipher text with the shared symmetric key used for encryption. This gives the verifier/receiver the composite message consisting of the original plaintext plus the MAC.

Verifying the MAC is simple. The verifier/receiver takes the plaintext and appends the symmetric key used for authentication. The verifier/receiver then hashes the plaintext plus key using the same hashing algorithm the applicant/sender used. This should give the MAC transmitted with the message.

If this process successfully reproduces the MAC, then the sender must know the symmetric key used for authentication. Only the true party and the verifier/receiver should know this key. The MAC must have been created by the true party.

## Benefits and Issues

### Benefits

Like digital signatures, MACs provide authentication. Also like digital signatures, MACs provide message integrity. If the message is altered en route either deliberately or by transmission errors, the verification process will not reproduce the MAC, and the message will be discarded.

### Issues

MACs really prove that someone who knows the symmetric authentication key created the MAC. Obviously, this could be the true party acting as the applicant/sender.

However, although it is easy to overlook the fact, the verifier/receiver could also have created the MAC because the verifier/receiver also knows the symmetric authentication key. Why would a verifier/receiver fabricate a MAC? The answer is that the verifier/receiver may be dishonest and wish to claim that the true party sent a message that the true party never sent, for instance, a message agreeing to a dubious contract.

Thanks to the possibility of verifier/receiver misbehavior, MACs cannot provide nonrepudiation. A dishonest

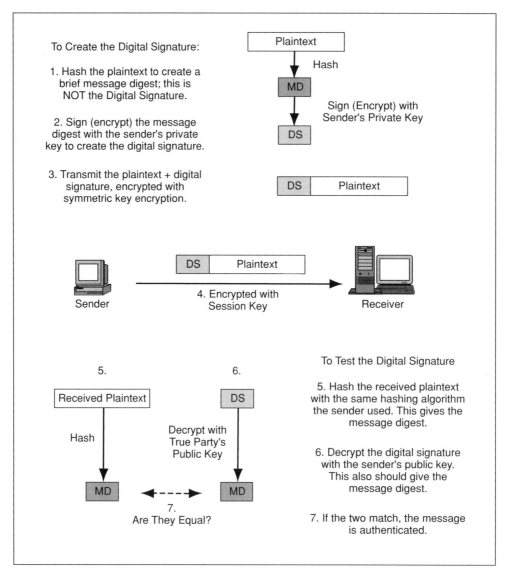

**Figure 2:** The creation, transmission, and verification of message authentication codes (MACs). From *Corporate Computer and Network Security* (p. 255), by R. Panko, 2004, Upper Saddle River, N.J.: Prentice-Hall. Reprinted with permission.

true party can repudiate a legitimate message claiming that the verifier/receiver really created it. In court cases, jurors would have to decide who to believe—hardly an easy undertaking.

Where nonrepudiation is an issue, MACs are dangerous.

## IPsec

One reason to consider MACs is that they are the default message-by-message authentication mechanism in IP security (IPsec) standards. These are increasingly being used in virtual private networks (VPNs) to ensure confidentiality, authentication, message integrity, and other benefits in dialogs between partners. If IPsec does become very widely used and if MACs continue to be the default authentication/integrity method, the lack of nonrepudiation could become a serious problem for business transactions.

## OTHER ELECTRONIC SIGNATURE TECHNOLOGIES

Digital signatures accompanied by digital certificates are the gold standard in electronic signature technologies, and MACs are good despite their lack of nonrepudiation. However, quite a few other types of e-signature technologies are possible and may make sense in particular situations.

## Typed Signatures and Scanned Physical Signatures

In the simplest e-signature methods, the sender merely types his or her name at the end of a message or includes a scanned copy of his or her written signature. Although typed signatures and scanned physical signatures are allowed under most e-signature regulations, they are not likely to stand up in court because they are so easily forged.

## Click Agreements

When you purchase software, you typically are required to click on a dialog box button to show that you accept the user licensing agreement. Click agreements generally are difficult to enforce in court because of the difficulty proving who actually clicked on the button.

However, enforceability often is not the goal. Rather, click agreements often serve primarily to create a ceremony in which the person formally makes a commitment. This brings the seriousness of the situation to the person's attention. In addition, when people make explicit commitments, they may be more likely to keep them.

## Authenticated Sessions

Many transactions are sessions in which the two parties exchange a long series of messages. With various mechanisms, it is possible to authenticate the user at the beginning of the session and perhaps occasionally during the session to ensure that the person is still there. Although less secure than digital signatures and MACs, which authenticate every message, authentication at the beginning of a session (initial authentication) provides some assurance that a certain party is sending the messages.

Most initial authentication systems rely on reusable passwords, which people (or software processes) use each time they log in for a certain period of time.

The problems with reusable passwords are well known. Unless the system enforces strong passwords, people tend to use easily guessed passwords that can be cracked in a few seconds by a password-cracking program. People also tend to write their passwords somewhere, often on their computer monitors.

A more subtle problem is lost passwords. About a quarter of all calls to help desks are for lost passwords. The help desk operator can perform a "password reset," giving the account a new password. However, there is danger in giving out new passwords over the telephone. The caller may be an impostor, not the real account holder. Although some password reset systems require the caller to answer questions that only the true account holder should know, most of these questions are easily guessed if the impostor has done his or her research.

Another means of authentication is access cards and token. If you have stayed at a hotel room recently, you probably were given an access card that allowed you into your room. Most such access cards have magnetic stripes containing information that allows access to the room; smart card versions have microprocessors and memory for more sophisticated identity checking.

Even if you get a key, the key is likely to be a physical token that contains access information. Plugging it into the door allows the door reader to query a central system for access permission. There also are tokens that plug into the USB ports of personal computers for access to those machines.

Another type of token requires the user to enter a PIN number on a small (generally) numerical keypad. The token then shows a temporary password on its display. The user must use this temporary password to log into a computer system.

Access cards and tokens provide good security, but they are easily lost or stolen. There must be a quick way to disable lost access devices as well as a way to reissue them in ways that impostors cannot exploit.

Another approach to handling authenticated access sessions at Web sites is visit traces, recording the paths users take through them, including click agreements they have made. Documentation that a person saw certain information can be convincing evidence in court and may prompt a person to drop repudiation claims. However, visit trace logs must be secured against tampering by the logkeeper if they are to be useful in court.

## Biometrics

One form of authenticated session technology is biometrics. It is new and complex, so we will give it its own section.

Biometrics comes from the words *bio*, meaning *biological life*, and *metrics*, meaning *measurement*. Some types of biometrics measure bodily dimensions, such as fingerprints, iris patterns in the eye, and facial features. Other types measure activities, such as motions and pressures involved when signing a name or the temporal patterns of password typing.

The advantage of biometric authentication is that it does not require the applicant to carry something that can be lost and (usually) does not require the applicant to remember anything. Despite jokes to the contrary, we never actually forget our heads at home. A major hope is that biometrics will replace reusable passwords as the dominant form of authentication.

A major problem with biometrics, however, is that there are serious disagreements over the error rates involved in biometric measurements. Many vendors make impressive claims about accuracy, but these often are based on tests conducted under ideal conditions and may not be representative of accuracy in the real world.

There are two basic types of errors in biometrics, indeed in all access control methods. False acceptance rates (FARs) verify or identify someone who should be rejected. High FARs means impostors are getting in and forming a strong basis for repudiation. A failure to test FARs may make access data difficult to defend in court.

At the opposite end of the spectrum is false rejection rates (FRRs). FRRs tell you what percentage of legitimate applications is rejected. Although FRRs do not harm security, significant FRRs may make a system unacceptable to users. Many systems allow applicants to attempt to authenticate themselves several times to reduce FRRs.

Another issue in biometrics is user acceptability. For instance, some users may refuse to use a fingerprint system because of its criminal connotations. Others will reject systems they fear may harm them; for instance, some people believe that eye identification systems shoot laser beams into their eyes. Still others reject systems that are difficult to use, such as iris scanning systems, which require proper eye placement. In general, if a significant number of users refuse to use the system, the loss in revenues and other values may make the system completely cost ineffective.

Another problem with biometrics is that the different technologies vary widely in cost and accuracy. Selecting a biometric method is an important task. Not surprisingly, the most expensive methods tend to be the most accurate.

In addition, the cost of biometric readers and other system components may be prohibitive.

A final problem is that we do not yet have comprehensive standards for biometrics. As a consequence, choosing biometric authentication today generally means getting locked into a single vendor.

## None of the Above

The last alternative in e-signatures is simply not to use them. In many cases, the benefits may not be worth the costs and damaged user relationships.

## SELECTING AN ELECTRONIC SIGNATURE METHOD

Selecting an electronic signature method is not a technical decision. It is a business decision. Like any business decision, it requires the selector to understand the business situation before considering anything else.

Some e-signature systems serve closed communities, such as individual corporations or consortia of firms. Others serve open communities, such as a vendor and its customers. In open communities, it is difficult to impose stringent e-signature requirements. For instance, in consumer e-commerce, it is traditional in the SSL/TLS encryption methodology that is used in almost all transactions to require the merchant but not the consumer to have a digital signature and digital certificate. Note that e-signature implementation can be asymmetrical, with different requirements imposed on the two sides. In addition, in an open community, the general lack of e-signature and PKI standards and the need to coordinate rollouts in many firms tends to require long lead times.

There are two forms of authentication, verification, and identification. In verification, the person claims to be a particular person, for instance, by typing in an account name. The authentication system then only has to see whether the password typed or the other authentication data given is correct for the account. If so, the applicant is verified as the true account holder. In identification, the applicant does not claim a particular identity. The applicant provides authentication data, and the identification system matches that data against that of *all* the accounts in the identification database. If the best match that is selected meets closeness-of-fit criteria, the applicant is identified as that person (or software process) in the database. Identification is more difficult than verification and thus has higher error rates. It also may lack the intentionality that is normally present in signing activities and so may not be enforceable in court.

## Security Requirements

Signatures of any kind exist to validate agreements. To be effective, they must be safe from use by impostors and from other security threats.

In security, one must always consider threat severity, which is the likely cost of a security incursion times the probability an incursion will take place. It is, in other words, the expected value of loss from a threat. If the threat severity is low and is likely to remain smaller than the cost of implementing an e-signature system, then implementing the system will not make economical sense.

In general, e-signatures should be viewed as security techniques, and security always must consider risk management—the balancing of risks and countermeasure costs. Generally speaking, however, the more expensive the transaction, the more expensive the e-signature.

Key length is an important security concern when private keys are used to sign documents or message digests. Documents that must be kept secure for many years must be signed with longer keys than documents whose signatures only have to be verifiable for a few years. However, longer keys mean longer processing times and therefore higher costs. The period of sensitivity is a crucial determinant of key length.

## Legal Goals

Another consideration in selecting an electronic signature technology is a firm's legal goals. Many countries require that contracts worth over a certain amount of money be signed to be valid. In U.S. commercial law, for instance, contracts over $500 or lasting a year or more must be signed to be valid. If the goal is to meet this requirement, even the least secure e-signing methods may be acceptable.

As noted earlier in this article, one consideration is whether to create a ceremony of commitment, in which a person must explicitly, through an action, acknowledge ownership of a document. Again, if this is the main goal, even nonsecure e-signing methods may be acceptable.

If the goal is nonrepudiation, then a stronger e-signature method is needed. The only method available today that provides strong technical nonrepudiability is use of digital signatures, which require a PKI for digital certificates. As noted earlier, it is necessary to keep the cipher-text version of the digital signature so that the decryption can be tested in court.

Although technical nonrepudiability is good, juries are likely to decide contested cases. If the complainant is more believable than the defendant, the jury may disregard the defense's argument that the e-signature method used does not provide technical nonrepudiation. If the defendant is more believable, the jury may side with the defense even if a digital signature and digital certificate are used.

## Suitability

Another consideration in selecting an e-signature methodology is whether the system can be implemented. One question to ask when considering the various methods is what, in any given firm, is technically feasible. Some choices may not be feasible, and some that are may be outside the firm's resources to implement it. PKIs are especially problematic.

Of course, the firm must consider the cost of implementing a system, including the cost of the technology itself and the cost of installing it. In addition, electronic signature processing slows computer processing often enough to require upgrading to faster hardware. The last major consideration in determining the suitability of a method is whether users will accept it. As noted earlier, fingerprints, iris scanning, and other techniques may offend users or make them uncomfortable. The company must also consider the cost of lost business if some users refuse to use e-signatures and therefore stop doing business with the firm. Conversely, a firm may gain revenues if it develops a reputation for having strong security in general.

Obviously, individual home consumers are unlikely to be willing to get digital certificates unless they see strong benefits from doing so. As a result, most firms are unlikely to require consumers to use digital certificates for fear of losing business.

## LEGAL AND REGULATORY ENVIRONMENT

One consideration that is especially difficult to discuss cleanly is the legal and regulatory environment of electronic signatures. Laws vary around the world and even within countries. Few of these laws, furthermore, have been tested in court. Regulation of certificate authorities and other aspects of electronic signatures barely exist, even in countries that have begun to back legislation with regulation.

In the United States, a number of states created electronic signature laws before the federal government created the Electronic Signatures in Global and National Commerce Act, better known as E-SIGN, in 2000. As the name states, E-SIGN governs only national (interstate) commerce. No court cases have yet appeared to test this area.

Quite a few states have created their own electronic signature laws. In 1999, before Congress acted, the National Conference of Commissioners on Uniform State Laws adopted the Uniform Electronic Transactions Act (UETA), and a number of states based their laws on this act. However, past court rulings have found that many intrastate activities affect interstate commerce and so are governed by federal laws.

In 1999, the European Parliament and the Council of the European Union created Directive 1999/93/EC, On a Community Framework for Electronic Signatures. This directive did not create laws but rather directed the member countries to create e-signature regulation. The first country to do so was Ireland, in July 2000. Germany followed in May 2001.

The simplest element in electronic signature laws is whether legal validity has been established. As noted earlier, most jurisdictions require that contracts worth more than a certain amount of money be signed to be valid. Almost all e-signature laws provide the weak protection of saying that contracts cannot be invalid simply because they are signed electronically. This does not ensure that a particular e-signature methodology will stand up in court if one side repudiates the document.

One consideration in selecting an electronic signature technology is whether a country's e-signature law allows all types or only some types of electronic signatures. The U.S. E-SIGN Act is intentionally vague, not mentioning specific e-signature technologies. The EC Directive mentions several specific technologies but does not limit itself to them.

The EC Directive defines an electronic signature in general as "data in electronic form which are attached to or logically associated with other electronic data and which serve as a method of authentication." The EC Directive also specifies *advanced e-signatures,* which basically are digital signatures based on qualified certificates—the strongest type of electronic signature. These advanced signatures are given a certain degree of privileged status, which is reasonable because of their strength. Most important, advanced electronic signatures are viewed as equivalent to hand signatures in legal proceedings.

Another consideration is whether e-signatures are permitted for all types of documents or only some. For instance, in the United States, the federal E-SIGN law forbids certain documents to be signed electronically because of potential harm to consumers. These exclusions were not present in early versions of the laws, which failed to pass because of insufficient consumer protection. Among the documents excluded are wills, trusts, adoptions, divorces, other family court matters, court documents, utilities cancellation notices, notices of foreclosures, eviction notices, insurance cancellations, warnings about the transportation of hazardous materials, and the repossession of primary residences.

Another key consideration in selecting an electronic signature technology is whether one side can force the other side to accept electronic signatures or whether using e-signatures is voluntary. Early versions of the U.S. E-SIGN law were rejected by Congress because they failed to say explicitly that people cannot be forced to accept electronically signed documents. The final E-SIGN Act says that consumers must be notified of options, including the mandatory option of paper-only transactions, must give consent, and must demonstrate the ability to store and access digital documents.

Digital signatures require digital certificates from certificate authorities. A major issue is whether a country will regulate certificate authorities. The U.S. E-SIGN Act leaves everything to industry. The EC Directive, in contrast, specifies that each country should establish a regulatory framework within the country for certificate authorities and related services, such as registration services, time stamping services, and directory services (Article 1a).

## CONCLUSION

Electronic signatures exist for legal reasons. We have long been able to send documents electronically. However, many documents must be signed to be legal in court proceedings. Until recently, the legality of electronic signatures sent with documents was uncertain.

Now, however, most countries have adopted electronic signature legislation, which permits certain types of electric signing. The U.S. E-SIGN legislation is especially broad in terms of what forms of electronic signatures it will recognize.

One reason for signing documents is to provide nonrepudiation, which means that the signer cannot claim not to have signed the document if they really had done so. Only one form of electronic signature provides nonrepudiation. This is the digital signature, in which the sender encrypts (signs) a message digest with his or her private key. If this digital signature can be verified with the true party's public key provided by a digital certificate from a reliable certificate authority, the only rational basis for nonrepudiation is that the true party's private key was stolen. Similarly, if someone falsely claims that a person signed a contract, a digital signature will prove that assertion false because verification with that person's public key will fail. Consequently, although many forms of electronic signature are permitted by law, only digital signatures provide strong legal protections.

# GLOSSARY

**Access Cards**   Have magnetic stripes containing information that allows you into, for instance, a hotel room. Smart card versions have microprocessors and memory for more sophisticated identity checking.

**Advanced E-Signatures**   In the European Union electronic signature directive, digital signatures based on qualified certificates

**Applicant**   The party wishing to have his or her identity authenticated.

**Attacker in the Middle**   Party who may insert a single fabricated message into an ongoing dialog, delete a message, or replay an earlier message.

**Authentication Data**   Where an identification system matches user-supplied data against all accounts in the identification database to determine who the user is.

**Biometric Authentication**   The authentication of a person based on body measurements.

**Ceremony of Commitment**   Act of signing a document that results in heightened awareness of the gravity of the situation on the part of the signer.

**Certificate Authorities (CAs)**   Organizations that create and distribute digital certificates.

**Certificate Revocation List (CRL)**   List of a certificate authority's certificates that have been revoked before the termination date listed on the certificate.

**Click Agreements**   Electronic signatures created by the user clicking on a button that says, for example, "agree."

**Digital Certificates**   Documents that give a named party's public key and other information.

**Digital Signatures**   Signature blocks created with public key encryption. They are created by encrypting message digests with the applicant's private key.

**Directive 1999/93/EC**   European Union electronic signature directive to the EU member nations.

**Electronic Signature (E-Signature)**   Any signing method that is used with computers and networks.

**E-SIGN**   U.S. electronic signature law.

**False Acceptance Rates (FARs)**   Percentage of times a person is authenticated when he or she should not be.

**False Rejection Rates (FRRs)**   Percentage of times a person is not authenticated when he or she should be.

**Hashing**   A mathematical process that can be applied to a string of bits of any length and that will produce a result (called a hash) that has the same short length no matter how long the input string is.

**Identification**   Process in which the applicant does not claim a particular identity. When the applicant provides authentication data, the identification system matches the data against all the accounts in the identification database to determine who the applicant is.

**Message Authentication Codes (MACs)**   Per-message signature blocks, created using symmetric key encryption. MACs are also called key-hashed message authentication codes (HMACs).

**Message Digest**   The result of hashing a plaintext message. This is the first step in creating a digital signature.

**Message Integrity**   Proof that a message has not been tampered with en route to its destination.

**Nonrepudiation**   When the sender cannot plausibly claim that a message did not really come from him.

**Password Reset**   Gives an account a new password when a reusable password is forgotten.

**Period of Sensitivity**   Period of time during which a file must be kept confidential.

**Public Key Deception**   Process in which an impostor sends his own private key, claiming that it is the true party's public key.

**Repudiate**   When a party claims that she did not send a message apparently sent from her.

**Reusable Passwords**   Passwords used repeatedly. Most passwords are reusable passwords.

**Scanned Physical Signatures**   Electronic signatures formed by scanning a written signature and inserting the image in the document as a signature block.

**Signatory**   Party who actually signs the document. May be the true party or someone or something to which the true party delegates signing authority.

**Supplicant**   Another name for an applicant.

**Tokens**   Physical devices used to authenticate a person.

**True Party**   The person or object the applicant claims to be.

**Typed Signatures**   Electronic signatures in which the sender merely types his or her name.

**Validity**   Characteristic of a document that allows it to be presented as evidence in a court.

**Verification**   When the person claims to be a particular person, for instance, when typing in an account name.

**Verifier**   The party wishing to determine the identity of the applicant.

**Visit Trace**   A list of the locations a user has visited at a Web site.

# CROSS REFERENCES

See *PKI (Public Key Infrastructure); Internet Security Standards; Public Key Standards: PKCS (Public-Key Cryptography Standards); Encryption Basics; Hashes and Message Digests; Public-Key Algorithms*

# FURTHER READING

American Bar Association. (1996). *Digital signature guidelines: Legal infrastructure for certification authorities and electronic commerce*. Washington, DC: American Bar Association.

Ford, W. (2000). *Secure electronic commerce: Building the infrastructure for digital signature and encryption* (2nd ed.). Englewood Cliffs, NJ: Prentice-Hall.

Grant, G. L. (1997). *Understanding digital signatures: Establishing trust over the Internet and other networks (CommerceNet)*. Columbus, OH: McGraw-Hill Professional.

Hammond, B. (2002). *Digital Signatures*. Emeryville, CA: McGraw-Hill Osborne Media.

Panko, R. (2004). *Business Computer and Network Security*. Englewood Cliffs, NJ: Prentice-Hall.

Pfitzmann, B. (1996). *Digital signature schemes: General framework and fail-stop signatures*. New York: Springer-Verlag.

Piper, F., Blake-Wilson, S., & Mitchell, J. (2000). *Digital signature: Security and control*. New York: Information Systems Audit and Control Foundation, 2000.

# E-Mail Security

Jon Callas, *PGP Corporation*

## INTRODUCTION

Electronic mail, commonly called e-mail, is the most widely used form of communication today, surpassing even telephone calls. Yet very few of those messages are sent using any security mechanisms whatsoever. This chapter describes e-mail systems, e-mail security, and how they are used.

## Internal and Internet E-Mail Compared

E-mail grew in two separate paths, with systems designed for the Internet and with systems designed for communications within an organization. With the rise of the Internet, the internal systems were adapted for Internet use, as this became the best mechanism for people in one organization to send messages to people in other organizations, as well as to their own customers.

Meanwhile, the Internet itself had developed its own systems for sending and receiving e-mail. These systems were standardized in the *Internet engineering task force* (IETF) and became widely implemented on a number of systems.

The importance of the Internet standards led software makers who did not support these standards either to convert to them or to make adapters for their servers so that they can be used for sending and receiving e-mail using the standard protocols.

The proprietary, nonstandard protocols are still widely used. Two of the main mail servers, Microsoft's *Exchange* and IBM's *Domino*, are proprietary e-mail servers. However, each use standard protocols for communications to other e-mail systems. E-mail today can be thought of as made of islands that may be using standard or proprietary protocols all connected with the standard protocols over the Internet.

## Overview of Standard Protocols

The standard IETF protocols are defined in a series of documents called RFCs. RFC is an abbreviation for *request for comments*. RFCs are not all created equal; some RFCs are *standards track* RFCs and others are *informational track* RFCs. Informational RFCs are documents that carry no weight as standards; they merely exist to document a system or subsystem, often so that there is a place for standards track RFCs to reference them. In fact, you will note that the two major e-mail security standards each started life as information track documents before they joined the standards track.

Although RFCs have often been compiled into a book, they are all text documents formatted for easy reading. They can best be found on the Internet itself using a URL of the following syntax: http://www.ietf.org/rfc/rfcNNNN.txt.

### Mail Agents

Standard mail systems are divided between different types of processes. These processes are as follows:

- *Mail user agent* (MUA): An MUA is an e-mail client program. It is what the user uses to read and send their e-mail.

- *Mail transfer agent* (MTA): An MTA is an e-mail router. It takes a message from an MUA or MTA and passes it on to another MTA or stores it locally for an MUA to retrieve. Sometimes, an MTA locally stores the message by means of a *mail delivery agent* but so-called MDAs typically do not have a protocol interface and can be considered to be a subsystem of the MTA itelf.

**Table 1** Core SMTP-Related RFCs

| RFC | Name | Description |
|---|---|---|
| RFC 2821 | Simple mail transfer protocol | This RFC defines the SMTP protocol itself. |
| RFC 2822 | Internet message format | This RFC defines the format of an IETF-standard e-mail message. |
| RFC 2554 | SMTP service extension for authentication | This is an extension of SMTP to allow for authenticated connections between systems that use SMTP. |
| RFC 2476 | Message submission | This is a variant of SMTP that is designed specifically for MUA to MTA transactions, where an MUA submits message to the MTA. It requires RFC2554. |

## SMTP

*Simple mail transfer protocol* (SMTP) is the protocol that governs MTA-to-MTA communications. MUAs also often use SMTP to deliver an outgoing message to an MTA for further transport. Ideally, however, MUAs use a variant of SMTP called the *message submission protocol* to authenticate their connection to their authorized MTAs.

SMTP is a *store-and-forward* protocol. Unlike most network protocols, SMTP is designed to work on unstable, unreliable networks. Historically, it was often the case that a site's connection to the Internet would be intermittent. For example, it might be connected only during normal business hours or perhaps even for 10 min/hr. A store-and-forward protocol allows messages to migrate from one system to another, even if the source and destination are not ever mutually connected to the main network at the same time.

An important characteristic of SMTP is that it is a store-and-forward protocol. This gives it great flexibility and contributes to the ubiquitous use of e-mail. Many systems that use e-mail would not be possible without it being a store-and-forward system. However, this also adds many security wrinkles to e-mail that simply do not exist in systems that rely on direct connections. Any system that receives e-mail must take into account the possibility that the system they are directly talking to is merely a middleman in the transaction. It may have neither created the message, nor even have any idea who

did. This is also why transport encryption through secure sockets layer/transfer layer security (SSL/TLS) or a Virtual Private Network (VPN) is not sufficient for e-mail security. If a message is to be protected, its content must be protected directly. Protecting the network connection is not sufficient.

SMTP is defined in a number of RFCs. Table 1 lists the important RFCs that describe how SMTP works.

## POP

*Post office protocol* (POP) is a protocol that an MUA may use for retrieving mail from a mail server. It is primarily designed so that an MUA may pull all e-mail messages from a server and manage it on the client machine. However, POP also allows for messages to be left on the server for some period of time before they are deleted. The server might have some time period after which messages are deleted, and many POP clients allow the messages to be left on the server for some reasonable period before they're deleted. Contrast this with Internet message access protocol (IMAP), described below.

POP is principally defined in the RFCs listed in Table 2.

## IMAP

IMAP is a protocol that an MUA can use for managing e-mail that resides on a server. Unlike POP, it is more than a retrieval protocol. It is a full client-server protocol that allows a user to keep a mailbox synchronized across several clients.

**Table 2** Core POP-Related RFCs

| RFC | Name | Description |
|---|---|---|
| RFC 1939 | Post office protocol, version 3 | This RFC defines the POP protocol itself. |
| RFC 2449 | POP3 extension mechanism | This RFC defines a mechanism to announce support for optional commands, extensions, and unconditional server behavior. |
| RFC 2384 | POP URL scheme | This RFC defines a URL scheme for referencing a POP mailbox. |
| RFC 1957 | Some observations on implementations of the post office protocol (POP3) | This informational RFC describes some implementation quirks of some popular POP clients. |
| RFC 1734 | POP3 AUTHentication command | This RFC describes the optional AUTH command, which can be used for negotiating authentication mechanisms. |
| RFC 2195 | IMAP/POP AUTHorize extension for simple challenge/response | This RFC describes the CRAM-MD5 authentication mechanism used to authenticate by password without sending the actual password over the network. This is also used with SMTP authentication as well as with POP or IMAP. |

**Table 3** Core IMAP-Related RFCs

| RFC | Name | Description |
|-----|------|-------------|
| RFC 3501 | Internet message access protocol, version 4rev1 | This RFC describes the IMAP protocol itself. |
| RFC 2192 | IMAP URL scheme | This RFC defines a URL scheme for referencing an IMAP mailbox. |
| RFC 2195 | IMAP/POP AUTHorize extension for simple challenge/response | This RFC describes the CRAM-MD5 authentication mechanism used to authenticate by password without sending the actual password over the network. This is also used with SMTP authentication as well as with POP or IMAP. |

IMAP is a complex protocol that includes operations for creating, deleting, and renaming mailboxes; checking for new messages; permanently removing messages; setting and clearing flags; message and MIME parsing; searching messages; and selective fetching of message attributes, texts, and portions thereof.

IMAP is principally defined in the RFCs listed in Table 3.

### Using SSL/TLS

It is possible to use any of the standard protocols with TLS, the IETF standard name for what is commonly called SSL. TLS is a slightly different protocol than SSL, because some changes were introduced in the standardization process. Although they are separate protocols, they are still similar enough that systems that support TLS also support SSL. Also, it is common that colloquially, people still say *SSL* when they actually mean *TLS*, simply because SSL was so widely used and so well-known before TLS was standardized. The RFCs that describe using TLS are in Table 4.

## Overview of Proprietary E-Mail Systems

The most widely used proprietary e-mail systems are Microsoft's *Exchange* server, IBM's *Domino* server, and Novell's *Groupwise* server. These servers were designed for message, document, and calendar management for an organization. They all use SMTP for message transfer to the Internet at large. They may also provide POP or IMAP services as well. They all have their own client programs as well: Micrsoft's *Outlook*, IBM's (Lotus) *Notes*, and Novell's *Groupwise*.

## The Need for Security

None of the standard protocols were designed with security in mind. As a notable exception, *Domino/Notes* was designed with security from its very beginning and has its own mechanisms that predate any of the standard mechanisms described further in this document.

The standard protocols were originally designed with password authentication in plaintext as well as the protocols themselves completely in the clear. Consequently, an eavesdropper on a connection could not only read all messages but also could acquire users' passwords. Clearly, this was not a desirable state of affairs. As time went on, they were enhanced for nonplaintext passwords, other authentication extensions, and securing the network connection that the protocol flows over. There were also developed standards for securing the bodies of messages.

In 2004, there has been work done by various groups formed to solve the threats of junk and fraudulent e-mail. At this writing, neither has produced standards for these issues. Furthermore, the activity that has happened has been rapid and dramatic. By the time you are reading this, much will have changed. Nonetheless, this is relevant to this chapter and a short description is provided later in the chapter.

## SECURITY REQUIREMENTS

Securing messages has a number of facets. Because e-mail was not designed with security in mind, systems and standards for securing e-mail have had to be fit within the structure of the existing e-mail system.

**Table 4** Core TLS-Related RFCs

| RFC | Name | Description |
|-----|------|-------------|
| RFC 2246 | The TLS protocol version 1.0 | This RFC describes TLS itself. |
| RFC 3546 | Transport layer security (TLS) extensions | This RFC describes a generic, backward-compatible extension mechanism for TLS. |
| RFC 3749 | Transport layer security protocol compression methods | This RFC describes how ZIP (DEFLATE) data compression can be used within a TLS stream. |
| RFC 3207 | SMTP service extension for secure SMTP over TLS | This RFC describes the STARTTLS mechanism for using SMTP over TLS. |
| RFC 2595 | Using TLS with IMAP, POP3, and ACAP | This RFC describes STARTTLS for both POP and IMAP. |
| RFC 3268 | AES ciphersuites for TLS | This RFC describes how to use the AES with TLS. |

## Postcards versus Letters versus E-Mail

It is a widely used metaphor that unprotected e-mail is like a postcard in the physical postal system, not like a letter. There is no envelope protecting the content of the message. This is why we need security; we expect messages to have some degree of privacy and integrity to them.

However, like all metaphors, this can be stretched until it breaks. Although e-mail resembles postal mail in many ways, it is not postal mail and there is no direct correspondence of the components of an e-mail to that of a letter.

Not only is there no envelope that wraps an e-mail, but the address portions of each do not exactly correspond. (There is also no stamp on an e-mail, as some people have observed in spam fighting and this is what makes the problem of junk e-mail much worse than of junk mail, even if that is merely degree and not kind.) This means that although the postal system offers metaphors and analogies to e-mail systems designers, we simply cannot graft systems from the past onto those in the present.

## Transport and Message Security

Transport encryption is necessary and arguably sufficient to protect the network sessions of online protocols such as POP and IMAP. TLS not only guards against eavesdroppers but also protects a stream from being tampered with. It is also desirable to protect the message content because once data leaves TLS, it is in the clear. Many people would prefer to have messages stored on an e-mail server encrypted. Particularly with growing governance and security regulations and practices, it is *desirable* if not yet a *requirement* that e-mail be protected from the administrators of the e-mail servers.

Stepping back to e-mail transport, because SMTP is a store-and-forward protocol, transport encryption alone is not sufficient to protect an e-mail in transit. The actual content of the message itself must also be protected because neither the sender nor the receiver have any control on the number of intermediate servers that an e-mail will cross. Therefore, to protect SMTP transmission there must be standards for protecting message content.

However, because this security is layered on top of the existing, insecure e-mail system, there are portions of the message that are not protected by message encryption systems. Notably, the headers of the message such as the To, From, and Subject headers are not protected by the message encryption systems. Furthermore, any signatures on the message are on the content of the message rather than on its headers.

Mere transport security leaves three open problems, one easily solved. Using transport encryption on SMTP whenever and wherever possible protects the headers of the message from eavesdropping and modification in transit, however imperfectly.

Identifying the source of the message is a problem that has been taken on by new work described below. This leaves only one unaddressed message security problem, that of actually encrypted headers, particularly the metadata in a message that is completely unprotected.

## Encryption

We protect e-mails from prying eyes with encryption. Encryption is the metaphorical envelope. Unlike a physical envelope, a properly encrypted e-mail cannot be read by anyone not possessing the proper keys. Conversery, although it might be possible to open and reseal a physical letter without being detected on a single occasion, it is very difficult to undetectably read messages over an extended period of time for a large number of people. This is why we use strong encryption on mere e-mails.

## Signing

Signing a message with a public keypair does two things. First, it shows that the message has not been tampered with. It shows that the message, the whole message, and nothing but the message arrived at the destination. Second, it shows who signed the message, at least to the degree to which the private part of the keypair can be believed to be under the control of only one entity. Signed data can thus be thought to be *authenticated* data.

It is possible to do this without public key cryptography; *message authentication codes* (MACs) can do this with a symmetric key. However, a MAC cannot be verified without knowing a symmetric key, and revealing the key to some outside party to validate the message gives that party the ability to create a MAC for any arbitrary content. The value that public key integrity systems have over symmetric key systems is that the signature can be verified without giving away the signing key. Signatures also can travel with the message even after the encryption envelope has been removed.

## Digital Signatures and Meaning

There is, however, no mathematics that tells us what a digital signature means. Digital signatures are very flexible things and can mean a variety of things. Among these, in increasing semantic strength, are the following:

1. A digital signature can denote that the content is intact. It is thus a sort of tamper-evident seal.
2. A digital signature can mean that the signer has seen the content. It is thus a sort of notary seal or perhaps a time stamp.
3. A digital signature can mean that the signer has merely processed the content. The MASS effort is creating signatures of this form as a form of spam fighting.
4. A digital signature can mean that the signer is the originator of the content. Many organizational announcements are signed thusly and most signed messages fall into this category.
5. A digital signature can mean that the signer agrees to abide by the content of the message. This type of signature is most like a written signature. Note that in this usage, the signer very likely did not originate the content.

Signature systems themselves can have semantics built into them or can be general purpose. A payment system, for example, is a type 5 system, but an antispam system has weaker meaning, generally type 3.

# Nonrepudiation

Nonrepudiation is the property that a valid digital signature is arbitrarily hard to forge, and therefore the owner of the key cannot deny the legitimacy of one. Nonrepudiation has mathematical merit; it is indeed extremely difficult to create a valid digital signature without possession of the private key. However, operationally, this is not so simple.

There are many ways that a key can be compromised or suborned. Viruses and other malware are often created to hijack the normal operations of the system. In 1997, there was a virus that attacked PGP private keyrings. Presently, it is relatively common for there to be viruses and worms designed to send e-mails for any number of reasons, virus/worm propagation being one reason, and some worms are designed to be vectors for sending spam e-mails themselves. When there becomes an interesting reason for a virus to hijack a signing key, there will be malware that does it.

Even with keys in smart cards or similar secure storage, there are many opportunities for malware to trick the user into signing something unintended. It is certainly possible to have secure hardware with secure input (this author was an architect of such a system), but these devices are presently extremely unusual.

There is a huge problem here—the more that a user must sign, the more the users want shortcuts to signing. The more actual intervention that a user must do to make a signature, the more they will want shortcuts or will avoid making signatures at all. Yet the more shortcuts there are to signing, the lower the overall security of the system and the less actual nonrepudiation it contains.

Consequently, although nonrepudiation is a goal and exists in the mathematical sense, the real-world situation is that a digital signature is evidence, rather than proof, of the signer's involvement, let alone intent (which, alas, cannot be mathematically demonstrated). This is one reason why some cryptographic systems such as antispam systems move signatures away from end users and toward the servers. Automated systems controlled by skilled people are more reliable for such purposes.

## Message Authenticity

Message authenticity systems are forms of weaker authentication. For example, you may want to know that a message comes from your bank and is not a fraudulent message sent by some impostor. However, this message may have also been modified by an intermediate handler—perhaps an antivirus system that adds a trailer saying the message has been scanned and found to be malware-free or an antispam system that gives a judgment of the content of the e-mail. This is a weaker form of authentication; the message need not and indeed cannot be completely specified in the signature.

There are both cryptographic and noncryptographic message authenticity systems. As of this writing, they are still new systems going through the standards processes as well as deployment and real-world use. They are discussed in more detail under Authenticity Systems.

# ENCRYPTION AND SIGNING OPTIONS

There are two main standards for message security, as well as the ongoing work for message authentication. They are OpenPGP and S/MIME. Although they differ in data layout, the core systems work the same way at a high level. This section describes how these mechanisms work, more about the specifics of the two main standards, and also how they vary.

## Relevant Encryption Mechanisms

Public key cryptography is the center of these systems and how they gain the ability to direct a message to a specific user. However, public key cryptography is not suitable for encrypting large amounts of data. It is a relatively slow operation; it runs four or more orders of magnitude slower than symmetric key encryption. The exact ratio depends on the public key size, as well as the symmetric algorithm. However, as time goes on, symmetric algorithms tend to get faster [advanced encryption standard is, for example, faster than Data Encryption Standard (DES)], and users tend to use larger public keys. This means that as time goes on, the disparity magnifies. Consequently, the public key operation encrypts a *session key* that is a symmetric key. That key is used with a bulk encryption algorithm, which encrypts the message itself. Thus, the public key wraps the session key. This has the advantage of being much faster. Key wrapping itself is a useful mechanism itself. This allows a single message to be encrypted to multiple *cryptographic recipients*. The recipients can be either public keys, or even a symmetric key as might be derived from a passphrase. Table 5 lists common algorithms used for public key encryption.

Note that the identifiers that denote the cryptographic recipients are not encrypted. Consequently, an eavesdropper can always see the recipients. This permits the eavesdropper to know who the recipients are, even if the eavesdropper cannot read the message. There is a branch of security called *traffic analysis* that derives information based on who is talking to whom, even if the content of the conversations cannot be read. Of course, this can be countered by having the recipient identifiers contain no information (for example, they could be a constant), but this complicates the cryptosystem. Typically, e-mail is already a prime candidate for traffic analysis, as an eavesdropper knows who the message is being delivered to—it is, after all, the recipient's e-mail address—and this limitation has little, if any, effect. Nonetheless, it is important to realize that although cryptographic mechanisms prevent an eavesdropper from knowing the contents of communication, they can actually make it easier for the eavesdropper to know that communication is taking place. This is why it is good security to secure messages superfluously. It is not necessary to secure a message that says, *"Let's have lunch,"* but if an adversary knows that only important messages are secured, this not only helps the attacker know which messages to devote attention to breaking but also makes traffic analysis trivial.

Inside the symmetric key encrypted data are found the data itself. However, the data can also be compressed.

**Table 5** Common Symmetric Key Cipher Algorithms

| Cipher Name | Usual Key Size | Explanation |
|---|---|---|
| DES | 56 bits | The *data encryption standard* was developed in 1997 by IBM and the United States government as a standard cipher for government and business. It has been replaced by AES, the *advanced encryption standard.* |
| Triple-DES | 112 or 168 bits | Triple-DES is an improvement to DES created by performing the basic DES operation three times, encrypting, then decrypting, then encrypting again. Triple-DES can implemented with either two or three 56-bit keys, giving a total key size of 112 or 168 bits. Like DES, its use is now replaced by AES. |
| AES | 128, 192, or 256 bits | The *advanced encryption standard* is the present U.S. government standard cipher for government and business use. |
| RC2 | 40 or 128 bits | RC2 is a block cipher most commonly used in S/MIME messages. |
| RC4 | 40 or 128 bits | RC4 is a stream cipher most commonly used in TLS sessions. |
| Blowfish | 128 bits | Blowfish is a block cipher used in a variety of applications, including OpenPGP messages. |
| CAST-128 | 128 bits | CAST-128 is a block cipher commonly used in OpenPGP and S/MIME messages. |
| IDEA | 128 bits | IDEA is a block cipher used in a variety of applications, most notably pre-OpenPGP versions of PGP. Its use is limited today not because of any security issues, but rather that it is patented, but without a free-use license. |

Compressing the encrypted data is desirable because it makes the resulting message smaller (typically). Compressed messages are also less regular in structure, which gains some small modicum of increased security.

If a message is both encrypted and signed, the signature may be either encrypted itself or unencrypted. An encrypted signature is said to be *inside the envelope*, whereas an unencrypted signature is said to be *outside the envelope*. Signatures inside the envelope are more secure because an eavesdropper cannot see them. A signature outside the envelope allows the eavesdropper even more information for traffic analysis. The eavesdropper now knows not only the cryptographic recipient but also the signer, who is likely to be the sender—and the eavesdropper has cryptographic confirmation of the sender's certificate. Conversely, a signature outside the envelope can permit systems such as a whitelist system based on the signatures to work with encrypted messages. Table 5 lists common algorithms used for public key signatures.

One last wrinkle is that there are interesting properties to signature placement. If a signature is inside the envelope, the recipient(s) can decrypt the message and then reformat the signed message as a plaintext, signed message. This possibly is not what the originator wanted. As an example, suppose Alice sent Bob a message that is encrypted and signed and describes Charlie in less than flattering terms.

This is the basic structure of an encrypted message. All public key cryptosystems follow this basic structure. The specifics of any given cryptosystem can differ wildly, and in the next sections are how they are then built into e-mail security and then more detailed looks at OpenPGP and S/MIME. Figure 1 shows the basic structure of a generic secure message, with the signature inside the envelope.

## Notes on Cryptographic Strength

Mathematically, a cipher can be said to be secure if there is no better way to break a message than a *brute force attack*

on the key; if the best possible attack is to try every possible key in sequence, then the cipher is mathematically secure. However, security is a practical pursuit, and in all things practical, mathematics is not sufficient.

A cipher must also be practically secure, meaning that the total number of possible keys (called the key space) is large enough that an attacker cannot practically try all the possible keys in a reasonable amount of time. Imagine a cipher with a three-bit key space, and assume that it is mathematically secure. This cipher has eight possible keys and is thus easily broken with pencil and paper—just try all eight possible keys. The amount of effort that is needed to break a given cipher or other component is called the *work factor* needed to break it. Our example above is a cipher with a work factor of three bits.

Some ciphers were considered secure in the past but are no longer considered secure. For example, the DES

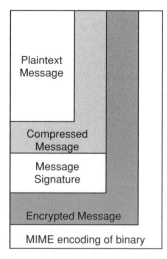

**Figure 1:** Structure of a secure message.

cipher has a 56-bit key space and is no longer considered secure. Ideally, a system's work factor grows exponentially with the key size. Generally this is true for symmetric ciphers. If a 56-bit key can be broken in a day (on average), then a 66-bit key can be broken in about 3 years (1024 days, to be exact). Thus, a 76-bit key can be broken (on average) in 3,072 years or by a distributed network of a thousand computers working for 3 years. And so on. These days, we consider a 128-bit key to be sufficient for all practical purposes.

Work factor grows exponentially with key size, and it is often difficult for us to estimate this sort of exponential growth. Burt Kaliski of RSA gives the following example of the strength of a 128-bit key: imagine a computer the size of a grain of sand that can iteratively test a decryption of a 128-bit key. Imagine that it can do one test in the amount of time that it takes light to cross it. Now imagine a distributed network of these computers that consists of these computers distributed over the surface of the Earth in a layer that is 1 m high. On average, this network will take 1000 (yes, 1000) years to exhaust the keyspace of a single 128-bit key. This is why we consider a 128-bit key to be practically secure. An attacker literally needs a spare planet full of computers to break a 128-bit key by brute force.

The AES can operate in 128-, 192-, and 256-bit versions. The stronger versions were created as a hedge against unforeseen advances in mathematics and technologies, as well as some foreseen advances.

For example, an area of active development is that of *quantum computers*. Our best estimate of what effect a quantum computer would have on algorithms is that it would effectively halve the key size of a symmetric cipher. Thus, a 128-bit key would be as vulnerable to an attack by a network of quantum computers as a 64-bit key is to an attack by a network of today's computers. Similarly, given a world with ubiquitous quantum computers, ciphers with 256-bit keys would be as strong as today's world with ubiquitous Von Neumann computers and 128-bit keys. The stronger versions of the AES are hedges against this hypothetical future.

## Cryptographic Balance

A cryptographic system also has the notion of *cryptographic balance*. A balanced cryptosystem has its various components with roughly equivalent strengths. For example, if a digital signature scheme is using a 160-bit hash function, then the matching public key should be approximately 1024 bits long. The hash function and the public key algorithm have approximately the same work factor. It would be gilding the lily to make a signature with a 2048-bit key and a 160-bit hash, as an attacker would attack the hash function.

Table 6, courtesy of the U.S. NIST, gives a measure of the balance between various cryptographic components. Note, however, that these are estimates. These measurements are something that people can and do disagree on, particularly when debating public key strength against symmetric key strength. In fact, this author believes the NIST comparison between public and symmetric keys to be pessimistic. However, the NIST estimates

**Table 6** Security Equivalences in Cryptographic Algorithms

| Comparable cryptographic strengths size in bits | | | | | | |
|---|---|---|---|---|---|---|
| Symmetric key | 56[a] | 80 | 112 | 128 | 192 | 256 |
| Hash function | | 160 | | 256 | 384 | 512 |
| MAC | 64[a] | 160 | | 256 | 384 | 512 |
| RSA/DSA | 512[a] | 1024 | 2K[b] | 3K[b] | 7.5K[b] | 15K[b] |
| Elliptic curve | | 160 | 224 | 256 | 384 | 512 |

[a] Not presently considered secure.
[b] FIPS parameters and standard currently under development.
Table courtesy U.S. NIST.

are valuable and authoritative, and conservative mathematical estimates are no crime (see Table 9).

## Standards for Secure E-Mail

The core cryptographic protocols give data objects that are encrypted, signed, or both. The RFC 1847 describes *security multiparts*, MIME-encoded objects for encrypted and signed parts within an e-mail message. More simply, the cryptographic object (such as an encrypted file) can merely be sent as an attachment to a message, or the cryptographic object can merely be the body of the message itself. Both S/MIME and OpenPGP have RFC 1847–compliant mechanisms for encoding a secure message.

## OpenPGP Overview

OpenPGP has at its roots the original PGP[1] written by Philip Zimmermann in 1991. It was the first widely deployed cryptosystem and was originally designed for use on Bulletin Board System (BBS) systems for encrypting files and messages on the BBS. OpenPGP itself comes out of work done by Zimmermann's team in creating a version of PGP free of intellectual property entanglements. The original PGP used the then-patented RSA algorithm for public key cryptography and the still-patented (in 2004) IDEA algorithm for symmetric cryptography. OpenPGP was designed to not require an algorithm with intellectual property constraints.

The Web page for the IETF's OpenPGP working group is http://www.ietf.org/html.charters/openPGP.html. OpenPGP is defined in the RFCs found in Table 7.

OpenPGP defines its own certificate format and data structure format. Furthermore, it describes a text-only coding for these objects called ASCII armor. This allows any system that can manipulate text to send an OpenPGP object. It also defines an all-intact coding for a signed text message called a *clearsigned* message. This allows any system that can manipulate text to send a message that is signed, yet readable, by a human being with no cryptographic software.

## S/MIME Overview

S/MIME is a descendant of some previous cryptosystems, *privacy enhanced mail* (PEM), *MIME object*

---

[1] PGP, Pretty Good Privacy, and Pretty Good are registered trademarks of PGP Corporation.

**Table 7** Core OpenPGP-related RFCs

| RFC | Name | Description |
|---|---|---|
| RFC 1991 | Pretty Good Privacy | This informational RFC describes the original PGP cryptosystem as implemented in PGP 2.6.2. |
| RFC 2440 | OpenPGP Formats | This RFC describes the coding for the data structures needed for OpenPGP certificates and cryptographic objects. |
| RFC 3156 | MIME Security with OpenPGP | This RFC describes OpenPGP/MIME, the RFC 1847 security multipart coding system for OpenPGP. |

*security services* (MOSS), and *message security protocol* (MSP).

The Web page for the IETF's S/MIME working group is http://www.ietf.org/html.charters/smime-charter.html. S/MIME is defined in the following RFCs (standards track only, except for the base S/MIME V2 RFCs) listed in Table 8.

Similarly to the way that OpenPGP has a predecessor, IETF-standard S/MIME is built on a previous S/MIME system, S/MIME V2. When this chapter talks about S/MIME, it refers to the IETF-standard S/MIME V3 unless otherwise noted.

S/MIME uses X.509 certificates for public key transport. Like it, its message structure is based on the ASN.1 data structure system. That data structure system is called *cryptographic message syntax* (CMS), which is itself a descendant of the PKCS7 encoding.

## Certificates, Trust, and Fine Differences

OpenPGP and S/MIME each use different certificate types, OpenPGP certificates and X.509 certificates. Syntactically, they are different, but there is no particular advantage to either. They both have mechanisms to describe all needed certificate attributes, and each has a generalized extension mechanism for expansion into new uses.

The term *key* is often colloquially used for OpenPGP certificates. The term predates X.509 certificates and the term certificate. It was created by Whitfield Diffie to be a short, euphonious way to talk about a key and all the data that is needed to use it effectively. It persists because he succeeded.

OpenPGP certificates are the more general form. They contain multiple certifications, as well as multiple names and even multiple use-directed keys. In contrast, an X.509

**Table 8** Core S/MIME-Related RFCs

| RFC | Name | Description |
|---|---|---|
| RFC 2311 | S/MIME version 2 message specification | This informational RFC describes S/MIME V2 message syntax. |
| RFC 2312 | S/MIME version 2 certificate handling | This informational RFC describes S/MIME V2 certificate semantics. |
| RFC 3850 | S/MIME V3.1 certificate handling | This RFC describes S/MIME's use of X.509 certificates. |
| RFC 3851 | S/MIME V3.1 message specification | This RFC describes the MIME wraping of CMS messages to make S/MIME messages. |
| RFC 3852 | Cryptographic message syntax (CMS) | This RFC describes the CMS standard for coding binary cryptographic objects. |
| RFC 2631 | Diffie–Hellman key agreement method | This RFC describes S/MIME's use of the ANSI X9.42 variant of Diffie–Hellman. |
| RFC 2634 | Enhanced security services for S/MIME | This RFC describes option S/MIME services for signed receipts, security labels, secure mailing lists, and signing certificates. |
| RFC 2984 | Use of the CAST-128 encryption algorithm in CMS | This RFC describes S/MIME's use of CAST-128. |
| RFC 3185 | Reuse of CMS content encryption keys | This RFC describes how a single symmetric key can be used for multiple data packets within a CMS blob. |
| RFC 3274 | Compressed data content type for CMS | This RFC describes how CMS uses compressed data within an encrypted message. |
| RFC 3370 | CMS algorithms | This RFC describes the conventions for specifying core algorithms in CMS. |
| RFC 3537 | Wrapping a hashed message authentication code (HMAC) key with a triple-DES key or an AES key | This RFC shows how an authenticated data type can wrap an HMAC key with AES or triple-DES. |
| RFC 3560 | Use of the RSAES-OAEP key transport algorithm in the CMS | This RFC shows how CMS uses OAEP for RSA encryption. |
| RFC 3565 | Use of AES within CMS | This RFC describes how AES encryption is specified in CMS. |
| RFC 3854 | Securing X.400 content with S/MIME | This RFC describes how S/MIME can be used to protect X.400 data. |

**Table 9** Algorithms Used for Public-Key Encryption and Digital Signatures

| Name | Key sizes | Explanation |
|---|---|---|
| RSA | No limit, typically 1024-4096 bits | RSA may be used for both signing and encryption. The signature size of an RSA signature is proportional to the size of the key. |
| DSA | 512-1024 bits | DSA is a signing-only algorithm. As of this writing, it is limited to 1024-bit key, but the U.S. NIST is finalizing the standard parameters for longer key sizes. The size of DSA signatures is proportional to the size of the hash function used with it. The U.S. NIST is expected to release the parameters for DSA keys larger than 1024 bits in early 2005. |
| Elgamal | No limit, typically 1024-4096 bits | Elgamal is a variant of Diffie–Hellman that can be used as a public key encryption algorithm similar to the way that RSA is used. Elgamal signatures are possible, but not generally used, as DSA, as DSA produces smaller signatures with similar security parameters. |
| ANSI X9.42 | No limit, typically 1024-4096 bits | X9.42 is a variant of Diffie–Hellman that can be used for public key encryption similar to the way that RSA and Elgamal can be used. |
| Elliptic Curve | No limit, typically 160-512 bits | Elliptic curve public key ciphers are variants of Diffie–Hellman-based algorithms. They differ from the typical algorithms in that they are mathematically exercised over a different set than the integers. Thus, the parameters are not integer numbers, but some point on a given elliptic curve. There are elliptic curve versions of DSA, Elgamal, and X9.42. Elliptic curve keys are smaller than integer keys for an equivalent cryptographic strengths. |

certificate has a single key, name, and certification. The OpenPGP usage is equivalent to having a collection of X.509 certificates that are the same on one or more attribute. For example, if a single certificate authority (CA) issues a certificate for signing and another for encryption, this is equivalent to the OpenPGP use of having two keys in a single certificate. Two X.509 certificates from different CAs that share the same key material are equivalent to the OpenPGP use of multiple certifications in a single certificate. Thus, the differences are smaller than advocates of either type might have you believe.

Semantically, there are also differences that are smaller than one is lead to believe. OpenPGP traditionally uses the so-called *web of trust*, whereas X.509 was designed to be used with a single hierarchy. Consequently, each has its strengths; there is no better way for two people who want to start sending secure e-mail than to use OpenPGP just as there is no better way to issue certificates in scales as large as telephone numbers. Each technology excels at its intended function and this is why each thrives to this day.

As each scales in its respective direction, the differences blur. Each system has grown beyond its simplest implementation to incorporate aspects of the other. OpenPGP has within it the notion of a *meta-introduce*, which is nothing more than a traditional CA root that delegates to sub-CAs. In the X.509 world, the lack of a single hierarchy has led to OpenPGP-like uses. The so-called *Bridge CA*, which enables a hierarchy made of competing subhierarchies (e.g., the U.S. government or any corporation that has had a merger), was created specifically to be equivalent to an OpenPGP *trusted introducer*.

However, some of these certificate use models that reflect into the implemented systems themselves. There is, for example, no reason why S/MIME must use certificates that come from a given hierarchy. However, nearly all S/MIME implementations work well only with certificates issued by a CA that is built into the implementation. Usually, these are the same CAs with root certificates installed into the browser. This means that it is difficult to use S/MIME with self-signed certificates or a local hierarchy. (There is no difference between the two; because a root certificate is a self-signed certificate, a lone self-signed certificate is a hierarchy of one.) Although most implementations allow a user to import certificates or root certificates,

**Table 10** Algorithms Used for Hashing Messages

| Name | Hash size | Explanation |
|---|---|---|
| MD5 | 128 bits | MD5 has been found to have cryptographic flaws, and is being phased out of existing cryptographic systems, but may still be used in some signatures. |
| SHA-1 | 160 bits | SHA-1 is an improved version of MD5, designed by the U.S. NIST. It is the most commonly used hash function today. |
| SHA-256 | 256 bits | SHA-256 is a recent hash function of a new design. It was developed by the U.S. NIST. |
| SHA-384 | 384 bits | SHA-384 is a recent hash function, developed by the U.S. NIST along with SHA-256 and SHA-512. It is typically not used, because it requires the same work as SHA-512 and consequently need only be used when more security is needed than SHA-256, but the data structures do not allow a full SHA-512 hash. |
| SHA-512 | 512 bits | SHA-512 is a recent hash function, developed by the U.S. NIST along with SHA-256 and SHA-384. |

it is often significantly more difficult to do this than it should be. Many otherwise security-savvy people (such as this author) have tried and failed to set up local certificate hierarchies. See Table 8 for S/MIME-related RFCs.

Conversely, the Open Group's *S/MIME Gateway* specification uses S/MIME and X.509 syntactically, but its use model is for a single self-signed certificate per domain. The gateways have a list of other participating gateways and are keyed by administrators telling each other the fingerprint of their certificates. Semantically, this is a direct trust system as one conventionally thinks of an OpenPGP system, but it operates at the domain rather than user-to-user.

There is even more direct syntax matching going on. Work is going on in the IETF to specify how to denote that an S/MIME certificate is in OpenPGP format. There is also an extension to OpenPGP used by PGP Corporation that permits an X.509 certificate to be rewrapped as an OpenPGP certificate with the same key material. The PGP products also allow an OpenPGP certificate to create an X.509 certificate request, which can then be sent to any X.509 CA, thus completely blurring the line between the syntax of the certificate formats.

As time goes on, these hybrid systems that mix elements of distributed and centralized semantics and agile syntax will continue to be more and more common. The apparent differences will in time be as irrelevant as the differences between various picture standards such as GIF, PNG, and JPEG.

## Comparisons Between OpenPGP and S/MIME

Both OpenPGP and S/MIME are secure cryptosystems. However, there are a number of differences between them. Here is a selection:

- Both the S/MIME and OpenPGP working groups are working on revisions to their respective standards. If you are seriously interested in either standard, you should check the RFC library at http://www.rfc-editor.org/rfcsearch.html for revisions and additions to the standards.

- Although both S/MIME and OpenPGP have a binary cryptographic blob specification and then successions of data wrappers around them. However, OpenPGP starts from the basic blob and then wraps the MIME system around it. In contrast, S/MIME starts from the MIME wrappers and and defines CMS under it. Some standards that use CMS objects in them say that they are "S/MIME-coded" when it would be more technically proper to say that they are "CMS-coded." This is because S/MIME was designed with the RFC 1847 codings in mind, and OpenPGP predates them. This means that there is no simple text encoding in S/MIME for an equivalent of OpenPGP's *cleartext* messages that are signed, human readable text with no MIME wrappers. Additionally, one does not typically (if ever) see a CMS equivalent to an OpenPGP detached signature.

- When OpenPGP specifies a cryptographic recipient, it is 64-bit truncation of the actual recipient fingerprint.

S/MIME recipients are the issuer id and certificate serial number of the recipient's X.509 certificate. Issuers are permitted to number X.509 certificates as they please, but typically, this is itself a cryptographic hash of the certificate.

Additionally, OpenPGP permits a *speculative* recipient, that is one that is in fact zero. This permits a message to be generated with no information in it that can be used for traffic analysis. Of course, when a speculative message decrypted, the implementation must do more work to tell what to do with a speculatively encrypted message.

- When OpenPGP bulk-encrypts data, it uses cipher feedback (CFB) mode, whereas S/MIME uses cipher block chaining (CBC) mode.

- Both OpenPGP and S/MIME allow the use of the RSA public key algorithm, as well as discrete logarithm systems. Both allow DSA for signing; OpenPGP uses Elgamal encryption, whereas S/MIME uses a similar variant of Diffie–Hellman as described in ASNI X9.42. Discrete logarithm certificates are not only common but also usual in OpenPGP systems. Conversely, DSA X.509 certificates are rare, and X9.42 certificates are almost unheard of. This disparity owes to the fact that the patents on discrete logarithms expired in 1997, whereas the RSA patent expired in 2000. OpenPGP's heritage in open systems led its implementers to prefer discrete-logarithm cryptography over RSA for those 3 years.

- Both OpenPGP and S/MIME allow the core message to be compressed. However, compressed messages are the rule with OpenPGP and unusual with S/MIME. This is because compression was a basic function in pre-OpenPGP versions of PGP and added into S/MIME as part of the IETF standardization process.

- S/MIME requires that an implementation be interoperable with S/MIME V2. This means that some implementations that claim to be S/MIME V3 systems are actually V2 systems.

- OpenPGP mandates that messages that are both encrypted and signed have the signatures inside the cryptographic envelope. S/MIME permits signatures either inside the envelope or outside the envelope.

- S/MIME sends with a message the certificate of the sender. OpenPGP does not, but relies on external mechanisms such as directories and databases for finding certificates. The S/MIME behavior has the advantage that you can always reply to an encrypted message and verify a signature in situ, even if you have no network connection. Conversely, this increases the size of an S/MIME message, and if all messages in a system are S/MIME messages, this can add up. In contrast, OpenPGP messages are frequently smaller than unencrypted messages because they are compressed. Many people, including this author, find this to be a nit—disk space is cheap and getting exponentially cheaper as time progresses, and e-mail is bloated by more things than encryption. However, it is a concern to some people and to those people, it is a major concern. Consequently, it must be stated.

- S/MIME limits the size of a public key in a certificate to 1024 bits, but many implementations allow keys up to 2048 bits. OpenPGP limits the size of a multiprecision integer to 65,535 bits, and this is reflected through the rest of the system, including maximum key size. However, most implementations limit public key size to 4096 bits.

- OpenPGP certificates contain information about the user's preferences and the features that the user's implementation supports. For example, the certificate contains a list of supported cipher algorithms, compression algorithms, and new features. In contrast, S/MIME codes this information into a mail message. This means that an OpenPGP user always knows how to code a message to the preferences and support level of the recipient's system. An S/MIME user, however, must first send a message to a correspondent before that person knows how to optimally encode a message. The S/MIME working group is working on a capabilities system to correct this issue.

- S/MIME V2 was based on 40-bit, U.S.-exportable cryptography. Today, this is not considered acceptable security by anyone, but it was a subject of debate before export regulations were liberalized in 2000. Because S/MIME requires backward compatibility with V2, there is a risk that any given message may use 40-bit cryptography, especially when initiating secure communications with someone else. The aforementioned capabilities system is also being created to correct this problem.

# AUTHENTICITY SYSTEMS

There are two in-progress systems in the IETF for message authenticity as antispam systems. Neither has produced a standard as of this writing in fall 2004, and there is even drama going on as we prepare this for press about patent licensing in MARID. However, these efforts are of such import that they should be described at a high level.

## The MARID Protocols for Authenticity

The MARID working group is producing a standard presently also called *Sender ID*. Sender ID itself is a merge between previous proposals, *Caller ID* and *sender policy framework (SPF)*. It is a noncryptographic authenticity system, using network information to validate e-mail senders. Here is how it works at a high level:

1. The owner of an Internet domain creates a DNS record that describes the servers that domain will use for sending mail.

2. When an e-mail server receives a message, it looks up the purported MARID record in the DNS and checks to see if the sending IP address is specified as one of the sending addresses.

3. Depending on the above check, the receiver takes some appropriate action. If there is no match, the receiver might consider the message to be bogus and reject it then and there, or merely weight it more strongly to be considered bogus. If the sending server is legitimate, further processing is still necessary, as there is nothing

to stop a spammer from registering their own domain and putting in the proper MARID records.

A complication in MARID is how to deal with systems that forward mail. Systems that participate in MARID must rewrite some of the e-mail headers so as to make sure that e-mail sent on behalf of one domain gets the proper attribution so that the DNS checks will work correctly.

As of this writing, there have been difficulties in MARID. Microsoft has not given licenses to its parts of MARID that are acceptable to parties that would license it. This means that those implementing MARID may be implementing SPF rather than the full Sender ID.

You can find information on the MARID working group, including the in-progress documents, at http://www.ietf.org/html.charters/marid-charter.html. The situation doubtlessly will have changed by the time you are reading this.

## The MASS Protocols for Authenticity

MASS is the name of an as-yet-unformed working group to produce a standard to check message authenticity based on digital signatures. Presently, the work is based on unifying Yahoo!'s *DomainKeys* system and Cisco's *Identified Internet Mail* system. Each of these systems sign some subset of the message's headers, as well as some subset of the message's content. They differ on issues of key management and verification, as well as some internal details, but the basic approach is nearly identical between the two proposals. A cross-industry group is working on the unification of the two systems so that an acceptable result can become a standard, without the difficulties that have presently dogged MARID.

It is necessary to allow for some changes in the e-mail message. Some headers may be added, removed, or altered as the message moves through the network. Some of these changes are significant, some are not. The message content itself might change in ways that are not significant. For example, an antivirus scanner might append a trailer to the message saying that the message has been scanned. This is not a significant change.

These systems are the cutting edge of e-mail security because they explore reasonable relaxation of a cryptographic system. A signature scheme that did not allow an antivirus text trailer would fail in the real world. However, a signature scheme that permits criminals to forge bank documents also fails.

## How MARID and MASS Work Together

MARID and MASS work together in a number of ways. Each of them relies on both evidence about a message's sender, and a scoring system for evaluating that information. Consequntly, policy and reputation information can be shared between them in many cases. MARID can be considered to be a blacklist system, easily finding invalid senders. MASS can be considered a whitelist system, easily finding valid messages. Authenticity cannot be solved by either blacklists or whitelists; both are needed for good results.

# IMPLEMENTIONS

No list of implementations is accurate or complete by the time it is printed. Here is an incomplete list of implementations of the standard systems:

## Client-Based Solutions

- S/MIME is built into a number of MUAs, including Mozilla, Microsoft Outlook, Novell Groupwise, and Apple's Mail. The IBM/Lotus Domino system can use S/MIME for outgoing mail as well.

- There is an open source S/MIME toolkit in the OpenSSL toolkit including a small certificate authority.

- An open source OpenPGP implementation, *Gnu Privacy Guard*, runs on Windows and most UNIX-like systems. There are also a number of open source GUI wrappers for it, as well as support for most UNIX-like mailers.

- PGP Corporation makes a number of OpenPGP and S/MIME compatible products, including support for many MUAs, including Outlook, Outlook Express, IBM/Lotus Notes, Novell Groupwise, Qualcomm Eudora, and Apple Mail. It is also supported within a number of other MUAs, including MailSmith, Pegasus Mail, and others.

- Articsoft make an OpenPGP implementation for file handling.

## Server-Based Solutions

- The Open Group have a set of standards for an S/MIME e-mail gateway. It is intended to be a single-certificate, server-to-server system. Tumbleweed and Net IQ have products that comply with this specification.

- Tovaris makes an S/MIME e-mail gateway.

- PGP Corporation makes *PGP Universal*, an OpenPGP and S/MIME compliant server system that can operate on SMTP, POP, and IMAP, as well as Exchange and Domino servers.

- *Anubis* is an open source OpenPGP gateway for SMTP.

- Forum Systems make an OpenPGP enhanced file transfer server.

- McAfee make an OpenPGP implementation for server-based file handling and server management.

# SUMMARY

We have seen how e-mail security works with cryptography to secure messages. We have examined the core security problems with message security and looked over the two standard cryptosystems. We have also described ongoing work in message authenticity. This is an ongoing process and there is always more work to be done.

# GLOSSARY

**Asymmetric Cipher**    A cipher that uses separate keys for encryption and decryption. Asymmetric ciphers are also called *public key* ciphers, because the encryption key can be freely distributed without compromising the security of the system.

**Authenticity**    The property that a message comes from the source that it purports to come from.

**Certificate**    A digitally signed object that binds together a public key and human-readable information about that key, such as a name, e-mail address, authorizations, and so on.

**Cipher**    An algorithm that takes readable data and makes it unreadable without possession of another piece of data, called the key.

**Cryptographic Balance**    The practice of using cryptographic algorithms that have equivalent strengths in concert.

**Digital Signature**    An asymmetric cryptographic object made with a public key pair that allows arbitrary entities to know if the signed data has been modified.

**DomainKeys**    A message authenticity protocol based on digital signatures. DomainKeys is developed by Yahoo! and is being unified with a similar proposal from Cisco called *Internet identified mail*.

**Domino**    IBM's server for the Notes e-mail and collaboration system.

**Envelope**    A colloquialism for the actual encryption in data that contains both encrypted and unencrypted parts. For example, in an encrypted e-mail message, the unencrypted sender and recipient names as well as the subject are said to be outside the envelope, but the encrypted data is said to be inside the envelope.

**Exchange**    Microsoft's server for the Outlook e-mail and collaboration system.

**Groupwise**    Novell's e-mail and collaboration system.

**Hash Function**    A cryptographic algorithm that takes a string of different lengths and produces fixed-length outputs. Hash functions are used as building blocks in digital signatures and MACs. Hash functions are also called *message digest* functions.

**Internet Engineering Task Force**    Standards body that produces many Internet standards.

**Internet Identified Mail**    A message authenticity protocol based on digital signatures. Internet identified mail is developed by Cisco and is being unified with a similar proposal from Yahoo! called *DomainKeys*.

**Internet Message Access Protocol**    A protocol that an MUA can use for managing e-mail that resides on a server.

**Mail Transport Agent**    An e-mail server.

**Mail User Agent**    An e-mail client.

**Message Authentication Code**    A cryptographic object that can be used to tell that data has not been modified. A MAC may be considered to be the symmetric key equivalent of a digital signature.

**OpenPGP**    IETF standard for encrypting data, one of two NIST standards, along with S/MIME.

**Post Office Protocol**    A protocol that an MUA may use for retrieving mail from a mail server.

**Request For Comments**    Document produced by the IETF. RFCs may be either informational or standards.

**S/MIME**    IETF standard for encrypting data, one of two NIST standards, along with OpenPGP.

**Secure Sockets Layer**    A protocol for protecting a connection-oriented network connection.

**Sender Policy Framework** An e-mail authenticity protocol that has e-mail senders publish which servers send their e-mail, so that a receiver can vet an e-mail based on the sending server. SPF is also sometimes called "sender preferred from." It is also a part of a similar system, *Sender ID*.

**Simple Mail Transfer Protocol** The protocol that governs MTA-to-MTA communications.

**Symmetric Cipher** A cipher that uses a single key for both encryption and decryption.

**Transport Layer Security** The IETF standardization of SSL.

## CROSS REFERENCES

See *Digital Signatures and Electronic Signatures; Encryption Basics; PGP (Pretty Good Privacy); S/MIME (Secure MIME); Secure Sockets Layer (SSL); SMTP (Simple Mail Transfer Protocol)*.

## FURTHER READING

Many of the references in this article are the RFCs that define the various protocols. These are provided in the tables in this document. Further reading is provided below:

Daemen, J., Rijmen, V. (2002). *The design of Rijndael: AES—The advanced encryption standard (information security and cryptography)*. New York: Springer-Verlag.

Diffie, W., Landau, S. (1999). *Privacy on the line: The politics of wiretapping and encryption*. Cambridge, MA: MIT Press.

Ferguson, N., Schneier, B. (2003). *Practical cryptography*. New York: John Wiley & Sons.

Garfinkel, S. (1995). *PGP: Pretty Good Privacy*. San Francisco: O'Reilly.

Kaufman, C., Perlman, R., Speciner, M. (2002). *Network security: Private communication in a public world* (2nd ed.), Upper Saddle River, NJ: Prentice Hall.

Menezes, A., Van Oorschot, P., Vanstone, S. (1996). *Handbook of applied cryptography*. Boca Raton, FL: CRC Press.

Rescorla, E. (2000). *SSL and TLS: Designing and building secure systems*. Boston: Addison-Wesley.

Schneier, B. (1995). *Applied cryptography* (2nd ed.). New York: John Wiley & Sons.

Stallings, R. (2002). *Cryptography and network security: Principles and practice* (3rd ed.). Upper Saddle River, NJ: Prentice Hall.

Viega, J., Messier, M., Chandra, P. (2002). *Network security with OpenSSL*. San Francisco: O'Reilly.

# Security for ATM Networks

Thomas D. Tarman, *Sandia National Laboratories*

## INTRODUCTION

Asynchronous transfer mode (ATM) is a networking technology that was selected by the International Telecommunication Union (ITU) to implement the broadband integrated digital services network, which promised integrated delivery of a variety of application traffic, including voice, video, and data. During the peak of ATM standards activity in the mid-1990s, a group of researchers and vendors started thinking about the need to supplement the ATM protocol standard suite with additional standards that provided cryptographically strong security services, including confidentiality, authentication, and access control. As a result, a working group was started in the ATM Forum that worked to develop a set of specifications for security services, and the ATM Security 1.1 specification was approved by the ATM Forum in 2001.

This chapter provides a brief overview of the security mechanisms that are defined in Security 1.1. However, because there is more to ATM security than the Security 1.1 mechanisms, this chapter first provides a basic introduction to ATM network protocols, followed by a discussion of how ATM devices can be configured to implement noncryptographic security mechanisms such as virtual private networks. Next, this chapter delves into the Security 1.1 services, including mechanisms that exist to support those services. A discussion of mechanisms for securing ATM infrastructure protocols follows. This chapter then concludes with some final remarks.

## ATM OVERVIEW

The purpose of this section is to provide the reader with sufficient background of ATM protocols with which to understand the various ATM security mechanisms described in this chapter. If more detail is desired, then the reader is urged to consult any of a variety of available ATM networking texts.

Relative to transmission control protocol/Internet protocol (TCP/IP), ATM is considered a link level technology in that it provides data transport services for connectionless IP datagrams. However, unlike most link level protocols such as Ethernet, ATM is a connection-oriented technology. As such, ATM data communications occur within the context of a connection, which must be established end to end through the ATM network before data transfer occurs.

To support ATM connection establishment and data transfer in an interoperable fashion, a number of protocols have been developed by international standards bodies (such as the ITU) and industry consortia (such as the ATM Forum). These protocols are organized along the ATM reference model, which is depicted in Figure 1.

This reference model represents each ATM protocol function (and security function) within a different plane as follows:

- user plane (responsible for user data transport),
- control plane (responsible for network control and establishment of user data connections), and
- management plane (responsible for managing connections and traffic).

Furthermore, the ATM reference model defines a set of layers within each plane. These layers provide abstract functionality that can be specific to an individual plane (e.g., adaptation of application data to ATM cells in the user plane ATM adaptation layer), or they can provide functionality that is common across all planes (e.g., ATM and physical layers).

In addition, the mechanisms that are described by this reference model may change, depending on where in the network a given protocol may operate. For example, the control plane protocol interactions between an end user and the ATM network over a user–network interface (UNI) differs from the protocol interactions between ATM switches over a network–network interface (NNI).

The following sections describe the ATM protocol functions provided by each ATM plane in more detail.

## User Plane

The ATM user plane is responsible for transporting user data traffic from one end system to another. The basic unit of data transfer for ATM is the cell, which is a small, fixed

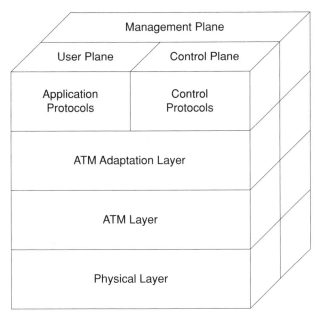

**Figure 1:** ATM reference model.

length "packet" that is composed of a 5-byte header and 48-byte payload. The header contains fields that indicate to ATM switches how to forward the cell along an ATM virtual circuit or path (described later). The header fields that carry this information are the virtual path identifier (VPI) and virtual circuit identifier (VCI). In addition, another header field identifies the type of information (i.e., user data or management information) contained in the cell payload. This field is called the payload type identifier (PTI).

Because ATM cells are so small, a mechanism is required to segment larger application protocol data units (PDUs) to ATM cells. This is accomplished by the ATM adaptation layer (AAL) function, which is depicted in Figure 2.

When a cell is transmitted into an ATM network, it is switched along a given virtual path or circuit that is configured end to end through the network. When an ATM switch receives the cell, it performs the following functions to switch the cell along the virtual circuit:

1. It notes the interface over which the cell is received and records the VPI and VCI values it finds in the cell's header.

2. Using the incoming interface ID, VPI, and VCI, it consults a switching table to determine the outgoing interface ID, VPI, and VCI.

3. It modifies the VPI and VCI header fields according to the contents of the switching table.

4. It sends the cell out the outgoing interface.

Central to the operation of an ATM switch is its switching table. This table must be configured correctly for a switch to successfully forward each ATM cell that it receives. This table can be configured manually via management configuration of each switch to form a permanent virtual circuit (PVC). Alternatively, control plane protocols can be used to establish a dynamic switched virtual circuit (SVC).

ATM provides a mechanism that allows virtual circuits that share a common VPI value (as shown in Figure 3) to be switched in aggregate along a common path. In this case, when an ATM switch receives a cell, it uses only the incoming interface ID and VPI value to extract the outgoing interface ID and VPI from the switching table. The benefit of virtual path switching is that the aggregation of virtual circuits simplifies configuration of PVCs, especially over many switches and between many sites.

## Control Plane

Although ATM virtual circuits or paths can be established manually, this method does not scale well for large ATM networks that contain many end systems and switches. As a result, the likelihood of human error in configuring many table entries in many switches becomes considerable. For this reason, the international standards bodies developed protocols for establishing SVCs across multivendor ATM networks. Generally, these protocols fall into two categories: virtual circuit (or path) signaling and virtual circuit routing.

As shown in Figure 4, when one end system (the calling party) wishes to establish a virtual connection to another end system (the called party), the calling party uses UNI signaling to instruct the network to establish the connection. To do so, the calling party issues a UNI SETUP message, which contains information fields such as a globally unique destination address, source address, requested network quality of service (QoS), and desired security attributes and parameters

When the first switch receives the SETUP request, it checks to see if it can support the request, it checks its

**Figure 2:** ATM user plane data segmentation.

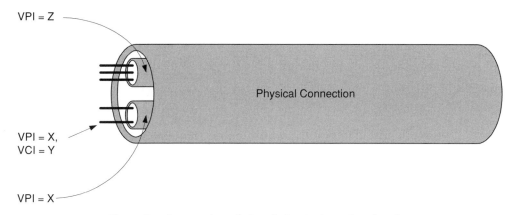

**Figure 3:**   Aggregation of virtual circuits into virtual paths.

local routing tables, and it sends an NNI SETUP request message to the next-hop switch. This process repeats for each switch in the path between the calling and called parties.

When the last switch processes the SETUP request, it issues a UNI SETUP request to the called party, which examines the SETUP message contents to determine if it wishes to accept the connection. If so, then it sends a UNI CONNECT response back to the network, and each switch allocates resources for the virtual circuit as it propagates the CONNECT message back to the calling party. This message may include additional information about the connection, including security attributes.

Recall that during the connection SETUP process, each switch along the path must decide which next-hop switch is "closest" to the called party. This decision is made using current network link state and topology information that is distributed through the ATM network via the private network–network interface (PNNI) protocol. Although this protocol is based on the open shortest path first (OSPF) protocol that was designed for IP routing, PNNI extends OSPF by providing many more levels of address aggregation (which makes the protocol more scalable) and by supporting QoS as a network link state attribute and routing metric. Thus, when a switch needs to decide which interface is the next-hop interface, it considers not only the current topology of the ATM

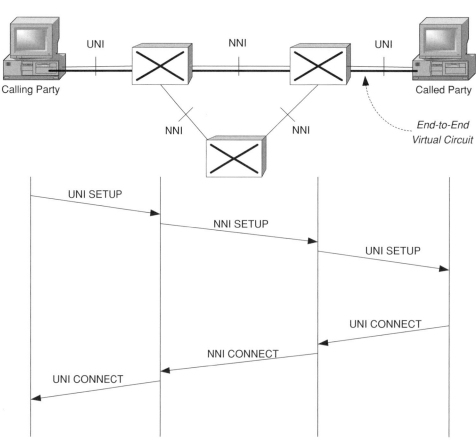

**Figure 4:**   ATM SVC connection establishment signaling.

network, but also how resources are allocated within the network.

## Management Plane

The ATM management plane is responsible for managing network entities such as the end points of a physical connection, virtual circuits, and virtual paths. In addition, the management plane is also responsible for reporting network congestion, which allows the end points to control the rate at which they send traffic into the ATM network.

One mechanism that is used for communicating network management information for a virtual circuit is the operation and maintenance (OAM) cell. OAM cells are special ATM cells that are used for detecting and isolating network faults, monitoring performance, and implementing security management functions. Because OAM cells report management information for a given virtual circuit (VC) or virtual path (VP), these cells are switched along with other cells (e.g., data cells) on the specified VC or VP. On a VP, F4 OAM cells (cells that report virtual path information) are differentiated from other cells through special values in the VCI field in the cells' headers. On a VC, F5 OAM cells (cells that report virtual circuit level information) are differentiated using the PTI field in the ATM cell header. Because these cells are switched along with user data cells, the relative ordering between user data and OAM cells is maintained. As discussed later, this is an important property for maintaining synchronization between ATM encryption devices.

Another management plane function that is provided by ATM is the integrated layer management interface (ILMI). This function allows devices that are directly connected to each other to exchange interface configuration information such as device and network addresses and physical layer attributes. This information is exchanged between the two devices via the simple network management protocol (SNMP).

## NONCRYPTOGRAPHIC ATM VPNS

In the previous section, the basic protocol mechanisms employed by ATM for connection establishment and data transfer were described. In this section, methods for applying these mechanisms to construct noncryptographic virtual private networks (VPNs) are described. An ATM VPN is considered here to be a noncryptographic technique for enforcing policies that govern whether ATM end systems or networks can connect to each other. VPNs are widely supported by ATM switch gear and are implemented via a number of mechanisms.

Regardless of which mechanism is used, the effectiveness of ATM VPNs is limited by the fact that they do not use cryptographic mechanisms for data confidentiality and authenticity. Therefore, although ATM end users are generally precluded from violating connection policy via these techniques, VPNs do not provide protection of ATM traffic from network operations personnel or others who have access to the ATM switching infrastructure. Furthermore, because VPNs rely on correct ATM switch configuration, configuration errors can negate the policy.

Given these caveats, VPNs are still useful because they are widely supported by modern ATM switch gear and

because they provide effective connection policy controls. The following sections describe different mechanisms for implementing VPNs.

## Permanent Virtual Circuits/Paths

The simplest mechanism for implementing ATM VPNs is to manually establish the allowed connections via permanent virtual circuits (PVCs) and to disable signaling support within the ATM network to ensure that only the PVCs will be used for carrying data traffic. This technique ensures that the only connections that exist in the ATM network are those that have been explicitly configured by network operations staff.

As described earlier, PVCs are configured by manually inserting entries in the switching tables within all switches that exist between each pair of hosts. The problem with this approach is that it does not scale well. That is, as the network diameter increases, the number of switch configuration actions also increases and reliability decreases. One way to reduce the amount of configuration and increase reliability is to use soft permanent virtual circuits (SPVCs) instead. With SPVCs, the connections are still "permanent" at the network edge, where the end systems attach (making them look like PVCs to the end systems). However, the connections are signaled and routed automatically in between the ATM edge switches. Because SPVC connections are initiated and maintained by the edge ATM switches, connection policy is still enforced by the network, but the configuration is confined to the edge switches.

With ATM PVCs or SPVCs, connection policy is enforced at the per-host level. If this level of granularity is too fine, a coarser level of granularity can be implemented using permanent virtual paths (PVPs). This approach, which is shown in Figure 5, can be used to enforce connection policies between ATM subnetworks rather than individual hosts.

With PVPs, each site's border switch (i.e., the switch that connects to the core or public ATM network) is configured to terminate each PVP tunnel that connects it to another site, as allowed by the connection policy. With a PVP mesh in place, each of the border switches acts as a signaling and routing peer with each of the other switches in the PVP mesh, allowing the hosts behind each border switch to establish SVCs through the PVP tunnels with hosts in other sites. Because the border switches at each site are peers with border switches at other sites, the sites that are served by these border switches trust all of the other sites. However, the border switches must not peer with the core or private network. Otherwise, connections can be established from the public network into a site's private network. Although this method minimizes necessary configuration to the border switches, it still requires cooperation (and increased service costs) from the core or public network provider.

## ATM Address Filtering

Most ATM switches provide the capability to permit or deny UNI connection requests based on the source and destination ATM addresses (and also other attributes) that accompany the SETUP message. To implement VPNs

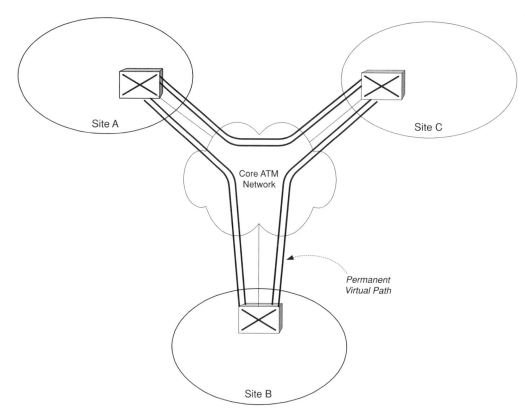

**Figure 5:** ATM connection policy enforcement using PVPs.

using this strategy, all edge ATM switches that connect to VPN hosts must be configured to permit connection requests to all other hosts that belong to the VPN.

For example, consider the VPN shown in Figure 6, which includes nodes A, B, and C, but not node D.

To implement this connection policy, the following filters are applied via network management operations on the edge switches:

| Switch | Interface | Incoming Policy | Outgoing Policy |
|---|---|---|---|
| SW1 | To Node A | Allow to B | Allow from B |
| | | Allow to C | Allow from C |
| | | Deny to all others | Deny from all others |
| SW2 | To Node B | Allow to A | Allow from A |
| | | Allow to C | Allow from C |
| | | Deny to all others | Deny from all others |
| SW3 | To Node C | Allow to A | Allow from A |
| | | Allow to C | Allow from C |
| | | Deny to all others | Deny from all others |
| SW3 | To Node D | (any policy) | (any policy) |

Although this example implements connection filtering at the host level of granularity using complete addresses, it may also be provided at the network level using addresses and address masks.

Address filtering has two advantages over PVCs. The first advantage is that the configuration required to implement a filtering policy needs only to be applied at the edge switches. The second advantage is that it leverages the flexibility provided by SVC signaling to establish connections. However, because filtering decisions may be based on source address information contained in the SETUP message, source address spoofing becomes a concern with this approach. To mitigate the possibility of source address spoofing, source address filters should be applied on the ingress ports of the edge switches. These filters would ensure that the source address that is claimed by the end system matches what is configured in the switch. From the earlier example, the following filters are added to prevent source address spoofing:

| Switch | Interface | Incoming policy |
|---|---|---|
| SW1 | To Node A | Allow from A |
| | | Deny from all others |
| SW2 | To Node B | Allow from B |
| | | Deny from all others |
| SW3 | To Node C | Allow from C |
| | | Deny from all others |

As described earlier, noncryptographic VPNs are useful because the mechanisms that implement them are widely supported by ATM equipment. However, if stronger mechanisms are required, then the use of cryptographic mechanisms must be considered.

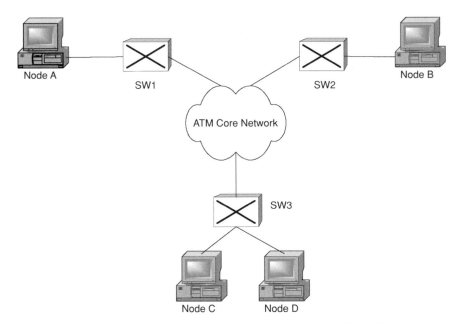

**Figure 6:** ATM connection policy enforcement using address filtering.

# CRYPTOGRAPHIC ATM SECURITY MECHANISMS

The ATM security mechanisms described in the previous section are widely supported by today's ATM switches. However, if stronger mechanisms are required by a network's security policy, then the cryptographic mechanisms defined in the ATM Forum Security 1.1 specification (ATM Forum, 2001a) may be required. This specification defines interoperable security mechanisms that perform the following functions:

- initial entity authentication,
- negotiation of security services and parameters,
- key exchange,
- confidentiality,
- data origin authentication and integrity, and
- changeover of encryption and authentication keys.

In addition, other ATM Forum specifications exist that define the following mechanisms:

- ATM control plane security and
- renegotiation of security parameters.

Although the following sections describe these security services in more detail, the reader should consult ATM Forum (2001a) and Tarman and Witzke (2001) for more detail on the implementation and use of these mechanisms.

## Connection Initiation Security

Security services for all or a portion of an ATM virtual circuit are provided by *security agents* (SAs), which are logical entities that may reside in specialized equipment (e.g., ATM encryption gear), ATM switches, or in ATM end systems. The logical pairing of two SAs to provide a security service is called a *security association*. Security associations apply whenever security services are performed, including initial security services that are performed during virtual circuit establishment and traffic security services that are performed during data transfer.

During the connection initiation phase of a cryptographically secured ATM virtual circuit, certain security services must be performed. First, before a security association can be established, common parameters for the security association must be configured in each SA. For example, if encryption is applied to a virtual circuit, the encryption devices must be configured with the encryption algorithm, mode of operation, and keying information that they must use. Although encryption parameters and keys may be configured manually, this approach quickly becomes unmanageable when virtual circuits are created and destroyed frequently.

For this reason, a protocol that communicates the security association parameters between participating SAs is the preferred mechanism. However, these parameters must be communicated securely. This requires strong authentication of the SAs that are involved in the security service and secure key exchange protocols. To address the need for secure parameter negotiation, authentication, and key exchange, the ATM Forum Security 1.1 specification defines a security message exchange (SME) protocol that implements these services. The SME protocol, which is performed at connection initiation before user data is carried by the virtual circuit, is implemented in one of two ways, using ATM SVC signaling or within the user plane virtual circuit.

An example of SME protocol operations within ATM signaling is shown in Figure 7.

In this approach, when SA1 sees a request for a new VC and it decides to secure the VC, it appends a special security services information element (SSIE) to the virtual circuit SETUP message and propagates the message toward

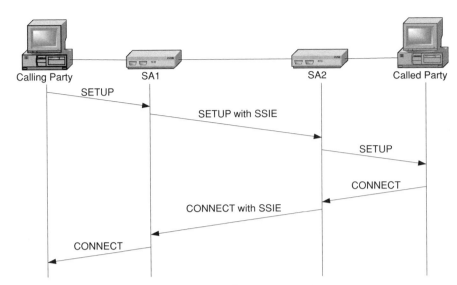

**Figure 7:** SME within ATM signaling.

the called party. This SSIE contains authentication, key exchange, and security association parameters for negotiation. When SA2 receives the SETUP message with the SSIE, it removes the SSIE, examines its contents, and decides whether the connection should continue. If so, it propagates the SETUP message toward the called party. When the CONNECT message comes back, SA2 adds another SSIE for the reverse direction, which is processed by SA1 upon receipt.

Although SVC signaling is the most obvious technique for transporting SME information during connection establishment, it has a number of limitations, including the following:

- **No support for exchange of public key certificates**: the signaling channel is limited to the amount of information it can carry, which precludes carrying large data objects such as public key certificates.

- **Security agents must maintain synchronized clocks**: authentication flows must be unique to prevent replay attacks, and the uniqueness of each flow must be verifiable by the receiver. However, the two-way nature of the SVC signaling protocol precludes the use of challenge–response mutual authentication, which requires three end-to-end flows. To implement mutual authentication with two flows, Security 1.1 specifies the use of time stamps that must be synchronized within a 5-min window. Upon receipt, the receiving device examines the time stamp to ensure it is within the time window with respect to the receiver's clock and that the time stamp is greater than any time stamp that has been previously received from the same sender.

- **Network support of SSIE is required**: this is the most serious limitation of the signaling-based approach. Because SVC signaling considers the SSIE to be optional, intermediate switches may be configured to discard the SSIE, preventing SME altogether.

- **No support for PVCs**: because this technique works with SVC signaling, PVCs (which are established outside of signaling) are not supported.

For the reasons listed above, the Security 1.1 specification defines an alternate SME transport mechanism that operates within the virtual circuit after it has been established but before user data is allowed to flow. This mechanism is depicted in Figure 8.

In this example, the SETUP message is propagated by the SAs as if they are ATM switches, with no security attributes added to the message. When the CONNECT message traverses the ATM network, it is held by SA1, and SA1 and SA2 perform the SME protocol within the portion of the new virtual circuit that connects them. If SME completes successfully, then SA1 allows the CONNECT message to continue to propagate to the calling party and subsequent data traffic on the virtual circuit is secured between the two SAs.

Because this variant of the SME protocol uses the data virtual circuit instead of the ATM signaling channel, all of the limitations listed earlier do not apply in this case. However, this mechanism does introduce additional delay in SVC establishment process, which can cause the ATM switches and end systems to time out the connection request prematurely. Therefore, care must be exercised if this option is selected.

## Label-Based Access Control

"Access control" in general implies the acceptance or rejection of a request for network services (e.g., an ATM virtual circuit) based on some policy. Policy criteria may include *implicit* criteria, such as the time of day at which the request is made, and *explicit* criteria, that is, information that is contained in the request. Examples of explicit access control criteria include the source address, destination address, higher layer protocol information, and quality of service attributes.

The ATM Forum Security 1.1 specification extends the list of explicit access control criteria by providing support for labeling an ATM virtual circuit request with the sensitivity of the data that the virtual circuit will carry. The data sensitivity is encoded according to the Federal Information Processing Standards (FIPS)

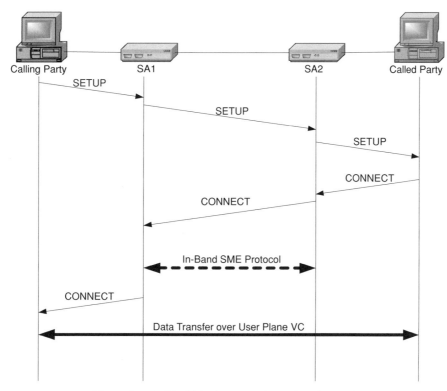

**Figure 8:** SME within the user plane virtual circuit.

Publication 188 (National Institute of Standards and Technology, 1994). This encoding scheme represents information sensitivity in two ways—the sensitivity *level* and the sensitivity *compartment*. An example of the relationship between level and compartment is shown in Figure 9.

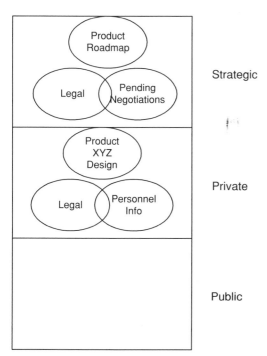

**Figure 9:** Example data sensitivity levels and compartments.

As the example shows, the data sensitivity level is an ordered, partitioned set arranged in a hierarchy from least sensitive data to most sensitive data. Within each sensitivity level there may exist one or more compartments, which are not necessarily partitioned and may be found within multiple sensitivity levels. These compartments further restrict the dissemination of information that is found within a level. Note that, as shown in the example, a sensitivity level need not contain any compartments.

When an ATM device (such as an end system, switch, or security appliance such as a firewall) labels a connection during connection establishment, it encodes the label according to FIPS 188 and includes the label in an SSIE that accompanies the connection SETUP message. When another device receives the labeled SETUP message, it checks that the level is less than or equal to the level that the receiver allows. If so, then the receiver checks for any compartment information that is contained in the message, and it verifies that it is configured to process one or all of the compartments specified in the label. (The selection of "one" or "all" is determined by site policy.) If both of these tests pass, then the receiver allows the connection.

Clearly, the existence of a sensitivity label does not necessarily imply that the sender correctly applied it or that the receiver will correctly honor it. Therefore, this access control technique requires all devices that apply, handle, or examine sensitivity labels to be trusted to correctly do so. If *any* device cannot be trusted to process labels correctly, then end-to-end cryptographic measures (e.g., ATM encryption and strong authentication) are required.

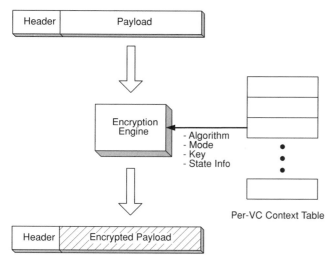

**Figure 10:** ATM encryption processing.

## Traffic Security

Whereas the initial security services described earlier are performed by the SME protocol when the connection is initiated, the traffic security services provided by the Security 1.1 specification operate on the user plane data traffic after the ATM virtual circuit or path is established. Specifically, two traffic security services are defined by Security 1.1: confidentiality (i.e., ATM cell encryption) and data origin authentication (i.e., data signatures using keyed message authentication codes).

### Encryption

If a pair of SAs is selected to provide encryption services on a portion of a virtual circuit, then they must first be configured with a specific encryption algorithm, mode of operation, and shared symmetric key. This configuration information, which is stored in a per-virtual circuit encryption context table, is retrieved each time an ATM cell is received and used to encrypt the ATM cell payload, as shown in Figure 10.

ATM networks present a few unique challenges and opportunities for data encryption. One obvious challenge is that ATM is specified to operate at link rates up to OC-192 (10 Gb/s). As a result, to achieve fast encryption, only symmetric block ciphers that lend themselves to implementation in hardware (such as the Data Encryption Standard) are specified in Security 1.1. However, unlike datagram-oriented protocols such as IP, ATM cell payloads are always 48 bytes in length (an integer multiple of most ciphers' block sizes), which circumvents the need to pad data before encryption. This simplifies encryptor implementation, allowing for faster designs.

Another property of ATM that enables efficient encryption is the fact that ATM maintains cell sequence integrity (i.e., cell ordering) within an ATM virtual circuit or path. Therefore, encryption synchronization information such as the state vector for counter mode or the initialization vector for cipher block chaining (CBC) is not included with each ATM cell. Rather, synchronization information is maintained within the encryptor and decryptor for each

virtual circuit or path that it processes. The advantage of this property is that it reduces the overhead of encryption. However, because the encryptor and decryptor must use the same state for each cell, if an encrypted cell is dropped, then all subsequent cells that are encrypted using counter mode will be decrypted improperly because the sender's state vector (cell count) is different from the receiver's. (However, this problem is not as severe with CBC mode. Because CBC is self-synchronizing, only the next cell is decrypted improperly. After that, synchronization is recovered and decryption occurs correctly.) As a result, virtual circuits and paths that are encrypted using counter mode must also carry session key changeover cells (described later), which carry resynchronization information.

### Data Origin Authentication

Another traffic security mechanism provided by the Security 1.1 specification is data origin authentication. This service provides the assurance that the data that are sent by one end system have not been maliciously modified in transit to the other end system. In addition, this service provides an option to detect whether the data have been maliciously retransmitted or reordered. The data origin authentication mechanism defined in Security 1.1 uses symmetric message authentication codes (MACs) that use shared secret keys to sign AAL 3/4 or AAL 5 data, as shown in Figure 11.

In the sending system, a MAC is calculated over the AAL service data unit (SDU) using the shared symmetric authentication key for the virtual circuit. Upon receiving the SDU containing the MAC, the receiving end system performs the same steps, and checks its locally computed MAC against the one contained in the received SDU. Because this service operates on AAL information, which is segmented into and reassembled from ATM cells, this service can be implemented only within the end systems that terminate the virtual circuit. Data origin authentication on virtual paths and within network devices such as switches is not supported in Security 1.1.

## Supporting Mechanisms

In addition to the security and traffic security mechanisms described earlier, ATM security specifications also provide supporting mechanisms for changing keys and for changing the parameters corresponding to a security association.

When an ATM traffic security mechanism is applied to user data on a virtual path or virtual circuit, security considerations require that the shared symmetric encryption and authentication keys be changed periodically; either at periodic intervals of time or after a specified amount of data has been processed under a given key. Either way, when a security agent decides that the shared symmetric key (also known as the *session key*) needs to be changed, it randomly generates a new session key, encrypts it using a shared symmetric *master key*, and sends the resulting key to the peer security agent using a session key update (SKU) OAM cell.

To coordinate the change to the new key, another special OAM cell called the session key changeover (SKC) cell is used to indicate to the peer SA that the next user

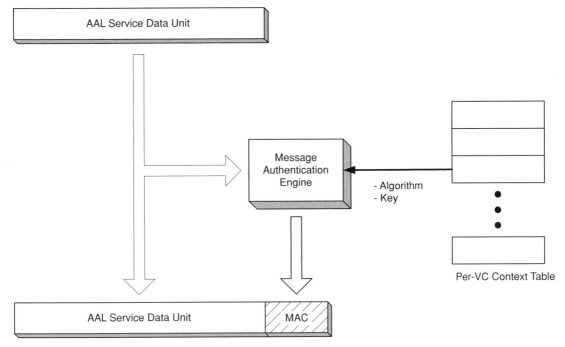

**Figure 11:** ATM data origin authentication processing.

data cell was encrypted using the new session key. (This cell is sent multiple times to increase the probability of reception should cell loss occur in the network.) Because the SKC cell contains keying and synchronization information, its contents affect how subsequent user data cells are processed. Therefore, its sequencing with respect to the user data cells must be preserved. As described earlier, because ATM OAM cells are switched with the user data cells for a given virtual circuit, OAM cells maintain cell sequence integrity with the data cell, allowing OAM cells to be used for cryptographic maintenance functions such as key changeover and resynchronization.

However, in situations where virtual circuits remain active for very long periods of time (e.g., circuits in a PVP mesh that remain up for months at a time), it may be necessary to renegotiate any of the parameters of a security association, including algorithms, master keys, and the set of security services that are applied to the security association. To support this need, an ATM Security 1.1 companion specification (ATM Forum, 2002) describes a mechanism for embedding the SME protocol into OAM cells to renegotiate the security association parameters. This specification also provides a coordinated security association changeover process similar to the SKC approach in that it uses OAM cells to signal to the peer security agent that the new security association parameters will be activated on the next user data cell.

## CONTROL PLANE SECURITY MECHANISMS

When one considers applying ATM security mechanisms, the most obvious need that comes to mind is protection of user data via mechanisms such as initial authentication, data encryption, and data origin authentication.

However, in certain environments, additional mechanisms are needed to protect the ATM switching infrastructure from other security risks that lead to service degradation or malicious redirection of ATM virtual circuits. For this reason, ATM security specifications include methods for securing control plane communications among devices. In addition, mechanisms have been developed in the research and development context that monitor control plane activities in an ATM network to look for suspected ATM infrastructure attacks and respond appropriately.

In the ATM Security 1.1 specification, a mechanism is defined that protects ATM control plane communications from a malicious modification attack. In this mechanism, each pair of ATM switches that communicate control plane information with each other is configured to implement the data origin authentication service described earlier using manually configured, preshared symmetric keys. Because this mechanism is configured manually, it is not meant to be widely distributed in an ATM network. Rather, its usefulness is limited to control plane communications across untrusted links or network spans, such as a PVP tunnel between two sites.

Because of this limitation, a companion specification (ATM Forum, 2001b) was developed to make control plane security more manageable. In addition, this specification added mechanisms to address a need to encrypt control plane messages to prevent disclosure of information about a virtual circuit (e.g., source and destination ATM addresses and QoS information) when it is established. This mechanism specifies the use of the SME protocol or the Internet key exchange (IKE) protocol to implement initial authentication and key exchange and specifies AAL-level encryption and data origin authentication using the encapsulating security payload (ESP) packet format to apply traffic security mechanisms to control plane

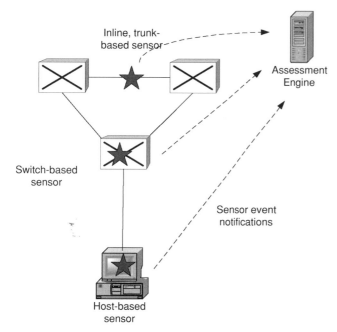

**Figure 12:** ATM infrastructure intrusion detection architecture.

messages. The result of this specification is a more robust approach to control plane security that simplifies management and allows it to be applied to all switches in an ATM network.

Securing control plane communications against man-in-the-middle attacks on the integrity and confidentiality of messages is an excellent start to securing the ATM infrastructure. However, should an ATM switch be compromised, another mechanism is required to detect that compromise and, if possible, respond to it. An example of an attack by a compromised switch is described in Smith, Hill, and Robinson (1999). A more comprehensive list of ATM control plane and data plane attacks are found in Ghosh (2002).

One mechanism for detecting compromised switch activity, which is described in Tarman et al. (2001), is shown in Figure 12.

In ATM infrastructure intrusion detection, sensors are deployed on hosts, switches, and links that filter certain network events such as connection attempts and forward event notifications to an assessment engine. When the assessment engine receives event notifications, it compares the event stream against one or more attack signatures to determine whether a suspected attack is occurring. If an attack signature is triggered, then a response may be generated to alert a network operator or to reconfigure a network device.

As with ATM user plane data security, there are many options available to the network designer for implementing security in the control plane, ranging from very basic protections against malicious message modifications to elaborate security protections backed up by extensive control plane monitoring and intrusion detection. As with the user plane mechanisms, the selection of control plane mechanisms must be based on a realistic assessment of

the security risks that require mitigation and the costs of implementing those protections.

## CONCLUSION

There are many mechanisms available to the ATM network engineer for implementing security protections once he or she has performed the prerequisite security analysis, which includes an analysis of the assets that need to be protected and the ATM network-borne threats to those assets. Depending on the outcome of this analysis, the protections that the engineer may consider implementing range from simple VPN implementations that do not require any special equipment to cryptographic mechanisms that are implemented commercially by a few vendors for protection of user data. If the security analysis calls for additional protection that must be afforded to the ATM switching infrastructure itself, then mechanisms such as control plane message security and control plane monitoring mechanisms are available. As with other security standards, the range of options available for implementing ATM security protections is wide; therefore, a careful security analysis and analysis of network design goals and constraints is imperative before deployment of available ATM security mechanisms.

## GLOSSARY

**Asynchronous Transfer Mode** A network technology for switching fixed-length data cells along a virtual circuit or path.
**Cell** A fixed-length packet of ATM data, with 5 bytes of header and 48 bytes of payload
**Data Origin Authentication** The cryptographic binding of ATM data to its source.
**Entity Authentication** The cryptographic binding of attributes (e.g., addresses, security parmeters, etc.) to the ATM connection endpoints.
**Key Changeover** An ATM security mechanism for assigning new keys for data encryption and data origin authentication.
**Label-Based Access Control** An ATM security mechanism for assigning data sensitivity attributes to a connection.
**Network–Network Interface (NNI)** The set of ATM protocols that operate between switches to perform connection establishment and routing.
**Permanent Virtual Circuit** A manually configured ATM virtual circuit.
**Security Agent** An ATM device that implements one or more security services.
**Security Association** The logical pairing of SAs to perform a security service.
**Security Message Exchange** An ATM security protocol for authenticating endpoints, exchanging keys, and negotiating security association parameters.
**Security Renegotiation** An ATM security mechanism that allows parameters for a security association to be changed without tearing-down and reestablishing the ATM connection.

**Switched Virtual Circuit** An ATM virtual circuit that is automatically configured by the ATM network via a signaling protocol.

**User–Network Interface** The set of ATM protocols that operate between an ATM endpoint and the first-hop switch to perform connection establishment.

**Virtual Private Network** A set of ATM connection policies that implement a closed community of ATM endpoints.

## CROSS REFERENCES

See *Computer and Network Authentication; Encryption Basics; Intrusion Detection Systems Basics; Key Management; VPN Basics.*

## REFERENCES

ATM Forum. (2001a). *ATM security specification version 1.1 (af-sec-0100.002)*. Retrieved February 8, 2004, from http://www.atmforum.com

ATM Forum. (2001b). *Control plane security (af-sec-0172.000)*. Retrieved February 8, 2004, from http://www.atmforum.com

ATM Forum. (2002). *Security services renegotiation addendum to security, version 1.1* (af-sec-0180.000). Retrieved February 8, 2004, from http://www.atmforum.com

Ghosh, S. (2002). *Principles of secure network systems design*. New York: Springer-Verlag.

National Institute of Standards and Technology. (1994). *Standard security label for information transfer*. Federal Information Processing Standards Publication 188.

Smith, R., Hill, D. W., & Robinson, N. P. (1999). ATM peer group leader attack and mitigation. In *Proceedings of IEEE MILCOM '99* (pp. 729–733). Piscataway, NJ: Institute of Electrical and Electronics Engineers.

Tarman, T. D., & Witzke, E. L. (2001). *Implementing security for ATM networks*. Boston, MA: Artech House.

Tarman, T. D., Witzke, E. L., Bauer, K. C., Kellogg, B. R., & Young, W. F. (2001). Asynchronous transfer mode (ATM) intrusion detection. In *Proceedings of IEEE/AFCEA MILCOM 2001*. Piscataway, NJ: Institute of Electrical and Electronics Engineers.

## FURTHER READING

Chuang, S. (1996). Securing ATM networks. In *Proceedings of the Third ACM Conference on Computer and Communications Security*, (pp. 19–30). New York: Association for Computing Machinery.

dePrycker, M. (1993). *Asynchronous transfer mode: Solution for broadband ISDN*. New York: Ellis Horwood Ltd.

Händel, R., Huber, M. N., & Schröder, S. (1998). *ATM networks—Concepts, protocols, applications*. Reading, MA: Addison-Wesley.

Laurent, M., et al. (1999). Secure communications in ATM networks. In *Proceedings of the 15th Annual Computer Security Applications Conference* (pp. 84–93). Piscataway, NJ: Institute of Electrical and Electronics Engineers.

McDysan, D. E., & Spohn, D. L. (1998). *ATM theory and applications*. New York: McGraw-Hill.

Patiyoot, D., & Shepherd, S. J. (1999). Security issues in ATM networks. *Operating Systems Review, 33*(4), 22–35.

Simon, C., & Torok, A. (2000). ATM security with firewalls. In *Proceedings of the Fifth IEEE Symposium on Computer and Communications* (pp. 186–191). Piscataway, NJ: Institute of Electrical and Electronics Engineers.

Stevenson, D., Hillery, N., & Byrd, G. (1995). Secure communications in ATM Networks. *Communications of the ACM, 38*(2), 45–52.

# VPN Basics

G. I. Papadimitriou, *Aristotle University*

M. S. Obaidat, *Monmouth University*

C. Papazoglou and A.S. Pomportsis, *Aristotle University*

## INTRODUCTION

The best way to come up with a definition of the term virtual private network (VPN) is to analyze each word separately. Having done that, Ferguson and Huston (1998) came up with the following definition: A VPN is a communications environment in which access is controlled to permit peer connections only within a defined community of interest and is constructed through some form of partitioning of a common underlying communications medium, where this underlying communications medium provides services to the network on a nonexclusive basis. Ferguson and Huston also provided a simpler and less formal description. A VPN is a private network constructed within a public network infrastructure, such as the global Internet. Others define a VPN as a network that allows two or more private networks to be connected over a publicly accessed network. It is similar to wide area networks (WAN) or a securely encrypted tunnel. The chief feature of VPNs is that they use public networks like the Internet rather than using expensive, private-leased lines while having similar security and encryption features as a private network.

VPNs have evolved as a compromise for enterprises desiring the convenience and cost-effectiveness offered by shared networks but requiring the strong security offered by private networks. Whereas closed WANs use isolation to ensure data are secure, VPNs use a combination of encryption, authentication, access management, and tunneling to provide access only to authorized parties and to protect data while in transit (Hunt & Rodgers 2003). To emulate a point-to-point link, data is encapsulated, or wrapped, with a header that provides the routing information, allowing it to traverse the shared or public internetworks to reach its end point. To emulate a private link, the data being sent are encrypted for confidentiality. Packets that are intercepted on the shared or public network are indecipherable without the encryption keys (Arora, Vemuganti, & Allani, 2001).

To enable the use of VPN functions, special software can be added on top of a general computing platform, such as a UNIX or Windows operating system. Alternatively, special hardware augmented with software can be used to provide VPN functions. Sometimes, VPN functions are added to a hardware-based network device such as a router or a firewall. In other cases, VPN functions are built from the ground up, and routing and firewall capabilities are added. A corporation can either create and manage the VPN itself or purchase VPN services from a service provider (Strayer & Yuan, 2001).

VPNs first appeared in 1984, when the service was offered to U.S. users by Sprint, with MCI and AT&T producing competing products soon after. In their initial form, VPNs were offered as a flexible, cost-effective approach to the problem of connecting large, dispersed groups of users. Private networks were the main alternative, and although equivalent functionality could be achieved via the public switched telephone network (PSTN), this was a limited solution because of the length of full national telephone numbers and the lack of in-dialing capabilities from the PSTN. Such a VPN acted as a PSTN emulation of a dedicated private network, using the resources of the PSTN in a time-sharing arrangement with other traffic (Hunt & Rodgers, 2003).

Many forms of VPNs have existed in the technology's relatively short lifetime. The level of variety has resulted from the distinct domains of expertise of the companies developing and marketing VPN solutions. For example, hardware manufacturers may offer customer-premise equipment-based solutions, whereas an Internet service provider (ISP) would be more likely to offer a network-based solution (Hunt & Rodgers, 2003).

The level of confusion and lack of interoperability between competing products lead to the submission of a

VPN framework to the Internet Engineering Task Force (IETF) in 2000, which defined VPNs as "the emulation of a private WAN facility using IP facilities" (Gleeson et al., 2000). A number of VPN implementations have been proposed to operate over a variety of underlying infrastructures and protocols, including asynchronous transfer mode (ATM), multiprotocol label switching (MPLS), Ethernet, Internet protocol (IP), and heterogeneous backbones (Hunt & Rodgers, 2003).

Traditional private networks facilitate connectivity among various network entities through a set of links comprising dedicated circuits. These are leased from public telecommunication carriers as well as privately installed wiring. The capacity of these links is available at all times, albeit fixed and inflexible. The traffic on these private networks belongs only to the enterprise or company deploying the network. Therefore, there is an assured level of performance associated with the network. Such assurances come with a price.

The drawbacks of this approach are as follows (Arora et al., 2001):

Traditional private networks are not cheap to plan and deploy. The costs associated with dedicated links are especially high when they involve international locations and security concerns are exacerbated due to the international transport of information. The planning phase of such networks involves detailed estimates of the applications, their traffic patterns, and their growth rates. Also, the planning periods are long because of the work involved in calculating these estimates.

Furthermore, dedicated links take time to install. It is not unusual that telecommunication carriers take about 60 to 90 days to install and activate a dedicated link. Such a long waiting period adversely affects the company's ability to react to the quick changes in these areas (Arora et al., 2001).

Another recent trend is the mobility of today's workforce. Portable computing facilities such as laptops and palm-based devices have made it easy for people to work without being physically present in their offices. This also allows for less investment in real estate (Arora et al., 2001).

To support the increase in home offices, companies need to provide a reliable information technology (IT) infrastructure so that employees can access company's information from remote locations. This has resulted in large modem pools for employees to dial in remotely. The cost keeps increasing because of the complexity of managing and maintaining the large modem pools. An additional cost with the mobile users is the long-distance calls or toll-free numbers for which the company pays. The costs are much higher if we consider international calling. For companies with large mobile workforce, these expenses add up to significant numbers (Arora et al., 2001).

Additionally, in the case of the private network, the company has to manage the network and all its associated elements, invest capital in network-switching infrastructure, hire trained staff, and assume complete responsibility for the provisioning and ongoing maintenance of the network service. Such a dedicated use of transport services, equipment, and staff is often difficult to justify for many small to medium-sized organizations, and although the functionality of a private network system is required, the expressed desire is to reduce the cost of the service through the use of shared transport services, equipment, and management (Ferguson & Huston, 1998).

In this direction, VPNs promise to help organizations support sales over the Internet more economically, tying business partners and suppliers together, linking branch offices, and supporting telecommuter access to corporate network resources. A VPN can reduce costs by replacing multiple communication links and legacy equipment with a single connection and one piece of equipment for each location (Younglove, 2000). To extend the reach of a company's intranet(s), a VPN over the Internet promises two benefits: cost efficiency and global reach. There are, however, three major concerns about VPN technology: security, manageability, and performance (Günter, 2001).

Security: For VPNs to be private, the transmitted data must be encrypted before entering the Internet because the Internet is considered an untrusted network. Everybody can connect to the Internet, and there is no guarantee that users stick to any policy or rule. Protecting the traveling data will not protect the information inside the intranet from unauthorized access (Günter, 2001).

Manageability: A company's telecommunication requirements and equipment evolve at a high speed. VPN managers must be able to cope with these changes avoiding high expenses. VPNs are connected to many entities that even by themselves are hard to manage and that constantly evolve. Such entities include the company's physical network (eventually featuring unregistered IP addresses), security policy, electronic services, and ISPs (Günter, 2001).

Performance: Because ISPs deliver IP packets still on a "best effort" basis, the transport performance of a VPN over the Internet cannot be predicted and is variable. Furthermore, security measures (encryption and authentication) can decrease transport performance significantly. This also points out two management problems: The clients must be enabled to (a) measure the performance and (b) customize the VPN (e.g., the security options) to optimize it (Günter, 2001).

A VPN solution consists of multiple, appropriately configured VPN devices that are placed in the appropriate locations within the network. As with any network, after all the VPN devices are installed and configured, the network should be continually monitored and managed (Strayer & Yuan, 2001).

The most common VPN device is the VPN gateway, which acts as the gatekeeper for network traffic to and from protected resources. Tunnels are established from the VPN gateway to other appropriate VPN devices serving as tunnel end points. A VPN gateway is usually located at the corporate network perimeter, and it acts on behalf of the protected network resources within the corporate intranet to negotiate and render security services. The gateway assembles the tunneling, authentication, access control, and data security functions into a single device. The details of how these functions are integrated within a VPN gateway are specific to a vendor's implementation. Sometimes these functions can be integrated into existing router or firewall products. Sometimes a VPN gateway can be a stand-alone device that performs pure VPN functions, without firewall or dynamic routing exchange capabilities (Strayer & Yuan, 2001).

The data traffic coming from the public interfaces (inbound traffic) is thoroughly examined by the gateway according to the security policies. Usually, only the traffic from the established secure tunnels should be processed by the VPN gateway. If no secure tunnel is found, the traffic should be dropped immediately, unless its purpose is to negotiate and establish a secure tunnel. Depending on the implementation, an alert or alarm can be generated to notify the network management station (Strayer & Yuan, 2001).

The data traffic coming from the private interfaces and exiting to the public interface (outbound traffic) is deemed secure a priori, even though many network attacks are generated within a corporate network. The outbound traffic is examined according to a set of policies on the gateway. If secure tunneling is required for the traffic, the VPN gateway first determines whether such a tunnel is already in place. If it is not, the gateway attempts to establish a new tunnel with the intended device—either another VPN gateway or simply some other device with secure tunneling capabilities. After the tunnel is established, the traffic is processed according to the tunnel rules and is sent into the tunnel. The traffic from the private interface can also be dropped if a policy cannot be found. Depending on how quickly a secure tunnel can be established, the VPN gateway may buffer the outbound packet before the secure tunnel is in place (Strayer & Yuan, 2001).

The VPN client is software used for remote VPN access for a single computer or user. Unlike the VPN gateway, which is a specialized device and can protect multiple network resources at the same time, the VPN client software is usually installed on an individual computer and serves that computer only. Generally, VPN client software creates a secure path from the client computer to a designated VPN gateway. The secure tunnel enables the client computer to obtain IP connectivity to access the network resources protected by that particular VPN gateway.

VPN client software also must implement the same functions as VPN gateways—tunneling, authentication, access control, and data security—although these implementations may be simpler or have fewer options. For example, the VPN software usually implements only one of the tunneling protocols. Because the remote computer does not act on behalf of any other users or resources, the access control can also be less complex.

Unlike the VPN gateway, in which all of the gateway's hardware and software is geared toward the VPN functionality, VPN client software is usually just an application running on a general-purpose operating system on the remote computer. Consequently, the client software should carefully consider its interactions with the operating system.

One of the important concerns regarding VPN client software is the simplicity of installation and operation. Because client software is expected to be deployed widely on end users' machines, it must be easily installed and easily operated by regular computer users who may not know much about the operating system, software compatibility, remote access, or VPNs. A VPN gateway, on the other hand, is usually deployed on the company's corporate network site and is managed by information technology professionals.

VPN client software must work within the constraints of host computers' operating systems, whether the software is deeply integrated with the operating system or runs as an application. Because networking is a major function of today's computers, almost all modern operating systems have built-in networking functionality. Few, however, have strong support for VPN capabilities integrated into the operating system. As a result, separate VPN client software must be written for those operating systems that lack the VPN functionality. Furthermore, the same VPN client software may need to be ported to different operating systems, even for different release versions of the same operating system (Yuan, 2002).

Two fundamental architectures are available for implementing network-based VPNs: virtual routers (VR) and piggybacking. The main difference between the two architectures is in the model used to achieve VPN reachability and membership functions. In the VR model, each VR in the VPN domain is running an instance of routing protocol responsible for disseminating VPN reachability information between VRs. Therefore, VPN membership and VPN reachability are treated as separate functions, and separate mechanisms are used to implement these functions. VPN reachability is carried out by a per-VPN instance of routing, and a range of mechanisms is possible for determining membership. In the piggyback model, the VPN network layer is terminated at the edge of the backbone, and a backbone routing protocol (i.e., extended border gateway protocol-4 [BGP-4]) is responsible for disseminating the VPN membership and reachability information between provider edge (PE) routers for all the VPNs configured on the PE (Brahim et al., 2003).

# TYPES OF VPN SERVICES

A variety of VPN implementations and configurations exists for various needs. Organizations may require their VPN to offer dial-up access or to allow third parties such as customers or suppliers to access specific components of their VPN (Hunt & Rodgers, 2003). VPNs can be classified into three broad categories: intranet, extranet, and remote access VPNs (Figure 1).

## Intranet VPNs

An intranet VPN connects a number of local area networks (intranets) located in multiple geographic areas over the shared network infrastructure. Typically, this service is used to connect multiple geographic locations of a single company (Arora et al., 2001). An intranet VPN enables the sharing of information and resources among dispersed employees. For example, branch offices can access the network at the head office, typically including key resources such as product or customer databases. Intranet access is strictly limited to these networks, and connections are authenticated. Differing levels of access may be allocated to different sites on the Intranet depending on their purpose (Hunt & Rodgers, 2003). Because an Intranet VPN is formed by connecting two or more trusted sites (corporate

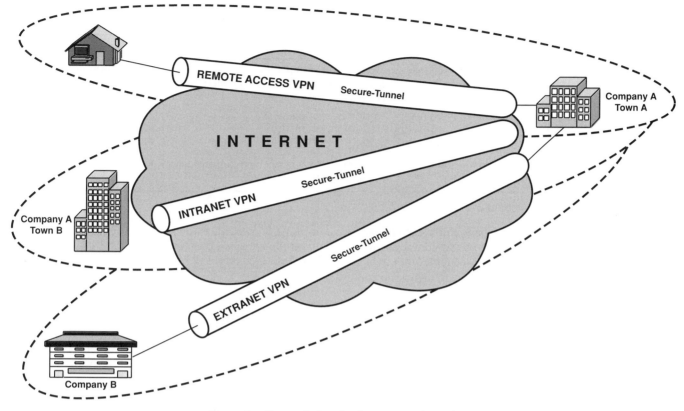

**Figure 1:** Types of virtual private network services.

LANs), which will certainly be protected by firewalls, most security concerns are alleviated.

## Extranet VPNs

An extranet VPN extends limited access to corporate computing resources to business partners, such as customers or suppliers, enabling access to shared information (Wright, 2000). Such users are restricted to specific areas of the intranet, usually denoted as the demilitarized zone (DMZ). It is the responsibility of the firewall and authentication and access management facilities to identify company employees and other users and differentiate their access privileges accordingly; employee connections should be directed to the company intranet, whereas recognized third-party connections should be directed to the DMZ (Hunt & Rodgers, 2003). An extranet VPN helps provide connectivity to new external suppliers and customers within a short period of time. Additionally, an extranet VPN supports a number of important e-commerce initiatives, providing opportunities for significant cost savings and efficiency gains.

A number of possible extranet configurations exist, which vary in their level of security and access. The most common examples, ordered from most to least secure, are the following (Hunt & Rodgers, 2003):

1. **Private extranet.** Access to a private extranet is strictly for members only, with no use made of shared networks. Such a configuration cannot be considered a VPN because it is physically private.

2. **Hybrid extranet.** This is equivalent in operation to a private extranet, except that it uses one or more shared network to provide connectivity. Membership is restricted, and access to private resources is limited to relevant resources only.

3. **Extranet service provider.** This configuration is offered by an ISP, which builds extranet services based on its backbone network. This is a type of provider-provisioned VPN.

4. **Public extranet.** A public extranet provides data that is globally accessible. An example is a company that provides a public Web site and possibly a public file transfer protocol (FTP) site that Web users are free to access. Such facilities are normally distinct and separate from private file servers, so that public servers cannot be used as staging points for compromising the private component of the extranet.

## Remote Access VPNs

A remote access VPN connects telecommuters and mobile users to corporate networks. An ideal VPN enables remote users to work as if they were at a workstation in the office. Deployment of a remote access VPN can result in considerable cost savings, eliminating the need for the company to manage large modem pools, and replacing the need for toll calls to these modems with calls to local ISP accounts. By taking advantage of a high-speed access infrastructure such as DSL (digital subscriber lines), cable modems, or ISDN (Integrated Services Digital Network), some of the performance limitations typically associated

**Table 1** Types of Virtual Private Network Services

| | Intranet | Extranet | Remote Access |
|---|---|---|---|
| Typical Scenario | Multiple geographic locations of a single company | Two or more companies have networked access to a limited amount of each other's corporate data | Mobile users connecting to corporate networks |
| Typical Users | Employees working in branch offices | Customers, suppliers | Employees working at home or on the road |
| Security Concerns | Minor | Medium | Major |
| Implementation | Two or more connected LANs | A company LAN connected to the other company's DMZ | Remote users dial up to the corporate network |

DMZ = demilitarized zone; LAN = local area network.

with remote access can be diminished (Hunt & Rodgers, 2003). In addition, wireless networks enable computers to achieve network connectivity with a reasonable amount of bandwidth without a physical connection (Ribeiro, Silva, & Zuquete, 2004).

The deployment of remote access VPNs also gives rise to several security concerns. Precautions must be taken to ensure that the corporate network is not compromised by an insecure remote user. The enforcement of company security policies on remote users is a necessary step in this direction, especially regarding virus protection. It must be noted that the increased flexibility of wireless networks raises additional security issues. On one hand, given the ubiquitous nature of the communication channel, clients of the infrastructure must be authenticated to avoid unauthorized users gaining access to network resources. On the other hand, because any wireless device may listen on the communication channel, data encryption must be enforced if some level of data protection and confidentiality is desired. The security concerns relating to VPNs are discussed in more detail in the following sections.

Table 1 summarizes the characteristics of the types of VPN.

## TUNNELING

Tunneling is defined as the encapsulation of a certain data packet (the original or inner packet) into another data packet (the encapsulating or outer packet) so that the inner packet is opaque to the network over which the outer packet is routed (Strayer & Yuan, 2001).

The need for tunneling arises when it is not appropriate for the inner packet to travel directly across the network for various reasons. For example, tunneling can be used to transport multiple protocols over a network based on some other protocol, or it can be used to hide source and destination addresses of the original packet. When tunneling is used for security services, an unsecured packet is put into a secure, usually encrypted packet (Strayer & Yuan, 2001).

Tunneling allows network traffic from many sources to travel via separate channels across the same infrastructure, and it enables network protocols to traverse incompatible infrastructures. Tunneling also allows traffic from many sources to be differentiated, so that it can be directed to specific destinations and receive specific levels of service (Wright, 2000). Two components can uniquely

determine a network tunnel: the end points of the tunnel and the encapsulation protocol used to transport the original data packet within the tunnel (Strayer & Yuan, 2001).

Tunneling is the most important mechanism used by VPNs. The idea behind this concept is that a part of the route between the originator and the target of the packet is determined independent of the destination IP address. The importance of tunneling in the context of access VPNs in broadband access networks is twofold (Cohen, 2003). First, the destination address field of a packet sent in an access VPN may indicate a non–globally unique IP address of a corporate internal server. Such an address must not be exposed to the Internet routers because these routers do not know how to route such packets. Second, often a packet sent by a user of an access VPN should be forwarded first to the user's ISP, and only then from the ISP toward the corporate network. In such a case, the first leg of the routing between the host and the ISP cannot be performed based on the destination IP address of the packet, even if this address is globally unique (Cohen, 2003).

The devices at one or both ends of a tunnel could be network address translation (NAT) devices. NAT is another important mechanism employed by VPNs. The need for IP address translation arises when a network's internal IP addresses cannot be used outside the network either because they are invalid for use outside or because the internal addressing must be kept private from the external network. Address translation allows hosts in a private network to transparently communicate with destinations on an external network and vice versa. NAT is a method by which IP addresses are mapped from one address realm (i.e., network domain) to another, providing transparent routing to end hosts (Srisuresh & Holdrege, 1999).

VPNs employ two main types of tunneling techniques (Hunt & Rodgers, 2003):

- **End-to-end tunneling,** also known as "transport model" tunneling: The VPN devices at each end of the connection are responsible for tunnel creation and encryption of the data transferred between the two sites, so the tunnel may extend through edge devices such as firewalls to the computers sending and receiving the traffic. Secure sockets layer/transaction layer security (SSL/TLS) is an example of a protocol that employs end-to-end tunneling. This solution is extremely secure, because the data never appears on the network in clear-text

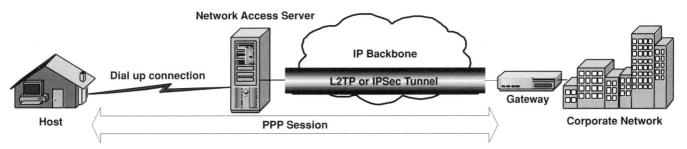

**Figure 2:** Compulsory tunneling scenario.

form. Performing encryption at the end hosts increases the complexity of the process of enforcing security policies. The network gateways, which would normally be responsible for enforcing security policy, are used only for forwarding the packets to their destination in this scenario, and as such they possess no knowledge of the content or purpose of the traffic. This is particularly problematic for filtering programs installed at the gateway.

- **Node-to-node tunneling.** Creation and termination of a node-to-node tunnel occurs at the gateway devices comprising the edge of the networks, which are typically firewalls. Under this model, transport within the LANs remains unchanged because it is assumed that internal traffic is inaccessible from outside the LAN. Once traffic reaches the gateway, it is encrypted and sent via a dynamically established tunnel to the equivalent device on the receiving LAN, where the data is decrypted to recover its original format and transmitted over the LAN to the intended recipient. This has an additional security advantage in that an attacker operating a network analyzer at some point on the network between the two tunnel servers would see IP packets with the source and destination addresses corresponding to those two servers—the true source and destinations are hidden in the encrypted payload of these packets. Because this information is hidden, the would-be attacker does not have any indication as to which traffic is heading to or from a particular machine and so will not know what is worth attempting to decrypt. This also eliminates the need for NAT to convert between public and private address spaces and moves the responsibility for performing encryption to a central server, so intensive encryption work does not need to be performed by workstations. This is especially important when using costly encryption

algorithms such as 3-DES (triple data encryption standard), which requires hardware encryption support to operate without limiting the effective bandwidth.

There are two main drawbacks associated with node-to-node tunneling (Hunt & Rodgers, 2003):

1. **Poor scalability:** The number of tunnels required for a VPN increases geometrically as the number of VPN nodes increases, and this has serious performance ramifications for large VPNs.
2. **Suboptimal routing:** Because tunnels represent only the end points and not the path taken to reach the other end of the tunnel, the paths taken across the shared network may not be optimal, which may cause performance problems.

One can also distinguish two tunneling modes: compulsory and voluntary tunneling (Figure 2). Compulsory tunneling is when the tunnel is created without any action from the user and without allowing the user any choice in the matter, and voluntary tunneling is when the tunnel is created at the request of the user for a specific purpose (Ferguson & Huston, 1998). The concepts of compulsory and voluntary tunneling are illustrated in Figures 2 and 3, respectively. In both figures, a host is attempting to connect to a corporate network using a dial-up connection to a network access server.

Desirable characteristics for a VPN tunneling mechanism include (Rosenbaum, Lau, & Jha, 2003):

- **Multiplexing:** There are cases in which multiple VPN tunnels may be needed between the same two IP end points, for instance, cases in which the VPNs are network based, and each end point supports multiple customers. Traffic for different customers travels over

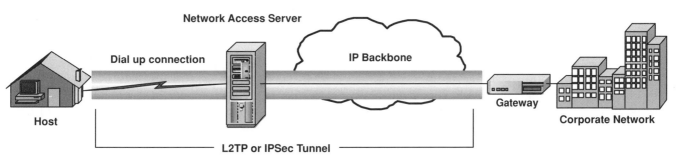

**Figure 3:** Voluntary tunneling scenario.

separate tunnels between the same two physical devices. A multiplexing field is needed to distinguish which packets belong to which tunnel. Sharing a tunnel in this manner may also reduce the latency and processing burden of tunnel setup.

- **Signaling protocol:** There is some configuration information that must be known by an end point in advance of the tunnel establishment, such as the IP address of the remote end point and any relevant tunnel attributes required, such as the level of security needed. Once this information is available, the actual tunnel establishment can be completed in one of two ways: via a management operation or via a signaling protocol that allows tunnels to be established dynamically. Using a signaling protocol can significantly reduce the management burden however, and as such, is essential in many deployment scenarios. It reduces the number of configurations needed, and also reduces the management coordination needed if a VPN spans multiple administrative domains.

- **Data security:** A VPN tunneling protocol must support mechanisms to allow for whatever level of security may be desired by customers, including authentication and/or encryption of various strengths. If some form of signaling mechanism is used by one VPN end point to dynamically establish a tunnel with another end point, then there is a requirement to be able to authenticate the party attempting the tunnel establishment.

- **Multiprotocol transport:** In many applications of VPNs, the VPN may carry opaque, multiprotocol traffic. As such, the tunneling protocol used must also support multiprotocol transport.

- **Frame sequencing:** Sequencing may be required for the efficient operation of particular end-to-end protocols or applications. To implement frame sequencing, the tunneling mechanism must support a sequencing field.

- **Tunnel maintenance:** The VPN end points must monitor the operation of the VPN tunnels to ensure that connectivity has not been lost and to take appropriate action, such as route recalculation, if there has been a failure.

- **Support for large maximum transmission units (MTUs):** If the tunnel's MTU is larger than the MTU of one or more individual hops along the path between tunnel end points, some form of frame fragmentation will be required within the tunnel. If the frame to be transferred is mapped into one IP datagram, normal IP fragmentation will occur when the IP datagram reaches a hop with an MTU smaller than the IP tunnel's MTU. This can have undesirable performance implications at the router performing such midtunnel fragmentation. An alternative approach is for the tunneling protocol itself to incorporate a segmentation and reassembly capability that operates at the tunnel level. This avoids IP-level fragmentation within the tunnel itself.

- **Minimization of tunnel overhead:** Minimizing the overhead of the tunneling mechanism is beneficial, particularly for the transport of jitter and latency sensitive traffic such as packetized voice and video. On the other hand, the security mechanisms that are applied impose their own overhead; hence, the objective should be to minimize overhead over and above that needed for security and not to burden those tunnels in which security is not mandatory with unnecessary overhead.

- **Quality of service (QoS)/traffic management:** Customers are expected to require that VPNs yield similar behavior to physical leased lines or dedicated connections with respect to such QoS parameters as loss rates, jitter, latency, and bandwidth guarantees. How such guarantees could be delivered will, in general, be a function of the traffic management characteristics of the VPN nodes themselves, and the access and backbone networks across which they are connected.

Three major tunneling protocol suites have been developed for building VPNs: point-to-point tunneling protocol, layer 2 tunneling protocol, and Internet protocol security. These protocols are discussed later.

## SECURITY CONCERNS

Security concerns that arise when transmitting data over shared networks can be divided into the following categories (Hunt & Rodgers, 2003):

1. **Privacy:** Can unauthorized parties gain access to private VPN traffic? Privacy can be achieved through the use of encryption.

2. **Integrity:** Can VPN traffic be altered without detection? Integrity is generally achieved through the use of checksums.

3. **Authentication:** Can I be certain that senders and recipients are really who they claim to be? Authentication is usually performed by confirming that the other party has knowledge or is in possession of some shared secret or unique key.

4. **Nonrepudiation:** Can senders or receivers later deny their involvement in a transaction? Nonrepudiation, also known as data origin verification, is often achieved through the use of digital signatures. When nonrepudiation measures are in place, the recipient cannot deny having received the transaction, nor can the sender deny having sent it (Hunt & Rodgers, 2003).

Two main trust models are applicable to the use of a shared backbone network (Hunt & Rodgers, 2003):

1. **Untrusted service provider:** In this scenario, customers do not trust their service provider to provide security for VPN traffic, preferring instead to employ devices that implement firewall functionality, passing data between these devices using secure tunnels. The role of the service provider in this scenario is solely that of a connectivity provider.

2. **Trusted service provider:** In this scenario, the customer trusts the service provider to provide a secure, managed VPN service. Specifically, the customer trusts that VPN packets will not be misdirected and that their contents will not be inspected or modified while in transit or subjected to traffic analysis by unauthorized parties.

# Cryptography

Cryptographic algorithms are essential for achieving secure communications over shared networks because a would-be attacker may obtain and store all the packets of a data stream belonging to a specific communication as it traverses the shared network. A number of different encryption algorithms are available, many of which support varying levels of security. The algorithms most commonly applied to VPNs are the data encryption standard (DES) and Triple DES (3-DES). DES has been the de facto standard in data communications for a number of years, but the ever-increasing processing capacity of computers has reached the point where only the larger key lengths supported by DES should be considered secure (Hunt & Rodgers, 2003).

Increased security generally comes at the cost of reduced performance, so a balance between efficiency and security must be achieved when applying encryption; the expected time for an attacker to complete a brute-force cipher attack should exceed the length of time for which the data remains valuable. If this requirement cannot be met effectively, alternative options such as dynamic key renegotiation within a given data stream may improve security without necessarily having a significant impact on performance. Such a process forces an attacker to decrypt small blocks of data at a time, dramatically increasing the difficulty of retrieving the clear-text for the entire message (Hunt & Rodgers, 2003).

# Integrity Checksums

A checksum is a series of bits of fixed length, the value of which is derived from a given block of data. Checksums are often appended to a block of data before transmission, so that the receiver can verify that the data was received in the exact condition in which it was sent (Hunt & Rodgers, 2003). Simple checksums are merely a count of the number of bits in a transmission unit, which is insufficient for security purposes because it provides no means of verifying the integrity of the received data, but only that it is of the correct size. Hash functions introduce a greater computational overhead than a simple tally but allow verification that the transmission was received successfully, free from transmission errors or deliberate tampering en route. The hash value, also known as a message digest, concisely represents the longer message or document from which it was derived. A message digest acts as a form of "digital fingerprint" of the original document and can be made public without revealing the contents of the corresponding document (Hunt & Rodgers, 2003).

# Authentication

Authentication of VPN users is generally performed by confirming the knowledge of some shared secret. Passwords are the most user-friendly option, although the process may incorporate tokens or smart cards if enhanced security is required. Digital certificates are a reliable way of providing strong authentication for large groups of users (Hunt & Rodgers, 2003). Because passwords can be cracked or sniffed, authentication methods that use static password authentication should be considered insecure,

particularly if the authentication session is not encrypted (Hunt & Rodgers, 2003).

Three distinct factors relate to authentication (Hunt & Rodgers, 2003):

1. What do you know? This fact should be known only by the user and the verifier and should be impossible to guess or derive. A common application of this factor in VPNs is an alphanumeric password, which is verified by an authentication server using an authentication protocol.

2. What do you have? In VPNs, this factor will typically be some form of identification card, smart card, or token. Such items should be unique and difficult to forge.

3. What you are? This refers to some unique attribute of the user, such as a fingerprint or voiceprint, which is impractical to forge or imitate. Such authentication methods are rarely used in VPNs at this time.

# Access Management

It is not always sufficient merely to authenticate a user; too often it is assumed that once a user has been granted access, he or she should have widespread access to almost all resources on the VPN (Hunt & Rodgers, 2003). This is a potentially dangerous assumption because insiders can pose as great a threat to the security of an organization as outsiders; they may have various advantages beyond privileges and access rights, such as a superior knowledge of system vulnerabilities and the whereabouts of sensitive information. Despite the risks involved, the problem of protecting a VPN and its resources from insiders is often assigned a relatively low priority, if not ignored altogether (Hunt & Rodgers, 2003).

This is where access management techniques can be a valuable tool. Using access management tools, such as Kerberos (a hardware or software implementation), an enterprise can ensure that insiders are granted access only to resources for which they have been explicitly assigned access rights. Usually, the process of managing and restricting access to VPN resources involves maintaining an access control list (ACL) for each of the resources for which use is restricted to specific users or groups of users. When a user attempts to access a given resource, the access management tool consults the ACL for that resource and will subsequently grant access only if that user is represented in the list (Hunt & Rodgers, 2003).

Security concerns relating to VPNs are summarized in Table 2.

# VPN IMPLEMENTATIONS

One can distinguish between two fundamental VPN models: the peer and the overlay model. In the peer model, the network layer forwarding path computation is implemented on a hop-by-hop basis, in which each node in the intermediate data transit path is a peer with a next-hop node. In contrast, in the overlay model, the network layer forwarding path computation is not implemented on a hop-by-hop basis, but rather, the intermediate link layer network is used as a "cut-through" to another edge node on the other side of a large cloud (Ferguson & Huston,

**Table 2** Virtual Private Network (VPN) Security Concerns

| Security Concern | Privacy | Integrity | Authentication | Nonrepudiation |
|---|---|---|---|---|
| Relevant Question | Can unauthorized parties gain access to private VPN traffic? | Can VPN traffic be altered without detection? | Can I be certain that senders or recipients are really who they claim to be? | Can the senders or receivers later deny involvement in a transaction? |
| Solution | Encryption | Checksums | Possession of secret key | Digital signatures |

1998). The overlay model introduces some serious scaling concerns when large numbers of egress peers are required. This is because the number of adjacencies increases in direct relationship with the number of peers, and thus the amount of computational and performance overhead required to maintain routing state, adjacency information, and other detailed packet forwarding and routing information for each peer becomes a liability in very large networks. If all egress nodes in a cut-through network become peers, in an effort to make all egress nodes one "layer 3" hop away from one another, this limits the scalability of the VPN overlay model quite remarkably (Ferguson & Huston, 1998).

A number of approaches to the problem of providing VPN links and services may be taken. In particular, a VPN may be implemented and secured at various layers of the transmission control protocol (TCP)/IP stack. The most significant of the currently available approaches are now described.

*Network layer VPNs* (Hunt & Rodgers, 2003), based primarily on IP, are implemented using network layer encryption and possibly tunneling. Packets entering the shared network are appended with an additional IP header containing a destination address, which corresponds to the other end of the tunnel. When this node receives the packet, the header is removed and the original packet, which is addressed to some location within the given network, is recovered. Because of this encapsulation, the original packets could be based on any network layer protocol without affecting their transport across the shared network.

*Data link layer VPNs* (Hunt & Rodgers, 2003) employ a shared backbone network based on a switched link layer technology such as frame relay (FR) or ATM. Links between VPN nodes are implemented as virtual circuits, which are inexpensive, flexible, and can offer some level of assured performance. Link layer VPNs are most appropriate for providing Intranet services; dial-up access is not well supported because most ISPs provide connectivity using IP. Most of the cost savings associated with VPNs are the result of use of ISPs. Therefore, IP-based network layer VPNs are more attractive than link layer VPNs if dial-up access is required. Virtual-circuit based VPNs face similar scalability issues to those of node-to-node tunneled VPNs, so a full-mesh architecture may not be possible. Alternatives such as partial meshes or hub-and-spoke configurations address this limitation to some extent, but these solutions may produce suboptimal behavior, especially for routing, introducing performance concerns.

*Application layer VPNs* (Hunt & Rodgers, 2003) are implemented in software, whereby workstations and servers are required to perform tasks such as encryption, rather than deferring these tasks to specialized hardware. As a result, software VPNs are inexpensive to implement but can have a significant impact on performance, limiting network throughput and producing high CPU usage, particularly over high-bandwidth connections.

In the case of *non-IP VPNs* (Ferguson & Huston, 1998), it is widely recognized that multiprotocol networks may also have requirements for VPNs. The most pervasive method of constructing VPNs in multiprotocol networks is to rely on application layer encryption, and as such, these are generally vendor proprietary, although some would contend that one of the most pervasive examples of this approach was the mainstay of the emergent Internet in the 1970s and 1980s—that of the UUCP (UNIX-to-UNIX copy protocol) network, which was (and remains) an open technology.

## Hardware Components

A number of hardware devices are required to implement the various types of VPNs just discussed. Many of these devices are common to standard networks, but some have additional burdens and responsibilities placed on them when applied to VPNs and their specific requirements. The main hardware devices employed by VPNs, and the implications of any additional processing that they must perform, are as follows (Hunt & Rodgers, 2003):

- **Firewalls:** VPNs must be protected from other users of the backbone network. This is typically achieved using a firewall, which provides critical services such as tunneling, cryptography, and route and content filtering (Hunt & Rodgers, 2003).

- **Routers:** Adding VPN functionality to existing routers can have an unacceptable performance impact, particularly at network stress points. Specifically, MPLS VPNs address this problem by making only the perimeter routers VPN-aware, so the core routers need not maintain the multiple routing tables that introduce so much overhead on perimeter routers (Hunt & Rodgers, 2003).

- **Switches:** Some switches offer facilities for increased separation of traffic by allowing a physical network to be partitioned into a number of virtual LANs (V-LANs). On a normal switch, all ports are part of the same network, whereas a V-LAN switch can treat different ports as parts of different networks if desired (Hunt & Rodgers, 2003).

- **Tunnel servers:** This service may be provided by a VPN router or a firewall. Assigning an existing network component this additional responsibility may have a serious impact on performance (Hunt & Rodgers, 2003).

- **Cryptocards:** Encryption algorithms that provide strong encryption, such as 3-DES, are computationally expensive and can limit effective bandwidth to around 100 Mbps unless specialized cryptographic hardware is used. On a workstation, this specialized hardware is provided in the form of an expansion card, which may be separate or integrated with the network interface card. Some firewalls also offer hardware support for various encryption algorithms (Hunt & Rodgers, 2003).

# PROTOCOLS EMPLOYED BY VPNs
## Point-to-Point Tunneling Protocol

The point-to-point tunneling protocol (PPTP; Pall, Verthein, Taarud, Little, & Zorn, 1999) allows the point-to-point protocol (PPP; Network Working Group, 1994) to be tunneled through an IP network. PPTP does not specify any changes to the PPP protocol, but describes a new vehicle for carrying PPP. The PPTP network server (PNS) is envisioned to run on a general purpose operating system while the client, referred to as a PPTP access concentrator (PAC), operates on a dial access platform. PPTP specifies a call-control and management protocol that allows the server to control access for dial-in circuit switched calls originating from a PSTN or ISDN or to initiate outbound circuit- switched connections. A network access server (NAS) provides temporary, on-demand network access to users. This access is point-to-point using PSTN or ISDN lines.

PPTP uses an extended version of the generic routing encapsulation mechanism (Hanks, Li, Farinacci, & Traina, 1994) to carry user PPP packets. These enhancements allow for low-level congestion and flow control to be provided on the tunnels used to carry user data between PAC and PNS. This mechanism allows for efficient use of the bandwidth available for the tunnels and avoids unnecessary retransmissions and buffer overruns. PPTP does not dictate the particular algorithms to be used for this low-level control, but it does define the parameters that must be communicated to allow such algorithms to work (Pall et al., 1999). PPTP allows existing NAS functions to be separated using a client–server architecture. Traditionally, the following functions are implemented by a NAS (Pall et al., 1999):

1. Physical native interfacing to PSTN or ISDN and control of external modems or terminal adapters
2. Logical termination of a PPP link control protocol (LCP) session
3. Participation in PPP authentication protocols
4. Channel aggregation and bundle management for PPP multilink protocol
5. Logical termination of various PPP network control protocols
6. Multiprotocol routing and bridging between NAS interfaces.

PPTP divides these functions between the PAC and PNS. The PAC is responsible for Functions 1, 2, and possibly 3. The PNS may be responsible for Function 3 and is responsible for Functions 4, 5, and 6. The decoupling of NAS functions offers the following benefits (Pall et al., 1999):

- **Flexible IP address management:** Dial-in users may maintain a single IP address as they dial into different PACs as long as they are served from a common PNS.
- **Support of non-IP protocols for dial networks behind IP networks.**
- **A solution to the "multilink hunt-group splitting" problem:** Multilink PPP, typically used to aggregate ISDN B channels, requires that all of the channels composing a multilink bundle be grouped at a single NAS. Because a multilink PPP bundle can be handled by a single PNS, the channels comprising the bundle may be spread across multiple PACs.

PPTP is implemented only by the PAC and PNS. No other systems need to be aware of it. Dial networks may be connected to a PAC without being aware of PPTP. Standard PPP client software should continue to operate on tunneled PPP links. PPTP can also be used to tunnel a PPP session over an IP network. In this configuration the PPTP tunnel and the PPP session runs between the same two machines with the caller acting as a PNS (Pall et al., 1999).

A tunnel is defined by a PNS–PAC pair. The tunnel protocol is defined by a modified version of generic routing encapsulation (GRE). The tunnel carries PPP datagrams between the PAC and the PNS. Many sessions are multiplexed on a single tunnel. A control connection operating over TCP controls the establishment, release, and maintenance of sessions and of the tunnel itself (Pall et al., 1999).

The security of user data passed over the tunneled PPP connection is addressed by PPP, as is authentication of the PPP peers. Because the PPTP control channel messages are neither authenticated nor integrity protected, it might be possible for an attacker to hijack the underlying TCP connection. It is also possible to manufacture false control channel messages and alter genuine messages in transit without detection. The GRE packets forming the tunnel itself are not cryptographically protected. Because the PPP negotiations are carried out over the tunnel, it may be possible for an attacker to eavesdrop and modify those negotiations. Unless the PPP payload data is cryptographically protected, it can be captured and read or modified (Pall et al., 1999).

PPTP is limited in usage. It offers remote connections to a single point. It does not support multiple connections nor does it easily support network-to-network connections. PPTP's security is also limited. It does not offer protection from substitution or playback attacks, nor does it provide perfect forward secrecy. PPTP has no clear mechanism for renegotiation if connectivity to the server is lost (Günter, 2001).

## Layer-2 Tunneling Protocol (L2TP)

Layer-2 tunneling protocol (L2TP; Townsley, Valencia, Rubens, Pall, Zorn, & Palter, 1999) facilitates the tunneling of PPP packets across an intervening network in a way that is as transparent as possible to both end users and applications. PPP defines an encapsulation mechanism for transporting multiprotocol packets across layer 2 (L2) point-to-point links. Typically, a user obtains a L2 connection to an NAS using one of a number of techniques (e.g., dial-up through the telephone system, ISDN, asymmetric DSL [ADSL], etc.) and then runs PPP over that connection. In such a configuration, the L2 termination point and PPP session end point reside on the same physical device (i.e., the NAS; Townsley et al., 1999).

L2TP extends the PPP model by allowing the L2 and PPP end points to reside on different devices interconnected by a packet-switched network. With L2TP, a user has an L2 connection to an access concentrator (e.g., modem bank, ADSL access multiplexer, etc.), and the concentrator then tunnels individual PPP frames to the NAS. This allows the actual processing of PPP packets to be divorced from the termination of the L2 circuit. One obvious benefit of such a separation is that instead of requiring the L2 connection terminate at the NAS (which may require a long-distance toll charge), the connection may terminate at a (local) circuit concentrator, which then extends the logical PPP session over a shared infrastructure such as frame relay circuit or the Internet. From the user's perspective, there is no functional difference between having the L2 circuit terminate in a NAS directly or using L2TP (Townsley et al., 1999).

L2TP has inherent support for the multiplexing of multiple calls from different users over a single link. Between the same two IP end points, there can be multiple L2TP tunnels, as identified by a tunnel-id, and multiple sessions within a tunnel, as identified by a session-id. Signaling is supported via the inbuilt control connection protocol, allowing both tunnels and sessions to be established dynamically (Rosenbaum, Lau, & Jha, 2003).

L2TP transports PPP packets (and only PPP packets) and thus can be used to carry multiprotocol traffic because PPP is multiprotocol. L2TP also supports sequenced delivery of packets. This is a capability that can be negotiated at session establishment and that can be turned on and off during a session. Concerning tunnel maintenance, L2TP uses a keep-alive protocol to distinguish between a tunnel outage and prolonged periods of tunnel inactivity (Rosenbaum et al., 2003).

L2TP as used over IP networks runs over the user datagram protocol UDP and must be used to carry PPP traffic. This results in a significant amount of overhead both in the data plane, with UDP, L2TP, and PPP headers, and in the control plane, with the L2TP and PPP control protocols (Rosenbaum et al., 2003). An L2TP header contains a 1-bit priority field, which can be set for packets that may need preferential treatment during local queuing and transmission. Also by transparently extending PPP, L2TP has inherent support for such PPP mechanisms as multilink PPP and its associated control protocols, which allow for bandwidth on demand to meet user requirements (Rosenbaum et al., 2003).

### Security Considerations

The L2TP tunnel end points may optionally perform an authentication procedure of one another during tunnel establishment. This authentication provides reasonable protection against replay and snooping during the tunnel establishment process. This mechanism is not designed to provide any authentication beyond tunnel establishment; it is fairly simple for a malicious user to inject packets once an authenticated tunnel establishment has been completed successfully (Townsley et al., 1999).

Securing L2TP (Patel, Aboba, Dixon, Zorn, & Booth, 2001) requires that the underlying transport make available encryption, integrity, and authentication services for all L2TP traffic. This secure transport operates on the entire L2TP packet and is functionally independent of PPP and the protocol being carried by PPP. As such, L2TP is only concerned with confidentiality, authenticity, and integrity of the L2TP packets between its tunnel end points. L2TP is similar to PPTP and they both target the remote access scenario. L2TP delegates security features toward IP security (IPsec; presented later. Additionally, it suffers from the same drawbacks as PPTP (Günter, 2001).

The choice between PPTP and L2TP for deployment in a VPN depends on whether the control needs to lie with the service provider or with the subscriber (Ferguson & Huston, 1998). Indeed, the difference can be characterized as to the client of the VPN in which the L2TP model is one of a "wholesale" access provider who has a number of configured client service providers who appear as VPNs on the common dial access system, and the PPTP model is one of distributed private access in which the client is an individual end user and the VPN structure is that of end-to-end tunnels. One might suggest too that the difference is also a matter of economics, because the L2TP model allows the service provider to provide a "value-added" service beyond basic IP-level connectivity and charge their subscribers accordingly for the privilege of using it, thus creating new revenue streams. On the other hand, the PPTP model enables distributed reach of the VPN at a much more atomic level, enabling corporate VPNs to extend access capabilities without the need for explicit service contracts with a multitude of NAPs (Ferguson & Huston, 1998).

## IP Security

IPSec is an open architecture for IP-packet encryption and authentication, thus it is located in the network layer. IPSec adds additional headers and trailers to an IP packet and can encapsulate (tunnel) IP packets in new ones (Cohen, 2003). A number of security services are provided by IPSec, including access control, connectionless integrity, nonrepudiation, protection against replay attacks, confidentiality and limited traffic flow confidentiality. These services are provided at the transport layer, offering protection for IP and upper layer protocols (Hunt and Rodgers, 2003). There are three main functionalities of IPSec separated in three protocols. One is the authentication through an Authentication Header (AH); the other is the encryption through an Encapsulating Security Payload (ESP) and finally automated key management through the Internet Key Exchange (IKE) protocol. IPSec provides an architecture for key management, encryption, authentication and tunneling (Cohen, 2003). IPSec was designed to be algorithm independent. It supports several encryption and authentication algorithms, which allow the companies using VPN to select the desired security level for each VPN (Younglove, 2000).

IPSec is an optimum solution for trusted LAN-to-LAN VPNs (Günter, 2001). IPsec can ensure authentication, privacy, and data integrity. It is open to a wide variety of encryption mechanisms. It is an application transparent and a natural IP extension, thus ensuring interoperability among VPNs over the Internet. Router vendors and VPN hardware vendors support IPsec. Nevertheless, there are disadvantages of IPsec. It is bound to the TCP/IP stack. IP addressing is part of IPsec's authentication algorithm. This is less secure than higher layered approaches, and it is a problem in dynamic address environments, which are common to ISPs. Moreover, it requires a public key infrastructure, which is still subject to current research, and it does not specify a methodology for access control beyond simple packet filtering (Günter, 2001).

### The Encapsulating Security Payload

The Encapsulating Security Payload (ESP) protocol is responsible for packet encryption. An ESP header is inserted into the packet between the IP header and the packet contents. The header contains a security parameter index (SPI), which specifies to the receiver the appropriate security association SA for processing the packet. Also included in the ESP header is a sequence number, which is a counter that increases each time a packet is sent to the same address using the same SPI and indicates the number of packets that have been sent with the same group of parameters. The sequence number provides protection against replay attacks, in which an attacker copies a packet and sends it out of sequence to confuse communicating nodes. Packet data is encrypted before transmission. ESP allows multiple methods of encryption, with DES as its default. ESP also can be used for data authentication. Included in the ESP header is an optional authentication field, which contains a cryptographic checksum that is computed over the ESP packet when encryption is complete. The ESP's authentication services do not protect the IP header that precedes the ESP packet.

ESP can be used in two modes. In transport mode, the packet's data, but not the IP header, is encrypted and optionally authenticated. Although transport mode ESP is sufficient for protecting the contents of a packet against eavesdropping, it leaves the source and destination IP addresses open to modification if the packet is intercepted. In tunnel mode, the packet's contents and the IP header are encrypted and, optionally, authenticated. Then, a new IP header is generated for routing the secured packets from sender to receiver. Although tunnel mode ESP provides more security than transport mode ESP, some types of traffic analysis are still possible. For example, the IP addresses of the sending and receiving gateways could still be determined by examining the packet headers.

### Key Management

There are two ways to handle key management within IPSec's architecture: manual keying and Internet key exchange (IKE). Manual keying involves face-to-face key exchanges (e.g., trading keys on paper or magnetic disk) or sending keys via a bonded courier or e-mail. Although manual keying is suitable for a small number of sites, automated key management is required to accommodate on-demand creation of keys for security associations (SAs). IPSec's default automated key management protocol is IKE. IKE was formed by combining the Internet security association key management protocol (ISAKMP), which defines procedures and packet formats to establish, negotiate, modify, and delete SAs, with the Oakley key determination protocol, which is a key exchange protocol based on the Diffie–Hellman algorithm.

Because key exchange is closely related to the management of security associations, part of the key management procedure is handled by SAs, and the security parameter index (SPI) values that refer to the SAs, in each IPSec packet. Whenever an SA is created, keys must be exchanged. IKE's structure combines these functions by requiring the initiating node to specify:

- an encryption algorithm to protect data
- a hash algorithm to reduce data for signing
- an authentication method for signing the data
- information about the material needed to generate the keys, over which a Diffie–Hellman exchange is performed.

A pseudo-random function used to hash certain values during the key exchange for verification purposes may also be specified.

### Packet Authentication

In IPSec's architecture, the authentication header (AH) provides data integrity and authentication services for IP packets. The data integrity feature prevents the undetected modification of a packet's contents while the packet is in transit, and the authentication feature prevents address spoofing and replay attacks and enables the receiver to authenticate the application and filter traffic accordingly (Wright, 2000). Like the ESP header, the AH is inserted into the packet between the IP header and the packet contents. The AH also contains an SPI, which specifies to the receiver the security protocols the sender is using for communications. The authentication provided by the AH differs from that provided by the ESP. AH services protect the external IP header that precedes the ESP header, along with the entire contents of the ESP packet. The AH contains authentication data, obtained by applying the hash algorithm defined by the SPI to the packet's contents. Two algorithms are supported: Hash-based Message Authentication Code with Message Digest version 5 (HMAC-MD5) and Secure Hash Algorithm version 1 (SHA-1) (Wright, 2000).

The authentication header can be used in the same two modes as ESP. In transport mode, the packet's data and the original IP header are authenticated. In tunnel mode, the entire IP packet—data, original IP header, and outer IP header—are authenticated. In addition to applying either AH or ESP to an IP packet in transport or tunnel modes, IPSec supports combinations of these modes. Several combinations are possible, among them (Wright, 2000):

- ESP could be used in transport mode without the authentication option (to encrypt the packet's data), then

AH could be applied in transport mode (to authenticate the ESP header, the packet's data, and the original IP header).

- AH could be used in transport mode to authenticate the packet's data and the original IP header, then ESP could be applied in tunnel mode to encrypt the entire, authenticated inner packet and to add a new IP header for routing the packet from sender to receiver.
- ESP could be used in tunnel mode to encrypt and, optionally, authenticate a packet and its original header, then AH could be applied in transport mode to authenticate the packet's data, original IP header, and outer IP header.

## User Authentication

A VPN must be able to authenticate users reliably to control access to enterprise resources and keep unauthorized users out of corporate networks (Wright, 2000). Three protocols are described here: password authentication protocol (PAP), challenge handshake authentication protocol (CHAP), and Remote Authentication Dial-In User Service (RADIUS).

PAP was originally designed as a simple way for one computer to authenticate itself to another computer when PPP is used as the communication's protocol. PAP is a two-way handshaking protocol. When the PPP link is established, the client system sends the plaintext user ID and password pair to the destination system (the authenticator). The authenticator either accepts the pair or the connection is terminated. PAP is not a secure means of user authentication. The authentication information is transmitted in the clear, and there is nothing to protect against playback attacks or excessive attempts by attackers to guess valid user ID–password pairs (Wright, 2000).

CHAP, a three-way handshaking protocol, is a more secure method for authenticating users. Instead of the simple, two-step user ID–password approval process used by PAP, CHAP uses a three-step process to produce a verified PPP link (Wright, 2000):

1. The authenticator sends a challenge message to the client system.
2. The client system calculates a value using a one-way hash function and sends the value back to the authenticator.
3. The authenticator acknowledges authentication if the response matches the expected value.

CHAP removes the possibility that an attacker can try repeatedly to log on over the same connection (a weakness inherent in PAP). PAP and CHAP share some disadvantages, however. Both protocols rely on a secret password that must be stored on the remote user's computer and on the local computer. If either computer comes under the control of a network attacker, the secret password will be compromised. Also, both PAP and CHAP allow only one set of privileges to be assigned to a specific computer. This prevents different network access privileges from being assigned to different remote users who use the same remote host (Wright, 2000).

RADIUS protocol provides greater flexibility for administering remote network connection users and sessions. RADIUS uses a client–server model to authenticate users, determine access levels, and maintain all necessary audit and accounting data. The RADIUS protocol uses an NAS to accept user connection requests, obtain user ID and password information, and pass the encrypted information securely to the RADIUS server. The RADIUS server returns the authentication status (approved or denied), along with any configuration data required for the NAS to provide services to the user. User authentication and access to services are managed by the RADIUS server, enabling a remote user to gain access to the same services from any communications server that can communicate with the RADIUS server (Wright, 2000).

The services and protocols of IPSec are summarized in Figure 4.

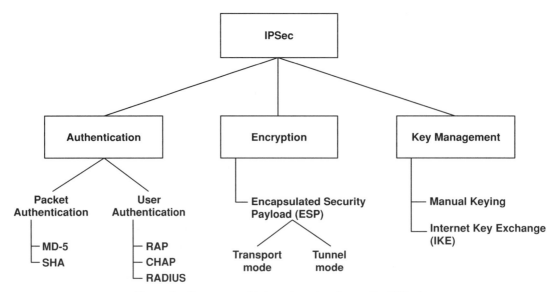

**Figure 4:** Summary of Internet protocol security (IPSec).

## SOCKS v5 and SSL

SOCKS v5 was originally approved by the IETF as a standard protocol for authenticated firewall traversal (Günter, 2001). When combined with the Secure Socket Layer (SSL) it provides the foundation for building highly secure VPNs that are compatible with any firewall. SOCKS v5 strength is access control. SOCKS v5 controls the flow of data at the session layer (OSI-layer 5). It establishes a circuit between a client and a host on a session-by-session basis. Thus it can provide more detailed access control than protocols in the lower layers without the need to reconfigure each application. SOCKS v5 and SSL can interoperate on top of IPv4, IPsec, PPTP, L2TP, or any other lower level VPN protocol. A session layer solution does not have to interfere with the networking transport components, thus the clients are nonintrusive. SOCKS v5 provides plug-and-play capabilities including access control, protocol filtering, content filtering, traffic monitoring, reporting, and administration applications. On the minus side, SOCKS v5 decreases performance. Also, client software is required to build a connection through the firewall to transmit all TCP/IP data through the proxy server (Günter, 2001).

## Multiprotocol Label Switching

MPLS is deployed in a ISP's IP backbone network that uses IP routers at the edges of the network and ATM switches controlled by a MPLS component in the inside (Günter, 2001). The basic idea is to do (intelligent) layer 3 routing at the edges of the backbone network and to do fast layer 2 forwarding inside the backbone network. Incoming IP packets get an attached MPLS header, they are labeled according to IP header information (mainly the target address, but also type of service and other fields). A label switched path is set up for each route or path through the network. Once this is done, all subsequent nodes may simply forward the packet along the label-switched path identified by the label at the front of the packet. Negotiations of labels between nodes are done by the label distribution protocol of MPLS. An ATM connection is set up for each label-switched path. Thus, MPLS can support quality of service. MPLS makes the underlying backbone infrastructure invisible to the layer 3 mechanisms. This lightweighted tunneling provides an extendible foundation that provides VPN and other service capabilities. Furthermore, the MPLS architecture enables network operators to define explicit routes (Günter, 2001). MPLS technologies are useful for ISPs that want to offer their customers a wide band of IP services. The ISPs add value to their service, for example, by offering the complete management of the customers VPN. Obviously, the more the customers outsource their VPN management, the more crucial network management becomes to the ISP (Günter, 2001).

MPLS VPNs provide a highly scalable technology for ISPs that want to offer layer 3 VPN services to their customers. The border gateway protocol (BGP-4) (Rekhter, Watson, & Li 1995) is a scalable protocol and is widely accepted in the industry. Furthermore, it is also well suited to carrying additional information in its routing updates, which is required in the MPLS VPN architecture (Tomsu & Wieser, 2002).

## QUALITY OF SERVICE SUPPORT

Apart from creating a segregated address environment to allow private communications, the VPN environment is also expected to be in a position to support a set of service levels (Zeng & Ansari, 2003). Such per-VPN service levels may be specified either in terms of a defined service level that the VPN can rely on at all times or in terms of a level of differentiation that the VPN can draw on the common platform resource with some level of priority of resource allocation (Ferguson & Huston, 1998). Efforts within the Integrated Services Working Group of the IETF have resulted in a set of specifications for the support of guaranteed and controlled load end-to-end traffic profiles using a mechanism which loads per-flow state into the switching elements of the network. There are a number of caveats regarding the use of these mechanisms, in particular relating to the ability to support the number of flows that will be encountered on the public Internet. Such caveats tend to suggest that these mechanisms will not be the ones that will ultimately be adopted to support service levels for VPNs in very large networking environments (Ferguson & Huston, 1998).

The differentiated services (DiffServ) approach tries to provide a solution for QoS support with better scalability than integrated services (IntServ). Differentiated services can provide two or more QoS levels without maintaining per-flow state at every router. The idea of DiffServ approach is to use the DiffServ field in the IP header to designate the appropriate DiffServ level that the packet should receive. DiffServ can provide scalability by aggregating the flows into a small number of DiffServ classes and by implementing traffic conditioning at the boundary routers of a network or an administrative domain (Cohen, 2003).

It must be noted that QoS and VPN techniques introduce new challenges. They need extensive configurations in the routers. The local configurations have to be consistent across the network. Many companies may not have the knowledge and resources to deploy and manage enhanced Internet services by themselves. Rather, they will outsource the service management to their ISP (Braun, Guenter, & Khalil, 2001).

The traditional model for specifying QoS arrangements involves drawing a set of network service requirements between an ordered pair of customer sites. The ordered pair defines a direction of data flow, and the whole set is called "traffic matrices." The traffic matrices model gives the customer fine granularity of control over the traffic flows between customer sites, and the network provider can offer stringent service guarantee for each data flow. Maintaining the traffic matrices can become complicated as the VPN grows, however (Harding, 2003).

Recent developments in VPN technologies have introduced a new QoS specification model, the hose model, that maybe desirable to the VPN customers. In this model, two hoses are given to the customer with one hose used for sending traffic out of the network and the other hose for receiving traffic from the network. This means that network provider offers aggregate traffic service to the customer in which all traffic going toward the customer site must fit within the receiving hose capacity and all the traffic going out of the customer site must be within the sending hose capacity (Harding, 2003). The hose specification contains the egress bandwidth (outbound traffic) and the ingress bandwidth (in-bound traffic) pair for every customer site that takes part in the VPN. The major advantages of this model from the customer perspective are that specification is made simple and there is a high potential for multiplexing gain for using aggregate requirements rather than traffic matrices. The simple specification allows changes to be made easily including changes in the VPN membership. However, the customer in this model loses control of the data flow between sites, and the service guarantee is on an aggregate basis, meaning coarser service guarantee level (Harding, 2003). From a network provider's perspective, the traffic matrices model specifies heavy constraints, which restrict the network optimization that can be achieved. The hose model specifies aggregate requirements that are lighter in constraints, thus giving the network provider more flexibility to perform network optimization. Network optimization involves mechanisms to improve bandwidth efficiency, load balancing, and traffic multiplexing (Harding, 2003).

## CONCLUSIONS

People increasingly depend on remote access to do their jobs, and demand is growing for access to large volumes of corporate information. Moreover, the upsurge of e-commerce means companies are implementing business applications that share information among sites, extending the reach of their business to partners, contractors, and supply chain. In all these areas, VPNs promise to reduce recurring telecommunications charges, minimize the amount of access equipment required, and give managers better control over their networks (Younglove, 2000). Organizations are struggling to meet the escalating demand for remote connectivity, and they are having difficulty dealing with the resulting increase in network complexity and end-user support costs. VPNs offer a more affordable, scalable way to meet the demands of a growing community of remote users and to manage branch office connectivity. They can help to accommodate the pace and unpredictability of business by linking customers and business partners into extranets on an ad hoc basis. VPNs can provide access to networked resources without compromising security. Virtual private networking offers the capability of enhanced and secure corporate communications with the promise of future cost savings (Wright, 2000).

The pertinent conclusion here is that although a VPN can take many forms, VPNs are built to solve some basic, common problems. These are virtualization of services and segregation of communications to a closed community of interest, while simultaneously exploiting the financial opportunity of economies of scale of the underlying common host communications system. Each solution has a number of strengths and also a number of weaknesses and vulnerabilities. There is no single mechanism for VPNs that will supplant all others in the months and years to come; instead we will continue to see a diversity of technology choices in this area of VPN support (Ferguson & Huston, 1998).

## GLOSSARY

**Border Gateway Protocol (BGP)** A routing protocol that facilitates the exchange of network reachability information between systems.

**Challenge Handshake Authentication Protocol (CHAP)** A three-way handshaking authentication protocol that can be applied to produce a verified PPP link. CHAP is a more secure authentication protocol compared to PAP.

**Extranet VPN** A VPN that extends limited access to corporate computing resources to business partners, such as customers or suppliers.

**Generic Routing Encapsulation (GRE)** A simple, general purpose encapsulation mechanism.

**Internet Key Exchange (IKE)** The default automated key management protocol of IPSec.

**Intranet VPN** A VPN that connects a number of local area networks located in multiple geographic areas over a shared network infrastructure.

**IP Security (IPSec)** An open architecture for IP-packet encryption and authentication and key management. IPSec adds additional headers and trailers to an IP packet and can encapsulate (tunnel) IP packets in new ones.

**Layer 2 Tunneling Protocol (L2TP)** A tunneling protocol that facilitates the tunneling of PPP packets across an intervening network in a way that is as transparent as possible to both end-users and applications.

**Network Address Translation (NAT)** A method by which IP addresses are mapped from one address realm (i.e., network domain) to another, providing transparent routing to end hosts.

**Password Authentication Protocol (PAP)** A simple two-way handshaking authentication protocol that allows one computer to authenticate itself to another computer when the point-to-point protocol is used as the communication's protocol.

**Point-to-Point Protocol (PPP)** A protocol that defines an encapsulation mechanism for transporting multiprotocol packets across layer 2 point-to-point links.

**Point-to-Point Tunneling Protocol (PPTP)** A tunneling protocol employed by VPNs that allows the Point-to-Point Protocol to be tunneled through an IP network.

**Remote Access VPN** A VPN that connects telecommuters and mobile users to corporate networks.

**Remote Authentication Dial-In User Service (RADIUS)** A user authentication protocol that uses a client–server model to authenticate users, determine access levels, and maintain all necessary audit and accounting data.

**Virtual Private Network (VPN)** A private network constructed within a public network infrastructure, such as the global Internet.

## CROSS REFERENCES

See *Encryption Basics; IP-Based VPN; Secure Sockets Layer (SSL); Security and Web Quality of Service; VPN Architecture.*

# REFERENCES

Arora, P., Vemuganti, P. R., & Allani, P. (2001). Comparison of VPN protocol—IPSec, PPTP, and L2TP. Project Report ECE 646, Retrieved September 10, 2003 from http://ece.gmu.edu/courses/ECE543/reportsF01/arveal.pdf

Brahim, H. O., Wright, G., Gleeson, B., Bach, R., Sloane, T., Young, A., et al. (2003, May). Network based IP VPN architecture using virtual routers. Internet draft <draft-ietf-l3vpn-vpn-vr-00.txt>. Retrieved September 1, 2003 from http://www.ietf.org/proceedings/03jul/I-D/draft-ietf-l3vpn-vpn-vr-00.txt

Braun T., Guenter M., & Khalil I. (2001, May). Management of quality of service enabled VPNs. *IEEE Communications Magazine*, 90–98.

Cohen, R. (2003, February). On the establishment of an access VPN in broadband access networks. *IEEE Communications Magazine*, 156–163.

Ferguson, P., & Huston, G. (1998). What is a VPN? Retrieved August 5, 2003 from http://www.employees.org/~ferguson

Gleeson, B., Lin, A., Heinanen, J., Armitage, G., & Malis, A. (2000, February). A framework for IP based virtual private networks, Request for comment (RFC) 2764. Retrieved August 20, 2003 from http://www.ietf.org/rfc/rfc2764.txt

Günter, M. (2001). Virtual private networks over the Internet. Retrieved September 10, 2003 from http://citeseer.nj.nec.com/480338.html

Hanks, S., Li, T., Farinacci, D., & Traina, P. (1994, October). Generic routing encapsulation (GRE). RFC 1701. Retrived August 12, 2003 from http://www.ietf.org/rfc/rfc1701.txt

Harding, A. (2003). SSL virtual private networks. *Computers & Security, 22*, 416–420.

Hunt, R., & Rodgers, C. (2003). Virtual private networks: Strong security at what cost? Retrieved August 25, 2003 from http://citeseer.nj.nec.com/555428.html

Network Working Group. (1994, July). The point-to-point protocol (PPP) (W. Simpson, Ed.). RFC 1661. Retrieved September 1, 2003 from http://www.ietf.org/rfc/rfc1661.txt

Pall, G., Verthein, W., Taarud, J., Little, W., & Zorn, G. (1999, July). Point-to-point tunneling protocol (PPTP). RFC 2637. Retrieved September 1, 2003 from http://www.ietf.org/rfc/rfc2637.txt

Patel B., Aboba B., Dixon W., Zorn G., & Booth S. (2001, November). Securing L2TP using IPsec. RFC 3193. Retrieved September 1, 2003 from http://www.ietf.org/rfc/ rfc3193.txt

Rekhter Y., Watson T. J., & Li, T. (1995, March). A border gateway protocol 4 (BGP-4). RFC 1771. Retrieved September 1, 2003 from http://www.ietf.org/rfc/rfc1771.txt

Ribeiro S., Silva F., & Zuquete A. (2004, June). A roaming authentication solution for wifi using IPSec VPNs with client certificates. Presented at the TERENA Networking Conference, Rhodes, Greece.

Rosenbaum, G., Lau, W., & Jha, S. (2003, September). Recent directions in virtual private network solutions. Presented at the IEEE International Conference on Networks (ICON 2003), Sydney, Australia.

Srisuresh, P., & Holdrege, M. (1999, August). IP network address translator (NAT) terminology and considerations. RFC 2663. Retrieved September 1, 2003 from http://www.ietf.org/rfc/rfc2663.txt

Strayer, W. T., & Yuan, R. (2001, May). Introduction to virtual private networks. Retrieved March 17, 2003 from http://www.awprofessional.com/articles/article.asp?p=167809&rl=1

Tomsu, P., & Wieser, G. (2002). MPLS-based VPNs—designing advanced virtual networks. Prentice-Hall.

Townsley, W., Valencia, A., Rubens, A., Pall, G., Zorn, G., & Palter, B. (1999, August). Layer two tunneling protocol. RFC 2661. Retrieved September 1, 2003 from http://www.ietf.org/rfc/rfc2661.txt

Wright, M. A. (2000, July). Virtual private network security. *Network-Security*, 11–14.

Younglove, R. (2000). Virtual private networks: Secure access for e-business. *IEEE Internet Computing, 4*, 96.

Yuan, R. (2002, January). The VPN Client and the Windows operating system. Retrieved September 10, 2003 from http://www.awprofessional.com/articles/article.asp?p=25042

Zeng, J., & Ansari, N. (2003, April). Toward IP virtual private network quality of service: A service provider perspective. *IEEE Communications Magazine*, 113–119.

# FURTHER READING

Braun, T., Günter, M., Kasumi, M., & Khalil, I. (1999, January). Virtual private network architecture. CATI Project Deliverable. Retrieved from http://www.tik.ee.ethz.ch/~cati/deliverables.html

# VPN Architecture

Stan Kurkovsky, *Central Connecticut State University*

## INTRODUCTION
### Motivation for Virtual Private Network (VPNs)

Ever since people started communicating effectively with one another, the issue of privacy has been a cornerstone. How do we protect our communication from being accessed by those who do not need to know about it? The Internet environment, in which most modern communication takes place, adds its own specifics to the nature of communication: it is conducted in a public medium. Virtual private networks (VPNs) provide the means for conducting private communications in the public Internet (Cohen & Kaempfer, 2000; Herscovitz, 1999; Tuomenoksa, 2002). A VPN merges the concept of a *virtual network* that exists on top of the Internet with the concept of a *private network* that provides confidentiality.

In the modern world dominated by business communication, VPNs provide an irreplaceable tool that enables businesses to communicate with customers and other businesses effectively and securely. In particular, a VPN has the following advantages (Gupta, 2003):

- *Worldwide coverage.* Because a VPN is not bounded by the physical limitations of a private network, it can be accessible at any place that has Internet connectivity. That explains the "virtual" part of the VPN term.
- *Cost effectiveness.* Although corporate VPN solutions are typically expensive, they are still much cheaper than purchasing and maintaining several special-purpose solutions covering the entire range of functionality of a single VPN solution.
- *Secure communication.* A VPN provides tools for user authentication, access control, and data encryption that guarantee the confidentiality of transmissions and data integrity.
- *Business infrastructure support.* In business-to-business (B2B) transactions, where products, services, or information is exchanged between businesses, it is very

important to establish trusted communication channels with business partners. Physical private networks are too impractical to be a common and effective solution for B2B transactions. VPNs, in contrast, provide a flexible and secure tool for such transactions.

## VPN Functionality and Technologies

*Tunneling* in VPNs is a process of encapsulating an original data packet into another packet by repeating one or more protocol layers. It is typically used as one of the tools to implement security: tunneling enables unsecured packets to be put into secure encrypted packets. Frequently, tunneling is used to hide the real source and destination addresses of the original data packet. It can also be used when there is a need to transport data packets and protocols over networks that only support other network protocols. Each VPN tunnel is uniquely identified by two components: its endpoints (where the tunnel starts and where it ends) and the encapsulation protocol transporting the data packets inside the tunnel (Yuan & Strayer, 2001).

*Authentication* in VPNs is a process of identity verification between the two networks on the opposite endpoints of the tunnel. This process ensures that the data are coming exactly from the source identified in the encapsulated data packets. There are two general types of authentication methods. Two-party authentication methods include password, challenge/response method, token cards, and smart cards; protocols and schemes used in this method include PAP, CHAP, EAP, RADIUS and OTP (see the following chapters of the *Handbook*: Access Control: Principles and Solutions, and Password Authentication). Trusted third-party authentication methods and tools include Kerberos, public key infrastructure (PKI), and Pretty Good Privacy (PGP; Northcutt, Zeltser, Winters, Frederick, & Ritchey, 2003; also see the following chapters of the *Handbook*: Kerberos, PKI (Public Key Infrastructure), and PGP (Pretty Good Privacy).

The access control procedure follows the authentication phase and allows the entities on a VPN to decide whether to allow each other the authorized access to resources. An access control decision is usually made based on the identity of the requester, the requested resources, and the rules of their access. Such a decision can be made by the server that hosts security services or by a separate policy server. Usually, a good solution is to administer all policies at a centralized server at each VPN endpoint.

Data security is the cornerstone of any VPN solution. VPN uses a public infrastructure to transport private data, which can potentially be intercepted, decrypted, read, and altered by others. Therefore, data integrity procedures and encryption must be applied to every network packet. A VPN solution must also be immune to a replay attack, which occurs when authentic packets are recorded by others and retransmitted at a later time. Such packets may pass the cryptography safeguards, but will render the entire message invalid if inserted into an incoming data stream. Over-the-air rekeying, a technique of changing encryption in the middle of a communication session, improves data security and helps prevent hazardous effects of replay attacks.

## VPN Solutions

A good VPN solution must comprise multiple and properly configured VPN devices and services placed in appropriate physical and network locations. After their installation and initial configuration, these devices and services must be monitored and maintained constantly.

A VPN gateway typically serves as an endpoint of a VPN tunnel and acts as a gatekeeper for all network packets coming to and from the resources protected by a VPN. Usually located at the perimeter of a corporate network, VPN gateways typically combine access control, authentication, and data security within a single hardware device. There are many stand-alone VPN gateways available; however, some vendors integrate them into routers or firewalls. Typically, any VPN gateway has at least one network interface for the inbound traffic (coming from the public Internet) and at least one for the outbound traffic (coming from the secure private network).

A VPN client is software that is used by a single user to remotely access the VPN. Although VPN gateway hardware is designed to serve multiple secure network resources, a VPN client is a program that is usually designed to work with a single computer. Similar to a VPN gateway, a VPN client provides authentication and data security and creates a tunnel between the computer on which it is installed and an endpoint of a VPN, on which a VPN gateway is usually installed.

## VPN ARCHITECTURE
### Types of VPN Architectures

In the discussion of VPN architecture, this chapter follows the following classification of building VPN solutions (Mairs, 2002; Yuan & Strayer, 2001): site-to-site intranet VPNs, remote access VPNs, and extranet VPNs.

Site-to-site intranet VPN solutions are typically used when two or more geographically dispersed corporate sites must be interconnected securely. Site-to-site VPNs are especially useful when it is not feasible to use a dedicated private network to interconnect the sites, but a public Internet connection is readily available. In a typical site-to-site VPN solution, VPN gateways are placed on the boundaries between the intranets local to each site and the public Internet. Encrypted VPN tunnels exist between each VPN gateway participating in this solution. Figure 1 presents a scenario in which there are three corporate sites, each with its own intranet and a VPN gateway placed at each intranet's network perimeter. There are three VPN tunnels formed through the public Internet interconnecting each pair of the VPN gateways.

A remote access VPN offers a secure and reliable way for telecommuters to connect to their main offices and corporate networks. A popular and older alternative to this solution is to use a remote access server at a centralized location that provides (mostly dial-up) connectivity for the remote users. However, this alternative suffers from two major drawbacks: dial-up modems are slow, and telephone connectivity frequently entails significant toll charges. Remote access VPNs provide a streamlined IP-based access for remote users regardless of how they connect to the Internet—whether they use dial-up, broadband, or Ethernet at any location. Figure 2 demonstrates a remote access VPN solution in which a VPN gateway provides a number of VPN tunnels for two (and possibly more) remote users, such as telecommuters. Each remote user must have VPN client software installed on his or her computer. In such a solution, the endpoints of the VPN

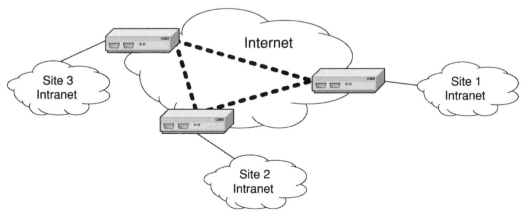

**Figure 1:** A site-to-site intranet VPN.

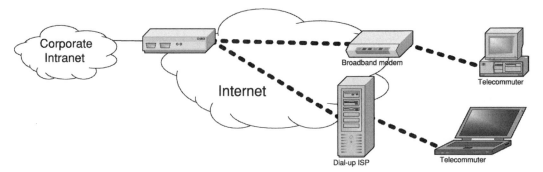

**Figure 2:** A remote access VPN.

tunnels are the corporate VPN gateway and the respective computers of the telecommuters.

An extranet VPN offers a solution by which a corporation can establish a secure channel of communication with its partners and large customers, as shown in Figure 3. This solution may be viewed as a kind of hybrid between a site-to-site intranet and a remote access VPN, but there are two major differences. First, extranet VPNs are used to connect the main corporate network with other networks, which belong to other companies or individuals. Second, extranet VPNs should not allow all traffic from the tunnel to pass through into the corporate network. Only the traffic pertaining to the relevant business transactions should be allowed to access a specially designated portion of the corporate extranet, which can be governed by special access rules and filters applied to the tunnel.

## Types of VPNs

Based on the way a particular VPN solution is implemented, it can be either a software-based or a hardware-based VPN (Mairs, 2002).

Software-based VPNs are best suited for situations in which the same organization does not control both of the VPN tunnel endpoints. Most software-based VPN products allow the traffic to be tunneled based on the source or destination Internet protocol (IP) address or the protocol used in communication. The ability to select specific traffic types to be tunneled presents an advantage when the remote VPN users see network traffic of many different types. Such a situation is typical for remote users of remote access VPNs. Software-based VPN solutions are reasonably inexpensive because they require no special hardware. However, they are not the most efficient solution and do not scale well as the number of users increases. Secure sockets layer (SSL) VPNs present an interesting implementation of software-based VPNs; they are discussed in detail in Araujo (2003) and Netilla Networks (2003).

Hardware-based VPNs consist of VPN concentrators and/or VPN-capable routers. The advantages of hardware-based VPNs include their ease of use and installation, their high network throughput, and their ability to support multiple VPN tunnels and high levels of encryption. However, hardware-based VPN solutions bear high upfront equipment costs, and they are less flexible than software-based VPN solutions. Unlike software-based VPNs, hardware-based VPNs typically tunnel all network traffic.

## VPN GATEWAYS

The main purpose of a VPN gateway is to separate a secure private network from the public Internet or other untrusted networks, which is achieved by the following:

- enabling the designated packets to enter and leave the private network securely
- keeping the undesired outside packets from entering the private network
- keeping the private network packets from unintentionally leaving the network

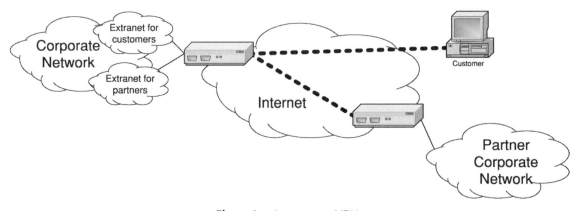

**Figure 3:** An extranet VPN.

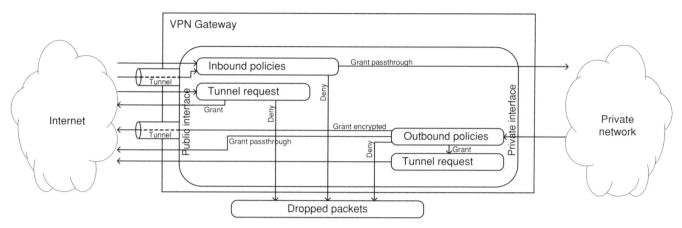

**Figure 4:** A VPN gateway.

Figure 4 shows the flow of IP packets coming in and out of a typical VPN gateway.

VPN gateways are designed to implement the following basic classes of functions: tunneling, authentication, access control, and data integrity and confidentiality. Although many techniques exist to implement each of those functions, as a rule, a well-designed VPN gateway should support at least one (and sometimes more than one) technique for each implementation. The specifics of how these functions are implemented and configured usually depend on the type of VPN in which a VPN gateway is used: site-to-site intranet, remote access, or extranet VPNs.

## Site-to-Site Intranet VPN Gateway Functionality

As shown in Figure 1, a site-to-site VPN connects, through a tunnel, two or more gateways situated in different physical locations. A sample set of requirements for such a VPN may include the following:

- *All VPN gateways must use digital certificates for authentication.* This implies that the VPN gateways must support PKI, as well as a set of digital certificate support functions in the Internet key exchange (IKE). IKE is further discussed in chapter IPsec: IKE (Internet Key Exchange of this *Handbook*. Certificate enrollment, renewal, and revocation options are flexible and are left to the VPN designer.

- *All private packets originating from either of the three intranet sites must be encrypted.* Such a solution must be implemented by tunneling with strong encryption and dynamically generated keys, which can be provided by using IPSec and IKE (Doraswamy & Harkins, 2003). IPsec is further discussed in chapters IPsec: AH (Authentication Header) and ESP (Encapsulating Security Payload) and IPsec: IKE (Internet Key Exchange) of this *Handbook*.

- *All intranet sites are allowed to communicate with one another only through the VPN.* All packets destined from one site to another must be encapsulated fully. Whether or not the different sites of the corporate network share the same address space, IPsec encapsulating security

payload (ESP) in tunnel mode offers a good solution to satisfy this requirement.

## Remote Access VPN Gateway Functionality

As presented in Figure 2, telecommuters use a remote access VPN to connect to a corporate network through a VPN tunnel that runs over a dial-up, broadband, or a local area network connection over the public Internet. Telecommuters may use a variety of different Internet service providers (ISPs) and very likely do not have fixed IP addresses. Most ISPs use dynamic host configuration protocol (DHCP) to dynamically assign IP addresses to their subscribers. VPN gateways must be capable of coping with the remote IP addresses that change frequently. In addition, for the IP packets to be routed correctly within the secure corporate network, it is important for the remote users to have IP addresses that are different from those assigned by their ISPs. To facilitate the task of serving as a remote access server, a VPN gateway must implement an address allocation and assignment scheme. In cases when a dynamic address allocation scheme is chosen, DHCP can be used as a solution. In addition to the VPN-assigned IP address, remote VPN clients must acquire additional information needed to connect to and communicate with the secure corporate network. For example, such information may include domain name system (DNS) and Windows Internet service (WINS) server IP addresses necessary to obtain access to their services.

A sample set of requirements for a remote access VPN may include the following:

- *All remote users must use digital certificates for authentication with the VPN gateway.* A standard solution is to use PKI, as well as a set of digital certificate support functions in IKE, as in the site-to-site intranet VPNs.

- *All private packets between the secure corporate network and the remote users must be encrypted.* Similar to the site-to-site intranet VPNs, such a solution can be provided by tunneling with strong encryption and dynamically generated keys using IPsec and IKE.

- *All remote users must be able to have access both to the corporate network through a VPN tunnel and to the public Internet, in which case no tunneling should be used.* Because remote telecommuting users must use a VPN client to connect to the corporate VPN, separating the network traffic based on its destination is the responsibility of the VPN client. However, because such remote users can access both secure and public networks, a special measure should be in place at both the VPN client and VPN gateway to prevent the unauthorized traffic from entering the private network.

In a typical large-scale remote access VPN, different remote users may have different access rights in the private corporate network. For example, one group may be allowed to use all network resources, whereas another group may only be allowed to use the corporate mail server. Granting different access rights can be achieved by assigning the remote users to different groups according to their access privileges. Then different access control rules may be assigned to each of the groups.

## Extranet VPN Functionality

Figure 3 illustrates that a typical extranet VPN is used to create secure communication channels among two or more private corporate networks or between a private corporate network and its customer. In a situation when an extranet VPN is used to connect two private corporate networks, a sample set of requirements for the VPN may include the following:

- *Digital certificates must be used by both VPN gateways for authentication.* A standard solution is to use PKI, as well as a set of digital certificate support functions in IKE, as in the site-to-site intranet VPNs.
- *All private packets between the two secure corporate networks must be encrypted.* Similar to the site-to-site intranet VPNs, such a solution can be provided by tunneling with strong encryption and dynamically generated keys using IPsec and IKE.
- *Traffic from each private network will be able to access only a limited set of resources on the other network.* Because there are two companies involved in this VPN solution, there are different access rules for the intranetwork traffic within each company and for the traffic that travels across the VPN from the network of one company to the other.

## Additional Functionality of VPN Gateways

In addition to their main functionality, VPN gateways, as a rule, support a wide array of extended functions.

- *Packet routing.* Typically, VPN gateways provide some basic packet routing capabilities. To increase the robustness of the security features of regular routing protocols, many existing VPN gateways prefer not to rely on automatic route discovery. Instead, they use manually configured static routes. Even though a VPN gateway does not use routing information to update its own routing table, it must be capable of relaying this routing information to other routers on the network. Such routing update data exchanges are typically sent as broadcast packets, and therefore VPN gateways must be able to send them through their tunnels.
- *Firewall functions.* To further limit access to the private networks at the perimeter of which they are located, VPN routers usually implement some firewall functions, including packet filtering and network address translation (NAT). It is necessary to use NAT because it is not uncommon to have two sites on the opposite sides of the tunnel with private addresses that share the same address space. In such a situation these addresses may overlap, and the VPN gateway would have to use NAT functions to replace the original source and destination IP addresses with new non-overlapping IP addresses before tunneling. Another firewall function frequently implemented in VPN gateways is packet filtering, which restricts the packets going into and coming out of a VPN tunnel. One of the desirable features in a VPN gateway is the ability to enable the packet filtering capability that applies to several encrypted tunnels at the same time. Firewalls are discussed further in the following chapters of this *Handbook*: Firewall Basics, Firewall Architectures, Packet Filtering and Stateful Firewalls, and Proxy Firewalls
- *Quality of service (QoS).* QoS is a principle of measuring and guaranteeing that data on packet-switched networks arrive at their destination within an acceptable amount of time. For a VPN to have a full QoS support, every single hop and link within the VPN tunnel must have QoS considerations (Ben-Ameur & Kerivin, 2003). However, simply having QoS support at the two endpoints of a VPN tunnel is still sometimes helpful. A VPN gateway supporting QoS must have the capability to classify and mark the packets based on the type of service quality that the traffic should receive. Such a VPN gateway should also have the capability to perform QoS negotiations with other routers.
- *Redundant failover.* Redundant failover implies that, if a VPN gateway hardware or software fails, there should be another gateway ready to seamlessly begin operating and to start tunneling packets for critical applications. Another implementation of redundant failover would assume that two or more gateways share the load of the same endpoint of a VPN tunnel. One of the major issues in the specifics of redundant failover implementation is how to determine whether a given VPN gateway is still operational. This is typically solved by querying the gateway periodically. Another issue is how to maintain the state information within a VPN gateway. If one VPN gateway fails, another gateway should assume operation as soon as possible to ensure the seamlessness of the VPN channel functions. The most practical way of maintaining this state of information is to send it periodically to the VPN gateway in reserve so that it could use it whenever it is determined that the main gateway is not functioning.

## VPN Gateway Provisioning

The operation of configuring a VPN gateway by network personnel is known as provisioning. The details of this configuration are vendor-specific, and it can be made through a Web-based interface, command-line interface, or a special graphical user interface (GUI) or application programming interface (API; Napier, 2002). However, all the configuration parameters can be divided into the following three components:

- *Gateway identity*. As a network device, a VPN gateway has a public and a private network interface, each of which may have several IP addresses. In addition to the IP addresses for each interface, a VPN gateway typically has a full host name and one or more digital certificates used for authentication purposes. Additionally, a VPN gateway may have several identities (additional IP addresses) for network-management functions.
- *External devices*. Because VPN gateways have packet forwarding capabilities, they must have information about the routers attached to each network interface. As network devices, VPN gateways should also be aware of many other network devices and services available to them, such as, for example, DNS, DHCP, and WINS servers.
- *Security policies*. The main goal of a VPN gateway is to provide secure communication between the two points of a VPN tunnel. The VPN gateway must be able to distinguish between the sites' network requests that should be granted and those that should be denied. Moreover, different trusted sites may have different access rights to different protected resources inside the private network guarded by the VPN gateway. Security policies describing these access rights are usually separated into two classes. Site-to-site policies determine the properties of the local secure tunnel, such as the tunneling mechanism, IP address of the public interface of the local VPN gateway, and local inbound and outbound access control filters. Because there is another VPN gateway on the other end of the VPN tunnel, that gateway's identity information is always readily available. This is not the case with the remote access clients, whose IP addresses are usually assigned dynamically. Therefore, remote access policies must incorporate secure authentication mechanisms to identify the remote clients.

## VPN Gateway Management

After the initial provisioning of a VPN gateway, network personnel must continuously manage the VPN gateway to make sure that the entire VPN solution meets its objectives. VPN gateway management encompasses the following areas of activity:

- *VPN configuration management*. After a VPN solution has been deployed and put into operation, modifying the configuration of the entire solution in general, and of a VPN gateway in particular, is known as configuration management. Obviously, it is a more difficult task than provisioning a VPN gateway before deployment. Typically, VPN gateways support one or more of the following four methods to access their configuration settings: Web-based graphical user interface (GUI) accessible through an Internet browser, command line interface (CLI), direct configuration file manipulation,

and application programming interface (API). An example of the Web-based management interface for Cisco VPN 3000 Concentrator Series is shown in Figure 5.

- *Network Monitoring*. Network monitoring provides a way to quickly find a failure of a network device if it occurs and to take steps to resolve the problem. Several methods exist by which centrally located network operations personnel can monitor network health. These methods include (1) using request-response protocols, such as the simple network management protocol (SNMP) to poll a VPN gateway's current status information; (2) using Internet control message protocol (ICMP) ping to check the responsiveness and the round-trip delay time that the IP packets need to travel to the VPN gateway; (3) using traceroute to map the current path to the VPN gateway and obtain the latency information corresponding to every hop along the path; and (4) using VPN gateway logs.
- *VPN accounting*. Logging the usage information for every user accessing a private network through a VPN gateway provides useful information about the gateway overall usage statistics, as well as usage statistics for individual users. This information can be used to bill each user for the use of the VPN. Typically, for every connected user, a VPN gateway creates a session and logs all accounting information for each session. Specific logged information about each session may include the user ID, session start and end time, remote and local IP addresses, and the number of inbound and outbound bytes and/or packets transmitted during the session.

## VPN Gateways and VPN Design

Most modern corporate networks are protected by firewalls. Many of these networks also employ some kind of VPN solution. Because the functionality of VPN gateways and firewalls overlaps, there is a definite trend to combine the VPN gateway and firewall functionality within the same physical device. However, if two separate devices are used and located on a corporate network perimeter, network designers may have to choose from several available scenarios, which are discussed in detail in Yuan and Strayer (2001).

VPN gateway solutions are employed when there is a need to interconnect two or more sites with a secure network. In a situation when there are many sites, the network designer has to make a decision about the VPN tunnel topology. As shown in Figure 6, a full mesh topology allows each network site to be connected with every other site; however, it is rather complex and does not offer enough scaling capabilities. A hub-and-spoke topology is simpler, but as shown in Figure 6, Site 6 may easily become a bottleneck in the tunneled communications. A partial mesh topology offers a reasonable compromise, allowing for more scalability and minimizing the possibility of degraded network performance caused by bottlenecks.

Because of the current IP address shortage, many private networks are using private IP addresses. Network address translation (NAT) is used to facilitate the hiding of these addresses and the routing of IP packets through the public Internet. Because NAT functionality must be enabled when the outbound packets are leaving the private

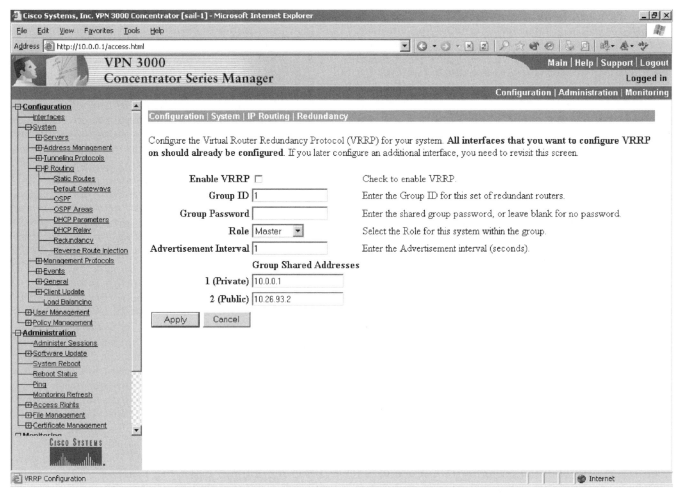

**Figure 5:** Web-based GUI management interface for Cisco VPN 3000 Concentrator Series.

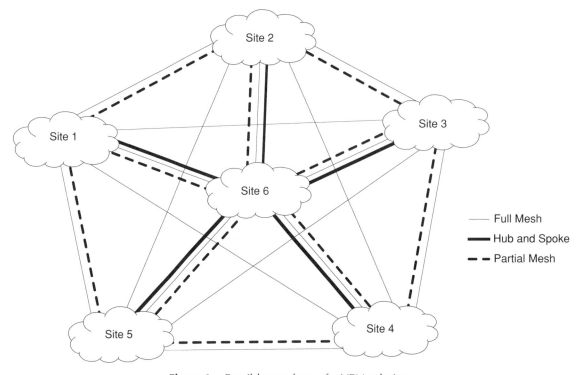

**Figure 6:** Possible topology of a VPN solution.

network perimeter and when the inbound packets are entering the private network perimeter, it is best to place NAT functionality within a VPN gateway device. Additionally, if IPsec is used as a tunneling technology by the VPN, address translation must be applied before packets are processed by IPsec.

The issue of scalability is inherent to many network solutions and applications. As the demand for more bandwidth grows and the amount of network traffic increases, VPN solutions must be able to scale according to these new requirements. Issues in network topology, load balancing, and bandwidth provisioning must be addressed to ensure the scalability of a VPN solution.

# VPN CLIENTS

A VPN client can be viewed as an oversimplified software implementation of the VPN gateway functionality that is designed to work on a single computer and enable the applications running on this computer to access the resources on a corporate network through a VPN tunnel.

## VPN Client Functionality

As with the VPN gateways, VPN clients must implement the following four classes of functionality of a VPN solution: tunneling, authentication, access control, and data integrity and confidentiality. Being an oversimplified implementation of the VPN gateway functionality, VPN clients usually implement only one technology needed to achieve the goals of each of these functions, whereas VPN gateways usually support several technologies. Because VPN clients are software applications running on stand-alone computers, they should be simple to install and operate and not too resource-consuming. Users who install VPN clients on their computers typically are not network administrators and would not want to deal with an overly complex software application that requires a lot of technical skills to install and maintain.

Typically, a VPN client implements only one tunneling protocol and can only connect to a VPN gateway on the other end of the tunnel as long as that device also supports that protocol. Implementing more than one tunneling protocol in a VPN client would increase its complexity and would require more skills to install and configure it.

Unlike the tunneling protocols, a typical VPN client usually supports several authentication protocols. Although this feature may increase the overall complexity of the VPN client application, there is a good reason for it. Several different authentication methods may be used within the same secured private network to which the VPN client connects. Therefore, such a VPN client must support all of these authentication protocols to enable its user to access all of these resources successfully. Although the complexity of the VPN client implementation does increase with the number of supported authentication protocols, this increase is usually negligible and by far is outweighed by the benefits.

Typical technologies used for user authentication in VPN clients include shared secret passwords, RADIUS authentication, and digital certificates. To reduce their complexity, in some cases VPN clients can partially rely on the operating system's functionality to implement a part of the authentication routine. For example, to implement the digital certificate authentication, a VPN client must support PKI, which to some extent is supported by many operating systems (Cross, 2001). However, PKI implementation in many operating systems is often too primitive, and the developers of the VPN clients have to implement it from scratch. The users of the VPN clients do not want to see the complexities of the certificate authentication mechanism. To them, the process of connecting to a VPN must appear as seamless as simply logging onto their computer. Therefore, many developers of the VPN clients provide their own implementation of digital certificate management and retrieval interfaces.

One of the roles of a VPN gateway is to restrict access to private network resources. VPN clients, in contrast, must enable their users to access the resources of a private network, which limits their access control role to a certain extent. This creates a situation in which the client host computer could serve as a "window" to the corporate network, possibly compromising its security. It is important to protect the host computer running a VPN client from any unauthorized users who could potentially gain access to the private network. To achieve this objective, the VPN client application must block access to the VPN from the public Internet by other hosts.

Frequently, the users of the VPN clients want to access the public Internet and the VPN at the same time. The VPN client software has three choices for routing these two categories of network traffic:

1. *Routing through the VPN gateway*. Route all traffic through the tunnel and let the VPN gateway make the routing decisions.
2. *Routing through the VPN client*. Route all public traffic directly to the Internet and all private traffic to the VPN tunnel.
3. *Treating the VPN client as a local resource*. Treat the VPN client as a device located inside the private network perimeter, and apply all traffic restrictions to it as if its host is a local network resource.

Data integrity and confidentiality functions of the VPN client must be adequate to those implemented by the corresponding VPN gateway. Otherwise, the VPN client and gateway would not be able to operate with one another. When a VPN client establishes the secure tunnel with the VPN gateway, that VPN client must be assigned a separate IP address, which will be used for routing within the corporate network. DHCP is typically used for these purposes.

## Additional Functionality of VPN Clients

The users of VPN clients are typically not specialized network personnel. They expect their experience of using the VPN to be as seamless and transparent as possible. In the best-case scenario, a VPN client user would only need to establish and terminate the VPN session; the rest of the process of accessing secured resources of the private corporate network should be free from extra and specialized procedures visible to the end user. The VPN client software must be robust and simple in operation. However, providing secure communication brings a significant overhead to many aspects of the host computer network functionality. Below is a sample of some issues that VPN clients may encounter:

- *NAT*. Similar to VPN gateways, VPN clients may also face the situation when private IP addresses must be translated into public IP addresses. Different vendors have different solutions to address the compatibility of IPsec and NAT.

- *MTU*. Because of the IP packet encapsulation, the possibility of packet fragmentation should be minimized. Fragmentation occurs when the size of the entire packet exceeds the value of the maximum transmission unit (MTU). This issue is of more concern with dial-up connections because their MTUs are set to optimal values to maximize the connection throughput. The number of bytes added by IPsec would force these packets to be fragmented; therefore, most VPN clients offer an option to change the MTU value for each network connection available to the host computer. Figure 7 illustrates how the MTU value can be changed in a Cisco VPN client application.

- *DNS*. In most realistic scenarios, public DNS servers have no data about the hosts located inside private networks. In contrast, private DNS servers that have the data about the hosts on their private network may not have the information located in public DNS servers. When a computer hosting a VPN client establishes an Internet connection (but before the VPN client itself is connected to the VPN), this computer normally uses a public DNS server. However, when a VPN connection is established, DNS entries on that computer are replaced completely or partially with those from the private DNS server.

## VPN Clients for Specific Operating Systems

Whether a VPN client runs as a stand-alone application or is deeply integrated into the core of the operating system, it must be bound by the architectural constraints of the host computer operating system. The three operating

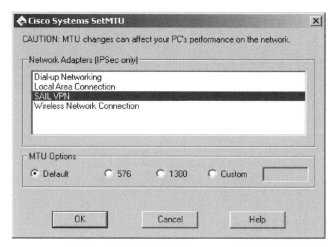

**Figure 7:** Setting the MTU value in a Cisco VPN client.

system families considered here are Microsoft Windows (in particular, XP Professional and 2003 Server), UNIX and its flavors, and Mac OS X. Most, if not all of the existing operating systems have built-in networking support, but not all of them have sufficient support of VPN functionality built into the operating system. Even for those operating systems that have strong built-in VPN support, vendors of VPN clients may choose to provide their own implementation of the VPN capabilities instead of using those provided by the operating system. Furthermore, these implementations may be different for different versions of the same operating system.

Typically, any operating system supports the following subset of IP layer functionality (Braden, 1989):

- Set the fields that were not set by the transport layer.
- Fragment the datagram to satisfy the MTU requirements.
- Set routing information by identifying the first hop.
- Pass the packet to the link layer.

Obviously, these steps must be augmented to support the VPN functionality and the associated security requirements.

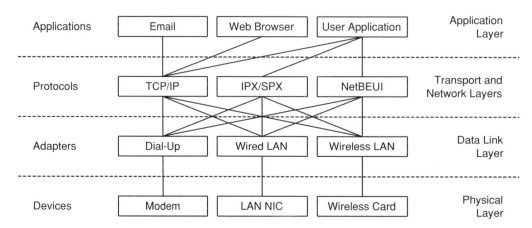

**Figure 8:** Network architecture in Windows operating systems.

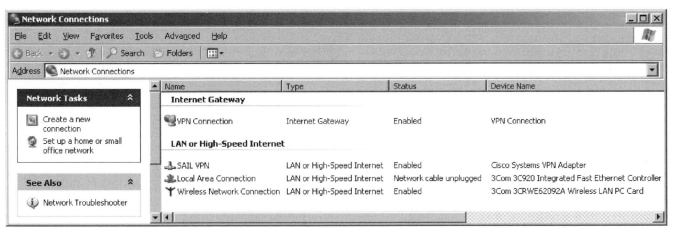

**Figure 9:** Network connections in Windows XP.

Networking architecture in Microsoft Windows operating systems is layered, as illustrated in Figure 8 (Microsoft 4). All physical devices, such as modems or wired and wireless local area network (LAN) cards, are controlled by the corresponding device drivers. Protocol-specific modules bind with the adapters according to their configuration. Modern Microsoft operating systems, such as Windows XP and Windows Server 2003, implement VPN functionality as a virtual adapter (Microsoft 1, 2, 3, & 5). Figure 9 illustrates the network connections in Windows XP: a Cisco Systems virtual VPN adapter is present among two other adapters to physical devices. In this scenario, VPN connection exists over a wireless network connection provided by a 3COM wireless LAN PC card (Zahur & Yang, 2004).

Figure 10 shows a Cisco VPN client for MS Windows connected to the "SAIL VPN" virtual private network. Figure 11 shows a Cisco VPN client for Mac OS

X displaying a list of fictitious VPNs used in Cisco VPN manuals.

Most implementations of UNIX and Linux provide an option to install a special device driver that enables the VPN functionality. Such a driver works directly below the IP network layer. Typically, such drivers are added as a so-called loadable kernel module, which does not require recompiling of the operating system's kernel. The implementation of VPN functionality in Mac OS is somewhat similar to that of UNIX. Mac OS allows the inserting of loadable modules into the networking protocol stack at run time.

## SUMMARY

This article presents the basics of modern VPN architectures. It is very difficult to cover all aspects and specifics of each particular implementation because of the space

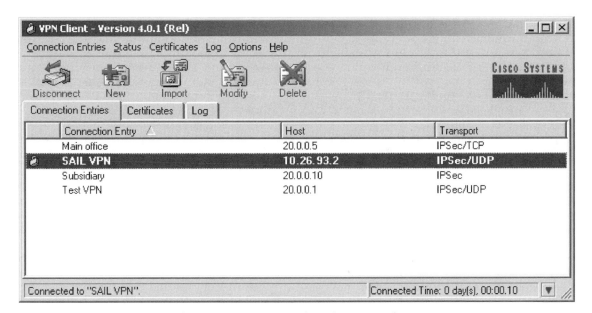

**Figure 10:** Cisco VPN client for MS Windows.

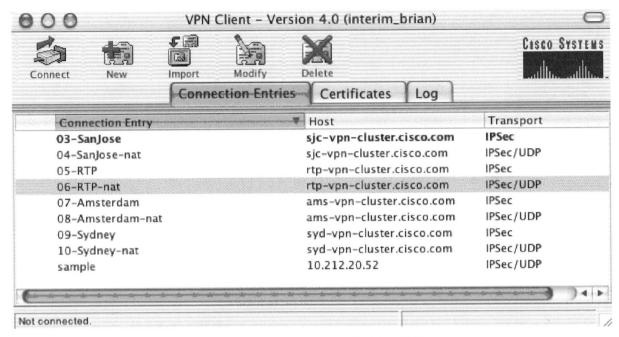

**Figure 11:** Cisco VPN client for Mac OS X.

limitations of this article. The book by Yuan and Strayer (2001) provides an excellent and in-depth treatment of the foundations of all aspects of the architecture of virtual private networks.

The Virtual Private Network Consortium (VPNC) unites the vast majority of the manufacturers of VPN hardware and software. It is impossible to list all of them here, but VPNC provides a list of all manufacturers and standard VPN features supported by their product (http://www.vpnc.org/vpnc-features-chart.html).

# GLOSSARY

**Challenge-Handshake Authentication Protocol (CHAP)** A secure authentication protocol.

**Domain Name System (DNS)** A way to locate and translate the Internet domain names into their corresponding IP addresses.

**Dynamic Host Configuration Protocol (DHCP)** A network protocol that handles a centralized and automated assignment of IP addresses.

**Encapsulating Security Payload (ESP)** A security protocol that provides data privacy services, optional data authentication, and anti-replay services.

**Extensible Authentication Protocol (EAP)** An authentication framework that supports multiple authentication methods.

**Internet Control Message Protocol (ICMP)** A message control and error-reporting network protocol between a host and a gateway to the Internet.

**Internet Key Exchange (IKE)** A protocol used to ensure security for VPN negotiation and remote host or network access.

**Internet Protocol (IP)** A standard that defines how data are transmitted over the Internet.

**Internet Protocol Security (IPsec)** A framework for a set of security protocols at the network or packet processing layer of network communication.

**Internet Service Provider (ISP)** A company that provides dial-up or broadband Internet connectivity to its individual or corporate subscribers.

**Maximum Transmission Unit (MTU)** The largest size of an IP packet specified in octets that can be sent over the network.

**Network Address Translation (NAT)** Translation of an IP address used within one network to a different IP address known within another network.

**One-Time Password (OTP)** A simple authentication technique in which each password is used only once.

**Password Authentication Protocol (PAP)** An authentication protocol allowing the peers using the point-to-point protocol to authenticate each other.

**Pretty Good Privacy (PGP)** A public-key encryption method that provides a secure file and message exchange.

**Public Key Infrastructure (PKI)** A system of public key encryption using digital certificates from certificate-issuing and registration authorities that verify and authenticate the validity of each party involved in an electronic transaction.

**Remote Authentication Dial-In User Service (RADIUS)** A protocol that enables remote access servers to communicate with a central server to authenticate dial-in users and authorize their access to the requested system or service.

**Simple Network Management Protocol (SNMP)** A protocol for network management and monitoring of network devices and their functions.

**Virtual Private Network (VPN)** A technology enabling secure data transmission between two computers across a shared or public network.

**Windows Internet Naming Service (WINS)** A technology used by Windows operating systems to manage the association of workstation names and locations with their IP addresses.

## CROSS REFERENCES

See *Encryption Basics; IP-Based VPN; Secure Sockets Layer (SSL); VPN Basics.*

## REFERENCES

Araujo, K. (2003). SSL VPN gateways: a new approach to secure remote access. Retrieved May 6, 2005, from http://www.continuitycentral.com/feature038.htm.

Ben-Ameur, W., & Kerivin, H. (2003). Networks new economical virtual private. *Communications of the ACM, 46*(6), 69–73.

Braden, R. (Ed.). (1989, October). RFC 1122: requirements for Internet hosts–communication layers. Retrieved May 6, 2005, from http://rfc.net/rfc1122.html.

Cohen, R., & Kaempfer, G. (2000). On the cost of virtual private networks. *IEEE/ACM Transactions on Networking, 6*(3), 775–784.

Cross, D. (2001). PKI enhancements in Windows XP Professional and Windows Server 2003. Retrieved from http://www.microsoft.com/technet/prodtechnol/winxppro/plan/pkienh.mspx on May 6, 2005.

Doraswamy, N., & Harkins, D. (2003). *IPSec: the new security standard for the Internet, intranets, and virtual private networks* (2nd ed). Englewood Cliffs, NJ: Prentice Hall PTR.

Gupta M. (2003). *Building a virtual private network.* Boston, MA: Premier Press.

Herscovitz, E. (1999). Secure virtual private networks: The future of data communications. *International Journal of Network Management, 9*(4), 213–220.

Mairs, J. (2002). VPNs: A beginner's guide. New York: McGraw Hill/Osborne.

Microsoft (N/A, Microsoft 1). Virtual private networking with IPSec. Retrieved May 6, 2005, from http://www.microsoft.com/resources/documentation/windows/xp/all/proddocs/en-us/sag_ipsectunnel.mspx.

Microsoft (March 24, 2003, Microsoft 2). Virtual private networking with Windows Server 2003: Overview. Retrieved May 6, 2005, from http://www.microsoft.com/windowsserver2003/techinfo/overview/vpnover.mspx.

Microsoft (N/A, Microsoft 3). Virtual private networks for Windows Server 2003. Retrieved May 6, 2005, from http://www.microsoft.com/windowsserver2003/technologies/networking/vpn/default.mspx.

Microsoft (N/A, Microsoft 4), Windows network architecture. Retrieved from May 6, 2005, http://www.microsoft.com/resources/documentation/windows/2000/server/reskit/en-us/tcpip/part4/tcpappb.mspx.

Microsoft (N/A, Microsoft 5). Virtual private networking in Windows XP Professional. Retrieved May 6, 2005, from http://www.microsoft.com/resources/documentation/windows/xp/all/proddocs/en-us/conn_vpn.mspx.

Napier, D. (2002). Setting up a VPN gateway. *Linux Journal, 93*, Retrieved May 6, 2005, from http://www.linuxjournal.com/article/4772.

Netilla Networks. (2003). A comparison of VPN solutions: SSL vs. IPSec. Retrieved May 6, 2005, from http://www.netilla.com/downloads/wp_ipsec-vs-ssl.pdf.

Northcutt S., Zeltser L., Winters S., Frederick K. K., & Ritchey R. W. (2003). *Inside network perimeter security.* Indianapolis, IN: New Riders Publishing.

Tuomenoksa, M. (2002) Demystifying VPN. Retrieved from http://www.openreach.com/white_papers/white_paper2.PDF.

Yuan R., & Strayer W. T. (2001). *Virtual private networks: technologies and solutions.* Boston, MA: Addison Wesley.

Zahur, Y., & Yang, T. (2004). Wireless LAN security and laboratory designs. *Journal of Computing in Small Colleges, 19*(3), 44–60.

# IP-Based VPN

David E. McDysan, *MCI Corporation*

## INTRODUCTION TO IP-BASED VPNs

An IP-based virtual private network (VPN) may provide service at layer 2 or layer 3. The focus of this chapter is on layer 3 VPNs, specifically those using the Internet protocol (IP). RFC 3809 (Nagarajan et al., 2004) covers requirements and aspects that are common to both layer 2 and layer 3 VPNs.

## Applications of IP VPNs

The public Internet plays an important role for many enterprises (McDysan, 2000). Users can exchange information with individuals anywhere in the world via e-mail, Web sites, transaction systems, file sharing, and file transfer. Furthermore, the Internet is rapidly growing as a means for commercial enterprises to conduct business and to advertise their goods and services. The Internet can help reduce administrative costs by placing the data entry, verification, and think-time aspects of order entry and service parameter selection in the hands of the end user. This replaces the older, less efficient paradigm of people in enterprises interacting over the postal system and/or the telephone and fax to place an order, update records, or complete a business transaction. The Web provides the automated means for the end user to peruse the choices at his or her own speed and convenience, requiring the expenditure of energy and time of only one person. Furthermore, careful design of the Web site by experts allows many more people access to the best set of information. In the classic telephone or fax method, the level of expertise depended on the particular agent whom the caller reached.

The tremendous volume of such information on public Web sites continues to grow and increase in quality based on real world experience and user feedback. When the Web sites contain enterprise-specific information that is sensitive for one reason or another, then we call the application an *intranet*. One level of security is that of user IDs and passwords. This is the same level of security used on many public domain Web sites. The next level of security is that of encryption and firewalls, topics covered in the next section. A more challenging activity is the use

by multiple enterprises of the Internet in a virtual private fashion in an application called an *extranet*. The premier example to date is probably that of the Automotive Network eXchange (ANX), which connects major automotive manufacturers and their suppliers, as described at the end of this chapter.

In addition to providing control over who may communicate with whom as described previously, VPNs have a number of additional important requirements. Of course, providing verifiable authentication that specific sites and users are part of a specific intranet or extranet VPN is an important requirement. In addition, keeping the administrative cost of VPNs under control requires automation of membership discovery in conjunction with this authentication. Furthermore, customer networks will make use of private IP addresses or nonunique IP address (e.g., unregistered addresses).

## Drivers for IP-Based VPNs

Progress marches ever onward, and the world of networking is no different (McDysan, 2000). In a manner similar to the way that enterprises constructed private data networks over the telecommunications infrastructure developed for telephony, the industry is developing a new wave of technologies overlaying the basic suite of Internet protocols to construct VPNs. When the public network infrastructure of a VPN matches that of the enterprise equipment, then significant savings can occur. This is a recurring theme in the history of communication networks, with the Internet being simply the latest frontier.

Successful enterprises are cost conscious. Even large government programs are subject to public scrutiny. In the highly competitive world of commercial enterprises, those that are not cost conscious fail on a predictable and regular basis. Standing still is simply not good enough. The maturation of computing hardware and the supporting software has ushered in the postindustrial information age. Now, enterprises need to interconnect employees, databases, servers, affiliates, and suppliers in a rapidly changing business environment. Flexibility becomes an overarching requirement. Those enterprises that do not adapt will not survive.

Increased competition breeds the need for innovation. With traditional services and products, new smaller companies grab market share by offering new and innovative services more rapidly or by offering traditional services or products at a lower cost. The incumbents sometimes cry foul, claiming that the newcomers are "cream skimming" the lucrative market segments. The newcomers counter that the incumbents are the "fat cats" who have all the cream. Although some monopolies do exist, either regulated or de facto, the pace of change is ever accelerating.

The worldwide adoption of the Web is a great equalizer. Even a small enterprise can have a large impact and presence via the electronic Web that never sleeps. The user-friendly Web browser with downloadable plug-ins empowers the distribution of new paradigm-shifting applications within days to weeks. The rapid adoption of electronic commerce will forever change the way business operates and government administers. Enterprises are rapidly deploying Web-based intranet and extranet technology to reduce internal costs, in many cases replacing legacy mainframe-based systems.

Communication networks continue to shrink the distances among nations, cultures, and time zones. The introduction of each new type of communication technology empowers the nearly instantaneous dissemination of new media types around the globe. Beginning with the first transatlantic telephone cable in 1956, the speed of transfer of news and breaking information has fallen from days to minutes. Communication satellites ushered in the era of video and multimedia distribution in the 1960s on the heels of the space age. In the late $20^{th}$ century, high-capacity fiber optic transoceanic and transcontinental cables wire connected the planet, bringing the benefits of digital transmission to the corridors used by most enterprises. This increase in high-performance connectivity enables enterprises to scale beyond national boundaries, particularly in the commercial and nonprofit sector, and also has an impact on governmental enterprises. Witness the lowering of national barriers in the European Union as an example.

Most enterprises have some sensitive information that would be of value to competitors or other parties. Enterprises trust the implicit security in private leased-line networks. In fact, a major impediment to the adoption of VPNs is the ability to ensure that this new technology delivers a level of privacy and security that enterprises have come to expect from private lines. Toward this end, the fundamental security requirements of any VPN are as follows (Kosiur, 1998; McDysan, 2000; Schneier, 1995):

- Authentication: validating that the originator is indeed who it claims to be
- Access control: the act of allowing only authorized users admission to the network
- Confidentiality: ensuring that no one can read or copy data transmitted across the network
- Integrity: guaranteeing that no one can alter data transferred by the network

VPN approaches employ different methods to meet these requirements. These methods are sometimes implicit and in other cases are explicit. Security is a fundamental requirement for customer edge-based VPNs operating over the shared Internet infrastructure. Of course, good security begins with secure practices. For example, if the employees of an enterprise leave their user IDs, passwords, or encryption keys lying about, then all of the security technology in the world will not be able to protect sensitive information.

Most enterprises believe that quality of service (QoS), traffic management, and prioritized or differentiated service will become increasingly important drivers in their evolving VPN communication needs. Although much of the following applies to the Internet at large, it applies to a VPN as well. Some applications, such as voice and video, have rigid required amounts of capacity and minimum levels of quality to operate acceptably. Other applications, such as Web browsing, file transfers, and e-mail, are elastic and can adapt to available capacity to a certain extent. However, even elastic applications result in lowered productivity and increase effective cost to the enterprise when certain minimum capacity and quality guidelines are not met. Normally, an enterprise may also need to prioritize or differentiate between these categories of applications to handle intervals of congestion.

The primary QoS measures are loss, delay, jitter, and availability. Voice and video applications have the most stringent delay, jitter, and loss requirements. Interactive data applications, such as Web browsing and electronic collaboration, have less stringent delay and loss requirements. Non-real-time applications, such as file transfer, e-mail, and data backup, work acceptably across a wide range of loss rates and delay. Availability requirements vary across enterprises.

Capacity, also referred to as bandwidth, is fundamental to the traffic engineering of a VPN that will enable it to deliver the required QoS. Some applications require a minimum amount of capacity to work at all, for example, voice and video. The performance of elastic protocols that adaptively change their transmission rate in response to congestion in the network improves as the capacity allocated to them increases. The Internet's transmission control protocol (TCP) that carries Web traffic and file transfers is an example of an elastic protocol. Other applications are elastic up to a certain point, after which adding capacity does not improve performance.

Many network providers guarantee specific QoS and capacity levels via service level agreements (SLAs). An SLA is a contract between the enterprise user and the network provider that spells out the capacity provided between points in the network that should be delivered with a specified QoS. If the network provider fails to meet the terms of the SLA, then the user may be entitled to a refund. These have become popular capabilities offered by network providers for the private line, frame relay, asynchronous transfer mode (ATM), network-based IP VPNs or Internet infrastructures employed by enterprises to construct VPNs.

Several approaches have been standardized for delivering one or more of the previous aspects of QoS. The oldest is the Integrated Services (Intserv) architecture (Braden, Clark, & Shenker, 1994) that uses the resource reservation protocol (RSVP; Wroclawski, 1997). Intserv/RSVP allows a host to request one of several levels of QoS at a specified level of capacity for a flow of packets specified by the IP address, transport protocol port numbers, and/or protocol type. The RSVP messages normally follow the same hop-by-hop routed path as other packets, and if the reservation is successful then the network provides the requested QoS for the level of capacity reserved. However, because RSVP signaling occurs at the individual flow, there is a significant scalability issue in a provider's backbone network caused by the signaling load for a large number of flows. For this reason, Intserv/RSVP is not supported in service provider networks and has seen only limited use in enterprise networks.

In response to these issues, the IETF defined another approach that addresses the scalability issues of Intserv/RSVP by treating only aggregates of flows using a convention called Differentiated Services (Diffserv; Blake et al., 1998). Diffserv redefines the type of service (TOS) byte in the IP packet header in terms of a small number of Diffserv code points (DSCPs) that indicate the type of QoS that the packet should receive. Capacity reservation at the individual flow level of Intserv/RSVP is avoided altogether and replaced by classification and traffic conditioning (e.g., policing) performed only at the edge of a DiffServ domain, for example, a customer network or a provider network. Furthermore, because Diffserv operates only on the contents of the IP packet header, it can coexist with IP security protocols, whereas Intserv/RSVP may not because it may rely on higher-layer protocol fields (e.g., TCP numbers) to identify an individual flow.

Most backbone IP networks use DiffServ, possibly using a so-called bandwidth broker, which incorporates policy server functions and also deals with customer traffic contract and network resource allocation. A bandwidth broker maps service level specifications to concrete configurations of edge routers of a DiffServ domain. However, Intserv/RSVP or next generation reservation signaling protocols still might have a role to play in signaling reservations in enterprise networks and at the edge of a service provider network, especially for such applications as digital audio and video, which would benefit from reservations for relative long-lived, high-bandwidth flows (Braun, Guenter, & Khalil, 2001).

## Introduction to VPN Technologies

A VPN attempts to draw from the best of both the public and private networking worlds. Such a network is private in the sense that the data an enterprise transfers over the VPN are separated from that of other enterprises or the public and may also be transferred securely. It is virtual in the sense that the underlying public infrastructure is partitioned to provide some level of service for each enterprise. A VPN enables communication among a set of sites by making use of a shared network infrastructure as contrasted with that of a private network, which has dedicated facilities connecting the set of sites in an enterprise. To a great extent, the intent is that the logical structure of the VPN, such as topology, addressing, connectivity, reachability, and access control, is equivalent to part of or all of a conventional private network.

A good VPN has the low-cost structure of a ubiquitous public network, but retains the capacity guarantees, quality, control, and security of a private network. How can a network design achieve these apparently contradictory goals? The answer lies in software-defined networking technology and sophisticated communication protocols, as well as good old-fashioned capitalism.

Frame relay, ATM, multiprotocol label switching (MPLS), and Ethernet are all forms of layer 2 label switching protocols (McDysan, 2000). A label is contained in the header field of a packet, frame, or cell and is unique only to an interface on a device, such as an enterprise user equipment or a network switch. Figure 1 illustrates the operation of a simple two-port label switch. Starting from the left-hand side, a label switch uses the label from the packet received on an interface as an index into a look-up table in the column marked "In." The look-up table returns the outgoing label from the column marked "Out" and the outgoing physical interface from the column marked "Port." The switch routes the packet, frame, or cell to the outgoing physical interface using an internal switching fabric and "switches" the label to the outgoing label retrieved from the look-up table. The example in Figure 1 uses patterns for the packets to trace the result of the label switching operation implemented by the look-up tables on the input side of each port. Of course, contention may occur for the output port in a label switch if multiple packets

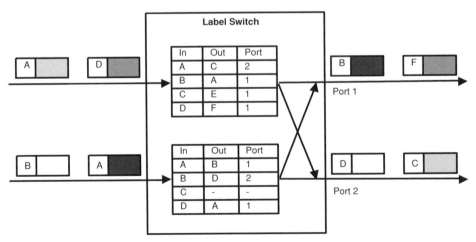

**Figure 1:** Layer 2 label switching.

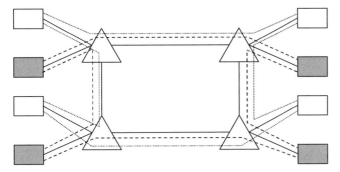

**Figure 2:** Two connection-oriented VPNs in a shared public network.

are destined for the same output. Typically, label switches must implement some form of queuing to handle this situation.

A layer 2 network comprises a number of label switches implementing the previous basic function. Typically, these switches also implement other features related to connection establishment, traffic control, QoS, congestion control, and the like. Some form of routing, signaling, and/or network management protocol establishes a consistent sequence of label switching mappings in the look-up tables to form a logical connection that can traverse multiple nodes. When the network is connection oriented, for example, in frame relay ATM, the pair-wise communication is usually called a virtual circuit or connection (VC). MPLS is also signaled and connection oriented, but employs unidirectional communication. For a connectionless L2 network, such as the Ethernet, the set of sites that are allowed to communicate is called a virtual local area network (VLAN).

Figure 2 illustrates a public connection-oriented network supporting two disjoint VPNs. As in Figure 1, shaded boxes represent equipment from different enterprises, and triangles represent provider edge label switches. The label-switched connection-oriented network implements disjoint virtual connections (either permanent or switched) between different enterprise nodes as indicated via dashed lines of different styles. A connection-oriented label-switched network operates very much like a private line network, but uses virtual connections instead of real ones. The important difference is that the service provider switches use label switching instead of time division multiplexing (TDM) cross-connects to logically share trunk circuits between multiple enterprise VPNs.

Thus, a connection-oriented VPN can be a plug-compatible replacement for a private line-based network. This has several advantages. First, the granularity of capacity allocation is much finer with a label switch than that implemented in the rigid TDM hierarchy. Second, if the traffic offered by the enterprises is bursty in nature, the service provider network can efficiently multiplex many traffic streams together. Finally, the shared public network achieves economies of scale by utilizing high-speed trunk circuits that have a markedly lower cost per bit per second (bps) than lower-speed links do.

X.25 was the first connection-oriented layer 2 data VPN, but it is now being phased out. It pioneered a VPN concept called a closed user group (CUG), which

is similar to that of an intranet or extranet. Frame relay followed X.25 by simplifying the protocol and hence improving the price–performance ratio in the late 1980s. Frame relay pioneered the important VPN concept of per connection traffic management and some simple responses to congestion. ATM was the successor to frame relay in the mid-1990s, focusing on a fixed cell size to ease hardware implementation and achieve high performance. ATM borrows heavily from the signaling protocols of the narrow-band integrated services digital network (ISDN), the traffic management concepts of frame relay, and automatic topology discovery from IP. ATM standards significantly extended the concept of QoS and defined traffic management more precisely, these being the hallmarks of ATM.

In some ways, MPLS is an enhancement of ATM: it provides most of the same capabilities, but also adds some useful extensions and refinements tailored to the support of IP. MPLS overcomes the inefficiency caused by the partial fill of the last fixed-length ATM cell when carrying variable-length packets in AAL5. MPLS also supports a more flexible hierarchical aggregation of connections and supports loop detection. The design of MPLS also allows tighter integration than ATM did of connection-oriented traffic engineering with IP routing protocols in service provider backbones. Extensions of these capabilities are also quite useful in support of network-based VPNs.

A connectionless protocol like IP does not require a signaling protocol because it does not use connections to forward user traffic. Instead, a routing protocol distributes topology information such that each node can make an independent, yet coordinated, decision about the next hop on which to forward packets that have a particular destination address prefix in the packet header. Unlike label switching, the addresses in packet headers must be unique throughout a set of interconnected networks, such as the Internet. Therefore, the forwarding look-up table has the same set of prefixes in every node in a simple connectionless network. Because each address must be unique, the forwarding table could become quite large. The Internet scales to large sizes by carefully administering address assignments so that their forwarding tables need only process the high-order prefix bits of the address.

In a connectionless network, a VPN is a logical overlay on a shared IP network of a different type. A shared IP network may be the public Internet or a network that supports IP routing protocols implemented specifically for use by enterprise customers. A secure IP VPN utilizes the concept of an encrypted tunnel implemented at the enterprise equipment connected to the IP network. A tunnel may exist at the link layer or the network layer, as an association between two endpoints attached to a public network, therefore making it virtual. Encryption is a technique that scrambles information such that only the intended receiver can decode it, thereby achieving privacy. Because an IP network is connectionless, the packets between enterprise nodes may take different paths depending on such conditions as link failures or the configuration of routing parameters. IP routing protocols synchronize the forwarding tables in all the nodes whenever the state of the network changes. This fundamental

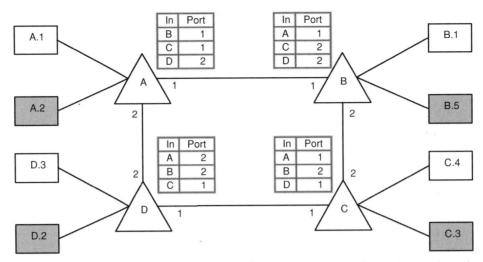

**Figure 3:** Two connectionless VPNs. "In" indicates the incoming destination packet address prefix, and "Port" indicates the outgoing physical port.

difference in paradigms is what has allowed the Internet to scale the way it has in response to the tremendous demand that arose in the latter half of the 1990s.

Figure 3 illustrates a connectionless IP-based VPN for two enterprises. The enterprise nodes are shaded boxes, each with an IP address that has a prefix (e.g., A.1 or B.5) associated with a triangle indicating the network router to which the access line attaches (e.g., A or B). For example, the gray-shaded enterprise node has an address prefix A.2 connected to the network router with address prefix A. Figure 3 illustrates the forwarding tables next to each network router. Each table contains an entry labeled "In" for the incoming packet address prefix, which is used to look up the next hop outgoing port. For example, at router A, a packet received with destination address prefix B is sent out on port 1. Note how these tables contain only the address prefix and the next hop link number, and not the enterprise node address prefixes. Therefore, the enterprise equipment at the edge of the network implements the IP VPN functions. This architecture has two fundamental advantages. First, configuration changes to the enterprise VPN do not require changes in the core Internet. Second, because the Internet is a global public network, a tunneled enterprise VPN can be implemented across multiple Internet service provider (ISP) networks.

Now we look at a categorization of logical VPN types and the terminology used to describe them.

## Taxonomy of IP-Based VPNs

The taxonomy of VPN types is primarily determined by whether the tunnels that provide the service terminate on customer edge (CE) or on provider edge (PE) devices (Callon et al., 2004; Carugi et al., 2005; Nagarajan et al., 2004). Figure 4 illustrates a VPN in which the tunnels terminate on the CE. A CE-based VPN is one in which knowledge of the service aspects of the customer network is limited to CE devices. Customer sites are interconnected via tunnels or hierarchical tunnels. The service provider network is unaware of the existence of the VPN because it operates exclusively on the headers of the tunneled packets. Specifically, a CE-based L2 VPN is link-layer (i.e., layer 2) service provided by CE equipment at the customer sites, for example, Ethernet. In a similar manner, a CE-based L3 VPN is a network layer (i.e., layer 3) service provided by CE devices at customer sites, with IP being the most widely implemented L3 protocol. This chapter focuses on L3 VPNs.

Figure 5 illustrates a VPN where the tunnels terminate on the PE. A PE-based VPN is one in which the service provider network maintains state information for each customer VPN such that packets are forwarded between customer sites in an intranet or extranet context using the customer's address space. Often, a hierarchical tunnel is used between PEs with the outermost tunnel being implemented by a provider (P) router, which provides PE-PE connectivity. (Note that the P and PE functions are

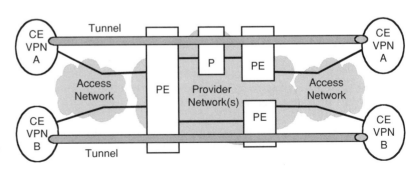

**Figure 4:** A generic customer equipment (CE)-based VPN.

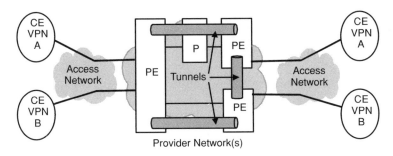

**Figure 5:** A generic provider edge (PE)-based (also called network-based) VPN.

logical and that a single router may implement both functions.) These tunnels may be dedicated to separate VPNs or shared among multiple VPNs by the PEs, which use label stacking to isolate traffic among VPNs. These inner tunnels interconnect a layer 3 virtual forwarding (or layer 2 switching) instance (VFI/VSI) for each VPN instance in a PE switching router. A PE-based L2 VPN provides a layer 2 service that switches link-layer packets between customer sites using the customer's link-layer identifiers, for example, Ethernet. A PE-based L3 VPN provides a layer 3 service that routes packets between customer sites using the customer network's address space, for example, IP. This chapter focuses on L3 VPNs. The IETF l2vpn working group is developing specific protocol solutions for L2 VPNs that support services that implement quite similar functions to that of frame relay, ATM virtual connections, or an Ethernet broadcast domain in a service called a virtual private LAN-like service (VPLS).

The CE-based approach is the simplest from the service provider backbone perspective, but does require a fair amount of configuration and management of the CE. In contrast, the PE-based approach provides greater control of traffic engineering and performance, but incurs additional complexity in the service provider network to achieve these benefits. The layer 3 VPN framework document (Callon et al., 2004) further describes these concepts in the context of a reference model that defines layered service relationships between devices and one or more levels of tunnels (Nagarajan et al., 2004). The next sections cover some specifics of CE- and PE-based VPNs as they relate to IP intranets and extranets.

# CUSTOMER EDGE (CE)-BASED VPNs

As defined earlier, CE-based VPNs partition sites by tunnels established between CE devices. Routing in the customer network often views the tunnels as simple point-to-point links or sometimes as broadcast LANs. For customer-provisioned CE-based VPNs, provisioning and management of the tunnels are done by the customer network administration, which is also responsible for operation of the routing protocol between CE devices. In provider-provisioned CE-based VPNs, service providers perform provisioning and management of the tunnels and may also configure and operate routing protocols on the CE devices. Of course, routing within a site is always under the control of the customer.

There are two primary types of IP, or L3, CE-based VPNs, distinguished by the type of tunnel employed. The first is older and is used primarily to construct intranets by using CE routers connected via FR or ATM virtual connections. The second is newer and is based on tunnels implemented by cryptographic methods over the public Internet using either dedicated or dial-up access.

## CE VPNs over Virtual Connection Networks

The frame relay and ATM connection-oriented VPN alternatives largely apply only to a single service provider. In order to connect each site to every other site in a fully meshed network of *n* sites, the service provider must provision on the order of *n*-squared virtual connections (VCs). Note that each VC must be provisioned at every intermediate FR or ATM switch in the service provider network. As the number of sites grows, service providers often interconnect the sites in what is called a hub-and-spoke architecture, as shown in Figure 6. Often, the hub sites are connected in a full mesh with branch sites dual-homed to a primary and secondary hub site as shown. Another motivation for implementing the hub-and-spoke design is that, with a full mesh of sites, the addition of a new site requires configuration not only of the new site but also of each of the other VPN sites.

The traffic forwarded between the sites in a VPN is isolated from all others by the logical separation provided by the virtual connections, which perform label switching as configured by a provisioning system. What results is for all practical purposes a private network with intersite communication occurring via virtual connections instead of private lines. Such a connection-oriented VPN is a good approach for intranets because the isolation and site-to-site traffic engineering provided to the approach are quite good. On the other hand, configuring such a network for extranets can be quite complex and inflexible. For these reasons, a number of enterprise users tend to use IP security protocols as the foundation for CE-VPNs that are used by many intranet and extranet applications.

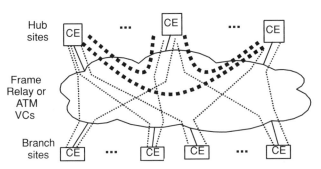

**Figure 6:** CE-based VPN over a partial mesh of L2 hub-and-spoke VCs.

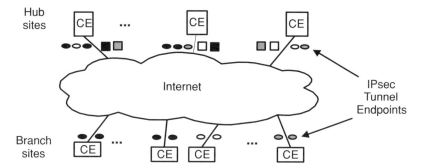

**Figure 7:** CE-based VPN using IPsec tunnels over the Internet. Circles are spoke-to-spoke tunnel endpoints, whereas squares are hub-to-hub tunnel endpoints.

## IPsec-based CE VPNs

An analogous IP-based VPN network has the same number of hub and branch sites, but requires the addition of overlay IP security (IPsec) tunneling and/or encryption functions in the CE devices. There is no explicit connection through the devices in the service provider network; instead all of the tunnel functions are implemented in the CE devices. Scaling issues similar to those in CE devices overlaid on virtual connections arise in IPsec-based CE VPNs, but here the limits are the number of IPsec tunnels and of routing adjacencies that a CE router can support. For these reasons, large IPsec CE-based VPNs also have a hub-and-spoke architecture. Figure 7 illustrates the same hub-and-spoke network example with shaded circles showing the hub-spoke tunnels, whereas the hub-hub tunnels are shown as shaded squares. The shading illustrates the logical connectivity, for example, the lower left-hand spoke CE site is connected to the top left and middle CE hub sites as indicated by the black-filled circle and square, respectively. Similar to the VC overlay approach, adding a new site to a full mesh requires configuration of a tunnel to every other site. Furthermore, the CE devices may also include network address translation (NAT) functions if the enterprise does not use globally unique, routable IP addresses. NAT is a function that maps IP packets with nonunique addresses to a unique, routable IP address, often mapping the higher-layer protocol (e.g., TCP or UDP) port numbers as well. In addition, in some cases even higher-layer protocol usage of IP addresses (e.g., HTTP, SNMP, SIP) must be also mapped. When a single ISP provides the network for an IP-based VPN, then guarantees on quality and performance are feasible. Beware that an IP-based VPN built on top of the public Internet using services provided by several ISPs may not provide the quality necessary for telephone-grade voice or multimedia applications.

The IETF designed the IPsec protocol suite to address the known issues involved with achieving secure communications over the Internet (McDysan, 2000). It reduces the threat of attacks based on IP address spoofing and provides a standardized means for ensuring data integrity, authenticating a data source, and guaranteeing confidentiality of information. Furthermore, it tackles head on the complex problem of key management. The Internet can be trusted based on this set of standards when a public key management infrastructure is used. IPsec plays an important role not only in enterprise VPNs but also in electronic commerce, as well as in secure individual end user communication.

IPsec refers to a suite of three interrelated security protocols implemented by modification to, or augmentation of, an IP packet in conjunction with an infrastructure that supports key distribution and management. An interrelated set of RFCs published by the IETF specifies the details of IPsec. Kent and Atkinson (1998) describe the overall IP security architecture, whereas Thayer et al. (1998) gives an overview of the IPsec protocol suite and the documents that describe it. Three protocols make up IPsec, with the names identifying the function performed. The two primary protocols involved in the transfer of data are called the authentication header (AH) and the encapsulating security payload (ESP). The AH protocol provides source authentication and data integrity verification using a header field, but does not provide confidentiality. AH also supports an optional mechanism to prevent replay attacks. The ESP protocol uses both a header and trailer field to provide confidentiality via encryption. ESP may also provide data integrity verification, source authentication, and an antireplay service. Because both the AH and ESP protocols use cryptographic methods, secure distribution and management of keys are a fundamental requirement. IPsec specifies that key management may be manual or automatic. The automatic key management protocol specified for IPsec is called Internet key exchange (IKE) and involves the mechanism for creating a security association (SA) between a source and a destination for the AH and ESP protocols.

The AH and ESP protocols operate in either transport or tunnel mode as defined by the parameters of an SA. In *transport mode*, they provide security by creating components of the IPsec header at the same time the source generates other IP header information. This means that transport mode can only operate between host systems. In *tunnel mode*, IPsec creates a new IP packet that contains the IPsec components and encapsulates the original unsecured packet. Because tunnel mode does not modify the original packet contents, it can be implemented using hardware or software located at an intermediate security gateway (SG) between the source or destination host system.

Figure 8 illustrates a pure IP-based VPN design that has a cost structure essentially independent of the traffic pattern. Here, every site has a firewall (shown as a brick wall in the figure) and SG so that any site may directly access the Internet or any other site. Furthermore, it shows a network access server (NAS), remote authentication dial-in user service (RADIUS) server, Web server, and extranet database located at three separate sites. Dial-in

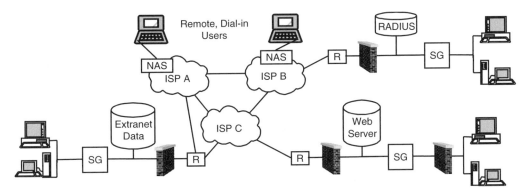

**Figure 8:** Pure IP distributed VPN design.

users are secured using the RADIUS authentication server and the security gateway. This design also reduces access costs because traffic for the Internet need not traverse a firewall at a headquarters site, as shown in the previous hierarchical example. Sites may also be dual-homed to different ISPs or to different sites within the same ISP for resiliency purposes, as necessary. This design is better suited to extranet applications and electronic commerce because communication via the public Internet is more interoperable and rapidly deployable than any other communication service.

## PROVIDER EDGE (PE)-BASED L3 VPNs

A PE-based L3 VPN is one in which PE devices in the SP network provide the partitioning of forwarding and routing information to only those (parts of) sites that are members of a specific intranet or extranet. This allows the existence of the VPN to be hidden from the CE devices, which can operate as if they were part of a normal customer network. As described earlier, PE-based VPNs use tunnels set up between PE devices. These tunnels may use one of a number of encapsulations to send traffic over the provider network(s), for example, MPLS, generic routing encapsulation, IPsec, or IP-in-IP. As sites for new VPNs are added or removed, PE-based VPN solutions provide a means to distribute membership information

automatically. There are two principal methods defined in the IETF (Callon et al., 2004) for implementing these types of PE-based L3 VPNs: aggregated routing and virtual routers.

## Aggregated Routing VPNs

The *aggregated routing approach* is one in which a separate forwarding table exists for each VPN on every PE that connects to a site in that VPN, but the exchange of routing information between the PEs is multiplexed, or aggregated together. The BGP/MPLS VPN (Rosen & Rekhter, 1999) approach uses extensions to the border gateway protocol (BGP) to implement this generic architecture. Figure 9 illustrates an aggregated routing approach that connects sites from three VPNs, A, B, and C, together in an extranet. Each PE has a separate virtual forwarding table for each VPN site that it serves, but the forwarded traffic and exchanged routing information use a set of shared tunnels, as shown in the center of Figure 9. Often these types of solutions are implemented on a single service provider network. However, there are an increasing number of implementations that operate across more than one provider network.

This approach alleviates some of the scaling issues involved with the connection- or tunnel-oriented CE-based approaches described earlier when full communication

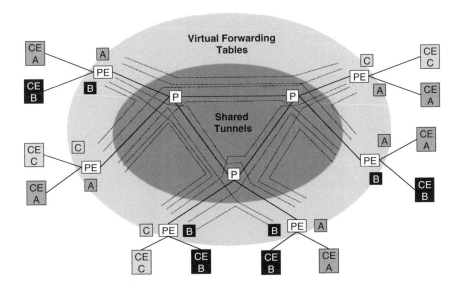

**Figure 9:** Aggregated routing and shared tunnel network-based L3 VPN.

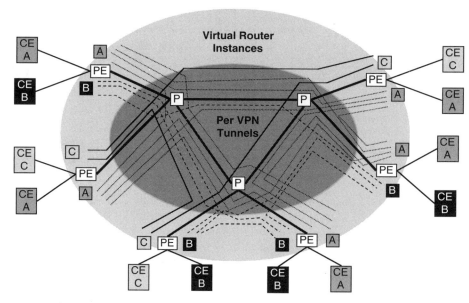

**Figure 10:** PE-based L3 VPN with virtual routers with tunnels per VPN.

between a set of sites is desired. Specifically, when adding or removing a site, only the PE involved with that site need be reconfigured; the BGP/MPLS protocols automatically take care of the rest. Furthermore, the protocols have the capability to advertise more than one route for the same destination address. This can be useful in an extranet to force traffic exchanged between different enterprises through additional devices, such as firewalls, filters, or other security-oriented devices.

## Virtual Router VPNs

Although the *virtual router (VR) based approach* (Muthukrishnan & Malis, 2000) also uses PE and P routers, there are several important differences, as illustrated in Figure 10. This example uses the same CE sites from the three VPNs discussed in Figure 9, the aggregated routing example. In a VR VPN, an instance of a virtual router is dedicated to each VPN in every PE that supports a site for that VPN. This means that each enterprise can manage its own routing instance on the PE. This approach works very well in cases where the enterprise network has other forms of connectivity between its sites, and then the VR instances look like just another (well-connected) router to the enterprise network. Usually, a separate set of tunnels is allocated in a full mesh between the VR instances, as shown by different line styles in the center of Figure 10. This allows excellent control of capacity allocation and control of QoS between the VPN sites.

The VR PE-based VPN is best suited for intranets. It is not frequently used in an extranet because one enterprise would have to exchange routing information with another. This could lead to undesirable security holes, instability of the routing and hence a greater likelihood of an outage, and more difficult coordination in the event of the inevitable moves, adds, and changes. It could be used, however, as a backbone network provided by one partner for connecting a number of other enterprises together, for example, using CE-based VPNs overlaid on a managed VR PE-based network.

## DESIGN CONSIDERATIONS AND EXAMPLE VPN DEPLOYMENT

This section summarizes some important considerations when choosing a VPN approach and gives an example of a CE-based IPsec VPN used for electronic commerce.

## Considerations in Choosing a VPN Approach

Establishing a set of goals and a plan to meet them is critical to success in most human endeavors, and virtual private networking is no exception (McDysan, 2000). The steps here are similar to that of any large-scale project. First, doing research on requirements, drivers, and needs is necessary to establish goals. Developing several candidate designs and then analyzing them in the harsh light of commercial business reality are the next crucial steps. A VPN may not be right for the enterprise under consideration at this time, and timing is important. Once the decision is made to implement a new type of VPN or to migrate existing private network applications to a VPN, the work is still not done. Detailed planning and a well-thought-out migration strategy are essential for an enterprise to achieve the goals set out at the beginning of the process.

A number of enterprises have already implemented VPNs of the types described in this chapter. A good starting point is to look at an enterprise that is similar to yours in some way, and read case studies, papers, and books about what worked and what did not. However, beware that the needs of each enterprise are unique and different, and therefore basing a decision on other's experiences, although helpful, is not sufficient to guarantee delivery of maximum benefit. It is important to analyze potential security threats and essential performance metrics. Formulating a threat model and considering what would happen if important information were stolen, made public, or corrupted are essential steps. Determining the performance required by applications is also important. Consider what would happen if a site is disconnected for a long period of time. Assess what the impact of network congestion would be. Discriminate between nice-to-have performance and what is absolutely necessary — this can make quite a difference in qualifying network designs and their eventual cost.

Some general guidelines for the choice of a L3 VPN approach are as follows. A PE-based L3 VPN provides an infrastructure that is separate from the Internet, which may avoid or mitigate a denial of service attack or other degradations experienced on the Internet. IP QoS mechanisms have more meaning in a PE-based L3 VPN context because the community of senders is that of the VPN, and not the entire Internet. Therefore, overload of a particular Diffserv QoS class is less likely. A CE-based VPN that uses IPsec cryptographic methods provides authenticated communication that may also be resistant to eavesdropping if encryption is also used. However, when tunneled over the Internet, denial of service, other attacks, or overloads may disrupt a CE-based L3 VPN. A combination of a PE-based L3 VPN and CE encryption may cost more, but provides separation from the Internet and tighter QoS control, as well as true security in the sense of avoiding eavesdropping and confirming the sender identity.

Although a generic framework may not apply to all enterprises, there are some helpful guidelines when categorizing types of requirements. One way to analyze VPN requirements is to consider the community of interest and access methods:

- Cost-effective remote and mobile user access
- An infrastructure for intranets that keeps resources secure within a single enterprise
- An infrastructure for extranets for controlling resource sharing between two or more enterprises

The economic crossover point regarding enterprise dial-in versus ISP-provided access services centers around the number of users that require dial-in access and the type as well as amount of activities that these users conduct. In general, a remote user population that generates bursty activity during relatively long duration sessions is a good candidate for ISP access. As described earlier, most

VPN techniques differ in the degree of traffic separation and control that an enterprise can have in an intranet context. On the other hand, if a driving requirement for the enterprise is extranet connectivity, then an IPsec-based solution is one of the few choices available. For more information, see the Virtual Private Network Consortium Web site (http://www.vpn.org). Because VPNs are so important to the world of electronic commerce, this chapter describes an example where a few large enterprises worked with a number of small to medium enterprises to create a successful model for extranet deployment.

## Deployment of a CE-Based VPN in E-Commerce

Unless your enterprise is the first to try a new technology, protocol, or architecture, there will likely be case studies available for review. A frequently documented extranet case study is the ANX (McDysan, 2000). This extranet VPN involves a few large enterprises (automotive manufacturers) and a significant number of small to medium enterprises (their suppliers). Initiated by the Automotive Industry Action Group (AIAG) in 1994, the IPsec-based ANX network had Chrysler, Ford, and General Motors as the founding network participants. These companies and other major automotive manufacturers use parts and services from a large number of common original equipment manufacturers, such as Bosch, Delta, Fisher, ITT, and TRW. After the completion of successful trials in 1997 and 1998, ANX launched into production in November 1998. By the end of 1999, ANX had nearly 500 registered trading partners. As an example of a quantifiable goal achievable by an extranet, the AIAG estimates that a collaborative planning, forecasting, and replacement tool running over the ANX network may save up to $1,200 per vehicle. This savings results from a reduction in length of the delivery cycle of parts and supplies and the associated inventory levels.

The ANX architecture is based on a set of interconnected certified service providers (CSPs), certified exchange point operators (CEPOs), and certificate authority service providers, to which ANX trading partners subscribe, as illustrated in Figure 11. Telcordia (formerly

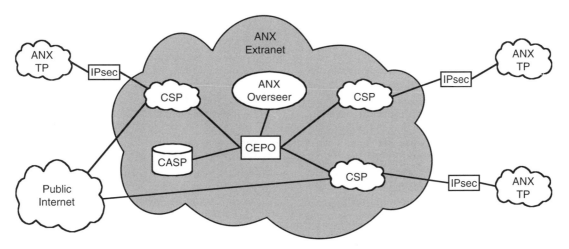

**Figure 11:** ANX extranet architecture.

Bellcore) has been chosen as the ANX overseer, which awards certification to CSPs and CEPOs. The ANX service quality certification categories are the following: network service features, interoperability, performance, reliability, business continuity and disaster recovery, security, customer care, and trouble handling. ANX has also specified the International Computer Security Association (ICSA) to certify IPsec-compliant equipment. Equipment that has the ICSA stamp of approval is a good place to start when looking for IPsec-compliant vendors.

This network is effectively a partitioned set of interfaces running on top of the public Internet infrastructure offered by the selected set of certified commercial ISPs. It replaces the prior complex arrangement of physical and logical connections among trading partners with one logically administered, cryptographically secured connection to the ANX extranet. Choice of the TCP/IP protocol suite provides access to a broad range of file transfer, electronic document interchange, e-mail, and other application software. This is especially important in the automotive industry where computer-based techniques are now used in almost every stage of the design, manufacturing, delivery, and maintenance aspects of the business. Although the benefits of ANX apply primarily to medium to large enterprises in the automotive industry, the drive toward interoperability will benefit other industry segments in the longer term (see http://www.anx.com for more information).

## GLOSSARY

**Customer edge (CE)**  A CE device is connected to a PE device via an access network for the purpose of communicating with users at different sites within the VPN.

**Enterprise**  A single organization, corporation, or government agency that administratively controls and sets policy for communication among a set of sites.

**Extranet**  An extranet allows communication between a set of sites that belong to different enterprises, as controlled by the enterprise administrators and/or a third party. These enterprises have access to a specified subset of each other's sites. Examples of extranets include companies performing joint software development, a group of suppliers and their customers exchanging orders and delivery tracking information, or different organizations participating in a consortium that has access to important information.

**Generic routing encapsulation (GRE)**  A general protocol for encapsulating a network layer protocol over another network layer protocol (Farinacci, Li, Hanks, Meyer, & Traina [RFC 2784], 2000).

**Intranet**  An intranet restricts communication to a set of sites that belong to one enterprise and via policy may further restrict communication between groups within these sites. For example, communication between marketing and engineering may be limited.

**IP security protocol (IPsec)**  A set of IETF standards that defines a suite of security protocols that provide confidentiality, integrity, and authentication services (Kent & Atkinson [RFC 2401], 1998).

**Layer 2 tunneling protocol (L2TP)**  An IETF standardized protocol defined initially for support of dial-in connections (Townsley et al. [RFC 2661], 1999). A successor to the proprietary Microsoft PPTP and Cisco L2F protocols, L2TP gives mobile users the appearance of being on an enterprise LAN.

**Multiprotocol label switching (MPLS)**  A switching technique that forwards packets based on a fixed-length label inserted between the link and network layer or use of a native layer 2 label, such as frame relay or ATM (Rosen, Viswanathan, & Callon [RFC 3031], 2001). Similar to frame relay and ATM in function, MPLS differs from these protocols by virtue of its tight coupling to IP routing protocols.

**Provider edge (PE)**  A PE device faces the service provider core network on one side and interfaces via an access network to one or more CE devices.

**Site**  A set of users that have connectivity without use of a service provider network. For example, a site may be the users that are part of the same enterprise in a building or campus.

**Tunnel**  A tunnel is formed by encapsulating packets with a header used to forward the encapsulated payload to the tunnel endpoint. In VPN applications, tunnel endpoints may be a CE or a PE device. Encapsulating one tunnel within another forms a hierarchical tunnel, which is useful to reduce the number of tunnels in the core of networks. Examples of protocols commonly used for forming a tunnel are MPLS, L2TP, GRE, IPsec, and IP-in-IP tunnels.

**User**  Someone or something that has been authorized to use a VPN service; for example, a human being using a host or a server.

**Virtual private network (VPN)**  A specific set of sites, configured as either an intranet or an extranet to allow communication. A set of users at a site may be a member of one or many VPNs.

## CROSS REFERENCES

See *Extranets: Applications, Development, Security and Privacy; Internet Architecture; Internet Security Standards; TCP/IP Suite; VPN Architecture; VPN Basics.*

## REFERENCES

Blake, S., Black, D., Carlson, M., Davies, E., Wang, Z., & Weiss, W. (1998, December). *An architecture for differentiated services, IEFT1998* (RFC 2475). Retrieved May 2, 2005, from http://ietf.org/rfc/rfc2475.txt

Braden, R., Clark, D., & Shenker, S. (1994, June). *Integrated services in the Internet architecture: An overview, IETF1994* (RFC 1633). Retrieved May 2, 2005, from http://ietf.org/rfc/rfc1633.txt

Braun, T., Guenter, M., & Khalil, I. (2001, May). Management of quality of service enabled VPNs. *IEEE Communications Magazine*, 90–98.

Callon, R., Suzuki, M., DeClerq, J., Gleeson, B., Malis, A., Muthukrishnan, K., et al. (2004). A framework for layer 3 provider provisioned virtual private networks. Retrieved May 2, 2005, from http://ietf.org/internet-drafts/draft-ietf-l3vpn-framework-00.txt

Carugi, M., McDysan, D., Fang, L., Nagarajan, A., Sumimoto, J., & Wilder, R. (2005). Service requirements for Layer 3 provider provisioned virtual private networks. Retrieved May 2, 2005, from http://ietf.org/rfc/rfc4031.txt

Farinacci, D., Li, T., Hanks, S., Meyer, D., & Traina, P. (2000, March). *Generic routing encapsulation (GRE), IETF 2000* (RC 2784). Retrieved May 2, 2005, from http://ietf.org/rfc/rfc2784.txt

Kent, S., & Atkinson, R. (1998, November). *Security architecture for the Internet protocol, IETF 1998* (RFC 2401). Retrieved May 2, 2005, from http://ietf.org/rfc/rfc2401.txt

Kosiur, D. (1998). *Building and managing virtual private networks*. New York: Wiley.

L3VPN charter. (n.d.). IETF Working Group charter page. Retrieved May 2, 2005, from http://ietf.org/html.charters/l3vpn-charter.html

McDysan, D. (2000). *VPN applications guide*. New York: Wiley.

Muthukrishnan, K., & Malis, A. (2000, September). *A core MPLS IP VPN architecture, IETF 2000* (RFC 2917). Retrieved May 2, 2005, from http://ietf.org/rfc/rfc2917.txt

Nagarajan, A., et al. (2004). *Generic requirements for provider provisioned virtual private networks (PPVPN),*

*IETF 2004* (RFC 3809). Retrieved May 2, 2005, from http://www.ietf.org/rfc/rfc3809.txt

Rosen, E., & Rekhter, Y. (1999, March). *BGP/MPLS VPNs, IETF 1999* (RFC 2547). Retrieved May 2, 2005, from http://ietf.org/rfc/rfc2547.txt

Rosen, E., Viswanathan, A., & Callon, R. (2001, January). *Multiprotocol label switching architecture, IETF 2001* (RFC 3031). Retrieved May 2, 2005, from http://ietf.org/rfc/rfc3031.txt

Schneier, B. (1995). *Applied cryptography: Protocols, algorithms, and source code in C*. New York: Wiley.

Thayer, R., Doraswamy, N., & Glenn, R. (1998, November). *IP security document roadmap, IETF 1998* (RFC 2411). Retrieved May 2, 2005, from http://ietf.org/rfc/rfc2411.txt

Townsley, W., Valencia, A., Rubens, A., Pall, G., Zorn, G., & Palter, B. (1999, August). *Layer two tunneling protocol L2TP, IETF1999* (RFC2661). Retrieved May 2, 2005, from http://ietf.org/rfc/rfc2661.txt

Wroclawski, J. (1997, September). *The use of RSVP with IETF integrated services, IETF1997* (RFC 2210). Retrieved May 2, 2005, from http://ietf.org/rfc/rfc2210.txt

# Identity Management

John Linn, *RSA Laboratories*

## INTRODUCTION

Today's network users are accessing ever-growing numbers of sites. Their accesses involve a widening set of attributes, such as shipping addresses, personal preferences, and authorization rights. Users and their administrators want the ability to control this information conveniently and consistently, according to security and privacy policies. Target sites want standard facilities that enable them (given suitable authorization) to obtain users' identity information without burdening the users involved. In response to these motivations, as of 2004, several initiatives are defining specifications concerned with identity management technologies.

In this chapter, we examine digital identity and its management, from an architectural perspective. We consider the pros and cons of management technologies, particularly regarding their influences on the security and privacy of user data. We examine the distributed components and functions that constitute identity management architectures and investigate their relationships with other elements of networking environments. We survey characteristics of several current activities that are specifying identity management approaches, such as the Organization for Advancement of Structured Information Standards (OASIS), Security Services Technical Committee (SSTC), and the Liberty Alliance.

## IDENTITY MANAGEMENT: MOTIVATION, GOALS, AND ISSUES

A traditional view of identity management is one centered within enterprises, where administrators configure accounts and rights associated with employees to enable and control their access to enterprise resources. As users' computer interactions have broadened from transactions with individual systems, managed locally, to wide-ranging interactions with large numbers of network sites under heterogeneous administration, elements of the users' digital identities have also broadened and have become dispersed. Different sites authenticate users independently and in different ways and maintain different contexts describing their views of information describing the users. This proliferation of nonnormalized data introduces many risks, including inconvenience, inconsistency, and confusion. Management and use of identity information across jurisdiction boundaries raises interdomain trust issues.

Emerging identity management technologies seek to address these concerns by applying explicit controls to the representation and management of digital identities. In technical terms, identity management depends on security. In terms of the results it achieves, identity management introduces both benefits and risks to the security and privacy of the users the identities represent. In this chapter, we consider the goals of identity management technologies, their constituent components, and the issues they raise.

### Broadening and Distributing Digital Identity

As time and technology advance, digital identities' scopes are expanding. A principal is the core of an identity and may be linked to an identified user or may represent an anonymous entity. An identity may be represented using different identifiers at different places. It may have associated attributes that are releasable selectively to different audiences. The need to control release of identity data implies a need for policy elements, which can themselves be considered as aspects of the identities.

A digital identity's contents may be contained within a single computer or may represent a distributed, linked set of data stored at many different places. Identity information may be stored in a variety of directories, databases, or other repositories. A single principal may have multiple distinct identities; this can occur as a side effect of technology or of deployment of separate information stores by different organizations. It may also be selected explicitly, as when a principal wishes to separate his or her activities undertaken in a business role from those undertaken in a personal role.

### Principals

Principals are the identity holders that employ and motivate identity management. Although principals are most commonly human users, they may also be users' devices, agents, or server systems. To deliver managed identities securely, principals are generally authenticated, using mechanisms such as passwords, hand-held tokens, and biometrics, and with cryptographic methods such as X.509 certificates (Housley, Polk, Ford, & Solo, 2002). Even when principals' identities are represented to information consumers in pseudonymous or anonymous form, it is common for a principal to be identified and authenticated to an identity management system, which then converts the identity into an appropriate form for delivery.

### Identity Attributes

Various sorts of attributes, suited to different purposes, can be linked to a principal's identity. For many years, computer operating systems (OSs) have managed specific attributes, such as group memberships, clearances, and designated privileges, and have exchanged these attributes with peers in trusted domains. Such attributes are often used in conjunction with the authorization services that the systems provide to mediate access to stored data. Identity management systems can support these elements but can also broaden the set of managed attributes to cover aspects of a principal that may be useful to conduct transactions or provide services to the principal, beyond the scope of OS-mediated authorization. Some examples include shipping address, contact information, credit card numbers, and preferences such as language and travel reservation choices.

### Identity Services

The scope of digital identity can be generalized still further to include active identity-related services as well as more passive attributes. Some potential examples include interactive calendar services and electronic wallets. These may be hosted on shared servers and/or on personal devices. Identity management for such environments extends to incorporate means to identify the services that correspond to a particular principal and perhaps also to encompass facilities mediating access to those services according to policies shaped by the principal.

## User Experience and Convenience

The advent of identity management systems promises increased convenience for users as they navigate the Web and may also enhance their security. Many Web sites request or require that their users establish accounts with passwords, to enable controlled access to valuable content, personal information, order processing data, and the like. Today, some users maintain large lists of usernames and passwords corresponding to different sites where they hold accounts. Given the annoyances that this process entails, it seems likely that many others may select a single password, perhaps one that is easily memorable and guessable, and reuse it across multiple sites. If, instead, a user only needs to authenticate to a single site, use of better-managed passwords or stronger authentication methods may become practical with that site.

### Single Sign-On

Methods that enable a user to log in once, whether with a password or other authentication method, and subsequently to gain access to multiple protected resources without reauthenticating, are known as single sign-on (SSO). As is discussed in subsequent sections, SSO can be achieved with a range of approaches, some of which are local to users' client systems and others that are distributed in nature.

### Single Attribute Entry

As digital identities have grown to incorporate attributes rather than just identifiers, the burden of reentering their contents at multiple sites has also grown. Consider, for example, the need to provide a shipping address each time an order is placed at a new Web merchant or to revise all such entries upon moving to a new home. Identity management technologies can enable such information to be entered once, maintained at a single place, and released to information consumers in accordance with authorization and privacy policies.

## Security, Privacy, and Control

Relative to ad hoc, fragmented representations of digital identities, identity management systems can enhance security and privacy protection for the information they contain. Among other benefits, this may help to safeguard the data against identity thieves. Four fair information practice principles, as cited in a report by the U.S. Federal Trade Commission (2000), are widely recognized as appropriate in the processing of personally identifiable information:

- notice of information practices,
- choices regarding the uses that may be made of collected information,
- user access to collected information, with provisions to change incorrect data or delete undesired entries, and
- appropriate security to protect collected data.

Control of identity information via a single interface to an identity management system can afford a direct means to address the first three principles. Storage of identity information within designated, protected systems, trusted to release sensitive information only as permitted by policy controls, can provide significant security for the data.

In a related activity, the Authentication Privacy Principles working group convened by the Center for Democracy and Technology (2003) has issued an interim report recommending principles in additional areas including the following:

- support for choice among alternative authentication tools, providers, and services;

- selective use of authentication, only when required to complete transactions; and
- minimizing collection and storage of data to that which is necessary to provide intended services.

Although use of identity management technology can enable and support enhanced security and privacy, it does not guarantee it. Mismanagement or compromise of identity management components can compromise the data they manage, perhaps even with a more concentrated effect than could arise if identity data is dispersed in an ad hoc fashion. An important, and yet unanswered, question is whether the convenience of SSO and the protection that centrally directed attribute control may offer will motivate principals to entrust their personal data to identity management systems.

### Principal Perspective

From a principal's perspective, a trusted identity management system can act as the principal's delegate, releasing information according to policies agreed upon by the principal without requiring unnecessary intervention by the principal. If the principal does not trust the system, however, or if the policies it enforces do not satisfy the principal's needs, these factors may limit the principal's ability to control sharing of identity data.

### Provider Perspective

From a provider's perspective, an identity management system can offer a uniform method for obtaining data about the principals that access it, without inconveniencing the principals involved.

### Operator Perspective

An identity management system's operator can establish attributes, such as authorization rights and group memberships, and can associate those attributes with the identities the system manages. In this manner, it can support authorization policies mediating access to provider resources. By concentrating the attributes under an identity management system's control, it becomes more practical to validate that the authorizations granted to different users are consistent with each other and with organizational policies. These capabilities can be particularly valuable when identity management technology is applied within an enterprise or between closely cooperating providers and identity managers.

## IDENTITY MANAGEMENT ELEMENTS

Identity management architectures include a number of functions, which may be decomposed across components in different ways. Commonly, users are identified and authenticated, and the authenticated results are represented in distinct forms to different consumers. Additionally or alternately, attributes corresponding to the users may be delivered. Data consumers need to be able to reference the information they require, and the users holding the identities need to be able to manage the information their identities contain. This section examines the elements of identity management systems, considering design alternatives and issues.

Figure 1 illustrates entities and dataflows in a generic identity management architecture. Not all actual systems necessarily include all listed elements, organize the elements into components in the same manner, or refer to the elements using the same terms. Generally, principals authenticate themselves to an identity provider; having done so, they can invoke its facilities to manage their identity information, and this information can be made selectively available to data consumers. Data consumers receive identifiers from the identity providers and can also receive references enabling them to obtain principal-related attributes from attribute services. Attribute data can be provided both by principals and administrators.

## Centralized and Distributed Systems

The functions of an identity management system can be decomposed in various ways. At one extreme, all identity and attribute information can be stored at a single site, which serves requests from locations throughout the

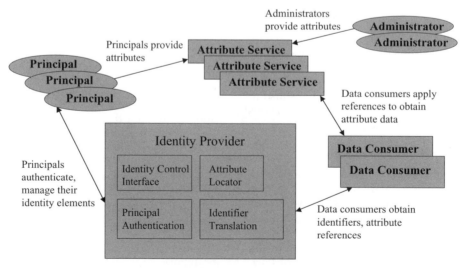

**Figure 1:** Generic identity management architecture.

Internet. This offers simplicity but also creates a single point of failure, affords an attractive target for attackers, and requires that principals and data consumers place extensive trust in the management site. These considerations may be acceptable within the boundaries of an enterprise but are likely to prove more contentious when the set of entities using the system crosses organizational boundaries.

Many identity management architectures allow multiple instances of their components to exist and interact, enabling different information to reside at different places. This helps to constrain the degree of trust that principals must place in particular providers and allows those providers to develop and operate independently. It also implies additional complexity, as it becomes necessary to provide facilities and services to locate information associated with principals. It may also complicate interoperability, because multiple interactions may be required to transfer data across processing entities and not all operators may be willing to undertake transactions with one another.

Identity information can be stored in a variety of repositories, including both directories and databases. Commonly, directories (e.g., those accessed using the Lightweight Directory Access Protocol [LDAP; Hodges & Morgan, 2002]) are used to publish information that changes relatively infrequently, making it available to a relatively broad set of authorized clients. Databases, in contrast, are often oriented to management of more dynamic data but generally make their data directly accessible only to a more constrained set of accessors; they are often found on the "back ends" of identity-related servers, which receive and mediate requests from other entities for operations to be performed. At the limit, identity information can be dispersed to personal devices under the direct control of individual principals. This approach reduces the need for trust in shared facilities but implies that the personal devices must be available and accessible whenever requests for identity information are to be processed.

## Identity Providers

An identity provider is an identity management architecture's core. It authenticates principals and provides control interfaces through which principals and/or their administrators can manage federations and other aspects of digital identities. In response to authorized requests, it provides data consumers with identifiers corresponding to the principals and references that the data consumers can employ to obtain associated attribute data.

### Personal and Distributed Authentication Mechanisms

In distributed computing environments, it is important to distinguish methods for authenticating human users (e.g., passwords, token devices, biometrics) from methods used to transfer authenticated identities between networked systems. Significantly, people cannot be expected to perform cryptographic processes to access their computers, although the systems they access can perform such operations. Human authentication is often based on an established relationship and the sharing of secret information with a system that is trusted to authenticate that user. Because sharing a secret more broadly would increase the chances of its exposure, it is desirable from a security perspective to confine its scope to a single verifier. In a representative identity management environment, the identity provider would authenticate the user and would then employ cryptographically protected mechanisms to deliver a representation of the user's identity to interested data consumers.

### Types of Identifiers

Users can be represented with identifiers of different types and markedly different properties of persistence and traceability. At one extreme, a user's identifier could persist for the lifetime of the user's association with the system and could be in a form directly and recognizably corresponding to the user's name. At the other extreme, a user could be identified to a system using an identifier uniquely generated for an individual communication and that does not visibly correspond to an identifiable person. In the middle, a persistent pseudonym permits a data consumer to recognize that a sequence of requests come from the same principal but not to identify the corresponding human individual.

### Identity Federation

Identity federation concerns linkages among multiple identifiers used to represent a principal to different relying parties. Commonly, identity providers manage such linkages, which may be established through protocol exchanges and/or by administrative configuration. There would be little motivation to incur the complexity of federation if all relying parties could receive the same identifiers to represent their accessing principals without need for further controls, but such cases may be exceptions, not rules. Federated identities have utility in cases that cross enterprise boundaries but also offer benefits for intraenterprise cases where different internal applications require different names. The value of federated identity is particularly evident in cases where one or more of the following conditions arise:

- Where a principal holds different identifiers for use with different relying parties, whether as a result of incompatible naming conventions or of inconsistent or uncoordinated administration, and wishes to link these identifiers for reasons of convenience.
- Where a principal wishes to specify the use of pseudonymous or anonymous identifiers with some or all relying parties, for privacy reasons.
- Where central control over the linkages between principals and relying parties is desired.

### Identity Lifecycle Management

Identity providers are central actors in managing the establishment, maintenance, and termination of identity elements. In this role, they can act on behalf of their principals and/or their organizations, coordinating consistent views of identities. A corporation may link its employee database and identity provider, thereby establishing managed identities corresponding to its employees.

When a principal's relationship with an identity provider terminates, the identity provider can inform each of the entities with which the principal's identity has been federated.

## Attribute Services

As the name implies, attribute services are responsible for managing access to attributes associated with identities. In some cases, or for certain attributes, it may be convenient to combine the attribute service function with an identity provider. In other cases, it may be appropriate for an identity's attributes to be distributed among one or more distinct services. Such decentralization may also imply a need for a further tier of services, used to locate the attribute services corresponding to an identity.

## Data Consumers

Data consumers receive the identifier and attribute information that an identity management system provides. Generally, they must generate authenticated requests so that their own identities can be securely determined. These identities can comprise inputs to authorization and privacy policies, used to mediate whether information should be released to a particular requesting consumer.

## NETWORKING AND APPLICATION INTEGRATION ISSUES

This section examines relationships between identity management and the protocols and components that carry and process users' interactions in networking environments. Pragmatic challenges arise today as results of the constraints of existing, deployed applications. If and as distributed identity management protocols and infrastructures are commonly deployed, and growing numbers of applications are integrated with them, more powerful and flexible forms of user interactions will become practical.

### Single Sign-On Approaches

Various approaches have been developed to achieve single sign-on in network environments. In one familiar approach, implemented within many Web browsers and other software products, a module on a user's client system monitors data streams to and from remote sites, looking for character sequences representing login dialogs. When such a sequence is detected, a stored username and password can be inserted, so the user need not enter the data manually. Usernames and passwords can be collected for an arbitrary set of sites, which need have no organizational relationship with one another. Problems with this approach include the following:

- not all login request interactions can be detected easily and robustly,
- stored passwords may be subject to compromise within the client system, and
- a user's password cache is not generally accessible if the user employs another client, unless, for example, portable smart cards are used for password storage.

A key advantage, however, is that this method can be applied without modifying server applications; applications, in fact, need not know that this form of single sign-on is being used.

Another form of single sign-on can be applied in Web environments, typically allowing accessors of a set of affiliated sites to authenticate once, without need for reauthentications to access other sites in the set. When one of the sites receives a request from an unauthenticated user, the site either performs an authentication itself or redirects the user's browser to another site that is designated to act as an authentication server. In either case, an authenticated user's browser receives an HTTP (Fielding et al., 1999) cookie that is automatically returned on subsequent requests to sites in the same domain, indicating the user's authentication state. In some implementations, authentication and cookie processing are performed in a front-end module or separate system to limit the need for modifications to the application servers behind them. Although this approach is convenient and popular, it has two particular limitations:

- It allows single sign-on only within an affiliate community of sites and does not simplify users' access to sites outside that community.
- In its basic form, the approach is vulnerable to interception of cookies on the network or in storage. Absent additional protective measures, an entity obtaining a user's cookie can use it to impersonate the user.

Kristol and Montulli (2000) provide further discussion about cookies and their usage.

Some contemporary architectures identity management architectures apply another approach. Here, a user's SSO session in a domain begins with authentication to the user's identity provider. The user may either navigate to the identity provider directly or may be redirected to it from another site. When a site wishes to determine an accessor's identity, it sends a request to the identity provider; the identity provider responds by indicating the associated principal's identity (or a corresponding pseudonym) and authentication state. This approach avoids the use of broadly shared cookies as a means to reflect authentication throughout a domain and therefore is less directly vulnerable to cookie interception. It depends, however, on the identity provider's ability to maintain state about the users it has authenticated and to associate them with access requests received by the sites it serves. Often, though not necessarily, this linkage is managed through use of a cookie shared between the identity provider and the user's browser; such a cookie need not be transferred to (and, potentially, exposed at) other systems.

### Browser Capabilities

Today, many SSO and identity management systems are being deployed to serve human principals accessing network resources via HTTP-capable browsers. These browsers generate requests and display data received in responses but are not equipped to respond to requests presented to them by other entities. As a result, for example, it is not feasible for an ordinary browser to act as its owner's attribute service, providing attribute information in response to direct queries. A user may maintain an appointment calendar on his or her desktop, but his or her browser's capabilities do not enable other sites to query the calendar for a free meeting time. If and as browser and device features evolve toward Web services, as discussed in a subsequent subsection, principals' attributes and services may migrate from separate platforms to modules or devices that are directly controlled by the principals involved.

Even though many browsers cannot provide services in the general sense, they do transfer data without direct human command in certain special and important cases. Browsers can be redirected from one site to another, and information can be transferred within the Uniform Resource Locators (URLs) employed. Scripting capabilities can be used to trigger a browser to post data items to a target site. HTTP cookies are commonly used to maintain state information between a browser and a single site or an affiliated set of sites, piggybacking their transfers on user-driven requests to the same destinations. Each of these methods plays an important role in the toolboxes of designers of Web-based systems, but some raise controversy. Cookies and scripting have been used in ways that compromise users' privacy and/or security, and some users elect to restrict their operations. It is functionally desirable, although sometimes challenging, to construct SSO and identity management systems that do not depend on these features being available and active in users' browsers.

## Identifying and Delimiting Sessions

A primary goal of SSO is user convenience. Once a user has logged in at an identity provider, it should be possible to access the sites that identity provider serves without further login-related dialogs. This simplicity may carry unintended implications, however. Consider the case of a user with an active SSO session enabling authenticated access to a range of sites but who wishes to visit a health insurance site anonymously to browse disease information. Although that user might find automatic SSO to that site convenient under other circumstances, as to conveniently retrieve stored information about processed claims, some explicit control should be available so that SSO-based propagation of user identities can be suppressed when desired. Similarly, it should be possible to distinguish among a user's different roles (e.g., personal vs. business accesses).

It can be complicated to indicate such distinctions in a clear fashion. One relatively coarse approach would require terminating a user's SSO session and then establishing a new one under different operating parameters. Alternately, an identity provider could offer its principals an interface through which they can adjust the scope of identity information that is to be delivered to their federated sites. Both of these examples illustrate the importance of facilities enabling principals to control sharing of their identity information in conjunction with particular sessions.

When SSO is provided silently, ambiguities can arise about the lifetime of sessions. It is reasonable to consider that an SSO session begins at the point when a principal authenticates. It also seems reasonable to consider that a session should end if the principal directs an identity provider to terminate it; upon such an event, the identity provider may be able to notify the other sites that the principal has accessed. The situation is less clear, however, if the principal does not explicitly notify the identity provider to end the session. Ordinarily, it should be possible to end a local session with an individual accessed site without ending an SSO-level session that may also span other sites. Additionally, timeouts may be provided so that no new sites may be accessed as a result of an SSO session that has been in place for more than a designated length of time.

## Identity Management and Web Services

Many of today's identity management designs and deployments are oriented to user-driven environments, where users make requests through browsers and view information received in responses. Many designers, however, are also looking toward environments where Web protocols are used to exchange data structured using the Extensible Markup Language (XML) between systems. These can provide a basis for machine–machine transactions, which can proceed autonomously without explicit user command. In such environments, for example, a user might enable a local agent that would obtain data from other sites, interpret and process that data, and apply the result on the user's behalf as the basis of subsequent requests. Collectively, technologies and protocols designed to enable such interactions in HTTP-based environments are described as providing Web services.

How do identity management and Web services relate to each other? There are two basic answers, both of which are valid. At one level, identity management systems can be constructed using Web service technologies. An attribute service, for example, could expose Web service interfaces to enable access to the data it stores. At another level, it is important to note that Web service transactions will generally be carried out on behalf of identities, whether of human users, server computers, or other forms of devices. These identities must be reflected appropriately, sometimes in pseudonymous form for privacy reasons, and may have associated attributes. These information elements, maintained and delivered by identity management systems, must be securely incorporated into Web service protocols.

## SECURITY AND PRIVACY ISSUES

This section explores the relationships among identity management, security, and privacy. It examines benefits and risks and considers the properties on which identity management systems must depend to offer strong protection to their users.

## Benefits of Identity Management
### Explicit Control and Policy Enforcement Points

An identity management system can make it easier for principals to understand and control the storage and sharing of their identity information. If an identity provider is implemented in a sound fashion and is operated by an organization that a principal trusts, it can act as the principal's delegate to enforce strong protection for sensitive identity information. Operating in conjunction with associated attribute services and other components, it can support consistent authorization policies, defining the set of destinations with which identity information can be shared. Additionally, it can act as a focal point for management of privacy policies (e.g., the Platform for Privacy Preferences, commonly known as P3P; World Wide Web Consortium, 2002), which afford control over additional dimensions such as data usage. Berthold and Köhntopp (2000) have further proposed the use of P3P as a basis to construct a general architecture to manage identity information.

### Segregation of Identity and Linkage Information

By supporting federated identities, an identity management system can represent a principal to different data consumers under different identifiers. This allows convenience, as by masking different user names a principal may have been assigned at different sites. It can also enhance privacy by providing a pseudonym to represent a principal to a data consumer instead of an identifier that can be easily traced to the principal or correlated with identifiers provided to other data consumers.

### Strengthening Authentication

When an identity management system is used, principals need authenticate themselves only to the identity provider rather than individually to multiple data consumers. This can strengthen the quality of authentication, for a combination of reasons:

- The identity provider is specifically dedicated to performing security-related processing and may be well equipped and administered for this purpose.
- Within the context of a relationship between a principal and a single identity provider, it may be practical to undertake a registration procedure that affords more opportunity for checking and validation than can be achieved on transient registrations with multiple data consumers.
- Between a principal and an identity provider, it may be practical to employ higher-strength authentication methods (e.g., cryptographically based devices, frequently changed passwords) than can be established with multiple data consumers, each of which may be accessed only relatively infrequently.

## Risks of Identity Management

### Single Point of Failure

As previously noted, use of identity providers for centralized authentication may allow higher assurance than would be practical with multiple independent data consumers. If, however, an attacker can compromise a principal's authentication at an identity provider, this enables the attacker to penetrate the principal's accounts at multiple destinations. As a result, identity providers may become attractive targets. It is important, therefore, that identity providers be implemented and operated securely

and that they employ relatively strong methods to authenticate their principals.

### Loss of Data Ownership

When identity information is fragmented, principals are explicitly aware of each site to which they provide particular identity elements. A principal might reasonably hesitate, for example, to provide attributes that could support identity theft to a site that had no clear reason to request such data. If such information is placed under an identity management system's control, however, a known path exists through which the data could be transferred to an undesired destination, without explicit data entry or knowledge by the principal. Similar concerns arise "behind the scenes" between sites even in fragmented environments, but any individual site can provide only the identity data it has obtained, which may be only a subset of an overall identity.

In an identity management environment, principals must rely on the management system's technical and administrative integrity and on its enforcement of policies suited to their requirements. Unless a principal is personally confident in the system's technology and operators, he or she may consider that providing identity data to the system represents a significant and unpredictable loss of ownership and control over the data. At this writing, deployment and use of identity management technologies has not yet become pervasive, and it remains to be seen what organizations will operate identity provider services. As identity providers emerge, the set of service choices available may have a significant influence on acceptance of the technologies involved.

## Dependencies and Assumptions

Identity management systems depend on security and privacy aspects of a number of supporting technologies. Without appropriate deployment and management of those technologies, identity management systems cannot deliver the protections that their users require. In this section, we examine some of these dependencies and consider how they can be satisfied in practice.

### Trust Management

An identity management system's distributed components must achieve trust in one another before sharing sensitive information and must share a common basis for secure communication. In contemporary architectures, the administrative decision to establish trust in one or more peer systems is often manifested technically through use of public key infrastructure (PKI) methods. Once entities can rely upon keys that are trusted to represent their communicating peers, the data they exchange can be secured for purposes of authentication, integrity, confidentiality, and, if needed, non-repudiation.

### Data Protection Within End Systems

Identity management systems must often rely on the capabilities that their components' local platforms and operating systems provide to protect and segregate data belonging to different users. As such, it is important that these mechanisms be resistant to compromise.

### Principal Consent Semantics

Principals must be able to designate permitted and/or prohibited accesses to elements of their identities. In some cases, particularly for sensitive requests, this may take place directly; a principal may be prompted to authorize a specific request to be fulfilled. In other cases, principals may select or configure policies that will be enforced when access requests are mediated. In either paradigm, end systems must be trusted to provide accurate information to the principal describing the access(es) being requested and to correctly reflect the principal's inputs as authorization decisions are enforced.

### Noncolluding Data Consumers

Today's identity management systems often support features that insulate data consumers from traceable linkages to principals. Typically, this is accomplished by providing indirect references to the principals, using pseudonyms. This is a valuable measure from a privacy perspective, as the identifiers that different data consumers receive from the identity management system do not enable the consumers to determine whether the identifiers correspond to the same principal. It is important to recognize, however, that these facilities cannot prevent data consumers from drawing inferences about principal identities based on other information that they can observe along with requests, such as protocol addresses and browsing patterns. If shared between data consumers, such data could enable those consumers to infer (to some probability) correlations among identifiers and principals. If it can be safely assumed that data consumers will not collude, this can strengthen the breadth and quality of privacy protection.

## ARCHITECTURE EXAMPLES

This section examines several proposed examples of identity management architectures, which are described in a variety of published standards and specifications. The first three activities are closely interrelated. The Security Assertion Markup Language (SAML) provides building blocks that are important in constructing identity management systems, and Liberty Alliance's Identity Federation Framework (ID-FF) and Shibboleth (developed by Internet2 and its Middleware Architecture Committee for Education (MACE)) both make use of SAML. The Liberty Alliance's Identity Web Services Framework (ID-WSF) layers on top of ID-FF, defining means to manage and access attributes and services associated with identities. WS-Federation defines an alternate approach, offering similar functions to some of the other specifications but with a broader orientation that places more emphasis on generalized Web service environments.

### Security Assertion Markup Language (SAML)

SAML, defined in Mishra, Philpott, & Maler (2005) is a work item of the Security Services Technical Committee (SSTC) within the Organization for Advancement of Structured Information Standards (OASIS). SAML defines XML-based facilities to represent and transfer several types of statements related to security-oriented operations:

- authentication statements,
- attribute statements, and
- authorization decision statements.

One or more of these statements can be combined into an object known as an assertion; for simplicity, for example, an assertion bearing only an authentication statement is commonly described as an authentication assertion.

It is important to recognize that authentication interactions with principals lie outside SAML's scope. Commonly, a server performs the steps needed to authenticate a principal and then issues SAML assertions representing the principal's authentication status. As such, SAML provides a level of indirection, insulating assertion consumers from the processing associated with particular authentication mechanisms.

### Liberty Alliance's Identity Federation Framework (ID-FF)

The Liberty Alliance Project was formed in 2001 and includes participants from a broad range of technology providers, Web site operators, and other organizations. Liberty has adopted SAML as a basis for SSO and has extended it to support federated identities. Its Identity Federation Framework (ID-FF) specifications (Wason, 2003) define additional usage profiles beyond those previously specified by OASIS, provide federation capabilities, and add an authentication context facility to describe aspects of user authentication. As of late 2003, ID-FF specifications had been contributed to the OASIS Security Services Technical Committee (TC). Many aspects of their contents were incorporated into subsequent versions of SAML specifications.

### Shibboleth

The Internet2/MACE Shibboleth project (Erdos & Cantor, 2002) seeks to manage identities across a network of universities. Like Liberty ID-FF, it provides SSO with federated identities, using SAML protocol elements as a basis. Information privacy and selective control over release of attributes are important design priorities. When an access request arrives at a Shibboleth-mediated destination, the target site communicates with a service at the principal's source domain and obtains an opaque handle corresponding to the requestor. This handle is used to request identifiers and/or other attributes from the source domain's attribute authority. The attributes received, in turn, can be used to determine the requestor's authorization to access the desired resource.

### Liberty Alliance's Identity Web Services Framework (ID-WSF)

Subsequent to its initial ID-FF work, the Liberty Alliance has defined a Web service framework (ID-WSF) (Tourzan & Koga, 2004) to support Web services based on individual identities. ID-WSF is layered over ID-FF and also uses facilities of Web Services Security: SOAP Message Security (Nadalin, Kaler, Hallam-Baker, & Monzillo, 2004). ID-WSF's central element is a discovery service, which requestors consult to locate identity-related services associated with a principal. The discovery service may also perform an authorization function, issuing tokens to requestors that reflect their permission to access a particular service. If designated by policy, access to an identity's attributes or services may be made contingent on explicit and active confirmation by the principal that owns the identity.

## WS-Federation

The WS-Federation (Bajaj et al., 2003a) specification, released by a group of companies, includes approaches to enable federation of identities. Its concept of federation also extends beyond identities to include relationships between realms. WS-Federation relies on several other specifications, such as Web Services Security: SOAP Message Security and WS-Trust (Anderson et al., 2004), and has not been contributed to a standards body at this writing. In contrast to other cited approaches, WS-Federation does not directly employ SAML, although SAML is one of several alternative approaches that may be used for authentication in the underlying Web Services Security: SOAP Message Security layer.

WS-Federation profiles have been defined for SOAP-based Web service environments (Bajaj et al., 2003b) and for use of WS-Federation with redirects and conventional HTTP browsers (Bajaj et al., 2003c). WS-Federation provides many of the same capabilities as are offered by the Liberty Alliance specifications, although some aspects of its architecture are structured differently. For example, WS-Federation can manage pseudonyms within a special case of attribute service rather than as an integral part of its identity provider function.

## CONCLUSIONS

Identity management offers the potential to unify and simplify control and access to digital identity data in network environments and to mediate its use according to policy-based controls. It is attracting significant interest from technology providers and Web site operators and is the subject of extensive specification and implementation activity. As its deployment increases, it may enable users to access network resources in a manner that is convenient while also preserving or enhancing protection of their private information. To satisfy these goals, however, systems must be designed, implemented, and operated with suitable technical and procedural assurance and must be administered by organizations that the users are willing to trust.

## GLOSSARY

**Attribute Services**   Attribute services are elements of an identity management system devoted to storing attributes of principals' identities, making those attributes accessible to authorized requestors, and enabling management of their contents and access permissions on behalf of the principals involved.

**Authentication**   In the context of identity management, authentication describes methods through which an entity can demonstrate its correspondence with a particular principal and identity. Authentication can be achieved using a range of methods, including passwords, token devices, and cryptographic mechanisms.

**Identity**   In the context of identity management, an identity comprises one or more identifiers representing a principal, possibly accompanied by a set of attributes and/or services related to the principal.

**Identity Attributes**   Identity attributes are elements of a principal's identity describing characteristics associated with the principal, over and beyond the principal's identifiers.

**Identity Federation**   Identity federation concerns linkages among different identifiers corresponding to a principal.

**Identity Management**   Identity management concerns methods that control the storage, linking, and access to elements that constitute principals' digital identities.

**Identity Provider**   An identity provider is a central element of an identity management architecture. It authenticates principals and provides control interfaces through which they and/or their administrators can manage their federations and other aspects of their digital identities. In response to authorized requests, it provides data consumers with identifiers corresponding to the principals and may offer references that the data consumers can employ to obtain associated attribute data.

**Identity Services**   An identity service is an active element of a principal's identity, responding on behalf of the principal to requests for information or actions.

**Principal**   In the context of identity management, a principal is an entity that can authenticate itself as the holder of a particular identity. Principals may be human users, computers, or other devices.

**Single Sign-On**   Single sign-on (SSO) describes methods that enable principals to access multiple sites as a result of a single authentication event.

## CROSS REFERENCES

See *Computer and Network Authentication; Cryptographic Privacy Protection Techniques; Digital Identity; Privacy Law and the Internet; Web Services.*

## REFERENCES

Anderson, S., Bohren, J., Boubez, T., Chanliau, M., Della-Libera, G., Dixon, B., et al. (2004). *Web Services Trust Language (WS-Trust) version 1.1.* Retrieved April 8, 2005, from http://www.ibm.com/developerworks/library/ws-trust/index.html

Bajaj, S., Della-Libera, G., Dixon, B., Dusche, M., Hondo, M., Hur, M., et al. (2003a). *Web Services Federation Language (WS-Federation).* Retrieved April 14, 2005, from http://www.ibm.com/developerworks/library/ws-fed/

Bajaj, S., Della-Libera, G., Dixon, B., Hondo, M., Hur, M., Kaler, C., et al. (2003b). *WS-Federation: Active Requestor Profile.* Retrieved April 14, 2005, from http://www.ibm.com/developerworks/library/ws-fedact/

Bajaj, S., Dixon, B., Dusche, M., Hondo, M., Hur, M., Lockhart, H., et al. (2003c). *WS-Federation: Passive Requestor Profile*. Retrieved April 14, 2005, from http://www.ibm.com/developerworks/library/ws-fedpass/

Berthold, O., & Köhntopp, M. (2000, July). *Identity management based on P3P*. Paper presented at the Workshop on Design Issues in Anonymity and Unobservability, Berkeley, CA.

Center for Democracy and Technology. (2003). *Authentication Privacy Principles Working Group interim report (privacy principles for authentication systems)*. Retrieved November 21, 2003, from http://www.cdt.org/privacy/authentication/030513interim.shtml

Erdos, M., & Cantor, S. (2002). *Shibboleth-architecture draft v05*. Retrieved November 21, 2003, from http://shibboleth.internet2.edu/draft-internet2-shibboleth-arch-v05.html

Fielding, R., Gettys, J., Mogul, J., Frystyk, H., Masinter, L., Leach, P., et al. (1999). *Hypertext transfer protocol–HTTP/1.1* (RFC 2616). Retrieved November 21, 2003, from http://www.ietf.org/rfc/rfc2616.txt

Hodges, J., & Morgan, R. (2002). *Lightweight directory access protocol (v3): Technical specification* (RFC 3377). Retrieved March 15, 2004, from http://www.ietf.org/rfc/rfc3377.txt

Housley, R., Polk, W., Ford, W., & Solo, D. (2002). *Internet X.509 public key infrastructure certificate and certificate revocation list (CRL) profile* (RFC 3280). Retrieved March 15, 2004, from http://www.ietf.org/rfc/rfc3280.txt

Kristol, D., & Montulli, L. (2000). *HTTP state management mechanism* (RFC 2965). Retrieved November 21, 2003, from http://www.ietf.org/rfc/rfc2965.txt

Mishra, P., Philpott, R. & Maler, E. (Eds.) (2005) *Conformance requirements for the OASIS Security Assertion Markup Language (SAML) V2.0*. OASIS Standard. Retrieved April 13, 2005, from http://docs.oasis-open.org/security/saml/v2.0/saml-conformance-2.0-os.pdf

Nadalin, A., Kaler, C., Hallam-Baker, P., & Monzillo, R. (Eds.), (2004). *Web services security: SOAP Message Security 1.0. (WS-Security 2004)* OASIS Standard. Retrieved April 14, 2005, from http://docs.oasis-open.org/wss/2004/01/oasis-200401-wss-soap-message-security-1.0.pdf

Tourzan, J., & Koga, Y. (Eds.). (2004). *Liberty ID-WSF Web Services Framework overview, version 1.0-errata-v1.0*. Retrieved April 14, 2005, from http://www.projectliberty.org/specs/draft-liberty-idwsf-overview-1.0-errata-v1.0.pdf

U. S. Federal Trade Commission. (2000). *Privacy online: Fair information practices in the electronic marketplace: A Federal Trade Commission report to Congress*. Retrieved November 21, 2003, from http://www.ftc.gov/reports/privacy2000/privacy2000.pdf

Wason, T. (Ed.). (2003). *Liberty ID-FF architecture overview, version 1.2*. Retrieved April 14, 2005, from http://www.projectliberty.org/specs/liberty-idff-arch-overview-v1.2.pdf

World Wide Web Consortium (W3C). (2002). *The Platform for Privacy Preferences 1.0 (P3P1.0) specification* (W3C Recommendation). Retrieved November 21, 2003, from http://www.w3.org/TR/P3P/

# The Use of Deception Techniques: Honeypots and Decoys

Fred Cohen, *University of New Haven*

## BACKGROUND AND HISTORY

Honeypots and other sorts of decoys are systems or components intended to cause malicious actors to attack the wrong targets. Along the way, they produce potentially useful information for defenders.

### Deception Fundamentals

According to the *American Heritage Dictionary of the English Language* deception is defined as the act of deceit and deceit is defined as deception.

Fundamentally, deception exploits errors in cognitive systems for advantage. It is achieved by systematically inducing and suppressing signals entering the target cognitive system. There have been many approaches to the identification of cognitive errors and methods for their exploitation, and some of these are explored here; for more thorough coverage, see Cohen, Lambert, Preston, Berry, Stewart, & Thomas (2001a). Honeypots and decoys achieve deception by presenting targets that appear to be useful targets for attackers. To quote Jesus Torres, who worked on honeypots as part of his graduate degree at the Naval Postgraduate School: "For a honeypot to work, it needs to have some honey."

Honeypots work by providing something that appears to be desirable to the attacker. The attacker, in searching for the honey of interest, comes across the honeypot and starts to taste of its wares. If they are appealing enough, the attacker spends significant time and effort getting at the honey provided. If the attacker has finite resources, the time spent going after the honeypot is time not spent going after other things the honeypot is intended to protect. If the attacker uses tools and techniques in attacking the honeypot, some aspects of those tools and techniques are thereby revealed to the defender.

Decoys—like the chaff used to cause the information systems employed in missiles to go after the wrong objective—induce some signals into the cognitive system of their target (the missile) that, if successful, cause the missile to go after the chaff instead of its real objective. Although some readers might be confused for a moment about the relevance of military operations to the normal civilian use of deceptions, this example is particularly useful for two reasons: it shows how information systems are used to deceive other information systems, and it is an example in which only the induction of signals is applied. Of course in tactical situations, the real object of the missile attack may also take other actions to suppress its own signals, and this makes the analogy even better suited for this use. Honeypots and decoys only induce signals; they do not suppress them. Although other deceptions that suppress signals may be used in concert with honeypots and decoys, the remainder of this chapter focuses on signal induction as a deceptive technique, shying away from signal suppression and combinations of signal suppression and induction.

### Historical Deceptions

Since long before 800 B.C. when Sun Tzu wrote *The Art of War* (1983), deception has been key to success in warfare. Similarly, information protection as a field of study has been around for at least 4,000 years (Kahn, 1967). And long before humans documented the use of deceptions, even before humans existed, deception was common in nature. Just as baboons beat their chests, so did early humans, and of course who has not seen the films of Khrushchev at the United Nations beating his shoe on the table and stating, "We will bury you!" Although this chapter is about deceptions involving computer systems, understanding the cognitive issues involved in deception is fundamental to understanding any deception.

## Cognitive Deception Background

Many authors have examined facets of deception from both an experiential and cognitive perspective. Chuck Whitlock has built a large part of his career on identifying and demonstrating these sorts of deceptions. His book, *Scam School* (Whitlock, 1997), includes detailed descriptions and examples of scores of common street deceptions. Fay Faron (1998) points out that most such confidence efforts are carried as specific "plays" and details the anatomy of a "con." Bob Fellows (2000) takes a detailed approach to how magic and similar techniques exploit human fallibility and cognitive limits to deceive people. Thomas Gilovich (1991) provides an in-depth analysis of human reasoning fallibility by presenting evidence from psychological studies that demonstrate how several human reasoning mechanisms result in erroneous conclusions. Charles K. West (1981) describes the steps in the psychological and social distortion of information and provides detailed support for cognitive limits leading to deception.

Al Seckel (2000) provides about 100 excellent examples of various optical illusions, many of which work regardless of the knowledge of the observer and some of which are defeated after the observer sees them only once. Donald D. Hoffman (1998) expands this discussion of optical illusions into a detailed examination of visual intelligence and how the brain processes visual information. It is particularly noteworthy that the visual cortex consumes a great deal of the total human brain space and that it has a great deal of effect on cognition. Deutsch (1995) similarly provides a series of demonstrations of the interpretation and misinterpretation of audio information.

First Karrass (1970) and then Cialdini (2001) have provided excellent summaries of negotiation strategies and the use of influence to gain advantage. Both also explain how to defend against influence tactics. Cialdini (2001) presents a simple structure for influence and asserts that much of the effect of influence techniques is built in and occurs below the conscious level for most people. Robertson and Powers (1990) have worked out a more detailed low-level theoretical model of cognition based on perceptual control theory (PCT), but extensions to higher levels of cognition have been highly speculative to date. They define a set of levels of cognition in terms of their order in the control system, but beyond the lowest few levels they have inadequate data for asserting that these are orders of complexity in the classic control theoretical sense. Their higher-level analysis results have also not been shown to be realistic representations of human behaviors.

David Lambert (1987) provides an extensive collection of examples of deceptions and deceptive techniques mapped into a cognitive model intended for modeling deception in military situations. These are categorized into cognitive levels in Lambert's cognitive model. Charles Handy (1993) discusses organizational structures and behaviors and the roles of power and influence within organizations. The National Research Council (NRC; 1998) presents models of human and organizational behavior and how automation has been applied in this area. The NRC report includes scores of examples of modeling techniques and details of simulation implementations based on those models and their applicability to current and future needs. Greene (1998) describes the 48 laws of power and, along the way, demonstrates 48 methods that exert compliance forces in an organization. These can be traced to cognitive influences and mapped out using models like those of Lambert (1987), Cialdini (2001), and the one we describe later in this chapter.

Closely related to the subject of deception is the work done by the CIA on the MKULTRA project. A good summary of some of the pre-1990 research on the psychological aspects of self-deception is provided in Heuer's (1999) book published by the CIA on the psychology of intelligence analysis. Heuer goes one step further in trying to assess ways to counter deception, and he concludes that intelligence analysts can make improvements in their presentation and analysis process. Several other papers on deception detection have been written and substantially summarized in Vrij's book on the subject, *Detecting Lies and Deceit* (2000).

All of these books and papers are summarized in more detail in "A Framework for Deception" (Cohen et al., 2001a), which provides much of the basis for this chapter's discussion of historical issues, as well as other related issues in deception not limited to honeypots, decoys, and signal induction deceptions. In addition, most of the computer deception background presented next is derived from this paper.

## Computer Deception Background

The most common example of a computer security mechanism based on deception is the response to attempted logins on most modern computer systems. When a user first attempts to access a system, he or she is asked for a user identification (UID) and password. Regardless of whether the cause of a failed access attempt was a nonexistent UID or an invalid password for that UID, a failed attempt is met with the same message. In text-based access methods, the UID is typically requested first, and even if no such UID exists in the system, a password is requested. Clearly, in such systems, the computer can identify that no such UID exists without asking for a password. Yet, these systems intentionally suppress the information that no such UID exists and instead induce a message designed to indicate that the UID does exist. In earlier systems where this was not done, attackers exploited the result to gain additional information about which UIDs were on the system, which dramatically reduced the difficulty of attacking the system.

Suppressing the information that a UID does not exist is a very widely accepted practice, and when presented as a deception, many people who otherwise object to deceptions in computer systems indicate that this somehow does not count. Some authors assert that the password example is not a deception at all, but rather something else. This assertion reflects two commonly held viewpoints.

1. Deceptions are considered "bad" things so whenever they are used widely they are renamed so they can be

thought of as "good" things. A honeypot is a good thing, but a deception is a bad thing. That is why the name "honeypot" is more popular than the name "jail," even though they are both names for the same basic item used at different points in time.

2. People want to believe that they are good, so when faced with labeling something they think of as good as a deception, they fight hard to reduce their feelings of guilt by asserting that it is not a deception but something else.

Deeper inspection will find that many deceptions are named other things. However, this should not sway us from understanding them in terms that are common and accurate. Here is an excellent but all too common response from one reviewer to the assertion that it is deceptive to fail to differentiate between the two different causes of access failure, as described above: "It's not deceptive to wait to answer a request until the request is complete. Would you see a person asked a question who doesn't answer immediately is being deceptive? I would think not."

This response from the reviewer, as it is from most who have not thought through deception at length, is that a user ID without the password is an incomplete response, and therefore it is not deceptive to fail to reply that the user ID is not valid as soon as it is known. So when I log in to a system that first asks for a user ID and then, only after I answer, asks for a password, this practice is not deceptive. However, if a request comes in for access to a Web server and the Web server provides a password page when there is no real login permitted from that remote IP address, this is considered a deception. The two situations are precisely analogous, but most people choose to view the former as legitimate and the latter as illegitimate because of their predisposition in this regard. This is a self-deception that this chapter cannot support.

### Long-Used Computer Deceptions

Examples of deception-based information system defenses that have been in use for a long time include concealed services, encryption, feeding false information, hard-to-guess passwords, isolated subfile system areas, low building profile, noise injection, path diversity, perception management, rerouting attacks, retaining confidentiality of security status information, spread spectrum, steganography, and traps. In addition, because criminals seem to seek certainty in their attacks on computer systems, increased uncertainty caused by deceptions may have a deterrent effect (Cohen, 1999d).

Not everyone immediately accepts that these are deceptive techniques; however, a few examples may help clarify the point. Spread spectrum is a good example in which the spreading of the signals across a large spectrum using pseudo-randomly generated next frequency values causes the attacker to miss the signals of interest. It is a deception in that it attempts to fool the listener into the belief that no signal is present and to trick the listener who is convinced that one is present that he or she cannot tell the signal from the noise. It conceals the true nature of the message behind its eternal change of signal carrier.

Steganography is a much simpler example to understand, and most readers take little time to accept that it is a deception. Steganography conceals messages inside other messages, such as concealing written material inside a file that is in a valid image format. Clearly the intent is to cause the observer not to notice that there is a signal present other than the obvious one of the image.

### Honeypots

In the early 1990s, the use of honeypots and decoys as a deception in the defense of information systems came to the forefront with a paper about a "jail" created in 1991 by AT&T researchers in real time to track and observe an attacker (Cheswick, Bellovin, D'Angelo, & Glick 1991). An approach to using deceptions for defense by customizing every system to defeat automated attacks was published the next year (Cohen, 1992), and in 1996, descriptions of Internet lightning rods (Cohen, 1996a) and an example of the use of perception management to counter perception management in the information infrastructure were given (Cohen, 1996b). More thorough coverage of this history was given in a 1999 paper on the subject (Cohen, 1999a).

Since that time, deception has increasingly been explored as a key technology area for innovation in information protection. Although some researchers do not view some of these techniques as deceptions, they certainly meet the definitions used in this chapter. The jail provided false information to attackers while the defenders tracked them down, provided records of their attempts, and kept them from entering other systems by entertaining them while they were in the jail. The lightning rods provided false information that caused attackers to go down the wrong paths for their attacks, thus shunting them away from their intended target while convincing them that these false targets were worth their while.

### Deception ToolKit, D-WALL, Invisible Router, Responder, and Execution Wrappers

The public release of the Deception ToolKit (DTK; Cohen, 1998a) led to a series of follow-up studies, technologies, and the increasing adoption of technical deceptions for the defense of information systems. There is now a small but growing industry with several commercial deception products: HoneyD from the HoneyNet project, the RIDLR project at the Naval Postgraduate School, National Security Agency–sponsored studies at RAND, the D-Wall technology (Cohen, 1999b, 2000b), the Invisible Router (IR), Responder (Cohen, 2001), and a number of studies and commercial developments now under way. DTK was made available on a bootable Linux CD in the late 1990s as part of the White Glove Linux distribution. HoneyD is also now provided on a bootable CD from the HoneyNet project.

DTK creates sets of fictitious services using Perl and a deception-specific finite state-machine specification language to implement input, state, and output sequences that emulate legitimate services to a desired level of depth and fidelity. Although any system can be emulated with this technology at the application layer, in practice the complexity of finite state machines is fairly limited. On the other hand, by the time the attacker is able to differentiate legitimate from DTK services, DTK has already alerted response processes, and with automated responses, other real services can be turned to deceptions to counter further attacks. Low-level deceptions that emulate operating systems at the protocol level are implemented in the White Glove version of DTK by setting kernel parameters using the /proc file system to emulate time to live (TTL) and other fields to increase the fidelity of the deception; however, these effects are somewhat limited.

D-WALL uses multiple address translation to allow a small number of computers to behave as if they were a larger number of computers. In the D-WALL approach to deception, a large address space is covered by a small set of computers of different types that are applied selectively to different applications depending on the addresses and other control factors. D-WALL provides the means for translating and selectively invoking services so that each physical machine used as a high-fidelity deception can be applied to a large number of addresses and can appear to be a variety of different configurations. The translation is done by D-WALL, whereas the high-fidelity deception is done by a computer of the same type as the computer being projected to the attacker.

The IR extends deception to the protocol level by creating predefined sets of responses to packets that could be controlled by a rule set similar to router rules. The IR enables packets to be routed through different interfaces so that the same IP address goes to different networks depending on measurable parameters in the language of the IR. The IR first introduced mirroring, an effect that is highly successful at causing higher-skilled attackers to become confused; it also introduced limited protocol-level deceptions, such as dazzlements and "Window zero" responses, to force TCP sessions to remain open indefinitely. This particular mechanism had also been implemented at around the same time in special-purpose tools. The IR implemented the "Wall" portion of the D-WALL technology in a single box, something described in the D-WALL patent but first implemented in the IR.

Responder is a Lisp-based tool that handles raw packets directly and uses a combination of a router-like syntax and the ability to add Lisp statements at any part of the packet-handling process. It also adds hash tables to various fields to increase performance and provides interfaces to higher-level controls so that graphic interfaces and external controls can be applied. The advantage of the Responder technology is that arbitrary changes can be made to packets via the Lisp programming interface. Thus, in addition to emulation of protocol elements associated with various machines and operating systems, Responder can allow arbitrary programmed responses, complex state machines, and interfaces to DTK-like services, all in a single machine that covers arbitrary address spaces. Because it operates at line speed, it can emulate arbitrary network conditions, including the ability to model complex infrastructures. The Responder technology also provides playback and packet-generation mechanisms that enable the creation of deceptions against local passive sniffers and can coordinate these activities with other deceptions so that they work against both proximate and distant attackers.

Execution wrappers augment the overall deception mechanisms by creating operating-system-level deceptions that are invoked whenever a program is executed.

The first execution wrapper implementation was done in White Glove Linux and applied to enable pairs of computers that acted in concert to provide highly effective deceptions against insiders with systems administrator access. In this particular case, because a bootable CD-based operating system was used, identical configurations could be created on two computers, one with content to be protected and the other with false content. The execution wrapper was then used to execute unauthorized programs on the second computer. The decision where to execute a program was based on system state and process lineage, and a series of experimental developments were used to demonstrate that this technology was capable of successfully deceiving systems administrators who tried to exceed their mandate and access content they were not authorized to see. The technology was then applied to a deception in which a Responder was used at the network level to control where attackers were directed based on their behavior; once legitimate users gained access to protected computers, they were again deceived by execution wrappers when they attempted unauthorized usage.

These deceptions were quite successful in the limited experiments undertaken, and the combined effects of external and internal deceptions provided a far greater range of options for the deception designer than had previously been available. The advantage of more options is that more error mechanisms can be exploited under better control.

### The HoneyNet Project

The HoneyNet project is dedicated to learning about the tools, tactics, and motives of the "blackhat" community and sharing the lessons learned. The primary tool used to gather this information is the Honeynet, a network of production systems designed to be compromised. Unlike most historic honeypots, the Honeynet project is not directed so much at deception to defeat the attacker in the tactical sense as at intelligence gathering for strategic advantage.

A substantial number of individual researchers have joined this project, which has had a great deal of success in providing information on widespread attacks, including the detection of large-scale denial of service worms prior to the use of the "zombies" for attack. At least one master's thesis was completed in 2002 based on these results. The Honeynet project has grown over the years into a global effort involving scores of researchers and has included substantial tool development in recent years.

HoneyD is the main line tool of this project. It consists of a program that creates sets of personalities associated with different machines based on known machine patterns associated with the detection mechanisms of "nmap," a network mapping program that does active fingerprinting. This is a variation on the D-WALL patent. Like Responder and IR, it can emulate an arbitrary number of hosts by responding to packets, and like DTK it can create more in-depth fictions associated with specific services on ports for each of those machines. It also does a passable job of emulating network structures. HoneyD on Open BSD and Arpd in a CD (HOACD) is the implementation of a low-interaction honeypot that runs directly from a CD and stores its logs and configuration files on a hard disk. The "honeydsum.pl" tool turns HoneyD logs into text output and can be used to correlate logs from multiple honeypots. Such tools as mydoom.pl and kuang2.pl provide emulations of systems attacked by specific worms so that attackers who use residual exploits associated with these attacks can be traced.

### RIDLR and Software Decoys

The RIDLR is a project launched by the Naval Postgraduate School and designed to test out the value of deception for detecting and defending against attacks on military information systems. RIDLR has been tested on several occasions at the Naval Postgraduate School, and software decoys were created in another set of projects there. In this case, an object-oriented architecture was augmented to include fictitious objects designed to provide specific responses to specific attempts to exploit potential system weaknesses (Michael, Rowe, Rothstein, Auguston, Drusinsky, & Riehle, 2002).

### The Rand Studies

In 1999, RAND completed an initial survey of deceptions in an attempt to understand the issues underlying deceptions for information protection (Gerwehr, Rothenberg, & Anderson, 1999). This effort included a historical study of issues, limited tool development, and limited testing with reasonably skilled attackers. The objective was to scratch the surface of possibilities and assess the value of further explorations. It predominantly explored intelligence-related efforts against systems and methods to conceal content and create large volumes of false content. It sought to understand the space of friendly defensive deceptions and gain a handle on what was likely to be effective in the future.

The follow-up RAND study (Gerwher, Weissler, Medby, Anderson, & Rothenberg, 2000) extends the previous results with a set of experiments on the effectiveness of deception against sample forces. The researchers characterize deception as an element of "active network defense." Not surprisingly, they conclude that more elaborate deceptions are more effective, but they also find a high degree of effectiveness for select superficial deceptions against select superficial intelligence probes. They conclude, among other things, that deception can be effective in protection, counterintelligence, against cyber-reconnaissance, and in gathering data about enemy reconnaissance. This is consistent with previous results that were more speculative. Counterdeception issues are also discussed, including structural, strategic, cognitive, deceptive, and overwhelming approaches.

### Deception in GOLEM

GOLEM is a system of software "agents" (programs) that are designed to perform goal-directed activities with specific behaviors. Because these behaviors interact, the researchers who developed these systems experienced the effect of incorrect answers and ultimately came to understand that deceptions could be effective in inducing a wide range of malicious and benevolent behaviors in their system. By exploiting these results they were able to generate helpful responses from otherwise unfriendly programs, showed some mathematical results about their simulation environment, and were able to classify several different sorts of effects (Castelfranhi, Falcone, & de Rosis, 1998).

### Older Theoretical Work

One historical and three current theoretical efforts have been undertaken in this area, but all are currently quite limited. Cohen looked at a mathematical structure of simple defensive network deceptions in 1999 (Cohen, 1999a) and concluded that, as a counterintelligence tool, network-based deceptions could be of significant value, particularly if the quality of the deceptions could be made good enough. Cohen suggested that the use of rerouting methods combined with live systems of the sorts being modeled would yield the highest fidelity in a deception. He also expressed the limits of fidelity associated with system content, traffic patterns, and user behavior, all of which could be simulated with increasing accuracy for increasing cost. In this paper, networks of up to 64,000 IP addresses were emulated for high-quality deceptions using D-WALL (Cohen, 2000b).

Glen Sharlun of the Naval Postgraduate School recently finished a master's thesis on the effect of deception as a deterrent and as a detection method in large-scale distributed denial of service attacks. Deceptive delays in program response were used by Somayaji to differentiate between human and automated mechanisms. Error mechanisms were identified for passive and active attack methods, and these error mechanisms were used to derive a theoretical approach to systematically creating deceptions that affect the cognitive systems of computers, people, and organizations (Cohen & Koike, 2003). This theoretical model describes the methods used to lead attackers through attack graphs with deceptions (Cohen & Koike, 2004).

### Contentions Over the Use of Deception

There is some contention in the world community surrounding the use of these and other deceptive techniques in defense of information systems. The contention seems to be around a few specific issues: (1) the morality of "lying" by presenting a false target for attacks, (2) legal liabilities that might be associated with deceptions, (3) the potential that legitimate users might be deceived and thus waste their time and fall under suspicion, and (4) the need for deceptions as opposed to other "legitimate" approaches to defending those systems.

Issue 4 is specious on its face. Presumably the market will settle the relative value of different approaches in terms of their utility. In addition, because deception systems have proven effective in many arenas, there seems little doubt as to the potential for the effective use of deception. Presumably defenders will not have to start telling attackers that they have guessed an invalid user identity before they try a password because, as a deception, this is somehow not legitimate.

Issue 3 is certainly a legitimate concern, but experimentally the deception of legitimate users has never been a real issue. For large classes of deception systems, the "distance" between legitimate users and the deceptions is so large that they never substantially interact. Significant effort must be undertaken in creating effective deceptions to determine what will have the greatest effect while minimizing the potential for undesired side effects. In this sense, amateur approaches to deception are likely to be less effective than those undertaken by experienced professionals, but everyone gets experience somewhere. There is a need for an appropriate place for those who wish to learn to do so in relative safety.

Issue 2 depends on the specifics of the legal climate and the deceptions in use. Clearly there are limits to the use of deception within any present legal framework; however, these limits are relatively easily avoided by prudent application of due diligence with regard to legality within each jurisdiction. A good example was the use of a mirroring with dazzlement approach to defending against worms. Because this crashed the attacking computers, liability was a concern, and after it was shown effective, it was stopped to prevent lawsuits.

Issue 1, the morality of deception, depends on a social structure that varies greatly and seems to have more to do with presentation and perception than with specific facts. In particular, when presented as a honeypot, deceptions are widely accepted and often hailed as brilliant, whereas the same deceptions presented under other names, such as deceptions, are viewed negatively. To avoid the negative connotation, different verbiage seems to be adequate.

# THEORETICAL RESULTS ON DECEPTIONS

Deception theory has been undertaken in a number of arenas. Although most of the real understanding of deceptions from an implementation point of view stems from the notion that deceptions exploit cognitive errors, most of the theoretical work has been oriented in a more mathematical domain. As a result of various research efforts, some interesting issues have come to light. Some features of deception seem to apply to all the targets of interest. Although the detailed mechanisms underlying these features may differ, the commonalities are worthy of note.

## Core Issues

Some core issues seem to recur in most deceptions (Cohen et al., 2001a). These issues should be addressed to ensure that deceptions operate effectively and without undue hazard.

## Error Models

Passive and active intelligence models have been created to explain how people and the systems they use to gather information operate in the information technology arena. These models have produced two structures for cognition and cognitive errors. Figure 1 shows error types in a set of models in which the attacker of the system can observe a system under attack passively or actively. Just as visual perception is formed from the analysis of sequences of light flash–inducing signals that enter the brain, perception of computer situations is formed by analysis of

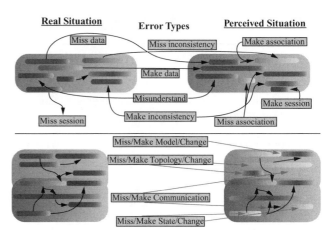

**Figure 1:** Error types in network attacks.

sequences of observables that flash into other computers, is analyzed by those computers, and produces depictions for the user. Errors include making and missing data, consistencies, inconsistencies, sessions, and associations. In the active case, where the attacker is able to provide information and see how the defender responds to that information, additional errors include making and missing models, model changes, topologies, topology changes, communications, communications changes, states, and state changes. The target of the deception in the case of a honeypot is an active attacker who can be presented with information that induces errors of these sorts.

For each error type, specific mechanisms have been identified in computers, humans, organizations, and combinations of these, and these mechanisms have been exploited systematically to drive attackers through attack graphs designed by defenders (Cohen & Kroike, 2004). In line with the basic theory of deceptions, deceptions can be designed by (1) identifying error types, (2) identifying and implementing mechanisms that induce those error types, and (3) selectively applying those mechanisms to cause desired effects in the target of the deception. The experiments described later in this chapter were used to confirm or refute this underlying theory, as well as the specific error mechanisms and the specific deception mechanisms used to induce these sorts of errors. Although only a relatively small number of experiments have been performed, the theoretical underpinning seems to be strong, and the general methodology has worked effectively when applied systematically.

## Models of Deception Effectiveness

A mathematical structure was developed in 1999 for understanding the implications of deception on attacker and defender workload and timing issues (Cohen, 1999a). This effort resulted in the characterization of certain classes of deceptions as having the following properties (Cohen, 1999b):

- Deception increases the attacker's workload.
- Deception allows defenders to better track attacks and respond before attackers succeed.
- Deception exhausts attacker resources.

**Table 1** Common Features of Deception

| | |
|---|---|
| Limited resources lead to controlled focus of attention | By pressuring or taking advantage of preexisting circumstances, the focus of attention can be stressed. In addition, focus can be inhibited, enhanced, and, through the combination of these, redirected. |
| All deception is a composite of concealments and simulations | Concealments inhibit observation, whereas simulations enhance observation. When used in combination they provide the means for redirection. |
| Memory and cognitive structure force uncertainty, predictability, and novelty | The limits of cognition force the use of rules of thumb as shortcuts to avoid the paralysis of analysis. This provides the means for inducing desired behavior through the discovery and exploitation of these rules of thumb in a manner that restricts or avoids higher-level cognition. |
| Time, timing, and sequence are critical | All deceptions have limits in planning time, time to perform, time until effect, time until discovery, sustainability, and sequences of acts. |
| Observables limit deception. | Target, target allies, and deceiver observables limit deception and deception control. |
| Operational security is a requirement. | Determining what needs to be kept secret involves a trade-off that requires metrics to be addressed properly. |
| Cybernetics and system resource limitations | Natural tendencies to retain stability lead to potentially exploitable movement or retention of stability states. |
| Deception has a recursive nature | Recursion between parties leads to uncertainty that cannot be resolved perfectly, but that can be approached with an appropriate basis for association to ground truth. |
| Large systems are affected by small changes | For organizations and other complex systems, finding the key components to move and finding ways to move are tactics for the selective use of deception to great effect. |
| Even simple deceptions are often quite complex | The complexity of what underlies a deception makes detailed analysis quite a substantial task. |
| Simple deceptions are combined to form complex deceptions | Big deceptions are formed from small subdeceptions, and yet they can be surprisingly effective. |
| Knowledge of the target is key | Knowledge of the target is one of the key elements in effective deception. |
| Legality | There are legal restrictions on some sorts of deceptions, and these must be considered in any implementation. |
| Modeling problems | There are many problems associated with forging and using good models of deception. |
| Unintended consequences | You may fool your own forces, create misassociations, and create misattributions. Collateral deception has often been observed. |
| Counterdeception | The target's capabilities for counterdeception may result in deceptions being detected. |

From Cohen et al. (2001a).

- Deception increases the sophistication required for attack.
- Deception increases attacker uncertainty.

Different deceptions produce different mathematical properties; however, for a class of deceptions involving honeypots and other related decoys, deception can be thought of in terms of their coverage of a space. These notions are based on an implied model of an attacker that was subsequently detailed in Cohen and Koike (2004) using the model provided in Figure 2.

In this model, an attacker is assumed to be undertaking an overall attack effort involving intelligence gathering, entries, privilege expansions, and privilege exploitations. In response there is an attack graph in which deceptions create additional alternatives for the attacker. Specifically, deception can suppress signals, thus causing the attacker to fail to find a real target, or in the case of honeypots and decoys, it can induce signals to cause the attacker to find false targets. As the attacker attempts to differentiate

deceptions from nondeceptions, successful honeypots and decoys consume attacker resources, and in some cases cause the erroneous belief that the false targets are real. The result of deceptions that are this successful is that the attacker goes further through the attack tree in the examination of false targets. An additional side effect seen in experiments is that real targets may be misidentified as false targets, thus causing attackers to believe that real systems are in fact honeypots. The model shown in Figure 2 is also recursive and has other properties of interest to the serious student of computer-related deception.

Examples of specific mechanisms that can drive attackers through these attack graphs are easy to come by. For example, the creation of large numbers of fictitious services and addresses in an Internet Protocol (IP) network results in a large number of cases of finding false targets, and because of the increased cognitive workload, it also causes attackers, particularly less detail-oriented attackers, to miss real targets. This is readily achieved by such technologies as D-WALL, the IR, HoneyD, DTK, and

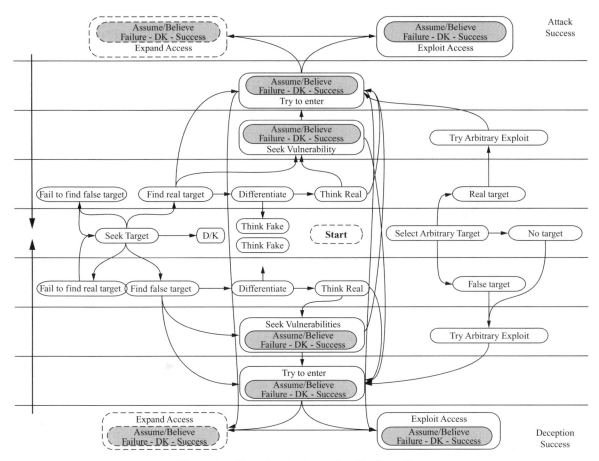

**Figure 2:** Generic attack graph with deception.

Responder. Similarly, mechanisms like execution wrappers have proven effective in causing attackers to move from a successful position after entry to a deception when they seek to exploit access. As a result they recursively go down the deceptive attack graph, making the transition from the highest level of "attack success" to "deception success."

Progress in the attack graph over time has also proven to be a valuable metric in assessing the effectiveness of defenses of all sorts. It was first applied to deception experiments in which positive and negative values are associated with increased travel up the real attack graph and increased travel down the deceptive attack graph, respectively. Thus in the example above, the attacker went from +4 to level −4 under the execution wrapper; in contrast, network-level deceptions tend to cause attackers to remain at level 0 and −1 for extended periods of time. In a nondeception environment, progress can only go in a negative direction under self-deception. The specific error types exploited in the execution wrapper case are missed and made topology, state, and state change. The errors made in the network deception cases are missed and made topology, sessions, and associations.

In the mathematical characterizations of deception workload, the effort expended by the attacker depends on the relative number of paths through the attack graph for deceptions and nondeceptions. When no deceptions are present, all paths are real, and the attacker always gains information as he or she explores the space of

real systems. With deceptions in place, a portion of the exploration produces false results. As the total space of attacker options grows large, if far more deceptions than actual systems are presented, the workload of the attacker for detecting real targets and differentiating between real and deception systems increases. Depending on the specifics of the situation, very high workloads can be attained for the attacker. At the same time, the defender who is able to observe attacker activity gains rapid knowledge of the presence of an attacker and their characteristics and can direct further deceptions toward the attacker. Specifically, the characteristics identified with the attacker can be used to present deceptions, even for real services.

Attackers can, in turn, seek to present different characteristics, including characteristics closely associated with legitimate users, to make it harder for the deception system to detect them, differentiate between attackers and legitimate users, and increase defender workload. However, attackers also have finite resources. As a result, the relative resources of attacker and defender, the number of deceptions versus nondeceptions, and the time and complexity of attacker and defender efforts play into the overall balance of effort. For typical Internet-based intelligence efforts using common tools for network mapping and vulnerability detection, defenders using deceptions have an enormous mathematical advantage. With the addition of rapid detection and response, which the defender gains with deception, the likelihood of attacker success and cost of defense can both be greatly reduced from situations where there are no deceptions.

## Honeypots

Although simplistic deceptions used in DTK and the HoneyNet project involve very low-fidelity deceptions, typical honeypots involve a small number of high-quality deceptions. These systems are typically oriented toward specific target audiences.

In broad-scale detection, deceptions gain effect by their large-scale deployment at randomly selected locations in a large space. For example, to rapidly detect widespread computer worms that enter certain classes of systems through random or pseudo-random sweeps of the IP address space, a number of systems are deployed at random locations where they await the appearance of malicious activity. If multiple systems detect similar activities, it is very likely to be a widespread attack. The more systems are placed, the sooner the attack will likely be detected, but the timeliness is not linear with the number of systems. Rather, the probability goes up with the number of deceptions placed in proportion to the size of the total space, whereas the time to detect is a function of the probability of encountering one or more of the deceptions systems as a function of the way the worm spreads. This is the hope of the HoneyNet project and proposals made to DARPA and other agencies for large-scale deception-based detection arrays for the rapid detection of large-scale worms.

For more targeted deceptions aimed at specific audiences, a different approach is undertaken. For example, the RIDLR project at the Naval Postgraduate School placed select systems on the Internet with specific characteristics that caused those systems to be noticed by specific audiences. These deceptions are more demanding in terms of deception system fidelity because they typically have to fool human attackers for enough time to gain the advantage desired by their placement. In one experiment, a system was placed with information on a specific subject known to be of interest to an opposition intelligence agency. The system was populated with specific information and had a regular user population consisting of students who were working on deception-related research. These users had created fictitious identities with specific characteristics of interest and were regularly interacting with each other based on those identities. The deception system included a specially placed, typical but not too obvious vulnerability specifically designed to allow an attacker to enter after targeting the system. It was identified in Internet search engines by one of its fictitious users and was thus probed by those engines and found in searches by people interested in the specific topics. The execution wrappers systems described above are examples of mechanisms that have been used successfully in high-fidelity deceptions oriented toward specific targets.

## Decoys

Decoys are typically thought of as larger-scale, lower-fidelity systems intended to change the statistical success rate of tactical attacks. For example, Deception ToolKit,

D-WALL, the IR, HoneyD, and Responder are designed to produce large numbers of deceptive services of different characteristics that dominate a search space. The basic idea is to fill the search space of the attacker's intelligence effort with decoys so that detection and differentiation of real targets becomes difficult or expensive. In this approach, the attacker seeking to find a target does a typical sweep of an address space looking for some set of services of interest. D-WALL and Responder are also useful for high-fidelity deceptions, but these deceptions require far more effort.

Tools like "nmap" map networks and provide lists of available services, whereas more sophisticated vulnerability testing tools identify operating system and server types and versions and associate them with specific vulnerabilities. Penetration-testing tools go a step further and provide live exploits that allow the user to semiautomatically exploit identified vulnerabilities and do multistep attack sequences with automated assistance. These tools have specific algorithmic methods of identifying known systems types and vulnerabilities, and the characteristics of the tools are readily identified by targets of their attacks if properly designed for that purpose. The defender can then simulate a variety of operating systems and services using these tools so that the user of the attack tools makes cognitive errors indirectly induced by the exploitation of those tools' cognitive errors. The deceived attacker then proceeds down defender-desired attack graphs while the defender traces the attacks to their source, calls in law enforcement or other response organizations, or feeds false information to the attacker to gain some strategic advantage. In at least one case, defenders included Trojan horse components in software placed in a honeypot with the intent of having that software stolen and used by the attackers. The Trojan horse contained mechanisms that induced covert channels in communication designed to give the so-called defenders an attack capability against the so-called attackers' systems.

Of course, not all decoys are of such high quality. Simple decoys, such as Deception ToolKit, are simple to detect and defeat. Yet after more than 7 years of use, simple decoys are still effective in detecting and defeating low-quality attackers who dominate the attack space. Such tools are completely automatic and inexpensive to operate, do not interfere with normal use, and provide clear, detailed indications of the presence of attacks in a timely fashion. Although they are ineffective against high-skilled attackers, they do free up time and effort that would otherwise be spent on less-skilled attackers. This is similar to the use of decoys in military systems. Just as typical chaff defeats many automated heat- or radar-seeking attack missiles, simple informational deceptions defeat automated attack tools. And just as good pilots are able to see past deceptions like chaff, so skilled information attackers are able to see past deceptions like Deception ToolKit. Finally, just as chaff still defeats missiles despite its limitations, so should simple deceptions be used to defeat automated attack tools despite their limitations. As long as the chaff costs less than the risks it mitigates, it is a good defense, and as long as simple deceptions reduce risk by more than the cost to deploy and operate them, they are good defenses as well.

Higher-quality decoys are also worthwhile, but as the quality of the decoy goes up, so does its cost. Although some of the more complex decoy systems like D-WALL provide more in-depth automation for larger-scale deceptions, the cost of these systems is far greater than Deception ToolKit. For example, a single D-WALL implementation can cost $100,000 to set up, as well as substantial operating costs to cover a few tens of thousands of IP addresses. Lower-fidelity systems like IR or Responder cost under $10,000 and cover the same-sized address space. Although Responder and IR can be used to implement the D-WALL functions, they also require additional hardware and programming to achieve the same level of fidelity. At some point the benefits of higher-fidelity decoys are outweighed by their costs.

## A Model for Deception of Computers

In looking at deceptions used in computers it is fundamental to understand that a computer is an automaton. Anthropomorphizing a computer into an intelligent being is a mistake in this context—a self-deception. Fundamentally, deceptions must cause systems to do things differently based on the systems' inability to differentiate a deception from a nondeception. Computers cannot really yet be called "aware" in the sense of people. Therefore, when we use a deception against a computer we are really using a deception against the skills of the humans who design, program, and use the computer.

In many ways computers should be better at detecting deceptions than people because of their tremendous logical analysis capability and the fact that the logical processes used by computers are normally quite different than the processes used by people. This provides some level of redundancy, and, in general, redundancy is a way to defeat corruption. Fortunately for those of us looking to do defensive deception against automated systems, most of the designers of modern attack technology have a tendency to minimize their programming effort and thus tend not to include a lot of redundancy in their analysis.

People use shortcuts in their programs just as they use shortcuts in their thinking. Their goal is to get to an answer quickly and in many cases without adequate information to make definitive selections. Computer power and memory are limited just like human brain power and memory are limited. To make efficient use of resources, people write programs that jump to premature conclusions and fail to verify content completely. In addition, people who observe computer output have a tendency to believe it. Therefore, if we can deceive the automation used by people to make decisions, we may often be able to deceive the users and avoid in-depth analysis.

A good example of this phenomenon is the use of packet sniffers and analyzers by attackers. The analysis tools in widespread use have faults that are not obvious to their users in that they project depictions of sessions even when the supposed sessions are not precisely accurate in the sense of following the protocol specifications correctly. Transmission control protocol (TCP) packets, for example, provide ordering and other similar checks; however, deceptions have been used successfully to cause these systems to project incorrect character sequences to their users, providing inaccurate user identification and authentication information for unencrypted terminal sessions. The net effect is that the attacker receives the wrong user identification and password, attempts to log into the system under attack, and is given access to a deception system. The combination of "Make Data" and "Miss Inconsistency" errors by the program and the user cause the deception to be effective.

Our model for computer deception starts with a model presented in "Structure of Intrusion and Intrusion Detection" (Cohen, 2000c). In this model, a computer system and its vulnerabilities are described in terms of intrusions at the hardware, device driver, protocol, operating system, library and support function, application, recursive language, and meaning versus content levels. The levels are all able to interact, but they usually interact hierarchically, with each level interacting with the ones just above and below it. This model is depicted in Figure 3.

This model is based on the notion that, at every level of the computer's cognitive hierarchy, signals can either be induced or inhibited. The normal process is shown in black, inhibitions are shown as grayed-out signals, and induced signals are shown in dark. All of these affect memory states and processor activities at other, typically adjacent levels of the cognitive system. Because deception detection and response capabilities are key issues in the ability to defend against deceptions, the following discussion focuses on the limits of detection.

- Hardware-Level Deceptions: Although some honeypots and decoys use hardware-level deceptions for local area networks from remote sites, these deceptions are problematic because the hardware-level information associated with systems is not generally available to remote locations.
- Driver-Level Deceptions: Driver-level deceptions are used by some decoys. For example, both the IR and Responder are able to create protocol disruptions to remote drivers by forcing them to stay engaged in sessions. For large-scale worms and remote network scanners, drivers on attacking systems that strictly follow protocols sometimes are unable to break free of their remote sessions and, after attempting more than a small finite number of connections, become permanently stuck and unable to scan further. Typically the programs operating these drivers then fail to make progress, and the system or application crashes.
- Protocol-Level Deceptions: Defensive protocol-level deceptions have proven relatively easy to develop and hard to defeat. Deception ToolKit (Cohen, 1998a) and D-WALL (Cohen, 1999a) both use protocol-level deceptions to great effect, and these are relatively simplistic mechanisms compared to what could be devised with substantial time and effort. HoneyD uses a similar mechanism. This appears to be a ripe area for further work. Most intelligence gathering today starts at the protocol level, overrun situations almost universally communicate with other systems at the protocol level, and insiders generally access other systems in the environment through the protocol level. Most remote driver deceptions are actually protocol-level deceptions that occur

## Model of computer deceptions

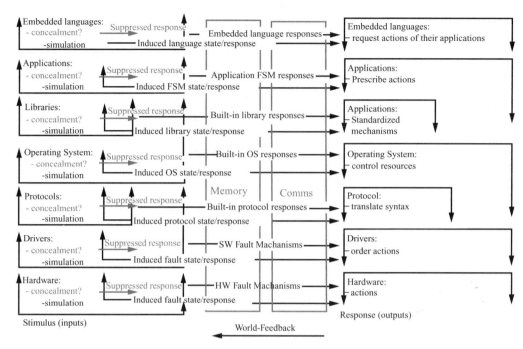

**Figure 3:** Model of computer cognitive failure mechanisms leading to deceptions.

because protocols are embedded in drivers. They also operate at the protocol level against systems that do not have such driver problems. One of the best examples is the use of mirroring (switching source and destination IP address and port numbers and emitting the input packet on the same interface on which it arrived). Mirroring in buffer overrun attacks reflects the original attack against its source, which causes human attackers to attack themselves, sometimes to great effect. If randomization is added toward the end of the packets, automated input buffer overrun attacks tend to crash the remote machines launching the attacks. These defenses have the potential to induce significant liability on the defender who chooses to use them.

- Operating-System-Level Deceptions: To use defensive deception at the target's operating system level requires offensive actions on the part of the deceiver and yields only indirect control over the target's cognitive capability. This control has to then be exploited to affect deceptions at other levels, and this exploitation may be very complex depending on the specific objective of the deception. This is not something done by honeypots or decoys on the market today; however, some honeypots have included software-based Trojan horses designed to attack the attacker by exploiting operating system and application weaknesses. The liability issues are such that this form of deception would only be suitable for governments.

- Library and Support-Function-Level Intrusions: Using library functions for defensive deceptions offers a great opportunity, but like operating systems, there are limits to the effectiveness of libraries because they are at a level below that used by higher-level cognitive functions. Thus, it is very difficult to produce just the right effects without providing obvious evidence that something is

not right. Library weaknesses have been exploited in the same manner as protocol weaknesses to cause attackers to become temporarily disabled when their intelligence software becomes unable to handle the responses.

- Application-Level Deceptions: Applications provide many new opportunities for deceptions. The apparent user interface languages offer syntax and semantics that may be exploited, whereas the actual user interface languages may differ from the apparent languages because of programming errors, back doors, and unanticipated interactions. Internal semantics may be in error or may fail to take all possible situations into account, or there may be interactions with other programs in the environment or with state information held by the operating environment. They always trust the data they receive so that false content is easily generated and efficient. These include most intelligence tools, exploits, and other tools and techniques used by severe threats. Known attack detection tools and anomaly detection have been applied at the application level with limited success. Network detection mechanisms also tend to operate at the application level for select known application vulnerabilities. A good example is the presentation of false information in response to application-generated network probes. The responses generate false information that reaches the user and appears to be accurate and in keeping with the normal operation of the tool. This is the class of deceptions exploited in most of the experiments that lead attackers through attack graphs.

Application-level defensive deceptions are very likely to be a major area of interest because (1) applications tend to be driven more by time to market than by surety and (2) applications tend to directly influence the decision processes made by attackers. For example, a defensive deception would typically cause a network scanner to make wrong decisions and report wrong results to the intelligence operative using it. Similarly, an application-level deception might be used to cause a system that is overrun to act on the wrong data. For systems administrators the problem is somewhat more complex, and it is less likely that application-level deceptions will work against them.

- Recursive Languages in the Operating Environment: Recursive languages are used in many applications including many intelligence and systems administration applications. In cases where this language can be defined or understood or where the recursive language itself acts as the application, deceptions against these recursive languages should work in much the same manner as deceptions against the applications themselves. This is suitable only to government-level operations because of the potential liabilities associated with its use.

## Commentary

Unlike people, computers do not typically have egos, but they do have built-in expectations and in some cases automatically seek to attain "goals." If those expectations and goals can be met or encouraged while carrying out the deception, the computers will fall prey just as people do.

There are three basic approaches to being very successful at defeating computers through deception. One approach is to create as high-fidelity a deception as you can and hope that the computer will be fooled. Another is to understand what data the computer is collecting and how it analyzes the data provided to it. The third is to alter the function of the computer to comply with your needs. The high-fidelity approach can be quite expensive, but should not be abandoned out of hand. At the same time, the approach of understanding enemy tools can never be done definitively without a tremendous intelligence capability. The modification of cognition approach requires an offensive capability that is not always available and is quite often illegal, but all three avenues seem to be worth pursuing.

1. **High Fidelity:** High-fidelity deception of computers with regard to their assessment, analysis, and use against other computers tends to be fairly easy to accomplish today using tools like D-WALL, the IR, and Responder in conjunction with such tools as execution wrappers. Although doing so is effective in the generic sense, for specific systems, additional efforts must be made to create the internal system conditions indicative of the desired deception environment. These efforts can be quite costly. These deceptions tend to operate at a protocol level and are augmented by other technologies to affect other levels of deception.

2. **Defeating Specific Tools:** Many specific tools are defeated by specific deception techniques. For example, nmap and similar scans of a network seeking services to exploit are easily defeated by such tools as the Deception ToolKit and HoneyD. More specific attack tools, such as Back Orifice (BO), can be countered directly by specific emulators, such as "NoBO," a PC-based tool that emulates a system that has already been subverted with BO. Some deception systems work against substantial classes of attack tools. HoneyD and the HoneyNet project attempt to create specific deceptions for widely spread worms.

The intelligence requirements of defeating specific tools may be substantial, but the extremely low cost of such defenses makes them appealing. Against off-the-Internet attack tools, these defenses are commonly effective and, at a minimum, increase the cost of attack far more than they affect the cost of defense. Unfortunately, for more severe threats, such as insiders, overrun situations, and intelligence organizations, these defenses are often inadequate. They are almost certain to be detected and avoided by an attacker with skills and access of this sort. Nevertheless, from a standpoint of defeating the automation used by these types of attackers, relatively low-level deceptions have proven effective.

3. **Modifying Function:** Modifying the function of computers is relatively easy to do and is commonly used in attacks. The question of legality aside, the technical aspects of modifying function for defense fall into the area of counterattack and are thus not a purely defensive operation. The basic plan is to gain access, expand privileges, induce desired changes for ultimate compliance, leave those changes in place, periodically verify proper operation, and exploit as desired. In some cases privileges gained in one system are used to attack other systems as well. Modified function is particularly useful for obtaining feedback on target cognition.

However, the problems in modifying function become more severe in the case of more severe threats. Insiders are using your systems, so modifying them to allow for deception allows for self-deception and enemy deception of you. For overrun conditions you rarely have access to the target system, so unless you can do very rapid and automated modification, this tactic will likely fail. For intelligence operations this requires that you defeat an intelligence organization that aims to deceive you. The implications are unpleasant, and inadequate study has been made in this area to make definitive decisions.

There is a general method of deception against computer systems that are being used to launch fully automated attacks against other computer systems. It analyzes the attacking system (the target) in terms of its use of responses from the defender and creates sequences of responses that emulate the desired responses to the target. Because all such mechanisms published or widely used today are quite finite and relatively simplistic, with substantial knowledge of the attack mechanism, it is relatively easy to create a low-quality deception that will be effective. It is noteworthy, for example, that Deception ToolKit, which was made publicly available in source form in 1998, is still almost completely effective against automated intelligence tools attempting to detect vulnerabilities. It seems that the widely used attack tools are not yet being designed to detect and counter deception.

That is not to say that red teams and intelligence agencies are not beginning to look at this issue (Cohen, 1999b). For example, in private conversations with defenders against select elite red teams, the question often comes up of how to defeat the attackers when they undergo a substantial intelligence effort directed at defeating their attempts at deceptive defense. The answer is to increase the fidelity of the deception. This has associated costs, but as the attack tools designed to counter deception improve, so will the requirement for higher fidelity in deceptions.

## Effects of Deceptions on Human Attackers

Attackers facing deception defenses do not go unscathed, as indicated by early experiments. Negative impacts included reduction in group cohesion, reduced desire to participate in attack activities, reduced enjoyment of activities, increased backtracking even when not under deception, and reduction in performance levels (Cohen & Koike, 2004). There was even evidence that one high-quality attack team became unable to perform attacks after having been exposed to deception defenses. Even a year later they had problems carrying out effective attacks because they were constantly concerned that they might be under deception. In the later section of this chapter on experiments, more details are provided on these results. What appears to be clear at this time is that the cognitive mechanisms used for tactical deception are not the only mechanisms at play. Long-term effects of deception on a strategic level are not yet as well understood.

## Models of Deception of More Complex Systems

Larger cognitive systems can be modeled as being built up from smaller cognitive subsystems through some composition mechanism. Using these combined models we may analyze and create larger-scale deceptions. However, to date there is no really good theory of composition for these sorts of systems, and attempts to build theories of composition for security properties of even relatively simple computer networks have proven rather difficult. We can also take a top-down approach, but without the ability to link top-level objectives to bottom-level capabilities and without metrics for comparing alternatives, the problem space grows rapidly, and results cannot be compared meaningfully. Unfortunately, honeypots and decoys are not oriented toward group deceptions, so the work in this area does not apply to these systems.

### Criminal Honeypots and Decoys

Criminals have moved to the Internet environment in large numbers and use deception as a fundamental part of their efforts to commit crimes and conceal their identities from law enforcement. Although the specific examples are too numerous to list, there are some common threads, among them that the same criminal activities that have historically worked person to person are being carried out over the Internet with great success.

Identity theft is one of the more common deceptions based on attacking computers. In this case, computers are mined for data regarding an individual and that individual's identity is taken over by the criminal, who then commits crimes under the assumed name. Innocent victims of the identity theft are often blamed for the crimes until they prove themselves innocent. Honeypots are commonly used in these and similar deceptions.

Typically a criminal will create a honeypot to collect data on individuals and use a range of deceptive techniques to steer potential victims to the deception. Child exploitation is commonly carried out by creating friends under the fiction of being the same age and sex as the victim. Typically a 40-year-old pedophile will engage a child and entice the youngster into a meeting outside the home. In some cases there have been resulting kidnappings, rapes, and even murders. Some of these individuals create child-friendly sites or exploit friendly sites to lure in children.

Larger-scale deceptions have also been carried out over the Internet. For example, one of the common methods is to engage a set of "shills" in a chat room who make different contributions to the conversation but toward the same goal. These shills are a form of decoy. Although the chat room is generally promoted as being even handed and fair, the reality is that anyone who says something negative about a particular product or competitor will get lambasted. This has the social effect of causing distrust of the dissenter and furthering the goals of the product maker. The deception is that the seemingly independent members are really part of the same team, or in some cases, even the same person. In another example, a student at a California university invested in derivatives of a stock made false postings to a financial forum that drove down the stock price. The net effect was a multimillion-dollar profit for the student and the near collapse of the stock. This is another example of a decoy.

The largest-scale computer deceptions tend to be the result of computer viruses. Like the mass hysteria of a financial bubble, computer viruses can cause entire networks of computers to act as a rampaging group. The most successful viruses today use human behavioral characteristics to induce the operator to foolishly run the virus, which, on its own, could not reproduce. An attacker typically sends an e-mail with an infected program as an attachment. If the infected program is run, it then sends itself in e-mail to other users with whom this user communicates, and so forth. The deception is the method that convinces the user to run the infected program. To do this, the program might be given an enticing name, or the message may seem like it was really from a friend asking the user to look at something, or perhaps the program is simply masked so as to simulate a normal document.

## EXPERIMENTS AND THE NEED FOR AN EXPERIMENTAL BASIS

One of the more difficult things to accomplish in the deception arena is to conduct meaningful experiments. Although a few authors have published experimental results in information protection, far fewer have attempted to use meaningful social science methodologies in these experiments or to provide enough testing to understand real situations. This may be because of the difficulty and high cost of such experiments and the lack of funding and motivation for such efforts. There is a critical need for future work in this area.

If one thing is clear, it is the fact that too few experiments have been done to understand how deception works in defense of computer systems; more generally, too few controlled experiments have been done to understand the computer attack and defense processes and to characterize them. Without a better empirical basis, it will be hard to make scientific conclusions about such efforts. Although anecdotal data can be used to produce many interesting statistics, the scientific utility of those statistics is very limited because they tend to reflect only those examples that people thought worthy of calling out.

Repeatability is also an issue in experiments. Although the experiments carried out at Sandia were repeated readily, initial conditions in social experiments are not easy to attain. Even more important, nobody has apparently sought to do repetitions of experiments under similar conditions or with similar metrics. For example, some experiments to determine the effectiveness of address rotation were carried out, but the same methodologies were not used in the subsequent experiments, so no direct comparison could be undertaken. In many cases, the expectations of sponsors are that defenses will be perfect or they are not worth using. However, deception defenses are essentially never perfect nor can they ever be. They change the characteristics of the search space, but they do not make successful attack impossible. Another major problem is that many experiments tend to measure ill-defined things, presumably with the intent of proving a technique to be effective. Yet, experiments that are scientific in nature must seek to refute or confirm specific hypotheses, and they must be measured using some metric that can be fairly measured and independently reviewed.

## Experiments to Date

Since the time that the first results on honeypots were published, there have been only a very small number of published experiments. Although there have been hundreds of published experiments by scores of authors in the area of human deception, refereed articles on computer deception experiments can be counted on one hand.

### Experiments on Test Subjects at Sandia National Laboratories

Originally, a few examples of real-world effects of deception were provided (Cohen, 1999b), but no scientific studies of the effects of deception on test subjects were performed. Although there was a mathematical analysis of the statistics of deception in a networked environment, there was no empirical data to confirm or refute these results (Cohen, 1999a). Subsequent experiments (Cohen & Kroike, 20004; Cohen, Marin, Sappington, Stewart, & Thomas, 2001) produced a series of results that have not been independently verified, but appear to be accurate based on the available data. In these experiments, forensically sound images of systems and configurations were used to create repeatable configurations that were presented to groups of attackers.

These attack groups were given specific goals for their efforts, and the results were measured by several metrics using a combination of observation by experiment monitors, videotaping of sessions that were then analyzed, and

**Experiment 3 Attack Graph**

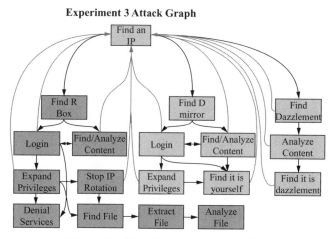

**Figure 4:** Experiment 3 attack graph.

forms that were filled out as individuals and then as a group at the end of each 4-hour session.

Attack progress was measured over time relative to an attack graph (Figure 4), with progress toward the deception light indicated as negative progress and progress toward the real objective dark indicated as positive progress. The experiments were all open ended and designed so that the attack group would never be able to complete the task but progress could still be measured. One result shows attackers not under deception and attackers under deception (Figure 5).

In the example provided here, the deception was extremely effective, but it was not as effective in all examples. Nevertheless, deception was shown to be very effective in all of the experiments, with attackers generally taking longer to make progress and making less progress over time under deception than attackers not under deception.

However, the results were far more interesting when a single experiment was repeated with the same groups for three weeks in a row. After the first week, one of the groups undergoing deception decided they did not wish to continue their work in this area. The experimenters allowed

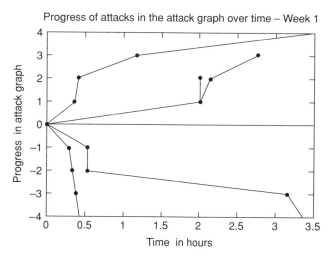

**Figure 5:** An example of one result in Experiment 3.

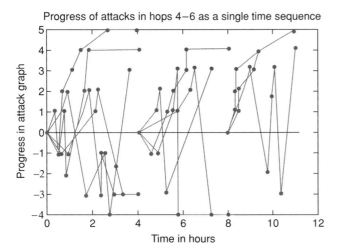

**Figure 6:** Progress of repetitions of experiment 4.

them to resign, thinking that this was to be expected after 4 straight weeks of 4-hour sessions. However, the next week, the same thing happened again with a second attack group undergoing deception. By the end of the third week of this sequence, of 25 original attackers—10 in two groups under no deception and 15 in three groups under deception—only 11 remained. Of the 11 remaining attackers, only 2 were under deception. Subsequent analysis of forms filled out by the groups and behavioral analysis of the motions and actions of individuals indicated that several psychological factors were present. Groups under deception started out enjoying the work equally with other groups, but ended up enjoying the work less, maintained less group cohesion, had reduced trust in leadership, and generally went slower and slower over time, despite the learning that was successful in improving progress over time for groups not under deception. These results seem to be consistent with those on learning in children for whom inconsistent feedback reduces performance.

### The HoneyNet Project

The HoneyNet Project (http://www.honeynet.org) is a substantial effort aimed at placing deception systems in the open environment to detect and track attack techniques. These deception systems have been largely effective in luring attackers. These lures are real systems placed on the Internet for the purpose of being attacked so that attack methods can be tracked and assessed. The only thing deceptive about them is that they are being watched more closely than would otherwise be apparent, and known faults are intentionally not being fixed to allow attacks to proceed. These lures are highly effective in allowing attackers to enter because they are extremely high-fidelity lures, but only for the purpose they are intended to provide. They do not, for example, include any user behaviors or content of interest. They are quite effective at creating sites that can be exploited for the attack of other sites.

For all of its potential benefit, however, the HoneyNet project has not performed any controlled experiments to understand the issues of deception effectiveness. In addition, over time the attackers appear to have learned about honeypots, and now many of them steer clear of them by using indicators of honeypot computers as differentiators

for their attacks. For example, they look for user presence in the computers and processes reminiscent of normal user behavior. These deceptions have not apparently been adapted quickly enough to ward off these attackers by simulating a user population.

### Red Teaming Experiments

Red teaming—finding vulnerabilities at the request of defenders (Cohen, 1998b)—has been performed by many groups for quite some time. The advantage of red teaming is that it provides a relatively realistic example of an attempted attack. The disadvantage is that it tends to be somewhat artificial and reflective of only a single run at the problem. Real systems get attacked over time by a wide range of attackers with different skill sets and approaches. Although many red teaming exercises have been performed, they tend not to provide the scientific data desired in the area of defensive deceptions because they have not historically been oriented toward this sort of defense.

Several red teaming experiments against simplistic defenses were performed under a DARPA research grant in 2000; these showed that sophisticated red teams were able to detect and defeat simplistic deceptions rapidly. These experiments were performed in a proximity-only case and used static deceptions of the same sort as provided by Deception ToolKit. As a result this was a best-case scenario for the attackers. Unfortunately, the experimental technique and data from these experiments were poor, and there were inadequate funding and attention paid to detail. Defenders apparently failed even to provide false traffic for these conditions, a necessity in creating effective deceptions against proximate attackers and a technique that was used in the Sandia experiments when proximate or enveloped attackers were in use. Only distant attacker models can possibly be effective under these conditions. Nevertheless, these results should be viewed as a cautionary note about the use of low-quality deceptions against high-quality attackers and should lead to further research into the range of effectiveness of different methods for different situations.

### RAND Experiments

War games played out by the armed services tend to ignore information system attacks because the exercises are quite expensive and successfully attacking information systems with their command-and-control capabilities defeats many of the other purposes of these war games. Although many recognize the importance of portraying effects realistically, we could say the same thing about nuclear weapons, but that does not justify dropping them on our forces for the practice value.

The most definitive experiments to date on the effectiveness of low-quality computer deceptions against high-quality computer-assisted human attackers were performed by RAND (Gerwehr et al., 2000). Their experiments with fairly generic deceptions operating against high-quality intelligence agency attackers demonstrated substantial effectiveness for short periods of time. These results imply that under certain conditions (i.e., short time frames, high tension, no predisposition to consider deceptions, etc.) these deceptions may be effective.

## Experiments We Believe Are Needed at This Time

The total number of controlled experimental runs to date involving deception in computer networks seems to be less than 50, and the number involving the use of deceptions for defense is limited to the 10 or so from the RAND study and 35 from the Sandia studies. Furthermore, the RAND studies did not use control groups or other methods to differentiate the effectiveness of deceptions. Clearly there is not enough experimental data to gain much in the way of knowledge, and just as clearly, many more experiments are required to gain a sound understanding of the issues underlying deception for defense.

The clear solution to this dilemma is the creation of a set of experiments that use social science methodologies to create, run, and evaluate a substantial set of parameters that will provide a better understanding, specific metrics, and accurate results in this area. For these experiments to be effective, we must not only create defenses but also come to understand how attackers work and think. For this reason, we need to create red teaming experiments in which we study both the attackers and the effects of defenses on the attackers. In addition, to isolate the effects of deception, we need to create control groups and experiments with double-blinded data collection. Although the Sandia studies had those features and their results are interesting, they are not adequate to draw strong or statistically valid conclusions, particularly in light of the results from subsequent DARPA studies without these controls.

## SUMMARY, CONCLUSIONS, AND FURTHER WORK

This chapter has summarized a great deal of information on the history of honeypots and decoys for use in the defense of computer systems. Although there is a great deal to know about how deception has been used in the past, it seems quite clear that there will be far more to know about deception in the future. The information protection field has an increasingly pressing need for innovations that change the balance between attack and defense. It is clear from what we already know that deception techniques have the demonstrated ability to increase attacker workload and reduce attacker effectiveness while decreasing defender effort required for detection and providing substantial increases in defender understanding of attacker capabilities and intent.

Modern defensive computer deceptions are in their infancy, but they are moderately effective, even in this simplistic state. The necessary breakthrough that will turn these basic deception techniques and technologies into viable long-term defenses is the linkage of social sciences research with technical development. Specifically, we need to measure the effects and known characteristics of deceptions on the systems comprised of people and their information technology to understand and exploit the psychological and physiological bases for the effectiveness of deceptions. The empirical basis for effective deception in other arenas is simply not available in the information protection arena today, and to attain it, there is a crying need for extensive experimentation in this arena.

To a large extent this work has been facilitated by the extensive literature on human and animal deception that has been generated over a long period of time. In recent years, the experimental evidence has accumulated to the point where there is general agreement in the part of the scientific community that studies deception about many of the underlying mechanisms, the character of deception, the issues in deception detection, and the facets that require further research. These same results and experimental techniques need to be applied to deception for information protection if we are to design effective and reliable deceptions.

To make progress, the most critical work is the systematic study of the effectiveness of deception techniques against combined systems with people and computers. This goes hand in hand with experiments on how to counter deceptions and the theoretical and practical limits of deceptions and deception technologies. In addition, codification of prior rules of engagement, the creation of simulation systems and expert systems for analysis of deceptions sequences, and a wide range of related work would clearly be beneficial as a means to apply the results of experiments once empirical results are available.

## GLOSSARY

**Dazzlement** A display intended to cause cognitive dissonance.
**Deception** Signal induction or suppression designed to cause cognitive errors in the target.
**Decoy** A deception intended to temporarily distract an attacker from the target.
**Honeypot** A deception system intended to be attacked.
**Perception Management** The exploitation of cognitive processes to control perceptions of the target.
**Steganography** Hidden writing (from Latin). Typically designed to conceal the presence of content.

## CROSS REFERENCES

See *Active Response to Computer Intrusions; Hackers, Crackers, and Computer Criminals; Intrusion Detection Systems Basics; Network Attacks.*

## REFERENCES

Castelfranhi, C., Falcone, R., & de Rosis, F. (1998). *Deceiving in GOLEM: How to strategically pilfer help.* Retrieved from http://www.istc.cnr.it/T3/download/aamas1998/Castelfranchi-et-alii.pdf
Cheswick, B., Bellovin, S., D'Angelo, D., & Glick, P. (1991, September). An evening with Berferd. *Proceedings of the Third Usenix UNIX Security Symposium.*
Cialdini, R. B. (2001). *Influence: Science and practice.* Boston: Allyn and Bacon.
Cohen, F. (1992). Operating system protection through program evolution. *Computers and Security.*
Cohen, F. (1996a, July). Internet holes—Internet lightning rods. *Network Security Magazine.*
Cohen, F. (1996b). A note on distributed coordinated attacks. *Computers and Security.*

Cohen, F. (1998a, March). *Deception Toolkit*. Retrieved from http://www.all.net/

Cohen, F. (1998b, March). Red teaming and other aggressive auditing techniques. *Managing Network Security*.

Cohen, F. (1999a). *A mathematical structure of simple defensive network deceptions*. Retrieved from http://www.all.net (InfoSec Baseline Studies)

Cohen, F. (1999b). A note on the role of deception in information protection. *Computers and Security, 18*(6). 479–518. Retrieved from http://www.ingentaconnect.com/content/els/01674048/1999/00000018/00000006

Cohen, F. (2000a, July). Managing network security: What does it do behind your back? *Network Security Management Magazine*.

Cohen, F. (2000b, October). *Method and apparatus for network deception/emulation* (No. PCT/US00/31295). Wahington, DC: International Patent Application.

Cohen, F. (2000c, May). *The structure of intrusion and intrusion detection*. Retrieved from http://www.all.net/ (InfoSec Baseline Studies)

Cohen, F. (2001). *Responder manual*. Retrieved from http:/www. /all.net/ (White Glove Distributions).

Cohen, F., & Koike, D. (2003, January). *Errors in the perception of computer-related information*. Retrieved from http://www.all.net/journal/deception/Errors/Errors.html

Cohen, F., & Koike, D. (2004, June). *Leading attackers through attack graphs with deceptions*. Retrieved from http://www.all.net/journal/deception/Agraph/Agraph.html

Cohen, F., Lambert, D., Preston, C., Berry, N., Stewart, C., & Thomas, E. (2001). *A framework for deception*. Retrieved from http://www. all.net/ (Deception for Protection)

Cohen, F., Marin, I., Sappington, J., Stewart, C., & Thomas, E. (2001). *Red teaming experiments with deception technologies*. Retrieved from http:/lwww/all.net/journal/deception/experiments/experiments.html

Deutsch, D. (1995). *Musical illusions and paradoxes*. La Jolla, CA: Philomel.

Faron, F. (1998). *Rip-off: A writer's guide to crimes of deception*. Cincinnati: Writers Digest Books.

Fellows, B. (2000). *Easily fooled*. Minneapolis: Mind Matters.

Gerwehr, S., Rothenberg, J., & Anderson, R. H. (1999, October). *An arsenal of deceptions for INFOSEC (OUO)* (PM-1167-NSA). Santa Monica, CA: RAND National Defense Research Institute Project Memorandum.

Gerwehr, S., Weissler, R., Medby, J. J., Anderson, R. H., & Rothenberg, J. (2000, November). *Employing deception in information systems to thwart adversary reconnaissance-phase activities (OUO)* (PM-1124-NSA). Santa Monica, CA: RAND National Defense Research Institute.

Gilovich, T. (1991). *How we know what isn't so: The fallibility of human reason in everyday life*. New York: Free Press.

Greene, R. (1998). *The 48 laws of power*. New York: Penguin Books.

Handy, C. (1993). *Understanding organizations*. New York: Oxford University Press.

Heuer, R. J., Jr. (1999). *Psychology of intelligence analysis*. Langley, VA: History Staff Center for the Study of Intelligence, Central Intelligence Agency.

Hoffman, D. D. (1998). *Visual intelligence: How we create what we see*. New York: Norton.

Kahn, D. (1967). *The code breakers*. New York: Macmillan Press.

Karrass, C. R. (1970). *The negotiating game*. New York: Thomas A. Crowell.

Lambert, D. (1987, October). *A cognitive model for exposition of human deception and counter-deception* (NOSC Tech. Rep. 1076).

Michael, J. B., Rowe, N. C., Rothstein, H. S., Auguston, M., Drusinsky, D., & Riehle, R. D. (2002, December). *Phase I report on intelligent software decoys: Technical feasibility and institutional issues in the context of homeland security*. Monterey, CA: Naval Postgraduate School.

National Research Council. (1998). *Modeling human and organizational behavior*. Washington, DC: National Academy Press.

Robertson, R. J., & Powers, W. T. (Eds.). (1990). *Introduction to modern psychology: The control-theory view*. Gravel Switch, KY: The Control Systems Group, Inc.

Seckel, S. (2000). *The art of optical illusions*. Carlton Books.

Sun Tzu. (1983). *The art of war* (J. Clavell, Trans.). New York: Dell Publishing.

Vrij, A. (2000). *Detecting lies and deceit*. New York: Wiley.

Weiner, N. (1954). *Cybernetics*.

West, C. K. (1981). *The social and psychological distortion of information*. Chicago: Nelson-Hall.

Whitlock, C. (1997). *Scam school*. New York: MacMillan.

## FURTHER READING

Chandler, D. (2001). *Personal home pages and the construction of identities on the Web*.

Cohen, F. (1998, April). The unpredictability defense. *Managing Network Security*.

Cohen, F. (1999). Simulating cyber attacks, defenses, and consequences. *Computers and Security*.

Cohen, F. (2000, August). Understanding viruses biologically. *Network Security Magazine*.

Cohen, F. *A theory of strategic games with uncommon objectives*

Cohen, F., Phillips, C., Swiler, L. P. Gaylor, T., Leary, P., Rupley, F., et al. (1999). A preliminary classification scheme for information system threats, attacks, and defenses: A cause and effect model and some analysis based on that model. In *The encyclopedia of computer science and technology*.

Danial, D., & Herbig, K. (Eds.). (1992). *Strategic military deception*. New York: Pergamon Books.

Dunnigan, J. F., &. Nofi, A. A. (1995). *Victory and deceit: Dirty tricks at war*. New York: William Morrow and Co.

Dewar, M. (1989). *The art of deception in warfare*. David and Charles Military Books.

Huber, R. E. (1983, September–October). Information warfare: Opportunity born of necessity. *Systems Technology, IX*(5), 14–21.

Hughes-Wilson, J. (1999). *Military intelligence blunders*. New York: Carol & Graf.

Ito, M. (1993). *Cybernetic fantasies: Extended selfhood in a virtual community*.

Kalbfleisch, P. J. (1994, December). The language of detecting deceit. *Journal of Language & Social Psychology, 13*(4), 469–487.

Keegan, J. (1993). *A history of warfare*. New York: Vintage Books.

Knowledge Systems Corporation. (1987, December). *C3CM Planning Analyzer: Functional description (draft) first update* (RADC/COAD Contract F30602-87-C-0103). Cary, NC: Author.

Mackay, C. (1989). *Extraordinary popular delusions and the madness of crowds*. West Conshohocken, PA: Templeton Publications.

Mitchell, R. W., & Thompson, N. S. (1986). *Deception: Perspectives on human and nonhuman deceit*. Albany, NY: SUNY Press.

National Technical Baseline. (1996, December). *Intrusion detection and response*. Albuquerque, NM: Lawrence Livermore National Laboratory, Sandia National Laboratories.

Peace, M. (2000). *A chat room ethnography*, Ph.D. diss.

Pekarske, B. (1990, September). Restoration in a flash—Using DS3 cross-connects, telephony.

Ratey, J. J. (2001). *A user's guide to the brain*. New York: Pantheon Books.

SSCSD. *Tactical decisionmaking under stress*. SPAWAR Systems Center.

Stein, G. (1993). *Encyclopedia of hoaxes*. Farmington Hills, MI: Gale Research, Inc.

Vanderheiden, H. (n.d.). *Gender swapping on the Net?* Retrieved from http://web.aq.org/~tigris/loci-virtualtherapy.html

Western Systems Coordinating Council. (1996, August). *WSCC Preliminary System Disturbance Report Aug 10, 1996—DRAFT*. Salt Lake City: Author.

Whaley, B. (1969). *Stratagem: Deception and surprise in war*. Cambridge, MA: MIT Center for International Studies.

Wilson, A. (1968). *The bomb and the computer*. New York: Delacorte Press.

# Active Response to Computer Intrusions

David Dittrich, *University of Washington*
Kenneth Einar Himma, *Seattle Pacific University*

## INTRODUCTION: THE CONCEPT OF ACTIVE RESPONSE

The *active response continuum* defines a category of digital response to unauthorized digital intrusions[1] and hence falls within a wide spectrum of potential responses by private entities.[2] At one end of the spectrum is the wholly passive, unknowing victim who relies entirely on just the inherent capabilities of the software that comes with the computer he or she purchased and who does not know when it is being attacked. At the other is the active, fully engaged victim who deliberately pursues a series of discrete tactics with a set of well-defined objectives in mind. As the term *active* indicates, active response measures fall toward the latter end of the spectrum.

As defined in this chapter, measures falling within the active response continuum have the following characteristics. First, these measures are, of course, digitally based; physically assaulting someone who is committing a digital trespass would not be an instance of active response. Second, they are reactive in the sense that they are implemented following detection of an unwanted digital intrusion and are intended to counter the intrusion; as such, they are contrived to serve investigative, defensive, or punitive purposes. Third, they are noncooperative in at least the minimal sense of being implemented without the consent of at least one of the parties involved in or affected by the intrusion. Finally, they usually have causal impacts on remote systems (i.e., those owned or controlled by some other person). These tactics range from more benign information-gathering measures (e.g., tracebacks) that have an impact on remote systems without impairing their ongoing operations and functions to more aggressive measures (e.g., denial of service counterattacks) expressly intended to inhibit or even stop the operations and functions of remote systems.

At an intuitive level, the definition of *active response* attempts to pick out digital acts that would be characterized as hacking if performed without provocation. Theorists and policymakers have become concerned with the phenomena discussed in this chapter precisely because of their resemblance to hacker attacks; it is, for this reason, that active response measures are sometimes referred to as *counterhacking* or *hacking back*. Although the definition of active response picks out some acts (e.g., scanning ports) that are not fairly characterized as hacking, even those acts are minimally intrusive. Indeed, although they might very well be morally justified all things considered, they raise, at least initially, the same sorts of privacy and property concerns that are raised by acts that *are* fairly characterized as hacking.

The definition also attempts to incorporate the idea that these measures are taken in response to an unauthorized intrusion. The idea that such measures are reactive implies that measures intended to detect the occurrence of an intrusion do not fall within the active response continuum. Reactive measures, as defined previously, are deliberately contrived as a response to an intrusion that has previously been detected—though it is true, of course, that detection and response might sometimes proceed together as the intrusion continues.

Although many measures taken in response to computer intrusions fall within the active response

---

[1] Other terms used to pick out such measures are *active defense, counterhacking,* and *hacking back.*

[2] This chapter is limited to private intrusion responses. The response by public entities to digital intrusions raises very different technical, ethical, and legal issues.

continuum, not all do. Measures reasonably calculated to stop either an ongoing attack or the harm it is causing are typically characterized as defensive; however, active response measures can serve a variety of purposes that are not, strictly speaking, defensive in either of these respects. For example, information-gathering efforts can be related to efforts to adopt measures calculated to stop an attack or its harmful effects, but they can also be directed at providing law enforcement agencies with sufficient evidence to prosecute culpable parties. In addition, some measures characterized as active response are motivated by a desire to punish or retaliate against an attack—with little regard for whether such measures actually bring about its cessation. Accordingly, although active response tactics are sometimes adopted for defensive purposes, they are also frequently adopted for investigatory and offensive purposes—and, indeed, can be employed in ongoing information warfare.[3]

Thus conceived, measures falling within the active response continuum are compatible with the efforts of law enforcement agencies to investigate and prosecute computer crimes. As is readily apparent, efforts by private victims to gather and preserve information about the attack can assist law enforcement efforts to investigate and prosecute an attack. Such information can provide not only helpful investigatory leads but can also form the foundation for the evidentiary base needed to prosecute culpable parties successfully.

Even so, it is worth emphasizing at the outset that active response measures are increasingly adopted by private firms as a substitute for involving law enforcement agencies. There are a variety of reasons for this practice. First, the resources available to law enforcement agencies for responding to digital intrusions have simply not kept pace with the frequency and severity of digital intrusions. The perceived decreasing success rate of law enforcement has led to a sense among private victims that it is far more efficient to respond without involving law enforcement. Second, and equally important, many commercial victims worry about the effects that publicizing an attack might have on their relationships with customers. The concern is that their customers would become alarmed after learning of security breaches and would ultimately respond by taking their business elsewhere. Therefore, such firms believe that the best way to minimize the risk of publicity and such deleterious effects is to respond internally to digital intrusions without involving law enforcement.

This chapter provides an overview of the active response continuum and considers the morality and legality of such tactics. It defines various levels of intrusion response in relation to the level of the victim's conscious involvement and posture, describes various technical barriers to active responses and the various ways in which law enforcement might be involved, characterizes active response measures along a spectrum ranging from benign to aggressive measures, and considers the ethicality and legality of responses falling along that spectrum.

It is important to keep in mind that the topic of active response is a novel one, with an academic and popular literature that is exceedingly small compared to the literature available for other security-related topics. As such, many of the descriptive and normative issues are currently being worked out by theoreticians and practitioners. As one might expect, then, theoreticians and practitioners disagree on a number of these issues. Such disagreements are not limited, however, to the usual ethical disagreements; they also encompass the descriptive classificatory claims that seek to distinguish the various levels and characteristics of active response.[4]

For this reason, the analysis in this chapter should not be considered the final word on any of the issues considered herein. As the topic of active response continues to attract more interest from practitioners, theoreticians, and ultimately lawmakers, one should expect that new descriptive taxonomies will emerge that may well change the normative landscape—changes that undoubtedly will result in changes in the content of existing law. Even so, this chapter is intended to provide a plausible conceptual and normative foundation for understanding the descriptive, ethical, and legal issues of active response and to enable the reader to follow the conversation as it evolves.

# LEVELS OF INTRUSION RESPONSE

As a first step toward understanding active response, it is important to get a sense of the range of potential responses to digital intrusions. At least five different levels of intrusion response can be distinguished along a spectrum according to the degree of the victim's deliberative engagement.[5] The spectrum begins at Level 0 where the victim has almost no knowledge of the intrusion and is hence wholly unengaged and ends at Level 4 where the victim is fully engaged and is acting independently of other involved parties (Table 1). Active response occurs primarily at this fourth level, which is itself divided into sublevels defining a subspectrum that progresses from less intrusive to more intrusive, less risky to more risky, and less disruptive to more disruptive sublevels of involvement.

## Level 0—Unaware

The defining attribute of a Level 0 response is the utter lack of involvement of the attack victim: the victim has no knowledge of the intrusion and takes no action whatsoever. At Level 0, the victim (construed to include both the owner/operator of the computer system and the organization to which he or she reports) takes no active role in responding either directly or indirectly to an ongoing attack. Indeed, at Level 0, the victim does not so much as

---

[3] For a general discussion of information warfare, see "Wireless Information Warfare" in this *Handbook*.

[4] This is because both the concept and the class of phenomena it attempts to pick out are novel; for this reason, there are simply no established conventions governing the use of the concept-term *active response*. Accordingly, the concept is likely to evolve as researchers identify more salient features shared by measures plausibly characterized as active response.

[5] We are indebted to attendees at the First Agora Workshop on Active Defense for this taxonomy and supporting analysis. The Agora, an information security group in Seattle, Washington, founded and led by Kirk Bailey (currently University of Washington CISO), has held three workshops on the topic of active response, the first of which was held in June 8, 2001. Much of the terminology and description of the active response continuum here was derived by workshop participants through the assistance of Captain Jake Schaffner (USN Ret.), who co-moderated this first workshop with Nick Multari.

**Table 1.** Levels of Intrusion Response

| Level | Victim Posture | Characteristic Actions |
|-------|----------------|------------------------|
| 0 | Unaware | None: Passive reliance on inherent software capabilities |
| 1 | Involved | Uses and maintains antivirus software and personal firewalls |
| 2 | Interactive | Modifies software and hardware in response to detected threats |
| 3 | Cooperative | Implements joint tracebacks with other affected parties |
| 4 | Noncooperative (active response) | Implements invasive tracebacks, cease-and-desist measures, and retaliatory counterstrikes |

even augment or alter the defensive capabilities inherent in the hardware, firmware, and/or software as delivered from the manufacturer or installer.

An example of a Level 0 response is the typical home-broadband customer who purchases a computer through a retail outlet and knows very little about security issues or technologies. These naïve users pay little, if any, attention to patches, antivirus software, settings on Web browsers, and have no comprehension of plaintext password and other vulnerabilities. Such users lack the ability to discover when their computers are compromised by worms or viruses. In the event of an intrusion of some sort, they simply continue to operate their computers as usual.

This category of user is a common target for attackers wishing either to (1) retain anonymity through the use of stepping stones or proxies; (2) install malicious software that permits remote control of the computer for use in distributed attacks or intrusions (e.g., distributed denial of service attacks or distributed spam transmission); or (3) steal disk space for storage of stolen content (e.g., pirated software, data stolen from other compromised hosts, and as a cache for malicious software).

## Level 1—Involved

Level 1 responses involve minimal engagement on the part of the victim. The victim establishes (either directly or via proxy) a day-to-day defensive posture involving only resources within his or her ownership or operational control. Such resources may include (1) use and maintenance (i.e., updating to keep current) of commercial antivirus products; (2) use of personal firewall software to limit remote access to services installed as part of the operating system (e.g., Windows System Message Block and NetBIOS name services); or (3) use of a hardware firewall between the network attach point and hosts in a local area network (e.g., a home LAN on a broadband cable). At this level, there is little interaction between the victim and the operations of these resources.

Level 1 responses are fairly characterized as passive, prophylactic, and silent. They are prophylactic in the sense that they are intended primarily to prevent attacks and do little to respond in an efficacious manner when an attack is detected. They are silent in the sense that the victim receives little input from the operation of these resources; for example, victims at this level might not even have set up an antivirus program to alert them when a virus is detected. They are passive in the sense that the victim does not actively respond in any thoughtful way

to the discovery of an intrusion. Even in instances where antivirus software alerts victims to a threat of some kind, their response at this level is usually limited to accepting, without any significant deliberation, the recommendations made by the antivirus software for cleanup.

## Level 2—Interactive

This level is characterized by the beginning of an active engagement with the threat. At Level 2, victims respond to evidence of an intrusion by taking minimally deliberative measures to modify resources under their ownership or control. A minimal Level 2 response, for example, may involve adjusting the security settings on a personal firewall to respond to a specific kind of detected threat—perhaps configuring software to ignore pings. A more fully engaged Level 2 response may involve looking up domain registry information for the Internet protocol (IP) of the "attacking system"[6] and reporting the attempted intrusion or actual compromise to the site that owns this IP. In some cases, the victim at this level may go so far as to report these events to incident coordination sites, such as CERT/CC,[7] and/or to law enforcement.

Though Level 2 responses actively engage the threat in some way, the extent of engagement is comparatively unsophisticated. These victims make little effort to investigate the intrusion or to perform a forensic analysis of compromised hosts and are content to rely on others to take action (e.g., the victim's incident response team or law enforcement agencies). At this level, victims typically respond to a successful intrusion by formatting the drive and reinstalling the operating system.

## Level 3—Cooperative

Level 3 is distinguished from lower levels in that it involves an attempt on the part of victims to reach out beyond those resources owned or operated by them. At Level 3, the victim attempts to enlist the cooperation of other organizations/systems in taking joint measures intended to attribute, mitigate, or eliminate the threat. It is important to note that the causal effects of action at

---

[6] Typically, the attacking site is the last hop in a potential chain of stepping stones located at a distance from the culpable source of the attack.

[7] On its Web page, CERT/CC is described as "a major reporting center for Internet security problems. Staff members provide technical advice and coordinate responses to security compromises, identify trends in intruder activity, work with other security experts to identify solutions to security problems, and disseminate information to the broad community" (see http://www.cert.org/).

this level extend for the first time beyond the victim's own resources.

There are a variety of Level 3 responses available to victims. Victims can, for example, identify an attacking site either by using domain registry information or by tracing the routing path to the site. Victims can then contact the attacking site itself or the upstream provider (e.g., in cases where it is suspected that the attacking site is potentially hostile, under the attacker's control, or unresponsive to previous communications). When contacting the attacking site or upstream provider, the victim may seek to share information about the intrusion, preserve critical information, or request that the other site contact local law enforcement agencies.

The efficacy of a Level 3 response obviously depends on quality cooperation from essential parties. For example, a successful Level 3 traceback is possible only if each of the parties acts with proper speed and shares needed information with other parties (and with law enforcement).

A coordinated cooperative response, however, is not always easy to achieve. Such a response is less likely when parties (1) are unable to get in touch with each other, (2) do not speak the same language, (3) have different skill levels, or (4) have different understandings of what is occurring and how best to respond. Any one of these inhibiting factors can contribute to an ineffective response and hence to a situation where the attacker is essentially unimpeded and at little risk of being caught.

A final important point to understand is that a multisite intrusion will not be entirely resolved, taking all compromised systems out of the hands of the attacker(s) unless *each and every site involved* is able to effectively work at Level 3, identifying all compromised hosts within their own network boundaries and doing so at roughly the same time. If this cannot be achieved, sites that have "cleaned up" can be and often are, immediately re-compromised by way of exploitation of trust relationships at sites that have not yet cleaned up. These trust relationships were the vector for compromise in the first place and are very difficult to entirely identify and clean up adequately, which leads to multisite intrusions sometimes lasting several months. (In some cases, compromised hosts are never identified and cleaned up.)

## Level 4—Noncooperative

A Level 4 response is characterized by deliberately unilateral steps—that is, without cooperative support from other parties—to identify, mitigate, or eliminate the threat by means that involve causal interaction with remote systems. These steps might be taken against an uncooperative perpetrator; or they might be taken against an organization or system that could (if cooperative) attribute, mitigate, or eliminate the threat. Such steps include noncooperative intelligence gathering, noncooperative "cease-and-desist" measures, counterstrikes designed to retaliate against attackers and deter future attacks, and preemptive measures.

### Noncooperative Intelligence Gathering

Noncooperative intelligence gathering involves unilateral attempts by one victim site to gather information from another victim site without the latter's permission by means that might be regarded as intrusive. For example, victims can scan ports in an attempt to obtain information from enabled and non-access-controlled services on the attacking host, such as Windows NetBIOS information (e.g., host name, Windows domain, login accounts, and services enabled), NFS mount points, process information, and last login information. Though there is controversy about whether port scans should be characterized as intrusive, many persons feel they impinge privacy and hence would regard them as intrusive—whether rightly or wrongly.

Noncooperative intelligence gathering can cause conflicts among victim sites. Suppose, for example, that site A takes it upon itself to scan the network of site B, attempting, say, to identify back doors or similar systems to those compromised at site A. Even if A attempts to cooperate with B by providing it with the results of the analysis to help B improve its understanding of the attack, B might still consider A's action objectionably intrusive if B feels its privacy has been threatened.

Such measures can also have the unintended effect of providing useful information to the attacker. If the attacker notices that A is scanning an attacked system, the attacker may respond by attempting to eliminate evidence of his or her presence in the system by deleting files and re-initializing hosts being used as stepping stones (including routers.) The effects of noncooperative measures in such circumstances not only make it more difficult to identify the attacker but can also result in further damage to the compromised system if the attacker deletes valuable files.

### Noncooperative Cease-and-Desist Measures

Noncooperative cease-and-desist measures are contrived to stop an attack by rendering the attacking machines inoperable and, hence, unlike the measures previously discussed, are intended to have a causal impact on someone else's computers in a direct and functional way. For example, a victim might attempt to shut off distributed denial of service (DDoS) agents by using vulnerabilities in those programs to inject commands or by targeting known vulnerabilities (e.g., the Windows RPC/DCOM vulnerability exploited by the MSBlast and Nachi worms) in ways that cause infected systems to crash. Noncooperative cease-and-desist measures, then, are expressly contrived to impair the operation and functioning of remote systems, causally affecting them in a much more intrusive way than the measures discussed previously.

### Retribution or Counterstrike

Retributive or counterstrike measures are fairly characterized as the most aggressive active-response tactics. As the name suggests, these measures are contrived to retaliate against attacking machines by inflicting something that is likely to be perceived as damage or harm of some kind by the attacker (or unknowing agents). The structure of a counterstrike may mirror the structure of the attack or it may differ in key respects. However, in every case, the immediate point is to inflict harm and is usually motivated ultimately by a desire to either stop or punish the attack. Like noncooperative cease-and-desist measures, retributive counterstrikes are intended to have a causal impact on the operations and functioning of remote systems.

There have been many cases where victims have responded to an attack by counterattacking the suspected attacker. A few years ago, for example, e-hippies launched a denial of service (DoS) attack on WTO servers hosted by Conxion.[8] Conxion responded by redirecting the incoming packets back to the attacking network (Radcliff, 2000a). The counterstrike succeeded in stopping the attack and is fairly characterized as defensive in part, but it was also partly punitive because Conxion could have ended the attack by simply dropping the packets at the router.

Though Conxion's counterstrike succeeded in ending the attack, it is generally imprudent (i.e., likely to harm one's own interests)[9] to respond to an attack with such aggressive measures. First, such measures are more likely to escalate a conflict than end it. Someone who initiates an attack is likely to respond to a counterattack with more force if it can be mustered. Unfortunately, even novice hackers can find a way to deploy a substantial number of machines (either by getting direct control over them or by enlisting the help of other parties) to stage large-scale DDoS attacks. In such cases, the numbers of hosts attacking the victim site may number in the tens of thousands,[10] significantly complicating incident response.

Second, as is discussed in more detail herein, such measures are of highly dubious legality. Shutting down attacking hosts is a heavy-handed measure that can have negative consequences that require a significant expenditure of resources on the part of the sites who own the hosts being attacked. In an increasingly litigious international culture, the unwanted cost of such measures might be expensive legal action against *you* for taking aggressive action.

### Preemptive Response

A recent development in the law of Singapore suggests the possibility of taking *legal* action to preempt an attack before it is staged. In November 2003, Singapore enacted changes to its Computer Misuse Act that allow the government to take preemptive action against hackers. The old law, as with computer-abuse statutes in every other nation, allowed authorities to act only after a hacker had committed a crime. The changes to Singapore's law allow the Singapore government to take unspecified actions to prevent an imminent attack by hackers against critical national infrastructures, imposing a maximum of three years in jail or a fine of up to 10,000 Singapore dollars (US$5,750) if convicted of preparing to stage a digital attack.[11]

Public preemptive response poses a host of practical difficulties. The state must have sufficient intelligence capabilities to be able to detect and identify potential attacks accurately before they are staged. These capabilities are, of course, very expensive to maintain and deploy,[12] but also have a variety of other social costs. For example, the public may perceive a decrease in its personal privacy without a reasonable increase in security against terrorist actions. Further, law enforcement agencies may begin arresting the wrong people, negatively affecting the overall law enforcement effort, as well as diminishing the public's sense that it is treated fairly and justly by law enforcement agencies.

## POTENTIAL TECHNICAL BARRIERS FOR INTRUSION RESPONSE

Several factors can complicate efforts to implement an effective response to a digital intrusion. First, digital evidence is somewhat less durable than material evidence, complicating efforts to understand an attack and identify its ultimate source. Second, the victim must understand the structure of an attack to determine an appropriate response. Third, digital attackers have a variety of sophisticated tools for effectively concealing their identities and frustrating efforts by victims to understand an attack.

### Volatility of Digital Information

In *Guidelines for Evidence Collection and Archiving*, Dominique Brezinski and Tom Killalea (2002) elaborate several "best practices" for collecting information during an intrusion that take into account the durability of digital evidence. In particular, they recommend attempting to collect information according to "order of volatility"; that is, collecting information in order of durability starting, of course, with the information that is least durable. Brezinski and Killalea characterize the following sources of information in a hierarchy from most to least volatile:

- registers, cache
- routing table, ARP cache (host route information), process table, kernel statistics, memory
- temporary file systems
- disk
- remote logging and monitoring data that are relevant to the system in question
- physical configuration, network topology
- archival media

Understanding this order is important in considering an active response because much of the data needed by the victim to understand an attack are extremely volatile. For example, an analysis of network flows and actual packets, which are at the top of the hierarchy, is crucial to understanding the structure and methodology of an intrusion.

---

[8] *Hack back*, by Deborah Radcliff, Network World, 05/29/00, http://www.nwfusion.com/

[9] Prudential considerations are distinct from ethical or legal considerations—though they may overlap. What is in one's self-interest may not be either ethical or legal, and conversely.

[10] A Scotland Yard detective has stated that "small groups of young people creating a resource out of a 10,000- to 30,000-strong computer [bot] network are renting them out to anybody who has the money" (Scotland Yard, 2004).

[11] There exist no other comparable laws at the time of writing, and it is not clear under what circumstances a justification could be made that taking

preemptive action against an attacker by government or private sector owner/operators was warranted.

[12] Typically, these resources are only available at the highest levels within federal level law enforcement agencies, and at that level only a very few high-priority cases can be handled at one time.

## Understanding Attack Methodology

A victim of a digital attack cannot mount an appropriate response of any kind beyond Level 1 without having some understanding of the attack's structure and methodology. Even an effective interactive response (Level 2) requires some understanding of the basic characteristics of the attack; a victim cannot modify software and hardware in a genuinely responsive way without understanding the attack's methodology and structure.[13] Similarly, a victim cannot implement an appropriate Level 4 response without understanding the attack; one cannot determine whether a response is both legally permissible and likely to meet legitimate objectives without some such understanding.

In addition to understanding the attack methodology and structure, there are other skills and resources required to engage in a meaningful and complete defense. It is important to have an up-to-minute "view of the battle space" to see how it changes during the conflict. Advanced attacks typically require reconnaissance of the network and take advantage of knowledge about the network topology and trust relationships between hosts of which most defenders are unaware.[14] For example, a defender may have two options for obtaining a piece of information about the attack, one that is detectable by the attacker and one that is not. If the defender is not aware that there are two options or unknowingly chooses the detectable option, thinking it to be the only appropriate one, the attacker may learn of the defender's pursuit and avoid the defensive action, return through remaining back doors, and possibly do significant damage as he or she "bugs out" of the network.

## Attribution

Preparing an active response that is both appropriate and likely to be efficacious depends on identifying both the immediate (i.e., innocent agents) and ultimate (i.e., culpable attacker) sources of an attack; that is, it depends on an accurate "attribution" of the attack to all the parties that are responsible either immediately or ultimately for the attack. Accurate attribution is obviously important because the responses by the military, the intelligence community, federal law enforcement, and the business community will differ radically depending on who is responsible for the attack.

Unfortunately, attribution can be extremely difficult. First, there are always a large number of possible culprits in any substantial Internet attack. The ultimate source of an attack could be (1) an unskilled "script-kiddie" using ready-made tools he or she downloaded from the Web, (2) a "black hat by night" employee of a large security company trying to increase market demand for his or her company's products, (3) a nation-state actor developing and testing an information warfare capability, (4) a spammer's hired gun who is trying to attack those who want to end spam or who is trying to establish a massive spam delivery network of compromised hosts, or (5) a terrorist organization trying to find a way to affect the economy by disrupting important businesses. Second, reasonably sophisticated attackers typically conceal their identities by using stepping stones, open wireless access points, stolen credit card numbers, cell phones with built-in modems, and dial-in services without caller-ID. These factors make reliable traceback and accurate attribution extremely challenging.

## INVOLVING LAW ENFORCEMENT AGENCIES

Law enforcement agencies are best able to respond effectively to a computer crime when they have a comprehensive, organized package of information, including damage estimates. Most law enforcement agencies have standard forms for reporting cybercrimes. For example, the Department of Homeland Security's Information Analysis and Infrastructure Protection Directorate (IAIP, formerly the National Infrastructure Protection Center, or NIPC) has both an online form and a PDF file for reporting cybercrimes (see http://www.us-cert.gov/).

It can also be useful to contact law enforcement agents to alert them when large-scale or technologically unusual computer network attacks are underway. Doing so provides agents with advance warning of potential workload, as well as allowing them to correlate incidents involving multiple sites. Law enforcement agents may have access to information not readily available to the general public that reveals the larger picture, but that picture cannot be appreciated fully if victim sites do not recognize attacks above the level of "script-kiddies" and report them to law enforcement. Understanding and using their standard reporting forms when communicating with law enforcement can facilitate an efficacious response.

## LEVELS OF FORCE: BENIGN THROUGH AGGRESSIVE RESPONSES

This section classifies various intrusion responses according to levels of "force." Although there are clear differences between physically forceful actions and digitally intrusive actions, there are sufficient similarities to justify characterizing the latter as involving force of some kind. Despite the probable limits to the analogy between digital and physical force, these limits are of little importance here and can be disregarded safely. Table 2 shows the levels of force.

---

[13] However, knowledge sufficient to enable a Level-2 response is still quite limited, potentially putting a victim with sensitive customer information in a position of increased liability for negligence in handling sensitive information. Such issues have not yet been addressed by the courts.

[14] See, for example, Col. John Boyd, *OODA Loop* http://www.mindsim.com/MindSim/Corporate/OODA.html. OODA stands for Observe, Orient, Decide, and Act and describes a complex relationship among the following variables: (1) observation, (2) prior experience, (3) an innate understanding of options that one can take at any given point to counter an attacker's moves, (4) an equal understanding of the expected outcome of those actions, and (5) the ability to come back to observations that confirm whether the expected outcome was obtained. The OODA Loop is neither a simple loop containing one path nor a "play book" that can be consulted and acted out without thought. The OODA Loop relates the attacker's and defender's abilities to see the battlefield, their understanding of the options for action, and knowledge of how to act appropriately in response to the attack.

**Table 2.** Levels of Force

| Level | Causal Impacts | Characteristic Actions |
|---|---|---|
| Benign | Limited to victim's own systems | Sniffing, scanning, readdressing hosts, honeypots |
| Intermediate | Affects remote systems but not calculated to produce damage | Invasive tracebacks, remote evidence collection |
| Aggressive | Impacts calculated to produce damage in remote systems | Remote exploitation, corruption of data, denial of service |

# Benign

Benign activities are those involving operations that have no direct causal effects on remote systems and are not adopted from a self-consciously noncooperative posture or attitude. Such measures include operations intended to gather information, as well as to address or correct vulnerabilities in the victim's networks.

Most benign measures do not fall within the active response continuum as that concept was defined previously, but some do—for an interesting reason. Some benign measures potentially affect the legitimate interests of other persons even if, strictly speaking, they do not have a causal impact on remote systems. Third parties may have legitimate privacy interests implicated by measures that have a causal impact on only those systems owned or controlled by the victim. If, for example, the victim is an Internet service provider renting Internet access and storage to a third party, measures that have a causal impact on only those resources within the victim's ownership or control may affect the legitimate moral interests of the victim. Insofar as the victim takes unilateral action without obtaining consent from interested third parties in situations in which consent is required ethically or legally, such action is fairly characterized as "noncooperative"—as opposed to "uncooperative." Although the latter term presupposes a deliberate refusal to behave in a cooperative way, the former notion does not. Thus, behaviors that are not cooperative in circumstances in which cooperation is required are "noncooperative" even if the failure to cooperate is unknowing. Unilateral benign measures that potentially infringe the legitimate interests of third parties, then, are fairly characterized as noncooperative and hence as active response.

## Sniffing

Sniffing (i.e., monitoring of network traffic) can occur only on LAN segments. This requires access to a device on the LAN on which you wish to sniff (e.g., connected to a wall port in a switched network, or ability to associate with a wireless access point). Attackers using sniffers typically take over a computer and use its interface to promiscuously capture all traffic that is accessible to that host. Using techniques that manipulate link-level traffic management functions, such as ARP cache poisoning and MAC table overflowing in switches, switches and virtual local area networks (VLANs) can sometimes be bypassed to increase the traffic that can be sniffed. Routers themselves are sometimes compromised and used to sniff traffic as well. Laws that prohibit monitoring of electronic communications typically have exemptions for owners and operators of networks or telecommunications systems and for those with authority for the investigation of breaches in network security; these exceptions allow such persons to monitor traffic. The main requirement is that the activity be done for protection of the network and computers involved.

## Readdressing Hosts or Networks

Attackers commonly attempt to map out network infrastructure to determine how to achieve their objectives inside the target network—a process that can take months or even years to complete if an attacker is trying to do it with stealth (a so-called low and slow scan). If the victim can rapidly readdress hosts and devices on its network after the commencement of an attack, the victim can effectively blind the attacker and force him or her to rescan the network. This may enable victims to detect the systems from which attackers are implementing scans and to identify hosts that are being used as stepping stones.

## Deception Using Honeypots

*Honeypots*, as commonly defined, are computer resources installed for the purpose of being compromised (see "The Use of Deception Techniques: Honeypots and Decoys" in this *Handbook;* http://project.honeynet.org/papers/honeynet/index.html). Honeypots can be used to augment existing firewalls and intrusion detection systems to identify malicious activity. Some honeypots not only appear to provide services desired by an attacker but can also mimic the operating-system fingerprint that results when an attacker scans the network with certain tools. In that attack situation, a defender can readdress certain hosts on the network, configure a system running those honeypots to replace the existing systems, and make it look like there are many more on the network just like it.

## Scanning

The attacker uses scanning to learn about the topology of the network and the devices being used, and the victim can do the same. Understanding the vulnerabilities being exploited by an attacker is essential to an effective response; scanning can help the victim find vulnerable and compromised hosts, thereby facilitating cleanup and evidence preservation. Indeed, a victim can continually scan his or her network to build an historical database of operating systems, listening ports, and services that can be queried on demand when investigating an attack to find all hosts matching a known exploitable profile. By performing a continual comparison of this same information, changes over time can be detected, which may signal intrusion activity. There are passive ways of gaining this same intelligence through monitoring network flows, although this monitoring only identifies hosts that are actively "talking" on the network.

### Session Hijacking/TCP Session "Sniping"

There are tools that enable a victim to hijack and terminate established transmission control protocol (TCP) sessions, as well as prevent new connections from being established. The careless and sporadic use of such tools is, however, likely to be noticed by the attacker—though an attacker could always misinterpret the results as having been caused by intermittent network failures. However, it is important to note that these tools are generally efficacious only if used on the same LAN segment as the hosts the attacker is using.

## Intermediate

Activities in this category involve causal interaction with remote systems outside a defender's network, but are neither intended nor reasonably likely to cause harm to those systems. It is worth noting that noncooperative measures falling in this category are fairly characterized as active response as this notion was defined previously—though, again, the reader is cautioned not to draw any substantive normative conclusions merely on the strength of a characterization of something as involving, or not involving, active response. This taxonomy can assist a normative analysis but is no substitute for such an analysis.

### Following Attack Paths in Reverse

Victims can attempt to follow attack paths back to the ultimate source of an attack. If a victim knows (1) the attacker's methodology for using back doors and exposed network services for establishing stepping stones or proxy relays, (2) the passwords and/or account names favored by the attacker, and (3) the IP addresses used for entry/exit from the victim's network, he or she can follow the attacker's trails backwards through the network. Tracing attack paths through systems within the victim's own network can be done without much worry if there are policies that allow this activity. Tracing attack paths through systems not directly owned or controlled by the victim might be ethically or legally problematic insofar as such actions have a causal impact on innocent parties. In either event, there is always a danger of destroying the time-line of events by changing the Modify-Access-Change (MAC) time stamps on affected systems.

### Remote Evidence Collection

Victims who enter a remote system have the same evidence-gathering abilities as they have on their own networks. This evidence can be in the form of output of commands that show running processes, last logins, and network connection states or can be in the form of contents of directories or even entire file-system bit images. Such measures are problematic if criminal codes (involving, say, stored electronic communications) apply.[15]

## Aggressive

Actions defined here as *aggressive* are reasonably likely to interfere with the availability, integrity, confidentiality, or authenticity of information systems outside one's own network. Aggressive measures include those intended or highly likely to result in something that the target would regard as harm or damage. Aggressive actions are all fairly characterized as active response since, as a conceptual matter, only a noncooperative act can be aggressive.

### Remote Exploitation

One class of aggressive measures involves victim penetration and exploitation of remote systems. Understanding a remote system's vulnerabilities can allow the victim to penetrate those systems using exploit programs (i.e., programs that take advantage of vulnerabilities in a computer system to gain access). These programs may include exploits used by the attacker within the victim's own system.[16]

There are several serious risks here that counsel against use of such measures. First, remote exploitation can cause major disruption to the host if the exploit crashes servers, network stacks, or the operating system itself. Second, it can leave digital tracks that the attacker would notice. Third, it can be detected by the site's incident handlers and treated as though it were a separate computer crime.

### Corruption of Data

Another class of aggressive measures involves alteration of data being used by the attacker. In a case where it is known that the attacker is using a file-system cache to store sniffer or vulnerability scanner logs, an effective response can involve the targeted editing or destruction of some or all of these files. Because it can take significant time for an attacker to successfully identify new hosts to attack, such measures can force the attacker to return to certain hosts or networks. At the very least, they can delay the attacker for long enough to allow the victim to finish an analysis of malware artifacts or system images and to gather new network flow information. However, it is important to realize that these actions can also destroy evidence that could be used in a criminal prosecution and may themselves violate criminal prohibitions on digital intrusions.

### Disabling Services on Remote Systems

Knowledge of services being used by the attacker on remote systems, together with the possession of accounts/passwords or knowledge of remotely exploitable vulnerabilities in these services, can enable a victim to disable them. The risks here are that (1) disabling the service could have a negative impact on the host or its users; (2) the service would simply be restarted as a normal course of system operation (e.g., through a monitoring daemon,

---

PATRIOT Act, however, allows law enforcement to monitor and use such communications if, among other things, relevant to an ongoing criminal investigation.

[16] Victims should always have a healthy distrust of programs in an attacker's possession, unless they have thoroughly reverse engineered them or verified their integrity from known trusted public sources.

---

[15] In the United States, for example, the Electronic Communications Privacy Act prohibits "interception and disclosure" of certain "wire, oral, or electronic communications." See 18 U.S.C., Section 2501 et seq. The USA

a scheduled process, or manually by the system administrator); and (3) the attacker has a means for restarting the service. Many rootkits include multiple back doors and/or remote command execution facilities that can be used to restart services; for this reason, a sound understanding of the malware involved and of success probabilities are needed to obtain the desired goal (i.e., shutting down access to the attacker), as well as to avoid alerting attackers that such measures are being pursued.

### Denial of Service

Another possibility is to use remotely exploitable vulnerabilities to cause hosts or the network infrastructure itself to fail at the other site, thereby taking control of remote systems out of the hands of the attacker, or overwhelming the network bandwidth of the site to the same end. The effect of such measures is to deny users access to the contents of the other site and hence to "deny service" to them.

Denial of service (DoS) responses are highly aggressive measures that are problematic for several reasons (see "Denial of Service" in this *Handbook*). First, such responses can have unforeseeable catastrophic effects on remote sites that are not unreasonably characterized as "collateral damage." For example, it is conceivable that disrupting a system that is involved in critical patient care could potentially result, directly or indirectly, in harm or even the death of a patient.[17] Similarly, it could be that a DoS response might result in financial losses that well exceed the value of the resources the victim is attempting to defend and in the worst-case scenario result in the losses of jobs of innocent persons. Second, it is rarely clear that DoS will accomplish the goal of removing access to the compromised systems. In large-scale attacks where the attacker controls tens or hundreds of thousands of systems, the victim typically lacks the ability to deny service to all of them.[18] Third, there is the possibility that the counterattack would simply be filtered out somewhere between the attacking network and the target networks. Not only will the counterattack fail as a means of removing control of these systems by the attacker, it may even disrupt the victim's own network connectivity as a result.

## THE ETHICS OF ACTIVE RESPONSE

This section is concerned with whether it is ethically permissible for private parties to adopt the various active response measures described herein in response to a digital attack. The structure of the analysis is as follows. The first section attempts to identify each of the substantive ethical principles potentially relevant in evaluating whether a particular active response strategy is permissible. The second section identifies an additional ethical principle that states an evidentiary precondition for justifiably acting on other substantive ethical principles (e.g., those identified in the first section). Finally, the third section applies these principles to aggressive, intermediate, and benign active response measures.[19]

One preliminary observation is in order here. As is standard in the area of applied ethics, the analysis here does not presuppose any particular general ethical theory like utilitarianism or Kantianism. Instead, the analysis purports to be grounded in general principles, and specific case judgments that figure prominently in ordinary ethical judgments and practices. Accordingly, the analysis begins by identifying ethical principles that are commonly accepted in Western industrialized nations[20] and proceeds by attempting to identify the implications of those widespread commitments with respect to the various levels of active response.

### Relevant Ethical Principles

#### Allowing Force in Defense of Self and Others

It is generally accepted in Western nations that a person has a moral right to use proportional force when necessary to defend against an attack. If, for example, A is shooting at B without provocation and B cannot save his or her own life without shooting A, it is permissible, according to ordinary judgments, for B to shoot A. If, however, A starts hitting B without provocation, it would be impermissible for B to shoot at A; because B's right of self-defense is limited to directing proportional force at A, it is permissible for B only to hit A.

The first ethical principle considered here, then, is a familiar one that allows a person to use proportional force when necessary to defend against an attack:

> **The Defense Principle:** It is morally permissible for one person to use force to defend him- or herself or other innocent persons against an attack provided that (1) such force is proportional to the force used in the attack, (2) such force is necessary either to repel the attack or to prevent the attack from resulting in harm of some kind, and (3) such force is directed at and is reasonably likely to harm only those persons who are responsible for the attack.

Although the term *force* has traditionally been used to describe violent physical attacks in which one person

---

[17] Arguably, the hospital would be negligent for having linked critical life-saving functions to a network that can be easily crashed by a remote DoS attack; however, this does not diminish the culpability of the party who performed the DoS attack as an active response measure in the first place—or the severity of the consequences.

[18] It is not uncommon for an attacker to control 10,000 hosts in a DDoS network or networks. In 2003, CERT/CC reported they were tracking a bot network of over 140,000 hosts (CERT Advisory, 2003). In 2004, a network of Phatbot "blended threat" bots (which include DoS capability) involving 400,000 hosts was observed by Symantec (Krebs, 2004), and the Association of Realtime Gambling Operators reported to the British All Party Internet Group that 518,000 hosts were used to attack one of their members (ARGO, 2004).

[19] There are two reasons for structuring the analysis this way. First, each of the various levels of active response must be evaluated under each of the ethical principles. Second, each of the various substantive principles is qualified by the evidentiary precondition discussed in the second section. For this reason, the analysis must begin by identifying all of the relevant substantive and evidentiary principles before considering how any one might apply to some active response measure.

[20] It is worth noting that the principles identified here are incorporated into the law of every Western industrialized nation. To the extent that most people accept those laws as legitimate, it is reasonable to conclude that most people believe they are just—and hence reflect the content of morality.

attempts to inflict physical harm on another person, it is reasonably construed here as applying to both physical *and* digital attacks.

Each of the elements of the Defense Principle states a *necessary* condition for the use of force. First, it justifies only force that is proportional to that used in the attack. Second, force must be necessary in the sense that the victim cannot stop the attack or prevent further harm to him- or herself without resorting to force. Third, the Defense Principle justifies the use of force only against persons directly responsible for the attack. Although some (but by no means all) theorists believe this element allows the use of force against an attacker who is innocent of wrongdoing (perhaps because he or she is clinically insane), all agree that the Defense Principle does not justify force against an innocent bystander.

At this juncture, it is worth noting that the Defense Principle will hence justify, at most, forceful active response measures directed at the owners of innocent agent machines; such machines are fairly characterized as "innocent attackers" rather than "innocent bystanders." Active response measures that have significant impacts on innocent bystanders will likely face difficulties under the Defense Principle.

## Allowing Otherwise Wrongful Acts to Secure the Greater Moral Good

It is also generally accepted in Western nations that morality allows the *infringement* (as opposed to *violation*) of an innocent person's rights when necessary to secure a significantly greater good.[21] For example, if A must enter onto the property of B without permission in order to stop a murderer from escaping, it is morally permissible for A to do so. Though such an act constitutes a *prima facie* trespass and hence infringes B's property rights, it does not violate B's property rights because it is morally justified.

There are four considerations that explain this judgment. First, stopping a dangerous murderer from escaping into the general population where he or she is likely to do more harm has great moral value. Second, it is not possible for A to achieve such moral value without coming onto B's land without permission. Third, the threat to the interests of the public is, from a moral point of view, significantly greater than the threat to B's interests. Fourth, A's intent in committing the putative trespass is morally respectable (i.e., to save the public from such a grave risk) and is hence properly respectful toward B.

Putting these four features together suggests a second general principle that might be applicable in evaluating active response:

**The Necessity Principle:** It is morally permissible for one person A to infringe a right $\rho$ of a person B if and only if (1) A's infringing of $\rho$ would result in great moral value; (2) the good that is protected by $\rho$ is significantly less valuable, morally speaking, than the good A can bring about by infringing $\rho$; (3) there is no other way for A to bring about this moral value that does not involve infringing $\rho$; and (4) A's attitude toward B's rights is otherwise properly respectful.

Like the Defense Principle, the Necessity Principle is construed here as applying in the context of both physical and digital attacks.

The Necessity Principle augments the Defense Principle by allowing acts that would infringe the rights of even innocent bystanders: the Necessity Principle seems to allow one person A to infringe the right of an innocent bystander B if necessary to defend A or some other person from a culpable attack that would result in a significantly greater harm than results from infringing B's right. However, insofar as the Necessity Principle requires the achievement of a *significantly* greater good, it does not allow a person to direct at an innocent bystander force that is fully proportional to the force of the attack.

The Necessity Principle is, thus, dissimilar to the Defense Principle in one respect that is significant for the evaluation of active response. Unlike the Defense Principle, the Necessity Principle potentially allows active response measures that have significant impacts on innocent bystanders. Even so, it is clear that the Necessity Principle will allow impacts on innocent bystanders only if the moral value of using the relevant active response measure significantly outweighs the moral disvalue of such impacts.

## Punitive or Retaliatory Principles

It might be thought that victims of an attack have a moral right to retaliate against or punish their attackers by inflicting a morally proportional harm on their attackers. If, for example, A hits B in the face and then turns and runs away in an obvious attempt to escape, it is ethically permissible, in this view, for B to catch A and then hit him back in the face. B's retaliatory act is justified because it gives A what A deserves and thereby restores the balance of justice that was disturbed by A's morally wrongful act. Applied to the present context, such an analysis would permit the victim of a digital attack to respond with force as a means of "evening the score."

Nevertheless, it is generally accepted that, in any society with a morally legitimate government, it is ethically impermissible for citizens to punish or retaliate against wrongdoing. Mainstream political theorists are unanimous in holding that it is the province of government—and not the individual—in such societies to punish wrongdoers after they have been found guilty in a fair trial. Indeed, vigilantism is universally condemned as wrong: so long as the state is reasonably effective in prosecuting and punishing wrongdoing, citizens are morally prohibited from forceful self-help.[22] As a general matter, it is

---

[21] By definition, to say that a right has been "infringed" is to say only that someone has acted in a way that is inconsistent with the holder's interest in that right; strictly speaking, then, the claim that a right has been infringed is a purely descriptive claim that connotes no moral judgment as to whether the infringement is wrong. In contrast, to say that a right has been "violated" is to say that the right has been infringed by some act and that the relevant act is morally wrong. Accordingly, it is a conceptual truth that it can be permissible for an individual or entity to infringe a right, but it cannot be permissible to violate a right.

[22] Such an analysis is presupposed by Jayawal, Yurcik, and Doss (2002). The assumption is that self-defense is legitimate but not retaliatory measures (which are implicitly condemned as "vigilantism").

wrong for private victims to even the score by retaliating or punishing attackers.[23]

## An Evidentiary Restriction for Justifiably Acting under Ethical Principles

Most theorists and laypersons agree that we have a duty to ensure we have correctly identified the facts and applicable ethical principle before taking action against a person on the strength of that principle. Suppose, for example, that A believes without good reason that B has wronged A in some way. If A takes action against B under a principle P without having a minimally adequate reason for thinking that P applies (say, because A lacks a minimally adequate reason to think that B has committed a wrong), then A has committed a wrong against B. A has a duty to be at least minimally justified in believing that P governs the situation; if A does not satisfy this duty, then A must give B the benefit of the doubt before acting on P until A has better evidence that P does, in fact, apply.

There is thus a third principle that is relevant with respect to evaluating active response measures—one that is evidentiary or, as theorists of knowledge put it, "epistemic" in character:

> **The Evidentiary Principle:** It is morally permissible for one person A to take action under an ethical principle P only if A has adequate reason for thinking that all of the necessary conditions for applying P are satisfied.

The Evidentiary Principle defines a moral duty to ensure that one is epistemically justified in acting under the relevant moral principles. If one person A takes aggressive action against another person B without having sufficient reason for believing the application conditions of the relevant principle have been satisfied, A has wronged B.

Accordingly, the victim of a digital attack can permissibly adopt active response measures only if he or she has adequate reason to think the application conditions of at least one of the relevant principles are satisfied. Under the Defense Principle, the victim must have adequate reason to believe that (1) whatever force is employed is proportional to the force used in the attack, (2) such force is necessary either to repel the attack or to prevent the attack from resulting in harm of some kind, and (3) such force is directed only at persons who are responsible for the attack. Under the Necessity Principle, the victim must have adequate reason to believe that (1) the relevant moral value significantly outweighs the relevant moral disvalue, (2) there is no other way to achieve the greater moral good than to do A, and (3) doing A will succeed in achieving the greater moral good. If the victim lacks reason to think the application conditions of both rules are satisfied and if these are the only relevant rules, then it would be wrong for him or her to adopt active response measures that infringe the rights of any innocent person.

## Evaluating Active Response under the Relevant Ethical Principles

In evaluating active response under the Defense, Necessity, and Evidentiary Principles, it is important to realize that the risk that active response measures will affect innocent persons is not purely "theoretical." Sophisticated attackers usually conceal their identities by staging attacks from innocent machines that have been compromised through a variety of mechanisms. Most active responses will have to be directed, at least in part, at the agent machines used to stage the attack. Given that innocent persons enjoy a general moral immunity against force, the likelihood of affecting innocent persons with active response occupies a central role in evaluating those responses under the Defense, Necessity, and Evidentiary Principles.

### Aggressive Measures

In many instances, aggressive active response cannot be justified by the Defense Principle. Consider Conxion's DoS response to the attack by E-hippies on World Trade Organization servers a few years ago. Because dropping the packets at the router would have stopped the harmful effects of the E-hippies attack, Conxion's response was not "necessary" to defend against those attacks and was not justified under the Defense Principle.

Indeed, characterizing such measures as "defensive" radically mischaracterizes them. Conxion's aggressive response cannot accurately be characterized as defensive because it was not needed to stop either the attack or the harmful effects of the attack. Indeed, the reason why Conxion adopted the more aggressive response was that it wished to inflict exactly the same kind of harm on the E-hippies' servers that the e-hippies intended to inflict on the WTO servers. For this reason, Conxion's objective was at least partly punitive or retaliatory in character. Because, as we have seen, it is generally impermissible for private parties (as opposed to the state) to punish an attack or forcefully retaliate against it, Conxion's response was unethical.

Additional ethical issues are raised by aggressive defense measures directed against attacks staged from innocent agent machines. Because the identity of the culpable attacker is generally unknown in such cases, any aggressive response will be directed at the innocent agents compromised by the attacker, which compounds the harms done to the owners of those machines. Although the agent machines are more plausibly characterized as "innocent attackers" than as "innocent bystanders," theorists disagree about whether the Defense Principle allows a forceful response to an innocent attacker. This disagreement, however, suggests that a victim of a digital attack lacks adequate reason to think that the Defense Principle would allow aggressive measures against innocent parties. Because it follows that the victim lacks adequate reason to think the application conditions of the Defense Principle are satisfied, aggressive responses should be presumed unethical under the Evidentiary Principle.

Aggressive defense is also problematic under the Necessity Principle. Even assuming an aggressive response is

---

[23] This line of analysis, however, presupposes that the state is reasonably effective in protecting against such attacks. See the following discussion of this issue and how it bears on the ethics of active response.

necessary to achieve the greater moral good of preventing the damage caused by an attack, an aggressive response may result in unpredictable harms that outweigh the relevant moral goods. Machines can be linked via a network to one another in unpredictable ways, making it impossible to identify all the harmful effects of an aggressive response in advance. Ethically significant "collateral damage" can be ruled out reliably in only a small class of exceptional cases.

Indeed, a variety of intranational and international worst-case scenarios are unfortunately possible. Suppose, for example, that an attacker compromises machines on a university network linked to a university hospital. If hospital machines performing a life-saving function are linked to the network, an aggressive response against that network might result in a loss of human life. Even worse, suppose that an attacker compromises machines used by one nation's government to attack private machines in another nation. If the two nations are hostile toward each other, an aggressive response by the private victim could raise international tensions—a particularly chilling prospect if the two nations are nuclear powers.

The point here is not that we have reason to think that these worst-case scenarios are very likely; rather, we do not have any reliable way to determine how likely they are. A victim contemplating an aggressive response has no reliable way to estimate the probabilities of such scenarios in the short time available to him or her. Because the victim cannot reliably assess these probabilities, he or she lacks adequate reason to think that the application conditions of the Necessity Principle are satisfied. Thus, under the Evidentiary Principle, the victim may not justifiably adopt aggressive measures under this principle.

## Intermediate Responses

Intermediate active responses typically include exploratory tracebacks that attempt to identify culpable attackers by following attack paths in reverse through innocent agent machines (if any) to the ultimate source of the attack, as well as devices that allow entry into a remote system for the purpose of gathering information. Though such responses are neither intended nor reasonably likely to cause harm, they are ethically problematic insofar as they are invasive in the following sense: to the extent that the use of a traceback results in an unauthorized entry onto innocent agent machines, it would appear to constitute a trespass—something that is presumptively impermissible.

One might think that such trespasses can be justified under the Necessity Principle.[24] To the extent that intermediate responses can be used reliably to identify the culpable source of a digital attack for the purpose of prosecuting the responsible parties,[25] they function to secure

the important moral good of restoring the public peace by bringing wrongdoers to justice—a good that seems important enough to justify comparatively minor trespasses onto the property of innocent persons.[26]

Unfortunately, it is frequently unclear whether intermediate responses are likely to succeed in identifying culpable parties. A sophisticated attacker can insulate him- or herself from discovery by compromising one set of innocent machines to control another set of innocent machines that will be used to stage the attack—a process that can be iterated several times. However, the greater the number of "hops in the chain" between attacker and victim, the less likely that intermediate responses will succeed in identifying the culpable party. Indeed, it is fair to say that the likelihood of identifying the culpable parties in such attacks by intermediate responses is morally negligible.

This means that the expected moral value (i.e., the magnitude of the good multiplied by the probability of realizing it) to be achieved by using invasive tracebacks is a lower value than is desirable. In contrast, the expected moral disvalue (i.e., the magnitude of the bad multiplied by the probability of realizing it) is significant; although it may be difficult to precisely quantify the magnitude of the evil involved in a trespass, the probability of committing a trespass in using invasive tracebacks against any reasonably sophisticated attack will be close to 1. This militates against the claim that the good that will be achieved by using invasive tracebacks is significantly greater than the bad that will be done.

Moreover, the use of intermediate responses can also have significant collateral impacts that are undesirable from a moral point of view. The use of invasive tracebacks can result in damage to a variety of important trust relationships. A private firm that implements a traceback in an attack staged from the machines of other competing businesses can damage not only trust relationships between those businesses but could also precipitate a response that damages trust relationships between consumers and businesses, potentially resulting in economic losses that are passed on to the public in the form of lost jobs. Even worse, the use of invasive tracebacks by a private firm in response to an attack staged from machines used by state officials of another nation could result in an international incident that damages the relationship between those nations.

Again, the point here is not that we have reason to think that these worst-case scenarios are very likely; rather, a victim contemplating an intermediate response cannot reliably estimate the probabilities of such scenarios in such a short period of time. Because the victim cannot reliably assess these probabilities, there is inadequate reason to think that the application conditions of the Necessity Principle have been satisfied. The Evidentiary Principle seems to preclude adopting intermediate responses in ordinary cases in which the victim lacks fairly detailed knowledge about the source and routing of an attack.

---

[24] Because intermediate responses neither punish nor defend against attacks, the ethical principles allowing defense or punitive measures are irrelevant.

[25] Not all intermediate responses are motivated by a desire to prosecute the wrongdoer. Many firms would prefer to avoid prosecuting intrusions to escape the unfavorable publicity that might result from the disclosure of security breaches. This reasoning would not justify intermediate responses in these cases.

---

[26] If the only way that a private security officer can apprehend a robbery suspect is to commit a trespass against the property of an innocent person, it seems clear that he or she is justified in doing so under the Necessity Principle.

Thus, in most cases, private parties cannot justify adopting intermediate responses on the strength of the Necessity Principle.

Nevertheless, it is important to emphasize that the analysis here is limited to current traceback technologies with their limitations. Many researchers are making considerable progress in improving the reliability and efficacy of traceback technologies (see, e.g., http://footfall.csc.ncsu.edu, which documents some intriguing advancements in these technologies).

Indeed, one might reasonably expect that researchers will eventually improve these technologies to the point where they are sufficiently efficacious in identifying culpable parties. Then, they could generally be justified under the Necessity Principle as bringing about the greater moral good of identifying culpable parties to an attack. Thus, although presumptively unjustified under the Necessity Principle at this juncture, this may not be the case for long.

### Benign Responses

One might think that benign responses are ethically unproblematic because, by definition, they affect only those physical resources owned by the victim. According to this line of argument, a person has a moral liberty to dispose of property as he or she sees fit. Other things being equal, the property owner has a liberty to make physical alterations in his or her property; thus, for example, I have a liberty to make my home safer by installing a new lock in my door. It might be true that one's obligations to, say, support one's family preclude damaging one's own property in circumstances where doing so renders one unable to support one's family; however, these constraints are exceptional. Persons are at considerable liberty to use or modify their property as they see fit.

This argument is problematic in a couple of ways. First, the party implementing a benign measure may be a non-owner who has authorized control over the owner's resources. The scope of the owner's liberty to dispose of his or her property does not extend in an unrestricted fashion to agents of the owner. What the agent may permissibly do depends on other factors including the terms of the agreement he or she has with the owner.

Second, and more important, the scope of a person's moral liberty with property is limited by the rights of other persons. For example, the fact that an employer E owns a workspace does not imply that E has a right to install cameras in the bathroom to monitor employees. In this case, E's liberty to dispose of E's property is outweighed by the right of E's employees to privacy.

Accordingly, the mere fact that benign measures affect only the property of the victim is not by itself sufficient to imply that they are ethically justified; if there are other persons, for example, who have privacy rights (such as might be true of an ISP) that might be violated by benign measures, then such measures are not clearly permissible. Indeed, users of a system might have a reasonable expectation of privacy in the contents of their files or communications that give rise to privacy rights that would be violated even by benign measures. Such expectations might arise, for example, among users of a university or corporate network.

For this reason, it is not possible to draw any general conclusions about the permissibility of benign responses to digital attacks. Because they will be impermissible in cases where they violate the rights of third parties, it is necessary in any given instance to determine whether there are third parties who have rights that might be violated by the adoption of even benign responses.

## The Inadequacy of Law Enforcement Efforts

There is, however, one powerful argument that can be made in defense of the view that it is permissible for private individuals to undertake active response. The argument rests on the idea that the state may legitimately prohibit recourse to self-help measures in dealing with a class of wrongful intrusions or attacks only insofar as it is providing minimally adequate protection against such attacks. If (1) digital intrusions are resulting in significant harm or injury of a kind that the state ought to protect against, and (2) the state's protective efforts are inadequate, then private individuals, in this line of reasoning, are entitled to adopt active response measures that conduce to their own protection.

Both antecedent clauses appear to be satisfied. Depending on the target and sophistication of the attack, an unauthorized digital intrusion can result in significant financial losses to its victims. For example, an extended DDoS attack that effectively takes a major online retailer offline for several hours might result in hundreds of thousands of dollars of business going to one of its online rivals. In the worst-case scenario, these financial losses can result in the loss of value to shareholders and ultimately the loss of jobs. It seems clear that the harms potentially resulting from digital intrusions fall within a class that the state ought to protect against.

Further, there is good reason to think that the state's protective efforts are inadequate. At this point in time, law enforcement agencies lack adequate resources to pursue investigations in the vast majority of computer intrusions. Even when there are sufficient resources to justify the state in intervening, the response is likely to come long after the damage is done. That law enforcement has just not been able to keep pace with the rapidly growing problems posed by digital attackers is not a matter of controversy.

There are a variety of reasons for this inadequate response. Most obviously, the availability of resources for combating cybercrime is constrained by fiscal and political realities; if the public is vehemently opposed to tax increases that would increase the resources for investigating cybercrime, then the growth of those resources will not keep pace with an increasing rate of intrusions. Equally important, there are special complexities involved in investigating and prosecuting digital intrusions. First, according to Mitchell and Banker (1998), investigation of digital intrusions is resource-intensive: "[w]hereas a typical (non-'high-tech') state or local law-enforcement officer may carry between forty and fifty cases at a time, a high-tech investigator has a full-time job handling three or four cases a month." Second, most sophisticated attacks pose jurisdictional complexities that increase the expense of law enforcement efforts because such attacks frequently involve crossing jurisdictional lines. For example, an attacker in one country might compromise machines in another country in order to stage an attack on a network in yet a third country.

Though such considerations show that the growing problem associated with digital intrusions demands an effective response of some kind, they fall short of showing that it is permissible, as a general matter, for private parties to undertake intermediate or aggressive active response measures. The previous argument assumes that private individuals can do what the state cannot—namely protect themselves adequately from the threats posed by digital intrusion. That is to say, the argument assumes that private active response is likely to be efficacious in achieving legitimate objectives.

At this time, however, there is very little reason to think that this underlying assumption is correct. For starters, invasive intermediate measures intended to collect information are likely to succeed in identifying culpable parties, as noted previously, in only direct attacks staged from the attacker's own computer or by unskilled or careless attackers; such measures are not likely to succeed in identifying parties culpable for intrusions that are staged from innocent machines or where a high degree of preparation and sophistication is involved.[27] Because an attacker sophisticated enough to stage an attack likely to result in significant damage is also likely to be sophisticated enough to interpose at least one layer of innocent machines between attacker and target, there is little reason to think that invasive investigatory measures are likely to achieve their legitimate objectives in precisely those attacks that are likely to result in the sort of damage that the state is obligated to protect against.

Moreover, aggressive measures are not likely to succeed in protecting the victim in any reasonably sophisticated attack. As noted previously, aggressive countermeasures are not usually calculated to result in the cessation of the attack and can instead frequently result in escalating the attack; for this reason, such countermeasures are not likely to succeed in achieving legitimate objectives that are purely defensive in character. Further, aggressive countermeasures cannot succeed in achieving legitimate punitive objectives in attacks staged from innocent machines. Punitive measures directed at the innocent agents do nothing by way of either punishing the ultimate source of the attack or deterring future attacks. A reasonably sophisticated attacker who knows the target will respond with aggressively punitive measures can simply interpose an additional layer of innocent machines to insulate him- or herself from the target.

Yet, if this argument fails to justify active response by private victims, it succeeds in showing that the problem of digital intrusions needs an effective coordinated solution of some kind—one that involves, at the very least, the sanction and cooperation of the state. One notable proposal deserves mention here. Mitchell and Banker (1998) have suggested a private-public solution that involves state

licensing of security professionals who are trained in responding to digital intrusions and who are authorized to do so subject to certain constraints. It is reasonable to hypothesize that an evaluation of such proposals will become the focus of normative research on active response in the near future.

## THE LEGALITY OF ACTIVE RESPONSE

Although no Western nation has any statutes that explicitly address the legality of active response, there are a number of laws that potentially apply to it. This section discusses some of these laws and their potential application to the various levels of active responses. Nevertheless, it should be emphasized that the discussion in this section is tentative (and should not in any event be construed as authoritative legal advice). It is clear only that the legality of the various active responses remains unsettled at this time in every Western nation.

### The United States

The federal law most likely to create liability for active response is Section 1030(a)(5) of the Computer Crime and Fraud Act (i.e., 18 U.S. Code Section 1030), which provides as follows:

> Whoever... (A)(i) knowingly causes the transmission of a program, information, code, or command, and as a result of such conduct, intentionally causes damage without authorization, to a protected computer; (ii) intentionally accesses a protected computer without authorization, and as a result of such conduct, recklessly causes damage; or (iii) intentionally accesses a protected computer without authorization, and as a result of such conduct, causes damage; and (B) by conduct described in clauses (i), (ii), or (iii) of subparagraph (A), caused (or in the case of an attempted offense, would, if completed, have caused)—(i) loss to 1 or more persons during any 1-year period... aggregating at least $5,000 in value; (ii) the modification or impairment, or potential modification or impairment, of the examination, diagnosis, treatment, or care of 1 or more individuals; (iii) physical injury to any person; (iv) a threat to public health or safety; or (v) damage affecting a computer system used by or for a government entity in furtherance of the administration of justice, national defense, or national security... shall be punished as provided in subsection (c) of this section.

Subsection (c) authorizes fines and imprisonment of up to twenty years for specified violations of the quoted provision.

Although the relevant provisions apply only to "protected computers," the definition of that category is potentially broad. In particular, it includes any "computer... used in interstate or foreign commerce or communication." Construed literally, this provision would include any computer that has been used to send

---

[27] Just as in physical crimes, however, it is nearly impossible to eliminate all traces of an intruder's presence and all tracks from all involved systems. As the attacker's skill increases, so must the skills of the defender in order to find and understand the significance of the latent traces.

an e-mail from a person in one state to a person in another state or used to access any Web page that is published on a network in a different state from the user—which would seem to include every computer capable of being attacked.

As the statute does not make exceptions for active response, persons adopting active responses to hacker attacks could potentially be prosecuted under the Act. For starters, it is highly likely that any computer being used in a hacker attack will satisfy the definition of a "protected computer"; if an active response measure results in statutorily sufficient damage, it could result in liability. It is true, of course, that the Act is most likely to apply to aggressive measures as these are intended to inflict damage or harm on the attacker. However, it could also apply to intermediate responses, such as invasive tracebacks, that deliberately trespass against external machines to identify attack paths. In the event that such measures proximately result in damage to those machines, they can give rise to liability under the Act.

Indeed, even benign measures might give rise to liability under certain circumstances. The mere fact that the user has property rights in a network does not, *by itself*, imply that the user is legally authorized to access computers on that network because computer users may have privacy rights that insulate their computers from certain kinds of access. To the extent that network owners access computers or files on those computers protected by such rights without appropriate authorization, they might be subject to liability for even benign measures that result in the right kinds of damage.[28]

## Canada

Canada has several statutes potentially applicable to active response. For example, Section 342.1(1) of the Canadian Criminal Code provides:

> Every one who, fraudulently and without colour of right (*a*) obtains, directly or indirectly, any computer service, (*b*) by means of an electromagnetic, acoustic, mechanical or other device, intercepts or causes to be intercepted, directly or indirectly, any function of a computer system, (*c*) uses or causes to be used, directly or indirectly, a computer system with intent to commit an offence under paragraph (*a*) or (*b*) or an offence under section 430 in relation to data or a computer system, or (*d*) uses, possesses, traffics in or permits another person to have access to a computer password that would enable a person to commit an offence under paragraph (*a*), (*b*) or (*c*) is guilty of an indictable offence and liable to imprisonment for a term not exceeding ten years, or is guilty of an offence punishable on summary conviction.

Another statute that is potentially applicable to active response is Section 430 (1.1), which defines the crime of

mischief as follows: "Every one commits mischief who willfully (*a*) destroys or alters data; (*b*) renders data meaningless, useless or ineffective; (*c*) obstructs, interrupts or interferes with the lawful use of data; or (*d*) obstructs, interrupts or interferes with any person in the lawful use of data or denies access to data to any person who is entitled to access thereto."

Literally construed, the language of both sections seems applicable to the most aggressive active response measures. Section 430 requires that destruction, alteration, obstruction, or interruption of data be "willful" as is true of the most aggressive active response measures: after all, such measures are, by definition, calculated to inflict harm or damage on those computers from which digital attacks are staged. Section 342.1 not only applies to these measures by incorporating the requirements of Section 430 but also by setting a less stringent standard for violation: merely obtaining unauthorized access (a necessary precondition for inflicting the sort of damage intended by aggressive active response) seems sufficient to subject a person to liability.

In contrast, only Section 342.1 seems applicable to intermediate responses; because intermediate responses are not intended to result in damage or destruction to targeted systems, Section 430 would not seem to apply. Section 342.1 is potentially applicable to a large range of intermediate responses precisely because there is no minimum damage requirement. In the absence of an applicable defense, unauthorized access of some kind seems sufficient to support liability for intermediate responses under Section 342.1.

The legality of benign responses under Section 342.1 turns on the same issues as discussed previously in connection with the Computer Crimes and Fraud Act.

## The European Union

On November 8, 2001, the Committee of Ministers of the Council formerly adopted the Convention on Cybercrime, which states guidelines for the various members of the European Union in formulating law regarding computer misuse (Council of Europe, 2001). Section 1 of Chapter II of the Convention states guidelines for formulating substantive criminal law as it pertains to unauthorized access to computers, unauthorized interception of data, data interference, system interference, misuse of computing devices, computer fraud, child pornography, and copyright infractions. Article 2 of the Convention is of particular relevance for our purposes as it defines the relevant guidelines for criminalizing unauthorized access of computer technologies. Article 2 provides as follows:

> Each Party shall adopt such legislative and other measures as may be necessary to establish as criminal offences under its domestic law, when committed intentionally, the access to the whole or any part of a computer system without right. A Party may require that the offence be committed by infringing security measures, with the intent of obtaining computer data or other dishonest intent, or in relation to a computer system that is connected to another computer system.

---

[28] State laws may also be applicable. A growing number of states are enacting statutes that criminalize various forms of computer misuse that include but are not limited to unauthorized computer intrusions.

Insofar as the defining characteristic of a hacker attack is the attempt to gain unauthorized access, Article 2 purports to guide the adoption of criminal laws regarding hacker attacks—and potentially active response.

Notably, the Convention on Cybercrime is also motivated by a concern to address the problems that arise out of the transnational character of cyberspace: "Given the cross-border nature of information networks, a concerted international effort is needed to deal with such misuse." Chapter III defines the guidelines for international co-operation. Article 23 expresses the general tenor of the principles governing international cooperation: "The Parties shall co-operate with each other, in accordance with the provisions of this chapter, and through application of relevant international instruments on international co-operation in criminal matters, arrangements agreed on the basis of uniform or reciprocal legislation, and domestic laws, to the widest extent possible for the purposes of investigations or proceedings concerning criminal offences related to computer systems and data, or for the collection of evidence in electronic form of a criminal offence." Remaining Articles define principles of extradition and other principles requiring mutual assistance among nations.

## Legal Analogues of the Defense and Necessity Principles

The criminal law of most, if not all, Western nations incorporates principles that allow for the forceful defense of innocent persons and that allow for an otherwise wrongful act when necessary to secure a good that is significantly greater than the evil created by the commission of that act.

For example, the penal statutes of New York State contain analogues of both the Defense and Necessity Principles. Section 35.15 states the analogue of the Defense Principle: "A person may . . . use physical force upon another person when and to the extent he reasonably believes such to be necessary to defend himself or a third person from what he reasonably believes to be the use or imminent use of unlawful physical force by such other person."[29] Section 35.05 states the analogue of the Necessity Principle: "conduct which would otherwise constitute an offense is justifiable and not criminal when . . . [it] is necessary as an emergency measure to avoid an imminent public or private injury which is about to occur by reason of a situation occasioned or developed through no fault of the actor, and which is of such gravity that, according to ordinary standards of intelligence and morality, the desirability and urgency of avoiding such injury clearly outweigh the desirability of avoiding the injury sought to be prevented by the statute defining the offense in issue."

These defenses, however, do not *necessarily* apply to the active response continuum. First, such statutes typically incorporate an evidentiary precondition for acting justifiably under the relevant defenses. Section 35.15 allows force only where the agent "reasonably believes" it is necessary. Similarly, Section 35.05 allows an otherwise wrongful act only when the moral goods "clearly outweigh" the moral evils. Even assuming that the courts in any particular jurisdiction are willing in principle to apply these sorts of provisions to active response contexts, the same sort of epistemic problems arise in the criminal context as in the ethical context.

Second, these statutes have been enacted with certain paradigmatic offenses in mind that do not include digital attacks. Consider, for example, the Model Penal Code's comment on the necessity defense:

> Under this section, property may be destroyed to prevent the spread of a fire. A speed limit may be violated in pursuing a suspected criminal. An ambulance may pass a traffic light. Mountain climbers lost in a storm may take refuge in a house or may appropriate provisions. Cargo may be jettisoned or an embargo violated to preserve the vessel. An alien may violate a curfew in order to reach an air raid shelter. A druggist may dispense a drug without the requisite prescription to alleviate grave distress in an emergency.[30]

As is readily evident, these examples do not anticipate the application of the necessity defense to digital contexts. For such reasons, it is simply not clear that courts are willing to apply these defenses to the digital context.

## CONCLUSION

The active response continuum comprises a variety of noncooperative measures that are intended to respond to a digital intrusion in ways that have a causal impact on remote machines. Such measures include acts that would fairly be characterized as hacking in circumstances in which they were unprovoked by an intrusion. They range from more benign measures intended to inflict no damage to highly aggressive measures intended to inflict the same kind of damage on the attacker that he or she is attempting to inflict on the victim. These tactics include sniffing, scanning, tracebacks, corruption of data, remote exploitation, and DoS attacks.

Because of their invasive quality, active response measures raise a variety of normative issues. DoS counterattacks, for example, raise prudential, ethical, and legal issues. Responding to a DoS attack with proportional force might actually result in increased harm to the victim insofar as it evokes an escalation of the attack; it might thus adversely affect the victim's own interests. Further, if the attack is distributed, the counterattack will necessarily be directed at innocent agent machines, raising serious ethical and legal issues. For all these reasons, such aggressive measures are ill-advised.

Nevertheless, the growing frequency of hacker attacks and the increasing inability of law enforcement agencies to respond adequately suggest the need for a coordinated solution involving both public and private elements. The key to keeping owners/operators from resorting to noncooperative, invasive active response measures might be for

---

[29] Penal Code, New York State Consolidated Laws (http://assembly.state.ny.us/leg/?cl=82&a=12).

[30] Model Penal Code and Commentaries (Official Draft and Revised Comments) pt. I, vol. 1, at 9–10.

governments to provide resources that would allow sites to enlist the support of trained and trusted regional incident response teams, thereby decreasing the differential in skills/resources/information that is driving the private sector to resort to active response.

There is now an opportunity for government policymakers, the military, the law enforcement community, and the private sector to work together and develop effective cooperative relationships, operational resources and training, and a clear and streamlined legal framework that will level the playing field between attackers and defenders. The hope is that this will happen before a massive cyberattack occurs.

## GLOSSARY

**Active Response** A variety of reactive, noncooperative responses to a digital intrusion that are typically calculated to affect remote systems and are intended to investigate, defend, repel, or punish the intrusion. Such measures range from benign measures that implicate the legitimate interests of innocent persons without affecting remote systems to aggressive measures that are intended to inflict harm or damage on the intended targets. Also referred to as "hacking back" and "counterhacking."

**Agent Machines** Machines belonging to innocent parties that are compromised by an attacker and used to stage a digital attack or intrusion of some kind.

**Cybercrime** Criminal activity that involves unauthorized use of computer technology in an essential way.

**Cyberterrorism** Hacking activity that attempts to harm innocent persons and thereby create a general sense of fear or terror among the general population for the purpose of achieving a political agenda.

**Denial of Service** A digital attack that is calculated to shut down a Web site, server, or network, usually by overwhelming it with sham requests for information.

**Digital Intrusion** An act intended to gain unauthorized access to the digital contents (e.g., files or programs) of another person. Such access can be for comparatively benign purposes (e.g., merely to look at files) or can be for malicious purposes (e.g., to destroy files).

**Honeypots** Computer resources installed for the purpose of being compromised that are used as decoys that permit users to identify malicious activity.

**Intrusion Response** Measures adopted by the victim of a digital intrusion intended to investigate, repel, or punish the intrusion.

**Kantianism** Ethical theory that assesses action according to whether the underlying principle can consistently be universalized; acts, in this view, are intrinsically right or wrong.

**Order of Volatility** Ranking of sources of digital information according to stability and durability.

**Sniffers** Programs that are designed to monitor network traffic on local area network segments.

**Tracebacks** Actions attempting to follow the path of an ongoing attack in reverse in order to identify its ultimate and hence culpable source.

**Utilitarianism** A consequentialist moral theory that holds that the goodness or badness of an action is determined entirely by its consequences on well-being, happiness, the number of preferences satisfied, or pleasure in the community; acts, in this view, are right or wrong in virtue of extrinsic characteristics (i.e., their effects), and not in virtue of intrinsic characteristics.

## CROSS REFERENCES

See *Hackers, Crackers, and Computer Criminals; Intrusion Detection Systems Basics; Legal, Social, and Ethical Issues of the Internet; Network Attacks.*

## REFERENCES

Association of Realtime Gambling Operators. (2004). Submission to APIG. Retrieved May 26, 2005, from http://www.apig.org.uk/ARGO%20Evidence.doc

Brezinski, D., & Killalea, T. (2002, February). *Guidelines for evidence collection and archiving* (RFC 3227). Retrieved May 26, 2005, from http://rfc3227.x42.com/

CERT Advisory. (2003, March 11). Increased activity targeting Windows shares (CA-2003-08, 2003). Retrieved May 26, 2005, from http://www.cert.org/advisories/CA-2003-08.html

Council of Europe. (2001). *Convention on cybercrime.* Retrieved May 26, 2005, from http://conventions.coe.int/Treaty/en/Reports/Html/185.htm

Honeynet Project. (n.d.). *Know your enemy: Honeynets.* Retrieved from http://project.honeynet.org/papers/honeynet/index.html

Jayawal, V., Yurcik, W., & Doss, D. (2002, June). Internet hack back: Counter attacks as self-defense or vigilantism? [Electronic version]. *Proceedings of the IEEE International Symposium on Technology and Society, 5.* Retrieved from http://www.sosresearch.org/publications/ISTAS02hackback.PDF

Krebs, B. (2004). "Sasser" worm tip of the PC bug invasion. *Security Focus.* Retrieved from http://www.security-focus.com/news/8573

Mitchell, S. D., & Banker, E. A. (1998, Spring). Private intrusion response. *Harvard Journal of Law & Technology, 11,* 699.

OODA Loop (n.d.). Retrieved from http://www.mindsim.com/MindSim/Corporate/OODA.html

Radcliff, D. (2000, May 29). Can you hack back? *Network World.* Retrieved from http://www.nwfusion.com/research/2000/0529feat2.html

Radcliff, D. (2000, November 13). Should you strike back? *ComputerWorld.* Retrieved from http://www.computerworld.com/governmenttopics/government/legalissues/story/0,10801,53869,00.html

Scotland Yard and the case of the rent-a-zombies. (2004, July 7). Retrieved from http://zdnet.com.com/2100-1105_2-5260154.html.

## FURTHER READING

American Bar Association, Privacy & Computer Crime Committee. (2003). *International guide to combating cybercrime.* Retrieved from http://www.abanet.org/abapubs/books/5450030I/

Computers under attack can hack back, expert says. (2002, August 3). *SiliconValley.com*. Retrieved from http://www.siliconvalley.com/mld/siliconvalley/3795332.htm

Dasgupta, D., & Gonzalez, F. A. (2001). An intelligent decision support system for intrusion detection and response. In V. I. Gorodetski, et. al. (Eds.), *Proceedings of MMM-ACNS*. Springer-Verlag.

Dittrich, D. (2005). Articles/papers related to the active response continuum. Retrieved from http://staff.washington.edu/dittrich/activedefense.html

Himma, K. E. (2004, January). Targeting the innocent: Active defense and the moral immunity of innocent persons from aggression. *Journal of Information, Communication, and Ethics in Society, 2*(1).

Himma, K. E. (2004, August). The ethics of tracing hacker attacks through the machines of innocent persons. *International Journal of Information Ethics*.

Legal Foundations. (1997). Approaches to cyber intrusion response. *Report to the President's Commission on Critical Infrastructure Protection*. Retrieved from http://www.timeusa.com/CIAO/resource/pccip/lf12.pdf

Mirkovic, J., Dietrich, S., Dittrich, D., & Reiher, P. (2005). *Internet Denial-of-Service: Attacks and Defense Mechanisms*. Englewood Cliffs, NJ: Prentice-Hall PTR.

Otsuka, M. (1994). Killing the innocent in self-defense. *Philosophy and Public Affairs, 23*(1), 74–94.

Putnam, T. L., & Elliot, D. D. *International responses to cybercrime*. Retrieved from http://www.google.com/url?sa=U&start=1&q=http://www-hoover.stanford.edu/publications/books/fulltext/cybercrime/35.pdf&e=7207

Strassman, P. (2003, December 1). New weapons of information warfare. *ComputerWorld*. Retrieved from http://www.computerworld.com/securitytopics/security/story/0,10801,87554,00.html

Wang, X., Reeves, D., & Wu, S. F. (n.d.). Tracing based active intrusion response. Retrieved from http://arqos.csc.ncsu.edu/papers/2001-09-sleepytracing-jiw.pdf

Yurcik, W. Information warfare survivability: Is the best defense a good offense?

# PART 3

# Detection, Recovery, Management, and Policy Considerations

# Intrusion Detection Systems Basics

Peng Ning, *North Carolina State University*
Sushil Jajodia, *George Mason University*

## INTRODUCTION

Intuitively, *intrusions* in an information system are the activities that violate the security policy of the system, and *intrusion detection* is the process used to identify intrusions. Intrusion detection has been studied for more than 20 years since Anderson's report (Anderson, 1980). It is based on the beliefs that an intruder's behavior will be noticeably different from that of a legitimate user and that many unauthorized actions will be detectable.

Intrusion detection systems (IDSs) are usually deployed along with other preventive security mechanisms, such as access control and authentication, as a second line of defense that protects information systems. There are several reasons why intrusion detection is a necessary part of the entire defense system. First, many traditional systems and applications were developed without security in mind. In other cases, systems and applications were developed to work in a different environment and may become vulnerable when deployed in the current environment. For example, a system may be perfectly secure when it is isolated, but become vulnerable when it is connected to the Internet. Intrusion detection provides a way to identify and thus allow responses to attacks against these systems. Second, because of the limitations of information security and software engineering practice, computer systems and applications may have design flaws or bugs that could be used by an intruder to attack the systems or applications. As a result, certain preventive mechanisms (e.g., firewalls) may not be as effective as expected.

Intrusion detection complements these protective mechanisms to improve system security. Even if the preventive security mechanisms can protect information systems successfully, it is still desirable to know what intrusions have happened or are happening, so that we can understand the security threats and risks and thus be better prepared for future attacks. Ideally, intrusion detection can be used as the foundation for reactive measures. For example, when a denial of service (DoS) attack is detected, a firewall may be reconfigured to filter out the attack traffic. Moreover, intrusion detection can also be used to enforce accountability and compliance with security policy. This is particularly important when dealing with threats from inside attackers, who are authorized to access the information system but may misuse their privileges to perform actions that violate the security policy.

In spite of their importance, IDSs are not replacements for preventive security mechanisms, such as access control and authentication. Indeed, IDSs themselves cannot provide sufficient protection for information systems. As an extreme example, if an attacker erases all the data in an information system, detecting the attacks cannot reduce the damage at all. Thus, IDSs should be deployed along with other preventive security mechanisms as a part of a comprehensive defense system.

Denning (1986) presented the first intrusion detection model, which has six main components: subjects, objects, audit records, profiles, anomaly records, and activity rules. *Subjects* refer to the initiators of activity in an information system; they are usually normal users. *Objects* are the resources managed by the information system, such as files, commands, and devices. *Audit records* are those generated by the information system in response to actions performed or attempted by subjects on objects. Examples include user login, command execution, and so forth. *Profiles* are structures that characterize the behavior of subjects with respect to objectives in terms of statistical metrics and models of observed activity. *Anomaly records* are indications of abnormal behaviors when they are detected. Finally, *activity rules* specify actions to take when some conditions are satisfied; these rules update profiles, detect abnormal behaviors, relate anomalies to suspected intrusions, and produce reports.

Since Denning's model (Denning, 1986), intrusion detection techniques have evolved into two classes: anomaly detection and misuse detection. *Anomaly detection* is based on the normal behavior of a subject (e.g., a user or a system); any action that significantly deviates from the normal behavior is considered intrusive. Denning's intrusion detection model is an example of anomaly detection. *Misuse detection* catches intrusions in terms of the characteristics of known attacks or system vulnerabilities; any action that conforms to the pattern of a known attack or vulnerability is considered intrusive. The rationale of misuse detection is that, with additional knowledge of known attacks or vulnerabilities, we can potentially detect these attacks more precisely and more quickly.

Alternatively, IDSs may be classified into host-based IDSs, distributed IDSs, and network-based IDSs according to the sources of the audit information used by each IDS. Host-based IDSs obtain audit data from host audit trails and usually aim at detecting attacks against a single host; distributed IDSs gather audit data from multiple hosts and possibly the network that connects the hosts, aiming at detecting attacks involving multiple hosts. Network-based IDSs use network traffic as the audit data source, relieving the burden on the hosts that usually provide normal computing services.

This chapter starts with an overview of current intrusion detection techniques. Next, it reviews the various types of anomaly detection methods, such as statistical models and machine learning methods, followed by an overview of various types of misuse detection methods, including rule-based languages, the colored Petri-net-based method, and the abstraction-based method. The section following that discusses additional techniques for intrusion detection in distributed systems, including distributed IDSs, network-based IDSs, and interoperation between (heterogeneous) IDSs. Finally, this chapter reviews intrusion alert correlation techniques. More details on host-based IDSs, network-based IDSs, and applying agent technology to intrusion detection can be found in other chapters in this *Handbook*.

# ANOMALY DETECTION
## Statistical Models

Statistical modeling is among the earliest methods used for detecting intrusions in electronic information systems. It is assumed that an intruder's behavior is noticeably different from that of a normal user, and statistical models are used to aggregate the user's behavior and distinguish an attacker from a normal user. The techniques are applicable to other subjects, such as user groups and programs. In some cases, a simple threshold value is used to indicate the distinction (as with the common rule of raising an alarm if the password is mistyped three times); alternately, more complex statistical models may be employed. Here, we discuss two statistical models that have been proposed for anomaly detection: NIDES/STAT and Haystack.

### NIDES/STAT

The Stanford Research Institute's next-generation real-time intrusion detection expert system statistical component (NIDES/STAT) observes behaviors of subjects on a monitored computer system and adaptively learns what is normal for individual subjects, such as users and groups (Axelsson, 1999). The observed behavior of a subject is flagged as a potential intrusion if it deviates significantly from the subject's expected behavior.

The expected behavior of a subject is stored in the profile of the subject. Different measures are used to measure different aspects of a subject's behavior. When audit records are processed, the system periodically generates an overall statistic, $T^2$, which reflects the abnormality of the subject. This value is a function of the abnormality values of all the measures comprising the profile. Suppose that $n$ measures $M_1, M_2, \ldots, M_n$ are used to model a subject's behavior. If $S_1, S_2, \ldots, S_n$ represent the abnormality values of $M_1$ through $M_n$, then the overall statistic $T^2$ is evaluated as follows, assuming that the $n$ measures are independent of each other:

$$T^2 = S_1{}^2 + S_2{}^2 + \cdots + S_n{}^2.$$

The profile of a subject is updated to reflect the changes in the subject's behavior. So that the most recently observed behaviors influence the profile more strongly, NIDES/STAT multiplies the frequency table in each profile by an exponential decay factor before incorporating the new audit data. Thus, NIDES/STAT adaptively learns a subject's behavior patterns. This keeps human users from having to adjust the profiles manually; however, it also introduces the possibility of an attacker gradually "training" the profile to consider his or her intrusive activities as normal behavior.

### Haystack

Haystack used a different statistical anomaly detection algorithm, which was adopted as the core of the host monitor in the distributed intrusion detection system (DIDS; Axelsson, 1999). This algorithm analyzes a user's activities according to a four-step process.

First, the algorithm generates a session vector to represent the activities of the user for a particular session. The session vector $\mathbf{X} = <x_1, x_2, \ldots, x_n>$ represents the counts for various attributes used to represent a user's activities for a single session. Examples of the attributes include session duration and number of files opened for reading.

Second, the algorithm generates a Bernoulli vector to represent the attributes that are out of range for a particular session. A threshold vector $\mathbf{T} = <t_1, t_2, \ldots, t_n>$, where $t_i$ is a tuple of the form $<t_{i,\min}, t_{i,\max}>$, is used to assist this step. The threshold vector is stored in a user's profile. The Bernoulli vector $\mathbf{B} = <b_1, b_2, \ldots, b_n>$ is generated so that $b_i$ is set to 1 if $x_i$ falls outside the range $t_i$, and $b_i$ is set to 0 otherwise.

Third, the algorithm generates a weighted intrusion score, for a particular intrusion type, from the Bernoulli vector and a weighted intrusion vector. Each group and intrusion type pair has a weighted intrusion vector $\mathbf{W} = <w_1, w_2, \ldots, w_n>$, in which each $w_i$ relates the importance of the $i$th attribute in the Bernoulli vector to detecting the particular intrusion type. The weight intrusion score is simply the sum of all weights, $w_i$, where the $i$th attribute falls outside the range $t_i$. That is,

$$\text{the weighted intrusion score} = \sum_{i=1}^{n} b_i \cdot w_i.$$

Finally, the algorithm generates a suspicion quotient to represent how suspicious this session is compared with all other sessions for a particular intrusion type. Specifically, the suspicion quotient is the probability that a random session's weighted intrusion score is less than or equal to the weighted intrusion score computed in the previous step.

Unlike NIDES/STAT, the Haystack algorithm has a step that determines resemblance to known attacks. The advantages of Haystack are that more knowledge about the possible attacks can be derived from this step and more effective responses can follow the alarms. However, extra knowledge about possible intrusion types is required: it is necessary to understand the impact of the intrusion types on the attributes of the session vectors and assign appropriate weights to these attributes to reflect the impact. In reality, the process of generating the weighted intrusion vectors is time consuming and error prone.

## Machine Learning and Data Mining Techniques

A number of machine learning and data mining techniques have been investigated for the purpose of anomaly detection. The focus of these approaches is to "learn" the normal behaviors of the system automatically from the historic normal data. Such normal behaviors are represented in various forms and are used as the basis for future anomaly detection. In this section, we discuss several approaches in this category.

### Time-Based Inductive Machine

Teng, Chen, and Lu (1990) proposed the use of a time-based inductive machine (TIM) to capture a user's behavior pattern. As a general-purpose tool, TIM discovers temporal sequential patterns in a sequence of events. The sequential patterns represent highly repetitive activities and are expected to provide predication. The temporal patterns, which are represented in the form of rules, are generated and modified from the input data using a logical inference called *inductive generalization*. When applied to intrusion detection, the rules describe the behavior patterns of either a user or a group of users based on past audit history. Each rule describes a sequential event pattern that predicts the next event from a given sequence of events. An example of a simplified rule produced in TIM is

$$E1 - E2 - E3 \rightarrow (E4 = 95\%; E5 = 5\%),$$

where $E1$, $E2$, $E3$, $E4$, and $E5$ are security events.

This rule says that if $E1$ is followed by $E2$, and $E2$ is followed by $E3$, then there is a 95% chance (based on the previous observation) that $E4$ will follow and a 5% chance that $E5$ will follow. TIM can produce more generalized

rules than that. For example, it may produce a rule in the form

$$E1 - * \rightarrow (E2 = 100\%),$$

where an asterisk matches any single event. Any number of asterisks is allowed in a rule.

The limitation of TIM is that it only considers the *immediately following* relationship between the observed events. That is, the rules only represent the event patterns in which events are adjacent to each other. However, a user may perform multiple tasks at the same time. For example, a user may check e-mail while editing a document. The events involved in one application, which tend to have strong patterns embedded in the sequence of events, may be interleaved with events from other applications. As a result, it is very possible that the rules generated by TIM cannot precisely capture the user's behavior pattern. Nevertheless, TIM may be suitable for capturing the behavior patterns of such entities as programs that usually focus on single tasks.

### Instance-Based Learning

Lane and Brodley (1998) applied *instance-based learning* (IBL) to learn entities' (e.g., users) normal behavior from temporal sequence data. IBL represents a concept of interest with a set of instances that exemplify the concept. The set of instances is called the instance dictionary. A new instance is classified according to its relation to stored instances. IBL requires a notion of "distance" between the instances so that the similarity of different instances can be measured and used to classify the instances.

Lane and Brodley did several things to adapt IBL to anomaly detection. First, they transformed the observed sequential data into fixed-length vectors (called *feature vectors*). Specifically, they segmented a sequence of events (e.g., a sequence of user commands) into all possible overlapping sequences of length $l$, where $l$ is an empirical parameter. Thus, each event is considered the starting point of a feature vector, and each event is replicated $l$ times. Second, they defined a similarity measure between the feature vectors. For a length $l$, the similarity between feature vectors $\mathbf{X} = (x_0, x_1, \ldots, x_{l-1})$ and $\mathbf{Y} = (y_0, y_1, \ldots, y_{l-1})$ is defined by the functions

$$w(X, Y, i) = \begin{cases} 0, & \text{if } i < 0 \text{ or } x_i \neq y_i \\ 1 + w(X, Y, i-1), & \text{if } x_i = y_i \end{cases}$$

and

$$Sim(X, Y) = \sum_{i=0}^{l-1} w(X, Y, i).$$

The converse measure, distance, is defined as $\text{Dist}(\mathbf{X}, \mathbf{Y}) = \text{Sim}_{max} - \text{Sim}(\mathbf{X}, \mathbf{Y})$, where $\text{Sim}_{max} = \text{Sim}(\mathbf{X}, \mathbf{X})$. Intuitively, the function $w(\mathbf{X}, \mathbf{Y}, i)$ accumulates weights from the most recently consecutively matched subsequences between $\mathbf{X}$ and $\mathbf{Y}$ at position $i$, whereas $\text{Sim}(\mathbf{X}, \mathbf{Y})$ is the integral of total weights.

A user profile is built to contain a collection of sequences, $\mathbf{D}$, selected from a user's observed actions (e.g., commands). The similarity between the profile and a newly observed sequence, $\mathbf{X}$, is defined as

$Sim_D(X) = max_{Y \in D}\{Sim(Y, X)\}$. That is, the similarity between $X$ and $D$ is defined as the similarity between $X$ and a vector in $D$ that is most similar to $X$. Then a threshold $r$ is chosen. If the similarity between an observed sequence $X$ and the profile $D$ is greater than $r$, $X$ is considered normal; otherwise, $X$ is abnormal.

To reduce the storage required by the profile, Lane and Brodley used the least-recently used pruning strategy to keep the profile at a manageable size. As new instances are acquired and classification is performed, the profile instance selected as most similar is time stamped. Least-recently used instances are removed when the profile is constrained to the desired size. In addition, they applied a clustering technique to group the instances in the profile, and they used a representative instance for each cluster.

IBL shares a problem found in TIM; that is, it tries to find patterns from sequences of consecutive events. As the authors have noted, a user may interrupt normal work (e.g., programming) and do something different (e.g., answer an urgent e-mail) and thus yield a different sequence of actions from his or her profile. Their solution (Lane & Brodley, 1998) is to use a time average of the similarity signals; however, such a solution may make real anomalies unnoticeable. In addition, the least-recently used pruning strategy gives an attacker a chance to train the profile slowly, so that intrusive activities are considered normal ones.

## Neural Networks

Fox, Henning, Reed, and Simmonian (1990) were the first to attempt modeling system and user behaviors using neural networks. Their choice of neural network is Kohonen's *self-organizing map* (SOM), which is a type of unsupervised learning technique that can discover underlying structures of the data without prior examples of intrusive and nonintrusive activities.

They used SOM as a real-time background monitor that alerts a more complex expert system. In their prototype system, 11 system parameters accessible from the system's statistical performance data are identified as the input to the SOM model: central processing unit (CPU) usage, paging activity, mailer activity, disk accesses, memory usage, average session time, number of users, absentee jobs, reads of "help" files, failed logins, and multiple logins. However, their study showed the results of only one simulated virus attack, which are not sufficient to draw serious conclusions.

In another attempt to apply a neural network to anomaly detection, Ghosh, Wanken, and Charron (1998) proposed using a *back-propagation* network to monitor running programs. A back-propagation network is developed for supervised learning. That is, it needs examples of intrusive and nonintrusive activities (called *training data*) to build the intrusion detection model. Such a network consists of an input layer, at least one hidden layer (neurons that are not directly connected to the input or output nodes), and an output layer. Typically, there are no connections between neurons in the same layer or between those in one layer and those in a previous layer.

The training cycle of a back-propagation network works in two phases. In the first phase, the input is submitted to the network and propagated to the output through the network. In the second phase, the desired output is compared with the network's output. If the vectors do not agree, the network updates the weights starting at the output neurons. Then the changes in weights are calculated for the previous layer and cascade through the layers of neurons toward the input neurons.

Ghosh and colleagues (1998) proposed using program input and the program internal state as the input to the back-propagation network. One interesting result is that they improved the performance of detection by using randomly generated data as anomalous input. By considering randomly generated data as anomalous, the network obtains more training data that are complementary to the actual training data.

As in statistical anomaly detection models, deciding the input parameters for neural network anomaly detectors is a difficult problem. In addition, assigning the initial weights to the neural networks is also an unresolved question. The experiments by Ghosh et al. (1998) showed that different initial weights could lead to anomaly detectors with different performance. Nevertheless, research on applying neural networks to anomaly detection is still preliminary; more work is needed to explore the capability of neural networks.

## Audit Data Analysis and Mining

Audit data analysis and mining (ADAM) proposes applying data mining techniques to discover abnormal patterns in large amounts of audit data; for example, network traffic collected by TCPdump, which is a program used to sniff and store packets transmitted in the network (Barbara, Couto, Jajodia, & Wu, 2001, 2002; Lee & Stolfo, 2000, use data mining techniques for automatically generating misuse models; we discuss their work in the section on misuse detection). In particular, the existing research focuses on the analysis of network audit data, such as the transmission control protocol (TCP) connections. Using data mining techniques, ADAM has the potential to provide a flexible representation of the network traffic pattern, uncover some unknown patterns of attacks that cannot be detected by other techniques, and accommodate a large amount of network audit data, which keeps growing in size.

ADAM uses several data-mining-related techniques to help detect abnormal network activities. The first technique ADAM uses is inspired by association rules. Given a set $I$ of items, an association rule is a rule of the form $X \rightarrow Y$, where $X$ and $Y$ are subsets (called item sets) of $I$ and $X \cap Y = \phi$. Association rules are usually discovered from a set $T$ of transactions, where each transaction is a subset of $I$. The rule $X \rightarrow Y$ has a *support s* in the transaction set $T$ if $s\%$ of the transactions in $T$ contain $X \cup Y$, and it has a *confidence c* if $c\%$ of the transactions in $T$ that contain $X$ also contain $Y$.

However, ADAM does not use association rules directly; instead, it adopts the item sets that have large enough support (called *large item sets*) to represent the pattern of network traffic. Specifically, it assumes that each network event (e.g., a TCP connection) is described by a set of attribute values, and it considers each event a transaction. The large item sets discovered from the network traffic then represent the frequent events in the network traffic. The power of such a mechanism lies in the flexible representation of events.

ADAM builds a profile of normal network activities in which the frequent events (represented by large item sets) are stored. During the detection time, it adopts a sliding-window method to incrementally examine the network events. Within each window, ADAM looks for the large item sets that do not appear in the profile and considers them suspicious.

The second technique ADAM uses is called *domain-level mining*. Intuitively, it tries to generalize the event attribute values used to describe a network event. For example, an IP address that belongs to the subnet *ise.gmu.edu* can be generalized to *ise.gmu.edu, gmu.edu,* and *edu*. Then it discovers large item sets using the generalized attribute values. An advantage of this approach is that it provides a way to aggregate the events that share some commonality and may enable the discovery of more attacks. However, the scheme used to generalize the attribute values is ad hoc; only generalization from IP addresses to subnets and from smaller subnets to larger subnets is studied.

The third technique ADAM uses is classification. ADAM is innovative in its use of classification for the output of the mining of large item sets. Four classification algorithms have been studied to date: C4.5 decision tree, naive Bayes, cascading classifier (which uses decision tree followed by naive Bayes and vice versa), and inductive rule learner. The results show that classification is quite effective in reducing false alarms.

Finally, ADAM uses the pseudo-Bayes estimator to accommodate unknown attacks. It is assumed that unknown attacks are the attacks that have not been observed. The training data are represented as a set of vectors, each of which corresponds to an event and is labeled as normal or as a known class of attacks. An additional class is then considered to represent the unknown attacks. Because the unknown attacks have not been observed in the training data, the probability $P(\mathbf{x}|class = \text{unknown})$, where $\mathbf{x}$ is a training vector, is zero. The pseudo-Bayes estimator is used to smooth all the conditional probabilities $P(\mathbf{x}|class)$ so that $P(\mathbf{x}|class = \text{unknown})$ is assigned a (small) probability. These conditional probabilities are then used to build a naive Bayes classifier.

The limitation of ADAM is that it cannot detect stealthy attacks. In other words, it can detect an attack only when it involves a relatively large number of events during a short period of time. This limitation occurs because ADAM raises an alarm only when the support of an unexpected rule (i.e., association of event attributes) exceeds a threshold. Indeed, this limitation is not unique to ADAM; most of the anomaly detection models and many of the misuse detection models suffer from the same problem.

## Computer Immunological Approachs

The computer immunological approach is based on an analogy of the immune system's capability of distinguishing self from nonself (Hofmeyr, Forrest, & Somayaji, 1998). This approach represents self as a collection of strings of length $l$, where $l$ is a system-wide parameter. A string of length $l$ is considered nonself if it does not match any string belonging to self. To generate detectors that can distinguish nonself from self, a naive approach is to randomly generate a string of length $l$ and check whether it matches any self-string. If yes, the generated string is discarded; otherwise, it is used as a detector. However, the naive approach takes time exponential to the number of self-strings. To address this problem, Hofmeyr et al. (1998) proposed a *"r-contiguous-bits"* matching rule to distinguish self from nonself: two $l$-bit strings match each other if they are identical in at least $r$ contiguous positions. As a result, detectors can be generated more efficiently for this particular matching rule.

Hofmeyr et al. (1998) proposed using short sequences of system calls to distinguish self from nonself for anomaly detection. Given a program in a particular installation, the immunological approach collects a database of all unique system call sequences of a certain length made by the program over a period of normal operation. During the detection time, it monitors the system call sequences and compares them with the sequences in the aforementioned database. For an observed sequence of system calls, this approach extracts all subsequences of length $l$ and computes the distance $d_{\min}(i)$ between each subsequence $i$ and the normal database as $d_{\min}(i) = \min [d(i, j)]$ for all sequences $j$ in the normal database), where $d(i, j)$ is the Hamming distance between sequences $i$ and $j$ (i.e., the number of different bits in sequences $i$ and $j$). The anomaly score of the observed sequence of system calls is then the maximum $d_{\min}(i)$ normalized by dividing the length of the sequence. This approach raises an alarm if the anomaly score is above a certain threshold.

The advantage of this approach is that it has a high probability of detecting anomalies using a small set of self-strings based on short sequences of system calls. In addition, it does not require any prior knowledge about attacks. The disadvantage is that it requires self to be well understood. That is, it requires a complete set of self-strings in order not to mistake self for nonself. This requirement may be trivial for such applications as virus detection, but it is very difficult for intrusion detection, where some normal behaviors cannot be foreseen when the detectors are being generated.

Sekar, Bendre, Dhurjati, and Bollineni (2001) further improved the computer immunological method by using an automaton to represent a program's normal behavior. The program counter is used as the state of the automaton, and the system calls made by the program are used as the events that cause the state transitions. As a result, the automaton representation can accommodate more information about the programs' normal behavior and thus reduce the false alert rate and improve the detection rate. In addition, the automaton representation is more compact than the previous alternative. Consequently, such automata are easier to build and more efficient to use for intrusion detection.

## Specification-Based Methods

Ko, Ruschitzka, and Levitt (1997) proposed a specification-based approach for intrusion detection. It is based on the use of *traces*, ordered sequences of execution events, to specify the intended behaviors of concurrent programs in distributed systems. A specification describes valid operation sequences of the execution of one or more programs, collectively called a (monitored) subject. A sequence of operations performed by the subject that does not conform to the specification is considered a security violation. Each specification is called a *trace policy*. A grammar called *parallel environment grammars* (PE grammars) was developed for specifying trace policies.

The advantage of this approach is that, in theory, it should be able to detect some new types of attacks that intruders will invent in the future. In particular, if a new attack causes a program to behave in a way outside the specification, then it will be flagged as a potential attack. The drawback of this approach is that substantial work is required to specify accurately the behavior of the many privileged system programs, and these specifications will be operating-system specific. To address this issue, Ko (2000) proposed the use of inductive logic programming to synthesize specifications from valid traces. The automatically generated specifications may be combined with manual rules to reduce the work involved in specification of valid program behaviors.

Wagner and Dean (2001) further advanced the specification-based approach. The basic idea is to automatically generate the specification of a program by deriving an abstract model of the programs from the source or binary code. Wagner and Dean studied several alternative models, including the call-graph model and the abstract stack model. Central to these models is the control flow graph of a program; these models adopt different ways to represent the possible system call traces according to the control flow graph. Attractive features of this approach are that it has the potential to detect unknown patterns of attacks and that it has no false alerts, although it may miss some attacks. Moreover, the specification-based methods also offer an opportunity to stop ongoing attacks. For example, it is possible to automatically embed code—for example, embedded sensors by Zamboni (2001)—in to an existing program, which forces the program to quit when certain specifications are violated.

## Information-Theoretic Measures

Lee and Xiang (2001) proposed the use of information-theoretic measures to help understand the characteristics of audit data and build anomaly detection models. The well-known concept *entropy* is the first information-theoretic measure. Given a set of classes $C_X$ and a data set $X$, where each data item belongs to a class $x \in C_X$, the entropy of $X$ relative to $C_X$ is defined as

$$H(X) = \sum_{x \in C_X} P(x) \log \frac{1}{P(x)},$$

where $P(x)$ is the probability of $x$ in $X$. For anomaly detection, entropy reveals the regularity of audit data with respect to some given classes.

The second information-theoretic measure is *conditional entropy*. The conditional entropy of $X$ given $Y$ is the entropy of the probability distribution $P(x|y)$; that is,

$$H(X|Y) = \sum_{x,y \in C_X, C_Y} P(x,y) \log \frac{1}{P(x|y)},$$

where $P(x,y)$ is the joint probability of $x$ and $y$ and $P(x|y)$ is the conditional probability of $x$ given $y$. The conditional entropy is proposed to measure the temporal or sequential characteristics of audit data. Let $X$ be a collection of sequences where each is a sequence of $n$ audit events and where $Y$ is the collection of prefixes of the sequences in $X$ that are of length $k$. Then $H(X|Y)$ indicates the uncertainty that remains for the rest of the audit events in a sequence $x$ after we have seen the first $k$ events of $x$. For anomaly detection, conditional entropy can be used as a measure of regularity of sequential dependencies.

The limitation of conditional entropy is that it only measures the sequential regularity of contiguous events. For example, a program may generate highly regular sequences of events; however, if these events are interleaved with other sequences of events, the conditional entropy will be very high, failing to reflect the regularity embedded in the interleaved sequences.

The third information-theoretic measure, *relative entropy*, measures the distance of the regularities between two data sets. The relative entropy between two probability distributions $p(x)$ and $q(x)$ that are defined over the same $x \in C_X$ is

$$\text{relEntropy}(p|q) = \sum_{x \in C_X} p(x) \log \frac{p(x)}{q(x)}.$$

The fourth information-theoretic measure, *relative conditional entropy*, measures the distance of the regularities with respect to the sequential dependency between two data sets. The relative entropy between two probability distributions $p(x|y)$ and $q(x|y)$ that are defined over the same $x \in C_X$ and $y \in C_Y$ is

$$\text{relCondEntropy}(p|q) = \sum_{x,y \in C_X, C_Y} p(x,y) \log \frac{p(x|y)}{q(x|y)}.$$

Viewing intrusion detection as a classification problem, Lee and Xiang proposed the fifth information-theoretic measure, *information gain*, to measure the performance of using some features for classification. The information gain of attribute (i.e., feature) $A$ on data set $X$ is

$$\text{Gain}(X, A) = H(X) - \sum_{v \in \text{Values}(A)} \frac{|X_v|}{|X|} H(X_v),$$

where $\text{Values}(A)$ is the set of values of $A$ and $X_v$ is the subset of $X$ where $A$ has value $v$. This measure can help choose the right features (i.e., the features that have high information gain) to build intrusion detection models. The limitation of information gain is that it requires a relatively complete data set. Nevertheless, an intrusion detection model cannot be better than the data set from which it is built.

## Limitation of Anomaly Detection

Although anomaly detection can accommodate unknown patterns of attacks, it also suffers from several drawbacks. A problem common to all anomaly detection approaches, with the exception of the specification-based approach, is that the subject's normal behavior is modeled on the basis of the (audit) data collected over a period of normal operation. If undiscovered intrusive activities occur during this period, they will be considered normal activities. In addition, because a subject's normal behavior usually changes over time (for example, a user's behavior may change when moving from one project to another), the IDSs that use the above approaches usually allow the subject's profile to change gradually. This gives an intruder the chance to gradually train the IDS and trick it into accepting intrusive activities as normal. In addition, because these approaches are all based on summarized information, they are insensitive to stealthy attacks. Finally, because of some technical reasons, the current anomaly detection approaches usually suffer from a high false-alarm rate.

Another difficult problem in building anomaly detection models is how to determine which features are to be used as the input of the models (e.g., the statistical models). In the existing models, the input parameters are usually decided by domain experts (e.g., network security experts) in ad hoc ways. There is no guarantee that either all the features or only the features related to intrusion detection will be selected as input parameters. Although missing important intrusion-related features makes it difficult to distinguish attacks from normal activities, having nonintrusion-related features could introduce "noise" into the models and thus affect the detection performance.

## MISUSE DETECTION

Misuse detection is considered complementary to anomaly detection. The rationale is that known attack patterns can be detected more effectively and efficiently by using explicit knowledge of them. Thus, misuse detection systems look for well-defined patterns of known attacks or vulnerabilities; they can catch an intrusive activity even if it is so negligible that the anomaly detection approaches tend to ignore it. Commercial systems often combine both misuse and anomaly detection approaches.

The major problems in misuse detection concern the representation of known attack patterns and the difficulty of detecting new attacks. The second problem is an inherent limitation of misuse detection: although misuse detection algorithms may sometimes detect variations of known attacks, they cannot identify truly new attacks because no pattern may be provided for them. Existing work on misuse detection is mostly aimed at the first problem, the representation of known attacks. The detection algorithms usually follow directly from the representation mechanisms. In this section, we discuss the typical ways to represent attacks.

## Rule-Based Languages

The rule-based expert system is the most widely used approach to misuse detection. The patterns of known attacks are specified as rule sets, and a forward-chaining expert system is usually used to look for signs of intrusions. Here we discuss two rule-based languages, rule-based sequence evaluation language (RUSSEL; Mounji, Charlier, Zampunieris, & Habris, 1995) and production-based expert system tool set (P-BEST; Lindqvist & Porras, 1999). Other rule-based languages exist, but they are all similar in that they all specify known attack patterns as event patterns.

### RUSSEL

RUSSEL is the language used in the advanced security audit trail analysis on the UNIX (ASAX) project. It is a language specifically tailored to the problem of searching arbitrary patterns of records in sequential files. The language provides common control structures, such as conditional, repetitive, and compound actions. Primitive actions include assignment, external routine call, and rule triggering. A RUSSEL program simply consists of a set of rule declarations that are composed of a rule name, a list of formal parameters and local variables, and an action part. RUSSEL also supports modules sharing global variables and exported rule declarations.

When intrusion detection is being enforced, the system analyzes the audit records one by one. For each audit record, the system executes all the active rules. The execution of an active rule may trigger (activate) new rules, raise alarms, write report messages, or alter global variables, for example. A rule can be triggered to be active for the current or the next record. In general, a rule is active for the current record because a prefix of a particular sequence of audit records has been detected. When all the rules active for the current record have been executed, the next record is read, and the rules triggered for it in the previous step are executed in turn. User-defined and built-in C-routines can be called from a rule body.

RUSSEL is quite flexible in describing sequential event patterns and corresponding actions. The ability to work with user-defined C-routines gives the users the power to describe almost anything that can be specified in a programming language. The disadvantage is that it is a low-level language. Specifying an attack pattern is similar to writing a program, although it provides a general condition-trigger framework and is declarative in nature. The feature that rules can share global variables introduces the possibility of bugs along with the convenience of sharing information among different rules.

### P-BEST

P-BEST was developed for the multiplexed information and computing service (Multics) intrusion detection and alerting system (MIDAS) and later employed by the intrusion detection expert system (IDES), NIDES, and the event monitoring enabling responses to anomalous live disturbances (EMERALD). The P-BEST toolset consists of a rule translator, a library of run-time routines, and a set of garbage collection routines. Rules and facts in P-BEST are written in production-rule specification language. The rule translator is then used to translate the specification into an expert system program in C language, which can then be compiled into either a stand-alone, self-contained executable program or a set of library routines that can be linked to a larger software framework.

The P-BEST language is quite small and intuitive. In P-BEST, the user specifies the structure of a fact (e.g., an audit record) through a template definition referred to as a *pattern type*. For example, an event consisting of four fields—*event type* (an integer), *return_code* (an integer), *username* (a string), and *hostname* (a string)—can be defined as ptype[event *event_type*: int, *return_code*: int, *username*: string, *hostname*: string].

Thus, P-BEST does not depend on the structure of the input data. One important advantage of P-BEST is that it is a language preprocessor (i.e., it generates a precompiled expert system) and can extend its ability by invoking external C functions. However, it shares a similar problem with RUSSEL: it is a low-level language. Specification of attack patterns in P-BEST is time consuming. Although many related rules are included in a system, correctness of the rules is difficult to check because of the interaction of these rules.

## State Transition Analysis Toolkit

Though rule-based languages are flexible and expressive in describing attack patterns for misuse detection, in practice, they are usually difficult to use. As Ilgun, Kemmerer, and Porras (1995) observed, "In general, expert rule-bases tend to be non-intuitive, requiring the skills of experienced rule-base programmers to update them." STAT was developed to address this problem.

In STAT, state transition analysis technique was adopted to facilitate the specification of the patterns of known attacks (Ilgun et al., 1995). It is based on the assumption that all penetrations share two common features. First, penetrations require the attacker to possess some minimum prerequisite access to the target system. Second, all penetrations lead to the acquisition of some ability that the attacker did not have prior to the attacks. Thus, STAT views an attack as a sequence of actions performed by an attacker that leads from some initial state on a system to a target-compromised state, where a *state* is a snapshot of the system representing the values of all memory locations on the system. Accordingly, STAT models attacks as a series of state changes that lead from an initial secure state to a target-compromised state.

To represent attacks, STAT requires some critical actions, called *signature actions*, to be identified. Signature actions refer to the actions that, if omitted from the execution of an attack scenario, would prevent its successful completion. Using the series of state changes and the signature actions that cause the state changes, an attack scenario is then represented as a state transition diagram, where the states in the diagram are specified by assertions of certain conditions and the signature actions are events observable from, for example, audit data.

STAT has been applied for misuse detection in UNIX systems, distributed systems, and networks. USTAT is the first prototype of STAT, which is aimed at misuse detection in UNIX systems (Ilgun et al., 1995). It relies on Sun Microsystems' C2- Basic Security Module (BSM) to collect audit records. In addition to detecting attacks, USTAT is designed to be a real-time system that can preempt an attack before any damage can be done. USTAT was later extended to process audit data collected on multiple UNIX hosts. The resulting system is called NSTAT. On the hosts being protected, NSTAT runs multiple daemon programs that read and forward audit data to a centralized server, which performs STAT analysis on all data.

A later application of STAT to network-based misuse detection resulted in another system, named NetSTAT (Vigna & Kemmerer, 1999). In this work, the network topology is further modeled as a hypergraph. Network interfaces, hosts, and links are considered the constituent elements of hypergraphs, with interfaces as the nodes, and hosts and links as hyperedges. Using the network topology model and the state transition description of network-based attacks, NetSTAT can map intrusion scenarios to specific network configurations and generate and distribute the activities to be monitored at certain places in a network.

STAT was intended to be a high-level tool to help specify attack patterns. Using STAT, the task of describing an attack scenario should be easier than using rule-based languages, although the analysis required to understand the nature of attacks remains the same. In the implementations of STAT techniques (i.e., USTAT, NSTAT, and NetSTAT), the attack scenarios are transformed into rule bases, which are enforced by a forward-chaining inference engine.

## Colored Petri Automata

Kumar and Spafford (1994) and Kumar (1995) viewed misuse detection as a pattern-matching process. They proposed an abstract hierarchy for classifying intrusion signatures (i.e., attack patterns) based on the structural interrelationships among the events that compose the signature. Events in such a hierarchy are high-level events that can be defined in terms of low-level audit trail events and used to instantiate the abstract hierarchy into a concrete one. A benefit of this classification scheme is that it clarifies the complexity of detecting the signatures in each level of the hierarchy. In addition, it also identifies the requirements that patterns in all categories of the classification must meet to represent the full range of commonly occurring intrusions (i.e., the specification of context, actions, and invariants in intrusion patterns).

Kumar and Spafford adopted colored Petri nets to represent attack signatures, with guards to represent signature contexts and vertices to represent system states. User-specified actions (e.g., assignments to variables) may be associated with such patterns and then executed when patterns are matched. The adapted colored Petri nets are called *colored Petri automata* (CPA). A CPA represents the transition of system states along paths that lead to intruded states. A CPA is also associated with pre- and postconditions that must be satisfied before and after the match, as well as invariants (i.e., conditions) that must be satisfied while the pattern is being matched. CPA has been implemented in a prototype misuse detection system called Intrusion Detection in Our Time (IDIOT).

CPA is quite expressive; it provides the ability to specify partial orders, which in turn subsume sequences and regular expressions. However, if improperly used, the expressiveness may lead to potential problems: If the intrusions are described in every detail, the attacker may be able to change the attacking strategy and bypass the IDSs. Nevertheless, CPA is not the root of the problem.

## Automatically Built Misuse Detection Models

Lee and Stolfo (2000) looked at intrusion detection as a data analysis process and applied several data mining techniques to build misuse detection models. The research efforts were conducted under a project entitled Jam, the Java Agent for Meta-learning (meta-learning is a general strategy that provides the means of learning how to combine and integrate a number of separately learned classifiers or models). In particular, association rules and frequent episodes are used to automatically discover features that should be used to model a subject's behavior, and the metaclassification is used to combine the results of different classifiers to obtain better classification results.

Lee and Stolfo extended the original association rules to take into account the "order of importance" relations among the system features (the notion of association rule was discussed above regarding ADAM). *Axis* refers to the features that are important to intrusion detection; only the association rules involving axis features are considered. For example, in the shell command records, the command is likely to reflect the intrusive activities and thus be identified as an axis feature. In some sense, axis features incorporate expert knowledge into the system and thus improve the effectiveness of association rules.

To represent frequent sequential patterns of network events, Lee and Stolfo extended frequent episodes to represent the sequential interaudit record patterns; this was originally proposed by Mannila, Toivonen, and Verkamo (1995). Their algorithm finds frequent sequential patterns in two phases. First, it finds the frequent associations among event attributes using the axis attributes, and then it generates the frequent sequential patterns from these associations. The algorithm also takes advantage of the "reference" relations among the system features. That is, when forming an episode, the event records covered by the constituent item sets of the episode share the same value for a given feature attribute. The mined frequent episodes are used to construct temporal statistical features, which are used to build classification models. Thus, new features can be derived from the training data set and then used for generating better intrusion detection models.

Another innovation of the JAM project is metaclassification, which combines the output of several base classifiers and generates the best results from them. Specifically, from the predictions of base classifiers and the correct classes, a metaclassifier learns which base classifier can make the best prediction for each type of input. It then chooses the prediction of the best base classifier for different input and combines the powers of the base classifiers.

Lee and Stolfo (2000) further advanced the state-of-the-art knowledge of intrusion detection by introducing the Mining Audit Data for Automated Models for Intrusion Detection (MADAMID) framework that helps generate intrusion detection models automatically. The limitation is that the framework depends on the volume of the evidence. That is, intrusive activities must generate a relatively noticeable set of events so the association of event attributes or frequent episodes can reflect them. Thus, the generated models must work with some other complementary systems, such as STAT.

## Abstraction-Based Intrusion Detection

The implementation of many misuse detection approaches shares a common problem: each system is written for a single environment and has proved difficult to use in other environments that may have similar policies and concerns. The primary goal of abstraction-based intrusion detection is to address this problem.

The initial attempt of the abstraction-based approach was a misuse detection system named the adaptable real-time misuse detection system (ARMD; Lin, Wang, & Jajodia, 1998). ARMD provides a high-level language for abstract misuse signatures, called MuSigs, and a mechanism to translate MuSigs into a monitoring program. The high-level language specifies a MuSig as a pattern over a sequence of abstract events, which is described as conditions that the abstract event attributes must satisfy. The gap between abstract events and audit records is bridged by an audit subsystem, which transforms the actual audit records into abstract events. In addition, on the basis of MuSigs, the available audit trail, and the strategy costs, ARMD uses a strategy generator to automatically generate monitoring strategies to govern the misuse detection process.

ARMD is a host-based misuse detection system. In addition to the features mentioned above, it also employs database query optimization techniques to speed up the processing of audit events. The experiences with ARMD show that knowing the characteristics of the audit trail helps estimate the cost of performing misuse detection and gives the security officers the opportunity to tune the misuse detection system.

A limitation of ARMD is that it requires users to have a precise understanding of the attacks and to make careful plans for the abstraction of events. This planning is not an easy job, especially when a user does not know how his or her MuSigs may be used. In particular, unforeseen attacks may invalidate previously defined abstract events and MuSigs, thus forcing the redevelopment of some or all of the MuSigs.

The work by Ning, Jajodia, and Wang (2001) further extended ARMD to address the aforementioned limitation. It provides a framework for distributed attack specification and event abstraction. In this framework, abstraction is considered an ongoing process. The structures of abstract events are represented as system views, and attack signatures are represented as generic patterns on the basis of system views. This new approach allows the semantics of a system view to be modified by defining new signatures and view definitions without changing the specifications of the views or the signatures specified on the basis of the system views. As a result, signatures in this model can potentially accommodate unknown variants of known attack patterns. Although the specification of attack signatures and the choice of right abstraction still partially depend on the users' skill, this framework provides guidance and alleviates the burden of writing and maintaining signatures.

## Limitation of Misuse Detection

Current misuse detection systems usually work better than anomaly detection systems for known attacks. That is, misuse detection systems detect patterns of known attacks more accurately and generate much fewer false alarms than do anomaly detection systems. This better performance occurs because misuse detection systems take advantage of explicit knowledge of the attacks.

The limitation of misuse detection is that it cannot detect novel or unknown attacks. As a result, the computer systems protected solely by misuse detection systems face the risk of being compromised without detecting the attacks. In addition, because explicit representation of attacks is required, misuse detection requires the nature of the attacks to be well understood. This implies that human experts must work on the analysis and representation of attacks, which is usually time consuming and error prone. Lee and Stolfo (2000) have improved this process by automatically building an intrusion detection model; however, identification of attacks in past events is still required.

# INTRUSION DETECTION IN DISTRIBUTED SYSTEMS

The rapid growth of the Internet not only provides the means for resource and information sharing but it also brings new challenges to the intrusion detection community. Because of the complexity and the amount of audit data generated by large-scale systems, traditional IDSs that were designed for individual hosts and small-scale networked systems cannot be applied directly to large-scale systems.

Research on intrusion detection in distributed systems is currently focusing on two essential issues: *scalability* and *heterogeneity*. The IDSs in large distributed systems need to be scalable to accommodate the large amount of audit data in such systems. In addition, such IDSs must be able to deal with heterogeneous information from component systems of different types and large distributed systems, as well as being able to cooperate with other types of IDSs.

Research on distributed intrusion detection is being conducted in three main areas. First, people are building scalable, distributed IDSs or are extending existing IDSs to make them capable of being scaled up to large systems. Second, network-based IDSs are being developed to take advantage of the standard network protocols to avoid heterogeneous audit data from different platforms. Third, standards and techniques are being developed to facilitate information sharing among different, possibly heterogeneous IDSs.

## Distributed Intrusion Detection Systems

Early distributed IDSs collected audit data in a distributed manner, but analyzed the data in a centralized place; for example, DIDS (Snapp et al., 1991) and ASAX (Mounji,

Charlier, Zampuniéris, & Habra, 1995). Although audit data were usually reduced before being sent to the central analysis unit, the scalability of such systems was still limited. When the size of the distributed system grows large, not only might audit data have to travel long distances before arriving at the central place but the central analysis component of the IDS may also be overwhelmed by large amount of audit data being generated.

Recent systems, such as EMERALD (Lindqvist & Porras, 1999), graph-based intrusion detection systems (GrIDS; Axelsson, 1999), and the autonomous agents for intrusion detection system (AAFID; Spafford & Zamboni, 2000), pay more attention to the scalability issue. To scale up to large distributed systems, these systems place IDS components in various locations in a distributed system. Each of these components receives audit data or alerts from a limited number of sources (e.g., hosts or other IDS components), so the system is not overwhelmed by large amounts of audit data. Different components are often organized hierarchically in a tree structure; lower-level IDS components disseminate their detection results to higher-level components, so the intrusion-related information from different locations can be correlated together.

Although most of the recent distributed IDSs are designed to be scalable, they only provide a partial solution to the scalability problem. The IDS components are either coordinated in an ad hoc way or are organized hierarchically. Although coordinating the IDS components in an ad hoc way is certainly not a general solution, organizing the components hierarchically is not always efficient, especially when the suspicious activities are spread out in different, unpredictable locations in a large system. In a hierarchical system, when the activities involved in a distributed attack fall beyond the scope of one IDS component, the audit data possibly related to the attack will have to be forwarded to a higher-level IDS component to be correlated with data from other places. In a worst-case scenario, the audit data may have to be forwarded several times before arriving at a place where the data can finally be correlated with the related information. This process not only wastes the network's bandwidth but it also limits the scalability of the detection of distributed attacks.

Abstraction-based intrusion detection (Ning, Jajodia, & Wang, 2001) addresses this problem by generating a hierarchy of IDS components dynamically, rather than statically. Intuitively, this method defines attack signatures as generic patterns (called *generic signatures*) of abstract events that may be observed in different places in a distributed system. When a particular type of attack is to be detected in a distributed system, the corresponding generic signature is mapped to the specific systems. The resulting signature is called a *specific signature*. This method then decomposes the specific signature into components called *detection tasks*, each of which corresponds to the intrusion detection activities required to process a type of event involved in the attack. A coordination mechanism is developed to arrange the messages passing between the detection tasks, so the distributed detection of attacks is equivalent to having all events processed in a central place. The abstraction-based method is more flexible and more efficient than the previous methods;

however, it is limited in that it is applicable only to misuse detection.

## Network-Based Intrusion Detection Systems

Network-based IDSs collect audit data from the network traffic, as opposed to host-based IDSs, which usually collect audit data from host audit trails. Examples of network-based IDSs include Network Security Monitor (NSM; Axelsson, 1999), NetSTAT (Vigna & Kemmerer, 1999), and Bro (Axelsson, 1999).

One challenge that network-based intrusion detection is facing is the speed of high-performance networks. This great speed makes it very difficult to capture the network traffic, let alone perform intrusion detection in real time.

Several efforts have addressed intrusion detection in high-speed networks. Snort, an open source IDS that specializes in network intrusion detection (Snort, 2002), was developed by Roesch (1999). It employs a fast pattern-matching algorithm to detect network misuse. However, early versions of Snort detected attacks individually, and its performance degrades when the number of attack signatures (rules) increases. Since version 1.9, Snort has incorporated new pattern-matching algorithms to address this problem.

Sekar, Guang, Verma, and Shanbhag (1999) developed a high-performance network IDS based on efficient pattern-matching algorithms. A distinguishing feature is that the performance of the system is independent of the number of misuse rules (signatures).

Kruegel, Valeur, Vigna, and Kemmerer (2002) proposed a partition approach to intrusion detection that supports misuse detection on high-speed network links. This approach is based on a slicing mechanism that divides the overall network traffic into subsets of manageable size. Thus, each subset can be processed by one or several misuse detection systems. The traffic partitioning is done such that each subset of the network traffic contains all of the evidence necessary to detect a specific attack.

Network-based IDSs offer several advantages. First, they can take advantage of the standard structure of network protocols, such as TCP/IP. This is a good way to avoid the confusion resulting from heterogeneity in a distributed system. Second, network-based IDSs usually run on a separate (dedicated) computer; thus, they do not consume the resources of the computers that are being protected.

Conversely, network-based IDS are not silver bullets. First, because these IDSs do not use host-based information, they may miss the opportunity to detect some attacks. For example, network-based IDSs cannot detect an attack launched from a console. Second, the standard network protocols do not solve the entire problem related to the heterogeneity of distributed systems because of the variety of application protocols and systems that use these protocols. For example, network-based IDSs must understand the UNIX shell commands if their goal is to monitor intrusive remote logins. As another example, network-based IDSs usually describe the suspicious network activities using the structure of the packet that standard network protocols such as TCP/IP support, which makes the specification of the suspicious activities to be detected very difficult.

Network-based IDSs have the same scalability problem as do general distributed IDSs. For example, existing network-based IDSs analyze network traffic data in a centralized place, as was done by the early distributed IDSs, although they may collect data from various places in the network. This structure limits the scale of the distributed systems that such IDSs can protect.

## Sharing Information Among Intrusion Detection Systems

With the deployment of so many commercial IDSs, these IDSs must be able to share information so that they can interact and thus achieve better performance than if operating in isolation. Research and development activities are currently under way to enable different, possibly heterogeneous IDSs to share information.

The common intrusion detection framework (CIDF) was developed to enable different intrusion detection and response (IDR) components to interoperate and share information and resources (Porras, Schnackenberg, Staniford-Chen, Stillman, & Wu, 1999). It began as a part of the Defense Advanced Research Project Agency (DARPA) Information Survivability program, with a focus on allowing DARPA projects to work together. CIDF considers IDR systems to be composed of four types of components that communicate via message passing: event generators (E-boxes), event analyzers (A-boxes), event databases (D-boxes), and response units (R-boxes). A communication framework and a common intrusion specification language are provided to assist the interoperation among CIDF components.

Researchers involved in CIDF started an Intrusion Detection Working Group (IDWG) in the Internet Engineering Task Force (IETF) in an attempt to bring CIDF to a broader community. The IDWG has been working to develop data formats and exchange procedures for sharing information among IDSs, response systems, and management systems. The extensible markup language (XML) has been chosen to provide the common format, and an intrusion detection message exchange format (IDMEF) has been defined in an Internet draft. The IDWG uses the blocks extensible exchange protocol (BEEP) as the application protocol framework for exchanging intrusion detection messages between different systems; an intrusion detection exchange protocol (IDXP) is specified as a BEEP profile, and a tunnel profile is provided to enable different systems to exchange messages through firewalls. At the time of this writing, these Internet drafts are under consideration for being adopted as IETF requests for comments (RFCs).

A negotiation protocol for CIDF components has been developed as part of the intrusion detection intercomponent adaptive negotiation (IDIAN) project (Feiertag et al., 2000). It allows distributed IDS components to discover the intrusion detection services of other components and to negotiate, manage, and adjust the use of those services. In particular, the notion of a filter was introduced to assist the negotiation process. A filter is essentially a pattern of CIDF messages, and the negotiation process helps determine one or several filters between two CIDF components. A CIDF component sends a CIDF message to another component only when the message matches the filters of the receiver. Similarly, a receiving CIDF component accepts an incoming CIDF message only if the message matches one of its filters. IDIAN partially addresses the information-sharing problem by enabling different IDS components to discover, negotiate, and adjust the use of services from each other.

Another effort in sharing information among different IDSs is the Hummer project (Frincke, Tobin, McConnell, Marconi, & Polla, 1998). In particular, the relationships among different IDSs (e.g., peer, friend, manager/subordinate) and policy issues (e.g., access control policy, cooperation policy) were studied, and a prototype system, HummingBird, was developed to address these issues. A limitation of the Hummer project is that it only addresses the general data-sharing issue; what information needs to be shared and how the information would be used are out of its scope. Thus, it should be used along with such mechanisms as IDIAN (Feiertag et al., 2000) and the decentralized coordination mechanism in the abstraction-based approach (Ning et al., 2001).

# INTRUSION ALERT CORRELATION

Traditional IDSs focus on low-level attacks or anomalies and raise alerts independently, though there may be logical connections between them. In situations where there are intensive attacks, not only will actual alerts be mixed with false alerts but the amount of alerts will also become unmanageable. As a result, it is difficult for human users or intrusion response systems to understand the alerts and take appropriate actions. Therefore, it is necessary to develop techniques to correlate IDS alerts and construct attack scenarios (i.e., steps that attackers use in their attacks) to facilitate intrusion analysis.

In this section, we first give a brief overview of the techniques for intrusion alert correlation and then present in more detail one approach that correlates intrusion alerts based on prerequisites and consequences of known attacks.

Techniques for intrusion alert correlation can be divided into several classes. The first class of approaches—for example, Spice (Staniford, Hoagland, & McAlerney, 2002), and probabilistic alert correlation (Valdes & Skinner, 2001)—correlates IDS alerts based on the similarities between alert attributes. These approaches usually require a distance function to measure the similarity between two IDS alerts based on the alert attribute values, and they correlate two alerts together if the distance between them is less than a certain threshold. Though they are effective for clustering similar alerts (e.g., alerts with the same source and destination IP addresses), they cannot fully discover the causal relationships between related alerts.

The second class of methods—for example, based on STATL (Eckmann, Vigna, & Kemmerer, 2002)—performs alert correlation based on attack scenarios specified by human users or learned from training datasets. Such methods are essentially extensions to misuse detection. Similar to misuse detection, intrusion alert correlation based on known scenarios is effective in recognizing known attack scenarios, but is also restricted to those scenarios or those that can be generalized from known scenarios. A variation in this class uses a consequence mechanism to specify what types of attacks may follow a given attack, partially addressing this problem (Debar & Wespi, 2001).

The third class of methods—for example, JIGSAW (Templeton & Levitt, 2000), the MIRADOR correlation method (Cuppens & Miege, 2002), and the correlation method based on prerequisites and consequences of attacks (Ning, Cui, & Reeves, 2002)—targets recognition of multistage attacks; it correlates alerts if the prerequisites of some later alerts are satisfied by the consequences of some earlier alerts. Such methods can potentially uncover the causal relationship between alerts and are not restricted to known attack scenarios. We discuss one such method in detail later.

The fourth class of methods attempts to correlate alerts (including IDS alerts) from multiple sources, using potentially complementary information to improve the understanding of possible intrusions. A formal model named M2D2 was proposed by Morin and colleagues (Morin, Mé, Debar, & Ducassé, 2002) to correlate alerts by using multiple information sources, including the characteristics of the monitored systems, the vulnerability information, the information about the monitoring tools, and information about the observed events. Because of the multiple information sources used in alert correlation, this method can potentially yield better results than those simply looking at intrusion alerts. A mission-impact-based approach was proposed by Porras, Fong, and Valdes (2002) to correlate alerts raised by INFOSEC devices, such as IDSs and firewalls. A distinguishing feature of this approach is that it correlates the alerts with the importance of system assets so that attention can be focused on critical resources. Though methods in this class are still in their preliminary stage, we believe techniques in this class will eventually provide the most support for intrusion alert analysis.

## Intrusion Alert Correlation Based on Prerequisites and Consequences of Attacks

To further illustrate intrusion alert correlation techniques, we give additional details about the alert correlation method based on prerequisites and consequences of attacks (Ning et al., 2002), which one of us was involved in developing.

The alert correlation model is based on the observation that, in series of attacks, the component attacks are usually not isolated, but are related as different stages of the attacks, with the early ones preparing for the later ones. For example, an attacker has to install distributed denial of dervice (DDoS) daemon programs before launching a DDoS attack. To take advantage of this observation, this method correlates alerts using prerequisites and consequences of the corresponding attacks. Intuitively, the *prerequisite* of an attack is the necessary condition for the attack to be successful. For example, the existence of a vulnerable service is the prerequisite of a remote buffer overflow attack against the service. Moreover, an attacker may make progress (e.g., install a Trojan horse program) as a result of an attack. Informally, the possible outcome of an attack is called the *consequence* of the attack. In a series of attacks where earlier ones are launched to prepare for later ones, there are usually connections between the consequences of the earlier attacks and the prerequisites of the later ones. Accordingly, this method identifies the prerequisites (e.g., existence of vulnerable services) and the consequences (e.g., discovery of vulnerable services) of attacks and correlates detected attacks (i.e., alerts) by matching the consequences of previous alerts and the prerequisites of later ones.

Predicates are used as basic constructs to represent prerequisites and consequences of attacks. For example, a scanning attack may discover UDP services vulnerable to certain buffer overflow attacks. We can use the predicate *UDPVulnerableToBOF* (*VictimIP*, *VictimPort*) to represent this discovery. In general, a logical formula (i.e., logical combination of predicates) is used to represent the prerequisite of an attack. Thus, we may have a prerequisite of the form *UDPVulnerableToBOF* (*VictimIP*, *VictimPort*) ^ *UDPAccessibleViaFirewall* (*VictimIP*, *VictimPort*). Similarly, a set of logical formulas is used to represent the consequence of an attack.

With predicates as basic constructs, a *hyper-alert type* is used to encode our knowledge about each type of attacks. A *hyper-alert type T* is a triple (*fact, prerequisite, consequence*) where (1) *fact* is a set of attribute names, each with an associated domain of values, (2) *prerequisite* is a logical formula whose free variables are all in *fact*, and (3) *consequence* is a set of logical formulas such that all the free variables in *consequence* are in *fact*. Intuitively, the *fact* component of a hyper-alert type gives the information associated with the alert, *prerequisite* specifies what must be true for the attack to be successful, and *consequence* describes what could be true if the attack indeed happens. For brevity, we omit the domains associated with attribute names when they are clear from context.

Given a hyper-alert type $T$ = (*fact, prerequisite, consequence*), a *hyper-alert* (instance) $h$ of type $T$ is a finite set of tuples on *fact*, where each tuple is associated with an interval-based time stamp [begin_time, end_time]. The hyper-alert $h$ implies that *prerequisite* must evaluate to True, and all the logical formulas in *consequence* might evaluate to True for each of the tuples. The *fact* component of a hyper-alert type is essentially a relation schema (as in relational databases), and a hyper-alert is a relation instance of this schema. A hyper-alert *instantiates* its *prerequisite* and *consequence* by replacing the free variables

in *prerequisite* and *consequence* with its specific values. Note that *prerequisite* and *consequence* can be instantiated multiple times if *fact* consists of multiple tuples. For example, if an IPSweep attack involves several IP addresses, the *prerequisite* and *consequence* of the corresponding hyper-alert type will be instantiated for each of these addresses.

To correlate hyper-alerts, this method checks if an earlier hyper-alert contributes to the prerequisite of a later one. Specifically, it decomposes the prerequisite of a hyper-alert into parts of predicates and tests whether the consequence of an earlier hyper-alert makes some parts of the prerequisite True (i.e., makes the prerequisite easier to satisfy). If the result is positive, then the hyper-alerts are correlated together. In the formal model, given an instance $h$ of the hyper-alert type $T$ = (*fact, prerequisite, consequence*), the *prerequisite set* (or *consequence set*, respectively) of $h$, denoted $P(h)$ [or $C(h)$, respectively], is the set of all such predicates that appear in *prerequisite* (or *consequence*, respectively) whose arguments are replaced with the corresponding attribute values of each tuple in $h$. Each element in $P(h)$ [or $C(h)$, respectively] is associated with the time stamp of the corresponding tuple in $h$. A hyper-alert $h_1$ *prepares for* hyper-alert $h_2$ if there exist $p \in P(h_2)$ and $C \subseteq C(h_1)$ such that for all $c \in C$, $c$.end_time $< p$.begin_time and the conjunction of all the logical formulas in $C$ implies $p$.

Given a sequence $S$ of hyper-alerts, a hyper-alert $h$ in $S$ is a *correlated hyper-alert* if there exists another hyper-alert $h'$ such that either $h$ prepares for $h'$ or $h'$ prepares for $h$. A *hyper-alert correlation graph* is used to represent a set of correlated hyper-alerts. Specifically, a *hyper-alert correlation graph* $CG = (N, E)$ is a connected graph, where $N$ is a set of hyper-alerts and for each pair $n_1$, $n_2 \in N$, there is a directed edge from $n_1$ to $n_2$ in $E$ if and only if $n_1$ prepares for $n_2$.

Figure 1 shows one of the hyper-alert correlation graphs discovered in an experiment with the 2000 DARPA intrusion detection evaluation datasets. Each node in Figure 1 represents a hyper-alert, where the label inside the node is the hyper-alert type followed by the hyper-alert ID. This hyper-alert correlation graph shows an attack scenario in which the attacker probes for vulnerable *Sadmind* service, compromises the vulnerable service using a buffer overflow attack, copies some file with *Rsh*, starts a DDoS daemon program named *mstream*, and finally launches a DDoS attack.

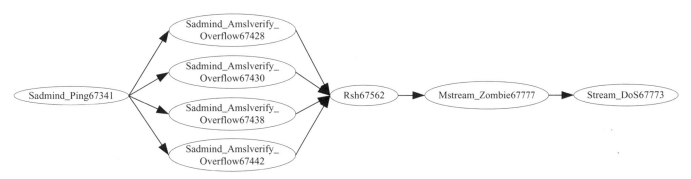

**Figure 1:** A hyper-alert correlation graph.

# CONCLUSION

Intrusion detection continues to be an active research field. Even after more than 20 years of research, however, the intrusion detection community still faces several difficult problems. How to detect unknown patterns of attacks without generating too many false alerts remains an unresolved problem, although recently, several results have shown there is a potential resolution to it. The evaluation and benchmarking of IDSs are also important issues that, once addressed, may provide useful guidance for organizational decision makers and end users. Some recent results in evaluating IDSs can be found in McHugh (2000). Moreover, reconstructing attack scenarios from intrusion alerts and integration of IDSs will improve both their usability and performance. Because many researchers and practitioners are actively addressing these problems, we expect intrusion detection to become a practical and effective solution for protecting information systems.

It is not possible to cover everything about intrusion detection in one chapter. Additional topics related to intrusion detection (e.g., host-based and network-based IDSs, intrusion detection using agent systems) are discussed in other chapters of this *Handbook*.

# GLOSSARY

**Anomaly Detection**   One of the two methodologies of intrusion detection. Anomaly detection is based on the normal behavior of a subject (e.g., a user or a system); any action that significantly deviates from the normal behavior is considered intrusive. More generally, anomaly detection refers to the identification of potential system security policy violations based on observation that some action or other characteristics deviate from normal. The underlying philosophy is that normal or acceptable behaviors and other features can be described and deviations from them recognized. The other methodology is misuse detection.

**Audit Trail**   A chronology of system resource usage that includes user login, file access, other various activities, and whether any actual or attempted security violations occurred.

**False Negative**   An actual misuse action that the system allows to pass as nonmisuse behavior.

**False Positive**   Classification of an action as anomalous (a possible instance of misuse) when it is legitimate.

**IDS**   Intrusion detection system.

**Intrusion**   Any activity that violates the security policy of an information system, normally ascribed to a system outsider who "enters" the system to perform this behavior but sometimes used more generally to cover any violation of policy. Also referred to as "misuse."

**Intrusion Alert Correlation**   The process of identifying related intrusion alerts and the relationship among them. The goal is often to reconstruct the attack scenarios (i.e., steps of attacks) from the intrusion alerts reported by IDS; alternately it may be used to recognize broad-based attacks even without regard to specific steps.

**Intrusion Detection**   The process of identifying intrusions or other misuses by observing security logs, audit data, or other information available in computer systems and/or networks.

**Misuse Detection**   One of the two methodologies of intrusion detection, often but not necessarily used to scrutinize representations of behavior. This method catches intrusions in terms of the characteristics of known patterns of attacks or system vulnerabilities; any action that conforms to the pattern of a known attack or vulnerability is considered intrusive. More generally, misuse detection refers to identification of system security policy violations based on recognizing actions or other characteristics known to be associated with such violations. The philosophy behind misuse detection is that inappropriate activities or behaviors can be characterized and used to detect policy violations. The other methodology is anomaly detection.

**Misuse Signature**   A known pattern or attack or vulnerability, usually specified in a certain attack specification language.

**Profile**   A set of parameters used to represent the pattern of a subject's (e.g., a user or a program) normal behavior. It is normally used to conduct anomaly detection.

**Security Policy**   A set of rules and procedures regulating the use of information, including its processing, storage, distribution, and presentation.

# CROSS REFERENCES

See *Computer Viruses and Worms; Host-Based Intrusion Detection Systems; Network-Based Intrusion Detection Systems; Security Policy Guidelines; The Use of Agent Technology for Intrusion Detection.*

# REFERENCES

Anderson, J. P. (1980). *Computer security threat monitoring and surveillance* (Technical Report). Fort Washington, PA: James P. Anderson Company.

Axelsson, S. (1999). *Research in intrusion-detection systems: A survey* (Technical Report TR 98-17). Göteborg, Sweden: Chalmers University of Technology, Department of Computer Engineering.

Barbara, D., Couto, J., Jajodia, S., & Wu, N. (2001). ADAM: A testbed for exploring the use of data mining in intrusion detection. *ACM SIGMOD Record, 30*(4), 15–24.

Barbara, D., Couto, J., Jajodia, S., & Wu, N. (2002). An architecture for anomaly detection. In D. Barbara & S. Jajodia (Eds.), *Applications of data mining in computer security* (pp. 63–76). Boston: Kluwer Academic.

Cuppens, F., & Miege, A. (2002). Alert correlation in a cooperative intrusion detection framework. In *Proceedings of the 2002 IEEE Symposium on Security and Privacy* (pp. 202–215). Los Alamitos, CA: IEEE Computer Society.

Debar, H. & Wespi, A. (2001). Aggregation and correlation of intrusion-detection alerts. In *Proceedings of Recent Advances in Intrusion Detection (Lecture Note in Computer Science 2212)* (pp. 85–103). Springer-Verlag.

Eckmann, S., Vigna, G., & Kemmerer, R. (2002). STATL: An attack language for state-based intrusion detection. *Journal of Computer Security, 10*, 71–104.

Feiertag, R., Rho, S., Benzinger, L., Wu, S., Redmond, T., Zhang, et al. (2000). Intrusion detection intercomponent adaptive negotiation. *Computer Networks, 34*, 605–621.

Fox, K. L., Henning, R. R., Reed, J. H., & Simonian, R. P. (1990). A neural network approach towards intrusion detection. In *Proceedings of 13th National Computer Security Conference* (pp. 125–134). Baltimore: National Institute of Standards and Technology (NIST).

Frincke, D., Tobin, D., McConnell, J., Marconi, J., & Polla, D. (1998). A framework for cooperative intrusion detection. In *Proceedings of the 21st National Information Systems Security Conference* (pp. 361–373). Baltimore: National Institute of Standards and Technology (NIST).

Ghosh, A. K., Wanken, J., & Charron, F. (1998). Detecting anomalous and unknown intrusions against programs. In K. Keus (Ed.), *Proceedings of the 14th Annual Computer Security Applications Conference* (pp. 259–267). Los Alamitos, CA: IEEE Computer Society.

Hofmeyr, S., Forrest, S., & Somayaji, A. (1998). Intrusion detection using sequences of system calls. *Journal of Computer Security, 6*, 151–180.

Ilgun, K., Kemmerer, R. A., & Porras, P. A. (1995). State transition analysis: A rule-based intrusion detection approach. *IEEE Transactions on Software Engineering, 21*(3), 181–199.

Ko, C. (2000). Logic induction of valid behavior specifications for intrusion detection. In M. Reiter & R. Needham (Eds.), *Proceedings of 2000 IEEE Symposium of Security and Privacy* (pp. 142–153). Los Alamitos, CA: IEEE Computer Society.

Ko, C., Ruschitzka, M., & Levitt, K. (1997). Execution monitoring of security-critical programs in distributed systems: A specification-based approach. In G. Dinolt & P. Karger (Eds.), *Proceedings of 1997 IEEE Symposium of Security and Privacy* (pp. 175–187). Los Alamitos, CA: IEEE Computer Society.

Kruegel, C., Valeur, F., Vigna, G., & Kemmerer, R. (2002). Stateful intrusion detection for high-speed networks. In M. Abadi & S. Bellovin (Eds.), *Proceedings of 2002 IEEE Symposium on Security and Privacy* (pp. 285–293). Los Alamitos, CA: IEEE Computer Society.

Kumar, S. (1995). *Classification and detection of computer intrusions*. Unpublished doctoral dissertation, Purdue University, West Lafayette, IN.

Kumar, S., & Spafford, E. H. (1994). A pattern-matching model for misuse intrusion detection. In *Proceedings of the 17th National Computer Security Conference* (pp. 11–21). Baltimore: National Institute of Standards and Technology (NIST).

Lane, T., & Brodley, C. E. (1998). Temporal sequence learning and data reduction for anomaly detection. In L. Gong & M. Reiter (Eds.), *Proceedings of 5th Conference on Computer and Communications Security* (pp. 150–158). New York: ACM Press.

Lee, W., & Stolfo, S. J. (2000). A framework for constructing features and models for intrusion detection systems. *ACM Transactions on Information and System Security, 3*(4), 227–261.

Lee, W., & Xiang, D. (2001). Information-theoretic measures for anomaly detection. In R. Needham &

M. Abadi (Eds.), *Proceedings of 2001 IEEE Symposium on Security and Privacy* (pp. 130–143). Los Alamitos, CA: IEEE Computer Society.

Lin, J., Wang, X. S., & Jajodia, S. (1998). Abstraction-based misuse detection: High-level specifications and adaptable strategies. In S. Foley (Ed.), *Proceedings of the 11th Computer Security Foundations Workshop* (pp. 190–201). Los Alamitos, CA: IEEE Computer Society.

Lindqvist, U., & Porras, P. A. (1999). Detecting computer and network misuse through the production-based expert system toolset (P-BEST). In L. Gong & M. Reiter (Eds.), *Proceedings of the 1999 IEEE Symposium on Security and Privacy* (pp. 146–161). Los Alamitos, CA: IEEE Computer Society.

Mannila, H., Toivonen, H., & Verkamo, A. I. (1995). Discovering frequent episodes in sequences. In U. Fayyad & R. Uthurusamy (Eds.), *Proceedings of the 1st Conference on Knowledge Discovery and Data Mining* (pp. 210–215). Menlo Park, CA: AAAI Press.

McHugh, J. (2000). Testing intrusion detection systems: A critique of the 1998 and 1999 DARPA intrusion detection system evaluations as performed by Lincoln laboratory. *ACM Transactions on Information and System Security, 3*(4), 262–294.

Morin, B., Mé, L., Debar, H., & Ducassé, M. (2002). M2D2: A formal data model for IDS alert correlation. In *Proceedings of the 5th International Symposium on Recent Advances in Intrusion Detection* (pp. 115–137). Springer-Verlag. Zurich, Switzerland.

Mounji, A., Charlier, B. L., Zampuniéris, D., & Habra, N. (1995). Distributed audit trail analysis. In D. Balenson & R. Shirey (Eds.), *Proceedings of the ISOC '95 Symposium on Network and Distributed System Security* (pp. 102–112). Los Alamitos, CA: IEEE Computer Society.

Ning, P., Cui, Y., & Reeves, D. S. (2002). Constructing attack scenarios through correlation of intrusion alerts. In *Proceedings of the 9th ACM Conference on Computer and Communications Security* (pp. 245–254). Washington, DC: ACM Press.

Ning, P., Jajodia, S., & Wang, X. S. (2001). Abstraction-based intrusion detection in distributed environments. *ACM Transactions on Information and System Security, 4*(4), 407–452.

Porras, P., Fong, M., & Valdes, A. (2002). A mission-impact-based approach to INFOSEC alarm correlation. In *Proceedings of the 5th International Symposium on Recent Advances in Intrusion Detection* (pp. 95–114). Springer-Verlag. Zurich, Switzerland.

Porras, P., Schnackenberg, D., Staniford-Chen, S., Stillman, M., & Wu, F. (1999). *Common intrusion detection framework architecture*. Retrieved February 13, 2003, from http://www.isi.edu/gost/cidf/

Roesch, M. (1999). Snort—lightweight intrusion detection for networks. In D. Parter (Ed.), *Proceedings of the 13th Systems Administration Conference*. Retrieved February 13, 2003, from http://www.usenix.org/publications/library/proceedings/lisa99/technical.html

Sekar, R., Bendre, M., Dhurjati, D., & Bollineni, P. (2001). A fast automaton-based method for detecting anomalous program behaviors. In R. Needham & M. Abadi

(Eds.), *Proceedings of 2001 IEEE Symposium on Security and Privacy* (pp. 144–155). Los Alamitos, CA: IEEE Computer Society.

Sekar, R., Guang, Y., Verma, S., & Shanbhag, T. (1999). A high-performance network intrusion detection system. In J. Motiwalla & G. Tsudik (Eds.), *Proceedings of the 6th ACM Conference on Computer and Communications Security* (pp. 8–17). New York: ACM Press.

Snapp, S. R., et al. (1991). DIDS (distributed intrusion detection system)—motivation, architecture, and an early prototype. In *Proceedings of 14th National Computer Security Conference* (pp. 167–176). Baltimore: National Institute of Standards and Technology (NIST).

*Snort—The open source intrusion detection system.* (2002). Retrieved February 13, 2003, from http://www.snort.org

Spafford, E. H., & Zamboni, D. (2000). Intrusion detection using autonomous agents. *Computer Networks, 34,* 547–570.

Staniford, S., Hoagland, J., & McAlerney, J. (2002). Practical automated detection of stealthy portscans. *Journal of Computer Security*, 105–136.

Templeton, S., & Levitt, K. (2000). A requires/provides model for computer attacks. In *Proceedings of New Security Paradigms Workshop* (pp. 31–38). New York: ACM Press.

Teng, H. S., Chen, K., & Lu, S. C. (1990). Adaptive real-time anomaly detection using inductively generated sequential patterns. In *Proceedings of 1990 IEEE Symposium on Security and Privacy* (pp. 278–284). Los Alamitos, CA: IEEE Computer Society.

Valdes, A., & Skinner, K. (2001). Probabilistic alert correlation. In *Proceedings of the 4th International Symposium on Recent Advances in Intrusion Detection* (pp. 54–68). Springer-Verlag. Davis, CA: USA.

Vigna, G., & Kemmerer, R. A. (1999). NetSTAT: A network-based intrusion detection system. *Journal of Computer Security, 7*(1), 37–71.

Wagner, D., & Dean, D. (2001). Intrusion detection via static analysis. In R. Needham & M. Abadi (Eds.), *Proceedings of 2001 IEEE Symposium on Security and Privacy* (pp. 156–168). Los Alamitos, CA IEEE Computer Society.

Zamboni, D. (2001) *Using internal sensors for computer intrusion detection.* Unpublished doctoral dissertation, Purdue University, West Lafayette, IN.

# Host-Based Intrusion Detection Systems

Giovanni Vigna, *Reliable Software Group*
Christopher Kruegel, *Technical University, Vienna, Austria*

## INTRODUCTION

Intrusion detection (Crothers, 2002; Schultz, Endorf, & Mellander, 2003) is the process of identifying and responding to suspicious activities targeted at computing and communication resources. An intrusion detection system (IDS) monitors and collects data from a target system that should be protected, processes and correlates the gathered information, and initiates responses when evidence of an intrusion is detected. Depending on their source of input, IDSs can be classified into network-based systems and host-based systems.

Network-based intrusion detection systems (NIDSs) collect input data by monitoring network traffic (e.g., packets captured by network interfaces in promiscuous mode). Host-based intrusion detection systems (HIDSs), on the other hand, rely on events collected by the hosts they monitor.

HIDSs can be classified based on the type of audit data they analyze or based on the techniques used to analyze their input. We chose a characterization based on the type of audit data and, in the following, present the two most common classes: operating system–level intrusion detection systems and application-level intrusion detection systems. For each class, we describe how audit data are gathered and what type of techniques are used for its analysis.

## OPERATING SYSTEM–LEVEL INTRUSION DETECTION

Host-based IDSs in this class use information provided by the operating system (OS) to identify attacks. This information can be of different granularity and level of abstraction. However, it usually relates to low-level system operations such as system calls, file system modifications, and user logons. Because these operations represent a low-level event stream, they usually contain reliable information and are difficult to tamper with, unless the system is compromised at the kernel level.

In the following, some OS-level auditing data-gathering mechanisms are presented. Then, different analysis techniques that use this type of information are described.

## Audit Data Gathering

Auditing is a mechanism to collect information regarding the activity of users and applications. To be useful, audit mechanisms have to be both tamper-resistant and non-bypassable. The OS is usually regarded as a trusted entity because it controls access to resources, such as memory and files. Therefore, most existing audit mechanisms are implemented within the OS.

OS audit data are not designed specifically for intrusion detection. Therefore, in many cases, the audit records produced by OS-level auditing facilities contain irrelevant information and sometimes also lack useful information. As a result, IDSs often have to access the OS directly to gather required data.

In past years, researchers have attempted to identify what type of information should be provided to an IDS to be able to detect intrusions effectively. For example, Lunt (1993) suggested the use of IDS-specific audit trails. Daniels and Spafford extended this initial idea and identified the audit data that OSs need to provide to support the detection of attacks against the TCP/IP stack (1999).

The availability of OS-level auditing mechanisms depends on the operating system considered. For example, Sun's operating systems (first SunOS and later Solaris) provide auditing information through the Basic Security Module (BSM). The BSM is a kernel extension that allows one to log events at the system call level. Different auditing levels can be specified, and, in addition to system calls, security-relevant higher-level events can be generated as well (e.g., login events). Unfortunately, auditing can be disabled by the `root` user, making this particular facility vulnerable to abuse by an attacker who gains administrative privileges on the monitored host.

BSM produces audit records that are stored in audit files in a binary format (to be more space efficient). The contents of such an audit file can be printed in human-readable format using the `praudit` tool. Figure 1 shows an example of records contained in a BSM audit file, as printed by the `praudit` tool. In this example, the records represent the execution of commands performed by invoking the `execve` system call.

```
Thu Aug 10 22:01:29 2004 -> UID:root EUID:root RUID:root - From machine:log1
execve() + /usr/bin/sparcv7/ps + cmdline:ps,-ef + success
Thu Aug 10 22:01:50 2004 -> UID:root EUID:root RUID:root - From machine:log1
execve() + /usr/bin/tail + cmdline:tail,/etc/system + success
Thu Aug 10 22:11:18 2004 -> UID:root EUID:root RUID:root - From machine:log1
execve() + /usr/bin/pwd + cmdline:pwd + success
Thu Aug 10 22:11:20 2004 -> UID:root EUID:root RUID:root - From machine:log1
execve() + /usr/bin/ls + cmdline:ls,-l + success
Thu Aug 10 22:11:33 2004 -> UID:root EUID:root RUID:root - From machine:log1
execve() + /usr/bin/ls + cmdline:ls,-l + success
```

**Figure 1:** BSM audit records.

Similar information is provided by other auditing facilities for different OSs. For example, for the Linux OS, SNARE and LIDS provide kernel-level auditing information.

SNARE (System Intrusion Analysis and Reporting Environment) wraps system calls in routines that gather and log information about processes that execute security-relevant system calls. It also supports simple pattern-matching operations on the audit records produced, which can be used as a rudimentary form of intrusion detection. A graphical tool that allows for the filtering of the collected information is provided as well.

LIDS (Linux Intrusion Detection System), despite its name, is not an intrusion detection system per se. Instead, it provides, in addition to its auditing capabilities, an access control layer that complements the standard UNIX access control mechanisms. This access control layer allows one to specify access control for files, processes, and devices. In particular, LIDS does not grant complete control to the root user. Therefore, it is possible to guarantee the protection of critical system parts (e.g., the kernel) even when the root account has been compromised. Access control is managed with the help of *capabilities*. Examples of such capabilities include CAP_LINUX_IMMUTABLE, which protects files or complete file systems from being overwritten when marked as "immutable," and CAP_NET_ADMIN, which prevents tampering with the network configuration (e.g., prevents route table entries from being changed, and prevents firewall entries from being tampered with). Other capabilities are provided to control the insertion and removal of kernel modules, raw disk/device I/O, and a range of other system administration functions.

Another place where audit and security information is stored are operating system log files. For example, almost all UNIX systems offer the *syslog* logging facility. The syslog facility is accessible through an API (Application Programming Interface) that sends a log message to syslogd, the logging daemon. Each log entry is composed of the identity of the logging process (usually the program name), the entry's level (i.e., the importance of the message), its facility (i.e., the source of the message), and the actual textual message.

Unfortunately, the syslog system has a number of shortcomings. For example, it logs textual messages with arbitrary formats, and, as a result, automated analysis of syslog output is very difficult. Also, the syslog facility encourages the use of multiple log files as a method for classifying events. Therefore, classifications are arbitrary and static, and related events are often sent to different log files. As a result, important context information might be lost. Finally, this facility provides limited notification and response mechanisms (e.g., sending mail to operators or administrators). Other event-logging implementations (e.g., syslog-ng, SDSC-syslog) exist that have addressed some of these limitations. Usually, these implementations support the syslog() function for backward compatibility but feed the syslog-generated messages into a more flexible logging system.

Microsoft Windows also provides an auditing system that can be leveraged to perform host-based intrusion detection. The auditing facility produces three event logs, namely the *system log*, the *security log*, and the *application log*.

1. The system log (SYSEVENT.EVT) contains events pertaining to Windows services and drivers. It tracks events during system startup, as well as hardware and controller failures (e.g., services that hang upon starting). In a networked setting, there will often be "browser" events in this log, because the machines on the network vote on which one will maintain the browser list.

2. The security log (SECEVENT.EVT) tracks security-related events such as logons, logoffs, changes to access rights, and system startup and shutdown, as well as events related to resource usage, such as creating, opening, or deleting files. Note that by default the security log is turned off and has to be explicitly enabled by the administrator.

3. The application log (APPEVENT.EVT) is used for events generated by applications. For example, a database program might record in this log a file access error or a problem with the application configuration. The events to be recorded are determined by the developer. This log can grow quite large in size when certain applications such as MS SQL Server or MS Exchange Server are running.

All three logs can be viewed using the native Windows Event Viewer and accessed via the Windows32 API. In addition, there are a number of third-party applications available to examine event logs or to collect log events from multiple Windows machines. The operating system offers built-in mechanisms to search and filter events using several different criteria (e.g., time, source, or category).

## Misuse-Based Approaches

Misuse detection systems contain a number of attack descriptions (or *signatures*) that are matched against the stream of audit data and compared to look for evidence that one of the modeled attack is occurring (Ilgun, Kemmerer, & Porras, 1995; Lindqvist & Porras, 1999).

Misuse detection systems usually provide an *attack language* that is used to describe the attacks that have to be detected. These languages provide mechanisms and abstractions for identifying the manifestation of an attack. Well-known examples of detection languages for host-based intrusion detection systems are P-Best (Lindqvist & Porras, 1999), which is the rule-based component of SRI's EMERALD, UCSB's STATL (Eckmann, Vigna, & Kemmerer, 2000), which is used by the STAT Toolset, and RUSSEL (Mounji, 1997), which is the language used by ASAX (Habra, Le Charlier, Mounji, & Mathieu, 1992).

All these languages provide a number of basic mechanisms to describe sequences of events and maintain some sort of intermediate state between different event matchings. In the following, we present in more detail the STATL language as an example of a language that is able to model complex attacks.

The STATL language provides constructs to represent an attack as a composition of *states* and *transitions*. States are used to characterize different snapshots of a system during the evolution of an attack. Obviously, it is not feasible to represent the complete state of a system (e.g., all volatile memory, file system); therefore, a STATL scenario uses variables to record just those parts of the system state needed to define an attack signature (e.g., the value of a counter or the ownership of a file). Each transition has an associated *action*, which is a specification of the events that cause the transition to be taken (i.e., the scenario moves into a new state). Examples of actions are the opening of a file or the execution of an application. The space of events that are relevant for an action is constrained by a *transition assertion*, which is a filter condition on events that may match the action. For example, an assertion may require that a file be opened with a specific mode (e.g., read-only) or that an application being executed is part of a predefined set of security-critical applications.

It is possible that several occurrences of the same attack are active at the same time. Thus, a STATL attack scenario has an operational semantics in terms of a set of *instances* of the same scenario *prototype*. The scenario prototype represents the scenario's definition and global environment, and the scenario instances represent individual attacks currently in progress.

The evolution of the set of instances of a scenario is determined by the type of transitions in the scenario definition. A transition can be *consuming, nonconsuming,* or *unwinding*. A nonconsuming transition is used to represent a step of an occurring attack that does not prevent further occurrences of attacks from spawning from the transition's source state. Therefore, when a nonconsuming transition is taken, the source state remains valid and the destination state becomes valid, too. For example, if an attack has two steps that are the creation of a link named "-i" to a SUID (Set User ID) shell script and the execution of the script through the created link, then the second step does not invalidate the previous state. That is, another execution of the script through the same link may occur. Semantically, the firing of a nonconsuming transition causes the creation of a *new* scenario instance.

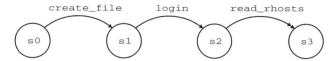

**Figure 2:**  *ftp-write* state transition diagram.

The original instance is still in the original state, whereas the new instance is in the state that is the destination state of the fired transition. In contrast, the firing of a consuming transition makes the source state of a particular attack occurrence invalid. Semantically, the firing of a consuming transition does not generate a new scenario instance; it simply changes the state of the original one. Unwinding transitions represent a form of "rollback" and are used to describe events and conditions that invalidate the progress of one or more scenario instances and require the return to an earlier state. For example, the deletion of a file may invalidate a condition needed for an attack to complete, and, therefore, the corresponding scenario instances may be brought back to a previous state, such as before the file was created.

The STATL language is used to describe scenarios in a host-based intrusion detection system called USTAT. USTAT uses Sun Microsystems' BSM as a source of audit data. For example, consider an *ftp-write* attack, where an attacker uses the *ftp* service to create a bogus `.rhosts` file in a world-writable *ftp* daemon home directory. Using the created file, the attacker is then able to open a remote session using the *rlogin* service without being required to supply a password. A generalization of this attack is that an attacker creates a bogus `.rhosts` file in any other user's home directory and then uses it to be allowed to login without providing a password. This generalization of the *ftp-write* attack is depicted schematically in the state transition diagram in Figure 2. The different types of arrows are used to denote different types of transitions: a solid arc with a single arrowhead denotes a nonconsuming transition and a solid arc with a double arrowhead denotes a consuming transition. A text-based STATL specification of the attack is given in Figure 3.

The sequence of events detected by this scenario is that a file is created (or written to) by a non-root user who does not own the directory containing the file, and then the login program runs and reads the suspicious file. WRITE, EXECUTE, and READ are abstractions of BSM-specific event types. The predicate `match_name()` and procedure `userid2name()` are helper functions that perform matching and user ID translation.

## Anomaly-Based Approaches

Anomaly-based techniques (Barbera & Jajodia, 2002; Denning, 1987; Ghosh, Wanken, & Charron, 1998; Javitz & Valdes, 1991) follow an approach that is complementary to misuse detection. In their case, detection is based on models of normal behavior of users and applications, which are called *profiles*. Any deviations from established profiles are interpreted as attacks.

The main advantage of anomaly-based techniques is that they are able to identify previously unknown attacks. By defining an expected, normal behavior, any abnormal

```
use bsm, unix;
scenario ftp_write
{
  int user;
  int pid;
  int inode;

  initial state s0 { }

  transition create_file (s0 -> s1)
    nonconsuming
  {
    [WRITE w] : (w.euid != 0) && (w.owner != w.ruid)
    { inode = w.inode; }
  }

  state s1 { }

  transition login (s1 -> s2)
    nonconsuming
  {
    [EXECUTE e] : match_name(e.objname, "login")
    {
      user = e.ruid;
      pid = e.pid;
    }
  }

  state s2 { }

  transition read_rhosts (s2 -> s3)
    consuming
  {
    [READ r] : (r.pid == pid) && (r.inode == inode)
  }

  state s3
  {
    {
      string username;
      userid2name(user, username);
      log("remote user %s gained local access", username);
    }
  }
}
```

**Figure 3:** Example attack scenario specified in STATL.

action can be detected, whether it is part of the threat model or not. The advantage of being able to detect previously unknown attacks is usually paid for with a high number of false positives (i.e., legitimate events are classified as malicious).

In the past, a number of host-based anomaly detection approaches have been proposed that build profiles using system calls (Forrest, Hofmeyr, Somayaji, & Longstaff, 1996; Wagner & Dean, 2001). More specifically, these systems rely on models of legitimate system call sequences issued by the application during normal operation. During the detection process, every monitored sequence that is not compliant with previously established profiles is considered part of an attack.

One technique to create the necessary models of legitimate system call sequences is the analysis of system call invocations during normal program execution. That is, the anomaly detection system "learns" normal behavior by monitoring system call traces of legitimate application runs. These systems, which do not rely on any a priori assumptions about applications, are thus called learning-based anomaly detectors.

An example of a learning-based anomaly detector that is based on system call analysis is described by Forrest et al. (1996). During the learning phase (also called training phase), this system collects all distinct system call sequences of a certain specified length. During detection, all actual system call sequences are compared to the set of legitimate ones and an alarm is raised if no match is found. The approach has been further refined by Lee, Stolfo, and Chan (1997) and Warrender, Forrest, and Pearlmutter (1999), where the authors study similar models and compare their effectiveness to the original technique. In Sekar, Bendre, Bollineni, and Dhurjati (2001), a deterministic system call automaton for a program is learned by associating each system call with its corresponding program counter. This model, however, does not take into account context information, which denotes the history of function calls stored on the program stack, and may miss attacks because of this imprecision. An extension that includes the context provided by the program call stack was described by Feng et al. (2003).

Another group of system call–based anomaly detection systems (Kruegel, Mutz, Valeur, & Vigna, 2003; Provos,

2003) focus on the analysis of system call arguments instead of using sequence information. In (Kruegel et al., 2003), the input to the detection process consists of an ordered stream $S = \{s_1, s_2, \ldots\}$ of system call invocations recorded by the OS. Every system call invocation $s \in S$ has a return value $r^s$ and a list of argument values $<a_1^s, \ldots, a_n^s>$. For each system call, a distinct profile is created. This profile captures the notion of a "normal" system call invocation by characterizing "normal" values for one or more of its arguments.

The expected "normal" values for individual arguments are determined with the help of models. A model is a set of procedures used to evaluate a certain feature of a system call argument, such as the length of a string. A model can operate in one of two modes, learning or detection. In learning mode, the model is trained and the notion of "normality" is developed by inspecting examples. Examples are values that are considered part of a regular execution of a program and are either derived directly from a subset of the input set $S$ (learning on the fly) or provided by previous program executions (learning from a training set).

In detection mode, the task of a model is to return the probability of occurrence of a system call argument value based on the model's prior training phase. This value reflects the likelihood that a certain feature value is observed, given the established profile. The assumption is that feature values with a sufficiently low probability (i.e., abnormal values) indicate a potential attack. To evaluate the overall anomaly score of an entire system call, the probability values of all models are aggregated.

An example of a model is the *string length* model. Usually, system call string arguments represent canonical file names that point to an entry in the file system. These arguments are commonly used when files are accessed (open, stat) or executed (execve). Their length rarely exceeds a hundred characters and they mostly consist of human-readable characters.

When malicious input is passed to programs, it is often the case that this input also appears in arguments of system calls. For example, consider a format string vulnerability in the log function of an application. Assume further that a failed open call is logged together with the file name. To exploit this kind of flaw, an attacker has to carefully craft a file name that triggers the format string vulnerability when the application attempts and subsequently fails to open the corresponding file. In this case, the exploit code manifests itself as an argument to the open call that contains a string with a length of several hundred bytes.

The goal of the string length model is to approximate the distribution of the lengths of a string argument and detect instances that significantly deviate from the observed normal behavior. To characterize normal string lengths, the mean $\hat{X}$ and the variance $\hat{\sigma}^2$ of the real string length distribution are approximated by calculating the sample mean $\overline{X}$ and the sample variance $\sigma^2$ for the lengths $l_1, l_2, \ldots, l_n$ of the argument strings processed during the learning phase. Then, in the detection phase, the actual values of system calls parameters are compared to the established profiles to determine if the observed value is within the range of legitimate values.

Another example of a model is the *character distribution* model. This model captures the concept of a "normal"

string argument by looking at its character distribution. The approach is based on the observation that large percentage of characters in such strings is drawn from a small subset of the 256 possible 8-bit values (mainly from letters, numbers, and a few special characters). As in English text, the characters are not uniformly distributed but occur with different frequencies.

This model learns the "normal" character distribution during a training phase. For each observed argument string, its character distribution is stored. The "normal" character distribution is then approximated by calculating the average of all stored character distributions. Then, during detection, a statistical test is used to determine the probability that the character distribution of an argument is an actual sample drawn from its established profile.

In contrast to signature-based approaches, the character distribution model has the advantage that it cannot be evaded by some well-known attempts to hide malicious code inside a string. In fact, signature-based systems often contain rules that raise an alarm when long sequences of $0 \times 90$ bytes (the nop operation on Intel $\times 86$-based architectures) are detected. An intruder may substitute these sequences with instructions that have a similar behavior (e.g., add rA, rA, 0, which adds 0 to the value in register A and stores the result back to A). By doing this, it is possible to prevent signature-based systems from detecting the attack. Such sequences, nonetheless, cause a distortion of the string's character distribution, and, therefore, the character distribution analysis still yields a high anomaly score.

The models described previously are just examples of how it is possible to create a learning-based anomaly detection system. There are a number of possible variations on this scheme and this field is still the object of active research.

A somewhat different approach is followed by RAD (Apap et al., 2002), a system that uses as input the registry access events on MS Windows hosts. RAD uses an attack-free history of accesses to the Windows registry to build a statistical model of the normal behavior of applications with respect to registry interaction. The model is then used to detect malicious applications that perform anomalous operations on the registry. A major drawback of this approach is that malicious software can damage the operating system without modifying the registry at all. Therefore, this system can only detect a subset of the possible attacks.

In general, evasion is a problem of all intrusion detection systems but it becomes more relevant in the case of anomaly detection techniques. The reason is that it is difficult to define models that prevent an intruder from performing attacks that stay within the limits of what is considered "normal." Such attacks, often called *mimicry attacks*, can be possible because of design problems (Tan & Maxion, 2002; Tan, Killourhy, & Maxion, 2002) or because of the poor quality of the input event stream. For example, user modeling based on command line analysis is well-known for being prone to evasion attacks, in which commands and application binaries are renamed (or replaced) by an attacker to create a session that conforms perfectly to the established normal profiles (Maxion & Townsend, 2002; Wang & Stolfo, 2003; Shonlau et al., 2001). In general, if the auditing mechanism relied upon by an intrusion detection system can be bypassed or modified by the attacker, then the design of the system will detect only attackers who are not aware of the existence of the intrusion detection system or who are not careful enough to cover their tracks.

## Specification-Based Approaches

Whereas learning-based anomaly detection systems build models by monitoring application traces, specification-based approaches define models a priori without using dynamic program information. In their case, the models are written manually or built by statically analyzing application code.

An early specification-based technique that was based on written specifications for events in distributed systems was presented by Ko, Ruschitzka, and Levitt (1997). It was later refined by Bernaschi, Gabrielli, and Mancini (2002) and Chari and Cheng (2002). Another system, called Janus (Goldberg, Wagner, Thomas, & Brewer, 1996), creates a restricted environment (called sandbox) for processes in which all system call invocations are intercepted and verified with respect to a manually written specification. The idea is to limit the potential damage that an attacker can cause after successfully compromising a process. Yet another approach, which is related to system call policies, are software wrappers (Fraser, Badger, & Feldman, 1999; Ko, Fraser, Badger, & Kilpatrick, 2000). Software wrappers define policies based on state machines that operate in kernel space. Whenever a system call is invoked, a number of wrappers are called to check whether the system call itself and its arguments are permitted. Because the wrappers dispose of state, it is possible to base decisions on a series of system calls.

The use of static analysis techniques to determine system call models was introduced by Wagner and Dean (2001) and Wagner and Soto (2002). In this approach, a call-graph model based on automata is used to characterize the expected system call sequences. The initial approach was extended by Giffin, Jha, and Miller (2004), who present an alternative, more efficient model to represent "legal" system call sequences. The price that has to be paid is the need to insert additional "checkpoint" system calls into the program, which is realized via binary rewriting. Another system that uses static analysis to extract a model of acceptable system calls is presented by Feng et al. (2004). In this case, the call stack information is used to better model the context in which normal system calls are executed.

Techniques that use specifications are usually not as prone to reporting false alarms as their anomaly-based cousins. That is, given a complete and accurate policy, these systems perform very well. Unfortunately, the task to produce such a policy for realistic applications and scenarios is not trivial.

## APPLICATION-LEVEL INTRUSION DETECTION

An important source of audit data for host-based intrusion detection systems is the information provided directly by applications. In the traditional sense, these data are read from log files or other similar sources. However, other techniques were developed where the integration between the IDS and the monitored application is tighter. Application audit data are rich, reliable, and very focused. Therefore, it is easy to determine which program is responsible for a particular event. On the downside, application data are also very specific and different applications have to be dealt with on an individual basis by the HIDS.

In the following section, we present application-level audit data-gathering techniques. Then, different analysis techniques that are based on this type of information are described.

## Audit Data Gathering

Most operating systems use centralized log files to provide a central repository for both operating system and application audit data. Besides the operating system log files (discussed in the previous section), audit information is also found in application-specific log files. Of particular interest are error logs, because malicious activity often causes side effects that are detected by an application's error-checking routines.

Application log files have the advantage that they can contain very detailed information. However, their format differs significantly among programs and intrusion detection systems need to be adapted to each individual application. Another disadvantage is the fact that, by the time the information is written to the log, the application has completed the operation in question. Thus, the IDS cannot act preemptively. In addition, the information available is often limited to a summary of a complete transaction. Consider, for example, a Web request that is logged in the common logfile format (CLF) as follows (taken from Almgren & Lindqvist, 2001):

```
10.0.1.2 - - [02/Jun/1999:13:41:37 -0700]
"GET /a.html HTTP/1.0" 404 194
```

This log entry describes a request from the host with IP address 10.0.1.2 that asked for the document a.html, which, at that time, did not exist. The server sent back a response containing 194 bytes. The log entry might not contain all the information an IDS needs for its analysis. Were the headers too long or otherwise malformed? How long did it take to process the request? How did the server parse the request? What local file did the request get translated into? In some applications, logging can be customized and can contain much more information. Nevertheless, in most systems not all internal information that is needed to understand the interpretation of an operation is available for logging. Furthermore, by enabling all log facilities, the risk of running out of storage space for the logs or incurring in performance degradation is increased.

To remove some of the limitations of log files with regard to audit data collection, application-integrated systems have been proposed (Almgren & Lindqvist, 2001). In such systems, the IDS monitors the inner workings of the application and analyzes the data at the same time as the application interprets it. This offers an opportunity to detect (and possibly stop) malicious operations before their execution. By tightly integrating the IDS with the application, more information can be accessed (e.g., local information that is never written to a log file). Furthermore, one can expect an application-integrated monitor to generate fewer false alarms, because it does not have to guess the interpretation and outcomes of malicious operations.

For example, a module in a Web server can see the entire HTTP request, including headers. The module can determine to which file within the local file system the request was mapped, and it can also determine if this file will be handled as a CGI (Common Gateway Interface) program (which is not visible in either the network traffic or the log files), even without parsing the configuration file of the Web server.

To successfully integrate an IDS into an application, the application must provide a suitable interface. To this end, some applications provide APIs or appropriate hooks for call-back routines. In case the application is open-source, another possibility is to extend the application with suitable IDS functionality.

Taking the idea of application-integrated audit data collection even further, honeypots were introduced. Spitzner (2004) defines a honeypot as "an information system resource whose value lies in unauthorized or illicit use of that resource." In general, a honeypot is a host or network intentionally configured with known vulnerabilities that are deliberately exposed to a public segment of the network so as to invite an intrusion attempt. Honeypots are useful in studying the behavior of attackers and they are a way to delay and distract intruders away from more valuable targets.

Honeypots are traditionally classified as low-interaction or high-interaction honeypots, which specifies the level of activity an attacker is allowed to perform. Low-interaction honeypots have limited interaction, and they normally work by emulating services and operating systems. For example, an emulated file transfer protocol (FTP) service listening on port 21 may just emulate at FTP login, or it may support a few additional FTP commands. The advantage of low-interaction honeypots is their simplicity. These honeypots tend to be easier to deploy and maintain, because the attacker never has access to a fully functional operating system to attack or harm others. The main disadvantage of low-interaction honeypots is that they log only limited information and are designed to capture known activity. Also, it is easier for an attacker to detect a low-interaction honeypot. No matter how good the emulation is, a skilled attacker can eventually detect their presence. A well-known open-source low-interaction honeypot is honeyd (Provos, 2004).

High-interaction honeypots are different from low-interaction honeypots in that they attempt to fully emulate the functioning of real OSs and applications. High-interaction honeypots offer two advantages over low-interaction honeypots. First, they can capture extensive amounts of information and so make it possible to learn the full extent of the intruder's behavior, be it the installation of new rootkits or the establishment of internet relay chat (IRC) sessions. Second, because high-interaction honeypots make no assumptions about how an attacker will behave, they provide an open environment that captures all activity and so make it possible to trap and learn from unanticipated behavior. On the downside, high-interaction honeypots can be more complex to deploy and maintain.

## Misuse-Based Approaches

One of the simplest signature-based systems that monitors application audit data is Swatch. Swatch, the *Simple Watch* daemon, is a program for UNIX system logging and was written to monitor messages as they are written to a log file via the UNIX `syslog()` utility. The idea is to keep system administrators from being overwhelmed by large quantities of log data. The tool monitors log files, filters out unwanted data, and takes one or more user-specified actions based upon patterns in the log. Swatch can monitor information as it is being appended to the log file and alert system administrators immediately about serious system problems as they occur. The patterns are specified as regular expressions.

A very similar system is LogSentry, which extends the monitoring to other system log files such as the ones produced by Psionic's PortSentry and HostSentry, system daemons, Wietse Venema's TCP Wrapper and Log Daemon packages, and the Firewall Toolkit by Trusted Information Systems (TIS).

Another tool that also works by monitoring system log files but that allows the specification of more complex attack scenarios is logSTAT (Vigna, Valeur, & Kemmerer, 2003). Using the same STATL language previously introduced, logSTAT applies the state transition analysis technique to the contents of syslog files.

WebSTAT (Vigna, Robertson, Kher, & Kemmerer, 2003), a tool related to logSTAT, extends the state transition analysis to application-specific log files, in particular, the Web server log files created by Apache. Several attack scenario have been implemented that include a malicious Web crawler scenario, a pattern-matching scenario, a repeated failed-access scenario, and a buffer-overflow detection scenario.

One interesting attack scenario included with WebSTAT is the cookie-stealing scenario. Cookies are a state management mechanism for HTTP (defined in RFC 2965, Kristol & Montulli, 2000) that is often used by Web application developers to implement session tracking. The cookie-stealing scenario detects if a cookie used as a session ID is improperly utilized by multiple users. This is often a manifestation of a malicious user attempting to hijack the session of a legitimate user to gain unauthorized access to protected Web resources.

The scenario begins by recording the issuance or initial use of a session cookie by a remote client by mapping the cookie to an IP address. In addition, an inactivity timer is simultaneously set. Subsequent use of the session cookie by the same client results in a reset of the timer, whereas a cookie expiration or session timeout results in the removal of the mapping for that cookie. If, however, a client uses the valid session cookie of another client, then an attack is assumed to be underway and an alarm is raised.

The cookie-stealing scenario is interesting because it underlines the need for *state* to detect certain classes of attacks. Most intrusion detection systems are *stateless*, meaning that each event is treated independently of others. However, certain attacks only manifest themselves as multiple steps in which each individual step is not intrusive *per se*. In the cookie-stealing scenario, the use of a cookie by each client appears benign. Only by detecting that two different clients share a single cookie malicious behavior can be identified.

As mentioned in the previous section, systems that operate on application log files have only a limited view of the operations performed by an application. This shortcoming is addressed by application-integrated systems. Almgren and Lindqvist have developed an integrated monitor to detect Web-based attacks against the Apache Web server (2001). The tool is directly attached to the Apache request pipeline, which consists of several stages that a client request runs through. Each stage possesses so-called hooks or callbacks that are used by the monitor to give feedback to the server as to whether it should continue executing the request.

The presented approach makes evasion techniques less effective, because the view of the intrusion detection system and the view of the server application are tightly integrated. On the other hand, a disadvantage of this approach is that by "in-lining" intrusion detection analysis, the performance of the Web server is affected. In addition, the proposed solution is tailored to a specific Web server (in this case, Apache) and cannot be easily ported to different servers.

## Anomaly-Based Approaches

An application-based anomaly detection system creates a profile of application behavior based on normal application activity. This activity is usually expressed as operations that an application performs. A profile can be created by observing traces of normal activity or by specifying all operations that an application is allowed to perform. This section deals with learning-based systems that establish a description of normal behavior by monitoring actual program executions. The following section discusses approaches in which profiles are specified a priori, based on policies that determine acceptable behavior.

An example of a system that monitors application behavior to create a profile of normal behavior is DIDAFIT (Detecting Intrusions in DAtabases through Fingerprinting Transactions; Lee, Low, & Wong, 2002). This system works by fingerprinting access patterns of legitimate database transactions and using them to identify database intrusions (in particular, standard query language (SQL) injection attacks). The work addresses the problem of learning the set of legitimate fingerprints from database trace logs that contain the SQL statements of benign transactions. To this end, the authors developed algorithms that perform useful generalization of the training set. That is, the system summarizes SQL statements into more general fingerprints and is capable of deriving possibly legitimate fingerprints that are missing from the training data. In addition, it can identify possibly malicious (so called "high-risk") SQL statements even in the training set.

Another example is a system that analyzes the interaction of Web clients with Web-based applications (Kruegel & Vigna, 2003). More precisely, this system analyzes client queries that reference server-side programs, and it creates models for a wide-range of different features of these queries. Examples of such features are access patterns of server-side programs or values of individual parameters in their invocation. Similar to the system call–based analysis presented previously, the tool derives automatically the parameter profiles associated with Web applications (e.g., the length and structure of request parameters). In addition, the relationship between queries and the access patterns of applications over time are also modeled.

Changes in access patterns can indicate attacks. When an application is usually accessed infrequently but is suddenly exposed to a burst of invocations, this increase could be the result of an attacker probing for vulnerabilities or the result of an exploit that has to guess parameter values. A single determined attacker can evade detection by executing his actions slowly enough to keep the frequency low. However, most tools used by less skilled intruders execute brute force attacks without stealthiness in mind. Also, when the knowledge of a vulnerability becomes more widespread, many attackers independently attempt to exploit the vulnerability and raise the total frequency to a suspicious level.

Another pattern focuses on the order in which programs are accessed. Web-based applications are often composed of a set of server-side programs, which, together, implement the application functionality. For example, a shopping application may have a login program to authenticate a user, a program to access a catalog, a program to add items to a virtual cart, and a program to perform checkout/payment. The nature of a Web-based application may impose a well-defined ordering over the invocation of its component programs. For example, a user has to first login before being able to perform any other transaction. Unusual order of program accesses can indicate malicious behavior, such as an attacker attempting to bypass a login check and access a privileged program directly.

## Specification-Based Approaches

The specification of application behavior is usually done at the system call interface (as described previously). However, there have been also suggestions to formally specify the normal behavior of an application by defining the input and output data that it exchanged with its users.

For example, in Cheung and Levitt (2002), the specification language VDM is used to create formal specifications that characterize the normal behavior of domain name service (DNS) clients and servers. The aim was to define a security goal of the DNS service, which states that a name server should only use DNS data that are consistent with data from name servers that manage the corresponding domain (i.e., authoritative name servers). Based on these specifications and to enforce the security goal, a DNS wrapper was implemented that examines the incoming and outgoing DNS traffic between name servers and resolvers. To detect messages that violate the security goal, cooperation with the authoritative name servers is required. Whenever a violating message is detected, it is dropped. Using their wrappers, the authors were successful in detecting DNS cache poisoning and spoofing attacks. Of course, the approach can be extended to specify the format and content of messages exchanged by other network service daemons.

Similar to wrappers for system calls, there are application-based techniques that verify arguments of shared library function calls (Balzer & Goldman, 1999). Using mediators, it is possible to prevent library functions from being called, to modify their arguments, and to adjust their return values.

## RELATED TECHNIQUES

A family of host-based tools that are considered related to intrusion detection systems are *integrity checkers*. The task of these tools is to detect whether certain monitored files were tampered with. Although these systems are not intrusion detection systems in the classic sense, they are often used to identify the activities of an intruder after a successful compromise. A well-known integrity checker is Tripwire (Kim & Spafford, 1994). Tripwire is a program that monitors key attributes of files that should not change, including binary signature, size, and expected change of size. To do so, file information and file content hashes are stored in a custom database. Similar to Tripwire, RedHat's package management system rpm can also be used for integrity-checking tasks.

The limit of file system integrity checkers is the fact that the analysis can only be reliably performed in an offline fashion. That is, the file system has to be mounted by an operating system that is known to be not compromised. The reason is that integrity checkers rely on operating system routines to access the file system. If the operating system itself is modified on a compromised host, the integrity checkers could be provided with incorrect information that can lead them to conclude that no modifications have occurred. Once the kernel is infected, it is very hard to determine if a system has been compromised without the help of hardware extensions such as the trusted platform module (TPM).

A common occurrence after a successful intrusion is the installation of a *rootkit* (Black Tie Affair, 1989). A rootkit is a collection of "easy-to-use" tools that help an intruder to hide her presence from the system administrator (e.g., log editors), to gather information about the system and its environment (e.g., network sniffers), and to ensure access at a later time (e.g., backdoored servers). Often, these rootkits include modified versions of system-auditing programs. These modified programs do not return any information to the administrator that involves specific files and processes that are used by the intruder.

Rootkits that simply replace or modify system files or intruders that manually change files can be detected by file integrity checkers. Recently, however, kernel-level rootkits have emerged that can bypass file integrity checks by modifying the kernel directly. Such rootkits (e.g., knark or Adore; Stealth, 2003) operate within the kernel by modifying critical data structures such as the system call table. No modification of program binaries to conceal malicious activity takes place anymore.

To detect kernel-level rootkits, a number of detection tools have been developed that could also be considered host-based intrusion detection systems. The most basic techniques used by these systems include searching for modified kernel modules on disk, searching for known strings in existing binaries, or searching for configuration files associated with specific rootkits. The problem is that when a system has been compromised at the kernel level, there is no guarantee that these detection tools will return reliable results. This is also true for signature-based rootkit detection tools such as chkrootkit that rely on operating system services to scan a machine for indications of known rootkits.

To circumvent the problem of a possibly untrusted operating system, rootkit scanners such as kstat, rkscan, and St. Michael follow a different approach. These tools are either implemented as kernel modules with direct access to kernel memory, or they analyze the contents of the kernel memory via /dev/kmem. Both techniques allow the programs to monitor the integrity of important kernel data structures without the use of system calls. For example, by comparing the system call addresses in the system call table with known good values (taken from the /boot/System.map file), it is possible to identify hijacked system call entries.

Another group of related tools, which have had the most commercial success, are virus scanners. A computer virus is a piece of software designed to make additional copies of itself and spread from location to location, typically without user knowledge or permission. Virus scanners are tools that scan a binary for the occurrence of viruses (code fragments) that are known to perform malicious actions. With the tremendous increase of Internet virus activity, the importance of scanners has increased dramatically. As a result, virus scanners are now virtually ubiquitous, especially on Microsoft Windows platforms.

## HOST-BASED IDSs VERSUS NETWORK-BASED IDSs

Host-based IDSs have both advantages and disadvantages when compared with network-based intrusion detection systems. One advantage is that HIDSs can access semantically rich information about the operations performed on a host, whereas NIDSs that analyze network traffic have to reassemble, parse, and interpret the application-level traffic to identify application-level actions. This is even more evident when application-level traffic is encrypted. In this case, a network-based monitor has to be equipped with the key material needed to decrypt the traffic; otherwise, the application-level information is not accessible. Also, the amount of information that HIDSs have to process is usually more limited, because the rate at which events are generated by the OS and applications is smaller than the rate at which network packets are sent over busy links. A third advantage is that HIDSs are less prone to evasion attacks because it is more difficult to desynchronize the view that the intrusion detection system has of the status of a monitored application with respect to the application itself. Finally, a host-based intrusion detection system has a better chance of performing a focused response because the process performing an attack can sometimes be easier identified and terminated.

On the other hand, host-based IDSs suffer from a set of limitations. A major disadvantage of HIDSs with respect to NIDSs is that the compromise of a host may allow an attacker to disable or tamper with the auditing system or even to disable the intrusion detection system altogether. This problem is caused by the all-or-nothing approach to privilege management followed by most operating systems. Once a process obtains administrative privileges, it is able to change any aspect of the system, including the kernel configuration and the code stored in programmable hardware. The other major disadvantage of HIDSs is that the intrusion detection process may affect substantially the performance of the operating system, and, as a consequence, of the applications running on a monitored host. A single network-based IDS can monitor a number of host without affecting their performance. In addition, a NIDS that monitors many hosts may detect attacks that span multiple hosts. The evidence associated with such attacks might be unavailable when monitoring only a single host. The limited view of host-based systems can be compensated for by combining information gathered from different host-based sensors at a central location. When data from different hosts is available, it is possible to correlate host-based data to get a more global view (Kruegel, Valeur, & Vigna, 2004). However, for this correlation process, a dedicated infrastructure is required. One of the first systems that used correlation of data produced by multiple host-based sensors was DIDS (Snapp et al., 1991). Finally, there is a maintenance cost associated with the deployment and maintenance of host-based IDSs, which tends to be higher than the cost associated with NIDSs because of the need to install an IDS on each protected host and of the heterogeneity of most environments (different operating systems, and different versions of the same operating system).

## FUTURE TRENDS

In the past, host-based IDSs have not been considered a viable solution to detect intruders because of their performance overhead and their inability to deliver reliable information in the case of a compromise. In addition, the problem of the large number of false positives produced by anomaly detection systems made it impossible to perform effective intrusion response (e.g., killing a process that is misbehaving) without the risk of hurting legitimate users of the system.

Recently, the interest in this class of intrusion detection systems has been boosted by increasingly more efficient detection techniques and the introduction of new hardware-based mechanisms that guarantee the integrity of a system even in the face of the compromise of a privileged account. This trend is also supported by firewall technology, which, in the past few years, has gradually moved from the gateway of a network to each single host (e.g., the popular ZoneAlarm tool for Windows). These new host-based firewalls are actually host-based intrusion detection systems that analyze network data.

The next generation of HIDSs will probably integrate host-based firewall technology, as well as other technologies, such as virus scanners and integrity checkers. The resulting intrusion detection system will monitor several event streams (e.g., network traffic directed to the host and system calls executed by applications) and will be able to correlate evidence that belongs to different domains. These hybrid systems will be able to provide effective detection and very focused response at a reasonable performance cost.

Another trend in host-based intrusion detection is the progressive integration of intrusion detection mechanisms into the kernel of the operating systems. Currently, the OS is extended to gather auditing information but the actual intrusion detection process is performed outside the kernel, in user space. By integrating intrusion detection within the kernel itself, it is possible to perform much more effective response, blocking suspicious operations before they cause any actual harm. This type of systems may be able to foil a wide range of attacks in an effective manner.

There are still many challenges in developing systems that are tightly integrated with the operating system kernel. The critical nature of the kernel leaves very little room for mistakes and the failure of a single kernel component can render the whole system unusable. Therefore, kernel-level solutions have to be implemented following a high-quality development process to meet the expectation of the user in terms of reliability and performance.

## CONCLUSIONS

For the past decade, network-based intrusion detection systems have clearly dominated host-based systems. The ease of maintenance and the possibility to monitor several targets with a single IDS installation has tipped the scales toward the network-based solution. However, the increasing use of very fast network links and encrypted connections have changed the situation. The quality of audit data that are available at the operating system and application levels, the increasing security awareness of end users, and the improved accuracy of host-based techniques have all contributed to a higher acceptance of such detection mechanisms.

This chapter discussed host-based intrusion detection systems and related techniques such as file integrity checkers and virus scanners. The main sources of audit data (operating system and application) were introduced and different approaches to analyze the data were presented. In addition, we analyzed the advantages and limitations of host-based solutions with regard to network-based techniques and outlined possible future developments in the field.

## GLOSSARY

**Anomaly-Based Intrusion Detection**   Intrusion detection techniques that rely on models of normal system behavior to identify intrusions.

**Audit**   A procedure used to validate that controls are in place and adequate for their purposes. This includes recording and analyzing activities to detect intrusions or abuses in an information system.

**Audit Data**   Data produced by an audit procedure.

**File Integrity Checker**   A system that verifies that the attributes and contents of files have not been modified by unauthorized subjects.

**Honeypot**   A host or network with known vulnerabilities deliberately exposed to a public network.

**Host-Based Intrusion Detection**   An intrusion detection system that uses audit data produced by the operating system and applications.

**Intrusion Detection Evasion**   An attempt to perform an attack such that it is not detected by an intrusion detection system.

**Intrusion Detection System**  A system that tries to identify attempts to hack or break into a computer system or to misuse it.

**Mimicry Attack**  An evasion attack in which the intruder attempts to make the attack appear like legitimate behavior.

**Misuse-Based Intrusion Detection**  Intrusion detection techniques that rely on specifications (signatures) of attacks to identify intrusions.

**Network-Based Intrusion Detection**  An intrusion detection system that uses data extracted from the network.

**Operating System Call**  The services provided by the operating system kernel to application programs and the way in which they are invoked.

**Program Context**  The context at a certain point in the program's execution that is the history of function calls stored on the program stack.

**Rootkit**  A collection of tools that allows a hacker to mask the fact that the system is compromised and to collect additional information.

## CROSS REFERENCES

See *Computer Viruses and Worms; Intrusion Detection Systems Basics; Network-Based Intrusion Detection Systems; Security Policy Guidelines; The Use of Agent Technology for Intrusion Detection.*

## REFERENCES

Almgren, M., & Lindqvist, U. (2001). Application-integrated data collection for security monitoring. In *Proceedings of the Symposium an Recent Advances in Intrusion Detection (RAID)* (LNCS, pp. 22–36). Davis, CA: Springer.

Apap, F., Honig, A., Hershkop, S., Eskin, E., & Stolfo, S. (2002). Detecting malicious software by monitoring anomalous Windows registry access. In *Proceedings of the Symposium on Recent Advances in Intrusion Detection (RAID)*. Zurich, Switzerland.

Balzer, R., & Goldman, N. (1999). Mediating connectors: A non-bypassable process wrapping technology. In *19th IEEE International Conference on Distributed Computing Systems*. Austin, Texas, pp. 73–77.

Barbera, D., & Jajodia, S. (Ed.). (2002). *Applications of data mining in computer security.* Kluwer.

Bernaschi, M., Gabrielli, E., & Mancini, L. V. (2002). REMUS: A security-enhanced operating system. *ACM Transactions on Information and System Security, 5*(36), pp. 36–61.

Black Tie Affair. (1989). Hiding out under UNIX. *Phrack Magazine, 3*(25).

Chari, S., & Cheng, P., (2002). BlueBoX: A policy-driven, host-based intrusion detection system. In *Proceedings of the Symposium on Network and Distributed System Security (NDSS)*, San Diego, CA.

Cheung, S., & Levitt, K. (2002, June). A formal specification based approach for protecting the domain name system. In *Proceedings of the International Conference on Dependable Systems and Networks*, New York, NY.

Crothers, T. (2002). *Implementing intrusion detection systems: A hands-on guide for securing the network.* New York: John Wiley & Sons.

Daniels, T., & Spafford, E. (1999). Identification of host audit data to detect attacks on low-level IP vulnerabilities. *Journal of Computer Security, 7*(1), pp. 3–35.

Denning, D. (1987, February). An intrusion detection model. *IEEE Transactions on Software Engineering, 13*(2), pp. 222–232.

Eckmann, S., Vigna, G., & Kemmerer, R. (2000, November). STATL: An attack language for state-based intrusion detection. In *Proceedings of the ACM Workshop on Intrusion Detection Systems*, Athens, Greece.

Feng, H., Giffin, J., Huang, Y., Jha, S., Lee, W., & Miller, B. (2004, May). Formalizing sensitivity in static analysis for intrusion detection. In *Proceedings of the IEEE Symposium on Security and Privacy*, Oakland, CA. pp. 194–204.

Feng, H., Kolesnikov, O., Fogla, P., Lee, W., & Gong, W. (2003). Anomaly detection using call stack information. In *Proceedings of the IEEE Symposium on Security and Privacy*, pp. 62–74.

Forrest, S., Hofmeyr, S., Somayaji, A., & Longstaff, T. (1996, May). A sense of self for UNIX processes. In *Proceedings of the IEEE Symposium on Security and Privacy* (pp. 120–128), Oakland, CA.

Fraser, T., Badger, L., & Feldman, M. (1999). Hardening COTS software with generic software wrappers. In *Proceedings of the IEEE Symposium on Security and Privacy* (pp. 2–16), Oakland, CA.

Ghosh, A., Wanken, J., & Charron, F. (1998, December). Detecting anomalous and unknown intrusions against programs. In *Proceedings of the Annual Computer Security Application Conference (ACSAC)* (pp. 259–267), Scottsdale, AZ.

Giffin, J., Jha, S., & Miller, B. (2004, February). Efficient context-sensitive intrusion detection. In *Proceedings of the Network and Distributed System Security Symposium (NDSS)*, San Diego, California.

Goldberg, I., Wagner, D., Thomas, R., & Brewer, E. (1996). A secure environment for untrusted helper applications. In *Proceedings of the Usenix Security Symposium*, San Jose, CA. pp. 1–13.

Habra, N., Le Charlier, B., Mounji, A., & Mathieu, I. (1992, November). ASAX: Software architecture and rule-based language for universal audit trail analysis. In *Proceedings of the European Symposium on Research in Computer Security (ESORICS)*, Toulouse, France. pp. 435–450.

Ilgun, K., Kemmerer, R., & Porras, P. (1995). State transition analysis: A rule-based intrusion detection system. *IEEE Transactions on Software Engineering, 21*(3), 181–199.

Javitz, H. S., & Valdes, A. (1991). The SRI IDES statistical anomaly detector. In *Proceedings of the IEEE Symposium on Security and Privacy*. pp. 316–326.

Kim, G., & Spafford, E. (1994). The design and implementation of tripwire: A file system integrity checker. In *Proceedings of the ACM Conference on Computer and Communications Security (CCS)* (pp. 18–29), Fairfax, VA.

Ko, C., Ruschitzka, M., & Levitt, K. (1997). Execution monitoring of security-critical programs in distributed systems: A specification-based approach. In *Proceedings of the IEEE Symposium on Security and Privacy* (pp. 175–187), Oakland, CA.

Ko, C., Fraser, T., Badger, L., & Kilpatrick, D. (2000). Detecting and countering system intrusions using software wrappers. In *Proceedings of the Usenix Security Symposium*. Denver, CO, pp. 145–156.

Kristol, D., & Montulli, L. (2000, October). *HTTP state management mechanism* (RFC 2965).

Kruegel, C., Mutz, D., Valeur, F., & Vigna, G. (2003, October). On the detection of anomalous system call arguments. In *Proceedings of the European Symposium on Research in Computer Security (ESORICS)*, (LNCS, pp. 326–343). Gjøvik, Norway, Springer-Verlag.

Kruegel, C., Valeur, F., & Vigna, G. (2004). *Intrusion detection and correlation: Challenges and solutions*. Norwell MA: Springer Verlag.

Kruegel, C., & Vigna, G. (2003, October). Anomaly detection of Web-based attacks. In *Proceedings of the ACM Conference on Computer and Communication Security (CCS)* (pp. 251–261). Washington, DC: ACM Press.

Lee, S., Low, W., & Wong, P. (2002). Learning fingerprints for a database intrusion detection system. In *Proceedings of the European Symposium on Research in Computer Security (ESORICS)*. Zurich, Switzerland. pp. 264–280.

Lee, W., Stolfo, S., & Chan, P. (1997, July). Learning patterns from unix process execution traces for intrusion detection. In *Proceedings of the AAAI Workshop: AI Approaches to Fraud Detection and Risk Management*.

Lindqvist, U., & Porras, P. A. (1999, May). Detecting computer and network misuse with the production-based expert system toolset (P-BEST). In *Proceedings of the IEEE Symposium on Security and Privacy* (pp. 146–161). Oakland, California.

Lunt, T. (1993). Detecting intruders in computer systems. In *Proceedings of the Annual Symposium and Technical Displays on Physical and Electronic Security*.

Maxion, R., & Townsend, T. (2002, June). Masquerade detection using truncated command lines. In *Proceedings of the International Conference on Dependable Systems and Networks (DSN)* (pp. 219–228). Washington, DC.

Mounji, A. (1997). *Languages and tools for rule-based distributed intrusion detection*. Unpublished doctoral dissertation, Facultés Universitaires Notre-Dame de la Paix, Namur, Belgium.

Provos, N. (2003). Improving host security with system call policies. In *Proceedings of the Usenix Security Symposium*. Washington, DC. pp. 257–272.

Provos, N. (2004). A virtual honeypot framework. In *Proceedings of the Usenix Security Symposium*. pp. 1–14, San Diego, CA.

Schonlau, M., DuMouchel, W., Ju, W., Karr, A., Theus, M., & Vardi, Y. (2001). Computer intrusion: Detecting masquerades. *Statistical Science, 16*(1) 57–74.

Schultz, G., Endorf, C., & Mellander, J. (2003). *Intrusion detection and prevention*. New York: McGraw-Hill Osborne Media.

Sekar, R., Bendre, M., Bollineni, P., & Dhurjati, D. (2001, May). A fast automaton-based method for detecting anomalous program behaviors. In *Proceedings of the IEEE Symposium on Security and Privacy*. Oakland, CA. pp. 144–154.

Snapp, S. R., Brentano, J., Dias, G., Goan, T., Heberlein, T., Ho, C., et al. (1991). DIDS (distributed intrusion detection system)—Motivation, architecture, and an early prototype. In *Proceedings of the National Computer Security Conference*. pp. 167–176.

Spitzner, L. (2004). *Honeypots: Tracking hackers*. Boston, MA: Addison-Wesley.

Stealth. (2003, August). Kernel rootkit experiences and the future. *Phrack Magazine, 11*(61).

Tan, K., & Maxion, R. (2002). "Why 6?" Defining the operational limits of stide, an anomaly-based intrusion detector. In *Proceedings of the IEEE Symposium on Security and Privacy* (pp. 188–202). Oakland, CA.

Tan, K. M. C., Killourhy, K. S., & Maxion, R. A. (2002). Undermining an anomaly-based intrusion detection system using common exploits. In *Proceedings of the International Symposium on Recent Advances in Intrusion Detection* (RAID) (pp. 54–73).

Vigna, G., Robertson, W., Kher, V., & Kemmerer, R. A. (2003). A stateful intrusion detection system for World Wide Web servers. In *Proceedings of the Annual Computer Security Applications Conference (ACSAC)* (pp. 34–43).

Vigna, G., Valeur, F., & Kemmerer, R. A. (2003). Designing and implementing a family of intrusion detection systems. In *Proceedings of the European Software Engineering Conference and ACM SIGSOFT Symposium on the Foundations of Software Engineering (ESEC/FSE 2003)*. pp. 88–97.

Wagner, D., & Dean, D. (2001, May). Intrusion detection via static analysis. In *Proceedings of the IEEE Symposium on Security and Privacy* (pp. 175–187). Oakland, CA.

Wagner, D., & Soto, P. (2002). Mimicry attacks on host-based intrusion detection systems. In *Proceedings of the ACM Conference on Computer and Communications Security (CCS)* (pp. 255–264). Washington, DC.

Wang, K., & Stolfo, S. (2003). One class training for masquerade detection. In *Proceedings of the ICDM Workshop on Data Mining for Computer Security (DMSEC)*. Melbourne, FL, pp. 2–7.

Warrender, C., Forrest, S., & Pearlmutter, B. A. (1999). Detecting intrusions using system calls: Alternative data models. In *Proceedings of the IEEE Symposium on Security and Privacy* (pp. 133–145). Oakland, CA.

# Network-Based Intrusion Detection Systems

Marco Cremonini, *University of Milan, Italy*

## INTRODUCTION

This chapter focuses on the characteristics of *network-based intrusion detection systems* (*NIDSs*). NIDSs collect data from packets in transit on a network segment for the purpose of identifying and preventing inappropriate network uses. NIDSs have several fundamental functional components:

- *Source of observed events:* The source-of-event information used to determine whether an intrusion has taken place. The most common sources are recorded from an individual computer system (in host-based IDSs) or by capturing network packets in transit (in network-based IDSs).

- *Analysis methodology:* The methods for analyzing observed events, signs of suspicious activities, or the evidence of intrusions. Data analysis may require one to preprocess raw data before performing the analysis task. For instance, it is common to perform *data reduction* operations to lessen the amount of data and to conduct *data normalization* when heterogeneous data sources are considered. In addition to the identification of malicious activity, the analysis often calls for *data correlation*: for example, to associate logs showing attacks occurring at different targets with a common source or to associate system vulnerabilities with the evidence of intrusion.

- *Response to alerts:* The set of actions that a NIDS takes once it detects signs of an intrusion. The most common response is to alert the network security staff. Alert techniques range from displaying alerts on monitoring consoles to sending e-mails or messages to intrusion analysts. An effective response depends on the completeness and clarity of the alert report, whether the

alert classification is based on the severity of the alarm, and the ability to remotely monitor data streams in real time as soon as an alert has been raised. Another important consideration is the ability to aggregate results based on common attributes, such as attack source, targets, or type of vulnerability exploited. Although several techniques for automatically responding to alerts have been attempted, they have met with limited acceptance because of some significant shortcomings.

One important metric for NIDSs is the rate of false alarms, also called *false positive*. All NIDSs (and actually all IDSs), regardless of the technology and approach on which they are built, experience some false positive alarms. A related metric is the rate of missed alarms or false negative alerts. In keeping with the terminology, NIDS alarms that correspond to actual intrusions are sometimes referred to as *true positives*. It is important to note that the dominant factor that most affects the performance and effectiveness of a NIDS is not its ability to correctly identify intrusions, but rather its ability to limit the rate of false alarms (Axelsson, 2000).

## NETWORK INTRUSION DETECTION MODELS
### Anomaly Detection

NIDSs that rely on *anomaly detection* (sometimes called *behavior-based*) look for anomalous events, such as unusual data in a collected data set or abnormal activities of monitored systems. The prior knowledge of normal system behavior when exposed to legal data patterns is used to decide whether a certain event is to be considered anomalous. Hence, the key factor for establishing the effectiveness of anomaly-based NIDSs is the reliability, expressiveness, and accuracy of the definition of normal system behavior. For this reason, this definition is traditionally the object of intensive research and testing in the field of anomaly detection. Anomaly detection systems are particularly interesting NIDSs because they are able to flag suspicious variations from normal system behavior as evidence of intrusion without specific knowledge of system vulnerabilities.

Statistical anomaly detection was one of the first techniques applied to intrusion detection. It has its roots in the work of Anderson (1980), who focused on detecting illegal computer usage by analyzing statistical discrepancies in audit trail data. The underlying assumption of the statistical approach is that the distribution of observed events fits a particular pattern, possibly inferred from a set of historical values.

In 1987, Denning published a seminal paper (Denning, 1987) describing four different statistical anomaly detection models: the operational model, which defines operational thresholds to compare against observed events; the mean and standard deviation model, which uses thresholds defined under the assumption that observed events are normally distributed; the multivariate model, which extends the mean and standard deviation model by correlating different attributes—for example, CPU time and input/output (I/O) usage—in the definition of thresholds; and the Markov process model, which adopts a probabilistic approach based on Markov processes to spot anomalous events. The statistical anomaly detection approach first advanced by Denning (1987) is commonly used to monitor host-based events; for instance, CPU usage, I/O usage, commands invoked; files/directories accessed; and system errors generated. Since Denning's paper, many other research projects have explored the possibilities provided by a statistical approach to anomaly detection. These projects further developed Denning's approach or proposed new models; see for example Anderson, Frivold, and Valdes (1995) and Porras and Neumann (1997). The statistical anomaly detection approach has also been studied extensively and applied to network-based systems. The work by Lee and Stolfo (2000) is one example among many others.

More recently, anomaly detection studies have concentrated on the application of alternate techniques for the definition of normal system behavior and the analysis of observed events. In particular, many efforts have shied away from the traditional approach based on statistics generated from historical values. Instead, these systems usually start from one or more safe and reliable data sets representing normal system behavior. Then, these data sets are used to instruct the NIDS about normal behavior patterns in what is often called the *training phase* of the system. Because of the training, the anomaly detection NIDS is better able to estimate the probability that an observed event is anomalous, either by comparing thresholds or algorithmically.

Other techniques that have been tested for analyzing data and inferring abnormal behavioral patterns include neural networks (Fox, Henning, Reed, & Simonian, 1990), expert systems (Lunt et al., 1992), and data mining (Lee

et al., 2000). Some research proposals have enlarged the set of system attributes potentially useful for anomaly detection, for example by modeling system behavior by means of sequences of system calls (Hofmeyr, Somayaji, & Forrest, 1998).

These considerable efforts notwithstanding, anomaly detection IDSs have not achieved large-scale acceptance in the commercial arena. This is because they often produce a large number of false alarms, as normal patterns of user and system behaviors can present unforeseen variations. In other words, the notion of "normal behavior" has turned out to be much too complex to be defined precisely and to be kept in sync with the dynamics of actual systems. The various techniques and models that have been proposed address these problems by trying to develop a methodology that is sufficiently powerful and expressive to depict normal behavior precisely and at the same time is manageable when the NIDS needs to be trained, deployed, and operated. The results are extremely interesting from a research standpoint, but do not provide the simplicity and automation required by commercial products. For this reason, commercial implementations have adopted only some simplistic forms of anomaly detection based on general usage thresholds and statistical patterns.

In sum, the principal advantages and disadvantages of anomaly-based NIDSs are the following:

□ Because they are able to detect unanticipated behaviors, they thus have the ability to detect evidence of intrusions without specific knowledge of system vulnerabilities and attack methods.

□ They often produce a large number of false-positive alarms because of the unpredictable ordinary behaviors of users and systems and the simplifications taken in modeling otherwise extremely complex system behaviors.

□ They often require an extensive training phase with large safe data sets in order to characterize normal behavior patterns. Here again, incomplete data sets and simplifications in inferring normal behavior from training data lead to poor results.

In practice, the complexity of characterizing reliable normal system behavior, which is so critical for the functioning of anomaly-based NIDSs, seems overwhelming, and instead other approaches have gained acceptance in real-world environments. These include misuse detection, the largest and most successful category of NIDSs today.

## Misuse Detection

*Network-based misuse detection systems* (sometimes called *knowledge-based*) analyze network activity looking for events that match a predefined pattern of activity representing a known attack (Bace & Mell, 2000). Often the patterns corresponding to known attacks are called *signatures*, and correspondingly, misuse-based NIDSs take the name of *signature-based* NIDSs.

Usually, each known attack is described by a corresponding signature. Thus, misuse-based NIDSs rely on a database of signatures representing their whole knowledge of illegal patterns of activity that the system is capable of detecting. As a result, the completeness, accuracy, and effectiveness of the collection of signatures in the database are key to a signature-based NIDS. Given this fact, it is perhaps not surprising that some commercial products keep their signature databases as secret as possible. Some vendors consider those data a critical asset in market competition. Others may fear that, by permitting a public scrutiny of their database, it could become relatively easy to evaluate the effectiveness of the NIDS, with potentially disappointing outcomes.

More sophisticated approaches to misuse detection have been proposed, in particular regarding the way signatures are expressed and the way a misuse is flagged. Some examples are the notion of context signatures of the BRO system (Sommer & Paxson, 2003); the STAT system (Ilgun, Kemmerer, & Porras, 1995), which uses transitions on a set of system states as signatures; and its companion system NetSTAT (Vigna & Kemmerer, 1999), which extends the STAT approach to network-based events. However, these sophisticated detection methods are still limited to research systems and have not yet been implemented in commercial NIDSs.

The principal advantages and disadvantages of misuse detection techniques are the following:

☐ They are effective in detecting attacks while (possibly) generating considerably less false alarms than anomaly-based systems.

☐ They can help in the identification of specific attack tools or techniques, thus permitting security managers to prioritize corrective measures.

☐ They can only detect attacks that are represented in the signature database; constant updating with signatures of new attacks is therefore a vital requirement of these NIDSs.

☐ They are often designed to use precisely defined signatures, which keep them from detecting variants of common attacks or the effects of new releases of known attack tools.

Finally, it must be stressed that the greatest advantage of anomaly-based systems—being independent from the knowledge of systems' vulnerability—has been lost with misuse detection systems. This is because they depend upon prior knowledge of all vulnerabilities that can afflict all monitored systems and networks, an unrealistic requirement in some modern complex environments. This dependency represents the principal disadvantage of this approach and could, in principle, undermine severely its future diffusion and acceptance. For this reason, anomaly detection is still a very active research area. The integration of anomaly and misuse detection features is a promising area for future advances in this field; for example, intrusion detection applied to Web applications.

# SIGNATURE-BASED NIDSs

A signature is a string-based pattern of a known attack or of an abnormal network event. Most NIDSs work by matching observed network events against a comprehensive collection of signatures. Signature definition may range from very simple, such as matching an illegal combination of transmission control protocol (TCP) flags, to complex, such as protocol-specific and stateful signatures. The degree of complexity in signature definition may be related to the types of application- or protocol-specific anomalous events to be detected; the requirement to detect correlated events, classes of vulnerabilities, and mutations of known attacks; or even detection based on decision trees for optimization purposes. In the end, the degree of sophistication of attacks that should be caught, as counterbalanced by performance considerations, is what most determines the complexity of the definition of signatures.

## Signature Examples

As our reference tool, we use Snort (Caswell, Beale, Foster, & Posluns, 2003; Snort, 2003), a signature-based open source and freeware NIDS. It is used widely in real-world intrusion detection because of its simple and straightforward rule definition that is publicly available. Snort is thus a good choice for discussing signatures.

An example of a simple signature available from Snort's rule set that is useful for the detection of SYN-FIN scans is shown below. In Snort, the reserved "\" character is used to write instructions on multiple lines. Line numbers have been added only for clarity of the presentation:

```
1. alert tcp $EXTERNAL_NET any -> $HOME_NET any \
2. (msg:"SCAN SYN FIN"; \
3. flags:SF,12; \
4. reference:arachnids,198; classtype: attempted-recon;
   sid:624; rev:2;)
```

As seen in the example, in general, a Snort rule is divided into a rule header (line 1) and rule options written inside parentheses (lines 2–4). A rule header contains the action triggered by the rule (e.g., *alert*), the network protocol (e.g., *tcp*), the source and the destination IP addresses, and the application ports (e.g., *any*). The key word *any* means that all values are matched. For convenience and manageability, these parameters of a rule header can be stored into local variables; note *$EXTERNAL_NET* and *$HOME_NET* are used in the example.

Rule options are the core of Snort rules. They are divided by semicolons and are made up of a *key word* that is itself separated with a colon from *arguments* (e.g., line 3: flags:SF, 12;). The msg keyword is typical of all rules (apart from a few exceptions not discussed here) and represents the text message to be printed by the alerting mechanism when an intrusion has been detected: it describes the reason for the alarm.

However, many other options can be used within a Snort rule. This chapter uses some Snort example rules to discuss different issues. These rules are presented entirely as they appear in the official rule set, but only options related to the presentation are discussed. Interested readers are directed to the *Snort User Manual* (Roesch & Green, 2004) and to Caswell, Beale, Foster, and Posluns (2003) for a detailed description of every option. In addition, readers interested in additional practical examples of intrusion analysis based on signatures are directed to Cooper, Northcutt, Fearnow, and Frederick (2001) and GIAC (2004).

The Snort example above is designed to trap an incoming SYN-FIN scan. Line 3 checks whether both TCP flags SYN and FIN are active simultaneously. Line 4 carries some more information about the source of the rule (i.e., arachnids, 198), the type of attack (i.e., attempted reconnaissance, being a scan), and the identifiers of the rule within the official Snort rule base (i.e., sid 624). Often, vulnerabilities matched by Snort rules have been already classified into the Computer Vulnerability and Exposures (CVE) database (CVE, 2003). In these cases, the CVE reference is provided in the informational part of the rule.

The signature for the SYN-FIN scan, as implemented by the rule in the example above, has its shortcomings. The principal one is that it, correctly, catches all SYN-FIN packets of a scan. The problem with this is that, if for each packet caught an alarm is reported to the network security staff, the staff will rapidly be flooded by these reports. Moreover, reports of scan packets are not really significant when taken singularly. What network security staff members are most interested in is aggregated information about the source, type, and frequency of the scan. Hence, for similar misuses, it is fundamental that the NIDS preprocess data and aggregate results before reporting. Additional features aimed at efficient monitoring and reporting are extremely valuable for an effective intrusion detection task.

A more elaborate example of signature is presented below. In this case, the scan wants to catch attempts to create a new database instance:

```
1. alert tcp $EXTERNAL_NET any -> $SQL_SERVERS
   $ORACLE_PORTS \
2. (msg:"ORACLE create database attempt"; \
3. flow:to_server,established; content:"create
   database"; nocase; \
4. classtype:protocol-command-decode;
   sid:1696; rev:3;)
```

Line 1, the rule header, states that interesting packets are flowing from external IP addresses to internal IP addresses for database servers responding on Oracle ports. In this example, the signature was specifically defined for Oracle databases, but could be modified easily to serve other database specifications. Line 2 is the text alert to be reported. Line 3 defines two additional matching conditions: first, packets must be directed to a server and must be part of an already established TCP connection, and second, the case-independent string "create database" must be contained in the packet payload.

This rule, we immediately observe, could easily result in false positives if the creation of databases from selected external sources is legitimately authorized. In such cases, stricter requirements would have to be implemented to restrict the source of this traffic. Another problem with this rule is that there is no conceivably valid reason for permitting a database system to be accessed from the outside and be instructed to create new database instances or similar major tasks.

Database creation is a critical task that needs to be addressed with care and precautions. Thus, if it is absolutely necessary to allow it from external sources, specific security measures must first be put in place—at a minimum for authenticating the source of the request, keeping the channel encrypted, validating the request syntactically and semantically, and uncoupling the request generated from outside entities from the actual request eventually addressed to the database system. Otherwise, it would be best to simply block the request at the perimeter by enforcing a rule that the database server cannot be used to create new databases from the external net. If this is the case, as normally it would be, the rule described could raise alerts for attempts that cannot be successful because, for instance, a firewall will have been configured to block them anyway. In such cases, again, the false-positive rate would increase, and the network security staff would eventually be overwhelmed by meaningless alerts. However, some network security operations are intent on monitoring all attempted attacks, even those with no chance to success.

In turn, the scenario would be completely different if packets that have traversed a firewall trigger this rule. In this case, the NIDS could fire off an alert about what would consist of a severe misconfiguration and serious vulnerability in the perimeter protection, in that it was supposed to block such attempts. Often then, for NIDSs, the location where a network event is observed is the key to evaluating a signature; in this example, the alert would have totally different meanings depending on whether it is triggered in front or behind a perimeter firewall.

The next example of an alert signature shows how response traffic, in addition to the stimulus traffic seen in previous rules, could be inspected to collect signs of unauthorized network activity. In this example, the rule catches responses to a failed authentication attempt due to an invalid user name. The responses may be an intelligence gathering activity or an attempt to connect to a concurrent version system (CVS) server on ports 2401/tcp and 2401/udp using the credentials of a user having escalated privileges (Snort, 2003).

```
1. alert tcp $HOME_NET 2401 -> $EXTERNAL_NET any \
2. (msg:"MISC CVS invalid user authentication
   response"; \
3. flow:from_server,established;content:"E Fatal
   error,aborting.";\ content:"|3a|nosuchuser";\
4. classtype:misc-attack; sid:2008; rev:3;)
```

In this example, the traffic tracked by the NIDS flows from the monitored network, specified by the variable $HOME_NET, with 2401/tcp as the source port, to the external network $EXTERNAL_NET. Packets matched by this rule are sent by servers during an established connection and must carry in their application payloads a string specifying the error generated by the invalid user authentication. In other words, actually two possible string patterns are specified in the rule. One possible shortcoming of this rule is that the misuse is recognized by means of string patterns that are strictly dependent on a specific syntax of authentication error routines. Moreover, all user authentication errors are caught—both fraudulent and common mistakes from legal users. Again, this uncertainty may cause an unwarranted increase in the number of false positives and thus impair the effectiveness of the intrusion detection task.

## Tuning Signatures

We learned from the earlier examples that a signature rule base needs to be carefully administered by the organization that makes use of it. There are several reasons why this care is needed. For one, a signature rule base must be kept up-to-date and needless signatures eliminated. Then, the remaining signatures must be *tuned*; that is, each signature must be analyzed and modified to optimize its efficacy in minimizing the number of false positives and maximizing its ability to catch true positives, as well as unduly suspicious behaviors. This tuning task depends largely on the specific context, resources, and goals of the organization that wishes to benefit from the intrusion detection features of the NIDS.

The pruning of unnecessary rules in the rule base is an important tuning activity. Although notable improvements in the algorithms for string matching have been achieved (Coit, Staniford, & McAlerney, 2003), NIDS performance still could be impaired strongly by an unnecessarily large rule base. Broad criteria that could be used in selecting signatures worth retaining in a rule base include the following:

□ Signatures covering individual exploits and shell code: these signatures usually generate few false positives, although they could be evaded by variants of known exploits or worm mutations.

□ Signatures catching traffic originating from within the enterprise network: such traffic is a strong indicator of successful system compromise.

□ Signatures based on several matching conditions: using such signatures reduces the number of false positives.

□ Signatures for nonexistent services: these signatures can be removed safely.

□ Signatures that turn out to be triggered too easily by legal packets and do not have a more precise formulation: these signatures should be considered among the first candidates for removal.

Although these last two criteria may seem obvious, they call for closer examination because some important hidden subtleties are often involved in their application. Eliminating signatures for nonexistent services means that the network security staff must know exactly which services are actually deployed. Doing so usually requires that the network security staff be informed in a timely and accurate fashion when new services and systems are put into operation. The coordination between the network security staff and the staff in charge of deploying new applications and services requires a serious organizational commitment to be effective, and sometimes these coordination efforts are flawed, unreliable, or not timely. The consequences of any such disconnects are generally severe for intrusion detection because entire new classes of vulnerabilities might not be detected by the NIDS, leaving entire systems exposed to risks, with potentially disastrous consequences.

The necessity for caution when removing broadly ineffective signatures that lack a more precise definition can be explained with an example taken from the Snort's rule base:

```
alert tcp $EXTERNAL_NET any -> $HOME_NET 111 \
(msg:"RPC portmap status request TCP"; \
flow:to_server,established; \
content:"|00 01 86 A0|"; offset:16; depth:4; \
content:"|00 00 00 03|"; distance:4; within:4; \
byte_jump:4,4,relative,align; byte_jump:4,4,
    relative,align; \
content:"|00 01 86 B8|"; within:4; \
reference:arachnids,15; classtype:rpc-portmap-
    decode; \
content:"|00 00 00 00|"; offset:8; depth:4;
    sid:2016; rev:5;)
```

This rule traps a remote procedure call (RPC) status request. This request may not be an attack against a host by itself; instead, it could be a form of intelligence gathering activity that must be monitored and curtailed. At the same time, when the NIDS is deployed internally so that $HOME_NET is set to a specific subnet and $EXTERNAL_NET includes other corporate subnets, this rule could be often triggered by legitimate intranet RPC-based traffic.

## Active Responses

Many NIDS systems have the ability to run some countermeasures proactively in the event of a detected intrusion. For instance, once a NIDS has detected an ongoing exploitation of a given vulnerability, it cannot limit its reaction to logging some data for postmortem analysis and sending an e-mail to the system administrator, because the time frame from detection to manual enforcement of some countermeasure might permit the attacker to complete or propagate the intrusion. The solution is to have the NIDS intervene actively by dropping the exploit connection. As shown in the next example, Snort provides such a feature:

```
alert tcp $EXTERNAL_NET any -> $HTTP_SERVERS $HTTP_PORTS \
(msg:"WEB-IIS cmd.exeaccess";flow:to_server,established; \
content:"cmd.exe"; nocase; react: block; \
classtype:web-application-attack; sid:1002; rev:5;)
```

The active response mechanism in the example is implemented with the key word `react`, which instructs Snort to actively close offending connections with a block. Active NIDS responses involving blocks are popular and generally take the name of *session sniping*. The connection is dropped by the NIDS by sending a properly forged TCP RESET packet to both ends of the connection. A properly forged TCP RESET means that those packets, one for each end of the connection, must appear as sent by the corresponding party and not by an intermediary. This requirement in turns means that the packets must also contain all the correct TCP attributes, such as sequence and acknowledgment numbers.

Unfortunately, several underhanded techniques have been developed to bypass NIDS session sniping mechanisms. The trick is to get the machine that is the victim of the intrusion to ignore the RESET packet. If successful, the NIDS will think it has torn down the session, and the attack can merrily proceed entirely unfettered. For the trick to succeed, the key factor is timing: the attacker must be able to deliver the next packet in the TCP session to the victim *before* the RESET packet is generated by the NIDS. In most TCP stacks, a RESET, to be processed, must match the current pointer (CP), which is the pointer to the next piece of data the stack expects to receive. Given this, if the network packet that triggered the alarm is immediately followed by another packet that arrives at the victim machine before the RESET and moves the CP, then there is a good chance that the RESET packet will be considered malformed and so be ignored by the victim's TCP stack, to its own detriment. Some variants of this basic technique exist. They are more complex to execute than the example given here, but are even more difficult to neutralize. Larsen and Haile (2002) have described these variant mechanisms in more detail. Consider for example the following Snort rules:

```
1. alert udp $EXTERNAL_NET any -> $HOME_NET 1434 (msg:
   "MS-SQL Worm propagation attempt"; content:"| 04| ";
   depth:1; content:"| 81 F1 03 01 04 9B 81 F1 01| ";
   content:"sock"; content:"send"; reference:bugtraq,
   5310; classtype:misc-attack; reference:bugtraq,5311;
   sid:2003; rev:2;)
2. alert udp $EXTERNAL_NET any -> $HOME_NET 53 (msg:"DNS
   EXPLOIT named tsig overflow attempt"; content:"| 80
   00 07 00 00 00 00 00 01 3F 00 01 02| "; classtype:
   attempted-admin; sid:314; rev:6; reference:cve,
   CVE-2001-0010; reference:bugtraq,2303;)
3. alert icmp $EXTERNAL_NET any -> $HOME_NET any (msg:
   "ICMP Large ICMP Packet"; dsize: >800; reference:
   arachnids,246; classtype:bad-unknown; sid:499; rev:3;)
```

These rules describe, respectively, (1) an attempt made by the MS-SQL worm to propagate itself from outside to inside the monitored network, (2) a buffer overflow attack toward a domain name system (DNS) service, and (3) the delivery of an abnormally large Internet control message protocol (ICMP) packet. These are just few examples of network traffic showing two characteristics that could completely impair session sniping countermeasures. First, harmful packets will have already passed through the NIDS before it is able to raise the alarm; the large ICMP packet detected by rule (3) will already be on its way to cause damage at the destination. Second, in UDP and ICMP communications, there is no session to be reset by a NIDS session sniping active response.

Circumstances like the one just described are clearly a strong limitation to session sniping efficacy. This is why another class of NIDS active responses has been introduced: *firewall updates*. Here again, the idea is simple: if we assume that the organization is operating a firewall for the protection of the network perimeter–and this is true for more than 80% of today's corporate networks–then filtering capabilities of firewalls can be exploited to block attacks detected by an active response NIDS. In other words, the NIDS active response could be used to update the firewall's security policy automatically. This way, the countermeasure is not limited to create TCP RESETs, but it is much stronger because a new firewall rule could block the malicious traffic better and more fully; for example, by filtering based on a certain undesirable IP source and destination port. The benefit of reconfiguring the firewall in

an NIDS active response is that any subsequent attempts from the attacker can be blocked early, at the firewall itself.

However, firewall updates tied to NIDS active responses are not without their limitations. As before, time could be an ally of the attackers. Given that triggering the NIDS alarm and updating firewall rules take time, sometimes a window of opportunity remains that is long enough to exploit a vulnerability fully and for example install a back door. Once the back door is in place, there is no way to know whether the updated firewall rule will block the attacker from remotely administering the compromised machine. In the absence of significant technological improvements, there will always remain a race between the two processes, one detecting intrusions and updating firewall rules and the other exploiting a vulnerability and installing a back door.

Another limitation of NIDS active responses tied to firewall updates is that attackers able to spoof IP addresses could activate the feature purposely, resulting in a denial of service condition. The net effect could be, for example, the disabling of network addresses corresponding to well-known Web sites, producing a flood of disgruntled calls to the network operation staff from all over the company and eventually resulting in the termination of the firewall update NIDS mechanism. In addition, there could be undetectable variants in the way that attackers forge packets that trigger the firewall updates mechanism. For example, if the attacker spoofs attacks from the network's upstream router or its DNS servers, the entire connection can be lost, with possible severe adverse effects to the company. In addition, motivated attackers could spoof selected IP addresses (e.g., commercial partners, customers, affiliates etc.) in an aim to produce specific business losses for the victim.

Overall, the traditional NIDS active response mechanisms—namely, session sniping and firewall updates—offer benefits circumscribed by clear limitations and possible unacceptable side effects. Thus, they should be used with care and not used to replace the proactive monitoring and analysis performed by network security staff. Advances in this area of NIDSs are expected, especially in terms of integration between NIDS and firewall features and more sophisticated methods for filtering out connection based on more selective alarms generated by a NIDS.

# PROTOCOL-BASED INTRUSION DETECTION
## Understanding Protocol Semantics

A significant development in signature-based NIDSs is their awareness of protocol semantics and consequently their ability to implement techniques for protocol analysis. Network protocols, corresponding to layers 3 (network) and 4 (transport) of the open systems interconnection (OSI model), which contain IP, TCP, and UDP, are analyzed by NIDSs by looking for out-of-specs packets, such as the ones carrying improper combinations of TCP flags, illegal IP addresses and ports, invalid header's attribute values, or unusually large payloads. Some NIDSs are now able to analyze application protocols, corresponding to layer 7. Often this means that modern NIDSs are now aware, within the context of both Requests for Comments (RFCs) and real-world implementations, of the specifications of some popular protocols, such as HTTP, SMTP, DNS, FTP, and Telnet; these can now be decoded and examined for violations and abnormalities. This capability allows a much larger range of signatures to be created than would be possible through simpler signature techniques. Such protocol-based signature sets are often called *packet grepping signatures* to emphasize that they emulate the execution of common Unix `grep` commands for string matching.

A limitation of some protocol-analysis-enabled NIDSs is that their inspection capabilities are restricted to single requests or responses without reference to the context of their exchange. Unfortunately, many attacks can be detected only by looking at the whole message exchange pattern between communicating parties, so that such anomalies as inconsistent responses, unexpected values, or odd options can be flagged as possible signs of intrusions. The best way to detect such attacks is by adding stateful inspection to protocol analysis. With *stateful protocol analysis*, the NIDS sensor can store communication actions and data for the duration of the application session. This allows the NIDS to find correlations among different events within a session, identifying attacks with multiple components that cannot be detected by other means.

## From Packet-Grepping to Protocol-Based Intrusion Detection

Protocol analysis techniques are indeed a notable advance in intrusion detection. Ranum (2002) characterizes protocol-based intrusion detection signatures as *decision tree structures*. The basic form of such a decision tree structure is a flat, one-level string pattern, which represents the elementary `grep`-like signature. Thereafter, additional conditions to be matched by the decision tree can be introduced easily; for example, by matching network protocol attributes and application ports. Furthermore, by adding additional protocol state conditions, based on who is sending which message; which command, option, or value is being specified; and which type of response is produced, more involved decision trees can be created. Intrusion detection would consist then simply of pruning the different branches of the tree and applying algorithm optimizations to improve evaluation performances.

The example provided by Ranum (2002), although expressed in an informal syntax and not codified in any real system, provides a clear and straightforward demonstration of the approach. First, using a flat, grep-like match, two suspicious strings from an attack signature, ".*WIZ.*" and "DEBUG", possibly extended by regular expressions, are compared with the payload of the packet. Next, conditions for the exchange of messages on port 25 are added, as follows:

```
Port 25: {
        Client-sends: ".*WIZ.*"
        Client-sends: "DEBUG"
    }
```

Lastly, state information and enhanced semantic awareness are added to port 25

```
Port 25:{
        state command-dialog client-sends ".*WIZ.*"
        | state command-dialog client-sends "DEBUG"
        client-sends "DATA" enter state message-body.
        state command-dialog client-sends line greater
        than 1024
        alert possible overflow attack
    }
```

Protocol analysis approaches can be used in NIDSs for the following different purposes:

☐ recognize whether certain attacks succeeded or failed by correlating an illegal stimulus with the status code of the application server response

☐ reveal brute force attacks, such as password guessing, by keeping track of large numbers of failed requests during a communication session

☐ discover abnormal messages, such as buffer overflow attempts, by correlating requests with responses and finding pairings that are incoherent with application semantics

An interesting example is described by Frederick (2002). The file-renaming feature of FTP involves two commands issued in sequence: (1) a "rename from" (RNFR) command reads the old file name, and (2) after the server's response to this command is received, a "rename to" (RNTO) command is issued. Some FTP implementations have been found vulnerable to intrusions carried out by issuing many consecutive RNTO commands. With stateful protocol analysis, any message carrying a RNTO command not preceded by a RNFR could be flagged as suspicious by the NIDS, and if the number of such messages increases above a certain threshold, an alert would be raised.

Overall, the benefits of stateful protocol analysis are clear and for this reason widely exploited in other fields of network security in addition to NIDSs, such as in firewalling technology. The possibility of extracting values and managing states within a session permits the correlation of network events and the identification of attacks that involve two or more message exchanges. Another benefit of tracking state is that a NIDS could check whether commands are issued in the proper sequence, according to the specifications of a certain protocol.

Clearly then, stateful protocol analysis is a significant improvement in intrusion detection techniques. At the same time, this technology has some drawbacks that must be taken into account. The main one is that the definition of stateful protocol-based signatures is more difficult than the definition of simple packet-grepping signatures, and consequently the definition of a whole rule base of signatures composed of multilevel decision trees could easily become a very complex task. This complexity could lead to inconsistencies, errors, redundancies, and so forth, thus impairing the potential gain in terms of NIDS efficacy and performance optimization. The other shortcoming of protocol analysis is that there are real systems using protocol implementations that do not fully follow RFCs or de facto standard specifications. This is indeed a serious problem for stateful protocol intrusion detection because systems that implement out-of-specs protocols may induce protocol analysis NIDSs to generate inconsistent results. As a remedy, a protocol analysis rule base must be customized according to the particulars of these out-of-specs protocols. The result is a growth in the rule base, an increase in rule base complexity, and almost certainly a negative impact on performance.

# EVASION TECHNIQUES
## Weaknesses of String Matching

The goal of NIDS evasion techniques is to obfuscate an illegal request so as to keep a signature from matching. In other words, a NIDS evasion technique consists not only of concealing an attack but also disguising an attack to make it appear less threatening than it really is. The exploitation of *string matching weaknesses* is the traditional way of obfuscating an evasion attack. A simple example is provided by the following Snort signature:

```
alert tcp $EXTERNAL_NET any -> $HTTP_SERVERS $HTTP_PORTS \
(msg:"WEB-MISC /etc/passwd"; flow:to_server,established; \
content:"/etc/passwd"; nocase; \
classtype:attempted-recon; sid:1122; rev:4;)
```

The key condition of this rule is based on trapping the attempted access to the `/etc/passwd` file by matching the "/etc/passwd" string contained in the packet payload to the condition in the signature. The problem is that the "/etc/passwd" string can be written in any number of different equivalent formats. For example, some of the easiest alternative syntaxes could be: "/etc//\//passwd" or "/etc/rc.d/../.\passwd," to name just two of the countless variants. If the NIDS does not decode the syntax into a normalized form before matching the string, the result could be unsuccessful, and thus the packet collected from live network traffic would not be recognized as malicious.

The Snort rule base does provide a signature that matches each generic attempt to implement a *directory traversal* technique (e.g., the one exploited with the "/etc/rc.d/../.\passwd" signature just discussed). Strings like these are always suspicious because there is no reasonably legitimate motivation to specify a path formatted in such a way. Here is the Snort signature:

```
alert tcp $EXTERNAL_NET any -> $HTTP_SERVERS $HTTP_PORTS \
(msg:"WEB-MISC http directory traversal"; flow:to_server,
established; \  content: "..\ \ "; \
reference:arachnids,298; classtype:attempted-recon;
sid:1112; rev:4;)
```

## Techniques

This section looks at the principal NIDS signature evasion techniques implemented in Libwhisker (2003):

□ *Method matching*: Some NIDSs fail because they incorrectly assume all HTTP requests use the GET method by hard-coding it in signatures such as "GET /cgi-bin/some.cgi." The illegal request can defeat the NIDS signature by using a different HTTP method, such as "HEAD /cgi-bin/some.cgi."

□ *URL encoding*: In this signature evasion technique, the URI is encoded as its escaped equivalent. The HTTP protocol specifies that arbitrary binary characters can be passed within the URI by using "%xx" notation, where "xx" is the hex value of the character. Thus, the "cgi-bin" string could be encoded to become the string "%63%67%69%2d%62%69%6e," which is thus still a legal representation of "cgi-bin." The encoding technique could even be applied more than one time, recursively. Today, almost all NIDSs decode encoded URIs before matching against string patterns.

□ *Directory traversal, self-reference traversal, and multiple slashes*: The tactic of traversing directories has been described before. In similar fashion, self-references and multiple slashes could be used to obfuscate an illegal access attempt; for instance, by using `/./././cgi-bin/./phf` and `//cgi-bin//some.cgi`. Decoding URIs before matching against string patterns is the countermeasure adopted by the great majority of NIDSs.

□ *Premature request ending*: This tactic exploits the curious choice of some NIDS to check only the beginning of an HTTP request instead of the whole message so as to optimize performance. A typical HTTP request looks like this:

```
GET /some.file HTTP/1.0\ r\ n
```

and is followed by some HTTP header blocks. If the analysis performed by a NIDS only focuses on the GET statement and ignores the ensuing headers, the request could be compromised in the following way:

```
GET /%20HTTP/1.0%0d%0aHeader:%20/../../cgi-bin/
   some.cgi
HTTP/1.0\ r\ n\ r\ n.
```

This translates into the following otherwise legal request, which would be inappropriately ignored by a NIDS:

```
GET / HTTP/1.0\ r\ n
Header: /../../cgi-bin/some.cgi HTTP/1.0\ r\ n\ r\ n
```

□ *Parameter hiding*: Even parameters of an HTTP request could be used to conceal an illegal access attempt. As in the previous case, some NIDSs, for performance optimization, do not analyze those parameters. Thus, an inappropriate request could be coded as follows:

```
GET /index.htm%3fparam=/../cgi-bin/some.cgi
HTTP/1.0
```

which translates to

```
GET /index.htm?param=/../cgi-bin/some.cgi
HTTP/1.0
```

and is perfectly valid. The access to the CGI could slip by undetected if the NIDS signature analysis stops at the "?" character that represents the beginning of the recklessly ignored parameter request list.

☐ *Long URLs*: Another performance optimization measure applied by some NIDSs is to look only at a specified maximum number of bytes in the message payload. This is reasonable in most cases unless it is exploited to let attack code pass undetected.

☐ *Out-of-specs systems*: HTTP RFC specifications require the use of "/" (forward slash) as the character separator in paths. In contrast, in the Microsoft Windows world the "\" (backslash) character is adopted. Despite this, Microsoft web servers must accept both formats, and for compatibility reasons internally they convert "\" into "/." This creates an easy opportunity to obfuscate strings, for example as /cgi-bin\some.cgi.

☐ *Session splicing*: A tricky evasion tactic exploits the possibility of splitting a request into multiple network packets. The receiving server will reassemble all packets received in a session and will process the resulting request. Some NIDSs do not perform the same reassembling because it would require the NIDS to remain aware of protocol semantics at the cost of a large computational overhead. Instead, they try to find signs of attacks in each packet singularly. For example, the request GET / HTTP/1.0 could be hidden as a sequence of packets reading "GE", "T ", "/", ' H", "T", "TP", "/1", and ".0."

Other evasion techniques have been developed. The *polymorphic shell code*, for example, is a well-known method used in virus evasion techniques. Consider the following Snort rule:

```
alert tcp $EXTERNAL_NET any -> $HOME_NET 22 \
(msg:"EXPLOIT ssh CRC32 overflow NOOP"; flow:to_server,
established; \
content:"| 90 90 90 90 90 90 90 90 90 90 90 90 90 90
90|"; \
reference:bugtraq,2347; reference:cve,CVE-2001-0144; \
classtype:shellcode-detect; sid:1326; rev:3;)
```

The overflow attempt against a vulnerability of the secure shell (SSH) service is detected with the usual signature that checks the presence of an overly long sequence of NO-OP (no operation) characters (i.e., hex 90s in this rule). The problem is that there are some dozen possible replacements to this particular sequence of NO-OP that provide the same effects. These alternative NO-OP characters could even be combined in a pseudo-random manner. In the absence of otherwise promising research advances, such techniques like this could be very effective in bypassing most NIDSs. An in-depth discussion of polymorphic shell code and its usage to defeat NIDS was published by the *Phrack* online magazine (2003).

Ptacek and Newsham (1998) have published a seminal paper about insertion, evasion, and denial of service techniques intended to subvert intrusion detection-systems. They discuss such tactics as session splicing, as well as even more sophisticated methods, including packet fragmentation and time-to-live attribute (TTL) manipulation. The presence of fragmented packets is traditionally cumbersome for network security tools because reassembling fragments while analyzing live network traffic could dramatically degrade performance and so curtail the ability of NIDSs to catch packets. In addition, when fragmentation is maliciously used by means of overlapping and overwriting fragments, and particularly when it is combined with the selective expiration of TTL counters, then the complexity of intrusion detection grows very quickly. In such a scenario, efficient reassembling features alone would not be sufficient because the analysis tool needs also to be aware of the network architecture on which it is deployed; that is, it has to recognize whether a TTL value associated with a certain packet will expire before it gets to the destination host. Issues related to the normalizing of network traffic prior to NIDS analysis are discussed by Handley, Kreibich, and Paxson (2001).

Another form of NIDS evasion arises from the fact that NIDS sensors themselves could be the targets of denial of service attacks. If NIDS sensors are blinded by an unmanageable number of purposely triggered alerts, real attacks to corporate systems could slip undetected by the system or by the security personnel.

# TESTING NIDS
## Approaches and Difficulties

Once a NIDS has been deployed and its rule base tuned, it is appropriate to test the quality of the tool and verify the effectiveness of the installed rule base. Testing a NIDS is a challenging task. The most common test procedures run a few selected attacks and analyze the results. However, modern NIDSs may have thousands of signatures, and conducting only a few test attacks is likely to result in testing just a few signatures in a way that is not necessarily representative of the overall quality of the NIDS or of its configuration. Conversely, the brute force testing of the entire rule base by running attacks corresponding to all signatures is extremely cumbersome, if not unfeasible in practice. Therefore, testing a NIDS is a process that should be tailored to the needs of each organization. A preliminary risk analysis must be done, threats prioritized, and tests performed on a selected list of corresponding attacks. Selecting meaningful test attacks may depend on several aspects, including the number and location of NIDS sensors, the presence of other security measures, the goals of intrusion detection (e.g., to verify which traffic goes through a firewall, to inspect which traffic travels on a network segment to some critical assets, etc.), the corporate network architecture, the extent of the provided networked services, and the type and quality of network traffic exchanged.

The combination of a precise knowledge of the threats with a methodology for classifying attacks permits one to select a well-balanced attack suite. One approach is to start from protocols, either network or application protocols, to classify attacks. This way, it is possible to develop a list of protocols that are of interest in the NIDS environment and then to use the list as the first step in choosing which attacks to run. The next step is to determine which attacks should be used for each classification. Here, the first point to be considered is whether one is more interested in attacks that match system characteristics only or in all attacks directed to one's corporate network. The former case is simpler and permits the use of a smaller rule set. The latter, in contrast, gives network administrators more information that is especially useful when planning the deployment of new technologies and platforms.

The remaining step is to mount the selected attacks against a test system. Retrieving representative exploit source code scripts and executables on the Web is straightforward. However, some problems may arise with this approach: (1) exploits collected from the Web might claim to have certain effects and instead result in others; (2) because exploits are often provided in executable form, they are difficult to inspect or reverse-engineer; (3) all too often, the published versions of exploits are purposely unsuccessful; and (4) running exploits correctly and producing the desired effects that makes tests meaningful can be a difficult and labor-intensive task.

In practice then, performing intrusion detection signature testing with real exploits is often time and resource intensive. Such tests cannot be performed on live systems, because no matter how many precautious have been taken; serious damage could be caused easily, even if inadvertently. For this reason, tests on NIDSs must be executed in safe and isolated environments and definitely require written authorizations from corporate management (Ranum, 2001). In almost every case, NIDS testing tools and test methodologies should prove very useful for guiding this testing process. These testing tools put together generally relevant exploits and largely automate the attack process. Often, they also have additional helpful features, such as creating customized attacks, providing user-friendly graphical user interfaces (GUIs), generating automatic reports, and opening the door to the possibility of testing live systems safely. Two interesting vulnerability scanners used to test NIDS among the many available are *Nessus* (2003) and *Nikto* (2004), which is a Web vulnerability scanner based on *Libwhisker* (2003).

## Guidelines and Test Criteria

The open security evaluation criteria (OSEC) test suite from Neohapsis (2003) offers one of the best available guideline and selection criteria sets for the testing of NIDSs. Test criteria employed by OSEC, as reported by Neohapsis (2003), are the following:

☐ *Device integrity checking (sensor)*: Verifies that the sensor itself is not easily subject to compromise or denial of service attacks

☐ *Signature baseline test*: Checks that the sensor catches the basic attacks used throughout the testing suite under minimal background traffic conditions

☐ *State test*: Establishes that the sensor has a stable state table, one that is reasonably sized for the traffic levels it is designed to monitor. A NIDS should be able to track a number of "sessions" at setup and at tear-down, at rates equivalent to what a stateful inspection firewall in a similar speed class can track.

☐ *Discard test*: Determines that the sensor does not expend significant resources while handling traffic that does not match any monitoring rule. To achieve high speeds, most NIDS sensors employ a quick discard mechanism for traffic that falls outside their signature

set. This suite tests the ability of the sniffing portion of the NIDS to hand off possibly significant traffic to the signature or rule-processing portion of the solution while experiencing various less significant traffic loads.

☐ *Engine flex test*: Tests the sensor's ability to recognize attacks when under maximal legitimate traffic stress. These tests are designed for stressing inspectors/decoders with background application-based traffic while valid attacks are injected.

☐ *Evasion test*: Rates the sensor's ability to recognize attacks that are sent through various obfuscation or evasion mechanisms. These tests are designed to verify the sensor's ability to deal with published means to evade network-based IDS sensors.

☐ *Inline engine test*: Gauges the sensor's ability to recognize attacks when reading traffic in-line or from a tap. These tests verify the engine's ability to reintegrate directional streams and to cope with traffic that exceeds half-duplex fiber speeds.

A useful essay about testing intrusion detection systems has been written by Mell, Hu, Lippmann, Haines, and Zissman (2002). The National Institute of Standards and Technology (NIST) has also published a comprehensive *Guideline on Network Security Testing* (Wack, Tracy, & Souppaya, 2003). This work aims to identify network testing requirements and to help set priorities when testing activities with limited resources. Furthermore, the NIST guidelines suggest a tailored approach by offering different levels of network security testing as appropriate to each organization's mission and security objectives. The NIST work is aimed at more systems than just NIDS, including firewalls, routers and switches, Web servers, mail servers, and application servers in general. It also includes a list of well-known security tools, both freeware and commercial, that could be useful as a reference list.

# NIDS DEPLOYMENT AND MANAGEMENT

The need for intrusion detection systems should not be regarded in isolation. Instead, it must be considered as one measure of a general defense-in-depth strategy. All security measures, NIDSs among others, should be deployed in a coherent model, wherein each component provides for some specific features and no single security measure represents the only line of defense of corporate assets. Thus, controls should be multiple and may overlap. Systems typically involved in defense-in-depth are routers, firewalls, public key infrastructures, virtual private networks, virus scanners, and intrusion detection systems. The architectural design of physical networks should assist the optimal deployment of these security components to ensure the protection of all critical assets. To this end, corporate networks are often compartmentalized based on the definition of security zones at different security levels.

## Basic Requirements for Large Organizations

Large organizations pose difficult problems for NIDS deployment because the network topology may be sparse and be made up of many decentralized subsidiaries or branches. Corporate networks may comprise many dozen of subnets with many different entry points, heterogeneous systems, and a vast variety of communication technologies. Among the most challenging tasks to be accomplished is the efficient coordination among network, system, and security administrators; application developers and maintainers; commercial personnel; and contractors, among other providers. To address these complex network architectures effectively, NIDS deployments must satisfy certain important requirements:

☐ *Centralized administration*: Distributed NIDSs should be centrally administered to help reduce costs, simplify maintenance, and enable more efficient controls and responses. Centralized administration calls for properly trained personnel exclusively dedicated to these tasks.

☐ *Data correlation*: The correlation of the data collected by sensors is a key task, the effectiveness of which affects the overall quality of the entire intrusion detection effort. Some commercial tools facilitate the various data correlation chores, but these chores still remain largely dependent on human analysis and expertise.

☐ *Incident response*: Incident response encompasses the set of procedures that must be followed in the event of an intrusion. It calls for an organizational process that has been planned carefully and documented in advance and is always ready to be activated. The efficiency of the incident response process greatly affects the duration of any induced downtime, the turn-around for the restoration of data and resources, and the outcomes of the ensuing forensic investigations.

Frinke (2000) has addressed extensively and formally the issue of detection of distributed attacks across cooperating enterprises, which represents a further level of management involving cooperation among different organizations.

## Physical Deployment

NIDS sensors should be configured with two network interface cards (NICs), one for system administration and one for passive traffic sniffing. The NIC used for system administration is configured with an ordinary TCP/IP address. It is used to send attack notifications, SNMP information, and system resets to the NIDS. The NIC that is configured for monitoring traffic usually does not have an IP address assigned to it so that it cannot be contacted or otherwise operate on the network. This NIC is set to promiscuous mode and uses a special driver that does not reveal any protocol addresses. It can only be used for passive traffic monitoring and profiling. Figure 1 shows the schema for this standard dual-NIC NIDS configuration.

The decision where to position NIDSs on a corporate network should be guided by the objectives of the organization (i.e., which connections should be monitored) and the costs and administration efforts involved. Figure 2 shows an example of a corporate network that includes several possible NIDS sensor positions.

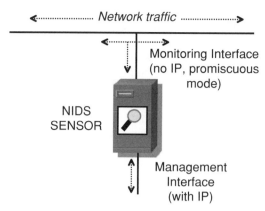

**Figure 1:** Recommended configuration of a NIDS sensor.

The NIDS sensors in Figure 2 have been numbered from 1 to 5, as follows:

*Sensor 1.* This position, outside the border router and facing the Internet, enables it to monitor all Internet network traffic unfiltered. In particular, incoming traffic is seen entirely, and all attempted attacks can be analyzed. The processing load for this capturing device is the highest, and it also has the highest rate of false-positive alarms.

*Sensor 2.* Here the NIDS sensor is positioned between the border router and the first-level firewall. This sensor sees traffic that is similar to Sensor 1, except that the router possibly will have been configured to filter out some of the incoming traffic with ingress and egress policies intended to drop some simple types of undesirable traffic. Compared to the position of Sensor 1, this position is useful in reducing the procession burden on the NIDS and incidentally the number of false alarms.

*Sensor 3.* This position in the DMZ is useful in several different ways. It can be used to check firewall rules by tracking which packets pass through the perimeter defenses. It can also be used to control traffic flowing internally (internal attackers are always an important source of security risks) and to perform specific

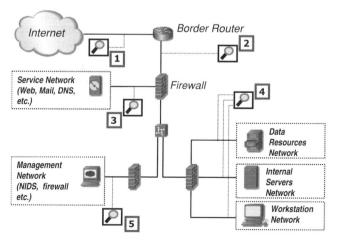

**Figure 2:** Example of NIDS sensor deployment.

monitoring activities related to connections used by particular devices, protocols, or network services. The NIDS rule set for a sensor in this network position is normally tuned to these particular services so as to reduce the NIDS processing load, lower the number of false positives, and thereby improve the overall effectiveness of the NIDS.

*Sensor 4.* This position enables it to collect data from multiple subnets simultaneously. Here again the rule set can be tuned to serve specific devices, protocols, and services more precisely. Centralized *syslog* servers could be used as well.

*Sensor 5.* In this last case, the NIDS is physically independent from the rest of the network to enable it to protect some of the network's most critical resources. Monitoring consoles used with this NIDS sensor may include ones for the administration of NIDSs and firewalls and for any other mission-critical network appliances and servers. This sensor position is particularly helpful when data collected from multiple NIDS sensors, as well as from firewalls and other systems, must be accessible from a centralized analysis console for system-wide inspection and correlation purposes.

## ECONOMICS OF NIDSs
### General Measurements

In large companies, the deployment and management of a security infrastructure present many difficulties, not just technical and organizational ones. Cost is certainly a critical factor. The expenses associated with NIDS-based security schemes must be evaluated from the standpoint of cost effectiveness just as with any other technological investment. Before purchasing or implementing NIDS-based security solutions, administrators must understand how NIDS-based solutions would help mitigate business risks. To do so effectively, security experts need to know what the company's risk profile is. This profile can be created by inventorying the assets, threats, and vulnerabilities that exist in the environment in which the company operates and estimating the adverse impact that a loss could have on its daily functioning and survivability. Once the risk profile has been determined, the impact of any of these risks on operations must be calculated.

Fortunately, general business measurements that have been adopted for IT investments can be applied to determine the value of security in quantifiable terms and assess their business impact. These include the following: business risk, return on investment (ROI), and total cost of ownership (TCO). Return on security investment (ROSI) is an example of a specific metric that has been introduced for security technology, although it is not conceptually different from ROI. Business risk is a financial calculation in which a monetary value is assigned to the loss or disruption of a business process. Soft costs, such as damage to the company's reputation after a security incident, must also be considered. ROI is a financial calculation that estimates the result of an investment over a given period of time. This ROI calculation requires that security problems and corresponding countermeasures be quantified.

Unfortunately, not all security problems can be quantified easily. Events with a low probability of occurrence but a catastrophic impact can contribute a great measure of risk uncertainty and so make ROI calculations unreliable.

This is the traditional decision problem of disaster recovery: how to quantify a reasonable expenditure for an event that might not happen at all, but can have catastrophic consequences if it does. When applied to intrusion detection, the degree of uncertainty is even greater. The victims of intrusions could suffer catastrophic consequences, severe ones, or just mildly negative effects. Catastrophic events are less probable, and most organizations never experience them. Mild ones are more probable and sometimes are almost a daily experience, but what is the definition and likelihood of a severe event?

One approach to improve on the reliability of ROI is to use more inclusive measures of cost. Total cost of ownership (TCO) is one such approach, taking into account that every purchase has costs that extend beyond the initial price tag, such as licensing and maintenance fees, training, new hardware or software, consulting, new internal resources, and organizational changes. Kinn and Timm (2002a; 2002b) have written a good description of the ROI analysis as applied to intrusion detection systems. Conry-Murray (2003) has published a paper about how to justify-security spending before management.

### Evaluating Investments

After years of fear, uncertainty, and doubt (FUD) tactics to convince companies to invest in security, increasingly the economic impact argument has been gaining momentum in the marketing press and in publications targeted at CIOs and CEOs. A surprising number of products and marketing-oriented analyses are claiming that whatever security expenses are incurred are justified on the basis of roughly estimated measurements and conjectural ROSI calculations. Sometimes, they make overly simplistic economic statements, such as claiming that the cost-benefit ratio of a security investment can be calculated by subtracting the security investment from the damage prevented; if this results in a positive number, then there is a positive ROSI—marginal costs and marginal benefits are to be considered, not absolute values, and the optimal investment occurs when the difference between benefits and costs is maximized, which means that at that point the marginal benefit is equal to the marginal cost of the investment. The reality is that any such simplistic calculations are unreliable.

A better approach is to consider that the greatest impact of a security investment that must be included in the calculation of a ROI is the change in organizational processes. The key is to recognize that significant positive effects brought about by the optimization of organizational processes following the adoption of new security technologies (e.g., better coding practices, better software engineering, better monitoring, etc.) could influence the ROI results dramatically.

Expansive and unsubstantiated ROI claims must be avoided. The analyses produced in the past in classic works about the advent of computers and their early impact on office and production environments—for example, such studies as *Beyond the Productivity Paradox* and *Beyond Computation*, by Brynjolfsson and Hitt (1998, 2000) still have important lessons to teach that are important to the understanding of the economics of investments in security technologies.

More recently, both economists and computer scientists have published interesting studies on the economics of security technology and of intrusion detection in particular. Wei, Frinke, Carter, and Ritter (2001), for instance, have written an essay on cost-benefit analysis for NIDSs. Gordon and Loeb (2002) have published "The Economics of Information Security Investment," a noteworthy study about this topic. Their analysis shows that security breach probability functions belong to different broad classes and that the optimal amount of spending follows different rules tied to the particular probability class of the risk. In particular, for one class of security breach probability functions that Gordon and Loeb (2002) analyzed, the optimal amount to spend on information security is a function of the level of vulnerability of such information. In contrast, for a second broad class of probability functions, the optimal amount to spend increases initially, but ultimately decreases with the level of vulnerability of such information. According to Gordon and Loeb (2002) then, there is strong evidence that managers responsible for allocating an information security budget should focus on information that falls into the midrange of their estimated vulnerability to security breaches. In this view, managers should carefully consider that some information sets might be so expensive to protect that only a moderate level of technology-based security investments is justified. Instead, Gordon and Loeb (2002) suggest that organizational countermeasures, instead of technical, would be more appropriate and should be at the ready in the event of a security incident.

Experienced information security managers argue that actual expected losses are typically an order of magnitude smaller than potential losses. Unfortunately, all too often the marketing press and security consultants play shamelessly on FUD (fear, uncertainty, and doubt). These unscrupulous elements stress the possibility of extravagant potential losses from security breaches so as to justify the exorbitant cost of their security products and services. Their security solutions would not otherwise survive a rational economic evaluation. Gordon and Loeb (2002) provide some interesting figures for two broad classes of security breach probability functions. They claim that the optimal amount to spend on information security never exceeds 37% of the expected loss resulting from a security breach and is typically much less than 37%. Their main conclusion, albeit still incomplete and in need of further investigation, is that the optimal amount to spend on information security should typically be only a small fraction of the expected loss from a security breach.

Some authors have argued that the optimal security expenditure must maximize the perceived, but not necessarily the actual, level of security of the individuals within an organization. For example, Anderson (2001) states that the perception of information *in*-security is due to what he describes as "perverse incentives," and thus many of the key issues related to the justification of security costs could be explained more clearly by considering microeconomic issues related to network externalities, asymmetric information distributions, moral conundrums, adverse selection, and liability dumping.

# LIMITATIONS OF NIDSs AND INNOVATIVE RESEARCH EFFORTS

Current NIDS technologies and functionalities have clear limitations that in earlier parts of this chapter were described together with the benefits and features of each solution. To summarize, NIDSs produce large amounts of data that need to be analyzed, aggregated, and correlated with audit data produced by others network components, such as routers and firewalls, to obtain the whole picture. They are prone to a significant ratio of false-positive alarms. Thus, NIDSs need to be operated by expert analysts. In addition, their effectiveness depends partially on the specific design of the network infrastructure. Automatic response mechanisms can be circumvented and exploited against the NIDS owner to provoke denial of service conditions. Many techniques exist that are able to evade detection.

In short, NIDSs are able to catch *many* but not *all* intrusions, are able to properly avoid alarms for *almost all* but not *all* legal connections, and in general are not able to block intrusions. These characteristics, for the most part, are not defects of current NIDSs; instead, they are intrinsic to the nature of detecting intrusions over a network.

Therefore, these systems must in no way be considered in isolation. NIDSs are a precious layer of security protection within a defense-in-depth strategy, but their shortcomings will have to be mitigated by further security layers and technologies.

Moreover, new technologies for building systems and for communicating are being developed, bringing new functionalities and services, as well as new security risks. Intrusion detection systems must evolve too to keep pace with the changing environment and with new or mutated threats. In the following section, some examples of new challenges to NIDS technology are discussed.

## Intrusion Detection for Web-Based Applications

Studies on NIDS technologies are addressing the new challenges that Web-based interactive architectures pose to security. Protocol analysis, for instance, is a first improvement in this direction because it extends the scope and expressiveness of traditional signature-based NIDSs. Of interest in this context is the recent proposal by Sommer and Paxson (2003), which introduces the concept of *contextual signatures*. These extend the mechanisms of NIDS protocol analysis by providing matching functions within a semantically characterized operational context. The need for semantic awareness is already manifest in the firewall area, where alongside traditional firewalling technologies and products, new tools now address security problems at the application level. These

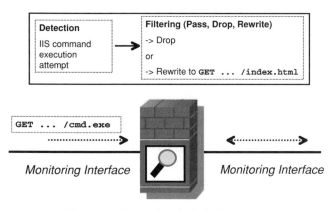

**Figure 3:** Example of a hybrid system.

firewalls are variously called Application Firewall, XML Gateways, SOAP Proxies, and Layer 7 Switches. These advances in firewall technology are relevant to NIDSs for at least two reasons. First, it is possible that some of the techniques and methods developed for semantics-aware firewalls could be adopted or could inspire innovations for semantics-aware intrusion detection systems, given the several commonalties between the two classes of systems. Second, there are currently attempts to develop hybrid systems that integrate intrusion detection features within firewalls, as discussed next.

## Hybrid Systems

Some innovative NIDS systems integrate intrusion detection features with filtering capabilities; for example, new appliances from Internet Security Systems (www.iss.net), Netscreen (www.netscreen.com), Radware (www.radware.com), and Entercept (www.entercept.com), to mention just a few well-known vendors. This integration enables intrusion detection to be proactive instead of merely reactive. Often the approach followed by these novel hybrid systems is to collocate, on the same hardware, intrusion detection features; that is, signature matching with firewalling features (i.e. policy-based packet filtering). Figure 3 shows a simplified and very general example of a hybrid system that combines a detection step (e.g., an illegal attempt to run `cmd.exe`) and a filtering step (e.g., the message could be accepted, rejected, or rewritten).

The ability to rewrite a message flagged as illegal and to turn it into an innocuous one is an unusual feature that traditionally firewalls do not offer. However, it is present in a tool called Hogwash (2004). Hogwash is based on Snort and represents an interesting example of a hybrid system. The rewriting feature is also a key element of anticipated Web service nodes soon to be found acting as intermediaries between a Web service requester and a Web service endpoint provider. Intermediaries are supposed to rewrite part of the SOAP payload (Mitra, 2002) for reasons related to routing, quality of service, or message-level security (OASIS, 2004). It seems not unreasonable to presume that intrusion detection and even firewalling at the XML/SOAP application level might benefit from an integrated approach, although scenarios like this one are still hypothetical and unexplored. A good introduction to hybrid systems can be found in Desai (2003).

## Combining Anomaly-Based and Signature-Based Intrusion Detection

The call for more semantic awareness in intrusion detection so as to enable NIDSs to neutralize Web-based attacks, like *SQL injection* for example (Spett, 2002), has encouraged several new research initiatives that combine anomaly-based and signature-based detection techniques. The underlying bottleneck is that Web-based misuse is much more difficult to characterize than traditional forms of network misuse. There is the added difficulty that Web-based attacks could be embedded in protocols such as SOAP, which are encapsulated inside the HTTP payload, which may themselves include application-dependent customizations. In such cases, Web-based intrusions that exploit application-based deficiencies can be very difficult to trap with tell tale signatures-archived in a NIDS rule base. Instead, these intrusions can only be defeated by a precise understanding of application semantics and of application implementation details. Alternatively, anomaly detection methods may prove to be helpful because they rely on defining legal actions and flagging as suspicious everything else. Anomaly-detection approaches could reduce considerably the complexity of intrusion detection for certain classes of vulnerabilities. A number of interesting works have appeared recently; see, for example Kruegel and Vigna (2003) and Kruegel, Toth, and Kirda (2002).

## NIDSs in Wireless Networks

Another area that is the subject of interesting research is mobile computing in wireless networks. Wireless local area networks (WLANs) have exhibited many different security flaws in past years, ranging from misconfiguration of wireless access points (WAPs) to unreliable cryptographic algorithms. Although some of these threats are probably due to the immaturity of the technology–for instance, the flawed wired equivalent privacy (WEP) algorithm–and others are common to the wired context, such as denial of service or session hijacking attacks, the wireless scenario presents new security issues that are of interest for intrusion detection.

Mobile ad hoc networks are particularly vulnerable because of their openess, variable topology, and lack of centralized management. To achieve an acceptable degree of security, Zhang, Lee, and Huang (2003), among others, argue that intrusion detection functionalities will become more useful and integrated more widely in mobile computing contexts.

However, although NIDSs may be even more valuable in mobile computing than in wired networks, the difference between the two types of networks makes it very difficult to apply current intrusion detection techniques to the wireless scenario. The most important difference is that today's NIDSs rely on real-time traffic analyses upon a fixed infrastructure and so cannot function well in the mobile computing environment. In wired networks, traffic is usually monitored at network edges–collecting data through network devices, such as switches, routers, and gateways–that are not present in the mobile ad hoc scenario. Therefore, audit data in an ad hoc mobile network can be collected only within the radio range or from individual hosts and not from nodes that concentrate the network traffic.

Another big difference between the two types of network is that the operational mode in the ad hoc mobile environment is subject to greater variability than in the wired one. For example, an anomalous behavior, such as false routing information, might be caused either by a temporary out-of-sync host or by a compromised host in an ad hoc mobile network. This increased complexity is likely to affect dramatically the quality of intrusion detection based on current technology.

The solution proposed by Zhang, Lee, and Huang (2003) is based on the integration of intrusion detection fuctionalities into all nodes of an ad hoc network. Effective cooperation and coordination among nodes acting as NIDSs become key to the success of such a distributed intrusion detection system.

## CONCLUSION

In conclusion, intrusion detection must not be separated from human expertise and management, whether when performing the task of detecting authentic intrusions or deploying intrusion detection systems within security architectures. In general, there is certainly a need for better management of distributed NIDSs, including reporting, production of statistics, correlation among observed events, and worldwide coordination. New threats require more sophisticated solutions, and so the automation of certain features could be extremely helpful. Yet, projects or products aimed at making intrusion detection a transparent task needing few human interventions have generally failed poorly. It appears very unlikely that this will change. The human analyst is a necessary component of an NIDS and a cost that cannot be eliminated. In the absence of a human analyst, intrusion detection and acceptable levels of security are simply not achievable.

There were recent comments in the literature claiming that intrusion detection systems are an ineffective technology (Vijayan, 2003). This harsh verdict was based on well-known drawbacks of many intrusion detection systems, such as significant management requirements, the need for full-time monitoring, the huge amount of false positives, and the necessity of data correlation. None of the arguments presented by Vijayan (2003) is new, and as a matter of fact the polemic represents perfectly the difficulties and exemplifies the need to manage intrusion detection at all levels: technical, economic, organizational, and process management. Thus, although technological advances are certainly needed and perhaps current NIDS tools will evolve and eventually combine with other security technologies, the current negative tendency to believe that, given the right tool, intrusion detection can become an automated commodity should be dismissed.

## GLOSSARY

**Brute force attack**   An attack is performed in a brute force style when all possible successful solutions are tried sequentially.

**Detection**   The act of identifying signs of intrusions.

**False negative**   The act of not detecting an intrusion when the observed event is illegal.

**False positive**   The act of erroneously detecting an intrusion caused by a legitimate observed event.

**Firewall**   A system or a collection of systems that enforce a security policy by filtering network packets. Usually, a firewall implements a perimeter security policy because it is physically disjoint from application systems and acts as an intermediary between service requesters and service providers belonging to the protected network.

**Grep**   The Unix command `grep` searches a given input file for lines containing a match to a given string pattern.

**Intrusion**   The term "intrusion" is used in a broad sense, because it is meant to identify each abnormal, illegal, or unauthorized network event. It is not limited to those actions that permit an intruder to get control of some machines; instead it encompasses all malicious network events. The term "attack" is used as a synonym for intrusion in this chapter.

**IP spoofing**   The act of forging a network packet with an IP address stored into the IP header that does not correspond to the actual IP address of the sender. The packet then looks like it was delivered by someone (i.e., the owner of the IP address illegally forced into the IP header) different from the real originator.

**Monitoring console**   An administration tool that lets security administrators observe and analyze detection results. It represents one of the most important features of a NIDS, given the difficulty of correlating and analyzing data.

**Network response**   Networked services react to incoming connections or requesting messages by generating responses. Responses are of different types: service providers can create corresponding application responses to application requests or faults when the request is incorrect or not understandable. Even no response is a way of responding to a certain stimulus. Intermediaries (e.g., routers, firewalls) generate other types of responses

**Network stimulus**   Network packets that attempt to communicate with a destination (e.g., attempt to establish a connection to a service provider) in order to perform some subsequent network activity or simply trigger a response.

**NIC**   Network interface card.

**Policy-based packet filter**   Systems that filter network traffic (i.e., accept or deny, usually) by matching packet attributes against a security policy. A security policy is a collection of rules, in which each rule defines a type of network traffic that must be allowed or dropped.

**Raw data**   Data logged by sensors or by systems in their native format, not processed or normalized.

**RFC**   The foundation documentation for Internet technologies.

**Scan**   A network activity aimed at acquiring information about a target, such as listening services, network accessibility, platform characteristics, and so forth. It is often realized by sending out-of-specs packets that might slip under filtering mechanisms.

**SOAP**   Simple object access protocol. It is a standard application protocol for sending XML-based structured messages. The W3C publishes SOAP specifications; the current version is 1.2.

**SYN, FIN, and RESET**   Standard TCP flags contained in each TCP header (together with ACK, URG, and PUSH).

**True negative**   The act of properly not detecting an intrusion when the observed event is legitimate.

**True positive**   The act of properly detecting an actual intrusion.

# CROSS REFERENCES

See *Computer Viruses and Worms; Host-Based Intrusion Detection Systems; Intrusion Detection Systems Basics; Security Policy Guidelines; The Use of Agent Technology for Intrusion Detection.*

# REFERENCES

Anderson, D., Frivold, T., & Valdes, A. (1995). *Next-generation intrusion detection expert system (NIDES): A summary (Tech. Rep. SRI-CSL-95-07)*. Menlo Park, CA: SRI International.

Anderson, J. P. (1980). *Computer security threat monitoring and surveillance (Tech. Rep. Contract 79F26400)*. Fort Washington: James. P. Anderson Co.

Anderson, R. (2001). Why information security is hard–An economic perspective. *Proceedings of 17th Annual Computer Security Applications Conference*. New Orleans, LA.

Axelsson, S. (2000). The base-rate fallacy and the difficulty of intrusion detection. *ACM Transactions on Information and System Security, 3*(3), 186–205.

Bace, R., & Mell, P. (2001). *Intrusion detection systems* (NIST Special Publication 800-31, National Institute of Standards and Technology). Retrieved May 26, 2004, from http://csrc.nist.gov/publications/nistpubs/800-31/sp800-31.pdf

Brynjolfsson, E., & Hitt, L. M. (1998). Beyond the productivity paradox. *Communications of the ACM. 41*(8), 49–55.

Brynjolfsson, E., & Hitt, L.M. (2000). Beyond computation: Information technology, organizational transformation and business performance. *Journal of Economic Perspectives, 14*(4), 23–48.

Caswell, B., Beale, J., Foster, J.C. & Posluns, J. (2003). *Snort 2.0 intrusion detection*. New York: Syngress Publishing.

Coit, C. J., Staniford, S., & McAlerney, J. (2003). Towards faster string matching for intrusion detection. *Proceedings of the DARPA Information Survivability Conference and Exposition (DISCEX II'01)*. Los Alamitos, CA: IEEE Computer Society.

Common vulnerabilities and exposures (CVE). (2003). *The standard for Internet security vulnerability names*. Retrieved May 26, 2004, from http://cve.mitre.org/

Conry-Murray, A. (2003). Strategies and issues: Justifying security spending. *Network Magazine*. Retrieved May 26, 2004, from http://www.networkmagazine.com/article/NMG20030305S0012

Cooper, M., Northcutt, S., Fearnow, M., & Frederick, K. (2001). *Intrusion signatures and analysis*. Indianapolis: New Riders Publishing.

Denning, D.E. (1987). An intrusion-detection model. *IEEE Transactions on Software Engineering, SE-13*(2), 222–232.

Desai, N. (2003). Intrusion prevention systems: The next step in the evolution of IDS. *Infocus, SecurityFocus*. Retrieved May 26, 2004, from http://www.securityfocus.com/infocus/1670

Fox, K. L., Henning, R. R., Reed, J. H., & Simonian, R. P. (1990). A neural network approach towards intrusion detection. *Proceedings of the 13th National Computer Security Conference*. Baltimore: NIST.

Frederick, K. K. (2002). Network intrusion detection signatures (Part Five). *Infocus, SecurityFocus*. Retrieved May 26, 2004, from http://www.securityfocus.com/infocus/1569

Frinke, D. (2000). Balancing cooperation and risk in intrusion detection. *ACM Transactions on Information and System Security, 3*(1), 1–29.

GIAC (Global Information Assurance Certification). (2004). *GIAC certified professionals*. Retrieved May 26, 2004, from http://www.giac.org/GCIA.php

Gordon, L.A., & Loeb, M.P. (2002). The economics of information security investment. *ACM Transactions on Information and System Security, 5*(4), 438–457.

Handley, M., Kreibich, C., & Paxson, V. (2001). Network intrusion detection: Evasion, traffic normalization, and end-to-end protocol semantics. *Proceedings of the USENIX Security Symposium 2001*, 115–131.

Hofmeyr, S.A., Somayaji, A., & Forrest, S. (1998). Intrusion detection using sequences of system calls. *Journal of Computer Security. 6*, 151–180.

Hogwash. (2004). Retrieved May 26, 2004, from http://sourceforge.net/projects/hogwash/

Ilgun, K., Kemmerer, R. A., & Porras, P. A. (1995). State transition analysis: A rule-based intrusion detection approach. *IEEE Transactions on Software Engineering. 21*(3), 181–199.

Kinn, D., & Timm, K. (2002a). Justifying the expense of IDS. Part One: An overview of ROIs for IDS. *Infocus. SecurityFocus*. Retrieved May 26, 2004, from http://www.securityfocus.com/infocus/1608

Kinn, D., & Timm, K. (2002b). Justifying the expense of IDS. Part Two: Calculating ROI for IDS. *Infocus. SecurityFocus*. Retrieved May 26, 2004, from http://www.securityfocus.com/infocus/1621

Kruegel, C., & Vigna, G. (2003). Anomaly detection of web-based attacks. *Proceedings of the ACM Conference on Computer Security*, 251–261.

Kruegel, C., Toth, T., & Kirda, E. (2002). Service specific anomaly detection for network intrusion detection. *Proceedings of the ACM Symposium on Applied Computing*.

Larsen, J., & Haile, J. (2002). Understanding IDS active response mechanisms. *Infocus, SecurityFocus*. Retrieved May 26, 2004, from http://www.securityfocus.com/infocus/1540

Lee, W., & Stolfo, S., (2000). A framework for constructing features and models for intrusion detection systems. *ACM Transactions on Information and System Security, 3*(4), 1–33.

Lee, W., Nimbalkar, R. A., Yee, K. K., Patil, S. B., Desai, P. H., et al. (2000). A data mining and CIDF based approach for detecting novel and distributed intrusions. *I Proceedings of RAID 2000*.

Libwhisker (2003). Retrieved May 26, 2004, from http://www.wiretrip.net/rfp/lw.asp

Lunt, T., Tamaru, A., Gilham, F., Jagannathan, R., Neumann, P., Javits, H., et al. (1992). *A real-time intrusion detection expert system (IDES) - Final technical report* (Tech. Rep.). Menlo Park, CA: SRI International

Mell, P., Hu, V., Lippmann, R., Haines, J., & Zissman, M. (2002). *An overview of issues in testing intrusion detection* (NIST IR 7007, National Institute of Standards and Technology). Retrieved May 26, 2004, from http://csrc.nist.gov/publications/nistir/nistir-7007.pdf

Mitra, N. (2002). SOAP Version 1.2 Part 0: Primer. World Wide Web Consortium (W3C). Retrieved May 26, 2004, from http://www.w3.org/TR/soap12-part0/

Neohapsis Open Security Evaluation Criteria. (2003), *NIDS OSEC v1.0*. Retrieved May 26, 2004, from http://osec.neohapsis.com/criteria/

Nessus (2003). *Nessus open source vulnerability scanner project*. Retrieved May 26, 2004, from http://www.nessus.org

Nikto (2004). Retrieved May 26, 2004, from http://www.cirt.net/code/nikto.shtml

OASIS (2004). *Web services security: SOAP message security (WS-Security 2004). OASIS Standard 200401*. Retrieved May 25, 2004, from http://docs.oasis-open.org/wss/2004/01/oasis-200401-wss-soap-message-security-1.0.pdf

Phrack (2003). Polymorphic shellcode engine using spectrum analysis. *Phrack Magazine, 61*. Retrieved May 26, 2004, from http://www.phrack.org/show.php?p=61&a=9

Porras, P. & Neumann, P. (1997). EMERALD: Event monitoring enabling responses to anomalous live disturbances. *Proceedings of the National Conference on Computer Security Systems*, 719–729.

Ptacek, T. H., & Newsham, T. N. (1998). Insertion, evasion, and denial of service: Eluding network intrusion detection (Tech. Rep.). *Secure Networks Inc*. Retrieved May 26, 2004, from http://secinf.net/info/ids/idspaper/idspaper.html

Ranum, M. (2001). Experiences benchmarking intrusion detection systems. *NFR Security Technical Publications*. Retrieved May 26, 2004, from http://www.snort.org/docs/Benchmarking-IDS-NFR.pdf

Ranum, M. (2002). Signature vs. protocol analysis. *Focus-IDS Archive, SecurityFocus*. Retrieved May 26, 2004, from http://www.securityfocus.com/archive/96/260234/2002-03-03/2002-03-09/2/

Roesch, M. & Green, C. (2004). *Snort user manual – Snort release: 2.3.3*. Retrieved May 26, 2004, from http://www.snort.org/docs/snort_manual/

Snort (2003). *Snort–The open source network intrusion detection system*. Retrieved May 26, 2004, from http://www. snort.org/

Sommer, R., & Paxson, V. (2003). Enhancing byte-level network intrusion detection signatures with context. *Proceedings of the ACM Conference on Computer Security*, 262–271.

Spett, K. (2002). SQL injection: Are your web application vulnerable? SPI Dynamics Inc., Atlanta, GA. Retrieved May 26, 2004, from http://www.spidynamics.com/papers/SQLInjectionWhitePaper.pdf

Vigna, G., & Kemmerer, R. A. (1999). NetSTAT: A network-based intrusion detection system. *Journal of Computer Security, 7*(1), 37–71.

Vijayan, J. (2003). IDS criticisms kindle debate. *Computerworld*. Retrieved May 26, 2004, from http://www.computerworld.com/securitytopics/security/story/0,10801,82391,00.html

Wack, J., Tracy, M., & Souppaya, M. (2003). *Guideline on network security testing* (NIST Special Publication 800-42, National Institute of Standards and Technology). Retrieved May 26, 2004, from http://csrc.nist.gov/publications/nistpubs/800-42/NIST-SP800-42.zip

Wei, H., Frinke, D., Carter, O., & Ritter, C. (2001). Cost-benefit analysis for network intrusion detection systems. *Proceedings of the CSI 28th Annual Computer Security Conference*.

Zhang, Y., Lee, W., & Huang, Y. (2003). Intrusion detection techniques for mobile wireless networks. *ACM/Kluwer Wireless Networks Journal, 9*(5), 545–556.

## FURTHER READING

Northcutt, S., & Novak, J. (2003). *Network intrusion detection* (3rd. ed.). Indianapolis: New Riders Publishing.

# The Use of Agent Technology for Intrusion Detection

Dipankar Dasgupta, *University of Memphis*

## INTRODUCTION

With the growing use of Internet applications and automated scripts, it has become very difficult to keep track of all cyber activities. In particular, it is hard to track each and every application, such as Jscript, VBScript, ActiveX, Outlook, Outlook Express, etc. However, it is possible to monitor their effects on the system and its resources. Moreover, it is necessary to analyze monitored network data efficiently for faster attack detection and response.

Intrusion/anomaly detection is an important part of cyber security. This is the process of identifying computer or network activity that is malicious or unauthorized. Most of the intrusion detection systems (IDSs) have a similar structure and component set. Each IDS consists of some sensors or agents that monitor one or more data source, apply some type of detection algorithm, and then send alerts or take responses when an attack or anomaly is detected. There are many commercially available IDSs; a detailed survey and taxonomy of practical IDSs may be found elsewhere (Allen et al., 2000; Debar, Dacier, & Wepsi, 1999). Some IDSs are anomaly based and some are signature based, whereas others combine both approaches. Security researchers have formed working groups to develop a common framework, methodology and description language for IDSs (Curry, 2000;Porras, Schnackenberg, Staniford-Chen, Stillman, & Wu, 1998). Recent works on building next-generation IDSs highlight new areas of research, which include artificial intelligence (Dasgupta & Gonzalez, 2002; Gomez & Dasgupta, 2002; Warrender, Forrest, & Pearlmutter, 1999), data mining (Lee, Stolfo, & Mok, 2000), statistical techniques, agent

frameworks (Asaka, Taguchi, & Goto, 1999a,b; Helmer, Wong, Honavar, & Miller, 2003), etc. There are many approaches used in agent technologies, such as autonomous agents (Barrus & Rose, 1998; Brian & Dasgutpa, 2001; Spafford & Zamboni, 2000), intelligent agents (Carver, Hill, Surdu, & Pooch, 2000), and mobile agents (Asaka, Okazawa, Taguchi, & Goto, 1999a,b; Bernardes & dos Santos, 2000; Dasgupta, 1999; Jansen, Mell, Karygiannis, & Marks, 1999; Jayazeri & Lugmayr, 2000: Krugel & Toth, 2001; Queiroz, Costa Carmo, & Pirmez, 1999) for distributed detection.

For example, an intrusion detection system using autonomous agents with a hierarchical architecture (called AAFID) has been proposed (Spafford & Zamboni, 2000). At its lowest level are agents, which perform data collection and analysis tasks; transceivers and monitors are the major components of this IDS. Each host has an agent that senses the activity and reports any abnormality to the transceivers. Transceivers are used to control these agents, and they report the results to the monitors. These monitors then perform high-level correlations among several hosts and thus across the entire network. An extension to AAFID uses intelligent agents that are capable of detecting attacks in a timely manner. These software agents can be treated as mobile agents if they are able to migrate from one computer to another computer. Even if the host machine, which launched the agents, is removed from the network, the agents can still work (Gopalakrishna & Spafford, 2001). Mobile agents are very efficient in performing remote execution even in the absence of the machine that initiated them. After completion of their assigned tasks, the mobile agents report the results or else they simply terminate (Karygiannis, 1998).

Brian and Dasgupta (2001) have applied mobile agents for network traffic analysis using mobile agent architecture, called SANTA. Here, the application of agents can be seen at several levels down the hierarchy, where each agent performs individual tasks. Some of the mobile agents collect the data from the network to analyze the traffic pattern. Others use ART-2 neural networks as the decision-support module to make appropriate decisions. This IDS uses on-line learning and subsequent detection of different kinds of attacks.

## Categories of Intrusive Attacks, Identification, and Detection

IDSs not only monitor and detect security breaches but also analyze a wide variety of malicious activities (Axelsson, 2000; Mell, Marks, & McLarson, 2000). Cyber attacks can be categorized in several ways:

- Passive attack: An attack that is aimed at gaining access to the critical system resources by using a personal tool or a publicly available tool for performing automated searches and indirectly breaking into the system
- Active attack: An attack that results in an unauthorized state change of a computing system or subsystems, such as vulnerability exposure, fabrication, denial of service, and erroneous outputs
- Internal misuse: An attack that occurs when someone inside an organization exceeds his or her privileges in accessing and/or using computing resources (e.g., when low-end customers exceed their privileges)
- External misuse: An attack that usually comes from an outside or unknown and unreliable source that might have a wide variety of intents

Two articles by Kazienko and Dorosz (2003, 2004) state that the following types of attacks can be identified by IDSs:

- Those related to unauthorized access to resources:
  - Password cracking and access violation
  - Trojan horses
  - Interceptions, modification, and fabrication
  - Network packet listening
  - Stealing confidential information
  - Unauthorized network connections
  - Illegal usage of IT resources for private purposes
  - Unauthorized access to system resources by taking advantage of the system's weakness
  - Unauthorized alteration of resources (after gaining unauthorized access)
  - Maliciously using the identity of others, for example, to obtain system administrator rights
  - Information modification, deletion, and addition
  - Modification of the system configurations
- Denial of service (DoS; Mardini, 2002; Mell, Marks, & McLarson, 2000) attack, which is unlike a virus, which bears a distinctive signature, but rather is a method that attackers use to prevent or deny legitimate users access to a computer.
- Flooding the system by sending huge amounts of useless information to block legitimate traffic and deny services.

- Ping flood—sending a large number of Internet control message packets (ICMP) packets to a broadcast address.
- Flood with mails—sending hundreds of thousands of messages in a short period of time; also post office protocol (POP) and simple mail transfer protocol (SMTP) relaying.
- SYN flood—sending many TCP requests and not handling handshakes as required by the protocol.
- Distributed denial of service (DDoS)—attacks coming from multiple sources in the network.

IDSs use the following detection methodologies:

- The most novel intrusion detection activities are discussed in CISCO Systems (http://www.cisco.com/en/US/products/sw/secursw/ps2113/products_white_paper09186a0080092334.shtml; Kazienko & Dorosz, 2004). The detection methodologies include simple pattern matching, stateful pattern matching, protocol decode-based signatures, heuristic-based signatures, and anomaly-based and application-behavior-based detections.
  - The most comprehensive detection mechanisms are discussed in Juniper Networks (http://www.juniper.net/products/intrusion/detection.htm); namely stateful signatures, protocol anomaly, backdoor detection, traffic anomaly, and network honeypots.

## Agent Technology

A software agent can be a program or a process that performs the tasks of a user. These agents can be autonomous and can operate without external control. Agents can also be classified into static agents and mobile agents. Static agents, as the name implies, remain in the host machine and cooperate with other such agents to perform specific tasks. Mobile agents have the capability to move from one host to the other in the network. They mostly address the security issues in the network.

The differences between these two types of agents can be explained using an example of how an e-mail agent works. A client using post office protocol (POP) and communicating with the server using simple mail transfer protocol (SMTP) can be considered as an example of a static agent. A POP client collects mail from the SMTP server at regular intervals, and the SMTP server stores the incoming mail at particular places for each client. Therefore, this type of communication involves agents that are static; the network is just used for data transfer. However, the same kind of transaction can be implemented using mobile agents. In this case, one mobile agent collects the new mail messages and goes around the network handing over the corresponding message at each node to the respective agents.

There are a number of compelling reasons to use software agents on the Internet. The following arguments justify the use of agent technology:

- Agents are consistent with the object-oriented paradigm and efficient agent software.
- The idea of intelligent entities communicating and coordinating with each other over wide area networks is a common concept in the Internet community.

- Multiagent systems can be designed to be self-configuring and decentralized.
- Agents can be added and subtracted from the system while it is running without requiring external intervention.
- A system with autonomously functioning components will not collapse when one or more of the components fail or malfunction.
- Multiagent architectures are inherently scaleable, modular, and fault tolerant.

# NETWORK INTRUSION DETECTION

A *network intrusion detection system* (NIDS) is a tool that acts as a network sensor or spy, listening to all the traffic on a given segment (Kazienko & Dorosz, 2004; Mardini, 2002). The packets are analyzed and compared to known attack signatures. The identified attacks are logged, and countermeasures can be taken ranging from paging the administrator to ending the connection or hardening a firewall.

## Tracking Network Traffic

In today's networks, bandwidth and traffic are increasing daily. Until recently, commercially available network-based IDS products simply could not keep pace with the increasing speed of networks. Checking the contents of each packet, performing pattern matching, and seeing if it matched any of the known signatures and rules in the database took a lot of time and consumed valuable resources. Today, local area networks (LANs) are clocking a speed of over 100 Mbps (Mardini, 2002), and network speeds keep growing faster than the technology for high-speed packet signature analysis. The network IDSs are unable to examine more than 20 Mbps of traffic, so there has recently been a risk of losing data or being unable to verify the various types of attacks. However, with the security market brimming with products, such as the Dragon Network Sensor from Enterasys, which claim a performance rating of over 1 Gbps or 1.4 million packet per second (http://www.enterasys.com/products/ids.), Cisco IDS series sensors (http://www.cisco.com/en/US/products/hw/vpndevc/ps4077/index.html), and Proventia Intrusion Detection from RealSecure Network Internet Security Systems (http://www.iss.net/products_services/enterprise_protection/proventia/a_series.php), IDS technology is taking on the network challenges. One widely used open source IDS called Snort is briefly described below.

## Snort Intrusion Detection System

Snort IDS is an open source, lightweight network IDS that has the capacity to perform real-time background traffic analysis and packet logging on IP networks. It supports writing custom rules (attack signatures), as well as managing and upgrading these rules. Further flexibility is provided to the users, allowing them to enable or disable specific protocol decoders, detect advanced attacks by matching against a defined rule set, and choose among several actions. This level of flexibility prevents data loss brought about by missing an actual attack and also lessens the likelihood of huge irrelevant alerts. Snort also performs protocol analysis, content searching/matching (Eanes, 2003). It can be used to detect various attacks and probes, such as buffer overflows, stealth port scans, CGI attacks (Exploit Common Gateway Interface binaries to attack web servers), SMB probes (Monitors SAMBA or Windows file server for specific or available file shares), and open systems (OS) fingerprinting attempts. It is equipped with a detection engine that utilizes a modular plug-in architecture and provides flexible language rules support.

Snort has five major components that work together to detect specific attacks and generate output in a required format by way of the detection system:

1. The packet decoder readies the incoming network packets for processing.
2. Preprocessors are input plug-ins that perform packet and TCP stream reassembly, normalization of packet headers, and anomaly detection.
3. The detection engine is a modular plug-in architecture that applies defined rules to packets.
4. The logging and alerting system generates logs and alert messages found by the detection engine with the packets.
5. Output modules control the final processing of logs and alerts in the specified output format.

## Probability of False Alarms

A false positive or false alarm is an alert caused by normal nonmalicious background traffic (Howell, 2002; Mell, Hu, Lippmann, Haines, & Zissman, 2002). It is difficult to measure false alarms because an IDS may have a different false-positive rate in each network environment, and there is no such thing as a "standard" network." In addition, it is difficult to determine aspects of network traffic or host activity that will cause false alarms. As a result, it may be difficult to guarantee the production of the same number and type of false alarms in an IDS test as are found in real networks. Finally, IDSs can be configured and tuned in a variety of ways to reduce the false-positive rate. This makes it difficult to determine which configuration of an IDS should be used for a particular false-positive test.

The probability of false alarms is the rate of false positives produced by an IDS in a given environment during a particular time frame. A receiver operating characteristic curve (ROC Chart) is an aggregate of the probability of false alarms and the probability of detection measurements. This is an important measure in the IDS testing community. This curve summarizes the relationship between two of the most important IDS characteristics: false positives and detection probability.

## Proactive IDS Agents

Currently, intrusion detection software is still highly reactive; that is, it can only detect attacks after they occur and have done some damage, even paralyzing the network. In contrast, intrusion prevention software actually prevents attacks, rather than only detecting their occurrence (Doty, 2002). Intrusion prevention security software is the next generation of network security software that proactively strengthens systems against damage from the different types of malicious attacks that signature-based technologies cannot detect.

Intrusion prevention has many advantages over intrusion detection. Unlike traditional intrusion detection products, intrusion prevention software actually restricts the attacks on internal resources by restricting the behavior of potentially malicious code without impeding business operations; it also provides a record of the attack and notifies security personnel when an attack is repelled. This software can also deal with DoS and other hostile attacks.

## Limitations of IDS Without Agent Technology

The use of mobile agents gives current IDSs these capabilities:

- to run continuously with minimal human interaction
- to withstand any crashes made intentionally or accidentally.
- to constantly monitor any malicious modifications
- to have lower overhead on the machine on which it is running
- to be adaptable to changes in the monitored environment
- to be able to scale well to monitor huge networks without compromising timely results
- to monitor the network even when some components of IDSs fail
- to have provision for run-time configuration
- to perform end-to-end encryption and high-speed communication

IDSs that do not employ mobile agents have the following drawbacks:

- Most IDSs tend to use a central controller, in which all the controls rest. This central controller can be a single point of failure. The intruder can discover the central point by some means and try to crash it.
- Some custom-made IDSs do not scale well for large networks or tend to process entire data at a single point. This results in limiting the size of the network to be monitored.
- Some IDSs do not allow run-time reconfiguration of the system. In some systems, it is sometimes achievable, but it involves the tedious task of editing a configuration file, which requires special knowledge. In addition, sometimes the IDSs have to be restarted to incorporate these changes.
- The rate of false alarms is high in current IDSs because they detect attacks based on the information from a single host or a single application.

Different types of hierarchical IDS that are vulnerable to attacks are described in Krugel and Toth (2001).

# INTRUSION DETECTION USING AGENTS

IDSs may use autonomous agents, intelligent agents, mobile agents, or some combination of these agents. Mobile agent technology uses the principles of different fields, such as artificial intelligence, neural networks, fuzzy logic, genetic algorithms, etc. to make them intelligent. Examples of some agent-based IDSs are given below:

- **Autonomous agents:** The Autonomous Agents for Intrusion Detection (AAFID; Brian & Dasgupta, 2001; Spafford & Zamboni, 2000) software is based on the principle of distributed intrusion detection, rather than building a single monolithic architecture that does almost all the data collection and analysis. This design employs a hierarchy of agents that work collectively. Each software agent performs a specific security-monitoring task at a host. The higher-level entities do the analysis on a per-host and per-network basis.

  The Fuzzy Intrusion Recognition Engine (FIRE; Dickerson, Juslin, Koukousoula, & Dickerson, 2001) is a network intrusion detection system that makes use of AAFID agents and fuzzy systems for analyzing and monitoring intrusive activity against computer networks.

- **Mobile agents:** Software agents can be treated as mobile agents, as they are able to move from one computer to another computer (Helmer, Wong, Slagell, Honavar, Miller, & Lutz, 2002; Jansen, 2002.; Jansen & Karygiannis, 1999; Mell & McLarson, 1999). Even if the host machine that launched the agents is eliminated from the network, they can still work. Thus, mobile agents are very powerful programs that can act even in the absence of the machine that initiated them. After completion of their assigned tasks, the mobile agents return to the host machine to report the results or else they simply terminate.

- **Intelligent agents:** Agent mobility allows various types of intelligent agents that employ classifier algorithms to travel among collection points, referred to as *data* cleaners, and uncover suspicious activities. The agent algorithms are standard sequence identification methods and feature the vector approach for data representation (Helmer, 2000). Helmer, Wong, Honavar, and Miller (2003) have implemented an intelligent system using distributed lightweight intelligent agents on which data mining is performed. These agents accomplish essential tasks with minimal code and are dynamically updatable, upgradable, smaller, and simpler and support faster transportation. Mehdi and Ghorbani (2002) have developed a fuzzy adaptive survivability model using intelligent agents that use fuzzy sets. The Cougaar Intrusion Detection System (CIDS) uses agents in the form of decision modules (implemented as plug-ins) such as the fuzzy inference system (FIS) with a knowledge base.

- **Java Agents for Meta-Learning:** Java Agents for Meta-Learning (from http://www1.cs.columbia.edu/~sal/JAM/PROJECT/) employs a distributed and scalable agent-based data mining system by providing a set of meta-learning agents for combining multiple models learned from various sites (remote and/or local). These intelligent agents apply various artificial intelligence techniques to model knowledge and reasoning, as well as behavior, in multiagent societies or domains.

Much research has been conducted in the area of applying agents to IDSs. Most studies describe the drawbacks associated with traditional IDSs (those that do not employ agent technology) and highlight the advantages obtained by using mobile agents.

Intrusion detection using autonomous agents is proposed by Spafford and Zamboni (2000), who have developed a new hierarchical architecture called AAFID (see above). At the lowest level are agents that perform data collection and analysis. Transceivers and monitors are higher-level entities. An agent is assigned to each host to perform the monitoring activity and report any abnormality to the transceivers. Transceivers control these agents and report the results to the monitors. These monitors then perform high-level correlation among several hosts and thus to the entire network. Spafford and Zamboni also discuss the importance of communication mechanisms among the network entities to ensure that the network is not overloaded. The AAFID architecture collects data from several sources and builds an IDS that is more capable of detecting intrusions than the centralized systems.

An extension to the above work is reported by Allen et al. (2000). Their work uses intelligent agents, which draw intelligence from artificial intelligence techniques. An intelligent agent is defined as an agent capable of detecting attacks in a timely manner; it should also be able to detect unknown intrusions and to communicate its knowledge to other agents. The system is trained for known attacks with neural networks. Thus, this work provides an extension to AAFID but with intelligence added to the system.

Debar, Dacier, and Wepspi (2000) also employ mobile agents (called D'Agents) to detect intrusions. These agents have the capability to move around the network and search for information on any server. They are provided with a document index to connect to Serval, a scalable information retrieval server. There are several phases in which the Serval agent operates. In the incident handling phase, it can identify all the operations performed by the attacker. In the forensic analysis phase, it provides correlation among logs from different machines. In the response phase, it is possible to stop the intrusion at early stages.

Brian and Dasgupta (2001) apply mobile agents to network traffic analysis in a mobile agent architecture, which is used in a project called SANTA. Here, agents are applied at several levels down the hierarchy. Each agent performs individual tasks, that help the entire IDS work by learning and detecting different kinds of attacks in a modular fashion. They also describe the application of ART-2 neural networks for decision-support modules needed to make appropriate decisions. One of the mobile agents collects the data from the network, which then are used to analyze the network traffic by SANTA. Figure 1 shows the architecture of a mobile agent.

Lee, Stolfo, and Mok (2000) describe the application of data mining concepts with mobile agents. Their work is mostly an extension to existing IDSs that use intelligence modules but do not make use of mobile agents. They were able to classify the network file system (NFS) and rlogin

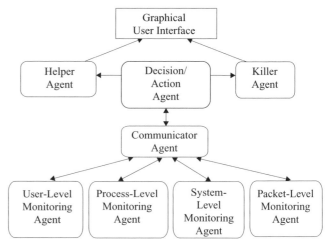

**Figure 1:** Mobile agent architecture—SANTA.

attacks by monitoring the system call sequences. Their work proved that using intelligent mobile agents would result in a more efficient means of attack detection than in the traditional IDS.

Mobile agents have also found their way into wireless networks. Kachirski and Guha (2002) and Krügel and Toth (2001) describe the use of mobile agents for detecting intrusions in dynamic mobile networks. They present Sparta, a mobile-agent-based IDS that detects intrusions even in a changing dynamic environment. The main feature of Sparta is that the agents do not view the network topology globally and hence are naturally suited for operating in a dynamic environment. Because of this ability to manage the sensors remotely and to provide automatic updates and integration of new devices, Sparta can overcome the challenges faced by the traditional IDS when they are used in mobile environments. The IDS architecture proposed by Krügel and Toth (2001) thwarts the attempts of hackers to use passive sniffing or active probing to detect an IDS. They employ a strategy where the critical IDS hosts are invisible to the attacker. The architecture is based on the ability of mobile agent technology to provide communication among different types of IDS components.

An important work on mobile agents is reported by Asaka, Okazawa, Taguchi, and Goto (1999a,b). Their work, which focuses on using mobile agent technology, provides a new taxonomy for IDSs, including such elements as agent tasks, description of the attack scenarios, how to relate information from different sources, and persistence of agents. Based on the new taxonomy, they incorporate mobile-agent-based IDS into Sparta and use public key infrastructure (PKI) authentication to provide secure communication among mobile agents. These researchers also highlight the advantages and disadvantages of using mobile agents and describe several IDSs that use mobile agents.

## Advantages of Using Mobile Agents in Intrusion Detection

Several advantages related to mobile agent usage are described in the literature (Bass, 1999; Gomez & Dasgupta, 2002; Helmer, Wong, Slagell, Honavar, Miller, & Lutz,

2002; Jansen, 2002.; Mell & McLarson, 1999) and are presented below:

- **Delay caused by networks:** When using hierarchical IDSs in a network results in a slower response when an attack occurs. This is because the central controller (machine) has to send the information about the attack to every participating host and the response must be made by each particular host throughout the network. This may not always result in an immediate response, as it might take too much time for the information to reach the destination host. Thus, traditional hierarchical IDSs may not be successful in achieving a timely detection of attacks. In contrast, if mobile agents are used, they can respond faster as they are directly dispatched from the central controller to the target host.

- **Minimizing network traffic:** Traditional IDSs employ different data collection mechanisms to collect data both at the host and network level. These data are later used to track any intrusions. Generally, there is a very huge amount of collected data, and for an intrusion to be detected, data from different hosts have to be collected and processed by the central controller. This increases network traffic, creating an overhead on the network. By employing mobile agents, the load on the network can be reduced as these mobile agents employ efficient search mechanisms, thereby reducing the necessity for data traffic among several hosts.

- **Persistency:** Because mobile nodes operate autonomously and asynchronously, they are not prone to failure even if the machine that hosts them fails. In centralized machines, when the central controller fails, the entire IDS is considered to be down because there is no communication among other hosts.

- **Structure and platform independence:** Mobile agents can be used in IDSs with a flexible structure. For example, one agent can be designated to collect the data in the network, another agent can be used to detect and report anomalies, and the rest can be used to take appropriate action. Because of this structure, mobile agents find tremendous application in IDSs. In addition, mobile agents from different vendors can be used to build IDSs, and it is possible to write your own mobile code to make it applicable to the existing environment.

- **Dynamic nature:** The dynamic nature of mobile agents enables them to be moved around the network. This also makes it possible to reconfigure the system during run time. Mobile agents can be cloned, dispatched, or put to sleep when the network configuration has to be changed. In addition, they can sense their execution environment and dynamically adapt to the situation.

- **Heterogeneous environment:** Mobile agents can be interoperable on multiple platforms because of the virtual interpreter installed on the host machine. Mobile agents are generally computer and transport-layer independent and are dependent only on the execution environment. This feature enables mobile agents to be used on several different platforms without compatibility problems.

- **Robust in nature:** Even if one of the agents fails, the other agents in the IDS can take over the tasks of the failed agent and continue the detection. This robust

behavior of mobile agents makes them more applicable in large environments where several agents and their interaction are needed for proper monitoring of the network.

- **Scalability:** By employing distributed mobile-agent IDSs, it is easier to handle large networks. Agents have the capability to clone and distribute themselves to the new machines when they are added to the network.

## Drawbacks of Using Mobile Agents

The main problem in using mobile agents involves security. Mobile agents require administration rights because they initiate a response when an intrusion is identified. Granting a mobile agent all permissions to the host on which it is operating can enable an intruder to induce any virus easily. Some preliminary measures can be taken to alleviate these security problems, including providing limited access control to important resources, applying cryptographic methods to exchange information, etc. Another potential problem occurs when the mobile agent contains credit card details of the user. Some hosts might try to obtain this private information from the mobile agents.

One downside when mobile agents detect attacks immediately and report them spontaneously is that it reduces the performance of the entire network. The network is also slowed when the code size of the IDS is large. This is because whenever the mobile agent has to go round the network, the entire code has to be moved along with it, and additionally source codes might have more bugs.

Though there are drawbacks associated with using mobile agents, they still find potential application in industry, academics, and research institutes.

## ANALYSIS TECHNIQUES, TESTING AND VALIDATION, AND PERFORMANCE OF IDS AGENTS
### Analysis Techniques

Three analysis techniques have been refined recently. Misuse detection is the oldest technique for detecting intrusions (Biege, 2001; Placek & Newsham, 1998). This procedure uses a pattern matching approach that matches event box data with attack signatures from a database; if the comparison results in a positive match, the system recognizes that there is some violation in the security policy and reacts accordingly. This procedure is easy to implement and use, and it is not very prone to false alarms. However misuse detection has one major disadvantage in that it can only recognize known attacks. Consequently, new attack patterns that are not added to the database go unrecognized by misuse detection.

To overcome the drawback of misuse detection, a new approach evolved to solve the problem known as *anomaly detection*. Anomaly detection is based on the premise that anything that does not match the "normal" behavior is, by definition "abnormal" (i.e., it is an anomaly) and therefore constitutes an attack. Compared to misuse detection (Biege, 2001), this method has the advantage of being able to recognize new attacks because they are defined as abnormal behavior. In addition, there is no need to implement and maintain a database of attack patterns. However, anomaly detection has its own drawbacks. Anomaly detection approaches must first acquire knowledge of what constitutes "normal" behavior for a network or computer system by creating user and system profiles. This phase alone is an obstacle and could be exploited by a malicious attacker who could teach the IDS to classify attacks as normal behavior. Thus, in the future, the IDS system might no longer recognize that type of attack as an unauthorized intrusion. Another drawback is the high rate of false positives triggered by the malfunctioning of normal system activities that are not actually attacks. Moreover, compared to misuse detection, the implementation of anomaly detection is more difficult, because it involves many complex procedures.

Another approach that is currently in the initial stages is known as *burglar alarm, passive trap,* or *strict anomaly detection* (Biege, 2001; Placek & Newsham, 1998). The premise is that anything that is not "good" must be "bad." In contrast to anomaly detection, the recognition of attacks is based on pattern recognition, just like misuse detection. This means that the system's normal, known behavior is stored in a database as a signature. Any kind of system activity that does not match a pattern in the database is classified as abnormal behavior and indicates an attack.

## Testing and Validation Approaches

IDS testing approaches can be classified into four categories with regard to their use of background traffic: tested using no background traffic/logs, tested using real traffic/logs, tested using sanitized traffic/logs, and testing using simulated traffic/logs (Mell, Hu, Lippmann, Haines, & Zissman, 2002).

### Testing Using No Background Traffic/Logs
In this type of testing, an IDS is set up on a host or network on which there is no network activity. Then, computer attacks are launched to determine whether an IDS can detect them. This technique can determine an IDS hit rate and which signature attacks an IDS can verify, but nothing about false positives because IDSs are used in different environments.

### Testing Using Real Traffic/Logs
Another way to test IDSs is by injecting attacks into a stream of real background activity. This approach is useful in determining the hit rates of IDS in different background activities, and because background activity is real, it contains all of the anomalies and subtleties of background activity. Furthermore, this approach compares IDS hit rates at different levels of background activity (Mell, Hu, Lippmann, Haines, & Zissman, 2002).

## Testing Using Sanitized Traffic/Logs

In this approach, real background activity is prerecorded and then sanitized to remove any sensitive data. Then, the attack data are injected within the sanitized datastream. Examples of sanitized traffic are cleansed TCP packet headers that were recorded with data during background traffic and were not used to test the IDS. The advantage of this approach is that the test data can be freely distributed and the test is repeatable.

## Testing by Generating Traffic on a Testbed Network

This is one of the most common approaches used to test IDS. In this technique, traffic is generated by complex traffic generators that model actual network traffic statistics. Network traffic and host audit logs can be recorded in such a testbed for later playback, or evaluations can be performed in real time. One of the advantages of this approach is that data can be freely distributed across the network. Because attacks have been created in the testbed network, there will be no other unknown attacks that could cause disruption. Lastly, IDS tests using generated traffic are usually repeatable because one can either replay previously generated background activity or have the simulator regenerate the same background activity that was used in a previous test. This kind of test would appear to be one of the best available because it tests both hit rates and false-positive rates and uses them to create ROC curves.

## Performance

The quantitative performance measurements such as coverage, probability of false alarms, probability of detection, ability to correlate events, ability to detect unseen attacks, etc. are some important evaluation criteria to determine IDS performance and effectiveness.

The system performance of intrusion detection may usually consume some system resources, so system resource use is an important metric for evaluating a local intrusion detection tool. Many experiments (Li, Song, & Zhang, 2004) show that the increase in resource (CPU, memory etc.) use of the monitored host is so light after running the host monitor agent that the user cannot perceive a difference. Generally, the use time of the CPU is less than 1%, and approximately 5% of the memory is exhausted. The detail system performance data are related to the CPU performance, memory capacity, operating system, current process number, etc. In fact, the amount of additive network traffic imposed by an IDS, is one of the main factors for evaluating that system. Host monitor agents and mobile agents all have the advantage of lessening network traffic. The network traffic generated by this system is less than 100 kB/sec. As we know, the size of the mobile agent affects the speed of its migration. Big mobile agents may cause system performance degradation.

# A DISTRIBUTED SECURITY AGENT SYSTEM

This section describes an autonomous agent system that uses intelligent decision-support modules for robust detection of anomalies and intrusions. The Cougaar-Based Intrusion Detection System (CIDS) provides a hierarchical security agent framework, in which a security node houses four different agents: manager agents, monitor agents, decision agents, and action agents. The activities of these agents are coordinated through the manager agent during sensing, communicating, and generating responses. Each agent performs unique functions in coordination with each other to address various security issues of the monitored environment.

The decision agent uses multiple intelligent decision support modules (such as fuzzy inference module, classifier system, knowledge base) and a bidding system to make a robust decision in the case of any abnormalities/intrusions. Because the differences between the normal and abnormal activities are not distinct, but rather fuzzy, the fuzzy inference module can reduce false alarms by using imprecise and heuristic knowledge to determine an appropriate response.

In the current implementation, the action agent reports the state of the monitored environment in intrusion detection message exchange format (IDMEF; Curry, 2000). Accordingly, the action agent generates IDMEF objects that represent intrusion/anomalous state, diagnosis, and recommended actions. The purpose is to send these objects to other system management agents to take necessary action, which may include killing a process, disabling access to a user who is a potential intruder, alerting the administrator about the intrusion, and the like.

## Cougaar: A Cognitive Agent Architecture

The Cougaar software was initially developed under DARPA sponsorship for the purpose of Military Logistics and is now available as open source (http://www.cougaar.org). The Cougaar is an excellent software architecture that enables distributed agent-based applications in a manner that is powerful, expressive, scalable, and maintainable. Cougaar is a large-scale workflow engine built on component-based, distributed agent architecture. The agents can communicate with one another through a built-in asynchronous message-passing protocol. Cougaar agents cooperate with one another to solve a particular problem, storing the shared solution in a distributed fashion across the agents. They are composed of related functional modules that are expected to rework the solution dynamically and continuously as the problem parameters, constraints, or execution environment change.

Agents are the prime components in the Cougaar architecture. An agent has two major components: a distributed blackboard (called Plan) and plug-ins. Each blackboard contains such elements as tasks, assets, and plan elements. Plug-ins are self-contained software components (*compute engine*) that can be loaded dynamically into agents. Plug-ins interact with the agent infrastructure according to a set of rules and guidelines (as binders), providing unique capabilities and behavior to complete given tasks. They come and talk to the Plan through the blackboard to perform agent operations and operate by publishing and subscribing objects onto the Plan. Plug-ins bring functionality to the agents, whereas the society of agents (node) provides structure and order of operations. Agents can also have special plug-ins called plan service plug-ins (PSPs). Programmers can develop HTML/ standalone JAVA user interfaces that communicate with PSPs. However, in the latest Cougaar versions, the PSPs are replaced by servlets, and communication among the agents is encrypted, making it secure.

## Cougaar-Based Security Agent Infrastructure

The Cougaar framework provides an effective base agent architecture that we used to develop a distributed security agent system called CIDS. In CIDS, a security node comprises manager agents, monitor agents, decision agents, and action agents, and a number of such nodes form a security community. The advantage of having an individual agent for each functional module is that it makes future modifications easy. According to software engineering principles, having different functionalities modularized makes for simplified development of a large software project.

In each security node, the control flow mainly occurs between the manager and subordinate agents to assign tasks and feedback accomplishments, whereas the data flow occurs among subordinate agents to transfer data. The control flow and data flow within a node and among various nodes use the same message-passing mechanism, which is provided by Cougaar. In the Java implementation, a particular class of objects is reserved

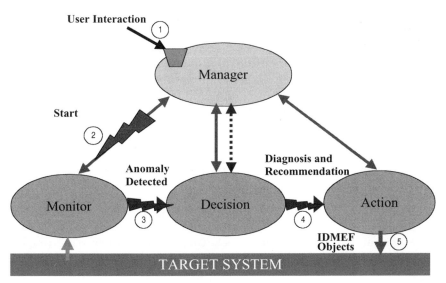

**Figure 2:** Sequence of activation of different agents.

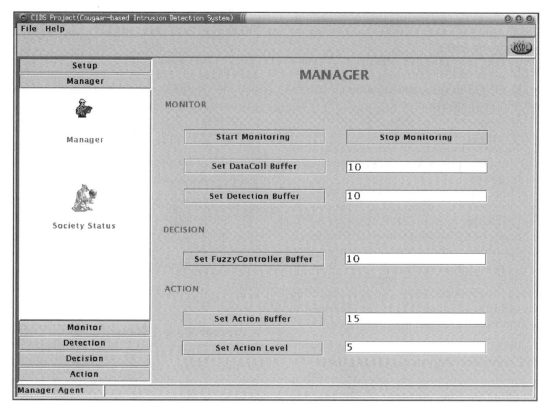

**Figure 3:** Snapshot of a manager agent control panel.

for control flow, and a different class of objects is reserved for the data flow.

## Security Node Society

The communication among communities is accomplished through manager agents, which share information among different security nodes in a network (Figure 2). The communications among various nodes use the same message-passing mechanism that is provided by the Cougaar framework.

In a symmetric arrangement of multiple security nodes, one security node (with four agents) may be placed in each host in the subnet. However, the flexible security agent architecture may also allow asymmetric configurations; for example, putting a monitor agent in one host and the remaining three agents in different hosts(s). The purpose of such an arrangement may be to reduce the load on the crucial monitored machine.

## Sequence of Operations

To explain the operation of the multiagent security system, the sequence of activation of these four agents is described below.

The user makes a request to start monitoring through the interface (PSP in the manager agent; Figure 3). The manager agent receives the user request and sends the command (task) to the monitor agent. The monitor agent starts collecting multilevel information from the target system and tries to detect deviations from the normal. If any deviation is detected, information on deviated parameters is sent to the decision agent, which processes

the anomalies and uses a fuzzy inference engine to classify different anomalies/attacks through rules generated previously using a normal profile. The action agent receives the messages and creates appropriate IDMEF objects.

## Experimentation and Evaluation of CIDS

Since the creation of the first version of Cougaar, several prototypes have been developed with added capabilities, transforming a very basic structure into a fully functional system. The current version of CIDS (CIDS 1.4) is built on Cougaar 8.8 and is compatible with Java 1.3, which can monitor machines in a LINUX/UNIX environment. To test the performance of CIDS 1.4, we have conducted a number of experiments with various port scans and simulated attacks.

The CIDS allows the monitoring of parameters at different levels (process, user, network) of target computer networks (Figure 4). Twenty parameters can be monitored using CIDS, including the following:

- Network level: local_sent_bytes, local received_bytes, etc.
- Process level: number of processes, running processes, etc.
- System level: CPU usage, physical RAM, etc.

In our experiments, two attacks were performed on the target host, a probe (PRB) attack using the *nmap* scan tool and user-to-remote (U2R) attack by using a secure shell (SSH) hacking tool. The total number of data samples collected was 1800 (300 for the PRB attack and 400 for the U2R attack, rest considered normal). Figure 5 shows

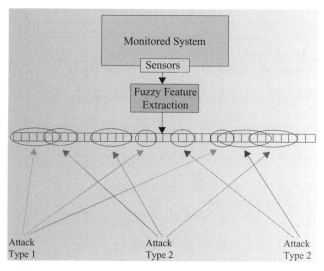

**Figure 4:** The effect of attacks on monitored parameters.

**Table 1** Binarization class ordering used in the CIDS experimentation

| INDEX | CLASS |
|-------|-------|
| 1 | PRB |
| 2 | U2R |
| 3 | Normal |

*Method:* using a simple port scanner written with "BSD sockets" at time of run
The network traffic is 14–19K.
The test scanned the first 6000 ports on the target machine.
Start = 13:06:52 End = 13:07:35
Found ports 22, 80, 111, 1024, 1115, 1117, 5555, 5556, 5557, 5558, 6000 open

the statistical values of the data collected by CIDS after 1000 seconds (100 samples).

The training data were preprocessed (i.e., the collected data were normalized), and the fuzzy space shown in Figure 5 was used for all monitored parameters. Different classes of attack in the data were sorted; Table 1 shows the binarization ordering applied to the training classes.

In this case of using the simple port scanner, we noticed that during the scanning, the number of received packets was spiking at the same time as the number of sent packets. This is a clear indication of port scan.

The fuzzy rules for the evolutionary algorithm parameters were fixed as shown in Table 2, and the number of samples used per individual was fixed at 100%. This percentage is appropriate because data samples are very small (1800).

We calculated the effectiveness of the evolved classifier over the training data set. It yielded a detection rate of 83.33% and a false alarm rate of 0.0%. The detection rate is low compared to the KDD-cup data set (knowledge discovery and data mining, a standard data set available from UCI Kdd archive at http://kdd.ics.uci.edu/) because the training data set was not cleaned (i.e., there were some samples that were classified in the training data set as attack classes but they corresponded to normal behavior

| | Max | Min | Average | Std Dev |
|---|---|---|---|---|
| LOCAL_SENT_BY... | 1501680.04 | 0.0 | 49034.7115 | 209676.7252 |
| LOCAL_RECEIVE... | 1501680.04 | 0.0 | 49034.7115 | 209676.7252 |
| LOCAL_SENT_PA... | 30031.0155 | 0.0 | 968.2621 | 4192.9019 |
| LOCAL_RECEIVE... | 30031.0155 | 0.0 | 968.2621 | 4192.9019 |
| REMOTE_SENT_... | 157736.2834 | 69.1597 | 2061.4408 | 15759.2544 |
| REMOTE_RECEIV... | 38155.6599 | 109.0445 | 1303.7547 | 4361.3567 |
| REMOTE_SENT_... | 236.5627 | 0.716 | 5.9258 | 24.1544 |
| REMOTE_RECIEV... | 175.3269 | 0.9421 | 5.4264 | 18.0581 |
| PROCESSES | 168.0 | 145.0 | 158.92 | 2.3428 |
| PROCESSES_ROOT | 33.0 | 31.0 | 31.63 | 0.9063 |
| PROCESSES_USER | 137.0 | 114.0 | 127.29 | 2.1192 |
| PROCESSES_BLO... | 0.0 | 0.0 | 0.0 | 0.0 |
| PROCESSES_RUN... | 4.0 | 1.0 | 1.22 | 0.561 |
| PROCESSES_WAI... | 166.0 | 143.0 | 157.7 | 2.3377 |
| PROCESSES_ZOM... | 0.0 | 0.0 | 0.0 | 0.0 |
| USED_PHYSICAL_... | 5.19225344E8 | 4.87841792E8 | 5.141676032E8 | 4803105.7715 |
| USED_SWAP_RAM | 278528.0 | 278528.0 | 278528.0 | 0.0 |
| LOGINS | 5.0 | 5.0 | 5.0 | 0.0 |
| FAILED_LOGINS | 0.0 | 0.0 | 0.0 | 0.0 |
| REMOTE_LOGINS | 0.0 | 0.0 | 0.0 | 0.0 |
| CPU_USERS | 106.8 | 6.2 | 12.337 | 14.8012 |

X-A CIDS Project(Cougaar-based Intrusion Detection System)
File  Help
Get Data  Policy File: Avg +/– StdDev ▼ 1.0  Generate
Setup
Manager
Monitor
Data Collection
Statistics
Training Data Generator
Detection
Decision
Action

**Monitor Agent Statistics**
Number of samples: 100

**Figure 5:** Statistical values collected by CIDS after 1000 seconds (100 samples).

**Table 2** Evolved classifier system in a sample run.

| Classifier System | Fuzzy Rules |
|---|---|
| PRB General | **IF** REMOTE_RECEIVED_PACKETS is high AND CPU_USERS is low OR USED_SWAP_RAM is medium **THEN** RECORD is PRB |
| | **IF** LOCAL_SENT_BYTES is low OR REMOTE_RECEIVED_PACKETS is not high **THEN** RECORD is not PRB |
| PRB Checking | **IF** PROCESSES_BLOCKED is low OR PROCESSES_WAITING is not high **THEN** RECORD is PRB |
| | **IF** PROCESSES_BLOCKED is high AND DEVIATION is low **THEN** RECORD is not PRB |
| U2R General | **IF** PROCESSES_RUNNING is medium-low OR PROCESSES_ROOT is medium **THEN** RECORD is U2R |
| | **IF** (PROCESSES_RUNNING is not medium-low OR CPU_USERS is medium) AND PROCESSES_ROOT is not medium **THEN** RECORD is Normal |
| U2R Checking | **IF** PROCESSES_ROOT is not medium AND PROCESSES_RUNNING is medium-low **THEN** RECORD is Normal |
| | **IF** PROCESSES_ROOT is medium OR REMOTE_RECEIVED_PACKETS is high OR PROCESSES_RUNNING is not medium-low **THEN** RECORD is Normal |

when the attack was stopped temporarily to distribute the attack in time) or because they (training data set samples) belonged to the fuzzy region of normal-abnormal (when the attack is starting or ending). Amazingly the false alarms rate was zero.

When CIDS was executed with the evolved classifier system the results were very impressive. Under normal conditions it did not generate any false alarms. Figure 6 shows the decision module under normal conditions.

When attacks are launched, the decision module raises an alarm. Table 2 shows the rules used to detect PRB and U2R attacks. Clearly, the fuzzy rule corresponds to the behavior shown for the parameters monitored.

When the U2R attack was executed, the decision module raised an alarm and showed the rule used to detect the attack. Figure 4 shows the monitoring and decision modules under a U2R attack. Although this attack was hard to detect because the monitored parameters under this attack behaved almost the same as under normal conditions, the classifier system was able to detect it in almost 90% of the cases.

## CONCLUSIONS

This chapter surveyed agent-based intrusion detection systems and illustrated the pros and cons of using such

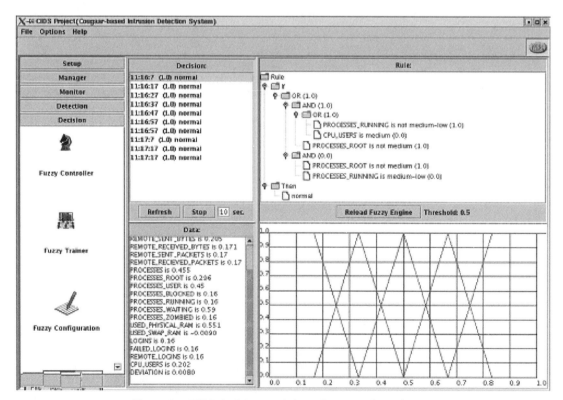

**Figure 6:** CIDS decision module under normal conditions.

a technology. It described a Cougaar agent-based system (called CIDS) for intrusion detection. Some experimental results were reported that indicated that CIDS could detect a wide variety of anomalies and intrusive activities.

CIDS has many advantages. A four-agent security node infrastructure is implemented on the Cougaar framework with unique functionality for each agent. The CIDS is a modular design, which allows the easy and independent inclusion of new detection, decision, and action plug-ins. A swing-based GUI provides a user-friendly interface that can run on the same computer or remotely. The monitored parameters, normalized values, and detected deviations are displayed in textual and graphical form. Cougaar also provides tools to generate automatically the normal profile (of the monitored environment) and to update the knowledge base of the decision module.

CIDS can be used not only as an anomaly/intrusion detection tool but also as a monitoring tool, because its data gathering and visualization can help evaluate the behavior of any monitored network. Experiments with the current prototype show that it could detect various types of probing and DoS attacks successfully. However, these are only tests, they are neither exhaustive nor demonstrate the capabilities of a full-fledged CIDS.

The long-term goal of CIDS research is to develop an intrusion detection system that will have the following characteristics:

- be flexible, scalable, and adaptable, which can provide a certain level of security assurance
- be able to identify irregularities that are linked to attempted or successful attacks, which may result in system failure or compromise
- be able in a systematic fashion to detect security breaches that are internal, external, accidental, or intentional

## ACKNOWLEDGEMENTS

This work was supported by the Defense Advanced Research Projects Agency (no. F30602-00-2-0514). The views and conclusions of this work in no way reflect the opinions or positions of the Defense Advanced Research Projects Agency or the U.S. government. The author would like to acknowledge the contribution of the members of ISSRL, F. Gonzalez, J. Gomez, K. Yallapu, M. Kaniganti, J. Rodriguez, and S. Balachandran.

## GLOSSARY

**AAFID** Acronym for Autonomous Agents for Intrusion Detection, a distributed monitoring and intrusion detection system that employs small stand-alone programs (agents) to perform monitoring functions in the hosts of a network.

**Agents** A program that performs some information gathering or processing task in the background. Typically, an agent is given a very small and well-defined task.

**Anomaly Detection** Anomaly detection compares observed activity against expected normal usage profiles, which may be developed for users, groups of users, applications, or system resource usage. Audit event records that fall outside the definition of normal behavior are considered anomalies.

**ART-2** A neural network model that belongs to the adaptive resonance theory developed by G. A Carpenter and S. Grossberg at the CNS (University of Boston). It is able to deal with analogue patterns, and it has three processing stages.

**CGI Attack** Attack due to vulnerabilities in CGI scripts run on HTTP servers.

**DoS Attack** Denial of service attack, which is designed to consume computing resources by flooding the network with useless traffic.

**Intelligent Agents** Programs used extensively on the Web that perform such tasks as retrieving and delivering information and automating repetitive tasks.

**Intrusion Detection System (IDS)** A security system for computers and networks for detecting inappropriate, incorrect, anomalous, or hacking activity. A system that operates on a host is a host-based IDS, whereas one that operates on network data flows is a network-based IDS. There are hybrid systems that combine both techniques.

**False Negatives** An attack or an event that is either not detected by the IDS or is considered not to be harmful by the system.

**False Positives/False Alarm** An event that is picked up by the IDS and declared an attack but is actually not harmful.

**Misuse Detection** Misuse detection checks for "bad activities over network" in comparison to abstracted descriptions of undesired activity.

**Mobile Agents** These agents can physically travel across a network and perform tasks on machines that provide agent hosting capability.

**NFS** Network file system, a client/server application designed by Sun Microsystems that allows all network users to access shared files stored on computers of different types.

**PKI** Acronym for public key infrastructure, a system of digital certificates, certificate authorities, and other registration authorities that verify and authenticate the validity of each party involved in an Internet transaction. A PKI is also called a trust hierarchy.

**POP** Acronym for post office protocol, which is used to retrieve e-mail from a mail server.

**PRB Attack** Probe attack, at the preattack stage, sensing open ports.

**Signature-based IDS** These systems search for a known identity—or signature—for each specific intrusion event.

**SMTP** Acronym for simple mail transfer protocol, a protocol for sending e-mail messages between servers.

**U2R Attack** User-to-root attack, a process in which a normal user gains root (superuser) privileges through an illegal way.

## CROSS REFERENCES

See *Computer Viruses and Worms; Host-Based Intrusion Detection Systems; Intrusion Detection Systems Basics; Mobile Code and Security; Network-Based Intrusion Detection Systems; Security Policy Guidelines.*

# REFERENCES

Allen, J., et al. (2000, January). *State of the practice of intrusion detection technologies* (Tech.Report. CMU/SEI-99-TR-028, CMU/SEI).

Asaka, M., Okazawa S., Taguchi A., & Goto, S. (1999a, June). A method of tracing intruders by use of mobile agents. *Proceedings of INET'99.*

Asaka, M., Taguchi A., & Goto, S. (1999b, June). The implementation of IDA: An intrusion detection agent system. *Proceedings of the 11th Annual FIRST Conference on Computer Security Incident Handling and Response (FIRST'99).*

Axelsson, S. (2000). *Intrusion detection systems: A survey and taxonomy.* Goteburg, Sweden: Chalmers Institute of Technology.

Barrus, J., & Rose, N. C. (1998, June). A distributed autonomous-agent network-intrusion detection and response system. *Proceedings of the Command and Control Research and Technology Symposium,.* Monterey, CA. Also available at http://www.cs.nps.navy.mil/people/faculty/rowe/barruspap.html.

Bass,T. (1999, May). Multisensor data fusion for next generation distributed intrusion detection systems. *Proceedings of the 1999 IRIS National Symposium on Sensor and Data Fusion.* Symposium conducted at The Johns Hopkins University Applied Physics Laboratory.

Bernardes, M. C., & Moreira, E. dos Santos. (2000). Implementation of an intrusion detection system based on mobile agents. *International Symposium on Software Engineering for Parallel and Distributed Systems,* 158–164.

Biege, T. (2001, April). Virtual burglar alarm—Intrusion detection systems. Retrieved January, 2005, from http://elibrary.fultus.com/technical/index.jsp?topic=/com. fultus.suse.howtos/howtos/suse/ids/cover.html.

Brian, H., & Dasgupta, D. (2001). Mobile security agents for network traffic analysis. *Proceedings of DARPA Information Survivability Conference and Exposition II (DISCEX-II),* Vol.2 (pp. 332–340). Los Alamitos, CA: IEEE Computer Society.

Carver, C. A., Hill, J. M. D., Surdu, J. R., & Pooch, U. W. (2000, June). A methodology for using intelligent agents to provide automated intrusion response. *IEEE Systems, Man, and Cybernetics Information Assurance and Security Workshop.* Symposium conducted at West Point, NY.

CISCO Systems. (n.d.). *The science of intrusion detection system attack identification.* Retrieved January 20, 2005, from http://www.cisco.com/en/US/tech/tk869/tk769/technologies_white_paper09186a008014f945.shtml.

CISCO IDS Series Sensors. (n.d.). Retrieved January 20, 2005, from http://www.cisco.com/en/US/products/hw/vpndevc/ ps4077/index.html

Cougaar. (n.d.). *A cognitive agent architecture.* Retrieved January 20, 2005, from http://www.cougaar.org

Curry, D. (2000). *Intrusion detection message exchange format. extensible markup language (xml) document type definition* (Intrusion Detection Working Group IETF Internet Draft 'draft-ietf-idwg-idmef-xml-01.txt').

Dasgupta, D. (1999). Immunity-based intrusion detection systems: A general framework. *Proceedings of the 22nd National Information Systems Security Conference (NISSC),* Page(s): 147–160, October 18–21, 1999.

Dasgupta, D., & Gonzalez, F. (2002, June). An immunity-based technique to characterize intrusions in computer networks. *IEEE Transactions on Evolutionary Computation, 6*(3).

Debar, Dacier, H. M., & Wepspi, A. (2000). *A revised taxonomy for intrusion detection systems.* Annales des Telecommunications, volume 55, (no. 7–8), pages 361–78.

De Mara, R., & Rocke, A. J. (2004, February). Mitigation of network tampering using dynamic dispatch of mobile agents. *Computers & Security, 23*(1), 31–42.

Dickerson, J., Juslin, J., Koukousoula, O., &. Dickerson, J. (2001, July). Fuzzy intrusion detection. *IFSA World Congress and 20th North American Fuzzy Information Processing Society (NAFIPS) International Conference: Vol. 3* (pp. 1506–1510). Vancouver, British Columbia.

Doty, T. (2002, January). New approach to intrusion detection: Intrusion prevention. *TECS, 23.*

Eanes, M. (2003, October 15). *Wanted dead or alive: Snort intrusion detection system.* GSEC Practical Assignment, Version 1.4b, Option 1. Retrieved May 26, 2004, from http://cnscenter.future.co.kr/resource/security/ids/1275.pdf

Enterasys. (n.d.). *Host-and network-based Intrusion defense for the entire enterprise.* Retrieved January 21, 2005 from http://www.enterasys.com/products/ids

Gomez, J., & Dasgupta D. (2002, June). Evolving fuzzy classifiers for intrusion detection. *Proceedings of the 3rd Annual IEEE Information Assurance Workshop,* New Orleans, Lousiana, June 17–19, 2002.

Gopalakrishna, R., & Spafford, E. A. *Framework for distributed intrusion detection interest driven cooperating agents.* Recent Advances in Intrusion Detection (RAID 2001), Oct. 2001.

Helmer, G. (2000). *Intelligent multi-agent system for intrusion detection and countermeasures.* Unpublished doctoral dissertation, Iowa State University, Ames.

Helmer, G., Wong, J. S. K., Honavar, V., & Miller, L (August 2003). Lightweight agents for intrusion detection. Journal of Systems and Software, Volume 67, Issue 2, Pages: 109–122.

Helmer, G., Wong, J., Slagell, M., Honavar, V., Miller, L., and Lutz, R. (2002) *A Software Fault Tree Approach to Requirements Specification of an Intrusion Detection System.* Requirements Engineering. Vol. 7(4) (2002) pp. 207–220.

Howell, D. (2002, June 30). Hackers often choose their corporate targets. *Investors Business Daily*

Internet Security Systems. (n.d.). *Proventia intrusion detection.* Retrieved January 21, 2005 from http://www. iss.net/products_services/enterprise_protection/proventia/a_series.php.

Jansen, W. Intrusion detection with mobile agents (2002, September). Computer Communications 25(15), Special Issue on Intrusion Detection, Elsevier, pp. 1392–1401, September 2002.

Jansen, W., & Karygiannis, T. (1999, August). *Mobile agent security* (Special Publication). Baltimore: National Institute of Standards and Technology.

Retrieved January, 2005, from http://csrc.nist.gov/mobilesecurity/Publications/sp800-19.pdf

Jansen, W., Mell, P., Karygiannis, T., & Marks, D. (1999, October). *Applying mobile agents to intrusion detection and response* (NIST Interim Report IR–6416). Baltimore: National Institute of Standards and Technology Computer Security Division.

Jansen, W., Mell, P., Karygiannis, T., & Marks, D. (2000, June). Mobile agents in intrusion detection and response. *Proceedings of the 12th Annual Canadian Information Technology Security Symposium.* Symposium conducted in Ottawa, Canada.

Java Agents for Meta-Learning. *(n.d.). Fraud and intrusion detection in financial information systems.* Retrieved January 20, 2005, from http://www1.cs.columbia.edu/~sal/JAM/PROJECT/.

Jazayeri, M., & Lugmayr, W. (2000, January). Gypsy: A component-based mobile agent system. *Eighth Euromicro Workshop on Parallel and Distributed Processing.* Symposium conducted in Greece.

Juniper Networks. (n.d.). *Attack detection.* Retrieved January 21, 2005, from http://www.juniper.net/products/intrusion/detection.html.

Kachirski, O., & Guha, R. (2002, July). Intrusion detection using mobile agents in wireless ad hoc networks. *IEEE Workshop on Knowledge Media Networking (KMN'02)*, Kyoto, Japan.

Karygiannis, T. (1998, March). Network security testing using mobile agents. *Third International Conference and Exhibition on the Practical Application of Intelligent Agents and Multi Agent technologies.* Symposium conducted in London.

Kazienko, P., & Dorosz, P. (2003). *Intrusion detection systems (IDS) Part 1: Classification; methods; techniques.* Retrieved January, 2005, from http://www.windowsecurity.com/articles_tutorials/intrusion_detection/.

Kazienko, P., & Dorosz, P. (2004). *Intrusion detection systems (IDS) Part 2: Classification; methods; techniques.* Retrieved January, 2005, from http://www.windowsecurity.com/articles_tutorials/intrusion_detection/.

Krügel, C., & Toth, T. (2001). *Applying mobile agent technology to intrusion detection.* Vienna: Distributed Systems Group, Technical University.

Lee, W., Stolfo, S., & Mok, K, (2000, December). Adaptive intrusion detection: A data mining approach. *Artificial Intelligence Review, 14*(6), 533–567.

Li, C., Song, Q., & Zhang, C. (2004). IDS architecture for distributed intrusion detection using mobile agents. *Proceedings of the second International Conference on Information Technology for Application* (ICITA-2004), HARBIN, CHINA 9–11 January 2004.

Mardini, Maged. (2002, May). *Case study in firewall and intrusion detection integration.* GSEC 1.4.

Mehdi, S., & Ghorbani, A. A. (2002). *Application of belief-desire-intention agents in intrusion detection & response.* Retrieved March, 2004, from http://dev.hil.unb.ca/Texts/PST/pdf/shajari.pdf

Mell, P., & McLarson, M. (1999, September). Mobile agent attack resistant distributed hierarchical intrusion detection systems. *Proceedings of the Second International Workshop on Recent Advances in Intrusion Detection (RAID99).* Symposium conducted at Purdue University.

Mell, P., Hu, V., Lippmann, R., Haines, J., & Zissman, M. (2002). *An overview of issues in testing intrusion detection* (NIST IR 7007, National Institute of Standards and Technology). Retrieved May 26, 2004, from http://csrc.nist.gov/publications/nistir/nistir-7007.pdf

Mell, P., Marks, D., & McLarson, M. (2000, November). A denial-of-service resistant intrusion detection architecture. *Computer Networks* [Special issue on intrusion detection]., Elsevier Science BV, November 2000.

Porras, P., Schnackenberg, D., Staniford-Chen, S., Stillman, M., & Wu, F. (1998, October). *The common intrusion detection framework architecture (CIDF).* Paper presented at the Information Survivability Workshop, Orlando FL.

Ptacek, T.H., & Newsham, T.N. (1998). Insertion, evasion, and denial of service: Eluding network intrusion detection (Tech. Rep.). *Secure Networks Inc.* Retrieved May 26, 2004, from http://secinf.net/info/ids/idspaper/idspaper.html

Queiroz, J. D. de, Costa Carmo L. F. R. da, & Pirmez, L. (1999, September). An autonomous mobile agent system to protect new generation networked applications. *Second Annual Workshop on Recent Advances in Intrusion Detection.* Symposium conducted in Rio de Janeiro, Brazil.

Spafford, E. H., & Zamboni, D. (2000, October). Intrusion detection using autonomous agents. *Computer Networks 34*(4), 547–570.

Warrender, C., Forrest, S., & Pearlmutter, B. (1999, May). Detecting intrusions using system calls: Alternative data models. *Proceedings of IEEE Symposium on Security and Privacy.* Los Alamitos, CA: IEEE Computer Society.

## FURTHER READING

Barriere L., Flocchini, P., Fraigniaud, P., & Santoro, N. (2002, August). Capture of an intruder by mobile agents. *Proceedings of the Fourteenth Annual ACM Symposium on parallel Algorithms and Architectures*, 200–209, ACM Press, Winnipeg, Canada.

Chari, S.N., & Cheng. P.C. (2003, May). BlueBox: A policy-driven host-based intrusion detection system. *ACM Transactions on Information and System Security*, 6(2), 173–200.

Helmer, G., Wong, J., Slagell, M., Honavar, V., Miller, L., & Lutz, R. (2002) *A Software Fault Tree Approach to Requirements Specification of an Intrusion Detection System.* Requirements Engineering. Vol. 7(4), pp. 207–220.

Roesch, M. (1999, November). Snort: Lightweight intrusion detection for networks. *Proceedings of LISA '99:13th Systems Administration Conference.* Symposium conducted in Seattle, WA.

# Contingency Planning Management

Marco Cremonini and Pierangela Samarati, *University of Milan, Italy*

## INTRODUCTION

*Disaster recovery* (DR) comprises a set of activities aimed at recovering and restoring critical business assets after the occurrence of an unforeseen event that has impaired corporate functions. From the 1970s era of EDP mainframes and centralized data centers until recently, DR has been associated with protecting against the consequences of external catastrophic events (e.g., floods, fires, or earthquakes). In turn, recovery and restoration activities were mostly focused on *physical facilities* and *IT assets* (data storages in particular) that could have been damaged.

However, the way in which companies are organized and managed has changed dramatically in recent years. Even the very nature of business assets has changed with the advent of Internet-based service-oriented companies, shifting from the provision of physical tangible goods alone to providing functions and services that could be operated in a wide range of different ways. DR has changed accordingly to meet the new business requirements, although mainframes and data centers have not disappeared and physical disasters may still occur.

Therefore, the field of DR has grown in complexity to handle both old and new requirements and to comply with newer business models that coexist with traditional industrial processes. For these reasons, the focus today has shifted from such tasks as effectively backing up data, recovering data centers, and rerouting telecommunications to ensuring the *continuous availability of entire business processes* – with the technology infrastructure taking a critical but no longer exclusive role (Rothstein, 2003). Setting this objective as the overall goal gives an enormous importance to the time factor: if downtime periods must be the shortest possible, then recovery and restoration must be faster and faster. In the old days of DR, a 72-hour downtime period was a reasonable *recovery-time*

*objective* (RTO). Today, a 24-hour RTO is considered the minimum acceptable standard for every DR plan, with requirements for RTOs in the range of a few hours or even minutes for those industrial sectors that are more exposed to economic losses as consequences of downtime periods. Sometimes, even planning for minutes of downtime as an acceptable objective seems insufficient today; the concept of recovery-time itself is questioned in favor of the goal of no downtime, planned or unplanned. In some cases–for example, financial services completely based on Internet connections–even the shortest downtime could result in severe losses, possibly reinforced by growing legal and contractual mandates. Hence, continuous availability is often a requirement to be taken literally when DR solutions are planned.

Given this new scenario, redundancy requirements of data and processes have migrated from DR alone, which involves an IT solution for recovering the existing infrastructure after a disaster, to *business continuity planning*, which includes not only recovery but also continuous implementation of best practices for data and process replication.

In this chapter, we discuss issues related to DR planning, which today should be considered one of the essential parts of *business continuity management* (BCM). In particular, the focus of DR planning is to restore the operability of systems that support mission-critical activities and critical business processes. The objective is for the organization to return to normal operations as soon as possible. Because many mission-critical business processes depend on a technology infrastructure consisting of applications, data, and IT hardware, the DR plan should be an IT-focused plan.

This chapter is organized as follows. First, we discuss the effects on BCM of the growing dependence of business-critical activities on the IT infrastructure and how this issue has changed the requirements for an effective DR plan. The causes of downtime are then explored, and in particular, we point out that modern organizations are mostly concerned with so-called small disasters (e.g., system failures, power outages, telecommunication interruption, and so on) and their management, which has modified the BCM focus in most cases. After that, we present the principal characteristics of BCM planning and introduce the importance of a business impact analysis as a fundamental activity for understanding the business needs of an organization and thus providing sound technical measures for DR. In the context of BCM, we introduce the notion of risk management, which includes the need for analyzing, mitigating, and transferring risks. The chapter then presents backups and alternate sites as the main techniques for data recovery and business continuity after the advent of failures. We also discuss failure issues in the emerging Web-hosting service scenario. To conclude the discussion, we provide a reference template for BCM/DR planning. Finally, the chapter ends with a short analysis of an important issue that is often overlooked in BCM literature: how BCM solutions relate to technology investments and, in particular, to a period of global economic difficulties. We suggest that BCM solutions should be made modular and suitable for the needs of small and mid-sized companies.

## GROWING DEPENDENCE ON THE IT INFRASTRUCTURE

For many years, corporations have placed most of their critical information assets into automated systems, and more recently, they have adopted business models largely based on the Internet. Although providing more efficiency, cost reduction, and competitive advantage, these developments have also increased corporations' dependence on the information technology (IT) infrastructure and therefore the potential economic losses caused by its failure. More than ever, a loss of access to the IT infrastructure will prove to be, in many cases, fatal for the business of affected companies. It is therefore crucial for companies to consider precise plans for counteracting possible events that may cause such interruptions. Examples of companies that failed to recover their businesses after a prolonged interruption of IT functions, caused by floods or fires, for example, are well known and documented (Hiles, 2002; Kaye, 2001; Noakes-Fry & Diamond, 2001; Toigo, 1999, 2001a).

E-business and Internet connections are shortening recovery-time requirements and changing the way we think about DR planning; full 24/7 operations and zero downtime are now commonly seen as business necessities. Although traditional countermeasures to natural disasters should still be provided (e.g., keeping backup data in locations out of the area possibly affected by natural disasters), a wide spectrum of other risks (e.g., cyber attacks) has to be considered. In addition, critical business processes must be analyzed and recovered much faster than in the past: downtimes of days (the usual time window for natural disasters) are definitely no longer sustainable for Internet-based businesses.

Nevertheless, many enterprises still have minimal contingency plans in place to ensure business continuity for their business requirements. Managers fail to plan for DR in the new project development life cycle, which results in more risks and exposures than in the past. From a technological standpoint, some managers and planners still do not understand the intrinsic fragility of the new architectures for the e-business to which they are migrating. Consequently, they do not understand fully the increased requirements for business continuity, do not plan for the inevitable failures, do not mitigate the risks, and are not prepared to sustain the consequences.

Especially since the year 2000, companies have made massive investments in reengineering their business processes and have realized that those investments need protection from events other than natural disasters, including outages, power failures, information security incidents, and misconfigurations. New methodologies, techniques, and commercial products have been developed to manage backups and to speed up recovery. It is now possible to plan for a recovery time of just a few hours or even minutes for many of the most common "small disasters" from which a massively network-based company may suffer frequently. The "zero downtime" goal, however, still sounds more like a utopian dream than a real-world objective or like something that resembles the "100% secure" promise of certain security solutions: a misleading commercial strategy that does not tackle the real difficulties of managing complex systems and diverges from the most realistic approach, which is made up of efforts to analyze, prevent, and mitigate threats; reduce losses; accept a certain level of risk; and in general manage security issues.

## CAUSES OF DOWNTIMES: THE PREVALENCE OF SMALL DISASTERS

Downtimes in business services might be caused by several reasons:

- equipment failure (e.g., disk crashes)
- disruption of power supply or telecommunications (e.g., blackouts or digging in road works)
- application failures or database corruption (e.g., misconfigurations or improper maintenance)
- human error (e.g., improper technical actions)
- insufficient technical staff (e.g., strikes or coincident emergencies)
- malicious software (e.g., viruses or worms)
- hacking and Internet intrusions (e.g., random targets or specifically selected targets)
- fire
- natural disasters (e.g., floods, earthquakes, or hurricanes)

Clearly, downtimes might be the effect of or worsened by a combination of causes; for instance, an emergency that could have been managed well without losses for the company may become catastrophic if it happens when key technical personnel are unavailable or are already busy solving another failure. Problems may even arise as a

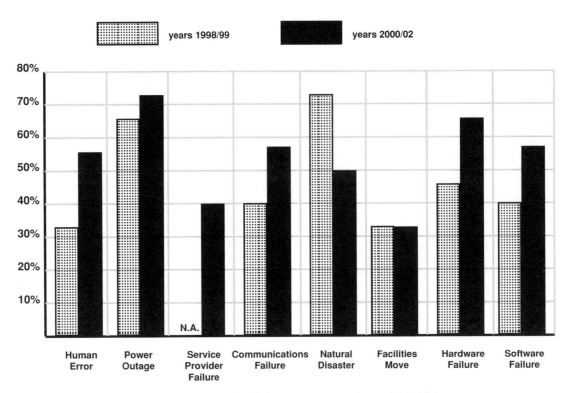

**Figure 1:** Causes of IT failures, years 1998/99 and 2000/02.

side effect of events that do not affect a company directly. For instance, if a company has an emergency, this event may impair the proper functioning or physical access to all locations in a certain area (e.g., incidents in chemical plants).

Causes of failure can be characterized further based on two aspects: (1) the *likelihood of occurrence* and (2) the *potential damage* that they can provoke. These two properties reflect, respectively, a *probabilistic* and a *quantitative* description. For instance, such events as sabotage, floods, or fire, which are usually considered in traditional DR plans, are rare, but when they happen, they are often catastrophic. On the other hand, such events as equipment failures or software errors are less catastrophic in nature, but may occur frequently and represent almost day-to-day problems for system administrators. In the BCM literature, these second types of failures are often informally called *small disasters* to point out their different nature and impact than the traditional disasters taken into account in early DR plans.

Usually, these small disasters are not devastating for a company, and in past years (in the pre-Internet age), they were not included in DR planning. However, with today's companies relying more and more on networked systems, complex distributed multicomponent architectures, and the Internet as a primary business enabler, short but frequent downtime periods can become a major problem in terms of competition, reputation, and revenue losses (Bounds, 2003; Toigo, 2001b).

How to strike a balance in investing decisions between prevention measures focused on rare but catastrophic events and those focused on small disasters is one of the most difficult challenges faced by modern BCM plans. In the old days, DR was focused only on the former; modern

information security and system/network administration techniques are focused only on the latter. BCM should encompass both, thereby planning for all risks that may affect a company.

To this end, the *2002 CPM/KPMG Business Continuity Benchmark Survey* (Hagg, 2002) presented some interesting findings for the year 2002. These results are similar to those of year 2000 and have been aggregated for the purpose of this chapter. The aggregated results shown here are only indicative of certain trends and do not reflect any statistical interpolation made by the author. Compared to these findings are those obtained in years 1998 and 1999 (again, results obtained by CPM/KPMG for these years are similar and for presentation purposes they are shown in aggregated form). Figure 1 summarizes these statistics.

These results demonstrate how business continuity can be impaired by multiple causes that range from human errors, such as misconfigurations or mere operational mistakes, to problems coming from the power supply that a UPS cannot sustain, communications interruptions that rapidly increase the harm suffered in the most damaging failures, and hardware/software failures that might happen frequently in huge IT infrastructures. Considering the relatively short time period between the two sets of results, the differences between causes of IT failures in 1998/99 and those in 2000/02 are notable. Traditional DR issues connected to natural disasters are now perceived and experienced as considerably less important than other issues. The most prevalent causes of failure that respondents of the CPM/KPMG survey point out as priorities are infrastructural facilities needed for supporting all business functions (power supply and communications), hardware/software components needed for running business services together with the essential human factor,

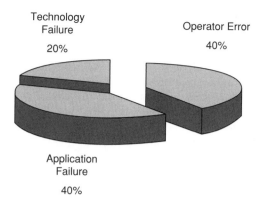

**Figure 2:** Humans versus hardware versus software as downtime causes.

and the increasing reliance upon external parties (e.g., service providers) that involves contractual obligations and service-level agreements (SLAs). It is easy to recognize in these results the changing nature of organizations and processes, which are oriented more and more toward networked, distributed, and Internet-based business models.

Other studies confirm the results of the CPM/KPMG survey and even add some more information, such as comparing how often a downtime is caused by a human error instead of a technology or application failure; in short, this measure compares humans versus hardware versus software. Figure 2 shows the results of this study by the Gartner Group (Scott & Natis, 1999).

According to this study, only 20% of downtime is caused by technology failures including hardware (servers and network devices), environmental factors (e.g., cooling and power outages), and natural disasters. By contrast, 40% of downtime is caused by application failures, which include software bugs, operating system crashes, performance slowdowns, incorrect updates, and changes to software. The remaining 40% of failures is due to human errors. In other words, according to these results, failures are mainly due to people and process issues, including software, whereas infrastructural components are more robust and reliable (Kaye, 2001; Noakes-Fry & Diamond, 2001, 2002).

These results should come as no surprise; actually, all technicians know that the most frequent causes of outages are application bugs and connectivity failures. Applications frequently fail because of all sorts of problems, including code bugs, bad design, weak requirement analysis, inconsistent tests, misconfigurations, erroneous installation or deployment, incompatibility with the run-time environment, and conflicts with other applications. Connectivity instead fails due to misconfiguration of such devices as routers, switches, or DNSs, sometimes caused by the company's staff and other times by Internet service providers (ISPs) and application service providers (ASPs).

Based on these figures, many experienced BCM planners suggest that organizations select products and vendors with a good reputation of robustness and be skeptical about the latest products because they often provide exciting new features but at the price of less reliability.

Adopting a prudent approach is important for software products because they have been one of the principal causes of small disasters, but is of particular significance for infrastructural hardware components whose robustness and reliability impact on the whole organization.

## THE COST OF DOWNTIME

To evaluate how much downtime periods may cost, companies must consider all the components that comprise their business and how each may be affected by system failures, including not only lost current revenues but also the loss of any future or potential revenues. Because many companies today have structured their organization across interdependent business units and have extended their supply chains, the impact of downtime may spread through many interconnections and hence grow rapidly. No longer restricted to a core business, businesses may experience the effects of downtime on related businesses, partners, and customers all along the value chain.

Moreover, companies' increasing reliance on a few business-critical technologies is another aspect that increases the severity of downtime impact. Internet-based companies, which require connectivity and availability of their Web sites 24 hours a day, 7 days a week, 365 days a year, are in such a situation—they are completely based on Internet connectivity for their business, which has made them the victim of unforeseen problems. In the last few years they have suffered all sorts of system and/or network outages and have been threatened by distributed denial of service attacks.

Downtime may have the following effects, with their attendant costs and losses:

- brand image recovery
- loss of share value
- loss of interests on overnight balances
- delay in customer accounting
- loss of control over debtors
- loss of credit control and increased bad debt
- delayed benefits of profits from new projects or products
- loss of revenue for service contracts
- cost of replacement of building, plant, equipment, and software
- loss of customers
- loss of profits
- liability claims
- additional costs for advertising and marketing

A classification of costs should divide them into tangible and intangible costs (Merchantz, 2002), which we discuss next.

### Tangible Costs

Tangible costs are easily identified and are often (though not always) easily measured and may include the following:

- *Lost revenue* – This is the most obvious cost, as the company cannot conduct business and balance sheets state that unmistakably. Just looking at normal hourly sales and then multiplying that figure by the number of hours of downtime provides a good estimate of lost revenues. However, as said, this must be regarded as only one component of the total cost of downtime and, taken singularly, normally underestimates the true loss greatly. E-business amplifies the problem because a company normally has no alternative way of conducting business and depends entirely on system availability.

- *Lost productivity* – During downtime, production is blocked, and productivity lowers to zero. The same applies even when production is not blocked completely, but is just impaired because employee productivity is still affected. Evaluating lost productivity is difficult because production normally does not stop completely and employees might then engage in different duties. One way to obtain an estimate is to compute the cost of salaries and wages for the downtime time frame. Productivity value is normally higher than labor costs; hence, this figure represents a conservative evaluation of what a company has lost during downtime. In addition to pure labor costs during downtime hours, one should consider that, after the recovery effort is completed, employees will not simply go back to their normal duties, but some will probably be in charge of other recovery actions (e.g., data reentry). This represents either additional costs (e.g., if done on an overtime basis) or less productivity (e.g., if done subtracting time to usual work).

- *Late fees and penalties* – Some companies work under contracts that include penalties for late deliveries. If system downtime causes them to miss their contracted delivery dates, the penalties incurred are another cost of downtime.

- *Legal costs* – Depending on the nature of the affected systems, there could be legal costs associated with downtime. For example, a drop in the share price may induce shareholders to initiate a class-action suit if they believe that management was negligent in protecting vital assets. Other examples of legal costs are cases of business partnerships in which the failure of one company affects the business of the others or of defective products delivered as a consequence of a system failure. In addition, some public utility companies could be considered legally responsible for the suspension of a public service due to the lack of sufficient precautions and failure prevention. Evaluating possible legal costs is extremely difficult because legal aspects are complex and are strictly related to the specificities of any single case. Experiences or historical data from companies in the same business sector could give a broad estimate. For a more specific evaluation, a legal consultant should analyze in detail the risks the company may face.

- *Other costs* – Many other costs could arise, which are often specific to the particular industrial sector. For example, a fresh food producer could be forced to discard perishable goods, a manufacturer may incur costs when restarting automatic machines, a construction company may have leased machines for which the leasing period must be prolonged, and so forth.

## Intangible Costs

Intangible costs by nature are neither easy to identify nor easy to measure, but they affect the business just like tangible ones and have been the most critical cost factor in recent years in the BCM field. Think for instance about the impact of a system failure on the company's brand and reputation. The brand value does not appear in any balance sheet, but it is often one of a business's most valuable assets. There are statistics and analyses (Hiles, 2002) that correlate how the devaluation of a reputation of a company suffering a disaster affects the share price. According to these studies, the share price of a corporation suffering a disaster falls by around 5% to 8% within the first few days after a disaster. This decline is reasonable because stakeholders may consider their investments to be in danger.

What is interesting is how recovery of the share price depends on the efficiency in recovering critical business functions. Past cases have shown that efficient recovery has enabled companies to regain the confidence of financial analysts quickly, and their share values have climbed back to the prices preceding the disaster, even increasing by 10% to 15% in the following 100 days. Companies that recovered with many difficulties, instead, were penalized with declining share values, around 15% on average (Hiles, 2002). These facts demonstrate how a company's reputation affects such tangible items as the share price, not only permitting a company to rapidly regain share prices held before a disaster but even improving on those quotes. An inefficient recovery, in contrast, harms the company's reputation, which may have a perverse effect on share prices.

Another intangible cost is lost opportunities. During a downtime period, potential customers who would have been conducting business with the company suffering the failure may choose a competitor. This lost opportunity not only causes an immediate loss but also may have persistent negative effects because those customers could be lost forever. Calculating such loss of future revenue is very difficult. Historical data showing the rate of new customers in a given period could provide a broad estimate.

After recovery, the company's management might be forced to initiate an expensive corporate image and marketing campaign and a promotional campaign with significant price discounts to regain the confidence of customers and rebuild its reputation. The cost of such promotional and marketing campaigns can be evaluated precisely and must be taken into account as possible additional costs of downtime. Statistics have shown that an organization may spend three or more times its normal annual marketing budget in the aftermath of a disaster to retain customer confidence and to retain or regain market share.

## BCM PLANNING

*Business continuity management (BCM) planning* consists of a set of activities aimed at identifying the impact of potential losses, defining and realizing viable recovery strategies, and developing recovery plans for ensuring the continuity of business services. Disaster recovery planning is one of the components of a BCM plan and encompasses a set of activities aimed at reducing the *likelihood* and the *impact of disaster events* on critical business assets (NIST, 2002; Toigo, 1999; Wold, 2002a, b,c). BCM and DR planning are as complicated as any major system development project, with many stages of analysis and an overall activity set encompassing all critical assets, business functions, and technological solutions.

Convincing corporate management to invest in BCM planning is often a challenge greater than dealing with the technical problems of backing up critical systems, minimizing downtime, and maintaining network connectivity. To complicate matters, investing in DR capabilities is not a one-time event, but must be sustained over time, because every DR plan needs to be tested, reviewed, and updated regularly to be effective. In addition, DR planning needs to be managed, improved, and updated in sync with modification of the IT infrastructure and of critical assets. For these reasons, management consensus is vital for every BCM plan that, in the best of circumstances, will enable failure avoidance, detecting and reacting to potential problems before they become disasters.

In their efforts to convince senior management to invest in BCM planning, experienced BCM planners have found that several typical issues are key. Among them, the most relevant is a careful *justification of the plan's expenditures*. BCM plans should be documented adequately with an in-depth analysis of the risks addressed in the plan, the benefits for the corporation, the possible impact on revenues of an insufficient BCM plan, the estimates of the cost of downtime, and the possible savings on insurance costs (Kaye, 2001; Toigo, 1999).

The process of managing business continuity, in a classification scheme inspired by the *Business Continuity Management–Good Practice Guidelines* (BCI, 2002) of the Business Continuity Institute, has these five phases:

1. understanding the company's business
2. recognizing the risks to business activities
3. developing recovery strategies, such as backup, alternate site, or replication
4. exercising, rehearsing, and periodically reviewing the DR-BC plan
5. creating a BCM management plan

## Understanding the Company's Business

Understanding a company's business requires an analysis of the operational aspects of the company. This analysis should determine what are the key business objectives and the products or services of the business objectives, when the business objectives should be achieved, who is involved in the achievement of business objectives, and how the business objectives are achieved. This analysis should result in the clear identification of *mission-critical activities*, and they should be the focus of BCM planning. Elements of mission-critical activities are human resources, stakeholders, suppliers, customers, facilities, functions, processes, materials, technology, telecommunications,

and data. In addition, for each mission-critical activity, it is necessary to identify *single points of failure*, which means that there are no alternatives to certain elements or components; therefore, more attention must be given to them in the BCM planning process.

After producing the outcomes of the initial analysis—mission-critical activities and single points of failure—this first phase proceeds with two distinct but complementary subprocesses: the *business impact analysis* (BIA) and a *risk assessment and analysis* (RA).

## Business Impact Analysis

The BIA encompasses activities aimed at identifying, quantifying, and qualifying the business impact and other effects of a mission-critical activity failure on a company. The fundamental outcome of the BIA is the identification of the minimum level of resources needed to accomplish the company's business objectives in terms of an acceptable recovery time—recovery-time objectives (RTO)—and an acceptable recovery status of assets: recovery-point objectives (RPO). The process that permits achieving such results is commonly called *business impact resource recovery analysis* (BIRRA). The outcomes of the BIA can then be summarized as the following:

- Identification of mission-critical activities, along with their dependencies and single points of failure
- Financial and nonfinancial impacts of a disruption, failure, or loss of one or more mission-critical activities for a given time frame
- Resources recovery priorities for each mission-critical activity based on the criticality of resources and on the associated sustainable time window and cost considerations; prioritizing recovery strategies can optimize allocations and expenditures for the recovery process
- Recovery objectives in terms of recovery-time objectives (RTO), recovery-point objectives (RPO), and the minimum level of acceptable business continuity to sustain the company's operations
- Business impact recovery resources analysis (BIRRA), which identifies the minimum level of resources necessary to achieve the recovery objectives according to the resource recovery objectives of each mission-critical activity

The BIA should involve staff members from several areas of the company. For instance, business managers are better able to analyze business impacts, either financial or nonfinancial, whereas senior management should be involved in determining recovery priorities among mission-critical activities. On the contrary, the operational and technical staff members who usually work with the company's resources might be better able to do the BIRRA.

## RISK MANAGEMENT

Risk is defined as the possibility of suffering harm or loss, and risk management is the process of planning for such eventuality (Wold & Shriver, 2002). The goal of risk management is not to eliminate all risks (which would be impossible in practice), but rather to find an *acceptable balance between reducing risk and preparing the organization for losses*. The risk management process has three steps:

1. *Risk analysis*: identify the types of losses that may occur, determine the causes and the likelihood that a loss will occur, and estimate the resulting cost for the organization
2. *Risk mitigation*: identify actions to reduce or eliminate the likelihood of occurrence of each risk, determine the cost of those actions, and produce a cost-benefit analysis of the actions for each risk and loss
3. *Risk transfer*: address the losses that may occur despite preventive actions and consider transferring those losses to insurers or third parties, such as service providers, vendors, or outsourcers in general

## Risk Analysis

A risk analysis includes these activities:

- *Identify existing risks* to mission-critical activities resulting from the BIA. For each mission-critical activity, threats and their possible sources should be identified.
- *Establish the likelihood and impact* of each possible threat. This analysis is needed for defining priorities and planning for preventive measures and recovery actions. The clear identification of the relationship between the likelihood and the impact of each risk is a key component.

Define BCM strategies for each failure cause, which means that the BCM planner must define approaches to manage the risk and estimate the trade-off between sustaining the possible losses and implementing a preventive strategy.

## Risk Mitigation

Risk mitigation is a process aimed at limiting the likelihood of risks and the potential losses those risks can cause (Kaye, 2001). The process of mitigating risks can be summarized in the following steps:

- *Avoid the causes*. Make conservative and prudential technology choices for critical assets: avoid technology risks by developing services in a robust manner and with the support of reliable platforms instead of adopting the latest technology without testing it for reliability (usually riskier), unless it has been proven to give a sensible competitive advantage.
- *Reduce the frequency*. All IT infrastructure components should be chosen based on their ability to ensure a low rate of failure. Operating systems and software/hardware platforms of different vendors (or different versions produced by the same vendor) often have different failure frequencies. To enforce the risk management strategy, reliability, and not just performance and features, should be evaluated carefully when purchasing technology.
- *Minimize the impact*. Because the frequency of failures and outages can never be reduced to zero, a risk

mitigation strategy should analyze all the possible single points of failure, the failure of which may cause major losses in terms of downtime and extent of service interruption. Redundancy is the typical strategy that can be applied to servers, network devices, and internal components.
- *Reduce the duration*. Minimizing the duration of downtime is the ultimate goal of every DR plan—the longer the downtime, the greater the loss of revenue. Many strategies can be adopted to speed up the recovery of data and functions. These may involve on-site hardware spares, on-site staff, efficient backup solutions, and alternative operative locations.

## Risk Transfer

Risks that cannot be sustained by a company can be transferred to a third-party that then assumes the risks in exchange for a service fee (Kaye, 2001). Hiles (2002) estimated that, in average, up to 40% of actual losses could be transferred, but no more than that. Risk transfer can assume two forms: insurance or outsourcing.

*Insurance* is the traditional way of transferring risks that cannot be mitigated with in-house solutions or transferred by purchasing the service outside. Most insurers offer coverage even for risks related to Internet-based threats, such as intrusions or denial of service attacks. With *outsourcing*, a third party provides a specific service in place of an in-house solution. This third party can then assume the risk of losses that the company may incur, either by refunding the fee paid by the company (as in case of Web-hosting services) or reimbursing the losses (as in case of vendors). Risk transfer is established via a contract that usually includes a service-level agreement (SLA) that should guarantee the company that purchases the service.

Risk transfer is a suitable solution in many situations, but the trade-off between the cost of possible downtime, if the service is realized in-house, and the cost of the purchased service with a certain quality level should be evaluated carefully. A careful evaluation of the return on the outsourcing investment should therefore be done to determine whether the strategy is convenient (downtime costs *versus* service fees). Consider, for example, networked services, Web hosting, and mainframe hosting, for which outsourcing is the common choice today.

When purchasing a critical service from a vendor instead of managing it in-house, the company signs an agreement concerning the level of service guaranteed. The parties agree on a certain uptime guarantee, expressed as a percentage of time of availability (usually a value between 99% and 100%) of the purchased service. Clearly, the higher the uptime guarantee, the more costly the service, and after a certain percentage of uptime guarantee, the cost that a company would pay for a given service level is not worth the benefit gained. Penalty clauses are normally defined in the SLA, which charges the Internet service provider (ISP) with monetary fines if it is unable to comply with the uptime guarantee. However, because there are loopholes in SLAs that can be exploited for the benefit of the service provider, legal clauses defined in the SLA should be reviewed carefully. Many ISPs promise an uptime of 99.99%, but do not actually comply with their claim because of a host of limitations related to infrastructure, government policies, inefficient resources, etc.

# RECOVERY STRATEGIES: BACKUP AND RECOVERY OF DATA

Key to an effective recovery of business functions is the availability of all the company's data, as well as the reconfiguration of all critical components of the IT infrastructure (e.g., backup of servers and network devices configuration, patches, passwords, routing tables, and firewall rules).

Backup and recovery of data should achieve two fundamental goals:

1. Backup should be done with a minimal impact on the production environment and, ideally, should be performed without blocking transaction execution.
2. Recovery should be efficient so to minimize the time frame necessary to restore the data and bring the system back to its operational state. The efficiency of the recovery process is a key factor for the effective restoration of the company's business functions as a delay in recovery could cause a severe loss of market share.

Although the need to maintain backup copies of data is well recognized, many companies overlook the need to make a copy of the system configurations. This requirement is overlooked so frequently because of its intrinsic organizational nature: system management and day-to-day administration of the IT infrastructure, such as a change in routing tables or firewall rules, installation of patches, or the like, must always be documented fully to be backed up. In addition, procedures should be put in place to make sure that every modification to system components—the ones needed by mission-critical activities and identified in the BIRRA, at least—is reported in backup copies. Effective recovery also requires that media for custom and purchased software together with their license information be kept off-site. Last, but not least, all documentation related to the BCM and DR plan should be backed up. It may seem obvious that BCM documentation and plans need to be available when an emergency calls for its activation, but this might not be the case if they were not kept in a safe and reachable place (e.g., off-line at an alternate site).

Some considerations should be devoted to the particular backup requirements of desktop computers and portable systems, which have some peculiarities with respect to servers. Often the PC data backup process is not automated (e.g., saving data on backed-up file servers), so it is a duty of users to manually save critical data on backed-up servers. This good practice should be governed by an appropriate usage policy (i.e., a documentation possibly subscribed to by each user stating, among other things, that each user should take care of saving his or her critical data on a backed-up server and not locally). Intermediate managers should enforce this policy, devoting particular attention to having training sessions during which users should be instructed about the importance of this recovery requirement. Providing an automatic backup and restoration process for PCs requires *interoperability and platform standardization*. Usually recommended are homogeneous platform operating systems, configurations, and applications among the organization's PCs and portable devices (NIST, 2002).

Backups should be kept in a safe place, where they cannot be affected by the consequences of a disaster; doing so enable their recovery in the event of a disaster that compromises or makes their original data unavailable. This has been for decades DR's golden rule, especially for mainframe-centric IT infrastructures. Traditionally, backup has been seen as a batch process, running during night hours, which stores on tapes all relevant information produced during that workday. Although this process is still used and is necessary for the majority of organizations, in many others cases it is now outdated. With the increase in Web-based services and service-oriented architectures (SOA), applications and business processes tend to be active on a 24/7 basis. Therefore, there is no longer the notion of "night hours," which was meant to be that window of inactivity of business transactions perfectly suited to take a snapshot of data. In many real-world scenarios, transactions are always running, and information is always accessed and possibly updated. In addition, the amount of data to be managed is growing every year at a terrific rate. Many commentators refer to the ever-growing amount of data that need to be managed, backed up, and restored as "the explosion of data" to emphasize both its impressive growth and chaotic nature (Campbell, 2000; Kaye, 2001; Nicolett & Berg, 1999; Toigo, 2001a).

## Techniques for Data Backup and Recovery

The development of data recovery strategies requires that effective backup strategies be in place. These in turn, should be based on priorities identified in the BIA and BIRRA processes. For backup purposes, business-critical data can be classified as follows:

- *Critical* – These are data that must be preserved for legal reasons or for use in business-critical processes and must be restored as soon as possible in the event of a disaster.
- *Vital* – These data are needed for important, but not critical, business processes. A loss of these data would represent a severe damage and economic loss for the company. These data may have privacy requirements.
- *Sensitive* – These data are used in normal business operations; they could be reconstructed from alternative sources in the event of loss but at some cost.
- *Noncritical* – These data could be reconstructed with minimal cost in the event of loss. They have no privacy or security requirements.

Such a classification should drive the organization of backup precedence and priorities, optimize recovery, and therefore minimize downtime.

Some of the main strategies and technologies for backing up data are summarized by Toigo (1999) as follows:

- *Server image backup.* Image backup creates a physical image of an entire disk. It operates at the physical disk level by transferring sectors of physical data storage blocks from hard disk to tape. It has fast transfer rates and provides complete server backup by transferring the entire content of the hard disk as a single unit. This technology requires the system to be inactive during the backup.
- *Snapshot or versioning backup.* This technique is fast because, after an initial complete image backup, it proceeds incrementally by backing up the modifications only. It works with block-level copies on a partition basis. It is widely used in traditional tape-based backup systems.
- *Full volume backup on a file-by-file basis.* Complete data sets are copied over the production network to backup devices. A process controlled by the server initiates the transfer to backup devices.
- *Incremental or differential file backup.* Files are compared with their version in the preceding backup, and only the changed files are backed up again. Differential backup keeps separate versions of the same backed-up files, whereas incremental backup just keeps the newer version.
- *Backup using object replication.* Software defines logical objects, including disk partition tables, boot volume, security information, system volume, and user data volumes. Logical objects are regarded as a single logical unit, and all data can be copied at once.
- *Electronic tape vaulting.* This process replaces the manual procedures for handling tapes stored in off-site storage facilities and for moving tapes between locations. To provide for immediate access to data stored on tapes, it exploits a wide area network (WAN) connection between the company facility and the off-site storage facility where the tapes are stored. Such technologies as shadowing and multiplexing controllers allow the simultaneous duplication of backup data streams in two or more tape devices. This way a company could make both a local backup (for complete recovery in the event of a disaster) and an electronic vaulting on a remote storage facility (to preserve data from a disaster, such as a flood or fire that affects the company site).
- *Remote disk mirroring.* It is another alternative to handling tapes physically. The content of disks is duplicated in near real time to a remote disk volume. The same concept is applied to redundant array of inexpensive disks (RAID) technology as a means of fault tolerance, rather than disaster recovery.

Making use of an off-site storage facility is the safest choice for preserving backups. The remote storage facility should be in a location that is unlikely to be affected by the same disasters that might affect the main company site. It could be a branch of the company or a commercial system recovery facility offering this service. Although companies with decentralized sites could choose to keep backups in their different sites, commercial storage facilities offer backup storage as a service, including media transportation, safe storage, and recovery (Nicolett & Berg, 1999; NIST, 2002; Toigo, 1999).

When selecting an off-site storage facility and vendor, there are some key factors to keep in mind:

- *Geographic area:* Distance from the organization and the possibility of the storage site being affected by the same disaster as the organization (locations geographically close to the organization are likely to be affected by the same natural disasters–setting up the DR site at a distance of at least 100 miles from the main site is recommended).
- *Accessibility:* Length of time to retrieve the data from storage and the storage facility's operating hours
- *Security:* Security capabilities of the storage facility and employee confidentiality, according to the data's sensitivity and security requirements
- *Environment:* Structural and environmental conditions of the storage facility, such as temperature, humidity, fire prevention, and power management control
- *Cost:* Cost of shipping, operational fees, and recovery services
- *Connectivity:* Robust, reliable WAN links between the primary and secondary sites

## ENSURING CONTINUITY OF OPERATIONS: ALTERNATE SITES STRATEGY

DR plans traditionally account for natural disasters as the first threat to an organization. Hence, in addition to the safe storage of data backups, it is necessary to provide an organization with a plan for the continuation of its business functions while occurred to its site and hardware assets suffer severe damage. A DR plan should then include a strategy to recover and perform system operations at an alternate facility. Generally, three types of alternate site strategies are possible (NIST, 2002):

1. dedicated site owned or operated by the organization
2. reciprocal agreement with an external entity (e.g., a business partner)
3. commercial leased facility

As prospective alternate sites are evaluated, the DR planner should ensure that the system's security, management, operational, and technical controls are compatible with the prospective site. Controls may include measures for network security, such as firewalls and intrusion detection systems, and physical access controls. If the service is purchased from a vendor, an SLA must be negotiated carefully. It must clearly state all conditions, such as testing time; workspace; security, hardware, and telecommunication requirements; support services; and recovery time frame.

The DR planners should be aware that a commercial facility usually hosts many customers, which may all be affected by the same natural disaster simultaneously. Hence, the commercial facility could be asked to recover several customers simultaneously, but might not have enough resources to do so properly. In that case, the commercial facility would tend to set priorities among its

**Table 1** Alternate site characteristics.

| Site | Cost | Hardware Equipment | Telecomm- unications | Setup Time | Location |
|------|------|--------------------|----------------------|------------|----------|
| **Cold** | Low | None | None | Long | Fixed |
| **Warm** | Medium | Partial | Partial/Full | Medium | Fixed |
| **Hot** | Medium/High | Full | Full | Short | Fixed |
| **Mobile** | High | Dependent | Dependent | Dependent | Not Fixed |
| **Mirrored** | High | Full | Full | None | Fixed |

customers and not treat all of them at the same level of service. Unfortunately, this scenario is realistic, and for this reason it is extremely important to negotiate a clear and extremely detailed SLA with the commercial vendor, with defined legal and penalty clauses that address how possible disasters will be handled and how priority status is determined.

Regardless of the type of alternate site strategy used, commercial facilities provide different services and have different levels of readiness with respect to the goal of immediate resumption of all business functions. The following classification of facilities also reflects the different commercial services offered on the market (NIST, 2002; Nicolett & Berg, 1999; Toigo, 1999):

- A *cold site* typically consists of a facility with adequate space and infrastructure (electric power, telecommunication connections, and environmental control) to support the IT infrastructure. However, the cold site contains neither IT equipment nor office automation equipment, such as telephones, fax machines, or copiers. The organization leasing a cold site needs to provide all the necessary equipment.
- A *warm site* is a partially equipped office space containing some hardware, software, telecommunication connections, and power sources. The warm site is kept in an operational status so it can be promptly made fully operative in the event of a disaster at the company's main site.
- A *hot site* is a fully functional and immediately ready facility equipped with all the needed hardware, software, telecommunication connections and equipment, and power sources. Hot sites are usually staffed 24 hours a day, 7 days a week. Recovery of business functions is guaranteed to be extremely fast.
- A *mobile site* is a self-contained, transportable shell equipped to restore immediately the subset of the most critical business functions, including telecommunication facilities. Major commercial vendors lease these mobile sites and keep them located in strategic places to enable them to reach most of the industrial plants in a relatively short time. However, to guarantee an on-time recovery, a company should sign agreements with vendors to have the mobile site ready in a time frame compatible with its business requirements.
- A *mirrored site* maintains an almost exact replica of the IT infrastructure of the company's main site and is always ready to recover all the business functions. Recovery is almost immediate through a mirrored site.

It is usually owned and operated by the company, given the high degree of customization and specificity required.

The *Contingency Planning Guide for Information Technology Systems*, published by the NIST (2002) summarizes the characteristics of the different alternate sites, as shown in Table 1.

The above solutions differ in terms of their cost and timeliness. Cold sites are less expensive to maintain, but require that the business expend considerable time to acquire and install the necessary equipment. Going down the list, we find solutions that are more expensive, but provide greater availability. Mirrored sites are the most expensive DR solution and provide almost 100% availability (i.e., minimal downtime). Because remote mirroring has gained a great deal of popularity as a reliable DR solution, we discuss it in more detail in the next section.

## Remote Mirroring

Remote mirroring techniques form the basis of many commercial systems aiming at safeguarding corporate data and providing fast recovery. However, sometimes the expectations that planners place on remote mirroring solutions are not realistic. In addition, solutions based on remote mirroring tend to be complex, both architecturally and in data management, so they can satisfy the high requirements from companies. This complexity may lead to a lack of robustness of the recovery system, misconfiguration, and improper array maintenance. The consequence could be the loss of synchrony between arrays or the storage of corrupted data. If this happens, a recovery could result in a multiplication of the disaster because it runs the risk of recovering corrupted or incoherent data (Kaye, 2001; Toigo, 2001a, b). In addition, remote mirroring does not provide for zero downtime, which is considered a requirement by some senior managers. Remote mirroring, if configured properly and implemented with high-level technology, can be much faster than many other recovery alternatives, but it cannot reduce the downtime to zero. Hence, remote mirroring is not the panacea that makes the nightmare of downtime disappear: risk management and DR planning are still mandatory. Moreover, remote mirroring is subject to data gaps, because some sort of asynchrony is usually implemented (e.g., the mirroring between the secondary and the tertiary arrays of Figure 3). Possible consequences of incoherent recovered data should be analyzed carefully in the planning stage. Such data may provoke the loss

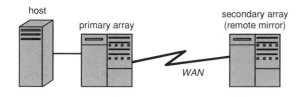

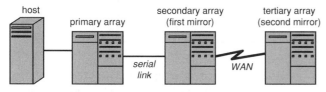

**Figure 3:** Remote mirroring configurations.

of commercial orders, payments, or shipments, if data gaps are not identified and handled properly. Solutions designed to be completely synchronous do exist, but come at high prices in terms of performances and system latency. In fact, the problem in remote mirroring has been traditionally the latency caused by the distance, possibly many hundreds of miles, between the sites, in particular when the mirroring is synchronous (i.e., writes to production disks waits for the mirrored writes to be completed and acknowledged).

Starting from the mid-1990s, the cost of high-speed bandwidth WAN decreased and vendors realized architectures that made remote mirroring one of the best solutions at an affordable cost for many companies. The typical improvement provided for three arrays, adding an intermediate site between the company and the final remote storage facility (Toigo, 1999). Figure 3 shows the traditional and the enhanced schema for remote mirroring. The benefit of the enhanced schema is twofold. First, the link between the company site and the secondary array could be a high-speed serial one, thus reducing the latency in synchronous mirroring. Second, the mirroring between the secondary and the final arrays, connected with a WAN, could be realized asynchronously, hence optimizing the mirror operation while not affecting the robustness of the DR solution.

## BACKUP AND RECOVERY FOR WEB-BASED HOSTING SERVICES

Web-hosting service providers (WHSPs) are commercial vendors that may store hundreds of Web sites in their infrastructures. Moreover, the hosted service may be complex and not merely a Web site. WHSPs can be composed of n-tier architectures with Web portals, application servers, middleware layers, and community services. Because of this increasing complexity, today it is common for an organization to purchase Web management and hosting service instead of implementing it in-house. However, like other outsourced services, customers should evaluate carefully how the service is provided and consider which guarantees the vendor provides in the event of an outage.

The primary deployment option for Web-based applications is an *Internet data center*. A growing number of enterprises are considering dual-site application architectures that split application traffic between two active sites. The active sites could be corporate data centers, commercial data centers, or both. One factor to consider carefully when purchasing services from commercial data centers is the large number of simultaneous recoveries that they will need to provide for all their customers in the event of an outage. Thus, as with hot site vendors, the customers of a Web hosting service should make sure that the outsourcer has a robust DR plan and, through clear SLAs, that it has a contractual responsibility to execute it effectively (Kaye, 2001; Toigo, 2001b).

Different technological options can be used for storage management of Web sites and Internet applications (Kaye, 2001):

- *Direct attached storage (DAS)*. The disk drives or arrays are directly connected to an individual server.
- *Network attached storage (NAS)*. High-performance general-purpose file servers are connected to Web sites via LANs.
- *Storage area networks (SAN)*. High-performance special-purpose storage systems are connected to Web servers via dedicated fiber optical links.
- *Global storage Systems (GSS)*. This is a technology for geographically replicated file systems.

Table 2 summarizes the principal characteristics of each storage solution (Kaye, 2001).

Networked storage solutions, however, can pose special difficulties that significantly degrade the speed of most tape-based solutions. For instance, in a SAN, domain servers, routers, and software delivering virtual volumes to SAN servers often manage physical disk devices. This networked infrastructure poses an increased management burden on the IT staff and is more prone to failures than the simpler DAS.

**Table 2** Web-hosting storage technologies.

| Capacity | For Static Content | For Shared Reads/Writes | For Databases |
|---|---|---|---|
| **DAS** <= 200 GB | Yes (very few Web servers) | No | Yes (good reliability using RAID) |
| **NAS** <= 10 TB | Yes (more Web servers) | Yes | Yes (very good reliability if clustered) |
| **SAN** 100 GB–100 TB | No (too expensive) | No | Yes (high reliability) |
| **GSS** 300 GB–100 TB | Yes (more locations) | Yes | No |

Most e-business applications hosted in Internet data centers are based on n-tier architectures. These multitier platforms typically include one or more Web servers, applications servers used to integrate Web technology with legacy systems, connectors and adapters, database servers storing raw data, and authentication and authorization servers filtering the user accesses and incoming connections. This complex architectural design and the interconnection of several components make these platforms clearly more prone to failures than centralized monolithic systems. These failures, often resulting in short but frequent outages, must be handled carefully in the planning stage or in negotiating SLAs with vendors. Components and replication strategies should be selected with the goal of minimizing downtime.

In addition to this class of system failures, e-business needs to face the growing rate of network attacks and denial of service. A concept that is often discussed today is "the convergence of DR and network security" for e-business applications, meaning that the two areas have much in common and more and more interdependencies. From a DR planning viewpoint, intrusions and security incidents are another cause of downtime to be considered in the risk management stage, in the BIA, and in the selection of vendors. Internet data centers should provide high-level staff skilled in network security and provide for robust security architectures and policies (Kaye, 2001; Toigo, 2001a, b).

## Storage Area Networks

Among storage technologies, the storage area network (SAN) in particular has gained wide acceptance—SANs amount to almost 50% of the current storage solutions on the market—and is today often deployed as an efficient DR technology. Tate, Cole, Gomilsek, and Van der Pijil (2000) provide a detailed presentation of SAN technology.

A SAN is a specialized, high-speed network attaching servers and storage devices using network devices, such as routers, gateways, hubs, and switches. Its main benefit is to eliminate dedicated connections between servers and storage devices. Moreover, a SAN also eliminates all restrictions on the amount of data that a server can access. A server is enabled to share a common storage environment, which may comprise many storage devices, including disk, tape, and optical storage. SAN solutions often utilize a dedicated network behind the servers, based primarily on Fiber Channel architecture. Fiber Channel provides a highly scalable bandwidth over long distances with the ability to offer full redundancy, high availability, and high performance. A SAN normally supports direct high-speed transfers between servers and storage devices in the following ways:

- *Server to storage.* This is the common method of interaction with storage devices. The SAN advantage is that the same storage device may be accessed serially or concurrently by multiple servers.
- *Server to server.* In this case, a SAN is used to enable high-speed and high-volume communications between servers.

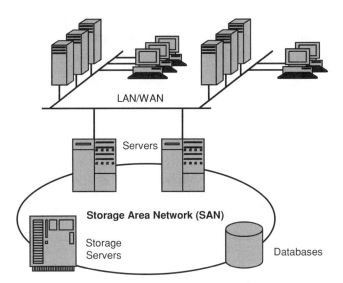

**Figure 4:** Storage area network (SAN) reference architecture.

- *Storage to storage.* With this configuration, a disk array could back up its data directly to tape across the SAN without processor intervention. Alternatively, a device could be mirrored remotely across the SAN

Figure 4 shows the typical SAN architecture.

## TRAINING, EXERCISING, AND REVIEWING THE PLAN
### Training and Exercising

Operational continuity, emergency response, and security plans should be exercised at least once a year. For example, many companies, such as Texas Instruments and Hewlett Packard, operate out of their backup data centers periodically, so that security experts are prepared for any disasters that may hamper normal business operations. Updated plans alone are not enough to ensure continuity if recovery team members do not exercise them and therefore do not know exactly what they are supposed to do. Team members should receive training in recovery concepts in general and their team's functions in particular. This way, needed improvements in strategies and plans are discovered, and team members may acquire valuable experience in dealing with their duties in the event of a recovery scenario.

An organization should review the following plan elements during the exercise:

- *Recovery team alert list*—This is contact information for all personnel assigned to the team. Because this list can change frequently, team leaders should update it regularly and communicate changes to each team member.
- *Critical functions list*—This is a list of critical functions that each team must accomplish in a recovery scenario.
- *Team recovery steps*—Strategies for recovery of critical functions must be reviewed to ensure that they meet the objectives stated in the BIA.
- *Functional recovery steps*—Procedures to complete all operational recoveries must be reviewed and validated to determine effectiveness and efficiency.

- *Vendor and customer list*—This contact information for critical vendors and customers must be reviewed to determine its accuracy and completeness.
- *Off-site storage list*—Critical facilities or resources stored off-site must be reviewed to determine their operational status and completeness.

## Testing

To determine which business processes to test and in which order, the BIA analysis should be at hand, because it is the BIA that states mission-critical activities and defines recovery requirements, such as the RTO and RPO. The most challenging aspect of exercising and testing a BCM plan is devising a testing methodology and implementation schedule such that the following occur:

- The BCM and DR plans are tested to the fullest extent possible, according to the BIA.
- The costs are sustainable and well documented.
- Interruptions of normal business operations are minimal or nonexistent.
- The tests provide a high degree of assurance in recovery capability.
- Evaluation of test results provides quality feedback to BCM and DR plans maintenance.

One of the most common methodologies for testing BCM and DR plans involves using checklists, performing simulations, checking the procedures in parallel between the main and an alternate site, and fully testing the DR plan by interrupting operations.

### Checklist Testing

Checklists are the primary tools for testing a plan, because they are inexpensive to implement and maintain. A checklist should be subdivided into groups of checklists dedicated to the different business units or organization areas involved in the DR plan. They should be specific and appropriate for each business unit and for those phases of mission-critical activities in which they are involved. In addition, the experience of each business unit should be used in preparing and updating checklists. A checklist test can be used to validate multiple components of the DR plan; for example, key procedures validation, hardware and software configuration, documentation completeness and update status, availability of process-specific resources, and data backup correctness and reliability.

### Simulation Testing

The purpose of simulating a failure is to evaluate the effectiveness of the BCM plan without interfering with normal business operations. Hardware, software, personnel, communications, procedures, documentation, transportation, utilities, and alternate site processing should be included in a simulation test. Such factors as traveling, moving equipment, or coordinating activities with external agencies may not be feasible during a simulated test. However, checklists can provide a reasonable level of assurance for many of these scenarios.

### Parallel Testing

In parallel tests, historical transactions, such as the prior business day's transactions, are processed against the preceding day's backup files at the replicated or hot site. All reports produced at the alternate site should agree with those produced at the main site.

### Full-interruption Testing

A full-interruption test activates the DR plan in its entirety. It is clearly the most meaningful test and also the most expensive and intrusive. It could disrupt normal operation and provoke losses to the company.

## BCM/DR PLANNING TEMPLATE

This section provides a reference template for BCM/DR planning derived from the MIT Business Continuity Plan (MIT, 1995). It is only one possible example of a BCM/DR plan template, because an actual plan should meet the peculiar requirements of every organization according to the entire BCM process. Among others, Brooks, Bedemjak, Juran, and Merryman (2002) provide another complete example and extensive comments, as well as the University of Toronto (2003), which has published its full plan outline. Further examples and interesting reading can be found in Toigo (1999) and DRJ (2002).

Our reference plan has the following schema.

Part I Introduction

Part II Design Of The Plan

1. Overview of the BCM plan
   a. Purpose
   b. Assumptions
   c. Development
   d. Maintenance
   e. Testing
2. Organization of Disaster Response and Recovery
   a. Administrative Computing Steering Committee
   b. Business Continuity Management Team
   c. Technical Support Teams
   d. Disaster Response
   e. Disaster Detection and Determination
   f. Disaster Notification
3. Initiation of the Business Continuity Plan
   a. Activation of an Alternate Site
   b. Dissemination of Public Information
   c. Disaster Recovery Strategy
4. Scope of the Business Continuity Plan
   a. Critical Functions
   b. Essential Functions
   c. Necessary Functions
   d. Desirable Functions

Part III Team Descriptions

1. Business Continuity Management Team
2. Company Support Teams
   a. Damage Assessment/Salvage Team
   b. Physical Security Team
   c. Public Information Team
   d. Telecommunication Team

Part IV Recovery Procedures

1. Notification List
2. Action Procedures

## BUSINESS CONTINUITY AND INVESTMENT SHORTAGE

BCM and DR solutions are usually expensive. For comprehensive solutions, costs were high in the old days of data centers and continue to be high today in the world of networked resources, replicated servers, and mirrored sites. A review, which recently appeared in *Network Computing* (Toigo, 2004), presented solutions from some vendors that address the needs of a reference fictional retailer taken as the test case. Costs for those solutions began at approximately $300,000, rose to $700,000, surpassed $1 million, and reached $6 million for the most expensive. Indeed, business continuity is not compatible with low budgets, especially because by its nature business continuity is organization wide and not modular.

Suzanne Widup (2003) raises an interesting question in her SANS Institute GSEC Practical: because economic difficulties have severely affected the development of BCM plans, why is BCM still proposed as an organization-wide plan instead of developing less monolithic and more modular approaches and less comprehensive and more affordable projects to comply with reduced investments? This is more a business than a technical trade-off that is rarely addressed in the BCM literature and on-line publications. Often statistics are presented about the percentage of companies that do not have any kind of BCM plan in place, do not perform any kind of testing and maintenance of plans, or do not invest in BCM planning. This is evidence that the perceived importance of BCM importance has diminished rather than increased. For instance, Widup (2003) discussed the results of a poll conducted by *InformationWeek* (D'Antoni, 2003) that of the 300 business technology executives interviewed about their 2003 budget plans and IT strategies, 65% said that BCM planning and improved disaster preparedness are priorities. This is a decrease from 77% in the previous year. Moreover, some 61% of executives at small companies reported a continued commitment to BCM planning, a drop of 14% compared with the year before. Responses among managers at midsize companies showed a similar decline, and larger-sized sites were down just 7% from the previous year.

Given the costs presented in Toigo (2004) and the current economic difficulties, it is no surprise that small and mid-sized companies have cut spending on BCM plans severely. Nevertheless, the BCM field seems to have no adequate proposal to face this situation. This demonstrates a weakness of BCM planning, which has found it very difficult to formulate proposals well suited for small and mid-sized companies that often simply rely on basic tape-based backups and other low-cost precautions.

One way to make BCM solutions more attractive to small and mid-sized companies is to make them more modular; for example, there should be different modules for different business functions, instead of imposing an organization-wide approach. Modular solutions are easier to integrate with existing infrastructures and technology.

Most of the expense of BCM solutions comes from the purchase of dedicated equipment, substitution of existing technology/components, and impossibility of preserving previous IT investments that often are cannot be integrated or reused with BCM solutions. Moreover, initial expenditures are not the only barrier to adopting BCM solutions. If those solutions are not made less expensive to maintain and update, the natural consequence of each period of economic difficulty will be the reduction of investments in BCM and in the maintenance and development of existing plans. Floods, fire, and power outage become secondary thoughts, and BCM budgets get smaller. We should admit openly that from a risk management perspective it does make sense when the risk of going out of business due to financial problems gains the first position in the rank of risks.

However, it is clear that modularizing a BCM plan and supporting only some functions instead of *all* mission-critical functions means having plans that are generally inadequate to sustain business continuity in the event of severe disasters. The coherence of an enterprise-wide plan, based on enterprise-wide analyses, developments, and tests, would be lost, as well as the performance and effectiveness of the more sophisticated technology in place today that is able to satisfy continuous availability requirements. Nevertheless, BCM analysts should consider that in most cases, cutting expenditures on BCM is not merely done because of the shortsightedness of a company's management; instead it may be the result of a realistic calculation in situations where financial shortages are the primary reason why a company goes out of business.

In these situations, BCM analysts and vendors should make efforts to demonstrate the cost effectiveness of solutions, to consider the trade-off between BCM investments and other technologies from the perspective of corporate management, and to be able to scale down solutions when circumstances need it.

Finally, to foster the adoption of complex BCM solutions, some BCM literature, especially on-line literature and marketing communications, seems sometimes to stress excessively the potential consequences of catastrophic and tragic events on business. Unfortunately, these consequences are sometimes presented without a corresponding realistic analysis of the likelihood of occurrence of those events, which actually is extremely low for the great majority of organizations. This literature has much in common with many marketing campaigns about cyber attacks in the information security area: both tend to focus on short-term emotional reactions instead of demonstrating cost effectiveness and the technical soundness of solutions. Information to enable a correct cost-benefit analysis is not provided to the customers, which turns out to be a shortsighted strategy in the mid- to long-term period when economic considerations become paramount for investment decisions.

## CONCLUSIONS

Internet connections have driven the development of new business models that have enlarged and modified the scope of DR since the days of mainframe-based data centers. This amplified discipline has taken the name of business continuity management, of which DR is today one aspect of a greater process aimed at assuring the continuity of mission-critical business activities. A requirement that follows this evolution in business models is the need for immediate recovery and continuous operations with zero downtime as their ultimate goal. Although the zero downtime goal is still impossible to achieve, and this should be stated clearly in each BCM project, the BCM field has developed new planning methodologies and techniques to match these requirements. As a consequence, the process of putting in place an effective BCM plan uses sophisticated technologies, but the many interconnections with both the IT infrastructure and the business functions of a company make it more complex. Companies could suffer severe losses if they experience one of the many risks, not just traditional disasters, but even so-called small disasters, which include failures of the IT infrastructure, telecommunications, power outages, and human errors. E-business models can no longer sustain those frequent downtimes or network outages as in the past, when companies accepted RTOs of some days in the event of an IT failure and RPOs that restored resources to the previous status.

Processes that enable a more efficient recovery phase in the event of a disaster, such as the business impact analysis, the business impact resource recovery analysis, risk management, and the innovative backup and recovery techniques, therefore assume great importance.

## GLOSSARY

**Activation**  The implementation of business continuity procedures, activities, and plans in response to an emergency, disaster, or incident.

**Alternate Site**  A location, other than the normal facility, used to process data and conduct critical business functions in the event of a disaster.

**Backup**  The process of copying data (paper-based or electronic) so as to be available and used if the original data are lost, destroyed, or corrupted.

**Business Continuity Management (BCM)**  A management process that identifies potential impacts that threaten an organization and provides a framework for assuring the continuity of business operations in the event of a disaster, failure, or unplanned incident.

**Business Continuity Plan**  A clearly and formally defined plan to use in the event of an emergency, incident, or failure. Typically, it includes the description of all key personnel, resources, services, and actions required to manage a BCM process.

**Business Continuity Planning**  The process of planning for the identification of potential losses, prevention measures, viable recovery strategies, and training/testing/maintenance activities provided by the BCM process.

**Business Impact Analysis (BIA)**  The management analysis that addresses financial and nonfinancial effects that might result in the event of a disaster or failure. The BIA represents the basis for every BCM strategy and solution.

**Business Impact Resource Recovery Analysis (BIRRA)**  The identification of the minimum level of resources (e.g., personnel, hardware, software, data, or telecommunications) required after a failure that permits an organization to still conduit its mission-critical activities at a minimum level of service. The BIRRA is normally a fundamental part of the BIA.

**Data Mirroring**  A process that permits the copying of data instantaneously to another location.

**Disaster**  Any event that can cause an organization to be unable to provide critical business functions for a certain period of time.

**Disaster Recovery**  An integral part of the BCM plan aimed at recovering and restoring organization's capabilities (e.g., IT and telecommunications) after a disaster.

**Electronic Vaulting**  Transfer of data to an off-site storage facility via a communication link or a different portable media.

**Facility**  Location containing equipment and infrastructure to perform normal business functions.

**Loss**  The financial or nonfinancial consequence resulting from a disaster/failure.

**Mission-Critical Activities**  The critical operational or business activities necessary to the organization's ability to achieve its business objectives.

**Network Outage**  The interruption of system availability as a result of a communication failure affecting a network.

**Off-site Storage Facility**  A secure and remote location where backups of hardware, software, data files, documents, or equipment are stored.

**Risk Assessment**  The overall process of risk identification, analysis, and evaluation.

**Risk Management**  The processes and structures put in place to effectively manage negative events to minimize adverse effects and reduce damages or losses to an acceptable level.

**Service-Level Agreement (SLA)**  A formal agreement between a service provider and the client that specifies all conditions of service provision.

**System Outage**  An unplanned interruption in system availability resulting from operational problems or hardware/software failures.

## CROSS REFERENCES

See *Implementing a Security Awareness Program; Managing a Network Environment; Risk Management for IT Security; Security Policy Guidelines; Web Hosting.*

## REFERENCES

BCI. (2002). Business continuity management—Good practice guidelines (Version BCI DJS). *The Business Continuity Institute.* Retrieved July 15, 2004, from http://www.thebci.org/BCI%20GPG%20-%20 Introduction.pdf

Bounds, G. (2003). Preparing for the worst: A best practices guide to disaster recovery planning. *Contingency Planning Magazine.* Retrieved July 15, 2004, from http://www.contingencyplanning.com/archives/2003/ apr/5.aspx

Brooks, C., Bedernjak, M., Juran, I., & Merryman, J. (2002). Appendix A: DR and business impact analysis planning templates. In *Disaster recovery strategies with Tivoli storage management* (IBM Redbook SG24-6844-00). Retrieved July 15, 2004, from http://www.redbooks.ibm.com/redbooks/SG246844.html

Campbell, R. (2000). *Continuity planning in the new millenium—The convergence of disciplines.* Retrieved July 15, 2004, from http://www.disaster-resource.com/cgi-bin/article_search.cgi?id='16'

D'Antoni, H. (2003). Business continuity slides down the priority scale. *InformationWeek.* Retrieved July 15, 2004, from http://www.informationweek.com/story/IWK20030109S0002

DRJ (2002). DRJ's sample DR plans and outlines. *Disaster Recovery Journal.* Retrieved July 15, 2004, from http://www.drj.com/new2dr/samples.htm

Hagg, A. (2002). Benchmark report: BCP in 2002. *Contingency Planning & Management.* Retrieved July 15, 2004, from http://www.contingencyplanning.com/archives/2002/julaug/1.aspx

Hiles, A. (2002). *Business impact analysis: What's your downside?* Retrieved July 15, 2004, from http://www.rothstein.com/articles/busimpact.html

Kaye, D. (2001). *Strategies for Web hosting and managed services.* New York: John Wiley & Sons.

Merchantz, B. (2002). The true cost of downtime. *Contingency Planning & Management.* Retrieved July 15, 2004, from http://www.contingencyplanning.com/archives/2002/mayjun/1.aspx

MIT (1995). MIT business continuity nlan. *Massachusetts Institute of Technology.* Retrieved July 15, 2004, from http://web.mit.edu/security/www/pubplan.htm

NIST (National Institute for Standard and Technology). (2002). *Contingency planning guide for information technology systems* (NIST Special Publication 800-34). Retrieved July 15, 2004, from http://csrc.nist.gov/publications/nistpubs/800-34/sp800-34.pdf

Nicolett, M., & Berg, T. (1999). *Storage backup and recovery for distributed systems* (Strategic Analyses Report R-09-3148). Stamford, CT: Gartner Group.

Noakes-Fry, K., & Diamond, T. (2001). *Business continuity recovery planning and management: perspective* (Technology Overview DPRO-100862). Stamford, CT: Gartner Group.

Noakes-Fry, K., & Diamond, T. (2002). *Business continuity planning software: Perspective* (Technology Overview DPRO-100469). Stamford, CT: Gartner Group.

Rothstein, P. J. (2003). *Averting disaster.* Retrieved July 15, 2004, from http://www.rothstein.com/articles/averting.html

Scott, D., & Natis, Y. (2000). *Building continuous availability into e-applications* (Research Note COM-12-1325). Stamford, CT: Gartner Group.

Tate, J., Cole, G., Gomilsek, I., & van der Pijll, J. (2000). Retrieved July 15, 2004, from http://www.redbooks.ibm.com/redbooks/pdfs/sg245758.pdf

Toigo, J. W. (1999). *Disaster recovery planning: Strategies for protecting critical information sssets* (2nd ed.). Englewood Cliffs, NJ: Prentice Hall PTR.

Toigo, J. W. (2001a). *Fighting fires on the Web.* Retrieved July 15, 2004, from http://www.esj.com/Features/article.aspx?EditorialsID=60

Toigo, J. W. (2001b). Storage disaster: Will you recover? *Network Computing.* Retrieved July 15, 2004, from http://www.networkcomputing.com/1205/1205f1.html

Toigo, J. W. (2004). Natural selection. *Network Computing.* Retrieved July 15, 2004, from http://www.nwc.com/showitem.jhtml?articleID=17301530&pgno=6

University of Toronto (2003). *Disaster recovery planning: Project plan outline.* Retrieved July 15, 2004, from Computing & Networking Services, University of Toronto Web site: http://www.utoronto.ca/security/drp.htm

Widup, S. (2003). *Business continuity planning in difficult economic times* (GSEC Practical, Security Reading Room, SANS Institute). Retrieved July 15, 2004, from http://www.sans.org/rr/papers/index.php?id=1114

Wold, G. H. (2002a). Disaster recovery planning process–Part I. *Disaster Recovery Journal.* Retrieved July 15, 2004, from http://www.drj.com/new2dr/w2_002.htm

Wold, G. H. (2002b). Disaster recovery planning process–Part II. *Disaster Recovery Journal.* Retrieved July 15, 2004, from http://www.drj.com/new2dr/w2_003.htm

Wold, G. H. (2002c). Disaster recovery planning process–Part iiI. *Disaster Recovery Journal.* Retrieved July 15, 2004, from http://www.drj.com/new2dr/w2_004.htm

Wold, G. H., & Shriver, R. F. (2002). Risk analysis techniques. *Disaster Recovery Journal.* Retrieved July 15, 2004, from http://www.drj.com/new2dr/w3_030.htm

# FURTHER READING

Takemura, R., & Taylor, R. M. (1996). *The increasing need for client/server contingency planning.* Retrieved July 15, 2004, from http://www.disaster-resource.com/cgi-bin/article_search.cgi?id='36'

# Computer Security Incident Response Teams (CSIRTs)

Raymond R. Panko, *University of Hawaii, Manoa*

## INTRODUCTION

Almost all corporations today protect themselves with layered defenses consisting of firewalls, antivirus systems, hardened hosts, and other protections. Even so, security incidents (also called security breaches) sometimes occur.

The firm's on-duty staff may be tasked to handle minor incidents because they can respond immediately and generally effectively. For major incidents, however, such as a major virus attack, a major denial-of-service attack, or the hacking (takeover) of important servers, the firm needs a team approach to stop the breach and get the firm back to normal. To handle major incidents, many firms create computer security incident response teams (CSIRTS), also known as computer emergency response teams (CERTs) and computer incident response teams (CIRTs). The term *computer emergency response team* (CERT) is a registered trademark of the CERT/Coordination Center at Carnegie-Mellon University (http://www.cert.org) and may only be used with permission.

A critical success factor for any CSIRT is speed of response. During a major security breach, a corporation's operations are likely to be disrupted. This can result in the loss of immediate revenues and the imposition of penalties by business partners and regulators and by a loss in customer or investor confidence. During the intense stresses of major security incidents, CSIRTs must be able to act rapidly but correctly.

During emergencies, humans often are not at their best cognitively. Instead of ensuring that they understand the situation well, they often fixate on a single possible solution that eventually turns out to be fatally flawed. They also tend to make mistakes and work slowly when they are handling complex and difficult tasks for the first time. In addition, teams with members who are unfamiliar with the way their coworkers operate often have communication breakdowns.

Consequently, it is extremely important for CSIRTs to be organized before an incident and to conduct live rehearsals regularly. Although first attempts may not be satisfactory, live rehearsals will identify problems that can be corrected so that performance is good during real incidents.

Once a real security breach occurs, the CSIRT's work must proceed through a series of well-considered steps (Panko, 2004). These are the discovery of an incident and its escalation to the status of major incident, the analysis of the incident to understand it, the containment of the attack to stop the spread of damage, repair to get damaged systems cleaned up and operational, possible punishment of the attacker, hardening of damaged systems against new attacks, and postmortem analysis.

## BEFORE THE INCIDENT
### Justifying the CSIRT

CSIRTs are expensive. It is important to be able to justify the cost of having one to senior management. It is also important to be able to justify requiring participation from a number of departments, including during live rehearsals, which are very time consuming.

The normal way to justify a CSIRT is to collect data on the frequency of attacks and the damage caused by attacks. One excellent general source is the Computer Emergency Response Team/Coordination Center (http://www.cert.org). Other good general sources are SecurityFocus (http://www.securityfocus.com) and SANS (http://www.sans.org). The Federal Bureau of Investigation (FBI) and the Computer Security Institute conduct an annual survey of corporations to assess the frequencies of various kinds of attacks (http://www.gocsi.com). A good source of data on viruses and spam is MessageLabs (http://www.messagelabs.com). In presenting summary information to top management, it is good to have data on both general trends and some examples of serious problems caused by incidents in specific corporations.

This information should be combined with estimates of how much major attacks of various types would cost the firm and, if possible, how having rapid detection and containment through the use of a CSIRT could reduce these costs.

## Organizing the CSIRT

The first step is to create the CSIRT. Information technology (IT) security incidents can affect several functional groups in a firm. It usually also takes the staff from several functional areas to handle major IT security incidents. Consequently, the CSIRT must draw on several functional areas for its membership (Panko, 2004): the IT security staff, the IT staff, functional line managers, public relations, the legal department, and external organizations, such as outsourcers and law enforcement agencies.

### The IT Security Staff

Obviously, the IT security staff needs to be involved and may lead the CSIRT. Most firms have very small IT security staffs, and for these firms, it is normal for the entire IT security staff to be on the CSIRT.

### The IT Staff

Sometimes, the IT security staff is under the information technology director. This arrangement is not ideal because a large fraction of all IT security breaches are committed by the IT staff. It is better for accountability if IT security is a parallel operation. Another reason for keeping the IT security staff separate is that the IT staff sometimes focuses primarily on technology, whereas the IT security staff must focus more broadly on organizational issues. On the negative side, separating IT security from IT can result in friction between the two groups in terms of the ownership of server logs and other important matters. In addition, a separated IT security staff cannot "order" the IT staff to take action, and separation frees the IT department from accountability for security.

In CSIRTs, it is important to have members of the IT staff be involved however IT security and IT relate organizationally. It is also important to have operational levels of IT represented as well as IT management because operational employees often have a better picture of what is happening at a detailed level, whereas IT managers have the broader perspective needed to understand what is happening across systems and the corporate implications of IT security breaches and alternative remedies.

### Functional Line Managers

Fixing an IT security breach is not simply a technical matter. For example, the simplest and most effective way to contain a hacking intrusion is to terminate a victim computer's network or Internet connection. The business implications of "pulling the plug" can be horrendous, however. Functional line managers in critical areas must be involved in and approve the CSIRT's actions.

### Public Relations

One non-IT group that needs to be strongly involved in an adverse incident is the company's public relations department. If there is a serious problem, the company will want to manage communication with the outside world to produce as little damage as possible to public relations. Under no circumstances should an IT or IT security employee talk to the media directly. Many firms also work with external public relations companies, and there are even public relations companies that specialize in incident handling.

### Legal Department

It is critical to have members of the legal department on the CSIRT. Lawyers have the specialized knowledge needed for prosecution and to defend the company against liability. (If an attacker compromises a corporate computer and uses it to attack another corporation, the company whose computer was compromised and used may be liable.)

### IT Outsourcers

Most companies outsource at least some of their IT activities, and many companies outsource most of their IT. In such cases, the IT outsourcing vendor will have to work closely with the CSIRT. Beyond that, the IT outsourcer must have good internal incident response capabilities, and expertise in incident handling may be a factor in selecting an outsourcer.

Some firms turn to IT security outsourcers to detect problems in internal systems and to provide expertise and actual work in the case of security incidents. One advantage of using IT security outsourcers is that they have constant experience with handling attacks, whereas internal CSIRTs may handle only a handful of attacks each year.

In any IT outsourcing, it is important to have outsourcers intimately connected to the CSIRT, including participating in rehearsals for security incidents.

### Software Contractors

Many information systems today are developed by contractors. In some cases, systems are custom built. In other cases, they are commercial off-the-shelf (COTS) products. In many cases, they are COTS products customized to a corporation's needs. During an incident, the CSIRT may need help from software developers. The CSIRT should have contact information for the contractors of all major systems, and in the case of pervasive organization-wide tools, such as enterprise resource planning (ERP) systems, a contractor employee may rehearse with the CSIRT during major planning exercises.

### Law Enforcement Agencies

Although law enforcement agencies will not actually be part of the CSIRT, their expertise is invaluable if action is to be taken against the attacker. It is important for the CSIRT to understand how to interact with law enforcement agencies and to know what services law enforcement agencies can provide, such as the copying and protection of evidence. Law enforcement officers may even participate in CSIRT rehearsals.

### Live Rehearsals

Once the CSIRT is formed, it must engage in live rehearsals that take it through realistic emergencies. During these tests, the CSIRT's members may discover that they are missing representation from an important functional area, that their approaches to recovery are not viable, that they have misunderstandings about authority and terminology, and so forth. Live rehearsals also build confidence and speed.

## Technology Base

The CSIRT will need some technology to do its job. Some of it the firm already has; some must be purchased separately.

### Protection Technology

By definition, incidents occur when protection technology (firewalls, antivirus, server hardening, etc.) breaks down. Good protection technology may, however, be able to reduce the severity of an attack. Protections are discussed extensively in other chapters in this encyclopedia.

### Intrusion Detection Systems (IDSs)

Technologies can also help in the response phase of incidents. Most obviously, intrusion detection systems can alert firms to attacks. In addition, IDS log files can help the firm analyze what has happened during an attack. This chapter does not look at IDSs because they are covered in detail elsewhere in the encyclopedia.

### File Integrity Checkers

To respond to an incident involving a server compromise, it is important to be able to know what changes the attacker has made. File integrity checkers periodically create message digests of important system programs. Tripwire is a popular file integrity checker. After an attack, message digests are again computed and compared with message digests before the attack to see which programs had been changed. Unfortunately, few firms use file integrity checkers because they are difficult to employ successfully. A serious problem with these tools is that many critical system files change during normal operation. Consequently, it takes a great deal of knowledge to select the specific system files to which file integrity checkers should be applied.

### Evidence Collection Technology

Evidence collection technology allows a firm to capture evidence during an attack. If evidence is not collected rapidly and carefully, it will become almost impossible to prosecute attackers or even to understand the attack well. One action is to back up the hard drive on the compromised computer. In addition, transient information stored in RAM (random access memory) during an attack may be crucial to understanding the attack and prosecuting attackers. Special-purpose software can handle backups and capture this transient information in ways that will preserve evidence for presentation in court if necessary. Again, this chapter does not discuss evidence collection technology because this topic is covered in several chapters dealing with forensics in this encyclopedia.

## The Problem of Communication

One inevitable problem in CSIRTs is communication. During an attack, e-mail may be compromised, and even if it is not, it is likely to be too slow for important functions. The CSIRT organizer must maintain up-to-date lists of office telephone numbers, home telephone numbers, pager numbers, short message service cellular telephone numbers, e-mail addresses, and other contact information for each member of the CSIRT. This contact information changes so rapidly that it must be updated frequently and aggressively.

In the same vein, each CSIRT member must designate an alternate team member if he or she is unavailable. The CSIRT leader needs to maintain up-to-date contact information for these alternates as well. Ideally, alternates should participate in tests.

## The Decision to Prosecute

One issue should be considered carefully before any incident occurs: whether to attempt to punish the attacker. For internal employees, this usually is a fairly straightforward decision because termination and lesser punishments are easy and usually legally safe to administer.

For external hackers, however, prosecution is difficult, especially if the attacker is a minor. Furthermore, pursuing prosecution may open up the firm to negative publicity and consequent losses in customer and investor confidence. Before attacks occur, the company should develop a policy regarding external (and internal) prosecution with the aid of the corporate legal department and senior managers.

One consideration in developing prosecution policies is that successful prosecution will require the CSIRT to take certain actions discussed later in this chapter. Evidence must be carefully protected and preserved. In addition, during the attack, it may be necessary to allow the attack to continue long enough to gather sufficient evidence for conviction instead of cutting off the attacker as soon as possible.

## DURING THE ATTACK

Although preparation before a security incident is important, how well the CSIRT responds to actual security incidents is the litmus test for success.

## Discovery and Escalation

First, the attack must be discovered. Often, the employee who discovers the attack is a low-level IT employee or an employee in a functional area such as marketing. A key question to ask any firm to assess its state of security is, "Do your employees know the telephone number for reporting security concerns?" A sticker with this number should be on every telephone in the organization. Often, this is the telephone number of the firm's general security office. Delays in reporting suspected security breaches often result in severe damage before the CSIRT can even start its work.

In other cases, the IT security or general IT staff detects the incident. Often, the firm's intrusion detection system sets off an alarm when there is suspicious activity in the system.

In addition, the IDS maintains log files of events relevant to security. During the later analysis phase, the analysis of these log files is crucial in understanding the nature of the incident.

The on-duty IT and IT security staff members typically handle small incidents. However, the on-duty staff manager must have clear guidelines for when to escalate an incident—that is, when to declare the situation sufficiently dangerous or damaging to convene the CSIRT. In particular, the firm must have good guidelines for classifying attacks as minor or major.

## Initial Analysis (Triage)

The first action of the CSIRT must be to analyze the situation. There is a tendency to act precipitously even when little information is available. A short initial period of incident analysis is critical for later success. This is similar to the medical concept of triage (the initial analysis of a patient's condition) and is, in fact, often called triage.

The first step is to classify the security incident. Typically, there are three types of security incidents—widespread virus or worm outbreaks, denial-of-service attacks, and hacking attacks. Hacking is the access of a protected resource without authorization or in excess of authorization. Hacking, in other words, is breaking into a client, server, switch, router, or other computer.

The second step is to understand the attack. What vulnerability allowed the hacker to break into the computer? What has he or she already done? How sophisticated does the attack appear to be? In the case of virus or worm outbreaks, how is the virus or worm propagating, and how rapidly is it propagating?

Although analysis typically focuses on internal data in computer and intrusion detection system log files, the CSIRT may also contact other organizations, including the Computer Emergency Response Team/Coordination Center (http://www.cert.org), which maintains information about common hacking breaches and virus attacks. There is a good chance that the current attack uses a method that is common in recent attacks, is well understood, and for which good defenses and recovery techniques are known.

## Containment

The next step is containment, which means stopping the attack. As noted earlier, the simplest approach to containment is to unplug affected computers. Although this is effective and may even prove to be necessary, it is a drastic step that can have important implications for the firm as a whole if an affected server is vital to the firm's operations. Effectively, unplugging a computer is a self-administered denial-of-service attack.

In addition, it may be desirable to allow the attacker to continue working so that the attack can be better understood. Containing attackers too soon may simply keep them out for a few minutes, after which they may be able to get back in using the same exploit they used to gain entry in the first place. In a virus or worm attack, containment before understanding may result in immediate reinfection through the same vulnerability.

If legal prosecution is a goal, furthermore, it may be important to continue gathering evidence. On the negative side, if hackers are given sufficient time, they can scatter backdoor attack programs throughout a server's directories, read sensitive information, and take steps to make themselves difficult to detect. Consequently, containment should be initiated as soon as possible.

## Recovery

Recovery, also called repair, means getting the computer system back to the state it was in before the attack. This means removing programs the attacker placed on the computer and cleaning up any altered data files.

Recovery usually focuses on program files, because hackers, and virus, and worms often litter the computer with attack programs that must be rooted out. Attackers also Trojanize legitimate system programs by replacing them with an attack program but keeping the name the same. To recover the system of program files on the computer, there are three main options: repair during continued operation, restoration from backup tapes, and reinstallation from original installation media.

### Repair During Continued Operation

If a company has a good way to recognize attack programs, it may be able to make program file repairs while the computer is still operational. However, this presumes that the firm has done such things as keep message digests for all program files so that changes can be detected. This seldom is done.

### Recovery from Backup Tapes

It is more common to reinstall all system and other program files from the last clean backup tape. This can be effective, but it is important to know when the attack began or the backup files may themselves be suspect. In addition, the restoration of program files from backup tapes often requires the system to be taken offline at least temporarily.

### Reinstallation from Original Installation Media

In the worst case, the computer's software will have to be reinstalled using original software installation media. It is important to have these media readily available for such eventualities. It is also important to document all configuration changes made during and since the last installation. For instance, patches frequently need to be applied to remove known vulnerabilities, and there usually are many company-specific and computer-specific configuration changes made for other reasons. Reinstallation from original media typically takes the computer down for several hours.

### Data Files

The CSIRT will face special nightmares if the attack damaged (or may have damaged) data files. Although restoration from the last clean backup tape will work for older files, all data entered since the last backup will be lost unless a real-time journal of changes has been maintained (which is rare). Laboriously, online files can be compared with backup files to identify safe files and files that must be looked at carefully.

## Protection Against Subsequent Attacks

The last action of any CSIRT during an attack is to protect the firm against subsequent attacks. Obviously, the specific vulnerability that allowed the attack to succeed must be fixed. In addition, firewalls should be tuned to stop such attacks if possible, and intrusion detection systems must get filters to warn of subsequent attacks conducted the way the current breach was created.

Second, and more subtly, the server that was attacked must be especially hardened against reattacks. Hardening involves the application of all patches to the system and the general configuring of the system for maximum security.

Internet hackers, to demonstrate their successes, often invite other hackers to get into your system. For some period of time after an attack, your "famous" server will continue to be attacked by hackers. If you repair the specific exploit used in the first place, hackers will attempt to find other vulnerabilities to prove that they could break into the server in ways that the original hacker could not.

# AFTER THE ATTACK
## Sanctions

Sanctions are punishments that a firm directs at attackers. Although anger usually makes a firm eager to sanction attackers, it is not always practical to do so.

### Punishing Employees

If the attacker is a current employee, the firm must weigh the benefits of prosecution against the simple expedient of firing the employee. (For minor incidents, more mild sanctions may be appropriate.) Firing an employee typically can be done with no publicity, especially if the employee agrees to keep quiet or face legal prosecution. In addition, although prosecution is difficult, employees usually can be terminated fairly easily for attacking IT resources, and it usually is legally safe to terminate them (although state laws differ in the United States, international laws vary greatly, and union agreements may make sanctions difficult to apply in some firms).

### Prosecuting Attackers

Prosecuting employees, ex-employees, or other outside attackers in courts of law requires a firm to prove that a particular person committed the attack. This can be difficult, especially if the attacker is using a spoofed IP address or attacked indirectly from a computer previously compromised instead of his or her own computer.

In addition, as noted earlier, the attacker must be traced doing a series of actions (individual actions may not convince a jury), and this may require allowing the attack to continue longer than it would if prosecution were not a goal.

Successful prosecution will depend heavily on the quality of evidence collected. As soon as possible, crucial information on the attacked computer must be documented or backed up. Otherwise, the defense will argue that the evidence is tainted and that many things could have caused later changes.

In addition, the CSIRT needs to document carefully how and by whom evidence was collected. The firm also must maintain a clear chain of evidence documenting who had the evidence at all times and how it was collected and protected after collection. Any breakdown in documentation can ruin a case. Judges often will not even allow a jury to see evidence that does not meet strict legal evidence requirements.

For prosecution, it is critical to train the CSIRT beforehand in evidence collection and preservation. In fact, it is highly desirable to call in local authorities or the FBI. They can make backups of your hard drives and collect other information in a way likely to get a conviction. Other chapters in this encyclopedia contain detailed discussions of forensic data collection.

### Lawsuits

For attacks that produce only modest amounts of damage, the authorities often are reluctant to prosecute. A firm may still be able to act through the legal system by suing the attacker for actual damages and perhaps for punitive damages as well. These damages and the attacker's cost of legal defense may be a satisfactory way to exact some measure of revenge. However, lawsuits are expensive and reveal the attack to public. In addition, if the hacker community views the lawsuit as "lame," the firm may become a popular target of revenge attacks by other hackers.

### Reprisal Attacks

One option is to attack the attacker in return—essentially, hacking the attacker's computer. This may seem attractive, but it is almost always a very bad idea. First, attackers often use intermediate victim computers to launch attacks. Reprisal attacks are likely to hurt an innocent victim. (If a firm feels that companies that allow their computers to be hacked are not innocent, it should keep in mind that it has just been hacked itself.)

Of course, more fundamentally, reprisal attacks are almost always illegal. The jailing of members of the CSIRT is not a goal of incident response. Also, a CSIRT is an official organization within the firm; liability for a reprisal attack is likely to extend to senior officers and even the board of directors. The chapter, Active Response to Computer Intrusions, gives a comprehensive analysis of reprisal attacks.

## Postmortem Analysis

After things have stabilized, it is important to conduct a postmortem analysis to review what happened during the incident. The goal is to improve future responses to incidents. Things that worked well should be noted, but problems also should be highlighted and fixes created for the future. After the exhaustion of an incident and the need to catch up on work postponed during the incident, it is difficult to motivate the CSIRT team members to undertake a postmortem analysis. However, given the valuable information gained during the actual incident, as opposed to simple live rehearsals, the information gathered in the postmortem analysis can produce strong benefits.

There should also be a follow-up analysis 1 to 6 months later to determine which recommendations made during a postmortem analysis have been implemented and which have not.

## CONCLUSION

When major IT security incidents happen, companies cannot sit back and wonder what they should do. Before the attack, companies need to organize and train cross-disciplinary computer security incident response teams—also called computer emergency response teams. Training using realistic rehearsals is important for ensuring adequate and rapid CSIRT responses during an emergency.

During an attack, once an incident is discovered and escalated by the on-duty staff to a major incident, the CSIRT is activated. The CSIRT analyzes the attack so that appropriate responses can be made, contains the attack to prevent further damage, recovers program files and perhaps data files, gathers information needed for internal punishment or legal prosecution, hardens the system to prevent reattacks, and conducts a postmortem analysis to refine its incident response abilities.

## GLOSSARY

**Analysis**   Incident response phase just after discovery phase. The CSIRT determines how the attack was made and what was done to affected systems.

**Breach**   Another name for a security incident.

**Computer Emergency Response Team (CERT)**   Another name for computer security incident response team.

**Computer Incident Response Team (CIRT)**   Another name for computer security incident response team.

**Computer Security Incident Response Team (CSIRT)**   Cross-disciplinary team created to respond to major security incidents.

**Containment**   The phase in incident response in which the damage to systems is stopped.

**Discovery**   The phase in incident response in which a security incident is first discovered and reported.

**Escalation**   The act of determining that a particular security incident is a major breach and that the CSIRT must be activated.

**Forensics**   The application of science to criminal investigations.

**Hacking**   Taking over a computer; intentionally using a computer without authorization or in excess of authorization.

**Hardening**   Removing vulnerabilities from a host computer and configuring the computer for high security.

**Incident**   Another name for a security incident.

**Incident Response**   The multiphase process of responding to a security incident.

**Information Technology (IT)**   Computer hardware, computer software, networking, and data.

**Intrusion Detection System**   Tool that signals that an attack appears to be underway and that collects data in log files for analysis during and after an incident.

**IT Security**   Security of the IT function, as opposed to physical and building security.

**IT Security Staff**   The IT security staff given responsibility for IT security, as opposed to physical and building security.

**Outsourcer**   External company that provides IT services to the firm.

**Postmortem Analysis**   Assessment conducted after a security incident to determine how to respond better in the future.

**Prosecution**   The attempt to convict an attacker in a court of law.

**Public Relations**   Department in a firm charged with communicating with the public and the media on behalf of the firm.

**Punishment**   Taking action against an attacker; both sanctioning employee attackers and prosecuting and suing external attackers.

**Repair**   Phase in incident response in which the damaged system is brought back to correct operation.

**Reprisal Attack**   Attacking the attacker (usually illegal).

**Security Breach**   Another name for a security incident.

**Security Incident**   A virus attack, denial-of-service attack, or hack (computer break-in).

**Trojanize**   To replace a legitimate file by an attacker's file, giving the attacker's file the same name as the legitimate file.

## CROSS REFERENCES

See *Active Response to Computer Intrusions; Combating the Cyber Crime Threat: Developments in Global Law Enforcement; Computer Forensic Procedures and Methods; Cybercrime and the U.S. Criminal Justice System; Cyberlaw: The Major Areas, Development, and Information Security Aspects; Digital Courts, the Law, and Evidence; Evidence Collection and Analysis Tools; Forensic Computing; Global Aspects of Cyberlaw; Intrusion Detection Systems Basics; Law Enforcement and Digital Evidence.*

## REFERENCES

Panko, R. R. (2004). *Corporate computer and network security*. Upper Saddle River, NJ: Prentice Hall.

## FURTHER READING

CERT (Computer Emergency Response Team), Carnegie-Mellon University. Retrieved April 2005, from http://www.cert.org. Provides a broad range of information services for CSIRTs, including detailed reports on specific aspects of CSIRT management and operation.

Kruse, W. G., II, & Heiser, J. G. (2002). *Computer forensics: Incident response essentials*. Boston: Addison-Wesley.

Lucas, J., & Moeller, B. (2004). *The effective incident response team*. Boston: Addison-Wesley.

Mandia, K., & Prosise, C. (2001). *Incident response*. New York: Osborne/McGraw-Hill.

Northcutt, S., & Novak, J. (2001). *Network intrusion detection: An analyst's handbook*. Indianapolis, IN: New Riders.

Prosise, C., & Mandia, K. (2001). *Incident response: Investigating computer crime*. Emeryville, CA: McGraw-Hill Osborne Media.

Schultz, E. E., & Shumway, R. (2002). *Incident response*. Indianapolis, IN: New Riders.

Schweitzer, D. (2003). *Incident response: Computer forensics toolkit*. Upper Saddle River, NJ: Prentice Hall.

West-Brown, M. J., Stikvort, D., Kossakowski, K. P., Killcrece, G., Ruefle, R., & Kajicek, M. (2003). *Handbook for computer security incident response teams* (2nd ed.). Pittsburgh, PA: Carnegie-Mellon Software Engineering Institute. Retrieved April 2005, from http://www.cert.org/archive/pdf/csirt-handbook.pdf

# Implementing a Security Awareness Program

K. Rudolph, *Native Intelligence, Inc.*

## AWARENESS AS A SURVIVAL TECHNIQUE

At 8:46 a.m. on September 11, 2001, the first of four hijacked passenger jets was deliberately crashed into the World Trade Center. Shortly after, two more planes were crashed: one, a second blow to the World Trade Center and the other into the Pentagon. The fourth plane crashed in a Pennsylvania field less than 90 minutes after the first plane was destroyed. Awareness is the reason why the fourth hijacked plane of the terrorist attack on September 11, 2001, crashed in a Pennsylvania field rather than into its probable target, the White House. Awareness (knowing what is going on around you) has an impact on the actions that you take to improve security.

Awareness of the situation came when passengers, reacting to the takeover of the aircraft, used their cell phones to communicate with the outside world. Speaking with relatives and business associates, they became aware of the World Trade Center and Pentagon attacks. At least three passengers indicated that they were planning to retake control of the plane from the hijackers. It is likely that their resistance led to the plane crashing before it reached its intended target. A black box recording retrieved from the crash site supports this scenario and suggests that the passengers succeeded in entering the cockpit. The plane most likely crashed while a struggle for the controls was underway or with a passenger at the controls (Wikipedia, n.d.).

The events of 9/11 raised awareness of security concerns worldwide. Business, government organizations, and individuals reexamined and resolved to improve their security measures to address the escalation in threats. Recognizing the importance of individuals in maintaining adequate levels of protection, the U.S. Department of Homeland Security (DHS) asked people to be aware of their environments and to report any suspicious or unusual activities. There is now a greater awareness of the interconnectedness and vulnerability of our virtual and physical infrastructures and the roles that individuals can and must play to protect them.

In the animal kingdom, awareness—being alert to danger signals and responding quickly—can be the difference between survival and death. Bats and dolphins use sonar to detect and avoid dangers, and cats use whiskers and keen senses of hearing, smell, and night-vision to probe their environments. Being alert to danger signals and responding quickly is also important for organizations. An organization's staff can similarly function as an organization's detection instruments, automatically recognizing things that are "out of place" and reflexively taking preventive and mitigating actions. Awareness activities can build and support this reflexive behavior.

Awareness among an organization's staff (used here to include contractors and partners and, in some cases, customers) is a cost-effective security countermeasure; that is, one that costs less than the impact that it addresses. When determining the cost effectiveness of controls, a general rule is that prevention costs less than cure. "Controls designed to prevent breaches from occurring are more cost-effective than those designed to identify and/or correct breaches after the fact—the main reason being that preventive controls reduce or eliminate the impact costs" (IsecT, 2003). The cost of security controls can include upfront expenses (e.g., purchase price, maintenance, or license fees), implementation and management costs, and costs associated with using or operating the controls. "Cutting-edge high technology security controls are, generally speaking, substantially more expensive across all three categories than low-tech service or procedural controls" (IsecT, 2003).

Members of an organization's workforce are generally the first to be affected by a security incident. Their compliance with security policy can make or break a security program. A staff that is security-aware can detect and prevent many incidents and mitigate damage when incidents do occur. To reap these benefits, awareness must be a critical part of an organization's security program.

Many industries, including health care and finance, as well as the U.S. government, are "finding that security education and awareness are no longer optional" (Ludwig, 2003). The Federal Information Security Management Act (FISMA), the Health Insurance Portability and Accountability Act (HIPAA), Sarbanes-Oxley Act, and the Gramm-Leach-Bliley Act (GLBA) require the federal government, the health care industry, and financial institutions, respectively, to provide mandatory security awareness for staff. "As this type of legislation becomes reasonable and customary, negligence and due diligence law come into play. Therefore, security awareness training is likely to become mandatory for all industries" (Ludwig, 2003).

## Awareness versus Training

Learning is a continuum; it starts with awareness, builds to training, and evolves into education (NIST, 2003). Security awareness differs from security training in purpose, approach, and results.

Awareness has the following characteristics:

- It is intended to focus attention on security and to change attitudes. Awareness sets the stage for training by changing individual perceptions and the organizational culture so that security is recognized as critical. Security failures can keep individuals from completing their work successfully and can threaten organizational survival. "Awareness activities are intended to allow individuals to recognize Information Technology (IT) security concerns and respond accordingly" (NIST, 2003).
- Learning tends to be short term, immediate, and specific.
- Learners are information recipients.
- It reaches broad audiences with attractive, attention-getting techniques.

Training exhibits different characteristics:

- It is more formal than awareness. The purpose of training is to build knowledge and skills to facilitate job performance.
- Training takes longer and involves producing skills and competency for those involved in functional specialties other than IT security (e.g., management, systems design, and acquisition).
- It is provided selectively based on an individual's roles (job functions) and needs.
- Learners have an active role.

## IT Security Is a People Problem

In 1952, UNIVAC, the first commercial computer, was used to predict the outcome of the U.S. presidential election. The human operators refused to believe its prediction, a landslide for Eisenhower, so they reprogrammed it to come up with a different solution. The actual result was, in fact, a landslide for Eisenhower. The operators' actions caused some to declare, "The trouble with machines is people."

Computer security is often viewed as a technology problem. Sophisticated hardware and software solutions are used to control access, detect potential intrusions, and prevent fraud. Yet, security incidents are occurring with increasing frequency. The reality is that computer security is both a human and a technological problem: people do not perform work consistently; they get tired and may perform tasks erratically; they may get angry (at the organization, their spouse, their boss, or at work in general) and intentionally try to disrupt or compromise operations; they may cause system failures by independently "improving" business processes; or they just do not follow established policies and procedures. Connecting computers into networks significantly increases risk because network security depends on the cooperation of every user. A single individual who allows a desktop computer to be compromised places every interconnected system and its associated assets at risk.

"Computers alone don't implement information security policies and standards—human beings purchase and configure the systems, switch on the control functions, monitor the alarms, and run them" (IsecT, 2003). In addition, people are more perceptive and adaptive than hardware/software components. Thus, if properly trained and motivated, they can be the strongest and most effective security countermeasure. Investments in technology to improve information security must be accompanied by investments in people. An awareness program is a needed complement to technical controls, not an alternative.

## Overnight Success Takes Time

Like exercise, security awareness requires time and repetition. If the audience is bombarded with the total awareness arsenal at one time, they become overwhelmed and reject or fail to assimilate much of the information presented. If the same volume of information is presented over an extended time frame, information retention and assimilation into daily business processes are increased. Effective awareness programs are long-term activities that bring about gradual improvement. Management must consistently support the security program and not change approaches from year to year for the sake of change. Awareness activities must consistently reinforce the awareness message, rather than replacing it with each new management interpretation. An effective security awareness program uses techniques similar to those used for a social marketing campaign, repeating a consistent message (e.g., "Don't drink and drive," "Buckle up," "Smoking kills," "Loose lips sink ships") and may need two to five years to produce measurable results (Zimmerman, 1997).

## CRITICAL SUCCESS FACTORS

A security awareness program needs a successful launch for maximum impact. A "preflight" checklist can facilitate a successful launch by ensuring that the following critical program elements are not overlooked:

- an information security policy that establishes the security "rules of behavior" for the organization
- senior-level management support and buy-in to demonstrate the importance of security
- destinations and road maps to guide and monitor program activities
- visibility and audience appeal to ensure that all subgroups within the workforce are addressed

## In-Place Information Security Policy

Security objectives must be embodied in policies that clarify and document management's intentions and concerns. Policies are an organization's "laws." They set expectations for employee performance and guide behaviors. An effective information security policy includes statements of goals and responsibilities and delineates what activities are allowed, what activities are not allowed, and what penalties may be imposed for failure to comply.

Effective information security policies show that management expects a focus on security ("This is important,

pay attention"). Well-defined security policies facilitate compliance and make it easier to take disciplinary action against those who compromise security. Established policies are also useful in dealing with personality types who will not do something until "management tells me to."

A cohesive information security awareness policy, tailored to the organizational culture, gives the total information security program credibility and visibility. It shows that management recognizes that security is important and that individuals will be held accountable for their actions.

An awareness policy should address three basic concepts:

1. Participation in the awareness program is required for everyone, including senior management, part-time and full-time staff, new hires, contractors, or other outsiders who have access to the organization's information systems. For example, new hires might be required to receive an information security awareness briefing within a specific time frame (e.g., 30 days after hire) or before being allowed system access. Existing employees might be required to attend an awareness activity or take a course within one month of program initiation and periodically thereafter (e.g., quarterly or annually). Existing employees might also be required to refresh their security awareness when the organization's IT environment changes significantly.

2. Everyone will be given sufficient time to participate in awareness activities. In many organizations, security policy also requires that employees sign a statement indicating that they understand the material presented and will comply with security policies.

3. Responsibility for conducting awareness program activities is assigned. The program might be created and implemented by one or a combination of the following: the training department; the security staff; or an outside organization, consultant, or security awareness specialist.

## Senior-Level Management Support

Senior management must be committed to information security and must visibly demonstrate that commitment by example (e.g., attending awareness briefings), by providing an adequate budget, and by supporting the security staff.

### Example

Senior management must lead by example. If senior managers do not take security seriously, the program will lack credibility. For example, if the security policy prohibits employees from bringing software from home for use on the organization's PCs and senior executives are seen using personal software on their office system to evaluate their stock portfolios, employees will perceive the policy as inconsistent, unfair, and not universally applicable.

## Budget

Demonstrated, documented top-management support prevents middle managers from denying requests to fund information security. Managers often do not allocate employee time for security awareness activities because they do not see a direct connection to the bottom line for which they are held accountable.

Some security analysts recommend that 40% of an organization's security budget be spent on awareness measures (McBride, 2000). The National Institute of Standards and Technology (NIST) offers four approaches to identifying funding requirements for awareness and training programs: percent of overall training budget, allocation per user by role, percent of overall IT budget, or explicit dollar allocations by component based on overall implementation costs (NIST, 2003).

## Security Staff Backing

Senior managers must stand behind the organization's policies and the security staff charged with enforcing those policies. This is especially important in areas where security and convenience conflict, such as enforcing a control that removes system access for users whose records show that they have not completed a required awareness refresher activity.

# Destination and Road Maps

Ideally, the goals (destination) of an awareness program should be specific, realistic, and measurable. Employees often know much of what an awareness program conveys, but the program serves to reinforce this knowledge and to produce automatic security behaviors. Thus, a goal could be to make "thinking security" a natural reflex for everyone in the organization. Just as martial artists practice many hours to reinforce techniques until responses to physical threats become automatic, awareness programs use repetition to reinforce desired security behaviors and attitudes.

An assessment of relevant legal and organization security policy requirements will help identify goals that can be used to rate performance and progress of the awareness program. Such requirements might include the HIPAA for those concerned with personal health data, the GLBA for those who deal with personal financial data, and the Sarbanes-Oxley Act for publicly-held companies, or the FISMA for federal government personnel. Once the goals are identified, metrics should be established to measure performance against those goals. Possible metrics include the following:

- Answers to survey questions, such as, "In the past three months, have you seen a password on a sticky note in your work area?" If the answer to this question is "yes," there is a compliance problem.
- Number of reported incidents. This number should increase as more people become aware of the reporting requirement and then stabilize or fall as preventive measures are improved.
- Attendance at previous awareness activities. Actions can be taken to encourage organizations whose staff members have not participated in awareness activities.
- Percent of staff who have completed an online security awareness course. One hundred percent should always be the expected norm for awareness activities.
- Estimated dollar value of losses experienced due to security incidents.
- Number of reported instances of lack of compliance with policy (e.g., failure to activate a secure screen saver when leaving the desktop unattended). Most compliance issues may be addressed with training.
- The quantity and quality of interactions between security personnel and end users (e.g., requests for help, specific questions). An increase in this area indicates an increase in user awareness.

Reaching an identified security awareness destination is easier with a road map or plan. An anecdotal story about Abraham Lincoln tells of his statement that if he had 8 hours to chop down a tree, he would spend the first 6 sharpening his ax. Lack of planning usually means that time is spent reacting to events, rather than being proactive and prepared. It takes great effort to chop down a tree with a dull ax. Similarly, it is much harder to create, manage, or measure the effect of an unplanned awareness program than a planned program with defined objectives, assigned responsibilities, and management direction.

Like Lincoln sharpening his ax, planning promotes awareness activities that are carefully designed to elicit specific, positive responses. Plans should also be flexible to address changes in organizational structure, organizational objectives, and applicable threats and vulnerabilities. This flexibility should also allow incorporation of particularly relevant current events. For example, an awareness activity might emphasize the offering of rewards by Microsoft for help in capturing virus writers as evidence that security issues are getting high-level attention.

The security awareness plan can be as short as three to five pages and should contain the following elements:

- a description of the organization and its IT culture
- the status of the organization's current efforts
- program goals and objectives and how progress will be measured
- a schedule showing actions to be completed and who is responsible for ensuring their completion

A security awareness program should be an ongoing effort. Some organizations offer a security awareness orientation to new employees and regular reinforcement for all employees at various times throughout the year. Doing so provides spaced repetition of the material and reinforces learning. Some organizations address security awareness on a monthly basis with newsletters, posters, screen savers, contests, surveys, and online modules. Other organizations offer awareness courses that are updated annually and provide reinforcement at various times, such as on November 30 International Computer Security Awareness Day. NIST SP 800-50 (2003) presents a detailed awareness approach for establishing and maintaining a security program, including an appendix with a sample awareness and training program plan template.

## Visibility and Audience Appeal

An effective awareness program cultivates a professional, positive, and visible image. A visible program demonstrates the value of the awareness activities, raises employee morale, and encourages the support of the general workforce. Security awareness programs that show the organization's concern for employees' IT security well-being at home (for telecommuters and others who use computers at home) and while traveling are better received than programs that ignore such issues. This is because the radio station that most people are tuned to is "WII FM," or What's In It For Me? Whether the target audience is all end users or senior management, showing them how they will personally benefit from improved security awareness contributes to program success. Viewing security as a service with the entire organization as a customer highlights the importance of marketing security to management and staff.

Joseph A. Grau, former chief of the Information Security Division at the Department of Defense Security Institute, believed in the importance of marketing security and often pointed out that customers actually pay for security services. For example, managers pay for enforcing the requirement to lock a classified document in a safe, rather than leaving it on a desk, with labor hours. Other methods of payment are in the form of energy, attention, and concern for security matters, such as taking time to identify and report a potential security incident. Even egos are part of the payment for security when "scientists, researchers, technical specialists, engineers, and management personnel must refrain from communicating their successes to friends, family, and peers to protect sensitive, company private, or classified information" (Hall & SE SIG Steering Committee, 2002).

# OBSTACLES AND OPPORTUNITIES

Starting an awareness program is not as easy as one might expect. Although senior managers seem to recognize the benefits of an awareness program when asked, they may still be reluctant to devote financial resources and staff time to it. It is relatively easy to identify the cost of an awareness program but difficult to quantify its benefits. This is a primary reason why the U.S. government has made maintenance of a computer security awareness program mandatory (FISMA, 2002).

The basic challenges faced when starting and maintaining an effective awareness program include gaining management support, gaining union support (where applicable), overcoming audience resistance, and addressing the diffusion of responsibility.

## Gaining Management Support

Management provides essential ingredients to a security awareness program: credibility, resources, and advocacy. Credibility comes when management complies with the security rules. If managers do not comply, then there

is no reason to expect anyone else to comply. Management allocates resources for the awareness program, visibly demonstrating that their support for the program is genuine. Managers must also support the program by supporting the security staff and showing that computer security is good business. If management does not show that awareness has a positive return, it will be difficult to justify consistent funding. To assist management in these tasks, it is important to keep management informed, speak their language, and provide proof of impact.

### Keep Management Informed

Managers need enough information to allow them to understand security concerns, make informed comments, and respond knowledgably to questions. To get this information to management, identify management reporting and communication mechanisms, such as progress reports, management briefings, and program reviews, and contribute information on security awareness program activities. Include updates with metrics that show performance measured against program goals. Metrics might include the number of violations or reported incidents, the number of incidents caused by internal user behaviors or items addressed in the security awareness materials, surveys of user perceptions about IT security, customer satisfaction surveys, self-assessments, audits, percent of compliance with requirements, and the like (Hall & SE SIG Steering Committee, 2002).

### Speak Their Language

To communicate with management, the IT staff concerned with awareness should consider the following:

- Present realistic information rather than either overstating threats or fears or providing a false sense of security by overemphasizing positive aspects in an attempt to keep the program from being seen as a "problem child."
- Present reasonable suggestions for solutions, along with problems and concerns.
- Prepare a written and verbal presentation so that if the allotted time is cut, you will be able to condense the verbal presentation and leave the written one, thereby delivering the complete message.
- Remember the budget—include costs involved and, where possible, reflect the anticipated benefits (e.g., fewer violations, temporary increase in reported incidents, increased compliance, better audit findings, reduction in misuse of IT assets or personnel time).
- Remember the ecology—ecology is the study of the relationship between organisms (e.g., users, systems) and their environment (e.g., hardware, physical access control). "The ecological aspects of security assert that you cannot afford to focus on one portion of the system without keeping track of the impact of each decision on the health of the ecosystem" (Bace, 2000). Be aware of the impact of the program on the entire organization and its mission. Management concerns include the amount of time that staff spend away from their jobs to satisfy administrative requirements.
- Management resistance is often based on expending funds on something perceived as a low priority or

on concerns about balancing security with operational needs. Although the time and effort to build a strong security program are not trivial, it is far less by comparison with the time and effort required to deal with just one serious incident. Some security professionals recommend pointing out that insurance policies require continuous funding but are not often used; however, few organizations choose to forego those costs (Bace, 2000). Another incentive for organizations is that many contracts require information security programs—especially when the contract is with the federal government or if it deals with intellectual property belonging to customers (e.g., contracts for hardware or software design services).

## Gaining Union Support

John Ippolito, CISSP and co-author of NIST SP 500-16, says, "Mention unions when developing an awareness program and the response ranges from a quizzical look to a sneer. People with a quizzical look have generally never worked with a union and fail to see their role in an awareness program. Those who sneer at the mention of union participation have typically had past efforts blocked by union action" (Ippolito, personal communication, 2003).

Unions can be a partner or an impediment to an awareness program or anything in between. Often, their role depends on how they are approached. Unions look after the best interests of their membership. An awareness program is trying to communicate computer security roles and responsibilities to that membership. Thus, union and program objectives, although different, are not in conflict. To gain union support, sell (present) your program as being in the best interests of union membership. Tips to accomplish this objective include the following:

- Bring in the union representatives early in the program-development phase. Union representatives do not like to be ignored, especially when their membership is involved. If union representatives are presented with a fully developed program, their first response may be to think that it is detrimental to the membership; otherwise, you would have given them more of an opportunity to contribute to its development. This thinking may then result in a micro review, in which union representatives look for anything, no matter how small, that might be interpreted as contrary to the interests of union members.

- Be sure that the representatives understand that the objective of the computer security awareness program is to create within the workforce an understanding that there is a problem (i.e., the potential for a security incident) that can adversely affect the ability of their membership to "get their job done." Thus, program participation is beneficial to their members, and it will help them reduce operating costs without staff reductions.

- Make it clear that the awareness program creates no new responsibilities. The awareness program is intended to help the workforce members recognize potential problems and follow existing security procedures. Ask the union representatives for examples of work situations that might be appropriate to highlight potential security issues.

- Be careful when suggesting any employee testing. Unions often interpret testing, especially when results are recorded, as a management mechanism used to limit the ability of their members to advance. Even a simple pass/fail test can create a union issue as the union will seek clarification about what happens if a person does not pass the test. At the awareness level, recording test or quiz results can be counterproductive and can create anxiety. The best approach is often to ask challenging questions and allow for safe failure, in which students can learn from their mistakes without penalties. Often, a goal of an awareness program is to take away some of the fear and ignorance that have traditionally surrounded IT security by allowing people to learn in a nonthreatening environment.

## Overcoming Audience Resistance

Another common obstacle is audience resistance. A story about a millionaire who threw a large pool party at his mansion illustrates this issue. The pool contained four alligators, and the millionaire announced that he would give $100,000 or a new Ferrari to anyone who would swim the length of the pool. A large splash immediately followed his announcement. The crowd watched a man frantically swimming to the other end. "Well done!" said the millionaire. "Which will you have, the money or the car?" The wet and angry man answered, "I don't care about your prize; I just want to know who pushed me." This is how some end users feel about mandatory awareness courses and activities. It does not matter how good the activity or reward; they just do not want to be told that they have to do it.

In many organizations, a positive approach is more effective than a negative one. Programs that rely on the "FUD factor" (motivation by fear, uncertainty, and doubt) or use negative phrases such as "failure to attend" may not be as effective, because such statements are viewed by some employees as challenges, whereas others see them as empty threats. In addition, such statements can be offensive to those employees who are always cooperative. It is often better "to encourage participation, expect compliance, and deal with the no-shows later" (Hall & SE SIG Steering Committee, 2002).

An awareness program must be formulated to address the total organization. This includes the naïve user, the new user, the power user, and even those who think that computer security is worthless and does not apply to them. Given this audience diversity, the content must be structured so that the same level of awareness can be communicated using a variety of techniques. For example, password protection might be best communicated to the naïve user through a computer-based "war story," whereas the same concepts might be best communicated to the power user with a brief statement of the organizational requirements on a poster or reminder memo.

Although the basic technology components may be similar from one organization to the next, the manner in which they are configured is often different, as is the terminology used to refer to them. For example, some organizations use the term "desktop" and others the term "workstation" to refer to the computer installed at an end user's location. These seemingly trivial differences can make a "one size fits all" awareness approach fail.

## Addressing the Diffusion of Responsibility

One result of addressing the entire organization with a single message is a diffusion of responsibility. When people are in a group, responsibility for acting is diffused. The security awareness program must convey that each individual is responsible for taking action to prevent or report breaches, regardless of how many others may have noticed the same symptoms or other factors.

To illustrate the diffusion of responsibility, researchers conducted an experiment where a student alone in a room staged an epileptic fit. When there was just one person listening next door, that person rushed to the student's aid 85% of the time. However, when subjects thought there were four others also overhearing the seizure, they came to the student's aid only 31% of the time. In another experiment, people who saw smoke seeping out from under a doorway reported it 75% of the time when they were on their own, but only 38% percent of the time when they were in a group (Darley & Latane, 1968). Providing individual reinforcement in addition to group activities may mitigate this diffusion of responsibility.

## APPROACH

### Awareness as Social Marketing

Raising awareness is similar to social marketing, which uses advertising techniques to inform the public of societal concerns, such as the campaigns to reduce smoking or decrease the use of alcohol on college campuses. The marketing concepts of message, product, and market apply in a security awareness campaign. The message is the need for security, the product is the practice of security, and the market is all employees. Communication is the essential tool, and the information disseminated becomes the foundation on which behavioral change is built.

Research and planning are essential and should result in a clear strategy that does the following:

- defines program objectives
- identifies primary and secondary audiences
- defines information to be communicated
- describes approaches that fit the organizational culture and structure
- describes benefits that accrue to the audience

Research may be conducted by observation, surveys, tests, and interviews. Review help desk statistics and trends for indications of actual and potential security incidents and evidence of training needs. For example, a large number of password resets might indicate that password procedures need to be reviewed or that users need additional training. Ask the staff how they would break into the system—the people closest to the system ought to know its vulnerabilities and should be thinking about how to fix them. Ask them to consider such questions as, "Are security breaches predictable?"

Pretest materials before distributing them. Pretesting provides evidence that materials are reaching your target audience with the intended message. It can also avoid embarrassing situations, such as occur after distributing a poster on which punctuation or the lack of punctuation changes the message (e.g., "Slow Work Zone" instead of "Slow, Work Zone"). Pretesting may be accomplished using focus groups, providing materials to a single unit within the organization or through group or individual interviews. In all cases, the evaluation should include a set of multiple-choice or ranking questions with one or two open-ended questions. This analysis approach facilitates data comparison and aggregation. The question set should be structured to determine the message received and the level of experience (novice, beginner, user, power user) required to understand the material and receive the intended message. The questions should also be structured to avoid leading the respondent.

## The Art of Motivation

An awareness program seeks to change attitudes and behaviors that may have been practiced for a long time in company procedures or become habits that are now part of the organizational culture. Change is often met with resistance simply because people do not like change. An awareness program must consider this natural workforce resistance to change by appealing to complementary attitudes or preferences. For example, the practice of password sharing with new employees to "get them on the system sooner" may be widespread. By showing that people are respected and recognized in the organization for protecting system access, rather than placing system assets at risk, the awareness campaign may change this behavior.

Hackers are often viewed as "cool" or as technical prodigies who deserve encouragement and nurturing, not punishment. Thus, an awareness program must communicate this anti-hacker message: hackers are not "cool," they lack an appreciation for ethical conduct, many are not technical experts (Trowbridge, 2003), and, most important, their actions (intentional or unintentional) hurt people. For example, the damage done when a person's identity or personal data are stolen is significant both in terms of dollars and disruption to that person's life: just think of the hours lost notifying creditors of the deception, changing credit cards and other financial documents, and proving that someone else signed the second mortgage on your house. An awareness program must deglamorize hackers by focusing on the victims and the harmful results of hacking. When people are aware that hackers hurt people, they may be better motivated to act to reduce hacking activity.

Security controls are generally viewed as an impediment to getting work done. The workforce needs to be motivated to comply through an awareness message that makes it clear that the need for security has been balanced against its impact on business processes. This message must be carried forward to system designers so that they also understand that cumbersome controls that are too disruptive to business processes will create an environment hostile toward security and are an incentive to bypass controls to meet schedules and production objectives.

Audience perceptions and cultural characteristics are factors that may be used in structuring motivational materials. Some of these factors are as follows:

- People want to conform to the organizational performance norm (i.e., they generally do not want to "stand out in a crowd"). Thus, show that security compliance results in positive feedback, whereas prosecution of violators is "noisy" and intended to cause embarrassment. Recent trends show that co-workers are reacting with less empathy toward those whose machines have become infected with viruses. Reactions to people who had their computers infected with the MyDoom virus in February 2004 included such statements as "For shame!" and "It takes affirmative action on the part of the clueless user to become infected" (Harmon, 2004).
- People are superstitious. That is one reason they pass on chain letters and often open or read e-mails with a subject line that indicates bad luck will follow if they do not continue the chain. Motivate your audience to change their perception of the superstition such that a negative outcome will be the result of following it (e.g., negative consequences will follow if you do open the chain letter and don't break the chain).
- People are curious. That is the primary reason why so many virus attacks are successful. People open an e-mail because the subject line makes them curious about the message contents. For example, the message "Your Account is Overdrawn," will make many people open a message to see what account, how much over, or what is this scam. Awareness techniques can take advantage of people's curiosity by creating multilevel messages, such as this one patterned on the Burma Shave model of stretching a message over a series of signs:

> Hackers send e-mail
> With subjects enticing
> To open the message
> And the virus it's hiding

Fear is often used as a motivator; however, the primary value of scare tactics is to attract audience attention. Learning communicated through fear is generally retained only in the short term. People follow messages communicated through fear, but their compliance quickly falls off when nothing bad happens. For example, if the message is, *"Open an e-mail attachment and you may get a virus that destroys your hard disk,"* every time an e-mail attachment is opened and nothing happens, the fear associated with this message is reduced. Eventually, opening an e-mail attachment will be performed without concern — until a virus actually does strike.

Therefore, fear should not be used as a primary motivator. However, if you do decide to use fear as a motivator, be prepared to back it up with consequences and publicity regarding every security incident. Although you may use fear to attract attention, a more effective delivery approach will have a positive spin. There should be more emphasis on how security measures can help your audience get the job done than on how many days they will be suspended if they fail to comply. Demonstrate that the courage and independence it takes to resist appeals from friends and co-workers to share copyrighted materials illegally are rewarded (i.e., those who follow the rules are seen as praiseworthy and not as weaklings).

Failure to properly tailor motivating techniques to your audience often results in the following:

- Loss of the audience's attention—The awareness message is never communicated; thus, workforce behavior remains unchanged.
- Alienation of the audience—The awareness message is communicated, but the workforce perceives the message as an incentive to work against security objectives.
- Trying to do too much—Awareness is not training or education. If the awareness audience is bombarded with everything that a security officer or system administrator should know about security, the awareness message will be lost and the audience turned off. Like an exercise program, awareness material is best when delivered in small increments, over an extended time frame, and is targeted to establishing the basic understanding that there is a security problem.

## CONTENT

Awareness is intended to change individuals' behaviors so that they recognize potential security incidents and react appropriately. Awareness materials are generally broad in coverage but limited in depth (i.e., awareness covers a lot of ground, but does not dig very deep holes). Using such materials avoids encroaching on training, which is in-depth, but is also role-based (i.e., provides the security training specific to an individual's organizational responsibilities).

NIST recommends the following 27 topics for security awareness programs:

- password use and management,
- protection from malicious code,
- policy (implications of noncompliance),
- unknown e-mail attachments,
- Web use,
- spam,
- data backup and storage,
- social engineering,
- incident response,
- shoulder surfing (watching over someone's shoulder as he or she types),
- changes in system environment,
- inventory and property transfer,
- personal use and gain issues,
- hand-held device security issues,
- encryption and transmission of sensitive data,
- laptop security while on travel,
- personally owned systems and software at work,
- timely application of system patches,
- software license restriction,
- supported/allowed software on organization systems,
- access control,
- individual accountability,

- user acknowledgment statements,
- visitor control and physical access to spaces,
- desktop security,
- protection of information throughout the life cycle, and
- e-mail list etiquette

(NIST, 2003). To avoid overwhelming the audience, NIST also recommends that these topics be explained one or a few at a time: "Brief mention of requirements (policies), the problems that the requirements were designed to remedy, and actions to take are the major topics to be covered in a typical awareness presentation" (NIST, 2003).

An awareness program should address three basic questions:

1. Why am I important to security?
2. What does a security incident look like?
3. What do I do about it (security)?

## Why Am I Important to Security?

Why am I important to security? It seems like this would be an easy concept to address in an awareness program, but it is not. People tend to believe the best of others (no one would want to break into my system), downplay the value of their work (I don't have anything that someone else would want or nothing I do really affects the organization), and are ignorant of their role in the security solution (I can't do anything; it's the IT staff's job). These audience perceptions must all be addressed and changed, and the best way to do that is through an awareness campaign.

"All individuals in the workforce are important to fulfilling organizational goals" is a message that needs to be communicated through an awareness program. People need to be reminded of the value of their work because they often do not understand how their work contributes to the business process. In addition, organizations provide their workforce with significant assets in the form of equipment, software, and data. Compromise or loss of these assets could cause significant harm to the organization's solvency and make it subject to legal liability due to data compromise.

Individuals often are the first to detect security incidents. The actions they take or fail to take subsequently determine the level of damage. Further, individual compliance with established security policies and procedures can "make or break" a security environment. For example, an individual leaving an unattended desktop connected to the corporate network places all the interconnected assets at risk.

## What Do Security Incidents Look Like?

What do security incidents look like? What does a criminal look like? Both questions have no single answer. There is no single criminal profile, and there is no single set of characteristics that fits a security incident.

An awareness program needs to communicate that individuals are not expected to report only verified security incidents. The determination as to whether a particular event is or is not a security incident is an after-the-fact decision made by the technical staff after evaluating the event, its cause, and impact. Individuals are expected to report anything that "might be" a security incident. Thus, the awareness materials should explain that individuals should report erratic or abnormal system behavior or such occurrences as phone calls from "equipment vendors" asking for user passwords, unusual processing slowdowns, dial-in circuits that are always busy, or anything else that appears strange or differs from the normal processing environment.

## What Do I Do About Security?

Explaining the role of the entire workforce (i.e., it is everybody's responsibility) in security comprises the bulk of the awareness program. The material communicated must be coordinated with organizational policies, and it must be limited in depth—do not cross over into training, or you will lose your audience. The material should also be tailored to the organization's technical architecture and configuration (e.g., do not explain the threats to wireless communications if wireless is not present; do not talk about mainframe security when there is no mainframe).

### Basic Security Concepts

Risks, threats, and vulnerabilities are basic concepts of security that must be generally understood so that security and the individual's relation to security can be placed in its proper perspective.

- Risk—The entire workforce should generally understand the concept of risk. The basic understanding that should be communicated is that no useful system is without risk and that security controls provide reasonable levels of protection, not absolute protection. It is therefore critical that individuals report anomalies that may indicate an attack or security incident.
- Threat—A threat is always present, and neither the individual nor the organization can affect when or if a threat will affect/attack their organization (i.e., threats are always there and you cannot change that). This is a simple but often misunderstood concept. Awareness programs need to address threats so that the workforce will understand that systems operate in an unfriendly environment and that is why it is so important for everyone to help maintain and strengthen the security environment.
- Vulnerabilities—Threats cannot have an impact on a system unless there is a vulnerability. Vulnerabilities include failure to change passwords, update/patch operating systems, or report potential incidents; lack of a surge suppressor; verbose information broadcasts on networked servers; and many others. Individuals can identify vulnerabilities (e.g., a desktop without a surge suppressor). Awareness material should provide examples of how to identify a vulnerability and the reporting process to ensure that the vulnerability is addressed.

### Technical Issues

Technical issues are the specific threats, system components, controls, or control techniques that should be considered for inclusion in an awareness program, including the following:

- Access control and passwords (password creation, change, resets, deletion)

- Social engineering (include specific examples of scripts that might be used)
- "Malware" (e.g., malicious mobile code, viruses, and worms), how it can damage an information system, and how the organization handles viruses, hoaxes, and spam
- Data sensitivity, including privacy issues (vulnerability of payroll, medical, and personnel records)
- Data handling, including transmission (wireless or hard-wired), storage, and backups
- Appropriate use of the Internet, including the World-Wide Web, peer-to-peer file sharing, and e-mail
- Mobile computing (for those who work from home or on travel)
- Home PCs (personally owned PCs)
- Laptops, PDAs/hand-held devices, and mobile phones

Each item included should be tailored to the specific user environment and organizational policy.

### Reporting

The primary responsibility of all individuals within the workforce is to comply with security policies and procedures and report potential vulnerabilities and potential security incidents. This section presents the topics that should be addressed regarding reporting in an awareness program.

- Who: Individuals within the workforce should be given the contact information, such as telephone and pager numbers, e-mail, and Web site URLs (addresses), of the security staff, the incident response team, and help desk personnel.
- What: The most critical information is who is reporting the incident; its symptoms, date, and time; and actions taken. Other types of information that are helpful when reporting a suspected problem include the affected system(s) or site(s), hardware and operating system, duration of incident, connections with other systems that were active, damage, and assistance needed.
- When: Users need to know that, with security events, time is of the essence. Reporting the problem immediately can often prevent or limit the scope and severity of the damage. Users should know not to delay reporting.
- How: Workers should be given instructions for reporting suspected problems by telephone or by e-mail using a system that is not suspected of being under attack.

## TECHNIQUES AND PRINCIPLES

Presentation of awareness materials is crucial. If the employee's reaction is "I knew that" or "So what?," the program is not effective. Desired responses include the following:

- "I never thought of it that way."
- "That surprises me!"
- "That's a great idea!"
- "I'd almost forgotten about that...."
- "I can use this."

### Start with a Bang—Make It Attention-Getting and Memorable

Experienced, in-demand speakers do not start a presentation with a long, dry, boring introduction that lists every law, regulation, policy, standard, guideline, or other requirement that relates to information security. If there were such a thing as a deadly sin in an awareness program, it would be to bore the audience. For an awareness message to be effective, the audience must identify with the idea, concept, or vision.

### Appeal to the Target Audience

A U.S. Critical Infrastructure Assurance Office publication states: "The level of security awareness required of a summer intern program assistant is the same as that needed by the Director, Chief, or Administrator of the agency" (Office of Personnel Management [OPM] regulation: 5 CFR Part 930, RIN 3205-AD43), and U.S. federal employees must attain this security awareness within 60 days of starting work. Although workers at all levels need to have security awareness, the methods for effectively reaching different employees with the awareness message may need to be different. It is easier to hit the bull's-eye when one can focus on a specific target.

There are different audiences within all organizations, with different characteristics based on their needs, roles, and interests:

- Needs. Audiences with similar needs will have similar levels of computer knowledge and experience. End users with minimal computer experience may be intimidated by and not respond well to technical jargon. Analogies and examples are more appropriate for audiences with little in-depth computer expertise.
- Roles and Interests. Awareness programs that appeal to the existing values and motivations of the target audience will be more successful than ones that try to change them. End users are usually interested in getting their job done with as little obstruction as possible. They are usually interested in knowing about the effect of security on their workload, delays, and job-performance evaluations. Managers are usually interested in the bottom line and measurable results. They want to know, "How much will this security control cost?" and "What kind of benefits will it bring?" Technical staff should receive materials with correct technical term usage. Otherwise, they may conclude that the information is beneath them or that it has been prepared by persons who lack technical knowledge.

To create an awareness program, first identify the audiences and conduct research to find out what they know and what questions about security they ask most often. Surveys and questionnaires can be used to reveal the starting level of awareness of security issues. They will also be useful for measuring progress after the awareness program is implemented.

Historical information can provide clues about what the audience knows and does not know. Asking, "What security-related problems has the organization experienced?" may reveal information that can be used to tailor the awareness program.

## Address Personality and Learning Styles (Provide Options)

Trainers often describe three primary learning styles: auditory, visual, and kinesthetic. An auditory learner picks up information from hearing or reading it and is effectively reached by lectures and written material. A visual learner wants to see what is being taught and prefers diagrams, charts, and pictures. A kinesthetic learner responds well to tactile input and wants to walk through the steps or learn by physically doing the task.

Yet, personality styles are arguably more important than learning styles. Some people will not follow a procedure until they understand the reason for it. To reach these people, present the "whys." If an exercise is included as part of an awareness course, once a question is answered, give learners the choice of trying again or receiving the answer. Some people learn best and have better retention when they figure out something for themselves. Others just want to see the result and move on to the next topic or exercise.

## Keep It Simple—Awareness Is Not Training

Awareness efforts should be simple. An objective of an awareness program is to take away the fear and ignorance that have traditionally surrounded information security. Effective awareness activities make people recognize that there is a problem and that they are part of the solution.

## Use Logos, Themes, and Images

Attention is a prerequisite to learning. This was recognized at least 80 years ago: "The person who can capture and hold attention is the person who can effectively influence human behavior" (Overstreet, 1925). Awareness activities and materials should be designed to attract attention in a positive way. Clever slogans and eye-catching images contribute to the program's success.

Well-designed security logos and mascots can be a source of pride and a showpiece for the organization. Images have greater impact than words. Color and design, as well as the uniqueness of the image, add to its effectiveness. The careful use of animated images in presentations, computer- and Web-based courses, and screen savers can enhance the message. A Web-based course used by many U.S. government organizations opens with the words, "What would happen if someone changed your data?" The words are an animated image that changes a few characters at a time until the message becomes completely unreadable: "Wyad ciunx safper ef stmxune khopgel joor deko?" This image makes a dramatic point about data integrity and availability.

Themes can be used to unite several concepts into a related message. The theme of "Prevention Is Better than Cure" would be appropriate for organizations that process medical data. Give-away items, such as first-aid kits with security slogans and contact information imprinted

on them, could tie in to a medical theme, as could the concepts of virus checking software and backups being similar to health insurance cards in that they must be current to be of value.

The U.S. Nuclear Regulatory Commission (NRC) celebrates International Computer Security Day each year with a different theme. The theme of a recent celebration was "Keep It Clean"; an NRC computer security officer (CSO) dressed as Mr. Clean (complete with a bald head and gold hoop earring) passed out antivirus software to employees who attended the event. A large, signed color photograph of the official Mr. Clean was on display. Another year, the celebration introduced the agency's new security mascot, Cyber Tyger. Cyber Tyger was featured on posters, on the cover of the antivirus software CD, and on buttons. Again, one of NRC's CSOs arrived in costume and delighted the visitors. In other years the themes have been "It's a Bug's Life" and "PC Doctor," in which a "sick" PC was wheeled into the lobby on a gurney while the CSO, dressed in surgical scrubs and mask, explained the symptoms of a virus infection to visitors.

Awareness posters can be developed around a common theme, with common design elements, or a phrase or logo. A staged campaign of posters might include a series with numbers on them; for example, "85" on one and "3 million" on another. No explanation of the numbers would be given, and a mystery would develop. Later, new posters could explain that 85 is the number of reported incidents at the organization in the past year and that 3 million is the number of dollars of lost business from a DDoS attack.

## Use Stories and Examples—Current and Credible

Stories about real people and real consequences (people being praised, disciplined, or fired) are useful in presentations and courses. Sources of stories include individuals who have been with the organization for a long time and have a "corporate memory," news events, Internet special interest bulletin boards, and security personnel who attend special interest group meetings and conferences.

The stories should relate to situations and decisions the audience may face. Stories about hackers accessing medical records would be useful to organizations that process medical data, whereas stories about fraud or identity theft would be of interest to personnel involved in the financial industry or the accounting function of an organization.

Awareness material must be fresh and not stale. Chef Oscar Gizelt of Delmonico's Restaurant in New York said, "Fish should smell like the tide. Once they smell like fish, it's too late." If awareness material is not changed frequently, it too begins to smell old and becomes boring, or less credible.

Credibility is crucial for an awareness program to be effective. The message should be clear, relevant, and appropriate to the real world. If the audience is required to use 15 different passwords as a part of day-to-day functions, prohibiting them from writing their passwords may not be as realistic as providing strategies for protecting the written list.

## Use Failure

"Expectation failure" is a most important learning accelerator (Schank, 1997). People often do not pay attention to information they are expecting to hear or see. When an employee takes a computer-based awareness quiz and gets an answer wrong, he or she pays more attention. Yet, failure should be safe and private. For this reason, computer-based awareness questions and quizzes should provide immediate feedback but should not record answers. At the awareness level, it is more important to give staff members something to think about than to have them get every answer correct. To remove anxiety, inform staff members that their answers will not be recorded.

## Involve the Audience—Buy-In Is Better Than Coercion

People who have contributed to the awareness program with suggestions, contest entries, or focus group testing are more likely to accept and follow security controls. This assumes that feedback is given for every suggestion submitted. No feedback implies "no management interest."

Awareness activities that are active and involve the audience are more memorable than passive ones. Whether in person, on a poster, or through a Web-based awareness course, involving the audience with questions such as "Did you know... ?" and "What would you do if... ?" is an effective awareness technique.

Trivia questions and unexpected or counterintuitive facts are good attention getters. For example, asking this question,

"In the United States, which of the following activities is illegal?

    A.   Creating a virus that spreads through e-mail
    B.   Disrupting Internet communications
    C.   Failing to make daily backups of data"

usually results in people choosing the first answer. The question is designed to be thought-provoking, because creating a virus is not actually illegal. Releasing a virus is, but that is not one of the answers. The correct answer is "Disrupting Internet communications." The question is designed to get people to think about security in new ways.

Another good awareness technique is to use unusual or psychologically compelling questions designed to engender thought. Such questions can be given during live presentations or over the Web. For example, logic professor Rick Garlikov suggested the following sequence of questions to help end users realize that it is not only the probability of a bad thing happening but also the damage that could occur that determines how much precaution is needed.

Start out asking the audience, "How many of you see security as just being a nuisance to your doing your real work?" If people raise their hands, call on them and ask "How so?" or "In what way?" or "Why is that?" Then see what they say, and go from there with "What if... ?" types of questions.

Ask how many believe that "an ounce of prevention is a pain in the neck" or "an ounce of prevention is a lot of trouble."

Agree that we all hate to take precautions when risk does not seem likely. However, there are two factors in determining the potential damage caused by any risk situation: probability and impact. Most people only take probability into account. Offer to try a Socratic demonstration to show that probability is not the only factor to take into account:

Ask, "How many of you would play Russian roulette?"

We assume most/all will not. If someone does say he would play, ask why. See whether his reason makes any sense. If not, just laugh and go on.

Ask those who won't play, "Why not?"

Presumably someone will say something like, "You can get killed," or "It's not good odds."

Then say, "Yes, and the odds are one in six, which are not good odds. But, I'll tell you what, let's make the odds a lot better. We'll just put one bullet in one chamber of one of 100 revolvers, so that your odds will only be 1 in 600. And we will sweeten the pot by letting you win $10 if the gun does not go off when you shoot it at your head? Now how many will play?"

If some would play under those conditions, ask them why, and let others agree or disagree.

The point is that no matter how much you increase the odds, the risk is not worth the game because you have too much to lose and not nearly enough to gain.

To wrap up this line of questions, explain, "The idea is that it is not just the odds that matter; it is what you can win versus what you can lose, along with the odds that need to be taken into account. So even if the risk of being hacked might be small, what will it cost you or your company if it happens? And what is the cost in trying to prevent it by just being a little more careful in ways we will teach you—such as changing your password more frequently, or being suspicious of anyone needing your password, or never hooking up a modem just to have slightly more convenience, etc.?"

## Be Surprising (The Unexpected Is Memorable)

Well-crafted awareness material is like a piñata; when the audience breaks it open, it should be full of surprises. An activity that often results in wonderful surprises and learning is role playing. Role playing (live or by means of computer- or Web-based simulations) is an excellent way to show the target audience what is expected of them. At a recent security educators' conference, two educators did an impromptu role play of a worker dealing with a boss who wanted to tail gate—to follow the employee through a secure door that had been opened with the employee's cardkey. The audience was entertained and learned by example how to handle such a situation and how to teach others to do the same. Audience members will remember the role play long after they have forgotten material presented on slides.

To attract attention in an awareness campaign, Richard Heron, Manager of Information Security for the Royal Bank of Canada in Sydney, Australia, handed out fortune cookies with security messages in them. He bought

20 boxes of fortune cookies, printed some key security messages (e.g., regarding passwords, not discussing confidential company information in public) on strips of paper, placed the security messages into the 400 cookies (using plastic gloves), took them to work, and handed them to the 300+ bank employees.

He describes these benefits of this approach: getting his message across in a memorable way, having the opportunity to meet and talk with staff so that they know who he is and how to reach him with security concerns, sharing his message in a positive nonconfrontational way, and sparking employees' interest and discussions about security. He found that staff began to query others: "What message did you get? I got 'If you fail to plan, you plan to fail.'" In the future he plans to include 10 messages in red or gold paper that will entitle the 10 recipients to win a prize (e.g., movie tickets).

## Use Competition

One federal organization uses a Web-based awareness course that is updated annually. Each year, the course shows the number of people in each area and office who are registered to take the course and the percent who complete it, also by area and office, in a real-time bar chart with animations. The office or area that reaches a 100% completion rate first wins a trophy that stays with that area's security officer for the entire year. All course takers can view the contest from any page in the course. In addition, the course includes a poster idea contest with monthly winners, whose ideas are rendered by a professional artist and then provided in downloadable PDF format. A grand winner is picked from the 12 monthly winners, and that poster is printed in an 11 × 17 format and provided to the organization. All winning posters display the name and office of the winners. The program allows end users to earn from one to three gold stars on their course completion certificates by answering bonus questions. Additionally, the first 10% of course takers to complete the course receive a certificate that has a blue rosette at the top with the words, "First ten percent."

Another organization also has teams of people whose job is to break into their own systems. These penetration testers leave tracks in the system audit trails, and system, network, or LAN administrators who find and report the "intrusions" win T-shirts that say, "I caught the test team" and coffee mugs or other prizes. An additional benefit realized is that some of the administrators also caught real intrusion attempts during this activity.

## Incorporate User Acknowledgment and Sign-Off

A technique for getting people to pay attention is to hold them personally responsible for their actions and choices. Many organizations have established policies requiring that individuals' system access be removed if participation in documented awareness orientations or refreshers is not recorded for them by the end of each fiscal year.

"Noisy prosecutions," which publicly shame security policy violators, are an excellent way to discourage security breaches. An example would be listing violators on the organization's intranet. Organizations may be reluctant to report security incidents out of concern for losing public confidence. Reporting incidents, however, allows trends to be tracked and may result in faster identification and response to problems.

## Use Analogies

Analogies, metaphors, and similes help learners associate new concepts with their previous knowledge or experience. These figures of speech create pictures that connect the teacher and learner to the same idea. The famous U.S. trial lawyer, Gerry Spence (1995) says, "Words that do not create images should be discarded." For example, saying that an organization that has a firewall but does not prevent users from installing modems in their desktop PCs is "like putting a steel door on a straw house" allows readers to visualize the concept.

Analogies can make complex topics easier to understand. They form a bridge between what the learners already know and the new concept or idea that the learners are expected to understand. For example, a common analogy used to explain password protection techniques is that passwords are like toothbrushes (change them often; never share). Another analogy is that passwords are like bubble gum (strongest when fresh; should be used by an individual, not a group; and if left lying around, will create a sticky mess). A memorable analogy, especially if accompanied by an illustration, is that passwords are like long underwear: they should be long and mysterious, should protect the owner, should be used by one person and not a group, and should be changed periodically.

The more creative or unusual the analogy, the more likely it is to be remembered. For example, sensitive data are like prescription medicines: they should be used only by those who need them and who are authorized to have them; they should not be transferred, sold, or given to those for whom they are not authorized; and they can cause damage if they are given to people who do not have a legitimate need for them. Cars, medieval castles, and American Indian and European folklore, among other topics, have been used successfully to present information-security concepts.

## Use Humor

Humor is an effective attention getter and can be used to motivate people and influence an organization's culture. It also helps people relax, which facilitates learning. Here are two rules for using humor in awareness presentations, courses, and materials:

1. Use humor that is relevant and complements or augments the message. Humor must be used for a purpose; otherwise, it is a distraction and will cause a loss of credibility.
2. Do not use humor that will offend your audience. Avoid sexist, ethnic, religious, political, and bathroom humor. Do not make fun of something that cannot be changed, such as a physical or social characteristic (e.g., an extra limb or stuttering).

It is often more acceptable to use humor involving oneself or those in positions of power, such as management and auditors. For example, a presenter might say, "The auditor is the one who arrives after the battle and bayonets the wounded," to an audience of managers. Or, a consultant for disaster recovery sites might explain about having a one-page disaster plan: "The plan is simple. It has only two steps: First, I always keep a copy of my resume up to date; and second, I store a backup copy in a secure, off-site location." The possibility of having this use of humor backfiring should be considered carefully.

Sources of humor include the following:

- cartoons, especially those that deal with organizational and technology humor
- humorous definitions; for example, "the Arnold Schwarzenegger virus—it'll be back"
- security-related poems or lyrics written to the tunes of popular songs or in a specific style, such as an information security rap
- a security haiku, a 17-syllable poem composed in three lines of 5, 7, and 5 syllables, such as the following:

> Computer virus,
> destroyer of files, survives
> through lack of scanning.

- David Letterman-style "Top Ten" lists, such as the Top Ten excuses for not making a backup or for not reporting a suspected incident

## Show Consequences

Some organizations send memos to all staff that describe specific examples of personnel who have violated policy. The memos cover a set time period—for example, the previous quarter—and include the number of individuals; the nature of the violations; and the penalties, such as loss of Internet privileges or two months without pay (also displayed in dollars, based on the average salary).

## Take Advantage of Circumstances

Current events can be an excellent source of material and can add credibility to an awareness program. Several Internet security and technology sites offer subscriptions to electronic security alerts and news clippings. Some organizations have established a "news hawk" program, in which rewards are given to the first employee to bring in a new relevant story that can be used as part of the awareness program. This is also a good technique to gain buy-in from the end-user community.

## TOOLS

When choosing tools to convey an awareness message, three questions should be addressed:

1. What tools are most appropriate for the message?
2. What methods are most likely to be credible to and accessible by the target audience?
3. Which methods (and how many methods) are feasible, considering the available budget and the time frame?

Using as many methods and tools as possible, with a consistent message, reinforces the message and increases the likelihood that the audience will be exposed to it often enough or long enough to absorb it.

## Web-Based Courses (Lessons Learned)

Browser-based tools include Web sites on the Internet, on the organization's Intranet, and Web-based courses. E-mail can be used to send alerts or electronic newsletters (e-zines). Web sites (public or private) can be used in the following ways:

- as a research tool for gathering information
- to present policies and other documents
- to post alerts
- to collect data for security awareness surveys or incident reporting
- for self-assessments to identify at-risk security practices
- for anonymous reporting of security concerns
- for Web casts of security conferences or presentations

Web-based awareness courses are useful for staff members who are geographically dispersed and who need to take the refresher or course at a time that is convenient for them. Such courses are especially well suited for use by individuals who have diverse backgrounds and experience with technology. Online courses offer the following advantages over traditional place-based and instructor-led training:

- Feedback is immediate, so learners do not build on early misunderstandings. Well-designed Web-based training takes cultural and personality differences into account and reassures timid trainees while allowing more confident ones to progress at a faster pace. "Why" buttons or links, "How" buttons, "Show me an example" buttons, and "Give me an alternative" buttons can be set up to let learners with different needs and personalities use the course to learn in ways that are comfortable for them.
- Because a Web-based awareness course can be taken at any time, it is convenient for the trainees. It does not have to be scheduled, so those with variable or hectic schedules can arrange to take the course at a time that is good for them.
- Web-based courses allow users to make mistakes and learn from them in a safe, nonthreatening environment.
- Web-based courses are flexible and can be customized to accommodate learners with different levels of experience and different interests. By placing detailed information in subordinate, linked pages, users are able to choose between the "need to know" main pages and the "nice to know" hyperlinked pages.
- Web-based courses can reduce costs and training time. Placing updates to courses on the Web eliminates the work involved with distributing the current version and materials to multiple locations. This can be more efficient and consistent because the content has

been reviewed, edited, and tested to make it clear and concise.

- Web-based courses are self-paced, so that more experienced users can race through without getting bored while novice users can ponder and explore.

Exciting and effective Web-based courses should have the following characteristics:

- Start with a bang. Begin with a story, an image, a headline, or something that immediately engages the learner's attention. Courses should never start with a dull, "why you need this training..." introduction. Writer Paul O'Neil offers some excellent advice to writers that applies to creators of awareness programs: "Always grab the reader by the throat in the first paragraph, sink your thumbs into his windpipe in the second, and hold him against the wall until the tag line."
- Be goal-based, allowing learners to choose how and when they will meet the course requirements.
- Be active and involve learning by doing.
- Address multiple learning styles and personalities. Appealing to multiple senses increases retention. Appealing to different personality styles ensures that the message will reach a wider audience.
- Challenge the learner's beliefs and expectations and allow learners to fail in interesting and safe ways.
- Use scenarios, examples and analogies—people learn best from real situations where they can relate the learning to prior knowledge.
- Provide feedback, such as immediate answers to questions. Feedback is essential to motivation and performance.
- Be memorable. People tend to remember things that are unusual or unexpected or that carry a visceral impact. Repetition also contributes to how memorable an idea is.
- Include stories. Stories grab people's attention. Organizations should collect stories about security incidents, security heroes, mistakes made, and lessons learned.
- Be accessible. Guidelines for creating Web pages that are accessible to people with vision or hearing impairments are published by the World Wide Web Consortium (W3C). To be accessible, the Web pages should not rely on vision or sound alone to impart meaning. For example, all graphics should be labeled with text that explains the graphic, and the contrast between the text and the background should be maximized.

A potential problem to watch for in Web-based courses is the tendency to get carried away by the technology. Just because an awareness course could have three dozen animated, singing computers decorating the pages does not mean that it should. The technology must be used appropriately; bigger buildings do not make better scholars, and more impressive technology does not necessarily result in a better learning experience. A Web-based course that is overloaded with animations and graphics that do not relate to course content or that has a poorly designed user interface will set the awareness program back.

## In-Person Briefings (and Brown Bag Lunches)

At a brown bag lunch, people who attend security-related workshops, conferences, or seminars can share a summary of the information presented with those who did not attend. Guest speakers can present material on current topics or their areas of expertise.

## Contests

Contests are a good way to motivate people. Vince Lombardi, former head coach of the Green Bay Packers, understood this. He once said, "Winning isn't everything. It's the only thing." After criticizing him for this statement, some of his critics put together a new kind of baseball league for children in a Texas community: "It was like the Little League—the same ball, same bat, same number of innings, same playing field—everything was the same except that they didn't keep score. The idea was that there wouldn't be any losers because nobody would know who won." The game lasted one and a half innings. After that "the kids went across the street to play sand lot ball where they could keep score" (Coonradt, 1997).

Security trivia contests, poster contests, security fact or fiction contests, first group to complete a security activity contest, and the like are all ways to increase audience participation and motivation.

## Intranet and/or Internet

Security awareness activities that use the Internet or an Intranet offer the advantages of ease of use, scalability (can be used for various audience sizes and in distributed locations), accountability (e.g., they can capture use statistics, quiz or test scoring, and other metrics), accommodation of individual learning rates, and even interaction among members of a community or among students and instructors.

## Posters

A poster series with themes or related designs can be used to highlight specific security issues. A poster should be colorful and should present a single message or idea. Using a professional artist to design the posters will increase their impact. Posters should be larger than standard letter size to stand out and gain attention. They should be changed or rotated regularly and placed at eye level in many locations. Posters can be printed on both sides of the paper, saving paper and shipping costs for organizations with multiple locations. The graphics shown in this chapter are illustrations by professional cartoonist, Charles A. Filus.

## Awareness Coupons

Awareness coupons are rewards given out to people for following security policy. When a recipient displays the coupon or tells others about it, people think more about security, thus enhancing awareness.

**Figure 1:** Example of a security awareness poster, artwork by Charles A. Filius

## Videos

Videos can be delivered on DVDs, VHS tapes, CD-ROMs, or over the Web. Most security awareness videos are less than 20 minutes long. They can be used at orientation briefings and brown bag lunches for staff where popcorn can be provided in bags preprinted with security messages. Videos are useful starting points for discussions and for briefings. They provide a consistent message

**Figure 2:** Example of Security By Wandering Around (SBWA) coupons, artwork by Charles A. Filius

throughout the organization and can be shown to staff at distributed locations, saving instructor travel time and costs. They can also be used to demonstrate cost effectively the impact of security failures (e.g., a fire at a data center or how sensitive data were found in the trash). Security awareness videos are available commercially for various fees and from the U.S. government often at no charge or for a nominal fee.

Although they are effective training tools, videos have their drawbacks. They can be expensive to produce, with costs averaging $4,000 or more per finished minute. In addition, as rapidly as technology and threats change, videos can quickly become outdated. An option is to produce an awareness video in digital format in segments that allow for updates as the environment or organizational needs change.

## Trinkets and Give-Aways

Various give-away items can be imprinted with a security slogan and contact information, such as security staff phone numbers or the organization's security Web site address. Give-aways that the recipient places in a visible location increase the exposure time of the message. Examples of give-away items are the following:

- Pencils, pens, and highlighters—"Report security breaches—it's the 'write' thing to do."
- Erasers—"Wipe out password sharing."
- Notepads—"Note who should be in your area and challenge strangers."
- Frisbees—"Our information security program is taking off."
- Mouse pads and inserts—mouse pads may be specially printed or have removable paper inserts, making the cost to change the message far less than the cost of printing new mouse pads.
- Key chains—"You are the key to information security."
- Flashlights—"Keep the spotlight on security."
- Cups or mugs—"Awareness—the best part of SecuriTEA" (when the campaign has explained that TEA stands for training, education, and awareness).
- Magnets, buttons, and stickers—"Stick with security."
- First-aid kits—"Be prepared for security."
- Rulers and calculators—"Security counts."
- Coasters, toys, hand exercisers, informational cards, posters, virus scanning software, and screen savers.
- Calendars with security images and messages.
- Candy bars with wrappers printed with security messages.

Larger, more expensive items, such as T-shirts, tote bags, and gift certificates, can be used as prizes for raffles at security events. The more useful, beautiful, or cleverly designed the item, the greater the likelihood that it will be kept.

## Publications (Newsletters)

Publications, such as newsletters and magazines in paper and electronic format may be devoted to security or may contain articles on security-related events or items of interest. Memos and alerts concerning security issues can be distributed to staff. To attract attention, consider stapling a facial tissue to stressful memos, such as ones that may be perceived as adding inconvenience or an additional burden on users. Brochures, pamphlets, and comic books can be targeted to specific audiences.

## Screen Savers

Screen savers are a graphic form of communication and, like posters, should be eye-catching for maximum impact. Involving a professional artist will improve message delivery. Screen savers should contain contact information for the organization's security and incident-handling functions. Animations or trivia questions and answers may make the screen saver more interesting. Screen savers should be updated periodically to keep the message fresh. Commercially produced security screen savers are available as are screen savers that can be easily tailored to deliver a security message.

## Sign-On Screen Messages

With some systems, it is possible to add a text message to the log-on or sign-on screen. These messages should be short, to the point, and changed frequently.

## Surveys and Suggestion Programs

Surveys, suggestion programs, and contests help achieve buy-in. Contests to suggest or name a security mascot, to provide poster ideas, or even ways to improve security can boost morale and contribute to team spirit. At presentations, speakers can tape prizes or awards under seats in the front row to encourage people to come early and sit up front.

## Inspections and Audits

Inspections and audits raise awareness among the staff being reviewed, at least for the duration of the inspection. However, additional audits and inspections, although useful techniques, create a negative perception. Another technique, called "SBWA" for **s**ecurity **b**y **w**andering **a**round, identifies staff members doing something correctly. A security staff member can tour the work area at the end of the day and leave certificates of congratulations, thank-you notes, or trinkets on the desks of people who have locked all sensitive information in cabinets before leaving. Randomness is more effective than regularly scheduled inspections. Another possibility would be to have the security personnel periodically demonstrate social engineering by attempting to "smooth talk" users into providing their passwords. Users who refuse would be rewarded. The number of users from a specific department or group who fall for the scheme might be used as an example in the next awareness session.

## Events, Conferences, Briefings, and Presentations

Participation in events, such as the International Computer Security Day on November 30th when it falls on a workday, or in any of the various information security conferences raises awareness. Here are other events that can contribute to awareness:

- A "Grill Your Security Officer Cook-Out" where food is served and staff are encouraged to bring any questions about security to the security officer.
- Lectures by dynamic speakers. A boring speaker will hurt the program's credibility, but a talented professional speaker can be eye-opening. Sometimes, personnel are more accepting of information presented by an independent subject-matter expert. Some organizations sponsor a monthly lecture series or lunch presentations on relevant topics.
- Security awareness briefings. Briefings are typically given to senior executives who have little time to spare and to new arrivals who need an overview of the organization's information security awareness policy before being granted system access.

## MEASUREMENT AND EVALUATION

It's wise to measure and evaluate the impact of security awareness programs. Managers provide funds to the security staff to pursue security goals. In turn, the security staff measures results and shares the measurements with management so that managers can assess performance. A common measurement is the number of people who participated in awareness orientations and refreshers. This figure can be determined through attendance sheets, course registrations or completion notifications for online courses, and signed user "acceptance of responsibilities" statements.

A better type of measurement is based on the techniques used to evaluate the effectiveness of advertising. A random sample of employees (or specific groups such as managers, program developers, or system administrators) could be selected for a survey or quiz on security awareness. The semiannual administration of such a survey could establish a basic statistical value for the "awareness level" in an organization. Follow-up security awareness efforts could then be directed at maintaining or improving on this established awareness level. Questions in the survey should address awareness of security policies and procedures, how to report an actual or suspected incident, behaviors related to security and perceptions about security. For example, a survey question might ask, "Do you suspect that you have taken a call from a social engineer?"

As with training, an awareness program that does not reach the intended audience is expensive, even if its per capita cost is low. Several measurements and methods may be used to assess the impact of an awareness program. Empirical evidence, such as feedback from presenters, audiences, and supervisors, is one of the most useful sources of measurement information. Some aspects of the awareness program that can be measured include, audience satisfaction, ease of access, ease of understanding, ease of use, retention, and learning or teaching effectiveness.

## Audience Satisfaction

Audience satisfaction can be measured after the fact with course or presentation evaluations or surveys about the awareness program. "Smiley face" evaluations, where the audience is asked to rate the program or activity on a scale, measure how well the audience liked the course, activity, or materials. User feedback may be requested on the presentation's relevance and effectiveness. Asking for suggestions is also a good approach. The volume and content of suggestions provided are good indicators of message impact.

## Audience Involvement

Attendance statistics from sign-in sheets, head counts, or evaluations or the number of trinkets given away at an event can be used to measure involvement in presentations and events. Web-based courses can measure the number and percent of people who started and completed the course and the amount of time spent on modules and pages and can record feedback questions and answers provided.

If contests are used, the number and quality of entries can be measured.

## Changes in Behavior

Changes in behavior can be measured through personal statements, such as feedback solicited from a survey or Web-based course question that asks, "What aspects of your behavior have you changed as a result of recent awareness activities?" Behavioral change can also be measured by the number of calls to the help desk for certain actions (e.g., assistance with security settings, requests for licensed versions of software, assistance with password changes or turning on locking screen savers). Adding a "yes or no" check box to the help desk or incident reporting forms that asks "Was this issue addressed in the security awareness materials or course?" can help to identify problem areas that need additional emphasis in awareness materials.

## Changes in Volume of Reported Incidents

An increase in reported incidents is usually a sign of success in newly implemented awareness programs. After users are more accustomed to what should be reported and as security controls are increased or compliance with policy improves, the number of reported incidents would be expected to decrease.

## Learning or Teaching Effectiveness

Pre- and post surveys and tests are useful in determining what the audience remembered and therefore in tailoring more effective future programs. Unless a preprogram test or preliminary survey is conducted, objectively measuring improvement is difficult, if not impossible. However, subjective measurement, such as surveying users on what they learned, is also useful and does not require a pretest.

## Audience Performance

This type of evaluation goes beyond the learner to gather input from an outside evaluator, such as a supervisor, security practitioner, incident response team, or help desk personnel. Follow-up interviews, walk-through testing, help desk and incident-reporting statistics, and audit findings can be used to measure improvements in awareness and job performance.

For example, before presenting an awareness campaign on password construction and management, a password-cracking program could be run to identify passwords that are subject to guessing or compromise. The same program could be run after the awareness activities and the results compared. Or an evaluator could walk though the work areas at lunchtime, looking for terminals that are unattended but not logged off. The same inspection could be performed at various times after the awareness program is initiated. Similarly, a survey of attitudes and specific knowledge could be taken before awareness efforts are initiated. Staff might be asked to whom they should report an incident or if they may take older versions of upgraded software home for use once newer versions have been licensed by the organization. Similar questions could be asked at intervals after the awareness program is implemented and the results compared. Regardless of the specific measurement used, a comparison baseline is needed. Data for the baseline should be gathered before the awareness program is implemented.

As with any awareness campaign, a security awareness effort requires repetition and consistency from year to year to achieve and maintain the desired impact and changes in workforce behavior.

# CONCLUSION

Awareness among an organization's staff is vital to maintaining the integrity of data and systems. Although organizations often view computer security as a technological problem and use sophisticated hardware and software solutions to control access, detect potential security incidents, and prevent fraud, the reality is that computer security is as much a people problem as a technological problem. End users are closer to potential problems; therefore, they need to be aware of potential risks, threats, vulnerabilities, and their own security responsibilities.

People are major contributors to the IT security problem, and they are also crucial to its solution. People are perceptive and adaptive, and if trained and motivated to be aware, they can be the strongest and most effective security countermeasure. Individuals often are the first to detect security incidents. The actions they take or fail to take determine the level of damage. An aware workforce can often compensate for deficiencies in technical controls. The intent of the awareness program is to make recognition of and reaction to security threats a reflexive behavior.

Awareness takes time. It also requires the organization to have an in-place information security policy, the support of the senior-level managers, and clear goals and plans for achieving awareness. The importance of establishing measurable goals cannot be overestimated and is critical to obtaining support and funding.

The goal of an awareness program is often to change attitudes and behaviors that may be embedded in long-term procedures or habits. To effect awareness, the program must appeal to the audience and be tailored to the workforce and to the technology of the organization.

The primary message of a security awareness program should be that security is everyone's responsibility. Actions taken by end users make a significant difference; thus, a well-trained and motivated workforce is a critical and necessary security control.

## GLOSSARY

**Awareness**  Being aware of what is going on around one; security awareness specifically focuses attention on security.

**Awareness Campaign**  The activities associated with conveying a specific awareness message (e.g., telling people "log off when away from your computer").

**Awareness Program**  The planned implementation and control of a mix of awareness activities over a period of time, with measurable goals and multiple topics. An awareness program may encompass several campaigns.

**Education**  The process of integrating all security skills and competencies into a common body of knowledge, adding a multidisciplinary study of concepts, issues, and principles.

**End User**  (Also computer user or user) Any person who uses an information system.

**FISMA**  The Federal Information Security Management Act of 2002.

**Focus Group**  A small group of end users (or of individuals from the target audience) who review and discuss awareness activities, courses, products, and the like, often under the guidance of an awareness material developer or training specialist.

**FUD Factor**  The effects of Fear, Uncertainty, and Doubt (FUD).

**Malicious Code (also malware)**  Hardware, software, or firmware that is intentionally included in a system for an unauthorized purpose (e.g., a Trojan horse).

**Orientation Briefing**  A presentation that provides new employees, contractors, and others with basic security information and information on the organization's security policies/programs. Usually these presentations are conducted on arrival or shortly thereafter.

**Refresher**  An awareness activity, such as a briefing, intended to reinforce and update awareness of security controls and policies and to remind individuals of their security responsibilities.

**Safe Failure**  The opportunity to learn from mistakes privately, such as with a computer simulation or course.

**Security Basics and Literacy**  A transitional stage between awareness and training.

**Shoulder Surfing**  Stealing a computer password or access code by peering over a person's shoulder while he or she types in the characters.

**Social Engineering**  Social engineering has been used in the information technology field to mean the art of conning a naive person into revealing sensitive data on a computer system, often on the Internet. The majority of security compromises are now done by exploiting the profusion of poorly secured computers with known security holes that are connected to the Internet. However, social-engineering attacks remain extremely common and are a way to attack systems protected against other methods; for instance, computers that are not connected to the Internet. It is an article of faith among experts in the field that "users are the weak link." A contemporary example of a social engineering attack is the use of e-mail attachments that contain malicious payloads (that, for instance, use the victim's machine to send massive quantities of spam). After earlier malicious e-mails led software vendors to disable automatic execution of attachments, users now have to explicitly activate attachments for this to occur. Many users, however, blindly click on any attachments they receive, thus allowing the attack to work. Training users about security policies and ensuring that they are followed are the primary defenses against social engineering.

**Social Marketing**  An approach to security awareness using attraction and persuasion techniques designed to encourage a group of people to alter old ideas, understand and accept new ideas, and value their new awareness enough to change attitudes and take positive actions to improve IT security.

**Target Audience**  A specified audience or demographic group for which a security-awareness message is designed.

**Threat**  Anything that can potentially harm a system or its associated assets (hardware, software, data, operations). Threats may be man-made or natural occurrences. Awareness programs do little to address threats; instead, they seek to reduce vulnerabilities.

**Training**  The process of producing relevant and needed security skills and competency, where security awareness is the "what," training is the "how."

**Vulnerability**  A weakness in automated system security procedures, administrative controls, physical layout, internal controls, and so forth that could be exploited by a threat to gain unauthorized access to information or disrupt critical processing. A goal of security-awareness programs is to reduce behavior-related vulnerabilities.

## CROSS REFERENCES

See *E-Mail and Internet Use Policies; Guidelines for a Comprehensive Security System; Security Policy Guidelines; The Asset-Security Goals Continuum: A Process for Security.*

## REFERENCES

Bace, R. (2000). *Intrusion detection*. Indianapolis: Macmillan Technical Publishing.

Coonradt, C. (1997). *The game of work*. Park City: Game of Work.

Darley, J., & Latane, B. (1968). Bystander intervention in emergencies: Diffusion of responsibility. *Journal of Personality and Social Psychology, 8,* 377–383.

FISMA. (2002). *The Federal Information Security Management Act of 2002, Sec. 3544. Federal agency responsibilities*. Retrieved from http://www.fedcirc.gov/library/legislation/FISMA.html

Hall, K., & the SE SIG Steering Committee (2002). *A system for gaining management support for your safeguards and security awareness program*. Retrieved from http://www.orau.gov/se/Products/SE%20SIG%20Gaining%20Mgmt%20Support.doc

Harmon, A. (2004, February 5). Geeks out the unsavvy on alert: Learn or log off. *New York Times*.

IsecT, Ltd. (2003). *Human factors in information security*. Retrieved from http://www.noticebored.com/html/human_factors.html

Ludwig, T. (2003, February). *Think secure: Building your security-minded workforce*. Retrieved from http://redsiren.com/02_00_01.html

McBride, P. (2000, November 9). How to spend a dollar on security. *ComputerWorld*. Retrieved from http://www.computerworld.com/security/story/0,10801,53651,00.html Accessed October 12, 2005

National Institute of Standards and Technology (NIST) (1998). *Information technology security training requirements: A role- and performance-based model* (Special Publication 800-16).

NIST. (2003). *Building an information technology security awareness and training program* (SP 800-50).

Overstreet, H. (1925). *Influencing human behaviour*. New York: Norton & Company.

Schank, R. (1997). *Virtual learning*. New York: McGraw Hill.

Schneier, B. (2003). *Beyond fear*. New York: Copernicus Books.

Spence, G. (1995). *How to argue and win every time*. New York: St. Martin's Press.

Trowbridge, J. (2003). *An overview of remote operating system fingerprinting*. Retrieved from http://www.sans.org/rr/whitepapers/testing/1231.php Accessed October 6, 2005

Wikipedia. (n.d.). Timeline of the September 11, 2001 terrorist attacks. Retrieved from http://en.wikipedia.org/wiki/September_11,_2001_Terrorist_Attack/Timeline

Zimmerman, R. (1997). *Social marketing strategies for campus prevention of alcohol and other drug problems*. Washington, DC: Higher Education Center for Alcohol and Other Drug Prevention.

# Risk Management for IT Security

Rick Kazman and Daniel N. Port, *University of Hawaii*
David Klappholz, *Stevens Institute of Technology*

## INTRODUCTION

According to Carr, Konda, Monarch, Ulrich, & Walker (1993), risks must be managed, and risk management must be part of any mature organization's overall management practices and management structure. They identify these primary activities for managing risk:

*Identify*: Risks must first be identified before they can be managed.

*Analyze*: Risks must be analyzed so that management can make prudent decisions about them.

*Plan*: For information about a risk to be turned into action, a detailed plan, outlining both present and potential future actions, must be created. These actions may mitigate the risk, avoid the risk, or even accept the risk.

*Track*: Risks, whether they have been acted upon or not, must be tracked, so that management can continue to exercise diligence.

*Control*: Even if a risk has been identified and addressed, it must be continually controlled to monitor for any deviations.

The key activity tying all of these activities together is *assessment*. Assessment is considered central to the risk management process, underlying all of the other activities.

For the purposes of exposition, we follow the generic risk taxonomy shown in Figure 1[1] (Boehm, 1991). In this taxonomy, the activity of risk management has two major

subactivities: risk assessment and risk control. Risk assessment is further divided into risk identification, risk analysis, and risk prioritization. Risk control is divided into risk management planning, risk resolution, and risk monitoring. Although we broadly discuss several areas of risk management, our focus in this chapter is primarily on risk assessment, as it applies to IT security. Assessment is the starting point and forms the fundamental basis for all risk management activities. Many risk assessment methods and techniques have directly analogous application to risk control. In such cases, we note this application without elaboration.

The terminology used in the field of risk management varies somewhat among the different business and engineering areas in which it is used; for example, see Boehm (1991), Carr et al. (1993), and Hall (1998). It even varies among writers in the field of IT security risk management. The generic risk management concepts that we just introduced were created for software development (of which security is one attribute). The reader familiar with other works on IT security risk management should have little trouble seeing the direct applications. In this section, we define terms informally with examples; in later sections, we formalize these definitions.

Although most people are unaware that they are doing it, we all engage in risk management on a daily basis. Consider, as an example, a decision, made on the way out the door, whether or not to stuff an umbrella into an uncomfortably heavy bag that will be taken on a 30-minute train ride, followed by a 10-minute walk[2] to the office. The

---

[1] In Figure 1, for application to security the examples listed for Risk Analysis might include Security Models, Threat Analysis, and Vulnerability Factor Analysis.

[2] This example, as well as a number of others in this section, is taken, albeit with considerably more detail, from NIST (2002).

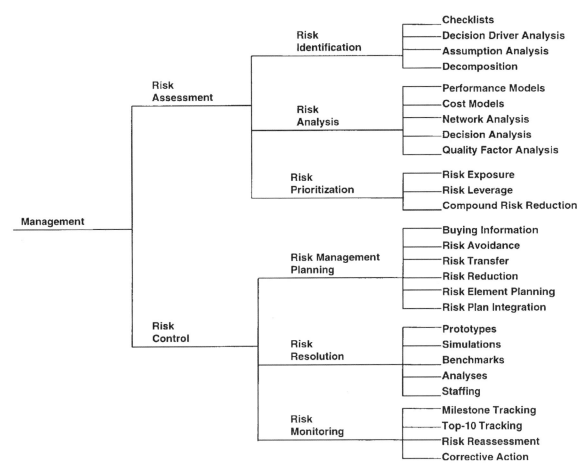

**Figure 1:** Boehm's Risk Management Taxonomy.

decision is based on a quick, often almost unconscious assessment of the risks involved and how to control them.

On the one hand, there is the probability that the rain predicted by the TV forecaster will actually materialize, that it will be in progress during the drive to the train station and/or during the walk, and, if all goes as badly as it might, that it will cause damage, from the point of view of both walking in drenched clothing and possibly losing work time during the drying-out period. Balanced against all these risks, on the other hand, is the discomfort of carrying the extra weight, of the possibility of having the precariously situated umbrella drop out of the bag and, as it did last week, causing a spillage of hot carry-out coffee during the effort to pick it up. An additional consideration is the probability that carrying the umbrella will solve the problem, a consideration that depends upon the expected strength of prevailing winds; if the wind proves to be too strong, the umbrella will provide no relief from the rain. An alternative possibility to consider, assuming it is an option, is to work at home all morning and to go to the office only after the rain or its unmaterialized threat has abated.

## Security Risk Assessment

In its typical definition, IT security involves protection of the *confidentiality*, *integrity*, and *availability* of data/information critical to the success of a business or government organization. Naturally, it also involves protection, from injury and death, of the people involved in dealing with that information. The following are examples of consequences that can result from the materialization of risks in the areas of confidentiality, integrity, and availability:

- Loss of confidentiality
  - personal embarrassment resulting from theft and publication of personal financial, health, or other data and possible prosecution and fine for individuals and the organization responsible for maintaining confidentiality
  - corporate loss of earnings resulting from theft of prepatent technical data
  - loss of life of a covert intelligence agent resulting from theft and revelation of name and address
- Loss of integrity
  - personal embarrassment and possibly fine and imprisonment resulting from insertion into database of false financial data implicating the subject in fraud or embezzlement
  - loss of corporate auditors' ability to detect embezzlement and the attendant loss of funds, resulting from deliberate corruption of financial data by embezzler
  - loss of life resulting from changes to database indicating that a subject is a covert agent when he or she is not

- Loss of availability
  - personal embarrassment caused by an inability to keep appointments resulting from temporary inability to use electronic calendar
  - temporary inability of corporation to issue weekly paychecks to employees, with attendant anger and loss of productivity, resulting from temporary unavailability of hours-worked data
  - loss of initiative, armaments, and lives resulting from battlefield commander's inability to connect to field-support database

The terms *threat*, *threat source*, *vulnerability*, *impact*, and *risk exposure* are in common use in the field of IT security risk assessment. Their application to the trip-to-work scenario is as follows:

- The *threat*, or *threat source*, is the onset of rain, at a sufficiently strong level, during an exposed part of the trip to work.
- The *vulnerability* is the fact that the person involved will get drenched if the threat materializes and the person has no form of shelter (e.g., an umbrella).
- The *impact* is the damage, measured in terms of discomfort and possibly of loss of productivity or even health, that will occur if the threat materializes.
- The *risk exposure* is an assessment, on either a numerical, perhaps monetary, scale or an ordinal scale (e.g., low, medium, or high), of the expected magnitude of the loss given the threat, the vulnerability to it, and its impact, should the threat materialize. In this example, the risk exposure might change if the person is wearing a water-resistant coat.

The first step in risk assessment is *risk identification*—the identification of potential threats, vulnerabilities to those threats, and impacts that would result should they materialize—all of which we presented for the scenario under discussion.

In the trip-to-work scenario, we are concerned with such intangibles as the threat of rain, the vulnerability of getting drenched, and the impact of discomfort, as well as with such tangibles as umbrellas. In the field of IT security, we are concerned with systems that store, process, and transmit data/information. Information systems are sometimes localized and sometimes widely distributed; they involve computer hardware and software, as well as other physical and human assets. Tangibles include the various sorts of equipment and media and the sites in which they and staff are housed. Intangibles include such notions as organizational reputation, opportunity or loss of same, productivity or loss of same, and so forth.

Threat sources are of at least three varieties: natural, human, and environmental:

1. *Natural*: electrical storms, monsoons, hurricanes, tornadoes, floods, avalanches, volcanic eruptions
2. *Human*: incorrect data entry (unintentional), forgetting to lock door (unintentional), failure to unlock door to enable confederate to enter after hours (intentional), denial of service attack (intentional), creation and propagation of viruses (intentional)

3. *Environmental*: failure of roof or wall caused by the use of bad construction materials, seepage of toxic chemicals through ceiling, power outage

Vulnerabilities have various sources, including technical failings such as those reported in the public and professional presses on a daily basis.[3] Fred Cohen (2004) provides an excellent, extensive taxonomy of threats and vulnerabilities in his Security Database. One unique aspect of this database is that threats (or causes) are cross-referenced against attack mechanisms to provide a linkage between the cause and the mechanisms used. The attack mechanisms are also cross-referenced against defense mechanisms to indicate which such mechanisms might be effective in some circumstances.

The second step in risk assessment is *risk analysis*, the estimation and calculation of the risk likelihoods (i.e., probabilities), magnitudes, impacts, and dependencies. This analysis is easy in the case of monetary impacts arising from threat-vulnerability pairs for which the probability of materializing can reasonably be computed, but is considerably harder in most other cases. Special care must be taken when assigning likelihoods as the quality of the entire risk assessment is strongly dependent on the accuracy and realism of the assigned probabilities.

The final step in risk assessment is *risk prioritization*; that is, prioritizing all risks with respect to the organization's relative exposures to them. It is typically necessary to use techniques that enable *risk comparison*, such as calculating risk exposure in terms of potential loss. In the trip-to-work scenario, risks other than the ones discussed herein might include those associated with not buckling the seatbelt during the drive to the station, the risk of an accident during the drive, the risk of missing the train, and so on. A meticulous person, one who always leaves the house earlier than necessary and who is very conscious of taking safety precautions, will likely rate these new risks as having far lower exposures than the rain risk: a less meticulous person might do otherwise. In a highly simplified version of a business situation, three threats might be volcanic eruption, late delivery of raw materials, and embezzlement. An organization located in Chicago would likely assign a lower priority to volcanic eruption than would one in southwestern Washington; an organization with suppliers that have never before been late would likely assign a lower priority to late delivery than would an organization using a supplier for the first time. Because there may be threats or vulnerabilities that you may not have included in your analysis, you should draw upon the experiences of others to help build a library of threats and vulnerabilities.

## IT Security Risk Control

During the risk control phase of the risk management process, we are concerned with *safeguards*, also known as *controls*. Safeguards fit into at least three categories—technical, management, and operational:

---

[3] A compilation of technical threats may be found at http//:icat.nist.gov or http://www.cert.org

1. *Technical*: authentication (prevention), authorization (prevention), access control (prevention), intrusion detection (detection), audit (detection), automatic backup (recovery), and so on.

2. *Management*: assign guards to critical venues (prevention) and institute user account initiation and termination procedures (prevention), need-to-know data access policy (prevention), periodic risk reassessment policy (prevention), organization-wide security training (prevention and detection), and so on.

3. *Operational*: secure network hardware from access to any but authorized network administrators and/or service personnel (prevention); bolt desktop PCs to desks (prevention); screen outsiders before permitting entry (prevention); set up and monitor motion alarms, sensors, and closed-circuit TV (detection of physical threat); set up and monitor smoke detectors, gas detectors, fire alarms (detection of environmental threats)

In the trip-to-work scenario, the safeguard that we have considered has a (fairly low-tech) technical component (i.e., the umbrella) and an operational component (i.e., carrying the umbrella). An alternative operational safeguard would be to work at home all morning, if that is an option, and to go to the office only after the rain or the threat of rain has abated.

During the risk-control phase of the risk-management process, we do the following:

• consider alternative individual safeguards and/or complexes of safeguards that might be used to eliminate/reduce/mitigate exposures to the various identified, analyzed, and prioritized threats (risk management planning)

• perform the cost-benefit analysis required to decide which specific safeguards to employ and institute the relevant safeguards (risk resolution)

• institute a process for continuous monitoring of the IT security situation to detect and resolve problems as they arise and to decide, where and when necessary, to update or change the system of safeguards (risk monitoring)

In business and government organizations, there may be many alternative possible safeguards, including different vendors' hardware and/or software solutions to a particular threat or cluster of threats, alternative management or procedural safeguards, and alternative combinations of technical, management, and procedural safeguards. Complicating matters is the likelihood that different combinations of safeguards address different, overlapping clusters of threats.

Risk resolution begins with the cost-benefit analysis of the various possible safeguards and controls in lowering, to an acceptable level, the assessed risk exposures resulting from the various identified threats, vulnerabilities, and attendant impacts. Just as we had to consider threats, vulnerabilities, and impacts during risk assessment, we must consider safeguards, their costs, and their efficacies during risk resolution. In the trip-to-work scenario, the marginal cost of the technical component of the umbrella-carrying safeguard is likely nil as most people already own umbrellas; the operational cost is the discomfort of carrying a heavier bag. Even in this simple example, the safeguard's efficacy must be considered. For example, if the wind proves to be too strong, the umbrella will not reduce the exposure effectively.

## Risk Management in Practice

The potential consequences of the materialization of a significant threat to a business or government organization and the obvious fact that risk management can greatly reduce those consequences make it eminently clear that no such organization can afford not to engage in a serious risk management effort. The smaller the organization and the simpler the threats, the less formal the organization's risk management effort need be. For the small organization, such as a single retail store belonging to a family, very informal risk management may suffice. In many situations, legal statutes and acquisition policies give an organization no choice—see this chapter's section on information security standards. The Hawthorne Principle states that productivity increases as a result of simply paying attention to workers' environments. It is likely, by analogy, that a simple concern with risk management produces significant, though certainly not optimal, results.

However, clearly risk management is rarely easy. In the case of the rare threat–vulnerability pair for which the probability can easily be assigned a numerical value, the impact can be assigned a precise monetary value, and there exists a safeguard with a cost and efficacy that can be pinned down numerically, there is no problem. In other cases, those in which one or more of the parameters can at best be placed on an ordinal scale, matters are more complicated and approximate methods must be used. Consider as examples the quantification of the impact of the following:

• personal embarrassment resulting from theft and publication of personal financial, health, or other data; insertion into database of false financial data implicating the subject in fraud or embezzlement; inability to keep appointments resulting from temporary inability to use electronic calendar

• corporate loss of earnings resulting from theft of prepatent technical data

• loss of corporate auditors' ability to detect embezzlement and attendant loss of funds, resulting from deliberate corruption of financial data by embezzler

• temporary inability of corporation to issue weekly paychecks to employees, with attendant anger and loss of productivity, resulting from temporary unavailability of hours-worked data

• loss of life of covert intelligence agent resulting from theft and revelation of name and address caused by changes to the database indicating that subject is a covert agent when he or she is not or by the battlefield commander's inability to connect to the field-support database

To aid in the identification and management of risks, a number of risk-management methods and risk

**Table 1:** Taxonomy of Software Development Risks (from Carr et al., 1993)

| A. Product Engineering | B. Development Environment | C. Program Constraints |
|---|---|---|
| 1. Requirements<br>  a. Stability<br>  b. Completeness<br>  c. Clarity<br>  d. Validity<br>  e. Feasibility<br>  f. Precedent<br>  g. Scale<br>2. Design<br>  a. Functionality<br>  b. Difficulty<br>  c. Interfaces<br>  d. Performance<br>  e. Testability<br>  f. Hardware Constraints<br>  g. Non-Developmental SW<br>3. Code and Unit Test<br>  a. Feasibility<br>  b. Testing<br>  c. Coding/Implementation<br>4. Integration and Test<br>  a. Environment<br>  b. Product<br>  c. System<br>5. Engineering Specialties<br>  a. Maintainability<br>  b. Reliability<br>  c. Safety<br>  d. Security<br>  e. Human Factors<br>  f. Specifications | 1. Development Process<br>  a. Formality<br>  b. Suitability<br>  c. Process Control<br>  d. Familiarity<br>  e. Product Control<br>2. Development System<br>  a. Capacity<br>  b. Suitability<br>  c. Usability<br>  d. Familiarity<br>  e. Reliability<br>  f. System Support<br>  g. Deliverability<br>3. Management Process<br>  a. Planning<br>  b. Project Organization<br>  c. Management Experience<br>  d. Program Interfaces<br>4. Management Methods<br>  a. Monitoring<br>  b. Personnel Management<br>  c. Quality Assurance<br>  d. Configuration Management<br>5. Work Environment<br>  a. Quality Attitude<br>  b. Cooperation<br>  c. Communication<br>  d. Morale | 1. Resources<br>  a. Schedule<br>  b. Staff<br>  c. Budget<br>  d. Facilities<br>2. Contract<br>  a. Type of Contract<br>  b. Restrictions<br>  c. Dependencies<br>3. Program Interfaces<br>  a. Customer<br>  b. Associate Contractors<br>  c. Subcontractors<br>  d. Prime Contractor<br>  e. Corporate Management<br>  f. Vendors<br>  g. Politics |

taxonomies have been created. The Software Engineering Institute's (SEI) risk taxonomy, for example, divides risk into three classes: product engineering, development environment, and program constraints. The first level of decomposition of each of these classes is given in Table 1.

This taxonomy is used to "drive" a risk assessment method. For each class (e.g., Product Engineering), and for each element within that class (e.g., Design) and for each attribute of that element (e.g., Performance), there are a set of questions that guide the risk analyst. Depending on the answers to these questions, the analyst might be guided to still further questions that probe the nature of the risk. For example, an analyst looking at performance risks would first ask whether a performance analysis has been done. If the answer is "yes," a follow-up question would ask about the level of confidence in this analysis. Note that security is just one attribute, located under the Engineering Specialties element. Clearly, to be able to manage security risks, we need to delve more deeply into the elements and attributes that are particular to security. We give some examples of risk-management methods tailored for security in the next section.

## RISK ASSESSMENT METHODOLOGIES

According to the ISO 17799 Information Security Standard (ISO, 2000), risk assessment is the assessment of threats to, impacts on, and vulnerabilities of information and information-processing facilities and the likelihood of their occurrences. Risk management is the process of identifying, controlling, and minimizing or eliminating risks that may affect information systems, for an acceptable cost.

The bulk of this chapter thus far has addressed IT security risk assessment. Now we turn to the broader topic of integrating security risk assessment with security risk management. The notion of risk management was introduced in the first section. In this section, we examine and compare some of the most common and widely used risk assessment methods for security management: Microsoft's Security Risk Management Discipline (SRMD; 2004); the Operationally Critical Threat, Asset, and Vulnerability Evaluation (OCTAVE, 2004) method, developed by SEI and the Computer Emergency Response Team (CERT) at Carnegie Mellon University (Alberts & Dorofee, 2002); and the Facilitated Risk Assessment

Process, developed by Peltier (Peltier, Peltier, & Blackley, 2003). To facilitate comparison of these methods, we look at their steps and their organization, examining how they do the following:

*establish a context and *goals* for the analysis
**focus* the inquiry
*perform the *analysis*
**close the loop*, tying analysis outcomes back to their original goals

By mapping these categories onto the activities and the analysis methods, we can see where each method places its emphasis.

## OCTAVE

The OCTAVE approach (2004) describes a family of security risk evaluation methods that, unlike many other security analysis methods, are aimed at finding *organizational* risk factors and strategic risk issues by examining an organization's security practices (Alberts & Dorofee, 2002). Its focus is not on finding specific security risks within specific systems, but rather to enable an organization to consider all dimensions of security risk so that it can determine strategic best practices. The OCTAVE approach thus needs to consider not only an organization's assets, threats, and vulnerabilities as any security method would, but it also asks the stakeholders to explicitly consider and evaluate the organizational impact of security policies and practices. For this reason, an organization's evaluation team must be multidisciplinary, comprising both technical personnel and management.

The OCTAVE process is organized into three phases that are carried out in a series of workshops. In Phase 1—Build Asset-Based Threat Profiles—the team first determines the context and goals for the analysis by describing the information-related assets that it wants to protect. The team does this via a set of structured interviews with senior management, operational management, IT staff, and general staff. The team then catalogues the current practices for protecting these assets. The OCTAVE approach then focuses the inquiry by selecting the most important of these assets as *critical assets*, which are the subject of the remainder of the analysis. For each critical asset, the evaluation team identifies a set of threats.

In Phase 2—Identify Infrastructure Vulnerabilities—the analysis team performs the analysis by first identifying a set of components that are related to the critical assets and then determining the resistance (or vulnerability) of each component to being compromised. They do this analysis by running tools that probe the identified components for known vulnerabilities.

Finally, in Phase 3—Develop Security Strategy and Plans—the team closes the loop. It examines the impact of the threats associated with each of the critical assets based on the Phase 2 analysis, using a common evaluation basis (e.g., a determination of high, medium, or low impact). Based on these evaluations, the team determines a course of action for each: a risk mitigation plan. Instead of merely determining a tactical response to these

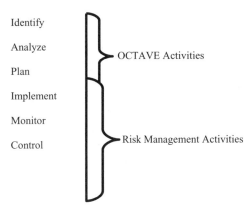

**Figure 2:** The OCTAVE Life Cycle.

risks, the goal of the OCTAVE analysis is to determine an organizational "protection strategy" for the critical assets.

As an approach that is aimed at strategic organization-wide risk reduction, OCTAVE also includes activities to ensure that the organization monitors and improves its process. These risk-reduction activities revolve around planning in detail how to implement the protection strategy, implementing the plans, monitoring the plans as they are being implemented to ensure that they are on schedule and are effective, and, finally, correcting any problems encountered. Thus, the three phases of the OCTAVE approach can be seen as part of a larger picture, encompassing the activities shown in Figure 2.

The OCTAVE approach has been instantiated in two methods to date: OCTAVE and OCTAVE-S. OCTAVE is aimed at large organizations with large, complex information-security requirements and infrastructures. OCTAVE-S, on the other hand, is aimed more at smaller organizations (or smaller subunits of large organizations) with simpler information-security needs.

## SRMD

The Security Risk Management Discipline (SRMD, 2004) provided by Microsoft Corporation combines ideas from Microsoft's solutions framework (a set of process guidelines for delivering effective software technology-centric solutions) and their operations framework, which guides organizations to make their systems more manageable, available, and supportable. The SRMD, as its name implies, is meant to assess and mitigate or manage security risks over a system's entire life cycle. As such, the SRMD is meant to be proactive and continuous and to permeate all decision-making, rather than being a method that one enacts periodically.

The SRMD, like the OCTAVE methods, is divided into three "primary processes." The first process, entitled Assessment, focuses first on identifying the assets that are of value to an organization and then assigning a specific value to each of those assets. This process establishes the context and goals for the analysis. Next, security risks that might have an impact upon those assets are brainstormed and analyzed. This process involves identifying threats, vulnerabilities, and exploits and then considering any available countermeasures. During this process, the impact of a potential threat must be quantified, as must the cost of any potential countermeasure against the risk. Given this basis of information, the security risks can be prioritized by their risk exposure (RE), although the SRMD does not use that term, so that strategic decisions can be made about which risks will receive the most attention and in what order. Therefore, both the *focusing* of the inquiry and the *analysis* occur in the first phase.

In Phase 2 of the SRMD—Development and Implementation—the risks found in Phase 1 are addressed, and for each one, a remediation strategy is created, implemented, and tracked. Every remediation strategy needs to be tested, including in a production environment, and the results of the tests are reported to ensure institutional learning. This phase thus handles *closing the loop*.

The third and final phase of the SRMD—Operation— recognizes that moving new processes and new assets into day-to-day operation requires effort and attention. This is another part of *closing the loop*. Creating new processes starts with a well-defined change-management process, which includes not only moving the new assets into production but also accompanying those new assets with new procedures as appropriate. These new and changed assets must be stabilized, and all personnel must become familiarized with them to ensure a successful transition and operation.

The SRMD, like the OCTAVE approach, emphasizes that security must have its place in the software and system-development life cycle and so has described a security framework process model. This model consists of six major processes and milestones:

1. initiation of the project definition, in which a vision scope is approved
2. security assessment and analyses, in which a project plan is approved
3. security remediation development, in which the identified scope of the remediation is covered
4. security remediation testing and resource functionality testing, in which release readiness is approved
5. security policies and countermeasure deployment, in which deployment is completed
6. deployment complete, in which preparations are made for the next iteration

The SRMD also identifies a security risk management discipline that aids an organization in planning a strategy to minimize the risks associated with security breaches. This discipline provides guidance on how to assess risk probabilities and losses; analyze and prioritize risks; and plan, schedule, and report on security risks.

For example, to determine a risk probability, the SRMD walks a user through a series of steps for determining (1) the probability of a threat, (2) the criticality of the asset, (3) the effort required to exploit the vulnerability, (4) the vulnerability factor, and (5) the asset priority. The first three steps allow one to determine the threat level, and the final two steps allow one to determine the impact or loss factor. By multiplying these together, we get a RE value.

Similarly, the SRMD provides a set of steps and factors to consider in valuing assets.

## FRAP

The Facilitated Risk Assessment Program (FRAP) is a qualitative process developed by Thomas Peltier. In the FRAP, a system or a segment of a business process is examined by a team that includes both business/managerial and IT personnel. The FRAP guides them to brainstorm potential threats, vulnerabilities, and potential damages to data integrity, confidentiality, and availability. Based on this brainstorming, the impacts to business operations are analyzed, and threats and risks are prioritized. The FRAP is purely *qualitative*, meaning that it makes no attempt to quantify risk probabilities and magnitudes. It has the following three phases.

### Phase 1: The Pre-FRAP Meeting
In Phase 1, the initial team members are chosen, and the team determines the scope and mechanics of the review. This process establishes the context and goals of the inquiry. The outputs of Phase 1 are a scope statement, an identification of the team members (typically between 7 and 15 people), a visual model of the security process being reviewed, and a set of definitions. These definitions serve as an anchor to the rest of the process. The FRAP recommends that the team agrees on the following terms: integrity, confidentiality, availability, risk, control, impact, and vulnerability. Finally, the mechanics of the meeting need to be agreed upon in Phase 1: location, schedule, materials, and so forth.

### Phase 2: The FRAP Session
Phase 2 is itself divided into three parts. These three parts serve as the focusing activity, as well as the front end of the analysis activity. The first activity is to establish the logistics for the meeting: who will take what role (owner, team leader, scribe, facilitator, team member). Once this is done, the team reviews the outputs from Phase 1—the definitions, scope statement, and so forth—to ensure that all team members start from a common basis of understanding. The second activity is brainstorming, in which all of the team members contribute risks that are of concern to them. The third and final activity of Phase 2 is prioritization. Prioritization is ranked along two dimensions: vulnerability (low to high) and impact (low to high). When the risks are documented, the team also contributes suggested controls for at least the high-priority risks.

### Phase 3: The Post-FRAP Meeting(s)
Phase 3 may be a single meeting or may be a series of meetings over many days. In this phase, the bulk of the analysis work is done, as well as closing the loop. The outputs from the phase are a cross-reference sheet, an identification of existing controls, a set of recommendations on open risks and their identified controls, and a final report. Producing the cross-reference sheet is the most time-consuming activity. This sheet shows all of the risks affected by each control, as well as any trade-offs between controls that have been identified. In addition to documenting

everything that has been learned in the FRAP, the final report contains an action plan, describing the controls to implement.

## Quantitative versus Qualitative Approaches

The security risk management methods described herein differ in whether they attempt to quantify security risks or to assess and prioritize risks qualitatively. The SRMD and the OCTAVE process approach the problems of identifying, analyzing, planning for, and managing security risks quantitatively (in the OCTAVE approach, quantitative analysis of risks is an optional element of Phase 3). The FRAP and OCTAVE-S, on the other hand, are purely qualitative. What are the costs and benefits of each approach?

Neither approach is obviously superior to the other. Quantitative methods tend to be more expensive and time-consuming to apply and require more front-end work, but they can produce more precise results. Such methods tend to be associated with higher-process maturity organizations. Qualitative methods, on the other hand, are less time-consuming (and therefore more agile to apply) and require less documentation. In addition, specific loss estimates are often not needed to make a determination to embark upon a risk-mitigation activity.

In the next section, we show how a quantitative security risk assessment practice can be implemented that is not unduly time- or resource-consuming.

## MANAGEMENT OF INFORMATION SECURITY STANDARDS

Guidelines and standards exist for developing and acquiring (technical) IT security products and operation-oriented and management-oriented IT security procedures. Along a second dimension, there are guidelines and standards that are associated with mechanisms for certification, those that are associated with laws that require due diligence, and those that are purely for "guidance." Finally, there are capability maturity models (CMMs) that are characterized most easily as being at one level higher than any of the aforementioned guidelines and standards. In this section, we introduce the most important IT security guidelines and standards in each of these categories. For each, we indicate its type, briefly describe its history and purpose, describe its major areas of concern, and indicate what it has to say about IT security risk management.

### TCSEC, ITSEC, CTCPEC, Common Criteria, and ISO 15408

TCSEC, ITSEC, CTCPEC, Common Criteria, and ISO 15408 (1999) constitute a family of standards in the sense that the first three are ancestors of the final two, and ISO 15408 is the ISO standard based on Common Criteria. All deal with security-related COTS (Commercial Off-The-Shelf) products. TCSEC stands for Trusted Computer System Evaluation Criteria, ITSEC for IT Security Evaluation and Certification Scheme, and CTCPEC for Canadian Trusted Computer Product Evaluation Criteria.

The original TCSEC document, often referred to as the "orange book," was published in 1985 by the National Computer Security Council (NCSC), a branch of the National Security Agency (NSA). TCSEC, which deals with both security requirements and assurance (evaluation) requirements, has three objectives:

1. to provide users with a yardstick with which to assess the degree of trust that can be placed in computer systems for the secure processing of classified or other sensitive information
2. to provide guidance to manufacturers as to what to build into their new, widely available trusted commercial products to satisfy trust requirements for sensitive applications
3. to provide a basis for specifying security requirements in acquisition specifications

Here is a description of TCSEC's scope from its foreword:

> This publication is effective immediately and is mandatory for use by all DoD [United States Department of Defense] Components in carrying out Automatic Data Processing [ADP] system technical security evaluation activities applicable to the processing and storage of classified and other sensitive DoD information and applications as set forth herein.

The precursors to ITSEC, TCSEC's United Kingdom counterpart, were developed by two government agencies. In 1985, the Communications Electronics Security Group (CESG) created facilities for performing security evaluations of government computer systems. A few years later, the Department of Trade and Industry (DTI) established the Commercial Computer Security Centre to evaluate security-related COTS products. The documents that resulted are known as "the Green Books." In December 1989, CESG and DTI issued a joint scheme, the UK IT Security Evaluation and Certification scheme, or, for short, the UK ITSEC scheme. The scheme went into effect on May 1, 1991. According to ITSEC's mission statement

> The objectives of the Scheme are to meet the needs of Industry and Government for cost effective and efficient security evaluation and certification of IT products and systems. The Scheme also aims to provide a framework for the international mutual recognition of certificates.

Work on TCSEC; ITSEC; the CTCPEC, which was developed by the Canadian Communications Security Establishment (CSE); and several European initiatives eventually led to development of the Common Criteria for Information Technology Security Evaluation, usually simply referred to as the Common Criteria and often further abbreviated to CC. The organizations that participated in the development of the Common Criteria and that are involved in certifying evaluation laboratories are AISEP (Australia and New Zealand), CSE (Canada), SCSSI (France), BSI (Germany), NLNCSA (Netherlands), CESG (United Kingdom), NIST (United States), and NSA (United States). An eminently readable discussion of CC's scope of applicability and how it works may be found in a report published on the Web site of Canada's Communication Security Establishment (CSE; http://www.csecst.gc.ca/en/documents/services/ccs/brochure.pdf).

In June 1999, Common Criteria became ISO 15408. A detailed view of the development of the Common Criteria and ISO 15408 may be found in Annex A of Common Criteria for Information Technology Security Evaluation (1999).

CC/ISO 15408 works as follows: A security-related product to be evaluated is referred to as a target of evaluation (TOE). The inputs to a TOE's Common Criteria evaluation are a security target (ST) package, a set of producer-supplied evidence about the TOE, and the TOE (hardware and/or software) itself.

The ST consists of the following:

- a list of security threats with which the TOE is intended to deal
- the TOE's objectives in dealing with those threats
- the TOE's functional requirements
- a specification of the TOE's implemented security functions and assurance measures.

The following are CC's 11 functional requirements classes:

1. Class FAU: Security audit
2. Class FCO: Communication
3. Class FCS: Cryptographic support
4. Class FDP: User data protection
5. Class FIA: Identification and authentication
6. Class FMT: Security management
7. Class FPR: Privacy
8. Class FPT: Protection of the TSF
9. Class FRU: Resource utilization
10. Class FTA: TOE access
11. Class FTP: Trusted path/channels

Each class is subcategorized into a number of "families" and each family into a number of "components." Some classes consist of few families; for example, Class FCS: Cryptographic support consists of just two families:

1. Cryptographic key management (FCS_CKM)
2. Cryptographic operation (FCS_COP)

Other classes consist of considerably more families; for example, Class FDP: User data protection includes 13 families:

1. Access control policy (FDP_ACC)
2. Access control functions (FDP_ACF)
3. Data authentication (FDP_DAU)
4. Export to outside TSF control (FDP_ETC)
5. Information flow control policy (FDP_IFC)
6. Information flow control functions (FDP_IFF)
7. Import from outside TSF control (FDP_ITC)
8. Internal TOE transfer (FDP_ITT)
9. Residual information protection (FDP_RIP)
10. Rollback (FDP_ROL)
11. Stored data integrity (FDP_SDI)
12. Inter-TSF user data confidentiality transfer protection (FDP_UCT)
13. Inter-TSF user data integrity transfer protection (FDP_UIT)

The following are CC's seven assurance requirements classes:

1. Class ACM: Configuration management
2. Class ADO: Delivery and operation
3. Class ADV: Development
4. Class AGD: Guidance documents
5. Class ALC: Life cycle support
6. Class ATE: Tests
7. Class AVA: Vulnerability assessment

An important part of a TOE's ST is the protection profile (PP), which details requirements that the product purports to satisfy or that the potential consumer must have. Common Criteria includes a set of "requirements of known validity" from which the preparer of the ST may choose in preparing the PP; consumers and/or developers may specify, in the PP, additional requirements that they deem necessary in a particular product or product category.

Common Criteria evaluation works as follows. In the United States, the National Information Assurance Partnership's (NIAP) Common Criteria Evaluation and Validation Scheme (CCEVS) Validation Body is jointly run by the National Institute of Standards and Technology (NIST) and the National Security Agency (NSA); according to the Common Criteria (1999), the process is as follows:

The Validation Body approves participation of security testing laboratories in the scheme in accordance with its established policies and procedures. During the course of an evaluation, the Validation Body provides technical guidance to those testing laboratories, validates the results of IT security evaluations for conformance to the Common Criteria, and serves as an interface to other nations for the recognition of such evaluations. IT security evaluations are conducted by commercial testing laboratories accredited by the NIST's National Voluntary Laboratory Accreditation Program (NVLAP) and approved by the Validation Body. These approved testing laboratories are called Common Criteria Testing Laboratories (CCTL).

Similar arrangements are in effect in the other countries involved in the Common Criteria.

A positive CC evaluation of a product yields a confirmation that the TOE satisfies the ST together with an indication of the evaluation assurance level (EAL) at which the ST is satisfied; there are seven EALs, ranging from EAL1 (functionally tested) and EAL2 (structurally tested) to EAL6 (semiformally verified design and testing) and EAL7 (formally verified design and testing).

As far as risk is concerned, Common Criteria assumes that the organization contemplating the purchase and use of a security-related product will use the results of the product's evaluation when performing the risk analysis required to determine whether the product meets the organization's IT security-related requirements. Although it naturally addresses threat/risk-related issues in depth, Common Criteria, being product centered rather than management or operationally centered, does not address the issue of the how an organization goes about performing that risk analysis. The following quotations from Common Criteria for Information Technology Security Evaluation Part 1 (2004) make this point very clearly:

> The evaluation process establishes a level of confidence that the security functions of such products and systems and the assurance measures applied to them meet these requirements. The evaluation results may help consumers to determine whether the IT product or system is secure enough for their intended application and whether the security risks implicit in its use are tolerable (p. 8).

> Consumers can use the results of evaluations to help decide whether an evaluated product or system fulfils their security needs. These security needs typically identified as a result of both risk analysis and policy direction. Consumers can also use the evaluation results to compare different products or systems. Presentation of the assurance requirements within a hierarchy supports this need (p. 19).

> The owners of the assets will analyze the possible threats to determine which ones apply to their environment. The results are known as risks. This analysis can aid in the selection of countermeasures to counter the risks and reduce it to an acceptable level (p. 25).

Types of product that have received Common Criteria certification include operating systems, database management systems, firewalls, switches and routers, certificate management software, public key infrastructure (PKI/key management infrastructure software, and so on.

The three parts of the Common Criteria Standard are available on these Web pages:

1. Part 1 of the CS Standard version 2.2, January 2004: Introduction and general model: http://www.commoncriteriaportal.org/public/files/ccpart1v2.2.pdf
2. Part 2 of the CC Standard version 2.2, January 2004: Security functional requirements: http://www.commoncriteriaportal.org/public/files/ccpart2v2.2.pdf
3. Part 3 of the CC Standard version 2.2, January 2004: Security assurance requirements: http://www.commoncriteriaportal.org/public/files/ccpart3v2.2.pdf

The three parts of the latest (1999) version of ISO 15408 may be ordered from the International Organization for Standardization.

## BS 7799, ISO 17799, and ISO TR 13335 (GMITS)

British Standard 7799 (BS 7799) and ISO 17799 form a family in the sense that the latter is the ISO standard version of the second of BS 7799's two parts, the first of which is best characterized as guidelines and the second of which as a standard against which certification is possible. ISO TR 13335 (GMITS) is included in this section because it provides additional guidance, especially in the area of risk management, for organizations seeking ISO 17799 certification. All three deal with operational—including, of course, site-related physical—and management aspects of IT security; as might be expected, they all deal with both the implementation and the ongoing operation of IT security activities.

BS 7799 Part 1 is entitled "Information Technology—Code of Practice for Information Security Management," and BS 7799 Part 2 is entitled "Information Security Management Systems—Specification with Guidance for Use." ISO 17799 is entitled "Code of Practice for Information Security Management," and ISO TR 13335 "Guidelines for the Management for IT Security," or GMITS for short.

The earliest precursor of ISO 17799 was created by the UK Department of Trade and Industry's (DTI) Commercial Computer Security Centre (CCSC), the organization that developed ITSEC (see above). Its first incarnation was the "Users Code of Practice," published in 1989. Its second incarnation was British Standard's guidance document PD 0003, "A Code of Practice for Information Security Management," developed by the National Computing Centre (NCC) with the aid of representatives from industry. In 1995, PD 0003 evolved into British Standard BS7799:1995. A second part of the standard, BS7799-2:1998 was published in February 1998. In September 2002, BS7799-2:1998 was updated to BS7799-2:2002 to make it consistent with ISO 9001:2000, ISO 14001:1996, and policies of the Organization for Economic Cooperation and Development (OECD). As of this writing, BS7799 Part 2 has not become an ISO standard, and there seems to be no effort to move it in that direction.

ISO 17799:2000 describes 127 security controls, each with numerous subsections, within the following 10 domains:

1. **Security Policy**—to provide management direction and support for information security
2. **Organizational Security**—to manage information security within the organization
3. **Asset Classification & Control**—to maintain appropriate protection of organizational assets
4. **Personnel Security**—to reduce the risks of human error, theft, fraud, or misuse of facilities
5. **Physical Security**—to prevent unauthorized access, damage, and interference to business premises and information

6. **Communication and Operation Management**—to ensure the correct and secure operation of information-processing facilities
7. **Access Control**—to control access to information
8. **System Development and Maintenance**—to ensure that security is built into information systems
9. **Business Continuity Management**—to counteract interruptions to business activities and to protect critical business processes from the effects of major failures or disasters
10. **Compliance**—to avoid breaches of any criminal and civil law; statutory, regulatory, or contractual obligations; and any security requirements

Although it is extremely thorough in its coverage, ISO/IEC 17799:2000 does not address the issues of evaluation or certification; it is, in the strict sense, a set of guidelines rather than a standard. It stresses risk assessment and risk management but, as a set of guidelines, does not specify a particular approach. BS 7799-2:2002 is, on the other hand, a standard in the strict sense. It specifies, in great detail, what is expected of an organization for the achievement of certification and what is expected of an assessor in the assessment of an organization for compliance. ISO 17799:2000 is intended to be used as a set of Code of Practice guidelines for organizations desirous of working toward BS 7799-2:2002 certification.

BS 7799-2:2002 certification is based on an organization's creation of a documented information security management system (ISMS). The ISMS is based on the continuous-improvement Plan, Do, Check, Act (PDCA) feedback-loop cycle invented by Walter Shewhart (1986) of Western Electric's Hawthorne Plant in the late 1930s and later popularized by W. Edwards Deming. The idea behind the cycle is to develop, implement, and continuously improve the organization's control and management of security.

As can be seen from BS 7799-2:2002's high-level definition of PDCA, the management of risk drives the entire process:

PLAN

- Define the scope of the ISMS
- Define the ISMS policy
- Define the approach to risk assessment
- Identify the risks
- Assess the risks
- Identify and evaluate options for the treatment of the risks
- Select control objectives and controls
- Prepare a Statement of Applicability (SOA)

CHECK

- Execute monitoring procedures
- Undertake regular reviews of ISMS effectiveness
- Review level of residual and acceptable risk
- Conduct internal ISMS audits
- Perform regular management reviews of the ISMS
- Record actions and events that impact on the ISMS

DO

- Formulate a risk treatment plan
- Implement the risk treatment plan
- Implement controls
- Implement training and awareness programs
- Manage operations
- Manage resources
- Implement procedures to detect and respond to security incidents

ACT

- Implement identified improvements
- Take corrective/preventive action
- Apply lessons learned
- Communicate results to interested parties
- Ensure that improvements achieve objectives

ISO TR 13335-3:1998, "Techniques for the Management of IT Security," and ISO TR 13335-4:2000, "Selection of Safeguards," describe in detail the topics of risk assessment and risk management, respectively. The British Standard Institute's (BSI) PD 3002, "Guide to BS 7799 risk assessment," and PD 3005, "Guide on the selection of BS 7799-2 controls," detail how GMITS Part 3 and GMITS Part 4 may be applied, respectively, to the risk assessment and risk management aspects of ISO/IEC 17799 and BS 7799 Part 2 (see http://www.bsi-global.com/ICT/Security/pd3002.xalter and http://www.bsi-global.com/ICT/Security/pd3005.xalter).

Assessment for BS7799-2:2002 certification is done by an assessor working for a *certification body*. A list of certification bodies may be found at the Web site of the International ISMS User Group (http://www.xisec.com/), as may a list of all certified organizations.

To be eligible to perform BS7799-2:2002 assessments, an organization must be accredited as a certification body by a *national accreditation body*. Different national accreditation bodies maintain reciprocal recognition agreements. Identities of and contact information for national accreditation bodies in Europe may be found at the European (cooperation for) Accreditation (EA) Web site at http://www.european-accreditation.org/, as can non-European accreditation bodies with which EA has contracts of cooperation; accreditation guidelines may be found there as well (EA, 2000).

The ISMS International Users Group lists the following as accredited certification bodies:

| | |
|---|---|
| BM TRADA Certification Limited | National Quality Assurance |
| BSI | Nemko (Norway) |
| BVQI (Bureau Veritas Quality International) | PSB Certification (Singapore) |
| Certification Europe CIS (Austria) | RINA S.p.A. (Italy) SAI Global Limited (Australia) |
| DNV (Det Norske Veritas) | SFS Certification (Finland) |
| DQS GmbH (Germany) | SGS ICS Limited |
| JACO-IS (Japanese Audit and Certification Organisation) | SQS (Swiss Quality System) |

| JQA (Japanese Quality Assurance) | STQC Certification Services (India) |
| KEMA (Netherlands) | Teknologisk Institutt Sertifisering AS (Norway) |
| KPMG Audit plc | TÜV Rheinland Group (Germany) |
| KPMG SA | UIMCert (Germany) |
| LRQA | United Registrar of Systems Limited |

A BS7799-2:2002 certification comes with a "scope," which specifies the part of the organization that is, in fact, certified–either the entire organization or one or more of its parts or activities.

## HIPAA

The U.S. Health Insurance Portability and Accountability Act of 1996 (HIPAA) is not a standard against which an organization is certified but rather is a statute with which relevant organizations are required to comply and which dictates government audit, with possible severe consequences, in case of complaints of violations. HIPAA's purpose, as stated in the act itself, is

> to improve portability and continuity of health insurance coverage in the group and individual markets, to combat waste, fraud, and abuse in health insurance and health care delivery, to promote the use of medical savings accounts, to improve access to long-term care services and coverage, to simplify the administration of health insurance, and for other purposes.

The desired results are intended to result from improved utilization of IT, which accounts for the act's inclusion of a privacy standard/rule and a security standard/rule. The act applies to protected health information (PHI)—anything to do with a patient or patients—that is *electronically* stored and *electronically* transmitted by a "covered entity" (i.e., a health plan, a health care provider, or a health care clearinghouse). The term *health plan* includes health insurers, health benefit plans, HMOs, other managed care organizations, and so on. The term *health care clearinghouse* includes billing services, health information providers, and the like. The final version of the Security Rule was enacted in February 2003; large organizations are required to comply by April 2005 and small ones by April 2006.

The HIPAA Security Rule is broken down into three areas: administrative (management and operational) safeguards, physical (operational) safeguards, and technical safeguards. The three safeguards are further broken down as follows:

### – Administrative Safeguards

- Security Management Process
- Security Responsibility
- Workforce Security
- Information Access Management
- Security Awareness and Training
- Security Incident Procedures
- Contingency Plan
- Evaluation
- Business Associate Contracts and Other Arrangements

### – Physical Safeguards

- Facility Access Controls
- Workstation Use
- Workstation Security
- Device and Media Controls

### – Technical Safeguards

- Access Controls
- Audit Controls
- Integrity
- Person or Entity Authentication
- Transmission Security

HIPAA's Security Rule specifies identification of the relevant IT systems—that is, scoping of the compliance effort as a necessary precursor to risk identification—followed by risk assessment and risk management planning.

Because HIPAA requires that a covered entity's implementation of the Security Rule be "comprehensive and coordinated," "scalable," and "technology neutral"—that it be updated regularly as technology changes—the act's provisions are general rather than specific. In May 2004, NIST issued a resource guide for implementing the Security Rule to aid the large number of organizations covered by HIPAA (NIST, 2004).

As indicated herein, there is no notion of HIPAA certification or accreditation. Rather, the U.S. Department of Health and Human Services (DHHS) has assigned its Office of Civil Rights (OCR) the responsibility for enforcing HIPAA by responding to complaints of violations.

An overview of HIPAA may be found at http://privacy.med.miami.edu/glossary/xd_hipaa.htm.

## SSE-CMM and ISO/IEC 21827

Up to this point, we have discussed standards/guidelines for IT security-related products and for the management of IT security programs. In general, an IT security standard/guideline can relate to the technical side of IT security, to the management side, or to both. A guideline/standard can simply be informational, it can specify a mechanism for certification, or it can specify due diligence and provide for complaint-driven audit, with penalties for noncompliance.

A capability maturity model (CMM) fits into none of these categories. Rather, it deals with the process whereby an activity is performed. A CMM is used to certify the process that an organization uses to produce its products rather than to certify the results of the application of that process (i.e., the products produced).

Some activities for which CMMs exist are software engineering (Paulk, Weber, Curtis, & Chrissis, 1995) and systems engineering (Bate et al., 1995). These CMMs apply to the development of arbitrary (not necessarily IT security-related) software applications or systems in the first case and of hardware/software systems in the second.

The philosophy behind a CMM is that if the process used by an organization in the production of products is sufficiently "mature," then it is safe to assume the following:

*The organization's existing products are of sufficient high quality—in the case of software, as an example, it meets functional requirements/specifications to a sufficient degree and has a sufficient high level of performance, reliability, availability, maintainability, and so on.

*A new product, yet to be developed, will be of sufficient high quality and will additionally be completed sufficiently close to schedule and to the projected budget.

A further aspect of the CMM notion is that an organization can be assigned a maturity level, typically on a scale of 1 to 5, which, in some sense, qualifies the notion of "sufficient," with Level 5 representing a very high level of sufficiency, Level 1 representing a low level, and Levels 2-4 being in between.

**Capability Level 1—Performed Informally:** Base practices of the process area are generally performed. The performance of these base practices may not be rigorously planned and tracked. Performance depends on individual knowledge and effort. Work products of the process area testify to their performance. Individuals within the organization recognize that an action should be performed, and there is general agreement that this action is performed as and when required. There are identifiable work products for the process.

**Capability Level 2—Planned and Tracked:** Performance of the base practices in the process area is planned and tracked. Performance according to specified procedures is verified. Work products conform to specified standards and requirements. Measurement is used to track process-area performance, thus enabling the organization to manage its activities based on actual performance. The primary distinction from Level 1, Performed Informally, is that the performance of the process is planned and managed.

**Capability Level 3—Well Defined:** Base practices are performed according to a well-defined process using approved, tailored versions of standard, documented processes. The primary distinction from Level 2, Planned and Tracked, is that the process is planned and managed using an organization-wide standard process.

**Capability Level 4—Quantitatively Controlled:** Detailed measures of performance are collected and analyzed. This leads to a quantitative understanding of process capability and an improved ability to predict performance. Performance is objectively managed, and the quality of work products is quantitatively known. The primary distinction from the Well Defined level is that the defined process is quantitatively understood and controlled.

**Capability Level 5—Continuously Improving:** Quantitative performance goals (targets) for process effectiveness and efficiency are established, based on the business goals of the organization. Continuous process improvement against these goals is enabled by quantitative feedback received from performing the defined processes and from piloting innovative ideas and technologies. The primary distinction from the quantitatively controlled level is that the defined process and the standard process undergo continuous refinement and improvement, based on a quantitative understanding of the impact of changes to these processes.

Considering the definitions of Levels 4 and 5, it should be no surprise that the development of the first CMM, the Software Engineering CMM, was influenced strongly by Shewhart and Deming's ideas on statistical process control (Shewhart, 1986).

According to the SSE-CMM Model Description Document, Version 3.0 (editorial comments in square brackets and references to risk management concepts in italics; http://www.sse-cmm.org/docs/ssecmmv3final.pdf) the System Security CMM (SSE-CMM) is extremely flexible—so flexible, in fact, that it applies to all the following:

***Product Developers:** The SSE-CMM includes practices that focus on gaining an understanding of the customer's security needs. Interaction with the customer is required to ascertain them. In the case of a [noncustom, noncontracted] product, the customer is generic as the product is developed a priori independent of a specific customer. When this is the case, the product marketing group or another group can be used as the hypothetical customer, if one is required. In this case, the product is hardware/software/other physical product to be used for IT security.

***Countermeasure Developers:** The model contains practices to address determining and analyzing security *vulnerabilities*, assessing operational *impacts*, and providing input and guidance to other groups involved (e.g., a software group). The group that provides the service of developing countermeasures needs to understand the relationships between these practices. In this case, the product is the countermeasures themselves.

***Security Service Providers:** To measure the process capability of an organization that performs *risk assessments*, several groups of practices come into play. During system development or integration, one would need to assess the organization with regard to its ability to *determine and analyze security vulnerabilities* and *assess the operational impacts*. In the operational case, one would need to assess the organization with regard to its ability to *monitor the security posture* of the system, *identify and analyze security vulnerabilities*, and *assess the operational impacts*. [This means assessing the entire IT security system—its technical, operational, and management aspects. Note that the provider can be an outside organization/consultant/integrator or an IT security implementation and/or management group within the very organization that will be using the system.]

The previous references to risk management concepts make it clear how critical risk management is to SSE-CMM. According to the same document (http://www.sse-cmm.org/docs/ssecmmv3final.pdf), SSE-CMM's history is as follows:

> The SSE-CMM initiative began as an NSA-sponsored effort in April 1993 with . . . investigation of the need for a specialized CMM to address security engineering. During this Conceive Phase, a straw-man Security Engineering CMM was developed to seed the effort.

> The information security community was invited to participate in the effort at the First Public Security Engineering CMM Workshop in January 1995. Representatives from over 60 organizations reaffirmed the need for such a model. As a result of the community's interest, Project Working Groups were formed at the workshop, initiating the Develop Phase of the effort.

> Development of the model and appraisal method was accomplished through the work of the SSE-CMM Steering, Author, and Application Working Groups with the first version of the model published in October 1996 and of the appraisal method in April 1997.

> To validate the model and appraisal method, pilots occurred from June 1996 through June 1997 . . . The pilots addressed various organizational aspects that contributed to the validation of the model . . .

> In July 1997, the Second Public Systems Security Engineering CMM Workshop was conducted . . . The workshop proceedings are available on the SSE-CMM web site . . . the International Systems Security Engineering Association (ISSEA) was formed to continue the development and promotion of the SSE-CMM . . . ISSEA continues to maintain the model and its associated materials as well as other activities related to systems security engineering and security in general. ISSEA has become active in the International Organization for Standardization and sponsored the SSE-CMM as an international standards ISO/IEC 21827 (2002).

The "base practices" for which CMM assesses security engineering maturity are divided into two groups. The groups, along with their process areas are as follows:

| SECURITY BASE PRACTICES | PROJECT AND ORGANIZATIONAL BASE PRACTICES |
|---|---|
| PA01—Administer Security Controls | General Security Considerations |
| PA02—Assess Impact | PA12—Ensure Quality |
| PA03—Assess Security Risk | PA13—Manage Configurations |
| PA04—Assess Threat | PA14—Manage Project Risk |
| PA05—Assess Vulnerability | PA15—Monitor and Control Technical Effort |
| PA06—Build Assurance Argument | PA16—Plan Technical Effort |
| PA07—Coordinate Security | PA17—Define Organization's Systems Engineering Process |
| PA08—Monitor Security Posture | PA18—Improve Organization's Systems Engineering Processes |
| PA09—Provide Security Input | PA19—Manage Product Line Evolution |
| PA10—Specify Security Needs | PA20—Manage Systems Engineering Support Environment |
| PA11—Verify and Validate Security | PA21—Provide Ongoing Skills and Knowledge |
| | PA22—Coordinate with Suppliers |

SSE-CMM provides documentation of both the basic model and of the appraisal method. According to SSE-CMM Appraisal Method Version 2.0 (http://www.sse-cmm.org/docs/SSAM.pdf), any organization wishing to evaluate the capability of another organization to perform systems security engineering activities should consider using the system security appraisal method (SSAM). The SSAM can be used to evaluate the processes of product developers, service providers, system integrators, system administrators, and security specialists to obtain a baseline or benchmark of actual practices against the standards detailed in the SSE-CMM (http://www.sse-cmm.org/docs/ssecmmv3final.pdf, October 1, 2004).

The International Systems Security Engineering Association (ISSEA: http://www.sse-cmm.org/issea/issea.asp ) "is a non-profit membership organization dedicated to the advancement of Systems Security Engineering as a defined and measurable discipline. Established in 1999, ISSEA and its members are tasked with the maintenance of the SSE-CMM." According to the ISSEA Web site, an appraiser certification program is currently being developed.

## NIST Guidance Documents

The U.S. National Institute on Standards and Technology (NIST) has taken a significant role in developing IT security guidelines and standards, with a special emphasis on IT security risk management. The following is a list of NIST IT security guidelines, very few of which do not have general applicability and all of which may be obtained through NIST's Web site, http://csrc.nist.gov/publications/nistpubs/:

*NIST *Computer Security Handbook*, February 7, 1996

*NIST Special Publication (SP) 800-12: *An Introduction to Computer Security*

*NIST SP 800-16: *Information Technology Security Training Requirements: A Role- and Performance-Based Model*, April 1998

*NIST SP 800-18: *Guide for Developing Security Plans for Information Technology Systems*, December 1998

*NIST SP 800-30: *Risk Management Guide for Information Technology Systems*, January 2002

*NIST SP 800-35: *Guide to Information Technology Security Services*

NIST SP 800-31: *Intrusion Detection Systems*, November 2001

*NIST SP 800-32: *Introduction to Public Key Technology and the Federal PKI Infrastructure*, February 2001.

*NIST SP 800-33: *Underlying Technical Models for Information Technology Security*, December 2001

*NIST SP 800-34: *Contingency Planning Guide for Information Technology Systems*, June 2002

*NIST SP 800-36: *Guide to Selecting Information Technology Security Products*, October 2003

*NIST SP 800-42: *Guideline on Network Security Testing*, October 2003

*NIST SP 800-48: *Wireless Network Security*, October 2003

*NIST SP 800-50: *Building an Information Technology Security Awareness and Training Program*, October 2003

*NIST SP 800-55: *Security Metrics Guide for Information Technology Systems*, July 2003

*NIST SP 800-64: *Security Considerations in the Information System Development Life Cycle*, October 2003

*NIST SP 802.11: *Bluetooth and Handheld Devices*, November 2002

## RISK MODELS

In the first section of this chapter, we introduced the fundamental techniques of risk assessment and risk management. In this section, we discuss how risk assessment applies to risk management *decision making*. Our focus is on strategic methods—methods that plan from the outset to achieve particular goals regardless of the circumstances—rather than tactical methods that attempt to make the best response in a given circumstance. To do this, we need to take some of the terms that we defined informally in the first section and give them more precise definitions.

### Definitions

A *risk*, from the security perspective, is the probability that some threat will successfully exploit a vulnerability in a system, along with the magnitude of this loss. The higher the probability that a threat will succeed and the greater the magnitude of the potential loss, the greater the risk for the organization.

A *threat*, then, is a stimulus for a risk; it is *any* danger to the system, an undesirable event. A threat, however, might not be a person. A *threat agent* is a person who initiates or instigates a threat.

Typically, a threat takes advantage of some system *vulnerability*, a condition in which the system is missing or applying a safeguard or control improperly. The vulnerability thus increases the likelihood of the threat or its impact or possibly both. It is important to note that the system includes people, not just hardware, software, and networks.

The net effect of a vulnerability being exploited by a threat agent is to expose the organization's assets to a potential loss. This loss might be in the form of a loss or disclosure of information, a corruption of the organization's information (a loss of *integrity*), or a denial of service.

In the language of risk, we need to consider the magnitude of all risk exposures to which an organization is susceptible. This leads to the *basic risk formula*, which attempts to quantify risk in terms of risk exposure (RE; Boehm, 1991):

$$RE = \text{probability(loss)} * \text{magnitude(loss)}$$

This formula is frequently written as follows $RE = P(L) * S(L)$.

For example, if organization A calculates the probability of a key server being down for 2 hours as 10% due to denial of service attacks, and the loss due to this downtime to be \$20,000, then the risk exposure facing A due to this loss is \$2,000.

Frequently, this formula is presented as a summation of all such risks to which a system is exposed, therefore:

$$\text{Total RE} = \sum P(L_i) * S(L_i)$$

where $L_i$ is the loss due to the $i^{th}$ risk.

For example, if organization A has two other risks that they are facing, one with a probability of 50% and a loss of \$1,000 and another with a probability of 0.1% and a loss of \$1,000,000, then A's Total RE is:

$0.1 * \$20,000 + 0.5 * \$1,000 + 0.001 * \$1,000,000$
$= \$2,000 + \$500 + \$1,000$
$= \$3,500$

Related to the notion of RE is *risk reduction leverage* (RRL). RRL is a way of gauging the effectiveness or desirability of a risk-reduction technique. The formula for RRL is:

$$RRL = (RE_{before} - RE_{after})/RRCost$$

where RRCost stands for risk-reduction cost. A similar formula can be used to compare the relative effectiveness of technique A with respect to B:

$$RRRL_{A,B} = (RE_B - RE_A)/(RRCost_A - RRCost_B)$$

where $RE_A$ and $RE_B$ are the risk exposures after using A and B, respectively (we assume that the RE before applying the techniques is the same for both techniques). We see that when $RRRL_{A,B} > 0$, technique A is more cost effective than technique B.

Let us consider an example. Say an organization is considering ways of lowering its defect risk on a safety-critical system and has identified two possible ways of finding defects and hence reducing the system risk: a structured walkthrough or an IV&V (independent validation and verification) activity. First, it must establish a cost for each risk-reduction technique. Next, it must evaluate its current RE (which is its $RE_{before}$) and the RE that will result from the application of the technique (the $RE_{after}$). Assume that the organization is interested in the risk involved if the safety-critical system fails. Such a failure would result in a loss to the company of \$10,000,000; currently, the company believes that there is a 5% likelihood of such an occurrence. Structured walkthroughs have, in the past, found 80% of the outstanding problems, reducing the probability of a loss to 1%. IV&V has been even more effective at finding problems, and it is expected that this technique will reduce the probability of a loss to 0.01%. However, the structured walkthrough is relatively inexpensive, costing just \$5,000 (the time of the employees involved). The IV&V, because it is independent, requires the hiring of a consultant, which will cost \$100,000. The RRL for each technique can now be calculated as follows:

$$\begin{aligned}
RRL_{inspection} &= (0.05^*10,000,000 - 0.01^*10,000,000)/5,000 \\
&= (500,000 - 100,000)/5,000 \\
&= 80 \\
RRL_{IV\&V} &= (0.5^*10,000,000 - 0.0001^*10,000,000) \\
&\quad /100,000 \\
&= (500,000 - 1,000)/100,000 \\
&= 4.99
\end{aligned}$$

Clearly, in this case, the organization will want to choose to do the inspection first, as its RRL is far greater than the IV&V activity. However, this could also be directly seen using the following calculation:

$$\begin{aligned}
RRRL_{inspection,IV\&V} &= (0.0001^*10,000,000 - 0.01^*10,000,000) \\
&\quad /(5,000 - 100,000) \\
&= (1,000 - 100,000)/(-95,000) \\
&= (-99,000)/(-95,000) = 1.042 > 0
\end{aligned}$$

Often, a technique reduces only the likelihood of a risk and not its magnitude. In this case, the RRL reduces to the cost-benefit (CB):

$$\begin{aligned}
CB &= [P_{before}(L) - P_{after}(L)]^*S(L)/RRCost \\
&= \Delta P(L)^*S(L)/RRCost
\end{aligned}$$

Finally, using RE, it is possible to develop a *risk profile* (or *RE profile*) with respect to some measure of interest. For example, one can evaluate RE as a function of a monotonically increasing quantity, such as elapsed time, cumulative effort, or cumulative cost. An example of a risk profile is given in Figure 3.

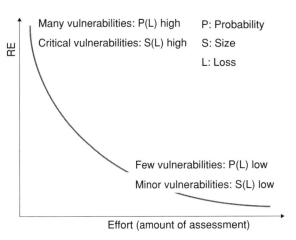

**Figure 3:** An Idealized Risk Reduction Profile.

Given this basis of understanding, we are now in a position to begin looking at specific techniques for strategic risk management.

## Strategic Risk Models

Every IT system in operation has some degree of security risk (Boehm, 1991). Recall that security risks are possible situations or events that can cause harm to a system and incur some form of loss. Security risks range in impact from trivial to fatal and in likelihood from certain to improbable. Thus far, we have only discussed risks that are either identified in that they arise from anticipated threats and known vulnerabilities; however, there are also unidentified risks where this is not the case. Similarly, the impact of an identified risk is either known where the expected loss-potential has been assessed or unknown where the loss-potential has not or cannot be assessed. Risks that are unidentified or have unknown impacts are sometimes loosely labeled as *risks due to uncertainty*. In the case of IT system security, risk considerations often must focus on uncertainty because by design, identified known risks are either addressed or accepted as within a "tolerable" level. Managing risks due to uncertainty is essentially the focus of sound risk management. Finally, note that a risk model describes risks and their impacts for a particular system.

We consider risk profile models because risks are generally not static. Likelihoods and impacts change with a number of factors, such as time, cost, system state, and so forth. As a consequence, it is often desirable to consider risks with respect to a planned set of events, such as assessment effort, system operation time, development investment, and so on. *Strategic risk models* represent risks that dynamically change over planned activities, and they can be used to promote effective risk management.

As introduced previously, this analysis makes use of risk profiling. Recall RE is the product of the probability of loss and the size of that loss as summed over all sources for a particular risk. Because security-risk considerations greatly affect a system's operational value, it is important that these risks be investigated candidly and completely. Expressing system development and operation considerations in terms of risk profiles enables quantitative assessment of attributes that are typically specified only qualitatively. A useful property of RE is that, if it is computed entirely within a particular system (i.e., there are no external loss sources), we may assume all RE sources are additive. This is true regardless of any complex dependencies and is analogous to mathematical expectation calculations within classic probability theory.

The additivity of RE can be exploited to analyze strategies for managing risk profiles for IT system security. Such analyses enable cost, schedule, and risk trade-off considerations that help identify effective risk-management strategies. In particular, this approach can help answer these difficult questions: what particular methods should be used to assess these vulnerabilities, which method should be used first, and how much is enough (risk assessment, risk mitigation, or risk control)? As in previous sections, our focus is on risk assessment while noting that the methods presented often have analogous counterparts in risk control.

## Strategic Risk Management Methods

The purpose of risk modeling is to aid in risk management decision-making. Management of risk does not necessarily result in removing risk; this is not always possible or even economically feasible. For any risk, there is usually only a limited degree to which that risk can be controlled or mitigated (i.e., the reduced expected loss). As indicated earlier, some risks due to uncertainty cannot be mitigated or even assessed. As such, *risk management* is the collection of activities used to address the identification, assessment, mitigation, avoidance, control, and continual reduction of risks within what is actually feasible *under particular conditions and constraints*. As such, the goal of risk management is one of "enlightened gambling" where we seek an expected outcome that is positive regardless of the circumstances. Assessment is the key starting point and, as stated earlier, the focus of this chapter. Assessment allows one to gain insight into the following factors:

- what the risks are and where is there risk due to uncertainty
- differentiating between development risks and operation risks
- differentiating between avoidable and unavoidable risks
- differentiating between controllable and uncontrollable risks
- cost and benefits of risk mitigation, avoidance, and control

Assessment enables the choice of a strategy for the mitigation and control of risk. However, it is not obvious from the outset that any given assessment strategy will be effective (or even feasible). In fact, a poorly chosen strategy may actually increase overall risk. A *strategic risk management method* is one that produces a risk-management strategy that reduces overall risk with respect to a particular goal (e.g., most risk reduction at lowest cost). Having a particular goal here is firmly predicated on having acceptable, well-defined strategic risk models as described earlier.

Models and methods for the strategic risk management of IT system security aid in making important "pre-crisis" risk management decisions by determining how much effort (or time) should be invested assessing security risks with respect to project risk factors, such as cost, schedule, launch (or operation) window, available skills and technology, uncontrollable external events, and so forth. In this way, assessment lays the foundation for a practical, economically feasible, empirically based approach for the strategic planning of risk-management efforts.

To illustrate the need for strategic risk management, we consider a general IT security risk assessment. The risk exposure corresponding to the cumulative potential loss from security violations in the operational system (e.g., system intrusions) will be called $RE_{security}$. The more assessment that is done, the lower is the $RE_{security}$ that results from unforeseen or uncontrolled vulnerabilities (i.e., uncertainty) such as those listed in Table 1. Assessing security attributes reduces both the size of loss due to surprises and the probability that surprises still remain. Before embarking on a security risk assessment, the system will likely contain many potential vulnerabilities, either known or from uncertainties. This results in an initially high (relative to the project) probability of loss—P(L)—value. In some systems, this may be critical, and so S(L), the size of the loss, will be high. Thus, without any assessment, $RE_{security}$ initially will be high. After an assessment has been done, the likelihood of unidentified vulnerabilities will be reduced. If the assessment is done thoroughly and identified vulnerabilities are addressed, most vulnerabilities remaining are likely to be minor, and $RE_{security}$ will be low.

It is generally not feasible to be totally exhaustive when performing a system assessment. As a result, the ideal assessment risk reduction profile as illustrated in Figure 3 is where $RE_{security}$ decreases as rapidly as possible at the beginning. This profile is ideal because it provides the maximum risk reduction for any given amount security assessment effort. As stated previously, this profile is not a given for any strategy.

To give a concrete example of how a nonideal risk reduction profile may occur, consider the data in Figure 4 taken from a space systems ground-control project. The

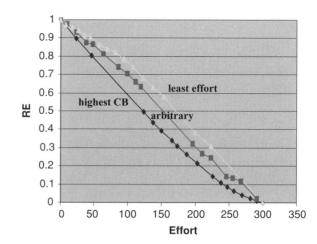

**Figure 4:** Examples of several $RE_{security}$ profiles.

**Table 2:** Examples of Security Attributes

| | |
|---|---|
| A1: Denial of Service | A8: File Deletions |
| A2: System Crash | A9: Access to Private Data |
| A3: Message Queue Overflow | A10: Hardware Failure |
| A4: System Fault | A11: Access to Code |
| A5: Misled Operator | A12: Resource Utilization |
| A6: Unauthorized Access | A13: Requirement Consistency and Completeness |
| A7: Unauthorized Administrator | A14: Understandability |

data are generated by assessing each relevant security attribute in Table 2 for S(L) in terms of the percentage of the project value lost that would result from the exploitation of a vulnerability in this attribute and for $\Delta$P(L) for the corresponding change in probability (as a percentage) of an exploitation occurring. These, in turn, are used to calculate the corresponding RE reductions if the attribute is assessed fully. The RE has been normalized to the fractional portion of the total known RE that can be reduced through assessment. The cost is effort in hours used to perform the assessment of the attribute, and CB is the cost-benefit ratio (the more specific form of RRL, as mentioned earlier). The attributes were assessed using an extensive security review checklist.

We see that some care must be taken in choosing the order (i.e., strategy) to perform the assessments so as to achieve the ideal risk-reduction profile indicated in Figure 3. Figure 4 compares three different ways to order the assessments. Each tick mark on the graph for each RE profile corresponds to the assessment of a particular attribute. Note that if the attributes are assessed in an arbitrary order, the curve will typically look like the approximately linear curve indicated in the middle of Figure 3, which clearly does not achieve the ideal. Another strategy is simply to do the least-effort assessments first. Doing so generally results in the even less desirable "supralinear" RE$_{security}$ reduction profile indicated in the topmost curve in Figure 4. Performing the assessments in the order of highest cost-benefit (CB) will achieve the desired RE$_{security}$ reduction profile. It can be shown that under fairly general circumstances, this will always be true.

Although we illustrated the strategic method using only risk assessment, analogous methods exist for risk control.

The important point here is that without a strategic approach, you are likely to end up with a less-than-ideal RE$_{security}$ reduction profile, as indicated in Figure 4. The consequences are real and significant because frequently all assessment tasks are not or cannot be performed. A less-than-ideal profile may occur when there are arbitrarily defined budgets, when people "feel" as if enough risk has been reduced, or more commonly when higher priority is given to tasks other than risk management. The result is a system with a high-degree of risk due to uncertainty with the usual consequences for "blind" risk taking (Basili & Boehm, 2001; Tran & Liu, 1997).

## PRACTICAL STRATEGIC RISK MODELS

In this section, we look at how strategtic methods can be applied in practice. We describe the use of strategic models to help make complex planning decisions, such as determining how much is enough risk assessment, and extend the strategic method to account for multiple techniques.

### Multitechnique Strategic Methods

To begin with, note that in our particular example the differences between risk reduction strategies do not appear very pronounced. One reason for this is purely an artifact of the normalization of the RE scale. If *absolute* RE is used (i.e., actual risk removed rather than relative risk reduction), the difference becomes more pronounced. There is a small concern that the absolute risk-reduction profile may not be consistent with the relative risk reduction profile. However, under general circumstances, an optimal relative risk reduction implies an optimal absolute risk-reduction profile.

In the example from Figure 4, the differences in RE and, to a lesser extent, in the effort expended between the attributes are relatively small when using a single assessment technique (in this example, vulnerability checklists). Using multiple assessment techniques can make a profound difference. Consider in our example if several different assessment techniques are employed.

A comparison of maximum cost-benefit versus arbitrary ordered assessment strategies using multiple assessment techniques is shown in Figure 5. The significant difference in strategies here is clear. The same amount of risk can be reduced for one third the effort.

AT1:   Analysis Using Formal Model
AT2:   API TEST
AT3:   Model Checking
AT4:   Code Review
AT5:   Lessons Learned
AT6:   Test Suites
AT7:   Vulnerability Checklist
AT8:   Static Analysis of Code
AT9:   Estimation
AT10: Interview Vendor
AT11: Investigation of Past Data
AT12: Test on Emulator
AT13: Benchmark Test
AT14: Attack Simulation

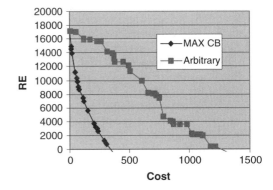

**Figure 5:** Absolute RE for Multiple Assessment Techniques on Example System.

This difference can be critical to a successful risk-management effort. The practical application of a strategic method assumes we are able to generate realistic strategic-risk models. From the previous discussion, it is clear that we want to apply the most appropriate risk management approach for each risk. Using multiple assessment techniques greatly increases the risk reduction cost-benefit yet has its complications. For example, in generating a multiattribute strategy, we must account for the possibility that, for some attributes, a particular assessment technique may not apply (e.g., API test for Misled Operator) or may not be cost-effective (e.g., Model Checking for Unauthorized Administrator).

We now present an algorithm that generates a practical, cost-effective strategic method (maximum risk reduction with respect to costs) with multiple assessment techniques for each attribute:

*Step 1: Identify the most significant system assessment attributes. Label them $1, \ldots, n$.

*Step 2: Identify the most significant assessment techniques (e.g., product testimonials, prototyping), applicable to the project, available resources (e.g., staff skills, tools). Label them $1, \ldots, m$.

*Step 3: Estimate the relative $S_i(L)$ quantities for attributes $i = 1, \ldots, n$ before any assessment.

*Step 4: Estimate the effort $C_{ij}$, size $S_{ij}(L)$, and change in risk exposures $\Delta RE_{ij}(L) = S_i(L) *P_i(L) - S_{ij}(L) *P_{ij}(L)$ resulting from assessing attribute i using technique j. Henceforth, we associate ij with the pair (attribute i, technique j).

*Step 5: Calculate the RRL matrix $RRL_{ij} = \Delta RE_{ij}(L) / C_{ij}$. Let $T(k) = (r_k, c_k)$ be the values for the corresponding attribute $r_k$, technique $c_k$ index of the $k^{th}$ largest element in the matrix. For each k, remove $RRL r_k c_k$ for $i = 1, \ldots, n$, then define $T(k + 1)$ until all n attributes are covered. Set $C_{T(k)}$ to be the corresponding $C_{ij}$ and $\Delta RE_{T(k)}$ to be the corresponding $\Delta RE_{ij}(L)$.

*Step 6: Graph the cumulative RE drop, $RE(n) = RE_{total} - \sum_{k=1}^{n} \Delta RE_{T(k)}$ versus cumulative effort $C(n) = \sum_{k=1}^{n} C_{T(k)}$.

This process produces an ideal $RE_{security}$ risk-reduction strategy, and it generalizes easily to risk control management activities. The strategy dictates that one perform T(k) for $k = 1,2,3,\ldots$ until the cost outweighs the benefit (i.e., $RRL_{T(k)} < 1$) unless other risk-reduction goals are desired (this is discussed further in the next section). The algorithm assumes that the entire effort allocated for each T(k) will be expended, and then the attribute will not be assessed further. As a result, there may be more optimal strategies that allow for partial effort using multiple techniques per attribute. Multiattribute optimization techniques, such as the use of simulated annealing, could potentially be applied to find these strategies, but are not discussed further here. Because the algorithm is somewhat involved, an example to illustrate it is presented in Tables 3a,b,c,d,e, resulting in the $RE_{security}$ reduction

misop : misled operator

syscr : system crash

sysft : system fault

unacc : unauthorized access

denos : denial of service

pdt = product testimonials

rvc = review checklist

ppy = product prototyping

**Table 3a:** Attribute Loss Size (Steps 1,2,3)

| misop | syscr | sysft | unacc | denos |
|-------|-------|-------|-------|-------|
| 50 | 40 | 40 | 70 | 50 |

**Table 3b:** (attribute i, technique j) Effort (Step 4)

| $C_{ij}$ | misop | syscr | sysft | unacc | denos |
|------|-------|-------|-------|-------|-------|
| pdt | 10 | 10 | 10 | 10 | 10 |
| rvc | 30 | 20 | 20 | 30 | 30 |
| ppy | 70 | 70 | 1 | 80 | 73 |

**Table 3c:** (attribute i, technique j) RE Reduction (Step 4)

| $\Delta P_{ij}(L)$ | misop | syscr | sysft | unacc | denos |
|------|-------|-------|-------|-------|-------|
| pdt | 40 | 10 | 60 | 11 | 20 |
| rvc | 70 | 30 | 55 | 30 | 30 |
| ppy | 90 | 90 | 0 | 90 | 90 |

**Table 3d:** (attribute i, technique j) Cost-Benefit (Step 5)

| $CB_{ij}$ | misop | syscr | sysft | unacc | denos |
|------|-------|-------|-------|-------|-------|
| pdt | 200 | 40 | 240 | 77 | 100 |
| rvc | 117 | 60 | 110 | 70 | 50 |
| ppy | 64 | 51 | 0 | 79 | 62 |

**Table 3e:** Highest Cost-Benefit Sorted (attribute i, technique j) (Step 5)

| T(n) | $CB_{ij}$ sorted | $\Sigma E_{T(k)}$ | $\Delta P_{T(k)}$ | $RE_{total} - \Sigma \Delta RE_{T(k)}$ |
|------|------|------|------|------|
| 1 | 240.00 | 10 | 240 | 896 |
| 2 | 200.00 | 20 | 40 | 656 |
| 3 | 116.67 | 50 | 70 | 616 |
| 4 | 110.00 | 70 | 55 | 546 |
| 5 | 100.00 | 80 | 20 | 491 |
| 6 | 78.75 | 160 | 90 | 471 |
| 7 | 77.00 | 170 | 11 | 381 |
| 8 | 70.00 | 200 | 30 | 370 |
| 9 | 64.29 | 270 | 90 | 340 |
| 10 | 61.64 | 343 | 90 | 250 |
| 11 | 60.00 | 363 | 30 | 160 |
| 12 | 51.43 | 433 | 90 | 130 |
| 13 | 50.00 | 463 | 30 | 40 |
| 14 | 40.00 | 473 | 10 | 10 |
| 15 | 0.00 | 474 | 0 | 0 |

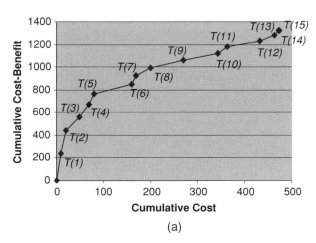

(a)

**Figure 6a:** Cost-Benefit T(k).

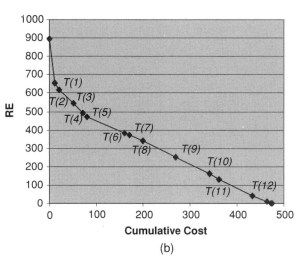

(b)

**Figure 6b**: $RE_{security}$ reduction T(k) (Step 6).

strategy displayed in Figures 6a,b. For simplicity of exposition in this example, we assume that the techniques only change the probability and not the size of the risks. That is, we consider CB and not RRL; however, the example easily generalizes. As such, we calculate $\Delta P_{ij}(L)$ and $CB_{ij}$ rather than $RRL_{ij}$.

Although it appears to be somewhat complex at first blush, the algorithm is actually fairly straightforward to implement and use. For example, the authors performed all analyses for this example and the example in Figure 5 completely within one spreadsheet.

## Strategic Decision-Making and Competing Risks

With a collection of strategic risk models, the strategic method can be used to provide meaningful answers to such questions as how much is enough risk assessment, mitigation, or control effort in which to invest. This question is critically important as in practice it is not feasible to implement exhaustive risk reduction because of constraints on resources (e.g., budget, personnel schedule, technology limitations). Even without such constraints, it is frequently impossible to reduce a risk to zero or even determine all possible risks for any given system. The best we can strive for is to reduce risk as much as possible within the given resources and uncertainties.

Recall from previous sections that ordering risk-reduction activities from highest to lowest RRL results in the "ideal" risk-reduction profile as indicated in Figure 3. It can be shown that, with respect to cost considerations, this is the optimal ordering for reducing risk when only a fraction of the risk-reduction activities will be performed. That is, if risk-reduction activity is stopped at any point, there is no other ordering that reduces more risk and leaves less total risk when the remaining activities are not done. In this model, if cost is the only consideration, then a natural answer to how much is enough is when the cost exceeds the risk-reduction benefit. Because the ordering of RRL is decreasing, there will be no activity beyond this point that would decrease the risk more than the cost for any of the previous activities.

The difficulty with using this stopping point is that it only accounts for cost with respect to the investment in risk-reduction activities. Furthermore, it assumes that cost and risk are equally exchangeable. In practice, this is not usually the case and, moreover, management activities always imply direct or collateral risks. For example, a system patch may do a marvelous job plugging a critical system vulnerability to a type of operating system virus, but if it takes too long to implement and disseminate the patch, the virus may propagate and cause unacceptable amounts of damage to the installed base. A more prudent action may be to quickly release a means of identifying and removing the particular virus threat at hand and perhaps delay the development of a patch. In this example, the risk-reduction activity of developing and disseminating a patch may indirectly increase the overall system risk despite the worthy, cost-effective investment in its development. The challenge here is of *competing risks*. That is, while one activity is reducing risk, there is another (event or activity) that is increasing risk. When the cumulative decreasing risk falls below the cumulative increasing risk, the overall system risk increases. When risk due to management activities is simply proportional (e.g., to effort, cost, schedule), it can be easily accounted for in $RE_{security}$ as an additional factor. This however, is generally not a realistic assumption to make with competing risks, as is elaborated next.

## Risk of Delay

Our example is only one indication of competing risks. There are a host of others. However, for this exposition, we refer to these considerations collectively as *risk due to delay* or $RE_{delay}$; these risks are of a fundamentally different nature than $RE_{security}$. We assume that a system starts out with no risk of delay and that any risk management effort expended contributes to the overall delay risk. Such risks can negatively affect or even paralyze a system to the point that it will fail to meet its intended operational goals. $RE_{delay}$ may result in losses due to nonuse of the system when required or expected, dissatisfied customers, or productivity losses when system capabilities are inaccessible or unreliable. $RE_{delay}$ will monotonically increase because it represents the cumulative RE due to delays.

To illustrate $RE_{delay}$, let us consider our operating system patch example again. We use this example only because the $RE_{delay}$ model is particularly straightforward; many other models are possible. For our example, because of the compounding of factors, it has been empirically suggested that once an operating system vulnerability is identified, the risk that it will be exploited increases supralinearly. Therefore, a reasonably good approximation to the $RE_{delay}$ risk profile can be generated through the identification of a few well-chosen data points. Here, we consider the following three critical points to be relevant:

**Point 1:** Vulnerability identified (or identifiable)—Once a system vulnerability has been identified, it is assumed that a malicious party may also have identified the vulnerability and will attempt to exploit it, thereby increasing overall security risk.

**Point 2:** Vulnerability exploited—when it is known (or very likely) that a system vulnerability has been exploited, losses are already being realized.

**Point 3:** Vulnerability exploits result in total loss.

Total loss occurs when the vulnerability has been exploited (e.g., massive dissemination of a highly destructive virus) to the point that the system no longer can, in confidence, operate to realize its intended value. When realized losses due to the exploits are unrecoverable (e.g., virus destroys or corrupts data or shuts out users, operating system must be reinstalled), then it is considered a "total loss."

The schedule for Points 1, 2, and 3 is necessarily sequential, and the time in terms of effort expended to arrive at these points is cumulative; hence, $RE_{delay}$ is successively nondecreasing at these points. Moreover, the change in $RE_{delay}$ between Points 1 and 2 can never be less than that between the starting point and Point 1; the same goes for Points 2 and 3. The critical points for our example project are shown in Table 4, and the resulting $RE_{delay}$ profile is illustrated in Figure 7.

As is evident in our example, creating appropriate risk models (e.g., $RE_{security}$, $RE_{delay}$) requires an organization to accumulate a fair amount of calibrated experience on the nature of the risks, their probabilities, and their magnitudes with respect to risk-management effort (e.g., cost, duration). In general, doing so can be challenging and costly. However, there are many practical approaches and software tools that address these topics specifically; see for example, Boehm (1991), Hall (1998), Tran and Liu (1997), and Ochs, Pfahl, Chrobok-Diening, and Nothelfer-Kolb (2001). We touch on some of these topics in the next section.

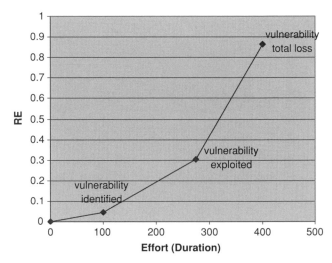

**Figure 7:**  Example $RE_{delay}$ Profile.

## Balancing Competing Risks for Strategic Planning

The general approach in answering a "how much is enough" question in the face of competing risks is to optimize $RE_{security}$ with respect to $RE_{delay}$. Depending on the models used, doing so balances the risk-reduction benefit of risk management and control activities with risk increases due to cost expenditures of dollars, effort, schedule, accessibility, and so forth.

Consider again our risk-assessment example. We have noted previously that it is important to have an efficient assessment strategy for reducing $RE_{security}$ and that such a strategy may be generated by assessing the attribute-technique pairs with the highest RRL first. We have indicated that assessment reduces $RE_{security}$ while simultaneously increasing $RE_{delay}$ due to the delay in removing system vulnerabilities. Too much assessment will put the system increasingly at risk as it exceeds the $RE_{delay}$ critical points. However, too little assessment will leave the system with too much risk due to uncertainty in the unassessed attributes. The ideal assessment strategy decreases $RE_{security}$, but does not expend so much effort that this reduction is dominated by $RE_{delay}$. This is a formal response to the question of how much is enough security assessment. Note that it derives directly from the general (often misunderstood) risk-management principle:

> If it's risky to not manage, DO manage (e.g., uncertain, high loss potential, unprecedented). If it's risky to manage, DO NOT manage (e.g., well established, well known, highly tested).

The goal is to apply this principle to balance $RE_{security}$ and $RE_{delay}$, thereby determining a strategic amount of assessment to perform before committing to a particular management or control strategy. Assuming we have generated a strategic $RE_{security}$ profile, the optimal assessment effort to expend will be that which minimizes the $RE_{security}$ + $RE_{delay}$. Doubtless, there are many dependencies among the risk factors, but recall that as mentioned earlier, the REs will be additive. As shown in Figure 8a, the decreasing

**Table 4**: Example $RE_{delay}$ Critical Points

| Point | S(L) | P(L) | RE | C |
|---|---|---|---|---|
| identified | 30 | 15 | 0.045 | 100 |
| exploited | 65 | 40 | 0.26 | 275 |
| total loss | 80 | 70 | 0.56 | 400 |

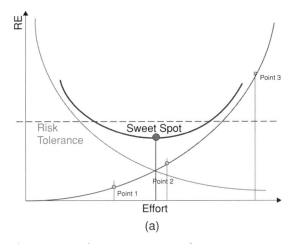

(a)

**Figure 8a:** Balancing $RE_{security}$ and $RE_{delay}$.

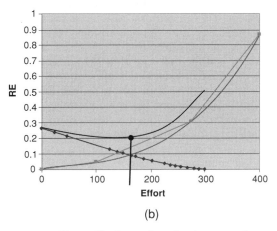

(b)

**Figure 8b:** Sweet Spot for the example.

$RE_{security}$ and increasing $RE_{delay}$ will have a minimum—the "sweet spot"—at some intermediate effort point. Assuming the ideal $RE_{security}$ reduction strategy discussed earlier, a strategic stopping point for assessment is when this intermediate effort point has been reached.

Note that the location of the sweet spot varies by type of organization. For example, in a dot.com company where $RE_{delay}$ increases rapidly because of market pressures, the resulting sweet spot is pushed to the left, indicating that less assessment should be done. By contrast, a safety-critical product such as for a nuclear power plant will have greater $RE_{security}$ because of larger potential losses. The sweet spot is pushed to the right, indicating that more assessment should be done. The sweet spot determination for the examples previously discussed is shown in Figure 8b. A third-order polynomial (shown in the figure) was used to interpolate between the critical points so that the $RE_{security} + RE_{delay}$ could be estimated numerically.

## Unsuitable Sweet Spots

There are situations where the sweet spot is not an acceptable determination of how much assessment to perform. Acceptability is achieved only when (as indicated in Figure 8a) the RE at the sweet spot is below a given risk tolerance and the effort at the sweet spot is less than the effort at critical Point 2. Although ideally the assessment effort should be less than the effort at Point 1, for most projects the additional risk incurred by passing this point is tolerable (Basili & Boehm, 2001). This risk is softened by the fact that the effort at the sweet spot cannot be far from the effort at Point 1. The effort beyond Point 1 to complete the assessment is small enough that the exploitability of the vulnerability will mostly be settled before passing Point 1. The exception occurs if $RE_{delay}$ increases very gradually, but then in turn the increase in risk would be much less pronounced.

What can be done in the event that the sweet spot is above an acceptable risk tolerance? There are two solutions: find another assessment approach that can lower $RE_{security}$, or mitigate potential losses (e.g., insurance policy) due to project delay to lower $RE_{delay}$. It is best if both solutions are applied. If the sweet spot effort exceeds

the effort for Point 2, the only reasonable approach is to find another assessment approach that can lower $RE_{security}$ faster. Paradoxically, if $RE_{delay}$ were increased, say by imposing greater cost, schedule, or effort constraints, this too could potentially move the sweet spot effort in front of Point 2. However, the price to pay for this is a large increase in the overall project risk, which likely will exceed a tolerable level. As with previous examples, there are analogous methods for other types of security risk assessments, mitigation, and control activities.

## PRACTICAL RISK EXPOSURE ESTIMATION

A risk management program relies critically on the ability to estimate representative risk exposures. It is tempting to expend a large amount of effort to obtain precise results; however, doing so may prove untenable or impractical. Fortunately for strategic method applications, estimates do not have to be precise. In this section, we describe one practical approach to estimating risk exposures.

## Qualitative Methods

Recall that calculating RE for a given risk involves estimating the probability of a potential loss P(L) and the size of that possible loss S(L). The challenge of estimating S(L) lies in quantifying intangibles, such as loss of reputation. There are numerous techniques that claim the ability to address this challenge, but in our experience we have found that estimating highly subjective loss potentials is best accomplished by choosing a tangible "standard" within the particular context at hand and then establishing the remaining values relative to this standard. For example, an organization determined that it lost $1,000 due to lost sales for every minute its central sales system was down. If the sales system was down for more than 4 hours, their reputation as an "easy to buy from" company would be degraded and fewer customers would return. The minimum loss of 4*60*$1,000 = $240,000 was considered a "3" on a scale from 0 to 10 in terms of loss magnitude, and the loss of return customers was considered a 5 relative to this monetary loss. These size estimates can be used for RE calculations so long as all loss potentials are translated into loss magnitudes from 0 to 10 relative to the system downtime.

In general, it is difficult to calculate P(L) directly. This is primarily because of a lack of representative models that are able to generate an appropriate probability distribution. Even though there are many wonderful candidate parametric-based models, frequently there are not enough available data to calibrate and validate them. One alternative to parametric models is to make use of a qualitative-based "betting analogy," as described in the following steps:

*Step 1:* For the risk under consideration, define a "satisfactory" level.

*Step 2:* Establish a personally meaningful amount of money, say, $100.

*Step 3:* Determine how much money you would be willing to risk in betting on a satisfactory level.

*Step 4:* Establish proposition (e.g., using virus checker will avoid infection and loss of data).

*Step 5:* Establish betting odds (e.g., no loss of data: you win $100; infection and loss of data: you lose $500).

*Step 6:* Determine willingness to bet:

Willing: low probability

Unwilling: high probability

Not sure: there is risk due to uncertainty, so need to buy information

*Step 7:* Express your willingness to bet with respect to the risk under consideration (e.g., we are likely to take this bet).

For whatever qualifies your willingness to bet statement (in our example, the qualification is "likely"), use an adjective calibration chart such as the one in Table 5 to obtain an estimate of the risk probability.

## Empirical Approaches

Empirical methods rely on generating RE estimates based on observations, historical data, or experiments. One of the attractive properties of RE is that it represents the expectation (or mean value) of the potential losses associated with a risk event. Under quite general conditions, this value can be approximated with the *sample mean*. Say

you have losses $L_1, L_2, \ldots, L_n$ associated with a particular risk area, then:

$$RE \approx \frac{1}{n} \sum_{i=1}^{n} L_i$$

Consult any college-level statistics book for further details on this concept. We can make use of this result in several ways depending on whether or not *historical risk loss data* and *risk event models* are available. Historical risk loss data are the recorded losses realized from actual projects that were exposed to the risk (i.e., the risk actually occurred) under consideration. A risk-event model is a dynamic representation of all the possible losses and conditions under which those losses would occur.

### Delphi Studies: no historical data, no risk event model

You may have noticed that the betting analogy relies on having a credible adjective calibration table. These tables might have been based on information obtained from surveying local experts. This technique can be used directly to estimate risk exposures. If a representative group of experts are available, a *Delphi study* (Helmer, 1966) often provides workable risk exposure estimates. Such a study would survey experts to estimate risk exposure values and then calculate the sample mean as an estimate for the actual risk exposure. To avoid obtaining erroneous results, Delphi studies should not be undertaken haphazardly. There are a variety of well-documented methodologies for conducting Delphi studies that should be followed to ensure valid results.

### Risk Sampling: historical data available, no risk event model

If there is a reasonable amount of historical loss data available that is representative (unbiased), then *risk sampling* may be an effective means of estimating REs. Calculate the estimated RE by taking the sample mean of the historical data. However, it is likely that the data set will be small, and the estimate may be poor. Under these conditions, bootstrapping and jack-knifing methods (Effron & Gong, 1983) may be used to improve estimates.

### Risk Event Simulation: no historical data available, risk event model available

When historical data are lacking or nonexistent and you are able to model the particular risk events under consideration, then *risk event simulation* may provide a means of estimating risk exposures. Usually, this method amounts to creating a series of random events to run through the risk model and then calculating the sample mean to estimate the RE. The idea here is to create a dynamic simulation of the risk events and run a series of experiments to get a representative collection of loss values. There is a host of powerful tools that can be of great use in creating and running these simulations. Two examples are the Simulink package for Matlab (http://www.mathworks.com) and Modelica for Dymola (http://www.dynasim.com).

**Table 5** Probability Adjective Calibration Table

| Statement | Assigned Probability Range |
| --- | --- |
| Almost Certainly | 85–100% |
| Highly Likely | 85–100% |
| Very Good Chance | 55–85% |
| Likely/Probably | 55–85% |
| Better Than Even | 50–55% |
| Unlikely | 15–45% |
| Probably Not | 15–45% |
| Little Chance | 0–15% |
| Highly Unlikely | 0–15% |

## Pitfalls to Avoid

As indicated in the previous discussions, there are many possible complications in estimating REs, such as using insufficient or biased data. Of all the potential complications, perhaps the most common and troublesome one is the problem of *compound risks*. A compound risk is one that is a dependent combination of risks. Some examples are the following:

- addressing more than one threat
- managing threats with key staff shortages
- vague vulnerability descriptions with ambitious security plans
- untried operating system patches with an ambitious release schedule

You must watch out for compound risks. The problem is that the dependencies complicate the probabilities in difficult-to-determine ways. When you identify a compound risk, it is best to reduce it to a noncompound risk if possible. If the dependencies are too strong or complex, then this may not be possible. In this case, you should plan to devote extra attention to containing such risks.

## SUMMARY

In this chapter, we have described a number of IT security risk-assessment and management techniques and standards. This is a rich and growing field of inquiry, and it reaches deep into technical as well as organizational and managerial practices. The key insights that the reader should take away from this chapter are that (1) security risk management is only effective to the degree that risk assessment is effective, and (2) it is not obvious how to go about applying individual security techniques (of which there are many) to ensure an optimal result at the level of the organization.

To address these issues, we described and demonstrated a strategic method for quantitatively assessing IT security risk that is provably optimal with respect to cost-benefit. It gives a manager a powerful tool for managing IT security risk.

## GLOSSARY

**BS 7799** British Standard 7799; consists of BS 7799 Parts 1 and 2.
**BS 7799 Part 1** Information Technology—Code of Practice for Information Security Management.
**BS 7799 Part 2** Information Security Management Systems—Specification with Guidance for Use.
**Common Criteria** Short for Common Criteria for Information Technology Security Evaluation, a standard for dealing with security-related COTS products and a descendant of ITSEC, CTCPEC, and TCSEC.
**CTCPEC** Canadian Trusted Computer Product Evaluation Criteria, a standard for dealing with security-related COTS products and an ancestor of Common Criteria and ISO 15408.
**FRAP** The Facilitated Risk Assessment Program, a qualitative process developed by Thomas Peltier.

**HIPAA** (U.S.) Health Insurance Portability and Accountability Act of 1996, a statute with which relevant organizations are required to comply and which dictates government audit, with possible severe consequences, in case of complaints of violations.
**ISO/IEC 21827** International Organization for Standardization/International Electrotechnical Commission 21827, the ISO/IEC version of SSE-CMM.
**ISO 15408** The ISO version of Common Criteria.
**ISO 17799** International Organization for Standardization 17799 Code of Practice for Information Security Management.
**ISO TR 13335 (GMITS, for short)** International Organization for Standardization Technical Report 13335 Guidelines for the Management for IT Security.
**ITSEC** IT Security Evaluation and Certification Scheme, a standard for dealing with security-related COTS products and an ancestor of Common Criteria and ISO 15408.
**NIST** (U.S.) National Institute of Standards and Technology. Founded in 1901, NIST is a nonregulatory federal agency within the U.S. Commerce Department's Technology Administration. NIST's mission is to develop and promote measurement, standards, and technology to enhance productivity, facilitate trade, and improve the quality of life.
**OCTAVE** Operationally Critical Threat, Asset, and Vulnerability Evaluation, a method developed by the Software Engineering Institute (SEI) and the CERT (Computer Emergency Response Team) at Carnegie Mellon University.
**Orange Book** See TCSEC.
**SRMD** Microsoft's Security Risk Management Discipline.
**SSE-CMM** System Security Capability Maturity Model.
**TCSEC** Trusted Computer System Evaluation Criteria. Often referred to as the "orange book," it was published in 1985 by the National Computer Security Council (NCSC), a branch of the National Security Agency (NSA). TCSEC is a standard for dealing with security-related COTS products and an ancestor of Common Criteria and ISO 15408.

## CROSS REFERENCES

See *Risk Management for IT Security: Managing a Network Environment; Security Insurance and Best Practices; The Asset–Security Goals Continuum: A Process for Security.*

## REFERENCES

Alberts, C., & Dorofee, A. (2002). *Managing information security risks: The OCTAVE approach.* Boston: Addison-Wesley.

Basili, V., & Boehm, B. (2001, May). COTS-based systems Top 10 list. *IEEE Computer, 34*(5).

Bate, R., et. al. (1995, November). *Systems engineering capability maturity model* (version 1.1). Pittsburgh: Software Engineering Institute, Carnegie Mellon University.

Boehdm, B. (1991, January). Software risk management: Principles and practices. *IEEE Software, 1*(8), 32–41.

Carr, M. J., Konda, S. L., Monarch, I., Ulrich, F. C., & Walker, C. F. (1993, June). *Taxonomy-based risk identification* (Tech. Rep. CMU/SEI-93-TR-6). Pittsburgh: Software Engineering Institute, Carnegie Mellon University.

Cohen, F. (2004). *Fred Cohen and Associates—Security database*. Retrieved from http://www.all.net, October 1, 2004.

Common Criteria for Information Technology Security Evaluation. (1999, August). *Part 1: Introduction and general model, Version 2.1* (CCIMB-99-031). Retrieved from http://www.commoncriteriaportal.org/public/files/ccpart1v21.pdf, October 1, 2004.

Common Criteria for Information Technology Security Evaluation. (2004, January). *Part 1: Introduction and general model, Version 2.2*. Retrieved from http://www.commoncriteriaportal.org/public/files/ccpart1v2.2.pdf, October 1, 2004.

Communication Security Establishment. (n.d.). *Common Criteria: An introduction*. Retrieved from http://www.cse-cst.gc.ca/en/documents/services/ccs/brochure.pdf, October 1, 2004.

Efron, B., & Gong, G. (1983). A leisurely look at the bootstrap, the jackknife, and cross-validation. *The American Statistician, 37*, 36–48.

European Co-operation for Accreditation (EA). (2000, February). *Guidelines for the accreditation of bodies operating certification/registration of information security management systems (EA-73)*. Retrieved from http://www.european-accreditation.org, October 1, 2004

Hall, E. M. (1998). *Managing risk*. Boston: Addison Wesley Longman.

Helmer, O. (1966). *Social technology*. New York: Basic Books.

ISO15408. (1999). *ISO/IEC Information technology—Security techniques—Evaluation criteria for IT security* (ISO/IEC 15408). Retrieved from http://www.iso.org/iso/en/CatalogueDetailPage.CatalogueDetail?CSNUMBER=27632&ICS1=35&ICS2=40&ICS3=, October 1, 2004.

ISO17799. (2000). *Information technology—Code of practice for information security management* (ISO/IEC 17799:2000). Retrieved from http://www.iso.org/iso/en/CatalogueDetailPage.CatalogueDetail? CSNUMBER=33441&ICS1=35&ICS2=40&ICS3=, October 1, 2004.

ISO21827. (2002). *ISO/IEC Information technology—Systems security engineering—Capability maturity model (SSE-CMM)* (ISO/IEC 21287). Retrieved from http://www.iso.org/iso/en/CatalogueDetailPage.atalogueDetail?CSNUMBER=34731&ICS1=35&ICS2=40& ICS3=, October 1, 2004.

NIST. (2004, May). *An introductory resource guide for implementing the Health Insurance Portability and Accountability Act (HIPAA) Security Rule* (Special Publication SP 800-66). Retrieved from http://csrc.nist.gov/publications/nistpubs/800-66/SP800-66.pdf )

Ochs, M., Pfahl, D., Chrobok-Diening, G., & Nothelfer-Kolb, B. (2001, April). A method for efficient measurement-based COTS assessment and selection: Method description and evaluation results. *Proceedings of the Seventh International Software Metrics Symposium METRICS 2001*, pp. 285–297.

Operationally Critical Threat, Asset, and Vulnerability Evaluation (OCTAVE). (2004). *OCTAVE CERT Coordination Center, Software Engineering Institute at Carnegie Mellon University*. Retrieved from http://www.cert.org/octave/, October 1, 2004.

Paulk, M. C., Weber, C. V., Curtis, B., & Chrissis, M. B. (1995). *The capability maturity model: guidelines for improving the software process*. Boston: Addison-Wesley.

Peltier, T., Peltier, J., &. Blackley, J.A. (2003). *Managing a network vulnerability assessment*. Philadelphia, PA: Auerbach Publications.

Privacy Data Protection Project. (n.d.). *HIPAA*. Retrieved from http://privacy.med.miami.edu/glossary/xd_hipaa.htm, October 1, 2004.

SEE-CMM. (1999, April). *Appraisal method, Version 2.0*. Retrieved from http://www.sse-cmm.org/docs/SSAM.pdf, October 1, 2004.

SEE-CMM. (n.d.). *Model description document, Version 3.0*. Retrieved from http://www.sse-cmm.org/docs/ssecmmv3final.pdf, October 1, 2004.

Shewhart, W. A. (1986). *Statistical method from the viewpoint of quality control*. Mineola, NY: Dover Publications.

SRDM. (2004). Understanding the security risk management discipline. In *Microsoft solution for Securing Windows 2000 Server*. Retrieved from http://www.microsoft.com/technet/Security/prodtech/win2000/secwin2k/default.mspx, October 1, 2004.

Tran, V., & Liu, D-B. (1997, January). A risk-mitigating model for the development of reliable and maintainable large-scale commercial-off-the-shelf integrated software systems. *Proceedings of the 1997 Annual Reliability and Maintainability Symposium*, pp. 361–367.

## FURTHER READING

Abts, C., Boehm, B., & Clark, E. B. (2001, April). COCOTS: A software COTS-based system (CBS) cost model. *Proceedings, ESCOM 2001*, pp. 1–8.

Alves, C., & Finkelstein, A. (2002, July). Challenges in COTS-decision making: A goal-driven requirements engineering perspective. *Workshop on Software Engineering Decision Support, in conjunction with SEKE'02*. Symposium conducted in Ischia, Italy.

# Security Insurance and Best Practices

Selahattin Kuru, Onur Ihsan Arsun, and Mustafa Yildiz, *Isik University, Turkey*

## INTRODUCTION

Insurance is a common tool for risk transfer. Individuals and organizations use this tool to transfer the risk of potential losses to another party, namely an insurance company. However, individuals and organizations have different motivations for purchasing insurance. In one classic example, a ship owner insures a ship and receives payment if the ship is damaged or destroyed. This example is one of the earliest uses of insurance. Interestingly, ships are now insured more often through risk pooling and spreading organizations, such as Lloyd's of London, because the loss of a large ship is too great for one insurer to accept. In contrast, individuals purchase health insurance toward which they pay a monthly or a yearly premium to an insurance company. If the insured gets ill, the insurance company provides the money required for the treatment under the conditions of the agreed policy. As a tool for risk transfer, insurance holds an important place in risk management and should be considered one of its main components.

Cyberinsurance, which is insurance related to Internet and other information technologies areas, is discussed in this chapter. Some of the components of traditional insurance coverage apply to cyberinsurance, but it has its unique properties as well. As a new and rapidly changing area, both insurers and the insured should give extra attention to cyberinsurance policies.

## INSURANCE AND RISK TRANSFER BASICS

The concept of risk transfer first appeared around 3000 B.C. Chinese merchants upon undertaking a dangerous voyage would disperse their cargo equally among several ships so as to minimize the potential overall risk of loss. The concept was further refined by the Babylonians. The Code of Hammurabi legalized a lending practice know as bottomry, whereby merchants/traders obtained loans from a group of investors. If a ship foundered or a caravan fell victim to thieves, the loans would be cancelled. The practice proved profitable through the combination of a high percentage of safe voyages and the interest paid on the loans.

The merchants of Rhodes also contributed to the development of risk transfer when they codified the concept of the general average. Ever the superstitious lot, sailors would often assign the blame for bad luck experienced during a voyage to a particular piece of cargo, not being satisfied until the "unlucky" goods were heaved overboard. To avoid the total loss to that merchant whose cargo had just been sacrificed for the greater good, Rhodian law required that those who benefited from the sacrifice contribute *pro rata* to compensate the owner for his "cursed" goods. The concept was further refined by Justinian, who expounded on salvage rights.

The next major developments in transferring risk do not appear until the 11th and 12th centuries when the navigators of Denmark began establishing guilds, one purpose of which was to indemnify its members against losses at sea. Not long thereafter in 1255, the merchants of Venice began pooling premiums to pay for loss due to piracy, spoilage, or pillage—essentially inventing the concept of mutual insurance. These basic concepts came to northern Europe and England with the Lombards in the 13th century, where they continued to evolve.

The modern insurance industry as we know it today traces its roots in large part to the rise of London as a center of trade in the 17th century. With an increase in trade came a commensurate need for a way to transfer the risk of those ventures. Although not the only venue for such activity, the coffee house opened by Edward Lloyd in 1688 was more successful at it than most, and Mr. Lloyd took pains to encourage a clientele of ships' captains, merchants, and owners. Not surprisingly, this earned Lloyd's coffee house the reputation of being the place to obtain trustworthy shipping news, which in turn ensured that it became recognized as the place for obtaining marine insurance. Much as they do today, a merchant seeking insurance would request that a broker approach wealthy merchants—substitute financially sound companies today—until the risk was fully placed or insured.

Insurance is defined by the Insurance Institute of America in three different ways. First, insurance is a transfer technique whereby the insured transfers the risk of financial loss to another party, the insurance company or insurer. Second, it is a contract between the policyholder and the insurer that states what financial consequences of loss are transferred and expresses the insurer's promise to pay for those consequences. Third, insurance is a business and, as such, needs to be conducted in a way that earns profit for its owners.

Insurance enables those who suffer a loss or accident to be compensated for the effects of their misfortune. The payments come from a fund of money contributed by all the holders of individual insurance policies. In other words, individual risks are pooled and shared, with each policyholder making a contribution to the common fund.

The money a policyholder pays an insurer is small compared to the potential for loss. If a family's house were to burn down, it probably could not afford to replace it without insurance. The insurance system enables someone to transfer the financial consequences of this loss to an insurance company.

The insurance company, in turn, pays for covered losses and distributes the costs among all of its policyholders. In that way, your fellow policyholders share the cost of your loss, as you share in theirs.

One other important term is *reinsurance*. Reinsurance can be defined as the transfer of some or all of an insurance risk to another insurer. Insurance companies have a limited amount of capital, and to protect it, they often limit the losses they may incur by purchasing reinsurance. The company transferring the risk is called the *ceding company*; the company receiving the risk is called the *assuming company* or reinsurer. Many reinsurance actions are not placed with a single reinsurer, but are shared among a number of reinsurers. The reinsurer who sets the terms for the reinsurance program is called the *lead reinsurer*; the other companies subscribing to the program are called *follow reinsurers*.

The most important key word in the insurance domain is *risk*. Because insurance is a means of transferring risk, the insurance process involves assessing, evaluating, and managing risk.

## Risk Management

Risk has many definitions; one of the most common is in the Australian/New Zealand Standard 4360:1999. It defines risk as "the chance of something happening that will have an impact upon objectives." It is measured in terms of consequences and likelihood. Risk management is defined as "the culture, processes and structures that are directed towards the effective management of potential opportunities and adverse effects."

*Risk management* is the term applied to a logical and systematic method of establishing a context and identifying, analyzing, evaluating, treating, monitoring, and communicating risks associated with any activity, function, or process in a way that will enable organizations to minimize losses and maximize opportunities. Risk management is as much about identifying opportunities as avoiding or mitigating losses (Hammesfahr, 2002).

In the information technology (IT) domain, there is an ongoing transition from trust management to risk management (Geer, 1998). Traditionally, IT security staff placed emphasis on building trusted systems for users through such measures as using encryption firewalls and the like (Whitman & Mattord, 2003). In contrast, risk management focuses on identifying and quantifying potential losses and the uncertainties surrounding them (Baer, 2003). Using a quantitative estimation of IT security risks, enterprise managers can decide how much to invest in security measures to mitigate them and/or whether to package them in forms that others will assume. The latter option depends on the availability of well-functioning markets for insurance that cover the risks that the enterprise wants to dismiss. Applying risk management principles to IT can bring IT security within the more familiar and workable paradigms of insurance, risk sharing, and risk securitization

## Risk Assessment

Managers have to consider a range of possible events that could take place in the life of the enterprise. Each of these events could have a material effect on the goals of the enterprise. The negative effects of risk are called threats, and the positive effects are called opportunities. McNamee classifies assets under risk into the following four groups:

1. financial assets, such as cash and investments
2. physical assets, such as land, buildings, and equipment
3. human assets, including knowledge and skills
4. intangible assets, such as reputation and information

One famous method for risk assessment is the Committee of Sponsoring Organization's (COSO) model, which has done a great deal to advance a simple set of clear guidelines on how to think about risk in the organization and risk in planning the audit. The COSO model is widely recognized as the definitive standard against which organizations measure the effectiveness of their internal control systems. It has three steps:

1. Establish the organization's objectives.
2. Assess risk.
   - Identify risks.
   - Measure risks.
   - Prioritize risks.
3. Determine the controls required.

One measure to prevent loss is to transfer the risk to another body or share it with other bodies. Insurance is a way to transfer potential losses that may be caused by risk to another party—an insurance company—to take advantage of economies of scale.

## Moral Hazards

The moral hazards problem deals with the lack of motivation by the insured to take actions to reduce the probability of a loss subsequent to purchasing insurance. The most common example comes from fire insurance. A company who owns fire insurance may be less willing to take necessary actions to prevent a fire and might even have an incentive to commit arson in times of cash shortage. In the IT domain, the moral hazards problem is much larger.

One way to address the moral hazards problem is through the use of deductibles. By using deductibles, the insured will suffer some amount of loss if the risk is realized. A more applicable way of protecting the cyberpolicy insurer is offering the insured reductions in the overall insurance price for taking protective actions to reduce the probability of a loss. Insurers have dealt with the moral hazards problem successfully by mandating protective measures and procedures designed to reduce losses.

As an example, an insured might claim large damages from database corruption resulting from an unknown hacker's breach of IT security. The insurer might then respond that the covered loss is actually much lower because the insured should have had backup records that the hacker could not reach. The insurer's argument would be that the hacking event was fortuitous, but that the resulting data corruption was not fortuitous, requiring the insured to take active protective measures. Unfortunately this is a case open for discussion and may lead to legal action. If the insured and the insurer had previously agreed to reduce the insurance price if protective actions were taken by the insured, both parties would benefit from the result.

# CYBERSECURITY AND CYBERINSURANCE
## Cybersecurity Threats

Today corporations use the Internet in many different forms, such as publishing Web sites, using electronic data exchange tools, transmitting e-mail, and selling goods on the Internet. The use of the Internet requires a server, which may store critical data of the corporation and is connected to a network to which many unknown parties are also connected (Tulloch, 2003). In addition to Internet-related functions, many processes are carried on throughout the corporation with the full or partial aid of computer software and hardware.

The benefits of using electronic systems and networks are obvious and include broadening the company's reach to larger areas and enabling business to be conducted more quickly and effectively. Much of the potential risks of the intensive use of the Internet and IT are not unique to cyberspace. For example, copyright infringements also occur in more traditional media, such as televisions or newspapers. However, unique perils, some of which are greater than many people might realize, come along with those benefits. Every year the Computer Security Institute/ Federal Bureau of Investigation (CSI/FBI) releases a Computer Crime and Security Survey on cyberthreats, cybercrime incidents, and their financial effects on the corporation. In 2004, 491 corporations responded to the survey (Power, 2004); its major findings are presented below:

- Hacking and computer viruses caused $1.6 trillion loss for the last 12 months.
- 64% of the respondents spent 1% to 5% of their total IT budget for security.
- Firms with annual sales under $10 million spent an average of approximately $500 per employee ($334 in operating expense and $163 in capital expenditures) on computer security, whereas the largest firms (those with annual sale over $1 billion) spent an average of about $110 per employee ($82 in operating expense and $30 in capital expenditures).
- 63% of the respondents did not outsource any of their IT security functions, whereas 25% outsourced up to 20% of those functions.
- Only 28% of the respondents had some kind of external insurance policies to help manage cybersecurity risks.
- More than 50% of the respondents confirmed that unauthorized use of computer systems had occurred in the last 12 months; this compares to about 70% in the year 2000.
- The types of attacks or misuse detected in the last 12 months in descending order were viruses (78%), insider abuse of net access (59%), laptop/mobile theft (49%), system penetration (39%), unauthorized access to information (37%), denial of service (17%), theft of proprietary information (10%), financial fraud (10%), and telecommunications fraud (5%).

As discussed above, although cyberrisk shares many common characteristics with traditional business risks, some cyberrisks are unique in terms of location, degree, and visibility. We can categorize cyberthreats into six distinct peril types (Clark, 2002):

1. **Content Risk:** A company is liable for any information that appears on its Web site. Web content can be found to violate copyrights or trademarks. It can

be considered libelous. If customers' personal information is seen by others, a company may be liable for violating privacy. Furthermore, Web content appears worldwide and may be subject to different laws in different jurisdictions. For example, competitive advertising is against the law in Germany, and Muslim countries prohibit the publication of interest rates in advertising.

2. **Viruses/malicious code/Trojan horses:** Any company that is connected to the Internet is susceptible to viruses that can cripple its systems. Viruses can result in legal liabilities, as well as cause damage to or destruction of a company's information assets. The notoriously infamous Melissa virus in 1999 caused an estimated $80 million worth of damage. The next year, the Love Bug virus resulted in an estimated $10 billion in damage. It infected 45 million e-mail users on its first day. The Love Bug originated in the Philippines, where there is no law against spreading viruses. Trojan horses are another risk. Computer users run software that appears to be harmless, but is actually doing something malicious to the system.

3. **Theft of proprietary information or customer data:** Generally, you do not know your information is stolen until it appears somewhere else. In March 2001, FBI reports show that one million credit card numbers have been stolen from 40 e-banking and e-commerce web sites in 20 states in the United States. Almost all of the sites had firewalls and similar technology to protect the systems from intruders. Loss of customer information can subject a company to lawsuits from customers, shareholders, and others, as well as to potential regulatory investigations. Companies have lost their competitive advantage when trade secrets or proprietary information was stolen by a competitor. In addition, a company's intellectual property, such as trademarks and copyrights, is more vulnerable when it is open to the Internet.

4. **Cyberextortion:** Cyberextortion occurs when hackers steal or threaten to steal your information for the purpose of selling it back to you. CD Universe, a music e-retailer, was approached by a hacker who had stolen the credit card numbers of 300,000 of their customers. For a "consulting fee" of $100,000, the hacker offered to tell the company how he broke in and to destroy the credit card numbers. The company refused to pay, and the extortionist posted 25,000 of the credit card numbers on the Internet.

5. **Distributed Denial of Service (DDoS) Attacks:** In a DDoS attack, a hacker uses several computers that are connected to the Internet to send streams of data to a company's server or Web site in quantities hundreds or thousands of times greater than the site was designed to handle. The Web site is unable to keep up with the flood of data and becomes unavailable. DDoS attacks can cause hours or days of lost revenue from business interruption. An e-retailer Web site that is out of service would not be able to handle buying customers. Sites can also make money through ads posted on their Web pages. When these sites are disrupted, every minute costs advertising revenues. As more people remain connected to the Internet 24 hours a day through cable modems or DSL lines, DDoS attacks are becoming more prevalent. In February 2000, *The New York Times* reported that DDoS attacks crippled some of the country's most well-known sites, including Amazon.com, eBay.com, and CNN.com, among others (http://query.nytimes.com/gst/abstract.html?res=F4071FF73E5A0C7A8CDDAB0894D8404482&incamp=archive:search).

6. **Internal risks:** Companies face more than the risk of an external computer attack. A company's employees can use technology to destroy company information or steal it to sell for a profit. Employees with access to e-mail can harm a company by sending messages with illicit content, for which the company may be liable. Internal risks have the highest probability of going undetected. For example, an employee may use company resources to run a side business and still go unnoticed.

## E-risk Management

Risk management is a process that enables enterprise managers to balance operational and economic costs of protective systems with the desired gain in mission effectiveness. For IT security, risk management is the process of assessing risk, taking steps to reduce risk to an acceptable level, and maintaining that level of risk (Gordon, Loeb, & Sohail, 2003). IT systems store, process, and transmit mission-critical information. The risk management process must take this into account and seek a workable balance between the costs of countermeasures and the threats to the information system. No risk management function can eliminate every risk to the information system, but with the appropriate application of risk management practices during the IT system's life cycle, risks with a high likelihood of occurring can be prioritized and addressed properly such that the residual risk is acceptable to the overall mission.

The first key principle of security is that no network is completely secure—information security is really about risk management. In the most basic of terms, the more important the asset is and the more it is exposed to security threats, the more resources you should put into securing it. Thus, it is imperative that the company understands how to evaluate an asset's value, the threats to it, and the appropriate security measures.

The e-risk management strategy should follow the definition given above. First, assess the risk, then reduce the risk to an acceptable level by technical and financial (insurance) means, and last maintain the risk at an acceptable level by investing in contingency plans or intrusion detection systems.

Organizations should begin the risk management process by assessing the threats to and vulnerabilities associated with their information systems. Managing security risks can be an incredibly daunting task, especially if you fail to do so in a well-organized and well-planned manner. Risk management often requires experience with financial accounting and budgeting, as well as the input of business analysts. Conducting a risk assessment of an organization's security can take months and generally involves many people from many parts of the company. Here is

| Value | Vulnerability | | |
|---|---|---|---|
| | High | Medium | Low |
| High | 9 | 6 | 3 |
| Medium | 6 | 4 | 2 |
| Low | 3 | 2 | 1 |

**Figure 1:** Value-vulnerability matrix

a simple seven-step process to follow for assessing and managing risk (Tulloch, 2003):

1. **Set the scope:** Trying to assess and manage all security risks in the organization is a huge and critical task. So before starting the risk assessment, setting its scope helps one estimate the time and costs involved more accurately and document and follow the results more easily.

2. **Identify assets and determine their value:** The second step in assessing risk is identifying assets and determining their value. When determining an asset's value, there are three important factors to take into account: (1) the financial impact of the asset's compromise or loss, (2) the nonfinancial impact of the asset's compromise or loss, and (3) the value of the asset to competitors

   In this step it is most helpful to produce a value-vulnerability matrix (Gordon et al., 2003). This grid shown in Figure 1 categorizes information from high to low for both value and vulnerability. The assets with values equal to or higher than 4 require the greatest attention.

   The financial impact of an asset's compromise or loss includes revenue and productivity lost because of downtime, costs associated with recovering services, and direct equipment losses. The nonfinancial impact of an asset's compromise or loss includes resources used in managing the public perception of a security incident. The value of the asset to the organization should be the main issue in determining how you secure the resource.

3. **Predict threats and vulnerabilities to assets:** The process of predicting threats and vulnerabilities to assets is known as *threat modeling*. Threat modeling uses a structured approach to address the severest threats that will cause the biggest losses to a company. It allows you to mitigate risk proactively, rather than having to react to it after a security incident.

4. **Document the security risks:** After completing the threat model, it is essential to document the security risks using a common template so that they can be reviewed by all relevant people and addressed systematically. When documenting the risks, it is a good practice to rank them. Risks can be ranked either quantitatively or qualitatively. Quantitative rankings use actual and estimated financial data about the assets to assess the severity of the risks. Qualitative rankings use a system to assess the relative impact of the risks. These methods of risk assessment complement each other. Quantitative ranking often requires acute accounting skills, whereas qualitative ranking often requires acute technical skills.

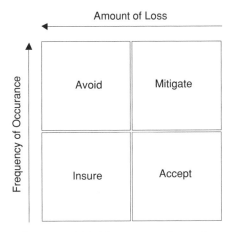

**Figure 2:** Risk Management Strategies

5. **Determine a risk management strategy:** After finishing the risk assessment, determine what general risk management strategy to follow and what security measures to implement in support of the risk management strategy. A risk management plan should clearly state the risk, threat, impact on the organization, risk management strategy, and security measures that will be taken. It will probably follow one of the four general categories of risk management shown in Figure 2.

   - **Accepting the risk:** This means taking no proactive measures and accepting the full exposure and consequences of the security threats to an asset. Use this strategy only as a last resort when no other rational options exist or when the costs associated with mitigating or transferring the risk are unaffordable or unreasonable. If this strategy is chosen, it is useful to create a contingency plan. A contingency plan details a set of actions that will be taken after the risk is realized and will lessen the impact of the compromise or loss of the asset.

   - **Mitigating the risk:** This is the most common method of securing computers and networks. Taking proactive measures either to reduce an asset's exposure to threats or the organization's dependence on the asset mitigates the security risk. Generally, reducing an organization's dependence on an asset is beyond the scope of a security administrator's control; however, reducing the exposure to threats is the primary job function of a security administrator. A common way to mitigate risk is to use antivirus software or firewalls to protect the IT infrastructure of the company. It is obvious that none of these trust management actions is adequate to eliminate possible damages so the company should create a contingency plan to follow if the risk is realized.

     When deciding to mitigate risk, one of the key financial metrics to consider is how much your organization will save because of that action minus the cost of implementing the security measure. If the result is a positive number and no other prohibitive factors exist, such as major conflicts with business operations, implementing the security measure is generally a good idea. On occasion, the cost of implementing the security measure will exceed the amount of money saved but will still be worthwhile; for example, when human life is at risk. In addition, if transferring the risk is chosen along with mitigating the risk, the protective measures taken would probably help reduce the cost of the cyberinsurance policy.

- **Insuring the risk:** An increasingly common method of addressing security risks is to transfer some of the risk to a third party. You can transfer a security risk to another party to take advantage of economies of scale, such as insurance, or to take advantage of another organization's expertise and services, such as a Web hosting service. With insurance, you are paying a relatively small fee to recover or lessen financial losses if the security risk should occur. This is especially important when the financial consequences of your security risk are abnormally large, such as making your organization vulnerable to class action lawsuits. If the need for cyberinsurance is recognized, a decision plan of action should be produced, as is explained below.

- **Avoiding the risk:** The opposite strategy to accepting risk is avoiding the risk entirely. To avoid risk, you must remove altogether the source of the threat, exposure to the threat, or your organization's reliance on the asset. Generally, avoid risk when there are little to no possibilities for mitigating or transferring the risk or when the consequences of realizing the risk are far more important than the benefits gained from undertaking the risk.

6. **Monitor the assets:** Once the actions defined in the risk management plan have been implemented, monitor the assets for comprehension of the security risks. Trigger the actions defined in contingency plans, and start investigating the security incident as soon as possible to limit the damage to your organization.

7. **Track changes to risks:** In time, changes to the organization's IT infrastructure, personnel, and business processes will most probably add new security risks and make some old ones obsolete. Similarly, threats to assets and vulnerabilities will evolve and increase in complexity. Track these changes and update the risk management plan and the associated security measures on a regular basis.

## Challenges Associated with Assessing Information Security Risks

Reliably assessing information security risks can be more difficult than assessing other types of risks because the data on the likelihood and costs associated with information security risk factors are often more limited and because risk factors are constantly changing.

- Data on risk factors are limited, such as the likelihood of a sophisticated hacker attack and the costs of damage, loss, or disruption caused by events that exploit security weaknesses.

- Some costs, such as a loss of customer confidence or disclosure of sensitive information, are inherently difficult to quantify.

- Although the cost of the hardware and software needed to strengthen controls may be known, it is often not possible to estimate precisely the related indirect costs, such as the possible loss of productivity that may result when new controls are implemented.

- Even if precise information were available, it would soon be out of date due to frequent changes in technology and such factors as improvements in tools available to would-be intruders.

## Cyberinsurance

Technology has continued to astound the world's electronic culture by reacting with mechanisms to defend and protect against the unknown. One new mechanism is cyberinsurance, which protects against potential losses from a cybercrime.

Cyberinsurance has experienced many challenges and at the same time has evolved into a more complex tool to protect companies. The insurance industry is attempting to gain more understanding of cybercrime issues and how to design insurance policies more accurately. It has perplexed those who had thought that with protection from the cybersecurity risk, they would be safe. The discussion here offers insight into the implications of insurance and cybercrime coverage and raises awareness of the uncertainties within the cyberinsurance arena.

In an effort to protect against unlawful electronic or physical activity, organizations are now taking a closer look at the effectiveness of their security measures and what is needed to protect confidential assets. Recent national and international regulations make it even more challenging for organizations to ensure that information assets and those environments that house critical information are proactively protected against unauthorized breaches. At the same time, covering such breaches has proven costly to the insurance industry and has encouraged it to define more efficient controls to mitigate the burden of settlement. Insurance companies are realizing the need to implement more refined assessment capabilities to determine the state of an organization's security infrastructure when examining its request for coverage (Drouin, 2004).

For a risk to be insurable, it should have the following characteristics:

- a noncatastrophic loss
- an accident (not the fault of the insured)
- nonintentional
- large exogenous exposure
- measurable

A quality cyberinsurance program should have three components. First, the program should assist the applicant with its risk assessment. Thus, the carrier should offer robust and free loss prevention services. Some of these services should be available regardless of whether the applicant decides to buy insurance. Second, the policy itself should cover the general coverage needs, including both first-party and third-party coverage. Third, the carrier should provide postincident funding for such expenses as public relation fees and criminal reward funds.

Technology is changing, and the effects it will have on organizations over time will change how insurance awards or denies reparation. Liability is a very complex issue when it comes to insurance-related matters. In many instances liability is tested through the lengthy legal process and a final ruling of judgment.

Because the cyberinsurance concept is relatively new, the industry is facing several important barriers. One of the most important ones is the lack of agreement on policy terminology and language. The frequent changes in IT result in ambiguity about what the policy covers. Insurers have relatively little experience with cybersecurity claims on which to base premiums, both because the field is new and because firms have resisted revealing losses from security breaches. Because reinsurers are concerned about the possibility of attacks by organized criminals or terrorists that may lead to greater losses than have occurred to date, lack of available reinsurance is also a concern. Policy exclusions are yet another barrier to the widespread use of cyberinsurance. Like other property/causality policies, cyberinsurance policies exclude claims from acts of war, riot, small disasters, etc. These risks, however, are the most feared ones. For example, it is difficult in cyberinsurance to distinguish organized attacks from terrorist attacks that may be under exclusion terms. There is also inadequate accountability for cybersecurity flaws and vulnerabilities. Even in the United States, the case law has not yet clarified who will be responsible for losses when a breach occurs.

Another issue is adverse selection. An adverse selection problem occurs when the loss to be insured contains private information that is not available to the insurer at the time the insurance is purchased. A common example is in health insurance when a person tries to purchase a health insurance while in a sick state. To deal with this problem, insurers require a medical examination before insuring individuals. However, in cyberinsurance cases, an adverse selection problem manifests in terms of probability of a security breach. Therefore, insurers require security audits before issuing a policy. As we have stated above, the frequent technological advances of the IT industry make it difficult to overcome the problem of adverse selection.

Once a company recognizes the need for cyberinsurance, it should follow this four-step decision plan (Clark, 2002):

1. *Conduct an information security risk audit*: We described this process in the e-risk management section. An information security risk audit identifies the company's information security risk exposure and values the assets.
2. *Assess current insurance coverage*: In this step existing property and liability insurance policies are examined to gain a better understanding of their coverage. This examination enables companies to notice the differences between their requirements and expectations and to determine the gaps in the policies.
3. *Examine and evaluate available policies*: In this step the company should examine and evaluate the available cyberinsurance policies. As there are varying policies

that differ in coverage and price, the company should use the results gained from the security audit to evaluate them.
4. *Select the policy*: The selected policy should have the desired coverage at a reasonable price. The trade-off between reducing the risk and the cost of insurance should be considered.

# LEGAL PRINCIPLES AND REGULATIONS
## Gramm-Leach-Bliley Act (GLBA)

The Gramm-Leach-Bliley Act (GLBA), signed into law in November 1999, is the U.S. government's response to the need to keep customer records secure in an era of online banking, e-commerce, and electronic records. GLBA requires banks to protect customer privacy and to prove they are doing so. Together, the requirements for security and privacy converge to position network and system integrity—and the ability to remediate quickly—as the foundation of a bank's IT policies and procedures.

Title V of GLBA imposes new requirements on the ways in which consumer data are handled by financial services companies. The primary focus of Title V, and the area that has received the most attention, is the sharing of personal data between organizations and their nonaffiliated business partners and agencies. Consumers must be given notice of the ways in which their data are used and of their right to "opt out" of any data sharing plan. Title V also requires financial services organizations to provide adequate security for systems that handle customer data. Security guidelines require the creation and documentation of detailed data security programs addressing both physical and logical access to data, risk assessment and mitigation programs, and employee training in the new security controls. Third-party contractors of financial services firms must also comply with the GLBA regulations.

On February 1, 2001, the Department of the Treasury, Federal Reserve System, and Federal Deposit Insurance Corporation issued interagency regulations in part requiring financial institutions to do the following:

- Develop and execute an information security program.
- Conduct regular tests of key controls of the information security program. These tests should be conducted by an independent third party or staff independent of those who develop or maintain the program.
- Protect against destruction, loss, or damage to customer information, including encrypting customer information while in transit or storage on networks.
- Involve the board of directors or an appropriate committee of the board to oversee and execute all of the above.

Because the responsibility for developing specific guidelines for compliance was delegated to the various federal and state agencies overseeing commercial and financial services, and some of these guidelines are still being issued, it is possible that guidelines for GLBA compliance may vary by states and financial services industries.

A similar action to the GLBA, the New Basel Capital Accord (Basel II) was drafted in January 2001 by the Basel Committee on Banking Supervision, proposes changes to improve "capital adequacy" (minimal capital requirements), enhance risk measurement and management capabilities, and promote accurate and transparent reporting to encourage banks to improve their risk management processes and reduce the risk of bank failures.

Basel II introduces a new capital charge related to the operational risks of financial institutions, defined as "the risk of direct or indirect loss resulting from inadequate or failed internal processes, people and systems or from external events," and creates improved supervisory processes and public disclosure requirements.

Currently in its third draft, the accord is expected to be adopted by all major financial regulators and supervisors by the end of 2006 and to have significant implications for all financial institutions worldwide. Institutions with advanced internal controls and processes will be able to benefit from the accords provisions for internal, ratings-based approaches to reduce minimum capital requirements and increase the funds available for cash flow, investment, and profit creation.

## Health Insurance Portability and Accountability Act of 1996 (HIPAA)

Best practices for assuring both data and network integrity differ little from industry to industry. Any organization managing critical electronic information understands the importance of protecting their data and networks from intrusion and abuse.

Health care providers face particularly difficult challenges because of the sensitive nature of the data they are responsible for safeguarding. In their environment, corrupted data can have grave consequences. Recognizing this gravity, legislators have taken steps to make the security and privacy of health care data a legal requirement.

The result of their concern is a broad new regulatory initiative that protects the confidentiality and integrity of electronically stored personal health information. The Health Insurance Portability and Accountability Act of 1996 (HIPAA) set in motion the process of establishing privacy and security standards for individually identifiable health information. Meeting these standards demands due diligence from data and network managers throughout the health care industry.

As part of HIPAA regulations, health care providers, health plans, and clearinghouses are responsible for protecting the security of client health information. As with GLBA, customer medical data are subject to controls on distribution and usage, and controls must be established to protect the privacy of customer data. Data must also be classified according to a standard classification system to allow greater portability of health data between providers and health plans. Specific guidelines on security controls for medical information have not yet been issued. HIPAA regulations are enforced by the Department of Health and Human Services.

As of April 14, 2003, health care providers and health plans are required to be in compliance with the HIPAA Privacy Regulation. Both the 1996 Congress and the two recent administrations agree that a privacy law is needed to ensure that sensitive personal health information can be shared for core health activities, with safeguards in place to limit the inappropriate use and sharing of patient data. The HIPAA privacy rule takes critical steps in that direction by requiring that privacy and security be built into the policies and practices of health care providers, plans, and others involved in health care.

## Sarbanes-Oxley Act (SOA) of 2002

The Sarbanes-Oxley Act (SOA) of 2002 mandates that corporations establish strict controls over business conduct and addresses how they manage their finance and accounting processes. In general, it applies to publicly held companies and their audit firms. Key technical components include data center operations, system software maintenance, application development and maintenance, business continuity, and application software integrity. Business requirements are controlled by the Audit Committee, which is responsible for reporting and certifying the organization's statements of corporate information and internal IT controls. If these specifics are not adhered to and the organization is found negligent in reference to fraud, then those implicated or found in violation of the Corporate and Fraud Accountability title of the SOA may face severe fines and possible imprisonment of 10 to 20 years.

Worthy of particular note is that the SOA's focus is on accounting reform and investor protection and its applicable to all private and public companies. Respectively, HIPAA and GLBA address health care and banking. At first, this legislation seems to have little to do with information security, but there are certain sections of the law that create rules for documenting financial reporting controls and processes. The logical progression from a weak information security program to noncompliance with the financial controls and processes of SOA is a short one. It is also one that is likely to come under increasing scrutiny.

On the international front, in 1995, the European Union passed the Data Protection Directive, which requires that international data exchanges that use European Union (EU) citizens' personal data be accorded the same level of protection that their home country would afford them. This means that U.S. companies must ensure that when they use EU citizens' personal data they provide the same level of protection these citizens are afforded within the EU.

## U.S. Food and Drug Administration (FDA) 21 CFR11

The U.S. Food and Drug Administration (FDA) has issued a set of regulations, collectively called 21 CFR111, that provide criteria for the acceptance of electronic records and electronic signatures as equivalent to paper records and handwritten signatures executed on paper.

These regulations, which apply to all FDA program areas, are intended to permit the widest possible use of electronic technology, compatible with the FDA's responsibility to promote and protect public health. Though electronic submissions are currently optional, the FDA is paving the way, with 21 CFR11, for routine and eventually mandatory electronic submission of clinical trial records.

The 21 CFR11 provides in-depth guidelines and criteria for ensuring authenticity and integrity of digital records and for documenting and validating authorized change processes to systems and software involved in the creation of digital records. The goal is the ability to discern invalid or altered records and, conversely, to assure accuracy, reliability, and validity of electronic records and signatures. Typical FDA-regulated activities that can accept 21 CFR11-compliant validated electronic records and signatures include new drug applications (NDAs), medical product license applications (PLAs), and biologics license applications (BLAs).

## Federal Information Security Management Act (FISMA)

Designed to enhance electronic government services and processes and transform agency operations by utilizing best practices from public and private sector organizations, the Federal Information Security Management Act (FISMA) is part of the E-Government Act and requires that agencies secure their enterprise architecture software.

FISMA states, "Each federal agency shall develop, document, and implement an agency-wide information security program to provide information security for the information and information systems that support the operations and assets of the agency, including those provided or managed by another agency, contractor, or other source."

FISMA introduces a legal definition for the term "information security," which is as follows:

> "The term 'information security' means protecting information and information systems from unauthorized access, use, disclosure, disruption, modification, or destruction in order to provide (A) integrity, which means guarding against improper information modification or destruction, and includes ensuring information nonrepudiation and authenticity; (B) confidentiality, which means preserving authorized restrictions on access and disclosure, including means for protecting personal privacy and proprietary information; and (C) availability, which means ensuring timely and reliable access to and use of information. All Federal information and information systems require some degree of security under one or more of the three elements of the forgoing definition."

In addition, FISMA requires that each government agency not only develop its own proprietary system configuration requirements but also then ensure compliance with those requirements. "Simply establishing such configuration requirements is not enough. It must be accompanied by adequate ongoing monitoring and maintenance."

## COVERAGE TYPES
### Conventional Coverage Types Applicable to Cybersecurity
#### General Liability

Traditional commercial general liability policies cover two basic areas of risk: first, bodily injury and damage to tangible property, and second, advertising and personal security. Liability claims arising out of transmission of a computer virus, theft of client information, denial of service, or other types of cyberrisk simply do not fall within these parameters of bodily injury or damage to tangible property. There have been several cases on this issue, the most notable being America On-Line (AOL) *versus* St. Paul. The coverage afforded in the advertising injury and personal injury (AI/PI) section has been subject to similar restrictions, as carriers have moved either to exclude Web-based content specifically or exclude the coverage altogether for businesses that have a significant Internet presence—thereby removing coverage for both online and offline content. Perhaps the only positive news is that these policies also typically include an Advertising Injury provision that might apply to some types of Web advertising-related claims. However, even here, caution is needed as the applicability of this provision to Web-based advertising has never been truly tested, and there are a number of restrictions and limitations in the insurance policy that could call into serious question coverage even in this narrow area.

#### Business Interruption

Many businesses purchase business-interruption insurance as part of their first-party property insurance. Unlike first-party property insurance, which covers damage to insured property, business-interruption insurance applies to the policyholder's consequential loss of business due to damage to property, including loss of business income. Business-interruption insurance policies generally limit coverage to the business income lost during the time required to restore the business or to a period of 12 months following the loss or damage and the additional cost associated with a covered business interruption. Other time limitations may apply to certain aspects of the coverage.

For example, contingent business-interruption coverage pays for losses resulting from property loss at the location of a key vendor or supplier, even in the absence of physical damage at the policyholder's premises. Other extensions of coverage may protect a policyholder's loss of leasehold interest, valuable papers, computers, and electronic data and media. A related coverage, called event cancellation coverage, is extended to pay a policyholder's losses from events that are cancelled for reasons specified in the policies.

#### Property

Cyberinsurance may provide protection against damage to hard assets caused via the Internet, machinery taken down, or equipment programmed to operate erratically. Typically, this policy does not acknowledge "data" as property. Most policies do not recognize a nonphysical peril as a covered risk. Most current carriers have placed a mandatory "data corruption" exclusion on policies for the last few years.

Property coverage can be divided into two segments in the business policy—fixed property (buildings, fixtures, etc.) and contents (equipment, inventory, etc.)—or purchased as a combined single limit. Property can be covered either as all risk or as specified peril.

Almost all policies exclude such events as wear and tear, as insurance is intended to cover sudden and accidental occurrences. The most widely known application of property coverage to cybersecurity is insuring IT equipment, such as computers.

### Errors and Omissions (Professional) Liability

Errors and omissions insurance (E&O) is one portion of a comprehensive professional liability insurance package. It protects business owners and professionals against liability claims or lawsuits for damage caused by errors (something they did) or omissions (something they failed to do). For example, if you are an accountant doing tax preparation work for a client and you mistakenly claim a deduction to which your client is not entitled, your client might sue you to recover the penalties imposed by the IRS (plus damages for the mental anguish caused by the audit). Errors and omissions insurance could protect you against such a lawsuit.

E&O policies can be quite expensive and are typically customized to meet the needs of a specific professional group. Professionals who purchase E&O policies include lawyers, accountants, engineers, bankers, employee benefit managers, architects, stockbrokers, insurance agents, travel agents, and others who manage money and property for others. The technology E&O policies are regularly bought by hardware and software companies, as well as by technological consulting firms.

Most states have several insurers who specialize in business insurance. These insurance companies generally sell E&O policies, as well as other types of professional and commercial liability insurance. Many professional and trade organizations also offer E&O insurance.

### Directors and Officers Liability

Directors and officers liability insurance provides financial protection for the directors and officers of your company in the event they are sued in conjunction with the performance of their duties as they relate to the company. Think of this as a management E&O policy.

This type of insurance usually includes employment practices liability and sometimes fiduciary liability. The former involves harassment and discrimination suits and is where the majority of your exposure lies.

Directors and officers insurance is often confused with E&O insurancem but the two are not synonymous. E&O is concerned with performance failures and negligence with respect to products and services, not the performance and duties of management. Generally it is a good idea to carry both types of insurance.

### Group Personal Liability

Group personal excess liability insurance is a comprehensive benefit for key personnel, managers, and employees. It provides personal liability coverage for each employee in a defined group and helps assure that the most valued staff members' personal assets are protected. In addition, it awards a cost-competitive insurance product to valued employees. Group personal excess liability insurance is a true "group" policy; the insurance company will not individually underwrite or decline any individual in the designated group.

### Employment Practices

Employment practices liability insurance is a relatively new form of liability insurance. It provides protection for an employer against claims made by employees, former employees, or potential employees. It covers discrimination (age, sex, race, disability, etc.), wrongful termination of employment, sexual harassment, and other employment-related allegations. It covers a firm, including its directors and officers.

Employment practices liability insurance is needed as soon as you start to hire employees. Most investors and directors require this coverage as part of the directors and officers liability insurance because they can also be held liable in suits relating to employment practices.

### Key Person Life Coverage

Key person life coverage is designed to protect your business upon the loss of a key employee. The tax-free proceeds from this policy can be used to find, hire, and train a replacement; compensate for business lost during the transition; or finance any number of timely business transactions.

### Intellectual Property

Intellectual property insurance protects companies against copyright, trademark, or patent infringement claims arising out of the company's operation. The insurance covers such items as all working papers, records, trade secrets, data, methodologies, drawings, software, documents, or other writings created, developed, or acquired by the company or supplied to or made available to it.

### Fidelity or Crime

Fidelity/crime insurance protects organizations from the loss of money, securities, or inventory resulting from crime. Common fidelity/crime insurance claims allege employee dishonesty, embezzlement, forgery, robbery, safe burglary, computer fraud, wire transfer fraud, counterfeiting, and other criminal acts.

These schemes involve every possible angle, taking advantage of any potential weakness in your company's financial controls and range from fictitious employees, dummy accounts payable, and nonexistent suppliers to the outright theft of money, securities, and property. Fraud and embezzlement in the workplace are on the rise, occurring in even the best work environments.

### Patent Coverage

Patent coverage is a policy that reimburses the insured for defense expenses and damages paid by the insured resulting from allegations that the insured has infringed on a patent, copyright, or trademark of a third party. Associated with this coverage is the "Defense of a Patent" coverage, which funds the legal process.

## Coverage Types Specific to Cybersecurity

The following types of coverage are specific to cyberinsurance:

- **General Internet Crime Liability:** This addresses the first- and third-party risks associated with e-business, the Internet, networks, and informational assets. Limitations exist with this level of coverage. It is important to review your business activities to ensure appropriate coverage.

- **Web Content Liability:** This provides coverage for claims arising out of the content of a Web site (including the invisible metatags content), such as libel, slander, copyright, and trademark infringement. This liability also covers third-party material that exists on the insured's Web site (e.g., banner advertisements).

- **Hacker Coverage:** This coverage is provided on a claims-made basis by insurers operating in the surplus lines market. The policy covers all electronic communication systems, including computer systems, telephone switches, or satellite relays. It is ideally suited for any small to mid-sized business that would be affected by an invasion of their telephone, satellite, facsimile, or computer systems.

- **Internet Professional Liability:** This provides coverage for claims arising out of the performance of professional services. Coverage usually includes both Web publishing activities and pure Internet services, such as being an Internet service provider, host, or Web designer. Any professional service conducted over the Internet can usually be added to the policy.

- **Network Security Third-Party Coverage:** This provides liability coverage arising from a failure of the insured's security system to prevent unauthorized use or access of its network. This important coverage would apply, subject to the policy's full terms, to claims arising from the transmission of a computer virus (such as the popular "Love Bug" or NIMDA virus), theft of a customer's information (most notably including credit card information), and so-called denial of service (DoS) liability. In 2004 alone, countless incidents of this type of misconduct have been reported.

- **Network Security First-Party Coverage:** This coverage provides, upon a covered event, reimbursement for loss arising out of the altering, copying, misappropriating, corrupting, destroying, disrupting, deleting, damaging, or theft of information assets, criminal or not. Typically the policy covers the cost of replacing, reproducing, recreating, restoring, or recollecting data. In the case of theft of a trade secret (a broadly defined term), the policy either pays or is capped at the endorsed negotiated amount.

- **Network Security First-Party Business-Interruption Coverage:** This coverage provides reimbursement for lost revenue as a result of a covered event. The policy provides coverage for the period of recovery plus an extended business-interruption period. Some policies also provide coverage for dependent business interruption, meaning the loss of e-revenue as a result of a computer attack on a third-party business (such as a supplier) upon which the insured's business depends.

- **Cyberextortion:** This provides reimbursement of investigation costs and sometimes of the extortion demand itself, in the event of a covered cyberextortion threat. These threats, which usually take the form of a demand for "consulting fees" to prevent the release of hacked information or to the threatened shutdown of the victim's Web site, are all too common.

- **Media Liability Coverage:** This coverage protects against claims arising out of the gathering and communication of information. It provides very valuable coverage against defamation and invasion of privacy claims, as well as copyright and/or trademark infringement. Investigate and clarify the level of privacy coverage before purchasing this insurance.

## A TYPICAL POLICY

A policy generally contains four chapters: an *insuring agreements* chapter where the coverage of the policy is explained, a *definitions* chapter where the formal definitions of the key words are given, an *exclusions* chapter where cases that are not covered by the policy are stated explicitly, and a *general conditions* chapter where valid mechanisms that apply to the policy are stated.

The insuring agreements chapter, which contains clauses that state the coverage of the policy, is usually broken into three sections: first-party liability, third-party liability, and rehabilitation expenses. A sample outline of an insurance agreements chapter is given below.

### Section One: First-Party Liability

| | |
|---|---|
| Insuring Agreement | 1. etwork Security First-Party Business-Interruption Coverage |
| Insuring Agreement | 2. Network Security First-Party Coverage |
| Insuring Agreement | 3. Cyberextortion |
| Insuring Agreement | 4. General Internet Crime Liability |

### Section Two: Third-Party Liability

| | |
|---|---|
| Insuring Agreement | 6. Network Security Third-Party Coverage |

### Rehabilitation Expenses

| | |
|---|---|
| Insuring Agreement | 7. Rehabilitation Expenses (Applicable to Sections One and Two) |

The general conditions chapter explains the mechanisms that are applicable to the policy. This chapter may also be broken into three sections. A sample outline for a general conditions chapter is given below.

### General Conditions Applicable to Section One

1. Discovery, Notice, and Proof of Loss
2. Valuation of Loss
3. Calculation of Business Interruption Loss and Extra Expense
4. Ownership
5. Interim Payments

*General Conditions Applicable to Section Two*
6. Notice and Reporting Claims and Circumstances
7. Defense, Settlement, and Cooperation
8. Extended Reporting Period

*General Conditions Applicable to Sections One and Two*
9. Policy Limits
10. Additional Offices, Computer Systems—Consolidation, Merger, or Purchase of Assets—Notice
11. Change of Control—Notice
12. Subrogation and Recoveries
13. Other Insurance or Indemnity
14. Termination or Cancellation
15. Representations, Fraud, and Entire Contract
16. Annual Inspection and Audit
17. Named Insured as Agent
18. Assignment
19. Legal Proceedings against Underwriters
20. Service of Suit
21. Governing Law

# HYPOTHETICAL CASE

Acme Incorporated runs an online electronic shop that sells different kinds of food of various cuisines to individual customers. Acme's e-commerce site keeps a list of registered restaurants and cafes located in the neighborhoods of many major cities. The customer selects the restaurant, orders the food, and uses his or her credit card to pay for it online. Acme has a special arrangement for Christmas meals, which are very popular and are a major source of income for the company.

Several weeks before Christmas, Acme Incorporated's CEO received an e-mail warning message from a hacker. The hacker indicated his opposition to Acme's fat-making Christmas meal arrangement and stated that the company is promoting obesity throughout the country. The hacker added that he had infiltrated Acme's computer system and stolen more than 100,000 credit card numbers from its database. If the CEO would deposit $100,000 into a specified Swiss bank account, the hacker would erase the credit card numbers and reveal the method he followed, as he only hacked into Acme's system. However, if the CEO did not pay the $100,000, the hacker would publicize the credit card numbers on the Web and also launch a denial of service (DoS) attack against Acme's servers, causing its computer system and Web site to shut down for a noticeable amount of time. Acme receives 40% of its income during the Christmas season. Furthermore, Acme expected to receive $10 million in online revenue between the date of the e-mail and December 28th.

Despite the potential loss of revenue, Acme's CEO decided not to give in to the hacker's demands. A few days after the e-mail was received, Acme's computer systems and Internet site suffered a distributed DoS attack and shut down. Furthermore, 20,000 of Acme's customers' credit card numbers were publicized on the Web by the hacker. It took 7 days for Acme to get its Web site up and running again. This downtime prevented customers from purchasing their special Christmas meals, and the fact that their credit cards were revealed on the Web increased customers' displeasure with the company. In addition, credit card issuers, who spent approximately $150 per card to reissue them; credit card holders who had to pay up to $50 of the fraudulent charges; and several other merchants who suffered financial losses after accepting the stolen credit card numbers filed suits against Acme.

Acme suffered the following financial losses:

- Cost to investigate extortion threat: $10,000
- Cost to retrieve damaged data: $50,000
- Cost of lost online revenue during week shutdown: $700,000
- Cost of lost online revenue after site recovery: $60,000 per week (12 weeks)
- Defense expenses of four lawsuits: $30,000 per week for 52 weeks of litigation before settlement, totaling $1,540,000.
- Expected settlement of four lawsuits: $2,500,000
- Cost of hiring outside public relations agent after crisis: $25,000

## Coverage of Hypothetical Case

Acme Incorporated suffered at least five types of financial loss in this hypothetical case: extortion expenses, property (data) damage, e-revenue business interruption, third-party litigation costs (defense and settlement), and public relations expenses.

Subject to the specific terms, conditions, and exclusions of the policy, all of these financial losses would be covered if Acme had a cyberinsurance policy.

Once the threatening e-mail was received, the carrier might well hire an expert cyberextortionist investigator to find out the level of the hacker's threat and the potential financial loss to Acme, if the threat was to be realized. After this investigation the investigator might recommend that Acme pay the extortion demand and then post a criminal reward for the hacker's capture and detention. It is most probable that the costs associated with this approach would have been much lower than the financial costs Acme ended up suffering.

The first-party coverage section of the cyberinsurance policy would generally cover both the costs of restoring the damaged data ($50,000) and the lost revenue during the 7 days that the Acme's Web site was down due to the DoS attack ($700,000), assuming that Acme could not have practically gotten its site up and running in a shorter period of time. The policy will also cover the future lost of revenue ($60,000 per week) up to the period of the "extended period of recovery," which is up to 90 days in a typical policy. Keep in mind that the carrier would not pay those amounts incurred during the policy's "waiting period retention," a period of between 12 to 48 hours depending upon the policy. Thus, if Acme's $700,000 loss was spread evenly over the week, the first $50,000 to $200,000 would be charged to the insured.

Assuming that the claims were reported properly and the other terms and conditions of the policy were satisfied, the policy would respond to the three lawsuits, hiring counsel and paying legal expenses, as well as any settlement or judgment. Again, the loss would be paid excess of the applicable retention. The total litigation cost if all three claims were settled after a year of litigation was $4,060,000.

Finally, a quality cyberinsurance policy would also recommend a public relations firm for Acme and would pay the $25,000 public relations fee.

In sum, the total policy payments would be more than $5,000,000.

# BEST PRACTICES
## Information Technology Infrastructure Library (ITIL)

The IT Infrastructure Library (ITIL) is a series of modules that help organizations achieve optimal use of their IT resources. These ITIL modules create a complete set of best practices for IT service provision and enable organizations to offer high-quality IT delivery and support services to their end users. As the industry-wide default standard for IT best practices, ITIL is increasingly being adopted by organizations all over the world to facilitate the increased effectiveness and efficiency of IT services and the reduction of risk.

ITIL was initially developed in the late 1980s and is still owned by the Office of Government Commerce (OGC) in the United Kingdom. OGC's customer base was the central government of the United Kingdom, but it soon became clear that its requirements were no different from the general needs of other organizations, whether in the public or private sector, large or small, centralized or distributed.

The ITIL has 7 components:

1. Service Support: This ensures appropriate services are in place to support business functions. Service Support includes Configuration Management, Service Desk, Incident Management, Problem Management, Change Management, and Release Management.
2. Service Delivery: This ensures that business functions receive adequate services to accomplish goals. Service Delivery includes Availability Management, Capacity Management, IT Services Continuity Management, IT Services Financial Management, and Service Level Management.
3. Security Management: This ensures that Security Management requirements are implemented as outlined in the Service Level Agreement. Security Management is the only process included in this section.
4. Application Management: This ensures that the appropriate software development life cycle is followed. Application Management includes Software Lifecycle Support and Testing of IT Services.
5. ICT Infrastructure Management: This section covers Network Service Management, Operations Management, Management of Local Processors, Computer Installation and Acceptance, and Systems Management.
6. Business Perspective: This section includes Business Continuity Management, Partnerships and Outsourcing, Surviving Change and Transformation of Business Practices through Change, and Understanding and Improving.
7. Planning to Implement Service Management: This explains how to implement ITIL and what benefits organizations may gain from it. This section covers Continuous Process Improvement.

Presently ITIL has come to represent rather more than just these modules alone, and the term "ITIL" is now being used to describe a plethora of ITIL-related goods and services that have grown into a comprehensive industry. As a nonproprietary public domain, ITIL-related fields today include the following:

- training
- certifications
- consultancy
- software tools
- user groups

Most organizations spend more on IT service provision, including maintenance of those services, than on IT development projects. It is imperative that users of those IT services obtain value for their money. The services must, of course, be matched to business needs and customer requirements as they change; they must be provided economically, making optimum use of scarce IT skills. There is a continual pressure in any organization to reduce cost while maintaining or improving IT services.

The ITIL provides a systematic approach to help organizations deliver well-managed IT services in the face of many constraints, such as lack of finances and time, more exacting and unpredictable business requirements and user demands, and the growing complexity of information systems.

ITIL currently offers three levels of qualifications:

1. Foundation-level: This tests understanding of the underlying ITIL principles and of the terms and concepts embodied within ITIL.
2. Practitioner-level: This is aimed at IT professionals who are practicing in one or more of the specific ITIL functions.
3. Service Manager-level: This is an advanced level and tests an understanding of the ITIL philosophy, including the reasons for adopting ITIL guidelines, the management implications, the costs, and the benefits.

The ITIL offers a systematic, professional approach to the management of IT service provision and can yield such benefits as the following:

- customer satisfaction with IT services that meet their needs
- reduced risk of being unable to meet the business requirements for IT services
- reduced costs of developing procedures and practices within an organization
- better communication and information flows between IT staff and customers
- assurance to the IT Director that staff are provided with appropriate standards and guidance

- greater productivity and better use of staff members' skills and experience
- a quality approach to IT service provision

ITIL also provides benefits to the customer of the IT services, such as the following:

- reassurance that IT services are provided in accordance with documented procedures, which can be audited
- the ability to depend upon IT services, enabling the customer to meet business objectives
- the provision of clearly defined contact points within IT services for inquiries or discussions about changing requirements
- the knowledge that detailed information is produced to justify charges for IT services and to provide feedback from monitoring of service-level agreements

The ITIL emphasizes the importance of providing IT services to satisfy business needs in a cost-effective manner. Many IT organizations are attempting to become more customer oriented, and ITIL can help organizations make this transition.

Because IT service management is a set of integrated and coordinated processes, organizations are likely to gain most benefit in the longer term from implementing all of the processes.

## Control Objectives for Information and Related Technology (COBiT)

Control Objectives for Information and related Technology (COBiT) is designed to be an IT governance aid to management in their understanding and managing of the risks and benefits associated with information and related technology. It is intended to provide clear policy and good practice for IT governance throughout the organization.

With IT often being critical to the success and survival of an entity, it is essential that IT be managed effectively. COBiT is designed to fit in between the overall business control models (e.g., COSO, CoCo, Cadbury, and King) and the various IT-focused models that include best practice guidelines, baseline controls, and specific industry standards (e.g., ISO 9000 TickIT scheme, ISO 7498, ITSEC Common Criteria, etc.).

COBiT creates the link between the business objectives of an entity and the specific IT and IT management tasks via statements about the control objectives. It classifies IT resources into three levels of effort: domains, processes, and tasks. Domains are groups of IT processes that are in line with the management cycle or life cycle applicable to IT processes. There are four broad domains:

1. planning and organization
2. acquisition and implementation
3. delivery and support
4. monitoring

COBiT aims to provide management with answers to the following traditional questions:

- What is the issue/problem?
- What is the solution?
- What does it consist of?
- Will it work?
- How do I do it?

COBiT identifies 34 IT processes grouped into 4 domains and is supported by 318 detailed control objectives. Each one of the 34 processes is related to IT resources and the quality, fiduciary, and security requirements of information.

COBiT provides a generally applicable and accepted standard for good IT security and control practices and enables management to determine and monitor the appropriate level of IT security and control for their organizations. Further, the COBiT Management Guidelines are generic and action oriented, addressing the following types of management concerns:

- Performance measurement—What are indicators of good performance?
- IT control profiling—What is important? What are critical success factors for control?
- Awareness—What are the risks of not achieving our objectives?
- Benchmarking—What do others do? How do we measure and compare?

COBiT's third edition has five parts:

1. Executive Overview
2. Framework
3. Management Guidelines
4. Implementation Tool Set
5. Audit Guidelines

### Benefits

COBiT is a framework that will guide management in deciding on the level of risk to accept, the most appropriate control practices, and the path to follow when it is necessary to improve the level of control. It addresses business objectives in a process-oriented manner.

COBiT links specific IT control models to overall business control models (e.g., COSO, Coco, Cadbury, and King). It defines high-level and detailed control objectives for the 34 IT process that are grouped in four domains. These processes guide management in selecting critical success factors (CSF)— the most important issues or actions that management need to control so that IT can be effective in enabling the entity's business objectives.

With the CSFs in mind, COBiT guides management in deciding on key goal indicators, those measurements that indicate that the required outcomes from the CSFs have been achieved. Thereafter, management is directed to determine the meaningful measures that indicate how well the IT processes are doing in enabling the achievement of the goals set by IT management.

The conceptual framework can be approached from three vantage points: (1) information criteria, (2) IT resources, and (3) IT processes. For example, managers may

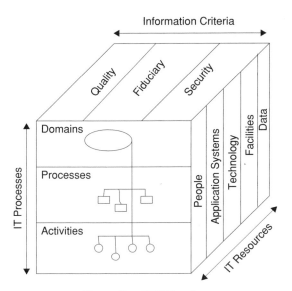

**Figure 3:** COBiT cube

want to look at CSFs from a quality, fiduciary, or security perspective (included in the Framework as seven specific information criteria). An IT manager, on the other hand, may want to consider IT resources for which he or she is accountable. Process owners, IT specialists, and users may have a specific interest in particular processes or activities/tasks. Auditors may wish to approach the Framework from a control coverage point of view. These three vantage points are depicted in the CobiT cube (Figure 3).

Using the COBiT as the framework, the domains are identified using wording that management would use in their day-to-day activities, not auditor jargon. Thus, four broad domains are identified: planning and organization, acquisition and implementation, delivery and support, and monitoring.

- **Planning and Organization**: This domain covers strategy and tactics; it focuses on how IT can best contribute to the achievement of the business objectives. Furthermore, the realization of the strategic vision needs to be planned, communicated, and managed for different perspectives. Finally, a proper organization as well as technological infrastructure must be put in place.

- **Acquisition and Implementation**: To realize the IT strategy, IT solutions need to be identified, developed, or acquired, as well as implemented and integrated into the business process. In addition, changes in and maintenance of existing systems are covered by this domain to make sure that the life cycle is continued for these systems.

- **Delivery and Support**: This domain is concerned with the actual delivery of required services, which range from traditional security and continuity operations to training. To deliver services, the necessary support processes must be implemented. This domain includes the actual processing of data by application systems, often classified under application controls.

- **Monitoring**: All IT processes need to be regularly assessed over time for their quality and compliance with

control requirements. This domain thus addresses management's oversight of the organization's control process and independent assurance provided by internal and external audit or obtained from alternative sources.

These processes can be applied at different levels within an organization. For example, some of these processes will be applied at the enterprise level, others at the information services function level, others at the business process owner level, etc.

It should also be noted that the effectiveness criterion of processes that plan or deliver solutions for business requirements will sometimes cover the criteria for availability, integrity, and confidentiality; in practice, these criteria have become business requirements. For example, the process of "identify solutions" has to be effective in providing the Availability, Integrity, and Confidentiality requirements.

## ISO 17799/BS 7799

ISO 17799 is an extremely comprehensive and detailed standard. Compliance with it therefore requires both a methodical and measured approach. It also requires commitment, as well as access to appropriate tools and products.

ISO 17799 is intended to serve as a single reference point for identifying a range of controls needed for most situations in which information systems are used in industry and commerce. It is organized into 10 major sections, each covering a different topic or area:

1. **Business Continuity Planning**: The objectives of this section are to counteract interruptions to business activities and to critical business processes from the effects of major failures or disasters.

2. **System Access Control**: The objectives of this section are (1) to control access to information, (2) to prevent unauthorized access to information systems, (3) to ensure the protection of networked services, (4) to prevent unauthorized computer access, (5) to detect unauthorized activities, and (6) to ensure information security when using mobile computing and tele-networking facilities

3. **System Development and Maintenance**: The objectives of this section are (1) to ensure security is built into operational systems; (2) to prevent loss, modification, or misuse of user data in application systems; (3) to protect the confidentiality, authenticity, and integrity of information; (4) to ensure that IT projects and support activities are conducted in a secure manner; and (5) to maintain the security of application system software and data.

4. **Physical and Environmental Security**: The objectives of this section are to prevent unauthorized access, damage, and interference to business premises and information; to prevent loss, damage, or compromise of assets and interruption to business activities; and to prevent compromise or theft of information and information-processing facilities.

5. **Compliance**: The objectives of this section are (1) to avoid breaches of any criminal or civil law, statutory,

regulatory, or contractual obligations, and of any security requirements; (2) to ensure compliance of systems with organizational security policies and standards; and (3) to maximize the effectiveness of and to minimize interference to/from the system audit process.

6. **Personnel Security**: The objectives of this section are to reduce risks of human error, theft, fraud, or misuse of facilities; to ensure that users are aware of information security threats and concerns and are equipped to support the corporate security policy in the course of their normal work; and to minimize the damage from security incidents and malfunctions and to learn from such incidents.

7. **Security Organization:** The objectives of this section are (1) to manage information security within the company, (2) to maintain the security of organizational information-processing facilities and information assets accessed by third parties, and (3) to maintain the security of information when the responsibility for information processing has been outsourced to another organization.

8. **Computer & Operations Management**: The objectives of this section are (1) to ensure the correct and secure operation of information-processing facilities; (2) to minimize the risk of systems failures; (3) to protect the integrity of software and information; (4) to maintain the integrity and availability of information processing and communication; (5) to ensure the safeguarding of information in networks and the protection of the supporting infrastructure; (6) to prevent damage to assets and interruptions to business activities; and (7) to prevent loss, modification, or misuse of information exchanged between organizations.

9. **Asset Classification and Control**: The objectives of this section are to maintain appropriate protection of corporate assets and to ensure that information assets receive an appropriate level of protection.

10. **Security Policy**: The objective of this section is to provide management direction and support for information security.

## Common Criteria (CC)

The Common Criteria's (CC) official name is the Common Criteria for Information Technology Security Evaluation, though it is normally just called the Common Criteria. The CC document has three parts: the introduction, which describes the overall CC; security functional requirements, which list various kinds of security functions that products might want to include; and security assurance requirements, which list various methods of assuring that a product is secure. There is also a related document, the Common Evaluation Methodology (CEM), which guides evaluators in applying the CC to formal evaluations; in particular, it amplifies what CC means in certain situations.

Although it can be used in other ways, the CC is typically used to create two kinds of documents, a *protection profile* (PP) or a *security target* (ST). A PP is a document created by group of users (for example, a consumer group or large organization) that identifies the desired security properties of a product. Basically, it is a list of user security requirements, described in a very specific way defined by the CC. If you are building a product similar to other existing products, it is quite possible that there are one or more PPs that define what some users believe are necessary for that kind of product (e.g., an operating system or firewall). An ST is a document that identifies what a product or a subset of it actually does that is security relevant. An ST does not need to meet the requirements of any particular PP, but an ST could meet the requirements of one or more PPs.

Both PPs and STs can go through a formal evaluation. An evaluation of a PP simply ensures that the PP meets various documentation rules and sanity checks. An ST evaluation involves not only examining the ST document, but more important it also involves evaluating an actual system, which is called the *target of evaluation* (TOE). The purpose of an ST evaluation is to ensure that, to the level of the assurance requirements specified by the ST, the actual product (the TOE) meets the ST's security functional requirements. Customers can then compare evaluated STs to PPs describing what they want and so determine if the products meet their requirements and, if not, where the limitations are.

To create a PP or ST, the organization goes through a process of identifying the security environment; namely, its assumptions, threats, and relevant organizational security policies (if any). From the security environment, it derives the security objectives for the product or product type. Finally, it selects the security requirements so that they meet the objectives. There are two kinds of security requirements: functional requirements (what a product has to be able to do) and assurance requirements (measures to inspire confidence that the objectives have been met). Actually creating a PP or ST is often not a simple straightforward process as outlined here, but the final result needs to show a clear relationship so that no critical point is easily overlooked. Even if the organization does not plan to write an ST or PP, the ideas in the CC can still be helpful, as is the process of identifying the security environment, objectives, and requirements.

The vast majority of the CC's text describes standardized functional requirements and assurance requirements. In essence, most of the CC is a general listing of possible security requirements that someone might want. PP authors pick from the various options to describe what they want, and ST authors pick from the options to describe what they provide.

Because many people might have difficulty identifying a reasonable set of assurance requirements, pre-created sets of assurance requirements called *evaluation assurance levels* (EALs) have been defined, ranging from 1 to 7. EAL2 is simply standard shorthand for the set of assurance requirements defined for EAL 2. Products can add additional assurance measures; for example, they might choose EAL2 plus some additional assurance measures (if the combination is not enough to achieve a higher EAL level, such a combination would be called EAL2 plus). There are mutual recognition agreements signed between many of the world's nations that will accept an evaluation done by an accredited laboratory in the other countries as long as all of the assurance measures taken were at the EAL 4 level or lower.

In writing an ST or PP, an open source software program, the CC Toolbox, can be of help. It can make sure that dependencies between requirements are met, suggest common requirements, and help you quickly develop a document, but it obviously cannot do your thinking for you. The specifications of exactly what information must be in a PP or ST are in CC part 1, annexes B and C, respectively.

To have a product (or PP) evaluated by an accredited laboratory, be prepared to expend money, time, and work throughout the process. In particular, higher levels of assurance become more expensive quickly. Simply believing the product is secure is not good enough; evaluators require evidence to justify any claims made. Thus, evaluations require documentation, and usually the available documentation has to be improved or developed to meet CC requirements (especially at the higher assurance levels). Every claim has to be justified to some level of confidence, so the more claims that are made, the stronger the claims; the more complicated the design, the more expensive the evaluation. Obviously, when flaws are found, they will usually need to be fixed. Note that a laboratory is paid to evaluate a product and determine the truth. If the product does not meet its claims, then there are basically two choices: fix the product or change (reduce) the claims.

It is important to discuss with customers what they want before beginning a formal ST evaluation; an ST that includes functional or assurance requirements not truly needed by customers will be unnecessarily expensive to evaluate, and an ST that omits necessary requirements may not be acceptable to the customers (because that necessary piece will not have been evaluated). PPs identify such requirements, but make sure that the PP accurately reflects the customer's real requirements (perhaps the customer only wants a part of the functionality or assurance in the PP, or has a different environment in mind, or wants something else instead for the situations where your product will be used). Note that an ST need not include every security feature in a product; an ST only states what will be (or has been) evaluated. A product that has a higher EAL rating is not necessarily more secure than a similar product with a lower rating or no rating; the environment might be different, the evaluation may have saved money and time by not evaluating the other product at a higher level, or perhaps the evaluation missed something important. Evaluations are not proofs; they simply impose a defined minimum bar to gain confidence in the requirements or product.

## Visa Cardholder Information Security Program (CISP)

In April 2000, Visa announced the launch of its Cardholder Information Security Program (CISP); it was launched in June 2001. CISP defines a standard of due care for securing Visa cardholder data, wherever it is located, and CISP compliance is required of all entities storing, processing, or transmitting Visa cardholder data. Members must comply with CISP and are responsible for ensuring the compliance of their merchants and agents—whether they support issuing or acquiring activity—for all payment channels, including retail (brick-and-mortar), mail/telephone-order, and e-commerce.

There are 12 basic security requirements with which all Visa payment system constituents need to comply:

1. Install and maintain a working firewall to protect data.
2. Keep security patches up to date.
3. Protect stored data.
4. Encrypt data sent across public networks.
5. Use and regularly update antivirus software.
6. Restrict access by "need to know."
7. Assign unique ID to each person with computer access.
8. Do not use vendor-supplied defaults for passwords and security parameters.
9. Track all access to data by unique ID.
10. Regularly test security systems and processes.
11. Implement and maintain an information security policy.
12. Restrict physical access to data.

Since its launch, CISP has been supported by ever-expanding operating regulations. The CISP requirements help Visa members, merchants, and service providers protect their information assets and meet the obligations to the Visa payment structure by doing the following:

- providing assurance to customers that their financial information is safe.
- minimizing the threats to an organization's financial stability and goodwill that can result from a compromise of data
- assessing fines, restrictions, and other penalties in the event of noncompliance

## GLOSSARY

**Act** a statute passed by a legislature or a planned statute that a legislature has not yet enacted.

**Asset** The organizational resource that is being protected. An asset can be logical, such as a Web site of information owned or controlled by the organization, or it can be physical, such as a computer system or another tangible object.

**Asset Valuation** The process of assigning financial value to each asset.

**Attack** An act that is an intentional or unintentional attempt to compromise the information and/or the systems that support it.

**Best Practices** Procedures that provide a superior level of security for an organization's information.

**Computer Security Institute (CSI)** An organization that focuses on information protection, especially policy development, risk analysis, and security awareness (http://www.gocsi.com)

**Contingency Planning** The program developed to prepare for, react to, and recover from events that threaten the security of the information assets of an organization.

**Denial of Service (DoS)**   An attack type in which the abuser sends a large number of connection or information requests to overwhelm and cripple a target.

**Distributed Denial of Service (DDoS)**   An attack type in which a coordinated stream of connection requests is launched against a target from many locations at the same time.

**Exploit**   A technique used to compromise a system.

**Firewall**   A dedicated computer that interfaces with computers outside a network and has special security precautions built into it to protect sensitive information on computers inside the network. All traffic to and from the network passes through the firewall, so that unauthorized data can be blocked.

**Hacker**   A person who uses and creates computer software for enjoyment or to gain access to information illegally.

**Incident**   An attack on an organization's information assets.

**Information Security**   The protection of information and the systems and hardware that use, store, and transmit the information.

**Information System**   The entire set of software, hardware, data, people, and procedures necessary to use information as a resource in the organization.

**Intruder**   An individual who gains or attempts to gain unauthorized access to a computer system or to gain unauthorized privileges on that system.

**Laws**   Rules adopted for determining expected behavior in modern society and drawn from ethics.

**Liability**   The legal obligation of an entity that includes responsibility for a wrongful act and the legal obligation to make restitution.

**Malicious Code**   Software designed to damage, destroy, or deny service to a target system.

**Privacy**   The state of being free from unauthorized observation.

**Quantitative Assessment**   The evaluation of an organization's assets, estimated values, and formulas.

**Risk**   The probability that something can happen.

**Risk Assessment**   The analysis of a danger so as to assign a risk rating or score to an information asset.

**Risk Management**   The process of identifying vulnerabilities in an organization's information system and taking steps to assure its confidentiality, integrity, and availability.

**Security**   To be protected from adversaries—from those who would do harm, intentionally or otherwise.

**Standards**   Detailed statements of actions that comply with policy.

**Threat**   An object, person, or other entity that represents a danger to an asset.

**Virus**   Software that attaches itself to another program that can cause damage when the host program is activated.

**Vulnerability**   Weakness or fault in a system or protection mechanism that exposes information to attack or damage.

**Worm**   Program that can replicate itself and send copies from computer to computer across network connections. Upon arrival the worm may be activated to replicate and propagate again. In addition to propagation, the worm usually performs some unwanted function.

## CROSS REFERENCES

See *Hackers, Crackers and Computer Criminals; Network Attacks; Risk Management for IT Security*.

## REFERENCES

Baer, W. S. (2003). Rewarding IT security in the marketplace. *Contemporary Security Policy*. pp. 4.

Clark, D. L. (2002). *Enterprise security: The manager's defense guide*. Boston: Addison-Wesley.

Drouin, D. (2004). *Cyber risk insurance, A Discourse and Preparatory Guide*. SANS Institute. Retrieved from http://www.sans.org/rr/papers/index.php?id=1412

Geer, D. E. (1998, November). Risk management is where the money is. *The Risk Digest: Forum on Risks to the Public in Computers and Related Systems*, The Risk Digest, Forum on Risks to the Public in Computers and Related Systems. Retreived from http://catless.ncl.ac.uk/Risks/20.06.htm

Gordon, L. A., Loeb, M. P., & Sohail, T. (2003, March). A framework for using insurance for cyber-risk management. *Communications of the ACM, 46*, 81.

Hammesfahr, R. W. (2002). *@Risk version 2.0*. London: Reactions Publishing.

McNamee D. (1996). *Assessing risk asssessment*.

Power, R. (2004, January). 2004 CSI/FBI Computer Crime and Security Survey. *Computer Society Issues and Trends, 8*(1).

Tulloch, M. (2003). *Microsoft encyclopedia of security*. Redmond, WA: Microsoft Press.

Visa. (2001). *Cardholder information security program*. Retrieved from http://usa.visa.com/business/accepting_visa/ops_risk_management/cisp.html

Whitman, M. E., & Mattord, H. J. (2003). *Principles of information security*. Thompson Publishing, Boston, MA, USA.

# Auditing Information Systems Security

S. Rao Vallabhaneni, *SRV Professional Publications*

# WHY AUDIT INFORMATION SYSTEMS AND SECURITY?

This section presents the criteria for auditing information systems (IS) and their security. It includes a brief discussion of government laws, directives, and regulations; professional auditing standards; risks and exposures, including computer crime and fraud; and good business practices.

## Government Laws, Directives, and Regulations: The Sarbanes-Oxley Act of 2002

Laws, directives, and regulations exist to protect consumers, industries, and the society as a whole. Many laws and regulations affect information systems and their security. Here, we discuss the Sarbanes-Oxley Act of 2002; other laws and regulations are presented in the Appendix. This Act has had a significant impact on the audit profession.

### Overview

As a result of recent corporate scandals resulting from management's lack of integrity, management fraud, accounting firms' negligence, and questionable use of earnings management techniques, both investors and creditors have lost confidence in corporate America. In light of this financial crisis and credibility gap, the U.S. Congress passed the Sarbanes-Oxley Act of 2002 to reform the accounting profession and corporate management and governance.

Essentially, the Act creates a five-member Public Company Accounting Oversight Board (PCAOB), which has the authority to set and enforce auditing, attestation, quality control, and ethics (including independence) standards for auditors of public companies. It also is empowered to inspect the auditing operations of public accounting firms that audit public companies and to impose disciplinary and remedial sanctions for violations of its rules, securities laws, and professional auditing and accounting standards.

Other provisions affecting the accounting profession include requiring the rotation of the lead audit partner and reviewing the audit partner every 5 years and extending the statute of limitations for the discovery of fraud to 2 years from the date of discovery and 5 years after the act. The law restricts the consulting work that auditors can perform for their publicly traded audit clients and establishes harsh penalties for securities law violations, corporate fraud, and document shredding. Fines range from $100,000 for individual negligent conduct to $15 million for a firm for knowing or intentional conduct, including recklessness and repeated acts of negligence.

The Act also requires CEOs and CFOs to certify their company's financial statements as part of the annual report to stockholders. They also have a greater duty to communicate and coordinate with corporate audit committees who are now responsible for hiring, compensating, and overseeing the independent auditors. There are new requirements regarding enhanced financial disclosures as well.

### Provisions of the Act

Those sections of the Act that apply to IS auditors are Sections 301, 302, 404, and 409. Section 301 focuses on public company audit committees. Section 302 deals with quarterly CEO/CFO certification of financial statements and disclosure controls. Section 404 addresses annual evaluation of internal controls over financial reporting. Section 409 focuses on real-time issuer disclosure requirements. Sections 404 and 409 are addressed below in more detail.

Section 404 of the Act requires the IT auditor to document and test the effectiveness of internal controls over IT and computer application systems. The scope of this review includes general computer controls, application controls, and systems software controls. Specifically, it can include security controls, a disaster recovery and business continuity plan, and IT infrastructure. Compliance with Section 404 requires companies to establish an infrastructure designed to protect and preserve vital records and data from destruction, loss, unauthorized alteration, or other misuse. This infrastructure is designed to ensure there is no room for the unauthorized alteration of records vital to maintaining the integrity of data and availability of business processes. Because CEOs and CFOs need to certify the financial statements, it is more important to ensure the integrity of financial data and availability of financial systems. The documentation effort should not be viewed as a sunk cost; instead it should be treated as a return on investment yielding a decreased reputation cost.

Note that Section 404 substantially increases the role and importance of IS auditors in the audit; whereas before internal controls over transaction cycles (e.g., sales and collection cycle) were performed on a rotational basis, now all controls over all cycles must be tested every year.

Section 409 of the Act requires that the issuer (firm) disclose to the public on a rapid and current basis additional information concerning material changes in their financial condition or operations, in plain English. Such information may include trend and qualitative information and graphic presentations. The purpose of the section is to require firms to inform investors in a timely, clear, and easier manner.

### Professional Auditing Standards

In the United States, audits are conducted according to the professional standards promulgated by the respective professional associations, including the American Institute of Certified Public Accountants (AICPA), the Institute of Internal Auditors (IIA), the U.S. Government Accounting Office (USGAO), and the Information Systems Audit and Control Association (ISACA). These standards require auditors to review the IS function just as they do with any

other business function, such as manufacturing, marketing, accounting and finance, and human resources. Auditing IS security is part of the IT audit. Auditors are bound by the standards issued by these associations. Violation of the standards or not adhering to them can lead to legal actions and loss of professional credentials issued by the associations. Note that the PCAOB is taking over the role of promulgating auditing standards as a result of the Sarbanes-Oxley Act.

### Risks and Exposures, Including Computer Crime and Fraud

Auditors are required to report to management actual or potential risks and exposures facing their organizations. Many risks and exposures exist in IT, including risks to hardware, to applications and data, and to operations. Examples of risks to hardware include natural disasters, such as flood and fire; blackouts and brownouts; and vandalism. Examples of risks to application and data include theft of information, data alteration and destruction, and Web site defacement. Examples of risks to IT operations include denial of service and spoofing. Examples of computer crime and fraud include data diddling, use of the salami technique, data leakage, computer viruses, and logic/time bombs. Security controls can reduce or eliminate these risks and exposures.

### Good Business Practices

It is good business practice to audit the IS function similar to any other business function. In fact, it is more important to audit the IS function because many other business functions depend on it. Most business functions are now automated, and this, in turn, increases the concentration of risks and exposures in the IS function. This is similar to putting all eggs in one basket.

## WHAT IS THE SCOPE OF THE INFORMATION SECURITY AUDIT?

This section discusses the scope of an information security audit, which varies from organization to organization. The six audit areas and the scope of each are presented below:

1. Information Protection Audit: review of logical access controls, user identification and authentication methods, and cryptographic techniques.

2. Telecommunications and Computer Network Audit: review of network security policies and practices, network attacks, and security in e-mail.

3. Application System Development, Acquisition, and Maintenance Audit: review of system development methodology, system acquisition process, system maintenance policies and practices, and system development project management controls.

4. Information Systems Operations Audit: review of problem and change management system, capacity management and service levels, system performance metrics, and hardware maintenance policies and practices.

5. Disaster Recovery and Business Continuity Audit: review of business impact analysis, contingency

strategies, application system priorities, backup and recovery alternatives, and participating in contingency test exercises.

6. Physical Security Audit: review of access to equipment, buildings, data centers, offices, mobile and portable computers, and network servers, as well as environmental controls (dust, heat, humidity, and air conditioning).

# WHO PERFORMS THE INFORMATION SYSTEMS SECURITY AUDITS?

This section focuses on the types of auditors available in the private and public sector and their roles and responsibilities in conducting these audits. It also presents the types of audits performed by these auditors.

## Types of Auditors Available

External auditors, internal auditors, and government auditors can perform the IS security audits in addition to other audits. They all do audit work differently based on their organization's mission, charter, and professional standards.

### External Auditors

External auditors perform external auditing, which is defined as a systematic process of (1) objectively obtaining and evaluating evidence regarding assertions about economic actions and events to ascertain the degree of correspondence between those assertions and established criteria and (2) communicating the audit results to interested parties.

External auditing work is conducted by independent, public accountants working for a private organization, using professional standards and complying with generally accepted auditing standards. Basically, external auditors perform financial audit work. The audit report is the auditor's formal means of communicating to interested parties a conclusion about the audited financial statements. External auditors are bound by the Professional Standards issued by AICPA, PCAOB, and the Financial Accounting Standards Board (FASB).

### Internal Auditors

Internal auditors perform internal auditing, which is defined as an independent, objective assurance and consulting activity designed to add value and improve an organization's operations. This activity helps an organization accomplish its objectives by bringing a systematic, disciplined approach to the evaluation and improvement of the effectiveness of risk management, control, and governance processes.

Internal auditing work is conducted by internal auditors working for an organization who are bound by the Professional Standards established by IIA. Esssentially, internal auditors perform operational audit work.

### Government Auditors

Government auditors perform government auditing in local, state, or federal governmental agencies. They conduct financial and nonfinancial audit work. Government auditors adhere to separate auditing standards issued by the USGAO. They are bound by the laws, regulations, and directives issued by various agencies.

## Types of Audits Performed

Audits performed by external, internal, or government auditors can be divided into two categories: financial and nonfinancial. The four types of nonfinancial audits are (1) operational audits, (2) compliance audits, (3) information technology audits, and (4) performance and program audits. Each type of audit is presented next.

Basically, *financial audits* focus on balance sheets and income statements, the two primary outputs of the financial reporting process. The statement of cash flows and retained earnings is also produced during the financial reporting process. External auditors perform financial audits.

An *operational audit* determines whether the entity is managing and utilizing its resources economically and efficiently. To gain the auditee's cooperation, it is good to allow the auditee to participate in the development of recommendations for improvement. Mostly, internal auditors perform operational audits.

An operational review ensures the following:

- reliability and integrity of information;
- compliance with policies, plans, procedures, laws, and regulations;
- safeguarding of assets (e.g., inventories);
- economical and efficient use of resources; and
- accomplishment of established objectives and goals for operations or programs.

One objective of operational auditing is most likely to be the determination of cost. Other operational auditing objectives include determining (1) whether purchasing management procures the right materials at the right time in the right quantities at the right price, (2) that proper measures of performance are used for a governmental agency providing service to the citizens, and (3) whether the marketing department has the organizational status needed to accomplish its objectives and operations in a manner that is cost beneficial to the company.

A *compliance audit* determines whether the entity complies with laws and regulations. External auditors, internal auditors, and governmental auditors perform compliance audits. Examples of compliance audit objectives include (1) determining whether expenditure of restricted funds at a government-supported university should be approved; (2) evaluating the propriety of the accounting for and use of customer deposits at a public utility; (3) determining whether purchases are approved at the proper level of authorization on the basis of dollar amount, as designated by company policy; and (4) determining whether employee benefit programs are operating in accordance with corporate policy and government regulations.

An *information technology audit* determines the security, availability, and integrity of information systems processing and the data they generate along with computer operations and telecommunications. External auditors, internal auditors, and government auditors perform IT audits in addition to other audits. They are bound by the Professional Standards issued by AICPA, PCAOB, IIA, USGAO, and ISACA. The ISACA specializes in the IT auditing field.

Government auditors in the public sector primarily conduct *performance and program audits*. Performance audits are similar to operational audits conducted by auditors in the private sector. According to the 1994 U.S. GAO's Government Auditing Standards, a performance audit is an objective and systematic examination of evidence for the purpose of providing an independent assessment of the performance of an existing or proposed government organization, program, or activity in order to provide useful information to improve public accountability and decision-making. Performance audits generally focus on efficiency and effectiveness, with an emphasis on effectiveness. Program audits focus on achieving program goals.

# WHAT IS THE AUDIT PROCESS?

Auditors use a systematic process or methodology to conduct audits in the field. This section discusses audit tasks starting with audit planning and ending with audit reporting. The audit process can be broken down into four phases or stages.

## Phase 1. Audit Planning

The audit plan is driven by the risk the organization faces either at the present time or in the future. The audit function identifies potential auditable areas within the organization; each audit area is then labeled as high, medium, or low risk using a risk assessment methodology. High-risk audit areas are reviewed first, followed by medium or low-risk areas depending on the audit resources available. The output of the audit planning is a list of auditable areas for the forthcoming year.

A written audit plan should be prepared for each auditable area and is essential to conducting audits efficiently and effectively. The form and content of the written audit plan vary among audits. The plan generally should include an audit work program and a memorandum or other appropriate documentation of key decisions regarding the objectives, scope, and methodology of the audit and of the auditors' basis for those decisions.

Documenting the audit plan provides the opportunity for the auditors to review the work done in planning the audit to determine whether (1) the proposed audit objectives are likely to result in a useful report, (2) the proposed audit scope and methodology are adequate to satisfy the audit objectives promptly, and (3) sufficient staff and other resources have been made available to perform the audit.

## Phase 2. Audit Fieldwork

During the fieldwork phase, auditors collect evidence to support their findings, conclusions, and recommendations. Two types of evidence exist: audit evidence and legal evidence. Legal evidence includes best evidence, secondary evidence, direct evidence, circumstantial evidence, conclusive evidence, corroborative evidence, opinion evidence, and hearsay evidence. Legal evidence is used in forensic work. There are seven types of audit evidence.

## Types of Audit Evidence

In deciding which audit procedures to use, there are seven broad categories of evidence from which the auditor can choose: physical examination, confirmation, documentation, observation, inquiry, reperformance, and analytical procedures. One or more of these categories are used in gathering and testing the audit evidence. Where applicable, examples are given for both the financial and computer environments because they become interrelated during a financial audit.

*Physical examination* is the inspection or count by the auditor of a tangible asset (e.g., inventory, cash, securities). The IS auditor can do a physical inspection of computer equipment, such as terminals, microcomputers, and printers.

*Confirmation* describes the receipt of a written response from an independent third party verifying the accuracy of information that was requested by the auditor. For example, the IS auditor would be involved in selecting a sample of accounts receivable from an accounts receivable master file maintained on the computer.

*Documentation* is the auditor's examination of documents and records to substantiate the information that is or should be included in the financial statements. Some document examples are customer orders, shipping documents, and sales invoices. Documents can be conveniently classified as internal and external. Some examples of internal documents are employee time cards and reports and inventory receiving reports. Vendors' invoices and insurance policies are two examples of external documents.

The primary determinant of the auditor's willingness to accept a document as reliable evidence is whether it is generated internally or externally. If internal, the auditor should determine whether it was created and processed under conditions of a good internal control structure. Internal documents created and processed under conditions of a weak internal control structure may not constitute reliable evidence. Usually, external documents are regarded as more reliable evidence than internal ones. For example, the IS auditor needs to make sure that the computer-based payroll system is processing all employee time card data in a proper, secure, and controlled manner. Similarly, he or she must ensure that the computer-based accounts payable system is processing all vendor invoices in a proper, secure, and controlled manner.

*Observation* is the use of the senses to assess certain activities. For example, the financial auditor may tour the plant to obtain a general impression of the facilities, observe whether equipment is rusty to evaluate obsolescence, and watch individuals perform accounting tasks to determine whether the person assigned a responsibility is actually performing it. Observation is rarely sufficient by itself; it is often supplemented by other corroborative evidence. Similarly, the IS auditor observes the cleanliness of equipment and general housekeeping procedures when touring the computer room.

*Inquiry* is the process of obtaining written or oral information from the auditee in response to questions from the auditor. Inquiry cannot be regarded as conclusive because the information obtained is not from an independent source and may be biased in the auditee's favor. Therefore, it is normally necessary to obtain further corroborating evidence through other procedures. For example, the financial auditor may ask the client's accounting management how the internal control structure records and controls accounting transactions. Later, the auditor performs tests of transactions to determine whether the transactions are recorded and authorized in the manner stated. Similarly, the IS auditor may ask both accounting and IS management how the computer system controls and processes the accounting transactions and then may test such assertions.

The IS auditor needs to understand both manual and automated parts of the system before explaining to the financial auditor how the total system works. Then, actual testing of controls and procedures can be split, with the financial auditor performing manual testing and the IS auditor doing the computer system testing. However, breaking the inquiry activity into manual and computer system is not meaningful initially because of the highly integrated nature of online and database application systems. If inquiry about the manual part is left solely to the financial auditor, he or she may not ask the right questions or may not understand how the manual activities interface with automated activities.

*Reperformance*, the testing of mathematical accuracy, involves rechecking a sample of the computations and transfers of information made by the client during the period under audit. Rechecking of computations includes such procedures as extending sales invoices and inventory, adding journals and subsidiary ledgers, and checking the calculation of depreciation expense and prepaid expenses. Often, these activities are called reperformance procedures. The IS auditor can test the mechanical accuracy of computations with the use of computer audit software for mathematical extensions or through the footing and cross-footing of certain data fields in a data file of interest to the financial auditor.

*Analytical procedures* use comparisons and relationships to determine whether account balances appear reasonable. An example is comparing the gross margin percent in the current year with that in preceding years. Another example is comparing the current period's total repair expense with a previous year's expense and investigating the difference, if material, to determine its cause. Analytical procedures should be performed early in the audit to aid in deciding which accounts do not need further verification, and which audit areas should be more thoroughly investigated. The IS auditor can support the financial auditor in selecting the financial audit accounts of interest from computer data files and can perform analytical comparisons using computer audit software.

### Standards of Audit Evidence

All audit evidence should meet the standards of sufficiency, competence, and relevance. Evidence is sufficient if it is based on facts and is in appropriate quantity (e.g., sample size). Competent evidence is reliable evidence. Relevance refers to the relationship of the information to its use. When audit evidence does not meet these three

standards, additional (corroborative) evidence is required before expressing an audit opinion.

## Phase 3. Audit Assessment

Audit assessment involves testing and evaluating the audit evidence through the performance of independent tests. Two types of audit tests exist: compliance and substantive. *Compliance testing (tests of control)* provides auditors with evidence concerning whether internal controls are in place and policies and procedures are operating effectively. *Substantive testing* provides auditors with evidence about the validity and propriety of the accounting treatment of transactions and balances. Both compliance and substantive tests have inherent sampling risks.

Compliance test sampling risks result from (1) an overreliance on controls indicating that the sample results support the auditor's planned degree of reliance upon the control when the true compliance rate does not justify such a conclusion and (2) an underreliance on controls indicating that the sample results do not support the planned degree of reliance on the control when the true compliance rate supports such reliance.

Compliance reviews and/or tests as they relate to the IS environment determine the following:

- whether passwords are changed periodically,
- whether a disaster recovery plan was tested,
- whether program changes are approved,
- whether system logs are reviewed, and
- whether controls are functioning as prescribed.

Substantive test sampling risks result from (1) an incorrect acceptance that the sample supports the conclusion that the recorded amount is not materially misstated when it is materially misstated and (2) an incorrect rejection that the sample supports the conclusion that the recorded amount is materially misstated when it is not.

Some examples of substantive reviews and/or tests as they relate to the IS environment include the following: (1) conducting system outage analysis, (2) performing system storage media analysis, (3) comparing book computer inventory to actual count, (4) conducting system availability analysis, and (5) reconciling account balances.

Compliance reviews and/or tests determine the degree to which substantive reviews and/or tests may be limited. Strong controls revealed in the compliance review can limit the need for substantive review.

## Phase 4. Audit Reporting

An audit report is a tangible product (output) of the audit work. It is a communication tool to inform all the affected parties in the organization about the audit work that was just completed. The content and format of audit reports vary between internal and external auditors because of their different responsibilities.

Written audit reports serve multiple purposes. Reports communicate the results of the audit work to auditees and others, make the results less susceptible to misunderstanding, and facilitate follow-up reviews to determine whether appropriate corrective actions have been taken (USGAO, 1994).

To be of maximum use, the report must be timely. A carefully prepared report may be of little value to decision makers if it arrives too late. Therefore, the audit organization should plan for the prompt issuance of the audit report and conduct the audit with this goal in mind.

The auditors should consider interim reporting, during the audit, of significant matters to appropriate auditees. Such communication, which may be oral or written, is not a substitute for a final written report, but it does alert auditees to matters needing immediate attention and allows them to correct problems before the final report is completed.

Summary reports highlighting audit results may be appropriate for levels of management above the auditee. They may be issued separately from or in conjunction with the final report.

The contents of the audit report should include some if not all of the following: objectives, scope, and methodology; audit findings, conclusions, and recommendations; compliance with standards, regulations, and laws; management (auditee's) responses; and auditee's noteworthy accomplishments. For example, the independent (external) auditor's report on financial statements does not include management response, which is discussed later.

Audit findings have often been characterized as containing the elements of criteria, condition, and effect, as well as cause when problems are found (USGAO, 1994). However, the elements needed for a finding depend entirely on the objectives of the audit. This means that the elements "cause" and "effect" may be optional for a compliance audit, but are a must for an operational audit. Thus, a finding or set of findings is complete to the extent that the audit objectives are satisfied and the report clearly relates those objectives to the finding's elements. A deficiency finding should have four elements or attributes– criteria, condition, cause, and effect—with recommendations being optional. The audit report should be complete, accurate, objective, convincing, and as clear and concise as the subject permits.

The final report should be distributed first to auditees directly interested in the audit work results and those responsible for acting on its findings and recommendations. Higher-level members in the organization may receive only a summary report. Reports may also be distributed to other interested or affected parties, such as external auditors and the board of directors.

Certain information may not be appropriate for disclosure to all report recipients, because it is privileged, proprietary, or related to improper or illegal acts. Such information, however, may be disclosed in a separate report. If the conditions being reported involve senior management, report distribution should only extend to the board of the organization.

Written summary reports are generally intended for high-level management and/or the audit committee. On the other hand, a detailed audit report dealing with a payroll department with significant control weaknesses would be most useful to the payroll department manager.

In some circumstances, it might be appropriate for auditors to issue oral reports. If they do so, the auditors should keep a written record of what they communicated and the basis for not issuing a written report. An oral report may be most appropriate when emergency action is needed. Before issuing an oral report, auditors should determine that both of the following conditions exist: (1) an oral report would effectively meet decision makers' needs for information about the results of the audit and (2) it is unlikely that parties other than those who would receive the oral report would have a significant interest in the results of the audit.

## WHAT IS THE MANAGEMENT'S RESPONSE TO THE AUDIT RESULTS?

The internal audit report includes audit results labeled as findings (problems) and recommendations (solutions). Management needs to decide whether to accept or reject the auditor's findings and recommendations. If management accepts some or all of the findings, they have a responsibility to submit a corrective action plan to correct the problems identified in the audit report. If management decides to reject some or all of the findings, management assumes the responsibility for not taking corrective action and the resulting risks. The external auditor's report presents findings, not necessarily recommendations.

One of the most effective ways to ensure that a report is fair, complete, and objective is to obtain advance review and comments from responsible management and others, as may be appropriate. By including the views of the auditees, a report shows not only what was found and what the auditors think about it but also what the responsible persons think about it and what they plan to do about it.

Auditors should normally request that the responsible auditees' views on significant findings, conclusions, and recommendations that adversely affect the audited entity be submitted in writing. When written comments cannot be obtained, oral comments should be requested.

Advance comments should be evaluated and recognized objectively, as appropriate, in the report. A promise or plan for corrective action should be noted, but should not be accepted as justification for dropping a significant finding or a related recommendation.

When the comments oppose the report's findings, conclusions, or recommendations and are not, in the auditors' opinion, valid, the auditors may choose to state their reasons for rejecting them. Conversely, the auditors should modify their report if they find the comments valid.

## AUDIT OBJECTIVES, AUDIT WORK PROGRAMS, AND AUDIT TOOLS AND TECHNIQUES

Before discussing audit objectives, one needs to understand control objectives because both audit objectives and control objectives should be aligned with each other. Control objectives provide the basis for the audit work.

A control, in general, is any action taken by management that would result in the accomplishment of the organization's goals, objectives, and mission. Controls also reduce or eliminate risks and exposures. *Control objectives* are management's intentions of what controls should be accomplishing to enable organizational goals to be achieved. Control practices and procedures help achieve the desired control objectives, which are aimed at preventing, detecting, and correcting errors, irregularities, and omissions occurring in IS and functional business areas.

Control practices can also help the auditor in understanding the control concerns and estimating the consequences of a lack of adequate controls. This awareness can provide the basis for recommendations to management about strengthening overall internal controls. The auditor may note that a single control practice or procedure may affect more than one control objective.

There are several detailed IS control objectives that an internal control structure must meet to prevent, detect, and correct errors, omissions, irregularities, and computer intrusions, such as viruses and worms, and to recover from such activities to ensure continuity of business operations. Here, the term "system" includes hardware, data, software, people, documentation, and the associated procedures, whether manual or automated. Next, 17 system control objectives are presented.

1. **System assets are safeguarded.** An organization's technology assets and resources, such as computer facilities, computer equipment, people, programs, and data, are to be safeguarded at all times to minimize waste and loss.

2. **System functionality is assured.** The computer-based application system supports business needs and the system's requirements for the maintenance of data confidentiality, integrity, and availability.

3. **System assurance is provided.** The computer system provides confidence to the user/customer of the system as to how well the functionality has been implemented. Assurance is a combination of correctness and effectiveness of the system functions.

4. **Software safety is guaranteed.** The objective is to develop and maintain the software correctly to protect against failure of the software. The software must have provisions to mitigate the consequences of its failure. For example, airline and medical systems should protect human life and prevent bodily injuries resulting from unsafe code in the computer system.

5. **System reliability is assured.** The objectives are to ensure that the hardware, software, and data are stable and that people can be trusted to carry out the organization's mission.

6. **System serviceability is provided.** The objective is to correct hardware and software problems in a timely manner to meet service-level guidelines.

7. **System security is assured.** An organization's assets and information resources are to be protected from unauthorized access and use.

8. **Data integrity is maintained.** Integrity deals with controls over how data are entered, communicated, processed, stored, and reported. The objective is to ensure that data are authorized, complete, accurate, consistent, and timely.

9. **System availability is assured.** The objective is to ensure that the system (hardware, software, and data) and its components are available when they are needed, where they are needed, and for whom they are needed.

10. **System confidentiality is assured.** The objective is to ensure that sensitive data are disclosed only to authorized people.

11. **System controllability is maintained.** Adequate manual and automated controls and procedures regarding hardware, software, data, and people should be available.

12. **System maintainability is assured.** The system, which includes hardware and software, should be maintained with existing resources at minimum cost and time.

13. **System auditability is provided.** The objective is to develop a chronological record of system activities that is sufficient to enable the reconstruction, review, and examination of the sequence of activities (i.e., audit trail).

14. **System usability is assured.** For example, the application system is appropriately user friendly, or the system design invites rather than inhibits the authorized user.

15. **System effectiveness is ensured.** System effectiveness is measured by determining that the system performs the intended functions and that users get the information they need in the right form and in a timely fashion.

16. **System economy and efficiency are maintained.** An economical and efficient system uses the minimum number of information resources to achieve the output level that the system's users require. Economy and efficiency must always be considered in the context of system effectiveness.

17. **System quality is maintained.** This is an overall goal. In addition to the above 16 objectives, the computer system should have built-in quality-related features, such as testability, portability, convertability, modifiability, readability, reliability, reusability, structuredness, consistency, understandability, and, above all, adequate documentation.

Auditors develop audit work programs and identify audit tools and techniques needed during the audit work. Audit work programs are the detailed audit procedures intended solely for the auditor's use. An audit program serves as a road map for the auditor. It lists the types of audit steps to be performed and evidence to be collected in order to determine whether audit objectives are met. The audit work program focuses on reviewing major activities and identifying key controls within and around such activities. It also includes the audit tools and techniques to be used during the audit work.

Manual audit tools and techniques include observations, interviews, checklists, inquiries, meetings, and questionnaires. In addition, use of computer-assisted audit tools and techniques should be explored to analyze data for trends, patterns, and anomalies.

For each of the six auditable areas discussed earlier in the section on the scope of the audit report, audit objectives are presented below to help nonauditors understand the nature and extent of the auditors' work.

### Audit Area 1. Information Protection Audit Objectives

1. Ensure that logical access controls are in place and are working as intended.
2. Ensure that data integrity and availability controls are established and maintained properly.
3. Ensure that user identification and authentication methods are current and are achieving their intended control objectives.
4. Ensure that key management practices are proper in the cryptographic and encryption methods.

### Audit Area 2. Telecommunications and Computer Network Audit Objectives

1. Ensure that controls over telecommunications software and hardware provide reasonable assurance that messages and transactions are secure, accounted for, and error free.
2. Ensure that network security and e-mail security policies and practices are adequate to prevent network attacks and computer fraud and/or to detect unauthorized transactions and users.
3. Ensure that controls over changes to telecommunications software are adequate and that backup and recovery controls ensure business continuity of online transactions and services.

### Audit Area 3. Application System Development, Acquisition, and Maintenance Audit Objectives

1. Ensure that application system integrity is established during its development, acquisition, and maintenance.
2. Ensure that appropriate security controls and audit trails are designed and built into the application system during its development or acquisition.

### Audit Area 4. Information Systems Operations Audit Objectives

1. Ensure that controls over problems and the change management system are adequate and are working properly.
2. Ensure that computer capacity is managed properly and that service levels to users are appropriate to the functional user needs.
3. Analyze system performance metrics to identify trends and patterns for improvement.
4. Ensure that operations management is adhering to hardware maintenance policies and that its practices are economical, efficient, and effective.

### Audit Area 5. Disaster Recovery and Business Continuity Audit Objectives

1. Ensure that business operations can be resumed normally after a disaster has occurred using backup programs and data.

2. Ensure that production work or customer service work continues properly without severe interruption or disruption.
3. Ensure that the entire contingency plan testing methodology is documented and communicated to all affected parties for learning and educational purposes.

### Audit Area 6. Physical Security Audit Objectives

1. Ensure that proper physical security devices and controls are in place and are working as intended.
2. Ensure that environmental controls over heat, humidity, and air conditioning are maintained according to vendor-suggested guidelines and are periodically tested for accuracy.

## CONCLUSIONS

Auditing the IS function and its security is similar to auditing any other business function, such as manufacturing, marketing, human resources, accounting, and finance. The work of the auditors benefits the organization because they try to uncover problems, suggest solutions, identify risks, suggest controls to reduce risks, pinpoint operationally inefficient and ineffective policies and practices, and recommend remedial actions. In this regard, auditors are supposed to think and act as the eyes and ears of senior management.

## GLOSSARY

**Audit Evidence**  A collection of documents, data, and information to support audit findings, conclusions, and recommendations.

**Audit Objectives**  Organizational goals that an auditor is planning to accomplish in the audit.

**Audit Planning**  A written plan that is essential to conducting audits efficiently and effectively.

**Audit Reporting**  A tangible product (output) of the audit work.

**Audit Tests**  Independent tests performed by auditors to confirm audit evidence.

**Audit Tools and Techniques**  Manual or automated approaches to conduct the audit in an efficient and effective manner.

**Audit Work Programs**  Documented audit work steps or procedures, which guide the auditor during the audit.

**Compliance Audits**  The scope of work includes determining whether an organization is complying with laws and regulations.

**Control Objectives**  Management's intentions of what controls should be accomplishing to achieve organizational goals and audit objectives.

**Data Diddling**  This involves hanging data before or during input to computers or during output from a computer system.

**External Auditors**  Audit professionals working for public accounting firms who primarily conduct financial audits.

**Financial Audits**  The scope of work includes review of the balance sheets and income statements of an organization.

**Government Auditors** Audit professionals working for local, state, or federal governmental agencies performing financial, operational, compliance, IT audits, and performance and program audits.

**Information Technology Audits** The scope of work includes determining the adequacy and effectiveness of security, and the availability and integrity of information systems.

**Internal Auditors** Audit professionals working for private firms who primarily conduct operational audits.

**Operational Audits** The scope of work includes review of business functions and operations for efficiency and effectiveness.

**Performance and Program Audits** The scope of work includes focusing on efficiency and effectiveness of governmental programs and activities.

**Salami Technique** Theft of small amounts of assets (primarily money) from a number of sources (e.g., bank accounts).

# APPENDIX: GOVERNMENT LAWS, DIRECTIVES, AND REGULATIONS
## The Clinger-Cohen Act of 1996

The Clinger-Cohen Act of 1996 is intended to improve the productivity, efficiency, and effectiveness of U.S. federal programs through the improved acquisition, use, and disposal of IT resources. Among other provisions, the law (1) encourages federal agencies to evaluate and adopt best management and acquisition practices used by both private and public sector organizations; (2) requires agencies to base decisions about IT investments on quantitative and qualitative factors associated with the costs, benefits, and risks of those investments and to use performance data to demonstrate how well the IT expenditures support improvements to agency programs through such measurements as reduced costs, improved employee productivity, and higher customer satisfaction; and (3) requires executive agencies to appoint CIOs to carry out the IT management provisions of the act and the broader information resources management requirements of the Paperwork Reduction Act. The Clinger-Cohen Act also streamlines the IT acquisition process by eliminating the General Services Administration's central acquisition authority, placing procurement responsibility directly with federal agencies and encouraging the adoption of smaller, modular IT acquisition projects.

## U.S. Computer Security Act of 1987

The U.S. Computer Security Act of 1987 requires federal agencies to identify sensitive systems, conduct computer security training, and develop computer security plans. The Act, which focuses on protecting computer-related assets, requires the following:

- identification by federal agencies of existing systems and new systems under development that contain sensitive information,
- development of a security plan for each identified sensitive computer system, and

- mandatory periodic training in computer security awareness and accepted computer security practice for all employees involved with the management, use, or operation of federal computer systems within or under the supervision of a federal agency.

The Computer Security Act of 1987 addresses the importance of ensuring and improving the security and privacy of sensitive information in the U.S. federal computer systems. It requires that the National Institute of Standards and Technology (NIST) develop standards and guidelines for computer systems to control loss and unauthorized modification or disclosure of sensitive information and to prevent computer-related fraud and misuse. It also requires that all operators of federal computer systems, including both federal agencies and their contractors, establish security plans.

## U.S. Privacy Act of 1974

This law was enacted to provide for the protection of information related to individuals that is maintained in federal information systems and to grant access to such information by the individual. The law establishes criteria for maintaining the confidentiality of sensitive data and guidelines for determining which data are covered.

The Act imposes numerous requirements upon federal agencies to prevent the misuse of data about individuals, to respect their confidentiality, and to preserve their integrity. Federal agencies can meet these requirements by the application of selected managerial, operational, and technical control procedures that, in combination, achieve the objectives of the Act.

The major provisions of the Act (1) limit disclosure of personal information to authorized persons and agencies; (2) require accuracy, relevance, timeliness, and completeness of records; and (3) require the use of safeguards to ensure the confidentiality and security of records.

Although the Act sets up legislative prohibitions against abuses, technical and related procedural safeguards are required to establish a reasonable confidence that compliance is indeed achieved. It is thus necessary to provide a reasonable degree of protection against unauthorized disclosure, destruction, or modification of personal data, whether intentionally caused or resulting from accident or carelessness.

The Privacy Act of 1974 protects the privacy of individuals identified in IS maintained by U.S. federal agencies by regulating the collection, maintenance, use, and dissemination of information by such agencies.

## U.S. OMB Circular A-130, Management of Federal Information Resources

Office of Management and Budget (OMB) Circular A-130, Appendix III, Security of Federal Automated Information Systems, has specific requirements for establishing an agency computer security program. The program should include application security, personnel security, IT installation security, and security awareness and training programs. Federal agencies are required to address security in their annual internal control report required under OMB.

## Circular A-123.U.S.OMB Circular A-123, Internal Control Systems

Office of Management and Budget (OMB) Circular A-123 details specific policies and standards for federal agencies for establishing and maintaining internal controls in their programs and administration activities. It includes requirements for vulnerability assessments and internal control reviews. The main provisions of A-123 became law through the enactment of the Federal Manager's Financial Integrity Act of 1982.

## Paperwork Reduction Act

The Paperwork Reduction Act (PRA) of 1995 applied life-cycle management principles to information management and focused on reducing the U.S. government's information collection burden. To this end, PRA designated senior information-resources manager positions in the major departments and agencies with responsibility for a wide range of functions. PRA also created the Office of Information and Regulatory Affairs within the OMB to provide central oversight of information management activities across the federal government.

## U.S. Freedom of Information Act

The Freedom of Information Act of 1966 established the right of public access to government information by requiring U.S. federal agencies to make information accessible to the public, either through automatic disclosure or upon specific request, subject to specified exemptions.

This law makes federal information readily available to the public. It also establishes the conditions under which information may be withheld from the public to ensure that certain information such as trade secrets be protected.

## Security and Freedom Through Encryption (SAFE) Act

The SAFE Act, which was approved in May 1997, guarantees the rights of all U.S. citizens and residents to use or sell any encryption technology. The purpose is to relax export controls on encryption. The bill specifically makes it legal for any person to use encryption, regardless of encryption algorithm, key length, or implementation technique; makes it legal for any person to sell encryption software, regardless of encryption algorithm, key length, or implementation technique; and prohibits state and federal governments from requiring anyone to surrender control of an encryption key. Note that the bill specifies legal, not illegal, usage of encryption.

The Act, for example, potentially escalates a minor crime to felony status if the person committing the minor crime used encryption in carrying it out. The Act allows the U.S. software industry to provide the data security features that consumers require to protect their data. In the past, government restrictions on encryption prevented this opportunity. The Act gives the American software users the freedom to use software with unlimited encryption strengths, prohibits mandatory key escrow requirements, and allows for export of encryption software.

## Electronic Communications Privacy Act (ECPA)

The Electronic Communications Privacy Act (ECPA) governs how investigators can obtain stored account records and contents from network service providers, including Internet service providers (ISPs), telephone companies, cell phone service providers, and satellite services. ECPA issues arise often in cases involving the Internet: any time investigators seek stored information concerning Internet accounts from providers of Internet service, they must comply with this statute.

## The Promotion of Commerce Online in the Digital Era Act and the Encryption Communications Privacy Act

Both Acts significantly liberalize export restrictions on software with strong encryption and seek to protect both privacy and security on the Internet. Both give software users the freedom to use data security software with no government intervention.

## The Economic Espionage and Protection of Proprietary Economic Information Act of 1996

This Act addresses the problem of industrial and corporate espionage work. It allows the Federal Bureau of Investigation (FBI) to investigate cases in which a foreign intelligence service attacks American firms to gather proprietary information to benefit companies in their own countries. High technology and defense industries are the primary targets. The Act redefines *stolen property* to include proprietary economic information.

The Act supplements state trade secret laws and defines a trade secret as financial, technical, business, engineering, scientific, or economic information, whether tangible or intangible and regardless of how it is stored. In addition, the Act specifies that the owner must take "reasonable measures" to keep the information secret.

Penalties under the Act are up to $500,000 and 15 years in prison (10 years if a foreign government's interest is not involved). The Act also gives the government the right to seize any proceeds from the sale of trade secrets or property obtained as a result of espionage.

## U.S. Federal Sentencing Guidelines

The U.S. federal sentencing guidelines for organizational defendants became effective in November 1991. These guidelines provide judges with a compact formula for sentencing business organizations for various white-collar crimes. Included are federal securities, antitrust, and employment and contract laws, as well as the crimes of mail and wire fraud, kickbacks and bribery, and money laundering.

The federal sentencing guidelines are equally applicable to the computer and IS security function of a business organization by requiring that security plans, policies, procedures, and standards be developed and implemented. It is important to ensure that these policies and procedures reflect the actual controls and practices being used and enforced.

## Organization for Economic Cooperation and Development (OECD)

OECD developed "Guidelines for the Security of Information Systems" in 1980 covering data collection limitations, quality of data, limitations on data use, IS security safeguards, and accountability of the data controller.

## U.S. Computer Fraud and Abuse Act

The Act, amended in 1996, deals with computers used in interstate commerce and makes it a crime to alter, damage, or destroy information; to steal passwords; or to introduce viruses or worms. It covers classified defense or foreign relations information, records of financial institutions or credit reporting agencies, and government computers. Unauthorized access or access in excess of authorization is a felony for classified information and a misdemeanor for financial information. The Act provides for imprisonment for unintentional damage limited to 1 year and civil penalties in terms of compensatory damages or other relief.

## U.S. Foreign Corrupt Practices Act of 1977

The Foreign Corrupt Practices Act of 1977, among other things, requires certain procedures by which a public corporation preserves its records. A vital records program must follow legal, regulatory, and business requirements. Internal accounting controls of a corporation should provide reasonable, cost-effective safeguards against the unauthorized use or disposition of company assets. This requires executives of public companies to preserve computer records, which requires disaster recovery planning. Hefty penalties can be assessed against executives found to be negligent in this area.

## ISO Standard 17799

The ISO Standard 17799, formerly known as the British Standard (BS) 7799, is a comprehensive set of controls addressing information security. It is intended to serve as a single reference point for identifying controls needed for most situations in which information systems are used in industry and commerce for large, medium, and small organizations. The standard has three major components: confidentiality, integrity, and availability.

ISO 17799 points out how organizations are dependent on information systems and technologies and the need to comply with laws and contractual terms. It makes the point that advances in information technology have increased the range of possible threats to information security, including such things as fraud, unauthorized access, damage, and system failures.

The standard recommends the following controls at the system specification and design stages:

- information security policy document;
- allocation of security responsibilities;
- information security education and training;
- reporting of security incidents;
- virus controls (prevention, detection, and correction);
- business continuity planning process;
- control of intellectual property;
- safeguarding of company records and equipment;
- compliance with data protection laws and regulations; and
- compliance with the organization's security policy.

### U.S. Computer Software Piracy

The purpose of the U.S. Executive Order on computer software piracy (intellectual property) is to prevent and combat computer software piracy by observing the relevant provisions of international agreements in effect in the United States, including applicable provisions of the World Trade Organization Agreement on Trade-Related Aspects of Intellectual Property Rights, the Berne Convention for the Protection of Literary and Artistic Works, and relevant provisions of U.S. federal law, including the Copyright Act.

## CROSS REFERENCES

See *Risk Management for IT Security; The Legal Implications of Information Security: Regulatory Compliance and Liability.*

## REFERENCES

U.S. General Accounting Office. (1994). *How to get action on audit recommendations*. Washington, DC: Author.

## FURTHER READING

Bayuk, J. L. (2000). *Stepping through the IS audit, Information Systems Audit and Control Association (ISACA)*. Rolling Meadows, IL: Information Systems Audit and Control Association.

Gallegos, M., & Allen-Senft. (1999). *Information technology control and audit*. Boca Raton, FL: CRC Press.

Vallabhaneni, S. R. (1989). *Auditing computer security*. New York: John Wiley & Sons.

Vallabhaneni, S. R. (2001). *CISA examination textbooks. 1: Theory* (3rd ed.). Retrieved June 7, 2005, from https://www.srvbooks.com/index.html

Vallabhaneni, S. R. (2002). *CISSP examination textbooks. 1: Theory* (2nd ed.). Retrieved June 7, 2005, from https://www.srvbooks.com/index.html

Vallabhaneni, S. R. (2004). *Certified Business Manager (CBM) examination preparation guides. 3: Theory*. Retrieved from http://www.apbm.org/

Weber, W. (1999). *Information systems control and audit*. Englewood Cliffs, NJ: Prentice Hall.

# Evidence Collection and Analysis Tools

Christopher L. T. Brown, *Technology Pathways*

## INTRODUCTION

In today's digital age, evidence of improprieties often lies deep within the corporate information technology infrastructure in such places as personal data assistants, the lowest levels of computer hard disks, and a litany of other storage devices. The old cliché, "the right tool for the job," has never been so fitting than when selecting tools for the conduct of computer forensics.

This article intends to do more than simply list various tools and their use. It provides readers with a discussion of the unique natures of different types of computer forensics tools and selection criteria for each. Information on tool testing and certifications is also provided to assist readers in their own tool selection and testing. Self-validation of tools is considered a "best practice" in the computer forensics field.

After the discussion on tool testing and classes of computer forensics tools, the article addresses specific tools and their capabilities. Although it does not present an exhaustive list, this article provides readers with a good sampling of best-of-breed computer forensics tools.

This article, by its very nature, discusses many companies and their products. Each company's or product's site URL is cited in the References.

## TYPES OF INVESTIGATIONS AND TOOL SELECTION

Until recently, there were very few tools created specifically for the conduct of computer forensics and evidence collection. Investigators would often need to improvise or create custom applications to get the job done. This is no longer the case in today's digital age. The needs of law enforcement and the legal community, as well as information technology incident response teams, are beginning to foster competition and the subsequent development of new applications by tool manufacturers. Additionally, new companies have entered the marketplace, creating more tightly focused tools and thereby allowing the type of investigation to drive tool selection. Three high-level areas of specialization in investigations are corporate misuse, civil discovery, and criminal investigations. Although certainly there is a wide cross-section of tools that may be indicated in all three areas, each has its own focus and therefore may call for specialized tools.

1. Corporate misuse investigations can be proactive or reactive and often involve investigators from several areas including the Information Technology and Human Resources departments. Tools used for these investigations are focused on the ability to conduct live monitoring of user activity, as well as the reconstruction of user actions after the fact.

2. Civil discovery can often involve thousands or even hundreds of thousands of pages of data. As a result, the civil discovery process requires extensive and varied filtering, categorization, reporting, and indexing measures. Tool selection for use in civil discovery should focus on the ability to conduct fast and varied searches while producing large and detailed reports.

3. Criminal investigations delve deep into hard disk and data devices, piecing together the smallest fragments to find evidence. Although uncovering graphics in child pornography is often one of the first capabilities that come to mind in tool selection for criminal investigations, virtually any type of crime can involve a computer or data storage device. Tool selection for criminal investigations can be considered a superset of all computer-forensics-related tools.

## TOOL TESTING, ADMISSIBILITY, AND STANDARDS
### Tool Testing and Standards

Even though tool testing, admissibility, and standards are a hotly debated area, most computer forensics experts agree that conducting your own tool testing and verification is paramount. That said, the Computer Forensics Tool Testing Program (CFTT) has embarked on a mission to provide a measure of assurance that the tools used in computer forensics investigations produce accurate results. The CFTT is a joint project of the National Institute of Justice, the National Institute of Standards and Technology (NIST), and other agencies, such as the Department of Defense and the Technical Support Working Group.

Although the CFTT testing and certification process is still somewhat slow, several very useful documents have been developed by the program to outline desired requirements for forensics disk imaging tools. The first document is appropriately titled "Disk Imaging Tool Specification." The second useful document from the CFTT project is the "Hard Disk Write Block Tool Specification." Both specifications have gone through extensive peer review and clearly outline how respective software and devices should and should not perform. Both documents are available on the NIST Web site (http://www. cftt.nist.gov).

In the spirit of the NIST CFTT project, the Computer Forensics Tool Testing list server was created on Yahoo Groups and is frequented by forensic tool manufactures testing various aspects of their products. The following caption is used to describe the group:

> "This group is for discussing and coordinating computer forensics tool testing. Testing methodologies will be discussed, as well as, the results of testing various tools. The ultimate goal of these tests is to ensure that tools used by computer forensics examiners are providing accurate and complete results.
>
> This discussion group is open to all individuals in the field who are interested in participating in the testing of computer forensics tools."

Brian Carrier (2004) is an active member of the Yahoo CFTT group and often posts disk images to test tool capabilities to the list. Brian also keeps a tool testing Web page with information on his test (http://www.digital-evidence.org).

To learn more about the CFTT group or to subscribe, visit their Web site (http://groups.yahoo.com/group/cftt).

## Admissibility of Digital Evidence

Admissibility of evidence in court can be a complex area of computer forensics and the law. Although some practitioners believe they are scientists using scientific tools, others believe they are technicians providing a technical work product. The truth is both can be correct depending on the case, evidence, and circumstances. Definitions aside, this discussion brings to light what is often referred to as "Daubert/Fry" or "Kelly/Fry," cases that apply to the admissibility of scientific evidence.

In a nutshell the Daubert, Kelly, and Fry rulings state that for scientific evidence and therefore digital evidence, if it is considered scientific, to be admissible in court, the following principles should be met:

- Has the scientific theory or technique been tested empirically, or is it falsifiable?
- Has the theory or technique been subjected to peer review and publication?
- What is the known or potential error rate?
- Is the theory or technique generally accepted within the relevant scientific community?

Kenneally (2001) presents interesting points on the use of open source software tools to quickly meet admissibility requirements set forth in the courts. All legal discussions aside, the goals of the principles above are to ensure that technical evidence is grounded in knowledge derived from the methods and procedures of science. In summary these principles are hard to argue with and are a useful benchmark for tool selection.

## CLASSES OF TOOLS

Computer forensics tools can be divided into three tool classes: collection, analysis, and presentation. These tool classes coincidentally cover three of the four phases of computer forensics, leaving out only the "preservation" phase (see below).

The first computer forensics tool most people think about is a disk imaging tool. Although such a tool may be the cornerstone of computer investigations, most investigators quickly find out that many tools are required in even the simplest of investigations. Once a disk is imaged (bit-stream image), the image must be analyzed. The complexity of analyzing an image is directly proportional to the varied number of applications and data formats on the disk image. Then, the results of the analysis must be presented.

Collection tools can include hardware or software and be disk focused or network data focused. Although not all investigators will need to capture live network data, most will find several hardware and software collection tools to be indispensable.

Collecting the most up-to-date analysis tools is a seemingly never-ending effort. This is because application data files continue to change over time, requiring investigators to continually seek out new ways to process the evidence they gathered using collection tools. E-mail is a perfect example of an area where investigators will need to invest in several tools.

Presentation tools can include report generation, data transfer, and CD-ROM/DVD burning tools. Staging the final filtered evidence files, indexing the files, and providing viewing directions and/or applications can be a major undertaking for some cases.

The following sections of this article discuss integrated imaging and analysis tools, as well as specialized tools for e-mail and Internet history analysis.

## INTEGRATED COLLECTION (IMAGING) AND ANALYSIS TOOLS

Before the late 1990s computer forensics investigators used a grab bag of individual specialized tools for every phase of processing a case. Then consumer demand led to the development of integrated collection, analysis, and reporting tools for computer forensics.

To understand the basic philosophy behind the design of these integrated applications, it is necessary to review what most forensics practitioners consider to be the four phases of computer forensics: collection, preservation, filtering, and presentation. Each product described here offers the user some level of support for each or all of these four phases.

Several of the key features required in a computer forensics collection and analysis tool are the following:

- The tool should collect data as least intrusively as possible. Although many people use the term "nonintrusively," the act of connecting to a suspect disk in any way is somewhat intrusive. Remember this scientific principle: the act of observing changes that are being observed.

- Bit-stream images are normally desirable when performing analysis, but not always practical. For situations where imaging is indicated, the tool should create bit-stream images of the original disk to allow investigators to work from the images.

- The tool should perform all work with evidence in a read-only manner. For computer forensics disk tools, this normally means reading the evidence disk at the sector level and then providing any viewing and analysis operations through its own read-only implementation of the specific file system. Even with this level of protection, a hardware disk protection (write blocker) should be considered essential to prevent damage to original evidence caused by software or firmware outside the investigator's control.

- The tool should be able to maintain cryptographic hashes of files and data and later be able to verify these hash values and thus file integrity. Keep in mind that the nature of cryptographic hashes states that "no matter how small the changes in the original data, the hash value should be significant." In other words, you can never identify what has changed in the original—only that at least one bit did change. An event as simple as a single disk sector going bad after the original disk image hash was created could cause subsequent hash comparisons to fail.

- The tool should include automated reporting features that allow the user to accurately represent the evidence in a reproducible fashion.

Although integrated computer forensics tools generally support various file systems and operating systems, the consoles normally run on either Windows platforms or UNIX and UNIX-like platforms. Note that since the introduction of Macintosh OS X, which is based on the BSD UNIX platform, Macintosh can now be considered a UNIX-Like platform.

## Windows-Based Tools

Three Windows-based integrated forensics tools that lead the market today are ProDiscover, EnCase, and FTK (Forensics Tool Kit). Each tool approaches integration, tool set, and case management in a slightly different way, but offers some unique feature or user interface.

A Windows-based integrated forensics application called ILook was intentionally omitted from this listing because the tool is only available to law enforcement users. Interestingly ILook was originally developed commercially. It was then purchased by the criminal investigations division of the U.S. Internal Revenue Service and subsequently made available only to law enforcement agencies.

ProDiscover was developed by Technology Pathways in late 2001 and is not a single application, but rather a family of forensics applications, with each product differing slightly based on its intended user and focus, whether criminal, civil or corporate. Additionally in corporate-focused computer forensics, both human resources departments and information technology departments may perform computer forensics, each with a slightly different focus.

The current ProDiscover family comprises ProDiscover for Windows, ProDiscover Forensics, ProDiscover Investigator, and ProDiscover Incident Response. One of the most prominent differences among the four current products is that ProDiscover Investigator and ProDiscover Incident Response include the capability to conduct live analysis and imaging over transmission control protocol/Internet protocol (TCP/IP) networks, whereas ProDiscover for Windows and ProDiscover Forensics are intended for forensics workstation use only.

All editions of ProDiscover allow the user to collect computer disk evidence in a variety of ways, including disk-to-disk bit-stream images and disk-to-image file bit-stream images. Users can also view directly connected disks in a read-only fashion and directly. When using ProDiscover Incident Response and ProDiscover Investigator, users have the same capabilities with remote systems over any TCP/IP network.

The ProDiscover image format is a metaformat that includes collection information in a header and trailer. ProDiscover collects the disk image much like UNIX "dd," then places header information in front of the image with case and investigator information, and places a log file at the end of the image with any input/output (I/O) errors that were encountered during collection. Because the ProDiscover image format is similar to UNIX "dd," ProDiscover can read images in "dd" format and export its images to "dd" format for use with other tools.

Figure 1 shows the ProDiscover console connected to a remote system, viewing two redundant array of independent devices (RAID) volumes in a Windows New Technology File System (NTFS) dynamic disk set.

In addition to imaging, ProDiscover allows the user to perform an array of common forensic tasks, such as searching for key words, checking for file type extension mismatches, and viewing data in cluster slack space.

ProDiscover offers an easy way to perform remote and live disk analysis. If the remote agent is placed in the CD-ROM, floppy, or USB slot of the target system, it will automatically run in memory and allow the investigation console to connect over the TCP/IP local area or wide area network. When the ProDiscover Console chooses to connect, all session setup information is passed using 256-bit TwoFish encryption, and globally unique identifiers are set up on both sides of the connection. At this point the

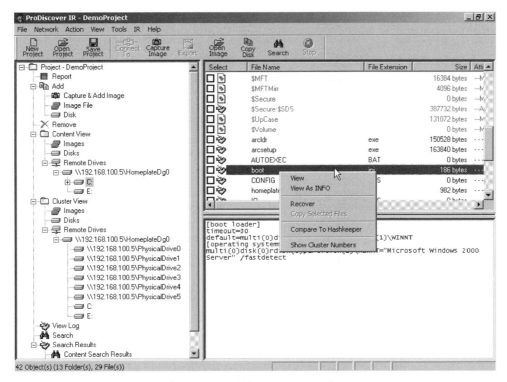

**Figure 1:** ProDiscover screen shot.

investigator can add a disk from the remote system directly to the current project and perform all normal forensic operations on the remote system, such as hash filtering, file header comparisons, and key word searching, all in a read-only forensically sound fashion.

In addition to the other forensic functions, ProDiscover Incident Response and ProDiscover Investigator have the ability to find hidden files, create and compare baseline file hashes, and search for suspect files.

One unique and patent-pending feature offered in all versions of ProDiscover is its ability to temporarily reset the host-protected area on an ATA 4 and above hard disk, thereby allowing access to any hidden files.

ATA Specifications added the "protected area" as a means for PC distributors to ship diagnostic utilities with PCs. Simply put, the ATA protected area is an area of the hard drive that is not reported to the system BIOS and operating system. Because the protected area is not normally seen, most disk forensics imaging tools do not image the area. Initially computer forensics analysts were not concerned greatly by the inability to image the protected area, largely because the feature was thought to be used only by PC distributors. There is now a growing level of interest and concern related to end user implementation of the protected area to hide data. The concern has been highlighted by the release of consumer-marketed utilities to implement the protected area to hide user data.

The ProDiscover project format, containing all report and case data, is an open standard XML format that can easily be accessed with such applications as Microsoft Excel for further processing.

EnCase was introduced in the late 1990s by Guidance Software Inc. and is one of the original Windows-based

integrated computer forensics tools It uses a case methodology in which users create a proprietary case file from which to work. In what has become the standard for tools of this class, users can add and manage multiple directly attached disks or disk images to a case. Within the case, users perform further analysis, such as hash filtering, timeline analysis, and reporting. One unique feature of EnCase is its image file format. Although it uses a meta image format similar to ProDiscover—adding a header and footer to the image of the hard disk—EnCase also adds a proprietary cyclic redundancy code (CRC) value every 32 sectors or 64 bytes of the image.

There has been much debate on computer forensics image formats, and one authority (Scott, 2003) offers an interesting analysis of common forensics imaging tools and their image formats. In his paper Scott suggests that forensics imaging can cause confusion because the resulting images can differ in type. Scott makes the proposal that forensic images be referred to as Bit-Copies or Bit.Plus-Copies, where a Bit-Copy is a RAW image and a Bit.Plus-Copy is a meta image.

The relative longevity of the EnCase product has allowed it ample time to support a wide assortment of file system formats, including NTFS, FAT 12/16/32, EXT 2/3, UFS, FFS, Reiser, CDFS, UDF, JOLIET, ISO9660, HFS, and HFST.

Another unique capability of EnCase is its use of EnScript, which is a macro-programming language for automating functions within EnCase. EnScript is object oriented and looks much like a blending of Visual Basic and C++ from a syntax stance. A collection of prewritten and supported EnScripts can be found on the Guidance Software Web site (http://www.guidancesoftware.com).

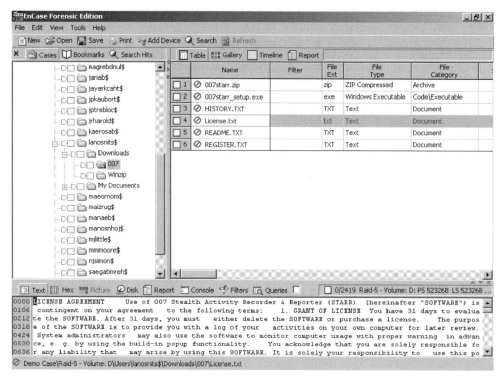

**Figure 2:** EnCase screen shot.

The EnCase user interface is similar to ProDiscover in layout, but differs in features and capabilities. The EnCase version 4 screen layout is shown in Figure 2.

In 2003 EnCase released a new version of their product dubbed "EnCase Enterprise Edition" and renamed the original EnCase product as the "EnCase Forensics Edition." The Enterprise Edition comprises three components to perform network-based investigations and forensics:

1. Examiner software, which is essentially a console used by the examiner.
2. SAFE (Secure Authentication for EnCase) server, which is used to authenticate users, administer access rights, and retain logs
3. Servlet, which is installed on network workstations and servers to act as a server between the EnCase console and the system being investigated

Guidance Software appears to be focusing its marketing efforts on its enterprise version of EnCase and network investigations. With the growing volume of data and places to store data around corporate networks, remote imaging and analysis will certainly play a key role in corporate security.

Forensics Tool Kit® (FTK) by Access Data (http:www.accessdata.com) is one of the leading Windows-based integrated forensics disk analysis applications (Figure 3). When FTK entered the computer forensics market, it initially focused on indexed-based searching found in another commercial application and software development library, dtSearch. By taking the time to create a comprehensive index of the search data up front, FTK enabled all subsequent searches to be accomplished faster. Considering that extended key word searching occupies a major part of the time taken by computer forensics investigations, this approach has immediate benefits to the investigator.

In addition to its focus on indexed searching, FTK has the ability to filter files using the National Institute Standards and Technology (NIST) RDS 28 hash value database and the National Drug Intelligence Center (NDIC) Hashkeeper database. Another notable feature of FTK is its ability to work closely with the Access Data password cracking tools: Password Recovery Toolkit and Distributed Network Attack.

Access Data recently added the ability to read compound files, such as e-mail databases and the Windows Registry. The ability to view many file formats was also added using Stellent's Outside In viewer technology.

FTK has not focused on the ability to capture disk images, but rather implements the ability to read other disk imaging formats, such as EnCase, SMART, Snapback, Safeback (up to but not including v.3), and Linux DD. Despite the earlier lack of native imaging capabilities, Access Data has been a long-time computer forensics industry insider, and FTK is easily considered one of the top three integrated computer forensics tools for the Windows platform.

## UNIX-Based Tools

The Sleuth Kit and Autopsy Forensic Browser are UNIX-based investigation tools for Windows and UNIX systems (http://www.sleuthkit.org). Both Autopsy and the Sleuth Kit are free, open source software and are maintained by Brian Carrier.

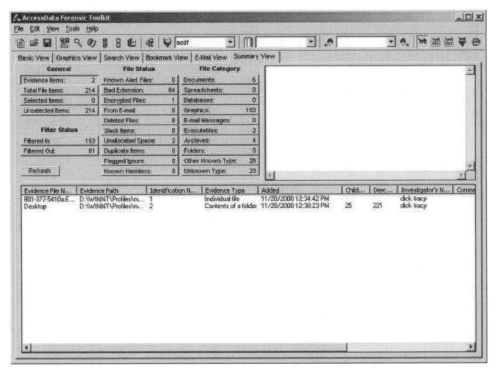

**Figure 3:** FTK screen shot.

Autopsy is a HTML-based graphical interface that allows an investigator to examine the files and unallocated areas of disks, file systems, and swap space (Figure 4). It uses the command line tools included in the Sleuth Kit: NTFS, FAT, UFS, and EXT2FS / EXT3FS file system tools; DOS, Macintosh, Sun, and BSD partition tools; and other tools to manage hash databases and sort files based on

their structure. Autopsy allows the investigator to interpret the contents of a hard disk or file system at several layers. At the lowest level, the investigator can view every block or sector in these forms: raw, hexidecimal, or with only the ASCII strings extracted. The investigator can also examine the file system from the "metadata" layer, where the data structures used to organize the files can be

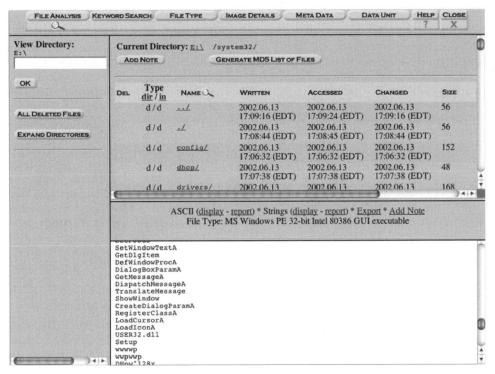

**Figure 4:** Autopsy screen shot.

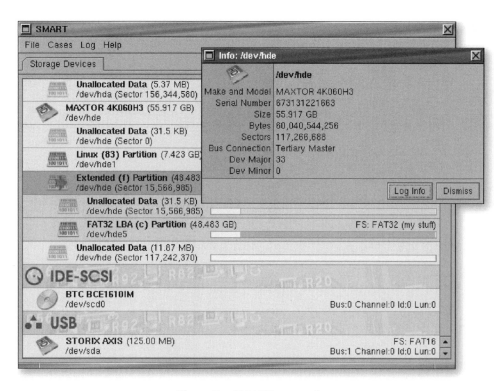

**Figure 5:** SMART screen shot.

viewed. Last, and most commonly used, is the file layer where the investigator can view the files and directories in the file system and see the names of deleted files. Autopsy also allows the investigator to perform key word searches, create time-lines of file activity, and sort files based on their internal structure.

The Sleuth Kit contains 18 command line tools and is based on the Coroner's Toolkit (TCT) by Dan Farmer and Wietse Venema. The tools are organized in a layered approach. The media management layer analyzes the partitions used in UNIX and x86-based disks; the file system layer analyzes the superblock and other general file system data structures; the data unit layer analyzes the individual sectors and blocks in a file system; the metadata layer analyzes the file data structures, such as NTFS MFT entries or UFS inode structures; and the file name layer analyzes the file name structures that create the file names and directories with which people are familiar. Within each layer are standard tools that allow the investigator to view details about a given object or to find mappings between the different layers. Although the individual tools in the Sleuth Kit allow the investigator to create custom scripts and view low-level details, it is most commonly used in conjunction with an interface, such as Autopsy.

F.I.R.E. was originally named Biatchux and is sometimes still referred to as such (http://fire.dmzs.com). F.I.R.E. is a relatively young and evolving source forge project, but has been very useful since its first release. It has two basic uses: as a (1) bootable Linux CD-ROM containing a variety of forensics and incident response tools, all accessible via an easy-to-use menu system, and (2) a collection of Windows-based tools for forensics and incident response. Although still not feature-complete at the time of this writing, F.I.R.E. offers its users an easy way

to collect evidence in a forensics environment. Even more attractive is that F.I.R.E. is free to use.

SMART is manufactured by ASR Data, which originally released an integrated imaging and analysis platform for Windows in 1992 called Expert Witness. Expert Witness for Windows95 then sold under the name EnCase by Guidance Software and eventually became one of the leading integrated imaging and analysis platforms for the Windows environment.

In keeping with the Expert Witness history, SMART has become one of the top integrated computer forensics environments for the Linux platform (Figure 5). SMART offers investigators a wide assortment of imaging and analysis capabilities including remote live preview, acquisition, authentication, searching, and reporting.

One advantage of SMART is its rich user interface, despite being a Linux-based tool. Throughout the application, users find extensive right-click and drill-down capabilities. SMART uses a modular design philosophy implemented through the use of plug-ins. Through plug-ins, additional feature sets, such as newly supported file systems, can be added, and fixes can be rolled out to users without an entire application upgrade.

Notably the network-enabled version of SMART is also available on the Be OS platform and can be placed on a bootable CD-ROM for field preview applications.

## DOS/Command Line Tools

Most of today's computer forensics tools have rich graphical user interfaces (GUIs) and all the flexibility that type of user interface provides. However, despite the advantages of a GUI, there is a performance trade-off for the windowing overhead. Sometimes processing large volumes of data can be streamlined with the use of a 32-bit command line application without the overhead of its GUI. For occasions where this performance advantage is warranted, Mares and Company (http://www.dmares.com) sells a comprehensive suite of command line utilities that are fast and efficient. The wide assortment of Mares and Company utilities offer accelerated performance for scripted processing of large volume data sets and repetitive tasks.

# DATA RECOVERY UTILITIES

In the context of computer forensics, data recovery utility discussions normally go well beyond that of simple file recovery. In fact, most of the integrated forensics tools already mentioned automatically recover deleted files without user action. Data recovery utilities are normally needed when entire disks or tapes are damaged and require repair. Other issues arise when boot partition tables become corrupt. These types of recoveries often involve making changes to the hard disk or media to correct the corrupted data, which places the procedures used in contention with preserving the original evidence. For these reasons the recovery is almost always performed on bit-stream duplicates of the original evidence. This type of low-level recovery can be done using manual or automated procedures. Manual procedures often involve finding a disk HEX editor, tracking down the offending disk locations, and then manually correcting the problem. One such disk editor is WinHex made by X-Ways software (http:www.x-ways.net/winhex/index-m.html).

WinHex has been around for many years and includes such forensics features as slack space extraction and hashing. One of its most useful features is its ability to apply templates to data areas, thus mapping out boot sectors, file tables, etc.

Automated recovery tools often take the research out of disk repair by providing pre-established templates and wizards for reassembling files, partition tables, and other disk structures. Data Recovery Software sells several products to automatically scan and repair partition tables, as well as redundant array of independent devices (RAID) volumes (http://www.datarecoverysoftware.us/index.html).

Ontrack, which was recently purchased by Kroll, Inc., provides unique data recovery software called the Easy Recovery™ family of products for file and disk recovery (http://www.ontrack.com). Additionally, Ontrack provides data recovery services and software to repair large broken e-mail databases, such as Microsoft Outlook and Exchange databases.

eMag Solutions makes a product called Media Merge that can handling thousands of tape format variations (http://www.emaglink.com/MMPC.htm). Media Merge provides PC users the capability to manage and manipulate data residing on tapes, optical disks, CDs, and hard drives. It runs on most Microsoft platforms and connects via SCSI to the tape drive.

# SPECIALIZED TOOLS FOR E-MAIL AND INTERNET HISTORY ANALYSIS

Many people feel a shield of anonymity when using a computer as a communications tool and are therefore inclined to be less inhibited when using it. Not surprisingly,

this makes e-mail communications and Internet activity history high on the list of desirable data to be recovered when analyzing a computer.

Because e-mail communications and Internet history information are often maintained in compound files, metafiles, or databases, analysis can require specialized tools for reading the specific files or databases. Some of the complexities in individual database formats have made it hard for any one vendor to create a tool to read all formats. Initially (and sometimes still) forensics investigators utilized applications created to convert e-mail box formats from one format to another as a means to extract and analyze the individual e-mails. Normally this process included extracting individual e-mails from a format, such as Microsoft Outlook's PST format, to flat text files or possibly Web-based HTML format for easy searching and presentation. Although this type of conversion is often a pivotal point of the forensics analysis process, newer applications created specifically for the forensics process have been produced, such as Paraben Software's Email Examiner (Figure 6; http://www.paraben-forensics.com).

Although still a young application, Paraben Software's Email Examiner has become the leader in e-mail extraction and processing of e-mail communications as evidence. Because Email Examiner was created as a forensics mail processing application, it includes extensive search and reporting capabilities, as well as message-by-message hashing for later verification.

At the time of this writing, Email Examiner could read 16 mailbox formats, including various versions of Microsoft Outlook and Eudora. Notably missing are America Online and IBM's Lotus Notes mail formats. A product called ForMorph Message Converter from Fkeeps.com (http://www.fkeeps.com) and another titled UniAccess from ComAxis Technology (http://www.comaxis.com) are able to convert AOL e-mail boxes to a variety of formats for analysis. For Lotus Notes, a product called Notes the Ripper was created by MyKey Technology specifically for forensics investigators (Figure 7; http://www.mytech.com).

Notes the Ripper is a Lotus Notes plug-in that allows the user to extract all messages from the Lotus Notes database to text, rich text, or HTML files, enabling easy subsequent processing utilizing other search tools.

Processing e-mail from servers can prove extremely challenging. In most cases the server operator does not want the server taken down, and processing the data from backup tapes can be time consuming at best. One accepted method for processing Microsoft Exchange Server databases is to use a tool called Exmerge from the Microsoft Exchange Server Resource Kit to extract mailboxes from a live Exchange Server to individual Microsoft Outlook database files called PST files. Once the mailboxes are segregated into PST files, they can easily be processed with an application, such as Email Examiner. Although this method is effective for smaller cases and servers, it does not scale very well for larger corporate environments. Even when processing mail servers from medium-sized networks with 400 or so users, the method above can become tedious.

Newer tools, such as Power Control Tools from Ontrack, allow automated processing of live Microsoft Exchange Servers or easy extraction of mail database files

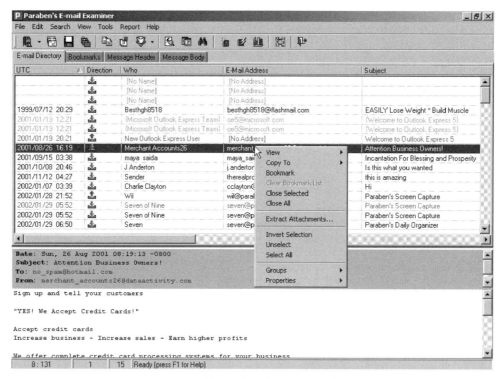

**Figure 6:** Email Examiner screen shot.

from backup tapes. Paraben Software also offers an e-mail server extraction product called Network Email Examiner that extracts e-mail from a Lotus Notes mail server, in addition to Microsoft Exchange Server.

Although Microsoft's Internet Explorer is without a doubt one of the more pervasive browsers found today, both Netscape Communicator and Opera are also used heavily. All of these browsers keep a wealth of information about activities in data files, as well as locally cached versions of Web pages visited. Most of the database and history file formats are well documented and publicly available.

Although several small utilities allow investigators to examine Internet history databases, Netanalysis by Digital

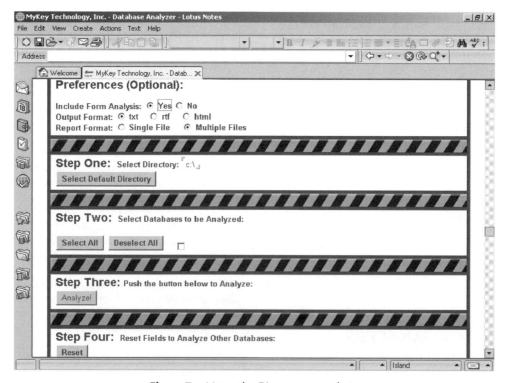

**Figure 7:** Notes the Ripper screen shot.

Detective stands out as a must-have tool for this type of investigation (http:www.digital-detective.co.uk). It allows investigators to extract the Internet history files from Microsoft Internet Explorer, Netscape, and Opera browsers. After extraction these databases can be searched and reported on in a multitude of ways. Netanalysis also offers investigators the ability to extract deleted Internet history from unallocated space and binary files.

## PDAs AND OTHER DEVICES

Digital evidence is plentiful in today's information age and can be found in many places other than a computer's hard disk. One of the first such devices that usually comes to mind is the personal digital assistant or PDA. Although PDAs often contain plentiful information just as in a computer's hard disk, their data are much more volatile. The golden rule for handling PDAs and such other devices as cell phones and pagers is to keep them charged after seizure. Although some personal devices contain nonvolatile ready access memory (RAM) for permanent storage, most data are usually stored in volatile RAM where they will be lost if the batteries are discharged. Often these types of batteries discharge within a day's time.

Paraben Software offers a Windows-based product specifically for the conduct of PDA forensics called PDA Seizure. Using PDA Seizure, investigators can collect images of PDA memory for Palm and Microsoft products. Although other products, such as EnCase, advertise the capabilities to perform PDA forensics, the Paraben product is the current leader.

For Palm PDAs, At Stake provides a product called "pdd" (Palm dd), which is a Windows-based tool for Palm OS memory imaging and forensic acquisition (http://www.atstake.com/research/tools/forensic/). Using this tool and the Palm OS Console Mode, investigators can create a bit-stream image of the selected memory. Full source code is available for pdd on the At Stake Web site (http://www.atstake.com/research/tools/forensic/).

Because WinHex by X-Ways software offers a method of capturing memory and data from almost any device connected to the system, this is a useful tool for PDAs, cameras, phones, and other devices that can be connected to a PC through a data cable.

One authority (Burnette, 2002) describes the process he underwent analyzing a RIM Blackberry device for the first time. In his paper, Burnette describes using the Blackberry development environment to view data from a PC as the user would have seen it on the PDA. Development environments for specialized PDAs such as the Blackberry are often available for free from the manufacturers and are often downloadable from their Web sites.

Every day, new devices are becoming available to users that may contain valuable data for an investigation. With the proper cable and a little innovation, the investigator can usually analyze the data if collected. Normally, the difficult step is not obtaining the data but rather identifying the device used. For instance, MP3 players are simple data storage devices that can contain documents and applications just as easily as MP3 files. Personal video recorders, such as Tivos, are nothing more than a PC running a specialized operating system and storing data on a hard disk. Some of the newest TV monitors have flash memory card

slots for direct viewing of picture files. Recently USB flash drives have been released in the form of a watch and a pen. The list goes on and on.

## EVIDENCE COLLECTION HARDWARE

Evidence collection hardware can mean many things to many people and can include anything from a screw driver to a cable or target hard disk. This section focuses on what are generally referred to as hand-held disk imagers or duplicators and stand-alone write blockers.

### Disk and Media Imagers

Logicube is the manufacturer of the Forensics SF-5000 imager (http://www.logicube.com). The imager when purchased as a system includes a lightweight hand-held main unit that houses a target Integrated Drive Electronics (IDE) evidence disk. The original evidence disk can then be connected externally via a direct IDE connection, an IDE to USB converter, or a CloneCard Pro PCMCIA adapter for capturing a notebook computer hard disk without cracking the case. The kit is all housed in a rugged carrying case and includes a portable printer for imaging reports and power supply. Logicube recently introduced the Forensic MD5, which is modeled after the SF-5000, but also includes MD5 hashing capabilities, as well as a removable compact flash disk for storing key word lists for live file searching among other uses. The Forensics MD5 also includes a thumb keyboard for data entry and the capability to create a UNIX style "dd" image in addition to the standard disk-to-disk image. Logicube also manufactures an assortment of hardware write blockers for use with or without their hand-held imagers.

Intelligent Computer Solutions' (ICS) primary forensics product for hand-held imaging is the SoloMaster Forensics (http://ics-iq.com). The SoloMaster is very similar to Logicube's SF-5000, but also has the ability to use an Adaptec SCSI PC card to capture SCSI evidence drives to an IDE target disk. In addition to the SoloMaster Forensics, ICS also resells the Guidance Software Fast Block write-blocking device and the Road MASSter portable forensics workstation. The Road MASSter is a self-contained portable workstation for field collection and on-site analysis using the Windows 98 SE platform. Recently ICS has produced a wide assortment of notebook hard disk adapters that have become quite useful as notebook vendors stray away from standard 2.5" hard disk and their associated connectors.

MyKey Technology recently introduced the DriveCopy, which is an easy-to-use, stand-alone drive imager with built-in write blocking (http://www.mykeytech.com). With the optional thermal printer, a report can be printed containing model number, S/N number, firmware, size, max speed, configuration, as well as the drive's features for both the source and target drive. The report will also include the results of the image process along with a report of bad sectors.

Corporate Systems Center makes a very good low-cost SCSI to IDE imaging system that has a forensics mode for write blocking, logging, and secure disk wiping (http://www.corpsys.com). The Portable Pro Drive Service/Test/Duplication Workstation provides many features enabling users to image, test, and repair a wide assortment of drive combinations.

## Write Blockers

Because extensive circuitry is not involved in developing hardware write blockers, many are now starting to become available. The increasing numbers of write blockers coupled with the importance of the device in evidence collection makes it imperative that investigators use reputable write blockers that have been tested extensively locally and by third parties. The following is a short list of some of the more reputable write blockers available today.

MyKey Technology manufactures several write blockers for IDE disks and flash disks. The NoWrite, their original write blocker, has several notable features including providing volatile access to the hardware-protected area of a disk. The NoWrite was designed to be fail-safe in that all failures prohibit any writes to the evidence drive. MyKey Technology calls this safety mechanism "Absolute Write Blocking."

The DriveCopy disk-to-disk duplicator from MyKey Technology is also the only drive duplicator to automatically address host-protected areas and device control overlay features. In addition, when duplicating a smaller drive onto a bigger drive, the DriveCopy automatically sets the Host Protected Area (HPA) on the bigger drive so that it will have the same number of sectors as the smaller source drive.

Another unique write blocker from MyKey Technology is the NoWrite FlashBlock, which protects compact flash or other digital media during collection and analysis. The FlashBlock is a single unit designed to accept Compact-Flash type I & II, Memory Stick, SmartMedia cards, and MultiMediaCards.

The ACARD SCSI-to-IDE Write Blocking Bridge (AEC7720WP) is one of the more widely used write blockers primarily due to its low cost (less than $100; http://www.microlandusa.com). Because the ACARD write blocker is a small open circuit card, it is not well suited for field write blocking. This card is, however, a good component to consider for a forensics workstation.

Intelligent Computer Solutions manufactures the DriveLock and DriveLock USB and distributes the Guidance FastBlock. It also provides a DriveLock built into a removable drive caddy that is very useful for forensics workstations.

Digital Intelligence, Inc., the makers of forensics workstations, also makes the FireFly write blocker (from http://www.digitalintelligence.com). The FireFly is a compact hardware-based write blocker that allows an IDE hard drive to be connected to a IEEE 1394 compliant FireWire device chain. Digital Intelligence also markets a kit containing a variety of write blockers that include capabilities for SCSI and IDE write blocking.

## COLLECTION AND ANALYSIS WORKSTATION

The current trend of computers getting smaller does not apply to most collection and analysis workstations. A collection and analysis workstation needs to be a fast, highly configurable machine and ready to connect to a wide assortment of disk and media. If you are the type of reader who likes to tinker, building a forensics workstation can be challenging and fun. Here are a few items to consider when building a forensics workstation.

- Select the tallest case you can find. Six full-sized bays are not too many.
- Place all drives in removable drive bays. Even the boot disk should be in a removable bay because you may want to secure the disk or have several operating systems to boot from.
- Pick the fastest processor and possibly a multiprocessor system, if within your budget.
- Do not skimp on RAM area, as forensics processing can be very resource intensive. Luckily, RAM is much less expensive these days.
- Enable at least one of your drive bays to be write blocked.
- Add a fast SCIS card and at least one drive bay for processing SCIS drives.
- Make sure you have USB 2.0; Firewire is a big plus.
- Add a multiformat media connector for analyzing SmartMedia, CompactFlash, SD Cards, etc. Even though these types of media usually have write protect switches, a write blocking connector is preferred.
- Test and label all external bays and access ports to ensure accuracy when adding drives and components.

Once the forensics workstation is built, there is still more to do. Most users continue to collect a never-ending array of adapters, converters, cables, and specialty connectors needed for computer forensics. Just think of all the different types of SCSI connectors in use during the last 10 years.

Tape media is another issue to consider. Even when performing computer forensics for a single corporation, tape formats and file systems can be numerous. Fortunately, most data retrieval companies can manage data conversions and are normally familiar with forensics methodologies.

It is easy to underestimate the hours required to build and test a computer forensics workstation, much less collecting the numerous adapters, cables, and support supplies. Digital Intelligence, Inc. has been making specialized computer forensics workstations for years beginning with the Forensics Recovery of Evidence Device (F.R.E.D.). The F.R.E.D. is one product in a wide assortment of specialized forensics devices created by Digital Intelligence. One of its significant components is its tool box filled with adapters, cables, and specialized tools. A typical comment by people when they see the tool box is that they may buy a F.R.E.D. for that alone.

Today, the F.R.E.D. comes in many versions, with the specifications of each changing as technology changes. For those without the time or inclination to build a forensics workstation themselves, the F.R.E.D is a good alternative.

Forensic Computers, much like Digital Intelligence, Inc., is a manufacturer of specialized computers for the computer forensics disk collection and analysis process (http://www.forensic-computers.com/products/html). Several products that make Forensic Computers stand out are their series of portable computer forensics workstations—the Air-Light—and their large-volume data storage towers.

The Air-Light is a portable, full-powered computer forensics workstation designed to fit into a rugged briefcase for air travel. Forensics Computers sells several versions of the Air-Light; each comes with an assortment of options fitting most customer needs.

Forensic Computers' line of "Data Monster" storage towers are manufactured in both SCSI and IDE versions and are designed to store more than a terabyte of data. Each Data Monster is capable of handling up to eight hot-swappable drives and has redundant power supplies for added reliability. Large-volume data storage towers are becoming a growing need in even small computer forensics labs.

Forensics Computers also builds multiprocessor-capable full tower computer forensics workstations. Multiprocessor workstations can become very helpful in cases involving extensive key word searches or brute force password cracking.

## EVIDENCE COLLECTION FIELD KIT

An evidence collection field kit is often referred to as the "black bag" or "fly-away-kit" and contains specialized tools for your own and possibly other environments. This list of field kit contents should be considered as a boiler plate for creating a personalized field kit.

- One forensic drive imager – Some investigators are using powerful notebook or cube-style computers that are fully outfitted as forensics workstations to conduct field images. Others choose to conduct the imaging on site with a hand-held imager, such as the Forensics Solo-Master Kit (SCSI) or LogiCubes F-FORENSIC-KIT and CLONECARD.
- Several large, fast, forensically clean and sealed hard disks. Forensically clean is a term used to describe a hard disk where every sector on the disk has been wiped with a specific and known or verifiable data pattern.
- Various adapters
  - USB to IDE adapter
  - USB to IDE portable drive enclosure with removable drive bay
  - SCSI II (50 Pin) to every other type of SCSI
  - SCA to SCSI III
  - IDE 40 Pin (notebook) to standard IDE
  - serial ATA adapter
- Several hardware-based write-blockers for IDE and USB. MyKey Technology, Inc. makes a wide assortment of write blockers and drive imagers.
- Several new composition books for field notes

  *Tamper-proof evidence bags (http://www.chiefsupply.com/fingerprint.phtml), labels, and tape.

- Sharpie or other permanent marker
- Blank floppies, CD-ROMs and DVDs as needed.

- Digital camera
- Adaptec SCSI PC card.
- A big bag to carry it all in

Each field kit will differ slightly based on the specific organization's needs. In some cases an assortment of specialized kits may be created for specific platforms or technologies. A Macintosh kit is an example of a specialized kit with an array of specialized tools for opening Macintosh computers and imaging or analyzing their disks.

## CONCLUSION

Computer forensics is one of the few professions where obtaining best-of-breed tools often means selecting and using more than one tool in each category. Most practitioners agree that it is best to have many tools to validate results and get the job done. The many tools vary greatly in terms of features and price points. This article has presented many specific tools, but is by no way exhaustive. The reader is encouraged to evaluate each tool based on his or her needs and budget and to conduct self-validation tests, as well as to seek independent validation of any tools used.

The number one challenge to digital evidence is authenticity or accuracy. Focusing on this challenge as well as determining how a tool will support the four phases of computer forensics—collection, preservation, filtering, and presentation—is the best guide in tool selection.

## GLOSSARY

**Bit-Stream image** Each disk drive's size or layout, sometimes called its geometry, can be different. Despite any differences in the disk geometry the bits of data from the first to the last bit on disk are what eventually make up the user-readable form. A bit-stream image is the process of taking each bit from one disk and laying it out in the exact same order on the destination disk despite any differences in disk size or geometry.

**Civil discovery** During civil litigation each party to a law suit has an opportunity to request information that may become or lead to evidence about the case. Civil discovery is the overall process of discovering information (evidence or something that leads to evidence) during civil litigation.

**Computer forensics** With forensics meaning "to aid the law" computer forensics is the practice of applying computer science to aid the legal process.

**Hash Value** A cryptographic hash is an algorithm used to produce fixed-length character sequences based on input of arbitrary length. Any given input always produces the same output, called a hash. If any input bit changes, the output hash will change significantly and in a random manner. Additionally there is no way the original input can be derived from the hash. Two of the most commonly used hashing algorithms are MD5 and SHA1.

**RAID** (Redundant Array of Independent Devices) RAID arrays can come in many shapes and sizes. A RAID array is a way, through the use of firmware or software or both, to make multiple physical drives appear as one or more logical drives. In some cases the RAID set offers fault tolerance, such as RAID 5 where pieces of data are striped across all the drives of a set and parity bits are also scattered throughout the other drives to allow regeneration of data if a drive is lost. In other cases, such as RAID 0, no fault tolerance is offered, but overall performance is increased by striping only the data across multiple drives with no parity bits.

## CROSS REFERENCES

See *Computer Forensic Procedures and Methods; Digital Courts, the Law and Evidence; Digital Evidence; Forensic Computing; Law Enforcement and Digital Evidence.*

## REFERENCES

Access Data. (n.d.). *Computer forensics software.* Retrieved February 15, 2004, from http://www.accessdata.com

*At Stake Forensics Research Tools.* (n.d.). Retrieved February 16, 2004, from http://www.atstake.com/research/tools/

*Autopsy & Sleuthkit.* (n.d.). Retrieved February 21, 2004, from http://www.sleuthkit.org

Burnette, M. (2002). Forensic examination of a RIM (Blackberry) wireless device. Retrieved May 21, 2004 from http://www.rh-law.com/ediscovery/Blackberry.pdf

Carrier, B. (n.d.). *File system forensic analysis.* Retrieved June 27, 2004, from http://www.digital-evidence.org

Chief Supply. (n.d.). *Evidence gathering and crime scene supplies.* Retrieved February 15, 2004, from http://www.chiefsupply.com/fingerprint.phtml

*Com Axis Technology.* (n.d.) Retrieved February 15, 2004, from http://www.comaxis.com

Corporate Systems Center. (n.d.). *Dealer wholesale headquarters.* Retrieved February 21, 2004, from http://www.corpsys.com/

CS Electronics. (n.d.). *Drive adapters.* Retrieved February 15, 2004, from http://www.scsi-cables.com/index.htm

*Data Recovery Software Services.* (n.d.). Retrieved February 15, 2004, from http://www.atarecoverysoftware.us/index.html

Digital Detective. (n.d.). *Forensic computing tools & utilities.* Retrieved February 15, 2004, from http://www.digital-detective.co.uk

Digital Detective. (n.d.). *Netanalysis.* Retrieved February 16, 2004, from http://www.digital-detective.co.uk/intro.asp

Digital Intelligence, Inc. (F.R.E.D./FireFly). (n.d.). *Software, hardware, training casework solutions for the computer forensic community.* Retrieved February 21, 2004, from http://www.digitalintelligence.com/

eMag Solutions. (n.d.). *MediaMerge for PC.* Retrieved February 15, 2004, from http://www.emaglink.com/MMPC.htm

*F.I.R.E. bootable forensics system on CD.* (n.d.). Retrieved February 21, 2004, from http://fire.dmzs.com/

*Fkeeps.com.* (n.d.). Retrieved February 15, 2004, from www.fkeeps.com

*Forensic Computers.* (n.d.). Retrieved February 29, 2004, from http://www.forensic-computers.com/products.html

*Guidance Software.* (n.d.). Retrieved February 15, 2004, from www.guidancesoftware.com

ILook Investigator. (n.d.). Toolsets. Retrieved February 15, 2004, from http://www.ilook-forensics.org/

Intelligent Computer Solutions, Inc. (n.d.) *Information technology.* Retrieved February 15, 2004, from http://www.ics-iq.com/

Kenneally, E. E. (2001). Gatekeeping out of the box: Open source software as a mechanism to assess reliability for digital evidence. *Virginia Journal of Law and Technology, 6*, 13.

Logicube. (n.d.). *Solitaire Forensics.* Retrieved February 15, 2004, from http://www.logicube.com/

Mares and Company. (n.d.). *Computer forensics and data analysis.* Retrieved February 21, 2004, from http://www.dmares.com/

Microland Electronics. (n.d.). *ACARD SCSI-to-IDE write blocking bridge (AEC7720WP).* Retrieved February 21, 2004, from http://www.microlandusa.com/microland/

*MyKey Technology, Inc.* (n.d.). Retrieved February 15, 2004, from http://www.mykeytech.com/

National Institute of Justice. (n.d.). *The Computer Forensic Tool Testing Project.* Retrieved February 7, 2004, from http://www.ojp.usdoj.gov/nij/sciencetech/cftt.htm

*NIST Disk Imaging Tool Specification 3.1.6.* (n.d.). Retrieved February 7, 2004, from http://www.cftt.nist.gov/DI-spec-3-1-6.doc

*NIST Hard Disk Write Block Tool Specification.* (n.d.). Retrieved February 7, 2004, from http://www.cftt.nist.gov/WB-spec-assert-1-may-02.doc

*Ontrack Data Recovery.* (n.d.). Retrieved February 15, 2004, from http://www.ontrack.com/

Paraben. (n.d.). *Forensic tools.* Retrieved February 15, 2004, from http://www.paraben-forensics.com/

*SANS Reading Room.* Retrieved February 15, 2004 from http://www.sans.org

Scott, M. (2003). *Independent review of common forensics imaging tools.* Retrieved February 22, 2004, from http://mtgroup.com/papers.htm

Technology Pathways, LLC. (n.d.). *ProDiscover computer forensics.* Retrieved February 15, 2004, from http://www.techpathways.com

X-Ways Software. (n.d.). *WinHex: Computer forensics & data recovery software, hex editor & disk editor.* Retrieved February 15, 2004, from http://www.x-ways.net/winhex/index-m.html

Yahoo CFTT List Server. (n.d.) *Computer forensics tool testing.* Retrieved February 15, 2004, from http://groups.yahoo.com/group/cftt

## FURTHER READING

Casey, E. (2001). *Handbook of computer crime investigation: Forensic tools & technology.* New York: Academic Press.

Kruse, W. G. II, & Heiser, J. G. (2001). *Computer forensics: Incident response essentials.* Boston: Addison-Wesley.

# Information Leakage: Detection and Countermeasures

Phil Venables, *Goldman Sachs*

## INTRODUCTION

Although information leakage can be the result of failings of security controls such as encryption and access control, in this context we use it specifically to mean the result of illegitimate use of legitimate authority over information, specifically, to obtain information in a legitimate way but subsequently use it in a way not intended by the granted access or organizational policies. For example, an employee leaving the company and taking his client list in electronic form, an employee leaking company financial statements, an analyst taking proprietary spreadsheet models upon suspecting his employment is likely to be terminated, use of an Internet Web site that discloses (as a result of a query) likely business actions, and so forth. This chapter focuses on the detective, protective, and corrective approaches to such activities in a practical, business-oriented way. The common thread is that it is explicit or implicit action by someone who has legitimate access to that information already. It may also include the primary actor being duped into leaking information directly, for example, by being a victim of social engineering, or indirectly by letting their environment fall foul to spyware or other malevolent objects.

Information leakage in this context, although obviously related, is considered distinct from more precise problems such as the well-studied domains of covert channels (Pfleeger, 2002), inference (Domingo-Ferrer, 2002), and traffic analysis, all of which are more serious issues in classified or otherwise high-assurance systems. The notion of this chapter is that such problems are at the extreme and that there are many more easily practiced threats that need to be addressed. Each of the exposures discussed in this chapter could be cast in the context of more theoretical models or explored through security models such as Bell–La Padula and Clark–Wilson (Denning, 1982) but rather we keep this to a less theoretical discussion for the sake of immediate practical applicability.

The concepts are explored as a loose bundling of analysis based around a protect, detect, and correct loop. A more thorough and linked taxonomy could well be developed but we leave that for other works; in this context we prefer a more applied stance. The chapter is built around the following structure:

- Scope of Illegitimate Use of Legitimate Authority in the Context of Leakage provides a background to the nature of this problem and why it is of increasing concern.

- Leakage Channels Overview defines a rough taxonomy for how the problem will be explored across physical, electronic, and human channels and explains the nature of leakage in each.

- Countermeasures covers a detailed analysis of a range of controls across detection, protection, and correction.

# SCOPE OF ILLEGITIMATE USE OF LEGITIMATE AUTHORITY IN THE CONTEXT OF LEAKAGE

Many aspects of how we define information security today are about providing a degree of assurance that the confidentiality, integrity, and availability of information is maintained and that accountability for people's actions is sustained. The focus of much of information security practice today is about identifying information assets, analyzing threat and vulnerability levels, and then making a risk decision as to what extent to protect those assets. In most cases this type of analysis assumes a known, or bounded unknown, set of threat actors and an authorized set of users.

In the context of information leakage as explored in this chapter, we step beyond this and examine the problem of direct or indirect leakage of information by, or from, an otherwise authorized actor. We do not explore information leakage as a result of direct attack against a security system with a well-defined and implemented policy, except insofar that other techniques can be used to dupe a user into disclosing things inadvertently. We demonstrate, however, that the boundaries are increasingly blurred.

More and more of the world's critical assets are represented digitally. Encoded in these digital forms are increasing amounts of valuable information from privacy-critical information to intellectual property that encodes future wealth. There is tremendous value in bits. Exponential growth of storage capacity and communications capability continues. Storage is becoming higher capacity, physically smaller, more reliable, faster, and much more portable that it once was. Communications capability continues to increase with highly reliable and prevalent systems including e-mail, instant messaging, and Web services that increasingly span traditional corporate boundaries.

This combination of events (information increasing in value and an increase in capability to copy such information and hence steal it) is, and will continue to be, a continued challenge. Using traditional security techniques we can analyze risk and establish adequate protective regimes for sensitive information but at some point someone somewhere needs to access and process this information. These authorized individuals are the vulnerability we explore as they can decide to take the information, can be duped physically or electronically into taking it, or, courtesy of the tools they use, can inadvertently disclose that information. This is not a new problem, and, as discussed, this is just a set of relaxed cases of covert channel, traffic analysis, and inference control problems.

It might be tempting to think, as you read this, that we are facing a losing battle. The overriding force of *compartment diffusion* (Venables, 2004) or the effect of entropy in action means that whenever we set up a barrier, things will gradually cross. This has been evident in the way corporate perimeters are tunneled and the way copy protection is routinely broken all the way through to the blurring of ownership of mobile devices and their contained information. We demonstrate that it is by no means futile to try to protect most things as there is an array of protective, detective, and corrective measures to take regarding the broad problem of information leakage.

## LEAKAGE CHANNELS OVERVIEW

Leakage channels can be considered in three broad categories:

- **Physical.** The movement of a physical asset or a physical object that encodes or store digital assets. Moving atoms.
- **Electronic.** The movement of a digital asset over a communications medium. Moving bits.
- **Human.** The movement of what an asset encodes through human interaction. Moving thoughts and ideas.

Leakage channels can be exploited directly or indirectly:

- **Direct.** An explicit action by an authorized person to abuse their otherwise legitimate authority to move assets in physical, electronic, or human form, for example, e-mailing sensitive information outside of the protection domain. This is overt action by the first party.
- **Indirect.** An implicit action by an authorized person that causes the unauthorized movement of assets in physical, electronic, or human form now or at some point in the future, for example, leaving copies of sensitive documents in a photocopier memory or inadvertently allowing spyware on a system. This is covert action by a third party.

Figure 1 diagrams these channels. Clearly there can be some overlap here: a USB attached portable disk drive is electronic but is considered physical because the means of taking the information from one place to another is physical. We are not going to struggle for taxonomical purity in this chapter where that would result in repetition in the discussion.

There can also be an overlap between direct and indirect methods of attack and there can, in fact, be defenses an attacker can use to disavow activities because of the prevalence of indirect attacks ("it wasn't me, some spyware must have done it").

## PHYSICAL CHANNELS

Physical leakage channels are probably the most familiar to people. People have been stealing things this way for years, taking documents home, faxing things, or smuggling diskettes out of the building. That was hard to stop, except in the most extremely protected government or military environments, and is not getting any easier given the scope/scale of the means of physically carrying bits and the digitization of most technologies.

### Good, Old-Fashioned Ways

Printed documents, folders full of information, and briefcases loaded with material can easily be sequestered and are hard to detect short of inspecting everyone. Even then, who can tell, at least in any normal commercial

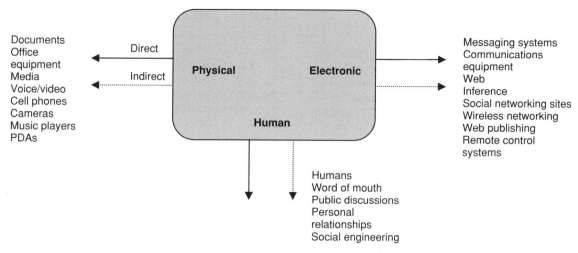

**Figure 1:** Leakage channels.

environment, that the material is not legitimately being removed to work on at home. This has always been an inefficient means of leaking information given that it is inherently low bandwidth; however, with increasingly high-quality scanners and OCR (optical character recognition) software bits can be rendered on paper, transported, and reconstituted into bits somewhere else with relative ease. If leakage is contained, on other, easier to exploit, and higher capacity channels, then you can expect regression to these good, old-fashioned ways.

## Office Equipment

Office equipment such as photocopiers, printers, scanners, and fax machines are increasingly functional and digital in nature. The risks here are now fairly common, including such scenarios as copiers storing copy jobs in memory after the initial copy has been made for someone to later simply trigger copy from memory, thereby indirectly leaking information. Fax machines, printers, and scanners can also suffer from this same indirect memory leakage problem. This can be compounded by the increasing tendency of these devices to be networked and to present, in many cases, weak security in how their management interfaces can be accessed. Some networked copiers for example have a neat Web-accessible interface that by default lets anyone retrieve digitized copies of copy jobs. There have even been incidents where devices such as shredders that have been designed to destroy information have been illicitly compromised and have an optical scanner in the shredding input feed that scans material to be shredded to a memory card for later retrieval by an attacker.

## Media

The exponentially increasing capacity and decreasing size of electronic, magnetic, or optical storage devices coupled with the prevalence of their read/write devices in most personal computers has introduced some tremendous means of stealing information. Diskettes, CDs, DVDs,

USB-attachable flash memory (such as pen drives, compact flash, or other digital media cards), through to high-capacity and high-speed USB and Firewire portable hard drives means that anything up to hundreds of gigabytes of information can be taken in a flash (no pun intended). Microsoft and other operating system vendors have done a wonderful job of making Universal Plug and Play recognize these storage systems and be ready for use in an instant.

## Voice and Video Communications

Another example of indirect attacks on communications, albeit in this case usually to do with stealing ideas expressed by people communicating, is in the increasingly rich functionality of voice and video communications equipment. This can be from simple attacks such as dialing into voice conference calls using a personal identification number (PIN) code that has not changed for a long time and setting conference room handsets to auto-answer on zero rings if you want to listen in what is going on in a conference room (assuming they are not using the phone). As with office equipment, the digitization and networked capability of these types of communications equipment are not without their issues; for example, there are certain video conferencing systems that when networked can be managed through a Web interface, and through this interface you can see and hear what is going on in a particular location or in a particular conference session. Even with equipment such as Web cams attached to personal computers, it is relative easy, if protective steps have not been taken, to seize control of the camera and observe what is going on around that computer, often to the embarrassment of the person at the computer.

Newer technologies such as IP telephony and IP video bring additional threats compounded by their network integration and digitization. Unless configured correctly, IP phones and their exchanges can be rigged to dupe caller id systems and can be prone to interception with voice stream reconstruction tools such as VOMIT (Voice Over Misconfigured Internet Telephony).

## Cell Phones, Cameras, Music Players, and PDAs

Most people carry a cell phone, many carry a personal digital assistant (PDA), and an increasing number of people carry compact digital cameras. All of these can be used to take information. A Bluetooth-enabled cell phone, for example, can be used to interface with a similarly enabled personal computer to retrieve, store, or relay information either directly in its storage or by acting as a digital modem. PDAs, especially those with higher storage capacities or interfaces to high-capacity memory cards, can likewise be used as physical transport devices for stolen bits. At the extreme, cameras can take pictures of sensitive information and digital cameras and music/video players can be used like PDAs as USB or Firewire interfaces to their embedded high-capacity flash memory or disk drives. Even companies banning cameras or camera cell phones on premises are increasingly finding enforcement a tough proposition as it is going to be hard to buy a cell phone without a camera soon. Besides, cameras and storage interfaces are turning up in many places from watches to pens.

Attacks against wireless-enabled devices, often configured insecurely by default, are feasible and have in many cases been demonstrated, from using Bluetooth to steal the contents of someone's phone or PDA to intercepting wireless local area network (LAN) sessions to indirectly steal information.

## Classic Spy Equipment

Let's not forget good old-fashioned bugs and other illicit retrieval devices that can indirectly attack or be used by an insider for direct information theft. These are, like most digital technology, getting more and more sophisticated, of greater capacity, better at operating stealthily, and capable of operating at a higher relay range. Increasingly, such physical interception devices are targeting personal computers in the form of hardware key loggers aiming at recording key strokes on an attached device for later physical or network-based retrieval.

## Emanations

At the risk of opening up a Tempest (the collected name, originating from the name of the study that first analyzed this, for the whole subject of electromagnetic radiation from devices inadvertently disclosing information) discussion, we have to mention the ease of which, in certain cases, information can leak from a particular location either through communications or output device (screen) leakage.

## Media and Equipment Disposal

Often the biggest source of leakage is the indirect, but still serious, result of the ineffective disposal of sensitive documents, media (disks, disk arrays, etc.), or computer equipment from large servers, desktop PCs, and PDAs. There are many cases of recovery of information, even where it has been supposedly deleted, from equipment disposed of or donated to other entities much to the embarrassment of the originators.

## Laptops and Corporate PDAs

Finally, let's not forget the high-capacity devices we permit people to legitimately move around with that contain synchronized copies of all their authorized information. These can easily be attached to home networks and the content copied out to a home PC or other environment, or in the case of PDAs, simply synchronized to a different host.

Even in the case of unauthorized laptops and PDAs, few large corporate networks yet implement internal network admission control to restrict unauthorized device connectivity, which can subsequently be used with authorized credentials to retrieve information to a device that can later be removed.

# ELECTRONIC CHANNELS

Since the advent of the Internet, electronic leakage channels have become significantly more prevalent and easy to exploit and use. Even prior to Internet-based communications, exploits were still feasible. Every year new communications systems are blended into existing ones. New channels are opened as a particular Web site implements a new feature and existing communication systems evolve to bypass previously effective control measures.

## Messaging Systems

Corporate e-mail is not the only high capacity and extremely efficient means of transporting information; in recent years it has been joined by other related technologies such as instant messaging and Web-based e-mail. These systems are typically characterized by the fact that they are intended for use in such a way that leakage is hard to distinguish from the authorized sharing of information to intended recipients. Even if corporate messaging systems are heavily monitored, and access to public mail systems such as Hotmail are blocked, it is a cat and mouse game to find and keep control over the daily emergence of new messaging systems, remailers, and anonymous mailers.

One of the main problems here is that a messaging system in the context of the Web is really only what the owner of a Web site intends. Bulletin boards, discussion groups, Web-accessible Usenet news, and the like can be easily utilized as messaging systems or leakage channels. Those entities running messaging systems are keenly aware of the restrictions often put in place and actively work out ways that their communications capability cannot be blocked at corporate boundaries.

## Communications Equipment

We covered communications equipment in the previous section, given the various physical exploits that can befall them, but they are also obviously an electronic communications challenge as well. Faxes, modems, cell phone digital modems, DSL lines, and cable lines can all be installed within the enterprise and provide an outbound conduit for the flow of information, as well as a potential inbound conduit for attackers.

## The Web

The Web can be thought of as one giant information channel. Any site courtesy of what it chooses to be can be a place where information is uploaded and downloaded. This can range from Web conferencing systems, bulletin boards, blogs, wikis, through to Internet storage and backup sites. Control of the flow to and from the Web can be problematic as often it is hard to distinguish the legitimate from the illegitimate. The use of SSL or other encryption/tunneling techniques can further challenge perimeter-based policy enforcement.

## Indirect Inferential Disclosure

In many cases the use of the Web, even when information is not moved, can disclose some information. For example, the fact of one corporation aiming to buy another maybe disclosed by an unusual pattern of hits to the target's Web site, or, as has happened on several occasions, a preemptive domain name registration can disclose an impending merger that is still not in the public domain. Additionally, use of information gathering or research Web sites when someone is researching a problem can disclose the very nature of why they are doing the research, which may be a corporate secret or otherwise nonpublic information. This can include both business disclosure (large number of hits from one company to another that is about to be the target of a takeover) and technical disclosures (technical staff posting queries to news groups that contain too much detailed information and that can inadvertently disclose a technical vulnerability).

## Social Networking and Contact Management Sites

There are a growing number of Web sites devoted to managing the relationships between people. These social networking sites such as LinkedIn or Web-based contact management services such as Plaxo or Cardscan.net present a useful and legitimate set of services that can be used to overtly leak information courtesy of their messaging and information management capability or indirectly leak information through their use, that is, leak the identity of your clients as they are represented in your network of connections.

### Wireless Networking

Even if corporate wireless LANs are protected from unauthorized entry, end points such as laptops unless properly configured can be used as outbound relay points onto other wireless LANs (WLANs) in the vicinity. The concentration of most corporations in major commercial districts and the increasing range and reliability of WLAN technology, coupled with the laggardly approach to WLAN security in most environments, can result in a viable outbound leakage channel.

## Web Publishing, Blogs, and Bulletin Boards

Many desktop tools such as Microsoft Office 2003 are optimized for Web-based interaction and utilization. This can be from automated Web publishing to external Web sites, cross-corporate-perimeter calendaring and scheduling information exchange, to automated population and synchronization with so-called blogs and bulletin boards. This can conspire to be an overt channel for leakage or an indirect channel for the unwary. This is another example of compartment diffusion in action—where any logical or physical barrier erected to separate information flows inevitably comes under pressure directly or is simply bypassed over time.

## Remote Control, Anonymizers, and Tunneled Protocols

Although the corporate network may be well protected from the outside in, there can be plenty of opportunity for connections from the inside out, ranging from remote control software such as GoToMyPC.com to anonymizers and firewall tunneling software such as Firethru.com, all designed to install with minimal privilege and to embed or tunnel themselves through authorized protocols such as http or https. Although these can be controlled, they are difficult to control absolutely without affecting legitimate services or capabilities on the end points within the enterprise.

## Credential Sharing

Access to protected information, granted to legitimate users or clients, may be shared beyond the initial point of authorization if the outside party abuses the information in their possession, say, by posting it to a bulletin board, or abuses their credentials (user id and password or other authenticator) in their possession by posting to one of the multitude of WareZ (sic), password-sharing sites, or indeed any bulletin board.

## Malware

There is an increasing variety of malware (spyware, adware, and Trojans) that unlike viruses or worms have the primary aim of stealing information or recording and relaying behaviors such as the names of Web sites visited.

## Phishing

Finally, we have seen a rise in the past couple of years of attacks classified as "phishing" whereby unsuspecting people are duped using a variety of electronic and social techniques into visiting fake Web sites that ultimately lead to the leakage of information. In most cases these are fake financial Web sites where the aim of the attacker is to convince someone to electronically disclose their bank account numbers, online banking passwords, or ATM PIN codes. The ease with which the virtual world can be mimicked and the nature of trust people seem to place in the online environment, despite suspicions to the contrary, would seem to indicate that this type of threat will get worse before it gets better.

## HUMAN CHANNELS

The human channel of leakage is perhaps the most difficult to manage because you cannot control what is in people's heads and what they will be willing to talk about inadvertently or otherwise.

## Word of Mouth

People will always talk. If they know something sensitive, if there is some advantage to sharing it, and if they are inclined to malevolence, then there is little that can be done to stop them, other than potentially detect it after the fact.

## Use of Communications Technology in Public Places

Inadvertently people share a lot of things. Whether it is a confidential phone call on a cellphone in a public place or a conversation in a crowded place, someone somewhere will be listening. Attackers know this and will hang out in the places where people are relaxed and prone to talk about things they should not such as hotel common areas, airport lounges, bars, and so forth.

## Personal Relationships

Most people tend to have friends, acquaintances, and even spouses who work in other environments where information inadvertently shared could be useful. Of course, most of the time people are either careful or otherwise trustworthy.

## Social Engineering

Another threat seemingly on the increase is that of social engineering, which is really nothing more than an updated term for confidence trickery or duping people into disclosing information or granting capabilities that otherwise would not be granted. This could be the unsuspected caller brandishing some knowledge of corporate structure to dupe the insider into helpfully disclosing sensitive information or, if not that, then at least information that would further add credibility to the attacker to then obtain sensitive information. People are regularly inadvertently abused in this way.

## Misdirection of Communications

Arguably an indirect electronic exposure, modern messaging systems such as e-mail clients are rich in features to enable ease of communication to individuals or groups. Distribution lists could be used to send information without really understanding membership of that group; this could be inadvertent or in some cases a cover excuse in case direct information leakage is discovered. Newer e-mail clients tend to have e-mail address autocomplete features that for the less than fastidious person can result in sensitive material being sent to someone with a similar name. Additionally, a recipient could have autoforwarding of e-mails enabled that would, unbeknown to the sender, result in all e-mail to that person ending up in the hands of someone else against the express wishes of both sender and, often, recipient. It seems, by luck of the draw, the information ends up with the person you would least like to receive it.

## Use of Public Facilities

Again, arguably an electronic exposure, but often repeated because of human fallibility, information is exposed in many public places such as airports or hotel business facilities where corporate systems may be accessed (by clientless SSL VPNs or other methods) and information downloaded and printed but then left on the hard drives of personal computers. These can then be easily retrieved directly or often remotely as the security of such public facilities is often lax. In fact, it can be beyond lax as these public facilities are often overtly compromised with key loggers, password sniffers, and other malware.

# COUNTERMEASURES

We have outlined a range of exposures to direct or indirect information leakage in the connected world in which we live. It is not comforting to think that this is not even a thorough analysis of all the channels and exploits that are possible, but rather just a flavor of the challenges we face today. The countermeasures we explore can be broken out into detective controls that would detect leakage after the fact, protective controls that would either stop an exploit or render an exploit ineffective, and corrective approaches showing the options of how to deal with situations when detected.

In this exposition of potential countermeasures, we are not going to rigorously map countermeasures to exposures because this would lead to a lot of duplication, given the many ways countermeasures cover the exposures. The countermeasures are sufficiently complementary and self-explanatory to be applied easily enough anyway.

It is worth stressing at this stage that all these measures are by definition incomplete. The nature of the problem of information leakage, in that it is direct or indirect illegitimate use of legitimate authority, means that like most aspects of information security we can simply reduce the risk but not eliminate it. At the extreme, even if all possible protective measures were applied, you still could not stop the idea in someone's head walking out of the door at the end of the working day.

## Detection

Detective techniques are, given the nature of the problem, our mainstay of controls. At one level this can be seen as not particularly satisfactory as it does not necessarily stop bad things from happening; however, diligent and speedy action of detected infractions can stop frequent recurrence from a particular threat actor and in many cases can uncover exposures that can be systemically countered using protective approaches.

### External Open Source Intelligence

It is surprising just how much information is available in the public domain, on Web sites, bulletin boards, Usenet news groups, and the like. Much internal leakage can be discovered by judicious scanning of open sources to detect documents that should not be in public places, detect Web sites containing leaked sensitive information, or simply to detect inappropriate information sharing in bulletin boards or similar shared environments. Detection techniques can be as simple as using Google or other search engines, and in particular their more advanced search facilities to target searches to particular document types by looking for specific phrases such as "SSN" (Social Security number) in Excel (spreadsheet) files on Web sites. Even richer ways of doing this would be to use a number of service providers who crawl the Web for leaked information, inappropriately shared information, or signs of brand infringement.

## Internal Intelligence Detection

In a similar fashion, an internal search engine can be used to profile easily accessible information within the corporation, on the assumption that sensitive information easily accessible can be obtained and leaked by more people. Regular use of an internal search engine looking for key words encoding sensitive terms, for example, password, SSN, and "company confidential," can be used to put in place a detect-and-correct feedback loop continuously applied to confine sensitive information to places where access control is enforced. Of course, this will not stop the abuse of legitimate access but it will confine the problem. It is important to do this kind of searching, given the increasing ease by which information can be published and shared using Intranet Web publishing technologies available on most corporate desktops.

## Messaging and Communications Analysis

The mainstay of leakage detection occurs by directing surveillance at electronic messaging channels, in particular e-mail, Web-based e-mail, and other Web messaging and instant messaging (IM) systems.

Such surveillance can be applied in three main ways, although other combinations can be envisaged:

- **Ingress/egress monitoring.** Monitoring of communications at the point of entry and exit into the environment including corporate firewalls, Internet e-mail gateways, or corporate instant messaging relays. This surveillance may be accompanied by intermediate monitoring at internal mail servers particularly where these represent a demarcation point for boundaries or domains within an enterprise, including those between divisions in a company that need to be separated for some business or regulatory purpose. The advantage of this is that a smaller number of places can be subject to surveillance and, given that detection is in the messaging flow, fast reaction can be enacted to block identified troublesome communications. The disadvantage is that this cannot always catch communications that may be encrypted end-to-end, as in the case of S/MIME encrypted e-mail, protected IM sessions, https-encoded Web traffic, or otherwise encoded or tunneled communication protocols. Of course if this is the only option open to a corporation, then capabilities may be limited to ensure the effectiveness of ingress/egress monitoring such as limiting e-mail encryption to be edge to edge or edge to end, or terminating https traffic with SSL proxies. The other advantage with this type of approach is to coalesce the variety of work to be done on communication flows at the perimeter, such as virus checking, quarantining, and spam filtering, to a smaller number of message-handling gateways.

- **End point monitoring.** Monitoring of communication flows at the closest point to the user, that is, desktop/laptop. This involves applying the same surveillance techniques but executed from an active agent. The advantage here is the reduction of the need to compromise end-to-end capabilities such as encryption by conducting surveillance before the protection of information together with the potential for more richness in surveillance techniques resulting from the lesser performance constraints operating one on one at the end point. The disadvantage is the number of agents and the resulting complexity of management. Additionally the security of the end point needs to be considered, especially if the end point is not sufficiently trusted such that the user could disable surveillance or otherwise obscure their activities.

- **Retention monitoring.** On the assumption that a company is retaining copies of communications for some period, then surveillance can be applied, offline, to the repository of retained communications. The advantage here is that surveillance could be richer given the relative reduction in time/processing constraints resulting from moving from real-time to batch operation. The corresponding disadvantage, of course, is that there is limited scope to turn this detective control into a fast reacting protective control should the need arise. However, you could easily imagine a combination of rich batch-oriented surveillance coupled with lesser but faster real-time in-flow detection and reaction.

As we have implied, surveillance can be made active after a suitable period of "training" to avoid false positives, thereby stopping communication flows that would violate whatever corporate policy has been established. However, herein lies the problem of how to decide whether a particular communication is violating what is often a hard-to-prescribe policy.

There are various techniques here, and I would think there will be many new techniques and variations on a theme appearing in the coming years as the problem of information leakage is tackled:

- **Extreme detection with human inspection.** This is where some criteria are established to filter communications at the extremes of reasonableness and then use human investigators to examine the flows. An example of this would be large e-mail reviews where, say, any e-mail of greater than 2 MB leaving the corporation would be copied to a queue for later manual inspection. This is straightforward to do, but depends on resources, skills, and judgment too much to be a suitable detection technique and is, naturally, far from real-time.

- **Statistical methods.** This is where communications are flagged as suspicious based on deviating from some learnt baseline. For example, a spike of hundreds of e-mail messages to one e-mail address within a short time frame is a good indicator of a person sending large amounts of information to a personal e-mail account, especially if that e-mail account is some heuristically detectable variant on their name.

- **Behavioral methods.** Arguably similar to statistical methods, behavioral methods apply deeper intelligence based on learnt rules or explicitly encoded rules. For example, flag all communications from employees communicating with competitors if they are not in a business area with known counterparty relationships to that company.

- **Policy- or lexicon-derived methods.** If there are known means to flag communications then these can be applied explicitly. For example, if a group of people should not be communicating certain document types to another group then flag the flow, or if messages contain certain red-flag phrases that can easily identify suspicious behavior. As with other methods, one has to be careful of false positives when making detection react to enforce protection. Of course, this is a variable stance depending on the posture you are seeking to enforce, and you may want to trade some manual postinspection work (to free captured false positives) in return for eliminating false negatives.

- **Data driven.** Perhaps the most precise of all, this is where the surveillance environment is programmed with the data you want to detect leaving the environment or at a higher level the patterns of data for which you want to look. For example, find all instances of messages containing things that look like account numbers. To further reduce false positives, you could even provide the system with the list of all your real account numbers. This is a risky proposition especially if you are placing surveillance at the edge of your network. However, many vendors have worked around this by using hash matching rather than direct matching of source data.

### Web Log Analysis

In the vein of pure detection, a valuable source of intelligence are your outbound Web logs, that is, activities of employees surfing the Web. Here, like message flow surveillance, the combination of points of surveillance can be applied from inline with the outbound firewall or proxies to postfact sifting of captured logs. Again, the various techniques of policy-driven inspection to statistical detection can be applied. Some examples of what to look for could be the following:

- "What are the top 10 Web sites this week to which we have sent the most information?" Given most Web traffic is request/reply, or is in volume downloaded to the enterprise, this will quickly show large external data transfers.

- "What are the top 10 Web sites with long-lived SSL connections?" This will likely show accesses to sites that operated hidden protocols such as SSL tunneling of remote control or other embedded traffic.

- If there are detective or protective technologies in use such as "deep packet inspection" (which enables examination within multiple embedded protocols), then these too should be examined. Rarely is it the case that weird multiple embedding is not the sign of something bad or at least of something worth correcting.

- Particularly important is analyzing hits against blocked Web sites (if you block categories of Web sites) as this can be a good indicator of internal machines compromised by spyware that bounces against the internal firewalls.

- Similarly, end point system logs rather than Web access logs can be sifted and analyzed for other strange behaviors such as excessive printing, anomalous out-of-hours use, and so forth.

### Account Misuse Detection

Although this is more akin to classic intrusion detection, it is important to profile and monitor access to corporate Web sites, particularly ones offering up sensitive or otherwise proprietary information. Explicitly monitoring for access from multiple locations by the same credentials in a short period of time would, for example, lead to a conclusion that a client's credentials had been willingly or inadvertently made available to third parties.

### Network and System Anomaly Detection

In many cases anomalous behavior detected at network or system level can be indicative of trouble happening at other layers in the environment and so we should look to make use of all our detective infrastructure. For example, a network anomaly-detection system could flag a large amount of traffic to an end point on one subnet from a server in another subnet, indicating an insider who discovered and downloaded internally available information for later removal. Of course, the implied authorization here would likely mean a high number of false positives. However, appropriate tuning to minimize the number of false negatives would still be a minimal form of egregious anomaly detection that when combined with other measures could still be useful.

### Environment Discovery

In the absence of precise and rigorous network admission control (such as 802.1x), it is likely that most complex and large environments are susceptible to the introduction of transient or permanent unauthorized devices such as laptops, desktops, access points, and servers. It is important to scan the environment for unexpected devices or services on a regular basis as part of normal corporate health and hygiene. These scans could also lead to the discovery of other unintended surprises, such as Web servers running on printers or exposed services running on video conference systems, that will likely need examining and locking down.

### Physical Inspection

At the extremes, if other detection is proving effective, then malevolent actors may seek traditional methods of taking information in document or portable media form. In this case you will likely have to resort to physical inspection of people and equipment leaving the corporation. For any corporation that cares about the 99.99% of its workforce that are honest and hardworking, this is likely to be an unacceptable option and the remaining risk will be simply accepted.

### Human Behavior Detection

For the outside threat intended to induce internal leakage such as social engineering attacks, the corporation's own employees are the best distributed neural network–based detection system you can imagine, if trained correctly, of course. People should be trained about social engineering, acceptable means of handling suspicious queries without overreacting (and harming the odd real customer inquiry), and how to report behavior to increase the likelihood of investigators or law enforcement catching the perpetrator.

## Protection and Prevention

Prevention of leakage is difficult. At the risk of belaboring the point, the problem is deciding on the legitimate versus illegitimate use of otherwise-authorized access by an individual. In other words it is not so much about whether they have access but what they do once they have access. Fortunately, there is an emerging set of technologies designed to solve this problem and to counter exposures that would otherwise indirectly compromise information in the realm of otherwise trusted access.

### Clean Rooms

This is, perhaps, the most extreme form of protection that will likely protect against most exposures. However, it comes at the expense of flexibility and usability and so is only applicable in certain circumstances. This control is the maintenance of so-called clean rooms, in other words logically or physically isolated environments in which access can be made but information cannot leave. An extreme form of this would be a physical clean room that was not accessible logically and at which there was tight control around what could be brought in and taken out. Examples of this exist in government or military secure installations and in some cases major corporations that have significant requirements for access restriction or intellectual property protection. For most enterprises in most circumstances this is not practical. However, a logical version of this can be workable using a terminal services approach whereby data is kept in a central server environment and access to it is logically projected by remote views using remote control or terminal services (e.g., Microsoft Terminal Services, Citrix, or a variety of Java technologies) whereby the end points are controlled so as to not permit the uploading, downloading, or printing of information. This type of clean-room approach has seen a lot of applicability in many corporations either to logically isolate internal environments or to support offshore outsourcing in locations that would otherwise not be trusted to permit full-scale access to the corporate data assets.

### Enterprise/Digital Rights Management

A technology that has been around for a number of years that is now reaching broad usage is that of digital rights management. Originally conceived to protect copyrighted content such as music, pictures, and video, we are now seeing this applied in corporate environments to enforce "protection with information not to information" (in other words, to have information be permanently wrapped in a protected cryptographic envelope and carry rights with it wherever it travels). Such enterprise rights management systems can also enforce other capabilities such as restrictions on cut and paste within documents and the ability to print or otherwise transport information. Most, if not all, rights management systems are known to be ultimately fallible given that any software control running on anything other than trusted hardware is capable of being compromised. Many of the vendors in this space do a reasonable job of making this sufficiently difficult that routine compromise would not be worth it for anything other than extremely valuable content. Even then the side effect of rights management can often be effective in that they show the intent to protect and make people think twice about compromising information. Given that a determined attacker can likely get something with enough time, this is not an unreasonable level of protection. As PC hardware evolves, with hardware security support available and increasing functionality at chip level, it is conceivable that at some point an even higher degree of trust will be possible as a foundation for stronger enterprise rights management systems.

Implementation of rights management is not straightforward because it requires a thorough understanding and analysis of the types of information to be protected and what policies should govern this. This will require, over time, a thorough taxonomy of information classification and categorization to apply the corporate rights policies. As this, in many cases, can be seen as a shift from discretionary access control to label-driven mandatory access controls, to use some standard terminology, you can expect to see an upward shift in centralized policy management resources to manage this environment.

Rights management can also be used with other protection regimes; for example, a clean room could be permitted to export information only if it was rights management protected.

There are also other problems resulting from the lack of standard implementations and the multiplicity of vendor solutions that limit interenterprise sharing of rights management protected data. Often accessing protected information needs a standard software agent that is vendor specific. The problem here is most major corporations have very little desire to further complicate or add to the amount of desktop software in their environments. There is a catch-22 to overcome, but for intraenterprise rights protection that is unlikely to be an issue. For information that does need to be shared externally then it can be subsequently forced to be exposed through a corporate secure document-sharing Web site because other unofficial means of sharing (such as e-mail) will not be effective unless the recipient has the rights agent and the authentic rights to the protected information.

In either case, it would seem implementation of a pervasive enterprise rights management system as a means to move focus from the protection of containers of information to the protection of information itself is the only tenable approach to dealing with the potential of information leakage. As we see in other protective controls, rights management needs to be complemented with technology to reinforce trust in the end points that support the rights management software. Additionally, this should be surrounded by comprehensive surveillance to assure the trusted channels and protective techniques are being used.

## Authentication and Authorization

Access must be constrained to authorized and authentic individuals, otherwise our problem of illegitimate use of legitimate authority becomes a much broader problem of anyone can access anything. Therefore, much more could be leaked by many more people.

## End Point Behavior Control

A key support control for other controls both preventative and detective is to have secured and, at least somewhat, trusted end points. This includes the following measures:

- Restrict the general user population that has local administrator privileges. Most people can get by with standard privileges and even system developers can usually be comfortable with power user privileges (to make an assumption, we are talking about Microsoft Windows). Even where people need administrator privileges, these can usually be granted temporarily or made irrelevant by attacking the root cause of privilege requirements such as better software distribution or better policy configuration of printer or wireless support. Reduction in administrator privileges means, overall, fewer spyware issues, less unauthorized software, and less potential for other controls to be disabled or attacks obfuscated.
- Patch systems and run a personal firewall (if appropriate). Also, running a suitably configured personal firewall can stop connectivity to home networks to upload information from the corporate laptop. Similarly, enforcement of firewall policies can stop Web surfing except when connected by VPN to the corporate network so that Internet site blocking is effective.
- Run antivirus software, keep it up to date, and take advantage of heuristic detection and any antispyware capability even at the expense of some potential false positives.
- Lock diskette drives and CD/DVD burners and lock down USB and other peripheral connectivity to reduce the risk of information being taken via high-capacity media.
- More advanced environments or those with higher security requirements can run network admission control systems to authenticate the identity and integrity of end points and can run behavior control or end point intrusion prevention systems to further protect systems.
- Configure browsers, IM, and e-mail clients to operate in as secure a way as feasible, subject to any flexibility constraints.

## Internet and Communications Access Blocking

As we have covered, one of the biggest sources of leakage is due to Internet access coupled with e-mail or other messaging access. Some of the more appropriate and easily deployed techniques to reduce the risk from these channels are as follows:

- Block access to whole categories of Internet sites such as Web-based e-mail and chat, storage sites, anonymizers,

and any other category of site that may be used to bypass other controls.
- In this way, and other ways, aim to reduce the number of communication channels and flows to those that you explicitly authorize and then know to monitor.
- Quarantine, that is, do not permit, whole classes of message attachment types that maybe used to embed information beyond the reach of surveillance systems. This may well include, paradoxically, prohibiting encrypted e-mail or password-protected files if you are surveilling at ingress/egress points. You could still meet security objectives to a degree by deploying edge-to-edge or edge-to-end messaging-protection systems.
- Again, paradoxically given the previous point, there may well be some use for anonymizers for a subset of your user population that is considered trusted (but additionally surveilled) if that subset's Internet access behavior would leak inferred information about the future intent of the corporation.
- Finally, all of this should be implemented in tandem with an effective end-user security awareness campaign to explain the rationale behind these controls.

## Portable Secure Environments

If you have a mobile population that accesses the corporate environment from untrusted end points such as public Internet terminals, then consider equipping people with some of the new variety of USB tokens that contain PIN-protected vaults, launch a secure browser from the token, and do a scan of the end point for spyware, keystroke loggers, and so forth prior to enabling connectivity. An alternative to this would be running a logical service projected from the corporate remote access gateways that would check the integrity of the remote device prior to permitting connectivity and that would likely disclose information if the remote device was in fact compromised. The prevalence of keystroke loggers in these environments, often in place to steal passwords, is another driver for two-factor authentication devices such as code word generators.

## Pervasive Surveillance, Education, and Training

Again, virtually all people in most corporations are diligent and trustworthy so it is important not to alienate people through these controls. This can be difficult but through constant training and awareness, people cannot only be led to understand the need for controls but can also become an important part of your sensory apparatus. Many people who are doing bad things will often give away their activities by behavioral clues or even through outright bragging. An aware workforce trained how to deal with this can be a vital first line of defense. In addition to this, surveillance done effectively and with some degree of sensitivity can increase the sense of diligence and reduce opportunistic leakage significantly.

Training and education can also assist in reducing indirect threats or threats resulting from errors or omissions. For example, a common channel of leakage in many firms that is hard to regulate is sensitive or otherwise embarrassing information being contained in tracked changes in Word or other documents. There is little that can be done here without draconian controls other than keeping people aware and diligent.

### Keeping Clear of Bad People

Finally, the other fairly obvious control to reduce the risk from bad people is to not employ bad people or let them access the things you care about. There are various well-worn techniques that mainly originate with comprehensive background checks of all individuals who have access to your environment. However, this is often not as simple as it may sound, given the complex web of privacy and other limiting legislation on an international basis that in many locations would restrict the ability to do this. Sometimes keeping clear of bad people is not enough if you are subject to good people turning bad. Employee codes of conduct, nondisclosure agreements, and other contractual terms can, to a degree, be a good deterrent in this case.

## Correction

Correction, or postincident reaction, can take many forms. It is important to be swift, consistent, and above all to seek to learn from every detected infraction to put in motion a feedback loop that constantly improves the environment either in terms of detection, protection, or correction/reaction. Such correction techniques can include the following:

- Maintaining an appropriately trained forensic investigations team, or have an outside provider that can act in this capacity. Evidence associated with the infraction may need to be used in a prosecution. It is beyond the scope of this chapter to cover all that is involved here; suffice to say, it is important to get this right if you would ever want to secure a conviction or other remedy in some dispute.
- Incident learning. Put in place feedback loops to take incidents and conduct postmortems or after-action activities to feed back lessons learnt into all aspects of your program.
- Include education and revisions to user training as a result of any incident.

## CONCLUSIONS

Detecting, preventing, and reacting to information leakage, especially by trusted insiders, is a difficult problem. It is important to recognize that without draconian measures, which are often counterproductive to the vast majority of your corporation's honest workers, any controls will ultimately be prone to defeat by a determined attacker. However, by applying some basic security measures and some more targeted techniques, the risk can be reduced substantially. Basic measures include these:

- Protect information by only permitting access by authentic and authorized users.
- Keep access authority current to people's roles.
- Terminate access as roles change or as someone leaves.

- Lock down end points, especially peripheral usage such as disk, CD/DVD, and USB-accessible drives.
- Keep and examine logs, or in large environments sift logs electronically, for anomalies.
- Seek executive support and ownership for this being a worthy problem.
- Establish clean rooms or secure zones for the most critical information while you are figuring out the more advanced measures.
- As much as you can, put in place an environment that by default denies communication channels and Web access.

More advanced measures include these:

- Block access to Internet sites that may cause problems, for example, Web-based e-mail and Internet storage sites.
- Perform high levels of surveillance on all communication flows.
- Classify or categorize information and implement an enterprise rights management system progressively across your organization to protect your most sensitive information.
- Interrelate and combine efforts with other areas in your company that have a need for some level of oversight. This would likely be at least the legal department, compliance department, and human resources department.

Finally, recognize the fundamental principle of *compartment diffusion*: that whenever we erect physical or logical barriers to a flow of anything then there will be forces at work to provide means to cross that barrier. That is a fancy way of saying this is yet another class of problem that will need continued focus and iterative control improvement based on incident learning. Above all, keep in mind that most people are honest and a badly designed or psychologically offensive control system will both harm the flexibility of the corporation and will turn your most important allies, the hardworking and honest vast majority, against the system. The former destroys the objective of protecting value, the latter creates more enemies, neither of which any of us can afford to do.

## GLOSSARY

**Blog (Web Log)**  A Web site constructed to permit easy development and maintenance of an online, diary-style personal Web site.

**S/MIME (Secure Multipart Internet Mail Extension)**  A standard for encrypting and signing MIME content of Internet e-mail.

**VOMIT (Voice Over Misconfigured Internet Telephony)**  A tool to reconstruct datagram streams of IP telephony traffic into wave/sound files for listening to conversations.

**WareZ**  Hacker slang for pirated or otherwise illicit content such as music, video, and software.

## CROSS REFERENCES

See *Corporate Spying: The Legal Aspects; Digital Rights Management; Legal, Social, and Ethical Issues of the Internet; Physical Security Measures; Physical Security Threats.*

## REFERENCES

Denning, E. (1982). *Cryptography and data security.* Boston: Addison-Wesley.

Domingo-Ferrer, J. (2002). *Inference control in statistical databases: From theory to practice.* Lecture Notes in Computer Science, 2316. Berlin: Springer-Verlag.

Pfleeger, C. (2002). *Security in computing.* Upper Saddle River, NJ: Prentice Hall.

Venables, P. (2004). *Information security and complexity.* Paper presented at the Burton Group Catalyst Conference 2004. Retrieved from http://www.burtongroup.com

## FURTHER READING

Anastatis, J. (2003). *The new forensics: Investigating corporate fraud and the theft of intellectual property.* Hoboken, NJ: John Wiley & Sons.

Boni, W., & Kovacich, G. (2000). *Netspionage: The global threat to information.* Burlington, MA: Butterworth-Heinemann.

Poon, A., Pearce, B., Comber, P., & Fletcher P. (2003). *Practical Web traffic analysis: Standards, privacy, techniques and results.* Berkeley, CA: APress.

# Digital Rights Management

Renato Iannella, *National ICT, Australia (NICTA)*

## INTRODUCTION

Digital rights management (DRM) covers the broad area of intellectual property management and enforcement by providing secure and trusted services to control the use and distribution of content. The "digital age" has seen both sides of DRM exposed. From the content owner's point of view, the secure aspects of DRM content control have been a blessing. However, from the consumer's point of view, the same secure aspects of DRM content control have been seen as a hindrance and impediment to open content use.

The majority of this dichotomy has been attributed to the initial effects of the first-generation DRM systems that primarily promoted an *enforcement-centric* view, that is, a view that limited and controlled the distribution of content. Newer generations of DRM now hold a more comprehensive *value chain* view that manages intellectual property rights and secures content at all stages of the content lifecycle, including less emphasis on limited use.

An example of this has been the successful iTunes/iPod music download service offered by Apple. In this particular case, the DRM involved, called "FairPlay," allows the end user unlimited play rights and rights to copy the music a fixed number of times to other devices for personal use. It is important to note that although the FairPlay DRM system technically can support these features, they would not be possible without the appropriate negotiation of these rights from the content owners by the service provider. This shows a much overlooked aspect of DRM in that the negotiated rights will dictate what is offered and not about what technically is capable by the underlying DRM system.

DRM consists of a mix of business models, social issues, legal conformance, and technical capabilities. A typical case is the scenario of purchasing an e-book as a gift for your niece. The business model has to be firstly created by the e-book publisher together with the rights to sell the

e-book from the content rights holder, which may include renegotiating rights under current copyright laws. Then, the publisher of the e-book needs to consider the mechanisms to enforce the personal use on the consumer's end device. Finally, as a "social" right that is normal in the traditional book world, the act of "giving" needs to be enabled as part of the original rights acquired. This then leads to some technical issues as to how and when to identify the end recipient (ie the niece) and what type of compatible systems must be used to enforce the end-user rights.

This brief example has shown another key aspect of DRM systems. They are an integral part of the entire end-to-end content lifecycle, not just a single service that exists in isolation. The key to a successful DRM system is that it is not seen as a separate "DRM system," but as part of typical content management and consumption systems with which users are familiar.

Others (e.g., Samuelson, 2003) have argued that in fact DRM is not about rights management and protection, but about "changing consumer expectations about what they are entitled to do with digital content." So, in the previous scenario, e-book purchasers must change their perception of buying "books" because the technology may not allow them to do what they are used to anymore. This also implies a strong requirement from the vendors to ensure that consumers are aware of what they are allowed, and more importantly, not allowed to do when acquiring digital content. Camp (2003) also concludes that "technology, by its nature, alters society as it diffuses throughout it" and argues that DRM systems must not be solely designed from law but must include technological and economic factors.

As DRM systems are now evolving from proprietary systems to open standards, the effects and influence of DRM will start to appear in more common desktop services. This will be the big test for DRM acceptability by the mass market and will show how well it has balanced the needs of the business, social, legal, and technical aspects.

This chapter provides a comprehensive overview of DRM by positioning it within the context of content management and showing the evolving steps of DRM. Next, the Systems Architecture section shows the core functional modules for DRM, followed by the Information Model section, showing the key semantic relationships. The standardization of DRM technologies also showcases the effects of DRM interoperability in the mobile sector. The latter also serves as a case study of how DRM systems and standards have evolved recently to meet the needs of the wider community.

## OVERVIEW

The primary objectives of DRM are to provide mechanisms for the control and management of the distribution of content including the processes that lead to the content being made available—all under the framework of intellectual property management. That is, the objective is to provide a mechanism for the complete content management lifecycle, focusing on aspects that deal with and include the management of rights information and usage.

This implies a dependent relationship between the functions of content management and DRM systems because both deal with the production and supply of digital content and share common technologies and techniques. Most important, both are necessary to have a valuable and practical marketplace that brings content and relevant rights from original creators to end consumers.

Typically, content management (CM) is inward focused and DRM is outward focused. For example, a CM system will support version control of a digital asset within an enterprise environment, and DRM will support the downstream usage of the digital asset after it is traded to a consumer. The objectives of CM are strongly related to DRM (Iannella & Higgs, 2003) but there has been little evidence of merging of the two into comprehensive single systems and services.

More formally, DRM involves the description, layering, analysis, valuation, trading, and monitoring of the rights over an enterprise's assets, both in physical and digital form and of tangible and intangible value. DRM covers the digital management of rights, be they rights in a physical manifestation of a work or rights in a digital manifestation of a work (Iannella, 2001). Although DRM can cover physical and intangible assets, these are unlikely to be under any rights enforcement system but instead under a mainly rights management system.

Systems that manage and supply content need to interface with, or be closely coupled with, systems that manage rights. Figure 1 shows the logical relationship between CM and DRM. As content is created and managed (e.g., version control, digitization), traded via an e-commerce exchange, and delivered to the consumer, appropriate rights information are also captured and managed in parallel.

In many cases the CM functions and the DRM functions have strong dependencies, such as the protection of the content at the consumer's end of the transaction. The terms and conditions agreed on in the trade will need to inform the content consumption systems to ensure that the content is only used for the purposes acquired.

At the point of trading, all the rights information managed is termed "upstream" and conversely "downstream" after that event. Current DRM technologies are focused on managing downstream rights. That is, the flow of content from a publishing organization to consumers. This flow is predominantly of relative simple usage consumption, for example, the trading of e-books in which the end consumer can only display or print the document. Upstream rights management is more complex because the value chain of agreements among contributors to the content needs to managed and controlled. The combination of all the intellectual effort and agreements needs to be amalgamated and made available to downstream offers. To discuss and define DRM, it is advantageous to separate it into two clear segments: rights management and rights enforcement.

### Rights Management

Rights management (RM) is concerned with managing intellectual property of content, including:

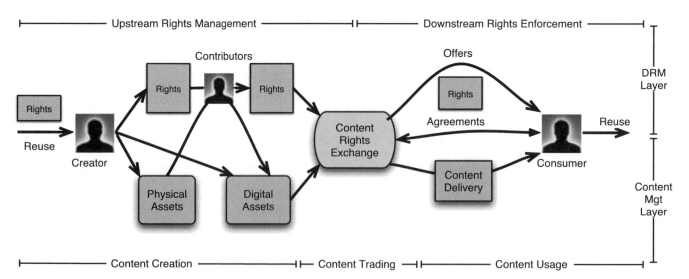

**Figure 1:** CM and DRM relationship.

- The rights holders of content and any existing terms of agreements.
- The creation of offers to consumers that include the terms and conditions for use of content.
- The creation of agreements (or contracts) for usage licenses to downstream users for content.
- Interfacing with party and identity management systems to authenticate users.
- Interfacing with e-commerce systems for billing and payments.
- Reporting on license activity and disbursing revenue (e.g., royalties) for the usage of rights.

A method for achieving RM is the use of a rights expression language (REL) for describing the terms and conditions of offers, agreements, and rights holder information. These computer-readable agreements, when embedded or associated with the content, enable the management and tracking of asset usages when distributed in controlled environments.

## Rights Enforcement

Rights enforcement (RE) is the process of ensuring that content is only used under the terms and conditions for which it was acquired. These include such functions as the following:

- Ensuring that only the allowed usage permissions are enabled
- Ensuring that any constraints on usage (such as time-based or count-based) are honored
- Ensuring that tracking of content (for example, to support per-use fees) is reported
- Supporting the encryption and authorised decryption of digital content, including public key management. This may include others forms of RE, such as watermarking

RE is the "public face" of DRM systems to which the majority of end users are exposed and is what typically concerns the content industry the most. As such, the "enforcement" approach to DRM has left many with serious concerns about usability and long-term interoperability of encrypted content. Additionally, RE is constantly under attack from members of the community who are keen to break "unbreakable" encryption techniques; most of the major systems have been cracked. DRM security is an area that is still an unsolved problem. The most obvious strategy is therefore to apply the best or most appropriate RE mechanism (that is, separate from the RM system) that may require updating in future versions.

There are also two aspects of RE that affect the overall security level of a DRM system. First is the actual specification (or architecture) of the encryption system and the second is the actual implementation of that specification. This may lead to cases where there is a strong encryption algorithm defined but which may be poorly implemented in a operational system.

## Framework

Now that rights expression languages are becoming standardized and the role of rights is better understood, RM functionality will be provided by much more capable but specialized modules that interface with open content management systems and identity systems.

A complete framework—shown in Figure 2—consists of the three core managed entities: content, parties, and rights. The separation of functionality into these three specialized management entities is critical to allow future flexibility in the types of usages able to be offered, the level of content protection provided, and the range of supported business models. Within these managed entities, there are numerous and overlapping systems, such as metadata, discovery, repository, and agreement systems. Many of these systems, such as identity and rights holders, will be closely coupled.

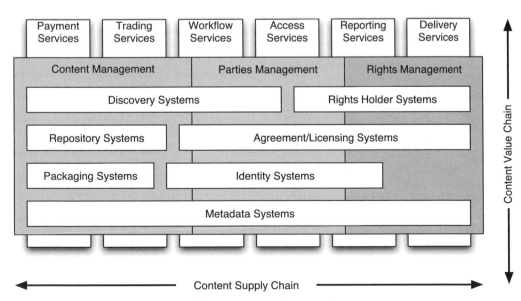

**Figure 2:** DRM framework.

Supporting all these systems is a collection of services that provide the operational instances to enable the service offerings, such as delivery, trading, reporting, and payment services. Again, some of these are common across the systems and also need to support interoperability across the three core managed entities.

The *content supply chain* extends across the breadth of the three core managed entities with the support of some of the services, such as workflow and delivery, for example. The greater the scope, from content creation, trade, use, and reuse, the more capable the supply chain.

The *content value chain* extends across the depth of the three core managed entities with the support of some of the systems, such as agreement/licensing and packaging. The greater the provision of such services for the end-user experience, the greater the value created by the supply chain. However, a very large value chain could be inefficient and costly so a balance would be needed to make overall business sense.

## Evolution

Like all technologies, DRM is constantly evolving. Three generations of DRM have been identified.

First-generation DRM approaches primarily stated the rights holders' names and usually claimed all rights over a work when it was provided to a customer. This statement could be in metadata or a "shrink wrap" license. In essence, the license details are simply textual information aimed for the end consumer to read.

Second-generation *downstream* DRM approaches utilized RE technologies to ensure that the permissions the creator or trader wanted to make available were not breached. For example, a media file is encrypted to a cryptographic key that is specific to a device to lock the two together. The key can permit certain functionality, such as display of an e-book, only on that device. This obviated the need to clearly state and manage the provenance and rights holders of a work because only simple consumption rights were available to acquirers.

Second-generation *upstream* DRM approaches extended CM systems to include some unstructured information about rights holders and the rights held over each media asset. New versions of a media asset are often managed by "version control" features, but the linkages between the rights and the versions can easily be lost or become meaningless as multiple assets are combined and reused.

Third-generation DRM approaches manage the upstream and downstream rights separately from the content and the parties. In such systems, dedicated and interoperable systems manage the rights, content, and identity aspects of the total system. Such advanced third-generation DRM systems would manage the following:

- The agreements or offers separately from the content that are the subject of the agreement/offer
- Complex rights holders' relationships and royalty allocations
- Rights over multiple content and content with multiple parts
- Changing rights over time that may affect previous agreements and/or result in revocation of rights
- Linkages with the identity of parties and supporting authentication and authorization services for both rights holders and end consumers
- Linkages with CM systems for encryption and delivery of content

Third-generation DRM systems require significant interoperability opportunities among the core entities mentioned. We are now seeing open standards in the area of identity management (Liberty Project, 2004) but there is still a large requirement for open standards to interface with content management systems.

## Legal Implications

As mentioned previously, DRM has significant legal issues and implications. The DRM relationship to copyright law is obvious and of primary concern because it covers intellectual property, the rights of creators, and exceptions available under certain conditions (e.g., "fair use" or "fair dealing").

New legal updates, such as the Digital Millennium Copyright Act (USA) and the WIPO Copyright Treaty have focused on the anticircumvention implication of DRM systems. In effect, they make it illegal to attempt to, or provide services that, purposely break DRM systems, even for such lawful activities as security research and fair use. Some have argued that such new laws and treaties are seriously impeding scientific progress and lack the fair balance required by intellectual property legislation (Samuelson, 2003).

Not so obvious is the DRM relationship with contract law, as rights licenses are contractually binding agreements between parties. The license makes explicit what the consumer is allowed to do with the content using a machine-based language. Interpreting the rules will need to lead to unambiguous behavior by the computer systems to allow the contract terms to be honored. Owens and Akalu (2004) point out that such licenses may force users to give up some rights under common copyright laws, but users may see more appropriate direct benefits.

One of the major deficiencies in current DRM systems is support for the wide range of copyright exceptions. There are a number of reasons for this, such as the fact that such exceptions vary across jurisdictions, but the main reason is that the law is purposely vague, complex, and indeterminate when defining these exceptions. Typically, copyright exceptions need to be dealt with at an individual level, looking at all the circumstances and context of use. And, of course, in computing systems, such characteristics are inefficient and difficult to program and support.

Because the legal implications are serious and considerable, we will probably see more support in future fourth-generation DRM systems.

# DRM-ARCHITECTURES

The architecture for DRM consists of a number of functional modules, each pertaining to specific roles and responsibilities.

## Functional Architecture

Figure 3 shows a DRM functional architecture, highlighting the relationship among three main layers: rights holders, service providers, and consumers.

The rights holders own and create content. This content is "offered" under various business rules (i.e., rights expressions) to service providers for ultimate sale or access to end consumers. The offers are made available to trusted service providers that enter into agreements to offer the content for retail sale. In return, rights holders expect royalties and other rewards.

Rights holders may create static content or "live" content (e.g., a football match) and this content needs to be managed and associated with all the parties that provide intellectual input or other services.

The service providers act as intermediaries to expose the content to consumers. Content they have agreed to provide (under the terms of the agreements with rights holders) may reside in their local repository or with the rights holders.

Consumers interact with the service provider to discover or preview the content offerings and to enter into agreements to receive content. Depending on the consumers' devices, the content may be transformed by various processes for delivery. These transformations may take into account these factors:

- The rendering formats, limits, or sizes of the end device
- The DRM client capabilities of the end device
- The location/network of the end device
- The security capabilities of the end device

The consumers receive content and licenses that they have acquired (either immediately or at a later stage). Their client manages the enforcement side of the agreement, including any decryption, constrained use monitoring, and tracking usage.

In some circumstances, content may be forwarded by consumers to other consumers. In this case, the receiving consumer will be redirected to obtain a license to use the content. Additionally, such licenses may entitle the sending consumer to receive benefits (e.g., "loyalty points") and this is also tracked.

The DRM functional architecture in Figure 3 does not highlight some of the technical issues with DRM to do with security of content and trust of parties. A DRM architecture needs the support of a system to manage the cryptographic keys of content, individual parties, and the physical devices. These keys are used to lock and unlock content by authorized parties and to digitally sign agreements. For example, a public key infrastructure (PKI) is such a system.

Also, across the three layers, there is a significant need for an interoperable "identity management" framework

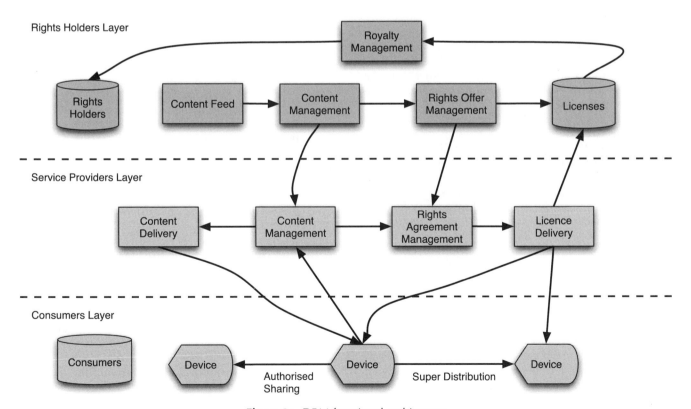

**Figure 3:** DRM functional architecture.

that can work with the security services to authenticate and authorize use of the content based on a party's credentials.

## Systems Architecture

Figure 4 shows some of the common DRM infrastructure components. The three roles of the parties (rights holders, service providers, and consumers) access the three core DRM functions (identity, content, and rights management) via specific service interfaces. The three DRM functions would interact with specific systems interfaces. For example, some interfaces may be tailored for delivery of content to a mobile device.

The identity management module would need to interface with the authentication/authorization system to provide necessary functions to identify all the parties in the relationship. The functions provided by identity management include these:

- Allocation of unique party identifiers
- User profile and preferences
- User's device management
- Public key management

A number of current standards are aimed at identity management, including the Liberty Project and directory services. However, many current DRM systems use other methods to identify parties, such as the cyptographic information used to secure content.

The content management and rights management modules provide the common services as discussed in the Overview section.

The security/encryption module provides the necessary services to encrypt the content and to sign license agreements, all under a "trust" mechanism. The strength of encryption algorithms are critical to the overall security level and may vary depending on the risk of hacking from the community. To express the encryption and signing, standards such as W3C XML encryption and W3C XML digital signatures are widely used. The most common trust mechanisms are provided by PKI. One of the most critical aspects of PKI is the establishment of a third-party organization that authorizes and issues certificates that establish which parties and devices can be trusted. The technical aspects of this process are well established, but the policies and procedures of the third-party organization need to meet the expectations of content providers.

## Example DRM Architecture: e-Learning

An emerging technology is the trading of learning objects via "content exchange" services or brokers. Current work has focused on managing the trading of learning content via their rights information (Erickson, 2001), as opposed to trading based on the digital media alone. An online e-learning DRM project investigated the end-to-end use of DRM in the learning content creation, management, and delivery services with the higher education and vocational training sectors (Iannella, 2004a). Figure 5 shows the generalized architecture used in this project.

There were five systems that interacted in the following way:

- The Learning Object eXchange (LOX) stored the learning content and managed the information about the learning object rights offers (i.e., terms and conditions of use). Users could then acquire the learning objects, which would then create the rights agreement and embed this license into the final content for delivery to the downstream systems.
- The eLibrary was a repository of metadata about traditional library items and also populated with metadata about the learning objects in LOX. Users can then search the eLibrary system and find learning objects in LOX with appropriate linkages to the object.
- The Learning Content Management System (LCMS) managed the acquired learning objects from LOX and provided mechanisms to access the resources within the learning objects for additional manipulation for instructor use. The LCMS would then act as a host of the content to ensure controls over the terms and conditions were met by the requesting systems.
- The Learning Management System (LMS) managed the interactions between the students and the learning object content, which it requested from the LCMS.
- The Identity system was a common sign-on service managed by a directory and proxy server. This enabled the users to transparently move between the systems without being challenged each time for their username and password. In the case of learning objects acquired that were constrained to specific student groups, the Directory was then checked to ensure that the student credentials appeared in the rights agreement for the content.

These projects used the ODRL rights expression language (ODRL, 2002) because its simple and extensible model was appropriate for learning applications. This finding was also supported by Guth and Koeppen (2002). The ODRL rights expression language (REL) is used to support expressing both rights offers and agreements over learning objects. A rights offer is a collection of permissions and constraints under which the rights holder is making the content available. The offer will usually also include some payment for these rights. In the education sector, payments may not always be required. Once accepted by an end consumer, the offer migrates to an agreement stipulating the exact parties involved and the agreed permissions and constraints. This agreement is then used by downstream systems to verify what can (and cannot) be performed on the content.

Figure 6 shows an example screen from the eLearning projects that enabled a rights holder to specify the terms and conditions for the learning object offer. The interface allows the user to select the permissions, constraints, and requirements that will make up the rights offer. This particular interface also allowed more complex relationships to be created. For example, the time range constraint for 1 year only applies to the adaptation permissions, and hence the usage permissions have no such constraints.

These projects demonstrated the current state of the art and were early examples of the emerging third-generation DRM systems. They also highlighted the need for interoperability across systems via open standards to enable the commercial trading of content via rights information.

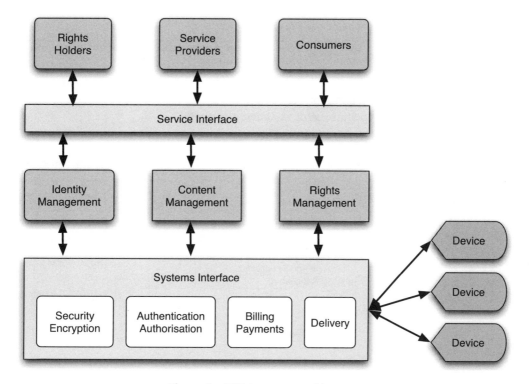

**Figure 4:** DRM systems architecture.

## INFORMATION MODEL

DRM requires the capture and management of significant and important information about the ownership of content and the allowable usages. This implies strong semantic relationships between the three core entities: rights, parties, and content.

The basic DRM information model (shown in Figure 7) relates these three entities for maximum flexibility: parties create content; parties own rights over content; parties use content. Each of these three core entities are further extrapolated to greater levels of detail.

## Rights

The rights entity captures the specific details of the offers and agreements between the parties and the content. This is usually expressed via a REL. A REL will provide details on

- Permissions: actual usages allowed over the content, such as play, print, sell.
- Constraints: limits to these permissions, such as count and time-based restrictions.

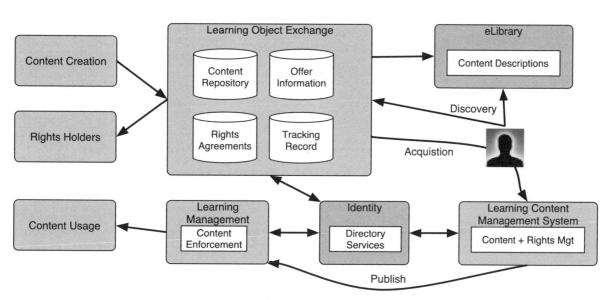

**Figure 5:** eLearning DRM architecture.

| Rights Offer Overview | Name | Rights Offer Type A5 |
| --- | --- | --- |
| | Description | Offer to Use/Adapt the content in Australia for public education. Adaption can only occur for 12 months after acquisition. |

**Permission Groups**

☑ Usage  (display, print, play, execute)
☑ Adaptation  (modify, excerpt, annotate, aggregate)
☐ Transfer [Republish]  (give, sell)

**Constraints**

| | | | Apply to Permission Groups: |
| --- | --- | --- | --- |
| ☐ Count | 1 ▼ | | ☐ Usage  ☐ Adaptation  ☐ Transfer |
| ☑ Territory | Australia ▼ | | ☑ Usage  ☑ Adaptation  ☐ Transfer |
| ☑ Time Range | One Year ▼ | | ☐ Usage  ☑ Adaptation  ☐ Transfer |
| ☑ Purpose | Public Education ▼ | | ☑ Usage  ☑ Adaptation  ☐ Transfer |
| ☐ Group | Group ID must be specified at Agreement time | | ☐ Usage  ☐ Adaptation  ☐ Transfer |
| ☐ Contextualise | Remarks | | ☑ Usage  ☑ Adaptation  ☐ Transfer |

**Requirements**

| ☐ Accept | Text to Accept |
| --- | --- |
| ☑ Attribution | Remarks |
| ☑ Payment | $200.00 ▼ |

**Figure 6:** Rights offer example screen.

- Requirements: obligations needed to exercise the permission such as payments.
- Conditions: global exceptions to control permissions, such as the need to have a valid credit card during the term of the agreement.

A REL should also provide the linkages to the parties and the content, usually via identifiers to instances of these entities. In some cases, the parties will be marked as rights holders or end consumers.

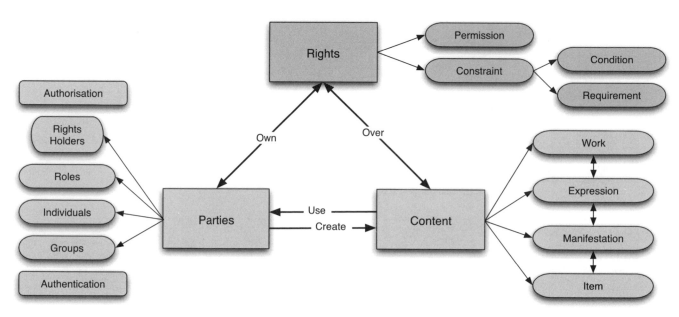

**Figure 7:** DRM information model.

## Content

Clearly the model needs to identify the content that is part of the rights expression. This is usually via formal identification systems. Content that is encrypted also requires information on how to decrypt the content.

An interesting aspect, yet overlooked by DRM systems, of content is the "layers" of content, as defined by the International Federation of Library Associations (Plassard, 1998), to enable works, expressions, manifestations, and items of the same content bundle to be identified and assigned rights. This is critical in that it shows the relationships among various stages (from abstract to concrete) and versions of content over its lifetime and links them together to clearly show how the rights have been assigned.

As an example, consider *Clear and Present Danger*. The abstract work, by Tom Clancy, would be the idea of the events that took place on Air Force One involving the president and including descriptions of the concepts and main ideas, features, or characters. The particular expressions of the work could then include

- The original novel text by Tom Clancy.
- the movie screenplay by Donald Stewart.

The general manifestations of the "original novel text" expression could include

- The hardcover book published by Putnam Pub Group.
- The audio CD published by Simon & Schuster.

The individual items of the "hardcover book" manifestations could include the single physical hardcover book purchased from a retail store.

The important point in this style of content modeling is that at any (and all) of the layers in the IFLA content model, different rights holders can be recognized and semantic relationships formed. In effect, the "chain of title" can be established and maintained throughout the lifetime of the content if this model is adopted.

## Parties

The parties entity enables the model to express which individuals, groups of individuals, organizations, or role types are rights holders or consumers of content. As with content, the parties are usually indicated via formal identification systems. Within a trusted environment, there is an obvious need for the parties identified in the model to be authenticated and then authorized to perform the functions expressed in the rights, such as display content or receive royalty payments for usage. There are emerging open standards in this area, in particular the Liberty Project, that can enable a framework for single sign-on and, potentially, manage a set of authorized operations to which users may be entitled.

Because the DRM model relies heavily on the identification of parties, it raises serious concerns about privacy. In many cases, it would be difficult to support anonymous and pseudoanonymous transactions because this, to some extent, goes against the requirements of effective rights management. However, there may be some cases where the content/rights provider does not care who acquires their content, as long as their use is managed at the consumer end correctly.

A number of DRM and privacy workshops and reports have highlighted privacy issues and proposed some potential solutions. For example, Vora et al. (2001) propose that all consumers should be treated as "first-class participants" and, hence, given complete control as to how their personal information is treated and used by all third parties. Kravitz, Yeoh, and So (2001) argue for a "trust server that mediates the conferral and revocation of trust relationships between consumers and providers" to address the privacy interest of consumers. Choen (2003) argues that "DRM controls can be designed to be 'leaky' allowing users greater flexibility to access and use information goods within private spaces."

Specific privacy technical solutions, such as the platform for privacy preferences (Marchiori, 2002), have yet to be demonstrated as an integral part of DRM systems but are an obvious and potential next step.

Privacy is an important issue and DRM standards and DRM designers do need to address technical measures that can support a balance with the social and policy needs of privacy protection.

## STANDARDS

Numerous standards groups, both formal and informal, have been involved in the standardization of DRM technologies. These are now emerging and showing excellent results for acceptance from content owners and wide adoption by consumers. There also have been occasions when DRM standard solutions have not been very successful, such as the Secure Digital Media Initiative (Wu, Craver, Felten, & Liu, 2001).

The Open Mobile Alliance (OMA) has produced comprehensive standards for DRM for content security and delivery. This is covered in depth in the next section. The REL used by OMA DRM is based on ODRL, which was created by the ODRL Initiative (2004).

The ISO/MPEG standards group has also been working on DRM standards for audio and video content. The MPEG-21 recommendation consists of numerous parts, of which three are directly related to DRM (Burnett, Van de Walle, Hill, Bormans, & Pereira, 2003):

- Part 4: Intellectual Property Management and Protection
- Part 5: Rights Expression Language
- Part 6: Rights Data Dictionary

Only Parts 5 and 6 have reached the formal standards level. The REL used by MPEG-21 is based on XrML, which is owned by ContentGuard (XrML, 2004).

Other standards groups, such as OASIS, the OpenE-Book Forum, and the IEEE Learning Technology Standards Committee are reviewing the RELs for adoption according to their specific community requirements.

One of the more ironic issues with the standardization of DRM technologies has been the use of patents by companies to try and gain a financial and technical edge over participants in the DRM sector. This has affected the standardization of DRM noticeably because it has created some "fear and uncertainty" in the potential costs of utilizing DRM standards in products and services (Guth & Iannella, 2005). With numerous existing DRM patents, the uptake may still be slow from smaller scale vendors and organizations as the patent holders may, or may not, attempt to enforce their "rights" over their claimed intellectual property. This is an issue that faces many standard-setting organizations (Lin, 2003).

On the other side of the fence is the more open Creative Commons (2004) project that is designed for rights holders who want to make their content freely available, with little more than the acknowledgment of their attribution for use of their content. Creative Commons only supports the expression of simple rights, such as attribution, noncommercial use, no derivative works allowed, and "share-a-like," so it is still first generation and does not support any enforcement behavior.

## Interoperability

One of the claimed advantages of open standards is to enable interoperability across different systems. This is fundamental and critical for the DRM community, as highlighted from a recent European Union Report (Commission of the European Communities, 2004): "A prerequisite to ensure Community-wide accessibility to DRM systems and services by rights holders as well as users and, in particular, consumers, is that DRM systems and services are interoperable" (p. 4).

The implication for disparate DRM systems to be compatible is that a major part of the content distribution and rights management chain must be open and standardized. Even the two existing international standards (OMA DRM and MPEG-21) are technically incompatible, so there will also need to be content and rights conversions.

Apart from the standards mentioned here, there are three major proprietary DRM systems on the market currently. These are Microsoft Windows Media DRM, Apple FairPlay, and Real Networks Helix. These commercial systems do not completely implement any of the formal DRM standards and hence are all incompatible. This will lead to potentially chaotic implementation scenarios if content owners wish to deliver to the broadest possible consumer base and consumers wish to maximize content usage. The Opera Project (Wegner, 2003) has concluded that there still are many technical obstacles to building interoperable DRM systems.

A short-term solution would be to identify the core but abstract functions required in a media- and system-independent fashion, then build appropriate "translation" functions (that are media-system proprietary) that would provide the actual data conversions and delivery to the consumers' proprietary DRM systems, including support for a number of trusted environments. Time will tell if this makes business sense and if the large commercial vendors fully adopt the international DRM standards.

## CASE STUDY: MOBILE DRM

The first OMA DRM specification (OMA, 2003) enabled simple business models for the distribution and control of content in the mobile sector. The second version of the OMA DRM specification (OMA, 2004) provides significant new features for premium content consumption and increases the security of content distribution by providing an industry standard trust mechanism.

OMA DRM Version 2.0 consists of four parts:

- OMA DRM architecture
- OMA DRM rights expression language
- OMA DRM content format
- OMA DRM specification

Version 2.0 introduces the OMA DRM specification, which includes a range of new advanced secure operations and trusted DRM communications, and revised content format and expanded rights expression language.

## OMA DRM Architecture

The basic model for OMA DRM consists of the following entities (shown in Figure 8):

- DRM agents: trusted entities in a device that control access to content objects
- Content objects: encrypted content
- Content issuers: trusted entities that deliver content objects to DRM agents
- Rights objects: terms and conditions for use of content objects (i.e., agreements and licenses)
- Rights issuers: trusted entities that deliver rights objects to DRM agents to enable access to content objects
- Users: human entities who interact with DRM agents to access content objects
- Devices: trusted entities that host DRM agents, either connected or unconnected to a network
- Domains: collections of devices that can share content and rights objects

A device can be any physical device, such as a mobile phone, computer, or even a storage device. The key criterion is that the device contain a trusted DRM agent. If the device is not connected to any network then a connected device may acquire the content object on its behalf. In this particular case, both devices must belong to the same domain.

All content objects are encrypted into DRM content format (DCF), and thus can be freely distributed (i.e., super distributed) over any transport protocol because they are inherently secure. DCFs can either contain discrete content (such as images and applications) or continuous media (such as audio, video, and streaming media).

The DCFs may include multiple containers, creating a multipart DCF. Each part must have a unique identifier (i.e., a ContentID) that enables a single rights object to refer to different parts of a content object and potentially assign different permissions.

Content objects require corresponding rights objects, which express the permissions and constraints over the use of the content object. A rights object is cryptographically bound to a DRM agent, hence ensuring that only those users who have properly acquired the rights object can have access to the content object.

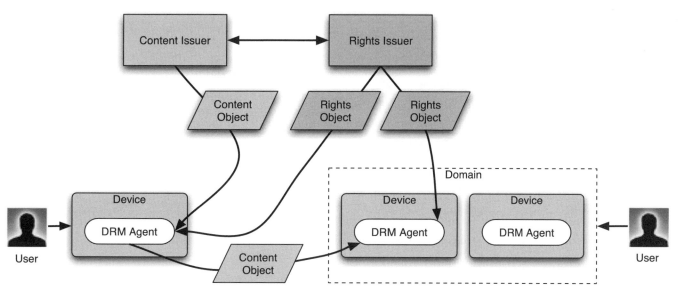

**Figure 8:** OMA DRM version 2.0 architecture.

A domain allows a user to use content and rights objects on any of the devices registered in the domain. Hence, as shown in Figure 8, a user has forwarded a content object to his friend's device. The friend has a number of devices in his domain and uses one of them to request and obtain a rights object to use the content object. In this case, the rights object will be a domain rights object and will allow any device in the domain to use the content object.

The trust model used in OMA DRM version 2 is based on PKI mechanisms. This means that the DRM agent has to be trusted by the rights issuer. The DRM agent is provisioned with a certificate that enables the rights issuer to make decisions on this trust level (e.g., based on the manufacturer of the device.) This is where third-party organizations, such as the Content Management License Administrator (2004), will play a significant role. This group will be the trusted source that issues keys and certificates to device manufacturers that are to be trusted in terms of adherence to a level of secure DRM behaviors. The CMLA is independent from OMA.

Other security aspects include protection to stop the replay of rights objects as well as trusted time sources to ensure that date and time constraints are always correctly enforced.

## OMA DRM Rights Expression Language

The OMA DRM REL is an application profile of ODRL with a defined a subset of ODRL's complete semantic functionality (ODRL, 2002). The profile includes the standard ODRL permission terms of "play," "display," "execute," and "print" and the standard ODRL constraint terms of "count," "datetime," "interval," "accumulated," and "individual."

The OMA REL profile also includes some extensions beyond the standard ODRL data dictionary terms. These include "export," "timed-count," and "system."

The "export" permission allows the content/rights object to be transformed to another non–OMA DRM system with compatible features and the same enforcement capabilities as OMA DRM.

The "timed-count" constraint has the same semantics as ODRL's "count" constraint with the added ability to specify how many seconds to wait after the content has been consumed (e.g., played) to decrement the counter.

The "system" constraint works with the "export" permission to specify a non–OMA DRM system to which the content/rights object will be exported. The "individual" constraint uses formal identifiers (i.e., the IMSI or WIM) of the end user that must be checked on the device before the content can be consumed.

For examples of the XML used by ODRL and the OMA DRM REL extensions, see Iannella (2004b).

The OMA DRM REL also supports referring to multiple permissions for multiple content objects in the same agreement (rights object). This means permissions can be grouped and linked to specific assets (content objects) in the ODRL agreement. The permissions could apply to just one asset or to all assets depending on the link information. To support subscriptions to content objects, the OMA DRM REL supports inheritance of rights objects.

Content objects may also include multiple DCF containers to enable multipart content. Each part is uniquely identified and can be referenced in the REL from a single rights object with different sets of permissions and constraints.

The example shown in Figure 9 includes a rights object with multiple permission groups and a multipart content object with various media parts. The rights object has direct and explicit links between the permissions and the separate media parts in the content object. For example, Media Image1 and Media Image2 can both be displayed five times but only Media Image1 can be printed.

The OMA DRM REL security model supports content object confidentiality by encrypting the content encryption key (CEK) to ensure the CEK is confidential. The CEK can be used to decrypt the content object. (Hence, this then relies on keeping the CEK secret from all unauthorized users.) The security model also ensures the integrity between the rights object and the content object by including a hash of the content object inside the rights object.

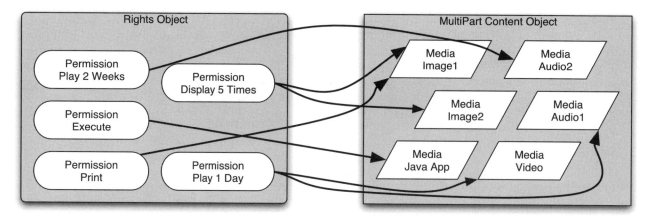

**Figure 9:** Multiple rights and multipart content objects.

The rights object is then digitally signed to prevent tampering with the content object identifier. The OMA DRM specification utilizes the W3C XML encryption and digital signatures recommendations to undertake the security model features.

## OMA DRM Specification

The OMA DRM specification outlines a number of new features for version 2.0 to manage the trusted communications between the core entities (as shown in Figure 8). This includes the format and semantics of the cryptographic protocol, key management, messages, processing instructions, and certificate profiles.

### Rights Object Acquisition Protocol (ROAP)

The ROAP is a suite of protocols for communications between a rights issuer and a DRM agent. This is a major new addition to the OMA DRM version 2.0 specification.

The ROAP protocols include

- The 4-pass protocol for the registration of devices with a rights issuers, which is usually only performed once at first contact to establish trust between a device and rights issuer.
- The 1- and 2-pass rights objects acquisition protocol, which includes mutual authentication and integrity-protected request and delivery of a rights object.
- Two-pass join and leave domain protocol, which initiates a request/response protocol whereby a device can leave or join a domain and receive the appropriate domain key.
- The ROAP trigger, which is sent to an entity to initiate one of these protocols.

There are numerous transport protocols for ROAP communications and data to be transmitted between devices and rights issuers. These include HTTP and Bluetooth.

### Protection of Content and Rights Objects

Content objects are protected by symmetric key encryption. The content encryption key (CEK) used to encrypt the content object (now a DCF) is inserted into the rights object by the rights Issuer. For integrity protection of the DCF, a cryptographic hash is generated of the DCF and also inserted into the rights object.

Rights objects are always digitally signed by the rights issuer and assigned a unique identifier. This ensures that the rights object cannot be modified during transmission and, because it contains the DCF cryptographic hash value, can ensure its integrity.

Rights objects containing count- and some time-based constraints (i.e., interval and accumulated) require the DRM agent to store and manage the current state of the usage. These "stateful" rights objects need to be protected from replay attacks as this may lead to the rights object being reinstated with the zero state. The 2-pass rights objects acquisition protocol supports this by including a nonce in the request/response that can be used to verify that the rights object is not being replayed.

The OMA DRM specifications have demonstrated some of the ideal characteristics of third-generation DRM systems and have shown significant maturity for a new standard. In particular, they have addressed the need for a trusted environment and high levels of advanced encryption. The rights agreements (rights objects from rights issuers) use a flexible REL and have been separated from the content issuers. Content can be identified to the subpart level with support for identification in the rights objects. Finally, the domain feature will allow end consumers to share content (for example, with family members) and help support some level of "social use."

## SUMMARY

It is clear that DRM has evolved rapidly over the past years with both open standards and proprietary systems. Obviously, the critical factor leading to wide adoption will be interoperability, as this enables rights owners to provide content to a wider audience. The key standard leading the way in this area is the OMA DRM specifications that are based on Internet protocols, and so have an opportunity to provide a single open standard for both wireless and wired sectors. OMA DRM has addressed the need for trust mechanisms and has provided a simple yet effective rights model supporting the majority of business cases.

The other critical adoption factor is the usability from the consumer's end. Apple has proven, with the iPod/iTunes service, that keeping the interface and access options as simple as possible will not deter users of DRM-managed content.

Finally, we still are only seeing the beginning of the DRM sector now evolving. Future DRM systems and standards will incorporate wider-ranging REL semantics and greater coupling to identity and e-commerce systems to capture more of the content and rights "transaction space."

## ACKNOWLEDGMENTS

The author acknowledges the support of IPR Systems and Live Events Wireless in the production of this chapter and the valuable feedback from reviewers.

## GLOSSARY

**Agreement** A formal contract (or license) between parties for the use of content including all terms and conditions.

**Client** A device or system capable of consuming and processing DRM content objects.

**Constraints** Limits to the use of content expressed in an agreement.

**Content Management** Processes and functions needed to manage the content lifecycle.

**Content Object** Encrypted content available to be consumed by clients with appropriate rights objects.

**Digital Rights Management (DRM)** Processes and functions needed to manage intellectual property rights.

**Domains** A group of client devices able to share content and rights.

**Encryption** Process to secure content and rights information for private use.

**eXtensible Rights Markup Language (XrML)** A REL used by the MPEG-21 standard.

**Identity** Mechanism to uniquely identify entities such as parties and content.

**Interoperability** Process of disparate systems transparently interchanging content and rights.

**MPEG** An international standards group developing specifications for audio and video.

**Offer** An expression of available rights over content to consumers from the content issuers.

**Open Digital Rights Language (ODRL)** A REL used by the OMA DRM standard.

**Open Mobile Alliance (OMA)** An international standards group developing specifications for the mobile sector.

**Parties** Human entities and roles such as rights holders and end consumers.

**Permissions** The actions or usages allowed over content.

**Privacy** The act of ensuring personal information is kept secret.

**Rights Enforcement** Processes and functions needed to control limits on content usage by clients.

**Rights Expression Language (REL)** A machine-readable language for expressing offers and agreements.

**Rights Management** Processes and functions needed to manage rights, rights holders, and associated requirements.

**Rights Object** An encrypted agreement.

## CROSS REFERENCES

See *Copyright Law; Legal, Social, and Ethical Issues of the Internet; Privacy Law and the Internet; Security Policy Enforcement.*

## REFERENCES

Burnett, I., Van de Walle, R., Hill, K., Bormans, J., & Pereira, F. (2003). MPEG-21: Goals and achievements. *IEEE Multimedia*, October–December, 60–70. 2003.

Camp, L. J. (2003). First principles of copyright for DRM design. *IEEE Internet Computing*. May–June, 59–65.

Cohen, J. E. (2003). DRM and privacy. *Communications of the ACM, 46*(4).

Commission of the European Communities. (2004, April 16). *The management of copyright and related rights in the Internal market*. Retrieved May 1, 2004, from http://europa.eu.int/eur-lex/en/com/cnc/2004/com2004 _0261en01.pdf

Content Management Licensing Administrator. (2004). Retrieved November 1, 2004, from http://www.cm-la.com/

Creative Commons. (2004). Retrieved October 1, 2004, from http://creativecommons.org/

Erickson, J. S. (2001). Information objects and rights management. *D-Lib Magazine*, 7(4). Retrieved September 1, 2004, from http://www.dlib.org/dlib/april01/erickson/04erickson.html

Guth, S., & Iannella, R. (2005) Critical review of MPEG LA software patent claims. *INDICARE News*, 23 March. Retrieved April 1, 2005, from http://www.indicare.org/tiki-read_article.php?articleId=90

Guth, S., & Köeppen, E. (2002). Electronic rights enforcement for learning media. Proceedings of the IEEE International Conference on Advanced Learning Technologies. IEEE Computer Society, Kazan, Russia, 9–12 Sept 2002. Retrieved November 1, 2004, from http://lttf.ieee.org/icalt2002/proceedings/t1503_icalt045_End.pdf

Iannella, R. (2001). Digital rights management (DRM) architectures. *D-Lib Magazine*, 7(6). Retrieved September 1, 2004, from http://www.dlib.org/dlib/june01/iannella/06iannella.html

Iannella, R. (2004a). Online trading of rights-enabled learning objects. *International Journal of Electronic Commerce, 8*(4), 99–113.

Iannella, R. (2004b). The open digital rights language: XML for digital rights management. *Information Security Technical Report, 9*(3), 47–55.

Iannella, R., & Higgs, P. (2003, April 9). *Driving content management with digital rights management* (IPR Systems White Paper). Retrieved February 1, 2004, from http://www.iprsystems.com/whitepapers/CM-DRM-WP.pdf

Kravitz, D., Yeoh, K.-E., & So, N. (2002). *Secure open systems for protecting privacy and digital services*. ACM Workshop on Security and Privacy in Digital Rights Management. *Lecture Notes in Computer Science 2320.*

Liberty Project. (2004). Retrieved March 1, 2004, from http://www.projectliberty.org/

Lin, D. (2003). Dual tragedies: IP rights in industry standards. *IEEE Computer, 36*(2), 25–27.

Marchiori, M. (2002, April 16). *The platform for privacy preferences 1.0 (P3P1.0) specification* (W3C Recommendation). Retrieved April 1, 2004, from http://www.w3.org/TR/P3P/

ODRL. (2002). *Open digital rights language, version 1.1.* ODRL Initiative. Retrieved May 1, 2003, from http://odrl.net/1.1/ODRL-11.pdf> and <http://www.w3.org/TR/odrl/

ODRL Initiative. (2004). Retrieved February 1, 2004, from http://odrl.net/

OMA. (2003). *Open mobile alliance digital rights management v1.0 approved enabler*. Retrieved February 1, 2004, from http://www.openmobilealliance.org/release_program/drm_v1_0.html

OMA. (2004). *Open mobile alliance digital rights management v2.0 candidate enabler*. Retrieved February 1, 2004, from http://www.openmobilealliance.org/release_program/drm_v2_0.html

Owens, R., & Akalu, R. (2004). Legal policy and digital rights management. *Proceedings of the IEEE, 92*(6), 997–1003.

Plassard, M. F. (Ed.). (1998). *International Federation of Library Associations and Institutions, functional requirements for bibliographic records: Final report, Vol. 19: UBCIM—New series*. Munich: Saur. Retrieved March 1, 2003, from http://www.ifla.org/VII/s13/frbr/frbr.pdf

Samuelson, P. (2003). DRM {and or vs} the law. *Communications of the ACM, 46*(4), 41–45.

Vora, P., Reynolds, D., Dickinson, I., Erickson, J., & Banks, D. (2001). *Privacy and digital rights management*. W3C Workshop on Digital Rights Management, January. Retrieved February 1, 2003, from http://www.w3.org/2000/12/drm-ws/pp/hp-poorvi2.html

Wegner, S. (Ed.). (2003). *OPERA—Interoperability of DRM technologies—Prototype description of an open DRM architecture*. Retrieved March 1, 2004, from http://www.eurescom.de/~pub/deliverables/documents/P1200-series/P1207/D3/P1207-D3.pdf

Wu, M., Craver, S., Felten, E. W., & Liu, B. (2001). Analysis of attacks on SDMI audio watermarks. Proceedings of the IEEE International Conference on Acoustics, Speech, and Signal Processing, May. Retrieved May 1, 2004, from http://www.ece.umd.edu/~minwu/public_paper/icassp01_sdmi.pdf

XrML. (2004). Retrieved June 1, 2004, from http://www.xrml.org/

# Web Hosting

Doug Kaye, *IT Conversations*

## INTRODUCTION

Web-hosting services (like Web sites) come in all shapes and sizes. The chart in Figure 1 shows the distribution of annual Web-hosting budgets for U.S. businesses. The average budget is on the order of $1,200 to $1,800 per year ($100 to $150 per month), but note that more than 10% of all businesses surveyed spend more than $100,000 per year.

Because of this tremendous range of offerings, one might think that the services at one end of the spectrum are very different from those at the other end. In fact, these services are far more alike than they are different. For example, all Web sites, no matter how small or how large, require Web servers, domain name services, backup and recovery, and connections to the Internet. It would be nearly impossible to analyze as a single group this wide range of offerings that fall under the Web-hosting umbrella. To keep our analysis more manageable, we segregate the vendors into categories and examine each category in detail.

## CATEGORIES

After a few years of confusion over the various types of Web hosting available, the vendors have settled into four distinct service categories as illustrated in Figure 2. Nearly everyone in the Web-hosting industry and the trade press has accepted these categories. As a result, the categories are now consistent and helpful in distinguishing the many vendors.

In the least expensive, or low-end, category are *shared servers*. As their name implies, these are computer systems that are shared by more than one Web site, and hence are appropriate for small, simple, low-traffic sites.

Next on the list are *dedicated servers*. These are nearly identical to shared servers with the obvious exception that they are not shared but rather dedicated to a single Web site or to multiple Web sites owned and controlled by the same business entity. Compared with shared servers, dedicated servers offer more capacity and flexibility and better security but at a higher price.

The next category is significantly different from the previous categories but in some ways substantially more limited. Instead of offering more support than is available from shared- and dedicated-server Web-hosting services, *colocation* is a rather bare-bones service that merely houses servers in a data center and connects those servers to the Internet. It does not include the server hardware or any of the software and services necessary to operate a Web site. Colocation by itself is aimed at customers who want to supply and manage their own Web site hardware and software but who do not want to provide the physical facilities and may not want to manage their links to the Internet.

*Managed service providers* (MSPs)—the fourth and final category—address the huge gap between the bare-bones offerings of colocation services and the needs of major Web site owners. Colocation services and MSPs have developed truly symbiotic relationships in which one could not succeed without the other, and the combination of these two services is often the choice of high-end Web sites. Figure 3 illustrates the range of features and services offered by the four major categories of web-hosting vendors relative to the costs of those services.

## COMPONENTS OF WEB HOSTING

The *service component pyramid* in Figure 4 illustrates the relationships of the separate components of Web hosting. Each layer generally supports the layers above it and depends on the layers below it. For example, operating-system software provides an environment for

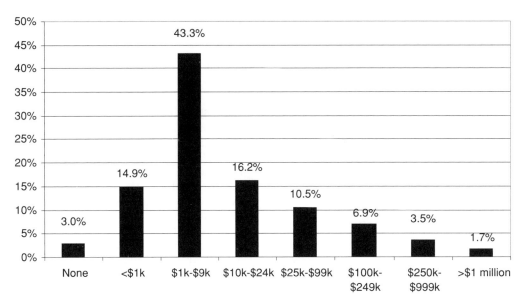

**Figure 1:** Annual Web-hosting budgets.
Source: ActivMedia Research (http://www.activmediaresearch.com).

application servers yet requires hardware on which to run.

Note the following:

The service components available from shared- and dedicated-server Web-hosting services are essentially the same and have, therefore, been combined into a single group.

Colocation, on the other hand, includes very few service components—just those at the lowest levels of the pyramid. Most notably, colocation rarely includes security services. When colocation is combined with managed services, however, the service components actually exceed those available with shared and dedicated servers.

The incremental difference between the shared/dedicated and colocation/managed service provider (MSP) combinations is the MSPs' support of application servers and databases. This is because the Web sites outsourced to MSPs are typically the largest and most complex. They are often based on application servers that, in turn, depend on high-end database packages.

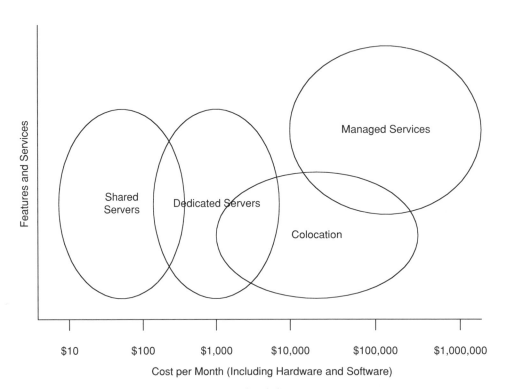

**Figure 2:** Cost comparison of web-hosting service categories.

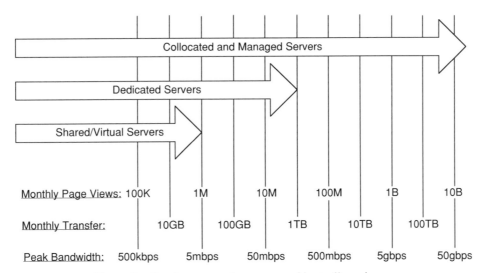

**Figure 3:** Service categories compared by traffic volume.

# SHARED AND DEDICATED SERVERS

A *shared server* (also referred to as a *virtual server*) is a single computer system on which a Web-hosting service runs multiple small Web sites owned by separate customers. The software for each Web site runs in a *virtual operating environment* that protects it from other Web sites running on the same physical server and vice versa.

Shared servers are used for the vast majority of all Web sites. Because these Web sites require relatively low levels of computer resources, multiple sites—sometimes thousands—can be run on a single server. This means, in turn, that a shared-server hosting provider can offer Web hosting for as little as $19.95 per month and still make money. Low-cost shared-server hosting can be an excellent choice for simple, *brochureware* sites (i.e., those that contain only marketing and promotional content and do not support complex e-commerce). Major Web-hosting services that specialize in shared servers typically build large *server farms*—Internet data centers with rows upon rows of racks filled with shared servers—which is how these vendors achieve the economies of scale necessary to offer shared-server hosting at low monthly prices. However, because prices are low and profit margins are therefore slim, shared-server hosting includes very little in the way of value-added services such as help troubleshooting or configuring of a customer's Web site.

Shared-server hosting is sold in packages that typically range in cost from $20 to $250 per month. Most vendors offer more than one package and allow customers to migrate or upgrade to a larger or more expensive package as the customers' needs increase.

Although the details of shared-server packages can vary greatly, the standard means by which vendors define their packages are the following:

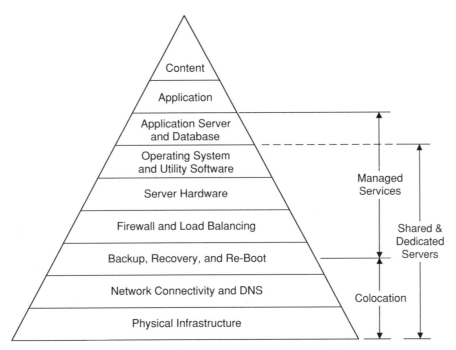

**Figure 4:** The service component pyramid.

- monthly fee (recurring)
- setup fee (one-time or nonrecurring)
- monthly data transfer cap (maximum)
- maximum disk storage
- number of e-mail accounts (e.g., info @yourdomain.com)

## Volume and Standardization

The computer hardware on which shared Web sites run varies greatly. Some shared-server vendors use a small number of large servers, each of which can host thousands of sites on a single computer system. Increasingly, however, shared-server vendors are turning to larger numbers of less powerful compact servers that are physically only 1 U in height. (A "U" or *rack unit* is 1¾ inches.)

To support such a large number of sites at such a low price, shared-server hosting is necessarily based on a very high degree of standardization. All components of shared-server hosting are treated as though they were part of assembly lines.

Shared-server hosting vendors typically offer menus of features and components from which a customer can select when building a Web site. Fortunately, because of intense competition in the shared-server hosting business, these menus include a large number of features and it is relatively easy to compare vendors' offerings to one another.

The following is a typical menu of shared-server hosting features:

- daily backup to tape
- offsite tape storage
- e-mail accounts (mailboxes)
- outbound e-mail relaying
- e-mail redirectors
- e-mail autoresponders (e.g., for automated responses to info@yoursite.com)
- Microsoft FrontPage extensions
- discussion forum software
- anonymous FTP
- administrative access via telnet or secure shell (SSH)
- electronic shopping cart software
- Secure Socket Layer (SSL) for secure Web pages and forms
- credit card merchant accounts and transaction processing
- log file processing and analysis tools
- support for scripting languages such as Perl and PHP
- Web-based control panels or access to configuration files for managing Web sites
- simple database software such as MySQL
- firewall protection of the Web server
- streaming media servers (optional, at additional cost)

In addition to providing these site components, a shared-server hosting vendor maintains all of the hardware and software.

## Three Tiers of Shared-Server Vendors

The ranks of shared-server vendors are actually divided into three different *tiers* (or subcategories), and each tier offers advantages in certain situations.

**Facility-owner vendors.** Vendors that own their servers and also operate their own data centers.
**Tenant vendors.** Vendors that own their servers but rent space within colocation facilities.
**Resellers.** These vendors do not even own the hardware but rather act as agents of facility-owner or tenant vendors.

### Facility-Owner Vendors

Today, the state of the art for data centers is quite high, and very few vendors (shared-server or otherwise) have the capitalization or borrowing power required to build and operate such facilities. On the other hand, these first-class facilities do exist, and there is no reason that a Web site—no matter how small it may be—should not reap the benefits of being located in one. Most of the owners of first-class data centers, however, do not directly offer shared-server hosting, because they are more likely to offer services at the high end of the hosting spectrum. The vendors that own large data centers are more experienced in dealing with customers who have Web-hosting budgets on the order of $10,000 per month or more.

### Tenant Vendors

Many smaller Web-hosting services came to realize over time that their second-class infrastructure not only was insufficient but was also causing them to lose customers to competitors who had better Internet connectivity, power, air conditioning, and physical security. The smart ones—those who realized they would otherwise be at a competitive disadvantage—adopted an "if you can't beat 'em, join 'em" attitude and opted out of providing any of the physical aspects of Web-site hosting. They themselves are customers (or *tenants*) of colocation facilities, but because they, in turn, offer shared-server hosting, they are *tenant vendors*. A tenant vendor can be an excellent alternative for a shared-server customer. The customer gets the advantages of a first-class data center and of having someone who is focused entirely on the operation of the shared-server systems.

### Resellers

Resellers are the third tier of shared-server vendors. A reseller bundles shared-server Web hosting from a third party with the reseller's own value-added services.

At first, the practice of reselling was considered deceptive, and today there are still some resellers who attempt to hide what they are doing from their customers by giving them the impression that they are facility-owner vendors. The better resellers, however, recognize that both they and the parent Web-hosting service are providing value to the end customer, and these resellers understand that it makes more sense for the customer to be aware of exactly what is happening.

From one perspective, resellers are simply salespeople who sign up customers and collect money. However, there are some resellers who actually provide a substantial level of service above and beyond the services provided by the parent vendors for whom they resell. For example, some resellers (like some tenant vendors) provide the site design, setup, and maintenance services that a high-volume shared-server vendor does not offer.

Likewise, some resellers and tenant vendors have particular *vertical application expertise* that may be of substantial value and importance. Vertical application expertise means experience with shared-server hosting to specific industry groups. There might be a reseller or tenant vendor, for instance, that offered shared-server hosting for realtors. Such a vendor might include a number of services that are unique to getting a real estate brokerage site online.

## Dedicated Servers

*Dedicated servers* are essentially the same as shared servers (i.e., they are owned by the hosting service and come with a standard suite of software and tools), but each Web site gets its own server and does not have to share it with other sites. In fact, the same companies that offer shared-server Web hosting typically offer dedicated servers as well, and some treat the two categories as virtually identical.

As compared with shared servers, dedicated servers offer the following advantages:

**Increased capacity**. Dedicated servers can handle substantially more of everything than a shared server can. Some dedicated servers can handle up to the following limits:

- 100 GB disk space
- 1 TB (a terabyte, or 1,000 gigabytes) monthly data transfer
- peak data transfer rates approaching 100 Mbps

**Improved security.** Dedicated servers eliminate the risks associated with sharing hardware with other Web sites.

**Improved reliability.** A dedicated server is less subject to outages and slowdowns caused by interactions with other Web sites.

**Additional configurations**. Some Web-hosting services allow customers to build sites using multiple dedicated servers that can be configured in a variety of ways to increase reliability, capacity, functionality, or all three.

### Two Tiers of Dedicated-Server Vendors
Unlike the shared-server business, where such relationships are common, few resellers or tenant vendors are in the dedicated-hosting business. There are, however, two distinct types of dedicated-server vendors.

**Shared/dedicated vendors.** Vendors that offer both services. In most cases, their dedicated-server business grew out of their shared-server business. As their shared-server customers' requirements increased, these vendors moved those customers to dedicated hardware.

**Dedicated-only vendors.** Vendors that are part of a somewhat newer breed. They do not offer any shared-server hosting.

Shared/dedicated vendors tend to treat both categories of customers (shared or dedicated) alike. Because these vendors evolved from the shared model, that is how they tend to view all Web sites. Many of the issues regarding shared servers discussed earlier in this chapter also apply to this tier of dedicated-server vendors. For example, shared/dedicated vendors are committed to standardization and the self-service model.

Because dedicated-only vendors are comparatively new, they began with a fresh start. These vendors tend to offer somewhat higher levels of customization and professional services than are available from the shared/dedicated vendors and, not surprisingly, they tend to do so for a higher price.

Shared and shared/dedicated vendors generally offer their support services in a depersonalized manner. Typically, shared and shared/dedicated vendors build call centers into which all e-mail messages, calls, and alerts are funneled through a single queue, with the one possible exception of segregating NT and UNIX/Linux issues because the skill sets necessary to support Web sites based on these two families of operating systems are so different.

Because the average revenues per customer are substantially higher for dedicated-only vendors, these vendors tend to incorporate at least some level of personalized service into their offerings.

## Shared- and Dedicated-Server Security
On one hand, Web sites hosted on shared servers are potentially the least secure. They are vulnerable to a unique class of attacks—malicious or unintentional—from other sites on the same server. Furthermore, they are susceptible to bad security practices by other Web site owners. If someone gains access to the system through one site, he is that much closer to being able to reach the other resources on the box. On the other hand, because shared-server vendors realize these inherent weaknesses, they are more likely to protect these boxes than are dedicated-server vendors. If a customer's site is compromised by an attack, the customer does not care whose fault it is; the effect is the same.

As similar as they may be in other ways, dedicated servers are notably different from shared servers when it comes to security. Dedicated-server customers are essentially in a do-it-yourself situation similar to that of colocation customers, as described in the next section. Unlike shared-server vendors, a dedicated-server vendor has little incentive to provide security services to individual customers. That is an option reserved for managed services. Furthermore, dedicated servers are typically offered without external firewall or other protective devices. In other words, whatever security services are required will have to be provided within the server itself. The options come down to a list of best practices: hardening the system (disabling unnecessary access) and running internal firewalls (e.g., the *iptables* facility in Linux). If you need more advanced services than those provided by dedicated-server vendors, consider using an MSP.

# COLOCATION

Now that we have covered shared and dedicated hosting, let us look at *colocation* (or *colo*). This is the oldest and most basic of the four Web-hosting services and, unlike shared or dedicated hosting, it is aimed at high-budget, sophisticated customers. Colocation vendors supply the fundamental services that are sometimes referred to as "power, pipe, and ping," a catchy phrase that includes, at the bare minimum, the following services:

- "real estate" (equipment racks, cabinets, or cages)
- electrical power (including battery and/or generator backup)
- air conditioning
- physical security
- fire suppression
- connectivity to the Internet

Some colocation vendors provide the following ancillary services:

- domain name service (DNS)
- "remote hands" to reboot servers or to cycle them off/on
- basic Web site monitoring and alert notification (pagers, phone calls)
- swapping of backup tapes (i.e., the customer manages the backup, but the colocation service removes and replaces tapes from the drives)
- hardware installation services
- spares management (i.e., management of spare parts made available to hardware repair technicians)

Three types of facilities are available from colocation services: open racks, cabinets, and cages. The variations in pricing for colocation real estate are primarily based upon the type of space provided.

## Open Racks

*Open racks* are best for sites that do not have enough servers to fill an entire rack or cabinet. Originally called "relay racks" because they held mechanical telephone relays before the advent of semiconductors, these come in standard 19- and 24-inch widths and are typically 6 or 7 feet tall.

The charges are based on the percentage of the rack used, or the number of inches or *rack units*. For example, some vendors charge for each half or quarter rack, whereas others charge by the inch, foot, or "U." (One U or *rack unit* is equal to 1.75 inches. A server or other piece of rack-mountable equipment that is 4 U in height, for instance, requires 7 inches of vertical rack space.)

## Locked Cabinets

*Locked cabinets* are an alternative to open racks. Not only do they reduce the number of problems that occur as a result of maintenance to neighboring systems, but they also improve security. In addition, a locked cabinet can be used as a place to keep tools and spare parts—something that cannot be done with open racks.

## Cages

Finally, *cages* can be used to create small, private data centers. Data center cages look very much like those in a zoo. They are typically made from a material that resembles cyclone fencing but is much tougher. They are fully enclosed (i.e., they go all the way to the ceiling) and have doors with padlocks. The smallest cages are approximately 7 by 10 feet and can hold three or four open racks. Larger cages can hold hundreds of racks. (Open racks are not a problem when they are used inside a private cage. In fact, it is much easier to cable and maintain servers installed in open racks than when they are installed inside enclosed cabinets.)

Most Web site owners find that cages are particularly attractive if they need more than five or six racks or cabinets and expect to manage their own servers or use an MSP independent from the colocation vendor. A cage gives the user the ultimate in isolation from other customers. Because users have floor space in addition to the rack space, they can store even more tools, spare parts, and servers than they can store in cabinets.

## Colocation Security

As with dedicated servers, colocation customers are confronted with a do-it-yourself security challenge. But unlike dedicated-server hosting, colocation also allows customers to deploy additional hardware such as firewalls to further secure their sites.

As described, many of the colocation security solutions are associated with physical security. In the case of shared, dedicated, and managed services, customers rarely have physical access to their servers. Because only the vendor's staff has access to the hardware, one customer's systems are somewhat protected from access by potentially malicious or clumsy other customers. Clearly, locked cabinets and cages go a long way toward securing collocated servers.

Colocation can, in some cases, offer the highest degree of physical-access security, which can be appropriate for sites that must store highly sensitive data such as personal financial information. Some colocation vendors allow high-security customers to keep their systems within locked cages to which even the hosting vendor has no access.

# MANAGED SERVICES

For many years, if customers opted for colocation, they had no choice but to manage their colocated servers themselves. Over time, more and more Web site owners found themselves in this position. Because those owners tended to have the largest budgets, a new market opportunity appeared for someone who was willing and able to come in and manage the high-end Web sites housed at colocation facilities.

To exploit this opportunity, a new Web-hosting service category, managed service providers, was born. Managed services are specifically designed to work in conjunction with colocation and to provide those services that are not addressed by colocation vendors themselves.

Many colocation vendors now offer managed services in reaction to the success of the MSPs, some of which were acquired by the colocation vendors. However, for years, although customers screamed that they needed such help, colocation vendors simply could not provide managed services themselves. The reason comes back to a recurring issue: the skills that are required to provide good power, pipe, and ping (colocation) are very different from those required to support and manage servers and applications. Even the cultures of such organizations are very different. (Just imagine calling a phone company's service center for help with a database performance problem, to understand the difference.)

## MSP Segmentation

When we covered shared, dedicated, and colocation Web hosting, we were able to further break down those classifications into subcategories. Because of the relative newness of the managed service business, the breakdown of vendors and the definitions of services are not as precise or as widely accepted as with shared, dedicated, and colocation hosting. The jargon has not yet stabilized, and an extraordinarily wide range of companies now call themselves MSPs.

Rather than creating categories that are not already in use in the MSP industry, our approach is to identify the raw criteria that distinguish one MSP from another. The criteria we explore include the following:

**Flexibility.** Some MSPs support a very limited (rigid) set of software and hardware products, whereas others are quite flexible in this regard. As we discuss, flexibility is not necessarily a good thing.

**Facility neutrality.** Some MSPs own their own data centers, whereas others are *portable* or data-center independent.

**Service levels and pricing models.** MSPs offer different levels of service and use pricing models that range from time-and-materials to flat-rate (component) pricing.

We examine each of these criteria in more detail and discuss how to select an MSP.

## Vendor Flexibility

The first MSPs approached the task of managing Web sites in much the same way as the classical IT staff outsourcers. They simply provided a staff that was skilled in Web operations on a professional services basis and billed by the hour. Such MSPs still exist and are referred to here as *flexible* MSPs, for reasons that will become clear shortly.

Other MSPs recognized, however, that they could achieve certain economies of scale, and perhaps even offer services of superior quality, by standardizing on a specific, limited set of hardware and software products and repeatable processes and procedures to support those products. These are referred to as *rigid* MSPs ("rigid" is not a derogatory term, and it is the best word to describe this class of

**Figure 5:**  Rigid versus flexible MSPs.

vendors). Figure 5 illustrates the polarized attributes of flexible and rigid MSPs.

### Flexible Model

At one end of the spectrum, fully flexible MSPs are essentially contract-staffing organizations that will support any technology, hardware, platform, and application. They are in the professional services business, providing system administrators, database administrators, and others either on a full-time (dedicated) basis or on an on-call basis and shared with other clients.

Most flexible MSPs add additional value in two ways. First, they tend to specialize in certain technologies, either companywide or by employing individuals with specialized skills and experience. Second, they implement a variety of processes and systems that are shared by all of their customers. These systems include monitoring a Web site's uptime and performance, as well as customer relationship management (CRM) components such as call center and incident-tracking systems.

The general approach of a flexible MSP is to provide services *the customer's way* and to try to function as an extension of the customer's own in-house staff. The primary advantage of working with a flexible MSP is that customers can build their Web sites using any hardware and software. If it is a combination of applications and hardware the MSP has never encountered before, it will ramp up on it and do whatever is necessary to make it work.

However, the real benefit of using a flexible MSP shows up later, when customers decide to enhance their sites by adding new features and systems that they could not have anticipated at the time they selected their MSPs and designed their initial configurations. If an organization tends to live on the cutting edge of Web and Internet technologies, it might do well to work with an MSP that can commit to this type of flexibility.

Flexibility does not come without a downside. As we will see, more rigid MSPs can sometimes achieve higher levels of efficiency and reliability because of their focus on repeatability and scalability. Although a flexible MSP can and will do whatever customers need, it may cost more in dollars, time, and reliability.

### Rigid Model

"Do one thing—but do it better than anyone else" could be the mantra for the more rigid MSPs. By limiting the number of hardware and software technologies they support, they can do a better job than if they had to spread their resources across a broader range. This is not marketing fluff but a very real advantage of this model. By doing the same things day in and day out, and creating economies of scale, a rigid MSP can simultaneously improve quality and keep costs down.

By working with a rigid MSP that is committed to a predefined and limited set of products, the customer not only shares staff with other customers (which is the case with flexible MSPs as well, of course) but also shares the cost of training their staff, because customers are all using the same technology. Furthermore, when a new problem occurs with a given component or combination, there is a good chance that another customer will have experienced the problem first, giving the benefit of a preventive fix, before the problem shows up on a given customer's Web site.

The rigid model is not perfect, either. The obvious disadvantage is that customers often cannot have things entirely their way. If an MSP supports only Oracle databases, for instance, but a customer wants to use Sybase, they will have to go to another vendor or manage the database themselves.

## Facility Neutrality

The primary value of an MSP is its ability to manage Web sites and keep them running. The physical infrastructure of the data center—the air conditioning, power, and security—is not the forte of most MSPs. Yet, these things are still required. Each MSP, therefore, has a way to provide such infrastructure for its customers. How they do so, however, varies greatly, and this is another important criterion for an evaluation of MSPs.

Figure 6 is a family tree of MSPs, illustrating how they can be further divided into groups according to their relationships to data-center facilities.

The first group—*facility-owner* MSPs—comprises those that own their data centers. In addition to being MSPs, these vendors are also in the colocation business, and they manage Web sites and servers that are located in their own facilities.

The other MSPs all belong to the *facility-neutral* group. MSPs in this category do not own data centers. Instead, they provide management services for sites and servers that are colocated at third-party facilities.

The facility-neutral group is further split into two subgroups according to whether the MSPs work only with specific colocation vendors or are entirely independent of the hosting location. The first subgroup (*tenant MSPs*) rent dedicated space within the data centers of one or more

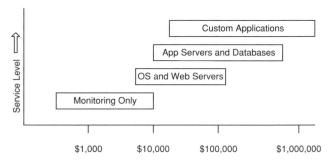

**Figure 7:**  MSP monthly pricing ranges.

colocation vendors and require that their customers' sites be housed at data centers operated by one of those partners. Tenant MSPs have these special relationships with one or a small number of colocation vendors.

*Portable MSPs*, members of the other subgroup of facility-neutral MSPs, are *entirely* neutral and will manage sites located anywhere in the world, even in their customers' own corporate facilities. MSPs in this group neither own nor rent data-center space.

## Service Levels

The range of services offered by vendors that call themselves managed service providers and the range of fees paid by their customers vary greatly. As a group, MSPs are generally aimed toward the high end of the overall Web-hosting marketplace, with contracts starting at $1,000 per month. Some managed-service contracts exceed $1 million per month—a 1,000:1 range.

The range of services and the associated monthly prices are illustrated in Figure 7. The monthly fees shown are in addition to the capital expenses of hardware and software.

### Monitoring

Note that at the very low end, starting at about $500 per month, MSPs provide only monitoring services. This means that for the established price (up to as much as $10,000), they will monitor a site and notify the Web site owner or specified third parties in case of outages.

The only reason MSPs offer such a basic service is to provide an entry point for customers that they hope will upgrade to higher cost services. The difference between monitoring for $500 per month and $10,000 per month depends on the number of the servers monitored and the complexity of the Web site.

### Platform Management

Basic monitoring does not include services to diagnose or resolve problems. The first level of service at which MSPs take responsibility and agree to meet service levels is in the management of the *platform*. At this level, an MSP will take responsibility for infrastructure, server hardware, the operating system software, other highly generic components (e.g., Web server software), and backup and recovery.

Platform management starts at about $5,000 per month. The high end ($100,000 per month) represents a site that includes 10 cabinets, at a higher ($10,000 per cabinet) price point.

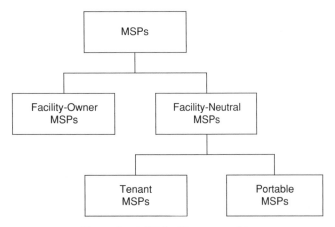

**Figure 6:**  MSP facility ownership.

### Application Management

Managing applications (databases and application servers) is the goal for most MSPs. For that purpose, they hope to generate $10,000 or more per cabinet per month in revenues. The chart in Figure 7 includes a low end at this price with a single-cabinet customer. A four-cabinet customer paying $15,000 per cabinet will spend $60,000 per month.

## MANAGED SECURITY PROVIDERS

Many of the security issues we address in this chapter raise one additional question: Who should be responsible for the security of your Web site? There are three possible answers: You can manage security yourself; you can let your Web-hosting service or MSP take care of it; or you can outsource security to a third-party Managed Security Service (MSS).

What is right for you is based on what you can afford and the extent of your risk. You can use your budget as a guideline, because it is also a reasonable indicator of the financial losses you might incur if your Web site were to be brought down by an attack. The more a company spends on its Web site, the more it usually stands to lose when the site is compromised.

If you are running on a shared server or a low-end dedicated server, your risks are likely very low, and third-party services will cost more than the threats they could help you avoid. Your best bet in this situation is to use whatever services your Web-hosting vendor provides as part of its standard package. Just make sure you have good backups (as we discussed previously in this chapter) to cover you in case an attack wipes out your code and content. Keep in mind that shared-server hosting will always be inherently vulnerable.

If you are using an MSP, but the *total* budget for your Web site is below $1 million per year (about $75,000 per month), the optional security services provided by your MSP may be worthwhile. You may also want to pay an independent security guru for periodic audits, but be careful to avoid the false sense of security that audits may give you. (Some security experts believe things change so quickly that an audit is invalid in as little as one week.) Neither your budget nor your total risk exposure (up to the amount that is covered by your worst-case scenario recovery plan) justifies the minimum $5,000 or so per month that it would cost to use an independent MSS.

If your total Web site budget is $1 million per year or more, *and* you have risks substantially greater than the loss of your static content, you should consider using an independent MSS in addition to your colo and/or MSP.

## SECURITY AUDITS

There is a lot of controversy surrounding security audits. Even the best audits are only valuable for a very short period of time. Once you or your Web-hosting vendor make a change to your Web site or to the routers and other devices connecting your site to the Internet, you have invalidated the audit. All bets are off.

Another arguable practice is using simulated attacks to audit a Web site. You are likely to find vulnerabilities using this approach but, once again, you may develop a false sense of security. It's easy to find *some* vulnerabilities. It is impossible to find them all.

One type of audit that may have value is one performed not on your Web site but on your Web-hosting vendor's processes. An *SAS 70* audit allows service organizations to disclose their control activities and processes to their customers and their customers' auditors in a uniform reporting format. *Statement on Auditing Standards (SAS) No. 70, Service Organizations,* is an auditing standard developed by the American Institute of Certified Public Accountants (AICPA).

SAS 70 is a widely recognized standard. It signifies that a service organization has had its control objectives and control activities examined by an independent accounting and auditing firm. A formal report including the auditor's opinion ("Service Auditor's Report") is issued to the service organization at the conclusion of a SAS 70 examination. A *Type I* report describes the service organization's description of controls at a specific point in time. A *Type II* report includes not only the service organization's description of controls but also detailed testing of the service organization's controls over a minimum six-month period.

Ask your hosting company if it has passed a SAS 70 Level I or Level II audit. Even if you don't use your MSP's security services, you will get the benefit, because the requirements to obtain SAS 70 certification apply to all of the systems under the MSP's control, even yours.

An MSS does not replace your MSP's security services but rather works with them. For example, an MSS does not take on the responsibility of most threat-avoidance activities. Most MSSs expect that you or your MSP will track and install security patches as if the MSS were not involved. What an MSS will do, however, is monitor your site on an ongoing basis and provide the following services:

**On-call intrusion detection response.** If something is caught by your intrusion detection system, your MSS will be notified by e-mail and pager and respond immediately, 24/7.

**Security logs review.** An MSS will scour the daily logs of your IDS and firewalls (if any), looking for anomalies and recommending courses of action as appropriate.

**Review your MSP's activities.** An MSS will constantly be looking over your MSP's shoulder to make sure your MSP does everything right, including the timely and correct installation of security-related patches.

Your MSP may try to convince you that it can provide all of the security services you need. However, when done right, security is a specialty that goes beyond what most MSPs are willing to invest in. If yours is a high-budget/high-risk Web site (i.e., at least a $1 million per-year budget *and* a potential for significant losses), you should consider working with independent experts.

Another reason to use a third party to manage security is to leverage the healthy tension that is created between the independent security specialists and the system administrators and technicians that work for your MSP. It is a lot like the tension that exists between programmers and quality assurance (QA) engineers. Like programmers, an MSP's system administrators and technicians are under pressure to get things done quickly, to respond to deadlines, and to move on to other tasks. Security experts, like QA staff, are there to occasionally put on the brakes to guarantee that things are done right. It is important to have advocates of both positions on your team, if you can afford it.

The same tensions that exist at the staff level ripple all the way up to senior management. MSS executives understand that it is their company's role to act as independent auditor of your system's security. As auditors, their responsibility actually exceeds that of your MSP.

If your total annual Web site budget is greater than $1 million, and your risks are substantially greater than just the loss of your static content, use an MSS to add knowledge, experience, and objectivity beyond what an MSP can provide.

Attacks are like hardware failures—they *will* happen. You have got to assume that the bad guys will get in no matter what you do, so you must practice risk management—not just threat avoidance—to deal with the attacks that do get through.

As you develop and update your security plan, do not lose sight of your customers and your business. Avoid spending money to tighten security only to make your Web site so unusable that visitors are needlessly discouraged. Sure, banks could dramatically reduce robberies by strip-searching everyone that come through their doors, but not too many customers would come back for more.

Refer to the bibliography in the appendix for recommendations of books that address this important topic in greater detail.

## ROOT ACCESS

*Root access* is a specific privilege in UNIX-based systems, but the concept applies to Windows/NT systems as well. Someone with full root access to a server has the ability to change any aspect of that server's software and configuration. Anyone with the ultimate responsibility for maintaining a server needs unrestricted ability to log in as the *root* or *admin* user.

Customers who want or need root access to their Web servers present a particular challenge to an MSP. If the MSP is to assume full responsibility for the operation of your servers, it does not want you or your staff snooping around inside those servers, making changes, and potentially causing trouble that the MSP then must resolve. Even if your intentions are honorable, you have all of the required skills, and you are extremely careful, your MSP may have different ways of doing things. What is standard operating procedure to you may not be to the MSP.

MSPs handle requests for root access in five ways:

**No root access, ever.** Some simply don't permit it. The logic (and it really can't be faulted) is that if you want the MSP to take responsibility for a server, the MSP must have full and exclusive control over that server.

**Root access with a reduced service level agreement (SLA).** Many MSPs will grant you root access to the servers, but they will insist on reducing their obligation and responsibility to determine and resolve problems associated with those servers. This is a common although rather draconian solution.

**Unrestricted root access.** Other MSPs (particularly those that do not offer rigorous SLAs) will allow you and your staff to have full root access to your servers. You should be realistic (even if your MSP is not) and remember that sharing root access fundamentally increases the likelihood that problems will occur.

**Restricted root access.** Programs such as *Sudo (super-user do)* for UNIX systems allow someone with unrestricted root access to grant specific individuals or group certain subsets of root privileges.

**Root access as a service.** A few progressive MSPs not only recognize that some customers need root access to their own servers but also that there is *value* associated with sharing root access. These MSPs offer root access as an add-on service under an extended SLA. The MSP's level of responsibility does not decrease, but there is an additional charge to the customer to cover the MSP's increased risk and liability.

Do not ask for root access unless you need it; but if you do, make sure it does not reduce your service level or the responsibility of your vendor.

## SECURITY AND WEB-HOSTING ARCHITECTURES

"I can improve the security in a bank by strip-searching every customer."

—Bruce Schneier, CTO and cofounder,
Counterpane Internet Security, Inc.

As Bruce Schneier's intentional sarcasm suggests, it does not make sense to eliminate all threats at all costs. You have got to make some very conscious decisions as to which threats are worth living with and which ones are not. Managing risks means first determining your potential losses and then having a plan that is based on sound risk/reward analysis to deal with them.

Risk is not necessarily a bad thing. We knowingly take risks all the time. There is a risk that by driving your car tomorrow you might have an accident. A strategy based solely on threat avoidance would suggest that you stay home. Good risk management, however, tells you that the benefits of driving outweigh the risks, so you decide to take your chances and drive your car anyway. To cover the eventuality of an accident, you buy insurance and thereby share the risks with other drivers.

In business, one often needs to take risks to generate profits. When you were hired for your current job, your employer took a risk. The company knew it would be paying your salary for some time before you did anything useful. (It was a worthwhile risk, was it not?)

Credit card companies are examples of good risk managers. Just think about all the risky things they do. They generously issue cards to people of questionable creditworthiness. When customers do not pay on time, the credit card companies extend them even more credit. Their credit loss rates are in the 5% range, but does that really concern them? No. They *manage* their risk. They know exactly what it would cost them to reduce that 5% loss rate to 4%, and they know that doing so would reduce their profits more than it would save them.

How about retail merchants? Have you ever thought about the grocery store that leaves beautiful fresh produce out in front of the market where anyone can just pick up an apple and walk away with it? How about the bookstore that has bins of not-too-popular books sitting out in front? What are these businesspeople thinking? Are they fools? No, they are managing their risk. They know that the losses they incur from these promotions will be outweighed by the profits from the incremental business they attract.

The same risk-management approach should be applied to Web site security. In the rest of this chapter, we use this strategy as we evaluate the risk/reward trade-offs of security technologies such as firewalls, intrusion detection systems, passwords, administrative networks, and encryption.

## DATA RECOVERY: AN IMPORTANT DEFENSE

A good backup and recovery plan is an important cornerstone of any Web site security strategy, because as long as you have a complete and uncorrupted copy of your Web site's data and content, you can recover from *any* attack. Good backups will not prevent the initial losses you may suffer, nor will they prevent collateral damage such as loss of goodwill, or liability for the disclosure of your customer's confidential data, but they will minimize the effect of *cascading losses* resulting from extended Web site downtime.

You should know (with your Web-hosting vendor's help) how long it would take you to restore your site from backups after a complete loss of all code and data. Once you have that information, you can compute the potential loss resulting from the downtime during which you would accomplish a recovery.

In many cases, you will find that no additional security-related actions prove to be worthwhile, and that you get the most bang for the buck by doing nothing more than maintaining good backups. For example, if your site contains only static content and perhaps a few forms, good backups could be the entire extent of your security plan. Certainly, if your Web site is a small one (e.g., running on a shared server), you are not going to spend thousands of dollars for a firewall or fancy intrusion detection system. Even if your site is large and complex, you may find that you do not need many of the security products and services that are being pitched to you.

Consider a good backup and recovery plan as the starting point for any security defense. Anything more should be justified on a cost–benefit basis.

## FIREWALLS

One of the first options you will have to consider is if and where to use firewalls—perhaps the most hotly debated Web site security topic of all.

Too many Web site owners and system administrators install firewalls (correctly or otherwise) and stop there. They believe they have adequately secured their Web sites. Firewalls are perceived (and sold) as a panacea. There is something about them—particularly those that come as dedicated *appliances*—that make people believe in them. It is very easy to look at the firewall logs every morning and pride yourself on the fact that your firewall prevented so many attacks the day before. It is very reassuring, but it is a false sense of security. Remember, most of the bad guys know how firewalls work. The logs only show you what the firewall caught; they do not even hint at the more sophisticated attacks that went right through the firewall.

There is only one good way to deploy firewalls: configure your Web site as though you did not have a firewall and then add one anyway.

Once you have *hardened* your servers (the process of removing or at least disabling all unnecessary or known hackable software), you can consider where to place firewalls. The conventional wisdom is to place them at the so-called point of maximum leverage, where your Web site connects to the Internet. The theory is that if you can keep someone from getting past your first line of defense, it is much easier to defend the next level. This makes sense if your Web site is for authenticated "members" only. Here is a reality check: most major Web sites do not use firewalls in front of their Web servers.

To see why, let's return to the bank analogy. As with a multitier Web site architecture, a bank has multiple levels of security. To enter the branch, you need virtually no authentication. Strangers are encouraged to walk in the door; they may want to open an account. It does not take much more authentication to make a deposit. If you know the account number and you have the money, the bank is happy to take it. Withdrawals, however, require that you show some identification. If you want to get into the vault, you are going to need even more robust authentication: a safe-deposit-box key and your signature.

A traditional strategy suggests that the bank could increase security by moving the robust authentication requirement from the vault to the front door of the branch. After all, some proponents would suggest, if you keep unauthenticated people from even entering the branch, you not only protect the vault, you also keep them from harassing the tellers (just think how secure we could make a bank if it were not for those darned customers!). However, not only would moving robust authentication to the front door discourage visitors, it would also be very expensive. The bank would have to issue keys to every customer and hire staff to check everyone's signature. By authenticating only when necessary (e.g., for access to the vault), the cost scales with the risk, and the solution is applied only where needed.

The same applies to a firewall in front of your Web site. Is it the Web servers you are trying to protect (like the front door of the bank) or is it your data (the vault)? Certainly you are not trying to protect your HTML pages or images. These are the very files you are encouraging visitors to access. Your risk of losing these files is relatively low.

And what about the cost? Firewalls in front of Web, cache, and streaming content servers are very expensive because the processing power required by a firewall to thoroughly examine packets is often greater than what it takes to create and transmit those packets in the first place. Even firewalls built using expensive servers are slow, sometimes much slower than the less-expensive servers they're trying to protect. So, protecting your front-line servers with firewalls will likely reduce the performance of your site, cost you more than they are worth, or both.

Do not use a firewall in front of your Web servers unless access to your static content is restricted to authenticated visitors and unauthorized access would cause a substantial loss.

## Back-End Firewalls

Although it does not make sense to require that visitors authenticate themselves to enter a bank branch, it is still important to do so for access to the vault. If your Web site is large and complex enough for you to even be thinking about a firewall (i.e., you have something worth protecting), the chances are good that you are also using at least a two-tier (and perhaps a three-tier) architecture. If so, there is probably no valuable data stored on your Web servers; it is most likely in a separate database. So, although it usually does not make sense to use firewalls in front of your Web, cache, and streaming servers, it may be a good idea to use them at points *within* your configuration that contain more valuable data and that receive a lower volume of traffic—for instance, in front of your application servers. Such a configuration is illustrated in Figure 8.

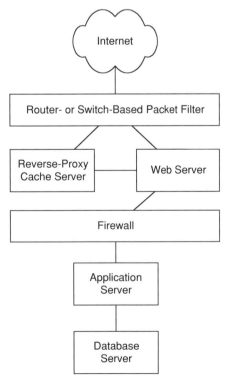

**Figure 8:** Back-end firewall.

Like the number of bank visitors who require access to the vault, the amount of traffic in and out of the application servers is much less than the volume of traffic in and out of the front door to your Web site. Therefore, a firewall in front of the application servers requires far less computer power than one that sits in front of the external servers.

In three-tier architectures, install a firewall between your Web servers and your application servers.

Note that in place of a full-fledged firewall in front of the Web and cache servers, the configuration shown in Figure 8 includes a *packet filter* running in a router, intelligent switch, or load balancer. A packet filter is simpler, faster, and less expensive than a full-fledged firewall. It restricts access by IP address and port number. This technology is virtually mandatory as basic defenses against certain attacks. (For more information on packet filtering, refer to any good book on Internet security, some of which are listed in Further Reading.)

Always use packet filtering in the switches, routers, and load balancers that connect your Web site to the Internet.

## Shared Firewalls

Some dedicated-server vendors and MSPs offer *firewall services* that enable you to connect your Web servers to their firewalls rather than purchase or lease firewalls of your own. These services may sound like a good option, but they make even less sense than installing your own firewall in front of your Web servers.

As discussed previously, placing a firewall in front of a Web server adds little value, and it creates a false sense of security. A *shared firewall* in this manner has the additional disadvantage that the performance of your Web site will be affected by the load placed on the firewall by other Web sites.

Do not even *think* of using a shared firewall between your Web server and your application servers or in any other back-end position. A shared firewall used in this way creates a potential path between your application servers and the servers of the other sites using the firewall. This path leaves you susceptible to weaknesses in your neighbors' security practices. If there happens to be even a one-line error in the firewall configuration file (an easy mistake to make and overlook), and if someone breaks into a neighboring Web site's server, he or she can get to your application servers through the firewall. Your risk increases with each site that is added to the shared firewall, because each additional site increases the chance that an error will be made or exploited. Yes, firewalls can be broken into, just like servers.

Do not use shared firewalls under any circumstances.

## ADMINISTRATIVE NETWORKS

To support remote management of your Web site, you may want to implement an *administrative network* (also called a *back-door network*). It will allow you to reach the servers that are normally inaccessible to the outside world, such as your application and database servers. An administrative network can be based on either a physical network connection (such as a T1) or by creating a *virtual private network* (*VPN*) superimposed on the public Internet. In

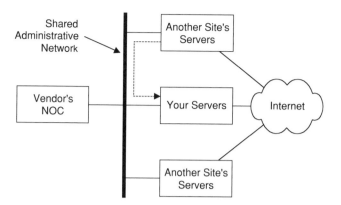

**Figure 9:** Multisite administrative network.

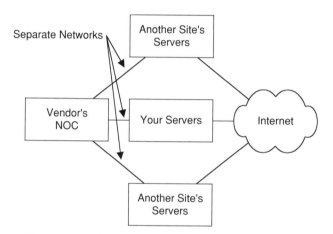

**Figure 10:** Administrative network star configuration.

general, a well-designed private administrative network (i.e., one that's available only to your organization, not to your Web-hosting vendor) is a good way to reach your servers.

Although it is okay for you to have a private administrative network, it is a potentially dangerous practice when a Web-hosting vendor or MSP uses a single back-door network to reach more than one customer's Web site by linking each customer's site to the vendor's NOC. As with a shared firewall, such a shared network link creates a potential path by which hackers can gain access to your servers by first breaking into those of other Web sites. This risky configuration is illustrated in Figure 9.

A better design is a configuration in which the network itself is not shared by multiple Web sites. Instead, each site has a separate dedicated connection to the vendor's NOC, as illustrated in Figure 10.

Be wary of vendors' shared administrative networks. Configurations in which the network itself is not shared are safer.

Some Web-hosting services and MSPs use their administrative networks for backup and recovery by connecting each of their customers' systems to a centralized backup server. This creates yet another path by which hackers can reach your site through the back door. It is important to watch out for this configuration as well.

## Back-Door Firewalls

No matter what topology you use for a back-door network (even if it is used only by you and not by a Web-hosting vendor), it is a good idea to use a firewall between the back-door network and your servers, as shown in Figure 11. Because the volume of traffic is quite low as compared with that which comes in through the front door of your

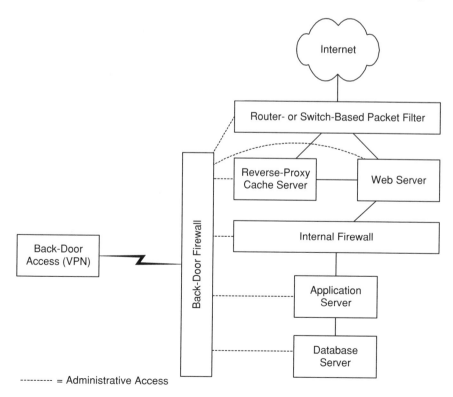

‑‑‑‑‑‑‑‑‑‑ = Administrative Access

**Figure 11:** Back-door access.

Web site, a firewall in this application does not need to be of particularly high performance. You can typically use a low-cost firewall appliance in this application.

Also, as shown in Figure 11, a back-door link through a firewall is a good way to gain administrative access to your routers, switches, and internal firewalls, in addition to your servers. If you have an administrative network, secure it with a firewall.

## CONCLUSION

In this chapter, we looked at a few of the classic myths of Web-hosting security: things that people think and do—with honorable intentions—that give them a false sense of security. In the process of exposing these myths, we supported four recommendations:

**Do not try to avoid all threats.** You will not succeed anyway. Find the right balance between threat avoidance and risk management.

**Watch out for a false sense of security.** Firewalls, intrusion detection systems, and audits can lull you into complacency.

**Beware of risky Web-hosting practices.** Vendors' use of administrative (back-door) networks and their poor management of software updates and patches increase your risk of security breaches.

**Make sure you have good backups.** They will not keep the bad guys from getting in, but good backups and archives will reduce the effect of attacks by ensuring that you can get a pre-attack version of your Web site up and running as quickly as possible.

## GLOSSARY

**Colocation** A bare-bones hosting service in which the vendor provides only physical space, power, air conditioning, and Internet connectivity.

**Facility-Owner Vendors** A class of Web-hosting vendors that own and operate their own data centers.

**Managed Service Provider (MSP)** A Web-hosting vendor that takes responsibility for ongoing management of a Web site's hardware and software.

**95th Percentile Rule** A method for measuring bandwidth utilization in which samples are taken at regular intervals, and the highest 5% are discarded. The next highest value is used.

**Nonrecurring Expenses (NRE)** One-time expenses such as installation and provisioning costs.

**Peak Bandwidth** The highest volume of data transmission used or required by a Web site.

**Rack Unit** A standard measure of the height of equipment when rack-mounted. One "U" equals 1.75 inches.

**Remote Hands** A service in which a Web-hosting vendor will perform basic tasks such as cycling a server's power off and on.

**Resellers** A class of Web-hosting vendors that act as sales agents for larger vendors.

**Tenant Vendors** A class of Web-hosting vendors that own their servers but colocate them in data centers owned by other vendors.

## CROSS REFERENCES

See *Contingency Planning Management; Firewall Basics; Managing a Network Environment; Security Architectures.*

## FURTHER READING

Burnham, C. (2001). *Web hosting.* Berkeley: Osborne/McGraw-Hill.

Kaye, D. (2002). *Strategies for Web hosting and managed services.* New York: Wiley.

Kaye, D. (weekly). *The IT Strategy Letter.* Kentfield, CA. Weekly. Available at http: www.rds.com

Netcraft. Available at http://www.netcraft.com

Schneier, B. (2000). *Secrets and lies: Digital security in a networked world.* New York: Wiley.

Stokeley Consulting. Available at http://www.stokely.com/unix.sysadm.resources/

*The Web Host Industry Review.* Available at http://www.thewhir.com

# Managing a Network Environment

Jian Ren, *Michigan State University*

## INTRODUCTION

Network management, in general, is a service that employs a variety of protocols, tools, applications, and devices to assist human network managers in monitoring and controlling the proper network resources, both hardware and software, to address service needs and the networks objectives.

When transmission control protocol/Internet protocol (TCP/IP) was developed, little thought was given to network management. Prior to the 1980s, the practice of network management was largely proprietary because of the high development cost. The rapid development in the 1980s of larger and more complex networks caused a significant diffusion of network management technologies. The starting point in providing specific network management tools was November 1987, when the simple gateway monitoring protocol (SGMP) was issued. In early 1988, the Internet Architecture Board (IAB) approved simple network management protocol (SNMP) as a short-term solution for network management. Standards such as SNMP and common management information protocol (CMIP) paved the way for standardized network management and development of innovative network management tools and applications.

*A network management system* (NMS) refers to a collection of applications that enable network components to be monitored and controlled. In a network environment, as shown in Figure 1, a managing device is called a *management station* or a *manager*, and the managed device is called a *management agent* or simply an *agent*. Management station and management agent are two key elements in an NMS. A management station serves as the interface between the human network manager and the network management system. It is also the platform for management applications to perform management functions through interactions with the management agents. The management agent responds to the requests from the management station and also provides the management station with unsolicited information.

Given the diversity of managed elements, such as routers, bridges, switches, hubs, and so on, and the wide variety of operating systems and programming interfaces, a management protocol is critical for the management station to communicate with the management agents effectively. SNMP and CMIP are two well-known network management protocols. A network management system is generally described using the open system interconnection (OSI) network management model. As an OSI network management protocol, CMIP was proposed as a replacement for the simple but less sophisticated SNMP; however, it has not been widely adopted. For this reason, we focus on SNMP in this chapter.

## OSI Network Management Model

The OSI network management comprises four major models (Subramanian, 2000):

- **Organization model** defines the manager, agent, and managed object. It describes the components of a network management system, the components' functions, and infrastructure.

- **Information model** is concerned with the information structure and storage. It specifies the information base used to describe the managed objects and their relationships. The structure of management information (SMI) defines the syntax and semantics of management information stored in the management information base (MIB). The MIB is used by both the agent process and the manager process for management information exchange and storage.

- **Communication model** deals with the way that information is exchanged between the agent and the manager and between the managers. There are three key elements in the communication model: transport protocol, application protocol, and the actual message to be communicated.

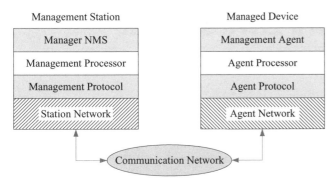

**Figure 1:** Manager–Agent Model.

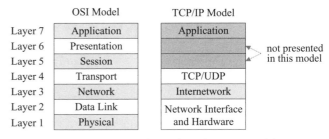

**Figure 2:** OSI and TCP/IP reference models.

- **Functional model** comprises five functional areas of network management, which are discussed in more detail in the next section.

## Network Management Layers

Two protocol architectures have served as the basis for the development of interoperable communications standards: the International Organization for Standardization (ISO) OSI reference model and the TCP/IP reference model, which are compared in Figure 2 (Tanenbaum, 2003). The OSI reference model was developed based on the premise that different layers of the protocol provide different services and functions. It provides a conceptual framework for communications among different network elements. The OSI model has seven layers. Network communication occurs at different layers, from the application layer to the physical layer; however, each layer can only communicate with its adjacent layers. The primary functions and services of the OSI layers are described in Table 1.

The OSI and TCP/IP reference models have much in common. Both are based on the concept of a stack of independent protocols. Also, the functionality of the corresponding layers is roughly similar.

However, differences do exist between the two reference models. The concepts that are central to the OSI model include service, interface, and protocol. The OSI reference model makes the distinction among these three concepts explicit. The TCP/IP model, however, does not clearly distinguish among these three concepts. As a consequence, the protocols in the OSI model are better hidden than in the TCP/IP model and can be replaced relatively easily as the technology changes. The OSI model was devised before the corresponding protocols were invented. Therefore, it is not biased toward one particular set of protocols, which makes it quite general. With TCP/IP, the reverse is true: the protocols came first, and the model was really just a description of the existing protocols. Consequently, this model does not fit any other protocol stacks (Tanenbaum, 2003).

## ISO NETWORK MANAGEMENT FUNCTIONS

The fundamental goal of network management is to ensure that the network resources are available to the designated users. To ensure rapid and consistent progress on network management functions, ISO has grouped the

**Table 1** OSI Layers and Functions

| Layer | Functions |
|---|---|
| Application | Provides the user application process with access to OSI facilities. |
| Presentation | Responsible for data representation, data compression, data encryption, and decryption. |
| | Ensures communication between systems with different data representation. |
| | Allows the application layer to access the session layer services. |
| Session | Allows users on different machines to establish sessions between them. |
| | Establishes and maintains connections between processes and data transfer services. |
| Transport | Provides reliable, transparent data transfer between end systems or hosts. |
| | Provides end-to-end error recovery and flow control. |
| | Multiplexes and demultiplexes messages from applications. |
| Network | Establishes, maintains, and terminates connections between end systems. |
| | Builds end-to-end routes through the network. |
| Data Link | Composed of two sublayers: logical link control (LLC) and media access control (MAC). |
| | Provides a well-defined service interface to the network layer. |
| | Deals with transmission errors. |
| | Regulates data flow. |
| Physical | Handles the interface to the communication medium. |
| | Deals with various medium characteristics. |

management functions into five areas: (a) configuration management, (b) fault management, (c) accounting management, (d) security management, and (e) performance management. The ISO classification has gained broad acceptance for both standardized and proprietary network management systems. A description of each management function is provided in the following subsections.

## Configuration Management

*Configuration management* is concerned with initializing a network, provisioning the network resources and services, and monitoring and controlling the network. More specifically, the responsibilities of configuration management include setting, maintaining, adding, and updating the relationship among components and the status of the components during network operation.

Configuration management consists of both device configuration and network configuration. Device configuration can be performed either locally or remotely. Automated network configurations, such as dynamic host configuration protocol (DHCP) and domain name services (DNS), play a key role in network management.

## Fault Management

*Fault management* involves detection, isolation, and correction of abnormal operations that may cause the failure of the OSI network. The major goal of fault management is to ensure that the network is always available and that a fault can be fixed as rapidly as possible after it occurs.

Faults should be distinct from errors. An error is generally a single event, whereas a fault is an abnormal condition that requires management attention to fix. For example, the physical communication line cut is a fault, whereas a single bit error on a communication line is an error.

## Security Management

*Security management* protects the networks and systems from unauthorized access and security attacks. The mechanisms for security management include authentication, encryption, and authorization. Security management is also concerned with generation, distribution, and storage of encryption keys as well as other security-related information. Security management may include security systems such as firewalls and intrusion detection systems that provide real-time event monitoring and event logs.

## Accounting Management

*Accounting management* enables the charge for the use of managed objects to be measured and the cost for such use to be determined. The measure may include the resources consumed, the facilities used to collect accounting data, billing parameters for the services used by customers, the maintenance of the databases used for billing purposes, and the preparation of resource usage and billing reports.

## Performance Management

*Performance management* is concerned with evaluating and reporting the behavior and the effectiveness of the managed network objects. A network monitoring system can measure and display the status of the network, such as gathering the statistical information on traffic volume, network availability, response times, and throughput.

# NETWORK MANAGEMENT PROTOCOLS

In this section, different versions of SNMP and RMON are introduced. SNMP is the most widely used data network management protocol. Most of the network components used in enterprise network systems have built-in network agents that can respond to an SNMP network management system. This enables the new components be automatically monitored. Remote network monitoring is, on the other hand, the most important addition to the basic set of SNMP standards. It defines a remote network monitoring MIB that supplements MIB-II and provides the network manager with vital information about the Internet work.

## SNMP

The objective of network management is to build a single protocol that manages both OSI and TCP/IP networks. Based on this goal, SNMP, or SNMPv1 (Case, Fedor, Schoffstall, & Davin, 1990; McCloghrie & Rose, 1991; Rose & McCloghrie, 1990) was first recommended as an interim set of specifications for use as the basis of common network management throughout the system, whereas the ISO CMIP over TCP/IP (CMOT) was recommended as the long-term solution (Cerf, 1988; 1989).

SNMP consists of three specifications: the SMI, which describes how managed objects contained in the MIB are defined; the MIB, which describes the managed objects contained in the MIB; and the SNMP itself, which defines the protocol used to manage these objects.

### SNMP Architecture

The model of network management that is used for TCP/IP network management includes the following key elements:

- **Management station:** Hosts the network management applications.
- **Management agent:** Provides information contained in the MIB to management applications and accepts control information from the management station.
- **Management information base:** Defines the information that can be collected and controlled by the management application.
- **Network management protocol:** Defines the protocol used to link the management station and the management agents.

The architecture of SNMP, shown in Figure 3, demonstrates the key elements of a network management environment. SNMP is designed to be a simple message-based application-layer protocol. The manager process achieves network management using SNMP, which is implemented

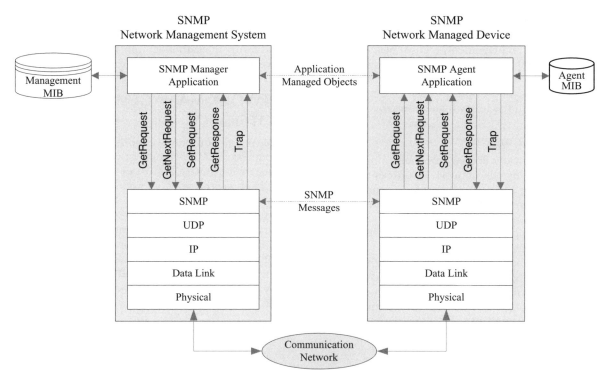

**Figure 3:** SNMP network management architecture.

over the user datagram protocol (UDP) (Bidgoli, 2005; Postel, 1980). The SNMP agent must also implement SNMP and UDP protocols. Because UDP is a connectionless protocol, SNMP is itself a connectionless protocol. No outgoing connections are maintained between a management station and its agents. This design minimizes the complexity of the management agents.

Figure 3 also shows that SNMP supports five types of protocol data units (PDUs). The manager can issue three types of PDUs on behalf of a management application: `GetRequest`, `GetNextRequest`, and `SetRequest`. The first two are variations of the Get function. All three messages are acknowledged by the agent in the form of a `GetResponse` message, which is passed up to the

management application. Another message that the agent generates is `trap`. A trap is an unsolicited message and is generated when an event that affects the normal operations of the MIB and the underlying managed resources occurs.

### SNMP Protocol Specifications

The SNMP message package communicated between a management station and an agent consists of a version identifier indicating the version of the SNMP protocol, an SNMP community name to be used for this message package, and an SNMP PDU. The message structure is shown in Figure 4 and each field is explained in Table 2.

| Version | Community Name | SNMP PDU |
|---------|----------------|----------|

(a) SNMP message

| PDU Type | RequestID | ErrorStatus | ErrorIndex | VariableBindings | | | | |
|----------|-----------|-------------|------------|--------|---------|-----|--------|---------|
| | | | | Name 1 | Value 1 | ... | Name N | Value N |

(b) `Get/Set` Type of PDUs

| PDU Type | Enterprise | Agent-Address | Generic-Trap | Specific-Trap | Timestamp | VariableBindings | | | | |
|----------|------------|---------------|--------------|---------------|-----------|--------|---------|-----|--------|---------|
| | | | | | | Name 1 | Value 1 | ... | Name N | Value N |

(c) `Trap` PDUs

**Figure 4:** SNMP message formats.

**Table 2** SNMP Message Fields

| Field | Functions |
|---|---|
| Version | SNMP version (RFC 1157 is version 1). |
| Community name | A pairing of an SNMP agent with some arbitrary set of SNMP application entities. (Community name serves as the password to authenticate the SNMP message.) |
| PDU type | The PDU type for the five messages is application data type, which is defined in RFC 1157 as `GetRequest (0)`, `GetNextRequest (1)`, `SetRequest (2)`, `GetResponse (3)`, `trap (4)`. |
| RequestID | Used to distinguish among outstanding requests by the unique ID. |
| ErrorStatus | A nonzero `ErrorStatus` is used to indicate that an exception occurred while processing a request. |
| ErrorIndex | Used to provide additional information on the error status. |
| VariableBindings | A list of variable names and corresponding values. |
| Enterprise | Type of object generating trap. |
| AgentAddress | Address of object generating trap. |
| GenericTrap | Generic trap type; values are `coldStart (0)`, `warmStart (1)`, `linkDown (2)`, `linkUp (3)`, `authenticationFailure (4)`, `egpNeighborLoss (5)`, `enterpriseSpecific (6)`. |
| SpecificTrap | Specific trap code not covered by the `enterpriseSpecific` type. |
| Timestamp | Time elapsed since last reinitialization. |

## Structure of Management Information

Figure 3 shows the information exchange between a single manager and agent pair. In a real network environment, there are many managers and agents. The foundation of a network management system is a management information base (MIB) containing a set of network objects to be managed. Each managed resource is represented as an object. The MIB is, in fact, a database structure of such objects in the form of a tree (Stallings, 1998). Each system in a network environment maintains a MIB that keeps the status of the resources to be managed at that system. The information can be used by the network management entity for resource monitoring and controlling. SMI defines the syntax and semantics used to describe the SNMP management information (McCloghrie, Perkins, & Schoenwaelder, 1999).

**MIB Structure.** For simplicity and extensibility, SMI avoids complex data types. Each type of object in an MIB has a name, syntax, and an encoding scheme. An object is uniquely identified by an OBJECT IDENTIFIER. The identifier is also used to identify the structure of object types. The term OBJECT DESCRIPTOR may also be used to refer to the object type (McCloghrie & Rose, 1991). The syntax of an object type is defined using abstract syntax notation one (ASN.1; ISO, 1987). Basic encoding rules (BER) have been adopted as the encoding scheme for data-type transfer between network entities.

The set of defined objects has a tree structure. Beginning with the root of the object identifier tree, each object identifier component value identifies an arc in the tree. The root has three nodes: itu (0), iso (1), and joint-iso-itu (2). Some of the nodes in the SMI object tree, starting from the root, are shown in Figure 5. The identifier is constructed by the set of numbers, separated by a dot that defines the path to the object from the root. Thus, the Internet node, for example, has its OBJECT

IDENTIFIER value of 1.3.6.1. It can also be defined as follows:

```
internet   OBJECT IDENTIFIER ::= { iso (1)
org (3) dod (6) 1 }.
```

Any object in the internet node will start with the prefix 1.3.6.1 or simply internet.

SMI defines four nodes under internet: directory, mgmt, experimental, and private. The mgmt

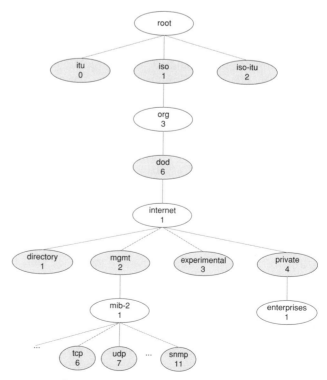

**Figure 5:** Management information tree.

subtree contains the definitions of MIBs that have been approved by the IAB. Two versions of the MIB with the same object identifier have been developed, `mib-1` and its extension `mib-2`. Additional objects can be defined in one of the following three mechanisms (Case et al., 1990; Stalling, 1998):

1. The `mib-2` subtree can be expanded or replaced by a completely new revision.
2. An experimental MIB can be constructed for a particular application. Such objects may subsequently be moved to the `mgmt` subtree.
3. Private extensions can be added to the private subtree.

**Object Syntax.** The syntax of an object type defines the abstract data structure corresponding to that object type. ASN.1 is used to define each individual object and the entire MIB structure. The definition of an object in SNMP contains the data type, its allowable forms and value ranges, and its relationship with other objects within the MIB.

**Encoding.** Objects in the MIB are encoded using the BER associated with ASN.1. Although it is not the most compact or efficient form of encoding, BER is a widely used, standardized encoding scheme. BER specifies a method for encoding values of each ASN.1 type as a string of octets for transmitting to another system.

### Management Information Base
Two versions of MIBs have been defined: MIB-I and MIB-II. MIB-II is a superset of MIB-I, with some additional objects and groups. MIB-II contains only essential elements; none of the objects is optional. The objects are arranged into groups in Table 3.

### Security Weaknesses
The only security feature that SNMP offers is through the community name contained in the SNMP message as shown in Figure 4. Community name serves as the password to authenticate the SNMP message. Without encryption, this feature essentially offers no security at all because the community name can be readily eavesdropped as it passes from the managed system

to the management system. Furthermore, SNMP cannot authenticate the source of a management message. Therefore, it is possible for unauthorized users to exercise SNMP network management functions and to eavesdrop on management information as it passes from the managed systems to the management system. Because of these deficiencies, many SNMP implementations have chosen not to implement the Set command. This reduces their utility to that of a network monitor and no network control applications can be supported.

## SNMPv2
SNMP was originally developed as an interim management protocol and CMIP over TCP/IP (CMOT), which essentially enables the OSI system management protocols to operate on top of the TCP protocol, as the ultimate network management protocol. However, the latter never came about in reality. At the same time, SNMP has been incorporated widely and enhancement is expected. SNMPv2 was developed when it was obvious that the OSI network management standards were not going to be implemented in the foreseeable future.

### Major Changes in SNMPv2
The SNMPv2 system architecture is essentially the same as that of SNMP. The key enhancement in SNMPv2 can be summarized as follows:

- **Bulk data transfer capability:** The most noticeable change in SNMPv2 is the inclusion of two new PDUs. The first PDU is the `GetBulkRequest` PDU, which enables the manager to retrieve large blocks of data efficiently and therefore speeds up the `GetNextRequest` process.
- **Manager-to-manager capability:** The second PDU is the `InformRequest` PDU, which enables one manager to send the trap type of information to another and thus makes network management systems interoperable.
- **Structure of management information:** The SMI defined in SNMP has been consolidated and rewritten.

### SNMPv2 Protocol Specifications
To improve the efficiency and performance of message exchange between systems, the PDU data structure in

---

**Table 3** Objects Contained in MIB-II

| Groups | Description |
|---|---|
| `system` | Contains system description and administrative information. |
| `interfaces` | Contains information about each of the interfaces from the system to a subnet. |
| `at` | Contains address translation table for Internet-to-subnet address mapping. This group is deprecated in MIB-II and is included solely for compatibility with MIB-I nodes. |
| `ip` | Contains information relevant to the implementation and operation of IP at a node. |
| `icmp` | Contains information relevant to the implementation and operation of ICMP at a node. |
| `tcp` | Contains information relevant to the implementation and operation of TCP at a node. |
| `udp` | Contains information relevant to the implementation and operation of UDP at a node. |
| `egp` | Contains information relevant to the implementation and operation of EGP at a node. |
| `transmission` | Contains information about the transmission schemes and access protocols at each system interface. |
| `snmp` | Contains information relevant to the implementation and operation of SNMP on this system. |

| PDU Type | Request ID | Error Status | ErrorIndex | Variable Bindings | | | | |
|---|---|---|---|---|---|---|---|---|
| | | | | Name 1 | Value 1 | ... | Name N | Value N |

(a) All but Bulk Type of PDUs

| PDU Type | Request ID | NonRepeaters | MaxRepetitions | Variable Bindings | | | | |
|---|---|---|---|---|---|---|---|---|
| | | | | Name 1 | Value 1 | ... | Name N | Value N |

(b) `GetBulkRequest` PDU

**Figure 6:** SNMPv2 PDU formats.

SNMPv2 has been standardized to a common format for all messages, given in Figure 6. In the `GetBulkRequest` PDU, `NonRepeaters` field indicates the number of nonrepetitive field values requested, and the `MaxRepetitions` field designates the maximum number of table rows requested.

### SNMPv2 Structure of Management Information

The SMI for SNMPv2 is based on the SMI for SNMP. It is nearly a proper superset of the SNMP SMI. The SNMPv2 SMI is divided into three parts: module definitions, object definitions, and notification definitions.

*Module definitions* are used to describe information modules. An ASN.1 macro, `MODULE-IDENTITY`, is used to concisely convey the semantics of an information module. *Object definitions* are used to describe managed objects. `Object-Type` is used to concisely convey both syntax and semantics of a managed object. *Notification definitions* are used to describe unsolicited transmissions of management information. Notification in SNMPv2 is equivalent to trap in SNMP SMI. `NOTIFICATION-TYPE` conveys both syntax and semantics.

### SNMPv2 Management Information Base

The SNMPv2 MIB defines objects that describe the behavior of an SNMPv2 entity. It consists of three groups:

- **System group:** An expansion of the original MIB-II `system` group. It includes a collection of objects that allow an SNMPv2 entity to act in an agent role and to describe its dynamic configurable object resources.
- **SNMP group:** A refinement to the original MIB-II `snmp` group. It consists of objects that provide the basic instrumentation of the protocol activity.
- **MIB objects group:** A collection of objects that deal with `SNMPv2Trap` PDUs and that allow several cooperating SNMPv2 entities, each acts in a manager role, to coordinate their use of the SNMPv2 set operations.

### Security Weaknesses

Similar to SNMP, SNMPv2 fails to provide any security services. The security of SNMPv2 remains the same as SNMP. Therefore, it is still vulnerable to security attacks such as masquerade, information modification, and information disclosure.

### SNMPv3

The security deficiency in SNMP and SNMPv2 significantly limits their utility. To remedy this problem, SNMPv3 was developed (Blumenthal & Wijnen, 2002; Case, Harrington, Presuhn, & Wijnen, 2002; Harrington, Presuhn, & Wijnen, 2002; Levi, Meyer, & Stewart, 2002; Wijnen, Presuhn, & McCloghrie, 2002). The SNMPv3 configuration can be set remotely with secure communication links. SNMPv3 also provides a framework for all three versions of SNMP and future development in SNMP with minimum effects on existing operations.

### SNMPv3 Architecture

An SNMP management network consists of a distributed, interacting collection of SNMP entities. Each entity consists of a collection of modules that interact with each other to provide services. The architecture of an entity is defined as the elements of that entity and the names associated with them. There are three kinds of naming: naming of entities, naming of identities, and naming of management information.

**SNMP Entities.** The elements of the architecture associated with an SNMP entity, shown in Figure 7, consist of an SNMP engine, named `snmpEngineID`, and a set of applications that use the services provided by the SNMP engine. A brief definition of each of the modules is described here:

- **Dispatcher:** Allows for concurrent support of multiple versions of SNMP messages in the SNMP engine. It performs three sets of functions. First, it sends and receives SNMP messages from the network. Second, it determines the version of the message and interacts with the corresponding message-processing model. Third, it provides an abstract interface to SNMP applications to deliver an incoming PDU to the local application and to send a PDU from the local application to a remote entity.
- **Message Processing Subsystem:** Responsible for preparing messages for sending and responsible for extracting data from received messages.
- **Security Subsystem:** Provides security services such as authentication and privacy of messages. It potentially contains multiple security models.
- **Access Control Subsystem:** Provides authorization services by means of one or more access control models.

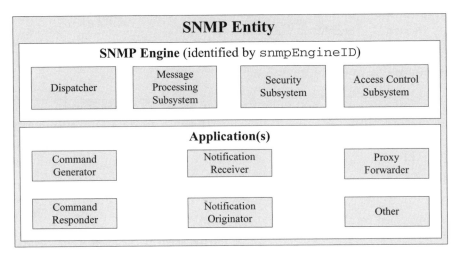

**Figure 7:** SNMP entity.

**SNMP Names.** The names associated with the identities include principal, securityName, and a model-dependent security ID. A principal indicates to whom services are provided. A principal can either be a person or an application. A securityName is a human-readable string that represents a principal. A model-dependent security ID is the model-specific representation of a security-Name within a particular security model.

A management entity can be responsible for more than one managed object. Each object is called a context and has a contextEngineID and a contextName. A scopePDU is a block of data containing a context EngineID, a contextName, and a PDU.

**Abstract Service Interfaces.** Abstract service interfaces describe the conceptual interfaces among the various subsystems within an SNMP entity and are defined by a set of primitives and the abstract data elements. A primitive specifies the function to be performed and the parameters to be used to pass data and control information. Table 4 lists the primitives that have been defined for the various subsystems.

### SNMPv3 Applications

SNMPv3 formally defines five types of applications. These applications make use of the services provided by the SNMP engine. SNMPv3 defines the procedures followed by each type of application when generating PDUs for transmission or processing incoming PDUs. The procedures are defined in terms of interaction with the dispatcher by means of the dispatcher primitives.

**Command Generator.** The command generator application makes use of the sendPdu and processResponse Pdu dispatcher primitive to generate GetRequest, Get-NextRequest, GetBulk, and SetRequest messages. It also processes the response to the command sent. The sendPdu provides the dispatcher with information about the intended destination, security parameters, and the actual PDU to be sent. The dispatcher then invokes the message processing model, which in turn invokes the security model, to prepare the message. The dispatcher delivers each incoming response PDU to the correct command generator application, using the processResponsePdu primitive.

**Command Responder.** A command responder application makes use of four dispatcher primitives (register ContextEngineID, unregisterContextEngineID, processPdu, and returnResponsePdu) and one access control subsystem primitive (isAccessAllowed) to receive and process SNMP Get and Set requests. It also sends response messages. The dispatcher delivers each incoming request PDU to the correct command responder application, using the processPDU primitive. The command generator uses returnResponsePdu to deliver the message back to the dispatcher.

**Notification Originators.** A notification originator application follows the same general procedures used for a command generator application to generate either a trap or an Inform. If an Inform PDU is to be sent, both the sendPDU and processResponse primitives are used. If a trap PDU is to be sent, only the sendPDU primitive is used.

**Notification Receiver.** A notification receiver application follows a subset of the general procedures as for a command responder application to receive SNMP notification messages. Both types of PDUs are received by means of a processPdu primitive. For an Inform PDU, a returnResponsePdu primitive is used to respond.

**Proxy Forwarder.** A proxy forwarder application makes use of dispatcher primitives to forward SNMP messages. The proxy forwarder application handles four types of messages: messages containing PDU types generated by a command generator application, messages containing PDU types generated by a command responder application, messages containing PDU types generated by a notification originator application, and messages containing a report indicator.

**Table 4** List of Primitives

| Component | Primitive | Service Provided |
|---|---|---|
| Dispatcher | sendPdu | Sends an SNMP request or notification to another SNMP entity. |
| | processPdu | Passes an incoming SNMP PDU to an application. |
| | returnResponsePdu | Returns an SNMP response PDU to the PDU dispatcher. |
| | processResponsePdu | Passes an incoming SNMP response PDU to an application. |
| | registerContextEngineID | Registers responsibility for a specific contextEngineID for specific pduTypes. |
| | unregisterContextEngineID | Unregisters responsibility for a specific contextEngineID for specific pduTypes. |
| Message process subsystem | prepareOutgoingMessage | Prepares an outgoing SNMP request or notification message. |
| | prepareResponseMessage | Prepares an outgoing SNMP response message. |
| | prepareDataElements | Prepares the abstract data elements from an incoming SNMP message. |
| Access control subsystem | isAccessAllowed | Checks if access is allowed. |
| Security subsystem | generateRequestMsg | Generates a request or notification message. |
| | processIncomingMsg | Processes an incoming message. |
| | generateResponseMsg | Generates a response message. |
| User-based security model | authenticateOutgoingMsg | Authenticates an outgoing message. |
| | authenticateIncomingMsg | Authenticates an incoming message. |
| | encryptData | Encrypts data. |
| | decryptData | Decrypts data. |

## SNMPv3 Management Information Base

Three separate MIB modules have been defined by Levi, Meyer, and Stewart (2002) to support SNMPv3 applications: the management target MIB, the notification MIB, and the proxy MIB.

The SNMP-TARGET-MIB module contains objects for defining management targets. It consists of two tables. The first table, the snmpTargetAddrTable, contains information about transport domains and addresses. The second table, the snmpTargetParamsTable, contains information about SNMP version and security information to be used when sending messages to particular transport domains and addresses.

The SNMP-NOTIFICATION-MIB module contains objects for remote configuration of the parameters used by an SNMP entity for the generation of notifications. It consists of three tables. The first table, the snmpNotifyTable, selects one or more entries in snmpTargetAddrTable to be used for notification generation. The second table, the snmpNotifyFilterProfileTable, sparsely augments the snmpTargetParamsTable to associate a set of filters with a particular management target. The third table, the snmpNotifyFilterTable, defines filters used to limit the number of notifications generated for a particular management target.

The SNMP-PROXY-MIB contains objects for the remote configuration of the parameters used by an SNMP entity for proxy forwarding operations. It contains a single table, snmpProxyTable, which is used to define the translations among management targets for forwarding messages.

## SNMPv3 Message Format

Each SNMPv3 message includes four data groups: msgVersion, msgGlobaGata, msgSecurityParameters, and msgPDU, as shown in Figure 8.

The msgVersion field is set to snmpv3 (3) and identifies the message as an SNMP version 3 message. The msgGlobaGata field contains the header information. The msgSecurityParameters field is used exclusively by the security model. The contents and format of the data are defined by the security model. The msgData is the scoped PDU field containing information to identify an administratively unique context and a PDU.

## Security Enhancement

One of the main objectives of SNMPv3 is the addition of security services for network management. SNMPv3 is intended to address four types of security threats: modification of information, masquerade, disclosure, and message-stream modification. The first two are identified as principal threats, whereas the last two are identified as secondary threats. A user-based security model (USM) is proposed in SNMPv3. This model reflects the traditional concept of a user identified by a userName (Blumenthal & Wijnen, 2002).

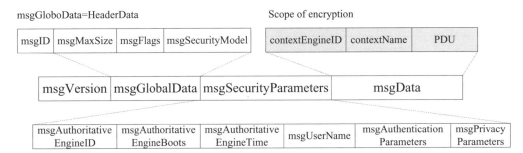

**Figure 8:** SNMPv3 message format.

**User-Based Security Model (USM).** The USM encompasses three different security modules: the *authentication module*, the *timeliness module*, and the *privacy module*.

To protect against message replay, delay, and redirection, when two management entities communicate, one of the SNMP engines is designated as the *authoritative SNMP engine*. Particularly when an SNMP message contains a payload that expects a response, the receiver of such messages is authoritative. When an SNMP message contains a payload that does not expect a response, then the sender of such a message is authoritative.

The message process model invokes the USM in the security subsystem. Based on the security level set in the message, the USM in turn invokes the authentication modules, privacy modules, and timeliness modules. The USM allows for different protocols to be used instead of or concurrent with the protocols described by Blumenthal and Wijnen (2002) and Wijnen, Presuhn, and McCloghrie (2002).

**Authentication.** USM uses one of two alternative authentication protocols to achieve data integrity and data origin authentication: HMAC-MD5-96 and HMAC-SHA-96. HMAC uses a secure hash function and a secret key to produce a message authentication code (Krawezyk, Bellare, & Canetti, 1997; Stallings, 1998). In this case, the secret key is the localized user's private authentication key `authKey`. The value of `authKey` is not accessible via SNMP. For HMAC-MD5-96, MD5 is used as the underlying hash function. The `authKey` is 16 octets in length. The algorithm produces a 128-bit output, which is truncated to 12 octets (96 bits). For HMAC-SHA-96, the underling hash function is SHA-1. The `authKey` is 20 octets in length. The algorithm produces a 20-octet output, which is again truncated to 12 octets.

**Encryption.** USM uses CBC-DES symmetric encryption protocol to protect against disclosure of the message payload (Krawezyk, Bellare, & Canetti, 1997; Stallings, 1998). A 16-octet `privKey` is provided as the input to the encryption protocol. The first eight octets (64 bits) of this `privKey` are used as a DES key. Because DES uses only 56 bits, the least significant bit in each octet is disregarded. For CBC mode, a 64-bit initialization vector (IV) is required. The last eight octets of the `privKey` contain a value that is used to generate this IV.

To ensure that the IVs for two different packets encrypted by the same key are not identical, an 8-octet string called "salt" is XOR-ed with the pre-IV to obtain the IV.

**View-Based Access Control Model (VACM).** The access control subsystem of an SNMP engine has the responsibility for checking whether a specific type of access (read, write, notify) to a particular object (instance) is allowed.

Access control occurs in an SNMP entity when processing SNMP retrieval or modification request messages from an SNMP entity and when an SNMP notification message is generated.

The VACM defines a set of services that an application can use for checking access rights. It is the responsibility of the application to make the proper service calls for access checking.

**Elements of the VACM Model.** VACM defined by Wijnen, Presuhn, and McCloghrie (2002) comprises five elements: group, security level, context, MIB view, and access policy.

- **Group:** A group is a set of zeros or more < `securityModel`, `securityName` > tuples on whose behalf SNMP management objects can be accessed. A group defines the access rights afforded to all `securityNames` that belong to that group. The combination of a `securityModel` and a `securityName` maps to at most one group identified by a `groupName`.
- **Security Level:** The access rights for the members of a group may vary depending on the security levels. The level of security is set by the msgFlags given in Figure 8.
- **Context:** An SNMP context is a collection of management information accessible by an SNMP entity. An SNMP entity potentially has access to many contexts.
- **MIB View:** For security reasons, it is often desirable to restrict the access rights of a particular group to only a subset of the MIB. To provide this capability, access to a context is via an MIB view, which details the specific set of managed object types as a set of view subtrees, with each view subtree being included in or excluded from the view.
- **Access Policy:** The VACM determines the access rights of a group (identified by `group-Name`) for a particular context (identified by

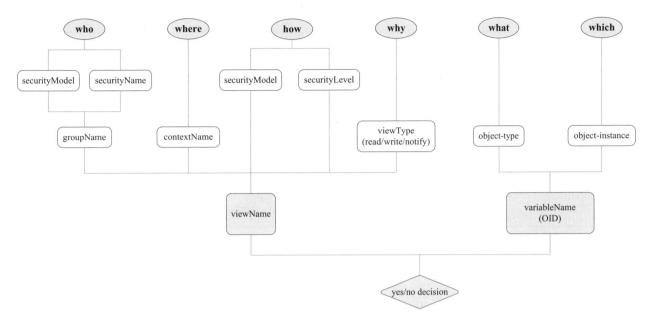

**Figure 9:** VACM access control logic.

contextName) based on securityModel and securityLevel. The access rights include a read view, a write view, and a notify view.

**The VACM Process.** An SNMP application invokes VACM via the isAccessAllowed primitive with the input parameters, including securityModel, securityName, securityLevel, viewType, contextName, and variableName. The VACM decision for access control is shown in Figure 9.

## Remote Network Monitoring (RMON)

Remote network-monitoring devices, often called *monitors* or *probes*, are instruments that exist for the purpose of managing a network. The RMON can produce summary information of the managed objects, including error statistics, performance statistics, and traffic statistics. Based on the statistics information, the status of the managed objects can be observed and analyzed.

### RMON1 Groups

The RMON1 specification is primarily a definition of a MIB defined by Waldbusser (2000; 1993). RMON1 delivers management information in nine groups of monitoring elements; each provides specific sets of data to meet common network-monitoring requirements. Some RMON1 groups require support of other RMON1 groups to function properly. Table 5 summarizes the nine monitoring groups specified by Waldbusser (1997).

### RMON2

RMON2, defined by Waldbusser (1997), enables network statistics and analysis to be provided from the network layer up to the application layer. The most visible and most beneficial capability in RMON2 is monitoring above the MAC layer, which supports protocol distribution and provides a view of the whole network rather than a single local area network (LAN) segment. RMON2 also enables host traffic for particular applications to be recorded. The

**Table 5** RMON1 MIBs

| RMON group | Function |
|---|---|
| Statistics | Contains statistics measured by the probe for each monitored interface on this device. |
| History | Records periodic statistical samples from a network and stores them for later retrieval. |
| Alarm | Takes statistical samples periodically from variables in the probe and compares them with previously configured thresholds. If the monitored variable crosses a threshold, an event is generated. |
| Host | Contains statistics associated with each host discovered on the network. |
| HostTopN | Prepares statistics about the top *N* hosts on a subnetwork based on the available parameters. |
| Matrix | Stores statistics for conversations between sets of two addresses. As the device detects a new conversation, it creates a new entry in its table. |
| Filters | Enables packets to be matched by a filter equation. These matched packets form a data stream that may be captured or may generate events. |
| Packet capture | Enables packets to be captured after they flow through a channel. |
| Events | Controls the generation and notification of events from a device. |
| Token ring extensions | Contains four groups to define some additional monitoring functions specified for token ring. They are the ring station group, the ring station order group, the ring station configuration group, and the source routing statistics group. |

**Table 6** RMON2 MIBs

| RMON2 MIB Group | Functions |
|---|---|
| Protocol directory | Presents an inventory of protocol types capable of monitoring. |
| Protocol distribution | Collects the relative amounts of octets and packets. |
| Address mapping | Provides address translation between MAC addresses and network addresses on the interface. |
| Network layer host | Provides network host traffic statistics. |
| Network layer matrix | Provides traffic analysis between each pair of network hosts. |
| Application layer host | Reports on protocol usage at the network layer or higher. |
| Application layer matrix | Provides protocol traffic analysis between pairs of network hosts. |
| User history collection | Provides user-specified history collection on alarm and configuration history. |
| Probe configuration | Controls the configuration of probe parameters. |
| RMON conformance | Describes the conformance requirements to RMON2 MIB. |

managed objects in RMON2 are arranged into groups as shown in Table 6.

# POLICY-BASED NETWORK MANAGEMENT; SOLUTIONS FOR THE NEXT GENERATION

*Policy-based network management* (*PBNM*; Strassner, 2004) is a way to manage the configuration and behavior of one or more entities based on business needs and policies. PBNM systems enable business rules and procedures to be translated into policies that configure and control the network and its services. PBNM can also be defined as a condition-action response mechanism. The general form is as follows:

```
ON <event>
IF <conditions>
THEN <actions>
```

PBNM enables an automatic response to conditions in the network according to predefined policies. By automating the network management, the entire network can be managed as an entity. The essence of PBNM can be portrayed in Figure 10.

## What Is a Policy?

*Policy* is typically defined as a set of operating rules that manage and control access to network resources. It allows a network to be managed through a descriptive language. Policy can be represented at different levels, ranging from business goals to device-specific configuration parameters.

*Policy management* is the usage of operating rules to accomplish decisions. It forms a bridge between a service level agreement (SLA) and the network entities. Business goals and policies can be defined as a separate business management layer on top of the service management layer that provides services such as quality of service (QoS), as shown in Figure 11 (Erfani, Lawrence, Malek, & Sugla, 1999).

With the growth in scale and complexity of computer networks, QoS and security are becoming very challenging management issues. PBNM is emerging as a promising solution in simplifying the management of QoS and security.

## Benefits of PBNM

The appealing part of PBNM is that through abstractions, the network management QoS and security mechanisms can be simplified so that the majority of network management tasks are simple in nature. PBNM also enables system behavior to be changed without modifying implementation. More specifically, the benefit of PBNM can be summarized as follows (Hewlett, Packard, 1999; Strassner, 2004):

- **Optimizes network resources intelligently:** The automation of management tasks intelligently optimizes both the use of network infrastructure and the network policies. PBNM reduces the need for adding bandwidth to congested links.

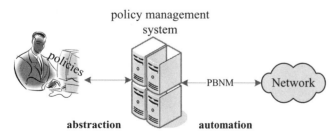

**Figure 10:** The basic model of policy-based management.

**Figure 11:** Network management layered view.

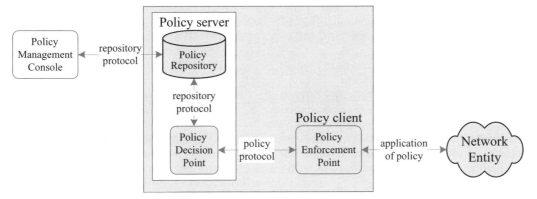

**Figure 12:** Logic architecture for PBNM.

- **Simplifies network and service management:** PBNM users are no longer required to be specialists to perform network management functions. Another aspect is that changes in business policies do not necessarily require any low layer development, which makes management updating painless.
- **Manages complex traffic and services intelligently:** PNBM can manage applications with competing demands for shared resources using the predicated traffic information. Unauthorized and unwanted applications can be controlled or eliminated, and mission-critical applications can be assigned with special priority.
- **Performs time-critical functions efficiently:** PBNM can simplify and better implement time-critical functions, such as changing device configurations within a specific time window and performing scheduled provisioning functions.
- **Provides better security:** PBNM can help categorize traffic into expected and unexpected types and assign rules to deal with each type. PBNM can also be used to determine whether a particular user can access a resource.

### Architecture of a PBNM System

The general architecture for a policy management system is shown in Figure 12. This architecture contains four major components (Hewlett-Packard, 1999; Westerinen et al., 2001):

- **Policy Management Console:** The user interface to construct policies, deploy policies, and monitor the status of policy-managed environment.
- **Policy Repository:** A database that stores the policy rules, their conditions and actions, and related policy data. It can also be defined as a model abstraction representing an administratively defined, logical container for reusable policy elements.
- **Policy Decision Point (PDP):** A logical process that makes decisions based on the policy rules and the conditions under which the policy rules are applied.
- **Policy Enforcement Point (PEP):** A logical entity that executes policy decisions and/or makes a configuration change.

- **Policy Communication Protocols:** Needed for data exchange among entities in the policy management system. The common object policy service protocol (COPS) is often mentioned to support the communication between the PDP and the PEP.

## CONCLUSION

In this chapter, after a brief introduction to the network management system, the evolution of the two most widely used network management standards, SNMP and RMON, and the rapid development in computer and communication networks were reviewed. As a promising solution for the next generation of network management, the architecture of PBNM has also been briefly discussed. The popularity of SNMP and RMON is largely due to their simplicity in architecture and implementation. However, the simplicity has its price; the versatile expertise required for the administrators and the reality that even a slight change in business policy may require complex development at lower layers prevent these standards from further development. To overcome these disadvantages, PBNM is proposed to ensure efficient network management and smooth network services upgrade. Although PBNM is still not fully mature yet, these promising features make it very appealing.

## GLOSSARY

**Account Management**  One of the five OSI systems management functional areas. Consists of facilities that enable cost allocation based on the use of network resources.

**Common Management Information Protocol (CMIP)**  An object-oriented OSI standard management protocol.

**Configuration Management**  One of the five OSI systems management functional areas. Consists of facilities that set and change the configuration of networks and network components.

**Fault Management**  One of the five OSI systems management functional areas. Consists of facilities that detect, isolate, and correct the abnormal operation of the OSI environment.

**HMAC Protocols**  Message authentication protocols used for the authentication scheme in security management. It uses a hashing algorithm to derive the message access code (MAC). Two common algorithms used in SNMP security management are HMAC-MD5-96 and HMAC-SHA-96.

**Managed Object**    A network device that can be managed remotely by a network management system.

**Management Information Base (MIB)**    An abstract definition of the management information available through a management interface in a system.

**Network Management System (NMS)**    The platform that houses the network manager module. It monitors and controls the network components from a centralized operation.

**Performance Management**    One of the five OSI systems management functional areas. Consists of facilities that evaluate the behavior of managed objects and the performance of network activities.

**Policy-Based Network Management (PBNM)**    Manages the configuration and behavior of networks based on business needs and policies.

**Remote Network Monitoring (RMON)**    Remotely monitoring of the network with a probe.

**Security Management**    One of the five OSI systems management functional areas. Consists of facilities that provide security services essential to operate OSI network management correctly and to protect managed objects.

**Simple Network Management Protocol (SNMP)**    An application-layer protocol that facilitates the exchange of management information among network devices.

**Structure of Management Information (SMI)**    Defines managed objects and their characteristics, as well as the relationships among the objects.

**Trap**    An alarm or an event generated by a management agent and sent in an unsolicited manner to a network management system.

**User-Based Access Control Model (UACM)**    The access control scheme defined in SNMPv3. It is more secure and flexible than the simple access policy defined in SNMP.

# CROSS REFERENCES

See *Contingency Planning Management; Security Architectures; TCP/IP Suite; Web Hosting.*

# REFERENCES

Bidgoli, H. (Ed.). (2005). *The handbook of information security,* Vol. 1. Hoboken, NJ: John Wiley & Sons.

Blumenthal, U., & Wijnen, B. (2002). *User-based security model (USM) for version 3 of the simple network management protocol (SNMPv3)* (RFC 3414). Retrieved from http://www.rfc-editor.org/rfc/rfc3414.txt

Case, J., Fedor, M., Schoffstall, M., & Davin, J. (1990). *A simple network management protocol (SNMP)* (RFC 1157). Retrieved from http://www.rfc-editor.org/rfc/rfc1157.txt

Case, J., Harrington, D., Presuhn, R., & Wijnen, B. (2002). *Message processing and dispatching for the simple network management protocol (SNMP)* (RFC 3412). Retrieved from http://www.rfc-editor.org/rfc/rfc3412.txt

Cerf, V. (1988). *IAB recommendations for the development of internet network management standards* (RFC 1052). Retrieved from http://www.rfc-editor.org/rfc/rfc1052.txt

Cerf, V. (1989). *Report of the second ad hoc network management review group* (RFC 1109). Retrieved from http://www.rfc-editor.org/rfc/rfc1109.txt

Erfani, S., Lawrence, V., Malek, M., & Sugla, B. (1999). Network management: Emerging trends and challenges. *Bell Labs Technical Journal,* October–December.

Harrington, D., Presuhn, R., & Wijnen, B. (2002). *An architecture for describing simple network management protocol (SNMP) management frameworks* (RFC 3411). Retrieved from http://www.rfc-editor.org/rfc/rfc3411.txt

Hewlett-Packard Company (1999, September 24). *A primer on policy-based network management.* Retrieved from http://www.openview.hp.com/Uploads/primer_on_policy-based_network_mgmt.pdf

International Organization for Standardization (ISO). (1987, December). *Specification of abstract syntax notation one (ASN.1)* (International Standard 8824).

Krawczyk, H., Bellare, M., & Canetti, R. (1997). *HMAC: Keyed-hashing for message authentication.* (RFC 2104). Retrieved from http://www.rfc-editor.org/rfc/rfc2104.txt

Levi, D., Meyer, P., & Stewart, B. (2002). *Simple network management protocol (SNMP) applications* (RFC 3413). Retrieved from http://www.rfc-editor.org/rfc/rfc3413.txt

McCloghrie, K., Perkins, D., & Schoenwaelder, J. (1999). *Structure of management information version 2 (SMIv2)* (RFC 2819). Retrieved from http://www.rfc-editor.org/rfc/rfc2819.txt

McCloghrie, K., & Rose, M. (1991). *Management information base for network management of TCP/IP-based internets: MIB-II* (RFC 1213). Retrieved from http://www.rfc-editor.org/rfc/rfc1213.txt

Postel, J. (1980). *User datagram protocol* (RFC 768). Retrieved from http://www.rfc-editor.org/rfc/rfc768.txt

Rose, M., & McCloghrie, K. (1990). *Structure and identification of management information for TCP/IP-based internets* (RFC 1155). Retrieved from http://www.rfc-editor.org/rfc/rfc1155.txt

Stallings, W. (1998). *SNMP, SNMPv2, SNMPv3 and RMON 1 and 2 (3rd ed.).* Boston: Addison-Wesley.

Strassner, J. (2004). *Policy-based network management—Solutions for the next generation.* Morgan Kaufmann.

Subramanian, M. (2000). *Network management—principles and practice.* Boston: Addison-Wesley.

Tanenbaum, A. (2003). *Computer networks (4th ed.).* Upper Saddle River, NJ: Prentice Hall.

Waldbusser, S. (1993). *Token ring extensions to the remote network monitoring MIB* (RFC 1513). Retrieved from http://www.rfc-editor.org/rfc/rfc1513.txt

Waldbusser, S. (1997). *Remote network monitoring management information base version 2 using SMIv2* (RFC 2021). Retrieved from http://www.rfc-editor.org/rfc/rfc2021.txt

Waldbusser, S. (2000). *Remote network monitoring management information base* (RFC 2819). Retrieved from http://www.rfc-editor.org/rfc/rfc2819.txt

Westerinen, A., Schnizlein, J., Strassner, J., Scherling, M., Quinn, B., Herzog, S., et al. (2001). *Terminology for Policy-Based Management* (RFC 3198). Retrieved from http://www.rfc-editor.org/rfc/rfc3198.txt

Wijnen, B., Presuhn, R., & McCloghrie, K. (2002). *View-based access control model (VACM) for the simple network management protocol (SNMP)* (RFC 3415). Retrieved from http://www.rfc-editor.org/rfc/rfc3415.txt

# E-Mail and Internet Use Policies

Nancy J. King, *Oregon State University*

## INTRODUCTION

Recent surveys highlight the importance for employers of having a well-drafted e-mail and Internet use policy. These surveys show the majority of employers adopt e-mail and Internet use policies for important business reasons that range from addressing employee productivity to preventing hostile work environments. For example, the American Management Association's *E-Mail Rules, Policies and Practices Survey* (2003) reported that 75% of the organizations in their survey had written policies concerning e-mail. More than one third of the respondents in this survey reported that they had experienced problems related to their e-mail systems including having their computer systems disabled for a time, having their businesses interrupted for a time, and having computer viruses enter their systems through e-mail. The average respondent in this survey reported spending about 107 minutes on e-mail every day—about 25% of the workday. Ninety percent of respondents in the survey reported sending and receiving personal e-mail at work, but the vast majority stated that personal e-mail amounts to less than 10% of all their e-mail correspondence. Eighty-six percent of respondents claimed e-mail makes them more efficient at work. Other surveys have demonstrated that employees' misuse of Internet access may also be a serious business concern for employers. It has been reported that many employees use the Internet at work for nonbusiness reasons such as viewing pornography, analyzing their investment portfolios, making personal travel arrangements, locating friends, following sports teams, and shopping for merchandise (Burgunder, 2004). Clearly the use of e-mail and Internet access by employees in the workplace calls for well-designed e-mail and Internet policies to prevent abuse of work time and to minimize other business and legal risks.

Although there are valid business reasons for employers to carefully craft e-mail and Internet use policies to avert abuses by some employees, it is likely that the vast majority of employees do not engage in misconduct or abuse the privilege of using the employers' communications equipment. Furthermore, employers benefit from employees' enhanced productivity made possible by e-mail and Internet access in the workplace. Additionally, employees have legal rights related to the workplace that need to be considered when employers draft e-mail and Internet policies. This chapter endeavors to help employers draft and enforce e-mail and Internet use policies that achieve an appropriate balance between preventing abuses and protecting employees' rights in the workplace.

## PURPOSE AND FUNCTION OF E-MAIL AND INTERNET USE POLICIES

An employer's policy covering e-mail and Internet use is a key workplace management tool. When the policy is properly drafted, effectively communicated to employees, and consistently enforced, it enables the employer to establish guidelines for acceptable and unacceptable workplace behavior involving the use of e-mail and Internet access (Page, 2002). An employer's e-mail and Internet access policy should notify employees of acceptable and unacceptable workplace behavior (Page, 2002). Another advantage of an effective policy is that it may prevent losses to the employer that may result from employees deliberately or carelessly misusing e-mail and Internet access. These losses may include misappropriations of intellectual property and employer liability for civil damages or criminal sanctions. An effective e-mail and Internet use policy helps an employer achieve legal compliance with a myriad of workplace laws that protect employee rights and restrict the employer's and employees' actions related to e-mail and Internet systems, provided the employer follows the policy, applies it fairly, and trains its managers on implementation of the policy (Harmon, 1982). Finally, an effective e-mail and Internet use policy reserves the employer's property and management rights, including the right to monitor the employer's equipment and systems for a variety of business reasons and the right to discipline or terminate employees for violating the policy (Harper Business, 1990). See Table 1, Drafting E-Mail and Internet Use Policies, for a chart describing important policy issues and drafting suggestions.

# SCOPE OF E-MAIL AND INTERNET USE POLICIES

An important strategic decision that an employer must make when drafting an e-mail and Internet use policy is the scope of the policy. The scope of the policy will be expanded or limited by the employer's decisions regarding whether to permit personal use of its e-mail and the Internet systems, limit application of the policy to employer-provided equipment and systems, cover off-premises use of its e-mail and Internet systems, and include wireless e-mail and Internet use under the policy.

## Business Use versus Personal Use

An important question for employers to answer is whether to limit employees' use of the employer's e-mail and Internet systems to "business use only," thus excluding any personal use of these systems provided by the employer. Generally employees in the United States have no legal "right" to use the employer's e-mail and Internet systems for personal reasons, so an employer's policy may lawfully adopt a business-use-only policy (King, 2003b). However, in view of the fact that many people work long hours, some advocates for privacy in the workplace argue it has become accepted that there will be a certain amount of personal business that will be done during business hours including personal e-mail communications (Sidbury, 2001). Realistically, some employees will use e-mail and Internet communications for some personal use regardless of any policy that is drafted (Anandarajan & Simmers, 2003).

Advantages of permitting some personal use are that employees may be better able to balance work and family conflicts by having access to e-mail and Internet systems for some personal uses, such as family emergencies,

monitoring the after-school activities of children, checking in with a spouse, and so forth. Personal use of e-mail and Internet access for these types of reasons may be less disruptive in the workplace than employees' use of telephones and/or cell phones, because the communications are generally "silent" and less likely to disrupt the work of other employees. Furthermore, allowing reasonable personal use of e-mail and Internet access may result in less loss of work time by reducing absenteeism at little or no additional cost to the employer. Allowing reasonable personal use of the employer's e-mail and Internet access may generate positive employee morale and may also encourage employees to keep abreast of technological developments. Some current research supports the conclusion that there are some positive beneficial side effects of permitting employees to surf the Web at work (Anandarajan & Simmers, 2003).

On the other hand, limiting e-mail and Internet access to "business-use only" may discourage employee abuse of work time for personal reasons; reduce the need for management to supervise employees' use of e-mail and the Internet to prevent excessive personal use; and limit the likelihood that employees opening personal e-mail on their employer's systems will infect the employer's system with computer viruses.

## Blurring of Workplace Boundaries

One of the advantages of e-mail and Internet technology is that it permits work to be done by employees from just about anywhere. A challenge for the policy drafter, however, is that blurred workplace boundaries may require the drafter to clearly define the scope of the policy. Should the employer's e-mail and Internet use policy also cover e-mail and Internet access by an *employee using his home computer system* and made on his own time? If on his own time, and from his home, an employee uses his laptop and his Internet service provider (ISP), such as America Online, to send an e-mail message to a coworker's personal e-mail account, should the employer's policy apply? If one assumes the employee's e-mail message exposes the employer's trade secrets in an insecure environment, the employer's business interest in applying its policy is obvious and valid. What if an employee uses her own laptop and Internet service provider to chat online and in so doing makes derogatory statements about her boss that members of the public may access, potentially harming the employer's reputation with its customers? In both of these situations, the employee is not using the employer's systems or equipment or making the communication on work time, but the online conversation arguably relates to the workplace and involves legitimate employer interests. From a management perspective, considering the potential harm to the employer's business, these types of communications probably should be covered by the employer's policy. However, caution should be exercised when drafting a policy that regulates employees' personal speech outside the workplace. In some states, private sector employees have constitutional free speech rights or rights to engage in lawful off-duty conduct that an employer may not regulate. Additionally, public sector employees have free speech rights under the federal constitution.

**Table 1**  Drafting E-Mail and Internet Use Policies

| Important Policy Issues | Drafting Suggestions |
|---|---|
| 1. Establishing the purpose of providing employee access to Company-provided e-mail and Internet access. | Company-provided e-mail and Internet access and related systems and equipment are provided to employees for the purpose of conducting Company business. |
| 2. Defining the scope of the e-mail and Internet use policy broadly. | This policy covers e-mail access and the contents of e-mail messages, Internet or intranet communications, records of Internet or intranet access, and other electronic communications, files, and data of any kind stored or transmitted by or on Company-owned or leased systems or equipment. The policy covers wireless access to the Company's equipment and systems. It also covers remote access to Company systems and equipment. |
| 3. Establishing Company ownership of electronic communications, files, and data. | Electronic communications, files, and data covered by this policy remain Company property even when transferred to equipment that is not owned by the Company. |
| 4. Clarifying that employees have no expectation of privacy in their use of Company-provided e-mail or Internet access and that all information communicated on the Company's systems is Company property. | Employees should *not* consider any communications made using Company-provided e-mail or Internet access to be private, even if those communications are personal in nature. Except as provided by law, all information communicated on any of the Company's systems or equipment, including e-mail or use of Internet access, is Company property. |
| 5. Establishing a standard for employees' use of Company-provided e-mail and Internet access. | Employees are authorized to use e-mail and Internet access for Company work-related purposes and consistent with company policies and procedures. Employees are expected to use good judgment and act courteously and professionally when using Company-provided e-mail and Internet access. |
| 6. Permitting employees to make reasonable personal use of Company-provided e-mail and Internet access while protecting Company business interests. | Employees may make reasonable personal use of Company-provided e-mail and Internet access so long as the use does not interfere with the work duties of any employee, violate Company policy, or unduly burden the Company's equipment or systems, and does not undermine the Company's business interests. The permission to make reasonable personal use of Company-provided e-mail and Internet systems may be revoked or revised at any time. |
| 7. Prohibiting employees from using Company-provided e-mail and Internet access for unlawful reasons. | Employees may not use Company-provided e-mail and Internet access for any illegal purpose. Uses that are illegal include violating [copyright or trade secret laws; child pornography laws; antitrust laws; laws restricting exports of information or other products for national security reasons; laws prohibiting online gambling, etc.]. |
| 8. Requiring employees to follow security procedures regarding use of e-mail and Internet Access. | Employees must follow security procedures established by the Company related to the use of Company-provided information systems and equipment including e-mail and Internet access. No person shall use any other user's identification or password or attempt to bypass security features to access information that the person is not authorized to access. |
| 9. Prohibiting employees from using Company-provided e-mail and Internet access for reasons that violate Company policy. | Employees may not use Company-provided e-mail and Internet access for any reason that violates Company policy. Company policy prohibits viewing, storing, or distributing pornography, sexually offensive materials, or other materials inappropriate for the workplace. It is also a violation of Company policy to make or distribute harassing or discriminatory communications related to sex, gender, race, religion, national origin, age, or disability. In all communications including e-mail and Internet chat, employees must follow Company policies regarding improper disclosures of confidential or proprietary information. |
| 10. Prohibiting employees from sending mass e-mail for personal reasons that may burden the Company's information technology systems. | Employees may not send spam or other mass e-mails that are not related to their work. A mass e-mail is a message sent simultaneously to more than __ recipients. |

*(Continued)*

**Table 1** (*Continued*)

| Important Policy Issues | Drafting Suggestions |
|---|---|
| 11. Reserving the Company's right to access or to retrieve communications, files, and other electronic data, use of computer forensics, or use of blocking software. | The Company may access, monitor, intercept, block access, inspect, copy, disclose, use, destroy, delete, recover using computer forensics or other techniques, and/or retain any communications, files, or other data covered by this policy, except as required by law. Such Company actions may occur at any time and no advance notice is required. Employees are required to provide passwords requested by the Company to enable access to Company property. |
| 12. Anticipating the Company's obligations to respond to government requests for electronic communications and other documents. | The Company may access, monitor, intercept, and/or disclose communications, files, or other data covered by this policy in relation to government investigations for national security or law enforcement purposes, without further notice. |
| 13. Reserving the Company's right to discipline or terminate employees for violations of the e-mail and Internet use policy. | Violations of this policy may result in immediate termination of employment or other discipline that the Company determines is appropriate under the circumstances. |
| 14. Reserving the right to take action against Company contractors whose employees violate this policy. | This policy applies to the employees of contractors who are authorized by the Company to use Company-provided e-mail and Internet access. Contractors are responsible for ensuring compliance with this policy by their employees. The Company reserves the right to exclude contractor's employees who violate this policy from further dealings with the Company. |

Note: This table has been prepared from the perspective of a private-sector, nonunion employer in the United States that employs at-will employees, referred to here as "Company." The information in the table does not provide legal advice for policy drafters. All workplace policies should be reviewed by the organization's legal counsel.

Many e-mail and Internet use issues also involve employees using their own computer systems and Internet service providers to access the employer's computer systems. This was the case in *Smyth v. Pillsbury Co.* (1996), where an employee sent an e-mail from his home to another employee by accessing the company's e-mail system. In his e-mail message, the employee made derogatory references about another manager that included a threat to "kill the backstabbing bastard" and compared an upcoming holiday party to a "Jim Jones Kool-Aid Affair." The employer obtained copies of the employee's e-mail and not surprisingly terminated him for inappropriate use of the company's e-mail system. In this type of situation, *both employer and employee-provided equipment and systems are being used* and the communication may be either personal or work-related. To protect the employer's interests, an employer's policy may, and probably should, cover any use of employer-provided computer equipment, e-mail, or Internet access, even if employee-provided equipment and/or systems are also utilized, and even if the communications are "personal." The employer's interest in including these types of communications within its e-mail and Internet use policy is stronger because the employer has provided at least some of the e-mail and Internet equipment or systems and because contemporary workplace violence and harassment concerns merit a broadly worded policy.

The determination of whether the scope of the employer's policy should include e-mail and Internet access involving employee-provided equipment, communications made outside the employee's work time, and personal as opposed to work-related communications involves weighing management as well as legal concerns.

For a discussion of legal constraints on the scope of e-mail and Internet use policies, see the discussion of Complying with Laws Protecting Employee Rights found later in this chapter, including invasion of privacy, federal labor law, and the rights of government or non-U.S. employees.

## Anticipating New Technologies

An employer should also consider the expanding forms of technology that can be used by employees to send and receive e-mail and access the Internet, including the availability of wireless technology and instant messaging capability (Honda & Martin, 2002). To avoid having its policy become technologically outdated, the employer's policy should be worded to encompass new technologies as they become available even if wireless or other e-mail and Internet access capabilities are not currently provided by the employer for its employees' use. This is because wireless technology permits employees to access e-mail and the Internet from the workplace with or without using the employer's e-mail or Internet access equipment or systems. For example, employees with a personal cell phone or personal digital assistant (PDA) with Internet capability can send or receive e-mail or access the Internet to chat and send instant messages while in the workplace and without using the employer's systems or equipment (Honda & Martin, 2002). This capability enables employees on the job to download pornography or copyrighted music or to send messages containing the employer's trade secrets to a competitor.

A recent survey reports that around 65% of employees in the United Kingdom (but less than one in five U.S.

employees) use instant messaging (that may be communicated with or without using wireless devices) to flirt with colleagues, scheme against the boss, gossip about coworkers, or even send sensitive information about major corporate projects. Many employees that use instant messaging wrongly assume instant messages cannot be monitored by the boss (Reuters, 2003). *Newsweek* recently reported that instant messaging technology may surpass e-mail as a business communication tool within three years. Also troubling for employers is the risk that employees will use instant messaging in unprofessional or even discriminatory ways, such as logging on as "cutelilpixiechick" or sending sexual jokes through instant messaging (McLure, 2003, p. 31). Thus, the use of wireless technology and/or instant messaging should be covered by an employer's e-mail and Internet use policy and raises valid productivity and legal risk considerations for employers.

At a minimum, the employer's e-mail and Internet use policy should cover the use of wireless technology by employees while they are at work, including the use of wireless technology provided by either the employer or employees. In the policy, the employer should also address the scope issues in the context of wireless devices including whether to permit reasonable personal e-mail and Internet access on the job using wireless devices, apply the policy to e-mail and Internet access using wireless devices if employees are not on the employer's premises, or cover wireless access that also involves use of the employer's systems and equipment. In the policy, the employer also should anticipate that new ways of communicating electronically will be used by employees, such as instant messaging capability. See the next section of the chapter for a discussion of some important legal constraints on imposing a policy with a broad scope.

## COMPLYING WITH LAWS PROTECTING EMPLOYEE RIGHTS

There are many legal issues that relate to drafting and enforcing e-mail and Internet use policies. This section of the chapter addresses legal concerns that relate to employee rights with respect to drafting and enforcing e-mail and Internet use policies. A well-drafted policy will serve as a legal compliance mechanism for management, such that following the policy will avoid violating laws that protect employee rights. A well-drafted policy will be enforceable legally because it will at least provide the minimum protection for an employee that is required by a multitude of laws regulating the employment relationship. A well-drafted policy will also minimize inadvertent creation of additional employee rights beyond those rights already found in existing laws.

### Contract Law Concerns

The critical contract law issue is that employment policies may create implied contracts that give employees legal rights they would not otherwise have under existing laws. Absent a contract of employment, employees who work for private businesses are "at will." At-will employees may be disciplined or terminated without advance notice for any lawful reason. Unlawful reasons include discipline or termination prohibited by state or federal discrimination statutes. Unlawful reasons also include a

number of exceptions to at-will employment that have been fashioned over time by courts or legislatures. These exceptions mitigate the harshness of at-will employment and protect employees from many forms of unfair terminations. They also encourage employers to fairly fashion and enforce workplace policies. Currently, the major categories of exceptions to at-will employment include implied covenants of good faith and fair dealing in employment contracts, implied contracts in the employment relationship, and prohibitions on wrongful discharge of at-will employees in violation of public policy (Garrison & Stevens, 2003). For example, promises made in workplace policies established by employers may be enforced as "implied contracts" by the courts (*Toussaint v. Blue Cross & Blue Shield of Michigan*, 1980; *Berube v. Fashion Centre Ltd.*, 1989). Discipline or termination of employees for reasons that violate implied contracts may be a breach of those contracts and a violation of the legal rights of employees, and gives employees the right to recover damages or perhaps seek reinstatement. To illustrate, if an employer's e-mail and Internet use policy promises employees that their personal communications will not be read by the employer, the policy may create a contractual promise of personal privacy in the workplace—a privacy right that at-will employees in U.S. workforces do not otherwise have (King, 2003a). If the employer then violates its own policy by reading the personal e-mail of employees and terminates employees for the contents of the e-mail, the employees may be able to successfully argue in court that their termination is a breach of an implied employment contract.

Although implied contracts have been enforced in employment situations, employees have not prevailed on this claim in any reported case that relates to e-mail and Internet access. One court even disregarded an oral promise of privacy made by an employer, finding the promise created no privacy rights or, even if it did, the employer acted reasonably in the circumstances. In this case, the employer suspended the employee for investigation of misconduct. The employer then successfully bypassed a password set by the employee that protected his personal files stored on the employer's computers, read the files, discovered evidence of misconduct, and then terminated the employee for misconduct (*McLaren v. Microsoft Corporation*, 1999). Employees have, however, prevailed in similar cases involving implied contracts based on other types of workplace policies (*Woolley v. Hoffmann-La Roche, Inc.*, 1985). For this reason, employers should be careful not to make promises in e-mail and Internet use policies that they are not prepared to fulfill. It is also a good idea to add a disclaimer in a policy, or in a handbook containing policies, to make it clear that the employer's policy does not create contractual rights for employees (*Federal Express Corp. v. Dutschmann*, 1993).

### Discrimination and Harassment Issues

An important component of an e-mail and Internet use policy is to prohibit unlawful discrimination and harassment. The risk that employees will harass or make discriminatory statements using e-mail or in an Internet chat room is significant and has been the focus of several lawsuits against employers. In *Blakey v. Cont'l Airlines*,

*Inc.* (2000), an airline captain complained of sexual harassment and a hostile work environment after coworkers placed derogatory messages referring to her gender on an electronic bulletin board that the employer provided for its employees' use. The fact that the electronic bulletin board was operated by CompuServe, a third-party provider, was not necessarily a defense for the employer—an appellate court ordered the trial court to consider whether the electronic bulletin board was so closely related to the workplace that it should be regarded as part of the workplace.

An employer's policy may also be a proactive tool to avoid liability for harassment and discrimination if it prohibits harassment or discrimination on the part of coworkers and the employer takes prompt remedial action to remedy any harassment once a complaint is made. For example, in *Schwenn v. Anheuser-Busch, Inc.* (1998), an employee lost a sexual harassment suit based on receipt of sexually harassing e-mail from coworkers on her office computer. Shortly after she complained, Anheuser-Busch investigated the complaint and took corrective action—it conducted two employee meetings to tell employees that its company sexual harassment policy prohibited harassment via e-mail and advised employees it would monitor e-mail messages and would discipline or discharge employees who violated the policies. In another case, an employee lost a lawsuit claiming that the employer negligently allowed employees to use the company e-mail system to send racially harassing e-mail (*Daniels v. Worldcom Corp.*, 1998). The employer in *Daniels* was found not to have been negligent because, upon learning of misuse of its e-mail system, it organized employee meetings to discuss proper use of the e-mail system and disciplined the employees who had improperly used the e-mail system.

All forms of unlawful discrimination and harassment prohibited by state and federal laws applicable to the employer should be prohibited in the employer's e-mail and Internet use policy. Actually, unlawful harassment is a form of unlawful discrimination. For example, unwanted derogatory comments about a person's gender or pregnancy, sexual jokes, and comments of a sexual nature are forms of sex discrimination that are prohibited by law when they generate a hostile work environment. Federal law prohibits discrimination and harassment in the workplace on the basis of gender or sex, race or color, national origin, religion, age, and disability (Title VII of the Civil Rights Act of 1964; the Age Discrimination in Employment Act of 1967; the Americans with Disabilities Act of 1990). An employer may also be required to prohibit other forms of discrimination and harassment, such as sexual orientation discrimination or harassment, because they are prohibited by state law (e.g., *Tanner v. OHSU*, 1998), or because the employer has adopted a voluntary policy to prohibit such forms of harassment.

## Disability and Medical Confidentiality Issues

The primary source of federal law that requires employers to protect the confidentiality of medical information related to employees is the Americans with Disabilities Act of 1990 (ADA). The ADA applies to all employment practices and policies of employers with more than 15 employees, including workplace e-mail and Internet use policies. The ADA's medical confidentiality rules protect all applicants and employees of a covered employer, even if the individual does not have a disability as defined by the ADA. The ADA requires employers to keep "disability-related" information confidential. In essence, the ADA prohibits companies from disclosing information about applicants' and employees' medical conditions, physical or mental impairments, and medical treatments to anyone inside or outside the company, except when permitted for specified purposes set out in the ADA. (United States Equal Opportunity Commission, 2000). The ADA also limits the inquiries that an employer may lawfully make about an applicant's or an employee's medical condition or disability. For example, an employer is prohibited from asking job applicants any questions that would reveal a physical or mental disability prior to making a conditional offer of employment. After employment begins, an employer is prohibited from asking employees any questions about their medical conditions or disabilities unless the questions are job-related and necessary. Details of an employee's medical treatment or condition are rarely job-related or necessary, and the ADA generally prohibits employers from prying into the employee's medical condition beyond assessing the employee's ability to perform job functions, need for accommodation, or need for time away from work. Family and medical leave laws also restrict the amount of information that an employer may request from the employee or the employee's doctor to substantiate an employee's leave request and require employers to keep an employee's medical reasons for taking family and medical leave confidential (see, e.g., Federal Family and Medical Leave Act of 1993).

An employer's e-mail and Internet use policy should prohibit uses of the employer's systems that would violate disability discrimination laws. In the policy or training related to the policy, employers should train supervisors on appropriate use of e-mail in light of the ADA and family and medical leave laws. Such training should include instruction not to use e-mail to ask applicants or employees for "disability-related" information prohibited by the ADA or for medical information that would violate family and medical leave laws. Employers also need to be cognizant that the digital form of electronic communications creates significant additional litigation risk for employers. For example, e-mail records of improper disability-related inquiries may exist in the employer's computer systems and files for lengthy periods. These electronic records may also be recoverable using computer forensics techniques. Electronic records may provide damaging evidence of ADA violations in disability discrimination or family and medical leave claims and lawsuits.

Another concern is whether e-mail or Internet communications from applicants or employees contain confidential medical information. The ADA or family and medical leave laws require employers to keep this type of information in separate confidential files and not to disclose it except as authorized by law. There is the potential for the employer to violate medical confidentiality laws whenever employees communicate with their supervisors about their medical conditions. For example, a supervisor may send an e-mail to ask the employee for information that the employer is not entitled to request, such as details about an employee's medical diagnosis or prognosis that are unnecessary to determine if the employee is currently able to do her job or to process a request for a family or medical leave. Or, an employee may voluntarily provide confidential medical information to a supervisor by e-mail, but the supervisor may unlawfully forward the e-mail message containing confidential medical information to coworkers or clients who are not entitled to have access to the information. The employer should also be concerned with the security of electronically stored e-mail and Internet communications, particularly the need to protect confidential medical information from snooping coworkers or hackers.

Health care providers, including self-insured employers who provide medical insurance directly for their employees, should also be aware of the medical confidentiality rules of the Health Insurance Portability and Accountability Act of 1996 (HIPAA). Administrative rules interpreting HIPAA require privacy for customers of health care providers including employees covered by self-insured plans (HIPAA Privacy Regulations, 2004). The HIPAA Privacy Regulations apply when a health care provider transmits health care information electronically. Under these regulations, the data subject is required to give permission for use or disclosure of health care data unless a statutory exclusion applies (Manny, 2003).

## Privacy Tort Concerns

Tort laws give employees only limited privacy rights in private sector workplaces. The privacy tort that is most frequently applied to workplace privacy issues is the tort of intrusion into seclusion, or into employees' private affairs (Rothstein, 2000). If an employer intentionally intrudes, physically or otherwise, upon the solitude or seclusion of the employee in his private affairs or concerns, and a reasonable person would find the intrusion was highly offensive, the employee may be able to recover damages for invasion of privacy under tort law (Rothstein, 2000). However, U.S. private sector employees generally have no reasonable expectation of privacy that prevents their employers from engaging in intrusive behavior in the workplace, such as monitoring and other surveillance, because courts have held employees give up workplace privacy rights by agreeing to work for the employer. In the rare cases where employees have been found to have reasonable expectations of privacy in their workplaces, employers still generally win most privacy tort cases. Employers win these cases because courts often find the employers' alleged privacy intrusions are not unreasonable. Sound business reasons often are found to justify employers' actions that are viewed by employees as invasions of privacy, such as investigating complaints that employees have used the employers' e-mail systems to harass other employees. Microsoft won a privacy tort case when it read an employee's e-mail messages stored in personal folders on Microsoft's computer system under a password created by the employee (*McLaren v. Microsoft Corporation*, 1999). The court rejected the employee's privacy tort claim, holding he had no reasonable expectation of privacy with respect to e-mail messages stored on his office computer. Further, the court held, even if he did have a reasonable expectation of privacy, a reasonable person would not consider Microsoft's interception of these communications to be a highly offensive invasion under these circumstances, in which the employer was investigating a sexual harassment complaint.

When an employer has a company policy that prohibits misuse of its e-mail or Internet system, the policy may serve to reduce expectations of privacy by employees in their use of e-mail or Internet systems, thus helping the employer defend privacy tort cases. For example, in *Garrity v. John Hancock Mutual Life Insurance Company* (2002) the court dismissed employees' claims of invasion of privacy based on their employer's reading of their e-mail on the employer's computer system. The court held the employer's policy prohibited using the employer's e-mail system to send or receive sexually explicit material and the employees had violated the employer's policy by sending and receiving sexually explicit e-mail messages.

Unless private sector employees have statutory or contractual rights to privacy, private sector employees have no privacy rights that limit their employers' ability to impose e-mail or Internet use policies or to engage in electronic monitoring of e-mail and Internet use in the workplace (Cottone, 2002). In contrast to private sector employees, employees covered by collective bargaining agreements may have contractual rights to privacy that arise from collective bargaining agreements. Collective bargaining agreements may also restrict employers' rights to terminate employees without just cause, notice, and procedural process (Cottone, 2002; National Labor Relations Act of 1935). Also in contrast to private sector employees, public employees may have rights to privacy and protections from arbitrary termination that are based on civil service legislation and state or federal constitutions (Cottone, 2002; *U.S. v. Simmons*, 2000). For a discussion of the additional privacy rights of nonunion employees covered by employment contracts other than at-will contracts, employees covered by collective bargaining agreements, and public sector employees, see the section of this chapter on Special Issues Related to Employment Status. See also the section of this chapter on Special Issues Related to Multinational Employers for a discussion of foreign laws that may confer greater privacy rights for private sector employees working in other countries.

## Electronic Communications Privacy Act

The Electronic Communication Privacy Act of 1986 (ECPA) is a federal law that protects the privacy of electronic communications, including the contents of e-mail and the contents of other Internet communications such as Internet chat. The ECPA prohibits wiretapping and unauthorized access to communications in electronic storage (*Konop v. Hawaiian Airlines*, 2002). Under these federal privacy statutes, it is unlawful for anyone, including an employer, to intentionally "intercept" the content of a wire, oral, or electronic communication (Title I violations) (ECPA, 1986). It is also a federal crime for anyone to "access" a facility providing electronic communication service without "authorization" and thereby obtain access to a wire or electronic communication while it is in electronic storage (Title II violations) (ECPA, 1986).

Unless the interception or unauthorized access of a wire, oral, or electronic communication is covered by one of several statutory exemptions or authorized or required by law or a government order, violation of these statutes is a federal crime. Fortunately for employers, there are many exceptions to the ECPA that permit employers to adopt e-mail and Internet use policies and reserve the rights to monitor the use of their equipment and systems. For example, Title I contains exceptions for "business use in the ordinary course of business," "providers of communication systems," and "consent" (Kesan, 2002; Sidbury, 2001). Title II contains exceptions for "providers of communications" and "authorization by users of communications systems" (Kesan, 2002; Sidbury, 2001).

Employers who want to reserve the right to monitor their employees' use of e-mail and Internet access systems need to consider the ECPA and its exemptions. However, keep in mind that the ECPA only restricts access to the *contents of electronic communications*. The ECPA does not restrict the employer's access to information about e-mail or Internet communications that is analogous to the *addressing information* on the outside of a letter sent through the U.S. mail. However there is some dispute over whether the subject line of an e-mail is content or addressing information. Also, a federal circuit court of appeals recently held that interception of personal information that was part of Internet search queries is covered by the ECPA (*In re Pharmatrak, Inc. Privacy Litigation*, 2002). For example, an Internet search query containing the key word "breast cancer" reveals a lot about the subject of an employee's Internet search particularly if it is captured along with personally identifying information about the sender of the query, for example the sender's name. Fortunately for Pharmatrak, the case was remanded to the district court to determine whether Pharmatrak intended to intercept the contents of electronic communications, a necessary element of an ECPA violation. The District Court found there was no evidence that Pharmatrak intentionally intercepted the electronic communications, and dismissed the case. Based on the *In re Pharmatrak, Inc. Privacy Litigation*, employers would be wise to view personal information contained in Internet queries as contents of employees' communication, rather than mere addressing information that would not be covered by the ECPA.

Additionally, adopting an e-mail and Internet use policy helps an employer fit within the ECPA's exemptions and may constitute express or implied "consent" by employees allowing the employer to intercept electronic communications. A workplace policy may also provide express or implied "authorization" by employees for the employer to access stored e-mail or Internet chat. Tips for compliance with the ECPA exemptions are also found in the section in this chapter on Reserving the Employer's Right to Conduct Electronic Monitoring. Finally, the exemption for interceptions of electronic communications in the ordinary course of business also permits some employer monitoring of e-mail and Internet access. However, in the context of telephone communications, courts have held this exemption does not permit the employer to listen to personal conversations, and the employer must stop listening when a communication is found to be personal (*Fischer v. Mt. Olive Lutheran Church*, 2002). Thus, the exceptions to Title I and Title II exempt much employer monitoring of employees' e-mail and Internet communications in the workplace from the ECPA's prohibitions.

The ECPA sets a minimum privacy protection for electronic communications, including those of employees. State wire-tapping statutes may be more protective of electronic communications privacy rights (United States Government Accounting Office, 2002) and should also be reviewed when drafting a policy. For example, Florida's Security of Communications Act is stricter than the ECPA and prohibits intercepting or disclosing the contents of any electronic communication without obtaining the consent of both the sender and the recipient. The Florida statute covers interceptions and disclosures of workplace communications even when the employer provides the e-mail system (Florida Statute, 2004, §934.01 et seq.; Safon, 2000). Additionally, some states have statutes that specifically restrict the employer's ability to monitor e-mail without employee consent (Burgunder, 2004; Safon, 2000). These workplace-specific laws are discussed next in this chapter.

## State Workplace Privacy Statutes

In addition to state tort laws related to privacy and state wiretapping statutes similar to the ECPA, some states have specific statutes that affect employment policies such as e-mail and Internet policies. For example, Connecticut has a state statute that prohibits employers from electronically monitoring employees' e-mail without giving employees prior written notice, except in certain circumstances. One of the exceptions allows employers to electronically monitor employees' e-mail when there are reasonable grounds to believe an employee has violated the law or engaged in conduct that creates a hostile work environment (Connecticut General Statutes, 2004, §31–48d). Other states have statutes that prohibit monitoring e-mail without employee consent (Burgunder, 2004; Safon, 2000 [collecting state laws that restrict employer e-mail monitoring, p. 101, 102]). California also passed a law restricting workplace monitoring in 2001, but it was vetoed by the governor (Burgunder, 2004; Safon, 2000). Finally, some states have statutes that prohibit employers from using employees' lawful, off-duty conduct as a reason for termination (see, e.g., Cardi, 2004). It is not a far stretch to imagine a court invalidating discipline or discharge of employees for violating an employer's e-mail and Internet use policy when that policy prohibits lawful off-duty use of e-mail and Internet access. Under these statutes, employees discharged for off-duty conduct that violates employers' e-mail and Internet use policies may have a remedy for wrongful termination. At the federal level, bills have been introduced in Congress to restrict U.S. employers from monitoring employee e-mail; however, to date none of these bills has been passed. Even where state laws exist that restrict workplace e-mail monitoring, the employer's e-mail and Internet use policy may help the employer show it has provided the notice or obtained the consent required by these state workplace privacy laws.

## Constitutional Restrictions

Generally, employers in the private sector may adopt e-mail and Internet policies without worrying about federal or state constitutional restrictions because private sector employment practices are not covered by the federal Constitution or by most state constitutions

(Burgunder, 2004). A few states have constitutions that protect the privacy of employees in private sector workplaces (Safon, 2000). California is one of these states (California Constitution, 2004, Article 1, Section 1). For issues of constitutional law that relate to government workplaces, see the discussion of this topic in Policies Covering Public Sector Employees in this chapter.

## Federal Labor Law Issues

Most employees working for private businesses have some protections under Section 7 of the federal National Labor Relations Act of 1935 (Section 7 and NLRA), regardless of whether they are represented by a union (King, 2003b). If nonunion or union-represented employees in private sector workplaces communicate with each other about their workplaces, including discussions about wages or other terms and conditions of employment, Section 7 of the NLRA may protect their communications from employer interference as "protected concerted activity" (King, 2003b). If an employer's e-mail and Internet use policy is broadly worded to prohibit employees from engaging in Section 7 activities, it will violate the NLRA. A policy that violates Section 7 of the NLRA is not enforceable and gives employees the right to file unfair labor practices charges against the employer with the National Labor Relations Board. Employees are entitled to seek remedies such as back pay and reinstatement if they are disciplined or discharged under policies that violate the NLRA. Employment policies such as confidentiality policies and wage-secrecy policies also are unenforceable under Section 7 if they are too broadly worded. For example, workplace policies that prohibit nonsupervisory employees from talking with each other about their wages generally violate Section 7. Therefore, e-mail or Internet use policies that include overly broad confidentiality or wage-secrecy provisions may violate Section 7.

An issue that is hotly debated is whether an employer's e-mail and Internet use policy may prohibit all nonbusiness use of the employer's systems, even use by employees to communicate about matters that would be protected by Section 7 of the NLRA. Current federal labor law seems to support the view that the employer may prohibit employees from engaging in *all* personal use of its e-mail or Internet access. In other words, an employer may have a business-use-only e-mail and Internet access policy, providing it enforces the policy in a nondiscriminatory way and prohibits all personal use, not just use for union-related matters or Section 7 protected matters (King, 2003b). However, if the employer's e-mail and Internet use policy permits some personal use of the employer's systems by employees, it must also permit employees to use the employer's systems and equipment to discuss matters that fall under the umbrella of "protected concerted activity." Protected concerted activity includes discussion between employees of union matters, wages, or other matters of mutual concern to employees.

Employers may have valid business reasons to limit personal e-mail or Internet use by employees, even when the employer's policy permits reasonable personal use. For example, if the employer can show that certain types of personal e-mail or Internet use by employees unduly burdens its systems, the employer can restrict the personal use for valid business reasons. Mass e-mails sent by employees that overburden an employer's computer systems and personal e-mails that expose the employer's systems to computer viruses are valid business reasons for an employer to limit employees' personal use of a company's systems. Also, even if an employer permits employees to make reasonable personal use of its e-mail and Internet systems, it need not permit employees to use work time for this purpose. The employer has a legitimate right to prevent loss of work time by employees sending and receiving e-mails for personal reasons (King, 2003b).

For a discussion of issues related to bargaining and enforcing a policy covering union employees, see Policies Covering Union-Represented Employees in this chapter.

## PROTECTING THE EMPLOYER'S TRADE SECRETS AND OTHER PROPRIETARY INFORMATION

An e-mail and Internet use policy is an important tool to protect a company's trade secrets such as marketing strategies, customer lists, price lists, expansion plans, and other company documents containing confidential and proprietary information that a company would like to keep secret from its competitors. When a company's trade secrets have been made publicly available, the information may lose its protection under trade secret law because it is no longer secret. This is because an essential component of the law's protection for a company's proprietary information is that the information is in fact not public knowledge. The employer's e-mail and Internet use policy should also prohibit employees from pirating trade secrets from former employers or competitors, thus exposing the company to litigation for trade secret infringement lawsuits under state trade secret laws. Trade secret theft is also a federal crime under the Economic Espionage Act of 1996, which provides for fines up to five million dollars against corporations as well as imprisonment and hefty fines for individuals.

An e-mail and Internet use policy is often supplemented by other preventive steps that may reduce the risk loss of the company's trade secrets and the risk of liability for infringing the trade secrets of other companies. For example, an employer may develop written nondisclosure and confidentiality agreements for employees to sign. An employer may also require job applicants or new employees to sign statements that they are not bound by noncompete or confidentiality agreements related to former employers and to agree that they will not use information that belongs to others, including information protected by trade secret laws.

## PREVENTING EMPLOYEES FROM ENGAGING IN CRIMINAL ACTIVITY

A company's e-mail and Internet policy should also prohibit use of company systems and property for criminal activity including violation of criminal laws. For example, criminal laws prohibit acquiring or distributing child pornography and make downloading copyrighted material without permission and in excess of "fair use" exemptions a criminal act.

## Unlawful Access to Child Pornography

A recent survey revealed that nearly half of human resource professionals reported that they have discovered pornography on company computers used by employees (Bachman, 2003). Although employees' access to pornography involving adults is generally not a crime, it is a serious risk for employers because it may create a hostile work environment, lead to embarrassing public relations problems, and may constitute a waste of work time when employees view pornography on the job. However, when employees view or distribute pornography involving children using company e-mail and Internet access, they violate criminal laws that prohibit viewing child pornography. A Boeing worker was recently arrested on suspicion of participating in child pornography through a Web cam streamed over the Internet (Biggs, 2003). The Boeing worker was arrested by police after security staff from Boeing told police they suspected the employee had been viewing child pornography via the Internet while at work. Acquiring or distributing child pornography violates state and federal laws that prohibit the exploitation of children. For example, a federal criminal statute prohibits the sexual exploitation of children including receiving, distributing, or reproducing child pornography (Sexual Exploitation of Children, 2004, 18 U.S.C.S. §2251 et seq.).

## Downloading Copyrighted Material Without Permission

With the advent of MP3 technology that enables easy downloading of music, video, and other electronic files, there is an increase in the ability of employees to engage in copyright-infringing activities using the employer's computer systems and Internet access. Infringement can result in civil suits for damages against employers that may be found vicariously liable for copyright infringement by employees. Copyright violations may also lead to criminal penalties under federal copyright laws. The No Electronic Theft Act of 1997 expanded the criminal remedies for copyright violations to include circumstances where copyright infringements are not motivated by financial gain, as long as the unlawful copies made have a total retail value of more than $1000 in any 180-day period. Today, even employees who are ignorant of the copyright laws can be criminally responsible for making unauthorized copies of music, videos, or other copyrighted works in the workplace. Likewise, employees who manage to circumvent copyright protection systems that are designed to control access to copyrighted work may violate the Digital Millennium Copyright Act of 1998. Thus, an employer's e-mail and Internet use policy should prohibit "hacking" into copyright protected materials as well as copying those materials without authorization. An effective policy alone may not be enough to deter copyright infringement by employees. A recent survey revealed that employees are still swapping music and other files on peer-to-peer applications at work, despite threats of lawsuits for copyright infringement by the music industry

(Reuters, 2004). Careful hiring, proper training of employees and supervisors, and monitoring to detect violations are also necessary steps employers should take to prevent copyright violations.

## RESERVING THE EMPLOYER'S RIGHT TO CONDUCT ELECTRONIC MONITORING

Electronic monitoring allows an employer to observe what employees do on the job and review employee communications, including e-mail and Internet activity, and enables employers to capture and review communications that employees consider private. Electronic monitoring also includes the use of computer forensics, a relatively new science, and an important advancement in the broader field of electronic monitoring and computer evidence. There are many good business justifications for employers to electronically monitor employees in the workplace. Key reasons for monitoring are to assess worker productivity, to protect company assets from misappropriation, and to ensure compliance with workplace policies. The importance of electronic monitoring to enforcement of the employer's e-mail and Internet use policy is the focus of this section of this chapter.

The term electronic monitoring is used in this chapter to encompass three different concepts. First, it includes employer use of *electronic devices to review and measure the work performance* of employees. For example, an employer may use a computer to retrieve and review an employee's e-mail messages sent to and received from customers to evaluate the employee's performance as a customer service representative. Second, it includes *electronic surveillance* in the form of an employer's use of electronic devices to observe the actions of employees while employees are not directly engaged in the performance of work duties, or for a purpose other than to measure their work performance. For example, an employer may electronically review an employee's e-mail messages as part of an investigation of a sexual harassment complaint. Third, it includes employer use of *computer forensics*, the electronic recovery and reconstruction of electronic data after deletion, concealment, or attempted destruction of the data (New Technologies, 2003). For example, an employer may use specialized computer forensics software to retrieve or recover e-mail messages stored on the employer's computer hard drive that relate to an investigation of alleged theft of its trade secrets by an employee. Recovery may be possible even if the employee has deleted the messages or reformatted the hard drive.

An e-mail and Internet use policy should reserve the right of the employer to conduct electronic monitoring for the following business reasons:

1) to investigate employee or former employee misconduct,

2) to investigate complaints by employees or former employees, and

3) to respond to litigation discovery requests and requests by government administrative agencies for information and documents.

The policy should also reserve the right of the employer to use a broad range of electronic monitoring techniques and technology including the following:

1) to conduct historical and real-time monitoring,
2) to use computer forensics techniques, and
3) to monitor off-site communications related to the employer's business.

By reserving the full panoply of employer rights to conduct electronic monitoring, the employer makes it clear that employees do not have expectations of privacy related to workplace use of e-mail and Internet access. This is a critical component of preventing and defending invasion of privacy claims by employees and others who may be covered by the policy, including former employees and independent contractors.

## RESPONDING TO GOVERNMENT REQUESTS FOR ELECTRONIC INFORMATION

Government requests for electronic information may come in a variety of forms. For example, government administrative agencies may request or subpoena information, including electronic documents and other information, in relation to discrimination, workplace safety, environmental, and other complaints. The information requested may include digital documents and electronic communications such as e-mail and Internet chat.

Recently, because of national security concerns, an important concern for employers is the possibility of being required to respond to government requests for information about its employees or customers that relates to criminal and foreign intelligence investigations. Electronic monitoring of computer systems, including workplace e-mail and Internet access, can be used to discover electronic evidence related to terrorism, computer hacking, and other crimes (King, 2003a). However, there are important privacy issues for employees that relate to employer monitoring for national security concerns (King, 2003a). In October 2001, the Uniting and Strengthening America by Providing Appropriate Tools Required to Intercept and Obstruct Terrorism Act (USA PATRIOT Act) amended provisions of the ECPA that prohibit interception of oral, wire, and electronic communications and restrict access to stored wire and electronic communications. As a result of the USA PATRIOT Act's amendments to these federal laws, employers may likely be asked, and in some cases compelled, to provide private information about employees and former employees to law enforcement and other government agencies (King, 2003a). The employers' expanded legal obligations include the possibility of employers receiving government requests to produce information about a former or current employee in conjunction with a criminal investigation or government intelligence surveillance of potential terrorism activities. Government orders and requests can take various forms including search warrants, court wiretap orders, pen-register and trap and trace orders, and subpoenas. The expanded employer legal obligations under the USA PATRIOT Act are essentially obligations to engage in electronic monitoring and/or to produce electronic communications, raising workplace privacy concerns. In some cases, the government order to conduct electronic monitoring of an employer's electronic communications system requires the employer to keep its participation secret even from the employee who is being monitored (King, 2003a).

For these reasons, an employer's e-mail and Internet policy should anticipate that the employer may be required to monitor its system and to secretly produce electronic communications and documents to the government under government order. Accordingly, an employer should not promise that it will notify employees if their e-mail or Internet access is disclosed to the government because current federal law may make it unlawful to keep this promise.

## RESERVING THE EMPLOYER'S RIGHT TO DISCIPLINE EMPLOYEES UNDER THE POLICY

An important component of an e-mail and Internet use policy is to reserve the employer's right to discipline employees for violation of the policy. The policy should provide employees with a warning that violations of the policy may lead to discipline up to and including termination from employment, thus serving to notify employees of the consequences of violating the policy. Certainly some misconduct or criminal activity engaged in by employees in violation of the employer's e-mail and Internet use policy will lead to immediate discharge. For example, an employee found to have distributed child pornography using the employer's computer system may face criminal prosecution as well as discipline for violating the employer's policy. Such a policy violation may clearly merit discharge from employment. However, other violations of the employer's policy may appear less serious and merit discipline short of discharge but that is designed to punish the offender and to set an example for other employees that may deter similar policy violations. For example, an employee found to have engaged in excessive personal, but lawful, use of the employer's e-mail or Internet access may be warned, placed on probation, or otherwise disciplined for the policy infraction, but would rarely be discharged for a first offense. A well-drafted e-mail and Internet use policy will reserve the right of the employer to discipline employees appropriately under the circumstances.

A number of important issues have been discussed thus far in the chapter that relate to drafting an effective e-mail and Internet use policy. A summary of some of these issues is provided in Table 1. Table 1 also includes drafting suggestions for policies covering at-will employees in private sector, nonunion workplaces. The next section discusses special issues related to policies covering at-will employees, union-represented employees, and public sector employees. Employers with employees working in countries other than the United States should also refer to the section of this chapter covering special issues for multinational employers.

# SPECIAL ISSUES RELATED TO EMPLOYMENT STATUS
## Policies Covering At-Will Employees

This chapter is primarily written from the primary perspective of private employers in the United States who have employees who are "at will." Under employment at will, employers may discipline or discharge an employee for almost any reason or for no reason, as long as the discharge is not contrary to law (including law established by statutes, court decision, or contracts) (Cottone, 2002). Many exceptions to at-will employment have been developed in statutes or by the courts, and these exceptions limit the employer's prerogatives to discipline and terminate employees. For example, it is unlawful under federal *discrimination laws* for an employer to treat employees differently with respect to terms and conditions of employment based on their sex, race, color, national origin, religion, age, or disability (Title VII of the Civil Rights Act of 1964,; Age Discrimination in Employment Act of 1967; Americans with Disabilities Act of 1990). At-will employees are also protected from *wrongful discharge for reasons that violate public policy*, such as exercising a legal right to file a workers' compensation claim, to serve on jury duty, or to come to the aid of a person known to be in serious danger (*Frampton v. Central Indiana Gas Co.*, 1973; *Garner v. Loomis Armored, Inc.*, 1996). Another exception to at-will employment protects employees covered by *individual employment contracts* that provide contractual rights greater than at-will employment, such as a right to be discharged only for just cause (Cottone, 2002; Leonard, 1988).

Unless an at-will employee has statutory or contractual rights to the contrary, the at-will employee has no privacy or other employment rights that limit an employer's ability to impose an e-mail or Internet use policy or engage in electronic monitoring of the workplace (Cottone, 2002). In contrast, an employer may not be able to unilaterally impose an e-mail or Internet use policy in a unionized workplace, at least if union employees may be disciplined for violations of the policy. Additionally, union employees who are covered by collective bargaining agreements may have contractual rights to privacy that arise from the collective bargaining agreement, and the collective bargaining agreement may also restrict an employer's right to terminate employees without just cause, notice, and procedural process, including arbitration to resolve any disputes (Cottone, 2002; National Labor Relations Act of 1935). Also in contrast to at-will employees, public employees may have rights to privacy and protections from arbitrary termination that are based on civil service legislation and state or federal constitutions (Cottone, 2002; *U.S. v. Simmons*, 2000).

When drafting an e-mail and Internet use policy, at-will employers often include wording in the policy to document the at-will employment relationship and a disclaimer designed to limit the likelihood that a court will interpret the policy to create contractual obligations other than at-will employment. Sometimes, the at-will language and the disclaimer will be included in the e-mail and Internet use policy itself. In other cases, an e-mail and Internet use policy is included with other policies in an employee handbook. Often, the at-will language and a disclaimer will be found in an introduction to the handbook to avoid repetition in individual policies. At-will language typically states that employment at the company is at-will and means that either the employer or the employee may terminate the employment relationship at any time, without advance notice, and for any reason except one prohibited by law. The disclaimer statement for at-will employees generally states that the policy and/or handbook is a guideline for employees and supervisors and does not create contractual relationships other than at-will employment.

Although at-will employment is common in private sector employment in the United States, it is not the only type of employment relationship that is possible. Therefore, the remaining discussion in this section of the chapter explores different legal requirements of which employers need to be aware when designing e-mail and Internet use policies for employees who are not at-will. It covers union-represented employees and government employees. The next section of the chapter covers e-mail and Internet use policies for employees of multinational companies who may work in countries that do not recognize at-will employment relationships and may have laws that provide greater legal rights for employees, including privacy rights, than those provided for employees in the United States.

## Policies Covering Union-Represented Employees

In workplaces where employees are represented by a labor union, the employer generally must bargain with the employees' union representative before introducing a new or a substantially revised policy regarding employees' use of informational technologies when employees may be disciplined under the policy (*King Soopers, Inc.*, 2003). This is because imposition of a new or substantially revised workplace policy that establishes a basis for employee discipline is a mandatory subject of bargaining under the National Labor Relations Act. Although there is little definite guidance on the topic, imposition of new e-mail or Internet policy covering union employees must be bargained if employees may be disciplined for failing to follow the policy (Lieber, 1998). A requirement to bargain with the union does not require the employer and union to agree on the terms of the policy. However, the employer is required to bargain in good faith about the effects of imposing the policy until a bargaining impasse is reached; only then may the employer may unilaterally impose its proposed workplace policy. An employer may also have an obligation to bargain with the union over imposition of electronic monitoring or other surveillance practices or policies that are designed to detect violations of the e-mail and Internet policy. For example, an employer was required to bargain with union representatives over the imposition of new package inspection practices designed to prevent employee theft (*Edgar P. Benjamin Healthcare Center*, 1996). So, by analogy, an employer may be required to bargain about electronic monitoring practices designed to prevent employee abuse of its computer systems and violations of its e-mail and Internet use policy.

If an employer implements a workplace policy without bargaining with the union or obtaining the union's waiver of its right to bargain, either the union or employees may file an unfair labor practice charge with the NLRB. Also, even if the policy is lawfully implemented, when disputes about e-mail and Internet use or employer monitoring arise, employers may have obligations under collective bargaining agreements to arbitrate these disputes. Such disputes may include disputes about employee discipline for violating the e-mail and Internet use policy or disputes about whether the employer's electronic monitoring violates the collective bargaining agreement.

## Policies Covering Public Sector Employees

Public employees may have constitutional rights to privacy under federal or state laws that employees in the private sector generally do not have, including a Fourth Amendment right to be free from unreasonable searches and seizures by the government (*O'Connor v. Ortega*, 1987). However, even where a constitutional right to privacy claim may be made, employers have generally prevailed on invasion of privacy claims. In *Kelleher v. City of Reading* (2002), a city employee lost a claim for invasion of privacy against the City of Reading for allegedly publicizing her e-mails and other purportedly private information relating to her suspension by the City Council, and in *U.S. v. Simmons* (2000), the federal government used electronic monitoring to examine the records of Web sites visited by a federal employee and then examined files saved on his computer. The court in *U.S. v. Simmons* recognized that public sector employees may have privacy rights in e-mail communications in some circumstances. However, the court said this employee did not have an objectively reasonable expectation of privacy in electronic communications made in the workplace in light of the employer's monitoring policy. The employer's policy specified the types of data that would be monitored, including e-mail, Internet, and electronic file transfers, and specified the ways in which the data would be retrieved, including audit and inspection. However, even if public employees' e-mail messages are public records that a public employer may monitor, courts have issued injunctions to prevent public disclosure of the contents of personal e-mail as personal information (*Tiberino v. Spokane County*, 2000). Although most invasion of privacy claims relate to public employees, states such as California have also extended state constitutional rights to privacy to *private sector employees*.

## SPECIAL ISSUES FOR MULTINATIONAL EMPLOYERS

Multinational employers face special challenges when designing e-mail and Internet use policies. The challenges for a private business that is a multinational employer include designing a policy that will provide the required privacy protections for employees working in countries other than the United States. The European Union (EU) is

recognized as the leader in this area, providing the greatest level of privacy protection for employees in the workplace (George, Lynch, & Marsnik, 2001). Because the EU has the most rigorous privacy protections for employers, it is helpful to understand the EU privacy rules when drafting an e-mail and Internet use policy for a multinational employer. Because of the increasingly global nature of business today, employers in the United States may be eventually be required to provide privacy protections for workplace communications consistent with the privacy principles found in EU privacy law.

There are two sources of privacy laws for employees working in the EU: a) privacy protections required under Directive 95/46/EC of the European Parliament and of the Council of 24 October 1995 (EU Privacy Directive) and b) privacy protections under workplace-specific privacy laws that relate to e-mail and Internet use policies (Delbar, Mormont, & Schots, 2003). A recent study in the EU titled "New Technology and Respect for Privacy at the Workplace" examines the use of e-mail and Internet use at work and respect for privacy in the workplace and summarizes laws that regulate workplace privacy rights in the EU (Delbar, Mormont, & Schots, 2003).

## Complying with the EU Privacy Directive

The EU Privacy Directive protects the privacy of individuals (referred to as "data subjects" in the EU Privacy Directive) when their personal data is processed. The EU Privacy Directive regulates the quality of personal data, requiring that it be processed fairly and lawfully, be collected for legitimate purposes, be relevant, be accurate, and be kept in a form that permits identification of data subjects for no longer than is necessary for the purposes of the collection (George, Lynch, & Marsnik, 2001). The EU Privacy Directive also sets criteria for legitimate processing of personal data. To process personal data of employees, employers are required to obtain consent from the data subject in some cases. In other cases, consent is not required but the employer may process personal data only when it is necessary for performance of a contract with the data subject, necessary for the controller of the personal data to meet its legal obligations, or allowed for other specified reasons. There are special rules that severely limit the processing of special categories of personal data that would reveal race, ethnic origin, political opinions, religious or philosophical beliefs, trade union membership, health, or sex life. The EU Privacy Directive requires collectors of personal data to inform the person about the processing of data and to give the person access to data about themselves. The party responsible for processing personal data must make sure the processing is confidential and secure and notify a designated government monitoring authority prior to processing. In addition to the processing restrictions, there are restrictions on the transfer of personal data outside the EU.

Currently, fifteen EU member nations have national legislation in place to implement the EU Privacy Directive (Delbar, Mormont, & Schots, 2003). Ten new EU members were admitted in 2004, and these new member nations also have or will be adopting national legislation to implement the EU Privacy directive. For an example of a global privacy policy adopted by a multinational employer with operations in the EU, see Hewlett-Packard's global master privacy policy (Hewlett-Packard, 2004). This global privacy policy is not specific to the context of e-mail and Internet use.

Although the EU Privacy Directive does not directly address the processing of personal data in the employment context, it is viewed as applying to the employment context (Delbar, Mormont, & Schots, 2003; George, Lynch, & Marsnik, 2001). However, the EU Privacy Directive does not expressly address a) the protections for personal data of employees in workplaces that results from using e-mail and Internet access, b) the effects of its provisions on workplace policies for e-mail or Internet use, or c) the lawfulness of employer monitoring of e-mail and Internet systems (Lasprogata, King, & Pillay, 2004). Because this is the case, multinational employers will also need to examine other laws of the countries where its employees are working, as described in the next section. The EU Commission is planning to issue a draft directive in 2004 or 2005 that will include a framework of employment-specific rules on personal data protection.

## Complying with Other Foreign Workplace Laws

In addition to the EU Privacy Directive, many EU member countries have their own laws that protect the privacy of employees and their communications in the workplace. These protections of privacy are found in the national laws of EU member countries including constitutions, personal data protection acts that implement the EU Privacy Directive, and workplace-specific laws (Lasprogata, King, & Pillay, 2004). Workplace-specific laws in EU member countries that protect the privacy of employees' e-mail and Internet communications are found in

- labor statutes,
- labor agreements (which may be national in scope),
- criminal statutes that protect the secrecy of private e-mail messages (as opposed to business enterprise-related messages) and may require consent for monitoring,
- civil statutes that apply when an employer has permitted private e-mail and Internet use by employees, and
- court decisions (including those requiring employers to have issued clear policies or instructions on e-mail and Internet use before disciplining employees for misuse).

In some countries, works councils and other employee representatives may have legal rights to agree or to be informed and consulted before new technology including monitoring equipment is introduced in a workforce.

Because there is little employment-specific legislation related to workplace privacy and e-mail or Internet use, multinational employers drafting a workplace e-mail or Internet use policies may also consult guidance and opinions issued by government bodies in the EU on privacy in the workplace and employees' e-mail and Internet use (Lasprogata, King, & Pillay). For example, the Information Commissioner in the United Kingdom published *The Employment Practices Data Protection Code* to provide guidance to employers on the process of complying with the United Kingdom's personal data protection act and offers good practice recommendations for employers (see United Kingdom Information Commissioner, 2004).

When a multinational employer has employees working in the EU and in other countries, it may choose to adopt a global e-mail and Internet use policy that provides the greater privacy protections required in the EU to all its global employees. This may make sense because other countries are also adopting privacy laws consistent with the EU, including Canada, Australia, New Zealand, South America, and parts of Asia (Scheer, 2003). Additionally, because the EU Privacy Directive applies to personal data that is transferred out of the EU to other countries, there are legal as well as business reasons to make sure an employer's global e-mail and Internet use policy satisfies the EU Directive. For example, General Motors Corporation recently found its plan to update its electronic company phone book to include office phone numbers for employees around the world was covered by the EU Privacy Directive because it involved sending the employees' office phone numbers outside the EU (Scheer, 2003). To comply with the EU Privacy Directive, General Motors Company ("GMC") was required to get the approval of the government privacy agency in the European countries where its employees worked and to satisfy rigorous personal data transfer rules before issuing the global phone book. Among other obligations under the EU Privacy Directive, GMC would be required to make disclosures to employees whose personal data would be included in the phone book and to consult with employees' labor representatives where appropriate. There is no reason to believe that employees' e-mail addresses would be treated differently than their office phone numbers, so the EU Directive would apply to global e-mail directories as well.

# COORDINATING E-MAIL AND INTERNET USE POLICIES WITH OTHER POLICIES

E-mail and Internet use policies typically involve issues that are related to other business practices and policies. The most obvious connection is between e-mail and Internet use policies and the company's *privacy practices and policies*. Because of the number of privacy issues related to e-mail and Internet use policies, a company should consider drafting a company privacy policy that covers employee privacy. With a general privacy policy in place, a company may refer to it in its e-mail and Internet use policy.

Another area of coordination between company practices and policies involves the retention of stored e-mail and Internet access records and a company's *document retention policies*. There are obvious risks related to retaining e-mail and Internet use records indefinitely, including the risk that the company will be required to sort and produce e-mail and Internet use records in litigation that may be filed in the future against the company. On the other hand, the company needs to be able to retain and produce e-mail and Internet use records related to discovery requests in pending or threatened litigation. For these reasons, a company's e-mail and Internet use policy should be consistent with its document retention policies for electronic documents and records.

A company's e-mail and Internet use policy also involves issues of *confidentiality of employee records*, including policies for granting access to e-mail communications and Internet access information. Employees are often concerned about the privacy of their e-mail communications and favor limiting their employer's access to records about their e-mail and Internet use. The employer often favors broad employer access to employees' electronic communications and records of Internet access for valid business reasons. Valid business reasons to reserve employer access to employees' electronic communications and Internet access records include investigating complaints of misconduct, responding to discovery requests related to litigation, and monitoring misuse of e-mail and Internet systems. If the company has a separate policy regarding confidentiality of employee records, it should be consistent with the company's e-mail and Internet use policy.

A serious concern of businesses today is *violence in the workplace and national security threats*. Many companies have separate policies prohibiting violence in the workplace and requiring employees to report threats of violence in the workplace and other threats. It is important to consider that threats of violence may be communicated by e-mail or Internet chat, and the employer and/or law enforcement may need access to e-mail and Internet systems to respond to threats of violence. On a broader scale, national security threats may also involve use of e-mail and Internet systems. Coordination of e-mail and Internet use policies with workplace violence policies and national security interests is crucial to enable appropriate responses to threats of violence and other security issues.

## COMMUNICATING E-MAIL AND INTERNET USE POLICIES TO EMPLOYEES

A critical component of being able to enforce an e-mail and Internet use policy is to communicate the policy to employees and others covered by the policy, such as independent contractors. There are various ways to communicate an e-mail and Internet use policy to the people who will be covered by the policy. A traditional way to communicate a workplace policy is to distribute a paper copy of the policy and to require written acknowledgement from the user that he or she has read and understands the policy. The user's acknowledgement generally becomes part of company records. Some employers electronically distribute their e-mail and Internet use policy to users of their e-mail and Internet use systems on a regular basis. To proceed and use the e-mail or Internet system, users of the system may periodically be required to scroll through the policy and to "click" on a statement indicating that the user has read and understands the employer's e-mail and Internet use policy. Electronic records of the user's acknowledgement of receipt of the policy may then be kept.

Another method of communicating an employer's e-mail and Internet use policy is to provide training for users of the system. The training may be part of new employee orientation. Training may also be provided for existing employees and other systems users on a periodic basis. The possibility of providing online training about using the employer's e-mail and Internet systems should also be considered. Certainly managers and supervisors responsible for implementing the e-mail and Internet use policy should receive training on administering the policy. A key component of training for managers and supervisors is to communicate the employer's philosophy about respecting employees' privacy consistent with protection of the employer's legitimate interests.

A critical issue regarding communication of the employer's e-mail and Internet use policy is to make sure it is communicated to all covered users of the employer's systems, including the employees of independent contractors that use the company's systems. Compliance with the employer's e-mail and Internet use policy should be referenced in any written agreements with independent contractors, staffing services, or other users of the employer's systems.

## ENFORCING THE POLICY

A key point related to designing and implementing effective e-mail and Internet use policies is that even the best designed policy will fail if it is not enforced consistently and fairly. A policy that is not followed consistently by the employer may lead to discrimination complaints when an attempt is made to enforce the policy. Such discrimination complaints may protest inconsistent enforcement of a policy against members of any legally protected class, including classes of persons based on race, sex, national origin, disability, or age. Additionally, even in nonunion workplaces, employees may file unfair labor practices complaints when an employer enforces an e-mail or Internet use policy in a way that discriminates against employees who are engaging in collective action related to their terms and conditions of employment. For example, selective discipline of an e-mail "griper" who sends an e-mail to coworkers complaining about the employer's new vacation policy may turn into an unfair labor practice complaint. If the employer's e-mail and Internet use policy prohibits all nonbusiness use of its e-mail and Internet systems, this type of e-mail message would violate the policy. If the employer disciplines the "griper" for sending personal e-mails but has not disciplined other employees for making personal use of its systems, it has inconsistently enforced the policy. In these types of situations, a court or administrative agency may reverse the discipline and order damages, effectively preventing the employer from enforcing its policy. See the discussion of discrimination and harassment concerns and federal labor law issues found in this chapter in the section on complying with laws protecting employee rights.

## CONCLUSION

The reassuring news for employers about drafting e-mail and Internet use policies is that well-drafted policies educate employees about the proper ways to use e-mail and the Internet, help protect employers' property and trade secrets, and help prevent expensive lawsuits related to misuse of the employers' systems. One of the challenges for employers is to comply with the multitude of laws that protect employee rights in this situation. It is true that private sector employers in the United States have the most latitude to draft policies that do not expand employee privacy and other legal rights, yet reserve employer rights to monitor and enforce their policies. Multinational employers with employees in the EU and other countries that have adopted privacy laws similar to those of the EU face the greatest challenges as they seek to comply with laws protecting the privacy of electronic communications, while preserving employer rights to monitor their systems and enforce their policies.

A key challenge for policy drafters is to keep abreast of the developments in laws that protect employee rights in the workplace. Because business is increasingly global, the development of workplace privacy laws related to e-mail and Internet use is a looming challenge for multinational employers. The EU is expected to issue a draft of a directive for workplace data protection in 2004 or 2005 that will specifically address privacy issues related to employees' use of e-mail and the Internet at work (Delbar, Mormont, & Schots, 2003). Countries other than the EU are following the lead of the EU in establishing workplace privacy rights for employees' e-mail and Internet communications, including e-mail and Internet communications.

A well-drafted e-mail and Internet use policy also needs to be effectively communicated to users who will be required to follow the policy. However, having a policy is no substitute for good management practices and consistent enforcement of the policy. Finally, all e-mail and Internet use policies should be reviewed by the company's legal counsel. Although this chapter provides much insight into the legal issues of which policy drafters and enforcers should be aware, it does not provide specific legal advice for any company related to its e-mail and Internet use policy and is not a substitute for consulting legal counsel.

# GLOSSARY

**At-Will Employment**  An employment relationship in which either the employee or the employer may terminate the employment at any time, without advance notice, and for any lawful reason. There are many exceptions to at-will employment that have been created in contracts, statutes, constitutions, or in some cases by courts. The major exceptions include prohibitions on the termination of an at-will employee for reasons that violate public policy (prohibit termination for serving on jury duty, filing workers' compensation claims, etc.); for reasons that violate discrimination statutes (prohibiting race, color, sex, religion, national origin, age, disability, pregnancy, harassment, and other forms of unlawful discrimination); for engaging in protected concerted activity under federal or state labor laws; for reporting unsafe working conditions; and for reporting criminal or other wrongful activity in the workplace ("whistle blowing"). Employees in the private sector are presumed to be at-will in the United States unless they are covered by an employment contract that promises employees greater protection from discipline or termination, such as a promise to be terminated only for "just cause." Union-represented employees covered by collective bargaining agreements generally have a right to be disciplined or terminated only for "just cause" and thus are not at-will employees.

**Computer Forensics**  The electronic recovery and reconstruction of electronic data after deletion, concealment, or attempted destruction of the data, generally from the hard drive of a computer.

**Contract**  An agreement between two or more parties creating obligations that a court will enforce. The agreement may be oral or written and may also be implied from the parties' conduct rather than their words. For example, an implied employment contract may be based on an employment handbook or employment policy that has been communicated to employees.

**Copyright**  A property right by an author of an original work that has been fixed in a tangible medium, including literary, musical, artistic, photographic, or film works. The holder of a copyright has the exclusive right to reproduce, distribute, perform, and display the work.

**Disabled Person**  A person is protected by federal disability laws if that person has a physical or mental impairment that substantially limits one or more major life activities, has a record of a substantially limiting physical or mental impairment, or is perceived by others as having such impairment. Under federal disability laws, all applicants and employees are entitled to medical confidentiality from their employers even if they are not otherwise disabled.

**Disclaimer**  A statement repudiating or renouncing the legal rights of another. For example, an employer may include a disclaimer in an employment policy or handbook to disavow the creation of any contractual rights on the part of employees and to attempt to retain an at-will employment relationship.

**Electronic Workplace Monitoring**  Use of electronic devices and/or computer software to measure or observe the work performance of employees, to conduct electronic surveillance of the workplace, including observation of the actions and communications of others, and the use of computer forensics to recover or reconstruct evidence of the actions or communications of employees and others related to the workplace.

**European Privacy Directive**  Requires member states of the European Union to enact national laws consistent with the European Privacy Directive (Directive 95/46/EC of the European Parliament and of the Council of 24 October 1995) to protect the privacy of personal data when it is processed by another person or company, including an employer. Requires that processing of personal data be fair and lawful, be collected for legitimate purposes, be relevant, be accurate, and be kept in a form that permits identification of data subjects for no longer than is necessary for the purposes of the collection of the data. Provides that data subjects are entitled to access data about themselves and have rights to correct data about themselves.

**Fair Use**    An exception under the U.S. Copyright Act that allows one who does not own a copyright to make "fair use" of the copyrighted work for such purposes as criticism, comment, news reporting, teaching, scholarship, or research without being liable for copyright infringement.

**Family and Medical Leave**    A form of protected leave from employment that is protected by federal and some state laws. The leave is available for an employee's serious health condition, for the birth or adoption of a child, and for the serious health condition of a family member, defined as a parent, spouse, or child. A person is not required to be disabled within the meaning of federal or state law to qualify for family and medical leave. Persons on family and medical leave are entitled to medical confidentiality from their employers.

**Hostile Work Environment**    A form of harassment prohibited by U.S. federal and state discrimination laws. A hostile work environment is unlawful when it is based on an employee's sex (or gender), race, color, national origin, religion, age, or disability (prohibited classifications). Although federal laws do not protect employees from sexual orientation or marital discrimination, state and local laws may prohibit harassment and discrimination for these reasons. Words or conduct of coworkers, supervisors, managers, or third parties that occurs in or associated with the workplace are unlawful discrimination when the words or conduct are based on one or more of the prohibited classifications, are unwelcome, and are either sufficiently serious or pervasive to constitute a hostile work environment.

**Tort**    The breach of a legal duty established by law that causes injury or damage to another. This is a civil wrong that does not arise from a contract. One who violates a civil duty and injures another may be required to pay damages to the person injured. Examples of torts include defamation, assault, battery, wrongful interference by a third party with a contractual relationship, and invasion of privacy.

**Trade Secret**    A formula, process, device, or other business information that is kept confidential to maintain a competitive advantage.

## CROSS REFERENCES

See *Copyright Law; Medical Records Security; Online Contracts; Privacy Law and the Internet.*

## REFERENCES

Age Discrimination in Employment Act of 1967. (1967). 29 U.S.C.S. §§621 et seq.

American Management Association. (2003). *2003 E-mail rules, policies and practices survey.* Retrieved March 15, 2004, from http://www.amanet.org

Americans with Disabilities Act of 1990. (2004). 42 U.S.C.S. §§12101 et seq.

Anandarajan, M., & Simmers, C. A. (2004). *Personal Web usage in the workplace: A guide to effective human resources management.* Hershey, PA: Information Science Publishing.

Bachman, J. (2003, October 23). Survey: Porn found often on work computers. *SiliconValley.com.* Retrieved March 15, 2004, from http://www.siliconvalley.com

*Berube v. Fashion Centre Ltd.* (1989). 771 P.2d 1033, Utah.

Biggs, P. (2003, September 23). Mesa man accused of molestation via Web cam. *The Arizona Republic*, B5.

*Blakey v. Cont'l Airlines, Inc.* (2000). 751 A.2d 538, New Jersey.

Burgunder, L. (2004). *Legal aspects of managing technology* (3rd ed., pp. 616, 619). Mason, OH: Thomson Corporation/West Legal Studies in Business.

California Constitution. (2004). Article 1, Section 1.

Cardi, M., Employer control of employee's off-duty conduct. (2004). *West's Colorado Practice Series, Methods of Practice*, §19.21 (4th ed.). Retrieved March 21, 2005, from http://web2.westlaw.com/signon/default.wl?bhcp=1&newdoor=true

Connecticut General Statutes. (2004). §31-48d.

Cottone, E. R. (2002). Employee protection from unjust discharge: A proposal for judicial reversal of the terminable-at-will doctrine. *Santa Clara Law Review, 42,* 1259.

*Daniels v. Worldcom Corp.* (1998). No. CIV.A.3:97-CV-0721-P, 1998 WL 91261 at *4, Northern District of Texas.

Delbar, C., Mormont, M., & Schots, M. (2003). *New technology and respect for privacy at the workplace* (EU Study). Institut des Sciences du Travail, European Industrial Relations Observatory Online. Retrieved March 21, 2005, from http://www.eiro.eurofound.eu.int/2003/07/study/TN0307101S.html

Digital Millennium Copyright Act of 1998. (2004). Pub. L., 17 U.S.C.S. §1201.

Directive 95/46/EC of the European Parliament and of the Council of 24 October 1995 on the protection of individuals with regard to the processing of personal data and on the free movement of such data. (1995). Council Directive 95/46, Arts. 22-23, O.J. (L281) 31 (EU Privacy Directive).

Economic Espionage Act of 1996. (2004). 18 U.S.C.S. §1831 et seq.

*Edgar P. Benjamin Healthcare Center* (1996). Case 1-CA-32505, 322 N.L.R.B. No. 128.

Electronic Communications Privacy Act of 1986 (ECPA). (2004). Pub. L. No. 99-508, 100 Stat. 1848 (1984) (Title I of the ECPA amended the Wiretap Act of 1968 and is codified at 18 U.S.C.S. §§2510 et seq. (2004); Title II of the ECPA created the Stored Communications Act and is codified at 18 U.S.C.S. §§2701–2711.

*Federal Express Corp. v. Dutschmann.* (1993). 846 S.W. 2d 282, Texas.

Federal Family and Medical Leave Act of 1993. (2004). 29 U.S.C.S. §2601 et seq.

*Fischer v. Mt. Olive Lutheran Church.* (2002). 207 F. Supp. 2d 914, 922, 928, W. D. Wisconsin.

Florida Statute. (2004). §934.01 et seq.

*Frampton v. Central Indiana Gas Co.* (1973). 260 Ind. 249, 297 N. E. 2d 425.

*Garner v. Loomis Armored, Inc.* (1996). 913 P.2d 377, 1996 Wash. LEXIS 109.

Garrison, M. J., & Stevens, C. D. (2003). Sign this agreement not to compete or you're fired! Noncompete agreements and the public policy exception to employment at will. *Employee Responsibilities and Rights Journal, 15*(3), 105.

*Garrity v. John Hancock Mutual Life Insurance Company* (2002). 2002 WL 974676 at *1, D. Massachusetts.

George, B. C., Lynch, P., & Marsnik, S. F. (2001). U.S. multinational employers: Navigating through the "safe harbor" principles to comply with the EU Data Privacy Directive. *American Business Law Journal, 38,* 735.

Harmon, R. E. (1982). *Improving administrative manuals* (p. 23). N.Y., N.Y: American Management Association.

Harper Business. (1990). *The company policy manual: A complete guide to legal and effective company policies* (pp. 340–342). N.Y., N.Y: HarperCollins Publishers.

Health Insurance Portability and Accountability Act of 1996. (2004). Public Law 104-191, codified at 42 U.S.C.S. §201 et seq.

Hewlett-Packard. (2004). Global master privacy policy. Retrieved March 21, 2005, from http://www.hp.com /hpinfo/globalcitizenship/privacy/masterpolicy.html

HIPAA Privacy Regulations. (2004). *Privacy of individually identifiable health information.* 45 C.F.R. §164.101 et seq.

Honda, G., & Martin, K. (2002). *The essential guide to Internet business technology* (pp. 36, 37). Upper Saddle River, NJ: Prentice Hall.

*In re Pharmatrak, Inc. Privacy Litigation.* (2002). 220 F.Supp.2d 4, D. Massachusetts.; reversed by 329 F.3d 9 (1st. Cir. 2003); on remand, 292 F.Supp.2d 263 (D. Massachusetts 2003) (dismissing the case on summary judgment).

*Kelleher v. City of Reading.* (2002). 2002 WL 1067422, E. D. Pennsylvania.

Kesan, J. P. (2002). Cyber-working or cyber-shirking?: A first principles examination of electronic privacy in the workplace. *Florida Law Review, 54,* 296.

King, N. J. (2003a). Electronic monitoring to promote national security impacts workplace privacy. *Employee Responsibilities and Rights Journal, 15*(3), 127.

King, N. J. (2003b). Labor law for managers of non-union employees in traditional and cyber workplaces. *American Business Law Journal, 40*(4), 827.

*King Soopers, Inc.* (2003). 27-CA-16965, 340 N.L.R.B. No. 75.

*Konop v. Hawaiian Airlines.* (2002). 302 F.3d 868, 870, 9th Cir.

Lasprogata, G., King, N. J. & Pillay, S. (2004). Regulation of electronic employee monitoring: identifying fundamental principles of employee privacy through a comparative study of data privacy legislation in the European Union, United States and Canada, *Stanford Technology Law Review,* 2004, 4, ¶24 et seq.

Leonard, A. S. (1988). A new common law of employment termination. *North Carolina Law Review, 66,* 631.

Lieber, E. (1998). Picketing the information superhighway: Must employers bargain with a union over their e-mail policy? *1998 Annual Survey of American Law,* 517.

Manny, C. (2003). Privacy protection for health information transferred between the European Union and the U.S.: A comparison of legal frameworks. *Business Law Review, 36,* 107.

McClure, J. (2003, November 17). U R hereby fired!. *Newsweek,* 31.

*McLaren v. Microsoft Corporation.* (1999). 1999 WL 339015, Texas App. (unpublished opinion).

National Labor Relations Act of 1935. (2004). 29 U.S.C.S. §§151–169.

New Technologies. (2004). Computer forensics defined. Retrieved March 21, 2005, from http://www.forensics-intl.com/def4.html

No Electronic Theft Act of 1997. (2004). PL 105-147 (HR 2265), codified at 17 U.S.C.S. §506.

*O'Connor v. Ortega.* (1987). 480 U.S. 709.

Page, S. B. (2002). *Establishing a system of policies and procedures* (pp. 2–9). Westerfield, OH: Process Improvement Publishing.

Reuters. (2003). Survey: Forget work, IM is for flirting, gossip. *CNN.com.* March 12, 2004, http://www.CNN.com

Reuters. (2004). Employees still swapping files at work. *Reuters.com.* March 4, 2004, http://www.reuters.com

Rothstein, L. E. (2000). Privacy or dignity: Electronic monitoring in the workplace. *New York Law Journal of International and Comparative Law, 19,* 379.

Safon, D. M. (2000). *Workplace privacy, real answers and practical solutions,* pp. 101–103, 105–112. Tampa, FL: Thompson Publishing Group.

Scheer, D. (2003, October 10). Europe's new high-tech role: Playing privacy cop to world, U.S. firms run afoul of EU laws on sharing and collection of data. *The Wall Street Journal,* section A, page 1, column 5.

*Schwenn v. Anheuser-Busch, Inc.* (1998). No. CIVA95CV716, 1998 WL 166845 at *1, N. D. New York.

Sexual Exploitation of Children. (2004). 18 U.S.C.S. §2251 et seq.

Sidbury, B. F. (2001). You've got mail…and your boss knows it: Rethinking the scope of the employer e-mail monitoring exceptions to the Electronic Communications Privacy Act. *U.C.L.A. Journal of Law and Technology,* 5.

*Smyth v. Pillsbury Co.* (1996). 914 F. Supp. 97, E.D. Pennsylvania.

*Tanner v. OHSU.* (1998). 971 P.2d 435, 437, Oregon App.

*Tiberino v. Spokane County.* (2000). 13 P.3d 1104, Washington Ct. App.

Title VII of the Civil Rights Act of 1964, as amended. (2004). 42 U.S.C.S. §2000d.

*Toussaint v. Blue Cross & Blue Shield of Michigan.* (1980). 292 N.W.2d 880, Michigan.

United Kingdom Information Commissioner. (n.d.). *Codes of practice* (employment parts I–IV). Retrieved March 21, 2005 from http://www.informationcommissioner. gov.uk/eventual.aspx?id=437

United States Equal Employment Opportunity Commission. (2000, July 27). *EEOC enforcement guidance: Disability-related inquiries and medical examinations* of employees under the Americans with Disabilities Act, number 915.002. Retrieved March 21, 2005, from http://eeoc.gov

United States Government Accounting Office (2002). Employee privacy, computer-use monitoring practices and policies of selected companies (Report to the Ranking Minority Member, Subcommittee on 21st Century Competitiveness, Committee on Education and the Workforce, House of Representatives.) Retrieved March 21, 2005, from http://www.gao.gov/new.items/d02717.pdf

Uniting and Strengthening America by Providing Appropriate Tools Required to Intercept and Obstruct Terrorism Act of 2001 (USA PATRIOT Act). (2001, October 26). Pub. L. No. 107-56, 115 Stat. 272.

*U.S. v. Simmons.* (2000). 206 F.3d 392, 4th Cir.

*Woolley v. Hoffmann-La Roche, Inc.* (1985). 491 A.2d 1257, New Jersey; modified, 499 A.2d 515, New Jersey.

# Forward Security
# Adaptive Cryptography: Time Evolution

Gene Itkis, *Boston University*

## SECURITY AND SECRET KEYS

As our world is growing increasingly dependent on digital systems, security of these systems is becoming increasingly critical. In addition to accidental failures, threats of malicious attacks must be addressed by the security systems of today and tomorrow.

Connectivity of the digital systems has become an integral part of their functionality. However, connectivity could also provide malicious attackers with an easy access to the system, in particular allowing them to mount their attacks even from the other side of the globe.

Physical isolation is hardly ever an option in achieving protection, and so most systems must rely on other mechanisms for their security. These mechanisms, be they simple passwords authentication or sophisticated cryptographic tools, generally depend on maintaining some secrets (keys).[1]

Thus, security of a system hinges on the condition that the attackers cannot gain access to its secret keys. This condition may be difficult to satisfy, especially because these keys must be actively used by the system. One might try to make it harder for an adversary to expose the secret keys. To this end, one might utilize special devices (e.g., smart cards), multiple factor mechanisms (e.g., regular passwords, combined with smart cards, and biometric mechanisms), and so on. But our experience shows that

no matter how strong the protection of the secret keys, it is very likely that a sufficiently motivated adversary will succeed sooner or later and expose these keys. Thus, an experienced security systems designer will plan *explicitly* for the event of key exposures.

Therefore, the goals for a security system design can be formulated as threefold: (1) make key exposures as difficult and as expensive for adversaries as possible; (2) if/when the keys are exposed, minimize the damage; and (3) recover from the exposures.

Modern cryptography offers a number of tools and techniques to assist in these tasks. These tools include threshold/proactive and forward secure schemes. More recently, intrusion-resilient cryptography has been introduced, combining the proactive and forward secure approaches. Key evolution is one common theme in these techniques.

In this chapter, we review these techniques, focusing on forward security.

The rest of the chapter is structured as follows: Introduction by Example: Forward Secure Signatures discusses digital signatures and their limitation. Signatures schemes are then used throughout the survey as a default example for illustrations. Key Security discusses various strategies for addressing security of the secret keys. Threshold and Forward Security: Overview surveys the literature and history of the key concepts. The definitions for the key evolving schemes are given under Key Evolution: Functional Definitions for Forward Security. Forward

---

[1] Auguste Kerckhoffs advocated that the security of the system be dependent only on the secrecy of these keys as early as 1883.

Secure Pseudorandom Generators, Forward Secure Signatures, and Forward Secure Public Key Encryption survey various forward secure schemes. Finally, Conclusion presents some open problems and other research directions related to forward security.

# INTRODUCTION BY EXAMPLE: FORWARD SECURE SIGNATURES

We use digital signatures as our standard example throughout the following survey. So, in the next subsection we introduce this important cryptographic tool.

## Digital Signatures

Digital signatures are an important tool, critical to applications ranging from the widely used SSL/TLS to the more futuristic e-commerce, digital checks, and digital cash. Digital signatures are discussed in greater detail in Sections 112 and 177 in this *Handbook*, as well as in much of the cryptographic literature.

Intuitively, digital signatures are used to authenticate digital documents, much as handwritten signatures are used to authenticate documents written on paper. In the case of traditional paper documents, the document contents and signature are bound together physically—by the paper that contains both. Even in the physical world, the security of this binding can be questioned. But in the digital domain, such physical binding is simply nonexistent. Thus, in the digital world, the signature must be bound directly to the document content.

In both the physical and digital case, there are two separate tasks: *signing* and *verifying*. The task of signing on behalf of a particular user should ideally be possible only for the user himself.[2] The verification typically should be possible for any member of the public.

The digital signature is thus characterized by the two algorithms: **Sign** and **Ver**. Both must take the document text (message) $m$ as the input. The first generates a signature $\sigma$, and the second takes that signature as the input.

It is convenient to use the same signing and verifying algorithms for all the users. Thus, both algorithms must also take as input some information that is unique to the particular user. For the case of the verification, this information should be public and is thus referred to as the user's *public key* (PK). Because only the particular user should be able to generate his signatures, the unique per-user information for signing must be secret and is thus referred to as *secret* (or *private*) *key* (SK).

Some systems allow the PK to be simply the user's ID (Gentry & Silverberg, 2002; Girault, 1990; Shamir, 1985). However, such identity-based schemes are often harder to construct, and therefore the association between the users and their public keys is often left out to public key

infrastructures (PKIs) (see, e.g., Internet Security Standards in this *Handbook*). In either case, the pair PK, SK must be generated (perhaps from some additional parameters); this is done by the algorithm **KeyGen**.

Thus, the following triplet gives the functional description of a signature scheme:

**KeyGen** $(1^k) \rightarrow$ (SK,PK): *key generation*
    Input: a security parameter $k \in \mathrm{N}$ (given in unary)
    Output: a pair (SK,PK), the secret key and public key

**Sign** (SK, $m$ ) $\rightarrow \sigma$: *signing*
    Input: the secret key SK and the message $m$ to be signed
    Output: signature $\sigma$ of $m$

**Ver** (PK, $m, \sigma$ ) $\rightarrow$ **valid**|**fail**: *verification*
    Input: the public key PK, a message $m$, and an alleged signature $\sigma$
    Output: **valid** or **fail**. Usually, it is required that **Ver** (PK, $m$, **Sign** (SK, $m$)) $\rightarrow$ **valid**.

Intuitively, a signature scheme is secure if it is infeasible for an adversary without SK to compute any signature $\sigma$ for a message $m$, such that **Ver** (PK, $m, \sigma$) outputs **Valid**. This remains infeasible even if the adversary adaptively obtains legitimate signatures for many other messages of the adversary's choice. See Goldwasser, Micali, and Rivest (1988; or many subsequent papers and books) for precise definitions of signature security.

## Limitations of Signatures

Ordinary digital signatures have a fundamental limitation: if the secret key of a signer is compromised, all the signatures (past and future) of that signer become suspect. Even though the *signer* might know which signatures were issued by him and which by the impostor (using the stolen key), there is no way for the *verifier* to distinguish them.

Thus, upon such a secret-key compromise, the signer should revoke his public key (itself a nontrivial problem) and obtain a fresh key pair. But what to do with the already issued signatures (i.e., those issued before the compromise—in good faith)? Reissuing them with the new key is expensive or even impossible (imagine having to do this for a certification authority, or in the absence of reliable and exhaustive records of the past signatures). What is even worse, a dishonest signer may see a key compromise as a golden opportunity to repudiate (some) previously signed documents. In fact, he or she might even fake a compromise him- or herself (e.g., by anonymously posting his secret key on the Internet and claiming to be the victim of a computer break-in).

# KEY SECURITY

This makes clear the importance of the security of the signer's secret key both to prevent the actual key compromise as well as make the "faked" key compromises less believable.

---

[2] It may be possible and desirable for the user to delegate authority vested in the signature to another party. In the physical world, this is usually achieved by explicit delegation of authority (e.g., power of attorney). Such delegations are also possible in the digital scenarios as well. But digital signatures potentially allow a stronger notion: a limited delegation of ability to generate signatures themselves. For example, using intrusion-resilient signatures (Itkis & Reyzin, 2002), the user can enable another party to generate his signatures but only if they are tagged with a particular date.

## Threshold Crypto: Space Dimension

One way to improve the security of the secret keys is to distribute it among different computers in such a way that breaking into individual computers would not affect security of the key, at least until sufficiently many of these computers have been compromised. This approach has been explored by *threshold* cryptography. For example, similar to the secret-sharing scheme of Shamir (1979), for any integers $n \geq t > 0$, the signing key SK can be shared among $n$ computers, so that any $t$ of them, working together, can generate valid signatures. But breaking into any $t-1$ of them gives *no* information about SK to the adversary (i.e., adversary learns *nothing* from these break-ins); in fact, any $t-1$ shares of SK look completely random. The signing algorithm would then become a protocol executed by a sufficiently large subset ($t$ or more) of these shareholding computers. The security definitions would have to be adjusted correspondingly—in particular, the SK cannot be reconstructed from the shares in any of these computers, because then it might be exposed (stolen) there.

## Proactive Crypto: Time Evolution of Sharing

A particularly strong, *proactive* version of the threshold cryptography tolerates even compromises of all the computers—as long as they were not simultaneous. This is achieved by introducing an aspect of time evolution: although the threshold cryptography shared a secret key statically, the proactive cryptographic schemes would constantly reshare the keys. Thus, the exposed key shares would not help the adversary after that key sharing changed. To apply this to the threshold signatures example, assume that at some point after an adversary breaks into a computer, the computer is completely "cleaned up," so the adversary loses control over that computer and access to the information on it (except the information that the adversary already stolen). Then, the proactive techniques allow the signature scheme to be strengthened to tolerate the adversary eventually breaking into *all* $n$ computers, as long as $<t$ are corrupted at a time.

## Limits of Proactive Security

However, even in the case of proactive security, the "combined" state of the system remains unchanged—the secret key being shared is the same, only the specifics of how it is stored evolve with time. Therefore, in the case of the total exposure (e.g., simultaneous compromise of all the computers holding key shares), the issue of past signatures remains.

## Price of Proactive/Threshold Security

A major drawback of the threshold and proactive systems is that any transaction—such as generating a signature—requires at least $t$ parties (i.e., participating computers) to perform joint computation: by executing a particular protocol to achieve the desired result. Such a communication can be inconvenient, inefficient, and sometimes even impossible. It also increases vulnerability of the participating computers.

## Key Evolution

### Exploring Time Dimension

A radically different approach to protecting the keys is to securely erase them—a *securely erased* key cannot be stolen. So, the signatures generated with such a key cannot be repudiated by a fallacious claim of exposure (assuming that the key was not exposed prior to the erasure).[3] Then the signatures generated with the secret key before it was erased should remain trustworthy forever—even after the signer's computer is compromised. This approach motivates an essential evolution of the whole system to occur in time, where the past is fundamentally irreproducible.

### Frequent Rekeying

The problem with erasing the secret key, of course, is that the signer can no longer produce signatures with it. With ordinary signatures, this means that the corresponding public key is now useful only for past signatures, and a new public key needs to be issued (and appropriately certified and disseminated) for the future ones. This makes such an approach expensive and inconvenient.

### Forward Secure Signatures

The goal of *forward secure* signature schemes is to provide the benefits of frequent rekeying without incurring the costs of changing public keys (and associated overhead). They enable the signer to frequently erase the secret key while maintaining the same public key. The notion of a forward security originated from the notion of "perfect forward secrecy" for key agreement (Günther, 1989), which protects past traffic even after long-term keys are compromised.[4]

To be more precise, in a forward secure signature scheme, the total time that the public key is valid (e.g., 1 year) is divided into $T$ *time periods* (e.g., 365 days). At the end of each time period, the signer computes the next secret key from the current one (via a *key update* algorithm) and erases the current secret key. Each signature includes an essential new component: the time period during which the signature is issued. The forward security property means that even if the adversary obtains the

---

[3] This assumption should not be taken lightly, of course. But it does offer a significant extra level of comfort. For example, imagine that a user decides to abbrogate a contract he signed a year earlier by claiming that the secret key used to sign the contract has been stolen and the other party of the contract forged the signature using this stolen key. This claim would look much more dubious if the only way the alleged key compromise could have occurred is if it took place at least a year earlier. It is even more dubious if the signer has not discovered the key compromise until the terms of the contract began to look less attractive than they did at the time of the signing (and alleged key exposure!). Although no fool-proof security for the signatures appears to be possible, the secure erasure of the relevant key does seem to offer a greater degree of comfort. A slight further improvement of this comfort level is offered by other models, such as key-insulated and intrusion-resilient cryptography (Dodis, Katz, Xu, & Yung, 2003; Itkis & Reyzin, 2002a), where the only time the key could have been stolen was on the day of the contract signing.

[4] The term *forward* in *forward security* and *forward secrecy* is viewed by many as confusing. One can argue that "backward" would be more appropriate because such schemes protect transactions that happened *before* a key exposure. Conversely, *forward* can be justified, because if a transaction occurs when the key is secure, then it will remain secure in the *future*, even after future key exposures.

current secret key, she still cannot forge signatures for past time periods.

## Limitations of Forward Security

Just as for ordinary signature schemes, for the forward secure signatures the signer is still expected to promptly *detect* key compromise. The sooner the determination is made and key revoked, the less damage the adversary can do. Thus, in particular, forward security does not remove the need for intrusion detection and for prompt key revocation (which both are rather problematic in practice).

## Beyond Forward Security

These limitations motivate research into extending the forward security approach. Some extensions, such as intrusion-resilient and key-insulated schemes (Dodis, Franklin, Katz, Miyaji, & Yung, 2003; Dodis, Katz, Xu, & Yung, 2002; Dodis, Katz, Xu, & Yung, 2003; Itkis, 2002; Itkis & Reyzin, 2002), aim to protect *future* as well as past signatures, thus making prompt detection of key compromise and key revocation less crucial for many applications. In particular, intrusion-resilient schemes allow to reduce the reliance on the revocation. Another extension, cryptographic tamper evidence (Itkis, 2003), addresses the issue of detection of key compromises. This extension capitalizes on the dynamically evolving nature of some of the schemes. Such evolution may enable detection of *use* of exposed keys even after a total compromise of the system (i.e., after *all* the secrets in the system have been exposed). Forward security focuses on the evolution of the secret keys. However, there may be some benefits in evolution of the public keys as well (e.g., to allow a controlled repudiation of signatures generated with secret keys extorted from the user). This problem was considered in Naccache, Pointcheval, and Tymen (2001) and then further developed in Itkis and Xie (2003), which not only restricted the possible repudiation to avoid its abuse but also provided more efficient solutions. This was achieved by explicit generalization of the key-evolving schemes to include both secret key and public key evolution.

# THRESHOLD AND FORWARD SECURITY: OVERVIEW

In this section, we provide the survey of the bibliographic references to the main results in the areas of threshold and forward security. We view these as the two dimensions along which the cryptography developed in response to the need to address key exposures.

## Threshold and Proactive Cryptography

Much of the work focused on distributing secrets and computation in such a way that an adversary must commit multiple breaches before security of the system fails. Examples include the general and fascinatingly powerful (albeit inefficient in practice) multiparty computation methods (e.g., Ben-Or, Goldwasser, & Wigderson, 1988; Chaum, Crfiepeau, & Damgfiard, 1998; Goldreich, Micali, & Wigderson, 1986; Goldreich, Micali, & Wigderson, 1987) and the more specific (and thus more efficient) *threshold* cryptography methods (Boneh & Franklin,

1997; Desmedt, 1997; Desmedt & Frankel, 1989; Gennaro, Jarecki, Krawczyk, & Rabin, 1996; Malkin, Wu, & Boneh, 1999; Pedersen, 1991; Shoup, 2000; Wu, Malkin, & Boneh, 1999).

*Proactive* security takes this approach further by forcing the adversary not only to break into many computers to learn anything but also to accomplish all these breaks nearly simultaneously (Barak, Herzberg, Naor, & Shai, 1999; Canetti, Gennaro, Jarecki, Krawezyk, & Rabin, 1999; Canetti, Halevi, & Herzberg, 2000; Desmedt, 1997; Frankel, Gemmell, MacKenzie, & Yung, 1997; Herzberg et al., 1997; Ostrovsky & Yung, 1991).

However, both threshold and proactive approaches require the cooperation of multiple parties for every cryptographic operation (even when there are some semitrusted parties involved, as in Beaver, 1999). It is difficult to apply them routinely in many settings, where the amount of data and processing demand greater efficiency and applications demand greater usability.

Another common approach to protecting secrets has been to keep them on computationally weak portable devices, such as smart cards. To make them usable for computationally intensive cryptographic tasks, approaches such as "server aided" (e.g., Beguin & Quisquater, 1995; Jakobsson & Wetzel, 2001; Laih, Yen, & Harn, 1991; Merkle, 2000; Nguyen & Stern, 1998; Pfitzmann & Waidner, 1993) and "remotely keyed" (e.g., Blaze, 1995, 1996; Blaze, Feigenbaum, & Naor, 1998; Lucks, 1997, 1999; Weis, Bakker, & Lucks, 2001) have been proposed (all-or-nothing transforms have been proposed as another solution to this problem; see Boyko, 1999, 2000; Rivest, 1997; Stinson, 2001). Furthermore, the devices can be made less likely to succumb to off-line attacks using the techniques of MacKenzie and Reiter (2001a, 2001b).

The security against *partial* key exposures—when only some portion of a secret key gets into the adversary's hands—has been addressed in Canetti et al. (2000), Dodis (2000), and Dodis, Sahai, and Smith (2001). This approach may be useful in the cases when learning all the bits of a key is difficult for the adversary (e.g., for some devices, such as smart cards, malicious probing of some bits might damage other bits—allowing the adversary to extract only partial information from the device).

None of these approaches, however, addressed what happens in the case when the secret key is exposed: they simply increase the difficulty of stealing the secrets.

## Forward Secure Cryptography

### Origins

Traditionally, forward security (including the term itself) is traced back to the work of Christoph Günther (1999) on key exchange protocols. This work in particular proposes a notion of "perfect forward secrecy." This property essentially requires that the confidentiality of the past messages is not compromised even after the long-term secrets are exposed. This definition, however, does not in any way imply the key evolution, which we believe is fundamental to forward security.

Continuing to focus on the forward secrecy (i.e., confidentiality of the past messages), Adam Back in cypherpunk e-mail discussion proposed the idea of a public key cryptosystem, which would generate a sequence of private and corresponding public keys $SK_i$, $PK_i$ (Back, 1996). That is, ideally Back wished for two "nonreversible" functions $f_1$, $f_2$ such that $f_1(SK_i) = SK_{i+1}$ and $f_2(PK_i) = PK_{i+1}$. Of course, the messages encrypted for public key $PK_i$ would still be decrypted with the private key $SK_i$. But now, an adversary would not be able to decrypt those messages if she had only $SK_i + 1$. So, Bob could certify and advertise his public key $PK_0$, and every day he could generate a new private key from the old one, securely erasing the old keys. Then Alice could send Bob a message on day $i$ using key $PK_i = f_2^i(PK_0)$. Then, even if Bob's key is exposed any time after day $i$, the message would remain confidential.

We can simplify this notation to make it look more modern (i.e., matching the notation of Bellare & Miner, 1999): without loss of generality, set $PK_i$, $\langle PK, i \rangle$, where PK is *the* public key of Bob. Then the $PK_i$ as defined by Back could be computed from $\langle PK, i \rangle$ "on the fly" as $f_2^i(PK)$. This computation could be integrated into the decryption or signature verification algorithms as needed.

In the same draft, Back proposed a scheme that was not quite as good as the previous ideal: although coming up with $f_1$ was easy, $f_2$ turned out to be much harder.[5] So, instead of computing new public keys from the previous ones, Back's scheme computed them from the corresponding private keys. Then, the sender of the message would simply be provided with all the public keys. In this case, $f_1$ could be any pseudorandom function, and the ElGamal/DH encryption (Diffie & Hellman, 1976; ElGamal, 1984) would use the key $PK_i = g^{SK_i} \bmod p$, for some large prime $p$ and a generator $g$ of $Z_p^*$.

In the subsequent year, Ross Anderson (1997) proposed applying the same approach to signatures. He also observed that *identity-based* cryptosystems (those where the identity of a user served as his public key) can be adopted to provide forward security: simply use a combination of the public key and the date as the identity.

## Key Evolving Schemes and Forward Secure Signatures

These initial ideas were formalized and further developed by Bellare and Miner (1999). In particular, they provided the formal definitions for the key evolving signature schemes and their security. The definitions we use herein are closely base on the definitions of Bellare & Miner (1999). New forward secure signature schemes were proposed in the same article, followed by more constructions (Abdalla & Reyzin, 2000; Itkis & Reyzin, 2001; Kozlov & Reyzin, 2002; Krawezyk, 2000; Malkin, Obana & Yung, 2002).

## Generic and Concrete Schemes

All the proposed schemes can be divided into two general categories: the generic and concrete.

A generic scheme is constructed from any ordinary (nonforward secure) scheme used as a black box. The security of the forward secure scheme is then reduced to the security of the underlying ordinary scheme (i.e., if some adversary can efficiently compromise the forward secure scheme, then we can construct an adversary compromising the security of the underlying ordinary scheme). The efficiency of a generic scheme is usually measured in terms of the number of the invocations of the underlying ordinary scheme, the number of the ordinary keys, and so on. Both Back's and Anderson's schemes, although originally presented as concrete schemes, could be generalized to generic ones.

A concrete scheme usually starts from a specific ordinary scheme and modifies it to achieve desired properties. A concrete scheme security is thus reducible to the specific cryptographic assumption, such as the strong RSA assumption, hardness of discrete log, bilinear Diffie–Hellman assumption, and so on. The efficiency of the concrete schemes is measured in terms of the number of specific operations used (e.g., modular multiplications). As with many ordinary schemes, this necessitates expressing the costs in terms of two security parameters. For example, for the ordinary schemes such as Fiat–Shamir (Fiege, Fiat, & Shamir, 1998; Fiat & Shamir, 1986), Guillou–Quisquater (1988), and many others, one security parameter $l$ characterizes the length of the modulus, whereas the other $k$ determines the number of rounds, the length of the query, or the length of a hash function output. Typically, these differ by an order of magnitude: $k$ is typically in the range 128–160, and $l$ is usually in the 1024–2048 range.

Of these schemes, Bellare & Miner (1999) proposed both generic and concrete schemes; Anderson (1997), Back (1996), Krawezyk (2000), and Malkin et al. (2002) proposed generic constructions (though originally described as concrete); the constructions of Abdalla and Reyzin (2000), Canetti et al. (2003), Itkis and Reyzin (2001), and Kozlov and Reyzin (2002) are concrete.

## Forward Secure Public Key Encryption

Forward secure public key encryption proved harder to achieve, and the first—and so far the only—result in that area was obtained only recently (Canetti et al., 2003); although some "approximations" of forward secure encryption were put forward by Dodis, Katz, Xu, & Yung (2002) and Tzeng & Tzeng (2001).

## Forward Security for All Tasks

So far we really surveyed forward security only for public key signatures and encryption. Providing forward security for other tasks has also been considered.

For example, Krawczyk (2000) constructed a generic forward secure pseudorandom number generator, which he then used to construct a forward secure public key signature scheme. Bellare and Yee (2001) also provide definitions, careful analysis, and constructions for forward secure pseudorandom generators as well as for forward secure symmetric signature and encryption schemes.

Forward secure versions of group (Song, 2001), threshold (Abdalla, Miner, & Namprempre, 2001; Liu, Chu, & Tzeng, 2003; Tzeng & Tzeng, 2001), and blind (Duc, Cheon, & Kim, 2003) signature schemes were defined and constructed (these are concrete constructions). One

---

[5] Indeed, only some seven years later this problem would be resolved, and even then only based on a less common bilinear Diffie–Hellman assumption (Canetti, Halevi, & Katz, 2003). Forward secure public key encryption based on the standard DH, discrete log, or factoring assumptions remains an open problem to the day of this writing.

may also observe that the typical group key management schemes (also referred to as secure multicast) generally include forward security in their definitions (see Caronni, Waldvogel, Sun, Weiler, & Plattner, 1999; Wallner, Harder, & Agee, 1999; and Weis et al., 2001, and subsequent work); these, however, are traditionally considered as a separate topic.

Also Abdallah, Bellare, and Namprepre (2001) generalized and analyzed the Fiat–Shamir paradigm of turning ID schemes into signatures. They extend their analysis to include forward security.

# KEY EVOLUTION: FUNCTIONAL DEFINITIONS FOR FORWARD SECURITY

The main functional distinction of forward-secure versions of cryptographic tools is the explicit use of time in all algorithms (e.g., encrypting or signing). In addition, because the secret key in forward secure schemes can evolve, there are procedures to handle such an evolution.

We outline the functional definitions for general key evolving schemes that can include some mechanisms beyond forward security. These definitions are based on Itkis and Xie (2003), which in turn generalized the definitions of Bellare and Miner (1999), where *key evolving schemes* were introduced formally. We also separate the key evolution aspect from the specifics of the cryptographic mechanism (e.g., key evolution is functionally independent from whether we deal with forward secure signatures or forward secure encryption).

## Common Procedures

### Key Generation

Key-generation procedure generates typically a pair of keys $(PK_0, SK_0)$, for the initial time period 0. For symmetric cryptography schemes, the public key PK can be assumed to be null. This procedure is essentially similar to the corresponding one without evolution as under "Digital Signatures": setting $T = 0$ makes the two completely identical.

**KeyGen** $(1^k, T) \rightarrow (SK_0, PK_0)$: *key generation*
> Input: a security parameter $k \in N$ (given in unary) and the total number of periods, $T$
> Output: a pair $(SK_0, PK_0)$, the initial secret key and public key

The maximum number of updates—the total number of time periods $T$—is required for some forward secure schemes. Different approaches for eliminating this bound are considered in Itkis (2002) and Malkin, Micciancio, and Miner (2002).

### Key Evolution

Key evolution procedure changes key $K_t$ (which can be either SK or PK) for the current period $t$ into the key $K_t + \Delta$ for the next time period $t + \Delta$ (typically, $\Delta = 1$, so the next time period is $t + 1$). This evolution can be either deterministic or randomized. This procedure is the one that is germane to the forward secure (and other key evolving) schemes.

**(KUp**$(K_t[, \mu][, \Delta]) \rightarrow K_{t+\Delta}[, \mu_t]$: *key update*
> Input: the current key $K_t$ [and optionally, the update message $\mu$] [and, optionally, the number $\Delta > 0$ by which to increment the time period; by default $\Delta = 1$]
> Output: The new key $K_{t+\Delta}$ [and, optionally, the update message $\mu_t$]

Previously, only $\Delta = 1$ has been considered and unless stated otherwise, we will assume $\Delta = 1$ below. However, in some cases, it might be beneficial to skip computing some of the keys. Naturally, for $\Delta > 1$, the update can be achieved by $\Delta$ successive key updates incrementing time by 1. But in some cases, more efficient updates are possible and desired.

The key evolution is typically done in a coordinated fashion: private and public keys evolve synchronously. For the ordinary forward security, the public key $PK_t$, $\langle PK, t \rangle$ always consists of the invariant part PK and the current time period number $t$. Thus, the public key evolution is trivial: it simply increments the time period number. Evolution of the secret keys is usually more complex, for security reasons, and depends on the specific scheme.

For some schemes, such as in Itkis and Xie (2003), it may be useful to allow greater freedom of the secret key evolution (e.g., make it randomized). This can increase the sophistication of the public key updates and require a greater level of coordination between the public and private key evolutions. The optional parameter/output $\mu$ in the **KUp** provides the mechanism for such coordination: the private key update in this case generates an update message $\mu_t$, which is then used as the optional input argument $\mu$ for the public key update.

Addition of time into the functional definitions of the standard cryptographic procedures is straightforward. We include as an example such definitions for the case of the signatures.

## Specific Example: Forward Secure Signatures

### Functional Definition for Signing and Verifying

Finally, here we include the functional definition of the standard signing and verifying procedures for signatures, adapted for the forward security.

**Sign** $(SK_t, m) \rightarrow \sigma_t$: *signing*
> Input: the secret key $SK_t$ for the current period $t$ and the message $m$ to be signed
> Output: signature $\sigma_t$ of $m$ (the time period $t$ of the signature generation is included in $\sigma_t$)

**Ver** $(PK_t, m, \sigma) \rightarrow$ **valid|fail**: *verification*
> Input: the public key $PK_t$, a message $m$, and an alleged signature $\sigma$ (including the signing time period $t'$)
> Output: **valid** or **fail**

The verification procedure may impose additional conditions depending on the public key time period and the time of the signature generation (e.g., $t \geq t'$).

Thus, the full functional definition for the forward secure signatures is obtained by combining the **KeyGen**, **Sign**, **Ver** procedures with KUp applied to the $SK_t$ (with no optional argument $\mu$) at the end of each period $t$ (no update message $\mu_t$ is generated in this case either). The public key update, which in this case simply increments the date, is usually not considered explicitly in the literature. But implicitly it is also assumed to be performed at the end of each time period (also without the optional input and output).

Note that functional definition for ordinary (not forward secure) signatures can be obtained by eliminating all subscripts (denoting time) and omitting the key evolution **KUp**, leaving only the **KeyGen**, **Sign**, and **Ver** procedures.

## Security Definitions

The modern definitions of security tend to be based on an adversary trying to distinguish certain inputs (e.g., encryptions of two known messages, or random versus pseudorandom strings) or generate some output (e.g., a valid signature). A scheme is secure if no adversary could succeed with a probability significantly different than for a very simplistic adversary guessing at random.

The different types of security (e.g., known plaintext, chosen ciphertext, and chosen-message) are captured by the specific powers of the adversary, including the information given to her. In this respect, forward security introduces two issues into these security definitions: First, adversary queries are now to include references to the time period for which the query is made (e.g., for which an adversary-chosen message is to be signed in the chosen message attack).

Second, and more important, the adversary is given the secret key $SK_t$ for the time period $t$ of her choice. But then the adversary's attack, to be considered successful, is restricted to the time period $< t$.

This restriction is quite intuitive: because the key evolution algorithm is known, the adversary can use it to obtain secret keys $SK_{t' > t}$ from the exposed $SK_t$. Thus, the restriction simply requires an adversary to succeed in the period that is not trivially compromised. The details of which periods exactly are not "trivially compromised" might get more complicated in some other key-evolving models such as intrusion resilient or key insulated.

Next, we consider different specific schemes. For each, we sketch the security definitions and outline and/or survey the main constructions.

# FORWARD SECURE PSEUDORANDOM GENERATORS
## Definitions

### Notation

For any set $S$, we write $x \xleftarrow{R} S$ to denote that $x$ is chosen from the set $S$ with the uniform probability (i.e., $x$ chosen randomly from $S$). For strings $a, b$, let $a||b$ denote their concatenation, and $|a|$ the length of string $a$. Let adversary $A$ be any probabilistic polynomial time (ppt) algorithm.

### Pseudorandom Generators Definition

Intuitively, for parameters $k, m > k$, a function $G: \{0, 1\}^k \to \{0, 1\}^m$ is a pseudorandom generator (PRG) if it is infeasible to distinguish its output from random. More precisely, set $s \xleftarrow{R} \{0, 1\}^k$, $x_0 \leftarrow G(s)$, $x_1 \xleftarrow{R} \{0, 1\}^m$, and $b \xleftarrow{R} \{0, 1\}$. Then $A$'s (distinguishing) advantage is defined as $|\text{Prob}[A(x_b) = b] - 1/2|$. $G$ is a PRG for any ppt adversary $A$, if her distinguishing advantage is small[6] for sufficiently large $k$.

### Forward Secure PRG Definition

To extend this to the forward secure setting, we use the **KeyGen** and **KUp** procedures to generate and update the secret keys (seeds) $SK_t$ for periods $t$. Without essential loss of generality and for the sake of avoiding extra notation, let the pseudorandom bits generated from $SK_t$ in the period $t$ be denoted as $PK_t$.[7]

To define the advantage, for some period $i$, set $x_0 \leftarrow PK_0||\ldots||PK_{i-1}$, $x_1 \xleftarrow{R} \{0, 1\}^{|x_0|}$, and $b \xleftarrow{R} \{0, 1\}$. Similarly, the advantage of $A$ is $|\text{Prob}[A(x_b, SK_i) = b] - 1/2|$ (note that $A$ is also given $SK_i$, so assuming deterministic key evolution, $A$ can generate all $SK_{t > i}$ and thus $PK_{t > i}$ on her own). And similarly, a key evolving PRG is forward secure if the advantage is small for all the ppt adversaries.

The period $i$ can be adaptively determined by the adversary, but choosing it at random would reduce the adversary's advantage at most by a factor of $1/T$.

## Schemes

Many of the classical PRG schemes implicitly provide forward security. However, this is not the case for some PRG schemes. For example, Bellare and Yee (2003) show that the alleged RC4 PRG is not forward secure.

### Hard-Core Iteration

A common approach to PRG constructions is to iterate a one-way permutation on the initial seed, at each iteration outputting a hard-core bit (Blum & Micali, 1984; Goldreich & Levin, 1989; Yao, 1982). [Intuitively, a bit $b()$ is hard-core (or hidden) for a function $f()$ if $b(x)$ is not predictable from $f(x)$; see Blum & Micali, 1984; Goldreich & Levin, 1989, for full definitions.] The security proofs for such PRGs can usually be easily extended to include forward security.

Indeed, let **KUp**$(SK_t)$ be a pseudorandom permutation and let $PK_t = b(SK_t)$, where $b()$ is a hard-core bit for **KUp**$()$. Then, the hybrid proof of Yao (1982) implies the forward security of the scheme.

---

[6] We leave the details of defining what exactly is to be considered small. Popular choices include exponential or superpolynomial.

[7] If the number of pseudorandom bits for each period is too large (e.g., if we wish to extend the definition to pseudorandom *functions*), then $PK_t$ can be treated as the "daily seed" (i.e., to be used as the seed for [another] pseudorandom generator/function [forward secure or not] used to generate the bits for the period $t$). Of course, in this case $PK_t$ must be sufficiently long and kept secret and erased at the end of the period $t$. This case is trivially reducible to the main case.

Similarly, the proofs for the more general PRG of Hfiastad, Impagliazzo, Levin, and Luby (1999) based on any one-way function can be extended to include forward security as well. In other words, their PRG is a fsPRG as well.

## PRG Iteration

Bellare & Yee (2003) and Krawczyk (2000) propose a construction of a fsPRG from any PRG. This construction is similar to the previous one based on the one-way permutations, except two parts of the pseudorandom generator output is used in place of both the one-way permutation and hard-core bit (indeed, for a random $x$, one-way permutation $f$ with a hard-core bit predicate $b$, the string $f(x)||b(x)$ is pseudorandom). We present their construction in a slightly generalized form.

Let $G : \{0, 1\}^k \to \{0, 1\}^{2k}$, and let $G_0$ denote the first $k$ bits output by $G$, whereas $G_1$ is the last $k$ bits [thus $G(s) = G_0(s)||G_1(s)$ for all $s$]. For any bit $b$, define $F_b(s)$, $G_b(s)$ and $F_{xb}(s)$, $G_b(F_b(s))$.

## Tree View

This can be viewed as in terms of trees: consider a binary tree with each node having a label and a value. The root is labeled with an empty string; a left child of any node extends the parent's label with 0, whereas a right child extends it with 1. Let $s$ be a value stored at the root, and let a node labeled $l$ store $F_l(s)$. Clearly, the value of the left child of any node is computed by applying $G_0$ to the parent's value (respectively, $G_1$ for the right child).

Consider a completely unbalanced tree where each leaf has label $1^t0$. This tree corresponds to the fsPRG construction of Bellare and Yee (2003) and Krawczyk (2000). Namely, $SK_t = F_{1^{t+1}}(s)$ and $PK_t = F_{1^t0}(s) = G_0(SK_{t-1})$.

## General Tree, Prefixless Construction

It is easy to generalize this construction, if desired, to other trees, including infinite ones. Specifically, consider any (possibly infinite) set of finite prefixless labels $L$: if $x, y \in L$, then $x$ is not a prefix of $y$. Let $l_i$ be the $i$-th smallest label in $L$. We can also refer to it as the prefixless (or self-delimiting) encoding of $i$ according to $L$. Now we set $PK_t$, $F_{l_t}(s)$. The secret key $SK_t$ must contain all the values from which the $PK_{t'>t}$ can be derived. For a node labeled $l$, define the *ancestor set* $P(l)$ to be the set of all the ancestors of $l$ (excluding $l$). In other words, $P(l)$ are the nodes on the path from $l$ to the root.

Define the *right set* $R(l)$ of $l$ to be the set of all the right children of $P(l)$ that are not in $P(l)$. $R(l)$ is the minimal set of nodes such that for any $l' \leq l$ $R(l)$ contains no ancestors of $l'$, but for each $l'' > l$, it contains exactly one ancestor of $l''$. In other words, $R(l_t)$ is the minimum set of nodes from which the values for all $l_{t''>t}$, but for no $l_{t'\leq t}$ can be derived. Thus, as before, for each leaf $l_t$, we set $PK_t$, $F_{l_t}(s)$. Now, the $SK_t$, $\{\langle F_l(s), l \rangle | l \in R(l_t)\}$.

This completely unbalanced tree is one example of prefixless encodings—essentially writing $i$ in unary notation and marking its end with 0. Then for any leaf $l_t = 1^t0$, $R(l_t) = \{1^{t+1}\}$. Thus, that construction is a special case of our more general tree construction, using a very simple and inefficient prefixless encoding.

The efficiency of the encoding does not influence much the fsPRG constructions under consideration. More efficient schemes can be beneficial in the cases when many intermediate values need not be computed; that is, when $\Delta > 1$ in the key update **KUp** (see "Common Procedures").

Moreover, essentially similar constructions are used later for other schemes (e.g., signatures) and will be able to benefit from better encodings.

## Prefixless (Self-Delimiting) Encodings

Self-delimiting encodings are a well-known concept, playing an important role, in particular, in Kolmogorov Complexity (Levin, 1973, 1974; Li & Vitfianyi, 1993) and in some scheduling problems (e.g., in Itkis & Levin, 1989). In the context of forward security, they were utilized for the first time in Itkis (2002) in a way similar to the one described here.

Various prefixless encodings abound. The simplest one handling infinite sets of inputs is probably to view each string $t$ as an integer represented in unary (using only 1s) and delimited with a single 0: $l_t = 1^t0$. That is, the one implicitly used in the schemes of Bellare and Yee (2003) and Krawczyk (2000). Of course, such an encoding is very inefficient: $|l_t| = 2^t$. However, a simple bootstrapping strategy can make it much more efficient: $l_t$ can consist of the length $|t|$ of $t$, encoded in a prefixless notation, followed by $t$ itself. In this case, $|l_t| = 2|t| = 2\lg t$. Iterating this one more time, we can get a prefixless encoding for which $|l_t| = \lg t + 2\lg\lg t = (1 + o(1))\lg t$. For practical purposes, it probably makes sense to stop here, though further iteration may yield better asymptotics (e.g., iterating $\lg^* t$ times, we can get $|l_t| = \lg t + \lg\lg t + \cdots + \lg^{\lg^* t} t + \lg^* t$).

Another approach to achieve prefixless encoding (instead of using unary notation at the base step) can represent each bit as two bits, 0 as 00, 1 as 01, and use 11 to mark the end of the string. Clearly, this encoding can be easily improved by encoding $t$ in ternary and using 10 to represent the ternary digit 2. Then $|l_t| = 2\log_3 t < 1.6\lg t$. Further reductions are possible: essentially, for any monotone function $f$ such that $\sum 1/f \leq 1$, it is possible to achieve an encoding such that $l_t \leq f(t)$. In particular, for any $\varepsilon > 0$, there exists a prefixless encoding such that $|l_t| \leq (1 + \varepsilon)\lg t + O(1)$. These methods can also be used in the same bootstrapping strategy.

## Symmetric Cryptography: From fsPRG to fsMAC, Audit Logs, and Encryption

It is possible to define a forward secure version of message authentication codes (MAC) and symmetric encryption (see Bellare & Yee, 2003). Intuitively, the concepts are fairly straightforward: the functional definition is obtained by adding the corresponding MAC or encrypt/decrypt functions to the common forward security **KeyGen**, **KUp** functions under "Common Procedures."

The forward secure constructions use the ordinary MAC or encrypt/decrypt functions and follow from the fsPRG directly: the key for each period is generated by the fsPRG and then used by the ordinary (nonforward secure) functions. Namely, in this notation, $PK_t$ is used as an ordinary MAC or encryption/decryption key for the period $t$.

Another nice application for the forward secure MACs—audit logs authentication—is suggested in Bellare and Yee (2003) (a similar but more heuristic solution was also proposed in Schneier & Kelsey, 1999). The basic idea is to authenticate a computer log using a forward secure MAC. In this case, an intruder cannot modify the past entries into the log without being detected (having all entries numbered and equating the entry number with the time period eliminates undetected deletions as well). The log's verification, however, can be done on a separate machine that stores the original $SK_0$ and can thus verify the log. In fact, forward securely encrypting the logs may offer even better security.

Our more efficient prefixless construction can be beneficial in this application—many times an inspector may not be interested in accessing the log in a linear fashion. Rather, it may be desired to extract specific log entries as fast as possible. In such cases, computing the desired $PK_t$ from the root $SK_0$ in the time logarithmic—rather than linear—in $t$ would improve efficiency significantly.

## Forward Secure Public Key Crypto: Naive Generic Construction

Before we move on to discuss specific forward secure public key cryptosystems, we discuss a simple but inefficient way of constructing a forward secure cryptosystem (whether public key signatures, encryption, or anything else) out of any ordinary one (same task, but no forward security). Refer to the ordinary cryptosystem (and all its functions) used in the construction as the basic one(s). We use it as a black box in our construction.

First, using the basic key-generation function, generate $T$ public/secret key pairs $\langle p_t, s_t \rangle$ for all $t \in \{0, T-1\}$. Then publish all public keys $p_t$. For time period $t$, use the ordinary scheme with the public/secret keys $p_t$ and $s_t$. The forward secure secret key $SK_t$ for time period $t$ is then $SK_t = \{\langle i, s_i \rangle | i \geq t\}$. The forward secure public key in general must contain all $PK_t = \{\langle i, p_i \rangle | 0 \leq i < T\}$. Such a naive scheme is very inefficient: it requires both public and secret storage to store $T$ ordinary keys (for the secret storage, this number is decreasing with time as $T - t$ keys stored at time $t$).

We can reduce the secret storage to one key plus whatever is required by the fsPRG: use fsPRG to provide the pseudorandom bits for the key generation. Now, generate key pairs $\langle p_t, s_t \rangle$ twice: after the first generation, publish all the $p^t$. Then use the fsPRG to regenerate the secret (and public) keys as needed for each period. This idea is further extended to obtain some of the following generic signature constructions.

## FORWARD SECURE SIGNATURES

Forward secure signature schemes can be divided into two categories: those that use (in a black-box manner) arbitrary signature schemes and those that modify specific signature schemes. We refer to the first category as *generic* or *black box* constructions and to the second as *concrete* or *explicit* constructions. The ordinary scheme(s) used as a black box in the generic constructions is referred to as the *basic* scheme. We consider these two groups separately.

## Generic Constructions

In the generic constructions, typically a master public key is used to certify (perhaps via a chain of certificates) the basic public key used for each time period. Usually, this requires increase in storage space (compared to the basic scheme) by a noticeable—at least logarithmic—factor: to maintain the current (public) certificates and the (secret) keys for issuing future certificates.

Generic forward secure schemes also require longer verification times than the ordinary signatures do: the verifier must verify the certification of the basic key for the current time period in addition to verifying the actual signature with that basic key. The verification of the basic key can require multiple signature verifications—for each step of the certification chain. There is, in fact, a trade-off between storage space and verification time.

### Static Schemes

The scheme proposed by Anderson (1997) is the first scheme of this type. It uses a flat—one level—certification hierarchy. The public key PK for his scheme is the certification key. All the basic keys and their certificates are generated at the key-generation stage (certificate for each basic public key includes the time period for which this key is to be used). The certification secret key is then destroyed. The rest of the scheme is then much the same as under "Forward Secure Public Key Crypto: Naive Generic Construction," except each signature is augmented by the certificate for the corresponding public key. Thus, for this scheme, the public key is just a single basic public key. However, the secret key must contain $T$ basic secret keys and as many certificates.

Krawczyk (2003) improves this construction, reducing the secret key storage to only the secret key of a fsPRG (in his construction, a single secret). This is achieved by recomputing the secret keys with the help of the fsPRG as described under "Forward Secure Public Key Crypto: Naive Generic Construction." This still leaves the storage of as many as $T$ certificates.

Further optimization (also suggested in Krawczyk, 2000) is to use the standard Merkle tree-hash construction (Merkle, 1989). Consider a finite binary tree; let each leaf store arbitrary value and each nonleaf store a hash of its children, for some cryptographic hash function. Then the root can serve as the certification key, where each leaf $l$ is certified with the values in the nodes adjacent to its path to the root $P(l)$. This construction reduces both the secret and public key sizes to 1. However, its signature verification requires an additional $T$ hash function evaluations, and an update at time $t$ takes time linear in $T - t$.

These two variants illustrate the trade-off between the storage space on the one hand and verification and update times on the other. However, using the recent results on traversing Merkle trees (Szydlo, 2004), it is possible to reduce all these costs—storage, verification, and update—to logarithmic.

In all these schemes, all the basic public keys are generated at the setup time—that is why we group them under the heading of static schemes. In particular, these schemes must have a known upper bound $T$ on the number of time periods. Moreover, the setup time is proportional to $T$ (for some of the schemes, even the update time or storage are linear in $T$). Next, we consider schemes that remove this limitation.

## Dynamic Schemes

These schemes constructed their certification tree completely at the setup time—next, we consider schemes that construct the certification hierarchy on the "as needed" basis. That is, at each time the signer maintains the current basic key as well as (the minimal set of) the basic keys required to certify all the future (but not the past) basic keys.

The first such scheme was proposed by Bellare and Miner (1999). Essentially, they used a certification tree of height $\lg T$. This resulted in the verification needing to check additional $\lg T$ certification signatures. It was observed in Merkle (1988) for standard (and in Abdalla & Reyzin, 2000, for the forward secure schemes, which use similar certificates) that each certifying public key is used only for authenticating a single message—the corresponding certificate of the children's public keys—and thus one-time signatures (Lamport, 1979; Merkle, 2002) are sufficient for this purpose. These signatures offer greater efficiency (see, e.g., Reyzin & Reyzin, 2002, and references there).

A few different certification topologies have been considered. A balanced $\lg T$ height tree used in Bellare and Miner (1999) limits the total number of periods. This limit was extended to be exponential in a security parameter $k$ by Malkin et al. (2002). Their tree consists of a relatively small balanced tree, each leaf of which is a root of another balanced tree. The height of a tree rooted at the $i$-th leaf of the top tree is $i$. Thus, for a top tree of height $\lg k$, it contains $k$ trees (for simplicity, assume $k$ is a power of 2). Thus, the whole tree contains $T = 2^k - 1$ leaves.

As pointed out in Itkis (2002), both of these tree structures represent special cases of prefixless encoding, and any other prefixless encoding will work for this purpose and may offer greater efficiency. In particular, using this approach, $T$ is truly unbounded and the signatures at time period $t$ require checking $\lg t + o(\lg t)$ certifications.

The same prefixless coding construction can be applied to the static schemes to reduce the signature length and verification time at time $t$ to be logarithmic in $t$ (as opposed to $T$ in the original constructions). The cost of update is still likely to require time (and probably storage) logarithmic in $T$. This motivates a further study of applying the techniques of Jakobsson, Leighton, Micali, and Szydlo (2003) and Szydlo (2003) to traversing "slanted" Merkle trees (e.g., corresponding to the prefixless encodings).

Although we can achieve compatible or even lower costs of running (but not setup) for the static schemes, the dynamic schemes still have the advantage of being able to support an unbounded number of periods (i.e., $T = \infty$), whereas the static schemes cannot handle even very large values of $T$, because the setup still takes $\Omega(T)$.

## Concrete Constructions

A number of forward secure schemes based on a specific number of theoretic assumptions and ordinary signature schemes have been proposed. As most of the practical ordinary signature schemes, most of the proposed concrete forward secure schemes are in the random oracle model. Clearly, any security proof in the random oracle model is no more than a "heuristic evidence" of security when the random oracle is instantiated by some cryptographic hash function, as is the common practice.[8] Forward secure signature scheme, whose security is proven based only on a strong RSA assumption (i.e., without the random oracle), was recently proposed by Camenisch and Koprowski (2003). In addition to not relying on random oracles, their construction allows a finer grain of forward security. Namely the signatures can be numbered within each period; then, even the signatures issued during the exposure period but prior to the exposure remain secure. The other schemes in this section are proven secure in the random oracle model.

The forward secure signature schemes based on factoring include those by Bellare and Miner (1999), based on the Fiat–Shamir scheme (Fiat & Shamir, 1986), and by Abdalla and Reyzin (2000), based on the $2^t$-th root scheme (Micali, 1994; Ohta & Okamoto, 1998; Ong & Schnorr, 1990). The schemes by Itkis and Reyzin (2001) based on the GQ signatures (Guillou & Quisquater, 2002), and Kozlov and Reyzin (2002) also require factoring to be hard, but it is not sufficient—strong RSA assumption is used (see Barific & Pfitzmann, 1997; Fujisaki & Okamoto, 1997; Itkis & Reyzin, 2001; Kozlov & Reyzin, 2002). We are not aware of any forward secure signature schemes based on discrete logarithms or DH assumptions.

These concrete schemes are sufficiently sophisticated that the in-depth coverage of these schemes is impractical in this survey. The reader is referred to the original articles for the details of the constructions and proofs. Here, we restrict ourselves to the high-level discussion and comparison of the schemes. Both Bellare and Miner (1999) and Abdalla and Reyzin (2000) require signing and verification times that are linear in $T$.

The scheme of Itkis and Reyzin (2001) reduces the signing and verifying times, signature sizes, and storage costs to be essentially the same as for the ordinary GQ signatures. However, the update time of the Itkis–Reyzin scheme is proportional to $T$ if the storage is kept minimum (one extra key). Increasing the storage to be logarithmic in $T$, the update costs can be reduced to logarithmic as well.

The Kozlov–Reyzin signature scheme improves the update time to just a single modular squaring but at a high price: the verifier must now perform $2(T - t)$ multiplications per period (in addition to verifying each individual signature—the cost of that operation is compatible with the Itkis–Reyzin scheme, though is slightly greater). Thus, this scheme can be efficient for the signer, especially for the case of frequent updates (see Kozlov & Reyzin, 2002, for the detailed performance comparison), but not for verifier (in fact, the verifier's cost exceeds the signer's cost of Itkis and Reyzin [2001], making it more compatible

---

[8] Use of random oracles in cryptography is a topic of ongoing debate. For example, Koblitz and Menezes (2004) survey some of the recent results intended to cast doubt on the random oracle model, but interpret them as actually supporting the model.

to (but better than) the costs of the Bellare–Miner and Abdalla–Reyzin.

## Time Period Bound

All these schemes require at least some computation (at least in the setup stage) to be linear in $T$. Therefore, none of the current nongeneric constructions have the advantage of the dynamic generic schemes that allow an unbounded number of time periods.

## Time–Space Trade-off: Pebbling

Both the Itkis–Reyzin and Kozlov–Reyzin scheme use an interesting technique of pebbling (suggested in Itkis & Reyzin, 2001) to optimize certain computation costs at a modest (logarithmic) increase in storage cost. This technique is of independent interest and in particular inspired (and is essentially equivalent to) the research into hash-chains computation (Coppersmith & Jakobsson, 2002; Jakobsson, 2002; Sella, 2003).

## FORWARD-SECURE PUBLIC KEY ENCRYPTION

We outlined under "Forward Secure Public Key Crypto: Naive Generic Construction" a trivial way of constructing various public key schemes (including encryption). That approach, however, is largely impractical, because it incurs linear in $T$ costs even in the most fundamental parameters, most importantly, the public key.

The only scheme to date that overcomes such high costs is provided by Canetti, Halevi, and Katz (2003). This scheme builds on the hierarchical identity-based encryption (HIBE) of Gentry and Silverberg (2002), which in turn is based on Boneh and Franklin's identity based encryption (Boneh & Franklin, 2001, 2003). All of these schemes are based on the bilinear Diffie–Hellman assumption (BDH). As was the case for the concrete signature schemes, it is impractical to describe the construction and the proofs for the schemes, so we restrict ourselves to only the high-level discussion and the reader is referred to the original articles for details.

Obtaining nontrivial public key encryption schemes based on more standard assumptions such as factoring, RSA, discrete log, or Diffie–Hellman (DDH or CDH) are still an open problem.

Intuitively, HIBE schemes define a tree (possibly non-binary) such that the tree has a single "master" public key associated with the whole tree and a secret key associated with each node. The encryption algorithm using the "master" public key and the ID of any tree node $v$ can encrypt a message so that it can be decrypted using the secret key for any of the ancestors of $v$. Moreover, the secret key for a node can be derived from the secret key of its parent. This derivation is one way: the parent's secret key cannot be derived from a child's key.

The IBE and HIBE constructions of Boneh and Franklin (2001, 2003) and Boyko (1999) needed to be extended slightly (which was achieved by some relaxation of security, which did not affect the forward security scheme), resulting in a slightly different version of HIBE.

The new HIBE scheme proposed in Canetti et al. (2003) had an additional advantage of being secure in the standard model (without the random oracles required in the previous constructions). Furthermore, the previous constructions were extended in Canetti et al. (2003) to (binary) trees of arbitrary depth.

With these tools, the forward secure encryption can use any of the prefixless encodings techniques much as under "Generic Constructions" to obtain the costs proportional to $\lg t$ for any operation at time $t$ (encryption, decryption, or key update). The ciphertext and secret keys similarly grow linearly in $\lg t$.

## CONCLUSION
### Forward Security: Open Problems

Forward secure cryptography is a fairly well-studied field, as might be seen even from this survey. However, a number of interesting open questions remain.

### Forward Secure Public Key Encryption Based on RSA or DH

The forward secure public key encryption schemes discussed under "Forward Secure Public Key Encryption" is based on the BDH assumption, which is somewhat less "standard" than some of the other assumptions such as RSA, strong RSA, decisional or computation DH assumptions, and so on. Although groups where the BDH assumption appears to hold are known, these groups are not as simple as the $Z_n^*$. Therefore, it would be very interesting to find forward secure encryption schemes that work in such groups and are based on the more common assumptions mentioned herein.

### Forward Secure Signatures: Efficiency and Removing Random Oracles

"Concrete Constructions" described some forward secure signature schemes, whose signing and verifying is as efficient as for ordinary (GQ) signatures. However, some of the other operations costs for these schemes depended on $T$: although the memory and update costs were only logarithmic in $T$, the key generation was $\Theta(T)$. Can these overheads be reduced or even removed? Some generic schemes do achieve independence from $T$ at the cost of introducing logarithmic (in current time period $t$) overhead in the signature size and the verification cost (there is no overhead for signing, and the update overhead can be amortized to be just an additive constant). This may be acceptable in practice, but avoiding such overhead altogether would be much more appealing.

Most of the signature schemes deployed in real systems do not have a full security proof: their security proofs rely on using random oracles in the constructions. In real life, these oracles do not exist and are replaced with "cryptographic hash functions" or pseudorandom functions, such as MD5 or SHA1. This renders the security proofs inapplicable (see, e.g., Goldwasser & Kalai, 2003, and the bibliography there). Signature schemes whose security proofs do not rely on random oracles have been proposed (e.g., the classic Goldwasser, Micali & Rivest, 1988, or more recent and more efficient Cramer & Shoup, 2000; Naccache, Pointcheval, & Stern, 2001). Are there forward secure variants of these schemes that have similar performance characteristics?

## Static Generic Schemes: Traversing Slanted Merkle Trees

The recent algorithms for the efficient traversal of the Merkle trees (Szydlo, 2002) can improve performance of the static generic constructions for the forward secure signatures. However, these still have the $\Theta(\lg T)$ overhead. The verification overhead of such static schemes can be improved to lg t for the current time period $t$ by using the prefixless encodings constructions. Can the Merkle tree traversal algorithms be adjusted for these prefixless trees? What is the best performance that can be obtained for such "slanted" trees traversals?

## Evolving Cryptography: Beyond Forward Security

As discussed under "Key Security," forward security provides an important tool for protecting the key and in a way represents a new fundamental development of cryptography: making it more resilient.

A number of articles (including those mentioned under "Forward Secure Crytography") have addressed adding forward security to other schemes. For more examples of such combinations—solved and open—the reader is referred to Bellare (1989). Although many of such combinations are very important, we focus on what we see as building on a more fundamental aspect of forward security.

We also discussed the time evolution aspect of the forward security. This trend had a number of subsequent developments.

## Cryptographic Tamper Evidence

No matter which security tools are utilized, a prudent security architect will always consider the case that the security is broken. In such cases, it is often desired to revoke the key or undertake other similarly dramatic recovery steps (this might be required even for forward secure systems, as discussed under "Key Evolution"). Thus, it is important to detect when the security is broken.

Until recently, this tamper detection was mainly achieved by heuristic methods, such as intrusion-detection systems. Indeed, it might seem that cryptography is powerless against an adversary who steals all the secrets. However, evolving cryptography opens some possibilities.

Any cryptographic system undergoes an important change after the adversary steals the secret keys of a user: the system would now have two players, where there is supposed to be one (the legitimate user and the adversary with the stolen secrets, both playing the same role). These two players would actually "diverge" if at least one of them evolves in a randomized fashion. Furthermore, in some scenarios—such as signatures—both of these players might produce some output (e.g., legitimate and forged signatures). This makes it possible to detect the divergence.

More specifically, Itkis (2003) defines *tamper evident signature schemes* offering an additional procedure *Div*, which detects tampering: given two signatures, Div can determine whether one of them was generated by the forger (essentially, Div detects divergence of the legitimate user and the forger). Surprisingly, this is possible even after the adversary has inconspicuously learned some—or even *all*—of the secrets in the system. In this case, it might be impossible to tell which signature is generated by the legitimate signer and which by the forger, but at least the fact of the tampering will be made evident.

Itkis (2003) defines several variants of tamper evidence, differing in the power to detect tampering. In all of these, an equally powerful adversary is assumed: he or she *adaptively* controls *all* the inputs to the legitimate signer (i.e., all messages to be signed and their timing) and observes *all* of his or her outputs (i.e., all signatures); he or she can also adaptively expose *all the secrets* at arbitrary times.

Itkis (2003) provides tamper-evident schemes for all the variants and proves their optimality by showing tight lower bounds. These lower bounds are perhaps more surprising than the constructions. The lower-bound proofs are information theoretic and thus cannot be broken by any methods (including by introducing any number of theoretic or algebraic complexity assumptions).

## General Key Evolution: Recovery

As mentioned previously, a seasoned security architect will always address the case of security compromise. The first issue to address—detecting the compromise—is discussed previously. But then recovery mechanisms from such compromises are required. For digital signatures, such a recovery should ideally—and when possible—include invalidation of the signatures issued with the compromised keys.

Recovery from one special case of compromises—extortion—were considered in Naccache et al. (2001). There, so-called *monotone signatures* were defined. In monotone signatures, a user can be forced (e.g., at gun point) to release the secret key. In this case, the user releases a "fake" secret key. This key generates signatures which look perfectly valid under the current public key. However, at a later time (once out of the danger), the user updates his public key. Under the new public key, all the signatures generated by the user before or after the extortion remain valid. But the signatures generated by the adversary using the extorted key become invalid under the new public key.

Itkis and Xie (2003) generalizes this work. It considers two models for key exposures: full and partial reveal. In the first, a key exposure reveals *all* the secrets currently existing in the system. This model is suitable for the pessimistic inconspicuous exposures scenario. The partial reveal model permits the signer to conceal some information under exposure (e.g., under coercive exposures, the signer is able to reveal a "fake" secret key). The monotone signatures assume the partial reveal model in this terminology.

Itkis and Xie (2003) propose a definition of *generalized key evolving signature scheme*, which unifies forward security and security against the coercive and inconspicuous key exposures (previously considered separately in Bellare & Miner, 1999; Itkis, 2003; Naccache et al., 2001). We based our definitions in this review in part on the definitions of Itkis and Xie (2003).

The new models helped to address certain repudiation problems inherent in the monotone signatures (Naccache et al., 2001) and achieve performance improvements.

### Intrusion-Resilience: Space–Time Combination

Forward secure cryptography protects the past time periods even when the current secret key is exposed. But what about protecting the future? Key-insulated cryptography (Dodis, Katz, Xu, & Yung, 2002, 2003) attempted to provide some security to the future. In that model the user is partitioned into two modules: *actor* and *base*. This is somewhat akin to the threshold cryptography model. However, unlike the threshold model, all the transactions are performed by the actor alone. Only the updates require the base to communicate with the actor, sending it an update message. Without such a message, the actor cannot update itself to the next period—thus, an adversary who steals the actor's secret key but does not receive the update message loses her advantage at the end of the time period, as the stolen secret key expires. Exposures of the base alone do not provide any useful information to the adversary. However, if the adversary exposes both base and actor at arbitrary times (and in some variants, even with sufficiently many exposures of only the actor), all the security is lost, including the past. The intrusion-resilient model (Itkis & Reyzin, 2002a) eliminated these security limitations. This model also uses the two modules: actor and base. However, it really combines all the benefits of the forward security and proactive crypto (see "Threshold and Proactive Cryptography"). Thus, the intrusion-resilient model can truly be considered as a time–space combination. In particular, the intrusion-resilient model tolerates arbitrarily many break-ins into both actor and base in arbitrary order. As long as these break-ins are not simultaneous, the only time periods that are compromised are those for which the actor was exposed.[9] Moreover, if a simultaneous exposure does occur, then the past periods remain secure (the future in this case obviously cannot be protected, because the adversary now knows the full state of the system).

The granularity of the exposures is determined by the frequency of *refresh* messages, similar to those used in the proactive security. Namely if there is at least one refresh message not seen by an adversary between two exposures, then these exposures are not considered to be simultaneous. If the update message must be sent from the base to the actor exactly once in a time period, the refresh messages can be sent as frequently as desired—more when the user feels his system is under the attack.

Intrusion-resilient schemes for signatures (Itkis, 2002; Itkis & Reyzin, 2002a) and for public key encryption (Dodis et al., 2003; Dodis, Franklin, Katz, Miyaji, & Yung, 2004) have been proposed. Itkis and Reyzin (2002a) build on the concrete construction of Itkis and Reyzin (2001), whereas Itkis (2002) proposes a generic scheme based on an arbitrary ordinary signature scheme. Similarly, for

the public key encryption, Dodis et al. (2003) propose a scheme based on specific algebraic assumptions, whereas Dodis et al. (2004) present a generic construction based on any *forward secure* encryption scheme with certain homomorphic properties.

Interrelations among intrusion-resilient, key-insulated, forward-secure, and so-called proxy signatures were recently studied in Malkin, Obana, & Yung (2002).

## From Theory to Practice

Key evolving cryptographic schemes offer potential benefits in a number of practical areas. Applications to PKI for intrusion-resilient and key-insulated signatures were suggested in Itkis and Reyzin (2002) and Le, Ouyang, Ford, and Makedon (2004), respectively. Other applications could be timed commitments, bidding, time-stamped delegation, and many others.

Many of these applications can have a significant practical impact. This is especially true for the case of PKI-related applications, because PKI is already widely deployed and used.

This transfer from theory to practice could be facilitated in particular by extending various cryptographic standards to accommodate key evolving cryptography. Additionally, integrating the key evolving cryptographic tools into the popular protocols (e.g., SSL/TLS) would also increase security and potentially even offer infrastructure savings.

In fact, most of the cryptographic tools deployed today already include (implicitly and/or "out of band") some form of key evolution in the form of key revocation, periodic changes of the secret keys (e.g., as in pay-TV data streams), or even password changes. Explicit integration of key evolution promises to leverage existing key evolving crypto tools, as well as enable and stimulate future productive research and progress in this direction.

## GLOSSARY

**Authentication**  Typically, assurance that a message was sent (authorized) by the purported author (and was not modified in transmission). Authentication mechanisms include *public key* (*digital signatures*) and *symmetric* (*MACs*) cryptography tools.

**Certificate**  A document associating a particular *public key* with a particular entity (e.g., user, corporation, privilege). Certificate is typically a record containing a *public key* and the entity it is associated with, *signed* by a *certification authority*. The entity (or its representative) typically holds the secret *private key* corresponding to the certified public key.

**Certification Authority**  An authority trusted within the appropriate *PKI* to issue and manage *certificates*.

**Certificate Revocation**  A mechanism to revoke certificates: identify those certificates that should not be trusted (e.g., if the corresponding private key has been *exposed*).

**Cryptographic Hash**  An efficiently computable function $h$, for which it is infeasible to find $x \neq y$ such that $h(x) = h(y)$. Cryptographic hash must be a *one-way function*, but a one-way function is not necessarily a cryptographic hash.

---

[9] The concept of exposure must be extended to include the trivial indirect exposure: When the actor is exposed at time period $t$ and the adversary intercepts all the messages from the base, including the next update message, then clearly the actor should be considered exposed at time $t + 1$ as well.

**Hash Tree**   A tree where the leaves are associated with some input values, and for each internal node, its value is the cryptographic hash of its children.

**Key Exposure**   An event of an adversary learning the secret (private) key.

**Message Authentication Code**   A symmetric cryptography mechanism for message *authentication*. Typically implemented as a keyed *one-way function* or *cryptographic hash*.

**Nonrepudiation**   A cryptographic service that (legally) prevents the originator of a message from denying authorship/authorization at a later date. This service can be generalized to other transactions.

**Merkle Tree**   See *hash tree*.

**One-Way Function**   An efficiently computable function but whose inverse is not efficiently computable.

**Private Key**   A value kept secret by its owner and used to perform operations that are intended to be available only to him/her (e.g., digitally sign his/her messages and/or documents, or read [decrypt] secret messages intended only for this private key owner). A private key is typically associated with a *public key*.

**Pseudorandom**   Indistinguishable from random.

**Pseudorandom number generator**   An algorithm computing a pseudorandom string from a random (but shorter) *seed*.

**Pseudorandom function**   A function of a seed and an index, such that for a random seed the string of the function outputs for all the indices is pseudorandom.

**Public Key**   A publicly available value associated with a particular secret *private key* and used to perform operations that are intended for the general public (e.g., verifying a digital signature or encrypting a message for a particular user [the holder of the corresponding private key]). A public key is often associated with the owner of the corresponding *private key* (e.g., by means of a *certificate* within a particular *PKI*).

**Public Key Cryptography**   A collection of algorithms and protocols utilizing related pairs of *public* and *private keys*, used for complementary operations: e.g., signing with the private key while verifying the signature using the corresponding public key; or encrypting using the public key and decrypting using the corresponding private key. Computing outputs of private key operations should be infeasible without the proper private key.

**Public Key Infrastructure**   A mechanism for associating public keys with entities such as users, corporations, privileges, authorizations, and so on. PKI typically includes servers and logistical mechanisms and policies and implies particular trust relations. PKI typically consists of a set of *certification authorities* administering *certificates*: their issuing, maintaining, and revoking.

**Random Function**   A function whose outputs are random: unpredictable for any input value, even when given the outputs for all the other input values.

**Random Oracle**   A random function given as a "black box." Random oracle is an abstract construct, in practice often emulated using a cryptographic hash. Proofs of security of some cryptographic mechanisms assume access to a random oracle; such proofs of security may not apply when the random oracle is implemented as an actual algorithm. Security of such mechanisms is a subject of much debate and research.

**Repudiation**   An attempt to disavow a prior commitment, authorization, or transaction (e.g., an attempt to deny *signing* a particular document).

**Signature**   A value used to authenticate a message as authorized by the *signer*. The *signer* computes the signature as a function of the message being signed and the signer's *secret (private) key*. The signature can be *verified* using the *public key* associated with the signer's private key. Computing a valid signature (the one that verifies as valid with a proper public key) should be infeasible without the private key.

**Symmetric Cryptography**   A collection of algorithms and protocols utilizing a single secret key, such that complementary operations, such as encrypting and decrypting, use the same key. This is in contrast to *public key cryptography* where analogous complementary operations require different keys.

## CROSS REFERENCES

See *Digital Signatures and Electronic Signatures; Encryption Basics; PKI (Public Key Infrastructure)*.

## ACKNOWLEDGMENT

This material is based on work supported by the National Science Foundation under Grant 0311485.

## REFERENCES

Abdalla, M., An, J. H., Bellare, M., & Namprempre, C. (2002). From identification to signatures via the Fiat–Shamir transform: Minimizing assumptions for security and forward-security. In L. Knudsen (ed.), *Lecture notes in computer science, vol. 2332: Advances in Cryptology—EUROCRYPT '2002* (pp. 418–433). Berlin: Springer-Verlag.

Abdalla, M., Miner, S., & Namprempre, C. (2001). Forward-secure threshold signature schemes. In D. Naccache (ed.), *Lecture notes in computer science, vol. 2020: Progress in Cryptology* (pp. 143–158). Berlin: Springer-Verlag.

Abdalla, M., & Reyzin, L. (2000). A new forward-secure digital signature scheme. In T. Okamoto (ed.), *Lecture notes in computer science, vol. 1976: Advances in Cryptology, ASIACRYPT 2000* (pp. 116–129). Berlin: Springer-Verlag.

Proceedings of the Twentieth Annual ACM Symposium on Theory of Computing, Chicago, Illinois, 2–4 May 1988.

Anderson, R. (1997). Invited lecture. In Fourth ACM Conference on Computer and Communication Security [1] (see also [8]).

Anderson, R. (2002). *Two remarks on public key cryptology* (Technical Report UCAM-CL-TR-549). Cambridge, UK: University of Cambridge, Computer Laboratory.

Back, A. (1996). *Non-interactive forward secrecy*. Retrieved June 9, 1996, from http://cypherpunks.venona.com/date/1996/09/msg00561.html

Barak, B., Herzberg, A., Naor, D., & Shai, E. (1999). The proactive security toolkit and applications. In G. Tsudik (ed.), *Proceedings of the 5th ACM Conference on Computer and Communications Security* (pp. 18–27). Singapore: ACM Press.

Barific, N., & Pfitzmann, B. (1997). Collision-free accumulators and fail-stop signature schemes without trees. In W. Fumy (ed.), *Lecture notes in computer science. vol. 1233: Advances in Cryptology, EUROCRYPT '97* (pp. 480–494). Berlin: Springer-Verlag.

Beave, D. (1999). Server-assisted cryptography. In *New Security Paradigms Workshop* (pp. 92–106). Association for Computing Machinery.

Beguin, P., & Quisquater, J. -J. (1995). Fast server-aided RSA signatures secure against active attacks. In *Lecture notes in computer science* (vol. 963).

Bellare, M. (1989). An automatic crypto research topic or paper title generator. Retrieved January 8, 2004, from http://www.cs.ucsd.edu/users/mihir/crypto-topic-generator.html

Bellare, M., & Miner, S. (1999). A forward-secure digital signature scheme. In M. Wiener, (ed.), *Lecture notes in computer science, vol. 1666: Advances in Cryptology, CRYPTO '99* (pp. 431–448). Berlin: Springer-Verlag.

Bellare, M., & Yee, B. (2001). *Forward security in private key cryptography*. Report 2001/035, Cryptology ePrint Archive. Retrieved January 4, 2004, from http://eprint.iacr.org/2001/035.ps.gz

Bellare, M., & Yee, B. (2003). Forward security in private key cryptography. In *CTRSA: CTRSA, The Cryptographers' Track at RSA Conference*.

Ben-Or, M., Goldwasser, S. & Wigderson, A. (1998). Completeness theorems for noncryptographic fault-tolerant distributed computation (extended abstract). In ACM [6], pages 1–10.

Blaze, M. (1995). *High-bandwidth encryption with low-bandwidth smartcards*. Technical report, AT&T Bell Laboratories. Retrieved October 12, 1995, ftp://research.att.com/dist/mab/cardcipher.ps

Blaze, M. (1996). High-bandwidth encryption with low-bandwidth smartcards. In D. Grollman (ed.), *Lecture notes in computer science, vol. 1039: Fast Software Encryption: Third International Workshop* (pp. 33–40). Berlin: Springer-Verlag.

Blaze, M., Feigenbaum, J. & Naor, M. (1998). A formal treatment of remotely keyed encryption. In *Advances in Cryptology—EUROCRYPT '98* (pp. 251–265).

Blum, M., & Micali, S. (1984). How to generate cryptographically strong sequences of pseudorandom bits. *SIAM Journal on Computing*, 13(4), 850–863.

Boneh, D., & Franklin, M. (1997). Efficient generation of shared RSA keys. In *Proceedings of the 17th International Advances in Cryptology Conference—CRYPTO '97* (pp. 425–439).

Boneh, D., & Franklin, M. (2001). Identity-based encryption from the Weil Pairing. In J. Kilian (ed.), *Advances in Cryptology—CRYPTO 2001, Lecture notes in computer science, vol. 2139:* (pp. 213–229). Berlin: Springer-Verlag.

Boneh, D., & Franklin, M. (2003). Identity-based encryption from the Weil pairing. *SIAM Journal on Computing*, 32(3), 586–615.

Boyko, V. (1999). On the security properties of OAEP as an all-or-nothing transform. In *Proceedings of the 19th International Advances in Cryptology Conference—CRYPTO '99* (pp. 503–518).

Boyko, V. *On all-or-nothing transforms and password-authenticated key exchange protocols*. Ph.D. thesis, Department of Electrical Engineering and Computer Science, MIT. Retrieved May 2000 from http://theory.lcs.mit.edu/cis/theses/victorphd.ps.gz

Brassard, G. (Ed.). (1990). *Lecture notes in computer science, vol. 435: Advances in Cryptology, CRYPTO '89* Berlin: Springer-Verlag.

Cachin, C., & Camenisch, J. (eds.). (2004). *Lecture notes in computer science vol. 3027: Advances in Cryptology, EUROCRYPT 2004, International Conference on the Theory and Applications of Cryptographic Techniques*. Berlin: Springer-Verlag.

Camenisch, J., & Koprowski, M. Fine-grained forward-secure signature schemes without random oracles. In *International Workshop on Coding and Cryptography*. INRIA and ENSTA, 2003.

Canetti, R., Dodis, Y., Halevi, S., Kushilevitz, E., & Sahai, A. Exposure-resilient functions and all-or-nothing transforms. In Preneel [110] (pp. 453–469).

Canetti, R., Gennaro, R., Jarecki, S., Krawczyk, H., & Rabin, T. (1999). Adaptive security for threshold cryptosystems. In *Proceedings of the 19th International Advances in Cryptology Conference—CRYPTO '99* (pp. 98–115).

Canetti, R., Halevi, S., & Herzberg, A. (2000). Maintaining authenticated communication in the presence of break-ins. *Journal of Cryptology*, 13(1), 61–105.

Canetti, R., Halevi, S., & Katz, J. (2003). A forward secure public key encryption scheme. In E. Biham (ed.), *Lecture notes in computer science, vol. 2656: Advances in Cryptology, Eurocrypt 2003*. Berlin: Springer-Verlag.

Caronni, G., Waldvogel, M., Sun, D., Weiler, N., & Plattner, B. (1999). The VersaKey framework: Versatile group key management. *IEEE Journal on Selected Areas in Communications*, 17(9), 1614–1631.

Chaum, D., Crfiepeau, C., & Damgfiard, I. (1998). Multiparty unconditionally secure protocols (extended abstract). In ACM [6], pages 11–19.

Coppersmith, D., & Jakobsson, M. (2002). Almost optimal hash sequence traversal. In *Lecture notes in computer science, vol. 2357: Proceedings of the Fourth Conference on Financial Cryptography* (FC '02). Berlin: Springer-Verlag.

Cramer, R., & Shoup, V. (2000). Signature schemes based on the strong RSA assumption. *ACM Transactions on Information and System Security*, 3(3), 161–185.

I. B. Damgfiard (Ed.). (1991). *Lecture notes in computer science, vol. 473: Advances in Cryptology, EUROCRYPT '90*. Berlin: Springer-Verlag.

Desmedt, Y. (1997). Some recent research aspects of threshold cryptography. In *Proceedings of the 1st International Information Security Workshop* (pp. 158–173).

Desmedt, Y., & Frankel, Y. (1989). Threshold cryptosystems. In Brassard [28], pages 307–315.

Diffie, W., & Hellman, M. E. (1976). New directions in cryptography. *IEEE Transactions on Information Theory*, IT-22(6), 644–654.

Dodis, Y., (2000). Exposure-resilient cryptography. Ph.D. thesis, Department of Electrical Engineering and Computer Science, MIT. Retrieved August 2000 from http://www.toc.lcs.mit.edu/yevgen/ps/phd-thesis.ps

Dodis, Y., Franklin, M., Katz, J., Miyaji, A., & Yung, M. (2003). Intrusion-resilient public-key encryption. In *Progress in Cryptology*, CT-RSA 2003 [2], pages 19–32.

Dodis, Y., Franklin, M., Katz, J., Miyaji, A., & Yung, M. (2004). A generic construction for intrusion-resilient public-key encryption. In *Lecture notes in computer science, vol. 2964: Progress in Cryptology, CT-RSA* (pp. 81–98). Berlin: Springer-Verlag.

Dodis, Y., Katz, J., Xu, S., & Yung, M. (2002). Key-insulated public key cryptosystems. In Knudsen [80].

Dodis, Y., Katz, J., Xu, S., & Yung, M. (2003). Strong key-insulated signature schemes. In *International Workshop on Practice and Theory in Public Key Cryptography*.

Dodis, Y., Sahai, A., & Smith, A. (2001). On perfect and adaptive security in exposure-resilient cryptography. In B. Pfitzmann (ed.), *Lecture notes in computer science, vol. 2045: Advances in Cryptology, EUROCRYPT 2001* (pp. 301–324). Berlin: Springer-Verlag.

Duc, Cheon, & Kim. (2003). A forward-secure blind signature scheme based on the strong RSA assumption. In *Lecture notes in computer science: International Conference on Information and Communications Security*.

ElGamal, T. (1985). A public key cryptosystem and a signature scheme based on discrete logarithms. In G. R. Blakley & D. Chaum (eds.), *Lecture notes in computer science, vol. 196: Advances in Cryptology: Proceedings of CRYPTO '84* (pp. 10–18). Berin: Springer-Verlag.

Feige, U., Fiat, A., & Shamir, A. (1988). Zero-knowledge proofs of identity. *Journal of Cryptology*, 1(2), 77–94.

Fiat, A., & Shamir, A. (1987). How to prove yourself: Practical solutions to identification and signature problems. In A. M. Odlyzko (ed.), *Lecture notes in computer science, vol. 263: Advances in Cryptology, CRYPTO '86* (pp. 186–194). Berlin: Springer-Verlag.

Fourth ACM Conference on Computer and Communication Security. ACM, Apr. 1–4 1997.

Frankel, Y., Gemmell, P., MacKenzie, P. D., & Yung, M. (1997). Proactive RSA. In *Proceedings of the 17th International Advances in Cryptology Conference—CRYPTO '97* (pp. 440–454).

Fujisaki, E., & Okamoto, T. (1997). Statistical zero knowledge protocols to prove modular polynomial relations. In B. S. Kaliski, Jr. (ed.), *Lecture notes in computer science, vol. 1294: Advances in Cryptology, CRYPTO '97* (pp. 16–30). Berlin: Springer-Verlag.

Gennaro, R., Jarecki, S., Krawczyk, H., & Rabin, T. (1996). Robust threshold DSS signatures. In U. Maurer (ed.), *Lecture notes in computer science, vol. 1070: Advances in Cryptology, EUROCRYPT '96* (pp. 354–371). Berlin: Springer-Verlag.

Gentry, X., & Silverberg, X. (2002). Hierarchical ID-based cryptography. In *Lecture notes in computer science: ASIACRYPT: Advances in Cryptology—ASIACRYPT: International Conference on the Theory and Application of Cryptology*. Berlin: Springer-Verlag.

Girault, M. (1990). An identity-based identification scheme based on discrete logarithms modulo a composite number. In Damgfiard [36] (pp. 481–486).

Goldreich, O., & Levin, L. (1989). A hard-core predicate for all one-way functions. In *Proceedings of the Twenty-First Annual ACM Symposium on Theory of Computing* (pp. 25–32).

Goldreich, O., Micali, S., & Wigderson, A. (1986). Proofs that yield nothing but their validity and a methodology of cryptographic protocol design (extended abstract). In *27th Annual Symposium on Foundations of Computer Science* (pp. 174–187).

Goldreich, O., Micali, S., & Wigderson, A. (1987). How to play any mental game or a completeness theorem for protocols with honest majority. In *Proceedings of the Nineteenth Annual ACM Symposium on Theory of Computing* (pp. 218–229).

Goldwasser, S. (ed.). (1990). *Lecture notes in computer science, vol. 403: Advances in Cryptology, CRYPTO '88*. Berlin: Springer-Verlag.

Goldwasser, S., & Kalai, Y. T. (2003). On the (in)security of the Fiat–Shamir paradigm. In *Proceedings of the 44th Symposium on Foundations of Computer Science*. IEEE Computer Society Press.

Goldwasser, S., Micali, S., & Rivest, R. L. (1988). A digital signature scheme secure against adaptive chosen-message attacks. *SIAM Journal on Computing*, 17(2), 281–308.

Guillou, L. C., & Quisquater, J. -J. (2002). A "paradoxical" indentity-based signature scheme resulting from zero knowledge. In Goldwasser [61] (pp. 216–231).

Günther, C. (1989). An identity-based key-exchange protocol. In Brassard [28].

Hfiastad, J., Impagliazzo, R., Levin, L., & Luby, M. (1999). Construction of pseudorandom generator from any one-way function. *SIAM Journal on Computing*, 28(4), 1364–1396.

Herzberg, A., Jakobsson, M., Jarecki, S., Krawczyk, H., & Yung, M. (1997). Proactive public key and signature systems. In Fourth ACM Conference on Computer and Communication Security [1], pages 100–110.

Itkis, G. (2002). Intrusion-resilient signatures: Generic constructions, or defeating strong adversary with minimal assumptions. In SCN02 [114].

Itkis, G. (2003). Cryptographic tamper evidence. In *10th ACM Conference on Computer and Communication Security*.

Itkis, G., & Levin, L. A. (1989). Power of fast VLSI models is insensitive to wires' thinness. In *30th Annual Symposium on Foundations of Computer Science* (pp. 402–407).

Itkis, G., & Reyzin, L. (2001). Forward-secure signatures with optimal signing and verifying. In J. Kilian (ed.), *Lecture notes in computer science, vol. 2139: Advances in Cryptology, CRYPTO 2001* (pp. 332–354). Berlin: Springer-Verlag.

Itkis, G., & Reyzin, L. (2002). SiBIR: Intrusion-resilient signatures, or towards obsoletion of certificate revocation. In Yung [129]. Available from http://eprint.iacr.org/2002/054/

Itkis, G., & Xie, P. (2003). Generalized key-evolving signatures, or how to foil an armed adversary. In *1st MiAn International Conference on Applied Cryptography and Network Security*. Berlin: Springer-Verlag.

Jakobsson, M., & Wetzel, S. (2001). Secure server-aided signature generation. In *Lecture notes in computer science PKC: International Workshop on Practice and Theory in Public Key Cryptography*.

Jakobsson, M. Fractal hash sequence representation and traversal. In Proceedings of the 2002 IEEE International Symposium on Information Theory (ISIT '02), pp. 437–444, July 2002.

Jakobsson, M., Leighton, T., Micali, S., & Szydlo, M. Fractal Merkle tree representation and traversal. In Progress in Cryptology—CT-RSA 2003 [2].

Kang Chu, C., Shan Liu, L., & Guey Tzeng, W. (2003). *A threshold GQ signature scheme*. Retrieved January 28, 2003, from http://eprint.iacr.org/2003/016

Kerckhoffs (von Nieuwenhof), A. (2004). La cryptographie militaire. (French) [Military cryptography]. *Journal des Sciences Militaires*, Jan. 1883. Retrieved January 1, 2004, http://www.petitcolas.net/fabien/kerckhoffs/

Knudsen, L. (ed.), *Lecture notes in computer science: Advances in Cryptology, EUROCRYPT 2002*. Berlin: Springer-Verlag.

Koblitz, N., & Menezes, A. (2004). Another look at "provable security." Cryptology ePrint Archive, Report 2004/152, 2004. Retrieved January 1, 2004, from http://eprint.iacr.org/

Kozlov, A., & Reyzin, L. (2002). Forward-secure signatures with fast key update. In SCN02 [114].

Krawczyk, H. (2000). Simple forward-secure signatures from any signature scheme. In *Seventh ACM Conference on Computer and Communication Security*.

Laih, C.-S., Yen, S.-M., & Harn, L. (1991). Two efficient server-aided secret computation protocols based on additional sequence. In *Proceedings of the Advances in Cryptology Conference—AISACRYPT '91* (pp. 450–459).

Lamport, L. (1979). *Constructing digital signatures from a one way function* (Technical Report CSL-98). SRI International, October 1979.

Le, Z., Ouyang, Y., Ford, J., & Makedon, F. (2004). A hierarchical key-insulated signature scheme in the ca trust model. In *Lecture notes in computer science, vol. 3225: Information Security* (pp. 280).

Levin, L. A. (1973). On the concept of a random sequence. Proceedings of National Academy of Science of USSR, *5*(14), 1413–1416 [in Russian].

Levin, L. A. (1974). Laws of information conservation (non-growth) and aspects of the foundations of probability theory. *Problemy Peredachi Informatsii*, *3*(10), 206–210.

Li, M., & Vitfianyi, P. (1993). *An introduction to Kolmogorov complexity and its applications*. Berlin: Springer-Verlag.

Liu, X., Chu, X., & Tzeng, X. (2003). A threshold GQ signature scheme. In *Lecture notes in computer science, vol. 1: International Conference on Applied Cryptography and Network Security*.

Lucks, S. (1997). On the security of remotely keyed encryption. In E. Biham (ed.), *Lecture notes in computer science, vol. 1267: Fast Software Encryption: 4th International Workshop* (pp. 219–229). Berlin: Springer-Verlag.

Lucks, S. (1999). Accelerated remotely keyed encryption. In L. Knudsen (ed.), *Lecture notes in computer science, vol. 1636: Fast software encryption: 6th International Workshop* (pp. 112–123). Berlin: Springer-Verlag.

MacKenzie, P., & Reiter, M. (2001a). Networked cryptographic devices resilient to capture. In *Proceedings of the IEEE Symposium on Research in Security and Privacy* (pp. 12–25). IEEE Computer Society, Technical Committee on Security and Privacy, IEEE Computer Society Press.

MacKenzie, P., & Reiter, M. K. (2001b). *Delegation of cryptographic servers for capture-resilient devices*. Technical Report 2001-37, DIMACS. Retrieved January 1, 2004, from ftp://dimacs. rutgers.edu/pub/dimacs/ TechnicalReports/TechReports/2001/2001-37.ps.gz

Malkin, M., Wu, T., & Boneh, D. (1999). Experimenting with shared generation of RSA keys. In Proceedings of the Symposium on Network and Distributed Systems Security (NDSS, '99), San Diego, CA, Feb. 1999. Internet Society.

Malkin, T., Micciancio, D., & Miner, S. (2002). Efficient generic forward secure signatures with an unbounded number of time periods. In Knudsen [80].

Malkin, T., Obana, S., & Yung, M. (2002). The hierarchy of key evolving signatures and a characterization of proxy signatures. In Cachin and Camenisch [29] (pp. 306–322).

Merkle, J. (2000). Multi-round passive attacks on server-aided RSA protocols. In S. Jajodia & P. Samarati (eds.), *Proceedings of the 7th ACM Conference on Computer and Communications Security* (pp. 102–107). ACM press.

Merkle, R. C. (1988). A digital signature based on a conventional encryption function. In C. Pomerance (ed.), *Lecture notes in computer science, vol: 293: Advances in Cryptology, CRYPTO '87* (pp. 369–378). Berlin: Springer-Verlag.

Merkle, R. C. (1998). A certified digital signature. In Brassard [28] (pp. 218–238).

Micali, S. (1994). *A secure and efficient digital signature algorithm*. Technical Report MIT/LCS/TM-501, Massachusetts Institute of Technology, Cambridge, MA, March 1994.

Naccache, D., Pointcheval, D., & Stern, J. (2001a). Twin signatures: An alternative to the hash-and-sign paradigm. In P. Samarati (ed.), *Proceedings of the 8th ACM Conference on Computer and Communications Security* (pp. 20–27). ACM Press.

Naccache, D., Pointcheval, D., & Tymen, C. (2001b). Monotone signatures. In P. Syverson (ed.), *Lecture notes in computer science, vol. 2339: Financial cryptography* (pp. 305–318). Berlin: Springer-Verlag.

Nguyen, P., & Stern, J. (1998). The Beguin–Quisquater server-aided RSA protocol from Crypto'95 is not secure. In *Lecture notes in computer science* (vol. 1514).

Ohta, K., & Okamoto, T. (1989). A modification of the Fiat–Shamir scheme. In Goldwasser [61], pages 232–243.

Ong, H., & Schnorr, C. P. Fast signature generation with a Fiat Shamir-like scheme. In Damgfiard [39] (pp. 432–440).

Ostrovsky, R., & Yung, M. (1991). How to withstand mobile virus attacks. In *10th Annual ACM Symposium on Principles of Distributed Computing* (pp. 51–59).

Pedersen, T. P. (1991). A threshold cryptosystem without a trusted party (extended abstract). In D. W. Davies (ed.), *Lecture notes in computer science, vol. 547: Advances in Cryptology, EUROCRYPT '91* (pp. 522–526). Berlin: Springer-Verlag.

Pfitzmann, B., & Waidner, M. (1993). Attacks on protocols for server-aided RSA computation. In *Lecture notes in computer science* (vol. 658).

Preneel, B. (ed.). (2000). *Lecture notes in computer science, vol. 1807: Advances in Cryptology, EUROCRYPT 2000*. Berlin: Springer-Verlag.

Progress in Cryptology—CT-RSA 2003, volume 2612 of *Lecture Notes in Computer Science*. Berlin: Springer-Verlag, 2003.

Reyzin, L., & Reyzin, N. (2002). Better than BiBa: Short one-time signatures with optimal signing and verifying. In *ACISP '02: 7th Australasian Conference on Information Security and Privacy*.

Rivest, R. (1997). All-or-nothing encryption and the package transform. In E. Biham (ed.), *Lecture notes in computer science, vol. 1267: Fast software encryption: Proceedings of the 4th International Workshop*. Berlin: Springer-Verlag.

Schneier, B., & Kelsey, J. (1999). Secure audit logs to support computer forensics. *ACM Trans. Inf. Syst. Secur.*, 2(2), 159–176.

Third Conference on Security in Communication Networks (SCN'02), volume 2576 of *Lecture notes in computer science*. Springer-Verlag, Sept. 12–13, 2002.

Sella, Y. (2003). On the computation-storage trade-offs of hash chain traversal. In *Lecture notes in computer science: Proceedings of the Fourth Conference on Financial Cryptography (FC '03)*. Berlin: Springer-Verlag.

Shamir, A. (1979). How to share a secret. *Communications of the ACM*, 22(11), 612–613.

Shamir, A. (1985). Identity-based cryptosystem and signature scheme. In G. R. Blakley & D. Chaum (eds.), *Lecture notes in computer science, vol. 196: Advances in Cryptology—CRYPTO '84* (pp. 120–126). Berlin: Springer-Verlag.

Shoup, V. (2000). Practical threshold signatures. In Preneel [110] (pp. 207–220).

Song, D. X. (2001). Practical forward secure group signature schemes. In *Eighth ACM Conference on Computer and Communication Security* (pp. 225–234).

Stinson, D. R. (2001). Something about all or nothing (transforms). *Designs, Codes, and Cryptography*, 22(2), 133–138.

Szydlo, M. (2002). Merkle tree traversal in log space and time. In Cachin and Camenisch [29] (pp. 541–554).

Tzeng, X., & Tzeng, X. (2001). Robust forward-secure signature schemes with proactive security. In *PKC: International Workshop on Practice and Theory in Public Key Cryptography*.

Tzeng, W. -G., & Tzeng, Z. -J. (2001). *Robust key-evolving public key encryption schemes*. Report 2001/009, Cryptology ePrint Archive. Retrieved January 1, 2004, from http://eprint.iacr.org/2001/009.ps.gz

Wallner, D. M., Harder, E. J., & Agee, R. C. (1999, June). *Key management for multicast: Issues and architectures*. RFC 2627, Internet Engineering Task Force.

Weis, R., Bakker, B., & Lucks, S. (2001). Security on your hand: Secure filesystems with a "non-cryptographic" JAVA-ring. *Lecture notes in computer science*, vol. 2041.

Wong, C. K., Gouda, M. G., & Lam, S. S. (1998). Secure group communications using key graphs. In *Proceedings of the ACM SIGCOMM '98 Conference on Applications, Technologies, Architectures, and Protocols for Computer Communication* (pp. 68–79).

Wu, T., Malkin, M., & Boneh, D. (1999). Building intrusion-tolerant applications. In *Proceedings of the 8th USENIX Security Symposium (SECURITY-99)* (pp. 79–92). Usenix Association.

Yao, A. C. (1982). Theory and application of trapdoor functions. In *23rd Annual Symposium on Foundations of Computer Science* (pp. 80–91).

Yung, M. (ed.). (2002). *Lecture notes in computer science: Advances in Cryptology, CRYPTO 2002*. Berlin: Springer-Verlag.

# Security Policy Guidelines

Mohamed Hamdi, *National Digital Certification Agency, Tunisia*
Noureddine Boudriga, *National Digital Certification Agency, Tunisia*
Mohammad S. Obaidat, *Monmouth University, NJ, USA*

## INTRODUCTION

Because computer system technologies are rapidly spreading from academic research to industrial applications, many security issues have been raised. This need for security is driven by the increasingly large proportion of losses caused to the enterprises by various security incidents. Security attacks may disturb the operation of the system, entail loss of secrets and privacy, and become a risk to the national security and economy. Several studies, such as the CSI/FBI survey (2004) and Campbell, Gordon, Loeb, & Zhou (2003) have analyzed the consequences of digital attacks on representative sets of organizations. It has been shown that, in most cases, severe economic losses result from these adverse events. Many organizations already had some protection mechanisms at the moment they were attacked. However, they are not 100% immune from possible damages caused by such attacks. Effectively, most security threats are not due to the lack of security equipments, but instead are due to breaches at the planning level. Clearly, there should be a strategic security plan for each organization. In fact, security controls are rarely acquired within the frame of a global security program.

To alleviate this problem, enterprises should consider computer system security as a means to achieve their business objectives. Hence, it should be subjected to a documentation activity just as is done for normal production processes. Strategies, policies, procedures, and guidelines should regulate the security management program.

Obviously, to reduce the security risks that threaten the communication infrastructure, the aforementioned documentation should be based on a set of security principles. This chapter attempts to cover various aspects related to

security policy (SP), which is the kernel of security documentation.

## Security Policy Fundamentals

The purpose of this section is to provide the basic concepts of several key considerations related to the SP. More precisely, we define the SP from the perspective that security rules can apply at many levels of the information system. Then, the objectives and the requirements that an SP should fulfill are presented. Finally, various key considerations and practical guidelines related to the SP components and the development process are discussed.

## Security Policy Definition

Finding a precise meaning for this term turns out to be a very arduous task because it is used to refer to numerous disparate aspects of information systems' security. The following examples give an idea of the different ways an SP can be defined depending on the context. The quoted sentences have been taken verbatim from the source documents so that the reader can concretely note this ambiguity.

1. Information system SP: For an organization that owns a set of networked assets, the SP constitutes the core of the security plan, which entails the design and the implementation of security measures as well as documentation of security incidents. The SP is the foundation for a security program that addresses the business needs of the organization. It should reflect the enterprise's strategic approach to coping with the security risks that characterize the environment. In Hare

(2002, pp. 353), the SP has been defined as a "high level statement that reflects organization's belief related to information security." The major purpose of the SP is to select the appropriate security solutions to face those threat events while ensuring that the cost of protecting the infrastructure does not exceed the benefit it provides. In business jargon, the rules of the SP should guarantee a return on investment (ROI).

2. Operating system (OS) SP: Because of the numerous security threats that exploit weaknesses at the OS level, a set of protection mechanisms should be implemented to plug up such vulnerabilities. The totality of the protection mechanisms related to an OS is called the trusted computing base (TCB). They concern the various resources of the computer system (e.g., hardware, software, processes). The most relevant example consists of the access control policy, which is enforced by secure OSs to protect the objects they handle. Obviously, for consistency and completeness purposes, those mechanisms should abide by a set of rules, which form the SP. The reference monitor is an entity that mediates accesses to objects by subjects. Among those accesses, only those that conform to the SP are allowed. The reference monitor basically guarantees that the OS respects several predefined security principles such as least privilege and continuous protection.

3. Key management SP: To establish a secure tunnel using the IPSec protocol suite, two end points should agree upon a set of mutually acceptable cryptographic parameters called security associations (SA). These security parameters are managed according to local security policies, which are set in each end node. For example, when creating a new SA in order to modify an older one, "deletion of the old SA is dependent on local security policy." Besides, a standard has been recently developed to administrate IPSec security policies; it defined the concept of IP security policy (IPSP).

These examples lead us to discuss the various SP types. It is noteworthy that rather than being conflicting, these definitions present the same concept from different angles. The attentive reader would have remarked that the first definition, related to information systems security, provides the broadest view in the sense that both OS security and the usage of secure protocols can be seen as specific components of the global security program. In our sense, the difficulty of defining an SP stems from the basic fact that security is related to many organizational aspects. For example, from a human resource perspective, the SP serves "to inform all individuals operating within an organization on how they should behave related to a specific topic" (Tudor, 2001). From a risk management point of view, "policies should be concerned with what assets to protect and why they need to be protected" (Canavan, 2001, pp. 239).

To unify all of these views, the SP can be defined as a set of rules that determines how a particular set of assets should be secured. This definition can in fact be applied to represent all SPs without delving into details concerning the context and the language to adopt (natural language or machine language).

Therefore, the SP is a multifaceted concept that can effectively be defined in various manners. Security specialists who addressed SPs mentioned this aspect. Most of them have agreed that "a suite of policy documents rather than a single policy document works better in a large corporate environment" (Canavan, 2003, p. 5). In fact, splitting the SP into fragments has multiple advantages:

1. All SP audiences can be addressed efficiently.
2. All security requirements can be addressed.
3. The security properties (e.g., confidentiality, integrity) of the various SP portions can be preserved more easily.

More concretely, a classification scheme should be considered to ensure that multiple policies are developed to address the same security context.

## SP Classes

Many SP classifications have been proposed in the literature. The most relevant ones are discussed in this subsection. As it has been pointed out, SPs can be classified according to their target audience, the security issues they treat, or their sensitivity (from a security point of view). Examples of such classifications are given here to highlight the importance, or even the necessity, of SP fragmentation.

1. Audience-based classification: Canavan (2003) argued that policies should be structured according to a hierarchical system with respect to the structure of roles. He proposed three policy types, which are governing policy, technical policy, and end-user policy.

2. Issue-based classification: Ensuring the security of a system is proportionally difficult to its complexity. Requirements related to security are defined with respect to the functionalities that the system provides. Depending on the assets to protect, some issues can be emphasized more than others. For example, an Internet service provider's (ISP) major need is to guarantee access to network services and to respect contracts, laws, and ethics. For this reason, ISPs concentrate their SPs on access control, authentication, and availability. However, because the data structures they handle are simple (compared with other types of organizations), developing an information classification policy (ICP) requires less effort. On the opposite end of the scale, a certification authority (CA) manages a richer data set. Cryptographic keys, digital certificates, and revocation lists are just examples of these data. Consequently, information classification becomes more complex than in the former case (ISPs). In the following, we attempt to list some of the security issues that would need a separate policy. The information security policy and the access control policy are discussed in particular detail. The remaining policies are discussed in later sections.

   a. Information classification policy (ICP): The amount of data managed by a typical organization is so large that security controls cannot be applied on a per-object basis. Consequently, the data to be handled should be divided into a finite set of classes so that the security measures can affect a whole class of objects instead of being applied to each individual piece of information. This classification can be performed according to many criteria, such as critical level and usage. Determining the critical level of a piece of information consists of assessing the amount of loss that could result from the violation of one of its security properties (i.e., confidentiality, integrity, and availability). For example, the documentation of a product, which is under development, is of utmost importance because if accessed by a competitor, the position of the organization would be affected. At this stage, it is important to point out that classification should not depend solely on the content of a piece of data, but also on the type of the enterprise. Effectively, sensitivity levels must be assigned on the basis of organization's requirements against the needs for confidentiality, integrity, or availability. This means that two identical records may have distinct classifications in two different environments. For instance, personal information (e.g., name, address) pertaining to employee X does not require specific controls when stored in the database of his employer. Nonetheless, if X is client of bank Y, its records must be classified as private because they are protected by laws.

    b. Access control policy (ACP): Once the sensitive objects have been determined and classified, measures to ensure a convenient protection should be defined. To this purpose, an ACP is created. An ACP is generally built around three basic activities: (a) identifying and authenticating users, (b) managing credentials (e.g., passwords, cryptographic keys), and (c) enforcing the application of good practices (such as least privileges and dual control). Of course, the ACP is strong related to the ICP. The nature of authentication credentials required to access a particular object is in fact determined bythe object's classification. Authentication mechanisms customary are grouped into three types: (a) knowledge-based authentication, (b) token-based authentication, and (c) characteristic-based authentication. For example, a password may be sufficient to protect ordinary files on a user machine. However, private keys used to sign digital documents should be kept on smart cards or cryptographic tokens to prevent those keys from being stolen. Practically, two main approaches can be followed to build an ACP: (a) discretionary access control, where the owner of data determines the objects that are allowed to access the data and the privileges they possess, (b) mandatory access control, where both the owner and the system define the access policy on the basis of subject privilege (or clearance) and subject sensitivity (or classification).

3. Sensitivity-based classification: Gaining knowledge about how a system is protected is often one of the primary goals for an attacker. Thus, the SP itself should be secured in the sense that it should not be accessed by unauthorized entities. This presumes that SP content is divided into pieces, each corresponding to a security level. The most trivial sensitivity-based classification consists of separating internal policies from external policies (Purser, 2004). Policies that address the secure functioning of the production process are internal. Their content should not be published outside the organization. Conversely, external policies are those that are intended to be published to an external audience. This classification can be improved by being more granular. For example, internal policies themselves can be split into many categories depending on the sensitivity of the concerned department.

## Security Policy Objectives

An enterprise's for a SP can be driven by various reasons, which depend essentially on the organization's nature and on the context in which it operates. As is outlined in this section, SPs can be directed toward the panoply of need. Thus, fixing a set of objectives to the SP development process would be very hard. However, what would be interesting at this level is to describe a spectrum of potential objectives and show how these can be ranked according to the enterprise characteristics. The objectives that we consider are listed here. They have been divided into two major categories: business-oriented objectives and regulatory objectives.

1. Business-oriented objectives: The reasons for developing and implementing SPs should align with the basic organizational objectives. The benefits of having an SP can be either direct or indirect. Some can be easily assessed in monetary terms (e.g., preventing critical assets from being attacked) whereas the others are abstract (e.g., preserving the reputation of the enterprise). The most important among the business-oriented objectives are as follows:

    a. Performing risk management: The measures of the SP should maintain the security of critical components at an acceptable level. In other terms, the SP should help the organization reduce the likelihood or the effects of harmful adverse events. Because perfect security cannot be actually reached, the organization should evaluate the risks that it faces and select the appropriate countermeasures. According to Swanson (1998), some of the main purposes of security plans are to "provide an overview of the security requirements of the system and describe the controls in place or planned for meeting those requirements," which constitute the essence of the risk management process. The SP is then one of the most important deliverables of the risk management cycle.

    b. Handling security incidents: The SP should outline the specific actions that would preserve the business activities when a devastating event occurs. This means that the key activities of the organization should not be disrupted by such events. In addition, the critical attacked components should be totally recovered once the event has passed. To this purpose, three SP components should be particularly focused upon: the monitoring policy, the recovery policy, and the forensics policy. These policies address the principal phases of the incident-response process, which are detection, reaction, and investigation. The monitoring policy primarily fixes the metrics used to define the system state. In addition, it defines the mechanisms that differentiate between normal and abnormal states. Attack signatures are also used in this context to detect the occurrence of security threats. The appropriate policy must describe how these signatures are handled (i.e., built, modified, and detected). It is noteworthy that the monitoring policy interferes with some other policies such as the data classification policy and the access control policy. Indeed a high proportion of the information needed to control the system state is sensitive. Consequently, the two policies must be considered when thinking about the means to gather the required data. Log files are among the most relevant examples because they constitute a rich source that provides views on the actions targeting the monitored system. Their integrity (and often confidentiality) should be strictly preserved. Moreover, administrators have to be authenticated conveniently when accessing these files. The recovery policy specifies how responses to security incidents should be conducted. These responses generally break into two categories: automated responses and manual responses. The former class concerns reactions that are mechanically executed by some components of the attacked system to stop the effect of a harmful event or to simply prevent it from happening. The latter category encompasses responses that cannot be triggered without the intervention of a human expert team. The interaction among the different members, including task scheduling and documentation handling, should be addressed in this context. Finally, the forensics policy should set the rules to determine the origin of a specific incident based on rigorous proofs. This requires procedures to gather, analyze, protect, store, and archive digital evidence.

c. Ensuring information integrity, confidentiality, and availability: Information is a crucial concern for successful enterprises. The SP should define the controls that protect appropriately the information assets. The three basic properties that must be preserved to avoid losses are integrity, confidentiality, and availability. Hare (2000) describes the SP as designed around two principal security goals, which are confidentiality and integrity. According to Hare, availability is generally not addressed by SPs. The main reason for this point of view is that only mathematical models of SPs have been studied in this reference. In our sense, none of those properties should be privileged. On one hand, if the integrity of critical business information is altered, several strategic organizational decisions could be seriously biased. On the other hand, if some piece of confidential information is divulged to competitors, the enterprise benefits might be considerably affected. Finally, availability is also a special concern to organizations that provide services through the means of their communication infrastructure. As it has been pointed out previously (handling security incidents), any disruption tackling a component of the information system can result in important losses.

d. Fixing individual responsibilities: The SP is designed so that all individuals operating within the target context know how they are intended to behave when interacting with the information system components. According to RFC 2196 (IETF, 1997), "the main purpose of a security policy is to inform users, staff and managers of their obligatory requirements for protecting technology and information assets." Likewise, according to Swanson (1998), SPs "delineate responsibilities and expected behavior of all individuals who access the system." Employees are asked to conform their actions to the content of the SP. Defining user responsibilities precisely is often useful to protect the enterprise's reputation. For example, if an employee does not act in conformance with the security rules, the organization can easily demonstrate that it did not approve the malicious actions.

2. Regulatory objectives: The security measures of the SP are often developed as a regulatory obligation. Organizations that operate in sensitive sectors are particularly concerned with this issue. In the following, we illustrate our reasoning by using two significant examples: banks and CAs. The former category is accountable for the operations it carries whereas the latter handles various types of critical information (e.g., key pairs, private user information). The following principles have to be respected, among others:

a. Duty of loyalty: When carrying his charges, an employee must place the employer's interest above his own. The relationship between the enterprise and the employee should be based on honesty and faith.

b. Conflict of interest: A conflict of interest corresponds to a situation where the effect of a given action is positive for a category of employees and negative for others. The SP should guarantee that the security rules do not include such discriminatory clauses.

c. Duty of care: The employees should proceed with caution when performing critical tasks. For example, the internal security auditing team should protect adequately the resources to which it has access (e.g., log files, personal information) to avoid divulgating confidential information.

d. Accountability: For accountability, the employees should be uniquely identified and authenticated. When the responsibility of an employee has a legal aspect, which is often the case, the identification and authentication have to be compliant with regulations. More precisely, credentials used for authentication purposes must conform to legislation. For instance, when asymmetric cryptographic keys are of use in this context, SP developers should verify that protocols (e.g., generation protocols, encryption protocols), format, and key lengths do not conflict with the regulatory framework.

Generally, the most important goals that might be achieved by a SP are these:

1. The measures of the SP should maintain the security of critical components at an acceptable level. In other

terms, the SP helps enterprises in reducing the amount of risk related to harmful adverse events.

2. The SP must include some response schemes that make the system recover if an incident occurs (e.g., security attack, natural disaster).

3. The SP must ensure the continuity of the critical processes conducted by an enterprise whenever an incident occurs.

4. Individual responsibilities and consequences must be defined.

Achieving these objectives instills a set of requirements that is presented in the next section.

## Policy Requirements

Following the discussion of the previous section, a SP must possess several properties to conform to the aforementioned objectives. The essence of these properties is given in the following.

1. Accountability: Every action performed on the system should leave a trace that can be monitored. This guideline is tightly related to the continuous control of the IT infrastructure. Practically, the most common accountability mechanism consists simply of recording traces into log files. Nonetheless, as resources dedicated to this activity are generally limited (in the sense that they do not allow the capture of all the attributes defining a system state), the security policy should clearly treat the following issues:
   a. Generation: What should be logged? Which are the relevant data with regard to the intrinsic characteristics of the system under analysis?
   b. Analysis: How should the captured information be analyzed to state whether the policy has been violated?
   c. Archiving and storage: The information that accounts for the interaction of various components of the system often has important security levels. Furthermore, archiving is a key consideration because of the fact that traces might be needed a long time after they were captured. Therefore, the security policy must discuss storage procedures, while stressing access control issues.

2. Awareness: Every user of the system should possess the appropriate knowledge to interact with the system in a secure manner. This principle is particularly important because most of the security attacks originate from the inside of the system or exploit vulnerabilities that exist in internal components (e.g., misconfigurations). In addition, awareness considerably reduces unintentional harmful actions. Training programs are often mentioned as a solution that fulfills these needs. However, we believe that a strong involvement of the human resources department is the best alternative for an enterprise to reach an acceptable security level. For instance, some investigations should be conducted to gather if the candidate caused security problems in his past jobs. Likewise, procedures that should apply when an employee leaves an organization have to be included

in the security policy to ensure that the employee no longer possesses his security privileges.

3. Proportionality: Security measures defined in the security policy must match the risks that threaten the system. In other terms, the value of critical information as well as the probability of security attacks (deduced from studying the environment of the system) should be taken into consideration when developing security policy. Obviously, overlooking these aspects would lead to grave consequences because of unrealistic views.

Some other requirements can also be added to the aforementioned ones. The most important, from a security point of view, are completeness and cost-effectiveness. In fact, for a SP to adequately protect a set of resources, all the adverse events that may decrease the security level of the system should be considered and thwarted. On the other hand, the rules of the SP should guarantee cost-effectiveness, meaning that the money and effort spent to reach an acceptable security level should not outweigh the benefit resulting from the application of those rules.

An intriguing point that might have been noticed by the reader is that the two latter objectives are, in some sense, conflicting. A complete SP is rarely cost-effective because the attacks corresponding to a generic environment are so numerous that mitigating all of them cannot be achieved with a reasonable budget. Another problem may arise from the fact that completeness is a utopia that can never be objectively reached. Effectively, the SP development team can never build a zero-uncertainty representation of the environment.

Consequently, the dependency between the SP requirements should be considered when fulfilling the objectives highlighted in the previous subsection. The major requirement for a SP is that it should be flexible enough by partially supporting all the elementary requirements that have been mentioned.

## SP Components

To fulfill these objectives and the requirements, the SP should cover some basic security elements. Canavan (2001) cited seven topics that should be addressed by a typical security policy: identification, authentication, access control, availability, confidentiality, integrity, and accountability.

Throughout the foregoing discussion, we found that the three first items can be merged into a single one called access control. Availability is addressed by the BCP and DRP whereas confidentiality and integrity are treated by both the DCP and ACP. Finally, accountability requires a backup policy for audit trails that constitute the output of the ACP.

The constituency of the SP is also a fundamental issue that is closely related to both objectives and requirements. The major components of a good SP should include the following:

1. An *access policy:* This defines privileges that are granted to system users to protect assets from loss or misuse. It should specify guidelines for external connections and adding new devices or software components to the information system.

2. An *accountability policy:* It defines the responsibilities of users, operation staff, and management. It should specify the audit coverage, operations, and the incident-handling guidelines.

3. An *authentication policy:* It addresses different authentication issues such as the use of operating system (OS) passwords, authentication devices, or digital certificates. It should provide guidelines for use of remote authentication and authentication devices.

4. An *availability policy:* It states a set of users' expectations for the availability of resources. It should describe recovery issues and redundancy of operations during downtime periods.

5. A *maintenance policy:* It describes how the maintenance people are allowed to handle the information technology systems and networks. It should specify how remote maintenance can be performed, if any.

6. A *violations reporting policy:* This describes all types of violations that must be reported and how reports are handled.

RFC 2196 proposes three other components that should be included in the SP (IETF, 1997):

1. A set of *computer technology purchasing guidelines:* These specify required or preferred security features.

2. A *privacy policy:* It defines the barrier that separates the security objectives from the privacy requirements. Ideally, this barrier must not be crossed in either direction.

3. A set of *supporting information:* It provides system users and managers with useful information for each type of policy violation.

Clearly, each of these points corresponds to a category of security services. We believe that this categorization is not the most appropriate scheme mainly because the SP should not necessarily include all of these categories. Therefore, a better approach consists of considering a dynamic set of components that differ from one environment to another. This ensures a better adaptation of the SP constituency to the enterprise needs. More concretely, the SP should be split into sections that represent the categories of the available assets (e.g., Web server, mail server, desktop workstation, private network). Then, a set of security requirements is associated with each asset category depending essentially on its nature. Hence, this reasoning can be seen as a mapping between the asset categories and the security requirements. These requirements can be ranked by order of importance for each asset category. For example, integrity is much more important than privacy and authentication when thinking about the security of a Web server. On the opposite, for a mail server, privacy should be carefully considered to ensure that the selected security measures preserve the secrecy of some private messages (or some message portions) while they are monitored. Moreover, authentication becomes essential in this case to avoid mail-spoofing attacks. To have a more concrete idea about the different security mechanisms that correspond to the most important resource categories, the reader is recommended to refer to the Computer Emergency Response Team (CERT) collection.

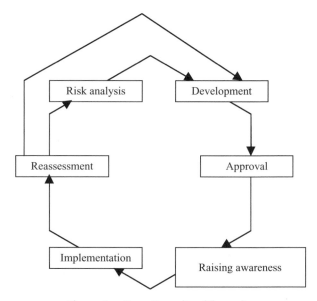

**Figure 1:** Security policy life cycle.

Obviously, more sophisticated approaches to determine the SP constituency can be evolved. However, the main point to retain from this discussion is that the SP components should be dynamically determined according to a sound methodology rather than being statically defined.

## SECURITY POLICY LIFE CYCLE

Developing a security policy should be done according to several steps that constitute a life cycle as represented in Figure 1.

These main steps are briefly explained:

1. Risk analysis: It includes essentially a mission statement, asset evaluation, and threat assessment. It is worth mentioning that some parts of the SP can be written in this step. In fact, the risk analyst needs some rules to assign a security level to each resource, meaning that the data classification policy should have already been constructed at this level.

2. Development: This step consists of selecting the security rules that best fit the requirements of the organization. The SP development team must use convenient languages to model and validate the SP. The main characteristic of this step is that it is performed progressively to move from an abstract representation toward a more concrete one.

3. Approval: It relies on a multidisciplinary committee that validates the security policy. At every layer (i.e., abstraction degree) of the development process, the SP should be validated against (a) the upper layer and (b) the security objectives.

4. Raising awareness: This ensures that the security policy is accessible to everyone who is authorized to access it. Thus, the SP is published correctly and every user of the secured system must possess the skills that are suitable to his or her responsibilities.

5. Implementation: It enforces the application of the security policy. During this step, operational and technical

controls are put in place. Operational controls are security mechanisms that are essentially implemented and executed by the users themselves, whereas technical controls include the automated security countermeasures.

6. Reassessment: It guarantees a continuous monitoring of the security policy through scheduled revisions and analyses. This process is essential to practically test the efficiency of the SP because new threats can occur.

Nevertheless, even if this life cycle is generic enough to represent the development steps of most SP types, it fails to model several specific cases. In fact, it is sometimes impossible to follow it rigorously. The life cycle architecture must change to adapt to system development. It should then be "flexible" enough to support such modifications. As for traditional systems, a security system life cycle consists of two principal phases: the acquisition phase and the utilization phase. Theoretically, the SP life cycle can be initiated at any point of the system development life cycle, even if it is always preferred that the SP evolve in parallel with the system (ISS, 2000; Grance, Stevens, 2003). As a result, some processes of the SP life cycle can be deleted, added, or modified. For example, when the information system is still in the acquisition phase, the implementation of the security controls cannot take place because some of the needed components are not available yet. Similarly, a cost-estimation activity should be performed initially to estimate the security budget and the human resources that would be necessary to apply the SP program. This task becomes unnecessary when doing a periodical review of the security policy.

Achieving the fixed security goals at the end of each step of the system's life cycle is crucial. If some SP components are not developed or not implemented during the appropriate phase, some security breaches might be left that would be hard to seal. This simply stems from the fact that the later a mistake is detected, the more difficult it is to repair.

## COST-EFFECTIVENESS: THE RISK ANALYSIS PROCESS

Security risk analysis is the process of identifying assets and threats, prioritizing the related vulnerabilities, and identifying appropriate measures and protections. A risk analysis activity has to be performed prior to the security policy development. It should take into account many factors such as the environment (e.g., existing assets, potential threats), the cost considerations, and the type of the security documents (BSI, 2000; Peltier, 2001). This section shows how risk analysis can be integrated in to the security policy life cycle.

### Integrating Risk Analysis Process into the SP Life Cycle

In this context, risk analysis is viewed as an activity generating data sets that will be used during the development of an SP. However, risk analysis itself is a discipline that has attracted great interest in the research community. Many models and methods have been built to support it.

Actually, risk analysis cannot be reduced to a preparatory step for the development of the SP because it has much more influence on the security process. It is generally conducted within the frame of the risk management cycle. The reader should be aware that in the present chapter, our discussion is focused on those aspects that are closely related to the SP development process.

Performing risk analysis allows us to (a) identify the important components of the system; (b) recognize the potential threats, risks, or issues related to the assets; (c) assess the risk degree related to each critical asset; (d) implement, for each risk, corrective countermeasures and controls, or accept the risk; and (e) measure the effectiveness of the countermeasures and controls. This assessment can be based on either a quantitative or a qualitative evaluation. The former assigns numerical values to the identified risks whereas the latter uses scales.

More simply, going through a risk assessment process allows the SP development team to determine what should be protected, how to protect it, and from what to protect it. Even more, this process ensures that the protection mechanisms are compliant with the available security budget, on one hand, and feasible, on the other hand. In fact, feasibility should be considered a major factor to enhance the efficiency of the resulting SP. For instance, requiring access codes (to a physical facility) to be changed daily is a security measure that cannot be concretely applied. Although it allows achieving a high protection level, the number of codes to be managed would be overwhelming. More generally, if a security process is difficult to apply, most of the employees will simply ignore it.

The advantages of performing risk analysis before constructing the SP stem from two major points:

1. Existing risk analysis methods can be often automated to a great degree through the use of software tools that considerably facilitate key tasks. Automation becomes very important, even necessary, in the case of large systems that have complex topologies. For a system including thousands of computers, which are also segmented into networks and subnetworks, the risk analyst would face substantial difficulties when trying to manually determine the threats related to each asset. Moreover, given that most of the available risk analysis methods are probabilistic, threat frequencies have to be kept up to date. This obviously requires the use of a learning mechanism. Thus, the use of databases, expert systems, and learning mechanisms are helpful to reduce decision time by mechanizing resource-demanding computations.

2. Including measures in the SP is equivalent to a decision-making process that might be affected by potential errors at the input stage. Risk analysis (RA), if conducted properly, should minimize these errors by providing a view that reflects accurately the security state of the system to be protected. Therefore, risk analysis makes the SP respect at least one of its major requirements, which is proportionality.

There are two types of security risk analysis: quantitative analysis and qualitative analysis. Quantitative RA attempts to assign independently objective numeric values to the elements of the risk analysis and to the level of potential losses. Even though it requires large amounts of preliminary work, quantitative RA generates efficient results that are expressed in management-based language.

Qualitative RA is subjective in nature and is based on scenarios and "what if" questions. Qualitative RA provides flexibility in the processing and reporting activities,;ut presents no basis for cost-benefit analysis of risk mitigation. Deciding which risk analysis process is appropriate for an enterprise is an important issue. Hybrid approaches are often used to combine the advantages of both approaches.

## Risk Analysis Steps

To be efficient, the risk analysis process should consist of the following steps:

1) Mission statement: Identifying the context is among the important tasks when developing a security policy. In fact, the content of the security policy depends essentially on two factors: (a) the objective of the security policy, which can be regulatory, informative, or advisory, and (b) the structure of the organization. (It has been stated previously that the SP content depends heavily on this factor.) Existing standards, regulatory policies, and guidelines should also be taken into account to ensure the compliance of the security policy with those documents. Moreover, the security objectives to be fulfilled by the potential countermeasures should be determined at this level. These should be balanced with the available human and monetary resources to schedule adequately the development, implementation, and review of the SP.

2) Asset analysis: This process consists essentially of gathering information about the different resources to classify them according to their criticality. The interdependency among the identified resources should be taken into consideration.

3) Threat analysis: The most important threats will be identified through a detailed analysis of the environment of the analyzed system.

Absolute security is unachievable and unrealistic. Nevertheless, potential losses must be weighed against risk factors, the value of the information, and its accessibility to the mission of the agency. In doing this, an enterprise must develop a risk mitigation plan through the use of risk analysis.

A risk analysis, when done by qualified evaluators and involving the application/data owners, is imperative to properly assess overall risk and determine a course of action to alleviate or minimize those risks identified.

Overall risk analysis considers (a) the likelihood that a threat will breach a vulnerability and (b) the value of the asset, that is, a quantification of the loss, possibly in dollars, resulting from that breach in terms of lost worker productivity (wages), cost of recovery from the problem, and even nonmonetary cost such as political exposure and other ramifications. Potential losses must be weighed, and the expenditure on security controls must be balanced against the value of the information resource and the consequences that could result from its loss or inaccessibility.

The information security officer should conduct periodic risk analyses to address any change in the organization's priorities and threats to information. The analyses should be conducted with sufficient regularity to ensure realistic responses to current risks (e.g., agencies with sensitive data should do this quarterly or semiannually, and agencies with minimal sensitive data may find annual reviews sufficient).

Results of risk analysis should be documented, and that documentation should be included as part of the enterprise's documented information security program. The documentation should be considered sensitive and potentially confidential and be treated accordingly.

The risk analysis may vary from an informal, but documented, review of a microcomputer or terminal installation to a formal, fully quantified risk analysis for a large computing environment.

At a minimum, risk analysis should involve consideration of the following factors:

- the nature of the information and systems,
- business purpose for which the information is used,
- environment in which the system is used and operated,
- protection provided by the controls in place,
- organizational consequences that would likely result from a significant breach of security,
- realistic likelihood of such a breach occurring in light of prevailing threats and controls, and
- determination of which information resources are to be protected and to what extent.

## WRITING EFFICIENCY: THE DEVELOPMENT PROCESS

After determining the major points that define the security needs of the target enterprise, a set of security rules have to be built to prevent the system from being jeopardized. To this end, a multidisciplinary team should be involved in the development process to reach an agreed-upon version of the SP. Development is, perhaps, the most critical task in the SP life cycle because it encompasses many seemingly unrelated aspects. The SP is certainly the cornerstone of the development of an efficient security program; however, it is not the only document that should be considered. It is a single component of a complex documentation hierarchy that should be developed in conjunction with the hierarchy. This section explores the concerns related to all of the security documentation and addresses particularly the following issues: (a) What are the documents that should accompany the development of the SP? (b) What are the steps that should be followed in the SP development process? (c) How to choose the appropriate language to express and validate the SP? (d) What is the role played by the security models in the SP development task? (e) What are the writing techniques that should be respected to ensure SP effectiveness? (f) What are the roles and the responsibilities that should be considered to develop the security documentation?

### SP and the Documentation Hierarchy

Before beginning to write the SP, the development team should carefully analyze the output of the risk analysis step to identify the documents that must be defined. This allows the team to build a global unified view about system security by taking into account the relationship among documents. To address this need, the classifications proposed in the first section are useful.

The problem at this stage is to organize the countermeasures selected throughout the risk analysis process into a complete and coherent documentation, which should be easy to use, easy to maintain, accurate and up to date, appropriate for target audiences, and self-contained. Raw security decisions must then be refined to have the appropriate format required for integratration into the SP. To respect the uniformity of the organization's approach to potential threats, the SP must be closely related to the whole security documentation. In the following, we outline the main document categories that should be used to build effective security architecture.

1. Standards: A standard is a document that defines how a specific task should be performed. It can concern, for instance, the development of a product or a protocol related to a secure process. Generally, standards are developed so that the community using the target system knows what should be done to interact with it securely.

2. Procedures: Procedures describe exactly how to use the standards and guidelines to implement the countermeasures that support the policy. These procedures can be used to describe everything from the configuration of operating systems, databases, and network hardware to how to add new users, systems, and software.

3. Baselines: Baselines are used to create a minimum level of security necessary to meet policy requirements. Baselines can be configurations, architectures, or procedures that might or might not reflect the business process, but that can be adapted to meet these requirements. They can be used as an abstraction to develop standards.

4. Guidelines: Sometimes security cannot be described as a standard or set as a baseline, but some guidance is necessary. These are areas where recommendations are created as guidelines to the user community as a reference to proper security. For example, your policy might require a risk analysis every year. Rather than requiring specific procedures to perform this audit, a guideline can specify the methodology that is to be used, leaving the audit team to work with management to fill in the details.

The SP classes defined in the first section can be hierarchically covered to cluster the security decisions (that will later become security rules). The SP development team must first determine the audience concerned by the countermeasure, then the issue it treats, and finally the sensitive data it might enclose.

## Language and Validation

From the previous discussion, we know that two important issues should be addressed: the SP language and the SP validation. Effectively, the SP is customarily written in a human natural language. When it is applied, the SP is translated into another language that is suitable to the secured process. To illustrate this idea, consider a policy describing the security of a networked system. To implement it, the administrator should configure the firewall, using its proper command set, in such a way that it will apply the SP. Even if the original SP substantially achieves its objectives, an error made by the administrator might make it deviate from these goals. Henceforth, the main problem at this stage is to prove that an expression of a SP in a given language conforms to another expression of the same SP in a different language. This issue is analogous to the software development process where many specifications corresponding to different levels of abstraction can be considered. These specifications that deal with the same problem are derived from each other by decreasing the abstraction level at each refinement. A key consideration is to test the conformance of each specification to the one it was derived from. On the other hand, an SP expressed through the use of a language must be validated to state whether it allows reaching the predefined security objectives (Cholvy & Cuppens, 1997; Siewe, Cau, & Zedan, 2003)

Many specification languages can be used to validate two key properties of the SP: consistency and completeness. Analyzing the SP consistency allows one to check whether the application of some security rules lead to conflicting situations. For example, in the case of an access control policy, an employee may have access to an object according to a specific measure, whereas another rule forbids this access. Completeness permits one to verify that the SP has covered all the environment of the organization.

In addition to this, the choice of the specification language often depends on the enterprise context, and more precisely, on the characteristic of the sensitive resources. For instance, the temporal aspect has not been investigated in early research activities that treated information access control. Nonetheless, recent works dealing with network security access control give great importance to this factor.

Consistency and completeness can be achieved while observing the following rules:

• The SP should be kept flexible. An SP should be made independent from specific hardware and software details. Mechanisms for updating the SP should be provided and be easy to use.

• Security services should be completely defined. This property can be achieved through the establishment of a complete list of the network services to be provided to the users who will be authorized to access the services and to the administrators of the services.

• Provided services should be separated and their real needs identified. Services should be isolated on dedicated hosts and filters be defined to cope with the services need.

## SP Development Phases

Throughout this discussion, it appears that the SP development can be viewed, from a certain angle, as an iterative process where two functions are repeatedly executed:

**Table 1** Example of Abstraction Levels

| Abstraction level | Target population | Security rule |
|---|---|---|
| High | SP validator | Each subject is allowed read access to objects that are less sensitive than it. |
| Medium | Security administrator | The financial and the production network must be put on two separate virtual local area networks (VLANs). |
| Low | High managerial | The employees of the financial department do not have read access to the production data. |

specification and validation. From one step to another, the specification used to model the SP becomes less abstract and closer to the reality. The process is stopped if a sufficient abstraction level is reached. This level may be adjusted according to the target population. In fact, the heterogeneity of the enterprise staff requires the development of different versions of the same SP. Each employee will have access to the version that fits with his or her position. Table 1 gives an illustrative example where the same security is expressed in three different manners. It shows how the same security statement can be expressed according to the audience. The last security rule (corresponding to low abstraction level) may seem close to the first one (corresponding to high abstraction level), but they exhibit important differences. The use of the term "each" confers an abstract aspect to the first rule. The last rule appears as an instantiation of the high-level one because abstract variables ("subject" and "object") have been substituted by concrete entities ("employees of the financial department" and "the production data").

The ITSEC defines three main abstraction levels for a SP:

- Corporate SP: Includes standards that apply to all the information systems of the enterprise as well as the relationship between these systems and the external ones.
- System SP: Defines the countermeasures that guarantee, for each category of sensitive resources, the respect of the corresponding security requirements.
- Technical SP: Defines the hardware and software mechanisms that should be used for a secure implementation of the system SP.

Using the documents issued at the RA analysis phase, the specification step applies the following guidelines to achieve a complete specification of an asset to protect:

- Identify all possible problems of the asset including misconfigurations, access points, and software bugs.
- Choose controls to protect the asset from the detected problems to reduce the related risk. Mulitple strategies should be used.
- Define appropriate procedures to identify unauthorized activity. These procedures should be based on an efficient monitoring of the system.
- Define the actions to be taken when a malicious activity is performed on the asset. Business activity and law enforcement should be involved in actions definition.

SP validation integrates several issues including formal validation, auditing, and testing. Formal validation should be achieved using formal models that allow proving ad hoc properties and checking whether the SP is consistent. Auditing process should be used to enhance system security, locate abuses, and control security procedures through logs and traces. Finally, testing can be realized in two phases: the first step generates case tests, and the second phase executes (or checks) the SP on the test cases.

In addition, SP validation may involve various departments in the company through a reviewing process. An SP may need to be reviewed by the legal department to provide advice on current relevant laws that may require certain types of information to be protected in specific ways. The human resources department also may need to review and approve or reject part of the SP depending on how it will relate to existing company policies. Finally, the internal audit department (IAD) in the company is likely to be involved in the SP validation. For instance, the IAD should conduct a companywide compliance of the SP with other policies, when implemented.

## Mathematical Models

The main advantage of representing an SP formally is to discard some relatively insignificant details. A mathematical model corresponds to an abstraction degree, giving an idea about the amount of the withdrawn details. A highly abstract formal framework provides a coarse view of the analyzed system. Actually, fixing this abstraction degree is often a delicate task. It should not drastically eliminate relevant details and it must simultaneously avoid rendering the SP development more complex by considering superfluous entities. Furthermore, mathematical modeling allows, through the application of a sequence of decreasing abstraction levels, the building of a set of views that represent the system in a fashion that is increasingly close to the reality. The language used at a given level can be enriched to refine the granularity of the representation. The model resulting from this process would clearly be more realistic. According to this reasoning, the development process can start with an abstract model and be refined gradually until it reaches an "acceptable" representation.

Generally, a formal modeling framework consists of (a) a set of entities that represent the elements of the analysis, (b) a logic allowing clauses and formulas, (c) a set of axioms that define the main properties of the system, and

(d) a set of deduction rules that show how logical formulas can be inferred ones from the others.

In the following, the concept of multilevel security (MLS) is defined. Particular importance is given to MLS because it is the basis of a wide range of policy models such as the Bell–La Padula (Bell & La Padula, 1976) model and the Biba (Biba, 1977) model. For space limitations, several more recent formalisms are not be treated in this chapter. The interested reader should refer to Ryan (2000) for more details.

## Multilevel Security Policies

These models consider a set of subjects $S$, objects $O$, and access modes $A$. A state of the system is represented by a matrix $M$ whose rows, columns, and entries correspond to the subjects, objects, and the access granted to the subject on the object, respectively. These access privileges belong to the set $A^*$, meaning that they are subsets of $A$. The matrix $M$ is often modeled by the following function $M: S \times O \to A$. Each element $e$ of $S \cup O$ possesses a clearance (or a security level) denoted $C(e)$. The mapping $C$ is then defined as function $C: S \cup O \to L$, where $L$ is the set of security levels, which is presumed to possess a lattice structure.

For instance, at the organization level, the set $L$ could be composed of *TopSecret*, *AD-Secret* (for administration department SECRET), *TD-Secret* (for technical department SECRET), *AD-confidential*, *TD-confidential*, and *Public*. The corresponding lattice is illustrated by Figure 2. This shows that *AD-Secret* dominates *AD-confidential* and *TD-confidential*. However, *AD-Secret* and *TD-Secret* cannot be compared and neither can *AD-confidential* and *TD-confidential*.

Multilevel security policies began to be used at the end of the 1970s to state what must and must not be done to guarantee the security of information flows. The most famous multilevel security models are Bell–La Padula (BPL) and Biba, which focus on confidentiality and integrity, respectively.

## SECURITY AWARENESS PROGRAM: THE PUBLICATION PROCESS

Hare (2002) argued that "the success of a given policy is based on the level of knowledge that the employees have about it." In fact, an awareness program has to be associated with the development of the security policy to ensure its efficiency. All the staff should understand (and apply) the directives of the security policy. To this purpose, the organization must communicate appropriately the content of the policy. To have an optimal efficiency to the awareness process, four main points should be addressed:

1. Which documentation should be developed to support the publication of the SP?
2. Which components of the SP should be communicated to each employee?
3. How to train accurately the organizations' staff?
4. How to ensure the cost-effectiveness of the awareness process?

Awareness programs should concentrate on all the organization's user population to achieve a successful IT security program. The program should focus on informing users of their responsibilities as documented in the SP.

## Documenting the SP

A set of documents should be created to allow all the staff to understand the SP. In the previous section, the problem of extracting procedures and guidelines from the SP has been highlighted. In fact, this seems to be the most relevant issue at this level because users of a given system often do not have access to the SP itself but only to some of its ramifications.

The issuing organization should therefore establish priorities to rank these documents according to their importance. Effectively, even several security plans can be extracted from the SP such as the BCP and the DRP. More practical documents, such as the code of conduct (CoC), can also be based on the SP. It is noteworthy that these documents should fulfill the same conditions as the SP. Recall that an SP must be

- *Simple and clear.* This can be attained by (a) ensuring that the documents writers have a consistent style, (b) using concrete rather than abstract language, (c) using easy-to-understand language, and (d) applying effective rules such as avoiding the use of very negative statements (Canavan, 2004).
- *Known to employees.* For this, documents should be published in such a way that they remain available to all company employees. The documents should be easily accessible for download and printing. Various tools can be used to inform employees about the SP (e.g., e-mail).
- *Supported and adhered to by top management.* SP documents include a single document called *governing policy*, which should cover information security concepts at a high level, to be read by managers. Governing policy should be closely aligned with existing and future human resource strategies and other company policies.

Moreover, SP updates need to be carefully undertaken by the personnel. Old versions must be correctly withdrawn and simple procedures have to be set for identifying the latest versions.

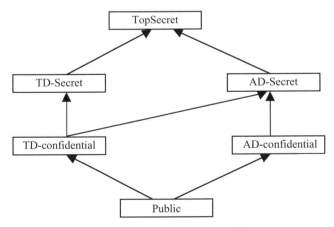

**Figure 2:** Organization security lattice.

## Distributing the SP

The SP often includes some critical data about the security of the organization that has issued it. Therefore, the awareness process should be role-dependent in the sense that distinction should be considered among the components that should be made accessible to various employee categories. Because of their diversity, managing the SP and the related security documents is a hard task. Documents should be stored in such a way that they can easily be retrieved by authorized people. Similarly, access should be denied to unauthorized entities. To illustrate this reasoning, consider the case where an information security policy is about to be published. The different roles that are customarily considered to categorize the people who handle classified data are given in the following:

- Originator: the person who creates the information.
- Authorizer: the person who manages access to the information.
- Owner: the person who might manage or have created the information.
- Custodian: the person who executes the rules fixed by the authorizer.
- User: the person who has access to the information in order to fulfill some job responsibilities.

It can be easily remarked that interferences between the policies concerning each of these roles would affect the overall system security. For instance, if an originator has a precise idea about how the authorizer and the custodian communicate, he would have more opportunities to build a successful attack strategy. The rules related to this communication would be indeed very helpful when an entity tries to substitute itself for the authorizer.

More generally, the content of the policy should be split into a number of fragments, each having a different security level. Every employee should have access only to the fragments that fit with his position in the organization. Furthermore, employees should acknowledge and accept the organization's defined security policies, procedures, and responsibilities.

## Training the Staff

Security awareness, including the training of information resource custodians, users, providers, and management, is one of the most effective means of reducing vulnerability to error and fraud and must be continually emphasized and reinforced. The training programs should suit the needs of the organization. In, three levels of complexity have been associated with training materials:

- Beginning level: for people who do not have any important technical knowledge.
- Intermediate level: for more experienced employees who have wider responsibilities.
- Advanced level: For experts whose jobs incorporate the highest level of trust. Security administrators, security officers, and network administrators are examples of people belonging to this category.

Security awareness and training programs can be described as a four-phase process (Wilson & Hash, 2003):

- Program design. During this phase, an assessment of the enterprise is conducted and a training strategy is developed and approved. Awareness and training program design must address the following main tasks: (a) how to structure the training activity, (b) how to conduct an assessment, (c) how to develop a training plan, (d) how to establish priorities, and (e) how to fund the program.
- Program development. This phase focuses on the availability of training resources, scope, content, and development of training material. The awareness and training program should develop material and identify the audiences and resources for each training course. It also should integrate useful tools to develop security training courses including methodologies such as those provided in. The first step in determining sources of training material to build a course is to decide if the material will be developed in-house or contracted out.
- Program implementation. This phase addresses effective communication for delivery of awareness and training program (ATP) material. Once the plan for implementing the ATP has been explained, the awareness material and messages can be presented and disseminated through the organization using messages, newsletters, computer-based sessions, and so forth. Techniques for effective delivery of training material should take advantage of technologies that support ease of use, scalability, and accountability.
- Program postimplementation. This step develops guidelines to keep the awareness and training program current and monitor its effectiveness. Continuous improvements should always be the theme for security ATP. Processes must be put into place to monitor compliance and effectiveness. An automated tracking system should be designed to capture key information regarding the program.

The ATP should include mechanisms for managing a security training function based on an understanding and assessment of budget and other resource-allocation mechanisms.

## Cost-Effectiveness of the Awareness Process

The needs related to awareness and training should be assessed to ensure the cost-effectiveness of the ATP. Determining these needs is very important because it must be shown that (a) the resources used in the frame of the awareness process have an *acceptable* cost and (b) the awareness process will have an *acceptable* efficiency. Obviously, part of these tasks should be conducted at the risk analysis step. However, some residual tasks can be achieved only after the SP has been developed. NIST guidelines for building the information technology security ATPs gave great importance to this topic. NIST requested that many roles be involved in the needed assessment. Executive managers, security personnel, system owners, system administrators, and operational managers should participate to this task, among others.

# SECURITY POLICY REASSESSMENT: THE AUDITING PROCESS

In the previous sections, we have described how to validate the SP during the different phases of its development. Meanwhile, such a priori validation is not sufficient. In fact, the starting point of the SP development often consists of a formal specification, which is gradually refined. The main shortcoming of this approach is that the specification, by nature, abstracts away some details that could turn out to be relevant. Even the refinement process does not allow a complete description of the environment. As a result, it is necessary to perform a postimplementation validation to verify whether the SP effectively achieves its objectives. This section discusses the SP reassessment by addressing the following key considerations:

- Which data are necessary for the SP assessment?
- How to scan the collected data?
- How to update the SP?

## Collecting Relevant Data

RFC 2196 states that "audit data should include any attempt to achieve a different security level by any person, process, or other entity in the network" (IETF, 1997). This document focuses on the login/logout procedure and does not discuss several important features that are highlighted in the following points:

- The auditing mechanisms, which are integrated in the OSs, do not offer the capability to gather sufficient information about the activity of different entities. For instance, log files containing login attempts are often corrupted by the attacker. Hence, more advanced monitoring tools are needed to give a clearer idea about the behavior of the system.
- When choosing the appropriate monitoring strategy, the following considerations should be thought of:
  1. Privacy: The monitoring process should not divulge private information to the security analysts. For example, the use of a file integrity checker should not give access to the content of the sensitive files to unauthorized users. This issue requires special attention because auditors generally have a lower security level than information owners.
  2. Cost: Information used during the monitoring process may become very voluminous if a high granularity is targeted. The auditors should take into consideration the available storage and processing capabilities before setting the monitoring infrastructure. For example, logging the activity of a firewall might require a dedicated log server. It must be checked whether the cost of this server is proportional to the importance of the information it generates.
  3. Efficiency: Each monitoring tool or procedure must substantially enhance the auditing capabilities. Potential redundancies should be removed.
  4. Security: The collected data includes sensitive information that should be maintained at a high security level. Audit trails must be secured to guarantee their integrity as well as their secrecy.
  5. Quality of service (QoS): Many data collection tools may have a negative effect on the production system of the enterprise. For instance, the sensors used by an IDS can slow the network activity when transmitting the collected data to the corresponding analyzers. Similarly, logging activity may require storage capabilities that cannot be offered by the available resources. Therefore, monitoring should not overwhelm the system with the data it generates.

## Assessing the SP Efficiency

Testing of the SP can be performed through the use of numerous mechanisms that vary according to the tested component. For instance, when testing an authentication policy, the security analyst should first see if an attacker did get through the access control system by spoofing the identity of an authorized user. This can be achieved by using data generated during the collection process. In addition, some penetration tests can serve to fulfill this goal. Many automated tools can be used by auditors in this context. A more interesting topic is the contingency plan.

A contingency plan should be tested periodically because there will undoubtedly be flaws in the plan and in its implementation. The plan will become dated as time passes and as the resources used to support critical functions change. Responsibility for keeping the contingency plan current should be specifically assigned. The extent and frequency of testing will vary among organizations and systems. There are several types of testing, including reviews, analysis, and simulations of disasters.

A *review* can be a simple test to check the accuracy of contingency plan documentation. For instance, a reviewer could check if individuals listed are still in the organization and still have the responsibilities that caused them to be included in the plan. This test can check home and work telephone numbers, organizational codes, and building and room numbers. The review can determine if files can be restored from backup tapes or if employees know emergency procedures.

An *analysis* may be performed on the entire plan or portions of it, such as emergency response procedures. It is advantageous if the analysis is performed by someone who did *not* help develop the contingency plan, but has a good working knowledge of the critical function and supporting resources. The analyst(s) may mentally follow the strategies in the contingency plan, looking for flaws in the logic or process used by the plan's developers. The analyst may also interview functional managers, resource managers, and their staff to uncover missing or unworkable pieces of the plan.

Organizations may also arrange *disaster simulations*. These tests provide valuable information about flaws in the contingency plan and provide practice for a real emergency. Although they can be expensive, these tests can also provide critical information that can be used to ensure the continuity of important functions. In general, the more critical the functions and the resources addressed in the contingency plan, the more cost-beneficial it is to perform a disaster simulation.

The ISO 17799 (BSI, 2000) provides a set of guidelines that can be used to evaluate the security documentation. It addresses a wide spectrum of security aspects including access control, backup and recovery, disaster recovery, risk management, physical security, security monitoring, and security awareness.

## Updating the SP

Several mechanisms must be subordinated to the policy itself to allow detecting events that require several changes in the policy. Also, the lifetime of the security policy is an important issue because it depends heavily on the type of the policy and on the context of the organization. Essentially, SP auditing should occur periodically to keep up with potential changes that may affect the system environment. Moreover, the update process should be triggered by the occurrence of security incidents. This stems from the fact that these incidents are often caused by weaknesses at the SP level.

Updating the SP often follows the same steps as its development (i.e., specification, validation). However, because the modifications are usually partial, in the sense that they touch only some fragments of the original SP, the process should take less time than the original development. Once it has been revised, the SP is then redistributed to the staff in a way that conforms to the awareness strategy.

## LEGAL ASPECTS

A strong interaction between the security policy and the regulatory framework must be considered. Some legal constraints can affect aspects of the security policy. The more important ones are highlighted here.

To take into account these considerations, the responsibilities that are incumbent upon each individual should be clearly defined. Moreover, the SP should be compliant with various laws related, for example, to digital investigation and digital crime penalties. In fact, one of the major benefits of structuring the security activity within the enterprise is to fix the appropriate penalties for someone who violates the SP. These penalties are often considered at the internal level. Administrative and disciplinary measures are defined proportionally to the security fault that has been committed. Nevertheless, some legal procedures can also be conducted to instill a criminal aspect to such faults if they have been previewed by the law of the corresponding country. In the United States, several legal acts (Electronic Confidentiality Act, Electronic Espionage Act, 1996) can illustrate this interaction between the SP and the legal framework. According to the Electronic Espionage Act, stealing sensitive data from an organization is a federal crime that may lead to fines and imprisonment. This Act encourages organizations to put in place the necessary mechanisms to appropriately protect their resources.

## GLOSSARY

**Cost-Effectiveness** The security rules that constitute the policy should contain measures that require an *acceptable* cost. Often, this cost is acceptable if it does not exceed the estimated benefit that would result from the implementation of those measures. Nonetheless, more sophisticated criteria can also be considered.

**Development Lifecycle** The process that should be followed during the development of several assets (e.g., pieces of software, network segments). Achieving the canonical security objectives requires the integration of the security policy within the development lifecycle.

**Formal Model** A mathematical framework that represents rigorously the security requirements and models the rules of a security policy. It allows verification of the consistency of the policy and checks whether it fulfills the security objectives.

**Policy Assessment** Because of the changes that affect the security of the target system, the security policy should be continuously monitored and updated. A periodical assessment of the security rules allows the detection of potential breaches. Moreover, the security policy should be evaluated every time it is violated.

**Risk Analysis (RA)** A process that aims at evaluating (either quantitatively or qualitatively) the threats corresponding to a specific system. It basically consists of determining the critical assets, listing the existing vulnerabilities, and deducing the potential threats. The main interest of risk analysis is that it guarantees cost-effectiveness. Others define RA as the process for measuring the relationship among frequency of attack, cost of attack, and cost of the asset involved.

**Security Awareness** The success of a security program heavily depends upon the level of knowledge that the employees have about it. An awareness program should therefore be conducted. More precisely, the security policy should be documented, distributed, and the staff should be appropriately trained.

**Security Policy** A set of rules that define how a process should be secured. These rules can be applied to a software development process, management of information systems, or communication protocols.

**Validation** The security policy has to be validated at more than one step. During the different phases of its development, every version of the policy should be proven to conform to the regulatory framework, the upper-level version, and the business objectives of the organization.

## CROSS REFERENCES

See *Contingency Planning Management; Implementing a Security Awareness Program; Risk Management for IT Security; The Legal Implications of Information Security: Regulatory Compliance and Liability*.

## REFERENCES

Bell, D. E., & La Padula, L. J. (1976). *Secure computer systems: Unified exposition and Multics interpretation* (Tech. Rep. ESD-TR-75-306). Bedford: MITRE Corporation.

Biba, K. J. (1977). *Integrity considerations for secure computer systems*. Technical Report MTR 3143. Bedford, MA: MITRE Corporation.

British Standard Institute (BSI). (2000). *ISO 17799 toolkit: Policy templates*. Retrieved September 13, 2004, from http://www.iso17799software.com

Campbell, K., Gordon, L. A., Loeb, M. P., & Zhou, L. (2003). The economic cost of publicly announced information security breaches: Empirical evidence from the stock market. *Journal of Computer Security, 11*, 431–448.

Canavan, J. E. (2001). *Fundamentals of network security* (pp. 239–259). Norwood, MA: Artech House.

Canavan, J. E. (2003). *An information security policy: Development guides for large companies*. Bethesda, MD: SANS Institute.

Cholvy, L., & Cuppens, F. (1997, July). *Analyzing consistency of security policies*. Paper presented at the IEEE Symposium on Security and Privacy, Oakland, CA.

CSI/FBI. (2004). *Computer crime and security survey*. Retrieved January 24, 2005, from http://www.gocsi.com

Hare, C. (2000). Policy development. In H. F. Tipton & M. Krause (Eds.), *Handbook of information security* (Vol. 3, Chap. 20, pp. 353–389). New York: Auerbach.

Internet Engineering Task Force (IETF). (1997). *Site security handbook* (RFC 2196). IETF Network Working Group. Retrieved August 24, 2004, from http://www.ietf.org/rfc/rfc2196.txt

Internet Security Systems (ISS). (2000). *Creating, implementing and managing the information security lifecycle*. Retrieved August 24, 2004, from http://documents.iss.net/whitepapers/securitycycle.pdf

Peltier, T. R. (2001). *Information security risk analysis*. New York: Auerbach.

Purser, C. (2004). *A practical guide to managing information security*. Norwood, MA: Artech House.

Ryan, P. Y. A. (2000). *Mathematical models of computer security* (pp. 1–62). Lecture Notes in Computer Science, 2171. Berlin: Springer-Verlag.

Siewe, F., Cau, A., & Zedan, H. (2003, October). *A compositional framework for access control policies enforcement*. Paper presented at the ACM Conference on Computer Security, FMSE '03, Washington, DC.

Swanson, M. (1998). *Guide for developing security plans for information technology systems* (NIST Special Publication 800-18). Retrieved September 4, 2004, from http://www.csrc.nist.gov/publications/nistpubs/800-18/Planguide.pdf

Tudor, J. K. (2001). Security policies, standards, and procedures. *In Information security architecture: An integrated approach to security in the organization* (pp. 79–100). New York: Auerbach.

Wilson, M., & Hash, J. (2003). *Building an information technology security awareness and training program* (NIST Special Publication 800-50). Retrieved September 4, 2004, from http://www.csrc.nist.gov/publications/nistpubs/800-50/NIST-SP800-50.pdf

## FURTHER READING

Swanson, M., Wohl, A., Pope, L., Grance, T., Hash, J., & Thomas, R. (2002). *Contingency planning guide for information technology systems* (NIST Special Publication 800-34). Retrieved September 4, 2004, from http://www.csrc.nist.gov/publications/nistpubs/800-34/op800-34.pdf

U.S. Department of Defense (DoD). (1985). *DoD trusted computer security system evaluation criteria* (*The Orange Book*; DoD 5200.28-STD). Retrieved September 13, 2004, from http://www.boran.com/security/tcsec.html

# Asset–Security Goals Continuum: A Process for Security

Margarita Maria Lenk, *Colorado State University*

## INTRODUCTION

This chapter models a process for a security team to utilize in designing, implementing, and maintaining Internet-related distributed systems security. The position taken by this chapter is that security is best framed as a complex, continuous process rather than as a one-time solution, product, or state. Security failures may occur from a variety of sources such as unauthorized access, unauthorized activities, restricted resources, changing technologies, human errors (fatigue, illness, lack of training or supervision, etc.), a lack of qualified IT staff, and poor communication between the IT staff and top management (Allen, 2001; Garfinkel & Spafford, 2001; IOMA, 2000; SANS, 2002; Stein, 1999). Security affects many different stakeholders who have unique priorities for and valuations of the assets that they desired to be secured. Finally, the effectiveness of security for a distributed system is often determined by the weakest link or piece in the system, rather than the sum of the system strengths. The task for security teams, then, involves not only designing an efficient and effective security system, but also continually assessing and testing the system in efforts to find and correct its weakest links. Anderson (2001) states that "building systems in the face of malice is one of the most important, interesting, and difficult tasks facing engineers in the twenty-first century."

## BUILDING YOUR SECURITY TEAM

Comprehensive security management should begin with the creation and delegation of authority to a knowledgeable, trusted security team. The size and membership of that team will depend on the size of the organization, the dependence of the organization and its business partners on their Internet-related networks for critical business processes (suppliers, customers, creditors, banks, etc.), and the level of risks associated with the organization's industry and practices (regulatory agencies, legal liabilities, etc.). Suggested membership for the comprehensive security team would include top management, a finance officer, an internal audit officer, systems and data administrators, major user group representatives, and major business partner representatives. Business part-ners may be suppliers, contract laborers, outsourced process providers, bankers, creditors, and customers. The many, new types of business affiliations and joint Web services are blurring the line between the organization, its partners, and their environment. These different stakeholders, whether in the organization or in the nexus of surrounding business partners, have varying priorities for and valuations of the assets involved in the distributed systems. Their needs and viewpoints, therefore, need to be included in the security process. Another chapter in this *Handbook* on *security policy guidelines* will help this team create some "ground rules" or guidance for all subsequent security-related decisions and policy creation.

The inclusion of top management representatives and a top financial officer on these security teams is important for several reasons. First, top management's attention typically first goes to issues of market, customer, and product or service quality and fulfillment. The provision of Internet-related network security does not directly bring in any new markets, new customers, or more revenue from existing customers. However, just as security failures can cause business failures or significant negative impacts on corporate image, the perceptions of security or lack thereof can have a sizable effect on customers' choices. Second, top management's influence on organizational culture affects management operating styles, the climate regarding competence, the delegation of authorities and responsibilities, and the policies and procedures for human resources (Greenstein & Vasarhelyi, 2002). Top management's explicit involvement and support is essential for the security policies, procedures, tools, and equipment to be taken seriously by the rest of the employees and other stakeholders. Participation in the security team is an efficient communication that management is willing to "walk the talk" of the importance of security for the organization.

The inclusion of a top finance officer in the security committee membership is important for two primary reasons. The officer can help establish the value, justification of the assets to be protected, the timing and amount of security-related cash outflows, and the metrics that will be used to measure the success or effectiveness of the security investments. Also, the officer can help make "benchmark" comparisons to the competitor's security-related cash outflows.

Internal auditors add the ability to verify vendor products before purchase as well as testing all security measures as to their effectiveness in some manner. The internal auditor will then know the level of internal control inherent to the electronic processes performed on the network. Collaborations with the internal auditors in this regard can result in cost efficiencies in the internal auditing department, as well as providing documentation that may result in cost efficiencies for the external independent audit process.

All policies and resolutions emerging from this team should be formalized in a written document that is signed by each of the team members. This document should be the source of guidance for subsequent security implementation and maintenance decisions.

## ASSET–SECURITY CONTINUUM

Figure 1 illustrates the asset–security continuum. This model has five individual elements: assets, risks, threats, controls, and security goals. Risks are defined as either the bad things that can happen to the assets or the likelihood of those bad things. Threats are defined as the sources of those risks. Controls are defined as the policies, procedures, and tools that reduce or eliminate the sources of risk. For example, business interruption is a serious risk, and power outages are one source or business interruption. A related control would be backup power supply. Another example: Fraud and embezzlement are serious risks, and unauthorized access to accounting records is one source for these risks. Maintained and protected access authorizations help reduce the ability to gain unauthorized access to accounting records.

Below the continuum, Figure 1 depicts four "dyads" representing the relationships among the individual elements of business' assets, risks, threats, controls, and security goals. The value of these dyads is that they break down the steps between assets and security goals into "discussion-able" dyads involving assets and their risks, risks and their threats (sources of risk), threats and controls, and controls and security goals.

Although the continuum may be "worked" from either endpoint, this chapter discusses an assets-to-security goals approach. The first step is to identify clearly the mission and primary strategies of the organization. Next, the security team identifies and prioritizes the assets that are critical to the execution of these strategies. All assets are to be considered, whether tangible or intangible, and physical or logical. An inclusive approach, involving assets from all areas of the organization, is recommended to avoid any political lock-jams.

Assets are the tangible and intangible aspects of a business that provide future value for the business. Examples of assets include servers, payroll systems, customer lists, patents, the database administrator's specific knowledge, or your organization's reputation for prompt, accurate responses to customers. Assets need to be identified and then dynamically categorized in terms of their priority with respect to the corporate mission and strategies. The dynamic categorization refers to the consideration of the timing of the risks and threats to those assets. For example, if the payroll application were to crash immediately after the electronic fund transfer instructions were sent to the bank, the corporation would have the time until the next payday to recover the payroll application. However, if the payroll application were to crash 1 hour before the normal fund transfer to employee accounts, the payroll system would have a much higher priority for the security system.

For each critical asset, the next step is to identify and prioritize the risks that may damage or negatively affect the organization's asset(s). Risks are defined in this model as events or circumstances that cause an organization to lose current or future market value. Examples of risks include business interruption or delay, excessive costs, theft or loss of assets, loss of revenues, loss of customer loyalty, loss of competitive advantage, legal or regulatory sanctions, and loss of intellectual property. Because of the political possibilities that may result from risk identification, these risks may have to be discussed at the lowest organizational unit level possible, and combined upward with regard to the organizational structure.

The next step involves identifying the specific threats to each asset–risk pair identified in the prior step. It is important to consider the factors and circumstances within the organization as well as in the external environment. Examples of threats from the external environment include malicious or curious hackers, new attack technologies, new regulatory standards, unexpected new competitors, misuse or abuse of your data by application service providers, earthquakes, floods, or war-related attacks. Examples of threats from the internal environment include malicious employees, software or hardware failures, outdated systems, undocumented systems, unintentional human error, and a lack of training, documentation, supervision, or review of employee activities.

For each identified threat from the prior step, a list of general and specific controls that may reduce or eliminate that threat is developed. Security controls are the policies, procedures, techniques, tools, habits, and leadership

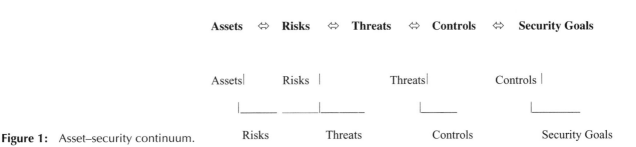

**Assets** ⇔ **Risks** ⇔ **Threats** ⇔ **Controls** ⇔ **Security Goals**

Assets|   Risks |   Threats|   Controls |

Risks        Threats        Controls        Security Goals

**Figure 1:**  Asset–security continuum.

structures and attitudes designed to reduce threats to an organization. An alternative framework for controls is to consider security-related controls to be those elements of an organization that contribute to the efficiency and effectiveness of operations, the safeguarding of assets, and compliance with legal and regulatory rules. Security controls can be pervasive throughout the organization (top management's attitude or the standard hiring practices) or as narrow-scoped and specific as a reasonableness check on one attribute of a table within in a database for a specific application.

Controls can be classified as preventative if they restrict the event from occurring, detective if they sound an alarm when the event is discovered, and corrective if they help restore the situation to that prior to the security-reducing event. Passwords are preventative controls because they are designed to keep unauthorized access from occurring. Logouts are detective controls that shut down login opportunities when a specific number of failed login attempts occur. Backups are corrective controls that restore the system to the state at the last time that the backups were made.

Controls can be required or discretionary, depending on the specifics of the situation or the judgment of the individual. Controls can be evaluated for effectiveness, which regards how the control helps increase the probability that a particular security goal is achieved. Also, controls can be categorized for efficiency, in terms of the number of threats mitigated by a particular control. Conversely, control redundancy (more than one control for a particular asset, process, or store) may be desired for highly vulnerable or valuable items for a business.

Security goals are the specific statements made by an organization to explain and communicate their security-related objectives. For example, organizations dependent on their Web commerce may want their Web servers functional 24 hours per day, 7 days per week. Companies with proprietary Web services may want to keep their code or methods confidential. Companies negotiating online with their suppliers or their customers may want to keep the negotiations secret so that none of the other competitors learn of their decisions. The security objectives should be stated in a manner that encourages assessment with specific confidence intervals and system reliability goals clearly articulated.

Comprehensive security for an organization is maximized when careful research and reflection occurs for each of the dyads in the asset–security continuum. The power of this model lies in the work within the individual dyad linkages rather than having a focus on the endpoints. Two examples are provided. First, consider purchasing negotiations with a primary supplier as the asset. Risks related to this asset include rising costs, for example, resulting from damages to the relationship with this supplier. Threats that increase this risk include errors in the online purchasing system, such as duplicate, erroneous, or unauthorized orders. Control procedures designed to mitigate these threats include automated field verification procedures, encryption, and digital signatures for all electronic communications with this supplier to achieve a security goal confidence that all communications have been confidential and authenticated.

A second example involves a business's customer database as the asset. A risk to this asset includes reduced customer service. Although there are several threats that could cause this risk, one of these could be a lack of integrity in the data regarding the customers (which could be due to hackers modifying the database, careless employees inputting errors, ineffective database design that does not allow important queries to be performed, etc.). Control plans that reduce these threats range from access controls (e.g., passwords and/or encryption) to application design and modification procedures and controls. The security goal for this example could be to have real-time accurate information on all customers. The next sections review each of the individual components of the asset–security continuum: assets, risks, threats, controls, and security goals.

## IDENTIFYING AND CLASSIFYING ASSETS

Organizations derive their current and future value from their assets. Their assets may be physical or digital, such as property, equipment, data, and software, or intangible, such as intellectual capital or a reputation of providing the best service. Security teams should first identify all value-providing assets and second, prioritize, or place a relative value that corresponds to the importance toward the organizational mission and strategies, on each asset. In this process, each stakeholder typically has a unique set of asset priorities that must be reconciled with the other members on the security team. Moreover, security teams must consider the dynamic nature of most environments and organizations; assets change for a variety of reasons (e.g., business restructurings, new technologies, and new partnerships). Finally, the priorities of different assets are sometimes a function of the timing of the threat. For example, consider a 2-week payroll application as the asset, and its inability to function as the risk. Threats related to this risk include hardware and software failure, malicious human actions, and even power outages. The priority of the payroll application asset will be much higher if the threat occurs immediately before direct deposits of employees' paychecks than if the threat occurs immediately after the employees get paid (which would provide you with 2 weeks in which to correct the problem).

Security teams need to develop a measure of the value of these assets to know what the ceiling, or maximum value to spend, in security controls for these assets. Most organizations have current or near-current lists of the physical assets related to the distributed systems: servers; motherboards; central processing units; memory modules; network interface, video, serial, and printer port cards; printers; scanners; multimedia devices; screens; power supplies; hard, floppy, and tape drives; CD-ROM readers; modems; and network cables, hubs, switches, bridges, and routers. Database administrators typically have lists and libraries containing descriptions of their system components and the logical assets within the databases. Proper documentation of the original copies of current software, service packs, and operating systems is recommended. For the physical assets (at least), a multiattribute classification scheme is recommended with the following categories: asset type (e.g., hardware, software, library references, communication equipment or channel wiring, wireless and portable tools); scope of asset utilization (general or specific application); organizational owner of the asset; physical or logical residence for the asset (with the physical asset identification number if relevant); relevant contract ancillaries (service level, warranties, updates, key contacts, etc.); sensitivity of data (e.g., personnel files, customer information); backups; and whether audit records are kept.

Oftentimes many organizations do not have lists of their other logical or intangible assets, such as branding; public image; customer service; product quality reputation; and information processing availability, confidentiality, and integrity. The security team may begin by reviewing the organizational mission, strategies, and tactics for operational goals. Then, for each goal, the security team can determine the assets that are required for these goals. Alternatively, the assets may be categorized first by their function to the organization, such as communication, staff responsibilities, supplier issues, data and property protection, and operational functionality (Lynn, 2001). Most information technology leaders recommend organizing assets by asset type as the best practice.

Once identified, the assets need to be prioritized in terms of their relative importance for security-related investments. These priorities can differ between stakeholders (e.g., a salesperson may value a customer database more highly than a purchasing agent). The participation of top management, finance officers, and internal auditors at this step will help keep this prioritization process focused on organizational goals. Most security system methodologies utilize a four- to six-level method for priorities, with a wide range of labels for each level. For example, the highest level of asset may be termed "strategic" or "critical" if impairment to the asset even for a small amount of time could cause serious interruption for the business. An example of a critical asset for an online bookstore would be its online shopping cart technology. The second highest level of priority could be labeled "tactical" or "sensitive" if the company could continue to function for the short run with that asset in an impaired state, yet the company would suffer significant losses in the long run without repair to these assets. The next level of priority may be termed "noncritical," indicating that the organization could function for a longer period without the asset; however, there may be cost or service effects in the long run that warrant consideration. The lowest level of asset priority could be labeled "nonsensitive," which means that if the asset is lost, the organization would easily find another way to create the value that the nonsensitive asset provided before the threat was realized.

The best practices for data classifications are those that indicate the level of criticality or sensitivity toward loss or disclosure to unauthorized audiences. Sensitive data have a higher than average need for assurance of accuracy and completeness (e.g., financial data). Confidential data have a higher than average need for confidentiality (e.g., customer lists and ordering history). Private data are items that could lead to legal consequences for the organization if accessed inappropriately (e.g., personnel health information). Public data are data that will not create a loss of value for the organization if it were to be inadvertently accessed, even if there is a policy to keep that information proprietary. Note that these dimensions are not a continuum, and any one asset may register on more than one dimension (Herrmann, 2002; Microsoft, 2003; NIST, 2004)

## IDENTIFYING RISKS, THREATS, AND PROBABLE LOSSES

There are many risks to our Internet-related wired and wireless networked environments. Threats can emerge from inside the organization as a result of a lack of leadership, poor utilization of technologies, human error or weaknesses, or physical environment problems. Threats can also result from external sources such as malicious independent parties, past/present business partners, or environmental changes (Rubin, 2001). Table 1 lists some of the sources of threats to an organization's distributed system security.

Significant risks can be caused by any of the stakeholders, employees, or unrelated hackers through viruses; manipulations of or errors/failures in software, hardware, telecommunications; or human error. Moreover, a comprehensive security team must discuss the importance of market or individual stakeholder perceptions of Internet-related risks, which may be higher than the actual risks.

It is important to remember that although a physical burglar can only enter one house at a time, a virtual burglar can enter many doors at one time, and it may be difficult to tell which doors have been opened.

Cisco (2001) identifies the primary perpetrators who reduce organizational security as unrelated hackers or snoops and unaware or disgruntled staff, either current or past employees. These perpetrators are interested in accessing, altering, damaging, copying, and stealing assets, whether digital or physical. Many times their most common vehicles include password guessing; introducing viruses, worms, and Trojan horses; reconnaissance attacks such as social engineering (whose purpose is information gathering); and the use of sniffers and scanners. System access points are the primary "targets" for security attacks. Common attacks include the modification of authentication services and file transfer protocol (FTP) functionality, data interception, packet replaying, packet modification, Internet protocol (IP) spoofing, denial of service, and manipulation of e-mail accounts and databases.

The security team should identify all of the possible threats that can access, alter, damage, destroy, or steal each asset. The threat assessment can be performed one asset at a time, each one considered independently or within groups of similar assets. For example, the asset of stored economic transaction information can face intentional and unintentional threats such as hardware or software errors; malicious programming such as viruses, Trojan horses, or worms; modifications made by authorized or unauthorized access, human error, negligence, or ignorance; changes in regulations or laws; natural disasters such as fires; or damage resulting from power surges, excess water or dust, or vandalism (Herrmann, 2002; Microsoft, 2003; NIST, 2004).

**Table 1** Sample Security Threats

| | |
|---|---|
| Advanced intrusion scanning techniques | Malicious Java applets |
| Airwave jamming techniques | Misconfiguration of e-mail protocols |
| Burglary and theft | Naming convention errors |
| Concurrency errors | Out-of-date hardware protection systems |
| Cracking techniques | Out-of-date intrusion detection systems |
| Cross-site scripting | Password mismanagement |
| Denial of service attacks | Phone "phreaking" |
| Digital payment alterations/fraud | Physical security threats |
| Disabled automated audit functions | Privacy violations |
| Distributed attack tools | Race conditions (multistage attacks) |
| Distributed denial of service attacks | Remote access violations |
| E-commerce vulnerabilities | Server and e-mail system bugs |
| Electronic and wave emissions | Side channel attacks |
| E-mail threats and vulnerabilities | Sniffing |
| Encryption key mismanagement | Spoofing |
| External events | Spyware |
| Fault tolerance errors, omissions, and attacks | Stack overflow attacks |
| Filtering technologies bugs | Stack smashing (memory overwrites) |
| Geographic separations from solutions | Staged attacks |
| Hacking techniques | SYN flooding |
| Hijacking sessions | Third-party services |
| Holes in operating system access controls | Turnover in IT administration |
| Identity theft | Viruses, worms, and Trojan horses (malicious code) |
| Intellectual property theft | Vulnerable CGI programs |
| Internal security threats | Weak SNMP protocol |
| Lack of employee training/supervision | Web bugs (attached to HTML) |
| Malicious human behavior | Wireless threats and attacks |

# CALCULATING THE MAXIMUM COST OF CONTROLS

Once the assets have been identified and prioritized, many organizations take the time to make classifications or categorizations to group these assets. The risks related to these categories of assets are then organized, and the threats that cause each category of risks are detailed. The next step is to calculate the maximum cost to spend on security-related controls. The maximum cost calculation is an expected-value algorithm based on the idea that the security costs for an asset (or asset category) should never be more than the value of the asset(s).

First, the security team should estimate the probability that the threats will occur. This estimation involves judgment, experience, and expertise. Best practices recommend that organizations hire independent, external experts, such as consultants or "red teams" for this task who can use prior event records and testimonies, past experiences, published reports, or data purchased from insurance or utility companies.

Second, the security team should estimate the conditional probability that a loss will occur given that the threats have occurred. The third step is to calculate the loss to the organization by estimating the loss in monetary terms. This estimate should include the replacement costs of the damaged assets but also the hours of time spent internally on the situation (time that could have been spent on productive tasks), as well as the intangible effects on relationships (e.g., the loss of trust or timeliness

and/or accuracy of customer orders). Again, internal past experiences, the viewpoints of current partners, and independent loss experts can assist with this estimation.

The fourth step is to calculate the expected value of the loss conditional on the threat occurring. This is the product of the monetary value estimate of the loss and the conditional probability that a loss will occur given that the threat has occurred. This multiplication product is the maximum cost that an organization should invest in security solutions for that asset for that threat/set of threats. For the entire security budget, these expected values should be summed up for all categories of risks and/or assets.

# TYPES OF SECURITY CONTROLS

Security controls are also called security tools. They include an extensive choice of administrative structures and a variety of technologies ranging from antivirus software to audit-tracking solutions to dedicated hardware such as firewalls and intrusion detection systems. Table 2 lists many of the most common types of comprehensive security system controls.

A common struggle is how to organize security controls. Controls can be organized by business unit, business strategy, by type of asset, by type of risk, and by type or source of threat. Controls may also be categorized by the nature of how they work: preventative controls, inspection controls, detection of internal failure controls, and correction of external failure controls. Other classification

**Table 2** Examples of Security Controls

| | |
|---|---|
| Access control | Medical records security |
| Ad blockers | Mobile code and agents |
| Antivirus technologies | Mobile code controls |
| Audit trails, logs, and alarms | Multicast data authentication |
| Backups | Overtly enforced security policies |
| Biometric technologies and authentication | Overall management style/support |
| Board of Directors audit committee | Passwords |
| Client-side security and digital certificates | Password authentication |
| Cluster server technologies | Physical security measures |
| Code-signing methods | Protection from malicious code |
| Configuration structures and policies | Protection of Web sites |
| Cookie crushers and other privacy protections | Quality service providers |
| Cryptography | RAID techniques (disk mirroring) |
| Database security | Redundant capacity |
| Deception techniques: honeypots and decoys | RFID tags |
| Digital signatures and electronic signatures | Securing Web sessions: SSL and other options |
| Disaster recovery planning | Securing automatic teller machine (ATM) networks |
| DNS protection | Server-side security |
| E-commerce safeguards | Smart card security |
| Encrypting email | SSL server certificates |
| Evidential issues | Tamper-resistant hardware |
| Firewalls and other packet-filtering technologies | User authentication |
| Identity management | Virtual private networks |
| Intrusion detection and response | Web application controls |
| Logging mechanisms | Web page content access control |

schemes separate the manual controls from the automated or computerized controls, or by whether the exercise of the control is mandatory or discretionary. Others organize controls with respect to where they apply to the distributed system asset components: hardware, software, mobile units, data, telecommunication channels, third-party issues, management, auditors, and employees. Yet others classify the controls according to their pervasiveness or specificity. Finally, many organizations classify their controls by the nature of the control (e.g., cryptography, firewall, intrusion detection system). The utilization of databases for asset–security continuum information allows organizations to efficiently retrieve queries on assets, risks, threats, controls, or security goals under a variety of viewpoints. Regardless of how an organization organizes their information regarding security controls, security team members must (a) define the cost and purpose (expected benefit) of each control, (b) distribute knowledge and responsibility for the control, and (c) regularly audit the efficiency and effectiveness of each control.

Security teams also develop and document organizational security policies regarding the culture toward security, top management's support for security, and the consequences of intentional internal violations of security policy. Security policies include rules about e-mail, Internet access, passwords, and remote access. Security policies for communication of suspected violations and adverse events are also included. From these policies, employees should be able to clearly understand the expectations for security-related behaviors, performance, and accountability. The three most common problems regarding security policies are (a) the policy is not written in a

manner that communicates clearly to non-IT employees, (b) the policy is not read or utilized by any employees, and (c) the security team does not "sell" the importance of security to employees in general. These problems typically result in less than organization-wide support for security. Oftentimes, a first step to improve the security culture involves having new employees read and sign the security policies upon hiring. Existing employees may be asked to read and sign the security policy at their next employee evaluation.

Oftentimes, the general security policies are written to be in compliance with the recommendations of the corporate attorney or the independent auditor. Management may utilize a variety of tools, such as security newsletters, lobby videos, and guest speakers on security issues followed by question-and-answer periods, to increase the visibility of and commitment to general security policies. Revision of security policies is warranted whenever there are new types of assets, risks, or threats (such as the publication of new software patches, etc.) or experiences as a result of incidents that warrant a change in policy (Garfinkel, Schwartz, & Spafford, 2003).

The security controls that involve human interaction must be analyzed closely for effectiveness and hidden costs. First, there needs to be a balance between the benefit of the control procedure and the effect on the individual performing the procedure. Many times, too many controls on a task will make the task inefficient and the employee may skip the controls that slow down his or her performance. If controls are too loose, on the other hand, then there may be security threats resulting from lack of control. An example of a frustrating control plan is having too many door keypads. Employees may be motivated to eliminate the control by propping the door open.

Cisco (2001) offers several "top" security controls to keep in mind as part of a comprehensive network security solution. First, they recommend the use of unobvious passwords that are changed every 3 months. Second, they support widespread security education for employees and business partners, especially with regards to the risks associated with e-mail attachments, and the use of the same current antivirus software throughout the organization(s). Third, immediate removal of network access is recommended when employees are terminated. Fourth, the use of centrally administrated servers for all remote access traffic is preferred. Fifth, the removal of all unutilized network services is an important Internet-related control for distributed systems. Sixth, Cisco also recommends maintaining current versions of Web server software. Finally, the establishment of a periodic review of the organizations' assets and risks is suggested to determine the current effectiveness of their security solutions.

Network configuration choices can dramatically affect the security issues within the network. Network services should only involve the minimum necessary functionality. Network administrator "back doors" should all be closed off. Network policies and procedures should be clearly stated, kept current, and periodically audited. Networks are in a state of continuous change, with new topographies, resources, and users. Network-level controls include integrity-checking utilities and documentation of registry changes, system development and maintenance records, and network-testing results. Network scanning software is a preventative control that can be utilized to locate security weaknesses before there is an adverse security incident. Cisco (2001) recommends that organizations hire professionals with demonstrated expertise, experience, and certifications for periodic security assessments on distributed systems.

IPs determine the security rules with regard to Web servers and clients (browsers). Threats can attack Web servers directly or indirectly and use the Web server to attack internal systems. Particularly vulnerable are Web servers' operating systems and Web server software. IP-based networks were originally engineered to be open systems, and efforts at maintaining openness while improving security can be inefficient. Even with sound security procedures, networks utilizing the IP protocols are still open to threats such as sniffing, man-in-the-middle, and spoofing attacks.

The most common forms of security control for Web servers are firewalls and intrusion detection systems, both of which filter users and packets coming in or going out to the Internet. These controls can be hardware, software, or hybrid solutions. Firewalls, for example, can stop unauthorized traffic both incoming and outgoing. They can direct allowed incoming traffic throughout the distributed system. They can protect network resources by hiding data and internal systems from inquiring entry requests. They can have audit functionalities for log requests and traffic. Types of firewalls include packet-filtering gateways, application gateways, and hybrid systems.

Intrusion detection systems can work at the network, host, or application levels. Both firewalls and intrusion detection systems work to restrict access to authorized users and authorized types of packets coming in to or going out from internal authorized sources or users. The functionality is similar to the use of physical locks and peepholes on doors: only those either recognized or with the appropriate key are allowed to enter.

Passwords are the most common access restriction control. Password policies should be developed by the network administrators. Policies should cover password creation, storage, utilization, change process, and deletion process. Access management is simplified when user groups are established, with policies written specifically for each user group. Employees should be trained to delete all stored items, especially passwords, after a session on a computer at cybercafes and airport lounges. Individuals should be allowed to try to log in with a password a few times before account lockout policies are activated. After lockout begins, the user must contact a system administrator for access.

Another essential control for networked environments is antivirus software. This software detects viruses entering or on a system, identifies the particular virus, and then removes the virus before, during, or after it executes. Antivirus software utilizes three types of detection tools. Static detection is the strongest tool of the three, detecting the virus before execution. Further downstream is the detection control by interception software. This software can catch a virus's attempts to infect boot sectors, applications, or data files. Another detection control is the practice of modification audits, which search for unexpected modification of executables. This control is the furthest downstream of the three methods, only detecting the virus well after it has been infecting the system. In this case, the antivirus software must systematically search through the system to remove all possible instances of the virus.

Controls related to validity and verification of identity involve authentication of the sender or receiver of transmitted messages. Controls related to authentication include digital certificates or public key certificates from certificate authorities, biometric devices, smart cards with private keys, and passwords. These authentication controls are recommended even in the situations where encrypted "tunnels" of secure traffic have been created on the Internet as virtual private networks. Other access measures include dual- and triple-item tests, challenge-response systems, and callback procedures for remote access attempts.

Encryption tools can scramble characters within messages and/or messages within Web sessions (e.g., SSL) to make it more difficult for unauthorized access. Encryption can be utilized to ensure data integrity through the use of digital signatures, which are message digests encrypted with the sender's private key, to be decrypted usually by the receiver with the sender's public key. Public trust is encouraged because the sender first registers with a certificate authority, who provides the sender with a private key for the encryption. The sender digests the message and then encrypts the message and its digest with the private, or secret, key. If the recipient of the message is doubtful about the sender, he or she can check with the certificate authority for validation of the identity of the sender.

Public key/private key dual encryption pairs are utilized to provide sender and receiver authentication and confidentiality. Pretty good privacy and S/MIME (secure/multipurpose Internet mail extensions) are two methods that can authenticate the originator and provide message confidentiality. S/MIME digitally signs and encrypts each e-mail message: sender authentication (validating the origin), message integrity (detecting whether any changes have been made to the contents), message confidentiality (no unauthorized recipients), and nonrepudiation (validating origin, receipt, timing, and contents). After transmission, files stored on a network server may also need to be secured. Microsoft's encrypting files systems is a Microsoft NT example of a symmetric key encryption for stored files.

Network auditing tools assist administrators to monitor activity to detect rather than prevent any problems. For example, audit logs contain records of logins, file accesses, password changes, and logoffs. Most audit software has extensive log files and audit trails that are useful to research the source of a bug or a break-in and to determine the amount and scope of the damage. Audit logs are also useful documentation for legal testimony and for claims toward insurance recoveries. Risks associated with auditing include unauthorized modification to the audit log tables and system performance degradation.

Recovery controls include the creation of backups and redundant processing capacity in the case of contingency or disaster recovery planning. Comprehensive security teams need to create backup policies, decide which files are backed up (e.g., databases, mail servers, user files, registries), how often they will be created, on which media, on which type of backup device (e.g., CD writers, tape drives, network shares), and when the backups will be periodically tested. Storage of backups can be onsite in a fireproof safe, or offsite, either in a hot site, cold site, or safety deposit box.

Disaster recovery plans typically identify an incident response team that is trained to know how to respond to an emergency. The location of reboot disks, the original software installation disks and license agreements, the names and addresses of vendor contacts, records of disk partition descriptions, and hardware configurations are all important to provide to the incident response team members.

Fault tolerance, disk mirroring, disk duplexing, and desk striping with parity are different types of redundant array of inline disks techniques, which are methods of backing up distributed system servers. Each method has its benefits and drawbacks. For example, disk mirroring backs up more of what is on the original disk than some of the other methods, but it is the least efficient in terms of disk storage utilization. Disk striping with parity separates data and parity information so that if there is a disaster, the information can be rebuilt with greater probability. This control works best when large database read operations are performed more often than write operations, and is weak when high-speed data retrieval is needed or when many write operations are required.

Cluster server technologies are groups of servers that have been programmed to act as a single, large unit. Resources and responsibilities are distributed among the servers within the cluster. One of the main advantages is the resulting low probability of downtime because if one server fails, the other servers continue to function. The more servers and backup systems that are added to the cluster, the lower the risk of system failure and the greater the likelihood of system availability. Another benefit of cluster server technologies is load balancing, which maximizes performance of the network by improving the throughput, a primary goal of Web, e-commerce, and FTP application servers (Cisco, 2001).

Additional design features include event handling, software patches, operating system weaknesses, architectural segregation of internal/external zones when using firewalls, and application development policies related to secure access. Best practices depend on the platform and software involved, and the creation, analysis, and maintenance of documentation regarding corporate "security tolerance" philosophy (e.g., the number and type of errors that are allowable or not).

Once the security controls have been determined, the security team must decide the specifics of the policies, methodologies, and technologies that will be utilized. Also, the security team must decide how to communicate the new or existing policies, changes, and security alerts to all of the stakeholders. Finally, the security team must design an implementation plan, execute the plan, and periodically audit and maintain the security system.

## SECURITY GOALS

The effectiveness of a comprehensive security system should be measured against previously stated and measurable security goals. Therefore, it is the responsibility of the security team to evaluate the mission and strategies of the organization along with the prioritized assets to develop a set of explicit security goals. These goals may be stated in terms of the organization's mission, operational goals, and strategies, or through the functions of prioritized assets, or through the mitigation of the threats that were avoided or reduced by the security system.

Lynn (2001) suggests security goals to be organized in terms of corporate communications to stakeholder (employees, insurance companies, suppliers, customers, regulatory agencies, technical support services, etc.), staff responsibilities (in terms of the chain of command, individual responsibilities, and checks for task coverage), supplier issues (order to run time), data protection (system performance, system of backups, and testing), property protection (equipment, furnishings, library, supplies, etc.), and operations (software, operating systems, emergency lighting, sprinklers, smoke detectors, extinguishers, utility shutoffs, backup generators, evacuation procedures, exit routes).

## CONCLUSION

The purpose of this chapter is to provide a process for comprehensive security in an organization. An asset–risk–threat–control–security goals continuum was presented along with the utilization of a multistakeholder security team as the best practice for organizational security. The first step involves the creation of a cross-functional security team with top management membership. The second step identifies both the priority assets (including property, data, and people) and risks affecting those assets. The third step evaluates the specific threats that create the risks and calculates the maximum cost of controls. The fourth step researches and plans appropriate controls for the priority assets and risks. The nature of these controls can range from general to specific, from preventative to corrective, and from manual to computerized. Finally, the security controls are matched to overall security goals for the organization.

This dyadic structure of the continuum emphasizes the important interrelationships among the consecutive elements of the asset–security model: assets and risks to those assets, risks and specific threats that cause those risks, threats and specific controls, and specific controls and overall security goals. The process of working through the four dyads within the model should develop a deeper understanding of the security relationships within the organization and lead to stronger security solutions. The importance of top management participation on the security team is emphasized for the validity, economic justification, and overall support for security programs to be taken seriously within an organization.

# GLOSSARY

**Access Control** A set of mechanisms and policies that restrict use of various computer resources.

**Account Lockout** A security feature that closes login access to a user account if a number of failed logon attempts occur within a specified duration of time. Lockout is based on security policy lockout settings.

**Antivirus Software** Used to prevent viruses from damaging a computer or to remove viruses from the computer.

**Application Gateway** An application gateway is an application program that runs on a firewall system between two networks. When a client program establishes a connection to a destination service, it connects to an application gateway, or proxy. The client then negotiates with the proxy server to communicate with the destination service. This creates two connections: one between the client and the proxy server and one between the proxy server and the destination. Once connected, the proxy makes all packet-forwarding decisions. Because all communication is conducted through the proxy server, computers behind the firewall are protected.

**Audit-Tracking Solution** A solution to determine through investigation the adequacy of, and adherence to, established procedures, instructions, specifications, codes, and standards or other applicable contractual and licensing requirements. Audit tracking is built into the operation of a system and ensures all interactions with the system are first authorized before being carried out and then recorded permanently in an operations log.

**Audit Trail** A record that shows who has accessed a computer system and where and what operations were performed during a given period of time. Audit trails are used for system reliability, accuracy, security, and recovery purposes.

**Authentication** The process of identifying an individual, usually based on a username and password. Authentication ensures that the individual is who he or she claims to be, but says nothing about the access rights of the individual.

**Authorization** The process of giving individuals access to system objects based on their identity.

**Biometric Devices** Devices and techniques used to identify and authenticate individuals or users through authentication techniques that rely on measurable physical characteristics that can be automatically checked, including computer analysis of fingerprints, speech, and facial characteristics.

**Boot Sector** The first sector on every floppy and hard disk, containing an executable program that is executed every time a PC is switched on or booted.

**Callback Procedure** A callback procedure is a validation measure that involves passing a procedure (or function) as a parameter to another procedure. When a certain event occurs in the procedure that was called, the callback procedure is triggered. When the callback procedure has completed execution, the control is passed back to the original procedure.

**Certificate Authority** A trusted third-party organization or company whose purpose is to issue digital certificates and create digital signatures and public–private key pairs. They are a critical component in data security and e-commerce because they guarantee the two parties exchanging information are really who they claim to be.

**Cluster** A collection of systems connected to share devices, whereupon all systems can read or write to all of the devices. The individual computers in a cluster are referred to as nodes.

**Cluster Server Technologies** Usually of two types—shared-disk and shared-nothing. The former implementation allows all cluster participants (nodes) to own and access cluster disk resources. In the latter, several nodes in the cluster may have access to a device or resource, but the resource is owned and managed by only one system at a time. Each node has its own memory, system disk, operating system, and subset of the cluster's resources.

**Cold Site** A disaster recovery service that allows a business to continue computer and network operations even in the face of computer or equipment failure by providing office space, but the customer provides and installs all the equipment needed to continue operations. It is less expensive but takes longer to get an enterprise in full operation after the disaster.

**Cross-Site Scripting (also called XSS)** Occurs when a Web application gets malicious data from a user, usually in the form of a hyperlink. The request looks less suspicious to the user when clicked on, but may lead to threats like account hijacking, changing of user settings, cookie theft/poisoning, or false advertising.

**Cryptography** The art of protecting information by transforming it (by encrypting it) into an unreadable format, called cipher text. Only those who possess a secret key should be able to decipher (or decrypt) the message into plain text.

**Cybercafé** A public or private location where one can connect via a computer to the Internet, typically for a flat fee plus a time-for-services fee.

**Database** A software application designed to help users organize information so that a computer program can quickly find and select desired information. Databases can be thought of as electronic filing systems.

**Digital Certificate** An attachment to an electronic message used for security purposes. The most common use of a digital certificate is to verify that a user sending a message is who he or she claims to be and to provide the receiver with the means to encode a reply.

**Digital Signature** Acts as the functional equivalent of a paper signature. A digital signature uniquely identifies a sender and can make a document binding. It can also be used to ensure that the original content of the message or document that has been conveyed is unchanged. They are becoming increasingly important in e-commerce as a component of authentication schemes.

**Disk Duplexing or Mirroring** A technique in which data is written to two duplicate disks simultaneously. If one of the disk drives fails, the system can instantly switch to the other disk without any loss of data or service. Disk mirroring is used commonly in online database systems where it is critical that the data be accessible at all times.

**Disk Striping** A technique for spreading data over multiple disk drives. The computer system breaks a body of data into units and spreads these units across available disks. Disk striping can speed up operations that retrieve data from disk storage.

**Distributed System** A distributed system is a collection of system resources that are physically at different locations but are shared among various users. The distribution is transparent to the user so that the system appears as one local machine.

**Encryption** The process or translation of data into a secret code. Encrypted data is called "cipher text" and unencrypted data is called "plain text."

**Fault Tolerance** The ability of a system to respond gracefully to an unexpected hardware or software failure. There are many levels of fault tolerance, from the ability to continue operation in the event of a power failure to performing every operation on two or more duplicate systems, so if one fails, the other can take over.

**Firewall** A system designed to prevent unauthorized access to or from a private network. Firewalls can be implemented in either hardware and/or software. All messages entering or leaving a network pass through the firewall, which examines each message and blocks those that do not meet specified security criteria.

**FTP (File Transfer Protocol)** Used on the Internet for sending or transferring files from one location to another.

**Host** A computer system that is accessed by a user working at a remote location.

**Hot Site** A commercial disaster recovery service that allows a business to continue computer and network operations even in the face of a failure. The affected enterprise can move all data processing operations to a hot site that has all the equipment needed for the enterprise to continue operation, including office space and furniture, telephone jacks, and computer equipment.

**Integrity** Data integrity refers to the validity or accuracy of stored data. Human errors, data transmission errors, software viruses or bugs, hardware malfunctions, and natural disasters may compromise data integrity.

**Integrity-Checking Utilities** Programs used for executing file system integrity checks on remote hosts from a server and sending reports via e-mail.

**Internet** The worldwide collection of interconnected networks and computers using and sharing information based on set rules defined by protocols such as TCP/IP.

**Intrusion Detection System** Inspection system checks all inbound and outbound network activities and identifies suspicious patterns.

**IP-Based Network** A network running on the Internet protocol. Each computer on the Internet (known as a host) has at least one IP address that uniquely identifies it from all other computers.

**IP Spoofing** A technique used to gain unauthorized access to computers. Here an intruder sends a message to a computer with an IP address indicating that the message is coming from a trusted host, thereby beguiling the user.

**Key** A string of bits used in cryptography that allows people to encrypt and decrypt data. The key determines the mapping of the plaintext to the ciphertext.

**Load Balancing** Distributing processing and communications activity evenly across a computer network with multiple servers so that a server is not overwhelmed. If one server starts to get swamped, requests are forwarded to other servers.

**Login** The recognition and authorization procedure used to connect a user to a computer system by using credentials such as username and password.

**Logout** The closing procedure used to disconnect from a computer system or formally end a session with the system. Once you log out, you must log back in to regain access.

**Network** A group of two or more computers connected together, usually to share resources.

**Network Administrator "Back Door"** An undocumented way of gaining access to a program, online service, or computer system. The back door, written by the original programmer, allows changes to be made. A back door is a potential security risk.

**Online Shopping Cart** A piece of software that acts as a catalog for an online store and also performs the ordering process. A shopping cart is an interface between a company's Web site and its infrastructure that allows consumers to select merchandise, review what they have selected, make necessary modifications or additions, and eventually purchase the items in the cart.

**Operating System** A software that serves as an interface between the system hardware and the users. The operating system is the most important program on a computer. Operating systems perform basic tasks, such as recognizing input from the keyboard, sending output to the display screen, keeping track of files and directories on the hard drive, and controlling peripheral devices such as disk drives and printers.

**Packet**   A piece of a message transmitted over a packet-switching network. In IP networks, packets are often called datagrams.

**Packet Filtering**   A method of controlling access to a network by analyzing incoming and outgoing packets and letting them pass or stopping them based on the IP addresses of the source and destination, thereby serving as one of the many techniques used for implementing security firewalls.

**Packet-Filtering Gateway**   A packet filter that analyzes each IP packet at the network layer and determines whether to pass or block it based on a set of rules. If it allows communication between two specific addresses, packets are allowed to travel through the firewall to the specified address. If no rule is available for a given address, the packet is rejected and not allowed to pass through the firewall.

**Packet Modification**   Modifying a packet that leads to sending incorrect or corrupted information across the network.

**Packet Replaying**   Replaying a packet to find out what was previously sent.

**Password**   A code used to log in or gain access to a locked or secure system.

**PGP (Pretty Good Privacy)**   A message encryption technique based on the public key method, which uses two keys—one public key that you share with anyone from whom you want to receive a message, the other a private key that you use to decrypt messages that you receive. PGP is one of the most common ways to protect messages on the Internet because it is effective, easy to use, and free.

**Phone Phreaking**   The act of cracking the phone network or entering it in an unauthorized manner to use it, for example, to make "free" phone calls.

**Private Key**   The undisclosed key in a matched key pair (that is, the private key and the public key) that each party must safeguard for public key cryptography. The private key is known only by the recipient of the message, whereas the public key is known to everyone.

**Proxy Server**   A server that operates between a client application, such as a Web browser, and another internal server. The purpose is to intercept all requests to the internal server for evaluation and to hide internal server identities.

**Public Key**   One part of a pair of asymmetric encryption keys that is distributed to all interested parties. Data encrypted by the public key can only be decrypted by the single private key that makes the other part of the pair of keys.

**Public Key Certificate**   A digitally signed document that serves to validate the sender's authorization and name. The document consists of a specially formatted block of data that contains the name of the certificate holder, the holder's public key, and the digital signature of a certification authority for authentication.

**Public Key Encryption**   A cryptographic system using two keys—a public key known to everyone and a private or secret key known only to the recipient of the message. For instance, when John wants to send a secure message to Jane, he uses Jane's public key to encrypt the message. Jane then uses her private key to decrypt it so that she can make sense out of it.

**Query**   A request for information to a database.

**RAID (Redundant Array of Independent [or Inexpensive] Disks)**   A combination of two or more drives (frequently on servers) used together for better fault tolerance and increased performance.

**Reboot**   Restarting a computer.

**Reboot Disks**   Disks used to reboot a system.

**Remote Access**   The ability to log on to a network from a different, distant, or remote location.

**Service Pack**   An update to a version of software that fixes an existing problem, such as a bug, or provides enhancements to the product. These enhancements and fixes will appear in the next version of the product.

**Smart Card**   A small electronic device about the size of a credit card that contains electronic memory and possibly an embedded integrated circuit (IC).

**S/MIME**   Multipurpose Internet mail extension (MIME) is originally a standard for defining the types of files attached to standard Internet mail messages. It is used in situations where one computer program needs to communicate with another program about what kind of file is being sent. Secure multipurpose Internet mail extension (S/MIME) describes how encryption information and a digital certificate can be included as part of the message body.

**Sniffer**   A program or device that monitors the flow of data in a network. Can be used for both legitimate network management functions and stealing information off a network. Sniffers are very dangerous because they are virtually impossible to detect and can be inserted almost anywhere.

**Software**   Computer instructions or data that are stored electronically. In contrast, storage devices and display devices that show or operate the instructions or data are hardware.

**SSL (Secure Sockets Layer)**   A program layer that manages the security of message transmission in a network.

**SYN Flooding**   Bombarding a system with dozens of false connection requests a minute that leads to degradation of the system's ability to give service to legitimate connection requests. This attack is also called the denial of service attack.

**System Access Point**   A physical location, hardware or software, from where one can connect to a system.

**System Administrator**   The individual responsible for maintaining a multiuser computer system. Small organizations may have only one system administrator, whereas large organizations and enterprises may have a team of system administrators.

**Trojan Horses**   Impostor files that claim to be something desirable but, in fact, are malicious. Unlike viruses, Trojan horse programs do not replicate themselves. Trojans contain malicious code that when triggered cause loss, or even theft, of data.

**Virtual Burglar**   A type of hacker that steals information on the Web.

**Virus**   A program or piece of code that is loaded onto your computer without your knowledge and runs against your wishes. Viruses can also replicate themselves. A simple virus can make a copy of itself over and over again and is very dangerous because it will quickly use all available memory and bring the system to a halt. An even more dangerous type of virus is capable of transmitting itself across networks and bypassing security systems.

**Web Commerce (E-Commerce or Electronic Commerce)** Business via the Internet, specifically, the electronic transfer of value across the Internet in exchange for the delivery of a service or product.

**Web Server** A computer that stores and delivers Web pages to other computers.

**Web Server Software** The software designed to be used on a Web server, for accepting, managing, and responding to Internet requests for sessions.

**Web Server's Operating System** The operating system that controls the functionality of a Web server.

**Wired Network** A network wired together through cables or physical connections as compared to a wireless network in which radio frequencies are generally used to make connections.

**Wireless Network** A network interconnected with radio waves or other signals instead of through cabling or physical connection.

**Worm** A program or algorithm that replicates itself over a computer network, usually performing malicious actions, such as shutting the system down or using up the computer's resources. Worms replicate themselves from system to system without the use of a host file, as opposed to viruses, which require the spreading of an infected host file. When capitalized as WORM, this term may refer to an acronym for "write once read many".

## CROSS REFERENCES

See *Auditing Information Systems Security; Computer Security Incident Response Teams (CSIRTs); Contingency Planning Management; Guidelines for a Comprehensive Security System; Risk Management for IT Security; The Common Criteria.*

## REFERENCES

Allen, J. (2001). *The CERT guide to system and network security practices*. New York: Addison-Wesley.

Anderson, R. (2001). *Security engineering: A guide to building dependable distributed systems*. New York: Wiley.

Cisco. (2001). *A beginner's guide to network security*. San Jose, CA: Cisco Systems.

Garfinkel, S., Schwartz, A., & Spafford, G.(2003) *Practical Unix & Internet security* (3rd ed.). Sebastopel, CA: O'Reilly.

Garfinkel, S., & Spafford, G. (2001). *Web security, privacy & e commerce*. Sebastopel, CA: O'Reilly.

Greenstein, M., & Vasarhelyi, M. (2002). *Electronic commerce: Security, risk management, and control*. New York: McGraw-Hill/Irwin.

Herrmann, D. (2002). *Using the common criteria for IT security evaluation*. Boca Raton, FL: Auerbach.

IOMA. (2000). *Outsourcing: How to know when to let someone else do the work* (Security Directors Rep. No. 00–8). New York: Institute of Management & Administration.

Lynn, J. (2001). Disaster planning: Are you prepared for the worst? *Commercial Law Bulletin, 16*(4), 30–31.

Microsoft. (2003). *Best practices for enterprise security*. Retrieved February 3, 2003, from http://www.microsoft.com/technet//security/bestprac/bpent/bpentsec.asp

National Institute of Standards and Technology (NIST). (2004). *FIPS PUB 199, standards for security categorization of federal information and information systems*. Retrieved March 3, 2004, from http://csrc.nist.gov/publications/fips/fips199/FIPS-PUB-199-final.pdf

Rubin, A. (2001). *White-hat security arsenal: Tackling the threats*. New York: Addison-Wesley.

SANS. (2002). *The twenty most critical Internet security vulnerabilities (updated): The experts' consensus*. Retrieved March 20, 2002, from http://www.sans.org/top20.htm

Scalet, S. (2002). How to plan for the inevitable. *CIO, 15*(11), 74–82.

Stein, T. (1999). Security starts with sound practices. *Electronic Commerce World, 9*(10), 46–47.

## FURTHER READING

CERT Coordination Center: http://www.cert.org

Internet Storm Center: http://isc.incidents.org

*Internetworking technologies handbook*, Chapter 51: Security technologies (pp. 1–12): http://www.cisco.com/univercd/cc/td/doc/cisintwk/ito_doc/security.htm

*Internet security policy: A technical guide*: http://www.packetstorm-security.org/docs/infosec/isptg/

# Multilevel Security

Richard E. Smith, *University of St. Thomas*

## INTRODUCTION

Many businesses and organizations need to protect secret information, and most can tolerate some leakage. Organizations that use multilevel security (MLS) systems tolerate no leakage at all. Businesses may face legal or financial risks if they fail to protect business secrets, but they can generally recover afterward by paying to repair the damage. At worst, the business goes bankrupt. Managers who take risks with business secrets might lose their jobs if secrets are leaked, but they are more likely to lose their jobs to failed projects or overrun budgets. This places a limit on the amount of money a business will invest in data secrecy.

The defense community, which includes the military services, intelligence organizations, related government agencies, and their supporting enterprises, cannot easily recover from certain information leaks. Stealth systems are not stealthy if the targets know what to look for, and surveillance systems do not see things if the targets know what camouflage to use. Such failures cannot always be corrected just by spending more money. Even worse, a system's weakness might not be detected until after a diplomatic or military disaster reveals it. During the Cold War, the threat of nuclear annihilation led military and political leaders to take such risks very seriously. It was easy to argue that data leakage could threaten a country's very existence. The defense community demanded levels of computer security far beyond what the business community needed.

## MLS Problem

We use the term *multilevel* because the defense community has classified both people and information into different levels of trust and sensitivity. These levels represent the well-known security classifications: Confidential, Secret, and Top Secret. Before people are allowed to look at classified information, they must be granted individual *clearances* that are based on individual investigations to establish their trustworthiness. People who have earned a Confidential clearance are authorized to see Confidential documents, but they are not trusted to look at Secret or Top Secret information any more than any member of the general public. These levels form the simple hierarchy shown in Figure 1. The dashed arrows in the figure illustrate the direction in which the rules allow data to flow: from "lower" levels to "higher" levels and not vice versa.

When speaking about these levels, we use three different terms:

- *Clearance level* indicates the level of trust given to a person with a security clearance, or a computer that processes classified information, or an area that has been physically secured for storing classified information. The level indicates the highest level of classified information to be stored or handled by the person, device, or location.
- *Classification level* indicates the level of sensitivity associated with some information, such as that in a document or a computer file. The level is supposed to indicate the degree of damage the country could suffer if the information is disclosed to an enemy.
- *Security level* is a generic term for either a clearance level or a classification level.

The defense community was the first and biggest customer for computing technology, and computers were still very expensive when they became routine fixtures in defense organizations. However, few organizations could afford separate computers to handle information at every different level: they had to develop procedures to share the computer without leaking classified information to uncleared (or insufficiently cleared) users. This was not as easy as it might sound. Even when people "took turns" running the computer at different security levels (a technique called *periods processing*), security officers had to worry about whether Top Secret information may have been left behind in memory or on the operating system's hard drive. Some sites purchased computers to dedicate exclusively to highly classified work, despite the cost, simply because they did not want to take the risk of leaking information.

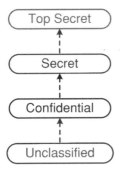

**Figure 1:** The hierarchical security levels.

Multiuser systems, like the early time-sharing systems, made such sharing particularly challenging. Ideally, people with Secret clearances should be able to work at the same time others were working on Top Secret data, and everyone should be able to share common programs and unclassified files. Although typical operating system mechanisms could usually protect different user programs from one another, they could not prevent a Confidential or Secret user from tricking a Top Secret user into releasing Top Secret information via a *Trojan horse*.

A Trojan horse is software that performs an invisible function that the user would not have chosen to perform. For example, consider a multiuser system in which users have stored numerous private files and have used the system's access permissions to protect those files from prying eyes. Imagine that the author of a locally developed word processing program has an unhealthy curiosity about others in the user community and wishes to read their protected files. The author can install a Trojan horse function in the word processing program to retrieve the protected files. The function copies a user's private files into the author's own directory whenever a user runs the word processing program.

When a user runs the word processing program, the program inherits that user's access permissions to the user's own files. Thus, the Trojan horse circumvents the access permissions by performing its hidden function when the unsuspecting user runs it (for further information, see the chapter about Trojan horse programs elsewhere in this *Handbook*). Viruses and network worms are Trojan horses in the sense that their replication logic is run under the context of the infected user. Occasionally, worms and viruses may include an additional Trojan horse mechanism that collects secret files from their victims. If the victim of a Trojan horse is someone with access to Top Secret information on a system with lesser-cleared users, then there is nothing on a conventional system to prevent leakage of the Top Secret information. Multiuser systems clearly need a special mechanism to protect multilevel data from leakage.

## Multiuser Operating Modes

In the United States, the defense community usually describes a multiuser system as operating in a particular mode. For the purposes of this discussion, there are three important operating modes:

- *Dedicated* mode: all users currently on the system have permission to access any of the data on the system. In dedicated mode, the computer itself does not need any built-in access control mechanisms if locked doors or other physical mechanisms prevent unauthorized users from accessing it.
- *System high* mode: all users currently on the system have the right security clearance to access any data on the system, but not all users have a need to know all data. If users do not need to know some of the data, then the system must have mechanisms to restrict their access. This requires the typical file access mechanisms of typical multiuser systems.
- *Multilevel* mode: not all users currently on the system are cleared for all data stored on the system. The system must have an access control mechanism that enforces MLS restrictions. It must also have mechanisms to enforce multiuser file access restrictions.

The phrase "need to know" refers to a commonly enforced rule in organizations that handle classified information. In general, a security clearance does not grant blanket permission to look at all information classified at that level or below. The clearance is really only the first step: people are only allowed to look at classified information that they *need to know* as part of the work they do.

In other words, if we give Janet a Secret clearance to work on a cryptographic device, then she has a need to know the Secret information related to that device. She does not have permission to study Secret information about spy satellites or Secret cryptographic information that does not apply to her device. If she is using a multiuser system containing Secret information about her project, other cryptographic projects, and even spy satellites, then the system must prevent Janet from browsing information belonging to the other projects and activities. On the other hand, the system should be able to grant Janet permission to look at other materials if she really needs the information to do her job.

A computer's operating mode determines what access control mechanisms it needs. Dedicated systems might not require any mechanisms beyond physical security. Computers running at system high must have user-based access restrictions similar to those typically provided in UNIX and in "professional" versions of Microsoft Windows. In multilevel mode, the system must prevent data from higher security levels from leaking to users who have lower clearances: this requires a special mechanism.

Typically, an MLS mechanism works as follows: users, computers, and networks carry computer-readable labels to indicate security levels. Data may flow from "same level" to "same level" or from "lower level" to "higher level" (Figure 2). Thus, Top Secret users can share data with one another, and a Top Secret user can retrieve information from a Secret user. It does not allow data from Top Secret (a higher level) to flow into a file or other location visible to a Secret user (at a lower level). If data are not subject to

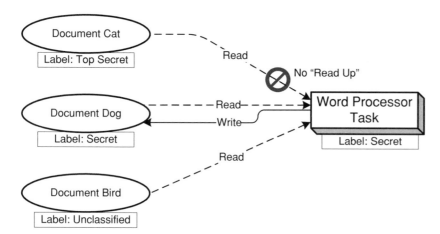

**Figure 2:** Data flows allowed by an MLS mechanism.

classification rules, that data belong to the "Unclassified" security level. On a computer this would include most application programs and any computing resources shared by all users.

A direct implementation of such a system allows the author of a Top Secret report to retrieve information entered by users operating at Secret or Confidential levels and merge it with Top Secret information. The user with the Secret clearance cannot "read up" to see the Top Secret result, because the data only flows in one direction between Secret and Top Secret. Unclassified data can be made visible to all users.

It is not enough to simply prevent users with lower clearances from reading data carrying higher classifications. What if a user with a Top Secret clearance stores some Top Secret data in a file readable by a Secret user? This causes the same problem as "reading up" because it makes the Top Secret data visible to the Secret user. Some may argue that Top Secret users should be trusted not to do such a thing. In fact, some would argue that they would never do it because it is a violation of the Espionage Act. Unfortunately, this argument does not take into account the risk of a Trojan horse.

For example, Figure 3 shows what could happen if an attacker inserts a macro function with a Trojan horse capability into a word processing file. The attacker has stored the macro function in a Confidential file and has told a Top Secret user to examine the file. When the user opens the Confidential file, the macro function starts running, and it tries to copy files from the Top Secret user's

directory into Confidential files belonging to the attacker. This is called "writing down" the data from a higher security level to a lower one.

In a system with typical access control mechanisms, the macro will succeed because the attacker can easily set up all of the permissions needed to allow the Top Secret user to write data into the other user's files. Clearly, the system cannot enforce MLS reliably if Trojan horse programs can circumvent MLS protections. There is no way users can avoid Trojan horse programs with 100% reliability, as suggested by the success of e-mail viruses. An effective MLS mechanism needs to block "write down" attempts as well as "read up" attempts.

## Bell–La Padula Model

The most widely recognized approach to MLS is the Bell–La Padula security model (Bell & LaPadula, 1974). The model effectively captures the essentials of the access restrictions implied by conventional military security levels. Most MLS mechanisms implement Bell–La Padula or a close variant of it. Although Bell–La Padula has accurately defined a MLS capability that keeps data safe, it has not led to the widespread development of successful multilevel systems. In practice, developers have not been able to produce MLS mechanisms that work reliably with high confidence, and some important defense applications require a "write down" capability that renders Bell–La Padula irrelevant (for an example, see the Sensor-to-Shooter section).

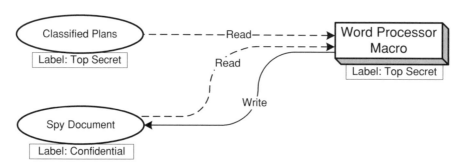

**Figure 3:** A macro function with a Trojan horse could leak data to a lower security level.

In the Bell–La Padula model, programs and processes (called *subjects*) try to transfer information via files, messages, I/O devices, or other resources in the computer system (called *objects*). Each subject and object carries a label containing its security level, that is, the subject's clearance level or the object's classification level. In the simplest case, the security levels are arranged in a hierarchy as shown in Figure 1. More elaborate cases involve *compartments*, as described in another section.

The Bell–La Padula model enforces MLS access restrictions by implementing two simple rules: the *simple security property* and the *\*-property*. When a subject tries to read from or write to an object, the system compares the subject's security label with the object's label and applies these rules. Unlike typical access restrictions on multiuser computing systems, these restrictions are *mandatory*: no users on the system can turn them off or bypass them. Typical multiuser access restrictions are *discretionary*, that is, they can be enabled or disabled by system administrators and often by individual users. If users, or even administrative users, can modify the access rules, then a Trojan horse can modify or even disable those rules. To prevent leakage by browsing users and Trojan horses, the Bell–La Padula systems always enforce the two properties.

Simple Security Property: A subject can read from an object as long as the subject's security level is the same as, or higher than, the object's security level. This is sometimes called the **no read up** property.

\*-Property: A subject can write to an object as long as the subject's security level is the same as or lower than the object's security level. This is sometimes called the **no write down** property.

The simple security property is obvious: it prevents people (or their processes) from reading data that has classifications exceeding their security clearances. Users cannot "read up" relative to their security clearances. They can "read down," which means that they can read data classified at or below the same level as their clearances.

The \*-property prevents people with higher clearances from passing highly classified data to users who do not share the appropriate clearance, either accidentally or intentionally. User programs cannot "write down" into files that carry a lower security level than the process they are currently running. This prevents Trojan horse programs from secretly leaking highly classified data. Figure 4 illustrates these properties: the dashed arrows show data being read in compliance with the simple security prop-

erty, and the lower solid arrow shows an attempted "write down" being blocked by the \*-property.

A system enforcing the Bell–La Padula model blocks the word processing macro in either of two ways, depending on the security level at which the user runs the word processing program. In one case, shown in Figure 4, the user runs the program at Top Secret. This allows the macro to read the user's Top Secret files, but the \*-property prevents the macro from writing to the attacker's Confidential files. When the process tries to open a Confidential file for writing, the MLS access rules prevent it.

In the other case, the Top Secret user runs the program at the Confidential level, because the file is classified Confidential. The program's macro function can read and modify Confidential files, including files set up by the attacker, but the simple security property prevents the macro from reading any Secret or Top Secret files.

## Compartments

Although the hierarchical security levels such as Top Secret are familiar to most people, they are not the only restrictions placed on information in the defense community. Organizations apply hierarchical security levels (Confidential, Secret, or Top Secret) to their data according to the damage that might be caused by leaking that data. Some organizations add other markings to classified material to further restrict its distribution. These markings go by many names: compartments, code words, caveats, categories, and so on, and they serve many purposes. In some cases, the markings indicate whether or not the data may be shared with particular organizations, enterprises, or allied countries. In many cases these markings give the data's creator or owner more control over the data's distribution. Each marking indicates another restriction placed on the distribution of a particular classified data item. People can only receive the classified data if they comply with *all* restrictions placed on the data's distribution.

The Bell–La Padula model refers to all of these additional markings as *compartments*. A security level may include compartment identifiers in addition to a hierarchical security level. If a particular file's security level includes one or more compartments, then the user's security level must also include those compartments or the user will not be allowed to read the file.

A system with compartments generally acquires a large number of distinct security levels: one for every legal

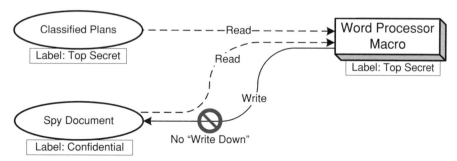

**Figure 4:** If the program can read Top Secret data, it can't write data to a lower level.

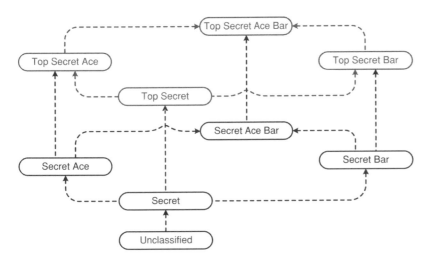

**Figure 5:** Lattice for Secret and Top Secret, including the compartments Ace and Bar.

combination of a hierarchical security level with zero or more compartments. The interrelationships between these levels form a directed graph called a *lattice*. Figure 5 shows the lattice for a system that contains Secret and Top Secret information with compartments Ace and Bar.

The arrows in the lattice show which security levels can read data labeled with other security levels. If the user Cathy has a Top Secret clearance with access to both compartments Ace and Bar, then she has permission to read any data on the system (assuming its owner has also given her "read" permission to that data). We determine the access rights associated with other security labels by following arrows in Figure 5.

If Cathy runs a program with the label Secret Ace, then the program can read data labeled Unclassified, Secret, or Secret Ace. The program cannot read data labeled Secret Bar or Secret Ace Bar, because its security label does not contain the Bar compartment. Figure 4 illustrates this: there is no path to Secret Ace that comes from a label containing the Bar compartment.

Likewise, the program cannot read Top Secret data because it is running at the Secret level, and no Top Secret labels lead to Secret labels.

## MLS and System Privileges

A high security clearance such as Cathy's shows that a particular organization is willing to trust Cathy with certain types of classified information. It is not a blank check that grants access to every resource on a computer system. MLS access rules always work in conjunction with the system's other access rules.

Systems that enforce MLS access rules always combine them with conventional, user-controlled access permissions. If a Secret or Confidential user blocks access to a file by other users, then a Top Secret user cannot read the file either. The "need to know" rule means that classified information should only be shared among individuals who genuinely need the information. Individual users are supposed to keep classified information protected from arbitrary browsing by other users. Higher security clearances do not grant permission to arbitrarily browse: access is still restricted by the need to know requirement.

Users who have Top Secret and higher clearances do not automatically acquire administrative or "superuser" status on multilevel computer systems, even if they are cleared for everything on the computer. In a way, the Top Secret security level actually restricts what the user can do: a program running at Top Secret cannot install an unclassified application program, for example. Many administrative tasks, such as installing application programs and other shared resources, must take place at the unclassified level. If an administrator installs programs while running at the Top Secret level, then the programs will be installed with Top Secret labels. Users with lower clearances would not be authorized to see the programs.

## Limitations in MLS Mechanisms

Despite strong support from the military community and a strong effort by computing vendors and computer security researchers, MLS mechanisms failed to provide the security and functionality required by the defense community. First, security researchers and MLS system developers found it to be extremely difficult, and perhaps impossible, to completely prevent information flow between different security levels in an MLS system. We will explore this problem further in the next section, Assurance Problem. A second problem was the virus threat: when we enforce MLS information flow we do nothing to prevent a virus introduced at a lower clearance level from propagating into higher clearance levels. Finally, the end user community found a number of cases where that the Bell–La Padula model of information flow did not entirely satisfy their operational and security needs.

Self-replicating software such as computer viruses became a minor phenomenon among the earliest home computer users in the late 1970s. Although viruses were not enough of a phenomenon to interest MLS researchers and developers, MLS systems caught the interest of the pioneering virus researcher Fred Cohen (1994). In 1984 he demonstrated that a virus inserted at the unclassified level of a system that implemented the Bell–La Padula model could rapidly spread throughout all security levels of a system. This particular infestation did not reflect a bug in the MLS implementation. Instead, it indicated a flaw in the Bell–La Padula model, which strives to allow information flows from low to high while preventing flows from high to low. Viruses represent a security threat that exploits an information flow from low to high, so MLS protection based on Bell–La Padula gives no protection against it.

Viruses represented one case in which the Bell–La Padula model did not meet the end users' operational and security needs. Additional cases emerged as end users gained experience with MLS systems. One problem was that the systems tended to collect a lot of "overclassified" information. Whenever a user created a document at a high security level, the document would have to retain that security level even if the user removed all sensitive information to create a less classified or even unclassified document. In essence, end users often needed a mechanism to "downgrade" information so its label reflected its lowered sensitivity.

The downgrading problem became especially important as end users sought to develop "sensor-to-shooter" systems. These systems would use highly classified intelligence data to produce tactical commands to be sent to combat units whose radios received information at the Secret level or lower (see the Sensor-to-Shooter section). In practice, systems would address the downgrading problem by installing privileged programs that bypassed the MLS mechanism to downgrade information. Although this served as a convenient patch to correct the problem, it also showed that practical systems did not entirely rely on the Bell–La Padula mechanisms that had cost so much to build and validate. This further eroded the defense community's interest in MLS based on Bell–La Padula products.

## ASSURANCE PROBLEM

Members of the defense community identified the need for MLS-capable systems in the 1960s, and a few vendors implemented the basic features (Hoffman, 1973; Karger & Schell, 1974; Weissman, 1969). However, government studies of the MLS problem emphasized the danger of relying on large, opaque operating systems to protect really valuable secrets (Anderson, 1972; Ware, 1970). Operating systems were already notorious for unreliability, and these reports highlighted the threat of a software bug that allowed leaks of highly sensitive information.

The recommended solution was to achieve high assurance through extensive analysis, review, and testing.

High assurance would clearly increase vendors' development costs and lead to higher product costs. This did not deter the U.S. defense community, which foresaw long-term cost savings. Karger and Schell (1974) repeated an assertion that MLS capabilities could save the U.S. Air Force alone $100 million a year, based on computing costs at that time.

Every MLS device poses a fundamental question: does it *really* enforce MLS or does it leak information somehow? The first MLS challenge is to develop a way to answer that question. We can decompose the problem into two more questions:

- What does it really mean to enforce MLS?
- How can we evaluate a system to verify that it enforces MLS?

The first question was answered by the development of security models, such as the Bell–La Padula model summarized earlier. A true security model provides a formal, mathematical representation of MLS information flow restrictions. The formal model makes the enforcement problem clear to nonprogrammers. It also makes the operating requirement clear to the programmers who implemented the MLS mechanisms.

To address the evaluation question, designers needed a way to prove that the system's MLS controls indeed work correctly. By the late 1960s, this had become a really serious challenge. Software systems had become much too large for anyone to review and validate: Brooks (1975) reported that IBM had more than a thousand people working on its ground-breaking system, OS/360. In the book *The Mythical Man-Month*, Brooks described the difficulties of building a large-scale software system. Project size was not the only challenge in building reliable and secure software: smaller teams, such as the team responsible for the Multics security mechanisms, could not detect and close every vulnerability (Karger & Schell, 1974).

The security community developed two sets of strategies for evaluating MLS systems: strategies for designing a reliable MLS system and strategies to prove the MLS system works correctly. The design strategies emphasized a special structure to ensure uniform enforcement of data access rules, called the *reference monitor*. The design strategies further required that the designers explicitly identify all system components that played a role in enforcing MLS; those components were defined as being part of the *trusted computing base*, which included all components that required high assurance.

The strategies for proving correctness relied heavily on formal design specifications and on techniques to analyze those designs. Some of these strategies were a reaction to ongoing quality control problems in the software industry, but others were developed as an attempt to detect *covert channels*, a largely unresolved weakness in MLS systems.

### System Design Strategies

During the early 1970s, the U.S. Air Force commissioned a study to develop feasible strategies for constructing and verifying MLS systems. The study pulled together significant findings by security researchers at that time into a report, called the Anderson (1972), report which heavily influenced subsequent U.S. government support of MLS systems. A later study (Nibaldi, 1979) identified the most promising strategies for trusted system development and proposed a set of criteria for evaluating such systems.

These proposals led to published criteria for developing and evaluating MLS systems called the *Trusted Computer System Evaluation Criteria* (TCSEC), or "Orange Book" (Department of Defense, 1985). The U.S. government established a process by which computer system vendors could submit their products for security evaluation. A government organization, the National Computer Security Center (NCSC), evaluated products against the TCSEC and rated the products according to their capabilities and trustworthiness. For a product to achieve the highest rating for trustworthiness, the NCSC needed to verify the correctness of the product's design.

To make design verification feasible, the Anderson report recommended (and the TCSEC required) that MLS systems enforce security through a "reference validation mechanism" that today we call the *reference monitor*. The reference monitor is the central point that enforces all access permissions. Specifically, a reference monitor must have three features:

- It must be *tamperproof*—there must be no way for attackers or others on the system to intentionally or accidentally disable it or otherwise interfere with its operation.
- It must be *nonbypassable*—all accesses to system resources must be mediated by the reference monitor. There must be no way to gain access to system resources except through mechanisms that use the reference monitor to make access control decisions.
- It must be *verifiable*—there must be a way to convince third-party evaluators (such as the NCSC) that the system will always enforce MLS correctly. The reference monitor should be small and simple enough in design and implementation to make verification practical.

Operating system designers had by that time recognized the concept of an operating system *kernel*: a portion of the system that made unrestricted accesses to the computer's resources so that other components did not need unrestricted access. Many designers believed that a good kernel should be small for the same reason as a reference monitor: it is easier to build confidence in a small software component than in a large one. This led to the concept of a *security kernel*: an operating system kernel that incorporated a reference monitor. Layered atop the security kernel would be supporting processes and utility programs to serve the system's users and the administrators. Some nonkernel software would require privileged access to system resources, but none would bypass the security kernel. The combination of the computer hardware, the security kernel, and its privileged components made up the *trusted computing base* (TCB)—the system components responsible for enforcing MLS restrictions. The TCB was the focus of assurance efforts: if it worked correctly, then the system would correctly enforce the MLS restrictions.

## Verifying System Correctness

Research culminating in the TCSEC had identified three essential elements to ensure that an MLS system operates correctly:

- Security policy—an explicit statement of what the system must do. This was based on a security model that described how the system enforced MLS.
- Security mechanisms—features of the reference monitor and the TCB that enforce the policy.
- Assurances—evidence that the mechanisms actually enforce the policy.

The computer industry has always relied primarily on system testing for quality assurance. However, the Anderson report recognized the shortcomings of testing by repeating Dijkstra's observation that tests can only prove the presence of bugs, not their absence. To improve assurance, the report made specific recommendations about how MLS systems should be designed, built, and tested. These recommendations became requirements in the TCSEC, particularly for products intended for the most critical applications:

- Top-down design—the product design should have a top-level design specification and a detailed design specification.
- Formal policy specification—there must be a formal specification of the product's security policy. This may be a restatement of Bell–La Padula that identifies the elements of the product that correspond to elements in the Bell–La Padula model.
- Formal top-level specification—there must be a formal specification of the product's externally visible behavior.
- Design correctness proof—there must be a mathematical proof showing that the top-level design is consistent with the security policy.
- Specification to code correspondence—there must be a way to show that the mechanisms appearing in the formal top-level specification are implemented in the source code.

These activities were not substituted for conventional product development techniques. Instead, these additional tasks were combined with the accepted "best practices" used in conventional computer system development. These practices tended to follow a "waterfall" process (Boehm, 1981; Department of Defense, 1985): first, the builders develop a *requirements specification*, from that they develop the top-down design, then they implement the product, and finally they test the product against the requirements. In the idealized process for developing an MLS product, the requirements specification focuses on testable functions and measurable performance capabilities while the policy model captures security requirements that cannot be tested directly. Figure 6 shows how these elements worked together to validate an MLS product's correct operation.

Product development has always been expensive. Many development organizations, especially smaller ones, try to save time and money by skipping the planning and design steps of the waterfall process. The TCSEC did not demand the waterfall process, but its requirements for highly assured systems imposed significant costs on development organizations. Both the Nibaldi study and the TCSEC recognized that not all product developers could afford to achieve the highest levels of assurance. Instead, the evaluation process identified a range of assurance levels that a product could achieve. Products intended for less critical activities could spend less money on their development process and achieve a lower standard of assurance. Products intended for the most critical applications, however, were expected to meet the highest practical assurance standard.

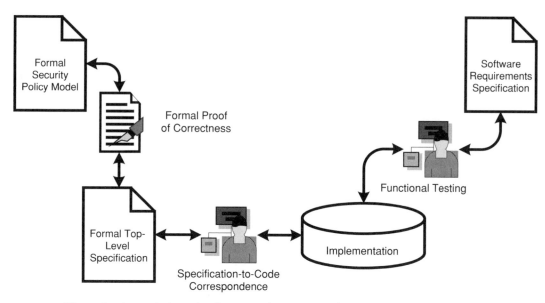

**Figure 6:** Interrelation of policy, specifications, implementation, and assurances.

## Covert Channels

Shortly after the Anderson report appeared, Lampson (1973) published a note that examined the general problem of keeping information in one program secret from another, a problem at the root of MLS enforcement. Lampson noted that computer systems contain a variety of channels by which two processes might exchange data. In addition to explicit channels such as the file system or interprocess communications services, there are *covert channels* that can also carry data between processes. These channels typically exploit operating system resources shared among all processes. For example, when one process can take exclusive control of a file, it prevents other processes from accessing the file, or when one process uses up all the free space on the hard drive, other processes will "see" this activity.

Because MLS systems could not achieve their fundamental objective (to protect secrets) if covert channels were present, defense security experts developed techniques to detect such channels. The TCSEC required a covert channel analysis of all MLS systems except those achieving the lowest assurance levels.

In general, there are two categories of covert channels: storage channels and timing channels. A *storage channel* transmits data from a "high" process to a "low" one by writing data to a storage location visible to the "low" one. For example, if a Secret process can see how much memory is left after a Top Secret process allocates some memory, the Top Secret process can send a numeric message by allocating or freeing the amount of memory equal to the message's numeric value. The covert channel consists of setting the contents of a storage location (the size of free memory) to a value by the "high" process that is readable by the "low" one.

A *timing channel* is one in which the "high" process communicates to the "low" one by varying the timing of some detectable event. For example, the Top Secret process might instruct the hard drive to visit particular disk blocks. When the Secret process goes to read data from

the hard drive itself, the disk activity by the Top Secret process will cause varying delays in the Secret program when it tries to use the hard drive itself. The Top Secret program can systematically impose delays on the Secret program's disk activities, and thus transmit information through the pattern of those delays. Wray (1991) describes a covert channel based on hard drive access speed and also uses the example to show how ambiguous the two covert channel categories can be.

The fundamental strategy for seeking convert channels is to inspect all shared resources in the system, decide if any could yield an effective covert channel, and measure the bandwidth of whatever covert channels are uncovered. Although a casual inspection by a trained analyst may often uncover covert channels, there is no guarantee that a casual inspection will find all such channels. Systematic techniques help increase confidence that the search has been comprehensive. An early technique, the *shared resource matrix* (Kemmerer, 1981, 2002), can analyze a system from either a formal or informal specification. Although the technique can detect covert storage channels, it cannot detect covert timing channels. An alternative approach, *noninterference*, requires formal policy and design specifications (Haigh & Young, 1987). This technique locates both timing and storage channels by proving theorems to show that processes in the system, as described in the design specification, cannot perform detectable ("interfering") actions that are visible to other processes in violation of MLS restrictions.

To be effective at locating covert channels, the design specification must accurately model all resource sharing that is visible to user processes in the system. Typically, the specification focuses its attention on the system functions made available to user processes: system calls to manipulate files, allocate memory, communicate with other processes, and so on. The development program for the LOCK system (Saydjari, 2002; Saydjari, Beckman, & Leaman, 1989), for example, included the development of a formal design specification to support a covert channel analysis. The LOCK design specification identified all system calls, described all inputs and outputs produced by these calls, including error results, and represented the internal mechanisms necessary to support those capabilities. The LOCK team used a form of noninterference to develop proofs that the system enforced MLS correctly (Fine, 1994).

As with any flaw detection technique, there is no way to confirm that all flaws have been found. Techniques that analyze the formal specification will detect all flaws in that specification, but there is no way to conclusively prove that the actual system implements the specification perfectly. Techniques based on less formal design descriptions are also limited by the quality of those descriptions: if the description omits a feature, there is no way to know if that feature opens a covert channel. At some point there must be a trade-off between the effort spent on searching for covert channels and the effort spent searching for other system flaws.

In practice, system developers have found it almost impossible to eliminate all covert channels. Although evaluation criteria encourage developers to eliminate as many covert channels as possible, the criteria also recognize that practical systems will probably include some channels. Instead of eliminating the channels, developers must identify them, measure their possible bandwidth, and provide strategies to reduce their potential for damage. Although not all security experts agree that covert channels are inevitable (Proctor & Neumann, 1992), typical MLS products contain covert channels. Thus, even the approved MLS products contain known weaknesses.

## Evaluation, Certification, and Accreditation

How does assurance fit into the process of actually deploying a system? In theory, one can plug a computer in and throw the switch without knowing anything about its reliability. In the defense community, however, a responsible officer must approve all critical systems before they can go into operation, especially if they handle classified information. Approval rarely occurs unless the officer receives appropriate assurance that the system will operate correctly. There are three major elements to this approval process in the U.S. defense community:

- Evaluation validates a set of security properties in a particular product or device. Product evaluation is not strictly required.
- Certification verifies that a specific installation and configuration of a system meets the requirements for that site. Although not absolutely required, systems are rarely approved for operation without at least an attempt at certification.
- Accreditation authorizes the installation to operate the system. The approval is almost always based on the results of the certification.

In military environments, a highly ranked officer, typically an admiral or general, must formally grant approval (*accreditation*) before a critical system goes into operation. Accreditation shows that the officer believes the system is safe to operate, or at least that the system's risks are outweighed by its benefits. The decision is based on the results of the system's *certification*: a process in which technical experts analyze and test the system to verify that it meets its security and safety requirements. The certification and accreditation process must meet certain standards (Department of Defense, 1997). Under rare, emergency conditions an officer could accredit a system even if there are problems with the certification.

Certification can be very expensive, especially for MLS systems. Tests and analyses must show that the system is not going to fail in a way that will leak classified information or interfere with the organization's mission. Tests must also show that all security mechanisms and procedures work as specified in the requirements. Certification of a custom-built system often involves design reviews and source code inspections. This work requires a lot of effort and special skills, leading to very high costs.

The product evaluation process heralded by the TCSEC was intended to provide off-the-shelf computing equipment that reliably enforced MLS restrictions. Although organizations could implement, certify, and accredit custom systems enforcing MLS, the certification costs were hard to predict and could overwhelm the project budget. If system developers could use off-the-shelf MLS products, their certification costs and project risks would be far lower. Certifiers could rely on the security features verified during evaluation, instead of having to verify a product's implementation themselves.

Product evaluations assess two major aspects: functionality and assurance. A successful evaluation indicates that the product contains the appropriate functional features and meets the specified level of assurance. The TCSEC defined a range of evaluation levels to reflect increasing levels of compliance with both functional and assurance requirements. Each higher evaluation level either incorporated the requirements of the next lower level or superseded particular requirements with a stronger requirement. Alphanumeric codes indicated each level, with D being lowest and A1 being highest:

- D—the lowest level, assigned to evaluated products that achieve no higher level; this level was rarely used.
- C1—a single-user system; this level was eventually discarded.
- C2—a multiuser system, like a UNIX time-sharing system.
- C3—an enhanced multiuser system; this level was eventually discarded.
- B1—the lowest level of evaluation for a system with MLS support.
- B2—an MLS system that incorporates basic architectural assurance requirements and a covert channel analysis.
- B3—an MLS system that incorporates more significant assurance requirements, including formal specifications.
- A1—an MLS system whose design has been proven correct mathematically.

Although the TCSEC defined a whole range of evaluation levels, the government wanted to encourage vendors to develop systems that met the highest levels. In fact, one of the pioneering evaluated products was SCOMP, an A1 system constructed by Honeywell (Fraim, 1983). Very few other vendors pursued an A1 evaluation. High assurance caused high product development costs; one project estimated that the high assurance tasks added 26% to the development effort's labor hours (Smith, 2001). In the fast-paced world of computer product development, that extra effort can cause delays that make the difference between a product's success or failure.

## Empty Shelf

To date, no commercial computer vendors have offered a genuine off-the-shelf MLS product. A handful of vendors had implemented MLS operating systems, but none of these were standard product offerings. All MLS products were expensive, special-purpose systems marketed almost exclusively to the military and government customers. Almost all MLS products were evaluated to the B1 level, meeting minimum assurance standards. Thus, the TCSEC program failed on two levels: it failed to persuade vendors to incorporate MLS features into their standard products, and it failed to persuade any vendors to produce products that met the A1 requirements for high assurance.

TCSEC evaluations were discontinued in 2000. The handful of modern MLS products are evaluated under the Common Criteria (Common Criteria Project Sponsoring Organizations, 1999), evaluation criteria designed to address a broader range of security products.

The most visible failure of MLS technology is its absence from typical desktops. As Microsoft's Windows operating systems came to dominate the desktop in the 1990s, Microsoft made no significant move to implement MLS technology. Versions of Windows have earned a TCSEC C2 evaluation and a more stringent EAL-4 evaluation under the Common Criteria, but it has never incorporated MLS. The closest Microsoft has come to offering MLS technology has been its Palladium effort, announced in 2002. The technology focused on the problem of digital rights management—restricting the distribution of copyrighted music and video—but the underlying mechanisms caught the interest of many in the MLS community because of potential MLS applications. The technology was slated for incorporation in a future Windows release codenamed "Longhorn," but was dropped from Microsoft's plans in 2004 (Orlowski, 2004).

Arguably several factors have contributed to the failure of the MLS product space. Microsoft demonstrated clearly that there was a giant market for products that omit MLS. Falling computer prices also played a role: sites where users typically work at a couple of different security levels find it cheaper to put two computers on every desktop than to try to deploy MLS products. Finally, the sheer cost and uncertainty of MLS product development undoubtedly discourage many vendors. It is hard to justify the effort to develop a "highly secure" system when it is likely that the system will still have identifiable weaknesses, such as covert channels, after all the costly, specialized work is done.

# MULTILEVEL NETWORKING

As computer costs fell and performance soared during the 1980s and 1990s, computer networks became essential for sharing work and resources. Long before computers were routinely wired to the Internet, sites were building local area networks to share printers and files. In the defense community, multilevel data sharing had to be addressed in a networking environment. Initially, the community embraced networks of cheap computers as a way to temporarily sidestep the MLS problem. Instead of tackling the problem of data sharing, many organizations simply deployed separate networks to operate at different security levels, each running in system high mode.

This approach did not help the intelligence community. Many projects and departments needed to process information carrying a variety of compartments and code words. It simply was not practical to provide individual networks for every possible combination of compartments and code words because there were so many to handle. Furthermore, intelligence analysts often spent their time combining information from different compartments to produce a document with a different classification. In practice, this work demanded an MLS desktop and often required communications via an MLS network.

Thus, MLS networking took two different paths in the 1990s. Organizations in the intelligence community continued to pursue MLS products. This reflected the needs of intelligence analysts. In networking, this called for *labeled networks*, that is, networks that carried classification labels on their traffic to ensure that MLS restrictions were enforced.

Many other military organizations, however, took a different path. Computers in most military organizations tended to cluster into networks handling data up to a specified security level, operating in system high mode. This choice was not driven by an architectural vision; it was more likely the effect of the desktop networking architecture emerging in the commercial marketplace combined with existing military computer security policies. Ultimately, this strategy was named *multiple single levels* or *multiple independent levels of security* (MILS).

## Labeled Networks

The fundamental objective of a labeled network is to prevent leakage of classified information. The leakage could occur through eavesdropping on the network infrastructure or by delivering data to an uncleared destination. This yielded two different approaches to labeled networking. The more complex approach used cryptography to keep different security levels separate and to prevent eavesdropping. The simpler approach inserted security labels into network traffic and relied on a reference monitor mechanism installed in network interfaces to restrict message delivery.

In practice, the cryptographic hardware and key management processes have often been too expensive to use in certain large-scale MLS network applications. Instead, sites have relied on physical security to protect their MLS networks from eavesdropping. This has been particularly true in the intelligence community, where the proliferation of compartments and code words have made it impractical to use cryptography to keep security levels separate.

Within such sites, the network infrastructure is physically isolated from any contact except by people with Top Secret clearances supported by special background investigations. Network wires are protected from tampering, though not from sophisticated attacks that might tempt uncleared outsiders. MLS access restrictions rely on security labels embedded in network messages. If cryptography is used at all, its primary purpose is to protect the integrity of security labels.

Standard traffic using the Internet protocol (IP) does not include security labels, but the Internet community developed standards for such labels, beginning with the IP security option (St. Johns, 1988). The U.S. Defense Intelligence Agency developed this further when implementing a protocol for the Department of Defense Intelligence Information System (DODIIS). The protocol, called DODIIS network security for information exchange (DNSIX), specified both the labeling and the checking process to be used when passing traffic through a DNSIX network interface (LaPadula, LeMoine, Vukelich, & Woodward, 1990). To increase the assurance of the resulting system, the specification included a design description for the checking process; the design had been verified against a security model that described the required MLS enforcement.

In the United States, MLS cryptographic techniques were exclusively the domain of the National Security Agency (NSA) because it set the standards for encrypting classified information. Traditional NSA protocols encrypted traffic at the link level, carrying the traffic without security labels. During the 1980s and 1990s the NSA started a series of programs to develop cryptographic protocols for handling labeled, multilevel data, including the Secure Data Network System, the Multilevel Network System Security Program, and the Multilevel Information System Security Initiative.

These programs yielded security protocol 3 (SP3) and the message security protocol (MSP). SP3 protects messages at the network protocol layer (layer 3) and has been used in gateway encryption devices for the DOD's Secret IP Router Network, which shares classified information at the Secret level among approved military and defense organizations. However, SP3 is a relatively old protocol and will probably be superseded by a variant of the IP security protocol that has been adapted for the defense community, called the high assurance IP interface specification. MSP protects messages at the application level and was originally designed to encrypt e-mail. The Defense Message System, the DOD's evolving secure e-mail system, uses MSP.

Obviously an MLS network uses encryption to protect traffic against eavesdropping. In addition, MLS protocols can use cryptography to enforce MLS access restrictions. The FIREFLY protocol illustrates this. Developed by the NSA for multilevel telephone and networking protocols, FIREFLY uses public key cryptography to negotiate encryption keys to protect traffic between two entities. Each FIREFLY certificate contains the clearance level of its owner, and the protocol compares the levels when negotiating keys. If the two entities are using secure telephones, then the protocol yields a key whose clearance level matches the lower of the two entities. If the two entities are establishing a computer network connection, then the negotiation succeeds only if the clearance levels match.

## Multiple Independent Levels of Security (MILS)

Despite the shortage of MLS products, the defense and intelligence communities dramatically expanded their use of computer systems during the 1980s and 1990s. Instead of implementing MLS systems, most organizations chose to deploy multiple computer networks, each dedicated to a security level they needed. This eliminated multiuser data sharing risks by eliminating the multiuser data sharing at multiple security levels. When necessary, less classified data was copied one way onto servers on a higher classified network from a removable disk or tape volume.

To simplify data sharing in the MILS environment, many organizations have implemented devices to transfer data from networks at one security level to networks at other levels. These devices generally fall into three categories:

- *Multilevel servers*—network servers implemented on an MLS system with individual network interfaces to connect to system high networks running at different security levels.
- *One-way guards*—devices that could transfer data from a network at a "low" security level to a network at a "high" level.
- *Downgrading guards*—devices that could transfer data in either direction between networks at different security levels.

In a multilevel server, computers on a network at a lower security level can store information on a server, and computers on networks at higher levels can visit the same server and retrieve that information. Vendors provide a variety of multilevel servers, including Web servers, database servers, and file servers. The Coalition Data Server is an example of a multilevel Web server that has been deployed by the U.S. Navy (McGovern, 2001). Although such systems are popular with some defense organizations, others avoid them. Most server products achieve relatively low levels of assurance, which suggests that attackers might find ways to leak information through them from a higher network to a lower one.

One-way guards implement a one-way data transfer from a network at a lower security level to a network at a higher level. The simplest implementations rely on hardware restrictions to guarantee that traffic flows in only one direction. For example, conventional fiber optic network equipment supports bidirectional traffic, but it is not difficult to construct fiber optic hardware that only contains a transmitter on one end and a receiver on the other. Such a device can transfer data in one direction with no risk of leaking data in the other. An obvious shortcoming is that there is no efficient way to prevent congestion because the low side has no way of knowing when or if its messages have been received. More sophisticated devices such as the NRL Pump (Kang, Moskowitz, & Lee, 1996) avoid this problem by implementing acknowledgments using trusted software. However, devices like the Pump can suffer from the same shortcoming as MLS servers: there are very few trustworthy operating systems on which to implement trusted MLS software, and most achieve relatively low assurance. The trustworthiness of the Pump will often be limited by the assurance of the underlying operating system.

Downgrading guards are important because they address a troublesome side effect of MILS computing: users often end up with overclassified information. A user on a Secret system may be working with both Confidential and Secret files, and it is simple to share those files with other users on Secret systems. However, he faces a problem if he needs to provide the Confidential file to a user on a Confidential system: how does he prevent Secret information from leaking when he tries to provide a clean copy of the Confidential file? There is no simple, reliable, and foolproof way to do this, especially when using commercial desktop computers.

The same problem often occurs in e-mail systems: a different user on a Top Secret network may wish to send an innocuous but important announcement to her colleagues on a Secret network. She knows that the recipients are authorized to receive the message's contents, but how does she ensure that no Top Secret information leaks out along with the e-mail message? The problem also appears in military databases: the database may contain information at a variety of security levels, but not all user communities will be able to handle data at the same level as the whole database. To be useful, the data must be sanitized and then released to users at lower classification levels. When a downgrading guard releases information from a higher security level to a lower one, the downgrading generally falls into one of three categories:

- Manual review and release—a trained and trusted operator carefully examines all files submitted for downgrading. If the file appears clean of unreleasable information, then it is released.
- Automated release—the system looks for indicators to show that an authorized person has reviewed the file and approved it for release. The indicators usually include cryptographic authentication, such as a digital signature.
- Automated review—the system uses a set of carefully constructed filters to examine the file to be released. The filters are designed to check for unreleasable data.

The traditional technique was manual review and release. A site would train an operator to identify classified information that should not be released, and the operator would manually review all data passing through the guard. This strategy proved impractical because it has become very difficult to reliably scan files for sensitive information. Word processors such as Microsoft Word tend to retain sensitive information even after the user has attempted to remove it from a file (Byers, 2004). Another problem is steganography: a subverted user on the high side of the guard, or a sophisticated piece of subverted

software, can easily embed large data items in graphic images or other digital files so that a visual review will not detect their presence. In addition to the problem of reliable scanning, there is a human factors problem: few operators would remain effective in this job for very long. Military security officers tell of review operators falling into a mode in which they automatically approve everything without review, partly to maintain message throughput and partly out of boredom.

The automated release approach was used by the Standard Mail Guard (SMG) (Smith, 1994). The SMG accepted text e-mail messages that had been reviewed by the message's author, explicitly labeled for release, and digitally signed using the Domain Name Service (DNS) protocol. The SMG would verify the digital signature and check the signer's identity against the list of users authorized to send e-mail through the guard. The SMG would also search the message for words associated with classified information that should not be released and block messages containing any such words. Authorized users could also transmit files through the guard by attaching them to e-mails. The attached files had to be reviewed and then "sealed" using a special application program: the SMG would verify the presence of the seal before releasing an attached file.

The automated review approach has been used by several guards since the 1980s, primarily to release database records from highly classified databases to networks at lower security levels. Many of these guards were designed to automatically review highly formatted force deployment data. The guards were configured with detailed rules on how to check the fields of the database records so that data was released at the correct security level. In some cases the guards were given instructions on how to sanitize certain database fields to remove highly classified data before releasing the records. Examples of automated review guards include Radiant Mercury, the Command and Control Guard, and the Imagery Support Server Guard (McGovern, 2001).

Although guards and multilevel servers provide a clear benefit by enabling data sharing between system high networks running at different clearance levels, they also pose problems. The most obvious problem is that it puts all of the MLS eggs in one basket: the guard centralizes MLS protection in a single device that undoubtedly draws the interest of attackers. Downgrading guards pose a particular concern because there are many ways that a Trojan horse on the "high" side of a guard may disguise sensitive information so that it passes successfully through the guard's downgrading filters. For example, the Trojan could embed classified information in an obviously unclassified image using steganography. Another problem is that the safest place to attach a label to data is at the data's point of origin: guards are less likely to label data correctly because they are removed from the data's point of origin (Saydjari, 2004). Guards that used an automated release mechanism may be somewhat less prone to this problem if the guard bases its decision on a cryptographically protected label provided at the data's point of origin. However, this benefit can be offset by other risks if the guard or the labeling process are hosted on a low-assurance operating system.

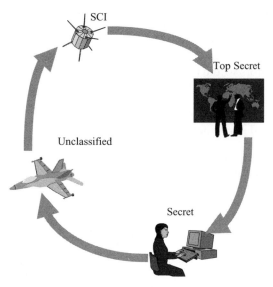

**Figure 7:** In sensor-to-shooter, data flows from higher levels to lower levels.

## Sensor-to-Shooter

During the 1991 Gulf War, the defense community came to appreciate the value of classified satellite images in planning attacks on enemy targets. The only complaint was that the imagery could not be delivered as fast as the tactical systems could take advantage of it (Federation of American Scientists, 1997). In the idealized state-of-the-art "sensor-to-shooter" system, analysts and mission commanders select targets electronically from satellite images displayed on workstations, and they send the targeting information electronically to tactical units (Figure 7). Clearly this involves at least one downgrading step, because tactical units probably will not be cleared to handle satellite intelligence. So far, no general-purpose strategy has emerged for handling automatic downgrading of this kind. In practice, downgrading mechanisms are approved for operation on a case-by-case basis.

## NONDEFENSE APPLICATIONS SIMILAR TO MLS

The following is a list of nonmilitary applications that bear some similarities to the MLS problem. Although this may suggest that there may someday be a commercial market for MLS technology, a closer look suggests this is unlikely. As noted earlier, MLS systems address a level of risk that does not exist in business environments. Buyers of commercial systems do not want to spend the money required to assure correct MLS enforcement. This is illustrated by examining the following MLS-like business applications:

- Protecting sensitive information—Businesses are legally obligated to protect certain types of information from disclosure. However, as noted earlier, the effects of leaking secrets in the defense community are far greater than the results of leaking secrets in the business world. Private companies have occasionally tried using MLS

to protect sensitive corporate data, but the attempt has usually been abandoned as too expensive.

- Digital rights management—To some extent, MLS protection is similar to the security problem of *digital rights management* (DRM). Typically, an organization or enterprise purchases computer equipment to benefit their business activities, and employees and associates use the computers to support the business activities. In both MLS and DRM, there is an absentee third party with a strong interest in restricting information disclosure, and this interest may in some cases interfere with the objectives of the computer's owners and users. In this case, as in the previous case, however, the trade-off in the business world will not justify the type of investment that MLS protection demands in the defense community.

- Secure server platforms—As more and more companies deploy e-commerce servers on the Internet, they face increased risks of losing assets to Internet-based crime. In theory, a hard-to-penetrate server built to military specifications would provide more confidence of safety to a company's customers and investors. In practice, however, neither the developers of these servers nor their customers have shown much interest in military-grade server security. Several vendors have offered such servers, notably Hewlett-Packard with its Virtual Vault product line, but vendors have found very little market interest in such products. Arguably it is for the same reason that MLS fails to excite interest in other applications: the risk is not perceived as being high enough to justify the expense of military-grade protection. Moreover, attacks on servers arrive in a variety of directions, many of which are not addressed by MLS protections.

- Firewall platforms—In the 1990s, many companies working on MLS systems developed and sold commercial firewalls that incorporated MLS-type protections, notably the Cyberguard and Sidewinder products. Although these products achieved some success in the defense community, neither competed effectively against products hosted on common commercial operating systems.

## CONCLUSION

Despite the failures and frustrations that have dogged MLS product developments for the past quarter-century, end users still call for MLS capabilities. This is because the problem remains: the defense community needs to share information at multiple security levels. Most of the community solves the problem by working on multilevel data in a system high environment and dealing with downgrading problems on a piecemeal basis. Although this solves the problem in some situations, it is not practical others, such as sensor-to-shooter applications.

The classic strategies intended to yield MLS products failed in several ways. First, the government's promotion of product evaluations failed when vendors found that MLS capabilities did not significantly increase product sales. The concept of deploying a provably secure system failed twice: first, when vendors found how expensive and uncertain evaluations could be, especially at the highest levels, and second, when security experts discovered how intractable the covert channel problem could be. Finally, the few MLS products that did make their way to market languished when end users realized how narrowly the products solved their security and sharing problems. The principal successes in MLS today are based on guard and trusted server products.

# GLOSSARY

**Accreditation** Approval granted to a computer system to perform a critical, defense-related application. The accreditation is usually granted by a senior military commander.

**Assurance** A set of processes, tests, and analyses performed on a computing system to ensure that it fulfills its most critical operating and security requirements.

**Bell–La Padula Model** A security model that reflects the information flow restrictions inherent in the access restrictions applied to classified information.

**Certification** The process of analyzing a system being deployed in a particular site to verify that it meets its operational and security requirements.

**Covert Channel** In general, an unplanned communications channel within a computer system that allows violations to its security policy. In an MLS system, this is an information flow that violates MLS restrictions.

**Evaluation** The process of analyzing the security functions and assurance evidence of a product by an independent organization to verify that the functions operate as required and that sufficient assurance evidence has been provided to have confidence in those functions.

**Labeled Network** A computer network on which all messages or data packets carry labels to indicate the classification level of the information being carried.

**Multilevel Security (MLS)** An operating mode in which the users who share a computing system and/or network do not all hold clearances to view all information on the system.

**Multiple Independent Levels of Security (MILS)** A networking and desktop computing environment that assigns dedicated, system high resources for processing classified information at different security levels. Users in a MILS environment may have two or more desktop computers, each dedicated to work at a particular security level.

**Reference Monitor** The component of an operating system that mediates all access attempts by subjects (processes) on the system and objects (files and other system resources).

**Security Model** An unambiguous, often formal, statement of the system's rules for achieving its security objectives, such as protecting the confidentiality of classified information from access by uncleared or insufficiently cleared users.

**System High** An operating mode in which the users who share a computing system and/or network all hold clearances that could allow them to view any information on the system.

**Trusted Computing Base** The specific hardware and software components on which a computing system relies when enforcing its security policy.

# CROSS REFERENCES

See *Access Control: Principles and Solutions; Information Leakage: Detection and Countermeasures; Multilevel Security Models; Security Policy Guidelines; The Common Criteria.*

# REFERENCES

Anderson, J. P. (1972). *Computer security technology planning study: Vol. 2* (ESD-TR-73-51, Vol. 2). Bedford, MA: Electronic Systems Division, Air Force Systems Command, Hanscom Field. Retrieved August 1, 2004, from http://csrc.nist.gov/publications/history/ande72.pdf

Bell, D. D., & La Padula, L. J. (1974). *Secure computer system: Unified exposition and multicsMULTICS interpretation* (ESD-TR-75-306). Bedford, MA: Electronic Systems Division, Air Force Systems Command, Hanscom Field. Retrieved August 1, 2004, from http://csrc.nist.gov/publications/history/bell76.pdf

Boehm, B. W. (1981). *Software engineering economics.* Englewood Cliffs, NJ: Prentice Hall.

Brooks, F. P. (1975). *The mythical man-month.* Reading, MA: Addison-Wesley.

Byers, S. (2004). Information leakage caused by hidden data in published documents. *IEEE Security and Privacy, 2*(2), 23–27. Retrieved October 1, 2004, from http://www.computer.org/security/v2n2/byers.htm

Cohen, F. C. (1994). *Short course on computer viruses* (2nd ed., pp. 35–36). New York: John Wiley & Sons.

Common Criteria Project Sponsoring Organizations. (1999). *Common criteria for information technology security evaluation, version 2.1.* Retrieved October 1, 2004, from http://csrc.nist.gov/cc/Documents/CC%20v2.1%20-%20HTML/CCCOVER.HTM

Department of Defense. (1985). *Trusted computer system evaluation criteria* (orange book, DOD 5200.28-STD). Washington, DC: Author. Retrieved October 1, 2004, from http://www.radium.ncsc.mil/tpep/library/rainbow/index.html#STD520028

Department of Defense. (1997). *DOD information technology security certification and accreditation* (DOD Instruction 5200.40). Washington, DC: Author. Retrieved October 1, 2004, from http://www.dtic.mil/whs/directives/corres/pdf/i520040_123097/i520040p.pdf

Federation of American Scientists. (1997). *Imagery intelligence: FAS space policy project Desert Star.* Retrieved August 1, 2004, from http://www.fas.org/spp/military/docops/operate/ds/images.htm

Fine, T. (1996). Defining noninterference in the temporal logic of actions. *Proceeding of the 1996 IEEE Conference on Security and Privacy* (pp. 12–21). Los Alamitos, CA: IEEE Computer Society Press.

Fraim, L. J. (1983). SCOMP: A solution to the multilevel security problem. *IEEE Computer, 16*(7), 26–34.

Haigh, J. T., & Young, W. D. (1987, February). Extending the noninterference version of MLS for SAT. *IEEE Transactions on Software Engineering, SE-13*(2), 141–150.

Hoffman, L. J. (1973). IBM's Resource Security System (RSS). In L. J. Hoffman (Ed.), *Security and privacy in computer systems* (pp. 379–401). Los Angeles: Melville.

Kang, M. H., Moskowitz, I. S., & Lee, D. C. (1996). A network pump. *IEEE Transactions on Software Engineering, 22*(5), 329–338.

Karger, P. A., & Schell, R. R. (1974). *MULTICS security evaluation, Vol. 2: Vulnerability analysis* (ESD-TR-74-193, Vol. 2). Bedford, MA: Electronic Systems Division, Air Force Systems Command, Hanscom Field. Retrieved August 1, 2004, from http://csrc.nist.gov/publications/history/karg74.pdf

Kemmerer, R. A. (1983). Shared resource matrix methodology: An approach to identifying storage and timing channels. *ACM Transactions on Computer Systems, 1*, 109–118.

Kemmerer, R. A. (2002). A practical approach to identifying storage and timing channels: Twenty years later. *Proceedings of the 18th Annual Computer Applications Security Conference*. Los Alamitos, CA: IEEE Computer Society Press.

Lampson, B. W. (1973, October). A note on the confinement problem. *Communications of the ACM, 16*(10), 613–615.

La Padula, L. J., LeMoine, J. E., Vukelich, D. F., & Woodward, J. P. L. (1990). *DNSIX detailed design specifications, version 2*. Bedford, MA: MITRE Corporation.

McGovern, S. C. (2001). *Information security requirements for a coalition wide area network*. Master's thesis, Naval Postgraduate School, Monterey, CA. Retrieved April 15, 2005, from http://cisr.nps.navy.mil/downloads/theses/01thesis_mcgovern.pdf

Nibaldi, G. H. (1979). *Proposed technical evaluation criteria for trusted computer systems* (M79-225). Bedford, MA: MITRE Corporation. Retrieved August 1, 2004, from http://csrc.nist.gov/publications/history/tniba79.pdf

Orlowski, A. (2004, May 6). MS Trusted Computing back to drawing board. *The Register*. Retrieved August 1, 2004, from http://www.theregister.co.uk/2004/ 05/06/microsoft_managed_code_rethink/

Proctor, N. E., & Neumann, P. G. (1992). Architectural implications of covert channels. *Proceedings of the Fifteenth National Computer Security Conference* (pp. 28–43). Retrieved November 15, 2004, from http://www.csl.sri.com/users/neumann/ncs92.html

Saydjari, O. S. (2002). LOCK: An historical perspective. *Proceedings of the 2002 Annual Computer Security Applications Conference*. Retrieved November 15, 2004, from http://www.acsac.org/2002/papers/classic-lock.pdf

Saydjari, O. S. (2004). Multilevel security: Reprise. *IEEE Security and Privacy, 2*(5), 64–67.

Saydjari, O. S., Beckman, J. K., & Leaman, J. R. (1989). LOCK Trek: Navigating uncharted space. *Proceedings of the 1989 IEEE Symposium on Security and Privacy* (pp. 167–175). Los Alamitos, CA: IEEE Computer Society Press.

Smith, R. E. (1994). Constructing a high assurance mail guard. *Proceedings of the 17th National Computer Security Conference* (pp. 247–253). Gaithersburg, MD: National Institute of Standards and Technology.

Smith, R. E. (2001). Cost profile of a highly assured, secure operating system. *ACM Transactions on Information System Security, 4*, 72–101.

St. Johns, M. (1988). *Draft revised IP security option* (RFC 1038). Retrieved October 1, 2004, from http://www.ietf.org/rfc/rfc1038.txt

Ware, W. H. (1970). *Security controls for computer systems (U): Report of Defense Science Board Task Force on Computer Security*. Santa Monica, CA: RAND Corporation. Retrieved August 1, 2004, from http://csrc.nist.gov/publications/history/ware70.pdf

Weissman, C. (1969). Security controls in the ADEPT-50 time-sharing system. *Proceedings of the 1969 Fall Joint Computer Conference*. [Reprinted in L. J. Hoffman (Ed.). (1973). *Security and privacy in computer systems* (pp. 216–243). Los Angeles: Melville.]

Wray, J. C. (1991). An analysis of covert timing channels. *1991 IEEE Symposium on Security and Privacy* (p. 27). Los Alamitos, CA: IEEE Computer Society Press.

# Multilevel Security Models

Mark Stamp and Ali Hushyar, *San Jose State University*

## INTRODUCTION

The United States Department of Defense (DoD) offers the following definition of multilevel security (Multilevel Security, 1995):

> Multilevel security, or MLS, is a capability that allows information with different sensitivities (i.e., classification and compartments) to be simultaneously stored and processed in an information system with users having different security clearances, authorizations, and needs to know, while preventing users from accessing information for which they are not cleared, do not have authorization, or do not have the need to know.

In other words, multilevel security (MLS) deals with issues related to access control. This chapter discusses many of the fundamental MLS models designed to address the issues surrounding MLS.

In its most basic form, an MLS model's access control restrictions are hierarchical. For example, an MLS system might classify information as Low or High, depending on its sensitivity. Each user would then be granted either High or Low access rights, corresponding to the classifications of the same name. A user with Low privileges could only access Low information, whereas a user with High privileges could access either High or Low information.

MLS has a long history—at least by the standards of information security—because it has been in use for many decades within classified government and military circles. This has led to considerable research into MLS systems and, consequently, the strengths and shortcomings of MLS are relatively well understood.

The access control concept embodied by MLS is of interest outside of military and government circles. For example, a corporation is likely to have information that only management is allowed to view, along with other information that all employees are allowed to access. One solution would be to create two separate information systems, one that is only accessible by management and one that is accessible by all employees. However, that would be an expensive and inconvenient solution. Instead, an MLS approach can be employed. With such a scheme, management would have High privileges (because they can view any document), whereas everyone else would have Low privileges.

Another, less obvious use for MLS is in a network firewall. Suppose that a firewall system is able to enforce High and Low privileges. Then, even if the security perimeter is breached, the resulting damage could be minimized, provided that the intruder can be held to Low privilege.

The outline of this chapter is as follows. In the next section, we discuss the MLS model used within the classified United States government and military bureaucracies. This is the best known use of MLS, and it is the basis for most research in the field. In the following section, we consider several security policy models that are intimately related to MLS. These include the well-known Bell–La Padula (BLP) model and the closely related Biba model. Although BLP has its critics, it provides a simple, intuitive, and analyzable model of MLS security requirements.

Any discussion of MLS inevitably leads to the complimentary concept of multilateral security (or compartments). Although it is possible to design a multilateral security system independent of MLS, and vice versa, in practice, multilevel and multilateral security are generally combined. For example, the classified United States government system includes numerous "compartments" within each classification level.

We then briefly discuss the covert channel problem, which arises in various contexts but is particularly acute in an MLS setting. This problem appears to be intractable, and hence the goal is to simply reduce the rate at which information can leak through such a channel.

We have also included an overview of the relationship of MLS models to certain applications. We conclude with a brief discussion of various other security models that are related to MLS models.

# MULTILEVEL SECURITY IN THE DoD

The United States Department of Defense (DoD) multilevel security model includes four security levels: Top Secret, Secret, Confidential, and Unclassified. The precise definition of each level can vary considerably between agencies within the DoD, but the general idea is that the release of Top Secret information would do grave harm to the interests of the United States, the release of Secret information would cause somewhat less harm, Confidential information would not cause significant damage if revealed, and Unclassified information is not officially protected.

In MLS, both information and users of the information have associated security levels. The security level of information is its classification, whereas the security level of a user is the user's security clearance. The same four security levels are used for both clearances and classifications.

A user with a Top Secret clearance can access information classified at any level, whereas a user with a Secret clearance can view information classified as Secret, Confidential, or Unclassified but has no access to Top Secret information. Similarly, a Confidential clearance gives access to Confidential and Unclassified information but not Secret or Top Secret. This simplified description yields a strictly hierarchical system. In the section Multilateral Security, we see that a lattice is actually used in place of this strict hierarchy.

To give some idea of the relative sensitivity of the various classifications, a Secret clearance requires a minimal background check (e.g., a check for a criminal record or financial mismanagement), whereas a Top Secret clearance requires a background check that includes a detailed investigation spanning the previous ten years, including interviews with associates, analysis of financial records, polygraph testing, and so on.

There are many practical problems associated with multilevel security. For example, the proper classification of information is not a trivial matter. One user might reasonably consider a document Secret, whereas another competent user considers it Confidential. Another concern is the level of granularity at which classifications are applied. One approach is to classify each paragraph of a written document and give the overall document the highest classification that appears on any paragraph. One reason for this approach is to aid in the declassification of documents (or parts thereof) resulting from, say, Freedom of Information Act (FOIA) requests.

Closely related to granularity is the problem of aggregation. Suppose we are required to classify source code (as is sometimes the case within the DoD). Individual pieces of code could each implement standard functionality (searching, sorting, etc.) and hence be Unclassified, yet in aggregate, the code might allow a knowledgeable attacker to deduce Top Secret information. These types of issues make the classification process far more subtle and subjective than is generally realized.

# CONFIDENTIALITY AND INTEGRITY POLICY MODELS
## Bell–La Padula Model

Confidentiality policies are intended to provide a precise description of the requirements needed to prevent the disclosure of confidential information. The purpose of the Bell–La Padula (BLP) security model is to capture the crucial features required of any MLS system. Here, we present a simplified discussion of BLP—see Bell and La Padula (1975), Bishop (2003), or Gollmann (1999) for a more thorough treatment.

Let S be a subject and let O be an object. S has a clearance and O has a classification. The security clearance of subject S is denoted by L(S), and the classification of object O is similarly denoted L(O). Then, L gives the security level of a subject or object.

Consider the DoD classification system discussed in the previous section. The classifications (and clearances) are ordered in the obvious way, namely, Top Secret > Secret > Confidential > Unclassified.

BLP can now be specified in terms of the following two properties.

***Simple Security Condition***
   S can read O if and only if $L(O) \leq L(S)$.

***\*–Property (Star-Property)***
   S can write O if and only if $L(S) \leq L(O)$.

These properties can be stated succinctly as "no read up" and "no write down," respectively. For obvious reasons, confidentiality policies such as BLP (and the corresponding integrity policies discussed in following sections) are referred to as information flow policies.

The simple security condition (no read up) is clearly a necessary part of any MLS system. The importance of the star-property (no write down) is a little more subtle. A nice example that shows the necessity of the star-property is found in the field of computer viruses. Without the star-property, viruses can break MLS systems by infecting a Top Secret account with a virus and having the virus "write down" classified information to an Unclassified account. Enforcing the star-property prevents this attack by preventing classified information from flowing down the MLS hierarchy.

Cohen, in his groundbreaking work on computer viruses (1994), used viruses to attack MLS systems of the day. Cohen was able to break MLS systems by infecting a Top Secret account with a virus and having the virus write down classified information to an Unclassified account using covert channels. Although Cohen employed covert channels, a similar approach could be used to write down information, in violation of the star-property. Such attacks still work on MLS systems today (F. B. Cohen, personal communication, June 30, 2004).

BLP can be enhanced by adding compartments (also known as categories) to the security levels. Compartments further restrict subjects to dealing with only those system resources that are necessary to accomplish their tasks and nothing more. This enforces the "need to know" principle within the MLS system. This topic is explored further in the section Multilateral Security.

It is perhaps surprising that the BLP's simply stated and intuitive properties can capture MLS requirements. However, BLP is not without its critics. McLean has argued that BLP is "so trivial that it is hard to imagine a realistic security model for which it does not hold" (1985, p. 47). To prove his point, McLean defined "system Z," which allowed a system administrator to temporarily reclassify an object, at which point it could be written down without violating the star-property. Defenders of BLP argued that system Z defied the assumptions underlying the BLP model. However, any such assumptions were unstated. To explicitly prevent the system Z attack, BLP was enhanced with a "tranquility property." This property states that security labels of subjects and objects, that is, L(S) and L(O), can never change.

The less restrictive "weak tranquility property" states that the security label of a subject or object can change only if it does not violate an established security policy. One advantage of the weak tranquility property is that in real world MLS systems, it is often desirable to give a user the least privilege needed for the current task. For example, when a user with a Top Secret clearance logs in to a system to check Unclassified e-mail, it is desirable to set his working clearance to Unclassified. The user's clearance can then be upgraded as needed for other tasks. This is known as the "high watermark" principle, and it is a way to assign default labels to new objects created by a user as well as a to minimize damage resulting from attacks or errors.

The weak tranquility property is also necessary if documents are ever to be declassified or reclassified. In the DoD MLS system, documents are regularly declassified.

For further information on BLP and, in particular, the controversy surrounding BLP, system Z, and so forth, see Bishop's excellent discussion (2003). Bishop nicely ties his discussion into fundamental questions about the nature of scientific modeling. Anderson (2001) provides an intuitive discussion of BLP and many related topics, with the emphasis on practical considerations.

## Biba's Integrity Policies

BLP aims to preserve data confidentiality. If data integrity is instead the concern, then a different model applies. This model must ensure that a data item can only be modified by a subject with the same or higher integrity level. The rationale here is that the data modified by a subject with a lower integrity level, the integrity of the data might be compromised. More generally, if an object includes components with multiple integrity levels, the overall integrity of the object can be no higher than the lowest integrity of any component it contains. This can be viewed as a "low watermark" principle, and it is a fundamental concept in Biba's model (1977). We show that Biba's model is, in a sense, the integrity counterpart of BLP.

Biba proposed three different integrity policies (1977, April): the low watermark policy, the ring policy, and what is known as Biba's model. Note that Biba's low watermark policy is not to be confused with the low watermark principle. The former describes how the integrity levels of subjects change in the policy, whereas the latter applies to the integrity level of objects. However, the low watermark principle is fundamental to all three of Biba's integrity policies.

The integrity level of a subject S and an object O are denoted as I(S) and I(O) respectively. Each policy allows a subject S to write to an object O only if the integrity level of S is at least as high as the integrity level of O, that is,

### Write Access Rule

S can write to O if and only if $I(O) \leq I(S)$.

This property places restrictions on the direct modification of data in the system. Biba's three policies differ in how they handle indirect modification of data. If a subject S can read an object O, then the integrity level of O may have an effect on the "trustworthiness" of S. The low watermark policy lowers the integrity level of S to that of the object it reads if the object O is at a lower integrity level. More precisely,

### Low Water Mark Policy

If S reads O, then the new integrity level of S, denoted I'(S), is the minimum of I(S) and I(O).

In contrast, the ring policy disregards indirect modification altogether and allows S to read any O with no affect on the subject's integrity level. Finally, Biba's model is the most restrictive. In Biba's model, subject S can read object O only if the integrity level of O is at least as high as the integrity level of S. That is,

### Biba's Model

S can read O if and only if $I(S) \leq I(O)$.

Biba's model, together with the write access rule stated previously, describes a "no read down" and "no write up" policy. This is the sense in which Biba's model is the integrity counterpart of BLP.

## Lipner's Model

Neither BLP nor Biba's model by themselves are sufficient to express the security requirements of many commercial policies. For example, it is often the case that both confidentiality and integrity are required simultaneously. Lipner's integrity matrix model is a combination of BLP and Biba's model. Lipner's model describes a software system that is accessible by subjects acting in different roles. These roles include application users and system controllers. An abridged description of Lipner's model is given here; see Bishop (2003) for a more thorough treatment.

Lipner incorporates BLP by describing a model that includes two security levels, High and Low, and the security categories Production Code (PC) and Production Data (PD), among others. The subjects that we consider are application users and system controllers. Subjects are given

**Table 1** Security Labels

| Subjects | Security Clearance |
|---|---|
| Application users | (Low, {PC, PD}) |
| System controllers | (Low, {<everything>}) |
| **Objects** | **Security Classification** |
| Production code | (Low, {PC}) |
| Production data | (Low, {PC, PD}) |
| System programs | (Low, {}) |
| System logs | (High, {<everything>}) |

security clearances in accordance with the specification of their jobs. Application users are given access to production code, PC, and production data, PD, because they need to be able to execute the application and modify production data via the application itself. System controllers on the other hand should have comprehensive read access to the system.

The relevant objects in the system include the production code, production data, system programs, and system logs entities. Production code and production data are at the Low security level, whereas system logs are at the High security level. In fact, system logs have the highest security label so that any subject can write to them. System programs are infrastructure programs that must be executable by any subject and hence are given the lowest security label, (Low, { }). All other objects are assigned security categories based on the data and on which subjects will be accessing them. For example, application users have the security clearance (Low, {PC, PD}) to read production code and production data. Therefore, production code has the classification (Low, {PC}). On the other hand, because application users must also write production data, the star-property forces production data to be classified as (Low, {PC, PD}). The security labels are summarized in Table 1.

There is one crucial issue that needs to be addressed with respect to the security model depicted in Table 1. The model must ensure that system programs can be modified by authorized subjects only, namely, the system controllers. To meet this requirement, Lipner augments security labels with integrity labels. The two integrity levels relevant to this example are denoted ILow and IHigh. There is one integrity category (IP) that distinguishes production entities from other categories in the system. One slight modification was made to the security labels by collapsing the PC and PD categories into a single Production (P) category. The resulting security and integrity labels are summarized in Table 2.

Lipner has shown that both integrity and confidentiality properties, as required in commercial policies, can be captured by combining security models. That is, policies expressing the authorized modification of data can be depicted by augmenting security labels with integrity labels. The next section introduces an alternative way to capture the security requirements of a commercial policy.

## Clark–Wilson Integrity Model

Many commercial integrity policies not only deal with the integrity of the data in the system but also with the integrity of the data access operations. By focusing on the transactions that are being executed in the system, the Clark–Wilson integrity model (CWM) closely models real commercial operating procedures. CWM places integrity controls on the data and the transactions that manipulate the data. CWM defines constrained data items (CDI) and unconstrained data items (UDI). The former are subject to strict integrity controls, whereas the latter are unchecked. System transactions are called transformation procedures (TP) and CWM ensures that each TP transitions the system from one secure state to another.

CWM achieves transaction integrity by using certification and enforcement rules on TPs. Certification rules are security policy restrictions on the behavior of transformation procedures, whereas enforcement rules are built-in system security mechanisms that achieve the objectives of the certification rules. There are three fundamental certification rules in CWM. The first requires that each TP preserve the integrity constraints of the CDIs on which it operates. Enforcement rules ensure this property by requiring that TPs only operate on a specified set of CDIs. Furthermore, specific users are associated with each TP, and the <user,TP,CDI> triple is known as a relation.

The second certification rule mandates that all relations obey the separation of duty principle. This is enforced by authenticating each user who wants to execute a TP. The third certification rule states that a system can accept a UDI as input and either reject the data or transform the data into a CDI. To enforce this restriction, all possible values for UDIs must be known a priori. This last certification rule is practical in the sense that it allows systems to process initially Low input data from external sources, which is not possible with the Biba model.

**Table 2** Security and Integrity Labels

| Subject | Security Clearance | Integrity Clearance |
|---|---|---|
| Application users | (Low, {P}) | (ILow, {IP}) |
| System controllers | (Low, {<everything>}) | (IHigh, {<everything>}) |
| **Objects** | **Security Classification** | **Integrity Classification** |
| Production code | (Low, {P}) | (IHigh, {IP}) |
| Production data | (Low, {P}) | (ILow, {IP}) |
| System programs | (Low, {}) | (IHigh, {IP}) |
| System logs | (High, {}) | (ILow, {}) |

CWM is similar to the Biba model in that both models assign integrity levels to subjects and objects. In CWM, subjects consist of high-level certified TPs and low-level transactions, and objects are either high-level CDIs or low-level UDIs. The Biba model, on the other hand, assumes that the subjects of the system are trusted in terms of the transactions they run, so there is no need for certification and enforcement rules. It is possible to express Biba's model using CWM by specifying the appropriate relations.

## MULTILATERAL SECURITY

Multilateral security (or compartments) deals with access control and information flow policies "across" rather than "up and down" security domains. Anderson (2001) describes two prominent systems that utilize multilateral security, namely, the United States classified intelligence system and professional environments such as investment houses. The former uses a variant of BLP (as discussed in the previous section) in which subjects and objects are classified using security labels complete with security levels and compartments. As mentioned previously, the use of compartments allows security models to express "need to know" policies within the system.

Together, security levels and compartments create a lattice structure that imposes a total ordering among all security labels, where a label consists of a security level together with a set of compartments. A lattice is a mathematical construct composed of a set of elements S and a relation R that is reflexive, antisymmetric, and transitive. In MLS systems, S consists of all possible security labels and the relation R is represented as "$\geq$."

Figure 1 gives an example of a lattice structure of security labels in a simple MLS system consisting of three of the four DoD security levels (Top Secret, Secret, and Unclassified), along with two compartments, Iraq and Canada. The arrows indicate a "$\geq$" relation on the labels in the system.

One practical concern with multilateral security systems is the tendency for security compartments to proliferate. For example, if a user in compartment A and a user in compartment B want to work together (within the same security level), a new compartment C combining parts of A and B could be created. As a result, the number of compartments can become unmanageable.

An interesting multilateral security model that combines both confidentiality and integrity is the Chinese wall model (CHW), which could, for example, be used to model conflict of interest situations in professional firms. In the context of an investment house, CHW would not allow a trader to represent two clients with conflicting interests. The investment house would maintain a database of objects, with all objects belonging to a single company grouped as a dataset (DS) for that company.

A conflict of interest class (CI) is defined as a collection of the DSs of all the companies that are in direct competition with one another. If a trader has read access to any object in the DS of one company, the trader will not be able to obtain read access to the DSs of any of the companies in the same CI. The condition for read access in CHW can be stated informally as

### CHW Simple Security Condition
A subject S can read an object O if O belongs to the DS that S is authorized to read, or for all objects that S has already read, the CI of each of those objects does not equal the CI of O.

One scenario that must be prevented in CHW is the flow of information among different CIs, as depicted in Figure 2. Suppose trader A has read access to DS 1 in CI 1 and trader B has read access to DS 2 in CI 1. In addition, trader B has read access to DS 3 in CI 2 and trader A has read/write access to DS 3 in CI 2. Then, it would be possible for trader A to read objects from DS 1 and write them to DS 3 where they can be read by trader B. This clearly violates the conflict of interest goal of the model.

The following write access condition is designed to prevent the undesirable information flow illustrated in Figure 2.

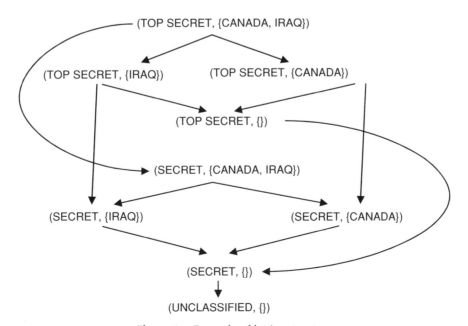

**Figure 1:** Example of lattice structure.

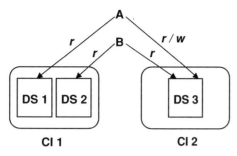

**Figure 2:** Flow of information between two CIs.

### CHW *–Property
A subject S can write to an object O if S can read O and, for all objects that S can read, the DSs of those objects are the same as the DS of O.

It is important to note the differences between the CHW and BLP models. Subjects in CHW do not have security clearances. More precisely, subjects initially do not have assigned security labels and are only constrained by the history of their actions. The fact that CHW records a subject's access history to evaluate new access requests is another essential difference between CHW and BLP.

## COVERT CHANNELS
Multilevel security policies place restrictions on legitimate channels of communication within a system. Other avenues of information flow may exist that are not accounted for by policies such as BLP. These communication channels can exist as a result of resources shared by users at different security levels.

Messages can be transmitted via covert storage channels by manipulating attributes of a shared resource. Suppose process A has write access to file F and process B has no access at all to F, except that B can read the metadata associated with file F. Then, process A can indirectly communicate with process B by varying the size of the file. For example, process A can delete the contents of the file F, resulting in a file of minimum size, to communicate a 0 to process B. Similarly, process A can add content to F to increase the file size to communicate a 1 to process B.

Messages can also be sent through covert timing channels by orchestrating temporal accesses to a shared resource. In MLS systems, Low processes can write to High objects. If acknowledgement messages are permitted in response to successful write operations, a High process could, for example, vary the acknowledgement response times to signal information to a Low process.

There are three conditions that need to be met to realize a covert channel. First, both the sending and receiving processes must have access to a shared resource or the ability to monitor its behavior. Second, the sending process must be able to modulate a property of the shared resource and have the receiving process observe the change. Finally, communication between the sending and receiving processes must be synchronized so that sequences of data signaling events can occur (National Computer Security Center, 1993).

As discussed in Anderson (2001), any serious attempt to eliminate all covert channels will inevitably result in a system that is unusable. In recognition of this fact, DoD policies only attempt to reduce the rate at which information can leak through a covert channel to no more than one bit per second (Department of Defense, 1993).

## APPLICATION-SPECIFIC MLS CONCEPTS
### MLS in Communication Protocols
Communication protocols and mechanisms are generally designed to achieve optimal performance and reliability. One method employed to ensure reliability is for a target entity to transmit acknowledgement (ACK) messages to a source entity indicating the successful reception of data. In secure MLS systems, communication can only travel from Low to High. As a result, the ACKs sent from High to Low must not be permitted because these messages can be manipulated to transmit sensitive information via a covert channel. However, removing ACKs from communication protocols compromises the reliability and performance of the communication channel. Kang and Moskovita (1995) explain how NRL pumps were designed to allow the secure communication of messages from Low to High without sacrificing the reliability of the underlying communication protocols.

Conventional communication from Low to High proceeds as follows: There are three buffers, a low buffer (LB) belonging to Low, a high buffer (HB) belonging to High, and an intermediate communication buffer (CB). Low sends data to its low buffer and if there is free space in the communication buffer (CB), it will receive an ACK from the low buffer. Only after receiving an ACK can Low send a subsequent message. High receives data from its high buffer and sends the corresponding ACK to the high buffer. This ACK removes the acknowledged data from the communication buffer.

Suppose that High does not acknowledge data. This will eventually cause the communication buffer to fill. When the communication buffer is full, Low will no longer receive ACKs from the low buffer. High can now dictate when Low will receive an ACK. When High sends an ACK, this will free space in the communication buffer for data that has not yet been acknowledged, which forces the low buffer to send an ACK to Low. This process yields a covert timing channel.

NRL pumps can be viewed as trusted communication mediators that sit between High and Low. The pump will control the behavior of the buffers, as illustrated in Figure 3. The rate at which Low sends data to the low buffer is called the send rate and the rate at which High receives data from the high buffer is called the service rate. $R_l$ is the rate at which Low receives an ACK from the low buffer and $R_H$ is the rate at which High sends an ACK to the high buffer.

If the send rate is greater than the service rate, then the communication buffer can be filled, resulting in the covert channel described above. To prevent this scenario, the pump can slow down the send rate by controlling $R_l$, the rate at which Low receives ACKs. Then, $R_l$ only needs to be decreased to match the service rate.

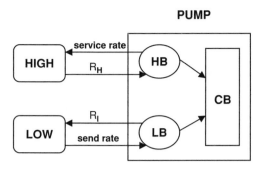

**Figure 3:** NRL pumps.

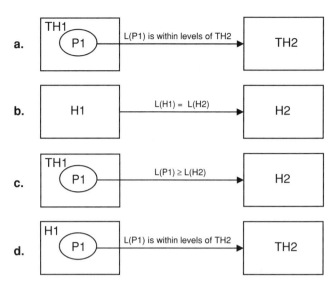

**Figure 4:** Connection scenarios.

NRL pumps are only designed to limit the rate at which High can send ACKs to Low. A limited threat from covert channels still exists with the NRL pump. It is generally believed that absolute security is—in the context of an MLS communication protocol—irreconcilable with reasonable performance and reliability. However, pumps do make it possible to build multilevel security systems because such pumps can be used to connect systems of different security levels.

## MLS in Computer Networks

There are many issues surrounding the problem of multilevel data sharing within a computer network and among different networks. The simplest case is when a network, with all its interconnected hosts and resources, operates under a single security level. Interconnections among networks with different security levels are achieved via the use of special-purpose guards that restrict information flow. These restrictions include allowing Low to High information flow and filtering or downgrading data as it flows from High to Low. These guards are essentially specialized firewalls that achieve MLS properties without using MLS mechanisms or products. This approach is known as multiple independent levels of security (MILS; Smith, 2003).

Alternatively, a computer network is said to be running in an MLS context if it can handle the multilevel classifications of its network elements and associated traffic. A network MLS system must apply access and information flow controls to the network as a whole instead of just within each network element. The network trusted computer base (NTCB)—which enforces the network security policy—works in conjunction with individual system TCBs. The primary goal of a NTCB is to determine which network elements can communicate with each other and then to regulate the flow of information between connections.

The nature of subjects and objects in a multilevel network security model varies depending on the layer in the network protocol stack. At the application layer, subjects are individual users whereas objects can be messages and files. At the network (i.e., IP) layer, subjects are hosts and processes on the network whereas objects are the packets and connections among the hosts. The following discussion is derived from Varadharajan (1990) and considers subjects and objects at the network layer.

A computer system or network is deemed "trusted" if it can handle information with different security labels.

Trusted networks can interconnect both trusted and untrusted systems. Because trusted networks deal with multilevel traffic, they assign security labels to the packets and sessions of a network connection. A trusted system can interact with another trusted network only if its security levels overlap with the security levels of the other network. A trusted system/trusted network configuration consists of individual system TCBs to ensure that the network only receives data within its range of security levels. It also consists of NTCBs to verify that a system receives traffic within its range of security levels. In an untrusted system/trusted network configuration, there is no TCB to make sure the network receives appropriately classified data. Because an untrusted system operates in a single classification mode, it is necessary that the corresponding security labels are within the security level range of the network.

Figure 4 illustrates different connection scenarios among trusted and untrusted hosts. If a process P1 on a trusted host TH1 wants to connect to a trusted host TH2, a NTCB verifies that the security clearance of the subject P1 is within the security range of TH2 (Figure 4a). If both hosts are untrusted, then H1 and H2 must have the same security label for a connection to be granted (Figure 4b). A process P1 on a trusted host TH1 can connect to an untrusted host H2 only if the security clearance of P1 is at least as high as the security label of H2 (Figure 4c). If a process P1 on untrusted host H1 wants to connect to trusted host TH2, the security clearance of P1 must be within the range of TH2 (Figure 4d). Finally, whenever a connection request is granted, information flow policies are enforced within the session.

## MLS in Database Management Systems

Relational database management systems can execute in the context of an MLS system (National Computer Security Center, 1993; Boebert & Kain, 1985). Security labels are assigned to subjects and objects, where objects can include tables, records, record fields, and so forth. In an MLS database, subjects have different views of the data in the database depending on their clearance. This means that the view of the database at the lowest security level is a subset of the view at the highest security level. A record can only be viewed by a subject with a security clearance at least as high as the record's highest field classification.

A "logical" record may be listed in a table many times depending on the number of views for that record. This potential problem is known as polyinstantiation. As a result, the concept of a primary key for a table in a MLS database model must be modified to take this view concept into consideration. The key for an MLS table not only includes the traditional primary key attribute (or attributes), but also the security label of the primary key. MLS databases introduce the problem of query ambiguity because the database handles queries that operate on these different record views. Furthermore, update commands invoke the creation of many records depending on the number of security levels that are involved in the system.

There are many MLS database models that deal with the semantic issues mentioned above—see Pranjic, Pertalj, & Jukic (2002) for more details. One such model is the Smith–Winslett model (SWM). SWM is structured as a set of relational database systems, one for each security level in the system. Security labels are assigned to primary keys and to records but not to record fields. All modification commands such as update can only be executed in the context of the subject's security clearance, thus reducing the resulting proliferation of records.

## MLS in Object-Oriented Systems

Black and Varadharajan (1990) provide an elegant description of MLS in object-oriented systems. The entities that comprise object-oriented systems are fundamentally different from those of the BLP model, for example. Recall that BLP associates security labels with "subjects" and "objects" that represent users and information, respectively. In contrast, object-oriented systems deal with classes, objects, methods, object variables, and messages. Here, classes denote the data type or template of an object and an object is an instantiation of a class. Objects contain state variables, which are manipulated by invoking an object's methods. Method invocation requires sending a message with the appropriate data to an object and having the receiving method send back a return message.

An important issue in object-oriented MLS systems is determining at what level of granularity to place security labels. Because information flow policies act on generic users and data, the counterparts in the object-oriented system are the object's methods and variables respectively. Messages are also classified as "user" entities because methods generate messages for remote method invocation. Given the method, message, and variable entities, there are many issues that must be addressed by an information flow policy such as BLP. The first is the relationship between an object's methods and its variables. Because a method can have read access to some variables and write access to others, the BLP model can be applied.

Managing the interactions between an object's methods and variables implies that there exists a mechanism to permit only valid access requests. This mechanism is

called a monitor and can be implemented in one of two ways. A monitor can regulate the access requests among methods and object variables only or among methods and all data including the data in a method's local storage. The former implementation results in a significant security vulnerability because a method can potentially store high-level data in local storage variables that is later leaked to unauthorized entities.

Objects communicate by invoking the methods of other objects. This invocation requires that messages be sent from one object to another. A message often carries with it object variables or other data that must be protected. A message carrying data is analogous to a user reading a data object. A message received by an object's sending method and a message received by an object's receiving method correspond to the access behavior of a user writing to a data object. Therefore, applying BLP to the message, variable, and method entities yields the following conditions:

1. The security label of a message must be $\geq$ the security label(s) of the data it encapsulates.
2. The security label of the sending method must be $\geq$ the security label of the message being sent.
3. The security label of the receiving method must be $\geq$ the security label of the message being received.

Because the value of an object variable can change during an object's lifetime, the security label associated with an object variable can also change to reflect the sensitivity of the data it holds. Object methods, however, are not associated with persistent data but instead deal with the access of object variables. Therefore, method security labels are immutable after object creation.

Objects create other objects by sending initialization data consisting of data values and associated security labels to object factories. However, if the security label of the data in the message does not dominate the security label of the message itself, it is possible for a message to carry high-level data and initialize low-level object variables with that data. As a result, the contents of a message must be at the same security classification as the message itself. This restriction can be checked by the object factory, which is assumed to be the core trusted component in the system. The factory must also be able to create and initialize variables with all security labels. Classifying methods is then a trivial issue that can be done after object creation.

## OTHER MODELS RELATED TO MLS
### Harrison–Ruzzo–Ullman Model

In 1976, Harrison, Ruzzo, and Ullman introduced the Harrison–Ruzzo–Ullman (HRU) protection model, which can express almost any protection policy. HRU is built on an access control matrix model where subjects and objects are the rows and columns of the matrix, respectively, and each element of the matrix indicates the access rights a subject has over an object. HRU recognizes that the protection state of a system changes over time; that is, processes execute procedures that transition the system from one protection state to another.

HRU defines six primitive commands that operate solely on the access control matrix: *create subject s, create object o, enter right r into, delete right r from, destroy subject s,* and *destroy object o*. These primitive commands are often combined together to create system commands. It is important to note that HRU handles the deletion of rights and the destruction of subjects or objects. These concepts are not dealt with in models such as BLP.

A fundamental issue regarding an HRU system is determining its security. That is, given an initial protection state (expressed as an access control matrix), does there exist a sequence of commands such that a specific right r is "leaked" by the system? However, not all "leaked" rights are considered insecure. For example, a subject can grant access rights to others for the objects he owns. Such legitimate transfers of rights must be accounted for in any HRU security analysis. It has been shown (Bishop, 2003) that the security of HRU is, in general, undecidable. Bishop gives a nice exposition on the restrictions that can be placed on access control models such as HRU to make the security question decidable.

## Type Enforcement Model

The type enforcement model (Boebert & Kain, 1985), also known as the Boebert–Kain model (BKM), is a table-based access control model similar to HRU. With BKM, there are three security factors that determine if and how a subject can access an object. In addition to the traditional multilevel security levels assigned to them, subjects have an attribute, called domain, whereas objects have an attribute called type. A subject's domain is the context or subsystem of which the subject is a part. An object's type refers to the kind of information it contains. The access control matrix is called the domain definition table (DDT), where the rows and columns of the table are the domains of the subjects and types of the objects respectively. Each cell of the DDT holds the access rights one domain has over a specific object type. An object also has a list of subjects who can access the object along with their capabilities. Access type evaluation is done by checking the mandatory access control policy enforced by the multilevel security levels, the discretionary access control policy enforced by the access control lists, and finally the DDT. Intuitively, this model restricts certain access types to specific domains rather than just specific users. This location dependence is the fundamental feature of BKM.

## Role-Based Access Control Model

Traditional access control models limit the ability of users to access objects in a system; that is, users are granted specific permissions that enable them to access certain system resources. A relatively new paradigm of access control is based on the roles that users assume in a system rather than their individual identity. Sandhu, Coyne, Feinstein, and Youman (1996) describe role-based access control (RBAC) models. These models define a role as a job function that is part of an organization's operational procedures. Permissions are granted to roles instead of to individual users and users are assigned to different roles according to their responsibilities.

RBAC allows system developers a great deal of flexibility. Relationships among roles, among permissions and roles, and among users and roles can be established to facilitate the implementation of security policy principles. For example, a system can define a mutual exclusion relation between two roles to enforce separation of duty policies or an inheritance relation between two roles to allow delegation of authority policies.

Managing security policies that associate permissions to users is tedious as permissions are likely to change over time. In RBAC, the permissions belonging to each role are considered more stable even though the users assigned to each role might change. Finally, relationships among users and roles are more manageable because adding and removing user membership in roles is easier than adding and revoking permissions from users.

Other security principles supported by RBAC include least privilege and data abstraction. Least privilege requires that only those permissions necessary for a user to execute a job function be assigned to the corresponding role. Data abstraction enables the creation of specific access operations apart from the generic read, write, and execute commands.

## Enforcing Least Privilege on Processes

Most access control policy implementations, including those in major operating systems such as some Windows and UNIX systems, operate at the level of the user. Although this prevents users from performing unauthorized actions, it does not prevent processes running on behalf of a user from performing unwanted actions. For example, a virus that has corrupted a user's process can send sensitive information to an attacker by opening a network connection without the user being aware of the information leakage. Karp (2003) explains that to limit the potential damage that a computer virus can cause to a system, the principle of least privilege should be applied at the process level. This way, a virus will only be able to take advantage of those capabilities that a process needs to perform its job and nothing more. For example, a virus in an e-mail client can disrupt the functionality of the client but will not be able to use network connections not granted to the client itself.

The major flaw in user-level access control systems is that any process a user invokes will run with all of the user's privileges. The alternative is to establish a mechanism that allows a user to grant different permissions to different processes. In such a system, a virus that takes over a process will not be able to operate outside of the set of permissions granted to the process. Implementing least privilege at the process level can be achieved by deploying operating systems that enforce the principle as part of their functionality or by writing applications in a programming language that support capability-based security.

## Steganographic File System

The steganographic file system discussed in Anderson, Needham, and Shamir (1998) can be implemented as part of a multilevel security system. This system includes an interesting "plausible deniability" feature, which insures that a user cannot be coerced into revealing information because the very existence of the information can be denied. A Linux implementation is available (McDonald & Kuhn, 2000).

# CONCLUSION

Two crucial properties of secure computing systems are confidentiality and integrity. In this chapter, we describe how MLS systems enforce these properties. The Bell–La Padula model (BLP) provided the foundation for security policy modeling, and Biba showed how to reconfigure the BLP framework to deal with integrity. More complex and flexible policies have been derived from BLP and Biba, including Lipner's model and lattice-based and multilateral policies that are designed to express the "need to know" principle. These models have been implemented in many systems ranging from operating systems to medical information systems.

An extraordinary amount of research has gone into MLS systems since the 1970s because of the importance of such systems to the military and government. Still, there are limitations to MLS models as they make many assumptions about underlying systems to provide a framework for security. Furthermore, the generic access control policies captured by BLP and Biba have been shown to be inadequate for expressing many relevant commercial policies. Nevertheless, MLS principles—as embodied by the MLS models discussed in this chapter—have been broadly applied to operating systems, databases, and computer networks, albeit with varying degrees of success. Successful implementation of the security principles expressed by MLS systems can, at the least, reduce the damage caused by successful attacks.

# GLOSSARY

**Access Control** The process of restricting access to information system resources to the appropriate and authorized users and systems.

**Communication Protocol** A set of rules that dictate the way in which two communicating parties exchange and interpret messages. The TCP/IP protocol suite is a collection of protocols that specify the manner in which data communication is conducted via the Internet.

**Computer Network** A collection of computer systems and network infrastructure components that enable the exchange of data electronically via telecommunication links.

**Computer Virus** A malicious program that replicates itself and infects other programs, often causing undesirable effects.

**Covert Storage Channel** A covert channel that uses a storage location to transmit information secretly from one party to another. In computer systems, a storage location such as a directory can be written to by one process and read by another, thus establishing a communication medium.

**Covert Timing Channel** A covert channel in which a process communicates information to another process by modulating a system resource, such as CPU time, of which the sending process has control.

**Firewall** A combination of hardware and software resources that monitor and prevent unauthorized network traffic from entering a protected internal network.

**Freedom of Information Act (FOIA)** A federal law that requires the United States government to disclose certain information to the public. The government must receive a written request for this information, which only applies to the executive branch of the federal government.

**Information System** A system that consists of people, computers, and procedures organized to use and communicate system information.

**Object-Oriented System** An architectural paradigm for building software systems by representing system components as objects. An object consists of internal data that represents an object's state and a set of methods that represent its computational logic. An object A can communicate with object B by invoking a method that object B defines.

**Security Policy** A statement that distinguishes between the secure and insecure modes of operation within a system as well as the procedures undertaken to protect the system.

**Trusted Computer Base (TCB)** The TCB refers to all of the protection mechanisms, hardware and software, within a computer system that enforce the security policy of the system.

**United States Department of Defense (DoD)** The federal department created in 1947 responsible for preserving the national security of the United States.

# CROSS REFERENCES

See *Access Control: Principles and Solutions; Information Leakage: Detection and Countermeasures; Multilevel Security; Security Policy Guidelines; The Common Criteria.*

# REFERENCES

Anderson, R. (2001). *Security engineering: A guide to building dependable distributed systems*. New York, NY: John Wiley & Sons, Inc.

Anderson, R., Needham, R., & Shamir, A. (1998). *The steganographic file system*. Retrieved April 8, 2005, from http://www.cl.cam.ac.uk/ftp/users/rja14/sfs3.pdf

Bell, D., & La Padula, L. (1975, July). *Secure computer systems: Unified exposition and Multics interpretation* (Technical Report MTR–2997). Bedford, MA: MITRE.

Biba, K. (1977, April). *Integrity considerations for secure computer systems* (Technical Report MTR–3153). Bedford, MA: MITRE.

Bishop, M. (2003). *Computer security: Art and science*. Boston, MA: Pearson Education.

Black, R., & Varadharajan, V. (1990, June). A multilevel security model for a distributed object–oriented system (HPL-90-74)., Hewlett–Packard Laboratories. Retrieved April 8, 2005, from http://www.hpl.hp.com/techreports/90/HPL-90-74.html

Boebert, W. E., & Kain, R. Y. (1985). A practical alternative to hierarchical integrity policies. In *Proceedings of the 8th National Computer Security Conference* (p. 18). Gaithersburg, MD: NIST.

Cohen, F. B. (1994). A short course on computer viruses (2nd ed.). New York, NY: John Wiley & Sons.

Department of Defense. (1993, November). A guide to understanding covert channel analysis of trusted systems (NCSC-TG-030). Fort George G. Meade, MD: Gligor, V. D.

Gollmann, D. (1999). *Computer security*. New York: John Wiley & Sons.

Harrison, M., Ruzzo, M. L., & Ullman, J. D. (1976). Protection in operating systems. *Communications of the ACM, 19*(8), 461–471.

Kang, M., & Moskovitz, I. S. (1995). A data pump for communication (NRL Memo Report 5540-957771). Washington, DC: Naval Research Laboratory.

Karp, A. H. (2003). Enforce POLA on processes to control viruses, *Communications of the ACM, 46*(12), 27–29.

McDonald, A., & Kuhn, M. (2000). *StegFS—A steganographic file system for Linux*. In *Proceedings of IH '99*, Lecture Notes in Computer Science 1768. Berlin: Springer-Verlag.

McLean, J. (1985, February). A comment on the 'Basic Security Theorem' of Bell and La Padula, *Information Processing Letters 20*(2), pp. 67–70.

*Multilevel security in the Department of Defense: The basics*. (1995, March). Retrieved April 8, 2005, from http://nsi.org/Library/Compsec/sec0.html

National Computer Security Center. (1993, November). A guide to understanding covert channel analysis of trusted systems. Retrieved April 8, 2005, from http://www.radium.ncsc.mil/tpep/library/rainbow/NCSC-TG-030.html

Pranjic, M., Pertalj, K., & Jukic, N. (2002). Importance of semantics in MLS database models. In *Proceedings of The 24th International Conference on Information Technology Interfaces* (pp. 51–56). Cavtat, Croatia.

Sandhu, R. S., Coyne, E. J., Feinstein, H. L., & Youman, C. E. (1996). Role based access control models, *IEEE Computer, 29*(2), 38–47.

Smith, R. (2003, September). The challenge of multilevel security. Retrieved April 8, 2005, from http://www.blackhat.com/presentations/bh-federal-03/bh-fed-03-smith.pdf

Varadharajan, V. (1990). A multilevel security policy model for networks. In *Proceedings IEEE INFOCOM '90* (Vol. 2, pp. 710–718). San Francisco.

# Security Architectures

Nicole Graf, *University of Cooprative Education, Germany*
Dominic Kneeshaw, *Independent Consultant, Germany*

## INTRODUCTION

*Webster's New Encyclopedic Dictionary* (1994) describes the word *architecture* as the "art or science of designing and building habitable structures." In its broadest sense, this meaning can also be applied to security architectures. The individual steps in the development of security architectures in an IT environment can be identified as follows:

- define the system's purpose in the context of an organization's business process,
- design technical structures and specifications,
- develop functional systems,
- deploy a tested and approved system,
- periodically audit the system, and
- continually improve the system.

This approach provides a clear framework with which to work but also gives rise to some significant questions. How should we define the system's purpose and what do we need to develop to fulfill that purpose? This chapter identifies the objectives of security architecture, the diversity of threats to IT security, and the implications these have for an organization.

The first step in the development of a security architecture is to define the system's purpose. This is driven by three factors, namely security criteria, security policy, and risk analysis.

### Security Criteria

Security criteria are primarily concerned with the privacy, availability, integrity, and authenticity of an organization's data and communications. Privacy means that a piece of information can only be made available to specific individuals. Availability ensures that information can be used at any agreed time, in agreed shape and quality. Integrity determines that information contains only approved or allowed changes. Authenticity covers the binding content, in which the originator's identity is confirmed.

The way in which individual organizations interpret and apply these criteria can vary according to their specific business environment and objectives. However, it is generally acceptable to assume that organizations need to conduct their affairs within the scope of these criteria to protect their intellectual property.

### Risk Analysis

The most simple and straightforward way of ensuring that one's property is protected would be to physically disconnect the network from the outside world, thus making it impossible for imposters to hack in to the network from a remote location. If one takes a moment to consider the implications of this scenario, then it becomes clear that this action is not discriminatory. Bona fide users, customers, and suppliers have also been denied access, putting an organization's business continuity and survival in jeopardy. Yet, neither human beings nor corporations choose domestic or business residences without windows and doors. The security risks in our homes and offices are addressed with the use of additional window locks, alarm systems, movement-sensitive security lights, and so forth. In this way, we aim to provide ample access to legitimate visitors, while providing adequate protection against undesired intrusion and abuse. Essentially the same doctrine applies to the application of IT security.

The analysis of risk provides extremely valuable input for the definition of a system's purpose. This process helps an organization to identify their vulnerabilities, the financial consequences of loss, and the relative costs of possible countermeasures.

## Security Policy

Users and IT teams alike are expected to adhere to all manner of corporate policies, and the security policy is no exception. As a consequence of security criteria and risk analysis, an organization will set out to document its rules, regulations, and guidelines for the use and protection of its IT environment. Thus, security policy becomes the driving force behind the planning, implementation, and evolution of an appropriate security architecture.

In an age where almost all aspects of information technology are governed by international standards, it is somewhat paradoxical that there is no such thing as an industry-standard security policy. As no two organizations or their networks are identical, security policy and the resulting architectures are virtually unique.

Because a preceding chapter of this *Handbook* has already dealt with security policies in considerable detail, this chapter concentrates on the architectures as the method of implementation.

## THREATS TO IT SECURITY

In the preceding section, we discussed that organizations will aim to ensure privacy, availability, integrity, and authenticity of their information and networks. Surely, if risk analysis, security policy, and security architecture are necessary to achieve this, then organizations must be facing some kind of threat?

It is irrelevant whether we consider a family personal computer (PC) in the home or a corporate PC in a network. Computers are under threat on a daily basis. Readers who monitor the events reported by a personal firewall while their home PC is online will appreciate that this statement is no exaggeration. The modern world of information technology gives rise to a variety of threats. Only by understanding the nature of these threats is it really possible to recognize the risks and account for them in security architecture.

The threats to IT security can largely be summarized in four categories, as follows:

1. spread of computer infection (e.g., viruses, spyware)
2. the human factor (malicious and inadvertent varieties)
3. technological threats (e.g., wireless local area network [WLAN] or Internet protocol [IP] telephony)
4. extraordinary events (e.g., acts of God, terrorism)

### Spread of Computer Infection

Computer-based infections are commonly referred to as *viruses*. However, this category is actually composed of a number of different types of threat, which can be summarized as follows.

### Adware

Adware programs secretly gather personal information and transmit it via the Internet to another computer. Adware is usually spread for advertising purposes and used to track information related to Internet browser usage and so forth. Adware is often downloaded in shareware or freeware from Web sites, e-mail messages, and instant messaging services.

### Dialers

Dialers are programs that use a system, usually without the user's permission or knowledge, to dial up the Internet connection via a premium rate number and accrue exorbitant online call charges. Dialers generally require a modem to dial up the Internet via a telephone line.

### Hacking Tools

These tools are used by a hacker to gain unauthorized access to a computer. One such example is a keystroke logger, which is used to record individual keystrokes (e.g., login or password entry) and to send this information to a hacker.

### Spyware

Spyware programs are stand-alone programs that can secretly monitor system activity, detect passwords or other confidential information, and transmit them to another computer. Spyware can be downloaded in a similar fashion to adware.

### Trojan Horses

Taken at face value, Trojan horses are files that are designed to appear desirable. However, they actually conceal a malicious purpose that a hacker can exploit. Trojan horses do not replicate or copy themselves, and they usually arrive by e-mail, for example, as an attachment, joke program, and so forth. Their glossy exterior disguises malicious code, which can cause loss of data or compromise the security of the computer.

### Viruses

A virus is a program or code that replicates itself by infecting a host. The host can be another program, boot sector, partition sector, or document that supports macros. Many viruses can do a large amount of damage to a computer. Because a virus replicates by attaching itself to a host, many detection tools are also able to remove a virus and leave the rest of the document intact.

### Worms

A worm is a program that spreads by making copies of itself from one disk drive to another or by copying itself using e-mail or another transport mechanism. A worm can usually be distinguished from a virus because it does not rely on a host to spread. A worm is able to copy and spread itself in its own right. It might arrive in the form of a joke program or other software and can compromise the security of the computer.

The various types of threat listed actually contain thousands of individual threats. The destructive nature of each threat can range from negligible to system critical. A particularly malicious virus can erase the contents of a hard disk in minutes and there is little that a user can do to stop the destruction. Detailed information relating to a specific threat can usually be obtained on the Web sites of commercial virus detection specialists (e.g., Symantec, McAfee, Computer Associates).

## Human Factor

There are many aspects of security that need attention, and a key element is the people inside and outside the organization. "Security continues to be, and probably will always be, a people problem. If you overlook that, you're in trouble" (R. H. Baker, 1991, Computer Security Handbook, PA: TAB Books, Blue Ridge Summit).

### Malicious Intent

Organizations can find themselves under attack from hackers, people who pride themselves in their ability to beat security systems. Some hackers might possess a completely benign intent, preferring to disappear from a network just as quietly as they came. However, for the purpose of this chapter, it is more appropriate to assume that hackers will wish to exercise their abilities to the disadvantage of an organization.

It is also necessary to consider that hackers are not the only malicious threat. An effective security architecture defines rules and implements systems to keep unauthorized users out and let legitimate users in. However, people within the organization often use exploits for the same reasons as external attackers. Employees can pose a serious threat, especially if they feel that they have an unresolved grievance with an organization. Such "internal attacks" represent a risk factor that should not be overlooked.

Regardless of motive, members of these groups might choose to harm an organization. They can do this by infiltrating the network, seeking access to sensitive documents, destroying sensitive documents, or simply putting a critical server out of action. Each of these scenarios can endanger the availability, integrity, privacy, and authenticity of information, and this is undesirable.

### Inadvertent Behavior

This essentially arises from the fact that human beings are sometimes quite lazy and prone to making errors. Most of us understand the implications of leaving the car unlocked in the street. Thus, we hide valuables out of sight and make sure that the vehicle is secure before leaving it unattended. However, many computer users are less aware of IT-related security issues. Lack of awareness of these issues provides a breeding ground for erroneous behavior.

As a result, login details get written down on sticky notes, people go to lunch without locking their user accounts, laptop computers are stolen from cars, and so forth. In another example, a major German automobile manufacturer discovered that a server was unexpectedly shutting down every day at the same time and after a while it would reboot. This caused a week of disruption until the problem was finally identified. There were no longer any power outlets free in the server room and the cleaning lady had been pulling a plug from the wall in order to connect the vacuum cleaner. Once she had finished cleaning the room, she reconnected the power cord and the server rebooted. This serves as a simple, yet poignant, example of the problems that "the human factor" can create for an IT team.

These instances can also endanger the security criteria, yet it is unfair to assume that an employee, or contractor, deliberately set out to harm the organization.

## Technological Vulnerabilities

Technology is actually a double-edged sword. On the one hand, technology can create a whole new series of vulnerabilities and threats for an organization. On the other hand, it can be used to provide the solution to those threats.

Technological issues can arise from known and accepted technologies that are already in use in the live, or production, environment. Unexpected hardware defects, such as failure of a network-switching component or a hard disk, can have considerable effect on the availability and integrity of information. Previously unknown loopholes in software programs and operating systems can be exploited by a hacker so that he can execute malicious code and modify, delete, or steal files.

Matters are complicated further because information technology does not stand still. In the highly competitive world of IT, manufacturers are under immense pressure to lead the market with new technological developments. This in turn drives ever-shorter development cycles for faster, more innovative, solutions. Unfortunately, it does not guarantee that new technologies or their components are threat-free.

New technologies are unknown quantities, and many organizations will be wise to test and verify new products and solutions in a laboratory environment before adopting them in the production network. Currently, there are two very good examples of emerging technologies that will influence the way organizations address the availability, privacy, and integrity of their networks. These are wireless local area networking (wireless LAN or WLAN) and IP telephony.

### Basics of Wireless LAN Technology

The charm of combining a broadband Internet access with a wireless internal network is promoted every day in the advertising media. Why install expensive cable-based networks if wireless LAN is an inexpensive and easy alternative? Salespeople can quickly access their network from anywhere without first having to locate a physical network socket. Warehouses can easily be provided with cable-free network coverage and so forth.

This sounds very convenient, but as a matter of engineering principles, wireless technology is inherently more vulnerable to unwanted interception, intrusion, and manipulation than wire line solutions, as a study project of Ernst & Young identified in 2003 (Ruediger, 2003).

In layman's terms, the wireless LAN signal can be likened to the broadcast of a television or radio signal. Anyone within range of the antenna and in possession of a corresponding receiver (e.g., radio, television) can switch on, tune in, and enjoy the broadcast.

Wireless transmissions of radio, television, mobile/cell phones, and WLAN services are not restricted to the traditional physical boundaries such as walls, floors, and ceilings of buildings. Because the typical range of a WLAN antenna (or access point) is approximately 50 m (150 ft) in free space, the implications for IT security are obvious. Eavesdroppers and hackers have an easy time because the signal is "hanging in the air," reaching beyond the confines of the building, and everyone within range of an antenna can access it. Indeed, if the corporate network has been configured with dynamic host configuration protocol (DHCP) for the provisioning of IP addresses, then the unwanted guest is even welcomed with a valid IP address and gateway configuration. Without appropriate security measures, a WLAN can endanger an organization's privacy and integrity.

### Basics of IP Telephony

IP telephony presents an organization with quite different challenges for its networking environment. Traditionally, voice and data were transmitted via physically separate networks. The computing LAN is an environment that comprises many distributed switches and intelligent computing clients (computers, printers, and servers). The classic telephony environment comprises a centralized switching system (the private branch exchange or PBX), connected directly by copper-wire pairs to the relatively "dumb" clients (telephone sets).

The migration from classic telephony to IP-based telephony is not that straightforward. There are a number of factors that warrant closer consideration before a data-oriented LAN can be used to accommodate telephony, or voice, as an application.

First, and perhaps most critical, telephony is a real-time application. This stems from the way the human brain and ear work. Simply put, a telephone conversation needs to flow, instantaneously and without interruption, for it to be understood by both parties. A delay of only 500 milliseconds can be frustrating to both parties and render them incapable of fluid conversation.

Yet, cell phone users will appreciate that the quality of the line and delivery of information can tail off marginally before the conversation becomes incomprehensible. In the "telephony world," real-time delivery is a necessity. Information loss is undesirable but can be tolerated to a limited extent because the brain can compensate for minor losses. However, the workings of the brain do not allow us to pause a conversation until every last piece of information has arrived and been sorted.

Conversely, the "data world" has been developed around an alternative trade-off. Personal computers are unable to compensate for missing information. As such, IP-based computer networks use mechanisms such as transmission control protocol (TCP) to ensure that missing packets of information are requested again. Once all packets are accounted for, they are sorted into order and the message is reconstructed. This process can take a number of seconds to complete, so generally computer applications are designed to tolerate considerable delay.

Another factor that differentiates the telephony and data worlds is the matter of power supply. In a classic telephony environment, the telephone sets are not only reliant on the PBX for its switching intelligence, but they also rely on it for their power. As a result, implementation of a battery backup system on a PBX means that telephony need not be affected by a power cut. In this manner, employees are still able to reach the outside world, send faxes, and conduct business during a power outage.

Again, this concept is at odds with a decentralized data network, where each client receives its power from the nearest wall socket, not from the LAN. Migration to IP telephony means that alternative power concepts need to be considered so that a power cut does not adversely affect the telephones as well as the computers.

These two very different worlds are almost at a tangent to each other. The migration of telephony to a predominantly data-oriented network requires careful planning and testing if it is to succeed.

In summary, new technologies can often represent one of the most serious threats to an organization's security. Careful research, analysis of the issues, and planning can ensure that an organization accounts for the pitfalls adequately.

## Extraordinary and Catastrophic Events

This category accounts for the less foreseeable threats that face an organization. These are generally considered to be "acts of God," for example, fires, floods, earthquakes, or lightning strikes. It should also be noted that since the tragic events of September 11, 2001, many organizations have also added terrorism to their list of extraordinary events.

Organizations might not be able to prevent acts of God or acts or terrorism. However, emergency precautions play a major role in preventing the loss of data and in restoring business continuity.

In contrast to the other threat categories listed, these are not everyday events. A building might be struck by lightning or catch fire only once in a lifetime, but such disasters can wipe out an organization's information and equipment in minutes. How much money, time, and other resources should an organization invest in IT security precautions for events that might never happen?

## ALL-EMBRACING ROLE OF SECURITY

The diversity of security threats and their effect on an organization's security criteria determine that security architecture is an almost boundless subject. As a result, a security architecture cannot be purchased as an "out of the box" or "one size fits all" solution. A comprehensive security architecture must encompass the broader aspects of organizational, technological, and physical security measures.

Figure 1 shows a graphical representation of an organizational structure from the perspective of information technology.

By taking a moment to consider the individual layers of this diagram, it will become clear that security is multifaceted and needs to address a variety of issues at every level of the organizational structure. It should be noted that not all matters are purely IT-centric in nature. For instance, the definition of rules, roles, and responsibilities is also a matter of organizational management. Protection of the server room against fire, flood, lightning, and other

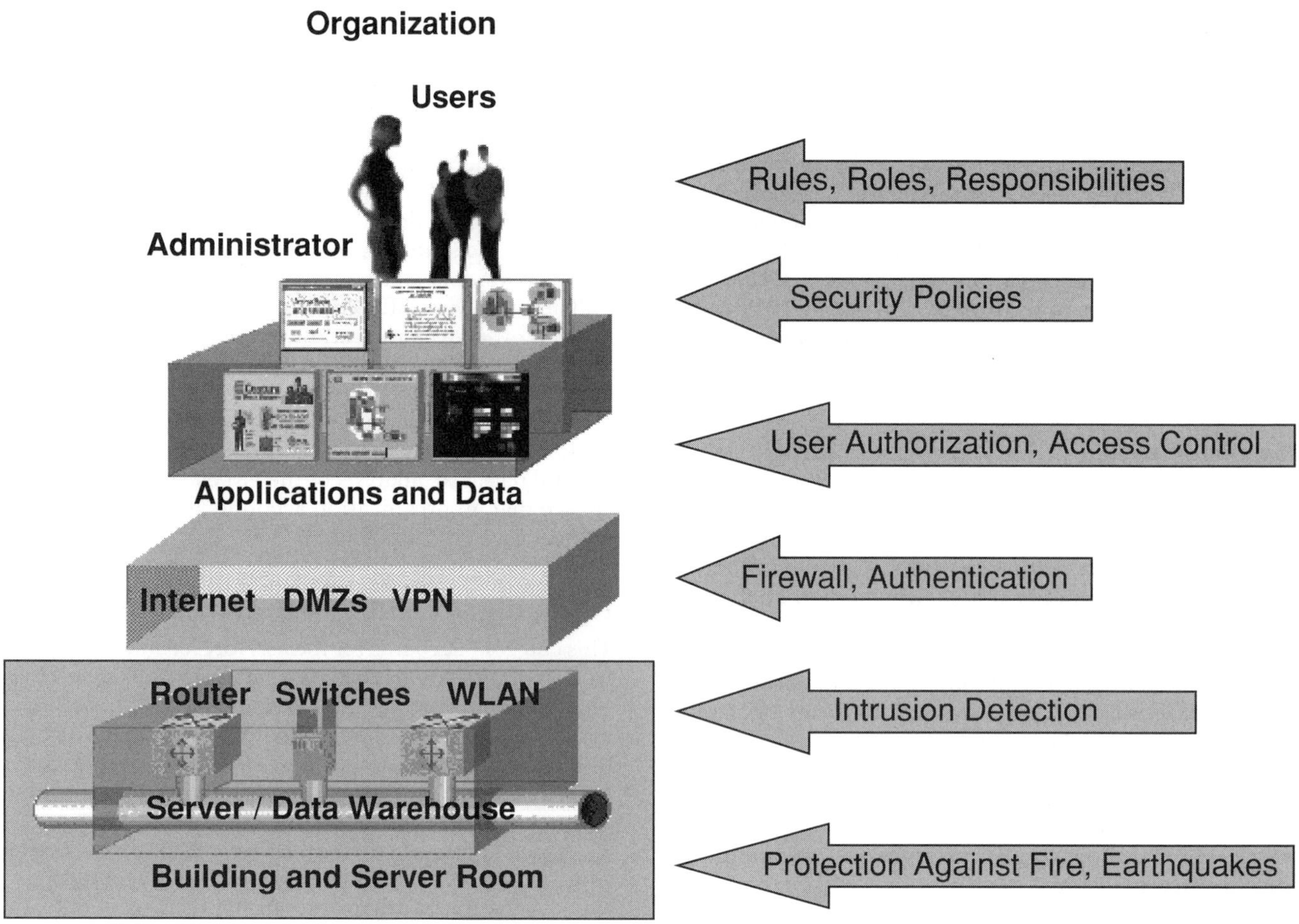

**Organization**

**Users**

**Administrator**

**Applications and Data**

**Internet   DMZs   VPN**

**Router   Switches   WLAN**

**Server / Data Warehouse**

**Building and Server Room**

Rules, Roles, Responsibilities

Security Policies

User Authorization, Access Control

Firewall, Authentication

Intrusion Detection

Protection Against Fire, Earthquakes

**Figure 1:** Essential components of security architectures.

disasters is also a matter of facilities management, and so on. In short, a comprehensive security architecture is a great deal more complex than simply installing a firewall. The following sections aim to make the reader aware of the broader issues and the ways in which these can be accounted for in a security architecture.

## Strategy

The main objective of a security architecture is to protect the intellectual capital, the lifeblood, of an organization. If information is tampered with, destroyed, or made available to competitors, the survival of an organization is put at considerable risk even in the short term.

However, as mentioned earlier in this chapter, the interpretation of security criteria, the outcome of risk analysis, and the content of security policy will vary from company to company. Differentiating factors can be the nature of the industry vertical (e.g., government, banking and insurance, health care, hospitality), organizational structures, communication needs with customers and suppliers, types of e-business applications, and so on.

An organization's strategy will be largely determined by its current situation and its objectives for the future. Thus, IT strategy will also be influenced by the current state of

the IT network and the ways it will need to develop to accommodate and support tomorrow's business goals.

## Management

A clear definition of roles and responsibilities needs to be established for employees and management, within the confines of the security architecture. Executive sponsorship and leadership of security will play an increasingly important role. In Germany, for instance, recently introduced legislation (BASEL II) states that executive management can be held liable with their personal wealth in the event that the company incurs damage caused by hackers, if the attacks are deemed to have been avoidable or preventable with the use of appropriate security measures. This might sound like a drastic measure. However, it will certainly encourage organizations to take the matter of IT security very seriously.

Executive-level management should be encouraged to assume responsibility for security expenditure within the framework of the IT budget and should lead the development and implementation of security policies and architectures. The approval of funds for security measures and systems takes a sizeable slice of the overall IT budget. "Security costs money, but lack of security costs much more" (translated from Koenig, 2004, p. 10). To reduce vulnerability and risks, companies sometimes have to deploy complex solutions, starting with the construction of their buildings and the selection and training of personnel.

## Definition and Maintenance of Access Permissions

An essential foundation of the security architecture is the definition of legitimate users. Should this be restricted to internal employees only, or opened up to partners, suppliers, and customers? This decision is an overriding factor, but inclusion should not give all authorized users the access rights to all facilities. In practice, each individual user should be granted access rights to a limited subset of systems, data, and applications. This procedure might not be easy or straightforward, but definitions of user groups, such as "finance," "sales," and "operations," can help categorize user rights. The maintenance of access rights will mean that a database needs to be continually monitored and updated. New employees come; other employees leave or are dismissed. New or modified business applications will also need to be reflected in the user access profiles as well.

## Training and Awareness of Employees

Security is also a question of awareness and acquaintance with the rules. Sensitivity of the employees can be promoted with training and other behavioral measures. Organizations might consider posting security guidelines on IT bulletin boards or Intranet pages. Periodic reminders of security policy can also be distributed to employees via e-mail. These measures can help but can also be ignored. As a result, an annual or biannual security briefing might also be a good way of ensuring that employees remain aware and alert to security issues.

## Rules Governing the Definition and Secrecy of Passwords

Many users handle their credentials with almost negligent disregard, writing passwords on sticky notes or using passwords that are all too easily cracked. This is almost understandable because many people typically have at least 8 or 15 passwords or personal identification numbers (PINs) for private and business use.

This practice need not be problematic, but one should take into account that so-called strong passwords (i.e., cryptic passwords containing 10 characters, including capital letters, small letters, numerals, and special characters) are harder for most users to remember.

In the event that a user becomes overloaded with 20, 30, or 40 such passwords, there is a risk of the password management process breaking down. A user might begin to note passwords down on paper or resort to using weak passwords, which are more easily remembered.

In an age where weak passwords can be found in lists that are available on numerous Web sites, it is imperative for training programs to cover password guidelines carefully so that employees are aware of the problems and can modify their behavior accordingly.

In addition to employee training in this area, there are a number of technology solutions available that serve to facilitate the administration and regular/forced changing

of passwords; this is covered in the section on access control.

## Prevention of Social Engineering

In the world of espionage, social engineering is a well-proven if somewhat lengthy and complex method of obtaining unauthorized access to information. A spy attempts to win the trust of an employee and subsequently finds out as much as possible about his victim. What is the name of his or her spouse; when is the victim's birthday; what are the victim's main interests, hobbies, or sporting activities; and so forth. From this information, it becomes possible to draw up a short list of potentially weak passwords.

The implications of this type of activity are obvious. While getting to know the victim better, the spy might even establish where it is that a victim hides passwords for safe keeping; for example, in a wallet or purse, on a personal digital assistant (PDA), and so forth. It is then immaterial whether the passwords themselves are strong (i.e., complex) or weak. The spy knows how and where to find them, and the rest is easy. The importance of a training program or seminar to alert employees to the risks can help them recognize the techniques and thwart this activity.

## Dealing with Security Systems and the Protection of Data

In principle, there should be clear guidelines for the storage and handling of information. Users must be comprehensively informed about their rights and their duties. Storing key information in public directories on generally accessible servers and even sending confidential and sensitive information (tenders, bids, designs, specifications) via the Internet without use of appropriate encryption techniques should be defined as strictly taboo. If a competitor manages to intercept these messages, he gains access to the sensitive information.

Furthermore, laptop and notebook computers are being stolen from cars and hotel rooms with increasing regularity. Although it is generally true that the hardware will be replaced by the insurance company, the loss of valuable and sensitive data is a serious problem.

Organizations can train their employees to make backup copies of the data stored on their PCs and notebooks at regular intervals. There are a number of software applications—for example, Second Copy—which can be implemented to facilitate and automate this for the user. The data is then backed up to a directory on a storage server and the permissions for this directory should be set such that only the corresponding user and an IT administrator can access the backup. In the event that a notebook is stolen, a wealth of information is not lost with it.

## Awareness of Supported and Unsupported Software

Attempts by employees to connect personal data-storage drives and download software or games are also common. Companies worldwide suffer billions of dollars of damage because of "infection" caused by games, screensavers, or similar programs.

Training should make employees aware of the risks associated with the use of the following items:

- third-party floppy disks and CD-ROMs (e.g., from computer magazines)
- software downloaded from the Internet (e.g., screensavers, files from peer-to-peer file sharing programs)
- dubious or unsolicited e-mails with attachments, regardless of whether the sender is known or unknown

Employees should understand that a violation or infringement of these guidelines and the installation or use of unsanctioned programs is strictly forbidden and can even lead to disciplinary action being taken.

### Recruitment of Security-Sanctioned Personnel

The human resources (HR) or personnel department usually plays a core role in the employee selection and recruitment process and should take account of the appropriate security parameters that apply to the advertised position. The screening of applicants during the interview procedure commonly focuses on the applicant's ability to fulfill the open position. Psychometric testing methods are often used to help identify an applicant's less obvious strengths and weaknesses. It is also appropriate at this stage to assess which applicants demonstrate a character of integrity and which ones may present more of a security risk.

This is true for all employees but especially for those employees who will frequently come into close contact with the physical network, servers, or data access devices. This includes maintenance personnel, cleaning teams, or IT teams. Finding the right personnel to run the network, which must be active 24 hours per day, 365 days per year, is a matter requiring diligence. The IT administrator often has such far-reaching authorization that an organization needs to afford him or her an extraordinary level of trust. An administrator or IT manager has to be selected carefully, as he or she could well become a target for ruthless fraud and social engineers.

### IT Outsourcing and IT Governance

The previous section assumes that all aspects of IT are managed "in house." However, it is worth noting that the outsourcing of IT services to third-party service providers has escalated rapidly since the mid-1990s.

Outsourcing can often serve a number of business goals, such as head-count reduction (number of employees), cost reduction and management, implementation of service level agreements and response times, and so forth. However, by definition, the outsourcing of these services also means that the selection and supervision of security-relevant personnel is often beyond the control of the organization (Gruender & Graf, 2004).

Although the personnel and day-to-day running of the network are now controlled by the outsourcing partner, it is still possible and generally necessary to retain control of the definition and implementation of policy. In this instance, an organization should retain a small number of IT personnel in the strategic role of IT governance. This department has the responsibility of working in partnership with the service provider to ensure satisfactory implementation and fulfillment of these items:

- security policy
- maintenance agreements
- service level agreements (SLAs)

In this manner, an organization is still able to manage exposure to vulnerabilities and the evolution of the network while enjoying the advantages of outsourcing.

### Dismissal

If an employee has found a new position with a competitor, then sensitive information could be at risk. Similarly, information can be at risk from a former employee who was fired or made redundant and has a score to settle. It goes without saying that authorized user accounts and corresponding access privileges should be frozen as soon as users leave or are dismissed. Failure to take appropriate action leaves a company open to a malicious attack and constitutes an inexcusable lapse of security.

## INFRASTRUCTURE

Security-sensitive areas of IT, such as the data center or server room, including the firewall, telephone system, and so forth, should always be locked and protected. Physical access to these facilities should be restricted to specific and approved personnel who have the keys or security codes to gain access. Physical access is relatively easy to control but needs to be complemented by a number of further measures.

## User Authentication

Another pertinent example of how the human factor gives rise to daily security challenges is the subject of password secrecy as previously described. The simple fact of the matter is that user authentication should be an integral part of the security architecture, in the same fashion that many organizations require their personnel to wear security passes to gain access to buildings. This is often achieved with a unique login name and password for each user. The password must only be known to the bona fide user and will be cross-referenced with a corresponding record on the server.

In small businesses with fewer than 100 desktops and a handful of servers, this procedure is manageable both for users and the IT team. However, as the size of the organization and the number of server applications increases, this potentially robust process can break down. Human beings, faced with a myriad of login names and passwords, begin to write them all down.

Technology cannot prevent users from writing down passwords, but technologies such as Passport exist that can reduce a variety of login names and passwords down to one pair for all services. This solution and others like it implement a centralized user account and password server. This coordinates the access privileges to other services such as remote access servers, VPN gateways, Citrix servers, e-mail servers, Windows domains, and so forth. In addition, the centralized server can be set to force a change of password at predetermined intervals (e.g., 30, 60, 90 days) and to reject the use of "weak" passwords that contain dictionary words, and so on.

These solutions serve to make password management extremely user friendly, encouraging the user to follow training principles and memorize credentials, while facilitating management of access privileges for the IT team.

## Fallback of the Data Network

The IT network is not only at the mercy of hackers and viruses. Sometimes a simple power cut, a hardware defect in a switch, or a damaged fiber optic cable can succeed in removing large portions of a LAN from service. Such events pose a threat to short-term business continuity and availability of information.

### Backup Power

So-called uninterruptable power supplies (UPSs) are nothing new and enable the near-instantaneous switchover to reserve (battery) power in the event of a power cut. Depending on the nature of the industry and customer transactions, many organizations consider it necessary to provide backup power to all critical devices in the data center, including Web/e-business servers, Internet routers, the firewall, the routing switch, and the telephone system. Typically, UPS systems can be engineered to provide up to 20 minutes of autonomy for the systems they support. Some telephone systems (PBXs) come with their own proprietary solutions capable of more than 2 hours of telephony service.

The advantages of backup power are twofold. On one hand, business continuity is maximized during short periods of power outage, yet if a power cut looks set to enter a prolonged phase, then the IT team is able to perform a graceful shutdown of critical servers before the UPS systems are exhausted. This greatly reduces the risk of key servers and applications failing to restart once power is restored.

### Hardware Fallback

Many established manufacturers of data-switching equipment offer a range of redundancy features and options in their components. These aim to limit the disruption of service in the event of a hardware failure.

### Redundant Features of Switching Components

Many switches can be configured with additional power supplies, or even dual-switching fabrics (CPUs). Such features, although costly, can go a long way to protecting a network from hardware failure. For particularly sensitive, mission-critical parts of the core network, an organization might also consider the redundant deployment of two or more routing switches. Fast spanning tree and virtual router redundancy protocol (VRRP) are industry standards that are able to facilitate this type of redundancy. If the primary (or master) routing switch in the LAN should fail, these protocols are able to reconfigure the network in less than 8 seconds. The secondary (or slave) switch can then ensure network availability while the other unit is out of service (see Figure 2).

It should not be forgotten that real-time applications, for example, IP telephony, do not tolerate an 8-second delay. "Sub second" fail-over is necessary to guarantee the continuity of such sensitive applications and this can be realized with proprietary solutions. A prime example of this is split multilink trunking, available on Nortel Networks' Ethernet Routing Switch 8600 platform.

### Redundant E-Business Servers

Companies with critical e-business applications may also consider the use of load-balancing switches in a server farm. In this manner, it is possible to run the same e-business application on a number of servers. The load-balancing switch assumes the responsibility for ensuring that each server is equally loaded with traffic and can dynamically switch sessions to the server that is currently experiencing the least load.

The advantages of this concept are twofold. First, if a server suffers a critical hardware failure or simply crashes, the load-balancing switch will compensate for the outage by diverting more traffic to the servers that are still in service. Second and perhaps less obvious, the very same action will be taken if the IT team removes a server from service. This is particularly useful if the servers are due for maintenance; for example, memory upgrade, software upgrade, installation of service packs, or component replacement.

### Redundant Internet Service Providers

Of course, load-balancing switches can help protect critical e-business applications from these server outages, but what happens to a company's Web site and e-business applications in the event that the Internet service provider (ISP) should fail?

This scenario is more common than one might think and is currently a frequent complaint of many German businesses, regardless of size or industry. Would it not be ideal if organizations were able to implement a redundant ISP concept, sharing their inbound and outbound Internet traffic across two or three fully autonomous ISPs?

Fortunately, equipment manufacturers such as F5 Networks have also developed load-balancing solutions specifically for this scenario. These types of solutions carry a pricetag in the region of US $15,000, which might make them prohibitive to smaller organizations. If, on the other hand, a company's business continuity is being crippled on a regular basis and many thousands of dollars in revenue are being wasted, then the business case begins to look most favorable.

## SOFTWARE

In recent history, the occurrence of virus attacks has been frequent and the nature of attacks has been remarkably diverse. This complicates the matter of defense. There are a number of factors to consider when deciding which operating systems, software, and programs should be implemented on an organization's servers, desktop PCs, and notebooks. These factors are greatly influenced by the purpose the server or PC should fulfill for an organization.

As far as PCs and notebooks are concerned, it can be useful to define and test standard images of approved operating systems, programs, and utilities. A standard image

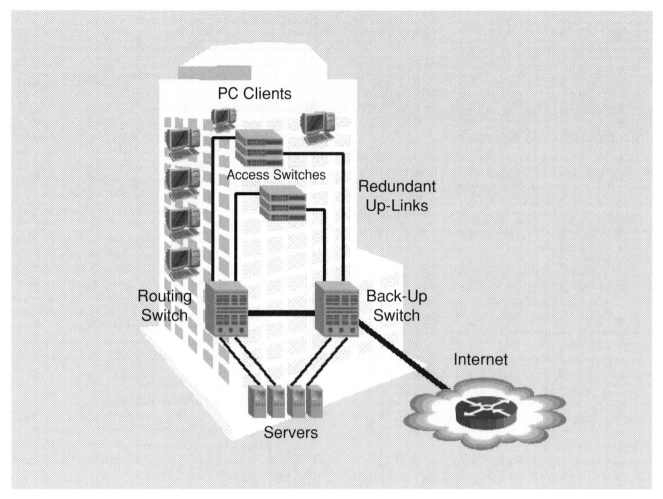

**Figure 2:** Redundant switching in the local area network.

should only contain vetted and tested programs, security utilities, and precautions that the users require to fulfill their daily business. Because desktop PCs and notebooks often serve different business purposes, it is usually the case that each requires its own approved software image.

## Software for Desktop PCs and Notebooks

These devices have to be used by families and employees who are usually familiar with an operating system and office suite from a market leader such as Microsoft. Practicality and user familiarity dictate that many organizations choose to base their PCs and notebooks on a Windows platform. This need not influence the choice of Web browser (alternatives include Netscape and Mozilla's Firefox), office suite (e.g., Sun's StarOffice or Ability Office), e-mail software (e.g., Lotus Notes), and so forth, all of which should be chosen on merit and can limit exposure to a variety of threats.

In addition, organizations should consider the following measures to protect their devices adequately.

### Virus Scanning Software

Virus detection tools really are a necessity for every PC and notebook. As new threats and their variants are dis-

covered on a daily basis, it is imperative that the virus scanning software on each device always contains the latest database of virus definitions or signatures. In medium and large organizations, with hundreds or thousands of PCs, it might be preferable to install a virus database on a server, which stores the virus-signatures and pushes them out to each PC in the network. This ensures timely, automated updates of every computer, while minimizing the long-term administrative effort and costs. Specialist companies such as Computer Associates, Symantec, McAfee, Norton, and others provide professional antivirus solutions.

### Security Updates

Companies such as Microsoft release security patches and service packs for their operating systems and applications on a frequent basis. However, with major releases (e.g., Service Pack 2 [SP2] for Windows XP), it can often be inappropriate to implement these updates in the field without laboratory testing and verification. Testing aims to verify that the update works in harmony with the existing programs and applications. In the instance of SP2, many IT teams have been aiming to ensure that their approved firewall and virus scanning software were able to work seamlessly with XP's new "security center." Problems that are discovered on the test bench can then be remedied and tested in isolation, without affecting the stability of the live business environment.

Once an update has been verified and approved, it then needs to be deployed to the appropriate computers in the field. This, of course, can be undertaken manually or with the use of automated systems. In similar fashion to the management of virus definitions, utilities such as System Management Services or Novell's zero effort networking (ZEN) can reliably automate this process and manage the rollout of the approved updates to each desktop.

As with many IT scenarios, organizations might first consider a cost analysis to determine whether the savings, in terms of time and wage bills, can justify the cost of deployment. However, in larger and geographically dispersed organizations, the business case can be most favorable for this type of solution.

### Personal Firewall Software

Desktop computers on the business premises should always be protected by a corporate firewall. Unfortunately, this is not always the case for notebook computers or domestic computers, which often use a public domain network such as a wireless LAN or a domestic broadband connection. In these instances, it is entirely feasible for a hacker to attempt access to the computer and the lack of a personal firewall will facilitate his task. Inclusion of personal firewall software in the standard image for these devices is a vital line of defense against malicious activity. The purpose of firewalls is described elsewhere in this chapter.

### VPN Software

Unless alternative measures are implemented, the communication between computers and servers in any IP network is conducted in clear text. Software tools such as sniffers are readily available for download on various Web sites, thus enabling even novices to seek out, eavesdrop, and record the exchange of information as it crosses the Internet in the public domain.

The art of cryptography, the encryption of information to make it useless to anybody other than the intended recipient, has been exercised by the human race for thousands of years. Cryptography has expanded its uses into a number of different areas of information technology, and virtual private networking (VPN) technology is one of them.

If a company has a need for remote users (e.g., home office users and small branch offices) to access its corporate network via the public domain, then a secure connection should be established to ensure privacy of the communication. One of the most common ways of achieving this is the use of IP-Sec technology, which is incorporated into VPN gateways and clients (see Figure 3). IP-Sec encapsulates or "tunnels" the encrypted information into normal IP packets with clear text headers that can still be read and understood by routers and switching devices in the Internet. In this manner, the packets can be routed from source to destination, but the payload of sensitive data is encrypted and secure. Manufacturers such as Nortel Networks, Cisco Systems, and others provide industry-leading solutions in the VPN arena.

### Cryptographic Storage

In previous sections, we established that regular backups of locally stored information can help prevent the loss of data in the event that a notebook should be stolen. The backup and restoration process is undoubtedly a valuable tool to prevent the loss of information. However, it does not prevent the information on a stolen computer from falling into the wrong hands.

Again, cryptography provides a solution to a serious problem. A few minutes research on the Internet will uncover companies such as Cypherix that offer cryptographic storage solutions. This solution and others like it create a secure "vault" on the local hard disk. The vault is password protected and any information stored in the vault is encrypted. Consequently, data can only be retrieved and deciphered once the vault is opened with the correct password.

This represents a robust solution to the problem, but there is one issue that should not be overlooked. Access to the vault is also reliant on a password, which gives rise to issues governing password complexity and secrecy as covered previously. In this regard, it should also be noted that cryptographic storage and information backup are complementary solutions, not mutually exclusive. Cryptographic storage prevents a third party from understanding and making use of the information. However, it is not able to restore information for the owners.

### Adware and Spyware Programs

These represent more recent categories of threat in the history of information technology. Adware and spyware have only really been discovered and recognized as undesirable programs within the past couple of years, and many people are still unaware of these types of threat. Although they do not usually present a risk to the integrity of stored information on a computer, many adware and spyware programs invade the individual's privacy by secretly reporting Web browser activity or login details to their originator. They can also hijack features of a user's Web browser and some varieties are known to tie up computer resources, resulting in a noticeable drop off in computing performance.

Fortunately, help is at hand. There are a number of commendable detection programs available that can detect such threats, remove them, and then immunize the system against possible reinfection. Two commonly used programs are freeware: Spybot Search & Destroy and Ad-Aware, both of which offer fuss-free protection for domestic users. As organizations might prefer to rely on an established mainstream software manufacturer, it is worth noting that companies such as Symantec have been busy updating their offerings to include these capabilities, and Computer Associates has recently purchased Pest Patrol, a well-known specialist in this arena.

## Software for Servers

The business-oriented selection, integration, and configuration of server-based applications is undoubtedly a vast topic. The types of server and applications that are installed will be very much determined by an organization's

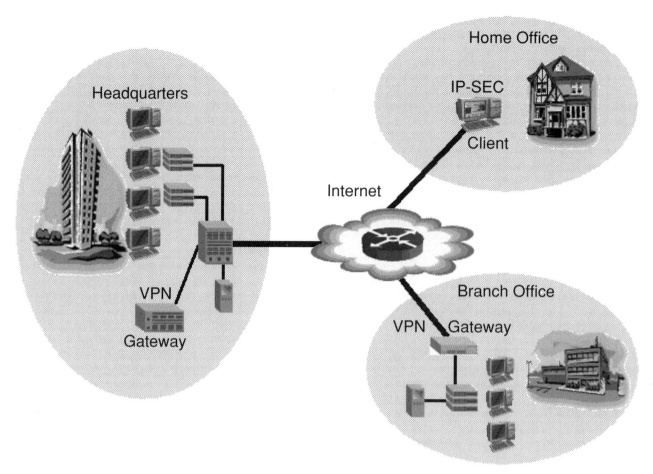

**Figure 3:** Virtual private networking.

business requirements and goals. Although it is difficult to summarize this topic in a few paragraphs, organizations might consider the following points.

### Web Hosting and E-Business Services

As far as Web hosting and e-business servers are concerned, these servers represent one of an organization's main interfaces to customers and suppliers who place their trust in the integrity of their transactions with the company. If e-business services suffer regular disruption, then this trust can be damaged beyond repair. UNIX-based servers are generally considered to be extremely robust and stable. Combined with the fact that UNIX operating systems are a less frequent target of viruses and worms, one can see the benefits for the relationship with customers and suppliers.

Regardless which platform an organization chooses for its e-business applications, one fact should not be overlooked. The customers and suppliers expect their online browser-based business transactions to be subject to the same security criteria that the organization sets for itself. As a result, authorized external users should be issued with login names and passwords. The access privileges afforded to these external users should be adequate to fulfill their transaction requirements, while keeping the external user at arms' length from other internal servers containing sensitive information. This takes care of

access control and authorization but does not address the problem of privacy.

Once again, cryptography provides an answer to this problem. Web browser technology is equipped with a feature called secure socket layer (SSL), which is capable of securing a browser-based session with the use of encryption. A secure session is denoted by "https://" in the address bar, and anyone who is familiar with Internet banking or pays for eBay goods via PayPal will also be familiar with the little yellow padlock that snaps shut at the bottom of the browser window. To adequately protect online transactions with customers and suppliers, a secure SSL-based session should be active from the login screen onward, so that the user name and passwords also remain confidential.

### Storage, Backup, E-Mail, and Other Applications

An organization will also require a host of other servers for applications such as e-mail, order processing, invoicing, centralized storage of product information, and corporate presentations, to name but a few. This raises questions for system administrators regarding integration of these services with desktop and notebook clients, administration of logins/passwords, and management of access privileges. Consequently, these services are often based on an operating system from the same stable as their desktop and notebook operating systems.

It is important to remember that servers are also subject to hacking and virus attempts. Although some servers in the network will not be performing business-critical functions, it might still be pertinent to maintain them with virus protection software, security patches, and other measures in a similar fashion to desktop computers. In this manner, organizations can avoid introducing a weak link into the security chain, and this can be a vital piece in the security jigsaw puzzle.

Prudence dictates that each server and application should be tested for compatibility with a software update before it is installed in the live business environment. As security updates and patches usually require a restart of the equipment to take effect, care should be taken to avoid loss of service for mission-critical applications. In the presence of load-balancing systems, this need not be a problem; otherwise, the servers should be updated outside of peak business hours to minimize outages.

# HARDWARE

When considering the capabilities of hardware platforms, it is all too easy to think in terms of speed and performance. Gigabits per second and gigaHertz are familiar buzzwords to most people. It is surely appropriate for organizations to consider performance in relation to business requirements when selecting network and computing components. However, it is just as important to consider security features and factors.

## New Technologies

Technological progress rapidly improves flexibility, scalability, and performance of equipment, but IT professionals should carefully analyze the security implications that new hardware and technologies can introduce. Issues surrounding new technologies such as wireless LAN have already been discussed. Some possible technology solutions for wireless LAN are considered in the following points.

## Securing the Wireless LAN

Today's digital mobile phone systems (e.g., GSM) incorporate a host of complex authentication and encryption procedures to ensure that each user can be identified and guaranteed privacy from other users and eavesdroppers. In a similar manner, the protection of wireless LANs will become ever more important for a company in today's age of remote users and widespread Internet access. A "state of the art" security architecture must take account of the use of wireless LANs.

Transmitting sensitive information in clear text, to and from a wireless access point, could pose a serious threat to the privacy of the organization. As mentioned earlier in this chapter, cryptography has an ever-increasing role to play in information technology, and the wireless LAN arena is no exception to this. Fortunately, help is at hand in the following forms.

## Encryption Using Wireless Equivalent Privacy (WEP)

Many wireless LAN antennas already support wired equivalent privacy (WEP), and this can make it an extremely budget-friendly solution. However, WEP technology is not as robust as its name suggests. WEP uses symmetric encryption and a single cipher key. A hacker needs no more than a notebook computer, a couple of wireless LAN cards, a variety of specialist software programs, and approximately 6 million packets of the encrypted data to determine the WEP cipher key. Once a hacker has this, he can access the network, eavesdrop, and even commence an attack.

Although the volume of data required to break WEP code might sound prohibitive initially, it is worth noting that a well-used corporate wireless LAN can provide the hacker with 6 million packets of data in less than two hours. If we now consider that the hacker can sit inconspicuously in his own vehicle outside of the premises, WEP begins to look like a rather uncertain and less desirable form of encryption. The risks associated with it might not justify the cost savings.

## Encryption Using Virtual Private Networks (VPNs)

The use of IP-Sec-based VPN technology presents an altogether more favorable cryptographic solution. This technology offers highly complex, 128-bit encryption techniques that can ensure the privacy of corporate communications. The costs of this need not be prohibitive either, because excellent industry solutions are available for less than $5,000 depending, of course, on requirements. In instances where a corporation already uses a VPN gateway for its home office and remote users, it is quite possible to use the same VPN gateway for the local wireless LAN. Sharing network resources for multiple uses in this manner speeds a company's return on investment and helps reduce ongoing maintenance costs.

## Radio Planning and Signal Strengths

A full-strength WLAN signal can reach up to 50 m (150 ft) in free space. However, characteristics of architecture and building materials can disturb the even distribution of the radio signal considerably, such that hot spots, weak spots, and even radio holes (small pockets of no signal) are inevitable. To maximize coverage and minimize disturbance of the signal, a professional radio survey is usually conducted prior to installation and will help determine the best locations for the wireless access points.

It is useful to keep in mind that many of today's wireless access points offer a variety of signal-strength settings to provide adequate control over transmission range. As such, it is possible to expand the scope of the radio survey, at minimal incremental cost, to optimize in-building coverage while minimizing the "leakage" of signals beyond the perimeter of the premises. It is also worth noting that radio planning and cryptography are not mutually exclusive. Organizations will ask themselves whether suppliers, customers, and maintenance personnel who visit the building should also have access to the wireless LAN, for instance.

The radio planning process can usually be facilitated by the equipment reseller or system house that is providing the wireless network. In this manner, radio planning and encryption can complement each other to ensure the privacy, availability, and security of a wireless network.

# ACCESS CONTROL

Twenty years ago, most companies had not yet migrated their IT environment from mainframes to PCs. The personal computer as we know it was very much in its infancy. As such, an organization's primary security objective focused on the ability to ensure that an internal member of staff could only see those data that where deemed appropriate and applicable to their function and role within the organization.

## Evolution of IT Platforms

The evolution toward decentralized computing, the explosive growth of personal/home computing, the birth of the "online society," and e-business have eliminated the traditional physical barriers that kept unwanted "guests" out of each other's computers and networks.

Earlier in this chapter, we saw that it is not practical for an organization to secure its network by completely cutting itself off from the outside world. Decentralized computing and networking, in form of Intranets, Extranets, and the Internet, bring new challenges for security systems. How can the organization open itself to the outside world while also fending off hackers and other criminals?

## Firewalls, the First Line of Defense

An access router connects the corporate network to the outside world, but it does not usually police the network boundary to check who, or what, is entering. Consequently, an attacker can gain access to an unprotected network quite easily. It follows that a multifaceted firewall needs to be installed to control access, police the data traffic, and foil unauthorized access.

There is a wide range of firewall solutions available on the market, from simple server-based software to complex hardware- and software-based solutions. Typically, professional firewall software will be designed to run in a "hardened" UNIX-based environment so that the firewall itself can be protected from hackers attempting to exploit weaknesses in the operating system of the firewall itself. Firewalls serve the following purposes for an organization.

### Demilitarized Zones (DMZs)

If an organization provides public services, then it should protect its servers with the use of demilitarized zones. DMZs are used to separate the corporate network from the Internet, thereby providing an additional area of security. The DMZ contains all public services that need to be reachable from outside (e.g., e-mail, Web sites, online ordering, and so forth) and is also protected by the firewall.

### Blocking and Filtering of Traffic

Individual types of traffic and services can be identified by specific ports that are addressed in transmission control protocol (TCP) or uniform datagram protocol (UDP). There are hundreds of TCP and UDP ports that identify individual traffic types and services. Although some of these services need to be accessible internally, it is not always desirable for the same ports and services to be accessible

by external users (or hackers). Simple examples of these are telnet on port 23 and file transfer protocol (FTP) on port 20.

In a network that is not protected by a firewall, generally all ports are open. If an attacker sends a connection request for port 20 (FTP), the server will open an FTP connection, and the attacker can initiate the next step in his attack.

The administrator can use firewalls to determine which ports can be opened or closed. This can usually be determined independently for externally and internally originating traffic. For example, if the firewall were to block TCP port 80 (HTTP session) for internal users, then none of a corporation's employees would be able to access Web sites with their browsers.

A few minutes of research on the Internet will also enable administrators to determine which ports are inherently dangerous because of a system vulnerability; for example, remote desktop protocol (RDP) on port 3389, and which ports have been targeted by Trojans, worms, or similar threats; for example, port 2283, which is registered for Lotus Notes and exploited by the worm "Dumaru.Y."

As a general rule, administrators should adopt the approach of "default deny," setting the firewall to block all ports with exception of those services that are required by clients, servers, and applications for approved business purposes. A correctly configured firewall represents a critical step in ensuring the fine balance between allowing and blocking access to the network.

### Event Logging

As per this explanation, a firewall will always be configured to leave a small subset of business-essential TCP ports open. It is not beyond the realm of possibility that a hacker will be able to design a new type of virus, worm, or other threat that is able to attack the network regardless.

Firewalls are also able to maintain logs of suspicious events. Although detailed analysis of logged events might take too long to thwart an attack that is in progress, the logs can be extremely valuable in the post-attack diagnosis. An IT team might then learn how to better protect the network against a similar form of attack in the future.

## Intrusion Detection

As we have discussed, firewalls play a crucial role in controlling the network boundary, but this does not ensure that a hacker is unable to gain access to a network. It should also be noted that firewalls do not monitor the corporate network for signs of suspicious activity. What happens if a hacker is able to exploit an approved TCP session or a loophole in an application and starts making inroads to the network?

Intrusion detection systems (IDS) can be deployed to scour the network for signs of potential break-ins. In the event that an IDS should identify suspicious activity, it can trigger alarms to the IT team and even initiate some countermeasures. There are two complementary approaches to intrusion detection and these are summarized as follows.

### Knowledge-Based Intrusion Detection

This is the most common form of intrusion detection. In general, this technique uses knowledge gained about specific attacks and system vulnerabilities. The IDS stores these in a database and monitors the network for attempts to exploit the recorded vulnerabilities. Activity that is not recorded in the database is deemed to be acceptable. If the IDS detects suspicious events, then it can initiate countermeasures, including the following examples:

- Insert temporary rules into the firewall, blocking traffic to and from the suspected attacker.
- Send reset packets in an attempt to end the appropriate TCP session.
- Trigger an alarm to alert the IT team or security officer.

In practice, this type of detection is considered to be good. The knowledge base is very focused, accounting for type of operating systems, types of applications, and so forth. Consequently, the IDS tool is very closely matched to the existing environment and the false-alarm rate in a well-maintained IDS is very low. However, this system is not flawless.

First, the IDS is permanently busy monitoring the network for thousands of variations of suspicious activity. By the time a suspicious event has been identified and the precautionary measures have been taken, a skilled hacker might have won the valuable seconds he needs to proceed to Step 2 or Step 3 of his attack, thus remaining a step or two ahead of the IDS.

Second, perhaps more critical, the system is reliant on the timely maintenance and accuracy of the knowledge database. Although the IDS knowledge base is very focused on the existing IT environment and known attacks, neither of these are constants. The introduction of new applications or operating system upgrades is a simple example of the variables that can influence the vulnerabilities in an IT environment. Furthermore, hackers do not always resort to previously used or known attack methods, priding themselves on their ability to develop something new. However, gathering required information on the latest forms of attack and relating these to the specific network environment is a time-consuming task. These factors serve to complicate maintenance of the knowledge base and hinder a 100% detection rate.

### Behavior-Based Intrusion Detection

As mentioned, knowledge-based and behavior-based detection should be treated as complementary to each other, not mutually exclusive. However, behavior-based detection is rarely implemented in current IDS tools.

Behavior-based intrusion detection works by learning a model of normal and accepted behavior in the network. The system uses this information as a benchmark, or reference, against which it monitors current network activities. The behavior-based technique then identifies an intrusion as behavior that deviates from the expected norm. Once it detects a suspicious behavior, it can sound the alarm.

Again, this system has advantages and disadvantages. On the one hand, this system is very good at discovering new and unforeseen vulnerabilities and is less dependent on changes that occur in the IT environment. However, it is difficult to predict the accuracy of the system. There tends to be a higher rate of false alarms. First, a totally legitimate behavior might not have been previously observed in the network during the learning phase. Second, behavior can change over time, meaning that the IDS might need to be retrained. It should also be noted that the IT network might be subject to an attack while the IDS is learning network behavior. In this instance, that particular attack is also reflected in the database of learned behavior and would not cause an alarm in the future.

## Protection of Remote Access Services (RAS)

In recent years, the number of RAS users has increased substantially in the majority of organizations. The corporate network is no longer confined to the campus itself. A large number of remote access pipes have to be set up, operated, and monitored for branch offices and mobile employees (Lipp, 2001). Salespeople and teleworkers require secure access to the corporate network via leased line, ISDN, DSL (broadband), or secure site-to-site VPNs.

Although authentication methods such as user name and password can be used to determine the identity of a remote user, this does not protect the data stream that is flowing across the public domain (the Internet) to the corporate network.

As already mentioned, highly complex cryptographic algorithms can be implemented to scramble and protect sensitive communication from eavesdroppers. Thus, two parties possessing the same encryption techniques and cipher key management are able to communicate with each other (Pohlmann, 2003).

We have established that SSL technology represents an excellent way of securing browser-based, online services among customers, suppliers, and the organization's e-business servers. Most online banking services rely on this technology, as do Web shops and online ticket-booking facilities, where it is necessary to transmit credit card details and other sensitive information. Ideally, browser-based sessions encrypted in this manner should be terminated on a so-called "SSL acceleration device," not on the content server itself. This serves not only to reduce the load on the server (SSL encryption is incredibly resource intensive), but also it means that an IDS is able to police the deciphered data stream on its way to the server.

We have also discussed the use of IP-Sec-based VPN technology as an excellent way of securing an employee's connection to the network via a wireless LAN or across the Internet from broadband DSL connection.

## EMERGENCY PRECAUTIONS

Until now, we have largely dealt with the need to ensure confidentiality of information, authenticate users, and prevent damage to the organization resulting from malicious activity. Previous sections already covered some of the issues surrounding the implications of hardware failure or power outage. These are not the only security threats that face an organization. We have identified extraordinary events as a possible threat to the organization's business continuity. A lightning strike, a fire, a flood, or an act of terrorism can all have disastrous consequences on the availability of the network and information. Although such occurrences are few and far between, some organizations feel it necessary to include appropriate contingencies in their security architecture.

## Backup of Local Hard Drives

A comprehensive security architecture provides for the backup of local hard drives to centralized drives on servers. Commercially available programs such as Second Copy can be used to facilitate this, and in this manner it is possible to automate the backup of data and subsequently restore it in the event of loss. Loss can mean many things in this context; for example, theft, fire damage, virus damage, or hard disk failure. Each of these realistic scenarios need not only afflict a desktop PC or notebook; they can also affect servers in the data center. How safe are the servers and the rooms in which they are located? This question becomes even more relevant when one realizes that other servers in the same room are running some of the company's most critical applications (e.g., e-business portals to customers, order processing, invoicing).

## Data Center Requirements

All the rooms containing technical equipment should be protected against physical damage (e.g., flood, fire, earthquake). Imagine a scenario where an organization owns the most expensive firewalls and security equipment and then a fire breaks out a few floors above the server rooms. The fire brigade managed to extinguish the fire. However, water from the fire hoses has run through the ceiling of the server room and ruined some mission-critical equipment such as servers, switches, and the telephone system.

In the absence of precautionary measures or contingencies, an organization then finds itself in an extremely uncomfortable situation:

- Where can it locate a fully functional server room inside of just a few hours?
- How can it restore the business-critical applications that where running on the servers at the time?
- How can it restore data for users who lost their PCs and notebooks in the fire or in the flood of water from the hoses?

From this perspective, the construction of a secure and safe server room can appear to be remarkably inexpensive in comparison with the price of a week's downtime, especially when a disaster can seriously jeopardize the survival of a company.

Organizations might also feel it appropriate to make regular (e.g., daily) backups of all servers in the data center. This helps to ensure that restoration of data is possible should the worst happen. It follows that the media on which the backups are held should not be stored in the same room, or even in the same building, wherever possible.

This process need not be problematic or costly for smaller organizations with a handful of servers to manage. Larger organizations that rely on a multitude of servers and critical applications might well be able to justify the cost of a second, fully redundant data center.

## Mirrored Data Centers

As the name suggests, this is essentially a carbon copy of the primary data center installed at a remote location (see Figure 4). The two data centers can be connected together with fiber optic technology. Current fiber optic-switching technology ensures that data can be transferred between the two sites at tens or even hundreds of gigabits per second. However, the following financial factors need to be carefully considered:

- cost of fiber optic-switching equipment
- cost of duplicate servers and other components
- monthly rental costs for the second premises
- monthly rental costs for the fiber-optic cables between the two centers
- maintenance costs for all of the above

Because this is a complex solution, often taking the IT department into "uncharted water," an organization can consider enlisting the services of a data security and storage specialist for this activity. Companies such as IBM, EMC, and others are extremely competent storage and data-center specialists.

Although this type of solution is not cheap, it brings many advantages to organizations that can justify it. In the event of a disaster at the main location, the server equipment, applications, and data are installed and ready for service in the secondary location. Consequently, critical services can be restored almost at the flick of a switch. Relationships with customers and millions of dollars of revenue are no longer at risk. This can decide the fate of a bank or an insurance company, for instance.

## SUMMARY

While attempting to illuminate the many issues that surround the matter of security architectures, this chapter has had to make generalizations. However, it should not be forgotten that a security architecture is not a mass-produced article that is available "off the shelf." It represents an organization's individual response to its environment and business objectives.

This chapter set out to provide readers with an overview of the issues to highlight some of the less obvious but important aspects of IT security. It has not been possible to cover every possible aspect in exhaustive detail. Subjects such as IP telephony, wireless LANs, and the protection of e-business servers are all examples that warrant further analysis and investigation.

Furthermore, it is acknowledged that not every solution presented herein suits every pocket. The types and complexity of solutions adopted by an organization will not only be determined by threats and

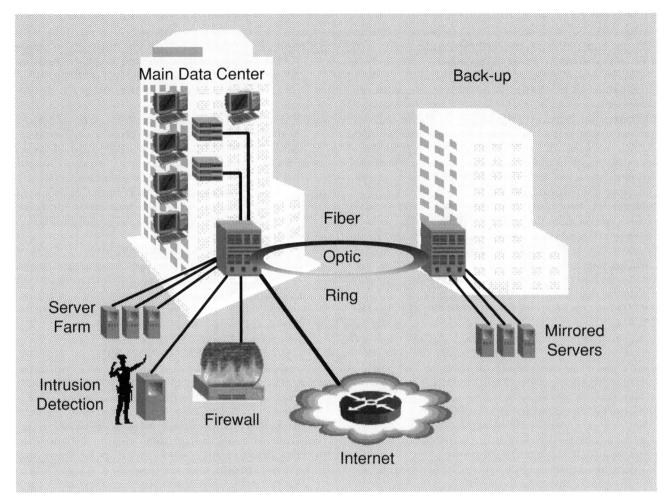

**Figure 4:** Fiber optic connection of data centers.

business strategy but also by the size of the IT security budget.

One thing is certain. Damage caused by hackers, crackers, viruses, computer sabotage, and loss of data show how mission-critical a fully integrated security architecture is. A study by the U.S. Computer Security Institute and FBI estimated the total damage from criminal IT activity in the United States in 1998 to be US $10 billion (Pohlmann, 2000). The losses that can be expected in 2005 may be many times higher.

The world of information technology is rapidly changing and so too are the problems it poses. Consequently, organizations should not let their security architectures stagnate. Continual improvement of protection mechanisms is necessary, but should only be undertaken in conjunction with sufficient laboratory testing and verification. This will help ensure that organizations protect themselves in the best possible manner.

## GLOSSARY

**DHCP (Dynamic Host Configuration Protocol)** Communications protocol that lets network administrators centrally manage and automate the assignment of IP addresses to devices in the network. Without DHCP, static IP addresses must be entered manually into each network device.

**DMZ (Demilitarized Zone)** A demilitarized zone is a computer host or small network inserted as a "neutral zone" between a private network and the public network. Servers that provide the company's Web site and Web pages to the outside world are usually located in the DMZ. Servers containing other corporate information are not. In this way, the DMZ prevents outside users from getting direct access to servers that store private company data.

**DSL (Digital Subscriber Line)** Technology for bringing high bandwidth information to homes and businesses via normal telephone lines.

**FTP (File Transfer Protocol)** An application protocol that uses the Internet's TCP/IP protocols as the simplest way of exchanging files between computers and servers. FTP is commonly used to download programs and documents.

**GSM (Global System for Mobile Communication)** A digital mobile telephone system that is the de facto standard in Europe and other parts of the world. GSM uses a variation of time division multiple access (TDMA) multiplexing. It digitizes and compresses data, then sends it down a channel with two other streams of user data, each in its own time slot. It operates at either the 900 MHz or 1800 MHz frequency band in Europe and 1900 MHz in North America.

**HTTP (Hypertext Transfer Protocol)** The set of rules for transferring text, graphical images, sound, and video via the World Wide Web to a computer's browser.

**IDS (Intrusion Detection System)** A type of security management system for computers and networks. An IDS gathers and analyzes information from various areas within a computer or a network to identify possible security breaches and report these to the IT administrator or security officer.

**IP (Internet Protocol)** A connectionless protocol, which means that there is no continuing connection between the end points that are communicating. Each packet is treated as an independent unit of data without any relation to any other unit of data (see also TCP). IP is the method by which data is sent from one computer to another on the Internet.

**ISDN (Integrated Services Digital Network)** A set of CCITT/ITU standards for connection-oriented digital transmission via ordinary telephone copper wire and other media. ISDN is made up of bearer, or b, channels and data, or d, channels. The b channels carry voice, video, and other services. The d channels carry control and signaling information.

**ISP (Internet Service Provider)** An ISP is a company that provides access to the Internet and other related services such as Web site building or hosting. An ISP has the equipment and the telecommunication line access required to have a point of presence on the Internet for the geographic area it serves.

**LAN (Local Area Network)** A group of computers and associated devices that share a common communication line or wireless link in a small geographic area (e.g., office building) to make use of printers and servers.

**PBX (Private Branch Exchange)** A PBX is a telephone system used to switch calls between users on local lines (or extensions) while allowing all users to share a certain number of external phone lines (or trunks). The main purpose of a PBX is to save the cost of renting a line for each user from the PTT or "telco." PBXs can also provide value-added services such as voice mail and automated call distribution for call centers.

**PDA (Personal Digital Assistant)** Small, mobile handheld device that provides computing and information storage and retrieval capabilities for personal or business use. PDAs often store calendar and address book information and can usually synchronize this data with programs, such as Outlook, on a personal computer.

**RTP (Remote Desktop Protocol)** The remote Windows terminal protocol used by Microsoft's Windows NT 4.0, Terminal Server Edition operating system, and Windows 2000 Terminal Services.

**SSL (Secure Sockets Layer)** A commonly used protocol for managing the security of a message transmission on the Internet. It uses a program layer located between HTTP and TCP.

**TCP (Transmission Control Protocol)** A set of rules used in conjunction with IP to send data in the form of message units (packets) between computers. TCP is responsible for keeping track of individual packets, requesting missing or lost packets, and reassembling them into complete messages at the other end.

**UDP (Uniform Datagram Protocol)** Uses IP to transfer message units (datagrams) from one computer to another. Unlike TCP, it does not keep track of the data or assemble it in the correct order. Thus, the application that uses the data must be able to determine that the entire message has arrived correctly. This is useful for IP telephony or other applications that need to save processing time and/or have small data units to exchange.

**UPS (Uninterruptable Power Supply)** A UPS provides short-term autonomy for network devices such as switches, routers, and servers. In the event that a UPS should detect a loss of primary power, it is able to instantly switch to battery-based backup power, thus providing enough time for network components to be gracefully shut down before the battery fails.

**VPN (Virtual Private Network)** A way to use a public telecommunication infrastructure (e.g., the Internet) to provide remote offices or individual user clients with secure access to their organization's network. This can avoid the deployment of costly leased lines.

**VRRP (Virtual Router Redundancy Protocol)** An Internet protocol that provides a way to have one or more backup routers when using a statically configured router network. A virtual IP address is shared among the routers, with one router designated as the master and the others designated as slaves or backups. If the master fails, the virtual IP address is mapped to the IP address of the next backup router.

**WEP (Wired Equivalent Privacy)** A security protocol specified by 802.11b and intended to provide wireless LANs with a level of privacy comparable to that of a normal wire-line LAN.

## CROSS REFERENCES

See *Access Control: Principles and Solutions; Computer and Network Authentication; Contingency Planning Management; Password Authentication; Risk Management for IT Security.*

## REFERENCES

Baker, R. H. (1991). *Computer security handbook*. TAB Professional reference books, Blue Ridge Summit.

Gruender, T., & Graf, N. (2004). *IT–outsourcing*. Berlin: Erich-Schmidt-Verlag.

Koenig, T. (2004). *Computerwoche* (Vol. 1, p. 10). IDG Business Verlag, Munich.

Lipp, M. (2001). *Virtual private networks* (p. 87). Munich: Addison-Wesley.

Pohlmann, N. (2003). *Firewall systeme*. MITP-Verlag (Extended ed.). Bonn, p. 518.

Pohlmann, N. (2000). *Firewall systeme*. MITP, 3 (Extended ed.). Bonn.

Ruediger, A. (2003). "Studio: W-lan Vernachlässign Sicherheit." *InformationWeek Germany, 11,* 20. CPA-Weka, Poing, Germany.

*Webster's new encyclopedic dictionary*. (1994). Koenemann-Verlag: Cologne.

## FURTHER READING

Pohl, H. (2001). *Informationssicherheit in Unternehmen*. IIR Conference S@fe IT, Munich.

Schulze, J. (2004). Computerwoche (Vol. 1, p. 12). IDG Business Verlag, Munich.

# Quality of Security Service: Adaptive Security

Timothy E. Levin and Cynthia E. Irvine, *Naval Postgraduate School*
Evdoxia Spyropoulou, *Technical Vocational Educational School of Computer Science of Halandri Greece*

## INTRODUCTION

The purpose of this chapter is to provide an overview, rationale, and motivation for understanding *quality of security service* (QoSS). Just as with the *quality of service* (QoS) mechanisms from which they are derived, QoSS mechanisms benefit both the subscriber (e.g., individual user or enterprise) and the overall distributed system. Users benefit by having reliable access to services, and the distributed systems whose resources are QoSS-managed may benefit by having more predictable resource utilization by users and more efficient resource allocation. Thus, the QoSS vision is to transform security from a performance obstacle into an adaptive, constructive network management tool.

### Motivation

Most of today's distributed and highly populated computing environments, as exemplified by the Internet, face challenges with security as well as with the management and availability of resources. Bandwidth in mobile and wireless environments is limited; batteries have limited lifetimes; Internet service providers must be proactive to constrain high bandwidth users; and many users struggle with download times and access to networks. Every day, we are reminded in our e-mail and in various news media about the significant security vulnerabilities in our computers and networks. Network administrators have a constant battle with the configuration of firewalls, routers, and user workstations. Furthermore, resource usage patterns and the security or threat environment of these general-purpose networks are in constant flux. Intelligent, adaptive, automated mechanisms are needed to help manage network resources for availability, performance, and security.

### Background

Historically, in a community of users with relatively homogeneous computing behaviors, resource usage load on multiuser systems could be understood, simplistically, to be a linear function of the number of users or the number of user terminals configured for the system.

Thus, a system administrator could govern the system resource usage load, to a large degree, by controlling the number of allowed simultaneous user input terminals (e.g., interactive terminals, modems, and card readers). In a distributed and internetworked environment, system administrators are often without recourse to such straightforward and simplistic resource-usage control approaches, because the number and type of user "terminals" and associated tasks may not be bounded by local (e.g., campus or enterprise) topographies and the resource requirements of different tasks may vary widely. In some cases, users of a given system resource may extend across the Internet. The QoS paradigm is designed to help address this problem by providing to users and administrators certain tools for managing resource usage and service levels.

QoS refers to the ability of a distributed system to provide network and computation services such that each user's expectations for timeliness and performance quality are met. There are several *dimensions* of QoS described in the literature (Chatterjee, Sabata, & Sydir, 1998; Vendatasubramanian & Nahrstedt, 1997), including accuracy, precision, and performance. For each QoS dimension, users can request or specify a level of service for one or more attributes, and the underlying QoS control mechanism (QoSM) is capable of delivering those services at the requested levels. Levels of service may be specified absolutely (e.g., megabytes of bandwidth) or statistically (e.g., 90% availability). The control mechanism must be able to modulate the level of the service to individual subscribers (e.g., users or enterprises). For example, a network-based multimedia application might be expected to deliver video frames so that the display is jitter-free to some requested level.

In addition to meeting individual user requirements, a QoSM makes choices that permit it to maximize overall benefit in accordance with its QoS policy. For example, one QoS policy might require that benefit be equally shared among all tasks. This would mean that if network resources were oversubscribed, all tasks would have a reduction in service. Another policy might be that no service is better than poor service, so that if resources were sufficiently oversubscribed, some tasks would be postponed or terminated. This policy could be extended so that certain tasks would be given priority for guaranteed service during times of resource congestion.

Users present their expectations to the QoS mechanism by way of service level requests. These requests can take the form of both hard and soft requirements (Stankovic, Supri, Ramamritham, & Buttazo, 1998). In essence, the system enters into a contract with the user to meet the hard and soft requirements. Hard requirements mandate fixed service levels that the QoSM must deliver if it is to accept the user's task, whereas a soft requirement can be considered to define a range of acceptable service, for example, in terms of bandwidth, response time, or image fidelity. Each soft requirement represents a variable that the QoSM can manipulate in balancing the needs of multiple users. Given latitude in the user's soft requirements, the more of these variables that the control mechanism has to manipulate, the easier will be its job of adapting to changing resource availability and satisfying the set of current users. Conversely, the QoSM can offer choices to the user (in response to which the user may enter hard or soft requests) only for aspects of the system that it controls and is willing to provide a range of service. For aspects in which there is no such control, only a fixed level of service can be delivered, thus adaptive QoS concepts do not apply.

## QUALITY OF SECURITY SERVICE

The purpose of this section is to provide an analysis of the role of security in a system designed to provide QoS. Security has long been a gleam in the eye of the QoS community: many QoS research and development "request for proposals" and QoS system-design presentation slides have included a placeholder for security, without defining security as a true QoS *dimension* (as discussed in the previous section). Some of these presentations have provided access control mechanisms within the QoS framework (Sabata, et al., 1997; Lee, et al., 1998), but they have only touched on security as a QoS dimension.

Inherently, QoS involves user requests for (levels of) services that are related to performance-sensitive variables in an underlying distributed system. For security to be a real part of QoS, then, security choices must be presented to users, and the QoS mechanism must be able to modulate related variables to provide predictable security service levels to those users. This raises the question of whether it makes sense within the context of coherent system security paradigms to provide such security choices to users. It is also of interest to understand how the limits on these choices are defined and how those limits relate to existing resource security policies.

The premise of QoSS is that QoS mechanisms can be more effective if variable levels of *security* services and requirements can be presented to users or network tasks. In this approach, the "level of service" must be within an acceptable range, may be absolute or statistical, and can indicate degrees of security with respect to assurance (integrity, confidentiality, privacy, authentication, etc.), mechanistic strength, administrative diligence, and so forth. For example,

- security level of user $\geq$ security level of resource,
- length of confidentiality encryption key $\geq$ 64 and $\leq$ 256, and
- percentage packets authenticated $\geq$ 50 and $\leq$ 90.

As described for QoS, these ranges result in additional parameters with which the QoSM can successfully meet overall user and system demands, as well as balance costs and projected benefits to specific users/clients (see the following discussion of QoSS cost framework). Furthermore, the broader solution space with which the QoSM has to work in the security realm means that it can adapt more gracefully to dynamic changes in resource availability and thereby do a better job at maintaining requested or required levels of service in all of its dimensions. The term *quality of security service* refers to the use of security as a quality of service dimension.

To recap, the enabling technology for both QoSS and a security-adaptable infrastructure is *variant security*, or the ability of security mechanisms and services to allow the amount, kind, or degree of security to vary within predefined ranges. This notion of network QoS has the potential to provide administrators and users with more flexibility and potentially better service, without compromise of network and system security policies.

## Security Ranges

For many, security is thought to be binary: either you have it or you do not. Without some minimum level of security, a system will be considered inadequate for user requirements. Yet, if a user's as well as the system's minimum requirements are met, can there not be some choice with respect to what is adequate? The answer is "yes." As an initial example, suppose that a user requires medium assurance of policy enforcement at any end system where a distributed task will be executed. If the assurance levels of potential target platforms range between medium and high assurance, there is a choice. In fact, if the medium assurance system is oversubscribed while the high assurance system is idle, the user may realize better overall service by electing to execute the task on the high assurance processor.

As with multimedia image resolution, users will generally desire the greatest amount of security (or image fidelity) available, but this desire is generally tempered by cost. The cost may take the form of monetary charges (unlimited bandwidth but at a high cost per byte) or performance degradation (for high resolution, processing and download times will be long), for example. When the cost is very high (e.g., slow response time), users may be willing to accept security that is less than their ideal level of service. Thus, the user/administrator's acceptable security would range from a minimum to an ideal. A system that is sufficiently flexible may be able to impose performance degradations on others when an application that is willing to pay enough or has the highest priority is introduced. By indicating a range within which they are willing to operate, the lower priced or lower priority tasks will still be able to run rather than being terminated or rejected. Yet, once a user (or security officer) decides on the minimum level of security required for a given application or scenario, why would they ever agree to more security, if it increases their cost? In general, the increase in cost will be acceptable to the user only if it is accompanied by a commensurate increase in some other associated level of service, such as

- likelihood of task completion;
- performance factors, such as latency and throughput;
- storage/output device features, such as supported media or format; and
- data features, such as color, accuracy, and precision.

In other words, more security and higher costs will be acceptable if it results in an increase or stasis in the overall satisfaction with the task invocation (see discussion of "benefit functions" in Irvine and Levin (2000), Jensen, Locke, & Tokuda (1985, and Kim, et al., (2000); thus, users could be motivated to consider security ranges above their established minimums. For example, an application may have variable data formats, which have correspondingly variable security requirements and costs. Perhaps a degraded image requires less security, and conversely, the enhanced image requires more security. Thus, a user might prefer heightened security if it is accompanied by greater image fidelity, even through the cost is higher.

An example taken from a popular military novel will help to illustrate our point. Suppose that high-, medium-, and low-resolution satellite images of enemy troop movements are available. A different type of optical equipment produces each type of image. To help keep confidential the optical technologies used to obtain the images, the images themselves are classified at high-, medium-, and low-sensitivity levels, respectively. For analysis of enemy troops in tactical planning, any resolution image will suffice, however, the low-resolution images are from old, slow equipment, and use of high-resolution images is restricted to emergencies (here, part of the cost of using the high resolution is the need to justify its usage at a later date). Therefore, the tactical commander issues a request for troop movement images with fidelity in the range of low to high, in the following priority order: medium, low, high (such that high would be used only when the other resolutions are not available). Thus, we have a situation in which the user would prefer medium security but will also accept low- or high-security images, depending on what is available.

An integrity example may also be useful. Suppose that a surgeon is performing a delicate brain operation remotely. To ensure that only the precise brain locations are affected, high fidelity is required. Additionally, there is a requirement for high integrity to ensure that the video stream is not tampered with by malicious entities who might wish to harm the patient. Secrecy is not a requirement, yet if the only secure communication channel available provides both a high level of secrecy and integrity, the operation is provided high secrecy as a bonus resulting from fidelity and integrity requirements. The following are some more examples of the use of real and hypothetical security ranges:

- Destination subnets could be classified by risk factor with respect to routing through, execution on, or logging on to nodes in those subnets (ISO, 1989). Users, applications, or enterprise-wide mechanisms could request of middleware control mechanisms that communications or tasks executed on the user's behalf utilize a specific *risk range* of subnets.

- Some environments may offer the user choices of logon authentication technology. For example, a user may log on with a standard password, a one-time password (crypto challenge–response), a public key smart card, a biometric device, or some combination of these. In these environments, the user could be granted greater access to resources (e.g., a higher classification of data) if he uses higher assurance authentication (Juneman, 1997).

- Some underlying systems support different *situational modes*. For some modes (e.g., normal, impacted, emergency), the user or administrator may be willing to accept more (or less) security. A commander under attack at a foreign embassy might require the highest communication security, whereas a commander under attack on the battlefield might declare, "damn the security, full speed ahead!" The Management System for Heterogeneous Networks (MSHN) resource management system is an example of a QoSM system in which the management of mode versus security requirement was designed to be handled automatically (Hensgen, et al., 1999; Irvine & Levin, 1999a).

- The security policy for a hypothetical commercial subnetwork requires outgoing IP packet encryption. In this environment, a multimedia application exports digital images (e.g., high-resolution fine art images). However, recognizing that the stakeholders in this specific environment can tolerate a media stream which is *partially* or *periodically* encrypted (viz., one yielding a suitably obscured image, which would render a stolen image unusable by the vast majority of its target market), the policy may only require that a range of from 80% to 100% of the packets should be encrypted. (Note that in some risk models, such a periodic encryption method might require fortified protection against cryptanalysis. In addition, care must be taken to ensure that the entire unencrypted image is not revealed in repeated transmissions.)

- Variable packet authentication (Schneck & Schwan, 1998) is a corollary to the preceding confidentiality scenario. In this case, the sender or recipient might be satisfied if (only) a certain percentage of the packets in an image stream were authenticated (e.g., 80% to 100%). Depending on the threat model and the packet-checking algorithm, to detect attacks, attention may need to be paid to the ratio of good to bad packets: if all of the packets were bogus and only 80% were checked (and consequently dropped), it might be possible for the display program to show a *completely* bogus image, utilizing the remaining 20%.

- The number of "rounds" performed in a cryptographic transformation algorithm, such as the advanced encryption standard, could be used as a QoSS variable, to the extent that more rounds consume more resources and provide more security.

- An administrator may choose to run an intrusion detection system (IDS) within an effectivity *range* rather than at a fixed level. There would be a minimal level of IDS processing below which the system would not be permitted to fall, but the IDS would be balanced against performance requirements of the organization's tasks. Thus, the IDS might perform more thoroughly (with deeper histories) when the system is lightly loaded than during peak hours. The administrator might also choose to set an upper limit to IDS processing to conserve resources.

- Another variable packet authentication scheme (Xie, Irvine, & Colwell, 1999) would be to authenticate only a certain percentage of each packet. The higher percentage of authentication could be used, for example, to protect against steganographic exfiltration of sensitive data.

From these examples, it is apparent that the notion of security ranges is useful and, in some cases, already evident in existing systems.

## QoSS MODEL

This section presents some observations about how variant security can be viewed in a distributed system that provides QoS support.

### Security Resources, Services, and Requirements

A *network system* is defined as the totality of network accessible resources. A *security service* is a high-level abstract resource providing security functionality, such as authentication, auditing, privacy, integrity, intrusion detection, nonrepudiation, and traffic flow confidentiality (Irvine & Levin, 1999b). A security service typically consumes other low-level *system resources* such as central processing unit (CPU) power, memory, disk space, and network bandwidth. For example, the common data security architecture (CDSA) (Sargent, 1998) describes modules, each of which contain specific security mechanisms to provide some of these services.

Each resource (including security services) may embody *security requirements* regarding its use. A requirement may restrict the availability of a resource to an external entity. Some restrictions might be the typical mandatory and discretionary requirements or other security constraints, for example, encryption available 9 p.m. to 5 a.m., range of available encryption algorithms, and range of required key lengths. To be general, we state that all security requirements define a *range* of permissible behavior. That is, a range may be unitary or degenerate, in which case it represents no choice. Where a range represents a choice, the requirement is called *security variant*.

### Task Sequences

Quality of service can be provided at several levels within the overall system. The notion of translucence, by which components can adapt to changing conditions at other system or network layers, results in a problem that is both horizontal, viz. distributed across the network, and vertical, viz. distributed within the layers of programs within a given network node. In the following discussion, the management of QoSS can be seen to have both horizontal and vertical interactions, depending on the implementation of the various components.

A *task* is an application invoked by a user or another task. The task utilizes various network system services and other resources. This utilization may be intermediated by different QoS middleware mechanisms, such as QoS-aware object request brokers and application servers, distributed resource management systems, and various network traffic managers. In these multiple-tiered environments, a task is invoked in a *task invocation sequence:*

- The user activates the application through some interface with an application manager (OS, browser, etc.).
- The application is intermediated by the QoSM.
- The QoSM submits the application to the system. Note that it is an implementation detail whether the QoSM returns advisory parameters to the application and the application invokes the system, or the QoSM submits the application with those parameters directly to the system. For simplicity, we assume, here, that the QoSM submits the application to the system.

More complex invocations are possible, such as chains of applications leading to the intermediation by the QoSM, chains of sequences, and so forth. However, the simplification of a user/application/QoSM/system model appears general enough to address the security concerns of the more complex cases.

Security requirements may be established or refined by any or all of the following: the user, the application, the QoSM, and the system; we call these entities *security requirement providers*. As an example of how a requirement can be refined within the task invocation sequence, consider how a typical application offers the user a choice for some service. If the user does not indicate a choice, the application may use a default value. If the user chooses a range, the application may invoke itself with a particular value within that range. Similarly, the QoSM may refine the application's choice, for example, to optimize the overall *system* (user population) performance, perform load balancing, and so forth.

### Security Limits and Choices

In a task invocation sequence, the request is passed from a previous requirement provider to the next provider. A security *choice* for each variant security requirement is logically included with each request step. The choice may be implicit or explicit. For example, if no explicit choice is made, then it may be implicit that the choice is to not limit or modify the security options proffered at that step. As with requirements, all security choices define a choice range, which may be unitary. Thus, each requirement provider specifies a choice range for each variant requirement in a given task invocation. For example, the user selects a range of 50–80% for packet authentication rate. This choice is passed to the next provider (viz., the application) in the sequence.

For each variant security requirement, each requirement provider may also have an explicit requirement *limit* range (again, unitary or variant) outside of which it will not accept a request. The limit applies to the request choice from the previous provider, for example, a given application will not accept a range greater than 60–100% from the user.

## Security Range Relationships

An important aspect of the notions of "range" and the relationship between ranges is how two elements of a range compare. In the packet authentication rate example, the "rate" variable is measured on a linear scale, so one choice, or element, has a natural relationship to another choice: one of greater than, less than, or equal. To be most general, we would also like to allow two choices within a range to be incomparable, resulting in a partial ordering. A natural interpretation of a security range is that the elements on one end of the range are "more secure than" the elements on the other end.

A *security requirement* is more formally defined, as follows: for each variant security requirement there is a set of elements, from which choices and limits are selected, that are partially ordered by a "security" relation. This relation is called "dominates," meaning that one element is more secure than a second if and only if the first element dominates the second. Each defined or selected security range for the requirement is a sublattice of that set such that the maximum of the range dominates the minimum. One range is contained "within" a second range, if and only if the maximum of the first dominates the maximum of the second, and the minimum of the second dominates the minimum of the first. For two ranges to intersect means that the maximum of each dominates the minimum of the other.

Table 1 shows the limits and choices of security requirement providers in a task invocation sequence.

Notice that the user does not have an effective limit range, as he has no previous provider upon whom to enforce such a range. Also, the system choice range is the level of service ultimately provided by the system in response to the request. This is a unitary range, because there is no next provider to whom a choice might be given. With so many requirement ranges at different points in the sequence, one may wonder how these ranges relate to each other.

The following relationships appear to be inherent in a task invocation sequence involving cooperating entities:

1. The maximum of each limit and choice range dominates the minimum of that range.
2. Each provider's choice range must be within its own limit range. This restriction reflects the natural protocol to respect one's own limits.
3. Each choice range must be within the previous choice range in the sequence. This reflects a natural protocol

to respect the choice of the previous requirement provider: a requirement provider will try to fulfill the request of a previous provider. For example, in a quality of service context, a service provider may accept a request if it can be realized, but it will not proceed with parameters that are divergent from (outside) the user's request.

4. Each choice range must be within the next limit range in the sequence. This restriction means that requests that are out of bounds will be rejected.
5. The limit ranges of each provider in a task sequence must all *intersect*. This is a consequence of the need for a choice to be within the provider's own limit and within the next limit, as well as within the previous choice. Obviously, if two ranges in a task invocation sequence do not intersect, there does not exist a value that could satisfy both ranges; this would disallow a task from being successfully invoked.

These relationships are illustrated in Figure 1. Because the choices and limits are partially ordered and thus functionally comparable, it is possible for a security service selection algorithm to be encoded. A QoSM would maintain databases of static and dynamic resource characteristics. In the static database, limits might be recorded, whereas the dynamic database could record current network conditions (e.g., available capacities) and choices. Thus, when a new task request enters the system, the QoSM can compute its execution strategy. Note that the complexity of this computation is "NP-complete" (Knuth, 1974), and extensive work exists on heuristic scheduling techniques, for example, that by Siegel and Ali (2000).

## QoSS APPLIED

In this section, two aspects of applying QoSS to distributed systems are presented: a framework for quantifying the cost of QoSS resource selections, such as would be utilized by a QoSM in making resource allocation decisions, and an examination of how a specific security mechanism can be modulated to provide differing levels of security service in response to QoSS requests.

## Costing

Security comes at a cost. If a particular security mechanism is "fixed" (i.e., always applied) then the overhead for the mechanism is part of the normal cost of running the task and the normal costing mechanism used by the QoSM will suffice. For variant security mechanisms, however, the security overhead will vary depending on the user's QoS request. Some task invocations will utilize little, if any, of the variant mechanism and other invocations may utilize the mechanism at an increased level. Also, the scheduler may adapt security support, while maintaining any minimum system security policy requirements, to schedule the tasks most efficiently. The QoSM must calculate how much the use of the security mechanism will increase the cost of the task, according to the specific security "level" requested. For this reason the QoSM must have access to detailed information about the resource cost (as well as the task's requested QoS) for each variant

**Table 1** Security Limits and Choices

|                        | User | Application | Middleware | System         |
|------------------------|------|-------------|------------|----------------|
| Choice range provided  | Yes  | Yes         | Yes        | Service level  |
| Limit range enforced   | No   | Yes         | Yes        | Yes            |

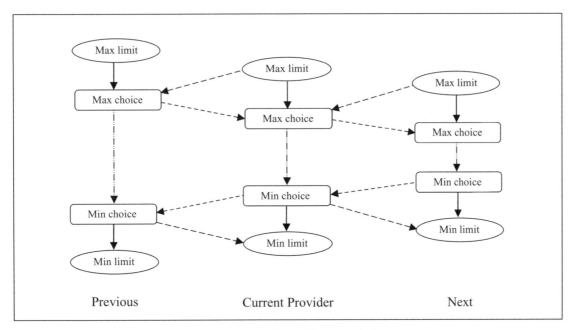

**Figure 1:** Relationships of limits and choices.

security mechanism. Near-optimal solution selection for task schedules depends on the accurate estimation of per-task, per-resource cost of security (Irvine & Levin, 1999a).

This approach for quantifying the costs related to a task's security requests (Spyropoulou, Levin, & Irvine, 2000) refers to costs relative to every security service invoked by the task. Each service may access CPU time, memory, bandwidth, disk space, and so forth. The resource usages may be temporary or persistent, providing discrimination between start-up and streaming costs.

For example, the Confidentiality on the Network Connection service, using a symmetric algorithm such as Twofish (Juneman, 1997) for data encryption, would require some extra processing during startup for the initialization of S boxes. This is a one-time cost during the establishment phase of the service. On the other hand, bandwidth costs for the confidentiality service are streaming costs only, in the form of extra bytes per packet because of the encryption algorithm.

In a QoS system every application would have its resource costs modeled as shown in Table 2, where cost expressions are functions of security variables. A given security variable may be a factor in more than one cost expression.

Units of measure can vary, for example, CPU costs can be measured in clocks (or clocks/packet), memory costs in bytes, and bandwidth costs in bytes (or bytes/packet). In another approach, all measures could be unitless and normalized within a common framework. A careful description of the semantics of the units with respect to each security service would then be required.

After the individual costs are calculated, their intended use is as input to a QoSM for efficient scheduling of tasks when treating security as a QoS dimension.

## Examination of Resource Modulation

For security to be a real part of QoS, security choices must be presented to users, and the QoS mechanism must be able to modulate related variables to provide predictable security service levels. Consider, for example, how a specific security mechanism, IPsec, can be externally modulated to provide different levels of security in response to QoSS requests from users or the QoSM. One approach is to manage detailed variant security attributes according to abstract *network mode* and user *security level* selections.

The variables associated with many security services are too complex for average users or application developers to understand or manage without assistance. A simplified abstraction of security, in the form of security level choices such as "high," "medium," and "low," can be provided. The applications, either alone or combined with the QoSM, can then manage a mapping of security levels to detailed variant attributes, and users will not have to contend with the complexity of these choices, as shown in Table 3.

**Table 2** Hypothetical CPU Cost Formulas for FTP Security

| | CPU Cost Types | |
| --- | --- | --- |
| **FTP Security Services** | **Startup (clocks)** | **Streaming (clocks/packet)** |
| Network integrity | $a * \text{KEY\_LENGTH} + b$ | $c * \text{INTEGRITY\_RATE}$ |
| User authentication | $d * e(\text{AUTHENTICATION\_TYPE}) + f$ | 0 |

**Table 3** Hypothetical Security Attributes per Security Level

|  | Security Level Choice | | |
| --- | --- | --- | --- |
|  | Low | Medium | High |
| Packet integrity rate | 0.6 | 0.8 | 1 |
| Symmetric key length | 56 | 96 | 128 |
| Type of authentication | None | Password | Biometric & password |

**Table 4** Hypothetical IPsec Security Attributes per Security Level

| Channel | Security Level | | |
| --- | --- | --- | --- |
|  | Low | Medium | High |
| telnet | No IPsec processing | ESP processing with DES | ESP processing with 3DES |
| finger | No IPsec processing | AH processing with HMAC-MD5 | AH processing with HMAC-SHA |
| ping | No IPsec processing | No IPsec processing | No IPsec processing |

Similarly, abstract policies regarding system limits for different situational modes and changing environments can be provided. For example, a military network or Internet service provider might have an "emergency" mode that indicates that there is a physical threat to the facility, or "congested" mode in which there is more traffic than the current capacity. In both of these cases, the system limits (and choices) for variant security attributes might be different than for a "normal" mode. Again, the applications, QoSM, and/or system could maintain a mapping from the abstract modes to specific security attribute settings, so that once the mapping has been established, users and administrators would not have to contend with the complexity of these choices.

Two entities that wish to communicate with each other using IPsec negotiate to establish IPsec *security associations* (SAs), which define the detailed security characteristics of the communication channels to be used, such as encryption and/or authentication algorithm, SA lifetime, and cryptographic keys. These SAs are used until their negotiated lifetime expires (assuming that no interruption or discard of the channel takes place). The two main issues for utilizing IPsec in a QoSS framework are as follows:

- The SAs should conform to the settings represented by the abstract QoSS parameters. The set of SA characteristics resulting from an SA negotiation should reflect the mappings determined for "network mode" and "security level."
- If there is a change in a QoSS parameter, currently active SAs should be stopped and renegotiated to conform to the new security mappings.

Although the usual IPsec management mechanisms have no provision for response to changing external requirements for a given communication channel, its framework is adaptable enough to allow for the dynamic management of SAs, such as would result from changes to network mode or security level selections.

One approach (described in detail in Spyropoulou, Agar, Levin, & Irvine, 2002) is to use a *trust management system* (Blaze, Feigenbaum, Ioannidis, & Keromytis, 1999) and an external *dynamic parameter console* to modulate the detailed IPsec security attributes. The dynamic parameter console interacts with the external environment, such as an administrator or an intrusion detection system, to receive the current selections for the network mode and security level, and to pass the selections to the trust management system. The trust management system keeps track of the current abstract settings, defines the mapping of levels and modes to detailed IPsec settings, and also acts as policy arbiter regarding allowed IPsec settings and connections (see Table 4). IPsec and the trust management system are instrumented to perform renegotiation of SAs when the abstract settings change.

If the network mode changes to reflect a modification in the system status, or if the user level changes to indicate a desire for higher security, then the dynamic parameter console notifies the trust management system and IPsec. The trust management system is updated with the new policy information for use with new SA negotiations. Furthermore, if there exist currently active SAs based on the changed policies, it removes them and initiates a renegotiation of those SAs.

## QoSS AND APPLICATION-CENTRIC SECURITY

The historical view of access control to resources was OS-centric with respect to the activities of applications and other programs that the OS hosted. The operating system enforced a policy, to the best of its ability, and ideally, objects never left the control domain of the OS. Policies that were enforced globally and persistently within this domain were considered to be "mandatory" and all others were considered to be "discretionary" (Brinkley & Schell, 1995). With the advent of distributed/heterogeneous applications, data storage objects, operating systems, and resources—and a plethora of middleware mechanisms for managing those distributed entities—*application-centric access control* has now become common, if not the norm (e.g., see Blaze, Feigenbaum, Ioannidis, & Keromytis, 1999). In this brave new world, the application itself (perhaps in concert with some middleware mechanisms) enforces access control on its objects, rather than depending for this function on an underlying (e.g., OS and hardware) control mechanism.

Thus, network applications have assumed some functions of the traditional OS. If the application's objects are completely encapsulated, such that the object never leaves the control domain of the application, then a global and persistent policy could be said to be enforced, assuming persistence on the part of the application. However, this is a necessary but not sufficient condition for effective policy enforcement. (Note that if the object is allowed to leave the application's domain, then it is more difficult to argue that a global policy is enforced. A component of one such argument for a distributed application is that objects in transit are protected, perhaps by cryptographic mechanisms, such that the object remains, logically, in the control domain of the application.)

Another aspect of traditional OS policy enforcement was the notion that, to be considered highly effective, access control should be performed at the lowest layers(s), including hardware, of a strictly layered system. The reason for allocating access control functions to the lower levels is that it is more feasible, then, to ensure that the mechanisms are unable to be bypassed, persistently enforced, and small enough to allow thorough analysis (e.g., see Anderson, 1972). Without understanding the dependency layering, it will not be clear on which other modules a module depends, nor will it be clear if there are fatal (e.g., circularly dependent) or semantically undefined execution sequences.

In the OS paradigm, regardless of how well formed or misused was an application, if the enforcement layers were well formed, the policy enforcement could be ensured. Modern distributed applications do not necessarily have these two properties (dependency layering and access control implemented at the lowest levels). For example, a network application, which has been allocated the responsibility for enforcing a security policy, typically depends on an untrusted operating system for access to resources, and dependency layering is not a fundamental design consideration in many modern distributed applications and systems.

Under the conditions described here for distributed systems, much more design analysis may be involved in understanding the degree to which a distributed system is capable of enforcing a security policy, than was required to analyze a traditional, nondistributed, layered system. The QoSS approach may be applicable in certain distributed systems that utilize application-centric access control concepts. This is not to say that this approach ameliorates the design analysis problems of application-centric access control. On the contrary, it is important to reiterate that each such system needs careful design review to understand the effectiveness of its security mechanisms. It is hoped that the security abstractions presented here will aid in such analyses.

## RELATED WORK

The *OSI Basic Reference Model Security Architecture* document (ISO, 1989) provides information and analysis about network communications security services and mechanisms, including a mapping of security services to mechanisms and OSI layers, and describes the behavior of lower layers when responding to security service requests. This analysis provides a good summary of network security services from the perspective of protection of communications. The QoSS approach is intended to include security services other than those specific to communications protection, and the QoSS service model is more oriented to the *n*-tier architectural framework rather than the OSI protocol stack. Additionally, the OSI work does not address the constructive management of security variability.

A *quality of protection* parameter is provided in the GSSAPI specification (Linn, 1993). This parameter is intended to manage the level of protection provided to a message communication stream by an underlying security mechanism (or service), "allowing callers to trade off security processing overhead dynamically against the protection requirements for particular messages." Another early reference to a variable security service is that of Schneck and Schwan (1998), which discusses variable packet authentication rates with respect to the management of system performance. The QoSS work presented here is intended to extend these efforts into a more general framework, which is applicable to a wide range of policy, processing, and networking contexts, as well as diverse security services.

References to security in the QoS literature can be found in Chatterjee, Sabata, and Sydir (1998), Aurrecoechea, Campbell, and Hauw (1996), and Welch, Shirazi, Ravindran, and Bruggeman (1998), although little is mentioned there of security variability or use of security as a functional QoS dimension. QoS itself has been extensively discussed in the literature, and the reader is referred to Aurrecoechea, Campbell, and Hauw (1996) for a thorough review of QoS definitions and architectures.

A *trust management system* (Blaze, M., Feigenbaum, J., Ioannidis, J., & Keromytis, 1999; 2001) provides a language and mechanism for specifying security policies and credentials, and may include a *policy server* or compliance checker to resolve questions about access control. The trust management system is not concerned with the nature of the specific policies (e.g., those involving variant security) that it stores and resolves, nor is the trust management system expressly concerned with QoS issues. However, a QoSS system could be built to utilize a trust management system to store and resolve security range relationships.

## CONCLUSION

This chapter provides an overview of QoSS and variant security and demonstrates that these concepts can be useful in improving security service and system performance in QoS-aware distributed systems. The general requirement for system attributes to participate in the provision of QoS, as well as an approach for how certain security attributes might meet these requirements, is described. Various forms of user and application security "ranges" are shown to make sense in relation to existing security policies when those ranges are presented as user choices.

It is evident that for a distributed multitiered system, security ranges can form a coherent system of relationships and security can be a semantically meaningful dimension of QoS without compromising existing security policies. Further study is needed to understand the effectiveness of QoSS in improving system performance in QoS-aware systems.

## GLOSSARY

**Quality of Service Dimension** A response attribute of a distributed system that a user or program can request or specify, and that the system is capable of delivering at or near those requested levels. Examples are bandwidth and response time.

**Quality of Security Service** Refers to the use of security as a quality of service dimension.

**Security Service** A high-level abstract resource providing security functionality such as authentication, auditing, privacy, integrity, intrusion detection, nonrepudiation, and traffic flow confidentiality. A security service typically consumes other low-level system resources and may be implemented by one or more security mechanisms.

**Variant Security** The ability of security mechanisms and services to allow the amount, kind, or degree of security to vary, within predefined ranges.

## CROSS REFERENCES

See *Auditing Information Systems Security; Computer and Network Authentication; Security and Web Quality of Service; Security Policy Guidelines.*

## REFERENCES

Anderson, J. P. (1972). *Computer security technology planning study* (Technical Report ESD-TR-73-51). Bedford, MA: Air Force Electronic Systems Division. Hanscom AFB. (Also available as Vol. 1, DITCAD-758206; Vol. 2, DITCAD-772806.)

Aurrecoechea, C., Campbell, A., & Hauw, L. (1996). A survey of quality of service architectures. *Multimedia Systems Journal*, 6(3), 138–151.

Blaze, M., Feigenbaum, J., Ioannidis, J., & Keromytis, A. (1999, September). *The KeyNote Trust-Management System version 2* (RFC 2704). Retrieved April 7, 2005, from http://ietf.org/rfc/rfc2704.txt?number=2704

Blaze, M., Feigenbaum, J., Ioannidis, J., & Keromytis, A. (2001). The role of trust management in distributed system security. In J. Vitek & C. Jensen (Eds.), *Secure Internet programming: Security issues for mobile and distributed objects* (pp. 185–210). New York: Springer-Verlag.

Brinkley, D. L., & Schell, R. R. (1995). Concepts and terminology for computer security. In M. Abrams, S. Jajodia, & H. Podell (Eds.), *Information security: An integrated collection of essays* (pp. 40–97). Los Alamitos, CA: IEEE Computer Society Press.

Chatterjee, S., Sabata, B., & Sydir, J. (1998). *ERDoS QoS architecture* (SRI Technical Report ITAD-1667-TR-98-075). Menlo Park, CA: SRI International.

Hensgen, D., Kidd, T., St. John, D., Schnaidt, M., Siegel, H. J., Braun, T., Kim, J.-K., et al. (1999). An overview of the management system for heterogeneous networks (MSHN). In V. Prasanna (Eds.), *Proceedings of the Heterogeneous Computing Workshop* (pp. 184–198). Los Alamitos, CA: IEEE Computer Society.

International Organization for Standardisation (ISO; 1989). *Information processing systems—open systems interconnection—basic reference model—part 2: Security architecture.* International Standard, no. 7498-2. Switzerland.

Irvine, C., & Levin, T. (1999a). *A note on mapping user-oriented security policies to complex mechanisms and services* (NPS Technical Report NPS-CS-99-008). Monterey, CA: Naval Postgraduate School.

Irvine, C., & Levin, T. (1999b). Toward a taxonomy and costing method for security metrics. *Proceedings of the Annual Computer Security Applications Conference* (pp. 183–188. Los Alamitos, CA: IEEE Computer Society.

Irvine, C., & Levin, T. (2000). Toward quality of security service in a resource management system benefit function. *Proceedings of the Heterogeneous Computing Workshop* (pp. 133–139). Los Alamitos, CA: IEEE Computer Society.

Jensen, E., Locke, C., & Tokuda, H. (1985). A time-driven scheduling model for real-time operating systems. In *Proceedings of the IEEE Real-Time Systems Symposium* (pp. 112–122). Los Alamitos, CA: IEEE Computer Society.

Juneman, R. R. (1997). Novell certificate extension attributes. In *Novel security attributes: Tutorial and detailed design, version 0.998.* Provo, UT: Novell.

Kim, J., Hensgen, D., Kidd, T., Siegel, H., St. John, D. Irvine, et al. (2000). A QoS performance measure framework for distributed heterogeneous networks. In *Proceedings of the Eighth Euromicro Workshop on Parallel and Distributed Processing* (pp. 18–27). Rhodes, Greece.

Knuth, D. E. (1974). A terminological proposal, SIGACT News 6(1), 12–18. ISSN:0163-5700. New York, NY: Association for Computing Machinery.

Lee, C. A., Stepanek, J., Michel, B. S., Kesselman, C., Lindell, R., Sonnwook Hwang, et al. (1998). The quality of service component for the Globus metacomputing system. In *Proceeding of the 1998 International Workshop on Quality of Service* (pp. 140–142). Los Alamitos, CA: IEEE Computer Society.

Linn, J. (1993). *Generic security service application program interface* (RFC 1508). Retrieved April 7, 2005, from http://ietf.org/rfc/rfc1508.txt?number=1508

Sabata, B., Chatterjee, S., Davis, M., Sydir, J., & Lawrence, T. (1997). Taxonomy for QoS specifications. In *Proceedings of the Third International Workshop on Object-Oriented Real-Time Dependable Systems* (pp. 100–107). Los Alamitos, CA: IEEE Computer Society.

Sargent, R. (1998). *CDSA explained: An indispensable guide to common data security architecture.* Reading, Berkshire, UK: The Open Group.

Schneck, P. A., & Schwan, K. (1998). *Dynamic authentication for high-performance networked applications* (Technical Report GIT-CC-98-08). Atlanta, Georgia: Georgia Institute of Technology College of Computing.

Siegel, H. J., & Ali, S. (2000). Techniques for mapping tasks to machines in heterogeneous computing systems. *Euromicro Journal of Systems Architecture*, 46(8), pp. 627–639.

Spyropoulou, E., Agar, C., Levin, T., & Irvine, C. (2002). IPsec modulation for quality of security service. In *Proceedings of the International System Security Engineering Association Conference.* Herndon, VA: International System Security Engineering Association.

Spyropoulou, E., Levin, T., & Irvine, C. (2000). Calculating costs for quality of security service. In *Proceedings of the 16th Computer Security Applications Conference* (pp. 334–343). Los Alamitos, CA: IEEE Computer Society.

Stankovic, J. A., Supri, M., Ramamritham, K., & Buttazo, G. C. (1998). *Deadline scheduling for real-time systems* (pp. 13–22). Norwell MA: Kluwer Academic Publishers.

Vendatasubramanian, N., & Nahrstedt, K. (1997). An integrated metric for video QoS. *Proceedings of the ACM International Multimedia Conference* (pp. 371–380). New York, NY: Association for Computing Machinery.

Welch, L., Shirazi, B., Ravindran, B. & Bruggeman, C. (1998). DeSiDeRaTa: QoS management technology for dynamic, scalable, dependable, real-time systems. In *Proceedings of the 15th Symposium on Distributed Computer Control* Systems (pp. 7–12). Internation Federation of Accountants, New York, NY.

Xie, G., Irvine, C., & Colwell, C. (1999). *A protocol for high speed packet authentication* (NPS Technical Report NPSCS-99-001). Monterey, CA: Naval Postgraduate School.

# Security Policy Enforcement

Cynthia E. Irvine, *Naval Postgraduate School*

## INTRODUCTION

Many chapters of this *Handbook* describe mechanisms that contribute to various facets of security. The arbitrary use of security mechanisms provides no prescription for the achievement of security goals. It is only in their application in the context of organizational objectives for the protection of information and computational assets that security can be assessed. This chapter is intended to discuss the policies that provide a rationale for those mechanisms and to broadly examine their enforcement mechanisms in computer systems. It is intended to focus primarily on fundamental concepts, which remain valid despite their longevity.

In a utopian world where nothing bad ever happened, information security would be unnecessary. There would be no accidents; all actions performed by users would be correct; no attackers would attempt to violate systems. Unfortunately, reality is dramatically different. Information owners are confronted with risks to their assets and, to address these risks, make statements regarding what needs to be protected and how well. These statements constitute the basis for information security policies.

Security policies for information and assets have been with us for centuries, but their application within computer systems requires examination. Sterne (1991) provides a useful guide to understanding how policy is expressed at several levels within an organization and how it is described in a technical context.

First, security policy applies to the protection of assets. Sterne points out that only tangible assets can be protected. Intangible assets may also be protected through the protection of tangible assets, but it is impossible to state and implement a policy to address intangible assets. For example, how can a bank protect its reputation? Not by putting guards around that "reputation." Instead it protects tangible assets such that its reputation is unsullied and enhanced. In contrast, the bank that inadequately protects funds transfers and financial records may be attacked with consequent damage to its reputation. Thus at the highest level, the company board of directors may state policy very abstractly: "important information and other assets must be protected." It will be up to management to translate that policy into more concrete terms and to establish the practices for its enforcement.

Policy is enforced through procedures and mechanisms. Prior to the information age, these procedures and mechanisms were manual: now they are automated. When computers are used to store and process information assets, technical policies are required to translate management strategies into engineering specifications. Even for a nontechnical asset, for example, a painting in a museum, a computer system may be used in conjunction with other protection, and a technical policy describing the policy to be enforced by that system will be required. Mechanisms within the system contribute to policy enforcement, but just as important, external technical and nontechnical procedures involving human interaction must be followed to ensure compliance with the enterprise policy. User account management provides an example where automated and procedural measures must be combined to achieve the desired result. At some nontechnical level, it must be determined whether a particular individual should have an account. Technical activities will ensure that the account, if granted, is created and maintained.

## Security as a Negative Requirement

In security, confidence in an information technology (IT) system comes from knowing that a broad range of bad things, many heretofore unknown, will not occur. For many enterprises, a lack of security can result in lost opportunity. This is due to the fact that fear of unknown security failures will prevent organizations from exploring new IT-based business models, where security is predicated on the fact that unauthorized access to critical information requires a level of effort that adversaries cannot mount. When security is good, a large number of bad things do not happen. Because it is impossible to enumerate all of the possible bad things (and few would choose to turn off security measures to discover even a partial list of these undesirable events), the notion of "measuring" security is not helpful. Because of this measurement problem, management is often reluctant to invest in security. It is more appropriate for management to ask, "In what activities are we unwilling to engage because we do not trust computer systems to adequately protect our assets?" Thus, security is enabling technology but is expressed as a negative requirement: do not let security breaches occur. Through a process of risk analysis, it is possible to create simple models and determine where within the enterprise various security measures will result in the highest return on investment.

## Security as a Constructive Effort

There are two approaches to achieving security policy enforcement, whether in individual systems or in networks of systems. The first is to apply various security measures to a system that is discovered to be insufficient after it has been deployed. Often such measures may be ad hoc. In the case of many commodity products, patches are used to remedy some flaw that has been revealed. Unfortunately, the cure may be worse than the original malady and can lead to additional flaws (Karger & Schell, 1974).

An alternative is to articulate the security policy and then construct a system sufficient to enforce it to some level of confidence. This approach allows system owners to better understand how various risks have been mitigated and those threats for which the system does not have sufficient protection. For example, if a system is intended for a student's database of favorite music, the assets are not of high value and lightweight mechanisms may be adequate to protect the information. A system intended to automate the processing of critical national security information will require considerably stronger security, because the threat posed by adversaries is much higher.

Security policies and the constructive techniques used to enforce them are the focus of what follows.

# KEY DEFINITIONS FOR DESCRIBING TECHNICAL POLICIES

Having provided a motivation for technical security, some terminology is required.

## Active Entities: Subjects

The heart of every computer is its central processing unit (CPU): a collection of registers and hardware mechanisms to execute code. Instructions are fetched and acted on with consequent changes to the system state. Although this is a rather simplistic description of modern processors, which in reality can be quite complex (Hennessy & Patterson, 1996), it is sufficient for this discussion. At any particular moment, the processor executes on behalf of a particular active entity. In a multiprocessing system, active entities are scheduled. These entities consist of the set of instructions being executed and some domain within the system address space that will be read, written, or both as the instructions are executed. These active entities are called *subjects* (Lampson, 1971). The people external to the computer, viz. users, are not subjects; subjects act within the computer on behalf of users. The notion of a subject is a term of art in computer security and should not be confused with threads. (See, for example, Tannenbaum, 2001, for a discussion of threads.) In many simple operating systems, subjects correspond to entire processes; however, some systems implement highly granular privilege policies such that a single process may support multiple subjects. Using hierarchical rings, Multics provided a highly granular privilege mechanism (Schroeder & Saltzer, 1972).

## Passive Entities: Objects

The passive entities of a system are called *objects* (Lampson, 1971). A set of objects comprise the domain of each subject. These objects possess security attributes such that the subject has some form of access to each object within its domain. It is possible for many subjects to share access to the same object. If an object can be written to by multiple subjects, as might occur in a database, some form of synchronization among subjects may be required. Because subjects execute within processes, a wide range of interprocess synchronization mechanisms (Maekawa, Oldehoft, & Oldehoft, 1987) may be useful. These can ensure that specific actions on resources are viewed as atomic.

The objective of security policy definition and enforcement is to control the ways subjects can share and affect the objects.

In a system lacking any sort of security policy, all subjects would have the same access rights to all objects. They would be expected to behave properly. Early operating system designers quickly recognized this as a recipe for chaos and instituted controls (a form of system-internal security policy) to protect processes from each other and from the operating system itself. Saltzer and Schroeder (1975) provide a review of many of these mechanisms. With the exception of certain specialized single-process systems (Weissman, 2003), today there is an expectation of controlled sharing of resources, for example, processor time, memory, and devices, among processes. Security policy is a major factor in determining the resource-sharing mechanisms.

# TYPES OF POLICIES

At a high level, an organization security policy may be expressed in terms of three objectives: confidentiality, integrity, and availability. These primary policies may be complemented by those for separation, least privilege, policy control, and other supporting policies.

## Confidentiality Policies

Confidentiality is focused on protecting information from unauthorized disclosure and may apply to requirements for secrecy and privacy. Confidentiality policies are implemented in most organizations. Businesses may wish to protect trade secrets, marketing plans, accounting information, proposals, and so forth from disclosure to the general public. In addition, they may be required to protect information regarding their personnel. In the health care industry, protection of personal information is of particular interest. Here, the disclosure of medical records to unauthorized individuals could have serious consequences. A number of laws and regulations articulate confidentiality policy requirements within various sectors of society.

## Integrity Policies

Integrity addresses the modification of information: it relates to the reliability or criticality of information. Information of high integrity might be considered to be either highly reliable, for example, from a highly trusted source, or intended for use in critical operations. For example, when a high integrity application is distributed, typical users might be permitted to inspect the source code or the binaries but would be prohibited from modifying either: those authorizations might be limited to certain engineers or programmers. A level of criticality might be associated with meteorological information prior to a space flight launch. As a consideration in a launch decision, such information must not be tampered with.

## Availability Policies

Both confidentiality and integrity policies can be implemented by mechanisms that determine whether a particular subject, which is ultimately executing on behalf of some user, may either observe or modify the information being protected. The decision is simple: either access is permitted or it is denied. Confidentiality and integrity can be reduced to a set of yes or no decisions. In contrast, policies regarding the availability of resources are notoriously difficult to characterize and even more challenging to enforce. This is due to the subjective nature of availability.

Availability policies, by their very nature, are subjective and must be addressed on a per-organization basis. Consider the following example. If an availability policy were to state that all users must have sufficient resources for arbitrary tasks, then when several users decided that they wanted to model colliding galaxies and molecular interactions on a small, general purpose computer (assuming these codes would execute on such a machine), the availability policy would not be met. This is a rather extreme scenario; however, it is easy to see how the tension for resources can result in service inadequacies.

As another example, suppose a user has a processor adequate for supporting a defined set of applications and also suppose that this system is not connected to any network. As long as the application suite is unmodified and there are no stresses imposed on the system by the network, the user is likely to find the system to be adequate. Now, introduce a new suite of applications that consume much larger amounts of system memory and require considerably more processing. Suddenly, the system that was once satisfactory is now inadequate. Connection to a network can further complicate the user's perception of system availability by taxing system resources to support network communications and data transfer, in addition to exposing the system to denial of service attacks in which adversaries deliberately consume system networking resources. Techniques to address the threat of denial of service attacks may entail the application of specially crafted confidentiality and integrity policies. Although availability can be addressed on a case-by-case basis, researchers have yet to develop a generally applicable model for system availability.

## Separation Policies

Separation systems enforce an internal policy that isolates processes from one another (Rushby & Randell, 1983). In general, absolute isolation is not particularly useful; therefore relaxation of absolute separation is usually required. This then leads to consideration of some combination of confidentiality and integrity policy enforcement. In the early years of this decade, hardware advances have allowed consideration of the practical construction of systems that employ a low-level separation kernel to create isolated blocks, where the term *block* is used in the mathematical sense. Through careful static configuration of the separation kernel, blocks represent equivalence classes. Within blocks, more granular mandatory policies may be enforced (Levin, Irvine, & Nguyen, 2004). If a set of common underlying processors supports the separation system, then issues such as availability and covert channels may emerge.

When absolute separation is required, but isolated Process A can perceive the presence of another presumably isolated process, B, then two problems arise. Process A may not have as many machine cycles with which to perform its task and thus may experience an availability problem. Second, through the manipulation of system-level resources, Process B may be able to signal to Process A in a manner not permitted by the overall separation policy. This creates a covert channel (Lampson, 1973; Levin & Clark, 2004).

## Least Privilege

The principle of least privilege (Saltzer & Schroeder, 1975) states that no entity within a system should be accorded privileges greater than those required to carry out its tasks. For example, the task of audit administrator does not require authorizations to manage user accounts or to configure new system devices, nor does a user who merely wishes to write a letter require the power to configure the operating system. To effectively apply the principle of least privilege within the context of an implementation, a policy must be articulated. Within a monolithic entity, the principle of least privilege can be used as a metric by which to structure the system based on information-hiding paradigms (Parnas, 1972). Among processes, the principle of least privilege can be realized by the application of integrity, and sometimes confidentiality, mechanisms. Among processes, the principle of least privilege can be implemented to protect the integrity of the operating system, libraries, and other reliable components from software of unknown provenance (Saltzer & Schroeder, 1975; Schroeder & Saltzer, 1972). This permits processes to be organized into a set of hierarchically ordered subjects, with the process integrity policy enforced by the underlying operating system. The domains having the least privilege depend on those of increasing privilege. Subjects in the former can be prevented from corrupting the data and software of the latter.

## Control Policies

The policies in the previous paragraphs describe the types of protection that may be required but do not address how those policies will be controlled. Control policies determine the ways in which policies can be modified, and fall into two categories: *discretionary* and *mandatory*. A discretionary control policy provides an interface whereby the access control policy can be modified at runtime by programs executing on behalf of users. A mandatory control policy may not be modified at runtime and instead is both global and persistent; a secret is secret no matter where the information is being accessed or what time of day it is. The difference between these control policies is of great importance. The fact that two kinds of control policies exist reflects fundamental differences in the way organizations want the policies themselves to be managed.

In organizations without computers, individuals are cognizant of all actions taken with respect to information being processed. These organizations may subdivide and compartmentalize their information. Certain individuals are vetted and authorized to handle specific, limited subsets of the information. Through the vetting and training process, each individual knows how to handle information of different sensitivities and is expected to exercise judgment so that sensitive information is not compromised.

When computers are used to augment and enhance productivity, a problem arises. Now, a program is executed on behalf of the individual. In general, software is written by third parties, be it commodity, open source, or custom. Although the software may properly perform its advertised functions, there is no guarantee that it does not contain additional, clandestine artifacts that attempt to modify, disregard, or circumvent the system security policy. Such malicious artifacts may take the form of Trojan horses or trapdoors, both of which are discussed further in the fifth section.

Figure 1 depicts a Trojan horse being executed by its victim, Alice. The access controls on her software do not permit Mallory to read her file; however, the access controls on Mallory's file permit Alice to write to his file. The Trojan horse, acting with Alice's permissions, is able to read her files and write their contents to Mallory's files in violation of Alice's intent to protect her information from access by Mallory. In a system with discretionary controls, the Trojan horse might also have used its control privileges to modify the access control list on Alice's information so that Mallory could read it.

If the intent of the policy is not correctly encoded into the underlying enforcement mechanisms, a Trojan horse can violate the policy. Another problem arises because in many systems, the policy can simply be modified, thus permitting the Trojan horse to carry out its malicious intent. When a system provides a general application interface

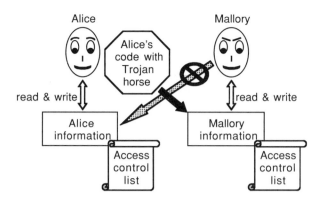

**Figure 1:** A Trojan horse executing in Alice's code is able to write to Mallory's information, thus circumventing Alice's intent to block Mallory's read access to her information.

that permits policy modification, the policy control mechanism is *discretionary*: users and programs can change the policy. This is useful when a requirement for dynamic policy modification exists and when the consequences of policy modification are insignificant. Thus, discretionary policies are appropriate in situations when a possible Trojan horse executing within an application will cause only minor, localized damage.

There are several ways that control over discretionary policies may be exercised (DoD, 1987). The most common form is *owner control*. Here, each object has an owner, a named user of the system, and that owner can change the access rights to the object, thus granting more or less access to various other users or collections of users called *groups*. *Centralized control* places an administrator in charge of granting and revoking access rights. Few systems take this approach, because the burden on the administrator may be too high. *Hierarchical control* systems organize the information objects in a tree-like structure, as in a typical file system, and provide diminishing control over access to objects as one moves from the root to the leaves. It could be useful in military or other highly structured, top-down organizations. Finally, *laissez-faire control* permits anyone to modify the policy on anything. Of the various approaches to discretionary control, owner control is the most common and is found in most variants of UNIX and Linux. Given sufficiently elaborate underlying control structures, an operating system can be configured to support any of these control policies.

The implementation of discretionary policies offers choices regarding access rights when objects are created. For example, an object might be created where all accesses were permitted until access by certain individuals is denied. Alternatively, objects could be initialized with all access denied and subsequent access to the object would be granted on a need-to-know basis. Lunt (1989) provides a detailed discussion of various approaches to discretionary access control.

Because of their fluidity, discretionary policies offer the opportunity to revoke the rights of subjects to objects. A problem associated with revocation is that although the right to an object may be revoked, the information itself may already have been accessed and copied. Another problem with revocation is that of its timing. If the permissions on an object are changed, should the system immediately locate and terminate access by subjects no longer authorized to access the object? One must find all, viz. the transitive closure, subjects with the revoked right that have active access. This would require examining all of the current accesses of all of the subjects, which, although feasible, could have a significant effect on system performance while the access control system conducts the search. Observers have noted that because the subject once had access to the object, it could have copied the information; hence access to the information that the object contained will not be prohibited. In addition, it might be considered somewhat impolite to cause an application to suddenly crash because access permissions were modified while the application was using the subsequently revoked object (especially because the application could have copied all of the information in the first place). As pointed out by Grossman (1995), immediate revocation may be particularly difficult to define and achieve in highly distributed systems.

Other dynamic changes in access rights can occur, for example, when the user represented by the process is dynamically changed as in the UNIX *setuid* permission mechanism. Code is stored in files and owned by individual system users. To execute new code, a system mechanism replaces the current executable of the process with a new one. Usually, the user identifier associated with the process remains the same; however, when the *setuid* permission is set, the process takes on the persona associated with the new executable. It would be possible to construct systems with this functionality that could grant access rights inappropriately. Checking for such behavior is not always possible. It has been proved that it is impossible to construct a mechanism that will determine whether an arbitrary system will leak information (Harrison, Ruzzo, & Ullman, 1976). Fortunately, there are systems constructed with nondiscretionary controls on the policy mechanism for which leakage of access rights does not occur.

Some systems support the notion of access permissions associated with various collections of job functions called roles. In a hospital, these might correspond to the functions of doctor, nurse, technician, administrator, and so forth. The benefits of access controls based on roles are realized in large organizations where administrators can assign users to roles and then change those roles as user responsibilities evolve. Many systems may be organized to support role-based access controls, a notion first introduced by Ferraiolo and Kuhn (1992). A survey of a large number of role-based access control models was conducted by Sandhu, Coyne, Feinstein, and Youman (1996).

Systems enforcing nondiscretionary, or mandatory, control policies do not provide a general interface for policy modification and are applied in cases when the policy is intended to be constant in both time and space. For example, if the secret formula to a popular cola drink is secret worldwide and at all times, it will be treated as such by both the company personnel and through the design and implementation of its IT systems.

A qualitative metric for determining when mandatory control policies are required can be found in the consequences of policy violation (Brinkley & Schell, 1995). If

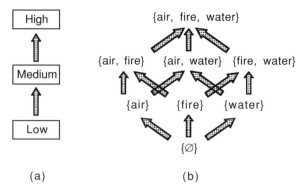

**Figure 2:** Lattice of access classes. A hierarchical ordering of classes is shown in (a). In (b), a set of noncomparable classes is shown. Arrows show the allowed direction of information flow.

grave harm would result and individuals would be fired or imprisoned for willfully violating the policy, then mandatory controls are probably appropriate.

In the context of mandatory policies, subjects and objects are allocated to equivalence classes that are partially ordered. Denning (1976) showed that a lattice provides a useful representation of the equivalence classes and their relationships with respect to the flow of information within a system enforcing a mandatory policy. Figure 2 shows both a hierarchical ordering of access classes and a set of classes created from noncomparable attributes: air, fire, and water. In the latter, any set of classes may receive information from a set of classes that is a subset of itself. The information flow policies depicted in the figure may be combined by taking their Cartesian product. The work of Denning also demonstrates that elaborate mandatory policies can be represented in a lattice through the introduction of additional equivalence classes so that a least upper bound and a greatest lower bound can be found for any pair of equivalence classes.

The Bell and LaPadula model provided a formal description of a mandatory confidentiality (secrecy) policy (Bell & LaPadula, 1973). Figure 3 illustrates the read and write accesses permitted to subjects when a mandatory confidentiality policy is enforced. Each subject may read

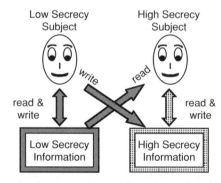

**Figure 3:** High confidentiality subjects have read access to low confidentiality information; at the same time confinement prevents the flow of high information to low.

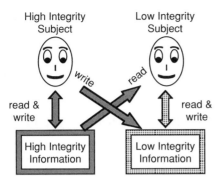

**Figure 4:** Confinement prevents the corruption of high integrity subjects with low integrity information; at the same time low integrity subjects benefit from high integrity information.

and write information at its own level. High secrecy subjects may read low secrecy information and low secrecy subjects may write high secrecy information, but low secrecy subjects may not read high secrecy information nor may high secrecy subjects write to low secrecy information. It is worth noting that although mandatory confidentiality policies generally permit low secrecy subjects to perform a blind write to high secrecy information, in practical implementations blind writes could result in chaos and are not generally permitted.

Figure 4 illustrates the read and write accesses permitted when a mandatory integrity policy is enforced, such as in the Biba model (Biba, 1977). Here, high integrity subjects may not be corrupted by low integrity information; at the same time low integrity information and subjects can be supplemented with high integrity information.

In the case of both confidentiality and integrity, the fact that the mandatory security levels are partially ordered makes comparison of access classes easy to implement.

It is worth noting that the Seaview model was the first to illustrate that a single set of equivalence classes could be used to enforce combined secrecy, integrity, and least privilege policies in a system with mandatory controls (Lunt et al., 1989). (Note that Seaview was a model for a database management system that allowed the enforcement of mandatory and discretionary policies. The formal name for the project was Secure Distributed Data Views.) The confidentiality policy model was similar to that formulated by Bell and LaPadula (1973). The integrity policy applied to access between processes, similar to that modeled by Biba (1977), whereas the least privilege policy, which was to be implemented using protection rings (DoD, 1994), applied to process-internal integrity (Shirley & Schell, 1981). The security levels were created by taking the Cartesian product of the partial orderings for the confidentiality and integrity policies.

The problem of characterizing security policies for the commercial sector where the integrity of information is often of equal or greater importance than its confidentiality was recognized in the early work of Lipner (1982), who described how the Biba model could be applied in commercial settings. Clark and Wilson (1987) described a more extensive commercial integrity model based on the

notion of transactions, which was shown to be feasible using existing technology by Shockley (1988). To describe conflict of interest regulations that arise in the business context, Brewer and Nash (1989) developed the Chinese Wall security model. Drawing on both confidentiality and integrity, active entities are not permitted to access information once a possible conflict of interest between two data sets has been established. For example, by accessing the protected information of a particular pharmaceutical company, access to the information of similar companies would be disallowed. A sanitization policy allows certain nonsensitive information to be released to the public.

## Supporting Policies

The policies discussed thus far relate to the access of subject to objects. In an operational system, supporting policies for user identification and authentication, as well as for audit, are required. The former allows a binding between the physical user external to the system and the subjects acting on the user's behalf within the system. First a user must identify himself to the system, then the user must demonstrate to the system that he is who he claims to be by presenting something that only comes from him. This might involve, for example, a password, a token, a biometric factor, or some combination of these.

Enforcement of discretionary policies generally takes the form of establishing rights to a particular object based on a name that is internally bound to each subject. For example, in many systems a user identifier is bound to the process, which also has a unique process identifier. Thus several processes may be acting on behalf of a particular user ID. The binding between the user's name and the user identifier is often found in the password file, which contains for each user a unique user name and user identifier.

For systems enforcing mandatory controls, the attribute associated with the subject will be its sensitivity level (equivalence class). This usually takes the form of a label. In a system enforcing mandatory policies, the password file might contain some maximum sensitivity level at which the user can log in. For example, a user cleared to TOP SECRET could select any one of the following levels for her current session: TOP SECRET, SECRET, or UNCLASSIFIED. Suppose a user logs on at SECRET, then, when a subject is instantiated on behalf of the user, one of its attributes will be the user's current session level, for example, SECRET.

Since the attributes bound to subjects acting on behalf of users are the basis for access control decisions, it should be clear that having a well-defined identification and authentication policy is required. For example, a system might require that each user have an individual password and be associated with a user group, that is, a set of common users such as *students* or *faculty*. Changes to groups might require additional passwords. Alternatively, a set of users might be associated with a particular activity or role for which they might authenticate. In a public library, it might be possible for anyone to access the system as a "library subscriber" and the purpose of the identification and authentication mechanism would be for accounting purposes rather than to track the individual reading habits of the population.

Audit provides a record of security-relevant events and can be used as a deterrent to such user malfeasance as white-collar crime. If bound to a rule-checking mechanism, audit may provide alerts of impending security violations and may evolve into elaborate intrusion detection systems. Policies must be established to determine what should be audited. For example, one might choose to audit all accesses to a particular file, but to no others; all activity on the system could be audited; the activities of a particular suspicious user might be recorded; the use of a particular set of system calls could be audited; and so forth. The choices regarding audit policy are extremely broad. Two important points should be noted, however. First, it is generally a good idea to audit the activities of the security administrator so that a record of security critical activities can be maintained. Second, policy makers should be aware that a voluminous audit record that is not accompanied by audit reduction tools is not likely to be particularly useful

In systems enforcing nondiscretionary policies, the management of labels and the labeling of information being transferred into and out of the system will be reflected in supporting policies. For example, there may be a requirement that all printed documents contain markings in their headers and footers indicating whether the document is "company proprietary" or "public."

System support is also required for the enforcement of administrative policies. These include user account management and security configuration, including the configuration of mandatory equivalence classes.

## Object Reuse

As noted previously, objects are the information containers in systems. They are constructed using system resources, usually primary and secondary memory, but devices must also be considered. When objects are deleted, the memory from which they were constructed is returned to a pool. To prevent inadvertent access to information previously stored in now defunct objects, an object reuse policy is applied to memory resources. Such policies usually stipulate that all information must be removed from resources prior to their reuse. The system implementation determines whether the information is purged immediately after object deletion or prior to its allocation to a new object.

With this overview of policies, it is now possible to describe the various techniques and mechanisms that may be used to provide for their enforcement.

## Policy Languages

Considerable work has been conducted in the area of defining languages for the expression of security policies. Only a few are presented here. An early example was KeyNote (Blaze, Feigenbaum, Ioannidis, & Keromytis, 1999). In highly networked organizations, databases accessible via Web interfaces provide a useful way to organize large quantities of information. Policies may be captured in the use of extensible markup language (XML) frameworks. Two emerging standards are SAML (Oasis, 2004) and XACML (Oasis, 2003). The former supports the exchange of security-relevant information between organizations, whereas the latter allows organizational security policies and access decisions to be expressed. A challenge for each of these standards is to create system architectures that provide a high assurance binding between security attributes and the information to be protected.

# POLICY ENFORCEMENT MECHANISMS

The mechanisms used to enforce primary confidentiality and integrity policies depend on the control policies. Mechanisms for the enforcement of discretionary and nondiscretionary policies are discussed.

## Mechanisms for Discretionary Policy Enforcement

Discretionary policies may be enforced in two ways: access control lists and capabilities.

### Access Control Lists

Access control lists (ACLs) are lists of permissions associated with each object such as a file, directory, or device. Each ACL entry consists of the name representing an entity, such as an individual user or group, and the rights accorded to that entity. Because access control lists for a large number of similar users (for example, all of the students enrolled in a particular class) may be burdensome, it is often convenient to organize users into groups so that access rights can be granted to a number of users simultaneously. The largest group is, naturally, everyone, also known as "public" on many systems.

The types of permissions contained in an ACL may include more than merely read, write, and execute. It is possible to list the users or groups that have control access to the object, that is, who can grant or deny permission for other access rights. Furthermore, an additional level of permission can be provided through control-of-control-access, an access right that permits administration of control accesses. Access modes may be combined to create specialized access modes. For example, *append* access can be created with a combination of read and write access and restricts all writing to the end of the target object. Sometimes, it may be necessary to explicitly deny access to a particular user or group. Thus, ACLs can be enlarged to support negative access rights. Using negative access rights, it is possible to deny an individual access to an object even though he is a member of a group that possesses that access right. These several levels of access rights along with their various combinations can be used to create a highly sophisticated system.

Two implementation considerations are of particular interest for ACL-based systems. First, the initial value of each object's ACL must be determined. It is possible to provide a template for an initial default ACL. This may be based on a template associated with the user or that is part of the parent directory. As noted earlier, Lunt (1989) provided an analysis of the defaults possible in systems with discretionary controls: no access (i.e., minimized access) or complete access. Where the principle of least privilege is to be observed, a limited or no access default would be appropriate.

The second implementation consideration is associated with the precedence of ACL entry interpretation. For example, suppose that there are conflicts between explicit user negative and positive permissions and those associated with one or more groups of which the user is a member. An organization may decide that negative ACLs take precedence, followed by positive user, group, and public permissions. This means that if an access right is explicitly denied, then the user will not be granted access despite the existence of positive access rights in other ACL entries.

The primary benefit of ACLs is that all permissions associated with a particular object are localized and can be easily managed. Revocation of access is achieved simply by changing the ACL. To "solve" the revocation problem described previously, implementations choose to have the revocation take effect on the next attempt to gain access to the object.

### Capabilities

An alternative implementation approach is *capabilities*. In a capability-based system, the access rights to objects are bound to the subjects executing on behalf of users, rather than the objects. At the time of login, an initial set of capabilities is bound to a subject. As execution progresses, additional capabilities may be gained by subjects. Once a subject possesses a capability for a particular object, that object may be accessed with the rights associated with the capability; all the subject needs to do is present the capability.

For capability-based systems, revocation presents challenges. This is because a capability-based system distributes the access rights to each object among many subjects. If subjects are able to copy and store capabilities, the revocation problem is further exacerbated. There is no central location that can be inspected to determine which subjects have potential access to a particular object. Instead, the capability list for each subject must be inspected. If one decided to revoke access to an object, potentially every capability list in the system would require inspection to ensure that the revocation was complete.

The implementation of highly granular capability mechanisms in operating systems has been attempted in several systems; one of the most notable was the CAP system (Wilkes & Needham, 1980). Although they can be implemented, the systems are notoriously complex and their lack of a conceptually simple policy enforcement mechanism caused this approach to be abandoned.

## Mechanisms for Enforcement of Nondiscretionary (Mandatory) Policies

As discussed previously, nondiscretionary policies provide no run-time interface for policy modification. Typical access control lists are unsuitable for the enforcement of mandatory policies. This is largely due to the enormous complexity of the management that would be required to ensure that all information and active entities have the proper security attributes and that those attributes cannot be modified via a run-time interface.

Two techniques are in common use for the enforcement of nondiscretionary policies. The first is physical and the second is logical. To discuss these policies, we introduce the notion of *sensitivity levels*. These are identifiers for equivalence classes of objects defined by the secrecy and integrity attributes associated with that set of objects. The choice of equivalence classes is up to the organization. For a private enterprise, the sensitivity levels might be PROPRIETARY, COMPANY CONFIDENTIAL, and PUBLIC, while a military organization might choose SECRET, CONFIDENTIAL, and UNCLASSIFIED.

To enforce policy using physical mechanisms, one must construct a separate network for each sensitivity level. All users must be authorized for the sensitivity level of the network and all information created and managed in that network must be considered to be at the network's sensitivity level. Such networks are described as being *single level*. The advantages of single-level systems or networks include the ability to identify and manage the access to information in a manner that is easy to understand. An isolated network may be maintained in a special facility and only users authorized to use that network may be granted access to the premises. The construction and maintenance of isolated networks and the facilities to house them can be costly, but when information is extremely critical the protection afforded by an isolated network may outweigh the cost.

There are serious disadvantages to physical isolation. Users must either move from room to room to access different networks, or they may have multiple systems on the desktop. The latter can lead to clutter and confusion when a user must access many networks in the course of daily activities. The user could use a KVM (keyboard, video, mouse) switch to minimize consumption of desktop space; however, multiple processors are still required and the possible advantage of seeing information at different sensitivity levels simultaneously is lost.

If nonsensitive information can be moved to networks of higher sensitivity, but without sensitivity labels associated with the information, it is impossible for users to distinguish nonsensitive information from that which is sensitive. To share the nonsensitive information with individuals having lesser authorizations, users must go back to the nonsensitive system. Alternatively, if a user wishes to transmit nonsensitive information directly from the more sensitive enclave, complex procedures are required to address the threat of unauthorized information flow resulting from the use of steganography (Kurak & McHugh, 1992) and other techniques for clandestine information hiding.

Logical isolation depends on an underlying mechanism that enforces the security policy. Because mandatory policies can always be characterized by comparisons between equivalence classes, it is possible to construct a relatively simple mechanism to determine whether a particular subject may have access to a given object. The Bell and LaPadula and Biba models permit read and write access by subjects at the same sensitivity level as the object; simultaneously, subjects are not permitted to read information of greater confidentiality, write to information of lesser confidentiality, write to objects of higher integrity, or read from objects of lesser integrity. Systems that enforce logical isolation can permit users to have a coherent view of all information at or below their sensitivity level. They also allow users to log into the system at any sensitivity level below their maximum authorization. Thus, from a single system, an authorized user is able to both access company proprietary information when logged in at "proprietary" and the Internet when logged in at the "public" sensitivity level.

# CRITICALITY OF CORRECT POLICY ENFORCEMENT

Failures in security policy enforcement may result from technical flaws in information systems or the failure of people to use the system as intended. Although the latter is of considerable concern and must be addressed through appropriate information security training and awareness programs, the former is of interest here.

A large number of failures in policy enforcement result from the presence of unspecified functionality in systems. Broadly defined, unspecified functionality is the set of system flaws and unintended artifacts that permit an adversary ultimately to bypass the policy enforcement mechanism of a system. Thus, failures in design and implementation, ranging from inadequate bounds checking of interface parameters to pathological interactions between synchronizing processes, can be exploited by adversaries intent on gaining system privileges for the purpose of avoiding the constraints of the protection mechanism. Such flaws were identified by Anderson (1972) and are still found in current systems (Karger & Schell, 2002). The Common Vulnerabilities and Exposures (MITRE, 2004) Web site lists more than 3000 unique entries. A complete enumeration is not possible here; however, a few of the major categories derived from Linde (1975) and Anderson (1972) are provided in Table 1.

A more insidious form of unspecified functionality occurs when a system is subverted (Anderson, Irvine, & Schell, 2004; Myers, 1980). In this case, a member of the system's development team intentionally adds clandestine functionality that permits the adversary to bypass system security mechanisms. The term subversion is generally applied to the operating system or kernel, whereas other

forms of malicious software, for example, Trojan horses, function in the context of applications. This permits several distinct characteristics of each to be identified. Trojan horses execute in the context of applications, thus they are constrained by the permissions and privileges of the user who is executing them. They can bypass the intended policy of the user but cannot bypass the policy enforcement mechanisms altogether. Trojan horses must be activated by the user. This gives the adversary less control over their execution.

In contrast, low-level subversion mechanisms execute within the operating system with full privileges and are unconstrained by policy enforcement mechanisms. They usually contain triggers for activation and deactivation, thus affording the adversary control over their execution as shown in Table 2.

It is useful to note that, generally, viruses execute in the context of applications, whereas other forms of malicious code can be placed either within applications or in the underlying system. In many cases, malicious code may be introduced into systems in the form of downloadable executables or scripts, updates, and patches. Thus, code of unknown provenance should be confined in a manner such that it does not result in pervasive damage.

## Assurance

As is the case with security, assurance is a term that is often misused. For example, some state that "software assurance" will improve the "security" of systems. Both of these terms are rather meaningless without context. For software assurance, some might say that a system possesses this quality if it functions as specified and if various tests indicate that the software behaves as expected over a set of inputs, but this definition assumes that there is no malicious intent involved in the construction of the system. If, on the other hand, one assumes a malicious adversary, then assurance means correct policy enforcement in the face of a sophisticated set of attacks specifically intended to misuse system interfaces or insert artifices into the system itself.

**Table 1** Examples of Errors Resulting in Security Flaws

| General error category | Example |
|---|---|
| System design errors | Absence of least privilege |
| | Inappropriate mechanism for shared objects |
| | Poor choice of data types |
| Design errors | Error recovery results in exploitable side effects |
| | System modifications that deviate original intent of security mechanisms |
| Implementation errors | Buffers sizes are not checked, resulting in "buffer overflow" |
| | Failure to initialize variables |
| | Absent parameters are erroneously assumed |
| User interface errors | Gratuitous active execution |
| | Passwords too short |
| | Default access control lists are too permissive |
| Configuration errors | Insecure defaults render the system vulnerable |
| | Critical resources remain unprotected because of bad configuration choices |

**Table 2** Comparison of Trojan Horse and System Subversion

| Trojan horse | System subversion |
|---|---|
| Requires activation and use by a victim user; the adversary cannot choose the time of activation. | No user is required. Activation and deactivation may be triggered remotely by the adversary. |
| Constrained by security controls imposed by the system on the victim. | Bypasses security controls. |
| Executes as an application. | Often executes within the operating system and, thus, has complete system privileges. |

For a system to have assurance of security, the security policy must be enforced at all times and the security mechanisms must be resistant to subversion and tamper. Given a particular security policy, an organization may seek more or less assurance that the policy is correctly enforced. For example, greater assurance might be required to show that only authorized individuals have access to trade secrets, whereas less assurance might be required for the protection of the agenda for the next staff meeting. As subsequent sections reveal, assurance of correct policy enforcement in the face of a malicious adversary is not easily achieved. The pressures of product development can lead to shortcuts that reduce assurance: a problem encountered in many security systems is that of vendor claims of correct policy enforcement, when these systems are, in fact, quite vulnerable to attack. Sometimes a vendor will claim to have a "secret" technique that makes a system secure (these claims seem to be most prevalent in the area of cryptography and key management), but close inspection by knowledgeable reviewers usually reveals serious flaws (Anderson, 1972; Karger & Schell, 1974). It is generally accepted that an objective third party must provide an independent assessment of system assurance. This is similar to the ratings provided by independent consumer organizations for a wide variety of products. The current framework for third-party evaluation of system assurance is that of the Common Criteria (ISO/IEC, 2004).

Established through an international treaty, the Common Criteria support the creation of high-level requirements documents called *protection profiles* for various classes of security products (NIST, 2004). Each protection profile includes both functional and assurance requirements, where the latter achieves one of seven levels of confidence through requirements imposed on the system lifecycle processes. For specific systems, developers can create a *security target*, which in addition to all of the requirements of the protection profile, includes more detailed system-specific requirements. Through a process of analysis and testing, product team evaluators use the protection profile and security target to establish whether the product meets both the functional and assurance security requirements. A second round of testing and analysis by independent evaluators validates the team's results. Completion of the process results in an official evaluated product.

A secure system should exhibit all of the characteristics of a classic reference monitor (Anderson, 1972): resistant to tamper, always invoked, and understandable. Threat analysis reveals that there are two broad classes of threats

to building a system that aspires to the objectives of the reference monitor concept. There are both developmental threats and operational threats to the system (Irvine et al., 2002). Developmental threats include the introduction of flaws into the system through mistakes in design and implementation and through deliberate system subversion. The former introduces exploitable flaws, whereas the latter introduces trapdoors. Hence, the system must be constructed using a methodology that will counter developmental threats, and it must be designed and implemented so that operational threats are mitigated.

Operational threats occur when the system is in use. Adversaries can include malicious insiders as well as external activities. The mechanisms that have been designed into the system are intended to counter operational threats; however, system security also depends on adequate user and administrator training, as well as good configuration management and system maintenance. In short, a well-constructed security system is of limited value if not used properly.

## CONSIDERATIONS FOR THE CONSTRUCTION OF SECURE SYSTEMS

Two challenges confront the developer who wishes to construct a secure system. The first is the problem of policy dependencies. Suppose that the elements of the system intended to enforce mandatory policy are built using constructs exported by mechanisms enforcing discretionary policy. We must ask: what sort of assurance is possible if a mandatory policy enforcement mechanism is constructed as a layer that depends on a discretionary policy enforcement mechanism? The discretionary mechanism will export the storage resources used by the mandatory layer to create its policy enforcement mechanism. Access to these storage resources is mediated by the discretionary mechanism, which, by definition, has a run-time interface that allows its policy to be modified. Thus, in this architecture the mandatory mechanism is subject to run-time modification: global and persistent policy enforcement cannot be ensured.

The second challenge is associated with system complexity. Assurance depends on the ability for evaluators, such as those using the Common Criteria (ISO/IEC, 2004) framework, to understand the system. It must be possible to state with some level of confidence that no malicious, unspecified functionality has been added to the system. As systems become more complex, they become less understandable. Although size is a factor when considering complexity, it is not the only consideration. The interactions between subsystems can be subtle and difficult to completely describe. An adversary may attempt to subvert a system by using internal synchronization, interrupt handling, and other mechanisms to compose a trapdoor or other clandestine artifice. Understandability of the system is essential. A metric for high assurance is that all components of the protection mechanism are both necessary and sufficient to enforce the security. No additional functionality, whether malicious or merely gratuitous, is included in such a system.

The problems of composition and complexity present even greater challenges for distributed systems. Composed systems may enforce the same policy with differing levels of assurance. When this is the case, the integrity and assurance of the overall system are forced to the greatest lower bound of the composed assurance levels (Irvine & Levin, 2002). Even when systems have the same level of assurance, sometimes when they are networked together the risk of unintended disclosure can be significantly increased. The cascade problem (Horton et al., 1993) represents a good example of this composition risk.

To create a distributed system, it is necessary to understand the various security policies to be enforced and to allocate those policies to components in a manner such that dependencies among the networked components are reasonable and a coherent distributed enforcement mechanism results. Unless an extensible distributed security architecture is described, the effect of the addition of new components usually requires complete reanalysis of the distributed system.

## Essential Elements for System Protection

Several key elements for the creation of an effective protection mechanism were identified by Saltzer and Schroeder (1975). These include a memory management mechanism that allows the memory resources used by applications to be distinguished from those of the underlying system. Memory management must be able to prevent applications from arbitrarily accessing system functions and databases. Unauthorized attempts to access these resources should result in a fault that can be handled by the underlying resource management mechanism. To permit applications to request services of the operating system, controlled entry points must be created. Not only must these entry points ensure the proper flow of control to the correct underlying function, but they should also validate all arguments so that misbehaving applications are unable to manipulate the called functions in unanticipated ways. The system should have at least two modes of operation: privileged and unprivileged. Hardware constructs are used by the operating system to set the mode. One or more protection bits can provide this service. The instructions for the management of the processor mode are restricted to the privileged mode. Instructions needed for primitive resource management must be privileged as well. Finally, it must be possible for the system to create an unambiguous binding between the user and processes that will execute on the user's behalf. A *trusted path* is used to both authenticate the system to the user and the

user to the system. It is constructed in such a way that both entities have confidence that neither interface is being spoofed.

## Constructive Security

Those building secure systems must be paranoid: someone intends to subvert the system and it may be a member of the core design team or someone else who has access to the system at some point during its lifecycle. Typical process-related and testing techniques described in software engineering are inadequate because they assume a benign development environment.

Security requirements engineering results in a description of the system to be built. As a start, it is important to understand that the system will be subject to both developmental and operational threats (Irvine et al., 2002). Operationally, the system must be demonstrated to be resistant to tamper and bypass of security mechanisms. Developmentally, one must construct the system through a process that demonstrates both the absence of malicious code and that the mechanisms to enforce policy are complete and correct. Construction of a secure system involves careful attention not only to the security architecture and its implementation, but also to lifecycle management issues. To avoid construction of what might be deemed a "secure brick," system designers must account for the various services it will provide and performance obligations the system will meet.

Although the formality of the Common Criteria (ISO/IEC, 2004) may not be needed for ad hoc systems, its systematic presentation of issues related to system assurance can be quite helpful in creating a set of requirements system developers must address. Consider, for example, the principle sections of a typical protection profile. After providing a set of definitions and conventions, a protection profile starts with a high-level description of the system to be constructed. Here, the developer is able to state whether a full, general-purpose operating system will be built or some less all-encompassing special purpose component. This leads to a presentation of the threats to the system through out its entire lifetime and the security policies it is expected to enforce. Based on threats, policies, and various usage assumptions, it is possible to develop a set of security objectives that both counter the threats and address the policies and assumptions. The objectives drive both the functional and assurance requirements for the system. Security functional requirements might include audit, identification and authentication, access control, enforcement of flow control in support of mandatory policies, administrative interfaces, and other functions. It is interesting to note at this point that not all of the functional requirements will map to the formal security policy model, which is called for in the assurance requirements of high assurance systems.

Assurance requirements dictate how the system will be constructed and may influence the way various mechanisms support functional requirements. Because system security must be addressed for the entire system lifecycle, assurance includes many activities beyond design and coding. It is necessary to ensure that the tools used to construct the system are protected, so that they do not become vectors for the insertion of malicious software by a highly skilled adversary (Karger & Schell, 1974). Also, it is necessary to ensure that the system is not modified en route to its end users and that unscrupulous installers or maintenance personnel do not corrupt the system. Before starting to construct the system, the development team must put into place all of the necessary mechanisms and procedures to ensure that the system is built in a manner that both identifies and eliminates flaws and prevents the inclusion of malicious functionality (Irvine et al., 2004). This high assurance development framework will include standards for system specification and design, review processes, configuration management, distribution procedures, user and administrator documentation, and maintenance and flaw remediation procedures. Separation of duty and multiperson oversight are an integral part of the effort.

## Secure System Development

As described in previous sections, dependencies are of great importance in designing a secure system. Consider the system to be organized as a set of hierarchical layers. Then, it must be organized so that each layer of the system depends only on layers that are of equal or higher assurance and that enforce equivalent or stronger policies. The raw resources of the hardware layer can be organized by low-level system software to export virtualized resources that are subject to a set of low-level policies. Primitives provided by the system might include memory, interrupt handling, and low-level scheduling, as well as synchronization. In a minimized system enforcing a separation policy, these may be the abstract data types exported at the system interface. For more traditional operating system kernels, additional operating system layers may be constructed that contain mechanisms to enforce the intended mandatory policies. The number and extent of these layers depend on whether the mandatory policy is void or richly populated, but it is important to recall that the dependencies must be such that the mandatory policy enforcement mechanisms do not depend on discretionary, viz. modifiable, policy components. It is important to note that a minimized kernel does not usually present a typical user-friendly application programming interface. A set of code libraries is usually superimposed on the operating system to hide the primitives described previously from typical programmers and users.

Once the system architecture has been delineated and policy has been allocated to its various layers, it is possible to focus on the construction of each layer. Here, the techniques used to develop a high assurance, low-level layer are sketched.

Because the objective in constructing the lowest layers of the system is to develop a coherent mechanism for the enforcement of the system's most critical policy, a combination of hardware and software is used to create the abstract machine that will be exported at this interface. Once the overall objectives of the system have been described, a formal security policy model is developed. The model provides a proof that if the system starts in a secure state then all operations will maintain that secure state. The formal model serves two important purposes:

first, it demonstrates that the intended policy is logically self-consistent and not flawed, and second, it provides a mathematical description of the system to which the implementation can be mapped. The objective of this mapping is to demonstrate that everything in the implementation is both necessary and sufficient for the enforcement of the policy and that no unspecified functionality, for example, possible subversion, is present.

The formal model is highly abstract, so two other documents are produced. One is a formal description of the system interface; the other is a high-level system interface description. Both describe the system interface in terms of inputs, outputs, effects, and exceptions. For the former, a formal proof is generated showing that the formal description maps to the formal security policy model. Thus, by transitivity, a proof that the formal interface also describes a system that maintains secure state is achieved. The latter is used as the starting point for the concrete implementation of the system.

Rigorous security engineering techniques employing the concepts of layering, modularity, and data hiding are used during development to ensure that the system has a coherent loop-free design and provides abstractions so that it is understandable. Within the system itself, the principle of least privilege can be applied as part of the engineering process. Ultimately, both the formal and informal efforts provide a mapping of the implementation to the formal security policy model as well as evidence that the system is correct and complete.

Because information flow is a concern, all of the processes described previously contribute to the ability of the developers to conduct a covert channel analysis of the system. Covert channels result from the manipulation of system interfaces in ways that cause unintended information flow and result from incomplete resource virtualization by the underlying protection mechanism. This means that some abstract data type presented at the system interface involves operating system constructs that can be manipulated to allow signaling to take place in violation of the system security policy. Covert channels fall into two classes: timing channels and storage channels. An effective technique for covert channel analysis is the shared-resource matrix method (Kemmerer, 1982). Using this technique, the effects of each system call on operating system–level data structures are analyzed and their visibility, perhaps through exceptions or timing delays, to other processes is identified. When the effects could result in unintended transmission of information, either a system flaw or a covert channel is present.

Although testing cannot prove that a system is secure, it is important to include testing in the development process. Traditional testing demonstrates that each function and module performs as specified. At the system level, traditional testing is supplemented by penetration testing. Here, the tester behaves as an adversary and attempts to abuse the system interfaces in an unexpected manner. A useful approach to penetration testing is the Flaw Hypothesis Methodology (Linde, 1975). This testing technique organizes testing in a way that allows the testing team to set goals by working with the customer. The team studies the target system and conducts extensive nonjudgmental brainstorming to hypothesize system flaws. Then, the flaws are prioritized according to a preestablished guideline. Desk checking or live testing allows the team to determine the feasibility of flaw exploitation. The process is iterative and encourages the generalization of flaws into broad categories from which additional flaws may be hypothesized. It is important to emphasize that this form of testing augments the careful development process described previously. No testing is exhaustive, so it cannot demonstrate the absence of flaws or subversion but merely lessen the likelihood of obvious flaws.

Once the system is built, its administrators and users must be provided with the documentation and training necessary to use it securely. When a system that contains useful security mechanisms is configured and used improperly, a false sense of security may result that may have consequences far worse than when management believed security was inadequate.

The processes sketched here must be thoroughly documented so that the system can be assessed with respect to its security requirements. Third-party evaluation provides a way for those who acquire the system to understand whether the system does, in fact, meet its security objectives. To date, no viable alternative to either the reference monitor concept or the need for third-party evaluation has been proposed. Future research may result in more streamlined approaches to secure system construction and assessment.

## Future Challenges

Many organizations enforce mandatory policies; however, operationally, they also require mechanisms where exceptions to these policies can be implemented. For example, consider a system that encrypts information before transmitting it on the network. The process of encryption can transform bits that represent proprietary sensitive information into bits that represent no information and, thus, can be seen by anyone (Shannon, 1949). In essence, encryption is *downgrading* the information, viz. changing its sensitivity level from high to low. Modern systems may require additional downgrading functions that move certain information from high networks or repositories to low ones. Sometimes the information is scanned for certain sensitive words that are then expunged from the data. This is called *sanitization*. All of these activities must be conducted using systems for which there is a very high confidence that only the correct actions will be taken. A danger in systems that do not involve human review is that of *steganography* (Kurak & McHugh, 1992). Steganography, the art of hidden writing, involves a secret encoded by malicious code in seemingly innocuous data so that it is not visible to the casual observer.

The components within a system that perform encryption, downgrading, and other operations that span mandatory sensitivity levels must be trusted to perform their tasks and nothing more—they must not contain unspecified functionality, for example, steganography, that would violate the intent of the system owners. The construction of *trusted systems* that, for most processes, enforce mandatory policies using underlying operating system controls and at the same time permit certain *trusted* applications to be subject to relaxed mandatory

constraints represents one of the great challenges in security modeling and engineering.

## CONCLUSION

Security policies are essential for computer and network security. Without a policy, security mechanisms are merely vacuous ad hoc functions that are combined to "do something," but what they might achieve, if anything, cannot be determined. At the management level, users must determine information assets that must be protected and must understand whether the authorizations for access to those assets are static or dynamic. This permits mandatory, discretionary, and supporting policies to be differentiated.

The nature of the policy will determine the mechanisms to be used for its enforcement. How those mechanisms are constructed addresses both developmental and operational threats. Assurance is derived from the rigorous security engineering process applied to its development and to the controls maintained over the system throughout its entire lifecycle. Independent assessment provides confidence that claims made regarding the correctness and completeness of the security policy enforcement mechanisms are valid.

## GLOSSARY

**Assurance** Basis for confidence that a system meets its security requirements. Increasing levels of assurance provide increasing confidence of the absence of flaws and malicious artifices.

**Covert Channel** A means to pass information in violation of the mandatory policy of a system through the manipulation of a system-internal object for which no explicit system interfaces are presented.

**Discretionary Security Policy** A security policy that may be modified through a functional interface presented at the run-time system interface.

**Least Privilege** The notion that an active system entity should operate with the privileges necessary to complete its job but no more.

**Nondiscretionary (Mandatory) Policy** A policy that is global and persistent, and that cannot be modified via run-time interfaces presented to applications.

**Object** A passive entity in a system that contains information.

**Security Policy** Rules, laws, and similar constraints used by an organization to define how its information is managed and disseminated.

**Subject** An active entity in a system that makes references to objects.

**Supporting Policy** Nonaccess control policies that must be adhered to in order to protect the information of an organization, including, but not limited to, audit, identification and authentication, regrading, and sanitization.

## CROSS REFERENCES

See *Access Control: Principles and Solutions; Information Assurance; Security Policy Guidelines.*

# REFERENCES

Anderson, E. A., Irvine, C. E., & Schell, R. R. (2004). Subversion as a threat in information warfare. *Journal of Information Warfare, 3*(2), 52–65.

Anderson, J. P. (1972). *Computer security technology planning study* (Tech. Rep. ESD-TR-73-51, Vols. 1 and 2, NTIS Document No. AD758206). Hanscom, MA: Hanscom Air Force Base, Air Force Electronic Systems Division.

Bell, D. E., & LaPadula, L. (1973) *Secure computer systems: Mathematical foundations and model* (Tech. Rep. No. M74-244). Bedford, MA: MITRE Corp.

Biba, K. J. (1977). *Integrity considerations for secure computer systems* (Tech. Rep. No. ESD-TR-76-372). Bedford, MA: MITRE Corp.

Blaze, M., Feigenbaum, J., Ioannidis, J., & Keromytis, A. D. (1999, September). *The KeyNote trust management system version 2* (RFC 2704). Internet Engineering Task Force. Retrieved November, 15 2002, from http://www.apps.ietf.org/rfc/rfc2704.html

Brewer, D. F. C., & Nash, M. J. (1989). The Chinese wall security policy. In *Proceedings of the 1989 IEEE Symposium on Security and Privacy* (pp. 219–230). Los Alamitos, CA: IEEE Computer Society Press.

Brinkley, D. L., & Schell, R. R. (1995). Concepts and terminology for computer security. In M. Abrams, S. Jajodia, & H. Podell (Eds.), *Information security: An integrated collection of essays* (pp. 40–97). Los Alamitos, CA: IEEE Computer Society Press.

Clark, D., & Wilson, D. (1987). A comparison of commercial and military security policies. In *Proceedings of the 1987 IEEE Symposium on Security and Privacy* (pp. 184–194). Los Alamitos, CA: IEEE Computer Society Press.

Denning, D. E. (1976). A lattice model of secure information flow. *Communications of the ACM, 19*(5), 236–243.

Department of Defense. (1987). *A guide to understanding discretionary access control in trusted systems.* Fort George Meade, MD: National Computer Security Center.

Department of Defense. (1994). *Final evaluation report of Gemini Computers.* Incorporated Gemini Trusted Network Processor, version 1.01. Fort George Meade, MD: National Computer Security Center.

Ferraiolo, D. F., & Kuhn, D. R. (1992). Role-based access control. In *Proceedings of the 15th national computer security conference* (pp. 554–563). Fort George Meade, MD: National Security Agency.

Grossman, G. (1995). Immediacy in distributed trusted systems. In *Proceedings of the eleventh annual computer security applications conference* (pp. 75–79). Los Alamitos, CA: IEEE Computer Society Press.

Harrison, M., Ruzzo, W., & Ullman, J. (1976). Protection in operating systems. *Communications of the ACM, 19*(8), 461–471.

Hennessy, J. L., & Patterson, D. A. (1996). *Computer architecture: A quantitative approach.* San Francisco, CA: Morgan Kaufmann.

Horton, J. D., Harland, R., Ashby, E., Cooper, R. H., Hyslop, W. F., Nickerson, B. G., Stewart, W. M., & Ward, O. K. (1993). The cascade vulnerability problem. In *Proceedings of the IEEE Symposium on Research in Security and Privacy* (pp. 110–116). Los Alamitos, CA: IEEE Computer Society Press.

Irvine, C. E., & Levin, T. (2002). A cautionary note regarding the data integrity capacity of certain secure systems. In M. Gertz, E. Guldentops, & L. Strous (Eds.), *Integrity, internal control and security in information systems* (pp. 3–25). Norwell, MA: Kluwer Academic.

Irvine, C. E., Levin, T., Wilson, J. D., Shifflett, D., & Pereira, B. (2002). An approach to security requirements engineering for a high assurance system. *Requirements Engineering, 7*(4), 192–208.

Irvine, C. E., Levin, T. E., Nguyen, T. D., & Dinolt, G. W. (2004). The trusted computing exemplar project. In *Proceedings of the 2004 IEEE systems, man and cybernetics information assurance workshop* (pp. 109–115). West Point, NY, & Los Alamitos, CA: IEEE Computer Society Press.

ISO/IEC. (2004, January). *15408—Common criteria for information technology security evaluation* (Rep. No. CCIMB-2004-01-001, Ver. 2.2, Rev. 256). Geneva, Switzerland: International Organization for Standardisation.

Karger, P. A., & Schell, R. R. (1974). *Multics security evaluation: Vulnerability analysis.* Bedford, MA: Hanscom Air Force Base, Information Systems Technology Application Office Deputy for Command and Management Systems Electronic Systems Division (AFSC).

Karger, P. A., & Schell, R. R. (2002). Thirty years later: The lessons from the Multics security evaluation. In *Proceedings of the annual computer security application conference* (pp. 119–126). Los Alamitos, CA: IEEE Computer Society Press.

Kemmerer, R. (1982). A practical approach to identifying storage and timing channels. In *Proceedings of the IEEE Symposium on Security and Privacy* (pp. 66–73). Los Alamitos, CA: IEEE Computer Society Press.

Kurak, C., & McHugh, J. (1992). A cautionary note on image downgrading. In *Proceedings of the eighth annual computer security applications conference* (pp. 153–59). Los Alamitos, CA: IEEE Computer Society Press.

Lampson, B. W. (1971). Protection. In *Fifth Princeton conference on information sciences and systems* (pp. 437–443). Reprinted in *ACM SIGOPS Operating Systems Review, 8*(1),18–24.

Lampson, B. W. (1973). A note on the confinement problem. *Communications of the ACM, 16*(10), 613–615.

Levin, T., & Clark, P. C. (2004). A note regarding covert channels. In *Proceedings of the sixth workshop on computer security education* (pp. 11–15). Monterey, CA: Naval Postgraduate School.

Levin, T. E., Irvine, C. E., & Nguyen, T. D. (2004). *A least privilege model for static separation kernels* (Tech. Rep. NPS-CS-05-003). Monterey, CA: Naval Postgraduate School.

Linde, R. R. (1975). Operating system penetration. In *Proceedings of the national computer conference* (pp. 36–368). Montvale, NJ: AFIPS Press.

Lipner, S. (1982). Non-discretionary controls for commercial applications. In *Proceedings of the 1982 IEEE Symposium on Security and Privacy* (pp. 2–20). Los Alamitos, CA: IEEE Computer Society Press.

Lunt, T. F. (1989). Access control policies: Some unanswered questions. *Computers and Security, 8,* 43–54.

Lunt, T. F., Neumann, P. G., Denning, D. E., Schell, R. R., Heckman, M., & Shockley, W. R. (1989, December). *Secure distributed data views security policy and interpretation for DMBS* for a Class A1 DBMS (RADC-TR-89-313, Vol 1). Griffiss Air Force Base, NY: Rome Air Development Center.

Maekawa, M., Oldehoft, A. E., & Oldehoft, R. R. (1987). *Operating systems.* Menlo Park, CA: Benjamin Cummings.

MITRE Corp. (2004). *Common vulnerabilities and exposures.* Retrieved December 22, 2004, from http://www.cve.mitre.org/

Myers, P. (1980). *Subversion: The neglected aspect of computer security.* Unpublished master's thesis, Naval Postgraduate School Monterey, CA.

NIST. (2004). *The common criteria evaluation and validation scheme.* Retrieved December 22, 2004, from http://niap.nist.gov/cc-scheme/index.html

Oasis. (2003). *Extensible access control markup language (XACML), version 1.0, Oasis standard.* In S. Godik & T. Moses (Eds.). Retrieved December 22, 2004, from http://www.oasis-open.org/committees/xacml/repository/

Oasis. (2004). *Conformance requirements for the OASIS security assertion markup language (SAML) v2.0* (Committee Draft 03). In P. Mishra, R. Philpott, & E. Maler (Eds.). Retrieved December 22, 2004, from http://www.oasis-open.org/committees/tc_home.php?wg_abbrev=security

Parnas, D. L. (1972). On the criteria to be used in decomposing systems into modules. *Communications of the ACM, 15*(12), 1053–1058.

Rushby, J., & Randell, B. (1983). A distributed secure system. *IEEE Computer, 16*(5), 55–67.

Saltzer, J. H., & Schroeder, M. D. (1975). The protection of information in computer systems. *Proceedings of the IEEE, 63*(9), 1278–1308.

Sandhu, R., Coyne, E. J., Feinstein, H. L., & Youman, C. E. (1996). Role-based access control models. *IEEE Computer, 29*(2), 38–47.

Schroeder, M. D., & Saltzer, J. H. (1972). A hardware architecture for implementing protection rings. *Communications of the ACM, 15*(3), 157–170.

Shannon, C. (1949). Communication theory of secrecy systems. *Bell Systems Technical Journal, 28,* 656–715.

Shirley, L. J., & Schell, R. R. (1981). Mechanism sufficiency validation by assignment. In *Proceedings of the IEEE Symposium on Security and Privacy* (pp. 26–32). Oakland, CA: IEEE Computer Society Press.

Shockley, W. R. (1988). Implementing the Clark/Wilson integrity policy using current technology. In *Proceedings of the 11th national computer security conference* (pp. 29–37). Fort George Meade, MD: National Security Agency.

Sterne, D. F. (1991). On the buzzword "security policy." In *Proceedings of the IEEE Symposium on Research in Security and Privacy* (pp. 219–230). Los Alamitos, CA: IEEE Computer Society Press.

Tannenbaum, A. (2001). *Modern operating systems* (2nd ed., pp. 81–100). Upper Saddle River, NJ: Prentice Hall.

Weissman, C. (2003). MLS-PCA: A high assurance security architecture for future avionics. In *Proceedings of the annual computer security application conference* (pp. 2–12). Los Alamitos, CA: IEEE Computer Society Press.

Wilkes, M. V., & Needham, R. M. (1980). The Cambridge model distributed system. *ACM SIGOPS Operating Systems Review, 14*(1), 21–29.

# Guidelines for a Comprehensive Security System

Hossein Bidgoli, *California State University, Bakersfield*

## INTRODUCTION

As has been discussed throughout this *Handbook*, security issues and threats in a network environment are varied and can be caused intentionally and unintentionally by both insiders and outsiders. Security issues and threats related to a network environment can be categorized as controllable, partially controllable, and uncontrollable. This final chapter presents a series of guidelines that identify various security issues and threats in a network environment and then offers a comprehensive security plan and guidelines for recovery if disaster strikes.

## FORMATION OF THE SECURITY TASK FORCE

For the continued success of a security system and to provide a "buy-in" environment, different users of the network and computer systems must have input in the design and implementation of the security system. Users' views must be highly regarded and nobody should feel left out. This issue is of considerable significance, because computer and network systems are being increasingly used by a wide variety of users. Generally speaking, computer and network systems have two groups of users: internal and external. Internal users are the employees within the organization who will use or interact with the system on a regular basis. These customers are the best source of information simply because they use the system on regular basis and could provide important input regarding the strengths and weaknesses of the security system. Another example of an internal user is a guest that might use a kiosk provided for system inquiries. External users are not the employees of the organization; however, they do interact with the system. They include customers, contractors, suppliers, and other business partners. In the case of e-commerce and Web-based systems, customers play a very important role. The e-commerce site must be easy to access, be informative, and have the answers to the important questions of a typical customer. At the same time, these systems must ensure the security and privacy of their users. The task force should include representatives

from these groups and individuals:

- users,
- top management,
- the top financial officer,
- the hardware group,
- the software group,
- the legal department, and
- the graphics or art department.

The representative from the top management is very important. In a nontechnical fashion, the advantages of the security system and the ways that the security system will improve the competitiveness of the organization should be explained to this group. The ways that the security system protects information resources throughout the organization and reduces the vulnerabilities, risk of data loss, and privacy issues should also be explained. The task force team should work to define the users' and customers' needs as precisely as possible. It also should define the risks and benefits associated with the security system.

Using a task force for the design of a security system is similar to joint application design, used by many system analysts for designing computer-based information systems. Joint application design (JAD) is a joint venture between users, top management, security specialists, and data processing professionals. It centers on a structured workshop (called a JAD session) where these users and security professionals come together to design a security system. It involves a detailed agenda, visual aids, a leader who moderates the session, and a scribe who records the agreed-upon specifications. It culminates in a final document containing definitions for data elements, workflows, screens, reports, and general security specifications. A significant advantage of using JAD is that different functional areas of corporations have different agendas when it comes to creating a security system. Using JAD, an organization can be assured that all executives representing various departments are together in group interviews. This helps to avoid collecting narrow and one-dimensional information requirements (Wood & Silver, 1989).

# IDENTIFICATION OF BASIC SECURITY SAFEGUARDS

Computer hackers, crackers, and criminals are making national and international news. It is no wonder that executives in private and public organizations are taking computer and network security very seriously. A comprehensive security system protects customers, buildings, terminals, printers, central processing units (CPUs), cables, and other hardware and software in an organization. Moreover, a comprehensive security plan protects data resources, the second most important resource (after human resources) in an organization. The data resources can be an e-mail message from a division supervisor to the CEO, an invoice being transferred using EDI, the blueprint for a new product design, the outline of a new advertising strategy, the credit card number of a customer, or financial statements. Security threats exceed merely stealing data; they include everything from sharing passwords with a coworker to leaving the system unattended while logged onto the network to spilling coffee on a keyboard. A comprehensive security system includes hardware, software, procedures, customers, and personnel that collectively protect the computing resources and keep intruders and hackers at bay. A comprehensive security system is broken down into three important aspects: secrecy, accuracy, and availability (Sanders, 1996). Let's briefly explain each aspect.

A *secret* system must not allow information to be disclosed to anyone who is not authorized to access it. In highly secure government agencies (Department of Defense, the Central Intelligence Agency, and the Internal Revenue Service, for example), secrecy ensures that only the users who are supposed to have access are granted that access. In business organizations, confidentiality ensures the protection of private information (payroll, personnel, and corporate data). In the e-commerce world, confidentiality ensures that customers' data is protected and will be used only for the intended purpose.

*Accuracy* ensures the integrity of data resources within the organization. This means that the security system must not allow the data to be corrupted or allow any unauthorized changes to the corporate database. Database administrators and webmasters must establish comprehensive security systems for corporate databases. Authorized users must be identified and they must be given proper access privileges. Just imagine that the addition or elimination of a zero would be the difference between $100,000 and $10,000. In e-commerce and financial transactions, accuracy and secrecy are important aspects of a security system, and they are the prerequisite for any data quality implementation throughout the organization.

*Availability* ensures the efficient and effective operation of a computer, network, and an e-commerce site. In a network environment, availability ensures that the system is always available and accessible. A secure system must make information available to authorized users. It should also ensure quick recovery of the system to its normal operation in the case of a disaster. In many cases, availability is the baseline security need for all authorized users. If the system is not accessible to its authorized users, the secrecy

and accuracy objectives of the system cannot be properly assessed.

In a network environment, a comprehensive security system must provide three levels of security:

- Front-end servers must be protected against unauthorized access (Level 1).
- Back-end systems must be protected to ensure privacy, confidentiality, accuracy, and integrity of data (Level 2).
- The corporate network must be protected against intrusion and unauthorized access (Level 3).

The goal in designing a comprehensive security system is first to design a fault-tolerant system and then take all the possible measures for protecting the organization data resources (Garfield, 1997). A fault-tolerant system is a combination of hardware and software techniques that improves the reliability of a network system. There are several techniques and tools that can improve the fault tolerance of a network system. The following are among the popular techniques:

- uninterruptible power supply (UPS),
- redundant arrays of independent disks (RAID), and
- mirror disks.

# IDENTIFICATION OF GENERAL SECURITY THREATS

*Computer and network security* is concerned with the unauthorized access to important data resources. Some threats are controllable, some are partially controllable, and some are completely uncontrollable. Some are intentional whereas others are unintentional (Bidgoli, 2002; 2003; Marion, 1995). Table 1 summarizes several potential computer and network disasters.

Some security threats such as earthquakes are natural and are uncontrollable (or are partially controllable). The damage from natural disasters is somewhat controllable. Buildings with special designs for earthquake protection are now available, and flood damage usually can be controlled. Frequently, computer rooms are designed separately from the rest of a structure to minimize

**Table 1** Potential Computer and Network Disasters

| Natural Disasters | Other Disasters |
| --- | --- |
| Cold weather | Blackouts and brownouts |
| Earthquakes | Fires |
| Floods | Gas leaks |
| Hot weather | Neighborhood hazards |
| Hurricanes | Nuclear attacks |
| Ice storms | Oil leaks |
| Ocean waves | Power failure |
| Severe dust | Power fluctuations |
| Snow | Radioactive fallout |
| Tornadoes | Structural failure |

**Table 2** Internal and External Threats and Vulnerability

| Type of Threat | Sources of Threats | | | | | |
|---|---|---|---|---|---|---|
| | I/O Operator | Supervisor | Programmer/ Webmaster | Systems Engineer/Technician | User | Competitor |
| Changing codes | x | | x | | | |
| Copying files | x | | x | | | |
| Destroying files | x | x | x | | x | x |
| Embezzlement | | | x | x | | x |
| Espionage | x | x | x | | | x |
| Installing bugs | | | x | x | | x |
| Sabotage | x | | x | x | | x |
| Selling data | x | x | x | | x | |
| Theft | | x | x | | x | x |
| Overwhelming the e-commerce site | | | | | x | x |

potential hazards. Wiring, air conditioning, and fire protection should be of special concern.

Some security threats are intentional, such as insiders or outsiders (for example, a hacker or a disgruntled employee) intentionally spreading a computer virus. Other security threats are unintentional, such as the accidental erasure of a computer file or the formatting of a data disk by an employee. A comprehensive security system should allow only authorized employees to have access to computing facilities. Locks and physical deterrents should prevent most computer thefts. Table 2 summarizes the threats posed by insiders and outsiders.

## IDENTIFICATION OF INTENTIONAL THREATS

Most of the intentional computer and network threats usually fall into one of the categories listed in Table 3. These threats and solutions for dealing with the majority of them have been discussed in several chapters of the *Handbook*. The table simply brings them to your attention once again.

The most highly publicized computer and network threat is computer viruses. A computer virus is a program or a series of self-propagating program codes triggered by a specified time or event within the computer system. When the program or the operating system containing the virus is used again, the virus attaches itself to other files and the cycle continues. The severity of computer viruses varies, ranging from springing a joke on a user to completely erasing or corrupting computer programs and data (Miastkowski, 1998).

In February 2000, computer hackers temporarily shut down several well-known sites, including Yahoo!, ZD.net, and Ameritrade, by bombarding them with bogus traffic. By estimating revenue losses at the affected Web sites, losses in market capitalization, and the amount that was spent upgrading security infrastructures as a result of the attacks, the Yankee Group estimated that these attacks cost the industry approximately $1.2 billion in 2000 (Niccolai, 2000).

Later the same year, the "I Love You" virus infected millions of e-mail users throughout the world. Viruses have brought the necessity of protecting computers from hackers, crackers, extremists, and computer criminals to the

**Table 3** Popular Intentional Threats

Computer viruses, worms, and Trojan horse programs
Virus hoaxes
Hostile Java applets
Logic bombs
Malicious software
Malware
Spyware
Mobile codes
Trap door (also called a back door)
Denial of service attacks
Password attacks
Password mismanagement
Session hijacking
Sniffing
Spoofing
Social engineering
Spam
Adware
Freeware
Cookies
Airwave jamming techniques
Cross site scripting
Phone phreaking
Server and e-mail bugs
Identity theft
Intellectual property theft
Stack overflow attacks
SYN flooding
Web bugs attached to HTML documents

**Table 4** Some Indications that a Computer May Have Been Infected by a Computer Virus

| Symptoms |
| --- |
| Certain programs are bigger than normal |
| Data disintegrates |
| Data or programs are damaged |
| Hard disk space diminishes significantly |
| Keyboard locks |
| Memory becomes constrained |
| Screen freezes (no cursor movement) |
| Sluggish disk access |
| Unexpected disk activity |
| Unusual messages appear on the screen |
| The computer takes too much time to boot |

**Table 5** Biometric Security Measures

| Biometric Measures |
| --- |
| Fingerprint |
| Hand geometry |
| Palmprint |
| Retinal scanning |
| Iris |
| Face |
| Signature analysis |
| Voice recognition |

forefront. The number of computer viruses is growing almost daily. Billions of dollars are stolen every year by computer criminals. According to Thomas Claburn (2002), worldwide economic damage from the Love Bug virus (in 2000) was $8.75 billion. The worldwide economic effect of all malicious code (in 2001) was $13.2 billion. Many organizations are reluctant to report their losses because they do not want to be recognized as vulnerable. With the popularity of e-commerce, e-mail applications, and various Internet applications, this problem will only worsen. Table 4 lists some indications that a computer may have been infected by a computer virus.

## IDENTIFICATION OF SECURITY MEASURES AND ENFORCEMENTS

A comprehensive security system should include the following:

- backups,
- biometric securities,
- nonbiometric securities,
- physical securities,
- software securities,
- electronic transaction securities, and
- the services of a computer emergency response team (CERT).

The first step toward securing a computer and a network is to generate a backup of each data file. The backup files must be kept in a location away from the computer room.

Biometric security measures involve a measurement of an element from the human body to enhance security measures. These security measures rely on the criteria that the unique part or characteristic of an individual cannot be stolen, lost, copied, or passed on to others. The user is always the intended user. A user will rarely lose his/her fingerprint or retinal characteristics. Some of the drawbacks of biometrics are their relative high cost, difficulty in gaining acceptance by users, and relative difficulty in installation. Biometric security measures are listed in Table 5.

Callback modems, firewalls, and intrusion detection systems are the three prominent nonbiometric security measures. When using a callback modem, the system tries to verify the validity of a particular access by logging the user off and calling the user back. By doing this, the system separates authorized users from unauthorized users.

A firewall is a combination of hardware and software that serves as a gateway between the private network and the Internet. Predefined access and scope of use are required, and all other requests are blocked. An effective firewall should protect both the export and import of data from and to the private network. Simply stated, a firewall filters unwanted traffic. If designed effectively, a firewall can look at packets of data that pass into or out of a private network and can decide whether to allow the passage based on the following (Garfield, 1997; Seachrist & Holzbaur, 1997):

- user identification,
- point of origin,
- point of destination,
- information content, and
- the specific port for traffic delivery.

There are different types of firewalls that can be used in different situations. Among the popular types discussed in the *Handbook* are application gateways, bastion host, circuit-level gateways and proxies, internal firewalls, packet-filtering firewalls, stateful firewalls, and network-based firewall services.

By careful examination of the packet that is trying to exit from or enter into the private network, a firewall can choose one of the following actions:

- reject the incoming packet,
- send a warning to the network administrator,
- send a message to the sender of the message stating that the attempt has failed, or
- allow the message to enter the private network.

Although firewalls protect networks from external access, they leave the network unprotected from internal intrusions.

Intrusion detection systems (IDS) can identify attack signatures, traces, or patterns; generate alarms to alert the network administrator and e-commerce site manager; and cause the routers to terminate the connection with the

**Table 6** Physical Security Measures

| |
|---|
| Cable shielding |
| Corner bolts |
| Electronic trackers |
| Identification badges |
| Proximity release door openers |
| Room shielding |
| Steel encasements |
| Tokens |
| Smart cards |

suspicious sources. These systems can also prevent denial-of-service attacks. Intrusion detection systems provide real-time monitoring of network traffic and implement the "prevent, detect, and react" approach to security. The network administrators should implement IDS in front of a firewall in every security domain. Although IDS are necessary for security, they have disadvantages that should be taken into account. Intrusion detection systems require significant processing power and can affect the performance of the network. They are relatively expensive and can sometimes mistake normal network traffic for a hacker attack and cause unnecessary alarms. Intrusion detection systems are in the early stages of development and more sophisticated systems are expected in the near future. There are a number of third-party tools available for intrusion detection.

Physical securities primarily address the concerns of access control to computers and networks as well as the devices available to secure computers and peripherals from acts of theft. Physical security is achieved through measures such as those listed in Table 6.

Cable shielding is accomplished by braiding layers of the conductors to form a braided shield. This scheme protects the data from electromagnetic emanations. This is done by either shielding or by using a conduit. Shielding is more difficult with hardware devices than with cables.

Corner bolts and steel bolts are inexpensive methods of securing a microcomputer or workstation to a desktop or counter. These devices are a combination of locks and cables. Steel bolts are used to secure workstations to a heavy-duty locking plate, which is then bonded to an anchor pad that has adhesive on both sides. The pad is then adhered to a desk or counter.

Electronic trackers are secured to the computer at the AC power insert point. If the power cord is disconnected, a coded transmitter sends a message to an alarm, which sounds, and/or a camera, which is activated to record the disturbance.

Identification badges are checked against a list of authorized personnel. Checks must be done on a regular basis so that any change in personnel is noted.

The proximity-release door opener is an effective way to control access to the computer room. Access to the computer area is gained through the use of a small radio transmitter located in the authorized employees' identification badges. When the authorized person comes to within a predetermined distance of the entry door, a radio signal sends a key number to the receiver, which unlocks the door for admittance.

Room shielding is spraying a nonconductive material in the computer room. This material reduces the number of signals being transmitted or completely confines the signals to the computer rooms.

Steel encasements are designed to fit over the entire computer. The encasement is made of heavy-gauge welded steel. The encasement is kept locked and the security administrator or another designated person has control of the key.

A token is a transmission device worn around the user's neck. The device activates the computer only when a user wearing a token is seated in front of the screen.

Smart cards have been in active use in European countries, Asia, and Australia for many years. They have been extensively used in the telecommunications industry for years. Because of their multipurpose functions, their popularity in the United Stated is also on the rise. A smart card is about the size of a credit card and is made of plastic with an embedded microprocessor chip that holds important financial and personal information. The microprocessor chip can be loaded with the relevant information and can be periodically recharged. Smart cards are broadly classified into two groups: contact and contactless. A contact smart card must be inserted into a special card reader to be read and updated. This type of smart card contains a microprocessor chip that makes contact with electrical connectors to transfer the data. A contactless smart card can be read from a short distance using radio frequency. This type of smart card also contains a microprocessor chip and an antenna that allows for the data to be transmitted to a special card reader without any physical contact.

Software securities are designed to protect the system from loss of data integrity, unauthorized access, and to provide data security. Software securities are accomplished by one of the following:

- access codes,
- data encryption,
- passwords,
- terminal resource security, and
- electronic transaction securities.

Access codes are the simplest form of access control, and the most basic security method is the missing-character code. Files and/or programs are listed in the directory incompletely. For the user to access the data, he/she must fill in the missing character(s). The challenge is that the authorized user must remember the missing characters.

Data encryption transforms original information called plaintext or cleartext into transformed information, called ciphertext or cipher, which usually has the appearance of random, unreadable data. The transformed information is called the cryptogram. The rules selected for encryption, known as the encryption algorithm, determine how simple or how complex the transformation process should be. The *Handbook* extensively discusses various cryptographic measures and protocols such as Kerberos, IPsec: AH and ESP, IPsec: IKE (Internet key exchange),

**Table 7** Guidelines for Improving the Effectiveness of Passwords as Security Measures

| |
|---|
| Change passwords frequently |
| Passwords should be six characters or longer |
| Passwords should consist of a combination of letters and numbers. The addition of capital letters can also be helpful to prevent password theft |
| Passwords should not be written down |
| Passwords should not be common names such as the first or last name of a user |
| Passwords should not be increased or decreased sequentially |
| Passwords should not follow any pattern |
| Before an employee is discharged, his/her password must be removed |

secure sockets layer (SSL), PKCS (public key cryptography standards), and secure shell (SSH).

Passwords are sets of numbers, characters, words, or combinations of these that must be entered into the system for access. Passwords are the most basic access controls, and their composition determines their vulnerability to discovery by unauthorized users. The human element, which plays a major role in the success of password control, is one of the most notable weaknesses of the password security system. For example, the user may simply forget the password or intentionally or unintentionally give the password to an unauthorized user. Table 7 provides a series of guidelines regarding improving the effectiveness of passwords as security measures.

Terminal resource security is a software capability that erases the screen automatically and signs the user off after a predetermined length of inactivity. There are also programs that allow the users to access data only during certain times. Any attempts to access the system other than during the predetermined times results in the denial of access.

Electronic transactions security are concerned with the following five key issues:

1) Confidentiality: How can we ensure that only the sender and the intended recipient can read the message?
2) Authentication: How can the recipient know that the data is from the intended originator?
3) Integrity: How can the recipient know that the contents of the data have not been changed during the transmission?
4) Nonrepudiation of origin: The sender cannot deny having sent the data and the content of that data.
5) Nonrepudiation of receipt: The recipient cannot deny having received the data or the content of that data.

In addition to firewalls and encryption techniques that are often used to protect the security of data over the private and public networks, there are other security measures that are often used for providing comprehensive

security over the Internet. These security measures include secure sockets layer (SSL), digital signatures, and electronic signatures.

# IDENTIFICATION OF COMPUTER EMERGENCY RESPONSE TEAM SERVICES

The Defense Advanced Research Projects Agency (DARPA) formed Computer Emergency Response Team (CERT) (pronounced SUHRT). This was the result of a worm attack in November 1988 that brought more than 6000 computers connected to the Internet to a halt. CERT is housed at Carnegie-Mellon University in Pittsburgh, where it is part of the Networked Systems Survivability program in the Software Engineering Institute, a federally funded research and development center. Currently, CERT focuses on security breach and denial-of-service incidents, providing alerts and guidelines on incident-handling and avoidance. CERT also conducts an ongoing public awareness campaign and engages in research aimed at improving security systems. Network administrators, webmasters, and e-commerce site mangers should always review the latest information provided by CERT. This information may assist in protecting vital e-commerce and network resources. Other sources that provide comprehensive information and guidelines on various network and e-commerce security issues include FedCIRC and CIAC. The Federal Computer Incident Response Capability (FedCIRC) is the central coordination and analysis facility dealing with computer security–related issues affecting the civilian agencies and departments of the federal government.

Computer Incident Advisory Capability (CIAC) provides on-call technical assistance and information to Department of Energy (DOE) sites faced with computer security incidents. This central incident-handling capability is one component of the all-encompassing service provided to the DOE community. The other services CIAC provides are awareness, training, and education; trend, threat, vulnerability, data collection issues, and analysis; and technology watch. CIAC is an element of the Computer Security Technology Center (CSTC) that supports the Lawrence Livermore National Laboratory (LLNL) (U. S. Department of Energy, 2005).

# THE FORMATION OF A COMPREHENSIVE SECURITY PLAN

Now that computer and network threats, vulnerabilities, security measures, and enforcements have been identified, this step introduces a comprehensive security plan. It should be noted that the amount of security budget and protection expenses is often dependent upon the value of the data (i.e., low risk or cost of data replacement would not justify a high cost for security). Some aspects of security measures can be improved and implemented with moderate expenses. Other technical aspects need capital investment in software, hardware, infrastructure, and technical expertise. An organization should carefully consider the security threats and issues presented in this chapter and examine those that are particularly related to a specific organization and try to integrate them into its security plan. To establish a comprehensive security plan, some or all of the following suggestions should be considered (Bidgoli & Azarmsa, 1989; Bidgoli, 2003; Forbes, 1998; Thayer 1998):

1) Organize a security committee. The participants of this committee could be some or all of the security task force members introduced earlier in this chapter. The committee should include representatives from user groups (including finance, accounting, marketing, manufacturing, and personnel), top management, the hardware group, the software group, security specialists, and the legal department. The committee will be responsible for the following:

   a) Setting security policies and procedures. A clear and precise security policy plays a significant role in an organization. A lack of such policies and procedures may result in the failure of employees to understand what undesirable activities are and, consequently, the inability of the organization to prosecute abusers. Many companies develop Business Control Procedure Catalogs or Business Control Process Guides in accordance with ISO 17799 to promulgate specific actions they will perform to provide security.

   b) Assessing the effectiveness of the security policies and procedures in the organization periodically and taking corrective actions.

   c) Distributing passwords and account numbers.

   d) Assigning users to specific groups with access limited to certain applications or data. These groups are often maintained by the network operating system (such as Windows) but applied to various other applications.

   e) Providing ongoing security training for key decision makers and computer users.

   f) Establishing the necessary protection plan for the computers and networks.

   g) Developing a regular audit procedure for login and system use.

   h) Obtaining employee and top management support for security policy enforcement.

   i) Evaluating and revising the security policies continually.

   j) Labeling hardware and software with warning stickers.

   k) Overseeing the security policy enforcement.

   l) Advocating the use of paper shredders for computer waste papers.

   m) Designing an audit trail procedure for both incoming and outgoing data.

   n) Designing a computer operation log to record the logon and logoff times for different users.

   o) Defining employee responsibilities related to security enforcement.

   p) Documenting and labeling all hardware and software components.

2) Post the organization's security policies in a visible place and/or in front of every entry port (workstation or PC). The signs should state the organization's policies on security.

3) Require all employees to sign an acceptable use policy. This would include appropriate and acceptable network and Web access as well as specify punishments as a result of misuse.

4) Encourage employees' sensitivity to security problems.

5) Revoke terminated employees' passwords and badges immediately so that a malicious ex-employee cannot be destructive.

6) Keep sensitive data, software, and printouts locked up to reduce the chance of accessing, stealing, or altering the information.

7) Exit from the programs and systems promptly. Log off and turn off the computer. This prohibits and minimizes unauthorized access to sensitive data.

8) Limit employee access to sensitive files to reduce temptation.

9) Limit computer access to authorized personnel only. Curious personnel must be kept away from the system.

10) Consider unlisted telephone numbers. An unlisted number deters hackers and intruders to some degree.

11) Compare the communication log with communication billing periodically. The log should contain all of the outgoing calls with the users' names and call destinations and time in and out. Also, keep a log of calls in and out. Billing discrepancies should be investigated.

12) Use cryptographic measures for sensitive data transfers as discussed in several chapters of the *Handbook*.

13) Be prepared for computer virus attacks by using the most recent version of the antivirus utility programs and consider the following:

   a) Boot the computer with a known, write-protected operating system floppy disk.

   b) Install only licensed software purchased from reputable vendors. After installation, store the original copies in a secure off-site location.

   c) Do not use software that arrives with its packaging open.

   d) Do not install software brought to the office from a home computer.

   e) Install only the needed software on each computer.

   f) Whenever downloading or copying a file (from the Web or from other sources), check it first with antivirus software.

   g) Do not allow employees to connect personal computing devices onto the organization's network without a thorough inspection for viruses and/or other harmful programs.

14) Observe the following against various computer threats:

   a) Install smoke detectors in the computer rooms.

   b) Keep fire extinguishers in and near computer rooms.

   c) Enforce "no smoking" policies.

   d) Install alarm systems for fire and smoke.

   e) Maintain a steady temperature in the computer rooms.

   f) Maintain humidity levels between 20 and 80%.

g) Equip the heating and cooling systems with air filters to protect against dust.

h) Keep computers away from glass windows and high surfaces, particularly if the computing facilities are in high-risk earthquake regions.

i) Secure computer equipment against strong vibrations and make sure that other objects will not fall on them in case of strong vibrations.

15) To minimize legal and social issues related to the Web and e-mail systems, design and distribute comprehensive e-mail and Web use policies.

16) Observe the following physical security measures:

a) The simplest way to keep someone from walking out the door with your computer is to bolt it down.

b) Use RAID, mirror disks, and UPS in all cases.

c) Use identification badges and tokens to screen out unauthorized users.

17) Install firewall and intrusion detection software and consider other electronic transaction security measures.

These steps should be used as guidelines. Not every organization will need to implement every step; however, some may need to include even more steps to fit their needs.

## PREPARING FOR A DISASTER

As discussed earlier, the sources of computer and network threats are numerous and are both controllable and uncontrollable, and damage can be done intentionally or unintentionally. In any event, an organization must be prepared to respond to a disaster if it occurs. One of the best security measures is to plan for disaster. The response process known as the disaster recovery planning or contingency planning system can play a major role in putting the organization back on its feet.

A disaster recovery plan is useful because it gives the organization a place to begin bringing the operation back to normal. It lists the tasks that must be performed and includes a map for recovery. Disaster may strike in one of the following forms:

- environmental contamination,
- hardware and software failures,
- human errors,
- natural and other disasters (see Table 1),
- power failure,
- sabotage, or
- theft.

It has been reported that more than half of all the traditional organizations throughout the world do not have a disaster recovery plan in place. Many of these organizations would not be able to return to normal operations after a disaster. To guard against disaster, all organizations should take the following steps before a disaster strikes:

- Back up all of your computer files. Store at least one generation of backups at an off-site facility.

- Periodically review security and fire standards for your computer facilities.

- Periodically review the information released by CERT and other security agencies.

- Make sure the staff is properly trained, and that they are aware of the consequences of possible disaster and what actions need to be taken to prevent such disasters.

- Regularly test your disaster recovery plan with trial data.

- Identify all of the vendors and manufacturers of the software and hardware used in the organization. Record their most recent addresses, phone numbers, Web sites, and e-mail addresses.

- Document all changes to the initial hardware and software.

- Get a comprehensive insurance policy for your computer and e-commerce facilities.

- Use hot sites—separate computer facilities with all the needed equipment.

- Use cold sites—rooms with raised floors, air conditioning, and humidity control without the computer itself.

- Share ownership of backup facilities.

- Use decentralized computer facilities.

- Arrange a reciprocal agreement with another installation.

- Check and recheck the sprinkler systems, fire extinguishers, and halon gas systems.

- Review the insurance policy to make sure that the coverage is adequate.

- Keep backups in off-site storage, periodically test the backups by testing the recovery procedures, and keep a detailed record of the machine-specific information such as model, serial number, and so forth.

- Keep a copy of the disaster recovery plan offsite.

- Go through a mock disaster.

### Steps to Take When Disaster Strikes

You have taken all the security measures, you have prepared for a disaster, and then disaster strikes. The following are some important steps that must be taken to bring the operation back to normal:

1) Contact the insurance company to confirm the agreement regarding the implementation of the recovery plan.

2) Restore the telephone lines and other communication systems.

3) Notify all the affected people including customers, suppliers, and employees.

4) Implement a help desk for assisting the affected people.

5) Put together a management crisis team to oversee the recovery plan.

6) Notify the affected people that the recovery is underway.

7) Document all the actions taken.

## CONCLUSION

A comprehensive security system can effectively protect the information resources of a company, improve its competitiveness, and minimize the potential social and legal issues. Security issues and threats in a network environment are varied and can be caused intentionally and unintentionally by insiders and outsiders. Security issues and threats in a network environment can be categorized as controllable, partially controllable, and uncontrollable. This chapter presented a series of guidelines that identified various security issues, threats, and enforcements and then offered a comprehensive security plan and steps for preparing for a disaster. These guidelines, if followed, should significantly improve the chances of success in protecting the integrity of information resources and keeping the hackers and crackers at bay.

## GLOSSARY

**Disaster Recovery** Also known as contingency planning. A formal plan for getting back to normal operations after disaster strikes.

**Intentional Threats** Those threats that are intentionally caused by insiders or outsiders, such as spreading a computer virus.

**Security Plan** A formal document that includes detailed descriptions and guidelines for protecting information resources including hardware, software, people, and data files.

**Security Task Force** Different users of the network and computer systems who are directly or indirectly affected by the security system, including a representative from the top management.

**Unintentional Threats** Those threats that are caused by mistakes, such as accidentally erasing a date file.

## CROSS REFERENCES

See *Contingency Planning Management; E-Mail and Internet Use Policies; The Asset-Security Goals Continuum: A Process for Security.*

## REFERENCES

Bidgoli, H. (2002). *Electronic commerce: Principles and practice.* San Diego, CA: Academic Press.

Bidgoli, H. (2003, fall). An integrated model for improving security management in the e-commerce environment. *Journal of International Technology and Information Management, 12*(2), 119–134.

Bidgoli, H., & Azarmsa, R. (1989, October). Computer security: New managerial concern for 80's and beyond. *Journal of Systems Management,* 21–27.

Claburn, T. T. (2002, April). By the numbers: Catch me if you can. *Ziff Davis Smart Business.* Retrieved February 1, 2005, from http://www.findarticles.com/p/articles/mi_zdzsb/is_200204/ai_ziff23929

Forbes, J. (1998, November 1). Let your fingers do the log-on. *Network World,* 12.

Garfield, M. J. (1997, winter). Planning for Internet security. *Information Systems Management,* 40–46.

Marion, L. (1995, February 15). Who's guarding the till at the cyber mall. *Datamation,* 38–41.

Miastkowski, S. (1998, March). Virus killers. *PC WORLD,* 189–204.

Niccolai, J. (2000, February 10). Web attacks could cost $1 billion. *PC World.com.* Retrieved March 24, 2005 from http://www.nwfusion.com/news/2000/0211hacker.html.

Sanders, S. (1996, January). Putting a lock on corporate data. *Data Communications,* 78–80.

Seachrist, D., & Holzbaur, H. (1997, June). Firewall software for NT and Unix. *Byte,* 130–134.

Thayer, R. (1998, March 21). Network security: Locking in to policy. *Security Policy,* 77.

U. S. Department of Energy. (2005). *Computer incident advisory capability on the WWW.* Retrieved February 1, 2005, from http://www.ciac.org/ciac/

Wood, J., & Silver, D. (1989). *Joint application design.* New York: John Wiley & Sons.

## FURTHER READING

McCarthy, V. (1996, May). Building a firewall. *Datamation,* 74–76.

Ning, P., & Jajodia, S. (2004). Intrusion detection techniques. In H. Bidgoli (Ed.), *The Internet encyclopedia* (Vol. 2, pp. 355–367). Hoboken, NJ: John Wiley & Sons.

Schultz, E. E. (2004). Denial of service attacks. In H. Bidgoli (Ed.), *The Internet encyclopedia* (Vol. 1, pp. 424–433). Hoboken, NJ: John Wiley & Sons.

Slade, R. (2004). Computer viruses and worms. In H. Bidgoli (Ed.), *The Internet encyclopedia* (Vol. 1, pp. 248–360). Hoboken, NJ: John Wiley & Sons.

# Reviewers List

Abdi, Ali New Jersey Institute of Technology

Abdu, Hasina University of Michigan, Dearborn

Aboelela, Emad University of Massachusetts, Dartmouth

Ackerman, Eric S. Nova Southeastern University

Ackermann, Ernest University of Mary Washington

Acquisti, Alessandro Carnegie Mellon University

Adigun, M. O. University of Zululand, South Africa

Aflaki, James Christian Brothers University

Agah, Afrand University of Texas, Arlington

Ahmad, Numan Deloitte & Touche (Middle East)

Aiman, Mark Purdue University

Akingbehin, Kiumi University of Michigan, Dearborn

Aksen, Deniz Koç University, Turkey

Albert, Raymond T. University of Maine

Ali, Sanwar Indiana University of Pennsylvania

Almgren, Magnus Chalmers University, Sweden

Aman, James R. Saint Xavier University

Anantharaju, Srinath North Carolina State University

Anjum, Forooq Telcordia

Antolovich, Michael Charles Sturt University

Apon, Amy University of Arkansas

Arbeláez, Harvey Monterey Institute of International Studies

Asadi, Mehran University of Texas, Arlington

Avoine, Gildas EPFL, Switzerland

Babad, Yair University of Illinois, Chicago

Backhouse, James London School of Economics and Political Science, UK

Baclawski, Kenneth Northeastern University

Bae, Benjamin B. Central Washington University

Bain, Jonathan Polytechnic University

Baker, Theodore P. Florida State University

Balfanz, Dirk Palo Alto Research Center

Balinsky, Alexander Cardiff University, UK

Ball, Nicholas L. University of Minnesota

Balthazard, Pierre A. Arizona State University West

Banks, William C. Syracuse University

Barlow, Judith Florida Institute of Technology

Baron, Jason R. University of Maryland

Barreto, Paulo LARC, Brazil

Barta, Dave University of Oregon

Bartos, Radim University of New Hampshire

Basham, Matthew J. St. Petersburg College

Baumgartner, Gerald Louisiana State University

Baxter, Steven R. Weber State University

Beck, James E. Carnegie Mellon University

Bell, Don R. Webster University

Benítez, Rubén Alvaro González Technical University of Catalonia, Spain

Bennette, Daniel University of Maryland, University College

Benyoucef, Morad University of Ottawa, Canada

Bergman, Clifford Iowa State University

Bergquist, Timothy M. Northwest Christian College

Bhatti, Arshad Saleem Institute of Information Technology, Pakistan

Bi, Xintong Mississippi State University

Biagioni, Edoardo S. University of Hawaii, Manoa

Bicakci, Kemal Vrije Universiteit Amsterdam, The Netherlands

Biham, Eli Technion, Israel

Birnhack, Michael University of Haifa, Israel

Bischof, H-P. Rochester Institute of Technology

Black, Sharon K. University of Colorado

Blanchette, Jean-François University of British Columbia, Canada

Blank, George New Jersey Institute of Technology

Blankenship, Jr. George C. The George Washington University

Blumer, Anselm Tufts University

Blustein, James Dalhousie University, Canada

Bockelman, Jay Oregon Institute of Technology

Bohner, Shawn Virginia Tech

Bohrer, Monty F. University of Sioux Falls

Boklan, Kent D. Queens College

Boldyreva, Alexandra Georgia Institute of Technology

Bollen, Johan Old Dominion University

Boncella, Robert J. Washburn University

Bonica, Ronald MCI, Inc.

Boostrom, Robert University of Southern Indiana

Booth, Lionel S. Tulane University

Borisov, Nikita University of California, Berkeley

Bortman, Eli C. Babson College

Boudriga, Noureddine University of Carthage, Tunisia

Bowie, Nolan A. Harvard University

Boyd, Kathy J. UMUC Europe

Boyd, Waldo T. CREATIVE WRITING (PTY)

Bradford, Phillip G. The University of Alabama

Braynov, Sviatoslav University of Illinois, Springfield

Brazel, Joseph F. North Carolina State University

Bremer, Oliver Nokia

Brenner, Susan W. University of Dayton

Bridges, Susan M. Mississippi State University

Britten, Jody S. Ball State University

Brown, Daniel Certicom Research

Brown, Eric Paul Department of Justice, BOP

Brown, Kevin F. Wright State University

Bruckman, Amy S. Georgia Institute of Technology

Brun, Todd A. University of Southern California

Bruß, Dagmar University of Hannover, Germany

Buchanan, Elizabeth A. University of Wisconsin, Milwaukee

Buell, Duncan A. University of South Carolina

Burns, Patrick C. Valdosta State University

Butler, Kevin AT&T Labs—Reserarch

Cai, Xiaomei University of Delaware

Caini, Carlo Università di Bologna, Italy

Calabresi, Leonello Advanced Systems S.r.l.

Callahan, Dale W. University of Alabama

Caloyannides, Michael Mitretek Systems

Canis, Randy L. Greensfelder, Hemker & Gale, P.C.

Cannady, James Nova Southeastern University

Cannistra, Robert M. Marist College

Cano, Jeimy J. Universidad de los Andes, COLOMBIA

**Caronni, Germano** Sun Microsystems Laboratories

**Carver, Blake** LISNews.com

**Carvin, Andy** EDC Center for Media & Community

**Cavanaugh, Charles D.** University of Louisiana, Lafayette

**Cedeño, Walter** Penn State, Great Valley

**Cervesato, Iliano** ITT Industries, Inc.

**Chakrabarti, Alok** New Jersey Institute of Technology

**Chan, Tom S.** Southern NH University

**Chan, King-Sun** Curtin University of Technology, Australia

**Chan, Susy S.** DePaul University

**Chan, Charles Siu-cheung** Queensland University, Australia

**Chan, Philip** Florida Institute of Technology

**Chandra, Surendar** University of Notre Dame

**Chandramouli, Ramaswamy** National Institute of Standards & Technology

**Chapin, Steve J.** Syracuse University

**Chatterjee, Samir** Claremont Graduate University

**Chen, Yu-Che** Iowa State University

**Chen, Thomas M.** Southern Methodist University

**Cheng, Xiuzhen** The George Washington University

**Cheng, Qi** University of Oklahoma

**Chepkevich, Richard A.** Hawaii Pacific University

**Chepya, Peter** Post University

**Chess, David M.** IBM Research

**Chiasson, Theodore** Dalhousie University, Canada

**Chigan, Chunxiao (Tricia)** Michigan Tech

**Christensen, Chris** Northern Kentucky University

**Chu, Chao-Hsien** Pennsylvania State University

**Chung, Ping-Tsai** Long Island University

**Ci, Song** The University of Michigan, Flint

**Clements, John L.** Titan Corporation

**Climek, David** State University of New York Institute of Technology

**Cocco, Gregory T.** Penn State University

**Cochran, J. Wesley** Texas Tech University

**Compatangelo, Ernesto** University of Aberdeen, UK

**Connelly, Kay** Indiana University

**Constantiou, Ioanna** Copenhagen Business School, Denmark

**Corazza, Giovanni E.** University of Bologna, Italy

**Cornell, Lee D.** Minnesota State University, Mankato

**Cosar, Ahmet** Middle East Technical University, Turkey

**Costello, Steven R.** McKendree College

**Cotter, Robert E.** University of Missouri, Kansas City

**Craiger, J. Philip** University of Central Florida

**Crawford, Walt** RLG

**Crawford, George W.** Penn State University

**Crispo, Bruno** Vrije Universiteit, Netherlands

**Cronin, Eric** University of Pennsylvania

**Crouch, Mary Lou V.** George Mason University

**Cruickshank, Haitham S.** University of Surrey, UK

**Cukic, Bojan** West Virginia University

**Cukier, Michel** University of Maryland

**Cunningham, Chet** Madisonville Community College

**Curry, Ann** The University of British Columbia, Canada

**CustódioFederal, Ricardo Felipe** University of Santa Catarina, Brazil

**Damian, Mirela** Villanova University

**Dampier, David A.** Mississippi State University

**Daoud, Moh** Las Positas College

**Darabi, Houshang** University of Illinois, Chicago

**Davies, Todd** Stanford University

**Davis, Mark Charles** University of Tulsa

**Davis, Scott C.** Old Dominion University

**Davis, James P.** University of South Carolina

**Davis, Diane** University of Texas, Austin

**Davis, Lloyd M.** University of Tennessee Space Institute

**Dawson, Linda** Monash University, Australia

**De, George Richard T.** University of Kansas

**de, Lara Eyal** University of Toronto, Canada

**Dean, Susan T.** UMUC, Europe

**Deaton, Russell** University of Arkansas

**Deflem, Mathieu** University of South Carolina

**Deibert, Ronald J.** University of Toronto, Canada

**DeJoie, Tony** Telcordia Technologies, Inc.

**Delugach, Harry S.** University of Alabama, Huntsville

**Demir, Tamer** Independent Consultant

**Deng, Jing** University of New Orleans

**DeNoia, Lynn A.** Rensselaer Polytechnic Institute

**Dent, Alexander W.** University of London, UK

**Desai, Raj** The University of Texas

**DeVries, Delwyn D.** The University of Tennessee

**Dhamija, Rachna** University of California, Berkeley

**Dhar, Subhankar** San Jose State University

**Dickinson, Ron B.** University of Maryland, European Division

**Dietz, Steven** Quintiles Transnational

**Dinda, Peter A.** Northwestern University

**Dingledine, Roger** Massachusetts Institute of Technology

**Dingley, Kate** University of Portsmouth, UK

**Doeppner, Thomas W.** Brown University

**Dogdu, Erdogan** Georgia State University

**Domingo-Ferrer, Josep** Rovira i Virgili University of Tarragona, Catalonia

**Dommel, Hans-Peter** Santa Clara University

**Dong, Yingfei** University of Hawaii

**Dooley, John F.** Knox College

**Dorsz, Jeff** Saddleback College

**Doss, David L.** Illinois State University

**Durbano, James P.** EM Photonics, Inc.

**Eagle, Christopher S.** Naval Postgraduate School

**Edelman, Benjamin** Harvard University

**Edmead, Mark T.** MTE Software, Inc.

**Edoh, Kossi Delali** Montclair State University

**Ellison, Robert J.** Carnegie Mellon University

**El-Said, Mostafa M.** The Pennsylvenia State University

**Emam, Ahmed** Western Kentucky University

**Endicott-Popovsky, Barbara** University of Idaho

**En-Nouaary, Abdeslam** Concordia University, Canada

**Ensmenger, Nathan L.** University of Pennsylvania

**Erbacher, Robert F.** Utah State University

**Ercetin, Ozgur** Sabanci University, Turkey

**Erickson, Carl B.** Atomic Object LLC.

**Esichaikul, Vatcharaporn** Asian Institute of Technology, Thailand

**Esmailzadeh, Riaz** Keio University, Japan

**Esparza, Charles R.** Glendale Community College

**Esser, Randy** Capitol College

**Esterline, Albert C.** North Carolina A&T State University

**Evans, David** University of Virginia

**Evans, Barry G.** University of Surrey, UK

**Evers, Pamela S.** University of North Carolina, Wilmington

**Ewert, Craig C.** UMUC-Europe

**Fahd, Wissam Boulos** Golden Gate University

**Fan, Guangbin** University of Mississippi

**Farwell, William L.** Deloitte & Touche LLP

**Fausch, Scott** Wright State University

**Fawcett, Tom** HP Laboratories

**Fay, David** International Planning & Research Corporation

**Fernback, Jan** Temple University

**Field, Jr. Thomas G.** Franklin Pierce Law Center

**Figg, Bill** Dakota State University

**Filiol, Eric** Army Signals School, France

**Fischer, Susanna** The Catholic University of America

**Fischer, Michael M. J.** Massachussets Institute of Technology

**Fitzpatrick, Robert B.** Robert B. Fitzpatrick PLLC

**Fogg, Stephen L.** Temple University

**Fortin, David R.** University of Canterbury, New Zealand

**Fox, Richard** Northern Kentucky University

**Franchitti, Jean-Claude** New York University

**Frank, Michael P.** FAMU-FSU College of Engineering

**Frankel, Mark S.** American Association for the Advancement of Science (AAAS)

**Frankland, Erich** Casper College

**Franklin, Edward N., Jr.** Golden Gate University

**Frater, Michael** University of New South Wales, Australia

**Freberg, John D.** Northwestern University

**Fredenberger, William B.** Valdosta State University

**Freedman, Michael J.** New York University

**French, Geoffrey S.** General Dynamics

**Frincke, Deborah A.** University of Idaho

**Fu, Huirong** North Dakota State University

**Fuchsberger, Andreas** University of London, UK

**Gabrielson, Bruce Clayton** Booz Allen Hamilton

**Gad, Gerges A.** University of Houston

**Galbraith, Steven** Royal Holloway, University of London, UK

**Gannod, Barbara D.** Arizona State University East

**Garrett, Kelly** University of Michigan

**Garrett, Paul** University of Minnesota

**Gartin, Timothy J.** KPMG

**Gasaway, Laura N.** University of North Carolina, Chapel Hill

**Gassko, Irene** Northeastern University

**Gast, Jim** University of Wisconsin, Platteville

**Gates, Carrie** Dalhousie University, Canada

**Gauvin, Tony** University of Maine, Fort Kent

**Gearhart, Deb** Dakota State University

**Gehrmann, Christian** Ericsson Mobile Platforms AB

**Geiger, Jeffrey H.** University of Richmond

**Gemmill, Laurie** Ohio Historical Society

**Genetti, Jon D.** University of Alaska, Fairbanks

**Genosko, Gary** Lakehead University, Canada

**Gerdes, Michael D.** RedSiren, Inc.

**Gleason, B. J.** University of Maryland, Asian Division-Korea

**Goel, Sanjay** University at Albany, SUNY

**Goff, Don** University of Maryland

**Goldman, Eric** Marquette University

**Golle, Philippe** Palo Alto Research Center

**Gomulkiewicz, Robert W.** University of Washington

**Gonder, John S.** Cisco Academy Manager

**Good, V. Nathaniel S.** University of California, Berkeley

**Goodman, Seymour E.** Georgia Institute of Technology

**Gopalakrishnan, Suresh** Tacit Networks Inc.

**Gordon, Sarah** Symantec Security Response

**Goss, Kay C.** Electronic Data Systems Corporation (EDS)

**Gouda, Mohamed** University of Texas, Austin

**Govindavajhala, Sudhakar** Princeton University

**Grabosky, Peter** Australian National University, Australia

**Grabowski, Barbara T.** Benedictine University

**Greenstadt, Rachel** Harvard University

**Greenwald, Michael** Lucent Technologies

**Grimaila, Michael R.** Air Force Institute of Technology

**Grimaila, Michael Russell** Texas A&M University, College Station

**Groth, Jens** University of Aarhus, Denmark

**Guan, Yong** Iowa State University

**Guevin, Paul R., III** Air University, United States Air Force

**Guha, Arup Ratan** University of Central Florida

**Guild, Kenneth** University of Essex, UK

**Gunkel, David J.** Northern Illinois University

**Guo, Jinhua** University of Michigan

**Gupta, Zijiang Yang Ajay** Western Michigan University

**Gurtov, Andrei** University of Helsinki, Finland

**Gutmann, Peter** University of Auckland, New Zealand

**Haas, Matthew** Corning Community College

**Hać, Anna** University of Hawaii, Manoa

**Hafner, William** Nova Southeastern University

**Hafner, Carole D.** Northeastern University

**Haigh, Tom J.** Adventium Labs Cyber Defense Agency

**Hailes, Stephen** University College, London, UK

**Halavais, Alexander M. C.** University at Buffalo

**Hanchey, Cindy Meyer** Oklahoma Baptist University

**Harapnuik, Dwayne** University of Alberta, Canada

**Harn, Lein** University of Missouri

**Harrison, Robert Wilson** Georgia State University

**Hart, Richard** University of New Hampshire

**Hartpence, Bruce** Rochester Institute of Technology

**Hassanein, Khaled** McMaster University, Canada

**Hauri, S. Ronald** Webster University

**Hay, Brian** University of Alaska, Fairbanks

**Hayne, Stephen C.** Colorado State University

**He, Ling** University of Florida

**Heikes, Deborah K.** University of Alabama, Huntsville

**Heim, Michael R.** Heim Seminars

**Helmer, Guy G.** Palisade Systems, Inc.

**Helms, Susan** University of Maryland, University College

**Hennekey, Jos. F.** Office of the Monroe County Sheriff

**Herman, Joseph** George Mason University

**Herring, Susan** Indiana University

**Heydari, Hossain** James Madison University

**Higgs, Bryan J.** Rivier College

**Hinke, Thomas H.** NASA Ames Research Center

**Hmimy, Hossam H.** Southern Methodist University

**Hohenberger, Susan** Massachusetts Institute of Technology

**Holden, Stephen H.** University of Maryland, Baltimore County

**Hole, Kjell Jørgen** University of Bergen, Norway

**Holschuh, Douglas R.** University of Georgia

**Homayounmehr, Farid** Stevens Institute of Technology

**Hong, Xiaoyan** University of Alabama

**Hosseini, Jinoos (Jean)** Northeastern University

**Hottell, Matthew** Indiana University

**Houssaini, Sqalli Mohammed** King Fahd University of Petroleum & Minerals, Saudi Arabia

**Howland, Brian M.** Boston University

**Hsieh, Bin-Tsan** National Cheng Kung University, Taiwan

**Hsiung, Pao-Ann** National Chung Cheng University, Taiwan

**Hu, Qing** Florida Atlantic University

**Huang, Chin-Tser** University of South Carolina

**Hura, Gurdeep S.** University of Idaho, Idaho Falls

**Hurstell, Mark G.** Tulane University

**Hutchinson, William** Edith Cowan University, Australia

**Huth, Michael** Imperial College, London, UK

**Hwang, Jenq-Neng** University of Washington

**Ibrahim, Hassan** University of Maryland, College Park

**Ingle, Henry T.** University of Texas, El Paso

**Ippolito, John B.** Allied Technology Group, Inc.

**Isburgh, Nathan** Austin Community College

**Jackson, Bill** Southern Oregon Unversity

**Jackson, David** Southern Oregon Unversity

**Jacobs, Andrew T.** SUNY Rockland

**Jacoby, Betty Anne** Montclair State University

**Jaffe, Joshua M. A.** Cryptography Research, Inc.

**Jaglom, Andre R.** Tannenbaum Helpern Syracuse & Hirschtritt LLP

**Jakes, Penny** University of Montana

**Jamalipour, Abbas** University of Sydney, Australia

**Jewell, Ronnie D.** Marshall University

**Jiao, Changli** University of Portland

**Johnson, Eric N.** Indiana University

**Johnson, Chris W.** University of Glasgow, UK

**Jones, Greg** University of North Texas

**Jones, Paul** The University of North Carolina, Chapel Hill

**Jörgensen, Peter E.** Florida State University

**Jung, Eunjin** The University of Texas, Austin

**Jurik, Mads** Independent Consultant

**Jurinski, James John** University of Portland

**Kabara, Joseph** University of Pittsburgh

**Kabay, M. E.** Norwich University

**Kain, Mike** Unisys Corporation and Drexel University

**Kaliski, Burt** RSA Laboratories

**Kaplan, Marilyn R.** University of Texas, Dallas

**Karush, Gerald** Southern New Hampshire University

**Karygiannis, Tom** National Institute of Standards and Technology (NIST)

**Katz, Jonathan** University of Maryland, University College

**Katzenbeisser, Stefan** Technische Universität München, Germany

**Kaufman, Billie Jo** American University

**Kavanaugh, Andrea L.** Virginia Tech

**Kellep, Charles A.** Capitol College

**Kelley, George** University of Cincinnati

**Kelley, Michael S.** Fidelity Information Services

**Kent, M. Allen, Jr.** Montana State University, Billings

**Keromytis, Angelos D.** Columbia University

**Keys, Anthony C.** University of Wisconsin, Eau Claire

**Khalil, Ashraf Khalil** Indiana University, Bloomington

**Khan, Ahmed S.** DeVry University

**Kiddoo, Jim** University of Alberta, Canada

**Kieff, F. Scott** Stanford University

**Kilford, Lloyd J.** California Institute of Technology

**Kim, Jong** Pohang University, Korea

**King, Nancy J.** Oregon State University

**Klappenecker, Andreas** Texas A&M University

**Kleist, Virginia Franke** West Virginia University

**Koç, Çetin K.** Oregon State University

**Kochtanek, Thomas R.** University of Missouri, Columbia

**Kohel, David R.** University of Sydney, Australia

**Kong, Jiejun** University of California, Los Angeles

**Korba, Larry** National Research Council, Canada

**Korkmaz, Turgay** The University of Texas, San Antonio

**Korpeoglu, Ibrahim** Bilkent University, Turkey

**Kozma, John Powers** Charleston County Public School System

**Krishnamachari, Bhaskar** University of Southern California

**Krishnamurthy, Prashant** University of Pittsburgh

**Krizanc, Danny** Wesleyan University

**Krzyzanowski, Paul** Rutgers University

**Kukowski, Stuart H.** Colorado School of Mines

**Kurgan, Lukasz** University of Alberta, Canada

**Kurkovsky, Stan** Columbus State University

**Kwiat, Kevin A.** Air Force Research Laboratory

**Kwiatkowska, Mila** University College of the Cariboo, Canada,

**Kwok, Yu-Kwong** The University of Hong Kong, Hong Kong

**LaBar, Martin** Southern Wesleyan University

**Lally, Ann** University of Washington Libraries

**Lamb, Annette** Purdue University

**Langford, Barry R.** Columbia College

**Larson, James G.** National University

**Lau, Daniel L.** University of Kentucky

**Lazarevic, Aleksandar** University of Minnesota

**LeBlanc, Cathie** Plymouth State University

**Lee, Yeuan-Kuen** Ming Chuan University, Taiwan

**Lee, Joohan** University of Central Florida

**Lee, Ronald M.** Florida International University

**Lee, Steven B.** San Jose State University

**Leitner, Lee J.** Drexel University

**Lekkas, Panos C.** Xstream Technologies LLC

**Leme, Luis P.** University of Maryland

**Lerner, Michah** Columbia University

**Letterio, Pirrone** EUTELSAT SA, France

**Levesque, Allen H.** Worcester Polytechnic Institute

**Levi, Albert** Sabanci University, Turkey

**Levy, Irvin** Gordon College

**Lewis, James** CSIS Technology

**Li, Xiangyang** University of Michigan

**Li, Kang** University of Georgia

**Libert, Benoît** UCL Crypto Group, Belgium

**Lim, James** City College of San Francisco

**Lin, Xia** Drexel University

**Lin, Shieu-Hong** Biola Univerity

**Lincke-Salecker, Susan** University of Wisconsin, Parkside

**Lineman, Jeffrey P.** Northwest Nazarene University

**Linton, Ronald C.** Columbus State University

**Liotine, Matthew** BLR Research

**Liotta, Antonio** University of Surrey, UK

**Liu, Hongfang** University of Maryland, Baltimore County

**Liu, Mei-Ling L.** California Polytechnic State University

**Liu, Peng** Penn State University

**Lobo, Andrea** Rowan University

**Lok, Simon** Columbia University

**Long, Cherie** Florida International University

**Longstaff, Thomas A.** Software Engineering Institute

**Loper, D. Kall** University of North Texas

**Lorenz, Pascal** University of Haute Alsace, France

**Lou, Kenneth Z.** Cerritos College

**Louzecky, David** University of Wisconsin

**Loy, Stephen L.** Eastern Kentucky University

**Luglio, Michele** University of Rome Tor Vergata, Italy

**Lunce, Stephen E.** Midwestern State University

**Lupu, Emil C.** Imperial College London, UK

**Lynch, Thomas J., III** Worcester Polytechnic Institute

**Lynn, Benjamin** Stanford University

**Mabrouk, Adam S.** Murray State University

**Macchiavello, Chiara** Università di Pavia, Italy

**MacDonald, Ian M.** The College of Saint Rose

**Machunda, Zachary Boniface** Minnesota State University,Moorhead

**Maclay, Colin M.** Harvard Law School

**Madison, Michael J.** University of Pittsburgh

**Magill, Evan** University of Stirling, Scotland

**Mahoney, Matthew V.** Florida Institute of Technology

**Mahoney, Jim** Marlboro College

**Makedon, Fillia S.** Dartmouth College

**Maloof, Marcus A.** Georgetown University

**Mal-Sarkar, Sanchita** Cleveland State University

**Mangold, Stefan** Swisscom Innovations, Switzerland

**Mano, Chad D.** University of Notre Dame

**Mao, Wenbo** Hewlett-Packard Laboratories

**Marchany, Randy** Virginia Tech

**Markantonakis, Konstantinos** Royal Holloway, University of London, UK

**Marshall, Christopher S.** Indianapolis-Marion County Public Library

**Martel, Normand M.** Medical Technology Research Corp.

**Marton, Christine** Global Health Informatics

**Marty, Paul F.** Florida State University

**Mashburn, Ronald Gene** West Texas A&M University

**Mason, Sharon** Rochester Institute of Technology

**Massey, Dan** Colorado State Universtiy

**Matalgah, Mustafa M.** The University of Mississippi

**Mateti, Prabhaker** Wright State University

**Mattord, Herbert J.** Kennesaw State University

**Mayes, Keith** Royal Holloway, University of London, UK

**Mazzei, James A.** University of Maryland

**McCord, S. Alan** Lawrence Technological University

**McCoy, Mark R.** University of Central Oklahoma

**McFarland, Daniel J.** Rowan University

**McGinn, Mark L.** St. Ambrose University

**McGraw, Gary** Cigital, Inc.

**McIver, Jr. William J.** State University of New York

**McKeever, Susan** Dublin Institute of Technology, Ireland

**McKeown, Jim** Dakota State University

**McNeill, Kevin M.** The University of Arizona

**Mead, Nancy R.** Carnegie Mellon University

**Mehta, Chirag** Santa Clara University

**Menz, Mark J.** Independendt Consultant

**Metzler, Jim** Ashton, Metzler & Associates

**Meunier, Pascal** Purdue University

**Meyer, Linda** Purdue University, Fort Wayne

**Mikeal, Rosa Leslie** University of Pennsylvania

**Mikhailov, Mikhail** GlovalSys Services (GSS)

**Mikkilineni, Rao** Golden Gate University

**Millard, Bruce R.** Arizona State University

**Miller, Brent A.** IBM Corporation

**Miller, Benjamin** Inside ID

**Miller, Holmes E.** Muhlenberg College

**Min, John** Northern Virginia Community College & Ruesch International

**Minow, Mary** LibraryLaw.com

**Mirchandani, Vinod** The University of Sydney, Australia

**Mirkovic, Jelena** University of Delaware

**Mohammed, Shaheed N.** Marist College

**Montgomery, Todd L.** West Virginia University

**Moran, Douglas B.** Tatzlwyrm Systems

**Morel, Benoit** Carnegie Mellon University

**Morneau, Keith A.** Northern Virginia Community College

**Morse, Fitzgerald** University of Evansville

**Morton, Russell S.** Winston-Salem State University

**Morton, L. P.** Northwood University

**Moul, Dennis** Carnegie Mellon University

**Mucchi, Lorenzo** University of Florence, Italy

**Muermann, Alexander** The Wharton School

**Mukherjee, Sumitra** Nova Southeastern University

**Mukkamala, Ravi** Old Dominion University

**Muma, Kimberly S.** Ferris State University

**Murray, Jr. Ottis L.** The University of North Carolina, Pembroke

**Mussulman, James E.** Southern Illinois University, Edwardsville

**Muthukumaran, B.** Sri Venkateswara College of Engineering, India

**Myers, Robert A.** Fairfield Resources International and Columbia University

**Naccache, David** Gemplus, France

**Nadal, Jacob** Craig Lab/Auxiliary Library Facility

**Nagle, Luz E.** Stetson University College

**Naimi, Linda L.** Purdue University

**Nair, Suku** Southern Methodist University

**Naldurg, Prasad G.** University of Illinois, Urbana-Champaign

**Nance, Kara L.** University of Alaska, Fairbanks

**Napjus, Chris N.** University of Maryland, University College

**Nath, Ravi** Creighton University

**Neal, Lisa** eLearn Magazine

**Neary, Pat** Central Michigan University

**Neely, Michael J.** University of Southern California

**Nemec, Carol R.** Southern Oregon University

**Newby, Gregory B.** Arctic Region Supercomputing Center

**Newman, J. Richard** Florida Institute of Technology

**Ngo, Hung Q.** SUNY, Buffalo

**Nicolay, John** Troy University

**Nieporent, Richard** Johns Hopkins University

**Ning, Peng** North Carolina State University

**Noubir, Guevara** Northeastern University

**Nyberg, Kaisa** Nokia Research Center, Finland

**Nystedt, Magnus** Francis Marion University

**O'Boyle, Todd** The MITRE Corporation

**O'Donnell, Jon** Clarion University of Pennsylvania

**O'Neal, Charles W.** Webster University

**O'Connell, Ian J.** University of Victoria, Canada

**Odlyzko, Andrew** The University of Minnesota

**Olan, Michael** Richard Stockton College

**Opderbeck, David W.** Seton Hall University

**Oppenheimer, Priscilla** Southern Oregon University

**Osborne, Lawrence J.** Lamar University

**Oswald, Elisabeth** Graz University of Technology, Austria

**Ouyang, Jinsong** California State University, Sacramento

**Ozok, A. Ant** University of Maryland, Baltimore County

**Pallithekethil, Vijay Oommen** Michigan Technological University

**Palmeri, Anthony J.** University of Wisconsin,Oshkosh

**Palombo, James** University of Maryland

**Pan, Yin** Rochester Institute of Technology

**Pappu, Ravikanth** ThingMagic LLC.

**Paprzycki, Marcin** Oklahoma State University

**Parisi, Jr. Robert A.** AIG eBusiness Risk Solutions

**Parker, James Byron** University of Maryland, Baltimore County

**Parks, Lance M.** Cosumnes River College

**Pastore, Raymond S.** Bloomsburg University

**Patel, Nilesh** University of Michigan, Dearborn

**Paterson, Kenneth G.** University of London, UK

**Patterson, David A.** The University of Tennessee

**Paulo, Anthony Leo** Aera Energy

**Payne, Jr. Charles N.** Adventium Labs

**Pearce, Charles** Gallaudet University

**Peavy, Don E.** Canyon College and University of Phoenix

**Penzhom, W. T.** University of Pretoria, South Africa

**Pepin, Madeleine** Our Lady of the Lake University

**Pernul, Günther** University of Regensburg, Germany

**Peslak, Alan** Penn State University

**Peterson, Gilbert L.** Air Force Institute of Technology

**Peterson, Victoria L.** Minnesota State University, Moorhead

**Phelps, Daniel C.** Florida State University

**Phifer, Lisa** Core Competence Inc.

**Phillips, Ronnie J.** Colorado State University

**Phonphoem, Anan** Kasetsart University, Thailand

**Pickering, Andrew J.** University of Maryland, University College

**Pickett, Michael C.** National University

**Piotrowski, Victor** University of Wisconsin, Superior

**Platt, Richard G.** University of West Florida

**Plum, Terry** Simmons Graduate School of Library and Information Science

**Plumer, Danielle Cunniff** The University of Texas, Austin

**Podgorski, Andrew S.** ASR Technologies Inc.

**Powers, Dennis M.** Southern Oregon University

**Prescott, John E.** University of Pittsburgh

**Prestage, Andrew** Kern County Superintendent of Schools

**Preston, Jon A.** Clayton College and State University

**Prettyman, Steve** Chattahoochee Technical College

**Prevatte, Tenette** Robeson Community College

**Prince, Matthew** John Marshall Law School

**Probst, David K.** Concordia University, Canada

**Provos, Niels** Google Inc.

**Pruitt-Mentle, Davina** University of Maryland

**Pucella, Riccardo** Cornell University

**Putnam, Elizabeth** Lucy Scribner Library

**Pyun, Jae-Young** Chosun University, Korea

**Rafaeli, Sandro** T&T, Brazil

**Raghavan, Vijay V.** Northern Kentucky University

**Ramage, Michael L.** Murray State University

**Ramasastry, Anita** University of Washington

**Rao, H. R.** SUNY, Buffalo

**Rao, Shrisha** Mount Mercy College

**Rauch, Jesse** Casper College

**Rawat, Surendra** Nortel Networks, Canada

**Reavis, David R** Texas A&M University, Texarkana

**Recor, Jeff** Olympus Security Group, Inc.

**Reis, Leslie Ann** The John Marshall Law School

**Rejman-Greene, Marek** British Telecommunications plc, UK

**Ren, Jian** Michigan State University

**Rhodes, Anthony (Tony)** Zayed University, Dubai

**Rice, Doug** Golden Gate University

**Richardson, Sherry** Clayton College & State University

**Rijmen, Vincent** Graz University, Austria

**Riley, O'Connor Thomas** North Carolina Wesleyan College

**Ritter, Terry** Independent Consultant

**Robbin, Alice** Indiana University

**Roberts, G. Keith** University of Redlands

**Robila, Stefan A.** Montclair State University

**Robin, J. Scott** Webster University

**Robinson, Wendy** Oakland University

**Rogers, Marcus K.** Purdue University

**Rogers, William** Biometric Digest

**Rogerson, Kenneth** Duke University

**Rose, Gregory M.** Washington State University

**Roselli, Diane Marie** Harrisburg Area Community College

**Rosenbaum, Joseph I.** Reed Smith LLP

**Rosenthal, Arnon** The MITRE Corporation

**Rosti, Emilia** Università degli Studi di Milano, Italy

**Roth, Volker** Fraunhofer IGD, Germany

**Rowe, Mark R.** Ohio University, Athens

**Rowe, Neil C.** U.S. Naval Postgraduate School

**Rowe, Kenneth E.** Purdue University

**Rubin, Bradley S.** University of St. Thomas

**Rucinski, Andrzej** University of New Hampshire

**Ryan, Julie J. C. H.** George Washington University

**Ryan, Mark** University of Birmingham, UK

**Ryutov, Tatyana** University of Sourthern California

**Sahin, Haydar T.** St. Philip's College & University of Texas, San Antonio

**Salomonsen, Gorm** Cryptomathic A/S, Denmark

**Sanghera, Kamaljeet** George Mason University

**Santos, Andre Luiz Moura dos** Georgia Institute of Technology

**Saroiu, Stefan** University of Washington

**Sarolahti, Pasi** Nokia Research Center, Finland

**Sarosdy, Randall L.** Akin Gump Strauss Hauer & Feld LLP

**Sarwar, Badrul M.** San Jose State University

**Satterlee, Brian** Liberty University

**Saunders, John H.** National Defense University

**Savoie, Michael J.** The University of Texas, Dallas

**Scacchi, Walt** University of California, Irvine

**Schaefer, Marcus** DePaul Unversity

**Schaefer, Guenter** Technische Universitaet, Berlin

**Scharlau, Bruce A.** University of Aberdeen, UK

**Scheets, George** Oklahoma State University

**Schiano, William T.** Bentley College

**Schlesinger, Richard** Kennesaw State University

**Schneider, Ed** Institute for Defense Analyses

**Schneider, Ryan A.** Troutman Sanders LLP

**Schonfeld, Tibor** George Washington University

**Schuldes, Michael H.** Dakota State University

**Schwaig, Kathy Stewart** Kennesaw State University

**Schwartz, Daniel G.** Florida State University

**Schwartz, Ray** The State University of New Jersey

**Schwarz, S. J. Thomas** Santa Clara University

**Schweik, Charles M.** University of Massachusetts, Amherst

**Schwerm, Marie** Marquette University

**Schwiebert, Loren** Wayne State University

**Schwimmer, Brian** University of Manitoba, Canada

**Scott, Michael** Dublin City University, Ireland

**Scottberg, Brian P.** COUNTRY Insurance and Financial ServicesSM

**Segall, Richard S.** Arkansas State University

**Seleznyov, Alexandr** University College, London

**Selig, Gad J.** University of Bridgeport & GPS Group, Inc.

**Sengupta, Arijit** Indiana University
**Senie, Daniel** Amaranth Networks Inc.
**Servetti, Antonio** Politecnico di Torino, Italy
**Shah, Rahul** Purdue University
**Shakir, Ameer H.** University of Maryland
**Sharif, Hamid R** University of Nebraska, Lincoln (Omaha Campus)
**Sheriff, Mohamed** Middlesex University, UK
**Sherman, Richard C.** Miami University
**Sheu, Myron** California State University, Dominguez Hills
**Shimeall, Timothy J.** Carnegie Mellon University
**Shmatikov, Vitaly** SRI International
**Shoemaker, DC** North Seattle Community College
**Shumba, Rose** Indiana University
**Shumway, Russell M.** Independent Consultant
**Sicker, Douglas C.** University of Colorado, Boulder
**Siegel, Eric V.** Prediction Impact
**Silverberg, Alice** Ohio State University
**Simco, Greg** Nova Southeastern University
**Simmons, Ken** Augusta Technical College
**Sivalingam, Krishna** University of Maryland, Baltimore County
**Smit, Lodewijk T.** University of Twente, The Netherlands
**Smith, Richard E.** University of St. Thomas
**Smith, Anthony H.** Purdue University
**Snow, Charles** George Mason University
**Sobol, Stephen** University of Leeds, UK
**Somasundaram, Siva** Stevens Institute of Technology
**Song, Min** Old Dominion University
**Song, Hongjun** The University of Memphis
**Spitzner, Lance** Honeynet Project
**Squibb, Jeffery L.** Southern Illinois University
**Stachurski, Dale** University of Maryland and Bowie State University
**Stackpole, Bill** Rochester Institute of Technology
**Staddon, Jessica** Palo Alto Research Center
**Stahl, Bernd Carsten** De Montfort University, UK
**Stamp, Mark** San Jose State University
**Stanley, Richard A.** Worcester Polytechnic Institute
**Steichen, Dean J.** Golden Gate University
**Stein, Andreas** University of Illinois, Urbana-Champaign
**Stevens, Kenneth J.** The University of New South Wales, Australia
**Stevens, Mark** North Carolina Wesleyan College

**Stewart, John N.** Independent Researcher
**Stewart, William G.** University of Maryland, University College
**Stiller, Evelyn** Plymouth State University
**Stolfo, Salvatore J.** Columbia University
**Strickland, Susan** Sam Houston State University
**Striegel, Aaron** University of Notre Dame
**Stucke, Carl H.** Georgia State University
**Styer, Daniel F.** Oberlin College
**Subramanian, Mani** Georgia Institute of Technology
**Suleman, Hussein** University of Cape Town, South Africa
**Sullivan, David** Oregon State University
**Sullivan, Grant** Dalhousie University, Canada
**Sun, Zhili** University of Surrey, UK
**Sussan, Fiona** Baruch College
**Swedin, Eric G.** Weber State University
**Tabor, Sharon W.** Boise State University
**Tan, Pang-Ning** Michigan State University
**Tang, Yuan-Liang** Chaoyang University of Technology, Taiwan, R.O.C.
**Tang, Zaiyong** Louisiana Tech University
**Tanner, Rudolf** UbiNetics, UK
**Tate, Stephen R.** University of North Texas
**Taylor, Luck Ann** The Pennsylvania State University
**Teixeira, Marvi** Polytechnic University of Puerto Rico
**Teng, Wei-Guang** National Taiwan University, Taiwan
**Tesi, Raffaello** University of Oulu, Finland
**Thomadakis, Michael E.** Texas A&M University,
**Thomas, William H.** Juniata College
**Thomsen, Dan** Tresys Technology
**Thrasher, Ward** Private Attorney
**Tian, Jeff** Southern Methodist University
**Tibbs, Richard W.** Radford University
**Tien, Lee** Electronic Frontier Foundation
**Tirenin, Wladimir (Walt)** Air Force Research Laboratory/Information Directorate (This is not an official endorsement by the U.S. Government.)
**Todd, Byron** Tallahassee Community College
**Toshio, Okamoto Garret** Santa Clara University
**Toth, Mihaly** Professor Emeritus
**Toumpis, Stavros** Telecommunications Research Center, Austria
**Townsend, Anthony** New York University

**Toze, Sandra L.** Dalhousie University, Canada
**Tracy, Kim W.** Lucent Technologies and North Central College
**Traore, Issa** University of Victoria, Canada
**Trappenberg, Thomas P.** Dalhousie University, Canada
**Trimmer, Ken** Idaho State University
**Troell, Luther** Rochester Institute of Technology
**Trolin, Mårten** Royal Institute of Technology, Stockholm
**Trostmann, Manfred F.** UMUC Maryland, Germany
**Tsiounis, Yiannis** InternetCash Corporation
**Tu, Feili** University of South Carolina
**Tucker, Terrell** Panama-Buena Vista Union School District
**Tung, Brian** USC Information Sciences Institute
**Turk, Daniel** Colorado State University
**Turner, Stephen Walter** The University of Michigan, Flint
**Tyre, James S.** Law Offices of James S. Tyre
**Upadhyaya, Shambhu** State University of New York, Buffalo
**Uysal, Murat** University of Waterloo, Canada
**Van, Camp Julie C.** California State University, Long Beach
**van, Wyk Kenneth R.** KRvW Associates, LLC
**Varma, Umesh C.** Campbell University
**Vaughn, Jr. Rayford B.** Mississippi State University
**Venables, Phil** Goldman Sachs
**Venema, Wietse** IBM T.J. Watson Research Center
**Verheul, Eric** PricewaterhouseCoopers Accountants N.V.
**Verma, Arvind** Indiana University
**Vert, Gregory** University of Nevada, Reno
**Vesperman, Jennifer K. L.** Author and Coordinator for LinuxChix
**Viehland, Dennis W.** Massey University, New Zealand
**Villagrá, Víctor A.** Technical University of Madrid, Spain
**Vincze, Eva A.** George Washington University
**Vrbsky, Susan V.** University of Alabama
**Vrij, Aldert** University of Portsmouth, UK
**Wagner, Paul J.** University of Wisconsin, Eau Claire
**Walden, James W.** The University of Toledo
**Walker, Jesse R.** Intel Corporation
**Wallace, Jonathan D.** Author and Attorney
**Walls, Noretta** University of South Alabama
**Walsh, J. M.** The University of North Carolina

**Walter, Colin D.** Comodo Research Lab, UK

**Wang, Yongge** University of North Carolina,Charlotte

**Wang, Xunhua** James Madison University

**Ward, David O.** Capitol College

**Wareham, Jonathan D.** Georgia State University

**Warren, Matt** Deakin University, Australia

**Waters, Brent** Princeton University

**Watro, Ronald J.** BBN Technologies

**Watson, John W.** Chipola College

**Watson, Keith** Purdue University

**Wayman, James L.** San Jose State University

**Wechsler, Harry** George Mason University

**Weil, Steven** Seitel Leeds & Associates

**Weiler, Nathalie** Swiss Federal Institute of Technolo, Switzerland

**Weinberger, George M.** Texas State University, San Marcos, Texas

**Weindling, Mark L.** Weindling Technology LLC

**Weippl, Edgar R.** University of Vienna, Austria

**Weis, Stephen A.** Massachusetts Institute of Technology

**Weiss, Jill C.** Florida International University

**Wenning, Rigo** W3C/ERCIM

**Wespi, Andreas** IBM Research Laboratory, Zurich

**West, Robert C.** U.S. Department of Homeland Security

**West-Brown, Moira** Independent Consultant

**Westby, Jody R.** American Bar Association

**Wheeler, Deborah L.** Oxford Internet Institute University of Washington, UK

**Whelan, Claire** Dublin City University, Ireland

**Whitehead, Chris** Columbus State University

**Whitlock, Charles R.** Experian

**Whyte, Bill** University of Leeds, UK

**Wiegand, Nathan** University of Alabama, Tuscaloos

**Wilbert, Janet M.** University of Tennessee, Martin

**Willette, William W.** University of Texas, Arlington

**William, William** Capitol College

**Wines, William A.** Miami University

**Winston, Thomas G.** Endicott College

**Wojciechowski, Pawel** EPFL, Switzerland

**Wolcott, Peter** University of Nebraska, Omaha

**Wolff, Richard S.** Montana State University

**Wool, Avishai** Tel Aviv University, Israel

**Workman, Michael** Florida State University

**Worona, Steven L.** EDUCAUSE

**Wright, Rebecca N.** Stevens Institute of Technology

**Wu, Chwan-Hwa** Auburn University

**Wu, Hsin-Tai** University of California, Los Angeles

**Wu, Ningning** University of Arkansas, Little Rock

**Wu, Hongyi** University of Louisiana, Lafayette

**Xie, Geoffrey G.** Naval Postgraduate School

**Xu, Shouhuai** University of Texas, San Antonio

**Xu, Jun** North Carolina State University

**Xu, Shouhuai** University of Texas, San Antonio

**Xue, Guoliang** Arizona State University

**Yampolskiy, Aleksandr** Yale University

**Yan, Li Tie** Institute for Infocomm Research, Singapore

**Yang, Cheer-Sun** West Chester University

**Yang, Kun** University of Essex, UK

**Yang, Zijiang** Western Michigan University

**Yang, Mei** University of Nevada, Las Vegas

**Yao, Tim S.** The University of Texas, El Paso

**Yasinsac, Alec** Florida State University

**Yetnikoff, Arlene S.** DePaul University

**Yin, Yiqun Lisa** RSA Laboratories

**Youman, Charles E.** Independent Consultant

**Young, Adam L.** Cigital, Inc.

**Young, Stewart M.** Stanford Law School

**Youssef, Mahmoud** Rutgers University

**Yu, Ting** North Carolina State University

**Yu, Peter K.** Michigan State University

**Yuan, Yufei** McMaster University, Canada

**Yue, Wei T.** University of Texas, Dallas

**Zachary, John** University of South Carolina

**Zamboni, Diego** IBM Zurich Research Laboratory, Switzerland

**Zeadally, Sherali** Wayne State University

**Zhang, N.** University of Manchester, UK

**Zhang, Fangguo** Sun Yat-sen University,China

**Zhang, Zhi-Li** University of Minnesota

**Zhong, Sheng** Stevens Institute of Technology

**Zhou, Jianying** Institute for Infocomm Research, Singapore

**Zhu, Sencun** George Mason University

**Zhu, Feng** Northeastern University

**Ziegenfuss, Douglas E.** Old Dominion University

**Zielonka, Larry** College of DuPage

**Zilic, Zeljko** McGill University, Canada

**Zillner, Thomas** University of Wisconsin

**Zimmermann, Han-Dieter** University of Muenster, Germany

**Zomaya, Albert Y.** The University of Sydney, Australia

**Zou, Xukai** Purdue University

**Zuniga-Galindo, W. A.** Barry University

# Index